Contents

ON THE ROAD

Contents

UNDERSTAND

SURVIVAL GUIDE

SPECIAL FEATURES

Welcome to Australia

Australia – the sixth-largest country on this lonely planet – is dazzlingly diverse: a sing-along medley of mountains, deserts, reefs, forests, beaches and multicultural melting-pot cities.

Hip Cities

Most Australians live along the coast, and most of these folks live in cities. In fact, Australia is the 18th-most urbanised country in the world: it follows that cities here are a lot of fun! Sydney is a glamorous collusion of beaches, boutiques and bars. Melbourne is all arts, alleyways and Australian Rules football. Brisbane is a subtropical town on the way up; Adelaide has festive grace and pubby poise. Boomtown Perth breathes west-coast optimism; Canberra transcends political agendas. And the tropical northern frontier town of Darwin and chilly southern sandstone city of Hobart couldn't be more different.

Arts & Culture

No matter which city you're wheeling into, you'll never go wanting for an offbeat theatre production, a rockin' live band, lofty art-gallery opening, movie launch or music festival mosh-pit. This was once a country where 'cultural cringe' held sway – the notion that anything locally produced simply wasn't up to scratch. But these days the tables have turned (and, if anything, Australian pride is a tad over-inflated). Aboriginal arts – particularly painting and dance – seem immune to such fluctuations and remain timelessly captivating.

Food & Drink

Australia plates up a multicultural fusion of European techniques and fresh Pacific-rim ingredients – aka 'Mod Oz' (Modern Australian). Seafood plays a starring role – from succulent Moreton Bay Bugs to delicate King George Whiting, there's variety in the ocean's bounty. And of course, beer in hand, you'll still find beef, lamb and chicken at Aussie barbecues. Don't drink beer? Australian wines are world-renowned: Barossa Valley shiraz, Hunter Valley semillon and Tasmanian sauvignon blanc. Need a caffeine hit? You'll find cafes everywhere, coffee machines in pubs and petrol stations, and baristas in downtown coffee carts.

It's a Wide Open Road

There's a heckuva lot of tarmac across this wide brown land. From Margaret River to Cooktown, Jabiru to Dover, the best way to appreciate Australia is to hit the road. Car hire is relatively affordable, road conditions are generally good, and outside of the big cities there's not much traffic. If you're driving a campervan, you'll find well-appointed caravan parks in most sizable towns. If you're feeling more adventurous, hire a 4WD and go off-road: Australia's national parks and secluded corners are custom-made for camping trips down the dirt road.

Why We Love Australia

By Charles Rawlings-Way and Meg Worby, Authors

We've both been living on this great southern land for 30-something years, and there are still places here that we haven't explored. This isn't to say that we've been sitting at home eating popcorn and watching David Attenborough – we're travel writers! It's just that Australia is so damn big. Even if we spent the next 30-something years on an endless round-Australia road trip, there'd still be surprises out there. And that, for a couple of restless road-addicts, is a very comforting reality.

For more about our authors, see p1112.

Above: Kakadu National Park, p841

Australia

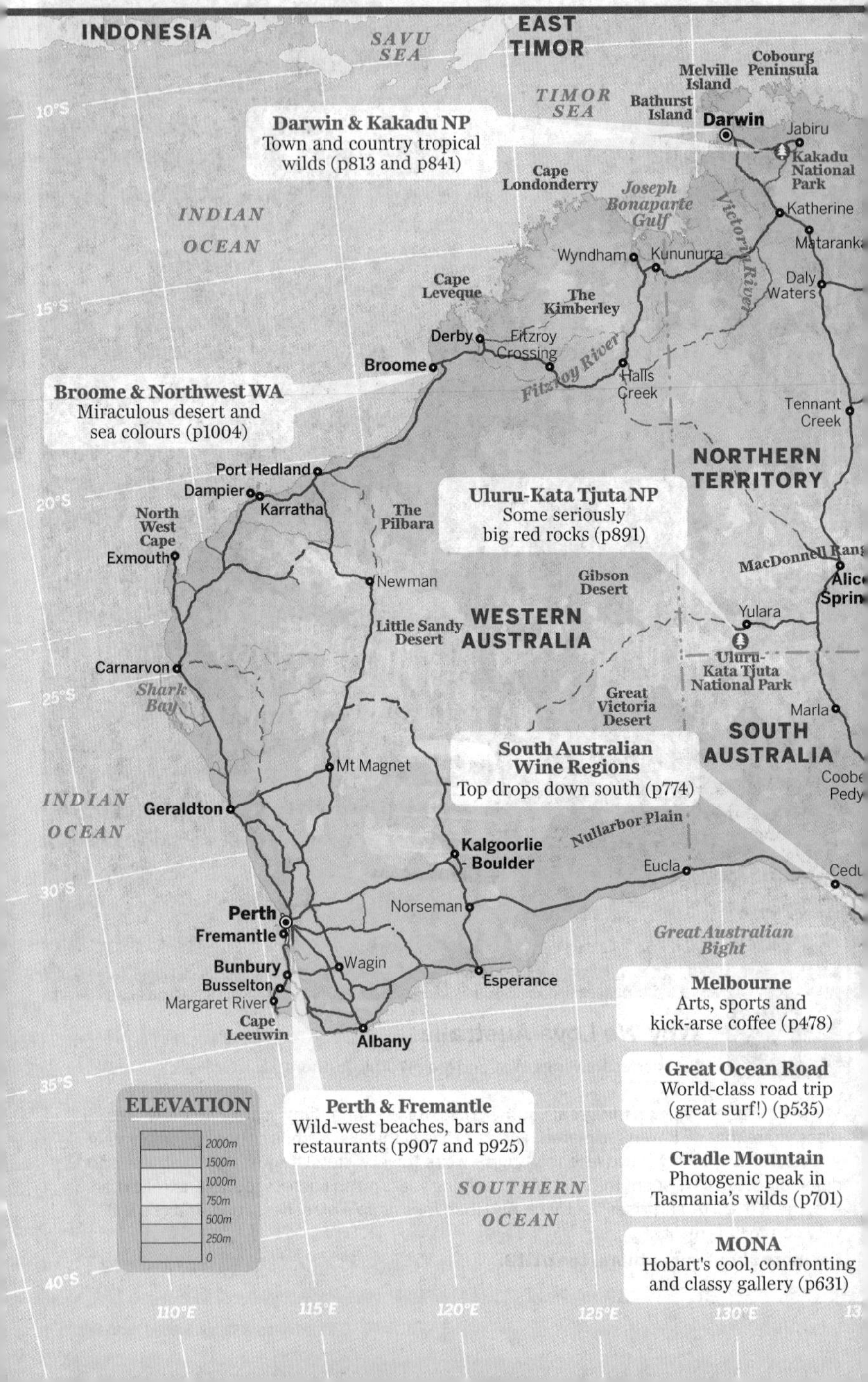
INDONESIA
SAVU SEA
EAST TIMOR
TIMOR SEA
Cobourg Peninsula
Melville Island
Bathurst Island
Darwin
Jabiru
Kakadu National Park
Darwin & Kakadu NP
Town and country tropical wilds (p813 and p841)
Cape Londonderry
Joseph Bonaparte Gulf
Victoria River
Katherine
Mataranka
INDIAN OCEAN
Wyndham
Kununurra
Daly Waters
Cape Leveque
The Kimberley
Derby
Fitzroy Crossing
Broome
Fitzroy River
Halls Creek
Broome & Northwest WA
Miraculous desert and sea colours (p1004)
Tennant Creek
NORTHERN TERRITORY
Port Hedland
Dampier
Karratha
North West Cape
Exmouth
The Pilbara
Uluru-Kata Tjuta NP
Some seriously big red rocks (p891)
MacDonnell Ranges
Newman
Gibson Desert
Little Sandy Desert
WESTERN AUSTRALIA
Yulara
Uluru-Kata Tjuta National Park
Carnarvon
Shark Bay
Great Victoria Desert
Marla
SOUTH AUSTRALIA
South Australian Wine Regions
Top drops down south (p774)
Mt Magnet
INDIAN OCEAN
Geraldton
Nullarbor Plain
Kalgoorlie-Boulder
Eucla
Perth
Fremantle
Norseman
Great Australian Bight
Bunbury
Busselton
Margaret River
Wagin
Esperance
Cape Leeuwin
Albany
Melbourne
Arts, sports and kick-arse coffee (p478)
Great Ocean Road
World-class road trip (great surf!) (p535)
ELEVATION
2000m
1500m
1000m
750m
500m
250m
0
Perth & Fremantle
Wild-west beaches, bars and restaurants (p907 and p925)
Cradle Mountain
Photogenic peak in Tasmania's wilds (p701)
SOUTHERN OCEAN
MONA
Hobart's cool, confronting and classy gallery (p631)
10°S
15°S
20°S
25°S
30°S
35°S
40°S
110°E
115°E
120°E
125°E
130°E

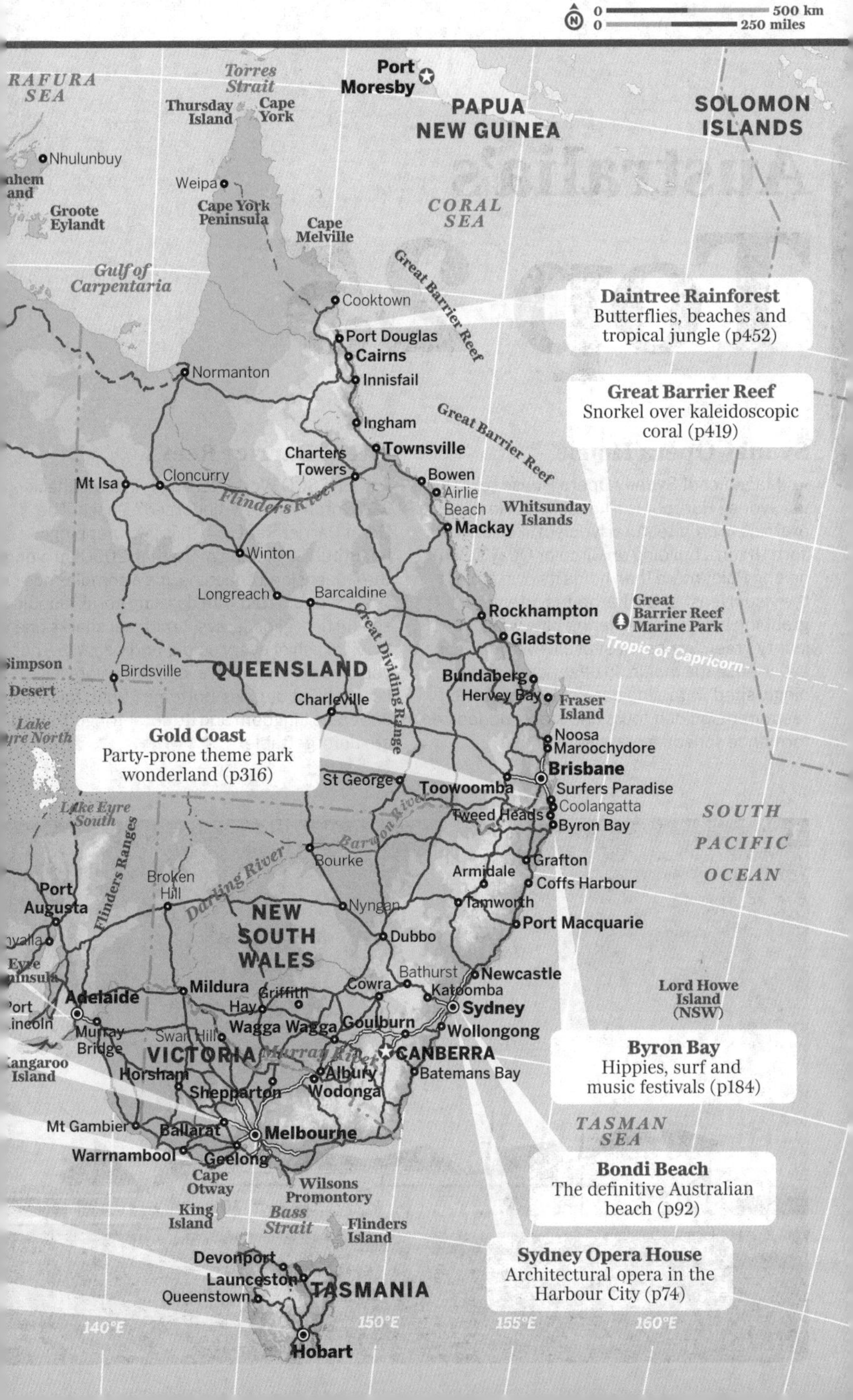
0 500 km
0 250 miles
Arafura Sea
Torres Strait
Thursday Island
Cape York
Port Moresby
PAPUA NEW GUINEA
SOLOMON ISLANDS
Nhulunbuy
Arnhem Land
Weipa
Cape York Peninsula
Groote Eylandt
Coral Sea
Cape Melville
Gulf of Carpentaria
Great Barrier Reef
Cooktown
Daintree Rainforest
Butterflies, beaches and tropical jungle (p452)
Port Douglas
Cairns
Normanton
Innisfail
Great Barrier Reef
Snorkel over kaleidoscopic coral (p419)
Ingham
Great Barrier Reef
Townsville
Charters Towers
Mt Isa
Cloncurry
Bowen
Airlie Beach
Flinders River
Whitsunday Islands
Mackay
Winton
Longreach
Barcaldine
Great Barrier Reef Marine Park
Rockhampton
Gladstone
Tropic of Capricorn
Great Dividing Range
Simpson Desert
Birdsville
QUEENSLAND
Bundaberg
Hervey Bay
Fraser Island
Charleville
Lake Eyre North
Gold Coast
Party-prone theme park wonderland (p316)
Noosa
Maroochydore
Brisbane
St George
Toowoomba
Surfers Paradise
Coolangatta
Tweed Heads
Byron Bay
Lake Eyre South
Flinders Ranges
Barwon River
South Pacific Ocean
Darling River
Bourke
Grafton
Broken Hill
Armidale
Coffs Harbour
Port Augusta
NEW SOUTH WALES
Nyngan
Tamworth
Port Macquarie
Dubbo
Eyre Peninsula
Bathurst
Newcastle
Lord Howe Island (NSW)
Adelaide
Mildura
Griffith
Cowra
Katoomba
Sydney
Port Lincoln
Hay
Murray Bridge
Swan Hill
Wagga Wagga
Goulburn
Wollongong
Kangaroo Island
VICTORIA
Murray River
CANBERRA
Byron Bay
Hippies, surf and music festivals (p184)
Horsham
Albury
Batemans Bay
Shepparton
Wodonga
Tasman Sea
Mt Gambier
Ballarat
Melbourne
Warrnambool
Geelong
Bondi Beach
The definitive Australian beach (p92)
Cape Otway
Wilsons Promontory
King Island
Bass Strait
Flinders Island
Devonport
Sydney Opera House
Architectural opera in the Harbour City (p74)
Launceston
TASMANIA
Queenstown
140°E
150°E
155°E
160°E
Hobart

Australia's Top 25

Sydney Opera House

1 Magnificent Sydney Opera House (p74) on Sydney Harbour is a headline act in itself. An exercise in architectural lyricism like no other, Jørn Utzon's building on Circular Quay's Bennelong Point more than holds its own amidst the visual feast of the harbour's attention-grabbing bridge, shimmering blue waters and jaunty green ferries. Best of all, everyone can experience the magic on offer here – a stunningly sited waterside bar, acclaimed French restaurant, guided tours and star-studded performance schedule make sure of that.

Great Barrier Reef

2 UNESCO World Heritage–listed? Check. Oprah Winfrey–endorsed? Check. The Great Barrier Reef (p419) is jaw-droppingly beautiful. Stretching more than 2000km along the Queensland coastline, it's a complex ecosystem populated with dazzling coral, languid sea turtles, gliding rays, timid reef sharks and tropical fish of every colour and size. Whether you dive on it, snorkel over it or explore it via scenic flight or glass-bottomed boat, this vivid undersea kingdom and its coral-fringed islands are unforgettable.

1

MONA

3 Occupying a riverside location a ferry ride from Hobart's harbourfront, Moorilla Estate's Museum of Old & New Art (MONA; p631) is a world-class institution. Described by its owner, Hobart philanthropist David Walsh, as a 'subversive adult Disneyland', three levels of underground galleries showcase more than 400 often controversial works of art. Visitors may not like everything they see, but it's guaranteed that intense debate and conversation will be on the agenda after viewing one of Australia's unique arts experiences.

Uluru-Kata Tjuta National Park

4 No matter how many times you've seen it on postcards, nothing prepares you for the grandeur of the Rock as it first appears on the outback horizon. With its remote desert location, deep cultural significance and spectacular natural beauty, Uluru is a special pilgrimage. But Uluru-Kata Tjuta National Park (p891) offers much more. Along with the equally captivating Kata Tjuta (the Olgas), there are mystical walks, sublime sunsets and ancient desert cultures to encounter. Below: Uluru

3

4

ALASTAIR POLLOCK PHOTOGRAPHY / GETTY IMAGES ©

STEVEN WARES / GETTY IMAGES ©

Melbourne

5 Why the queue? Oh, that's just the line to get into the latest hot 'no bookings' restaurant in Melbourne (p478). The next best restaurant/chef/cafe/food truck may be the talk of the town, but there are things locals would never change: the leafy parks and gardens in the inner city 'burbs; the clunky trams that whisk the creative northerners to sea-breezy St Kilda; and the allegiances that living in such a sports-mad city brings. The city's world-renowned street-art scene expresses Melbourne's fears, frustrations and joys. Above: Centre Place

Daintree Rainforest

6 Lush green rainforest replete with fan palms, prehistoric-looking ferns and twisted mangroves tumble down towards a brilliant white-sand coastline in the ancient, World Heritage–listed Daintree Rainforest (p452). Enveloped in a cacophony of birdsong, frog croaking and the buzz of insects, you can explore the area via wildlife-spotting night tours, mountain treks, canopy walks, 4WD trips, horse riding, kayaking, croc-spotting cruises, tropical-fruit orchard tours...Whew! If you're lucky, you might even spot an elusive cassowary.

Great Ocean Road

7 The Twelve Apostles – rock formations jutting out of wild waters – are one of Victoria's most vivid sights, but it's the 'getting there' road trip that doubles their impact. Take it slow while driving along roads that curl beside spectacular Bass Strait beaches, then whip slightly inland through rainforests alive with small towns and big trees. The secrets of the Great Ocean Road (p535) don't stop here; further along is maritime treasure Port Fairy and hidden Cape Bridgewater. For the ultimate in slow travel, walk the Great Ocean Walk from Apollo Bay to the Apostles.

ROBERT FRANCIS / ROBERT HARDING / GETTY IMAGES ©

Byron Bay

8 Up there with kangaroos and Akubra hats, big-hearted Byron Bay (just Byron to its mates; p184) is one of the enduring icons of Australian culture. Families on school holidays, surfers and sunseekers from across the globe gather by the foreshore at sunset, drawn to this spot on the world map by fabulous restaurants, a chilled pace of life, endless beaches and an astonishing range of activities on offer. More than that, they're here because this is one of the most beautiful stretches of coast in the country.

Gold Coast

9 Brash, trashy, hedonistic, over-hyped... Queensland's Gold Coast (p316) is all of these things, but if you're looking for a party, bring it on! Beyond the fray is the beach – an improbably gorgeous coastline of clean sand, warm water and peeling surf breaks. The bronzed gods of the surf, Australia's surf lifesavers, patrol the sand and pit their skills against one another in surf carnivals – gruelling events involving ocean swimming, beach sprints and surf boat racing. Also here are Australia's biggest theme parks – a rollercoaster nirvana! Top right: Surfers Paradise

Gourmet Food & Wine

10 Right across Australia you'll find gourmet offerings for all budgets: cool-climate wines and cheeses in Tasmania, coffee and fabulous Greek and Italian in Melbourne, oysters and seafood in Sydney, punchy red wines and riesling in South Australia, marron in Western Australia, and native meats and bush tucker in the Northern Territory. The nation's many wine regions have spawned a culture of fine cuisine using regional ingredients – if you're touring the cellar doors, you'll never be far from a starchy white tablecloth and a romantic lunch.

The Whitsundays

11 You can hop around a whole stack of tropical islands in this seafaring life and never find anywhere with the sheer tropical beauty of the Whitsundays (p392). Travellers of all monetary persuasions launch yachts from party town Airlie Beach and drift between these lush green isles in a slow search for paradise (you'll probably find it in more than one place). Don't miss Whitehaven Beach (p393) – one of Australia's best. Wish you were here?

Canberra's Museums & Galleries

12 Though Canberra (p258) is only a century old, Australia's purpose-built capital has always been preoccupied with history. Its big drawcard is a portfolio of impressive museums and galleries that focus on recounting the national narrative. Institutions such as the National Gallery of Australia, National Museum of Australia, National Portrait Gallery and Australian War Memorial offer a fascinating insight into the country's history and culture.
Below: National Museum of Australia (p261)

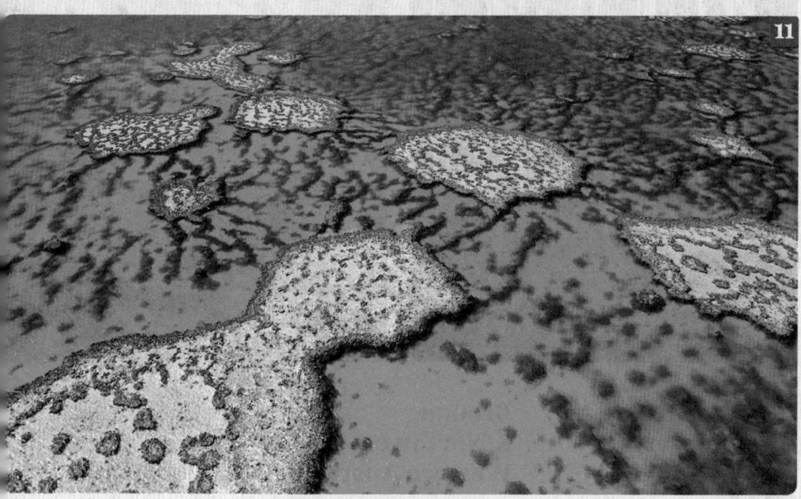

11

12

13

RICHARD I'ANSON / GETTY IMAGES ©

14

Wilsons Promontory

13 Victoria's southernmost point and finest coastal national park, Wilsons Promontory (or just 'The Prom'; p607) is heaven for bushwalkers, wildlife-watchers, surfers and photographers. The bushland and coastal scenery here is out of this world; even short walks from the main base at Tidal River will reveal views of stunning beaches and bays. But with more than 80km of marked walking trails, taking you through forests, marshes, low granite mountains and along squeaky beaches, the best of the Prom requires some serious footwork.

Broome & Northwest Western Australia

14 Harsh, remote and stunningly beautiful, Australia's final frontier promises unparalleled adventure. Scorched spinifex and boab plains hide plunging waterfalls, while pristine beaches and reefs fringe an inhospitable coast. Explore three World Heritage sites: Shark Bay (p983), Ningaloo (p996) and Purnululu (p1023), and Broome (p1008), one of the world's great travellers' crossroads, where every evening a searing crimson sun slips past camels and tourists into the turquoise Indian Ocean. Above: Broome

Perth & Fremantle

15 Perth (p907) may be isolated, but it's far from being a backwater. Sophisticated restaurants fly the flag for Mod Oz cuisine – some in restored heritage buildings in the CBD – and chic cocktail bars linger in laneways. Contrasting with the flashy front the city presents to the Swan River, Perth's more bohemian inner suburbs echo with the thrum of guitars and the sizzle of woks. Just down the river, the pubs of Fremantle (p925) serve some of Western Australia's finest craft beers, and colonial buildings punctuate a glorious Victorian townscape. Above far right: Perth

15

Cradle Mountain

16 A precipitous comb of rock carved out by millennia of ice and wind, crescent-shaped Cradle Mountain (p701) is Tasmania's most recognisable – and spectacular – mountain peak. It's an all-day walk (and boulder scramble) to the summit and back, for unbelievable panoramas over Tasmania's alpine heart. Or you can stand in awe below and fill your camera with the perfect views across Dove Lake to the mountain. If the peak has disappeared in clouds or snow, warm yourself by the fire in one of the nearby lodges...and come back tomorrow.

ANDREW BAIN / GETTY IMAGES ©

16

Darwin & Kakadu National Park

17 Levelled by WWII bombs and Cyclone Tracy, Darwin (p813) knows a thing or two about reinvention. This frontier city has emerged from the tropical steam to become a multicultural, hedonistic hotspot: the launch pad for trips into some of Australia's most remarkable wilderness. Two hours southeast, Kakadu National Park (p841) is the place to see Indigenous rock art under jagged escarpments and waterholes at the base of plummeting waterfalls. Below: Kakadu National Park

South Australian Wine Regions

18 Adelaide is drunk on the success of its three world-famous wine regions: the Barossa Valley (p774) to the north, with its gutsy reds, old vines and German know-how; McLaren Vale (p744) to the south, a Mediterranean palette of sea, vines and shiraz; and the Clare Valley (p779), known for riesling. Better-kept secrets are the cool-climate stunners from the Adelaide Hills (p740) and the cabernet sauvignon of the Coonawarra (p766). Below: Penfolds winery (p776), Barossa Valley

17

18

TOM COCKREM / GETTY IMAGES ©

RICHARD I'ANSON / GETTY IMAGES ©

Indigenous Art

19 Immersed in 'The Dreaming' – a vast unchanging network of life and land tracing back to spiritual ancestors – Aboriginal art (p1043) is a conduit between past and present, supernatural and earthly, people and land. Central Australian dot paintings are exquisite, as are Tiwi Island wood carvings and fabrics, Arnhem Land bark paintings and Torres Strait Islander prints, weavings and carvings. Most large galleries around Australia have Indigenous collections, or you can also make an informed purchase at a commercial gallery. Above: Aboriginal craftswomen, Arnhem Land (p855)

Sporting Obsessions

20 Australia is sports-mad! (p1060) Australian Rules football is the local religion: the pinnacle of the Australian Football League (AFL) season is Grand Final Day in Melbourne (September). Melbourne also hosts the Australian Open tennis championship (January), the Australian Formula One Grand Prix (March), the Melbourne Cup horse race (November), and the Boxing Day Test cricket match. In Queensland and New South Wales, catch a National Rugby League (NRL) match during winter. Above top right: AFL Grand Final (p501), Melbourne

Southwest Coast, Western Australia

21 The joy of drifting from winery to winery along country roads shaded by gum trees is only one of the delights of Western Australia's southwest. There are caves to explore, historic towns to visit and spring wildflowers to admire. Surfers flock to world-class breaks around Margaret River (p944), but it's not unusual to find yourself on a white-sand beach with nobody else in sight. In late winter and early spring, look offshore and chances are you'll spot whales cruising along the coast-hugging 'Humpback Highway'. Above: Lake Cave (p945)

Fraser Island

22 The world's largest patch of sand, Fraser Island (p346) is home to dingos, shipwrecks and all manner of birdlife. Four-wheel drive vehicles (regular cars are not allowed) fan out around epic camp spots and long white beaches. The wild coastline curbs any thoughts of doing much more than wandering between pristine creeks and freshwater lakes. Beach camping under the stars will bring you back to nature. A short ferry trip away is Hervey Bay, where humpback whales shoot along the coast in winter and spring.

Native Wildlife

23 Furry, cuddly, ferocious – you can find all this and more on a wildlife-watching journey around Australia. Head south for penguins and fur seals, and north for otherworldly cassowaries and dinosaur-like crocodiles. In between is a panoply of extraordinary animals found nowhere else on earth: koalas, kangaroos, wombats and platypuses. There's great whale-watching along the coast, the awe-inspiring sight of nesting sea turtles on Queensland beaches, plus the unforgettable cackle of the laughing kookaburra. Above: Wombat

Outback Tracks

24 Whether you're belting an old station wagon along South Australia's Oodnadatta Track (p805) or depreciating your 4WD on the Birdsville Track (p380), you'll know you're not just visiting the outback, you've become part of it. Out here, the sky is bluer and the dust redder than anywhere else. Days are measured in hundreds of kilometres and spinifex. Nights are spent in the five-zillion-star hotel. Less well-wheeled are WA's Gibb River Road (p1017) and Duncan Road (p1022) – outback epics. Above: Karijini National Park (p1000)

Bondi Beach

25 Definitively Sydney and irresistibly hip, Bondi (p92) is one of the world's great beaches. Surfers, models, skate punks and backpackers surf a hedonistic wave through the bars and restaurants along Campbell Pde, but the beach is a timeless constant. It's the closest ocean beach to the city, has consistently good (though crowded) waves and is great for a rough 'n' tumble swim. Don't miss a jaunt along the Bondi to Coogee Clifftop Walk, kicking off at the southern end of the beach. Above: Bondi to Coogee Clifftop Walk (p93)

Need to Know

For more information, see Survival Guide (p1066)

Currency
Australian dollar ($)

Language
English

Visas
All visitors to Australia need a visa, except New Zealanders. Apply online for an ETA or eVisitor visa, each allowing a three-month stay.

Money
ATMs widely available, especially in larger cities and towns. Credit cards accepted in most hotels and restaurants.

Mobile Phones
European phones will work on Australia's network, but most American or Japanese phones will not. Use global roaming or a local SIM card and pre-paid account.

Time
Australia has three main time zones: Australian Eastern, Central and Western Standard Time. Sydney is on AEST, which is GMT/UCT plus 10 hours.

When to Go

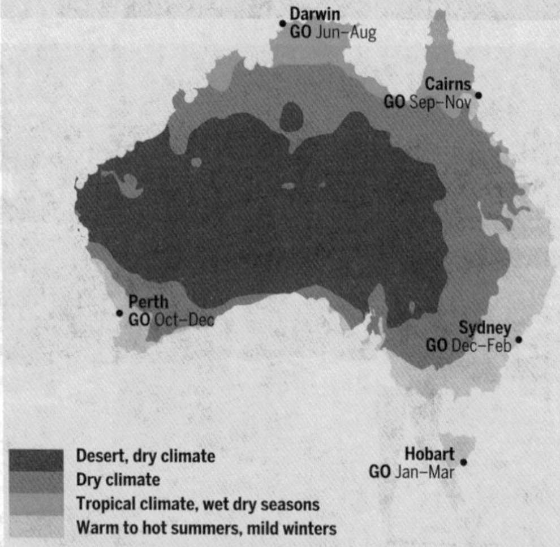

High Season
(Dec–Feb)

➡ Summertime: local holidays, busy beaches and cricket.

➡ Prices rise 25% for big-city accommodation.

➡ Central Australia experiences high season over winter (June to August) due to mild days and low humidity.

Shoulder Season
(Sep–Nov)

➡ Warm sun, clear skies, shorter queues.

➡ Local business people are relaxed, not yet stressed by summer crowds.

➡ Autumn (March to May) is also shoulder season: atmospheric in Victoria and Tasmania.

Low Season
(Jun–Aug)

➡ Cool rainy days down south; mild sunny skies up north.

➡ Low tourist numbers; attractions keep slightly shorter hours.

➡ Head for the desert, the tropical north or the snow.

Websites

Lonely Planet (www.lonelyplanet.com/australia) Destination information, hotel bookings, traveller forum and more.

Tourism Australia (www.australia.com) Government tourism site with visitor info.

Bureau of Meteorology (www.bom.gov.au) Nationwide weather forecasts.

The Australian (www.theaustralian.com.au) National broadsheet newspaper online.

Parks Australia (www.environment.gov.au/parks) Info on national parks and reserves.

Coastalwatch (www.coastalwatch.com) Surf reports and surf-cams.

Important Numbers

Regular Australian phone numbers have a two-digit area code followed by an eight-digit number. Drop the initial 0 if calling from abroad.

Country code	61
International access code	0011
Emergency (ambulance, fire, police)	000
Directory assistance	1223

Exchange Rates

Canada	C$1	$0.95
China	Y1	$0.18
Euro	€1	$1.41
Japan	¥100	$1.09
New Zealand	NZ$1	$0.85
South Korea	W100	$0.09
UK	UK£1	$1.64
US	US$1	$1.10

For current exchange rates see www.xe.com

Daily Costs

Budget: Less than $100

- Dorm bed: $25–$35
- Double room in a hostel: from $80
- Simple pizza or pasta meal: $10–$15
- Short bus or tram ride: $4

Midrange: $100– $280

- Double room in a midrange hotel: $100–$200
- Breakfast or lunch in a cafe: $20–$40
- Short taxi ride: $25
- Car hire per day: from $35

Top End: More than $280

- Double room in a top-end hotel: from $200
- Three-course meal in a classy restaurant: $80
- Nightclub cover charge: $10–$20
- Domestic flight Sydney to Melbourne: from $100

Opening Hours

Opening hours vary from state to state, but use the following as a general guide.

Banks 9.30am–4pm Monday to Thursday; until 5pm Friday

Bars 4pm til late

Cafes 7am–5pm

Pubs 11am–midnight

Restaurants noon–2.30pm and 6pm–9pm

Shops 9am–5pm Monday to Saturday

Supermarkets 7am–8pm; some 24 hours.

Arriving in Australia

Sydney Airport (p131)

AirportLink trains run to the city centre every 10 minutes from 4.50am to 12.40am. Prebooked shuttle buses service city hotels. A taxi into the city costs $40 to $50 (30 minutes).

Melbourne Airport (p1081)

SkyBus services (24-hr) run to the city every 10 to 30 minutes. A taxi into the city costs around $40 (25 minutes).

Brisbane Airport (p1081)

Airtrain trains run into the city centre every 15 to 30 minutes from 5.45am to 10pm. Prebooked shuttle buses service city hotels. A taxi into the city costs $35 to $45 (25 minutes).

Getting Around

Australia is the sixth-largest country in the world – so how you get from A to B requires some thought.

Car Travel at your own tempo, explore remote areas and visit regions with no public transport. Hire cars in major towns; drive on the left.

Plane Fast-track your holiday with affordable, frequent, fast flights between major centres. Carbon offset your flights if you're feeling guilty.

Bus Reliable, frequent long-haul services around the country. Not always cheaper than flying.

Train Slow, expensive and infrequent...but the scenery is great! Opt for a sleeper carriage rather than an 'overnighter' seat.

For much more on **getting around**, see p1081

What's New

Small Bars in Brisbane & Sydney

Brisbane has twigged to small-bar culture. Sassy new booze rooms here include Super Whatnot (p304), a split-level speakeasy down a nondescript city laneway, and The End (p305), a slender hipster hangout in the West End. Of course, Sydney has been doing small bars with style for years: head for Shady Pines Saloon (p124) in East Sydney, Jester Seeds (p125) in Newtown or the quirkily hip Stitch (p123) in the city centre.

Museum of Contemporary Art, Sydney

The $53-million renovation of MCA features a new entrance, exhibition spaces, rooftop cafe and sculpture terrace. Also new is ARTBAR, a hip performance event on the last Friday of the month. (p74)

National Library of Australia, Canberra

The new Treasures Gallery at the National Library features prized items collected over the past 100 years, including Lieutenant James Cook's journal from the *Endeavour*. (p264)

Magnetic Island Snorkelling, Queensland

Self-guided snorkelling tours have opened up off Nelly Bay and Geoffrey Bay, accessed from the beach and exploring shipwrecks and reefs. (p401)

Beechworth Gaol, Victoria

Operational until 2006, Beechworth's historic gaol – that once housed nefarious bushranger Ned Kelly – now hosts spooky guided tours through the guard towers, cells and gallows. (p595)

Gourmania Food Tours, Hobart

Explore Hobart's food scene on a walking tour: meet artisan producers, restaurateurs and wine experts, and make a list of places to return to later in your trip. (p633)

West Terrace Cemetery, Adelaide

Creepy? Well, just a bit. But the new self-guided tours of this old boneyard on Adelaide's CBD fringe make a great escape from the busy streets. (p719)

Waterfront Precinct, Darwin

Darwin's ever-evolving Waterfront Precinct now hosts a wave lagoon and a seawater recreation lagoon, patrolled by lifesavers and surrounded by lawns and eateries. (p911)

Brookfield Place, Perth

With multiple restaurants, cafes and bars, Perth's hottest new precinct for eating and drinking centres on the thoughtful restoration of a row of downtown heritage buildings. (p917)

Margaret River Gourmet Escape, Western Australia

Australia's – and the world's – best chefs, food writers and gourmands descend on Margaret River to celebrate the region's fine craft beers, wines and artisan produce. (p32)

For more recommendations and reviews, see **lonelyplanet.com/Australia**

If You Like...

Beaches

Bondi Beach An essential Sydney experience: carve up the surf or simply laze around and people-watch. (p92)

Wineglass Bay It's worth the scramble up and over the saddle to visit this gorgeous goblet of Tasmanian sand. (p663)

Whitehaven Beach The jewel of the Whitsundays in Queensland, with powdery white sand and crystal-clear waters. (p392)

Bells Beach Australia's best-known surf beach is near Torquay on Victoria's Great Ocean Road. (p540)

Hellfire Bay Sand like talcum powder in the middle of Western Australia's Cape Le Grand National Park, which is precisely in the middle of nowhere. (p963)

Carrickalinga Beach Southeast of Adelaide near the McLaren Vale wine region: good fishing, shallow aquamarine swimming and very few people. (p747)

Avalon The most photogenic of Sydney's gorgeous Northern Beaches. (p97)

Crowdy Head Untrammelled gold-sand New South Wales (NSW) beaches set against a backdrop of rugged rock formations. (p160)

Islands

Kangaroo Island A great spot in South Australia (SA) for wildlife-watching and some of Australia's freshest seafood. (p752)

Bruny Island A windswept, sparsely populated retreat south of Hobart, with magical coastal scenery. (p647)

Fraser Island The world's largest sand island has giant sand dunes, freshwater lakes and abundant wildlife. (p347)

Whitsundays Check yourself into a top resort or go sailing around this pristine Queensland archipelago. (p392)

North Stradbroke Island Brisbane's holiday playground, with surf beaches and passing whales. (p312)

Rottnest Island A ferry ride from Fremantle in Western Australia (WA) is this atmospheric atoll with a chequered history. (p932)

Lizard Island A real get-away-from-it-all isle in far north Queensland: splash out on resort perks or rough it with some camping. (p460)

Lady Elliott Island Ringed by the Great Barrier Reef, this remote Queensland island is the place to play castaway. (p362)

Wilderness

Australia is 15 times the size of the UK, with a third of the population: it's no surprise that there are plenty of wild places here.

Blue Mountains National Park The closest true wilderness to Sydney: canyons, cliffs and eucalypt forests. (p136)

Flinders Ranges National Park Treading a line between desolation and beauty, the ancient outcrops of SA's Wilpena Pound are mesmerising. (p793)

Nitmiluk (Katherine Gorge) National Park Tackle the epic five-day Jatbula Trail in this rugged Northern Territory (NT) wilderness, with plenty of cooling swim-spots on the way. (p861)

Cradle Mountain-Lake St Clair National Park Immerse yourself in Tasmania's sometimes forbidding, ever-photogenic landscape. (p701)

IF YOU LIKE...THEME PARKS

Head straight for Queensland's Gold Coast, home to half a dozen massive parks (Dreamworld, Warner Bros Movie World, Wet'n'Wild etc). Tacky, but great fun. (p319)

The Kimberley In northern WA you'll find pounding waterfalls, spectacular gorges, barren peaks and an empty coastline. (p1004)

Daintree Rainforest Explore Far North Queensland's ancient forest with lots of activities and few tourists. (p451)

Sturt National Park Rich in wildlife and deliciously remote, NSW's far northwest is an accessible slice of the outback. (p239)

Luxury Stays

Park Hyatt Sing about the Sydney Opera House views at this swanky harbourside hotel. (p103)

Hayman Island Still the swishest of Queensland's many resort islands. (p394)

Southern Ocean Lodge A remote architectural delight on SA's Kangaroo Island, attracting the fiscally elite. (p760)

Islington Hobart's best boutique bolt-hole is a reinvented 1847 manor. (p637)

Paperbark Camp Luxury tent-style accommodation in Jervis Bay: like a plush African safari in the NSW bush. (p247)

Acacia Chalets Spend your days in the wineries around Margaret River in WA, and your nights here. (p947)

Sails in the Desert Outback opulence at Yulara next to Uluru in the Northern Territory. (p898)

Wine

Australia's wine regions also cultivate a strong foodie culture and sustain some fabulous restaurants.

Barossa Valley Home to Australia's greatest reds, with 80-plus wineries around historic German-settled villages, in SA. (p774)

(Above) Art Gallery of South Australia (p717)
(Below) Hayman Island (p394)

McLaren Vale An hour south of Adelaide, this is Mediterranean-feeling shiraz heaven. (p744)

Tamar Valley One of Tasmania's key cool-climate wine areas, a short hop from Launceston. (p677)

Clare Valley SA's Clare Valley makes riesling that rocks – enough said. (p779)

Yarra Valley An hour from Melbourne is the place for syrupy whites and complex cabernets. (p526)

Hunter Valley Dating back to the 1820s, the Hunter Valley is Australia's oldest wine region – super semillon. (p143)

Pubs & Live Music

Northcote Social Club One of Melbourne's best live-music spots, with a buzzing front bar and a big deck out the back. (p517)

Venue 505 Sydney's best little jazz bar features top-notch performers in an edgy underground space. (p127)

Governor Hindmarsh Hotel A sprawling old Adelaide rocker with decent pub grub and all kinds of live tunes. (p736)

Knopwood's Retreat There's no sight more welcoming than the fire in 'Knoppie's' grate on a chilly Hobart evening. (p640)

Sail & Anchor A Fremantle pub sporting the tag line, 'In fermentation, there is truth'. (p931)

Corner Hotel Legendary rock room in Richmond, Melbourne. (p517)

Breakfast Creek Hotel So enduringly popular this Brisbane hotel is almost kitsch. (p305)

IF YOU LIKE...CLIMBING BRIDGES

Both Sydney (p71) and Brisbane (p291) offer bridge climbs – a magnificent way to see these cities from an eagle's-nest height.

Palace Hotel An extravagantly muralled old Broken Hill pub enjoying a revival. (p237)

Art Galleries

National Gallery of Australia This superb Canberra museum houses 7500-plus works by Aboriginal and Torres Strait Islander artists. (p259)

Museum of Old & New Art (MONA) Australia's newest and most thematically challenging fine-art gallery is the talk of Hobart town. (p631)

National Gallery of Victoria International home to travelling exhibitions par excellence (Monet, Dali, Caravaggio): queue up with the rest of Melbourne to get in. (p483)

Art Gallery of NSW This old-stager keeps things hip with ever-changing exhibitions, including the always-controversial Archibald Prize for portraiture. (p77)

Art Gallery of South Australia On Adelaide's North Tce, this art house does things with progressive style. (p717)

Ballarat Art Gallery Australia's oldest and largest regional gallery, crammed with works by noted Australian artists. (p571)

Museum & Art Gallery of the Northern Territory Darwin's classy art gallery is packed full of superb indigenous art. (p816)

Pro Hart Gallery In Broken Hill NSW there is a collection of works by this miner-turned-world-renowned painter. (p235)

Indigenous Culture

Kakadu National Park Extraordinary rock-art galleries dapple the cliffs at Nourlangie and Ubirr in the NT. (p841)

Koorie Heritage Trust In Melbourne: a great place to discover southeastern Aboriginal culture, with tours, and contemporary and traditional art. (p482)

Kuku-Yalanji Dreamtime Walks Guided walks through Mossman Gorge in Queensland with indigenous guides. (p451)

Uluru-Kata Tjuta Cultural Centre Understand local Aboriginal law, custom and religion on Uluru's doorstep. (p895)

Bookabee Tours Indigenous-run tours of Adelaide and the Flinders Ranges in SA. (p724)

Booderee National Park Award-winning tourism activities, gardens and walking trails overseen by the land's traditional owners in NSW. (p247)

Ingan Tours Entirely Aboriginal-owned and Aboriginal-run rainforest tours in tropical north Queensland. (p409)

Carnarvon Gorge Get a close-up view of stunning rock art inside these twisted gorges in Queensland. (p372)

Dampier Peninsula Interact with remote WA communities and learn how to spear fish and catch mudcrabs. (p1014)

Mungo National Park (p232)

Outback Adventure

Getting from A to B in Australia's outback can be a big adventure. If you hire a 4WD, be well prepared or take a tour with a well-informed guide.

4WD to Cape York One of the country's great wilderness adventures is the off-road journey to mainland Australia's northern tip: take a tour or go it alone. (p464)

The Red Centre Explore Uluru and Kata Tjuta in Australia's desert heart on a tour from Alice Springs. (p887)

Karijini National Park Scramble, abseil, slide and dive through gorges on an adventure tour in this remote WA park. (p1000)

Oodnadatta Track Tackle this historic former rail route in SA, passing Lake Eyre (Kati Thanda), remote pubs and plenty of emus and lizards. (p805)

Nullarbor Plain The ultimate outback road trip: 2700km from Adelaide to Perth across the long, wide, empty Nullarbor Plain. (p964)

Mungo National Park A wonderful outback destination in NSW, with amazing land formations, wildlife and Aboriginal cultural tours. (p232)

Arnhem Land Take a day tour of remote Arnhem Land from Jabiru in Kakadu National Park, NT. (p841)

Purnululu National Park Wander through these ancient eroded beehive domes in WA. (p1023)

Month by Month

TOP EVENTS

Adelaide Fringe, February

Sydney Gay & Lesbian Mardi Gras, March

Melbourne International Film Festival, July

Tropfest, February

AFL Grand Final, September

January

January yawns into action as Australia recovers from its Christmas hangover, but then everyone realises: 'Hey, this is summer!'. The festival season kicks in with sun-stroked outdoor music festivals; Melbourne hosts the Australian Open tennis.

Sydney Festival

(www.sydneyfestival.org.au) 'It's big' says the promo material. Indeed, sprawling over three summer weeks, this fab affiliation of music, dance, talks, theatre and visual arts – much of it free and family-focussed – is an artistic behemoth.

Big Day Out

(www.bigdayout.com) This touring one-day alt-rock festival visits Sydney, Melbourne, Adelaide, Perth and the Gold Coast. It features a huge line-up of big-name international artists (previously Metallica, The Killers and Red Hot Chilli Peppers have appeared) and plenty of home-grown talent. Think moshing, sun and beer.

MONA FOMA

(www.mofo.net.au) Brian Ritchie, bass player with the Violent Femmes, pulls the curatorial strings as MONA's adventurous spirit inspires an annual celebration of eclectic and exciting art, music and culture in Hobart. Launched in June 2013, Dark MOFO is the festival's moody winter sibling.

Tamworth Country Music Festival

(www.tamworthcountrymusicfestival.com.au) This late-January hoedown in northern New South Wales is all about big hats, golden guitars and some of the finest country music you'll hear this side of Nashville, Tennessee (mostly Australian acts, with a few world-class internationals).

Australia Day

(www.australia-day.com) Australia's 'birthday' (when the First Fleet landed in 1788) is 26 January, and Australians celebrate with picnics, barbecues, fireworks and, increasingly, nationalistic flag-waving, drunkenness and chest-beating. In less mood to celebrate are the Indigenous Australians, who refer to it as Invasion Day or Survival Day.

February

February is usually Australia's warmest month: hot and sticky up north as the wet season continues, but divine in Tasmania and Victoria. Everywhere else, locals go back to work, to the beach or to the cricket.

Tropfest

(www.tropfest.com.au) The world's largest short-film festival happens on Sydney's grassy Domain one Sunday in late February. To discourage cheating and inspire creativity, a compulsory prop appears in each entry (eg kiss, sneeze, balloon). Free screenings and celeb judges (Joseph Fiennes, Salma Hayek).

Adelaide Fringe

(www.adelaidefringe.com.au) All the acts that don't make the cut (or don't want to) for the more highbrow Adelaide Festival end up in the month-long Fringe, second only to Edinburgh's version. Hyperactive comedy, music and circus acts spill from the Garden of Unearthly Delights in the parklands.

March

March is harvest time in Australia's vineyards and in recent years it has been just as hot as January and February, despite its autumnal status. Melbourne's streets jam up with the Formula One Grand Prix.

Sydney Gay & Lesbian Mardi Gras

(www.mardigras.org.au) A month-long arts festival culminating in a flamboyant parade along Sydney's Oxford St on the first Saturday in March attracts 300,000 spectators. Gyms empty out, solariums darken, waxing emporiums tally their profits. After-party tickets are gold.

WOMADelaide

(www.womadelaide.com.au) Annual festival of world music, arts, food and dance, held over four days in Adelaide's luscious Botanic Park, attracting crowds from around Australia. Eight stages host hundreds of acts. It's very family friendly and you can get a cold beer too.

April

Melbourne and the Adelaide Hills are atmospheric as European trees turn golden then maroon. Up north the rain is abating and the desert temperatures are becoming manageable. Easter means pricey accommodation everywhere.

Apollo Bay Music Festival

(www.apollobaymusicfestival.com) On the gorgeous Great Ocean Road southwest of Melbourne (just far enough to make it an overnighter), this alt-pop, left-field fest spreads itself out along the foreshore. The town's churches, halls, and cafes become performance venues.

May

The dry season begins in the Northern Territory, northern Western Australia and Far North Queensland: relief from humidity. A great time to visit Uluru (Ayers Rock), before the tour buses arrive in droves.

Ord Valley Muster

(www.ordvalleymuster.com) For two weeks every May, Kununurra (far-north WA) hits overdrive during the annual Ord Valley Muster, a collection of sporting, charity and cultural events leading up to a large outdoor concert under the full moon on the banks of the Ord River.

Whale Watching

Between May and October along the southeastern Australian coast, migrating southern right and humpback whales come close to shore to feed, breed and calf. See them at Hervey Bay (Queensland), Warrnambool (Victoria), Victor Harbor (South Australia), Albany (WA) and North Stradbroke Island (Queensland).

June

Winter begins: snow falls across the Southern Alps ski resorts and football season fills grandstands across the country. Peak season in the tropical north: waterfalls and outback tracks are reasonable (accommodation prices less so).

Noosa Long Weekend Festival

(www.noosalongweekend.com) Noosa – that affluent little beach enclave on Queensland's Sunshine Coast – can get a bit self-centred and serious at times. This 10-day festival gives people a chance to get arty: food, music, dance, readings and workshops.

Laura Aboriginal Dance Festival

(www.lauradancefestival.com) Sleepy Laura, 330km north of Cairns on the Cape York Peninsula in Far North Queensland, hosts the largest traditional Indigenous gathering in Australia. Communities from the region come together for dance, song and ceremony. The Laura Races and Rodeo happen the following weekend.

Ski Season

(www.ski.com.au) When winter blows in, snow bunnies and powder hounds dust off their skis and snowboards and make for the mountains. Victoria and NSW have the key resorts; there are a couple of small runs in Tasmania too.

July

Pubs with open fires, cosy coffee shops and empty beaches down south; packed markets, tours and accommodation up north. Bring warm clothes for anywhere south of Alice Springs. Don't miss 'MIFF'.

Melbourne International Film Festival

(MIFF; www.miff.com.au) Right up there with Toronto and Cannes, MIFF has been running since 1952 and has grown into a wildly popular event; tickets sell like piping-hot chestnuts in the inner city. Myriad short films, feature-length spectaculars and documentaries flicker across city screens every winter.

Beer Can Regatta

(www.beercanregatta.org.au) The NT festival calender is studded with quirky gems like this one at Darwin's Mindil Beach, where hundreds of 'boats' constructed from empty beer cans race across the shallows. Much drinking and laughter: staying afloat is a secondary concern.

August

August is when southerners, sick of winter's grey-sky drear, head to Queensland for some sun. Last chance to head to the tropical Top End and outback before things get too hot and wet.

Cairns Festival

(www.cairns.qld.gov.au/festival) Running for three weeks from late August to early September, this massive art-and-culture fest brings a stellar program of music, theatre, dance, comedy, film, indigenous art and public exhibitions. Outdoor events held in public plazas, parks and gardens make good use of Cairns' tropical setting.

September

Spring heralds a rampant bloom of wildflowers across outback WA and SA and flower festivals happen in places such as Canberra. Football finishes and the spring horse-racing carnival begins.

Brisbane Festival

(www.brisbanefestival.com.au) One of Australia's largest and most diverse arts festivals (p296) runs for 22 days in September and features an impressive line-up of concerts, plays, dance performances and fringe events around the city. It finishes off with 'Riverfire', an elaborate fireworks show over the river.

AFL Grand Final

(www.afl.com.au) The pinnacle of the Australian Rules football season is this high-flying spectacle in Melbourne, watched (on TV) by millions of impassioned Aussies. Tickets to the game are scarce, but at half-time everyone's neighbourhood BBQ moves into the local park for a little amateur kick-to-kick.

October

The weather avoids extremes everywhere: a good time to go camping or to hang out at some vineyards (It's a dirty job, but someone has to do it...). After the football and before the cricket, sports fans twiddle their thumbs.

Jazz in the Vines

(www.jazzinthevines.com.au) There are lots of food-and-wine festivals like this across Australia's wine regions (Barossa, McLaren Vale, Yarra Valley...). The Hunter Valley's proximity to the Sydney jazz scene ensures a top line-up at Tyrrell's Vineyard.

November

Northern beaches may close due to 'stingers' – jellyfish in the shallow waters off north Queensland, the NT and WA. Outdoor events ramp up; the surf life-saving season flexes its muscles on beaches everywhere.

Melbourne Cup

(www.melbournecup.com) On the first Tuesday in November, Australia's (if not the world's) premier horse race chews up the turf in Melbourne. Country towns schedule racing events to coincide with the day and the country does actually pause to watch the 'race that stops a nation'.

Margaret River Gourmet Escape

(www.gourmetescape.com.au) Western Australia's contribution to the national circuit of fine food-and-wine fests. The line-up of celebrity chefs is impressive: dozens of culinary doyens plating up seriously good food. But it's the Margaret River wines that really steal the show.

Sculpture by the Sea

(www.sculpturebythesea.com) In mid-November the clifftop trail from Bondi Beach to Tamarama in Sydney transforms into an exquisite sculpture garden. Serious prize money is on offer for the most creative, curious or quizzical offerings from international and local sculptors. Also happens on Perth's Cottesloe Beach in March.

Wangaratta Jazz & Blues

(www.wangarattajazz.com) Wangaratta – population 17,000, in rural northeast Victoria – fills up with groovy, finger-snappin' beboppers for this esteemed annual jazz and blues fest.

December

Ring the bell, school's out! Holidays begin two weeks before Christmas. Cities are packed with shoppers and the weather is desirably hot. Up north, monsoon season is underway: afternoon thunderstorms bring pelting rain.

Sydney to Hobart Yacht Race

(www.rolexsydneyhobart.com) On Boxing Day (26 December), Sydney Harbour churns with competitors and onlookers for the start of the world's most arduous open-ocean yacht race (628 nautical miles!). When the yachties hit Hobart a few days later, this small city celebrates with feasting, drinking and dancing sea-legs (see p627).

Itineraries

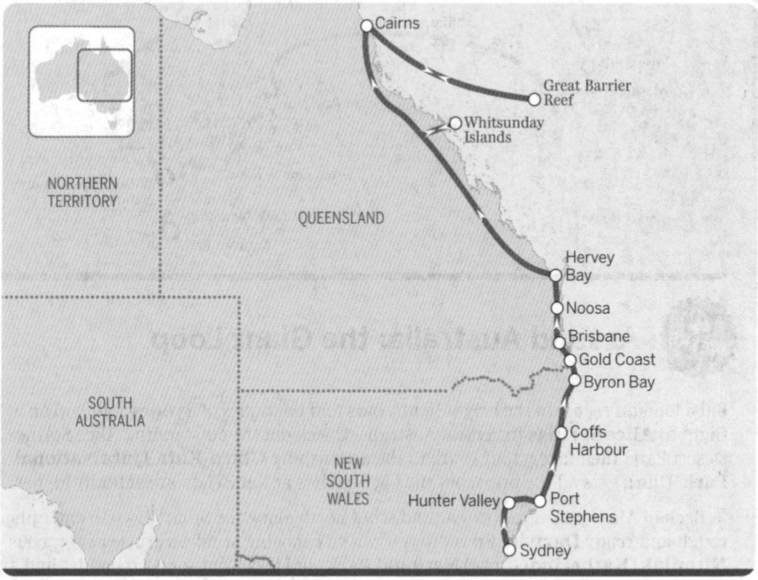

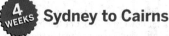

4 WEEKS Sydney to Cairns

Hugging the east coast between Sydney and Cairns for 2864km, this is the most well-trodden path in Australia. You could do it in two weeks, but why not take four and really chill out.

Start with a few days immersed in the bright lights and glitz of **Sydney**, then meander north along the Pacific Hwy through central and northern New South Wales (NSW). Hang out in the **Hunter Valley** for some fine vino-quaffing, and stop to splash in the sea at family-friendly **Port Stephens** and **Coffs Harbour**, home of the iconic/kitsch 'Big Banana'). Skip up to **Byron Bay** for New Age awakenings and superb beaches, then head over the Queensland border to the party-prone, surf-addled **Gold Coast**. Pause in hip **Brisbane** then amble up to affluent **Noosa** on the glorious Sunshine Coast.

The Bruce Hwy traces the stunning coast into Far North Queensland. Spot some passing whales off the coast of **Hervey Bay** and track further north to the blissful **Whitsunday Islands**, the coral charms of the **Great Barrier Reef** and the scuba-diving nexus of **Cairns**.

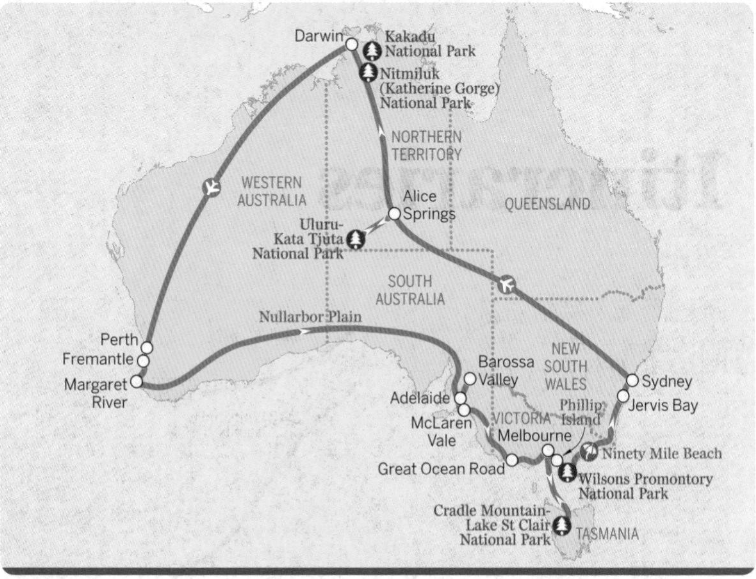

4 WEEKS Around Australia: the Giant Loop

Bid a fond *au revoir* to the bright lights, bars and boutiques of **Sydney** and hop on a flight to **Alice Springs** in central Australia. Check out the outstanding Alice Springs Desert Park, then take a tour south to the astonishing **Uluru-Kata Tjuta National Park**. Uluru gets all the press, but the big boulders at Kata Tjuta are actually higher.

Back in Alice, pick up a hire car and scoot north along the Stuart Hwy to emerging, rough-and-ready **Darwin**. En route you can go canoeing or take a cruise at gorgeous **Nitmiluk (Katherine Gorge) National Park**, and check out some crocodiles and ancient Aboriginal rock-art galleries at **Kakadu National Park**.

From Darwin, hop on a flight to **Perth** – a confident city that sets its own agenda – and the soulful old port town of **Fremantle**, not far down the road. Continuing south, wine away some hours around **Margaret River** until you're ready to tackle the flat immensity of the **Nullarbor Plain** – if you're not up for the epic drive to festival-frenzied **Adelaide**, the *Indian Pacific* train ride is unforgettable.

Check out the world-class wine regions around Adelaide (the **Barossa Valley** and **McLaren Vale** are both just an hour away), or traverse the impossibly scenic **Great Ocean Road** to sports-mad **Melbourne**. Don't miss a game of Australian Rules football or cricket at the cauldron-like Melbourne Cricket Ground.

If you have a few extra days, take the car ferry across to **Tasmania** – as 'English' as Australia gets. Australia's divine island state preserves some of the country's oldest forests and World Heritage–listed mountain ranges: **Cradle Mountain–Lake St Clair National Park** is accessible and absolutely beautiful.

From Melbourne, continue along the Victorian coast to the penguins and koalas on **Phillip Island** and white-sand seclusion of **Wilsons Promontory National Park**. Spend a couple of days somewhere along **Ninety Mile Beach** then cruise up the southern NSW coast to idyllic **Jervis Bay** (spot any whales?). Back in **Sydney**, there are so many beaches you're sure to find a patch of sand with your name on it.

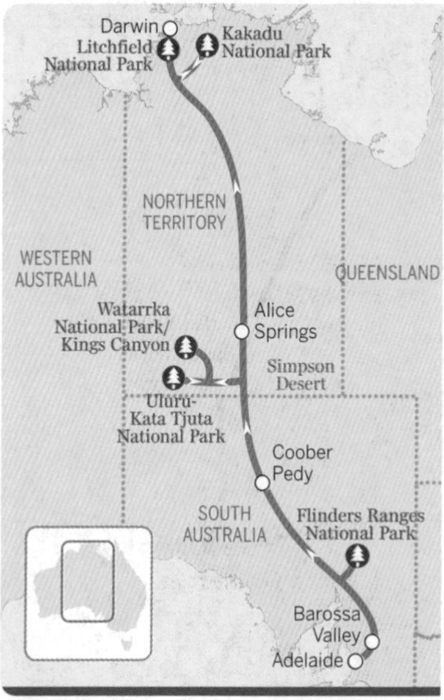

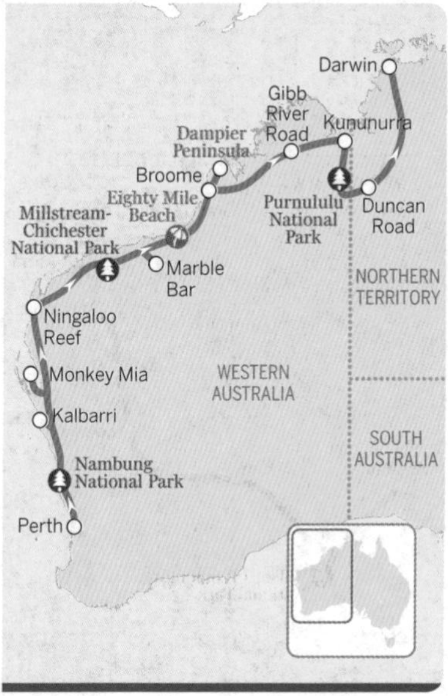

2 WEEKS Adelaide to Darwin

This classic 3000km dash up the Stuart Hwy takes you into Australia's desert heart.

From the eat-streets and old stone pubs of **Adelaide**, head north to the **Barossa Valley** for world-class red wines. Next stop is rust-coloured **Flinders Ranges National Park**, with Ikara (Wilpena Pound) jagging up from the semidesert.

Just off the Stuart Hwy are the opal-tinted dugouts of **Coober Pedy**. Continuing north into the Simpson Desert, the Lasseter Hwy delivers you to iconic **Uluru-Kata Tjuta National Park**. The desert chasm of **Watarrka (Kings Canyon) National Park** is 300km further north.

Overnight in the desert oasis of **Alice Springs**, then continue north to the waterfalls and swimming holes of **Litchfield National Park** and the wetlands and rock-scapes of World Heritage–listed **Kakadu National Park**.

Gone are the days when **Darwin** was just a redneck frontier town: now the city is multicultural, as a visit to the Mindil Beach Sunset Market will confirm. Don't miss the Deckchair Cinema and Museum & Art Gallery of the Northern Territory.

3 WEEKS Perth, the Pilbara & the Kimberley

Feeling adventurous? Purge your urban urges in progressive **Perth**, then steer your 4WD north into Western Australia's remote Pilbara and Kimberley regions.

First stop is the otherworldly **Nambung National Park**, followed by **Kalbarri** with its gorges and seacliffs. Meet dolphins at **Monkey Mia**, then hug the coast for superb snorkelling on **Ningaloo Reef**.

Inland are the red-iron hues of the Pilbara. Cool-off at **Millstream-Chichester National Park** then down a beer at **Marble Bar**, Australia's hottest town, before watching turtles at **Eighty Mile Beach**.

The Big Empty stretches north to **Broome**, a multicultural town with ritzy resorts along Cable Beach. Nearby **Dampier Peninsula** beckons with pristine beaches and laid-back camping. From here, veer east into the rough heart of the Kimberley and tackle the legendary **Gibb River Road**.

Restock in **Kununurra** before tracking south to the sandstone domes of **Purnululu National Park**. Take the exquisitely lonely **Duncan Road** into the Northern Territory: once you hit the asphalt, party-town **Darwin** isn't far away.

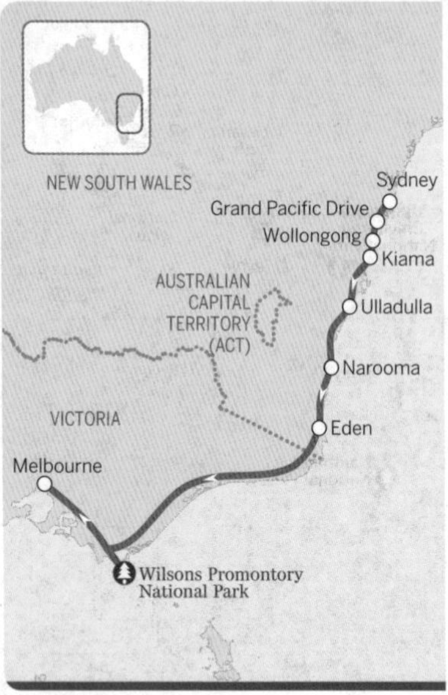

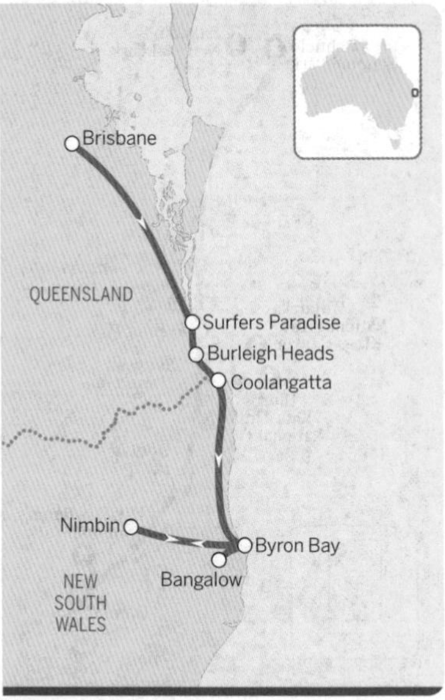

10 DAYS Sydney to Melbourne

Most people fly into Sydney, Australia's biggest city, but just under 1000km south is Melbourne, Sydney's arty rival.

Check out **Sydney** from its sparkling harbour: the gorgeous Sydney Opera House and colossal Sydney Harbour Bridge are unmissable. For a bird's-eye view, tackle the Bridge Climb over the great grey arch. Feel like a swim? The backpackers, beach breaks and bikinis make Bondi Beach a quintessential Australian experience.

Heading south, zip along the elevated **Grand Pacific Drive,** through **Wollongong** to the lovely coastal town of **Kiama**. Nearby, the Illawarra Fly Tree Top Walk jags through the rainforest canopy.

Continuing south, meander through **Ulladulla**, **Narooma** and the aptly named **Eden** near the Victorian border. The road from here to Melbourne is low-key: spice things up with bushwalks and beaches at **Wilsons Promontory National Park**.

Melbourne is a burgeoning bayside city famous for the arts, Australian Rules football and coffee. Wander the laneways, mooch around the galleries, grab a pub dinner and catch a live band.

1 WEEK Brisbane to Byron Bay

Strap a surfboard to the roof rack and cruise into your very own *Endless Summer*: this stretch of Australia's east coast is famous for its surf.

Once a sleepy river town, **Brisbane** is booming, growing so fast that it can be difficult to navigate. Its urban charms (great restaurants, arts scene, coffee and bars) meld seamlessly with the natural environment (cliffs, parklands and the serpentine Brisbane River).

Heading south to the Gold Coast, the cityscape of **Surfers Paradise** appears on the horizon. There are as many apartment towers here as shades of fake tan: check it out if you like casinos, theme parks and boozy backpackers. More low-key are the surfie town of **Burleigh Heads** and the surf life-saving mecca **Coolangatta**.

Despite big summer crowds and big development money, **Byron Bay** in northern NSW remains a happy hippie town with great pubs, restaurants, beaches and the famous Pass point break. Don't miss inland day-trips to pretty **Bangalow** and Australia's almost mythical alternative-lifestyle hangout, **Nimbin**.

Plan Your Trip

Your Reef Trip

The Great Barrier Reef, stretching over 2000km from just south of the Tropic of Capricorn (near Gladstone) to just south of Papua New Guinea, is the most extensive reef system in the world, and made entirely by living organisms. There are numerous ways to see the magnificent spectacle of the Reef. Diving and snorkelling are the best methods of getting up close and personal with the menagerie of marine life and dazzling corals. You can also surround yourself with fabulous tropical fish without getting wet on a semi-submersible or glass-bottomed boat, which provide windows to the underwater world below.

When to Go

High season is from June to December. The best overall visibility is from August to January.

From December to March northern Queensland (north of Townsville) has the wet season, bringing oppressive heat and abundant rainfall; from July to September it's drier and cooler.

Anytime is generally good to visit the Whitsundays. Winter (June to August) can be pleasantly warm, but you will occasionally need a jumper. South of the Whitsundays, summer (December to March) is hot and humid.

Southern and central Queensland experience mild winters – pleasant enough for diving or snorkelling in a wetsuit.

Picking Your Spot

There are many popular and remarkable spots from which to access the Reef but bear in mind that individual areas change over time, depending on the weather or any recent damage.

Best Wildlife Experiences

Sea turtles hatching on Lady Elliot Island or Heron Island; looking out for reef sharks, turtles and rays while kayaking off Green Island; spotting koalas on Magnetic Island; and Fraser Island wildlife.

Best Snorkelling Experiences

Head to Knuckle, Hardy and Fitzroy Reefs, Magnetic Island or the Whitsunday Islands.

Best Views from Above

Scenic chopper or plane ride from Cairns, Hamilton and the Whitsunday Islands. Skydiving over Airlie Beach.

Best Sailing Experiences

Sailing from Airlie Beach through the Whitsunday Islands; exploring Agincourt Reef from Port Douglas.

Useful Websites

Dive Queensland (www.divequeensland.com.au)

Great Barrier Reef Marine Park Authority (www.gbrmpa.gov.au)

Queensland Department of National Parks (www.nprsr.qld.gov.au)

Mainland Gateways

There are several mainland gateways to the Reef, all offering slightly different experiences or activities. Here's a brief overview, ordered from south to north.

Agnes Water & Town of 1770 are small towns and good choices if you want to escape the crowds. Tours head to Fitzroy Reef Lagoon, one of the most pristine sections of the Reef, where visitor numbers are still limited. The lagoon is excellent for snorkelling but also spectacular viewed from the boat.

Gladstone is a slightly bigger town but still a relatively small gateway. It's an exceptional choice for avid divers and snorkellers, being the closest access point to the southern or Capricorn reef islands and innumerable cays, including Lady Elliot Island.

Airlie Beach is a small town with a full rack of sailing outfits. The big attraction here is spending two or more days aboard a boat and seeing some of the Whitsunday Islands' fringing coral reefs. Whether you're a five- or no-star traveller, there'll be a tour to match your budget.

Townsville is a renowned gateway among divers. A four- or five-night live-aboard around the numerous islands and pockets of the Reef is a great choice. In particular, Kelso Reef and the wreck of the SS *Yongala* are teeming with marine life. There are also a couple of day-trip options on glass-bottomed boats. **Reef HQ**, which is basically a version of the Reef in an aquarium, is also here.

Mission Beach is closer to the Reef than any other gateway destination. This small, quiet town offers a few boat and diving tours to sections of the outer reef. Although the choice isn't huge, neither are the crowds.

Cairns is the main launching pad for Reef tours with a bewildering number of operators offering relatively inexpensive day trips on large boats to intimate five-day luxury charters. The variety covers a wide section of the Reef, with some operators going as far north as Lizard Island. Inexpensive tours are likely to travel to inner, less pristine reefs. Scenic flights also operate out of Cairns.

Port Douglas is a swanky resort town and a gateway to the Low Isles and Agincourt Reef, an outer ribbon reef featuring crystal-clear water and stunning corals. Diving, snorkelling and cruising trips tend to be classier, pricier and less crowded than in Cairns. You can also take a scenic flight from here.

Cooktown is close to Lizard Island but the town and its tour operators shut down between November and May for the wet season.

Islands

Speckled throughout the Reef are a profusion of islands and cays that offer some of the most stunning access to the Reef. Here is a list of some of the best islands, travelling from south to north.

For more information on individual islands, take a look at areas around the Whitsunday Coast, Capricorn Coast, Townsville to Mission Beach, Cairns and Port Douglas to Cooktown.

Lady Elliot Island has a coral cay that is awe-inspiring for birdwatchers, with some 57 species living on the island. Sea turtles also nest here and it's possibly the best location on the Reef to see manta rays. It's also a famed diving spot. There's a resort here, but you can also visit Lady Elliot on a day trip from Bundaberg.

Heron Island is a tiny, tranquil coral cay sitting amid a huge spread of reef. It's a diving mecca, but the snorkelling is also good and it's possible to do a reef walk from here. Heron is a nesting ground for green and loggerhead turtles and home to some 30 species of birds. The sole resort on the island charges accordingly.

Hamilton Island, the daddy of the Whitsundays, is a sprawling family-friendly resort laden with infrastructure. While the atmosphere isn't exactly intimate, there is a wealth of tours going to the outer reef. It's also a good place to see patches of the Reef that can't be explored from the mainland.

Hook Island is an outer Whitsunday island surrounded by reefs. There is excellent swimming and snorkelling here, and the island offers good bushwalking. There's affordable accommodation on Hook and it's easily accessed from Airlie Beach, making it a top choice for those on a budget.

Orpheus Island is a national park and one of the Reef's most exclusive, tranquil and romantic hideaways. This island is great for snorkelling – you can step right off the beach and be surrounded by the Reef's colourful marine life. Clusters of fringing reefs also provide plenty of diving opportunities.

Green Island is another of the Reef's true coral cays. The fringing reefs here are considered to be among the most beautiful surrounding any island, and the diving and snorkelling are quite spectacular. Covered in dense rainforest, the entire island is a national park. Bird life is abundant.

Reef Highlights

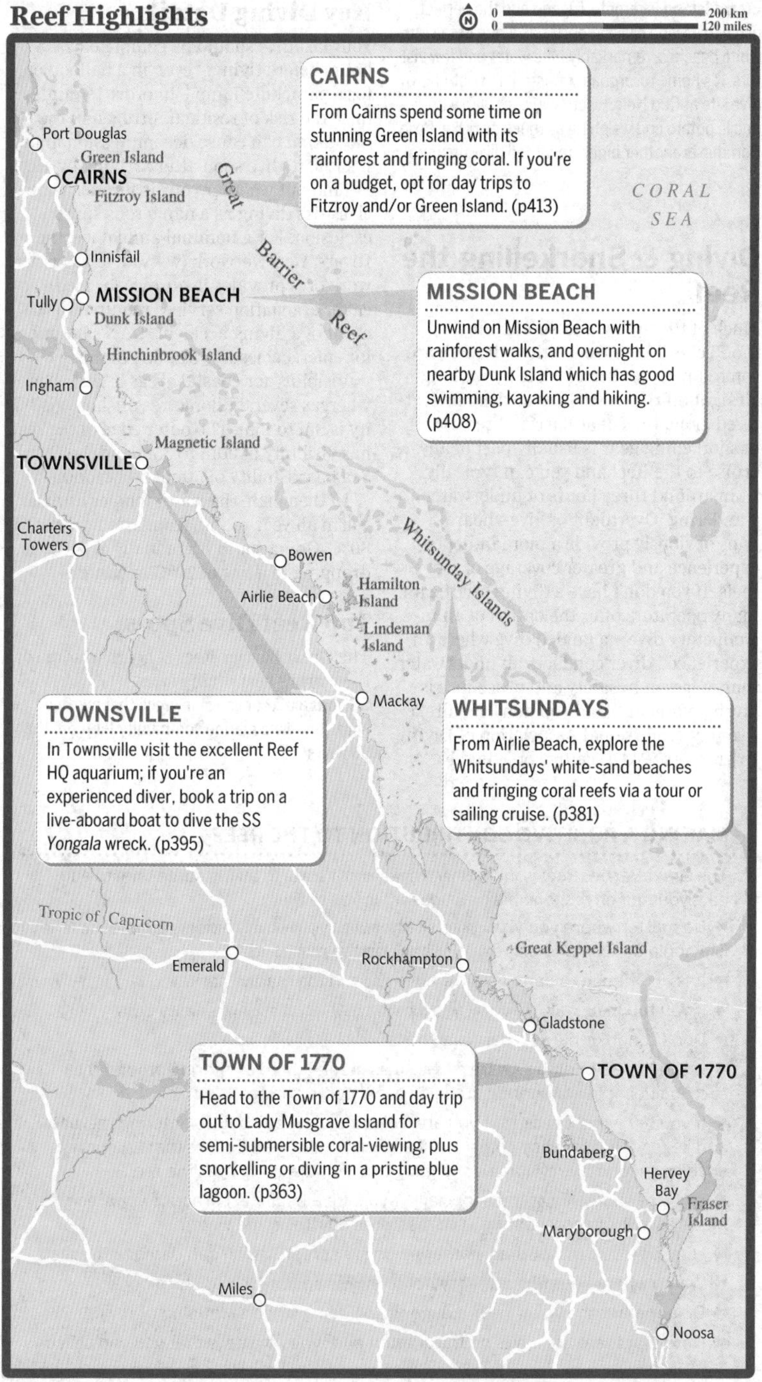
0 200 km
0 120 miles
CAIRNS
From Cairns spend some time on stunning Green Island with its rainforest and fringing coral. If you're on a budget, opt for day trips to Fitzroy and/or Green Island. (p413)
MISSION BEACH
Unwind on Mission Beach with rainforest walks, and overnight on nearby Dunk Island which has good swimming, kayaking and hiking. (p408)
TOWNSVILLE
In Townsville visit the excellent Reef HQ aquarium; if you're an experienced diver, book a trip on a live-aboard boat to dive the SS *Yongala* wreck. (p395)
WHITSUNDAYS
From Airlie Beach, explore the Whitsundays' white-sand beaches and fringing coral reefs via a tour or sailing cruise. (p381)
TOWN OF 1770
Head to the Town of 1770 and day trip out to Lady Musgrave Island for semi-submersible coral-viewing, plus snorkelling or diving in a pristine blue lagoon. (p363)
CORAL SEA
Great Barrier Reef
Whitsunday Islands
Port Douglas
Green Island
CAIRNS
Fitzroy Island
Innisfail
Tully
MISSION BEACH
Dunk Island
Hinchinbrook Island
Ingham
Magnetic Island
TOWNSVILLE
Charters Towers
Bowen
Airlie Beach
Hamilton Island
Lindeman Island
Mackay
Tropic of Capricorn
Emerald
Rockhampton
Great Keppel Island
Gladstone
TOWN OF 1770
Bundaberg
Hervey Bay
Fraser Island
Maryborough
Miles
Noosa

Lizard Island is remote, rugged and the perfect place to escape civilisation. It has a ring of talcum-white beaches, remarkably blue water and few visitors. It's home to, arguably, Australia's best-known dive site at Cod Hole, where you can swim with docile potato cod weighing as much as 60kg. Pixie Bommie is another highly regarded dive site here.

Diving & Snorkelling the Reef

Much of the diving and snorkelling on the Reef is boat-based, although there are some superb reefs accessible by walking straight off the beach of some islands scattered along the Great Barrier. Free use of snorkelling gear is usually part of any cruise to the Reef and you can typically fit in around three hours of underwater wandering. Overnight or 'live-aboard' trips obviously provide a more in-depth experience and greater coverage of the reefs. If you don't have a diving certificate, many operators offer the option of an introductory dive – a guided dive where an experienced diver conducts an underwater tour. A lesson in safety and procedure is given beforehand and you don't require a five-day Professional Association of Diving Instructors (PADI) course or a 'buddy'.

Key Diving Details

Your last dive should be completed 24 hours before flying – even in a balloon or for a parachute jump – in order to minimise the risk of residual nitrogen in the blood that can cause decompression injury. It's fine to dive soon after arriving by air.

Find out whether your insurance policy classifies diving as a dangerous sport exclusion. For a nominal annual fee, the Divers Alert Network (www.diversalertnetwork.org) provides insurance for medical or evacuation services required in the event of a diving accident. DAN's hotline for emergencies is ☎919 684 9111.

Visibility for coastal areas is 1m to 3m whereas several kilometres offshore visibility is 8m to 15m. The outer edge of the reef has visibility of 20m to 35m and the Coral Sea has visibility of 50m and beyond.

In the north, the water temperature is warm all year round, from around 24°C to 30°C. Going south it gradually gets cooler, dropping to a low of 20°C in winter.

Top Reef Dive Spots

The Great Barrier Reef is home to some of the world's best diving sites.

SS Yongala A sunken shipwreck that has been home to a vivid marine community for more than 90 years.

MAKING A POSITIVE CONTRIBUTION TO THE REEF

The Great Barrier Reef is incredibly fragile and it's worth taking some time to educate yourself on responsible practices while you're there.

- No matter where you visit, take all litter with you – even biodegradable material like apple cores – and dispose of it back on the mainland.
- It is an offence to damage or remove coral in the marine park.
- If you touch or walk on coral you'll damage it and get some nasty cuts.
- Don't touch or harass marine animals.
- If you have a boat, be aware of the rules in relation to anchoring around the reef, including 'no anchoring areas' to avoid coral damage.
- If you're diving, check that you are weighted correctly before entering the water and keep your buoyancy control well away from the reef. Ensure that equipment such as secondary regulators and gauges aren't dragging over the reef.
- If you're snorkelling (and especially if you are a beginner) practice your technique away from coral until you've mastered control in the water.
- Hire a wetsuit rather than slathering on sunscreen, which can damage the reef.
- Watch where your fins are – try not to stir up sediment or disturb coral.
- Do not enter the water near a dugong, including when swimming or diving.
- Note that there are limits on the amount and types of shells that you can collect.

TOP SNORKELLING SITES

Some nondivers may wonder if it's really worth going to the Great Barrier Reef 'just to snorkel'. The answer is a resounding yes. Much of the rich, colourful coral lies just underneath the surface (as coral needs bright sunlight to flourish) and is easily accessible. Here's a round-up of the top snorkelling sites:

- Fitzroy Reef Lagoon (Town of 1770)
- Heron Island (Capricorn Coast)
- Great Keppel Island
- Lady Elliot Island (Capricorn Coast)
- Lady Musgrave Island (Capricorn Coast)
- Hook Island (Whitsundays)
- Hayman Island (Whitsundays)
- Lizard Island (Cairns)
- Border Island (Whitsundays)
- Hardy Reef (Whitsundays)
- Knuckle Reef (Whitsundays)
- Michaelmas Reef (Cairns)
- Hastings Reef (Cairns)
- Norman Reef (Cairns)
- Saxon Reef (Cairns)
- Green Island (Cairns)
- Opal Reef (Port Douglas)
- Agincourt Reef (Port Douglas)
- Mackay Reef (Port Douglas)

Cod Hole Go nose-to-nose with a potato cod.
Heron Island Join a crowd of colourful fish straight off the beach.

Lady Elliot Island 19 highly regarded dive sites.

Pixie Bommie, Delve into the after-five world of the Reef by taking a night dive.

Boat Excursions

Unless you're staying on a coral-fringed island in the middle of the Great Barrier Reef, you'll need to join a boat excursion to experience the Reef's real beauty. Day trips leave from many places along the coast, as well as from island resorts, and typically include the use of snorkelling gear, snacks and a buffet lunch, with scuba diving an optional extra. On some boats a marine biologist presents a talk on the Reef's ecology.

Boat trips vary dramatically in passenger numbers, type of vessel and quality – which is reflected in the price – so it's worth getting all the details before committing. When selecting a tour, consider the vessel (motorised catamaran or sailing ship), the number of passengers (from six to 400), what extras are offered and the destination. The outer reefs are usually more pristine. Inner reefs often show signs of damage from humans, coral bleaching and coral-eating crown-of-thorns starfish. Some operators offer the option of a trip in a glass-bottomed boat or semi-submersible.

Many boats have underwater cameras for hire – although you'll save money by hiring these on land (or using your own waterproof camera or underwater housing). Some boats also have professional photographers on board who will dive with you and take high-quality shots of you in action.

Live-Aboards

If you're eager to do as much diving as possible, a live-aboard is an excellent option as you'll do three dives per day, plus some night dives, all in more remote parts of the Great Barrier Reef. Trip lengths vary from one to 12 nights. The three-day/three-night voyages, which allow up to 11 dives, are among the most common.

Check out the various options as some boats offer specialist itineraries following marine life, such as minke whales or coral spawning, or offer trips to remote spots like the far northern reefs, Pompey Complex, Coral Sea Reefs or Swain Reefs.

It's recommended to go with operators who are Dive Queensland members: this ensures they follow a minimum set of guidelines. Ideally, they are also accredited by **Ecotourism Australia** (www.ecotourism.org.au).

Popular departure points for live-aboard dive vessels, along with the locales they visit are:

Bundaberg The Bunker Island group, including Lady Musgrave and Lady Elliot Islands, possibly Fitzroy, Llewellyn and rarely visited Boult Reefs or Hoskyn and Fairfax Islands.

1770 Bunker Island group.

Gladstone Swain and Bunker Island groups.

Mackay Lihou Reef and the Coral Sea.

Airlie Beach The Whitsundays, Knuckle Reef and Hardy Reef.

Townsville *Yongala* wreck, plus canyons of Wheeler Reef and Keeper Reef.

Cairns Cod Hole, Ribbon Reefs, the Coral Sea and the far northern reefs.

Port Douglas Osprey Reef, Cod Hole, Ribbon Reefs, Coral Sea and the far northern reefs.

Dive Courses

In Queensland there are numerous places where you can learn to dive, take a refresher course or improve your skills. Dive courses are generally of a high standard, and all schools teach either PADI or Scuba Schools International (SSI) qualifications. Which certification you choose isn't as important as choosing a good instructor, so be sure to seek local recommendations and meet with the instructor before committing to a program.

A popular place to learn is Cairns, where you can choose between courses for the budget-minded (four-day courses from around $490) that combine pool training and reef dives, to more intensive courses that include reef diving on a live-aboard (five-day courses including three-day/two-night live-aboard start from $700).

Other places where you can learn to dive, and then head out on the Reef include Airlie Beach, Bundaberg, Hamilton Island, Magnetic Island, Mission Beach, Port Douglas and Townsville.

Camping on the Great Barrier Reef

Pitching a tent on an island is a unique and affordable way to experience the Great Barrier Reef. Campers enjoy an idyllic tropical setting at a fraction of the price of the five-star island resort that may be located down the road from the camp ground. Camp site facilities range from virtually nothing to showers, flush toilets, interpretive signage and picnic tables. Most islands are remote, so ensure you are adequately prepared for medical and general emergencies.

Wherever you stay, you'll need to be self-sufficient, bringing your own food and water (5L per day per person). Weather can often prevent planned pick ups, so have enough supplies to last an extra four days in case you get stranded.

Camp only in designated areas, keep to marked trails and take out all that you brought in. Fires are banned so you'll need a gas stove or similar.

National park camping permits need to be booked in advance online through Queensland Department of National Parks (www.nprsr.qld.gov.au). Our top picks:

Whitsunday Islands Nearly a dozen beautifully sited camping areas, scattered on the islands of Hook, Whitsunday and Henning.

Capricornia Cays Camping available on three separate coral cays including Masthead Island, North West Island and Lady Musgrave Island – a fantastic, uninhabited island that's limited to a maximum of 40 campers.

Dunk Island Equal parts resort and national park with good swimming, kayaking and hiking.

Fitzroy Island Resort and national park with short walking trails through bush and coral just off the beaches.

Frankland Islands Coral-fringed island with white-sand beaches off Cairns.

Lizard Island Stunning beaches, magnificent coral and abundant wildlife, but visitors mostly arrive by plane.

Orpheus Island Secluded island (accessible by air) with pretty tropical forest and superb fringing reef.

Plan Your Trip

Your Outback Trip

Australia's outback starts somewhere 'beyond the black stump'. Exactly where that is, is a little hard to pin down on a map. But you'll know you are there when the sky yawns enormously wide, the horizon is unnervingly empty, and the sparse inhabitants you encounter are incomparably resilient and distinctively Australian. Globalised sameness is yet to fully infiltrate the outback and so the enduring indigenous culture, unique wildlife and intriguing landscape awaits the modern day adventurer.

About the Outback

The Australian outback is a vast, imprecise region extending out from the centre of the continent. While most Australians live on the coast, that thin green fringe of the continent is hardly typical of this enormous land mass. Inland is the desert soul of Australia.

Weather patterns vary from region to region – from sandy arid deserts to semi-arid scrublands to tropical savannah – but you can generally rely on hot sunny days, starry night skies and mile after mile of unbroken horizon.

When to Go

Best Times

June through August is when southeastern Australia (where most of the population lives) is sniffling through rainy, cloudy winter days, the outback comes into its own. Rain isn't unheard of in central Australia – in fact there's been a hell of a lot of it in recent years – but clear skies, moderate daytime temperatures, cold nights and good driving conditions are the norm.

September and October is spring and is also a prime time to head into the outback, especially if you're into wildflowers. The MacDonnell Ranges near Alice Springs and the Flinders Ranges in northern South

The Best...

Season

Winter (June to August) Mild days, cool nights and low humidity.

Things to Pack

Sunscreen, sunglasses, a hat, insect repellent, plenty of water and some good tunes for the car stereo.

Outback Track

Oodnadatta Track (p805) 620km of red dust, emus, lizards, salt lakes and historic railroad remnants.

Indigenous Culture

Kakadu National Park (p841) Head into the tropical Top End wilderness for ancient rock art and cultural tours run by indigenous guides.

Outback National Park

Uluru-Kata Tjuta National Park (p891) Iconic Uluru (Ayres Rock) is simply unmissable, while nearby Kata Tjuta is less well known but just as impressive.

Outback Tracks: Off the Beaten Road

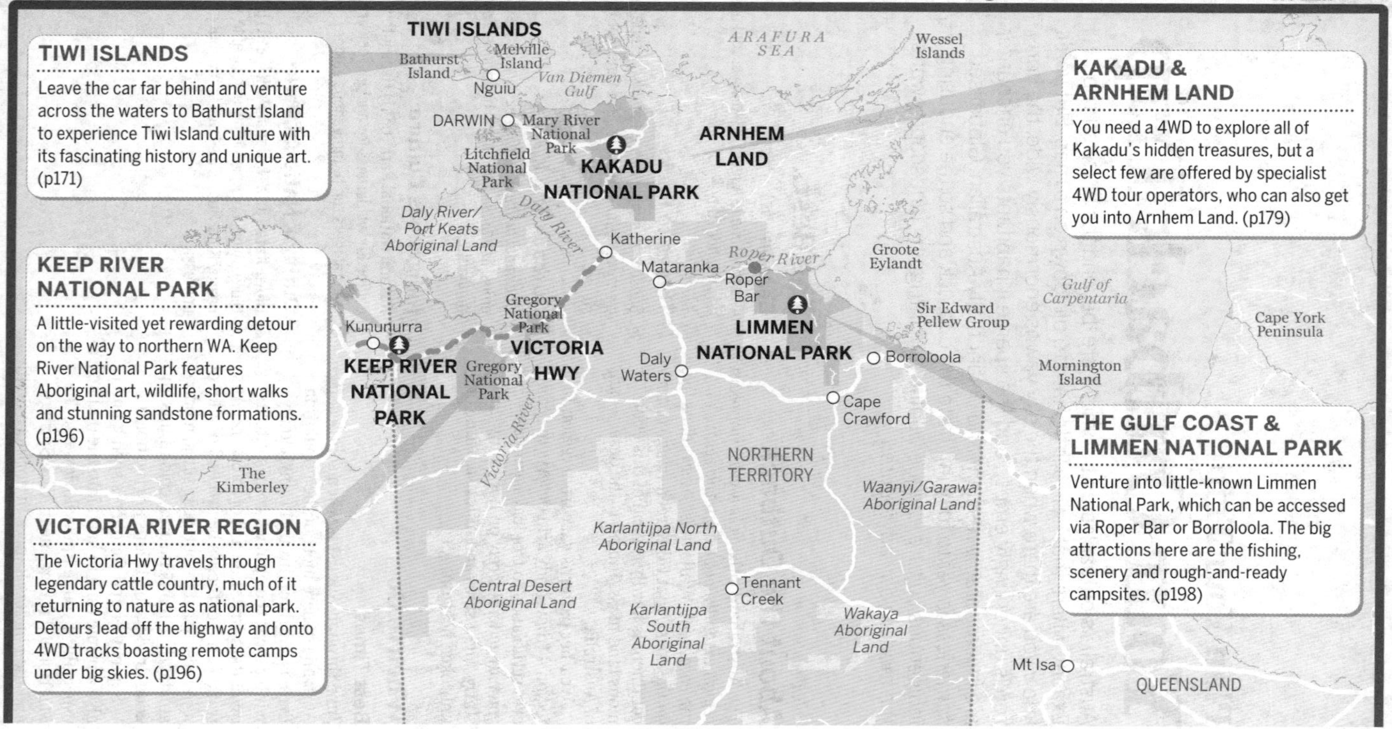

TIWI ISLANDS

Leave the car far behind and venture across the waters to Bathurst Island to experience Tiwi Island culture with its fascinating history and unique art. (p171)

KEEP RIVER NATIONAL PARK

A little-visited yet rewarding detour on the way to northern WA. Keep River National Park features Aboriginal art, wildlife, short walks and stunning sandstone formations. (p196)

VICTORIA RIVER REGION

The Victoria Hwy travels through legendary cattle country, much of it returning to nature as national park. Detours lead off the highway and onto 4WD tracks boasting remote camps under big skies. (p196)

KAKADU & ARNHEM LAND

You need a 4WD to explore all of Kakadu's hidden treasures, but a select few are offered by specialist 4WD tour operators, who can also get you into Arnhem Land. (p179)

THE GULF COAST & LIMMEN NATIONAL PARK

Venture into little-known Limmen National Park, which can be accessed via Roper Bar or Borroloola. The big attractions here are the fishing, scenery and rough-and-ready campsites. (p198)

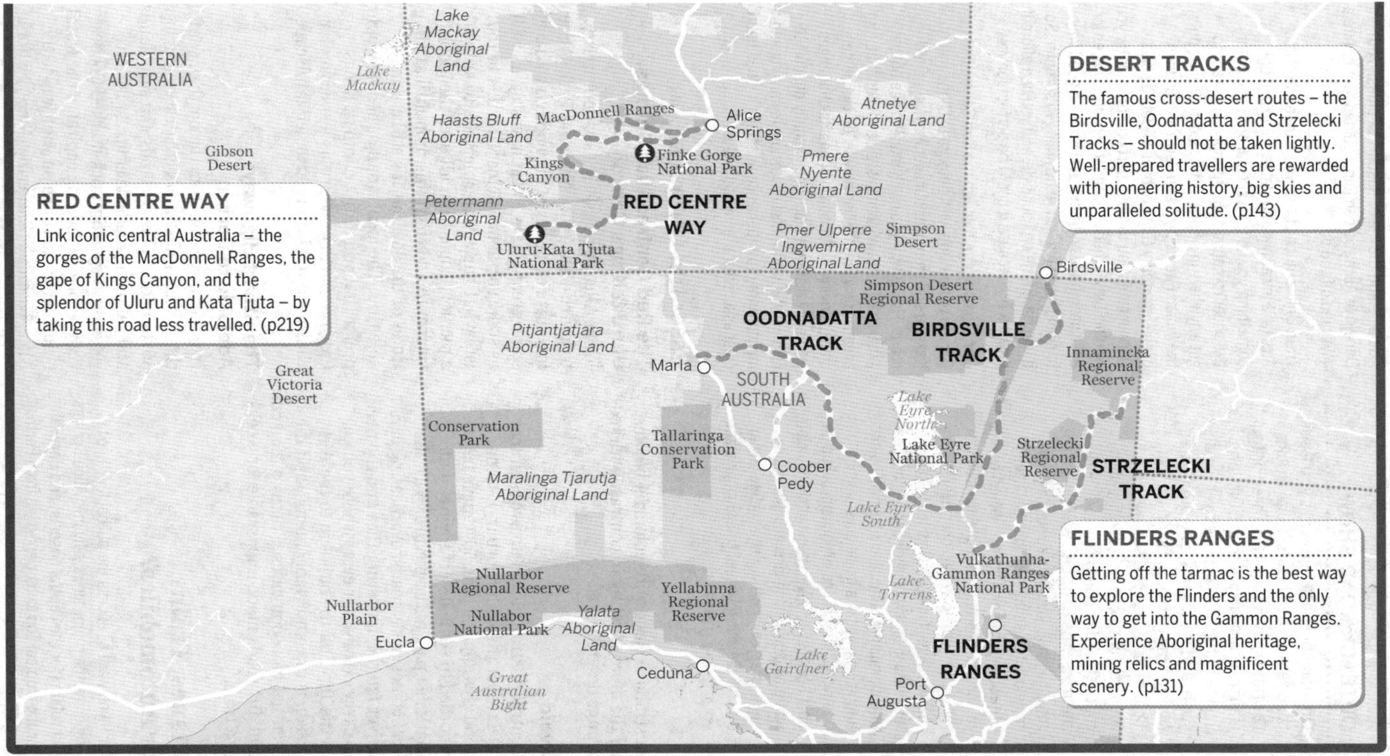

RED CENTRE WAY

Link iconic central Australia – the gorges of the MacDonnell Ranges, the gape of Kings Canyon, and the splendor of Uluru and Kata Tjuta – by taking this road less travelled. (p219)

DESERT TRACKS

The famous cross-desert routes – the Birdsville, Oodnadatta and Strzelecki Tracks – should not be taken lightly. Well-prepared travellers are rewarded with pioneering history, big skies and unparalleled solitude. (p143)

FLINDERS RANGES

Getting off the tarmac is the best way to explore the Flinders and the only way to get into the Gammon Ranges. Experience Aboriginal heritage, mining relics and magnificent scenery. (p131)

OUTBACK ROAD SHOW

On many outback highways you'll see thundering road trains: huge trucks (a prime mover plus two, three or four trailers) some more than 50m long. These things don't move over for anyone, and it's like a scene out of *Mad Max* having one bear down on you at 120km/h. When you see a road train approaching on a narrow bitumen road, slow down and pull over – if the truck has to put its wheels off the road to pass you, the resulting barrage of stones will almost certainly smash your windscreen. When trying to overtake one, allow plenty of room (about a kilometre) to complete the manoeuvre. Road trains throw up a lot of dust on dirt roads, so if you see one coming it's best to just pull over and stop until it's gone past.

And while you're on outback roads, don't forget to give the standard bush wave to oncoming drivers – it's simply a matter of lifting the index finger off the steering wheel to acknowledge your fellow motorist.

Australia explode with colourful blooms, all the more dazzling in contrast with red-orange desert sands.

Avoid

Central Australia heats up over summer (December through February) – temperatures approaching 50°C have been recorded in some desert towns – but that's just part of the picture. With the heat comes dusty roads, overheating cars, driver fatigue, irritating flies and the need to carry extra water everywhere you go. In the Top End the build-up to the Wet season is uncomfortably humid, and the eventual monsoon can see many a road cut and dirt roads made impassable for weeks at a time.

Planes, Trains or Automobiles?

Air If you want to access the outback without a long drive, the major airlines fly into Alice Springs and Yulara (for the central deserts) and Darwin (for the tropical Top End), departing from Perth, Adelaide and the major east-coast cities. From Darwin or Alice you can join a guided tour or hire a 4WD and off you go.

Train Unlike much of the world, train travel in Australia is neither affordable nor expedient. It's something you do for a special occasion or for the sheer romance of trains, not if you want to get anywhere in a hurry. That said, travelling on the *Indian Pacific* between Perth and Sydney or the legendary *Ghan* between Adelaide and Darwin takes you through parts of the country you wouldn't see otherwise, and it certainly makes for a leisurely holiday. Train travel is also a good way to beat the heat if you're travelling in summer. So if you have time on your side, and you can afford it, give it a try because it could be perfect for you.

Car You can drive through the Red Centre from Darwin to Adelaide with detours to Uluru and Kakadu and more without ever leaving sealed roads. However, if you really want to see outback Australia, there are plenty of side routes that breathe new life into the phrase 'off the beaten track'. Driving in the outback has its challenges – immense distances and occasionally difficult terrain – but it's ultimately the most rewarding and intimate way to experience Australia's 'dead heart' (rest assured, it's alive and kicking!).

Essential Outback

The Red Centre: Alice Springs, Uluru & Kings Canyon

From Alice Springs it's a six-hour drive to Uluru-Kata Tjuta National Park. Alice is a surprising oasis: big enough to have some great places to eat and stay, as well as some social problems. Uluru is to tourists what half a watermelon is to ants at a picnic: people from all over the globe swarm to and from this monolith at all times of the day. But it's still a remarkable find. The local Anangu people would prefer that you didn't climb it. Kings Canyon, north of Uluru, is a spectacular chasm carved into the rugged landscape.

The Stuart Highway: Adelaide to Darwin

In either direction, from the north or south, this is one of Australia's greatest road trips: 3020km of red desert sands, flat scrublands and galloping roadside emus. Make sure you stop at spookily pock-marked Coober Pedy – the opal-mining capital of the world – and detour to Uluru on your way to the Alice. Nitmiluk (Katherine Gorge) National

OUTBACK DRIVING & SAFETY CHECKLIST

You need to be particularly organised and vigilant when travelling in the outback, especially on remote sandy tracks, due to the lack of water, long distances between fuel stops and isolation. Here are a few tips:

Communication

➡ Report your route and schedule to the police, a friend or relative.

➡ Mobile phones are useless if you travel off the highway. Consider hiring a satellite phone, high-frequency (HF) radio transceiver equipped to pick up Royal Flying Doctor Service bases, or emergency position-indicating radio beacon (EPIRB).

➡ In an emergency, stay with your vehicle; it's easier to spot than you are, and you won't be able to carry a heavy load of water very far.

➡ If you do become stranded, consider setting fire to a spare tyre (let the air out first). The pall of smoke will be visible for miles.

Your Vehicle

➡ Have your vehicle serviced and checked before you leave.

➡ Load the vehicle evenly, with heavy items inside and light items on the roof rack.

➡ Consider carrying spare fuel in an appropriate container.

➡ Carry essential tools: a spare tyre (two is preferable), fan belt, radiator hose, tyre-pressure gauge and air pump, and a shovel.

➡ An off-road jack might be handy, as will a snatchem strap or tow rope for quick extraction when you're stuck (useful if there's another vehicle to pull you out).

Supplies & Equipment

➡ Carry plenty of water: in warm weather allow 5L per person per day and an extra amount for the radiator, carried in several containers.

➡ Bring plenty of food in case of a breakdown.

➡ Carry a first-aid kit, maps, a torch with spare batteries, a compass, and a GPS.

Weather & Road Conditions

➡ Check road conditions before travelling: roads that are passable in the Dry (March to October) can disappear beneath water during the Wet.

➡ Don't attempt to cross flooded bridges or causeways unless you're sure of the depth, and of any road damage hidden underwater.

Dirt-Road Driving

➡ Inflate your tyres to the recommended levels for the terrain you're travelling on; on desert sand, deflate your tyres to 20-25psi to avoid getting bogged. Don't forget to re-inflate them when you leave the sand.

➡ Reduce speed on unsealed roads as braking distances increase.

➡ Dirt roads are often corrugated: keeping an even speed is the best approach.

➡ Dust on outback roads can obscure vision, so stop and wait for it to settle.

➡ Choose a low gear for steep inclines and the lowest gear for steep declines. Use the brake sparingly and don't turn sideways on a hill.

Road Hazards

➡ Take a rest every few hours: driver fatigue is an all-too-common problem.

➡ Wandering cattle, sheep, emus, kangaroos, camels etc make driving fast a dangerous prospect. Take care and avoid nocturnal driving, as this is often when native animals come out. Many car-hire companies prohibit night-time driving.

➡ Road trains are an ever-present menace on the main highways. Give them a wide berth, they're much bigger than you!

Park is also en route, a photogenic series of sheer rocky gorges and waterholes. Kakadu National Park is next, with World Heritage listed tropical wetlands. When you get to Darwin, reward yourself with a cold beer and some nocturnal high jinks on Mitchell St.

The Tropics: Darwin, Kakadu & Katherine

The outback in the tropical Top End is a different experience to the deserts further south. Here, the wet and dry seasons determine how easy it is to get from A to B. In the Wet, roads become impassable and crocodiles move freely through the wetlands. But before you cancel your plans, this is also a time of abundance and great natural beauty in the national parks – plus Kakadu resorts approach half-price! Darwin isn't really an outback town these days, especially in the Dry when backpackers from around the world fill the bars and Mindil Beach market. Katherine, three hours to the south, is much more 'country', and the jumping-off point for the astonishing Nitmiluk (Katherine Gorge) National Park.

The Victoria Highway: Katherine to the Kimberley

The Victoria Highway is a significant section of the epic Savannah Way from Cairns to Broome, the classic 'across-the-top' route. Leaving Katherine it winds through classic cattle country, where farms can be as big as small European countries. There are 4WD and hiking opportunities, outback campsites, rock art, national parks, red gorges and crocodiles. And this region boasts some of the Top End's best barramundi fishing. The immense Gregory National Park, a former cattle station, is best explored with 4WD, however, in the Dry a 2WD will get you into most of the historic sites, campgrounds and Keep River National Park near the border with Western Australia.

PERMITS FOR ABORIGINAL LAND

In the outback, if you plan on driving through pastoral stations and Aboriginal communities you may need to get permission first. This is for your safety; many travellers have tackled this rugged landscape on their own and required complicated rescues after getting lost or breaking down.

Permits are issued by various Aboriginal land-management authorities; see destination chapters for details. Processing applications can take anywhere from a few minutes to a few days.

Facilities

Outback roadhouses emerge from the desert heat haze with surprising regularity. It always pays to calculate the distance to the next fuel stop, but even on the remote Oodnadatta Track you'll find petrol and cold beer every few hundred kilometres. Most roadhouses (many of them open 24 hours) sell fuel and have attached restaurants where you can get a decent steak and a fry-up feed. Just don't expect an epicurean experience. There's often accommodation for road-weary drivers out the back – including campsites, air-conditioned motel-style rooms, and basic cabins.

Resources

Tourism NT (www.travelnt.com) Bountiful info about the Northern Territory outback. Also produces *The Essential NT Drive Guide*, a terrific booklet with driving distances, national parks, and outback info and advice for 2WD and 4WD travellers.

Parks & Wildlife NT (www.nt.gov.au/parks) General advice on the NT's fabulous national parks: access, walking tracks, and camping etc.

South Australian Tourism Commission (www.southaustralia.com) The lowdown on the South Australian outback, from the Flinders Ranges to Coober Pedy.

Department of Environment, Water & Natural Resources (www.environment.sa.gov.au) Advice, maps and camping permits for SA's national parks.

Parks Australia (www.environment.gov.au/parks) Extensive information about the federally administered Kakadu and Uluru-Kata Tjuta National Parks.

OUTBACK CYCLING

Pedalling your way through the outback is not something to tackle lightly, and certainly not something you'd even consider in summer. But you do see the odd wiry, suntanned soul pushing their panniers along the Stuart Hwy between Adelaide and Darwin. Availability of drinking water is the main concern: isolated water sources (bores, tanks, creeks etc) shown on maps may be dry or undrinkable. Make sure you've got the necessary spare parts and bike-repair knowledge. Check with locals if you're heading into remote areas, and always tell someone where you're headed. And if you make it through, try for a book deal – this is intrepid travel defined.

Organised Tours

If you don't feel like doing all the planning and driving, a guided tour is a great way to experience the outback. These range from beery backpacker jaunts between outback pubs, to indigenous cultural tours and multiday bushwalking treks into remote wilderness.

Outback Tracks

The Australian outback is criss-crossed by sealed highways, but one of the more interesting ways to get from A to B is by taking a detour along historic cattle and rail routes. While you may not necessarily need a 4WD to tackle some of these roads, the rugged construction of these vehicles makes for a much more comfortable drive. Whatever the vehicle, you will need to be prepared for the isolation and lack of facilities.

Don't attempt the tougher routes during the hottest part of the year (December to February, inclusive); apart from the risk of heat exhaustion, simple mishaps can lead to tragedy in these conditions. There's also no point going anywhere on outback dirt roads if there's been recent flooding.

Red Centre Way & Mereenie Loop Road

Starting in Alice Springs this well-used track is an alternative route to the big attractions of the Red Centre. The route initially follows the sealed Larapinta and Namatjira Drives skirting the magnificent MacDonnell Ranges to Glen Helen Gorge. Beyond Glen Helen the route meets the Mereenie Loop Road. This is where things get interesting. The Mereenie Loop road requires a permit ($3.50) and is usually so heavily corrugated that it will rattle a conventional 2WD until it finds its weak spot. This is the rugged short cut to Kings Canyon, Watarrka National Park, and from Kings Canyon the sealed Luritja Road connects to the Lasseter Highway and Uluru-Kata Tjuta National Park.

Oodnadatta Track

Mostly running parallel to the old *Ghan* railway line through outback SA, this iconic track is fully bypassed by the sealed Stuart Hwy to the west. Using this track, it's 429km from Marree to Oodnadatta, then another 216km to the Stuart Hwy at Marla. As long as there is no rain, any well-prepared conventional vehicle should be able to manage this fascinating route, but a 4WD will do it in comfort.

Birdsville Track

Spanning 517km from Marree in SA to Birdsville just across the border of Queensland, this old droving trail is one of Australia's best-known outback routes - although it's not known for spectacular and varying scenery. Again it's feasible to travel it in a well-prepared, conventional vehicle but not recommended. Don't miss a beer at the Birdsville Hotel!

Strzelecki Track

This track covers much of the same territory through SA as the Birdsville Track. Starting south of Marree at Lyndhurst, it reaches Innamincka 460km northeast and close to the Queensland border. It was at Innamincka that the explorers Burke and Wills died. A 4WD is a safe bet, even though this route has been much improved due to work on the Moomba gas fields.

Nathan River Road

This road, which resembles a farm track in parts, is a scenic section of the Savannah Way, a cobbled together route which winds all the way from Cairns to Broome. This particular section traverses some remote country along the western edge of the Gulf of Carpentaria between Roper Bar and Borroloola, much of it protected within Limmen National Park. A high-clearance vehicle is a must and carrying two spare tyres is recommended because of the frequent sharp rocks. Excellent camping beside barramundi- and crocodile-filled streams and waterholes is the main attraction here.

Tanami Track

Turning off the Stuart Hwy just north of Alice Springs, this 1000km route runs northwest across the Tanami Desert to Halls Creek in WA. The road has received extensive work so conventional vehicles are normally OK, although there are sandy stretches on the WA side and it can be very corrugated if it hasn't been graded recently. Get advice on road conditions in Alice Springs.

Plenty & Sandover Highways

These remote routes run east from the Stuart Hwy, north of Alice Springs, to Boulia or Mt Isa in Queensland. The Plenty Highway skirts the northern fringe of the Simpson Desert and offers the chance of gemstone fossicking in the Harts Range. The Sandover Hwy offers a memorable if monotonous experience in remote touring. It is a novelty to see another vehicle. Both roads are not to be taken lightly; they are often very rough going with little water and with sections that are very infrequently used. Signs of human habitation are rare and facilities are few and far between.

Finke & Old Andado Tracks

The Finke Track (the first part of which is the Old South Rd) follows the route of the old *Ghan* railway (long since dismantled) between Alice Springs and the Aboriginal settlement of Finke (Aputula). Along the way you can call into Chambers Pillar Historical Reserve to view the colourful sandstone tower. From Finke the road heads east along the Goyder Creek, a tributary of the Finke River, before turning north towards Andado Station and, 18km further, the homestead. At Old Andado the track swings north for the 321km trip to Alice. The Old Andado Track winds its way through the Simpson Desert to link the Old Andado Homestead with Alice Springs. On the way you pass the Mac Clark Conservation Reserve, which protects a stand of rare waddy trees. A high-clearance 4WD is definitely recommended and you should be equipped with high-frequency (HF) radio or emergency position-indicating radio beacon (EPIRB).

Simpson Desert

The route crossing the Simpson Desert from Mt Dare, near Finke, to Birdsville is a real test of both driver and vehicle. A 4WD is definitely required on the unmaintained tracks and you should be in a party of at least three vehicles equipped with sat phones, HF radio and/or EPIRB.

Blue Mountains National Park (p136)

Plan Your Trip

Australia Outdoors

Australia offers up plenty of excuses to just sit back and roll your eyes across the landscape, but that same landscape lends itself to boundless outdoor pursuits – whether it's getting active on the trails and mountains on dry land, or on the swells and reefs offshore.

When to Go

September–October

Spring brings the end of football season, which means a lot of yelling from the grandstands. The more actively inclined rejoice in sunnier weather and warmer days, perfect for bushwalking, wildlife watching and rock climbing.

December–February

Australians hit the beach in summer. Now is the time for surfing, sailing, swimming, fishing, snorkelling, skydiving, paragliding...

March–May

Autumn is a nostalgic time in Australia, with cool nights and wood smoke: perfect weather for a bushwalk or perhaps a cycling trip – not too hot, not too cold.

June–August

When winter hits, make a beeline for the outback or the snow. Pack up your 4WD and head into the desert for a hike or scenic flight, or grab your snowboard and head into the mountains for some powdery fun.

On the Land

Bushwalking is a prime pastime in all Australian states and territories. Cycling is a great way to get around, despite the mammoth distances sometimes involved. There's also skiing in the mountains and wildlife watching pretty much everywhere.

Bushwalking

Bushwalking is supremely popular in Australia, with vast swathes of untouched scrub and forest providing ample opportunity. Hikes vary from 20-minute jaunts off the roadside to week-long wilderness epics. The best time to head into the bush varies from state to state, but as a general rule the further north you go, the more tropical and humid the climate gets: June to August are the best walking months up north; down south, summer and early autumn (December to March) are better.

Notable walks include the Overland Track and the South Coast Track in Tasmania, and the Australian Alps Walking Track, Great Ocean Walk and Great South West Walk in Victoria. The Bibbulmun Track in Western Australia (WA) is great, as is the Thorsborne Trail across Hinchinbrook Island and the Gold Coast Hinterland Great Walk in Queensland.

In New South Wales (NSW) you can trek between Sydney and Newcastle on the Great North Walk, tackle Royal National Park's Coast Track, the Six Foot Track in the Blue Mountains, or scale Mt Kosciuszko, Australia's highest peak. In South Australia (SA) you can bite off a chunk of the 1200km Heysen Trail, while in the Northern Territory (NT) there's the majestic 233.5km Larapinta Trail and remote tracks in Nitmiluk (Katherine Gorge) National Park.

Cycling

Cyclists in Australia have access to plenty of cycling routes and can tour the country for days, weekends or even multiweek trips. Or you can just rent a bike for a few hours and wheel around a city.

Standout longer routes include the Murray to the Mountains Rail Trail and the East Gippsland Rail Trail in Victoria. In WA the Munda Biddi Trail offers 900km of mountain biking, or you can rampage along the same distance on the Mawson Trail in SA.

Rental rates charged by most outfits for road or mountain bikes start at around \$20/40 per hour/day. Deposits range from \$50 to \$200, depending on the rental period. Most states have bicycle organisations that can provide maps and advice.

Wildlife Watching

The local wildlife is one of Australia's top selling points, and justifiably so. National

BEST BUSHWALKS

- Thorsborne Trail, Queensland
- Great South West Walk, Victoria
- Overland Track, Tasmania
- Heysen Trail, Deep Creek Conservation Park, South Australia
- Larapinta Trail, Northern Territory

Cycling the Murray to the Mountains Rail Trail (p597)

parks are the best places to meet the residents, although many species are nocturnal so you may need to hone your torch (flashlight) skills to spot them.

Australia is a twitcher's (committed bird-watcher) haven, with a wide variety of habitats and bird life, particularly water birds. Canberra has the richest bird life of any Australian capital city. Birds are also big business in the tropical north, particularly in Kakadu National Park in NT where the bird life is astonishing (...not to mention the crocodiles).

In NSW there are platypuses and gliders in New England National Park, and 120 bird species in Dorrigo National Park. Border Ranges National Park is home to a quarter of all of Australia's bird species. Willandra National Park is World Heritage-listed and encompasses dense temperate wetlands and wildlife, and koalas are a dime a dozen around Port Macquarie. WA also has ample birdwatching hot spots.

In Victoria, Wilsons Promontory National Park teems with wildlife – in fact, wombats sometimes seem to outnumber people.

In SA make a beeline for Flinders Chase National Park on Kangaroo Island (KI) to see koalas, kangaroos and platypuses; and Flinders National Park in the north for emus. In Queensland, head to Malanda for bird life, turtles and pademelons; Cape Tribulation for even better bird life; Magnetic Island for koala spotting; Fraser Island for dingoes; and the Daintree Rainforest for cassowaries. In Tasmania, Maria Island is another twitcher's paradise, while Mt William and Mt Field National Parks teem with native fauna, including Tasmanian devils.

Skiing & Snowboarding

Australia has a small but enthusiastic skiing industry, with snowfields straddling the NSW–Victoria border. The season is relatively short, however, running from about mid-June to early September, and snowfalls can be unpredictable. In NSW the top places to ski are within Kosciuszko National Park in the Snowy Mountains; in Victoria head for Mt Buller, Falls Creek or Mt Hotham in the High Country. Tasmania also has a few small ski fields.

Diving, Great Barrier Reef (p40)

On the Water

As Australia's national anthem will tell you, this land is 'girt by sea'. Surfing, fishing, sailing, diving and snorkelling are what people do here – national pastimes one and all. Marine-mammal watching trips have also become popular in recent years. Inland there are vast lakes and meandering rivers, offering rafting, canoeing, kayaking and (yet more) fishing opportunities.

Where to Surf in Australia

Bells Beach, Cactus, Margaret River, the Superbank...mention any of them in the right company and stories of surfing legend will undoubtedly emerge. The Superbank hosts the first event on the Association of Surfing Professionals (ASP) World Tour calendar each year, and Bells Beach the second, with Bells the longest-serving host of an ASP event. Cactus dangles the lure of remote mystique, while Margaret River is a haunt for surfers chasing bigger waves.

While the aforementioned might be jewels, they're dot points in the sea of stars that Australia has to offer. Little wonder – the coastline is vast, touching the Indian, Southern and South Pacific Oceans. With that much potential swell, an intricate coastal architecture and the right conditions, you'll find anything from innocent breaks to gnarly reefs not far from all six Australian state capitals.

New South Wales

- Manly through Avalon, otherwise known as Sydney's Northern Beaches
- Byron Bay, Lennox Head and Angourie Point on the far north coast
- Nambucca Heads and Crescent Head on the mid-north coast
- The areas around Jervis Bay and Ulladulla on the south coast

Queensland

- The Superbank (a 2km-long sandbar stretching from Snapper Rocks to Kirra Point)
- Burleigh Heads through to Surfers Paradise on the Gold Coast

Surfing, Burleigh Heads (p324)

- North Stradbroke Island in Moreton Bay
- Caloundra, Alexandra Heads near Maroochydore and Noosa on the Sunshine Coast

Victoria

- Bells Beach – this is the spiritual home of Australian surfing; when the wave is on, few people would argue, but the break is notoriously inconsistent
- Smiths Beach on Phillip Island
- Point Leo, Flinders, Gunnamatta, Rye and Portsea on the Mornington Peninsula
- On the southwest coast, Barwon Heads, Point Lonsdale, Torquay and numerous spots along the Great Ocean Road

Tasmania

- Marrawah, on the exposed northwest coast, can offer huge waves
- St Helens and Bicheno on the east coast
- Eaglehawk Neck on the Tasman Peninsula
- Closer to Hobart, Cremorne Point and Clifton Beach

South Australia

- Cactus Beach, west of Ceduna on remote Point Sinclair – internationally recognised for quality and consistency
- Streaky Bay and Greenly Beach on the western side of the Eyre Peninsula
- Pennington Bay – the most consistent surf on Kangaroo Island
- Pondalowie Bay and Stenhouse Bay on the Yorke Peninsula in Innes National Park
- Victor Harbor, Port Elliot and Middleton Beach south of Adelaide

Western Australia

- Margaret River, Gracetown and Yallingup in the southwest
- Trigg Point and Scarborough Beach, just north of Perth
- Further north at Geraldton and Kalbarri
- Down south at Denmark on the Southern Ocean

Diving & Snorkelling

The Great Barrier Reef has more dazzling dive sites than you can poke a fin at.

In WA Ningaloo Reef is every bit as interesting as the east-coast reefs, without the tourist numbers, and there are spectacular artificial reefs created by sunken ships at Albany and Dunsborough.

The Rapid Bay jetty off the Gulf St Vincent coast in SA is renowned for its abundant marine life, and in Tasmania the Bay of Fires and Eaglehawk Neck are popular spots. In NSW head for Jervis Bay and Fish Rock Cave off South West Rocks.

PLAY IT SAFE

Before you strap on your boots, make sure you're walking in a region (and on tracks) within your realm of experience, and that you feel healthy and comfortable walking for a sustained period. Check with local authorities for weather and track updates: be aware that weather conditions and terrain can vary significantly within regions, and that seasonal changes can considerably alter any track.

FLIP NICKLIN / GETTY IMAGES ©

Top: Fishing, Adaminaby (p216)

Bottom: Dolphin watching, Monkey Mia (p985)

Fishing

Barramundi fishing is hugely popular across the Top End, particularly around Borroloola in the NT, and Karumba and Lake Tinaroo in Queensland.

Ocean fishing is possible right around the country, from pier or beach, or you can organise a deep-sea charter. There are magnificent glacial lakes and clear streams for trout fishing in Tasmania.

Before casting a line, be warned that strict limits to catches and sizes apply in Australia, and many species are threatened and therefore protected. Check local guidelines via fishing equipment stores or through individual state's government fishing bodies for information.

Whale, Dolphin & Marine-life Watching

Southern right and humpback whales pass close to Australia's southern coast on their migratory route between the Antarctic and warmer waters. The best spots for whale-watching cruises are Hervey Bay in Queensland, Eden in southern NSW, the mid-north coast of NSW, Warrnambool in Victoria, Albany on WA's southwest cape, and numerous places in SA. Whale-watching season is roughly May to October. For whale sharks and manta rays try WA's Ningaloo Marine Park.

Dolphins can be seen year-round along the east coast at Jervis Bay, Port Stephens and Byron Bay in NSW; off the coast of WA at Bunbury and Rockingham; off North Stradbroke Island in Queensland; and you can swim with them off Sorrento in Victoria. You can also see fairy penguins in Victoria on Phillip Island. In WA, fur seals and sea lions can variously be seen at Rottnest Island, Esperance, Rockingham and Green Head, and all manner of beautiful sea creatures inhabit Monkey Mia (including dugongs!). Sea lions also visit the aptly named (though not technically correct) Seal Bay on South Australia's Kangaroo Island.

TOP FIVE WILDLIFE ENCOUNTERS

- Whales, Hervey Bay, Queensland
- Grey kangaroos, Namadgi National Park, Australian Capital Territory
- Penguins, Phillip Island, Victoria
- Tasmanian devils, Tasmania
- Dolphins, Monkey Mia, Western Australia

Planning & Resources

Bicycles Network Australia (www.bicycles.net.au) Information, news and links.

Bushwalking Australia (www.bushwalkingaustralia.org) Website for the national body, with links to state/territory bushwalking clubs and federations.

Coastalwatch (www.coastalwatch.com) Surf-cams, reports and weather charts for all the best breaks.

Lonely Planet (www.lonelyplanet.com) The *Walking in Australia* guide has detailed information about bushwalking around the country.

Dive-Oz (www.diveoz.com.au) Online scuba-diving resource.

Fishnet (www.fishnet.com.au) Devoted to all aspects of Australian fishing (nothing to do with stockings...).

Ski Online (www.ski.com.au) Commercial site with holiday offers plus snow-cams, forecasts and reports.

Regions at a Glance

Sydney & New South Wales

Surf Beaches
Food
Wilderness

Sydney Surf

Sydney's surf beaches can't be beaten. Bondi is the name on everyone's lips, but the waves here get crowded. Head south to Maroubra or Cronulla, or north to Manly for more elbow room.

Mod Oz Cuisine

Modern Australian, or 'Mod Oz', is the name of the culinary game here – a pan-Pacific fusion of styles and ingredients with plenty of Sydney seafood. Serve it up with a harbour view and you've got a winning combo.

National Parks

NSW has some of the best national parks in Australia. Around Sydney there's the Royal National Park, with fab walks and beaches; waterways and wildlife in Ku-ring-gai Chase National Park; and vast tracts of native forest in Wollemi National Park in the Blue Mountains.

p62

Canberra & Around

History & Culture
Wineries
Politics

Canberra Museums

Canberra offers the National Gallery, with its magnificent collections of Australian, Asian and Aboriginal and Torres Strait Islander art; the National Museum, whose imaginative exhibits provide insights into the Australian heart and soul; the moving and fascinating War Memorial; and the entirely impressive National Portrait Gallery.

Cool-Climate Wines

Canberra's wine industry is relatively new but is winning admirers with a consistent crop of fine cool-climate wines. The Canberra vineyards are an easy and picturesque drive from downtown.

Parliamant House

Politics is what really makes Canberra tick: find out for yourself at a rigorous session of 'Question Time' at Parliament House, or visit Old Parliament House and check out the Museum of Australian Democracy.

p256

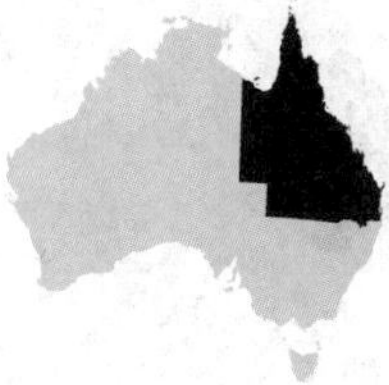

Queensland & the Great Barrier Reef

Diving & Snorkelling
Beaches & Islands
Urban Culture

Great Barrier Reef

Blessed with the fish-rich, technicolor Great Barrier Reef, Queensland is the place for world-class diving and snorkelling. Take a day trip, bob around in a glass-bottom boat, or just paddle out from the beach on a reef-fringed island.

The Whitsundays

There's great surf along Queensland's south coast, and reefs and rainforest-cloaked islands further north, but for picture-perfect white-sand beaches and turquoise seas, the Whitsundays are unmissable: get on a yacht and enjoy.

Booming Brisbane

Watch out Sydney and Melbourne, Brisbane is on the rise! Hip bars, fab restaurants, a vibrant arts culture and good coffee everywhere: 'Australia's new world city' is an ambitious, edgy, progressive place to be.

p274

Melbourne & Victoria

History
Sports
Surf Beaches

Gold-Rush Towns

Walk the boom-town streets of 1850s gold-rush towns. With their handsome, lace-fringed buildings, Melbourne, Bendigo and Ballarat are rich reminders of how good Victoria had it in those days.

Football & Cricket

Melbourne is the spiritual home of Australian Rules football: grab some friends and boot a ball around a wintry city park. Summer means cricket: local kids are either watching it on TV, talking about it or out in the streets playing it.

Southern Surf

With relentless Southern Ocean swells surging in, there's plenty of quality (if chilly) surf along Victoria's Great Ocean Road. Bells Beach is Australia's most famous break, and home to the Rip Curl Pro surf comp every Easter.

p473

Tasmania

Food
Wildlife
History

Gourmet Travel

Tasmania produces larders-full of fine food and drink. Chefs from all over Australia are increasingly besotted with Tasmania's excellent fresh produce, including briny fresh salmon and oysters, cool-climate wines, hoppy craft beers and plump fruit and vegetables.

Native Species

You might not spy a thylacine, but on a Tassie bushwalk you can see wallabies, possums, pademelons, iconic Tasmanian devils and possibly a snake or two. There's also whale-, seal- and penguin-spotting along the coast.

Colonial Times

Tasmania's bleak colonial history is on display in Port Arthur and along the Heritage Hwy, made all the more potent by dramatic landscapes seemingly out of proportion with the state's compact footprint.

p618

Adelaide & South Australia

Wine
Festivals
National Parks

SA Wine Regions

We challenge you to visit SA without inadvertently driving through a wine region. You may have heard of the Barossa Valley, Clare Valley and McLaren Vale, but what about the lesser-known Langhorne Creek, Mt Benson, Currency Creek or the Adelaide Hills regions? All top drops worth pulling over for.

Adelaide's Mad March

At the end of every summer Adelaide erupts with festivals: visual arts, world music, theatre, busking and the growl of V8 engines. The only question is, why do it all at the same time?

Flinders Ranges

The dunes and lagoons of Coorong National Park are amazing, but for sheer geologic majesty visit Ikara (Wilpena Pound), part of the craggy, russet-red Flinders Ranges National Park in central SA.

p710

Darwin to Uluru

Wildlife
Indigenous Culture
National Parks

Kakadu Critters

The further north you head in Australia, the more deadly, dangerous and just damn big the creatures become. Kakadu National Park has whopping crocs in the waterways, scrub pythons slithering across the land and brolgas prancing like pelicans on stilts.

Art in Alice Springs

The NT is home to the renowned indigenous Desert Art Movement: learn the stories behind the mesmerising paintings and make an informed purchase in Alice Springs.

Desert Landscapes

In terms of iconic Australian landscapes, it's hard to look past Uluru-Kata Tjuta National Park – the biggest boulders you'll ever see. Further north, West MacDonnell National Park and Watarrka (Kings Canyon) National Park have some truly gorgeous gorges.

p807

Perth & Western Australia

Coastal Scenery
Adventure
Wildlife

Ningaloo Marine Park

There are boundless beaches along WA's spectacular 12,500km-long coastline. But for sheer sandy delight, visit the isolated beaches leading down to the shallow lagoons of the World Heritage–listed Ningaloo Marine Park.

Kimberley Action

Bring it on: take the ride of your life along the bone-shaking Gibb River Road, to the exceptional Mitchell Falls and remote Kalumburu. Jump on a speedboat and head full throttle for the Horizontal Waterfalls, then grab a canoe and paddle down the mighty Ord River.

Native Species

You can spy sharks, rays, turtles and migrating whales along WA's central west coast. Inland, birds flock to the oasis pools of Millstream-Chichester National Park, and pythons and rock wallabies hide in the shadows of Karijini National Park.

p901

On the Road

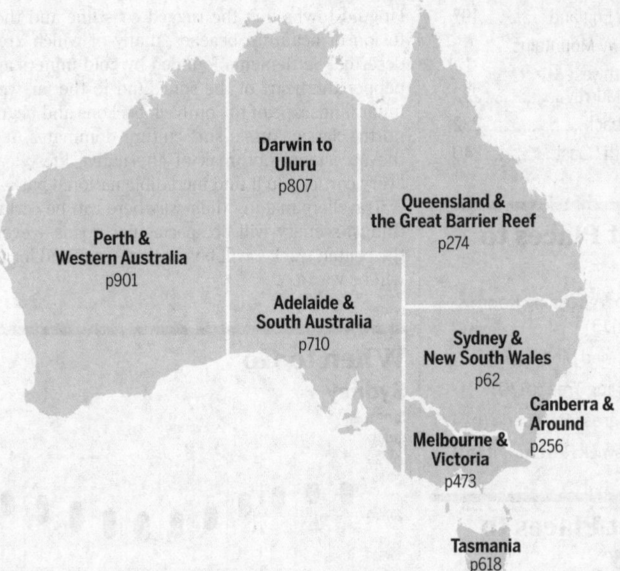
Darwin to Uluru p807
Queensland & the Great Barrier Reef p274
Perth & Western Australia p901
Adelaide & South Australia p710
Sydney & New South Wales p62
Canberra & Around p256
Melbourne & Victoria p473
Tasmania p618

Sydney & New South Wales

Includes ➡

Best Places to Eat

- Icebergs Dining Room & Bar (p113)
- Stunned Mullet (p165)
- Jaaning Tree (p170)
- Seagrass Brasserie (p247)
- Chiswick Restaurant (p112)

Best Places to Stay

- Crystal Creek Rainforest Retreat (p197)
- Byron at Byron (p189)
- Thistle HIll (p147)
- Sydney Harbour YHA (p103)
- Yamba YHA (p181)

Why Go?

The birthplace of the modern nation, New South Wales (NSW) is rich in history, landscapes and contrasts. It's also home to sophisticated Sydney, the nation's capital in all but name.

Here, diversity reigns supreme. South of the harbour, languid towns hug the rugged coastline and there's a profusion of beautiful beaches, many of which are idyllically deserted. Settlements founded by gold miners and graziers pepper the heart of the state, and to the far west the arid lunar landscape of the outback beckons and beguiles. In the north, classic Aussie surf culture dominates, tempered by the occasional outbreak of alternative lifestyle. In almost every corner you'll find incredible national parks to explore.

Travellers making their way here can be certain of three things: scenery will be spectacular, roads – even those off the beaten track – will be relatively easy and local welcomes will be warm.

When to Go

Sydney

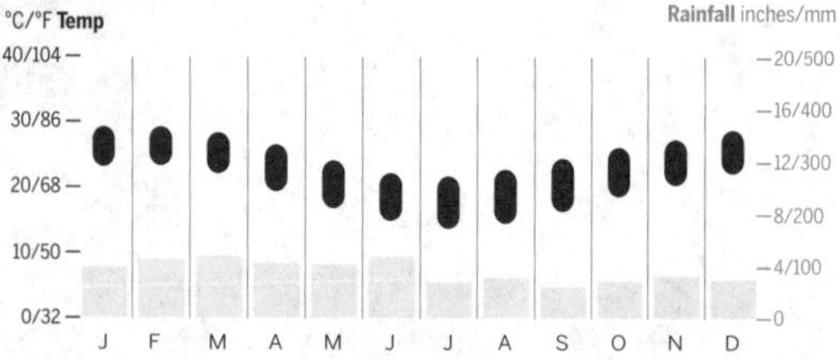

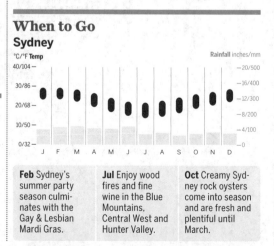

Feb Sydney's summer party season culminates with the Gay & Lesbian Mardi Gras.

Jul Enjoy wood fires and fine wine in the Blue Mountains, Central West and Hunter Valley.

Oct Creamy Sydney rock oysters come into season and are fresh and plentiful until March.

Wildlife Watching

Having a close encounter of the furry kind is a holiday highlight for many visitors to NSW. In Sydney, **Taronga Zoo**, **SEA LIFE Sydney Aquarium**, **WILD LIFE Sydney Zoo** and the **Manly SEA LIFE Sanctuary** offer the chance to see, pet and even dive with native species. Heading into the countryside, the state's coastal bush, state forests and 800+ national parks and reserves are home to kangaroos, wallabies, koalas, platypus, wombats and many other cute critters. See p169 for a guide to wildlife viewing opportunities across the state.

DON'T MISS

Rural NSW offers a treasure trove of eccentric festivals. In January, the town of Parkes in the central west is inundated by hundreds of middle-aged, jumpsuit-clad men during the Elvis Festival (p211), and at Easter the opal town of Lightning Ridge stages its annual **Great Goat Race** (p203).

In October, the town of Deniliquin holds its famous Ute Muster (p231), where blokes and sheilas compete for titles such as 'Chick's Ute' and 'Feral Ute'. Also in October is Wooli's Australian National Goanna Pulling Championships (p179), in which men and women, squatting on all fours, attach leather harnesses to their heads and engage in a cranial tug of war. Go figure.

The biggest rural festival of all is a serious music event, but has pronounced eccentric characteristics. Tamworth's Country Music Festival (p199) stages more than 800 events every January including its exuberant 'Longest Line Dance', the world record for which was set in 2009 when 3392 bootscooters participated.

Top Five Beaches

- **Tallow Beach, Byron Bay** (p185) An idyllic 7km stretch of sand stretching from Cape Byron to Broken Head.
- **Bondi Beach, Sydney** (p92) One of the world's most famous urban surf scenes – see and be seen!
- **Crowdy Head** (p160) Deserted beach and extraordinary views.
- **Jervis Bay** (p246) White sandy beaches, bushland, forest and a protected marine park.
- **Tomaree Peninsula** (p154) Near-deserted beaches, national parks and an extraordinary sand-dune system.

TOP TIP

MyMulti passes, the Family Funday Sunday pass and Pensioner Excursion travel passes can save you a bit of money when travelling on public transport. Off-peak daily return train tickets also offer good value.

Fast Facts

- Population: 6.9 million
- Area: 800,642 sq km
- Telephone area code: ☎ 02 (Broken Hill ☎ 08)
- Number of patrolled surf beaches: 176

Advance Planning

- Book your accommodation well in advance, particularly for the summer months.
- Work out how many national parks will be on your itinerary – if there are more than six, buy an annual multi-parks pass ($65).
- Make weekend fine-dining reservations well in advance.

Resources

- **City of Sydney** (☎ 9265 9333; www.cityofsydney.nsw.gov.au)
- **New South Wales** (www.visitnsw.com.au)
- **NSW National Parks & Wildlife Service** (NPWS; www.nationalparks.nsw.gov.au)

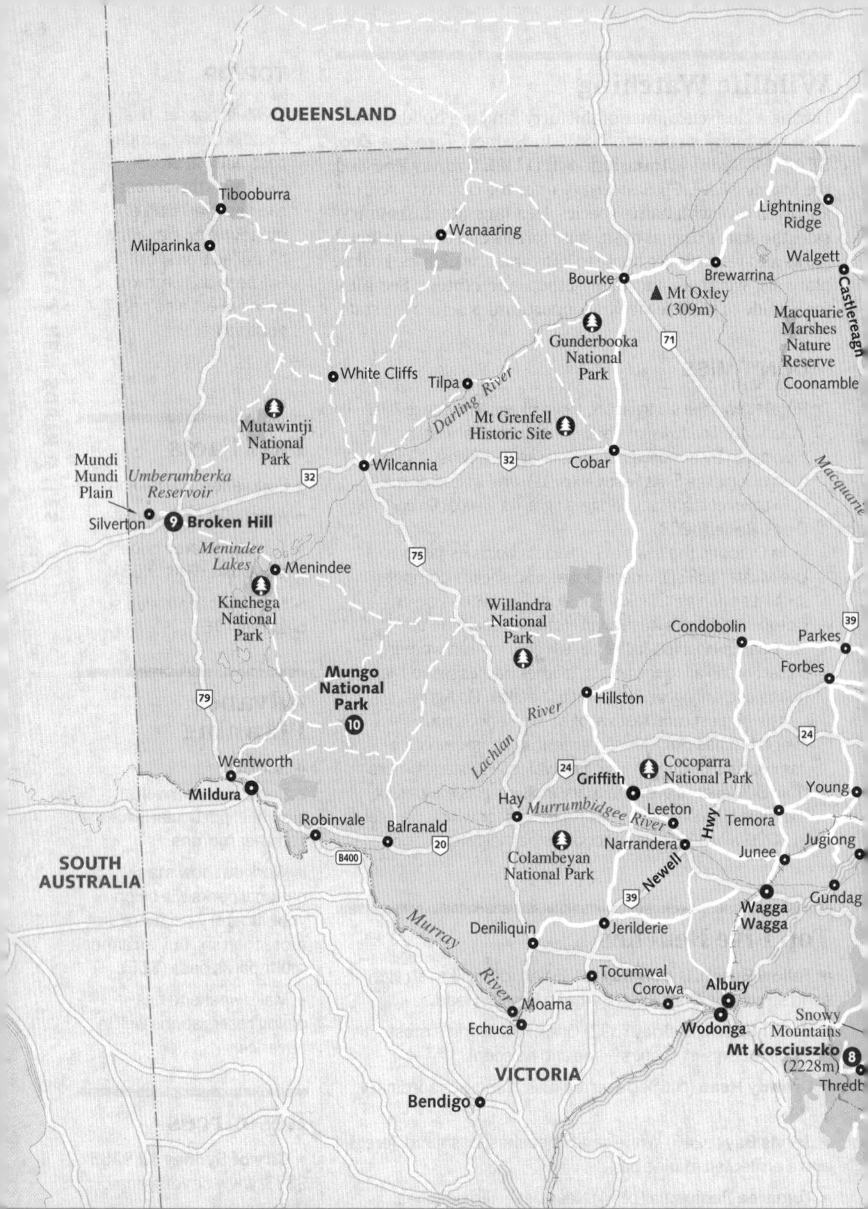

Sydney & New South Wales Highlights

1. Be seduced by Australia's sexiest city, **Sydney** (p70)
2. Follow a bush trail under dense and ancient forest canopies in the **Blue Mountains** (p136)
3. Broaden your palate and waistline in the **Hunter Valley** (p143)
4. Traverse the shifting sand dunes of the **Worimi Conservation Lands** (p155)
5. Drive from the coast to rainforests and historic towns along the **Waterfall Way** (p173)

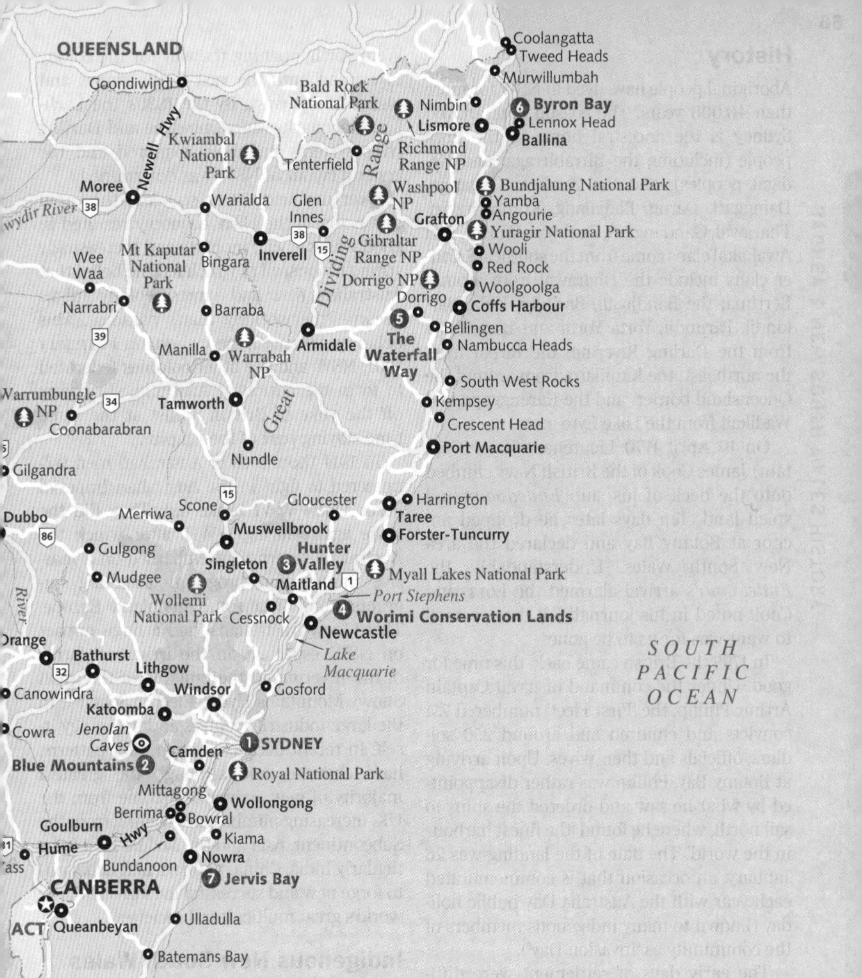

❻ Make a beeline for the beautiful beaches and laid-back lifestyle of **Byron Bay** (p184)

❼ Dip your toes in the pure white sand and sapphire waters of **Jervis Bay** (p246)

❽ Hike to the roof of Australia amid alpine scenery at **Mt Kosciuszko** (p219)

❾ Be inspired by the dramatic scenery and empty spaces of **Broken Hill** (p233)

❿ Encounter Aboriginal history and the Walls of China in **Mungo National Park** (p232)

History

Aboriginal people have lived in NSW for more than 40,000 years. The coastal area around Sydney is the ancestral home of the Eora people (including the Birrabirragal and Gadigal peoples), and the Anaiwan, Ngarigo, Dainggati, Darug, Badjalang, Kumbainggiri, Tharawal, Gandangara, Guringai, Worimi and Awabakal clans come from the southeast. Other clans include the Dharawal from around Berrima; the Bandjigali, Barindji, Kula, Barkindji, Parundji, Yorta Yorta and Baranbinja from the Darling Riverine; the Birpai from the northeast; the Kamilaroi from around the Queensland border; and the Karenggapa and Wadikali from the Lake Eyre area.

On 19 April 1770 Lieutenant (later Captain) James Cook of the British Navy climbed onto the deck of his ship *Endeavour* and spied land. Ten days later he dropped anchor at Botany Bay and declared the area New South Wales. Understandably, the *Endeavour*'s arrival alarmed the Eora, and Cook noted in his journal: 'All they seemed to want was for us to be gone.'

In 1788 the British came back, this time for good. Under the command of naval Captain Arthur Phillip, the 'First Fleet' numbered 751 convicts and children and around 250 soldiers, officials and their wives. Upon arriving at Botany Bay, Phillip was rather disappointed by what he saw and ordered the ships to sail north, where he found 'the finest harbour in the world'. The date of the landing was 26 January, an occasion that is commemorated each year with the Australia Day public holiday (known to many indigenous members of the community as 'Invasion Day').

The early days of settlement were difficult, with famine and lawlessness threatening the population, but by the early 1800s Sydney was a bustling port with new houses, warehouses and streets. The surrounding bushland was overtaken by vegetable gardens and orchards, ensuring that the threat of starvation no longer hung over the colony.

In 1793 Phillip returned to London and self-serving military officers took control of Government House. Soon, the vigorous new society that the first governor had worked so hard to establish began to unravel. Fortunately, London swiftly took action, dispatching Governor Lachlan Macquarie to restore the rule of law. Under his guidance the colony flourished.

In 1813 the Blue Mountains were penetrated by explorers Blaxland, Lawson and Wentworth, opening the way for the colony to expand onto the vast fertile slopes and plains of the west. By the 1830s the Lachlan, Macquarie, Murrumbidgee and Darling river systems had been explored and the general layout of NSW was determined.

Over the next 60 or so years the rapid expansion of the NSW economy resulted in good wages, social mobility and increasingly strong unions, all of which fed the belief that Australia's first and largest colony might become 'the working man's paradise'. This belief was strengthened when, on 1 January 1901, NSW and the other colonies federated to form the nation of Australia, shrugging off the yoke of Britain whilst at the same time staying part of the Empire.

In 1914 thousands of Australian men volunteered to fight in the Australian Imperial Force when WWI broke out. They did the same again during WWII, after which the Australian government embarked on a massive immigration program, attracting migrants from Britain and mainland Europe. These 'new Australians' had a huge impact on NSW, especially in the irrigation farms of the Riverina, in the building of the great Snowy Mountains Hydro-Electric Scheme, in the large industrial centres and in Sydney itself. In recent decades immigration patterns have changed, and although the greatest majority of new arrivals still come from the UK, increasing numbers are coming from the Subcontinent, Asia and the Middle East (particularly India, China, Vietnam and Lebanon) to forge new and successful lives in one of the world's great multicultural societies.

Indigenous New South Wales

Indigenous clans or bands in NSW have their own languages and identity. Traditionally, the clans were semi-nomadic, moving within their territories to fish, hunt and gather plants. As well as providing food, the land also formed the basis for their spiritual life and Dreaming (belief system), which is why its forced acquisition by the Europeans had such catastrophic consequences.

The colonists were swift to subject the local people to kidnappings and punishment, with the explicit aim of terrifying them into submission. Smallpox, introduced by the Europeans, also decimated the local population, which had no resistance to such a disease. But there was resistance in other forms: Aboriginal freedom-fighting groups began to spring up, led by indigenous warriors including Pemulwuy (1750–1802), a member of the Bidjigal clan from around Botany Bay, and Musquito (c1780–1825), a member of the Eora from the north shore of Port Jackson. The freedom fighters were eventually crushed as the settlers resorted to ever more barbaric methods to achieve total domination.

At the most recent national census (2011) there were an estimated 172,625 Aboriginal people in NSW (31.5% of the country's indigenous population and just over 1% of the total population of the state). Approximately 40% of the population lives in the Greater Sydney area.

There are a number of ways to gain an insight into the state's indigenous culture when you are here.

In Sydney, the Australian Museum, Art Gallery of NSW, Museum of Sydney, Powerhouse Museum, Rocks Discovery Museum and Royal Botanic Gardens all have exhibits and programs relating to Aboriginal life and culture.

For information on the ancient Aboriginal rock paintings and engravings around the harbour, check with the Sydney Harbour National Park Information Centre at Cadman's Cottage in The Rocks. You can see rock engravings up close on the Manly Scenic Walkway and in the Ku-ring-gai Chase National Park.

Unfortunately, there are very few companies offering tours concentrating on the city's Aboriginal culture. An easily accessible option is an Aboriginal Heritage Tour in the Sydney Royal Botanic Gardens.

Outside Sydney, there are many sites of Aboriginal heritage, including Brisbane Water National Park near Gosford; Gunderbooka National Park; the Pilliga Forest; the Murramarang Aboriginal Area in the national park of the same name; and the Mt Grenfell Historic Site.

Tour companies include Blue Mountains Walkabout, which runs guided adventurous treks with Aboriginal and spiritual themes; Muggadah Indigenous Tours, which runs guided walks viewing significant cultural sites on traditional land around Echo Point near Katoomba; and Aboriginal Cultural Concepts in Ballina, which offers an Aboriginal heritage tour along the Bundjalung Coast. Other options include Warrumbungle Tara Cave Walk in the wonderfully monikered Warrumbungle National Park, or visits to the remote Mungo National Park guided by the indigenous-owned and -operated Harry Nanya Tours.

Cultural centres include the Muru Mittigar Aboriginal Cultural Centre (p138) in Castlereagh near Penrith, the Aboriginal Cultural Centre & Keeping Place in Armidale, the Yarrawarra Aboriginal Cultural Centre in Red Rock, the Minjungbal Aboriginal Cultural Centre in Tweed Heads and the Umbarra Cultural Centre near Bermagui.

For more information about indigenous NSW, go to www.visitnsw.com.au and follow the links to Aboriginal NSW under Things to Do/Attractions, or go to www.indigenoustourism.australia.com for links to Indigenous-owned and -operated tour and accommodation operators, as well as artists and art organisations. Be warned, though, that the information available at both of these sites can be out of date.

National Parks

There are over 800 exceptionally diverse national parks and reserves in NSW, from the subtropical rainforest of the Border Ranges and white peaks of the Snowy Mountains to the haunting, fragile landscapes of the outback. In reasonable weather most of these parks and reserves are accessible by conventional vehicle; unfortunately, few can be accessed by public transport.

The **NSW National Parks & Wildlife Service** (NPWS; Map p80; www.nationalparks.nsw.gov.au) does an excellent job. Many parks have visitor centres with detailed information on the area, walking tracks and camping options. Where there isn't one, visit the nearest NPWS office for information.

Forty-six of the parks charge daily entry fees, generally $7 per vehicle; check the NPWS website for a list. If you plan on visiting a number of parks, consider purchasing an annual multi-park pass ($65), which gives unlimited entry to all the state's parks and reserves except Kosciuszko National Park and the Chowder Bay precinct of Sydney Harbour National Park.

Many parks have camp sites with facilities; some are free, others cost between $5 and $10 a night per person. Popular sites are often booked out during holidays. Bush camping is allowed in some parks; contact the NPWS office for regulations.

Activities

The state offers a huge array of activities suiting every level of fitness and fearlessness.

Birdwatching

Lord Howe Island is known for its bird life, as are Dorrigo National Park and the Macquarie Marshes Nature Reserve.

Bushwalking

Almost every national park has marked trails or wilderness-walking opportunities; these range from gentle wanders to longer, more challenging treks.

Near Sydney, the wilderness areas of Royal National Park hide dramatic clifftop walks including a 28km coastal walking trail. There are smaller bushwalks around the inlets of Broken Bay in Ku-ring-gai Chase National Park.

West of Sydney, the sandstone bluffs, eucalyptus forests and wildflowers of the Blue Mountains offer a breathtaking experience, as does the walk to the summit of Australia's highest peak, Mt Kosciuszko (2228m), in Kosciuszko National Park.

In the state's northwest, Warrumbungle National Park, with its volcanic peaks, has over 30km of trails to keep you busy.

The Yuraygir Coastal Walk is a 65km signposted walk from Angourie to Red Rock following the path of the coastal emu over a series of tracks, trails, beaches and rock platforms, and passing through the villages of Brooms Head, Minne Water and Wooli.

Keen trampers should try the 15km Syndicate Ridge Walking Trail near Bellingen, the 45km Six Foot Track from Katoomba to the Jenolan Caves and the 100km World Heritage Walk in Washpool National Park on the south coast. Those who can cope with steep ascents should consider taking the challenge of climbing the 980m-high Pigeon House Mountain.

There are also great walks on Lord Howe Island and Norfolk Island.

The NPWS website offers loads of information about walks within its parks and reserves, and the National Parks Association of NSW (www.npansw.org.au) publishes the highly regarded *Bushwalks in the Sydney Region Volumes 1 & 2* by S Lord and G Daniel; these can be purchased through the association's website. Also look out for *Sydney's Best Bush, Park & City Walks* (Veechi Stuart), which includes 50 walks and covers most of the major national parks; the highly regarded *Blue Mountains: Best Bushwalks* is by the same author. Another useful resource is the online bushwalking and camping resource Wildwalks (www.wildwalks.com), which provides free maps and track notes for over 900 walks and publishes three bushwalking guides: *The Great North Walk*; *Best River & Alpine Walks around Mt Kosciuszko*; and *Best Bush & Coastal Walks of the Central Coast*. Each can be purchased through the website.

Cycling

Sydney's ever-growing network of cycling paths is a pivotal component of Sydney City Council's praiseworthy Sustainable City 2030 initiative. See http://sydneycycleways.net/ for details.

Other popular cycling destinations include the Blue Mountains and the Great North Rd around the Hawkesbury River. In the southeast, mountain biking is a warm-weather favourite in Kosciuszko National Park and at Mt Canobolas, southwest of Orange.

You can access cycling guides and maps, a handy bike-shop finder, safety tips and the *PushOn* bikeriders' magazine through the Resources pages of the Bicycle NSW website (www.bicyclensw.org.au). Lonely Planet's *Cycling Australia* is another useful resource.

Diving & Snorkelling

North of Sydney, try Broughton Island near Port Stephens and Fish Rock Cave off South West Rocks. You can swim with grey nurse sharks at Narooma and with leopard sharks at Julian Rocks Marine Reserve off Byron Bay. Good dive schools can be found at Byron Bay and Coffs Harbour; the Coffs Harbour ones can organise dives in Solitary Islands Marine Park, where warm tropical currents and cooler southern currents meet, resulting in a wonderful combination of corals, reef fish and seaweeds.

On the South Coast popular diving spots include Jervis Bay, Montague Island and Bass Point near Shellharbour.

There's also great diving and snorkelling on Lord Howe Island.

Scenic Drives

Spectacular scenic drives include the Greater Blue Mountains Drive; the Bells Line of Road between Richmond and Lithgow; the Waterfall Way from just south of Coffs Harbour to inland Armidale; Loop Rd, which takes you from Gleniffer near Bellingen to the foot of the New England tableland; and the Alpine Way in the Snowy Mountains.

Skiing & Snowboarding

Snowfields criss-cross the NSW–Victoria border. The season usually runs from early June to late August, but sometimes snow lasts until early October; snowfalls can be unpredictable. Cross-country skiing is popular and most resorts offer lessons and equipment.

The Snowy Mountains boast popular resorts including Charlotte Pass, Perisher Blue, Selwyn and Thredbo.

Surfing

You can fine-tune your surfing skills (or indeed learn some) at Newcastle, Port Macquarie and Coffs Harbour. Crescent Head is the longboarding capital of Australia, and the gnarly swells at Angourie Point are for seasoned surfers and/or nutcases only. Further north, you can hang ten at Lennox Head and Byron Bay.

The South Coast is literally awash with great surf beaches, particularly around Wollongong, Batemans Bay and Bermagui.

For surf forecasts and other information, go to www.coastalwatch.com.

Whale & Dolphin Watching

Every year between late May and late November, southern right and humpback whales migrate along Australia's southern coast. Get up close to these magnificent creatures on a whale-watching cruise; good spots are Eden in southern NSW and along the mid-north coast at Coffs Harbour and Port Stephens. Eden even hosts a whale-watching festival in early November each year.

Dolphins can be seen year-round at many places along the NSW coast, including Jervis Bay, Port Stephens and Byron Bay. They're even occasionally seen off Sydney's Eastern Beaches.

White-Water Rafting, Kayaking & Canoeing

For rafting, try the upper Murray near Jindabyne.

There is stunning sea kayaking at Byron Bay, Lord Howe Island, Batemans Bay and Eden. You can also kayak around Sydney Harbour.

For canoeing, head to Barrington Tops National Park, Myall Lakes National Park, Bellingen, Coffs Harbour and the Kangaroo Valley.

For more information, check the Paddle NSW (www.paddlensw.org.au) and River Canoe Club of NSW (www.rivercanoeclub.canoe.org.au) websites.

Wine Regions

The oldest and best-known wine region in NSW is the Hunter Valley, which is known for its semillon and shiraz. Though it has long held the reputation as the state's premier wine-growing area, its claim to this accolade has been seriously challenged in recent decades by the Central Ranges Region, which comprises Cowra, known for its chardonnay; Mudgee, for its cabernet sauvignon and shiraz; and Orange, for a number of varietals including shiraz, cabernet sauvignon, chardonnay and sauvignon blanc.

Other wine regions include the Southern New South Wales Zone, made up of Gundagai (known for its chardonnay, shiraz and cabernet sauvignon); Hilltops (for its cabernet sauvignon and shiraz); and Tumbarumba (for its pinot noir, chardonnay and sparkling wines).

Smaller and less-renowned regions include the Riverina, Perricoota, Shoalhaven Coast, Southern Highlands, Hastings River, Northern Slopes and the Western Plains.

Oenophiles should consider visiting Orange in late October for its **Wine Week** (www.tasteorange.com.au/wine week), 10 days of events and activities highlighting the region's premium wines. Other wine-related events include the Hunter Valley Wine & Food Month in June, the **Mudgee Wine Festival** (www.mudgeewine.com.au) in September and the **UnWINEd in the Riverina Festival** (www.unwined-riverina.com) held in Griffith in early June.

Yoga & Alternative Therapies

There's only one place to go if you're keen to indulge in a spot of yoga or investigate some alternative therapies: Byron Bay.

Tours

NSW offers tours to suit all tastes and budgets: wineries, whale watching, bushwalking, Aboriginal heritage, surfing and more.

Seasonal Work

Most seasonal work is available in autumn, when the fruit and grapes harvests occur.

In winter, there are plenty of jobs available in the snowfields of the Snowy Mountains.

The Australian Government's **Harvest Trail** (☎1800 062 332; www.jobsearch.gov.au/harvesttrail) is an excellent resource for job hunters.

Getting There & Around

By car and motorcycle, you'll probably reach NSW via the Hume Hwy (Rte 31) if you're coming from the south, or via the Pacific Hwy (Rte 1) if you're coming from the north. The Princes Hwy heads south from Sydney along the state's southern coast.

AIR

Sydney Airport (p131) is the main gateway for most visitors to Australia and is also the country's major domestic hub.

Qantas (☎13 13 13; www.qantas.com.au), **Jetstar** (☎13 15 38; www.jetstar.com.au), **Virgin Australia** (☎13 67 89; www.virginaustralia. com) and **Tiger Airways** (☎03-9335 3033; www.tigerairways.com/au/en) have frequent domestic flights to/from Sydney. Qantas and smaller airlines, including **Rex** (Regional Express; ☎13 17 13; www.rex.com.au), **Brindabella Airlines** (☎1300 66 88 24; www.brindabellaairlines.com.au) and **Aeropelican** (☎13 13 13; www.aeropelican.com.au), fly to rural destinations throughout NSW.

BUS

Bus is the major form of transport to most towns in NSW. If you want to make multistop trips, look for cheap stopover deals rather than buying separate tickets. In remote areas school buses may be the only public-transport option; the drivers will usually pick you up, but they're not obliged to. Note that fares purchased online are marginally cheaper than over-the-counter tickets.

There are a number of bus companies servicing intra- and interstate routes.

Australia Wide (☎02-9516 1300; www.austwidecoaches.com.au) Sydney to Orange and Bathurst.

Busways (☎02-9625 8900; www.busways.com.au) Hundreds of local routes on the north and central coasts as well as in southwest Sydney.

Firefly (Map p80; ☎1300 730 740; www.fireflyexpress.com.au) Sydney to Adelaide via Canberra and Melbourne.

Greyhound (☎1300 4739 46863, 1300 GREYHOUND; www.greyhound.com.au) Services from Sydney to Canberra, Melbourne, Wagga Wagga, Newcastle, Coffs Harbour, Byron Bay, Surfers Paradise and Brisbane.

Murrays (☎13 22 51; www.murrays.com.au) Services between Sydney, Canberra and the South Coast all year, and between Canberra and the snow fields during the ski season.

Port Stephens Coaches (☎02-4982 2926; www.pscoaches.com.au) Sydney and Newcastle to Port Stephens.

Premier (☎13 34 10; www.premierms.com.au) Sydney to Coffs Harbour, Byron Bay, Gold Coast, Brisbane, Airlie Beach and Cairns.

Priors Scenic Express (☎1800 816 234; www.priorsbus.com.au) Parramatta to Moruya via Bowral, Nowra and Batemans Bay.

TRAIN

CountryLink (☎13 22 32; www.countrylink.info) The state rail service will take you to many sizeable towns in NSW, in conjunction with connecting buses. You need to book in advance by phone, online or in person at one of Sydney's CountryLink Travel Centres – these are listed on its website. CountryLink offers 1st- and economy-class tickets, as well as a quota of discount and multistop tickets: the Backtracker Pass, only available to international visitors, offers unlimited travel on the CountryLink network, including Sydney, country NSW, the Gold Coast, Brisbane, Canberra and Melbourne, from $218/251/273/383 for 14 days/one month/three months/six months.

CityRail (p133), the Sydney metropolitan service, runs frequent commuter-style trains south through Wollongong to Bomaderry; west through the Blue Mountains to Katoomba and Lithgow; north to Newcastle; and southwest through the Southern Highlands to Goulburn. For train information, visit a CityRail Information Booth at Circular Quay, Central Station, Town Hall Station or Kings Cross Station.

SYDNEY

POP 4.5 MILLION

More laid back than any major metropolis should rightly be, Australia's only truly international city (and one of the great ones at that) is home to three of the country's major icons – the Harbour Bridge, the Opera House and Bondi Beach – but her attractions definitely don't stop there. This is the country's oldest, largest and most diverse city, a sun-kissed settlement that is characterised by spectacular scenery and the charm of its residents.

Sights

Sydney Harbour

Stretching 20km inland from the South Pacific Ocean to the mouth of the Parramatta River, this magnificent natural harbour is the city's shimmering soul and the focus of every visitor's stay. Providing a serene and picture-perfect backdrop to Sydney's fast-paced urban lifestyle, the harbour's beaches, coves, bays, islands and wildlife-filled pockets of national park offer locals innumerable options for recreation, relaxation and rejuvenation. Exploring this vast and visually arresting area by ferry is one of Sydney's great joys.

Forming the gateway to the harbour from the ocean are **North Head** and **South Head**. The former fishing village of **Watsons Bay** nestles on South Head's harbour side, and the city's favourite day-trip destination, **Manly**, occupies a promontory straddling harbour and ocean near North Head. Into the harbour and roughly equidistant between the heads is the North Shore's **Middle Head**, characterised by sheltered coves and upmarket residential suburbs.

The focal point of the inner harbour and the city's major transport hub is **Circular Quay**, home to the Sydney Opera House and the recently renovated Museum of Modern Art (MCA). From here, you are able to access the central business district and catch ferries to destinations along both shores of the harbour and to some of the harbour islands.

Sydney Harbour National Park NATIONAL PARK

(www.npws.nsw.gov.au) Sydney Harbour National Park protects large swathes of bushland around the harbour shoreline, plus several **harbour islands**. In among the greenery you'll find walking tracks, scenic lookouts, Aboriginal carvings, beaches and a handful of historic sites. The park incorporates South Head and Nielsen Park south of the harbour, but most of it is on the North Shore – including Bradleys Head, Middle Head, Dobroyd Head and North Head. Free brochures, including self-guided tours, are available from the Sydney Harbour National Park Information Centre (p131) in The Rocks.

The park also includes five harbour islands: Clark Island off Darling Point, Shark Island off Rose Bay, Rodd Island in Iron Cover near Birkenhead, Goat Island off Balmain and the small, fortified Fort Denison off Mrs Macquaries Point. Three of these can be visited on daily tours – see the boxed text on p74 for details.

Sydney Harbour Bridge BRIDGE

(Map p80; Circular Quay, Circular Quay, Circular Quay) Sydneysiders adore their 'coathanger'. Thousands of them drive, walk and rollerblade across it every day, others clamour over it on the wildly popular BridgeClimb (p101) tour or sail under it on a Sydney ferry. Celebrated by the nation's poets, novelists, photographers and painters ever since its opening in 1932, it provides the harbour with a powerful and instantly recognisable visual signature.

The bridge's vital statistics are impressive: 134m high, 502m long, 49m wide and 53,000 tonnes. Linking the CBD with North Sydney at one of the harbour's narrowest points, it was the the world's widest long-span bridge when it was constructed and is still one of the largest bridges of its kind in the world.

The best way to experience the bridge is on foot – don't expect much of a view crossing by train or car (driving south there's a toll). Staircases access the bridge from both

SYDNEY IN...

Two Days

Start your first day at **Circular Quay**. Visit the **Museum of Modern Art (MCA)** and then follow the harbourside walkway to the **Art Gallery of NSW**. That night, enjoy a performance at the **Opera House** or check out the action in **Kings Cross** or **Darlinghurst**.

Next day, it's time to spend the day soaking up the sun and scene at **Bondi** – be sure to take the **clifftop walk** to Coogee and then make your way back to Bondi for a sunset drink at **Icebergs Dining Room & Bar**.

Four Days

On day three, board a ferry and sail through the Heads to **Manly**, where you can swim at the beach or follow the 10km Manly Scenic Walkway. That night, head to **Surry Hills** for drinks and dinner.

On day four, learn about Sydney's convict heritage at the **Hyde Park Barracks Museum** and then spend the afternoon shopping in **Paddington** or **Newtown**.

One Week

With a week, you can spare a couple of days to visit the majestic **Blue Mountains**, fitting in a full day of bushwalking before rewarding yourself with a gourmet dinner. Back in Sydney, explore **The Rocks**, **Sydney Harbour National Park** and the **Taronga Zoo**.

Sydney

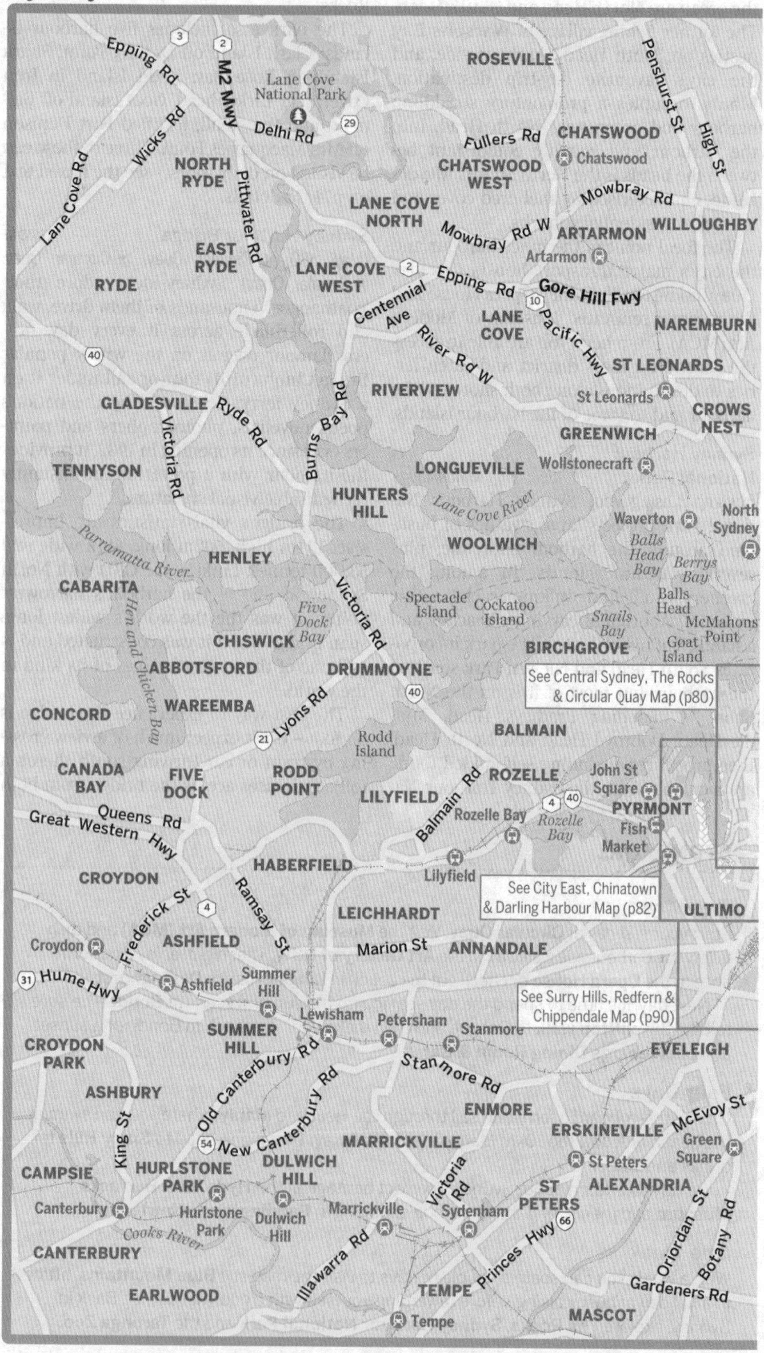

Epping Rd
M2 Mwy
Lane Cove National Park
Delhi Rd
ROSEVILLE
Penshurst St
High St
Wicks Rd
Lane Cove Rd
NORTH RYDE
Pittwater Rd
Fullers Rd
CHATSWOOD
Chatswood
CHATSWOOD WEST
LANE COVE NORTH
Mowbray Rd
Mowbray Rd W
ARTARMON
WILLOUGHBY
Artarmon
EAST RYDE
LANE COVE WEST
Epping Rd
Gore Hill Fwy
RYDE
Centennial Ave
LANE COVE
Pacific Hwy
NAREMBURN
River Rd W
ST LEONARDS
St Leonards
RIVERVIEW
CROWS NEST
GLADESVILLE
Ryde Rd
Burns Bay Rd
GREENWICH
Victoria Rd
TENNYSON
LONGUEVILLE
Wollstonecraft
HUNTERS HILL
Lane Cove River
Waverton
North Sydney
WOOLWICH
Balls Head Bay
Berrys Bay
Parramatta River
HENLEY
CABARITA
Hen and Chicken Bay
Five Dock Bay
Victoria Rd
Spectacle Island
Cockatoo Island
Balls Head
Snails Bay
McMahons Point
CHISWICK
Goat Island
BIRCHGROVE
ABBOTSFORD
DRUMMOYNE
See Central Sydney, The Rocks & Circular Quay Map (p80)
CONCORD
WAREEMBA
Lyons Rd
BALMAIN
Rodd Island
CANADA BAY
FIVE DOCK
RODD POINT
Balmain Rd
ROZELLE
John St Square
LILYFIELD
PYRMONT
Queens Rd
Rozelle Bay
Great Western Hwy
Fish Market
HABERFIELD
CROYDON
Lilyfield
Ramsay St
See City East, Chinatown & Darling Harbour Map (p82)
Frederick St
LEICHHARDT
ULTIMO
Croydon
ASHFIELD
Marion St
ANNANDALE
Hume Hwy
Ashfield
Summer Hill
See Surry Hills, Redfern & Chippendale Map (p90)
Lewisham
Petersham
Stanmore
SUMMER HILL
CROYDON PARK
Old Canterbury Rd
EVELEIGH
Stanmore Rd
ASHBURY
New Canterbury Rd
ENMORE
McEvoy St
ERSKINEVILLE
Green Square
King St
MARRICKVILLE
CAMPSIE
HURLSTONE PARK
DULWICH HILL
St Peters
Victoria Rd
ST PETERS
ALEXANDRIA
Canterbury
Hurlstone Park
Dulwich Hill
Marrickville
Sydenham
Cooks River
Illawarra Rd
Princes Hwy
Oriordan St
Botany Rd
CANTERBURY
TEMPE
Gardeners Rd
EARLWOOD
Tempe
MASCOT

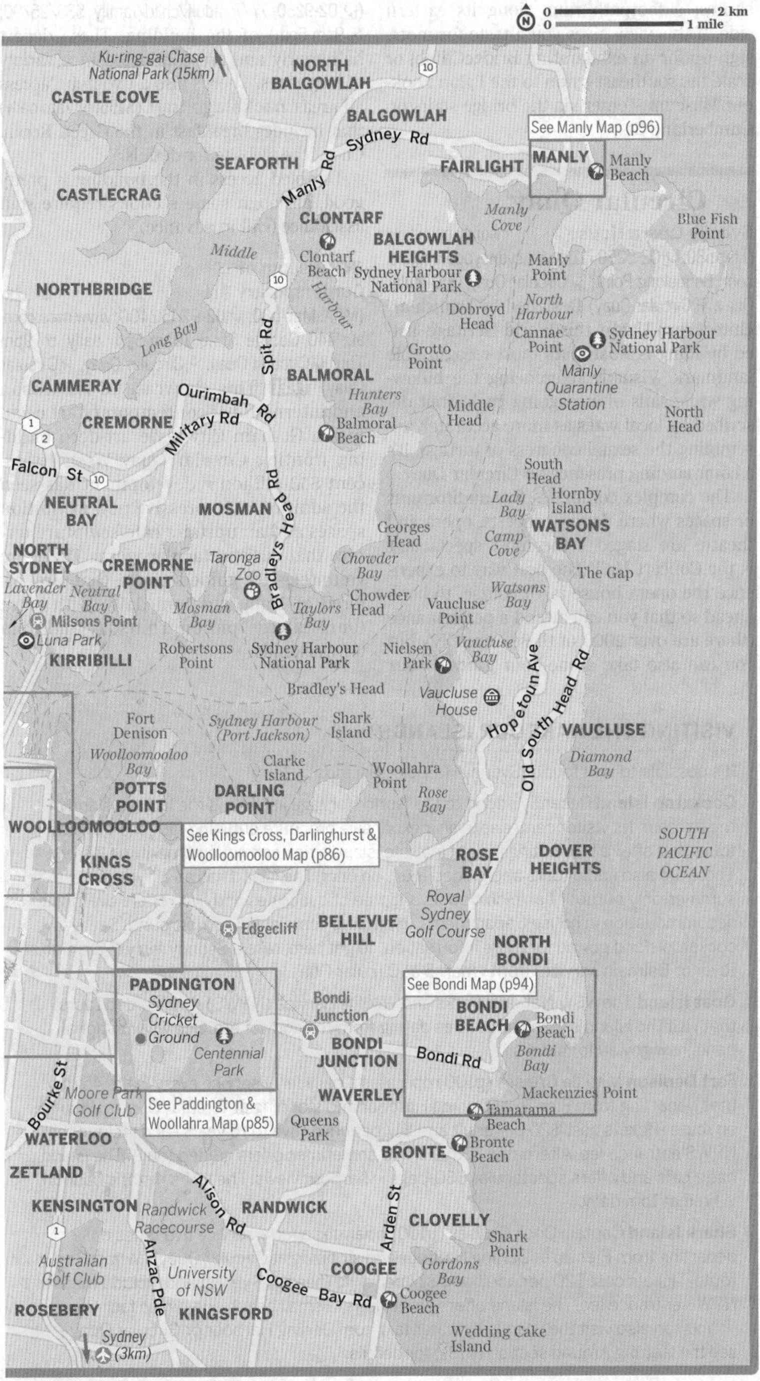
0
2 km
0
1 mile
Ku-ring-gai Chase National Park (15km)
NORTH BALGOWLAH
CASTLE COVE
BALGOWLAH
See Manly Map (p96)
Sydney Rd
Manly Rd
SEAFORTH
FAIRLIGHT
MANLY
Manly Beach
CASTLECRAG
CLONTARF
Manly Cove
Blue Fish Point
BALGOWLAH HEIGHTS
Middle
Clontarf Beach
Sydney Harbour National Park
Manly Point
NORTHBRIDGE
Harbour
Dobroyd Head
North Harbour
Long Bay
Spit Rd
Grotto Point
Cannae Point
Sydney Harbour National Park
Manly Quarantine Station
BALMORAL
CAMMERAY
Ourimbah Rd
Hunters Bay
Middle Head
North Head
CREMORNE
Military Rd
Balmoral Beach
Falcon St
South Head
NEUTRAL BAY
Lady Bay
Hornby Island
MOSMAN
Bradleys Head Rd
Georges Head
WATSONS BAY
Camp Cove
NORTH SYDNEY
CREMORNE POINT
Taronga Zoo
Chowder Bay
The Gap
Lavender Bay
Neutral Bay
Watsons Bay
Chowder Head
Vaucluse Point
Mosman Bay
Taylors Bay
Milsons Point
Luna Park
Vaucluse Bay
Robertsons Point
Sydney Harbour National Park
Nielsen Park
KIRRIBILLI
Hopetoun Ave
Old South Head Rd
Bradley's Head
Vaucluse House
Fort Denison
Sydney Harbour (Port Jackson)
Shark Island
VAUCLUSE
Woolloomooloo Bay
Diamond Bay
Clarke Island
Woollahra Point
POTTS POINT
DARLING POINT
Rose Bay
WOOLLOOMOOLOO
See Kings Cross, Darlinghurst & Woolloomooloo Map (p86)
SOUTH PACIFIC OCEAN
KINGS CROSS
ROSE BAY
DOVER HEIGHTS
Royal Sydney Golf Course
Edgecliff
BELLEVUE HILL
NORTH BONDI
PADDINGTON
See Bondi Map (p94)
Sydney Cricket Ground
Bondi Junction
BONDI BEACH
Bondi Beach
Centennial Park
BONDI JUNCTION
Bondi Rd
Bondi Bay
Bourke St
Moore Park Golf Club
See Paddington & Woollahra Map (p85)
WAVERLEY
Mackenzies Point
Tamarama Beach
Queens Park
WATERLOO
BRONTE
Bronte Beach
ZETLAND
Alison Rd
KENSINGTON
Randwick Racecourse
RANDWICK
Arden St
CLOVELLY
Shark Point
Anzac Pde
Australian Golf Club
Gordons Bay
COOGEE
University of NSW
Coogee Bay Rd
Coogee Beach
ROSEBERY
KINGSFORD
Wedding Cake Island
Sydney (3km)

shores; a footpath runs along its eastern side. If this view gives you a taste for more, sign up for an exhilarating BridgeClimb, or scale the southeast pylon to the Pylon Lookout Museum – enter via the bridge stairs on Cumberland St.

Circular Quay

Sydney Opera House NOTABLE BUILDING

(Map p80; ☎02-9250 7111; www.sydneyoperahouse.com; Bennelong Point; Circular Quay, Circular Quay, Circular Quay) Designed by Danish architect Jørn Utzon, this World Heritage–listed building is Australia's most recognisable landmark. Visually referencing the billowing white sails of a seagoing yacht (but described by local wags as more accurately resembling the sexual congress of turtles), it's a commanding presence on Circular Quay.

The complex comprises five auditoriums or spaces where dance, concerts, opera and theatre are staged – the most spectacular is the Concert Hall. The best way to experience the opera house is, of course, to book ahead so that you can attend a performance (there are over 2000 of these annually), but you can also take a one-hour **guided tour** (☎02-9250 7777; adult/child/family $35/25/90; 9am-5pm) of the building. These depart half-hourly and are conducted in a variety of languages. There's also a two-hour 'access all areas' **backstage tour** ($155; 7am daily) that includes breakfast in the Green Room. Check the website for details.

Disabled access in the building is pretty good, although some sections require staff assistance (call in advance).

★ **Museum of Contemporary Art** GALLERY

(MCA; Map p80; ☎02-9245 2400; www.mca.com.au; 140 George St; 10am-5pm daily, to 9pm Thu; Circular Quay, Circular Quay, Circular Quay) FREE This showcase of Australian and international contemporary art occupies a Gotham City–style art-deco building fronting Circular Quay West. Its recent $53-million redevelopment has seen the addition of impressive new exhibition spaces and an upstairs cafe/sculpture terrace that has spectacular views. There are volunteer-led guided tours that are offered at 11am and 1pm daily, with extra tours run at 7pm on Thursday and 3pm on weekends.

VISITING THE HARBOUR ISLANDS

It's possible to visit four of Sydney Harbour's islands by ferry:

Cockatoo Island Recently added to the World Heritage list, this is the largest island in the harbour. Its visitor centre sells an inexpensive brochure outlining four self-guided tours that offer a fascinating insight into the island's rich convict and maritime history. There are also audio tours and guided tours on offer. The island has an all-year cafe, a summer-only outdoor bar, picnic spots and free bbq facilities and even offers overnight accommodation in houses, apartments, 'glamping' tents and a campground. See www.cockatooisland.gov.au for more information. To get here, take a Sydney ferry (Paramatta River or Balmain service) from Wharf 5 at Circular Quay.

Goat Island The NSW National Parks and Wildlife Service (NPWS) runs guided tours that visit the island's many structures dating from the convict era. See www.nationalparks.nsw.gov.au for details.

Fort Denison Matilda Cruises (p100) operates a daily ferry service every 30 to 45 minutes departing from Pier 26 at Darling Harbour and stopping at Circular Quay's Wharf 6 en route. Tickets cost $20 per adult and $17 per child (five to 15 years) and include the NPWS entrance fee. Alternatively, the NPWS sometimes offers guided tours. The island has a cafe and offers spectacular 360-degree harbour views. The fort's historic cannon is fired at 1pm daily.

Shark Island Captain Cook Cruises (p100) operates a ferry service five times daily departing from Pier 26 at Darling Harbour and stopping at Circular Quay's Wharf 6 en route. Tickets cost $20 per adult and $17 per child (five to 15 years) and include the NPWS entrance fee. The island offers great views, a small beach and picnic facilities.

You can also visit the islands by water taxi from Darling Harbour or Circular Quay – see the Getting Around section (p131) for details.

DISCOUNT PASSES

History buffs should be sure to purchase a **Ticket Through Time** (☎02-8239 2211; www.hht.net.au/visiting/ticket_through_time; adult/concession & child/family $30/15/60), which gives access to 11 properties opened to the public by the Historic Houses Trust (HHT). The pass is valid for three months and is available online or at most HHT properties.

The **Ultimate Sydney Pass** (adult/child $95/70), available from the Sydney Tower Eye, is valid for 30 days and gives entry to the Sydney Tower Eye and Skywalk in Central Sydney and SEA LIFE Sydney Aquarium, WILD LIFE Sydney Zoo and Madame Tussaud's at Darling Harbour.

The **4 Attraction Combo Pass** (adult/child/family $67.50/49.50/216) gives entry to the Sydney Tower Eye, Manly SEA LIFE Sanctuary, SEA LIFE Sydney Aquarium and WILD LIFE Sydney Zoo. It's available from all four venues.

Australian Travel Specialists (ATS; ☎1800 355 537; www.atstravel.com.au; ticket booths at Wharf 6, Circular Quay & Harbourside Shopping Centre, Darling Harbour) also offer a number of discount passes to sights and attractions in and around Sydney, but these don't always offer a useful saving. Be sure to investigate fully before purchasing.

The museum's constantly changing exhibition program has a particularly strong multimedia focus, but painting and sculpture also feature prominently. Highlights include the annual 'Primavera' show held in spring, which showcases Australian visual artists under the age of 35, and the artist-curated ARTBAR event (adult/concession $20/15) held on the last Friday evening of every month. This showcases art, design, dance and performance and is one of the hottest arts tickets in town.

Entry to the permanent exhibitions is free, but charges are levied for special exhibitions.

Customs House HISTORIC BUILDING
(Map p80; ☎02-9242 8555; www.cityofsydney.nsw.gov.au/customshouse/thelibrary; 31 Alfred St; ⏲10am-7pm Mon-Fri, 11am-4pm Sat & Sun; 🚌Circular Quay, ⛴Circular Quay, 🚆Circular Quay) FREE Opposite the unforgivably dishevelled Circular Quay transport hub, this handsome 1885 building houses a branch of Sydney City Libraries where it's possible to access the internet via free wi-fi or the library's own terminals ($3 per 30 minutes), read a huge selection of newspapers and magazines, use toilet facilities and admire a 1:500 model of the inner city displayed under the foyer's glass floor.

Justice & Police Museum MUSEUM
(Map p80; ☎02-9252 1144; www.hht.net.au; cnr Albert & Phillip Sts; adult/child $10/5; ⏲10am-5pm Sat & Sun; 🚆Circular Quay) Occupying the former Water Police Station (1858), this small museum opposite Circular Quay East documents the city's dark and disreputable past through a constantly changing and often macabre series of exhibitions.

The Rocks

The site of Sydney's first European settlement has evolved unrecognisably from the days when its residents sloshed through open sewers and squalid alleyways. Here, sailors, whalers and larrikins boozed and brawled shamelessly in countless harbourside pubs and nearly as many brothels and opium dens.

The Rocks remained a commercial and maritime hub until shipping services moved from Circular Quay in the late 1800s. A bubonic plague outbreak in 1900 continued the decline. Construction of the Harbour Bridge in the 1920s caused the demolition of many buildings, with entire streets disappearing under the bridge's southern approach.

It wasn't until the 1970s that The Rocks' cultural and architectural heritage was recognised. The ensuing tourism-driven redevelopment saved many old buildings, but has turned the area east of the bridge highway into a tourist trap where kitsch cafes and shops hocking stuffed koalas and ersatz didgeridoos reign supreme. Nevertheless, it's a fascinating area to explore on foot.

Beyond the **Argyle Cut**, an impressive tunnel excavated by convicts, is **Millers Point**, a charming district of early colonial homes; stroll here to enjoy everything The Rocks is not. **Argyle Place** (Map p80; Argyle St; 🚆Circular Quay) is an English-style village green overlooked by **Garrison Church** (Map p80; 9247 1268; www.thegarrisonchurch.org.au; 62 Lower Fort St; 9am-5pm; Circular Quay), Australia's oldest house of worship (1848).

The wharves around Dawes Point are rapidly emerging from prolonged decay. Walsh Bay's Pier 4 houses the renowned Sydney Theatre Company and several other performance troupes. The impressive Sydney Theatre is across the road.

The Rocks Discovery Museum MUSEUM
(Map p80; 02-9240 8680; www.rocksdiscoverymuseum.com; 2-8 Kendall La; 10am-5pm; Circular Quay, Circular Quay, Circular Quay) FREE Divided into four chronological displays – Warrane (pre-1788), Colony (1788–1820), Port (1820–1900) and Transformations (1900 to the present) – this excellent museum digs deep into The Rocks' history and leads you on an artefact-rich tour. Sensitive attention is given to The Rocks' original inhabitants, the Gadigal people.

SH Ervin Gallery GALLERY
(Map p80; 02-9258 0173; www.shervingallery.com.au; Watson Rd; adult/concession/under 12 $7/5/free; 11am-5pm Tue-Sun; Wynyard) Perched high on Observatory Hill inside the old Fort St School (1856), this National Trust–operated gallery exhibits historial and contemporary Australian art, with an emphasis on works by women artists. There's a cafe here, too.

Sydney Observatory OBSERVATORY
(Map p80; 02-9921 3485; www.sydneyobservatory.com.au; Watson Rd; building & grounds free, telescope & 3D theatre adult/concession & child $8/6, night telescope & 3D theatre adult/concession $18/14; 10am-5pm; Circular Quay, Circular Quay, Circular Quay) FREE Built in the 1850s, Sydney's copper-domed observatory sits in gardens overlooking Millers Point and the harbour. Inside is a collection of vintage apparatus, including Australia's oldest working telescope (1874). Also on offer are AV displays, an interactive Australian astronomy exhibition including Aboriginal sky stories and modern stargazing, and a 3D Theatre. Bookings are essential for the night telescope & theatre sessions.

Susannah Place Museum MUSEUM
(Map p80; 02-9241 1893; www.hht.net.au; 58-64 Gloucester St; adult/child $8/4; guided tours 2pm, 3pm & 4pm daily; Circular Quay, Circular Quay, Circular Quay) Dating from 1844, this diminutive terrace of four houses and a shop selling historical wares is a fascinating time-capsule of life in inner-city Sydney since colonial times. After watching a documentary about the people who lived here (some until as recently as 1990), a guide will take you through the claustrophobic terraces, which are decorated to reflect different periods in their histories.

City East

Narrow lanes lead southeast from Circular Quay up the hill towards Sydney's historic parliament precinct on Macquarie St. Further east again are the wonderful Royal Botanic Gardens and a 34 hectare tract of parkland known as the Domain.

Royal Botanic Gardens GARDENS
(Map p80; 02-9231 8111; www.rbgsyd.nsw.gov.au; Mrs Macquaries Rd; 7am-sunset; Circular Quay, Circular Quay, Circular Quay or Martin Pl) FREE Before European settlement, the tidal area along Woccanmagully (Farm Cove) was used by the Gadigal (Cadigal) people as an initiation ground. It was then used by Governors Phillip and Macquarie as a private reserve. In 1816 Allan Cunningham arrived in the colony and was appointed the king's botanist. He was soon succeeded by Charles Fraser, who started planting a botanical garden next to the governor's vegetable garden in 1817. By 1821 Fraser was formally appointed Government Colonial Botanist and part of his duties includes being superintendent of the colony's new Botanic Gardens. By 1831 roads and paths had been constructed through the Domain to allow public access.

Highlights of this 30-hectare urban oasis include the rose garden, rainforest walk and palm grove. The Cadi Jam Ora display tells the story of the Gadigal people and features plants that grew on this site before European settlement – it's best explored on an **Aboriginal Heritage Tour** (02-9231 8134; adult/student & child $36.50/16.50; 10am Fri), which includes bush-food tastings. Advance bookings are essential.

At the northeastern tip of the gardens is a scenic lookout known as **Mrs Macquaries Point**. It was named in 1810 after Elizabeth, Governor Macquarie's wife, who ordered a chair chiselled into the rock from which she'd view the harbour. In summer the OpenAir Cinema (p126) operates here.

Volunteers conduct free 1½-hour **guided walks** of the gardens departing from the information counter at the garden shop at 10.30am daily; there are extra walks at 1pm on weekdays from March to November. To enjoy wonderful views of the harbour and gardens, follow the path from the Opera House around Farm Cove, past Mrs Macquarie's Point and along Woolloomooloo Bay to the Art Gallery of NSW and the Domain.

★ Art Gallery of NSW GALLERY
(Map p86; ☎1800 679 278; www.artgallery.nsw.gov.au; Art Gallery Rd, the Domain; ⏰10am-5pm Thu-Tue, to 9pm Wed; 🚆St James) FREE Magnificently located on an elevated site in The Domain, the state's flagship art gallery boasts an impressive collection of Australian and international art. Highlights include the Aboriginal and Torres Strait Islander art on display in the Yiribana Gallery on lower level 3, the contemporary galleries on lower level 2 and the Australian galleries on the ground floor. Temporary exhibition galleries host international and interstate touring exhibitions (entry charges often apply) as well as the annual and ever-controversial Archibald Prize, which showcases portraits of famous and not-so-famous Australians.

Popular gallery events include Art After Hours on Wednesday evenings, exhibition-related lectures, film screenings and free volunteer-guided tours – check the gallery's website for details. There's a cafe with outdoor terrace on lower level 1 and a restaurant with views across to Woolloomooloo Bay on the ground floor.

Government House HISTORIC BUILDING
(Map p80; ☎02-9931 5222; www.hht.net.au; Macquarie St; ⏰grounds 10am-4pm, tours 10.30am-3pm Fri-Sun; 🚌Circular Quay, ⛴Circular Quay, 🚆Circular Quay) FREE Encased in manicured grounds within the Royal Botanic Gardens, this Gothic sandstone mansion served as the home of NSW's governors from 1846 to 1996. The governor, who now resides in Admiralty House on the North Shore (Sydney's most prestigious address), still uses it for weekly meetings and when hosting visiting heads of state and royalty. The interior can only be visited on a guided tour; get your entry ticket from the gatehouse.

Around Hyde Park

Located at the southern end of Macquarie St, this much-loved civic park has a grand avenue of trees and a series of delightful fountains. Its dignified **Anzac Memorial** (Map p80; ☎9267 7668; www.rslnsw.com.au; Hyde Park; ⏰9am-5pm; 🚆Museum) FREE has an interior dome studded with one star for each of the 120,000 NSW citizens who served in WWI. **St Mary's Cathedral** (Map p80; ☎9220 0400; www.stmaryscathedral.org.au; cnr College St & St Marys Rd; ⏰6.30am-6.30pm; 🚆St James) overlooks the park from the eastern flank, while Sydney's **Great Synagogue** (Map p80; ☎9267 2477; www.greatsynagogue.org.au; 187a Elizabeth St; tours adult/child $10/5; ⏰tours noon Tue & Thu; 🚆St James), built in 1878, is on the western flank, and the city's oldest church, **St James'** (Map p80; ☎8227 1300; www.sjks.org.au; 173 King St; ⏰10am-4pm Mon-Fri, 9am-1pm Sat, 7.30am-4pm Sun; 🚆St James) (1819), overlooks the southern edge but is accessed via King Street.

Australian Museum MUSEUM
(Map p80; ☎02-9320 6000; http://australianmuseum.net.au; 6 College St; adult/child $12/8; ⏰9.30am-5pm; 🚆Museum) Occupying a prominent position opposite Hyde Park on the corner of William Street, this natural history museum stuffed its first animal and started collecting minerals just 40 years after the First Fleet dropped anchor and its curatorial philosophy and permanent exhibits don't appear to have changed much in the intervening centuries. The only exceptions are the changing exhibits in the Indigenous Australians gallery, which often showcases contemporary Aboriginal issues and art, and the blockbuster travelling exhibitions that the museum sources from overseas institutions.

AUSTRALIAN CONVICT SITES

The most recent Australian additions to the World Heritage List are 11 sites that are collectively known as the Australian Convict Sites (www.environment.gov.au/heritage/places/world/convict-sites). Four of these sites are in or around Sydney: Old Government House and Domain in Parramatta; Hyde Park Barracks in Sydney, Cockatoo Island at the junction of the Parramatta and Lane Cove Rivers in Sydney; and the Old Great North Road, which you can visit on your way to the Hunter Valley.

These sites are among a number in NSW dating back to early colonial times, including examples in Port Macquarie, Norfolk Island and Windsor.

Central Sydney

Sydney lacks a true civic centre, but **Martin Place** (Map p80; Martin Place) comes close. This grand pedestrian mall extends from Macquarie St to George St, and is lined with monumental financial buildings and the Victorian colonnaded general post office. There's a cenotaph commemorating Australia's war dead, an amphitheatre for lunchtime entertainment and plenty of places to sit and watch the weekday crowds. On weekends it's as quiet as a graveyard.

The 1874 **Town Hall** (Map p80; 9265 9189; www.cityofsydney.nsw.gov.au/sydneytownhall; 483 George St; 8am-6pm Mon-Fri; Town Hall) is a few blocks south of Martin Pl on the corner of George and Druitt Sts. The elaborate chamber room and concert hall inside match the fabulously ornate exterior. The neighbouring Anglican **St Andrew's Cathedral** (Map p80; 9265 1661; www.cathedral.sydney.anglican.asn.au; cnr George & Bathurst Sts; 10am-4pm Mon, Tue, Fri & Sat, 8am-8pm Wed, 10am-6.30pm Thu, 7.30am-8pm Sun; Town Hall) was built around the same time. Next to St Andrew's, occupying an entire city block, is the **Queen Victoria Building** (QVB; Map p80; 9264 9209; www.qvb.com.au; 455 George St; tours $15; 11am-5pm Sun, 9am-6pm Mon-Wed, Fri & Sat, 9am-9pm Thu; Town Hall), Sydney's most sumptuous shopping complex. Running a close second is the elegant Strand Arcade (p129) running between Pitt St Mall and George St, which has a strong representation of Australian designer fashion. On the corner of Pitt and Market Sts is Westfield Sydney (p130), the city's glitziest shopping mall. It's the access point for the Sydney Tower Eye (p78).

Breathing life into the southwestern zone is Sydney's much-loved **Chinatown** (Map p82; www.chinatown.com.au/eng; Dixon St; Town Hall), a vibrant district of restaurants, shops, street art and aroma-filled alleyways. Chinatown parties hard during Chinese New Year in late January/early February – streets throng with sideshows, digitally accompanied musicians and stalls selling everything from good-luck tokens to black-sesame ice-cream burgers (fear not: seeing jaunty, fire-breathing paper dragons after eating these is not a hallucinogenic effect).

Sydney Tower Eye TOWER
(Map p80; 02-9333 9222; www.sydneytowereye.com.au; 100 Market St; adult/child $26/15, Skywalk

City Walk
The Rocks

START THE ROCKS DISCOVERY MUSEUM
FINISH CADMANS COTTAGE
LENGTH 880M
DURATION 2 TO 3 HOURS

This area was where European settlers landed on 26 January 1788, and it remains the first port of call for most visitors to Sydney. Start this walk at **1 The Rocks Discovery Museum** (p76), where the exhibits offer an excellent overview of the area's rich and often disreputable history. From the museum, walk north up Kendall Lane to its junction with **2 Mill Lane**, named after a steam-powered flour mill that was once located here. The mill was demolished around 1920, one of many 18th- and 19th-century buildings in The Rocks to suffer the same fate during the 20th century. Turn left (west) into Mill Lane and then walk up to **3 The Rocks Square** on the corner of Playfair St where, in 1973, local residents, conservationists, social activists and members of trade unions clashed with police and put themselves in the path of bulldozers that were demolishing structures on this site. The protesters were intent on preserving the streets and buildings that had been home to local families for generations, and their fight became known in the national media as the 'Battle for The Rocks'. In 1975 the NSW State Government, which had initially backed the developers, bowed to popular opinion and declared that all remaining historic buildings north of the Cahill Expressway were to be retained, conserved and restored.

Turn left (south) into Playfair St and walk past **4 Argyle Terrace** (1877) and **5 Argyle Stores** (1828–1913) on your right. Then turn right and walk west up Argyle St to the impressive **6 Argyle Cut** (p75), a road cut through a sandstone ridge of rock to allow access between Circular Quay and the port at Millers Point. It was created between the 1830s and 1860s, initially by convicts and later by qualified stonemasons.

Turn left into Cumberland St until you see the 1914 **7 Australian Hotel** (p123) on the corner of Gloucester St. The **8 King George V Recreation Centre** op-

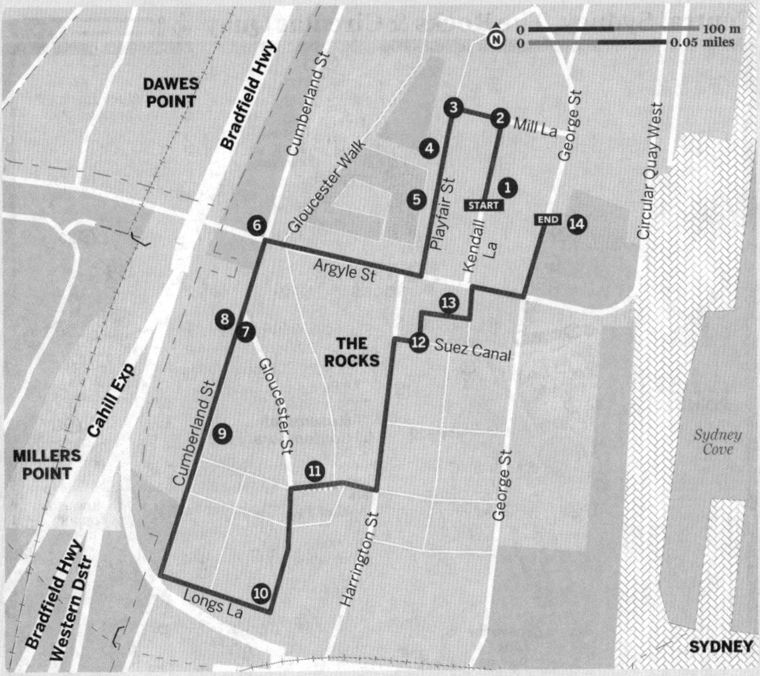

posite the hotel was designed by Lippmann Associates and opened in 1998; wedged between the historic street and the boundary wall of the elevated freeway, it's an interesting and popular contemporary architectural intervention in this historic precinct.

Continue along Cumberland St. On the left you'll find the ecofriendly 9 **Sydney Harbour YHA** (p103), an impressive building that incorporates an archaeological dig site. In 1994 the remains of over 30 houses, two laneways, shops and pubs were excavated here, along with over 750,000 artefacts.

Veer left into Longs Lane, which will take you through to Gloucester St. On the northwest corner of the lane is 10 **Jobbins Terrace**, constructed between 1855 and 1857. A handsome row of housing, it is one of only two extant Greek Revival–style terraces in NSW. The modest 1844 terrace now functioning as the 11 **Susannah Place Museum** (p76), opposite, presents an interesting contrast.

From the museum's shop, which sells a quirky range of Australiana souvenirs, walk down the stairs in Cumberland Pl to Harrington St, then veer left and walk north down to 12 **Suez Canal**, a narrow laneway on the right-hand side. In the 19th century this was one of the most infamous locations in Sydney, frequented by prostitutes and members of the infamous 'Rocks Push' larrikin gang that ruled the area from the 1870s to the end of the 1890s. Members were known for assault and battery against police and pedestrians; one of their tried and trusted techniques was to have female members of the gang entice drunks and seamen into dark areas to be assaulted and robbed.

Turn into Suez Canal and then left into the Well Courtyard, once used for dog baiting and cock fighting. Then walk down the steps to stone-paved Greenway Lane, named after famous convict architect Francis Greenway, who lived nearby on the corner of Argyle and George Sts.

Exit onto Argyle St; the building at No 45–47 is 13 **Gannon House**, built in 1839 as a residence and carpentry store by former convict Michael Gannon; he was known for the quality of his coffins.

Turn right, towards the harbour, and walk down to George St. In the park opposite is diminutive 14 **Cadmans Cottage**, built in 1815–16 for John Cadman, the Government Coxswain. It is the only remaining element of the city's original dockyard precinct, and is Sydney's oldest house.

Central Sydney, The Rocks & Circular Quay

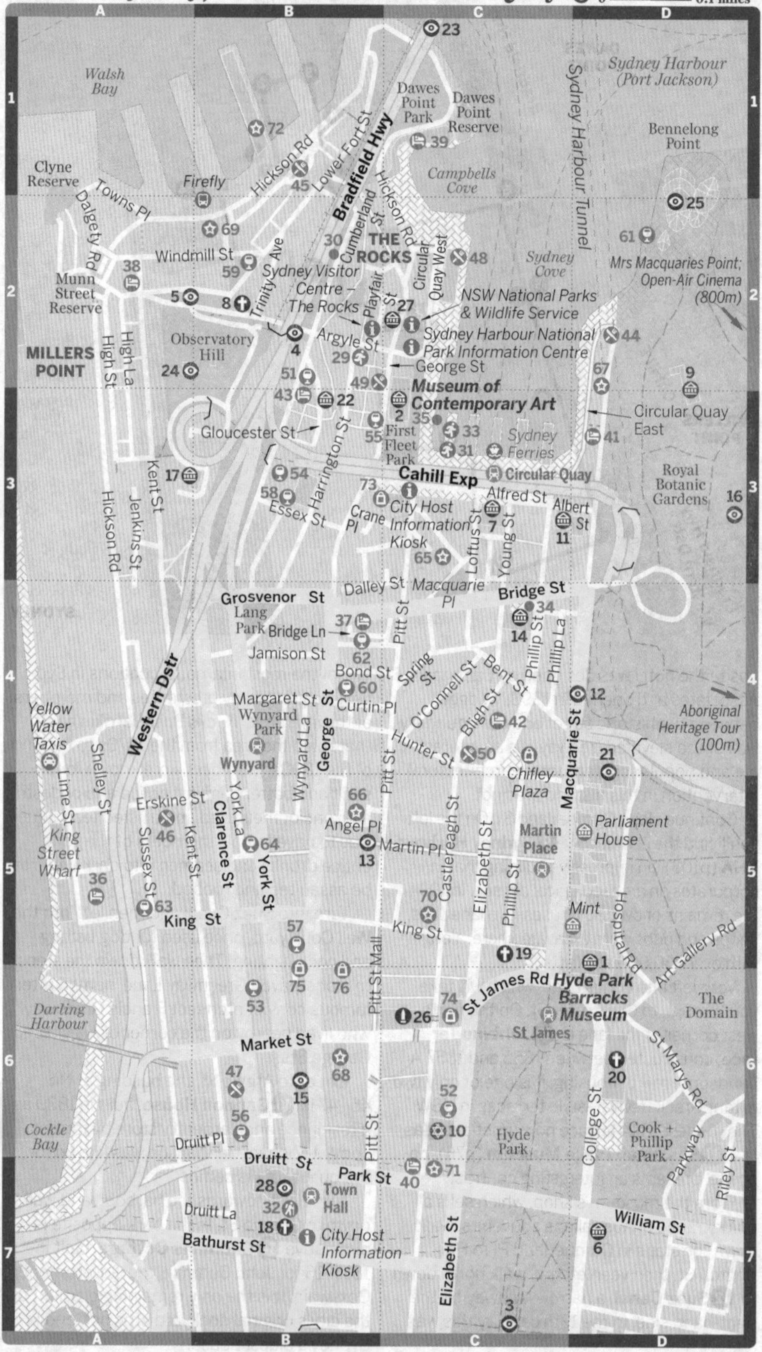

Central Sydney, The Rocks & Circular Quay

Top Sights
1 Hyde Park Barracks Museum D5
2 Museum of Contemporary Art C3

Sights
3 Anzac Memorial C7
4 Argyle Cut B2
5 Argyle Place A2
6 Australian Museum D7
7 Customs House C3
8 Garrison Church B2
9 Government House D2
10 Great Synagogue C6
11 Justice & Police Museum C3
12 Macquarie Street D4
13 Martin Place B5
14 Museum of Sydney C4
15 Queen Victoria Building B6
16 Royal Botanic Gardens D3
17 SH Ervin Gallery A3
18 St Andrew's Cathedral B7
19 St James' Church C5
20 St Mary's Cathedral D6
21 State Library of NSW D4
22 Susannah Place Museum B3
23 Sydney Harbour Bridge C1
24 Sydney Observatory A2
25 Sydney Opera House D2
26 Sydney Tower Eye C6
27 The Rocks Discovery Museum C2
28 Town Hall B7

Activities, Courses & Tours
29 Bonza Bike Tours B2
30 BridgeClimb B2
31 Captain Cook Cruises C3
32 I'm Free B7
33 Matilda Cruises C3
34 Sydney Architecture Walks C4
35 Whale Watching Sydney C3

Sleeping
36 Adina Apartment Hotel Sydney Harbourside A5
37 Establishment Hotel B4
38 Lord Nelson Brewery Hotel A2
39 Park Hyatt C1
40 Park8 .... C7
41 Pullman Quay Grand Sydney Harbour D3
QT Sydney .... (see 68)
42 Sofitel Sydney Wentworth C4
43 Sydney Harbour YHA B3

Eating
44 Aria D2
Cafe Sopra .... (see 37)
45 Cafe Sopra B1
46 Central Baking Depot A5
Guillaume at Bennelong .... (see 25)
47 Le Grand Café B6
48 Quay C2
49 Rockpool B2
50 Rockpool Bar & Grill C4
Spice Temple .... (see 50)

Drinking & Nightlife
51 Australian Hotel B2
52 Bambini Wine Room C6
53 Baxter Inn B6
54 Blu Bar on 36 .... B3
55 Fortune of War B3
56 Grandma's B6
57 Grasshopper B5
58 Harts Pub B3
59 Hero of Waterloo B2
60 O Bar B4
61 Opera Bar D2
62 Palmer & Co B4
63 Slip Inn & Chinese Laundry A5
64 Stitch B5

Entertainment
65 Basement C3
66 City Recital Hall B5
67 Dendy Opera Quays D2
68 State Theatre B6
Sydney Opera House .... (see 25)
69 Sydney Theatre B2
70 Theatre Royal C5
71 Ticketek C7
Ticketmaster .... (see 68)
72 Wharf Theatre B1

Shopping
73 Australian Wine Centre B3
74 David Jones C6
Queen Victoria Building .... (see 15)
75 RM Williams B6
76 Strand Arcade B6
Westfield Sydney .... (see 26)

adult/child $65/45; ⏲9am-10.30pm; St James) The 309m-tall Sydney Tower offers unbeatable 360-degree views from its observation level 250m up in the sky. On a clear day you'll see west to the Blue Mountains, south to Botany Bay, east across the harbour to the silvery Pacific and down onto the city streets. A visit here starts with the **4D Experience** – a short 3D film giving you a bird's-eye view (a parakeet's to be exact) of city, surf, harbour and what lies beneath the water, accompanied by mist sprays and bubbles; it's actually pretty darn cool.

Daredevils can don a spiffy 'skysuit' and take the **Skywalk**: shackle yourself to the safety rail and step onto two glass-floored

City East, Chinatown & Darling Harbour

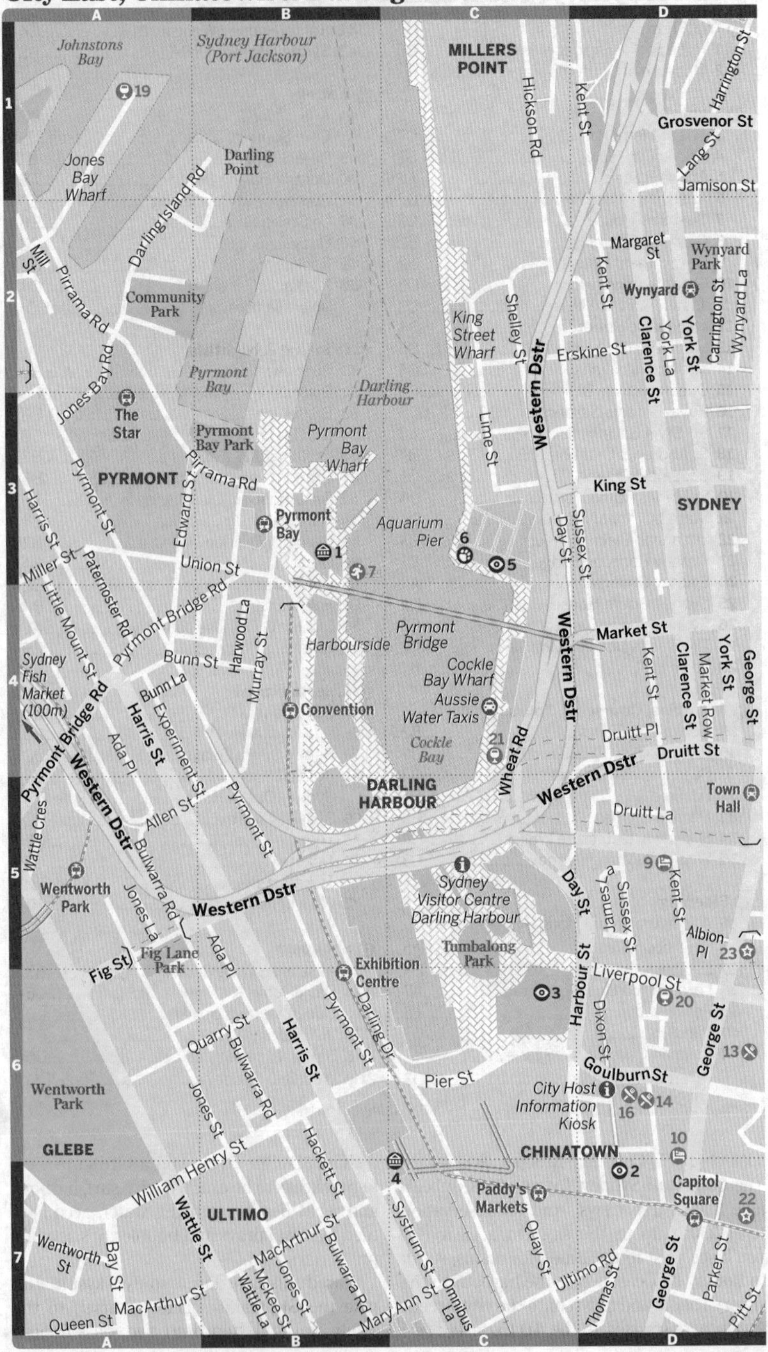

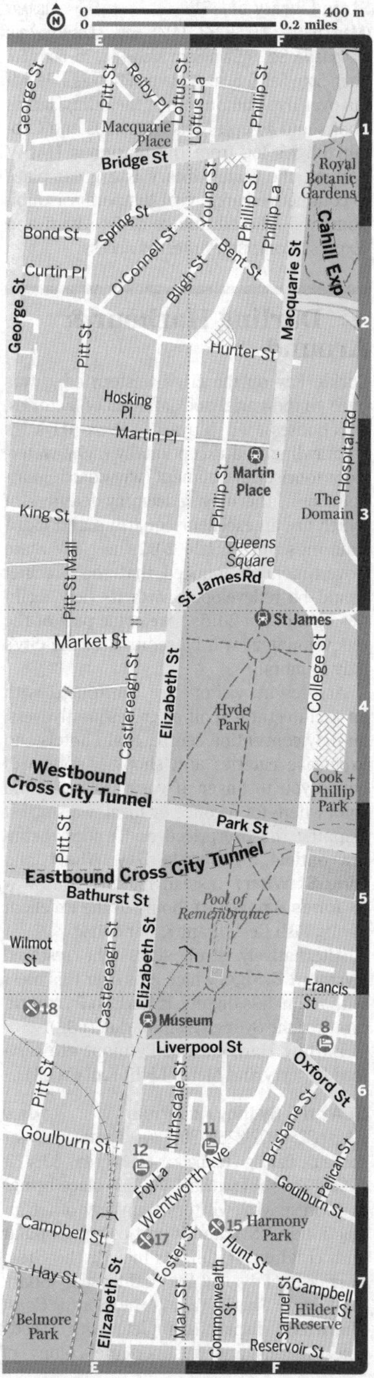

viewing platforms outside Sydney Tower's observation deck, 268m above the street; it's even possible to sign up for one of the yoga classes held here – see the website for details.

Note that we've cited walk-in prices; considerable savings can be made if you book online.

Museum of Sydney MUSEUM

(MoS; Map p80; ☎02-9251 5988; www.hht.net.au; cnr Phillip & Bridge Sts; adult/concession $10/5; ⏰10am-5pm; 🚌Circular Quay, ⛴Circular Quay, 🚆Circular Quay) Janet Laurence and Fiona Foley's evocative 1995 sculpture *Edge of the Trees* occupies pride of place in the forecourt of this sleek museum, marking the site of first contact between the British colonists and Sydney's original inhabitants, the Gadigal people. It's one of a number of important artworks here, including Gordon Bennett's 1991 painting *Possession Island*,

City East, Chinatown & Darling Harbour

Sights

1 Australian National Maritime Museum....B3
2 Chinatown....D7
3 Chinese Garden of Friendship....C6
4 Powerhouse Museum....C7
5 SEA LIFE Sydney Aquarium....C3
6 WILD LIFE Sydney Zoo....C3

Activities, Courses & Tours

7 Sydney by Sail....B3

Sleeping

8 150 Apartments....F6
9 Adina Apartment Hotel Sydney....D5
10 Pensione Hotel....D6
11 Travelodge Sydney....F6
12 Vibe Hotel Sydney....E6

Eating

13 Din Tai Fung....D6
14 Golden Century....D6
15 Longrain....F7
16 Mamak....D6
17 Spice I Am....E7
18 Sydney Madang....E6

Drinking & Nightlife

19 Flying Fish....A1
20 Good God Small Club....D6
21 Home....C4

Entertainment

22 Capitol Theatre....D7
23 Metro Theatre....D5

which greets visitors as they enter the foyer, and presents a very different interpretation of Captain Cook's 1770 arrival and claim of British sovereignty to that presented in most history books.

Built on the site of Sydney's first (and infamously pungent) Government House, the museum offers a modest array of permanent exhibits documenting Sydney's early colonial history – brought to life through oral histories, artefacts and state-of-the-art interactive installations – as well as a changing exhibition program in its two temporary galleries. Be sure to open some of the many stainless steel and glass drawers (they close themselves).

Macquarie Street HISTORIC PRECINCT

(Map p80) A swathe of splendid sandstone colonial buildings graces this street. Many of these buildings were commissioned by Lachlan Macquarie, the first NSW governor to envisage and plan for a settlement that would rise above its convict origins and become a place where prosperous futures could be forged. Macquarie enlisted convict architect Francis Greenway to help realise his plans, and together they set a gold standard for architectural excellence that the city has, alas, never since managed to replicate.

★**Hyde Park Barracks Museum** MUSEUM

(Map p80; 02-8239 2311; www.hht.net.au; Queens Sq, Macquarie St; adult/concession$10/5; 10am-5pm; St James) Francis Greenway designed this austerely elegant Georgian structure as housing for male convicts in the early 19th century, and 50,000 men and boys spent time here between 1819 and 1848. Most had been charged with property crimes in British courts and served terms of life, seven or 14 years transportation. From 1830 the building housed courts of General Sessions at which convicts and their employers put their complaints to visiting magistrates, who determined various penalties. Punishments could include the cruel treadmill, flogging, a stint in leg irons, solitary confinement, reassignment to a distant road gang or banishment to Cockatoo Island. The building housed new female migrants as well as the colony's destitute women from 1848, and then was converted into government departments. In 1990 it was transformed into this museum, which uses installations and exhibits to give an absolutely fascinating insight into everyday convict life.

State Library of NSW LIBRARY

(Map p80; 02-9273 1414; www.sl.nsw.gov.au; Macquarie St; 9am-8pm Mon-Thu, to 5pm Fri, 10am-5pm Sat & Sun; Martin Pl) FREE Holding over five million tomes, including James Cook's and Joseph Banks' journals and Captain Bligh's log from the mutinous HMAV *Bounty*, the State Library is a great place to conduct research, visit temporary exhibitions and take advantage of free wi-fi and 'Express Computer' internet access.

Darling Harbour & Around

Cockle Bay on the city's western edge was once an industrial dockland full of factories, warehouses and shipyards. These days it's a sprawling and exceptionally tacky waterfront tourist development (www.darlingharbour.com), the only redeeming features of which are an excellent aquarium and maritime museum. In late 2012 the NSW State Government announced that the precinct would be redeveloped, with its new facilities opening in 2016. A welcome part of the redevelopment will be removal of the city's ugly monorail.

At present, visitors are confronted with an architectural spoil of grotesque flyovers, an ugly convention centre, chain hotels and expensive eateries and shops – none will entice you to linger. If you're keen to find somewhere for a coffee or meal, we suggest skipping the overpriced and underwhelming outlets on **Cockle Bay Wharf** and **King St Wharf**, instead making your way to **Jones Bay Wharf**, home to the excellent Flying Fish Restaurant & Bar (p114).

Alternatively, stroll across the restored **Pyrmont Bridge**, which cuts over this mess with a timeless dignity. It leads to **Pyrmont**, home of the Sydney Fish Market (p88).

Darling Harbour and Pyrmont are serviced by ferry and Metro Light Rail (MLR).

SEA LIFE Sydney Aquarium AQUARIUM

(Map p82; 02-8251 7800; www.sydneyaquarium.com.au; Darling Harbour; adult/child $38/22; 9am-8pm; Town Hall) This place brings in more paying visitors than any other attraction in NSW, and is particularly popular with children. Highlights include the Great Barrier Reef display, the slightly scary Shark Walk and Shark Valley, the South Coast Shipwreck display (complete with Weedy Sea Dragons and a super-cute colony of

Little Penguins) and the Sydney Harbour Habitat (home to the Clown Anemonefish, aka Little Nemo). Arrive early to beat the crowds. Booking online will save you money.

WILD LIFE Sydney Zoo ZOO

(Map p82; ☎02-9333 9245; www.wildlifesydney.com.au; Darling Harbour; adult/child $36/20; ⏲9am-5pm; 🚉Town Hall) This indoor wildlife zoo next to the aquarium offers the chance to get up close to local critters, including koalas, kangaroos, rock wallabies, echidnas, Tasmanian devils, a hairy-nosed wombat, scrub pythons and plenty of bugs.

Powerhouse Museum MUSEUM

(Map p82; ☎02-9217 0111; www.powerhousemuseum.com; 500 Harris St, Ultimo; adult/child $12/6; ⏲10am-5pm; 🚉Paddy's Markets) A short walk from Darling Harbour, this museum is housed in the former power station for Sydney's once-extensive tram network. A sensational showcase for science and design, it's a huge hit with kids but is equally popular with adults. Visitors are encouraged to discover and be inspired by human ingenuity through exhibits that are always thoughtfully curated and often interactive.

Paddington & Woollahra

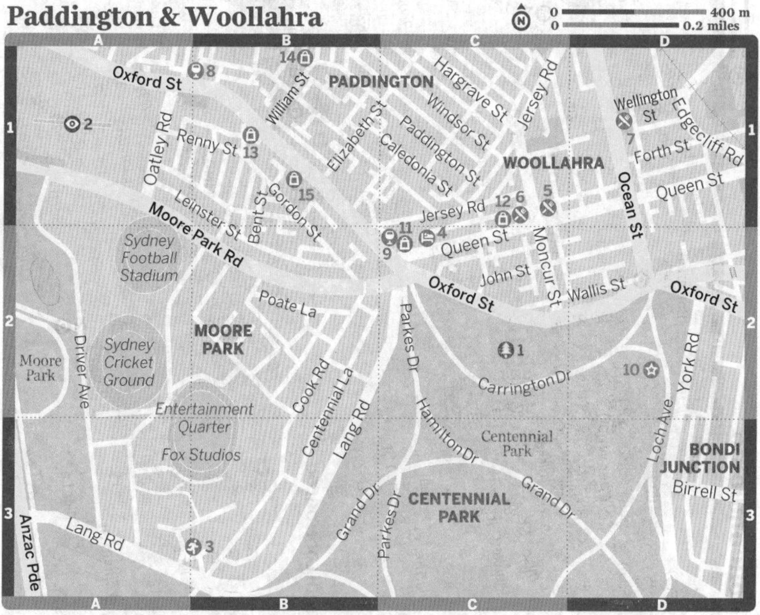

Paddington & Woollahra

Sights
1 Centennial Park C2
2 Victoria Barracks A1

Activities, Courses & Tours
3 Centennial Parklands Equestrian Centre B3

Sleeping
4 Kathryn's on Queen C2

Eating
5 bills C1
6 Bistro Moncur C1
7 Chiswick Restaurant D1

Drinking & Nightlife
8 Imperial Hotel B1
9 Wine Library C2

Entertainment
10 Moonlight Cinema D2

Shopping
11 Akira Isogawa C2
12 Collette Dinnigan C1
13 Dinosaur Designs B1
14 Leona Edmiston B1
15 Paddington Markets B1

Kings Cross, Darlinghurst & Woolloomooloo

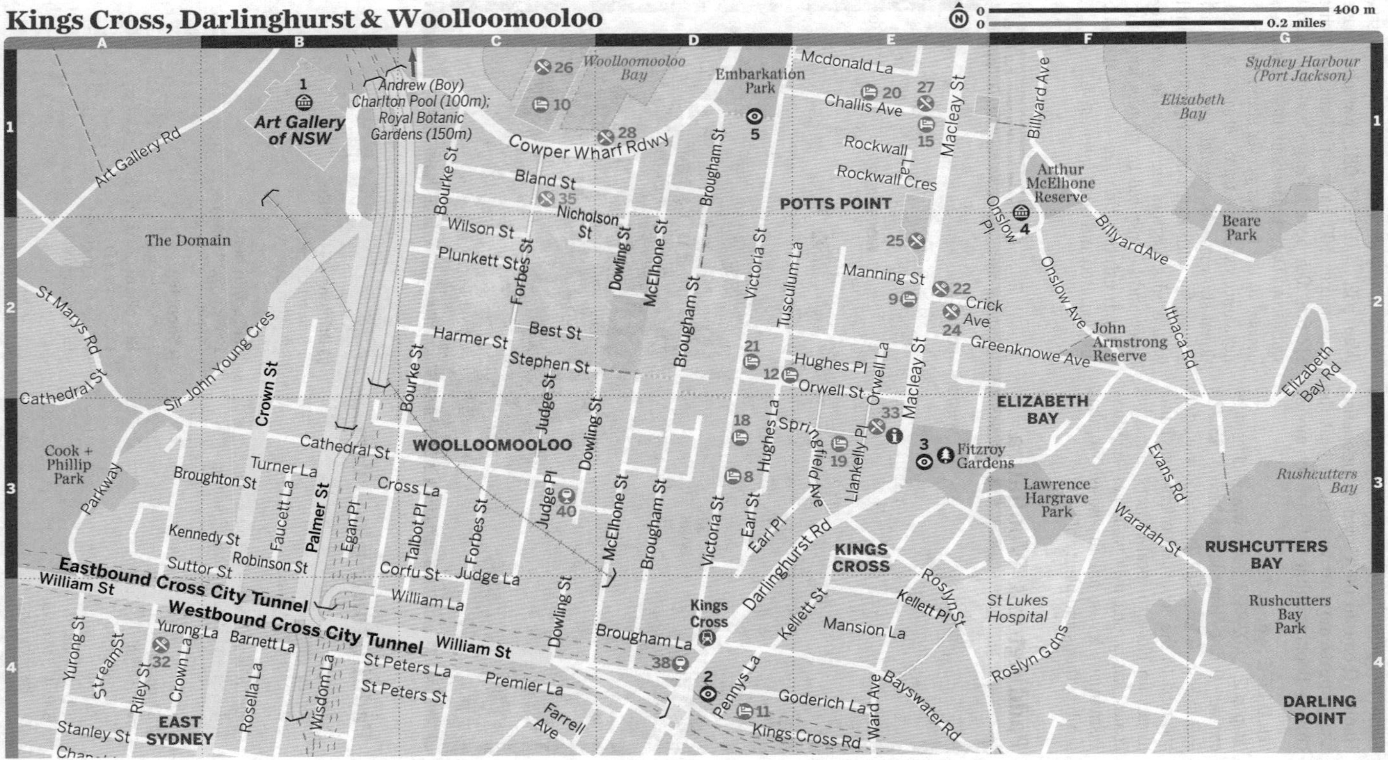

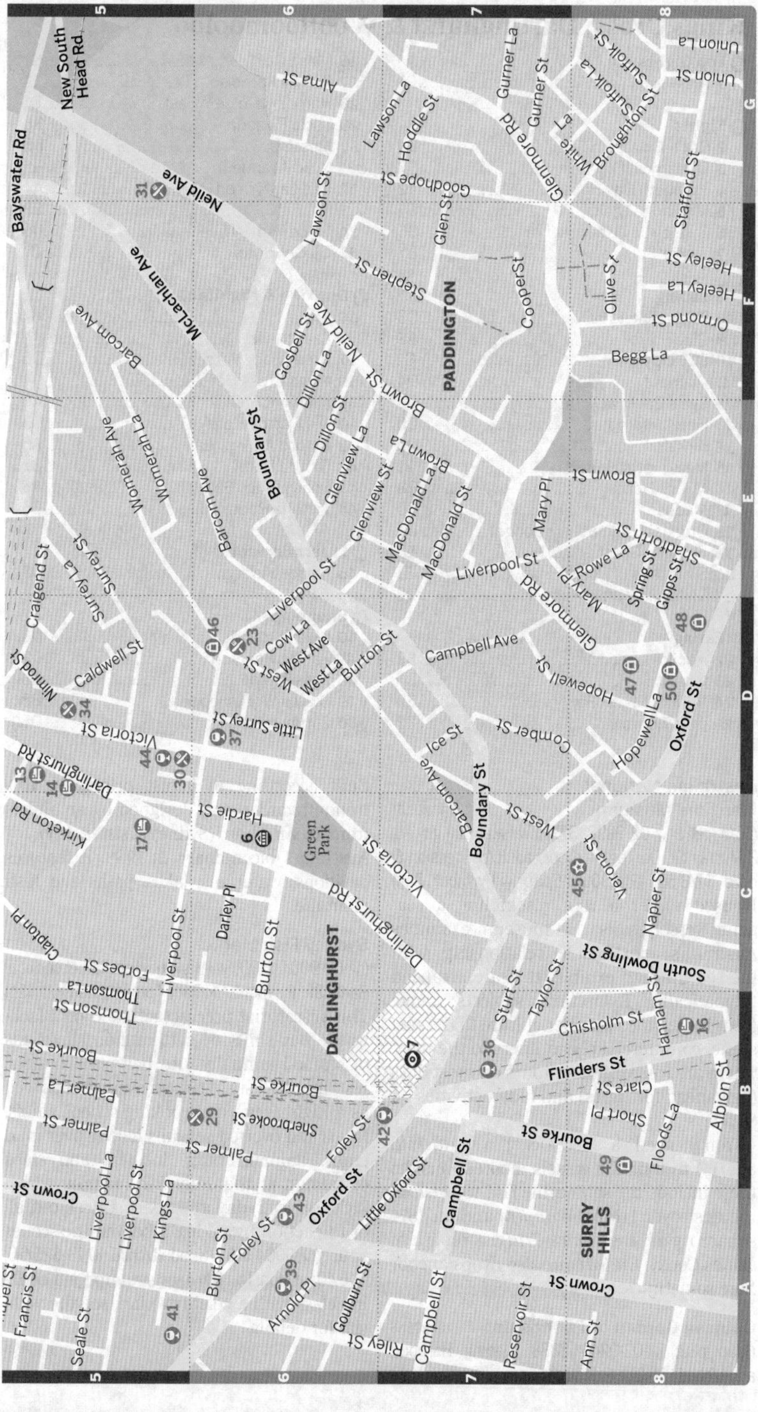

5
6
7
8
A
B
C
D
E
F
G
Bayswater Rd
New South Head Rd
Neild Ave
McLachlan Ave
Barcom Ave
Womerah Ave
Womerah La
Craigend St
Surrey La
Surrey St
Caldwell St
Nimrod St
Victoria St
Darlinghurst Rd
Kirketon Rd
Boundary St
Alma St
Lawson St
Lawson La
Hoddle St
Goodhope St
Glen St
Stephen St
Gosbell St
Dillon La
Dillon St
Brown St
Brown La
Glenview La
Glenview St
MacDonald La
MacDonald St
Liverpool St
Cow La
West Ave
West St
West La
Burton St
Little Surrey St
Campbell Ave
Ice St
Comber St
Hopewell St
Hopewell La
Oxford St
Gurner La
Gurner St
Glenmore Rd
White La
Broughton St
Suffolk La
Suffolk St
Union La
Union St
Stafford St
Heeley St
Heeley La
Ormond St
Olive St
Cooper St
Begg La
PADDINGTON
Mary Pl
Rowe La
Spring St
Gipps St
Shadforth St
Hardie St
Green Park
Darley Pl
DARLINGHURST
Forbes St
Thomson La
Thomson St
Clapton Pl
Bourke St
Palmer La
Palmer St
Sherbrooke St
Foley St
Crown St
Kings La
Liverpool La
Francis St
Seale St
Arnold Pl
Goulburn St
Riley St
Campbell St
Little Oxford St
Reservoir St
Ann St
SURRY HILLS
Floods La
Short Pl
Clare St
Albion St
Flinders St
Chisholm St
Hannam St
Taylor St
Sturt St
South Dowling St
Napier St
Verona St

Kings Cross, Darlinghurst & Woolloomooloo

Top Sights
1 Art Gallery of NSW ... B1

Sights
2 Coca-Cola Sign ... D4
3 El Alamein Fountain ... E3
4 Elizabeth Bay House ... F2
5 McElhone Stairs ... D1
6 Sydney Jewish Museum ... C6
7 Taylor Square ... B7

Sleeping
8 Backpackers HQ ... D3
9 Blue Parrot ... E2
10 BLUE Sydney ... C1
11 Diamant ... D4
12 Eva's Backpackers ... D2
13 Hotel Altamont ... D5
14 Kirketon Hotel ... D5
15 Maisonette Hotel ... E1
16 Manor House ... B8
17 Medusa ... C5
18 Original Backpackers Lodge ... D3
19 Regents Court ... E3
20 Simpsons of Potts Point ... E1
21 Victoria Court Hotel ... D2

Eating
22 Apollo ... E2
23 bills ... D6
24 Bourke Street Bakery ... E2
25 Cafe Sopra ... E2
26 China Doll ... C1
27 Fratelli Paradiso ... E1
28 Harry's Cafe de Wheels ... D1
29 Lucio Pizzeria ... B6
30 Messina ... D5
31 Neild Avenue ... G5
32 Red Lantern on Riley ... A4
33 Room 10 ... E3
34 Spice I Am - The Restaurant ... D5
35 Tilbury Hotel ... C1

Drinking & Nightlife
36 Arq ... B7
Eau-de-Vie ... (see 14)
37 Green Park Hotel ... D6
38 Kings Cross Hotel ... D4
39 Midnight Shift ... A6
40 Old Fitzroy Hotel ... C3
41 Oxford Art Factory ... A5
42 Oxford Hotel ... B7
43 Shady Pines Saloon ... A6
44 Victoria Room ... D5

Entertainment
45 Palace Verona ... C8

Shopping
46 Blue Spinach ... D6
47 Easton Pearson ... D8
48 Sass & Bide ... D8
49 Studio Workshopped ... B8
50 Zimmermann ... D8

Australian National Maritime Museum MUSEUM
(Map p82; ☎02-9298 3777; www.anmm.gov.au; 2 Murray St, Darling Harbour; adult/concession & child $7/3.50; ⏲9.30am-5pm; Pyrmont Bay) Housed under a roof resembling a sea-going vessel's sails, this museum examines Australia's inextricable relationship with the sea through exhibits that are arranged thematically. Exhibition subjects range from indigenous islander culture to the surf scene, commercial ocean liners to the navy. There are free volunteer tours on most days (call ahead for times) and kids' activities on Sundays.

You'll need a 'big ticket' (adult/child $25/15) to tour the vessels moored outside; these include the submarine HMAS *Onslow*, the destroyer HMAS *Vampire* and an 1874 square rigger, the *James Craig*. A replica of James Cook's *Endeavour* also drops anchor here sometimes.

Chinese Garden of Friendship GARDENS
(Map p82; ☎02-9240 8888; Darling Harbour; adult/child $6/3; ⏲9.30am-5pm; Town Hall) Built according to Taoist principles, this tranquil garden was designed by architects from Guangzhou (Sydney's sister city) for Australia's bicentenary in 1988. It features pavilions, waterfalls, lakes, paths and lush plant life.

Sydney Fish Market MARKET
(☎02-9004 1100; www.sydneyfishmarket.com.au; Bank St, Pyrmont; ⏲7am-4pm; Fish Market) This piscatorial precinct situated on Blackwattle Bay shifts over 15 million kilograms of seafood annually, and has retail outlets, restaurants, a sushi bar, an oyster bar as well as a highly regarded cooking school. Chefs, locals and overfed seagulls haggle over mud crabs, Balmain bugs, lobsters and slabs of salmon at the daily fish auction, which kicks off everyday at 5.30am. Check out all of the action by taking a behind-the-scenes **tour** (☎9004 1163/8; adult/child 10-13 $25/10; ⏲6.40am Mon, Thu & Fri), or sign up for a cooking class with a celebrity chef; see the website for details.

Kings Cross

Crowned by a huge illuminated **Coca-Cola sign** (Map p86) – Sydney's equivalent of LA's iconic Hollywood sign – 'the Cross' has long been the home of Sydney's vice industry. In the 19th and early 20th centuries the suburb was home to grand estates and stylish apartments, but it underwent a radical change in the 1930s when wine-soaked intellectuals, artists, musicians, pleasure-seekers and ne'er-do-wells rowdily claimed the streets for their own. The neighbourhood's reputation was sealed during the Vietnam War, when American sailors based at the nearby Garden Island naval base flooded the Cross with a tide of drug-fuelled debauchery.

Although the streets retain an air of seedy hedonism, the neighbourhood has recently undergone something of a cultural renaissance. Sleazy one minute and sophisticated the next, it's well worth a visit.

The gracious, tree-lined enclaves of neighbouring **Potts Point** and **Elizabeth Bay** have been popular residential areas ever since Alexander Macleay, Colonial Secretary of New South Wales, commissioned architect John Verge to design a mansion overlooking the water here in the 1830s.

Possibly the only word in the world with eight 'o's, the suburb of **Woolloomooloo**, down **McElhone Stairs** (Map p86; Victoria St; Kings Cross) from the Cross, was once a slum full of drunks and sailors (a fair few of whom were drunken sailors). Things are more genteel these days – the pubs are relaxed and **Woolloomooloo Wharf** is now home to a boutique hotel and a swathe of upmarket restaurants. Outside the wharf is the famous **Harry's Cafe de Wheels** (Map p86; 02-9347 3074; www.harryscafedewheels.com.au; Cowper Wharf Rd; pies $3-4; 9am-1am Sun, 8.30am-3am Mon-Sat; 311), where generations of Sydneysiders have stopped to sober up over a late-night 'Tiger' (beef pie served with mushy peas, mashed potato and gravy) on the way home from a big night at the Cross.

REINVENTING THE CROSS

In the early years of the colony, Kings Cross was home to the city's wealthy citizens, who were attracted by its harbour views and handy distance from the smells and noise of the central city. Its grand villas, farming estates and genteel atmosphere were worlds away from the rough-and-tumble scene around Circular Quay and The Rocks.

This bucolic idyll lasted until the early 20th century, when the estates were subdivided and most of the villas were demolished (Tusculum on Manning St and Elizabeth Bay House on Onslow Ave were exceptions). Blocks of apartments took their place and the city's bohemian set moved in, attracted by cheap rents and a modernist vibe. These bohemians were closely followed by Sydney's criminal underclass, who set up businesses selling sly grog (untaxed alcohol), running illegal betting shops and operating brothels. The streets were home to writers, actors, poets, journalists, artists, petty crims and infamous brothel owners such as Tilly Devine and Kate Leigh – it was a neighbourhood where the louche charm of this convict-established city was pronounced, and where creativity flourished alongside crime.

The local scene changed during the Vietnam War, when heroin was imported from Southeast Asia and drug lords took over the streets, distributing drugs, running prostitution rings and opening sleazy nightclubs where strippers and dealers plied their trades. The bohemians moved out and addicts, street prostitutes, petty crims and enforcers moved in, joined by Sydneysiders who came to walk on the wild side every Friday and Saturday night. The City of Sydney (p131) heritage walking tour gives a fascinating insight into this era.

But as the adage says, 'what goes around, comes around'. In recent years bohemians have returned, joined by upwardly mobile young professionals lured by the hip cafes, bars, restaurants and live-music venues that are mushrooming in the streets and laneways off Darlinghurst Rd. To experience the renaissance, head to Llankelly Pl (a laneway where drug deals once took place and where arty cafes such as Room 10 (p110) now preside), eat in the restaurants on Macleay St, sit by the recently restored and much-loved dandelion-shaped **El Alamein fountain** (Map p86; Macleay St, Fitzroy Gardens; Kings Cross) in the Fitzroy Gardens or party at the Kings Cross Hotel's edgy FBi Social (p124) venue.

Surry Hills, Redfern & Chippendale

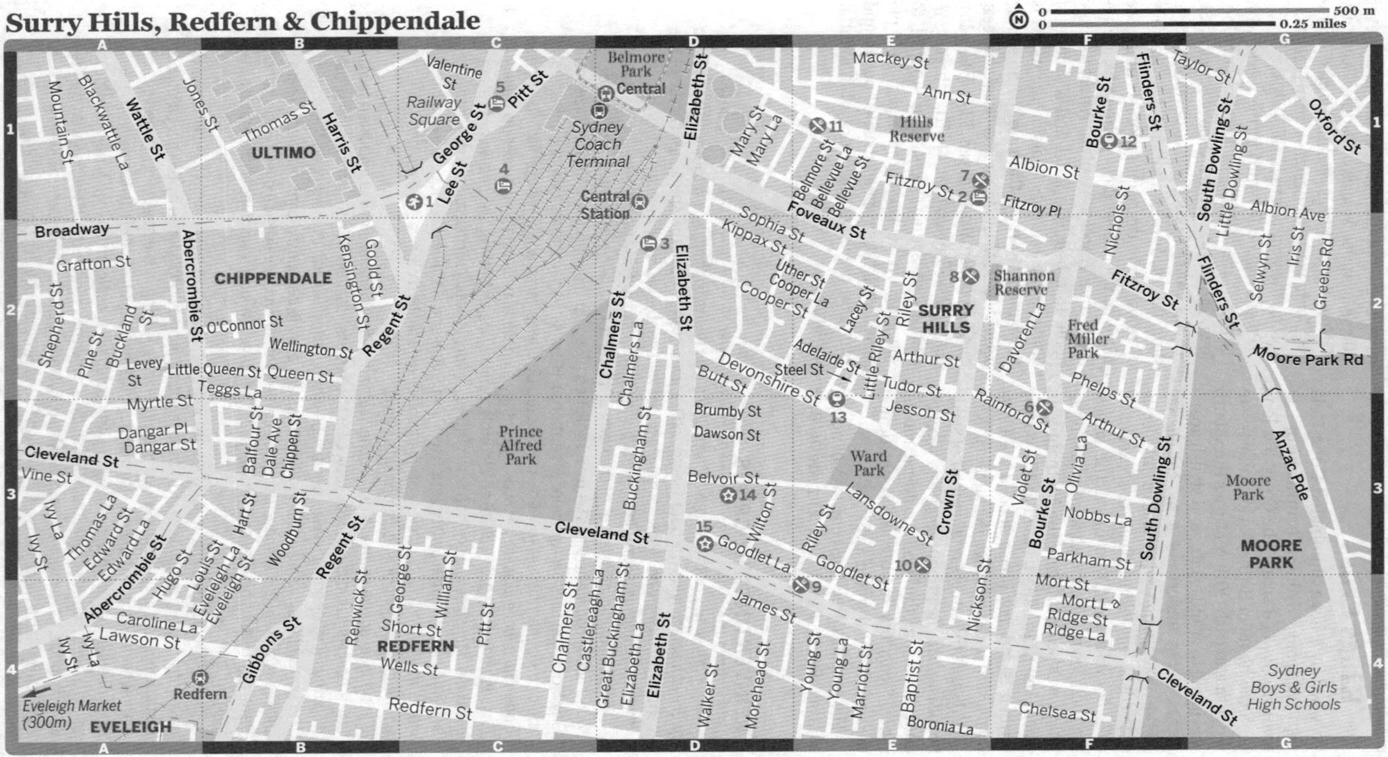

Surry Hills, Redfern & Chippendale

It's a 15-minute walk to the Cross from the city, or you could hop on a train. Buses 311 and 323-6 from the city also pass through here.

Elizabeth Bay House HISTORIC BUILDING
(Map p86; ☎02-9356 3022; www.hht.net.au; 7 Onslow Ave, Elizabeth Bay; adult/concession $8/4; ⏰11am-4pm Fri-Sun; 🚉Kings Cross) Now dwarfed by 20th-century apartments, Alexander Macleay's Greek revival–style mansion was one of the finest houses in the colony when it was completed in 1839. Its grounds – a sort of botanical garden for Macleay, who collected plants from around the world – extended from the harbour all the way up the hill to Kings Cross.The architectural highlight is an exquisite entrance saloon with a curved and cantileved staircase.

Inner East

Once the heart of Sydney's entertainment and shopping scenes, **Oxford Street** is now sadly tawdry. Most shopping action has moved onto side streets such as Glenmore Rd in Paddington and Queen St in Woollahra, while bars and restaurants have migrated to neighbouring **Surry Hills**. Despite this, the area around **Taylor Square** (Map p86; cnr Oxford & Bourke Sts; 🚉Museum) is still the decadent nucleus for the city's gay community – the Sydney Gay & Lesbian Mardi Gras famously gyrates through here every February, and gay-centric pubs and clubs do a brisk trade every weekend. To get here from the CBD, walk from Hyde Park or catch bus 378 from Railway Sq or bus 333, 380 or 389 from Circular Quay.

Wedged between Oxford and William Sts, **Darlinghurst** is home to cafes, pubs, restaurants and boutique hotels. Down the hill is **East Sydney**.

Paddington, aka 'Paddo', is an upmarket residential suburb of restored Victorian-era terrace houses, many with attractive iron 'lace' detailing. It's also home to one of the city's finest examples of Georgian architecture, **Victoria Barracks** (Map p85; ☎8335 5170; Oxford St; ⏰tours 10am Thu; 🚌380) FREE. Built between 1840 and 1848 on a huge block bounded by Greens, Oatley and Moore Park Rds and fronting Oxford St, it's still in operation as the headquarters of the Australian Army's Training Command.

The best time to explore Paddington's jacaranda-lined streets and laneways is on Saturday, when the Paddington Markets (p128) are held.

East of Paddington is the ritzy residential suburb of **Woollahra**. Just southeast, at the top end of Oxford St, is the 220-hectare **Centennial Park** (Map p85; ☎9339 6699; www.centennialparklands.com.au; Oxford St; ⏰vehicles sunrise-sunset; 🚉Bondi Junction), which has running, cycling, skating and horse-riding tracks, duck ponds, barbecue sites and sports pitches.

Sydney Jewish Museum MUSEUM
(Map p86; ☎02-9360 7999; www.sydneyjewishmuseum.com.au; 148 Darlinghurst Rd, Darlinghurst; adult/child $10/6; ⏰10am-4pm Sun-Thu, to 2pm Fri; 🚉Kings Cross) Created largely as a Holocaust memorial, this museum also has a modest display examining Australian Jewish history, culture and tradition from the time of the First Fleet (which included 16 known Jews) to the immediate aftermath of WWII (when Australia became home to the largest number of Holocaust survivors per capita after Israel) to the present day. Allow at least two hours to take it all in. Free 45-minute volunteer-led tours leave at noon on Monday, Wednesday, Friday and Sunday.

Eastern Suburbs

Handsome **Rushcutters Bay** is a five-minute walk east of Kings Cross; its harbourside park is a lovely spot for a walk or jog. The eastern suburbs extend out from here – a conservative conglomeration of elite private schools, European sedans, overpriced boutiques and heavily mortgaged waterside mansions. The harbour-hugging New South Head Rd passes through **Double Bay** and **Rose Bay**, and then climbs east into the gorgeous enclave of **Vaucluse**, where shady **Nielsen Park** (Vaucluse Rd; daylight hr; 325) is home to one of Sydney's best harbour beaches, complete with a netted swimming enclosure, crescent-shaped stretch of sand, picnic facilities and a popular cafe-restaurant. It's an idyllic spot to spend a day, preferably during the week – crowds are inevitable on weekends.

From the park, you can take an easy 10-minute loop walk along Bottle and Glass Rocks or make your way to the public park in the grounds of nearby **Strickland House**, built in 1856. The harbour views from here are wonderful.

At the entrance to the harbour is **Watsons Bay**, where you can enjoy blissful briny breezes and a postcard-perfect view of the city skyline while eating takeaway fish and chips from Doyles on the Wharf (p113) or taking tea in the genteel surrounds of Dunbar House (p113). Nearby **Camp Cove** is a lovely beach, and there's a nude beach (mostly male) near South Head at **Lady Bay**. **South Head** has great views across the harbour entrance to North Head and Middle Head. The **Gap** is an epic clifftop lookout where sunrises, sunsets, canoodling and suicide leaps transpire with similar frequency.

Buses 324 and 325 from Circular Quay service the eastern suburbs via Kings Cross (grab a seat on the left heading east to snare the best views) and bus 380 travels from Circular Quay via Paddington, North Bondi and Watsons Bay. The Watsons Bay ferry leaves from Wharf 4 at Circular Quay, stopping at Double Bay and Rose Bay en route.

Vaucluse House HISTORIC BUILDING
(02-9388 7922; www.hht.net.au; Wentworth Rd, Vaucluse; adult/concession $8/4; 11am-4pm Fri-Sun; 325) It's only a short walk from Neilsen Park to this imposing, turreted specimen of Gothic Australiana set amid 10 hectares of lush gardens. Between 1827 and 1853 it was the family home of explorer and political agitator William Charles Wentworth, one of the leaders of the first European expedition to cross the Blue Mountains in 1831 and a high-profile champion of individual rights and political freedom in the fledgling colony. There's a pleasant tearoom overlooking the garden.

Bondi

Flanked by rugged rocks and multi-million-dollar apartments, Bondi's famous golden crescent of sand and surf attracts a daily cast of sunburned backpackers and bronzed locals who swarm over the sand, surrounding clifftop paths and beachfront park. Perhaps it's the contradictions of the place that make it so compelling – everyone fits into the Bondi scene as long as they're wearing swimmers, sunblock and a smile. The suburb itself has a unique atmosphere due to its eclectic mix of traditional Jewish community members, dyed-in-the-wool Aussies, tourists who never went home and socially aspirational young professionals. Put simply, it's the type of place where everyone will feel comfortable and most will feel happy with the world and their immediate place in it.

The simply sensational 5.5km **Bondi to Coogee Clifftop Walk** (p93) leads south from Bondi Beach along the clifftops to Coogee via Tamarama, Bronte and Clovelly, interweaving panoramic views, patrolled beaches, sea baths, waterside parks and plaques recounting local Aboriginal myths and stories.

In Bondi, most of the decent pubs, bars and restaurants are found at the northern end of Campbell Pde, on Bondi Rd or on Glenayr Ave. The famous Bondi Icebergs Swimming Club (p99) with its beachfront pool is at the southern end of the beach where the clifftop walk starts.

To get here, take bus 389, 380 or 333 from Circular Quay. Alternatively, take a bus or train to the transport interchange at Bondi Junction and transfer to bus 382, 381, X84, X89 or one of the previously mentioned services there. All of these buses go North Bondi – to get to the beach you'll need to alight at the corner of Hall St and Glenayre Ave (look for the Bondi Picnic cafe) and walk east along Hall St or go to the terminus at the bus interchange on Brighton Blvd and walk downhill.

City Walk Bondi to Coogee Coastal Walk

START BONDI ICEBERGS SWIMMING CLUB
FINISH COOGEE BEACH
LENGTH 5.5KM
DURATION 2½ HOURS

Both ends of this fantastic walkway are well connected to bus routes, as are most points in between should you feel too hot and bothered to continue (a cooling dip at any of the beaches en route should cure that). There's little shade on this track, so make sure you apply sunscreen and don a hat before setting out.

Starting at **1 Bondi Beach**, take the stairs up the south end to Notts Ave, passing above the glistening **2 Icebergs swimming pool** (p99). Step onto the cliff-top trail at the end of Notts Ave.

Walk south past the small reserve known as Mark's Park; from here, the blustery sandstone cliffs and grinding Pacific Ocean couldn't be more spectacular (watch for dolphins, whales and surfers). Small but perfectly formed **3 Tamarama** has a deep reach of sand that is totally disproportionate to its width.

Descend from the cliff tops down onto **4 Bronte Beach**. Take a dip, lay out a picnic under the Norfolk Pines or head to a cafe for a caffeine hit. After your break, pick up the path on the southern side of the beach.

Some famous Australians are among the subterranean denizens of the amazing cliff-edge **5 Waverley Cemetery**. On a clear day this is a prime vantage point for whale-watchers.

Pass the locals enjoying a beer or a game of bowls at the Clovelly Bowling Club, then breeze past the cockatoos and canoodling lovers in **6 Burrows Park** to sheltered **7 Clovelly Beach**.

Follow the footpath up through the car park, along Cliffbrook Pde, then down the steps to the upturned dinghies that line **8 Gordons Bay**, one of Sydney's best shore-dive spots.

The trail continues past **9 Dolphin Point** then lands you smack-bang on glorious **10 Coogee Beach**. Swagger into the Coogee Bay Hotel and toast your efforts with a cold beer or two.

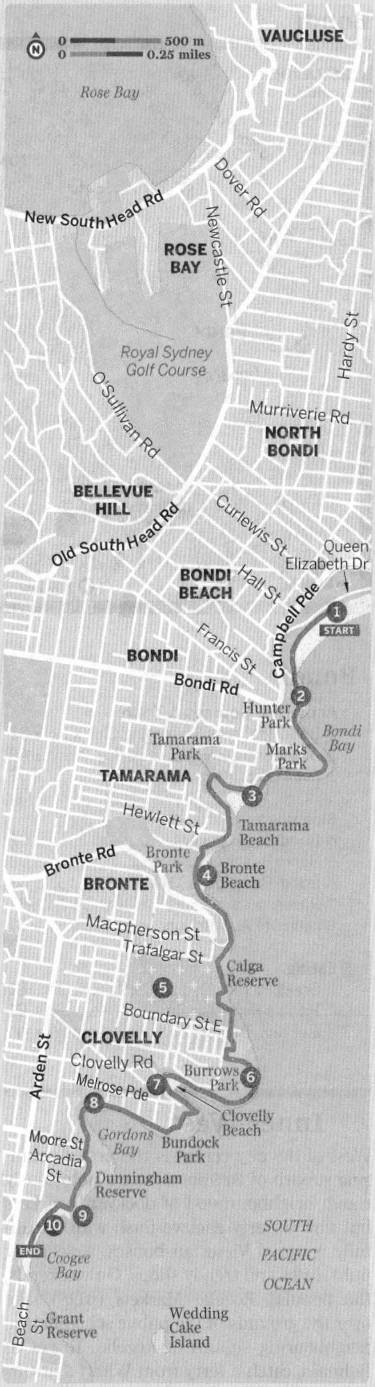

Bondi

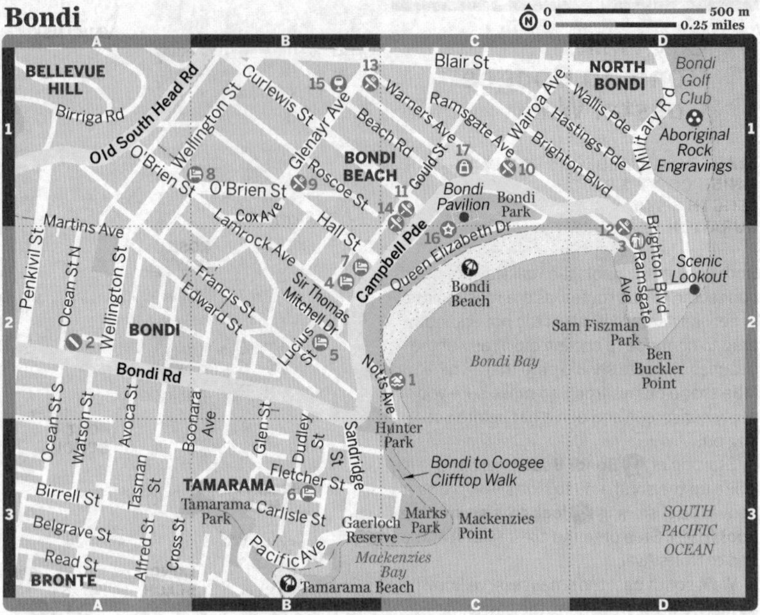

Bondi

Activities, Courses & Tours
1 Bondi Icebergs Swimming Club C2
2 Dive Centre Bondi A2
3 Let's Go Surfing D2

Sleeping
4 Bondi Backpackers B2
5 Bondi Beach House B2
6 Bondi Beachouse YHA B3
7 Ravesi's B2
8 Ultimate Apartments B1

Eating
9 Bondi Picnic B1
10 Harry's Espresso Bar C1
Icebergs Dining Room .... (see 1)
11 La Macelleria C1
12 North Bondi Italian Food D2
13 Organic Republic B1
14 Pompei's C1

Drinking & Nightlife
15 Beach Road Hotel B1
Icebergs Bar .... (see 1)
North Bondi RSL .... (see 12)

Entertainment
16 Bondi Openair Cinema C2

Shopping
17 Bondi Markets C1

Inner West

West of the city centre is the pretty peninsula suburb of **Balmain**, once a notoriously rough neighbourhood of dockyard workers but now an arty enclave flush with beautifully restored Victorian houses, welcoming pubs, cafes and trendy shops. On weekends, the popular Rozelle Markets (p128) take over the grounds of the public school in the neighbouring suburb of Rozelle. To get to Balmain, catch a ferry from Wharf 5 at Circular Quay to the wharf at East Balmain or hop on bus 433 at George St in The Rocks, or bus 442 from the QVB; both buses stop in Rozelle en route.

Once a busy bohemian destination, the now-somnolent suburb of **Glebe** lies just southwest of the centre of town, close to Sydney University. There are a couple of good hostels on Glebe Point Rd, as well as one of the city's best-loved bookshops, **Gleebooks** (☎02-9660 2333; www.gleebooks.com.au; 49 Glebe Point Rd; ⏲9am-7pm Sun-Wed, 9am-9pm

Thu-Sat; Glebe). For a refreshment break, head to the **bush tucker cafe** run by Beryl Van-Oploo (aka Aunty Beryl) in the historic gardener's lodge at Victoria Park, on the other side of Broadway/Paramatta Rd. On Saturdays the hippyish Glebe Markets (p128) overruns Glebe Public School. Glebe is a 10-minute walk from Central Station along side streets – avoid smoggy Broadway. Buses 431 and 433 run via George St along Glebe Point Rd; the 433 continues to Gladstone Park in Balmain. The MLR also stops here.

South of Sydney University is **Newtown**, a melting pot of social and sexual subcultures. King St, its main drag, is full of hip boutiques, bookshops, cafes and bars. Take the train, or bus 422, 423, 426 or 428 from Circular Quay or Castlereagh St to King St.

Southwest of Glebe is predominantly Italian **Leichhardt**. Norton St is the place for pizza, pasta and debates about the relative merits and demerits of the Ferrari 458 Italia. Buses 436, 438 and 440 from Circular Quay will get you there.

North Shore

At the northern end of the Harbour Bridge are the unexpectedly tranquil waterside suburbs of **Milsons Point** and **McMahons Point**. Both command astonishing city views and also overlook the shimmering waters of **Lavender Bay**.

Just east of the bridge is the stately suburb of **Kirribilli**, home to **Admiralty House** and **Kirribilli House**, the Sydney residences of the governor-general and prime minister respectively.

You can walk across the bridge to access Milsons Point, McMahons Point, Lavender Bay and Kirribilli, or take the short ferry ride from Wharves 4 and 5 at Circular Quay.

East of Kirribilli are the upmarket residential suburbs of **Neutral Bay**, **Cremorne** and **Mosman**, known for their coves, harbourside parks and ladies who lunch. On the northern side of Mosman is pretty-as-a-picture **Balmoral**, the beach of which fronts Hunters Bay. There's a netted swimming enclosure here, as well as the much-loved **Bathers' Pavilion** (02-9969 5050; www.batherspavilion.com.au; 4 The Esplanade, Balmoral Beach; restaurant mains $48, cafe $16-36; lunch & dinner; ; 245) restaurant, cafe and kiosk. The best way to visit all of these North Shore suburbs is by catching a ferry from Wharf 4 at Circular Quay.

Taronga Zoo ZOO
(02-9969 2777; www.taronga.org.au; Bradleys Head Rd, Mosman; adult/child 4-15 $44/22; 9.30am-4.30pm May-Aug, to 5pm Sep-Apr; Taronga Zoo) Sydneysiders often joke that the animals here are housed on the best tract of real estate in the city. Unfortunately, the zoo's knock-'em-dead harbour views and glorious profusion of trees go hand-in-hand with sadly cramped enclosures for some of the zoo's 4000 residents. Highlights include the nocturnal platypus habitat, the Great Southern Oceans section, the Asian elephant display and the seals.

Animal displays, feedings and 'encounters' happen throughout the day. Twilight concerts jazz things up in summer, and you can even sign up for a 'Roar and Snore' overnight camping experience. See the website for details.

Guided tours include **Nura Diya** (02-9978 4782; 90min tour adult/child $99/69; 9.45am Mon, Wed & Fri), where indigenous guides introduce you to native animals and share Dreaming stories about them, while giving an insight into traditional Aboriginal life. Advance bookings are essential.

From the ferry wharf, the Sky Safari cable car will whisk you to the main entrance, from where you can traverse the zoo downhill back to the ferry. This is included in the cost of your entrance ticket. A Zoo Pass (adult/child/family $51.50/25.50/144.50) includes a return ferry ride from Circular Quay plus zoo admission. Disabled access is good, even if arriving by ferry, and wheelchairs are available.

Wendy Whiteley's Secret Garden GARDENS
(Milsons Point/Luna Park) FREE Created and still maintained by the widow of high-profile Sydney artist Brett Whiteley, this lush public garden has replaced what was once a rubbish-filled railway siding at Lavender Bay. Accessed through Clark Park, off Lavender St, it features native plants, towering fig trees, a maze of paths and artworks. There are also wonderful views of the Sydney Harbour Bridge.

Luna Park AMUSEMENT PARK
(02-9922 6644; www.lunaparksydney.com; 1 Olympic Dr, Milsons Point; single-ride tickets $10, ride pass $20-50; 11am-10pm Fri & Sat, 10am-6pm Sun, 11am-4pm Mon; Milsons Point/Luna Park) A demented-looking clown sculpture forms the entrance to this amusement park overlooking Sydney Harbour and is one of

a number of original 1930s features. Others include the Coney Island funhouse, a pretty carousel and the nausea-inducing rotor. You can pay as you go, or buy a height-based unlimited ride pass (cheaper if purchased online). Extended hours during school and public holidays.

Manly

Refreshingly relaxed Manly occupies a narrow isthmus between ocean and harbour beaches near North Head. It's the only place in Sydney where you can catch a harbour ferry to swim in the ocean. The scene here is radically different to that at Bondi – locals outnumber foreign tourists, and bodyboards are considered far more important accessories than designer bikinis or show-off budgie smugglers (tight-fitting mens' swimming costumes).

Other than the beach, the suburb's greatest attraction is **Manly Scenic Walkway** (140, 143, 144, Manly). This has two major components: the 10km western stretch between Manly Cove and Spit Bridge in Mosman, and the 9.5km eastern loop from Manly Cove to North Head and back.

To walk the western stretch, take bus E68/70/71/78/79 or 169 from Wynyard station or bus 175, 178, 179, 180 or 189 from the Queen Victoria Building or Wynyard and alight at Spit Rd between Spit Junction and the Spit Bridge. From the bridge, follow the walkway around Middle and North Harbours, passing waterside mansions, harbour beaches and viewpoints, an Aboriginal engraving site and through the rugged Sydney Harbour National Park to Manly, where you

Manly

0 200 m
0 0.1 miles

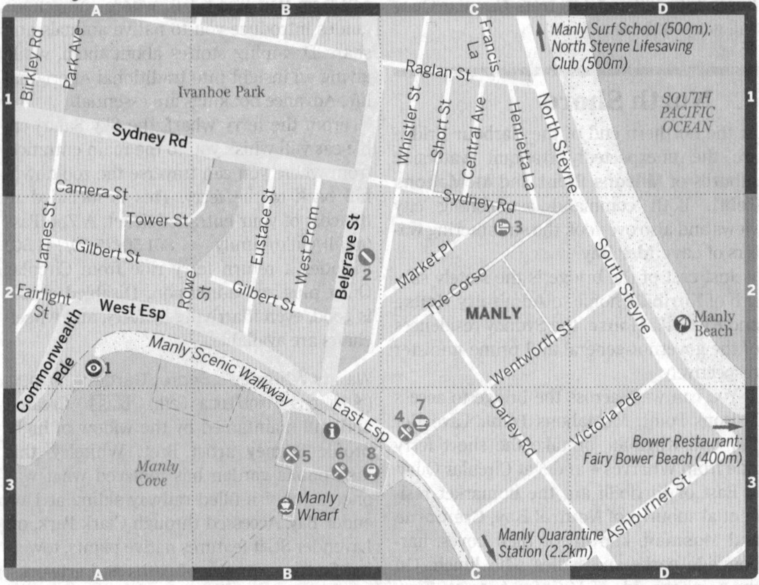

Manly

Sights
1 Manly SEA LIFE Sanctuary A2

Activities, Courses & Tours
2 Dive Centre Manly B2

Sleeping
3 Boardrider Backpacker C2

Eating
4 Adriano Zumbo C3
5 Hugos Manly B3
6 Manly Phoenix B3

Drinking & Nightlife
7 Barefoot Coffee Traders C3
8 Manly Wharf Hotel B3

can head to the beach or hop on a ferry back to the city. The walk takes approximately four hours.

The 9.5km eastern loop is known as the North Head Circuit Track, and takes between three and four hours. From the ferry wharf, follow Eastern Esplanade and Stuart St to Spring Cove, head into the North Head section of the Sydney Harbour National Park, and make your way through the bush to the spectacular Fairfax Lookout on North Head (approximately 45 minutes in total). If you're here in the middle of the year, you may see migrating whales from this vantage point. From the lookout, walk the Fairfax Loop (1km, 30 minutes) and then head back to the ferry wharf via the Cabbage Tree Bay Walk, which follows the sea-sprayed shoreline back to Manly via tiny Fairy Bower Beach and picturesque Shelly Beach.

Go to www.manly.nsw.gov.au/attractions/walking-tracks/manly-scenic-walkway/ to download a map of the full route. Information is also available from the helpful visitor centre in front of Manly Wharf.

Regular ferries travel between Circular Quay and Manly – it's one of Sydney's best-loved journeys.

Manly SEA LIFE Sanctuary AQUARIUM

(Map p96; ☎02-8251 7877; www.manlysealifesanctuary.com.au; West Esplanade; adult/child $24/12; ⏱10am-5.30pm, last admission 4.45pm; ⛴Manly) Keen to have a close encounter with a 3m Grey Nurse shark? Sign up for a **Shark Dive Xtreme** (☎02-8251 7878; introductory dives from $216) here and you can dive in their oceanarium (the reassuring news is that unlike Great White and Tiger Sharks, this species is unable to tear flesh with their teeth). Also here is an enclosure populated with Little Penguins (Manly is a breeding habitat for these cute-as-a-button critters) and an interactive rockpool exhibit that kids love to bits. Save money by pre-booking via the website.

Manly Quarantine Station HISTORIC SITE

(☎02-9466 1500; www.qstation.com.au; North Head Scenic Dr; ⏱visitor centre 10am-2pm Mon-Thu, to 4pm Sun, to 8pm Fri & Sat) Between 1832 and 1984 migrants suspected of carrying contagious diseases were isolated at this facility, and it's now a popular tourist attraction complete with visitor centre, cafe, bar and restaurant. Take a two-hour **Quarantine Station Story Tour** (adult/child $35/25; ⏱2pm Sat & Sun), a spooky adults-only **Ghost Tour** (adult/concession Wed-Fri & Sun $49/44, Sat $55/49; ⏱8pm Wed-Sun) or a '**Family Ghosty' Tour** (adult/child/family $36/28/120; ⏱7pm Fri & Sat in summer, 6pm Fri & Sat in winter). Bookings are essential for all three. For a full-immersion experience, you can even choose to overnight here. The website has details.

To get here, walk or take bus 135 from Stand J outside Manly Wharf.

Northern Beaches

The 20km-stretch of coast between Manly and well-heeled **Palm Beach** (where TV soap *Home and Away* is filmed) is often described as the most impressive urban surfing landscape in the world, and the sun-bronzed locals who swim and catch the waves at Manly, Collaroy, Freshwater, Dee Why, Narrabeen, Mona Vale, Newport, Bilgola, Avalon, Whale and Palm Beaches are uniformly proud to agree.

Each of these beaches has a markedly different atmosphere – for instance, Palm and Whale Beaches are glamorous and relatively secluded, Manly is egalitarian and ever-crowded, Avalon and Dee Why are favourites with families and Narrabeen is frequented by serious surfers.

To get to Collaroy, North Narrabeen (for Narrabeen), Mona Vale, Newport, Bilgola, Avalon, Whale and Palm Beaches from the CBD, catch bus L90 or 190 from the Queen Victoria Building. From Manly Wharf, bus 136 goes to Chatswood via Curl Curl, and Dee Why; bus 156 goes to McCarrs Creek via Dee Why, Collaroy, North Narrabeen and Mona Vale.

Ku-ring-gai Chase National Park NATIONAL PARK

(www.nationalparks.nsw.gov.au; admission per car per day $11, landing fee by boat adult/child $3/2) This spectacular 14,928-hectare park, 24km from the city centre, forms Sydney's northern boundary. It's a classic mix of sandstone, bushland and water vistas, taking in over 100km of coastline along the southern edge of Broken Bay where it heads into the Hawkesbury River.

Ku-ring-gai takes its name from its original inhabitants, the Guringai people, who were all but wiped out just after colonisation through violence at the hands of British settlers or introduced disease. It's well worth reading Kate Grenville's Booker-nominated *The Secret River* for an engrossing but harrowing telling of this story.

Remnants of Aboriginal life are visible today thanks to the preservation of more than 800 sites, including rock paintings, middens and cave art. To learn about these sites and about the park's flora and fauna, enter the park through the Mt Colah entrance and visit the **Kalkari Discovery Centre** (☎02-9472 9300; Ku-ring-gai Chase Rd; ⏲9am-5pm) FREE, which has displays and videos on Australian fauna and Aboriginal culture. There is a short self-guided walk around the centre on which you can see swamp wallabies, bush turkeys, native ducks and goannas.

From the Resolute picnic area at **West Head** you can amble 100m to **Red Hands Cave**, where there are some very faint ochre handprints. About another 500m along **Resolute Track** (after a short steep section) is an Aboriginal engraving site. You can turn around or continue to one more site and make a 3.5km loop that takes in **Resolute Beach**. The view from the **West Head Lookout** is truly spectacular – don't miss it.

Less than 3km west of the picnic area, along West Head Rd, is the **Basin Track**, which offers an easy stroll to a good set of engravings. Approximately 2.5km further along the track is the Basin, a shallow round inlet where there is a **campground** (www.nationalparks.nsw.gov.au/ku-ring-gai-chase-national-park/the-basin-campground/camping; adult/child per night $28/7) area with BBQs, showers and toilets. Access is via the Basin Track or by ferry or water taxi from Palm Beach.

For information, visit the **Bobbin Inn Visitor Centre** (☎02-9472 8949; Bobbin Head, Bobbin Inn; ⏲10am-noon & 12.30-4pm), operated by the NSW Parks and Wildlife Service. Also here are a marina, picnic areas, toilets, a cafe and a boardwalk leading through mangroves. EcoTreasures (p100) runs highly regarded guided tours in the park.

Access to the park is by car or the **Palm Beach Ferry** (☎02-9974 2411; www.palmbeachferry.com.au; adult/child $7.50/3.70; ⏲9am-7pm Mon-Fri, to 6pm Sat & Sun) run by Fantasea. This runs hourly from Palm Beach to Mackerel Beach, via the Basin (20 minutes).

If you are arriving by car, enter Ku-ring-gai Chase Rd off Pacific Hwy, Mt Colah; Bobbin Head Rd, North Turramurra; or McCarrs Creek Rd, Terrey Hills.

Activities

Cycling

Bicycle NSW (Map p90; ☎02-9218 5400; www.bicyclensw.org.au; Level 5, 822 George St; ⏲9am-5pm Mon-Fri; 🚉Central) publishes *Cycling Around Sydney*, a book detailing 30 city routes and paths; purchase it through the website. Sydney City Council offers cycling maps, a list of shops offering bike hire and plenty of other information on its excellent Sydney Cycleways (http://sydneycycleways.net) website.

Diving & Snorkelling

Sydney's best shore dives are at Gordons Bay, north of Coogee; Shark Point, Clovelly; and Ship Rock, Cronulla. Other destinations include North Bondi, Camp Cove and Bare Island. Popular boat-dive sites are Wedding Cake Island off Coogee, Sydney Heads, and off Royal National Park.

There's good snorkelling off Clovelly and Manly Beaches. EcoTreasures (p100), a company specialising in ecotourism, runs a popular Snorkel Walk & Talk tour in Manly.

Dive Centre Bondi DIVING
(Map p94; ☎02-9369 3855; www.divebondi.com.au; 198 Bondi Rd, Bondi; ⏲9am-6pm Mon-Fri, 7.30am-6pm Sat & Sun) This Professional Association of Diving Instructors (PADI) five-star centre offers learn-to-dive courses (one day $225, three days $495), guided shore dives ($120 for two dives) and fortnightly boat dives ($225).

Dive Centre Manly DIVING
(Map p96; ☎02-9977 4355; www.divesydney.com.au; 10 Belgrave St, Manly; ⏲9am-6pm Mon-Fri, 8am-6pm Sat & Sun) This is one of the largest dive shops in Sydney. A two-day learn-to-dive PADI adventure costs $495, daily guided shore dives cost $115/125 for one/two dives, and Friday, Saturday and Sunday boat dives cost $175.

Horse Riding

Centennial Parklands Equestrian Centre HORSE RIDING
(Map p85; ☎02-9332 2809; www.cpequestrian.com.au; 114-120 Lang Rd, Centennial Park; escorted park ride from $80; 🚌372-374 & 391-397) Take a one-hour, 3.6km horse ride around tree-lined Centennial Park, Sydney's favourite urban green space. Five stables within the centre conduct park rides – check the website for details.

Sailing

Sydney has dozens of yacht clubs and sailing schools.

EastSail SAILING
(☎02-9327 1166; www.eastsail.com.au; d'Albora Marina, New Beach Rd, Rushcutters Bay) Nobody

ever said that yachting was a cheap sport. Take the two-day, live-aboard Start Yachting course for $575, or arrange a charter.

Sydney by Sail SAILING
(Map p82; ☎02-9280 1110; www.sydneybysail.com; 2 Murray St, Darling Harbour) Departing daily from outside the Maritime Museum, Sydney by Sail offers harbour cruises (three hours $165, children half-price) and coastal sailing adventures on weekends (six hours, adult/child $190/80). It also runs sailing courses (weekend introductory sailing course $595).

Surfing

On the South Shore, get tubed at Bondi, Tamarama, Coogee, Maroubra and Cronulla. The North Shore is home to a dozen surf beaches between Manly and Palm Beach, including Curl Curl, Dee Why, Narrabeen, Mona Vale and Newport.

Let's Go Surfing SURFING
(Map p94; ☎02-9365 1800; www.letsgosurfing.com.au; 128 Ramsgate Ave, North Bondi) You can hire gear (board and wetsuit one hour/two hours/day/week $25/30/50/150) or learn to surf with this well-established school. It caters to practically everyone, with classes for grommets aged seven to 16 (1½ hours $49), adults (two hours $99, women-only classes available) and private tuition (1½ hours $175). North Bondi is a great beach for learners.

Manly Surf School SURFING
(☎02-9977 6977; www.manlysurfschool.com; North Steyne Surf Club, Manly) Offers group surf lessons (one/two lessons adult $70/110, child $55/90) as well as private tuition (adult/child $90/70 one hour lesson). Also runs surf safaris up to the Northern Beaches, including two lessons, lunch, gear and city pick-ups ($99).

Swimming

There are 100-plus public swimming pools in Sydney, and many beaches have protected rock pools. Harbour beaches offer sheltered and shark-netted swimming, but nothing beats Pacific Ocean waves. Always swim within the flagged lifeguard-patrolled areas, and never underestimate the surf.

Andrew 'Boy' Charlton Pool SWIMMING
(☎02-9358 6686; www.abcpool.org; 1c Mrs Macquaries Rd, The Domain; adult/child $6/4.50; ⏰6am-8pm mid-Sep–Apr) Sydney's best saltwater pool – smack bang next to the harbour – is a magnet for water-loving gays, straights, mums and fashionistas. Serious lap swimmers rule the scene. Five-star change rooms and a hip cafe.

Bondi Icebergs Swimming Club SWIMMING
(Map p94; ☎02-9130 4804; www.icebergs.com.au; 1 Notts Ave, Bondi; adult/child $5.50/3.50; ⏰6am-6.30pm Mon-Wed & Fri, 6.30am-6.30pm Sat & Sun) The city's most famous pool commands the best view in Bondi and has a cute little cafe. It's closed for cleaning on Thursdays.

Dawn Fraser Baths SWIMMING
(☎02-9555 1903; www.lpac.nsw.gov.au; Elkington Park, Fitzroy Ave, Balmain; adult/child $4.40/3.10; ⏰7.15am-6.30pm Oct-Nov, 6.45am-7pm Dec-Feb, 7.15am-6.30pm Mar-Apr) This late-Victorian tidal-flow seawater pool (1884) offers a small beach at low tide and yoga classes ($13.50) during summer.

North Sydney Olympic Pool SWIMMING
(☎02-9955 2309; www.northsydney.nsw.gov.au; Alfred St South, Milsons Point; adult/child $6.70/3.40; ⏰5.30am-9pm Mon-Fri, 7am-7pm Sat & Sun, creche 9am-noon Mon, Wed & Fri) Next to Luna Park and with extraordinary harbour views. Facilities include a 50m outdoor pool, a 25m indoor pool, a gym ($18.50 with pool and sauna access), a crèche ($4.10 per hour) and a cafe.

Wylies Baths SWIMMING
(☎02-9665 2838; www.wylies.com.au; Neptune St, Coogee; adult/child $4.50/1; ⏰7am-7pm Oct-Mar, 7am-5pm Apr-Sep) Superb ocean tidal pool (built 1907) that is more targeted to swimmers than general beachgoers. After your swim, take a yoga class ($15), enjoy a massage or have a coffee at the kiosk, which has magnificent ocean views.

Tours

There are countless tours available in Sydney. You can book many of them at the Sydney Visitor Centres at The Rocks or Darling Harbour.

Bicycle Tours

Bike Buffs CYCLING
(☎0414 960 332; www.bikebuffs.com.au) Offers a four-hour, two-wheeled tour (adult/child/family $95/70/290) around the harbourside sights (including jaunts over the Harbour Bridge), departing from its meeting point on the corner of Argyle & Lower Fort Sts in The Rocks at 10.30am every day. Bookings essential.

SYDNEY FOR CHILDREN

Organised kids' activities ramp up during school holidays (December/January, April, July and September); check www.sydneyforkids.com.au, www.kidfriendly.com.au, www.au.timeout.com/sydney/kids and www.webchild.com.au/sydneyschild/your-community for listings.

Most kids love the SEA LIFE Sydney Aquarium (p84), WILD LIFE Sydney Zoo (p85) and Australian National Maritime Museum (p88) at Darling Harbour and the Powerhouse Museum (p85) at neighbouring Ultimo. Also worth investigating are the 'Tours for Tots' and 'GalleryKids Sunday Performance Program' at the Art Gallery of NSW (p77) – details are on the gallery's website.

Elsewhere, Taronga Zoo (p95) and Luna Park (p95) are sure to please. Visits to swimming pools, surfing lessons and horse or pony rides are also popular.

Nielsen Park (p92) in Vaucluse is the perfect choice if the younger members of your entourage need to stretch their legs and burn up some energy. It's also a great spot for sandcastle building! Other kid-friendly beaches include Balmoral Beach, Shelly Beach and Dee Why on the North Shore, and Clovelly Beach, Bronte Beach and the North Bondi Children's Pool on the Eastern Beaches.

Bonza Bike Tours CYCLING
(Map p80; ☎02-9247 8800; www.bonzabiketours.com; 30 Harrington St, The Rocks; Circular Quay) These bike boffins run a 2½ hour City Highlights tour on Tuesday, Wednesday, Thursday and Sunday, and a four-hour Sydney Classic tour on Monday, Wednesday, Friday and Saturday. Both cost adult/child/family $99/79/290. Other tours tackle the Harbour Bridge, Manly and the city highlights.

Eco Tours

EcoTreasures SNORKELLING
(☎0415 121 648; www.ecotreasures.com.au) Small group tours include the Sydney Coastal Experience (eight hours, adult/child $145/125), which includes a one-hour paddleboard lesson, a guided 5km bushwalk in Ku-ring-gai Chase National Park, a swim, whale watching (in season) and lunch. Also offers coastal walks, a Snorkel Walk & Talk in Manly and a range of Aboriginal heritage tours lead by indigenous guides.

Harbour Cruises

Captain Cook Cruises CRUISE
(Map p80; ☎02-9206 1111, 1800 804 843; www.captaincook.com.au) This crew offers a Harbour Highlights cruise (adult/child/family $32/16/66) plus a 24-hour Harbour Explorer pass (adult/child/family $42/24/84) that is the aquatic version of a hop-on, hop-off bus tour stopping at Watsons Bay, Shark Island, Taronga Zoo, Fort Denison, Circular Quay, Luna Park and Darling Harbour. Both leave from Circular Quay's Wharf 6. It also runs whale-watching cruises in season.

Matilda Cruises CRUISE
(Map p80; ☎02-8270 5188; www.matilda.com.au) Matilda offers a variety of cruise options on sailing catamarans, motorised catamarans and high-speed executive rockets. It also runs a 24-hour hop-on, hop-off harbour circuit pass (adult/child $42/24) departing from Pier 26 at Darling Harbour before picking up more passengers at Circular Quay's Wharf 6.

Kayak Tours

Natural Wanders KAYAKING
(☎0427 225 072; www.kayaksydney.com; tours $65-150) Offers exhilarating morning tours around the Harbour Bridge, Lavender Bay, Balmain, Birchgrove, Kirribilli, Neutral Bay and Mosman for both novices and experienced kayakers. A private 2¼-hour tour costs $150 for one person or $240 for two; group tours start at $65 per person.

Sydney Harbour Kayaks KAYAKING
(☎02-9960 4389; www.sydneyharbourkayaks.com.au; Smiths Boat Shed, 81 Parriwi Rd, Mosman; 9am-5pm Mon-Fri, 7.30am-5pm Sat & Sun) Rents kayaks (per hour/five hours from $20/70) and leads half-day weekend eco-tours ($99) from near the Spit Bridge, which crosses Middle Harbour.

Scenic Flights

Sydney Seaplanes SCENIC FLIGHTS
(☎1300 732 752, 02-9974 1455; www.seaplanes.com.au) Scenic flights from the Rose Bay Marina in a restored de Havilland Canada DHC-2 Beaver or a 2007 Cessna Caravan. Choose from a 15-minute flight over Bondi Beach

and Sydney Harbour ($200) or a 30-minute flight over the Northern Beaches ($265).

Walking Tours

BridgeClimb WALKING TOUR
(Map p80; ☎02-8274 7777; www.bridgeclimb.com; 3 Cumberland St, The Rocks; adult $198-298, child $138-198; Circular Quay, Circular Quay) Don a headset, a safety cord and a dandy grey jumpsuit and you'll be ready to embark on an exhilarating climb to the top of Sydney's famous harbour bridge. Safety is taken seriously, as is the money-making potential of the photographic sessions at the top (personal cameras aren't allowed).

I'm Free WALKING TOUR
(Map p80; www.imfree.com.au; 10.30am & 2.30pm) FREE These tours are nominally free, but in reality are run by enthusiastic young guides for tips. There's a three-hour tour of the city departing from the anchor beside Sydney Town Hall at 10.30am and 2.30pm, and a 1½-hour tour of The Rocks departing from Cadman's Cottage at 6pm. No bookings taken – just show up and look for the guide in a bright green T-shirt. Check the website for timetable changes.

Sydney Architecture Walks WALKING, CYCLING
(Map p80; ☎0403 888 390; www.sydneyarchitecture.org; walk adult/concession $35/25, cycle $120/110) These bright young archi-buffs run a five-hour cycling tour and three themed two-hour walking tours (the city; Utzon and the Sydney Opera House; and harbour-edge architecture). The tours depart from the Museum of Sydney; call or email info@sydneyarchitecture.org for bookings and departure times.

The Rocks Ghost Tours WALKING TOUR
(☎02-9241 1283; www.ghosttours.com.au; adult $42; 6.45pm Apr-Sep, 7.45pm Oct-Mar) If you like your spine chilled and your pulse slightly quickened, join one of these two-hour tours, departing from Cadman's Cottage nightly. Tours run rain or shine (ponchos provided); bookings essential.

Whale-Watching Tours

Whale Watching Sydney CRUISE
(Map p80; ☎02-9583 1199; www.whalewatchingsydney.net) Humpback and southern right whales habitually shunt up and down the Sydney coastline, sometimes venturing into the harbour. This outfit offers a two-hour Adventure Cruise (adult/child $60/40) on a speedboat and a three-hour Discovery Cruise (adult/child/family $89/54/229) on a large catamaran. Departure points are Cockle Bar Marina at Darling Harbour and Campbells Cove, Circular Quay, and the season runs from May to November.

Festivals & Events

Sydney Festival ARTS
(www.sydneyfestival.org.au) This massive event in January floods the city with art and includes free outdoor concerts in the Domain.

Big Day Out MUSIC
(www.bigdayout.com) Open-air concert in mid-January featuring many local and international performers and bands.

Chinese New Year CULTURE
(www.sydneychinesenewyear.com) Colourful celebration featuring food, fireworks and much more. Actual dates vary according to the phases of the moon.

St Jerome's Laneway Festival MUSIC
(www.lanewayfestival.com.au) Indie music takes over the 'lanes' around Macquarie Pl in early February.

Sydney Gay & Lesbian Mardi Gras GAY, LESBIAN
(www.mardigras.org.au) The highlight of this world-famous festival held in February is the over-the-top, sequined Oxford St parade, culminating in a Bacchanalian party at the Entertainment Quarter in Moore Park.

Tropfest FILM
(www.tropfest.com) The world's largest short-film festival takes over the Domain for one night in February.

Biennale of Sydney CULTURE
(www.biennaleofsydney.com.au) High-profile festival of art and ideas held between March and June every even-numbered year.

Royal Easter Show AGRICULTURE
(www.eastershow.com.au) Ostensibly a kiddie-centric agricultural show, this wonderful Sydney tradition is a two-week fiesta of carnival rides, showbags and sugar-fuelled frivolity.

Vivid Sydney CULTURE
(www.vividsydney.com) Immersive light installations and projections in the city, live music, talks and debates during May and June.

City2Surf SPORT
(www.city2surf.com.au) Charity event when over 80,000 people run the 14km from Hyde

Park to Bondi Beach on the second Sunday in August.

Festival of the Winds KITES
(Queen Elizabeth Dr, Bondi Pavilion; 380) Held on the second weekend in September, this festival brings spectacular kites shaped like animals and aliens to Bondi Beach.

Art & About ART
(www.artandabout.com.au) Specially commissioned works by local and international artists pop up in unusual locations throughout the city between late September and late October.

Sculpture by the Sea ART
(www.sculpturebythesea.com) Between late October and early November, the clifftop trail from Bondi Beach to Tamarama transforms into a sculpture garden.

Homebake MUSIC
(www.homebake.com.au) Held on the first Saturday in December, this one-day music bash in the Domain is a showcase of the best Australian and New Zealand bands around.

Bondi Christmas Bash CELEBRATION
Sydney's international family of travellers traditionally heads to Bondi Beach on December 25. There's usually a party in the Pavilion.

Sydney to Hobart Yacht Race SPORT
(www.rolexsydneyhobart.com) On 26 December Sydney Harbour is a sight to behold as hun-

GAY & LESBIAN SYDNEY

Gay and lesbian culture forms a vocal and vital part of Sydney's social fabric. **Taylor Square** on Oxford St is the centre of arguably the second-largest gay community in the world after San Francisco; Newtown is home to Sydney's lesbian scene.

Sydney's famous **Gay & Lesbian Mardi Gras** (www.mardigras.org.au) draws over 300,000 spectators and involves over 10,000 participants; the Mardi Gras also runs the annual **Sleaze Ball** (02-9568 8600; www.mardigras.org.au; 1 Driver Ave, Hordern Pavilion; 339) held in late September/early October at the Horden Pavilion in Moore Park.

Free gay media includes *SX* (www.gaynewsnetwork.com.au), the *Star Observer* (www.starobserver.com.au), *Lesbians on the Loose* (www.lotl.com) and *DNA* (www.dnamagazine.com.au).

Most hotels, restaurants and bars in Darlinghurst and Surry Hills are very gay-friendly. To party, go for a wander along the city end of Oxford St, or check out the following:

Arq (Map p86; 02-9380 8700; www.arqsydney.com.au; 16 Flinders St; admission free-$25; 9pm-late Thu-Sun; Museum) Drag shows on Thursday from 9pm, clubbing over two floors on Friday and Saturday, caberet on Sunday (the main event of the week).

Chinese Laundry (p124) runs regular party events.

Beresford Hotel (p125) has a glam Sunday afternoon scene.

Fag Tag (www.fagtag.com.au) Organised takeovers of straight bars, usually in summer – lots of free fun.

Imperial Hotel (www.theimperialhotel.com.au; 35 Erskineville Rd; front bar free, cellar club before/after 10pm free/$10, cabaret bar Fri/Sat $10/15; 3pm-late; Erskineville) The drag acts at this art-deco pub inspired *Priscilla, Queen of the Desert* (the opening scene was filmed here). Come for caberet on Friday and Saturday, a DJ on Sunday and a range of events during the rest of the week.

In the Dark (www.inthedark.com.au) Runs various parties, including Homesexual and Queer Nation (both at Home) and DILF (who's your daddy?).

Midnight Shift (Map p86; 02-9358 3848; www.themidnightshift.com.au; 85 Oxford St; admission free-$10; noon-2am Mon & Tue, noon-4am Wed, Thu & Sun, noon-6am Fri & Sun; Museum) The grande dame of the Oxford St scene. The downstairs bar attracts an unpretentious mix of blokes, twinks and bears. Upstairs is a serious tits-to-the-wind club (open from 10pm Fridays and Saturdays) where lavish drag productions are staged.

Oxford Hotel (Map p86; 02-8324 5200; www.theoxfordhotel.com.au; 134 Oxford St; 10am-late; Museum) The basement miniclub spins pop and indie on weekends. Upstairs, the Supper Club and Polo Lounge play host to an eclectic program of cabaret and DJs.

dreds of boats crowd its waters to farewell the yachts competing in this gruelling race.

New Year's Eve FIREWORKS
(www.cityofsydney.nsw.gov.au/nye) The biggest party of the year, with a flamboyant firework display on the Harbour.

🛏 Sleeping

You'll sleep well (though not cheaply) in Sydney. The winter months sometimes deliver bargains, but between November and February you should expect prices to jump by as much as 40%. The reality is that the city is busy all year – we advise you to book ahead and shop around for the best price.

Rooms in the city centre are often discounted on weekends, whereas prices of those near the beaches rise. Breakfast isn't included in many room rates and can be expensive – consider checking out the local cafe scene instead. Wi-fi access and parking often cost extra, too.

In this chapter, budget ($) indicates a room costing under $120 per night, midrange ($$) between $120 and $250 per night and top end ($$$) over $250 a night. Prices skyrocket during the busy Christmas/New Year period.

🛏 Circular Quay & the Rocks

⭐ **Sydney Harbour YHA** HOSTEL $
(Map p80; ☑02-8272 0900; www.yha.com.au; 110 Cumberland St, The Rocks; dm $48-50, d $168-185, f $205; ❀@🛜; 🚇Circular Quay, 🛳Circular Quay, 🚉Circular Quay) The view from the rooftop terrace and deluxe rooms at this relatively new and exceptionally well-run YHA hostel is fabulous – right over Circular Quay to the Opera House. The modern four- and six-bed dorms and the private rooms are neat and comfortable; all come with private bathrooms. The building was designed to be environmentally sustainable and incorporates a major archaeological dig into its footprint.

Lord Nelson Brewery Hotel HISTORIC HOTEL $$
(Map p80; ☑02-9251 4044; www.lordnelson.com. au; 19 Kent St, Millers Point; r with/without bathroom $190/130; ❀🛜; 🚉Circular Quay) Pulling beers since 1841, this boutique sandstone pub has nine upstairs rooms with exposed stone walls and dormer windows. Most are spacious and have en suites; there are also cheaper, smaller rooms with shared facilities. The house-brewed Old Admiral Dark Ale is terrific, and goes down particuarly well with the hearty pub food served in the restaurant.

Pullman Quay
Grand Sydney Harbour APARTMENT $$$
(Map p80; ☑02-9256 4000; www.mirvachotels. com; 61 Macquarie St, Circular Quay East; 1-/2 bedroom apt from $409/699; ❀🛜; 🚇Circular Quay, 🛳Circular Quay, 🚉Circular Quay) Known locally as 'the Toaster', the architecturally uninspired building housing this apartment hotel has the city's best location – right next to the Opera House. Each of the apartments has contemporary decor and features a balcony, separate lounge and dining areas, bathroom with spa bath, and kitchen with integrated laundry. It's worth paying extra for a harbour view.

Park Hyatt LUXURY HOTEL $$$
(Map p80; ☑02-9256 1234; www.sydney.park. hyatt.com; 7 Hickson Rd, The Rocks; r from $795; ❀@🛜; 🚇Circular Quay, 🛳Circular Quay, 🚉Circular Quay) Luxury meets location at Sydney's poshest hotel. Bookending Circular Quay with the Opera House, its recently refurbished interiors, service levels and facilities are second to none. The in-house Dining Room restaurant is highly regarded.

🛏 City Centre

Bounce HOSTEL $
(Map p90; ☑02-9281 2222; www.bouncehotel. com.au; 28 Chalmers St; dm $37-45, d $139-149; ❀@🛜; 🚉Central) 🍴 Bounce positions itself as an upmarket hostel 'where budget and boutique meet', and we're pleased to concur. All dorms and rooms are air-conditioned, female-only dorms have private bathrooms, beds have inner-spring mattresses and bathrooms are sleek. Chuck another prawn on the roof terrace's barbie and soak up those skyline views.

Wake Up! HOSTEL $
(Map p90; ☑02-9288 7888; www.wakeup.com.au; 509 Pitt St; dm $34-40, s $98, d $108-118; ❀@🛜; 🚉Central) Flashpackers sleep soundly in this converted 1900 department store on top of Sydney's busiest intersection. It's a convivial, colourful, professionally run place with 520 beds, lots of activities, tour desk, 24-hour check-in, sunny cafe, bar and no excuse for neglecting your inner party animal.

Railway Square YHA HOSTEL $
(Map p90; ☑ 02-9281 9666; www.yha.com.au; 8-10 Lee St; dm $33-44, r $107-119; @ 🛜 ⊠; 🚇 Central) Clever renovations have turned this former parcel shed at Central Station into a hip hostel complete with platform. Sleep in dorms in converted train carriages (bring earplugs) or in the main building. There are also private rooms (some with private bathrooms).

Pensione Hotel BOUTIQUE HOTEL $$
(Map p82; ☑ 02-9265 8888; www.pensione.com.au; 631-635 George St; s from $110, d from $135; ✳ 🛜; 🚇 Central) This tastefully reworked post office features smart, neutrally shaded rooms with tea/coffee facilities and fridges. Guests can also use the laundry and communal lounge-kitchenette. It's a busy location, and even though the windows facing George St are double-glazed you should expect street noise. Good value at the lower end of its price scale, but overpriced at the upper end.

**Adina Apartment Hotel
Sydney Harbourside** APARTMENT $$
(Map p80; ☑ 02-9249 7000; www.adinahotels. com.au; 55 Shelley St, Kings Street Wharf, Darling Harbour; studio from $170, 1-bedroom apt from $200; P ✳ 🛜 ⊠; 🚊 Darling Harbour) A newish low-rise development just off King St Wharf where all apartments have kitchens, and all but the studios have laundry facilities and balconies. There's also a pool, a gym and a sauna.

**Adina Apartment Hotel
Sydney** APARTMENT $$
(Map p82; ☑ 02-9274 0000; www.adinahotels.com. au; 511 Kent St; studio from $180, 1-/2-bedroom apt from $240/280; ✳ 🛜 ⊠; 🚇 Town Hall) Near both Chinatown and Darling Harbour but with double-glazed windows to ensure a good night's sleep, this apartment hotel offers spacious, fully equipped apartments and smaller studio rooms with kitchenettes. The larger apartments offer the best value.

Vibe Hotel Sydney HOTEL $$
(Map p82; ☑ 02-8272 3300; www.vibehotels. com.au; 111 Goulburn St; d/ste from $180/210; ✳ @ 🛜 ⊠; 🚇 Central) The rooms are spacious and well priced at this handy midrange hotel near Museum and Central train stations and on the fringe of Surry Hills. All have a seating area, flat-screen TV, work desk and large closet. It has a ground-floor cafe and a gym, a sauna and a good-sized pool on the outdoor deck.

Travelodge Sydney HOTEL $$
(Map p82; ☑ 02-8267 1700; www.travelodge. au/travelodge-sydney-hotel/home; cnr Wentworth Ave & Goulburn St; d from $110; ✳ @ 🛜; 🚇 Museum, Central) A great location near Hyde Park (equidistant between Museum Station and Central Station) plus clean, comfortable and well-set-up rooms with basic kitchenette mean that this is a compelling albeit characterless choice, particularly if you can score one of the internet specials (look for the three- or five-night packages). Wi-fi is only available in rooms on the upper floors.

Establishment Hotel BOUTIQUE HOTEL $$$
(Map p80; ☑ 02-9240 3100; www.merivale.com. au; 5 Bridge La; r from $299; ✳ @ 🛜; 🚇 Wynyard) Hidden down a nondescript lane, this boutique hotel attracts discreet celebrities, style-conscious couples and cashed-up execs dreaming of a nooner with their assistants. What the hotel lacks in facilities it more than makes up for in glamour, but noise (from adjacent rooms, corridors and in-house bars and restaurants) is a real problem. If staying here, you'll have VIP access into all the 'it' bars of the Merivale empire.

QT Sydney BOUTIQUE HOTEL $$$
(Map p80; ☑ 02-8262 0000; www.qtsydney.com. au; 49 Market St; rm from $380; ✳ 🛜; 🚇 Town Hall) Nothing's being kept on the QT at this new boutique hotel. The ultra-theatrical decor and gregarious staff perfectly suit the location in the historic State Theatre buildings, and quirky touches such as the DIY martini kit in every room deserve applause. There's a spa complete with hamam and old-school barber, plus a bar and grill operated by one of the city's most fashionable restaurateurs, Robert Marchetti.

Park8 BOUTIQUE HOTEL $$$
(Map p80; ☑ 02-9283 2488; www.8hotels.com; 185 Castlereagh St; r $225-275; ✳ 🛜; 🚇 Town Hall) Hidden in plain sight behind a hole-in-the-wall cafe, this offering close to the city's major shopping action gets the balance of comfort and style just right. It's one of the impressive 8 Hotels portfolio (Kirketon, Diamont etc).

Sofitel Sydney Wentworth LUXURY HOTEL $$$
(Map p80; ☑ 02-9228 9188; http://sofitelsydney. com.au; 68-101 Phillip St; r from $390; P ✳ @ 🛜; 🚇 Martin Pl) One of a cluster of facility-rich five-star choices in the streets leading down to Circular Quay, the Sofitel is known for its spacious and luxuriously appointed rooms

and for the keenly priced weekend deals often found on online booking sites. Unfortunately, parking and wi-fi are mega-pricey.

Kings Cross, Potts Point & Woolloomooloo

★Blue Parrot HOSTEL $
(Map p86; ☎02-9356 4888; www.blueparrot.com.au; 87 Macleay St, Potts Point; dm $34-40; @; Kings Cross) If you're looking for a home away from home, this cracker of a hostel will fit the bill. Away from the seedy epicentre of the Cross, it's surrounded by the alluring cafes, bars and restaurants that Potts Point is known for, but is so comfortable that you'll probably decide to stay in, cook in the communal kitchen and then chill out in one of the hammocks strung between trees in the leafy rear courtyard. Dorms sleep between four and 10 and have lockers, fans and spring mattresses; most share bathrooms (one shower per 10 beds). The best of the bunch overlooks the courtyard. Wi-fi and internet are free, and there's a strong entertainment program.

Eva's Backpackers HOSTEL $
(Map p86; ☎02-9358 2185; www.evasbackpackers.com.au; 6-8 Orwell St, Kings Cross; dm $29-36, d with shared bathroom $85-96; ; Kings Cross) Eva's gets our vote as the cleanest hostel in Sydney (high praise indeed, as a number of its competitors are no slouches in this respect). Dorms are of a reasonable size and have lockers; a few have private bathrooms and air-con. Drawcards include free breakfast and wi-fi, a fab rooftop terrace complete with BBQs, and a sociable downstairs kitchen-dining room.

Original Backpackers Lodge HOSTEL $
(Map p86; ☎02-9356 3232; www.originalbackpackers.com.au; 160-162 Victoria St, Kings Cross; dm $22-34, s $65-85, d $70-95; Kings Cross) This huge place occupies two historic mansions, offering dozens of beds and a great (if noisy) central courtyard. Dorms have lockers, high ceilings, fridges, TVs, fans and shared bathrooms; they're generally more attractive than the single and double rooms, which are boxey. There's a huge communal kitchen, a TV room and a busy schedule of social activities including a $5 BBQ on Friday nights.

Backpackers HQ HOSTEL $
(Map p86; ☎02-9356 4551; www.backpackershq.com.au; 174 Victoria St, Kings Cross; dm $28-45, d without bathroom $85-99, d $95-110; ; Kings Cross) New owners have decided to banish the party vibe at this Victoria St old-timer, introducing a wannabe designer decor and encouraging a quiet atmosphere. Dorms sleep between four and 10; all have lockers and some have fridges and private bathrooms. The communal kitchen is small and basic, but the free internet and breakfast compensate.

Diamant HOTEL $$
(Map p86; ☎02-9295 8888; www.diamant.com.au; 14 Kings Cross Rd, Kings Cross; r $159-375, ste $315-425, apt $500-$3200; P; Kings Cross) Riding high behind the iconic Coca-Cola sign is this well-priced designer hotel. Rooms and apartments are slick and spacious, with king-size beds, quality linen, work desks, huge plasma screens and iPod docks; some are set up for disabled guests. Choose from bridge, harbour or city views.

Regents Court APARTMENT $$
(Map p86; ☎02-9331 2099; www.8hotels.com; 18 Springfield Ave, Kings Cross; studio apt from $185; ; Kings Cross) Nestled on a slowly gentrifying back street in the centre of the Cross, this apartment block has been reinvented as a boutique apartment hotel by Sydney stylemeisters 8 Hotels. There are 26 sparsely furnished, self-contained studio apartments up for grabs, all with cooking facilities. Communal facilities include a laundry and roof garden.

Victoria Court Hotel B&B $$
(Map p86; ☎02-9357 3200; www.victoriacourt.com.au; 122 Victoria St, Potts Point; s $99-132, d $110-280; ; Kings Cross) Chintzy charm reigns supreme at this faded but well-run B&B, which has 25 clean rooms spread over a pair of three-storey 1881 terrace houses. The more expensive rooms are larger and some have balconies.

Maisonette Hotel HOTEL $$
(Map p86; ☎02-9357 3878; www.sydneylodges.com/lodges/the-maisonette-hotel/; 31 Challis Ave, Potts Point; s/d from $59/98; ; Kings Cross) Wake up and smell the coffee above one of the city's most popular cafe strips. The rooms range from small, bright doubles with en suites to little singles with shared bathrooms; all have TVs and kitchenettes. Be warned: those overlooking the street can be noisy.

★BLUE Sydney LUXURY HOTEL $$$
(Map p86; ☎02-9331 9000; www.tajhotels.com/sydney; 6 Cowper Wharf Rdwy, Woolloomooloo; r from

$252; ❄@🛜≋; 🚌311) Originally opened by the chic W Hotels chain but now operated by the ultra-professional Taj Group, this outstanding hotel occupies the front section of the Woolloomooloo finger wharf. Although the common areas lack allure, most guests couldn't care less – they're too busy relaxing in their spacious, lavishly appointed rooms, swimming in the indoor pool, using the gym or wining and dining in one of the wharf's excellent restaurants.

Simpsons of Potts Point B&B **$$$**
(Map p86; ☎02-9356 2199; www.simpsonshotel.com; 8 Challis Ave, Potts Point; r from $235; P❄@🛜; 🚆Kings Cross) Occupying an 1892 red-brick villa at the quiet end of a busy cafe strip, this perennially popular place has an endearingly old-fashioned interior decoration. The downstairs lounge and breakfast room are lovely, and rooms are both comfortable and impeccably clean.

Inner East

Medusa BOUTIQUE HOTEL **$$**
(Map p86; ☎02-9331 1000; www.medusa.com.au; 267 Darlinghurst Rd, Darlinghurst; r $210-420; ❄@🛜; 🚆Kings Cross) There's not a serpent in sight at this theatrically decorated, gay-friendly designer hotel. Eighteen stylish and comfortable rooms with basic kitchenette are arranged around an internal courtyard featuring a surprisingly noisy water feature (fortunately, it's turned off at night). Staff will happily welcome your chihuahua, but don't encourage child guests.

Adina Apartment Hotel Sydney APARTMENT **$$**
(Map p90; ☎02-8302 1000; www.adinahotels.com.au; 359 Crown St, Surry Hills; apt from $190; P❄@🛜≋; 🚆Central) As one of the main pastimes in Surry Hills is eating out, you may find the well-equipped kitchenette of your spacious, well-appointed apartment doesn't get a lot of use – there are three highly regarded restaurants in the same complex. The gym, sauna and leafy pool area are plenty popular over Mardi Gras.

Kirketon Hotel BOUTIQUE HOTEL **$$**
(Map p86; ☎02-9332 2011; www.kirketon.com.au; 229 Darlinghurst Rd; r $160-280; ❄🛜; 🚆Kings Cross) You might feel like you're in a David Lynch movie as you wander the darkened, mirror-lined corridors to your room, one of 40 spread over two levels. Even the cramped standard rooms have classy trimmings such as gilt-edged mirrors, superior linen and plasma screens.

Hotel Altamont BOUTIQUE HOTEL **$$**
(Map p86; ☎02-9360 6000; www.altamont.com.au; 207 Darlinghurst Rd, Darlinghurst; d $99-190; ❄🛜; 🚆Kings Cross) Altamont flagged the end of '60s peace and love, but here in Darlinghurst the good times continue unabated. Sixteen well-priced rooms have a pleasant but slightly worn decor – opt for a deluxe version if possible. Staff are welcoming and the location is close – but not too close – to the Cross. Breakfast is included in the room rate.

Kathryn's on Queen B&B **$$**
(Map p85; ☎02-9327 4535; www.kathryns.com.au; 20 Queen St, Woollahra; r $180-260; 🚌380) Deftly run by the ever-smiley Kathryn, this grandiose 1888 Victorian terrace at the top end of Woollahra's gilded mile offers two rooms that are tastefully decorated in cream and white. The lavish breakfast can be enjoyed in the courtyard garden.

Manor House BOUTIQUE HOTEL **$$**
(Map p86; ☎02-9380 6633; www.manorhouse.com.au; 86 Flinders St, Surry Hills; r $160-245; ❄🛜; 🚆Central) Sashay from Taylor Sq into this time-tripping 1850s mansion, complete with extravagant chandeliers, moulded ceilings, Victorian tiling and fountains tinkling in the garden. It's filled to the gills around Mardi Gras time, being right on the parade route and within staggering distance of the party.

150 Apartments APARTMENT **$$$**
(Map p82; ☎02-9280 1087, 1300 246 835; www.apartmenthotel.com.au; 150 Liverpool St, East Sydney; apt from $339; P❄🛜; 🚆Museum) Designed by minimalist masters Engelen Moore, these ferociously fashionable two- and three-bedroom apartments near Hyde Park have kitchens and laundries and are fully equipped with designer furniture and appliances, although not all rooms have air-con. There are discount rates for long-term stays.

Bondi

As well as the options listed here, the new Boheme Bondi Beach development on Hall St is slated to include an Adina Apartment Hotel. Check www.adina.com.au for details.

Bondi Beachouse YHA HOSTEL $
(Map p94; ☎02-9365 2088; www.yha.com.au; 63 Fletcher St; dm $30-35, tw/d without/with bathroom $80/100, f without/with bathroom $170/180; ; 361 from Bondi Junction) A short but steep stroll from the beach, this 95-bed art-deco hostel offers facilities including a table-tennis table, air-conditioned TV rooms, communal kitchen, and a rooftop deck with views over Tamarama Beach. Bodyboards and snorkels are available at no cost; surfboard hire costs $15 for six hours. Dorms sleep between four and eight, and some of the private rooms have ocean views – all are clean and well maintained. The entertainment program includes a $5 BBQ dinner on Friday, and a Monday pancake night organised by Sydney's evangelical Christian Hillsong Church.

Bondi Backpackers HOSTEL $
(Map p94; ☎02-9130 4660, 1800 304 660; www.bondibackpackers.com.au; 110 Campbell Pde; dm $22-45, s without bathroom $45-65, d without bathroom $57-105; @; 389, 380 or 333) Coming a distant second to the YHA in the quality stakes, this run-down joint opposite the beach gets a mention for two reasons: its location directly across from the beach, and its highly professional and helpful manager, Cherie Nelson. The no-frills dorms, rooms and bathrooms are clean, and guests receive a free breakfast and 30 minutes' free wi-fi or internet per day.

Bondi Beach House GUESTHOUSE $$
(Map p94; ☎0417 336 444; www.bondibeachhouse.com.au; 28 Sir Thomas Mitchell Rd; s $80-135, d $120-300, ste $185-325; ; 389, 380 or 333) Tucked away in a tranquil pocket behind Campbell Pde, this charming place offers a real home-away-from-home atmosphere. Though only a five-minute walk from the beach, you may well be tempted to stay in all day – the rear courtyard and front terrace are great spots for relaxing. Six of the nine rooms have private bathrooms; of these, the suites are the nicest. No children under 12 and DIY breakfast. Book well in advance for the one available car space.

Ultimate Apartments APARTMENT $$
(Map p94; ☎02-9365 7969; www.apartmentsbondibeach.com; 59 O'Brien St; s&d $125-185; P; 389, 380 or 333) It may appear to be existing in a strangely parallel 1970s universe, but this relentlessly unfashionable motel is clean, secure and quiet. Every room has a kitchenette, there's plenty of free on-site parking, the beach is a short-ish walk away and facilities include a communal laundromat and swimming pool.

Ravesi's BOUTIQUE HOTEL $$$
(Map p94; ☎02-9365 4422; www.ravesis.com.au; 118 Campbell Pde; d $209-389, ste $289-549; ; 389, 380 or 333) Ravesi's fits into Bondi's shaggy surfer scene like a briefcase on a beach, but it's a popular choice for romantic weekends. The sleek chocolate-and-grey rooms are well sized, but their location above one of Campbell Pde's busiest bars means that they can be noisy. The best rooms have deep balconies with five-star ocean views. No breakfast.

Coogee

Coogee Beach House HOSTEL $
(☎02-9665 1162; www.coogeebeachhouse.com; 171 Arden St; dm $25-35, d without bathroom $80-95; @; 372, 374) Affable manager Daniel Harris is proud of his hostel, and for good reason. The dorms (four and six beds), private rooms and shared bathrooms are very clean, and the atmosphere is both welcoming and tranquil (guests go out to party). Beds aren't super comfortable and there were no lockers when we visited, but compensations include a barbecue terrace, a communal kitchen, free breakfast and complimentary use of surfboards, bodyboards and bikes.

Dive Hotel BOUTIQUE HOTEL $$
(☎02-9665 5538; www.divehotel.com.au; 234 Arden St; r $155-215, r with ocean view $220-315; P@; 372, 374) Plenty of hotels don't live up to their name ('grand', 'palace' and 'central' are often less than literal) and thankfully neither does this one. Its 14 rooms are spacious and each comes with a kitchenette. If possible, opt for one that faces the ocean. Breakfast is served in an extremely attractive indoor/outdoor lounge where two resident dogs hold court. No children under eight years old.

Glebe, Newtown & Enmore

Billabong Gardens HOSTEL $
(☎02-9550 3236; www.billabonggardens.com.au; 5-11 Egan St, Newtown; dm $26-28, s $55-95, d $75-115; @; Newtown) A location close to the King St action and Royal Prince Alfred

Hospital means that this excellent hostel attracts travellers, touring rock bands, medical students and urbanites of all persuasions. Rooms come with or without bathrooms; most are in the main building but some are in a nearby terrace house. The TV lounge, BBQ area and solar-heated pool are busy social hubs.

Glebe Village HOSTEL $
(☎02-9660 8878; www.glebevillage.com; 256 Glebe Point Rd, Glebe; dm $23-27, s/d $65/90; P@; 431) Spread over three Victorian-era houses, this global village in the middle of Glebe is a bit like a grungy collection of student flats – perfect for those less hung-up on comfort than good times. It offers a mix of shared bathrooms and en suites, plus lively indoor and outdoor communal areas. Breakfast (included) might be pancakes if you're lucky.

Glebe Point YHA HOSTEL $
(☎02-9692 8418; www.yha.com.au; 262-264 Glebe Point Rd, Glebe; dm $28-45, s without bathroom $70, d without bathroom $84-105; @; 431) A chilled-out, brightly painted place with decent facilities and simple, clean rooms with sinks. The main lure for party people is the rooftop terrace with its barbecue nights, speed-dating extravaganzas and salsa showdowns.

Tara Guest House B&B $$
(☎02-9519 4809; www.taraguesthouse.com.au; 13 Edgeware Rd, Enmore; d with/without bathroom $205/175, ste $205; ; Newtown) Hosts Julian and Brom ain't no Scarlett O'Hara and Rhett Butler – they work together happily and have a wonderful ability to make everyone feel at home, at their atmosphere-laden B&B near Newtown. Frankly, my dears, you won't give a damn that only one of the four bedrooms has an en suite; your only problems will be doing justice to the huge gourmet breakfast and eventually saying goodbye to resident border collie Oscar. Traffic noise means that light sleepers should bring earplugs.

North Shore

Lane Cove River Tourist Park CAMPGROUND $
(☎02-9888 9133; www.lcrtp.com.au; Plassey Rd, Macquarie Park, Lane Cove; unpowered/powered sites per 2 people $37/39, d/f cabins from $135/155; @; North Ryde) Have a back-to-nature experience in the middle of the city by staying in this national park campsite 14km northwest of the city centre. There are caravan and camp sites, cabins and a pool to cool off in when the city swelters. First-time campers are catered for with furnished sites (d $90) and there's even a 'glamping' option (d $200).

Vibe Hotel North Sydney HOTEL $$
(☎02-9955 1111; www.vibehotels.com.au; 88 Alfred St South, Milsons Point; r from $179; @; Milsons Point/Luna Park, Milsons Point) Dappled with Vibe's trademark lime and aubergine colour scheme, this slick hotel sports 165 rooms and 36 suites, the best of which offer a choice of Lavender Bay or Kirribilli views. During the week it pulls the business crowd and commands top dollar, but you can often nab a good deal on weekends.

Manly

Boardrider Backpacker HOSTEL $
(Map p96; ☎02-9977 6077; www.boardrider.com.au; Rear 63, the Corso; dm $26-40, d $97-150, d without bathroom $75-135; ; Manly) The best of the two hostels in Manly (by a long shot), Boardrider has a range of dorms and private rooms that are extremely popular with long-term guests. Be warned: cleanliness doesn't appear to be high on the priority list and the location right on the Corso will make noise a problem for light sleepers. There's a busy entertainment program, free wi-fi all week and free breakfast on weekdays.

101 Addison Road B&B $$
(☎02-9977 6216; www.bb-manly.com; 101 Addison Rd; r $160-170; P; Manly) At the risk of sounding like a Victorian matron, the only word to describe this 1880 cottage on a quiet street near Shelley Beach is 'delightful'. Two rooms are available, but single-group bookings are the name of the game (from one to four people) – meaning you'll have free reign of the antique-strewn accommodation, including a private lounge with grand piano and open fireplace.

Eating

As our selection of reviews indicates, Sydney is home to restaurants serving cuisines from every corner of the globe. This, combined with wonderful fresh produce and some of the world's best chefs, make it a hugely exciting foodie destination.

Booking is advisable where telephone numbers are listed.

City Centre, the Rocks & Circular Quay

Din Tai Fung CHINESE $
(Map p82; www.dintaifungaustralia.com.au; L1, World Sq, 644 George St; dumplings $11-20, steamed buns $3, noodles $12-19; 11.30am-2.30pm & 5.30-9pm; Museum) It also does noodles and buns, but it's the dumplings that have made this Taiwanese chain famous, delivering an explosion of fabulously flavoursome broth as you bite into their delicate casings (opt for the Xiao Long Bao). Come early, come hungry, come prepared to share your table. It also has stalls in the food court at Westfield Sydney.

Sydney Madang KOREAN $
(Map p82; 371a Pitt St; soups $12-17, pancakes $13-22, steam bowl $40-55; 11.30am-1am; Museum) Down a teensy Little Korea laneway is this backdoor gem – an authentic barbecue joint that's low on interior charisma but high on quality and quantity. Noisy, cramped and chaotic, yes, but the chilli seafood soup, korean pancakes and steam bowl banquets will have you coming back the next day.

Mamak MALAYSIAN $
(Map p82; www.mamak.com.au; 15 Goulburn St; roti $5.50-11.50, satays $9-16; 11.30am-2.30pm & 5.30-10pm daily, till 2am Fri & Sat; Town Hall) Get here early if you want to score a table without queuing, because this eat-and-run Malaysian joint is one of the most popular cheapies in the city. The satays are cooked over charcoal and are particularly delicious when accompanied by a flaky golden roti. No bookings and BYO alcohol.

Le Grand Café FRENCH, CAFE $
(Map p80; www.afsydney.com.au/about/le-grand-cafe; 257 Clarence St; mains $8-12; 8.30am-6.15pm Mon-Thu, to 5pm Fri, 8.30am-2.30pm Sat; Town Hall) All we can say about this popular cafe in the foyer of the Harry Seidler–designed Alliance Française building is *ooh la la*. The classic French snacks (think rich soups, quiche and croque-monsieur) are tasty, and the surrounds are extremely smart. No bookings and cash only.

Central Baking Depot BAKERY $
(CBD; Map p80; www.centralbakingdepot.com.au; 37-39 Erskine St; sandwiches $8-9, pies & quiches $4.50-5.50; 7am-4.30pm Mon-Fri, 8am-3pm Sat; Wynyard) Once upon a time the best bakeries were confined to the suburbs, but CBD has brought quality bread and baked goods into the heart of the city. Drop by for a savoury snack (pies, sausage rolls, croissants, pizza slices, sandwiches), or a sweet treat with coffee. Seating is limited to a modest scattering of tables and a window bench.

THE CULT OF THE CELEBRITY CHEF

Many Sydneysiders consider a sprinkling of celebrity to be an essential ingredient when it comes to dining out. There is a veritable constellation of chefs cooking around town who have attained local and international stardom courtesy of television cooking programs or cookbooks. These include the following:

- **Bill Granger** (Bills, p112) Lifestyle chef and author of 10 cookbooks whose food and style are thought by many to be quintessentially Sydney.
- **Kylie Kwong** (Billy Kwong, p112) Presents her own television programs (*My China* etc) and has written a number of cookbooks.
- **Luke Nguyen** (Red Lantern, p111) Presents his own television programs (*Luke Nguyen's Vietnam, The Songs of Sapa, Luke Nguyen's Greater Mekong*) and has written a number of cookbooks.
- **Matt Moran** (**Aria**, Map p80; 9252 2555; www.ariarestaurant.com; 1 Macquarie St; mains $48; lunch Mon-Fri, dinner daily; Circular Quay; Chiswick Restaurant, p112) Matt's portrait is on show at the National Portrait Gallery in Canberra and he is known to millions of Australians through regular appearances on *MasterChef Australia*.
- **Neil Perry** (Rockpool Bar & Grill, p110; **Rockpool**, Map p80; 9252 1888; www.rockpool.com; 107 George St; 2 courses $100; lunch Fri & Sat, dinner Tue-Sat; Circular Quay; and **Spice Temple**, Map p80; 8078 1088; www.rockpool.com; 10 Bligh St; dishes $15-45; lunch Mon-Fri, dinner Mon-Sat; Martin Place) The city's original rock-star chef (with ponytail to match) has a long list of cookbooks and appearances on television cooking programs to his credit.

Golden Century CHINESE, SEAFOOD **$$**
(Map p82; ☎02-9212 3901; www.goldencentury.com.au; 393-399 Sussex St; seafood mains from $23; ⊙noon-4am; Town Hall) The fish tank at this frenetic Cantonese place forms a window-wall to the street, signalling Golden Century's long-held credentials as one of Sydney's top seafood restaurants. Splash out on the whole lobster cooked in ginger and shallots, which follows a snappy tank–net–kitchen–customer trajectory.

Quay MODERN AUSTRALIAN **$$$**
(Map p80; ☎02-9251 5600; www.quay.com.au; L3, Overseas Passenger Terminal; set menu lunch/dinner from $125/175; ⊙noon-2.30pm Tue-Fri, 6-10pm daily; Circular Quay, Circular Quay, Circular Quay) Quay is guilty of breaking the rule that good views make for bad food. Chef Peter Gilmore has achieved international recognition for his exquisite mod-Oz food (Quay is in the San Pellegrino Top 50 list) and the view is extraordinary – as long as there's not a cruise ship in the way. Bookings essential.

Rockpool Bar & Grill STEAKHOUSE **$$$**
(Map p80; ☎02-8078 1900; www.rockpool.com; 66 Hunter St; mains $25-115; ⊙noon-3pm Mon-Fri, 6-11pm Mon-Sat; Martin Pl) You'll feel like a 1930s Manhattan stockbroker when you dine at this sleek operation in the art-deco City Mutual Building. The bar is famous for its dry-aged, full-blood wagyu burger (make sure you order a side of the hand-cut fat chips), and the grill specialises in succulent steaks cooked on the wood-fired grill and seafood dishes cooked in a charcoal oven.

Guillaume at Bennelong FRENCH **$$$**
(Map p80; ☎02-9241 1999; www.guillaumeatbennelong.com.au; Sydney Opera House; set menus $150-195; ⊙5.30pm-late Tue-Sat, noon-3pm Thu & Fri; Circular Quay, Circular Quay, Circular Quay) Enjoy magnificent views and the masterful cuisine of acclaimed chef Guillaume Brahimi. His contemporary French fare has fans hollering operatically all over town. There's a bargain pre-theatre deal (two/three courses $66/78) and a tapas menu (four/six/eight tapas $35/45/55) in the bar.

Kings Cross, Potts Point & Woolloomooloo

Room 10 CAFE **$**
(Map p86; 10 Llankelly Pl, Kings Cross; mains $8-12; ⊙7am-4pm Mon-Fri, 8am-4pm Sat, 9am-2pm Sun; Kings Cross) An exemplar of the current crop of hip cafes taking Sydney by storm (tiny space, laneway location, uncomfortable seating, excellent coffee, simple but delicious food), Room 10 is also a standout contributor when it comes to the reinvention of the Cross. Queue for a stool, or order your coffee to go.

Bourke Street Bakery CAFE **$**
(Map p86; www.bourkestreetbakery.com.au; 46a Macleay St, Potts Point; sandwiches $8, pies & quiches $5-6, pastries $3-5; ⊙7am-5pm Mon-Fri, 8am-5pm Sat & Sun; Kings Cross) Its flagship Surry Hills bakery is a Sydney institution, so locals in Potts Point were ecstatic when this new branch opened in one of their leafy side streets. Sit inside the bunker-like space or claim one of the streetside tables to enjoy a pie, quiche, sandwich, pastry or cake, accompanied by a good cup of coffee. Enter off Crick Ave.

Fratelli Paradiso ITALIAN **$$**
(Map p86; www.fratelliparadiso.com; 12-16 Challis Ave, Potts Point; mains $22-31; ⊙7am-11pm Mon-Sat, to 6pm Sun; Kings Cross) This underlit trattoria has them queuing at the door (especially on weekends). Showcasing perfectly cooked, seasonally inspired Italian dishes and serving excellent espresso coffee, it has plenty of Italian-style va va voom. No bookings.

Apollo GREEK **$$**
(Map p86; ☎02-8354 0888; www.theapollo.com.au; 44 Macleay St, Potts Point; meze $5-22, mains $16-34; ⊙6-10.30pm Mon-Thu, noon-10.30pm Fri & Sat, noon-9.30pm Sun; Kings Cross) An exemplar of modern Greek cooking, this taverna has fashionably minimalist decor, a well-priced menu of share plates and a bustling vibe. Starters are particularly impressive, especially the pita bread hot from the oven, the fried saganaki cheese with honey and oregano, and the wild weed and cheese pie.

Cafe Sopra ITALIAN **$$**
(Map p86; www.fratellifresh.com.au; 81 Macleay St, Potts Point; salads $18-20, pastas $18-26, mains $26-28; ⊙noon-10pm; Kings Cross) Attached to the mighty impressive Fratelli Fresh provedore, Sopra serves no-fuss, perfectly prepared Italian food in a bustling atmosphere. The huge menu changes seasonally, but some favourites (eg the fabulous *rigatoni alla bolognese*) are constants. There are other branches in Danks St, **Waterloo** (☎9699 3174; 7 Danks St; mains $18-26; ⊙breakfast Sat, lunch daily; M20, 355); Hickson Rd, **Walsh Bay** (Map p80; 16 Hickson Rd; mains

$18-26; ⌚lunch & dinner; 🚉Wynyard); and Bridge St in the **city** (Map p80; 11 Bridge Street, Sydney).

Tilbury Hotel GASTROPUB **$$**

(Map p86; www.tilburyhotel.com.au; 12-18 Nicholson St, Woolloomooloo; restaurant mains $28-36, bar mains $12-18; ⌚restaurant noon-3pm & 6-10pm Tue-Sat, noon-5pm Sun, bar 11am-11pm Mon-Thu, 11am-midnight Fri & Sat, noon-10pm Sun ; 🚌311) Once the dank domain of burly sailors and visiting ne'er-do-wells, the Tilbury now sparkles as one of the city's best gastropubs. It attracts a well-heeled crowd that eats mod-Med dishes in the airy restaurant and outdoor courtyard (lunch only) or noshes on steaks, gourmet burgers and fish & chips in the front bar.

China Doll MODERN ASIAN **$$$**

(Map p86; ☎02-9380 6744; www.chinadoll.com.au; 4-6 Cowper Wharf Rdwy, Woolloomooloo; mains $26-45; ⌚noon-2.30pm & 6pm-late; 🚌311) This doll lives in a sophisticated house overlooking the Woolloomooloo marina and city skyline. She's a busy entertainer (bookings are essential) and likes to experiment in the kitchen – dishes are sampled from across Asia and are designed to be shared, although waiters will arrange half serves for solo diners.

Inner East

★**Reuben Hills** CAFE **$**

(Map p90; http://reubenhills.com.au; 61 Albion St, Surry Hills; eggs & sandwiches $11-16, mains $11-18; ⌚7am-4pm Mon-Sat, 8am-4pm Sun; 🚉Central) An industrial fitout and Latin American menu await here at Reuben Hills (aka hipster central). Fantastic single-origin coffee and fried chicken star, but the eggs, tacos and *baleadas* (sandwiches) are no slouches, either.

Spice I Am THAI **$**

(Map p82; www.spiceiam.com; 90 Wentworth Ave, Surry Hills; mains $8-26; ⌚11.30am-3.30pm & 5.45-10pm; 🚉Central) The signature dishes at this mega-popular BYO eatery on the city edge of Surry Hills are fragrant, flavoursome and cheap, meaning that queues are inevitable. It's been so successful that it's opened other, more upmarket and licensed branches in **Balmain** (237 Darling St, Balmain; ⌚5.45-10.30pm Mon-Wed, 11.30am-3.30pm & 5.45-10.30pm Thu-Sun; ⛴East Balmain) and **Darlinghurst** (Map p86; ☎02-9280 0928; www.spiceiam.com; 296-300 Victoria St, Darlinghurst; mains $28-38; ⌚11.30am-3.30pm & 5.45-10.30pm; 🍷; 🚉Kings Cross).

Messina ICE CREAM **$**

(Map p86; www.gelatomessina.com; 241 Victoria St, Darlinghurst; cup or cone $4-7; ⌚noon-11pm; 🚉Kings Cross) Sicilian-style gelato is given a fashionable twist at Messina's laboratory and shop in Victoria St, and the locals can't get enough of flavours including salted caramel with white chocolate. There's another branch in **Surry Hills** (Map p90; 389 Crown St, Surry Hills; ⌚noon-11pm; 🚉Central).

Carrington SPANISH **$$**

(Map p90; ☎02-9360 4714; http://the-carrington.com.au/; 563 Bourke St, Surry Hills; breakfast dishes $6-20, tapas $8-19, mains $18-28; ⌚noon-10pm Mon-Fri, 9am-10pm Sat & Sun; 🚉Central) Many consider this to be Sydney's best gastropub, and there's no denying that the classic Iberian menu offerings deserve a heartfelt *olé*! Weekend breakfast might be a tortilla or baked egg, lunch could be a sandwich or salad and dinner can be chosen from an array of tapas, pintxos and mains.

Lucio Pizzeria PIZZA **$$**

(Map p86; www.luciopizzeria.com; Shop 1, Republic 2 Courtyard, 248 Palmer St, Darlinghurst; pizzas $17-22, antipasti $21.50-26; ⌚6-10pm Wed-Mon; 🚉Museum) One of a cluster of eateries in an attractive courtyard off Palmer St, Lucio's has impeccable Italian credentials: the pizzas are cooked in a wood-fired oven and are authentically Neopolitan, Peroni is the tipple of choice and statement sunglasses are much in evidence on the outdoor tables. No booking, so get here early or be prepared to queue.

Porteño ARGENTINIAN **$$**

(Map p90; ☎02-8399 1440; www.porteno.com.au; 358 Cleveland St, Surry Hills; sharing plates $8-46; ⌚from 6pm Tue-Sat; 🅿; 🚉Central) The lads who made their mark with the wildly popular Bodega tapas bar in Surry Hills have stepped up their robust homage to the foods of South America, and they've taken loads of fans along for the ride. Bring a huge appetite and a posse; you can only book for five or more. Don't miss the magnificent eight-hour wood-fired suckling pig.

Red Lantern VIETNAMESE **$$**

(Map p90; ☎02-9698 4355; www.redlantern.com.au; 545 Crown St, Surry Hills; mains $28-40; ⌚6-10pm Mon, Sat & Sun, noon-3pm & 6-10pm Tue-Fri; 🍷; 🚉Central) 🌿 Run by popular television presenter Luke Nguyen, this atmospheric eatery serves modern takes on classic Vietnamese dishes, and is deservedly popular. There's another branch in **East Sydney** (Map p86; ☎02-9698 4355; www.redlantern.com.au/riley; 60 Riley St, Darlinghurst; ⏰noon-3pm & 6-10pm Tue-Fri, 6-10pm Sat & Sun; 🚇Museum or Kings Cross).

Bills CAFE $

(Map p86; www.bills.com.au; 433 Liverpool St, Darlinghurst; breakfast $5.50-18.50, lunch $7.50-26; ⏰7.30am-3pm Mon-Sat, 8.30am-3pm Sun) Bill Granger almost single-handedly kicked off the Sydney craze for stylish brunch. His two most famous dishes – ricotta hotcakes and sweetcorn fritters – have legions of fans. This is where it all started, but there are also branches in **Surry Hills** (Map p90; ☎02-9360 4762; 359 Crown St, Surrey Hills; ⏰7am-10pm; 🚇Central) and **Woollahra** (Map p85; ☎02-9328 7997; www.bills.com.au; 118 Queen St, Woollahra; mains $14-26; ⏰breakfast & lunch; 🚌389).

Billy Kwong CHINESE $$

(Map p90; ☎02-9332 3300; www.kyliekwong.org; 3/355 Crown St, Surry Hills; mains $24-49; ⏰6-10pm Mon-Thu, 6-11pm Fri & Sat, 6-9pm Sun; 🖉; 🚇Central) 🍃 BK's sets aside most of its tables for walk-in customers – perfect for travellers who don't have the luxury of booking weeks ahead. Chef Kylie Kwong cooks up modern Chinese dishes using the best organic, sustainable and fair-trade ingredients (try the duck with orange sauce) and serves them in a cramped, noisy but convivial environment.

Longrain THAI $$$

(Map p82; ☎02-9280 2888; www.longrain.com; 85 Commonwealth St, Surry Hills; mains $33-44; ⏰6pm-11pm Mon-Thu, noon-3 & 6-10pm Fri, 5.30-11pm Sat, 5.30-10pm Sun; 🚇Central) Devotees flock here to feast on Longrain's fragrant modern Thai dishes and sip on delicately hued and utterly delicious fruit-flavoured cocktails. Sit at shared tables or the bar.

Marque MODERN AUSTRALIAN $$$

(Map p90; ☎02-9332 2225; www.marquerestaurant.com.au; 355 Crown St, Surry Hills; 5/8 courses $95/160; ⏰from 6.30pm Mon-Thu, from noon & 6.30pm Fri, from 6pm Sat; 🚇Central) It's Mark Best's delicious, inventive, beautifully presented food that has won Marque various best restaurant gongs in recent years; it's certainly not the somewhat stuffy ambience or insipid decor. There's an excellent-value, three-course set lunch on Friday ($45).

Paddington & Woollahra

★**Chiswick Restaurant** MODERN AUSTRALIAN $$

(Map p85; ☎02-8388 8688; www.chiswickrestaurant.com.au; 65 Ocean St, Woollahra; mains $28-38; ⏰noon-2.30pm & 6-10pm Mon-Thu, noon-3pm & 5.30-10pm Fri & Sat, noon-3pm & 5.30-9.30pm Sun; 🚌389) There may be a celebrity at centre stage (TV regular Matt Moran), but the real star of this show is the pretty kitchen garden, which wraps around the dining room and dictates what's on the menu. There are a decent number of options for vegetarians, but meat from the Moran family farm and local seafood feature prominently.

Bistro Moncur FRENCH $$

(Map p85; ☎02-9327 9713; www.bistromoncur.com.au; 116 Queen St, Woollahra; mains $30-45; ⏰noon-3pm & 6-10.30pm Tue-Sun, 6-10.30pm Mon; 🚌389) Mini-moguls and lunching ladies while away long afternoons beneath Bistro Moncur's vaulted ceilings and monochromatic mural. The menu changes seasonally but signature dishes such as grilled sirloin Cafe de Paris delight diners year-round. Meals on the upstairs terrace (mains $17 to $26) are more casual, with classic pub dishes dominating the menu. There's live music in the bar and on the terrace on most Thursday and Sunday evenings. Does not take bookings.

Four in Hand MODERN AUSTRALIAN $$$

(☎02-9362 1999; www.fourinhand.com.au; 105 Sutherland St, Paddington; restaurant mains $39; ⏰restaurant noon-2.30pm & 6.30pm-late Tue-Sun, bar noon-10pm Sun & Mon, to 11pm Tue-Sat; 🚇Edgecliff) You can't go far in Paddington without tripping over a beautiful old pub with amazing food. This is the best of them, famous for its slow-cooked and nose-to-tail meat dishes. The bar meals (mains $18 to $28) are popular with Paddo locals.

Bondi & Bronte

Bondi Picnic CAFE $

(Map p94; 101 Hall St, Bondi; breakfast $9-15, sandwiches $10; ⏰6.30am-4pm; 📶; 🚌389, 380 or 333) The indoor/outdoor window seats give this cruisy corner cafe a suitably alfresco feel, and the laid-back locals who breakfast here give it a big-thumbs up. Simple fresh food, free wi-fi and excellent coffee are on offer.

Organic Republic BAKERY $
(Map p94; cnr Glenayr & Warners Aves, Bondi; pastries $3-4, sandwiches $7-10; ⌚5am-6pm; 🚌389, 380 or 333) 🍃 Its motto 'let the bread speak' says it all – fabulous sandwiches on slabs of home-baked organic bread (including spelt) are the signature at this bakery cafe in a peaceful pocket of Bondi, but you can also enjoy delicious cakes, pastries, pies and biscuits accompanied by a free-trade coffee made with organic milk.

La Macelleria SANDWICHES $
(Map p94; cnr Curlewis & Gould Sts, Bondi; filled panini $9.90; ⌚10am-8pm; 🚌389, 380 or 333) The panini here are nearly as big as the breakers at the nearby beach, making it a popular take-away option. Owner Robert Marchetti makes his own Italian-style charcuterie, and his salami, bresaola (air-cured beef) and porchetta (roast pork) are used to excellent effect.

Harry's Espresso Bar CAFE $
(Map p94; 136 Wairoa Ave, North Bondi; mains $7-14; ⌚7.30am-5pm; 🚌389, 380 or 333) Harry's game is coffee and he's winning down this end of the beach (there's even a coffee window for beach-bound caffeine addicts). The food is so so. Everything comes with a side order of graffiti art.

★**North Bondi Italian Food** ITALIAN $$
(Map p94; 118-120 Ramsgate Ave, North Bondi; pastas $18-38, mains $18-34; ⌚6pm-midnight Mon-Thu, noon-midnight Fri-Sun, open from noon Thu summer only; 🚌389, 380 or 333) As noisy as it is fashionable, this terrific trattoria in the North Bondi RSL building has a casual vibe, simple but *molto delizioso* food and a democratic no-booking policy. Come early to snaffle a table overlooking the beach. The owners also operate a Paddington offshoot, **Neild Avenue** (Map p86; ☎02-8353 4400; 10 Neild Ave, Paddington; mains $35-42; ⌚noon-4pm & 6-10pm Fri-Sun, 6-10pm Mon-Thu; 🚆Edgecliff).

Pompei's ITALIAN $$
(Map p94; ☎02-9365 1233; www.pompeis.com.au; 126-130 Roscoe St, North Bondi; pizzas $19-24, mains $24-34; ⌚4.30-11pm Tue-Thu, 11.30am-11pm Fri-Sun; 🚌389, 380 or 333) The pizzas here are great, but it's the handmade pasta dishes and exquisite gelato (made daily using organic milk and fresh fruit) that are the real stars in the firmament.

Three Blue Ducks CAFE $$
(www.threeblueducks.com; 141-143 Macpherson St, Bronte; breakfast $7-19, lunch $16-26, dinner shared plates $17; ⌚7am-4pm Tue, 7am-4pm & 6-10pm Wed-Fri, 7.30am-3pm & 6-10pm Sat, 7.30am-3pm Sun; 🚌378) 🍃 These ducks are a fair waddle from the water but that doesn't stop queues forming outside the graffiti-covered walls for its famous weekend breakfast and lunch. The food's great, but we think the coffee is a huge let-down.

★**Icebergs Dining Room** ITALIAN $$$
(Map p94; ☎02-9365 9000; www.idrb.com; 1 Notts Ave, Bondi; mains $36-95; ⌚noon-4.30pm & 6.30pm-midnight Tue-Sun; 🚌389, 380 or 333) Icebergs' million-dollar view sweeps across the Bondi Beach arc to the sea. The menu features modern takes on classic Italian dishes and a dedicated menu of aged beef, perfectly cooked. Come for lunch so as to make the most of the view, or arrive in time to enjoy a sunset cocktail at the bar before your meal.

Eastern Beaches

Dunbar House BREAKFAST, CAFE $
(☎02-9337 1226; www.dunbarhouse.com.au; 9 Marine Pde, Watsons Bay; breakfast dishes $10-16; ⌚8am-3.30pm; ⛴Watsons Bay) This meticulously restored 1830s mansion is an idyllic breakfast or brunch destination, particularly if you can score one of the harbour-view tables on the verandah. Bookings are essential on weekends.

Doyles on the Wharf FISH & CHIPS $
(www.doyles.com.au; Fisherman's Wharf, Watsons Bay; fish & chips $14-19, half-dozen oysters $13.50; ⌚10.30am-5pm Sun-Thu, 10.30am-7pm Fri & Sat; ⛴Watsons Bay) The million-dollar view comes free of charge when you buy lunch from this kiosk at the front of Watsons Bay Warf, and there are plenty of vantage points in the adjoining park.

Inner West

Adriano Zumbo PATISSERIE $
(http://adrianozumbo.com; 114 Terry St, Rozelle; cake $9, pastry $3.50-4.50, zumbaron $2.50; ⌚6.30am-4pm Mon-Fri, 7.30am-4pm Sat & Sun; 🚌433, 442) Sugar-spinning genius Adriano Zumbo gets up at 3am every morning to bake his delectable cakes, '*zumbarons*' (aka macarons), pies and tarts. Located close to the Rozelle Markets, the cafe's nine stools are hot property on weekends. There are other branches (take-away only) in **Balmain** (296 Darling St, Balmain; items $3-18; ⌚8am-6pm;

Balmain) and **Manly** (Map p96; cnr East Esplanade & Wentworth St, Manly; 7am-7pm Mon-Fri, 8am-5.30pm Sat & Sun).

Black Star Pastry BAKERY $
(www.blackstarpastry.com.au; 277 Australia St, Newtown; pies $8, sandwiches $10, cakes $7; 7am-5pm; Newtown) Follow the lead of locals and head to this tiny cafe off King St to pay homage to its gourmet pies, sandwiches and cakes. There are a few stools out front, but most customers order their treats to go.

Riverview Hotel & Dining GASTROPUB $$
(02-9810 1151; www.theriverviewhotel.com.au; 29 Birchgrove Rd, Balmain; roast of the day $25, pizzas $20, mains $28-35; East Balmain) Sydneysiders are rightfully proud of their pub culture, and 'The Riv' is one of the best pubs in town. British expats flock here on Sundays to enjoy a roast of the day at lunch, and locals are equally keen on the pizzas served in the downstairs bar at night. Others (including us) always look forward to the modern European dishes served in the elegant upstairs dining room.

Bloodwood INTERNATIONAL $$
(www.bloodwoodnewtown.com; 416 King St, Newtown; mains $25-30; 5pm-late Mon, Wed & Thu, noon-late Fri & Sat, noon-10pm Sun; Newtown) Relax over a few drinks and a progression of globally inspired shared plates at this popular bar-bistro. The decor is industrial-chic and the vibe is alternative – very Newtown.

Flying Fish COCKTAIL BAR
(Map p82; 9518 6677; www.flyingfish.com.au; Jones Bay Wharf; noon-5pm Sun, 6-10.30pm Mon-Sat; The Star) Fancy the idea of a Sri Lankan-style barramundi curry eaten in a glamorous loft-style restaurant overlooking the water? Or maybe a glass of champagne enjoyed with freshly sucked oysters or A-grade sashimi in an outdoor bar? Flying Fish offers both options, and even has a kids' menu ($25).

North Shore & Manly

Bower Restaurant CAFE, MODERN AUSTRALIAN $$
(02-9977 5451; www.thebowerrestauarnt.com.au; cnr Marine Pde & Bower La, Manly; breakfast $7.50-23.50, lunch $20-33; 8am-3pm; Manly) Follow the scenic promenade east from Manly's ocean beach towards Shelly Beach and you will soon arrive at this cute cafe within spray's breath of the sea. Eat in, or grab takeaway fish & chips ($16) or a panino ($8).

Hugos Manly ITALIAN $$
(Map p96; 02-8116 8555; www.hugos.com.au; Manly Wharf, East Esplanade, Manly; pizzas $20-28, mains $30-40; noon-late; Manly) Occupying an altogether more glamorous location than its Kings Cross parent, this restaurant on the wharf serves the same acclaimed pizzas but tops them with harbour views. Expert bar staff concoct cocktails, or you can opt for an ice-cold beer.

Manly Phoenix CHINESE $$
(Map p96; 02-9977 2988; www.phoenixrestaurants.com.au/manly-phoenix; Manly Wharf, East Esplanade, Manly; yum cha $28, mains $19-49; 11am-11pm Mon-Sat, 10am-11pm Sun; Manly) A ferry ride followed by yum cha at Phoenix Manly has developed into a weekend habit for many Sydneysiders. Book ahead if you want a table with a view.

Palm Beach

Boathouse CAFE $$
(www.theboathousepb.com.au; Governor Phillip Park, Palm Beach; breakfast $8-23, lunch $16-45; 7.30am-4pm; L90, 190) Sit on the large timber deck facing Pittwater or grab a table on the lawn out front – either option is alluring at Palm Beach's most popular cafe. The food is nearly as impressive as the views, and that's really saying something.

Barrenjoey House MODERN AUSTRALIAN $$
(02-9974 4001; www.barrenjoeyhouse.com; 1108 Barrenjoey Rd, Palm Beach; mains $27-39; 11.30am-late; L90, 190) Overlooking picturesque Pittwater from opposite the ferry wharf, this showcase of Palm Beach style is perfect for a leisurely lunch. The menu is casual but assured, with a selection that will please most palates, even junior ones. It also has B&B rooms upstairs (from $180).

Drinking & Nightlife

Pubs are a crucial part of the Sydney social scene, and you can down a glass or schooner (NSW term for a large glass) of beer at elaborate 19th-century affairs, cavernous art-deco joints, modern recesses, and everything in between. Bars are generally more stylish and urbane, sometimes with a dress code.

There's a thriving live-music scene in pubs, pop-up venues and music halls, but good dance clubs are strangely thin on the ground.

(Continued on page 123)

KIMBERLEY COOLE / GETTY IMAGES © ARCHITECT: JORN UTZON

This Is Sydney

The shimmering harbour may be the city's most famous asset, but Sydney's glorious beaches and sybaritic nightlife are equally alluring. This is a destination with a perfect balance of outdoor and indoor, natural and contrived – one that miraculously manages to be even more than the sum of its magnificent parts.

Contents

Above Sydney Opera House (p74)

1

2

1. Sydney Harbour Bridge (p71) **2.** Luna Park (p95)
3. Sydney Harbour ferry

Sydney Harbour

It's called the Harbour City for good reason. Few places on earth are as defined by their geographical form as Sydney, and even fewer incorporate such a spectacular water feature.

Visitors have been writing odes to the harbour's beauty ever since the First Fleet landed here on 26 January 1788. Few have done it justice, though. After all, how can any writing match the exultation of a ferry trip across shimmering blue waters or the satisfaction of an afternoon spent lazing in a sheltered sandy cove?

Everything here revolves around the water – suburbs, recreation, traffic, even the collective consciousness.

At the heart of the city is Circular Quay, from where the city's famous flotilla of green-and-yellow ferries do five-minute dashes across to Milsons Point and Kirribilli, speedy sails to the Middle Harbour and majestic processions past the Opera House, Fort Denison and the Heads to the popular day-tripper destination of Manly.

To the east of Circular Quay, a genteel ribbon of suburbs unfurls, characterised by mansions, money and conservative mindsets. Harking west are former working-class neighbourhoods such as Balmain and Birchgrove that have been reinvented as arty residential enclaves.

Across the iconic Sydney Harbour Bridge is the somewhat stolid North Shore, residential location of choice for the city's conservative middle classes, whose leafy villas stretch from Neutral Bay to Manly. Traffic snarls are the norm here, as is the aspiration to own a yacht for weekend jaunts on the harbour.

An altogether different Sydney is found to the south, where a ring of trendy inner-city neighbourhoods surround the central business district and give the harbour a buzzing urban edge.

Sydney Harbour

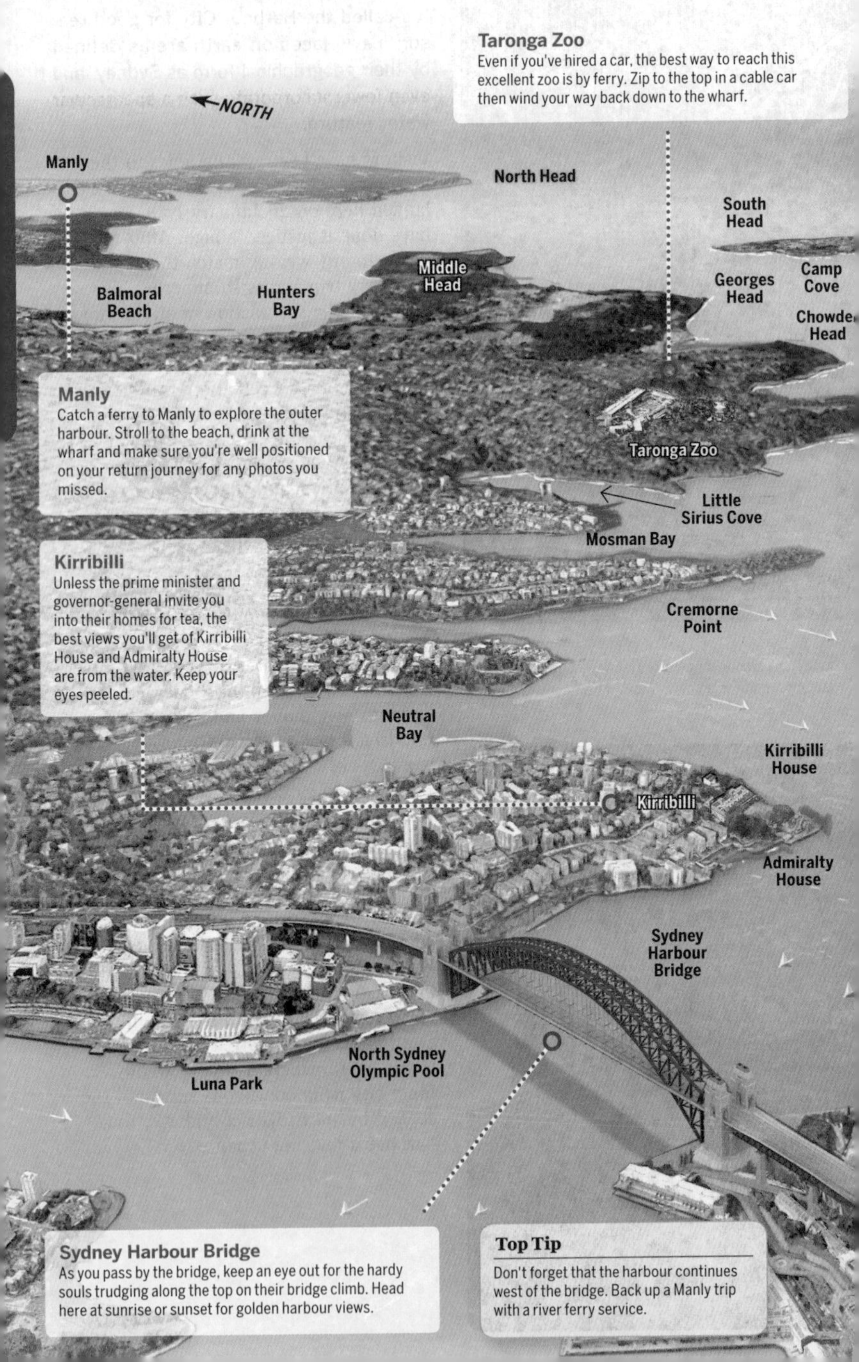

Taronga Zoo

Even if you've hired a car, the best way to reach this excellent zoo is by ferry. Zip to the top in a cable car then wind your way back down to the wharf.

Manly

Catch a ferry to Manly to explore the outer harbour. Stroll to the beach, drink at the wharf and make sure you're well positioned on your return journey for any photos you missed.

Kirribilli

Unless the prime minister and governor-general invite you into their homes for tea, the best views you'll get of Kirribilli House and Admiralty House are from the water. Keep your eyes peeled.

Sydney Harbour Bridge

As you pass by the bridge, keep an eye out for the hardy souls trudging along the top on their bridge climb. Head here at sunrise or sunset for golden harbour views.

Top Tip

Don't forget that the harbour continues west of the bridge. Back up a Manly trip with a river ferry service.

Watsons Bay
Imagine Watsons Bay as the isolated fishing village it once was as you pull into its sheltered wharf. Stroll around South Head for views up the harbour and over ocean-battered cliffs.

Fort Denison
Known as Pinchgut, this fortified speck was once a place of fearsome punishment. The bodies of executed convicts were left to hang here as a grisly warning to all; the local Aborigines were horrified.

PETE DRAGICEVICH ©

Ferries
Circular Quay is the hub for state-run Sydney Ferries; nine separate routes leave from here, journeying to 38 different wharves.

Sydney Opera House
You can clamber all over it and walk around it, but nothing beats the perspective you get as your ferry glides past the Opera House's dazzling sails. Have your camera at the ready.

Circular Quay
Circular Quay has been at the centre of Sydney life since the First Fleet dropped anchor here in 1788. Book your ferry ticket, check the indicator boards for the correct pier and get onboard.

Beaches

In Sydney, nothing beats a day at the beach. Sun, sand and surf dominate the culture for six months of every year, and locals wouldn't have it any other way.

The city's magnificent string of ocean beaches stretches north from the Royal National Park to Palm Beach, luring surfers, scenesters, swimmers and sunbathers onto their golden sands and into the powerful waves of the South Pacific Ocean.

There's none of that horrible European habit of privatising the beach here. Lay down a towel and you've claimed a personal patch of paradise for as long as you want it. Some locals enjoy a quick dip before or after work, while the lucky ones stay on the sand for the whole day – everyone makes the most of the time they have.

Ocean Beaches

Serious surfers head to Cronulla in the south; Maroubra, Bronte, Tamarama and North Bondi in the east; and Curl Curl, Narrabeen, Queenscliff, Harbord (Freshwater) and Manly on the Northern Beaches. Of these, Bronte and Manly are also popular with swimmers, joining Coogee, Clovelly, Bondi, Bilgola, Whale and Palm as regular entries on 'Best Beaches' lists. Each of these beaches has a devoted crew of regulars – families flock to Clovelly, Bronte and Whale Beach, while bronzed singles strut their stuff at Coogee and Palm Beach. The best-known beaches – Bondi and Manly – host an incongruous mix of pasty-skinned foreigners, weather-wizened surf gurus, grommets (beginner surfers) and geriatric locals who have been perfecting their body-surfing techniques for more than

OLIVER STREWE / GETTY IMAGES ©

KOKKAI NG / GETTY IMAGES ©

1. Bondi Icebergs Swimming Club (p99) **2.** Surfers, Bondi (p92)

half a century. Always crowded, these two beaches showcase the most endearing and eclectic aspects of Sydney's character, and shouldn't be missed.

Ocean Pools

Those who find surf off-putting should take advantage of Sydney's famous ocean pools. There are 40 man-made ocean pools up and down the coast, the most popular of which are Wylie's Baths, Giles Baths and the Ross Jones Memorial Pool in Coogee; the Bondi Icebergs Swimming Club; and the pool at Fairy Bower Beach in Manly.

Harbour Beaches & Pools

Lady Bay at South Head and Shark Beach at Nielsen Park in Vaucluse are the best of the harbour beaches (note that Lady Bay is a nude beach). There are netted swimming enclosures or pools at Cremorne Point on the North Shore and Balmoral Beach on the Middle Harbour.

BEACHES BY NEIGHBOURHOOD

- **Sydney Harbour** Lots of hidden coves; the best are near the Heads.
- **Bondi to Coogee** High cliffs frame a string of surf beaches, and an excellent coffee is always a short walk away.
- **Northern Beaches** A steady succession of spectacular surf beaches stretching for nearly 30km.

New Year's Eve fireworks, Sydney Harbour (p

After Dark

In the early years of the colony, enjoying a beaker or two of rum was the only form of entertainment available to Sydneysiders. Today, the situation couldn't be more different.

The festival calendar is a good case in point. The year kicks off with a frenzy of fireworks over Circular Quay and doesn't calm down for months. No sooner has the Sydney Festival, with its associated openings and events, finished than the biggest party of all kicks off: the famous Sydney Gay & Lesbian Mardi Gras. Winter brings fashion, literature, film and art to the fore, with opening nights, cocktail parties and literary soirées dominating everyone's datebooks. And then there's a slight hiatus until summer works its magic and everyone takes to the city's streets to make the most of daylight savings' long days and blissfully balmy nights.

Whatever your inclination, Sydney will indulge it. You can attend the theatre or the opera, drink in a beer garden or rooftop bar, take in a jazz performance or a drag show, watch films under the stars or club late into the night.

Put simply, this is a town that well and truly lives up to its hype when it comes to partying. So make your plans, dress sexy and get ready to paint the town red. You'll be in excellent company when you do.

(Continued from page 114)

The Rocks & Circular Quay

Opera Bar BAR, LIVE MUSIC

(Map p80; www.operabar.com.au; lower concourse, Sydney Opera House, Circular Quay; ⏲11.30am-midnight Sun-Thu, to 1am Fri & Sat; 🚌Circular Quay, ⛴Circular Quay, 🚆Circular Quay) Putting a totally different – and mighty sophisticated – spin on the concept of a beer garden, Sydney's most spectacularly sited bar is the perfect place to be on balmy evenings. There's live music from 8.30pm weekdays and 2pm on weekends.

Harts Pub PUB

(Map p80; www.hartspub.com; cnr Essex and Gloucester Sts, The Rocks; ⏲noon-midnight Mon-Wed, to 1am Thu-Sat, to 11pm Sun; 🚌Circular Quay, ⛴Circular Quay) Pouring a range of craft beers (small batch beer brewed using traditional methods), Harts is frequented by locals drawn by the beer, the rugby tipping competition and some of Sydney's best pub food.

Hero of Waterloo PUB, LIVE MUSIC

(Map p80; www.heroofwaterloo.com.au; 81 Lower Fort St, The Rocks; ⏲9.30am-11.30pm Mon-Sat, noon-10pm Sun; 🚌Circular Quay, ⛴Circular Quay, 🚆Circular Quay) Enter this rough-hewn 1843 sandstone pub to meet some locals, chat-up the Irish bar staff and grab an earful of the folk, old-time jazz and Celtic music performed live on Friday, Saturday and Sunday.

Fortune of War PUB, LIVE MUSIC

(Map p80; www.fortuneofwar.com.au; 137 George St, The Rocks; ⏲9am-late Mon-Fri, 11am-late Sat, 11am-midnight Sun; 🚌Circular Quay, ⛴Circular Quay, 🚆Circular Quay) This 1828 drinking den retains much of its original charm. There is live music here on Friday and Saturday nights from 8pm and on weekend afternoons from 2pm.

Australian Hotel PUB

(Map p80; www.australianheritagehotel.com; 100 Cumberland St, The Rocks; 🚌Circular Quay, ⛴Circular Quay, 🚆Circular Quay) Boasting a bonza selection of fair dinkum ocker beer and wine, the Australian keeps to the antipodean theme with its pizzas, which feature kangaroo, emu, saltwater crocodile and other unorthodox toppings ($17 to $26).

Blu Bar on 36 COCKTAIL BAR

(Map p80; www.shangri-la.com; Level 36, 176 Cumberland St, The Rocks; ⏲5pm-midnight Mon-Thu, to 1am Fri & Sat, 5-11pm Sun; 🚌Circular Quay, ⛴Circular Quay, 🚆Circular Quay) The drinks may be pricey, but it's well worth heading up to the top of the Shangri-La Hotel for the views, which seem to stretch all the way to New Zealand. The dress code is officially 'smart casual', but err on the side of smart if you can't handle rejection.

City Centre

Stitch BAR

(Map p80; www.stitchbar.com; 61 York St; ⏲4pm-midnight Mon-Wed, noon-2am Thu-Sat; 🚆Wynyard) The finest exemplar of Sydney's penchant for ersatz speakeasys, Stitch is accessed via swinging doors at the rear of what looks like a tailor's workshop. Hidden beneath is a surprisingly large but perpetually crowded space decorated with sewing patterns and wooden Singer sewing-machine cases.

Baxter Inn BAR

(Map p80; www.thebaxterinn.com; 152-156 Clarence St; ⏲4pm-1am Mon-Sat; 🚆Town Hall) Yes, it really is down that dark lane and through that unmarked door (it's easier to find if there's a queue; otherwise look for the bouncer lurking nearby). Whisky's the poison at this self-proclaimed and highly fashionable swillhouse.

Grasshopper BAR

(Map p80; www.thegrasshopper.com.au; 1 Temperance Lane; ⏲4pm-late Mon-Thu & Sat, noon-late Fri; 🚆St James) The first of many grungy laneway bars to open in the inner city couldn't have chosen a more darkly ironic location than Temperance Lane. The heart of the operation is the cool downstairs bar; hop upstairs for food.

Grandma's COCKTAIL BAR

(Map p80; www.grandmasbarsydney.com; basement, 275 Clarence St; ⏲3pm-late Mon-Fri, 5pm-late Sat; 🚆Town Hall) A stag's head greets you on the stairs and ushers you into a tiny subterranean world of parrot wallpaper and tiki cocktails. Billing itself as a 'retrosexual haven of cosmopolitan kitsch and faded granny glamour', Grandma's hits the mark.

O Bar COCKTAIL BAR

(Map p80; www.summitrestaurant.com.au; Level 47, Australia Sq, 264 George St; ⏲5pm-late Sat-Tue, noon-late Wed-Fri; 🚆Wynyard) Shoot up to this murderously cool revolving *Goldfinger*-esque bar, offering killer cocktails, comfortable chairs and views to die for.

Bambini Wine Room WINE BAR
(Map p80; www.bambinitrust.com.au; 185 Elizabeth St; 3-10pm Mon-Fri, 5.30-11pm Sat; St James) Don't worry, this bar doesn't sell wine to *bambini* – it's a very grown-up, European affair. The tiny dark-wood-panelled room is the sort of place where you'd expect to see Oscar Wilde holding court in the corner.

Palmer & Co BAR
(Map p80; https://merivale.com.au/palmerandco; Abercrombie Lane; 5pm-late Sat-Wed, 4pm-late Thu, noon-late Fri; Wynyard) Another self-consiously hip member of Sydney's speak-easy brigade, this 'legitimate importer of bracing tonics and fortifying liquid' is part of Justin Hemmes' trend-setting hospitality empire and has the cashed-up and fashionable clientele that this inevitably entails.

Ash Street Cellar WINE BAR, CAFE
(www.merivale.com/#/ivy/ashstreetcellar; 1 Ash St; 8.30am-11pm Mon-Fri) Part of the frighteningly fashionable Ivy complex, this European-flavoured wine bar in a pedestrianised laneway off George St largely caters to suits, but makes everyone feel welcome. There's excellent coffee during the day, and even better tapas ($8 to $32) and wine at night.

Chinatown & Darling Harbour

Good God Small Club CLUB, LIVE MUSIC
(Map p82; www.goodgodgoodgod.com; 55 Liverpool St, Chinatown; front bar free, club free-$20; 5pm-1am Wed, 5pm-2am Thu, 5pm-5am Fri, 6pm-5am Sat; Town Hall) In a defunct underground taverna near Chinatown, Good God's rear dancetaria hosts everything from live indie bands to Jamaican reggae, '50s soul, rockabilly and tropical house music. Its success lies in the focus on great music rather than glamorous surrounds.

Slip Inn & Chinese Laundry BAR, CLUB
(Map p80; www.merivale.com; 111 Sussex St, Central Sydney; club $15-25; 10am-midnight Mon-Thu, to 2am Fri, 5pm-2am Sat; Wynyard) Slip in to this warren of moody rooms on the edge of Darling Harbour and bump hips with the kids. There are bars, pool tables, a beer garden, dance floors and a menu including pizza and tapas. On Friday night the bass cranks up at the attached Chinese Laundry nightclub on the corner of King and Sussex Sts; on Saturdays there's a roster of international and local electro, house and techno DJs.

Home CLUB, LIVE MUSIC
(Map p82; www.homesydney.com; 1 Wheat Rd, Cockle Bay Wharf; admission free-$55; club Fri & Sat; Town Hall) Welcome to the pleasuredome: a three-level, 2100-capacity timber and glass 'prow' that's home to a dance floor, countless bars, outdoor balconies, and sonics that make other clubs sound like transistor radios. Catch top-name international DJs, plus live bands amping it up at Tokio Hotel downstairs from Tuesday to Saturday.

Kings Cross, Potts Point & Woolloomooloo

★**Kings Cross Hotel** PUB, LIVE MUSIC
(Map p86; www.kingscrosshotel.com.au; 244-248 William St, Kings Cross; noon-3am Sun-Thu, to 6am Fri & Sat; Kings Cross) With five floors above ground and one below, this huge pub is a hive of boozy entertainment that positively swarms on weekends. Best of all is FBi Social, an alternative radio station–led takeover of the 2nd floor bringing with it an edgy roster of live music. The roof bar has DJs on weekends and awesome city views.

Old Fitzroy Hotel PUB
(Map p86; www.oldfitzroy.com.au; 129 Dowling St, Woolloomooloo; 11am-midnight Mon-Fri, noon-midnight Sat, 3-10pm Sun; Kings Cross) Islington meets Melbourne in the back streets of Woolloomooloo: this totally unpretentious theatre pub is also a decent old-fashioned boozer in its own right. There are airy street-side tables, and an upstairs area with a pool table and scruffy lounges.

Inner East

★**Shady Pines Saloon** BAR
(Map p86; www.shadypinessaloon.com; shop 4, 256 Crown St, East Sydney; 4pm-midnight; Museum) With no sign or street number on the door and an entry from a shady back lane (look for the white door before Bikram Yoga on Foley St), this subterranean honky-tonk bar caters to the urban boho. Sip whisky-and-rye with the good ole hipster boys amid Western memorabilia and taxidermy.

Imperial Hotel PUB
(Map p85; www.imperialhotelpaddington.com.au; 252 Oxford St, Paddington; 10am-midnight Mon-Sat, to 10pm Sun; 380) Paddington is one of Sydney's golden suburbs, blessed with a great location, leafy streets, pretty houses

and wonderful pubs. This is the best of the neighbourhood watering holes, offering a stylish interior, solicitous service, an extensive list of regional wines, live acoustic music on Sunday afternoons and simply sensational pub grub (mains $17 to $29).

Shakespeare Hotel PUB
(Map p90; 200 Devonshire St, Surry Hills; Central) A classic Sydney pub (1879) with art-nouveau tiled walls, a skuzzy carpet, the horses on the TV and $12.50 bar meals. Not a hint of glitz or interior design. Perfect!

Wine Library WINE BAR
(Map p85; www.wine-library.com.au; 18 Oxford St, Woollahra; 11.30am-11.30pm Mon-Sat, to 10pm Sun; 380) An impressive range of wines by the glass, smart casual ambiance and Mediterranean-inclined bar menu make the Library a popular pitstop.

Eau-de-Vie COCKTAIL BAR
(Map p86; www.eaudevie.com.au; 229 Darlinghurst Rd, Darlinghurst; 6pm-1am; Kings Cross) Take the door marked 'restrooms' at the back of the Kirketon Hotel's Art Lounge (itself a ritzy bar) and enter this sophisticated black-walled speakeasy, where a team of dedicated shirt-and-tie-wearing mixologists concoct the sort of beverages that win best-cocktail gongs.

Green Park Hotel PUB
(Map p86; www.greenparkhotel.com.au; 360 Victoria St, Darlinghurst; 10am-2am Mon-Sat, noon-midnight Sun; Kings Cross) The ever-rockin' Green Park has pool tables, rolled-arm leather couches, a beer garden and a huge tiled central bar teeming with travellers, gay guys and pierced locals.

Victoria Room COCKTAIL BAR
(Map p86; 02-9357 4488; www.thevictoriaroom.com; Level 1, 235 Victoria St, Darlinghurst; 6pm-midnight Tue-Thu, to 1am Fri & Sat, high tea noon-5pm Sat & Sun; Kings Cross) Claim one of the chesterfields and relax over an expertly prepared cocktail or two at this sultry, Raj-style drinking den or book ahead to enjoy the weekend high tea ($45 to $65).

Beresford Hotel PUB, LIVE MUSIC
(Map p90; www.theberesford.com.au; 354 Bourke St, Surry Hills; noon-1am; Central) The once-grungy Beresford (circa 1870) now lures the bold, buffed and beautiful. The crowd will make you feel either inadequate or right at home, depending on how the mirror is treating you. There's a vast beer selection and an upstairs live music/club space.

Oxford Art Factory BAR, LIVE MUSIC
(Map p86; www.oxfordartfactory.com; 38-46 Oxford St, Darlinghurst; cover charge & opening hours vary; Museum) Indie kids party against an arty backdrop at this two-room multipurpose venue modelled on Warhol's NYC creative base. There's a gallery, bar and performance space that often hosts international acts and DJs. Check the website for what's on.

Newtown

Courthouse Hotel PUB
(202 Australia St; 10am-midnight Mon-Sat, to 10pm Sun; Newtown) What a brilliant pub! A block back from the King St fray, the 150-year-old Courthouse is the kind of place where everyone from pool-playing goth lesbians to magistrates can have a beer and feel right at home. A beer garden, beer specials, decent house red and good pub grub, too.

Jester Seeds COCKTAIL BAR
(www.jesterseeds.com; 127 King St; 4pm-midnight Tue-Sat, to 10pm Sun; Newtown) Jester Seeds is very Newtown. By that we mean a bit gloomy, a little grungy and very hip, with the requisite thrift-shop furniture, graffiti, obtuse name, astroturf 'garden' and classic but credible soundtrack.

Bank Hotel PUB, DJ
(02-8568 1900; www.bankhotel.com.au; 324 King St, Newtown; 10am-late; Newtown) There's been bags of cash splashed about the Bank, but it still attracts a kooky mix of lesbians (especially for Lady L on Wednesdays), students, sports fans, gay guys and just about everyone else. There's a rooftop terrace, cocktail bar, Thai restaurant and DJs.

Corridor COCKTAIL BAR
(www.corridorbar.com.au; 153a King St; 3pm-midnight Tue-Fri, 1pm-midnight Sat, 1-10pm Sun, happy hour 5-7pm Tue-Fri; Newtown) The name exaggerates this bar's skinniness, but not by much. Downstairs the bartenders serve old-fashioned cocktails and a good range of wine, while upstairs there's interesting art (for sale) and a tiny deck.

Bondi & Coogee

Icebergs Bar BAR
(Map p94; www.idrb.com; 1 Notts Ave, Bondi; noon-midnight Tue-Sat, to 10pm Sun; 380, 389, 333) Most folks come here to eat in the attached restaurant, but the bar is a brilliant

place for a drink. The hanging chairs, colourful sofas and ritzy cocktails are fab, but the view looking north across Bondi Beach is the absolute killer.

North Bondi RSL BAR
(Map p94; www.northbondirsl.com.au; 120 Ramsgate Ave, North Bondi; ⌚noon-midnight Mon-Thu, 10am-midnight Fri-Sun; 🚌380, 389, 333) This Returned & Services League bar ain't fancy, but with views no one can afford and drinks that everyone can, who cares? Bring ID, as non-members need to prove that they live at least 5km away. There are live bands most Saturdays, trivia on Tuesdays and cheap steaks on Wednesdays.

Beach Road Hotel PUB, DJ
(Map p94; www.beachroadbondi.com.au; 71 Beach Rd, Bondi; ⌚10am-1am Mon-Sat, to 10pm Sun; 🚌389, 380, 333) Weekends at this big boxy pub are a boisterous multilevel alcoholiday, with Bondi types (bronzed, buff and brooding) and woozy out-of-towners playing pool, drinking beer and digging live bands and DJs.

Coogee Bay Hotel PUB, CLUB
(www.coogeebayhotel.com.au; cnr Coogee Bay Rd & Arden St, Coogee; ⌚9am-3am Mon-Thu, to 5am Fri & Sat, to midnight Sun; 🚌372-374) This rambling, rowdy complex opposite the beach packs in the backpackers for live music, open-mic nights, comedy and big-screen sports.

Manly

Manly Wharf Hotel PUB
(Map p96; www.manlywharfhotel.com.au; Manly Wharf; ⌚11.30am-midnight Mon-Sat, 11am-10pm Sun; ⛴Manly) Tuck away a few schooners after a hard day in the surf, then pour yourself onto the ferry. Sports games draw a crowd and DJs liven up Sunday afternoons. Great pub food, too, with specials throughout the week.

Barefoot Coffee Traders CAFE
(Map p96; cnr East Esplanade & Wentworth St, Manly; ⌚6.30am-5.30pm Mon-Fri, 7.30am-5.30pm Sat & Sun; ⛴Manly) The suburb's best coffee (fair trade, organic beans from Toby's Estate) is served at the original location (p126) near the corner of Whistler St and Sydney Rd, and also at this new outlet conveniently (or should that be dangerously?) close to Adriano Zumbo's patisserie.

☆ Entertainment

Sydney has an eclectic and innovative arts, entertainment and music scene. Outdoor cinemas and sports stadiums cater to families, the city's theatre scene is healthy and dynamic, and live music is everywhere.

Pick up the 'Metro' section in Friday's *Sydney Morning Herald* for comprehensive entertainment details. Tickets for most shows can be purchased directly from venues or through the **Moshtix** (☎1300 438 849; www.moshtix.com.au), **Ticketmaster** (Map p80; ☎136 100; www.ticketmaster.com.au) or **Ticketek** (Map p80; ☎132 849; www.ticketek.com.au) ticketing agencies.

Cinemas

First-run cinemas abound and most have a cheap night when tickets are discounted by around a third. If you're in town over summer, try to attend one of the open-air cinemas – they're great fun.

OpenAir Cinema CINEMA
(☎1300 366 649; www.stgeorgeopenair.com.au; Mrs Macquaries Rd, Royal Botanic Gardens; tickets $35; ⌚Jan & Feb; 🚌Circular Quay, ⛴Circular Quay, 🚆Circular Quay) Right on the harbour, the outdoor three-storey screen here comes with surround sound, sunsets, skyline and swanky food and wine. Most tickets are purchased in advance, but a limited number of tickets go on sale at the door each night at 6.30pm – check the website for details.

Bondi Openair Cinema CINEMA
(Map p94; http://openaircinemas.com.au/bondi; Dolphin Lawn, next to Bondi Pavilion; tickets $17-40; ⌚Jan-Mar; 🚌380, 389, 333) Enjoy open-air screenings at the ocean's edge, with live bands providing prescreening entertainment. Bookings advisable.

Dendy Opera Quays CINEMA
(Map p80; ☎02-9247 3800; www.dendy.com.au; 2 Circular Quay East; 2-/3D adult $18/19; ⌚sessions 10am-9pm; 🚌Circular Quay, ⛴Circular Quay, 🚆Circular Quay) When the harbour glare and squawking seagulls get too much, follow the scent of popcorn into the dark folds of this plush cinema. Screening first-run, independent world films, it's augmented by friendly attendants, a cafe and a bar. There's another branch in King St, Newtown.

Moonlight Cinema CINEMA
(Map p85; ☎1300 551 908; www.moonlight.com.au; Belvedere Amphitheatre, cnr Loch & Broome Aves; adult $18; ⌚Dec-Mar; 🚆Bondi Junction)

Take a picnic and join the bats under the stars in magnificent Centennial Park; enter via Woollahra Gate on Oxford St. A mix of new-release blockbusters, art house and classics is programmed.

Palace Verona CINEMA
(Map p86; ✆ 02-9360 6099; www.palacecinemas.com.au; 17 Oxford St, Paddington; adult $11-18.50; ⊙ sessions 10am-9.30pm; ☐ 380) This urbane cinema has a wine and espresso bar where you can debate the artistic merits of the non-blockbuster flick you've just seen.

Live Music

Sydney Opera House PERFORMING ARTS
(Map p80; ✆ 02-9250 7777; www.sydneyopera-house.com; Bennelong Point, Circular Quay; ⊙ box office 9am-8.30pm Mon-Sat; ☐ Circular Quay, ☐ Circular Quay, ☐ Circular Quay) Yes, it's more than a landmark. As well as theatre and dance, there are performances by Opera Australia, the Australian Ballet, the Sydney Symphony and Bangarra Dance Theatre.

City Recital Hall CLASSICAL MUSIC
(Map p80; ✆ 02-8256 2222; www.cityrecitalhall.com; 2 Angel Pl, City Centre; ⊙ box office 9am-5pm Mon-Fri; ☐ Martin Pl) Based on the classic configuration of the 19th-century European concert hall, this custom-built 1200-seat venue boasts near-perfect acoustics. Catch top-flight companies such as Musica Viva, the Australian Brandenburg Orchestra and the Australian Chamber Orchestra here.

Metro Theatre PERFORMING ARTS
(Map p82; ✆ 02-9550 3666; www.metrotheatre.com.au; 624 George St; ☐ Town Hall) Easily Sydney's best venue to catch local and international alternative acts in well-ventilated, easy-seeing comfort. Other offerings include comedy, cabaret and dance parties.

Venue 505 LIVE MUSIC
(Map p90; www.venue505.com; 280 Cleveland St, Surry Hills; ⊙ from 7.30pm Mon-Sat; ☐ Central) Focusing on jazz, roots, reggae, funk, gypsy and Latin music, this small, relaxed venue is artist-run and thoughtfully programmed. The space features comfortable couches and murals by a local artist.

Basement LIVE MUSIC
(Map p80; ✆ 02-9251 2797; www.thebasement.com.au; 7 Macquarie Pl, Circular Quay; ☐ Circular Quay, ☐ Circular Quay, ☐ Circular Quay) Once solely a jazz venue, the Basement now hosts international and local musicians working in many disciplines and genres. Dinner-and-

show tickets net you a table by the stage, guaranteeing a better view than the standing-only area by the bar.

Annandale Hotel LIVE MUSIC
(✆ 02-9550 1078; www.annandalehotel.com; 17 Parramatta Rd, Annandale; ⊙ box office 9.30am-5.30pm Tue-Fri; ☐ 436-440) Long at the forefront of Sydney's live music scene, the Annandale coughs up alt-rock, metal, punk and electronica.

Enmore Theatre PERFORMING ARTS
(✆ 02-9550 3666; www.enmoretheatre.com.au; 130 Enmore Rd, Newtown; ⊙ box office 9am-6pm Mon-Fri, 10am-2pm Sat; ☐ Newtown) Originally a vaudeville playhouse, the elegantly dishevelled, 2500-capacity Enmore now hosts touring musicians, plus theatre and comedy.

Spectator Sports

On any given Sydney weekend there'll be all manner of balls being hurled, kicked and batted around. Sydneysiders are passionate about the **National Rugby League** (NRL; www.nrl.com.au; tickets through Ticketek from $25). The season kicks off in March in suburban stadiums and the ANZ Stadium, with September finals.

Over the same period, hometown favourites the Sydney Swans and Greater Western Sydney (the Giants) play in the **Australian Football League** (AFL; www.afl.com.au; tickets $20-40). The Swans play at the Sydney Cricket Ground (SCG) and the Giants at the Sydney Showground Stadium in Sydney's Olympic Park.

The **cricket** (http://cricket.com.au) season runs from October to March, the SCG hosting interstate Sheffield Shield and sell-out international Test, Twenty20 and One Day International matches.

Theatre

Head to the **Sydney Theatre** (Map p80; ✆ 02-9250 1999; www.sydneytheatre.org; 22 Hickson Rd; ☐ Wynyard), **Wharf Theatre** (Map p80; ✆ 02-9250 1777; www.sydneytheatre.com.au; Pier 4/5, 15 Hickson Rd; ☐ Wynyard) ⚓ and **Company B** (Map p90; ✆ 02-9699 3444; www.belvoir.com.au; 25 Belvoir St) for theatre; and to the **Capitol Theatre** (Map p82; ✆ 02-9320 5000; www.capitoltheatre.com.au; 13 Campbell St; ☐ Central), **Theatre Royal** (Map p80; www.theatreroyal.net.au; 108 King St, MLC Centre) and **State Theatre** (Map p80; ✆ 136 100; www.statetheatre.com.au; 49 Market St; ☐ St James) for musicals and other stage events.

Shopping

Most shops are open from 9.30am to 6pm Monday to Wednesday, Friday and Saturday, and until 9pm Thursday. Sunday trading is common but expect slightly shorter hours.

Serious shoppers should consider downloading the suburb-by-suburb shopping guides produced by Urban Walkabout (www.urbanwalkabout.com/sydney); free printed versions of the maps are also available at tourist information offices and booths across the city. There are dedicated guides (with handy map) covering the CBD, The Rocks, Chinatown, Paddington, Woollahra, Surry Hills, Darlinghurst, Potts Point/Kings Cross, Bondi, Pyrmont/Ultimo, Redfern/Waterloo, Balmain/Rozelle, Newtown, Redfern/Waterloo, Glebe, Double Bay, Mosman, the Lower North Shore and Manly.

The top end of Oxford St, Glenmore Rd in Paddington and Queen St in Woollahra are Sydney's premier fashion enclaves, but there are also plenty of boutiques in the CBD and in Newtown.

Aboriginal & Pacific Art ART & CRAFT
(www.2danksstreet.com.au; 2 Danks St, Waterloo; ⏲11am-5pm Tue-Sat; 🚌M20, 355) One of a number of commercial galleries under the same roof; this one represents community-based Aboriginal and Pacific Islander art.

Akira Isogawa CLOTHING
(Map p85; www.akira.com.au; 12a Queen St, Woollahra; 🚌380) This Japanese-born, resident

SYDNEY'S WEEKEND MARKETS

Sydneysiders enjoy going to local markets nearly as much as going to the beach (and that's really saying something). Many inner-city suburbs host weekend markets in the grounds of local schools and churches, and these sell everything from organic food to original designer clothing. You'll inevitably encounter some tragic hippy paraphernalia, appalling art and overpriced tourist tat, but there are often exciting purchases to be made, too. The best of the markets:

➡ **Bondi Markets** (Map p94; ☎02-9315 8988; www.bondimarkets.com.au; Bondi Beach Public School, Campbell Pde; ⏲9am-1pm Sat, 10am-4pm Sun; 🚌380) The kids are at the beach on Sunday as their school fills up with Bondi characters rummaging through secondhand clothes and books, jewellery, aromatherapy oils, old records and more. There's a farmers market in the school grounds on Saturdays between 9am and 1pm.

➡ **Eveleigh Market** (www.eveleighmarket.com.au; 243 Wilson St, Darlington; ⏲farmers market 8am-1pm Sat, artisans' market 10am-3pm 1st Sun of month, closed 1st half of Jan; 🚆Redfern) Over 70 regular stallholders sell their home-grown produce at Sydney's best farmers market, which is held in a heritage-listed railway workshop in the Eveleigh Railyards. There's also an artisans' market on the first Sunday of every month. When here, you can also visit the CarriageWorks arts and cultural precinct (www.carriageworks.com.au).

➡ **Glebe Markets** (www.glebemarkets.com.au; Glebe Public School, cnr Glebe Point Rd & Derby Pl; ⏲10am-4pm Sat; 🚌Glebe) Sydney's dreadlocked, shoeless, inner-city contingent beats an aimless course to this crowded hippy-ish market.

➡ **Kirribilli Markets** (www.kirribillimarkets.com; Burton Street Tunnel & Bradfield Park Bowling Green, Kirribilli; ⏲general market 7am-3pm 4th Sat of the month Jan-Nov, 1st & 3rd Sat Dec; art, design & fashion market 9am-3pm 2nd Sun of the month; 🚆Milsons Point/Luna Park) This harbourside market sells a jumble of products, with a strong emphasis on vintage clothes and accessories of every kind. It also holds an art, design and fashion market on the second Sunday of the month.

➡ **Paddington Markets** (Map p85; www.paddingtonmarkets.com.au; Paddington Public School, 395 Oxford St, Paddington; ⏲10am-4pm Sat; 🚌380) Originating in the 1970s when it was beloved by the alternative set, this market is more mainstream these days, but is still worth checking out for its new and vintage clothing, creative crafts and jewellery.

➡ **Rozelle Markets** (☎02-9818 5373; www.rozellemarkets.com.au; cnr Darling & National Sts; ⏲9am-4pm Sat & Sun; 🚌432-4) One of Sydney's best bargain-hunter markets, with very few tourists. Sift through hippie jewellery, vintage clothes, books and knick-knacks, with live folk music, palm readings and exotic food stalls as a backdrop.

Aussie designer produces meticulously tailored ensembles for women featuring gorgeous fabrics. There's another store in the Strand Arcade.

Annandale Galleries ART
(www.annandalegalleries.com.au; 110 Trafalgar St, Annandale ; 11am-5pm Tue-Sat; 436, 438, 439, 440) Highly regarded commercial gallery that represents Aboriginal artists from the communities of Maningrida and Yirrkala in North East Arnhem Land.

Australian Wine Centre WINE
(Map p80; www.australianwinecentre.com; Goldfields House, 1 Alfred St, Circular Quay; Circular Quay) This multilingual basement store is packed with quality Australian wine, beer and spirits. Pick up some Hunter Valley semillon or organise a shipment back home.

Blue Spinach CLOTHING, ACCESSORIES
(Map p86; 02-9331 3904; www.bluespinach.com.au; 348 Liverpool St, Darlinghurst; Kings Cross) High-end recycled clothes for penny-pinching label lovers of all genders. If you can make it beyond the shocking blue facade (shocking doesn't really do it justice), you'll find luxury labels at (relatively) bargain prices.

Collette Dinnigan CLOTHING
(Map p85; www.collettedinnigan.com.au; 104 Queen St, Woollahra; 380) The queen of Aussie couture delivers fabulously feminine frocks with exquisite trimmings.

David Jones DEPARTMENT STORE
(Map p80; www.davidjones.com.au; 86-108 Castlereagh St, Central Sydney; St James) DJs is Sydney's premier department store. The Castlereagh St store has women's and children's clothing; Market St has menswear and a high-brow food court. There's another store at **Westfield Bondi Junction** (02-9947 8000; www.westfield.com.au; 500 Oxford St; 9.30am-6pm Fri-Wed, to 9pm Thu; Bondi Junction).

Dinosaur Designs JEWELLERY, HOMEWARES
(Map p85; www.dinosaurdesigns.com.au; 339 Oxford St, Paddington; 380) If the Flintstones opened a jewellery store, this is what it would look like: oversized, richly coloured, translucent resin bangles and baubles sit among technicoloured vases and bowls. There's another store in the Strand Arcade.

Easton Pearson CLOTHING
(Map p86; www.eastonpearson.com; 30 Glenmore Rd, Paddington; 380) Brisbane designers who popularised ethno-chic in Australia and are particularly beloved by women of a slightly fuller figure.

Leona Edmiston CLOTHING, ACCESSORIES
(Map p85; www.leonaedmiston.com; 88 William St, Paddington; 380) Leona Edmiston knows frocks – from little and black to whimsically floral or all-out sexy. Also at Westfield Bondi Junction, Westfield Sydney, Chifley Plaza and the Strand Arcade.

Queen Victoria Building SHOPPING CENTRE
(QVB; Map p80; www.qvb.com.au; 455 George St, Central Sydney; Town Hall) The magnificent QVB takes up a whole block and boasts nearly 200 shops on five levels. It's a high-Victorian masterpiece – without doubt Sydney's most beautiful shopping centre.

RM Williams CLOTHING, ACCESSORIES
(Map p80; www.rmwilliams.com.au; 389 George St, Central Sydney; Wynyard) Urban cowboys and country folk can't get enough of this hard-wearing Aussie outback gear. Check out the Driza-Bone oilskin jackets, Akubra hats, moleskin jeans and leather work boots. There are other branches in The Rocks, Westfield Sydney and Chifley Plaza on the corner of Phillip and Hunter Sts.

Sass & Bide CLOTHING, ACCESSORIES
(Map p86; www.sassandbide.com; 132 Oxford St, Paddington; 380) Brisbane's Heidi Middleton and Sarah-Jane Clarke are known for their sassy low-cut women's jeans, body-hugging jackets and mini dresses. There are other branches in the Strand Arcade, Westfield Sydney and Westfield Bondi Junction.

Strand Arcade SHOPPING CENTRE
(Map p80; www.strandarcade.com.au; 412 George St, Central Sydney; St James) Constructed in 1891, the Strand competes with the QVB for the title of the city's most beautiful shopping centre. It has a particularly strong range of Australian designer fashion, and is home to Strand Hatters, a Sydney institution.

Studio Workshopped CRAFT
(Map p86; www.workshopped.com.au; 417 Bourke St, Surry Hills; 10.30am-6pm Wed-Sat; 380) After checking out the exhibitions in the upstairs exhibition spaces of the Object: Australian Design Centre (www.object.com.au), pop into the ground-floor retail outlet to source a handmade souvenir of your Sydney sojourn. There's usually an artisan in residence (the space doubles as a studio) and

BUYING INDIGENOUS ART & ARTEFACTS

There are plenty of shops and galleries around the state selling indigenous-made artworks, artefacts and products, but it's sadly common to encounter Chinese-made fakes, works that breach the cultural copyright of indigenous artists, and galleries that exploit artist poverty by buying their art unreasonably cheaply – wherever possible, look for products that are being produced and/or marketed by indigenous-owned, not-for-profit operators.

If you're buying from a gallery, make sure that it's a member of the Indigenous Art Trade Association (www.arttrade.com.au) or the Australian Commercial Galleries Association (www.acga.com.au).

there's always an array of tempting jewellery and homewares on offer.

Utopia Art ART
(www.utopiaartsydney.com.au; 2 Danks St, Waterloo; 10am-5pm Tue-Sat; M20, 355) Another gallery in the complex at 2 Danks St, Utopia exhibits Aboriginal and non-Aboriginal artists in a contemporary context.

Westfield Sydney MALL
(Map p80; www.westfield.com.au/sydney; cnr Pitt St Mall & Market St, Central Sydney) This huge shopping mall incorporates Sydney Tower and has an excellent food court plus main-street retailers such as Zara and Gap.

Zimmermann CLOTHING
(Map p86; www.zimmermannwear.com; 2-16 Glenmore Rd, Paddington; 380) Chic and cheeky women's street clothes and swimwear from sisters Nicky and Simone Zimmermann. There are other stores in Westfield Sydney and Westfield Bondi Junction.

Information

EMERGENCY

In the event of an emergency, call 000 to contact the police, ambulance and fire authorities.

Lifeline (13 11 14; www.lifelinesydney.org; 24hr) Round-the-clock phone counselling services, including suicide prevention.

Police Stations For a searchable list of all police stations in NSW, go to www.police.nsw.gov.au and click on 'your police' tab.

Rape Crisis Centre (1800 424 017; www.nswrapecrisis.com.au; 24hr) Offers 24-hour counselling.

INTERNET ACCESS

The vast majority of hotels and hostels offer their guests internet access, and often this is provided at no charge. The City of Sydney Libraries at Kings Cross, Haymarket, Newtown, Surry Hills, Glebe, Town Hall and the Customs House on Circular Quay all offer free wi-fi – go to www.cityofsydney.nsw.gov.au/explore/libraries/about-the-network/computers-and-internet for more information.

MEDICAL SERVICES

Kings Cross Clinic (02-9358 3066; www.kingscrossclinic.com.au; 13 Springfield Ave, Kings Cross; 9am-1pm & 2-6pm Mon-Fri, 10am-1pm Sat; Kings Cross) General practitioners with a travel medicine focus, offering vaccinations, dive medicals and sexual health advice.

Royal Prince Alfred Hospital (RPA; 02-9515 6111; www.sswahs.nsw.gov.au/rpa; Missenden Rd, Camperdown; 24hr emergency dept; Macdonaldtown)

St Vincent's Hospital (02-8382 1111; wwwsvh.stvincents.com.au; 390 Victoria St, Darlinghurst; 24hr emergency dept; Kings Cross)

Sydney Hospital (02-9382 7111; www.seslhd.health.nsw.gov.au/SHSEH; 8 Macquarie St, Central Sydney; 24hr emergency dept)

MONEY

There are plenty of ATMs throughout Sydney; foreign-exchange offices are found in Kings Cross and around Chinatown, Circular Quay and Central Station.

TOURIST INFORMATION

City Host Information Kiosks (www.cityofsydney.nsw.gov.au) Circular Quay (Map p80; cnr Pitt & Alfred Sts; 9am-5pm; Circular Quay); Town Hall (Map p80; George St, Town Hall; 9am-5pm; Town Hall); Haymarket (Map p82; Dixon St; 11am-7pm; Town Hall) Friendly and helpful staff supply maps, brochures and information.

Kings Cross Tourist Information Kiosk (Map p86; cnr Darlinghurst Rd & Macleay St, Kings Cross; 9am-5pm Sun-Thu, 9am-11pm Fri & Sat; Kings Cross) Supplies maps, brochures, walking-tour maps and transport information.

Manly Visitor Information Centre (Map p96; 02-9977 1430; www.manlytourism.com.au; Manly Wharf; 9am-5pm Mon-Fri, 10am-4pm Sat & Sun; Manly) Extremely helpful volunteer staff supply brochures, maps and transport information.

Sydney Harbour National Park Information Centre (Map p80; ☎02-9253 0888; www.environment.nsw.gov.au; Cadman's Cottage, 110 George St; ⏰9.30am-4.30pm Mon-Fri, 10am-4.30pm Sat & Sun; 🚆Circular Quay) Has maps of walks in different parts of the park and organises tours of the harbour islands.

Sydney Visitor Centres (☎02-9240 8788; www.sydneyvisitorcentre.com) Darling Harbour (Map p82; ☎9240 8788; www.darlingharbour.com; ⏰9.30am-5.30pm; 🚆Town Hall); The Rocks (Map p80; ☎9240 8788; www.sydney-visitorcentre.com; cnr Argyle & Playfair Sts; ⏰9.30am-5.30pm; 🚆Circular Quay) Both branches have a wide range of brochures and staff can book accommodation, tours and attractions.

USEFUL WEBSITES

Art Almanac (www.art-almanac.com.au) Comprehensive public and private gallery listings.

City of Sydney (☎02-9265 9333; www.cityofsydney.nsw.gov.au) Fantastic website chock-full of information about the city.

RealSurf (www.realsurf.com) Local surf reports.

Time Out Sydney (www.timeoutsydney.com.au) Listings and articles from the monthly magazine.

Sydney Morning Herald (www.smh.com.au) Good for upcoming events, restaurant and bar reviews, and to take the pulse of the city.

TwoThousand (www.twothousand.com.au) Snapshot of Sydney's subculture.

ℹ Getting There & Away

AIR

Sydney Airport (SYD; www.sydneyairport.com.au) is Australia's busiest, so don't be surprised if there are delays. It's only 10km south of the city centre, making access relatively easy. The T1 (international) and T2 and T3 (domestic) terminals are a 4km bus ($5.50, 10 minutes) or train ($5, two minutes) ride apart (the airport is privately run so transferring terminals – a service that's free in most of the world – is seen as a profit opportunity). If you are transferring from a Qantas international flight to a Qantas domestic flight (or vice versa), free transfers are provided by the airline. Virgin Australia offers a similar service.

BUS

All private interstate and regional bus travellers arrive at the **Sydney Coach Terminal** (Map p90; ☎9281 9366; Eddy Ave, Central Station; ⏰6am-6pm Mon-Fri, 8am-6pm Sat & Sun) on the corner of Eddy Ave and Pitt St in front of Central Station.

TRAIN

CountryLink (☎13 22 32; www.countrylink.info) runs services connecting Sydney with regional and interstate destinations. The major train hub is **Central Station** (☎24hr transport information 13 15 00, bookings 13 22 32; www.countrylink.info; Eddy Ave; ⏰staffed ticket booths 6.15am-8.45pm, ticket machines 24hr).

ℹ Getting Around

Your transport options may be many in Sydney but your journey won't always be easy. Spend more than a day in town and you won't be able to miss stories about the dire state of the overpatronised, underfunded system. Ferries, trains and many buses are operated by the same government department, but each mode seems to operate in blissful ignorance of the others, with only one integrated ticket, the MyMulti pass, available.

On Sundays families can take advantage of the 'Family Funday' ticket, which gives all-day travel on all Sydney transport for $2.50 per person (minimum one adult and one child). Australian

ℹ MYZONE TICKETS & PASSES

There are three discount options for travelling on Sydney's public transport network: MyMulti day passes, MyMulti weekly passes and TravelTen Tickets. You can purchase these at newsagencies, newsstands and bus/ferry/train ticket offices. For information, see www.myzone.nsw.gov.au.

MyMulti Day Pass This pass (adult/child $22/11) gives unlimited transport on government-operated buses, ferries, MLR and trains within Sydney, the Blue Mountains, Hunter Valley, Central Coast, Newcastle and Illawarra.

MyMulti Passes Gives unlimited transport in the metropolitan area for one week (adult $44 to $52, child $22 to $26), or across Sydney, the Blue Mountains, Hunter Valley, Central Coast, Newcastle, South Coast, Southern Highlands and Port Stephens (adult/child $61/30.50).

MyBus, MyTrain and MyFerry TravelTen Tickets These offer 10 discounted rides but can only be used on one mode of transport.

seniors are eligible for a $2.50 all-day excursion ticket.

For information on government-operated buses, ferries and trains try the **Transport Infoline** (☎13 15 00; www.131500.com.au).

TO/FROM THE AIRPORT

One of the easiest ways to get to and from the airport is with a shuttle company – most hotels and hostels will be able to organise this for you.

Airport Link (☎13 15 00; www.airportlink.com.au; one-way adult/child Domestic Station-Central Sydney $15.90/11.40, International Station-Central Sydney $16.70/11.80; ⏲4.30am-12.40am) is a strange service: it's a normal commuter train line, but you pay through the nose to use the airport stations (punters going to Wolli Creek, the next stop *beyond* the airport, pay $3.60). The trip from Central Station takes a mere 10 minutes or so.

Bus 400 travels from Bondi Junction to Burwood, stopping at both the domestic and international terminals en route. A ticket costs $4.60.

Taxi fares from the airport are approximately $40 to the city centre ($45 between 10pm and 6am), $40 to Bondi ($45 between 10pm and 6am) and $75 to Manly ($90 between 10pm and 6am).

BOAT

Ferry Harbour ferries and RiverCats (to Parramatta) operated by **Sydney Ferries** (Map p80; www.sydneyferries.info) depart from Circular Quay. Most ferries operate between 6am and midnight; those servicing tourist attractions operate shorter hours.

A one-way inner-harbour ride on a regular ferry costs adult/concession $5.80/2.90. A one-way ride to Manly or Parramatta costs $7.20/$3.60.

A one-way trip to Manly with **Manly Fast Ferry** (☎02-9583 1199; www.manlyfastferry.com.au) costs adult/child $9/6 one way. Services depart from Circular Quay's Wharf 6 between 6.40am and 7.30pm weekdays, 10.10am and 6.40pm weekends.

Water taxis ply dedicated shuttle routes; rides to/from other harbour venues can be booked.

Aussie Water Taxis (Map p82; ☎02-9211 7730; www.aussiewatertaxis.com; Cockle Bay Wharf) Darling Harbour to Circular Quay single/return adult $15/25, child $10/15; Darling Harbour to Taronga Zoo single/return adult $25/40, child $15/25; 45-minute Harbour and Nightlights Tours adult/child $35/25.

Yellow Water Taxis (Map p80; ☎02-9299 0199; www.yellowwatertaxis.com.au) Circular Quay to Darling Harbour adult/child $15/10; set price per four people for other trips – see the website for details.

BUS

Sydney Buses (☎131 500; www.sydneybuses.info) has an extensive network; you can check route and timetable information online. Nightrider buses operate infrequently after regular services cease around midnight.

The main city bus stops are Circular Quay, Wynyard Park (York St), the Queen Victoria Building (QVB; York St) and Railway Sq. Many services are prepay-only during the week – buy tickets from newsagents or Bus TransitShops. On weekends you can usually purchase your ticket on the bus. There are three fare zones: $2.20/3.60/4.60. There's a Bus TransitShop booth at Circular Quay, and there are others at the Queen Victoria Building, Railway Sq and Wynyard Station.

Bus routes starting with an X indicate limited-stop express routes; those with an L have limited stops. A free CBD shuttle (bus 555) departs every 20 minutes between 9.30am and 3.30pm Monday to Wednesday and Friday, till 9pm on Thursday and between 9.30am and 6pm Saturday and Sunday. Its route travels between Circular Quay and Central Station, stopping at Martin Pl, St James and Museum railway stations, Chinatown, Town Hall, QVB and Wynyard railway station en route.

CAR & MOTORCYCLE

Cars are good for day trips out of town, but driving one in the city is like having an anchor around your neck. Traffic is heavy and parking is both elusive and very expensive (expect $30 per day).

Buying or Selling a Car

The **Sydney Travellers Car Market** (www.sydneytravellerscarmarket.com.au; Level 2, Kings Cross Car Park, Ward Ave, Kings Cross; ⏲9am-4.40pm; 🚇Kings Cross) is based in the Kings Cross Car Park off Ward Ave. This provides useful information about the paperwork needed to buy, sell and register vehicles. Sellers can leave their vehicles in the market overnight between Monday and Thursday at no cost; usual carpark charges apply from Friday to Sunday. Note that it is illegal to sleep in the vehicle while it is in the carpark. It is also illegal to sell vehicles on the street anywhere in central Sydney.

Hire

The Yellow Pages (www.yellowpages.com.au) lists car-hire companies, some specialising in renting clapped-out wrecks at rock-bottom prices – read the fine print! For campervan hire, head towards William St in Kings Cross, where companies such as **Jucy** (☎1800 150 850; www.jucy.com.au) are located.

Road Tolls

There's a $4 southbound toll on the Sydney Harbour Bridge and Tunnel; a $6 northbound toll on the Eastern Distributor; tolls of $2.30 to

$4.90 on the Cross City Tunnel; and a $3 toll on the Lane Cove Tunnel. Sydney's main motorways (M2, M5 South-West and M7) are also tolled ($0.62 to $7.30). For information about the system, go to www.sydneymotorways.com.

The tolling system is electronic, meaning that it's up to you to organise an electronic tag or visitors' pass through any of the following websites: www.roamcom.au, www.roamexpress.com.au or www.myetoll.com.au. Note that most car-hire companies now supply etags.

METRO LIGHT RAIL (MLR)

The **Metro Light Rail** (MLR; www.metrolightrail.com.au) operates tram services between Central Station and the Sydney Convention Centre in Darling Harbour via Chinatown (zone 1) and then beyond Darling Harbour to Lilyfield via Pyrmont, Star City Casino, the Fish Markets, Glebe and Rozelle (zone 2). Services between Central and Star City run every 10 to 15 minutes 24 hours per day; others operate from 6am to 11pm (midnight on Friday and Saturday).

TAXI

Taxis and cab ranks proliferate in Sydney. Flag fall is $3.50, then it's $2.14 per kilometre (plus 20% from 10pm to 6am). The waiting charge is $0.92 per minute. Passengers must pay bridge, tunnel and road tolls (even if you don't incur them 'outbound', the returning driver will incur them 'inbound').

Major taxi companies offering phone bookings ($2.40 fee):

Legion (☎13 14 51; www.legioncabs.com.au)

Premier Cabs (☎13 10 17; www.premiercabs.com.au)

Taxis Combined (☎13 33 00; www.taxiscombined.com.au)

TRAIN

Sydney's suburban rail network is operated by **CityRail** (☎131 500; www.cityrail.info). Lines radiate from the underground City Circle (seven city-centre stations plus Kings Cross) but don't service the northern, southern or eastern beaches, Balmain/Rozelle or Glebe. All suburban trains stop at Central Station, and usually one or more of the other City Circle stations, too.

Trains run from around 5am to midnight. After 9am on weekdays you can buy an off-peak return ticket, valid until midnight, for 30% less than the standard fare.

Twenty-four-hour ticket machines occupy most stations, but customer service officers are usually available if you need help with the fares. If you have to change trains, buy a ticket to your ultimate destination, but don't exit the transfer station en route or your ticket will be invalid.

There is a handy fare calculator on the CityRail website.

AROUND SYDNEY

Sydney's extensive urban sprawl is fringed by bush. To the south, Royal National Park – the second-oldest national park in the world – shelters lost-to-the-world beaches, rainforest pockets and precipitous cliffscapes. To the west, the wooded foothills of the Great Dividing Range climb to the magnificent Blue Mountains National Park. And to the northwest the Hawkesbury River wends its way through the Dharug, Marramarra and Brisbane Waters National Parks.

Royal National Park

The 15,080-hectare **Royal National Park** (☎02-9542 0648; www.environment.nsw.gov.au; cars $11, pedestrians & cyclists free; ⏲ gates to park areas locked at 8.30pm daily) was established in 1879, making it the oldest national park in the world after Yellowstone in the USA. Here you'll find pockets of subtropical rainforest, wind-blown coastal scrub, sandstone gullies dominated by gum trees, fresh- and saltwater wetlands, and isolated beaches. This is traditionally the home of the Dharawal people, and there are numerous Aboriginal sites and artefacts.

The national park begins at Port Hacking, 32km south of Sydney, and stretches 20km further south. Its main road detours to Bundeena, a small town on Port Hacking, the starting point for kayaking tours of the park and the spectacular two-day, 26km-long **Coast Track**. See the website for details of other bushwalks in the park.

Within the park there's sheltered saltwater swimming at Wattamolla, Jibbon, Little Marley and Bonnie Vale, and freshwater swimming holes at Karloo Pool (around 2km east of Heathcote Station), Deer Pool and Curracurrang. Surfers should head for Garie Beach, North Era, South Era and Burning Palms on the park's southern coastline. At the historic **Audley Boat Shed** (☎02-9545 4967; www.audleyboatshed.com; 6 Farnell Ave) you can hire rowboats, canoes and kayaks ($20/45 per hour/day), aqua bikes ($15 per 30 minutes) and bicycles ($16/34 per hour/day) and make your way up Kangaroo Creek or the Hacking River.

The **park office** (☎02-9542 0648; 159 Farnell Ave, Audley Heights; ⏲9am-4.30pm Mon-Fri) can assist with maps, brochures, camping permits and bushwalking details.

Around Sydney

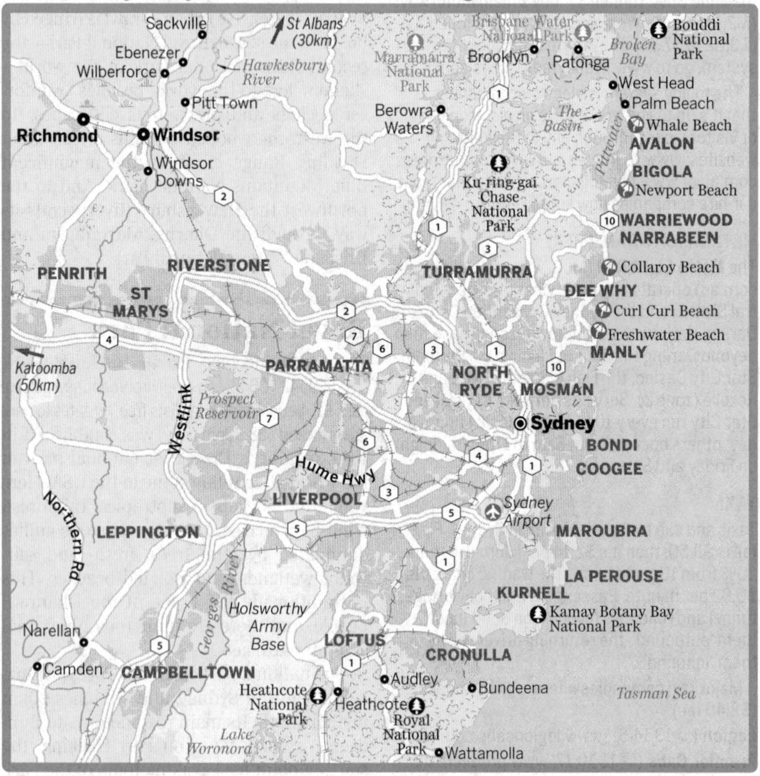

There's a drive-in **camp site** at Bonnie Vale near Bundeena, for which you'll need to book in advance through the park office (adult/child $28/7 per night). If you're walking, you can camp along the coastal trail at North Era and at Uloola Falls on the western side of the park; organise permits (adult/child $5/3 per night) through the park office.

Getting There & Away

From Sydney, take the Princes Hwy south and turn off at Farnell Ave, south of Loftus, to the park's northern end – it's about a 45-minute drive from the city. If you're driving north from Wollongong, don't miss the famous 665m-long curving Sea Cliff Bridge section of Lawrence Hargrave Dr between Clifton and Coalcliff.

The most scenic route into the park is to take the CityRail train (Eastern Suburbs and Illawarra line) to Cronulla (one way adult/child $5/2.50), and then jump aboard a **Cronulla National Park Ferry** (☎02-9523 2990; www.cronullaferries.com.au; Cronulla Wharf; adult/child one way $6.30/$3.15; ⏲hourly between 5.30am-6.30pm Mon-Fri, 8.30am-6.30pm Sat, 8.30am-5.30pm Sun) to Bundeena. Cronulla Wharf is off Tonkin St just below the train station.

Alternatively, Loftus, Engadine, Heathcote, Waterfall and Otford train stations are on the park boundary and have trails leading into the park. Loftus is closest to the park office (6km).

Hawkesbury River

Less than an hour from Sydney, the Hawkesbury River is a favourite weekend destination for city folk. The river – one of the longest in eastern Australia – flows past honeycomb-coloured cliffs, historic townships and riverside hamlets into bays and inlets and between a series of national parks.

The fertile farming country around the Hawkesbury sustains vineyards, vegetable farms, flower acreages and alpaca studs. Contact **Hawkesbury Harvest** (☎0406 237 877; www.hawkesburyharvest.com.au) for information on wine and farm trails.

Many artisans work in the area; contact the Hawkesbury Artists & Artisans Trail (www.haat.com.au) for information on visiting their galleries, shops and studios.

The **Riverboat Postman** (☎02-9985 9900, 0400 600 111; www.riverboatpostman.com.au; Brooklyn Public Wharf, Dangar Rd; adult/child/seniors $50/15/44; ⏲10am Mon-Fri), Australia's last operating mail boat, departs from the Brooklyn Wharf, beside the Hawkesbury River Railway Station, and chugs 40km up the Lower Hawkesbury as far as Marlow, returning to Brooklyn at 1.15pm. Senior citizens form the bulk of the passenger list, drawn by the views, morning tea and ploughman's lunch (all inclusive).

Near Brooklyn is the unique **Peats Bite** (☎02-9985 9040; http://peatsbite.com.au; Sunny Corner; set menu per person without wine $130; ⏲lunch Sat & Sun, closed Jul & Aug), which has been operated by the same family since 1981. A truly laid-back place, it offers a seven-course, four-hour set lunch and encourages guests to linger over their food, take a dip in the pool between courses and shimmy on the dance floor when owner Tammy gets up to sing. Access is by boat only, and you can book to stay overnight if you so choose (suite from $280). Boat transfers from the Kangaroo Point Public Wharf near Brooklyn take 10 to 15 minutes and cost $25 per person; call for details.

Further upstream a narrow forested waterway diverts from the Hawkesbury and peters down to the chilled-out river town of **Berowra Waters**, where a handful of businesses, boat sheds and residences cluster around the free, 24-hour ferry across Berowra Creek.

CityRail trains run from Sydney's Central Station to Berowra (one way adult/child $6.60/3.30, 45 minutes, roughly hourly) and on to Brooklyn's Hawkesbury River Station (one way adult/child $6.60/3.30, one hour). Note that Berowra train station is a solid 6km trudge from Berowra Waters. **Hawkesbury Water Taxis** (☎0400 600 111; www.hawkesburycruises.com.au; trips from $80) will take you anywhere along the river.

The lively riverside hamlet of **Wisemans Ferry** spills over a bow of the Hawkesbury River where it slides east towards Brooklyn. The surrounding area retains remnants of the convict-built **Great North Road**, originally constructed to link Sydney with the Hunter Valley and now part of the Australian Convict Sites listing on Unesco's World Heritage List. Today the road is a pretty back route to the north. Some 15km of the original road has been preserved and offers an excellent mountain-bike trail. To download a self-guided tour brochure, go to www.rta.nsw.gov.au and type 'convict trail' into the search box.

The social hub at Wisemans Ferry is the historic sandstone **Wisemans Inn Hotel** (☎02-4566 4301; www.wisemanshotel.com.au; Old Northern Rd; d & tw $75, f $90), which has basic pub rooms and a steakhouse (mains $13 to $30, open noon to 8.30pm) serving mediocre pub grub. There's live music (mainly country) and dozens of bikies at weekends. The prettiest access is from the east, via Old Wisemans Ferry Rd, which is wedged between Dharug National Park and the river.

HAWKESBURY HOUSEBOATS

The best way to experience the Hawkesbury is on a fully equipped houseboat. Rates skyrocket during summer and school holidays, but most outfits offer affordable low-season, midweek and long-term rental specials. To give a very rough guide, a two-/four-/six-berth boat for three nights costs from $650/740/1100 from September to early December, with prices doubling during the Christmas/New Year period and on weekends and holidays throughout the year.

Companies are based in Brooklyn, Wisemen's Ferry and Lower Portland. The following are some of the main players:

- **Able Hawkesbury River Houseboats** (☎02-4566 4308, 1800 024 979; www.hawkesburyhouseboats.com.au; 3008 River Rd, Wisemans Ferry)
- **Brooklyn Marina** (☎02-9985 7722; www.brooklynmarina.com.au; 45 Brooklyn Rd, Brooklyn)
- **Holidays Afloat** (☎02-9985 5555; www.holidaysafloat.com.au; 87 Brooklyn Rd, Brooklyn)
- **Ripples Houseboats** (☎02-9985 5555; www.ripples.com.au; 87 Brooklyn Rd, Brooklyn)

Two free 24-hour ferries connect the Wisemans Ferry riverbanks.

Largely unsealed but photogenic roads on both sides of the Macdonald River run north from Wisemans Ferry to tiny **St Albans** in Darkinung tribal country.

The **Hawkesbury Visitor Information Centre** (☎ 02-4578 0233; www.hawkesburytourism.com.au; Ham Common Park, Hawkesbury Valley Way, Clarendon; ⏲9am-5pm Mon-Fri, to 4pm Sat & Sun) opposite the RAAF base at Clarendon, between the towns of Richmond and Windsor, can supply information about the region.

Blue Mountains

A region with more than its fair share of natural beauty, the Blue Mountains was an obvious contender when Unesco called for Australian nominations to the World Heritage List, and its inclusion was ratified in 2000. The slate-coloured haze that gives the mountains their name comes from a fine mist of oil exuded by the huge eucalyptus gums that form a dense canopy across the landscape of deep, often-inaccessible valleys and chiselled sandstone outcrops.

The foothills begin 65km inland from Sydney, rising to an 1100m-high sandstone plateau riddled with valleys eroded into the stone over thousands of years. There are eight connected conservation areas in the region, including the **Blue Mountains National Park** (☎ 02-4787 8877; www.environment.nsw.gov.au/nationalparks; per car $7 in the Glenbrook area only), which has some truly fantastic scenery, excellent bushwalks, Aboriginal engravings and all the canyons and cliffs you could ask for. It's the most popular and accessible of the three national parks in the area. Great lookouts include the Evan's and Govett's Leap lookouts near Blackheath, Sublime Point in Leura and Echo Point and Cahill's Lookout in Katoomba.

Wollemi National Park (☎ 02-4787 8877; www.environment.nsw.gov.au/nationalparks), north of the Bells Line of Road, is NSW's largest forested wilderness area, stretching all the way to Denman in the Hunter Valley.

Six Aboriginal language groups treasure connections with the area that reach back into ancient time. They are the Dharawal and Gundungurra people (in the south), the Wiradjuri (in the west and northwest), and the Wanaruah, Darkinjung and Darug (in the northeast).

Although it's possible to visit on a day trip from Sydney, we strongly recommend that you stay at least one night so that you can explore a few of the towns, do at least one bushwalk and enjoy a dinner at one of the excellent restaurants in Blackheath or Leura.The hills can be surprisingly cool throughout the year, so bring a coat or wrap.

Sights

Glenbrook to Blackheath

Arriving from Sydney, the first of the Blue Mountains town you will encounter is Glenbrook (population 4945). From here, you can drive or walk into the Blue Mountains National Park; this is the only part of the park where entry fees apply. Six kilometres from the park entrance gate is the **Mt Portal Lookout**, which has panoramic views into the Glenbrook Gorge, over the Nepean River and back to Sydney. Kangaroos can often be spotted in this part of the national park.

Artist, author and bon vivant Norman Lindsay, infamous for his racy artworks but much loved for his children's tale *The Magic Pudding,* lived in Faulconbridge, 14km up the mountain from Glenbrook, from 1912 until his death in 1969. His home and studio have been preserved and are maintained by the National Trust as the **Norman Lindsay Gallery and Museum** (☎02-4751 1067; www.normanlindsay.com.au; 14 Norman Lindsay Cres, Faulconbridge; adult/child $12/6; ⏲10am-4pm), with a significant collection of his paintings, watercolours, drawings and sculptures.

Further up the mountain, the town of **Wentworth Falls** (population 5934) commands views to the south across the majestic Jamison Valley. One of the best bushwalks in the Blue Mountains – the National Pass Walk – has its starting point at the **Conservation Hut** (www.conservationhut.com.au; Fletcher St; lunch mains $21-29, sandwiches $8.50-18; ⏲9am-4pm Mon-Fri, to 5pm Sat & Sun), where maps, information, water and food are available. The track passes Queen Victoria lookout and then heads into the sublimely beautiful Valley of the Waters, home to the Empress, Silvia and Lodore waterfalls. It then leads up the historic Grand Stairway, built by hand in the early 1900s, and arrives at the Wentworth Falls and Jamison lookouts, both of which offer magnificent views.

Nearby **Leura** (population 4365) is a genteel town of undulating streets, herit-

Blue Mountains

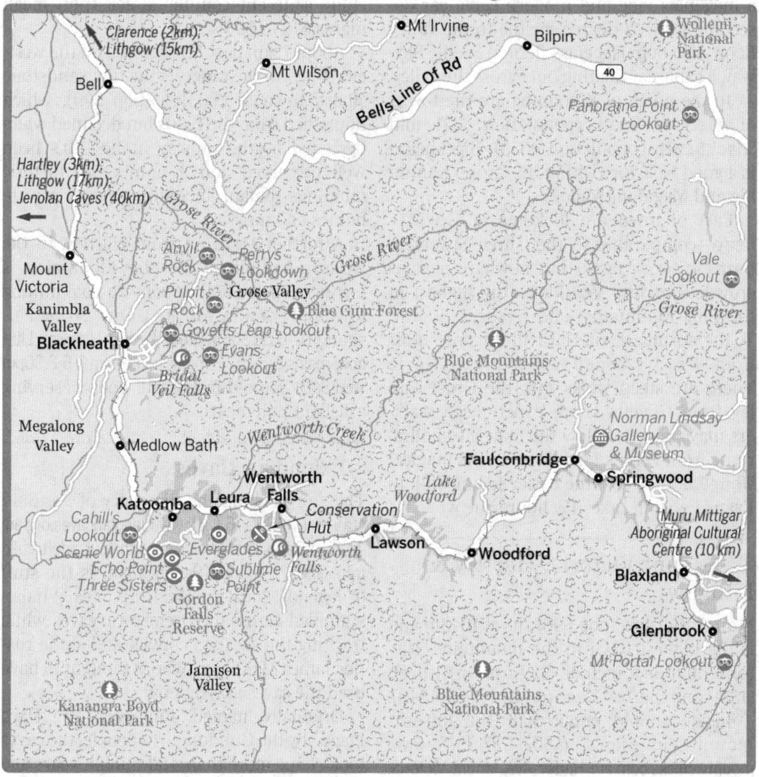

age houses and lush gardens. At its centre is the Mall, a tree-lined main street with boutiques, galleries and cafes. The town's major heritage property is the National Trust–owned **Everglades** (☎02-4784 1938; www.everglades.org.au; 37 Everglades Ave, Leura; adult/concession/child $10/8/4; ⏲10am-5pm spring & summer, 10am-4pm autumn & winter), which was built in the 1930s and has one of the country's foremost heritage gardens.

Just outside town is **Gordon Falls Reserve**, an idyllic picnic spot complete with barbeques. From here you can trek the steep Prince Henry Cliff Walk, or take the Cliff Drive 4km west past Leura Cascades to **Katoomba** (population 8016), the region's main town. The often-misty steep streets are lined with art-deco buildings and the local population is an odd mix of country battlers, hippies, mortgage refugees from the big smoke (Sydney) and members of a Tennessee-based messianic Christian sect called the Twelve Tribes (aka the Community of Believers), who live communally, believe in traditional lifestyle and operate the Common Ground Café in the main street. Extraordinarily, all of these locals seem to live together harmoniously. They also seem to cope with the huge numbers of tour buses and tourists who come here to ooh and aah at the spectacular view of the Jamison Valley and **Three Sisters** rock formation towers from the **Echo Point** viewing platforms.

There are a number of short walks from Echo Point that allow you to escape the bulk of the crowds. Parking is expensive ($3.80 for first hour, $4.40 for subsequent hours); if you're walking here from the town centre, Lurline St is the most attractive route.

Three kilometres from the centre of Katoomba you'll find **Scenic World** (☎02-4780 0200; www.scenicworld.com.au; cnr Violet St & Cliff Dr, Katoomba; cableway, walkway & skyway adult/child/family $28/14/70; 9am-5pm), with a megaplex vibe and modern cable car descending the 52-degree incline to the valley floor. Also here is a glass-floored Scenic Skyway, a cable car floating out across the valley.

To the north of Katoomba are the towns of **Medlow Bath** (population 517) and **Blackheath** (population 4353). Blackheath is a good base for visiting the Grose, Kanimbla and Megalong Valleys.

East of town are lookouts at **Govetts Leap** (comparable to the Three Sisters in terms of 'wow' factor but nowhere near as crowded), **Bridal Veil Falls** (the highest in the Blue Mountains) and **Evans Lookout**. To the northeast, via Hat Hill Rd, are **Pulpit Rock**, **Perry's Lookdown** and **Anvil Rock**. There are steep walks into the Grose Valley from Govetts Leap; experienced walkers may want to follow the 5km (5½ hours) route from Perry's Lookdown to the magical **Blue Gum Forest**; the easier 1.5km walk to Evans Lookout takes 1½ hours one way.

Mount Victoria, Hartley & Lithgow

Mount Victoria (pop 896) sits at 1043m and is the highest town in the mountains. Historic buildings include **St Peter's Church** (1874) and the **Toll Keepers Cottage** (1849).

Inside an old public hall, the 130-seat **Mount Vic Flicks** (02-4787 1577; www.mountvicflicks.com.au; Harley Ave, Mount Victoria; adult/child $11/9; Thu-Sun) is a wonderful step back in time complete with lolly bar selling sweet slices, choc tops and scones with jam and cream.

The best pub in the area by a mountain mile is the 1878 **Imperial Hotel** (02-4787 1878; 1 Station St; 11am-10pm), where you can enjoy a decent counter attack (pub meal; mains $18 to $23).

About 12km past Mt Victoria, on the western slopes of the range, is the tiny, sandstone 'ghost' town of **Hartley** (pop 299), which flourished from the 1830s but declined when bypassed by the railway in 1887. It's been well preserved and a number of historic buildings remain, including several private homes and inns.

A further 14km on from Hartley, in the western foothills of the Blue Mountains, is **Lithgow** (pop 5651), a sombre coal-mining town only of note for the **Donnybrook Hotel** (02-6351 3065; Great Western Highway, Lithgow; mains $15-25; meals noon-2pm & 6-8.30pm Wed-Sat), an old-fashioned boozer serving excellent pub meals.

Jenolan Caves

The story behind the discovery of **Jenolan Caves** (1300 763 311; www.jenolancaves.org.au; Jenolan Caves Rd; admission with tour adult/child from $30/21; tours 9am-5.30pm) is the stuff of legends: local pastoralist James Whalan stumbled across the prehistoric caves while tracking the escaped convict and cattle rustler James McKeown, who is thought to have used the caves as a hideout.

Originally named Binoomea or 'Dark Places' by the Gundungurra people, the caves took shape more than 400 million years ago and are one of the most extensive and complex limestone cave systems in the world.

There are over 350 caves in the region, although only a handful are open to the public. You must take a **tour** to see them; there's a bewildering array of options at dif-

WORTH A TRIP

MURU MITTIGAR ABORIGINAL CULTURAL CENTRE

If travelling from Sydney to the Blue Mountains, consider stopping in Castlereagh near Penrith to visit the **Muru Mittigar Aboriginal Cultural Centre** (02-4729 2377; www.murumittigar.com.au; 89-151 Old Castlereagh Rd, Castlereagh; 9am-4pm Mon-Fri), which was opened as an Aboriginal Meeting Place in 1998 to acknowledge the Darug people as the traditional custodians of the region. The centre showcases the art and stories of the Darug people as well as the rich diversity of indigenous peoples throughout Australia. Its four-hour cultural tour (adult/child $45/26) usually includes a talk about Aboriginal beliefs and stories, a hands-on boomerang throwing exercise, a bush-tucker walk, a painting demonstration and a didgeridoo playing experience. A cafe on site serves bush tucker morning teas ($9).

The centre is an hour's drive west of Sydney and an hour's drive east of Katoomba. Advance bookings are recommended.

ferent levels of difficulty; staff at the ticket office are happy to explain them all. You can also don a boiler suit and squeeze yourself through narrow tunnels with only a headlamp to guide you on a **Plughole Adventure Tour** ($80; ⏲1.15pm daily).

The caves are 30km from the Great Western Hwy (Rte 4), a 1¼-hour drive from Katoomba. The narrow Jenolan Caves Rd becomes a one-way system between 11.45am and 1.15pm daily, running clockwise from the caves out through Oberon.

Although there are a few accommodation options in Jenolan Village and the surrounding area, none are really worthy of recommendation.

Activities

Bushwalking

Explorers Wentworth, Blaxland and Lawson set off a craze for exploring the area when they became the first Europeans to traverse these majestic mountains in 1813. Fortunately, there are walks of every possible duration and level of difficulty on offer, so everyone can participate. The two most popular bushwalking areas are the Jamison Valley, south of Katoomba, and the Grose Valley, northeast of Katoomba and east of Blackheath. Other great walking opportunities can be found in the area south of Glenbrook, the Kanangra Boyd National Park (accessible from Oberon or Jenolan Caves) and the Wollemi National Park, north of Bells Line of Road. One of the most rewarding walks is the 45km, three-day **Six Foot Track** from Katoomba along the Megalong Valley to Cox's River and on to the Jenolan Caves. It has camp sites along the way.

The extraordinarily helpful **NPWS Visitor Centre** (☎02-4787 8877; bluemountains.heritagecentre@environment.nsw.gov.au; Govetts Leap Rd, Blackheath; ⏲9am-4.30pm) at Blackheath, about 2.5km off the Great Western Hwy and 10km north of Katoomba, can help you pick a hike, offer safety tips and advise about camping. Note that the bush here is dense and that it can be easy to become lost – there have been deaths as a consequence. Always leave your name and walk plan with the Katoomba Police, at the NPWS office or at one of the visitor centres; the Katoomba police station, Echo Point Visitor Centre and NPWS office also offer free use of personal locator beacons.

It's important to carry clean drinking water with you – the mountain streams are polluted due to their proximity to urban areas.

A range of NPWS walks pamphlets and maps ($3 to $7) are available from the NPWS office and from the visitor information centres at Glenbrook and Katoomba. All three centres also sell the Hema *Blue Mountains* walking map ($10.50) and Veechi Stuart's well-regarded *Blue Mountains: Best Bushwalks* ($32) book.

Cycling

The mountains are also a popular cycling destination, with many people taking their bikes on the train to Woodford and then cycling downhill to Glenbrook, a ride of two to three hours. Cycling maps ($7) are available from the visitor information centres at Glenbrook and Katoomba.

Driving

The Greater Blue Mountains Drive (www.greaterbluemountainsdrive.com.au) is a 1200km tour linking Sydney with the Blue Mountains region; it incorporates 18 'discovery trails' (stand-alone scenic drives), the most popular being the 36km, one-hour 'Blue Mountains Drive Discovery Trail' that starts in Katoomba and finishes at the Valley of the Waters picnic area at Wentworth Falls.

The best driving maps are Gregory's *Blue Mountains Touring Map* ($7.95) and the *Greater Blue Mountains Drive Touring Map* ($7.95). Both are available at the visitor information centres.

Adventure Activities & Tours

Most operators have offices in Katoomba – competition is fierce, so shop around for the best deal.

Australian School of Mountaineering ADVENTURE ACTIVITIES
(ASM; ☎02-4782 2014; www.asmguides.com; 166 Katoomba St, Katoomba) Full-day rock climbs ($195) and canyoning ($180 to $220), plus abseiling courses.

Blue Mountains Walkabout CULTURAL TOUR
(☎0408 443 822; www.bluemountainswalkabout.com; $95) Full-day indigenous-owned and -guided adventurous trek with a spiritual theme; starts at Faulconbridge train station and ends at Springwood station.

High 'n' Wild Mountain Adventures ADVENTURE SPORTS
(☎02-4782 6224; www.highandwild.com.au; 3/5 Katoomba St, Katoomba) Guided abseiling ($125 to $189), rock climbing ($249 to $349) and canyoning ($179 to $225).

Life's an Adventure ADVENTURE SPORTS
(☎02-9913 8939; www.lifesanadventure.com.au; half- & full-day tours adult $145-299, child $105-199) Runs guided full-day kayaking, hiking, 4WD and mountain-biking tours, plus a three-day guided camping hike along the Six Foot Track ($479 to $649).

Muggadah Indigenous Tours CULTURAL TOUR
(☎02-4782 2413, 0423 573 909; kathleen@muggadahtours.com.au; adult/child $50/25) These indigenous-operated guided walks view significant cultural sites on traditional land around Echo Point.

River Deep Mountain High ADVENTURE SPORTS
(☎02-4782 6109; www.rdmh.com.au; 2/187 Katoomba St, Katoomba) Offers half-day abseiling ($130), full-day canyoning ($190) and full-day canyoning and abseiling ($180) packages, plus a range of guided hikes and 4WD tours.

Tread Lightly Eco Tours ECOTOURS
(☎02-4788 1229; www.treadlightly.com.au) Has a wide range of day and night walks ($65 to $135) that emphasise the ecology of the region.

Festivals & Events

Yulefest CELEBRATION
(www.bluemts.com.au) Out-of-kilter Christmas-style celebrations between June and August.

Winter Magic COMMUNITY FESTIVAL
(www.wintermagic.com.au) This one-day festival on the day of the winter solstice in June sees Katoomba's main street taken over by market stalls, costumed locals and performances.

Leura Garden Festival GARDENING
(www.leuragardensfestival.com) Green-thumbed tourists flock to Leura during October, when Leura's many gardens are at their blooming best.

Sleeping

There's a good range of accommodation in the Blue Mountains, but you'll need to book ahead during winter and for every weekend during the year (Sydneysiders love coming here for romantic weekends away). Backpackers tend to stay in Katoomba, where the hostels are, but those with their own transport prefer Leura and Blackheath, where the restaurants and cafes are better.

Note that the famous **Hydro Majestic Hotel** (www.hydromajestic.com.au), an art-deco extravaganza perched on the escarpment at Medlow Bath, has been slated for renovation for years but works are yet to commence. It is closed in the interim.

No 14 HOSTEL $
(☎02-4782 7104; www.no14.com.au; 14 Lovel St, Katoomba; dm $25-28, d $75-85, d without bathroom $65-75; @📶) Resembling a cheery share house, this clean and tidy hostel has a friendly vibe but suffers from a lack of bathrooms (three showers for 26 beds). Dorms have three or four beds; attic-style doubles are comfy. A basic breakfast, internet and wi-fi are included in the room rate.

Flying Fox HOSTEL $
(☎02-4782 4226; www.theflyingfox.com.au; 190 Bathurst Rd, Katoomba; tent sites per person $19, dm $26-30, d without bathroom $74-82; @📶) Owners Ross and Wendy are travellers at heart, and have endowed this unassuming hostel with an endearing home-away-from-home feel. There's no party scene – just *glühwine* (mulled wine) and chocolate in the friendly lounge and a pasta night once per week. Guests can use the well-equipped communal kitchen and there's a social lounge with woodstove but no TV. Internet and wi-fi are free, which is a plus, but there aren't many bathrooms.

Blue Mountains YHA HOSTEL $
(☎02-4782 1416; www.yha.com.au; 207 Katoomba St, Katoomba; dm $30-32, d with/without bathroom $100/90, f with/without bathroom $140/126; @📶) Behind the austere brick exterior of this popular 200-bed hostel is a selection of dorms and family rooms that are comfortable, light and spotlessly clean. Facilities include a lounge with open fire, central heating, a huge TV room, pool table, excellent communal kitchen and outdoor space with barbecues. A DIY breakfast costs $3 to $6.50.

Glenella Guesthouse GUESTHOUSE $$
(☎02-4787 8352; www.glenellabluemountainshotel.com.au; 56-60 Govetts Leap Rd; r $110-170, f $220-260; 📶) Graceful Glenella has been functioning as a guesthouse since 1912 and is now operated with enthusiasm and expertise by a young couple who make guests feel very welcome. There are seven comfortable bedrooms, an attractive lounge and a stunning dining room where a truly excellent breakfast is served.

Waldorf Leura Gardens HOTEL $$
(☎02-4784 4000; www.leuragardensresort.com.au; 20-28 Fitzroy St, Leura; d $107-199; ❄📶🏊)

Resort facilities (heated pool and spa, table tennis, gym, squash courts, pool table and gym), a garden setting and a location opposite Leura's 18-hole golf course make this motel-style place a popular choice for families and retirees. Rooms are comfortable and clean, service is friendly and both advance-purchase and last-minute rates are highly affordable.

Broomelea Bed & Breakfast   B&B $$
(☑02-4784 2940; www.broomelea.com.au; 273 Leura Mall, Leura; r $160-225; @📶) Leafy Leura gets a bum rap for being snooty, but when B&Bs are as plush as this 1909 Edwardian specimen, who cares? Manicured gardens, cane furniture on the verandah, an open fire and a snug lounge are just a few of Broomelea's bonuses. There's also a self-contained cottage for families ($160 to $205).

Greens of Leura   B&B $$
(☑02-4784 3241; www.thegreensleura.com.au; 24-26 Grose St, Leura; r $162-205; @📶) On a quiet street parallel to the Mall, this pretty timber house set in a lovely garden offers five rooms named after English writers (Browning, Austen etc). All are individually decorated; some have four-poster beds and spas. The complimentary afternoon teas are a nice touch. Two-night minimum stay.

Lilianfels   LUXURY HOTEL $$$
(☑02-4780 1200; www.lilianfels.com.au; Lilianfels Ave, Katoomba; d $250-715; ste $425-725; ✳@📶🏊) Ah, if life could always be this sweet! This luxury resort offers 85 rooms, the region's best restaurant (Darley's; three-courses $125) and an indulgent array of facilities including a spa, heated indoor and outdoor pools, tennis court, billiard/games room, library and gym. Located in a historic homestead in manicured gardens next to Echo Point, it is regularly nominated as one of Australia's top hotels. Last-minute and room-only prices can be considerably reduced.

✗ Eating

Anonymous   CAFE $
(www.anonymouscafe.com.au; 237-238 Great Western Hwy, Blackheath; sandwiches $10, ploughman's lunch $14-17; ⊙6am-4pm Mon-Fri, 7am-5pm Sat & Sun) The groovy inner-city Sydney coffee thang has kicked off here in Blackheath courtesy of this cute cafe opposite the train station in Blackheath, and the locals are lovin' it. The coffee (blend and single origin) is made with care and expertise, and the menu changes each week according to what local produce is in season.

Sanwiye Korean Cafe   KOREAN $
(☑0405 402 130; 177 Katoomba St, Katoomba; noodle soups $10-12, dumplings $10-12, savoury pancakes $12-14; ⊙11am-9.30pm Tue-Sun) In the sea of overpriced mediocrity that is the Katoomba dining scene (and that's a generous description), this is the only place that deserves a recommendation. It's simple, sure, and it won't be winning awards any time soon, but the food is fresh and made with love by the Korean owners. Booking is advisable (it's tiny) and credit cards aren't accepted.

Blue Mountains Food Co-op   SELF-CATERING $
(www.bluemtnsfood.asn.au; Ha'penny Lane, shops 1 & 2, Katoomba; ⊙9am-6pm Mon-Fri, 8.30am-5pm Sat, 10am-4.30pm Sun) The perfect stop for hard-core self-caterers and bushwalkers in need of goodies for their backpacks, the Co-op stocks organic, vegan and gluten-free local foods and produce.

Solitary   MODERN AUSTRALIAN $$
(☑02-4782 1164; www.solitary.com.au; 90 Cliff Dr, Leura Falls; lunch dishes $15-32, sandwiches $14-18, scones $13; ⊙10.30am-4.30pm Wed, Thu, Sun & Mon, 10.30am-4.30pm & 6.30-10pm Fri & Sat, closed 2 weeks Jan) The seasonally driven menu tries hard to live up to this restaurant's setting atop the Leura Cascades. Sit in the old-fashioned dining spaces or on the front lawn to enjoy lunch or a Devonshire tea.

Leura Garage   MEDITERRANEAN $$
(☑02-4784 3391; www.leuragarage.com.au; 84 Railway Pde, Leura; breakfast $9-19, shared plates $9-31, pizzas $21-29; ⊙11.30am-late Mon, Thu & Fri, 8am-late Sat & Sun) Suspended mufflers and stacks of old tires signal the occupation of the former tenant of this hugely popular place off the top end of Leura Mall. The vibe is hipster-ish, the house wine is perfectly quaffable and the shared plates, including deli-laden pizza, are hefty in size.

Silk's Brasserie   MODERN AUSTRALIAN $$
(☑02-4784 2534; www.silksleura.com; 128 Leura Mall, Leura; lunch mains $24-39, dinner mains $30-39; ⊙noon-2.30pm & 6-9pm Mon-Sat) A warm welcome awaits at Leura's long-standing fine diner. Although the dishes can sometimes be overworked, the serves are generous and the flavours harmonious. There's a

two-course minimum on Friday and Saturday nights.

Ashcrofts MODERN AUSTRALIAN $$$
(02-4787 8297; www.ashcrofts.com; 18 Govetts Leap Rd, Blackheath; 2-/3-courses $78/88; 6-10pm Thu-Sat, noon-3pm & 6-10pm Sun) For the past decade, chef Corinne Evatt has been wooing locals and visitors alike with her flavoursome, globally inspired dishes. The wine list is among the best in the mountains and service is professional.

Escarpment MODERN AUSTRALIAN $$$
(02-47877269; www.escarpmentblackheath.com; 246 Great Western Hwy, Blackheath; dinner mains $31-39, 2-course fixed lunch $37; 6-10pm Fri & Mon, noon-3pm & 6-10pm Sat & Sun) The decor at this unassuming bistro features attractive artwork and an old-fashioned espresso machine. There's nothing old-fashioned or overly arty about the menu, though – it changes with the season and makes the most of local produce.

Drinking & Entertainment

Alexandra Hotel PUB
(www.alexandrahotel.com.au; 62 Great Western Hwy, Leura; meals noon-2pm & 5.30-9pm) The Alex is a gem. Join the punters at the pool comp on Monday, poker night on Wednesday, gay night on Friday and DJ on Saturday. For a rest, relax over an excellent pub meal in the restaurant (mains $18 to $27) or bar ($15 to $19).

Old City Bank Bar & Brasserie BAR
(Katoomba St, Katoomba; 7am-2am Mon-Thu, to 3am Fri & Sat, 10am-10pm Sun;) Run by the venerable Carrington Hotel, this popular place has a pleasant bar on the ground floor and a dining room upstairs serving pizzas ($15 to $19) and pub-style grub (mains $19 to $26). There's live music most Friday and Saturday nights.

True to the Bean CAFE
(123 Katoomba St, Katoomba; waffles $7; 7am-5pm Mon-Sat, 8am-4pm Sun) The Sydney obsession with single-estate coffee has made its way to Katoomba's main drag in the form of this tiny espresso bar. Consider a sweet side of waffles with maple syrup and icecream.

Edge Cinema CINEMA
(www.edgecinema.com.au; 225 Great Western Hwy, Katoomba; tickets $16; 9.30am-late) A giant screen (and we mean humungeous!) shows mainstream movies. Budget Tuesdays feature flicks for $10 per person.

Information

There are visitor information centres on the Great Western Hwy at **Glenbrook** (1300 653 408; www.visitbluemountains.org; Great Western Highway; 8.30am-4pm Mon-Sat, 8.30am-3pm Sun) and at Echo Point in **Katoomba** (1300 653 408; www.visitbluemountains.com.au; Echo Point, Katoomba; 9am-5pm). Both can provide plenty of information and will book accommodation, tours and attractions.

The **Blue Mountains District Anzac Memorial Hospital** (02-4784 6500; www.wsahs.nsw.gov.au/bluemountains/index.htm; cnr Woodlands Rd & Great Western Hwy, Katoomba; 24hr emergency) in Katoomba has a 24-hour emergency department.

Getting There & Around

To reach the Blue Mountains by road, leave Sydney via Parramatta Rd. At Strathfield detour onto the toll-free M4, which becomes the Great Western Hwy west of Penrith and takes you to all of the Blue Mountains towns. It takes approximately 1½ hours to drive from central Sydney to Katoomba.

Blue Mountains Bus (02-4751 1077; www.bmbc.com.au) Local buses travel from Katoomba to Wentworth Falls (buses 685 and 690K), Scenic World (bus 686), Leura (buses 685 and 690K) and Blackheath (bus 698). Fares cost between $2 and $4.30.

Blue Mountains Explorer Bus (1300 300 915; www.explorerbus.com.au; 283 Bathurst Rd, Katoomba; adult/child $38/19; 9.45am-4.54pm) Offers hop-on/hop-off service on a 26-stop Katoomba–Leura loop. Leaves from Katoomba station every 30 minutes to one hour.

Blue Mountains ExplorerLink (13 15 00; www.cityrail.info/tickets/which/explorerlink; 1-day pass adult/child from $49.60/24.80, 3-day pass adult/child from $71.60/35.80) Gives return train travel from Sydney to the Blue Mountains, plus access to the Explorer Bus service.

CityRail (13 15 00; www.cityrail.info) Runs to the mountains from Sydney's Central Station (one way adult/child $8.40/4.20, two hours, hourly). Off-peak return tickets cost $11.60/5.80. There are stations at towns along the Great Western Hwy, including Glenbrook, Faulconbridge, Wentworth Falls, Leura, Katoomba, Medlow Bath, Blackheath, Mt Victoria, Zig Zag and Lithgow.

Trolley Tours (4782 7999; www.trolleytours.com.au; 76 Bathurst Rd, Katoomba; ticket $25; 9.45am-5.42pm) Runs a hop-on, hop-off bus

WORTH A TRIP

BELLS LINE OF ROAD

This stretch of road between Richmond and Lithgow is the most scenic route across the Blue Mountains and is highly recommended if you have your own transport. There are fine views towards the coast from Kurrajong Heights on the eastern slopes of the range, there are orchards (mainly apple) around Bilpin and there's sandstone-cliff and bush scenery all the way to Lithgow.

Midway between Bilpin and Bell, the delightful **Blue Mountains Botanic Garden Mount Tomah** (☎02-4567 3000; www.rbgsyd.nsw.gov.au; Bells Line of Road; ⏱9am-5.30pm Mon-Fri, 9.30am-5.30pm Sat & Sun) FREE is a cool-climate annexe of Sydney's Royal Botanic Gardens. As well as native plants there are displays of exotic cold-climate species, including some magnificent rhododendrons. Parts of the park are wheelchair accessible.

If you're at Bilpin for lunch or dinner, make a beeline for **Apple Bar** (☎02-4567 0335; www.applebar.com.au; 2488 Bells Line of Road, Bilpin; pizzas $26-29, mains $30-43; ⏱noon-3pm & 6-10pm Fri-Sun, noon-3pm Mon), which is set in a weatherboard cottage amongst Bilpin's apple orchards and serves excellent pizzas and grills from its wood-fired oven. At other times, head to the charming rose garden cafe **Tutti Frutti** (http://tuttifruitti.com.au; 1917 Bells Line of Road, Bilpin; ⏱10am-4pm Thu & Mon, 9.30am-5pm Fri-Sun), where you can enjoy Devonshire teas, coffee, homemade pies (including a sensational apple version) and berry ice cream. The **Bilpin Markets** are held at the district hall every Saturday from 10am to noon.

To access Bells Line of Road, head out on Parramatta Rd from Sydney, and from Parramatta drive northwest on Windsor Rd to Windsor. Richmond Rd from Windsor becomes the Bells Line of Road west of Richmond. The road meets State Route 69 at Kurrajong, which can be followed through the Wollemi and Yengo National Parks to the Hunter Valley.

barely disguised as a trolley, looping around 29 stops in Katoomba and Leura.

HUNTER VALLEY

A filigree of narrow country lanes criss-crosses this verdant valley, but a pleasant country drive isn't the main motivator for visitors – sheer decadence is. The Hunter is one big gorge-fest: fine wine, boutique beer, chocolate, cheese, olives, you name it. Bacchus would surely approve.

Going on the philosophy that good food and wine will inevitably up the odds for nookie, the region is a popular weekender for Sydney couples. Every Friday they descend, like a plague of Ralph-Lauren-Polo-shirt-wearing locusts. Prices leap up accordingly.

The oldest wine region in Australia, the Hunter is known for its semillon and shiraz. Vines were first planted in the 1820s and by the 1860s there were 20 sq km under cultivation. However, the wineries gradually declined, and it wasn't until the 1960s that winemaking again became an important industry. If it's no longer the crowning jewel of the Australian wine industry, it still turns in some excellent vintages.

The Hunter has an important ace up its sleeve: these wineries are refreshingly attitude-free and welcoming of viticulturists and novices alike. Staff will rarely give you the evil eye if you leadenly twirl your glass once too often, or don't conspicuously savour the bouquet. Even those with only a casual interest in wine should be sure to tour around – it's a lovely area, surrounded by national parks and chock-full of things to do.

Sights & Activities

Most attractions lie in an area bordered to the north by the New England Hwy and to the south by Wollombi/Maitland Rd, with the main cluster of wineries and restaurants being on or around Broke Rd in **Pokolbin** (pop 694). The main town serving the area is **Cessnock** (pop 13,673), to the south. Wine Country Dr heads straight up from Cessnock to **Branxton** (pop 1826). To confuse matters, the bottom half of this route is sometimes labelled Allandale Rd and the top end Branxton Rd.

Hunter Valley

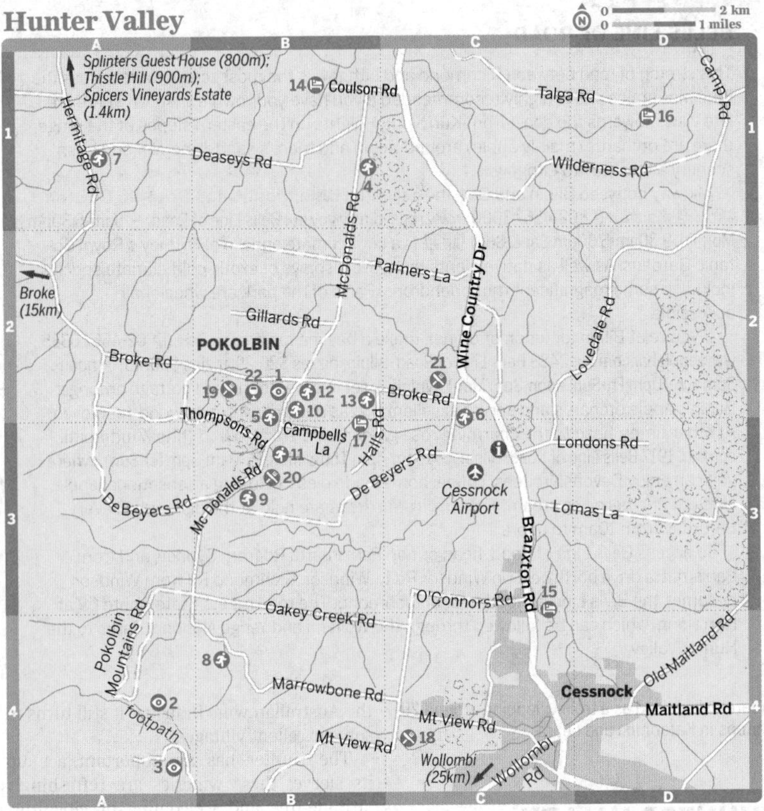

Hunter Valley

Sights
1 Hunter Valley Gardens B2
2 Lookout A4
3 Mt Bright Lookout A4

Activities, Courses & Tours
4 Bimbadgen Estate B1
5 Brokenwood B2
6 Hungerford Hill C2
7 Keith Tulloch Winery A1
8 McWilliams Mount Pleasant B4
9 Pooles Rock Wines B3
10 Small Winemakers Centre B2
11 Tamburlaine B3
12 Tempus Two B2
13 Tower Estate B2

Sleeping
14 Buffs at Pokolbin B1
15 Hunter Valley YHA C3
16 Tonic D1
17 Tower Lodge B3

Eating
18 Bistro Molines C4
19 Café Enzo B2
20 Hunter Olive Centre B3
Hunter Valley Cheese Company .... (see 1)
21 Hunter Valley Chocolate Company at Peterson House C2
Hunter Valley Smelly Cheese Shop .... (see 12)
Muse Restaurant .... (see 6)

Drinking & Nightlife
22 Harrigan's B2

To the northwest, there are further vineyards around the towns of **Broke** and **Singleton**.

Wineries

The valley's 140-plus wineries range from small-scale family-run affairs to massive commercial operations. Most offer free tastings, although a couple of the glitzier ones charge a small fee. Remember that the vineyards don't offer this service out of the goodness of their hearts. It's poor form if you don't buy at least the occasional bottle.

Grab a copy of the free *Hunter Valley Visitors Guide* from the information centre at Pokolbin and use its handy map to plot your course or just follow your nose, hunting out the tucked-away small producers.

Bimbadgen Estate WINERY
(☎02-4998 4600, restaurant 02-4998 4666; www.bimbadgen.com.au; 790 McDonalds Rd, Pokolbin; ⊙10am-5pm Sun-Thu, to 7pm Fri & Sat) Cresting a hill and with an exceptionally fine restaurant (mains $32 to $45, high tea $20; open lunch and high tea daily, dinner Thursday to Saturday) that sports spectacular views over the vines. It also offers accommodation in two houses; one sleeps eight and the other four. Contact the winery for details.

Brokenwood WINERY
(www.brokenwood.com.au; 401-427 McDonalds Rd, Pokolbin; ⊙9.30am-5pm Mon-Sat, 10am-5pm Sun) This is one of the Hunter's most acclaimed wineries.

Hungerford Hill WINERY
(www.hungerfordhill.com.au; 2450 Broke Rd, Pokolbin; ⊙10am-5pm Sun-Thu, to 6pm Fri & Sat) Shaped like a big barrel, with its 'lid' permanently propped open, this winery stands sentinel at the entry to Broke Rd. It's home to the highly regarded Muse Restaurant (p148).

Keith Tulloch Winery WINERY
(☎02-4998 7500; http://keithtullochwine.com.au; cnr Hermitage & Deasys Rds, Pokolbin; tastings $5 (redeemable when wine is purchased); ⊙10am-5pm) This winery also has a gourmet cafe (noon to 3pm Wednesday to Sunday) and offers one two-bedroom apartment ($320 to $860 per night) sleeping four adults.

Macquariedale Estate WINERY
(www.macquariedale.com.au; 170 Sweetwater Rd, Rothbury; ⊙10am-5pm) A boutique winemaker that's certified organic and biodynamic. It also grows garlic.

Margan WINERY
(www.margan.com.au; 1238 Millbrodale Rd, Broke; ⊙10am-5pm) Gorgeous setting, classy tasting room and the fabulous Margan restaurant (p147).

McWilliams Mount Pleasant WINERY
(www.mountpleasantwines.com.au; 401 Marrowbone Rd, Pokolbin; ⊙10am-4.30pm) One of the oldest (1880) and best-known vineyards in the valley.

Pooles Rock Wines WINERY
(www.poolesrock.com.au; DeBeyers Rd, Pokolbin; ⊙9.30am-5pm) A big player, producing the midpriced Cockfighter's Ghost range as well as its excellent flagship wines.

Small Winemakers Centre CELLAR DOOR
(www.smallwinemakerscentre.com.au; 426 McDonalds Rd, Pokolbin; ⊙10am-5pm) Acts as a cellar door for six boutique winemakers plus the Australian Regional Food Store.

Stonehurst Cedar Creek WINERY
(www.cedarcreekcottages.com.au; 1840 Wollombi Rd, Wollombi; ⊙10am-5pm) One of the six wineries in the picturesque Wollombi Valley. Uses organic practices and offers basic cabin accommodation.

Tamburlaine WINERY
(www.tamburlaine.com.au; 358 McDonalds Rd, Pokolbin; ⊙9am-5pm) An excellent producer focusing on sustainable viticulture.

Tempus Two WINERY
(www.tempustwo.com.au; cnr McDonalds & Broke Rds, Pokolbin; ⊙10am-5pm) This huge place is a favourite with tour buses, who descend upon its Thai and Japanese restaurants and purchase gourmet goodies from its Smelly Cheese Shop.

Tower Estate WINERY
(www.towerestatewines.com; cnr Halls & Broke Rds, Pokolbin; ⊙10am-5pm) Established by one of Australia's major wine industry figures, the late Len Evans, Tower is the classiest winery in the valley and also offers its most sophisticated accommodation option.

Wyndham Estate WINERY
(☎02-4938 3444; www.wyndhamestate.com; 700 Dalwood Rd, Dalwood; ⊙9.30am-4.30pm) Established in 1828, this winery at Dalwood near Branxton is known for its shiraz. It's also home to the highly regarded Olive Tree Restaurant (breakfast dishes $16 to $24, lunch

mains $32 to $35; open noon to 3pm Saturday and 10am to 3pm Sunday).

Other Attractions

Hunter Valley Gardens GARDENS
(www.hvg.com.au; Broke Rd; adult/child/family $25/15/65; ⏲9am-5pm) Although there's something a little Disney about it, this relatively young 24-hectare garden has impressive floral and landscape displays. It's the home of the valley's famous **Christmas Lights Spectacular** (⏲mid-Nov–early Jan), Australia's biggest Christmas lights display.

Adventure Activities & Tours

If no one's volunteering to stay sober enough to drive, there are plenty of winery tours available. Some operators will collect you in Sydney or Newcastle for a lengthy day trip. Staff at visitor centres and accommodation providers should be able to arrange a booking that suits your needs.

Aussie Wine Tours WINE
(☎0402 909 090; www.aussiewinetours.com.au) You can determine your own itinerary if you take one of these private, chauffeur-driven tours.

Balloon Aloft BALLOON FLIGHT
(☎1800 028 568, 02-4991 1955; www.balloonaloft.com; flights from $299) Sunrise flights over the vineyards.

Hunter Valley Boutique Wine Tours WINE
(☎02-4990 8989; www.huntervalleytours.com.au) Small-group tours; from $65 per person for a half-day tour and from $99 for a full-day tour including lunch.

Hunter Valley Wine Tasting Tours WINE
(☎02-9357 5511; www.huntervalleywinetastingtours.com.au) These full-day minvan tours from Sydney ($110 to $153), Newcastle ($80 to $105) or the valley ($75 to $100) visit five wineries.

Hunter Wine Helicopters HELICOPTER RIDES
(☎02-4991 7352; www.hunterwinehelicopters.com.au; from $80 per person) Hop aboard for a 10-minute 'Vineyard Spectacular' ($80) or 15-minute 'Brokenback Tour' ($110) ride. Also offers a range of lunch-and-fly packages.

Tex Tours WINE
(☎0410 462 540; www.textours.com.au) Offers entertaining full-day Hunter Valley winery tours (from $65, backpacker discounts available) from Newcastle and Maitland.

Wine Rover WINE
(☎02-4990 1699; www.rovercoaches.com.au) Coaches pick you up in Cessnock or Pokolbin ($45/55 weekdays/weekends), Branxton ($55/65), Newcastle ($60/70) or at Morisset train station ($55/65) for a day spent visiting wineries and other attractions.

> **SENSIBLE SUPPING**
>
> Australia's National Health and Medical Research Council recommends that people who are driving should drink no more than two standard drinks in the first hour and then no more than one per hour after that (women, who tend to reach a higher blood alcohol concentration faster than men, should consider drinking only one standard drink in the first hour). Wineries usually offer 20mL tastes of wine – five of these equal one standard drink.

Festivals & Events

During the warm months superstars regularly drop by for weekend concerts at the bigger vineyards. If there's something special on, accommodation books up well in advance. Check what's on at www.winecountry.com.au.

A Day on the Green MUSIC
(www.adayonthegreen.com.au) At Bimbadgen Estate during summer.

Lovedale Long Lunch FOOD
(www.lovedalelonglunch.com.au) Seven wineries and chefs serve huge lunches acompanied by with music and art, in May.

Hunter Valley Wine & Food Month WINE, FOOD
(www.huntervalleyuncorked.com.au/hunter-valley-food-and-wine) In June.

Jazz in the Vines JAZZ
(www.jazzinthevines.com.au) At Tyrrell's Vineyard in October.

Opera in the Vineyards OPERA
(www.4di.com.au) At Wyndham Estate in October.

Sleeping

Prices shoot up savagely on Friday and Saturday nights and two-night minimum stays are common. Many places don't accept child guests.

Hunter Valley YHA HOSTEL $
(☎02-4991 3278; www.yha.com.au; 100 Wine Country Dr, Nulkaba; unpowered campervan sites $15pp, dm $27-34, d with bathroom $86-95, d without bathroom $74-82; @ ≋) Set on a working vineyard, this family-run hostel is jammed-packed in February, when working-holiday-makers come to the valley to pick fruit. The reward at the end of their long day is a pool and sauna, clean facilities and plenty of bonhomie in the communal kitchen and around the barbeque and outdoor pizza oven; on weekends the hostel's winery tours ($45) are popular. Be warned that the rooms can get stiflingly hot. If you call ahead staff will collect you from the bus stop at Cessnock.

★**Thistle Hill** GUESTHOUSE $$
(☎02-6574 7217; www.thill.com.au; 591 Hermitage Rd, Pokolbin; d Sun-Thu $200, Fri & Sat $270, cottage Sun-Thu $210, Fri & Sat $520; ❄ 🛜 ≋) Peter and Carol's idyllic 25-acre property features rose gardens, a lime orchard, a vineyard, a self-contained cottage sleeping up to five and a luxurious guesthouse with six ensuite rooms. Rooms and common areas have trés elegant French Provincial decor and the pool pavilion (pool, guest lounge and breakfast room) is simply stunning.

Buffs at Pokolbin CABINS $$
(☎02-4998 7636; www.buffsatpokolbin.com.au; 47 Coulson Rd, Pokolbin; 1-bedroom cottage midweek/weekend $150/225; 2-bedroom cottage midweek $180-240, weekend $280-320; ❄ ≋) Set on a tranquil 40-hectare property where kangaroos hop under the gum trees and gentle cooling breezes come off the dam, Buffs' four spotlessly clean self-contained cottages are as comfortable as they are keenly priced. A fantastic choice for families and couples alike.

Splinters Guest House B&B $$
(☎02-6574 7118; http://splinters.com.au; 617 Hermitage Rd, Pokolbin; d $180-220, apt $240-280; ❄ 🛜 ≋) Gregarious owner Bobby Jory runs her B&B with great élan, offering plenty of advice about the region and treating guests to gourmet breakfasts, port and chocolates in rooms, and cheese and wine on the terrace after a day touring the wineries. There are three smart B&B doubles with comfortable beds, and two rustic self-catering cottages.

Tower Lodge LUXURY HOTEL $$$
(☎02-4998 7022; www.towerestatewines.com/tower-lodge; Halls Rd, Pokolbin; d midweek/weekend from $450/650; ❄ @ 🛜 ≋) There are 12 luxurious rooms to choose from at this vineyard hotel, each furnished with antiques and artworks. After a day spent touring the valley, you can enjoy a complimentary afternoon tea or aperitif in the magnificent lounge before kicking onto dinner at the estate's Roberts Restaurant (lunch mains $25 to $45, dinner mains $42 to $65).

Spicers Vineyards Estate RESORT $$$
(☎1300 192 868; www.spicersgroup.com.au; 555 Hermitage Rd, Pokolbin; ste $395-495; ❄ 🛜 ≋) Marketing itself as 'the ultimate intimately unique wine country estate', Spicers offers eight modern suites with king-size bed, lounge area with open fireplace and bathroom with spa. Facilities include the excellent Restaurant Botanica (dinner Wednesday to Sunday and lunch Saturday and Sunday, two-/three-courses $65/75), a pool with running-water spa, a tennis court and a short nine-hole golf course.

Tonic BOUTIQUE HOTEL $$$
(☎02-4930 9999; www.tonichotel.com.au; 251 Talga Rd, Lovedale; d incl breakfast $425, apt $850; ❄ 🛜 ≋) Sydney style-meisters adore this boutique hotel, which has six double rooms and a two-bedroom apartment. The decor is self-avowedly anti-chintz, with polished concrete floors, a vivid colour scheme and contemporary furnishings. DIY breakfast makings are provided.

Eating

Bookings are recommended midweek and essential on weekends. Don't expect any bargains – those on a tight budget should self-cater.

Many wineries have restaurants – as well as the reviews here, see the Wineries listings.

Café Enzo CAFE $$
(www.enzohuntervalley.com.au; Peppers Creek, cnr Broke & Ekerts Rds, Pokolbin; breakfast dishes $9-23, lunch mains $18-36; ⏰9am-4pm Mon-Wed, to 5pm Sat & Sun) Claim a table by the fireside in winter or in the garden in summer to enjoy the rustic, generously sized dishes served at this popular place in the Pepper Creek Village. There's a tempting produce shop next door.

★**Margan** MODERN AUSTRALIAN $$$
(☎02-6579 1372; www.margan.com.au; 1238 Milbrodale Rd, Broke; breakfast dishes $12-18, lunch mains $36-38, 2-/4-/5-course tasting menu $65/80/95; ⏰noon-3pm & 6-9.30pm Fri & Sat,

9-11am & noon-3pm Sun) Live up to the area's name and go for broke when it comes to ordering from the tempting array of dishes on offer at this vineyard restaurant. Much of the produce is sourced from the vineyard's kitchen garden; the rest comes from local providores whenever possible. Views are across the vines to the Brokenback Range.

Bistro Molines FRENCH $$$
(☎ 02-4990 9553; www.bistromolines.com.au; 749 Mt View Rd, Mt View; mains $35-41; ⏲ noon-3pm Thu & Mon, noon-3pm & 7-9pm Fri & Sat) Set in the Tallavera Grove winery, this French restaurant has a sensational, seasonally driven menu that is nearly as impressive as the view over the vines.

Muse Restaurant MODERN AUSTRALIAN $$$
(☎ 02-4998 6777; www.musedining.com.au; Hungerford Hill Vineyard, 1 Broke Rd, Pokolbin; lunch mains $26-36, set 2-/3-course dinner $75/95, 5-course tasting menu $110; ⏲ 10am-5pm & 6.30-10pm Wed-Sat, 10am-5pm Sun) Functioning as a sophisticated cafe during the day and a fine diner in the evening, Muse offers food that runs the gamut from mediocre to inspired to oh-my-god-why-is-that-dish-erupting? Sydney's food critics love it, but we think it promises more than it delivers.

Providores

Hunter Olive Centre OLIVE SHOP
(www.pokolbinestate.com.au; 298 McDonalds Rd, Pokolbin Estate Vineyard; ⏲ 10am-5pm) Olives, oil, tapanade, *dukkah* (a blend of ground nuts and spices), jams, chutney and lavender products.

Hunter Valley Cheese Company CHEESE SHOP
(www.huntervalleycheese.com.au; McGuigans Winery, 447 McDonalds Rd; ⏲ 9am-5.30pm) Staff will chew your ear about cheesy comestibles all day long, especially during the daily 11am and 3pm cheese talks. There's a bewildering variety of styles available for purchase.

Hunter Valley Chocolate Company at Peterson House CHOCOLATE SHOP
(www.hvchocolate.com.au; Peterson House, cnr Broke & Branxton Rds, Pokolbin; ⏲ 9am-5pm) Chocolates, fudge and other treats are made in a Lovedale factory and are sold there, here, and at a store in the Hunter Valley Gardens.

Hunter Valley Smelly Cheese Shop DELI
(www.huntervalleysmellycheeseshop.com.au; Tempus Two Winery, 2144 Broke Rd, Pokolbin; ⏲ 9am-5.30pm) A hugely popular place that's full to the rafters with produce from local suppliers and elsewhere. The climate-controlled cheese room is stacked with desirables, and you can also buy bread, relishes, meats and olives for Wine Country picnics. There's another branch at Pokolbin Village, 2188 Broke Rd.

Drinking

Wollombi Tavern PUB
(www.wollombitavern.com.au; Old North Rd, Wollombi; ⏲ 10am-late) Strategically located at the Wollombi crossroads, this fabulous little pub is the home of Dr Jurd's Jungle Juice, a dangerous brew of port, brandy and wine. The less adventurous (or should that read foolhardy?) can opt for a glass of excellent locally produced wine, including Stonehurst's chambourcin and Undercliff's semillon and shiraz. On weekends, the tavern is a favourite pit stop for motorbike clubs (the nonscary sort).

Harrigan's PUB
(Broke Rd, Pokolbin) A comfortable Irish pub with beef-and-Guinness pies on the menu, live bands most weekends and plenty of opportunities for a craic.

Information

Hunter Valley Visitor Information Centre (☎ 02-4990 0900; www.winecountry.com.au; 455 Wine Country Dr, Pokolbin; ⏲ 9am-5pm Mon-Sat, to 4pm Sun) The visitors centre has a huge stock of leaflets as well as information on valley accommodation, attractions and dining.

Getting There & Away

If you're driving from Sydney, consider exiting north from the M1 at the Peats Ridge Rd exit and making your way along the convict-built Great North Rd to the charming colonial town of Wollombi and then heading north to Broke or east to Cessnock via Wollombi Rd. Pokolbin can be accessed from both.

CityRail has a line heading through the Hunter Valley from Newcastle (adult/child $6.60/3.30, 55 minutes); get off at Morisset and catch a connecting Rover Coaches service to Cessnock (adult/child $4.50/2.20, 50 minutes). Trains from Sydney (adult/child $8.40/4.20, 3¾ hours) also stop at Morisset.

Rover Coaches (☎ 02-4990 1699; www.rovercoaches.com.au) has regular services between Cessnock and Newcastle ($4.50, 1½ hours). **Hunter Valley Day Tours** (☎ 02-4951 4574; www.huntervalleydaytours.com.au) operates a shuttle service from Newcastle Airport to Hunter Valley hotels ($125 for one to two persons).

Getting Around

Exploring without a car can be challenging. The YHA hostel hires bikes ($22 per day), as do **Grapemobile** (☎02-4998 7660, 0418 404 039; www.grapemobile.com.au; Pokolbin Brothers Wines, crn Palmers Lane & McDonalds Rd, Pokolbin; per day $25) and **Hunter Valley Cycling** (☎0418 281 480; www.huntervalley-cycling.com.au; tandem $50 per day, mountain bike $45 for 2 days).

The **Vineyard Shuttle** (☎02-4991 3655; www.huntervalleyclassiccarriages.com.au) offers a restaurant shuttle service.

NEWCASTLE

POP 308,308

Sydney may be blessed with glitz and glamour, but the state's second-largest city has down-to-earth larrikin charm instead. Newcastle is the kind of place where you can grocery shop barefoot, go surfing in your lunch hour and quickly become best buddies with the Novocastrian sitting next to you in the bar.

This easygoing, 'no worries' attitude is due to Newcastle's rough-and-tumble past, shaped by a cast of convicts and coal miners. Today it continues to be the largest coal export harbour in the world, and its famed pub and surf cultures continue to thrive.

Sights

Museums, Galleries & Historical Sites

Newcastle Regional Museum MUSEUM
(☎02-4974 1400; www.newcastlemuseum.com.au; Workshop Way, Honeysuckle Precinct; ⏲10am-5pm Tue-Sun) FREE Opened in May 2011 to great fanfare, this museum occupies the restored Honeysuckle rail workshops on the foreshore and focuses on the history and industrial heritage of the city. Exhibits are largely geared towards schoolchildren.

Newcastle Art Gallery ART GALLERY
(☎02-4974 5100; www.nag.org.au; cnr Laman & Darby Sts; ⏲10am-5pm Tue-Sun; free guided tours 11am Sat & Sun) FREE The city's main cultural institution is housed in a particularly ugly Brutalist building that was undergoing a major renovation when we visited. It has a small permanent collection of Australian works (look out for paintings by John Brack, Charles Blackman, Fred Williams and Euan Macleod as well as pieces from the gallery's growing Indigenous collection). It also hosts temporary exhibitions.

NOBBY'S HEAD

Originally an island (in 1770 Captain Cook described it as 'a small clump of an island lying close to shore'), this headland at the entrance to Newcastle's harbour was joined to the mainland by a stone breakwater built by convicts between 1818 and 1846; many of these poor souls were lost to the wild seas during its construction. The walk along the spit towards its historic **lighthouse** (open 10am to 4pm Sunday December to March) and meteorological station is truly exhilarating, with waves crashing about your ears and joggers jostling your elbows.

Fort Scratchley HISTORIC SITE
(☎02-4974 5033; www.fortscratchley.com.au; Nobby's Rd; admission to top area free, guided tour of full site adult/child $15/7.50; ⏲10am-4pm Wed-Mon, last tour departs 2.30pm) Originally constructed during the Crimean War to protect the city from possible invasion, this recently restored fort perched high above Newcastle Harbour was one of the few gun installations in Australia to fire a gun in anger during WWII. On 8 June 1942 a Japanese submarine suddenly surfaced, raining shells on the city. Fort Scratchley returned fire, negating the threat after just four rounds. Learn all about it on a guided tour of the fort and its underground tunnels.

Lock Up CULTURAL CENTRE
(☎02-4925 2265; www.thelockup.info; 90 Hunter St; ⏲10am-4pm Wed-Sun) FREE These days, artists-in-residence are incarcerated in this former police station (1861) rather than prisoners. There's a contemporary art gallery, artists studios and a small law-and-order museum.

Maritime Centre MUSEUM
(☎02-4929 2588; www.maritimecentrenewcastle.org.au; 3 Honeysuckle Dr, Lee Wharf; adult/child $10/5; ⏲10am-4pm Tue-Sun) Learn all about Newcastle's nautical heritage – including its still-working harbour – at this museum occupying a restored harbourfront wharf building.

Wildlife Reserves

Blackbutt Reserve NATURE RESERVE
(☎02-4904 3344; www.newcastle.nsw.gov.au/recreation/blackbutt_reserve; Carnley Ave, Kotara; ⏲9am-5pm) FREE Sitting in a tract of

Newcastle

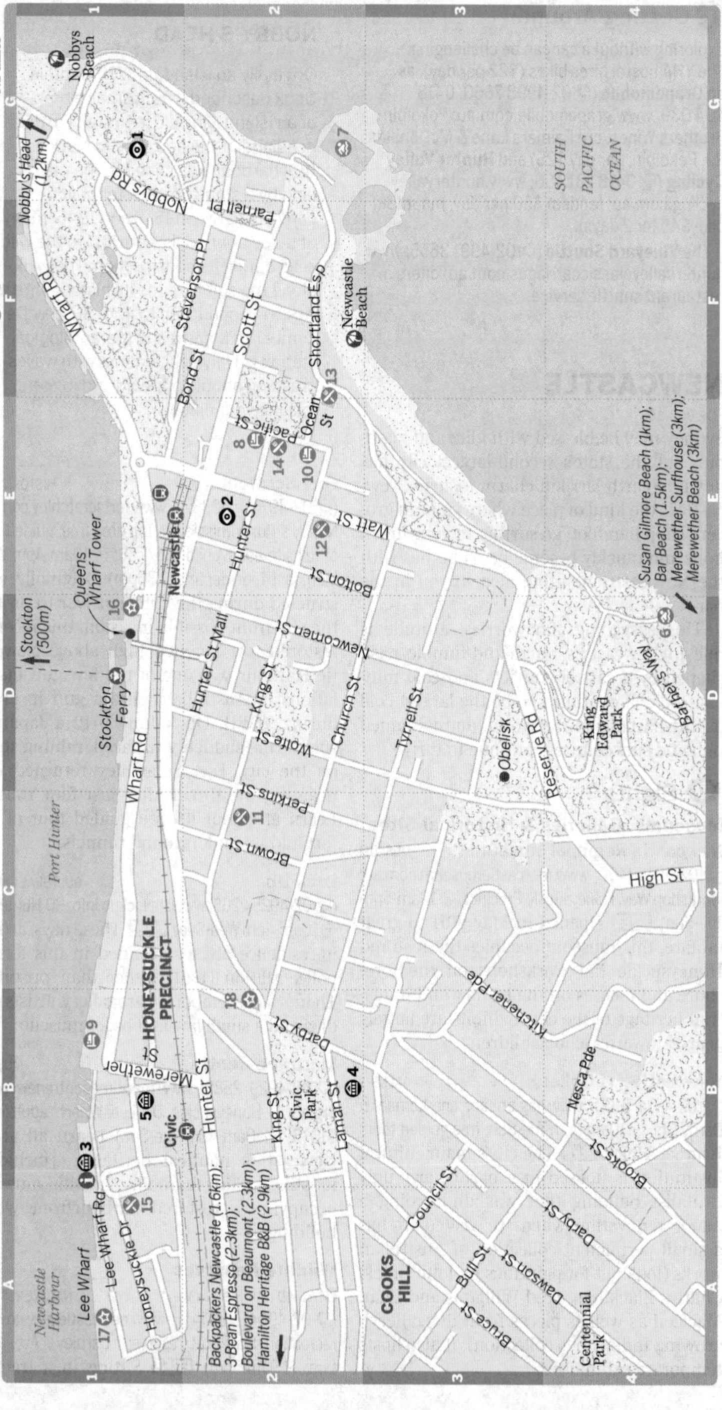
Nobbys Beach
Nobby's Head (1.2km)
Nobbys Rd
Parnell Pl
Wharf Rd
Stevenson Pl
Bond St
Scott St
Shortland Esp
Newcastle Beach
Pacific St
Ocean St
Hunter St
Watt St
Bolton St
Newcomen St
Hunter St Mall
King St
Church St
Tyrrell St
Wolfe St
Perkins St
Brown St
Darby St
Laman St
Civic Park
Council St
Bull St
Bruce St
Dawson St
Darby St
Brooks St
Nesca Pde
Kitchener Pde
High St
Reserve Rd
Obelisk
King Edward Park
Bather's Way
Susan Gilmore Beach (1km); Bar Beach (1.5km); Merewether Surfhouse (3km); Merewether Beach (3km)
SOUTH PACIFIC OCEAN
Stockton (500m)
Stockton Ferry
Queens Wharf Tower
Newcastle
Port Hunter
HONEYSUCKLE PRECINCT
Merewether St
Civic
Lee Wharf
Lee Wharf Rd
Honeysuckle Dr
Newcastle Harbour
Backpackers Newcastle (1.6km); 3 Bean Espresso (2.3km); Boulevard on Beaumont (2.3km); Hamilton Heritage B&B (2.9km)
COOKS HILL
Centennial Park
400 m
0.2 miles

Newcastle

Sights

1	Fort Scratchley	G1
2	Lock Up	E2
3	Maritime Centre	B1
4	Newcastle Art Gallery	B2
5	Newcastle Regional Museum	B1

Activities, Courses & Tours

6	Bogey Hole	D4
7	Ocean Baths	G2

Sleeping

8	Backpackers by the Beach	E2
9	Crowne Plaza	B1
10	Newcastle Beach YHA	E2

Eating

11	Bacchus	C2
12	Bocados	E2
13	Estabar	F2
14	Restaurant Mason	E2
15	Sprout Dining	A1

Entertainment

16	Brewery	D1
17	Honeysuckle Hotel	A1
18	MJ Finnegans	B2

bushland with plenty of walking trails and picnic areas, this council-run reserve has enclosures featuring native critters, including koalas, kangaroos, wallabies and wombats, along with a cacophonic chorus of native birds. Take bus 224 or 317 (30 minutes) to the park's edge then walk 1km to the entrance.

Hunter Wetlands Centre NATURE RESERVE
(☎02-4951 6466; www.wetlands.org.au; 412 Sandgate Rd, Shortland; adult/child $10/5; ⏲9am-4pm) This swampy wonderland is home to over 200 bird and animal species. You can explore via canoe ($14.90 for two hours) or dip in a net and examine the results under a magnifying glass. Bring mosquito repellent if you don't want to contribute to the ecosystem in ways you hadn't intended. Take the Pacific Hwy towards Maitland and turn left at the cemetery, or catch bus 106 or 107 (40 minutes) from the train station. Alight at King Street.

Activities

Swimming & Surfing

At the east end of town, the needs of surfers and swimmers are sated at **Newcastle Beach**, but if you're irrationally paranoid about sharks, the concrete **ocean baths** are a mellow alternative, encased in wonderful multicoloured 1922 architecture. There's a shallow pool for toddlers and a compelling backdrop of heaving ocean and chugging cargo ships. Surfers should goofy-foot it to **Nobby's Beach**, just north of the baths – the fast left-hander known as the Wedge is at its north end.

South of Newcastle Beach, below King Edward Park, is Australia's oldest ocean bath, the convict-carved **Bogey Hole**. It's an atmospheric place to splash about when the surf's crashing over its edge.

The most popular surfing break is at **Bar Beach**, 1km south. If your swimsuit is chafing, scramble around the rocks at the north end to the (unofficial) clothing-optional **Susan Gilmour Beach**, which is only accessible at low tide. At nearby **Merewether Beach** the opening of the winter swimming season is heralded at its ocean baths, where blocks of ice are dumped into the water so that the cold-blooded freaks from the Merewether Mackerels Winter Swimming Club can strut their stuff. Frequent local buses from the CBD run as far south as Bar Beach, but only buses 201, 225 and 310 continue to Merewether.

The city's famous surfing festival, **Surfest** (www.surfest.com), takes place in February or March each year.

Walking & Bicycle Tours

The visitor centre has plenty of brochures outlining self-guided themed walking and bicycle tours of the city. These include the **Bather's Way**, which leads between Nobby's and Merewether Beaches and is dotted with signs describing indigenous, convict and natural history, and the **Newcastle East Heritage Walk**,which heads past colonial highlights in the city centre.

The *Newcastle By Design* brochure, also available at the visitor centre, outlines a short stroll down and around Hunter St, covering some of the inner city's interesting architecture.

Sleeping

There's a thriving backpacker scene in Newcastle, with an extensive party program in city-centre pubs including the Great Northern and the Brewery. Believe it or not, the most popular activity is Tuesday night bingo at the Grand Hotel.

Newcastle Beach YHA HOSTEL $
(☎02-4925 3544; www.yha.com.au; 30 Pacific St, Newcastle East; dm/s/d/f $35/59/85; @ 🛜) This heritage-listed building is close to Newcastle Beach. Inside, it's a bit like an English public school (without the humiliating hazing rituals), featuring grand spaces and high ceilings. There's a wonderful lounge with pool table and big-screen TV, but modern amenities such as air-con, fans or effective heating are nowhere to be seen. Free bodyboard use.

Backpackers by the Beach HOSTEL $
(☎02-4926 3472, 1800 008 972; www.backpackersbythebeach.com.au; 34 Hunter St, Newcastle East; dm $34, d without bathroom $78) Close to the main beach, this small hostel has unadorned decor, cramped dorms and rooms, clean bathrooms, a communal kitchen and a friendly vibe. There's free use of body- and surfboards and free tea and coffee.

Backpackers Newcastle HOSTEL $
(☎1800 33 34 36, 02-4969 3436; www.backpackersnewcastle.com.au; 42-44 Denison St, Hamilton; dm $29, d $70, d without bathroom $55; @ 🏊) Uneasily located in a suburban street (the locals were trying to get it closed down when we visited), this rundown hostel spreads over two houses and has facilities including a small pool, courtyard with hammocks, basic communal kitchen and ping-pong and pool tables. The distance from the beach and the lack of lockers and wi-fi could be problematic.

Stockton Beach Holiday Park CAMPGROUND $
(☎02-4928 1393; www.stocktonbeach.com; 3 Pitt St, Stockton; unpowered site $28-44, powered site $33-55, d cabins $130-203, d villa $145-250; @ 🛜) The water almost laps at your toes when you emerge from your tent or campervan at this tourist park behind the dunes in Stockton. There are BBQs, a camp kitchen, kids' playground areas, a fully equipped laundry and free wi-fi and internet access. Cabins and villas are newly renovated and have facilities such as equipped kitchens and TV/DVD; villas also have air-con.

Hamilton Heritage B&B B&B $$
(☎02-4961 1242; www.accommodationinnewcastle.com.au; 178 Denison St, Hamilton; s $95, d $145-170, f $170-320; ❄ 🛜) It's all florals and frills in this Federation-era home near the Beaumont St cafe strip. The three rooms (two doubles and one family room sleeping up to five) have old-fashioned en suites, fridge, and tea-and-coffee making facilities. There's a communal lounge with TV, and guests can use the kitchen and barbecue. Pet friendly.

Boulevard on Beaumont APARTMENT $$
(☎02-4940 0088; www.boulevardonbeaumont.com.au; 131 Beaumont St, Hamilton; studio apt $159-179, 2-bedroom apt $189-210; P ❄ 🛜) Located in the busy suburb of Hamilton, north of the city centre, these serviced apartments come with a washing machine and dryer, kitchen with dishwasher and lounge/dining area. It claims to be boutique (which it certainly is not), but apartments are clean, comfortable and well priced.

Crowne Plaza HOTEL $$$
(☎02-4907 5000; www.crowneplaza.com.au/newcastle; cnr Merewether St & Wharf Rd, Newcastle; r $185-355; P ❄ @ 🛜 🏊) This large, beige modern hotel is right on the waterfront and is easily the best sleeping option in town. Service is excellent and the pool is a real plus. Breakfast costs $20-33.

Eating

Darby St in Cooks Hill is the main cafe strip, but the restaurants along its length are uninspiring. The same applies to the tacky joints along Honeysuckle Wharf and along the foreshore. The **Newcastle City Farmers Market** (www.newcastlecityfarmersmarket.com.au) is held at Newcastle Showground, Griffiths Rd, Broadmeadows most Sundays between 8am and 1pm.

Estabar CAFE $
(61 Shortland Esplanade, Newcastle East; breakfast dishes $6-15, light lunch dish $15; ⏲6.30am-6pm) Start the day with breakfast at this busy cafe overlooking Newcastle Beach. The sourdough toast is served with homemade jam made with seasonal fruit, and many of the other menu offerings feature local organic produce – check the blackboards for daily specials. It also sells gelato.

3 Bean Espresso CAFE $
(103 Tudor St, Hamilton; breakfast $7-16, lunch mains $18-21; ⏲6.15am-5pm Mon-Fri, to 3pm Sat) 🍃 Novocastrians love going out for a weekend breakfast, and this bustling cafe is one of their venues of choice. Innumerable variations of eggs are the main attraction, and both the coffee and fruit-laden iced tea are good. Enter off Beaumont St.

Bocados SPANISH **$$**
(☎02-4925 2801; www.bocados.com.au; 25 King St, Newcastle East; tapas $7-20, raciones $17-33; ⏰6pm-late Tue, noon-3pm & 6pm-late Wed-Sat, 5pm-late Sun) Only a castanet click away from Newcastle Beach, Bocado has a menu featuring tapas (small plates) and raciones (larger plates) that trawl the Iberian peninsula for their inspiration. There are plenty of Spanish drops on the menu, or you can BYO (Tuesday and Wednesday only, corkage $7 per bottle).

Restaurant Mason MODERN AUSTRALIAN **$$**
(☎02-4926 1014; www.restaurantmason.com; 3/35 Hunter St, Newcastle; mains $27-34; ⏰noon-3.30 & 6pm-late Tue-Thu, 8-11.30am & noon-late Fri, 8-11.30am & 6pm-late Sat, 8-11.30am & noon-3pm Sun) Newcastle's Mall isn't picturesque, but this breezy restaurant at its beach end provides a bit of an antidote. Tables are set under the plane trees outside, and the main dining space opens to the elements – it has a casual, summery feel. Dishes are available in full and half serves and are simply conceived, making the most of the colour and freshness of local produce.

Next-door **Cafe Mason** is a more affordable but no less satisfying option, serving homemade pastries, pies and quiches along with excellent coffee. It's open for breakfast and lunch daily.

Merewether Surfhouse MODERN AUSTRALIAN **$$**
(☎02-4918 0000; www.surfhouse.com.au; Henderson Pde, Merewether; restaurant mains $29-40, pizzas in bar $19, cafe meals $13-20, breakfast dishes $7-20; ⏰cafe 7am-3pm, restaurant noon-3pm & 6-9 Tue-Sun, terrace bar 11.30am-late) Watch the action on Merewether Beach from one of the many spaces in this newly built and architecturally notable complex. You can enjoy a pizza in the top-floor terrace bar, sophisticated Mod Oz dishes in the adjoining restaurant, breakfast or a fish & chip lunch in the cafe on the beach promenade or a gelato from the kiosk. Views are spectacular and it's perfectly acceptable to limit yourself to a drink in the bar or a coffee in the cafe.

Sprout Dining MODERN MEDITERRANEAN **$$**
(☎02-4023 3565; http://sproutcatering.com.au; 1/2 Honeysuckle Drive, Newcastle; mains $32; ⏰6-9pm Wed, noon-2pm & 6-9pm Thu-Sat, noon-2pm Sun) The menu changes weekly at this casually elegant bistro opposite the Maritime Museum at Honeysickle Wharf, but always features an array of delicious house-made pasta (small/large $16/27). Crowd-pleasing mains and desserts are complemented by a good range of regional wines.

Bacchus MODERN AUSTRALIAN **$$$**
(☎02-4927 1332; www.bacchusnewcastle.com.au; 141 King St, Newcastle; dinner mains $45-49, degustation $90-140; ⏰6-11pm Tue-Sat) A decadent Roman god has transformed this former Methodist mission into a very atmospheric place to splurge (not purge – this isn't ancient Rome, after all). The surrounds are extremely elegant, dishes are assured and the wine list is excellent.

Drinking & Entertainment

MJ Finnegans PUB
(www.finneganshotel.com.au; 21-23 Darby St, Newcastle; ⏰Mon-Sat) The place for backpacker meals, trivia, pool competitions and, on the weekends, live bands and DJs.

Brewery MICROBREWERY
(http://qwb.com.au; 150 Wharf Rd, Newcastle) Perched on Queens Wharf; the views and outdoor tables are sought after by both Novocastrian office workers and uni students. Has regular live music Wednesday to Sunday and decent food.

Honeysuckle Hotel PUB
(www.honeysucklehotel.com.au; Lee Wharf, Honeysuckle Dr, Newcastle; ⏰10am-11pm Mon-Thu, to midnight Fri & Sat, to 10pm Sun) The deck at this waterfront place, located in the trendy Honeysuckle precinct, is a perfect spot for a sundowner. A DJ takes centre stage on summer Sundays between 4pm and 7pm.

Information

If you've got a laptop with wireless capability, head to Beaumont St in Hamilton or to the Hunter St Mall between Tudor and Donald Sts, where you can access one hour of free wi-fi broadband.

John Hunter Hospital (☎02-4921 3000; Lookout Rd, New Lambton Heights) Has 24-hour emergency care.

Visitor Centre (☎1800 654 558; www.visitnewcastle.com.au; Lee Wharf, 3 Honeysuckle Dr, Newcastle; ⏰10am-4pm Tue-Sun) Located in the foyer of the Maritime Centre, this office is volunteer-operated and although well-intentioned, isn't particularly useful

Getting There & Away

AIR

Newcastle Airport (☎02-4928 9800; www.newcastleairport.com.au) is at Williamtown, 23km north of the city.

Virgin Australia (☎13 67 89; www.virgin-australia.com) and **Jetstar** (☎13 15 38; www.jetstar.com) both fly to Brisbane and Melbourne. Brindabella Airlines (p70) services Canberra, Aeropelican (p70) flies to Sydney and Rex (p70) flies to Ballina and Sydney.

BUS

Nearly all long-distance buses stop behind the Newcastle train station. **Greyhound** (☎1300 GREYHOUND, 1300 4739 46863; www.greyhound.com.au) heads to Forster ($51, three hours, daily) and Port Macquarie ($77, four hours,two daily). **Premier Motor Service** (☎13 34 10; www.premierms.com.au) runs a daily bus to/from Sydney ($34, 2½ hours) and Brisbane ($76, 14 hours).

Rover Coaches (☎02-4990 1699; www.rovercoaches.com.au) heads to Cessnock ($4.50, 1½ hours) in the Hunter Valley. **Port Stephens Coaches** (☎02-4982 2940; www.pscoaches.com.au) has regular buses between Nelson Bay and Newcastle ($4.60, 1¾ hours). **Busways** (☎1800 043 263; www.busways.com.au) operates services to/from Hawks Nest via Tea Gardens ($20, 1½ hours, three daily).

TRAIN

A better option than the buses, **CityRail** (☎13 15 00; www.cityrail.info) operates frequent servces between Newcastle and Sydney (adult/child $8.40/4.30, three hours).

Getting Around

TO & FROM THE AIRPORT

Port Stephens Coaches' (p154) service 130 heads to Williamtown airport frequently ($5, 40 minutes) en route to Nelsons Bay.

Shuttle bus services from the airport to Newcastle cost approximately $35 per person ($45 for two people). To book these or shuttles to other destinations in the area, contact **Newcastle Airport Information Services** (☎02-4928 9822; 7am-7pm).

A taxi to Newcastle city centre will cost around $65.

BUS

Newcastle has an extensive network of **local buses** (☎13 15 00; www.newcastlebuses.info). A fare-free shuttle bus (No 555) follows a 20-minute one-way loop from Newcastle railway station to the Honeysuckle precinct, the Hamilton cafe precinct and King St between 9am and 2.40pm (weekdays) and 9am and 5.40pm (weekends). Other fares are time-based (one hour/four hours/all day $3.60/7/10.50); tickets can be purchased from the bus driver. The main depot is next to Newcastle train station.

FERRY

The **Stockton ferry** (adult/child $2.50/1.20) leaves every half-hour from Queens Wharf between 5.15am and midnight on Friday and Saturday, until 11pm Monday to Thursday and until 10pm on Sunday. Purchase tickets on board.

TRAIN

Services terminate at Newcastle station after stopping at Broadmeadow, Hamilton, Wickham and Civic stations.

MID-NORTH COAST

Newcastle to Taree

From Newcastle and the nearby Hunter Valley, you can choose to zoom north along the Pacific Hwy or enjoy a far more pleasant trip by making a series of meandering diversions along the coast.

Port Stephens

POP 28,100

This stunning sheltered bay is about an hour's drive north of Newcastle, occupying a submerged valley that stretches more than 20km inland. Framing its southern edge is the narrow **Tomaree Peninsula**, blessed with near-deserted beaches, national parks and an extraordinary sand-dune system. The main centre, **Nelson Bay**, is home to both a fishing fleet and an armada of tourist vessels, capitalising on its status as the 'dolphin capital of Australia'.

Just east of Nelson Bay, and virtually merged with it, is the slightly smaller **Shoal Bay**, with a long beach that's great for swimming (but only in the morning, as winds come up in the afternoon). The road ends a short drive south from here at **Fingal Bay**, with another lovely beach on the fringes of **Tomaree National Park**. The park stretches west around clothing-optional **Samurai Beach**, a popular surfing spot, and **One Mile Beach**, a gorgeous semicircle of the softest sand and bluest water favoured by surfers, beachcombers and idle romantics.

The park ends at the somnolent surfside village of **Anna Bay**, which has as a backdrop the incredible Worimi Conservation Lands. Gan Gan Rd connects Anna Bay, One Mile Beach and Samurai Beach with Nelson Bay Rd.

WORIMI COUNTRY

The area from the Tomaree Peninsula to Forster and as far west as Gloucester is the land of the Worimi people, who have lived in this region for thousands of years. Very little of it is now in their possession, but in 2001 the sand dunes of the Stockton Bight were returned to them, creating the Worimi Conservation Lands. The Worimi people in turn entered an agreement to co-manage it with the NPWS.

Sacred places and occupation sites are scattered throughout the region. **Dark Point Aboriginal Place** in Myall Lakes National Park has been significant to the Worimi for around 4000 years. Local lore has it that in the late 19th century it was the site of one of many massacres of Aboriginal people at the hands of white settlers, when a group was herded onto the rocks and pushed off.

For more information, look out for the *Worimi Conservation Lands* brochure published by the NSW Department of Environment & Climate Change.

Sights

The **Worimi Conservation Lands** at Stockton Bight are the longest moving sand dunes in the southern hemisphere, stretching over 35km. In the heart of it, it's possible to become so surrounded by shimmering sand that you'll lose sight of the ocean or any sign of life. It's incredibly evocative. At the far west end of the beach, the wreck of the *Sygna* founders in the water.

Thanks to the generosity of the Worimi people, whose land this is, you're able to roam around (provided you don't disturb any Aboriginal sites), camp within 100m of the high-tide mark (you'll need a portable toilet), drive along the beach (4WD only; permit required) and mash up the sand dunes within the designated recreational-vehicle area. Get your permits ($10 for three days) from the Port Stephens Visitor Centre (p156) or NPWS office (p156) in Nelson Bay; allow seven days for the pass to be mailed to you.

Tomaree National Park NATIONAL PARK
(www.environment.nsw.gov.au/nationalparks) Tomaree National Park is a wonderfully wild expanse harbouring several threatened species, including the spotted-tailed quoll and powerful owl. If you keep your eyes peeled you're bound to spot a koala or wallaby. At the eastern end of Shoal Bay there's a short walk to the surf at unpatrolled **Zenith Beach** (beware of rips and strong undercurrents), or you can tackle the strenuous **Tomaree Head Summit Walk** (1km, one hour return) and be rewarded by stunning ocean views; birdwatchers should watch out for the Gould's petrel – the offshore islands of Cabbage Tree and Boondelbah are this endangered species' only nesting site in the world. Longer walks are detailed in *Bushwalks Around Port Stephens* ($5.95), a pamphlet available from the NPWS office and the visitor centre.

Heritage Light House Cottage HISTORIC BUILDING
(☎02-4984 2505; ⏲10am-4pm) FREE The restored 1875 Heritage Light House Cottage at Nelson Head has a small museum with displays on the area's history and a tearoom. The views of Port Stephens are suitably inspiring.

Activities

Imagine Cruises DOLPHIN WATCHING
(☎02-4984 9000; www.imaginecruises.com.au; Dock C, d'Albora Marinas) Eco-accredited trips, including 3½-hour Sail, Swim, Snorkel and Dolphin Watch trips (adult/child $60/30, December to March), 90-minute Dolphin Watch cruises ($26/14, December to April), three-hour Whale Watch cruises ($60/25, mid-May to mid-November); two-hour Seafood Dinner Cruise ($39/20; December to April) and 3½-hour Swim with the Dolphins experience ($229; weekends only).

Anna Bay Surf School SURFING
(☎0411 419 576; www.annabaysurfschool.com.au; Hannah Pde, One Mile Beach Holiday Park; introductory/2-/3-day lessons $60/110/165) Surf lessons and board hire (one/two hour $17/28).

Moonshadow DOLPHIN WATCHING
(☎02-4984 9388; www.moonshadow.com.au; shop 3, 35 Stockton St) Dolphin watching (adult/child $20.80/10.80), whale watching ($48/20, May to November) and dinner cruises ($69/25.50). Eco-accredited.

Blue Water Sea Kayaking SEA KAYAKING
(☎0405 033 518; www.kayakingportstephens.com.au) Offers a range of paddle-powered excursions, including hour-long beginner tours (adult/child $30/20), 1½-hour sunset tours ($35/25) and 2½-hour discovery tours ($45/35).

Port Stephens 4WD Tours 4WD
(☎02-4984 4760; www.portstephens4wd.com.au; shop 3, 35 Stockton St) Offers a 1½-hour beach and dune tour (adult/child $49/29) and a sandboarding experience ($26/19).

Sleeping

Consider staying at Anna Bay or One Mile Beach so you can take advantage of their tranquil settings near great beaches.

★Port Stephens YHA Samurai Beach Bungalows HOSTEL $
(☎02-4982 1921; www.samuraiportstephens.com; Frost Rd; dm $34-40, d $89-121; @ 🛜 🏊) These attractively furnished wooden-floored cabins are arranged around a swimming pool and set in koala-populated bushland dotted with Asian sculpture. There's a bush kitchen with BBQs and a ramshackle games shed with pool table.

★Melaleuca Surfside Backpackers HOSTEL $
(☎02-4981 9422; www.melaleucabackpackers.com.au; 2 Koala Pl; camp sites per person $20, dm $32-35, d from $100; @ 🛜) Architect-designed wooden cabins are set amid peaceful scrub inhabited by koalas and kookaburras at this friendly, well-run place. There's a welcoming lounge area and kitchen, and the owners offer dune surfing and other day trips.

Wanderers Retreat HOTEL $$
(☎02-4982 1702; www.wanderersretreat.com; 7 Koala Pl; d cabin $125-260, treehouse d $195-285; ❄ 🏊) 🍃 Guests can make like Robinson Crusoe in one of the three luxury treehouses at this tranquil retreat. There are also seven two-bedroom cottages.

Bali at the Bay APARTMENTS $$$
(☎02-4981 2964; www.baliatthebay.com.au; 1 Achilles St; d $260-300; ❄) Two exceedingly beautiful self-contained apartments, chock-full of flower-garlanded Buddhas and carved wood, do a good job of living up to the name. The bathrooms are exquisite and spa treatments are available.

Eating

Yikes! The eating options on this part of the coast are, for the most part, ridiculously pretentious (and overpriced). Fortunately, all of the accommodation options we have recommended have self-catering facilities.

Red Ned's Pies FAST FOOD $
(www.redneds.com.au; shop 3/17-19 Stockton St; pies $6-8; ⏲6am-5pm) Piemaker Barry Kelly learnt his trade in top-shelf international hotels and his philosophy is simple: he gets a kick out of watching people stare at his specials board, goggle-eyed (anyone for crocodile in parsley, shallot and white-wine sauce?).

Point MODERN AUSTRALIAN $$
(☎02-4984 7111; www.thepointrestaurant.com.au; Soldiers Point Marina, Sunset Blvd; lunch mains $19-28, dinner $34-45; ⏲lunch & dinner Tue-Sun) When locals celebrate romantic milestones, this restaurant on the marina at Soldiers Point is their number-one choice. Views from the balcony and glassed dining room are lovely, and the menu has loads of tempting seafood dishes. The mixed grilled seafood is a good order. It's 9km west of Nelson Bay.

Information

NPWS Office (☎02-4984 8200; www.nationalparks.nsw.gov.au; 12b Teramby Rd; ⏲8.30am-4.30pm Mon-Fri)
Visitor Centre (☎1800 808 900; www.portstephens.org.au; Victoria Pde; ⏲9am-5pm)

Getting There & Around

Port Stephens Coaches (☎02-4982 2940; www.pscoaches.com.au) regularly zip around Port Stephens' townships heading to Newcastle and Newcastle Airport ($4.60, 1¾ hours).

Port Stephens Ferry Service (☎0412 682 117) chugs from Nelson Bay to Tea Gardens and back three times a day (return fare adult/child $22/11, one hour each way).

Tea Gardens & Hawks Nest

POP 2100 (TEA GARDENS), 1123 (HAWKS NEST)

Opposite Nelson Bay, on the north shore of Port Stephens, are Tea Gardens and Hawks Nest. Sporting the most quaintly evocative names on the coast, this tranquil pair of towns in the Great Lakes district straddle the mouth of the Myall River, linked by the graceful, curved Singing Bridge. Tea Gardens has a quiet, laid-back charm; it's a river culture here, older and genteel. At Hawks Nest it's all about the beaches. **Jimmys Beach** fronts a glasslike stretch of water facing Nelson Bay, while stunning **Bennetts Beach** looks to the ocean and Broughton Island.

Sleeping & Eating

Tea Gardens Hotel Motel HOTEL $
(02-4997 0203; www.teagardenshotelmotel.com.au; cnr Marine Dr & Maxwell St; r from $65;) On the riverfront, this popular watering hole offers basic rooms set around a rear garden with a small kids' play area.

Tea Gardens Boat Shed CAFE $
(02-4997 0307; www.teagardensboatshed.com.au; 110 Marine Dr; breakfast dishes $5-17, lunch mains $17-27, dinner mains $16.50-29.50; 8.30am-11am, noon-2.30pm & 6-9pm Wed-Sat, 8.30am-11am & noon-2.30pm Sun-Tue) You'll have to cope with a few shrieks from the local pelicans when you choose to devour your meal at this former boatshed right on the water. And it's no wonder they're miffed – everything's delicious. The coffee is good and the deck is a lovely spot for a sunset drink.

Information

Tea Gardens Visitor Centre (02-4997 0111; www.greatlakes.org.au; Myall St; 10am-4pm) Near the bridge.

Getting There & Around

While only 5km from Nelson Bay as the cockatoo flies, the drive necessitates returning to the Pacific Hwy via Medowie and then doubling back – a distance of 81km. The alternative is the Port Stephens Ferry Service (p156).

If you're continuing north, the stunning scenic route through Myall Lakes National Park involves a short ferry crossing at Bombah Point.

Busways (1800 043 263; www.busways.com.au) operates services to/from Newcastle ($20, 1½ hours, three daily).

Myall Lakes National Park

On an extravagantly pretty section of the coast, this large **national park** (www.environment.nsw.gov.au/nationalparks; vehicle admission $7) incorporates a patchwork of lakes, islands, dense littoral rainforest and beaches. The lakes support an incredible quantity and variety of bird life, including bowerbirds, white-bellied sea eagles and tawny frogmouths. There are paths through coastal rainforest and past beach dunes at **Mungo Brush** in the south, perfect for spotting wildflowers, kangaroos, wallabies and bandicoots.

ABORIGINAL STORIES

One of the more interesting tourism initiatives of recent times in coastal NSW is the gathering together of numerous Aboriginal stories from the region. The stories range from tales from the Dreaming to narratives tied to far more recent events. They're available on www.pacificcoast.com.au – click on the 'Saltwater Freshwater Aboriginal Stories' tab.

The best beaches and surf are in the north around beautiful, secluded **Seal Rocks**, a bushy hamlet hugging Sugarloaf Bay. It has a great beach, with emerald-green rock pools, epic ocean views and golden sand. Take the short walk to the **Sugarloaf Point Lighthouse**, where the views are sublime. There's a water-choked gorge along the way and a detour to lonely **Lighthouse Beach**, a popular surfing spot. The path around the lighthouse leads to a lookout over the actual Seal Rocks – islets that provide sanctuary for Australia's northernmost colony of Australian fur seals. During summer breeding the seals are out in abundance and you'll do well to bring binoculars. **Humpback whales** swim past Seal Rocks during their annual migration and can sometimes be seen from the shore.

About a half-hour by boat from Nelson Bay, **Broughton Island** is uninhabited except for muttonbirds, little penguins and an enormous diversity of fish species. The diving is tops and the beaches incredibly secluded.

Sleeping & Eating

Camp Sites CAMPGROUND $
(www.nationalparks.nsw.gov.au; sites per adult $7.50-10, child $3.50-5) There are numerous campgrounds dotted around the park; none can be booked ahead of your visit.

Seal Rocks Holiday Park CAMPGROUND $
(02-4997 6164; www.sealrocksholidaypark.com.au; Kinka Rd, Seal Rocks; unpowered camp sites $28-35, powered camp & caravan sites $32-40, cabins $75-205;) This excellent place offers a range of budget accommodation styles

WORTH A TRIP

NORFOLK ISLAND

Norfolk Island (population 2302) is a pine-studded speck adrift in the South Pacific Ocean, 1600km northeast of Sydney and 1000km northwest of Auckland. It's the largest of a cluster of three islands emerging from the underwater Norfolk Ridge, which stretches from New Zealand to New Caledonia, the closest landfall, almost 700km north.

Polynesians were in Norfolk 800 years before it was first seen by Captain Cook in 1774. From 1788, only weeks after the First Fleet reached Port Jackson to settle Sydney, until 1855 it was twice used as a penal colony and became known as 'hell in the Pacific' after being declared 'a place of the extremest punishment short of death'.

After 1855 the prisoners were shipped off to Van Diemen's Land (Tasmania) and Queen Victoria handed the island over to the descendants of the mutineers from the HMS *Bounty*, who had outgrown their adopted Pitcairn Island. About a third of the present population is descended from the 194 Pitcairners and their Tahitian wives who arrived on 8 June 1856.

The island measures only 8km by 5km, with vertical cliffs defining much of the coastline. **Kingston** is on Slaughter Bay on the island's south coast. The service town of **Burnt Pine** is in the centre of the island, near the airport, while **Norfolk Island National Park** (www.environment.gov.au/parks/norfolk) encompasses the hillier northern part of the island.

Covering 650 hectares, the national park offers bushwalking, with awesome views from Mt Pitt (316m) and Mt Bates (318m). There's a sheltered beach at Emily Bay in the south, from where glass-bottom boats depart to ogle the coral below.

Snorkelling around the Kingston breakwall is worthwhile; hire gear in Burnt Pine. Alternatively, several companies arrange snorkelling, diving and fishing trips.

Kingston, built by convicts of the second penal colony, is Norfolk's star attraction. Many historic buildings have been restored – the best of these, along **Quality Row**, still house the island's administrators, as well as four small-but-engaging **museums** (www.museums.gov.nf; single/combined ticket $10/25, children free; ⌚11am-3pm Mon-Sat; Pier Store Museum also open Sun).

By the shore are the ruins of an early pentagonal prison, a lime pit (into which convict murder victims were sometimes thrown) and the **convict cemetery**.

Bounty Folk Museum (Middlegate Rd; admission $10; ⌚10am-4pm) is crammed with motley convict-era and *Bounty* souvenirs. **Fletcher's Mutiny Cyclorama** (www.norfolkcyclorama.nlk.nf; Queen Elizabeth Ave; per person from $11.50; ⌚9am-5pm Mon-Sat, 10am-3pm Sun) is a 360-degree panoramic painting depicting the *Bounty* mutiny and Norfolk Island history.

There is plenty of accommodation on Norfolk, though none of it is budget; check out www.norfolkisland.com.au/accommodation for listings. All accommodation must be booked in advance. Most visitors come on package deals, sometimes including car hire and breakfast.

The **visitor centre** (☎6723-22 147; www.norfolkisland.com.au; Taylors Rd, Burnt Pine; ⌚8.30am-5pm Mon, Tue, Thu & Fri, to 4pm Wed, to 3pm Sat & Sun) is next to the post office or check out the websites www.norfolkbedbank.com and www.gonorfolkisland.com.

The island is a 2½-hour flight from east-coast Australia, 1¾ hours from Auckland. **Air New Zealand** (☎in New Zealand 0800 737 000; www.airnewzealand.co.nz) flies from Auckland (from $475 return) once a week, with more frequent flights to/from Sydney (from $558), Melbourne (from $980), Newcastle (from $980) and Brisbane (from $508).

All visitors must have a valid passport and a return airline ticket. Australian and New Zealand passport holders don't require visas, but all other nationalities must obtain an Australian entry visa before flying.

Island time is GMT plus 11½ hours – 1½ hours ahead of Sydney (30 minutes ahead in summer).

including grassed camping and caravan sites that are right on the water.

Lighthouse Keepers' Cottages HISTORIC HOTEL $$$
(02-4997 6590; www.sealrockslighthouseaccommodation.com.au; cottage $340-450;) Spend a weekend in one of the three old lighthouse keeper's cottages at Sugarloaf Point lighthouse accommodation. If the crashing waves and wildlife aren't distracting enough, each cottage has queen beds, plasma televisions, DVD players and barbecues.

Bombah Point Eco Cottages BUNGALOW $$$
(02-4997 4401; www.bombah.com.au; 969 Bombah Pt Rd; d $220-275;) This is a cluster of architect-designed and attractive self-contained cottages. Each cottage sleeps between five and six guests. The 'Eco' in the name is well-deserved: sewage is treated on site using a bioreactor system, electricity comes courtesy of solar panels and filtered rainwater tanks provide water.

Getting There & Away

At Bombah Broadwater the **Bombah Point ferry** (per car $5) crosses every half-hour from 8am to 6pm; the trip takes five minutes. A 10km section of Bombah Point Rd, heading to the Pacific Hwy at Bulahdelah, is unsealed.

Pacific Palms

POP 685

Secreted between Myall Lakes and Booti Booti National Parks, Pacific Palms is one of those places that well-heeled city dwellers slink off to on weekends. If you're camping in either of the parks you might find yourself here when the espresso cravings kick in – there are a couple of excellent cafes.

Most of the houses cling to **Blueys Beach** or **Boomerang Beach**, both long stretches of golden sand popular with surfers. The most popular swimming beach in the area (and the only one that's patrolled) is **Elizabeth Beach**, on the southern edge of nearby Booti Booti National Park

Sleeping & Eating

Mobys Beachside Retreat RESORT $$
(02-6591 0000; www.mobysretreat.com.au; 4 Red Gum Rd, Boomerang Beach; apt 1-bedroom $180-240, 2-bedroom $250-300, 3-bedroom $300-380;) This holiday resort lies directly opposite Boomerang Beach and crams 75 self-contained holiday apartments with sleek decor and excellent amenities into a relatively small area. There's a tennis court, swimming pool and children's playground on site, as well as a good restaurant (mains $25 to $28).

Twenty by Twelve CAFE $
(shop 8, 207 Boomerang Dr; breakfast dishes $4-13, wraps $9.50, burgers & pies $14.50; 7.30am-3pm) Camping is all very well, but try getting a coffee like this out of a billycan. It also sells light meals, local organic produce and delicious deli treats.

Recky AUSTRALIAN $$
(The Lakes Way; mains $14-23; 11am-late) The Recky is actually the Pacific Palms Recreation Club and, yep, it's one of those sign-in clubs with cheap booze, a bistro and occasional live music. And be warned: its slogan is 'Get wrecked at the Recky'.

Information

Visitor Centre (02-6554 0123; Boomerang Dr; 10am-4pm)

Getting There & Away

To get here, **Busways** (1800 043 263; www.busways.com.au) stops at Blueys Beach on its journey between Taree/Forster and Newcastle.

Booti Booti National Park

This 1567-hectare **national park** (www.environment.nsw.gov.au/nationalparks; vehicle admission $7) stretches along a skinny peninsula with **Seven Mile Beach** on its eastern side and **Wallis Lake** on its west. The northern section of the park is swathed in coastal rainforest and topped by 224m **Cape Hawke**. At the Cape Hawke headland there's a **viewing platform**, well worth the sweat of climbing the 420-something steps.

Green Cathedral is an interesting space (consecrated in 1940) that consists of wooden pews under the palm trees, looking to the lake.

There's self-registration camping at the **Ruins Campground** (camping per adult $10-14, child $5-7), at the southern end of Seven Mile Beach. **Lakeside Escape B&B** (02-6557 6400; www.lakesideescape.com.au; 85 Green Point Dr, Green Point; s/d from $145/185; @) is located in the Green Point fishing village on the park's western edge. All three rooms overlook Wallis Lake and there's a heated spa on the outdoor deck. Children are not welcome.

WORTH A TRIP

BARRINGTON TOPS NATIONAL PARK

Lying on the rugged Barrington Plateau, this World Heritage–listed wilderness (www.environment.nsw.gov.au/nationalparks) rises to a height of almost 1600m. Northern rainforest butts into southern sclerophyll here, creating one of Australia's most diverse ecosystems, with giant strangler figs, mossy Antarctic beech forests, limpid rainforest swimming holes and pocket-sized pademelons (note: it is illegal to put pademelons in your pocket).

Bushwalks, mountain biking, horse riding, canoeing, fishing and 4WDing are the order of the day here. The **Barrington Trail** is particularly popular for 4WDing, but it's closed from June to September. Be prepared for cold snaps, and even snow, at any time.

Barrington Outdoor Adventure Centre (☎ 02-6558 2093; www.boac.com.au; 126 Thunderbolts Way; 1-/2-day kayaking tours $160/385, 1-day mountain-biking tour $170, 2-day mountain-bike/kayak tour $395) specialises in downhill mountain-biking adventures and white-water kayaking trips. It also hires out mountain bikes, canoes and kayaks (one-day hire mountain bike/canoe/kayak $60/85/65).

Camping is possible throughout the park (adult per night $5 to $10, child $3 to $5). You can access the camping grounds at Devils Hole, Wombat Creek, Polblue, Horse Swamp and Gloucester River in a 2WD, but you'll need a 4WD for those at Little Murray, Gummi Falls and Junction Pools.

Dam It Getaway (☎ 02-6558 4272; www.damitgetaway.com; 81 Kia Ora Hill Rd, Gloucester; 2-bed cabin from $170 plus $50/25 per extra adult/child) offers simple but well-maintained accommodation close to Gloucester.

The park can be accessed from Scone, Dungog and Gloucester. For more information contact the NPWS office in **Gloucester** (☎ 02-6538 5300; 59 Church St, Gloucester; ⏲ 8.30am-4.30pm Mon-Fri).

The **NPWS office** (☎ 02-6591 0300; ⏲ 8.30am-4.30pm) is at Ruins Campground.

Taree to Port Macquarie

From Forster-Tuncurry the Pacific Hwy swings inland to Taree in the fertile Manning Valley. Further west into the valley is **Wingham Brush Nature Reserve**, a patch of idyllic rainforest that is home to giant, otherworldly Moreton Bay figs and flocks of flying foxes. The nearby town of **Wingham** combines English county cuteness with a rugged lumberjack history – an intriguing combination. Consider stopping here for two reasons. One is to eat at **Bent on Food** (www.bentonfood.com.au; mains $9.90-25; ⏲ 8am-5pm Mon-Fri, 8am-3pm Sat, 9am-3pm Sun), one of the best cafes in rural NSW with great food such as the warm pork belly citrus salad with walnuts. The second is to stay overnight at the **Bank Guesthouse** (☎ 02-6553 5068; www.thebankandtellers.com.au; 48 Bent St; r $165-185; ❄ 📶), a friendly place offering stylishly decorated rooms in a 1920s bank manager's residence, as well as a self-catering guesthouse cottage in the rear garden. **CountryLink** (☎ 02-8202 2000; www.countrylink.info) trains from Sydney stop at Taree and Wingham ($57, 5½ hours, two daily). The train continues to Coffs Harbour ($38, 3½ hours, two daily).

Back on the Pacific Hwy, a half-hour drive north will bring you to the turn-off to the small village of **Harrington**, while **Crowdy Head** is an even smaller fishing village 6km northeast of Harrington at the edge of **Crowdy Bay National Park** (www.environment.nsw.gov.au/nationalparks; vehicle admission $7). It was supposedly named when Captain Cook witnessed a gathering of Aborigines on the headland in 1770. The views from the 1878 **lighthouse** are breathtaking – out to the limitless ocean, down to the deserted beaches and back to the apparent wilderness of the coastal plain and mountains. It's like Cook never arrived at all.

Known for its rock formations and rugged cliffs, the 10,001-hectare national park here backs onto a long and beautiful beach that sweeps from Crowdy Head north to **Diamond Head**. There's a lovely 4.8km (two-hour) loop track over the Diamond headland.

The roads running through the park are unsealed and full of potholes, but the dappled light of the gum trees makes it a lovely drive. There are basic **camp sites** (☎02-6582 3355; site per adult/child $10/5) at Diamond Head, Indian Head, Kylie's Hut and Kylie's Beach, as well as in the southern part of the park at **Crowdy Gap** (☎02-6552 4097; site per adult/child $10/5). You'll need to bring water in for all of them.

Leaving the national park via Diamond Head Rd, continue through to Laurieton and onto the tiny town of Kew, from where you can veer off the highway and follow Ocean Dr all the way to Port Macquarie. Along the way, you'll pass **Dooragan National Park**, dominated by **North Brother Mountain** with lookouts and incredible views. Nearby is **North Haven**, an absolute blinder of a surf beach.

Port Macquarie

POP 41,491

Pleasure has long replaced punishment as the main purpose of Port Macquarie. Formed in 1821 as a place of hard labour for those convicts who reoffended after being transported to Sydney, it was the third town to be established on the Australian mainland. These days, though, Port, as it's commonly known, is overwhelmingly holiday-focused, making the most of its position at the entrance to the subtropical coast, its beautiful surf beaches and its laid-back coffee culture.

Sights

Port is blessed with awesome beaches. Surfing is excellent at **Town**, **Flynns** and **Lighthouse Beaches**, all of which are patrolled in summer. The rainforest runs down to the sand at **Shelly** and **Miners Beaches**, the latter of which is an unofficial nude beach.

It's possible to walk all the way from the Town Wharf to Lighthouse Beach. On the way, the **breakwater** at the bottom of town has been transformed into a work of community guerrilla art. The elaborately painted rocks range from beautiful memorials for lost loved ones to 'party hard'-type inanities.

Away from the centre, between Miners and Lighthouse Beaches, little **Tacking Point Lighthouse** (1879) commands a headland offering immense views up and down the coast. It's a great spot to watch the waves rolling in to the long beautiful stretch of Lighthouse Beach.

In addition to the following sights, there's a **foreshore market** of crafts and foods from 8am to 1pm on the second Saturday of the month. It takes place in Westport Park, at the corner of Buller and Park Streets.

The visitor centre (p165) has a list of local wineries within a day's journey of town.

★ **Koala Hospital** NATURE RESERVE
(www.koalahospital.org.au; Lord St; admission by donation; 8am-4.30pm) Koalas living near urban areas are at risk from traffic and domestic animals, and more than 200 each year end up in this shelter. You can walk around the open-air enclosures any time of the day, but you'll learn more during the tours (3pm). Some of the longer-term patients have signs detailing their stories and you can sign up to 'adopt' one of the koalas. Check the website for details of volunteer opportunities.

★ **Sea Acres Rainforest Centre** NATURE RESERVE
(www.nationalparks.nsw.gov.au; Pacific Dr; adult/child $8/4; 9am-4.30pm) This 72-hectare pocket of coastal rainforest was recently declared a national park, protecting as it does the state's largest stand of coastal rainforest. It's alive with birds, goannas, brush turkeys and, so as to be truly authentic, mosquitoes (insect repellent is provided). The highlight is the outstanding wheelchair- and pram-accessible, 1.3km-long boardwalk through the forest. Fascinating one-hour guided tours by knowledgeable volunteers are included in the price. Call ahead for times of bush-tucker tours led by Aboriginal guides.

★ **Glasshouse Cultural Centre** ARTS CENTRE
(www.glasshouse.org.au; cnr Clarence & Hay Sts; 9am-5.30pm Mon-Fri, to 4pm Sat & Sun) The showpiece Glasshouse opened in July 2009 in the heart of Port. It was built on the site of

WORTH A TRIP

ONE FOR THE KIDS: TIMBERTOWN

Around 18km west of Port Macquarie, the small town of Wauchope is home to one of rural Australia's premier children's attractions. **Timbertown** (www.timbertown.com.au; Oxley Hwy, Wauchope; adult/child $19.50/16; 9.30am-4pm) is a reconstruction of a 19th-century inland Australian town with architecture faithful to the period, as well as volunteers in period dress, bullock teams, steam engines, a heritage playground and shops that recreate the early pioneer spirit.

Port Macquarie

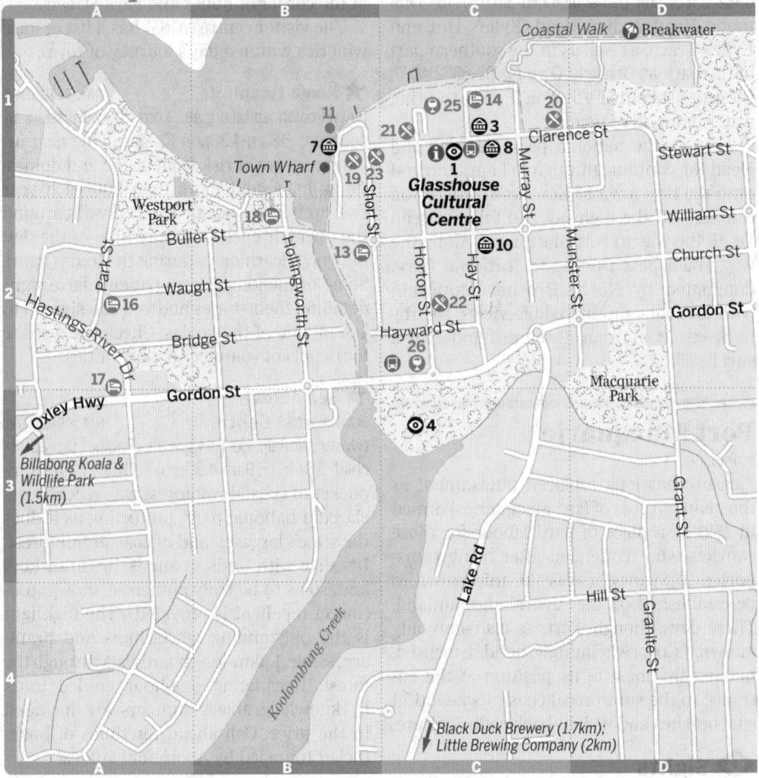

Port Macquarie

Top Sights
1 Glasshouse Cultural Centre C1
2 Koala Hospital E4

Sights
3 Courthouse C1
4 Kooloonbung Creek Nature Park C3
5 Maritime Museum E2
6 Observatory E2
7 Pilot's Boatshed Museum B1
8 Port Macquarie Historical Society Museum C1
9 Roto House E4
10 St Thomas' Anglican Church C2

Activities, Courses & Tours
11 Port Macquarie Cruise Adventures B1
12 Port Macquarie Surf School F4
Port Sea Kayak Adventures .... (see 18)

Sleeping
13 Mantra Quayside B2
14 Northpoint Apartments C1
15 Observatory E2
16 Ozzie Pozzie Backpackers A2
17 Port Macquarie Backpackers A2
18 Waters Edge Boutique Hotel B2

Eating
19 Cedro B1
20 Corner Restaurant Cafe C1
21 Crèma Espresso Bar C1
22 Fusion 7 .... C2
23 Macquarie Seafoods B1
Milkbar Town Beach .... (see 15)
24 Stunned Mullet E2

Drinking & Nightlife
25 Beach House C1
26 Finnian's C2

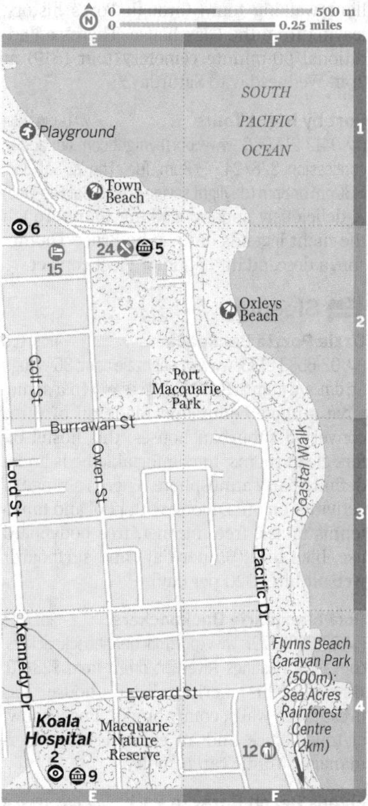

convict overseers' cottages; many archaeological artefacts from the original buildings are on display in the foyer. The funky building, modelled on environmental sustainability, houses the **regional art gallery**, a 600-seat theatre, the tourist information centre and a shop selling local arts and crafts museum and two theatres.

Billabong Koala & Wildlife Park NATURE RESERVE
(61 Billabong Dr; adult/child $22.50/13; ⏲9am-5pm) For more koala action head just west of the intersection of the Pacific and Oxley Hwys and make sure you're there for the 'koala patting' (10.30am, 1.30pm and 3.30pm). The park has a koala breeding centre, although if this facility is anything to go by, koala dating requires a lot of sitting around looking stoned. There are heaps of other Australian critters here, too.

Kooloonbung Creek Nature Park NATURE RESERVE
(cnr Gordon & Horton Sts) FREE Home to many bird species, this park close to the town centre encompasses 50 hectares of bush and wetland that can be explored via walking trails and wheelchair-accessible boardwalks. It includes the **Port Macquarie Historic Cemetery**.

Port Macquarie Historical Society Museum MUSEUM, HISTORIC BUILDING
(22 Clarence St; adult/child $5/2; ⏲9.30am-3.30pm Mon-Sat) In the town centre you'll find a host of colonial buildings including the 1836 ochre-brick Port Macquarie Historical Society Museum. Its labyrinth of rooms includes a costume gallery.

Courthouse HISTORIC BUILDING
(adult/child $2/0.50; ⏲10am-3.30pm Mon-Fri, to 1pm Sat) The courthouse was built in 1869 and is one of Port's loveliest buildings. It was used right up until 1986 and the 48th Regiment still parade around and fire off their guns here on the first Saturday of each month – ask at the visitor centre for timings.

St Thomas' Anglican Church HISTORIC BUILDING, CHURCH
(Hay St; admission by gold coin donation; ⏲9.30am-noon & 2-4pm Mon-Fri) This 1824, convict-built church is one of the oldest still-functioning churches in Australia. It still has its box pews and crenulated tower, echoing the Norman churches of southern England.

Roto House MUSEUM, HISTORIC BUILDING
(Lord St; admission by gold coin donation; ⏲10am-4.30pm subject to availability of volunteer staff) This period colonial-era home, next to the Koala Hospital in Macquarie Nature Reserve, is a lovely Victorian villa (1891) with interesting displays about its original owners who owned a swathe of land here that ran all the way to the sea.

Maritime Museum MUSEUM
(6 William St; adult/child $5/2; ⏲10am-4pm) The old pilot house above Town Beach has been converted into a small Maritime Museum. There's an even smaller extension of the museum in the 1890s **Pilot's Boatshed** (☎02-6584 2987; ⏲Tue & Thu) at the Town Wharf.

Observatory OBSERVATORY
(www.pmobs.org.au; William St; adult/child $8/5; ⏲7.30-8.30pm Wed & Sun, 8.15-9.15pm during daylight saving) For those looking for answers

beyond the horizon, sneak a peek through the telescope at the astronomical observatory on one of its public viewing and presentation nights.

Little Brewing Company BREWERY
(☎02-6581 3949; www.thelittlebrewingcompany.com.au; Unit 1/58 Uralla Rd; ⏰10am-4pm Mon-Sat) Cellar door tastings and sales from an award-winning boutique brewery.

Black Duck Brewery BREWERY
(www.blackduckbrewery.com.au; 6B Acacia Ave; ⏰10am-6pm Thu & Fri, to 4pm Sat & Sun) A well-regarded microbrewery with cellar-door sales.

Activities

Port Macquarie Surf School SURFING
(☎02-6584 7733; www.portmacquariesurfschool.com.au; lessons from $40) Offers a wide range of lessons and prices.

Port Sea Kayak Adventures SEA KAYAKING
(☎0409 776 566; www.portkayak.com.au; Buller St Bridge; 2-/6-hour guided trips $35/75) Runs a two-hour River & Mangrove trip and a six-hour Freshwater Rapids trip. It also rents kayaks ($15 per person per hour).

Port Macquarie Camel Safaris CAMEL RIDING
(☎0437 672 080; www.portmacquariecamels.com.au; Matthew Flinders Dr; 30-minute ride adult/child $30/25; ⏰9.30am-1pm Sun-Fri) Camel rides on the southern end of Lighthouse Beach.

River Cruises on Port Venture CRUISE
(☎1300 795 577; www.portventure.com.au; adult/child from $17/10) Twilight, lunch and eco history cruises with dolphin watching part of the fun. Some trips are aboard a replica Chinese junk.

Port Macquarie Cruise Adventures CRUISE
(☎0414 897 444; www.cruiseadventures.com.au; 74 Clarence St, Town Wharf; adult/child/concession from $25/10/22) Offers eco-cruises to national parks, Devonshire Tea cruises, lunch, sunset, river and everglades tours.

Soul Surfing SURFING
(www.soulsurfing.com.au; classes from $50) A good surf school that's especially good for beginners.

Tours

Historic Port Macquarie Walking Tours WALKING TOUR
(☎0447 429 016; www.pmheritage.com.au; per person $29; ⏰9.30am Wed-Sat) Two-and-a-half-hour walking tours through Port's history, leaving from the Glasshouse. There's an additional 90-minute cemetery tour ($19) at 2pm Wednesday to Saturday.

Port by Night Tours WALKING TOUR
(☎0412 217 060; www.portbynight.com.au; adult/concession $28/24; ⏰8pm Tue, Thu & Sat Jan, 6.30pm or 8pm (daylight saving) Thu & Sat Feb-Dec) A deliciously spooky walking tour through the night legends of town by Bruce Thompson, a descendant of a First Fleet convict.

Sleeping

Ozzie Pozzie Backpackers HOSTEL $
(☎02-6583 8133; www.ozziepozzie.com; 36 Waugh St; dm/s/d from $28/60/88; @📶🏊) In a somewhat strange compound made up of three converted suburban houses, this hostel offers clean rooms, uncomfortable beds and a definite party atmosphere. There's a range of activities on offer, along with pool and table-tennis tables, free internet, free bodyboard use, bike hire ($5 per day) and surfboard/wetsuit hire ($20 per day).

Port Macquarie Backpackers HOSTEL $
(☎02-6583 1791; www.portmacquariebackpackers.com.au; 2 Hastings River Dr; dm/d from $23/70; @📶🏊) This heritage-listed house has pressed-tin walls, comfy bunks, a new shower/toilet block and an enthusiastic owner-manager. Traffic can be noisy.

Flynns Beach Caravan Park CARAVAN PARK $
(☎02-6583 5754; www.flynnsbeachcaravanpark.com.au; 22 Ocean St; unpowered/powered sites $22/28, cabins from $80) An attractive, shady park at the southern end of town and across the road from Flynns Beach.

Observatory HOTEL $$
(☎02-6586 8000; www.observatory.net.au; 40 William St; r/apt from $145/169; ❄📶🏊) A friendly welcome is the norm at this excellent modern hotel opposite Town Beach. Rooms and apartments are comfortable and well equipped; many have balconies overlooking the water. The close proximity to the beach, good cafes and restaurants mean that you won't have to stray far from your room.

Waters Edge Boutique Hotel HOTEL $$
(☎02-6583 2955; www.watersedgeboutiquehotel.com.au; 1 Buller St; d $109-149; ❄📶🏊) A newish place just across the bridge, this well-priced place wears its 'boutique' tag pretty lightly but the rooms are nonetheless nicely turned

out, there's a fine pool and children's playground and a waterside bar-restaurant.

Mantra Quayside
APARTMENTS $$
(☑02-6588 4000; www.mantraquayside.com.au; cnr William & Short Sts; apt $150-240; ✳@📶🏊) This place is a favourite with visitors wanting a self-contained bolthole close to both the beach and the cafe strip.

Northpoint Apartments
APARTMENTS $$
(☑1800 210 222, 02-6583 8333; www.northpointapartments.com.au; 2 Murray St; 2-/3-bedroom apt from $180/220; ✳📶🏊) Large, classy and contemporary apartments, some with fabulous views (for which you pay extra).

✖ Eating

Milkbar Town Beach
CAFE $
(shop 2, 40 William St; lunch mains $9-16; ⊙7.30am-3pm Mon-Fri, to noon Sat & Sun) A casually chic cafe on the ground floor of a modern apartment block (the Observatory), Milkbar is known for its homemade icy poles, single-origin coffee and surfer clientele.

Cedro
CAFE $
(72 Clarence St; mains $10.50-18.50; ⊙7.30am-2.30pm Tue-Sat, 7.30am-noon Sun) On a sunny day you can sit on the street between the palm trees, order the generous house breakfast, sip a good coffee and plan your next move: the beach, or another coffee stop? While you decide, the corn, coriander and green-chilli fritters are memorable.

Macquarie Seafoods
FISH & CHIPS $
(☑02-6583 8476; 68 Clarence St; fish & chips from $12; ⊙11am-8.30pm) Everyone has their own favourite fish and chippery, but this place in the town centre wins our vote for the lightness of its batter.

Corner Restaurant Cafe
CAFE $$
(cornerrestaurant.com.au; cnr Clarence & Munster Sts; lunch mains $13-27, dinner mains $29-35; ⊙7am-9pm) On the ground floor of a holiday apartment block, this sleek operation has a definite Sydney-ish sheen and good cafe fare that could hold its own in Surry Hills. Think seafood tasting plates or pearl barley risotto.

Fusion 7
MODERN AUSTRALIAN $$
(☑02-6584 1171; www.fusion7.com.au; 124 Horton St; mains $29-35; ⊙6-9pm Tue-Sat) Chef Lindsey Schwab worked with the father of fusion cuisine, Peter Gordon, in London. Despite this pedigree and the restaurant's name, the food is more Mod Oz than fusion – try the

pan-fried saltwater barramundi. Desserts are particularly delicious.

Crèma Espresso Bar
CAFE $$
(cnr Horton & Clarence Sts; mains $10.50-16.50; ⊙7am-5pm Mon-Fri, 8am-5pm Sat, 8am-3pm Sun) The coffee here is so good that you fail to realise that its food is pretty tasty as well – we loved the Thai beef salad, while it also does sandwiches and service is good. Check out the old Space Invaders machine in the corner.

★ Stunned Mullet
MODERN AUSTRALIAN $$$
(☑02-6584 7757; www.thestunnedmullet.com.au; 24 William St; mains $28-38; ⊙noon-2.30pm & 6-8.30pm) Australian idiom lesson: to look like a stunned mullet is to wear an expression of bewilderment. It's exactly the sort of look you might adopt while struggling to choose between the delicious Mod Oz menu items and extensive wine-list offerings at Port's best restaurant. Asian and French influences make themselves heard but the emphasis is on fresh, top-quality ingredients cooked to perfection.

🍷 Drinking & Entertainment

Finnian's
PUB
(⊙11am-late) The backpacker's boozer of choice, this Irish tavern near the new bus depot offers raffles and trivia nights midweek but cranks up the party atmosphere on Fridays and Saturdays with live music from 8pm.

Beach House
PUB
(Horton St; ⊙11am-late) The enviable position right on the grassy water's edge makes this beautiful pub perfect for lazy afternoon drinks. As the wee hours draw near, folk fasten their beer goggles and mingle inside.

ℹ Information

Visitor Centre (☑02-6581 8000; www.portmacquarieinfo.com.au; The Glasshouse, cnr Hay & Clarence Sts; ⊙9am-5.30pm Mon-Fri, 9am-4pm Sat & Sun)

ℹ Getting There & Away

AIR
Port Macquarie Airport (☑02-6581 8111; Boundary St) is 5km from the centre of town ($18 to $20 in a taxi).

Both **Qantas** (☑13 13 13; www.qantas.com.au) and **Virgin Australia** (☑13 67 89; www.virginaustralia.com) have daily flights to Sydney. Brindabella Airlines (p70) has services to Brisbane, Coffs Harbour and Newcastle.

BUS

Greyhound (☎1300 4739 46863; www.greyhound.com.au) stops three times daily on its way between Sydney ($58 to $89, 6½ hours) and Brisbane ($74 to $122, 9½ hours).

Premier Motor Service (☎13 34 10; www.premierms.com.au) heads daily to Sydney ($60, 6½ hours), Newcastle ($47, four hours) and Brisbane ($67, 9½ hours).

Getting Around

The **Settlement Point Ferry** (per car $5) operates 24 hours. A 10-minute trip on a flat punt gives you access to North Beach.

Port Macquarie to Coffs Harbour

Kempsey

POP 10,374

About 45km north of Port Macquarie, Kempsey is a large rural town serving the farms of the Macleay Valley. There's little to draw you here but fans of unmistakeably Aussie icons will find two of them.

The fabled Akubra hat (www.akubra.com.au), the headwear of choice for generations of rural Australians, came from Kempsey and although the factory is not open to the public, the local department store will happily fit out those wanting an iconic Aussie souvenir.

Country-music legend the late Slim Dusty (who also favoured an Akubra) was born here. The wheels are in (very slow) motion for the opening of a **Slim Dusty Heritage Centre** (www.slimdustycentre.com.au; Old Kempsey Showgrounds).

The **Kempsey visitor centre** (☎02-6563 1555; www.macleayvalleycoast.com.au; Pacific Hwy) is at a rest stop on the south side of town, sharing space with a **sheep shearer's museum** (adult/child $5/2.50; ⏲10am-4pm).

WORTH A TRIP

DIRT ROADS & RIVERS

For a bit of adventure take the partly unsealed but well-kept Loftus Rd from Crescent Head to South West Rocks alongside the pretty-as-a-picture Belmore and Macleay Rivers. The road detours through gorgeous riverside **Gladstone** with a pub and quaint cafes.

The turn-off to Crescent Head is near the visitor centre in Kempsey. Alternatively, from the north take the very scenic Belmore Rd, which leaves the Pacific Hwy at Seven Oaks and follows the Macleay River.

Cavanaghs (☎02-6562 7800; www.cavanaghs.com.au) run buses to South West Rocks from Kempsey Medical Centre (Belgrave St).

Crescent Head & Around

POP 979

This little hideaway, 18km southeast of Kempsey, is the kind of sleepy place you'd come to write a book. Failing that, how about learning to ride a longboard? The town is one of Australia's surf longboarding capitals, and it's here that the Malibu surfboard gained prominence in Australia during the '60s.

Today many come just to watch the longboard riders surf the epic waves of **Little Nobby's Junction**. There's also good shortboard riding off Plomer Rd. Untrammelled **Killick Beach** stretches 14km north.

Sleeping & Eating

Crescent Head Holiday Park CAMPGROUND $
(☎02-6566 0261; Pacific St; camp sites/cabins from $22/92; @) Right on the beach, Crescent Head Holiday Park is a lovely spot to pitch a tent. The reception doubles as Creso Cafe with espressos, wraps and sandwiches as well as a heart-starting breakfast egg-and-bacon roll. It also rents out surfboards ($15/30/40 hour/half-day/full day).

★**Bush and Beach Motel** MOTEL $$
(Surfari Central; ☎1800 007 873, 02-6566 0009; www.surfaris.com; 353 Loftus Rd; dm $30 d $60-120; @) These guys started the original Sydney–Byron surf tours and have now based themselves in Crescent Head because 'the surf is guaranteed every day'. The rooms are clean and comfortable with bathrooms and some wicked wall murals. Surf-and-stay packages are a speciality.

Sun Worship Eco Apartments APARTMENTS $$$
(☎1300 664 757; www.sunworship.com.au; 9 Belmore St; apt $190-280;) Sun Worship Eco Apartments are new and funky rammed-earth villas featuring sustainable designs, including flow-through ventilation, solar orientation and solar hot water. They're spacious too.

WORTH A TRIP

LORD HOWE ISLAND

Shhh! Lord Howe Island (population 350) is one of Australia's best-kept coastal secrets – Lord how we love it! About 600km northeast of Sydney, at the same latitude as Port Macquarie, this gorgeous subtropical island remains remarkably pristine. World Heritage–listed for its rare bird and plant life, the island is a haven for ecotourists and those seeking a *real* holiday. Many visitors (numbers are limited to 400 at any one time) are repeat customers, returning for a dose of the island's barefoot, first-name hospitality, empty beaches and balmy vibes.

Crescent-shaped Lord Howe wraps itself around a lagoon, fringed by coral reefs. The island is lorded over by three peaks: Mt Lidgbird (777m) and Mt Gower (875m) in the south, and the astonishing spike of Ball's Pyramid (551m) jagging up from the sea 23km to the southeast.

Between September and April, Lord Howe becomes a rabbling gaggle of nesting seabirds. Check out the bird life on bushwalks along the coast and through the hills and rainforest. The summit climb up Mt Gower (eight to 10 hours return) is one of Australia's best one-day walks. The steep hike will either cure or initiate vertigo; you must be accompanied by a licensed guide.

Fish feeding causes a splash in the Ned's Beach shallows, and you can snorkel among vivid tropical fish and coral just offshore. Hire a mask, snorkel, fins and wetsuit at the beach using an honesty-box system. There's good surf at Blinky Beach, and off the island's western shore is the world's southernmost coral reef, sheltered by a wide lagoon popular for sea kayaking. You can also inspect the sea life from above via a glass-bottom boat or immerse yourself completely on a scuba dive.

The island is about 11km long by 3km wide; most accommodation and services are located in the flat area north of the airport. Island time is GMT plus 10½ hours – 30 minutes ahead of Sydney (the same as Sydney in summer). Unless you have a boat you'll have to fly here, and both food and accommodation are limited and pricey, although prices do fall considerably in winter

Camping is prohibited on the island, and all accommodation must be booked in advance. There are 18 lodge and self-contained apartment businesses here, some of which close in winter. Restaurant bookings are essential. Keep an eye out for 'Fish Fries' held on various nights at various resort restaurants, plus the bowls club and golf course – they offer all-you-can-eat seafood fresh off the boat (the local kingfish is brilliant).

The **visitor centre** (☎1800 240 937, 02-6563 2114; www.lordhoweisland.info; cnr Lagoon & Middle Beach Rds; ⏲9.30am-2.30pm Mon-Fri, to 2pm Sun) website has links to flight and accommodation packages. The centre is inside the **Lord Howe Island Museum**, a good source of island geography and natural history. It has internet access.

Near the corner of Ned's Beach and Lagoon Rds there's a post office, general store and two banks (no ATMs). Some businesses have Eftpos facilities. QantasLink (p165) has flights most days from Sydney (from $395 one way), and weekend flights from Brisbane (via Sydney). There are also seasonal weekly flights from Port Macquarie ($465 one way) and midweek flights from Brisbane from February to June, and September to December. Flight time from the mainland is around two hours.

★ **Mongrel's** SEAFOOD $

(7 Main St) Mongrel's sells a dozen of the freshest Sydney Rock oysters you can eat for $7, or $9.50 if you want them shucked – the perfect beach snack.

Crescent Tavern PUB, AUSTRALIAN $$

(www.crescentheadtavern.com.au; 2 Main St; mains $15-26; ⏲noon-2pm & 5.30-8pm) Crescent Tavern has cold beer, a sun-soaked deck and excellent food – what else could you want? Expect fish and chips, chilli garlic prawns and schnitzel.

ℹ Getting There & Away

Busways (☎1800 043 263; www.busways.com.au) Busways buses run from Crescent Head to Kempsey.

Hat Head National Park

This coastal **park** (www.environment.nsw.gov.au; per car per day $7) of 7458 hectares runs north from near Hat Head to **Smoky Cape** (south of Arakoon), protecting scrubland, swamps and some excellent beaches backed by one of the largest dune systems in NSW.

The wonderfully isolated village of **Hat Head**, surrounded by the national park, is much smaller and quieter than Crescent Head with its own natural beauty. At the end of town, a picturesque wooden footbridge crosses the aqua-green salt marsh ocean inlet. The water is so clear you can see fish darting around. **Hat Head Holiday Park** (☎02-6567 7501; www.4shoreholidayparks.com.au; camp sites from $21, cabins from $85) is close to the sheltered bay and footbridge and offers backpacker rates. You can camp (adult/child $5/3) at **Hungry Gate**, 5km south of Hat Head, or at Smoky Cape, just below **Smoky Cape Lighthouse**.

Hat Head and the national park are accessible from the hamlet of Kinchela, on the road between Kempsey and South West Rocks.

South West Rocks & Around

POP 4816

South West Rocks, at the end of a headland, is a pretty seaside place, perfect for weekenders, where brisk beach walks, bottomless bottles of red and top-notch food are the order of the day. The spectacular beach here is one of the few places on the east coast where you can watch the sun set over the water.

Sights & Activities

Imposing and profoundly historic, Trial Bay occupies the west headland of the town and the **Trial Bay Gaol** (☎02-6566 6168; adult/child $8/5; ⏲9am-4.30pm) dominates the area. The wretched souls incarcerated here during the 19th century had to endure breathtaking views of the ocean, forests and freedom. Actually it's been mostly unoccupied, aside from a brief interlude in WWII when it housed German prisoners. Today it's a worthwhile museum. The **Arakoon State Conservation Area** surrounds the gaol and has a popular campground.

Southeast of South West Rocks, **Smoky Cape Lighthouse** (☎02-6566 6301; www.smokycapelighthouse.com) is perched high above the ocean on a bracingly breezy cape. Phone ahead for tours.

The South West Rocks area is great for divers, especially **Fish Rock Cave**, south of Smoky Cape. **South West Rocks Dive Centre** (☎02-6566 6474; www.southwestrocksdive.com.au; 5/98 Gregory St; 1-/2-day double boat dives $130/250) and **Fish Rock Dive Centre** (☎02-6566 6614; www.fishrock.com.au; 134 Gregory St; 2/4 dives $130/250) both offer dives and accommodation.

Little Bay Beach is a good spot to have a swim with kangaroos looking on. It's the start of a couple of nice walks.

Sleeping

★ **Trial Bay Camping Area** CAMPGROUND $
(☎02-6566 6168; www.nationalparks.nsw.gov.au; camp sites per night from $28) Behind the gaol, this magnificent camp site sits on the peninsula affording generous beach views from most sites. Amenities include hot showers and coin-slot barbies.

★ **Smoky Cape Lighthouse** B&B $$
(☎02-6566 6301; www.smokycapelighthouse.com; s/d from $150/220, cottages per 2 nights from $500) Romantic evenings can be spent hearing the wind whip around the sturdy white lighthouse-keeper's building just a few metres from the lighthouse itself. The views are also fuel for passion.

Heritage GUESTHOUSE $$
(☎02-6566 6625; www.heritageguesthouse.com.au; 21-23 Livingstone St; r incl breakfast $120-175; ❄) This renovated 1880s house has lovely, old-fashioned rooms, some with spas. Choose from the simpler rooms downstairs or the more lavish versions upstairs with ocean views.

Eating & Drinking

Seabreeze Hotel PUB $$
(☎02-6566 6909; www.seabreezebeachhotel.com.au; Livingstone St; mains $13-23.50; ⏲noon-8.30pm) This place serves scrubbed-up pub nosh (everything from bangers and mash to Thai red curry) on pleasant decks. Watch for the daily $10 specials.

Geppys MEDITERRANEAN $$
(☎02-6566 6169; cnr Livingstone & Memorial Sts; mains $32; ⏲6.30-9pm) This cosmopolitan restaurant is signed up to the slow-food movement; tuck into veal medallions with a raspberry reduction or fresh fish with salsa verde. It's open for drinks, too.

Surf Club SURF CLUB
(⏲4-9pm Fri-Sun Dec-Feb) This club on Horseshoe Bay is the best place in town for a beer with an ocean view. Unpretentious meals, including roasts and shepherd's pie, are a Sunday must.

NEW SOUTH WALES GUIDE TO NATIVE AUSTRALIAN ANIMALS

For more information and a detailed list of sites, watch out for *The Complete Guide to Finding the Mammals of Australia*, due out in December 2013 and published by the CSIRO (www.csiro.au).

If you don't see these animals in the wild, Dubbo's Western Plains Zoo (p212) and Potoroo Palace (p253) near Merimbula have captive Australian species.

Kangaroos

➡ **Eastern grey kangaroos** are commonly found in any grassy woodlands in most national parks and at campgrounds along the coast, such as at **Jervis Bay** and **South West Rocks**. Sightings are almost guaranteed at **Pambula**, close to **Merimbula**.

➡ **Red kangaroos** are common in Outback NSW, for example **Mungo National Park** or **Sturt National Park**.

Wallabies

➡ **Black (swamp) wallabies** live in dense forest, especially near watercourses, and are common along the coast. **Red-necked wallabies** inhabit drier, more open forest. Both are often seen along roadsides, especially in the early morning on quiet backroads.

➡ **Potato Point** near Tuross (south of Bateman's Bay) has red-necked wallabies and grey kangaroos right down at the beach.

Koalas

Koala populations are larger along the coast from Sydney to the Queensland border, less so south of Sydney.

➡ **Gunnedah** (west of Tamworth) claims to be the koala capital of Australia; koalas can usually be seen near the visitor centre. The website www.visitnsw.com/destinations/country-nsw/tamworth-area/gunnedah/attractions/koalas-in-gunnedah gives a list of other sites.

➡ Other possibilities include Robinson's Lookout (p193) in Lismore, **Byron Bay** and **Port Macquarie**.

Platypus

Platypus are shy and best seen in the early morning, especially in winter when males are very active. Even so, there are some fairly reliable spots:

➡ Try Slacks Creek road, where it crosses the Murrumbidgee River about 10km. **northwest of Cooma**

➡ In the middle of **Bombala** (south of Cooma) from the Monaro Hwy bridge over the Bombala River, and at the Bombala Platypus Reserve 4.5 km south-west of Bombala on the Delegate road.

➡ **Tucki Tucki Creek** in Lismore is worth a look.

➡ In the Murrumbidgee River near the visitor centre in **Wagga Wagga**

Liquid Assets Adventure Tours (p175) in Coffs Harbour runs platypus tours.

Wombats

The best chance of seeing wombats is in the hilly, forested country of southeastern NSW, but they are rare on the coast. Possible sites:

➡ In the **Snowy Mountains** you might spot one, including along the Alpine Way between Jindabyne and Thredbo, and along mountain back roads at dusk, especially in winter.

➡ **Bendeela picnic spot** in Kangaroo Valley

Information

Visitor Centre (1800 642 480; www.macleayvalleycoast.com.au; Boatman's Cottage; 9am-4pm)

Getting There & Away

Busways (1300 555 611; www.busways.com.au) runs two or three times daily Monday to Saturday to/from Kempsey (Belgrave St, $13.50, 50 minutes).

Nambucca Heads

POP 6220

Nambucca is idyllically strewn over a dramatically curling headland interlaced with the estuaries of the Nambucca River. It is spacious, sleepy and unspoilt with one of the coast's prettiest foreshores.

Sights & Activities

From the visitor centre, **Gulmani Boardwalk** stretches 3km along the foreshore, through parks and bushland, and over pristine sand and waterways. It's the perfect introduction to the town.

Of the numerous lookouts, **Captain Cook Lookout**, with its 180-degree vista, best exploits the staggering views.

The only patrolled beach in town is **Main Beach**. **Beilby's** and **Shelly Beaches** are just to the south, closer to the river mouth – where the best surf is – and can be reached by going past the Captain Cook Lookout.

Located near the foreshore, the **V-Wall** is a clever snapshot of life. Here you can read graffitied memoirs from newlyweds, young people and travellers who have left their colourful mark. Pick up a paintbrush and make your mark.

Headland Historical Museum MUSEUM
(www.here.com.au/museum; Liston St; adult/child $3/0.50; 2-4pm Wed, Sat & Sun) Worth a visit, this museum has local-history exhibits, including a collection of more than 1000 photos.

Sleeping

White Albatross Holiday Resort CARAVAN PARK $
(02-6568 6468; www.whitealbatross.com.au; Wellington Dr; camp sites/vans/cabins from $39/65/80) Located near the river mouth with an adjacent lagoon to swim in, this large holiday park surrounds a sheltered lagoon. Beaches and the V-Wall Tavern are all close by.

Riverview Boutique Hotel GUESTHOUSE $$
(02-6568 6386; www.riverviewlodgenambucca.com.au; 4 Wellington Dr; s/d from $120/130;) Built in 1887, this old pub was, for many years, one of only a few buildings on the rise of a hill overlooking the foreshore. Today the old two-storey wooden charmer has eight stylish rooms (with fridges); some have stunning views.

Marcel Towers APARTMENTS $$
(02-6568 7041; www.marceltowers.com.au; Wellington Dr; d from $120; @) The decor at these holiday apartments might be somewhat passé, but the balcony views over a restaurant-studded foreshore soon make up for it. Apartments are clean and available for overnight or longer stays.

Eating

Bookshop Café CAFE $
(cnr Ridge & Bowra Sts; meals $8-16; 8am-5pm) The porch tables here are *the* place in town for breakfast. The fruit smoothies are rather excellent.

★**Jaaning Tree** MODERN AUSTRALIAN $$
(02-6569 4444; www.jaaningtree.com.au; Shop 8, 1 Wellington Drive; mains $23-38; noon-3pm & 6-9pm Fri & Sat, noon-3pm Wed, Thu & Sat) Right on the waterfront, this stunning restaurant is all about creative takes on Australian staples – how about the house speciality of kangaroo with chocolate jus and beetroot.

★**Matilda's** SEAFOOD $$$
(02-6568 6024; Wellington Dr; mains $28-42; 6-9pm Mon-Sat) Saved up for a seafood feast? Go no further. This cute little shack juggles good old-fashioned beachfront character with food and service know-how. BYO.

Information

Nambucca Heads Visitor Centre (02-6568 6954; www.nambuccatourism.com.au; cnr Riverside Dr & Pacific Hwy; 9am-5pm) This visitor centre doubles as the main bus terminal.

Getting There & Away

Long-distance buses stop at the visitor centre. **Premier** (13 34 10; www.premierms.com.au) charges $63 to either Sydney or Brisbane (both eight to nine hours). **Greyhound** (1300 GREYHOUND, 1300 4739 46863; www.greyhound.com.au) charges $106 to Sydney (nine hours) and $110 for a slightly quicker run to Brisbane.

Busways (☎1300 555 611; www.busways.com.au) runs two or three times Monday to Saturday to Bellingen ($9, one hour) and Coffs Harbour ($9.75, one hour) via Urunga.

CountryLink (☎13 22 32; www.countrylink.info) has three trains north to Coffs Harbour ($6, 40 minutes) and beyond, and south to Sydney ($81, eight hours).

Bellingen

POP 3038

Buried in foliage on a hillside by the banks of the Bellinger River, this gorgeous town dances to the beat of its own bongo drum, attracting a populace of artists, academics and those drawn to a more organic lifestyle. Thick with gourmet cuisine and accommodation, it is, as one visitor rightly stated, hippie without the dippy. From December to March a huge colony of flying foxes descends on **Bat Island**.

Sights & Activities

Hammond & Wheatley Emporium HISTORIC BUILDING
(Hyde St) First up, head to this magnificent shop, formerly an old department store. It has been beautifully restored and now houses a clothes shop, art gallery and cafe.

Markets MARKET
(www.bellingenmarkets.com.au) On the third Saturday of the month the community market in Bellinger Park is a regional sensation, with over 250 stalls. On the second and fourth Saturday of the month there's a growers market at Bellingen showgrounds.

Heartland Didgeridoos MUSIC
(www.heartlanddidgeridoos.com.au; 2/25 Hyde St) The first didg in space came from here. As such, the indigenous owners have a growing international reputation.

Old Butter Factory HISTORIC BUILDING
(www.bellingen.com/butterfactory; 1 Doepel St; ⌚9am-5pm) This historic place houses craft shops, a gallery, opal dealers, a masseur and a great cafe.

Bellingen Canoe Adventures CANOEING
(☎02-6655 9955; www.canoeadventures.com.au; 4 Tyson St; day tours per adult/child $90/60) This outfit has wonderful guided canoe tours on the Bellinger River, including full-moon tours (adult/child $25/20).

Festivals & Events

Camp Creative ARTS
(www.campcreative.com.au; ⌚mid-Jan) A week-long carnival of the arts.

Bellingen Jazz & Blues Festival JAZZ
(www.bellingenjazzfestival.com.au; ⌚mid-Aug) A strong line-up of jazz names.

Sleeping

★**Bellingen YHA** HOSTEL $
(☎02-6655 1116; www3.yha.com.au; 2 Short St; dm/d from $27/70; @📶) This renovated two-storey weatherboard, overlooking the pristine river valley, attracts backpackers via the grapevine and then keeps them here with its tranquil, engaging atmosphere. Camping also available.

Federal Hotel HOTEL $
(☎02-6655 1003; www.federalhotel.com.au; 77 Hyde St; dm/d with shared bathroom $40/80; ⌚Relish Bar & Grill lunch & dinner; ❄@) This beautiful old pub has refurbished weatherboard rooms that open onto a balcony with a sweeping view of the main street. Downstairs there is a lively pub scene, and an excellent restaurant.

Rivendell GUESTHOUSE $$
(☎02-6655 0060; www.rivendellguesthouse.com.au; 12 Hyde St; s/d from $130/150; 🏊) Unlike many, Rivendell is right in town. The three bedrooms have verandahs fronting lush gardens surrounding a freshwater pool. Decor is restrained yet homely, always a plus with a B&B.

Maddefords Cottages APARTMENTS $$
(☎02-6655 9866; www.maddefordscottages.com.au; 224 North Bank Rd; d $145; ❄) These polished mountain cabins have cosy interiors with country furnishings and big, sunny windows. Timber balconies overlook a tumbling private valley. Your first night includes a sizeable brekkie hamper. Overall, it's outstanding value.

Bellingen Valley Lodge LODGE $$
(www.bellingenvalleylodge.com.au; 1381 Waterfall Way; s/d/tw from $100/110/120; 🏊) This fine lodge has attractive hotel-style rooms, all with valley views, which makes it fine choice 1km from Bellingen. The restaurant has log fires in winter and the grounds make the most of the rural setting.

Eating & Drinking

★Vintage Nest Espresso CAFE $
(62 Hyde St; sandwiches $9; 7.30am-5pm Mon-Fri, 9am-1.30pm Sat) Sip on excellent coffee amid the eclectic curios of this vintage shop. One side is clothes-tastic, the other is a nudge at nostalgia with old books and records, used furniture and '70s kitchenware. Thankfully the hearty sandwiches are not preloved.

Tuckshop Bellingen CAFE $
(63 Hyde St; mains $8-15; 7.30am-1pm Mon-Sat) Great coffee and a delicious line-up of breakfast and good vegetarian options.

Bellingen Gelato Bar CAFE $
(101 Hyde St; 10am-6pm) A 1950s-America-styled cafe with homemade ice cream.

Lodge 241 CAFE, BAR $$
(www.bellingen.com/thelodge; Hyde St; mains $12-25; 8.30am-5.30pm Wed-Sun, dinner Fri & Sat) A pew at this excellent cafe is golden. Chess players gather here on a Sunday to soak up the atmosphere while locals line up along a communal table and imbibe great coffee. It's licensed so is good for a tipple too.

No 2 Oak St MODERN AUSTRALIAN, FRENCH $$$
(02-6655 9000; www.no2oakst.com.au; 2 Oak St; mains $35-45; 6.30-9.30pm Wed-Sat) The bounty of local produce is celebrated at this restaurant where host Toni Urquart provides the welcome while Ray Urquart works his kitchen magic. A table out on the verandah in the 1910 country house is a magical place to dine in the evening. Book ahead and just try and resist the Positano seafood stew...

Information

There's an excellent community website at www.bellingen.com.

Waterfall Way Visitor Centre (29-31 Hyde St; 9am-5pm)

Getting There & Away

Busways (1300 555 611; www.busways.com.au) runs two or three times Monday to Saturday from Nambucca Heads ($11, 40 minutes) and Coffs Harbour ($9.50, 70 minutes) to Bellingen via Urunga.

Keans (1800 625 587) has buses west to Dorrigo and Tamworth twice a week.

Around Bellingen

There are some beautiful spots waiting to be discovered in the surrounding valleys. The most accessible is the hamlet of **Gleniffer**, 6km to the north and clearly signposted from North Bellingen. There's a good swimming hole in the **Never Never River** behind the small Gleniffer School of Arts at the crossroads. Then you can drive around **Loop Road**, which takes you to the foot of the New England tableland – a great drive for which words don't do justice.

Dorrigo National Park

The most accessible of Australia's World Heritage–listed rainforests, this 11,902-hectare national park is simply stunning, encompassing around 120 bird species and numerous walking tracks. The turn-off to the park is just south of Dorrigo. The **Rainforest Centre** (Dome Rd; 8.30am-4.30pm Mon-Fri, 9am-4.30pm Sat & Sun), at the park entrance, has information about the park's various ecosystems and can advise you on which walk to conquer. The **Walk with the Birds Track** is an easy 400m stroll but the real highlight is the **Skywalk**, a walkway jutting over the rainforest canopy with jaw-dropping views of the ranges beyond.

Dorrigo

POP 1072

Arrayed around the T-junction of two wider-than-wide streets, Dorrigo is a pretty little place. One gets the sense that this might be the next Bellingen in terms of food and wine, but it hasn't quite happened yet. The winding roads that lead here from Armidale, Bellingen and Coffs Harbour, however, reveal rainforests, mountain passes and waterfalls – some of the most dramatic scenery in NSW.

Sights

The town's main attraction is the Dorrigo Rainforest Centre (p172) and **Dangar Falls**, which cascade over a series of rocky shelves before plummeting into a pristine gorge. An elevated skywalk leads to a stunning lookout, and you can swim beneath the falls if you have a yen for glacial bathing.

Red Dirt Distillery BREWERY
(☎02-6657 1373; www.reddirtdistillery.com.au; 51-53 Hickory St; ⊙8.30am-4.30pm Mon-Fri, to 2pm Sat) David Scott, the owner of the Red Dirt Distillery, gets creative with a range of vodka and liqueurs made with, for example, spuds grown in Dorrigo's red dirt. Buy a bottle, plus some of his deli snacks and you're talking picnic, or sit in for an antipasto platter.

Sleeping & Eating

★**Tallawarra Retreat B&B** B&B $$
(☎02-6657 2315; www.tallawalla.com; 113 Old Coramba Rd; s/d incl breakfast $105/140;) This peaceful B&B is set amid picturesque gardens and forest around 1km from Dorrigo town centre. Paul and Di are friendly hosts and the rooms are comfortable and blissfully quiet. There's also a beautiful summer-only tea house and cafe.

Dorrigo Hotel/Motel HOTEL $$
(☎6657 2017; www.hotelmoteldorrigo.com.au; cnr Cudgery & Hickory Sts; dm $35, d $60-95;) The bedrooms here, some with bathrooms, have been tastefully renovated to provide the merest hint of wholesome country hospitality. Double doors open onto the wide-girthed verandah for a sweeping main-street vista. There are motel rooms also.

Dragonfly CAFE $$
(18-20 Cudgery St; mains $10-20; ⊙8am-3.30pm Mon-Sat) The local foodies' hub and hangout is Dragonfly, a cafe-cum-bookshop set in a chic minimalist space with a large, sunny rear dining area. Creative salads, sandwiches and veggie specials entice even if service is a tad slow.

33 on Hickory PIZZA $$
(☎02-6657 1882; www.thirtythreeonhickory.com.au; 33 Hickory St; small/large pizzas from $15/20; ⊙5-9pm Wed-Sun) This is a gorgeous 1920s weatherboard cottage with stained-glass windows, tasteful antiques and a blossoming garden. The main game is organic sourdough pizza served in style with bright white tablecloths, sparkling silverware and a cosy wood fire.

Information

Visitor Centre (☎02-6657 2486; www.dorrigo.com; 36 Hickory Street; ⊙9am-5pm)

Getting There & Away

Twice a week **Keans** (☎1800 043 339) buses run to Bellingen, Coffs Harbour and Armidale.

Coffs Harbour

POP 45,580

Coffs Harbour has always had to work hard to tart up its image. Where other coastal towns have the ready-made aesthetic of a main street slap-bang on the waterfront, Coffs has an inland city centre, and much of

WORTH A TRIP

SCENIC DRIVE: COFFS HARBOUR TO ARMIDALE

The Waterfall Way is an awe-inspiring drive from just south of coasty Coffs Harbour to inland Armidale. The journey traverses the gamut of spectacular World Heritage–listed national parks and passes through characteristic old towns, including charm-your-socks-off Bellingen and sleepy hillside Dorrigo.

Begin in **Coffs Harbour** and head down the rather dull Pacific Hwy. After 22km, take the turn-off for **Bellingen**, which lies 12km and a world away from the coast and its towel-clad crowds. After spending as much time here as you can spare, continue northwest. Soon enough, the road starts to climb steeply, passing beneath glorious stands of rainforest as it snakes its way up the eastern wall of the Great Dividing Range. Around 27km after Bellingen, **Dorrigo** has numerous opportunities for drawing near to the rainforest.

Some 48km past Dorrigo (and 2km west of Ebor), consider a detour to spectacular **Ebor Falls**, where the Guy Fawkes River takes a big plunge. A further 7km past the turn-off is Point Lookout Rd, which leads to **New England National Park**, a World Heritage site. There are numerous walks into this misty rainforest off this access road. A further 30km on from the Point Lookout Rd, look for **Wollomombi Falls**, a highlight of the World Heritage–listed Oxley Wild Rivers National Park. Here the water plunges down 260m. From here, it's a pretty 32km-drive through rolling, lightly wooded hills into heritage-rich Armidale.

Coffs Harbour

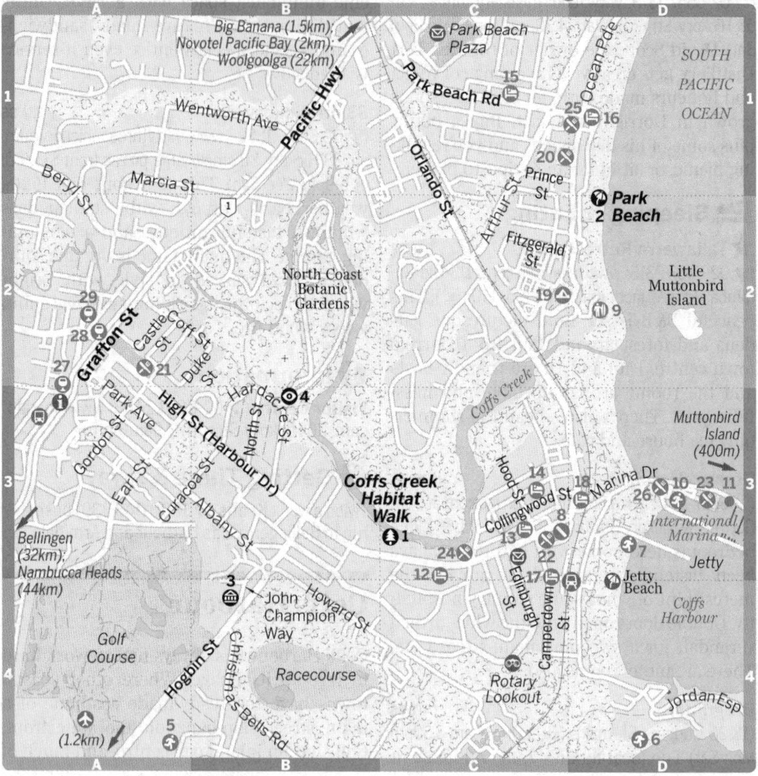

the town almost seems to turn its back on the sea. And yet, Coffs has a string of fabulous beaches and a preponderance of water-based activities, action sports and wildlife encounters, making it hugely popular with families, backpackers and the 'middle-Australian' market.

Sights

As well as Park Beach, the city's beaches include **Jetty Beach** which is more sheltered and better for families. **Diggers Beach**, reached by turning off the highway near the Big Banana, has a nude section. Surfers enjoy Diggers and **Macauleys Headland**, where swells average 1m to 1.5m.

★Park Beach BEACH

A long and lovely stretch of sand which has a picnic ground and is patrolled near the surf club at busy times – don't swim beyond the flags as there can be a strong undertow. The beach is backed by dense shrubbery and dunes that conceal the urban blight beyond – it's a lovely place for a sunset walk.

North Coast Botanic Gardens GARDEN

(www.coffsbotanicgarden.com.au; Hardacre St; admission by donation; 9am-5pm) Immerse yourself in the subtropical surrounds. Small stands of lush rainforest and numerous endangered species are some of the features. The 6km **Coffs Creek Habitat Walk** passes by, starting opposite the council chambers on Coff St and finishing near the ocean.

★Muttonbird Island NATURE RESERVE

Dramatically joined to Coffs Harbour by the northern breakwater in 1935, this eco treasure is occupied from late August to early April by some 12,000 pairs of muttonbirds, with cute offspring visible in December and January. The walk to the top (quite steep at the end) rewards with sweeping vistas along the coast. It marks the southern boundary

Coffs Harbour

of Solitary Islands Marine Park, a meeting place of tropical waters and southern currents. Evening tours of the island (adult/child $20/10) are possible – ask at the visitor centre or visit www.environment.nsw.gov.au/NationalParks.

Big Banana AMUSEMENT PARK
(www.bigbanana.com; Pacific Hwy; ⏲9am-4.30pm) Built in 1964, it actually started the craze for 'Big Things' in Australia (just so you know who to blame or praise). Admission is free, but there are for individual attractions such as ice skating, toboggan rides and a waterslide.

Bunker Cartoon Gallery GALLERY
(www.coffsharbour.nsw.gov.au; John Champion Way; adult/child $2/1; ⏲10am-4pm Mon-Sat) Rotating selections from the permanent collection of 18,000 cartoons on display in a WWII bunker.

Activities

For canoe, kayak and stand-up-paddle-board hire, try Mangrove Jack's (p177).

Jetty Dive Centre DIVING
(☎02-6651 1611; www.jettydive.com.au; 398 Harbour Dr; double dives from $125) Great-value PADI certification; the diving and snorkelling around Solitary Islands Marine Park is pretty spectacular. Also whale watching from roughly June to October.

Liquid Assets Adventure Tours ADVENTURE SPORTS
(☎02-6658 0850; www.surfrafting.com; 328 Harbour Dr; half-day tours from $60) Watery fun of all kinds is on offer: surf-kayaking, white-water rafting, kayaking in the marine park, platypus tours and more.

Valery Horse Trails HORSE RIDING
(☎02-6653 4301; www.valerytrails.com.au; 758 Valery Rd; 2hr ride adult/child $60/50) A stable of 60 horses and plenty of acreage.

Coffs Jet Ski JET SKIING
(☎0418 665 656; www.coffsjetskihire.com.au; Park Beach; 15/30/60min from $60/100/160) Jet skis for hire from Park Beach.

Coffs City Skydivers SKYDIVING
(☎02-6651 1167; coffsskydivers.com.au; Coffs Harbour airport; tandem jumps $229-495) Satisfies all urges to fling yourself from a plane, including courses.

Coffs Jetty Stand Up Paddle Board Hire WATER SPORTS
(☎0422 391 951; www.coffsjettysup.com.au; single/family per hr $20/50; ⏲9am-4pm Sat & Sun, daily in summer) Rent stand-up paddle boards at the jetty.

WATCHING WHALES

Whales travelling along Australia's east coast is one of the great marine migrations on the planet. Whales – particularly humpback whales – travel north to warmer waters closer to the equator to calve. They begin their return, southward journey in July and this continues until November. The season tends to end earlier in the north, but doesn't begin until September along New South Wales' far south coast. We have listed numerous whale-watching tours throughout this chapter. Otherwise, some of our favourite land-based vantage points include the following:

- Cape Byron Lighthouse, Byron Bay
- Diggers Headland or Brooms Head, Wooli
- Pilot Hill or Pippi Beach, Yamba
- Shelley Beach, Ballina
- Port Morton Lookout, Lennox Head
- Lookout, Eden

Lee Winkler's Surf School SURFING
(☎02-6650 0050; www.leewiklerssurfschool.com.au; Park Beach; from $50) One of the longest standing surf schools in Coffs.

East Coast Surf School SURFING
(☎02-6651 5515; www.eastcoastsurfschool.com.au; Diggers Beach; lessons from $55) This school is particularly female-friendly as it is run by noted east-coast surfer Helene Enevoldson. 'You will stand up!' is its motto.

Dorrigo Freefall ADVENTURE SPORTS
(☎0412 444 469; www.runningwild.com.au; ⌚half-day $97) This action company will pick you up in Coffs Harbour, transport you up to Dorrigo, take you to the Dorrigo Rainforest Centre and then drive down one of the steepest roads in coastal NSW, down to the coastal littoral. Bikes are provided.

Pacific Explorer Whale Watching WHALE WATCHING
(☎0422 210 338; www.pacificexplorer.com.au; 2-3hr from $40) A 10m catamaran limited to 23 passengers.

Coffs Coast Camel Rides CAMEL RIDE
(☎0448 822 635; www.coffscoastcamels.com.au; adult/child $30/25; ⌚daily Dec & Jan, Tue, Thu & Sat Feb-Apr, shorter hr rest of year) Camel rides along the beach.

Spirit of Coffs Harbour Cruises WHALE WATCHING
(☎02-6650 0155; www.gowhalewatching.com.au; shop 5, Coffs Harbour Marina; per person $45; ⌚9.30am May-Nov) Whale watching ($45) and cruises.

Festivals & Events

Pittwater to Coffs Yacht Race YACHT RACE
(www.pittwatertocoffs.com.au) New Year. Starts in Sydney, finishes here.

Sawtell Chilli Festival FOOD
(www.sawtellchillifestival.com.au) Early July.

Coffs Harbour International Buskers' Festival MUSIC
(www.coffsharbourbuskers.com) Late September and not to be missed. Also a Comedy Festival with plenty of live stand-up performers.

Sleeping

Motels cluster in two spots: out on the Pacific Hwy by the visitor centre where they can suck in road-trippers, and down by Park Beach where they can comfort beachgoers. There's no real reason to stay out by the Pacific Hwy.

One of many holiday-apartment agents is **Pacific Property & Management** (☎02-6652 1466; www.coffsaccommodation.com.au; 101 Park Beach Rd). The visitor centre has an accommodation booking service.

Coffs Harbour YHA HOSTEL $
(☎02-6652 6462; www3.yha.com.au; 51 Collingwood St; dm/d $27/77; @) The dorms and doubles with bathrooms are spacious and modern here, and the TV lounge and kitchen are immaculate. You can hire surfboards and bikes.

Aussitel Backpackers HOSTEL $
(☎02-6651 1871, 1800 330 335; www.aussitel.com; 312 Harbour Dr; dm/d $25/65; @) Don't be put off by the exterior. This capacious brick house, with homely dorms and a shady courtyard, is a hub for backpackers of all shapes and sizes, codes and creeds. Diving specialists are on site (PADI courses from $395).

Hoey Moey Pub HOSTEL $
(☎02-6652 3833; www.hoeymoey.com.au; 90 Ocean Pde; dm/d from $26/72) You can hear the waves roll in from these motel-style back-

packer rooms nicely located between the pub and the main beach. You can also hear your mates in the beer garden. Renovated rooms are slightly pricier.

Park Beach Holiday Park CARAVAN PARK $
(☎02-6648 4888; www.coffsholidays.com.au; Ocean Pde; camp sites/cabins from $30/69; @≋) Massive, with 332 sites and 55 cabins; located across the road from the beach. Kids are well catered for.

Observatory Holiday Apartments APARTMENTS $$
(☎02-6650 0462; www.theobservatory.com.au; 30-36 Camperdown St; apt $140-180, 3-bedroom townhouse $230; ❄☰≋) The one-, two- and three-bedroom apartments in this attractive modern complex are bright and airy, with chef-friendly kitchens. Some have spas with window views and all have balconies with ocean views. You're separated from the beach by a railway line.

Pacific Marina Luxury Apartments APARTMENTS $$
(☎1800 127 466, 02-6651 7955; www.pacificmarina.com.au; 22 Orlando St; 1-/2-/3-bedroom apt from $170/220/260; ❄☰≋) Large modern apartments in one of the best locations in town, close to shops, restaurants and the beach.

Caribbean Motel MOTEL $$
(☎02-6652 1500; www.caribbeanmotel.com.au; 353 Harbour Dr; d/apt from $128/161; ❄@☰≋) Close to Coffs Creek and the jetty, this 24-unit motel has been tastefully renovated and features a breakfast buffet and tables by the pool. The best rooms have balconies, views and spas plus there are great-value one-bedroom suites with kitchenettes.

Aanuka Beach Resort RESORT $$
(☎02-6652 7555; www.aanuka.com.au; 11 Firman Dr; r from $149; ❄@≋) It might be out of town, but this semi-luxurious resort, set amid luscious foliage, has excellent studios and apartments, all with spas and dishy interiors. It sits on a quiet neck of Diggers Beach and has tennis courts and an award-winning restaurant.

Novotel Pacific Bay RESORT $$$
(☎02-6659 7000; www.novotelpacificbayresort.com.au; cnr Pacific Hwy & Bay Dr; r from $155; ❄☰≋) Pacific Bay has all the features of a large resort: tennis courts, a golf course, walking trails, a kids' club, a spa and a fitness centre. The grounds are large and the 180 rooms have balconies, many with kitchens. It's 3km north of Coffs.

Eating

You can eat well down by the jetty, while the strip of eateries on Harbour Dr (High St) is a hungry browser's delight. The downtown area is good for lunch, or for coffee all day, but most places are closed in the evening.

Cocoa CAFE $
(36/35 High St; mains $8-13; ⏲breakfast & lunch) A hot spot for the business set and pram brigade. Great breakfasts.

Fisherman's Co-op FISH & CHIPS $
(www.coffsfishcoop.com.au; 69 Marina Dr; mains $8-15; ⏲9am-6pm winter, to 8pm summer) Fish fresh off the boats; perfect fodder for a Muttonbird Island picnic.

★ **Mangrove Jacks** MODERN AUSTRALIAN $$
(www.mangrovejackscafe.com.au; Promenade Centre, Harbour Dr; breakfast $10-15.50, lunch mains $15-26.50, dinner mains $21-30; ⏲breakfast & lunch daily, dinner Tue-Sat) One of two restaurants wonderfully located on a quiet bend of Coffs Creek, Mangrove Jacks uses almost exclusively local produce, has Coopers on tap, and offers tasty lunch dishes such as coconut seafood curry and more formal dinner options like char-grilled eye fillet served on potato and pumpkin roesti.

Urban Espresso Lounge CAFE $$
(www.urbanespressolounge.com.au; 384a Harbour Dr; mains $14-22.50; ⏲breakfast & lunch daily, dinner Thu-Sat) A stylish little outpost on the main dining strip, UEL opens out onto the street and is at once classy and casual. Both the food and service rarely miss a beat – try the honey-roasted beetroot, goat's cheese and pumpkin salad. Great coffee rounds out a great package.

Water Surf Art Cafe CAFE $$
(☎02-6651 4500; www.watersurfartcafe.com; 370 Harbour Dr; mains $9.50-13; ⏲7am-3pm) This could be the coolest cafe in town with contemporary art on the wall, friendly service and fresh tastes such as the Teriyaki chicken burger or the avocado and feta bruschetta.

Crying Tiger THAI $$
(☎02-6650 0195; 382 Harbour Dr; mains $18-27; ⏲dinner) Swimming in fragrant smells, the Crying Tiger keeps inquisitive diners happy

with dishes like red-duck curry, pork belly and jungle curry. You can set the chilli gauge as high or low as you like.

Yknot Bistro BISTRO $$
(www.yknotbistro.com.au; 30 Marina Dr; mains $18-39; breakfast, lunch & dinner) Part of the Coffs Harbour Yacht Club, this busy eatery has a bar serving pub-style seafood, steaks and pasta – we liked the seafood meze. There's also plenty of outdoor seating with ocean views – rare in Coffs.

Cafe Aqua CAFE $$
(02-6652 5566; www.cafeaqua.com.au; 57 Ocean Pde; mains $13-20; 7am-3pm) This lovely cafe at the northern end of Coffs does sunrise burgers or pancakes for breakfast, open roast beef sandwiches or grilled calamari for lunch.

OP81 MODERN AUSTRALIAN $$
(81 Ocean Pde; lunch mains from $15; breakfast & lunch Tue-Sun, dinner Fri) Modern decor, contemporary food and a big front deck.

Caffé Fiasco ITALIAN $$$
(fiascorestaurant.com.au; 22 Orlando St; mains $19-37; dinner Tue-Sat) Classic Italian fare is prepared in an open kitchen surrounded by widely spaced tables where they serve fabulous pasta and dishes like Millyhill slow-cooked lamb shoulder with soft polenta and broccolini puree. The gardens' herbs are used in the dishes. Servings could be larger.

Drinking & Nightlife

See Thursday's edition of the *Coffs Harbour Advocate* for live-music listings.

Coast Hotel PUB
(www.coasthotel.com.au; 2 Moonee St; 11am-late) Formerly the Old Fitzroy Hotel, this place has been purpose-renovated to supply lovers of a lazy afternoon in a beer garden with a venue. It has landscaped decking and cool breakaway areas so you can kick back on a couch if the mood takes you. The food is great, too.

Hoey Moey Pub PUB
(www.hoeymoey.com.au; 90 Ocean Pde; 10am-late) The massive inner beer 'garden' gives a good indication of how much this place kicks off in the summer. Pool comps, great live music and terrifying karaoke sessions are the norm.

Coffs Hotel PUB
(www.coffsharbourhotel.com; cnr Pacific Hwy & West Harbour Dr; 11am-late) Irish pub with bands, several bars, DJs and mad Friday nights.

Pier Hotel PUB
(www.pierhotelcoffs.com.au; 365 Harbour Dr) Renovated with a sunny rear terrace.

Plantation Hotel PUB
(www.plantationhotel.com.au; 11am-late) The Plantation is a pub at heart, so beer, live rock and decent steak are mainstays.

Information

Visitor Centre (02-6648 4990, 1300 369 070; www.coffscoast.com.au; Pacific Hwy; 9am-5pm)

Getting There & Away

AIR

Coffs Harbour Airport is just south of town. **Virgin Australia** (13 67 89; www.virginaustralia.com)and **Qantas** (13 13 13; www.qantas.com.au) fly to Sydney.

BUS

Long-distance and regional buses leave from a shelter adjacent to the visitor centre.

Premier (13 34 10; www.premierms.com.au) has several services a day north, including a middle-of-the-night bus to Byron Bay ($50, 5¼ hours), and an overnight service south to Sydney ($66, 8½ hours). **Greyhound** (1300 4739 46863; www.greyhound.com.au) offers more convenient but more expensive services in both directions.

Busways (1300 555 611; www.busways.com.au) runs two or three times daily, Monday to Saturday, to Nambucca Heads ($9.75, one hour) and Bellingen ($9.70, 50 minutes) via Urunga.

TRAIN

CountryLink (13 22 32; www.countrylink.info) has two trains daily north to Brisbane ($59, 6½ hours), and south to Sydney ($67, nine hours).

Getting Around

Hostel shuttles meet all long-distance buses and trains.

Coffs Bike Hire (02-6652 5102; cnr Orlando & Collingwood Sts; per day $30) rents mountain bikes.

Coffs District Taxi Network (13 10 08) operates a 24-hour cab service.

NORTH COAST

Coffs Harbour to Byron Bay

The Pacific Hwy runs near the coast – but not in sight of it – for 30km north of Coffs. Look for turn-offs to small beaches that are often quite uncrowded. The road then turns inland to Grafton, avoiding Yuraygir National Park and the isolated beach town of Wooli.

Woolgoolga

POP 4718

This coastal town just north of Coffs is a good small-town stop option. It's known for its surf-and-Sikh community – even if you're just driving by on the highway you're sure to notice the impressive Guru Nanak Temple, a Sikh *gurdwara* (place of worship).

Drive straight through town for a magnificent view of the group of five islands in the **Solitary Islands Marine Park**, the meeting point of warm tropical currents and cooler southern currents, making for a wonderful combination of corals, reef fish and seaweeds. Dive shops in Coffs Harbour organise tours.

SLEEPING & EATING

Woolgoolga Beach Caravan Park CARAVAN PARK $
(☎02-6654 1373; www.coffscoastholidayparks.com.au; Beach St; powered sites from $30, cabins $97-258) The caravan park is right on the beach.

Waterside Cabins CABIN $$
(☎02-6654 1644; www.watersidecabins.com.au; cnr Pacific Hwy & Hearnes Lake Rd; cabins from $93;) These luxury cabins are a lovely base for the Coffs Coast with stylish two-bedroom cabins, some of which overlook a lake. There's a private walkway to the beach, a half-sized tennis court and a barbecue area.

Bluebottles Brasserie CAFE, MODERN AUSTRALIAN $$$
(cnr Wharf & Beach Sts; mains $24-30; ⏲7.30am-3pm Sun-Thu, 7am-late Fri & Sat) Bluebottles Brasserie is a happening restaurant that serves fine seafood and also hosts live jazz sessions.

Red Rock

POP 310

Red Rock is a sleepy village with a gorgeous inlet and surrounds, 3km off the highway. It is a site sacred to the Gunawarri people. Soak up the sun or catch a fish while camping at **Red Rock Caravan Park** (☎02-6649 2730; www.redrock.org.au; 1 Lawson St, Red Rock; unpowered/powered sites $30/35, cabins $109-143). The **Yarrawarra Aboriginal Cultural Centre** (☎02-6640 7100; yarrawarra.org; 170 Red Rock Rd, Corindi Beach) has bush-medicine tours ($18 per person), traditional-basket-weaving and art classes as well as a bush-tucker cafe that serves crocodile, kangaroo and emu dishes. Ring ahead to find out about what's on.

The 53,502-hectare **Yuraygir National Park** (www.environment.nsw.gov.au; per car per day $7) covers the 60km stretch of coast north from Red Rock. The isolated beaches are best discovered on the **Yuraygir Coastal Walk**, a 65km signposted walk from Angourie to Red Rock following the path of the coastal emu over a series of tracks, trails, beaches and rock platforms, and passing through the villages of Brooms Head, Minne Water and Wooli.

Walkers can bush-camp at seven basic **camping areas** (per person from $10) along the route. It's best walked north to south with the sun at your back. Grafton **NPWS** (☎02-6641 1500; www.environment.nsw.gov.au; ⏲8.30am-4.30pm Mon-Fri) has info and a downloadable map.

Wooli

POP 493

Wooli, which is sitauted on a long isthmus, with a river estuary on one side and the ocean on the other side, has an isolated charm. It hosts the **Australian National Goanna Pulling Championships** (www.goannapulling.com.au) in early October. Rather than ripping the eponymous animal to shreds, participants, squatting on all fours, attach leather harnesses to their own heads and engage in a cranial tug of war.

Solitary Island Marine Park Resort (☎1800 003 031, 02-6649 7519; www.solitaryislandsresort.com.au; North St; campsites/beach shack/cabins from $28/48/99) has lovely cabins in a scrubby bush setting.

Grafton

POP 16,598

Grafton is a serene puff from an uncomplicated past. Nestled into a quiet bend of the Clarence River, the town's charming grid of wide streets has grand pubs and splendid old houses. It's also the 1963 founding home of hang-gliding, though you'll have to go elsewhere to partake in the sport.

Don't be fooled by the franchises along the highway, the main part of town is reached over an imposing 1932 double-decker (road and rail) bridge.

Sights & Activities

Victoria St is the town's historical focal point, providing fascinating glimpses of 19th-century architecture, including the **courthouse** (1862), **Roches Family Hotel** (1870) and the **Anglican Cathedral** (1884).

Susan Island, in the middle of the river, is home to the biggest fruit-bat colony in the southern hemisphere. Their evening departure is a spectacular summer sight.

The local arts scene drives **Grafton Artsfest** (graftonartsfestival.org), held twice yearly with workshops and exhibitions.

Grafton Regional Gallery GALLERY
(02-6642 3177; www.graftongallery.nsw.gov.au; 158 Fitzroy St; admission by donation; 10am-4pm Tue-Sun) The Grafton Regional Gallery hosts quality works from galleries around NSW.

Sleeping & Eating

Roches Family Hotel HOTEL $
(02-6644 2866; www.roches.com.au; 85 Victoria St; s/d incl breakfast with shared bathrooms $35/55) This fantastic, historic hotel has spruced-up pub rooms, a cafe and a beer garden. It's worth calling in just for a peek at the croc in the public bar.

Annies B&B B&B $$
(0421 914 295; www.anniesbnbgrafton.com; 13 Mary St; r $140-280;) This beautiful big old Victorian house on a leafy corner has private rooms set apart from the family home.

Clocktower Hotel PUB $$
(www.clocktowerhotel.com.au; 93 Princes St; mains $12-30; 10am-9pm) The Clocktower does an excellent range of Aussie staples such as steaks, burgers, pasta and chicken parma – it does them well and doesn't make you pay over the odds for them.

No 1 Duke Street PIZZA, MODERN AUSTRALIAN $$
(02-6643 1010; www.dukestreet.com.au; 1 Duke St; lunch mains $18-30, dinner mains $30-35; 8am-3pm Sat & Sun, 5-9pm Wed-Sat) Woodfired pizzas, occasional live jazz and a riverside location make this a welcome addition to Grafton's eating scene.

Georgies at the Gallery CAFE $$
(02-6642 6996; 158 Fitzroy St; mains $8-23; 10am-3pm & 6-10pm Wed-Sat, 10am-3pm Tue & Sun) At the Grafton Regional Gallery. This is Grafton's best cafe by a long shot. It occupies the gallery's internal courtyard where Grafton's cultured folk sip on good coffee and nibble on salads, quiche and cake.

Information

Clarence River Visitor Centre (02-6642 4677; www.clarencetourism.com; cnr Spring St & Pacific Hwy; 9am-5pm) South of town.

RUSSELL CROWE'S CURIOS

What is Russell Crowe's *Gladiator* costume doing in an old wooden barn in the tiny town of Nymboida, 30 minutes southwest of Grafton? How about Johnny Cash's gold albums and Don Bradman's caps? The answer: this is the 'Museum of Interesting Things', and Crowe owns it.

The Aussie superstar grew up in nearby Nana Glen where his parents still live. When he bought the adjoining **Coaching Station Inn** (02-6649 4126; www.coachingstation.com; 3970 Armidale Rd; s/d $110/140), he had the old barn refitted to house his considerable collection of boy's toys, from music and movie memorabilia to sporting paraphernalia and vintage motorbikes. The **museum** (11am-3pm Wed-Fri, 11am-5pm Sat, 10am-3pm Sun) FREE also acts as a repository for artefacts from local pioneering history, a nod to the day when horse-drawn Cobb & Co coaches stopped here on the woolpack road from Armidale to Grafton.

Aside from the photos that dot the inn's main bar, you're not likely to see the man himself. Then again, the barman reckons he sometimes pops in unannounced. After all, 'it's only 11 minutes by chopper from his mum and dad's house'.

NPWS Office (☎02-6641 1500; level 3, 49 Victoria St)

Getting There & Away

Busways (☎1300 555 611; www.busways.com.au) runs to Yamba ($13.50, 1¼ hours, six daily) and Maclean ($11.40, 45 minutes).

Greyhound (☎1300 GREYHOUND, 1300 4739 46863; www.greyhound.com.au) and **Premier** (☎13 34 10; www.premierms.com.au) stop at the train station on runs south to Sydney ($121, 11 hours) and north to Byron ($66, 3½ hours).

CountryLink (☎13 22 32; www.countrylink.info) stops here on its north coast route. Sydney ($87, 10 hours) is served three times daily.

Yamba & Angourie

POP 6032 (YAMBA), 184 (ANGOURIE)

Once a sleepy little fishing town, Yamba is slowly growing in popularity with a relaxed pace of life and excellent food.

Its southern neighbour, Angourie, a small chilled-out place, is home to NSW's first National Surfing Reserve and has always been a hot spot for experienced surfers. Apart from the surf, the only sign of development is the Pacific St mansion of Gordon Merchant, founder of the surf brand Billabong, who grew up here (and who, by all accounts, still gets around in boardshorts).

Sights & Activities

Surfing for the big boys is at **Angourie Point** but Yamba's beaches have something for everyone else. When the surf is flat **Pippi's** is decent, especially when dolphins hang around. **Main Beach** is the busiest with an ocean pool, banana palms and a grassy slope for those who don't want sand up their clacker. **Convent Beach** is a sunbaker's haven and **Turner's**, protected by the breakwall, is ideal for surf lessons.

The Yuraygir Coastal Walk begins in Angourie.

Iluka Nature Reserve NATURE RESERVE

World Heritage–listed Iluka is a short detour off the highway or a ferry ride away; it's the southern end of **Bundjalung National Park** (www.environment.nsw.gov.au; per car per day $7), largely untouched and best explored with 4WD. Highlights include the literally named Ten Mile Beach and the hopefully not-literally named Hell Hole Lagoon. The passenger-only **Clarence River Ferry** (☎02-6646 6423; www.clarenceriverferries.com; adult/child $7/3.50) runs at least four times daily.

> WORTH A TRIP
>
> **GRAFTON TO YAMBA**
>
> Heading north on the Pacific Hwy it's worth taking a small detour to **Ulmarra** (population 435), a heritage-listed town with a river port. There's the quaint old corner **Ulmarra Hotel** (☎02-6644 5305; www.ulmarrahotel.com.au; 2 Coldstream St; s/d from $40/60) with a wrought-iron verandah, pub rooms and a greener-than-green beer garden (mains $9 to $26) that stretches down to the river, which can be crossed by car ferry 1km north of town. Further on, **Maclean** (population 2600) is a picturesque little town with an unmistakeable Scottish heritage.

Blue Pools NATURE RESERVE

These spring-water-fed water holes are the remains of the quarry used for the breakwall. Locals and the daring climb the 'chalk-line', 'tree-line' or 'death-line' cliff faces and plunge to their depths. The saner can slip silently into clear water, surrounded by bush, only metres from the surf.

Yamba River Markets MARKET

Fourth Sunday of month on Clarence River.

Story House Museum MUSEUM

(☎02-6646 2316; www.pyhsmuseum.com.au; River St; adult/child $3/free; ⏱10am-4.30pm Tue-Thu, 2-4.30pm Sat & Sun) Maritime culture and shipwrecks.

Yamba-Angourie Surf School SURFING

(☎02-6646 1496; www.yambaangouriesurfschool.com.au; 2hr/3-day lessons $50/120) Classes here are run by former Australian surfing champion, Jeremy Walters.

Yamba Kayak KAYAKING

(☎02-6646 1137; www.yambakayak.com.au; Whiting Beach car park; 3/5hrs $70/90) Half- and full-day adventures are a speciality with forays into nearby wilderness areas.

Xtreme Cycle & Skate CYCLING, HIKING

(☎02-6645 8879; 34 Coldstream St; adult half-/full day $15/25, child half-/full day $10/15) Has bikes for rent.

Sleeping

★**Yamba YHA** HOSTEL $

(☎02-6646 3997; www3.yha.com.au; 26 Coldstream St; dm from $27; ❄@🛜≋) Spankingly modern and groovy, this is a purpose-built hostel with an excellent downstairs bar and restaurant (mains $9 to $29). Upstairs there's a rooftop deck, pool and barbecue area. It's family run and extremely welcoming. After sampling one of Shane's '10-buck' welcome tours, you're guaranteed to extend your stay.

Pacific Hotel PUB, HOTEL **$**
(☎02-6646 2466; www.pacifichotelyamba.com.au; 18 Pilot St; dm $20-35, r with/without bathroom $120/70) This is a fabulous pub overlooking the ocean, with bright bunk rooms and handsome hotel rooms. Great views but the food is also exceptional – a lofty step above the usual pub nosh.

Calypso Holiday Park CARAVAN PARK **$**
(☎02-6646 2468; www.calypsoyamba.com.au; Harbour St; camp sites from $28, cabins from $80; @ ≋) The best-located camping place, Calypso is a short walk from the town centre and all the beaches. There are 162 sites and 32 cabins, some quite posh, and all close to the water.

★**Angourie Rainforest Resort** RESORT **$$**
(☎02-6646 8600; www.angourieresort.com.au; 166 Angourie Rd; 1-/2-bedroom apt from $135/170; ❄ @ 🛜 ≋) A little piece of paradise sidled up to 600 hectares of flora. Luxuries include a pool, a tennis court, a restaurant and a day spa. Extras include a pristine rainforest aroma and resident birds and lizards.

Eating & Drinking

★**Beachwood** MIDDLE EASTERN **$$**
(☎02-6646 9781; www.beachwoodcafe.com.au; 22 High St; mains $15; ⏲7am-3pm Tue-Sun) Tipped as the best breakfast in town, its lunches also draw a regular crowd with fabulous Turkish-inspired flavours and good coffee.

Frangipan MEDITERRANEAN **$$**
(☎02-6646 2553; www.frangipan.com.au; 11-13 The Crescent; mains $19-32; ⏲6.30-10pm Tue-Sat) Surfing memorabilia overlooks a classy dining area and the two-course meal for $25 might just be coastal NSW's best deal. The crisp-skinned salmon wins our vote.

El Pirata TAPAS **$$**
(☎02-6646 3276; 6 Clarence St; dishes $9-18; ⏲6-9.30pm Tue-Sun) This is a fabulous tapas bar serving authentic hot and cold Spanish dishes, including *jamon* (ham), chorizo, oily garlic prawns and cheesy stuffed peppers. It's at its best during summer when the Sydney owners are back in town.

Yamba Bar & Grill STEAK **$$**
(☎02-6646 1155; 15 Clarence St; mains $15-34; ⏲6-9.30pm Tue-Sun) This stylish food den is spacious with a great rear deck and view. The menu is for serious steak lovers with sides right from the gastropub playbook: chips and rocket salad. Service can be a little slow when things are busy. There are a couple of other restaurants on this little strip.

Getting There & Away

Busways (☎1300 555 611; www.busways.com.au) buses go to Maclean ($6.75, 30 minutes) and Grafton ($12.50, 1¼ hours, several Monday to Saturday). **CountryLink** (☎13 22 32; www.countrylink.info) buses go to Byron Bay ($17, three hours, one daily) and to Grafton where they connect to Sydney ($91, 11½ hours). **Greyhound** (☎1300 GREYHOUND, 1300 4739 46863; www.greyhound.com.au) stops on runs south to Sydney ($142, 11½ hours) and north to Byron ($37, two hours).

Ballina

POP 15,963

At the mouth of the Richmond River, Ballina is spoilt for white sandy beaches and crystal-clear waters. If it weren't so close to Byron it would be a tourist haven in its own right.

Sights & Activities

Norton St boasts a number of impressive late-19th-century buildings from Ballina's days as a rich lumber town. For architecture of a different kind, the dilapidated Big Prawn is 1km west of town – someone should put it out of its misery.

White and sandy, like all good beaches, **Shelly Beach** is patrolled. Calm **Shaws Bay Lagoon** is popular with families. **South Ballina Beach** is a good excursion option via the car ferry on Burns Point Ferry Rd.

Naval & Maritime Museum MUSEUM
(☎02-6681 1002; www.ballinamaritimemuseum.org.au; Regatta Ave; admission by donation; ⏲9am-4pm) Behind the information centre, this museum is where you will find the amazing remains of a balsawood raft that drifted across the Pacific from Ecuador as part of the Las Balsas expedition in 1973.

Richmond River Cruises BOAT TOUR
(☎02-6687 5688; www.rrcruises.com.au; Regatta Ave; 2hr trip adult/child $30/15; ⏲10am & 2pm

Wed & Sun) The most established cruise service and also wheelchair friendly.

Aboriginal Cultural Concepts CULTURAL TOUR
(☎0405 654 280; www.aboriginalculturalconcepts.com; half-/full-day tours per person $80/160; ⏲10am-2pm Wed-Sat) Get an indigenous insight into the local area on these heritage tours exploring mythological sights along Bundjalung Coast. The three-hour bushtucker tour is popular.

Jack Ransom Cycles BICYCLE RENTAL
(16 Cherry St; per day $20) Bicycle rental for exploring the town and surrounds.

Sleeping & Eating

Ballina Travellers Lodge HOTEL $
(☎02-6686 6737; www.ballinatravellerslodge.com.au; 36-38 Tamar St; s/d/tw $65/95/115;) This lodge combines motel and hostel guests. It is clean and comfortable and the owners are a good source of info.

★**Ballina Manor** HISTORIC HOTEL $$$
(☎02-6681 5888; www.ballinamanor.com.au; 25 Norton St; r $165-377;) This grand old dame of hospitality was once a school but has since been converted into a luxurious guesthouse filled to the hilt with restored 1920s furnishings, carpets and curtains. All rooms are indulgent: the best room has a four-poster bed and spa.

La Cucina di Vino ITALIAN $$
(2 Martin St; mains $13-26; ⏲noon-3pm & 5-9pm Wed-Sun, 5-9pm Mon & Tue) Water views and an open corner locale make this Italian restaurant an excellent venue for a long lunch. There's pizza too.

Ballina Gallery Cafe CAFE $$
(☎02-6681 38888; www.ballinagallerycafe.com.au; 46 Cherry St; mains $14-29) Breakfasts, salads and sandwiches are the perfect complement to the light decorators touch of the former council chambers here. Ballina's best cafe.

Information

Ballina Visitor Centre (☎02-6686 3484; www.discoverballina.com; cnr Las Balsas Plaza & River St) At the eastern end of town.

Getting There & Away

If you're driving to Byron Bay, take the coast road through Lennox Head. It's much prettier than the Pacific Hwy and with less traffic.

AIR

Ballina's airport (BNK) is the best way to reach Byron Bay – only 30km to the north. It has car-rental desks and plenty of local transport options. Airline service is increasing.

Jetstar (☎13 15 38; www.jetstar.com.au) Serves Sydney.

Regional Express (☎13 17 13; www.regionalexpress.com.au) Serves Sydney.

Virgin Australia (☎13 67 89; www.virginaustralia.com) Serves Melbourne via Sydney.

BUS

Greyhound (☎1300 GREYHOUND, 1300 4739 46863; www.greyhound.com.au) heads north to Byron ($5.60, 40 minutes) and Brisbane ($61, four to five hours) and south to Sydney ($152, 12 hours). **Premier** (☎13 34 10; www.premierms.com.au) heads south to Sydney ($92, 13 hours).

Blanch's Bus Service (p193) operates several daily services from the airport and the Tamar St bus stop to Lennox Head ($7.80, 30 minutes), Byron Bay ($12, 70 minutes) and Mullumbimby ($11, 85 minutes).

SHUTTLE

Numerous shuttle companies meet flights and serve Ballina, Byron Bay and other nearby towns. Rates average $15 to $20.

Airport Express (☎0414 660 031; www.stevestours.com.au)

Byron Easy Bus (☎02-6685 7447; www.byronbayshuttle.com.au)

Lennox Head

POP 5764

A protected National Surfing Reserve, Lennox Head is home to picturesque coastline with some of the best surf on the coast, including long right-hander breaks. Its blossoming food scene combined with a laid-back atmosphere makes it a quieter alternative to its boisterous well-touristed neighbour Byron, 17km north.

Sights & Activities

Stunning **Seven Mile Beach** runs along parallel to the main street. The best places for a dip are at the north end near the surf club or at the southern end in the Channel. **Port Morton lookout** is a whale- and dolphin-spotting high point.

Lake Ainsworth, a lagoon just back from the surf club, is made brown by tannins from the tea trees along its banks, which also make swimming here beneficial to the skin. If the wind's up, **Wind & Water Action Sports** (☎0419 686 188;

www.windnwater.net; surf lessons per hr $80) has kite-boarding, windsurfing and surf lessons, plus hire equipment. **Seabreeze Hang Gliding** (☎0428 560 248; www.seabreezehang-gliding.com; tandem hanglide from $145) offers tandem flights off Lennox Headland.

Sleeping & Eating

The **Professionals** (☎02-6687 7579; www.lennoxheadaccom.net.au; 66 Ballina St) is good for holiday rentals.

Lennox Head Beach House HOSTEL $
(☎02-6687 7636; www.yha.com.au; 3 Ross St; dm/d $30.50/70; @) YHA-affiliated and only 100m from the beach, this place has immaculate rooms and a great vibe. For $5 you can use the boards, sailboards and bikes.

Lake Ainsworth Holiday Park CARAVAN PARK $
(☎02-6687 7249; www.ballinabeachside.com.au; Pacific Pde; powered sites $33, cabins from $80; wi-fi) Family-friendly, just opposite the beach.

O-pes MEDITERRANEAN $$
(☎02-6687 7388; 90-92 Ballina St; mains $25-32; ⊙noon-3pm & 5.30-9pm, also 9.30-11.30am Sat & Sun) Comfy couches and low-slung tables mix it with a beachfront vibe and vista. The menu balances casual tapas with more formal à la carte dishes.

Getting There & Away

Blanch's Bus Service (p193) operates a service to Ballina ($7.80), Mullumbimby ($10.50) and Byron Bay ($8.50).

Byron Bay

POP 4959

Bondi, Bell's Beach and Byron Bay. The reputation of this iconic Aussie beach precedes it: it's a gorgeous town where the trademark laid-back, New Age populace lives an escapist, organic lifestyle against a backdrop of

Byron Bay

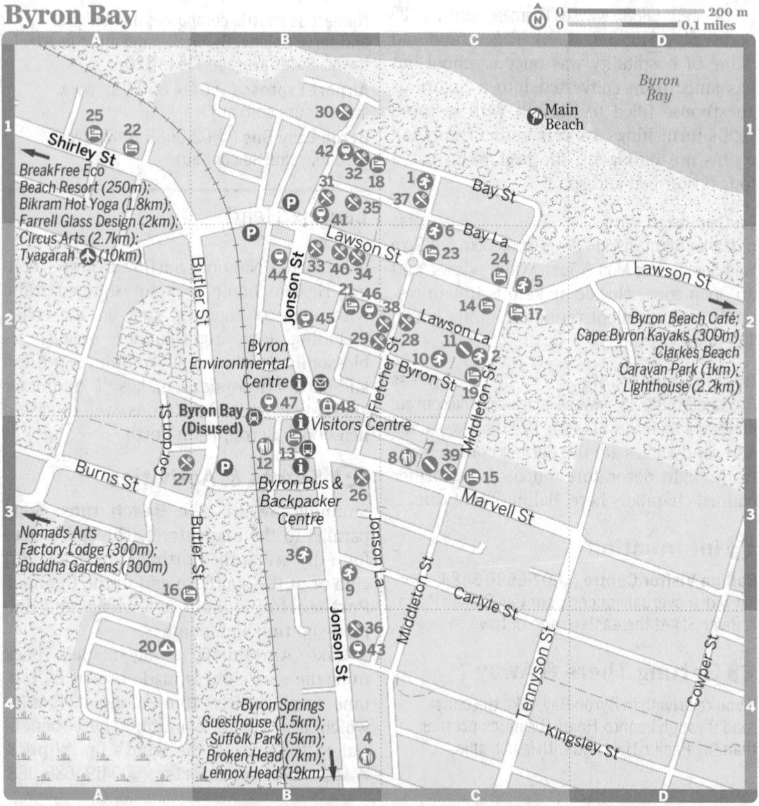

evergreen hinterland and endlessly surfable coastline.

The pitfall lies in arriving in this utopia along with every other backpacker on the coast, and wondering what all the fuss is about. But Byron's unique vibe has a way of converting even the most cynical with its long days, balmy weather, endless beaches, delightful accommodation, fine food, delirious nightlife and ambling milieu.

It's an addiction that's hard to kick; many simply don't. A weekend turns into a week, a week into a month...Before you know it, dreadlocks are a serious consideration.

Sights

Main Beach, immediately in front of town, is terrific for people-watching and swimming. At the western edge of town, **Belongil Beach** is clothing-optional. **Clarkes Beach**, at the eastern end of Main Beach, is good for surfing, but the best surf is at the next few beaches along: **Pass**, **Wategos** and **Little Wategos**.

Tallow Beach is an amazing stretch that extends 7km south of Cape Byron to a rockier patch around **Broken Head**, where a succession of small beaches dots the coast before opening onto **Seven Mile Beach**, which goes all the way to Lennox Head.

The suburb of **Suffolk Park** (with more good surf, particularly in winter) starts 3km south of town. **Kings Beach**, a popular gay beach, is just off Seven Mile Beach Rd near the Broken Head Holiday Park.

Cape Byron

The grandfather of the poet Lord Byron was a renowned navigator in the 1760s, and Captain Cook named this spot, mainland Australia's most easterly, after him.

The views from the summit are spectacular, particularly if you've just burnt breakfast off on the climbing track from Clarkes Beach. Ribboning around the headland, it dips and (mostly) soars its way to the lighthouse. The surrounding ocean also jumps to the tune of dolphins and migrating humpback whales in

Byron Bay

Activities, Courses & Tours
1 Bay Beach Hire ... C1
Blackdog Surfing ... (see 19)
2 Byron Ayurveda Centre ... C2
3 Byron Bay Bicycles ... B3
4 Byron Bay Surf School ... B4
5 Byron Surf & Bike Hire ... C2
6 Cocoon ... C2
7 Dive Byron Bay ... C3
8 Mojosurf Adventures ... C3
9 Relax Haven ... B3
10 Ruth Smith Healing ... C2
Shambala ... (see 9)
11 Sundive ... C2
12 Surfing Byron Bay ... B3

Sleeping
13 Accommodation Booking Office ... B3
14 Aquarius ... C2
15 Atlantic ... C3
16 Bamboo Cottage ... A3
17 Bay Beach Motel ... C2
18 Beach Hotel Resort ... B1
19 Cape Byron YHA ... C2
20 Glen Villa Resort ... A4
21 Nomads ... B2
22 Outrigger Bay Resort ... A1
23 Professionals ... C2
24 Waves ... C2
25 Wollongbar Motor Inn ... A1

Eating
Balcony ... (see 41)
26 Bay Leaf Café ... B3
27 Byron Farmers Market ... A3
28 Dip ... C2
29 Earth 'n' Sea ... B2
Espressohead ... (see 19)
30 Fishheads ... B1
31 Fresh ... B1
32 Italian at the Pacific ... B1
33 Kinoko Sushi Bar ... B2
34 Mokha ... B2
35 Mongers ... B1
36 One One One ... B4
Orgasmic ... (see 35)
37 Orient Express ... C1
Petit Snail ... (see 9)
38 St Elmo ... C2
39 Targa ... C3
40 Twisted Sista ... B2

Drinking & Nightlife
41 Balcony ... B1
42 Beach Hotel ... B1
43 Cheeky Monkeys ... B4
44 Cocomangas ... B2
45 Great Northern ... B2
46 La La Land ... B2
47 Railway Friendly Bar ... B2
St Elmo ... (see 38)

Shopping
Happy High Herbs ... (see 10)
48 Planet Corroboree ... B2

DON'T MISS

NAPPING IN NATURE

Located right at the Byron Bay Lighthouse, the historic 1901 **Lighthouse Keepers Cottages** (☎02-6685 6552; www.nationalparks.nsw.gov.au; 3-day rentals from $1200) have been renovated with polished wood floors and lovely furnishings so that guests can spend the night here. The views are swell and you have the place to yourself after dusk. There are other, similar possibilities elsewhere along the coast.

June and July. Towering over all is the 1901 **lighthouse** (☎02-6685 6585; Lighthouse Rd; ⏲8am-sunset), Australia's most easterly and powerful. The Cape Byron Walking Track continues around the northeastern side of the cape, delving into **Cape Byron State Conservation Park**, where you'll encounter Australian brush turkeys and wallabies. En route, there are fine views from **Captain Cook Lookout**. You can also drive right up to the lighthouse and pay $7 for the privilege of parking (or nothing at all if you park 300m below).

Activities

Adventure sports abound in Byron Bay and most operators offer a free pick-up service from local accommodation. Surfing and diving are the biggest draws.

Surfing

Byron Bay waves are often quite mellow. Many hostels provide free boards to guests. Half-day classes typically start at $60.

Blackdog Surfing SURFING
(☎02-6680 9828; www.blackdogsurfing.com; 4/5-11 Bryon St) Intimate group lessons and women's courses.

Byron Bay Surf School SURFING
(☎1800 707 274; www.byronbaysurfschool.com; 127 Jonson St) Surf camps too.

Byron Surf Kool Katz SURFING
(☎02-6685 5169; www.koolkatzsurf.com) Half-day lessons and more.

Mojosurf Adventures SURFING
(☎1800 113 044; www.mojosurf.com; Marvell St; 1/2 lessons $69/119, 2-/3-day trips $280/445) Epic surf trips.

Surfing Byron Bay SURFING
(☎02-6685 7099; www.gosurfingbyronbay.com; 84 Jonson St) Has courses for kids and, unlike some other operators, they surf in Byron Bay, not Ballina.

Soul Surf School SURFING
(☎1800 089 699; www.soulsurfschool.com.au) Recommended classes for beginners.

Surfaris SURFING
(☎1800 634 951; www.surfaris.com; 3-/4-/5-day tours $450/550/650) Fabulous multiday trips between Sydney and Byron Bay, including camping and meals.

Diving & Snorkelling

About 3km offshore, **Julian Rocks Marine Reserve** blends cold southerly and warm northerly currents, attracting a profusion of marine species and divers alike.

Dive Byron Bay DIVING
(☎02-6685 8333, 1800 243 483; www.byronbaydivecentre.com.au; 9 Marvell St) Rentals, sales, PADI courses from $495, dives from $95.

Sundive DIVING
(☎02-6685 7755; www.sundive.com.au; 8 Middleton St; snorkelling tour $55; ⏲tours 8am, 10.45am & 1pm) Scuba diving plus daily snorkelling.

Blue Bay Divers DIVING, SNORKELLING
(☎1800 858 155; www.bluebaydivers.com.au; double dive with tank hire $115) Small groups and the chance to dive or snorkel with dolphns and turtles.

Alternative Therapies

Byron is the alternative-therapy heartland – the visitor centre has a full list of options.

Ruth Smith Healing HEALTH & FITNESS
(Abundatia; ☎02-6685 8008; www.ruthsmithhealing.com; 6-7 Byron St; treatments from $150) Connect with your spirit to bring about healing.

Bikram Yoga YOGA
(☎02-6685 6334; www.bikramyogabyronbay.com.au; 8 Grevillea St; casual 90min class $20) One of the more respected yoga schools in Byron.

Buddha Gardens DAY SPA
(☎02-6680 7844; www.buddhagardensdayspa.com.au; 1 Skinners Shoot Rd, Arts Factory Village; massage from $120; ⏲10am-6pm) Balinese-style day spa.

Byron Ayurveda Centre HEALTH & FITNESS
(☎02-6632 2244; www.ayurvedahouse.com.au; shop 6, Middleton St; treatments from $45; ⏲10am-

5pm Wed-Sun) It's exfoliation all the way at this restful place aimed at the masses.

Relax Haven HEALTH & FITNESS
(☎02-6685 8304; www.relaxhaven.com.au; 3/107 Jonson St; ⏰9am-8.30pm) Massages, kinesiology and floatation tanks that get rave reviews from travellers.

Cocoon HEALTH & FITNESS
(☎02-6685 5711; 6/11 Fletcher St; massage from $70) Offers 'healthful retreats' from family holidays.

Shambala HEALTH & FITNESS
(☎02-6680 7791; www.shambala.net.au; 4 Carlyle St; treatments from $55; ⏰9am-7pm) Massage, reflexology and acupuncture.

Flying

Byron Airwaves HANG-GLIDING
(☎02-6629 0354; www.byronair.com) Tandem hang-gliding ($145) and courses (starting from $1500).

Byron Bay Ballooning BALLOONING
(☎1300 889 660; www.byronbayballooning.com.au; Tyagarah Airport; adult/child $325/175) Sunrise flights including gourmet breakfast.

Byron Gliding SCENIC FLIGHT
(☎02-6684 7627; www.byrongliding.com; flights from $120) Drift high above the earth in a glider.

Byron Bay Microlights MICROLIGHTING
(☎0407 281 687; www.byronbaymicrolights.com.au; Tyagarah Airport; 15-/30-/45-minute flight $100/180/245) A range of scenic flights.

Skydive Byron Bay SKYDIVING
(☎1800 800 840, 02-6684 1323; www.skydivebyronbay.com; Tyagarah Airport; tandem flights $264-504) Tandem dives are priced depending on altitude and time of freefall (20 to 60 seconds).

Skydive the Beach SKYDIVING
(☎1800 302 005; www.skydivethebeachbyronbay.com; per person $249-299) Tandem skydives from up to 14,000 feet.

Kayaking

Exhibitionist dolphins enhance scenic, half-day kayaking tours in and around Cape Byron Marine Park.

Cape Byron Kayaks KAYAKING
(☎02-6680 9555; www.capebyronkayaks.com; adult/child $59/69; ⏰tours 8.30am & 1pm) Cape Byron Kayaks offers great half-day kayaking tours in and around Cape Byron Marine Park. Exhibitionist dolphins are the main attraction (if you don't see one you get a free second trip).

Gosea Kayaks KAYAKING
(☎0416 222 344; www.goseakayakbyronbay.com.au; adult/child $69/59; ⏰tours 9.30am & 2pm) If you don't see a whale, turtle or dolphin, you kayak for free. Some tours go with Aboriginal guides.

Other

Byron Surf & Bike Hire BICYCLE RENTAL
(☎02-6680 7066; 1-3 31 Lawson St) Rents bikes ($20 per day), kayaks (half-day $45), surfboards ($30 per day) and other active gear.

Bay Beach Hire BICYCLE RENTAL
(☎1800 089 699; 3/14 Bay St; half-/full-day bike or surfboard rental $20/30) Bikes, surfboards, stand-up paddle boards, wetsuits and snorkels for hire.

Byron Bay Bicycles BICYCLE RENTAL
(☎02-6685 6067; www.byronbaybicycles.com.au; The Plaza, 85 Jonson St; 4/8hr $14/22; ⏰8.30am-5.30pm Mon-Fri, 9am-4pm Sat) Bikes for rent close to the town centre.

Circus Arts COURSE
(☎02-6685 6566; www.circusarts.com.au; 17 Centennial Circuit) About 2km west of town with holiday classes for kids.

Farrell Glass Design GLASS BLOWING
(☎02-6685 7044; www.farrellglassdesign.com; 6 Acacia St; ⏰10am-4pm Tue-Sun) Ring ahead for glass-blowing demonstrations.

☞ Tours

Numerous operators run tours to Nimbin (p194) and other interesting places in the hinterland. Most tour companies will pick you up from where you're staying.

Aboriginal Cultural Concepts CULTURAL TOUR
(☎0405 654 280; www.aboriginalculturalconcepts.com; half-/full-day tours $80/160; ⏰10am-1pm Wed-Sat) Heritage tours exploring mythological sights along Bundjalung Coast. Highly recommended.

Byron Bay Eco Tours ECOLOGICAL
(☎02-6685 4030; www.byron-bay.com/ecotours; tours $85; ⏰9am) Full-day tours to nearby rainforests with excellent commentary.

Byron Bay Wildlife Tours WILDLIFE
(☎0429 770 686; www.byronbaywildlifetours.com; adult/child $70/35) Seven mammals guaranteed

or your money back. Wildlife tours in summer (from November) then whale watching June to October.

Mountain Bike Tours   MOUNTAIN BIKING
(☑0429 122 504; www.mountainbiketours.com.au; half-/full-day tours $75/125; ☺9am) Environmentally friendly bike tours into the rainforest and along the coast.

Vision Walks   WILDLIFE
(☑02-6687 4237; www.visionwalks.com; adult/child night tour $99/75, other tours from $45/28) See nocturnal animals in their natural habitat on the Night Vision Walk; other excellent wildlife tours also possible.

Byron Bay Adventure Tours   TOUR, HIKING
(☑1300 120 028; www.byronbayadventuretours.com.au) Day walks and overnight tours to Mount Warning

✵ Festivals & Events

East Coast International Blues & Roots Music Festival   MUSIC
(www.bluesfest.com.au) Held over Easter, this international jam attracts high-calibre international performers and local heavyweights. Book early.

Byron Bay Writers Festival   LITERATURE
(www.byronbaywritersfestival.com.au) In late July/early August, this festival gathers together top-shelf writers and literary followers from across Australia.

Byron Bay Surf Festival   SURFING
(www.byronbaysurffestival.com) Late-October celebration of surf culture.

🛏 Sleeping

Don't turn up in January without having a reservation. Schoolies Week at the end of November is also one to avoid. During these periods, one-night-only bookings are rare.

Motels are clustered in town and south along Bangalow Rd. There are scores of B&Bs and apartments all along Belongil Beach.

The **accommodation booking office** (☑02-6680 8666; www.byronbayaccom.net), run by the visitor centre, is a great service for booking in advance.

For holiday houses check out **Professionals** (☑02-6685 6552; www.byronbaypro.com.au; cnr Lawson & Fletcher Sts).

Nomads Arts Factory Lodge   HOSTEL, CAMPGROUND $
(☑02-6685 7709; nomadsworld.com/arts-factory; Skinners Shoot Rd; camp sites $18, dm/d from $35/80; @🐾🛜🏊) For an archetypal Byron experience, bunker down here. The complex has didgeridoo lessons and yoga and meditation workshops delivered in a serene hippie-esque setting on a picturesque swamp. Choose from colourful six- to 10-bed dorms, a cottage, tepees or wagons. Couples can opt for aptly titled 'cube' rooms, island retreat canvas huts or the pricier love shack with bathroom.

Nomads   HOSTEL $
(☑02-6680 7966; www.nomadsbyronbay.com.au; 1 Lawson Lane; dm $25, d $90, d without bathroom $105; @🛜) Byron's biggest backpackers packs an edgy punch with its glossy designer-led decor and funky furniture. It is purpose-built so the 10 dorm rooms are squeaky clean, but they're not half as good as the king rooms, which have bathrooms, fridges and plasma televisions.

Aquarius   HOSTEL $
(☑02-6685 7663; www.aquarius-backpackers.com.au; 14-16 Lawson St; dm/d/motel d from $32/75/150; 🚽@🏊) This motel-style backpackers overflows with the comings and goings of hyperactive, excitable travellers. There's plenty of communal space – including a bar – ensuring those going it solo can find mates. Self-contained spa suites also available (doubles from $170).

Cape Byron YHA   HOSTEL $
(☑1800 652 627, 02-6685 8788; www3.yha.com.au; cnr Middleton & Byron Sts; dm/d from $32/105; 🚽@🏊) Modern, tidy, central.

Clarkes Beach Caravan Park   CARAVAN PARK $
(☑02-6685 6496; www.northcoastparks.com.au/clarkes; off Lighthouse Rd; unpowered sites/cabins from $42/140; @) Tightly packed cabins and sites in a bush setting.

Glen Villa Resort   CARAVAN PARK $
(☑02-6685 7382; www.glenvillaresort.com.au; Butler St; d cabin from $95; 🚽@🛜🏊) Slightly militant 'two people only' rule, but well maintained. It's off the main traffic route so is last to fill up.

Atlantic   GUESTHOUSE $$
(☑02-6685 5118; www.atlanticbyronbay.com.au; 13 Marvell St; r from $155; 🚽🛜🏊) What a difference a facelift makes. This little residen-

tial compound has been transformed into a shiny white seaside haven where Byron surf culture meets Caribbean style.

Bamboo Cottage GUESTHOUSE $$
(☎02-6685 5509; www.byron-bay.com/bamboocottage; 76 Butler St; r from $120; 📶) Featuring global charm and wall hangings, Bamboo Cottage treats guests to a choice of three individually styled rooms with Asian and Pacific island overtones in a home-away-from-home atmosphere. It's on the quiet side of the tracks. The cheaper rooms have shared bathrooms.

Oasis Resort & Treetop Houses APARTMENTS $$
(☎02-6685 7390, 1800 336 129; byronoasis.com.au; 24 Scott St; apt/treetop apt from $200/360; ❄🏊) Away from the town centre, this compact resort is engulfed by palms and has apartments with big balconies. Even better are those sitting atop the tree canopies with outdoor spas and ocean views.

Byron Springs Guesthouse GUESTHOUSE $$
(☎0457 808 101; www.byronsprings.com.au; 2 Oodgeroo Garden; s with shared bathroom from $75, d without/with bathroom from $95/110; ❄📶) Polished wood floorboards, white linen and a lovely leafy setting make this a good choice if you like to be removed from the throng. It's a 20-minute walk into the centre.

Bay Beach Motel MOTEL $$
(☎02-6685 6090; www.baybeachmotel.com.au; 32 Lawson St; r $140-200, 2-bedroom apt from $340; ❄📶🏊) Unpretentious but smart, this white-brick hotel with IKEA-esque furnishings is close to town and the beach, but not so close that partygoers keep guests awake.

BreakFree Eco Beach Resort SELF-CATERING $$
(☎02-6639 5700; www.ecobeachbyron.com.au; 35-37 Shirley St; d $186, 1-/2-bedroom apartment $219/404) At the upper end of midrange price and quality, this trim resort of fresh studios and one-bedroom apartments is like a gleaming shrine to Ikea with simple but contemporary interiors.

Wollongbar Motor Inn SELF-CATERING $$
(☎02-6685 8200; www.wollongbar.com; 19-21 Shirley St; s/d/f from $129/149/179) Interiors here are generously roomy and the family rooms have a box full of toys for the kids. The beach is a short walk through the bush (watch for brush turkeys).

★**Byron at Byron** RESORT $$$
(☎02-6639 2000, 1300 554 362; www.thebyronatbyron.com.au; r from $305; ❄@📶🏊) For the ultimate in luxury this 92-suite resort is set within 45 acres of subtropical rainforest. It is a hive of wildlife and endangered species and the resort maintains its sympathy to the environment with eco credentials listed online. When you're not lounging by the infinity pool take the 10-minute stroll to Tallow Beach via a series of wonderful boardwalks.

Beach Hotel Resort RESORT $$$
(☎02-6685 6402; www.beachhotelresort.com.au; Bay St; r incl breakfast from $440; ❄🏊) In Byron's hub, this beachfront icon attracts a classy crowd somewhat more reserved than that of the massive hotel beer garden next door. Ground-floor rooms open onto lush gardens and a heated pool where a family of lizards sunbakes; rooms in the upper storeys have ocean views.

Rae's on Watego's HOTEL $$$
(☎02-6685 5366; www.raes.com.au; Marine Pde; r from $540; ❄@📶🏊) This dazzlingly white Mediterranean villa was once rated one of the world's top 25 hotels. It's definitely one of Australia's. Rooms here have an artistic and casual elegance that lets the luxury sneak up on you. The restaurant is worth the trip alone.

Outrigger Bay Resort APARTMENTS $$$
(☎02-6685 8646; www.outriggerbay.com; 9 Shirley St; 2-/3-bedroom apt $223/284; ❄📶🏊) This apartment complex has one-, two- and three-bedroom units with open kitchens on a shady site overlooking a pool. The beach is only 50m away.

Waves APARTMENTS $$$
(☎1800 040 151; www.wavesresorts.com.au; 35 Lawson St; d apt $180-400; ❄📶) Cushy, central boutique penthouse and studio apartments.

Eating

Bay Leaf Café MODERN AUSTRALIAN $
(Marvell St; mains $9-17; ⏰6.30am-5pm) This tiny wedge-shaped bohemian cafe has a small but excellent menu prepared in a busy open kitchen. Best meal of the day is breakfast. That is, unless fresh homemade pasta takes your fancy.

Fishheads SEAFOOD, FISH & CHIPS $
(www.restaurantbyronbay.com; 1 Jonson St; mains $9.50-22; ⏰7.30am-9pm; 📶) Right on the beach, this fabulous takeaway shop sells

traditional battered fish and chips ($9.80) or take it up a notch with chilli and garlic squid with Asian coleslaw. The restaurant is fine too, but why wouldn't you dine on the beach?

Twisted Sista BAKERY $
(shop 1, 4 Lawson St; mains $10-19; ⏲7.30am-3pm) Bounteous baked goods include huge muffins, salmon bruschetta and overstuffed sandwiches on beautiful bread. Outdoor tables add to the slightly happy hungover vibe.

Mongers FISH & CHIPS $
(☎02-6680 8080; www.mongers.com.au; Bay Lane; mains $13-20; ⏲midday-9pm) Tucked behind the Beach Hotel, this fish-and-chips joint issues forth to tables of devotees. It's a narrow, back-alley space but the quality is all high-street. Lighten things up with a grilled calamari salad.

Espressohead CAFE $
(Shop 7, Middleton St) Locals flock to this place for its excellent coffees, bagels, fresh pasta and salads.

Byron Farmers Market SELF-CATERING $
(www.byronfarmersmarket.com.au; Butler St Reserve; ⏲7-11am Thu) An open-air temple to regional food.

Dip MEDITERRANEAN $
(21 Fletcher St; tapas $4.50-21; ⏲8am-3pm) Groovy bar with inspired menu.

Mokha MEDITERRANEAN, MIDDLE EASTERN $
(Shop 2, Lawson St; mains $9-32; 📶) Eclectic Euro-Middle Eastern menu and lengthy wine list.

★**St Elmo** MEDITERRANEAN, BAR $$
(☎02-6680 7426; www.stelmodining.com; cnr Fletcher St & Lawson Lane; mains $14.50-26; ⏲4pm-late Mon-Thu, noon-late Fri-Sun) Kartell stools nod to just how much design work it takes to get bums on seats. Sit on one to be served gourmet cocktails by extremely fit bronzed and accented barmen, or settle in for dinner; the shared plates ($23) make great date fodder. Dishes might include seared scallops with peppers stuffed with chorizo and prawn paella.

Kinoko Sushi Bar JAPANESE $$
(7/23 Jonson St; mains $13.80-25; ⏲noon-9pm) Choo choo choose something from the sushi train or let the Japanese chef slice up a plate of fresh sashimi. This is a lively place where the Asahi also goes down well.

Balcony MEDITERRANEAN $$
(☎02-6680 9666; www.balcony.com.au; cnr Lawson & Jonson Sts; lunch mains $13.50-25, dinner mains $24-32; ⏲8am-9pm; 📶) The eponymous architectural feature here wraps around the building and gives you tremendous views of the passing Byron parade and the always-clogged traffic circle. The food is Mediterranean fusion, with global influences – expect cheeseboards, tapas and seafood-accented dishes. The drink list is long.

Byron Beach Cafe CAFE $$
(☎02-6685 8400; www.byronbeachcafe.com.au; Lawson St, Clarkes Beach; mains $17-34; ⏲7.30am-10pm) This superb spot west of the main town and overlooking Clarks Beach is ideal for a beachside coffee, breakfast or later meals such as beach snapper pie or crispy pork belly, seared scallops and apple and cauliflour purée.

Italian at the Pacific ITALIAN $$
(☎02-6680 7055; italianatthepacific.com.au; Bay St; mains $26-35; ⏲6-10pm) Byron's best Italian restaurant is just back from the foreshore and the lovely setting is matched by some fine dishes such as the beetroot-cured kingfish carpaccio.

Orient Express THAI, VIETNAMESE $$
(☎02-6680 8808; www.orientexpresseatery.com.au; 1/2 Fletcher St; yum cha per item $7.50, mains $15-35; ⏲11am-9.30pm Fri-Sun, 5.30-9.30pm Mon-Thu) Easily mistaken for an Asian decorator's shop, or a teahouse, this is actually one of the best restaurants in Byron, helmed by Tippy Heng. The modern menu here is fairly brief but full of flavour and the weekend yum cha is outstanding. Expect to wait.

Targa CAFE, ITALIAN $$
(☎02-6680 9960; www.targabyronbay.com; 11 Marvell St; lunch meals $5-12, dinner mains $25-32; ⏲7am-11pm) A lovely Italian cafe and wine bar just far enough removed from main-street clamour, Targa is popular and casual for breakfast and lunch, while dinner is a slightly more serious affair.

Orgasmic MIDDLE EASTERN $$
(11 Bay Lane; mains $14-23; ⏲10am-10pm) Plop your bum on a cube cushion at this alley eatery that's one step above a stall. Takeaways include big mezze plates, ideal for quick picnics.

One One One MEDITERRANEAN $$
(☎02-6680 7388; 1/111 Jonson St; mains $22-36; ⏲8am-3pm daily, also 5.30-9pm Fri & Sat; 📶) HQ

for slow-food devotees locally, the ingredients here celebrate regional produce. The menu is mostly vegetarian with a largely Middle Eastern focus – try the traditional Yemeni pastries or an intriguing dish known as 'the priest fainted' (slow-cooked eggplant). Plates are good for sharing.

Earth 'n' Sea ITALIAN **$$**
(☎02-6685 6029; www.earthnsea.com.au; cnr Fletcher & Byron Sts; pasta $15-18, pizza from $17.50; ⊙noon-2.30pm & 5-9pm Mon-Fri, noon-9pm Sat & Sun) The pizza list at this old favourite is long and full of flavour. Pasta is on the menu too. Beers include several excellent microbrews from the Northern Rivers Brewing Co.

Fresh CAFE **$$**
(☎02-6685 7810; www.byronfresh.com.au; 7 Jonson St; meals $17-35; ⊙7am-11pm) Top spot for breakfast with excellent pancakes. At night, sit at open-air tables and chow down on menu offerings including the Zen Burger and Paradise Salad. People-watching is half the appeal. No reservations.

Petit Snail FRENCH **$$$**
(☎02-6685 8526; www.thepetitsnail.com.au; 5 Carlyle St; mains $31-45; ⊙6.30-9.30pm Wed-Sat) This intimate restaurant is off the main beat and is more Bordeaux than Byron. French staff serve up traditional red-white-and-blue fare such as steak tartare, wild rabbit terrine, duck *confit* and lots of fromage. There's outdoor dining on the verandah. Book ahead.

Rae's on Watego's MODERN AUSTRALIAN **$$$**
(☎02-6685 5366; www.raes.com.au; Marine Pde; mains $30-45; ⊙noon-5pm & 6-11.30pm) Exquisite cuisine on a terrace with the sound of surf providing an agreeable soundtrack. The menu changes daily but always surprises with its unconventional pairings of ingredients and spices. Book ahead.

Drinking & Nightlife

Byron Bay's nightlife is varied and runs late. Check the gig guide in Thursday's *Byron Shire News*, tune into Bay 99.9 FM or visit www.byronbayentertainment.com.

★**Balcony** BAR
(www.balcony.com.au; cnr Lawson & Jonson Sts; ⊙8am-11pm) With its verandah poking out amid the palm trees, this fine bar-cum-restaurant is the place to park yourself. Choose from stools, chairs or sofas while working through a cocktail list that will make you giddy just looking at it.

Railway Friendly Bar PUB
(Jonson St; ⊙11am-late) This indoor-outdoor pub draws everyone from lobster-red British tourists to acid-soaked hippies and high-on-life earth mothers. Its cosy interior is the old railway station. The front beer garden, conducive to boozy afternoons, has live music most nights.

Great Northern PUB
(www.thenorthern.com.au; Byron St; ⊙noon-late) You won't need your fancy duds at this brash and boisterous pub. It's loud and beery with live music most nights and even louder when hosting headline acts. Soak up the booze with a wood-fired pizza.

Beach Hotel PUB
(beachhotel.com.au; cnr Jonson & Bay Sts; ⊙11am-late) The mothership of all pubs is close to the main beach and is shot through with a fabulously infectious atmosphere that makes everyone your best mate. There's live music and DJs some nights.

St Elmo BAR
(www.stelmodining.com; cnr Fletcher St & Lawson Lane; ⊙4pm-late Mon-Thu, noon-late Fri & Sat, noon-10pm Sun) Gourmet cocktails.

Cocomangas NIGHTCLUB
(www.cocomangas.com.au; 32 Jonson St; ⊙9pm-3am Mon-Sat) Byron's oldest club. Mondays is backpacker night.

La La Land NIGHTCLUB
(www.lalalandbyronbay.com.au; 6 Lawson St; ⊙9pm-3am) One of Byron Bay's better nightclubs.

Cheeky Monkeys NIGHTCLUB
(www.cheekymonkeys.com.au; 115 Jonson St; ⊙7pm-3am) A backpackers bonanza – with wet T-shirt comps.

Shopping

Broadly speaking, Fletcher St, north of Marvell St, has artsy boutiques; frock shops hover around the Lawson and Fletcher Sts traffic circle; west of here and south on Jonson St you'll find a huge range – everything from lingerie to New Age.

Planet Corroboree ARTS & CRAFTS
(1/69 Jonson St; ⊙10am-6pm) Huge range of Aboriginal art.

WORTH A TRIP

BANGALOW

Boutiques, fine eateries, bookshops and an excellent pub, all a mere 14km from Byron Bay. Beautiful Bangalow (population 1520), with its character-laden main street, is the kind of place that turns Sydneysiders into tree-changers.

There's a good weekly **farmers market** (Byron St; ⏰8-11am Sat) and a praised **cooking school** (☎02-6687 2799; www.leahroland.com/bangalow-cooking-school).

Stately old **Bangalow Guesthouse** (☎02-6687 1317; bangalowguesthouse.com.au; 99 Byron St; r $165-285) sits on the river's edge ensuring guests see platypuses and oversized lizards as they take on breakfast. It's the stuff of B&B dreams.

About 4km north, **Possum Creek Eco Lodge** (☎02-6687 1188; www.possumcreeklodge.com.au; Cedarvale Rd; bungalows from $198;) has views across the lush valleys. The 'eco' in the name is not green-washing – water is recycled, stored from rain and otherwise conserved. Power is partially solar.

Located at Bangalow Hotel, **Bangalow Dining Rooms** (www.bangalowdining.com; Byron St; mains $17-36; ⏰noon-3pm & 5.30-9pm) is a classy place with just the right amount of cool. Reserve a table in the dining room or sit on the deck and order from the cheaper pub menu; gourmet burgers and the like.

Uptown (☎02-6687 2555; townbangalow.com.au; 33 Byron St; five-course set menu $85; ⏰6.30-9.30pm Thu-Sat) is one of coastal NSW's best restaurants with a designer set menu with seasonal local produce. Book ahead. Downstairs, **Downtown** (☎02-6687 1010; townbangalow.com.au; 33 Byron St; ⏰7.30am-3pm Mon-Sat, 9am-3pm Sun) is run by the same people and is perfect for cakes, coffees and breakfasts. Book ahead.

Blanch's Bus Service (p193) operates a service to Ballina ($9) and Byron Bay ($7.80).

Happy High Herbs HERBS
(☎02-6680 8856; www.happyhighherbs.com; 1/5-7 Byron St; ⏰11am-5pm Mon-Fri, 10.30am-5pm Sat, 11am-3pm Sun) Herbs and natural remedies. Adults only.

Information

The website www.byron-bay.com is helpful. The *Pink Guide* is a local publication aimed at gay and lesbian tourists; have a look at its useful website (www.byronbaypinkguide.blogspot.com.au).

INTERNET ACCESS

Byron has many internet-access places that cram customers together in tight, sweaty little pods to stare at tiny screens. They come and go with the seasons. Otherwise, many cafes and most hotels and hostels now have wi-fi or a public internet-enabled computer.

MEDICAL SERVICES

Bay Centre Medical Clinic (☎02-6685 6206; www.byronmed.com.au; 6 Lawson St; ⏰8am-5.30pm Mon-Thu, to 5pm Fri, to noon Sat) Full-service general surgery.

Byron Bay Hospital (☎02-6685 6200; www.ncahs.nsw.gov.au; cnr Wordsworth & Shirley Sts; ⏰24hr) For medical emergencies.

ChemCoast Pharmacy (☎02-6685 6274; 20 Jonson St; ⏰8am-8pm)

MONEY

Atlas Currency Exchange (www.atlascurrency.com.au; Central Arcade, 4/47 Byron St) Foreign exchange, cash and money transfers, internet access.

TOURIST INFORMATION

Backpackers World (☎02-6685 8858; www.backpackersworld.com.au; shop 6, 75 Jonson St) Primarily a travel agent.

Byron Bus & Backpacker Centre (☎02-6685 5517; 84 Jonson St; ⏰7.30am-7pm) Next to the coach stop; handles bus, train, accommodation and activity bookings. Also has left-luggage lockers ($7).

Byron Environmental Centre (www.byronenvironmentcentre.asn.au; Mullumbimby Railway Station, 2 Prince St) The hours are highly sporadic but the passions of these local environmentalists are not.

Visitors Centre (☎02-6680 8558; www.visitbyronbay.com; Stationmaster's Cottage, Jonson St; ⏰9am-5pm) Ground zero for tourist information. It can get a little overwhelmed at peak periods.

Getting There & Away

AIR

The closest airport is at Ballina and with its rapidly expanding service it is the best airport for Byron. The airport also has shuttle services and hire cars for Byron travellers.

Coolangatta airport on the Gold Coast has a greater range of services but can involve a traffic-clogged drive. **Byron Bay Shuttle** (www.byronbayshuttle.com.au) serves both Coolangatta ($36.10) and Ballina ($17.10) airports.

BUS

Long-distance buses for **Greyhound** (☎1300 4739 46863; www.greyhound.com.au) and **Premier** (☎13 34 10; www.premierms.com.au) stop on Jonson St. Approximate times and fares for both are as follows: Brisbane ($30, 2¾ hours), Coffs Harbour ($50, 5¼ hours) and Sydney (from $92, 12 to 14 hours).

Blanch's Bus Service (☎02-6686 2144; www.blanchs.com.au) operates several daily services from the airport to Lennox Head ($8.50, 25 minutes), Ballina (Tamar St stop, $12, 70 minutes) and Mullumbimby ($11.75, 35 minutes).

Other services:

- **Byron Easy Bus** (p183) Byron Bay to Brisbane ($54) or Gold Coast ($39) airports
- **Express Bus Service** (☎1300 363 123; www.byronbayexpress.com.au) Byron Bay to Coolangatta and Surfers Paradise (one way/return $30/55)

TRAIN

People still mourn the loss of the popular Country Link train service from Sydney. In fact a popular movie released in 2008, *Derailed*, documents this transport travesty.

Getting Around

There are car rental places at Ballina Airport.

Byron Bay Taxis (☎02-6685 5008; www.byronbaytaxis.com.au) On call 24 hours.

Earth Car Rentals (☎02-6685 7472; www.earthcar.com.au; 3a/1 Byron St) Claims to be Australia's first carbon-neutral car rental company.

For places that rent bicycles, see p187.

FAR NORTH COAST HINTERLAND

Just minutes from Byron, the greener-than-green undulating landscape is a crocheted rug of lush rainforest, pastoral lands, striped orchards and stands of eucalypt, all navigable via pretty winding roads.

The hippie haven of Nimbin is the most popular of the inland hamlets, but towns such as Bangalow, with its esteemed boutiques and gourmet restaurants, exemplify the trend for combining the laid-back lifestyle of the country with the creature comforts of the big smoke.

The hinterland also boasts the **Border Ranges**, **Wollumbin** (which now includes former Mt Warning National Park) and **Nightcap National Parks**, which form part of the World Heritage–listed rainforests of the Central Eastern Rainforest Reserves. With a combined total of 43,926 hectares, the parks are a haven for walking and camping, and a bounty of Aboriginal history and culture.

Lismore

POP 27,474

Lismore, the hinterland's commercial centre, appears to have been dropped into its green surroundings without ruffling the feathers of the pristine hinterland. The town itself sits on the Wilson River, though it has yet to take advantage of this, and is otherwise beautified by a liberal supply of heritage and art-deco buildings, and a thriving artistic community. Students from Southern Cross University add to the town's eclecticism.

Sights & Activities

To get a glimpse of platypuses, head to the northern end of Kadina St and walk up to **Tucki Tucki Creek** at dawn or sunset. You can also spot koalas at **Robinson's Lookout** (Robinson's Ave, Girards Hill).

Wilson River walking track starts in the CBD and skirts the river. Along the way you'll pass a **bush-tucker garden**, nurturing the once daily diet of the Widjabal people, the traditional owners of the land.

More than a half-dozen used-book stores are within a block of the intersection of Carrington and Magellan Sts.

The **farmers market** (⏲8-11am Sat) and **Organic Market** (⏲8-11am Tue) are held at the showground, off Nimbin Rd.

Lismore Regional Art Gallery GALLERY
(www.lismoregallery.org; 131 Molesworth St; ⏲10am-4pm Tue, Wed & Fri, to 6pm Thu, to 2pm Sat & Sun) FREE The diminutive Lismore Regional Art Gallery has just enough space for two visiting exhibitions, but they're usually excellent.

Koala Care Centre WILDLIFE REFUGE
(www.friendsofthekoala.org; Range Rd; per person/family $5/10; ⏲tours 10am & 2pm Mon-Fri, 10am

Sat) The worthy Koala Care Centre is home to recovering koalas.

Sleeping & Eating

Lismore Palms CARAVAN PARK $
(02-6621 7067; www.lismorepalms.com.au; 42 Brunswick St; camp sites/cabins from $22/72;) The best of Lismore's caravan parks, this one is right on the river and has 13 self-contained cabins.

Karinga MOTEL $$
(02-6621 2787; www.karingamotel.com; 258 Molesworth St; r $148;) The pick of the litter, the Karinga has had a tasteful facelift: the rooms have been fully refurbished and a funky pool and spa installed.

Fire in the Belly PIZZA $
(02-6621 4889; www.fireinthebelly.com.au; 109 Dawson St; mains $12-20, pizzas $14-34) Wood-fired, gourmet pizzas make this one of the best places to order a pizza in northern NSW.

Mecca CAFE, BAR $
(meccacafe.com.au; 80 Magellan St; meals $9-16; 7am-5pm Mon-Wed, to late Thu-Sat) A stodgy old caff has been reborn as a retro-hip scenester playground. Lots of local musicians hang out at the pavement tables sipping the excellent coffee by day and jamming till late weekend nights.

★**Howard's** CAFE, DELI $
(www.howardsdeli.com.au; 106 Keen St; mains $12-26; 7.30am-5pm Mon-Wed, 7.30am-6pm Thu & Fri, 7.30am-2pm Sat, 9am-1pm Sun) Go no further than this deli-cum-cafe-cum-butchery, a *Babette's Feast* of wholesome salads, meaty lasagnes and hearty frittatas. For picnics: gourmet chutney, oil and coffee. For camping: house-made snags.

Information

Lismore visitor centre (1300 369 795; www.visitlismore.com.au; cnr Molesworth & Ballina Sts) The centre has plenty on Lismore, Nimbin and surrounds, and a rainforest display ($1). Kids dig the Heritage Park playground and skate park, next to the centre.

Getting There & Away

Kirklands (02-6622 1499) runs to Byron Bay ($16.80, 50 minutes, two to three times daily). **Waller's** (02-6687 8550) buses run to Nimbin ($10.75, 70 minutes).

Nimbin

POP 468

Welcome to Australia's hippie capital, a strange little place and an ageing social experiment where anything goes. Reefers included. And dreadlocks and tie-dye. And enduring campaigns to legalise hemp. It's hard to know what to make of it all, espe-

WORTH A TRIP

TWEED HEADS

The Pacific Hwy continues north to the Queensland border at Tweed Heads. If it's a leisurely pace you're after take a detour through the towns of **Mullumbimby** ('Mullum'; population 3164) and **Brunswick Heads** (population 1450). The former is a serene coast-hinterland hybrid with lazy palms, typical tropical architecture and a cosmopolitan spread of cafes, bistros and pubs. There's also a trail along the Brunswick River in town that passes through tropical forest and is lined with signs relating Aboriginal stories. The **Mullum Music Festival** (www.mullummusicfestival.com; late Nov) is a prime time to visit.

Only slightly north of Mullum on the Old Pacific Hwy, beautiful Brunswick Heads reaps a bounty of fresh oysters and mud crabs from its peaceful Brunswick River inlets and beaches. The 1940s **Hotel Brunswick** (02-6685 1236; www.hotelbrunswick.com.au; Mullumbimby St; s/d/f $55/85/110) is a sight to behold and a destination unto itself with a magnificent beer garden that unfurls beneath flourishing poincianas. It has decent pub rooms and there's live music on weekends.

Tweed Heads (population 55,553) marks the southern end of the Gold Coast strip. Before you cross into the 'Sunshine State' check out the **Minjungbal Aboriginal Cultural Centre** (02-5524 2109; cnr Kirkwood & Duffy Sts; 9am-4pm Mon-Fri), set in a grove of old gum trees on the Tweed River. There's a Walk on Water Track and **boardwalk** through the mangroves.

THE NIMBIN STORY

Until the 1970s, Nimbin was a pretty if otherwise unremarkable village like so many in the hinterland of the northern New South Wales coast. That changed forever in May 1973 when the third (and final) Aquarius Festival was held here, drawing large numbers of students, hippies and devotees of sustainable living and alternative lifestyles. After the 10-day festival ended, some of the festival attendees stayed on in an attempt to live out the ideals expressed during the festival – Nimbin hasn't been the same since. The festival is also remembered for having been one of the first in Australia to formally request permission from the traditional indigenous inhabitants, the Bundjalung people, to hold the festival on their lands.

A lesser-known landmark in Nimbin's history came in 1979 with the Terania Creek Battle, a four-week stand-off between environmentalists and logging companies close to Nimbin. It was the first major conservation battle of its kind in modern Australian history and the victory by conservationists is often credited with ensuring the survival of NSW's vast tracts of rainforest.

cially if you're only here for the day – stay overnight to get a more rounded impression.

Sights & Activities

Despite the reticence of many locals to be pinned down on exact opening times, for fear of ruining Nimbin's image, most places open 10am to 5pm. Every fourth and fifth Sunday, Nimbin has its own **market** (Nimbin Community Centre; 9am-2.30pm), a spectacular affair of produce and art where locals revel in their culture.

Hemp Embassy NOVELTY SHOP
(www.hempembassy.net; 51 Cullen St) This place raises consciousness about marijuana legalisation, as well as providing all the tools and fashion items you'll need to get high (or at least attract more police raids). The embassy leads the Mardi Grass festival each May. Smokers are welcome at the tiny Hemp Bar next door (although you'll have to step outside to light up).

Nimbin Candle Factory ARTS & CRAFTS
(02-6689 1010; www.nimbincandles.com.au; 9am-5pm Mon-Fri) Just 400m down the hill from town and off the Murwillumbah road, the Old Butter Factory incubates a number of little businesses, including the candle factory where thousands of hand-dipped paraffin candles are on display.

Nimbin Museum MUSEUM
(www.nimbinmuseum.com; 62 Cullen St; admission by $2 donation) An interpretive and expressionistic museum that packs an eclectic collection of local art into a modest space. It's far more a work of art than of history.

Nimbin Artists Gallery GALLERY
(49 Cullen St; 10am-4pm) Nimbin is something of an artistic hub and you can find artists' work on display in this small gallery-cum-shop.

Nimbin Craft Gallery GALLERY
(02-6689 1375; www.nimbincraftgallery.com.au; 1 Sibley St; 10am-5pm) It's difficult to see where this stops being a gallery and becomes a shop, but that doesn't detract from the interesting local crafts on offer here.

Sleeping

There are nearly 100 local farms more than happy to host volunteers willing to yank weeds and perform other chores. The international Willing Workers on Organic Farms (www.wwoof.com.au) coordinates many such programs.

Nimbin Rox YHA Hostel HOTEL $
(02-6689 0022; www.nimbinrox.com; 74 Thornburn St; dm/tw/d from $23/50/61; @) Rox has hammocks, permaculture gardens, craft workshops, live bands, Thai massage, yurts, tepees and camping and a heated pool.

Rainbow Retreat Backpackers HOSTEL $
(02-6689 1262; www.rainbowretreat.net; 75 Thorburn St; camping/dm/s/d $15/25/40/60, bungalows from $120) Very basic, but totally in the age-of-Aquarius spirit. Relax, chill out, sleep in a funky little shack or gypsy van or camp out. There's a free courtesy bus from Byron Bay.

Nimbin Hotel & Backpackers HOTEL, HOSTEL $
(02-6689 1246; www.nimbinhotel.com.au; 53 Cullen St; dm/d $35/70; @) The two- and four-

bed rooms in the town's veteran pub are tidy and open onto the classic shaded verandah.

Granny's Farm HOSTEL $
(☎02-6689 1333; www.nimbingrannysfarm.com; 112 Cullen St; camping/dm/d/ste $15/25/50/60) Basic accommodation at Nimbin's backpackers of longest standing.

Black Sheep Farm GUESTHOUSE $$
(☎02-6689 1095; www.blacksheepfarm.com.au; d $195;) With a saltwater pool and Finnish sauna, guests might struggle to leave the self-contained cabin on the edge of a rainforest near Nightcap National Park. It sleeps up to seven people (per extra person $20). There's also a smaller and cheaper cottage available.

Eating & Drinking

Nimbin Hotel MODERN AUSTRALIAN $
(☎02-6689 1246; Cullen St; meals $12-18; ⏲10am-10pm Mon-Fri, 11am-11pm Sat & Sun) The classic local boozer has a surprisingly sophisticated restaurant out back. Called the Hummingbird Bistro, it serves up everything from a Tree-hugger's Salad to Barramundi. A vast covered porch overlooks a verdant valley. There's live music many Friday nights.

Rainbow Café CAFE $
(☎02-6689 1997; 64a Cullen St; mains $8-17; ⏲7.30am-3pm) Murals cover the walls of this thumping Nimbim institution serving generous burgers, wraps, nachos and salads. The leafy courtyard has a familiar whiff.

Nimbin Trattoria & Pizzeria ITALIAN $
(☎02-6689 1427; 70 Cullen St; mains $12-15, pizza $12-20; ⏲6-9pm) You'll find outstanding pizzas and delicious pastas at this dinner-only place, plus live music most Thursdays.

Information

Visitor Centre (☎02-6689 1388; www.visitnimbin.com.au; 46 Cullen St; ⏲10am-4pm) Has great local info.

Getting There & Away

Companies in Byron Bay offer day tours to Nimbin, sometimes with stops in the region. Most leave at 10am and return around 6pm. Companies include the following:

- **Nimbin Shuttle** (☎0413 217 153; www.nimbintours.com.au; one way/same-day return $14/25, open return $26)
- **Grasshoppers** (☎0438 269 076; www.grasshoppers.com.au; return incl BBQ lunch $45)
- **Jim's Alternative Tours** (☎0401 592 247; www.jimsalternativetours.com; tours $40; ⏲10am)

Buses leave twice daily from Monday to Friday for Murwillumbah ($14.40, one hour). Ask at the visitor centre for details.

Murwillumbah

POP 8523

Murwillumbah is gleefully free of precociousness. Sitting calmly, as it does, on the banks of the Tweed River, it's a great base for exploring the river country, Wollumbin-Mt Warning National Park and the surrounding NSW-Queensland Border Ranges. The town, an agricultural focal point for the region, is old school with a charming main street and hills flanked with heritage facades. Views of Wollumbin-Mt Warning peek around every corner.

Sights

Tropical Fruit World GARDEN
(☎02-6677 7222; www.tropicalfruitworld.com.au; Duranbah Rd; adult/child $44/25; ⏲10am-4.30pm) Just north of town, this place allegedly has the world's largest collection of tropical fruit, along with plantation safaris, tastings and a jungle cruise. Plan for at least half a day to make the most of the pricey entry.

Tweed River Regional Art Gallery ART GALLERY
(www.tweed.nsw.gov.au/artgallery; cnr Mistral Rd & Tweed Valley Way; ⏲10am-5pm Wed-Sun) FREE This exceptional gallery is an architectural delight, home to some of Australia's finest in a variety of media, with a particularly good portrait collection.

Murwillumbah Museum MUSEUM
(☎02-6672 1865; 2 Queensland Rd; adult/child $2/1.50; ⏲11am-3pm Wed-Fri & 4th Sun of month) This small museum is housed in a beautiful old building and features a solid account of local history and an interesting radio room.

Sleeping & Eating

Mount Warning-Murwillumbah YHA HOSTEL $
(☎02-6672 3763; www3.yha.com.au; 1 Tumbulgum Rd; dm/d from $29/64) This former river captain's home now houses a colourful waterfront hostel with eight-bed dorms. There's free ice cream at night plus canoe and

bike hire. Tours to Mt Warning are reason enough to bunk down here.

Murwillumbah Motor Inn MOTEL $$
(☎02-6672 2022; www.murwillumbahmotorinn.com.au; 17 Byangum Rd; s/d $102/112;) These clean and comfortable rooms are a great option away from the town centre. The deluxe rooms have flat-screen televisions. There's a pleasant courtyard out the back.

Sugar Beat CAFE $
(☎02-6672 2330; Shop 2, 6-8 Commercial Rd; mains $7-16; ⏲7.30am-5pm Mon-Fri, to 2pm Sat) Park yourself by the sunny window, settle into a corner of the long bench seating or take in the scene from one of the pavement tables. There's cafe-style fusion fare and locally famous baked goods.

New Leaf Café VEGETARIAN $
(☎02-6672 2667; shop 10, Murwillumbah Plaza; meals $12-25; ⏲8am-3.30pm Mon-Sat) The food here is creative and vegetarian, with plenty of Middle Eastern flavours and salads on offer. Dine inside, alfresco, or take away.

Information

Murwillumbah Visitor Centre (☎02-6672 1340; www.tweedcoolangatta.com.au; cnr Alma St & Tweed Valley Way; ⏲9am-4.30pm Mon-Sat, 9.30am-4pm Sun) Has national park info.

Getting There & Away

Greyhound (☎1300 GREYHOUND, 1300 4739 46863; www.greyhound.com.au) and **Premier** (☎13 34 10; www.premierms.com.au) have services several times daily on the Sydney ($92 to $108, 15 to 19¼ hours, via Byron Bay) and Brisbane ($25 to $33, two to 3¼ hours) route.

Waller's (☎02-6622 6266) has school-day buses to Nimbin (one hour) and Lismore.

FOREST RETREATS

Murwillumbah's coastal hinterland is exceptionally beautiful and two places deep in the forest immerse you in all that's good about these parts. **Crystal Creek Rainforest Retreat** (☎02-6679 1591; www.ccrr.com.au; Brookers Rd, Upper Crystal Creek; d $385-645), northwest of Murwillumbah, has luxury timber bungalows with spa baths and elevated balconies, while **Mount Warning Forest Hideaway** (☎02-6679 7277; www.foresthideaway.com.au; 460 Byrrill Creek Rd, Uki; d $90-200;) is more rustic but equally secluded.

NEW ENGLAND

New England misses out on the kind of exposure Australia's desert landscapes and vast coastlines attract, but the area's rolling green hills and farmland, autumnal foliage and vast tracts of bushland are worthy of exploration.

The verdant scenery prompted the original settlers to name the area New England in 1839. In the northern 'highlands' especially, images of Britain still raise their head. Mist settles in the cool-climate hilltops and valleys, little churches sit in oak-studded paddocks and winding roads navigate impossibly green landscapes.

The region has a string of national parks, home to more rugged landscapes including Bald Rock and Washpool National Parks in the north. On the Waterfall Way linking Armidale and Coffs Harbour, Guy Fawkes River, Cathedral Rock, New England and Oxley Wild Rivers National Parks feature granite outcrops, unforgettably deep gorges and waterfalls.

Amid all this greenery, the two main population centres of Tamworth and Armidale have plenty of heritage architecture – Tamworth is one of the country music capitals of the world, while Armidale has good places to eat.

Tamworth

POP 36,131

Country music kicks this town along like a line of bootscooters, especially during the festival in late January. Otherwise, this bustling provincial town doesn't have much more than a tree-filled main street, but echoes of country music are never far away. The wine scene is emerging but the food and cafe culture lags behind.

Dress codes are stricter in Tamworth than elsewhere in the region.

Sights & Activities

★**Australian Country Music Foundation** MUSEUM
(www.acmf.org.au; 93 Brisbane St; adult/child $6/4; ⏲10am-4pm Mon-Fri, to 2pm Sat) If the names Tex Morton, Buddy Williams and Smoky

WORTH A TRIP

THE FOSSICKERS WAY

You're now heading into gemstone territory. This scenic route (www.fossickersway.com) begins 60km southeast of Tamworth at Nundle and goes through Tamworth, 191km north to Warialda, then 124km east through Inverell to Glen Innes, 100km north of Armidale.

Nundle

This charming town (population 597) has a tranquil perch between the Great Dividing Range and Peel River. There's a mining museum, some cute little old wares shops and an intriguing **Woollen Mill** (1 Oakenville St; ⊙10am-4pm) FREE, one of only two in the country. **Peel Inn** (☎02-6769 3377; www.peelinn.com.au; s/d with shared bathroom $45/80, with bathroom $60/90) is an all-round great pub. Meals include delicious local trout. The **visitor centre** (☎02-6769 3026; www.nundle.info/nundle; Jenkins St; ⊙9am-4pm) is on Jenkins St.

Manilla

The **national paragliding championships** are held here in February. **Manilla Paragliding** (☎02-6785 6545; www.flymanilla.com) offers tandem flights. The town is a glimmer of its former glory, but the three remaining pubs stand defiantly on the main street. Grab your bait and licence from **North Manilla Store** just north of the bridge, before heading to **Lake Keepit** or **Warrabah National Park** (camp sites per adult/child $5/3) for the big bites. There's also a helpful **visitor centre** (☎02-6785 1207; 197 Manilla St; ⊙9am-4pm).

Barraba

Settled in the 1830s, Barraba, with its wide streets and elegant awnings, was put on the map during the gold fever of the late 1800s. Travel 3km north, turn right onto Woodsreef Rd and you'll come to **Ironbark Goldfield and Woodsreef Reserve**, where you can use a shovel, pick and pan. **Millie's Park Vineyard** has wines, a barbecue and a nature walk. Drop-ins are welcome at **Andy's Backpackers** (☎02-6782 1916; www.andysbackpackers.com.au; 98 Queen St; dm $28; @) whether for a bed, a meal, a game of chess or just a chat. The **visitor centre** (☎02-6782 1255; 116 Queen St; ⊙9am-4pm) has fossicking info.

Bingara

This small town straddling the Gwydir River is horse-riding country; try it at **Gwydir River Trail Rides** (Jackaroo Jillaroo; ☎02-6724 1562; www.jackaroojillaroodownunder.com.au; 17 Keera St; 2hr trail ride $55, half-day canoe hire $30). For fair-dinkum Aussieness, complete the five-day Jackeroo/Jillaroo Adventure ($670). **Fossickers Way Motel** (☎02-6724 1373; www.bingaramotel.com.au; 2 Finch St; s/d $75/85; ❄) is one of the few hotels on the main road between Tamworth and Warialda. The **visitor centre** (☎02-6724 0066; www.bingara.com.au; 74 Maitland St) is in the Roxy Theatre, a Greek-influenced, refurnished art-deco cinema still used today. Ask about tours.

Inverell

It might not be that aesthetically fabulous but its sapphires are. Pick up a fossicking map at the **visitor centre** (☎02-6728 8161; www.inverell.com.au; Campbell St; ⊙9am-4pm) and sample olive oil at **Olives of Beaulieu** (www.olivesofbeaulieu.com.au; 439 Copeton Dam Rd; ⊙11am-4pm Wed-Sun). An early-20th-century manor house, **Blair Athol Estate B&B** (☎02-6722 4288; www.babs.com.au/blairathol; Warialda Rd; d $90-150) has stunning grounds peppered with a rich mix of flora from Himalayan cedars to boabs.

Glen Innes

Businesses with names such as Glen This and Wee That hint at the Scottish heritage in Glen Innes (population 5173). The **visitor centre** (☎02-6730 2400; www.gleninnestourism.com; ⊙9am-5pm Mon-Fri, 9am-3pm Sat & Sun) is on the New England Hwy and there are **standing stones** off the Gwydir Hwy. **Land of the Beardies History House** (www.beardieshistoryhouse.info; cnr West Ave & Ferguson St; ⊙10am-noon & 1-4pm Mon-Fri, 1-4pm Sat & Sun) FREE fills an old hospital with eclectic artefacts. If you fancy saddling up, take a **pub crawl on horseback** (☎02-6732 1599; www.pubcrawlsonhorseback.com.au; Bullock Mountain Homestead; 2/3-day ride $465/685).

Dawson mean anything to you, then this will too. This country-music Hall of Fame has photographs, historic video and film footage, music and souvenirs.

Walk a Country Mile Museum   MUSEUM
(cnr Peel & Murray Sts; adult/child $5/4.50) One of Tamworth's better exhibitions on country music, this compact collection has video footage, photos, explanations about Tamworth's historical connection to country music and other memorabilia on all the major stars. It's in the visitor centre.

Big Golden Guitar Tourist Centre   MUSEUM
(☑02-6765 2688; www.biggoldenguitar.com.au; New England Hwy) This info hub has a cafe and a shop where you can stock up on all-important golden-guitar snow cones. When you've finished, check out the **Wax Museum** (adult/child $10/4).

Oxley Scenic Lookout   LOOKOUT
(Scenic Rd) Grab a bottle of wine and follow jacaranda-lined White St to the very top, where you'll reach this viewpoint. It's the best spot to watch the sun go down over Tamworth and the Liverpool Ranges.

Tamworth Regional Gallery   GALLERY
(www.tamworthregionalgallery.com.au; 466 Peel St; ⊙10am-5pm Tue-Fri, to 4pm Sat) FREE In purpose-built premises next to the library, the gallery has some interesting local bequeaths and more modern roving exhibitions.

Tamworth Marsupial Park   ZOO
(Endeavour Dr; ⊙8am-4.45pm) FREE Over-friendly cockatoos and other native animals live here alongside barbecues and picnic shelters. The park joins the **Kamilaroi walking track** – ask at the visitor centre for an information sheet on the track and map.

**Leconfield Jackaroo &
Jillaroo School**   OUTDOORS
(☑02-6769 4328; www.leconfield.com; 'Bimboola', Kootingal; 5-day course $625) Keen on mustering, milking, shearing and shoeing? This school will have you sorting the cowboys from the girls' blouses in no time.

✯ Festivals & Events

Country Music Festival   MUSIC
(www.tamworthcountrymusicfestival.com.au) Held at the end of January, New England's biggest annual party, the Country Music Festival, lasts 10 days. There are over 800 acts, of which a significant proportion are free.

Otherwise tickets range from $15 to $50. The visitor centre may be able to track down a bed, but can certainly sell you a full program. During the festival, the 'Festival Express' bus connects the various venues and most hotels for a one-off fee of $10.

🛏 Sleeping

Unless you book months in advance, you'll be lucky to find a bed or camp site during the festival when prices skyrocket. However, the council makes large areas of river land available to campers, where it's rough and rowdy but fun.

Tamworth YHA   HOSTEL $
(☑02-6761 2600; www.yha.com.au; 169 Marius St; dm/d from $26/58; ❄ @) On a busy street but neat as a pin. Contacts for Jackaroo & Jillaroo School.

★**Quality Hotel Powerhouse**   HOTEL $$
(☑02-6766 7000; www.qualityhotelpowerhouse. com.au; New England Hwy; r $172-219; ❄ ⊛ ⛱) The classy rooms here have an old-world style wedded to an impeccable attention to detail and stylish modern bathrooms. There's also an excellent restaurant.

Edward Parry Motel   MOTEL $$
(☑02-6765 9075; www.edwardparrymotel.com; 261 Goonoo Goonoo Rd; d/f $134/164, 2-bedroom

---

TAMWORTH COUNTRY MUSIC AT A GLANCE

Whether you're a bootscooter from way back or just keen to get a taste of what makes Tamworth tick, the following is our guide to making the most of your time in town:

➡ **Best time to visit**: Late January for the Country Music Festival (p199)

➡ **Best Museums**: Australian Country Music Foundation (p197) and Walk a Country Mile Museum (p199)

➡ **Best Place to Buy CDs**: Big Golden Guitar Tourist Centre (p199)

➡ **Best live music**: Check Thursday's *Northern Daily Leader*

➡ **Hands of Fame**: Over 200 hand prints of the stars at the corner of Kable Ave and Bridge St

➡ **Strangest Sight**: 'Noses of Fame' at Joe Maquire's Hotel, Peel St

apt from $205; ❄️📶🏊) This four-star motel has decent rooms, but this place is especially good for families with expansive two-bedroom apartments.

Retreat B&B $$$
(☎02-6766 3353; www.froogmoorepark.com.au; 78 Bligh St; r incl breakfast from $225; 📶) Individually styled rooms with names as varied as Moroccan Fantasy and The Dungeon, this avant-garde B&B is one of the quirkier and more luxurious places to stay in town. Rooms are large and brimful of personality, and the breakfasts could just be the best in town.

Eating

Tamworth Hotel PUB $
(☎02-6766 2923; 147 Marius St; mains $8.50-22) Heritage colours and a 1930s design make this one of Tamworth's more aesthetically pleasing pubs. Choose from a formal dining area with white tablecloths and shiny glasses, or the bistro/brasserie with chicken parma, steak sandwiches and roasts.

Rocks on Peel MODERN AUSTRALIAN $$
(Peel St; mains $17-27; ⏰11am-9pm Mon-Fri, 9am-9pm Sat & Sun) Set in a lovely high-ceilinged heritage building, this casual place is as good for a coffee as an order of prime Scotch fillet or salt and pepper squid.

Banjos AUSTRALIAN $$
(☎02-6765 7588; www.wtlc.com.au; Phillip St; mains $19-35; ⏰noon-2pm & 6-9pm) For a real slice of Aussie culture, try the bistro at the West Tamworth League Club. It's noisy, you have to sign in for a temporary membership and pass the poker machines to reach the bistro, but the food's good – we enjoyed a roast pumpkin and haloumi salad and the barramundi served on a lemon myrtle mash – and it's great for kids.

Information

Visitor Centre (☎02-6767 5300; www.visittamworth.com.au; cnr Peel & Murray Sts)

Getting There & Away

Qantas (☎13 13 13; www.qantas.com.au) flies to Sydney ($125, one hour).

Greyhound (☎1300 GREYHOUND, 1300 4739 46863; www.greyhound.com.au) has daily services along the New England Hwy to Armidale ($32, 1½ hours) and through to Sydney ($71, 6½ hours). **CountryLink** (☎13 22 32; www.countrylink.info) runs daily to Armidale ($14, two hours) and Sydney ($59, 6¼ hours).

Armidale

POP 19,818

Armidale's heritage buildings, gardens and moss-covered churches look like the stage set for a period drama. This old-world scenery coupled with spectacular autumn foliage plays a big part in attracting people to this regional centre which is surrounded by some of Australia's best grazing country. Excellent delis and coffee shops point to a food scene worthy of exploring, too. For the spectacular route down to the coast at Coffs Harbour, see the boxed text, p173.

Sights & Activities

Pick up the heritage-walking-tour pamphlet from the visitor centre.

New England Regional Art Museum MUSEUM
(www.neram.com.au; Kentucky St; ⏰10am-5pm Tue-Fri, 10am-4pm Sat & Sun) FREE At the southern edge of town, 'Neram' has a sizeable permanent collection and good contemporary exhibitions in pleasant grounds. It also houses the **Museum of Printing**, a cafe and souvenir shop.

Aboriginal Cultural Centre & Keeping Place GALLERY
(www.acckp.com.au; 128 Kentucky St; art exhibits $2-5; ⏰9am-4pm Mon-Fri, 10am-2pm Sat) Next door to the New England Regional Art Museum, this place will broaden your perception of indigenous art, and enable the kids to make their own with the help of a resident artist.

Heritage Bus Tours BUS TOUR
(☎1800 627 736, 02-6770 3888; ⏰10am) FREE Free 2½-hour tours of Armidale depart from the visitor centre; bookings essential.

Sleeping & Eating

Pembroke Tourist & Leisure Park & YHA HOSTEL $
(☎02-6772 6470; www.pembroke.com.au; 39 Waterfall Way; unpowered/powered sites $28/33, cabins $72-132; @🏊) Friendly and leafy with a hostel wing.

★**Lindsay House** B&B $$
(☎02-6771 4554; www.lindsayhouse.com.au; 128 Faulkner St; r $145-205; 📶) Immerse yourself

in a past when beds were four-poster, ceilings were ornate, furniture was beautifully crafted and port was served in the evening. This lovely old home is as restful and recuperative as it is grand.

★**Petersons Guesthouse** GUESTHOUSE $$$
(02-6772 0422; www.petersonsguesthouse.com.au; Dangarsleigh Rd; r from $200;) Beautifully restored to its former British opulence, this grand old estate has seven suites with period bathrooms and gorgeous antique furniture. The hosts wine and dine their guests fireside without impinging on privacy. Enjoy lunch under the trees at the weekends.

Bottega Café & Delicatezza CAFE, DELI $
(02-6772 6262; 2/14 Moore St; mains $12-22; breakfast & lunch Tue-Sat) A haunt not just for foodies, but for hungries too. This cafe has tables and shelves stocked with gourmet produce and a deli full of charcuterie and cheese. Breakfast doesn't get much better.

★**Bistro on Cinders** EUROPEAN, ASIAN $$
(02-6772 4273; www.bistrooncinders.com; 14 Cinders Lane; mains $18-34; 8.30am-3pm Mon-Sat) Behind the post office, this plain brick building with a little courtyard houses a fantastic eatery. It's contemporary but not pretentious – have a quick coffee or sit around all night admiring the groovy chandeliers and artwork.

Information

Visitor Centre (02-6772 3888; www.armidaletourism.com.au; 82 Marsh St; 9am-5pm) At the bus station.

Getting There & Around

The airport is 5km southeast of town. **Qantas** (13 13 13; www.qantas.com.au) flies to Sydney ($125, 1¼ hours).

Greyhound (1300 GREYHOUND, 1300 4739 46863; www.greyhound.com.au) runs to Tamworth ($32, 1½ hours) and Sydney ($107, eight hours).

CountryLink (13 22 32; www.countrylink.info) runs daily to Tamworth ($14, two hours), Newcastle ($56, 5¾ hours) and Sydney ($66, 8¼ hours).

Around Armidale

Dramatic, forested and wild, **Gibraltar Range** and **Washpool National Park** (www.environment.nsw.gov.au; per car per day $7) lie south and north of the Gwydir Hwy, about 80km east of Glen Innes on the road to Grafton. There are two camping areas; **Mulligans** (adult/child $10/5) is near Little Dandahra Creek, which is ideal for swimming. Of the many walks, the 100km **World Heritage Walk** is a standout.

Away to the northwest, **Kwiambal National Park** (admission free), pronounced kigh-*am*-bal, sits at the junction of the Macintyre and Severn Rivers. Largely undiscovered, it's an important conservation area for the tumbledown gum and Caley's ironbark.

Tenterfield & Around

POP 2997

At the junction of the New England and Bruxner Hwys, Tenterfield is the hub of a region boasting a smattering of characteristic villages and 10 national parks. In the town itself you can have fun wandering around historic buildings and checking out Australia's oldest cork tree.

There is plenty of work fruit picking on farms near town from October through to May. Ask at the visitor centre for details.

Sights & Activities

Tenterfield Saddler LANDMARK, SHOP
(www.tenterfieldsaddler.com; 123 High St; 10am-4pm) Celebrated by Peter Allen (who was born here) in his eponymous song, the saddler is still open for business.

Thunderbolt's Hideout LANDMARK
About 12km out on the road north to Lisbon, this is where bushranger Captain Thunderbolt holed up in hiding. On your way, check out the **Tenterfield Weather Rock** near the baths.

Kurrajong Downs Winery WINERY
(www.kurrajongdownswines.com; Kurrajong Downs Rd; 10am-4pm Thu-Mon) One of a handful of wineries in the district, Kurrajong has a restaurant and cellar door.

Bald Rock National Park NATURE RESERVE
(per car per day $7) About 29km northeast of Tenterfield, here you can hike to the top of Australia's largest exposed granite monolith (which looks like a stripy little Uluru) and camp (adult/child $10/5) near the base.

Richmond Range National Park NATIONAL PARK
(admission free) East of Tambulam, this 15,712-hectare park contains some of the best-preserved old-growth rainforest in

NSW. It's part of a World Heritage–listed preserve showing off what this part of Australia looked like before settlement.

Sleeping

Tenterfield Lodge & Caravan Park CARAVAN PARK $
(☎02-6736 1477; www.tenterfieldbiz.com/tenterfieldlodge; 2 Manners St; unpowered/powered sites $25/28, dm from $35, cabins $65-100; @) This friendly place has a range of accommodation options.

Tenterfield Cottage B&B $$
(☎0439 769 998; www.tenterfield.com.au; 121 Rouse St; r from $155; ❄) With wood fires, electric blankets on the beds and a kitchen, this cottage, which opened in 2010, has a wonderfully homely feel. It usually requires a two-night minimum stay but the issue is usually one of not wanting to leave, so that shouldn't be a problem.

Information

Visitor Centre (☎02-6736 1082; www.tenterfield.com; 157 Rouse St; ⊙9am-5pm Mon-Sat) Has bushwalking guides and can book tours to nearby national parks.

Getting There & Away

Buses leave Tenterfield from the **Community Centre** (Manners St). **Greyhound** (☎1300 GREYHOUND, 1300 4739 46863; www.greyhound.com.au) runs to Tamworth ($66, four hours) and Sydney ($138, 10½ hours). **Northern Rivers Buslines** (☎02-6626 1499; www.nrbuslines.com.au) has buses to Lismore ($39), with connections to Byron Bay.

CountryLink (☎13 22 32; www.countrylink.info) buses run south to Glen Innes ($12, 1¼ hours), and to Armidale ($25, 2¾ hours) where you can change for Sydney ($75, 8¼ hours).

NORTHWEST

People tend to race through this flat archetypal Australian landscape, possibly with Queensland beaches on their minds.

The Newell Hwy (Rte 39), the through-route from Victoria, passes through stargazing Coonabarabran and the burgeoning Aboriginal art hub of Moree, before hitting the border at Goondiwindi.

If Queensland isn't on the itinerary, chances are Lightning Ridge is. Like other Australian mining communities, the town throws up as many characters as it does gems.

West of Coonabarabran, Warrumbungle National Park is one of the most popular in NSW with camping, walking, stargazing and a wealth of Aboriginal culture and history. Similarly, Moree has some intriguing Aboriginal sites, largely undiscovered by tourists.

Castlereagh Highway

The Castlereagh Hwy (Rte 55) forks off the Oxley Hwy at pretty **Gilgandra** then runs to the Queensland border through **Walgett**, **Coonamble** and the rugged opal country of Lightning Ridge.

Just north of Gilgandra, pull off the highway at the spot where, in 1818, John Oxley spat the dummy. Expecting to find a giant inland sea, he instead discovered that the Macquarie River petered out into a boggy marsh. The town was also the starting point for the Coo-ee March, a WWI recruiting drive to Sydney, led by a butcher and his brother.

West of here, the prolific bird life of 19,824-hectare **Macquarie Marshes Nature Reserve** is best seen during breeding season (usually spring, but it varies with water levels).

Lightning Ridge

POP 1496

Know what a 'ratter', a 'rough' and a 'blower' are? Opal lingo, that's what. Near the Queensland border, this strikingly imaginative mining community (one of the world's few sources of black opals) has real frontier spirit, and is home to eccentric artisans, true-blue bushies and a general unconventional collective.

The 'Ridge' was named after an unfortunate event in 1963 when a flock of sheep, their drover and his faithful dog were struck down by lightning. Their singed woolly carcasses were still wafting with smoke when the town took its name from the event.

Sights & Activities

Several underground mines and opal showrooms are open to the public.

Black Queen MUSEUM
(☎02-6829 0980; www.blackqueen.com.au; adult/family $25/75) This is a quirky antique lamp museum in a building built from 14,000 bot-

tles, but the main attraction is the award-winning three-act 'outback theatre' performances (9am, 1pm and 3pm). Book ahead.

Chambers of the Black Hand ART GALLERY
(www.wj.com.au/whatto/blackhand.html; 3 Mile Rd, Yellow Car Door 5) Artist and miner Ron Canlin has turned a 40ft-deep claim into a cavernous gallery of carvings: dinosaurs, Aboriginal scenes, pharaohs, you name it.

Walk-In Mine MINE
(☎02-6829 0473; www.walkinmine.com.au; Bald Hill; adult/child $20/6; ⊙9am-5pm Apr-Oct, 8.30am-12.30pm Nov-Mar) Visit this mine to get a feel for the type of environment encountered by the average opal miner.

Black Opal Tours TOUR
(☎02-6829 0368; www.blackopaltours.com.au; adult/child $30/12; ⊙tours 8.30am, 9.30am & 1.30pm) You can do a bit of exploring with this outfit on its daily tours, including opal fossicking. Prices vary depending on how many things you wish to see.

Hot Artesian Bore Baths SPRING
(Pandora St; ⊙24hr) FREE Most visitors find time for a soak in the warm artesian water here. It is closed 10am to noon Monday, Wednesday and Friday for cleaning.

Festivals & Events

Though it's hard to work out how many – if any – opals are still being dug up, the town makes a show of it when fossicking season kicks off over the Easter long weekend. You can prove your worth at the **Great Goat Race**. Catch a feral beast, give it some racing lessons, let it go with 50 other goats, and bet money on it. There's a **gem festival** every July.

Sleeping & Eating

Glengarry Hilton HOTEL $
(☎02-6829 3983; per person incl breakfast $20) About 80km south of town, the opal fields of Grawin and Glengarry are also part of the experience. The Hilton is a tin shed of a pub, frequented by lots of local characters. There are four bunk rooms and a double room. It was up for sale last time we visited so things could change, although hopefully not too much.

Black Opal Holiday Units MOTEL $$
(☎02-6829 0222; www.blackopalholidayunits.com.au; Morilla St; r from $90; ❄) A range of accommodation here has decor that is either tired or retro – make up your own mind – but it's a decent base for a night or two.

Chats On Opal CAFE $
(4 Opal St; mains $8-17; ⊙7.30am-3pm) A colourful place serving gourmet sandwiches, cakes and decent coffee. It's a good place to watch the world go by.

Information

Visitor Centre (☎02-6829 1670; Morilla St; ⊙9am-4pm)

Getting There & Away

Air Link (☎02-6884 2435; www.airlinkairlines.com.au) has charter flights to Walgett, Coonamble and Sydney via Dubbo. **CountryLink** (☎13 22 32; www.countrylink.info) buses run to Dubbo ($47, 4½ hours).

Newell Highway

Coonabarabran

POP 2576

The Newell Hwy briefly joins the Oxley Hwy from Tamworth at Coonabarabran ('The Bran' to locals), the gateway to the Warrumbungles. The helpful **visitor centre** (☎02-6849 2144; www.coonabarabran.com/vic; Newell Hwy) is south of the clock tower. Motels dot the highway.

Head 27km west of town in the Warrumbungle Range for some of the world's major, and Australia's largest, telescopes at **Siding Spring Observatory** (☎02-6842 6211; National Park Rd; activity centre adult/child $6/4); ask at the visitor centre for access details.

Between Coonabarabran and Narrabri, the **Pilliga Forest** springs either side of the highway. For a closer look at this iconic semi-arid landscape featuring sandstone caves with Aboriginal rock engraving, contact the new **Discovery Centre** (☎02-6843 4011; 50-58 Wellington St), west of the highway at Baradine.

Moree

POP 7720

This large town on the Gwydir River has the **Hot Artesian Pool Complex** (cnr Anne & Gosport Sts; adult/child $7/4.50; ⊙6am-8.30pm Mon-Fri, 7am-7pm Sat & Sun), where locals frolic in 42°C water; opening hours can vary – ask

WORTH A TRIP

WARRUMBUNGLES

When the Warrumbungle Volcano erupted more than 13 million years ago it formed the spectacular granite domes of the **Warrumbungle National Park** (www.environment.nsw.gov.au; per car $7). Sitting 33km west of Coonabarabran, this 23,311-hectare park has 43km of bushwalking trails and explosive wildflower displays during spring. As such, this is one of the most beautiful parks in New South Wales, although sadly a serious bushfire swept through here in early 2013 so some areas of the park will take some years to fully recover.

Park fees are payable at the **NPWS visitor centre** (☎02-6825 4364) in the park; some sights also have camp fees (adult/child from $5/3). Walking tracks range from the 1.1km **Wambelong Nature Track** up to the peerless 12.5km **Breadknife and High Tops Walk**. Eastern grey kangaroos, red-knecked wallabies and emus are all possibilities along the trail, as well as prolific birdlife.

at the **visitor centre** (☎02-6575 3350; www.moreetourism.com.au). Many accommodation options also have artesian pools.

Moree Plains Gallery (www.moreeplainsgallery.org.au; cnr Frome & Herber Sts; ⏲10am-5pm Mon-Fri, 10am-1pm Sat) FREE has an inspiring collection of Aboriginal art by some of the country's best artists, including Arone Meeks, Dorothy Napangardi, Elizabeth Nyumi Nungurrayi and Judy Watson. For a more local take, check out **Yaama Maliyaa Arts** (29 Herber St); the friendly owner is also a good source of info on local Aboriginal sites.

Café 2400 (123 Balo St; mains $10-16; ⏲8am-5pm Mon-Fri, 8am-1pm Sat) would be at home in Sydney's groovier suburbs, with healthy (often gluten-free) dishes and good coffee.

Cotton-related work is available from March to May for skilled workers. Anyone can partake in cotton chipping from November to January or olive- and pecan-picking from April to August. The job application process had been put out for tendering when we passed through – ask at the visitor centre on where to start looking.

CENTRAL WEST

The Central West's relative proximity to Sydney and its population of eager tree-changers, weekend-awayers and holiday-homers has no doubt given many of the agricultural cities and towns just beyond the Blue Mountains a leg-up.

The university city of Bathurst is also a rev-head's haven, Orange has an inordinate number of lauded chefs and restaurants, Mudgee is a small town with a big nose for wine, and Dubbo has joined the milieu with a newish cultural centre.

The stately buildings, grandiose wide streets, parks, and vivid and well-tended English gardens align these cities with a past built on gold-mining and bushranger folklore. This history is best explored in the smaller hill towns where wide verandahs and old pubs are often coupled with a decent cafe or restaurant and local B&B.

Further west, Forbes and Parkes were united by the radio telescope made famous by the movie *The Dish* until Elvis fever gave the latter town something of its own to focus on. Drive further west and the harsher outback soil of the far west takes over.

Bathurst

POP 31,294

Bathurst is Australia's oldest inland settlement, boasting European trees, a cool climate and a beautiful manicured central square where formidable Victorian buildings can snap you back to the past. And then, in a dramatic change of pace, it's also the bastion of Australian motor sport, hosting numerous events.

Sights & Activities

Ask at the visitor centre for information about **wineries, hiking trails** and **scenic drives** in the region.

Australian Fossil & Mineral Museum MUSEUM
(www.somervillecollection.com.au; 224 Howick St; adult/child $10/5; ⏲10am-4pm Mon-Sat, to 2pm Sun) See Tyrannosaurus rex, Australia's

only complete skeleton. You'll also see the internationally renowned **Somerville Collection**, a remarkable private collection of over 6000 fossils from every period of the earth's history.

Bathurst Regional Art Gallery ART GALLERY
(www.bathurstart.com.au; 70-78 Keppel St; ⌚10am-5pm Tue-Sat, 11am-2pm Sun) FREE The gallery has a dynamic collection of work, featuring local artists as well as exciting touring exhibitions.

Courthouse HISTORIC BUILDING, MUSEUM
(www.bathursthistory.org.au; Russell St; Historical Museum adult/child $4/2; ⌚Historical Museum 10am-4pm Tue, Wed & Sat, 11am-2pm Sun) This extraordinary 1880 building is the most impressive of Bathurst's historical buildings and houses the small **Historical Museum**. Pick up the visitor centre's *Bathurst Courthouse* information sheet before you visit.

Chifley Home HISTORIC BUILDING
(www.chifleyhome.org.au; 10 Busby St; adult/child $10/6; ⌚tours 10am & noon Sat-Mon) Ben Chifley, prime minister from 1945 to 1949, lived in Bathurst, and the modest Chifley Home is on display. There's also an education centre.

Abercrombie House HISTORIC BUILDING
(www.abercrombiehouse.com.au; 311 Ophir Rd; adult/child $15/5; ⌚tours 11.15am Sat & Sun) This astonishing Tudor Gothic confection and 52-room mansion, north of the town centre, is one of Bathurst's more impressive structures. Take Durham St heading northwest then follow the signs.

National Motor Racing Museum MUSEUM
(www.nmrm.com.au; Pit Straight, Murrays Corner, Mt Panorama; adult/child/family $10.50/4.50/25.50; ⌚9am-4.30pm) Rev-heads will enjoy the 6.2km Mt Panorama Motor Racing Circuit, the venue for the epic **Bathurst 1000** in October. You can drive around the circuit, but only up to an unthrilling 60km/h. There's a good lookout and racing-themed children's playground at the top. All roads lead to the track, including southwest along William St. The visitor centre has some information sheets on the track and its racing history.

Sleeping

Jack Duggans Irish Pub HOTEL $
(☎02-6331 2712; www.jackduggans.com.au; 135 George St; dm/s/d $25/45/65) The recently renovated former Commerical Hotel, in the heart of town, has a lively restaurant and bar downstairs and small but inviting rooms upstairs, opening onto a verandah. Prices go up on weekends.

Big4 Bathurst Holiday Park CARAVAN PARK $
(☎02-63318286; www.bathurstholidaypark.com.au; Sydney Rd; 2-person powered sites/cabins from $34/98; ❄≋) This well-equipped park, with cute, red-topped, corrugated-iron miners cottages, is the main caravan and camping option. Prices increase when the races are on.

Accommodation Warehouse APARTMENTS $$
(☎02-6332 2801; www.accomwarehouse.com.au; 121a Keppel St; s/d $95/125) A soaring, historic brick building with arched windows and Juliet balconies, this place has three lovely self-contained apartments. A continental breakfast is included.

Rydges Mount Panorama HOTEL $$
(☎02-6338 1888; www.rydges.com/bathurst; 1 Conrod Straight; d/f $150/175;) This large, recently refurbished hotel is ideal for those keen for a view over the race track.

Eating

★**Church Bar** PIZZA $$
(www.churchbar.com.au; 1 Ribbon Gang Lane; pizzas $17-24; ⌚noon-late) This restored 1850s church now attracts punters praying to a different deity: the god of wood-fired pizza. The soaring ceilings and verdant courtyard off William St make it one of the region's best eating and socialising venues.

Hub CAFE $$
(52 Keppel St; mains $14-21; ⌚7am-5pm Mon-Sat, to 3pm Sun) A canopy of red umbrellas and green leaves makes this charming, popular spot the perfect place for alfresco lunch. The cajun chicken burger and Vietnamese prawn salad go down a treat, as does live jazz on Thursday nights.

Elie's Café MODERN AUSTRALIAN $$
(☎02-6332 1707; 108 William St; mains $28; ⌚7.30am-6pm Mon-Wed, 7.30am-late Thu-Sat, 7.30am-4pm Sun) Set in the ground floor of the stunning heritage building of the old Royal Hotel, this engaging spot has some tables out on the street and an attractive indoor area. Service is friendly and the food is creative without going too far – modern Australian cooking as it should be.

WORTH A TRIP

SCENIC DRIVE: BATHURST TO GULGONG

The region north of Bathurst is good driving territory with beautiful scenery, parks and reserves and a handful of quaint little towns.

Follow the signs towards Lithgow from **Bathurst** city centre, then take the turn-off for Sofala. An easy drive through increasingly rolling country dips down into a valley 43km northeast of Bathurst. Just before crossing the bridge, detour along the charming, ramshackle main street of **Sofala**, a pretty hangover from the region's gold-mining days. If you've endless time, consider the long, partially unpaved 105km detour to Mudgee via **Hill End**, another old gold-mining village. Otherwise, from Sofala continue for 28km to Ilford where you join the main Lithgow–Mudgee road. As you head northwest, you'll pass pretty **Lake Windamere** before reaching **Mudgee**. Ignore the town's untidy outskirts and head for the centre, taking Church St which becomes Ulan Rd, which in turn heads northwest of town past some of the best wineries. Some 11km out of Mudgee, consider a detour to the **Munghorn Lake Nature Reserve**, where there's the popular 8km-return Castle Rock walking trail; the reserve is home to the endangered Regent's Honeyeater.

Back on the main Ulan road, around 29km after leaving Mudgee, ignore for now the turn-off for Gulgong, and do the same for the national park another 3km on. Pass the scarred landscape of an open-cut mine for 10km, then take the turn-off for 'The Drip' in **Goulburn Ranges National Park**. This 3km-return walk along a narrow river valley is one of the prettier short walks in regional New South Wales. The trail begins at the car park around 200m down off the road, next to a popular swimming hole, and passes between a steepish escarpment and the riverbank; there are some Aboriginal rock paintings on the overhanging rocks across the creek around halfway along. Watch also for wallabies, kangaroos and wombats.

Return to your car and to Ulan, then follow the signs for historic **Gulgong**, which lies 24km away through dense, fire-scarred forest.

Thai Buddha THAI $$
(1/35 William St; mains $13-26; ⏲11am-9pm) Authentic Thai cooking with some Chinese dishes and sushi.

Information

Visitor Centre (☎1800 681 000; www.visitbathurst.com.au; Kendall Ave)

Getting There & Away

Rex (☎13 17 13; www.rex.com.au) flies to Sydney ($119, 45 minutes).

Australia Wide Coaches (☎02-6362 7963; www.austwidecoaches.com.au) *Sydney Express* leaves daily ($34, 3½ hours). **CountryLink** (☎13 22 32; www.countrylink.info) trains go to Sydney ($8.40, 4¼ hours via Lithgow). CountryLink's XPT train also stops here on the daily Sydney ($38, 3¾ hours) and Dubbo ($34, three hours) service.

Orange

POP 34,992

There might be pears, apples and stone fruit aplenty in the surrounding orchards, but it just so happens the town was named after Prince William of Orange. It's now a dedicated food-and-wine hub with four distinct seasons – and a food festival for each. The city's parks and gardens are a kaleidoscope of colours throughout the year, with cold winters bringing occasional snowfalls. Bush poet AB 'Banjo' Paterson was born here.

Sights & Activities

Mt Canobolas NATURE RESERVE
Southwest of Orange, this nature reserve encompasses waterfalls, views, walking trails and bike paths. **Lake Canoblas** is a good place to start with plenty of picnic areas and a lakeside children's playground – the turn-off to the lake is on the extension of Coronation Rd, 8km west of town.

Orange Regional Gallery GALLERY
(www.org.nsw.gov.au; Civic Sq; ⏲10am-5pm Tue-Sat, noon-4pm Sun) FREE Next to the visitor centre, the gallery has an ambitious, varied program of exhibitions and some Australian masters.

Festivals & Events

Testament to its 'foodie' reputation, Orange now has four seasonal festivals (www.tasteorange.com.au) where the region's producers make star appearances: **Slow Summer**, in early February, **F.O.O.D Week** (www.orangefoodweek.com.au) in mid-April, **Frost Fest** in early August and **Wine Week** in late October.

Local produce can be foraged at the popular **farmers market** (www.orangefarmersmarket.org.au; Orange Regional Gallery North Ct; ⏲8.30am-noon) held on the second Saturday of the month. From May to September, or when it's wet, the market is in the Orange Showground.

Sleeping

Stay Orange (www.stayorange.com.au) lists 31 places to stay in and around Orange.

★De Russie Suites BOUTIQUE HOTEL **$$**
(☎02-6360 0973; www.derussiehotels.com.au; 72 Hill St; r from $151; ❄📶) As good as anything in Sydney, this hotel has boutique written all over it. It has all the luxurious cons expected in a hotel plus self-contained facilities. Breakfast is included and comes in hamper format.

Templers Mill Motel MOTEL **$$**
(☎02-6362 5611; www.oesc.com.au; 94 Byng St; s/d from $102/126; ❄📶) This well-run motel has recently renovated and even vaguely stylish rooms. It's a short walk to restaurants and the main street.

Arancia B&B B&B **$$**
(☎02-6365 3305; www.arancia.com.au; 69 Wrights Lane; r from $200; ❄📶) Set in rolling green hills, this B&B has hotel-worthy facilities, including spacious rooms with big beds, en suites, cups of tea and classy furnishings. Breakfasts here are famous, but it's adults only. Check out its packages that include meals and even a winery tour.

Eating

★Byng Street Local Store CAFE **$**
(☎02-6369 0768; www.byngstreet.com.au; 47 Byng St; mains $6-18; ⏲6am-7pm Mon-Sat, 6am-4pm Sun) This fabulous little corner store could just be our favourite place to eat in Orange, and that's no small claim. The bread is freshly baked on site, its breakfasts are unusually tasty and it has a range of hot meals at lunchtime from a menu that changes with the seasons. The salads and sandwiches are highlights.

Mills Cafe CAFE **$**
(Byng St; mains from $5.80; ⏲6am-8pm Mon-Fri, to 3pm Sat) Part cafeteria, part groovy cafe, this busy place does Orange's best burgers, as well as fish and chips and salads.

WINERIES AROUND ORANGE

Orange has a reputation for distinctive cool-climate wines, with many award-winning vineyards. Pick up the *Orange & District Wine & Food Guide* from the visitor centre or www.tasteorange.com.au. For tours, try **Orange Taxi Tours** (www.orangetaxis.com.au; per vehicle from $60 per hour) or **Central West Getaways** (☎0413 551 212; www.centralwestgetaways.com; 2-/3-/4-hr tours per person $55/75/105). Some of the best wineries with cellar door sales:

- **Brangayne of Orange** (☎02-6365 3229; www.brangayne.com; 837 Pinnacle Rd; ⏲11am-1pm & 2-4pm Mon-Fri, 11am-5pm Sat, 11am-4pm Sun)
- **De Salis Wines** (☎0403 956 295; www.desaliswines.com.au; 125 Mount Lofty Rd; ⏲11am-5pm Sat & Sun)
- **Orange Mountain Wines** (☎02-6365 2626; www.orangemountain.com.au; cnr Forbes Rd & Radnedge Lane; ⏲9am-5pm Sat & Sun)
- **Printhie** (www.printhiewines.com.au; 439 Yuranigh Rd; ⏲10am-4pm Mon-Fri, noon-4pm Sat)
- **Stockman's Ridge** (☎02-6365 6212; www.stockmansridge.com.au; 21 Boree Lane; ⏲10am-5pm Sat & Sun)
- **Word of Mouth Wines** (☎02-6365 3509; www.wordofmouthwines.com.au; 790 Pinnacle Rd; ⏲10.30am-3pm Sun, Mon & Wed-Fri, to 5pm Sat)

Union Bank WINE BAR $$
(☎02-6361 4441; www.unionbank.com.au; cnr Sale & Byng Sts; mains $12-22; ⊙noon-3pm & 6-9pm Mon-Sat) This upmarket and rather groovy cellar door and wine bar has more than 500 wine labels, any of which can be enjoyed with a cheese platter or antipasto plate.

Racine at La Colline Winery MODERN AUSTRALIAN, FRENCH $$$
(☎02-6365 3275; www.racinerestaurant.com.au; 42 Lake Canobolas Rd; 2-/3-course set menu $65/75; ⊙noon-3pm & 6-9pm Fri & Sat, 6-9pm Thu, noon-3pm Sun) High-class cooking and a fine rural setting are a winning combination at this lovely vineyard off the road to Lake Canoblas. Dishes may include twice-cooked pork belly or dressed blue swimmer crab.

Lolli Redini MODERN AUSTRALIAN $$$
(☎02-6361 7748; www.lolliredini.com.au; 48 Sale St; 2-/3-course set menu $65/80, mains from $30; ⊙6-9pm Tue-Sat) A huge buzz surrounds this place and bookings are always essential. The matching of main courses with wines is always well thought out and some of its dishes (the gruyere and gorgonzola cheese souffle for entree, for example) are exceptional. But we found the mains to be a touch disappointing and hence overpriced.

Information

Orange Visitor Centre (☎02-6393 8226, 1800 069 466; www.visitorange.com.au; 151 Byng St; ⊙9am-5pm)

Verto (☎02-6361 5300; www.verto.org.au) Can help you find fruit-picking work in the area. Ask also at the visitor centre for orchards with accommodation.

Getting There & Away

Rex (☎13 17 13; www.rex.com.au) flies to Sydney (from $153, 50 minutes). The airport is 13km southeast of Orange.

Australia Wide Coaches (☎02-6362 7963; www.austwidecoaches.com.au) *Sydney Express* leaves daily ($38, 4¼ hours). **CountryLink** (☎13 22 32; www.countrylink.info) trains go to Sydney (from $31, five hours) and Dubbo ($22.50, 1¾ hours).

Millthorpe

Only 20 minutes from Orange, this pioneering village with heritage architecture is a little slice of the mid-1800s. Its cuteness is such that the National Trust has classified the whole place. It's a quieter alternative to staying in busy Orange.

Sights

Millthorpe Wine Centre WINERY
(www.millthorpewinecentre.com.au; Millthorpe Railway Station; ⊙10am-5pm Sat & Sun) The old railway station has been artfully converted into a showroom for two of the region's wines – Edgecome and Coffee Hill.

Angullong WINERY
(www.angullong.com.au; cnr Park & Victoria Sts; ⊙11am-5pm Sat & Sun) This versatile winemaker has cellar-door tastings and sales on weekends.

Sleeping & Eating

Millthorpe Bed & Breakfast B&B
(☎02-6366 3967; www.millthorpebedandbreakfast.com.au; 11 Morley St; r from $175) Hotel-standard rooms on a quiet Millthorpe street.

Old Mill Cafe CAFE $$
(☎02-6366 3188; 12 Pym St; mains from $15; ⊙9am-4.30pm) Coffee and cakes in a designer rustic setting is the staple here, but it also does hot lunch meals from Thursday to Monday.

Gerry's @ The Commercial MODERN AUSTRALIAN $$
(☎02-6366 3999; gerryatthecommercial@gmail.com; 29 Park St; mains $22-29; ⊙noon-3pm & 6-9pm Wed-Sat, 6-9pm Tue, noon-3pm Sun) Fabulous pub food, open fireplaces, local wines and not a TV or poker machine in sight. This is one of rural NSW's best pubs for a meal. Try the five-meat mixed grill or the bangers and mash and a local Angullong (p208) red.

Tonic MODERN AUSTRALIAN $$
(☎02-6366 3811; www.tonicmillthorpe.com.au; cnr Pym & Victoria Sts, Millthorpe; mains $30; ⊙10am-3pm & 6.30-9.30pm Sat, 10am-3pm Sun, 6.30-9.30pm Thu & Fri) White tablecloths, shiny glassware and contemporary food such as pan-fried barramundi or roast pork backstrap. Highly recommended for a classy night out.

Getting There & Away

From Orange, take the Bathurst road, then turn off to Millthorpe just after passing through Lucknow; Millthorpe is 8km from the turn-off.

Canowindra

POP 1424

The small town of Canowindra (the name means 'home' or 'camping place' in the local indigenous language) is the perfect laid-back weekender. It's 32km north of Cowra and has a heritage-listed main street where a surprising number of art galleries and old wares shops make for a leisurely meander.

Sights & Activities

Age of Fishes Museum MUSEUM
(www.ageoffishes.org.au; cnr Gaskill & Ferguson Sts; adult/child $10/5) This intriguing exhibition unravels the mysteries of a fossil site found nearby featuring the preserved remains of long-extinct fish pre-dating the dinosaurs.

Tom's Waterhole Winery WINERY
(www.tomswaterhole.com.au; Longs Corner Rd; ⏲10am-4pm) This winery has a cellar door and a cafe serving ploughman's lunches.

Swinging Bridge WINERY
(www.swingingbridge.com.au; 33 Gaskill St; ⏲11am-6pm Fri-Sun) Award-winning local winery with cellar-door sales.

Taste Canowindra WINERY
(www.tastecanowindra.com.au; 42 Ferguson St; ⏲10am-7pm Sun-Thu, to 10pm Fri & Sat) Taste Canowindra hosts regional wine tastings, art-and-craft exhibitions, and the occasional live band.

Aussie Balloontrek SCENIC FLIGHTS
(☎02-6361 2552; www.aussieballoontrek.com.au; Nanami Lane; 30-/45-/60min flight per person $180/230/320) Aussie Balloontrek can get you high with a champagne breakfast.

Balloon Joy Flights SCENIC FLIGHTS
(www.balloonjoyflights.com.au; adult/child $280/200) Balloon Joy Flights operates from Tom's Waterhole Winery.

Sleeping & Eating

Old Vic Inn HOTEL $$
(☎02-6344 1009; www.oldvicinn.com.au; 56 Gaskill St; r with/without bathroom incl breakfast from $130/90; ❄) The Old Vic Inn occupies a lovely old pub building, with a cosy restaurant (open Thursday to Saturday) and B&B accommodation.

Everview Retreat B&B $$$
(☎02-6344 3116; www.everview.com.au; 72 Cultowa Lane; d from $220; ❄) For a little more space and romance, this retreat has luxury stone cottages equipped with spas, DVDs, the works. It's just off the Canowindra-Cowra Rd.

Information

Visitor Centre (☎02-6344 1008; cnr Gaskill & Ferguson Sts; ⏲10am-4pm)

Cowra

POP 8107

History buffs will be prone to various states of excitability in Cowra, a town with a unique story. In August 1944 more than 1000 Japanese prisoners attempted to break out of a prisoner-of-war camp here (231 of them died, along with four Australians). Since the war, Cowra has aligned itself with Japan and the cause of world peace. The visitor centre (p210) shows an excellent nine-minute holographic film about the breakout scene – it has been praised by Bill Bryson no less.

Sights & Activities

At the corner of Darling and Kendall Sts, watch for the **World Peace Bell**, a replica of the bell that stands outside the United Nations and the only one of its kind in Australia.

Japanese Garden GARDENS
(www.cowragarden.com.au; Binni Creek Rd; adult/child $13.50/7.50; ⏲8.30am-5pm) Built as a token of Cowra's connection with Japanese POWs (but with no overt mention of the war or the breakout), the tranquil 5-hectare garden and attached cultural centre, with its collection of *ukiyo-e* paintings depicting everyday events in pre-industrial Japan, are well worth visiting. Audioguides are available to help with plant identification.

Australian & Japanese War Cemeteries CEMETERY
These well-kept cemeteries are well signposted off the Orange–Cowra road, around 5km south of town; many of those remembered here died very young.

POW Camp MEMORIAL
(Evans Rd) Easy-to-follow signs from the cemetery lead to the site of the Japanese breakout. A voiceover from the watchtower tells the story of the breakout, while you can still see the camp foundations.

Mill WINERY
(www.windowrie.com.au; 6 Vaux St; ⌚11am-5pm) In the heart of town, the Mill is Cowra's oldest building, where the millstone first turned in 1861. The region's chardonnay has tickled many a palate; enjoy it here with a cellar-door cheese platter.

Darby Falls Observatory OBSERVATORY
(☎02-6345 1900; Observatory Rd; adult/child $10/7; ⌚8.30-11pm during periods of daylight saving, 7-10pm rest of year) This is one of the darkest places for stargazing in all of Australia. From town, head out Darby Falls Rd for 22km, then follow the signs.

Cowra Regional Art Gallery ART GALLERY
(www.cowraartgallery.com.au; 77 Darling St; ⌚10am-4pm Tue-Sat, 2-4pm Sun) FREE The gallery has a permanent collection and exhibitions. For art alfresco, take a peek beneath Lachlan River bridge to see murals painted by Aboriginal artist Kim Freeman.

Festivals & Events

Cherry Blossom Festival TOWN FESTIVAL
(⌚3rd weekend in Sep) This *sakura matsuri* (cherry-blossom festival) is further evidence of Cowra's strong ties with Japan.

CHERRY-PICKING AT YOUNG

Young, 69km southwest of Cowra, is the cherry capital of Australia and one of the best places in the state to earn some money fruit-picking. The cherry harvest is in November and December, which coincides with the **Cherry Festival** on the first weekend in December. In January other stone fruits are harvested and in February the prune harvest begins. For help in finding a placement, try **Verto** (Harvest Labour Services; ☎1300 364 445; www.verto.org.au), or ask at the **visitor centre** (☎02-6382 3394; www.visityoung.com.au; Lovell St; ⌚9.30am-4pm). Accommodation can sometimes be found at the orchard where you're working, or try **Young Tourist Park** (☎02-6382 2190; Zouch St; powered camp sites per adult $30, cabins $55-91;). Otherwise, ask at the visitor centre. **CountryLink** (☎13 22 32; www.countrylink.info) has daily services to Sydney ($67, eight hours) via Cootamundra.

Cowra Cork & Fork FOOD & WINE
(⌚early Nov) Wine and food festival celebrating the region's produce.

Sleeping & Eating

Decent takeaways (including two Thai options) and cafes line the main (Kendal) street.

Vineyard Motel MOTEL $$
(☎02-6342 3641; www.vineyardmotel.com.au; Chardonnay Rd; s/d from $115/135;) The Lachlan Valley vineyard views from this quiet motel, 4km from town, are so mesmerising that the plastic flowers and lace doilies can be forgiven.

Breakout Motor Inn MOTEL $$
(☎02-6342 6111; www.breakoutmotel.com.au; 181 Kendal St; r from $115;) This is a modern and quite delightful place, at the eastern end of the town centre, with atmospheric slate, blue and beige decor. It has a handful of apartments.

Neila GREEK, CHINESE $$$
(☎02-6341 2188; www.neila.com.au; 5 Kendal St; mains $36; ⌚6.30-10pm Thu-Sat) On Cowra's main drag, this small gem is a tribute to the quality of food in the region and to the owners themselves who grow much of what ends up on the plate. It has received a chef's hat award 10 years running. BYO.

Quarry MODERN AUSTRALIAN $$
(☎02-6342 3650; www.thequarryrestaurant.com.au; 7191 Boorowa Rd; lunch mains $19-30, dinner mains $33; ⌚lunch Thu & Sun, lunch & dinner Fri & Sat) On the edge of town 4km along Boorowa Rd, the Quarry cellar-door restaurant is set amid the vineyards, and the cuisine is well regarded. For lunch we liked the Cowra lamb and mint sausages on creamy mash served with the Quarry chilli jam. Having gorged on this, we didn't make it to dinner, but if we had we would have ordered the slow-baked duck breast on wasabi-and-spinach mash with beetroot-and-orange relish.

Information

Visitor Centre (☎02-6342 4333; www.cowratourism.com.au; Olympic Park, Mid Western Hwy)

Getting There & Away

CountryLink (☎13 22 32; www.countrylink.info) has daily services to Sydney ($37, six hours) but you may have to change in Lithgow.

Parkes

POP 10,026

Parkes has two very different claims to fame. First, it's home to the massive radio telescope made famous by the film *The Dish*. Secondly, hundreds of Elvis impersonators celebrate the King's birthday in the second week in January, when the population doubles. Otherwise it's a fairly sleepy inland rural town.

Sights

Sir Henry Parkes Visitor Centre MUSEUM
(Newell Hwy; admission $10; 9am-5pm Mon-Fri, 10am-4pm Sat & Sun) There are four museums in one at the visitor centre with a walk through the 'moat cottage', a replica of **Sir Henry Parkes' birthplace**, the **King's Castle Elvis Exhibit**, a **motor museum** (including an Elvis Cadillac) and the **antique machinery museum**.

Radio Telescope TELESCOPE
Built by the Commonwealth Scientific & Industrial Research Organisation (CSIRO) in 1961, this telescope is 6km east of the Newell Hwy, 19km north of Parkes. As one of the world's most powerful telescopes it has helped Australian radio astronomers become leaders in their field, and brought pictures of the *Apollo 11* moon landing to an audience of 600 million people. The **Dish CSIRO visitor centre** (www.parkes.atnf.csiro.au; 8.30am-4.15pm) FREE has hands-on displays and visual effects; 3-D films (adult/child $7.50/5) screen throughout the day.

Festivals & Events

Elvis Festival ELVIS
(www.parkeselvisfestival.com.au) On the second weekend in January, this is one of the weirdest and wackiest festivals in the country. An influx of King lookalikes invade the town to celebrate his birthday with street parades, concerts, talent quests and busking. Don't forget your blue suedes!

Sleeping & Eating

Coachman Hotel Motel MOTEL $
(02-6862 2622; www.coachman.com.au; 48-54 Welcome St; s/d from $70/75;) The well-kept but otherwise fairly standard motel rooms here are just off the main street.

Old Parkes Convent B&B $$
(02-6862 2385; www.parkesconvent.com.au; 33 Currajong St; s/d $140/180;) This charming old heritage building has two impeccably attired apartments filled with antiques – one with an open fireplace. The first is in the old boarding house with the other in the main heritage building.

Bellas CAFE $$
(02-6862 4212; 245 Clarinda St; meals $17-25; 7.30am-3pm Tue, to 8.30pm Wed-Sat) An excellent eatery with vibrantly coloured booths and good pasta and pizza dishes. On-the-go brekkies include banana bread ($7) or come back later for heartier modern Oz-Italian fare and vino by the glass.

Dish Café CAFE $$
(02-6862 1566; Telescope Rd, Parkes Radio Telescope; lunch mains $14-20; 8.30am-3.30pm) In the shadow of the telescope, this cafe has close-up views of the dish and a healthy selection of breakfast and lunch dishes, including the Dish burger or the celestial-chicken wrap with brie and avocado. Eat indoors or out.

Information

Visitor Centre (1800 624 365; www.visitparkes.com.au; Newell Hwy) In a new purpose-built building along the Newell Hwy on the north side of town.

Getting There & Away

CountryLink (13 22 32; www.countrylink.info) runs three daily buses to Sydney (from $49, seven to 10 hours).

> WORTH A TRIP
>
> **HOLDEN UTES ART INSTALLATION**
>
> About 70km from Parkes on the Condobolin road, the **Holden Utes Art Installation** (www.utesinthepaddock.com.au; Mulgutherie Lane) is a peculiar tribute to life in the outback with the iconic vehicles given a creative makeover. Spot the bottle of Bundy and Dame Edna on the 'loo'.

Dubbo

POP 32,327

The important rural centre of Dubbo, on one of the main inland north–south driving routes and a gateway of sorts to the outback, has two main attractions: the Western Plains Zoo and the Western Plains Cultural Centre.

Sights

Western Plains Zoo ZOO
(☎02-6681 1400; www.taronga.org.au; Obley Rd; 2-day adult/child/family pass $45/22/109; ⊙9am-4pm) With over 1500 animals, this is Dubbo's star attraction, not to mention one of the best zoos in regional Australia. You can walk the 6km trail, hire a bike ($15) or join the crawling line of cars. Guided walks (adult/child $15/7.50) start at 6.45am every weekend and Wednesday and Friday in school holidays. Book ahead (☎02-6881 1488) for special animal encounters.

Western Plains Cultural Centre MUSEUM
(☎02-6801 4444; www.wpccdubbo.org.au; 76 Wingewarra St; ⊙10am-4pm Wed, Thu & Sat-Mon, to 8pm Fri) FREE Incorporating **Dubbo Regional Museum and Gallery**, the cultural centre is housed in a swanky architectural space cleverly incorporating the main hall of Dubbo's former high school. The combination befits the centre's exhibitions, both contemporary and historic. There's an innovative dedicated children's gallery.

Old Dubbo Gaol MUSEUM
(www.olddubbogaol.com.au; 90 Macquarie St; adult/child $15/5; ⊙9am-4pm, guided tours 3pm Mon-Fri, 11am, 2pm & 3pm Sat & Sun) This is now a museum where 'animatronic' characters tell their stories – you hear from a condemned man due for a meeting with the gallows. There are also characters in costume on weekends and moonlight tours are possible. Creepy but authentic.

Dubbo Observatory OBSERVATORY
(www.dubboobservatory.com.au; 17 Camp Rd; adult/child/family $20/10/50; ⊙9pm Dec-Feb, 8.30pm Mar, Oct & Nov, 8pm Apr, 7.30pm May-Sep) Advance bookings are essential for this fascinating chance to stargaze; visits are only possible when the weather's fine.

Dundullimal HISTORIC BUILDING
(☎02-6885 3022; 23L Obley Rd; adult/child $8/4; ⊙noon-4pm Tue-Fri, 11am-2pm Sat) About 2km beyond the Western Plains Zoo, this is a National Trust timber-slab homestead built in the 1840s showcasing some of the earliest forms of permanent European housing in NSW.

Sleeping

There are plenty of hotels on Cobra St.

Dubbo City Holiday Park CAMPGROUND $
(☎02-6882 4820; www.dubbocityholidaypark.com.au; Whylandra St; powered sites/cabins from $26/105; ❄≋) On the riverbank with cabins nestled between trees.

No 95 Dubbo MOTEL $$
(☎02-6882 7888; www.no95.com.au; 95 Cobra St; r $135; ❄@≋) This place has a hotel-standard facade but inside, the rooms are equipped with top-notch furniture, linen and appliances. It's one of the nicer options in town.

Westbury Guesthouse GUESTHOUSE $$
(☎02-6884 9445; www.westburyguesthouse.com.au; cnr Brisbane & Wingewarra Sts; s/d $125/150; ❄) This lovely old heritage home (1910) has spacious rooms, all with bathrooms, and a shared lounge and kitchen.

Eating & Drinking

Artology + Café CAFE $
(209 Darling St; mains $11-16; ⊙8am-4pm Mon-Fri, 9am-3pm Sat) A black-and-red-daubed terrace fronts Dubbo's latest ode to caffeine culture. Inside it's all funky spaces, Bodum coffee cups and cube stools. The fare is easy eats: rolls, quiches, muffins etc.

Red Earth Estate Vineyard VINEYARD $
(www.redearthestate.com.au; 18 Camp Rd; ⊙11am-5pm Thu-Tue) Around 4.5km past the Western Plains Zoo, Red Earth is one of four vineyards. It has lunchtime platters and free tastings.

Village Bakery Cafe CAFE & BAKERY $
(www.villagebakerycafe.com.au; 113a Darling St; ⊙6am-5.30pm) Award-winning pies (such as the kangaroo port and cranberry pie), sandwiches and a casual cafe setting make this a good choice if you're not after a full meal.

★**Two Doors Tapas & Wine Bar** TAPAS $$
(☎02-6885 2333; www.twodoors.com.au; 215b Macquarie St; lunch mains $12-15, dinner mains $16-28; ⊙10am-9pm Tue-Sat) Kick back with a drink in a leafy courtyard below street level, while munching on everything from paella to fried goat's cheese or slow roasted pork belly.

Information

Visitor Centre (☎1800 674 443, 02-6801 4450; www.dubbo.com.au; cnr Macquarie St & Newell Hwy; ⊙9am-5pm) At the northern end of town.

Getting There & Around

Rex (☎13 17 13; www.rex.com.au) and **Qantas** (☎13 13 13; www.qantas.com.au) fly to Sydney (from $137, one hour).

The **CountryLink** (☎13 22 32; www.countrylink.info) XPT trains run to Sydney (from $52, 6¾ hours).

Mudgee

POP 9830

Mudgee is an Aboriginal word for 'nest in the hills', a fitting name for this quaint little grid of a town with vineyards on its edge and rolling hills wherever you turn. The wineries come hand in hand with excellent cuisine, making it a popular weekend getaway where gastronomic exploration is central to the experience.

Sights

Mudgee's 44 vineyards are clustered in two groups north and southeast of town. This makes them ideal for cycling between, as long as you don't try too many wines en route... The vintage is later than the Hunter Valley because of Mudgee's higher altitude, but it's well regarded in wine circles. The region is well known for its shiraz, cabernet sauvignon and a blend of the two.

Logan WINERY
(www.loganwines.com.au; 33 Castlereagh Hwy; ⏲10am-5pm) An impressive cellar-door experience and great wines. Floor-to-ceiling windows, an extravagant deck, cheese platters and coffee, too.

Pieter Van Gent WINERY
(☎02-6376 3030; www.pvgwinery.com.au; 141 Black Springs Rd; ⏲9am-5pm Mon-Sat, 10.30am-4pm Sun & public holidays) Heavenly muscat, picnic-lunch wine tours by bike, tastings in the barrel room (11.30am Saturday) and accommodation.

Petersons of Mudgee WINERY
(www.petersonswines.com.au; Black Springs Rd; ⏲9am-5pm Mon-Sat, 10am-5pm Sun) Smallish, with a lovely deck overlooking vineyards.

Vinifera Wines WINERY
(www.viniferawines.com.au; 194 Henry Lawson Dr; ⏲10am-5pm Mon-Sat, 11am-5pm Sun) Croquet days, barbecues and tapas. Good tunes too.

Burnbrae Winery WINERY
(www.burnbraewines.com.au; 548 Hill End Rd; ⏲9am-5pm Mon-Fri, 10am-4pm Sun) Respected wines and lunch platters under an old peppercorn tree.

Willow Lane WINERY
(www.thewillowlane.com.au; Eurunderee Lane; ⏲11am-4pm Fri & Sun, 10.30am-5pm Sat) Known for its chardonnay and shiraz varieties.

Lowe Wines WINERY
(☎03-6372 0800; www.lowewine.com.au; 327 Tinja Lane) Organic wines and an unmistakeable passion for winemaking.

Sleeping

Wildwood Guesthouse GUESTHOUSE $$
(☎02-6373 3701; www.wildwoodmudgee.com.au; Henry Lawson Dr; r from $200) There are plenty of flash guesthouses and B&Bs in and around Mudgee. This luxury option, set amid the countryside, is highly recommended.

De Russie Suites BOUTIQUE HOTEL $$
(☎02-6372 7650; www.derussiehotels.com.au; cnr Perry & Gladstone St; ste from $151; ❄📶) Simply stunning apartment suites make a sophisticated choice in town.

Cobb & Co Boutique Hotel BOUTIQUE HOTEL $$
(☎02-6372 7245; www.cobbandcocourt.com.au; 97 Market St; r from $155) In the centre of town, this place has mod cons elegantly suited to its heritage style.

Mudgee Homestead Guesthouse GUESTHOUSE $$$
(☎02-6373 3786; www.mudgeehomestead.com.au; 3 Coorumbene Court; s/d incl breakfast from $195/220) Sweeping views dominate this beautifully appointed guesthouse set amid

MUDGEE WINES AT A GLANCE

- **Best source of information**: visitor centre (p214) – ask for its *Pull-Out Guide to the Wineries*
- **Best winery tours**: **Mudgee Wine & Country Tours** (☎02-6372 2367; www.mudgeewinetours.com.au; half-/full-day tours $50/95) and **Mudgee Tourist Bus** (☎0428 669 945; www.mudgeetouristbus.com.au; 5-/9-winery tour $40/60)
- **Best wine bar**: Roth's (p214)
- **Best time to visit**: September for the **wine festival** (www.mudgeewine.com.au).

40 acres five minutes from town. Prices rise on weekends, but fine dinners are included.

Eating & Drinking

★Butcher Shop Café CAFE $
(49 Church St; mains $10-17; ⊙8am-5pm Mon-Fri, to 4pm Sat & Sun) A hip eatery in an old butchery with stained glass, vintage decor and contemporary artwork on the walls. The delicious fare is understated and includes salads and gourmet burgers, and the coffee is roasted in-house.

High Valley Wine & Cheese Co CAFE, DELI $$
(www.highvalley.com.au; 137 Ulan Rd; mains $10-21; ⊙10am-5pm Mon-Fri, 8.30am-5pm Sat & Sun) Located in a beautiful stone-and-corrugated-iron building, this lovely foodie stop has a produce shop and a vine-laden verandah under which you can indulge in coffee, antipasto plates for two, fabulous cheese platters and a chai latte cheesecake for dessert.

Sajo's MODERN AUSTRALIAN $$
(☎02-6372 2722; www.sajos.com.au; 22 Church St; lunch mains $16-18, dinner mains $35; ⊙noon-2pm & 6-9pm Mon-Sat) With stained-glass-window character and a fine pedigree among the state's food critics, Sajo's is a fine place for a meal – for dinner try the seared spice-crusted kangaroo – but it's also a lounge bar of distinction.

Mudgee Brewery MICROBREWERY
(www.mudgeebrewery.com.au; Church St; ⊙8am-5.30pm Mon-Wed, 8am-late Thu-Sun) In addition to fine light meals throughout the day, this airy space hosts live music at 6.30pm Thursdays, 7pm Fridays and a very civilised 4.30pm on Sundays. Beers on tap include Mudgee Brewery Lite and Mudgee Mud Imperial Stout.

★Roth's WINE BAR
(www.rothswinebar.com.au; 30 Market St; ⊙5pm-late Wed-Sat) The oldest wine bar (1923) in NSW sits behind a small heritage facade, and serves up great local wines, fine bar food and excellent live music. Bliss.

Information

Visitor Centre (☎02-6372 1020; www.visitmudgeeregion.com.au; 84 Market St; ⊙9am-5pm) Pick up its *Mudgee Mud Map* visitor guide.

Getting There & Around

CountryLink (☎13 22 32; www.countrylink.info) buses to Lithgow connect with Sydney trains ($45, five hours). **Aeropelican** (☎02-4928 9600; www.aeropelican.com.au) has daily flights to Sydney (from $140, 50 minutes).

Countryfit (6-42 Short St; 1-4hr $25, 1 day $30) has bikes for hire.

Gulgong

POP 1866

This gorgeous time-warped town (www.gulgong.net) once featured alongside author Henry Lawson on the $10 note. Today the narrow, rambling streets, classified by the National Trust, are not so done-up that they have lost their charm.

The town also has a **Henry Lawson Heritage Festival** during the June long weekend, with concerts at the Opera House and other festivities.

Sights

Henry Lawson Centre MUSEUM
(147 Mayne St; adult/child $5/3; ⊙10am-3.30pm Mon-Sat, to 1pm Sun) Author Henry Lawson spent part of his childhood here, and the Henry Lawson Centre looks at his early memories of the town.

Gulgong Pioneer Museum MUSEUM
(www.gulgong.net/museum.htm; 73 Herbert St; adult/child $10/3.50) The huge Gulgong Pioneer Museum has one of the most eclectic and chaotic collections of artefacts in the state.

Opera House HISTORIC BUILDING, THEATRE
(☎02-6374 1162; 99-101 Mayne St) Originally built from bark, the Opera House is one of the oldest surviving theatres in Australia and still holds several performances a year. Ask at the visitor centre.

Sleeping & Eating

Ten Dollar Town MOTEL $$
(☎02-6374 1204; www.tendollartownmotel.com.au; cnr Mayne & Medley Sts; r from $110) Ten Dollar Town is a motel with a heritage facade and a rear garden and sitting area to make you feel at home.

Butcher Shop Café CAFE $
(113 Mayne St; mains $10-15; ⊙8am-4pm Mon-Fri, 8am-2pm Sat, 9am-2pm Sun) Butcher Shop Café is a delightful little, erm, former butcher shop, cleverly transformed. It serves a hearty array of food all chalked up on the blackboard. The melts and toasties are especially good.

Information

Gulgong Visitor Centre (02-6374 1202; 66 Herbert St; 10am-3pm Thu-Mon)

Getting There & Away

CountryLink (13 22 32; www.countrylink.info) Daily buses to Mudgee ($5, 30 minutes).

SNOWY MOUNTAINS

The Snowies, as they are known, form part of the Great Diving Range where it straddles the NSW-Victorian border and they lay claim to the highest mountain on the Australian mainland, Mt Kosciuszko (koz-zy-*os*-ko), at 2228m. This is Australia's only true alpine area, and as such can expect snowfalls from early June to late August, although the ski season can last from June to September.

Kosciuszko National Park, NSW's largest at 673,492 hectares, dominates the Snowies in all seasons. The Snowy Mountains Hwy and Alpine Way worm their way through the park providing spectacular scenery and access to the tiny towns of the famed Snowy Mountain Scheme. In winter, the bigger towns of Jindabyne and Cooma become hives of activity when day trippers and holidaymakers pass through on their way to Thredbo and Perisher Blue.

Getting There & Away

Cooma is the eastern gateway to the Snowy Mountains. If you are just going to one place to ski, then public transport is an option. Otherwise, you'll need a car, which does let you fully appreciate the region.There are restrictions on car use in the national park during the ski season; check with the NPWS or visitor centres at Cooma or Jindabyne before entering.

The airport, about 10km southwest of Cooma on the Snowy Mountains Hwy, is running again. Brindabella Airlines has flights to Sydney (from $120, 1¼ hours).

Murrays (13 22 51; www.murrays.com.au) buses run from Canberra via Cooma, Jindabyne and Bullocks Flat (all $55) to Thredbo ($60). It also has day returns to Thredbo ($85) and Perisher Blue ($65), with lift passes and equipment packages available. **Greyhound Ski Express** (1300 GREYHOUND, 1300 4739 46863; www.greyhound.com.au) has similar itineraries and package deals.

Snowliner Coaches (02-6452 1584; www.snowliner.com.au) does a public-accessible school run to Jindabyne (adult/child $15/8) and back.

SKI COSTS

- During peak season at Thredbo, an adult two-/five-/seven-day lift ticket costs $165/362/499. Children's tickets cost $90/209/291. Two-day group-lesson packages (including lift tickets) cost from $234/166 for adults/children.
- During peak season at Perisher Blue an adult two-/five-day lift ticket costs $230/415. Children's tickets cost $129/295.
- During peak season at Charlotte Pass an adult one-/three-day lift ticket costs $106/293. Children's tickets cost $65/180.
- Boots, skis and stocks, or snowboards and boots, can be hired for $55/45 per half-day rising incrementally to seven days $200/115 for adults/children.

CountryLink (132 232; www.countrylink.info) runs year-round to Canberra ($14, 1¼ hours) and Sydney Central ($53, seven hours). Snowboards and skis are not permitted on board.

Cooma

POP 6301

You could 'coo-ee' down the main street of Cooma in summer and not raise an eyebrow. But proximity to the snowfields keeps this little town punching above its weight during winter. It imbues the best of country town with good places to hang out, an attractive centre and a laid-back vibe.

Sights & Activities

On the Monaro Hwy, 2km north of the town centre, the **Snowy Mountains Scheme Information Centre** (1800 623 776; www.snowyhydro.com.au) FREE has the best info on this feat of engineering; the dams and hydroelectric plant took 25 years and more than 100,000 people to build.

Cooma Monaro Railway (02-6452 7791; www.cmrailway.org.au; Bradley St; 11am, 1pm & 2pm Sat & Sun Oct-Jun, 1pm & 2pm Sun mid-Jun-Sep) runs train rides to Snowy Junction (adult/child $6/4), Bunyan ($12/8) and Chakola ($18/12) aboard restored 1923 CPH rail motors. Ring ahead for midweek rides.

Next to functioning Cooma Gaol is the **NSW Department of Corrective Services Museum** (1 Vagg St; ⌚12.30-3.30pm Tue-Fri, 9.15am-3.30pm Sat) FREE, exhibiting artefacts from convict time through to the present prison system. Inmates conduct tours and sell their art and craft.

Sleeping

Royal Hotel HOTEL $

(☎02-6452 2132; www.royalhotelcooma.com; 59 Sharp St; s/d $45/75) The oldest licensed hotel in Cooma is a beautiful old sandstone place with decent pub rooms, open fires, shared bathrooms and a great verandah. Refurbished **Lambies Grill** is a fine place for a grilled steak and a beer.

Snowtels CARAVAN PARK $

(☎02-6452 1828; www.snowtels.com.au; 286 Sharp St; unpowered/powered sites $24/29, 1-/8-berth huts from $50/135, cabins from $65) On the highway, 1.5km west of town, this is a big, well-equipped place. Prices go up marginally in winter.

Alpine Hotel HOTEL $$

(☎02-6452 1466; www.alpinehotel.com.au; 170 Sharp St; d $145, s/d with shared bathroom $70/100) This newly renovated art-deco pub is as comfortable as budget rooms get. Downstairs the bistro is equally clean with lovely wooden fittings, classic pub meals and outdoor seating.

Eating

Kettle & Seed CAFE $

(☎02-6452 5882; 47 Vale St; mains from $7.50; ⌚7am-4pm Mon-Fri, 8am-4pm Sat) A coffee shop that wouldn't be out of place in an upmarket Sydney suburb, this place roasts its own beans and it shows. The light meals (sandwiches and spinach pies) are good, but almost incidental with coffee this great.

★**Lott Food Store** BAKERY, CAFE $$

(☎02-6452 1414; www.lott.com.au; 177 Sharp St; mains $13.50-17.50; ⌚7am-4pm Mon-Thu, 7am-

WORTH A TRIP

SCENIC DRIVE: THE HIGH COUNTRY

The high country around Cooma may be better known for its winter skiing, but we love it just as much in summer for the chance to drive around Australia's premier stand of Alpine forest. There are only two petrol stations (at Adaminaby and Khancoban) in the 247km from Thredbo to Cooma and prices can be up to 15 cents a litre above what you'll pay in Cooma. All distances listed here are from Cooma.

To begin, take Sharp St in Cooma west then take the turn-off to Tumut 7km out of town. Pass through gloriously named **Adaminaby** (51km; elevation 1017m), then 13km further on you leave behind rolling grazing country and enter the denser woodlands of **Koscuiszko National Park**. Soon enough, the landscape opens out a little and the first ghostly trunks (left by a 2003 fire) appear. At the 86km mark, at the sign for **Permanent Creek** (87km), leave the car by the roadside and climb to the poignant hillside graves of the **Kiandra Cemetery** – from 1891 to 1912, 47 people were buried at this remote gold-mining spot; 19 were aged under three and only six died of old age.

The road climbs past the ruins of **Kiandra** at 1400m above sea level, then take the turn-off for Cabramurra soon after at the 89km mark, with another turn-off for Cabramurra at 104km. **Cabramurra** itself is a further 4km on – this is Australia's highest town at 1488m. The steep descent from Cabramurra is one of the prettiest on the whole route, with a stunning honour guard of eerie white trunks before dropping down to the dam. Around 124km out of Cooma, stop to photograph the iconic corrugated iron **Bradleys & O'Briens Hut**. As you continue southwest, you'll pass a number of rest areas and trail heads, always following the signs to Khancoban. With the trip clock at 192km, pause for fine views at **Scammell's Ridge Lookout**.

At 204km, **Geehi Rest Area** has a lovely spot next to Swampy Plains Creek, while **Tom Groggin Rest Area**, a further 20km further on, is also riverside; we saw kangaroos here last time we visited. At 233km, in a patch of stunningly tall trunks, the **Leather Barrel Rest Area** also warrants a pause. After 243km you climb to one of the highest points of the road, a sign says 'Great Dividing Range 1580m', before dropping down the river valley into Thredbo.

9pm Fri, 8am-4pm Sat & Sun) In a kitted-out corner shop, Cooma's light-and-airy foodie hub has excellent coffee, hearty snacks, light lunches and pastries and is a provedore of all kinds of kitchenwares and gourmet goodies perfect for picnics.

Information

Visitor Centre (02-6455 1742; www.visitcooma.com.au; 119 Sharp St) Makes accommodation bookings.

Getting There & Away

Victoria's **V/Line** (13 61 96; www.vline.com.au) has a twice-weekly run from Melbourne to Canberra via Cooma (9¼ hours). The trip from Melbourne takes you by train to Bairnsdale, then by bus.

Jindabyne

POP 1727

Jindabyne has a split personality. As the closest town to Kosciuszko National Park's major ski resorts, it sleeps more than 20,000 visitors in winter. But in summer the crowds go elsewhere and the town reverts to its relatively peaceful small-town self, where fishing is the mainstay activity.

Sights & Activities

Paddy Pallin ADVENTURE SPORTS
(1800 623 459; www.paddypallin.com.au; cnr Kosciuszko & Thredbo Rds; 9am-4pm summer, 7am-7pm Sat-Thu, 7am-7pm Sat-Thu, 7am-midnight Fri winter) A kitted-out adventure centre 2.5km from Jindabyne, just past the Thredbo Rd turn-off.

Discovery Holiday Parks BOATING
(02-6456-2099; www.discoveryholidayparks.com.au; cnr Kosciuszko Rd & Alpine Way) Has motorboats, canoes and paddleboats for hire.

Sleeping

The influx of snow bunnies that comes here in winter sends prices through the roof, so book ahead. Agents for holiday rental include the **Jindabyne & Snowy Mountains Accommodation Centre** (1800 527 622; www.snowaccommodation.com.au) and **Visit Snowy Mountains** (02-6457 7132; www.visitsnowymountains.com.au). Many lodges have ski gear and accommodation packages.

HORSE RIDING IN THE SNOWY MOUNTAINS

One of the most popular ways for exploring the Snowy Mountains high country is on horseback. Options include the following:

Snowy River Horseback Adventure (02-6457 8393; www.snowyriverhorsebackadventure.com.au; half-/1-/2-day rides $120/215/780; Oct-May)

Reynella Kosciusko Rides (02-6454 2386, 1800 029 909; www.reynellarides.com.au; 669 Kingston Rd, Adaminaby; three-/four-/five-day treks from $1200/1555/1870)

Snowy Wilderness (1800 218 171; www.snowywilderness.com.au; Barry Way; one-/two-/seven-day treks $295/690/2080) Twenty-nine kilometres southwest of Jindabyne.

Snowy Mountains Backpackers HOSTEL $
(1800 333 468; www.snowybackpackers.com.au; 7-8 Gippsland St; summer dm/d $25/60, winter dm $30-50, d $90-140, family dm $180-240; @) Perhaps the best winter value in Jindabyne, this well-oiled machine has clean rooms, a cafe, internet, rooms with bathrooms, advice on activities and service with a smile. The way a backpackers should be.

Carinya Alpine Village SKI LODGE $
(02-6456 2252; www.carinya-village.com.au; Carinya Lane; winter bunkrooms per person $30-50, apt per person from $175) Off the Snowy River Way, this budget abode with four- to 10-bed apartments has no pretensions. It's homely and basic – ideal for those who prefer boarding to critiquing furniture. Skis and boards available for rent.

Banjo Paterson Inn HOTEL $$
(02-6456 2372; www.banjopatersoninn.com.au; 1 Kosciuszko Rd; r summer $100-130, winter $150-230) The best rooms at this place have balconies and lake views. Other facilities include a rowdy bar and brewery. It might look a little washed out in summer but it's a lively establishment come snowtime.

Lake Jindabyne Hotel/Motel HOTEL, MOTEL $$
(1800 646 818; www.lakejindabynehotel.com.au; Kosciuszko Rd; r $105-190;) A big place by the lake in the centre of town, this has a heated pool, a spa, a sauna and a bar.

Eating & Drinking

Angie's Italian Kitchen ITALIAN $$
(☎02-6456 2523; Snowy Mountains Plaza; mains $18-23; ⊙noon-2.30pm & 6-9pm) Ignore the nearby Italian competitors: this cosy eatery with an outdoor deck and water views has been around for over 20 years. Think black mussels with tomato and garlic, homemade ravioli and wood-fired pizzas.

Café Darya MIDDLE EASTERN $$
(☎02-6457 1867; Snowy Mountains Plaza; ⊙6-9pm Tue-Sat) Tucked away on Jindabyne's upper level, this Persian restaurant is a treat for those who find it. Fill up on slow-cooked lamb shank in Persian spices and rose petals or, for something lighter, a trio of dips.

Eboshi JAPANESE $$
(☎02-6456 1326; www.eboshi.com.au; Gippsland St; mains $12-27; ⊙11.30am-2pm & 6pm-late) Japanese beer, including Yebisu, and otherwise reliable Japanese staples. Takeaway bento boxes from noon.

Kosciuszko Brewery MICROBREWERY, BAR
(www.banjopatersoninn.com.au; 1 Kosciuszko Rd, Banjo Paterson Inn) Sample Kosciuszko Pale, a slightly cloudy ale.

Lake Jindabyne Hotel/Motel BAR
(www.lakejindabynehotel.com.au; Kosciuszko Rd) A massive bar, purpose-built for packing people in.

Information

Snowy Region Visitor Centre (☎02-6450 5600; www.environment.nsw.gov.au; Kosciuszko Rd; ⊙9am-4pm) Operated by the NPWS with display areas, a cinema and a good cafe.

Getting There & Away

Several coach companies operate shuttle services from the Snowy Region visitors centre to the ski fields.

Kosciuszko National Park

The jewel in NSW's national-park crown, covering 673,492 hectares and stretching 150km from north to south, has so many varied attractions that it takes visits in all seasons to really gauge its full potential.

Year-round, this is a wonderland of alpine and subalpine flora and fauna. This is the only place on the planet, for example, where you'll find the rare mountain pygmy possum. Come spring and summer, pristine walking trails and camp sites can be appreciated when spectacular alpine flowers are in full bloom. Mystical caves, limestone gorges, historic huts and homesteads are also ripe for discovery. The park is also popular for cyclists and mountain bikers.

If you're just driving through the park, no park fees are payable, but if you're overnighting or driving beyond Jindabyne up towards Charlotte Pass, you'll be liable for $16 per vehicle per 24 hours. For details of a scenic drive through the park, see the boxed text, p216.

Sleeping

Accommodation services include **Jindabyne & Snowy Mountains Accommodation Centre** (☎1800 527 622; www.snowaccommodation.com.au), **Snowy Mountains Holiday Centre** (☎1800 641 064; www.smhc.com.au), **Snowy Mountains Reservation Centre** (☎1800 020 622; www.snowholidays.com.au), **Thredbo Accommodation** (☎02-9929 7944; www.accommodationthredbo.com.au) and **Thredbo Resort Centre** (☎1300 020 589; www.thredbo.com.au).

Information

The main NPWS visitor centre for the park is at Jindabyne. There's an **education centre** (☎02-6451 3700) at Sawpit Creek (15km from Jindabyne), which runs programs during school holidays, and visitor centres at Khancoban in the west of the park, and Yarrangobilly Caves and Tumut in the north.

Entry to the national park costs $27 per 24 hours per car in winter and $16 at other times. If you intend to stay a while, buy the $190 annual parks permit – it gives you unlimited access to every national park in NSW.

Getting There & Around

Several coach companies operate shuttle services from the **Snowy Region visitors centre** (☎1800 004 439, 02-6450 5600; www.environment.nsw.gov.au) in Jindabyne to the ski fields.

In winter you can normally drive as far as Perisher Valley, but snow chains must be carried in 2WD vehicles – even when there's no snow – and fitted where directed. The penalty if you're caught without them is hefty. The simplest, safest way to get to Perisher Valley and Smiggin Holes in winter is to take the Skitube train.

CLIMBING AUSTRALIA'S HIGHEST MOUNTAIN

Australia's highest mountain is an easy one to climb, although getting to the top can still be a strenuous trek. The rewards are ample. Hiking is possible whenever there is no snow on the ground.

Guided options include the **Mt Kosciuszko Day Walk** (www.thredbo.com.au; adult/child/family $42/28/84; ⌚10am-3.30pm Sat, Sun, Tue & Thu late Oct-late Apr) or the once-in-a-lifetime **Sunset Tour** (www.thredbo.com.au; adult $85; ⌚3.30pm Wed late Dec-late Apr). Otherwise, the three main solo options are as follows:

Mt Kosciuszko Track From Thredbo, take the Kosciuszko Express Chairlift (day pass adult/child $32/17; 9.30am to 4pm). From the top of the lift, it's a steep, 13km-return climb to the summit and back again.

Summit Walk Drive to the end of the paved road above Charlotte Pass, then follow a wide gravel track (until 1976 it was possible to drive to the summit). It's a 9km climb to the summit (18km return). There's a steep final climb and, en route, Seaman's Hut is famous for expansive wildflower displays. Mountain bikers can ride as far as Rawson Pass.

Main Range Track Also begins above Charlotte Pass, this strenuous 20km loop takes you to the summit and back, climbing a handful of minor creeks en route.

Thredbo

POP 471

Thredbo is oft lauded as Australia's number-one ski resort. At 1370m it not only has the longest runs and some of the best skiing, the village itself is eye candy compared with other Australian ski villages, the blue, green and grey tones ensuring chalets and lodges blend with the surrounding snow gums and alpine flora. And, of course, Thredbo is an all-season resort.

Thredbo was also the scene of one of Australia's worst recent tragedies when, in July 1997, the Kosciuszko Alpine Way embankment, running across the upper edge of the village, collapsed, taking with it two snow lodges and 2000 cubic metres of liquefied soil. The only survivor, Stuart Diver, lay trapped under the rubble next to his dead wife for 65 hours. Eighteen people died and there are memorials to the tragedy dotted around the village.

Sights

Thredbo Ski Museum MUSEUM
(www.thredboskimuseum.com; ⌚1-5pm Jul, Aug & Jan, 1-5pm Sat & Sun Feb-Apr) FREE More a museum of the Snowy Mountains than a specifically ski-oriented museum, this little collection is nonetheles fascinating and a nice alternative to more active pursuits. It's at the northern end of the Thredbo Alpine Hotel.

Activities

Thredbo's skiing terrain is roughly 16% beginner, 67% intermediate and 17% advanced, with different snow 'parks' to suit each category. The **Supertrail** (3.7km) begins at Australia's highest lifted point, then drops 670m through some pretty awesome scenery. From up here you can also take the 5km easy **Village Trail** to Friday Flats, or black-run junkies can crank it up a notch on the 5.9km hair-raiser from **Karels T-Bar** right down to Friday Flats. These back-valley slopes are best in the morning; head to the front valley in the afternoon for more freestyle action.

There's free **twilight skiing** (with a valid lift ticket) from 4.30pm to 7.30pm on Thursdays and Saturdays during July and August at Friday Flats.

For advice on climbing Mt Kosciuszko, see the boxed text on p219.

Kosciuszko Express Chairlift CHAIRLIFT
(day pass adult/child return $32/17) Climbs 560 vertical metres over 1.8km for fabulous views. Climbing Mt Kosciuszko is possible from the top station.

Bobsled ADVENTURE SPORTS
(1/6/10 rides $7/34/48; ⌚10am-4.30pm) A 700m luge-style track winding down the mountain.

Thredbo Leisure Centre ADVENTURE SPORTS
(☎02-6459 4138; Friday Dr; adult/child $7.90/5.90, activities extra; ⌚7am-7pm peak periods, otherwise noon-7pm) Organises all sorts of activities, summer and winter, including hiking,

mountain biking, canoeing, white-water rafting, abseiling and horse riding.

Thredbo Snow Sports Outdoor Adventures ADVENTURE SPORTS
(☎ 02-6459 4044; www.thredbo.com.au) Has a diverse range of high-energy activities including snowshoeing, snow climbing, telemark and back-country alpine touring. It also hosts a cool five-star snow camping expedition where you snowshoe to a secret camp site, feast on gourmet cuisine and test your snow survival skills overnight.

Kosciuszko Cross Country Ski School ADVENTURE SPORTS
(☎ 0421 862 354; www.k7adventures.com) Cross-country skiing, ice-climbing, snow-shoeing, hiking, caving and more.

Festivals & Events

Thredbo Blues Festival MUSIC
(www.thredbo.com.au/thredboblues; ⌚ mid-Jan) This fine Blues festival wakes Thredbo from its summer slumber.

Sleeping

Thredbo YHA Lodge HOSTEL $
(☎ 02-6457 6376; www.yha.com.au; 8 Jack Adams Path; summer tw $83, dm/tw without bathroom $29/70; @) The best budget value on the mountain, this YHA is well appointed, with great common areas, a good kitchen and a balcony. Expect to pay five times this amount in peak season when adults must be full YHA members.

Candlelight Lodge LODGE $$
(☎ 1800 020 900, 02-6457 6318; www.candlelightlodge.com.au; 32 Diggings Tce; s/d winter from $190/250, summer from $110/150; 📶) Founded by Hungarian immigrants, this Tyrolean lodge has great rooms, all with views. The restaurant's fondue (winter only) is fabulous.

Lake Crackenback Resort RESORT, LODGE $$$
(☎ 02-6451 3000; www.lakecrackenback.com.au; 1650 Alpine Way; r from $250; ❄ @ 📶 🏊) Around halfway between Thredbo and Jindabyne, this spa resort run by the Novotel chain is one of the loveliest places to stay in the Snowy Mountains. Rooms (apartments or chalets) are large and classy, the restaurant is outstanding and the surroundings are stunning.

Thredbo Alpine Hotel HOTEL $$$
(☎ 1800 026 333; Friday Dr; winter/summer d incl breakfast from $199/169; ❄ @ 🏊) Suitably flash rooms.

Aneeki Lodge LODGE $$$
(☎ 0417 479 581; www.aneeki.com.au; 9 Bobuck Lane; winter d $300-375, summer d $90-175) Simple (sometimes pine-clad) rooms that are comfortable enough if a little bland.

Ski In Ski Out LODGE $$$
(☎ 02-6457 7030; www.skiinskiout.com.au; r from $380; 📶) Five-star lodge accommodation.

Eating & Drinking

Gourmet 42 CAFE $
(100 Mowamba Pl, Village Sq; mains $12-17; ⌚ 7.30am-3pm) Hungover boarders and sleepy bar staff rock up here for excellent coffee, soup and pasta.

Knickerbocker MODERN AUSTRALIAN, BAR $$
(☎ 02-6457 6844; www.theknickerbocker.com.au; Diggings Tce; mains $28-32; ⌚ 6-11pm) Thredbo's latest ode to good times; sit indoors for alpine cosiness or rug up on the deck with brilliant views and a 'log' fire. Seriously gourmet meals go down a treat after 'schnappy hour' (4pm to 6pm).

Altitude 1380 CAFE $$
(☎ 02-6457 6190; Village Sq; mains $14-18; ⌚ 7am-4pm) Reliable lively eatery.

Aprés Bar BAR
(☎ 02-6457 6222; www.thedenman.com.au; Diggings Tce, Denman Hotel; mains from $25; ⌚ 6pm-late) Cosy couches and crimson leather poufs are crammed together in this cosy over-25s atmosphere. The tunes are spot-on and vino by the glass is affordable.

Berntis Bar BAR
(☎ 02-6457 6332; 4 Mowomba Pl; tapas/mains from $11/28; ⌚ 6pm-late) The winter steakhouse and year-round tapas bar are the starting points for a good night out at this locals-recommend-it hang-out.

Information

Thredbo Visitor Centre (☎ 02-6459 4294; www.thredbo.com.au; Friday Dr; ⌚ 9am-5pm summer 8am-6pm winter) Good for finding accommodation.

Perisher Blue

ELEV 1680M

Perisher Valley, Smiggin Holes, Mt Blue Cow and Guthega make up the massive resort of **Perisher Blue** (☎ 02-6459 4495, 1300 369 909; www.perisherblue.com.au). Guthega (1640m) and Mt Blue Cow (1640m) are mainly day

SKIING

Thredbo has a short season (early June to late August) but it has just completed the final stage of its $6 million automated snowmaking machines (ensuring coverage across most of the middle and lower slopes), and Perisher Blue has upgraded its facilities to enable more reliable connections between major chairlifts. If the outcome is not exactly 100%-guaranteed snow, it's a pretty good start.

Off the slopes there's lively nightlife, excellent restaurants, and a plethora of facilities and activities catering for families. Both Thredbo and Perisher Blue have a designated kids' skiing program, crèches and day care.

On the downside, the resorts tend to be particularly crowded at weekends and the short season means operators have to get their returns quickly, so costs are high.

Sleeping

There's no longer a problem finding accommodation in summer, especially at the year-round resort of Thredbo. The Alpine Way between Jindabyne and Thredbo is similarly punctuated with cosy B&Bs and resorts. In all cases the off-season prices will be considerably lower, some less than half the peak-season prices.

The only formal camping area is **Kosciuszko Mountain Retreat** (☎02-6456 2224; www.kositreat.com.au; Sawpit Creek; unpowered/powered sites from $23/33, vans/cabins from $58/78), but there are 48 rough camp sites spread throughout the park, most of them accessible by 2WD and equipped with toilet, picnic and barbecue facilities. Many are run by the **NPWS** (www.environment.nsw.gov.au) who also have some historic homesteads.

Seasonal Work

Thredbo employs about 200 year-round full-time staff and close to 750 in winter. For job vacancies and info, **Snowy Staff** (☎02-8005 6219; www.snowystaff.com.au; Nuggets Crossing, Jindabyne) is a one-stop shop. Also check out www.totallyintoit.com.au. The noticeboard at Thredbo supermarket in the village centre also posts jobs and accommodation.

For seasonal job vacancies and information in Perisher Blue, check out www.perisherjobs.com.au. Foreign applicants need a working visa (www.immi.gov.au); however, Perisher Blue can apply for sponsored work visas. Winter job applications tend to close at the start of April.

Charlotte Pass also has jobs ops (www.charlottepass.com.au then click on the 'Employment' tab at the bottom of the page).

Information

For snow and road reports, contact the visitor centres at **Thredbo** (☎02-6459 4100; www.thredbo.com.au) and **Perisher Blue** (☎1900 926 664) or try www.rta.nsw.gov.au, www.bom.gov.au and www.ski.com.au. Also tune into 97.7 Snow FM locally or 96.3FM in the north of the park.

resorts, so they're smaller and less crowded. Mt Blue Cow is accessible via the **Skitube** (☎1300 655 822; same-day return adult/child $52/29, open return $79/40). The accessibility of the Skitube is Perisher's most underrated drawcard. Simply park the car at Bullocks Flat, buy a ticket, board the train and within 15 minutes you're on the slopes. Blue Cow doesn't have the village ambience of Thredbo, but there are alpine and cross-country runs, valley and bowl skiing and snowboarding areas (dude!).

Intermediate and above skiers and boarders can get to know the slopes on a **free tour** (10am Monday, Thursday and Saturday) with an orange-jacket-clad mountain host. Meet under the Trail Guide sign at the mid-station of Perisher Quad Express.

For something adventurous, **Wilderness Sports** (☎02-6456 2966; www.wildernesssports.com.au) are the back-country experts, with tours including one- to five-day expeditions.

Sleeping

Most accommodation is in Perisher Valley and Smiggin Holes. Most rates include either breakfast and lunch or breakfast and dinner. Winter only.

Sundeck Hotel HOTEL $$$
(☎02-6457 5222; www.sundeckhotel.com.au; Kosciuszko Rd; d & tw per person $210-350;) Australia's highest hotel, and one of Perisher's oldest lodges, has a comfy bar and great views over the Quad 8 Express – mountain-view rooms cost more. It's blissfully ski-in, ski-out.

Heidi's Chalet APARTMENTS $$$
(☎1800 252 668; www.heidis.com.au; Munyang Rd, Smiggin Holes; 2-night apt $1200-1800) Four-person apartments a short snowplough to the ski lifts.

Charlotte Pass

ELEV 1780M

At the base of Mt Kosciuszko, **Charlotte Pass** (www.charlottepass.com.au) is one of the highest, oldest and most isolated ski resorts in Australia, and in winter you have to 'snowcat' (use oversnow transport) the last 8km from Perisher Valley (about $55 each way; book ahead). Five lifts service rather short but uncrowded runs, and this is good ski-touring country. It's also marketing itself as a good base for summer activities.

Accommodation includes the grand **Kosciuszko Chalet** (☎1800 026 369; www.charlottepass.com.au; Fri & Sat r per person for 2 nights full board, transfer & lift tickets $769-1019) and the cheaper **Alitji Alpine Lodge** (☎02-6457 5024; www.ski.com.au; r per person 2 nights $465-720).

SOUTHWEST & THE MURRAY

Between Sydney and Albury, a string of atmospheric old inland towns straddle the Hume Hwy, each of them with a claim to some kind of fame, be it bushrangers, drought, rich grazing land or old money.

Northwest of the highway, the land flattens out, becoming incrementally redder and drier. The Murray and Murrumbidgee Rivers that make up the Riverina district not only offer respite in a harsh landscape, but an income through farming centred on irrigation and a growing tourism industry based around food in places like Griffith.

Hume Highway

Like all big swaths of four-lane bitumen, the Hume Hwy, running nearly 900km from Sydney to Melbourne, is somewhat lacking in aesthetic appeal. That said, it does provide an opportunity, via myriad signposted scenic routes, to visit small heritage towns just off the highway.

Much of the highway is speed limited to 110km/h, which is rigorously enforced by speed cameras and roadside police cars. Speeding fines are hefty.

Sydney to Goulburn

Mittagong & Bowral

POP 19,726 (MITTAGONG & BOWRAL)

The large towns of Mittagong and Bowral adjoin each other just off the Hume Hwy. Together with Moss Vale, they make up the main towns of the **Southern Highlands**, a pretty area still revelling in its Englishness.

Sights

International Cricket Hall of Fame MUSEUM
(☎02-4862 1247; www.internationalcrickethall.com.au; St Jude St, Bowral; adult/child $20/10; ⏲10am-5pm) Bowral is where the late great cricketer Sir Donald Bradman, Australia's greatest sporting hero and legendary to the point of sainthood, spent his boyhood. There's a cricket ground here and fans pay homage to the great man at the museum which has the **Bradman Museum of Cricket** (www.bradman.com.au), with an engrossing collection of Ashes and Don-centric memorabilia that even cricket-loathers tend to admit is worthwhile.

Festivals & Events

Bowral Tulip Time Festival
(www.tuliptime.net.au) Spring flower festival in late September and/or early October.

Sleeping & Eating

This pocket of the Hume is popular with Sydney day trippers and overnighters, and has a good dining and B&B scene. Top spots for lunch include **Centennial Vineyards** (☎02-4861 8700; www.centennialrestaurant.com.au; Centennial Rd; mains $33.50-42; ⏲10am-5pm Wed-Mon), which has a flash restaurant, or **Southern Highland Wines** (☎02-4686 2300; www.shw.com.au; Oldbury Rd; mains $28-

CAVES OF THE SOUTHERN HIGHLANDS

The convoluted but spectacular limestone **Wombeyan Caves** (☎02-4843 5976; www.nationalparks.nsw.gov.au; Wombeyan Caves Rd; Figtree Cave adult/child $18/12, 2 caves & tour 'Discovery Pass' $30/23; ⊙9am-4pm) are at the end of an unsealed mountain road 65km northwest of Mittagong. Nearby are walking trails, a campground with cabins (from $72 to $90), a dormitory ($65), a cottage (from $72 to $95) and plenty of wildlife.

The famous **Abercrombie Caves** (☎02-6368 8603; abercrombiecaves.com; self-guided/guided tours $15/20; ⊙9am-4pm) are reached via a turn-off 72km south of Bathurst. The complex has one of the world's largest natural tunnels, the Grand Arch.

About 57km southeast of Yass, along some partly dirt roads, the limestone **Careys Cave** (☎02-6227 9622; www.weejaspercaves.com; adult/child $15.40/9.90; ⊙tours noon, 1.30pm & 3pm Sat & Sun, noon & 1.30pm Fri & Mon) is at Wee Jasper. Phone ahead for tours.

The Jenolan Caves (p138) are also in the region.

40; ⊙noon-3pm Thu-Mon) with its tasty cafe. **McVitty Grove Estate** (☎02-4878 5044; www.mcvittygrove.com.au; Wombeyan Caves Rd; tapas $9-26, mains $26-32; ⊙10am-4pm Thu-Sun) scores points for its stunning views and weekend tapas.

Links Manor GUESTHOUSE **$$$**
(☎02-4861 1977; www.linkshouse.com.au; 17 Links Rd, Bowral; r $190-340; ❄📶) This boutique guesthouse has a lovely library, drawing room, garden courtyard and staff straight out of *Remains of the Day*. Prices are at their highest on Friday and Saturday nights.

Biota Dining MODERN AUSTRALIAN **$$$**
(☎02-4862 2005; biotadining.com; 18 Kangaloon Rd; mains $35-42; ⊙9am-2pm Sun, noon-2.30pm & 6-9.30pm Mon & Wed-Sat) Minimalist chic fuses perfectly here with a menu that has in the past included such glories as spatchcok in hazelnut crumbs. The wine list here is as good as the Sunday brunch.

ℹ Information

Southern Highlands Visitors Centre (☎02-4871 2888; www.southern-highlands.com.au; 62-70 Main St, Mittagong; ⊙9am-5pm Mon-Fri, to 4pm Sat & Sun)

Berrima & Bundanoon

POP 246 (BERRIMA), 2419 (BUNDANOON)

A little further south along the Hume from Mittagong, and also part of the Southern Highlands, is tiny but heritage-classified Berrima, founded in 1829. It's full of art galleries, tourist-trapping antique shops, historic buildings and fine food and wine. It's the best quick stop on this stretch of highway.

Sights & Activities

The Southern Highlands takes pride in its literary history and has plenty of bookshops to explore (www.booktown.com.au). One is 3km north of Berrima: **Berkelouw's Book Barn & Café** (☎02-4877 1370; www.berkelouw.com.au; Old Hume Hwy; ⊙9.30am-4.30pm Mon-Fri, to 5pm Sat & Sun) stocks over 200,000 secondhand and antiquated tomes and it has live jazz at 4pm Wednesdays.

South of Berrima is the small, appealing town of Bundanoon, one of the gateways to the vast and unruly **Morton National Park**, which has the deep gorges and high sandstone plateaus of the Budawang Range. The **NPWS visitor centre** (☎02-4887 7270; www.nationalparks.nsw.gov.au; Nowra Rd, Fitzroy Falls) is at the park entrance and has information on walking and hiking.

Sleeping & Eating

Bundanoon YHA HOSTEL **$**
(☎02-4883 6010; www.yha.com.au; 115 Railway Ave; dm/d $28/68.50) Bundanoon YHA occupies a fastidiously restored Edwardian guesthouse, complete with shady verandah and gallons of gingham.

Josh's Café CAFE **$$**
(☎02-4877 2200; 9 Old Hume Hwy; mains $25-32; ⊙noon-3pm Wed, noon-3pm & 6-9pm Thu-Sat, 9am-3pm Sun) This ecelectic cafe loves to char grill everything from mushrooms to meats while Turkish flavours sometimes get a run.

Eschalot MODERN AUSTRALIAN **$$$**
(☎02-4877 1977; www.eschalot.com.au; 24 Old Hume Hwy; mains $32-41; ⊙6-9pm Wed, noon-2.30pm & 6-9pm Thu-Sat, noon-2.30pm Sun) This heritage sandstone cottage is the perfect foil

WORTH A TRIP

BUNGONIA STATE CONSERVATION AREA

About 40km southeast of Goulburn and abutting Morton National Park, **Bungonia State Conservation Area** (02-4844 4277; www.nationalparks.nsw.gov.au; 838 Lookdown Rd) has a dramatic forested gorge, deep caves, well-signposted walking tracks and a cool camping area with hot showers, toilets, a communal kitchen and gas barbecues.

for modern Australian cooking at its best, from barramundi to Bangalow pork with all sorts of surprising little twists. Desserts are heavenly.

Getting There & Away

CountryLink (13 22 32; www.countrylink.info) runs from Bundanoon to Wollongong ($8.50, two hours) and Sydney Central ($21, two hours).

Goulburn & Around

POP 21,484

Goulburn lays claim to being Australia's first inland city and it now pats itself on the back for being one of the faster-growing regional centres. The old town centre, studded with historic buildings, is worth a stroll. There are plenty of alfresco cafes to choose from but not many gourmet ones.

Sights & Activities

Big Merino MUSEUM
(www.thebigmerino.com.au; cnr Hume & Sowerby Sts; 8.30am-5.30pm) FREE This three-storey-high celebration of Australian wool and shearing culture is near Goulburn's southern exit.

Old Goulburn Brewery BREWERY
(02-4821 6071; goulburnbrewery.servebeer.com; 23 Bungonia Rd; adult/child $15/free; 11am-4pm, tours 10am & 3pm Fri-Sun) Old Goulburn Brewery is where you can see the workings of a brewery and, more importantly, sip on a beer. It also has cheap and cheerful 1830s brewer's cottage accommodation.

Information

Goulburn Visitor Centre (02-4823 4492, 1800 353 646; www.igoulburn.com; 201 Sloane St; 9am-5pm Mon-Fri, to 4pm Sat & Sun) Ask about cellar-door wineries out of town.

Getting There & Away

Country Link has trains to Sydney ($28.50, 2¼ hours).

Yass & Around

POP 5591

Yass is pretty and quiet (thanks to the highway bypass). But it's also atmospheric, laced with heritage buildings, and shops and pubs of the wide-verandah variety.

Yass Valley visitor centre (02-6226 2557; www.yassvalley.com.au; 259 Comur St; 9.30am-4.30pm Mon-Fri, 10am-4pm Sat & Sun) is in Coronation Park. Next door, the **Yass & District Museum** (02-6226 2577; www.yasshistory.org; adult/child $5/1; 10am-4pm Sat & Sun summer) has a model reconstruction of the town in the 1890s. The 1835 **Cooma Cottage** (02-6226 1470; adult/child $7/5; 10am-4pm Thu-Sun) is on the Yass Valley Way on the Sydney side of town.

The **Hume & Hovell Walking Track**, which follows the route chosen by explorer Hamilton Hume and his sometime partner in exploration, William Hovell, has some half-day and longer walks that begin at Cooma Cottage. The visitor centre has brochures with other walking suggestions.

At the start of November the **Wine, Roses & All That Jazz Festival** features live music, gourmet food and wine tasting at 25 cellar doors.

The best place to stay is undoubtedly the graceful old **Globe Inn** (02-6226 3680; www.theglobeinn.com.au; 70 Rossi St; s/d from $130/160).

Gundagai

POP 1926

Gundagai, on the Murrumbidgee River, is relaxed and one of the more interesting small towns along (or bypassed by) the Hume, with fascinating bushranger and Aboriginal history. It's the perfect place to break up the long journey between Melbourne and Sydney.

Sights

The evocative **Prince Alfred Bridge** (closed to traffic, and to pedestrians since flood damage a few years back) is the star of Gundagai's sights. It crosses the flood plain of the Murrumbidgee River. Running alongside it is a stretch of the longest wooden railway track in NSW.

Green Dog Gallery (www.greendoggallery.com.au; Sheridan St; ⏲10.30am-5.30pm Thu-Sat Sep-Jul) and **Lannigan Abbey & Bandamora Art Gallery** (☎02-6944 2852; www.laniganabbey.com.au; 72 First Ave; ⏲9am-5pm) are worth a bo peep.

Gold rushes and bushrangers were part of the town's colourful early history. The notorious bushranger Captain Moonlite was tried in Gundagai's 1859 courthouse and is now buried in the town's **northern cemetery**. While you're in the cemetery, check out the grave of Yarri, an Aborigine who saved almost 50 locals when the area flooded in the early 1800s.

The **Mt Parnassus** lookout has picnic facilities and good 360-degree views over the town and surrounds; take the steep walk (or drive) up Hanley St. Ask at the visitor centre for directions to the equally scenic **Rotary Lookout** across the river in South Gundagai.

About 8km east of town, the **Dog on the Tuckerbox** is Gundagai's most famous monument. A sculpture of a dog from a 19th-century bush ballad, it is well known along the Hume Hwy. It is mostly a petrol-and-sausage-roll pit stop.

Just 6km out of town, **Gundagai Wines** (☎0419 220 711; www.gundagaiwines.com; Nangus Rd; ⏲10.30am-4.30pm Fri-Sun) cellar door is in an old woolshed set within a rose garden.

Festivals & Events

The **Snake Gully Cup**, in mid-November, is a highly prized local racing carnival that straddles two days.

On a Celtic note, the **Turning Wave** (www.turningwave.org.au) festival in September is a folksy folk favourite.

Sleeping & Eating

Gundagai River Caravan Park CARAVAN PARK, CABINS $
(☎02-6944 1702; www.gundagairivercaravanpark.com.au; unpowered/powered sites $18/28, cabins from $86) A lovely riverside location.

Poet's Recall MOTEL $$
(☎02-6944 1777; cnr West & Punch Sts; s/d $85/100; 📶🏊) Touches such as a swimming pool, spa and bar make Poet's Recall the best motel in town. The restaurant dishes up roasts and other homestyle meals.

Hillview Farmstay APARTMENTS $$
(☎02-6944 7535; www.hillviewfarmstay.com.au; Hume Hwy; 1-/2-/4-bedroom cottage $145/175/450; ❄) Around 34km south of town and signposted off the Hume Highway, these nicely turned out cottages inhabit a 1000-acre farm and are especially good for wildlife and birdwatching.

Gundagai Bakery BAKERY $
(184 Sheridan St; pies from $4; ⏲6am-4pm Mon-Sat, 9am-2pm Sun) This place along the main street claims to be the oldest working bakery in Australia. It dates back to 1864, although the shop at the front gives no signs of such an august heritage. The pies are decent as you'd expect with this much time to perfect them.

Family Hotel PUB $$
(213 Sheridan St; mains $15-24; ⏲noon-1.45pm Mon-Wed, noon-1.45pm & 6-8.30pm Thu-Sat) This old-style country pub does dishes such as chicken shnitzel and gravy or T-Bone steak.

Information

Visitor Centre (☎02-6944 0250; www.visitgundagai.com.au; 249 Sheridan St; ⏲8.30am-5pm) Housed within the centre is **Rusconi's Marble Masterpiece** (admission $5), an intricate marble model that relentlessly plays 'Along the Road to Gundagai', so that you'll likely hum it mindlessly for days.

Albury

POP 45,627

This major regional centre on the Murray River sits on the state border opposite its Victorian twin, Wodonga. Its a good launchpad for trips to the snowfields and high country of both Victoria and NSW and for exploring the upper Murray River. It's also a good spot to break the journey between Sydney and Melbourne.

Sights & Activities

Library Museum MUSEUM
(☎02-6023 8333; cnr Kiewa & Swift Sts; ⏲10am-7pm Mon, Wed & Thu, to 5pm Tue & Fri, to 4pm Sat, noon-4pm Sun) FREE Albury's fabulous state-of-the-art showpiece, dubbed the 'living room', blends book borrowing, magazine browsing and net surfing with exhibitions and local history, including Aboriginal culture and 20th-century migration into the area.

Albury Art Gallery ART GALLERY
(☎6043 5800; 546 Dean St; ⏱10am-5pm Mon-Fri, 10am-4pm Sat, noon-4pm Sun) FREE This gallery has a small permanent collection featuring works by Russell Drysdale and Fred Williams, contemporary Australian photography, a reading room and a shop.

Botanic Gardens GARDEN
This 4-hectare garden, at the northern end of Wodonga Pl, is old, formal and beautiful – a heritage walk is available from the visitor centre.

Ettamogah Pub NOTABLE BUILDING
(☎02-6026 2366; www.ettamogah.com; Wagga Rd, Tabletop) A real-life re-creation of a famous Aussie cartoon pub by Albury-born Ken Maynard.

Activities

Noreuil Park PARK
For a cleansing river swim, turn right into Albury, just before the Lincoln Causeway, where there are beautiful shady plane trees and a **river swimming pool**. Try the **loop**, a magical 20-minute float (on your back) around a big bend that ends close to where you began.

Wonga Wetlands NATURE RESERVE
(Riverina Hwy, Splitters Creek) See up to 154 bird species and an indigenous camp site established by local Wiradjuri people at this innovative project to restore local wetlands. There is some lovely red-gum scenery along the 0.5km, 1.2km and 2.5km trails. The reserve is 6km west of town along Padmore Drive.

Sleeping

Albury Motor Village YHA HOSTEL $
(☎02-6040 2999; www3.yha.com.au; 372 Wagga Rd; powered sites/dm/d $27/63/77; @ 🏊) About 4.5km north of the centre on the road to Sydney, this youth hostel has a range of cabins, vans and backpacker beds in clean dorms.

Briardale B&B B&B $$
(☎02-6025 5131; 396 Poplar Dr; r from $121; ❄) This elegant North Albury B&B has some beautifully decorated rooms with an understated antique style.

Quest Albury APARTMENTS $$
(☎02-6058 0900; www.questalbury.com.au; 550 Kiewa St; r from $155; ❄📶) Spacious studio suites, as well as two- and three-bedroom apartments could just be Albury's most comfortable deal. The look is classy, casual and contemporary with soothing tones and dark-wood furnishings.

Chifley MOTEL $$
(☎02-6021 5366; www.chifleyhotels.com; cnr Dean & Elizabeth Sts; r from $105-192; ❄📶🏊) Albury's tallest building is also its most popular hotel. It has all the expected mod cons plus a restaurant and cocktail bar. It's on the main street.

Eating & Drinking

Dean St is a long strip of takeaways, cafes, restaurants and nightlife.

Baan Sabai Jai THAI $
(☎02-6021 2250; 459 Smollett St; mains $15-23; ⏱lunch & dinner) This excellent restaurant with a traditional Thai street-food cart on the front pavement has stolen the hearts and appetites of locals with its authentic Thai dishes. Fly by or eat in.

★ **Green Zebra** CAFE $$
(☎02-6023 1100; www.greenzebra.com.au; 484 Dean St; mains $13-17.50; ⏱8am-6.30pm Mon-Fri) The homemade pasta, salads and other organic food are always a winner but everything's good here, from the walnut and pumpkin ravioli with blue cheese and fig chutney to the lamb and chickpea salad. The produce used from its own garden is chalked up on a board each day and it's a long and reassuring list.

Kinross Woolshed HOTEL $$
(www.kinrosswoolshed.com.au; Old Sydney Rd, Thurgoona; mains $11-26; ⏱breakfast & lunch Mon-Sat) It's worth taking a drive (or get the **shuttle bus** ☎02-6043 1155) to this excellent country pub in an old 1890s woolshed. It has live music (usually country) on Saturday night and the area's cheapest breakfast: $2 bacon-and-egg rolls (7am to 11am Saturday). Its specials might include the Tuesday 'Moo and Brew', a 300g Scotch fillet steak with a drink for $11.

Border Wine Room MODERN AUSTRALIAN $$
(www.borderwineroom.com.au; 492a Dean St; mains $29-37; ⏱4pm-midnight Tue-Sat) Albury's funkiest restaurant is upstairs with a bay of windows overlooking the main street. It's more a restaurant than a bar and dishes we enjoyed include Alsace-style three pork (kassler, hock and sausage).

Information

Albury Visitor Information Centre (☎1300 252 879; www.visitalburywodonga.com.au; Railway Pl; ⏲9am-5pm) Opposite the railway station.

Getting There & Away

The **airport** (Borella Rd) is 10 minutes out of town. **Rex** (☎13 17 13; www.rex.com.au), **Virgin Australia** (☎13 67 89; www.virginaustralia.com) and **Qantas** (☎13 13 13; www.qantas.com.au) share routes to Sydney (from $109, 1¼ hours) and Melbourne (from $106, one hour).

Greyhound (☎1300 GREYHOUND, 1300 4739 46863; www.greyhound.com.au) has coaches to Melbourne ($49, 3¾ hours), Wagga Wagga ($34, 2½ hours) and Sydney (from $75, 8½ to 10 hours).

CountryLink (☎13 22 32; www.countrylink.info) XPT trains run north to Wagga ($26.50, 1¼ hours) and Sydney (from $102.50, eight hours), and south to Melbourne ($67, 3½ hours). CountryLink buses run to Echuca ($45, 4¼ hours) three times a week (from the train station bus stop). **V/Line** (☎13 61 96; www.vline.com.au) trains run to Melbourne ($30, 3¾ hours).

Wagga Wagga

POP 46,913

The Murrumbidgee River squiggles around the northern end of 'Wagga' like a snake in an Aboriginal painting. Its wide-girthed eucalypts and sandy banks add an understated beauty to a place already prettied by wide tree-lined streets and lovely gardens. Meaning 'place of many crows' in the language of the local Wiradjuri people, 'Wagga' is the state's largest inland city.

Sights & Activities

Botanic Gardens GARDEN

(Macleay St; ⏲sunrise-sunset) These pretty gardens have a small **zoo** with kangaroos, wombats and emus, and there's a free-flight aviary. The nearby Lord Baden Powell Dr leads to a good lookout and the scenic **Captain Cook Drive**.

Museum of the Riverina MUSEUM

(www.wagga.nsw.gov.au/museum; Baden Powell Dr; ⏲10am-5pm Tue-Sat, noon-4pm Sun) FREE The museum operates from both the Civic Centre and the Botanic Gardens; the latter site focuses on Wagga's people, places and events and includes a **Sporting Hall of Fame**.

Wagga Wagga Art Gallery ART GALLERY

(☎02-6926 9660; www.waggaartgallery.org; Morrow St, Civic Centre; ⏲10am-5pm Tue-Sat, noon-4pm Sun) FREE The highlight of this excellent gallery of local and national artists is the wonderful **National Art Glass Gallery**.

Livestock Sales AGRICULTURE

(Boman industrial area) Wagga is a major centre for livestock sales; you can watch farmers sell cattle on Monday (7am to around noon) in an amphitheatre-style ring, and sheep by the thousands on Thursday (from 8am).

Wiradjuri Walking Track WALKING

(www.lands.nsw.gov.au) This great 30km circuit beginning from the visitor centre includes some good lookouts and places of Aboriginal significance. Watch out for platypus in the river, although you'd have to be both patient and fortunate to spot this elusive creature. There's a shorter 12km walk. Maps are available from the visitor centre.

Wagga Beach BEACH

At the end of Tarcutta St, this is a good swimming option by the river.

Sleeping

Romano's Hotel HOTEL $

(☎02-6921 2013; www.romanoshotel.com.au; cnr Fitzmaurice & Sturt Sts; d $85, s/d without bathroom $45/55) This is an airy old pub with high ceilings, OK rooms, grand beds and old bathrooms; ask for a room on the quieter 2nd floor.

WAGGA WINERIES & OILS

Harefield Ridge (www.cottontailwines.com.au; 562 Pattersons Rd; ⏲10am-close Thu-Sun) Cellar-door tastings, sales and meals.

Wagga Wagga Winery (☎02-6922 1221; Oura Rd; ⏲11am-10pm Wed-Sun) Cellar-door sales and good meals.

Charles Sturt University Winery (www.csu.edu.au/winery; McKeown Dr; ⏲11am-5pm Mon-Fri, to 4pm Sat & Sun) Award-winning wines, olive oil and cheese tastings.

Wollundry Grove Olives (☎02-6924 6494; www.wollundrygroveolives.com.au; 15 Mary Gilmore Rd) Award-winning extra virgin olive oil and table olives. Phone ahead for tours and tastings.

WORTH A TRIP

JUNEE

Some 33km north of Wagga Wagga, Junee is a small, friendly country town with numerous impressive buildings.

Built in 1884, the mansion of **Monte Cristo** (☎02-6924 1637; www.montecristo.com.au; Monte Cristo Rd; adult/child $9.50/free; ⏲10am-4pm) is open for self-guided tours and Devonshire tea. Rumour says it's haunted by its former owner. The town also has three fine old country pubs – the **Junee Hotel** (Seignior St) (1876), the **Commercial Hotel** (cnr Lorne & Waratah Sts) (1915) and the **Loftus on Humphreys** (6 Humphreys St); the latter, undergoing major renovations when we visited, was the town's grandest hotel, with a frontage running for an entire block. The film *The Crossing*, starring Russell Crowe, was filmed there.

Other attractions include the 1947 **Railway Roundhouse** (☎02-6924 2909; www.rhta-junee.org; Harold St; adult/child $6/4; ⏲noon-4.30pm Mon-Fri, from 9.30am Sat & Sun), a giant turntable with 42 train-repair bays and the only surviving, working one of its kind in Australia, and the **Junee Liquorice & Chocolate Factory** (☎02-6924 3574; www.greengroveorganics.com; 45-61 Lord St; adult/child $4/2.50; ⏲9.30am-4.30pm), which makes a show out of creating liquorice and chocolate in the old Junee Flour Mill (1935).

Get info from the small **visitor centre** (www.visitjunee.com.au; Lorne St, Aquatic Centre), although there's not always someone on duty.

Wagga Wagga Beach Caravan Park CARAVAN PARK $
(☎02-6931 0603; www.wwbcp.com.au; 2 Johnston St; sites per adult $22, cabins $65-120; ❄📶) This park has a swimming beach fashioned from the riverbank and plenty of grassy knolls and cabins.

Townhouse HOTEL $$
(☎02- 6921 4337; townhousewagga.com.au; 70 Morgan St; r from $139; ❄📶) This slick in-town option has the feel of a boutique hotel, and professional and friendly service that you'd expect of a business hotel. Rooms are large and stylish, although not all have exterior windows.

Dunns B&B B&B $$
(☎02-6925 7771; www.dunnsbedandbreakfast.com.au; 63 Mitchelmore St; s/d $130/140; ❄📶) A pristinely decorated federation home with three en suite rooms and the use of a private balcony and sitting room. It's out of the city centre near the Botanic Gardens.

✕ Eating

Mates Gully Organics CAFE $$
(www.matesgully.com.au; 32 Fitzmaurice St; mains $14-33; ⏲8am-4pm Sun-Tue, to 9.30pm Wed-Sat; 📶) Long wooden tables and wall art create a nice vibe in Wagga's coolest cafe. The owners have a farm-to-plate approach and much of the produce is home-grown. There's also occasional live music.

Three Chefs Cafe CAFE $$
(☎02-6921 5897; www.threechefs.com.au; 97 Fitzmaurice St; lunch mains $16-23, dinner mains $31-39; ⏲9am-9.30pm Tue-Sat) This popular cafe opens onto the street and draws a regular crowd for its light but substantive lunch meals and more formal dinner atmosphere. For lunch, try the wild mushroom and rocket risotto.

★ **Magpies Nest** MEDITERRANEAN $$$
(☎02-6933 1523; 20 Pine Gully Rd; mains $28-40, set menu $55; ⏲5.30-9pm Tue-Sat) A delightfully informal restaurant set in a restored 1860s stone stable overlooking the Murrumbidgee River flats and surrounded by olive groves and vineyards. The fare is regional with a hint of Tuscany, and my, it's good. When we passed through the menu included the intriguing 'shoulder of lamb, long and slow, spiced with mystery and in turmeric and rosewater pan reduction'...

ℹ Information

Visitor Centre (☎1300 100 122; www.visitwagga.com; 183 Tarcutta St; ⏲9am-5pm)

ℹ Getting There & Away

Qantas (☎13 13 13; www.qantas.com.au) flies to Sydney (from $85, one hour) and **Rex** (☎13 17 13; www.rex.com.au) flies to Melbourne (from $121, 1¼ hours) and Sydney (from $115, 1¼ hours).

CountryLink (☎13 22 32; www.countrylink.info) buses leave from **Wagga train station**

(☎13 22 32, 02-6939 5488), where you can make bookings. CountryLink's XPT train runs to Albury ($26.50, 1¼ hours), Melbourne ($89, five hours) and Sydney Central ($89, 6¾ hours).

Griffith

POP 17,616

You're almost as likely to see Indians as Italians in Griffith, a tribute to the cultural eclecticism in this small agricultural town. Its wide leafy main street might lack the heritage architecture of other regional centres, but behind the urbane shopfronts there's a culinary world that has made Griffith the wine-and-food capital of the Riverina.

Sights & Activities

Pioneer Park Museum MUSEUM
(☎02-6962 4196; cnr Remembrance & Scenic Drs; adult/child $10/6; ⏱9.30am-4pm) High on a hill north of the town centre is a re-creation of an early Riverina village, with an old hospital, a music room and other fascinating displays in original old buildings.

Sir Dudley de Chair Lookout LOOKOUT
Further along Scenic Dr, this pretty spot has a panoramic view and is near the **Hermit's Cave**, which was inhabited by an Italian-born man for decades in the early 20th century; watch out for snakes in the area.

McWilliam's Hanwood Estate WINERY
(www.mcwilliamswine.com; Jack McWilliam Rd, Hanwood; ⏱tastings 10am-4pm Tue-Sat) The region's oldest winery (1913).

De Bortoli WINERY
(www.debortoli.com.au; De Bortoli Rd; ⏱9am-5pm Mon-Sat, to 4pm Sun) One of Australia's best-known wines.

Catania Fruit Salad Farm FARM
(☎02-6963 0219; www.cataniafruitsaladfarm.com.au; Farm 43 Cox Rd, Handwood; ⏱1.30pm Feb-Nov) The friendly owners host enjoyable working farm tours that wind up with a session tasting pickles, relishes, plums and jam.

Festivals & Events

UnWINEd FOOD & WINE
(www.unwined-riverina.com) In early June, UnWINEd is a festival of food and wine with tutored tastings, languid lunches and live music at various venues.

Sleeping

★ **Myalbangera Outstation** HOSTEL $
(☎0428 130 093; Rankin Springs Rd, Farm 1646, Yenda; dm $19-25, d $40-45; ❄) An excellent backpacker option, located about 12km out of town in an iconic Australiana setting. The owners know the lay of the land and can assist with work and transfers from town.

Shearer's Quarters at Pioneer Park Museum HOSTEL $
(☎0429 300 126; Remembrance Dr; per person per night/week $23/130) Cheapest nightly option up at Pioneer Park.

Hotel Victoria HOTEL $
(☎02-6962 1299; www.hotelvictoria.com.au; 384 Banna Ave; s/d incl breakfast $90/105; ❄📶) The Victoria features bright corridors, cheerful rooms and good bathrooms. Downstairs is a bistro with a chargrill. Must be booked through the visitor centre.

Grand Motel MOTEL $$
(☎02-6969 4400; www.grandmotelgriffith.com.au; 454 Banna Ave; s/d from $125/135; ❄📶🏊) Griffith's snazziest sleep option has lofty ceilings, bright modern rooms and an impressive foyer. Parking, gym and spa facilites are nice extras, so too the in-room dining from Marco's Restaurant. Avoid the room without windows.

Eating

Banna Ave is lined with Italian pizza and pasta shops.

★ **La Scala** ITALIAN $$
(☎02-6962 4322; 455b Banna Ave; mains $26-30; ⏱dinner Tue-Sat) Hidden down steps and behind a couple of old brown doors, this huge cellar, covered in murals, is one of Griffith's institutions. There's nothing modern about the menu either; expect old-school recipes and house white for $5 a glass. Brilliant.

Marco's Restaurant MODERN AUSTRALIAN $$
(☎02-6964 3438; www.marcosgriffith.com.au; 10/454 Banna Ave; mains $19-27; ⏱noon-3pm & 6-9pm Tue-Fri, 6-9pm Mon & Sat) One of the snazzier options in town with a menu that includes grilled salmon, T-Bone steak and pavlova. It's hidden up a little staircase a few metres from the affiliated Grand Motel.

La Tavola ITALIAN $$
(☎02-6962 7777; 188 Banna Ave; mains $18-29; ⏱noon-2.30pm & 6-9pm) The tacky decor is all part of the Italian experience at this

restaurant dishing up favourites such as chicken *al funghi*, pepper steak, saltimbocca, a darn good La Tavola Special pizza and the like. Watch for cheaper lunch specials.

Shopping

Riverina Grove FOOD
(☎02-6962 7988; www.riverinagrove.com.au; 4 Whybrow St) This produce mecca has everything from marinated feta, pasta sauce and olive oils to homemade jams and chutney.

Information

Grapes and other crops provide year-round harvest jobs, but some periods are slower than others. Ask for advice at the visitor centre before doing the rounds. *Area News* is also a good source for jobs.

Riverina NPWS Office (☎02-6966 8100; www.nationalparks.nsw.gov.au; 200 Yambil St) Information on nearby national parks.

Visitor Centre (☎02-6962 4145; www.visitgriffith.com.au; cnr Banna & Jondaryan Aves)

Getting There & Around

Rex (☎13 17 13; www.rex.com.au) flies to Sydney (from $125, 1¼ hours).

All buses, except CountryLink (which stops at the train station), stop at the **Griffith Travel & Transit Centre** (☎02-6962 7199; Banna Ave), in the same building as the visitor centre. Services run daily to Melbourne ($98, 9½ hours) and Sydney ($88, 10¼ hours), both via Cootamundra, and Mildura ($72, six hours).

DON'T MISS

ITALIAN GREATS IN GRIFFITH

- Best cannoli pastry – **Bertoldo's Bakery** (324 & 150 Banna Ave; ⏲breakfast & lunch).
- Best foccacia – **La Piccola Italian Deli** (444a Banna Ave; ⏲8.30am-5.30pm Mon-Fri, 8.30am-1pm Sat, 9am-noon Sun) Huge and stuffed with ham, cheese, olives and semidried tomatoes.
- Best cappuccino – **Dolce Dolce** (449 Banna Ave; ⏲8am-4pm Wed-Sat, 8.30am-2pm Sun) In a row of art-deco inspired shops circa 1957.
- Best pizza – **Belvedere** (494 Banna Ave; pizzas from $12; ⏲noon-midnight Tue-Sun) Under new management, so the jury's out.

Deniliquin & Around

POP 7494

A quintessential inland Australian town, Deniliquin, or 'Deni' as it's known, lies along a wide bend of the Edwards River. Here you'll find an attractive river beach and some appealing riverside walks amid the red gums. There's also a famed and ever-growing festival dedicated to that curious Aussie obsession, the ute.

Sights & Activities

Island Sanctuary WILDLIFE RESERVE
(adult/child $180/135) The 16-hectare Island Sanctuary, at the junction of the Edwards River and Tarrangle Creek, has a fine walking track among the river red gums. It's home to plenty of wildlife, including eastern grey kangaroos, and almost one-fifth of all bird species recorded in Australia have been seen here. Entry is via footbridge off the southeastern end of the main Cressy St.

McLean Beach BEACH
At the northern end of town, McLean Beach is one of Australia's finest river beaches, with sand, picnic facilities and a walking track.

Festivals & Events

Blues & Roots Festival MUSIC
(denibluesfestival.com; ⏲Easter weekend) Begun in 2013 with a stellar line-up that included Santana, the Steve Miller Band and Chris Isaak, this music festival looks here to stay.

Deni Matchmakers Festival LOCAL FESTIVAL
(www.denimatchmakers.com.au) If you're single get along to this four-day festival in March.

Sleeping & Eating

Riverside Caravan Park CARAVAN PARK $
(☎03-5881 1284; www.deniliquinriversidecaravanpark.com.au; 20 Davidson St; cabins $75-130, unpowered/powered sites per person from $20/28;) This camp site on the river bank has comfortable cabins, a swimming pool and a couple of tiny children's playgrounds. It's a short walk from the main street.

Riverview Motel MOTEL $
(☎03-5881 2311; www.riverviewmotel.com.au; 1 Butler St; s/d $82/92;) Most of the fairly standard motel rooms here at the northern end of town have shared porches overlooking McLean Beach and the Edward River. It has one of the better restaurants in town,

Rinaldi's (mains $18 to 35), which does good steaks.

★ **Cottages on Edward** B&B $$
(☎0407 815 641; www.cottagesonedward.com.au; 304 River St; cottages incl breakfast $135 Sun-Thu, $165 Fri & Sat ❄) These two charming cottages, overseen by the equally charming Richard and Pat, make a fine alternative to the motels elsewhere. The rooms have understated antique furnishings, spa baths and a real sense of being a home away from home. It's across the river at the eastern end of town.

★ **Crossing Café** MODERN AUSTRALIAN $$
(☎03-5881 7827; 295 George St; mains $14-26; ⏲8am-4pm Tue-Thu, 8am-late Fri, 8.30am-late Sat, 8.30am-4pm Sun) This place has an outdoor deck overlooking an idyllic riverside setting. The menu focuses on quality rather than quantity. Think Thai beef salad or salt-and-pepper calamari.

Information

Visitor Centre (☎1800 650 712; www.denitourism.com.au; George St; ⏲9am-4pm)

Getting There & Away

Long-distance buses stop on Whitelock St, opposite Gorman Park. **CountryLink** (☎13 22 32; www.countrylink.info) buses run to Albury ($25.48, 3½ hours), linking with the XPT train to Sydney Central ($98, 12 hours). **V/Line** (☎13 61 96; www.vline.com.au) coaches run to Melbourne ($24.90, four hours).

CELEBRATING THE UTE

On the New South Wales Labour Day long weekend in October, Deniliquin celebrates the Aussie love affair with the ute during the **Ute Muster** (www.deniutemuster.com.au), which attracts people from across the country for an action-packed weekend in their utes – 10,152 of them at last record-breaking count in 2010! Events include rodeo, chainsaw sculpturing, woodchopping, helicopter rides and activities for kids. The muster is part of the **Play on the Plains Festival** (☎03-5881 3388) which draws some big names in Australian music – Cold Chisel, Hoodoo Gurus and Crowded House have all appeared in recent years. Events begin on Friday evening, with things winding up by Sunday lunchtime.

Wentworth

POP 1227

The colonial river port of Wentworth, at the confluence of the Murray and Darling Rivers, has a handful of attractive old buildings and serves as a gateway to Mungo National Park.

Sights

Historic Buildings ARCHITECTURE
The modest replica of the colonial-era **wharf** has a small customs shed; Wentworth was once New South Wales' third-largest port after Newcastle and Sydney. In the centre of town, the **Old Post Office** (1899) has a pretty picket fence, while the **Wentworth Court House** (1880) is a fine brick affair. At the northwestern end of town, **Old Wentworth Gaol** (☎03-5027 3337; Beverley St; adult/child $8/4; ⏲10am-5pm) is a fascinating step back in time. Across the road, the interesting **Folk Museum & Pioneer World** (☎03-5027 3160; adult/child $5/2; ⏲10am-4pm) has 176 photos of paddle steamers.

Murray-Darling RIVER
The point where the Darling River flows into the Murray is visible from the southwestern corner of town. The riverside park, accessible from Cadell St, has enormous river red gums shading the banks, and an elevated lookout.

Perry Sand Hills VIEWPOINT
Around 6km north of town, and signposted off the Broken Hill and then Renmark roads, these low but really rather pretty orange sand dunes date back 40,000 years. Curiously, the area just beyond the dunes was one of three final candidates for the site of Australia's new capital city in the early 20th century. The dunes are at their best at sunset or sunrise.

Tours

Harry Nanya Tours CULTURAL TOUR
(☎03-5027 2076; www.harrynanyatours.com.au; 384 Silver City Hwy; adult/child from $180/110) Harry Nanya Tours runs day (April to October) and sunset (November to March) eight-hour tours with Aboriginal guides into Mungo National Park. Pick-ups are available

or tag along with your own car (adult/child $90/45).

Discover Mildura CULTURAL TOUR
(☎0419 127 995; www.discovermildura.com.au; per person incl lunch $150) Guided day trips to Mungo National Park.

Wentworth River Cruises BOAT TOUR
(☎0408 647 097; www.wentworthcruises.com.au; adult $20-38, child $15-20; ⏰2pm & 8pm Wed, 12.30pm Sun) Three different weekly cruises make a nice alternative to watching the waters from the riverbank.

Sleeping & Eating

Houseboats are an interesting option. Try **Sunraysia Houseboats** (☎03-5027 3621; www.sunraysiahouseboats.com), **Adelora Houseboat** (☎03-5027 3512; www.adelora.com.au; 44 Cadell St) or **Murray Darling Houseboats** (☎03-5027 3235; www.murraydarling-houseboats.com.au; 6/58 Wentworth St). There are cheap eateries around the town centre, but one that stands out.

Wentworth Grande Resort HOTEL $$
(☎03-5027 2225; www.wentworthgranderesort.com.au; 61-79 Darling St; r $99-159, f/ste 160/200; ❄📶🏊) Easily the best option in the town centre, this large place has a range of large and well-maintained rooms next to the Darling River.

★**Avoca-On-Darling** HISTORIC HOTEL $$$
(☎03-5027 3020; sites.google.com/site/avocaondarling; off Low Darling Rd; homestead per person incl meals $140) A historical option is a room at this lovely guest house, an 1800s heritage homestead 26km from Wentworth on the gum-laden banks of the river junction. A self-contained cook's cottage ($160), jackeroo's quarters ($25 per person) and campsites (powered/unpowered $25/15) are also available. Travel 6km north of Wentworth along the Broken Hill road, then take the Lower Darling Rd, then turn off at the white wheel after a further 18.5km.

OUTBACK NEW SOUTH WALES: OUR TOP FIVE

- A game of Two-Up in the Main Bar of Broken Hill's Palace Hotel (p235)
- The long, lonely road to Tibooburra and Sturt National Park (p239)
- The Walls of China in Mungo National Park (p232)
- Historic Aboriginal sites in Mutawintji National Park (p238)
- Sleep underground in White Cliffs (p239)

Information

Visitor Centre (☎03-5027 5080; www.wentworth.nsw.gov.au; 66 Darling St; ⏰9am-5pm Mon-Fri, to 1pm Sat & Sun)

Getting There & Away

Busesrus (www.busesrus.com) has buses three times a week from Wentworth to Broken Hill (3½ hours, $84).

OUTBACK

NSW is rarely credited for its far-west outback corner but it should be. Grey saltbush and red sand make it easy out here to imagine yourself superimposed onto the world's biggest Aboriginal dot painting, a canvas reaching as far as the eye can see.

The mining town of Broken Hill is its unique heart-centre, close to much-photographed Silverton. The state's far west is also home to some of regional Australia's more beguiling national parks. And to truly fall off the map, there's Tibooburra and Cameron Corner at the impossibly remote intersection of NSW, Queensland and South Australia (SA). Further afield is White Cliffs, where there's more to do underground than above.

Mungo National Park

This remote, beautiful and important place covers 27,850 hectares of the Willandra Lakes World Heritage area and is one of Australia's most beautiful and accessible slices of the outback.

Sights

Lake Mungo is a dry lake and site of the oldest archaeological finds in Australia as well as being the longest continual record of Aboriginal life (the world's oldest recorded cremation site has been found here).

A 25km semicircle ('lunette') of huge sand dunes, the fabulous **Walls of China** has been created by the unceasing westerly wind. From the visitor centre, a good unsealed road leads across the dry lake bed to the Walls of China. Since heavy rains in 2011, getting up close and personal with the formations is the preserve of guided tours; everyone else must admire from the **viewing platform**. The road continues beyond the platform car park to the pretty **Red Top Lookout** which boasts fine views. Beyond that point, it's a one-way road that loops all the way back to the visitors centre, a 70km drive in all. There's a self-guided drive brochure at the visitor centre.

Ask at the visitor centre for details on the 2.5km **Grassland Nature Trail** direct from Main Camp, the 2.5km **Foreshore Walk** from the visitor centre, or the new **Heritage Trail** (a 6km walk or 12km cycle or drive).

Tours

The NPWS conducts 2½-hour 'Discovery' foreshore walks, tag-along tours and starry night adventures (adult/child $10/5). Ask at the visitor centre.

Harry Nanya Tours INDIGENOUS TOUR
(☎03-5027 2076; www.harrynanyatours.com.au; adult/child $180/110 from Wentworth or Mildura) Day (April to October) and sunset (November to March) eight-hour tours with Aboriginal guides.

My Country Enterprise Tours INDIGENOUS TOUR
(☎0401 919 275; www.mycountryenterprises.com) Indigenous-led walking tours through the park with multi-day options possible.

Sleeping

Main Camp CAMPGROUND $
(adult/child $5/3, car $7) Located 2km from the visitor centre.

Belah Camp CAMPGROUND $
(adult/child $5/3, car $7) Remote Belah Camp is on the eastern side of the dunes.

Shearers' Quarters HUT $
(s/d $50/60, child $10) These former shearers' quarters have five rooms, a communal kitchen and bathroom, and barbecue area. It's BYO bed linen.

Turlee Station Stay CAMPGROUND, GUESTHOUSE $
(☎03-5029 7208; www.turleestationstay.com.au; camping/shearers' huts/bungalow/cabins $8/50/80/150) Camping, basic shearers' quarters, simple bungalows and four-star cabins mean there's something for everyone at this well-run working station. It's on the unsealed road in from Balranald.

MUNGO NATIONAL PARK AT A GLANCE

When to Visit: Year-round but best April to October

Gateway Towns: Balranald, Wentworth and Broken Hill

Main attractions: Walls of China land formations; outback isolation; wildlife; Aboriginal sites

Transport: Unsealed roads into the park are accessible in 2WD vehicles except after rains.

Mungo Lodge LODGE $$$
(☎03-5029 7297; www.mungolodge.com.au; d from $270; ❄📶) Mungo Lodge, on the Mildura road, about 4km from the visitor centre has attractive cabins with all the mod cons and a flash restaurant (book ahead).

Information

There's a $7 per vehicle entry fee for the park, payable at the visitor centre.

Visitor Centre (☎03-5021 8900; www.visitmungo.com.au; ⏲approx 8am-4pm daily)

NPWS Office (☎03-5021 8900) On the corner of the Sturt Hwy at Buronga, near Mildura.

Getting There & Away

Mungo is 110km from Mildura and 150km from Balranald on good, unsealed roads that become instantly impassable after rain – a 2WD vehicle is generally fine in dry weather. The closest places selling fuel are at Balranald, Mildura, Wentworth and Menindee, but not Pooncarie.

Ask at the tourist offices in the gateway towns to see if the roads into Mungo are open *and* accessible by 2WD. You can also phone ☎132 701 or ☎03-5027 5090, or check online at wentworth.nsw.gov.au/services/roadclosures.php.

Broken Hill

POP 18,430

The massive silver skimp dump that forms a backdrop for Broken Hill's town centre accentuates the unique character of this desert frontier town. For all its remoteness, its fine facilities and appealing attractions can feel like an oasis somewhere close to the end of the earth. Some of the state's best national parks are also nearby, as is an intriguing ghost town.

Broken Hill

Broken Hill

Top Sights
1 Broken Hill Regional Art Gallery D2
2 Line of Lode Miners Memorial C4
3 Palace Hotel C3

Sights
4 Albert Kersten Mining & Minerals Museum C3
5 Silver City Mint & Art Centre C2

Activities, Courses & Tours
6 Silver City Tours D2
7 Tri State Safaris C1

Sleeping
8 Caledonian B&B C2
9 Imperial C2
Palace Hotel .... (see 3)
10 Red Earth Motel D2
11 Royal Exchange Hotel C3

Eating
12 Broken Earth Café & Restaurant C4
13 Café Alfresco's D2
Royal Exchange Hotel .... (see 11)
14 Thom, Dick & Harry's D3

Drinking & Nightlife
Palace Hotel .... (see 3)

History

A boundary rider, Charles Rasp, laid the foundations in Broken Hill that took Australia from an agricultural country to an industrial nation. In 1883 he discovered a silver lode and formed the Broken Hill Proprietary Company (which now goes by the name of BHP Billiton). It ultimately became

Australia's largest company and an international giant.

Early conditions in the mine were appalling. Hundreds of miners died and many more suffered from lead poisoning and lung disease. This gave rise to the other great force in Broken Hill, the unions. Many miners were immigrants, but all were united in their efforts to improve conditions. The Big Strike of 1919–20 lasted for over 18 months, but the miners achieved a 35-hour week and the end of dry drilling.

Today the world's richest deposits of silver, lead and zinc are still being worked here, although mining operations are slowly winding down.

Sights

Day Dream Mine MINING
(☎08-8088 5682; underground tours adult/child $30/10, surface $8/4; ⏰10am-3pm Mar-Nov, 10am & 11.30am Dec-Feb) The first mines were walk-in, pick-and-shovel horrors. For an amazing experience, tour this historic mine where you squeeze down the steps with your helmet-light quivering on your head. Sturdy footwear is essential. It's a scenic 20-minute dirt drive off the Silverton road, 28km from Broken Hill.

★**Line of Lode Miners Memorial** MEMORIAL & LOOKOUT
(Federation Hill; adult/child $2.50/free; ⏰10am-5pm) Teetering atop the huge silver skimp dump is this moving memorial. It houses the impressively stark Cor-Ten steel memorial to the 900 miners who have died since Broken Hill first became a mining town; it's an appalling litany of gruesome deaths. To get here, travel south along Iodide Street, cross the railway tracks then follow the signs.

★**Broken Hill Regional Art Gallery** ART GALLERY
(www.bhartgallery.com.au; 404-408 Argent St; admission by gold coin donation; ⏰10am-5pm) This must-see gallery is housed in the beautifully restored Sully's Emporium. It is the oldest regional gallery in NSW and holds 1500 works in its permanent collection.

Royal Flying Doctor Service MUSEUM
(☎08-8080 3714; www.flyingdoctors.org; aerodrome; adult/child $7/3.70; ⏰9am-5pm Mon-Fri, 10am-3pm Sat & Sun) This iconic Australian institution exhibition includes the fascinating **Mantle of Safety Museum**, with lots of quirky stories and things to see.

★**Palace Hotel** HISTORIC BUILDING & MURALS
(☎08-8088 1699; cnr Argent & Sulphide Sts) Star of the hit Australian movie *The Adventures of Priscilla, Queen of the Desert,* this impressive old pub (1888) has an elaborate cast-iron verandah – the longest in the state and now heritage listed by the National Trust – and overwhelming murals. The main bar was being renovated at the time of writing and there's no finer way to get a feel for the place by ordering a beer while you soak it all up. There are also rooms (p236).

★**Pro Hart Gallery** ART GALLERY
(www.prohart.com.au; 108 Wyman St; adult/child $4/2; ⏰9am-5pm Mon-Sat, 10am-5pm Sun) Pro Hart, who died early in 2006, was a former miner and is widely considered to be one of outback Australia's premier painters. His work is spread over three storeys, his studio has been re-created in replica with his last painting still on the easel, and there's a fascinating video presentation about his life and work. To get here, take Kaolin St north for 2km from Argent St.

Bells Milk Bar & Museum MILK BAR, MUSEUM
(www.bellsmilkbar.com.au; 60 Patton St; ⏰10am-5.30pm) In South Broken Hill (follow Crystal St west from the train station), this old milk bar is a slice of 1950s nostalgia. Sip on a 'soda spider' and soak up the memorabilia from one of the Formica tables. Truly authentic.

School of the Air CULTURAL BUILDING
(www.schoolair-p.schools.nsw.edu.au/; Lane St; admission $4.40; ⏰broadcasts 8.30am school days) For a back-to-school experience, sit in on a class that broadcasts to kids in isolated homesteads. Bookings must be made at least a day in advance at the visitor centre. Not surprisingly, the school is closed during school holidays.

Albert Kersten Mining & Minerals Museum MUSEUM
(cnr Bromide & Crystal Sts; adult/child $5/4; ⏰10am-4.45pm Mon-Fri, 1-4.45pm Sat & Sun) This is an interactive geology museum, with beautiful and rare minerals and crystals on display and lots of touch-and-feel exhibits. It's also home to a 42kg silver nugget.

Photographic Recollections GALLERY
(Eyre St, Old Central Power Station; adult/child $5/2.50; ⏰9.30am-1pm Mon-Fri, 1-4pm Sat) This wonderful exhibition in South Broken Hill is a pictorial history of Broken Hill; the images of Argent St down through the years are the

PHONES, TIMES & FOOTBALL

When the New South Wales government refused to give Broken Hill the services it needed, saying the town was just a pinprick on the map, the Barrier Industrial Council replied that Sydney was also a pinprick from where it was, and Broken Hill would henceforth be part of South Australia (SA). Since the town was responsible for much of NSW's wealth, Broken Hill was told it was to remain part of NSW. In protest, the town adopted SA time, phone area code, and football, playing Australian Rules from then on.

Tourists beware: time in Broken Hill is Central Standard Time (CST), 30 minutes later than the surrounding area on Eastern Standard Time (EST); you're in the 08 phone code region; and don't talk about rugby in the pub.

highlight. The owner, Cliff Braes, may have retired by the time you read this – ask at the visitor centre.

Silver City Mint & Art Centre ART GALLERY
(www.silvercitymint.com.au; Chloride St; admission to Big Picture $7; ⏲10am-4pm Mon-Sat, 1-4pm Sun) This is home to a chocolate factory and the Big Picture, the largest continuous canvas in Australia (they claim it's the biggest in the world), an amazing 100m-by-12m diorama of the Broken Hill outback.

Tours

Broken Hill Walk Tours WALKING TOUR
(by donation; ⏲10am Mon, Wed & Fri Mar-Dec) Walking tours around Broken Hill that leave from the visitor centre.

City Sights Outback Tours 4WD
(☎08-8087 2484, 1800 670 120; www.bhoutbacktours.com.au) Day and half-day tours of Broken Hill, Silverton, Menindee Lakes and White Cliffs.

Mine Tours MINE
(☎08-8087 2484) Day Dream Mine and Silverton tours depart daily at 9.30am. Call ahead for reservation and pick-up or ask at the visitor centre.

Tri State Safaris TOUR
(☎08-8088 2389; www.tristate.com.au) One- to 19-day tours to places such as Mutawinji National Park, Corner Country, Birdsville and the Simpson Desert.

Festivals & Events

St Pats Day Races HORSE RACING
(www.stpatricks.org.au) These races in March are an iconic annual event.

Sleeping

★**Caledonian B&B** B&B $
(☎08-8087 1945; www.caledonianbnb.com.au; 140 Chloride St; d $130, s/d with shared bathroom incl breakfast $79/89, self-catering cottages for 2 $140, additional $15 per person; ❄📶) This fine B&B is in a refurbished pub (1898) known as 'the Cally'. Hugh and Barb are welcoming hosts and the rooms are lovingly maintained. Wake up and smell Hugh's espresso coffee and you'll be hooked.

Imperial GUESTHOUSE $$
(☎08-8087 7444; 88 Oxide St; r/apt from $170/260; ❄📶🏊) One of Broken Hill's best, this converted heritage pub, with a spectacular wrought-iron verandah, has been exquisitely renovated and doesn't skimp on creature comforts with a full-size billiard table in the 'main bar'.

Palace Hotel HISTORIC HOTEL $$
(☎08-8088 1699; www.thepalacehotelbrokenhill.com.au; 227 Argent St; r $85-135, dm/s/d with shared bathroom $30/45/65, Priscilla Suite $135; ❄) This ageing icon is under new management and although it won't be to everyone's taste, a stay here is one of the great sleeping experiences in the outback. Rooms are proudly retro and the murals in the public areas are extraordinary. For the full experience, try the Priscilla Suite.

Red Earth Motel MOTEL $$
(☎08-8088 5694; www.redearthmotel.com.au; 469 Argent St; ste $140, 2-/3-bedroom apt $200/240; ❄📶🏊) One of the best motels in rural NSW, this family-run place has large and stylish rooms that outdo many hotels in town – every room has a large bed, separate sitting area, kitchen, fridge and microwave, there's a guest laundry and the apartments are ideal for longer stays.

Royal Exchange Hotel HOTEL $$$
(☎08-8087 2308; www.royalexchangehotel.com; 320 Argent St; r $89-150; ❄📶) This beautifully restored 1930s hotel with an art-deco bent is an accommodation oasis in the heart of town.

Eating & Drinking

Thom, Dick & Harry's CAFE $
(www.thomdickharrys.com.au; 354 Argent St; baguettes $8.50; ⏲9am-5.30pm Mon-Thu, to 6pm Fri, to 2pm Sat) A narrow shop cluttered with stylish kitchenware and gourmet produce. Sit in among it (or out on the street) for a decent coffee and delicious baguettes.

★**Broken Earth Café & Restaurant** MODERN AUSTRALIAN $$
(☎08-8087 1318; www.brokenearthrestaurant.com.au; Federation Hill; lunch mains $18.50-22, dinner mains from $37.50; ⏲10am-late) With its stunning views over Broken Hill, airy modern design and eclectic gourmet menu, this gets a big thumbs up. Try the king prawn risotto for lunch, while there's all-day coffee and cakes, too. Book ahead for dinner.

Café Alfresco's MODERN AUSTRALIAN $$
(☎08-8087 5599; 397 Argent St; mains $14-29; ⏲noon-2.30pm & 6-9pm) The service ticks along at an outback pace but this place still pulls an unfussy crowd pining for plates of pancakes, roasts, gourmet salads, pasta dishes and pizzas.

Royal Exchange Hotel MODERN AUSTRALIAN $$
(320 Argent St; mains $28-36; ⏲6-9.30pm Mon-Sat) For an upmarket dining experience, the Royal Exchange Hotel does gourmet takes on Australian staples, such as scallops wrapped in pancetta. Servings are smaller than they should be for this price.

★**Palace Hotel** PUB
(227 Argent St; ⏲10am-late) The main bar at this atmospheric place, one of the most storied pubs in the outback, was being refurbished when we passed through. When it reopens, they're hoping to have Australia's only licence for 'two-up' (gambling on the fall of two coins). It's that sort of place.

Information

NPWS Office (☎08-8080 3200; 183 Argent St; ⏲8.30am-4.30pm Mon-Fri) Road-closure updates and park accommodation bookings.

Visitor Centre (☎08-8088 3560; www.visitbrokenhill.com.au; cnr Blende & Bromide Sts)

Getting There & Away

Rex (☎13 17 13; www.rex.com.au) flies to Adelaide ($125, 1¼ hours), Sydney (from $205, 2¾ hours) and Melbourne (from $223, two hours).

Buses arrive at the visitor centre. **CountryLink** (☎13 22 32; www.countrylink.info) runs the *Broken Hill Outback Explorer* to Sydney ($118, 13½ hours). The **CountryLink booking office** (☎08-8087 1400; ⏲8am-5pm Mon-Fri) is at the train station.

The **Indian Pacific** (☎13 21 47; www.trainways.com.au) goes east to Sydney (from $128, 16 hours), south to Adelaide (from $123, 6¾ hours) and west to Perth (from $351, 47 hours).

Around Broken Hill

Silverton

POP ABOUT 100 PEOPLE & 2 DONKEYS

Silverton (www.silverton.org.au), an old silver-mining town and now an outback ghost town, is like walking inside a Drysdale painting. Silverton's fortunes peaked in 1885, when it had a population of 3000, but in 1889 the mines closed and the people (and some houses) moved to Broken Hill.

Silverton is the setting of films such as *Mad Max II* and *A Town Like Alice*. The popular **Silverton Hotel** (☎08-8088 5313; Layard St; ⏲9am-9pm) displays film memorabilia and a litany of miscellany typifying Australia's peculiar brand of larrikin humour. The replica Mad Max 'interceptor', which stood out the front for years, has moved next door.

It's hard to believe the tiny **Old Silverton Gaol** (adult/child $4/1; ⏲9.30am-4pm) housed 14 cells. Now it's a museum with photos and memorabilia of the early prison days. The **School Museum** (adult/child $2.50/1; ⏲9.30am-3.30pm Mon, Wed, Fri & Sat) is another history pit stop.

OUTBACK DUSK & DAWN

One of the most brilliant experiences at Broken Hill is a sunset or sunrise at the **Sculpture Symposium** (Nine Mile Rd; admission $5; ⏲6am-8.30pm) on the highest hilltop 9km from town. The sculptures are the work of 12 international artists who carved the huge sandstone blocks on site. The symposium is part of the 2400-hectare **Living Desert**, featuring a 2km cultural trail through protected native flora, a Sturt desert pea display, an Aboriginal story pole and picnic and barbecue area. You can drive up to the summit or park in the lower car park and climb up for 20 minutes.

Silverton Tea Rooms (☎08-8088 6601; mains $8; ⏲8am-5.30pm), with 'cafe' sprawled across the corrugated-iron roof, has a menu with staples such as Gun Shearers Pie, Bushman's Burger and quandong (a local native fruit) pie or ice cream. Next door, the **Mad Max 2 Museum** (adult/child $7.50/5; ⏲10am-4pm) is the culmination of Englishman Adrian Bennett's lifetime obsession with the theme.

Information

Visitor Centre (☎08-8088 7566) In the Beyond 39 Dips shop, a reference to the roller-coaster road from Broken Hill.

Getting There & Away

Silverton is 25km west of Broken Hill along a sealed road.

Mundi Mundi

The road beyond Silverton becomes isolated and the horizons vast almost immediately, but it's worth driving 5km to **Mundi Mundi Lookout** where the view over the Mundi Mundi Plain is so extensive it reveals the curvature of the Earth.

Mutawintji National Park

This exceptional 69,000-hectare park lies in the Byngnano Range – the eroded and sculptured remains of a 400-million-year-old seabed. Its stunning gorges and rock pools teem with wildlife, and the mulga plains here stretch to the horizon.

The Malyangapa and Bandjigali peoples have lived in the area for more than 8000 years, and there are important rock engravings, stencils, paintings and scattered remains of their day-to-day life. Most of these are only accessible via a guided tour – try **Silver City Tours** (☎08-8087 6956; www.silvercitytours.com.au; 380 Argent St) and Tri State Safaris (p236). The park brochure from the NPWS Office (p237) in Broken Hill includes a simple map and eight walks or drives through the park.

You can camp at **Homestead Creek** (adult/child $5/3), but you'll need to bring your own food.

In dry weather, the park is accessible in 2WD vehicles, but always come prepared and tell someone where you're travelling – a man died out here in 2012 when he became disoriented and strayed from his car. Check road-closure info on ☎08-8082 6660, ☎13 27 01 or ☎08-8091 5155.

Corner Country

Out here, it's a different world; both harsh and peaceful, stretching forever to the endless sky. This far-western corner of NSW is a semidesert of red plains, heat, dust and flies, a fascinating stretch of the outback that captures all the allure of the remote Australian bush.

Tibooburra

Tiny Tibooburra, the hottest town in the state, is a quintessential outback frontier town with two rough-around-the-edges

WORTH A TRIP

MENINDEE LAKES & KINCHEGA NATIONAL PARK

Menindee Lakes are a series of nine natural, ephemeral lakes adjacent to the Darling River; dead trees in the shallows make for some photogenic corners. There's a helpful **visitor centre** (☎08-8091 4274; www.menindeelakes.com; 27 Yartla St) in Menindee and **River Lady Tours** (☎0427 195 336; river.boat@bigpond.com; from $32.50 per person) has daytime cruises, sunset cruises and camp-oven dinner cruises, departing from Lake Wetherell weir.

Kinchega National Park (admission per car $7) is close to Menindee. There are three well-marked driving trails through the park or join the NPWS discovery tours (adult/child $10/5), including billy tea with Aboriginal elders. Accommodation is available at the **shearers' quarters** (adult/child $20/10), which can be booked at Broken Hill NPWS office (p237). There are also four riverside **camp sites** (adult/child $5/3). Just south of Kinchega National Park, glorious old **Bindara Station** (☎02-8091 7412; www.bindarastation.com; d half-board per person $95, cottage $110) is a working cattle property with B&B accommodation, camp sites, Jillaroos' quarters and a cottage.

sandstone pubs, a small drive-in cinema and a landscape of large red rock formations known as 'gibbers'. The **Keeping Place** (☎08-8091 3435) features indigenous artefacts and art from the Wadigali, Wangkumara and Malyangaba peoples. Ask at the visitor centre if it's not open.

Sturt National Park

North and northwest of Tibooburra, vast Sturt National Park encompasses 325,329 hectares of classic outback terrain. Just out of town in the park, glorious Mt Wood Historic Homestead provides the impetus for a real outback stay. Dead Horse Gully is a basic NPWS camping ground 1km north of town; you'll need to bring drinking water (as you should everywhere).

The park stretches northeast to Cameron Corner, reached by a well-signposted dirt road (allow two hours). A post marks the spot where Queensland, SA and NSW meet. In the Queensland corner, the vine-covered Cameron Corner Store has fuel, meals, accommodation and advice on road conditions.

Most tracks through the park are negotiable in a 2WD vehicle unless it has been raining. The only exception is Middle Rd, which is 4WD-only.

Sleeping & Eating

You can camp at **Mt Wood Homestead** (☎08-8091 3308; camping adult/child $5/3, cabin from $50), or try **Granites Motel & Caravan Park** (☎08-8091 3477; Brown St; unpowered/powered sites $6/18, cabins $55-90, motel s/d from $75/90), which has a range of accommodation options.

Information

NPWS Office (☎08-8091 3308; Briscoe St) Visit the large parks office with its adjoining Courthouse Museum.

Getting There & Away

The Silver City Hwy connects Tibooburra with Broken Hill (331km) via Milparinka. The road is a mixture of tarmac and unsealed – the road can be perilous (and even closed) after (rare) rains. Ask about road conditions at the visitor centre (p237) or NPWS Office (p237) in Broken Hill, or ring TJ's Roadhouse in Tibooburra on ☎08-8091 3477.

North of Tibooburra on the Silver City Hwy (Rte 79) it's mostly sealed but monstrous after rain. Along the Queensland border is the 5400km dingo-proof fence, patrolled daily by boundary riders.

White Cliffs

There are few stranger places in Australia than the tiny pock-marked opal-mining town of White Cliffs, located 93km northwest of Wilcannia. Surrounded by some of the harshest country the outback has to offer, many residents in this pot-holed landscape have moved underground to escape temperatures that soar to 50°C.

You can also try fossicking for the world-renowned local opals around the old diggings where you'll see interpretative signs, but watch the kids around those deep, unfenced holes.

East of town, **Paroo Darling National Park** covers 178,052 hectares and includes picturesque catchment from the Paroo and Darling Rivers. There's **camping** (adult/child $5/3) near the ruins of the Coach and Horses Pub.

Sleeping

PJ's Underground B&B B&B $$
(☎08-8091 6626; pjsunderground@bigpond.com; Dugout 72, Turley's Hill; s/d $130/170) This underground B&B is a clean and comfortable desert oasis with a serene garden. It also has a library, you can fossick for opals on the roof and it runs mine tours ($8 per person).

White Cliffs Underground Motel MOTEL $$
(☎08-8091 6677; www.undergroundmotel.com.au; r incl breakfast $135; @ ≋) This underground motel was custom-built with a tunnelling machine. It has wide corridors, a lively dining room and delightfully comfortable silent rooms. Claustrophobics can stay in the two above-ground rooms.

Information

NPWS Office (☎08-8083 7900; www.nationalparks.nsw.gov.au; Keraro St; tours adult/child $8/4)

Bourke

POP 2047

Australian poet Henry Lawson once said 'If you know Bourke, you know Australia'. Immortalised for Australians in the expression 'back of Bourke' (in the middle of nowhere), this town sits on the edge of the outback, miles from anywhere and sprawled along the Darling River. Crime can be a problem here, so keep a close eye on your valuables.

Sights

The impressive three-tiered wharf at the northern end of Sturt St is a faithful reconstruction of the original (built in 1897). Ask about paddlesteamer cruises at the **visitor centre** (02-6872 1222; www.visitbourke.com; Anson St; closed Sun summer). It also has an excellent leaflet called *Bourke Mud Map Tours*, detailing walks and drives in the area.

Contact the **NPWS office** (02-6872 2744; 51 Oxley St) for visits to the Aboriginal art sites at Gunderbooka National Park. There's camping at Dry Tank (adult/child $5/3) or try the shearer's quarters (doubles $80).

Back O' Bourke Exhibition Centre MUSEUM
(02-6872 1395; www.backobourke.com.au; Kidman Way; adult/child $20/10; 9am-4pm Mon-Fri) This worthwhile exhibition space follows the legends of the back country – both indigenous and settler – through interactive displays.

Bourke's Historic Cemetery CEMETERY
(Kidman Way) Bourke's cemetery is peppered with epitaphs saying 'perished in the bush'. Professor Fred Hollows, the internationally renowned eye surgeon, is buried here.

Sleeping & Eating

★ **Bourke Riverside Motel** MOTEL $$
(02-6872 2539; www.bourkeriversidemotel.com; 3 Mitchell St; s/d from $110/125;) An oasis in the desert, this rambling historic motel with an enchanting riverside garden has eclectic rooms with antique furniture and an array of good and bad artwork.

Morrall's Bakery BAKERY, CAFE $
(02-6872 2086; 37 Mitchell St; 6am-4pm Mon-Fri, to 2pm Sat) Tuck into a Back o' Bourke lamb pie, a drover's breakfast or a cappuccino here.

Getting There & Away

CountryLink (13 22 32; www.countrylink.info) buses run to Dubbo ($57, 4½ hours).

SOUTH COAST

If a road trip takes your fancy you've come to the right place. The south coast, breathtaking in the extreme, stretches 400km by road to the Victorian border through rolling dairy country, heritage towns, stunning national parks and rugged coastline. Though the main thoroughfare, the Princes Hwy (Rte 66), shadows the coast, the south coast is undoubtedly best experienced by dipping on and off the road well travelled. It's on the back roads and byways that isolated beaches, pristine camp sites and remote lighthouses reveal themselves.

The south coast's pit stops hold their own, too, among them the holiday-hectic, coastal hubs of Wollongong, Kiama, Batemans Bay, Narooma and Merimbula. Alternatively, put the brakes on the pace in the beautiful little beachside nooks of Jervis Bay, Bermagui and Eden, where the comforts of the city cater to a quieter crowd just as partial to a day's fishing as an espresso coffee. Inland, Kangaroo Valley manages to compete with its coastal counterparts with top-notch restaurants, heritage buildings and vineyards.

Whales are quite fond of the south coast, too, especially from September through to the end of November.

Wollongong

POP 245,942

The 'Gong', 80km south of Sydney, is the envy of many cities. Sure, it has restaurants, bars, arts, culture and entertainment, that's easy enough. But it also enjoys a laid-back, beachside lifestyle. Just to rub it in, Sydney is easily accessible by local rail.

There are 17 patrolled beaches and a spectacular sandstone escarpment that runs from the Royal National Park south past Wollongong and Port Kembla. The Grand Pacific Dr makes the most of the landscape and the whole combination makes for a host of outdoor activities: excellent surf, safe beaches, bushwalks and sky-high adventures to name a few. Our only complaint? Distant factories belching out smoke scar the middle distance along the main town beaches.

Sights

Wollongong's fishing fleet is based at the southern end of the harbour, **Belmore Basin**. There's a fishing cooperative here (with a fish market and a couple of cafes) and an 1872 **lighthouse** on the point. Nearby, on the headland, is the newer **Breakwater Lighthouse**.

Along the highway, **Nan Tien Buddhist Temple** (02-4272 0600; www.nantien.org.au; Berkeley Rd, Berkeley; 9am-5pm Tue-Sun) has

Wollongong

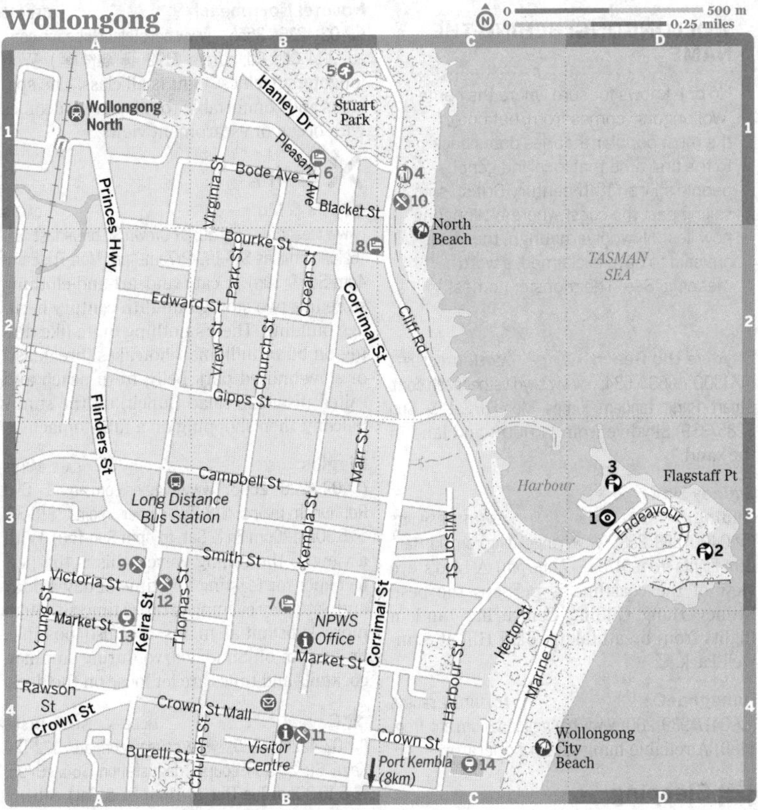

Wollongong

Sights
1 Belmore Basin D3
2 Breakwater Lighthouse D3
3 Old Lighthouse D3

Activities, Courses & Tours
4 Pines Surfing Academy C1
5 Skydive the Beach B1

Sleeping
6 Beach Park Motor Inn B1
7 Keiraleagh B3
8 Novotel Northbeach B2

Eating
9 Caveau A3
10 Diggies C1
11 Lee & Me B4
12 Lorenzo's Diner A3

Drinking & Nightlife
13 Hotel Illawarra A4
14 Illawarra Brewery C4

weekend retreats, vegetarian cooking classes, meditation and t'ai chi.

Activities

Taupu Surf School SURFING
(02-4268 0088; www.taupusurfschool.com; 1/3 lessons $65/160; Mon-Sat) Taupu Surf School runs courses at Thirroul and North Wollongong. Further south, Seven Mile Beach has surf camps.

Pines Surfing Academy SURFING
(pinessurfingacademy.com.au; North Beach; 3-day course $120, board hire 1/3hr $20/30; mid-Dec-late-Jan) Summer-only surf lessons.

WOLLONGONG: BEHIND THE NAME

No one knows for sure where the name 'Wollongong' comes from, but one of the most popular theories dates back to the first time that local indigenous people saw an 18th-century British ship sailing past the coast where Wollongong now lies. 'Nywoolyarngungh', the locals are said to have exclaimed, a word meaning 'See! The monster comes!'

Skydive the Beach ADVENTURE SPORTS
(☎1300 663 634; www.skydivethebeach.com; Stuart Park; tandem jumps Mon-Fri/Sat & Sun $285/339) Skydive from 14,000ft and land in the sand.

Sydney Hang Gliding Centre ADVENTURE SPORTS
(☎0400 258 258; www.hanggliding.com.au; tandem flights from $175; ⊙7am-7pm) A bird's eye view of the coastline is perhaps the best. Sydney Hang Gliding Centre has tandem flights from breathtaking Bald Hill at Stanwell Park.

HanggIideOz ADVENTURE SPORTS
(☎0417 939 200; www.hangglideoz.com.au; from $180) A reliable hang-gliding operator.

Sleeping

Coledale Beach Camping Reserve CAMPGROUND $
(☎02-4267 4302; www.coledalebeach.com.au; Beach Rd; unpowered/powered sites from $25/32) Small and right on the beach, this is one of the best urban camping spots on the coast.

Keiraleagh HOSTEL $
(☎02-4228 6765; www.backpack.net.au; 60 Kembla St; dm/s/d from $20/45/65; @ 🛜) This rambling heritage house is clogged with atmosphere, with pressed metal ceilings, roses in the cornices and festively painted rooms. The basic dorms are out the back, along with a sizeable Balinese-inspired garden and a BBQ.

Beach Park Motor Inn HOTEL $$
(☎02-4226 1577; www.beachparkmotorinn.com.au; 16 Pleasant Ave; r $88-185; ❄ 🛜) The friendly owners keep the slightly twee rooms in this white-brick establishment spick and span. It's in an urban setting, a short walk from the beach.

Novotel Northbeach HOTEL $$$
(☎02-4226 3555; www.novotelnorthbeach.com.au; 2-14 Cliff Rd; r from $199; ❄ @ 🛜 🏊) Wollongong's flashiest joint is all class. The spacious and comfortable rooms have balconies with ocean or escarpment views.

Eating

★**Lee & Me** CAFE $
(www.leeandme.com.au; 87 Crown St; breakfast $11-16, lunch mains $13-19; ⊙7am-4pm Mon-Fri, 8am-4pm Sat & Sun) A cafe and art-and-clothing store in a two-storey, late-19th-century heritage building. There's nothing quite like dining on buttermilk malt hotcakes (breakfast) or slow-braised pork belly, fresh peach and salted pistachio salad (lunch) on the sunny balcony, then shopping on a full stomach.

Diggies CAFE, BAR $$
(☎02-4226 2688; www.diggies.com.au; 1 Cliff Rd; lunch mains $18-25, dinner mains $18-32; ⊙6.30am-10pm Fri & Sat, to 4pm Sun-Thu) With a view to the rolling waves, this is the perfect spot for feasting any time of day. Friday and Saturday evening is tapas time although more substantial mains are also possible. From 4pm on Sunday arvo during summer, cocktails and tunes are let loose on the deck.

★**Caveau** MODERN AUSTRALIAN $$$
(☎02-4226 4855; www.caveau.com.au; 122-124 Keira St; 2-/3-/7-course degustation $64/79/95; ⊙6-10.30pm Tue-Thu, to 11pm Fri & Sat) Sitting unpretentiously on Keira St, this lauded restaurant washed in a soft amber glow serves gourmet treats such as roasted lobster tails or scallop gnocchi.

Lorenzo's Diner ITALIAN $$$
(☎02-4229 5633; www.lorenzosdiner.com.au; 119 Keira St; mains $38-45; ⊙noon-2.30pm & 6-9pm Thu & Fri, 6-9pm Tue, Wed & Sat) Seriously nice people run this upmarket modern Italian restaurant. The food (try the risotto di mare) matches the excellent service. Bookings are recommended.

Drinking & Nightlife

Hotel Illawarra PUB
(www.hotelillawarra.com.au; cnr Market & Keira Sts; ⊙11am-late) Best suited to the cocktail-sipping funky set, this complex has the red-hued Amber bar and Cucina Illawarra, which dishes up Mediterranean fare, tapas-style. It has a generous 5pm to 9pm happy hour.

Illawarra Brewery BAR
(www.brewery.net; WIN Entertainment Centre, cnr Crown & Harbour Sts; ⌚11am-midnight Mon-Thu, 10am-1am Fri & Sat, 10am-midnight Sun) This slick bar has six house beers on tap, plus one that changes every season. It's also opened up its taps to other microbreweries from across the country and the result is a fabulous array of beers. It also serves bistro-style meals.

Information

NPWS Office (☎02-4223 3000; Market St, ground fl, State Government Office Block; ⌚9am-3pm Mon-Fri)

Visitor Centre (☎1800 240 737; www.visitwollongong.com.au; 93 Crown St; ⌚9am-5pm Mon-Sat, 10am-4pm Sun)

Wollongong Visitors Centre (☎02-4227 5545; www.visitwollongong.com.au) Located 20 minutes from the CBD on the Princes Hwy at Bulli Tops. Books accommodation.

Getting There & Away

All long-distance buses leave from the **long distance bus station** (☎02-4226 1022; cnr Keira & Campbell Sts).

➡ **Premier** (☎13 34 10; www.premierms.com.au) has buses to Sydney ($18, two hours) and Eden ($69, eight hours).

➡ **Murrays** (☎13 22 51; www.murrays.com.au) travels to Canberra ($41, 3½ hours).

Getting Around

Bringing a bike on the train from Sydney is a great way to get around; a cycle path runs from the city centre north to Bulli and south to Port Kembla.

For taxis, call ☎02-4229 9311.

Wollongong to Nowra

This region has some great beaches, state forests and, in the ranges to the west, the big **Morton National Park**. **Lake Illawarra** is popular for water sports.

Kiama & Around

Right on the water's edge with good beaches and surf, Kiama hasn't had to work hard for its share of glory. What it has done is admirable and tasteful, making this one of the best stops on the south coast. The visitor centre is on Blowhole Point, so called because of a **blowhole** that can spurt water 60m.

Sights & Activities

There's a good **lookout** from the top of Saddleback Mountain, and waves at **Surf** and **Bombo Beaches**. A new 6km **coastal walk** with the requisite boulders, beaches, sea caves and cliff faces stretches from Love's Bay in Kiama Heights to the north end of Werri Beach.

Amid the flora and fauna of the Southern Highlands, about 14km inland from Kiama, the fabulous **Illawarra Fly Tree Top Walk** (☎1300 362 881; www.illawarrafly.com.au; 182 Knights Hill Rd, Knights Hill; adult/child/family $24/10/59; ⌚9am-5pm) takes visitors on a 500m elevated walk to the edge of the forest with spectacular Illawarra and ocean views.

Near the tree top walk, the **Minnamurra Rainforest Centre** has two stunning nature walks and a **NPWS visitor centre** (☎02-4236 0469) in beautiful **Budderoo National Park** (www.environment.nsw.gov.au; per car $11). On the way you'll pass through the old village of **Jamberoo**, which has a nice pub.

Sleeping & Eating

Grand Hotel PUB $
(☎02-4232 1037; www.grandhotelkiama.com.au; 49 Manning St; per person from $49) The Grand caters to backpackers with basic but clean rooms with shared bathrooms.

Bellevue GUESTHOUSE $$
(☎02-4232 4000; bellevueaccommodation.com.au; 21 Minnamurra St; r from $140) This charming house hosts guests in luxury serviced

> **SURFING NORTH BEACH & WOLLONGONG CITY BEACH**
>
> **North Beach** and **Wollongong City Beach** have breaks suitable for all visitors and are walking distance from the city centre. Look for the Acids Reef break on North Beach for more of a challenge. Up the coast, the options are varied and less crowded, with fun beach breaks at **Coledale** and **Bulli** beaches, and reef breaks at **Sharkies** (also at Coledale) and **Headlands**. The risk of meeting a finned friend at Sharkies is minimal, but surfers have occasionally encountered humpback whales surfacing close to shore. Check out www.wannasurf.com for a full rundown on local waves and a five-day forecast.

DON'T MISS

HERE'S TO THE VIEW

Built in 1886 and now heritage-listed, the grand old **Scarborough Hotel** (www.thescarboroughhotel.com.au; 383 Lawrence Hargrave Dr, Scarborough; ⏲9am-5pm Mon-Thu, 8.30am-9pm Fri & Sat, 8.30am-6pm Sun) has recently been renovated, reopened and reinvigorated so that punters can once again take advantage of one of the best beer gardens in New South Wales, if not Australia. The ocean view from the wooden bench seats and tables is so spectacular it wouldn't matter if the beer was warm. It's not, thankfully, and the gastro food (mains $15 to $35) gets the thumbs up too.

apartments in a two-storey 1890s heritage manor. It has ocean views and is a short walk to the main street. Rates rise appreciably on weekends.

★**Kiama Harbour Cabins** CABINS $$$
(☎02-4232 2707; Blowhole Point; 1/2/3-bedroom cabins from $210/225/285; ❄) These are in the best position in town and have barbecues on the front verandahs, which overlook the beach and the ocean pool. The cabins themselves are attractive.

Chachi's ITALIAN $$
(☎02-4233 1144; www.chachisrestaurant.com.au; 32 Collins St; mains $14-31; ⏲noon-2pm & 5.30-9pm Wed-Fri, 5.30-9pm Mon, Tue & Sat) Located in a historic strip of terraced houses, Chachi's is well loved among locals for its casual Italian alfresco dining and menu that changes with the seasons.

Information

Visitor Centre (☎02-4232 3322, 1300 654 262; www.kiama.com.au; Blowhole Point Rd; ⏲9am-5pm)

Getting There & Away

Premier (☎13 34 10; www.premierms.com.au) buses run twice daily to Berry ($18, 30 minutes), Eden ($69, six hours) and Sydney ($25, 2½ hours). **Kiama Coachlines** (☎02-4232 3466; www.kiamacoachlines.com.au) runs to Gerroa, Gerringong and Minnamurra (via Jamberoo).

Frequent **CityRail** (☎13 15 00; www.cityrail.info) trains run to Wollongong, Sydney and Bomaderry/Nowra.

Berry

POP 1690

Berry has metamorphosed from a small retiree kind of town into a popular inland south-coast stop. Is the chintz outweighing the heritage character these days? You decide. For information, try www.berry.net.au.

Sleeping & Eating

Hotel Berry HOTEL $
(☎02-4464 1011; www.berryhotel.com.au; 120 Queen St; s $50-75, d $80-100) This popular local watering hole has standard but large pub bedrooms. Its rear dining room serves grilled steaks and other pub grub. It organises short tours of local wineries.

Village Boutique MOTEL $$
(☎02-4464 3570; www.berrymotel.com.au; 72 Queen St; r $160-240; ❄📶🏊) Stylish rooms (some with a spa). The pool is more water-feature size.

Berry Woodfired Sourdough BAKERY $
(Prince Alfred St; mains $6-15; ⏲7am-4pm Wed-Sun) Delicious bread is baked here, or sit down for a light meal.

Hungry Duck ASIAN FUSION $$
(☎02-4464 2323; hungryduck.com.au; 85 Queen St; mains $17-34; ⏲6-9.30pm Wed-Mon) 🍃 Has a contemporary Asian menu served tapas-style. Try the tempura alpaca tenderloin or crab ravioli. Book ahead.

Getting There & Away

There are scenic roads from Berry to pretty Kangaroo Valley. **Premier** (☎13 34 10; www.premierms.com.au) has buses to Kiama ($18, 30 minutes), Nowra ($18, 25 minutes) and Sydney ($25, three hours, twice daily).

Frequent **CityRail** (☎131 500; www.cityrail.info) trains go to Wollongong ($6.60, 1¼ hours) from **Berry station** (☎02-4464 1022; Station Rd), with connections to Sydney.

Kangaroo Valley

POP 298

Unbelievably picturesque Kangaroo Valley is pegged in by a fortress of rainforest-covered cliffs and the valley floor is carpeted by pasturelands, river gums and gurgling creeks. The slow country town of Kangaroo Valley itself has an excellent pub, a bakery and a general store, plus the odd feel-good shop and gallery to satiate wealthy Sydneysiders who populate the town at the weekend.

The formal entry to the valley is the iron-and-sandstone **Hamden Bridge** (1898), a few kilometres north of the town. The beach just below the bridge is a good for a swim.

Sights & Activities

Pioneer Museum Park MUSEUM
(☎02-4465 1306; www.kangaroovalleymuseum.com.au; Moss Vale Rd, Hampden Bridge; adult/child $7/5; ⏲10am-4pm Fri-Mon Oct-Easter, 11am-3pm Fri-Mon Easter-Sep) Next to the bridge, the walkabout Pioneer Museum Park provides a visual encounter with rural life in the late 19th century.

Kangaroo Valley Explorer HIKING
(www.kvexplorer.com.au) information on self-guided walks in the region, including in the neighbouring Morton National Park and a 'Historic Walk' around the town itself.

Flavours of the Valley COOKING CLASS
(☎02-4465 2010; www.flavoursofthevalley.com.au; per person from $130) Mediterranean cooking classes and a range of tempting foodie experiences; it's signposted off the road to Bendeela picnic spot.

Kangaroo Valley Adventure Co ADVENTURE SPORTS
(☎02-4465 1372; www.kvac.com.au; Glenmack Park Camp Site) Combined hiking and biking (half-day $60), canoeing and camping (overnight from $75) and biking, hiking and kayaking (full day $100).

Kangaroo Valley Safaris ADVENTURE SPORTS
(☎02-4465 1502; www.kangaroovalleycanoes.com.au; 2210 Moss Vale Rd) Kangaroo Valley Safaris rents canoes and kayaks (per day $35 to $140) and runs overnight canoe ($105) and sea-kayak ($140) camping trips.

Sleeping

For a bush-camping experience head north out of town to **Bendeela picnic spot**. It's signed.

Glenmack Park CARAVAN PARK, CAMPGROUND $
(☎02-4465 1372; www.glenmack.com.au; 215 Moss Vale Rd; unpowered/powered sites $12/28, cabins $55-150) There's a carpet of grass to pitch a tent on at Glenmack Park or take the more comfortable option of a cabin. You can light a campfire (such a rarity!).

Kangaroo Valley Holiday Cabins CABINS $$
(☎02-4465 1628; www.bigbellfarm.com.au; 1666 Kangaroo Valley Rd; cabins $85-250) Simple cabins sleeping four on a 24-acre farm.

Hamden Cottage B&B $$$
(☎02-4465 1502; www.kangaroovalleyaccommodation.com.au; 2210 Moss Vale Rd; d incl breakfast Mon-Thu/Fri-Sun $210/265) Near the Hamden Bridge, the pretty little Hamden Cottage has a rear garden that attracts wallabies and has classy rooms with dark-wood furnishings.

Cloud Song B&B $$$
(☎02-4465 1194; www.cloudsonginkangaroovalley.com.au; 170 Moss Vale Rd; d from $220) Beautifully designed modern cabins with open fireplaces and some with balconies. It's just off the main road right in the centre of town.

Minimbah Farm Cottages GUESTHOUSE $$$
(☎02-4465 1056; www.minimbah.com.au; 48 Nugents Creek Rd; r $270-420) Sleep eight to 13 people in the hills 1.5km from the village.

Eating

Jing Jo MODERN AUSTRALIAN, THAI $$
(☎02-4465 1314; 2038 Moss Vale Rd; mains $13-25; ⏲10am-2.30am & 6-9pm Thu & Fri, from 9am Sat & Sun) Thoughtfully prepared Aussie dishes for lunch and authentic Thai cuisine at night – it's a winning combination at this attractive, wide-verandah-ed place just across the bridge from the main village.

Friendly Inn Hotel PUB $$
(☎02-4465 1355; 159 Moss Vale Rd; mains $15-23; ⏲11.30am-9pm) This is Kangaroo Valley's heartbeat, a classic country boozer, ever-so-subtly renovated to retain its local character. The rear grassy beer garden has gorgeous views, or sit on the sunny pub verandah to people watch.

Café Bella CAFE $$
(151 Moss Vale Rd; mains $9-21; ⏲noon-2.30pm Thu, 6.30-9.30pm Fri-Sun) A few doors up from the pub, Café Bella has books, nooks and crannies and is a homely place for no-fuss cafe cooking.

Getting There & Away

Kennedy's Bus Service (☎1300 133 477; www.kennedystours.com.au) Daily buses to Moss Vale via Fitzroy Falls, and Nowra via Cambewarra.

Nowra

POP 27,988

Nowra, around 17km from the coast, is the largest town in the Shoalhaven area. Although there are prettier beach towns, it's a handy base for excursions to beaches and villages around the region.

Sights

The relaxing **Ben's Walk** starts at the bridge near Scenic Dr and follows the south bank of the Shoalhaven River (6km return). North of the river, the circular 5.5km **Bomaderry Creek Walking Track** runs through sandstone gorges from a trailhead at the end of Narang Rd.

For surfing information, pick up the *Shoalhaven Surfing Guide* from the visitor centre – it describes 17 surfing spots along the coast.

Nowra Wildlife Park WILDLIFE RESERVE
(02-4421 3949; www.nowrawildlifepark.com.au; Rock Hill Rd, North Nowra; adult/child $18/10; 9am-5pm) The 6.5-hectare Nowra Wildlife Park, on the north bank of the Shoalhaven River, is a hang-out for mammals, birds and reptiles.

Shoalhaven City Arts Centre GALLERY
(www.shoalhavenartscentre.com.au; 12 Berry St; 10am-4pm Tue-Fri, 11am-3pm Sat) FREE Excellent local gallery with well-known artists such as Arthur Boyd, some Aboriginal artists and lesser-known names, as well as good temporary exhibitions.

WORTH A TRIP

SURF & TURF

East of Nowra, the Shoalhaven River meanders through dairy country in a system of estuaries and wetlands, finally reaching the sea at Crookhaven Heads, aka Crooky, where there's good surf. **Greenwell Point**, on the estuary about 15km east of Nowra, is a quiet, pretty fishing village specialising in **fresh oysters**. The little kiosk near the pier has fish and chips. Just north of the surf beach here is stunning **Seven Mile Beach National Park** stretching up to **Gerroa**. It's an idyllic picnic spot.

Just before Shoalhaven Heads you pass through **Coolangatta**, the site of the earliest European settlement on this coast. **Coolangatta Estate** (02-4448 7131; www.coolangattaestate.com.au; r from $140; winery 10am-5pm) is a slick winery with a golf course, a good restaurant and accommodation in convict-era buildings.

Shoalhaven River Cruises CRUISE
(0429 981 007; www.shoalhavenrivercruise.com; 2-/3hr cruise $29/44) Shoalhaven River Cruises has tours either up (two hours) or down (three to 3½ hours) the beautiful Shoalhaven River, leaving from the wharf just east of the bridge. Check the website for times.

Sleeping & Eating

George Bass Motor Inn MOTEL $$
(02-4421 6388; www.georgebass.com.au; 65 Bridge Rd; s/d from $109/129;) An unpretentious but well-appointed single-storey motor inn, the George Bass has clean and sunny rooms. The more expensive ones are slightly newer.

Whitehouse GUESTHOUSE $$
(02-4421 2084; www.whitehouseguesthouse.com; 30 Junction St; d/tr from $102/151;) Whitehouse is a homely and family-friendly guesthouse.

Red Raven MODERN AUSTRALIAN $$
(02-4423 3433; 55 Junction St; mains $21-32; 11.30am-2.30pm & 6pm-late Tue-Fri, 6pm-late Sat) In an old fire brigade building, Red Raven dishes up distinctly Aussie flavours such as roasted kangaroo fillets with polenta chips.

Information

NPWS Office (02-4423 2170; 55 Graham St)
Shoalhaven Visitor Centre (1300 662 808; www.shoalhavenholidays.com.au; Princes Hwy; 9am-5pm) Just south of Nowra bridge.

Getting There & Away

Premier (13 34 10; www.premierms.com.au) coaches stop on the run between Sydney ($25, three hours), via Berry ($18, 20 minutes), and Melbourne ($82, 14 hours), via Ulladulla ($18, one hour).

The train station is 3km north of town at Bomaderry. Frequent **City Rail** (131 500; www.cityrail.info) trains go to Wollongong ($8.40, 1¼ hours) via Berry ($4.40, 10 minutes), with connections to Sydney.

Jervis Bay

South of Nowra, Jervis Bay is a scenically opulent and unmissable stretch of coastline with white sandy beaches, bushland, forest and a protected marine park. **Huskisson** (population 1593), one of the oldest towns on the bay, is the main hub. It has a handful of excellent eating venues, delightful surrounds and plenty of adventure-based activity that make it a great place to spend a night or two.

Sights & Activities

Lady Denman Heritage Complex MUSEUM
(02-4441 5675; www.ladydenman.asn.au; Dent St; adult/child $10/5; 10am-4pm) This complex has interesting history on Jervis Bay, a maritime museum and a small visitor centre. On the first Saturday of each month it hosts a **growers market**.

Dolphin Watch Cruises BOAT TOUR, WILDLIFE
(02-441 6311; www.dolphinwatch.com.au; 50 Owen St; dolphin-/whale-/seal-watching tour $35/60/80) This place has the best reputation for dolphin-watching tours and whale-watching tours (June to November), with trips also to nearby seal cliffs.

Dive Jervis Bay DIVING & SNORKELLING
(02-4441 5255; www.divejervisbay.com; 64 Owen St; 1/2 dives $100/170) A reliable diving operator.

Hire Au Go-Go CYCLING
(02-4441 5241; hireaugogo.com; 1 Tomerong St; 1hr/day $19/60) Electric bike for exploring pathways around the water's edge.

Jervis Bay Kayaks KAYAKING
(02-4441 7157; www.jervisbaykayaks.com; 13 Hawke St; 3hr/1-day kayak hire $60/75, guided half-/full-day tour $96/150) Kayak rental in Huskisson.

JB Surf School SURFING
(0449 266 994; www.jbsurfschool.com.au; group/private lessons per person from $50/90) Surf classes at Jervis Bay and Sussex Inlet.

Jervis Bay Eco Adventures BOAT TOURS
(www.jervisbayecoadventures.com.au; 58 Owen St, Huskisson; per adult $55-85, per child $30-45; tours 10.30am & 1pm) Two-hour boat trips around Jervis Bay.

Sleeping & Eating

Jervis Bay is close enough to Sydney to get an influx of weekenders.

★ **Paperbark Camp** CAMPGROUND $$$
(1300 668 167; www.paperbarkcamp.com.au; 571 Woollamia Rd; s/d from $325/370; closed mid-Jun-Aug) Ecotourism at its luxury best: this five-star accommodation includes 12 safari-style tents with outdoor showers, plus **Gunyah Restaurant** (02-4441 7299; mains $35; dinner), which sits among the treetops.

DON'T MISS

BOODEREE NATIONAL PARK

Occupying Jervis Bay's southeastern spit, this stunning **park** (www.booderee.gov.au; 2-day car or motorcycle entry $10) combines heathland, small rainforest pockets, sparkling water, white sandy beaches and a botanic garden. In 1995 the Wreck Bay Aboriginal community won a land claim and now jointly administers the vast park. There are walks aplenty, basic camp sites and beaches, as well as a botanical garden containing coastal plant species once used for food and medicine by local indigenous groups. Get maps and information about other indigenous sites within the park from **Booderee visitor centre** (02-4443 0977; www.booderee.gov.au; Jervis Bay Rd) at the park entrance.

Huskisson B&B B&B $$$
(02-4441 7551; www.huskissonbnb.com.au; 12 Tomerong St; r $195-245;) A cute weatherboard with bright and airy eclectic rooms containing comfy beds and fluffy towels.

Supply CAFE $
(02-4441 5815; www.supplyjervisbay.com.au; shop 1, 54 Owen St; mains $12-17; 7.30am-5pm Mon-Sat, to 3pm Sun) The fresh and healthy fodder (think fresh sandwiches and a fine caesar salad) and juices found here are echoed in the floor-to-ceiling shelves of produce.

★ **Seagrass Brasserie** SEAFOOD $$$
(02-4441 6124; www.seagrass.net.au; 13 Currambene St; mains $34.50; 6-9pm) With its wooden louver windows and white tablecloths, this eatery combines indoor and outdoor deck dining. Seafood with Asian ingredients is a stand out, so too the bloody Mary oyster shots.

Wild Ginger ASIAN $$
(02-4441 5577; www.wild-ginger.com.au; 42 Owen St; mains $31.50; 4.30pm-late Tue-Sun) From the same people who brought you Seagrass Brasserie, this exciting new venture draws its inspiration primarily from Thailand but you'll also come across dishes from Japan and Southeast Asia.

Getting There & Around

Jervis Bay Territory (4423 5244) runs a bus around Jervis Bay communities, and from Huskisson to Nowra three times every weekday and once on Saturday and Sunday. **Nowra Coaches** (☎02-4423 5244; www.nowracoaches.com.au) runs a bus (route 733) around Jervis Bay and to Nowra (70 minutes) on Tuesdays and Fridays.

Around Jervis Bay

Ulladulla itself doesn't have much to offer, but there is good swimming and surfing nearby at **Mollymook beach**, just north of town.

★**Cupitt's Winery & Restaurant** (☎02-4455 7888; www.cupittwines.com.au; 60 Washburton Rd, Ulladulla; mains $32-38; ⊙noon-2.30pm Wed, Thu & Sun, noon-2.30pm & 6-8.30pm Fri & Sat) is a little piece of Provence that offers some of the most respected cuisine this side of Sydney. Wine tasting is in the restored 1851 creamery, creative dishes capture the essence of coastal Australia and there's boutique accommodation in the vineyard.

Batemans Bay

POP 11,334

The good beaches and a luscious estuary in this fishing port have given it a leg-up to become one of the south coast's largest holiday centres. But the town and waterfront are lacklustre, and the food scene is yet to take off.

Sights & Activities

Corrigans Beach is the closest patch of sand to the town centre. South of here is a series of small beaches nibbled into the rocky shore. Surfers flock to **Surf Beach**, **Malua Bay** and **Broulee**, which has a small wave when everywhere else is flat. For the experienced, the best surfing in the area is at **Pink Rocks** (near Broulee).

The visitor centre has pamphlets and advice on walks in the area.

Mogo Zoo ZOO
(☎02-4474 4855; www.mogozoo.com.au; 222 Tomakin Rd, Mogo; adult/child $28/15; ⊙9am-5pm) Around 10km south of Batemans Bay, this good zoo has a white lion, tigers, cheetahs and snow leopards, as well as the odd kangaroo.

Soulrider Surf School SURFING
(☎02-4478 6297; www.soulrider.com.au; 1hr adult/child $45/40) Good surf school with a range of packages.

Surf the Bay Surf School SURFING
(☎0432 144 220; www.surfthebay.com.au; group/private lesson $40/75) Surfing lessons at Bateman's Bay and Broulee.

Broulee Surf School SURFING
(☎02-4471 7370; www.brouleesurfschool.com.au; adult/child $45/40) Experienced surf school just down the coast at Broulee.

Total Eco Adventures WATER SPORTS
(☎02-4471 6969; www.totalecoadventures.com.au; 7/77 Coronation Drive, Broulee) Kayaking, snorkelling, stand-up paddling and surfing.

Merinda Cruises CRUISE
(☎02-4472 4052; Boatshed, Clyde St; 3hr cruise adult/child $28/15; ⊙11.30am) Cruises up the Clyde River estuary from the ferry wharf just east of the bridge. No credit cards.

Region X KAYAKING
(☎0400 184 034; www.seakayakingnsw.com.au; kayak rental for 1/2/3hr $20/30/40, tours $60-125) Rent a kayak to explore nearby waterways.

Bay & Beyond KAYAKING
(☎02-4478 7777; www.bayandbeyond.com.au; kayak tours per person $50-120) Guided kayak trips along the coast and into the nearby estuaries.

Sleeping

One quirky alternative to traditional forms of accommodation is to gather your mates and hire a houseboat. Try four-bedroom **Bay River Houseboats** (☎02-4472 5649; www.bayriverhouseboats.com.au; Wray St; 4 nights from $650), or **Clyde River Houseboats** (☎02-4472 6369; www.clyderiverhouseboats.com.au; 3 nights $700-1350), which leases six-/10-berth boats.

Shady Willow Holiday Park HOSTEL, CARAVAN PARK $
(☎02-4472 6111; www.shadywillows.com.au; cnr South St & Old Princes Hwy; powered sites $26, dm/d $28/58, caravan from $58; ❄📶🏊) YHA set amid static caravans and shady palms, with a boho ambience.

Lincoln Downs HOTEL $$
(☎1800 789 250; www.lincolndowns.com.au; Princes Hwy; r from $115; ❄📶🏊) Excellent motel-style rooms, many of which overlook a private lake. There's also a resident peacock.

Clyde River Motor Inn MOTEL $$
(☎02-4472 6444; www.clydemotel.com.au; 3 Clyde St; s $95-140, d $99-140; ❄📶🏊) This central

WORTH A TRIP

PIGEON HOUSE MOUNTAIN

Climbing Pigeon House Mountain (720m) in the far south of Morton National Park is one of the south coast's most rewarding hikes.

The main access road leaves the highway about 8km south of Ulladulla, then it's a rough and rocky 26km drive to the picnic area at the start of the track. The return walk takes three to four hours but plan for longer; the summit is barbaric-yawp territory where the rest of the world rolls out from under your feet in all directions.

On a clear day, Gulaga (Mt Dromedary) sticks its head up in the south and to the northwest is Point Perpendicular. In between, a canopy of stunning national park vegetation spreads out like a blanket, occasionally making creases in the steep gorges carved by the Clyde River and flattening out over the elongated plateaus of Byangee Walls and the Castle.

People with a fear of heights should avoid the final section; and be sure to take water.

motel is excellent value, with good river rooms and townhouses, and up to three-bedroom apartments.

Eating

★Innes Boatshed FISH & CHIPS $

(1 Clyde St; fish & chips $13; 9am-9pm Wed-Mon, to 3pm Tue) Around since the 1950s, this is one of the best-loved fish-and-chip joints on the south coast. It also does sushi and oysters, and has some fine tables out the back on the decking.

North St CAFE & BAR $

(02-4472 5710; 5 North St; mains $10-18; 8am-4pm Sun-Thu, 8am-late Fri & Sat) This refreshingly funky little den has decent coffee and a tasty selection of breakfasts, salads, sandwiches and light lunches. It's a neat place for a wine, too.

Blank Canvas MODERN AUSTRALIAN $$

(02-4472 5016; www.blankcanvasrestaurant.com.au; Annetts Arcade, Orient St; mains $15.50-23.50; noon-9pm Wed-Mon) Right on the water and with funky couches indoors, this cafe by day morphs into a more intimate dining experience in the evening. Try the coconut king prawn cocktail or the blue swimmer crab roulade. The restaurant is a block west of Orient St, from where it's signposted.

Starfish Deli AUSTRALIAN $$

(02-4472 4880; starfishdeli.com.au; 1 Clyde St; lunch mains $16-23, dinner mains $23-34; 9am-9pm) Fish and chips, mussels and wood-fired pizzas are the mainstays here at this waterfront place that seems to attract every hungry diner in town. Unless you don't mind waiting, booking ahead is a good idea for lunch and dinner in summer.

On the Pier SEAFOOD $$$

(02-4472 6405; onthepier.com.au; 2 Old Punt Rd; mains $28-35; 6-10pm Mon & Tue, noon-2.30pm & 6-10pm Thu-Sun) Batemans Bay's most celebrated restaurant and with dishes such as crispy skinned pork belly and grilled scallops it's not hard to see why.

Information

Visitor Centre (1800 802 528; Princes Hwy; 9am-5pm) Has local art for sale.

Getting There & Away

Murrays (13 22 51; www.murrays.com.au) services Batemans Bay with daily services to Canberra ($27, 2½ hours) and Narooma ($22, two hours). **Premier** (13 34 10; www.premierms.com.au) coaches stop here en route to/from Sydney ($45, six hours), Eden ($46, 3½ hours) and Wollongong ($43, four hours).

Narooma

POP 2409

Narooma is a sleepy little seaside town with a large number of retiree residents adding to its snail-paced leisurely atmosphere. It's also one of the prettier coastal towns, boasting the attractive Wagonga River inlet, a picturesque bridge and relatively little development.

Sights & Activities

Narooma is an access point for Deua, Gulaga and Wadbilliga National Parks.

Mystery Bay, between Cape Dromedary and Corunna Point, is rocky but good for surfing, as is **Handkerchief Beach**. More relaxing swims can be had at the south end of **Bar Beach**. On the other side of the Wagonga inlet entrance, 400m as the crow flies, **Bar Rock Lookout** has views of Montague Island. The clear waters around the island are good for diving, especially from February to June when you can snorkel with the fur seals.

Mills Bay Boardwalk WALKING
Heading north over the bridge, take the first two right turns to this 5km wheelchair- and pram-friendly track where you can spot seabirds, large schools of fish and stingrays.

Island Charters Narooma DIVING, WHALE WATCHING
(☎02-44761047; www.islandchartersnarooma.com; Bluewater Dr) This popular company offers diving ($95), snorkelling ($75) and whale watching (adult/child $77/60). Attractions in the area include grey nurse sharks, fur seals and the wreck of the SS *Lady Darling*. Book tours at the visitor centre.

Wagonga Princess CRUISE
(☎02-4476 2665; www.wagongainletcruises.com; adult/child $35/25; ⏲3hr cruise departs 1pm Sun, Wed & Fri Feb-Dec, daily Jan) Cruise on this century-old electric ferry up the Wagonga River.

Narooma Bike Hire BICYCLE RENTAL
(☎0403 157 290; 8 Noorooma Cres; half-/full-day hire $25/40) Bike rental for exploring the coast at reasonable prices.

Sleeping

Narooma YHA HOSTEL $
(☎02-4476 3287; www3.yha.com.au; 243 Princes Hwy; dm/d from $26/62; @) A YHA stalwart, this place has comfortable, clean motel-style rooms and fun hosts.

Horizon Holiday Apartments APARTMENTS $$
(☎02-4476 5200; www.horizonapartmentsnarooma.com.au; 147 Princes Hwy; 1-/2-bedroom apt from $119/179) Clean-lined modern apartments, some with partial ocean views.

Whale Motor Inn MOTEL $$
(☎02-4476 2411; www.whalemotorinn.com; 104 Wagonga St; d $125-215; ❄📶🏊) This place offers the best all-round views of Narooma and it's easily the pick of Narooma's motels. It has large, clean renovated rooms with balconies, and an excellent restaurant.

Eating

Taylor's Seafood FISH & CHIPS $
(Riverside Dr; mains $7-16; ⏲lunch & dinner Tue-Sun) Taylor's does Narooma's best fish and chips down by the water.

Quarterdeck Marina SEAFOOD $$
(13 Riverside Dr; mains $22; ⏲8am-3pm Thu-Mon) With its colourful, eclectic decor, Quarterdeck serves ah-me-hearties breakfasts and fresh seafood lunches on a great enclosed deck overhanging the river.

Na Siam THAI $$
(☎02-4476 5002; 1/26 Princes Hwy; mains $15-20; ⏲noon-2.30pm & 5-9.30pm Tue-Sun, open every day Dec-Apr) Better-than-average Thai cuisine on the main road through town.

Information

NPWS Office (☎02-4476 0800; www.nationalparks.nsw.gov.au; cnr Graham & Burrawang Sts)

Visitor Centre (☎02-4476 2881, 1800 240 003; www.eurobodalla.com.au; Princes Hwy; ⏲9am-5pm)

Getting There & Around

Premier (☎13 34 10; www.premierms.com.au) has buses to Eden ($41, 2½ hours), and to Sydney ($58, seven hours) via Wollongong ($56, five hours). Buses stop outside Lynch's Hotel. **Murrays** (☎13 22 51; www.murrays.com.au)runs to Batemans Bay ($20, two hours) and Canberra ($41.20, 4½ hours).

Around Narooma

On the Princes Hwy is **Cobargo**, an unspoilt old town. Near here is the main 2WD access point to rugged Wadbilliga National Park, a subalpine wilderness area of 98,530 hectares.

Montague Island

Around 10km offshore from Narooma, Montague Island was once an important source of food for local Aboriginal people (who called it Barunguba) and is now a nature reserve. Little penguins nest here; the best time to see them is spring. Many other seabirds and hundreds of fur seals also call the island home, and there's a historic lighthouse.

Montague Island Nature Reserve Tours (☎1800 240 003; per person $120-155) operates morning, afternoon and evening boat tours of two to four hours, depending on demand and sea conditions. Take the evening trip if you want to see the little penguins come ashore. Bookings can be made through Narooma's visitor centre (p250). It can also arrange overnight stays in the lighthouse cottages on the island for groups - check out www.montagueisland.com.au.

Tilba

Off the highway, 15km south of Narooma, Central Tilba is perched on the side of Gulaga (Mt Dromedary; 797m). It's a delightful 19th-century gold-mining boomtown, one of the loveliest of its kind anywhere in the state. There's information and a town guide at Bates Emporium, at the start of the main street pick up the excellent free brochure *Tilba - 175 Years of Living History*. Further along are several craft, antique and gift shops, galleries, and food venues. There are two parts to the village, separated by around 2km - Central Tilba is the prettiest part.

Tilba Valley Wines (☎02-4473 7308; www.tilbavalleywines.com; 947 Old Hwy; ⏲10am-5pm Oct-Apr, 11am-4pm Wed-Sun May-Jul & Sep) sits on the shores of Lake Corunna close to Tilba.

On the main street at Central Tilba, **ABC Cheese Factory** (www.southcoastcheese.com.au; ⏲9am-5pm) produces cheddar and lets you see how they do it.

Sleeping & Eating

For information about the town and at least 13 accommodation options in the area, visit www.tilba.com.au.

Green Gables B&B $$
(☎02-4473 7435; www.greengables.com.au; 269 Corkhill Drive; r from $160) Stunning rooms in a glorious setting.

Bryn at Tilba B&B $$
(www.thebrynattilba.com.au; 91 Punkalla-Tilba Rd; r $170-250) Beautiful rooms with dark wood offset by white linen.

Two-Storey B&B B&B $$
(☎02-4473 7290; www.tilbatwostory.com; Bate St; ⏲r from $150) Frilly, floral decor right on the main street.

Premium Cheese Shop CAFE $
(☎02-4473 7659; www.southcoastcheese.com; 1 Bate St; mains $5-13; ⏲9am-5pm) Light meals and dozens of locally produced cheeses to take home with you.

Bermagui

POP 1473

South of the beautiful bird-filled Wallaga Lake and off the Princes Hwy, Bermagui is a pretty fishing port with a main street that hums to the sound of small-town contentment. The architectural showpiece is the new whiz-bang **Fishermen's Wharf** (Lamont St), designed by renowned architect and local resident Philip Cox, with all the tempters city visitors expect.

There are several **walks** around Bermagui, including 6km north along the coast to **Camel Rock** and a further 2km to Wallaga Lake. There's good **surfing** at Camel Rock and Cuttagee beaches, or you could toss a mullet from the shops and hit **Shelly Beach**, a child-friendly swimming spot. A kilometre's wander around the point will bring you to the **Blue Pool**, a dramatic ocean pool built into the base of the cliffs.

Sleeping & Eating

For holiday rentals, try **Julie Rutherford Real Estate** (☎02-6493 3444; www.julierutherford.com.au).

Zane Grey Park CARAVAN PARK $
(☎02-6493 4382; www.zanegreytouristpark.com.au; Lamont St; powered/unpowered sites $28/25, cabins $80-220) This place has a prime position on Dickson's Point, a Frisbee throw from Horseshoe Bay.

★ **Bermagui Beach Hotel** HOTEL $$
(☎02-6493 4206; www.bermaguibeachhotel.com.au; 10 Lamont St; dm $35, d/ste from $80/95; ❄) This is a gorgeous old place with the best balcony views in town. Stay here to tap into the local scene. The suites have spas.

DON'T MISS

MURRAMARANG NATIONAL PARK

This beautiful, coastal **park** (www.environment.nsw.gov.au; per car per day $7) is home to wild kangaroos, rich birdlife and the protected **Murramarang Aboriginal Area**, which contains ancient middens and other indigenous cultural treasures. Inside the park, stunning **Pretty** (☎02-4457 2019; unpowered sites adult/child $10/5, powered sites $14/7), **Pebbly** (☎02-4478 6023; adult/child $10/5) and **Depot Beach** (☎4478 6582) camping grounds are idyllic locations close to the surf (Pebbly is the most popular for surfing). Pretty Beach is the most accessible. No caravans are allowed at Pebbly Beach.

Harbourview Motel MOTEL $$
(☎02-6493 5213; www.harbourviewmotel.com.au; 56-58 Lamont St; s $130-175, d $140-185;) Good standard motel rooms close to the water.

★**Bluewave Seafoods** FISH & CHIPS $
(☎02-6493 5725; www.bluewaveseafood.com.au; Fishermen's Wharf; fish & chips $12; ⏰9am-7.30pm Mon-Wed, 9am-8pm Thu-Sun) Has what could be the best fish and chips on the south coast.

Il Passaggio ITALIAN $$
(☎02-6493 5753; ilpassagio.com.au; Fishermen's Wharf; mains $29; ⏰noon-2pm Tue-Thu, noon-2pm & 6-9.30pm Fri-Sun) Dishes up excellent modern Italian using the freshest local ingredients in a contemporary dining room with white walls and red leather. It's a winning combination whether you order the blue-eye, steak or ricotta gnocchi.

Mimosa Dry Stone MODERN AUSTRALIAN $$$
(☎02-6494 0164; www.mimosawines.com.au; 2845 Bermagui-Tahtra Rd; mains $30-36, pizza $20-28; ⏰noon-3pm & 6-9pm Thu-Sat, noon-3pm Sun-Wed summer, shorter hr rest of year) Midway between Bermagui and Tathra, this winery has a respected restaurant in a stunning building that's often booked out months in advance for weddings. Ring ahead.

Drinking & Nightlife

Mister Jones CAFE
(www.misterjones.com.au; 1/4 Bunga St; ⏰7am-noon Mon-Sat) This cool espresso bar–cum–art studio would go unnoticed if it weren't for the coffee cogniscenti sitting outside sipping on cappuccinos topped with choc chunks.

Horse & Camel Wine Bar WINE BAR
(www.horseandcamel.com.au; Fishermen's Wharf; ⏰3-10pm Thu-Sun, daily in Jan) Order a wine from more than 200 choices. At its best on Sunday afternoon at 4pm when there's sometimes live music.

Information

Visitor Centre (☎02-6493 3054; www.bermagui.net; Bunga St; ⏰10am-4pm)

Getting There & Away

Premier (☎13 34 10; www.premierms.com.au) stops here once a day en route to/from Sydney ($60, 11 hours), Narooma ($11, 40 minutes) and Eden ($31, 1¾ hours) via Merimbula ($22, 1¼ hours).

South to the Victorian Border

Running along 20km of beautiful coastline, **Mimosa Rocks National Park** (admission free) is 5802 hectares of earthly paradise with dense and varied bush, caves, headlands and beaches with crystal-clear water. There are basic **camp sites** (adult/child $10/5) at **Aragunnu Beach**, **Picnic Point**, and **Middle** and **Gillards Beaches**. The Narooma **NPWS office** (☎02-4476 0800; www.nationalparks.nsw.gov.au) has more info.

Taking in most of the coast from Merimbula north to Tathra (on beautiful Sapphire Coast Dr), **Bournda National Park** (per car $7) is a 2654-hectare park with good beaches, freshwater lagoons and several walking trails. **Camping** (adult/child $10/5) is permitted at Hobart Beach, on the southern shore of the big **Wallagoot Lagoon**. Contact the **Merimbula NPWS office** (☎02-6495 5000) for more information.

Merimbula

POP 6873

The surplus of nondescript hotels and holiday apartments lining the sloping main street of Merimbula still manages to play second fiddle to the town's impressive inlet (or lake). The rocking boat masts and sky-blue water – catering to fisherfolk throwing in a line wherever they please – make this popular holiday place very easy on the eye.

Sights & Activities

Merimbula Aquarium AQUARIUM
(www.merimbulawharf.com.au; Lake St; adult/child $13/8; ⏰10am-5pm) At the wharf on the eastern point is this small aquarium. There are good views across the lake from near here and the jetty is a popular fishing spot.

Boardwalk WALKING
West of the bridge, just off the causeway, a magnificent 1.75km boardwalk takes nature lovers and morning people hopping and skipping around mangroves, oyster farms and melaleucas. Pick up the useful brochure at the tourist information centre.

Merimbula Divers Lodge DIVING
(☎02-6495 3611; www.merimbuladiverslodge.com.au; 15 Park St; 1/2 shore dives $77/120 plus $55 for equipment, PADI-certificate course $499) This place has courses and offers three wreck dives and a cave dive.

Coastlife Adventures SURFING
(☎02-6494 1122; www.coastlife.com.au; group/private surf lessons $60/90, 2-hr kayak tours $50-60) This place does morning surf and stand-up paddle lessons as well as marine kayak tours.

Cycle n Surf BICYCLE RENTAL
(☎02-6495 2171; Shop 1B Marine Pde; bicycles per 1/4/24hr $10/20/30, surfboard rental half-/full day $40/60) Rent bicycles and surfboards at this friendly place.

Merimbula Marina CRUISE
(☎02-6495 1686; www.merimbulamarina.com; Merimbula jetty; adult $45-69, child $20-40) The small kiosk here runs reef, dolphin- and whale-watching cruises

Sleeping

Wandarrah YHA Lodge HOSTEL $
(☎02-6495 3503; www3.yha.com.au; 8 Marine Pde; dm/f from $28/135; @) This clean place, with a good kitchen and hanging-out areas, is near the surf beach and the bus stop. Pick-ups by arrangement or let the staff know if you're arriving late.

Merimbula Beach Holiday Park CAMPGROUND, CARAVAN PARK $
(☎02-6495 3381; www.merimbulabeachholidaypark.com.au; 2 Short Point Rd; camp sites $30-43, cabins $110-315;) At Short Point Beach. Leafy and kid-friendly and it has an on-site cafe.

Coast Resort APARTMENTS $$
(☎02-495 4930; www.coastresort.com.au; 1 Elizabeth St; 1-/2-/3-bedroom apt from $170/195/240;) You could describe the decor of this huge upmarket apartment-style complex as ultramodern, although stark might be more apt. Still, comfort's not a problem and the two pools, tennis court and proximity to the beach are all very appealing.

Merimbula Lakeview Hotel MOTEL $$$
(☎02-6495 1202; www.merimbulalakeview.com.au; Market St; r from $85;) This waterfront establishment has stylish rooms with all the motel trimmings. Come summertime, it's close to the beer garden...which may be good or bad.

Eating

Original Fix CAFE $
(☎02-6495 3800; Shop 5/17 Merimbula Dr; light meals $9-15; 9am-5pm Sun-Thu, 9am-late Fri & Sat) Best known for its delicious handmade chocolates and ice creams, this place also does paninis, nachos, salads and roast pumpkin, bean and basil curry for lunch.

★ Zanzibar MODERN AUSTRALIAN $$
(☎02-6495 3636; zanzibarmerimbula.com.au; cnr Main & Market Sts; mains $25-33, 2-/3-course meal $60/75; 6-9pm Tue, Wed & Sat, noon-2pm & 6-9pm Fri & Sat) Don't leave town without an evening at this culinary gem, which prides itself on locally caught seafood and hand-picked produce. There's so much here that's good, from crab ravioli to shitake-and-pork-jowl consommé.

Waterfront Cafe CAFE, SEAFOOD $$
(☎02-6495 7684; www.thewaterfrontcafe.net.au; Shop 1, The Promenade; mains $19-30; 8am-10pm) One of few Merimbula eateries to take advantage of the town's lakeside location, the Waterfront is a local institution. Its oysters are among the best on the south coast.

Cantina SPANISH $$
(☎02-6495 1085; 56 Market St; tapas $7-15, mains $25-30; 11.30am-late Mon-Sat, 2.30-10pm Sun) This atmospheric little hidey-hole in the centre of town dishes up shared tapas plates, while the two-course lunch with a glass of wine for $25 is terrific value.

WILDLIFE AROUND MERIMBULA

In addition to whales from September to November, there are...

Kangaroos and wallabies Pambula-Merimbula Golf Course and Pambula Beach (follow the signs off the Princes Hwy along the road to Eden); sightings are possible throughout the day, but dusk and sunset (from 4.30pm) is the time for almost guaranteed sightings.

Other native animals Potoroo Palace (☎02-6494 9225; www.potoroopalace.com; 2372 Princes Hwy; adult/child $17/10; 10am-4pm) houses an impressive array of echidnas, kangaroos, dingos, koalas, potoroos and native birds. It's 9km north of Merimbula on the road to Bega.

Waterbirds Panboola (www.panboola.com) in Pambula incorporates walking trails through the Pambula Wetlands.

Information

NPWS Office (02-6495 5000; www.environment.nsw.gov.au; cnr Merimbula & Sapphire Coast Drs; 9am-4pm Mon-Fri)

Visitor Centre (02-6495 1129; www.sapphirecoast.com.au; cnr Market & Beach Sts; 9am-5pm)

Getting There & Away

AIR

The **airport** (www.merimbulaairport.com.au) is 1km out of town on the road to Pambula. **Rex** (13 17 13; www.rex.com.au) flies daily to Melbourne (from $155, 1½ hours) and Sydney (from $156, 1¾ hours).

BUS

Buses stop outside the Commonwealth Bank on Market St. **Premier** (13 34 10; www.premierms.com.au) has daily buses to Sydney ($69, 10 hours) via Narooma ($31, two hours). **CountryLink** (13 22 32; www.countrylink.info)runs a daily bus to Canberra ($33, four hours).

Deanes Buslines (02-6495 6452; www.deanesbuslines.com.au) runs to Bega ($11.50, one hour, six daily) and Eden ($9.25, 40 minutes, five daily).

Eden

POP 3043

Eden lives up to its namesake. Once a haven for fisherfolk and woodchippers, this charming seaside town is now squarely on the itinerary for those looking to laze a day away on the town's 1.5km beach or explore the surrounding national parks and wilderness areas. Whale watching is big on the agenda and Eden comes alive at the start of November with the annual **Whale Festival** (www.edenwhalefestival.com.au; Nov).

Sights Activities

Killer Whale Museum MUSEUM
(94 Imlay St; adult/child $9/2.50; 9.15am-3.45pm Mon-Sat, 11.15am-3.45pm Sun) The skeleton of Old Tom, a killer whale and local legend, is housed here.

Cat Balou Cruises CRUISE
(0427 962 027; www.catbalou.com.au; Main Wharf; adult/child $75/60) In October and November, Cat Balou Cruises has whale-spotting cruises. At other times, dolphins, fur seals and seabirds can usually be seen during the shorter bay cruise (adult/child $35/20).

Ocean Wilderness KAYAKING
(0405 529 214; www.oceanwilderness.com.au; 4/6hr tours from $80/100) Ocean Wilderness does half-day kayaking trips through Ben Boyd National Park and Twofold Bay and a day trip to Davidson Whaling Station. Ask about overnight trips.

Sapphire Coast Marine Discovery Centre HIKING, SNORKELLING
(02-6496 1699; www.sapphirecoastdiscovery.com.au; Main Wharf; adult/child $7/2; 10am-3pm Wed-Sat) See the sea through a rocky reef aquarium and sign up for a rocky shore ramble (adult/child $10/8) or group snorkelling trip ($25).

Sleeping & Eating

Great Southern Hotel HOTEL $
(02-6496 1515; www.greatsouthernninn.com.au; 121 Imlay St; dm/s/d from $30/70/90) The Great Southern Hotel has good-value shared pub rooms and newly renovated backpacker accommodation. The pub grub is hearty and the rear deck's a winner.

Eden Tourist Park CARAVAN PARK $
(02-6496 1139; www.edentouristpark.com.au; Aslings Beach Rd; unpowered/powered sites from $25/28, cabins from $65) This caravan park is neat, trim and in a prime position on a spit separating stunning Aslings Beach from Lake Curalo.

Seahorse Inn BOUTIQUE HOTEL $$
(02-6496 1361; www.seahorseinn.com.au; d from $175;) At Boydtown 6km south of Eden, the Seahorse Inn overlooks Twofold Bay. It's a lavish boutique hotel with all the trimmings.

Taste of Eden CAFE $$
(Main Wharf; mains $14-28; 8am-3pm) This is an atmospheric, tiny cafe with seafaring decor serving a good selection of seafood, including fresh local mussels with white wine, chilli and lemon.

Wharfside Café CAFE $$
(www.wharfsidecafe.com.au; Main Wharf; mains $11-27; 8am-3pm) The corner locale of the Wharfside Café makes it ideal for lazy coffee in the sun or seafood dishes. It does the simple things best, such as grilled fish.

Information

Visitor Centre (02-6496 1953; www.visiteden.com.au; Mitchell St; 9am-5pm Mon-Sat, 10am-4pm Sun)

Getting There & Away

Premier (☎13 34 10; www.premierms.com.au) has buses to Sydney ($71, nine hours) and most places in between. **Deane's** (☎02-6495 6452; www.deanestransitgroup.com.au) runs to Bega ($14.50, 1¼ hours) via Merimbula ($9.25, 40 minutes). It stops opposite the Caltex service station.

Ben Boyd National Park & Around

Protecting some relics of failed entrepreneur Ben Boyd's long-defunct whaling operations, this national park (10,485 hectares), stretching north and south along the coast on either side of Eden, has dramatic coastline, bush and walking territory. The southern access road is the sealed Edrom Rd, off the Princes Hwy 19km south of Eden.

Wonboyn Rd is 4km south of Edrom Rd, and gives access to **Nadgee Nature Reserve**, 20,671 hectares of remote wilderness stretching from the southern tip of Ben Boyd National Park to the Victorian border, and to **Wonboyn**, a small settlement on Wonboyn Lake at the northern end of the reserve. Many roads in the parks have unsealed sections that can be slippery after rain.

Canberra & Around

Includes ➡

Best Places to Eat

- Ottoman (p268)
- Silo Bakery (p268)
- Lanterne Rooms (p267)
- Italian & Sons (p267)
- Dieci e Mezzo (p268)

Best Places to Stay

- East Hotel (p266)
- Diamant Hotel (p266)
- Hyatt Hotel Canberra (p267)
- Canberra YHA Hostel (p266)
- Burbury Hotel (p266)

Why Go?

Established to showcase the expansive spaces, immense wealth and staunchly democratic aspirations of a newly-minted nation, the city of Canberra is where many of the decisions that shape Australia are made and where many of its major cultural institutions are located. It's odd, then, that the place is so lacking in personality – in many ways, time spent on a visit here is time that could better be spent elsewhere in the country.

The exception to this rule applies to domestic tourists, because this is a destination that every Australian should visit at least once. Its flagship museums and galleries – especially the Australian War Memorial, National Gallery of Australia, National Portrait Gallery and National Museum of Australia – are repositories of the artefacts and artworks that have shaped and defined Australia's modern history and character, making them guardians and storytellers of the national narrative.

When to Go

Canberra

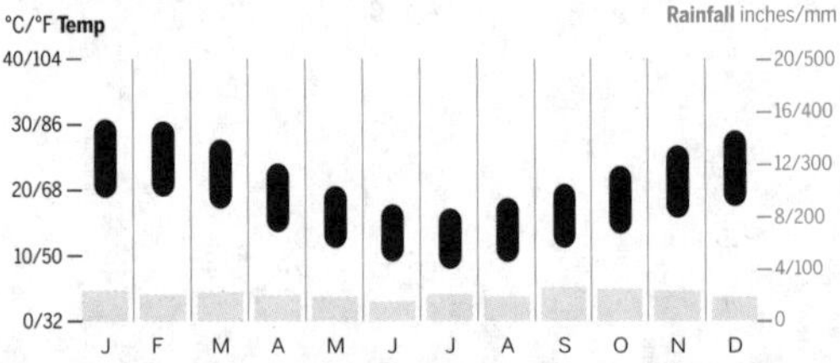

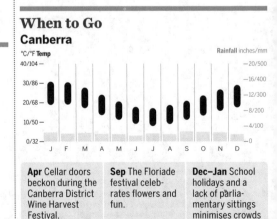

Apr Cellar doors beckon during the Canberra District Wine Harvest Festival.

Sep The Floriade festival celebrates flowers and fun.

Dec–Jan School holidays and a lack of parliamentary sittings minimises crowds and hotel prices.

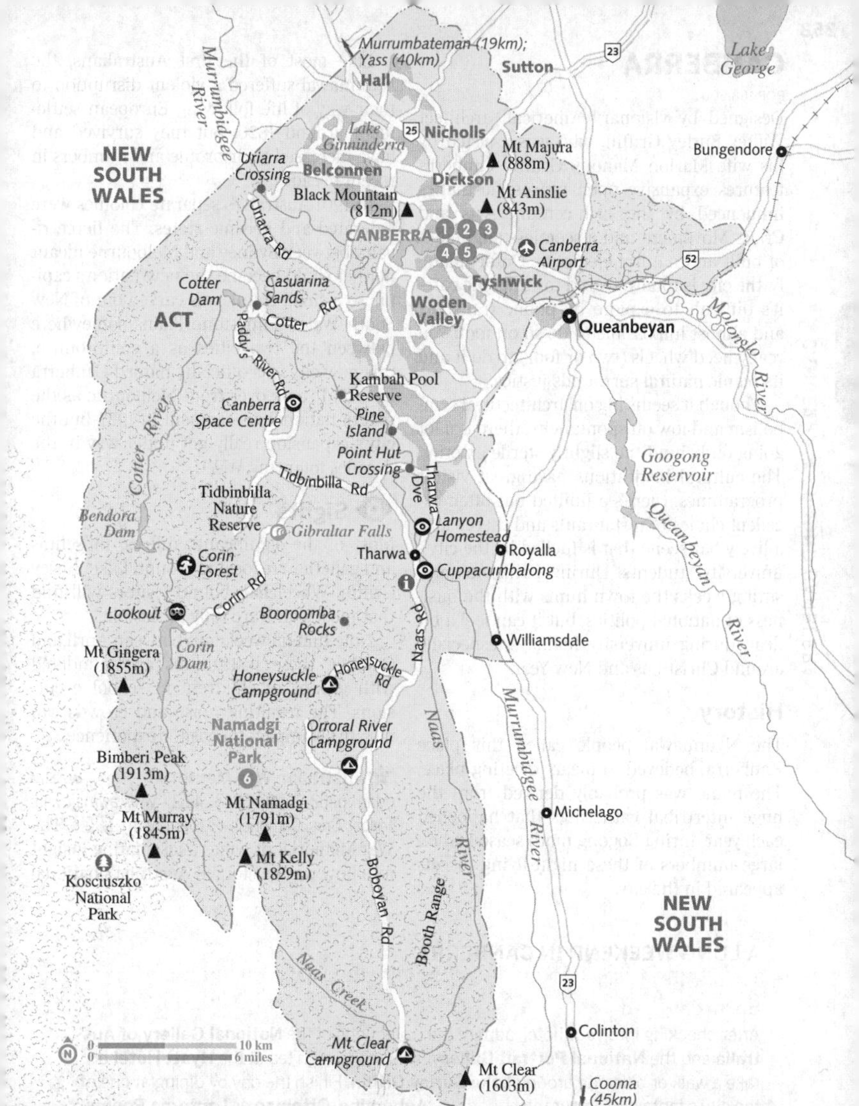

Canberra & Around Highlights

1. Admire Australian and international artworks at the **National Gallery of Australia** (p259)
2. Learn about Australia's nation-defining military history at the **Australian War Memorial** (p258)
3. Witness democracy in action at **Parliament House** (p260)
4. Paddle, cycle, skate, walk or run around **Lake Burley Griffin** (p259)
5. Ponder an eclectic array of portraits at the **National Portrait Gallery** (p260)
6. Spot kangaroos and Aboriginal rock art in **Namadgi National Park** (p273)
7. Sample the award-winning cold-climate drops being produced at the region's many **wineries** (p272)

CANBERRA

POP 168,500

Designed by visionary American architect Walter Burley Griffin, who was assisted by his wife Marion Mahony Griffin, Canberra features expansive open spaces, aesthetics influenced by the 19th-century Arts and Crafts Movement and a seemless alignment of built and natural elements. Unfortunately, the city is totally geared towards the car – it's difficult to explore by public transport and almost impossible to do so on foot. You really need wheels (two or four) to do it and its scenic natural surrounds justice.

Though it seems big on architectural symbolism and low on spontaneity, there is a lot going on behind the slightly sterile exterior. The cultural institutions have great visitor programmes, there's a limited but often excellent choice of restaurants and there's also a lively bar scene that is fuelled by the city's university students. During parliamentary-sitting weeks the town hums with the business of national politics, but it can feel a bit dead during university holidays, especially around Christmas and New Year.

History

The Ngunnawal people called this place Kanberra, believed to mean 'meeting place'. The name was probably derived from the huge intertribal gatherings that happened each year during Bogong moth season when large numbers of these night-flying insects appeared in the city.

Like most of the first Australians, the Ngunnawal suffered a violent disruption to their way of life following European settlement around 1820, but they survived and have increased their profile and numbers in recent decades.

In 1901 Australia's separate colonies were federated and became states. The fierce rivalry between Sydney and Melbourne meant neither could become the new nation's capital, so a small chunk was carved out of New South Wales' Limestone Plains somewhere between the two cities as a compromise; this new city was officially named Canberra in 1913. It took over from Melbourne as the seat of national government in 1927, but the city's expansion really got under way in the decades following WWII.

Sights

Most of the significant edifices, museums and galleries are located around Lake Burley Griffin. Wheelchair-bound visitors will find that most sights are fully accessible.

Note that on weekdays between April and October, these institutions are inundated with groups of children on school excursions. The resulting noise and crowds can negatively impact the visitor experience.

★ **Australian War Memorial** MUSEUM

(Map p262; ☎02-6243 4211; www.awm.gov.au; Treloar Cres, Campbell; ⏲10am-5pm) FREE The War Memorial provides a fascinating insight into how war has forged Australia's national

A LONG WEEKEND IN CANBERRA

Saturday

After checking into your hotel, admire the collections of the **National Gallery of Australia** and the **National Portrait Gallery**. Then enjoy high tea at the **Hyatt Hotel** or take a walk or bike ride around **Lake Burley Griffin**. Finish the day by dining at one of the city's fantastic restaurants – perhaps **Aubergine**, **Ottoman** or **Lanterne Rooms**.

Sunday

Have a delicious brunch at **Silo Bakery**, check out the **Old Bus Depot Markets** and then head to the **Australian War Memorial** for a powerful and moving glimpse into the nation's military history. At the end of the day, enjoy a casual Italian meal at **Bicicletta Restaurant**.

Monday

If today's a sitting day, book a ringside seat at the only game in town – **Parliamentary Question Time**. On your way to the afternoon session, browse the displays at the **Museum of Australian Democracy** at Old Parliament House and enjoy lunch at its **Kitchen Cabinet** cafe. Celebrate your final evening over dinner at **Italian & Sons** or **Dieci e Mezzo**.

identity, and in so doing delivers Canberra's most rewarding museum experience. Entry is via a **Commemorative Courtyard** where the names of the nation's war dead are memorialised on a roll of honour. Over the years family members have attached bright-red paper poppies to the names of their fallen relatives, imparting a melancholic beauty. These poppies of remembrance reference those that flowered on the battlegrounds of Belgium, France and Gallipoli in the spring of 1915.

Behind the courtyard is the mosaic-encrusted **Hall of Memory**. This is home to the **Tomb of the Unknown Australian Soldier**, who represents all Australians who have given their lives during wartime.

Inside the museum are halls dedicated to WWI, WWII and conflicts from 1945 to the present day. There's also an aircraft hall with plenty of exhibits that provides a perfect introduction to the sound-and-light shows that are staged in the impressive **Anzac Hall**. The most exciting of the shows are *Striking by Night*, a re-creation of a night operation over Berlin in 1943; and *Over the Front: the Great War in the Air*.

Free volunteer-led 90-minute guided tours leave from the **Orientation Gallery** next to the main entrance at 10am, 10.15am, 10.30am, 11am, noon, 1pm, 1.30pm, 2pm, 2.30pm and 3pm; 45-minute tours leave at 10.45am and 1.15pm. Alternatively, purchase the *Self-Guided Tour* leaflet with map ($5).

The memorial's **Terrace Cafe** (Treloar Cres, Australian War Memorial; breakfast $5-17, lunch $12-20; ⏲8.30am-4.30pm Mon-Fri & 8am-4.30pm Sat & Sun) occupies an attractive glass pavilion next door to the main building. It serves decent food and coffee in indoor and outdoor spaces.

Lake Burley Griffin LANDMARK

(Map p262) The 35km shore of this lake is home to most of the city's cultural institutions and to a high proportion of its leisure activities. It was filled by damming the Molonglo River in 1963 with the 33m-high Scrivener Dam and was named after American architect Walter Burley Griffin who, with the help of his wife and fellow architect Marion, won an international competition to design Australia's new capital city in 1911.

Built in 1970 to mark the bicentenary of Cook's landfall, the **Captain Cook Memorial Water Jet** near Regatta Point flings a 6-tonne column of water up into the air. There is also a **skeleton globe** at the Point on which Cook's three great voyages are traced.

On Aspen Island is the 50m-high **National Carillon**, a gift from Britain on Canberra's 50th anniversary in 1963. The tower has 55 bronze bells, weighing from 7kg to 6 tonnes each, making it one of the world's largest musical instruments. Daily recitals are held – check the monthly schedule at www.nationalcapital.gov.au.

CANBERRA FOR CHILDREN

Kids like Canberra because there's lots of cool stuff for them to do. Most of the museums and galleries have kids programmes, and many offer dedicated tours and events – check websites for details.

For hands-on fun, visit Questacon (p264), the National Museum of Australia (p261), the National Film & Sound Archive (p261), the Australian Institute of Sport (p264) and the Canberra Space Centre (p273). It's even possible to cuddle a cheetah and pat a panda at the National Zoo & Aquarium (p264).

For fresh air and exercise, go for a bike ride around Lake Burley Griffin or head to the Tidbinbilla Nature Reserve (p273) or Namadgi National Park (p273).

★National Gallery of Australia ART GALLERY

(Map p262; ☎02-6240 6502; www.nga.gov.au; Parkes Pl, Parkes; permanent collection admission free; ⏲10am-5pm) FREE On entering this impressive gallery you will be confronted with one of its most extraordinary exhibits, an Aboriginal Memorial from Central Arnhem Land that was created for the nation's bicentenary in 1988. The work of 43 artists, this 'forest of souls' presents 200 hollow log coffins (one for every year of European settlement) and is one of the gallery's many works by Aboriginal and Torres Strait Islander people.

Also on show is Australian art from the colonial to contemporary period and three galleries showcasing art from the Indian Subcontinent, Southeast Asia and China, Japan and Central Asia. Together, these form the country's most important and comprehensive collection of Asian art. There's also a notable collection of Pacific art and a collection of European and American works with a few knock-out pieces.

Canberra

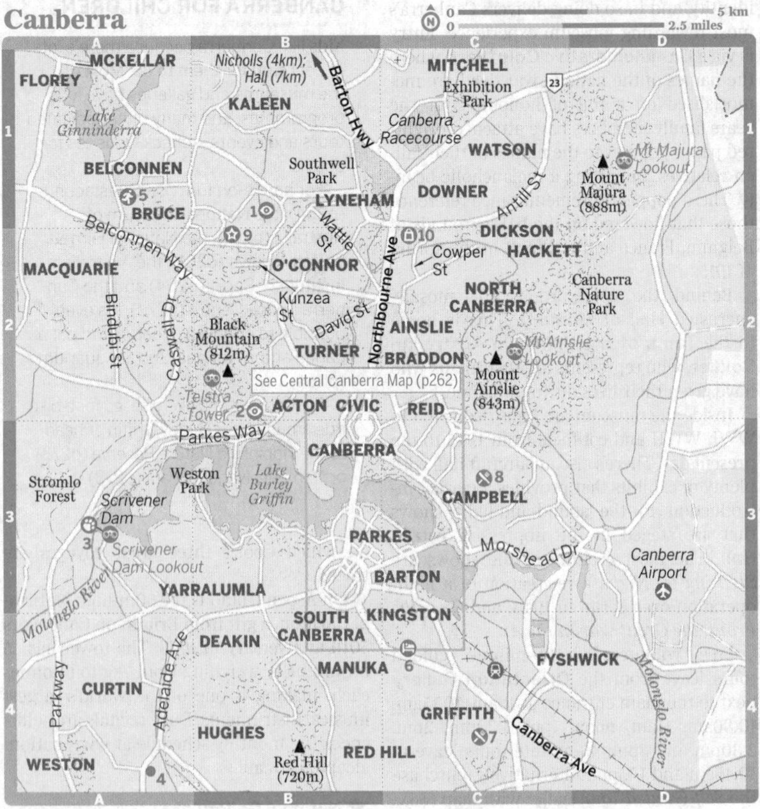

There is a ground-floor cafe and a gallery shop where you will be able to source a tasteful souvenir or two to take home. Behind the building is a somewhat scruffy sculpture garden and a restaurant (open noon to 2pm Wednesday to Sunday).

Consider taking advantage of a free guided tour – check the website for details. Note that visiting exhibitions usually attract an admission fee.

★Parliament House NOTABLE BUILDING

(Map p262; ☎02-6277 5399; www.aph.gov.au; ⏲from 9am Mon & Tue & from 8.30am Wed & Thu sitting days, 9am-5pm non-sitting days) FREE Opened in 1988 after a 10-year, $1.2 billion construction project, the national parliament building is dug into Capital Hill, its roof covered in grass and topped by an 81m-high flagpole. The rooftop lawns are easily accessible, encompass 23 hectares of landscaped gardens, and provide superb 360-degree views of the city. Underneath is a complex of five buildings that incorporate 17 courtyards, a striking entrance foyer, a Great Hall, the House of Representatives, the Senate and 2300km of corridors. All can be visited on a free guided tour (30-minutes on sitting days, 45 minutes on non-sitting days). These set off at 10am, 1pm and 3pm daily.

Visitors can self-navigate and watch parliamentary proceedings from the public galleries. Tickets for Question Time (2pm on sitting days) in the House of Representatives are free but must be booked through the **Sergeant at Arms** (☎02-6277 4889); tickets aren't required for the Senate chamber. See the website for a calendar of sitting days.

★National Portrait Gallery ART GALLERY

(Map p262; ☎02-6102 7000; www.portrait.gov.au; King Edward Tce, Parkes; ⏲10am-5pm) FREE This gallery tells the story of Australia through its faces – from wax cameos of Aboriginal

Canberra

Sights

Activities, Courses & Tours

Sleeping

Eating

Entertainment

Shopping

tribespeople to colonial portraits of the nation's founding families and contemporary works such as Howard Arkley's Day-Glo portrait of musician Nick Cave.

The purpose-built building was designed by architect Richard Johnson of Sydney firm Johnson Pilton Walker and all of its spaces – from exhibition rooms to the lovely terrace cafe – work extremely well.

Museum of Australian Democracy MUSEUM
(Map p262; 02-6270 8222; www.moadoph.gov.au; Old Parliament House, 18 King George Tce, Parkes; adult/concession/family $2/1/5; 9am-5pm) It was the seat of government from 1927 to 1988, so this building offers visitors a whiff of bygone parliamentary activity alongside its exhibits. These won't be particularly meaningful for non-Aussies, but all those who have studied Australian history or followed the histrionics and high-jinx in Canberra over the decades will be transported back to many significant events in the relatively short life of its parliamentary democracy. Displays cover Australian prime ministers, the roots of global and local democracy, and the history of local protest movements. You can also visit the old Senate and House of Representative chambers, the parliamentary library and the prime minister's office.

Off the entrance foyer is the Kitchen Cabinet (p268), a great little cafe serving pies, quiches, sandwiches and excellent coffee.

The lawn in front of Old Parliament House is home to the **Aboriginal Tent Embassy** – an important site in the struggle for equality and representation for Indigenous Australians. **Reconciliation Place**, where artwork represents the nation's commitment to the cause of reconciliation between Indigenous and non-Indigenous Australians, is down on the shore of Lake Burley Griffin.

National Museum of Australia MUSEUM
(Map p262; 02-6208 5000; www.nma.gov.au; Lawson Cres, Acton Peninsula; guided tours adult/child/family $10/5/25; 9am-5pm) FREE Dismantling and analysing a national identity is a laudable endeavour, and this museum makes a valiant effort to do just that. Cluttered with exhibits, it makes a point of avoiding standard curatorial conventions such as organising exhibits chronologically, which some visitors will find exhilarating and others will find annoying – kids tend to love it. Exhibits focus on environmental change, indigenous culture, national icons and more. Don't miss the introductory film, shown in the small rotating **Circa Theatre** at the start of the exhibition route.

Bus 7 runs here from Civic. There's also a free bus on weekends and public holidays, departing regularly from 10.30am from platform 7 in the Civic bus interchange along Alinga St, East Row and Mort St.

National Film & Sound Archive MUSEUM, CINEMA
(Map p262; 02-6248 2000; www.nfsa.gov.au; McCoy Circuit, Acton; 9am-5pm Mon-Fri, 10am-5pm Sat & Sun) FREE Set in a delightful art-deco building, this archive preserves Australian moving-picture and sound recordings for posterity. The *Sights + Sounds of a Nation* exhibition is great to visit if the place is quiet, but incredibly frustrating when it's busy, as there is no soundproofing around the audiovisual exhibits. There are also temporary exhibitions, talks and film screenings in the **Arc Cinema** (Map p262; adult/concession $11/9; 2pm & 7pm Thu, 2pm, 4.30pm & 7.30pm Sat & 2pm & 4.30pm Sun). Teatro Fellini Café serves coffee and simple lunches in the internal courtyard.

Australian National Botanic Gardens GARDENS
(Map p260; 02-6250 9540; www.anbg.gov.au; Clunies Ross St, Acton; 8.30am-5pm Feb-Dec, to 8pm Sat & Sun Jan, visitors centre 9.30am-4.30pm) FREE Devoted to the growth, study and promotion of Australian floral diversity, these

Central Canberra

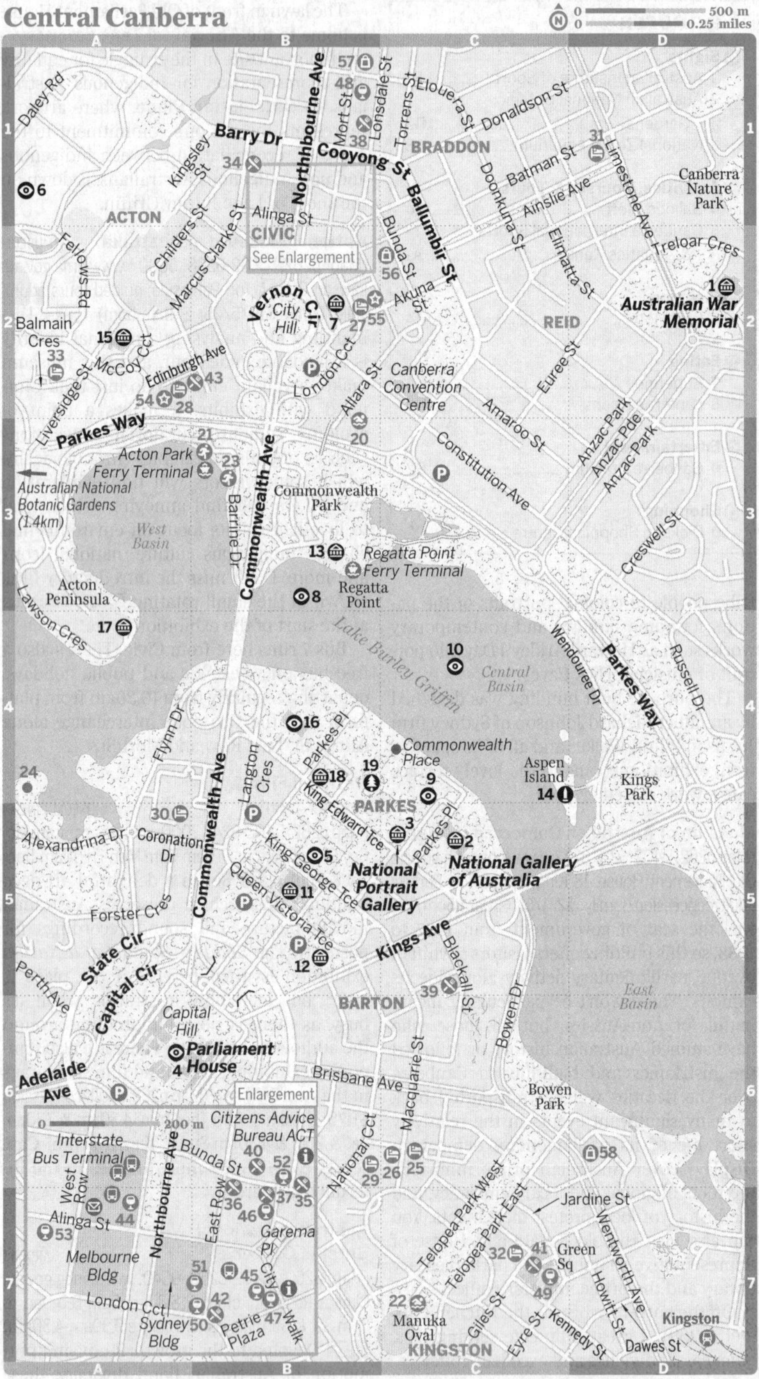

Central Canberra

Top Sights

1	Australian War Memorial	D2
2	National Gallery of Australia	C5
3	National Portrait Gallery	C5
4	Parliament House	A6

Sights

5	Aboriginal Tent Embassy	B5
6	Australian National University	A1
7	Canberra Museum & Gallery	B2
8	Captain Cook Memorial Water Jet	B3
9	High Court of Australia	C4
10	Lake Burley Griffin	C4
11	Museum of Australian Democracy	B5
12	National Archives of Australia	B5
13	National Capital Exhibition	B3
14	National Carillon	C4
15	National Film & Sound Archive	A2
16	National Library of Australia	B4
17	National Museum of Australia	A4
18	Questacon	B4
19	Reconciliation Place	B4

Activities, Courses & Tours

20	Canberra Olympic Pool	B3
21	Lake Burley Griffin Boat Hire	B3
22	Manuka Swimming Pool	C7
23	Mr Spokes Bike Hire	B3
24	Southern Cross Yacht Club	A4

Sleeping

25	Brassey	C6
26	Burbury Hotel	C6
27	Canberra City YHA	B2
28	Diamant Hotel	A2
29	Hotel Realm	B6
30	Hyatt Hotel Canberra	A5
31	Mercure Canberra	D1
32	The York Canberra	C7
33	University House	A2

Eating

	Artespresso	(see 32)
	Bicicletta Restaurant	(see 28)
34	Courgette	B1
35	Cream	B6
36	Dieci e Mezzo	B6
37	Gus' Café	B7
	Italian & Sons	(see 38)
	Kitchen Cabinet	(see 11)
38	Lonsdale Street Roasters	B1
	Malamay	(see 26)
39	Ottoman	C5
40	Sammy's Kitchen	B6
41	Silo Bakery	C7
	The Tea Lounge	(see 30)
42	Tosolini's	B7
43	Urban Food	B2

Drinking & Nightlife

	ANU Union Bar	(see 6)
44	Benchmark Wine Bar	A7
45	Cube	B7
46	Honky Tonks	B7
47	King O'Malley's	B7
48	Knightsbridge Penthouse	B1
49	Little Brussels Belgian Beer Cafe	C7
50	Mooseheads	B7
51	Phoenix	B7
52	Tongue & Groove	B6
	Transit Bar	(see 27)
53	Wig & Pen	A7

Entertainment

	Arc Cinema	(see 15)
	Canberra Theatre Centre	(see 7)
54	Palace Electric Cinema	A2
55	Ticketek	B2

Shopping

56	Canberra Centre	C2
	Craft ACT	(see 7)
57	Electric Shadows Bookshop	B1
	National Library Bookshop	(see 16)
58	Old Bus Depot Markets	D6

gardens are spread over 90 hectares on Black Mountain's lower slopes. Self-guided trails include the Joseph Banks Walk, which showcases colourful plants illustrating the diversity of Australian flora. There's also a 90-minute return trail branching from the main path near the eucalypt lawn (with 600 species of this quintessential Aussie tree) and leading into the higher areas of the gardens before continuing into the Black Mountain Nature Park and on to the summit.

The **visitor centre** is the departure point for free volunteer-led **guided walks** at 11am and 2pm. On weekends, a 12-seater electric bus leaves the visitor centre on a **Flora Explorer Tour** (adult/child $6/3; 1pm Sat & Sun).

Canberra Museum & Gallery MUSEUM, GALLERY
(Map p262; 02-6207 3968; www.museumsandgallery.act.gov.au; cnr London Circuit & Civic Sq, Civic; 10am-5pm Mon-Fri, noon-4pm Sat & Sun Sep-May) FREE This museum and gallery is devoted to Canberra's social history and visual arts, and has a collection of iconic works by Sidney Nolan, best known for his paintings of 19th-century bushranger Ned Kelly.

National Library of Australia LIBRARY
(Map p262; ☎02-6262 1111; www.nla.gov.au; Parkes Pl, Parkes; ⏲Treasures Gallery 10am-5pm) FREE This library has accumulated over six million items since being established in 1901, most of which can be accessed in the reading rooms. Don't miss the new **Treasures Gallery**, where artefacts such as Captain Cook's *Endeavour* journal and Captain Bligh's list of mutineers are among the regularly refreshed display – free 40-minute volunteer-led tours are held at 10.30am daily and 11.30am on Monday, Wednesday and Friday.

Australian Institute of Sport SPORTS INSTITUTE
(AIS; Map p260; ☎02-6214 1010; www.ausport.gov.au/tours; Leverrier St, Bruce; tours adult/student/child/family $18/13/10/49; ⏲tours 10am, 11.30am, 1pm & 2.30pm) The country's elite and aspiring-elite athletes hone their sporting prowess at the AIS. The 90-minute **tours** led by resident athletes have information on training routines and diets. There are displays on Australian champions and the Sydney Olympics, plus interactive exhibits where you can publicly humble yourself at a variety of sports or test the accuracy, speed and strength of your ball skills and reaction time.

Questacon MUSEUM
(Map p262; ☎02-6270 2800; www.questacon.edu.au; King Edward Tce, Parkes; adult/child & concession/family $23/17.50/70; ⏲9am-5pm) This hands-on science and technology centre is a child magnet due to its lively, educational and just plain fun interactive exhibits. Kids can explore the physics of sport, athletics and fun parks, cause tsunamis and take shelter from cyclones and earthquakes. Exciting science shows, presentations and puppet shows are included in the admission price.

National Capital Exhibition MUSEUM
(Map p262; ☎02-6272 2902; www.nationalcapital.gov.au; Barrine Dr, Commonwealth Park; ⏲9am-5pm Mon-Fri, 10am-4pm Sat & Sun) FREE Learn about the Indigenous people of the Canberra area and see copies of exquisite Burley-Griffin drawings of the city at this modest museum near Regatta Point.

National Zoo & Aquarium ZOO, AQUARIUM
(Map p260; ☎02-6287 8400; www.nationalzoo.com.au; 999 Lady Denman Dr, Yarralumla; adult/student & senior/child/family $38/31/21.50/105, tour weekends/weekdays $135/110; ⏲10am-5pm) Nestled behind Scrivener Dam, this zoo and aquarium is home to a roll call of fascinating animals. Book ahead to cuddle a cheetah ($165), have an up-and-relatively-personal encounter with a red panda, white lion or giraffe ($50), or take a **tour** behind the scenes to hand feed the lions, tigers and bears ($110). Bus 81 from the Civic interchange stops close by on weekends only.

Mount Ainslie LOOKOUT
In the northeast, 843m high Mt Ainslie has fine views day and night; walking tracks start behind the War Memorial, climb Mt Ainslie and end at **Mount Majura** (888m).

Activities

Canberra's lakes, mountains and climate offer abundant opportunities for bushwalking, swimming, cycling and other activities.

Boating

Lake Burley Griffin BOAT HIRE
(Map p262; ☎02-6249 6861; www.actboathire.com; Acton Jetty, Civic; ⏲9am-5pm Mon-Fri, 8.30am-6pm Sat & Sun, closed May-Aug) Canoe, kayak and paddleboat hire ($15 to $30 per hour).

Bushwalking

Tidbinbilla Nature Reserve (p273), southwest of the city, has walking and bicycle tracks, a eucalypt forest and a platypus habitat. Another great area for bushwalking is Namadgi National Park (p273), a 30-minute drive south of the city centre.

Cycling

Canberra has one of the most extensive cycle-path networks of any Australian city. The Canberra and Region Visitors Centre stocks two useful, free brochures: *Lake Burley Griffin Cycle Routes* and the *Walking & Cycling Map* published by **Pedal Power ACT** (http://pedalpower.org.au).

Mr Spokes Bike Hire BIKE HIRE
(Map p262; ☎02-6257 1188; www.mrspokes.com.au; Barrine Dr, Acton; ⏲9am-5pm Wed-Sun, daily during school holidays) Near the Acton Park ferry terminal; bike hire per hour/half day/full day costs $20/30/40.

Row'n'Ride BIKE HIRE
(☎0410 547 838; www.realfun.com.au) Delivers bicycles (hire per day/week $45/95) to your door.

Swimming

Canberra International Sports & Aquatics Centre AQUATICS CENTRE
(Map p260; ☎02-6251 7888; www.cisac.com.au; 100 Eastern Valley Way, Bruce; adult/child $5.50/4; ⏲6am-9pm Mon-Fri, 7am-7pm Sat & Sun) With

25m and 50m heated indoor swimming pools.

Canberra Olympic Pool SWIMMING POOL
(Map p262; ☎02-6248 6799; www.canberraolympicpool.com.au; cnr Allara St & Constitution Ave, Civic; adult/child $6/4; ⏰6am-8.30pm Mon-Thu, 6am-8pm Fri, 7am-6pm Sat, 8am-6pm Sun) Three pools (including one 50m heated pool), a cafe and a health club.

Manuka Swimming Pool SWIMMING POOL
(Map p262; ☎02-6295 1910; NSW Cres, Manuka; adult/child $5.50/4.50; ⏰6.30am-7pm Mon-Fri, 8am-7pm Sat & Sun Nov-Mar, usually closed Apr-Oct) Art deco–era 30m pool.

Tours

Balloon Aloft AERIAL TOUR
(Map p260; ☎02-6285 1540; www.canberraballoons.com.au; 7 Irving St, Phillip; rides from adult/child $290/210) Offers quiet aerial views over Canberra.

Canberra Day Tours CITY TOUR
(☎0418 455 099; www.canberradaytours.com.au; adult/child $35/20) This hop-on hop-off service on the Red Explorer bus leaves from the Melbourne Building, Northbourne Ave, Civic. The first service leaves at 9.30am, the last at 3pm. Check the website for the timetable.

Southern Cross Yacht Club CRUISE
(Map p262; ☎02-6273 1784; www.cscc.com.au; 1 Mariner Pl, Yarralumla) Provides Sunday lunch and Thursday dinner sightseeing cruises aboard the MV *Southern Cross* (adult/child $70/25), as well as a one-hour tour departing 3pm every Sunday (adult/child $15/9).

Lake Burley Griffin Cruises CRUISE
(☎0419 418 846; www.lakecruises.com.au; adult/child $15/8) Runs informative tours on the lake daily between mid-October and mid-May.

Festivals & Events

For a handy calendar of festivals and special events in the ACT, see www.events.act.gov.au.

Australia Day Live LIVE MUSIC
(www.australiaday.org.au) The annual 25 January live concert on the lawns of Parliament House.

National Multicultural Festival CULTURAL
(www.multiculturalfestival.com.au) Celebrated in February.

Royal Canberra Show AGRICULTURAL SHOW
(www.rncas.org.au/showwebsite/main.html) The country meets the city at the end of February.

Enlighten CULTURE
(www.enlightencanberra.com.au) In March, many of the city's cultural institutions open their doors after-hours to host events and experiences promoting 'Canberra in a whole new light'.

Canberra Festival ARTS, CULTURE
(www.events.act.gov.au) The city's extended birthday party on 12 March, with a day-long food, drinks and arts festival.

Canberra Balloon Spectacular HOT-AIR BALLOONING
The lawns in front of Old Parliament House are filled with hot-air balloons taking to the sky one weekend in March.

National Folk Festival ARTS, CULTURE
(www.folkfestival.asn.au) One of the country's largest folk festivals is held each Easter.

Canberra District Wine Harvest Festival WINE
(www.canberrawines.com.au) This weekend of wine, food and music at Canberra district wineries is organised by the Canberra District Wine Industry Association and is held in April.

Anzac Day MEMORIAL
National holiday held on 25 April, commemorating the armed services. Dawn services and marches are held at the Australian War Memorial.

Canberra International Music Festival MUSIC
(www.cimf.org.au) Local, interstate and international musicians perform in iconic architectural spaces around town in May.

Floriade FLOWER SHOW
(www.floriadeaustralia.com) Held in September/October, Canberra's headline festival is dedicated to the city's spectacular spring flowers.

Sleeping

Canberra's accommodation is busiest during parliamentary sitting days. At this time, hotels charge peak rates mid-week, but drop rates on weekends. Peak rates also apply during the Floriade festival.

In this chapter, budget ($) indicates a room costing under $120 per night, midrange ($$) between $120 and $250 per night and top-end ($$$) over $250 a night. Unfortunately, there are very few budget and lower-midrange options worthy of recommendation.

Most places don't include breakfast in their standard room rates. We've noted exceptions in the reviews.

North of Lake Burley Griffin

Canberra City YHA HOSTEL $
(Map p262; ☎02-6248 9155; www.yha.com.au; 7 Akuna St, Civic; dm $32-39, d & tw $110, f $175; ❄@📶🏊) School groups dominate the guest register of this well-run hostel. Most rooms and dorms use shared bathrooms, although the family rooms have private facilities. Dorms have bunks and lockers and private rooms have tea-and-coffee-making facilities. Services and facilities include bike hire ($25 per day), a small indoor pool, a sauna, a self-catering kitchen, an outdoor terrace hosting BBQs on Fridays, and a cafe.

★**Diamant Hotel** BOUTIQUE HOTEL $$
(Map p262; ☎02-6175 2222; www.diamant.com.au; 15 Edinburgh Ave, Civic; r $160-320, apt $350-650; P❄📶) Located in the up-and-coming New Acton precinct near Civic, the Diamant has a sheen of Sydney-style sophistication. Eight types of rooms and apartments occupy a 1926 apartment block, all renovated and featuring amenities including ipod docks, B&O CD players and spacious bathrooms with rain showers. Service is solicitous and facilities include a gym and the popular Library Bar and Bicicletta Restaurant.

University House HOTEL $$
(Map p262; ☎02-6125 5211; www.anu.edu.au/unihouse; 1 Balmain Cres, Acton; s without bathroom $99, d & tw with bathroom $144-159, apt $190; P❄📶) This 1950s-era building, with furniture and ambience to match, resides in the bushy grounds of the Australian National University (ANU) and is favoured by research students, visiting academics and the occasional politician. The spacious rooms and two-bedroom apartments are basic but comfortable enough. There's also a pleasant rear courtyard, a restaurant and a cafe.

Mercure Canberra HOTEL $$
(Map p262; ☎02-6243 0000; www.accorhotels.com; cnr Ainslie & Limestone Aves, Braddon; standard d $159-209, superior $189-269; ❄📶) The main wing of this busy business hotel occupies a 1927 National Trust–listed building very close to the War Memorial. Later additions have been built around a garden courtyard and house the best of the rooms – opt for a superior room with balcony if possible.

HALLS OF RESIDENCE

Some of the ANU's halls of residence, nestled in the campus' leafy grounds, rent out rooms from late November to late February during uni holidays. Most offer similar facilities; room prices start at around $65.

See www.visitcanberra.com.au/Accommodation/Residential-colleges.aspx for details.

South of Lake Burley Griffin

★**East Hotel** HOTEL $$$
(Map p260; ☎02-6295 6925, 1800 816 469; www.easthotel.com.au; 69 Canberra Ave, Kingston; studio r $265-320, apt $315-270; P❄@📶) Cleverly straddling the divide between boutique and business, this new hotel offers thoughtfully planned and stylishly executed spaces. The foyer is home to a multimedia installation, bank of Apple Macs, lounge area (complete with excellent magazine selection) and cafe; next door is the chic Ox Eatery and a bar. Rooms feature amenities including a work desk, ipod dock, espresso machine and equipped kitchenette – we were particularly impressed with the 'luxe studios' and with the family rooms, which come complete with X-box and beanbags.

Burbury Hotel HOTEL $$$
(Map p262; ☎02-6173 2700; www.burburyhotel.com.au; 1 Burbury Close, Barton; r $195-240, ste $210-300, 2-bed ste $240-380; P❄@📶) This business hotel offers rooms, one- and two-bedroom suites and access to leisure facilities at the neighbouring Realm Hotel. The decor of the rooms and suites is bland, but all are well set-up and pleasantly light. In-room technology is particularly impressive, offering Apple Mac-Minis and ipod docks. Breakfast costs $20 and is enjoyed on an upstairs terrace with a great view.

Brassey HOTEL $$$
(Map p262; ☎02-6273 3766; www.brassey.net.au; cnr Belmore Gardens & Macquarie St, Barton;

r $190-245, f $280-300; P ❄ @) Endearingly old-fashioned, the Brassey has a guesthouse feel and is very popular with conference groups and elderly tourists, who maintain a high profile in the in-house bar, restaurant and beer garden. Rooms lack even a skerrick of style, but are comfortable and clean. The lack of wi-fi will be a disincentive for some, but the generous complimentary breakfast buffet compensates.

Hyatt Hotel Canberra LUXURY HOTEL $$$
(Map p262; ☎02-6270 1234; www.canberra.park.hyatt.com; 120 Commonwealth Ave, Yarralumla; r $250-700, ste $695-1200; P ❄ @ ☰ ≋) Spotting visiting heads of state is a popular activity in the foyer of Canberra's most luxurious and historic hotel. Over 200 rooms, well-used meeting spaces and a popular tea lounge mean that a constant stream of visitors passes through the building. Rooms are large, recently refurbished and extremely well equipped, and facilities include an indoor pool, spa, sauna and gym.

The York Canberra APARTMENT $$$
(Map p262; ☎02-6295 2333; www.yorkcanberra.com.au; 31 Giles St, Kingston; r $250, 1-bed apt $275, 2-bed apt $350; P ❄ ☰) Located in the centre of Kingston's popular cafe and restaurant strip, the York is an excellent choice for business travellers and families. It offers a range of well-sized suites and apartments, some with fully equipped kitchens and washing machine/dryer, and the rest with kitchenettes. No breakfast, but there are plenty of cafe options close by.

Hotel Realm HOTEL $$$
(Map p262; ☎02-6163 1800; www.hotelrealm.com.au; 18 National Circuit, Barton; r $215-285, ste $250-315; ❄ ☰ ≋) This flashy joint aims to impress, from the soaring atrium lobby to the spacious double rooms overlooking Capital Hill. Mostly servicing business guests, it's an easy distance from Parliament House and the museums on King Edward Tce. There's a spa, a health club with lap pool, gym, sauna and steam room. The array of popular restaurants and bars downstairs will make choosing a dinner or drinking venue easy.

Eating

Dining hubs include Civic, Kingston, Manuka and Griffith. There's also a popular Asian strip on Woolley St in Dickson. Note that many restaurants are closed on Sunday and Monday.

North of Lake Burley Griffin

Lonsdale Street Roasters CAFE $
(Map p262; http://lonsdalestreetroasters.com; Shop 3, 7 Lonsdale St, Braddon; panini $6-13; ⏲6.30am-4pm Mon-Fri, 6.30am-3pm Sat) Ask a Canberran to nominate the cafe serving the best coffee in town and their answer will almost inevitably be this grungy-chic cafe. A range of gourmet panini are on offer, as is damn fine coffee made with freshly roasted beans.

Gus' Café CAFE $
(Map p262; ☎02-6248 8118; www.guscafe.com.au; cnr Garema Pl & Bunda St; breakfast $4-18; ⏲7.15am-9pm) Augustin Petersilka (aka Gus), a homesick Viennese, founded this cafe in 1967 and it has since become a Canberra institution. It serves sandwiches, wraps and burgers at lunch, but is best loved for all-day breakfast and its rich and delectable cakes (try the chocolate mud).

Urban Food CAFE $
(Map p262; cnr Marcus Clarke St & Edinburgh Ave, Civic; ⏲7.30am-3.30pm, produce store open until 8pm) Come here for a fresh juice, smoothie or organic, single-estate coffee while checking your email using the complimentary wi-fi. On your way out, you can go grocery shopping in the attached produce and liquor shop.

★ **Lanterne Rooms** MALAYSIAN $$
(Map p260; ☎02-6249 6889; http://lanternerooms.chairmangroup.com.au; Shop 3, Blamey Pl, Campell Shops; mains $30-34; ⏲noon-2.30pm & 6-10.30pm Tue-Fri, 6-10.30pm Sat) It may be located in a scruffy shopping centre in Campbell, but that's the only suburban trait apparent in this atmosphere-laden eatery. Serving expertly cooked Nyonya dishes in a colourful interior that references Penang farmhouses from the colonial era, it's sophisticated and welcoming in equal measure.

Italian & Sons ITALIAN $$
(Map p262; ☎02-6162 4888; www.italianandsons.com.au; Shop 7, 7 Lonsdale St, Braddon; mains $24-33; ⏲6-10pm Mon & Sat, noon-2.30pm & 6-10pm Tue-Fri) As hip as Canberra gets, this trattoria serves thin-crust pizzas, al dente pastas and one dish of the day to a loyal clientele. Book ahead.

Bicicletta Restaurant ITALIAN $$
(Map p262; ☎02 6262 8683; www.8hotels.com/canberra-hotel/diamant-hotel/bicicletta; Diamant Hotel, 15 Edinburgh Ave, Civic; panini $12-18,

pastas $20-28, pizzas $20-25; ⏲7-11am, noon-3pm & 6-10pm) The chefs at this casual restaurant inside the Diamant Hotel in the New Acton precinct make the most of seasonal, locally sourced and sustainable produce. Lunch is casual (panini, salads, pizza and pasta) and dinner is pretty much the same, albeit with the addition of a few grilled dishes to the menu. The indoor/outdoor eating arrangement works particularly well in summer, when the restaurant hosts an outdoor cinema on Tuesday evenings.

Cream CAFE, BAR $$
(Map p262; ☎02-6162 1448; www.creamcafebar.com.au; cnr Bunda & Genge Sts, Civic; breakfast $7-18, light lunches $11-24, mains $23-36; ⏲7.30am-10pm Mon-Fri, 8am-10pm Sat & Sun) Bunda St is Canberra's entertainment epicentre, and this huge art deco–inspired joint was the ruling monarch of the scene when we visited. Arranged around a central bar, its tables are filled with ladies lunching, businessmen closing deals and shoppers needing a rest. After work, cocktails reign supreme.

Tosolini's ITALIAN $$
(Map p262; ☎02-6247 4317; www.tosolinis.com.au; cnr London Circuit & East Row, Civic; breakfast $15-17, panini $9, pastas $20-28; ⏲7.30am-late) Well-worn Tosolini's has been keeping workers and shoppers replete and happy for decades, and shows no sign of losing its somewhat stolid allure. Toasted panini, bruschetta and focaccias are popular at lunch, but mamma-style pastas take centre stage for dinner.

Sammy's Kitchen MALAYSIAN $$
(Map p262; ☎02-6247 1464; Shop FG09 North Quarter, Canberra Centre, Bunda St, Civic; mains $10-25; ⏲11am-10pm) Sammy's is a long-standing local favourite serving up cheap and plentiful Chinese and Malay dishes. No frills, but lots of fun.

Dieci e Mezzo ITALIAN $$
(Map p262; ☎02-6248 3142; www.dieciemezzo.com.au; AGL House, cnr Bunda & Mort Sts; mains $29-34; ⏲8.30am-10pm Mon-Fri, 6-10pm Sat) Its office-foyer location is a bit strange, but the Scandinavian-influenced fit out at this restaurant is extremely stylish and the food is absolutely delicious. The derivation is Italian, but the execution is up-to-the-minute Oz, making the most of local, seasonal produce and matching it to a thoughtful list of Australian and international wines. The express lunch ($29/39/49 for 1/2/3 courses plus a glass of wine) is terrific value.

Courgette MODERN AUSTRALIAN $$$
(Map p262; ☎02-6247 4042; www.courgette.com.au; 54 Marcus Clarke St, Civic; 4-course set dinner menu $75, 3-course express lunch $55; ⏲noon-3pm & 6.30-11pm Mon-Fri, 6.30-11pm Sat) Locals wanting to celebrate major occasions often head to this restaurant in Civic, drawn by its French-influenced menu and wine list. The surrounds are uninspiring (particularly the side dining space) and the food may be overly fussy for some. Set menus are compulsory.

South of Lake Burley Griffin

★Silo Bakery BAKERY, CAFE $
(Map p262; ☎02-6260 6060; http://silobakery.com.au/; 36 Giles St, Kingston; breakfast $3.50-22, lunch $12-24; ⏲7am-4pm Tue-Sat) Why can't this place open a branch where we live? If it did, we'd be there all the time! Its soughdough bread, pies, pastries and tarts are perfect breakfast temptations, and an assortment of filled baguettes, rustic mains and cheese platters keep the customers happy at lunch. Good coffee and a thoughtful list of wines by the glass complete an almost perfect package. Book for lunch.

Kitchen Cabinet CAFE $
(Map p262; www.thekitchencabinet.com.au; King George Terrace, Parkes, Old Parliament House; sandwiches, pies & quiches $8; ⏲9am-5pm) Located in the foyer of Old Parliament House (hence the pun in its name), this cracker of a cafe serves sandwiches, pies, quiches, a daily dish of the day and truly excellent coffee to queues of staffers from parliament house and the galleries. There's a small internal dining area and a few tables on the terrace.

★Ottoman TURKISH $$
(Map p262; ☎02-6273 6111; www.ottomancuisine.com.au; cnr Broughton & Blackall Sts, Barton; mains $33, 7-course degustation menu $75; ⏲noon-3pm & 6-10pm Tue-Fri, 6-10pm Sat) A whimsically designed glass pavilion in the middle of Barton is a surprising location for this splendid Turkish restaurant. There are plenty of traditional dishes on the menu (mezes, dolma, kebabs) but most are given a cunning Mod Oz twist by chef Erkin Esen. The wine list is well-priced and thoughtfully constructed, and service is exemplary.

Artespresso MODERN AUSTRALIAN $$
(Map p262; ☎02-6295 8055; 31 Giles St, Kingston; breakfast dishes $6-20, mains $26-36; ⏲noon-2.30

&6-10pm Mon-Fri, 9am-2pm Sat & Sun) This bistro-style eatery has contemporary art on the walls, but the paintings get scant attention from diners elbow-deep in decadent eggy breakfasts or supping on delicious dinners.

Aubergine MODERN AUSTRALIAN **$$$**
(Map p260; ☎02-6260 8666; www.aubergine.com.au; 18 Barker St, Griffith; 2-/3-/5-course set menu $65/80/95; ⏲6pm-10pm Mon-Sat) It may be loved by food critics, but Aubergine isn't the type of restaurant to big-note itself. Frankly, it doesn't need to. After eating here everyone leaves with an appreciation of Ben Willis' great ability to deliver a menu that hits all the right buttons – delicious, exciting and perfectly balanced. Service and food presentation are assured, leaving the dining space with its huge windows to supply a theatrical touch.

Malamay CHINESE **$$$**
(Map p262; ☎02-6162 1220; http://malamay.chairmangroup.com.au; 1 Burbury Close, Barton, Burbury Hotel; lunch banquet $46.50, dinner banquet $68.50; ⏲noon-2.30pm & 6pm-10.30pm Tue-Fri, 6-10.30pm Sat) The spicy flavours of Sichuan cuisine entice at this new restaurant. A glamorous interior references Shanghai circa 1930 and is a perfect setting in which to enjoy a (mandatory) set banquet.

The Tea Lounge CAFE **$$$**
(Map p262; 120 Commonwealth Avenue, Parkes, Hyatt Hotel; high tea $43; ⏲2.30-5pm Sat & Sun) Put on your glad rags (boaters and feather boas are not unknown) and shimmy on down to the lounge in the Hyatt Hotel to enjoy a lavish spread of sandwiches, scones, cakes and slices accompanied by a glass of bubbly (included). Bookings are essential.

Drinking & Nightlife

Pubs and bars are mostly concentrated in Civic, but there are also some in the northern suburbs of Dickson and O'Connor and across the lake in Kingston. During the summer, when the university students are out of town, the bar scene pretty well collapses.

Knightsbridge Penthouse COCKTAIL BAR
(Map p262; ☎02-6262 6221; www.knightsbridgepenthouse.com.au; 34 Mort St, Braddon; ⏲5pm-midnight Tue & Wed, 4pm-1am Thu, 4pm-3am Fri & Sat) Its name may make it sound like an upmarket brothel, but this gin joint is a lot classier than that. It meets its self-stated aim of 'purveying good times', offering an arty, gay-friendly atmosphere and serving excellent cocktails.

Phoenix PUB
(Map p262; ☎02-6247 1606; www.lovethephoenix.com; 23 East Row, Civic; ⏲noon-1am Mon-Wed, noon-3am Thu-Sat) Regulars don't think twice about coming back to this pub after rising from the ashes of the night before. It's a staunch supporter of new local musicians, and has a mellow atmosphere, rustic decorations and armchairs that incline you towards pondering life for the night.

King O'Malley's IRISH PUB
(Map p262; ☎02-6257 0111; www.kingomalleys.com.au; 131 City Walk, Civic; ⏲11am-midnight) This backpacker favourite is one of a number of Irish-themed pubs in Canberra, and it lives up to its claim of being the best of the bunch. There's Guinness and Kilkenny on tap, as well as a busy entertainment programme (trivia night on Monday, Irish jam music on Sunday and Thursday, a French-speaking night on Wednesday, and live bands on Thursday, Friday and Saturday). No covers and definitely no attitude.

Tongue & Groove BAR, CLUB
(Map p262; www.tandg.com.au; cnr Genge & Bunda Sts, Civic; ⏲5.30pm-9.30pm Mon-Thu, noon-2am Fri & Sat, noon-9.30pm Sun) There's a different offering every night at T&G – tapas on Monday, pizza specials on Tuesday, live music on Thursday, a DJ spinning old-school mash-ups on Friday etc. The bar morphs into a club on Friday and Saturday nights.

Benchmark Wine Bar WINE BAR
(Map p262; ☎02-6262 6522; www.benchmark-winebar.com.au; 65 Northbourne Ave, Civic; ⏲11.30am-3pm & 5pm-late Mon-Fri, 5pm-late Sat) All-day tapas, a tasty brasserie menu and an annually adjusted wine menu listing over 500 bottles are the hallmarks here. Book if you're coming for dinner.

Honky Tonks BAR
(Map p262; www.drinkhonkytonks.com.au; 17 Garema Pl, Civic; ⏲4pm-late Mon-Thu, 2pm-late Fri-Sun) Canberra's compadres meet up here to eat tacos, drink margaritas and listen to eclectic sets from the DJ. It's loads of fun.

Mooseheads PUB, CLUB
(Map p262; www.mooseheads.com.au; 105 London Circuit, Civic; ⏲11am-3am Mon-Wed, 11am-5am Thu-Sat) Plenty of beers on tap (including the house brew) and cheap prices make this place popular. Pool tables and pub meals downstairs, dancefloor and DJ upstairs.

ANU Union Bar PUB

(Map p262; 02-6125 2446; www.anuunion.com.au; Union Ct, Acton; cover $5-20; gigs from 8pm) A mainstay of Canberra's music scene, the Uni Bar (on the ANU campus) has live music bouncing off its walls and into the ears of sozzled students up to three times a week during the semester. Student discounts usually apply to gigs. It's also a good place for a game of pool and a drink.

Wig & Pen PUB

(Map p262; 02-6248 0171; cnr Alinga St & West Row, Civic; noon-midnight Mon-Fri, 2pm-midnight Sat & Sun) This little brewery and pub has its two-room interior packed out on Friday nights by office workers who also enjoy the hearty pub grub. It produces several styles of beer, including real English-style ale.

Little Brussels Belgian Beer Cafe PUB

(Map p262; 02-6260 6511; http://belgiumbeercanberra.com.au; 29 Jardine St, Kingston; noon-10pm Mon & Sun, to 11pm Tue-Thu, to midnight Fri & Sat) Serving over 40 Belgian beers and offering a menu replete with Belgian dishes (mussels, anyone?), this is the place to quench a thirst and educate a palate.

Cube NIGHTCLUB

(Map p262; 02-6257 1110; www.cubenightclub.com.au; 33 Petrie Plaza, Civic; 10pm-late Thu-Sun) Revellers throw themselves onto the bed-sized lounges to take a break from the dance floor at this hetero-friendly gay club. Expect cheap drinks on Thursday and frisky male dancers on Friday.

Transit Bar BAR

(Map p262; 02-6162 0899; http://transitbar.com.au; 7 Akuna St, Civic; noon-10pm Mon-Sat, 2pm-8pm Sun) Tucked under a youth hostel, this bar hosts karaoke on Tuesday, trivia on Wednesday and live gigs at the end of the week.

☆ Entertainment

Canberra has always been curiously good at nurturing its music talent, and live gigs are always popping up around town. You'll find entertainment listings in Thursday's *Canberra Times* and on the **BMA website** (www.bmamag.com). **Ticketek** (Map p262; 02-6219 6666; www.ticketek.com.au; Akuna St, Civic) sells tickets to all major events.

Cinemas

Palace Electric Cinema CINEMA

(Map p262; 02-6222 4900; www.palacecinemas.com.au/cinemas/electric/; 2 Phillip Law St, New Acton Nishi) Art-house, documentary, independent and quality new release films are screened at this brand-new cinema in the glam NewActon complex.

Theatre

Canberra Theatre Centre THEATRE

(Map p262; box office 02-6275 2700; www.canberratheatre.org.au; London Circuit, Civic Sq, Civic; box office 9am-5pm Mon-Fri, 10am-2pm Sat) This centre is the hub of live theatre in Canberra and the dramatic goings-on range from Shakespeare to Circus Oz and Indigenous dance troupes.

Sport

The Canberra Raiders are the hometown rugby league side and during the season (from March to September) they play regularly at **Canberra Stadium** (Map p260; 02-6256 6700; www.canberrastadium.com; Battye St, Bruce). Also laying tackles at Canberra Stadium are the ACT Brumbies rugby union team, who play in the international Super 15 competition (February to May).

Shopping

For tasteful souvenirs, check out the gift shops in the National Gallery of Australia (p259), the National Portrait Gallery (p260) and the National Museum of Australia (p261). There is late-night city shopping on Friday.

Canberra Centre MALL

(Map p262; 02-6247 5611; www.canberracentre.com.au; Bunda St, Civic; 9am-5.30pm Mon-Thu, 9am-9pm Fri, 9am-5pm Sat, 10am-4pm Sun) The city's biggest shopping centre boasts fashion boutiques, food emporia, jewellery shops, a cinema complex and the David Jones and Myer department stores. The information desk can help with wheelchair and stroller hire.

Craft ACT HOMEWARES, JEWELLERY

(Map p262; 02-6262 9993; www.craftact.org.au; 1st fl, North Bldg, 180 London Circuit, Civic; 10am-5pm Tue-Fri, noon-4pm Sat) It's well worth visiting this venue for the wonderful exhibitions of contemporary work, including cutting-edge designs in the form of bags, bowls, pendants and prints.

Electric Shadows Bookshop BOOKSHOP

(Map p262; 02-6248 8352; www.electricshadowsbookshop.com.au; 40 Mort St, Braddon; 9am-7pm Mon-Thu, 9am-8pm Fri & Sat, 11am-6pm Sun) Canberra's best bookshop has a particularly strong selection of books on theatre and film, plus gay and lesbian books and an excellent range of art-house DVDs.

Old Bus Depot Markets MARKET
(Map p262; ☎02-6292 8391; www.obdm.com.au; 21 Wentworth Ave, Kingston; ⊙10am-4pm Sun) This popular, decade-old indoor market specialises in handcrafted goods and regional edibles, including the output of the Canberra district's 20-plus wineries.

National Library Bookshop BOOKSHOP
(Map p262; ☎02-6262 1424; http://bookshop.nla.gov.au; Parkes Pl, Parkes; ⊙9am-5pm) Stocks exclusively Australian books, including a superb range of fiction.

Information

EMERGENCY

Dial 000 for ambulance, fire or police.

Canberra Rape Crisis Centre (☎02-6247 2525; http://crcc.org.au) Help 24 hours.

Lifeline (☎13 11 14) Crisis counselling available 24 hours.

INTERNET ACCESS

There's free wi-fi in parts of the Canberra Centre – check its website for specific locations. You'll also find free access in the Canberra Museum and Gallery, the National Library of Australia, Parliament House and the cafe at the National Museum of Australia.

INTERNET RESOURCES

Canberra & Region Bed & Breakfast Network (www.canberrabandb.net.au) B&B options in and around Canberra.

Events ACT (www.events.act.gov.au) A guide to local festivals and events.

Visit Canberra (www.visitcanberra.com.au) What to eat, see, drink and do in Canberra. Also organises accommodation bookings.

MEDICAL SERVICES

Canberra Hospital (☎emergency dept 02-6244 2222; http://health.act.gov.au/health-services/canberra-hospital; Yamba Dr, Garran; ⊙24hr emergency dept)

Travel Doctor (☎02-6222 2300; www.traveldoctor.com.au; Suite 14, Lena Karmel Lodge, 1 Childers Ln, Civic; ⊙8.30am-5pm Mon & Fri, 8.30am-7.30pm Tue-Thu) For all travel vaccinations – appointments essential.

TOURIST INFORMATION

Canberra & Region Visitors Centre (☎1300 554 114, 02-6205 0044; www.visitcanberra.com.au; 330 Northbourne Ave, Dickson; ⊙9am-5pm Mon-Fri, to 4pm Sat & Sun) Head to this centre north of Civic for information about the city and the region. There's also a **City Information Booth** (Map p262; ⊙10am-4pm Mon-Sat) near Garema Pl in Civic, open from September to April.

Citizens Advice Bureau ACT (Map p262; ☎02-6248 7988; www.citizensadvice.org.au; Griffin Centre, 20 Genge St, Civic; ⊙10am-4pm Mon, Tue, Thu & Fri, to 1pm Wed) The helpful people here can provide you with plenty of information on the community services and facilities available in the ACT.

Getting There & Away

Air

Qantas (☎13 13 13, TTY 1800 652 660; www.qantas.com.au; Northbourne Ave, Jolimont Centre, Civic) and **Virgin Australia** (☎13 67 89; www.virginaustralia.com) flights connect **Canberra Airport** (Map p260; ☎02-6275 2226; www.canberraairport.com.au) with all Australian state capitals. **Brindabella Airlines** (☎1300 668 824; www.brindabella-airlines.com.au) services Newcastle.

Bus

The **interstate bus terminal** is at the Jolimont Centre and has showers, left-luggage lockers, public internet access, and free phone lines to the visitor information centre and some budget accommodation.

Inside is **Greyhound Australia** (Map p262; ☎1300 4739 46863, GREYHOUND 1300; ⊙Jolimont Centre branch 6am-9.30pm) with frequent services to Sydney ($36 to $42, 3½ hours to 4½ hours), Adelaide ($175, 19¾ hours) and Melbourne ($75 to $85, eight to nine hours). In winter there are services to Cooma, Jindabyne and Thredbo.

Also in the terminal is **Murrays** (Map p262; ☎13 22 51; www.murrays.com.au; ⊙Jolimont Centre branch 7am-7pm), which runs daily express services to Sydney (adult $33 to $39, 3½ hours) and also runs to Batemans Bay ($28, 2½ hours), Narooma ($42, 4½ hours) and Wollongong ($42, 3½ hours), as well as the ski fields.

Transborder (☎02-6241 0033; www.transborder.com.au) runs daily to Yass ($11, 50 minutes) and has a service to Thredbo via Jindabyne during the ski season.

Car & Motorcycle

The Hume Hwy connects Sydney and Melbourne, passing 50km north of Canberra. The Federal Hwy runs north to connect with the Hume near Goulburn, and the Barton Hwy (Rte 25) meets the Hume near Yass. To the south, the Monaro Hwy connects Canberra with Cooma.

Train

Kingston train station (Wentworth Ave) is the city's rail terminus. Book trains and connecting buses inside the station at the **CountryLink**

Travel Centre (☎13 22 32, 02-6295 1198; ⏲6am-5pm Mon-Sat, 10.30am-5.30pm Sun).

CountryLink trains run to/from Sydney ($29 to $40, 4½ hours, two to three daily). There's no direct train to Melbourne; a CountryLink coach to Cootamundra ($14, 2½ hours) links with the Sydney to Melbourne train service ($67, six hours). A daily **V/Line** (☎13 61 96; www.vline.com.au) Canberra Link service involves a train between Melbourne and Albury-Wodonga, then a connecting bus to Canberra ($54, 8½ hours).

Getting Around

To/From the Airport

Canberra Airport is in Pialligo, which is situated 8km southeast of the city. A taxi fare to the city centre costs around $35 ($37 between 9pm and 6am). **Airport Express** (☎1300 368 897; www.royalecoach.com.au; $10 one way) runs 20-minute shuttle-bus services between the airport and West Row in Civic between 7am and 5.50pm weekdays, and at 8.10am and 6.40pm on weekends.

Car & Motorcycle

Canberra's road system is as circuitous as a politician's answer to a straight question. That said, the wide and relatively uncluttered main roads make driving easy, even at so-called 'peak-hour' times. A map is essential.

Parking is plentiful and relatively inexpensive.

Public Transport

Canberra's public transport provider is the **ACT Internal Omnibus Network** (Action; ☎13 17 10; www.action.act.gov.au). The main bus stops are along Alinga St, East Row and Mort St. The **information kiosk** (East Row, Civic; ⏲7.30am-5.30pm Mon-Fri) has free maps and timetables.

You can buy single-trip tickets (adult/concession $4/2), but it's better value to buy a daily ticket (adult/concession $7.60/3.80). Prepurchase tickets are available from Action agents (including the visitors centre and some newsagents). You can also buy them on buses.

Services are regular on weekdays, but thin on the ground on weekends.

Action also offers several tourist routes (buses 33, 34, 40 and 80) that service most of Canberra's tourist attractions.

Taxi

Canberra Elite Taxis (☎13 22 27; www.canberracabs.com.au)

Cabxpress (☎02-6260 6011; www.cabxpress.com.au)

AROUND CANBERRA

For information and maps on sights around Canberra, including the unspoiled bushland just outside the urban limits, head to the Canberra & Region Visitors Centre.

WINERIES OF THE ACT

Canberra's wine region is finally attracting worldwide recognition for the high-country cool-climate wines produced here. In particular the area has wonderful riesling and shiraz.

For a list of cellar doors to visit, see www.canberrawines.com.au or pick up a *Canberra District Wineries Guide* map at the Canberra Visitors Centre. These are a good start:

Brindabella Hills Winery (☎02-6230 2583; www.brindabellahills.com.au; Woodgrove Cl, Hall; ⏲cellar door 10am-5pm Sat & Sun) This sizeable vineyard near Hall is set on a beautiful ridge and will suppy cheese platters to accompany your tasting on request.

Clonakilla Wines (☎02-6277 5877; www.clonakilla.com.au; Crisps Ln, Murrumbateman; ⏲cellar door 10am-5pm) Boutique winery producing some highly sought varieties, including an award-winning shiraz viognier.

Eden Road Wines (☎02-6226 8800; www.edenroadwines.com.au; 3182 Barton Hwy, Murrumbateman; cellar door 11am-4pm Wed-Sun) New winery producing fantastic shiraz.

Helm Wines (☎02-6227 5953; www.helmwines.com.au; 19 Butts Rd, Murrembateman ; ⏲cellar door 10am-5pm Thu-Mon) The best rieslings produced in the region can be tasted in the winery's pretty tasting room, a former schoolhouse dating from 1888.

Lark Hill (☎02-6238 1393; www.larkhillwine.com.au; 521 Bungendore Rd, Bungendore; ⏲cellar door 10am-5pm Thu-Mon) Set in the hills on the Lake George Escarpment overlooking Bungendore village, Lark Hill produces biodynamic wines and has a restaurant.

Wily Trout Vineyard (☎02-6230 2487; www.poacherspantry.com.au; 431 Nanima Rd, Hall; ⏲cellar door 10am-5pm, cafe noon-3pm & 6-10pm Fri, 10am-3pm & 6-10pm Sat, 10am-3pm Sun) Home to the Poachers Pantry and Smokehouse Café, the best eatery in the region.

Murrumbidgee River Corridor

About 66km of the **Murrumbidgee River** flows through the ACT, and along with major tributaries of the **Molonglo** and **Cotter Rivers**, it has great riverside picnic locations and swimming spots. Pick up a map and brochure at the Canberra Visitors Centre and explore the waters of: **Uriarra Crossing**, 24km northwest of the city, on the Murrumbidgee near its meeting with the Molonglo River; **Casuarina Sands**, 19km west of the city at the meeting of the Cotter and Murrumbidgee Rivers; **Kambah Pool Reserve**, another 14km upstream on the Murrumbidgee; **Cotter Dam**, 23km west of the city on the Cotter River and with a camping ground; **Pine Island** and **Point Hut Crossing**, upstream of Kambah Pool Reserve; and **Gibraltar Falls**, about 45km southwest of the city.

On the banks of the Murrumbidgee, 20km south of Canberra, is the lovely **Lanyon Homestead** (☎02-6235 5677; www.museumsandgalleries.act.gov.au/lanyon/; Tharwa Dr, Tharwa; adult/concession/family $7/5/15; ⏲10am-4pm Tue-Sun), a beautifully restored 1850s farming property. You can picnic in the rambling gardens or take a break in its cafe.

Tidbinbilla & Namadgi

Canberra Space Centre MUSEUM
(☎02-6201 7880; www.cdscc.nasa.gov; 421 Discovery Dr, off Cotter & Paddys River Rds, Tidbinbilla; ⏲9am-5pm) FREE The Canberra Space Centre resides in the grounds of the Canberra Deep Space Communication Complex, 35km southwest of the city. Pride of place goes to Deep Space Station 43, a 70m-diameter dish that has communicated with the likes of *Voyager 1* and *2*, *Galileo* and various Mars probes. There are displays of spacecraft and deep-space tracking technology, plus a piece of lunar basalt scooped up by *Apollo XI* in 1969. A theatre continuously screens short films on space exploration.

Tidbinbilla Nature Reserve NATURE RESERVE
(☎02-6205 1233; www.tidbinbilla.com.au; off Paddy's River Rd, via Cotter Rd, Weston Creek, or Point Hut Crossing, Gordon; day pass per car $10, concession driver $6.50; ⏲visitor centre 9am-4.30pm) Located just 45km southwest of the city, this nature reserve is full of bushwalking tracks. There are kangaroos and emus here and you can view platypuses and lyrebirds at dusk. Call for information on ranger-guided activities on weekends and school holidays.

Namadgi National Park NATIONAL PARK
(www.tams.act.gov.au/parks-recreation/parks_and_reserves/namadgi_national_park) Namadgi is the Aboriginal word for the mountains southwest of Canberra, and this park includes eight peaks higher than 1700m. It offers excellent opportunities for bushwalking, mountain biking, fishing, horse riding and viewing Aboriginal rock art. For more information, visit the **Namadgi Visitor Centre** (☎02-6207 2900; Naas Rd, Tharwa; ⏲9am-4pm Mon-Fri, to 4.30pm Sat & Sun), 2km south of the Tharwa township. **Camping** (unpowered sites per person $3-5) is available at Honeysuckle Creek, Mt Clear and Orroral River; book through the visitor centre.

Surrounding Towns & Villages

A number of NSW towns lie just over the border and are intrinsically linked to the national capital. Many of them offer country-style accommodation plus fine food and wine.

Just 15 minutes' drive from downtown Canberra along the Barton Hwy you'll find **Hall**, where the **Poachers Pantry** (☎02-6230 2487; www.poacherspantry.com.au; Nanima Rd, Hall; ⏲10am-5pm daily for tastings and sales) at Wily Trout Vineyard attracts foodies from all over the region for its cured meats.

There's a clutch of highly regarded wineries at **Murrumbateman** (30 minutes' drive from Canberra along the Barton Hwy). After a day of tastings, you may wish to check into the welcoming **Schönegg Guesthouse** (☎02-6227 0344; www.schonegg.com.au; 381 Hillview Dr, Murrumbateman; s $120-230, d $140-250; ❄📶) for the night.

Bungendore is a very attractive village 35km east of Canberra that bustles on weekends but sleeps during the week. There are galleries and antique stores aplenty to keep the cardigan crowd amused and bemused, but the highlight would have to be the **Bungendore Wood Works Gallery** (☎02-6238 1682; http://bungendorewoodworks.com.au; cnr Malbon & Ellendon Sts, Bungendore; ⏲9am-5pm), which showcases superb works crafted from Australian timber. If you opt to stay the night, the best accommodation option is the antique-laden, character-filled **Old Stone House** (☎02-6238 1888; www.theoldstonehouse.com.au; 41 Molonglo St, Bungendore; r $220; ❄).

Queensland & the Great Barrier Reef

Includes ➡

Off the Beaten Track

- Lizard Island (p460)
- Lamington National Park (p328)
- Torres Strait Islands (p471)
- Mt Isa (p374)
- Rainbow Beach (p352)

Best Places to Stay

- Azjure Studio Retreat (p344)
- Svendsen's Beach (p370)
- Bowen Terrace (p299)
- Reef House Resort & Spa (p436)
- Hillcrest Guest House (p459)

Why Go?

From the surf-soaked Gold Coast beaches to the tropical Daintree rainforest, this massive state offers a dizzying array of distractions. Queensland's big-ticket lure is the 2000km-long submarine kingdom of the Great Barrier Reef: fish, fish, coral and more fish... Islands are also a Queensland speciality: everything from photogenic coral-fringed beauties to rugged sand isles ripe for adventure.

Speaking of adventure, the 'Sunshine State' really delivers: snorkel or dive under warm ocean waves, go white-water rafting on grade-IV rapids, kayak the coastline, surf a classic point break, or bushwalk through rainforests and gorges. Wildlife-watching is superb here too, with tropical birds, whales, cassowaries and crocs filling your photo album.

When the sun sets, Queensland doesn't go to bed: seafood feasts, cool bars, live bands and pumping clubs await (especially in Brisbane, arguably Australia's hippest city). The hardest part is deciding where to begin...

When to Go

Cairns

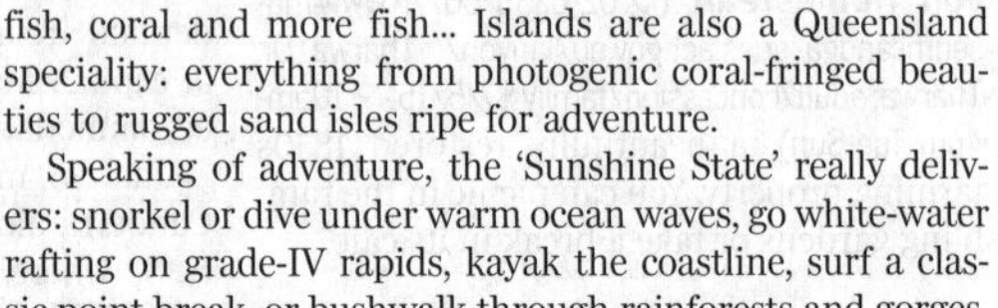

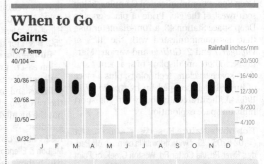

Jan The Wet brings heavy rains up north, and summer heat and humidity elsewhere.

Jun–Aug Peak tourist season in the tropics: mild days, cool nights (bring a jacket).

Sep Warm spring days: it's perfect in Brisbane, or beat the crowds to the Gold Coast.

Places to Stick Around

Sometimes you just need to find that quaint little beach town, put the backpack down and take a break from travelling. After long days on the road, Mission Beach is a perfect place to recharge, with beaut beaches, rainforest walks and an easygoing vibe. Cairns, Surfers Paradise and Airlie Beach are heaving with backpackers – if you're looking to party, look no further. Just north of Cairns, hip Port Douglas has a long, lovely shoreline and makes a relaxed base for exploring the area. Surf junkies may want to put down temporary roots further south: check out Noosa, which has a little of everything (beaches, surf, national parks, low- and high-end accommodation and restaurants) or Burleigh Heads and Coolangatta – even more laid-back, with plenty of great waves. In Brisbane, unwind in the West End for a few days: bars, bookshops and brilliant coffee (the pillars of civilised society).

REGIONAL TOURS

Queensland is absolutely humongous: taking an organised tour of the hot-spots (or off-the-beaten-track areas) is a great way to cover some territory.

Plenty of operators offer 4WD tours of Cape York Peninsula – mainland Australia's northern tip – often with the option of driving one way and flying or boating the other.

Tours of Fraser Island from Noosa and Hervey Bay are an easy way to see one of Queensland's natural wonders, especially if you don't feel like tackling the 4WD-ing alone (it's tough going, even for experienced drivers).

For sailing, few places rival the Whitsunday Islands. Many operators based in Airlie Beach offer cruises, or if you want to do your own thing, you can get a group together and charter a yacht.

Best Wildlife Watching

- **Humpback whales** See them off Hervey Bay during their annual migration (late July to early November).
- **Koalas** Spot them on Magnetic Island.
- **Cassowaries** Look for them wandering around Mission Beach and Cape Tribulation.
- **Platypuses** See them in Eungella National Park.
- **Sea turtles** From November to March on Mon Repos beach you can see nesting sea turtles lumbering up from the deep, followed weeks later by tiny hatchlings making a dash for the water.
- **Crocodiles** Saltwater (estuarine) crocodiles – the world's largest crocodile species – live along the tropical north Queensland coast. Snap some photos on a cruise along the Daintree River.

DON'T MISS

Farmers markets are great opportunities to sample Queensland's culinary riches and support local growers. Our faves are in Brisbane, Noosa and little Eumundi, which has a market almost bigger than the town.

Fast Facts

- Population: 4.56 million
- Area: 1,852,642 sq km (slightly larger than Alaska and Greece combined)
- Birds: 630 species

Top Tips

- Don't swim off northern beaches during the stinger (box jellyfish) season from November to May.
- If you're a sea-sickness sufferer, don't forget your ginger tablets before boating out to the Great Barrier Reef.

Resources

- Lonely Planet (www.lonelyplanet.com/australia/queensland) Tours, hotels, history, eating, drinking, getting-around info…the works!
- Courier Mail (www.couriermail.com.au) Brisbane's daily newspaper online. Who won the rugby?
- Queensland Holidays (www.queenslandholidays.com.au) Great for trip planning.

Queensland & the Great Barrier Reef Highlights

1 A perfect **Brisbane** day: coffee in the West End, the Gallery of Modern Art, and a few beers in Fortitude Valley (p282)

2 Hiking through gorges and rainforests in **Lamington National Park** (p328)

3 Chilling with a kangaroo at the eco-friendly **Australia Zoo** (p337)

4 Bushwalking, kayaking or surfing followed by a ritzy dinner in **Noosa** (p331)

5 Exploring the sand-scape scenery of **Fraser Island** (p347)

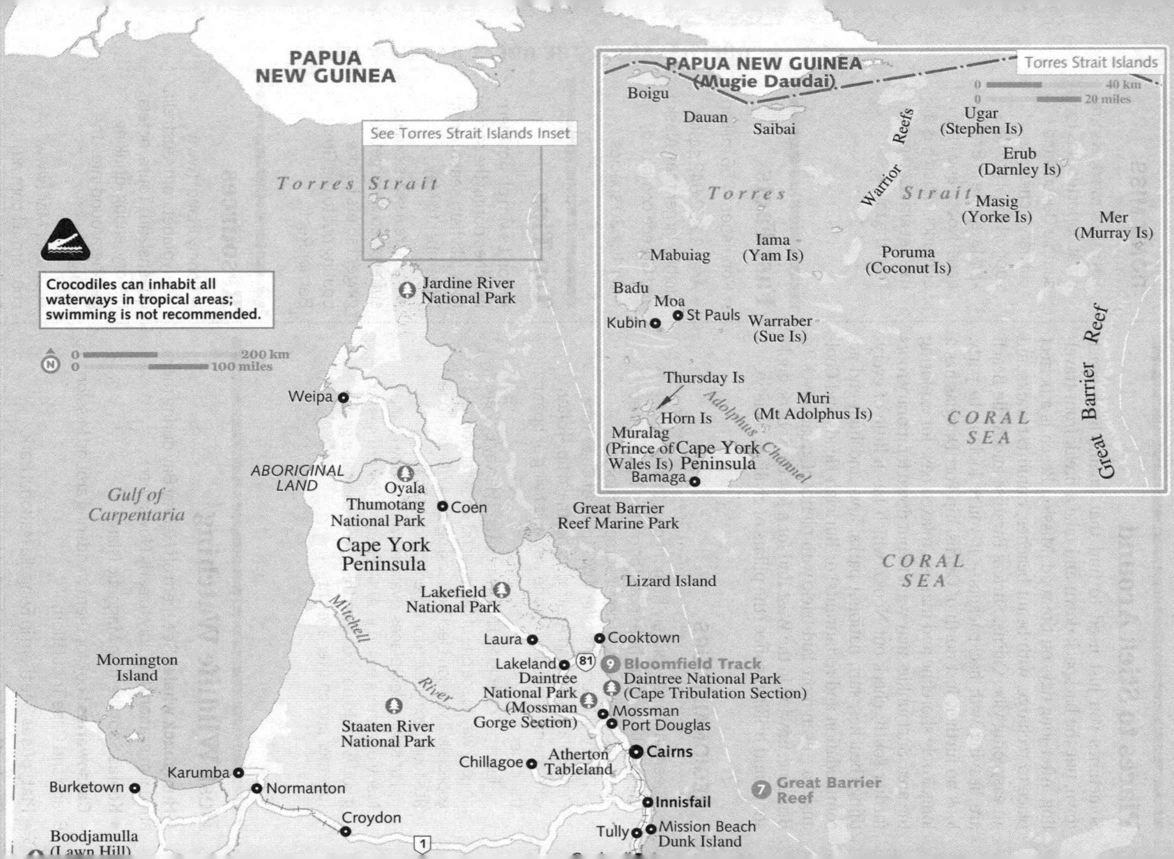

6 Steering a yacht around the azure seas off the **Whitsunday Islands** (p384)

7 Snorkelling over the fabled **Great Barrier Reef** off Cairns or Port Douglas (p417)

8 Discovering ancient rock art in the twisting sandstone canyon of **Carnarvon Gorge** (p372)

9 Tackling the rugged 4WD **Bloomfield Track** from Cape Trib to Cooktown (p457)

10 Getting up early to surf the point break at **Burleigh Heads** (p324)

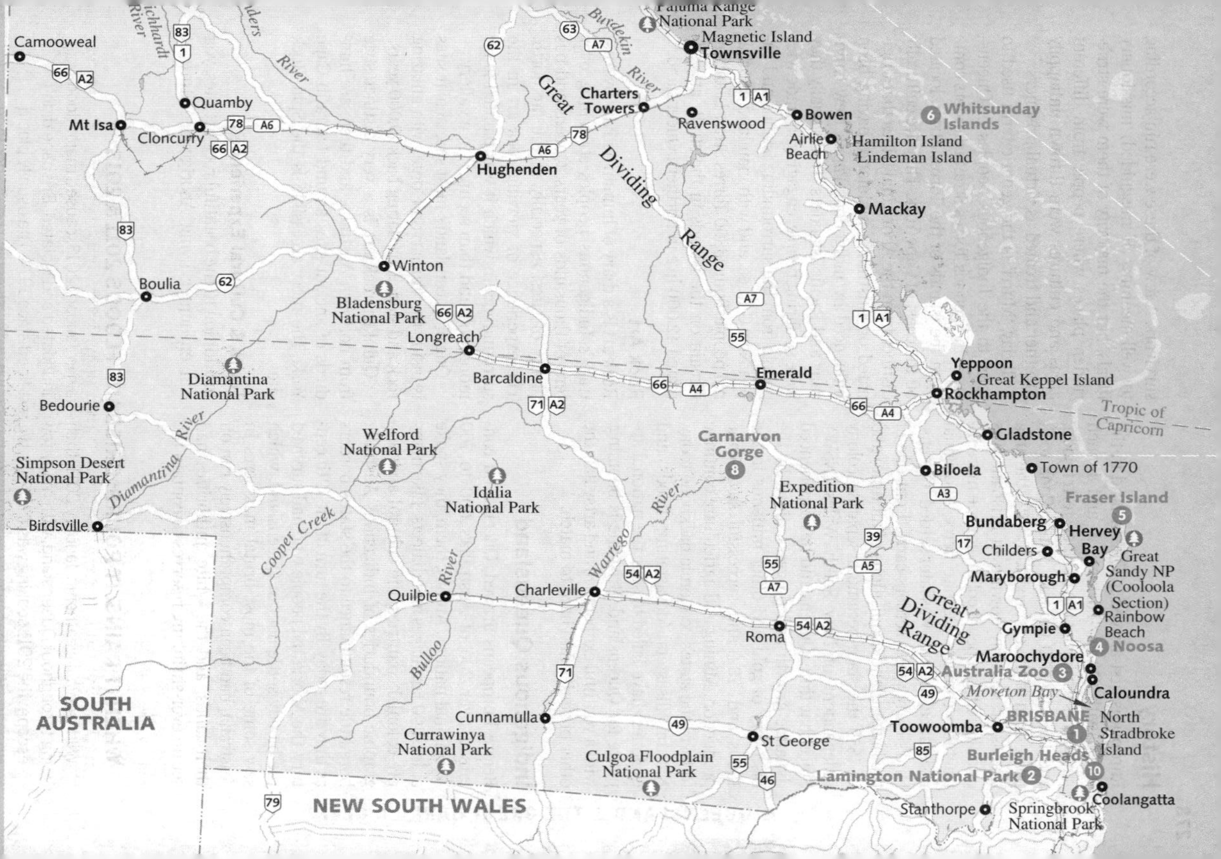

History

Europeans first arrived in Queensland in the 1600s with Dutch, Portuguese and French navigators exploring the northeastern region, and then in 1770 Captain James Cook took possession of the east coast. By 1825 the area that is present-day downtown Brisbane was established as a penal colony for the more intractable convicts. Despite fierce Aboriginal resistance, the area was later settled (Queensland's early white settlers carried out one of the biggest land acquisitions of all time) and in 1859 the state became a separate colony independent of New South Wales (NSW). Since that time, Queensland has experienced dynamic growth and progress, aided by the discovery of gold and other minerals in the 1860s and '70s, and successful sugar-cane production. Mining and agriculture continue to form the state's economic backbone today. Natural disasters (devastating floods and cyclones) have failed to sour the national appetite for Queensland. Brisbane is booming, with a youthful exuberance and artsy flair the other big cities find hard to match.

Indigenous Queensland

Before Europeans arrived, Queensland contained over 200 of Australia's 600 to 700 Aboriginal nations. Among them, they spoke at least 90 languages and dialects. Like many pre-colonial countries, the cultural and geographic boundaries of indigenous Australia bore little resemblance to the state's borders as they are today. By the turn of the 19th century, the Aboriginal people who had survived the bloody settlement of Queensland, which saw some of the most brutal massacres in Australia, had been comprehensively run off their lands, and the white authorities had set up ever-shrinking reserves to contain the survivors. A few of these were run according to well-meaning (if misguided) missionary ideals, but the majority of them were strife-ridden places where people from different areas and cultures were thrown unhappily together and treated as virtual prisoners.

Today, 'Murri' is the generic term used to refer to the Indigenous peoples of Queensland. Indigenous Torres Strait Islanders come from the islands of the Torres Strait, located off the coast of Cape York. They are culturally distinct from the Aboriginal tribes that originated on Australia's mainland, having been influenced by indigenous Papua New Guineans and Pacific Islanders. Traditionally they were seafaring people, engaging in trade with people from the surrounding islands and Papua New Guinea, and with mainland Aboriginal people. Some 6800 Torres Strait Islanders remain on the islands in the strait; an estimated 42,000 live in northern Queensland.

Rock Art

Rock art is a diary of human activity by Australia's Indigenous peoples stretching over tens of thousands of years. Queensland has plenty of sites, especially in the far north. The experience of viewing rock art in the surroundings in which it was painted is far more profound than seeing it in a gallery.

One of Queensland's most spectacular sites is inside the Carnarvon Gorge, with amazing rock and stencil art dating back 19,000 years.

Quinkan rock art is a very distinct style from northern Australia, and there are hundreds of ancient sites around Laura in Cape York. The most accessible is the Split Rock site.

Tours & Cultural Experiences

In addition to the beautiful rock-art sites, you can encounter living Aboriginal culture at

WHEN IT RAINS, IT POURS: BRISBANE FLOODS 2011 & 2013

Wild tropical weather in January 2011, then again in January 2013, caused major flooding throughout Queensland, with many towns inundated and isolated. Brisbane didn't escape: the 2011 soaking was the city's biggest flood since 1974. The usually placid Brisbane River became a swirling torrent of brown water, sweeping boats, pontoons and debris downstream. Flood water streamed into the CBD's riverfront areas, while in low-lying suburbs only rooftops remained above the waterline. The South Bank Parklands were drenched, ferry terminals were swept away, riverside restaurants and bars saturated, and the city's fabulous floating riverside pathway, the Riverwalk, was destroyed. In many parts of the city, little evidence of the floods remained a few months later, but in 2013 the rains came again – this time the tail-end of Tropical Cyclone Oswald – flooding many of the same areas. Damage was less dramatic this time, but caused heartbreak for those home- and business-owners who had just rebuilt after 2011.

the Hopevale community (check out Guurrbi Tours, 458) north of Cooktown. There are Aboriginal-led tours at Mossman Gorge and Malanda Falls. The Gab Titui Cultural Centre on Thursday Island is a unique development by Torres Strait Islander communities, and at the Tjapukai Cultural Park near Cairns an award-winning Aboriginal dance group performs most days for tourists. The annual Dreaming Festival, held as part of the Woodford Folk Festival, is a colourful showcase of indigenous arts from across the country.

Perhaps the most exciting event, however, is the Laura Aboriginal Dance Festival, held every odd-numbered year in June on the Cape York Peninsula.

National Parks

There are some 220 national parks and state forests dotted around Queensland, and while some comprise only a single hill or lake, others are major wilderness areas. Many islands, expanses of water and stretches of coast are also national parks.

Three of the most spectacular national parks inland are Lamington, on the forested rim of an ancient volcano on the NSW border; Carnarvon, with its dramatic 30km gorge southwest of Rockhampton; and, near Mackay, rainforested Eungella swarms with wildlife.

On the coast, the Great Sandy National Park (Cooloola) is a mesmerising tangle of mangroves, rivers and forest; and, of course, there's the jewel in Queensland's crown – the Great Barrier Reef Marine Park.

The Queensland Department of National Parks, Recreation, Sport & Racing website (www.nprsr.qld.gov.au) has details of all the national parks, including bushwalks and other activities, safety and history of the parks, plus permits for camping and off-road driving.

LOADS OF TOADS

Cane toads were introduced to Australia in 1935 in an attempt to control the pesky sugar cane beetle. They're not pretty: warty skin, heavy-ridged eyes, poisonous glands... Worse, they've proved to be absolutely useless: they ignore the cane grubs and instead focus on reproducing. Widely hated, there are now over 200 million cane toads around Australia – an invasion that has seen populations of native snakes and goannas decline. But not everyone loathes them: Queensland's representative rugby league team has the cane toad as its unofficial mascot, and the toad has been listed by the National Trust of Queensland as a state icon (warts and all).

Activities

Bushwalking

Queensland's bigger national parks have kilometres of marked year-round walking tracks, plus there are excellent bushwalking opportunities in smaller state and national parks. Many of the favourites are part of the Queensland government's **Great Walks of Queensland** network: 10 tracks designed to allow walkers to experience rainforests and bushland without disturbing the ecosystem. Walk locations include the Whitsundays, the Sunshine Coast, the Sunshine Coast hinterland, the Mackay highlands, Fraser Island, the Gold Coast hinterland, Carnarvon Gorge and tropical north Queensland. See www.nprsr.qld.gov.au/experiences/great-walks for more information.

Also around the state you can tackle Hinchinbrook Island's famed Thorsborne Trail; Wooroonooran, which contains Queensland's highest peak, Mt Bartle Frere (1657m); and the traditional walking trails of the Jirrbal and Mamu Aboriginal people.

Camping

There are some top camping spots in Queensland. Many of the state and national parks have camping grounds, with toilets, showers and sometimes electric barbecues. You'll also find privately run camping grounds, motels and lodges on national park fringes.

In order to camp in a national park you will need a permit. You can self-register at a handful of sites, but for the vast majority you will need to purchase a permit in advance: the easiest way is via the ParksQ service on the Queensland Department of National Parks, Recreation, Sport & Racing website (www.nprsr.qld.gov.au). Camping in national parks and state forests costs $5.45/21.80 per person/family per night. Popular parks fill up at holiday times – book well in advance.

Diving & Snorkelling

The Queensland coast is dotted with plenty of spectacular dive sites. The Great Barrier

Reef provides some of the world's best diving and snorkelling, and there are dozens of operators vying to teach you to scuba dive or provide you with the ultimate dive safari. There are also some 1600 shipwrecks along the state's coast, providing vivid and densely populated marine metropolises for you to explore. Most big towns along the coast have a dive school (or two), though the most popular places to learn are Airlie Beach, Cairns and Townsville.

You can snorkel just about everywhere in Queensland; it requires minimum effort and anyone can do it. Many diving locations are also popular snorkelling sites.

Diving is generally good year-round, although during the wet season – roughly December to March – floods can wash mud out into the ocean and visibility for divers and snorkellers is sometimes affected. Also, all water activities, including diving and snorkelling, are affected by stingers (box jellyfish), which are found along the Queensland coast from Agnes Water north between November and May.

Extreme Sports

Queensland has its fair share of activities to satisfy thrillseekers. Try bungee jumping at major tourist stops such as Airlie Beach and Cairns, or hit the rollercoasters at the Gold Coast theme parks. You can also try skydiving here: hurl yourself out of a perfectly good aeroplane at Caloundra, Airlie Beach or Mission Beach.

Sailing & Fishing

Nautical types will find plenty of places in Queensland with boats and/or sailboards for hire. Manly (near Brisbane) and Airlie Beach – gateway to the Whitsunday Islands – are probably the biggest centres, with all kinds of options for messing about in boats. The Whitsunday Islands, with their plentiful bays and calm waters, are especially popular. Day trips start at around $100, while overnight trips start at around $250. Bareboat charters (sailing yourself) are also possible from around $500 per day.

Fishing is one of Queensland's most popular sports: you can hire fishing gear and/or boats in many places. Fraser Island, Karumba, Cooktown and North Stradbroke Island are some good spots. The Great Barrier Reef has tight fishing regulations: for comprehensive information, contact the **Great Barrier Reef Marine Park Authority** (☎07-4750 0700; www.gbrmpa.gov.au), based in Townsville.

Surfing

There are some fantastic breaks along Queensland's southeast coast, most notably at Coolangatta, Burleigh Heads, Surfers Paradise, North Stradbroke Island, Noosa and Town of 1770. Surf shops in these areas generally offer board hire, or you can buy secondhand ones. If you've never hit the surf before, it's a good idea to have a lesson or two.

DIVING & SNORKELLING OUTSIDE THE GREAT BARRIER REEF

SITE	OPERATOR	WHAT YOU'LL SEE
North Stradbroke Island	Manta Lodge (www.mantalodge.com.au)	Manta rays, leopard and grey nurse sharks, humpback whales, turtles, dolphins, hard and soft corals
Moreton Island	Diveworld (www.diveworld.com.au)	Tangalooma Wrecks; good snorkelling site
Southport	Diving the Gold Coast (www.divingthegoldcoast.com.au)	Abundant marine life, including rays, sharks, turtles and 200 fish species
Mooloolaba	Scuba World (www.scubaworld.com.au)	Ex-HMAS *Brisbane*, a sunken warship off the coast
Hervey Bay	Dive Hervey Bay (www.diveherveybay.com.au)	Shallow caves, schools of large fish, wreck dives, turtles, sea snakes, stonefish, rays, trevally
Rainbow Beach	Wolf Rock Dive Centre (www.wolfrockdive.com.au)	Grey nurse sharks, turtles, manta rays and giant groupers amid volcanic pinnacles
Bundaberg	Bundaberg Aqua Scuba (www.aquascuba.com.au)	Wreck dives, groupers, turtles, rays, live-aboard dive boat

KAYAKING SITES

SITE	OPERATOR	WHAT YOU'LL SEE
North Stradbroke Island	Straddie Adventures (www.straddieadventures.com.au)	Lovely coastline, dolphins, sea turtles, rays, snorkelling sites
Great Sandy National Park	Elanda Point (www.elanda.com.au)	High-backed dunes, wildflowers, mangroves, rainforests
Whitsunday Islands	Salty Dog (www.saltydog.com.au)	Day and multi-day trips taking in South Molle Island and Whitehaven Beach, coral reefs, dolphins, turtles, sea eagles
Noosa	Noosa Ocean Kayak (www.noosa kayaktours.com)	Sea-kayak tours with dolphins and turtles; Noosa River kayaking
Magnetic Island	Magnetic Island Sea Kayaks (www.seakayak.com.au)	Exploring picturesque island bays
Mission Beach	Coral Sea Kayaking (www.coralseakayak.com)	Day paddles to and around Dunk Island, multi-day trips to Hinchinbrook Island

Swimming

North of Fraser Island the beaches are sheltered by the Great Barrier Reef: no surf, but great for swimming. There are also some fantastic freshwater swimming spots around the state in rivers and waterholes. Box jellyfish are a serious problem from Rockhampton north between October and April. Also be aware of saltwater crocs (salties) cruising in the coastal waters and rivers north of Rockhampton: heed any warning signs.

White-Water Rafting, Canoeing & Kayaking

The Tully and North Johnstone Rivers between Townsville and Cairns are the big ones for white-water rafting. You can do four-day rafting trips on the North Johnstone from about $1400, and day trips from $155 on the Tully, including transfers.

Kayaking and canoeing are also popular activities in Queensland: operators run paddling expeditions along inland waterways and lakes, and out through the protected Barrier Reef waters – sometimes from the mainland to offshore islands. There are also plenty of companies that operate guided tours around the Gold and Sunshine Coasts.

Wine Regions

Huh? Wineries in Queensland? Still under the radar in most parts of Australia (and virtually unknown abroad), the **Granite Belt Wine Country**, a few hours southwest of Brisbane, has slowly been carving a name for itself. Cooler than coastal Queensland owing to its higher elevation (topping out at 954m), the area attracted Sicilian immigrants in the 1800s who planted the first vines. Gateway town Stanthorpe now sustains 50-plus boutique wineries, which produce an impressive range of varietals. Grapes from Italy, South Africa, Portugal, Spain and France all do well here. Online, see www.granitebeltwinecountry.com.au.

Tours

Specialised tours abound in Queensland. Most are connected with a particular activity (eg bushwalking, horse riding) or area (eg Great Barrier Reef, 4WD tours to Cape York).

There are dozens of tours (mostly from Cairns and Port Douglas) out to the Great Barrier Reef. You can fly in a seaplane out to a deserted coral cay, take a fast catamaran to the outer reef and spend the day snorkelling, join a live-aboard dive boat to explore remote sections of the reef, or take a day trip to snorkel coral gardens and bask on pretty islands.

In Far North Queensland you can take the Kuranda Scenic Railway up to the Kuranda markets, tour the Atherton Tableland, visit Cape Tribulation on a 4WD tour, cruise along the Daintree River, go white-water rafting, and visit Aboriginal rock-art galleries in Cape York.

From the Gold Coast there are tours to Lamington and Springbrook National Parks, and numerous tours run out of Brisbane to the Sunshine and Gold Coasts, and the islands of Moreton Bay.

See regional sections for listings.

Seasonal Work

There's seasonal fruit- and vegetable-picking work aplenty around Stanthorpe, Childers, Bundaberg and even Cairns. During harvest times these towns attract backpackers by the bucket load, hoping to pick tomatoes in exchange for a bit of cash. Stanthorpe and Childers are basically one-traffic-light villages with little to do as far as nightlife goes: if you're only here to work, no problem, but if you're also looking for a bit of atmosphere, it's probably best to head to Bundaberg.

Most backpackers are usually hooked up with farm work directly through youth hostels, which also provide transport to and from the harvest site. This is a major plus, as there is no public transport to the farms. Being connected to a hostel can also be helpful if you end up having a problem with your farm boss.

ℹ Information

For comprehensive info about the state, get a hold of Lonely Planet's *Queensland & the Great Barrier Reef* guidebook. **Queensland Holidays** (www.queenslandholidays.com.au) is the official Queensland Tourism site – great for trip planning. There are also official tourist offices in most major Queensland towns. Other useful resources:

Sunlover Holidays (www.sunloverholidays.com) Accommodation and tour bookings.

Queensland Department of National Parks, Recreation, Sport & Racing (NPRSR; www.nprsr.qld.gov.au)

Royal Automobile Club of Queensland (RACQ; www.racq.com.au)

ℹ Getting There & Around

Brisbane is the main port of call for flights into Queensland and is the main international airport for the state, but Cairns and Gold Coast (Coolangatta) airports also handle international flights.

AIR

Within Australia, the big national carriers – **Qantas** (www.qantas.com.au), **Jetstar** (www.jetstar.com.au) and **Virgin Australia** (www.virginaustralia.com) – fly to Queensland's major cities.

Tiger Airways (www.tigerairways.com) connects Melbourne and Sydney with Brisbane, Cairns, Mackay and the Gold Coast (Coolangatta), and runs Maroochydore–Melbourne flights.

There are also smaller airlines, including charter flights, operating up and down the coast, across the Cape York Peninsula and into the outback. **Skytrans** (www.skytrans.com.au) and **Regional Express** (REX; www.rex.com.au) serve select towns in northern Queensland.

BUS

Greyhound Australia (www.greyhound.com.au) The largest bus company in Australia, with extensive coverage of Queensland and beyond. For extensive bus travel, Greyhound has various travel passes to save money.

Premier Motor Service (www.premierms.com.au) Covers the route between Melbourne, Sydney, Brisbane and Cairns, with fewer services than Greyhound but often cheaper fares.

CAR

The roads in Queensland are in good condition, particularly along the coastal highways and main thoroughfares in the hinterland and outback. However, they can often turn into badly maintained sealed roads or dirt tracks in the more remote areas of the state. Traffic between Brisbane and the Gold Coast can be hellish: avoid Friday and Sunday evenings. Brisbane generally has the cheapest car-hire rates.

TRAIN

Queensland Rail (www.queenslandrail.com.au) operates numerous services throughout Queensland. The main railway line is the Brisbane to Cairns run, which is serviced by the *Tilt Train*, a high-speed connection that operates three times weekly, and the *Sunlander*, a more leisurely option with three services weekly. There are also inland services from Brisbane to Charleville, Brisbane to Longreach, and from Townsville to Mt Isa, plus a more regular *Tilt Train* service between Brisbane and Rockhampton. Brisbane to Sydney services are run by the NSW-based CountryLink (p1091).

BRISBANE

POP 2.15 MILLION

Australia's most underrated city? Booming Brisbane is an energetic river town on the way up, with an edgy arts scene, pumping nightlife and great coffee and restaurants. Plush parks and historic buildings complete the picture, all folded into the elbows of the meandering Brisbane River.

Brisbanites are out on the streets: the weather is brilliant and so are the bodies. Fit-looking locals get up early to go jogging, swimming, cycling, kayaking, rock climbing or just walk the dog. But it's not all superficial: subcultural undercurrents run deep here too, with cool bookshops, globally inspired restaurants, cafes, bars and band rooms aplenty.

But perhaps it's the Brisbane River itself – which broke so many hearts when it flooded in 2011 and 2013 – that gives Brisbane its edge. The river's organic convolutions carve the city into a patchwork of urban villages, each with a distinct style and topography: bohemian, low-lying West End; hip, hilltop Paddington; exclusive, peninsular New Farm; prim, pointy Kangaroo Point. Move from village to village and experience this diverse, eccentric, happening capital.

History

Pre-colonial Aboriginal inhabitants knew this area as Mian-jin, meaning 'place shaped like a spike'. The first white settlement here was established at Redcliffe on Moreton Bay in 1824 – a penal colony for difficult convicts from the Botany Bay colony in NSW. After struggling with inadequate water supplies and hostile Aboriginal groups, the colony was relocated to safer territory on the banks of the Brisbane River, before the whole convict colony idea was abandoned in 1839.

Moreton Bay was opened to free settlers in 1842. This marked the beginning of Brisbane's rise to prominence and the beginning of the end for the region's Aboriginal peoples.

Sights

City Centre

Commissariat Store Museum MUSEUM
(Map p288; www.queenslandhistory.org; 115 William St; adult/child/family $5/3/10; 10am-4pm Tue-Fri) Built by convicts in 1829, this former government storehouse is the oldest occupied building in Brisbane. Inside is an immaculate little museum devoted to convict and colonial history. Don't miss the convict 'fingers' and the exhibit on Italians in Queensland.

Roma Street Parkland PARK
(Map p288; www.romastreetparkland.com; 1 Parkland Blvd; 24hr) FREE This beautifully maintained, 16-hectare downtown park is one of the world's largest subtropical urban gardens. Formerly a market and a railway yard, the park opened in 2001 and features native trees, a lake, lookouts, waterfalls, a playground, BBQs and many a frangipani. It's something of a maze: easy to get into, hard to get out.

QUT Art Museum MUSEUM
(Map p288; www.artmuseum.qut.edu.au; 2 George St; 10am-5pm Tue-Fri, noon-4pm Sat & Sun) FREE On the Queensland University of Technology campus is this excellent little museum, displaying regularly changing exhibits of contemporary Australian art and works by Brisbane art students.

City Botanic Gardens PARK
(Map p288; www.brisbane.qld.gov.au; Alice St; 24hr) FREE On the river, Brisbane's favourite green space is a mass of lawns, tangled Moreton Bay figs, bunya pines and macadamia trees descending gently from the Queensland University of Technology campus. Free guided tours leave the rotunda at 11am and 1pm Monday to Saturday.

Old Government House HISTORIC BUILDING
(Map p288; www.ogh.qut.edu.au; George St; 10am-4pm Sun-Fri) FREE This 1862 gem was designed by estimable government architect Charles Tiffin as an appropriately plush residence for Sir George Bowen, Queensland's first governor. Tour the lavish innards (restored in 2009), and check out some William Robinson landscapes in the gallery upstairs.

Parliament House HISTORIC BUILDING
(Map p288; www.parliament.qld.gov.au; cnr Alice & George Sts; tours 1pm, 2pm, 3pm & 4pm non-sitting days) FREE This lovely blanched-white stone French Renaissance–style building dates from 1868 and is one of Brisbane's treasured historical landmarks. Free tours leave on demand (2pm only when parliament is sitting).

City Hall HISTORIC BUILDING
(Map p288; www.brisbane.qld.gov.au; btwn Ann & Adelaide Sts) Overlooking King George Sq, this fine 1930s sandstone edifice is fronted by a row of sequoia-sized corinthian columns and has an 85m-high clocktower. Bells peal out across city rooftops every hour. By the time you read this a three-year renovation should be complete: see if the **observation platform** and **Museum of Brisbane** (Map p288; www.museumofbrisbane.com.au) are open yet.

Treasury Building HISTORIC BUILDING
(Map p288; www.treasurybrisbane.com.au; cnr Queen & William Sts; 24hr) FREE At the western end of the Queen St Mall is the magnificent Italian Renaissance–style Treasury Building, dating from 1889. No tax collectors inside – just Brisbane's casino.

Greater Brisbane

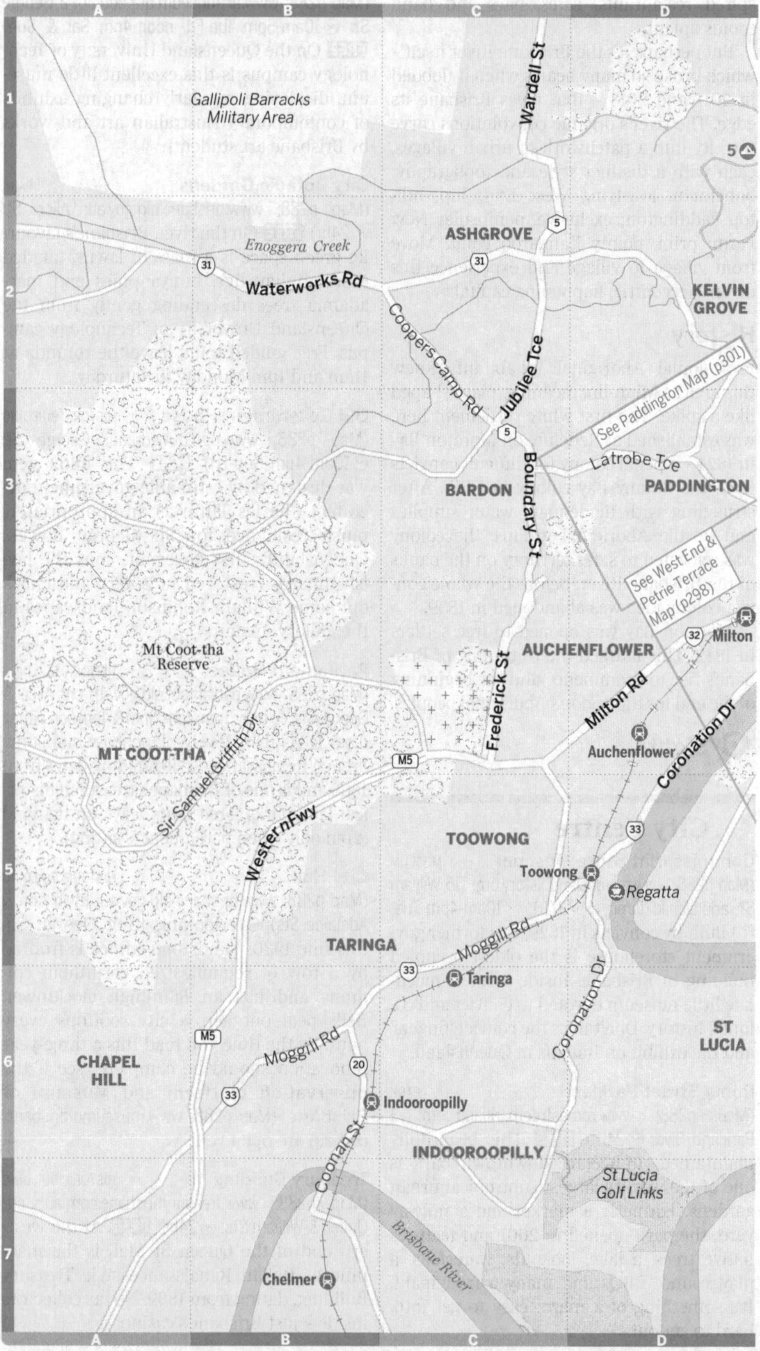
A
B
C
D
1
2
3
4
5
6
7
Gallipoli Barracks Military Area
Wardell St
5
ASHGROVE
Enoggera Creek
31
Waterworks Rd
KELVIN GROVE
Coopers Camp Rd
Jubilee Tce
See Paddington Map (p301)
Latrobe Tce
BARDON
Boundary St
PADDINGTON
See West End & Petrie Terrace Map (p298)
Milton
32
AUCHENFLOWER
Frederick St
Mt Coot-tha Reserve
Milton Rd
Coronation Dr
Auchenflower
M5
MT COOT-THA
Sir Samuel Griffith Dr
Western Fwy
TOOWONG
33
Toowong
Regatta
TARINGA
Moggill Rd
Taringa
Coronation Dr
ST LUCIA
Moggill Rd
20
CHAPEL HILL
Indooroopilly
INDOOROOPILLY
Coonan St
St Lucia Golf Links
Brisbane River
Chelmer

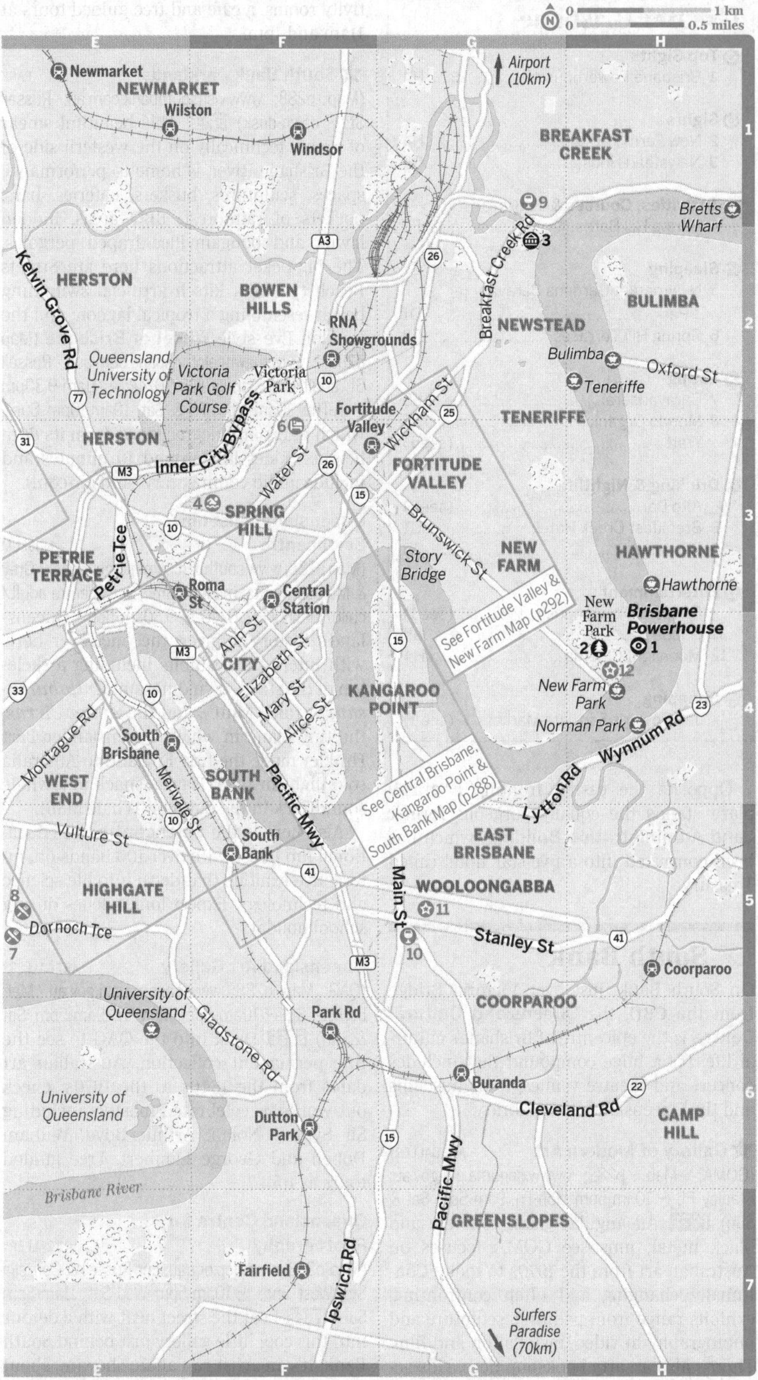
0 1 km
0 0.5 miles
E
F
G
H
1
2
3
4
5
6
7
Newmarket
NEWMARKET
Wilston
Windsor
Airport (10km)
BREAKFAST CREEK
9
Bretts Wharf
3
Breakfast Creek Rd
A3
26
HERSTON
Kelvin Grove Rd
BOWEN HILLS
BULIMBA
NEWSTEAD
RNA Showgrounds
Queensland University of Technology
Victoria Park Golf Course
Victoria Park
Bulimba
Oxford St
Teneriffe
77
10
Fortitude Valley
Wickham St
25
TENERIFFE
6
31
HERSTON
Inner City Bypass
M3
Water St
26
FORTITUDE VALLEY
4
SPRING HILL
15
Brunswick St
10
NEW FARM
HAWTHORNE
PETRIE TERRACE
Petrie Tce
Story Bridge
Hawthorne
Roma St
Central Station
See Fortitude Valley & New Farm Map (p292)
New Farm Park
Brisbane Powerhouse
2
1
Ann St
15
M3
CITY
Elizabeth St
12
33
10
Mary St
KANGAROO POINT
New Farm Park
23
Montague Rd
Alice St
Norman Park
South Brisbane
Wynnum Rd
WEST END
SOUTH BANK
Merivale St
Pacific Mwy
See Central Brisbane, Kangaroo Point & South Bank Map (p288)
Lytton Rd
10
Vulture St
South Bank
EAST BRISBANE
41
Main St
WOOLOONGABBA
HIGHGATE HILL
8
11
Dornoch Tce
7
Stanley St
41
10
M3
Coorparoo
University of Queensland
COORPAROO
Gladstone Rd
Park Rd
Buranda
22
University of Queensland
Cleveland Rd
CAMP HILL
Dutton Park
15
Pacific Mwy
Brisbane River
GREENSLOPES
Ipswich Rd
Fairfield
Surfers Paradise (70km)

Greater Brisbane

Opposite the casino fronting a grassy plaza stands the equally gorgeous former **Land Administration Building**, which has been converted into a five-star hotel called Treasury.

South Bank

On South Bank, just over Victoria Bridge from the CBD, the **Queensland Cultural Centre** is the epicentre of Brisbane's cultural life. It's a huge compound that includes concert and theatre venues, four museums and the Queensland State Library.

★**Gallery of Modern Art** ART GALLERY
(GOMA; Map p288; www.qagoma.qld.gov.au; Stanley Pl; 10am-5pm Mon-Fri, 9am-5pm Sat & Sun) FREE All angular glass, concrete and black metal, must-see GOMA focuses on Australian art from the 1970s to today. Continually changing and often confronting, exhibits range from painting, sculpture and photography to video, installation and film. There's also an arty bookshop here, kids activity rooms, a cafe and free guided tours at 11am and 1pm.

★**South Bank Parklands** PARK
(Map p288; www.visitsouthbank.com.au; Russell St; dawn-dusk) FREE This beautiful smear of green, technically on the western side of the Brisbane River, is home to performance spaces, sculptures, buskers, eateries, bars, pockets of rainforest, BBQ areas, hidden lawns and bougainvillea-draped pergolas. The big-ticket attractions here are Streets Beach (p291), a kitsch artificial swimming beach resembling a tropical lagoon; and the London Eye–style **Wheel of Brisbane** (Map p288; www.thewheelofbrisbane.com.au; Russell St; adult/child/family $15/10/42; 11am-9.30pm Mon-Thu, 10am-11pm Fri & Sat, 10am-10pm Sun), which offers 360-degree views from its 60m heights. Rides last around 10 minutes and include audio commentary (and air-con!).

Queensland Museum & Sciencentre MUSEUM
(Map p288; www.southbank.qm.qld.gov.au; cnr Grey & Melbourne Sts; museum free, Sciencentre adult/child/family $13/10/40; 9.30am-5pm) Queensland's history is given the once-over here, with interesting exhibits including a skeleton of the state's own dinosaur *Muttaburrasaurus* (aka 'Mutt'), and the *Avian Cirrus*, the tiny plane in which Queenslander Bert Hinkler made the first England-to-Australia solo flight in 1928. Have a snack to a whale soundtrack in the outdoor 'Whale Mall'.

Also here is the **Sciencentre**, an educational fun house with over 100 hands-on, interactive exhibits that delve into life science and technology. Expect long queues during school holidays.

Queensland Art Gallery ART GALLERY
(QAG; Map p288; www.qagoma.qld.gov.au; Melbourne St; 10am-5pm Mon-Fri, 9am-5pm Sat & Sun) FREE Duck into the QAG to see the fine permanent collection. Australian art dates from the 1840s to the 1970s: check out works by celebrated masters including Sir Sydney Nolan, Arthur Boyd, William Dobell and George Lambert. Free guided tours at 1pm.

Queensland Centre for Photography ART GALLERY
(Map p288; www.qcp.org.au; cnr Russell & Cordelia Sts, West End; 10am-5pm Wed-Sat, 11am-3pm Sun) FREE Beat the street heat with a detour into this cool little gallery just behind South Bank. It's an artist-run affair, showing about

10 Australian contemporary photography exhibitions per year.

Queensland Maritime Museum MUSEUM
(Map p288; www.maritimemuseum.com.au; Stanley St; adult/child/family $12/6/28; ⏲9.30am-4.30pm) On the southern edge of the South Bank Parklands is this quaint old museum, the highlight of which is the gigantic HMAS *Diamantina,* a restored WWII frigate that you can clamber aboard and explore.

Fortitude Valley & New Farm

★**Brisbane Powerhouse** ARTS CENTRE
(Map p284; www.brisbanepowerhouse.org; 119 Lamington St; ⏲9am-5pm Mon-Fri, 10am-4pm Sat & Sun) On the eastern flank of New Farm Park stands the Powerhouse, a once-derelict power station that's been transformed into a contemporary arts centre. Inside the brick husk are graffiti remnants, old industrial machinery and randomly placed headphones offering sonic sound-grabs. The Powerhouse hosts a range of performances (many free), and has two restaurants with killer river views.

Institute of Modern Art ART GALLERY
(IMA; Map p292; www.ima.org.au; 420 Brunswick St, Fortitude Valley; ⏲11am-5pm Tue-Sat, to 8pm Thu) FREE In the Judith Wright Centre of Contemporary Arts, this excellent noncommercial gallery with an industrial vibe has regular showings by local names. With risqué, emerging and experimental art for grown-ups, it's GOMA's naughty little cousin.

Chinatown NEIGHBOURHOOD
(Map p292; Duncan St) Brisbane's Chinatown occupies only one street, but is just as flamboyant and flavour-filled as its Sydney and Melbourne counterparts. Glazed flat ducks hang behind steamy windows; aromas of Thai, Chinese, Vietnamese, Laotian and Japanese cooking fill the air. There are free outdoor movies during summer, and it goes nuts over Chinese New Year in February.

Greater Brisbane

Mt Coot-tha Reserve NATURE RESERVE
(Map 284; www.brisbane.qld.gov.au; Mt Coot-tha Rd, Mt Coot-tha; ⏲24hr) FREE A 15-minute drive or bus ride from the city, this huge bush reserve is topped by 287m Mt Coot-tha (more of a hill, really). On the hillsides you'll find a botanic garden, planetarium and the eye-popping **Mt Coot-tha Lookout** (www.brisbanelookout.com; 1012 Sir Samuel Griffith Dr; ⏲24hr) FREE. On a clear day you can see

BRISBANE FOR CHILDREN

From toddlers to teenagers, there's no shortage of places to keep kids busy (and parents happy) in Brisbane.

Start with the city's leafy inner-city parks: South Bank Parklands (p286) has lawns, BBQs, playgrounds and the slow-spinning Wheel of Brisbane (p286) – a real mind-blower for anyone under 15. The lifeguard-patrolled Streets Beach (p291) is here too, with a shallow section for really small swimmers. **New Farm Park** is a beaut spot by the river, with a series of treehouse-like platforms interlinking huge (and shady) Moreton Bay fig trees.

Too humid for the park? Head for the air-con at the **Queensland Cultural Centre** on South Bank. Here the Queensland Museum (p286) runs some fab, hands-on programs for little tackers during school holidays. The incorporated **Sciencentre** has plenty of push-this-button-and-see-what-happens action. The Queensland Art Gallery (p286) has a Children's Art Centre which runs regular programs throughout the year, as does the State Library of Queensland (p309) and the Gallery of Modern Art (p286).

C!RCA (Map p292; ☎07-3852 3110; www.circa.org.au; L3, 420 Brunswick St, Fortitude Valley) offers action-packed 'circus classes' (tumbling, balancing, jumping, trapeze work) for budding young carnies at the Judith Wright Centre in Fortitude Valley.

The river is a big plus. Take a ferry ride around the bends of central Brisbane, or chug further afield to the Lone Pine Koala Sanctuary (p289), where they can cuddle up to a critter. If you're heading out Mt Coot-tha way, check out a show at the Sir Thomas Brisbane Planetarium (p289).

Day-care or babysitting options include **Dial an Angel** (☎1300 721 111, 07-3878 1077; www.dialanangel.com) and **Care4Kidz** (☎07-3103 0298; www.careforkidz.com.au).

Central Brisbane, Kangaroo Point & South Bank

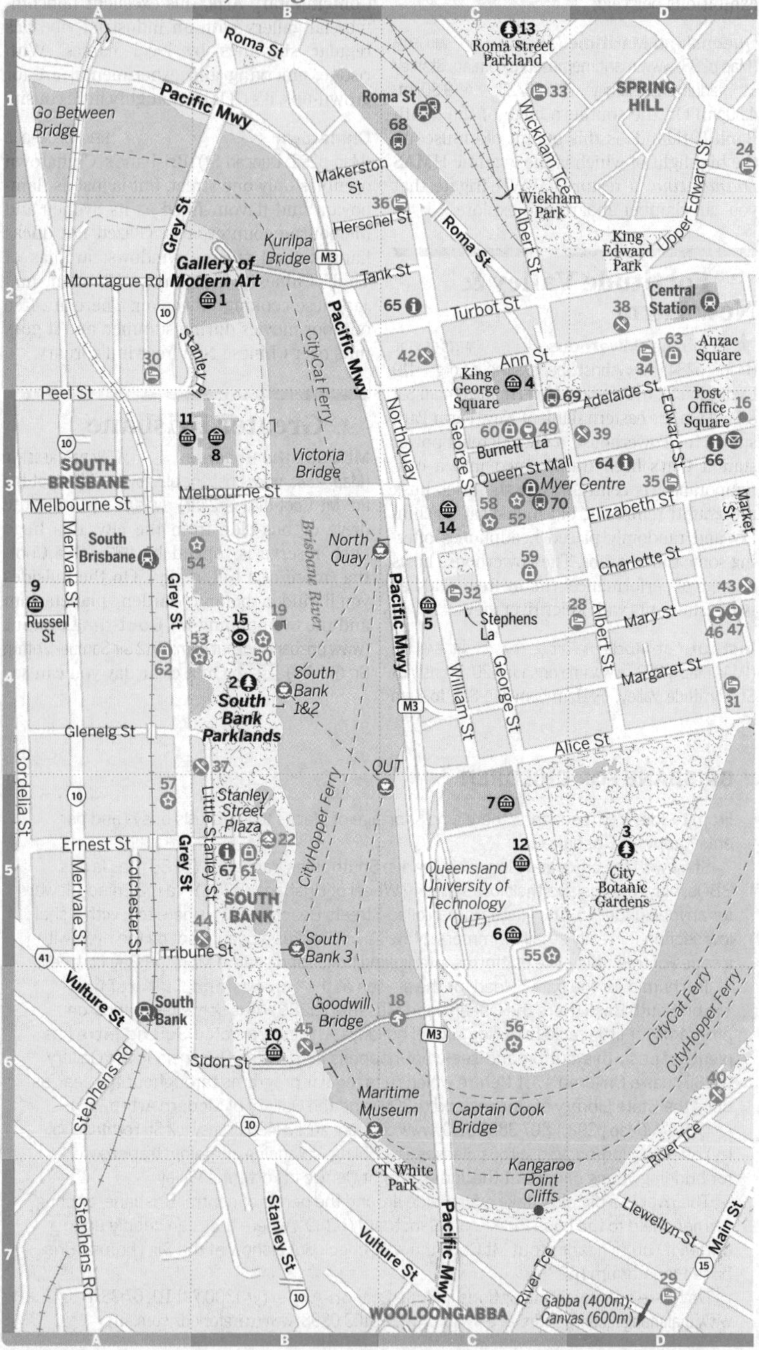

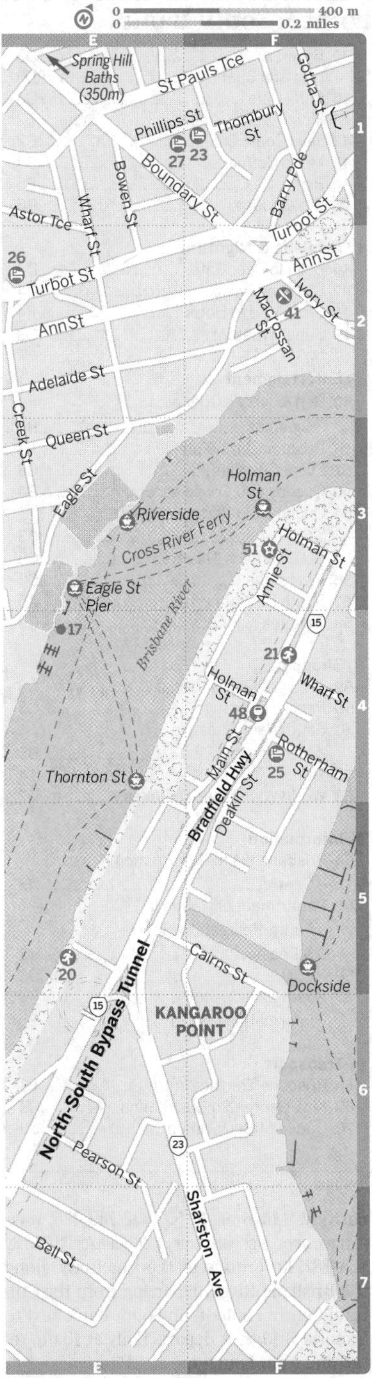

the Moreton Bay islands. There's a cafe and flashy restaurant at the lookout too.

Just north of the road to the lookout, on Samuel Griffith Dr, is the turn-off to **JC Slaughter Falls**, 700m along a walking track; plus a 1.5km **Aboriginal Art Trail**, which takes you past eight art sites with works by local Aboriginal artists. You can also hike to the lookout from JC Slaughter Falls (about 4km return – steep!).

At the base of Mt Coot-tha is **Brisbane Botanic Gardens** (www.brisbane.qld.gov.au/botanicgardens; Mt Coot-tha Rd; ⌚8am-5.30pm) FREE, which has a plethora of mini ecologies: cactus, bonsai and herb gardens, rainforests, arid zones... You'll feel like you're traversing the globe in all its vegetated splendour! There are free guided walks at 11am and 1pm Monday and Saturday, and free minibus tours at 10.45am Monday to Thursday.

Also in the gardens, **Sir Thomas Brisbane Planetarium** (☎07-3403 2578; www.brisbane.qld.gov.au/planetarium; Mt Coot-tha Rd) is Australia's largest. There's a great observatory here with regular starry shows. It was closed for renovations at the time of writing: call or check the website for new opening times and admission costs.

To get here via public transport, take bus 471 from Adelaide St in the city, opposite King George Sq ($4.80, 25 minutes). The bus drops you off in the lookout car park and stops outside the Brisbane Botanic Gardens en route.

Newstead House HISTORIC BUILDING
(Map p284; www.newsteadhouse.com.au; cnr Breakfast Creek Rd & Newstead Ave, Newstead; adult/child/family $6/4/15; ⌚10am-4pm Mon-Thu, 2-5pm Sun) On a breezy hill overlooking the river, Brisbane's oldest house dates from 1846 and is beautifully fitted out with Victorian furnishings, antiques, clothing and period displays. It's a modest, peach-coloured L-shaped affair, surrounded by manicured lawns with lovely river views. Wedding photographers do their best to avoid the big brick electrical substation in the gardens. Free Sunday afternoon concerts.

Lone Pine Koala Sanctuary NATURE RESERVE
(☎07-3378 1366; www.koala.net; 708 Jesmond Rd, Fig Tree Pocket; adult/child/family $33/22/80; ⌚9am-5pm) About 12km south of the city centre, Lone Pine Koala Sanctuary occupies a patch of parkland beside the river. It's home to 130 or so koalas, plus kangaroos, possums, wombats, birds and other Aussie

Central Brisbane, Kangaroo Point & South Bank

Top Sights
- 1 Gallery of Modern Art ... B2
- 2 South Bank Parklands ... B4

Sights
- 3 City Botanic Gardens ... D5
- 4 City Hall ... C2
- 5 Commissariat Store Museum ... C4
- Museum of Brisbane ... (see 4)
- 6 Old Government House ... C5
- 7 Parliament House ... C5
- 8 Queensland Art Gallery ... B3
- 9 Queensland Centre for Photography ... A4
- 10 Queensland Maritime Museum ... B6
- 11 Queensland Museum & Sciencentre ... A3
- 12 QUT Art Museum ... C5
- 13 Roma Street Parkland ... C1
- 14 Treasury Building ... C3
- 15 Wheel of Brisbane ... B4

Activities, Courses & Tours
- Brisbane Greeters ... (see 64)
- 16 CitySights ... D3
- 17 Kookaburra River Queens ... E4
- 18 Planet Inline ... C6
- 19 River City Cruises ... B4
- 20 Riverlife Adventure Centre ... E5
- 21 Story Bridge Adventure Climb ... F4
- 22 Streets Beach ... B5

Sleeping
- 23 Dahrl Court ... F1
- 24 Diamant Hotel ... D1
- 25 Il Mondo ... F4
- 26 Inchcolm Hotel ... E2
- 27 Kookaburra Inn ... E1
- 28 M on Mary ... D4
- 29 Queensland Motel ... D7
- 30 Riverside Hotel ... A2
- 31 Stamford Plaza Brisbane ... D4
- 32 Treasury ... C4
- 33 Urban Brisbane ... C1
- 34 X-Base Brisbane Central ... D2
- 35 X-Base Brisbane Embassy ... D3
- 36 X-Base Brisbane Uptown ... C2

Eating
- 37 Ahmet's ... B4
- 38 Bleeding Heart Gallery ... D2
- 39 Brew ... D3
- Cha Cha Char ... (see 17)
- 40 Cliffs Cafe ... D6
- 41 E'cco ... F2
- 42 Java Coast Cafe ... C2
- 43 Merlo Coffee ... D4
- 44 Piaf ... B5
- 45 Stokehouse ... B6

Drinking & Nightlife
- 46 Belgian Beer Cafe ... D4
- 47 Laneway ... D4
- 48 Story Bridge Hotel ... F4
- 49 Super Whatnot ... C3

Entertainment
- 50 Ben & Jerry's Openair Cinemas ... B4
- 51 Brisbane Jazz Club ... F3
- 52 Event Cinemas ... C3
- 53 Queensland Conservatorium ... B4
- 54 Queensland Performing Arts Centre ... B3
- 55 QUT Gardens Theatre ... C5
- 56 Riverstage ... C6
- 57 South Bank Cinema ... A5
- 58 Ticketek ... C3

Shopping
- 59 Archives Fine Books ... C3
- 60 Record Exchange ... C3
- 61 South Bank Lifestyle Markets ... B5
- 62 Title ... A4
- 63 World Wide Maps & Globes ... D2

Information
- 64 Brisbane Visitor Information Centre ... D3
- 65 Department of National Parks, Recreation, Sport & Racing ... C2
- 66 RACQ ... D3
- 67 South Bank Visitor Information Centre ... B5

Transport
- 68 Brisbane Transit Centre ... C1
- 69 King George Sq Bus Station ... C3
- 70 Queen St Bus Station ... C3

critters. The koalas are undeniably cute – most visitors readily cough up the $16 to have their picture snapped hugging one. There are animal presentations scheduled throughout the day.

To get here catch bus 430 ($6.70, 45 minutes) from the Queen St bus station. Alternatively, **Mirimar II** (☎0412 749 426; www.mirimar.com; incl park entry per adult/child/family $65/38/190) cruises to the sanctuary along the Brisbane River, departing from the Cultural Centre Pontoon on South Bank next to Victoria Bridge. It departs daily at 10am, returning from Lone Pine at 1.45pm.

Activities

Pick up the self-guided *Brisbane City Walk* brochure from info centres, which takes you through Roma St Parkland, South Bank Parklands and the City Botanic Gardens.

Swimming

Streets Beach SWIMMING
(Map p288; www.visitsouthbank.com.au; South Bank; ⏲daylight hours) FREE A central spot for a quick (and free) dip is the man-made, riverside Streets Beach at South Bank. Lifeguards, hollering kids, beach babes, strutting gym-junkies, ice-cream carts – it's all here.

Spring Hill Baths SWIMMING
(Map p284; www.bluefitbrisbane.com.au; 14 Torrington St, Spring Hill; adult/child/family $4.90/3.50/14.90; ⏲6.30am-7pm Mon-Thu, 6.30am-6pm Fri, 8am-5pm Sat & Sun) Opened in 1886, this quaint old 25m pool is encircled by cute timber change rooms.

Valley Pool SWIMMING
(Map p292; www.valleypool.com.au; 432 Wickham St, Fortitude Valley; adult/child/family $4.90/3.50/10.30; ⏲5.30am-7.30pm Mon-Fri, 7.30am-6pm Sat & Sun) Big clean outdoor pool, popular with glam types (of all persuasions).

Cycling

Brisbane has over 900km of bike trails, including routes along the Brisbane River. Check out the city website (www.brisbane.qld.gov.au) for maps and info. See also Riverlife Adventure Centre (p291) for bike hire.

Bicycle Revolution BICYCLE RENTAL
(Map p298; www.bicyclerevolution.org.au; 294 Montague Rd, West End; per day/week $35/100; ⏲9am-5pm Mon, 9am-6pm Tue-Fri, 8am-2pm Sat) Friendly community shop with a great range of recycled city bikes with reconditioned parts.

Gardens Cycle Hire BICYCLE RENTAL
(☎0408 003 198; www.brisbanebicyclehire.com; hire per day/week $40/90) Bikes delivered to your door.

CityCycle BICYCLE RENTAL
(☎1300 229 253; www.citycycle.com.au; hire per hour/day $2.20/165; ⏲hire 5am-10pm, return 24hr) To use Brisbane's bike-share program, subscribe via the website (per day/week/three months $2/11/27.50), then can hire a bike (additional fee) from any of the 100-plus stations around central Brisbane. Good for short hops; pricey by the day. BYO helmet and lock.

Climbing & Abseiling

Story Bridge Adventure Climb BRIDGE CLIMBING
(Map p288; ☎1300 254 627; www.sbac.net.au; 170 Main St, Kangaroo Point; adult/child from $99/85) A Brisbane must-do, the bridge climb offers unbeatable views of the city – either dawn, day, twilight or night. The 2½-hour climb scales the southern half of the bridge, taking you 80m above the twisting, muddy Brisbane River below. Minimum age 10. Bridge abseiling expeditions are also available.

Riverlife Adventure Centre ROCK CLIMBING
(Map p288; ☎07-3891 5766; www.riverlife.com.au; Naval Stores, Kangaroo Point Bikeway, Kangaroo Point; ⏲9am-5pm) Near the 20m Kangaroo Point cliffs, Riverlife runs rock-climbing sessions (from $49) and abseiling exploits ($39). They also offer kayaking river trips

WORTH A TRIP

D'AGUILAR RANGE NATIONAL PARK

Suburban malaise? Slake your wilderness cravings at the 50,000-hectare **D'Aguilar Range National Park** (www.nprsr.qld.gov.au/parks/daguilar; Mount Nebo Rd, The Gap), just 10km northwest of the city centre but worlds away. There are **walking trails** ranging from a few hundred metres to 13km, including the 6km Morelia Track at Manorina day-use area and the 4.3km Greene's Falls Track at Mt Glorious. Mountain biking is also an option. You can camp in the park too, in remote, walk-in bush **campsites** (☎13 74 68; www.qld.gov.au/camping; per person $5.45).

At the park entrance the **Walkabout Creek Visitor Information Centre** (☎07-3512 2300; www.nprsr.qld.gov.au; 60 Mt Nebo Rd, The Gap; wildlife centre adult/child/family $6.40/4.35/16; ⏲9am-4.30pm) has maps of the park. Also here is the South East Queensland Wildlife Centre where you can see a resident platypus up close, plus turtles, lizards, pythons and gliders. There's also a small but wonderful walk-through aviary, and a cafe.

To get here catch bus 385 ($6.70, 30 minutes) from Roma St Station to the visitor information centre; the last bus back to the city is at 4.48pm (3.53pm on weekends).

Fortitude Valley & New Farm

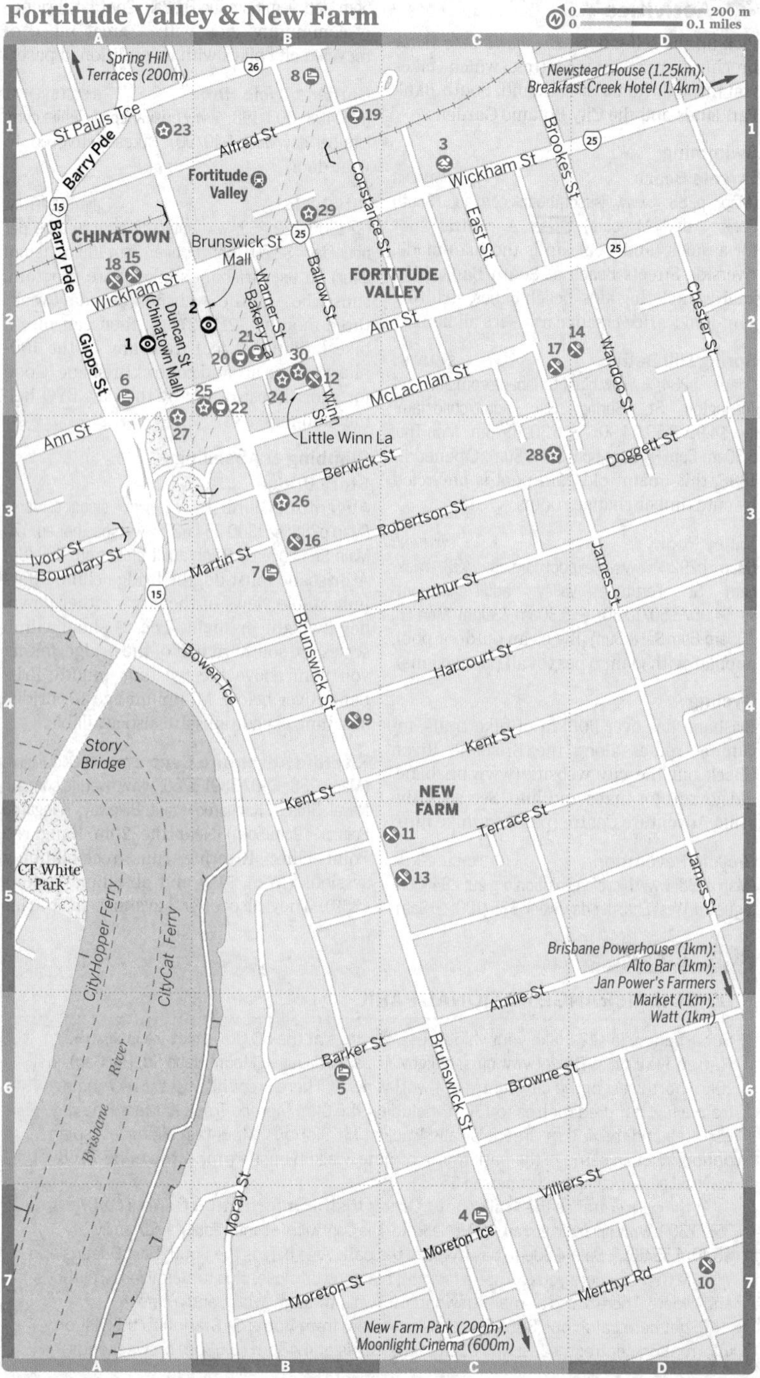

Fortitude Valley & New Farm

Sights
1 Chinatown A2
Institute of Modern Art .... (see 26)
2 Valley Walk of Fame B2

Activities, Courses & Tours
C!RCA .... (see 26)
3 Valley Pool C1

Sleeping
4 Allender Apartments C7
5 Bowen Terrace B6
6 Bunk Backpackers A2
7 Central Brunswick Apartments B3
8 Limes B1

Eating
9 Burger Urge B4
10 Cafe Bouquiniste D7
11 Café Cirque C5
12 Flamingo B2
13 Himalayan Cafe C5
14 James Street Market D2
15 Kuan Yin Tea House A2
16 Ortiga B3
17 Spoon Deli Cafe C2
18 The Vietnamese A2

Drinking & Nightlife
19 Alfred & Constance B1
20 Bowery B2
Cru Bar & Cellar .... (see 17)
21 La Ruche B2
22 Press Club B2

Entertainment
23 Alloneword A1
24 Beat MegaClub B2
Birdees .... (see 6)
25 Cloudland B2
26 Judith Wright Centre of Contemporary Arts B3
27 Oh Hello A3
28 Palace Centro C3
29 Wickham Hotel B1
30 Zoo B2

Shopping
Blonde Venus .... (see 30)

(from $39) and hire out bikes (per four hours $30), kayaks (per two hours $33) and in-line skates (per four hours $40).

Urban Climb ROCK CLIMBING, ABSEILING
(Map p298; ☎07-3844 2544; www.urbanclimb.com; 2/220 Montague Rd, West End; adult/child $18/16; ⏲noon-10pm Mon-Thu, noon-9pm Fri, 10am-6pm Sat & Sun) A large indoor climbing wall with 200-plus routes.

In-line Skating

You can hire skates and equipment from Riverlife Adventure Centre (p291).

Planet Inline SKATING
(Map p288; ☎07-3217 3571; www.planetinline.com; Goodwill Bridge; tours $15) Runs skate tours through the CBD, starting at 7.15pm Wednesdays from the top of the Goodwill Bridge. It also runs a Saturday-morning breakfast-club tour. Call in advance or book online.

Skydiving & Ballooning

Jump the Beach Brisbane SKYDIVING
(☎1800 800 840; www.jumpthebeachbrisbane.com.au; skydives from $344) Picks up from the CBD and offers tandem skydives over Brisbane, landing on the sand in Redcliffe.

Fly Me to the Moon BALLOONING
(☎07-3423 0400; www.brisbanehotairballooning.com.au; per person $299) One-hour hot-air balloon trips over Brisbane. Pick-up and breakfast included.

Tours

CityCat FERRY RIDES
(☎13 12 30; www.translink.com.au; one-way $5.60; ⏲5.25am-11.50pm) Ditching the car or bus and catching a sleek CityCat ferry along the river is the Brisbane sightseeing journey of choice! Stand on an open-air deck and glide under the Story Bridge to South Bank and the city centre. Ferries run every 15 to 30 minutes between the University of Queensland in the southwest to Apollo Rd terminal north of the city, stopping at 14 terminals in between, including New Farm Park, North Quay (for the CBD), South Bank and West End.

XXXX Brewery Tour TOUR
(Map p298; ☎07-3361 7597; www.xxxxbrewerytour.com.au; cnr Black & Paten Sts, Milton; adult/child $25/16; ⏲hourly 11am-4pm Mon-Fri, 12.30pm, 1pm & 1.30pm Sat, 11am, noon & 12.30pm Sun) Feel a XXXX coming on? Grown-up entry to this brewery tour includes a few humidity beating ales, so leave the car at home. Also on offer are beer-and-barbecue tours on Wednesday nights and Saturday during the day (adult/child $38/29), which include lunch. Book all tours in advance, online or by phone. There's

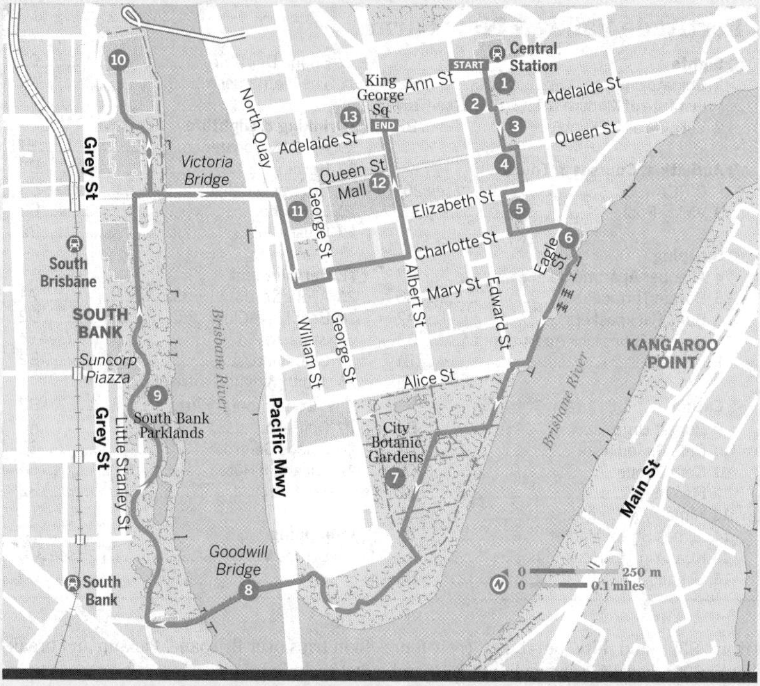

City Walk
CBD & South Bank Circuit

START CENTRAL STATION
FINISH KING GEORGE SQ
DISTANCE 5KM; TWO HOURS

Cross Ann St south of Central Station to the sobering 1 **Shrine of Remembrance** above the northern edge of 2 **Anzac Square**, with its bulbous boab trees and wandering ibises.

At the southern side of the square, scale one of the pedestrian bridges over Adelaide St, which lead to the elevated, manicured 3 **Post Office Square**. The square is fronted at its southern end by Brisbane's stately stone 4 **GPO**. Take the alley between the wings of the post office through to Elizabeth St. Cross the road and stick your head into beautiful white-stone 5 **St Stephen's Cathedral**.

Walk through the grassy courtyard behind the cathedral until Charlotte St. Take a left, cross Eagle St and duck through 6 **Eagle St Pier** on the river. Check the Story Bridge views to your left, then go down the steps to the riverside boardwalk and truck south.

At the corner of Edward and Alice Sts, detour through the 7 **City Botanic Gardens** (p283). Cast an eye across the river to the Kangaroo Point cliffs, then skirt around the back of the Brisbane Riverstage to the pedestrian-only 8 **Goodwill Bridge**: check out HMAS *Diamantina* in the Queensland Maritime Museum to your left. From here, jag north into the 9 **South Bank Parklands** (p286).

If time is on your side, duck into the outstanding 10 **Gallery of Modern Art** (p286). Otherwise, cross Victoria Bridge back into central Brisbane. Just south of the gorgeous 11 **Treasury Building** (p283) on William St, an unnamed alley cuts through to George St. Dogleg across George into Charlotte St, continue along Charlotte then turn left into Albert St in Brisbane's modern CBD.

Continue along Albert St, cross 12 **Queen Street Mall** – trashy and trad shopping in equal measure – and then Adelaide St into King George Sq, with 13 **City Hall** (p283) anchoring the southwest side. After taking in the scene, backtrack to the mall for a much-deserved pick-me-up.

also an alehouse here if you feel like kicking on. The brewery is a 20-minute walk west from Roma St Station, or take the train to Milton Station. Wear enclosed shoes.

CitySights GUIDED TOUR
(Map p288; www.citysights.com.au; day tickets per adult/child/family $35/20/80; ⊙9am-3.45pm) This hop-on-hop-off shuttle bus wheels past 19 of Brisbane's major landmarks, including the CBD, Mt Coot-tha, Chinatown, South Bank and Story Bridge. Tours depart every 45 minutes from Post Office Sq on Queen St. The same ticket covers you for unlimited use of CityCat ferry services.

Brisbane Greeters GUIDED TOUR
(Map p288; ☎07-3006 6290; www.brisbanegreeters.com.au; Brisbane Visitor Information Centre, Queen St Mall; ⊙10am) FREE Small-group, hand-held introductory tours of Brizzy with affable volunteers. Tours are themed: public art on Monday, Queenslander architecture on Tuesday, churches on Wednesday, the river on Sunday etc. Call to see what's running, or to customise a tour. Bookings essential.

Brisbane Lights Tours GUIDED TOUR
(☎07-3822 6028; www.brisbanelightstours.com; adult/child from $65/30) Three-hour nocturnal tours departing at 6.30pm nightly (hotel pick-ups included), covering a dozen city landmarks, with dinner (or a snack) at Mt Coot-tha Lookout and a 20-minute CityCat cruise.

River City Cruises CRUISE
(Map p288; ☎0428 278 473; www.rivercitycruises.com.au; South Bank Parklands Jetty A; adult/child/family $25/15/60) River City runs 1½-hour cruises with commentary from South Bank to New Farm and back. They depart from South Bank at 10.30am and 12.30pm (plus 2.30pm during summer).

Kookaburra River Queens CRUISE
(Map p288; ☎07-3221 1300; www.kookaburrariverqueens.com; Eagle St Pier; lunch/dinner cruises per person from $42/79) Chug up and down the river in a wooden paddle steamer. Meals are three-course seafood and carvery buffet affairs; there's live jazz on the Sunday lunch cruise.

Festivals & Events

Brisbane International TENNIS
(www.brisbaneinternational.com.au) Pro tennis tournament attracting the world's best, held in January at the Queensland Tennis Centre just prior to the Australian Open (in Melbourne).

Chinese New Year CULTURAL EVENT
(www.chinesenewyear.com.au) Held in Fortitude Valley's Chinatown Mall (Duncan St) in February. Firecrackers, dancing dragons and fantastic food.

Brisbane Comedy Festival COMEDY
(www.briscomfest.com) Four-week festival in March featuring local and international laugh-mongers at the Brisbane Powerhouse.

Urban Country Festival MUSIC
(www.urbancountry.com.au) Four-day country-music fest in May with up to 500 guitar twangers and nasally bards. Held 45 minutes north of Brisbane in Caboolture (where Keith Urban grew up...which has nothing to do with the festival name!).

Brisbane Winter Carnival HORSE RACING
(www.horseracinginfo.com.au) The state's major horse-racing carnival, held in May and June. The biggest day is the Stradbroke Handicap in early June.

Out of the Box ARTS
(www.outoftheboxfestival.com.au) Six-day biennial festival of performing and visual arts for kids, with lots of interactive and free events. Held in June in even-numbered years.

Brisbane International Film Festival FILM
(www.biff.com.au) Twelve days of quality films flicker across Brisbane screens in July.

Queensland Music Festival MUSIC
(QMF; www.queenslandmusicfestival.org.au) Statewide festival with styles ranging from classical to contemporary, held over two weeks in July in odd-numbered years. Most events are free.

'Ekka' Royal Queensland Show AGRICULTURE
(www.ekka.com.au) Country and city collide in August for Queensland's largest annual event, the Ekka (formerly the Brisbane Exhibition, which was shortened to 'Ekka'). Baby animals, showbags, spooky carnies, shearing demonstrations, rides and over-sugared kids ahoy!

Brisbane Festival ARTS
(www.brisbanefestival.com.au) Brisbane's major festival of the arts, held over three weeks in September. See the boxed text (p296).

Brisbane Pride Festival GAY & LESBIAN
(www.brisbanepridefestival.com.au) Brisbane's annual gay and lesbian celebration is held

BRISBANE FESTIVAL

In September, Brisbane's streets become a hurly-burly of colour, flair, flavour and fireworks during the city's biggest annual arts event – the Brisbane Festival. Running over three weeks, the festival involves over 300 performances and 60-odd events, enticing 2000-plus artists from across the planet. Art exhibitions, dance, theatre, opera, symphonies, circus performers, buskers and vaudeville acts generate an eclectic scene, with many free street events and concerts around town. Staged over the Brisbane River, with vantage points at South Bank, the city and West End, Riverfire is a highlight – a massive fireworks show with a synchronised soundtrack.

over four weeks in September (some events in June, including the fab Queen's Ball).

Brisbane Writers Festival ARTS
(BWF; www.brisbanewritersfestival.com.au) Queensland's premier literary event has been running for 50 years: words, books, and people who put words in books. Held in September.

Valley Fiesta MUSIC
(www.valleyfiesta.com.au) Rock bands and DJs take over Fortitude Valley's Brunswick St and Chinatown malls for three days in October. Brisbane's biggest free music fest.

Sleeping

Brisbane has an excellent selection of accommodation options. Most are beyond the business beds of the city centre, but they're usually within walking distance or have good public-transport connections. Head for Spring Hill for peace and quiet; Fortitude Valley for party nights; Paddington for cafes and boutiques; Petrie Terrace for hostels; gay-friendly New Farm for restaurants; and West End for bars and bookshops.

City Centre

X-Base Brisbane Central HOSTEL $
(Map p288; ☎07-3211 2433, 1800 242 273; www.stayatbase.com; 398 Edward St; dm $27-33, s/d/tw $55/70/70; ❄@📶) This colossal backpackers has basic rooms in a lace-fringed heritage building (once a Salvation Army budget hotel). There's a rooftop terrace with city views, a rickety old elevator, and a bar downstairs. Not all rooms have air-con. There are two other branches nearby: **X-Base Brisbane Embassy** (Map p288; ☎07-3166 8000; 214 Elizabeth St; dm $31-35, d with/without bathroom $99/79; ❄@📶), which is much quieter but a bit soulless; and the purpose-built **X-Base Brisbane Uptown** (Map p288; ☎07-3238 5888; 466 George St; dm $22-36, d & tw $130-140; ❄@📶), which falls somewhere in between (soundproofed rooms, all with bathroom).

Diamant Hotel BOUTIQUE HOTEL $$
(Map p288; ☎07-3009 3400; www.8hotels.com; 52 Astor Tce; d from $139; P❄📶) Behind an ultra-mod black-and-white facade, seven-storey Diamant has compact, contemporary rooms with natty wallpaper and thoughtful touches (original artwork, iPod docks, free wi-fi). The bigger suites have kitchenettes and lounge areas, and there's a bar-restaurant on the ground floor. Parking $28.

Urban Brisbane HOTEL $$
(Map p288; ☎07-3831 6177; www.hotelurban.com.au; 345 Wickham Tce; d from $150; ❄@📶🏊) Still looking sexy after a $10-million makeover in 2008, the Urban has stylish rooms with masculine hues, balconies and high-end fittings (super-comfy beds, big TVs, fuzzy bathrobes). There's also a heated outdoor pool, a bar, and lots of uniformed flight attendants checking in and out. Parking $15.

Inchcolm Hotel HERITAGE HOTEL $$
(Map p288; ☎07-3226 8888; www.theinchcolm.com.au; 73 Wickham Tce; r $160-250; P❄📶🏊) Built in the 1930s as doctors' suites, the heritage-listed Inchcolm (pronounced as per 'Malcolm') retains elements of its past (love the old elevator!), but the rooms have been overhauled. Those in the newer wing have more space and light; in the older wing there's more character. There's also a rooftop pool and in-house restaurant. Parking $30.

Treasury LUXURY HOTEL $$$
(Map p288; ☎07-3306 8888; www.treasury-brisbane.com.au; 130 William St; r from $230; P❄@📶) Brisbane's most lavish hotel is behind the equally lavish exterior of the former Land Administration Building. Each room is unique and awash with heritage features, and has high ceilings, framed artwork, polished wood furniture and elegant furnishings. The best rooms have river views. Super-efficient staff; parking $20.

Stamford Plaza Brisbane HOTEL $$$
(Map p288; ☎07-3221 1999; www.stamford.com.au; cnr Edward & Margaret Sts; r from $269; P❄@📶🏊) In the southern CBD, the towering Stamford has classical music in the lobby and rows of Mercedes in the driveway. Opulent rooms are a tad antiquey (not that there's anything wrong with that...), but have huge beds, and there are multiple on-site bars, eateries and salons. Park your Merc for $40.

M on Mary APARTMENTS $$$
(Map p288; ☎07-3503 8000; www.monmary.com; 70 Mary St; 1-/3-bedroom apt from $200/419; P❄📶) A stone's throw from the botanic gardens, this 43-storey tower has modern, comfortable one- and three-bedroom apartments (pricey, but with more affordable long-term rates). The best apartments have balconies; the not-so-good ones are a bit gloomy. Parking $30.

South Bank & West End

Brisbane Backpackers Resort HOSTEL $
(Map p298; ☎07-3844 9956, 1800 626 452; www.brisbanebackpackers.com.au; 110 Vulture St, West End; dm $27-34, tw/d/tr $110/120/135; P❄@📶🏊) Is there such a thing as 'backpacker kitsch'? If so, this hulking hostel probably qualifies, with dubious marketing relating to 'bad girls' and what they do and don't do...But if you're looking to party, you're in the right place. There's a great pool and bar area, and rooms are basic but generally well maintained.

Somewhere to Stay HOSTEL $
(Map p298; ☎07-3846 2858, 1800 812 398; www.somewheretostay.com.au; 47 Brighton Rd; dm $19-27, s $49-54, d $59-79; P@📶🏊) An enormous white Queenslander (actually, a couple of buildings) with more than 50 rooms and a very laid-back vibe. Cheap, casual and grungy: not for the pernickety.

Riverside Hotel HOTEL $$
(Map p288; ☎1800 301 101, 07-3846 0577; www.riversidehotel.com.au; 20 Montague Rd, South Bank; d/1-bedroom apt from $109/149; P❄📶🏊) This huge place spreads through several taupe-coloured buildings, and has surprisingly friendly staff for such a sprawling outfit. Right across the road from GOMA and South Bank, location is why you're here: don't expect too much from the motel-style rooms and you'll be fine.

Petrie Terrace

Aussie Way Backpackers HOSTEL $
(Map p298; ☎07-3369 0711; www.aussiewaybackpackers.com; 34 Cricket St; dm/s/d/f/q $26/55/68/78/104; ❄📶🏊) Set in a photogenic, two-storey timber Queenslander on the appealingly named Cricket St, Aussie Way feels more like a homely guesthouse than a hostel, with spacious, tastefully furnished rooms and a fab pool for sticky Brisbane afternoons. The doubles in the second building out the back are just lovely. All quiet after 10.30pm.

Brisbane City YHA HOSTEL $
(Map p298; ☎07-3236 1004; www.yha.com.au; 392 Upper Roma St; dm $33-38, tw & d with/without bathroom $114/97, f $132; P❄@📶🏊) This immaculate, well-run hostel has a rooftop pool and a sundeck with incredible river views. The maximum dorm size is six beds (not too big); most have bathrooms. Big on security, activities, tours and kitchen space (lots of fridges). The cafe/bar has trivia nights and happy hours, but this is a YHA, not party central. Parking $10.

Chill Backpackers HOSTEL $
(Map p298; ☎1800 851 875, 07-3236 0088; www.chillbackpackers.com; 328 Upper Roma St; dm $29-35, d/tr $89/105; P❄@📶) This garish aqua building on the CBD fringe has small, clean, modern rooms, and there's a roof deck with fab river views (just like the YHA up the road, but from a slightly reduced altitude). There are 150 beds here, but if they're full the affiliated Brisbane City Backpackers is a couple of doors away.

ROCK 'N' ROLL BRISBANE

It's a long way from Hollywood Blvd, but Fortitude Valley has its very own **Valley Walk of Fame** (Map p292) honouring the city's most successful musos. At the top end of Brunswick St Mall are 10 plaques celebrating artists that have called Brisbane home (at least for their formative years): the pre-*Saturday Night Fever* **Bee Gees**, punk legends the **Saints**, Queensland import **Keith Urban**, and 15-time ARIA award–winning rockers **Powderfinger**, just to name a few. Nineties electro-rockers **Regurgitator** and indie band **Custard** also get a mention. Brisbane rocks!

West End & Petrie Terrace

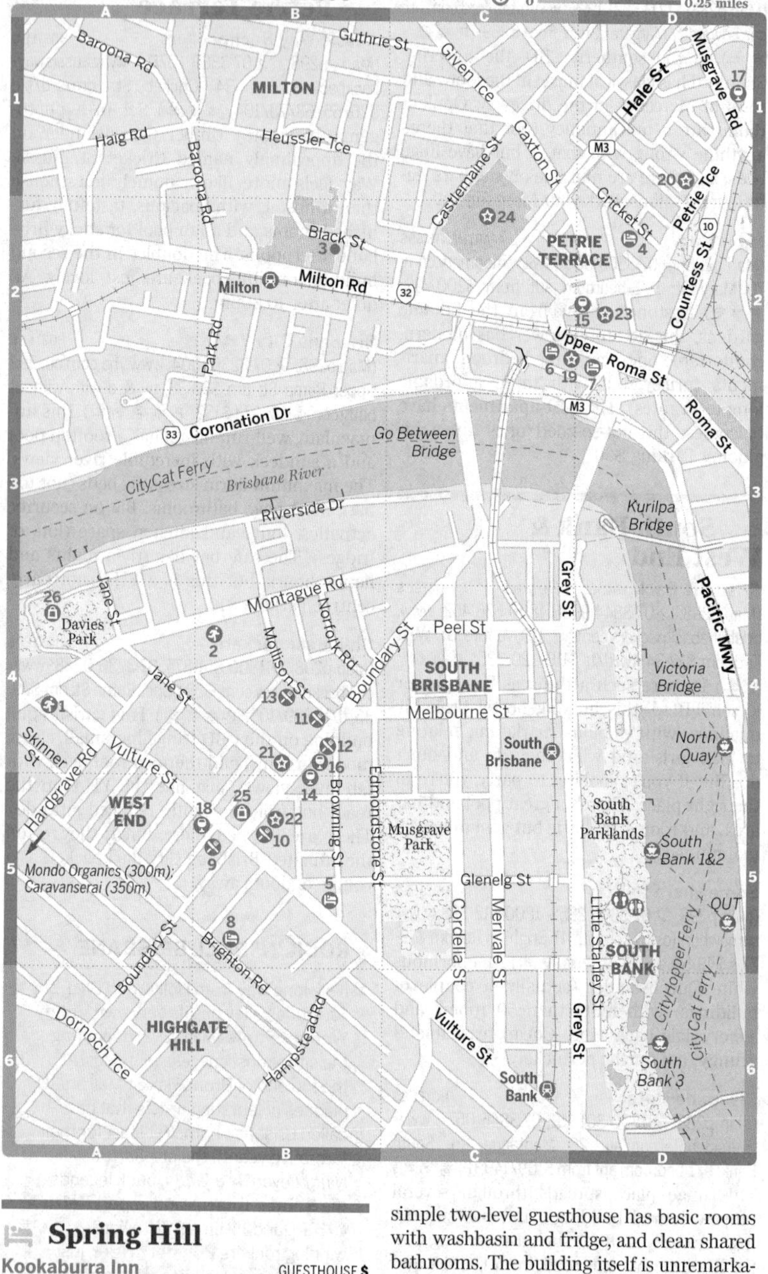

Spring Hill

Kookaburra Inn GUESTHOUSE $
(Map p288; ☎07-3832 1303, 1800 733 533; www.kookaburra-inn.com.au; 41 Phillips St; s/d without bathroom from $59/76; ❄@🛜) This small, simple two-level guesthouse has basic rooms with washbasin and fridge, and clean shared bathrooms. The building itself is unremarkable, but there's a lounge, kitchen and outdoor patio. A decent budget option if you've done dorms to death. Air-con in some doubles only.

West End & Petrie Terrace

Activities, Courses & Tours
1 Bicycle Revolution A4
2 Urban Climb B4
3 XXXX Brewery Tour B2

Sleeping
4 Aussie Way Backpackers D2
5 Brisbane Backpackers Resort B5
6 Brisbane City YHA C2
7 Chill Backpackers D2
8 Somewhere to Stay B5

Eating
9 Blackstar Coffee Roasters B5
10 George's Seafood B5
11 Gunshop Café B4
12 Little Greek Taverna B4
13 The Burrow B4

Drinking & Nightlife
14 Archive Beer Boutique B5
15 Cabiria D2
16 Lychee Lounge B4
17 Normanby Hotel D1
18 The End B5

Entertainment
19 Beetle Bar C2
20 Brisbane Arts Theatre D1
21 Hi-Fi B4
22 Lock 'n' Load B5
Loft West End .... (see 14)
23 Palace Barracks D2
24 Suncorp Stadium C2

Shopping
25 Avid Reader B5
26 Davies Park Market A4

Dahrl Court APARTMENT $$
(Map p288; ☎07-3831 9553; www.dahrlcourt.com.au; 45 Phillips St; apt from $155; P ❄ @) In a hushed, leafy pocket of Spring Hill, these 13 roomy apartments offer great bang for your buck. The heritage aesthetics might feel a bit kitsch, but there are lovely old timber ballustrades and art-deco ceilings, and all apartments have kitchens.

Spring Hill Terraces MOTEL $$
(Map p284; ☎07-3854 1048; www.springhillterraces.com; 260 Water St; d $95-145, units $175; P ❄ 📶 🏊) Offering good old-fashioned service, security and a tiny pool, Spring Hill Terraces has motel-style rooms and roomier terrace units with balconies and leafy courtyards. A 10-minute walk from Fortitude Valley.

Fortitude Valley

Bunk Backpackers HOSTEL $
(Map p292; ☎07-3257 3644, 1800 682 865; www.bunkbrisbane.com.au; cnr Ann & Gipps Sts; dm $21-33, s $60, d/apt from $80/180; P ❄ @ 📶 🏊) This old arts college was reborn as a backpackers in 2006 – and the party hasn't stopped! It's a huge, five-level place with 55 rooms (mostly eight-bed dorms), just staggering distance from the Valley nightlife. There's an in-house bar (Birdees, 305), a Mexican cantina, and some great apartments on the top floor.

Central Brunswick Apartments APARTMENT $$
(Map p292; ☎07-3852 1411; www.centralbrunswickhotel.com.au; 455 Brunswick St; r $140-180; P ❄ 📶) Emerging from the husk of an old brick brewery building, these 60 apartments are a hit with business bods. All have fully equipped kitchens, and there's an on-site gym, free wi-fi and rooftop BBQ. Parking $10 per night.

Limes BOUTIQUE HOTEL $$$
(Map p292; ☎07-3852 9000; www.limeshotel.com.au; 142 Constance St; d from $230; ❄ 📶) A slick slice of style in the Valley, Limes has 21 handsome rooms that make good use of tight space – each has plush furniture, kitchenettes and thoughtful extras (iPod docks, free wi-fi, free gym pass). The rooftop bar and cinema (!) are magic.

New Farm

★ **Bowen Terrace** GUESTHOUSE $
(Map p292; ☎07-3254 0458; www.bowenterrace.com.au; 365 Bowen Tce; dm/s/d without bathroom $35/60/85, d/f with bathroom $99/145; P @ 🏊) A beautifully restored, 100-year-old Queenslander, this guesthouse is in a quiet part of New Farm. There are TVs, bar fridges, quality bed linens and lofty ceilings with fans in every room. Out the back there's a deck overlooking the enticing pool. No air-con but real value for money, with far more class than your average hostel.

Allender Apartments APARTMENT $$
(Map p292; ☎07-3358 5832; www.allenderapartments.com.au; 3 Moreton St; d $135, 1-bedroom apt $160-170; ❄ 📶) Allender's apartments are a mixed bag. In the plain yellow-brick building are simply furnished but clean rooms.

More attractive are the heritage apartments in the adjoining Fingal House, a 1918 Queenslander with polished timber floors, oak furniture and access to a private verandah or courtyard.

Kangaroo Point

Il Mondo HOTEL $$
(Map p288; ☎07-3392 0111, 1300 665 526; www.ilmondo.com.au; 25 Rotherham St; r $160, 1-/3-bedroom apt $250/500; P ❄ @ 📶 🏊) In a beaut location near the Story Bridge, this postmodern-looking, seven-storey hotel has handsome rooms and apartments with minimalist design, high-end fixtures and plenty of space. The biggest apartments sleep six – good value for a full house.

Queensland Motel MOTEL $$
(Map p288; ☎07-3391 1061; www.queenslandmotel.id.au; 777 Main St; d/tr/f $120/150/185; P ❄ 📶 🏊) A no-frills, friendly, old-school motel near 'the Gabba' cricket ground and 20 minutes' walk to the city. Shoot for a room on the top floor, with palm trees rustling outside your window.

Paddington & Around

Newmarket Gardens Caravan Park CAMPGROUND $
(Map p284; ☎07-3356 1458; www.newmarketgardens.com.au; 199 Ashgrove Ave, Newmarket; unpowered/powered sites $38/39, on-site vans $56, budget r $64, cabins $125-150; P ❄ @ 📶) This upbeat caravan park doesn't have many trees (some of them are mangoes – beware falling fruit!), but it's just 4km north of the city, accessible by bus and train. There's a row of six simple budget rooms (no air-con), five tidy cabins (with air-con) and a sea of van and tent sites.

Casabella Apartment APARTMENT $$
(Map p301; ☎07-3217 6507; www.casabellaapartment.com; 211 Latrobe Tce, Paddington; apt $185; P 📶) The understorey of this fuschia-coloured house at the quiet end of Paddo's main drag has been converted into a very comfortable self-contained unit. There are two bedrooms (sleeps three), warm Mediterranean colour schemes, recycled timber floors and lots of louvres to let the cross-breeze through (no air-con). Lovely! Free street parking.

Fern Cottage B&B $$
(Map p301; ☎07-3511 6685; www.ferncottage.net; 89 Fernberg Rd, Paddington; s/d $135/165; P ❄ 📶) Fern Cottage is a renovated, mustard-coloured, three-suite Queenslander with splashes of chintzy ambience and a shared guest kitchen. The suites are cushy (two of which sleep three; plus one double), and there's a BBQ terrace out the back. Free street parking.

★**Latrobe Apartment** APARTMENT $$$
(Map p301; ☎0448 944 026; www.stayz.com.au/77109; 183a Latrobe Tce, Paddington; apt $200; P ❄ 📶) Underneath a chiropractor in affluent Paddington is this excellent two-bedroom apartment, sleeping four, with two bathrooms, polished floorboards, sexy lighting and a fabulous BBQ deck. It's a sleek, contemporary design, with quality everything: linen, toiletries, kitchenware, TV, iPod dock, leather lounge... Cafes and free parking up at street level.

Eating

Like most things in Brisbane, dining experiences can be broadly defined by which neighbourhood you're in. The city centre is the place for fine dining and coffee nooks. In Fortitude Valley you'll find cheap cafes and Chinatown. Nearby, New Farm has plenty of multicultural eateries and award winners. West End is littered with bohemian cafes. South Bank swings between mainstream and pricey eats. But no matter where you are, you'll always be able to eat outside!

City Centre

★**Brew** CAFE, WINE BAR $
(Map p288; ☎07-3211 4242; www.brewgroup.com.au; Lower Burnett La; mains $6-12; ⏲7am-5pm Mon, to 10pm Tue & Wed, to 11.30pm Thu & Fri, 9am-11.30pm Sat, 9am-3pm Sun) You'd expect to find this kind of subcultural underground cafe in Seattle or Berlin...but Brisbane? Breaking new coffee-cultural ground in Queensland, Brew takes the caffeine into the alleyways, serving simple food (tapas, pastas, sandwiches) to go with the black stuff. Serves wines and bottled beers if you feel like a different kind of brew.

Bleeding Heart Gallery CAFE $
(Map p288; ☎07-3229 0395; www.bleedingheart.com.au; 166 Ann St; mains $5-10; ⏲7am-5pm Mon-Fri; 📶) 🌿 Set back from hectic Ann St in an

Paddington

1865 servants' home (Brisbane's third-oldest building!), this spacious cafe/gallery has hippie vibes and hosts art exhibitions, occasional concerts and other events. All profits go into funding charitable community enterprises.

Merlo Coffee CAFE $
(Map p288; ☎07-3221 2616; www.merlo.com.au; 10 Market St; items $4-8; ⏰6.30am-4pm Mon-Fri) Keeping the downtown business bods firing, this roaster/cafe is one of several Merlos around Brisbane (a local success story). The food is fine (croissants, cakes, sandwiches), but what you're here for is the coffee: strong enough to get you through the next meeting.

Java Coast Cafe CAFE $
(Map p288; ☎07-3211 3040; www.javacoastcafe.com.au; 340 George St; mains $11-20; ⏰6.30am-3pm Mon-Fri) Behind a grungy downtown rollerdoor, a skinny alleyway leads to a hidden cafe garden with a fountain, subtropical plants and Buddha statues. An oasis on the Java coast! Good coffee, teas, sandwiches, salads and light meals with Asian accents.

E'cco MODERN AUSTRALIAN $$$
(Map p288; ☎07-3831 8344; www.eccobistro.com; 100 Boundary St; mains $43; ⏰noon-3pm Tue-Fri, 6-10pm Tue-Sat) One of the finest restaurants

Paddington

Sleeping
1 Casabella Apartment A1
2 Fern Cottage B2
3 Latrobe Apartment A1

Eating
4 Il Posto B2

Drinking & Nightlife
5 Lark C3

Shopping
6 Paddington Antique Centre B1

in the state, award-winning E'cco is a culinary must. Menu masterpieces from chef Philip Johnson include liquorice-spiced pork belly with caramelised peach, onion jam and kipfler potatoes. The interior is suitably swish: all black, white and stainless steel.

Stokehouse MODERN AUSTRALIAN $$$
(Map p288; ☎07-3020 0600; www.stokehouse.com.au; River Quay, Sidon St, South Bank; mains $34-62; ⏰10am-1am) Looking for a classy restaurant in which to pop the question? This angular, concrete and dark-timber bunker by the river is for you. Start with the spanner

crab with apple jelly, then move on to the Daintree barramundi with white clams and sauerkraut. Flashy Stoke Bar is next door (for champagne after she/he says 'Yes!').

Cha Cha Char STEAKHOUSE **$$$**
(Map p288; ☎07-3211 9944; www.chachachar.com.au; Shop 5, 1 Eagle St Pier; mains $38-95; ⊙noon-11pm Mon-Fri, 6pm-11pm Sat & Sun) Wallowing in awards, this long-running favourite serves Brisbane's best steaks, along with first-rate seafood and roast game meats. The classy semicircular dining room in the Eagle St Pier complex has floor-to-ceiling windows and river views.

South Bank & Kangaroo Point

Piaf FRENCH **$$**
(Map p288; ☎07-3846 5026; www.piafbistro.com.au; 5/182 Grey St, South Bank; breakfast mains $6-18, lunch & dinner $24-28; ⊙7am-late) A chilled-out but still intimate bistro with a loyal following, Piaf serves a small selection (generally just five mains and a few salads and other light options) of good-value, contemporary French-inspired food. French wines by the glass.

Cliffs Cafe CAFE **$$**
(Map p288; www.cliffscafe.com.au; 29 River Tce; mains $12-20; ⊙7am-5pm) A steep climb up from the riverside, this cliff-top cafe has superb river and city-skyline views. It's a casual, open-air pavilion: thick burgers, battered barramundi and chips, salads, desserts and good coffee are the standouts.

Ahmet's TURKISH **$$**
(Map p288; ☎07-3846 6699; www.ahmets.com; Shop 10, 168 Grey St, South Bank; mains $19-34, banquets per person $34-46; ⊙11.30am-3pm & 6pm-late; ☑) On restaurant-lined Grey St, Ahmet's serves delectable Turkish fare amid a riot of colours and Grand Bazaar/Bosphorus murals. Try a Sucuk *pide* (oven-baked Turkish bread with Turkish salami, egg, tomato and mozzarella). Deep street-side terrace and regular live music.

Fortitude Valley & Chinatown

James Street Market MARKET, SELF-CATERING **$**
(Map p292; www.jamesstmarket.com.au; 22 James St; ⊙8.30am-7pm Mon-Fri, 8am-6pm Sat & Sun) Paradise for gourmands, this small but beautifully stocked market has gourmet cheeses, a bakery/patisserie, fruit and veg, flowers, and lots of quality goodies. The fresh seafood counter serves excellent sushi and sashimi.

The Vietnamese VIETNAMESE **$**
(Map p292; ☎07-3252 4112; www.thevietnamese-restaurant.com.au; 194 Wickham St; mains $10-20; ⊙11am-3pm & 5pm-10pm) Aptly if unimaginatively named, this is indeed *the* place in town to eat Vietnamese, with exquisitely prepared dishes served to an always crowded house. Go for something from the 'Chef's Recommendation' list: crispy beef strips with honey and chilli, or clay-pot prawns with oyster sauce. Great value for money.

Flamingo CAFE **$**
(Map p292; ☎07-3252 7557; www.facebook.com/pages/flamingo-cafe/362822247134; 5b Winn St; mains $10-15; ⊙7.30am-4pm Mon-Sat, 8.30am-4pm Sun) Hiding down a tiny lane off Ann St, Flamingo is a buzzy little bolt-hole cafe with black and pink walls, a boho vibe and cheerfully profane wait staff. Winning vegie burgers and banana-and-date loaf.

Kuan Yin Tea House CHINESE, VEGETARIAN **$**
(Map p292; ☎07-3252 4557; www.kuanyintea-house.blogspot.com.au; 198 Wickham St; mains $6-12; ⊙11.30am-7.30pm Mon, Wed & Thu, to 8pm Fri, to 5pm Sat, to 3pm Sun; ☑) Kuan Yin is a small, garish BYO place with faux-wood panelling and a bamboo-lined ceiling. Food-wise it serves flavourful vegetarian noodle soups, dumplings and mock-meat rice dishes. Try the tofu salad. Great tea selection, too.

Ortiga SPANISH **$$**
(Map p292; ☎07-3852 1155; www.ortiga.com.au; 446 Brunswick St; tapas $6-50, mains $18-32; ⊙12.30-3pm Fri, 6pm-late Tue-Sun) One of Brisbane's best restaurants, Ortiga offers a stylish upstairs tapas bar (heavy on the meats) with a pressed-tin ceiling and window bench, and an elegant subterranean dining room with an open kitchen. Top picks include Basque pork sausage, *pulpo a gallega* (Galician-braised octopus) and whole slow-cooked lamb shoulder. Kick-ass cocktails, too.

Spoon Deli Cafe CAFE **$$**
(Map p292; ☎07-3257 1750; www.spoondeli.com.au; Shop B3, 22 James St; breakfast $7-20, mains $18-30; ⊙6.30am-6pm Mon-Fri, 7am-5pm Sat & Sun) Inside James St Market, this upscale

deli serves gloriously rich pastas, salads, soups, colossal paninis and lasagne slabs. The fresh juices are a liquid meal unto themselves. Walls are lined with deli produce: vinegars, oils, herbs and hampers. You'll feel hungry as soon as you walk in!

New Farm

Cafe Bouquiniste
CAFE $

(Map p292; 121 Merthyr Rd; mains $8-12; ⊙ 7.30am-5pm Mon-Fri, 8.30am-5pm Sat, 8.30am-1pm Sun; 🖋) Filling a tiny old side-street shopfront, this boho cafe and bookseller has buckets of charm (if not much space). The coffee is fantastic, service is friendly, and the prices are right for breakfast fare, toasted sandwiches, savoury tarts and cakes. Try the pumpkin, goats cheese and sage tart.

Himalayan Cafe
NEPALESE $

(Map p292; ☑ 07-3358 4015; 640 Brunswick St; mains $15-25; ⊙ 5.30-10pm Tue-Sun; 🖋) Awash with prayer flags and colourful cushions, this karmically positive, unfussy restaurant serves authentic Tibetan and Nepalese fare such as tender *fhaiya darkau* (lamb with vegies, coconut milk and spices). Repeat the house mantra: 'May positive forces be with every single living thing that exists'.

Burger Urge
BURGERS $

(Map p292; www.burgerurge.com.au; 542 Brunswick St; mains $10-21; ⊙ noon-late Mon-Thu, 11.30am-late Fri-Sun) One of several Burger Urges around town, serving brilliant buns: lamb, chicken, cheese, chilli, Greek, Turkish, steak and vegie options aplenty. Sit on the footpath under rock-blaring speakers, or inside with the comic-book wallpaper.

Café Cirque
CAFE $$

(Map p292; 618 Brunswick St; mains $14-17; ⊙ 7am-4pm; 🖋) One of the best breakfast spots (served all day) in town, buzzing Café Cirque serves rich coffee and daily specials, along with open-face sandwiches and gourmet salads for lunch. Little skinny room with foldback windows to the street.

Watt
MODERN AUSTRALIAN $$

(Map p284; ☑ 07-3358 5464; www.wattrestaurant.com.au; Brisbane Powerhouse, 119 Lamington St; mains $9-25; ⊙ 9am-late Mon-Fri, 8am-late Sat & Sun) On the riverbank level of the Brisbane Powerhouse is casual, breezy Watt. Order up some duck salad with sweet chilli, rocket and orange; or a smoked ham-hock terrine with lentils and cornichons. Wines by the

glass; DJ tunes on Sunday afternoons. The *flood* sculpture out the front has been a bit too relevant of late...

Paddington

Il Posto
ITALIAN $$

(Map p301; ☑ 07-3367 3111; www.ilposto.com.au; 107 Latrobe Tce; mains $20-29; ⊙ noon-4pm & 5.30-late Tue-Sun; 🖪) Pizza and pasta just like they make in Rome, served on an outdoor piazza (or inside if it's too humid). Pizzas come either *rosse* or *bianche* (with or without tomato base), and are thin and crispy. Great staff, Peroni beer on tap, and kid-friendly too.

West End

George's Seafood
FISH & CHIPS $

(Map p298; ☑ 07-3844 4100; 150 Boundary St; meals $8-10; ⊙ 9.30am-7.30pm Mon-Fri, 10.30am-7.30pm Sat & Sun) With a window full of fresh mudcrabs, Moreton Bay rock oysters, banana prawns and whole snapper, this old fish-and-chipper has been here forever. The $8 cod-and-chips is why you're here – unbeatable!

The Burrow
CAFE $

(Map p298; ☑ 07-3846 0030; www.theburrow-westend.com.au; 37 Mollison St; mains $10-20; ⊙ 7am-late Tue-Sun; 🖥) In the open-sided understorey of a shambling old Queenslander, casual Burrow is like a Baja California cantina crossed with a student share-house: laid-back and beachy with surf murals and wafting Pink Floyd. Try the hangover-removing El Desperados taco for breakfast – pulled pork, eggs and jalapeño salsa. Good coffee, too.

Blackstar Coffee Roasters
CAFE $

(Map p298; www.blackstarcoffee.com.au; 44 Thomas St; items $6-12; ⊙ 7am-5pm Mon-Sat, 7am-8pm Sun) A neighbourhood fave, West End's own bean roaster has excellent coffee, a simple breakfast menu (wraps, avocado on toast, eggs Benedict), wailing Roy Orbison and live jazz on Saturday evening. Try one of their cold-pressed coffees on a hot day.

★ Gunshop Café
CAFE, MODERN AUSTRALIAN $$

(Map p298; ☑ 07-3844 2241; www.thegunshopcafe.com; 53 Mollison St; mains $17-33; ⊙ 6.30am-2pm Mon, 6.30am-late Tue-Sat, 6.30am-2.30pm Sun) With cool tunes, interesting art and happy staff, this peaceably repurposed gun shop has exposed-brick walls, sculptural ceiling lamps and an inviting back garden. The locally sourced menu changes daily, but regulars include smoked chicken lasagne, a pulled pork baguette and wild-mushroom risotto. Boutique beers, excellent Australian wines and afternoon pick-me-ups available.

Mondo Organics MODERN AUSTRALIAN **$$**
(Map p284; ☎07-3844 1132; www.mondo-organics.com.au; 166 Hardgrave Rd; mains $25-36; ⏰8.30-11.30am Sat & Sun, noon-2.30pm Fri-Sun, 6pm-late Wed-Sat) Using the highest-quality organic and sustainable produce, Mondo Organics earns top marks for its delicious seasonal menu. Recent hits include duck breast with fig, sage and strawberry; and potato and parmesan gnocchi with golden shallots, zucchini and salsa verde. See the website for details on the attached cooking school.

Little Greek Taverna GREEK **$$**
(Map p298; ☎07-3255 2215; www.littlegreektaverna.com.au; Shop 5, 1 Browning St; mains $15-30, banquets per person $35-42; ⏰11am-9pm;) Up-tempo, eternally busy and in a prime West End location, the LGT is perfect for a big Greek feast and some people-watching. Launch into a prawn and saganaki salad or a classic lamb yiros, washed down with a sleep-defeating Greek coffee. Kid-friendly, too.

Caravanserai TURKISH **$$**
(Map p284; ☎07-3217 2617; www.caravanserai-restaurant.com.au; 1 Dornoch Tce; mains $25-35; ⏰noon-2.30pm Fri & Sat, 6pm-late Tue-Sun) Woven tablecloths, red walls and candlelit tables create a snug atmosphere at this standout Turkish restaurant. Share an Ottoman meze platter (haloumi, chorizo, almond-crusted goats cheese, garlic prawns and more good stuff), or tuck into the excellent braised lamb shank.

Drinking & Nightlife

The prime drinking destination in Brisbane is Fortitude Valley, with its lounges, live-music bars and nightclubs. Most clubs here are open from Wednesday to Sunday nights; some are free, others charge up to $20. Dress nice and bring your ID. In the CBD there's a bottoms-up after-work crowd, while West End has cool bars full of inner-city funksters.

City Centre

★Super Whatnot BAR
(Map p288; www.superwhatnot.com; 48 Burnett La; ⏰3pm-late Tue-Sat) Trailblazing Super Whatnot is a funky, industrial laneway space, with a mezzanine floor and sunken lounge. Drinks: bottled boutique Australian beers and cocktails (try the cure-all Penicillin). Food: American-inspired bar snacks (hotdogs, mini burritos, nachos). Tunes: vinyl DJs Thursday to Saturday spinning funk, soul and hip-hop; live acoustic acts Wednesday. Winning combo!

Laneway BAR
(Map p288; www.urbanerestaurant.com/the-laneway; 181 Mary St; ⏰noon-midnight Mon-Fri, 6pm-midnight Sat) Upstairs above the urbane Euro restaurant (walk through the restaurant to the stairs, or shuffle in the back door from the eponymous Spencer La), Laneway is a sassy cocktail bar full of upwardly mobile city fashionistas. Sip a Clementina (spicy mandarin and tequila) then order a wagyu burger to keep you upright.

Belgian Beer Cafe BAR
(Map p288; www.belgianbeercafebrussels.com.au; cnr Mary & Edward Sts; ⏰11.30am-late) Wood-panelled walls and art-deco lights lend an old-world charm to this buzzing space. Out the back, the beer garden has big screens and big after-work egos. Lots of Hoegaarden and Leffe and high-end bistro fare. Ignore the '80s-era Stevie Wonder.

Fortitude Valley

★Alfred & Constance BAR
(Map p292; www.alfredandconstance.com.au; 130 Constance St; ⏰10am-3am) Wow! Fabulously eccentric A&C occupies two old weatherboard houses. Inside, fluoro-clad ditch diggers, tattooed lesbians, suits and surfies roam between the tiki bar, rooftop terrace, cafe area and lounge rooms checking out the interiors: chandeliers, skeletons, surfboards, old hi-fi equipment... It's weird, and very wonderful. Great beers, cocktails and food.

Bowery COCKTAIL BAR
(Map p292; www.thebowery.com.au; 676 Ann St; ⏰5pm-late Tue-Sun) The exposed-brick walls, gilded mirrors, booths and foot-worn floorboards at this long, narrow bar bring a touch of substance to the valley fray. The cocktails and wine list are top-notch (and priced accordingly), and there's live jazz/dub Tuesday to Thursday. DJs spin on weekends.

Press Club COCKTAIL BAR
(Map p292; www.pressclub.net.au; 339 Brunswick St; ⏰5pm-late Tue-Sun) Amber hues, leather

sofas, ottomans, glowing chandeliers, fabric-covered lanterns... It's all rather glamorously Moroccan here (with a touch of that kooky cantina from *Star Wars*). Live music on Thursday (jazz, funk, rockabilly) and DJs on weekends.

La Ruche COCKTAIL BAR
(Map p292; www.laruche.com.au; 680 Ann St) French for 'the hive', La Ruche is indeed buzzing, with a dressed-up crowd bantering over bespoke cocktails and tapas plates. Interiors morph *Alice in Wonderland* with the Mexican Day of the Dead, while there's a smoking courtyard out the back and an intimate retreat upstairs.

Cru Bar & Cellar WINE BAR
(Map p292; www.crubar.com; 22 James St; ⏲11am-late Mon-Fri, 10am-late Sat & Sun) A mind-pickling menu of hundreds of wines (by the glass, bottle or half-bottle) is on offer at this classy joint, with confidently strutting staff, a glowing marble bar and fold-back windows to the street.

Birdees CLUB
(Map p292; www.birdees.com.au; 608 Ann St; ⏲4pm-late Mon-Thu, noon-5am Fri & Sat, noon-late Sun) Part of the sprawling Bunk Backpackers complex, Birdees fills, predictably, with backpackers going berserk. Big fun. The Aviary room upstairs has comedy on Thursday nights.

Oh Hello CLUB
(Map p292; www.ohhello.com.au; 621 Ann St; ⏲9pm-5am Thu-Sat) Oh hello! Fancy seeing you here! This convivial club is perfect if you like the idea of clubbing but find the reality a bit deflating. It's unpretentious (you can wear a T-shirt), there's a great selection of craft beers, and the cool kids here don't think too highly of themselves.

Cloudland CLUB
(Map p292; www.katarzyna.com.au/venues/cloudland; 641 Ann St; ⏲5pm-late Thu & Fri, noon-late Sat & Sun) Like stepping into a surreal cloud forest, this multilevel club has a huge plant-filled lobby with a retractable glass roof, a wall of water and wrought-iron birdcage-like nooks. Even if you're not a clubber, peek through the windows during the day: the interior design is astonishing!

Alloneword CLUB, BAR
(Map p292; www.alloneword.com.au; 188 Brunswick St; ⏲8pm-late Fri & Sat) On a seedy stretch of Brunswick, this whimsical underground spot bucks the beats in favour of old-school funk, soul and hip-hop. Beaut outdoor area; monthly indie music nights. We just wish it was open more often!

Beat MegaClub CLUB, GAY
(Map p292; www.thebeatmegaclub.com.au; 677 Ann St; ⏲9pm-5am Mon & Tue, 8pm-5am Wed-Sun) Five rooms + seven bars + three chill-out areas + hard house/electro/retro/techno beats = the perfect place for dance junkies. It's big with the gay and lesbian crowd, with regular drag performances.

Wickham Hotel CLUB, GAY
(Map p292; www.thewickham.com.au; 308 Wickham St; ⏲10am-late) Brisbane's most popular gay and lesbian venue, with rainbow flags, drag shows and blaring Gloria Gaynor.

West End

Archive Beer Boutique BAR
(Map p298; www.archivebeerboutique.com.au; 100 Boundary St; ⏲11am-late) Interesting beer, interesting place: welcome to Archive, a temple of beer with many a fine frothy on tap (try the Evil Twin West Coast Red Ale). Check out the bar made of books! Oh, and the food's good, too (steaks, mussels, pasta). Upstairs is **Loft West End** (Map p298; www.loftwestend.com), a sophisticated cocktail/food room.

The End BAR
(Map p298; www.73vulture.com; 1/73 Vulture St; ⏲3pm-midnight) This mod-industrial shopfront conversion is a real locals' hangout, with hipsters, cheese boards, Morrisey on the turntable, DJs and live acoustic troubadours. The Blackstar mocha stout (caffeine courtesy of the local roaster) will cheer up your rainy river afternoon.

Lychee Lounge COCKTAIL BAR
(Map p298; www.lycheelounge.com.au; 94 Boundary St; ⏲3pm-midnight Sun-Thu, 3pm-1am Fri & Sat) Sink into the lush furniture and stare up at the macabre doll-head chandeliers at this exotic oriental lounge bar, with mellow beats, mood lighting and an open frontage to Boundary St. Is that a *real* opium den?

New Farm & Around

Breakfast Creek Hotel PUB
(Map p284; www.breakfastcreekhotel.com; 2 Kingsford Smith Dr, Albion; ⏲10am-late) This historic 1889 pub is a Brisbane classic. Built in lavish

French Renaissance style, it has various bars and dining areas (including a beer garden and an art-deco 'private bar' where you can drink beer tapped from a wooden keg). The stylish Substation No 41 bar serves cocktails and super steaks.

Alto Bar BAR, RESTAURANT
(Map p284; www.baralto.com.au; Brisbane Powerhouse, 119 Lamington St, New Farm; ⏲11am-late Tue-Sun) Inside the arts-loving Powerhouse, this snappy upstairs bar/restaurant has an enormous balcony with chunky timber tables, overlooking the river – a mighty fine vantage point any time of day.

Kangaroo Point & Around

Story Bridge Hotel PUB
(Map p288; www.storybridgehotel.com.au; 200 Main St, Kangaroo Point; ⏲9am-late) Beneath the bridge at Kangaroo Point, this beautiful 1886 pub and beer garden is perfect for a pint after a long day exploring. Live jazz on Sundays (from 3pm); lots of different drinking and eating areas.

Canvas WINE BAR
(Map p284; www.canvasclub.com.au; 16b Logan Rd, Woolloongabba; ⏲3pm-midnight Tue-Fri, 11.30am-late Sat & Sun) In the shadow of the Gabba cricket ground, Canvas is hip, compact and artsy. Step down off Logan St – an emerging eating/drinking/antiques hub – pause to ogle the kooky mural, then order a 'Guerilla Warfare' from the moustachioed bartender.

Paddington & Petrie Terrace

Cabiria BAR
(Map p298; www.cabiria.com.au; 6 The Barracks, 61 Petrie Tce, Petrie Terrace; ⏲7-10.30am Mon, 7am-late Tue-Sat) Brisbane's old police barracks have been converted into a complex of bars and eateries, the pick of which is cool Cabiria. It's a skinny, dim-lit room with mirrors and shimmering racks of booze (35 different tequilas!). Awesome New York–style sandwiches.

Lark BAR
(Map p301; www.thelark.com.au; 267 Given Tce, Paddington; ⏲4pm-midnight Wed-Fri, 1pm-midnight Sat, 1-10pm Sun) Inside an intimate, two-level brick terrace, Lark serves up inventive fusion fare and artful cocktails. Tapas share-plates involve hits like wagyu sliders and parmesan-crusted mushrooms, washed down with international wines, crafty beers and cocktails (go for the Cherry Bourbon Smash). What a lark!

Normanby Hotel PUB
(Map p298; www.thenormanby.com.au; 1 Musgrave Rd, Brisbane; ⏲10am-3pm) A handsome 1889 redbrick pub on the end of Petrie Tce, with a beer garden under a vast fig tree. Goes nuts during 'Sunday Sessions' (boozy wakes for the weekend).

☆ Entertainment

Most big-ticket international bands have Brisbane on their radar, and the city's clubs regularly attract top-class DJs. Theatres, cinemas and other performing-arts venues are among Australia's biggest and best.

Free entertainment street-press includes *Time Off* (www.timeoff.com.au) and *Scene* (www.scenemagazine.com.au). *Q News* (www.qnews.com.au) covers the gay and lesbian scene. The *Courier Mail* (www.news.com.au/couriermail) also has daily arts and entertainment listings, or check the *Brisbane Times* (www.brisbanetimes.com.au).

Ticketek (Map p288; ☎13 28 49; www.ticketek.com.au; cnr Elizabeth & George Sts; ⏲9am-5pm) is a central booking agency that handles major events, sports and performances. Try **Qtix** (☎13 62 46; www.qtix.com.au) for loftier arts performances.

Live Music

Lock 'n' Load LIVE MUSIC
(Map p298; www.locknloadbistro.com.au; 142 Boundary St, West End; ⏲10am-late Mon-Fri, 7am-late Sat & Sun) This gastro-pub lures an upbeat crowd of music fans. Bands play the small front stage (jazz and originals). Catch a gig, then show up for breakfast the next morning (the grilled sardines go well with hangovers).

Hi-Fi LIVE MUSIC
(Map p298; www.thehifi.com.au; 125 Boundary St, West End) This mod, minimalist rock room has unobstructed sight lines and a great line-up of local and international talent (from the Gin Blossoms to Suicidal Tendencies). Retro Vinyl bar is out the front.

Zoo LIVE MUSIC
(Map p292; www.thezoo.com.au; 711 Ann St, Fortitude Valley; ⏲7.30pm-late Wed-Sun) The Zoo has surrendered a bit of musical territory to the Hi-Fi, but is still a grungy spot for rock, hip-hop, acoustic, reggae and electronic acts (lots of raw local talent).

Brisbane Jazz Club JAZZ
(Map p288; ☎07-3391 2006; www.brisbanejazzclub.com.au; 1 Annie St, Kangaroo Point; ⊙6.30-11pm Thu-Sat, 5.30-9.30pm Sun) Straight out of the bayou, this tiny riverside jazz shack has been Brisbane's jazz beacon since 1972. Anyone who's anyone in the scene plays here when they're in town. Cover charge $12 to $20.

Riverstage LIVE MUSIC
(Map p288; www.brisbane.qld.gov.au/facilities-recreation/arts-and-culture/riverstage; 59 Gardens Point Rd) Riverstage is a fab outdoor arena on the southern tip of the downtown Brisbane peninsula. Big internationals like the Stone Roses and guitar-god Slash grace the stage.

Beetle Bar LIVE MUSIC
(Map p298; www.beetlebar.com.au; 350 Upper Roma St; ⊙7pm-late Thu-Sat) Full of boozy backpackers from the surrounding hostels, Beetle Bar is the spot for up-and-coming local and national alt-rock acts. Look for the reconfigured VW Beetle on the roof.

Cinemas

Moonlight Cinema CINEMA
(Map p284; www.moonlight.com.au; Brisbane Powerhouse, 119 Lamington Rd, New Farm; adult/child $16/12; ⊙7pm Wed-Sun) New Farm Park behind the Powerhouse hosts alfresco flicks between December and February. Arrive early to get a good spot.

Palace Barracks CINEMA
(Map p298; www.palacecinemas.com.au; 61 Petrie Tce, Petrie Terrace; adult/child $17.50/13; ⊙10am-late) Near Roma St Station, plush, six-screen Palace Barracks shows Hollywood and alternative fare. And there's a bar!

Ben & Jerry's Openair Cinemas CINEMA
(Map p288; www.openaircinemas.com.au; Cultural Forecourt, South Bank Parklands, South Bank; adult/child online $17/12, at the gate $22/17; ⊙from 6pm Mon-Fri, from 4pm Sat & Sun) From mid-October to late November you can watch big-screen classics under the stars (or clouds) at South Bank. Hire a beanbag or bring a picnic rug.

Palace Centro CINEMA
(Map p292; www.palacecinemas.com.au; 39 James St, Fortitude Valley; adult/child $17.50/13; ⊙10am-late) Palace Centro screens art-house films and has a French film festival in March/April.

Event Cinemas CINEMA
(Map p288; www.eventcinemas.com.au; L3, Myer Centre, Elizabeth St; adult/child $17/12.50; ⊙10am-late) Also accessible from Queen St Mall; shows mainstream smash-'em-up blockbusters.

South Bank Cinema CINEMA
(Map p288; www.cineplex.com.au; cnr Grey & Ernest Sts, South Bank; adult/child from $9/5; ⊙10am-late) The cheapest complex for mainstream releases.

Performing Arts

Brisbane Powerhouse PERFORMING ARTS
(Map p284; www.brisbanepowerhouse.org; 119 Lamington St, New Farm) Nationally and internationally acclaimed theatre, music, comedy, dance... There are loads of happenings at the Powerhouse – many free – and the venue, with its cool bar-restaurants, enjoys a gorgeous setting overlooking the Brisbane River.

Queensland Performing Arts Centre PERFORMING ARTS
(QPAC; Map p288; www.qpac.com.au; Queensland Cultural Centre, cnr Grey & Melbourne Sts, South Bank; ⊙box office 9am-8.30pm Mon-Sat) Brisbane's main high-arts performance centre comprises three venues and features concerts, plays, dance and performances of all genres: anything from flamenco to the Australian Ballet and *West Side Story* revivals.

Queensland Conservatorium LIVE MUSIC
(Map p288; www.griffith.edu.au/music/queensland-conservatorium; 140 Grey St, South Bank; ⊙box office 7am-10pm Mon-Fri, 8am-6pm Sat & Sun) Part of Griffith University, the Conservatorium hosts opera, as well as touring artists playing classical, jazz, rock and world music. Many concerts are free.

Judith Wright Centre of Contemporary Arts PERFORMING ARTS
(Map p292; www.judithwrightcentre.com; 420 Brunswick St, Fortitude Valley; 📶) A medium-sized (300 seats max) space for cutting-edge performances.

Brisbane Arts Theatre THEATRE
(Map p298; www.artstheatre.com.au; 210 Petrie Tce) Intimate community theatre built in 1936; catch improvisation troupes, children's theatre or classic plays.

QUT Gardens Theatre THEATRE
(Map p288; www.gardenstheatre.qut.edu.au; Queensland University of Technology, 2 George St; ⊙box office 10am-4pm) On the university campus, but with productions that are anything but amateur. Expect to see Australia's best professional stage actors.

MARKET-LOVERS GUIDE TO BRISBANE

➡ **Jan Power's Farmers Market** (Map p284; www.janpowersfarmersmarkets.com.au; Brisbane Powerhouse, 119 Lamington St, New Farm; ⊙6am-noon 2nd & 4th Sat of month) Fancy some purple heirloom carrots or blue bananas? This fab farmers market, with more than 120 stalls, coughs up some unusual produce. Also great for more predictably coloured flowers, cheeses, coffees and fish.

➡ **Davies Park Market** (Map p298; www.daviesparkmarket.com.au; Davies Park, West End; ⊙6am-2pm Sat) Under a grove of huge Moreton Bay fig trees in the West End, this hippie riverside market features organic foods, gourmet breakfasts, herbs and flowers, bric-a-brac and buskers.

➡ **South Bank Lifestyle Markets** (Map p288; www.southbankmarket.com.au; Stanley St Plaza, South Bank; ⊙5-10pm Fri, 10am-5pm Sat, 9am-5pm Sun) It's a bit touristy, but this riverside market has a great range of clothing, craft, art, handmade goods and souvenirs (just ignore the lacquered boomerangs).

Sport

Like most other Australians, Brisbanites are sports-mad. Catch some interstate or international cricket at the **Gabba** (Brisbane Cricket Ground; Map p284; www.thegabba.org.au; 411 Vulture St, Woolloongabba), south of Kangaroo Point. The cricket season runs from October to March.

The Gabba is also the home ground for the Brisbane Lions, an **Australian Football League** (AFL; www.afl.com.au) team. Watch them in action, often at night under lights, between March and September.

Rugby league is also a big spectator sport. The Brisbane Broncos, part of the **National Rugby League** (NRL; www.nrl.com.au) competition, play home games over winter at **Suncorp Stadium** (Map p298; www.suncorpstadium.com.au; 40 Castlemaine St, Milton).

Also calling Suncorp home are the Queensland Roar football (soccer) team, part of the **A-League** (www.footballaustralia.com.au/aleague), attracting massive crowds in recent years. The domestic football season lasts from August to February.

Shopping

Queen Street Mall and the **Myer Centre** in the CBD have big chain stores, upmarket outlets and the obligatory touristy trash. Smaller independent and specialist shops are in Fortitude Valley and Paddington.

Title BOOKS
(Map p288; www.titlespace.com; 1/133 Grey St, South Bank; ⊙10am-6pm Mon-Sat, 10am-4pm Sun) Offbeat and alternative art, music, photography and cinema books, plus vinyl, CDs and DVDs – a quality dose of subversive, lefty rebelliousness (just what South Bank needs!).

Record Exchange MUSIC
(Map p288; www.recordexchange.com.au; L1, 65 Adelaide St, Brisbane; ⊙9am-5pm) Home to an astounding collection of vinyl, plus CDs, DVDs, posters and other rock memorabilia. 'Brisbane's most interesting shop' (self-professed).

Blonde Venus CLOTHING
(Map p292; www.blondevenus.com.au; 707 Ann St, Fortitude Valley; ⊙10am-6pm Mon-Sat, 11am-4.30pm Sun) One of the top boutiques in Brisbane, Blonde Venus has been around for 20-plus years, stocking a well-curated selection of both indie and couture labels. One of a string of great boutiques along this slice of Ann St.

Archives Fine Books BOOKS
(Map p288; www.facebook.com/archivesfinebooks; 40 Charlotte St, Brisbane; ⊙10am-7pm Mon-Fri, 9am-5pm Sat, 11am-5pm Sun) You could get lost in here for hours: rickety bookshelves, squeaky floorboards and upwards of half-a-million secondhand books.

Paddington Antique Centre ANTIQUES
(Map p301; www.paddingtonantiquecentre.com.au; 167 Latrobe Tce; ⊙10am-5pm) The city's biggest antique emporium is inside a 1929 theatre, with over 50 dealers selling all manner of historic treasure/trash: clothes, jewellery, dolls, books, '60s Hawaiian shirts, lamps, musical instruments, toys, WWII German helmets...

Avid Reader BOOKS
(Map p298; www.avidreader.com.au; 193 Boundary St, West End; ⊙8.30am-8.30pm Mon-Fri, 8.30am-6pm Sat, 8.30am-5pm Sun) Diverse pages, a little

cafe in the corner and frequent readings and bookish events: a real West End cultural hub.

World Wide Maps & Globes BOOKS
(Map p288; www.worldwidemaps.com.au; Shop 30, Anzac Sq Arcade, 267 Edward St, Brisbane; ⏲9am-6pm Mon-Thu, 9am-8pm Fri, 10am-4pm Sat) A good assortment of maps and travel guides (including camping and hiking guides).

Information

EMERGENCY

Ambulance, Fire, Police (☎000) Brisbane's police HQ is at 200 Roma St in the city.

Lifeline (☎13 11 14; www.lifeline.org.au) Crisis counselling.

RACQ (Map p288; ☎13 11 11; www.racq.com.au) Automotive roadside assistance.

INTERNET ACCESS

State Library of Queensland (www.slq.qld.gov.au; Stanley Pl, South Bank; ⏲10am-8pm Mon-Thu, 10am-5pm Fri-Sun) Quick 20-minute terminals and free wi-fi.

Brisbane Square Library (www.brisbane.qld.gov.au; 266 George St, Brisbane; ⏲9am-6pm Mon-Thu, 9am-7pm Fri, 10am-3pm Sat & Sun) Free internet terminals and wi-fi access.

MEDICAL SERVICES

Pharmacy on the Mall (☎07-3221 4585; www.pharmacies.com.au/pharmacy-on-the-mall; 141 Queen St, Brisbane; ⏲7am-9pm Mon-Thu, 7am-9.30pm Fri, 8am-9pm Sat, 8.30am-6pm Sun)

Royal Brisbane & Women's Hospital (☎07-3636 8111; www.health.qld.gov.au/rbwh; cnr Butterfield St & Bowen Bridge Rd, Herston) Has a 24-hour casualty ward.

CBD Medical Centre (☎07-3211 3611; www.cbdmedical.com.au; L1, 245 Albert St, Brisbane; ⏲7.30am-7pm Mon-Fri, 8.30am-5pm Sat, 9.30am-4pm Sun) General medical services and vaccinations.

Travel Doctor (TMVC; ☎07-3815 6900; www.traveldoctor.com.au; 75 Astor Tce, Spring Hill) Travellers' medical services.

MONEY

American Express (☎1300 139 060; www.americanexpress.com; 260 Queen St, Brisbane; ⏲8.30am-4pm Mon-Thu, 9am-5pm Fri) Located within the Westpac bank.

Travelex (☎07-3210 6325; www.travelex.com.au; Shop 149F, Myer Centre, Queen St Mall, Brisbane; ⏲9am-5pm Mon-Thu & Sat, 9am-8pm Fri, 10am-4pm Sun) Money exchange.

POST

Main Post Office (GPO; Map p288; www.auspost.com.au; 261 Queen St, Brisbane; ⏲7am-6pm Mon-Fri, 10am-1.30pm Sat)

TOURIST INFORMATION

Brisbane Visitor Information Centre (Map p288; ☎07-3006 6290; www.visitbrisbane.com.au; Queen St Mall, Brisbane; ⏲9am-5.30pm Mon-Thu, 9am-7pm Fri, 9am-5pm Sat, 10am-5pm Sun) Located between Edward and Albert Sts. Great info counter for all things Brisbane.

South Bank Visitor Information Centre (Map p288; www.visitsouthbank.com.au; Stanley St Plaza, South Bank; ⏲9am-5pm) Info on South Bank plus tours, accommodation and transport info and tickets to entertainment events.

Department of National Parks, Recreation, Sport & Racing (Map p288; ☎1300 130 372, 4WD permits ☎13 74 68; www.nprsr.qld.gov.au; L3, 400 George St, Brisbane; ⏲8.30am-4.30pm Mon-Fri) Maps, brochures and books on national parks and state forests, plus camping info and Fraser Island permits.

Getting There & Away

AIR

Brisbane Airport (www.bne.com.au) is about 16km northeast of the city centre at Eagle Farm, and has separate international and domestic terminals about 2km apart. These are linked by the **Airtrain** (☎07-3215 5000; www.airtrain.com.au), which runs every 15 to 30 minutes from 5.45am to 10pm (per person $5).

BUS

Brisbane's main terminus and booking office for all long-distance buses and trains is the **Brisbane Transit Centre** (Roma St Station; Map p288; www.brisbanetransitcentre.com.au; Roma St, Brisbane), about 500m west of the city centre. Booking desks for **Greyhound** (www.greyhound.com.au) and **Premier Motor Service** (www.premierms.com.au) are here.

Typical times and prices:

DESTINATION	DURATION (HR)	ONE-WAY FARE
Byron Bay	4	$30-35
Sydney	16-17	$105-180
Airlie Beach	19-24w	$220-240
Cairns	29-34	$290-340
Hervey Bay	5-7	$45-75
Mackay	16½-20	$205-215
Noosa	2½-3	$30-35
Rockhampton	11-16	$150-175
Surfers Paradise	1½	$20-25
Townsville	23-27	$255-275

CAR & MOTORCYCLE

Brisbane has five major motorways (M1 to M5) run by **Queensland Motorways** (☎13 33 31;

www.qldmotorways.com.au). If you're just passing through north–south/south–north, take the Gateway Motorway (M1), which bypasses the city centre ($4.05 toll; see the website for payment options, in advance or retrospectively).

Major car-hire companies – **Avis** (www.avis.com.au), **Budget** (www.budget.com.au), **Europcar** (www.europcar.com.au), **Hertz** (www.hertz.com.au) and **Thrifty** (www.thrifty.com.au) – have offices at Brisbane Airport and in the city.

Smaller rental companies with branches near the airport (and shuttles to get there):

Ace Rental Cars (☎1800 620 408; www.acerentals.com.au; 330 Nudgee Rd, Hendra)

Apex Car Rentals (☎1800 121 029; www.apexrentacar.com.au; 400 Nudgee Rd, Hendra)

East Coast Car Rentals (☎1800 028 881; www.eastcoastcarrentals.com.au; 504 Nudgee Road, Hendra)

TRAIN

Brisbane's main station for long-distance trains is Roma St Station (aka Brisbane Transit Centre). For reservations and information contact the **Queensland Rail Travel Centre** (☎13 16 17, 07-3235 1323; www.queenslandrail.com.au; 305 Edward St, Central Station) at Central Station. Intra-Queensland routes from Brisbane include the following:

Spirit of the Outback Brisbane–Longreach via Rockhampton (economy seat/triple sleeper/single sleeper $229/305/485, 24 hours, Tuesday and Saturday).

Sunlander Brisbane–Cairns via Townsville (economy seat/economy sleeper/1st-class sleeper $265/340/480, 31 hours, Tuesday, Thursday and Sunday).

Tilt Train Brisbane–Cairns (business seat $360, 24 hours, Monday and Friday).

Westlander Brisbane–Charleville (economy seat/triple sleeper/single sleeper $144/210/309, 17 hours, Tuesday and Thursday).

CountryLink (☎13 22 32; www.countrylink.info) Brisbane–Sydney (economy/1st class/sleeper $131/184/263, 13 to 14 hours, daily).

ℹ Getting Around

Brisbane's excellent public-transport network – bus, train and ferry – is run by **TransLink** (☎13 12 30; www.translink.com.au).

Fares Buses, trains and ferries operate on a zone system: most of the inner-city suburbs are in Zone 1, which translates into a single fare of $4.80/2.40 per adult/child.

Go Card To save around 30% on individual fares, buy a *Go Card* ($5 starting balance), which is sold (and recharged) at transit stations and newsagents, or by phone or online.

NightLink There are dedicated nocturnal NightLink bus, train and fixed-rate taxi services from the city and Fortitiude Valley: see www.translink.com.au for details.

TO/FROM THE AIRPORT

Airtrain (adult/child $15/7.50) runs every 15 to 30 minutes from 5.45am to 10pm from the airport to Fortitude Valley, Central Station, Roma St Station (Brisbane Transit Centre) and other key destinations. There are also half-hourly services to the airport from Gold Coast Citytrain stops.

If you prefer door-to-door service, **Coachtrans** (☎07-5556 9888; www.coachtrans.com.au) runs regular shuttle buses between the airport and CBD hotels (adult/child $20/10); it also connects Brisbane Airport to Gold Coast hotels (adult/child $46/23).

A taxi into the centre from the airport will cost $35 to $45.

BOAT

In addition to the fast CityCat (p293) services, Translink runs Cross River Ferries, connecting Kangaroo Point with the CBD, and New Farm Park with Norman Park on the adjacent shore (and also Teneriffe and Bulimba further north).

Free (yes free!) CityHopper Ferries zigzag back and forth across the water between North Quay, South Bank, the CBD, Kangaroo Point and Sydney St in New Farm.

These additional services start around 6am and run till about 11pm. For Cross River Ferries, fares/zones apply as per all other Brisbane transport.

BUS

Translink runs free City Loop and Spring Hill Loop bus services that circle the CBD and Spring Hill, stopping at key spots like QUT, Queen St Mall, City Botanic Gardens, Central Station and Roma St Parkland. It runs every 10 minutes on weekdays between 7am and 6pm.

The main stops for local buses are the underground **Queen Street Bus Station** (Map p288) and **King George Square Bus Station** (Map p288). You can also pick up many buses from the stops along Adelaide St, between George and Edward Sts.

Buses generally run every 10 to 30 minutes Monday to Friday, from 5am till about 11pm, and with the same frequency on Saturday morning (starting at 6am). Services are less frequent at other times, and cease at 9pm Sunday and at midnight on other days. CityGlider and BUZ services are high-frequency services along busy routes.

CAR & MOTORCYCLE

There is ticketed two-hour parking on many streets in the CBD and the inner suburbs. Heed the signs: Brisbane's parking inspectors take no prisoners. Parking is cheaper around South

Bank and the West End than in the city centre, but is free in the CBD during the evening.

A GPS unit could be your best friend: Brisbane's streets are organically laid-out and convoluted.

TAXI

In the city there are taxi ranks at Roma St Station and at the top end of Edward St, by the junction with Adelaide St. You might have a tough time hailing one late at night in Fortitude Valley: there's a rank near the corner of Brunswick St and Ann St, but expect long queues.

Black & White (☎13 32 22; www.blackandwhitecabs.com.au)

Yellow Cab Co (☎13 19 24; www.yellowcab.com.au)

TRAIN

The fast Citytrain network has six main lines, which run as far north as Gympie on the Sunshine Coast and as far south as Varsity Lakes on the Gold Coast. All trains go through Roma St, Central and Fortitude Valley Stations; there's also a handy South Bank Station.

MORETON BAY

Lapping at Brisbane's urban verges, shallow Moreton Bay is packed full of marine life, including the eponymous Moreton Bay bugs (crayfish-like crustaceans). The bay also has some startlingly beautiful islands, easily accessible from the mainland. North Stradbroke Island is a real stunner, with great surfing beaches, marine life and nonchalant holiday airs. On Moreton Island, wild dolphins and shipwrecks are the enticements.

☞ Tours

Humpback whales are a regular sight in the bay between June and November when they migrate to and from their southern feeding grounds. Moreton Bay also has the largest resident population of bottlenose dolphins in the world (more than 300).

Redlands Kayak Tours KAYAKING
(☎1300 529 258; www.redlandskayaktours.com.au; per person/family $69/246) Three-hour

Brisbane & Moreton Bay

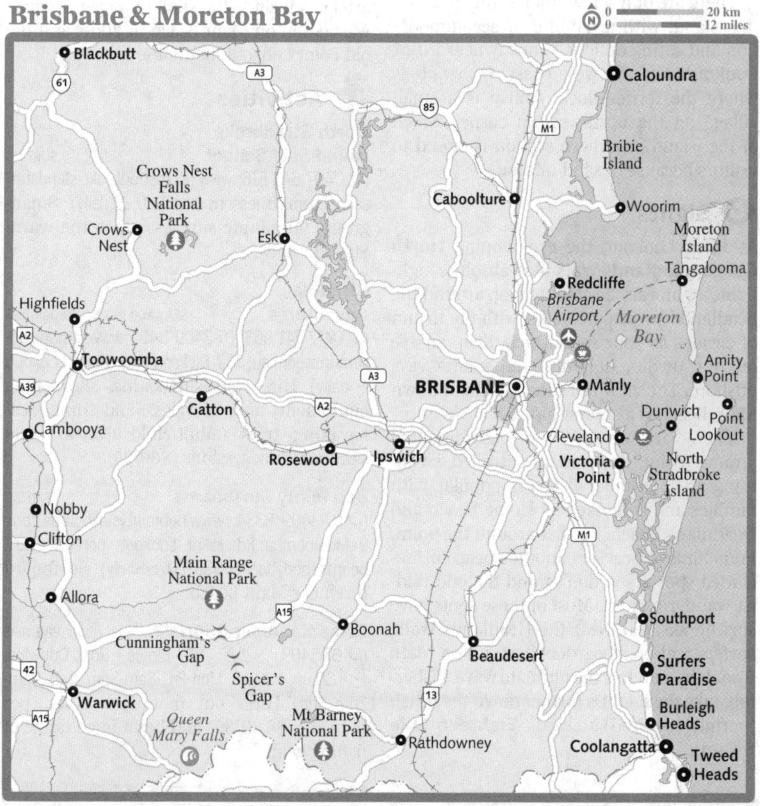

guided kayak tours of the bay for grown-ups and kids, departing various mainland locations. Shorter paddles also available.

Robinson Cruises CRUISE
(☎0408 872 316; www.robinsoncruises.com; Raby Bay Harbour, Cleveland; per person from $99) Two-hour evening yacht cruises of the bay, with wildlife-spotting and lots of sunset appreciation.

North Stradbroke Island

POP 2000

An easy 30-minute ferry chug from Cleveland, this unpretentious holiday isle is like Noosa and Byron Bay rolled into one. There's a string of glorious powdery white beaches, great surf and some quality places to stay and eat. It's also a hot-spot for spying dolphins, turtles, manta rays and, between June and November, hundreds of humpback whales. 'Straddie' also boasts freshwater lakes and 4WD tracks.

There are only a few small settlements on the island, with a handful of accommodation and eating options – mostly near **Point Lookout**. On the west coast, **Dunwich** is where the ferries dock. **Amity** is a small village on the northwestern corner. Much of the island's southern section is closed to visitors because of sand mining.

Sights

At Point Lookout, the eye-popping **North Gorge Headlands Walk** is an absolute highlight. It's an easy 20-minute loop around the headland along boardwalks, with the thrum of cicadas as your soundtrack. Keep an eye out for turtles, dolphins and manta rays offshore. The view from the headland down Main Beach is a showstopper.

There are several gorgeous **beaches** around Point Lookout. A patrolled swimming area, Cylinder Beach is popular with families and is flanked by Home Beach and Deadman's Beach. Further around the point, Frenchman's Beach is another peaceful, secluded spot if you don't mind the odd nudist wandering past. Most of these spots have surf breaks, too. Near the Headlands Walk, surfers and bodyboarders descend on **Main Beach** in search of the ultimate wave. Fisherfolk take their 4WDs further down the beach (permit required) towards **Eighteen Mile Swamp**.

About 4km east of Dunwich, the tanin-stained **Brown Lake** is the colour of stewed tea, but is completely OK for swimming. There are picnic tables, barbecues and a toilet at the lake. About 4km further along this road, take the 2.6km (40-minute) bush track to the sparkling **Blue Lake**, part of **Naree Budjong Djara National Park** (www.nprsr.qld.gov.au/parks/naree-budjong-djara). Look for forest birds and skittish lizards along the way. Further north towards Point Lookout, **The Keyholes** is a freshwater lake and lagoon system. There's 4WD access via the beach – a permit is required ($38.25 from Straddie Camping).

Once the 'Dunwich Benevolent Asylum' – a home for the destitute – the small but impressive **North Stradbroke Island Historical Museum** (☎07-3409 9699; www.stradbrokemuseum.com.au; 15-17 Welsby St, Dunwich; adult/child $3.50/1; ⏱10am-2pm Tue-Sat, 11am-3pm Sun) describes shipwrecks, harrowing voyages and an introduction to the island's rich Aboriginal history (the Quandamooka are the traditional owners of Minjerribah, aka Straddie). Island artefacts include the skull of a sperm whale washed up on Main Beach in 2004, and the old Point Lookout lighthouse lens.

Activities

North Stradbroke Island Surf School SURFING
(☎0407 642 616; www.northstradbrokeislandsurfschool.com.au; lessons from $50; ⏱daily) Small-group, 90-minute surf lessons in the warm Straddie waves.

Straddie Adventures SEA KAYAKING, SANDBOARDING
(☎0417 741 963, 07-3409 8414; www.straddieadventures.com.au; 132 Dickson Way, Point Lookout; ⏱daily) Hires out surfboards, snorkelling equipment and bicycles, and runs sea-kayaking trips (adult/child $60/45) and sandboarding sessions ($30/25).

Bob Minty Surfboards SURFING
(☎07-3409 8334; www.bobmintysurfboards.com; 9 Mooloomba Rd, Point Lookout; per day surfboards/bodyboards $35/20; ⏱daily) Surfboard hire near Main Beach.

Straddie Super Sports BIKE HIRE
(☎07-3409 9252; 18 Bingle Rd, Dunwich; ⏱8.30am-4.30pm Mon-Fri, 8am-3pm Sat, 9am-2pm Sun) Hires out mountain bikes (per hour/day $6.50/30) and has a huge range of fishing gear.

Manta Scuba Centre DIVING
(☎07-3409 8888; www.mantalodge.com.au; 132 Dickson Way, Point Lookout) Based at the YHA, Manta Scuba Centre runs snorkelling trips ($85), with a two-hour boat trip and all gear included. A two-dive trip with all gear for certified divers is $196. Scuba courses start at $253; snorkel gear hire is $25.

Tours

North Stradbroke Island 4WD Tours & Camping Holidays DRIVING TOUR
(☎07-3409 8051; www.stradbroketourism.com; adult/child half-day $35/20, full day $85/55) Offers 4WD tours around the Point Lookout area, with lots of bush, beaches and wildlife. Beach fishing is $45/30 per adult/child.

Straddie Kingfisher Tours DRIVING TOUR
(☎07-3409 9502; www.straddiekingfishertours.com.au; adult/child island pick-up $80/40, from Brisbane or Gold Coast $195/145) Operates six-hour 4WD and fishing tours; also has whale-watching tours in season. Ask about kayaking and sandboarding options.

Sleeping

Straddie Camping CAMPGROUND $
(☎07-3409 9668; www.straddiecamping.com.au; 1 Junner St, Dunwich; 4WD campsite from $16.50, unpowered/powered sites from $37/44, cabins from $115; booking office 8am-4pm) There are eight island campgrounds operated by this outfit, including two 4WD-only foreshore camps (permits required, $38.25). The best of the bunch are grouped around Point Lookout: the campgrounds at **Adder Rock** and the **Home Beach** both overlook the sand, while the **Cylinder Beach** campground sits right on one of the island's best beaches. Book well in advance; good weekly rates.

Manta Lodge YHA HOSTEL $
(☎07-3409 8888; www.mantalodge.com.au; 1 East Coast Rd, Point Lookout; dm/d $32/82; @) This three-storey, lemon-yellow hostel has clean (if unremarkable) rooms and a great beach-side location. There are jungly hammocks out the back and a dive school downstairs.

Straddie Views B&B $$
(☎07-3409 8875; www.northstradbrokeisland.com/straddiebb; 26 Cumming Pde, Point Lookout; r from $150) There are two spacious downstairs suites in this B&B, run by a friendly Straddie couple. Cooked breakfast is served on the upstairs deck with fab sea views.

Stradbroke Island Beach Hotel HOTEL $$$
(☎07-3409 8188; www.stradbrokehotel.com.au; East Coast Rd, Point Lookout; d from $235;) Straddie's only pub has 12 cool, inviting rooms with shell-coloured tiles, blonde timbers, high-end gadgets and balconies. Walk to the beach, or get distracted by the open-walled bar downstairs en route (serving breakfast, lunch and dinner; mains $15 to $36). Flashy three- and four-bed apartments also available.

Allure APARTMENT $$$
(☎1800 555 200, 07-3415 0000; www.allurestradbroke.com.au; 43 East Coast Rd, Point Lookout; apt from $216;) These large ultramodern apartments are set in a leafy compound. Each villa (or 'shack' as the one-bedrooms are called) features lots of beachy colours, original artwork and an outdoor deck with barbecue. There isn't much space between villas, but they're cleverly designed with privacy in mind. Much cheaper for stays of more than one night.

Pandanus Palms Resort APARTMENT $$$
(☎07-3409 8106; www.pandanuspalmsresort.com; 21 Cumming Pde, Point Lookout; 2-/3-bedroom apt from $350/450; @) High above the beach, the two- and three-bed townhouses here don't have air-con and are a bit '90s style-wise, but they're roomy and the best ones have ocean views, private yards and barbecues. There's a tennis court, too.

Eating

Oceanic Gelati GELATI $
(☎07-3415 3222; 19 Mooloomba Rd, Point Lookout; gelati from $3; 9.30am-5pm) 'OMG! This is the best gelati ever!' So says one satisfied customer, and we're in complete agreement. Try the dairy-free tropical, cooling lemon or classic vanilla.

Island Fruit Barn CAFE $
(16 Bingle Rd, Dunwich; mains $10-14; 7am-5pm Mon-Fri, 7am-4pm Sat & Sun;) On the main road in Dunwich, Island Fruit Barn is a casual little congregation of tables with excellent breakfasts, smoothies, salads and sandwiches using top-quality ingredients. Order a spinach-and-feta roll, then stock up in the gourmet grocery section.

Look MODERN AUSTRALIAN $$
(☎07-3415 3390; www.lookcafebar.com; cnr East Coast Rd & Mintee St, Point Lookout; mains $22-38; 8am-3pm daily, 6-9pm Thu-Sat) The hub of the Point Lookout scene during the day, with

funky tunes and breezy outdoor seating with water views. Lots of wines by the glass and smokin' chilli prawns.

Point Lookout Bowls Club PUB FARE **$$**
(☎07-3409 8182; www.pointlookoutbowlsclub.com.au; East Coast Rd, Point Lookout; mains $9-25; ⊙11.30am-2pm & 6-8pm) For casual pub grub meals that won't break the bank, head for the local bowls club. The chef is from France – could he be any further from home?

Fishes at the Point SEAFOOD **$$**
(www.fishesatthepoint.com.au; East Coast Rd, Point Lookout; mains $10-25; ⊙8am-8pm Sat-Thu, 8am-9pm Fri;) True to form, Fishes offers fresh fish and chips, plus outdoor seating across the road from the North Gorge Headlands Walk. A bit heavy on the batter, but you need that after a surf.

Information

Although it's quiet most of the year, the island population swells significantly at Christmas, Easter and during school holidays: book accommodation or camping permits well in advance.

If you plan to go off-road you can get information and obtain a 4WD permit ($38.25) from Straddie Camping (313).

Getting There & Away

The gateway to North Stradbroke Island is the seaside suburb of Cleveland. Regular **Citytrain** (www.translink.com.au) services run from Brisbane's Central and Roma St stations to Cleveland station ($9.50, one hour); buses to the ferry terminal meet the trains at Cleveland station ($4.80, 10 minutes).

Big Red Cat (☎1800 733 228, 07-3488 9777; www.bigredcat.com.au; return per vehicle incl passengers $146, walk-on adult/child $20/10; ⊙5.15am-6pm Mon-Sat, 7am-7pm Sun) In a tandem operation with Stradbroke Ferries, the feline-looking Big Red Cat vehicle/passenger ferry does the Cleveland–Dunwich run around eight times daily (45 minutes).

Stradbroke Ferries (☎07-3488 5300; www.stradbrokeferries.com.au; return per vehicle incl passengers $146, walk-on adult/child $20/10; ⊙5.15am-6pm Mon-Sat, 7am-7pm Sun) Teaming up with Big Red Cat, Stradbroke Ferries' passenger and passenger/vehicle services runs to Dunwich and back around 12 times daily (passenger ferries 25 minutes, vehicle ferries 45 minutes).

Gold Cats Stradbroke Flyer (☎07-3286 1964; www.flyer.com.au; Middle St, Cleveland; return adult/child/family $19/10/50) Gold Cat Stradbroke Flyer runs around a dozen return passenger trips daily between Cleveland and One Mile Jetty at Dunwich (30 minutes).

Getting Around

Straddie is big: it's best to have your own wheels to explore it properly. If not, **Stradbroke Island Buses** (☎07-3415 2417; www.stradbrokebuses.com) meet the ferries at Dunwich and run to Amity and Point Lookout ($9.60 return). The last bus to Dunwich leaves Point Lookout at 6.20pm. There's also the **Stradbroke Cab Service** (☎0408 193 685), which charges around $60 from Dunwich to Point Lookout.

Moreton Island

POP 250

You'll be reassured to learn that Moreton Island's cache of sandy shores, bushland, bird life, dunes and glorious lagoons are well protected – 95% of the isle is designated national park (see www.nprsr.qld.gov.au/parks/moreton-island).

The island has a rich history, from early Aboriginal settlements to the site of Queensland's first and only whaling station at Tangalooma, which operated between 1952 and 1962. These days, swimming, snorkelling and 4WD trails keep visitors occupied (in fact, the island is a 4WD-only destination). **Tangalooma** now hosts the island's sole resort, and there are three other small settlements on the west coast: **Bulwer** sits near the northwestern tip, **Cowan Cowan** between Bulwer and Tangalooma, and **Kooringal** is near the southern tip.

Sights & Activities

Dolphin feeding happens each evening around sunset at Tangalooma, halfway down the western side of the island. Around half-a-dozen dolphins swim in from the ocean and take fish from the hands of volunteer feeders. You have to be a guest of the Tangalooma Island Resort to participate, but onlookers are welcome. The resort also organises **whale-watching** cruises (June to October).

Just north of the resort, off the coast, are the rusty **Tangalooma Wrecks** – 15 sunken ships forming a sheltered boat mooring (and a brilliant **snorkelling** spot!). You can hire snorkelling gear from the resort, or **Tangatours** (☎07-3410 6927; www.tangatours.com.au; Tangalooma Island Resort) offers guided snorkelling trips around the wrecks ($45) as well as guided **paddleboarding** ($59) and dusk **kayaking** tours ($49).

Island **bushwalks** include a desert trail (two hours) leaving from the resort, as well as the strenuous trek up Mt Tempest (280m), 3km inland from Eagers Creek – worthwhile, but you'll need transport to reach the start.

Built in 1857 at the island's northern tip, **Cape Moreton Lighthouse** is the oldest operating lighthouse in Queensland, and is the place to come for great views if the whales are passing by.

☞ Tours

Dolphin Wild ADVENTURE TOUR
(☑ 07-3880 4444; www.dolphinwild.com.au; Newport Marina, Scarborough; per adult/child/family incl lunch $125/75/325) These full-day ecotours head out to Moreton Island with commentary from a marine naturalist and guided snorkel tours ($20/10 per adult/child) around the Tangalooma wrecks. Transfers from Brisbane and the Gold Coast available.

Adventure Moreton Island ADVENTURE TOUR
(☑ 1300 022 878; www.adventuremoretonisland.com; 1-day tours from $129) Operated in cahoots with Tangatours at Tangalooma Island Resort, these tours offer a range of activities (paddleboarding, snorkelling, sailing, kayaking, fishing etc), ex-Brisbane. Overnight resort accommodation packages also available (including tour from $288).

Sunrover Tours ADVENTURE TOUR
(☑ 07-3203 4241, 1800 353 717; www.sunrover.com.au; day tour adult/child $145/125, plus park fees $30) A 4WD-tour operator with full-day and longer (two- and three-day) camping tours. Snorkelling, shipwrecks, bushwalks and dolphin-spotting. Departs Brisbane.

Moreton Bay Escapes ADVENTURE TOUR
(☑ 1300 559 355; www.moretonbayescapes.com.au; 1-day tours adult/child from $179/129, 2-day camping tours $309/179) 🌿 A certified ecotour, the one-day 4WD tour includes snorkelling or kayaking, sand-boarding, marine-wildlife watching and a picnic lunch. Camp overnight to see more of the isle.

Micat DRIVING TOUR
(☑ 07-3909 3333; www.micat.com.au; 1-day tours adult/child from $159/130) Guided 4WD trips with either an eco or adventure bent.

🛏 Sleeping

There are a few holiday flats and houses for rent at Kooringal, Cowan Cowan and Bulwer: see listings at www.moretonisland.com.au.

There are 10 national-park **campgrounds** (☑ 13 74 68; www.nprsr.qld.gov.au/experiences/camping; sites per adult/child/family $5.45/3/21.80) on Moreton Island, all with water, toilets and cold showers; five campgrounds are on the beach. Book online or by phone before you get to the island.

Tangalooma Island Resort HOTEL, APARTMENTS $$$
(☑ 07-3637 2000, 1300 652 250; www.tangalooma.com; 1-night packages from $370; ✳ @ 🌐 🏊) This beautifully sited place has the island resort market cornered. There are abundant sleeping options, starting with simple hotel rooms. A step up are the units and suites, where you'll get beachside access and more contemporary decor. The apartments range from two- to four-bedroom configurations. The resort has several eating options; accommodation prices generally include return ferry fares and transfers.

ℹ Information

There's a small convenience store plus cafes, restaurants and bars at the resort; otherwise, bring food supplies from the mainland.

There are no paved roads on Moreton Island, but 4WDs can travel along the beaches and cross-island tracks (regular cars not permitted). Permits for 4WDs cost $42.15 and are available through ferry operators, online or via phone from the Department of National Parks, Recreation, Sport & Racing (p309). Ferry bookings are mandatory if you want to take a vehicle across.

Online, see www.visitmoretonisland.com.

ℹ Getting There & Around

Several ferries operate from the mainland. To explore once you get to the island, bring a 4WD on one of the ferries or take a tour (most tours are ex-Brisbane, and include ferry transfers).

Tangalooma Flyer (☑ 07-3268 6333, shuttle bus 07-3637 2000; www.tangalooma.com; adult/child return $45/25) Fast passenger catamaran operated by Tangalooma Island Resort. It makes the 75-minute trip to the resort three times daily from Holt St Wharf in Brisbane (see the website for directions). A shuttle bus (adult/child one way $20/10) scoots to the wharf from the CBD or airport; bookings essential.

Micat (www.micat.com.au; 14 Howard Smith Dr, Port of Brisbane; return passenger adult/child $50/35, vehicle incl 2 people $195-230) Vehicle ferries from Port of Brisbane to Tangalooma around eight times weekly (75 minutes); see the website for directions to the ferry terminal.

Amity Trader (☎0487 227 437, 07-3820 6557; www.amitytrader.com; vehicle & passengers one way/return $135/250) Island hopping? The vehicle ferry Amity Trader sails between Amity Point on North Stradbroke Island and Kooringal on Moreton Island's southern tip, around four times weekly (30 minutes).

Bribie Island

POP 16,200

Queensland's only offshore island linked to the mainland by bridge, Bribie is 70km north of Brisbane at the top end of Moreton Bay. Like Stradbroke and Moreton it's a sand island with protected bushland areas, but it's far more developed (read: suburban).

Still, there are some beaut beaches and remote campgrounds (p315) on the west and north coasts, administered by the Department of National Parks, Recreation, Sport & Racing; book ahead. You'll also need a 4WD to access these areas, and a 4WD permit ($40.35 per week): pick one up via the Department website (www.nprsr.qld.gov.au) or from **Gateway Bait & Tackle** (☎07-5497 5253; www.gatewaybaitandtackle.com.au; 1383 Bribie Island Rd, Ningi; ⏲5.30am-5.30pm Mon-Fri, 4.30am-6pm Sat, 4.30am-5pm Sun) on the mainland side of the bridge to the island. For general island info, head to the **Bribie Island visitor information centre** (☎07-3408 9026; www.bribie.com.au; Benabrow Ave, Bellara; ⏲9am-4pm).

If you're not camping, the flashy new multistorey **On the Beach Resort** (☎07-3400 1400; www.onthebeachresort.com.au; 9 North St, Woorim; 2-/3-bedroom apt from $205/275; ❄🏊) at Woorim out-luxes anything else on the island and has great beach views. For a superior spin on pub grub and bountiful cold beer, try the **Surf Club Bribie Island** (☎07-3408 2141; www.thesurfclubbribie.com.au; 2 First Ave, Woorim; mains $14-30; ⏲11.30am-3pm & 5.30-9pm).

Frequent Citytrain services run from Brisbane to Caboolture, from where **Bribie Island Coaches** (www.bribiecoaches.com.au) connects to Bribie Island; regular Brisbane Translink fares apply (one way $13.90).

GOLD COAST

You might rub your eyes and do a double-take as you approach the Gold Goast from afar: fronting onto this iconic ribbon of surf beaches is a towering city of high-rise apartments, totally at odds with the natural landscape. Down at street level are eateries, bars and theme parks that attract a perpetual stream of sunburnt holidaymakers. The undisputed fun capital is Surfers Paradise, where dizzying nightlife sucks you in and spits you back out exhausted. But the hype diminishes drastically away from Surfers: Broadbeach's chic style and Burleigh Heads' seaside charm mellow into Coolangatta's laid-back surfer ethos.

Festivals & Events

Big Day Out MUSIC
(www.bigdayout.com) Huge international music festival in late January.

Tropfest FILM
(www.tropfest.com/au/surfers-paradise) This international short-film fest comes to the Gold Coast in February.

Quicksilver Pro SURFING
(www.aspworldtour.com) The world's best surfers hit the waves in mid-March; the first comp of the annual world tour.

Surf Life-Saving Championships SURF LIFE-SAVING
(www.sls.com.au) In April: expect to see some incredibly fit people running about wearing very little.

UNEXPECTED TREASURE: ABBEY MUSEUM

On the road to Bribie Island, 6km from the Bruce Hwy turn-off, is an astonishing art and archaeology collection at the **Abbey Museum** (☎07-5495 1652; www.abbeymuseum.com; 63 The Abbey Pl, Caboolture, off Old Toorbul Point Rd; adult/child/family $8.80/5/19.80; ⏲10am-4pm Mon-Sat). The artefacts here span the globe and would be at home in any of the world's famous museums. Once the private collection of Englishman John Ward, the pieces – including Neolithic tools, medieval manuscripts and ancient Roman, Greek, Aztec and Japanese artefacts – will have you scratching your head in amazement. The on-site church has more original stained glass from Winchester Cathedral than what is actually left in the cathedral. If you're here in July, make merry with 37,000 other history boffins at Australia's largest medieval festival (see www.abbeytournament.com).

Gold Coast & Hinterland

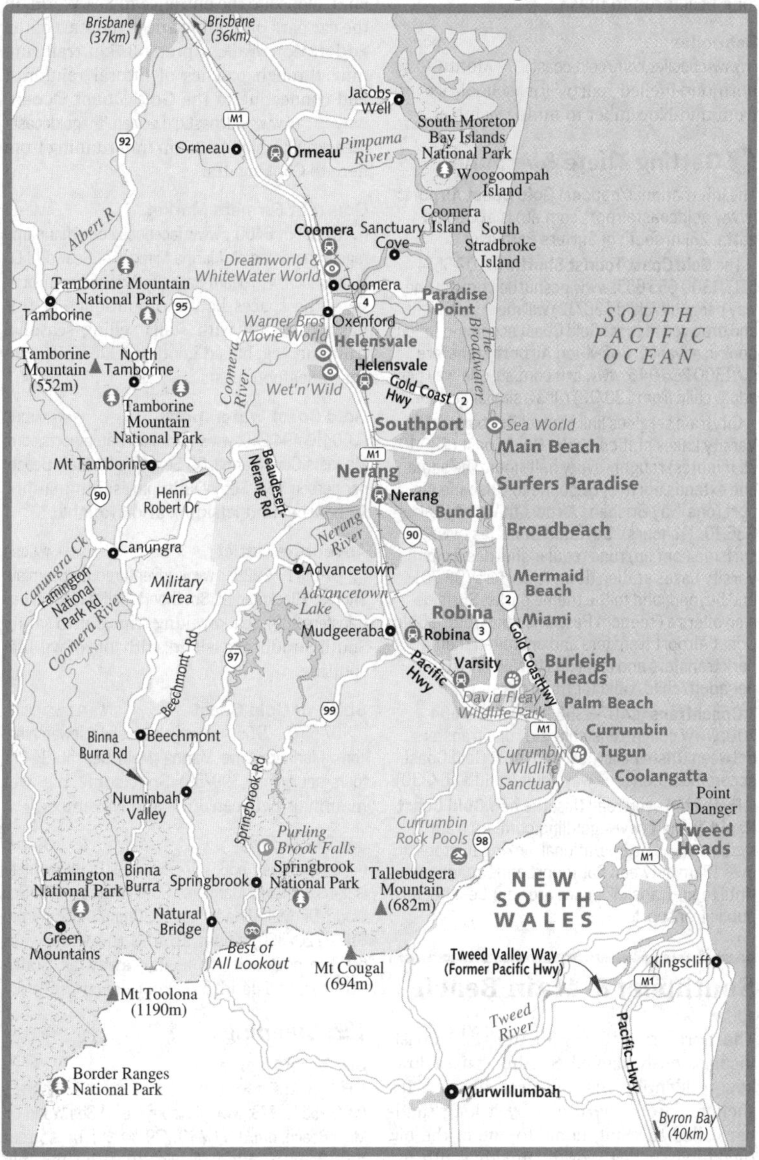

Gold Coast Marathon MARATHON
(www.goldcoastmarathon.com.au) Forty-two kilometres of pain in July.

Gold Coast 600 MOTORSPORTS
(www.surfersparadise.v8supercars.com.au) Three days in October: the streets of Surfers are transformed into a temporary race circuit for V8 Supercars.

Coolangatta Gold SURF LIFE-SAVING
(www.sls.com.au/coolangattagold) In October; gruelling competition with surf-ski paddle,

beach runs, ocean swim, board paddle and long beach run to finish.

Schoolies HOLIDAY
(www.schoolies.com/gold-coast) Month-long, hormone-fuelled party for school leavers from mid-November to mid-December.

Getting There & Around

The international/national **Gold Coast Airport** (www.goldcoastairport.com.au) is at Coolangatta, 25km south of Surfers Paradise.

The **Gold Coast Tourist Shuttle** (☎07-5574 5111, 1300 655 655; www.gcshuttle.com.au; one-way per adult/child $20/12) will meet your flight and drop you at most Gold Coast accommodation; book in advance. **Con-X-ion Airport Transfers** (☎1300 266 946; www.cxn.com.au; one-way per adult/child from $20/12) runs a similar service.

Citytrain services link central Brisbane with Varsity Lakes station on the Gold Coast ($20.10, 75 minutes) roughly every half-hour. The same line extends north of Brisbane to Brisbane Airport (one-way Brisbane Airport to Varsity Lakes $36.10, 1¾ hours). **Surfside Buslines** (www.surfside.com.au) runs regular shuttles from the Varsity Lakes station down to Surfers ($6.70) and beyond, and to the theme parks. Surfside also offers a Freedom Pass including return Gold Coast Airport transfers and unlimited theme park transfers and local bus travel for $70/36 per adult/child, valid for three days.

Coachtrans (☎07-3358 9700, 1300 664 700; www.coachtrans.com.au) runs transfers between Brisbane airport and most Gold Coast accommodation (one way adult/child $46/230).

By the time you read this, the new **Gold Coast Rapid Transit** (www.goldlinq.com.au) tram system might be operational, linking 16 stops over 13km between Southport and Broadbeach. Until then, Translink buses are your best bet for public transport.

Southport & Main Beach

POP 28,300

The northern gateway to the Gold Coast, incongruously named Southport is a low-key residential and business district. It's sheltered from the ocean by a long sandbar called the Spit, home to one of the big theme parks, Sea World. Directly southeast is glorious, golden Main Beach, where the apartment blocks begin their inexorable rise towards Surfers Paradise.

Sights & Activities

The ocean side of the Spit at Main Beach is a popular **fishing** spot: from here you can see across the channel to South Stradbroke Island. Opposite the entrance to Sea World, in the car park of Phillip Park, is the start of the **Federation Walk**, a pretty 3.7km trail running through patches of littoral rainforest and connecting to the **Gold Coast Oceanway** (www.goldcoast.qld.gov.au/thegoldcoast/oceanway-156.html), a 36km trail running from here to Coolangatta.

Gourmet Farmers Market MARKET
(☎07-5555 6400; www.facebook.com/marinamiragefarmersmarket; Marina Mirage, 74 Seaworld Dr, Main Beach; ⏲7-11am Sat) On Saturday mornings, the spaces between boutiques at this flashy mall fill with stalls selling seasonal fruit and veg, baked goods, pickles, oils, vinegars, seafood, pasta...

Gold Coast Watersports PARASAILING
(☎0410 494 240; www.goldcoastwatersports.com; Mariners Cove Marina, 60 Seaworld Dr, Main Beach; per person from $65) Daily parasailing jaunts. Jetboating and jetskiing also available.

Adventure Outlet SEA KAYAKING
(☎07-5571 2929; www.adventureoutlet.com.au; Shop 5, 3 Jackman St, Southport; half-day tours incl transfers $89) Sea kayaking trips out to sandy South Stradbroke Island, with lots of wildlife spotting.

Spirit of Gold Coast WHALE WATCHING
(☎07-5572 7755; www.goldcoastwhalewatching.com; Mariners Cove Marina, Main Beach; 2½-3hr tours adult/child $99/59) Spot some big wet mammals between June and November.

Jet Ski Safaris JETSKIING
(☎0409 754 538, 07-5526 3111; www.jetskisafaris.com.au; Mariners Cove Marina, 60 Sea World Dr, Main Beach; tours 30min/1hr/2hr from $120/220/360) Zoom around the waterways off Main Beach, or as far away as South Stradbroke Island. No experience required.

Sleeping

Surfers Paradise

YHA at Main Beach HOSTEL $
(☎07-5571 1776; www.yha.com.au; 70 Sea World Dr, Main Beach; dm/d & tw $31/79; @☎) In a great first-floor position overlooking the marina: drop down over the balcony to access a plethora of water sports, cruises and tours. There is a free shuttle bus, and barbecue nights every Friday, and the hostel is within wobbling distance of the Fisherman's Wharf Tavern (p320). Sky-blue dorms; very well organised.

GOLD COAST THEME PARKS

The gravity defying rollercoasters and waterslides at these American-style parks offer some seriously dizzy action – keeping your lunch down is a constant battle. Discount tickets are sold in most of the tourist offices on the Gold Coast; the VIP Pass (per person $110) grants unlimited entry to Sea World, Warner Bros Movie World and Wet'n'Wild. Tip: arrive early or face a long walk from the far side of the car park.

➡ **Dreamworld** (☎1800 073 300, 07-5588 1111; www.dreamworld.com.au; Dreamworld Pkwy, Coomera; adult/child $95/75, online $90/70; ⏲10am-5pm) Home to the 'Big 8 Thrill Rides', such as the Giant Drop and Tower of Terror II. Get your photo taken with Aussie animals or a Bengal tiger at Tiger Island. Access to WhiteWater World included in ticket price.

➡ **Sea World** (☎13 33 86, 07-5588 2222; www.seaworld.com.au; Sea World Dr, The Spit, Main Beach; adult/child $83/50; ⏲9.30am-5.30pm) See polar bears, sharks, seals, penguins and performing dolphins at this aquatic park, which also has the mandatory rollercoasters and waterslides. Animal shows throughout the day.

➡ **Warner Bros Movie World** (☎13 33 86, 07-5573 3999; www.movieworld.com.au; Pacific Hwy, Oxenford; adult/child $83/50; ⏲9.30am-5pm) Movie-themed shows, rides and attractions, including the Batwing Spaceshot, Justice League 3D Ride and Scooby-Doo Spooky Rollercoaster. Batman, Austin Powers, Porky Pig et al roam through the crowds.

➡ **Wet'n'Wild** (☎13 33 86, 07-5556 1660; www.wetnwild.com.au; Pacific Hwy, Oxenford; adult/child $60/35; ⏲10am-5pm) The ultimate waterslide here is the Kamikaze, where you plunge down an 11m drop in a two-person tube at 50km/h. This vast water park also has pitch-black slides, white-water rapids and wave pools.

➡ **WhiteWater World** (☎1800 073 300, 07-5588 1111; www.whitewaterworld.com.au; Dreamworld Parkway, Coomera; adult/child $95/75, online $90/70; ⏲10am-4pm) Connected to Dreamworld; has waterslide rides like the Temple of Huey and the Cave of Waves. You can learn to surf here too! Ticket price includes entry to Dreamworld.

Trekkers HOSTEL $
(☎07-5591 5616, 1800 100 004; www.trekkersbackpackers.com.au; 22 White St, Southport; dm/d & tw $30/75;) You could bottle the friendly vibes in this sociable old Queenslander and make a mint. The building is looking a bit tired, but the communal areas are homey and the garden is a mini-oasis. Fun and easy-going, not big or flashy.

Main Beach Tourist Park CARAVAN PARK $
(☎07-5667 2720; www.gctp.com.au/main; 3600 Main Beach Pde, Main Beach; powered sites/cabins & villas from $44/121;) Just across the road from the beach and backed by a phalanx of high-rise apartments, this caravan park is a family favourite. It's a tight fit between sites, but the facilities are decent.

Harbour Side Resort APARTMENT $$
(☎07-5591 6666; www.harboursideresort.com.au; 132 Marine Pde, Southport; 1-/2-bedroom apt $130/170;) 'Resort' is a bit of a stretch, and disregard the busy road: inside this facelifted, three-storey place you'll find motel-style units with well-equipped kitchens and a fab pool.

Eating & Drinking

★ **Providore** CAFE $
(☎07-5532 9390; www.facebook.com/miragemarket; Shop 27 Marina Mirage, 74 Sea World Dr, Main Beach; mains $9-16; ⏲7am-6pm Sun-Wed, 7am-10pm Thu-Sat) Floor-to-ceiling windows rimmed with Italian mineral water bottles, inverted desk lamps dangling from the ceiling, good-looking Euro tourists, wines by the glass, bread racks, cheese fridges and baskets overflowing with fresh produce: this excellent deli/cafe gets a lot of things right. Order some polenta and eggs or some Bircher muesli and start your day with aplomb.

Peter's Fish Market SEAFOOD, FISH & CHIPS $
(☎07-5591 7747; www.petersfish.com.au; Sea World Dr, Main Beach; meals $9-16; ⏲9am-7.30pm, cooking from noon) A no-nonsense fish market selling fresh and cooked seafood in all shapes and sizes (and at great prices), fresh from the trawlers moored out the front.

Sunset Bar & Grill MODERN AUSTRALIAN $$
(☎07-5528 2622; www.sunsetbarandgrill.com.au; Shop 31, Marina Mirage, 74 Sea World Dr, Main Beach;

dishes $12-28; ⏲7am-6pm Mon-Fri, 7am-7pm Sat & Sun) This umbrella-shaded, family-friendly place by the water serves reasonably priced (if predictable) steaks, salads, burgers and seafood dishes.

Fisherman's Wharf Tavern PUB
(☎07-5571 0566; www.fishermanswharftavern.com.au; Shop 40, Mariners Cove, Main Beach; ⏲10am-late) This boisterous harbourside pub – on a pier out over the water – is a beers-from-10am kinda joint, and gets raucous after dark on weekends. The kitchen (mains $15 to $29, breakfast on weekends, lunch and dinner daily) whips up reliable burgers and fish-and-chips, plus curries, steaks and big salads.

Surfers Paradise & Broadbeach

Some say the surfers prefer beaches elsewhere and paradise has been tragically lost, but there's no denying this wild and trashy party zone attracts a phenomenal number of visitors (20,000 per day!). Cashed-up tourists swarm to Surfers Paradise (population 19,670) for a heady cocktail of clubs, bars, malls and maybe a bit of beach-time when the hangover kicks in. It's a sexy place: lots of shirtless, tattooed backpackers and more cleavage than the Grand Canyon. But if you're looking for substance – with the notable exception of the Arts Centre – it's a case of 'Move along, nothing to see here'.

The decibel level is considerably lower directly south in Broadbeach (population 4650), which offers some chic restaurants and a gorgeous stretch of golden shore.

Sights & Activities

SkyPoint Observation Deck LOOKOUT
(www.skypoint.com.au; Level 77, Q1 Bldg, Hamilton Ave, Surfers Paradise; adult/child/family $21/12.50/54.50; ⏲7am-8.30pm Sun-Thu, 7am-11.30am Fri & Sat) Surfers' sights are usually spread across beach towels, but for an eagle-eye scope, zip up to this 230m-high observation deck near the top of Q1, the 27th tallest building in the world. You can also tackle the **SkyPoint Climb** up the spire to 270m high (adult/child from $69/49).

Cheyne Horan School of Surf SURFING
(☎1800 227 873; www.cheynehoran.com.au; 2hr lesson $49, 3/5 lessons $129/189; ⏲10am & 2pm) Learn to carve up the waves with former pro surfer Cheyne Horan. Board hire $30 per day.

Go Ride a Wave SURFING
(☎1300 132 441; www.gorideawave.com.au; Shop 189, Centro Centre, Cavill Ave, Surfers Paradise; 2hr lesson from $65, 3/5 lessons $180/260; ⏲9am-5pm) Learn to surf in Surfers. Also rents out surfboards (per day $45) and kayaks (per day $80) and runs kids' surf lessons.

Balloon Down Under BALLOONING
(☎07-5500 4797; www.balloondownunder.com; 1hr flights adult/child $299/240) Sunrise flights over the Gold Coast ending with a champagne breakfast.

Tours

Aqua Duck BOAT TOUR
(☎07-5539 0222; www.aquaduck.com.au; 36 Cavill Ave, Surfers Paradise; adult/child/family $35/26/95; ⏲every 75min 10am-5.30pm) Check out Surfers by land and water in a boat with wheels. One-hour tours depart from Surfers Paradise Blvd outside Centre Arcade.

Sleeping

Gold Coast Accommodation Service ACCOMMODATION SERVICES
(☎07-5592 0067; www.goldcoastaccommodationservice.com) Advice and bookings for GC accommodation (particularly useful during Schoolies!).

Sleeping Inn Surfers HOSTEL $
(☎07-5592 4455, 1800 817 832; www.sleepinginn.com.au; 26 Peninsular Dr, Surfers Paradise; dm $28-32, d & tw $68-114; @🛜🏊) This backpackers occupies an old apartment block away from the centre, so, as the name suggests, there's a chance you may get to sleep in. Pizza nights, barbecue nights and pick-ups in a vintage limo.

Backpackers in Paradise HOSTEL $
(☎07-5538 4344, 1800 268 621; www.backpackersinparadise.com; 40 Peninsular Dr, Surfers Paradise; dm $25-33, d $80; @🛜🏊) If you're in Surfers to wage war against sleep, this party backpackers is the place for you. Encircling a courtyard carpeted with astroturf, most rooms are freshly painted and have bathrooms. The bar does cheap dinners – fuel-up before you hit the town.

Surfers Paradise Backpackers Resort HOSTEL $
(☎07-5592 4677, 1800 282 800; www.surfersparadisebackpackers.com.au; 2837 Gold Coast Hwy,

LOCAL KNOWLEDGE

LUKE EGAN: FORMER PRO SURFER

The Gold Coast is one of the top five surfing destinations in the world. The most unique thing about the Goldy is that the waves break mostly on sand, so for sandy bottoms we get some of the most perfect waves in the world.

Best Surf Beaches

The length of ride on the famous points of Burleigh Heads, Kirra, Rainbow Bay and Snapper Rocks make the Goldy a must for every passionate surfer.

Where to Learn

The waves at Greenmount Point and Currumbin allow first-timers plenty of time to get to their feet and still enjoy a long ride. Learning to surf at these two places would be close to the best place to learn anywhere in Australia, and probably the world.

Best Experience

There isn't a better feeling than being 'surfed out' – the feeling you have after a day of surfing. Even though I no longer compete on the world surfing tour I still surf every day like it's my last.

When not Surfing

I love mountain-bike riding in the hills close to Mt Warning, and catching up with friends at one of the Gold Coast's great cafes and restaurants.

Surfers Paradise; dm/d & tw from $29/74; @ 🛜 🏊) This bricky, motel-like hostel – on a busy road and a fair hike from the action – has a sporty vibe (pool room, tennis court), dorms with bathrooms and surprisingly nice self-contained apartments. There's a free courtesy bus to and from the Transit Centre.

Vibe Hotel HOTEL **$$**
(☎07-5539 0444, 13 84 23; www.vibehotels.com.au; 42 Ferny Ave, Surfers Paradise; d $100-250; ❄ @ 🛜 🏊) Slick but affordable, this chocolate and lime-green high-rise on the Nerang River is a vibrant gem amongst Surfers' bland plethora of hotels and apartments. The rooms are subtle-chic and the pool is a top spot for sundowners. The aqua-view rooms have Nerang River views.

Chateau Beachside Resort APARTMENT **$$**
(☎07-5538 1022; www.chateaubeachside.com.au; cnr Elkhorn Ave & Esplanade, Surfers Paradise; d/1-bedroom apt from $170/200; ❄ @ 🛜 🏊) Less Loire Valley, more Las Vegas, this seaside 'chateau' (actually an 18-storey tower) is an excellent choice. All the renovated studios and apartments have ocean views and the 18m pool is a bonus. Minimum two-night stay.

Surfers International Apartments APARTMENT **$$**
(☎07-5579 1299, 1800 891 299; www.surfersinternational.com.au; 7-9 Trickett St, Surfers Paradise; 1-bedroom apt $100-180, 2br $150-250; 🛜 🏊) This 20-storey high-rise just off the beach has large, comfortable apartments, most with full ocean views. Decor is a bit early-2000s, but it's a solid option and close to everything.

Breakfree Cosmopolitan APARTMENT **$$**
(☎07-5570 2311; www.breakfree.com.au; cnr Surfers Paradise Blvd & Beach Rd, Surfers Paradise; 1-/2-bedroom apt from $125/155; ❄ 🛜 🏊) Set back from the beach but still central, this complex contains 55 privately owned, self-contained apartments, furnished by the owners (so, a bit stylistically hit-and-miss). There's also a barbecue area, two pools and free parking. Minimum two-night stay in summer.

Wave APARTMENT **$$$**
(☎07-5555 9200; www.thewavesresort.com.au; 89-91 Surf Pde, Broadbeach; 1-/2-/3-bedroom apt from $290/405/480; ❄ @ 🛜 🏊) Towering over glam Broadbeach, you can't miss this funky high-rise with its wobbly, wave-inspired facade. The plush pads here take full advantage of panoramic coastal views (especially good from the sky pool on the 34th floor). Minimum three-night stay.

Artique APARTMENT **$$$**
(☎1800 454 442, 07-5564 3100; www.artiqueresort.com.au; cnr Surfers Paradise Blvd & Enderley Ave, Surfers Paradise; 1-/2-bedroom apt from $240/290; ❄ 🛜 🏊) One of several slick new apartment towers at Surfers' southern end,

Surfers Paradise

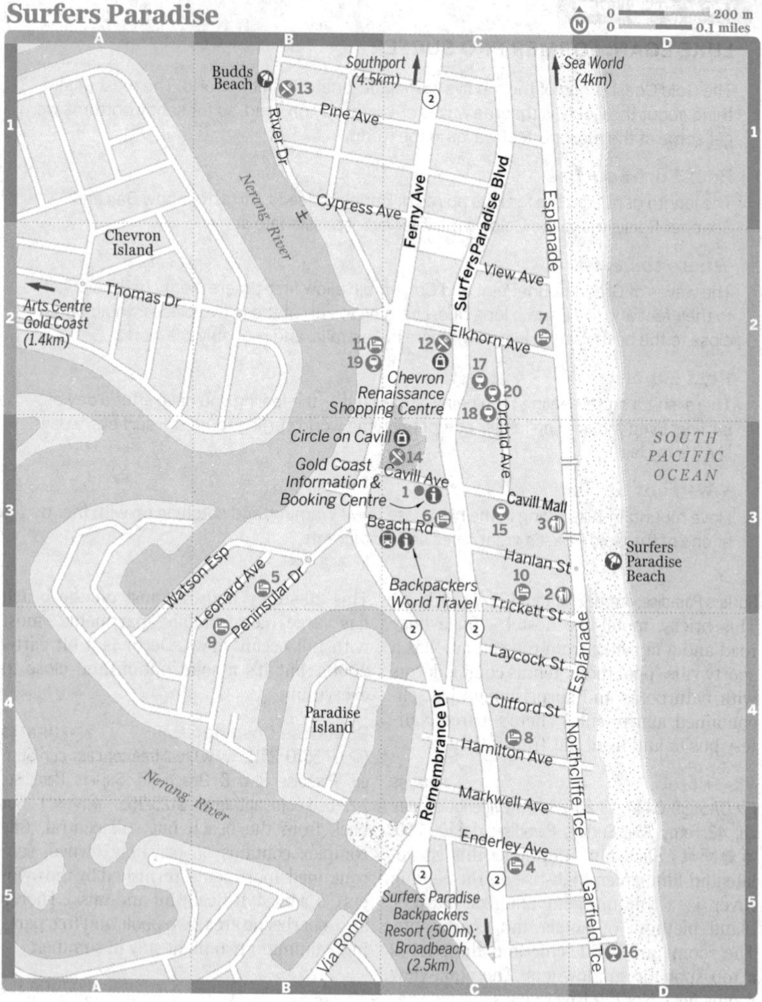

Artique (which is certainly not antique) features a curvy facade, glazed balustrades, muted charcoal-and-cream tones, classy kitchens and babbling fountains. Minimum stays apply (usually three nights).

Q1 Resort APARTMENT $$$

(☎07-5630 4500, 1300 792 008; www.q1.com.au; Hamilton Ave, Surfers Paradise; 1-/2-/3-bedroom apt from $318/325/666;) Spend a night in the world's 27th-tallest building! It's a slick resort with a mod mix of metal, glass and fabulous wrap-around views. All units have glass-enclosed balconies. There's a lagoon-style pool and a fitness centre if the beach doesn't exhaust you. The very sassy French restaurant **Absynthe** (☎07-5504 6466; www.absynthe.com.au; mains $48; ⏲6-10pm Tue-Sat) is here, too.

Eating

Broadbeach's culinary scene is a class above Surfers', where quantity often trumps quality.

Bumbles Café CAFE $

(☎07-5538 6668; www.bumblescafe.com; 21 River Dr, Surfers Paradise; mains $9-27; ⏲7am-3pm Fri-Wed, 7am-10pm Thu) Chilled-out, grey-painted

Surfers Paradise

Sights

	SkyPoint Observation Deck	(see 8)

Activities, Courses & Tours

1	Aqua Duck	C3
2	Cheyne Horan School of Surf	C3
3	Go Ride a Wave	C3

Sleeping

4	Artique	C5
5	Backpackers in Paradise	B3
6	Breakfree Cosmopolitan	C3
7	Chateau Beachside Resort	C2
8	Q1 Resort	C4
9	Sleeping Inn Surfers	B4
10	Surfers International Apartments	C3
11	Vibe Hotel	B2

Eating

	Absynthe	(see 8)
12	Baritalia	C2
13	Bumbles Café	B1
14	Kamikaze Teppanyaki	C3
	Surfers Sandbar	(see 7)

Drinking & Nightlife

15	Beergarden	C3
16	BMD Northcliffe Surf Club	D5
17	Shuffle	C2
18	Sin City	C2
19	Titanium Bar	B2
20	Vanity	C2

corner cafe opposite shallow Budds Beach on the Nerang River. Order a FAT (feta, avocado and tomato on toast) and enjoy a few minutes away from the fray.

Burrito Bar MEXICAN $
(07-5538 0370; www.theburritobar.com.au; Shop 113, Wave Bldg, 88-91 Surf Pde, Broadbeach; items $4-11; 10am-late;) Mexican street-food offerings: Baja fish tacos, pulled-pork nachos, chipotle steak burritos... Order a few things to fill up. Wicked murals inside!

Baritalia ITALIAN $$
(07-5592 4700; www.baritaliagoldcoast.com.au; Shop 15, Chevron Renaissance Bldg, cnr Elkhorn Ave & Surfers Paradise Blvd, Surfers Paradise; mains $15-35; 7.30am-late) Perfect for people-watching, this Italian bar and restaurant has a fab outdoor terrace and hip international staff. Go for the chilli seafood broth with Moreton Bay bugs, saffron and capers, or excellent pastas, pizzas and risotto. Decent wines by the glass (mostly from South Australia, Western Australia and New Zealand) and good coffee.

Surfers Sandbar MODERN AUSTRALIAN $$
(www.facebook.com/surferssandbar; cnr Elkhorn Ave & Esplanade, Surfers Paradise; mains $12-32; 6.45am-late) The menu is predictable – burgers, fish-and-chips, steak sandwiches, pizza – but beachside prominence gives this cafe/bar the edge over most Surfers eateries. Forgo the pubby indoor space and chow-down on the terrace (you can hear lifesavers berating absent-minded swimmers across the street).

Koi MODERN AUSTRALIAN $$
(07-5570 3060; www.koibroadbeach.com.au; Wave Bldg, cnr Surf Pde & Albert Ave, Broadbeach; mains breakfast $14-21, lunch & dinner $18-40; 7am-late) This cruisy cafe/bar is the pick of the Surf Pde eateries in Broadbeach. Fast-moving, black-clad waitstaff shuffle out plates of risotto, pasta, gourmet pizza, tapas, seafood and Koi beans (with poached eggs, chorizo, crispy onion and balsamic reduction).

Kamikaze Teppanyaki JAPANESE $$
(07-5592 0888; www.kamikaze.net.au; Shop 12A, Circle on Cavill, 55 Cavill Ave, Surfers Paradise; dishes $8-33; 11.30am-late) Popular alfresco Japanese restaurant. Sit next to the skillet and the egg-flippin' chef, or outside with big-screen sports views.

Moo Moo STEAKHOUSE $$$
(07-5539 9952; www.moomoorestaurant.com; Broadbeach on the Park, 2486 Gold Coast Hwy, Broadbeach; mains $29-69; noon-3pm & 6pm-late) A carnivorous mecca, Moo Moo's winning steaks include lots of wagyu and a 400g, 50-day dry-aged rib eye on the bone. There's also seafood and pasta on the menu. Love the cowhide-clad bar!

Drinking & Nightlife

Orchid Ave is Surfers' club strip. Cover charges are usually $10 to $20; Wednesday and Saturday are the big party nights. You can tag along with other boozy backpackers on club crawls organised by **Plan B Party Tours** (1300 721 570; www.planbtours.com; tickets $60): tickets get you in to five clubs and take the hassle out of the experience. **Big Night Out** (www.goldcoastbackpackers.net; tickets $30) and **Wicked Club Crawl** (07-5504 7025; www.wickedclubcrawl.com.au; tickets $30-50) are similar (but with four clubs).

Titanium Bar BAR
(www.titaniumbar.com.au; 30-34 Ferny Ave, Surfers Paradise; ⏲10am-late) Unless you like Irish pubs, this metallic-looking bar is the best drinking spot in town, perfect for a beer or six as the sun sets over the Nerang River.

Beergarden BAR
(www.surfersbeergarden.com.au; Cavill Ave, Surfers Paradise; ⏲10am-5am) Not so much a garden – more of a black-painted beer barn overlooking Cavill Ave. Steel yourself with a few cold ones before you hit the clubs, or catch live bands on Saturday nights or reggae on Sunday afternoons.

BMD Northcliffe Surf Club SURF CLUB
(www.northcliffesurfclub.com.au; cnr Garfield Tce & Thornton St, Surfers Paradise; ⏲7.30am-late) A little south of Cavill Mall, this surf club squats directly on the beach. It's big and brash with zero intimacy (like Surfers itself), but the sweeping surf views go well with a coldie on a hot day. Good food, too.

Sin City CLUB
(www.sincitynightclub.com.au; 22 Orchid Ave, Surfers Paradise; ⏲9pm-late) This Vegas-style sin pit is the place for wrongdoings: sexy staff, big-name DJs and visiting celebs trying not to get photographed.

Shuffle CLUB
(www.platinumnightclub.com.au/shuffle-nightclub; Shop 15b, The Forum, 26 Orchid Ave, Surfers Paradise) Shuffle into Shuffle for an intimate club experience, with dirty underground house and a backpacker-heavy crowd (less red carpet, more downmarket).

Vanity CLUB
(www.vanitynightclub.com.au; 26 Orchid Ave, Surfers Paradise; ⏲5am-5pm) 'Because it's all about you' at Vanity, one of the glammest clubs in town, which digs deep into the sexy marketing book of tricks. Dress to the nines; no visible tatts.

☆ Entertainment

Arts Centre Gold Coast THEATRE, CINEMA
(☎07-5588 4000; www.theartscentregc.com.au; 135 Bundall Rd, Surfers Paradise; ⏲box office 8am-9pm Mon-Fri, 9am-9pm Sat, 11am-7pm Sun) A bastion of culture and civility beside the Nerang River, the Arts Centre has two cinemas, a restaurant, a bar, the Gold Coast City Gallery and a 1200-seat theatre, which regularly hosts impressive productions (comedy, jazz, opera, kids' concerts etc).

ℹ Information

Gold Coast Information & Booking Centre (☎1300 309 440; www.visitgoldcoast.com; Cavill Ave, Surfers Paradise; ⏲8.30am-5pm Mon-Sat, 9am-4pm Sun) The main GC tourist information booth; also sells theme-park tickets and has public transport info.

Backpackers World Travel (☎07-5561 0634; www.backpackerworldtravel.com; Islander Resort, 6 Beach Rd, Surfers Paradise; ⏲10am-6.30pm Mon-Fri, 10am-5pm Sat, 10am-4pm Sun) Accommodation, tour and transport bookings and internet access.

Gold Coast Hospital (☎07-5519 8211; www.health.qld.gov.au/goldcoasthealth; 108 Nerang St, Southport)

Surfers Paradise Day & Night Medical Centre (☎07-5592 2299; 3221 Surfers Paradise Blvd, Surfers Paradise; ⏲6am-11pm) General medical centre and pharmacy. Make an appointment or just walk in.

Paradise Medical Centre (☎07-5592 3999; Centro Surfers Paradise, Cavill Mall, Surfers Paradise; ⏲8am-4pm Mon-Fri, 8.30am-11pm Sat) General medical services by appointment.

ℹ Getting There & Around

Long-distance buses stop at the **Surfers Paradise Transit Centre** (10 Beach Rd, Surfers Paradise). **Greyhound** (www.greyhound.com.au) and **Premier Motor Service** (www.premierms.com.au) have frequent services to/from Brisbane ($26, 90 minutes), Byron Bay ($30, 2½ hours) and beyond.

Bike Hire Gold Coast (☎1800 130 140; www.bikehiregoldcoast.com.au; bike hire per half/full day $25/30) Quality mountain bikes delivered to your door. Good weekly rates.

East Coast Car Rentals (☎1800 028 881, 07-5592 0444; www.eastcoastcarrentals.com.au; 80 Ferny Ave, Surfers Paradise) Car hire from around $35 per day.

Gold Coast Cabs (☎13 10 08; www.gccabs.com.au)

Red Back Rentals (☎07-5592 1655; www.redbackrentals.com.au; Transit Centre, 10 Beach Rd, Surfers Paradise) Car hire from around $50 per day.

Scooter Hire Gold Coast (☎07-5511 0398; www.scooterhiregoldcoast.com.au; 3269 Surfers Paradise Blvd, Surfers Paradise) Scooter hire (50cc) from around $65 per day.

Burleigh Heads

POP 9200

The true, sandy essence of the Gold Coast permeates the chilled-out surfie town of Burleigh Heads. With its cheery cafes and beachfront restaurants, famous right-hand point break, beautiful beach and little national park on the rocky headland, Burleigh charms everyone. Nearby Currumbin also has great waves.

○ Sights & Activities

Burleigh Head National Park NATIONAL PARK
(www.nprsr.qld.gov.au/parks/burleigh-head; Goodwin Tce; ⊙24hr) FREE A walk around the headland through Burleigh Head National Park is a must for any visitor – it's a 27-hectare rainforest reserve with plenty of bird life and several walking trails. Great views of the Burleigh surf en route.

Currumbin Wildlife Sanctuary WILDLIFE PARK
(☑07-5534 1266, 1300 886 511; www.cws.org.au; 28 Tomewin St, Currumbin; adult/child/family $49/33/131; ⊙8am-5pm) Currumbin Wildlife Sanctuary has Australia's biggest rainforest aviary, where you can hand-feed a technicolour blur of rainbow lorikeets. There's also kangaroo feeding, photo ops with koalas and crocodiles, reptile shows and Aboriginal dance displays. It's cheaper after 3pm. See the website for details on coach transfers from the north or south (return from $15).

David Fleay Wildlife Park WILDLIFE PARK
(☑07-5576 2411; www.nprsr.qld.gov.au/parks/david-fleay; cnr Loman La & West Burleigh Rd, West Burleigh; adult/child/family $19/9/48; ⊙9am-5pm) Opened by the doctor who first succeeded in breeding platypuses, this wildlife park has 4km of walking tracks through mangroves and rainforest and plenty of educational and informative shows throughout the day. It's an excellent opportunity to experience Australian fauna. It's around 3km inland from Burleigh Heads.

Jellurgal Cultural Centre INDIGENOUS CULTURE
(☑07-5525 5955; www.jellurgal.com.au; 1711 Gold Coast Hwy; ⊙8am-4pm Mon-Sat, 9am-2pm Sun) FREE This new Aboriginal cultural centre at the base of Burleigh's headland sheds some light on life here hundreds of years ago. There's lots of art and artefacts to look at, plus an interpretive multimedia boardwalk. Ask about daily tours (additional cost).

Currumbin Rock Pools SWIMMING
(www.gcparks.com.au/park-details.aspx?park=1751; Currumbin Creek Rd, Currumbin Valley; ⊙24hr) FREE The natural swimming holes at Currumbin Rock Pools are a cool spot during the hot summer months, with grassy banks, barbecues and rocky ledges from which

teenagers plummet. It's 14km up Currumbin Creek Rd from the coast.

Surfing Services Australia SURFING
(☑07-5535 5557; www.surfingservices.com.au; adult/child $35/25) Surfing lessons at Currumbin every weekend (daily during school holidays).

Hotstuff Surfboards SURFING
(☑07-5535 6899; www.goldcoastsurf.com.au; 1709 Gold Coast Hwy; ⊙9am-5pm) Hotstuff rents out surfboards (minimals, soft boards and bodyboards) per half/full day for $30/40.

Gold Coast Skydive SKYDIVING
(☑07-5599 1920; www.goldcoastskydive.com.au; tandem dives from $345) Plummet out of the sky from 12,000 feet up? Go on – you know you want to!

⊟ Sleeping

Burleigh Beach Tourist Park CARAVAN PARK $
(☑07-5667 2750; www.goldcoasttouristparks.com.au; 36 Goodwin Tce; unpowered/powered sites from $30/41, cabins $151-219; ❄@🐾🏊) This council-owned park is snug, but it's well run and in a great spot near the beach. Aim for one of the three blue cabins at the front of the park.

Burleigh Palms Holiday Apartments APARTMENT $$
(☑07-5576 3955; www.burleighpalms.com; 1849 Gold Coast Hwy; 1-bedroom apt per night/week from $150/550, 2-bedroom apt from $180/660; ❄🐾🏊) Even though they're on the highway, these large and comfortable self-contained units – a quick dash to the beach through the back alley – are solid value. The owners have a wealth of local info, and do the cleaning themselves to keep the accommodation costs down.

Hillhaven Holiday Apartments APARTMENT $$
(☑07-5535 1055; www.hillhaven.com.au; 2 Goodwin Tce; 2-bedroom apt from $180; @🐾) Right on the headland adjacent to the national park, these renovated apartments – the pick of which is the gold deluxe room at $300 per night – have awesome views of Burleigh Heads and the surf. It's ultra quiet and only 150m to the beach.

Wyuna APARTMENT $$
(☑07-5535 3302; www.wyunaapartments.com.au; 82 The Esplanade; 2-/3-bedroom apt per week from $675/950; 🐾) Large, old-fashioned apartments in a great location opposite the beach.

They're individually owned, so the decor is mixed. This was one of the first high-rises on the Gold Coast! Weekly stays preferred.

✗ Eating & Drinking

★ Borough Barista
CAFE **$**

(www.facebook.com/pages/borough-barista/ 236745933011462; 14 The Esplanade; mains $10-17; ⊙ 6am-2.30pm) A little open-walled caffeine shack with a simple menu of burgers and salads and an unmistakable panache when it comes to coffee. The grilled haloumi burger with mushrooms, caramelised onions and chutney will turn you vegetarian. Cool tunes and friendly vibes.

Bluff Café
CAFE **$$**

(☑ 07-5576 6333; Old Burleigh Theatre Arcade, 1/66 Goodwin Tce; mains $15-23; ⊙ 7am-3pm Mon & Tue, 7am-9pm Wed-Sun) Cheery, breezy cafe opposite the beach in the curious old Burleigh Theatre building. Excellent pizza, pasta and big breakfasts (try the Spanish eggs)...and you can wear your bathing suit!

Oskars
SEAFOOD **$$$**

(☑ 07-5576 3722; www.oskars.com.au; 43 Goodwin Tce; mains $38-43; ⊙ 10am-midnight) One of the Gold Coast's finest, this ooh-la-la restaurant right on the beach serves award-winning seafood and has sweeping views up the coast to Surfers. Go for the spanner crab souffle and the satay spiced green prawns.

Fish House
SEAFOOD **$$$**

(☑ 07-5535 7725; www.thefishhouse.com.au; 50 Goodwin Tce; mains $36-46; ⊙ noon-3pm & 6-9pm Wed-Sun) This stylish red-brick box across the road from the beach goes heavy on the underwater stuff: whiting, swordfish, trevalla, John Dory...all locally caught or imported fresh from interstate. Dress in decent duds and be prepared to speak loudly.

Pointbreak Bar & Grill
BAR

(☑ 07-5535 0822; www.pointbreakburleigh.com; 43 Goodwin Tce; ⊙ noon-late) Unwind with a sundowner and some tapas ($12 to $14) at this chic waterfront bar and restaurant. Dress nice.

Coolangatta

POP 5200

A laid-back seaside town on Queensland's southern border, Coolangatta has quality surf beaches and a tight-knit community. If you want to bypass the glam and party scene, catch some great waves or just kick back on the beach, 'Cooly' is for you. North of the point, Kirra has a beautiful long stretch of beach with challenging surf.

🏃 Activities

Cooly Surf
SURFING

(☑ 07-5536 1470; www.surfshopaustralia.com.au; cnr Marine Pde & Dutton St; ⊙ 9am-5pm) Cooly Surf hires out surfboards (half/full day $30/45) and stand-up paddleboards ($40/55), and runs two-hour surf lessons ($45).

Walkin' on Water
SURFING

(WoW; ☑ 0418 780 311, 07-5534 1886; www.walkinonwater.com; per person $50) Two-hour surf lessons on the main beach at Cooly.

Rainforest Cruises
CRUISE

(☑ 07-5536 8800; www.goldcoastcruising.com; 2hr cruises from $40) These guys have cruise options ranging from crab-catching to surf 'n' turf lunches on rainforest cruises along the Tweed River.

🛏 Sleeping

★ Komune
HOTEL, HOSTEL **$**

(☑ 07-5536 6764; www.komuneresorts.com; 146 Marine Pde; dm from $45, 1-/2-bedroom apt from $105/145, penthouse from $245; ⊛❄) With beach-funk decor, Bali-esque pool area and an ultra laid-back vibe, this eight-storey converted apartment tower is the ultimate surf retreat. There are budget dorms, apartments and a hip penthouse begging for a party. A different take on the hostel concept.

Kirra Beach Tourist Park
CARAVAN PARK **$**

(☑ 07-5667 2740; www.goldcoasttouristparks.com. au; 10 Charlotte St; unpowered/powered sites $30/37, cabins from $138; ⊛@❄❄) Large council-run park with plenty of trees, wandering ibises and a well-stocked open-air camp kitchen. Good-value self-contained cabins; a few hundred metres to the beach.

Coolangatta Sands Hostel
HOSTEL **$**

(☑ 07-5536 7472; www.coolangattasandshostel.com. au; cnr Griffith & McLean Sts; dm/d from $30/80; ⊛@❄) Above the boozy Coolangatta Sands Hotel, this hostel is a warren of rooms and corridors, but there's a fab wrap-around balcony above the street (no booze allowed – go downstairs to the pub). Red chesterfields in the TV room if it's raining.

Coolangatta YHA
HOSTEL **$**

(☑ 07-5536 7644; www.yha.com.au; 230 Coolangatta Rd, Bilinga; dm $27-34, s/d from $42/67;

(@ 📶 ≋) A *looong* 4km haul from the action in an industrial pocket next to the noisy airport, this YHA is redeemed by free breakfast, free transfers to Coolangatta and the beach across the road. You can also hire surfboards ($20 per day) and bikes ($25).

Nirvana APARTMENT $$$
(☎07-5506 5555; www.nirvanabythesea.com.au; 1 Douglas St; 2-/3-bedroom apt from $205/365) Attaining some sort of salty nirvana across from Kirra beach, this sleek new apartment tower comes with all the bells and whistles: two pools, gym, cinema room, ocean views and sundry salons.

Eating & Drinking

Burger Lounge BURGERS $
(☎07-5599 5762; www.burgerlounge.com.au; cnr Musgrave & Douglas Sts; mains $10-17; ⏲10am-9pm Thu-Tue, 11am-9pm Wed) Awesome bunfest in a triangular-shaped room at the base of the Nirvana apartment tower. The chicken and mango chilli burger is a winner! Lots of good beers, cocktails and wines too, and sangria by the jug.

Bread 'n' Butter TAPAS, BAR $$
(☎07-5599 4666; www.breadnbutter.com.au; 76 Musgrave St; tapas $13-22, pizzas $19-25; ⏲5.30-late) Head upstairs to the Bread 'n' Butter balcony, where moody lighting and chilled tunes make this tapas bar perfect for a drink, some pizza or some tapas (or all three). Uses local and home-grown produce and recycles precisely 78% of waste. DJs spin on Friday and Saturday nights.

Coolangatta Hotel PUB
(www.thecoolyhotel.com.au; cnr Marine Pde & Warner St; ⏲10am-late) The hub of Coolangatta's nocturnal scene, this huge pub right across from the beach has live bands (Grinspoon, the Reubens, Dinosaur Jnr), sausage sizzles, pool comps, trivia nights, acoustic jam nights, pub meals, the works. Big Sunday Sessions.

GOLD COAST HINTERLAND

Inland from the surf, sand and half-naked bods on the Gold Coast, the densely forested mountains of the McPherson Range feel a million miles away. There are some brilliant national parks here, with subtropical jungle, waterfalls, lookouts and rampant wildlife. Springbrook National Park is arguably the wettest place in southeast Queensland, with cool air and a dense sea of forest. Lamington National Park attracts birdwatchers and hikers; Tamborine Mountain lures the craft/cottage weekend set.

Tours

Bushwacker Ecotours ECOTOUR
(☎07-3848 8806, 1300 559 355; www.bushwacker-ecotours.com.au; tours adult/child from $125/95) Ecotours to the hinterland with rainforest walks in Springbrook National Park.

Mountain Coach Company TOUR
(☎1300 762 665, 07-5524 4249; www.mountain-coach.com.au) Daily tours from the Gold Coast to Tamborine Mountain (adult/child $59/49), Lamington National Park ($84/54) and Springbrook National Park ($89/57). Transfer-only prices also available ex-Gold Coast (Tamborine Mountain adult/child $30/20; Lamington National Park $50/20).

Araucaria Ecotours ECOTOURS
(☎07-5544 1283; www.learnaboutwildlife.com) Eco-attuned day tours including birdwatching ($154) and Tamborine Mountain ($165).

JPT Tour Group TOUR
(☎07-56301602; www.daytours.com.au; tours from adult/child $99/57) A variety of day tours ex-Brisbane or Gold Coast, including Lamington National Park via Tamborine Mountain and nocturnal glowworm tours to Natural Bridge.

Tamborine Mountain

Just 36km northwest of Southport is Tamborine Mountain (525m), a squat plateau known for its quaint/kitsch shops selling homemade sweets and tacky Australian souvenirs. There are a few winery cellar doors here too (though the wineries themselves are mostly in Stanthorpe, 200km southwest).

The **Tamborine Mountain visitor information centre** (☎07-5545 3200; www.tamborinemtncc.org.au; Doughty Park, Main Western Rd, North Tamborine; ⏲10am-4pm Mon-Fri, 9.30am-4pm Sat & Sun) is in North Tamborine.

Sights & Activities

Tamborine National Park NATIONAL PARK
(www.nprsr.qld.gov.au/parks/tamborine) There are some beautiful spots in the 1500-hectare Tamborine National Park, including impressive cascades at Witches Falls, Cedar Creek

Falls and Curtis Falls, accessed via easy-to-moderate walking trails.

Mt Tamborine Brewery BREWERY
(☎07-5545 2032; www.mtbeer.com; 165 Long Rd, Eagle Heights; ⏲9.30am-5pm Mon-Thu, 9.30am-late Fri-Sun) Thirsty? Swing by the Mt Tamborine Brewery for a Rainforest Lager or a tasting tray (four beer samples for $10). There's also a bistro here for lunch (mains $13 to $23).

Witches Chase Cheese Company CHEESEWRIGHT
(www.witcheschasecheese.com.au; 165 Long Rd, Eagle Heights; ⏲10am-4pm) In the same steel-and-dark-timber complex as the Mt Tamborine Brewery is Witches Chase Cheese Company, with free tastings or bread-and-cheese boards for $25. Try the triple-cream brie.

Skywalk WALKING
(☎07-5545 2222; www.rainforestskywalk.com.au; 333 Geissman Dr, North Tamborine; adult/child/family $19.50/9.50/49; ⏲9.30am-4pm) Take a wander out into the rainforest canopy at Skywalk, at its highest point 30m above the ground. The path descends to the forest floor and leads to Cedar Creek: keep an eye out for rare Richmond Birdwing butterflies along the way.

Sleeping

Tamborine Mountain Caravan & Camping CAMPGROUND $
(☎07-5545 0034; www.tamborine.info; Cedar Creek Falls Rd, Tamborine; unpowered/powered sites $20/28, safari tents $85-100) This wooded camping ground, with affable staff, nifty safari tents and a freshwater swimming hole, is a five-minute walk up Cedar Creek.

Polish Place CHALET $$$
(☎07-5545 1603; www.polishplace.com.au; 333 Main Western Rd, North Tamborine; chalets from $259; ❄📶) There's a distinctly tacky Bavarian or Polish vibe infusing much Tamborine Mountain commerce, but despite the marketing, the accommodation here is reasonably kitsch-free. The five timber-lined, self-contained chalets have loft bedrooms and superb views from their front decks.

Springbrook National Park

About a 40-minute drive west of Burleigh Heads, **Springbrook National Park** (www.nprsr.qld.gov.au/parks/springbrook) is a steep remnant of the huge Tweed Shield volcano that centred on nearby Mt Warning in NSW more than 20 million years ago. It's a wonderland for hikers, with excellent trails through cool-temperate, subtropical and eucalypt forests offering a mosaic of gorges, cliffs and waterfalls.

The park is divided into four sections. The 900m-high **Springbrook Plateau** section is laced with waterfalls and eye-popping lookouts, including the 106m Purling Brook Falls, Canyon Lookout and Best of All Lookout. Along the pathway to Best of All Lookout are some gnarled ancient Antarctic beech trees, and the view from the lookout itself is phenomenal (indeed, best of all). There's an unstaffed **visitor information centre** at the end of Old School Rd, and 11 grassy campsites nearby at **Settlement Campground** (☎13 74 68; www.nprsr.qld.gov.au/parks/springbrook/camping.html; per person/family $5.45/21.80); book in advance. Alternatively, try **Mouses House** (☎07-5533 5192; www.mouseshouse.com.au; 2807 Springbrook Rd, Springbrook; r from $250, 2 nights from $430; ❄📶) – 12 lovely timber chalets linked by rainforest boardwalks.

The scenic **Natural Bridge** section, off the Nerang–Murwillumbah road, has a 1km walking circuit leading to a huge rock arch spanning a water-formed cave – home to a luminous colony of glow-worms.

The **Mount Cougal** section, accessed via Currumbin Creek Rd, has several waterfalls and swimming holes (watch out for submerged logs and slippery rocks). The heavily forested **Numinbah** section to the north is the fourth section of the park.

Lamington National Park

West of Springbrook, the 20,500-hectare **Lamington National Park** (www.nprsr.qld.gov.au/parks/lamington) is a precious ecological giant – it's the largest undisturbed tract of subtropical rainforest in Australia. Most of the park sits on a 900m-high plateau studded with beautiful gorges, waterfalls, thick subtropical rainforests and 160km of bushwalking trails.

The two most accessible sections of the park are the **Binna Burra** and **Green Mountains** sections, both reached via long, narrow, winding roads from Canungra (not great for big campervans). Binna Burra can also be reached from Nerang.

Bushwalks within the park include everything from short jaunts to multi-day epics. For experienced hikers, the Gold Coast Hinterland Great Walk is a three-day trip along a 54km path from the Green Mountains section to the Springbrook Plateau. Other favourites include the excellent Tree Top Canopy Walk along a series of rope-and-plank suspension bridges at Green Mountains, and the 21km Border Track that follows the dividing range between NSW and Queensland and links Binna Burra to Green Mountains.

Walking guides are available from the **ranger stations** (7.30am-4pm Mon-Fri, 9am-3.30pm Sat & Sun) at Binna Burra and Green Mountains.

Sleeping & Eating

Green Mountains Campground CAMPGROUND $

(13 74 68; www.nprsr.qld.gov.au/parks/lamington/camping.html; sites per person/family $5.45/22) There's a tiered national parks campground as you head down the hill from O'Reilly's. There are plenty of spots for tents and caravans (and a toilet/shower block); obtain permits in advance by phone or online.

Binna Burra Mountain Lodge GUESTHOUSE $$$

(1300 246 622, 07-5533 3622; www.binnaburralodge.com.au; 1069 Binna Burra Rd, Beechmont; unpowered/powered sites $28/35, safari tents from $55, d incl breakfast with/without bathroom $300/190, apt from $295) Stay in the lodge, in rustic log cabins, flashy new apartments or in a tent surrounded by forest in this atmospheric mountain retreat. The central restaurant (mains $20 to $40) has good views over the national park, and is open for breakfast, lunch and dinner. Organised activities include abseiling, guided walks, flying-fox flights and nightly nature documentaries. Transport to and from the lodge can be arranged upon request. The lodge also runs the cafe-style Teahouse (mains $14 to $18) a few hundred metres up the road, open 9am to 3pm.

O'Reilly's Rainforest Retreat GUESTHOUSE $$$

(1800 688 722, 07-5502 4911; www.oreillys.com.au; Lamington National Park Rd, Green Mountains; s/d from $163/278, 1-/2-bedroom villas from $400/435; @) Established in 1926, this famous Green Mountains guesthouse is still run by the O'Reilly family. The original guesthouse is a tad faded but retains a certain rustic charm – and sensational views! – but there's also a choice of luxury villas and newish 'mountain view' doubles. The **Discovery Centre** runs daily activities, including guided rainforest walks, glow-worm walks and 4WD tours (all at added cost), and free nightly nature documentaries. There's also a day spa, cafe, bar and a restaurant (mains $25 to $40), which is open for breakfast, lunch and dinner.

NOOSA & THE SUNSHINE COAST

From the tip of Bribie Island, the 'Sunny Coast' stretches north for 100 golden kilometres to the Cooloola Coast, just beyond the exclusive, leafy resort town of Noosa. The coast is perfect for surfing and swimming, and Mooloolaba – with its popular beach, outdoor eateries and cafes – is a firm favourite with holidaying Australian families.

Forming a stunning backdrop to this spectacular coastline are the ethereal Glass House Mountains. A little further north is the Sunshine Coast hinterland, home to the forested folds and ridges, gorges and waterfalls, lush green pastures and quaint villages of the Blackall Range.

The Sunshine Coast is also home to one of the world's great wildlife sanctuaries, the iconic Australia Zoo.

Getting There & Away

AIR

The Sunshine Coast Airport is at Mudjimba, 10km north of Maroochydore and 26km south of Noosa. **Jetstar** (13 15 38; www.jetstar.com.au) and **Virgin Australia** (13 67 89; www.virginaustralia.com) have daily flights from Sydney and Melbourne.

BUS

Greyhound Australia (1300 473 946; www.greyhound.com.au) has daily services from Brisbane to Caloundra ($25, two hours), Maroochydore ($25, two hours) and Noosa ($29, 2½ hours). **Premier Motor Service** (13 34 10; www.premierms.com.au) also services Maroochydore and Noosa from Brisbane.

Getting Around

Several companies offer transfers from the Sunshine Coast Airport and Brisbane to points along the coast. Fares from Brisbane cost $40 to $50. From the Sunshine Coast Airport fares are around $20 to $25.

Sunshine Coast

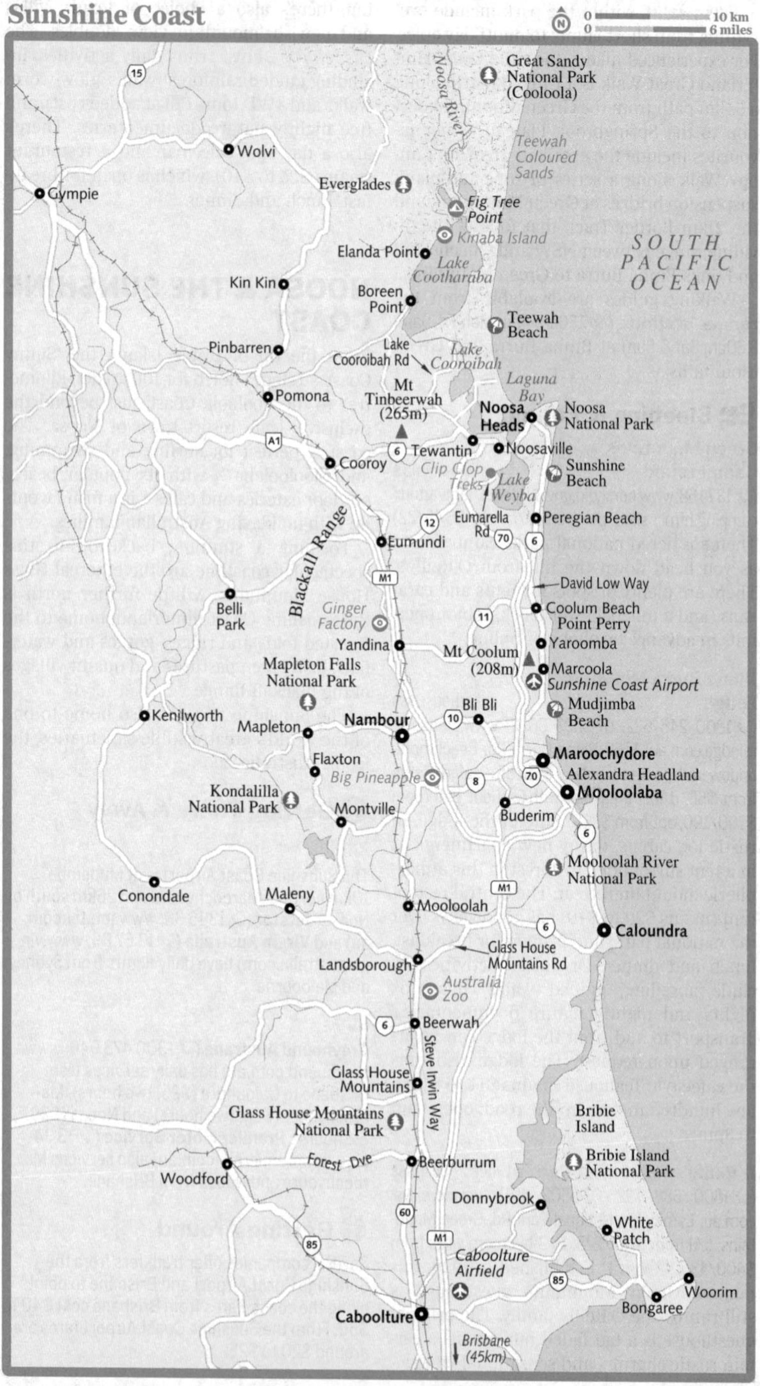
0 10 km
0 6 miles
Great Sandy National Park (Cooloola)
Noosa River
Teewah Coloured Sands
Wolvi
Gympie
Everglades
Fig Tree Point
Kinaba Island
Elanda Point
Lake Cootharaba
SOUTH PACIFIC OCEAN
Kin Kin
Boreen Point
Teewah Beach
Pinbarren
Lake Cooroibah Rd
Lake Cooroibah
Laguna Bay
Pomona
Mt Tinbeerwah (265m)
Noosa Heads
Noosa National Park
Tewantin
Noosaville
Cooroy
Clip Clop Treks
Lake Weyba
Sunshine Beach
Blackall Range
Eumarella Rd
Peregian Beach
Eumundi
David Low Way
Belli Park
Ginger Factory
Coolum Beach
Point Perry
Yandina
Mt Coolum (208m)
Yaroomba
Marcoola
Sunshine Coast Airport
Mapleton Falls National Park
Mudjimba Beach
Bli Bli
Kenilworth
Mapleton
Nambour
Flaxton
Maroochydore
Alexandra Headland
Big Pineapple
Mooloolaba
Kondalilla National Park
Montville
Buderim
Mooloolah River National Park
Conondale
Maleny
Mooloolah
Caloundra
Glass House Mountains Rd
Landsborough
Australia Zoo
Beerwah
Steve Irwin Way
Glass House Mountains
Glass House Mountains National Park
Bribie Island
Bribie Island National Park
Forest Dve
Woodford
Beerburrum
Donnybrook
White Patch
Caboolture Airfield
Woorim
Bongaree
Caboolture
Brisbane (45km)
15
A1
6
12
70
M1
11
10
8
60
85

The blue minibuses run by **Sunbus** (☎13 12 30) buzz frequently between Caloundra and Noosa. Sunbus also has regular buses from Noosa across to the train station at Nambour ($5, one hour) via Eumundi.

Col's Airport Shuttle (☎07-5450 5933; www.airshuttle.com.au)

Henry's (☎07-5474 0199; www.henrys.com.au)

Noosa Transfers & Charters (☎07-5450 5933; www.noosatransfers.com.au)

Sun-Air Bus Service (☎07-5477 0888, 1800 804 340; www.sunair.com.au)

TRAIN

Citytrain has services from Nambour to Brisbane ($22, two hours). Trains also go to Beerwah ($12, 1½ hours), near Australia Zoo.

Noosa

POP 9110

Once a little-known surfer hang-out, Noosa is now a stylish resort town and one of Queensland's star attractions. Noosa's stunning natural landscape of crystalline beaches and tropical rainforests blends seamlessly with its fashionable boulevard, Hastings St, and the sophisticated beach elite who flock here. On long weekends and school holidays, though, the flock becomes a migration, and narrow Hastings St a slow-moving file of traffic.

Beyond the glamour is a biosphere of gorgeous natural beauty where rugged bush and beach adventures are easy to find.

Sights

One of Noosa's best features, the lovely **Noosa National Park** (☎07-5447 3243; Hastings St; ⏲9am-3pm) covers the headland and offers fine walks, great coastal scenery and a string of bays with waves that draw surfers from all over the country. Clothes are optional at Alexandria Bay on the eastern side, an informal nudist beach.

The most scenic way to access the national park is to follow the boardwalk along the coast from town. Pick up a walking-track map from the **Queensland Parks & Wildlife Service (QPWS) centre** (⏲9am-3pm), at the entrance to the park. Sleepy koalas are often spotted in the trees near Tea Tree Bay and dolphins are commonly seen from the rocky headlands around Alexandria Bay.

For a panoramic view of the park, walk or drive up to Laguna Lookout (300m from Viewland Dr) in Noosa Junction.

Activities

Noosa River is excellent for canoeing and kayaking. It's possible to follow it north past beautiful homes through to Lakes Cooroibah and Cootharaba, and the Cooloola section of the Great Sandy National Park, just south of Rainbow Beach Rd. **Noosa Ocean Kayak Tours** (☎0418 787 577; www.noosakayaktours.com; 2hr tours $66, kayak hire per day $55) hires out kayaks and offers sea-kayaking tours around Noosa National Park and Noosa River.

For a more sedate experience, hop aboard the **Noosa Ferry** (☎07-5449 8442; per person $20), which cruises the waters of Noosa Sound on its popular BYO sunset cruise. It also has 90-minute round-trip cruises to Tewantin from the Sheraton jetty. A new ecologically minded 'biosphere' cruise ($45, 2½ hours) leaves on demand at 10am and includes a stop for morning tea.

Sunday morning sailing lessons are offered at **Noosa Yacht & Rowing Club** (☎07-5440 7407; www.nyrc.com.au; Chaplain Park, Gympie Tce) and further down-river at Boreen Point.

Numerous companies offer surf lessons and board hire, including **Merrick's Learn to Surf** (☎0418 787 577; www.learntosurf.com.au; 2hr lessons $60; ⏲9am & 1.30pm), **Go Ride A Wave** (☎1300 132 441; www.gorideawave.com.au; 2hr lessons $65, 2hr surfboard hire $25, 1hr stand-up paddleboard hire $30) and **Noosa Kite Surfing** (☎0458 909 012; www.noosakitesurfing.com.au; 2hr lessons $95).

Tours

A number of tour operators offer trips from Noosa to Fraser Island via the Cooloola Coast.

Fraser Island Adventure Tours ADVENTURE TOUR
(☎07-5444 6957; www.fraserislandadventuretours.com.au; day tours $165) The very popular day tour to Eli Creek and Lake McKenzie packs as much punch as a two-day tour.

Offbeat Ecotours ECOTOUR
(☎1300 023 835; www.offbeattours.com.au; full-day tours adult/child $155/110) These spirited day trips into the Noosa Hinterland – the 'oxygen tank' of Noosa – feature waterfall swimming, intimate encounters with ancient flora and a gourmet lunch to rival the Hastings St massive.

Noosa Heads

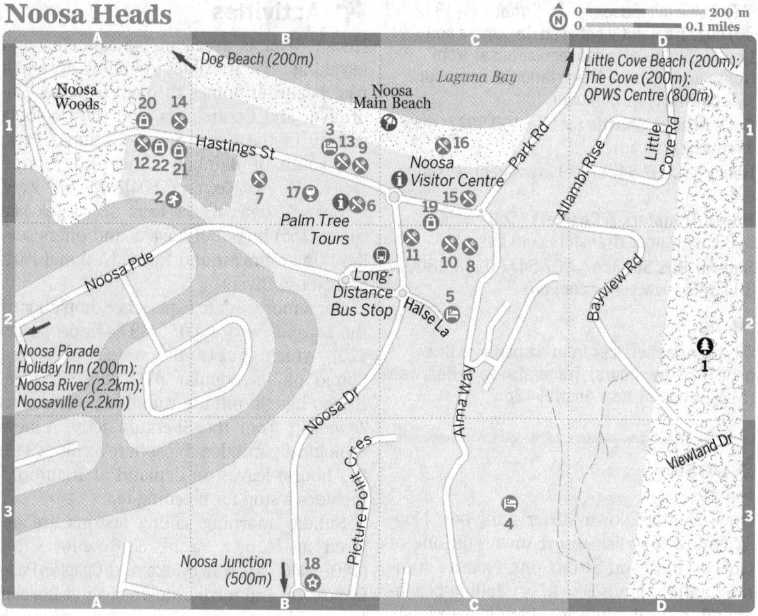

Noosa Heads

Sights
1 Noosa National Park ... D2

Activities, Courses & Tours
2 Noosa Ferry ... A1

Sleeping
3 Accom Noosa ... B1
4 Outriggers Little Hastings ... C3
5 YHA Halse Lodge ... C2

Eating
6 Aromas ... B1
7 Bay Village Shopping Centre Food Court ... B1
8 Berardo's ... C2
9 Bistro C ... B1
10 Café Le Monde ... C2
11 Gaston ... C2
12 Kaali ... A1
13 Laguna Bakery ... B1
14 Lindoni's ... A1
15 Massimo's ... C1
16 Noosa Heads SLSC ... C1

Drinking & Nightlife
17 Zachary's ... B1

Entertainment
18 Reef Hotel ... B3

Shopping
19 Dwyer's Bookstore ... C1
20 Lamington ... A1
21 Streets of Harlem ... A1
22 Summer & Salt ... A1

Sunset Safaris DRIVING TOUR
(☎1300 553 606; www.sunsetsafaris.com.au; 3-day safaris per person $389) A large operator that runs youth-oriented tours.

Discovery Group DRIVING TOUR
(☎07-5449 0393; www.thediscoverygroup.com.au; day tours adult/child $169/125) Visit Fraser island in a big 4WD truck. Includes a guided rainforest walk at Central Station and visits to Lakes Birrabeen and McKenzie. Also offers day tours exploring the Noosa everglades by 4WD and boat ($99/135 day/overnight).

Festivals & Events

Noosa Food & Wine Festival FOOD, WINE
(www.noosafoodandwine.com.au) May; a four-day tribute to great eating and drinking.

Noosa Long Weekend FOOD, FASHION
(www.noosalongweekend.com) June or July; 10 days of the arts, fashion and frivolity.

Noosa Jazz Festival JAZZ
(www.noosajazz.com.au) Late August; over four days, the festival draws talented musicians from across the globe.

🛏 Sleeping

Accom Noosa ACCOMMODATION SERVICES
(☑1800 072 078; www.accomnoosa.com.au; Shop 5, Fairshore Apartments, Hastings St, Noosa Heads) Accom Noosa is a good place to find short-term holiday rentals.

YHA Halse Lodge HOSTEL $
(☑1800 242 567; www.halselodge.com.au; 2 Halse Lane; members/non-members dm $29/32, d $78/86; @ 🛜) This restored Queenslander has survived the gentrification of Noosa Heads with indie reputation intact. Its elevated position amid scrub belies its close proximity to Main Beach, and the bar serves the best-value meals in town ($10 to 15). The dorms can feel stuffy but they are clean and staff are friendly.

Flashpackers HOSTEL $
(☑07-5455 4088; www.flashpackersnoosa.com; 102 Pacific Ave, Sunshine Beach; dm from $25, d from $65; ❄ 🛜 ❄) The Sunshine Beach backpacking scene has been given a boost by the arrival of this hip new family-run budget operation. Flashpackers challenges the flea-bitten status quo with pristine dorm rooms and an airy tropical design. Thoughtful touches include full-length mirrors, ample wall sockets and complimentary Friday-night sausage sizzle.

Nomads Backpackers HOSTEL $
(☑07-5447 3355; www.nomadshostels.com; 44 Noosa Dr; dm from $28; @ 🛜 ❄) At the notorious Nomads a good night's rest is not always an option; luckily the bar at this Noosa branch is a ripper. Dorms have a minimum of eight beds and while the kitchen facilities aren't the cleanest, staff are bubbly and knowledgeable and there's loads of shared space. The tour desk is helpful but we reckon you can just as easily book your own adventures.

Noosa River Holiday Park CARAVAN PARK $
(☑07-5449 7050; www.sunshinecoastholidayparks.com; 4 Russell St; unpowered/powered sites $34/42; 🛜) On the banks of the Noosa River, this is the closest camping facility to Noosa. Although it's a pretty spot, the strict regulations might make you reconsider camping here.

Anchor Motel Noosa MOTEL $$
(☑07-5449 8055; www.anchormotelnoosa.com.au; cnr Anchor St & Weyba Rd; r from $110; ❄ 🛜 ❄) Ships ahoy, this place is a bargain! There's nothing pretentious about the spotless, marine-themed rooms but all have bathrooms and small balconies, and some have king-sized beds. The shared space around the pool and barbecue are good launching pads for a night out in Noosaville.

Islander Noosa Resort RESORT $$
(☑07-5440 9200; www.islandernoosa.com.au; 187 Gympie Tce; 2-/3-bedroom villas $200/250; ❄ @ 🛜 ❄) A mainstay of Noosaville's tropical resort scene, the Islander is best suited to families with aquatic-minded kids or those looking to stay at home among lush gardens. Some rooms are a little tired but the three pools are classy and the on-site Moondoggy's Cafe is an institution (and welcomes pets).

The Cove APARTMENT $$
(☑5447 4111; www.thecovenoosa.com.au; cnr Park Rd & Little Cove Rd; 2-bedroom apt from $200;

QUEENSLAND & THE GREAT BARRIER REEF NOOSA

EUMUNDI

Sweet little Eumundi is a quaint highland village with a quirky New-Age vibe greatly amplified during its famous market days.

➜ The **Eumundi markets** (☉6.30am-2pm Sat, 8am-1pm Wed) attract thousands of visitors to their 300-plus stalls and have everything from hand-crafted furniture and jewellery to homemade clothes and alternative-healing booths, plus food and live music.

➜ **Hidden Valley B&B** (☑07-5442 8685; www.eumundibed.com; 39 Caplick Way; r $175-195; 🛜 ❄) is an attractive Queenslander 400m from Eumundi on the Noosa road, with wildly designed thematic rooms with balconies.

➜ **Gridley Homestead** (☑07-5442 7197; www.gridley.com.au; 1 Sale St, Eumundi; d from $185) is another semi-posh option in a beautiful home.

Sunbus runs hourly from Noosa Heads ($4.20, 40 minutes) and Nambour ($5.10, 30 minutes). A number of Noosa tour operators visit the Eumundi markets.

(P ❄ ≋) Opposite charming Little Cove Beach, this well-managed, low-key resort has spacious, bright apartments that suit longer stays. The bathrooms have been recently updated and the tiled floors and airy bedrooms are perfect for those hot summer days. There's an excellent pool in the internal courtyard and the popular penthouse suites have outdor spas. It's a five-minute walk downhill to Hastings St.

Noosa Parade Holiday Inn APARTMENT $$
(☎07-5447 4177; www.noosaparadeholidayinn.com; 51 Noosa Pde; r $125; ❄ ≋) A long way from the pages of glossy magazines but close enough to walk to Hastings St, these bright apartments are quiet and comfortable.

Noosa River Retreat APARTMENT $$
(☎07-5474 2811; www.noosariverretreat.net; cnr Weyba Rd & Reef St; studios $110; ❄ @ ≋) Excellent in-room and on-site facilities make this complex a decent place to stay despite the awkward location and traffic noise. Small native gardens surround the better corner units though all are spacious for the price.

Outriggers Little Hastings RESORT $$$
(☎07-5449 2277; www.outrigger.com; Viewland Dr, access via Little Cove Rd after 7pm; 1-/2-bedroom apt $269/339) The newest addition to the luxury scene is in a relatively secluded section – a dead-end road – on the Hastings St side of the national park. The Outriggers is typically stylish with clean lines and soft colours throughout. Balconies and windows look out on thick greenery, and there is ample space for a post-hill-climb cocktail party.

Eating

Noosa has a fabulous dining scene. For quick bites, you can eat well for around $10 at the **Bay Village Shopping Centre food court** (Hastings St, Noosa Heads). Self-caterers can stock up at the Noosa Fair Shopping Centre.

Noosa Heads & Hastings Street

Head to Hastings St and Noosa Heads for sophisticated dining. Noosaville is growing in stature, while Noosa Junction has more affordable options.

Laguna Bakery BAKERY $
(☎07-5447 2606; 3/49 Hastings St) Friendly bakery with strong coffee and yummy pastries to go.

Massimo's GELATI $
(Hastings St; gelati $2-4; ⊙9am-10pm) Definitely one of the best *gelaterias* in Queensland.

Café Le Monde MODERN AUSTRALIAN $$
(Hastings St; mains $15-28; ⊙breakfast, lunch & dinner) Opposite the surf club, but with plum street views, Le Monde offers classic Noosa dining: attractive and attentive staff, huge menu running throughout the day, family friendly yet still somehow hip. Food-wise, the pick is the burgers. Happy-hour drinks are a real scene and live music is a regular feature.

Bistro C MODERN AUSTRALIAN $$
(☎07-5447 2855; Hastings St, On the Beach Resort; mains $25-35; ⊙breakfast, lunch & dinner) While service can be a little hectic at peak times, the location and food consistency are still unrivalled in Noosa. It works just as well for breakfast – try the eggs Benedict with corn fritters – as it does for mocktails in the late afternoon or seafood pasta at night.

Noosa Heads SLSC INTERNATIONAL $$
(Hastings St; mains $12-33; ⊙breakfast Sat & Sun, lunch & dinner daily) While some may baulk at lining up for your food, the meals here are delicious, ranging from seafood to steak and stir fry. The turnover is incredible in high season and the perfect beach views from the deck are hard to resist.

Gaston MODERN AUSTRALIAN $$
(5/50 Hastings St; mains $17-25; ⊙breakfast, lunch & dinner) Less stuffy than some of the more frequented Hastings St restaurants, Gaston excels in uncomplicated bistro food. The lunch special ($17 for a main and a drink) and dinner special ($50 for two mains and a bottle of wine) are superb value.

Kaali INDIAN $$
(☎07-5474 8989; 2/2 Hastings St; mains $19-29) Popular Kaali adds a welcome subcontinental twist to the Hastings St dining scene. Dishes are fairly typical Indian fare with lively spice varieties and generous portions. The Goan fish curry and the lamb shanks are both excellent; otherwise, pay attention to the specials board.

Aromas CAFE $$
(32 Hastings St; mains $10-28; ⊙breakfast, lunch & dinner) Come to Aromas for coffee, cake and eavesdropping beneath the chandeliers. It's a great meeting place in the heart of the foot traffic, and the light meals are passable.

Lindoni's ITALIAN $$$

(☎07-5447 5111; Hastings St; mains $20-50; ⏲dinner) Faultless Italian romanticism could easily falter on the Sunshine Coast but this Hastings St favourite still draws attention for its fine service and dining. Think Positano and the Amalfi coast – with lashings of *amore*. Try the *saltimbocca* and anything from the wine list.

Berardo's MODERN AUSTRALIAN $$$

(☎07-5447 5666; Hastings St; mains $30-42; ⏲dinner) Still Noosa's most celebrated restaurant, Berardo's is a study in contemporary cuisine inspired by the decor of yesteryear. With its classically trained musicians and impeccable waitstaff, this is the place for intimate celebration. The produce is almost all sourced locally and highlights include free-range duck breast, Kilcoy eye fillet and tuna *tataki*.

Noosaville & Around

Check out the strip along Thomas St or Gibson St. Many places here are BYO, so stock up on wine and beer beforehand.

Burger Bar BURGERS $

(4 Thomas St; burgers $10-15; ⏲11am-9pm; ✎) This informal, quirky venue whips up hormone-free, vegetarian, and weird and wonderful burgerian delights. Try the chilli-laden Afterburner.

Gusto MODERN AUSTRALIAN $$

(☎07-5449 7144; 257 Gympie Tce; mains $25-35; ⏲lunch & dinner) Gusto matches Noosa's classy competition with effortless style, superior service and breezy river views. The Mod Oz menu includes Hervey Bay scallops, veal fillets, Mooloolaba prawns and local fried cuttlefish.

Humid MODERN AUSTRALIAN $$

(☎07-5449 9755; 195 Weyba Rd; mains $25-30; ⏲lunch & dinner Wed-Sun; ✎) In an unassuming location near the footy ground, Humid is in a double-storey warehouse conversion that serves booze downstairs before seducing you upstairs with delicious, affordable food. The female duo in charge are respected for their innovative fare, which features rabbit pie, roasted barramundi and a creative vegetarian menu.

Embassy XO CHINESE $$

(☎07-5455 4460; 56 Duke St, Sunshine Beach; mains $25-35) A classy addition to the humble Duke St precinct, Embassy XO is at least one hat above the usual Chinese fare. The exquisite banquet ($55 per person) or the weekend *yum cha* are good entry points into this hot new place that serves up inventive dishes like rice-encrusted snapper and five-spiced ocean trout.

Wasabi JAPANESE $$

(☎07-5449 2443; 2 Quamby Pl; mains $20-33; ⏲dinner Tue-Sun, lunch Fri & Sat) Choose between *oshinagaki* (starters) like tiger prawn tempura or raw venison, then proceed to *futari* (two-person dishes) such as charcoal soba noodles or spatchcock teriyaki. Wasabi is right on the Noosa River.

iPazzi ITALIAN $$

(☎07-5412 2841; 28-30 Sunshine Beach Rd, Noosa Junction; mains $16-30) A passionate Sicilian couple runs this authentic little restaurant in unfashionable Noosa Junction. A steady clientele of locals enjoys the homemade, mostly organic Italian food.

Thomas Corner MODERN AUSTRALIAN $$

(cnr Thomas St & Gympie Tce; mains $16-33; ⏲lunch & dinner) A much revered local chef has opened this relaxed diner on a prime Noosaville corner. It's a casual alfresco restaurant with concrete and wooden decor and the locally sourced food is similary understated: pork shoulder baguettes, wagyu brisket and marinated sardines are all delicious.

Drinking & Entertainment

Zachary's BAR

(30 Hastings St) With new venues in Noosaville and Peregian Beach, Zachary's has the late-night pizza and all-day cocktail crowd sewn up. The original on Hastings St is still the best.

KB's BAR

(44 Noosa Dr, Noosa Junction) The Koala Bar is still the venue of choice for young cosmopolitans who prefer their beer in plastic and their music in chorus-laden loops. Unpack your dirty laundry on the dance floor or reminisce about a time before you owned a suitcase.

Noosa Yacht Club YACHT CLUB

(Gympie Tce) The pub food is OK but anywhere you can drink cheap stubbies overlooking a natural body of water is a destination in its own right. Sailing lessons available on Sundays.

J LIVE MUSIC
(☎07-5455 4455; www.thej.com.au; 60 Noosa Dr, Noosa Junction) The J, aka the Junction, showcases a broad range of artistic, cultural and musical performances from world and rock to classical. Check the website for event details.

Reef Hotel LIVE MUSIC
(☎07-5447 4477; 9 Noosa Dr; ⊙11am-midnight Sun-Thu, to 3am Fri & Sat) The renovation may be a little soulless but there's live music during the week and the downstairs club cranks until 3am on Friday and Saturday nights.

Noosa Arts Theatre THEATRE
(www.noosaartstheatre.org.au; 163 Weyba Rd, Noosaville) High drama to ostentatious adaptation at this friendly community theatre.

Noosa 5 Cinemas CINEMA
(☎07-5447 5130; www.noosacinemas.com.au; 29 Sunshine Beach Rd, Noosa Junction) This plush, comfortable cinema screens the latest blockbusters.

Shopping

Summer & Salt CLOTHING
(7/14 Hastings St; ⊙9.30am-5pm) While most discerning beach bums would never be seen dead in a 'rashie', a local designer has released a stylish range of the sun-safe, skintight tops and opened a second store in Noosa.

Lamington GIFTS
(☎07-5447 5773; www.lamington.net.au; 1/5 Hastings St; ⊙9.30am-5pm) Find gifts you didn't know you needed at this charming store.

Streets of Harlem CLOTHING
(☎07-5455 4109; 8 Hastings St; ⊙9.30am-5pm) Urban youth fashion and excellent coffee. The industrial design is not exactly sunny but even the sun can be a drag sometimes.

Noosa Marina Sunday Markets MARKET
(⊙8am-2pm) Catch the Noosa River Ferry down to Tewantin for the buzzing weekend market for live music, local produce and cheap clothing.

Dwyer's Bookstore BOOKS
(Shop 5, Laguna, Hastings St) Good range of new fiction.

River Read BOOKS
(☎07-5473 0483; 6 Thomas St, Noosaville; ⊙9.30am-4.30pm) Friendly bookstore and cafe with excellent children's section.

Information

The forward-thinking council did away with traffic lights some years back, which has led to an unusual number of roundabouts, so know thy exit. Broadly speaking, Noosa encompasses three zones: Noosa Heads (around Laguna Bay and Hastings St), Noosaville (along the Noosa River) and Noosa Junction (the administrative centre).

Noosa Visitor Centre (☎07-5430 5020; www.visitnoosa.com.au; Hastings St, Noosa Heads; ⊙9am-5pm)

Palm Tree Tours (☎07-5474 9166; www.palmtreetours.com.au; Bay Village Shopping Centre, Hastings St; ⊙9am-5pm) Very helpful tour desk. Can book tours, accommodation and bus tickets.

Post Office (91 Noosa Dr)

Urban Mailbox (Ocean Breeze, Noosa Dr; per 15min $3; ⊙8am-8pm) Internet access.

Getting There & Around

Long-distance buses stop at the bus stop near the corner of Noosa Dr and Noosa Pde. Most hostels have courtesy pick-ups, except YHA Halse Lodge, which is 100m away. The state-of-the-art Noosa Junction station opened in 2012 and now acts as the bus hub for the region.

Sunbus has frequent services to Maroochydore ($5, one hour) and the Nambour train station ($5, one hour).

During peak holiday seasons (26 December to 10 January and over Easter), free shuttle buses travel between Weyba Rd (just outside Noosa Junction) and Tewantin, stopping just about everywhere in between.

Noosa Bike Hire (☎07-5474 3322; www.noosabikehire.com; per 4hr/day $23/39) hires out bicycles from several locations in Noosa, including Nomads Backpackers and Flashpackers. Alternatively, bikes are delivered free to your door.

Scooter Style (☎07-5449 7733; www.scooterstyle.com.au; 207 Gympie Tce, Noosaville; per day from $65) hires out zippy scooters.

Noosa Ferry operates ferries between Noosa Heads and Tewantin (one way adult/child/family $13/4.50/30, all-day pass $20/6/49, 30 minutes).

Car rental starts at about $50 per day with **Noosa Car Rentals** (☎0429 053 728; www.noosacarrentals.com.au).

Glass House Mountains

Rising high above the green subtropical hinterland are the 16 volcanic crags known as the Glass House Mountains. Mt Beerwah (556m), the highest of these ethereal cor-

CREATURE FEATURE: AUSTRALIA ZOO

Just north of Beerwah is one of Queensland's, if not Australia's, most famous tourist attractions. **Australia Zoo** (☎07-5494 1134; www.australiazoo.com.au; Steve Irwin Way, Beerwah; adult/child/family $59/35/172; ⏲9am-5pm) is a fitting homage to its founder, zany celebrity wildlife enthusiast Steve Irwin. As well as all things slimy and scaly, the zoo has an amazing wildlife menagerie and features a Cambodian-style Tiger Temple, the Asian-themed Elephantasia, as well as the famous Crocoseum. There are macaws, birds of prey, giant tortoises, snakes, otters, camels, and more crocs and critters than you can poke a stick at. Plan to spend a full day at this amazing wildlife park.

Various companies offer tours from Brisbane and the Sunshine Coast. The zoo operates a free courtesy bus from towns along the coast, as well as from the Beerwah train station (bookings essential).

nices, is the mother according to Dreaming mythology.

Hikers are spoilt for choice here. If you're in a hurry, the **Glass House Mountains lookout** provides a fine view of the peaks and the distant beaches. The **lookout circuit** (800m) is a short and steep walking track that leads through open scribbly-gum forest and down a wet gully before circling back.

For something more intense, check out the 1.4km (return) hike to the summit of **Mount Ngungun** (253m). It has impressive views of the four major peaks and a bit of challenging hiking – keep the kids close as the steep trail passes close to the cliff line and can be slippery.

For some mountainside parkour, otherwise known as 'bouldering', leg it up **Tibrogargan** (3km return) and **Beerwah** (2.6km return); you'll need good shoes and leg muscles to spring up the patches of loose rock.

Reach the Glass House Mountains National Park via a series of sealed and unsealed roads off Steve Irwin Way. Coming from the Bruce Hwy (Rte 1), take the Landsborough exit.

Sleeping & Eating

Glass House Mountains Ecolodge LODGE $$
(☎07-5493 0008; www.glasshouseecolodge.com; 198 Barrs Rd, Glass House Mountains; r $45-185) This novel retreat, overseen by a keen environmentalist, is close to Australia Zoo and offers a range of good-value sleeping options, including the cosy Orchard Room ($105) and the converted Church Loft ($175), each with polished floorboards and tremendous views of Mt Tibrogargan. It's the ideal base to explore the region. Pick-ups available from Glass House Mountains station.

Glasshouse Mountains Holiday Village CAMPING $
(☎07-5496 9338; www.glasshousemountainsholidayvillage.com.au; 778 Steve Irwin Way, Glass House Mountains; unpowered/powered sites $25/35, cabins from $110; ❄🏊) Accommodation in the park is limited. Glasshouse Mountains Holiday Village has comfortable, self-contained cabins, scrappy sites and spectacular mountain views.

Glasshouse Mountains Tavern PUB $$
(10 Reed St, Glass House Mountains; mains $15-25; ⏲lunch & dinner) This fine country swill hall serves good pub grub and icy-cold beer.

Caloundra

POP 20,200

The Sunshine Coast's southernmost suburb is a sprawling beach community of seven surf beaches linked up by a fine promenade running north to Currimundi. With loads of beachfront cafes – and a grand backdrop of the Glass House Mountains – Caloundra is popular with holidaying families and weekenders from Brisbane.

Sights & Activities

Caloundra's beaches curve around the headland so you'll always find a sheltered beach no matter how windy it gets. **Bulcock Beach**, just down from the main street and pinched by the northern tip of Bribie Island, captures a good wind tunnel, making it popular with kite surfers. There's a lovely promenade on the foreshore that extends around to **Kings Beach**, where there's a kiddie-friendly interactive water feature, and a free saltwater swimming pool on the rocks. Depending on the conditions, **Moffat Beach** and **Dickey Beach** have the best surf breaks.

Caloundra Surf School SURFING
(☎0413 381 010; www.caloundrasurfschool.com; lessons per person from $45) The pick of the surf schools, with board hire also available.

Blue Water Kayak Tours KAYAKING
(☎07-5494 7789; www.bluewaterkayaktours.com; half-/full-day tours minimum 4 people $80/150) Blue Water Kayak Tours runs an excellent day trip for active souls to the northern tip of Bribie Island.

Caloundra Cruise CRUISE
(☎07-5492 8280; www.caloundracruise.com; adult/child/family $20/10/52) Caloundra Cruise has a great 1½-hour eco-explorer cruise through the Pumicestone Passage.

Sunshine Coast Skydivers SKYDIVING
(☎07-54370211; www.sunshinecoastskydivers.com.au; Caloundra Aerodrome; tandem jumps from $249) Get a bird's-eye view of Caloundra with the popular Sunshine Coast Skydivers.

Sleeping

There's often a minimum three-night stay in high season.

Caloundra Backpackers HOSTEL $
(☎07-5499 7655; www.caloundrabackpackers.com.au; 84 Omrah Ave; dm/d $28/65; @ 📶) A practical budget option with a popular lounge and two decent kitchens. The dorms are a little bland but it's peaceful and well located. There is free bike, surfboard and stand-up paddleboard hire.

Dicky Beach Family Holiday Park CAMPING GROUND $
(☎07-5491 3342; www.dicky.com.au; 4 Beerburrum St; unpowered/powered sites $32/35, cabins from $90; ❄ 📶 🏊) You can't get any closer to one of Caloundra's most popular beaches. The brick cabins are as ordered and tidy as the grounds and there's a small swimming pool for the kids.

City Centre Motel MOTEL $$
(☎07-5491 3301; www.mymotel.net.au; 20 Orsovar Tce; d $109-129; ❄) The Golden Chain motel is the closest to the city centre. The seven rooms are basic and comfortable.

Rumba Resort RESORT $$$
(☎07-5492 0555; www.rumbaresort.com.au; Leeding Tce, Bulcock Beach; r from $260) This new five-star resort is ultra trendy for Caloundra. Staff are positively buoyant and the rooms and pool area live up to the hype.

Eating & Drinking

The Bulcock Beach esplanade has a number of alfresco cafes and restaurants, all with perfect sea views.

Saltwater@Kings CAFE $$
(☎07-5437 2260; 8 Levuka Ave, Kings Beach; mains $16-38; ⏲breakfast, lunch & dinner) The most established restaurant in town is on King's Beach. We loved the cheesy gnocchi pudding with crab and the chook breast pocket but others rave about the spoon-licking desserts.

La Dolce Vita ITALIAN $$
(☎07-5438 2377; Shop 1, Rumba Resort, 10 Leeding Tce; mains $20-35; ⏲breakfast, lunch & dinner) This modern Italian restaurant has a stylish black-and-white theme, but it's best to sit outdoors behind the large glass-windowed booth for alfresco dining with gorgeous sea views.

Tides SEAFOOD $$$
(☎07-5438 2304; 26 Esplanade, Bulcock Beach; mains $35-50; ⏲lunch & dinner) The views of the Pumicestone Passage are matched by the seafood and steak at this high-end restaurant, though you'll pay for the privilege.

CBX PUB
(12 Bulcock St) Live bands and DJs on weekends make this the local party scene. Pub meals available.

Information

Sunshine Coast Visitor Centre (☎07-5478 2233; 7 Caloundra Rd; ⏲9am-5pm) On the roundabout at the entrance to the town. There's also a kiosk in the main street.

Getting There & Away

The **bus terminal** (Cooma Tce) is one block back from Bulcock Beach. **Sunbus** (☎13 12 30) runs shuttles to Noosa ($6.60, 1½ hours) that stop in Maroochydore ($3.70, 50 minutes). **Greyhound** (☎1300 473 946; www.greyhound.com.au) has buses to/from Brisbane ($36, two hours).

Maroochy

POP 47,000

The Sunshine Coast suburbs of Maroochydore, Alexandra Headland and Mooloolaba, collectively known as Maroochy, were once bastions of the Australian surfing scene, but these days their coastal charm is giving way to a steady suburban sprawl and ugly high-rise development.

The beaches themselves are still captivating, though. Mooloolaba is perhaps the hippest of the bunch, having the longest beaches, the most consistent surf and a plethora of cafes, shops and colourful rental houses.

Maroochydore takes its name from the local Aboriginal word, *murukutchi-da*, meaning 'home of the black swan'.

Sights & Activities

Underwater World AQUARIUM
(☎07-5458 6280; www.underwaterworld.com.au; Wharf, Mooloolaba; adult/child/family $35/23/96; ⏰9am-5pm) New enclosures at Queensland's largest oceanarium include the Turtle Temple and Bay of Rays. There's also a touch tank, seal shows and educational spiels to entertain both kids and adults.

Scuba World DIVING
(☎07-5444 8595; www.scubaworld.com.au; Wharf, Mooloolaba; dives from $119; ⏰9am-5pm Mon-Sat, 10.30am-4pm Sun) These guys arrange shark dives (certified/uncertified divers $195/245) at Underwater World, coral dives off the coast and a wreck dive of the ex-HMAS *Brisbane*. Professional Association of Diving Instructors (PADI) courses are available.

Steve Irwin's Whale One WHALE WATCHING
(☎1800 942 531; www.whaleone.com.au; The Wharf, Parkyn Pde; adult/child/family $119/79/320) For those who can't make it north to Hervey Bay, these whale-watching cruises in September and October are held on a fairly luxurious vessel.

Robbie Sherwell's XL Surfing Academy SURFING
(☎07-5478 1337; www.robbiesherwell.com.au; 1hr lessons private/group $95/45) Book a lesson with surfing legend Robbie Sherwell at his established school based in Mooloolaba.

Sunshine Coast Bike & Board Hire SURFBOARD RENTAL
(☎0439 706 206; www.adventurehire.com.au) Hires out surfboards (per day $25), bikes (per day $30) and bodyboards (per day $30).

Hire Hut KAYAK RENTAL
(☎07-5444 0366; www.oceanjetski.com.au; Wharf, Parkyn Pde, Mooloolaba) Hires out kayaks ($25 per two hours), stand-up paddleboards ($35 per two hours), jet skis ($100 per hour) and boats ($42/75 per hour/half-day).

Sleeping

Mooloolaba Beach Backpackers HOSTEL $
(☎07-5444 3399; www.mooloolababackpackers.com; 75 Brisbane Rd; dm/d $28/70; @ 📶 🏊) Pretty rough around the edges but it's the only real backpackers in the area and it's only 500m to the beach. Avoid the self-catering facilities and concentrate on taking advantage of the free bikes, kayaks, surfboards and stand-up paddleboards.

Mooloolaba Beach Caravan Park CAMPING GROUND $
(☎07-5444 1201; www.maroochypark.qld.gov.au; Parkyn Pde; powered sites from $35) This little beauty fronts lovely Mooloolaba Beach.

Kyamba Court Motel MOTEL $$
(☎07-5444 0202; www.kyambacourtmotel.com.au; 94 Brisbane Rd; d Mon-Fri $95, Sat $130; ❄ 📶 🏊) Exceptional value for the over-inflated Mooloola region, Kyamba fronts the canal and has large, comfortable rooms. It's a short walk into town and to the beach.

Landmark Resort RESORT $$
(☎07-5444 5555; www.landmarkresort.com.au; cnr Esplanade & Burnett St; studios/1-bedroom apt from $170/230; ❄ @ 📶 🏊) A trusted skyrise with superlative views and a plum location 20m from Mooloolaba's cafe strip and beach. There's a heated lagoon-style pool, and a rooftop spa and barbecue.

Coral Sea Apartments APARTMENT $$
(☎07-5479 2999; www.coralsea-apartments.com; 35-37 Sixth Ave; 1-/2-bedroom apt from $160/190; ❄ @ 🏊) These tastefully furnished apartments with balconies occupy a lovely spot close to Maroochy Surf Club and the beach.

Eating

Nude CAFE $
(Shop 3, Mooloolaba Esplanade; dishes $6-18; ⏰breakfast & lunch) After a successful stint at Cotton Tree, this alfresco cafe has hit the Esplanade and makes the ideal spot for people-watching, and for ocean views with your latte or fresh sandwich.

Raw Energy CAFE $
(Mantra, Esplanade; dishes $6-18; ⏰breakfast & lunch) In this popular beachside cafe, pretty young things serve up tofu, tempeh and gluten-free meals with 'zinger' juices. Muffin addicts will think they've found The One.

Mojo's CAFE $
(☎07-5443 3341; 2/1 King St, Cotton Tree; sandwiches $6-9) Mojo's is one of those East Coast Oz surf cafes that churn out the health shakes, juices, salads and sandwiches. Everyone on both sides of the counter is pretty,

healthy and hungry for more. It's fairly organic and sensitive to dietary requirements.

Boat Shed SEAFOOD $$
(☎07-5443 3808; Esplanade, Cotton Tree; mains $25-35; ⊙lunch daily, dinner Mon-Sat) The location on the Maroochy River complements the enticing seafood starter menu but the service fell short when we visited. A safe bet is to drink cocktails at sunset under the cotton trees and maybe nibble at seared scallops or tuna carpaccio ($19 each) as the mood takes you.

Karma Waters MODERN AUSTRALIAN $$
(Mantra, Esplanade; mains $21-32; ⊙breakfast, lunch & dinner) Another outdoor eatery along the lively Esplanade, Karma Waters dishes up Mod Oz cuisine with a Portuguese influence.

Bella Venezia ITALIAN $$$
(☎07-5444 5844; 95 Esplanade; mains $25-38; ⊙lunch & dinner) Locals gather at this arcade restaurant and wine bar that serves delicious Aus-Italian food and strictly Italian wines. The duck salad, veal meatballs and the entire *secondi* menu are highly recommended.

Drinking & Nightlife

★**Mooloolaba SLSC** SURF CLUB
(Esplanade; ⊙10am-10pm Sun-Thu, to midnight Fri & Sat) Right on the beach, Mooloolaba's iconic surf club has floor-to-ceiling windows affording stunning views during the day and suntanned dance-floor antics by night. The food is also very good.

Club WT CLUB
(Wharf, Parkyn Pde; ⊙Tue & Thu-Sat) At this hi-tech club, formerly known as Friday's, the dance-floor antics are still the same. It's inside the otherwise family-friendly Wharf Tavern.

Information

Sunshine Coast Visitor Information Centre (☎1800 644 969; www.maroochytourism.com; ⊙9am-5pm) Maroochydore (cnr Sixth Ave & Melrose St); Mooloolaba (cnr Brisbane Rd & First Ave); Sunshine Coast Airport (Friendship Dr, Sunshine Coast Airport)

Getting There & Around

Long-distance buses stop in front of Maroochydore's Sunshine Coast visitor information centre. **Sunbus** (☎13 12 30) has frequent services between Mooloolaba and Maroochydore ($2) and on to Noosa. The local bus interchange is at the Sunshine Plaza.

Around Maroochy

Coolum Beach and **Peregian Beach** are both favourites with local surfers when there's a good swell. **Point Perry** is a wonderful vantage point for that quintessential Aussie summer snap, while intrepid photographers (and anyone else for that matter) can climb **Mount Coolum** (208m) for bird's-eye vistas. Get details at the **visitor information office** (David Low Way; ⊙9am-5pm Mon-Fri, 10am-4pm Sat) – look for it off the main drag from Maroochy towards Coolum and Peregian.

Sleeping

Villa Coolum MOTEL $
(☎07-5446 1286; www.villacoolum.com; 102 Coolum Tce, Coolum Beach; r $79-99;) Spacious motel-style rooms fronting a long balcony.

Coolum Beach Caravan Park CAMPING GROUND $
(☎1800 461 474; David Low Way, Coolum; sites unpowered/powered $32/35) Beachfront and basic with plenty of grass on which to shake the sand from your undies.

Retreat Beach Houses HOLIDAY HOUSE $$
(☎07-5448 1922; www.theretreat.com.au; 390 David Low Way, Peregian Beach; house from $165; P) These gorgeous modern houses nestled in sand dunes have their own private track to Peregian Beach.

Eating

Spirit House THAI $$
(☎07-5446 8977; www.spirithouse.com.au; 20 Nindery Rd, Yandina; mains $20-25;) This new contemporary Asian restaurant and cooking school is considered by foodies to be among the finest of its type in Australia.

Pitchfork MODERN AUSTRALIAN $$
(☎07-5471 3697; 5/4 Kingfisher Dr, Peregian Beach; mains $25-35) On the edge of the Peregian Beach square, Pitchfork is an unsung hero of the Sunshine Coast eating scene. Crispy fried soft-shell crab ($17) and hot smoked salmon linguini ($29) were both tremendous. Best of all, it's BYO and there's a bottle shop next door!

Cooloola Coast

Running from its southern tip at Noosa to Rainbow Beach in the north is 50km of gloriously undeveloped Cooloola Coast. Wildlife abounds, but a fair amount of 4WD through-traffic means your starry nights are not always spent in silence.

Nevertheless, travelling north here is a real buzz, as you forgo the bitumen for low tidal highways, passing the Teewah Coloured Sands and the wreck of the *Cherry Venture,* swept ashore in 1973.

Lake Cooroibah

Where the Noosa River widens into the wondrous Lake Cooroibah, you'll find surprisingly thick bushland – a popular base for engaging with the natural environment.

Lake Cooroibah is about 2km north of Tewantin. From the end of Moorindil St in Tewantin, you can catch the **Noosa North Shore Ferry** (07-5447 1321; per pedestrian/car one way $1/6; 5.30am-10.20pm Sun-Thu, 5am-12.20am Fri & Sat) up to the lake in a conventional vehicle and camp along sections of the beach.

Gagaju Backpackers (1300 302 271, 07-5474 3522; www.tripod.com/gagaju; 118 Johns Dr, Tewantin; unpowered sites/dm $10/15; @) is a riverside eco-wilderness camp with basic dorms constructed out of recycled timber. There's a somewhat hands-off managerial approach, unless a good party is involved! Don't forget to bring food and mozzie repellent. A courtesy shuttle runs to and from Noosa twice a day.

A touch more luxury is found at the **Noosa North Shore Retreat** (07-5447 1225; www.noosanorthshoreretreat.com.au; Beach Rd; unpowered/powered sites from $15/24, r from $145, cabins from $65; @). Choose from a tent or a shiny motel room, then break up your day with stints paddling around the lake, bushwalking or tracking marsupials.

There's also the recently overhauled **Great Sandy Bar & Restaurant** (Noosa North Shore Retreat; mains $15-25; lunch & dinner; P), a great place for a long lunch or to mark the beginning and end of a 4WD adventure.

Lake Cootharaba

A little further northwest of Tewantin is Lake Cootharaba, the gateway to the Noosa everglades, offering bushwalking, canoeing and bush camping. This pretty water reserve is some 10km long and 5km across. A good entry to the lake is at **Boreen Point**, a relaxed little community with several places to stay and to eat.

From Boreen Point, an unsealed road leads another 5km up to **Elanda Point**.

For kayaking enthusiasts, **Kanu Kapers** (07-5485 3328; www.kanukapersaustralia.com; 11 Toolara St, Boreen Point; kayak hire per day $65) offers guided or self-guided trips (per person $75, overnight trip $115) into the everglades. **Lake Escapades** (07-5641 4473; www.lakeescapades.com.au; 49 Laguna St, Boreen Point; canoe hire per day per person $99, 3-day camping safaris $139) hires out canoes and kayaks for self-guided trips. The company also operates a water taxi to Kinaba (one way/return $15/30).

On the river, the quiet and simple **Boreen Point Camping Ground** (07-5485 3244; Teewah St, Dun's Beach, Boreen Point; unpowered/powered sites $15/22) is dominated by large gums and native bush, while the two self-contained **Lake Cootharaba Gallery Units** (07-5485 3153; 64 Laguna St, Boreen Point; r from $99;) are homey and practical.

The **Apollonian Hotel** (07-5485 3100; Laguna St, Boreen Point; mains $12-30; lunch & dinner) is a gorgeous old pub with sturdy timber walls, shady verandahs and a beautifully preserved interior. The pub grub is tasty and popular, especially the Sunday spit-roast lunch which always features live local music. You can sleep very comfortably in restored railway quarters ($65).

Great Sandy National Park (Cooloola)

This 54,000-hectare national park sports a varied wilderness of mangroves, forest and heathland that is traversed by the Noosa River. You can navigate a 4WD through the park all the way north to Rainbow Beach. Activity options include kayaking and walking with some fantastic trails starting from Elanda Point on the shore of Lake Cootharaba, including the 46km Cooloola Wilderness Trail to Rainbow Beach and a 7km trail to an unstaffed QPWS information centre at Kinaba.

Before you go, pop into the **QPWS Great Sandy Information Centre** (07-5449 7792; 240 Moorindil St, Tewantin; 8am-4pm), which can provide information on park access, tide times and fire bans within the park. The centre issues car and camping permits for both Fraser Island and Great Sandy National Park.

NEW YEAR'S MUSIC AT WOODFORD

The famous **Woodford Folk Festival** (www.woodfordfolkfestival.com) features over 2000 national and international performers playing folk, traditional Irish, indigenous and world music, as well as buskers, belly dancers, craft markets, visual-arts performances, environmental talks and a visiting squad of Tibetan monks. The festival is held on a property near Woodford, 35km northwest of Caboolture, from 27 December to 1 January each year. Camping grounds are set up on the property but be prepared for a mud bath if it rains. Shuttle buses run regularly from the Caboolture train station to and from the festival grounds.

The most popular (and best-equipped) camping grounds are Fig Tree Point (at the northern end of Lake Cootharaba), Harry's Hut (about 4km upstream) and Freshwater (about 6km south of Double Island Point) on the coast. You can also camp (per person/family $5.85/21.80) at designated zones on the beach if you're driving up to Rainbow Beach. Apart from Harry's Hut, Freshwater and Teewah Beach, all sites are accessible by hiking or river only.

Sunshine Coast Hinterland

Inland from **Nambour**, the Blackall Range creates a scenic hinterland with rather chintzy rustic villages. The scenic Mapleton–Maleny road runs along the ridge of the range, past rainforests at **Mapleton Falls National Park**, 4km northwest of Mapleton. It's worth walking to the bottom for a spectacularly refreshing swim.

Kondalilla National Park is 3km northwest of Montville. Both Mapleton and Kondalilla waterfalls plunge more than 80m, and their lookouts offer wonderful forest views.

The largest town in the region is **Maleny**, a green and scenic mountain town famous for its bohemian spirit. **Maleny Lodge** (☎07-5494 2370; www.malenylodge.com.au; 58 Maple St; s/d from $180/200;) is a Victorian-era guesthouse accurately appointed with period furniture. **Up Front Club** (☎07-5494 2592; 31 Main St; dishes $12-24; ⏰breakfast, lunch & dinner) is a little folk music bolthole worth a visit.

Midway between Mapleton and Maleny is **Montville**, a dinky trinket town popular with short-term visitors escaping the steamy coast. There's an antique-clock emporium, candy-making display centre, cafes, pubs and a contender for 'best view from a car park'. The area is brimming with B&Bs – ask the **information centre** (☎07-5478 5544; 198 Main St; ⏰10am-4pm) for up-to-date listings and vacancies.

A little further west through the Blackall Ranges is **Kenilworth**, a friendly 'outdoorsy' village in the Mary River Valley.

DARLING DOWNS

Queensland's breadbasket is a rich pastoral tapestry of rolling greens and grainy hues that make a relaxing detour from the coast. The lush and picturesque countryside of the Granite Belt supports an up-and-coming wine region and a thriving fruit industry (ably supported by young itinerant workers). The dramatic boulder-and-bush landscapes of Girraween and Sundown National Parks attract walkers and wildflower hunters alike, while the stately city of Toowoomba is famed for its gardens.

Further north, the Bunya Mountains National Park is filled with high-altitude pines and prehistoric grasses that skirt the Great Dividing Range. Inland, huge sheep and cotton farms run west into the outback, where you can leave your ride in the highest gear and roll out into the great unknown.

Getting There & Away

Greyhound Australia (☎1300 473 946; www.greyhound.com.au) has connections from Brisbane to Toowoomba ($26, two hours), Roma ($86, eight hours) and Stanthorpe ($75, 4½ hours).

Crisps' Coaches (☎07-4661 8333; www.crisps.com.au) is the biggest local operator, offering services from Brisbane to Stanthorpe ($60, 3½ hours).

The **Queensland Rail** (☎13 22 32, 1300 131 722; www.traveltrain.com.au) *Westlander* runs twice weekly from Brisbane to Charleville (economy seat/sleeper $112/177, 17 hours) on Tuesday and Thursday, returning on Wednesday and Friday, stopping in Toowoomba (from $35, four hours) and Roma (economy seat/sleeper $82/148, 11 hours).

Stanthorpe

POP 5385

Queensland's coolest town (literally), at an altitude of 915m, Stanthorpe has a distinct four-season climate. It's a winter retreat where normally sweltering Queenslanders can relax in front of a fire or enjoy a red from one of the 50 boutique wineries in the region.

The annual **Brass Monkey Festival** is celebrated here from June to August with a parade of music events and food fiestas in town and at various wineries.

The **Strange Bird Alternative Wine Trail** sings a palatable tune. Sample tempranillo, barbera, viognier and other grapes more suited to the Granite Belt climate than more traditional varieties. Maps are available at the visitor centre, or check out www.granitebeltwinecountry.com.au.

Located 17km south of Stanthorpe, **Girraween National Park** is home to towering granite boulders, pristine forests and brilliant blooms of springtime wildflowers. There's a number of good trails here. The shortest path is a 3km walk and scramble up the 1080m Pyramids, while the granddaddy of Girraween walks is the 10.4km trek to the top of Mt Norman (1267m).

Sleeping

Country Style CABIN, CAMPGROUND $
(☎07-4683 4358; www.countrystyleaccommodation.com.au; 27,156 New England Hwy; camp sites/caravan sites/cabins $20/25/100; @) Amid 5 hectares of bushland, Country Style has basic motel-style cabins with small kitchens and wood-burning fires. Peaceful, unpowered camp sites overlook the Severn River. It's on the highway to Ballandean, 10km south of Stanthorpe.

Briar Rose Cottages COTTAGE $
(☎07-4683 6334; www.briarrosecottages.com.au; 66 Wallangarra Rd; d Sun-Thu $95, Fri & Sat $110) These cute cottages are small in size but big on romance.

Diamondvale B&B Cottages COTTAGE $$
(☎07-4681 3367; www.diamondvalecottages.com.au; 26 Diamondvale Rd; d from $170; wi-fi) Charming hosts and a bushland setting outside Stanthorpe make Diamondvale popular with return visitors. There are four cottages, each with charming old-fashioned details. You can follow the creek 2km and stroll into town.

TOP VINEYARDS & GRANITE BELT DELICACIES

Alongside the pinots and cabernets, the hot and dry Granite Belt region produces some less common Iberian varieties such as tempranillo and verdelho. With dozens of wineries offering free tastings, you could easily spend a week or more sampling the fruits of the region. The following are on the free map available at the Stanthorpe tourist office (p345).

- **Summit Estate** (☎07-4683 2011; www.summitestate.com.au; 291 Granite Belt Drive, Thulimbah; ⏲10am-4.30pm daily) Overseen by a reputed Argentinean winemaker and owned by a group of wine lovers from Brisbane. Don't miss the pinot noir.
- **Symphony Hill** (☎07-4684 1388; www.symphonyhill.com.au; 2017 Eukey Rd, Ballandean; ⏲10am-4pm) A family affair that produces a number of interesting reds.
- **Ballandean** (☎07-4684 1226; www.ballandeanestate.com; 354 Sundown Rd, Ballandean) One of Queensland's oldest wineries, with free tours (11am, 1pm and 3pm) and a restaurant.
- **Pyramids Road** (☎07-4684 5151; www.pyramidsroad.com; 25 Wyberba Rd, Balladean; ⏲10am-4.30pm Thu-Mon) On the road to Girraween National Park.
- **Robert Channon** (☎07-4683 3260; www.robertchannonwines.com; 32 Bradley Lane, Stanthorpe; ⏲11am-4pm Mon-Tue & Fri, 10am-5pm Sat-Sun) Trophy-winning verdelho and a fine lunch restaurant with lake views.
- **Vincenzo's** (☎07-4683 2033; New England Hwy, Stanthorpe; ⏲8.30am-5pm) An enormous deli emporium with a fine cafe.
- **Granite Belt Dairy** (☎07-4685 2277; 4 Duncan Lane, Thulimbah; ⏲10am-4pm) What's wine without cheese? It's all available for sampling, plus there are fantastic milkshakes, cheesecake, breads, chutneys and other picnic fare.
- **Bramble Patch** (☎07-4683 4205; 381 Townsend Rd, Stanthorpe; ⏲10am-4pm) Berry grower worth visiting for the ice cream with homemade berry compote, waffles with berries and fresh fruits (November to April).

Commercial Hotel HOTEL $$
(07-4681 2244; www.stanthorpeaccommodation.com; Maryland St, Stanthorpe; d $100; Fri & Sat only) Compact pub-style rooms with tasteful decor and small writing desks. Excellent for a dirty weekend; the wine bar 1915 is downstairs.

Ballandean Tavern Motel MOTEL $$
(07-4684 1044; www.ballandeantavern.com.au; cnr St Jude's Rd & Eukey Rd, Ballandean; d from $120; P ❄) This new brick motel alongside the excellent older pub is the best-value accommodation in town. The large double rooms have ensuite bathrooms and modern, highly functional furniture.

Murray Gardens MOTEL, CABIN $$
(07-4681 4121; www.murraygardens.com.au; 10 Pancor Rd; motel r $95-125, cottages $189-239; ❄) Set on 8 hectares of natural bushland on the outskirts of town, Murray Gardens is ideal for families with children. You can choose between a motel room or a fully self-contained cottage with a fireplace or gas heating.

★ **Azjure Studio Retreat** BOUTIQUE HOTEL $$$
(0405 127 070; www.azjure.com.au; 165 Sundown Rd, Ballandean; from $275; P ❄) Queensland country style meets contemporary design in these three spacious spa studios and a two-bedroom villa. Hot tubs overlook grazing kangaroos, the rooms are appointed well beyond the Granite Belt standard – including an excellent book and DVD collection – and the owners are very knowledgeable about the local wine scene.

Vineyard Cottages COTTAGE $$$
(07-4684 1270; www.vineyardcottages.com.au; 28126 New England Hwy, Ballandean; cottage from $230) Highly recommended cottages on the highway through Ballandean set in a converted church.

Girraween Environmental Lodge CABIN $$$
(07-4684 5138; www.girraweenlodge.com.au; Pyramids Rd; cabins $280;) An eco-friendly bushland retreat set on 162 hectares adjacent to the national park. There's an outdoor spa and plunge pool.

Eating & Drinking

Patty's on McGregor MODERN AUSTRALIAN $$
(07-4681 3463; 2 McGregor Tce; mains $28-36; dinner Thu-Sat) An intimate and artsy vibe resonates throughout this unassuming little place in a residential area. Prices are a little high but the service is excellent and the rotating menu features mostly organic fare.

Queensland College of Wine Tourism MODERN AUSTRALIAN $$
(07-4685 5050; cnr New England Hwy & Caves Rd; mains $15-34; 10am-3pm Tue-Sun) The elegant Varias features the delectable handiwork of student chefs at the college. The 'medley of mains' menu ($40) includes four courses, wine and coffee. Floor-to-ceiling windows overlook the vineyard.

Barrel Room MODERN AUSTRALIAN $$
(07-4684 1326; Ballandean Estate Wines, Sundown Rd; mains $18-29; 10am-4pm Wed-Mon, 6-8pm Fri & Sat) This cosy restaurant, framed by 140-year-old floor-to-ceiling wine barrels, is the pick of the many winery restaurants.

Anna's Restaurant ITALIAN $$
(07-4681 1265; cnr Wallangarra Rd & O'Mara Tce; mains $19-33; dinner Tue-Sat) A family-run Italian BYO restaurant set in a pretty Queenslander, Anna's is famous locally for its weekend buffets ($30 to $35).

Shiraz MODERN AUSTRALIAN $$$
(07-4684 1000; 28,200 New England Hwy; mains $33-35; lunch & dinner Wed-Sun) Hidden behind a hedge, opposite the Triceratops statue in Ballandean, Shiraz is a small restaurant with a deserved reputation for excellence. Wines are matched accordingly by the warm, relaxed staff. The Angus beef fillet and the fish dishes get a lot of attention but we loved the mushroom ravioli and desserts.

Bar 1915 WINE BAR
(Maryland St, Stanthorpe; 6pm-midnight Fri & Sat) An attractive wine bar in the wonderfully renovated Commercial Hotel. Dress standards apply.

OFF THE BEATEN TRACK

STORM KING DAM

To get to Storm King Dam, 10km south of Stanthorpe, turn left on Eukey Rd and zip between vineyards and granite boulders, around grassy hairpins and follow the old tin signs. When you get there, have a picnic, swim, leap off a pontoon, take it all in, then cut straight for the back entrance to Giraween National Park. By now the normal world feels very, very far away.

ℹ Information

Stanthorpe Visitors Centre (☑ 07-4681 2057; www.granitebeltwinecountry.com.au; 28 Leslie Pde; ☺ 9am-5pm)

Toowoomba

POP 96,568

On the edge of a plateau of the Great Dividing Range, some 700m above breathtaking Lockyer Valley, lies Toowoomba, Queensland's largest inland city. Despite its great location, there's not a lot to do, but the cooler climate produces an array of dazzling gardens, which are celebrated with particular fervour during the fabulous **Carnival of Flowers** in September.

Picnic Point, on the eastern outskirts of town, offers outstanding views and a decent walking trail.

◎ Sights

Cobb & Co Museum   MUSEUM
(27 Lindsay St; adult/child $12.50/6.50; ☺ 10am-4pm, tours 10.30am) The ever-expanding Cobb & Co Museum is more than a collection of carriages and traps from the horse-drawn age; it's also a showcase for Toowoomba's Indigenous and multicultural communities, and includes a children's play area.

Queen's Park   GARDENS
(cnr Lindsay & Campbell Sts) Queen's Park houses the botanic gardens. Its vast open spaces are popular with sporty types and there are plenty of shaded areas for the picnic set.

Ju Raku En Japanese Garden   GARDENS
(West St; ☺ 7am-dusk) A beautiful garden with 3km of walking trails, waterfalls and streams.

Toowoomba Regional Art Gallery   GALLERY
(☑ 07-4688 6652; 531 Ruthven St; ☺ 10am-4pm Tue-Sat, 1-4pm Sun) FREE This small gallery houses the Lionel Lindsay Art Collection of paintings, fine art and drawings, and an interesting collection of rare books.

🛏 Sleeping

Book well ahead if visiting during September's Carnival of Flowers festival.

Toowoomba Motor Village Tourist Park   CAMPGROUND, CABIN $
(☑ 07-4635 8186; www.toowoombamotorvillage.com.au; 821 Ruthven St; camp sites $20-31, cabins &

units $55-100) Excellent, modern park, 2.5km south of the centre, with terrific views.

Vacy Hall   GUESTHOUSE $$
(☑ 07-4639 2055; www.vacyhall.com.au; 135 Russell St; d $120-197; ☜) Just uphill from the town centre, this magnificent 1880s mansion offers 12 heritage-style rooms with loads of romantic old-world charm. The collection of artwork and antiques placed throughout befits a small gallery.

James Cottage   B&B $$
(☑ 07-4637 8377; www.jamescottage.com; 128 James St; d $150-165) An elegant B&B in an early-20th-century Queenslander, James Cottage has two fine guest bedrooms and an open fireplace. It's a short walk into town.

City Golf Club Motel   MOTEL $$
(☑ 07-4636 9999; www.citygolfmotel.com.au; 775 Ruthven St; d from $169; ⓟ❄☜≋) No need to like golf to stay here (thankfully!). The 45 new mini-apartments are laid out like a permanent residential complex with guest access to the fine lap pool, spa, wi-fi, BBQ area and golf course (at a discount). It's a short walk into town proper, though there is a good restaurant in the clubhouse.

Ecoridge Hideaway   CHALET $$
(☑ 07-4630 9636; www.ecoridgehideaway.com.au; 712 Rockmount Rd, Preston; r from $130) Ecoridge is a pleasant alternative to the fairly bland accommodation scene in town. It's 15km from Toowoomba on the road to Gatton and consists of three stylish self-contained chalets set in harmony with the surrounding Great Dividing Range.

Park Motor Inn   MOTEL $$
(☑ 07-4632 1011; www.parktoowoomba.com.au; 88 Margaret St; s/d $120/130; ❄) This comfortably furnished motel has a handy and quiet location opposite leafy Queens Park. It's close to a couple of popular cafes.

Central Plaza Hotel   HOTEL $$
(☑ 07-4688 5333; www.toowoombacentralplaza.com.au; 523 Ruthven St; apt from $175; ❄≋) Award-winning hotel complex with colourful, well-designed apartments, a rooftop pool, a cafe and exceptional executive suites.

🍴 Eating & Drinking

Park House Cafe   MODERN AUSTRALIAN $$
(☑ 07-4638 2211; 92 Margaret St; mains $19-29; ☺ breakfast & lunch daily, dinner Wed-Sat) Queensland simplicity reigns in this relaxed

cottage cafe. Burgers are the lunch of choice and dinner is dependable grilled meat, seafood and pasta. Choose between verandah and patio seating.

Qi'lin CHINESE $$
(☎07-4613 1233; Shop 29, 187 Hume St; mains $12-21; ⏲lunch & dinner Tue-Sun) A glitzy Chinese restaurant on the edge of a shopping centre parking lot. Absolutely delicious off the menu with clean, flavoursome seafood and tofu dishes the highlight. Buffet lunch ($19) and dinner ($29) are very popular with local gluttons.

Oxygen Café CAFE $$
(cnr Ruthven & Little Sts; mains $10-24; ⏲breakfast & lunch Tue-Sun, dinner Thu-Sat; ✍) Quality organic food on Ruthven St at this colourful cafe with a regular clientele. The breakfasts are tasty but smallish, but the burgers (vegetarian, grilled yellow fin tuna) and sandwiches are great for lunch. It has recently opened for dinner; try the Indian-influenced dishes.

Cube Hotel BAR, CLUB
(☎07-4632 4747; cnr Margaret & Neil Sts) This impressive entertainment complex features a 'stone grill' restaurant, all-day cafe, cocktail bar and two levels of nightclubbing. The decibels increase tenfold on weekends.

Spotted Cow PUB
(cnr Ruthven & Campbell Sts) A youth-oriented pub with a stack of different beers and good live rock music.

ℹ Information

The heart of downtown Toowoomba is around Ruthven St (part of the north–south New England Hwy, Rte 61) and Margaret St.

The helpful **Toowoomba Visitor Centre** (86 James St) is located southeast of the centre, at the junction with Kitchener St.

West of Toowoomba

About 45km west of Toowoomba is the **Jondaryan Woolshed Complex** (☎07-4692 2229; www.jondaryanwoolshed.com; 264 Evanslea Rd; adult/child $13/8; ⏲10am-4pm), which displays antique tractors and obscure farm machinery. There are daily blacksmithing and shearing demonstrations – check the website for times. To really get into the pioneering spirit, try spending a night in the shearers' quarters ($17) or one of the self-contained cabins ($95 to $150). Or you can pseudo-camp in pre-erected safari tents ($29 to $36), which come complete with mattress.

A further 167km west, on the main street in Miles, is **Dogwood Crossing** (☎07-4628 5566; www.dogwoodcrossing.com; ⏲9am-5pm Mon-Fri, 10am-4pm Sat & Sun), a $1.6-million community project that combines visual arts, social history and literature into a museum, gallery, library and multimedia resource centre. You can bed down for the night in a refurbished underground bunker or a converted troop train at **Possum Park** (☎07-4627 1651; Leichhardt Hwy; d from $90). Munitions were stored in these bunkers during WWII as part of Australia's prepared last line of defence against the advancing Japanese. There's also a campground.

Some 350km west of Toowoomba lies Roma, an early Queensland settlement that is today the centre of a sheep- and cattle-raising district. The town's major landmark is the **Big Rig Complex** (☎07-4622 4355; www.thebigrig.com.au; Warrego Hwy; adult/child $10/7, combined entry & night show $16/11; ⏲9am-5pm, night show 7pm daily Apr-Nov, Wed & Sun Dec-Mar), a museum of oil and gas exploration centred on the old steam-operated oil rig at the eastern edge of town. There's also a sound-and-light show. In the same spot, the **visitor information centre** (☎07-4622 8676; 2 Riggers Rd; ⏲9am-5pm) can help with accommodation, especially handy if you're stopping here en route to Carnarvon Gorge.

Easter in the Country is Roma's annual week-long celebration of country music and life in western Queensland. It's held in late March or early April.

FRASER ISLAND & THE FRASER COAST

World Heritage–listed Fraser Island is a mystical land of giant dunes, ancient rainforests and luminous lakes.

Across the calm waters of the Great Sandy Strait, Hervey Bay is the launching pad to Fraser. There's a whiff of burgeoning beach-cafe culture, but at heart it's a mellow coastal community riding on the back of the annual humpback-whale migrations. Further south, tiny Rainbow Beach is an unaffected seaside village and an alternative departure point for Fraser Island.

Inland, grazing and agricultural fields surround old-fashioned country towns.

Bundaberg, the largest city in the region, overlooks a sea of waving sugar cane and is famous for its golden rum – a fiery, gut-churning spirit guaranteed to scramble a few brain cells!

Fraser Island

POP 400

Fraser Island is the largest sand island in the world (measuring 120km by 15km) and the only place where rainforest grows on sand. The Butchulla people call it K'Gari (paradise) which was created over hundreds of thousands of years from sand drifting off the east coast of mainland Australia.

Inland, the vegetation varies from dense tropical rainforest and wild heath to wetlands and wallum scrub, with 'sandblows' (giant dunes over 200m high), mineral streams and freshwater lakes opening onto long sandy beaches fringed with pounding surf. The island is home to a profusion of bird life and wildlife, including the purest strain of dingo in Australia, while offshore waters teem with dugong, dolphins, sharks and migrating humpback whales.

An ever-increasing volume of 4WD traffic does detract from the experience somewhat. With over 350,000 people visiting the island each year, Fraser can sometimes feel like a giant sandpit with its own peak hour and congested beach highway.

Before crossing via ferry from either Rainbow Beach or Hervey Bay, ensure that your vehicle has suitably high clearance and, if camping, that you have adequate food, water and fuel. Driving on Fraser all looks pretty relaxed in the brochure, but a sudden tide change or an unseen pothole can set your wheels spinning perilously.

History

Fraser Island takes its European name from James and Eliza Fraser. The captain of the *Stirling Castle* and his wife were shipwrecked on the northwest coast in 1836. He died here, and she survived with help from the local Aboriginal people.

As European settlers awoke to the value of Fraser's timber, that same tribe of people was displaced (although not without a fight) and tracts of rainforest were cleared in the search for turpentine (satiny), a waterproof wood prized by shipbuilders. The island's mineral sands were also mined for many years.

In the late 20th century the focus shifted from exploitation to protection. Sand mining ceased in 1975 and logging ended in 1991. Fraser Island joined the World Heritage list in 1992.

Sights & Activities

Seventy-Five Mile Beach runs the length of the island's east coast and offers some captivating scenery along the way. From Fraser's southern tip, use the high-tide access track between Hook Point and **Dilli Village**, rather than the beach. From here on, the eastern beach is the main thoroughfare. Stock up at nearby **Eurong**, the start of the inland track, across to Central Station and Wanggoolba Creek (for the ferry to River Heads).

In the middle of the island is **Central Station**, the starting point for numerous walking trails. Signposted tracks head to the beautiful **Lakes McKenzie**, **Jennings**, **Birrabeen** (with fewer tourists) and **Boomanjin**, in effect giant rainwater puddles 'perched' atop a thin impermeable layer of decaying twigs and leaves. Lore has it that rich mineral sand lends the lakes anti-ageing properties.

About 4km north of Eurong along the beach is a signposted walking trail to **Lake Wabby**. An easier route is from the lookout on the inland track. Wabby is edged on three sides by eucalypt forest, while the fourth side is a massive sandblow, which is encroaching on the lake at a rate of about 3m a year. The lake is deceptively shallow and diving is extremely dangerous. You can

FRASER ISLAND GREAT WALK

The Fraser Island Great Walk is a stunning way to see this enigmatic island in all its diverse colours. The trail undulates through the island's interior for 90km from Dilli Village to Happy Valley. Broken up into sections of 6km to 16km, plus some side trails, it follows the pathways of Fraser Island's original inhabitants, the Butchulla people, and passes underneath rainforest canopies, through shifting dunes and alongside some of the island's vivid lakes.

Before you go, pick up the *Fraser Island Great Walk* brochure from a QPWS office (or download it from www.derm.qld.gov.au) and seek updates on the track's conditions and book in advance to camp.

Fraser Island

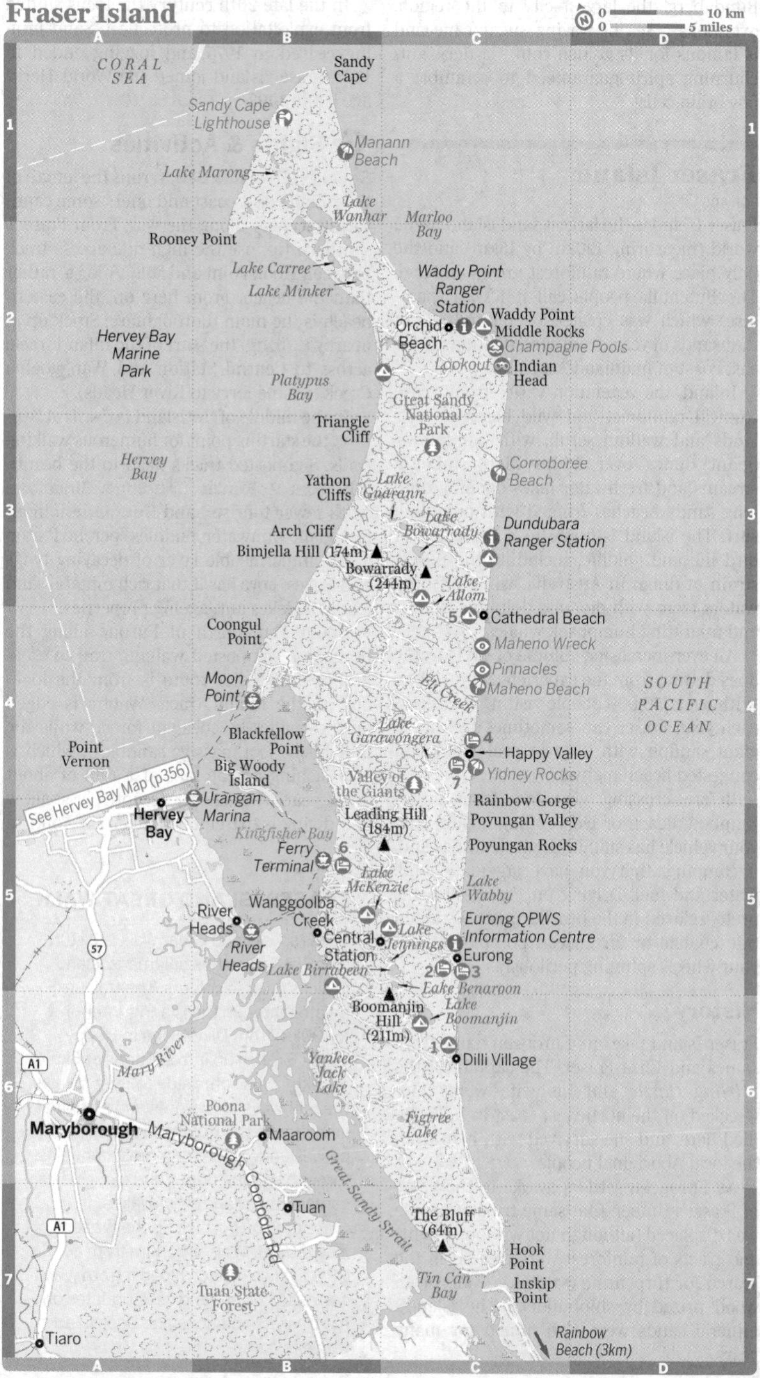

0 10 km
0 5 miles
CORAL SEA
Sandy Cape
Sandy Cape Lighthouse
Manann Beach
Lake Marong
Lake Wanhar
Marloo Bay
Rooney Point
Lake Carree
Lake Minker
Waddy Point Ranger Station
Waddy Point
Orchid Beach
Middle Rocks
Champagne Pools
Hervey Bay Marine Park
Lookout
Indian Head
Platypus Bay
Great Sandy National Park
Triangle Cliff
Hervey Bay
Corroboree Beach
Yathon Cliffs
Lake Guarann
Lake Bowarrady
Dundubara Ranger Station
Arch Cliff
Bimjella Hill (174m)
Bowarrady (244m)
Lake Allom
Cathedral Beach
Coongul Point
Maheno Wreck
Pinnacles
Eli Creek
Moon Point
Maheno Beach
SOUTH PACIFIC OCEAN
Blackfellow Point
Lake Garawongera
Point Vernon
Happy Valley
Big Woody Island
Yidney Rocks
See Hervey Bay Map (p356)
Valley of the Giants
Urangan Marina
Hervey Bay
Rainbow Gorge
Leading Hill (184m)
Poyungan Valley
Kingfisher Bay
Poyungan Rocks
Ferry Terminal
Lake McKenzie
Lake Wabby
Wanggoolba Creek
River Heads
Eurong QPWS Information Centre
Central Station
Lake Jennings
River Heads
Eurong
Lake Birrabeen
Lake Benaroon
Boomanjin Hill (211m)
Lake Boomanjin
Dilli Village
Mary River
Yankee Jack Lake
Poona National Park
Maryborough
Maaroom
Figtree Lake
Maryborough Cooloola Rd
Great Sandy Strait
Tuan
The Bluff (64m)
Hook Point
Tin Can Bay
Inskip Point
Tuan State Forest
Tiaro
Rainbow Beach (3km)

Fraser Island

Sleeping

often find turtles and huge catfish under the trees in the eastern corner of the lake.

Driving north along the beach you'll pass **Happy Valley**, with many places to stay, and **Eli Creek**. After rainfall this becomes a fast-moving, crystal-clear waterway that will carry you effortlessly downstream. Pretty much everyone wanders knee-deep along its pretty path. About 2km from Eli Creek is the wreck of the **Maheno**, a passenger liner that was blown ashore by a cyclone in 1935 while being towed to a Japanese scrapyard.

Roughly 5km north of the *Maheno* you'll find the **Pinnacles** (a section of coloured sand cliffs) and, about 10km beyond, **Dundubara**. Then there's a 20km stretch of beach before you come to the rocky outcrop of **Indian Head**, the best vantage point on the island. Sharks, manta rays, dolphins and (during the migration season) whales can often be spotted from the top of the headland.

From Indian Head the trail branches inland, passing the **Champagne Pools**, the only safe spot on the island for saltwater swimming. This inland road leads back to **Waddy Point** and **Orchid Beach**, the last settlement on the island. Many tracks north of this are closed for environmental protection. The 30km of beach up to **Sandy Cape** – the northern tip, with its lighthouse – is off-limits to hire vehicles. The beach from Sandy Cape to Rooney Point is closed to all vehicles, as is the road from Orchid Beach to **Platypus Bay** on the western coast.

On the island you can take a scenic flight with **MI Helicopters** (☎07-4125 1599, 1800 600 345; www.mihelicopters.com.au; 25min flights $230) or with **Air Fraser** (☎1800 600 345, 07-4125 3600; www.airfraserisland.com.au; same day return flight from Hervey Bay $125).

Sleeping & Eating

Camping is by far the best way to experience the island, but come prepared or pay through the nose for supplies. Permits are required at QPWS camping grounds and any public area (ie along the beach). Camping is permitted on designated stretches of the eastern beach, but there are no facilities. Fires are prohibited, except in communal fire rings at Waddy Point and Dundubara.

Dilli Village Fraser Island CAMPGROUND $
(☎07-4127 9130; unpowered/powered sites $20/30, bunkrooms $40, cabins $100) This tidy site perched on a gentle slope is run by the University of the Sunshine Coast.

QPWS Camping Grounds CAMPGROUND $
(per person/family $5.85/21.80) The most developed QPWS camping grounds, with coin-operated hot showers, toilets and barbecues, are at **Waddy Point**, **Dundubara** and **Central Station**. Campers with vehicles can also use the smaller camping grounds with fewer facilities at **Lake Boomanjin**, **Ungowa** and **Wathumba** on the western coast. Walkers' camps (for hikers only) are set away from the main campgrounds along the Fraser Island Great Walk trail. The trail map lists the camp sites and their facilities.

Fraser Island Retreat CABIN $$
(☎07-4127 9144; www.fraserisretreat.com.au; Happy Valley; cabins per 2 nights $330; @🛜≋) The nine timber cabins here are some of the best-value accommodation on the island. While lacking self-catering facilities, the cabins are airy, bright and sleep up to four. A former backpacker lodge, the site enjoys thickish tropical foliage and close proximity to the wilds of Happy Valley Beach. There's a restaurant and shop on-site.

Fraser Island Beachhouses RENTAL HOUSE $$
(☎07-4127 9205, 1800 626 230; www.fraserisland-beachhouses.com.au; Eurong Second Valley; per 2 nights studio $300, 2-bedroom house from $700; ≋) These are loads of fun for small groups who want an element of privacy. The sunny, self-contained units are kitted out with polished wood, cable TVs and ocean views.

Eurong Beach Resort RESORT $$
(☎07-4120 1600, 1800 111 808; www.eurong.com.au; Eurong; r $135, 2-bedroom apt $185, mains $18-40; ⊙breakfast, lunch & dinner; ❄@≋) Located on the east coast, Eurong is a friendly, middle-of-the-road resort that provides decent value in either motel rooms or apartments. Either way, ask for the Coral Sea location. The pub-style restaurant is pretty good and both the lagoon-style pool and Beach Bar are prime socialising areas. There's a bottle shop and petrol station on-site.

Kingfisher Bay Resort RESORT $$
(07-4194 9300, 1800 072 555; www.kingfisherbay.com; Kingfisher Bay; d $188, 2-bedroom villas $228;) A slightly overstretched resort that accommodates copious amounts of day visitors in high season. Still, the rooms are generously decked out, with private balconies and modern kitchens. The timber villas by the beach are a real treat. There's a three-night minimum stay in high season. The resort has restaurants, bars and shops and operates daily tours of the island (adult/child $155/105).

Frasers@Cathedral Beach CAMPGROUND $$
(07-4127 9177; www.cathedralsonfraser.com.au; Cathedral Beach; unpowered sites $39, powered sites $45, cabins with/without bathroom $220/180;) This spacious, privately run park – with its abundant, flat, grassy sites – is a fave with families.

Sailfish on Fraser APARTMENT $$$
(07-4127 9494; www.sailfishonfraser.com.au; d from $230-250, extra person $10;) A little faded but still a supremely comfortable collection of two-bedroom apartments, some with

SAND SAFARIS: EXPLORING FRASER ISLAND

The only way to explore Fraser Island is with a 4WD vehicle. For most travellers there are three transport options: tag-along tours, organised tours or 4WD hire.

Please be aware of your environmental footprint. When choosing how to visit this precious landscape, bear in mind that the greater the number of individual vehicles driving on the island, the greater the environmental damage.

Tag-Along Tours

Popular with backpackers, tag-along tours feature a group of travellers that pile into a 4WD convoy and follow a lead vehicle with an experienced guide and driver.

Advantages – flexibility; you can make new friends fast.

Disadvantages – if your group doesn't get along it's a loooong three days. Inexperienced drivers get bogged in sand all the time, but this can be part of the fun.

Rates hover around $300 to $320 for three-day/two-night packages, and exclude food, fuel and alcohol.

Organised Tours

Package tours leave from Hervey Bay, Rainbow Beach and Noosa and cover rainforests, Eli Creek, Lakes McKenzie and Wabby, the Pinnacles and the *Maheno* shipwreck.

Advantages – minimum of fuss, plus you can return to Rainbow Beach or Noosa, or vice versa. Expert commentary.

Disadvantages – during peak season you could share the experience with 40 others.
There are also tour companies based in Hervey Bay.

- **Fraser Explorer Tours** (1800 249 122, 07-4194 9222; www.fraserexplorertours.com.au; 1-/2-day tours $175/319) Popular budget option.
- **Dropbear Tours** (1800 061 156, 0487 333 606; www.dropbearadventures.com.au; 3-day tour $350) New operator out of Flashpackers (p333) with interesting three-day tour.
- **Fraser Experience** (1800 689 819, 07-4124 4244; www.fraserexperience.com; 1-/2-day tours $180/327) Small groups and more freedom about the itinerary.

4WD Hire

Hire companies lease out 4WD vehicles in Hervey Bay, Rainbow Beach and on the island. Reckon on covering 20km an hour on the inland tracks and 40km an hour on the eastern beach. Most companies will help arrange ferries and permits and camping gear.

Advantages – complete freedom to roam the island and escape the crowds.

Disadvantages – you may find you have to tackle beach and track conditions even experienced drivers find challenging.
Rates for multiday rentals start at around $185 per day depending on the vehicle. On the island, **Aussie Trax 4WD** (07-4124 4433, 1800 062 275; www.fraserisland4wd.com.au; Kingfisher Bay Resort; per day from $227) hires out 4WDs.

wall-to-wall glass doors. Space is no concern and all have spas and mod cons. There's a good pool and an area to wash your 4WD.

Information

General supplies and expensive fuel are available from stores at Cathedral Beach, Eurong, Kingfisher Bay, Happy Valley and Orchid Beach.

The main ranger station, **Eurong QPWS Information Centre** (☎07-4127 9128) is at Eurong. Others can be found at **Dundubara** (☎07-4127 9138) and **Waddy Point** (☎07-4127 9190).

The **Fraser Island Taxi Service** (☎07-4127 9188) operates all over the island. A one-way fare from Kingfisher Bay to Eurong is $80.

If your vehicle breaks down, call the **tow-truck service** (☎07-4127 9449, 0428 353 164) based in Eurong.

PERMITS

You will need permits for vehicles (per month/year $42.15/211.30) and camping (per person/family $5.85/21.80), and these must be purchased before you arrive. It's best to purchase the permits online at www.derm.qld.gov.au or contact **QPWS** (☎13 74 68). Permits aren't required for private camping grounds or resorts. Permit-issuing offices:

Bundaberg QPWS Office (☎07-4131 1600; 46 Quay St)

Great Sandy Information Centre (☎07-5449 7792; 240 Moorinidil St; ⏱8am-4pm) Near Noosa.

Marina Kiosk (☎07-4128 9800; Buccaneer Ave, Urangan Boat Harbour, Urangan; ⏱6am-6pm)

Maryborough QPWS (☎07-4121 1800; 20 Tennyson St; ⏱8.30am-5pm Mon-Fri)

Rainbow Beach QPWS (☎07-5486 3160; Rainbow Beach Rd)

River Heads Information kiosk (☎07-4125 8485; ⏱6.15-11.15am & 2-3.30pm) Ferry departure point at River Heads, south of Hervey Bay.

Getting There & Away

Vehicle ferries connect Fraser Island with River Heads, about 10km south of Hervey Bay, or further south at Inskip Point, near Rainbow Beach.

Fraser Island Barges (☎1800 227 437; www.fraserislandferry.com.au) makes the crossing (vehicle and four passengers $155 return, 30 minutes) from River Heads to Wanggoolba Creek on the western coast of Fraser Island. It departs daily from River Heads at 8.30am, 10.15am and 4pm, and returns from the island at 9am, 3pm and 5pm.

Kingfisher Vehicular Ferry (☎1800 072 555; www.fraserislandferry.com) operates a daily vehicle and passenger ferry (pedestrian adult/child $50/25 return, vehicle and four passengers $155 return, 50 minutes) from River Heads to Kingfisher Bay, departing at 6.45am, 9am, 12.30pm, 3.30pm, 6.45pm and 9.30pm and returning at 7.50am, 10.30am, 2pm, 5pm, 8.30pm and 11pm.

Coming from Rainbow Beach, the operators **Rainbow Venture & Fraser Explorer** (☎07-4194 9300; pedestrian/vehicle return $10/80) and **Manta Ray** (☎07-5486 8888; vehicle return $90) both make the 15-minute crossing from Inskip Point to Hook Point on Fraser Island continuously from about 7am to 5.30pm daily.

Air Fraser Island (☎07-4125 3600; www.airfraserisland.com.au) charges from $125 for a return flight (20 minutes each way) to the island's eastern beach, departing from Hervey Bay airport.

Gympie

POP 18,602

Gympie's gold once saved Queensland from near-bankruptcy, but that was in the 1860s and not much has happened since. A few period buildings line the main street, but most travellers on the Bruce Hwy bypass the town centre.

Every August the **Gympie Muster** (www.muster.com.au) is a place of pilgrimage for Australian country music fans and a wonderful initiation for first-time listeners. There's also a week-long **Gold Rush Festival** (www.goldrush.org.au) every October.

The **Woodworks Forestry & Timber Museum** (cnr Fraser Rd & Bruce Hwy; admission $5; ⏱10am-4pm Mon-Sat) on the highway south of town has some interesting logging memorabilia, while the **Valley Rattler** (☎07-5482 2750; www.thevalleyrattler.com; half-day tours per adult/child $34/10, day tours $50/25; ⏱half-day tours 9.30am, 11.30am & 1.45pm) is a restored 1923 steam train that leaves Tozer St every Wednesday and Sunday at 10am.

The **Royal Hotel** (☎07-5482 1144; www.theroyalgympie.com.au; 190 Mary St; d/t $120/130; P ❄ ☎) is a renovated pub with a popular bar and restaurant and beautiful rooms. **The Decks** (☎07-5483 8888; 250 Mary St; mains $12-34; ⏱breakfast & lunch daily, dinner Wed-Sat) serves homestyle breakfast and lunch to all walks of life.

Greyhound Australia (☎1300 473 946; www.greyhound.com.au) and **Premier Motor Service** (☎13 34 10; www.premierms.com.au) serve Gympie from Noosa ($28, two hours) and Hervey Bay ($31, 1¼ hours). Long-distance coaches stop at the bus shelter in Jaycee Way, behind Mary St. **Polley's Coaches** (☎07-5480 4500; Pinewood Ave) has buses from Gympie to Rainbow Beach ($18, 1¾ hours), departing from the Sovereign Cinema on Monkland St (at O'Connell St) at 1.15pm on weekdays.

Rainbow Beach

POP 1100

Gorgeous Rainbow Beach is a tiny town at the base of the Inskip Peninsula with spectacular multicoloured sand cliffs overlooking its rolling surf and white sandy beach. Still modestly touristed, the town has a relaxed vibe with plenty of options for the active soul. Convenient access to Fraser Island (only 15 minutes by barge) and the Cooloola section of the Great Sandy National Park has made it one of Queensland's real coastal beauty spots.

The town is named for the **coloured sand cliffs**, a 2km walk along the beach. A 600m track along the cliffs at the southern end of Cooloola Dr leads to the **Carlo Sandblow**, a spectacular 120m-high dune.

Activities

The Cooloola section of the **Great Sandy National Park** (p341) has a number of **national park camp sites** (www.derm.qld.gov.au; per person/family $5.15/20.60), including a wonderful stretch of beach camping along Teewah Beach. Book permits online. You'll also need a 4WD permit (www.derm.qld.gov.au; per day/week/month $10/25/40).

Bushwalkers will find tracks throughout the national park, including the 46.2km **Cooloola Wilderness Trail**, which starts at Mullens car park (off Rainbow Beach Rd) and ends near Lake Cooloola. Maps are available from the **QPWS** (☎07-5486 3160; Rainbow Beach Rd).

Surf & Sand Safaris DRIVING TOUR
(☎07-5486 3131; www.surfandsandsafaris.com.au; per adult/child $75/40) Excellent half-day tours to Double Island Point via the national park for those who want to explore further than the main Rainbow Beach but don't have the vehicular means.

Rainbow Beach Dolphin View Sea Kayaking KAYAKING
(☎0408 738 192; Shop 1, 6 Rainbow Beach Rd; 3hr tours per person $65) Leaves from the Rainbow Beach Surf Centre.

Rainbow Beach Surf School SURFING
(☎0408 738 192; www.rainbowbeachsurfschool.com; 3hr session $55) Same mob that runs the kayaking hangs ten on a long, safe beach break.

Rainbow Paragliding PARAGLIDING
(☎0418 754 157, 07-5486 3048; www.paragliding-rainbow.com; glides $180) Tandem jump with renowned paragliding outfit.

Skydive Rainbow Beach SKYDIVING
(☎0418 218 358; www.skydiverainbowbeach.com; 8000/14,000ft dives $299/369) As good a place as any in the world to try it for the first time.

Wolf Rock Dive Centre DIVING
(☎0438 740 811, 07-5486 8004; www.wolfrockdive.com.au; double dive charters from $210) Grey nurse sharks and plenty of spooky ledges in one of Australia's premier dive spots.

Sleeping

Beds are found mostly on Spectrum St and up the hill towards Carlo Sandblow. The three main hostels arrange 4WD tours to Fraser Island.

Rainbow Beach Hire-a-Camp CAMPING SUPPLIES
(☎07-5486 8633; www.rainbow-beach-hire-a-camp.com.au; per day/night $30/50) If you don't have your own gear, these guys can sort it out in style.

★ **Debbie's Place** B&B $
(☎07-5486 3506; www.rainbowbeachaccommodation.com.au; 30 Kurana St; d/ste from $99/109, 3-bedroom apt from $260; ❄) Pet and people friendly, Debbie's is an institution in Rainbow Beach for its terrific-value, self-contained rooms in a timber Queenslander. The namesake owner works hard to ensure guests are at ease. The outdoor areas with shared cooking facilities are a plus.

Pippies Beach House HOSTEL $
(☎1800 425 356; www.pippiesbeachhouse.com.au; 22 Spectrum St; dm/d $24/65; ❄@🛜🏊) Pippies is a family-run place that is great for mingling between outdoor pursuits. The free breakfast, wi-fi and boogie board hire are welcome additions. The bathrooms and kitchens, like most on this stretch, are cramped and a bit scruffy.

Fraser's on Rainbow YHA HOSTEL $
(☎1800 100 170; www.frasersonrainbow.com; 18 Spectrum St; dm/d from $25/65; @🏊) Fairly charmless inside the clean, tiled motel-style

rooms but the outdoor bar is popular most nights and all hours. Meals are available.

Rainbow Beach Holiday Village CAMPGROUND $
(☎1300 366 596; www.beach-village.com; 13 Rainbow Beach Rd; unpowered/powered sites from $27/34, cabins from $90; ❄ 🏊) This excellent and popular park spreads over 2 hectares overlooking the beach and ocean.

Plantation Resort APARTMENT $$$
(☎07-5486 9000; www.plantationresortatrainbow.com.au; 1 Rainbow Beach Rd; 1-bedroom apt from $199; ❄ @ 🏊) These swish apartments have perfect ocean views, and the outdoor cane settings and white plantation-themed rooms will have you reaching for the nearest gin and tonic. It's classy beach-chic and smack bang in the middle of town.

Rainbow Sea Resort APARTMENT $$$
(☎07-5486 3555; www.rainbowsea.com.au; 3 Oceanview Pde; d from $270; P ❄ 📶 🏊) This new split-level apartment complex, close to the beach, makes full use of its elevated position overlooking Rainbow Beach. The suites are spacious and bright with massive balconies though some of the furniture has the feeling it may soon fade.

Eating

Self-caterers will find a supermarket on Rainbow Beach Rd.

Creme de la Creme ICE CREAM $
(☎07-5486 8889; Shop 2, 1 Rainbow Beach Rd; $3 per scoop) Banana splits, slushies and spiders to end the perfect beach day.

Waterview Bistro MODERN AUSTRALIAN $$
(☎07-5486 8344; Cooloola Dr; mains $26-35; ⏲lunch & dinner Wed-Sat, lunch Sun) Sunset drinks are a must at this swish restaurant with sensational views of Fraser Island from its hilltop perch. Try the signature seafood chowder ($22) or the lunch special ($19 including glass of wine).

Rainbow Beach Hotel PUB $$
(1 Rainbow Beach Rd; mains $15-35; ⏲lunch & dinner) The spruced-up pub carries on the plantation theme with ceiling fans, palm trees, timber floors and cane furnishings. Go for the seafood paella ($28) or chilli spaghettini ($22). Have a sunset drink on the upstairs balcony.

Cafe Jilarty CAFE $$
(12 Rainbow Beach Rd; mains $10-30; ⏲breakfast, lunch & dinner) New name but the same delicious coffee, cake and light meals as the former proprietor.

Rainbow Beach SLSC SURF CLUB $$
(☎07-5486 3249; Wide Bay Esplanade; mains $15-25; ⏲lunch & dinner; P ❄) Classic dirty carpet ambience rules at this lifeblood of the local community. The food is very good too, featuring macadamia fish with mango sauce ($23), killer fish burgers ($15) and mixed fajitas ($26). Service can be slowish at times.

Getting There & Around

Greyhound Australia (☎1300 473 946; www.greyhound.com.au) and **Premier Motor Service** (☎13 34 10; www.premierms.com.au) have daily services from Brisbane ($46, five hours), Noosa ($30, three hours) and Hervey Bay ($26, two hours).

Most 4WD-hire companies will also arrange permits, barge costs and hire out camping gear, including **All Trax 4WD Hire** (☎07-5486 8767; www.fraserisland4x4.com.au; Rainbow Beach Rd, Shell service station; per day from $120) and **Rainbow Beach Adventure Centre 4WD Hire** (☎07-5486 3288; www.adventurecentre.com.au; Rainbow Beach Rd; per day from $150).

Maryborough

POP 1100

Born in 1847, Maryborough is one of Queensland's oldest towns, and its port was the first shaky step ashore for thousands of 19th-century free settlers looking for a better life in the new country. Heritage and history are Maryborough's fortes, the pace of yesteryear reflected in its beautifully restored colonial-era buildings and gracious Queenslander homes. Today, it's a modest old country town with depleted economic fortunes.

Maryborough is also the birthplace of PL Travers, creator of everyone's favourite umbrella-wielding nanny, Mary Poppins.

Thirteen heritage-listed buildings, parklands and museums in **Portside** (101 Wharf St; ⏲10am-4pm Mon-Fri, to 1pm Sat & Sun) paint a different story from Maryborough's colourful past – ruffians, brothels, opium dens and all. **Brennan & Geraghty's Store** (64 Lennox St; adult/child/family $5.50/2.50/13.50; ⏲10am-3pm) is a 19th-century general store converted into a museum.Free **guided walks** (9am Monday to Saturday) depart from the city hall every morning.

Every Thursday and on the last Sunday of the month in Queen's Park you can take a ride (adult/child $3/2) on the **Mary Ann**, a full-sized replica of Queensland's first steam locomotive, built in Maryborough in 1873.

Inside the 100-year-old city hall is the excellent **Maryborough/Fraser Island visitor centre** (Kent St; ⌚9am-5pm Mon-Fri, to 1pm Sat & Sun).

If you stay overnight, **Eco Queenslander** (☎0438 195 443; www.ecoqueenslander.com; 15 Treasure St; house $140) is an entire home for your convenience. **Wallace Caravan Park & Units Motel** (☎07-4121 3970; www.wallacecaravanpark.com; 22 Ferry St; unpowered/powered sites $20/25, cabins $75-85; ❄🏊) is a leafy and convenient option. **McNevin's Parkway Motel** (☎1800 072 000; www.mcnevins.com.au; 188 John St; r from $125; ❄@📶🏊) has well-lit, comfortable motel rooms and a very helpful reception.

Port Residence (☎07-4123 5001; Wharf St, Customs House; mains $15-30; ⌚breakfast, lunch & dinner Thu-Sun) is an elegant restaurant overlooking the Mary River, and **Milosc** (☎07-4122 1741; Level 3, 333 Kent St; coffee $3, cake $3; ⌚breakfast & lunch Mon-Sat) is the best cafe in town by far. **Lounge 1868** (116 Wharf St; ⌚Fri & Sat nights) at the Customs House Hotel is the starting point for a night out, while the **Post Office Hotel** (☎07-4121 3289; cnr Bazaar & Wharf Sts), in a lovely building designed by an Italian architect in 1889, is a fine post-work watering hole.

Maryborough West train station is 7km west of town on Lennox St. Here you'll find trains to Brisbane ($60, five hours, at least four weekly) and the main bus station next door.

If you just need to get to Hervey Bay ($8, one hour), catch one of the frequently departing Wide Bay Transit buses from outside city hall.

Hervey Bay

POP 76,403

As the main gateway to Fraser Island, Hervey Bay has matured from a welfare-by-the-sea escape into a low-key tourist destination thanks to its lovely sandy bay (and soothing sea breezes), steady resort development and huge pods of humpback whales.

The often sleepy, startlingly long Esplanade has an air of youthful anticipation as the bars fill up come nightfall.

From July to October humble fishing boats transform into high-tech whale-watching vessels in time for the mass humpback migration. This is reputedly the best viewing region in the world.

The gentle shallow bay itself is very safe for swimming and snorkelling (especially off the end of Zephyr St in Scarness), which means many mums, dads and kids also pay Hervey Bay a seasonal visit.

Sights

Reef World AQUARIUM
(☎07-4128 9828; Pulgul St, Urangan; adult/child $18/9, shark dives $50; ⌚9.30am-4pm) Fairly uninspired presentation but knowledgeable and passionate staff ensure a sound family experience. You can feed turtles or take a dip with lemon, whaler and other nonpredatory sharks.

Botanic Gardens GARDENS
(Elizabeth St, Urangan; ⌚6.30am-8.30pm) The gardens have dense foliage, walking tracks, a few lagoons and more than 80 species of bird.

Fraser Coast Discovery Sphere MUSEUM
(☎07-4197 4207; www.frasercoastdiscoverysphere.com.au; 166 Old Maryborough Rd, Pialba; adult/child/family $7.50/5.50/20.50; ⌚10am-4pm) Loads of educational activities inspired by the region. Ideal for kids and curious adults.

Activities

Fraser Island

Hervey Bay is great for arranging a 4WD adventure on Fraser Island. Some hostels put groups together in tag-along tours. A maximum of five vehicles follow a lead vehicle with an experienced guide and driver. Rates hover around $300 to $320 for a three-day/two-night camping trip, and exclude food, fuel and alcohol. Places that offer trips include **Colonial Village YHA** (☎1800 818 280; www.cvyha.com), **Fraser Roving** (☎1800 989 811, 07-4125 6386; www.fraserroving.com.au), **Nomads** (☎1800 354 535, 07-4125 3601; www.nomadshostels.com), **Next Backpackers** (☎07-4125 6600; www.nextbackpackers.com.au) and **Palace Adventures** (☎1800 063 168; www.palaceadventures.com.au).

If you prefer to go on your own (not recommended for inexperienced off-road drivers), consider hiring a car.

Water Sports

Aquavue WATER SPORTS
(☎07-4125 5528; www.aquavue.com.au; The Esplanade) Hires out SeaKarts (a cross between a windsurfer and a catamaran; $50 per hour),

kayaks ($20 per hour) and jet skis ($50 per 15 minutes). Guided Fraser Island jet-ski tours for $320. Be the first of your friends to try futuristic 'FlyBoarding'.

Enzo's on the Beach WATER SPORTS
(07-4124 6375) Kitesurfing ($130 per two-hour lesson) and paddleboarding ($30/40 per hour/two hours). Also hires out kayaks and surf skis.

Cruises

Krystal Klear CRUISE
(07-4128 9800; 5hr tours adult/child $90/50) Leaving from the Urangan marina, this day trip on a 40ft glass-bottomed boat includes snorkelling, coral viewing and an island tropical barbecue.

Fishing

The fishing in and around Hervey Bay is excellent and many vessels operate fishing safaris. **MV Fighting Whiting** (07-4124 6599; www.fightingwhiting.com.au; adult/child/family $70/35/170) offers expeditions that include lunch.

Other Activities

Skydive Hervey Bay SKYDIVING
(0458 064 703; www.skydiveherveybay.com.au) Tandem skydives for $325 from 12,000ft.

Susan River Homestead HORSE RIDING
(07-4121 6846; www.susanriver.com; Hervey Bay–Maryborough Rd) Located halfway between Maryborough and Hervey Bay. Two-hour rides cost $85.

Festivals & Events

Hervey Bay Whale Festival WHALES
(www.herveybaywhalefestival.com.au) In early August, the Hervey Bay Whale Festival celebrates the return of the whales.

Sleeping

★ **Flashpackers** HOSTEL $
(07-4124 1366; www.flashpackersherveybay.com; 195 Torquay Tce, Torquay; dm $25-30, d $70;) Here's a hostel worth exporting, with a comfortable, spacious dorm and rooms with bathrooms. Reading lights, numerous power

GIANTS OF THE SEA: WHALE WATCHING IN HERVEY BAY

Every year, from August to early November, thousands of humpback whales *(Megaptera novaeangliae)* cruise into Hervey Bay's sheltered waters for a few days before continuing their arduous migration south to the Antarctic. Having mated and given birth in the warmer waters off northeastern Australia, they arrive in Hervey Bay in groups of about a dozen (known as pulses), before splitting into smaller groups of two or three (pods). The new calves use the time to develop the thick layers of blubber necessary for survival in icy southern waters, by consuming around 600L of milk daily.

Viewing these majestic creatures is simply awe-inspiring. Showy aqua-acrobats, humpbacks wave their pectoral fins, slap their tails, breach and simply 'blow'. Many will roll up beside the whale-watching boats with one eye clear of the water, making those on board wonder who's actually watching whom.

Cruises go from the Urangan Marina out to Platypus Bay and then zip around from pod to pod to find the most active whales. In a very competitive market, vessels offer half-day (four-hour) tours that include breakfast or lunch and cost around $115 for adults and $60 for children. The larger boats run six-hour day trips and the amenities are better, but they take around two hours to reach Platypus Bay. Some recommended operators:

- **Spirit of Hervey Bay** (1800 642 544; www.spiritofherveybay.com; 8.30am & 1.30pm) The largest vessel with the greatest number of passengers. Has an underwater hydrophone and underwater viewing window.
- **That's Awesome** (1800 653 775; www.awesomeadventure.com.au; 7am, 10.30am & 2.30pm) This rigid inflatable boat speeds out to the whales faster than any other vessel. The low deck level means you're nearly eyeball-to-eyeball with the big mammals.
- **Freedom Whale Watch** (1300 879 960; www.freedomwhalewatch.com.au; adult/child $125/80, 8.30am) Award-winning operator runs six-hour trips.
- **MV Tasman Venture** (1800 620 322; www.tasmanventure.com.au; 8.30am & 1.30pm) Maximum of 80 passengers; underwater microphones and viewing windows.
- **Blue Dolphin Marine Tours** (07-4124 9600; www.bluedolphintours.com.au; adult/child $120/90; 7.30am) Maximum 20 passengers on a 10m catamaran.

Hervey Bay

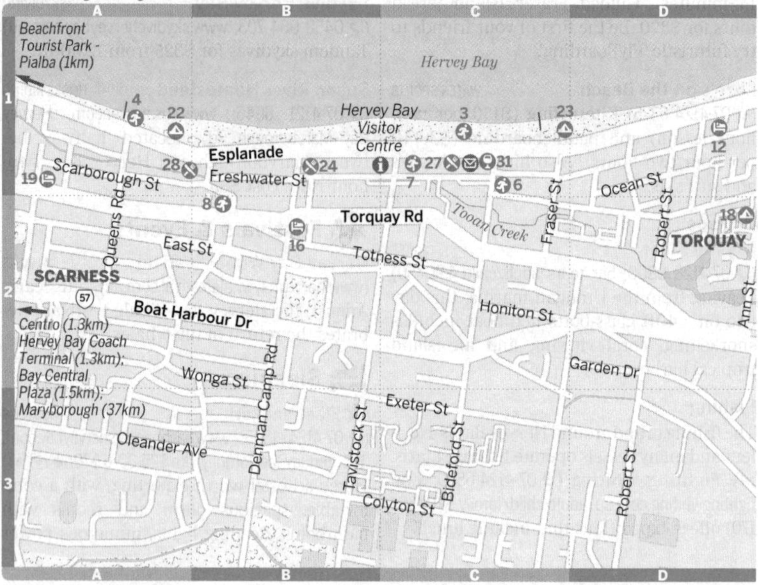

Hervey Bay

Sights

1 Botanic Gardens F2
2 Reef World H2

Activities, Courses & Tours

3 Aquavue C1
Blue Dolphin Marine Tours .... (see 9)
4 Enzo's on the Beach A1
5 Krystal Klear H3
MV Tasman Venture .... (see 9)
6 Next Backpackers C1
7 Nomads C1
8 Palace Adventures B2
9 Spirit of Hervey Bay H2
That's Awesome .... (see 9)

Sleeping

10 Akama H3
11 Alexander Lakeside B&B E2
12 Australis Shelly Bay Resort D1
13 Bay B&B F1
14 Boat Harbour Resort G3
15 Colonial Village YHA G3
16 Flashpackers B2
17 Grange Resort F1
18 Happy Wanderer Village D2
19 Mango Eco Hostel A1
20 Peppers Pier Resort G1
21 Quarterdecks Harbour Retreat G3
22 Scarness Beachfront Tourist Park A1
23 Torquay Beachfront Tourist Park C1

Eating

Aquavue .... (see 3)
24 Black Dog Café B1
25 Boat Club H3
26 Café Balaena H2
27 Café Tapas C1
Enzo's on the Beach .... (see 4)
28 Hoolihan's A1
29 Pavilion by the Pier G1
30 Pier Restaurant E1

Drinking & Nightlife

31 Viper C1

sockets, walk-in communal fridge, spotless (albeit brand new) communal areas and showers with power. Set a street back from the beach and now the new standard for backpacker accommodation in Hervey Bay.

Beachfront Tourist Parks CAMPGROUND $
(www.beachfronttouristparks.com.au; unpowered/powered sites $25/36) Pialba (☎07-4128 1399; The Esplanade, Pialba); Scarness (☎07-4125 1578; The Esplanade, Scarness); Torquay (☎07-4125

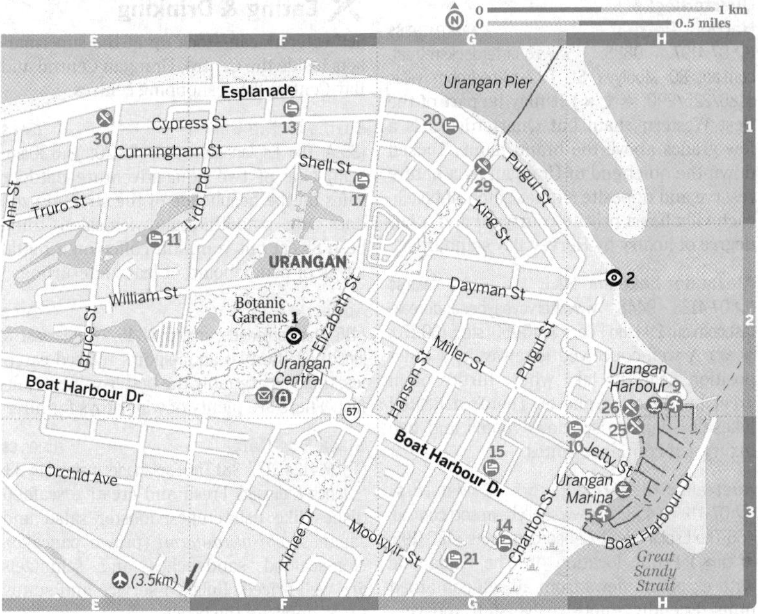

1578; The Esplanade, Torquay) Fronting Hervey Bay's exquisitely long sandy beach, all three of these shady parks have the best ocean views; the Torquay site is in the heart of the action.

Colonial Village YHA HOSTEL $
(☎1800 818 280; www.cvyha.com; 820 Boat Harbour Dr; dm/d/cabins from $32/56/70; ❄@≋) A very well-managed and executed hostel set on 8 hectares of tranquil bushland, close to the marina and only 50m from the beach. There's a positive, understated communal vibe, with good birdlife, music-filled common areas and extra facilities like basketball and tennis courts.

Mango Eco Hostel HOSTEL $
(☎07-4124 2832; www.mangohostel.net; 110 Torquay Rd, Mango Hostel; dm/d $28/60; P❄📶) Not for the package tourist, this small, colourful hostel is a kind of old-school travellers' haunt, both intimate and unusual. Run by a passionate local who readily shares his dismay about the exploitation of Fraser Island, Mango sleeps guests in a four-bed dorm room and two very homely doubles. The wraparound verandah and outdoor dining area add an atmosphere of tropicalismo.

Happy Wanderer Village CAMPGROUND $
(☎07-4125 1103; www.happywanderer.com.au; 105 Truro St; unpowered/powered sites from $30/35, cabins/villas from $64/121; ❄📶≋) The manicured lawns and profuse gum-tree cover at this large park make for great tent sites.

Akama APARTMENT $$
(☎07-4197 0777, 1800 770 661; www.akamaresort.com.au; 625 Charlton; 1-/2-bedroom apt from $175/220; P❄≋) A tall, modern complex overlooking a fairly busy road near the marina, Akama excels on the inside. The apartments are enormous, with white interiors, slick bathrooms and open-plan living straight from a design catalogue. There are distant views of Fraser Island from the spacious balconies and an excellent pool and barbecue area. Staff are exceptional.

Bay B&B B&B $$
(☎07-4125 6919; www.baybedandbreakfast.com.au; 180 Cypress St; s $100, d $125-140; ❄@≋) An honest B&B with enough charm to compete with the spread of resorts in the area. It's run by a friendly, well-travelled Frenchman, his wife (and their dog). Guest rooms are in a comfy annexe out the back, while the famed breakfasts are served in a tropical garden. Excellent value.

Quarterdecks Harbour Retreat APARTMENT $$
(07-4197 0888; www.quarterdecksretreat.com.au; 80 Moolyyir St; 1-/2-/3-bedroom villas $185/225/290;) It may be part of the Best Western chain but Quarterdecks is a few grades above the brand name. Tucked down the quiet end of Urangan by a nature reserve and opposite a quiet patch of beach, each villa has a private courtyard and a fair degree of luxury by Hervey Bay standards.

Alexander Lakeside B&B B&B $$
(07-4128 9448; www.herveybaybedandbreakfast.com.au; 29 Lido Pde; r $140-150, ste $160-170;) A well-conceived getaway in a quiet position near the lake where turtles often greet breakfasting guests. There's a heated lakeside spa, two spacious rooms and two luxury self-contained suites.

Australis Shelly Bay Resort APARTMENT $$
(07-4125 4533; www.shellybayresort.com.au; 466 The Esplanade; 1-/2-bedroom units $180/195; @) Prime location on The Esplanade with excellent views from all self-contained units. Friendly, unobstrusive staff and very good discounts on multiple night stays.

Boat Harbour Resort APARTMENT $$
(07-4125 5079; www.boatharbourresort.net; 651-652 Charlton St; studio from $120, bungalow from $150;) Close to the Hervey Bay marina, these timber studios and bungalows are set on attractive grounds. The studios have sizeable decks out the front, and the roomy two-bedroom bungalows are great for families.

Peppers Pier Resort RESORT $$$
(1300 737 444, 4194 9700; www.peppers.com.au/pier-resort; The Esplanade, Urangan; 1-/2-bedroom ste from $184/259; P) This new resort in a burgeoning strip down the end of the Esplanade is the centrepiece of Hervey Bay's high-end hotels. The serviced apartments are quite opulent, with the streamlined Peppers decor and smart use of space. The pool is the best in town but the street-facing restaurant is best only for sunset drinks.

Grange Resort RESORT $$$
(07-4125 2002; www.thegrange-herveybay.com.au; cnr Elizabeth & Shell Sts; 1-/2-bedroom villas $195/225;) Reminiscent of a stylish desert resort with fancy split-level condos and filled with life's little luxuries, this place is close to the beach and to town.

Eating & Drinking

Self-caterers can stock up at the supermarkets inside the Centro, Urangan Central and Bay Central Plaza shopping centres.

Enzo's on the Beach CAFE $
(351A The Esplanade; mains $8-20; 6.30am-5pm) One of two aqua-adventure outdoor cafes on the beach side of the street, Enzo's does the smoothie/sandwich/salad thing best. Sweat out your stiff coffee on a rental kayak or paddleboard or learn kitesurfing.

Aquavue CAFE $
(415 The Esplanade; mains $8-15; breakfast & lunch) Of the two aqua-sports relaxed eateries, this has arguably the better-value breakfast. There are plenty of water toys for hire.

Black Dog Café FUSION $$
(07-4124 3177; 381 The Esplanade; mains $14-33; lunch & dinner) Fresh and creative seafood dishes like fish crepes, lobster salad and Japanese *ebi okinoyami* (prawn pancake). Non-seafood sandwiches and schnitzels are well-priced. Relaxed service and sunny tunes opposite the beach.

Boat Club PUB $$
(07-4128 9643; Buccaneer Dve, Urangan; mains $17-29, lunch & dinner) An evening at The Hervey Bay Boat Club reminds the visitor that the cafe culture on The Esplanade will never overshadow the locals' love of multipurpose entertainment venues by a body of water with subsidised drink prices and chances for a big screen and a flutter. Take a number for huge pub-style meals that come with chips almost always.

Café Tapas TAPAS $$
(417 The Esplanade; tapas $7; lunch & dinner) Asian-inspired tapas and very good cocktail service. This slick venue has funky artwork, dim lighting, red couches, and low tables flickering with coloured lights.

Café Balaena CAFE $$
(07-4125 4799; Shop 7, Terminal Bldg, Buccaneer Ave; mains $10-25; breakfast & lunch daily, dinner Thu-Mon) Definitely the pick of the waterfront cafes at the marina. The menu ranges across the board with a good dose of fairly priced seafood and outstanding fruit juices.

Pier Restaurant SEAFOOD $$
(07-4128 9699; 573 The Esplanade; mains $20-40; dinner Mon-Sat) Although it sits op-

posite the water, à la carte Pier makes little use of its ocean views. However, it does have an interesting seafood menu (crocodile and Hervey Bay scallops), and is deservedly popular.

Hoolihan's PUB $$
(382 The Esplanade; mains $16-27) Like all good Irish pubs, Hoolihan's is wildly popular, especially with the backpacker crowd. Maybe it's got something to do with its hard-drinking ethos and carbo-laden meals.

Pavilion by the Pier MODERN AUSTRALIAN $$$
(☎07-4125 2288; 1 Pier St; mains $19-39; ⏲breakfast & lunch Tue, breakfast, lunch & dinner Wed-Sun) The Pavilion offers stylishly presented cuisine and an agreeable outlook from the parklands by the old Urangan pier. The classiest place for an evening meal.

Viper CLUB
(410 The Esplanade, Torquay; ⏲10pm-3am Wed, Fri & Sat) This new club is a rough diamond with cranking music and an energetic crowd, especially during summer.

Information

Hervey Bay Visitor Centre (☎1800 649 926; 401 The Esplanade; internet per hr $4) Friendly, privately run booking office with internet access.

Hervey Bay Visitor Information Centre (☎1800 811 728; www.herveybaytourism.com.au; cnr Urraween & Maryborough Rds) Helpful tourist office on outskirts of town.

Mad Travel (☎07-4125 3601; 408 The Esplanade; internet per hr $4) Located at Nomads. Offers internet access and is a booking agent for tours and activities.

Getting There & Away

BOAT

Boats to Fraser Island leave from River Heads, about 10km south of town, and Urangan Marina. Most tours leave from Urangan Harbour.

BUS

Long-distance buses depart from **Hervey Bay Coach Terminal** (☎07-4124 4000; Central Ave, Pialba). Regular services head to/from Brisbane ($70, 5½ hours), Maroochydore ($45, 3½ hours), Bundaberg ($25, 1½ hours) and Rockhampton ($92, six hours). **Wide Bay Transit** (☎07-4121 3719) has hourly services from Urangan Marina to Maryborough ($8, one hour) every weekday, with fewer services on weekends.

Getting Around

Seega Rent a Car (☎07-4125 6008; 463 The Esplanade) has small cars from $45 to $60 a day.

Plenty of rental companies make Hervey Bay the best place to hire a 4WD for Fraser Island:

Aussie Trax (☎1800 062 275; 56 Boat Harbour Dr, Pialba)

Fraser Island 4WD Hire (☎07-4125 6612; www.fraser4wdhire.com.au; 5 Kruger Ct, Urangan)

Hervey Bay Rent A Car (☎07-4194 6626) Also rents out scooters ($30 per day).

Safari 4WD Hire (☎1800 689 819; www.safari4wdhire.com.au; 102 Boat Harbour Dr, Pialba)

Childers

POP 1630

One of the sweeter stops on the heavily plied Bruce Hwy is pretty little Childers. This sugar-cane town, scattered with liquorice-coloured houses and fruit-picking youth, is used by most travellers to stretch their legs or take a cafe break in the country.

A little out of town, **Sugarbowl Caravan Park** (☎07-4126 1521; 4660 Bruce Hwy; unpowered/powered sites $20/22, cabins $66; @ ≋) has spectacular views over the surrounding countryside. There's plenty of space and a good scattering of foliage between sites. Many farm-working backpackers stay here, but a better option is the very clean and friendly **Childers Tourist Park & Camp** (☎07-4126 1371; 111 Stockyard Rd; rates for 2 people unpowered/powered sites $24/25, on-site vans $66) – you'll need a car.

For warm, country hospitality the cute cane-cutter cottages at **Mango Hill B&B** (☎07-4126 1311; www.mangohillcottages.com; 8 Mango Hill Dr; s/d $90/120; ≋), 4km south of town, are decorated with handmade wooden furniture, country decor and comfy beds that ooze charm and romance. There's an on-site organic winery.

Kape Centro (65 Churchill St; mains $10-18; ⏲breakfast & lunch) is a charming cafe in the old post office building. Reached via a turnoff south of town, **Mammino's** (115 Lucketts Rd; ⏲9am-5pm) makes real macadamia-nut ice cream.

Childers is 50km southwest of Bundaberg. **Greyhound Australia** (☎1300 473 946) and **Premier Motor Service** (☎13 34 10) both stop at the Shell service station north of town and have daily services to/from Brisbane ($84, 6½ hours), Hervey Bay ($17, one hour) and Bundaberg ($24, 1½ hours).

Bundaberg

POP 60,000

Boasting a sublime climate, coral-fringed beaches and waving fields of sugar cane, 'Bundy' is still overlooked by most travellers. Born out of these cane fields is the famous Bundaberg Rum, a potent, mind-blowing liquor and unsung national icon.

Hordes of backpackers flock to Bundy for fruit-picking and farm work. Keen divers, surfers and holidaying families quickly pass through on their way to nearby seaside villages like **Bargara**, 16km to the east, and a dazzling bank of coral near the Barolin Rocks in the Woongarra Marine Park

Massive floods in early 2013 decimated Bundaberg's peaceful, palm-lined streets and many residents are still dealing with the aftermath.

Sights

Bundaberg Rum Distillery DISTILLERY
(07-4131 2999; www.bundabergrum.com.au; Avenue St; self-guided tours adult/child $15/7.50, guided tours $25/12.50; 9am-3.30pm Mon-Fri, to 2.30pm Sat & Sun) Wake up and smell the molasses! Tours here follow the rum's production from start to finish and, if you're over 18, you get to sample the final product. The one-hour, wheelchair-accessible tours run every hour on the hour. Note, you must wear closed-toe shoes.

Botanic Gardens GARDENS
(Mt Perry Rd; 6am-6.30pm) The Botanic Gardens, 2km north of the centre, is a green oasis of tropical shrubs, towering trees and flowering gardens surrounding a few small lakes. Bring a picnic lunch!

Hinkler Hall of Aviation MUSEUM
(www.hinklerhallofaviation.com; Mt Perry Rd, Botanic Gardens; adult/child/family $15/10/40; 9am-4pm) Located within the Botanical Gardens, the museum has multimedia exhibits, a flight simulator, and informative displays about Bert Hinkler, the first pilot to fly solo between England and Australia, in 1928.

Sleeping

Bundaberg's hostels cater to working backpackers; most hostels arrange harvest work. Standards vary considerably.

Bundaberg Spanish Motor Inn MOTEL $
(07-4152 5444; www.bundabergspanishmotorinn.com; 134 Woongarra St; s/d $95/105;) The best-kept premises in its category is located on a quiet side street off the main drag. The hacienda style is a little ambitious but the self-contained units facing the pool are extremely comfortable.

Bigfoot Backpackers HOSTEL $
(07-4152 3659; www.footprintsadventures.com.au; 66 Targo St;) Comfortable and friendly hostel in town that also runs fabulous turtle tours to Mon Repos. A few dabs of fresh paint and a more chilled vibe raise this above the many competitors. There are ample fruit-picking opportunities available.

Cellblock Backpackers HOSTEL $
(1800 837 773; cnr Quay & Maryborough Sts; dm per night/week from $28/165, d $70;) This barely legal establishment is a heritage-listed former lock-up and hostel for the hardened traveller. The seven restored jail cells lack windows (of course) but are comfortable enough in a crisis. The real action, however, takes place poolside at the happening bar where the owner fraternises with guests until the wee hours. Know what to expect and you'll probably love it.

★**Inglebrae** B&B $$
(07-4154 4003; www.inglebrae.com; 17 Branyan St; r incl breakfast $120-150;) Inglebrae represents tremendous value. The glorious restored Queenslander is instilled with more than a touch of yesteryear: stained glass, antique bric-a-brac, raised four-poster beds. Toiletries, linen and breakfast on the verandah are also first class.

Burnett Riverside Motel MOTEL $$
(07-4155 8777; www.burnettmotel.com.au; 7 Quay St; d $150-200;) The most expensive accommodation in Bundaberg has a central position overlooking the river and a variety of inhouse facilities like sauna, gym and the popular H2O restaurant. Rooms, however, are a bit dank for the price and the furniture needs an overhaul.

Eating & Drinking

Rosie Blu DELI $
(07-4151 0957; 90A Bourbong St; mains $9-19) This narrow deli cafe in the heart of town offers delicious respite from the hot Bundy streets. Floral wallpaper and vintage furniture fill quickly with locals who nibble and whisper over homemade lasagna, sandwiches, pies and salads.

Spicy Tonight FUSION $
(07-4154 3320; 1 Targo St; dishes $12-20; lunch & dinner Mon-Sat;) A cornerside institution for fans of pan-Asian food, with hot curries, stir fries, tandoori and a host of vegetarian dishes. The high ceilings and well-spaced tables offer comfort in summer.

Indulge CAFE $
(80 Bourbong St; dishes $9-16; breakfast & lunch) Intoxicating pastries, fancy brekkies, decent coffee and consistently good food draw in the crowds.

Teaspoon CAFE $
(10 Targo St; mains $5-10; 8am-5pm Mon-Sat) This funky little cafe has the best coffee in town.

Les Chefs INTERNATIONAL $$
(07-4153 1770; 238 Bourbong St; mains $27; lunch Tue-Fri, dinner Mon-Sat) The most popular restaurant in town serves enormous plates of international fare. The large menu includes chicken enchiladas ($22), grilled fish ($24), veal schnitzel ($25) and yummy desserts. It's BYO and can get very busy so book ahead.

Spinnaker Restaurant & Bar MODERN AUSTRALIAN $$
(07-4152 8033; 1A Quay St; dishes $10-40; lunch Tue-Fri, dinner Tue-Sat) This riverside bar restaurant has made a post-flood resurgence with tasty pizzas, decent tapas and strong cocktails.

Restaurant MODERN AUSTRALIAN $$
(07-4154 4589; cnr Quay & Toonburra Sts; mains $25-35; dinner Tue-Sat) Once a rowing shed, this riverside bar and restaurant serves up simple Mod Oz cuisine. The interior can be a bit dim, but the outdoor tables on the timber deck make a lovely spot for a quiet drink. Live music plays on weekends.

Restaurant 55 ITALIAN $$
(07-4151 3038; 55-57 Walker St; mains $19-35; lunch & dinner Tues-Sat) Fine dining has arrived in Bundy, with 55 serving modern Italian cuisine to rival the big cities. Pasta made on the premises combines beautifully with fresh local seafood. Grilled fish and veal dishes are flavoursome and well-proportioned. Finish with the creme brulee ($13).

Club Hotel PUB
(cnr Tantitha & Bourbong Sts) The lounge bar has laid-back lounges and chill-out music.

GRAND DAMES OF THE DEEP

In the dead of night on the quiet beach of Mon Repos, 15km northeast of Bundaberg, female loggerhead turtles lumber laboriously up the sand, scoop a shallow hole with their flippers, lay 100 or so eggs, and then cover them up before returning to the ocean deep. About eight weeks later the hatchlings dig their way to the surface, and under cover of darkness emerge en masse to scurry to the water as quickly as their flippers allow. Egg laying and hatching takes place from November to March. The **Mon Repos Visitor Centre** (07-4153 8888; 271 Bourbong St) has information on turtle conservation and organises nightly tours (adult/child $10/5.25) from 7pm during the season. Bookings are mandatory and can be made through the Bundaberg visitor centre or at www.bookbundabergregion.com.au.

Central Hotel CLUB
(18 Targo St) Strut your stuff on the dance floor at Bundy's hottest nightclub.

Information

Bundaberg Email Centre (197 Bourbong St; per hr $4; 10am-10pm) Internet access.
Bundaberg Visitor Centre (07-4153 8888, 1300 722 099; www.bundabergregion.info; 271 Bourbong St; 9am-5pm)
QPWS (07-4131 1600; Targo St)

Getting There & Away

The coach terminal is in Targo St. Both **Greyhound Australia** (1300 473 946; www.greyhound.com.au) and **Premier Motor Service** (13 34 10; www.premierms.com.au) have daily services connecting Bundaberg with Brisbane ($95, seven hours), Hervey Bay ($24, 1½ hours) and Rockhampton ($75, four hours).

Duffy's Coaches (07-4151 4226) covers Bargara ($5, 35 minutes), leaving from the back of Target on Woongarra St.

Queensland Rail (13 12 30; www.queenslandrail.com.au) *Sunlander* ($68, seven hours, three weekly) and *Tilt Train* ($68, five hours, Sunday to Friday) services travel from Brisbane to Bundaberg on their respective routes to Cairns and Rockhampton.

Bundaberg's **Hinkler Airport** (Takalvan St) is about 4km southwest of the centre. There are three or four Bundaberg–Brisbane flights daily with **QantasLink** (13 13 13; www.qantas.com.au).

CAPRICORN COAST

The stunning powdery white beaches and aqua-blue waters of the tropical islands and coral cays of the Capricorn Coast fit the picture-postcard image perfectly. The peaceful islands of the southern Great Barrier Reef – Heron and Lady Elliot in particular – offer some of the best snorkelling and diving in Queensland, while remote beaches and windswept national parks can be found along the entire Capricorn coastline from lovely Byfield to charming 1770.

Rising above the inland plains, the weathered plateaus of the Great Dividing Range form spectacular sandstone escarpments, especially around the Carnarvon and Blackdown Tableland National Parks, where ancient Aboriginal rock art, deep gorges and waterfalls abound.

Southern Reef Islands

Some of the Capricorn Coast's finest moments lie 80km to the northeast of Bundaberg, on these lush green-and-gold islands atop a glassy azure sea. More and more savvy travellers are doing their Great Barrier Reef thing here – and for good reason. There's the diving wilderness of Lady Elliot and Lady Musgrave, while at secluded Heron Island you can literally wade into an underwater paradise.

The Town of 1770 is the most common stepping-off point; otherwise, use Hervey Bay or Bundaberg. Tours to the islands (from $175) stop at a number of beaches and snorkelling spots and include lunch. Alternatively, you can camp at Lady Musgrave, or stay overnight at the no-frills resort on Lady Elliot.

Lady Elliot Island

On the southern frontier of the Great Barrier Reef, Lady Elliot is a 40-hectare vegetated coral cay popular with divers, snorkellers and nesting sea turtles. The island is a breeding and nesting ground for many species of tropical seabirds, but its stunning underwater landscape is the main attraction. Divers can walk straight off the beach to explore an ocean bed of shipwrecks, coral gardens, bommies (coral pinnacles or outcroppings) and blowholes, and abundant marine life including barracuda, giant manta rays and harmless leopard sharks.

Lady Elliot Island is not a national park, and camping is not allowed.

Lady Elliot Island Resort (☎1800 072 200; www.ladyelliot.com.au; per person $147-350) may have a monopoly on the island's accommodation, but it's still great value for a bed on the edge of heaven. Accommodation is in tent cabins, simple motel-style units, or more expensive two-bedroom self-contained suites with the sand at stretching distance. Rates include breakfast and dinner, snorkelling gear and some tours.

Lady Musgrave Island

Wannabe castaways look no further. This tiny 15-hectare cay, 100km northeast of Bundaberg, sits on the western rim of a stunning, turquoise-blue reef lagoon renowned for its safe swimming, snorkelling and diving. A squeaky, white-sand beach fringes a dense canopy of pisonia forest brimming with roosting bird life, including terns, shearwaters and white-capped noddies. Birds nest from October to April, green turtles from November to February.

The uninhabited island is part of the Capricornia Cays National Park and there is a QPWS camping ground on the island's west side. The camping ground has bush toilets but little else and campers must be totally self-sufficient, even bringing their own water. Numbers are limited to 40 at any one time, so apply well ahead for a permit with the **QPWS** (☎13 74 68). Online bookings can be made through www.qld.gov.au/camping – search under Capricornia Cays National Park. Don't forget to bring a gas stove as fires are not permitted on the island.

Day trips to Lady Musgrave depart from the Town of 1770 marina.

Heron & Wilson Islands

With the underwater reef world accessible directly from the beach, Heron Island is famed for scuba diving and snorkelling, although you'll need a fair amount of cash to visit. A true coral cay, it is densely vegetated with pisonia trees and surrounded by 24 sq km of reef. There's a resort and research station on the northeastern third of the island; the remainder is national park.

The former five-star **Heron Island Resort** (☎07-4972 9055, 1800 737 678; www.heronisland.com; s/d incl buffet breakfast from $398/499) has seen better days but it is certainly not reason to stay away from the island. The Point Suites still have the best views and the family rooms are comfortable enough not to detract from the island experience. However, the restaurant (and only place to eat) might be considered below par in both service and food quality considering the high price. Guests will pay $200/100 per adult/child for launch transfer, or $790/430 for helicopter transfer. Both are from Gladstone.

Wilson Island (www.wilsonisland.com; s/d from $853/1100), also part of a national park, is an exclusive wilderness retreat with six permanent tents and solar-heated showers. The inclusive menu is superb, as are the beaches, especially for snorkelling. The only access is from Heron Island and you'll need to buy a combined Wilson-Heron package and spend at least two nights on Wilson Island.

Agnes Water & Town of 1770

Surrounded by national parks, sandy beaches and the blue Pacific, the twin coastal towns of Agnes Water and Town of 1770 are among Queensland's most appealing seaside destinations. The tiny settlement of Agnes Water has a lovely white-sand beach, the east coast's most northerly surf beach, while the even tinier Town of 1770 (little more than a marina!) marks Captain Cook's first landing in Queensland. This area provides good access to the southern end of the reef, including the Fitzroy Reef Lagoon. The 'Discovery Coast' is a popular nook for surfing, boating and fishing away from the crowds. To get here, turn east off the Bruce Hwy at Miriam Vale, 70km south of Gladstone. It's another 57km to Agnes Water and a further 6km to the Town of 1770.

Activities

The action around here happens on and in the water. Agnes Water is supposedly Queensland's northernmost surf beach. A surf lifesaving club patrols the main beach and there are often good breaks along the coast.

Reef 2 Beach Surf School SURFING
(☎07-4974 9072; www.reef2beachsurf.com; 1/10 Round Hill Rd, Agnes Water) Learn to surf on the gentle breaks of the main beach with this highly acclaimed surf school. A three-hour group surfing lesson is $17, and surfboard hire is $20 for four hours.

1770 Liquid Adventures KAYAKING
(☎0428 956 630; www.1770liquidadventures.com.au; 2hr kayak rental $40) Liquid runs a spectacular twilight kayak tour ($55).

1770 Underwater Sea Adventures DIVING
(☎1300 553 889; www.1770underseaadventures.com.au) Check availability prior to landing in town. Courses, reef trips and wreck dives all doable.

Scooteroo MOTORCYCLING
(☎07-4974 7696; www.scooterrootours.com; 21 Bicentennial Dr, Agnes Water; 3hr chopper rides $60) Irreverent and engaging 60km ride around the area.

Tours

1770 Larc Tours TOUR
(☎07-4974 9422; www.1770larctours.com.au; adult/child $148/88) A pink amphibious military vehicle emerging from the water around Bustard Head and Eurimbula National Park sounds counter-intuitive to eco-tourism yet somehow the whole spirit of the thing feels right. If a day is too long, the outfit also runs one-hour sunset cruises ($38) and sandboarding safaris ($120 per person).

Lady Musgrave Cruises CRUISE
(☎07-4974 9077; www.1770reefcruises.com; Captain Cook Dr; adult/child $175/85) Has excellent day trips to Lady Musgrave Island aboard the *Spirit of 1770*. Trips include snorkelling, fishing gear, coral viewing in a semisubmersible, lunch and snacks. Island camping transfers are also available for $320 per person.

ThunderCat 1770 ADVENTURE, TOUR
(☎0427 177 000; adult/child $85/65) Ride in a 4m inflatable surf racing craft across the waves or visit secluded beaches, learn some local history and explore 1770's pristine waterways and national-park coastline.

Sleeping

Backpackers 1770 HOSTEL $
(☎07-4974 9132; www.the1770backpackers.com; 7 Agnes St; dm/d $25/55; @) Small friendly backpackers 700m from the beach.

1770 Southern Cross Tourist Retreat HOSTEL $
(☎07-4974 7225; www.1770southerncross.com; 2694 Round Hill Rd; dm/d incl breakfast $25/85; @ ≋) There's an enlightened approach to budget accommodation at this retreat, with 6.5 hectares of bushland 2.5km out of town. Buddhist statues, a meditation *sala* and a fish-filled, swimmable lake are ideal for pensive reflection, or sleeping off a hangover. The rooms have a hint of southeast Asia and the dorms are the best for miles.

Capricorn Coast

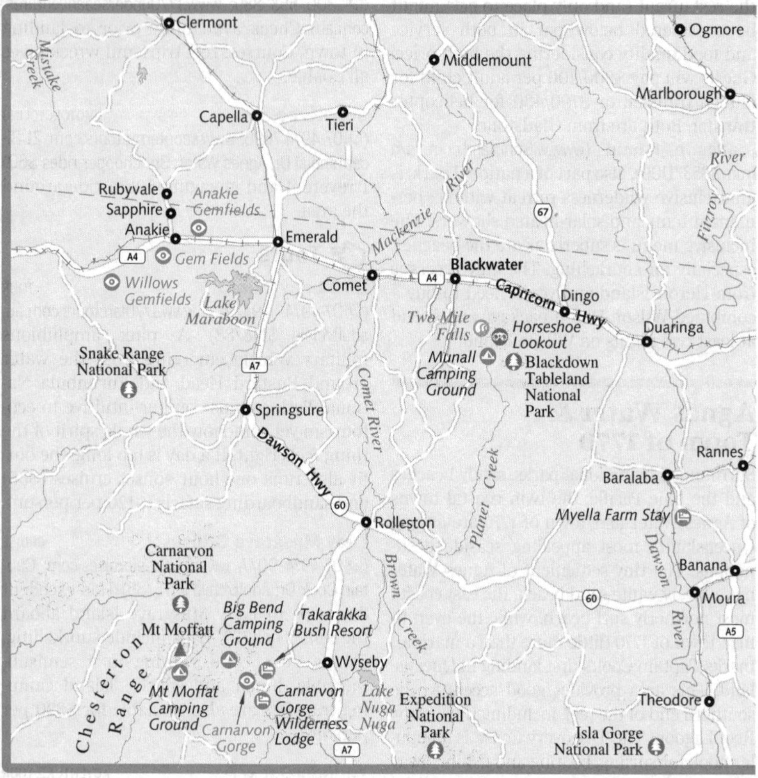

Cool Bananas HOSTEL $

(☎1800 227 660, 07-4974 7660; www.coolbananas.net.au; 2 Springs Rd; dm night/week $26/140; @) A short walk from Agnes main beach and shopping precinct is this chilled-out backpackers with very clean six- and eight-bed dorms. The greatest assets are the warm staff and the bright communal areas. It's especially popular with young Europeans.

1770 Camping Grounds CAMPGROUND $

(☎07-4974 9286; www.1770campinggrounds.com; Captain Cook Dr; unpowered/powered sites $33/38) A large peaceful park by the beach.

Agnes Water Beach Caravan Park CAMPGROUND $$

(☎07-4974 9132; www.agneswaterfirstpoint.com.au; Jeffrey Ct; unpowered/powered sites $30/59, cabins $160-$250) This park has tented cabins on stilts that offer excellent-value beachfront rooms. Each cabin comes with its own deck, equipped with gas barbecue.

LaLaLand Retreat RETREAT $$

(☎ 4974 9554; www.lalaland1770aw.com.au; 61 Bicentennial Dve, Agnes Water; cabin from $170; P❄) The four colourful cabins at this new guesthouse on the road into town are set in attractive bushland scrub and each sleeps four people easily. There is an excellent lagoon-style pool, wheelchair access and, aside from potential nosy neighbours, a sense of remove from civilisation.

Beach Shacks APARTMENT $$

(☎07-4974 9463; www.1770beachshacks.com; 578 Captain Cook Dr; d from $190) The best accommodation in the Town of 1770 proper is run by a charming Canadian lady. These 'shacks' are more than humble beach dwellings, with cane, bamboo and timber on the outside, and contemporary decor on the inside. Ask for the Light House.

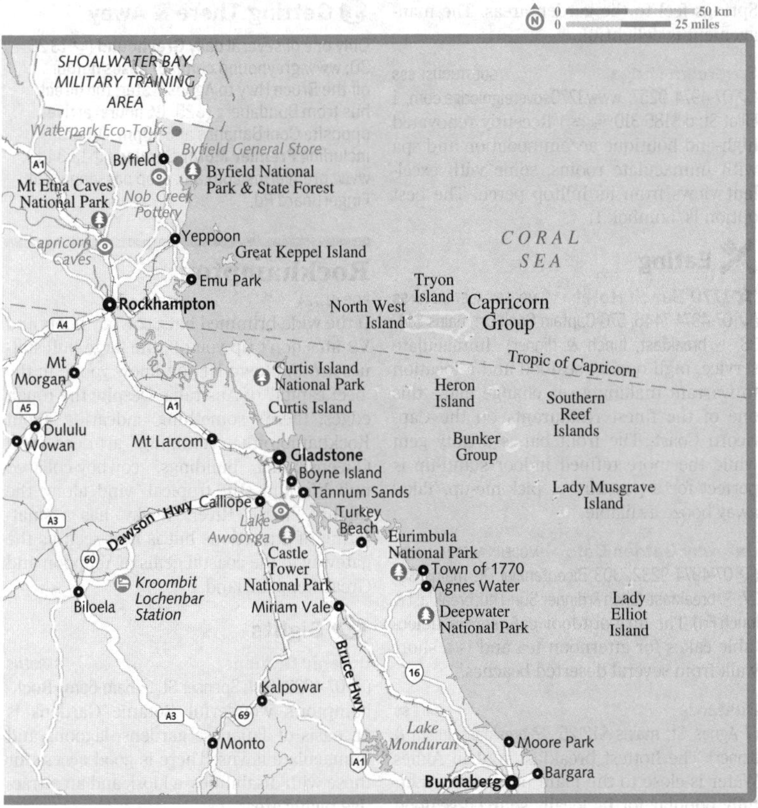

Captain Cook Holiday Village CAMPGROUND, CABIN $$
(☎07-4974 9219; www.1770holidayvillage.com.au; 384 Captain Cook Dve; unpowered/powered sites from $35/41, cabins from $109, villas from $149; P ≋) Equidistant to both 1770 and Agnes Water is this fine camping complex that gets very popular in summer. The cabins are comfortable and well-maintained, and represent the best value in town for couples or small groups.

Mango Tree Motel MOTEL $$
(☎07-4974 9132; www.mangotreemotel.com; 7 Agnes St; r from $140; ❄) Good-value motel with large rooms 100m from the beach.

Agnes Water Beach Club APARTMENT $$
(☎07-4974 7355; www.agneswaterbeachclub.com.au; 3 Agnes St; 1-/2-bedroom apt from $145/190; ❄ @ ≋) Brand-new luxury apartments with excellent facilities in a great location.

Sandcastles 1770 Motel & Resort MOTEL, RESORT $$
(☎07-4974 9428; www.sandcastles1770.com.au; 1 Grahame Colyer Dr; motel r from $120, villas & beach-home apt $160-650; ❄ @ ≋) Set on 4 hectares of landscaped gardens and subtropical vegetation, Sandcastles has a mix of motel-style rooms (from $90), luxury beach-home apartments and airy Balinese-themed villas. There's also a popular restaurant on-site.

Pavillions on 1770 APARTMENT $$$
(☎07-4902 1000; www.pavillionson1770.com.au; 4 Beaches Village Circuit; 1-/2-bedroom apt from $180/220; P ❄ ≋) This prime development on the site of the former Mantra looks a little like a retirement village on a rugged section of beach. Still, the apartments are brilliant: huge bathrooms, state-of-the-art kitchens, dual balconies and king-size beds. There are two exquisite swimming pools and a Palm

Springs feel to the garden areas. The management is delightful.

Sovereign Lodge GUESTHOUSE $$$
(☎07-4974 9257; www.1770sovereignlodge.com; 1 Elliot St; d $185-310; ❄ ✉) Recently renovated high-end boutique accommodation and spa with immaculate rooms, some with excellent views from its hilltop perch. The best option is 'Lombok 1'.

Eating

★1770 Beach Hotel MODERN AUSTRALIAN $$
(☎07-4974 7446; 576 Captain Cook Dr; mains $14-38; ⊙breakfast, lunch & dinner) Immaculate service, high quality seafood and a location to warrant making a sea change make this one of the finest restaurants on the Capricorn Coast. The front bar is a salty gem while the more refined indoor stand-up is perfect for a post-sunset pick-me-up. Takeaway booze available.

Getaway Garden Café MODERN AUSTRALIAN $$
(☎07-4974 9232; 303 Bicentennial Dr; mains $8-27; ⊙breakfast, lunch & dinner Sun-Thu, breakfast & lunch Fri) The airy outdoor cafe serves delectable cakes for afternoon tea and is a short walk from several deserted beaches.

Bustards CAFE $$
(7 Agnes St; mains $12-25; ⊙breakfast, lunch & dinner) The hottest breakfast spot in Agnes Water is close to the main beach and rightfully popular for its locally sourced seafood and light lunches. Service comes in buckets and spades.

Kahunas Pizza Bar & Grill MODERN AUSTRALIAN $$
(☎07-4974 9428; 1 Grahame Colyer Dr; mains $15-38; ⊙dinner) Located inside a small resort, Kahunas is a popular choice with locals, especially for beer and fabulous wood-fired pizza.

Agnes Water Tavern PUB $$
(☎07-4974 9469; 1 Tavern Rd; mains $15-30; ⊙lunch & dinner) Pleasant multi-purpose pub with plenty of outdoor seating. Lunch and dinner specials daily.

Information

Agnes Water Visitor Information Centre
(☎07-4902 1533; 71 Springs Rd; ⊙9am-4.30pm Mon-Fri) Very friendly and helpful staff at this brand-new $1-million community centre about 700m from the main intersection.

Getting There & Away

Only one of several daily **Greyhound** (☎13 20 30; www.greyhound.com.au) buses detours off the Bruce Hwy to Agnes Water; the direct bus from Bundaberg ($25, 1½ hours) arrives opposite Cool Bananas at 6.10pm. Others, including **Premier Motor Service** (☎13 34 10; www.premierms.com.au), drop passengers at Fingerboard Rd.

Rockhampton

POP 61,724

If the wide-brimmed hats, cowboy boots and V8 utes don't tip you off, the large bull statues around town let you know you're in the 'beef capital' of Australia. Despite the rough edges, there's something endearing about Rockhampton's crumbling art-deco and Queenslander buildings, cowboy-collared pub life and stiff tropical wind along the mighty Fitzroy River. 'Rocky' has a smattering of attractions but is best seen as the gateway to the coastal gems of Yeppoon and Great Keppel Island.

Sights

Botanic Gardens GARDENS
(☎07-4922 1654; Spencer St; ⊙6am-6pm) Rockhampton's wonderful Botanic Gardens is an oasis of Japanese gardens, lagoons and immaculate lawns. There is good access for those with disabilities, a kiosk and an attractive picnic area.

Rockhampton Zoo ZOO
(Botanic Gardens, Spencer St; ⊙8am-4.30pm) FREE There's Australian native flora and fauna on show with regular feeding tours.

Dreamtime Cultural Centre CULTURAL CENTRE
(☎07-4936 1655; www.dreamtimecentre.com.au; Bruce Hwy; adult/child $14/6.50; ⊙10am-3.30pm Mon-Fri, tours 10.30am) An easily accessible insight into Aboriginal and Torres Strait Islander heritage and history. The excellent 90-minute tours are hands on (boomerangs!) and appeal to all ages. It's about 7km north of the centre.

Rockhampton City Art Gallery GALLERY
(62 Victoria Pde; ⊙10am-4pm Tue-Fri, 11am-4pm Sat & Sun) FREE This gallery exhibits an impressive collection of Australian paintings, including works by Sir Russell Drysdale, Sir Sidney Nolan and Albert Namatjira.

Sleeping

Choose somewhere in the old centre, south of the river, if you want to stroll the more elegant streets overlooking the Fitzroy River.

Rockhampton YHA HOSTEL $
(07-4927 5288; www.yha.com.au; 60 MacFarlane St; dm/d $22/60;) This well-maintained hostel has a spacious lounge and dining area, dorms, private doubles and cabins. The hostel arranges tours, has courtesy pick-ups from the bus station, and sells coach tickets. There's also free bike hire.

Heritage Hotel HOTEL $
(07-4927 6996; www.theheritagehotel.com.au; 228 Quay St; dm/s/d $25/56/107;) This old pub with iron-lattice balconies has a stylish cocktail lounge with river views and outdoor tables. The rooms are decent for the price with shared bathrooms and a beautiful wraparound balcony. Can be noisy on weekends. Good place for a drink.

Southside Holiday Village CAMPGROUND $
(1800 075 911; www.sshv.com.au; Lower Dawson Rd; sites unpowered/powered/with bathroom $25/32/42, cabins $62-102;) This excellent caravan park has cabins, villas and large grassy camp sites about 3km south of the centre. There's a courtesy coach.

Criterion HOTEL $$
(07-4922 1225; www.thecriterion.com.au; 150 Quay St; r $60-85, motel r $130-160;) No longer haunted by that pesky chambermaid, apparently, the Criterion is a grand old hotel on the Fitzroy. The foyer is full of charm and the bar and bistro heave with locals. The period rooms upstairs are mixed, so see a few.

Denison Hotel BOUTIQUE HOTEL $$
(07-4923 7378; www.denisonhotel.com.au; 233 Denison St; r $105-165;) This freshly renovated 1885 Victorian home is an easy walk from Quay St. Its stately rooms come with four-poster beds and plasma TVs, and the hotel's Rolls Royce can pick you up from the airport or station.

The Bridge Motor Inn MOTEL $$
(07-4927 7488; www.thebridgemotorinn.com.au; 31 Bolsover St; r $95-130;) Found on the way into town, The Bridge is one of the better motor inns in Rocky. The pool is ideal for freshening up and the rooms are clean and quiet.

STINGERS

It mightn't look or feel pretty, but unless you stay out of the water a 'stinger suit' is your only real protection against Queensland's lethal jellyfish (and harmful UV rays). There are two to be aware of: the rare and tiny (1cm to 2cm across) irukandji and the box jellyfish, also known as the sea wasp or stinger. They're found in coastal waters north of Rockhampton (occasionally further south) from around October to April, although the danger periods can vary.

If someone has been stung, call an ambulance or get a lifeguard (artificial respiration may be required), douse the stings with vinegar (available on many beaches or from nearby houses) and seek medical aid.

Check with lifeguards whether the stingers are out. If so, stick to the hotel pool.

Coffee House MOTEL, APARTMENT $$
(07-4927 5722; www.coffeehouse.com.au; 51 William St; r $160-189;) The Coffee House features beautifully appointed motel rooms, self-contained apartments and spa suites. There's a popular and stylish cafe-restaurant–wine bar on-site.

Eating & Drinking

Saigon Saigon ASIAN $$
(07-4927 0888; www.saigonbytheriver.com; Quay St; mains $15-20; lunch & dinner Wed-Mon;) The only restaurant on the riverside of Quay St is in a two-storey bamboo hut. The Vietnamese and Chinese dishes are spot on, and any of the curries do the trick. Vegetarians have plenty to choose from.

Bistro 98 SEAFOOD, STEAKHOUSE $$
(07-4927 5322; www.98.com.au; 98 Victoria Pde; mains $18-46; breakfast daily, lunch Mon-Fri, dinner Mon-Sat) One of Rocky's finest, this licensed dining room features modern Australian versions of kangaroo, steak, lamb and seafood. Sit inside or on the terrace overlooking the river.

Pacino's ITALIAN $$$
(07-4922 5833; cnr Fitzroy & George Sts; mains $25-40; dinner Tue-Sun) Prices are a little steep for fairly typical Italian fare. The staff are excellent though and the stone floors,

wooden tables and potted fig trees create a touch of Roman charm.

Great Western Hotel BAR
(www.greatwesternhotel.com.au; 39 Stanley St) Drink rum and beer, eat superlative steak and – on Wednesday and Friday nights – practise your bullriding skills in the rodeo arena.

Shopping

Mavericks CLOTHING
(07-4921 0622; 161 Canning St) Mavericks sells quality belt buckles, Akubra hats, stockman whips and other countrified regalia.

Information

Rockhampton Visitor Information Centre (208 Quay St) is in the beautiful former Customs House.

Getting There & Away

AIR

Rockhampton is serviced by **Qantas** (13 13 13; www.qantas.com.au) and **Virgin Australia** (13 67 89; www.virginaustralia.com).

BUS

Greyhound Australia (13 20 30; www.greyhound.com.au) has regular services from Rocky to Mackay ($59, four hours), Brisbane ($151, 11 hours) and Cairns ($189, 18 hours). All services stop at the **Mobil roadhouse** (91 George St).
Premier Motor Service (13 34 10; www.premierms.com.au) operates a Brisbane–Cairns service, stopping at Rockhampton.

TRAIN

Queensland Rail (1800 872 467; www.queenslandrail.com.au) runs the *Tilt Train*, which connects Rockhampton with Brisbane (from $130, 7½ hours, Sunday to Friday) and Cairns (from $229, 16 hours, twice weekly). The train station is 450m southwest of the city centre.

Around Rockhampton

About 23km north of Rockhampton, in the Berserker Range, are the impressive **Capricorn Caves** (07-4934 2883; www.capricorncaves.com.au; 30 Olsens Caves Rd; adult/child $27/14; 9am-4pm). These deeply illuminated limestone passages are particularly spectacular during the summer solstice period (1 December to 14 January), when the sun beams vertical shafts of light through the roof of the Belfry Cave. Guided tours leave on the hour.

In bushland next to the caves, the excellent **Capricorn Caves Cabins** (07-4934 2883; www.capricorncaves.com.au; 30 Olsens Caves Rd; powered sites $34, cabins from $140) provide a novel experience. The camping facilities are fairly modest.

Myella Farm Stay (07-4998 1290; www.myella.com; Baralaba Rd; 2/4 days $260/480, day trips $120;) is a 1040-hectare beef property, 120km southwest of Rockhampton, with a fully renovated homestead fitted with hardwood floors and pine-scented mod cons. You can care for orphaned joeys at the on-site kangaroo rehab centre, ride horses or just unwind in the almost outback. Prices include free transfers from Rockhampton.

Kroombit Lochenbar Station (07-4992 2186; www.kroombit.com.au; dm $27, d with/without bathroom $84/68, 2-day & 2-night packages per person incl room, meals & activities $280;) is a fine farm stay, 35km east of Biloela.

Yeppoon

POP 13,500

The gateway to Great Keppel Island, Yeppoon is an attractive seaside village with pleasant beaches giving way to untapped rainforest around Byfield. Travelling south, you pass Rosslyn Bay, the departure point for Great Keppel, and lovely little Emu Park, before winding your way along scenic coastline.

Sleeping

Emu's Beach Resort & Backpackers HOSTEL $
(1800 333 349; www.emusbeachresort.com; 92 Pattison St, Emu Park; dm $25-28, d/tr/q $80/95/105;) Emu Beach Resort is a down-tempo seaside escape for young families after space and quiet or backpackers finished with the East Coast party scene. The dorms and doubles are well-presented and surround an attractive pool and barbecue area. If you can wrestle away from the new bar, the empty beach across the road is beautiful. It's 19km south of Yeppoon.

Beachside Caravan Park CAMPGROUND $
(07-4939 3738; Farnborough Rd; unpowered sites $25, powered sites $30-34) Very basic camping park north of the town centre, with a beachfront location its saving grace.

Surfside Motel MOTEL $$
(07-4939 1272; 30 Anzac Pde; r $110-140;) This 1950s strip of lime-green

WORTH A TRIP

BYFIELD

Diverse and beautiful, Byfield National Park consists of monstrous sand dunes, thick semi-tropical rainforest, wetlands and rocky pinnacles. It's superb Sunday-arvo driving terrain, with plenty of hiking paths and isolated beaches to warrant a longer stay. There are five **camping grounds** (☎13 74 68; www.derm.qld.gov.au/camping; per person/family $5.85/21.80) to choose from; all must be prebooked. Nine Mile Beach and Five Rocks campgrounds are on the beach and require a 4WD to access. When conditions are right, there's decent surf at Nine Mile Beach. **Byfield General Store** (☎07-4935 1190; Byfield Rd, Byfield; ⏰8am-6pm Wed-Mon, to 2pm Tue) doubles as an information centre. It also stocks fuel and famous vegie burgers ($10).

The area is also known for the highly controversial military training facility at Shoalwater Bay that borders the forest and park, and is strictly off-limits.

You can unfurl your senses in the rainforest on a silent, electric-boat tour with **Waterpark Eco-Tours** (☎07-4935 1171; www.waterparkecotours.com; 201 Waterpark Creek Rd; 2-3hr tours $25, cabins $120).

Nob Creek Pottery (☎07-4935 1161; 216 Arnolds Rd; ⏰9am-5pm) FREE is a working pottery and gallery nestled in leafy rainforest. The gallery showcases hand-blown glass, woodwork and jewellery, and the handmade ceramics are outstanding.

Built by the multi-faceted owners of Nob Creek Pottery, **Byfield Mountain Retreat** (☎07-4935 1161; www.byfieldmountainretreat.com; per night/week $220/1200) is a remarkable place to stay. Set on 66 acres of richly scented rainforest splendour, the house sleeps 12 and overlooks a working dam. The interior is influenced by Balinese aesthetics, and there's a log fire, walking trails and king-size beds. The verandah views of the hinterland are heady.

Signposted just north of Byfield, **Ferns Hideaway** (☎07-4935 1235; www.fernshideaway.com.au; 67 Cahills Rd, Byfield; unpowered sites $24, d $150; ❄🏊) is a secluded bush oasis with double rooms, a campground and canoeing and nature walks. The timber homestead has a quality à la carte restaurant (mains $18 to 32; open breakfast Sunday, lunch and afternoon tea Wednesday to Sunday and dinner Saturday) featuring live music on weekends.

Byfield Creek Lodge (☎07-4935 1117; www.byfieldcreeklodge.com.au; 32 Richters Rd, Byfield; d incl breakfast from $150; ❄) is an African-themed B&B set on 3.2 hectares of rainforest overlooking Byfield Creek.

motel units epitomises summer holidays at the beach. They are very popular due to their fair price, proximity to the beach (it's across the road) and friendly service.

Coast Motel MOTEL $$
(☎07-4930 2325; www.thecoastmotel.com.au; 52 Scenic Hwy; r from $135; P❄📶🏊) Located a few clicks from town but still on the beach, this brand new motel has minimalist, white rooms in a raised, old-style motor inn set-up.

While Away B&B B&B $$
(☎07-4939 5719; www.whileawaybandb.com.au; 44 Todd Ave; s/d incl breakfast $115/140; ❄) This B&B makes for a peaceful getaway, with four good-sized rooms and an immaculately clean house, as well as generous breakfasts.

Villa Mar Colina BOUTIQUE HOTEL $$$
(☎07-4939 3177; www.villamarcolina.com.au; 34 Adelaide St; villa from $210; P❄📶🏊) The views from high on Bluff Point are gobsmacking at this series of Mediterranean-style villas located a short, steep walk from the Yeppoon shops. The friendly owners – who made a sea-change from Victoria – maintain immaculate premises and have a contender for a 'Best View From a Pool' award.

Eating & Drinking

The Shore Thing CAFE $
(☎07-4939 1993; 1/6 Normanby St; mains $10-16; ⏰7.30am-5pm Sun-Thu) This bright, sure thing is the pick of the local cafes due to its prompt service and yummy breakfasts.

Shio Kaze JAPANESE $$
(☎07-4939 5575; 18 Anzac Pde; for 2 people about $70; ⏰lunch & dinner Wed-Sun) Delectable sushi opposite the beach, though it's not cheap ($25 for a smallish single-person platter)

and service was a little priggish when we visited. Lunchtime bento boxes ($22 to $29) are better value. BYO alcohol.

Thai Take-Away THAI $$
(24 Anzac Pde; mains $12-25; ⏲ dinner) A deservedly popular BYO restaurant where you can dine alfresco while satisfying those chilli and coconut cravings. There's a large selection of seafood dishes and snappy service.

Megalomania FUSION $$$
(☎ 07-4939 2333; Arthur St; mains $22-36; ⏲ lunch & dinner Tue-Sat, lunch Sun) An urban-island vibe permeates Yeppoon's best restaurant which serves a kind of Oz-Asian fusion cuisine, with emphasis on seafood. The barramundi spring rolls ($18) and coconut king prawn laksa ($36) set the tone (and the standard price range) for the lunch and dinner menus. Acoustic music and smooth cocktails round out the experience.

Strand Hotel PUB
(2 Normanby St) Threatened for redevelopment, the Strand is still a battered old beast serving $10 counter meals to some clientele who possess a certain battered charm.

Information

Capricorn Coast Information Centre (☎ 1800 675 785; www.capricorncoast.com.au; Scenic Hwy; ⏲ 9am-5pm) For info on the area, head to Capricorn Coast Information Centre.

Great Keppel Island

Great Keppel Island is a stunning island with rocky headlands, forested hills and a fringe of powdery white sand lapped by clear azure waters. Numerous 'castaway' beaches ring the 14-sq-km island, while natural bushland covers 90% of the interior. A string of huts and accommodation options sits behind the trees lining the main beach, but the developments are low-key and unobtrusive and the island itself is only 13km offshore.

The kiosk at Great Keppel Island Holiday Village has a few essentials, but if you want to cook bring your own supplies.

Sights & Activities

The beaches of Great Keppel rate among Queensland's best. Take a short stroll from **Fisherman's Beach**, the main beach, and you'll find your own deserted stretch of white sand. There is fairly good coral and excellent fish life, especially between Great Keppel and Humpy Island to the south. A 30-minute walk south around the headland brings you to **Monkey Beach**, where there's good snorkelling. A walking trail from the southern end of the airfield takes you to **Long Beach**, perhaps the best of the island's beaches.

There are several bushwalking tracks from Fisherman's Beach; the longest and perhaps most difficult leads to the 2.5m 'lighthouse' near Bald Rock Point on the far side of the island (three hours return).

Keppel Reef Scuba Adventures DIVING
(☎ 07-4939 5022, 0408 004 536; www.keppeldive.com; Putney Beach) Keppel Reef Scuba Adventures offers introductory dives for $200, snorkelling trips (per person $50), and also hires out snorkelling gear (per day $15).

Watersports Hut WATER SPORTS
(☎ 07-4925 0624; Putney Beach; ⏲ weekends & school holidays) The Watersports Hut is just one of a few places hiring sailboards, catamarans, motorboats and snorkelling gear. It can also take you waterskiing, parasailing or camel-riding.

Sleeping & Eating

★ **Svendsen's Beach** CABIN $
(☎ 07-4938 3717; www.svendsensbeach.com; cabins for 3 nights per person $330) From the moment the water-taxi collects you from Putney Beach, you will feel the worries of the mainland drift away. Bushwalking, snorkelling, bird watching and generally lazing about are all highly recommended. There are two luxury tent-bungalows on separate elevated timber decks, each with a small kitchen. BYO grub (food). Minimum three-night stay.

Great Keppel Island Backpackers & Holiday Village HOSTEL, CABIN $$
(☎ 07-4939 8655; www.gkiholidayvillage.com.au; dm $35, s & d tents $90, cabins $150, 2-bedroom houses for 5 nights from $850) Well-managed operation that acts as a sort of hub for the (modest) travel community on the island. The communal facilities are excellent and the entire premises is neat and orderly. Most guests choose the large 'tents' but the newly renovated houses are great value if you have a bit of a mob.

Keppel Lodge GUESTHOUSE $$
(☎ 07-4939 4251; www.keppellodge.com.au; Fisherman's Beach; d $110) A pleasant open-plan house with four large bedrooms branching

from a large communal lounge and kitchen. The house is available in its entirety ($440) or as individual motel-type suites.

Island Pizza PIZZA $
(☎07-4939 4699; The Esplanade; dishes $6-30) This friendly place prides itself on its gourmet pizzas with plenty of toppings. Check the blackboard for opening times.

Getting There & Away

Freedom Fast Cats (☎07-4933 6244, 1800 336 244; www.freedomfastcats.com) depart from the Keppel Bay marina in Rosslyn Bay (7km south of Yeppoon) for Great Keppel Island each morning, returning that same afternoon (call ahead for precise times). The return fare is $50/30/145 per adult/child/family. If you have booked accommodation, check that someone will meet you on the beach to help with your luggage.

Other Keppel Bay Islands

Although you can make day trips to the fringing coral reefs of Middle Island or **Halfway Island** from Great Keppel Island (ask your accommodation or at Great Keppel Island Holiday Village), you can also **camp** (per person/family $5.85/21.80) on several national park islands, including **Humpy Island**, **Middle Island**, **North Keppel Island** and **Miall Island**. You'll need all your own supplies, including water. For information and permits contact the **QPWS** (☎13 74 68; www.qld.gov.au/camping) or **Rosslyn Bay Marine Parks** (☎07-4933 6595).

The Queensland brewing giant XXXX has recently leased the very glamorous **Pumpkin Island** until 2015. So, unless you have any luck with a 'specially marked' box of beer, you are not allowed to visit the island.

From Rosslyn Bay, **Funtastic Cruises** (☎0438 909 502; cruises adult/child $90/75) offers day cruises exploring the islands and can also provide drop-offs and pick-ups for campers

Capricorn Hinterland

The Central Highlands, west of Rockhampton, are home to two excellent national parks. Blackdown Tableland National Park is a brooding, powerful place, while visitors to Carnarvon National Park come mostly for the spectacular gorge. At Emerald, 270km inland, you can break your back and your spirit fossicking for gems in the heat and rubble. Try to stick to the cooler months between April and November.

Blackdown Tableland National Park

Spooky, spectacular Blackdown Tableland is a 600m sandstone plateau that rises suddenly out of the flat plains of central Queensland. It's a bushwalker's heaven here, with unique wildlife and plant species and a strong Indigenous artistic and spiritual presence. The turn-off to Blackdown Tableland is 11km west of Dingo and 35km east of the coal-mining centre of Blackwater. The 23km gravel road, which begins at the base of the tableland, isn't suitable for caravans and can be unsafe in wet weather – the first 8km stretch is steep, winding and often slippery. At the top you'll come to the breathtaking **Horseshoe Lookout**, with picnic tables, barbecues and toilets. There's a walking trail to **Two Mile Falls** (2km) starting here.

Munall Camping Ground (☎13 74 68; www.qld.gov.au/camping; per person/family $5.45/21.80) is about 8km on from Horseshoe Lookout. It has pit toilets and fireplaces – you'll need water, firewood and/or a fuel stove. Bookings are essential.

Gem Fields

West of **Emerald** (named after Emerald Creek, in turn named after local prospector Jack Emerald) sit 640 sq km of gem fields that draw a regular trickle of heart-strong speckers who eke out a living until a jackpot – or sunstroke – arrives. Rare and precious rubies, sapphires and zircons do find their way to the surface from time to time, especially after a heavy rain.

To go fossicking you need a licence (adult/family $6.85/9.80) from one of the gem fields' general stores or post offices. If you just wish to dabble, you can buy a bucket of 'wash' (mine dirt in water) from one of the fossicking parks and hand-sieve and wash it.

Anakie, 42km west of Emerald, dubs itself the 'Gateway to the Gemfields'. As such, there is a feeling of neglect in the tired, empty streets, perhaps due to the one-track mindedness of local industry.

Another 18km on is **Rubyvale**, the main town on the fields, and 2km further is the excellent **Miners Heritage Walk-in**

Mine (☎07-4985 4444; Heritage Rd, Rubyvale; adult/child $13/5; ⌚9am-5pm). Informative 30-minute underground tours are available here throughout the day in which you descend into a maze of tunnels 18m beneath the surface.

There are caravan-camping parks at Anakie, Rubyvale and Willows Gemfields.

Run by a couple of experienced travellers, the spruced-up **Sapphire Caravan Park Retreat** (☎07-4985 4281; www.sapphirecaravanpark.com.au; 57 Sunrise Rd, Sapphire; unpowered/powered sites $25/29, miners hut/cottage/ste $75/115/125) is near the centre of town. It has a range of sleeping options, including fancy suites and miners huts. The shared facilities surpass the regional standard.

Pat's Gems (☎07-4985 4544; 1056 Rubyvale Rd; cabins $85; ⌚cafe 8.30am-5pm; ❄) has four clean cabins, which fill quickly with happy regulars and families. There's a camp barbecue, kitchen area and an on-site cafe. The proprietress and namesake is a delight.

Carnarvon National Park

Carnarvon Gorge is a dramatic rendition of Australian natural beauty. Escaped convicts often took refuge here among ancient rock paintings. The area was made a national park in 1932 after defeated farmers forfeited their pastoral lease.

The 30km-long, 200m-high gorge was carved out over millions of years by Carnarvon Creek and its tributaries twisting through soft sedimentary rock. What was left behind is a lush, other-worldly oasis, where life flourished, shielded from the stark terrain. You'll find giant cycads, king ferns, river oaks, flooded gums, cabbage palms, deep pools and platypuses in the creek.

For most people, Carnarvon Gorge *is* the Carnarvon National Park, because the other sections – including Mt Moffatt (where Indigenous groups lived some 19,000 years ago), Ka Ka Mundi and Salvator Rosa – have long been difficult to access.

Coming from Rolleston the road is bitumen for 75km and unsealed for 20km. From Roma via Injune and Wyseby homestead, the road is good bitumen for about 215km, then unsealed and fairly rough for the last 30km. After heavy rain, both these roads can become impassable.

The entrance road leads to an **information centre** (☎07-4984 4505; ⌚8-10am & 3-5pm) and scenic picnic ground. Limited camping is available by the entrance during school holidays. The main walking track also starts here, following Carnarvon Creek through the gorge, with detours to various points of interest. These include the **Moss Garden** (3.6km from the picnic area), **Ward's Canyon** (4.8km), the **Art Gallery** (5.6km) and **Cathedral Cave** (9.3km). Allow *at least* a whole day for a visit. Basic groceries and ice are available at Takarakka Bush Resort. Petrol is not available anywhere in the gorge – fill up at Rolleston or Injune.

You cannot drive from Carnarvon Gorge to other sections of the park, although you can reach beautiful Mt Moffatt via an unsealed road from Injune (4WD necessary).

Sunrover Expeditions (☎1800 353 717; www.sunrover.com.au; per person incl all meals $950) runs a five-day camping safari into Carnarvon Gorge between March and October.

For accommodation, book ahead before entering. **Big Bend Camping Ground** (☎13 74 68; www.qld.gov.au/camping; sites per person/family $5.85/21.80) is an isolated campground a 10km walk up the gorge. For **Mt Moffatt Camping Ground** (☎13 74 68; www.qld.gov.au/camping; sites per person/family $5.85/21.80), campers need to be self-sufficient and have a 4WD.

A little scrappy around the edges, **Takarakka Bush Resort** (☎07-4984 4535; www.takarakka.com.au; Wyseby Rd; unpowered/powered sites from $38/45, cabins $195-228) is still popular with families and bush whackers. The overpriced safari tents ($132) are OK for the ill-prepared. The ensuite cabins are tiring by the season but can sleep four and therefore represent decent value. Reception sells basic groceries, maps, booze, ice and fresh linen ($10). The resort is 5km from the entry to the gorge.

Outback chic is on offer at the attractive **Carnarvon Gorge Wilderness Lodge** (☎1800 644 150; www.carnarvon-gorge.com; Wyseby Rd; d from $220; ⌚closed Nov-Feb; ❄), set deep in the bush. Excellent guided tours are available, plus a full-board package (from $155 to $300 per person).

There are no bus services to Carnarvon, so the best way to get here is to hire a car or take an overnight tour from the coast.

OUTBACK

The outback is a mythological frontier where settler folk struck open the deep-red earth and bored out a nation through grit and verse. Past the Great Dividing Range the sky opens up over tough country, both relentless and beautiful, and the ancient song lines run deep. Travellers come for the exotic and intimate Australian experience, their restlessness tamed by the sheer size of the place, its luminous colours and its silence.

Although sparsely settled, the outback is well serviced by major roads, namely the Overlander's Way (Flinders and Barkly Hwys – Rtes 78 and 66) and the Matilda Hwy (Landsborough Hwy, Rte 71) and Burke Developmental Rd (Rte 83). Once you turn off these major arteries, however, road conditions deteriorate rapidly, services are remote and you need to be fully self-sufficient, carrying spare parts, fuel and water. Also do some planning, as some sights and accommodation options (in particular the outback stations) close from November to March, the outback's hottest period.

There are some very active and friendly local communities in the region and plenty on offer for adventurers.

Charters Towers to Cloncurry

The Flinders Hwy runs a gruelling 775km stretch of mostly flat road from Charters Towers west to little Cloncurry. The highway was originally a Cobb & Co coach run, and along its length are small towns established as coach stopovers. The main towns out here are Prairie (200km west of Charters Towers), Hughenden, Richmond and Julia Creek where you can pick up the sealed Wills Developmental Rd north to Burketown (467km).

The **Kronosaurus Korner** (☎07-4741 3429; www.kronosauruskorner.com.au; 91 Goldring St, Richmond; adult/child $20/10; ⏲8.30am-4pm) centre houses easily the best collection of marine fossils in the region, most found by local landholders. Pride of place goes to an almost complete 4.25m pliosaur skeleton – one of Australia's best vertebrate fossils – and a partial skeleton of *Kronosaurus queenslandicus*, the largest known marine reptile to have ever lived here.

The relatively lush **Porcupine Gorge National Park** (☎13 74 68; www.qld.gov.au/camping; camping per person/family $5.85/21.80) is an oasis in the dry country north of Hughenden. The best spot to go to is Pyramid Lookout, 70km north of Hughenden, where you can camp by a running creek and walk into the gorge.

At Prairie, located 200km west of Charters Towers, the friendly, supposedly haunted **Prairie Hotel** (☎07-4741 5121; Flinders Hwy; unpowered/powered sites $15/20, s/d from $60/90; ❄) is filled with memorabilia and atmosphere.

FJ Holden's (☎07-4741 5121; cnr Brodie St & Flinders Hwy, Hughenden; meals $5-24; ⏲8am-8pm Mon-Sat, 9am-8pm Sun) has an interesting display of dinosaur fossils and is an excellent car-themed burger joint.

Cloncurry

POP 3428

Lying 121km east of Mt Isa, the 'Curry' was the birthplace of the Royal Flying Doctor Service (RFDS). In the 19th century Cloncurry was the largest producer of copper in the British Empire. Today it's a busy pastoral centre with a reinvigorated mining industry. It's also the home of Bob Katter, a colourful and parochial politician who recently founded his own political party.

John Flynn Place (☎07-4742 4125; cnr Daintree & King Sts; adult/child $8.50/4; ⏲8am-4.30pm Mon-Fri, 9am-3pm Sat & Sun Apr-Oct) commemorates Flynn's work in setting up the invaluable Royal Flying Doctor Service. The building incorporates an art gallery, cultural centre and theatre.

OUTBACK FARM STAYS

One of the best ways to experience western Queensland is to stay on one of the area's vast cattle stations, where you can get a close-up look at the way of life – and the economic lifeblood – of the outback. Most offer station tours and other activities. Sadly, due to a range of economic factors, this is a dwindling tourist market.

Carisbrooke Station (☎07-4657 0084; www.carisbrookestation.com.au; Winton; unpowered sites d/f $17/25, d from $90) Carisbrooke Station, on the outskirts of Winton, is the pride of the Phillott Family. Incredible bush landscapes spread out from the self-contained accommodation. The property features endless walking trails and the chance to fossick for dinosaur bones.

The best place to sleep is the **Wagon Wheel Motel** (07-4742 1866; 54 Ramsay St; s/d from $85/96;), which is clean, comfortable and sports a friendly bar.

Mt Isa

POP 22,091

'The Isa' is one of the state's longest-running mining towns and a travel and lifestyle hub for central Queensland. At night the surrounding cliffs glow and zing with industry. The proud locals share the dusty heat and geographic isolation – often over multiple beers – and the sense of community is palpable.

The most pleasant surprise to first-time visitors to Isa is the stark red beauty of the place. Strange rocky formations – padded with olive-green spinifex – line the perimeter of town as deep-blue sunsets eclipse all unnatural light. Nearby are a number of under-visited camping spots and abandoned mine trails that make for fun day trips for those who like to return to 'civilisation' after dark.

Try to visit in mid-August for Australia's largest rodeo.

Sights & Activities

Outback at Isa MUSEUM
(1300 659 660; www.outbackatisa.com.au; 19 Marian St; 8.30am-5pm) The Australian Tourism Award–winning Outback at Isa is featured on most itineraries, and for good reason, too. The hands-on museum provides a colourful, articulate and air-conditioned overview of mining, pioneering and local history. It comprises a number of galleries and experiences like the Hard Times Mine and the fascinating Riversleigh Fossil Centre. It also houses the Outback park. There's a good-value, two-day DiscoveryTourPass ($59), which combines all the attractions.

Swimming Pool SWIMMING
(07-4743 2137; cnr Isa St & Fourth Ave; admission $4) Take refuge from the oppressive heat or cut some morning laps.

Sleeping

Travellers Haven HOSTEL $
(07-4743 0313; www.travellershaven.com.au; 75 Spence St; dm/s/d $29/50/66;) The rooms are fairly modest and the shared facilities a little tired but the pool is one of the best in Isa and the lounge is a great meeting place. The lovely British owner will share her passion for the region. Call ahead for pick-ups.

Mt Isa Caravan Park CARAVAN PARK $
(07-4743 3252; www.mtisacaravanpark.com.au; 112 Marian St; unpowered/powered sites $27/35, on-site caravans $70, villas $100;) Impressive tourist village with a swag of sleeping options, including self-contained units ($140). The pool is a big'un and there are plenty of shady grassed areas.

Fourth Avenue Motor Inn MOTEL $$
(07-4743 3477; www.fourthavemotorinn.com; 14 Fourth Ave; d from $135;) This friendly, colourful motor inn, in a quiet residential zone, has recently been renovated. The saltwater pool is set in a neat outdoor area and the rooms are a touch above the town average. Ask about long-term rates.

Spinifex Motel MOTEL $$
(07-4749 2944; www.spinifexmotel.com.au; 79 Marian St; r $160-200;) A brilliant little establishment with large tiled rooms, tasteful furniture, writing desks and private outdoor patios. The staff are considered and courteous. It's a few blocks along the Barkly Hwy.

Central Point Motel MOTEL $$
(07-4743 0666; www.centralpoint-motel.com; 6 Marian St; s/d $130/150;) A short, steamy walk from town, the Central Point has a tropical atmosphere and well-equipped kitchenettes in all the sunny rooms.

Red Earth Hotel HOTEL $$$
(1800 603 488; www.redearth-hotel.com.au; Rodeo Dr; d $180-250;) Owned by a respectable man-about-town, the Red Earth tips hats to the prosperous old west in its wide corridors, period-style furniture (including huge writing desks) and claw-foot bathtubs. It's worth paying the little extra for a private balcony, spa and huge TV. There's an excellent restaurant in the lobby.

Eating & Drinking

Livingstone's MODERN AUSTRALIAN $$
(1800 603 488; 26 Miles St; mains $15-38; lunch & dinner daily, breakfast Sat & Sun) The poshest joint in town is run by an ex-Sydney chef who knows his way around a souffle. There are gourmet sandwiches and salads at lunch while dinner is more formal. Scotch fillet with tiger prawns ($36) and the barramundi ($34) were both hits when we visited. Service and cocktails are awkwardly sweet.

Mt Isa

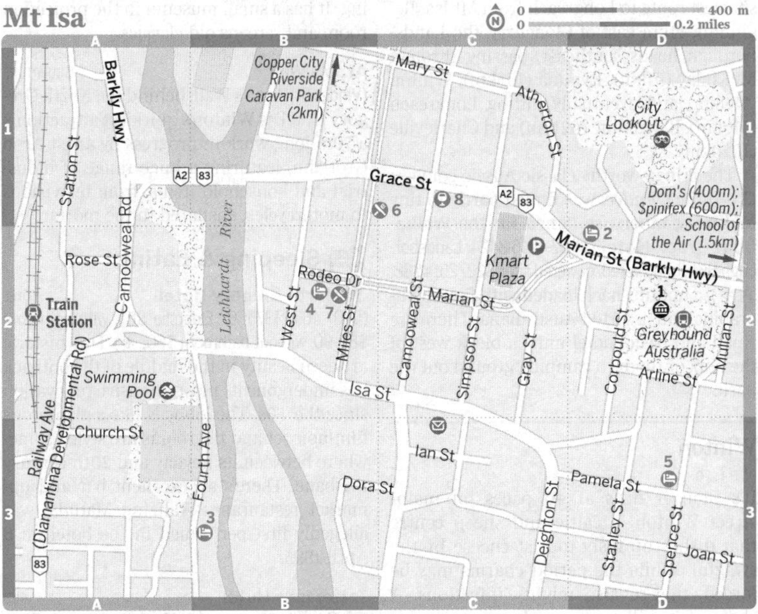

Rodeo Bar & Grill STEAKHOUSE $$

(☎07-4749 8888; Rodeo Dr; mains $25-32; ⊙10am-late) Downstairs in the newly renovated Isa Hotel, Rodeo Bar & Grill is a sanctuary for meatheads. Breakfast in a booth is surprisingly good, and there are pizzas and tapas-style snacks for munching on the outside deck.

Buffs Club BAR, CLUB

(www.buffs.com.au; cnr Grace & Camooweal Sts; ⊙10am-midnight Sun & Mon, to 2am Fri & Sat) Isa's most central nightspot, with the busy Billabong Bar, a sundeck and live entertainment on weekends.

Irish Club BAR, CLUB

(☎07-4743 5678; 1 Nineteenth Ave) A multipurpose venue with a cavernous bar, a tacky club that heaves on weekends, poker machines and a pretty good restaurant.

Mt Isa

Sights

1 Outback at Isa D2

Sleeping

2 Central Point Motel D2
3 Fourth Avenue Motor Inn B3
4 Red Earth Hotel B2
5 Travellers Haven D3

Eating

6 Livingstone's C1
7 Rodeo Bar & Grill B2

Drinking & Nightlife

8 Buffs Club C1

Getting There & Around

Rex (☎13 17 13; www.rex.com.au) flies direct from Mt Isa to Townsville.

Greyhound Australia (☎13 14 99; www.greyhound.com.au) has regular services to Townsville ($157, 11½ hours), Longreach ($113, 8½ hours) and Brisbane ($210, 26½ hours).

The **Queensland Rail** (☎1800 872 467; www.queenslandrail.com.au) *Inlander* runs between Mt Isa and Townsville (economy seat/sleeper $125/188, 21 hours).

The following car-hire firms have desks at the airport: **Avis** (☎07-4743 3733), **Hertz** (☎07-4743 4142) and **Thrifty** (☎07-4743 2911). For a taxi to town ($25 to $35), call **Mt Isa Taxis** (☎07-4743 2333).

Mt Isa to Charleville

Arguably the most popular road trip in outback Queensland runs east along the Barkly Hwy to the Landsborough Hwy. It's also the shortest route to Longreach from Mt Isa. Beginning 14km east of Cloncurry, the Landsborough heads southeast, passing through McKinlay (91km), Kynuna (168km), Winton (339km) and eventually hitting Longreach (516km), Barcaldine (621km) and Charleville (1020km).

The cringe-worthy classic Aussie comedy, *Crocodile Dundee*, was filmed partly in tiny McKinlay, otherwise famed for the **Walkabout Creek Hotel** (07-4746 8424; Landsborough Hwy; unpowered/powered sites $22/25, s $88; P ❄), a hot tin shack loaded with film memorabilia and assorted Australiana. There are small and basic motel units a block west of the pub, or there's a camping ground out the back.

Winton

POP 1320

It's pioneer days at 40 paces on main-street Winton, a cattle and sheep centre that dishes up tasty tourist cheese by the swagful. While the period charms may be forced, they're also mighty infectious. A short visit will have you happy-snapping at the heritage buildings and brushing up on your bush poetry. When you've run out of things to do in the town, plan your run with the dinosaurs (see the boxed text, p378).

The **Outback Festival** (www.outbackfestival.org) offers hilarious outback antics in late September.

Sights

Waltzing Matilda Centre MUSEUM
(07-4657 1466; www.matildacentre.com.au; 50 Elderslie St; adult/child/family $20/1/49; 9am-5pm) Doubling as the visitor information booth, there is a surprising number of exhibits here for a museum devoted to a song, including an indoor billabong complete with a squatter, troopers and a jolly swagman. The centre also houses the Qantilda Pioneer Place, which has a huge range of artefacts and displays on the founding of Qantas.

Royal Theatre THEATRE, MUSEUM
(07-4657 1296; 73 Elderslie St; adult/child $6.50/4; screenings 8pm Wed Apr-Sep) Find the world's biggest deck chair in the open-air Royal Theatre around the rear of the Wookatook Gift & Gem. There's an old-movie-world charm in the canvas-slung chairs, corrugated tin walls and star-studded ceiling. It has a small museum in the projection room and screens old classics.

Arno's Wall SCULPTURE
(Vindex St) Arno's Wall, behind the North Gregory Hotel, is Winton's quirkiest attraction – a 70m-long work-in-progress by artist Arno Grotjahn, featuring a huge range of industrial and household items, from televisions to motorcycles, ensnared in the mortar.

Sleeping & Eating

★ **North Gregory Hotel** HOTEL
(07-4657 1375; 67 Elderslie St; r with bathroom $80-90, without bathroom $60; ❄) This historic art-deco beauty in the middle of the outback has undergone its most extensive renovation since the '50s. The lobby is like a glamorous film-noir set and the rooms are styled somewhere between its heyday and 20th-century Brisbane. There's an excellent bar and upmarket restaurant. 'Waltzing Matilda' was allegedly first performed in the hotel on 6 April 1895.

Tattersalls Hotel PUB
(78 Elderslie St; mains $8-25; 11am-9pm) This friendly timber pub on the corner is an incongruous foodie destination with reasonably priced pub food cooked with bush spices and best served on the wooden verandah facing the street.

Getting There & Away

Greyhound Australia (13 14 99; www.greyhound.com.au) connects Winton with Brisbane ($178, 20 hours), Mt Isa ($98, six hours) and Longreach ($40, two hours).

Longreach

POP 3700

This prosperous outback town was the home of Qantas early last century, but these days it's equally famous for the Australian Stockman's Hall of Fame & Outback Heritage Centre, one of outback Queensland's biggest attractions. The Tropic of Capricorn passes through Longreach, and so do more than a million sheep and cattle.

Sights

Australian Stockman's Hall of Fame & Outback Heritage Centre MUSEUM
(07-4658 2166; www.outbackheritage.com.au; Landsborough Hwy; adult/child/family $29.50/15/70; 9am-5pm) Australian Stockman's Hall of Fame & Outback Heritage Centre is a

tribute to the early stockmen and explorers (check out the nifty maps), and has a range of galleries covering Aboriginal culture and European arrival. It's 2km east of town towards Barcaldine. Admission is valid for two days. It closes December to mid-February.

Qantas Founders Outback Museum
MUSEUM

(☑07-4658 3737; www.qfom.com.au; Landsborough Hwy; adult/child/family $21/11/49.50; ☉9am-5pm) Qantas Founders Outback Museum houses a life-size replica of an Avro 504K, the first aircraft owned by the fledgling airline. Interactive multimedia and working displays tell the history of Qantas. Next door, the original 1921 Qantas hangar houses a mint-condition DH-61. Towering over everything is a bright and shiny **747-200B Jumbo** (adult/child/family $19/10/45; museum & jumbo tours $34/18/75, wing walks adult/child $85/55; ☉tours 9.30am, 11am, 1pm & 3pm), whose wings you can walk (bookings essential).

🖐 Tours

Kinnon & Co Longreach
CRUISE, TOUR

(☑07-4658 1776; www.kinnonandco.com.au; 115a Eagle St) The main tour operator in Longreach runs a sunset cruise on the Thomson River, followed by dinner under the stars and campfire entertainment (adult/child/family $75/50/225). The Cobb & Co 'Gallop thru the Scrub' (adult/child/family $79/52/236) combines stagecoaching with a theatre show, lunch and a film.

Outback Aussie Tours
TOUR, TRAIN

(☑07-4658 3000; www.oat.net.au; Landsborough Hwy) On the railway platform, Outback offers a variety of multiday tours from the five-day Longreach and Winton tour (from $1699) to outback garden tours and rail journeys.

🛏 Sleeping & Eating

Eagle St has a number of pubs with good, cheap meals.

Longreach Tourist Park
CAMPGROUND $

(☑07-4658 1781; www.longreachtouristpark.com.au; 12 Thrush Rd; unpowered/powered sites $30/35, cabins $98, villa $135; ✳ ❄) A hot and dusty old site but friendly management and comfortable cabins if the caravan just doesn't cut it anymore.

Commercial Hotel
PUB, MOTEL $

(☑07-4658 1677; 102 Eagle St; s/d with bathroom $70/90, without bathroom $28/45, cabins $80-120;

✳ ❄) This hotel has basic but comfy rooms, and its friendly, bougainvillea-filled beer garden hosts bargain steak nights.

Old Time Cottage
RENTAL HOUSE $$

(☑07-4658 1550; 158 Crane St; r $105; ✳) A great choice for groups and families, this quaint little corrugated-iron cottage is set in an attractive garden. Fully furnished, the self-contained cottage sleeps up to five people.

Longreach Motor Inn
MOTEL $$

(☑07-4658 2322; 84 Galah St; r $124-134; ✳ ❄) Huge rooms with corresponding balconies and professional staff are the features of this popular motel on the edge of the shopping strip. The gated pool and shady garden kill an afternoon with ease. The on-site restaurant, Harry's (mains $20 to $30), is the best in Longreach.

Eagle's Nest Bar & Grill
MODERN AUSTRALIAN $$

(110 Eagle St; meals $20-33; ☉11am-9pm Wed-Sun, 8am-8pm Sat & Sun) Great for breakfast on weekends.

ℹ Information

There's a **Visitor Information Centre** (☑07-4658 3555; 99 Eagle St; ☉8.30am-5pm Mon-Fri, 9am-noon Sat & Sun, closed Sat & Sun Oct-Mar) on Eagle St.

ℹ Getting There & Away

Greyhound Australia (☑1300 473 946; www.greyhound.com.au) has a daily bus service to Brisbane ($169, 18 hours) via Charleville ($64, 6¾ hours) and Mt Isa via Winton and Cloncurry. Buses stop behind the Commercial Hotel.

Paradise Coaches (☑1300 300 156; www.paradisecoaches.com.au) makes the twice-weekly run to Rockhampton, returning via Emerald. Buses stop at Outback Aussie Tours next to the train station.

Queensland Rail (☑1300 131 722; www.traveltrain.com.au) operates the twice-weekly *Spirit of the Outback* service between Longreach and Brisbane via Rockhampton.

Barcaldine

POP 1500

Barcaldine (Bar-*call*-din) is a colourful little pub town at the junction of the Landsborough and Capricorn Hwys (Rte 66), 108km east of Longreach.

The town gained a place in Australian history in 1891 when it became the headquarters of a major shearers' strike. The confrontation led to the formation of the

THE DINOSAUR TRAIL

About 95 million years ago – give or take a few million – a herd of small dinosaurs got spooked by a predator and scattered. The resulting stampede left thousands of footprints in the stream bed, which nature remarkably conspired to fossilise and preserve. The **Lark Quarry Dinosaur Trackways** (☎07-4657 1188; www.dinosaurtrackways.com.au; guided 55min tours adult/child $11/6; ⊙tours 10am, noon & 2pm), 110km southwest of Winton, is outback Queensland's mini *Jurassic Park*, where you can see the remnants of the prehistoric stampede. Protected by a sheltered walkway, the site can only be visited by guided tour. There are no facilities to stay (or eat), but it's a well-signposted drive on the unsealed but well-maintained Winton–Jundah road, suitable for 2WD vehicles in the Dry. Contact the Waltzing Matilda Centre (p376) at Winton to book tours.

The **Australian Age of Dinosaurs** (☎07-4657 0778; http://aaodl.com; guided tours adult/child $22/11; ⊙8.30am-5pm, tours 9am, 11am, 1pm & 3pm) is a fascinating interactive research museum housed on a local cattle station atop a rugged plateau offering spectacular views. Fossil enthusiasts can book in advance for a day ($60) or a week's worth of bone preparation. To get there, follow the Landsborough Hwy 15km east of Winton (about 20 minutes' drive).

Australian Workers' Party, which is now the Australian Labor Party. The organisers' meeting place was the Tree of Knowledge, a ghost gum planted near the train station that long stood as a monument to workers and their rights. It was tragically poisoned in 2006 but a radical new monument now raises plenty of political ire.

The original inhabitants of Barcaldine were the Inningai, who 'disappeared' soon after explorer Thomas Mitchell arrived in 1824.

Sights & Activities

★Tree of Knowledge Memorial MEMORIAL
This $5m contemporary art installation – labelled by one disgruntled local as Ms Gillard's 'upside down milk crate' – is best seen at night when dappled light filters through the wooden wind chimes. Love it or not, it certainly makes art critics of the pubs' patrons across the road.

Australian Workers Heritage Centre MUSEUM
(☎07-4651 2422; www.australianworkersheritagecentre.com.au; Ash St; adult/child/family $12/7.50/28; ⊙9am-5pm Mon-Sat, 10am-5pm Sun) This centre provides a rundown on Australian social, political and industrial movements, and features the Australian Bicentennial Theatre.

Artesian Country Tours TOUR
(☎07-4651 2211; www.artesiancountrytours.com.au; adult/child $145/65; ⊙Wed & Sat, weather permitting) Runs a highly regarded historical tour to local Aboriginal rock-art sites, lava caves and cattle stations.

Sleeping & Eating

Blacksmith's Cottage COTTAGE $
(☎07-4651 1724; 7 Elm St; d/tr/q $70/80/90) The tiny wood-and-tin Blacksmith's Cottage dates from the late 19th century and is filled with antiques and quirky knick-knacks.

Barcaldine Country Motor Inn MOTEL $
(☎07-4651 1488; 1 Box St; s/d $89/99; ❄) The very homely rooms here are well presented, cool and clean. It's just around the corner from the main street's iconic pubs.

3ls Bar & Bistro PUB FOOD $$
(mains $15-25) Liars, larrikins and legends revel in the rustic, open-shed restaurant with wooden bench tables and stockmen's ropes and branding irons on the walls. Shut up and eat your steak, mate.

Information

The **Visitor Information Centre** (☎07-4651 1724; Oak St) is next to the train station.

Charleville

POP 3728

Lying 760km west of Brisbane, Charleville is the grand old dame of central Queensland and the largest town in Mulga country. Due largely to its prime locale on the Warrego River, the town was an important centre for early explorers – Cobb & Co had its largest coach-making factory here – but the town has maintained its prosperity as a major Australian wool centre.

Visitors can gain a spectacular view of the night sky via a high-powered telescope and an expert guide at the **Cosmos Centre** (07-4654 3057; www.cosmoscentre.com; single/family $7/21, night observatory sessions adult/child/family$27/18/65; 10am-4pm, observatory 7.30pm). The 90-minute sessions start soon after sunset. The centre lies 2km south of town, off Airport Dr.

Charleville's QPWS runs a captive-breeding program for the endangered bilby called the **Bilby Experience** (07-4654 4717; 1 Park St; admission $5; Apr-Oct). Book at the Cosmos Centre.

If you're planning an overnight stay, there's the **Hotel Corones** (07-4654 1022; 33 Wills St; r $40-95;). Bypass the motel rooms in favour of the Corones' resurrected upstairs interior where rooms feature fireplaces, leadlight windows and elegant Australian antiques. You can eat in the grandiose dining room (mains $15 to $20), or the public bar (mains $10 to $12) with the riff-raff.

The visitor information centre (07-4654 3057; Sturt St) is on the southeast side of town.

The Channel Country

You wanted outback, did ya? Well, here it is, mate – miles and bloody square miles of it! The Channel Country is an unforgiving, eerily empty region where red-sand hills, the odd wildflower and strange luminous phenomena run across prime beef-grazing land. The channels are formed by water rushing south from the summer monsoons to fill the Georgina, Hamilton and Diamantina Rivers and Cooper Creek. Avoid the summer months (October to April), unless you go for searing heat and dust.

Getting There & Around

There are no train or bus services in the Channel Country, and the closest car rental is in Mt Isa. Fools perish out here; roads are poorly marked and getting lost is easy. In fact, it's required that you write your name, destination and expected date of arrival on a blackboard at the station where you start. Some roads from the east and north to the fringes of the Channel Country are sealed, but between October and May even these can be cut off when dirt roads become quagmires. Visiting this area requires a sturdy vehicle (a 4WD if you want to get off the beaten track) with decent clearance. Always carry plenty of drinking water and petrol.

The main road through this area is the Diamantina Developmental Rd. It runs south from Mt Isa through Boulia to Bedourie, then east through Windorah and Quilpie to Charleville. It's a long and lonely 1340km along mostly sealed road, though some sections are single lane bitumen (pull over for the road trains). Take extra caution when driving at dusk, when the warm road attracts wild camels and kangaroos.

Mt Isa to Boulia

It's around 300km of sealed road from Mt Isa south to Boulia, and the only facilities along the route are at Dajarra, which has a pub and a roadhouse.

Boulia

POP 300

The unofficial 'capital' of the Channel Country is a neat little outpost on the cusp of the great Simpson Desert. It's from here that the world's longest mail run comes to an end, some 3000km from Port Augusta in South Australia. In mid-July, Boulia hosts Australia's premier camel-racing event, the **Desert Sands Camel Races**.

The most famous residents of Boulia are the mysterious Min Min Lights, a supposedly natural phenomenon that occurs when the temperature plummets after dark and erratic lights appear on the unusually flat horizon.

They're out there, perhaps, or at least there's sci-fi gadgetry and eerie lighting in an hourly 'alien' show at the **Min Min Encounter** (07-4746 3386; Herbert St; adult/child/family $15.60/12.50/36.50; 8.30am-5pm Mon-Fri, 8am-5pm Sat & Sun). Doubling as the information centre, this is classic travel kitsch.

The **Stone House Museum** (cnr Pituri & Hamilton Sts; adult/child $5/3; 8am-noon & 1-4pm Mon-Fri, 8am-noon Sat & Sun) has sheds full of outback stuff, space junk, local history, Aboriginal artefacts and the preserved 1888 home of the pioneering Jones family (the Stone House).

The best place to sleep is the **Desert Sands Motel** (07-4746 3000; www.desertsandsmotel.com.au; Herbert St; s/d $115/125;), with modern and spacious units.

The sealed Kennedy Developmental Rd (Rte 62) runs east from Boulia, 369km to Winton. The only stop along the way is **Middleton**, 175km from Boulia, where there's a pub and fuel.

OFF THE BEATEN TRACK

BIRDSVILLE, QUILPIE & AROUND

The Birdsville Developmental Rd heads east from Birdsville, meeting the Diamantina Developmental Rd after 277km of rough gravel and sand. Motorists must carry enough fuel and water to cover the 395km to the nearest town of Windorah.

Just west of Cooper Creek, **Windorah** has a pub, a general store and a basic caravan park. The **Western Star Hotel** (☎07-4656 3166; www.westernstarhotel.com.au; 15 Albert St; pub s/d $50/60, motel s/d $90/100; ❄), originally built in 1878, is a terrific country pub with delicious food and excellent motel units in a separate building. **Yabbie races** are staged here on the Wednesday before the Birdsville Races.

Quilpie is an opal-mining town and the railhead from which cattle are sent to the coast. South of Quilpie and west of Cunnamulla are the remote **Yowah Opal Fields** and the town of **Eulo**, which co-hosts the **World Lizard Racing Championships** with Cunnamulla in late August. **Thargomindah**, 130km west of Eulo, has a couple of motels and a guesthouse. **Noccundra**, another 145km further west, has just one hotel supplying basic accommodation, meals and fuel. If you have a 4WD you can continue west to Innamincka, in SA, on the rough and stony Strzelecki Track, via the site of the famous **Dig Tree**, where William Brahe buried provisions during the ill-fated Burke and Wills expedition in 1860–61.

Bedourie

POP 120

From Boulia it's 200km of mainly unsealed road south to Bedourie, the administrative centre for the huge Diamantina Shire Council. A big attraction is the free public swimming pool and **artesian spa**.

The charming adobe-brick **Bedourie Hotel** (☎07-4746 1201; www.bedouriehotel.com; Herbert St; r from $88; ❄) was built in the 1880s and is a social hub for the region. There are very cosy motel rooms out the back. Monstrous plates of steak and barramundi are served in the dining room.

There's also a caravan park and comfortable motel units at the **Simpson Desert Oasis** (☎07-4746 1291; 1 Herbert St; unpowered/powered sites free/$26, cabins $103-139, motel r $114-156; ❄), a roadhouse with fuel, a supermarket and a restaurant.

Birdsville

POP 120

Off-the-beaten-track travellers can't claim the title until they visit Birdsville, an iconic Australian settlement on the fringe of the Simpson Desert, and Queensland's most remote 'town'.

During the first weekend in September, the annual **Birdsville Cup** (www.birdsvilleraces.com) horse races draw up to 7000 fans from all over the country to drink, dance and gamble for three dusty days. Parking is free for all light aircraft.

At the **Birdsville Studio** (☎07-4656 3221; www.birdsvillestudio.com.au; Graham St; ⏲9am-10pm Jun-Sep), you can inspect and buy outback art by exceptional local artist Wolfgang John.

Standing strong in sandstone since 1884 is the much-loved **Birdsville Hotel** (☎07-4656 3244; www.theoutback.com.au; Adelaide St; s/d $140/160; ❄). When you've had a gutful, the motel-style units are tasteful and spacious, while the restaurant (mains $15 to 30) is surprisingly slick.

Birdsville Track

The 517km Birdsville Track stretches south of Birdsville to Maree in SA, taking a desolate course between the Simpson Desert to the west and Sturt Stony Desert to the east. The first stretch from Birdsville has two alternative routes, but only the longer, more easterly Outside Track is open these days. Before tackling the track, it's a good idea to keep friends or relatives informed of your movements so they can notify the authorities should you fail to report in on time.

Check in at the **Wirrarri Centre** (☎07-4656 3300) to learn the lay of the road, stock up on fuel and snacks, and email someone you wish was here.

Simpson Desert National Park

The waterless Simpson Desert occupies a massive 200,000 sq km of central Australia and stretches across the Queensland, NT and SA borders. The Queensland section, in the state's far southwestern corner, is protected as the 10,000-sq-km Simpson Desert National Park, and is a remote, arid landscape of high red sand dunes, spinifex and cane grass.

While conventional vehicles can just about tackle the Birdsville Track in dry conditions, the Simpson crossing requires a 4WD and far more preparation. Crossings should only be undertaken by parties of at least two 4WD vehicles equipped with suitable communications (such as an EPIRB) to call for help if necessary. Alternatively, you can hire a satellite phone from **Birdsville police** (☎07-4656 3220) and return it to **Maree police** (☎08-8675 8346) in SA.

Permits are required to camp anywhere in the park and can be obtained online (through www.qld.gov.au/camping) or at the **QPWS** (☎07-4650 1990) in Birdsville or Longreach, and Birdsville's service stations. You also need a separate permit to travel into the SA parks, and these are available through the **South Australian National Parks & Wildlife Service** (☎1800 816 078).

WHITSUNDAY COAST

Opal-jade waters and white sandy beaches fringe the forested domes of these 'drowned' mountains where you can camp in secluded bays as a modern-day castaway, laze in a tropical island resort, snorkel, dive or set sail through this stunning archipelago. Beneath the shimmering seas are swarms of tropical fish and the world's largest coral garden in the Great Barrier Reef Marine Park. The gateway to the islands, Airlie Beach, is a vibrant backpacker hub with a throbbing nightlife.

A little north are the natural unspoilt coastal gems of Hydeaway Bay and Cape Gloucester. South of Airlie is lush green hinterland at Finch Hatton Gorge and Eungella National Park where platypuses play in the wild.

Mackay

POP 85,399

An attractive country coastal town with art-deco buildings and national parks nearby, Mackay doesn't quite make the tourist hit-list. Instead, it caters more to the surrounding agricultural and mining industries. Located 6.5km northeast of the centre, the marina is a pleasant place to dine among the boating fraternity, while the northern beaches are largely unspoilt and empty.

Sights & Activities

Mackay's impressive **art-deco architecture** owes much to a devastating cyclone in 1918, which flattened many of the town's buildings. Enthusiasts should pick up a copy of *Art Deco Mackay* from the town hall visitor information centre.

There are good views over the harbour from **Mt Basset Lookout** and at **Rotary Lookout** in North Mackay.

Some fine beaches are within a short walk of the marina, but Mackay's best beaches, **Blacks Beach**, **Eimeo** and **Bucasia**, are about 16km north of town.

Artspace Mackay GALLERY

(☎07-4957 1775; www.artspacemackay.com.au; Gordon St; ⏲10am-5pm Tue-Sun) FREE Upholds the strong reputation of regional Queensland art galleries, showcasing local and visiting works on the edge of the civic precinct. Graze at **Foodspace** (⏲9am-3pm Tue-Sun), the licensed cafe on site.

Mackay Regional Botanical Gardens GARDENS

(Lagoon St) Three kilometres south of the city centre is this little piece of floral tropicana.

Bluewater Lagoon LAGOON

(⏲9am-5.45pm) FREE The pleasant artificial lagoon near Caneland Shopping Centre has water fountains, water slides, grassed picnic areas and a cafe.

Tours

Beyond Mackay's sugar-cane sea are a superb rainforest and national park.

Reeforest Adventure Tours CULTURAL TOUR

(☎1800 500 353; www.reeforest.com) Offers a wide range of tours, including a platypus and rainforest visit ($115) and trips to the Farleigh Sugar Mill ($22).

Farleigh Sugar Mill TOUR

(☎07-4959 8360; 2hr tours per person $22; ⏲9am, 11am & 1pm Jun-Nov) In the cane-crushing season you can see how the sweet crystals are made. The mill is 10km northwest of Mackay.

Whitsunday Coast

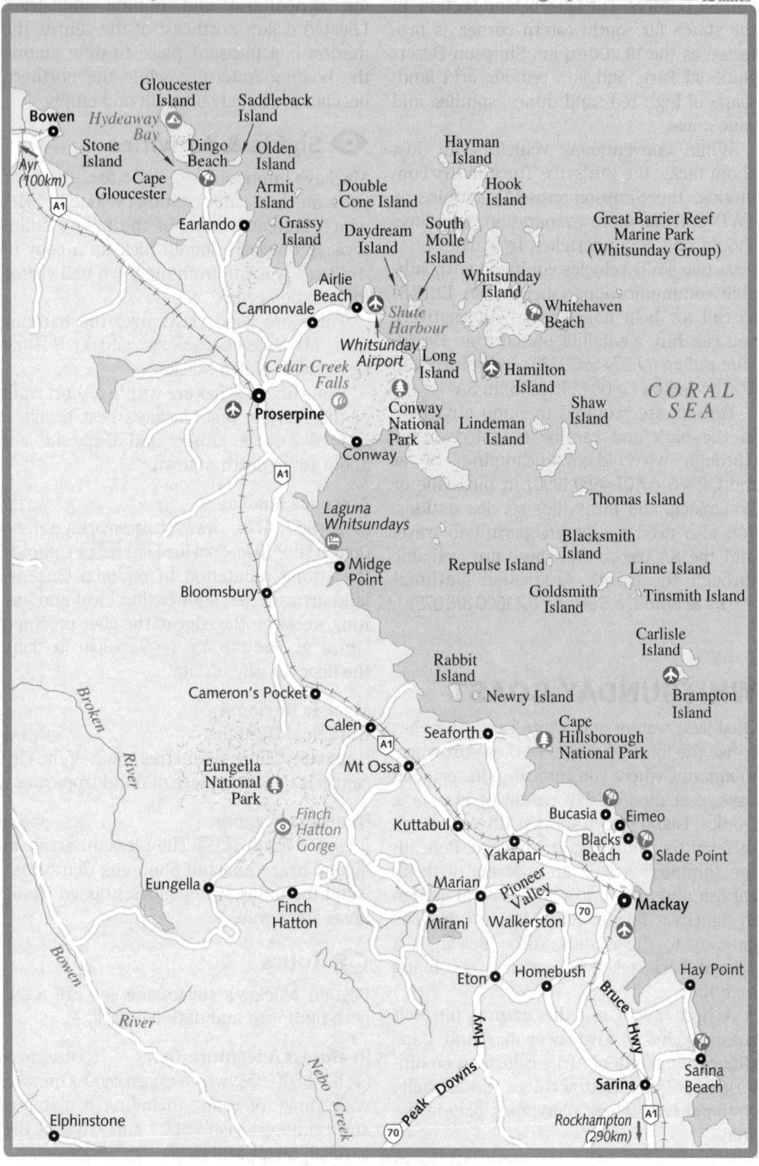

Festivals & Events

Wintermoon Folk Festival MUSIC
(07-4958 8390; www.wintermoonfestival.com; day tickets adult/child $90/free) Each year around May this folk festival is held at Cameron's Pocket, 70km north of Mackay.

Sleeping

Hotels in Mackay can fill up quickly due to a steady influx of mine workers – book ahead.

Stoney Creek Farmstay FARM STAY $
(07-4954 1177; www.stoneycreekfarmstay.com; Peak Downs Hwy; dm/cottage $25/145) Down

a rough track behind the Peak Downs Hwy is this tremendous little farm stay overseen by a handyman par excellence. You can stay at a secluded cottage or the charismatic Dead Horse Hostel. Three-hour horse rides cost $95 per person. Owners can pick you up if you ring ahead (minimum of two people). Willing Workers on Organic Farms (WWOOFers) welcome. It's 32km south of Mackay.

Gecko's Rest HOSTEL $
(07-4944 1230; www.geckosrest.com.au; 34 Sydney St; dm/d/f $24/55/90;) Gecko's is rough as guts and bursting with mine workers on the prowl. It's also the only hostel in town (entrepreneur wanted!) so the beds are very cheap and just clean enough. Enjoy the massive rooftop balcony and the location on the doorstep of clubs and restaurants.

Coral Sands Motel MOTEL $$
(07-4951 1244; www.coralsandsmotel.com.au; 44 Macalister St; r $130-165;) Terrific little place in the heart of the action with friendly management and tropical kitsch motel rooms.

Ocean Resort Village RESORT $$
(1800 075 144; www.oceanresortvillage.com.au; 5 Bridge Rd; apt $95-105, 2-bedroom apt $140;)

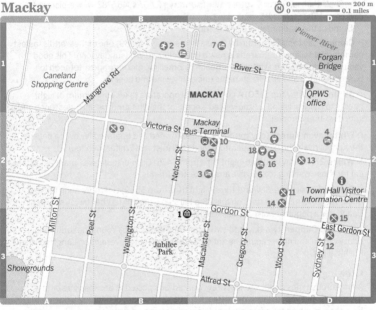

Mackay

Mackay

Sights
1 Artspace Mackay B3

Activities, Courses & Tours
2 Bluewater Lagoon B1

Sleeping
3 Coral Sands Motel C2
4 Gecko's Rest D2
5 Lanai Riverside Apartments B1
6 Mackay Grande Suites C2
7 Mid City Motor Inn C1
8 Quest C2

Eating
9 Austral Hotel B2
10 Bollywood Bites C2
11 Burp Eat Drink D2
Foodspace (see 1)
12 Global Burgers D3
13 Kevin's Place D2
14 Montezuma's C2
15 Oscar's on Sydney D3

Drinking & Nightlife
16 Gordi's Cafe & Bar C2
17 Mainstreet C2
18 Tryst C2

SAILING THE WHITSUNDAYS

Aside from day trips, most overnight sailing packages are for three days and two nights or two days and two nights. Check what you pay for. Some companies set sail in the afternoon of the first day and return by mid-morning of the last, while others set out early and return late. Be sure what you're committing to – don't set sail on a party boat if you're after a chilled-out cruise. If you're flexible with dates, last-minute stand-by rates can considerably reduce the price, and you'll also have a better idea of weather conditions.

Most vessels offer snorkelling on the fringing reefs (the reefs around the islands). The softer coral here is often more colourful and abundant than what you see on the outer reef. Check if snorkel equipment, stinger suits and reef taxes are included in the package. Diving usually costs extra.

Once you've decided what suits, book at one of the many booking agencies in town such as Whitsundays Central Reservation Centre (p392) or a management company such as **Whitsunday Sailing Adventures** (☎07-4940 2000; www.whitsundaysailing.com; Shute Harbour Rd) or **Explore Whitsundays** (☎07-4946 5782; www.explorewhitsundays.com; 4 The Esplanade).

Some of the recommended sailing trips:

➡ **Camira** (day trips $175) Run by Cruise Whitsundays (p389) one of the world's fastest commercial sailing catamarans is now a lilac-coloured Whitsunday icon. This good-value day trip includes Whitehaven Beach, snorkelling, morning and afternoon tea, a barbecue lunch and all refreshments (including wine and beer).

➡ **SV Domino** (day trip $150) A co-op of local operators takes a maximum of eight guests to Bali Hai island, a little-visited 'secret' of the Whitsundays. Includes lunch and a good two-hour snorkel.

➡ **Whitehaven Xpress** (day trip $160) Locally owned and operated for over a decade, the Xpress rivals the bigger operators for its Hill Inlet and Whitehaven tours.

➡ **Wings 2** (two-day-and-two-night trips from $475) Comfortable, well-maintained fast cat for those wanting to sail, dive and make new friends.

➡ **Solway Lass** (three-day-and-three-night trips from $559) Get more bang for your buck. You get a full three days on this 28m tall ship – the only authentic tall ship in Airlie Beach. It's a popular choice for backpackers.

➡ **Atlantic Clipper** (two-day-and-two-night trips from $455) Young, beautiful and boozy crowd and no escaping the antics. Snorkelling (or recovering) on Langford Island is a highlight.

Crewing

Adventurous types might see the 'Crew Wanted' ads posted in backpackers or at the marina and yacht club in Airlie Beach (p386) and dream of hitching a ride on the high seas. In return for a free bunk, meals, and a sailing adventure you get to hoist the mainsail, take the helm, and clean the head. You could have the experience of a lifetime – whether good or bad depends on the vessel, skipper, other crew members (if any) and your own attitude. Think about being stuck with someone you don't know on a 10m boat, several kilometres from shore, before you actually find yourself there.

This is a good-value beachside resort comprising 34 self-contained apartments set amid lush, tropical gardens. The cool, shady setting has two pools, barbecue areas and half-court tennis. It's located 4km southeast of the town centre (take Gordon to Goldsmith to Bridge).

Mid City Motor Inn MOTEL $$
(☎07-4951 1666; stay@midcitymotel.com.au; 2 Macalister St; r $114-180; ❄@🛜🏊) A real old-timer in an enviable riverside locale opposite a school. Good value by the city standard.

Mackay Grande Suites HOTEL $$$
(☎07-4969 1000; www.mackaygrandsuites.com; 9 Gregory St; r from $169; P❄🏊) Downtown Mackay finally got itself a posh hotel and the professional service to match. These centrally located suites may have delusions of grandeur but they are nonetheless comfort-

able and larger than most. The beds are very firm and the bathrooms expansive.

Clarion Hotel Mackay Marina LUXURY HOTEL $$$
(☎07-4955 9400; www.mackaymarinahotel.com; Mulherin Dr; d $189-275;) This welcoming luxury hotel down at the peaceful marina precinct has an excellent on-site restaurant and enormous swimming pool. It's located 6.5km northeast of the centre. (Take Sydney St north across the Forgan Bridge.)

Quest APARTMENT $$$
(☎07-4829 3500; www.questmackay.com.au; 38 Macalister St; studios $195, 1-/2-bedroom apts from $220/350;) A little pokey for the price, these Quest apartments are still very modern and well-maintained. The kitchenettes are only for basic food preparation and views from most rooms are of other rooms. The pool is the biggest tick.

Lanai Riverside Apartments APARTMENT $$$
(☎07-4957 4401; www.lanaiapartments.com.au; 20 River St; r from $220;) Plum location by the river and the interiors are shiny and new, though management works off-site, so the day-to-day housekeeping can be a little slack.

Eating

★Comet Coffee CAFE $
(☎0423 420 195; 43 Victoria St; sandwiches $7-9; 5.30am-2.30pm Mon-Fri, 9am-noon Sat &Sun) Our favourite coffee in Mackay is served in an old garage in the quiet end of town. Great magazine collection and couch-lounging section, and delicious muffins.

Global Burgers BURGERS $
(☎07-4951 4555; Sydney St; burgers $12-15; lunch & dinner) Mackay's branch of this small burger chain heaves with custom daily. The salads are also worth a run.

Kevin's Place ASIAN $$
(☎07-4953 5835; cnr Victoria & Wood Sts; mains $18-25; lunch & dinner Mon-Fri, dinner Sat) Fast-paced faux-colonial Singaporean restaurant covered in palm fronds and serviced by young staff who bark out orders for sizzling hawker food all day and half the night.

Bollywood Bites INDIAN $$
(☎07-4957 8785; 141 Victoria St; mains $12-25; lunch & dinner;) This is a fun and authentic little curry house on a brightly lit corner block. The usual Indian classics reign with loads of vegetarian options.

Montezuma's MEXICAN $$
(☎07-4944 1214; 94 Wood St; mains $12-24; lunch & dinner) Mexican-influenced restaurant with cosy atmosphere and snug booths.

Austral Hotel PUB $$
(☎07-4951 3288; 189 Victoria St; mains $17-31, steaks $23-41; lunch & dinner) Overpriced but very reliable pub fare and perfect atmosphere for families.

Oscar's on Sydney FUSION $$
(☎07-4944 0173; cnr Sydney & Gordon Sts; mains $10-21; breakfast & lunch) A real favourite with the Mackay coffee set. The delicious *poffertjes* (authentic Dutch pancakes with traditional toppings) are a hit.

Burp Eat Drink MODERN AUSTRALIAN $$$
(☎07-4951 3546; 86 Wood St; mains $32-40; lunch & dinner Tue-Fri, dinner Sat) Burp is a seriously flavoursome high-end joint that belies its casual tropical locale with a sophisticated shared menu. Celebrity-chef-in-the-making Adrian Connors presides over dishes such as white anchovies in lemon and honey-glazed duck. It gets noisy and busy but that's because it's good.

Drinking & Nightlife

Gordi's Cafe & Bar PUB
(85 Victoria St) Gordi's is a street-side watering hole with a reputation as the unrivalled pre-party or post-work meeting place.

Tryst CLUB
(99 Victoria St; 10pm-3am) Tryst hosts surprisingly classy underground dance music parties. Catch some handpicked maestros of the scene educating the masses.

Satchmo's at the Reef BAR
(Mulherin Dr) A classy wine-and-tapas bar full of boaties – it's down at the marina – and featuring live music on Sunday afternoon.

Sails Sports Bar BAR
(Mulherin Dr) This themed bar on the marina can get rowdy some nights, but it maintains the Sunday arvo tradition with live music and plenty of drink deals.

Mainstreet CLUB
(148 Victoria St; Thu-Sat) A staple on the 'big night out' itinerary for locals and seasonal workers, with live music and DJs.

Information

Mackay Queensland Parks & Wildlife Service (QPWS; ☎07-4944 7800; www.derm.qld.gov.au; 30 Tennyson St)

Mackay Visitor Centre (☎07-4944 5888; www.mackayregion.com; 320 Nebo Rd; ⊙9am-5pm Mon, 8.30am-5pm Tue-Fri, 9am-4pm Sat & Sun) About 3km south of the centre. Internet access.

QPWS office (☎07-4944 7800; fax 07-4944 7811; cnr Wood & River Sts)

Town Hall Visitor Information Centre (☎07-4951 4803; townhall@mackayregion.com; 63 Sydney St; ⊙9am-5pm Mon-Fri, to noon Sat & Sun) Also has internet access.

Getting There & Around

AIR

The airport is about 3km south of the centre. **Jetstar** (☎13 15 38; www.jetstar.com.au) and **Virgin Australia** (☎13 67 89; www.virginaustralia.com) fly to/from Brisbane; **Tiger Airways** (☎03-9999 2888; www.tigerairways.com.au) flies to/from Melbourne. **Qantas** (☎13 13 13; www.qantas.com.au) has direct flights most days between Mackay and Brisbane, Rockhampton and Townsville.

BUS

Buses stop at the **Mackay Bus Terminal** (☎07-4944 2144; cnr Victoria & Macalister Sts; ⊙7am-6pm Mon-Fri, to 4pm Sat), where tickets can also be booked. **Greyhound Australia** (☎13 20 30; www.greyhound.com.au) and **Premier Motor Service** (☎13 34 10; www.premierms.com.au) travel up and down the coast between Brisbane ($207, 17 hours) and Cairns ($152, 13 hours), stopping in Mackay.

TAXI

Mackay Taxis (☎13 10 08) will get you to the airport, marina or train station for about $25.

TRAIN

The **Queensland Rail** (☎1300 13 17 22; www.traveltrain.com.au) *Tilt Train* connects Mackay with Brisbane ($240, 13 hours), Townsville ($110, 5½ hours) and Cairns ($190, 12 hours). The slower *Sunlander* does the same: Brisbane (economy seat/sleeper $160/220, 17 hours). The train station is at Paget, 5km south of the city centre.

Airlie Beach

POP 3000

Airlie is the kind of town where humanity celebrates its close proximity to natural beauty by partying very hard. A relatively tiny town that can at times feel as busy as Brisbane, Airlie draws a stream of budget travellers, the sailing fraternity (who converge here for the mainland conveniences), families (who flock to the fine restaurants and boutique hotels) and shrewd, often short-sighted developers.

Abel Point Marina is about 1km west along a pleasant boardwalk, and Shute Harbour is about 12km east. The new Port of Airlie precinct had added an element of big city style.

Activities

Sailing is the leisure activity of choice here, in all its nautical variations. There are numerous **sailing tours**, but if you've got salt water in your veins, a **bareboat charter** might be more your style. Expect to pay between $500 and $800 a day in high season (September to January) for a yacht that will comfortably sleep four to six people. Airlie Beach is also a great place to learn to sail.

Air Whitsunday Seaplanes SCENIC FLIGHTS
(☎07-4946 9111; www.airwhitsunday.com.au) This outfit offers three-hour Reef Adventures (adult/child $360/280), a Whitehaven experience ($240/210) and the signature four-hour Panorama Tour ($475/390) where you fly to Hardy Lagoon to snorkel or ride a semisubmersible, then fly to Whitehaven Beach for a picnic lunch. It also runs day trips to exclusive Hayman Island ($245).

Charter Yachts Australia SAILING CHARTER
(☎1800 639 520; www.cya.com.au; Abel Point Marina) An excellent group to arrange your DIY yachting experience in the Whitsundays. Yachts from $500 per night, five night minimum.

Whitsunday Escape SAILING CHARTER
(☎1800 075 145; www.whitsundayescape.com; Abel Point Marina) Specialises in bareboat charters – charter boats that come without a skipper or crew, where you would skipper the boat yourself. The outfit can provide a sail guide, provisions and a cook if requested.

Scamper CAMPING
(www.destinationairliebeach.com.au) Provides island camping with a choice from dozens of island locations.

Island Transfers CAMPING
(☎07-4967 7355; www.islandtransfers.com) Transfers to a campsite of your choice on Whitsunday Island, Hook Island or one of the Molle Islands.

Airlie Beach

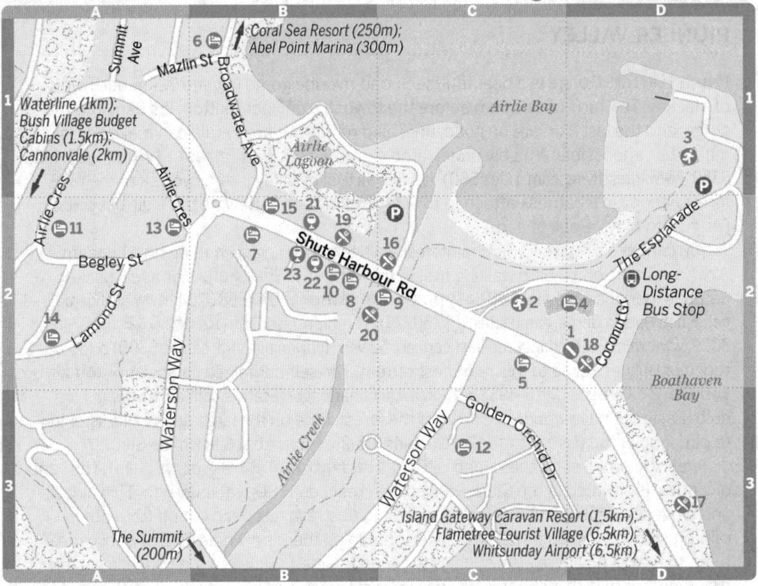

Airlie Beach

Activities, Courses & Tours

1 Whitsunday Dive Adventures D2
2 Whitsunday Marine Academy C2
3 Whitsunday Sailing Club D1

Sleeping

4 Airlie Beach Hotel D2
5 Airlie Beach YHA C2
6 Airlie Waterfront B&B B1
7 Base Airlie Beach Resort B2
8 Beaches Backpackers B2
9 Magnums Backpackers C2
10 Nomads Backpackers B2
11 Sunlit Waters A2
12 Water's Edge Resort C3
13 Waterview A2
14 Whitsunday Organic B&B A2
15 Whitsundays Central Reservation Centre B2

Eating

16 Airlie Supermarket C2
Deja Vu .... (see 12)
17 Denman Cellars Beer Cafe D3
18 Fish D'vine D2
19 Mr Bones B2
20 Village Cafe B2
Whitsunday Sailing Club .... (see 3)

Drinking & Nightlife

Magnum's .... (see 9)
21 Mama Africa B2
22 Paddy's Shenanigans B2
23 Uber B2

Whitsunday Rent A Yacht SAILING CHARTER
(☎1800 075 000; www.rentayacht.com.au; Trinity Jetty, Shute Harbour) Provides skipper-yourself cruises with a minimum charter period of five nights.

Whitsunday Marine Academy SAILING LESSONS
(☎1800 810 116; www.explorewhitsundays.com; 4 The Esplanade) Run by Explore Whitsundays.

Whitsunday Sailing Club SAILING LESSONS
(☎07-4946 6138; Airlie Point) Runs cruises and has a calendar of sailing events and learn-to-sail courses.

Whitsunday Dive Adventures DIVING, SNORKELLING
(☎07-4948 1239; www.whitsundaydivecentre.com; 303 Shute Harbour Rd) Offers a range of instruction, including PADI-certified open-water

WORTH A TRIP

PIONEER VALLEY

Finch Hatton Gorge is a beautiful, secluded riverine gorge located 32km northwest of Mackay. The turn-off is 1.5km before the township of Finch Hatton. It's 9km into the gorge, and the last 3km are on good, unsealed roads, but heavy rain can make access difficult or impossible. A highly underrated extreme activity is **Forest Flying** (☎07-4958 3359; www.forestflying.com; rides $60). It's like virtual monkey play as you skim the rainforest canopy in a harness attached to a 340m-long cable. Beware the fruit-bat colony (August to May). Book ahead.

You can take a relaxed 1.6km rainforest walk to a stunning swimming hole beneath **Araluen Falls**, or a 2.6km walking trail to the **Wheel of Fire Falls**. For a real back-to-nature experience, stay in the **Platypus Bushcamp** (☎07-4958 3204; www.bushcamp.net; Finch Hatton Gorge; camp sites/d $7.50/75). The high-end **Rainforest B&B** (☎07-4958 3099; www.rainforestbedandbreakfast.com.au; 52 Van Houweninges Rd; cabins $300) adds a touch of Balinese style to this rainforest retreat. The self-contained cabins at **Finch Hatton Gorge Cabins** (☎07-4958 3281; www.finchhattongorgecabins.com.au; d $95; ❄) are quite basic but have wonderful views of the forest. Dine on the large deck while listening to birdsong at the **River Rock Cafe** (mains $15-25; ⏲breakfast & lunch Tue-Sun).

Twenty kilometres further along is **Eungella National Park** (*young*-gulla). The 'land of clouds' is situated in the Clark Ranges, and reaches 1280m at its zenith. This oldest and longest stretch of subtropical rainforest in Australia has been cut off from other rainforest areas for roughly 30,000 years, meaning there's a whole host of freaky creatures that exist nowhere else, such as the orange-sided skink and the Eungella gastric brooding frog, which incubates its eggs in its stomach and gives birth by spitting out the tadpoles!

On the trails between Eungella and Broken River, the real star is the world's cutest, most reclusive monotreme (egg-laying mammal). You can be fairly sure of seeing platypuses from the viewing platform near the bridge. The best times are immediately after dawn and at dusk, but you must be patient, as sightings are very rare.

Resident goannas and brush-tailed possums enjoy the lovely **Broken River Mountain Resort** (☎07-4958 4000; www.brokenrivermr.com.au; d $105-160; ❄@📶🏊), which has cosy cedar cabins, and a wood-finished lounge.

There's also the **QPWS Fern Flat Camping Ground** (per person/family $5.15/21), which is reserved for walk-in campers only, near the (usually unstaffed) **QPWS office** (☎07-4958 4552). You need to self-register.

The beautiful little country cafe, **Pinnacle Coffee Devine** (☎07-4958 5167; Mackay-Eungella Rd, Pinnacle; ⏲8am-4pm), has a mesmerising view of the canefields.

Buses don't cover Finch Hatton or Eungella, so you'll need a car or an organised tour from Mackay.

dive courses ($660). Half-day dive trips cost $175. Many boat cruises.

Salty Dog Sea Kayaking KAYAKING
(☎07-4946 1388; www.saltydog.com.au; half-/full-day trips $80/130) Offers guided full-day tours and kayak rental ($50/70 per half-/full day), plus longer kayak/camping missions (the six-day challenge costs $1490). It's a charming and healthy way to see the islands.

Skydive Airlie Beach SKYDIVING
(☎07-4946 9115; www.skydiveairliebeach.com.au) Tandem skydives from $249.

HeliReef SCENIC FLIGHTS
(☎07-4946 9102; www.helireef.com.au) Offers helicopter flights to the reef and a picnic lunch on Whitehaven Beach ($349).

Tours

If snorkelling, lying on the beach or exploring the rainforests of the Whitsunday Islands appeals, then it's just a matter of hunting down the tour that will suit you.

Most cruise operators run out of Abel Point Marina, but those that run from Shute Harbour do pick-ups from Airlie Beach and Cannonvale. You can take a bus to Shute Harbour.

Voyager 4 Island Cruise BOAT TOUR
(☎07-4946 5255; www.wiac.com.au; adult/child $140/80) A good-value day cruise that includes snorkelling at Hook Island, beachcombing and swimming at Whitehaven Beach, and checking out Daydream Island. You can add a scenic flight for $60.

Cruise Whitsundays BOAT TOUR
(☎07-4946 4662; www.cruisewhitsundays.com) The biggest operator in town runs speedboat trips to the Barrier Reef Marine Base ($210), a pontoon located in Knuckle Reef Lagoon, where you can snorkel, dive or just cruise at sea.

Ocean Rafting BOAT TOUR
(☎07-4946 6848; www.oceanrafting.com.au; adult/child/family $124/81/374) Fast-paced day tours let you swim at Whitehaven Beach, view Aboriginal cave paintings at Nara Inlet and snorkel the reef at Mantaray Bay or Border Island.

Big Fury BOAT TOUR
(☎07-4948 2201; adult/child/family $130/70/350) Speeds out to Whitehaven Beach on an open-air sports boat followed by lunch and then snorkelling at a secluded reef nearby.

Whitsunday Crocodile Safari TOUR
(☎07-4948 3310; www.proserpineecotours.com; adult/child $120/60) Remarkable opportunity to spend time around crocodiles in the wild, explore secret estuaries and eat real bush tucker.

Sleeping

Whitsundays Central Reservation Centre ACCOMMODATION SERVICES
(☎1800 677 119; www.airliebeach.com; 259 Shute Harbour Rd) To take the hassle out of finding the right accommodation, Whitsundays Central Reservation Centre can be of enormous assistance.

Bush Village Budget Cabins HOSTEL $
(☎1800 8098 256; www.bushvillage.com.au; 2 St Martins Rd; dm from $30, d $93; ❄@≋) These boutique backpacker cabins, only 1.5km west of Airlie, have undergone a revamp and offer good-value budget accommodation. Dorms and doubles are in 17 self-contained cabins set in leafy gardens. There's a courtesy bus into town.

Magnums Backpackers HOSTEL $
(☎1800 624 634; www.magnums.com.au; 366 Shute Harbour Rd; camp sites/van sites $22/24, dm/d $22/56, cabins per person $24; ❄@📶) Magnums continues to grow like a beautiful noxious weed. The bar-side antics are pretty full on but luckily the majority of beds are way down the back in a tropical garden. Be patient with reception staff as there is serious demand in high season. The private rooms are surprisingly quiet.

Backpackers by the Bay HOSTEL $
(☎07-4946 7267, 1800 646 994; www.backpackersbythebay.com; 12 Hermitage Dr; dm/d & tw $27/70; ❄@≋) About a 10-minute walk from town is this excellent alternative to the frenetic cluster of hostels downtown. The clientele are decidedly low-key and the ambience is perpetuated by strung hammocks, a good pool and an absence of loud music. The air-conditioned rooms are very tidy and staff are very welcoming.

Base Airlie Beach Resort HOSTEL $
(☎1800 242 273, 07-4948 2000; www.stayatbase.com; 336 Shute Harbour Rd; camp site $12.50, dm from $26, s/d $45/90; P❄📶≋) The newish Base resort is a remarkably cost-effective, er, base from which to explore the Whitsundays. Housed on an impressive patch of land in among the Airlie hustle, there's a small pool (sporting all kinds of madness when we visited) and the best rooms at this price we could find. The staff could smile more but who really wants to work in the height of summer?

Nomads Backpackers HOSTEL $
(☎07-4999 6600; www.nomadsairliebeach.com; 354 Shute Harbour Rd; dm/d $29/92; ❄@📶≋) Some pleasant grassed areas give this Nomads branch a slight competitive edge in the budget market. The camping sites in particular enjoy some shady respite though the dorms are fairly primitive. The private rooms have TV, fridge and kitchenettes. The communal facilities were filthy when we visited.

Beaches Backpackers HOSTEL $
(☎1800 636 630; www.beaches.com.au; 356 Shute Harbour Rd; dm/d $22/70; ❄@📶≋) Warning: this is a party place. Under no circumstances should you complain about the relentless dirge pumping from the bar through your thin bedroom walls. Your concerns will fall on deaf ears. Sleep is for the weak. The food is pretty decent and you will meet fellow romantics with subliminal ease.

Flametree Tourist Village CARAVAN PARK $
(☎07-4946 9388; www.flametreevillage.com.au; Shute Harbour Rd; unpowered/powered sites $21/27,

cabins from $79; ❄@≋) Spacious sites are scattered through lovely bird-filled gardens, and there's a good camp kitchen and barbecue area. The park is 6.5km west of Airlie.

Airlie Beach YHA HOSTEL $
(☎1800 247 251, 07-4946 6312; airliebeach@yha.com.au; 394 Shute Harbour Rd; dm $26.50, d $69.50-77.50; ❄@≋) This central and reasonably quiet YHA outfit is nothing to email home about in terms of value, but the pool is above average.

Island Gateway Caravan Resort CAMPGROUND $
(☎07-4946 6228; www.islandgateway.com.au; Shute Harbour Rd; unpowered/powered sites $30/37, cabins $80-135, chalets $145-225; ❄☜≋) Large park 1.5km east of Airlie. A mixture of accommodation options means a mixed clientele.

★**The Summit** APARTMENT $$
(☎1800 463 417; www.summitairliebeach.com.au; 15 Flame Tree Court; 1-/2-bedroom apt from $160/190; P❄☜≋) Nestled high above Airlie Beach are these exceptional apartments with some of the best views of the Whitsundays and hinterland. Try to nab one in the 600s. The fittings and furnishings are equally top notch and the shaded recreation area by the pool has free wi-fi and a spectacular outlook.

Waterview APARTMENT $$
(☎07-4948 1748; www.waterviewairliebeach.com.au; 42 Airlie Cres; studios/1-bedroom units from $135/149; ❄☜) An excellent choice for location and comfort, this boutique accommodation overlooks the main street and has gorgeous views of the bay. The rooms are modern, airy and spacious and have kitchenettes for self-caterers.

Club Crocodile HOTEL $$
(☎07-4946 7155; www.clubcroc.com.au; d from $119; P❄≋) On the road between Cannovale and Airlie Beach is this excellent budget option that is really popular with domestic tourists and young families. The Olympic-sized swimming pool is the hub of the action and even features a waterfall. How lovely!

Sunlit Waters APARTMENT $$
(☎07-4946 6352; www.sunlitwaters.com; 20 Airlie Cres; studios from $92, 1-bedroom apt $115; ❄≋) One of the best-value options in Airlie Beach, these large studios have everything you could want, including a self-contained kitchenette and stunning views from the long balconies.

Airlie Beach Hotel HOTEL $$
(☎1800 466 233; www.airliebeachhotel.com.au; cnr The Esplanade & Coconut Grove; s/d $135/145, hotel r $179-289; ❄☜≋) The spacious hotel rooms with sea views are much better value than the drab motel unit. Reception closes at 9pm.

Water's Edge Resort APARTMENT $$$
(☎07-4948 4300; www.watersedgewhitsundays.com.au; 4 Golden Orchid Dr; 1-bedroom apt $210-260, 2-bedroom apt $275-345; ❄≋) It's easy walking distance to town for such an elegant retreat. The languid heat subsides upon entering reception and the rooms don't disappoint: pastels and creamy hues, cane headboards and cooling use of shutters maximise the tropical experience. The staggered pool area will subdue the most restless soul.

Coral Sea Resort RESORT $$$
(☎1800 075 061; www.coralsearesort.com; 25 Ocean View Ave; d $220-370, 1-bedroom apt $330, 2-bedroom apt $350-400; ❄@☜≋) At the end of a low headland overlooking the water just west of the town centre, Coral Sea Resort has one of the best positions around. Many of the rooms have stunning views.

Airlie Waterfront B&B B&B $$$
(☎07-4946 7631; www.airliewaterfrontbnb.com.au; cnr Broadwater Ave & Mazlin St; d $259-285; ❄@) With absolutely gorgeous views and immaculately presented from top to toe, this sumptuously furnished B&B oozes class and is a leisurely five-minute walk into town along the boardwalk.

Whitsunday Organic B&B B&B $$$
(☎07-4946 7151; www.whitsundaybb.com.au; 8 Lamond St; s/d $155/210) An element of hype surrounds this much-loved guesthouse but the organic breakfasts do live up to the billing. Peace is best found outside the small rooms and in the gardens brimming with life.

Eating

Marino's Deli DELI $
(Whitsunday Shopping Centre, Cannonvale; dishes $7-16; ⏲11am-8pm Mon-Sat) In a new premises in Cannonvale, Marino's is still the first choice for locals looking for delicious homemade pasta and huge salads. Affordable, high-quality Italian food is available for takeaway.

Village Cafe CAFE $
(☎07-4946 5745; 351 Shute Harbour Rd; mains $10-21; ⊙7.30am-9pm) Very reliable and well-priced eatery with famous breakfasts, strong coffee and the 'hot rock' ($26 to $34) sizzle plate at lunch or dinner.

Airlie Supermarket SUPERMARKET $
(277 Shute Harbour Rd) For self-caterers.

★ **Mr Bones** PIZZA, TAPAS $$
(☎0416 011 615; Shop 8, Lagoon Plaza, 263 Shute Harbour Rd; shared plates $12-17, pizza $15-23; ⊙9am-9pm Tue-Sat) Mr Bones is the new standard bearer in Airlie Beach for hip, affordable dining. The location opposite the lagoon is a gastronomic thoroughfare and diners here relish the prompt service and inventive cooking. The thin-based pizzas are tremendous – try the prawn and harissa – while the eggplant chips ($15) and spicy sardines ($17) suggest a playfulness that suits the holiday vibe.

Fish D'vine SEAFOOD $$
(☎07-4948 0088; 303 Shute Harbour Rd; mains $14-28; ⊙lunch & dinner) The mixture of sugary liquor and seafood is strangely palatable at this popular Airlie institution. A selection of over 200 different rums somehow complements big plates of barbecued tiger prawns ($26) and yummy four-fish tasting plates ($27).

Denman Cellars Beer Cafe TAPAS $$
(☎07-4948 1333; Shop 15, 33 Port Dr; mains $12-26; ⊙11am-10pm Mon-Fri, 8am-11pm Sat & Sun) Solid Mod-Oz food including lamb meatballs, very small shared seafood tapas and stock breakfast menu pales under the sheer weight of the beer menu. Lots of fun in the sun!

Waterline MODERN AUSTRALIAN $$
(☎07-4948 1023; 1 Shingley Dr; mains $20-30; ⊙lunch & dinner Wed-Sun, breakfast Sun) With stunning views over the marina, this restaurant at Shingley Beach Resort has one of the best locations for waterfront dining. The decor is tropical beach-chic. Recommended by the locals for its good service, great food and consistent quality.

Whitsunday Sailing Club PUB $$
(☎07-4946 7894; Airlie Point; mains $14-32; ⊙lunch & dinner) The sailing-club terrace (don't sit inside) is a great place for a meal and a drink and wonderful ocean views. Choose from the usual steak and schnitzel culprits.

Alain's Restaurant FRENCH $$$
(☎07-4946 5464; 44 Coral Esplanade; mains $25-35; ⊙dinner Thu-Sat) The region's most unpretentious high-end restaurant is this French doozy opposite Cannonvale beach. The six-course *table d'hôte* menu will please any palate. The service is considered and attentive. Book early in high season.

Deja Vu FUSION $$$
(☎07-4948 4309; Golden Orchid Dr; lunch mains $15-21, dinner mains $27-40; ⊙lunch Wed-Sun, dinner Wed-Sat) Rated as one of Airlie's best, this Polynesian-themed restaurant concocts contemporary dishes with Asian and Mediterranean influences. Be sure to while away a few hours at the famous long Sunday lunch (eight courses for $40 per person).

Drinking & Nightlife

According to the locals, Airlie Beach is a drinking town with a sailing problem. The bars at Magnums and Beaches, the two big backpackers in the centre of town, are always crowded.

Uber BAR
(350 Shute Harbour Rd; ⊙2-11pm Tue-Thu, to 2am Fri & Sat) This uber-cool bar and restaurant is the classiest in town. Come for cocktails, lounge in comfortable nooks on the alfresco deck, or just savour the uber-ambience.

Paddy's Shenanigans IRISH PUB
(352 Shute Harbour Rd; ⊙5pm-3am) Paddy's has live music late at night, and proudly encourages the Irish penchant for hard drinking.

Mama Africa CLUB
(263 Shute Harbour Rd; ⊙10pm-5am) Just a stumble across the road from the main party bars, this African-style safari nightclub throbs a beat that both hunter and prey find hard to resist.

Magnum's PUB
(☎07-4946 6266; Shute Harbour Rd; ⊙11am-midnight) Imagine five hundred sunburned 20-somethings jumping around in a vast outdoor venue with cheap champagne and cheap beds. Magnum's is a classic backpacker party; we say whack it on an ironic 'do-before-you-die' list.

Information

Private operators dish out tourist advice along Shute Harbour Rd – use your discretion and shop around.

Destination Whitsundays (07-4946 7172; 297 Shute Harbour Rd) Books tours.

QPWS (07-4967 7355; www.derm.qld.gov.au; cnr Shute Harbour & Mandalay Rds; 9am-4.30pm Mon-Fri) Situated 3km towards Shute Harbour. A must-visit for info on island camping and various hikes.

Whitsundays Central Reservation Centre (1800 677 119; www.airliebeach.com; 259 Shute Harbour Rd; 7am-7pm) Helpful family-run tour agency. Also has internet.

Getting There & Around

The closest major airports are at Proserpine and on Hamilton Island. The small **Whitsunday Airport** (07-4946 9180, 07-4946 9933) is about 6km southeast of town.

Greyhound (13 20 30; www.greyhound.com.au) and **Premier Motor Service** (13 34 10; www.premierms.com.au) have bus connections to Brisbane ($230, 19 hours), Mackay ($38, two hours), Townsville ($58, 4½ hours) and Cairns ($140, 11 hours). Long-distance buses stop on The Esplanade, between the sailing club and Airlie Beach Hotel.

Whitsunday Transit (07-4946 1800) connects Proserpine (Proserpine Airport), Cannonvale, Abel Point, Airlie Beach and Shute Harbour. Buses operate from 6am to 10.30pm.

Car-rental agencies include **Avis** (07-4951 1266), **Europcar** (07-4946 4133; 398 Shute Harbour Rd), **Fun Rentals** (07-4948 0489; 344 Shute Harbour Rd) and **Hertz** (07-4946 4687; 342 Shute Harbour Rd).

Whitsunday Islands

The 74 islands that make up this stunning archipelago are really the tips of mountains jutting out from the Coral Sea, and from their sandy fringes the ocean spreads towards the horizon. Sheltered by the Great Barrier Reef, the waters are perfect for sailing.

Of the numerous stunning beaches and secluded bays, Whitehaven Beach stands out for its pure white silica sand. It is undoubtedly the finest beach in the Whitsundays, and possibly one of the finest in the world.

Only seven of the islands have tourist resorts – catering to every budget and whim from the basic accommodation at Hook Island to the exclusive luxury of Hayman Island. Most of the islands are uninhabited, and several offer the chance of back-to-nature beach camping and bushwalking.

Sleeping

Most rates quoted for resorts are the standard rates, but look around for better-value package deals.

QPWS (www.derm.qld.gov.au) manages the Whitsunday Islands National Park camping grounds on several islands. Camping permits are available online, from the Whitsunday QPWS office and the Whitsunday Information Centre in Proserpine. Permits cost $5.85/21.80 per person/family.

You must be self-sufficient, and are advised to take 5L of water per person per day, plus three days' extra supply in case you get stuck. You should also have a fuel stove; wood fires are banned on all islands.

Get to your island with **Whitsunday Island Camping Connections – Scamper** (07-4946 6285; www.whitsundaycamping.com.au), which leaves from Shute Harbour and can drop you at South Molle, Denman or Planton Islands ($65 return); Whitsunday Island ($105 return); Whitehaven Beach ($155 return); and Hook Island ($160 return). Camping transfers also include complimentary snorkelling gear and water containers. You can also hire camp kits ($40 per night). A food drop-off service can be provided at extra cost.

Getting There & Around

The two main airports for the Whitsundays are at Hamilton Island and Proserpine, 36km southwest of Airlie Beach. **Virgin Australia** (13 67 89; www.virginaustralia.com) and **Jetstar** (13 15 38; www.jetstar.com.au) connect Hamilton Island with Brisbane, Sydney and Melbourne. **QantasLink** (13 13 13; www.qantas.com.au) flies there from Cairns.

Transfers between Abel Point Marina and Daydream, Long, Hamilton and South Molle Islands are provided by **Cruise Whitsundays** (07-4946 4662; www.cruisewhitsundays.com; adult/child one way $30/20).

Long Island

Long Island has some of the best beaches in the Whitsundays and some 13km of walking tracks. The island stretches 9km long by 1.5km wide; a 500m-wide channel separates it from the mainland. Day trippers can use the facilities at Long Island Resort.

There's a national-park **camp site** at Sandy Bay.

Paradise Bay (07-4946 9777; www.paradisebay.com.au; 3-night packages per person from $1500) is a secluded eco-friendly lodge on

CONWAY NATIONAL PARK

The mountains of this national park and the Whitsunday Islands are part of the same coastal mountain range. Rising sea levels following the last ice age flooded the lower valleys, leaving only the highest peaks as islands, now cut off from the mainland.

The road from Airlie Beach to Shute Harbour passes through the northern section of the park. Several **walking trails** start from near the picnic and day-use area. About 1km past the day-use area, there's a 2.4km walk up to the **Mt Rooper lookout**, which provides good views of the Whitsunday Passage and islands. Further along the main road, towards Coral Point (before Shute Harbour), there's a 1km track leading down to **Coral Beach** and **The Beak lookout**. This track was created with the assistance of the Giru Dala, the traditional custodians of the Whitsunday area; a brochure available at the start of the trail explains how the local Indigenous people use plants growing in the area.

To reach the beautiful **Cedar Creek Falls**, turn off the Proserpine–Airlie Beach road onto Conway Rd, 18km southwest of Airlie Beach. It's then about 15km to the falls; the roads are well signposted. This is a popular picnic and swimming spot – when there's enough water, that is!

Paradise Bay with 10 spacious bungalows made from Australian hardwood. There is a three-night minimum stay, and no children or motorised water sports allowed, so you are guaranteed peace and tranquillity. The tariff is inclusive of helicopter transfers from Hamilton Island, sailing tours, food and beer.

Long Island Resort (☎1800 075 125; www.oceanhotels.com.au/longisland; d incl all meals $260-380; ❄@≋) is a resort for everyone (kids welcome), with varying levels of comfort, the best being those on the beachfront. There are great short walks from here, and loads of activities.

South Molle Island

Lovers of birds and long, sandy beaches will enjoy the largest island of the Molle archipelago. Nearly 15km of splendid walking tracks traverse this mountainous 4-sq-km island; the highest point is Mt Jeffreys (198m), but the climb up Spion Kop is also worthwhile.

There are national-park **camping grounds** located at Sandy Bay in the south and at Paddle Bay near one very tired resort.

Daydream Island

Recently purchased by Chinese investors, Daydream Island feels more like a pontoon than a natural wonder. It's only a 15-minute ferry ride from the mainland so most appeals to families with kids, or day trippers. Loads of water-sports gear is available for hire.

The **Daydream Island Resort & Spa** (☎1800 075 040; www.daydreamisland.com; d from $328; ❄📶≋) feels a bit like an island theme park but it still prides itself on excellent service and remarkable building and grounds maintenance. There are three swimming pools, tennis courts, catamarans and faux-beaches. There's also a kids' club.

Hook Island

The second largest of the Whitsundays, the 53-sq-km Hook Island is predominantly national park and rises to 450m at Hook Peak. Hook boasts some of the best diving and snorkelling locations in the Whitsundays.

Those who don't mind roughing it book in at the **Hook Island Wilderness Resort** (☎07-4946 9380; www.hookislandresort.com; camp sites per person $20, d with/without bathroom $120/100; ❄≋), a battered place with basic quarters and a licensed restaurant (mains $16 to 27).

There are some good camping opportunities in national-park **camping grounds** at Maureen Cove, Steen's Beach, Bloodhorn Beach, Curlew Beach and Crayfish Beach.

Whitsunday Island

Whitehaven Beach, on Whitsunday Island, is a much-fabled, pristine 7km-long stretch of dazzling white sand bounded by lush tropical vegetation and a brilliant blue sea. From Hill Inlet, at the northern end of the beach, the swirling pattern of pure white sand through the turquoise and aquamarine water paints a magical picture. There's excellent snorkelling from its southern end.

There are national-park **camping grounds** at Dugong, Nari's and Joe's Beaches in the west; at Chance Bay in the south; at the southern end of Whitehaven Beach; and at Peter Bay in the north.

Hamilton Island

Hamilton Island is the most 'liveable' island in the Whitsundays. There's a school, a new marina, a golf course, a busy domestic airport and, despite the crowds, a sense of in-the-know exclusivity.

There are a few **walking trails** on the island, the best being from behind the Reef View Hotel up to Passage Peak (230m) on the northeastern corner of the island.

Hamilton Island Resort (07-4946 9999; www.hamiltonisland.com.au; d from $370;) has extensive options, including bungalows, luxury villas, plush hotel rooms and self-contained apartments. At the high-end, **Qualia** (07-4948 9222, 1300 780 959; www.qualia.com.au; d from $1510) regularly scoops international awards.

Hamilton is a ready-made day trip from Shute Harbour, and you can use some of the resort's facilities.

Lindeman Island

Lovely Lindeman is mostly national park, with empty bays and 20km of impressive walking trails. Nature photographers descend for the varied island tree life and the sublime view from Mt Oldfield (210m). **Boat Port** is the best spot for camping.

Hayman Island

The most northern of the Whitsunday group, Hayman is just 4 sq km in area and rises to 250m above sea level. It has forested hills, valleys and beaches, and a five-star resort.

An avenue of huge date palms leads to **Hayman Island Resort** (07-4940 1234, 1800 075 175; www.hayman.com.au; r incl breakfast $466-8000;), one of the most luxurious on the Great Barrier Reef.

For non-guests, flying is the only way to do day trips to Hayman. Check out **Air Whitsunday Seaplanes** (07-4946 9111; per person $195).

Other Whitsunday Islands

The northern islands of the Whitsunday group are undeveloped and seldom visited by cruise boats or water taxis. Several of these – Gloucester, Saddleback, Olden and Armit Islands – have national-park **camping grounds**. The **QPWS office** (07-4946 7022; www.derm.qld.gov.au), 3km south of Airlie Beach, can issue camping permits and advise you on which islands to visit and how to get there.

Bowen

POP 10,260

Bowen is a classic reminder of the typical small Queensland coastal towns of the 1970s – wide streets, low-rise buildings, wooden Queenslander houses, and laid-back, friendly locals. The foreshore, with its landscaped esplanade, picnic tables and barbecues, is a focal point. Fruit-picking is a major draw for long-term travellers between April and November and for everyone else there are stunning beaches and bays northeast of the town centre.

Hostels open and close fairly regularly depending on the season.

Sleeping & Eating

Barnacles Backpackers HOSTEL $
(07-4786 4400; www.barnaclesbackpackers.com; 18 Gordon St; dm from $30) Clean hostel but can have poor service; also the only one open in Bowen when we visited.

Rose Bay Resort RESORT $$
(07-4786 9000; www.rosebayresort.com.au; 2 Pandanus St; r $150-270;) In a beautiful location right on the beach, these spacious studios and comfy units will ensure plenty of quiet time. Good location and good value. Minimum two-night stay.

360 on the Hill CAFE $
(07-4786 6360; Margaret Reynolds Dr; mains $6-16; 8am-4pm Sat-Thu, 8am-9pm Fri) High atop Flagstaff Hill. Serves delicious food and features stunning 360-degree views.

Food Freaks CAFE $
(07-4786 5133; 18-20 Herbert St; mains $10-18; 8am-4pm) Best breakfast for miles and some of the friendliest service we experienced on the whole Queensland coast!

Smoothies, baguettes and muffins seem perennial favourites.

Cove CHINESE, MALAY **$$**
(☎07-4791 2050; Coral Cove Apartments, Horseshoe Bay Rd; mains $15-25; ⊙lunch & dinner Tue-Sun) Serves an interesting fusion of Chinese and Malay dishes with spectacular sea views from the timber deck.

Grandview Hotel PUB **$$**
(☎07-4786 6360; mains $8-25; ⊙11am-9pm) Huge corner pub consistently recommended by locals for its quality meals and sizeable portions.

Getting There & Away

Long-distance buses stop outside **Bowen Travel** (☎07-4786 2835; 40 William St), where you can book and purchase bus tickets. **Greyhound Australia** (☎13 20 30; www.greyhound.com.au) and **Premier Motor Service** (☎13 34 10; www.premierms.com.au) have frequent services to/from Rockhampton ($110, eight hours), Airlie Beach ($28, 1½ hours) and Townsville ($50, four hours).

TOWNSVILLE TO MISSION BEACH

North of the Whitsunday Coast you'll find mountain ranges, authentic outback towns and islands worth hopping to. Townsville's waterfront stretches for miles and is hugged by hotels and pubs. Magnetic Island lies just offshore and, with its 22 bays, makes an awesome place for isolated-beach-to-isolated-beach walking. Northwest of Townsville, the misty rainforest of the Paluma Range National Park stakes its claim as the southernmost part of the fantastic Wet Tropics World Heritage Area.

Other highlights include forested Hinchinbrook and Dunk Islands, and charming Mission Beach, surrounded by tropical rainforest.

Townsville

POP 189,931

Backed by a giant red hill, Townsville is an underrated regional centre that has undergone an extensive makeover on the back of mining and military coin. An endless esplanade fronts the Coral Sea where ferries shoot across to Magnetic Island and divers plum its depths.

A short stroll takes visitors past fine museums, colourful heritage buildings, a huge aquarium and sports-mad, sun-drenched locals. Townsville has an average of 320 days of sunshine per year. Undercover seating at Dairy Farmers Stadium was considered unnecessary because of the minimal rainfall during the rugby-league season.

The compact city centre is easy to get about on foot. Just east of the pedestrian-only Victoria Bridge (or the Dean St vehicle bridge), South Townsville is home to the city's premier drinking and dining precinct, centred on rejuvenated Palmer St.

Sights

★ **Reef HQ Aquarium** AQUARIUM
(www.reefhq.com.au; Flinders St E; adult/child $26.50/12.80; ⊙9.30am-5pm) Townsville's excellent aquarium is a living reef on dry land. A staggering 2.5 million litres of water flow through the coral-reef tank, which is home to sharks, rays and over 100 fish species, plus brilliantly hued coral. Kids will love seeing, feeding and touching turtles at the turtle hospital.

Castle Hill LOOKOUT
If the temperature's right (ie the asphalt's not melting) it's worth scrambling to the top of this striking 286m-high red hill (an isolated pink-granite monolith) for the view. Walk up via the rough 'goat track' (2km one way) from Hillside Cres. There's also a road (via Gregory St or Stanley St), if you're driving.

Botanic Gardens GARDENS
(⊙sunrise-sunset) FREE Townsville's botanic gardens are spread across three locations: each has its own character, but all have tropical plants and are abundantly green. Closest to the centre, the formal, ornamental **Queens Gardens** (cnr Gregory & Paxton Sts) are 1km northwest of town at the base of Castle Hill.

Billabong Sanctuary WILDLIFE RESERVE
(www.billabongsanctuary.com.au; Bruce Hwy; adult/child $30/19; ⊙9am-4pm) Just 17km south of Townsville, this eco-certified wildlife park offers up-close-and-personal encounters with Australian wildlife – from dingoes to cassowaries – in their natural habitat. There are feedings, shows and talks every half-hour or so.

Australian Institute of Marine Science RESEARCH INSTITUTE
(AIMS; ☎07-4753 4444; www.aims.gov.au) This marine-research facility at Cape Ferguson

Townsville

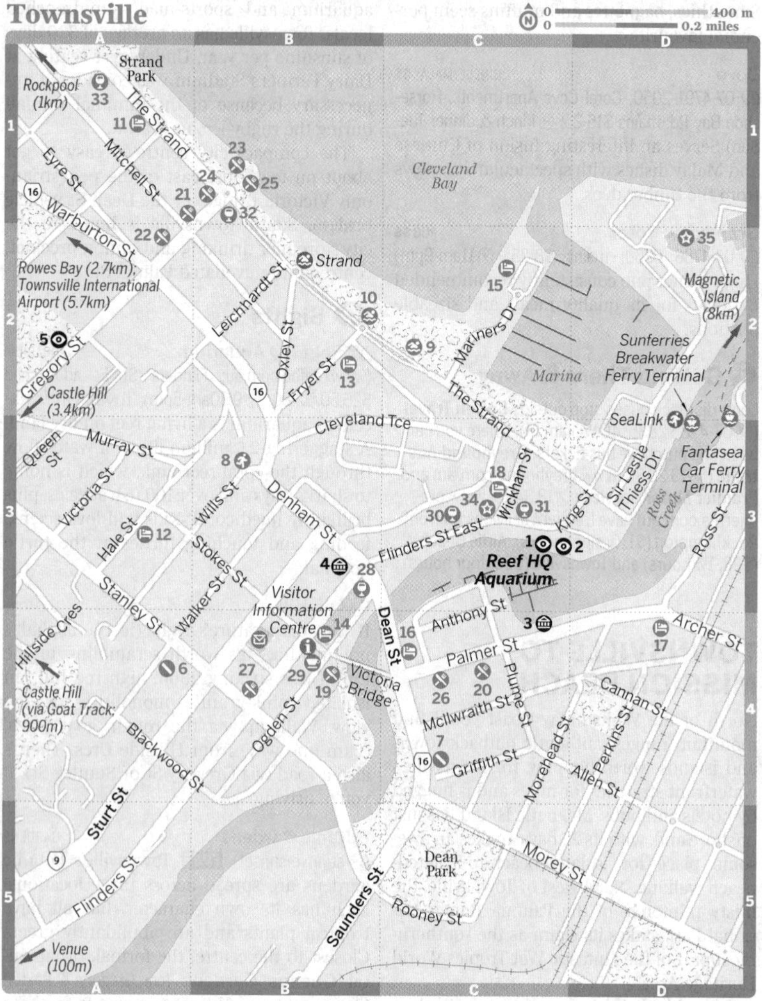

runs free two-hour tours (10am Fridays, March to November) covering the institute's research (such as coral bleaching and management of the Great Barrier Reef) and how it relates to the community; advance bookings are essential. The turn-off from the Bruce Hwy is 35km southeast of Townsville.

Museum of Tropical Queensland MUSEUM
(www.mtq.qld.gov.au; 70-102 Flinders St E; adult/child $15/8.80; ⏲9.30am-5pm) The MTQ reconstructs scenes using detailed models with interactive displays. At 11am and 2.30pm you can load and fire a cannon, 1700s-style; galleries include the kid-friendly MindZone science centre, displays on north Queensland's rainforests and a new exhibition on the animals of Gondwana (ancient Australia).

Maritime Museum of Townsville MUSEUM
(www.townsvillemaritimemuseum.org.au; 42-68 Palmer St; adult/child $6/3; ⏲10am-3pm Mon-Fri, noon-3pm Sat & Sun) A smaller affair, with lighthouse memorabilia and a *Yongala* shipwreck model and display. The HMAS *Townsville* is now permanently berthed here.

Townsville

Top Sights
1 Reef HQ Aquarium......C3

Sights
2 Cultural Centre......C3
3 Maritime Museum of Townsville......C4
Museum of Tropical Queensland......(see 2)
4 Perc Tucker Regional Gallery......B3
5 Queens Gardens......A2

Activities, Courses & Tours
6 Adrenalin Dive......A4
7 Remote Area Dive......C4
8 Sky Dive Townsville......B3
9 Tobruk Memorial Baths......C2
10 Water Playground......B2

Sleeping
11 Aquarius on the Beach......A1
12 Coral Lodge......A3
13 Historic Yongala Lodge Motel......B2
14 Holiday Inn......B4
15 Mariners North......C2
16 Oaks Gateway on Palmer......C4
17 Oaks Hotel M......D4
Orchid Guest House......(see 12)
18 Reef Lodge......C3

Eating
19 A Touch of Salt......B4
20 Benny's Hot Wok......C4
21 Bountiful Thai......A1
22 Cafe Bambini......A2
23 Cbar......B1
24 Harold's Seafood......B1
25 Longboard Bar & Grill......B1
26 Salt Cellar......C4
Souvlaki Bar......(see 24)
27 The Sweatshop......B4
TUBE......(see 21)

Drinking & Nightlife
28 Brewery......B3
29 Coffee Dominion......B4
30 Consortium......C3
31 Molly Malones......C3
32 Seaview Hotel......B1
33 Watermark Hotel......A1

Entertainment
34 Flynns......C3
35 Jupiters Casino......D2

Cultural Centre CULTURAL CENTRE
(07-4772 7679; www.cctownsville.com.au; 2-68 Flinders St E; 9.30am-4.30pm) Showcases the history, traditions and customs of the Wulgurkaba and Bindal people. Call for guided tour times.

Perc Tucker Regional Gallery GALLERY
(www.townsville.qld.gov.au; cnr Denham & Flinders Sts; 10am-5pm Mon-Fri, to 2pm Sat & Sun) A contemporary art gallery in a stately 1885 former bank. Exhibitions focus on north Queensland artists.

Activities

Stretching 2.2km, Townsville's palm-lined waterfront (the Strand) is interspersed with parks, pools and cafes. Its golden-sand beach is patrolled and protected by two stinger enclosures from November to May.

At the northern tip is the **rock pool** (24hr) FREE, an enormous artificial swimming pool surrounded by lawns and sandy beaches. Alternatively, head to the chlorinated safety of the heritage-listed Olympic-size swimming pool, **Tobruk Memorial Baths** (www.townsville.qld.gov.au; Strand; adult/child $2.50/1.50; 5.30am-7pm Mon-Thu, to 6pm Fri, 7am-4pm Sat, 8am-5pm Sun).

There's also a brilliant little **water playground** (10am-8pm Dec-Mar, to 6pm Sep-Nov, Apr & May, to 5pm Jun-Aug) FREE for kids.

Woodstock Trail Rides HORSE RIDING
(07-4778 8888; www.woodstocktrailrides.com.au; Jones Rd; 90-minute/half-day rides $80/100, cattle musters $175) Situated 43km south of Townsville, this huge property has full- and half-day horse-riding trips as well as **cattle musters** for aspiring cowboys and girls. Bookings essential.

Sky Dive Townsville SKYDIVING
(07-4772 4889; www.skydivetownsville.com.au; tandem dives from $395) Those curious to know Townsville from top to bottom can try a tandem dive, landing in the middle of the sandy Strand.

Diving

The visitor centre has a list of Townsville-based operators offering PADI-certified learn-to-dive courses. Prices start at about $615.

Adrenalin Dive DIVING
(07-4724 0600; www.adrenalinedive.com.au) Day trips to the *Yongala* (from $220) and Wheeler Reef (from $280), both including two dives. Also offers snorkelling (from

$180) on Wheeler Reef as well as live-aboard trips, and dive certification courses.

Remote Area Dive DIVING
(RAD; ☎07-4721 4424; www.remoteareadive.com; 16 Dean St) Runs day trips (from $220) to Orpheus and Pelorus islands. Also live-aboard trips and dive courses.

Salt Dive DIVING
(☎07-4721 1760; www.saltdive.com.au; 2/276 Charters Towers Rd, Hermit Park) *Yongala* and reef-diving day trips (from $199) aboard a fast boat; dive courses available.

SeaLink FERRY
(☎07-4771 3855; www.sealinkqld.gov.au; Sir Leslie Thiess Dr; per person from $145) Operates day trips to the Great Barrier Reef. A certified or introductory dive costs an additional around A$70.

Yongala Dive DIVING
(☎07-4783 1519; www.yongaladive.com.au; 56 Narrah St) *Yongala* wreck dives ($259 including gear) from Alva Beach, 104km southeast of Townsville. It only takes 30 minutes to get out to the wreck from here, instead of a 2½-hour boat trip from Townsville. Book ahead for backpacker-style accommodation at its onshore **dive lodge** (dm/d $25/60; @).

Tours

Kookaburra Tours GUIDED TOUR
(☎0448 794 798; www.kookaburratours.com.au) Highly recommended day trips include 'Heritage and Highlights' city tours (adult/child $50/25), Wallaman Falls (adult/child $125/55) and rainforest tours in Mount Spec National Park (adult/child $125/55).

Townsville Ghost Tours GUIDED TOUR
(☎0404 453 354; www.townsvilleghosttours.com.au) Five spooky options, from city haunts aboard the 'ghost bus' (from $65) to an overnight trip to Ravenswood ($250 including meals and accommodation).

Sleeping

Coral Lodge B&B $
(☎07-4771 5512; www.corallodge.com.au; 32 Hale St; s/d without bathroom $70/90, units from $85; ❄) At the base of Stanton Hill is a fun Aussie family home that has been used as lodging for nearly a century. Pay a bit extra for the self-contained units which are terrific value. The lodge is only a short walk from the sights of Townsville but you can call ahead for pick up.

Reef Lodge HOSTEL $
(☎07-4721 1112; www.reeflodge.com.au; 4 Wickham St; dm $22-26, d with/without bathroom $80/62; ❄@wifi) Townsville's best hostel does not have much to compete with, and keeps rooms and service pretty basic. However, there are thoughtful touches like Buddhist sculptures and hammocks strewn through the garden, pond sculptures and a kick-arse '80s-style games room.

Orchid Guest House GUESTHOUSE $
(☎07-4771 6683; www.orchidguesthouse.com.au; 34 Hale St; dm $27, with/without bathroom s $75/55, d $85/65; ❄) Bright and cheerful budget rooms await low-key backpackers and itinerant workers at this quiet, well-run guesthouse. The owners know their clientele and provide mountains of information on the area. You can't miss the sky blue exteriors.

Rowes Bay Caravan Park CAMPGROUND $
(☎07-4771 3576; www.rowesbaycp.com.au; Heatley Pde; unpowered/powered sites $26/36, cabins with/without bathroom from $98/65, villas $105; ❄@wifi pool) Leafy park directly opposite Rowes Bay's beachfront. Brand-new villas are smaller but spiffier than cabins.

Classique B&B B&B $$
(☎0407 699 748; www.classiquebnb.com.au; 495 Sturt St; r $165-185; P❄wifi pool) Multiple industry awards are no surprise for this beautifully maintained B&B on the way to Castle Hill. The historic Queenslander features high-pressed metal ceilings and hoop pine timber floors. There's a small pool and a snooker room. There are only three rooms, each with ensuite bathroom and a small living area.

Historic Yongala Lodge Motel MOTEL $$
(☎07-4772 4633; www.historicyongala.com.au; 11 Fryer St; motel r $99-105, 1-bedroom apt $115-120; ❄wifi pool) This late-19th-century heritage building is ideally located near the Strand and the CBD. The motel-style rooms are a little compact but the price is very fair and the on-site Greek restaurant (mains $20 to $38, open for dinner Monday to Sat)is popular with locals.

Aquarius on the Beach HOTEL $$
(☎1800 622 474; www.aquariusonthebeach.com.au; 75 The Strand; d $110-150; ❄@wifi pool) A few clicks from the city along the posh end of the Strand is this juggernaut of a building that offers choice views to Magnetic Island from

the full-width balconies. The decor is holding up pretty well considering the age of the place and service is astute. Ideal for families.

Oaks Gateway on Palmer
HOTEL **$$**

(☑ 07-4753 2900; www.oakshotelsresorts.com; 2 Dibbs St; r from $129; P❋🛜🏊) Excellent new Oaks franchise on the waterfront. Rooms are modern with views of either the water or the hinterland. There's an Infinity pool and the staff is very capable.

Holiday Inn
HOTEL **$$**

(☑ 07-4772 2477; www.townsville.holiday-inn.com; 334 Flinders St; d $110-189; ❋🛜🏊) This 20-storey, 1976-built circular building is a Townsville icon known as the 'sugar shaker'. The rooftop pool is worth the stay alone and the rooms are surprisingly lush given the concrete exterior.

Oaks Hotel M
HOTEL **$$**

(☑ 1800 760 144; www.oakshotelsresorts.com; 81 Palmer St; d $144-189; ❋🛜🏊) This 11-storey hotel has space-age rooms, excellent facilities and glittering views from the higher-priced rooms.

Mariners North
APARTMENT **$$$**

(☑ 07-4722 0777; www.marinersnorth.com.au; 7 Mariners Dr; 2-/3-bedroom apt from $250/390; ❋🛜🏊) Plum location at the city end of the Strand and an incredible poolside vista across the Coral Sea give this apartment complex a definite advantage. Perfect for families with kids though management can be a little forthright. Guests can access the Tobruk pool and gym.

✖ Eating

★ The Sweatshop
CAFE **$**

(☑ 0435 845 237; 181 Flinders St; jaffles $7, burgers $12, coffee $3.50; ☺ 7.30am-4pm Mon-Wed, 7.30am-8pm Thu, 7.30am-midnight Fri-Sat, 9am-3pm Sun) This tongue-in-cheek art space serves simple, high quality food and the best coffee in Townsville. If the stingers and the heat are combining to oppress your senses, reload here all day long.

TUBE
BURGERS **$**

(☑ 07-4772 2856; 2/58 The Strand, North Ward; burgers $10-14; ☺ 11am-8pm Mon-Thu, 11am-9pm Fri-Sat, 8am-10pm Sun) Straight-up burger bar with creative reinventions like the Reef & Beef and My Big Fat Greek Burger. 'The Ultimate Burger Experience' (TUBE) is the most appealing of the North Ward cheap eats. It's also licensed.

Cafe Bambini
CAFE **$**

(46 Gregory St; mains $11.50-20; ☺ 5.30am-5pm Mon-Fri, 6.30am-4pm Sat & Sun; 🖊) Four locations around the city and no sign of slowing down for this local catering mob who specialise in breakfasts and fresh take-away food.

Harold's Seafood
SEAFOOD **$**

(cnr The Strand & Gregory St; meals $4-10; ☺ lunch & dinner) This takeaway joint has bug burgers of the Moreton Bay variety.

Souvlaki Bar
GREEK **$**

(Shops 3 & 4, 58 The Strand; mains $6.50-17.50; ☺ 10.30am-9pm Mon-Fri, to 10pm Sat & Sun) Grab a big Greek breakfast of bacon, eggs, sausage, souvlaki, grilled tomatoes, haloumi and pita bread.

Coffee Dominion
CAFE **$**

(www.coffeedominion.com.au; cnr Stokes & Ogden Sts; ☺ 6am-5pm Mon-Wed, to 5.30pm Thu & Fri, 7am-1pm Sat & Sun) 🖊 Eco-conscious cafe.

Longboard Bar & Grill
MODERN AUSTRALIAN **$$**

(☑ 07-4724 1234; The Strand, opposite Gregory St; mains $15-34; ☺ 11.30am-3pm & 5.30pm-late) The only restaurant on the water's edge has been reincarnated as a brewery and grillhouse where seafood, steak and beer food such as buffalo wings and fish tacos are served up to huge crowds, especially on weekends.

Benny's Hot Wok
ASIAN **$$**

(☑ 07-4724 3243; 17-21 Palmer St; mains $14-29; ☺ lunch Fri & Sun, dinner daily) The cocktail bar and steamy, tropical setting are reason enough to visit this north Queensland favourite. The full gamut of Asian food is on offer, with mixed success, mind you.

A Touch of Salt
MODERN AUSTRALIAN **$$**

(☑ 07-4724 4441; cnr Stokes & Ogden Sts; mains $30-36; ☺ lunch Thu & Fri, dinner Tue-Sat) The less pretentious (and less interesting) of the two Salt establishments.

Cbar
CAFE **$$**

(The Strand, opposite Gregory St; mains $16-26; ☺ 7am-10pm; 🖊) Very reliable and agreeable venue serving full meals throughout the day, from coconut prawns with mango salsa to Moroccan-style beef tagines.

Bountiful Thai
THAI **$$**

(Shop 1, 52 Gregory St; mains $13-21; ☺ lunch Mon-Fri, dinner daily) Takeaway whipping up noodle and rice dishes, curries and soups in huge portions and quick time.

RAVENSWOOD & CHARTERS TOWERS

You don't have to venture too far inland for a taste of the dry, dusty Queensland outback, which is a stark contrast to the verdant coast. This detour is easily accessible on a day trip from Townsville, but it's worth staying overnight if you can.

Along the Flinders Hwy, a turn-off at Mingela, 88km southwest of Townsville, leads 40km south to the tiny gold-mining village of **Ravenswood** (population 150), with a couple of gorgeous turn-of-the-20th-century pubs with accommodation.

A further 47km west along the Flinders Hwy from Mingela is the historic gold-rush town of **Charters Towers** (population 8100). The 'towers' are its surrounding tors (hills). William Skelton Ewbank Melbourne (WSEM) Charters was the gold commissioner during the rush, when the town was the second-largest, and wealthiest, in Queensland. With almost 100 mines, some 90 pubs and a stock exchange, it became known simply as 'the World'.

Today, a highlight of a visit to the Towers is strolling past its glorious facades recalling the grandeur of those heady days, and listening to locals' ghost stories.

History oozes from the walls of the 1890 **Stock Exchange Arcade**, next door to the **Charters Towers visitor centre** (☎07-4752 0314; www.charterstowers.qld.gov.au; 74 Mosman St; ⊙9am-5pm). The visitor centre has a free brochure outlining the **One Square Mile Trail** of the town centre's beautifully preserved 19th-century buildings, and books all tours in town, including the **Venus Gold Battery** (Millchester Rd; tours adult/child $12/6; ⊙10am-3pm), where gold-bearing ore was crushed and processed; it cranks into action during mid-July's **Gold Fever Festival**.

Come nightfall, panoramic Towers Hill, the site where gold was first discovered, is the atmospheric setting for a free **open-air cinema** showing the 20-minute film *Ghosts After Dark* – check seasonal screening times with the visitor centre.

In-town accommodation includes period furniture–filled former pub the **Royal Private Hotel** (☎07-4787 8688; 100 Mosman St; s/d without bathroom $45/55, d with bathroom $90-115; ❄📶). A venture to Charters Towers is incomplete without scoffing one of the award-winning pies at **Towers Bakery** (114 Gill St; pies $3.90-4.30; ⊙5am-3pm Mon-Fri, to 1pm Sat).

Greyhound Australia (☎1300 473 946; www.greyhound.com.au) has four weekly services between Townsville and Charters Towers ($36, 1¾ hours).

The **Queensland Rail** (☎1300 131 722; www.traveltrain.com.au) *Inlander* runs twice weekly between Townsville and Charters Towers ($28, three hours).

Salt Cellar MODERN AUSTRALIAN $$$
(☎07-4724 5866; www.thesaltcellar.com.au; 13 Palmer St; mains $30-40; ⊙5.30pm-late Mon-Sat) The newest addition to the Salt emporium is now the darling of the Palmer St dinner set. An extensive wine cellar accentuates starters like pheasant tortellini ($21) and tamarind prawns ($19). For the main course, we loved the venison loin ($40). Service is first class.

Drinking & Nightlife

★**Brewery** MICROBREWERY
(252 Flinders St; mains $17-36; ⊙Mon-Sat, restaurant lunch & dinner Mon-Sat) A variety of brews, from wit bier to stout, are made on-site at Townsville's handsomely restored 1880s former post office. Soak them up with a meal at its refined restaurant.

Watermark Hotel BAR
(72-74 The Strand) Some serious Sunday sessions take place in the tavern bar, while there's also a more upmarket bar and an excellent Mod Oz restaurant (mains $28 to $36, open lunch and dinner daily, breakfast Sunday).

Seaview Hotel PUB
(cnr The Strand & Gregory St; restaurant mains $21-44; ⊙restaurant lunch & dinner) The sea views, fig-tree locale and occasionally loud live music win over pub-loving locals in this sprawling drinking hub.

Molly Malones PUB, CLUB
(87 Flinders St E; ⊙The Shed 8pm-5am Tue, Fri & Sat) This boisterous Irish pub stages live music on Friday and Saturday nights, or you can shake it on the dance floor of its adjacent nightclub, **The Shed**.

Consortium CLUB
(159 Flinders St E; ⌚9pm-5am Tue & Thu-Sun) Resident DJs, DJ comps and events like 'fetish and fantasy' balls make this big city–style venue Townsville's hippest nightclub.

☆ Entertainment

Flynns LIVE MUSIC
(101 Flinders St E; ⌚5pm-late Tue-Sun) A jolly Irish pub that doesn't try too hard to be Irish. Wildly popular for its $8 jugs and live music every night except Wednesday, when karaoke takes over.

The Venue LIVE MUSIC
(www.thevenue.com.au; 719 Flinders St W) Multi-level place with regular gigs by Aussie acts (Grinspoon et al) and four bars.

Jupiters Casino CASINO
(Sir Leslie Thiess Dr) Come here for a waterside flutter.

ℹ Information

Internet Den (277 Flinders St; per 90min $5; ⌚8am-10pm) Internet access.

QPWS (☎13 74 68; www.derm.qld.gov.au; 1-7 Marlow St)

Visitor Information Centre (☎07-4721 3660; www.townsvilleonline.com.au; cnr Flinders & Stokes Sts) Extensive visitor information on Townsville, Magnetic Island and nearby national parks.

ℹ Getting There & Away

AIR

Virgin Australia (☎13 67 89; www.virginaustralia.com), **Jetstar** (☎13 15 38; www.jetstar.com.au) and **Qantas** (☎13 13 13; www.qantas.com.au) all service Townsville.

BUS

Greyhound Australia departs from here. Buses pick up and drop off at Townsville's **Sunferries Breakwater ferry terminal** (2/14 Sir Leslie Thiess Dr; lockers per day $4-6).

DESTINATION	PRICE ($)	DURATION (HR)
Airlie Beach	71	4½
Brisbane	270	23
Cairns	83	6
Charters Towers	36	1½
Mackay	96	6
Mission Beach	63	4
Rockhampton	149	12

Premier Motor Service (☎13 34 10; www.premierms.com.au) has one service a day to/from Brisbane and Cairns, stopping in Townsville at the **Fantasea car ferry terminal** (Ross St, South Townsville).

ℹ Getting Around

Townsville's airport is 5km northwest of the city in Garbutt. A taxi costs $20, or the **Airport Shuttle** (☎07-4775 5544; one way/return $10/18) services all arrivals and departures, with pick-ups and drop-offs throughout the CBD (bookings essential).

Sunbus (☎07-4725 8482; www.sunbus.com.au) scoots around town; pick up info from the visitor information centre.

Taxis congregate near the Sunbus **bus interchange** (cnr Flinders & Stokes Sts), or call **Townsville Taxis** (☎13 10 08).

Magnetic Island

POP 2500

'Maggie', as she's affectionately called, is a 'real' island. Permanent residents live and work here and some even make the daily commute to Townsville. Over half of this mountainous, triangular-shaped island's 52 sq km is national park, with scenic walks and abundant wildlife, including one of the largest concentrations of wild koalas in Australia. Stunning beaches offer adrenalin-pumping water sports or just the chance to bask in the sunshine. Each of the four tiny beach villages has its own distinct personality, and the granite boulders, hoop pines and eucalypts are a change from your typical tropical-island paradise.

◉ Sights & Activities

There's one main road across the island, which goes from Picnic Bay, past Nelly and Geoffrey Bays, to Horseshoe Bay. Local buses ply the route regularly.

Walking tracks abound on Magnetic Island, and **DERM** (☎13 74 68; www.derm.qld.gov.au) produces a leaflet of the island's excellent bushwalking tracks. Walks are mainly along the east coast and vary in length from half an hour to half a day.

Fort Complex FORT
In 1942 Townsville became a major military base, and a **forts** complex was built on Magnetic Island to spot aircraft with its two 3-million-candle-power searchlights. If you're going to do just one walk, then the

forts walk (2.8km, 1½ hours return) is a must. It starts near the Radical Bay turn-off. Or head north to Radical Bay via the rough vehicle track. This has walking tracks to secluded **Arthur Bay** and **Florence Bay** (the northern sides of both offer the island's best snorkelling).

Picnic Bay BAY

Picnic Bay is slowly recovering from the loss of the ferry terminal a few years ago. Travellers are returning for its end-of-the-line seclusion, the elegant curlew birds close at hand and the night views of Townsville.

Activities in the area include **swimming** in the beach's stinger enclosure (November to May) or hitting balls around the nine-hole golf course at the **Magnetic Island Country Club** (07-4778 5188; www.magneticislandgolf.com.au; Hurst St; from 8am). West is **Cockle Bay**, site of the HMS *City of Adelaide* wreck, followed by **West Point** with its stunning sunsets and secluded beach. East round the coast is **Rocky Bay**, where a short, steep walk leads down to a beautiful sheltered beach.

Nelly Bay BAY

This bustling harbour is where the island experience begins and ends if you come by passenger or car ferry. Nelly Bay has a wide range of eating and sleeping options and a decent beach. There's a children's playground towards the northern end of the beach and good snorkelling on the fringing coral reef.

Arcadia Village VILLAGE

Arcadia village has the island's main concentration of shops, eateries and accommodation. Its main beach, **Geoffrey Bay**, has a reef at its southern end (DERM discourages reef walking). By far its prettiest beach is **Alma Bay cove**, with huge boulders tumbling into the sea. There's plenty of shade, along with picnic tables and a children's playground here.

If you head to the end of the road at Bremner Point, between Geoffrey Bay and Alma Bay, at 5pm, you can have **wild rock wallabies** literally eating out of your hand – they've become accustomed to being fed at the same time each day.

Radical Bay BAY

Radical Bay once housed a resort, and a replacement is in the pipeline. In the meantime it's a peaceful spot. You can walk across the headland to Horseshoe Bay, taking a detour down to the unofficial nudist beach of **Balding Bay** (3.4km return).

Horseshoe Bay BAY

The beach here is easily the best of the island's accessible beaches. It has a stinger enclosure, water-sports equipment for hire, a row of cafes and a good pub. Bungalow Bay Koala Village has a **wildlife park** (adult/child $19/10; 2hr tours 10am, noon & 2.30pm) where you can cuddle koalas ($14 including photos), or tuck into a **bush tucker gourmet breakfast** (adult/child $25/12.50). A monthly **craft market** (9.30am-2pm last Sun of month) sets up along the beachfront.

Pleasure Divers DIVING

(1800 797 797; www.pleasuredivers.com.au; 10 Marine Pde, Arcadia; open-water course per person $349) Teaches all PADI courses and offers reef, wreck and island dives.

Magnetic Island Hire Boats BOAT HIRE

(07-4778 5327) Rents out boats ($220 per day plus fuel) that can carry up to eight people – great for fishing, snorkelling or just finding your own private cove.

Horseshoe Bay Ranch HORSE RIDING

(07-4778 5109; www.horseshoebayranch.com.au; 38 Gifford St, Horseshoe Bay; 2hr rides $100) Memorable rides through bush and along the beach.

Tours

Providence V CRUISE

(07-4778 5580; www.providencesailing.com.au) Six-hour sailing trips aboard a 62ft schooner for $129 (including snorkelling gear); also 2½-hour champagne sunset cruises.

Magnetic Island Sea Kayaks KAYAKING

(07-4778 5424; www.seakayak.com.au; 93 Horseshoe Bay Rd; tours from $85) Eco-certified morning and sunset tours departing from Horseshoe Bay. Also offers kayak rental (per day from $75).

Reef Ecotours SNORKELLING

(0419 712 579; www.reefecotours.com; adult/child $80/70) Family-friendly one-hour snorkelling tours guided by a marine biologist.

Tropicana Tours DRIVING TOUR

(07-4758 1800; www.tropicanatours.com.au; full day adult/child $198/99) Offers 4WD tours taking in wildlife, as well as lunch at a local cafe and a sunset cocktail (all included in the price).

Sleeping

Much of the accommodation on the island is holiday rental cottages – contact **First National Real Estate** (07-4778 5077; 21 Marine Pde, Arcadia) or **Smith & Elliott** (07-4778 5570; 4/5 Bright Ave, Arcadia).

Picnic Bay

Tropical Palms Inn MOTEL $$
(07-4778 5076; www.tropicalpalmsinn.com.au; 34 Picnic St; s/d $100/110;) With a terrific little swimming pool situated right outside your front door, the self-contained motel units here are bright and comfortable. Reception can hire out 4WDs (from $75 per day).

Nelly Bay

Base Backpackers HOSTEL $
(1800 242 273; www.stayatbase.com; 1 Nelly Bay Rd; camping $12 per person, dm $25-30, d with/without bathroom from $120/70;) Come here for the Island Bar and full-moon parties rather than the fairly shoddy cabins and flippant service. If loitering in Townsville then take a package that includes lodging, food and transport.

Canopy Chalets CHALET $$
(0417 030 630; www.canopymagneticisland.com.au; 42 Yates St; d from $160;) This discreet couples-only lodging has some of the more modern interiors on the island including loft-style bedrooms and sleek kitchenettes. The pool is luxurious and the premises is a 10-minute walk from the Nelly Bay ferry terminal.

Shambhala Retreat RETREAT $$
(0448 160 580; www.shambhala-retreat-magnetic-island.com.au; 11-13 Barton St; d $115;) The entirely green powered property contains three small units with their own tree-screened patios for watching wildlife. Two have outdoor courtyard showers, and all have fully equipped kitchens and laundry facilities. Some of the best value on the island. There is a two-night minimum stay.

Grand Mercure Apartments APARTMENT $$$
(07-4758 2100; www.accorhotels.com; Sooning St; d from $260;) Slick high-end accommodation by the ferry terminal. Recently overhauled and some of the best views in the region.

Arcadia

Arcadia Beach Guest House GUESTHOUSE $$
(07-4778 5668; www.arcadiabeachguesthouse.com.au; 27 Marine Pde; dm $35-40, tents $55, d without bathroom $85-100, d with bathroom $130-160;) Once a hostel for nurses, this place is far from clinical. Choose between bright rooms, safari tents and shared dorms. You can turtle-spot from the balcony, or rent a canoe, Moke (buggy) or 4WD. Free ferry pick-ups.

Hotel Arcadia HOTEL $$
(07-4778 5177; www.hotelarcadia.com.au; 7 Marine Pde; r $99-145;) Fresh from a facelift, Hotel Arcadia has swish rooms; make sure you ask for one with an ocean view. The hub of Arcadia bay is on-site bistro and bar, the Island Tavern (mains $20 to $28, open lunch and dinner), which keeps punters happy with $10 jugs, cane-toad races every Wednesday night and a large swimming pool accessible to the public.

Horseshoe Bay

Bungalow Bay Koala Village HOSTEL $
(1800 285 577, 07-4778 5577; www.bungalowbay.com.au; 40 Horseshoe Bay Rd; unpowered/powered sites per person $12.50/15, dm $28, d with/without bathroom $90/74;) Not only a resort-style, YHA-associated hostel but a nature wonderland (with its own wildlife park). Less than five minutes' walk from the beach, A-frame bungalows are strewn throughout leafy grounds backing onto national park. Cool off at the outdoor bar, go coconut bowling, or tuck into a curry at the restaurant (mains $16 to $24, open lunch and dinner).

Shaws on the Shore APARTMENT $$$
(07-4778 1900; www.shawsontheshore.com.au; 7 Pacific Dr; 1-/2-/3-bedroom apt $175/265/320;) Shaws is not going to win any interior design awards but the location opposite Horseshoe Bay is unbeatable and the spacious apartments are among the best value on the island. Plus, they are easier to book than the many requiring agents.

Eating

Horseshoe Bay has the island's best eateries.

Picnic Bay

Bluelephant Thai THAI $$
(07-4758 1101; 4/8 The Esplanade; mains $11-18) This great-value, honest Thai food is drawing

the crowd back to Picnic Bay. Evenings can fill up so book ahead or be left dreaming of bowlfuls of lemongrass, coriander and chilli-infused goodness.

Picnic Bay Hotel PUB $$
(Picnic Bay Mall; mains $11-26; ⏲10am-late) Settle in for a drink with Townsville's city lights sparkling across the bay. Its R&R Cafe Bar has an all-day grazing menu and huge salads, including Cajun prawn.

Nelly Bay

Man Friday MEXICAN, INTERNATIONAL $$
(☎07-4778 5658; 37 Warboy St; mains $14-39; ⏲dinner Wed-Mon; ✎) Tex-Mex on an island may seem a little curious but the sizzling fajitas and spicy steaks are a hit with families and backpackers. Bring your own wine but book ahead or risk missing out.

Le Paradis FRENCH $$
(☎07-4778 5044; cnr Mandalay Ave & Sooning St; mains $20-35; ⏲11.30am-3pm Fri-Sun, 11.30am-9pm Tue-Sat) Attentive service and an elegant menu at this French restaurant which has an attached 'kiosk' selling fresh baguettes and more. It's BYO.

Arcadia

Butler's Pantry CAFE, DELI $
(Shop 2-3, 5 Bright Ave; mains $15-21; ⏲breakfast & lunch Wed-Mon; ✎) At this gourmet grocery store–cafe you'll find the island's best brekkies, including pancakes, eggs every which way, and stacks of veggie options. Great lunches too.

Caffè dell' Isola ITALIAN $$
(Shop 1, 7 Marine Pde; mains $15-26; ⏲breakfast & lunch Tue, Thu & Sun, breakfast, lunch & dinner Wed, Fri & Sat, daily during school holidays) A little brusque perhaps, but you will happily turn the other cheek when the crisp-crust pizzas arrive at your courtyard table. Cash only.

Banister's Seafood SEAFOOD $$
(☎07-4778 5700; 22 McCabe Cres; mains $10-22; ⏲lunch & dinner) You can do the whole sit-down thing and order off the menu chalked on the blackboard of this BYO-only seafood joint, or grab some takeaway and head to a nearby beach.

Arcadia Night Market MARKET $$
(Hayles Ave, Arcadia; ⏲5-8pm Fri) Small but lively night market next door to the RSL, with sizzling Indonesian food and seafood to cook up yourself.

Horseshoe Bay

Cafe Nourish CAFE $
(☎07-4778 1885; 3/6 Pacific Dr; mains $9-15) Very friendly cafe and popular with locals. Loads of magazines and games to choose from while you sip huge smoothies and munch on yummy wraps.

Beach Bar & Bistro CONTEMPORARY $$
(7 Pacific Dr; mains $12-25) The best restaurant in Horseshoe is an unassuming place with an eclectic menu and a highly skilled chef. The burgers are in fact grilled meals inside bread, while the pies and Asian dishes are spot on. Cool service and tunes made our half-day.

Marlin Bar PUB $$
(3 Pacific Dr; mains $16-24; ⏲lunch & dinner) Sunset stubbies at the Marlin are a rite of passage for travellers to Maggie and the hearty seafood, steak and late breakfast can mop up the damage caused by one too many. Can get rather busy on weekends.

Barefoot MODERN AUSTRALIAN $$
(☎07-4758 1170; 5 Pacific Dr; mains $16-30; ⏲lunch & dinner Thu-Mon) Maggie's most urbane restaurant has a long wine list, appealing lunch specials, superb seafood platters and tasty desserts. The art gallery provides welcome space for digestive contemplation. Service is beachy keen.

Information

There's no official visitor information centre on Magnetic Island, but Townsville's visitor information centre has comprehensive info and maps, and can help find accommodation.

ATMs are scattered throughout the island, although there are no banks. The **post office** (Sooning St, Nelly Bay) also has an ATM.

Getting There & Away

All ferries arrive and depart Maggie from the terminal at Nelly Bay.

Sealink (☎07-4726 0800; www.sealinkqld.com.au) operates a frequent passenger ferry between Townsville and Magnetic Island (adult/child return $29/15), which takes around 20 minutes. Ferries depart from Townsville from the Sunferries Breakwater Terminal at 2/14 Sir Leslie Thiess Dr.

Fantasea (☎07-4796 9300; www.magnetic-islandferry.com.au; Ross St, South Townsville) operates a car ferry crossing eight times daily (seven on weekends) from the south side of Ross Creek, taking 35 minutes. It costs $178 (return) for a car and up to three passengers, and $29/17 (return) for an adult/child foot passenger only. Bookings are essential. Bicycles are transported free.

Both Townsville terminals have car parking.

❶ Getting Around

BICYCLE

Magnetic Island is ideal for cycling although some of the hills can be hard work. Most places to stay rent bikes for around $20 a day and a number of places offer them free to guests.

BUS

The **Magnetic Island Bus Service** (☑ 07-4778 5130) ploughs between Picnic Bay and Horseshoe Bay at least 18 times a day, meeting all ferries and stopping at major accommodation places. A hop-on, hop-off day pass costs $6.

MOKE & SCOOTER

Moke (buggy) and scooter rental places abound around the island. Expect to pay around $75 per day for a Moke. You'll need to be over 21, have a current international or Australian driver's licence and leave a credit-card deposit. Scooter hire starts at around $35 per day. Try **MI Wheels** (☑ 07-4778 5491; 138 Sooning St, Nelly Bay) for a classic Moke or 'topless' (open-topped) car, or **Roadrunner Scooter Hire** (☑ 07-4778 5222; 3/64 Kelly St, Nelly Bay) for scooters and trail bikes.

North of Townsville

Paluma Range National Park

The Paluma Range National Park runs almost from Ingham to Townsville, and includes the must-see Mt Spec-Big Crystal Creek section, 62km north of Townsville. This is a pocket of rainforest with some awesome views of the coast and a variety of different walking trails.

From the Bruce Hwy, the 4km-long route (Spiegelhauer Rd) to **Big Crystal Creek** is located 2km north of Mt Spec Rd. It's an easy 100m walk from the car park to **Paradise Waterhole**, with its sandy beach on one side and great views of the mountains in the distance. The self-registration QPWS camping ground (per person/family $5.15/21) has gas barbecues, toilets and water (treat before drinking).

To get to **Jourama Falls**, travel 6km on a good, sealed road from the highway, though the creek at the entrance can be impassable. It's a steep walk up to the lookout; watch for Ulysses butterflies, nocturnal brown bandicoots and mahogany gliders (a threatened species). The rock pools are good for a dip, and there are plenty of turtles to check out. The QPWS camping ground has toilets and barbecues.

Up in the tiny village of Paluma is the cool **Paluma Rainforest Inn** (☑ 07-4770 8688; www.rainforestinnpaluma.com; 1 Mt Spec Rd; d $125; ❀), with stylish, well-designed rooms, lovely gardens and a recommended licensed restaurant (mains $19 to $29, open lunch Wednesday to Monday, breakfast and dinner by reservation).

About 14km west of Paluma (the last 4km along a bumpy unsealed road) is **Hidden Valley Cabins** (☑ 07-4770 8088; www.hidden-valleycabins.com.au; d without bathroom $89, cabins $159-229; ❀) ✿, a solar-powered, carbon-neutral eco-retreat. You'll find a clutch of log cabins grouped close together and new deluxe options. A range of two-hour tours ($20) including platypus-spotting safaris and night walks, run daily. Its restaurant (mains $24 to $31, open breakfast, lunch and dinner) serves country-style home cooking and is open to guests only.

There's no fuel in Paluma, so fill up before heading out this way.

Ingham & Around

Laid-back Ingham is the proud guardian of the ever-expanding **Tyto wetlands** (Tyto Wetlands Information Centre; ☑ 07-4776 4792; www.hinchinbrooknq.com.au; cnr Cooper St & Bruce Hwy; ⊙ 8.45am-5pm Mon-Fri, 9am-4pm Sat & Sun), which has 4km of walking trails and attracts around 230 species of bird, including far-flung guests from Siberia and Japan, as well as hundreds of wallabies at dawn and dusk. There's a fine regional gallery and library on-site.

In mid-May the **Australian Italian Festival** (www.australianitalianfestival.com.au) celebrates the fact that 60% of Ingham residents are of Italian descent, with pasta flying, wine flowing and music playing over three days.

Ingham is the jumping-off point for a trip out to magnificent **Wallaman Falls**, the longest single-drop waterfall in Australia at 305m. Located in **Girringun National Park**, 51km southwest of the town (sealed except for 10km; not suitable for caravans), the falls look their best in the Wet though are spectacular at any time. Nearby, the self-registration **QPWS campground** (per person/family $5.15/21) has showers and barbecues; the swimming hole is frequented by the occasional platypus. Two- and three-day walking trails start from the falls, with camp sites along the way – pick up a *Wallaman Falls Section Girringun National Park* leaflet from the Tyto Wetlands Information Centre.

Mungalla Station (07-4777 8718; www.mungallaaboriginaltours.com.au; Forrest Beach, Allingham; 2hr tours adult/child $40/10), 15km east of Ingham, runs insightful Indigenous-led tours, including boomerang throwing and stories from the local Nywaigi culture. Definitely book in for a traditional Kup Murri lunch (adult/child incl tour $80/20) of meat and vegies wrapped in banana leaves and cooked underground in an earth oven. If you have a self-contained caravan or campervan, you can camp (per van $10) overnight.

Once the domain of Italian cane cutters, Ingham's wonderful 1920s art-deco **Noorla Heritage Resort** (07-4776 1100; www.hotelnoorla.com.au; 5-9 Warren St; unpowered/powered sites $15/22, dm $28, d with/without bathroom $139/89) has magnificently restored high-ceilinged rooms, plus cheaper container-style rooms in the garden. A photo montage of local stories lines the walls, bringing the town's history to life, as do the stories told around the resort's aqua-tiled guests-only bar. Home cooking includes regular Kup Murri dinners (one-/two-course meals $24.50/33, dinner Monday to Saturday). Ask about transfers to Mungalla Station.

Lucinda is a sweet-as-pie port town with one massive attribute – a 6km-long jetty used for shipping sugar. **Lucinda Jetty Store & Take-Away** (07-4777 8280; 2 Rigby St; mains $15.50-19.50; 6am-7pm) serves great barramundi, crumbed steak and king salmon as well as takeaway fare like burgers and filled rolls.

Cardwell

POP 12,000

Spread along kilometres of crocodile-infested waters (even the public pool has a crocodile on its sign), Cardwell is the gateway to the sublime Hinchinbrook Island National Park but has its own unique seaside, prawn-burger-lovin' attitude that doesn't take long to get used to. Port Hinchinbrook Marina, 2km from the town, feels eerily quiet after Cyclone Yasi but still serves as the departure point for Hinchinbrook Island. Behind Cardwell is the 26km **Cardwell Forest Drive**, and you can dip into the springs and spas along the way.

The very modern warehouse-style **Cardwell Backpackers Hostel** (07-4066 8404; www.cardwellbackpackers.com.au; 6 Brasenose St; dm $20) run by charismatic locals and is well above the standard seasonal worker digs. Banana and pineapple farms provide work throughout the year.

Cardwell Beachcomber Motel & Tourist Park (07-4066 8550; www.cardwellbeachcomber.com.au; 43a Marine Pde; unpowered/powered sites $25/30, motel d $75-100, cabins & studios $90-110) is back to life after the storm and is a beautiful family-style resort with a range of accommodation options, including brand new ocean-front villas. Its licensed restaurant (mains $24.50 to $36.50; open breakfast daily, lunch and dinner Monday to Saturday) is the best in town, serving the likes of rosemary-crusted lamb, slow-roasted pork and sweet-and-sour flathead, as well as pizzas.

Over 1.2 green, tree-shaded hectares, accommodation options at the well-run **Kookaburra Holiday Park** (07-4066 8648; www.kookaburraholidaypark.com.au; 175 Bruce Hwy; unpowered/powered sites $22/29, dm/s/d without bathroom $25/45/50, cabins without bathroom $65, units $85-105) include airy dorms in a large Queenslander house at the back. You can borrow fishing rods, prawn nets and crab pots to catch dinner, and tents to head off for some bush camping.

Hand-built from mud bricks, natural timber and stone, **Mudbrick Manor** (07-4066 2299; www.mudbrickmanor.com.au; Lot 13, Stony Creek Rd; s/d $90/120) is a family home that has huge, beautifully appointed rooms grouped around a courtyard with fountain. Spend long, lazy evenings on the verandah or large lounge area. Rates include hot breakfast; book at least a few hours ahead for delicious three-course dinners (per person $30).

Port Hinchinbrook Resort (07-4066 2000; www.porthinchinbrook.com.au; Bruce Hwy; d $130-225) has cabins clustered around the wharf where boats depart for Hinchinbrook Island and are more like luxury open-plan villas, with front doors that slide wide open to catch the waterfront breezes. The resort's Marina Restaurant (mains $18 to $38, open lunch and dinner daily year-round, breakfast Easter to September) dishes up reef-and-beef-type fare along with views over the boats docked out front.

Vívia Café (135 Victoria St; mains $9-20; 7am-4pm;) is a lovely place to linger on a road trip over gourmet sandwiches, salads, pasta and seafood. Coffee is spot on, too. **Gourmet Grub** (93 Victoria St; mains $8-16; 8am-3pm Mon-Thu, to 8pm Fri, 9am-3pm Sat & Sun;) is a chilled cafe with a boho vibe serving good brekkies and icy soy smoothies.

The **Rainforest and Reef Centre** (07-4066 8601; www.portofhinchinbrook.com.au; 8.30am-5pm Mon-Fri, 9am-3pm Sat & Sun Apr-Oct, to 1pm Sat & Sun Nov-Mar), next to Cardwell's town jetty, has detailed info on island transfers, hiking transfers and cruises to Hinchinbrook Island and other nearby national parks.

Getting There & Away

Greyhound Australia (1300 473 946; www.greyhound.com.au) and **Premier Motor Service** (13 34 10; www.premierms.com.au) buses on the Brisbane–Cairns route stop at Cardwell. Fares with Greyhound/Premier are $48 to Cairns, and $36 to Townsville.

Cardwell is on the Brisbane–Cairns train line; contact **Queensland Rail** (1300 131 722; www.traveltrain.qr.com.au) for details.

Boats depart for Hinchinbrook Island from Port Hinchinbrook Marina, 2km south of town.

Hinchinbrook Island National Park

Australia's largest island national park remains a holy grail for walkers and lovers of solitary travel. Granite mountains rise dramatically from the sea; rugged Mt Bowen (1121m) is the island's highest peak. The mainland side is dense with lush tropical vegetation, while long sandy beaches and tangles of mangrove curve around the eastern shore. All 399 sq km of the island is national park, so there is plenty of wildlife, including the pretty-faced wallaby and the iridescent-blue Ulysses butterfly.

Hinchinbrook's highlight is the **Thorsborne Trail** (also known as the East Coast Trail), a 32km coastal track from Ramsay Bay past Zoe Bay, with its beautiful waterfall, to George Point at the southern tip. **DERM camp sites** (13 74 68; www.derm.qld.gov.au; per person $5.15) are interspersed along the route. It's recommended that you take three nights to complete the trail, allowing for swimming stops and quiet time. Return walks of individual sections are also possible. This is the real wilderness experience; you'll need to use plenty of insect repellent, protect your food from ravenous native rats, draw water from creeks as you go (water is reliably available at Nina, Little Ramsay and Zoe Bays), and be alert to the possible presence of crocs around the mangroves. The trail is ungraded and at times rough.

Only 40 people are allowed on the track at any one time, so book ahead. DERM recommends booking a year ahead for a place during the high season and six months ahead for other dates. If you're late but lucky you might get to replace a cancellation. Cardwell's Rainforest and Reef Centre stocks the imperative *Thorsborne Trail* brochure.

Thorsborne Trail walkers can pick up a one-way transfer ($50) back to the mainland with **Hinchinbrook Wilderness Safaris** (07-4777 8307; www.hinchinbrookwilderness-safaris.com.au) from George Point at the southern end of the trail.

Boats leave regularly from Port Hinchinbrook in Cardwell.

Tully

POP 2500

Surrounded by banana plantations, the sugar-mill town of Tully, 44km north of Cardwell, takes pride in its reputation as the wettest place in Australia. Its big 7.9m **golden gumboot** at the entrance to town boasts that Tully received 7.9m of rain in 1950. All that

TULLY RIVER RAFTING

The Tully River provides thrilling white water year-round thanks to all that rain and the river's hydroelectric floodgates. Rafting trips are timed to coincide with the daily release of the floodgates, resulting in grade-four rapids, with stunning rainforest scenery as a backdrop.

Day trips with **Raging Thunder Adventures** (07-4030 7990; www.ragingthunder.com.au/rafting.asp; standard/'xtreme' trips $185/215) or **R'n'R White Water Rafting** (07-4041 9444; www.raft.com.au; trips $185) include a barbecue lunch and transport from Tully or nearby Mission Beach. The cost is between $215 and $230, which includes transfers from as far north as Palm Cove.

rain ensures plenty of raftable rapids on the nearby Tully River.

The **Tully Visitor & Heritage Centre** (☎07-4068 2288; Bruce Hwy; ⏲8.30am-4.30pm Mon-Fri, 9am-2pm Sat & Sun) has a brochure outlining a self-guided **heritage walk** around town, with 17 interpretative panels including one dedicated to Tully's UFO sightings.

Book at the visitor centre for 90-minute **Tully Sugar Mill Tours** (adult/child $17/11; ⏲daily late Jun–early Nov) during the crushing season.

The visitor centre stocks walking maps for trails along former logging tracks in the Tully-accessed section of the **Misty Mountains** (www.mistymountains.com.au); 640m-high **Mt Tyson**; and **Tully Gorge National Park**, 40km west of town. Tully Gorge has picnic facilities, but crocs inhabit the area. If you want a swim, head to the croc-free (and alligator-free) **Alligator's Nest**, 7km north of town via Murray St.

Practically all accommodation in Tully is geared for banana workers, with cheap weekly rates and help finding farm work. The visitor centre has a list, or try the excellent **Banana Barracks** (☎07-4068 0455; www.bananabarracks.com; 50 Butler St; dm with/without bathroom $28/24, bungalows $40; @📶🏊), bang in the town centre, with lots of corrugated iron, pool tables, and decent dorms and bungalows out the back. It's also the hub of Tully's nightlife.

For non-workers, the only real option is the corporate-oriented **Tully Motel** (☎07-4068 2233; www.tullymotel.com; Bruce Hwy; d $89-110; ❄📶), with large, well-appointed rooms done up in heritage colours, and Tully's only restaurant, **Plantations** (mains $27-38; ⏲dinner Mon-Fri).

Greyhound Australia (☎1300 473 946; www.greyhound.com.au) and **Premier Motor Service** (☎13 34 10; www.premierms.com.au) buses on the Brisbane–Cairns route stop in town; fares with Greyhound/Premier are $29 to Cairns and $39 to Townsville.

Mission Beach

POP 4000

Less than 30km east of the Bruce Hwy's rolling sugar-cane and banana plantations, the hamlets that make up greater Mission Beach are hidden amongst World Heritage rainforest. The rainforest extends right to the Coral Sea, giving this 14km-long palm-fringed stretch of secluded inlets and wide, empty beaches the castaway feel of a tropical island.

Although collectively referred to as Mission Beach or just 'Mission', the area comprises a sequence of individual hamlets strung along the coast. **Bingil Bay** lies 4.8km north of **Mission Beach** proper (sometimes called North Mission). **Wongaling Beach** is 5km south; from here it's a further 5.5km south to **South Mission Beach**. Most amenities are in Mission Beach proper and Wongaling Beach; South Mission Beach and Bingil Bay are mainly residential.

Mission Beach is one of the closest access points to the Great Barrier Reef, and the gateway to Dunk Island. Fanning out around Mission are picturesque walking tracks, which are fine places to see wildlife, including cassowaries – in fact, Australia's highest density of cassowaries (around 40) roam the surrounding rainforests.

To avoid an unexpected meeting with a croc or stinger, don't swim in any of Mission Beach's creeks – stick to the swimming enclosures provided.

Sights & Activities

Adrenalin junkies flock to Mission Beach for extreme and water-based sports, including white-water rafting on the nearby Tully River.

The **walking** in the area is superb. The visitor centre stocks walking guides detailing trails. From David St in central Mission Beach, the **Ulysses Link** – named for the bright-blue Ulysses butterflies that flit through the area – is a gentle 2km stroll along the foreshore to Clump Point. Sweeping views unfold from the **Bicton Hill Track** (4km, two hours return) through Clump Mountain National Park. The superb coastal **Kennedy Track** (7km, four hours return) leads past secluded Lovers Beach and a lookout at Lugger Bay. **Licuala State Forest** has a number of rainforest walks, including a 10-minute children's walk marked with cassowary footprints, and the **Rainforest Circuit & Fan Palm Boardwalk** (1.2km, 30 minutes return), with interpretive signage and a cassowary display.

★ **Babinda Kayak Hire** KAYAKING
(☎07-4067 2678; www.babindakayakhire.com.au; 330 Stager Rd, Babinda; half-day/full day $42/75) Easy yet breathtakingly beautiful kayaking tours through permanently flowing mountain streams in Wooroonooran National Park. A bit of a must-do if you're in the area.

★ **Ingan Tours** INDIGENOUS TOUR
(☎1300 728 067; www.ingan.com.au; adult/child $120/60) An indigenous operator with impeccable credentials is causing a stir for its 'Spirit of the Rainforest' tour (adult/child $120/60, Tuesday, Thursday and Saturday).

Jump the Beach SKYDIVING
(☎1800 444 568; www.jumpthebeach.com.au; 9000/11,000/14,000ft tandem dives $284/345/369) Mission Beach is one of the most popular spots in Queensland to skydive. Jump the Beach claims to offer 'Australia's highest dive'.

Skydive Mission Beach SKYDIVING
(☎1800 800 840; www.skydivemissionbeach.com; 9000/11,000/14,000ft tandem dives $249/310/334) Skydive Mission Beach is part of a seasoned, nationwide operation.

Calypso Dive DIVING
(☎07-4068 8432; www.calypsodive.com.au; per person from $245) Experienced divers can join trips to the *Lady Bowen* wreck. Calypso also offers reef dives and PADI open-water courses ($625). Alternatively, you can snorkel the reef ($169).

Coral Sea Kayaking KAYAKING
(☎07-4068 9154; www.coralseakayaking.com; half/full day $77/128) Coral Sea Kayaking is run by a true travelling couple who excel in guiding paddlers to Dunk Island and back.

Fishin' Mission FISHING
(☎07-4088 6121; www.fishinmission.com.au; half/full day $130/190) Relaxed yet thoroughly professional fishing charters to either Dunk Island or a handful of 'secret' reefs.

Mission Beach Charters WATER TOURS
(☎07-4068 7009; www.missionbeachcharters.com.au; 1349c El Arish-Mission Beach Rd) Astute operator with a whole raft of flexible products including Dunk Island drop-offs (and all-important camping permits) and whale-watching tours in season.

Mission Beach Adventure Centre EQUIPMENT HIRE
(☎0429 469 330; www.missionbeachadventurecentre.com.au; Seaview St, Mission Beach) The 'hut on the beach' offers bike hire ($20 per half-day), kayak hire (singles/doubles $15/30 per hour), and, when the wind's up, blokarting ($30/50 per half-hour/hour).

Sleeping

The visitor centre has a list of booking agents for holiday rentals. Hostels have courtesy bus pick-ups.

Wongaling Beach

★ **Scotty's Mission Beach House** HOSTEL $
(☎1800 665 567; www.scottysbeachhouse.com.au; 167 Reid Rd; dm $24-29, d $61-71; ❄@📶🏊) Scotty's is run by the kind of crowd who legitimately love what they do and share that passion with their guests. Includes impeccable dorms and a lush pool area. A happening bar and restaurant, Scotty's Bar & Grill (mains $10 to $30, open dinner), welcomes the outside world.

Hibiscus Lodge B&B B&B $$
(☎07-4068 9096; www.hibiscuslodge.com.au; 5 Kurrajong Cl; r $105-120) Only three rooms but an abundance of grace from the hosts and a luxurious setting above a bird-filled garden remind you why you came to Mission in the first place. The only requirement is to rise for sunset drinks, and maybe the breakfast ,which is one of the best in town.

Licuala Lodge B&B $$
(☎07-4068 8194; www.licualalodge.com.au; 11 Mission Circle; s/d $99/135; 📶🏊) Licuala is a beautifully conceived B&B run by Mick and Sue. Standing proud on timber poles, there are five plush hotel-style rooms with floorboards that open onto a gorgeous shared verandah. Guests can enjoy complimentary beer, soft drinks and fruit juices.

Absolute Backpackers HOSTEL $
(☎07-4068 8317; www.absolutebackpackers.com.au; Wongaling Beach Rd; dm $22-26, d $58; ❄@📶🏊) This popular hostel close to the bus terminal is more like a low-key resort than a party joint. It's set in spacious grounds and run by attentive, professional staff. The kitchen is open 24 hours and the dorm rooms are impeccable.

Mission Beach

Mission Beach Retreat HOSTEL $
(☎07-4088 6229; www.missionbeachretreat.com.au; 49 Porters Promenade; dm $21-24, d $56; ❄@📶🏊) It's seen better days, but then again so have most properties in this cyclone-prone region. The bedding is excellent and there is a relaxed, intimate hostel vibe. The local hospitality is disarmingly warm.

Mission Beach Ecovillage CABIN $$
(07-4068 7534; www.ecovillage.com.au; Clump Point Rd; d $135-220;) Nestled on a 2-acre patch of banana tree–filled rainforest running to the beach, this quiet, family-friendly resort is a seductive introduction to Mission Beach. The restaurant (mains $19, open dinner Tuesday to Saturday) is deservedly popular. Some bungalows have spas.

Rainforest Motel MOTEL $$
(07-4068 7556; www.missionbeachrainforestmotel.com; 9 Endeavour Ave; s/d $98/119;) Terrific-value motel just a short walk from the Mission Beach shops, yet secreted away in rainforest foliage. The friendly owners take great pride in presenting the cool, tiled rooms. Free bikes available.

Castaways Resort & Spa RESORT $$$
(1800 079 002; www.castaways.com.au; Pacific Pde; d $145-185, 1-/2-bedroom units $205/295;) Castaways' cheapest rooms don't have balconies, so it's worth splashing out a bit more for one of the 'Coral Sea' rooms, with extended deck and day bed. Even the units are small, but perks include two elongated pools, a luxurious spa (www.driftspa.com.au) and live entertainment at the bar-restaurant (mains $12 to $32, open breakfast, lunch and dinner).

Sejala on the Beach CABIN $$$
(07-4088 6699; http://missionbeachholidays.com.au/sejala; 26 Pacific Pde; d $260;) Intimate rainforest chic in these three huts (go for one of the two facing the beach) that are perfect for couples. All have decks with private barbecues.

Bingil Bay

Sanctuary CABIN $
(1800 777 012, 07-4088 6064; www.sanctuaryatmission.com; 72 Holt Rd; dm $35, s/d huts $65/70, cabins $145/165; mid-Apr–mid-Dec;) You can sleep surrounded only by flyscreen on a platform in a simple hut, or opt for one of the cabins, whose glass-walled showers have floor-to-ceiling rainforest views. In addition to walks you can take a yoga class ($15) or indulge in a massage ($80 per hour). Cook in the self-catering kitchen or dine on wholesome fare at the restaurant (mains $19-33, open breakfast, lunch and dinner). Eco-initiatives include the resort's own sewerage system, harvesting rainwater and biodegradable detergents. The resort is reached by a steep 600m-long rainforest walking track from the car park (4WD pick-up available).

Treehouse HOSTEL $
(07-4068 7137; Frizelle Rd; unpowered sites $12, dm/d $25/55;) Musical instruments and no TV set the chilled-out scene at this timber YHA-associated hostel high in the rainforest.

Eating

Wongaling Beach

★**Cafe Rustica** ITALIAN $$
(07-4068 9111; Wongaling Beach Rd; mains $18-25; 5pm-late Wed-Sat, 10am-late Sun;) We loved the homemade pasta and traditional crispy-crust pizzas prepared by this friendly couple at the Wongaling beach shack.

Na Na Thai THAI $$
(07-4068 9101; 165 Reid St; mains $16-26; 5pm-8.30pm Tue-Sun) Na Na serves exquisite northern Thai food in a laid-back setting. It's run by a friendly Aussie bloke who graciously does the rounds and intimately knows his menu.

Mission Beach

Early Birds Cafe CAFE $
(Shop 2, 46 Porter Promenade; mains $6-15; 6am-3pm, closed Wed;) The pick of the breakfast joints and always busy.

New Deli CAFE, DELI $
(Shop 1, 47 Porter Promenade; mains $8-16; 9.30am-6pm Mon-Fri;) The place to stock up on goodies for a gourmet picnic.

The Garage MODERN AUSTRALIAN $$
(07-4088 6280; Donkin Lane; mezze plate $17; 7am-late;) The hottest new spot in the Village Green serves delicious 'sliders' (mini burgers), free-pour cocktails ($14), good coffee, cakes and tapas. Diners congregate around dark wooden tables in the courtyard. Live music rolls through the busy periods.

Shrubbery Taverna SEAFOOD $$
(07-4068 7803; David St; mains $19-36; 9am-9pm Mon-Thu, 9am-late Fri-Sun) The most dependable restaurant in South Mission is a real local hang-out that specialises in seafood. Service was a little slack when we visited but the shaded bamboo gardens are a delightful place to chill. Live music on Friday night and Sunday afternoon.

THE CASSOWARY

The flightless cassowary is as tall as a grown man, has three toes, a blue-and-purple head, red wattles (fleshy lobes hanging from its neck), a helmet-like horn and unusual black feathers, which look more like ratty hair. It could certainly be confused with an ageing rocker. Traditional gender roles are reversed, with the male bird incubating the egg and rearing the chicks alone. The Australian cassowary is also known as the southern cassowary, though it's only found in the north of Queensland. It makes sense when you realise that other species are found in Papua New Guinea – to the north of Australia.

The cassowary is a vital link in the rainforest ecosystem. It is the only animal capable of dispersing the seeds of more than 70 species of tree whose fruits are too large for other rainforest animals to digest and pass.

The cassowary is an endangered species; there are less than 1000 left. Its biggest threat is loss of habitat, and eggs and chicks are vulnerable to dogs and wild pigs. A number of birds are also hit by cars: heed road signs warning drivers to be cassowary-aware. You're most likely to see cassowaries around Mission Beach and the Cape Tribulation section of the Daintree National Park. They can be aggressive, particularly if they have chicks. Do not approach them; if one threatens you, don't run – give the bird right-of-way and try to keep something solid between you and it, preferably a tree.

Next to the Mission Beach visitor centre, there are cassowary-conservation displays at the **Wet Tropics Environment Centre** (07-4068 7197; www.wettropics.gov.au; Porter Promenade, Porter Promenade; 10am-4pm), which is staffed by volunteers from the **Community for Cassowary & Coastal Conservation** (C4; www.cassowaryconservation.asn.au). Proceeds from gift-shop purchases go towards buying cassowary habitat. The website www.savethecassowary.org.au is also a good source of info.

Bingil Bay

Bingil Bay Cafe CAFE $$
(29 Bingil Bay Rd; mains $14-23; breakfast, lunch & dinner;) You won't miss this colourful corner store with a positive vibe and a host of music and cultural activities buzzing from the porch. The food is eclectic and breakfast is the highlight. Don't sweat the casual service.

Information

The efficient **Mission Beach visitor centre** (07-4068 7099; www.missionbeachtourism.com; Porters Promenade; 9am-4.45pm Mon-Sat, 10am-4pm Sun) has reams of info in multiple languages.

Getting There & Around

Greyhound Australia (1300 473 946; www.greyhound.com.au) and **Premier Motor Service** (13 34 10; www.premierms.com.au) buses stop in Wongaling Beach next to the giant 'big cassowary'; fares with Greyhound/Premier are $26 to Cairns, $40 to Townsville.

Mission Beach Adventure Centre rents out bikes (per half-day/day $10/20).

Call 13 10 08 for a taxi.

You can catch a **water taxi** (07-4068 8310; 71 Banfield Pde, Wongaling Beach; $35 same day return, 3hr 3-island tour $50 Wed & Fri 12.30pm) from Wongaling Beach at 9am, 10am and 11am; depart from Dunk Island at noon and 3.30pm.

Dunk Island

Known to the Djiru Aboriginal people as Coonanglebah (the island of peace and plenty), Dunk is pretty much your ideal tropical island. The island's **rainforest walks** are invigorating, and while some people run the full island circuit (9.2km), taking the sometimes difficult track slowly lets you check out secluded beaches. See the fanning Hinchinbrook Channel from Mt Kootaloo (271m, 5.6km).

The island's resort is currently closed due to cyclone damage, though camping has reopened. Permits for the **DERM campground** (13 74 68; www.derm.qld.gov.au; per person $5.15) need to be organised through **Mission Beach Charters** (07-4068 7009; www.missionbeachcharters.com.au).

Mission Beach Dunk Island Water Taxi (07-4068 8310; Banfield Pde, Wongaling Beach; adult/child return $35/18), departing from Wongaling Beach, makes the 20-minute trip to Dunk Island.

Mission Beach to Cairns

Mountains, cane fields, cane-train tracks and forest run alongside the road from Mission Beach to Cairns. For variety, take the alternative 'Canecutter Way' route to Innisfail via the cute towns of Silkwood and Mena Creek – 42km of true sugar-cane country.

Mena Creek's main claim to fame is the unusual **Paronella Park** (07-4065 0000; www.paronellapark.com.au; Japoonvale Rd; adult/child $38/19; 9am-7.30pm), which features the ruins of a Spanish castle hand-built in the 1930s. Floods, fire and moist tropics have rendered these mossy remains almost medieval. Entry includes free camping in the adjacent caravan park and both a day and an evening tour. Timber cabins (doubles $80) are also available.

Further north at **South Johnstone**, the charming little art gallery, cafe and second-hand bookshop **Off the Rails** (Hynes St; mains $8-18; 10am-5pm Wed-Sun;) has great coffee and uses local produce in dishes like marinated-veggie platters.

Innisfail

POP 10,143

A wonderful main street meanders through this busy farming town to the wide Johnstone River. Art-deco buildings abound, as cyclones damaged many buildings in the 1920s and 1930s, and the replacements were constructed in the style of that time, turning Innisfail into the art-deco capital of Australia. You can get a self-guided art-deco tour map from the **visitor information centre** (07-4061 2655; www.innisfailtourism.com.au; cnr Eslick St & Bruce Hwy; 9am-5pm Mon-Fri, 10am-12.30pm Sat & Sun).

Innisfail's best lodging option, the **Barrier Reef Motel** (07-4061 4988; www.barrierreefmotel.com.au; Bruce Hwy; s/d $110/120, units $150-170;) has 41 airy, tiled rooms, a restaurant (mains $28 to $30.50, open breakfast and dinner) and a bar. The **Codge Lodge** (07-4061 8055; www.codgelodge.com; 63 Rankin St; dm $30;) is a cheerful hostel set in an atmospheric Queenslander with a wide timber verandah. Plenty of farm workers bunk down for an extended stay, but it also welcomes overnight travellers.

Everything is locally sourced or organic at **Monsoon Cruising** (0427 776 663; 1 Innisfail Wharf; mains $10-16; 10am-5pm Wed-Sat Mar-Dec;), a moored cruiser serving bread baked fresh on the boat and black tiger prawns straight off the trawlers. **Oliveri's Continental Deli** (41 Edith St; sandwiches $8-9; 8.30am-5.30pm Mon-Fri, to 1pm Sat;) is an Innisfail institution serving awesome sandwiches.

Greyhound Australia (1300 473 946; www.greyhound.com.au) calls into Innisfail on the Brisbane–Cairns route, with six services daily stopping at King George St. **Premier Motor Service** (13 34 10; www.premierms.com.au) has one daily service to Innisfail on the same route.

Around Innisfail

From Innisfail the Palmerston Hwy winds west up to the magical Atherton Tableland, passing through the rainforest of **Wooroonooran National Park**, which has creeks, waterfalls, scenic walking tracks and a self-registration **camping ground** (Henrietta Creek; per person/family $5.85/21.80) at Henrietta Creek (38km from Innisfail), just off the road.

About 27km along the Palmerston Hwy (signposted 4km northwest of Innisfail), the **Mamu Rainforest Canopy Walkway** (Palmerston Hwy; adult/child $20/10; 9.30am-5.30pm, last entry 4.30pm) gives you a bird's-eye perspective from its 100-step, 37m-high tower. Allow at least an hour to complete the 2.5km, wheelchair-accessible circuit.

At the southeastern corner of the park, **Crawford's Lookout** has views of the white water of the North Johnstone River, but it's worth the walk down to view it at closer range. Among the park's walks is the lovely **Nandroya Falls Circuit** (7.2km, three to four hours), which crosses a swimming hole. A number of platypus-viewing areas are marked in the park; first or last light of day are the best times to spot them.

For a more challenging walk, you might take on Queensland's highest peak, **Mt Bartle Frere** (1657m). Sitting inside Wooroonooran National Park, it falls within the dramatic Bellenden Ker range, which skirts the Bruce Hwy between Innisfail and Cairns. Experienced walkers can embark on the **Mt Bartle Frere Summit Track** (15km, two days return), which leads from the Josephine Falls car park to the summit. There's also a 10km (eight-hour) return walk to Broken Nose. Pick up a trail guide from the nearest visitor centre or contact **QPWS** (13 13 04; www.epa.qld.gov.au). Self-registration **camping** (per person/family $5.85/21.80) is permitted along the trail.

The Palmerston Hwy continues west to Millaa Millaa, passing the entrance to the Waterfall Circuit just before the town.

CAIRNS & AROUND

Cairns has a heady reputation as Australia's reef-diving capital, with dazzling marine life and coral-fringed islands a short boat ride offshore. It's also tropical north Queensland's party central. Yet lush rainforest, waterfalls, volcanic-crater lakes and beach communities lie just beyond the city limits, as do the Atherton Tableland's gourmet food producers, farms and orchards. The magnificent Daintree National Park stretches up the coast, its rainforest tumbling right onto white-sand beaches. Further north, the Bloomfield Track from Cape Tribulation to Cooktown is one of Australia's great 4WD journeys.

Cairns

POP 163,000

Cairns has come a long way from struggling cane town to international resort city. It may not have a beach, but the mudflats and mangroves along the Esplanade foreshore have been replaced with a multimillion-dollar development of parks and the dazzling saltwater lagoon, with top-quality restaurants overlooking the marina. And if you do want some sand, it's a short local bus ride or easy drive to Cairns' northern beaches.

For many visitors this is the end of the line on the east-coast jaunt (or the start for those flying into Cairns' international airport), and the city is awash with bars and nightclubs, as well as accommodation and eateries in all price ranges. It's a city that's more board shorts than briefcases, and you can walk straight from the nightclub to the pier and catch one of the many morning boats that make the daily island or reef, diving or snorkelling pilgrimage.

Sights

Cairns Foreshore & Lagoon WATERFRONT

(Lagoon 6am-10pm Thu-Tue, noon-10pm Wed) FREE In the absence of a beach, sunbathers flock around Cairns' shallow but spectacular saltwater swimming **lagoon** on the city's reclaimed foreshore. The artificial 4800-sq-metre lagoon is patrolled by lifeguards and illuminated at night.

Northwest from the lagoon, the boardwalk **promenade**, which stretches for almost 3km, has picnic areas, free barbecues and playgrounds lining the foreshore.

Flecker Botanic Gardens GARDENS

(www.cairns.qld.gov.au; Collins Ave; 7.30am-5.30pm Mon-Fri, 8.30am-5.30pm Sat & Sun, information centre 9am-4.30pm Mon-Fri, 10am-2.30pm

CAIRNS REGION IN...

Two Days

Rise early for a stroll through the **Flecker Botanic Gardens** and the **Tanks Art Centre**. Save the afternoon for an Aboriginal cultural experience at the **Tjapukai Cultural Park**. Afterwards, raise a glass with locals and travellers at the capacious outdoor bar at **Gilligan's**. Grab a snack there, or wander the city in search of your favourite cuisine.

On day two, head way out to the **Great Barrier Reef** on a full-day cruise. Get an eyeful of coral gardens and iridescent fish and marine life by snorkelling or diving, or stay dry in a glass-bottom boat. By night, mingle with newly christened reef lovers over dinner and drinks at the **Salt House**.

Four Days

Spend the third day basking on an island – snorkelling the reef and exploring the rainforest of **Green Island**, enjoying the view from the summit of **Fitzroy Island** or playing castaway on the coral-fringed **Frankland Islands**. Back on the mainland, take an early-evening stroll along **Cairns Esplanade**, followed by a decadent meal at **Ochre** or **Fetta's Greek Tavern**.

On day four, catch the Scenic Railway to **Kuranda**, walk into a flurry of winged beauties at the **Australian Butterfly Sanctuary** and get a bird's-eye rainforest view on the way back by returning on the **Skyrail**. Alternatively, take an eco-accredited tour to the **Atherton Tableland** or **Cape Tribulation** and the magical **Daintree rainforest**.

Cairns

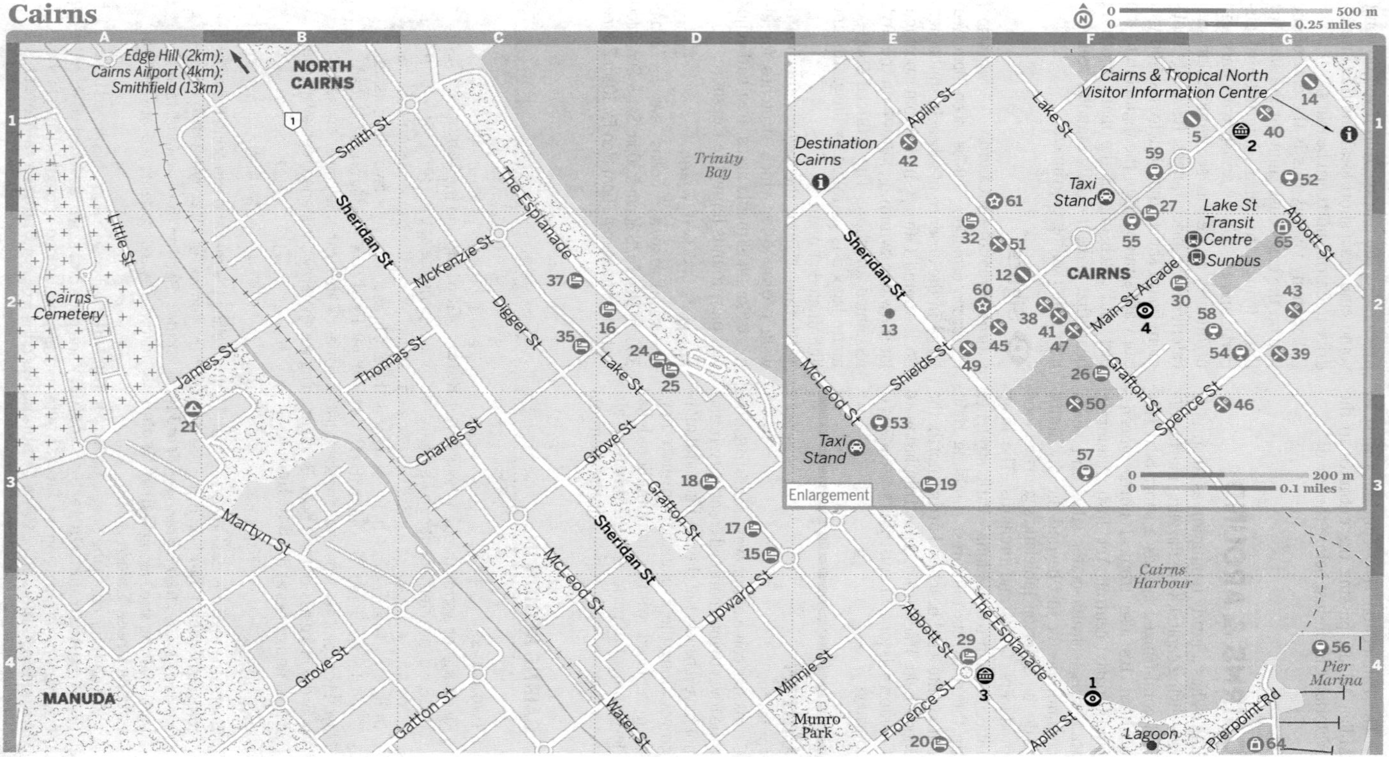
0 500 m
0 0.25 miles
A
B
C
D
E
F
G
1
2
3
4
Edge Hill (2km); Cairns Airport (4km); Smithfield (13km)
NORTH CAIRNS
MANUDA
Trinity Bay
Cairns Harbour
Pier Marina
Cairns Cemetery
Munro Park
Lagoon
Little St
James St
Smith St
Sheridan St
McKenzie St
Thomas St
Charles St
Digger St
The Esplanade
Lake St
Grove St
Grafton St
Martyn St
McLeod St
Upward St
Gatton St
Water St
Minnie St
Abbott St
Florence St
Aplin St
Pierpoint Rd
Enlargement
Destination Cairns
Cairns & Tropical North Visitor Information Centre
Taxi Stand
Lake St Transit Centre
Sunbus
CAIRNS
Main St Arcade
Shields St
Spence St
0 200 m
0 0.1 miles

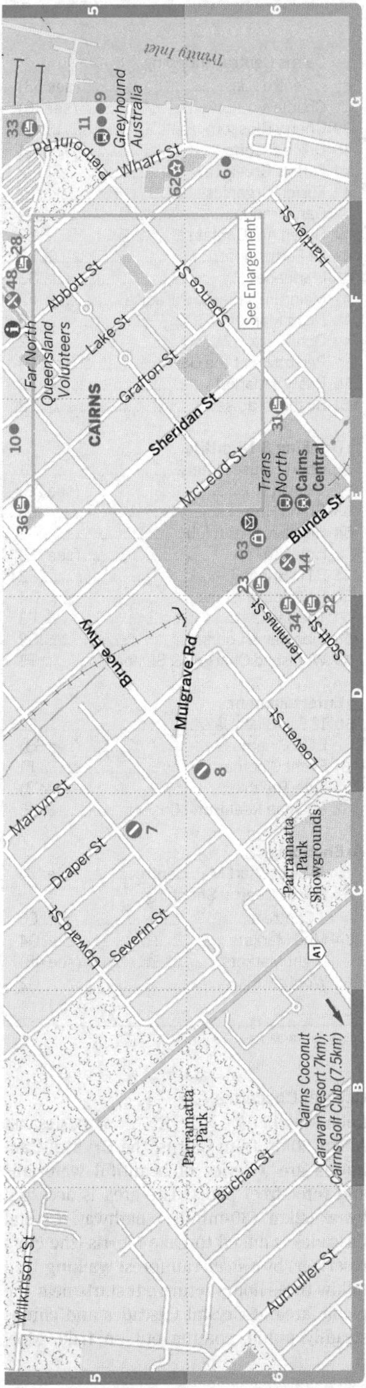

Sat & Sun) These beautiful tropical gardens are an explosion of greenery and rainforest plants. They include an area for bush-tucker plants and the Gondwanan Evolutionary Garden, which traces the 415-million-year heritage of tropical plants. Free guided walks depart from Tuesday to Friday at 10am from the **information centre**. There's a good **Wild Bean Cafe** (mains $9-18, ⌚7am to 4.30pm). Take bus 131 to get here.

Opposite the gardens the **Rainforest Boardwalk** leads to **Saltwater Creek** and **Centenary Lakes**. Uphill from the gardens, **Mt Whitfield Conservation Park** has two walking tracks through rainforest, climbing to viewpoints over the city; follow the Red Arrow circuit (1.5km, one hour) or the more demanding Blue Arrow circuit (6.6km, four to five hours).

Tanks Arts Centre GALLERY, THEATRE
(www.tanksartscentre.com; 46 Collins Ave; ⌚gallery 10am-4pm Mon-Fri) Three gigantic WWII fuel-storage tanks have been transformed into studios, galleries showcasing Australian artists' work and an inspired performing-arts venue (with some great bands), plus a lively **market day** (last Sun of month Apr-Nov).

Cairns Regional Gallery GALLERY
(www.cairnsregionalgallery.com.au; cnr Abbott & Shields Sts; adult/child under 16 $5/free; ⌚9am-5pm Mon-Fri, 10-5pm Sat, 10am-2pm Sun) In a colonnaded 1936 heritage building, Cairns' acclaimed regional gallery hosts exhibitions reflecting the consciousness of the tropical north region, with an emphasis on local and indigenous works and top-notch visiting exhibitions such as Goya's etchings.

Tjapukai Cultural Park CULTURAL CENTRE
(☎07-4042 9999; www.tjapukai.com.au; Kamerunga Rd; adult/child $36/18, Tjapukai by Night adult/child $99/49.50; ⌚9am-5pm, Tjapukai by Night 7-9.30pm) This indigenous-owned cultural extravaganza features the Creation Theatre, which tells the story of creation using giant holograms and actors, a dance theatre and a gallery, as well as boomerang- and spear-throwing demonstrations and didgeridoo lessons. A fireside corroboree is the centrepiece of the **Tjapukai by Night** dinner-and-show deal.

The park is about 15km north of the city centre, just off the Captain Cook Hwy near the Skyrail terminal; transfers are available for an extra charge.

Cairns

Sights

1 Cairns Foreshore F4
2 Cairns Regional Gallery G1
3 Centre of Contemporary Arts E4
4 Reef Teach F2

Activities, Courses & Tours

5 Cairns Dive Centre G1
6 Cairns Seaplanes G6
7 Deep Sea Divers Den C5
8 Down Under Dive D6
9 Great Adventures G5
10 Mike Ball Dive Expeditions E5
11 Passions of Paradise G5
12 Pro-Dive F2
13 Skydive the Reef Cairns E2
14 Tusa Dive G1

Sleeping

15 201 Lake Street D3
16 Acacia Court D2
17 Balinese D3
18 Bay Village D3
19 Cairns Central YHA E3
20 Cairns Girls Hostel E4
21 Cairns Holiday Park A3
22 Cairns Sharehouse D6
23 Dreamtime Travellers Rest E6
24 Floriana Guesthouse D2
25 Floriana Villas D2
26 Gilligan's F2
27 Global Backpackers F1
28 Global Backpackers (Waterfront) F5
29 Hotel Cairns E4
30 Inn Cairns F2
31 Mid City E6
32 Northern Greenhouse E2
33 Shangri-La G5
34 Travellers Oasis D6
35 Tropical Queenslander C2
36 Villa Vaucluse E5
37 Waterfront Terraces C2

Eating

38 Asian Foods Australia F2
Cairns Central Shopping Centre .... (see 63)
Charlie's .... (see 16)
39 Cherry Blossom G2
40 Dolce & Caffe G1
41 Fetta's Greek Taverna F2
42 Fusion Organics E1
43 Ganbaranba G2
44 Green Ant Cantina E6
45 La Fettuccina F2
46 Marinades G3
47 Meldrum's Pies in Paradise F2
48 Night Markets F5
49 Ochre E2
Perrotta's at the Gallery .... (see 2)
50 Rusty's Markets F3
51 Sushi Paradise F2

Drinking & Nightlife

52 Court House Hotel G1
Gilligan's .... (see 26)
53 Grand Hotel E3
54 Heritage Nightclub G2
Hotel Cairns .... (see 29)
55 PJ O'Briens F2
56 Salt House G4
57 The Jack F3
58 Vibe Bar & Lounge G2
59 Woolshed Chargrill & Saloon F1

Entertainment

60 12 Bar Blues Jazz E2
BCC Cinemas .... (see 63)
61 Event Cinemas Cairns F1
Jute Theatre .... (see 3)
62 Pullman Reef Hotel Casino G5

Shopping

Absells Chart Map Centre .... (see 4)
63 Cairns Central Shopping Centre E6
64 Mud Markets G4
Night Markets .... (see 48)
65 Woolworths G2

Centre of Contemporary Arts GALLERY, THEATRE

(www.coca.org.au; 96 Abbott St; ⏲10am-5pm Mon-Sat) FREE CoCA houses the **KickArts** (www.kickarts.com.au) galleries of local contemporary visual art, as well as the **Jute Theatre** (www.jute.com.au) and the **End Credits Film Club** (www.endcredits.com.au). The gift shop here has a stellar range of prints, craft and jewellery by Aussie artists...all at reasonable prices too.

Crystal Cascades & Lake Morris WATERFALLS, LAKE

About 20km from Cairns, the **Crystal Cascades** are a series of beautiful waterfalls and (croc-free) pools. The area is accessed by a 1.2km (30-minute) pathway. Crystal Cascades is linked to Lake Morris (the city's reservoir) by a *steep* rainforest **walking trail** (allow three hours return). It starts near the picnic area at Crystal Cascades and climbs steadily uphill, coming out on Lake Morris Rd, about 300m from Copperlode Dam (turn right).

Reef Teach INTERPRETIVE CENTRE
(☎07-4031 7794; http://reefteach.wordpress.com; 2nd fl, Main Street Arcade, 85 Lake St; adult/child $18/9; ⏲lectures 5.30-8.30pm Tue-Sat) Before heading out to the reef, take your knowledge to greater depths at this excellent and informative centre, where marine experts explain how to identify specific types of coral and fish and how to treat the reef with respect.

Activities

A plethora of tour operators runs adventure-based activities from Cairns, most offering transfers to/from your accommodation.

AJ Hackett Bungee & Minjin BUNGY JUMPING
(☎1800 622 888; www.ajhackett.com; McGregor Rd; bungy jumps $169, minjin swings $89, bungee & minjin swing combos $225; ⏲10am-5pm) Bungy from the purpose-built tower or swing from the trees on the minjin (a harness swing). Rates include transfers.

Cable Ski WATERSKIING
(☎07-4038 1304; www.cableskicairns.com.au; Captain Cook Hwy; adult/child per hr $39/34, per day $69/64; ⏲10am-6pm) Learn to waterski, wakeboard or kneeboard tethered to a cable (not a boat) at this water-sports park near the Skyrail.

Cairns Golf Club GOLF
(☎07-4037 6777; www.cairnsgolfclub.com.au; Grundy St, Woree) A scenic 18-hole course, 7km south of the city centre, established in 1923. Hires out equipment; rates depend on the day and tee time.

Fishing Cairns FISHING
(☎0448 563 586; www.fishingcairns.com.au) Arranges river, reef and game fishing trips.

Tours

A staggering 600-plus tours bus, boat, fly and drive out of Cairns each day. You'll see booking agencies on nearly every corner in the city. Popular tours include the ones to Green, Fitzroy and the Frankland Islands and day tours to Lizard Island.

Great Barrier Reef

Reef operators generally include transport, lunch and snorkelling gear in their tour prices. Many have diving options, including introductory dives requiring no prior experience. When choosing a tour, consider the vessel (catamaran or sailing ship), its capacity (from six to 300 people), what extras are offered and the destination. The outer reefs are more pristine; inner-reef areas can be patchy, showing signs of damage from humans, coral bleaching and crown-of-thorns starfish. In most cases you get what you pay for. Some operators offer the dearer option of a trip in a glass-bottomed boat or semisubmersible.

The majority of boats depart from the Pier Marina and Reef Fleet Terminal at about 8am, returning around 6pm. As well as the popular day trips, a number of operators also offer multiday live-aboard trips, which include specialised dive opportunities such as night diving. Dive-course companies also offer tours.

Several dive boats offer helmet diving (from $140). Hoses attached to the helmet deliver air, so you can breathe normally. Because you're 'walking' on a submerged platform, it's ideal for nonswimmers, kids over 12 and anyone who doesn't like to get their hair wet.

Coral Princess CRUISE
(☎1800 079 545, 07-4040 9999; www.coralprincess.com.au) Three- to seven-night cruises between Cairns, Pelorus Island and Lizard Island (return from $1347 per person, twin share).

Great Adventures SNORKELLING, TOUR
(☎07-4044 9944; www.greatadventures.com.au; Reef Fleet Terminal, 1 Spence St; adult/child from $201/101) Fast catamaran day trips to a floating pontoon for snorkelling, with an optional stopover on Green Island (from $222/111), as well as semisubmersibles and a glass-bottomed boat. Diving add-on available.

SEASONAL WORK

Cairns is one of the most popular places on the east coast to pick up casual work in the tourism and hospitality sectors. Those bilingual in Japanese, Mandarin, Korean and German can pick up tour-translating work. And, of course, Cairns is a magnet for dive instructors and the like.

For those planning to stick around in Cairns for a month or more to work, dive or study, look for a room via **Cairns Sharehouse** (☎07-4041 1875; www.cairns-sharehouse.com; 17 Scott St; s per week from $130, tw & d per person per week from $110; ❄📶🏊).

DIVE COURSES

Cairns is the scuba-diving capital of the Great Barrier Reef and a popular place to attain Professional Association of Diving Instructors (PADI) open-water certification. There's a plethora of courses on offer, from budget four-day courses that combine pool training and reef dives to five-day courses that include two days' pool theory and three days' living aboard a boat, diving less-frequented parts of the reef. Many operators are multilingual.

All operators require you to have a dive medical certificate, which they can arrange (around $60). A reef tax ($40 to $80) is payable as well. Many operators also offer advanced courses for certified divers. Dive schools include the following:

- **Cairns Dive Centre** (07-4051 0294; www.cairnsdive.com.au; 121 Abbott St) Long-running operator affiliated with Scuba Schools International (SSI) rather than PADI. Live-aboard courses (four/five days $680/820), live-aboard (from $310) and day tours ($180).
- **Deep Sea Divers Den** (07-4046 7333; www.diversden.com.au; 319 Draper St) Long-established school running multiday live-aboard courses and trips from $445.
- **Down Under Dive** (07-4052 8300, 1800 079 099; www.downunderdive.com.au; 287 Draper St) Four- and five-day live-aboard open-water courses from $450 to $660.
- **Pro-Dive** (07-4031 5255; www.prodivecairns.com; cnr Grafton & Shields St; live-aboard trips from $1250, open-water courses from $880) One of Cairns' most experienced operators with excellent staff. Runs a comprehensive five-day learn-to-dive course incorporating a three-day live-aboard trip for $880. Dive live-aboards available from $1250.
- **Tusa Dive** (07-4047 9100; www.tusadive.com; cnr Shields St & The Esplanade) Inexpensive four-day learn-to-dive courses ($670) including two day trips' diving.

Passions of Paradise DIVING, SNORKELLING
(1800 111 346, 07-4041 1600; www.passions.com.au; adult/child $139/89) Sexy sailing catamaran taking you to Michaelmas Cay and Paradise Reef for snorkelling or diving.

Silverswift DIVING, SNORKELLING
(07-4044 9944; www.silverseries.com.au; adult/child from $180/130) Popular catamaran for snorkelling/diving three outer reefs.

Spirit of Freedom DIVING
(07-4047 9150; www.spiritoffreedom.com.au; 3-/4-/7-day trips from $1475/1800/3025) Three-deck vessel with live-aboard trips to Cod Hole and Ribbon Reefs.

Sunlover DIVING, SNORKELLING
(07-4050 1333; www.sunlover.com.au; adult/child/family $180/65/425) Fast family-friendly catamaran rides to a snorkelling pontoon on the outer Moore Reef. Options include semi-submersible trips and helmet diving.

Scenic Flights

Great Barrier Reef Helicopters SCENIC FLIGHTS
(07-4081 8888; www.gbrhelicopters.com.au; 20/60min flight per person from $260/559) Helicopter flights departing from Green Island (10 minutes $148) to an hour-long reef and rainforest trip.

Cairns Seaplanes SCENIC FLIGHTS
(07-4031 4307; www.cairnsseaplanes.com; 2/3 Abbott St; 30min flights from $269) Scenic reef flights, including to Green Island.

White-Water Rafting

The excitement level of white-water rafting down the Barron, Russell and North Johnstone Rivers is hitched to the season: the wetter the weather, the whiter your water. The Tully River has rapids year-round (see p407). Trips are graded from armchair (grade one) to white knuckle (grade five).

Foaming Fury RAFTING
(07-4031 7460, 1800 801 540; www.foamingfury.com.au) Full-day trips on the Russell River ($149); half-day on the Barron ($129), with options for kids aged over 10.

Raging Thunder RAFTING
(07-4030 7900; www.ragingthunder.com.au; rafting trips from $133) Full-day Tully trips (standard $195, 'Xtreme' $225) and half-day Barron trips ($133).

Tubing

Aussie Drifterz TUBING
(0401 318 475; www.aussiedrifterz.net; half-day tours adult/child $69/49) Float in an inner tube along beautiful Behana Gorge.

(Continued on page 425)

The Great Barrier Reef

Each year, more than 1.5 million visitors come to this World Heritage–listed area that stretches across 2000km of coastline. Diving and snorkelling are just some of the ways to experience this wonderful and rich ecosystem. There's also sailing, scenic flights and idyllic days exploring the reef's gateway towns and stunning islands.

Contents

Above Aerial view of the Great Barrier Reef

Gateways to the Reef

There are numerous ways to approach Australia's massive undersea kingdom. You can head to a popular gateway town and join an organised tour, sign up for a multiday sailing or diving trip exploring less-travelled outer fringes of the reef, or fly out to a remote island, where you'll have the reef largely to yourself.

The Whitsundays

Home to turquoise waters, coral gardens and palm-fringed beaches, the Whitsundays have many options for reef-exploring: base yourself on an island, go sailing or stay on Airlie Beach and island-hop on day trips.

Cairns

The most popular gateway to the reef, Cairns has dozens of boat operators offering day trips with snorkelling as well as multiday reef explorations on live-aboard vessels. For the uninitiated, Cairns is a good place to learn to dive.

Port Douglas

An hour's drive north of Cairns, Port Douglas is a laid-back beach town with dive boats heading out to over a dozen sites, including more pristine outer reefs, such as Agincourt Reef.

Townsville

Australia's largest tropical city is far from the outer reef (2½ hours by boat) but has some exceptional draws: access to Australia's best wreck dive, an excellent aquarium, marine-themed museums, plus multiday live-aboard dive boats departing from here.

Southern Reef Islands

For an idyllic getaway off the beaten path, book a trip to one of several remote reef-fringed islands on the southern edge of the Great Barrier Reef. You'll find fantastic snorkelling and diving right off the island.

1

1. Clownfish **2.** Airlie Beach (p386) **3.** Reef HQ Aquarium (p395), Townsville

3

2

ULLA LOHMANN / GETTY IMAGES ©

1

2

TANYA PUNTTI / GETTY IMAGES ©

1. Whitehaven Beach (p393) 2. Helicopter scenic flight over Whitsunday Islands (p392) 3. Snorkelling, Cairns (p418)

3

Top Reef Encounters

Donning a mask and fins and getting an up-close look at this marine wonderland is one of the best ways to experience the Great Barrier Reef. You can get a different take aboard a glass-bottomed boat tour, on a scenic flight or on a land-based reef walk.

Diving & Snorkelling

The classic way to see the Great Barrier Reef is to board a catamaran and visit several different coral-rich spots on a long day trip. Nothing quite compares to that first underwater glimpse, whether diving or snorkelling.

Semi-submersibles & Boats

A growing number of reef operators (especially around Cairns) offer semi-submersible or glass-bottomed boat tours, which give cinematic views of coral, rays, fish, turtles and sharks – without you ever having to get wet.

Sailing

You can escape the crowds and see some spectacular reef scenery aboard a sailboat. Experienced mariners can hire a bareboat, others can join a multiday tour – both are easily arranged from Airlie Beach or Port Douglas.

Reef Walking

Many reefs of the southern Great Barrier Reef are exposed at low tide, allowing visitors to walk on the reef top (on sandy tracks between living coral). This can be a fantastic way to learn about marine life, especially if accompanied by a naturalist guide.

Scenic Flights

Get a bird's-eye view of the vast coral reef and its cays and islands from a scenic flight. You can sign up for a helicopter tour (offered from Cairns) or a seaplane tour (particularly memorable over the Whitsundays).

Sea turt

Nature's Theme Park

Home to some of the greatest biodiversity of any ecosystem on earth, the Great Barrier Reef is a marine wonderland. You'll find 30-plus species of marine mammals along with countless species of fish, coral, molluscs and sponges. Above the water, 200 bird species and 118 butterfly species have been recorded on reef islands and cays.

Common fish species include dusky butterfly fish, which are a rich navy blue with sulphur-yellow noses and back fins; large graphic turkfish, with luminescent pastel coats; teeny neon damsels, with darting flecks of electric blue; and six-banded angelfish, with blue tails, yellow bodies and tiger stripes. Rays, including the spotted eagle ray, are worth looking out for.

The reef is also a haven to many marine mammals, such as whales, dolphins and dugongs. Dugongs are listed as vulnerable, and a significant number of them live in Australia's northern waters; the reef is home to around 15% of the global population. Humpback whales migrate from Antarctica to the reef's warm waters to breed between May and October. Minke whales can be seen off the coast from Cairns to Lizard Island in June and July. Porpoises and killer and pilot whales also make their home here. One of the reef's most-loved inhabitants is the sea turtle. Six of the world's seven species (all endangered) live on the reef and lay eggs on the islands' sandy beaches in spring or summer.

(Continued from page 418)

Ballooning

The dawn skies above Cairns and the highlands see a multitude of balloons seemingly suspended in the air. Most flights take off from the Mareeba region in the Atherton Tableland and include champagne breakfast afterwards.

Hot Air Cairns BALLOONING
(☎07-4039 9900; www.hotair.com.au; 30min flights from $235) Balloon flights over the lush Atherton Tableland; prices include pick-up and drop-off.

Skydiving

Skydive the Reef Cairns SKYDIVING
(☎1800 800 840; www.skydivethereefcairns.com.au; 59 Sheridan St; tandem jumps 9000/14,000ft $264/349) A 9000ft jump gives you up to 28 seconds' freefalling, while jumping at 14,000ft gives you over 60 seconds plummeting back to earth.

Atherton Tableland

Food Trail Tours FOOD TOUR
(☎07-4041 1522; www.foodtrailtours.com.au; adult/child from $159/80; ⊙Mon-Sat) Taste your way around the tableland, visiting farms producing macadamias, tropical-fruit wine, cheese, chocolate and coffee.

On the Wallaby OUTDOORS
(☎07-4033 6575; www.onthewallaby.com; day/overnight tours $99/169) Excellent activity-based tours including cycling, hiking and canoeing.

Uncle Brian's Tours GUIDED TOUR
(☎07-4033 6575; www.unclebrian.com.au; tours $109; ⊙Mon-Wed, Fri & Sat) Lively small-group day trips covering forests, waterfalls and lakes.

Cape Tribulation & the Daintree

After the Great Barrier Reef, Cape Trib is the next most popular day trip – usually including a cruise on the Daintree River. Access is via a well-signposted sealed road, so don't discount hiring your own vehicle.

Billy Tea Bush Safaris ECOTOUR
(☎07-4032 0077; www.billytea.com.au; day trips adult/child $185/135) Exciting eco day tours to Cape Trib and along the 4WD Bloomfield Track to Emmagen Creek. Also offers tours to Chillagoe, Cooktown and Cape York.

BTS Tours OUTDOORS
(☎07-4099 5665; www.btstours.com.au; day trips adult/child $165/120) Small-group tours, including swimming and canoeing to the Daintree River and Mossman Gorge.

Cape Trib Connections GUIDED TOUR
(☎07-4032 0500; www.capetribconnections.com; day trips adult/child $119/99) Includes Mossman Gorge and Cape Tribulation Beach. Also overnight tours (from $135).

Trek North Safaris GUIDED TOUR
(☎07-4041 4333; www.treknorth.com.au; adult/child $160/110) Full-day tours include Mossman Gorge and a river cruise.

Tropical Horizons Tours ECOTOUR
(☎07-4035 6445; www.tropicalhorizonstours.com.au; day tours from $117) Day trips to Cape Trib and the Daintree; also overnight tours.

Tropics Explorer GUIDED TOUR
(☎07-4031 3460, 1800 801 540; www.tropics-explorer.com.au; day tours from $99) Fun Cape Trib day trips; overnight tours available.

Cooktown & Cape York

Adventure North Australia DRIVING TOUR
(☎07-4028 3376; www.adventurenorthaustralia.com; 1-day tours adult/child $250/200) Has 4WD trips to Cooktown via the coastal route, returning via the inland route. Also two- and three-day tours, fly-drive and Aboriginal cultural tours.

Undara Lava Tubes

Undara Experience GUIDED TOUR
(☎07-4097 1411; www.undara.com.au; 2-day tours adult/child from $289/195) Overnight coach and rail tours to the Undara lava tubes.

City Tours

Cairns Discovery Tours GUIDED TOUR
(☎07-4028 3567; www.cairnsdiscoverytours.com; adult/child $69/35; ⊙Mon-Sat) Half-day afternoon tours run by horticulturists; includes the botanic gardens and Palm Cove. Northern-beaches transfers are an extra $5.

Sleeping

Accommodation agencies have up-to-date listings and can assist in finding a suitable place to bed for the night. The **Accommodation Centre** (☎1800 807 730, 07-4051 4066; www.accomcentre.com.au) has information on a wide range of options, including hostels, apartments and hotels.

Cairns is a backpacker hot spot, with around 40 hostels – from intimate converted houses to hangar-sized resorts. The scene is so competitive that many hotels offer free daily dinner vouchers. The city's wealth of self-contained accommodation works well for groups or families, while dozens of virtually identical motels are lined up along Sheridan St. Most tour operators also pick up and drop off at Cairns' northern beaches accommodation.

Dreamtime Travellers Rest HOSTEL $

(☎07-4031 6753, 1800 058 440; www.dreamtime-hostel.com; cnr Bunda & Terminus Sts; d $24-26, tw without bathroom $59, d without bathroom $58-62; @ 📶 🏊) This chilled-out hostel at the edge of the city combines friendly staff with cozy rooms in an old Queenslander. The charming compound offers pockets of space to curl up with a book. Cheap pizza and barbecue nights round off the package.

Tropic Days HOSTEL $

(☎1800 421 521, 07-4041 1521; www.tropicdays.com.au; 26-38 Bunting St; camp sites $12, tents $16, dm $26-27, d without bathroom $64-74; ❄ @ 📶 🏊) Tucked behind the showgrounds (with a courtesy bus into town), this busy hostel is a haven of tropical gardens strung with hammocks, with a pool table and a chilled vibe that makes it easy to stay longer than planned. Three- to four-bed dorms are bunk-free, doubles share spotless bathrooms, the kitchen's stocked with spices, and even nonguests can book for Monday night's croc, emu and roo barbecue ($12 including a didge show).

Cairns Girls Hostel HOSTEL $

(☎07-4051 2016; www.cairnsgirlshostel.com.au; 147 Lake St; dm/tw $20/48; @ 📶) Sorry, boys! With three well-equipped kitchens, spacious lounge areas and a manager who looks after you as if you were a guest in her own home, this 1900s-built, white-glove-test-clean, female-only hostel is one of the most accommodating budget stays in Cairns.

Cairns Coconut Caravan Resort CAMPGROUND $

(☎07-4054 6644; www.coconut.com.au; cnr Bruce Hwy & Anderson Rd; sites powered/with bathroom $46/64, cabins with bathroom $130-175, villas $250-340; P ❄ @ 🏊) The last word in five-star caravan-park luxury, 8km south of the city centre. Spas, a waterpark, a playground, an outdoor cinema and a slew of accommodation options.

Travellers Oasis HOSTEL $

(☎07-4052 1377; www.travellersoasis.com.au; 8 Scott St; dm $27, s without bathroom $45, d without bathroom $64-74; ❄ @ 📶 🏊) Handmade timber furniture, sculptures, bright colours and a barbecue area make this soulful 50-bed backpacker hostel a laid-back place to hang out with like-minded travellers. Dorms are bunk-free; shared bathrooms are clean.

Global Backpackers HOSTEL $

(☎07-4031 7921, 1800 819 024; www.globalbackpackerscairns.com.au; 9b Shields St; dm from $18, d from $60; ❄ @ 📶 🏊) It's all about location, location, location at this flashy, centrally located hostel. Common areas are swathed in dark hues and rooms are cosy if not plain. It doesn't matter as most guests seem happy to chill-out on the balcony or by the pool. There's a similarly-priced **waterfront branch** (www.globalbackpackerscairns.com.au; 67 The Esplanade; dm from $18, d from $60; ❄ @ 📶).

Gilligan's HOSTEL $

(☎07-4041 6566; www.gilligansbackpackers.com.au; 57-89 Grafton St; dm $25-37, d $130; ❄ @ 📶 🏊) The 'G spot' is pricey, impersonal and very loud, but all rooms at this flashpacker resort have bathrooms and most have balconies; higher-priced rooms come with fridges and TVs. Party goers never have to leave thanks to nightly entertainment such as bogan bingo, jelly wrestling, live music and DJs. The complex houses several bars, a beauty salon, and a gym to work off all that beer.

Cairns Holiday Park CAMPGROUND $

(☎1800 259 977, 07-4051 1467; www.cairnscamping.com.au; 12-30 Little St; sites unpowered/powered/with bathroom $34/41/52, cabins with/without bathroom $88/63; P ❄ @ 📶 🏊) The closest to central Cairns, this caravan park is 3.5km north of the city centre. The smart and clean bathroom and camp-kitchen facilities accompany tidy cabins and free internet.

Cairns Central YHA HOSTEL $

(☎07-4051 0772; www.yha.com.au; 20-26 McLeod St; dm $25-30, s/d/f $40/80/117; ❄ @ 🏊) Bright, spotless and professionally staffed hostel with a good reputation. A great choice for location and for travellers who aren't necessarily here to party.

Northern Greenhouse HOSTEL $$

(☎07-4047 7200, 1800 000 541; www.friendlygroup.com.au; 117 Grafton St; dm/tw/apt $28/95/140; P ❄ @ 📶 🏊) It fits into the budget category with dorm accommodation and a relaxed attitude, but this friendly place is a cut above, with neat and large studio-style apartments with kitchens and balconies.

The central deck, pool and games room are great for socialising. Freebies include breakfast and a Sunday barbie.

Floriana Guesthouse GUESTHOUSE **$$**
(☑ 07-4051 7886; www.florianaguesthouse.com; 183 The Esplanade; s $75, d $89 & $140; ❋ @ 🛜 🏊) Run by charismatic jazz musician Maggie, Cairns-of-old still exists at this old-fashioned guesthouse, which retains its original polished floorboards and art-deco fittings. The swirling staircase leads to 10 individually decorated rooms, some with bay windows and window seats, others with balconies.

Floriana Villas APARTMENT **$$**
(☑ 0403 339 000; www.florianavillas.com.au; 187-189 The Esplanade; 1-bedroom apt $110-150, 2-bedroom apt $200; ❋ 🛜 🏊) Next to the Floriana Guesthouse, this distinctive white-and-blue complex – built by a Maltese family in the 1940s – has been converted into enormous, contemporary self-contained apartments. Minimum stay is three nights; extras include free bike hire, a shaded pool with spa jets and a landscaped barbecue area.

Inn Cairns APARTMENT **$$**
(☑ 07-4041 2350; www.inncairns.com.au; 71 Lake St; apt $125-188; P ❋ @ 🛜 🏊) Behind the unassuming facade, this is true inner-city apartment living. Take the lift up to the 1st-floor pool or to the rooftop garden for a sundowner. The elegant self-contained apartments have separate bedroom and living areas and friendly staff will make you feel at home 'Inn' Cairns.

Balinese MOTEL **$$**
(☑ 07-4051 9922, 1800 023 331; www.balinese.com.au; 215 Lake St; d from $110; ❋ @ 🛜 🏊) Bali comes to Cairns at this small low-rise complex: waking up among the authentic wood furnishings and ceramic pieces, you may be taken with the sudden urge to have your hair beaded.

Bay Village RESORT **$$**
(☑ 07-4051 4622; www.bayvillage.com.au; cnr Lake & Gatton Sts; d $150-330; ❋ @ 🏊) Smart units encircle a central pool at this sprawling resort. It's popular with package tours but no worse for that. Pricier rooms are self-contained, with kitchens and lounges; Balinese chefs cook up aromatic cuisine at the on-site **Bay Leaf Restaurant** (mains $16 to $31, lunch Monday to Friday, dinner daily). Free airport transfers.

Mid City APARTMENT **$$**
(☑ 07-4051 5050; www.midcity.com.au; 6 McLeod St; 1-/2-bedroom apt $175/225; ❋ @ 🛜 🏊) The immaculate, terracotta-tiled apartments in this arctic-white building are self-contained, with good kitchens, washing machines and dryers, and a balcony to enjoy balmy nights outside.

Villa Vaucluse APARTMENT **$$**
(☑ 07-4051 8566; www.villavaucluse.com.au; 141-143 Grafton St; 1-bedroom apt $258; ❋ 🛜 🏊) Mediterranean decor meets tropical influences, with central atrium, secluded saltwater swimming pool and rather sumptuous self-contained apartments. Online rates knock about 50% off rack rates.

Tropical Queenslander RESORT **$$**
(☑ 07-4051 0122; www.queenslanderhotels.com.au; 287 Lake St; apt from $130; ❋ @ 🛜 🏊) Double dip here in the two pools, and relax in the smart apartments with kitchenettes, bathrooms and balconies.

Acacia Court HOTEL **$$**
(☑ 07-4051 1501; www.acaciacourt.com; 223-227 The Esplanade; d $120-170; P ❋ 🛜 🏊) A stroll along the foreshore from town, this waterfront high-rise has dated rooms but you get Shangri-la views at budget rates if you book online. Most rooms have private balconies. Famed buffet restaurant Charlie's (p429) is downstairs.

★ **201 Lake Street** HOTEL **$$$**
(☑ 07-4053 0100, 1800 628 929; www.201lakestreet.com.au; 201 Lake St; r $120-260, apt $215-260) Lifted from the pages of a trendy magazine, this apartment complex has a lemongrass-scented reception area, stellar pool and a touch of exclusivity. Grecian white predominates and guests can choose from a smooth hotel room or contemporary apartments with an entertainment area, a plasma-screen TV and balcony.

Shangri-La HOTEL **$$$**
(☑ 07-4031 1411; www.shangri-la.com/cairns; Pierpoint Rd; r from $270; P ❋ @ 🛜 🏊) In an unbeatable waterfront setting, towering over the marina, Shangri-La is Cairns' top hotel, a swish five-star that ticks all the boxes for location, views, facilities (including a gym and pool bar) and attentive service. The Horizon Club rooms are top notch. Online bookings in low season can net you a room for as little as $170.

Hotel Cairns HOTEL $$$
(☎07-4051 6188; www.thehotelcairns.com; cnr Abbott & Florence Sts; d $195-265;) There's a real tropical charm to this sprawling bone-white hotel, built in traditional Queenslander plantation style. Modern rooms have an understated elegance and the huge 'tower' rooms and suites offer luxurious touches like wicker chaises longues and private balconies.

Waterfront Terraces APARTMENT $$$
(☎07-4031 8333; www.cairnsluxury.com; 233 The Esplanade; 1-/2-bedroom apt $212/289;) Set in lush tropical grounds, these low-rise luxury apartments have handsomely furnished separate tiled lounges and kitchen areas and all the trimmings, including big balconies looking out over the ocean.

Eating

Cairns' status as an international city is reflected in its multicultural restaurants, which often incorporate a tropical Aussie twist. Some of Cairns' pubs dish up amazingly cheap meals to the thrifty backpacker hordes and they're not half bad.

Along the waterfront outside the Pier Marketplace, half a dozen international restaurants share a boardwalk overlooking the marina – just wander along and take your pick. Similarly, a stroll along the Esplanade will turn up everything from seafood restaurants to steak houses.

Sushi Paradise JAPANESE $
(☎07-4028 3452; 111 Grafton St; sushi $3-15; 11am-6.30pm Mon-Sat) Cheap and cheerful is the order of the day at this popular takeaway sushi joint. Pull up a plastic chair outside, mix up the wasabi and soy sauce, and down freshly made handrolls, sashimi and sushi. The free-flow of green tea is a nice touch.

Ganbaranba JAPANESE $
(☎07-4031 2522; 12-20 Spence St; ramen $10-15; 11am-10pm daily) It's a good sign that regulars (on a first-name basis with the staff) keep returning for the filling bowls of handmade ramen. Choose from a range of toppings and broth...all prepared authentically by Japanese staff.

Meldrum's Pies in Paradise BAKERY $
(97 Grafton St; pies $4.70-5.90; 7am-5pm Mon-Fri, to 2.30pm Sat;) A Cairns institution, Meldrum's bakes some 40 inventive varieties of the humble Aussie pie – from chicken and avocado to pumpkin gnocchi or tuna mornay. Great for lunch on the (budget) run.

Fusion Organics CAFE $
(www.fusionorganics.com.au; cnr Aplin & Grafton Sts; dishes $4-19.50; 7am-3pm Mon-Fri, to 2pm Sat;) In the wicker-chair-strewn corner courtyard of a historic 1921 red-brick former ambulance station, hard-working chefs whip up Fusion's organic, allergy-free fare such as quiches, frittatas, corn fritters and filled breads you can finish off with fresh juice.

Vanilla Gelateria ICE CREAM $
(Pierpoint Rd; cone or cup $4-6; 9.30am-11pm) Icy scoops of gelati like Toblerone; lemon, lime and bitters – even Red Bull! Perfect for a hot day.

Night Markets FOOD COURT $
(The Esplanade; dishes $10-15; 5-11pm daily) If you want something cheap and quick, the Night Markets, between Alpin and Shields Sts, have a busy Asian-style food court.

Fetta's Greek Taverna GREEK $$
(☎07-4051 6966; www.fettasgreektaverna.com.au; 99 Grafton St; dishes $13-25; 11.30am-3pm Mon-Fri, 5.30pm-late daily) The white walls and blue-accented windows do a great job evoking Santorini. But it's the food that's the star of the show here, with classic Greek dishes. For the indecisive, the $35 set menu goes the whole hog – dip, saganaki, mousakka, salad, grilled meats, calamari, baklava AND coffee. The takeaway section offers great-value gyros topped with with zingy tzatziki for $9.

Ochre MODERN AUSTRALIAN $$
(☎07-4051 0100; www.ochrerestaurant.com.au; 43 Shields St; mains $23-37; 11am-3pm Mon-Fri, 6-10.30pm daily;) In an ochre- and plum-toned dining room, the changing menu at this innovative restaurant utilises native Aussie fauna (such as croc with native pepper, or roo with quandong-chilli glaze) and flora (wattle-seed damper loaf with peanut oil and native dukka; lemon-myrtle panacotta). Croc burgers and wallaby topside round off the menu. Can't decide? Try a tasting plate.

Green Ant Cantina MEXICAN $$
(☎07-4041 5061; www.greenantcantina.com; 183 Bunda St; mains $15-40; 6pm-late daily;) This funky little slice of Mexico behind the railway station is worth seeking out for its homemade quesadillas, enchiladas and Corona-battered barramundi. Great cocktail list, cool tunes and the occasional live band.

Marinades INDIAN $$
(☎07-4041 1422; 43 Spence St; mains $14-30; ⏰11am-2.30pm, 6-10pm Tue-Sun; 🖉) A long, *long* menu of aromatic dishes like lobster marinated in cashew paste, or Goan prawn curry, along with restrained decor in its dining room, make Marinades the pick of Cairns' Indian restaurants. Thali lunch sets ($10 to $12) are good value and you save 10% when doing takeaway.

Perrotta's at the Gallery MEDITERRANEAN $$
(☎07-4031 5899; 38 Abbott St; mains $14-36; ⏰8.30am-11pm daily; 🖉) This breezy spot adjoining the Cairns Regional Gallery tempts you onto its covered deck's wrought-iron furniture for tasty breakfasts, coffees, and a Med-inspired menu at lunch and dinner. The odd surly staff member blemishes the overall experience though.

Dolce & Caffe CAFE $$
(Shop 1, Mantra Esplanade, Shields St; dishes $6.50-18; ⏰6am-5pm daily; 🖉) A local 'see and be seen' fave for its good coffee and super-fresh salads.

La Fettuccina ITALIAN $$
(☎07-4031 5959; www.lafettuccina.com; 41 Shields St; mains $26-31; ⏰6-10.30pm daily) Homemade sauces and pasta are a speciality at this small, atmospheric Italian restaurant. Try for a seat on the tiny, internal wrought-iron mezzanine balcony. Licensed and BYO.

Charlie's SEAFOOD $$
(☎07-4051 5011; 223-227 The Esplanade; buffets $23.50; ⏰6-10.30pm daily) It's not the fanciest place in town, but Charlie's, at the Acacia Court Hotel, is known for its nightly all-you-can-eat 'quantity over quality' seafood buffet. Fill your plate with prawns, oysters, clams or hot food and eat out on the poolside terrace.

Cherry Blossom JAPANESE $$$
(☎07-4052 1050; cnr Spence & Lake Sts; mains $29-53; ⏰noon-2pm Tue-Fri, 5-11pm Mon-Sat) This 1st-floor restaurant is reminiscent of an *Iron Chef* cook-off, with two chefs working at opposite ends of the restaurant floor. Despite being in need of an interior update, the restaurant is popular for sushi, teppanyaki and plenty of theatre.

Self-Catering

Cairns' main fresh food market is **Rusty's Markets** (Grafton St; ⏰5am-6pm Fri, 6am-3pm Sat, 6am-2pm Sun), between Shields and Spence Sts.

Asian Foods Australia SELF-CATERING $
(101 Grafton St) Stocks a wide range of food products from all over Asia.

Cairns Central Shopping Centre SELF-CATERING
(www.cairnscentral.com.au; McLeod St; ⏰9am-5.30pm Mon-Wed, Fri & Sat, to 9pm Thu, 10am-4.30pm Sun) This huge shopping centre has a butcher and a couple of supermarkets including Coles.

Drinking

Cairns holds the mantle as the party capital of the north Queensland coast, with loads of options. Most venues are multipurpose, offering food, alcohol and some form of entertainment, and you can always find a beer garden or terrace to enjoy balmy evenings.

★**Salt House** BAR
(www.salthouse.com.au; 6/2 Pierpoint Rd; ⏰9am-2am Fri-Sun, 11am-2am Mon-Thu) Next to Cairns' yacht club, Salt House has a sleek nautical design that has seen it become the city's most sought-after bar. Killer cocktails are paired with occasional live music, or DJs hitting the decks. The restaurant serves up excellent modern Australian food including line-caught fish and succulent steaks, and is worth migrating to after sundowners.

Vibe Bar & Lounge BAR
(☎07-4052 1494; 39 Lake St; ⏰11am-late Mon, Wed & Fri, 5pm-late Sat, 6pm-late Sun) A fresh lick of paint has breathed life back into this medium-sized restaurant/bar. The pub grub is passable but it's the drinks list and pumping dance floor (from 9pm) that draw the punters in.

Gilligan's BAR, CLUB
(www.gilligansbackpackers.com.au; 57-89 Grafton St; ⏰9am-late) You're guaranteed a crowd at Cairns' biggest and busiest backpacker resort, with 400-odd backpackers staying here. But it's also popular with locals for its immense beer deck, live bands, DJs spinning house tunes, and cocktails in its upstairs lounge bar.

Court House Hotel PUB
(38 Abbott St; ⏰9am-late) In Cairns' gleaming white former courthouse building, dating from 1921, the Court House pub is replete with a polished timber island bar and Scales of Justice statue – and cane-toad races on Wednesday night. DJs spin on Fridays. On

any other day, park yourself in the quiet beer garden outside.

The Jack BAR
(☎07-4051 2490; www.thejack.com.au; 48 Spence St; ⏲to late daily) The huge beer garden with barrels for tables, big screens and a music stage is the stand-out at this marginally Irish-themed pub attached to a backpackers. The entertainment spans live bands, DJs, UFC telecasts and swimsuit competitions.

Pier Bar & Grill BAR
(www.pierbar.com.au; Pierpoint Rd; ⏲11.30am-late) A local stalwart for its waterfront location and well-priced meals. The Pier's Sunday sessions are packed to the gills and *the* place to be.

Grand Hotel PUB
(www.grandhotelcairns.com; 33 McLeod St; ⏲11am-1am) This laid-back local is worth a visit just so that you can rest your beer on the bar – an 11m-long carved crocodile!

PJ O'Briens IRISH PUB
(cnr Lake & Shields Sts; ⏲to late daily) There are sticky carpets and the smell of stale Guinness, but Irish-themed PJ's packs 'em in with party nights, pole dancing and dirt-cheap meals.

Woolshed Chargrill & Saloon BAR
(☎07-4031 6304; www.thewoolshed.com.au; 24 Shields St; ⏲to late daily) Another backpacker magnet (probably because many hostels offer Woolshed meal vouchers!) where a young crowd of travellers and diving instructors elect to get hammered and dance on the tables.

Hotel Cairns BAR
(www.thehotelcairns.com; cnr Abbott & Florence Sts; ⏲to late daily) This grand-dame hotel is a low-key alternative to Cairns' hurdy-gurdy party scene, with nightly piano and double-bass performances.

Heritage Nightclub CLUB
(☎07-4031 8070; www.theheritagecairns.com; cnr Spence & Lake Sts; ⏲9pm-3am Thu, 10pm-5am Sat & Sun) When the DJ starts revving, a high-energy crowd downs cocktails and shots and spills out onto the enormous 1st-floor balcony. It can get messy but you can't go wrong if you're looking for a party.

☆ Entertainment

Live music hits stages all over town; the Tanks Arts Centre hosts well-known pop, rock, indie and folk artists. Jazz buffs should check the weekly roster at www.tropicjazz.org.au. Nightclubs come and go; ask locally about what's hot (and not). Clubs generally close at 3am or later; cover charges usually apply.

The website www.entertainmentcairns.com and hostels generally stock free backpackers magazines listing the hot spots.

12 Bar Blues Jazz JAZZ
(☎07-4041 7388; 62 Shields St; ⏲7pm-late Wed-Sun) The best (perhaps only) place in Cairns for loungy live music, this intimate bar grooves to the beat of jazz, blues and swing. Songwriter open-mic night takes place on Thursday, and general open-mic night on Sunday.

Pullman Reef Hotel Casino CASINO, BAR
(www.reefcasino.com.au; 35-41 Wharf St; ⏲4-11pm Mon & Tue, 4pm-late Wed-Sun) Cairns' casino has table games as well as hundreds of poker machines. Also three restaurants and four bars, including **Vertigo Bar & Lounge**, with free live music and ticketed shows and a massive sports bar (screening free movies twice a week). Mum can take the kids to the inhouse **wildlife dome** while daddy gambles away the family fortune.

Starry Night Cinema CINEMA
(www.endcredits.org.au; Flecker Botanic Gardens, Collins Ave, Edge Hill; admission $10; ⏲Jun-Oct) Every third Wednesday of the month classic films screen from about 6.30pm in the tropical outdoors of the botanic gardens.

Jute Theatre THEATRE
(☎07-4050 9444; www.jute.com.au; CoCA, 96 Abbott St; tickets from $20) Stages contemporary Australian works and indie plays in the Centre of Contemporary Arts.

Rondo Theatre THEATRE
(☎07-4031 9555, 1800 855 835; www.cairnslittletheatre.com; Greenslopes St; tickets $18-22) Community plays and musicals at this theatre opposite Centenary Lakes. It's 4.5km northwest of the centre (take Sheridan St to Greenslopes St).

Event Cinemas Cairns CINEMA
(www.eventcinemas.com.au; 108 Grafton St) Mainstream flicks and occasional foreign and arthouse films; cheap tickets on Tuesdays.

BCC Cinemas CINEMA
(☎07-4052 1166; Cairns Central Shopping Centre, McLeod St) Mainstream films, cheap tickets on Tuesdays.

Shopping

Cairns offers the gamut of shopping, from high-end boutiques like Louis Vuitton to garishly kitsch souvenir barns. You'll have no trouble finding a box of macadamia nuts, some emu or crocodile jerky, fake designer sunglasses and tropical-fish fridge magnets.

Mud Markets MARKET
(Pier Marketplace; 9am-3pm Sat & Sun) Live entertainment, craft and organic produce are all on offer here. Of course, if your supply of 'Cairns Australia' T-shirts is running low...they have that, too.

Cairns Central Shopping Centre SHOPPING CENTRE
(www.cairnscentral.com.au; McLeod St; 9am-5.30pm Mon-Wed, Fri & Sat, to 9pm Thu, 10am-4.30pm Sun) Enormous centre with a huge range of speciality stores selling everything from books to bikinis.

Woolworths SUPERMARKET
(103 Abbott St; 9am-9pm daily) Chain supermarket with a massive selection geared towards Cairns' travellers (sunscreen, SIM cards etc).

Night Markets MARKET
(www.nightmarkets.com.au; The Esplanade; 4.30pm-midnight) Tacky souvenirs, trinkets and cheap massages are the order of the day here.

Absells Chart Map Centre BOOKS, MAPS
(Main Street Arcade, 85 Lake St) Absells carries an impressive range of quality regional maps, topographic maps and nautical charts.

Information

EMERGENCY

Ambulance, fire & police (000; 24hr)

Police Station (07-4030 7000; 5 Sheridan St)

INTERNET ACCESS

Most tour-booking agencies and accommodation places have internet-enabled PCs and wi-fi; dedicated internet cafes are clustered along Abbott St, between Shields and Aplin Sts.

MEDICAL SERVICES

Cairns Base Hospital (07-4050 6333; The Esplanade) Has a 24-hour emergency service.

Cairns City 24 Hour Medical Centre (07-4052 1119; cnr Florence & Grafton Sts) General practice and dive medicals.

Cairns Travel Clinic (07-4041 1699; www.ctlmedical.com.au; 15 Lake St; 8.30am-5.30pm Mon-Fri, 9am-noon Sat) Vaccinations and supplies such as anti-malarials.

MONEY

Most of the major banks have branches with ATMs and foreign exchange; private currency-exchange bureaus line The Esplanade and are open longer hours.

American Express (1300 139 060; 63 Lake St) In Westpac Bank.

Travelex (07-4041 6043; Shop 73, Cairns Central Shopping Centre; 9am-5pm Mon-Wed & Sat, 9am-7pm Thu, 10am-4pm Sun)

POST

Post Office (07-4051 3099; Shop 115, Cairns Central Shopping Centre; 9am-5pm Mon-Fri, 9am-noon Sat)

TOURIST INFORMATION

Plenty of places stick up 'i' signs and call themselves 'information centres', but they're basically tour-booking agencies. All hostels have a booking desk and can offer information.

Cairns & Tropical North Visitor Information Centre (1800 093 300; www.cairnsgreatbarrierreef.org.au; 51 The Esplanade; 8.30am-6.30pm daily) Government-run centre that doles out impartial advice and can book accommodation and tours.

Cairns Discount Tours (07-4055 7158; www.cairnsdiscounttours.com.au) Knowledgeable booking agent for day trips and tours, specialising in last-minute deals.

Destination Cairns (1800 807 730, 07-4051 4055; cnr Sheridan & Aplin Sts) Destination Cairns has wheelchair access and information and tour bookings.

Far North Queensland Volunteers (07-4041 7400; www.fnqvolunteers.org; 68 Abbott St) Arranges volunteer positions with nonprofit community groups.

Royal Automobile Club of Queensland (RACQ; 07-4042 3100; www.racq.com.au; 537 Mulgrave Rd, Earlville) Maps and information on road conditions state-wide, including Cape York. For a 24-hour recorded road-report service, call 1300 130 595.

Getting There & Away

AIR

Qantas (13 13 13; www.qantas.com.au), **Virgin Australia** (13 67 89; www.virginaustralia.com) and **Jetstar** (13 15 38; www.jetstar.com.au) all service Cairns, with flights to/from Brisbane, Sydney, Melbourne, Darwin (including via Alice Springs) and Townsville. There are international flights to/from places including China and Singapore.

THE BAMA WAY

From Cairns to Cooktown, you can see the country through Indigenous eyes along the **Bama Way** (www.bamaway.com.au). Bama (pronounced Bumma) means 'person' in the Kuku Yalanji and Guugu Yimithirr languages, and highlights include tours with Indigenous guides, such as the Walker family tours on the Bloomfield Track, and Willie Gordon's enlightening Guurrbi Tours in Cooktown. Pick up a Bama Way map from visitor centres.

Skytrans (☎1300 759 872, 07-4040 6799; www.skytrans.com.au) Skytrans services Cape York and remote north Queensland towns.

Hinterland Aviation (☎07-4040 1333; www.hinterlandaviation.com.au) Hinterland Aviation has one to three flights daily except Sunday to/from Cooktown (one way $410, 40 minutes).

BUS

Cairns is the hub for Far North Queensland buses.

Greyhound Australia (☎1300 473 946; www.greyhound.com.au) Has four daily services down the coast to Brisbane ($295, 29 hours) via Townsville ($59, six hours), Airlie Beach ($130, 11 hours) and Rockhampton ($190, 18 hours). Bus passes can reduce costs. Departs from Reef Fleet Terminal, at the southern end of The Esplanade.

Premier Motor Service (☎13 34 10; www.premierms.com.au) Runs one daily service to Brisbane ($205, 29 hours) via Innisfail ($19, 1½ hours), Mission Beach ($19, two hours), Tully ($26, 2½ hours), Cardwell ($30, three hours), Townsville ($55, 5½ hours) and Airlie Beach ($90, 10 hours). Departs from stop D, Lake St Transit Centre. Cheaper bus passes available.

Trans North (☎07-4095 8644; www.transnorthbus.com; Cairns Central Rail Station) Has five daily bus services connecting Cairns with the tableland, serving Kuranda ($8, 30 minutes, five daily), Mareeba ($18, one hour, one to three daily), Atherton ($23.40, 1¾ hours, one to three daily). Ask about connections to Ravenshoe and Chillagoe. Departs from Cairns Central Rail Station; buy tickets when boarding.

John's Kuranda Bus (☎0418 772 953) Runs a service between Cairns and Kuranda two to five times daily ($5, 30 minutes). Departs from Lake Street Transit Centre.

Sun Palm (☎07-4087 2900; www.sunpalmtransport.com) Runs northern services from Cairns to Port Douglas ($40, 1½ hours) via Palm Cove and the northern beaches (from $20) and Mossman ($45, 1¾ hours). Departures from the airport and CBD.

Country Road Coachlines (☎07-4045 2794; www.countryroadcoachlines.com.au) Runs a daily bus service between Cairns and Cooktown ($80) and Cape Tribulation ($50) on either the coastal route (Bloomfield Track via Port Douglas and Mossman) or inland route (via Mareeba), depending on the day of departure and the condition of the track. Departures from the Reef Fleet Terminal.

CAR & MOTORCYCLE

All major car-rental companies have branches in Cairns and at the airport, with discount car- and campervan-rental companies proliferating throughout town. Daily rates start at around $45 for a late-model small car and around $80 for a 4WD. The big boys such as **Hertz** and **Europcar** are located in **Cairns Square** (cnr Shields & Abbott Sts). If you're in for the long haul, check out the noticeboard on Abbott St for used campervans and ex-backpackers' cars.

Britz Australia (☎07-4032 2611, 1800 331 454; www.britz.com.au; 419 Sheridan St) Hires out campervans.

East Coast (☎1800 028 881, 07-5592 0444; www.eastcoastcarrentals.com.au; 146 Sheridan St)

Choppers Motorcycle Tours & Hire (☎0408-066 024; www.choppersmotorcycles.com.au; 150 Sheridan St) Hire a Harley (from $190 a day) or smaller bikes (from $75). Also offers motorcycle tours.

TRAIN

The *Sunlander* departs from Cairns' **train station** (Bunda St) on Tuesday, Thursday and Saturday for Brisbane (one way from $200, 31½ hours); the Scenic Railway runs daily to/from Kuranda. Contact **Queensland Rail** (☎13 16 17; www.traveltrain.com.au).

Getting Around

TO/FROM THE AIRPORT

The airport is about 7km north of central Cairns; many accommodation places offer courtesy pick-ups. Sun Palm (p432) meets all incoming flights and runs a shuttle bus (adult/child $12/6) to the CBD. You can also book airport transfers to/from Cairns' northern beaches ($20), Palm Cove ($20), Port Douglas ($40), and Mossman ($45). **Black & White Taxis** (☎13 10 08) charges around $30.

BICYCLE

Bike hire is also available from some accommodation places.

Bike Man (☎07-4041 5566; www.bikeman.com.au; 99 Sheridan St; per day/week $15/60) Hire, sales and repairs.

Cairns Bicycle Hire (☎07-4031 3444; www.cairnsbicyclehire.com.au; 47 Shields St; per day/week from $25/65, scooters per day from $85) Groovy bikes and scooters.

BUS

Sunbus (☎07-4057 7411; www.sunbus.com.au; Lake St Transit Centre) runs regular services in and around Cairns from the Lake St Transit Centre, where schedules are posted. Useful routes include: Flecker Botanic Gardens/Edge Hill and Machans Beach (bus 131), Holloways Beach and Yorkeys Knob (buses 112, 113, 120), and Trinity Beach, Clifton Beach and Palm Cove (buses 110, 111). Most buses heading north go via Smithfield. All are served by the late-running night service (N). Heading south, bus 140 runs as far as Gordonvale.

TAXI

Black & White Taxis has a rank near the corner of Lake and Shields Sts, and one on McLeod St, outside Cairns Central Shopping Centre.

Islands off Cairns

Cairns day trippers can easily head out to Green Island, as well as Fitzroy Island and Frankland Islands National Parks for a bit of sunning, snorkelling and indulging.

Around Cairns

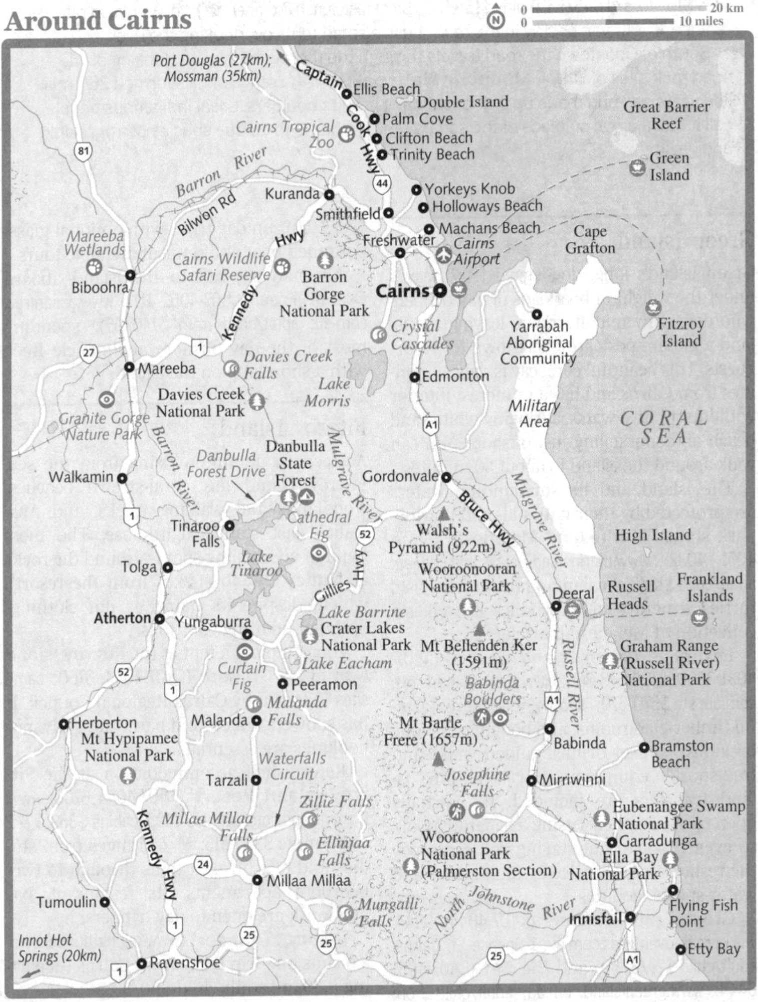

CAIRNS TO COOKTOWN – THE INLAND ROAD

It's 332km (about four hours' drive) from Cairns to Cooktown via this cattle, cockie 'n' croc route. You can either access the Mulligan Hwy from Mareeba, or via the turn-off just before Mossman. The road travels past rugged ironbarks and cattle-trodden land before joining the Cooktown Developmental Rd at Lakeland. From here it's another 80km to Cooktown.

The tiny town of **Mt Molloy** marks the start of the Mulligan Hwy. The **National Hotel** (07-4094 1133; www.mountmolloynationalhotel.com.au; Main St, Mt Molloy; s/d $40/80) has accommodation and pub grub (mains $12 to $24, open lunch and dinner), while **Mt Molloy Cafe & Takeaway** (07-4094 1187; mains $6-15), aka 'Lobo Loco', doles out everything from dim sums and burritos to boxes of cornflakes, or a shot of bourbon at its bar.

The Palmer River gold rush (1873–83) occurred about 70km to the west, throwing up boom towns Palmerville and Maytown; little of either remain today. You'll find food, fuel and road crews at the **Palmer River Roadhouse** (07-4060 2020; unpowered/powered sites $15/20, s/d $45/55, mains $15-25; breakfast, lunch & dinner; @). You can also pitch a tent, park your van or stay in the roadhouse's safari tents overlooking the river.

South of Cooktown the road travels through the thoroughly sinister-looking blackened rock piles of **Black Mountain National Park** – a range of hills formed 260 million years ago and made up of thousands of granite boulders. Local Indigenous people call it Kalcajagga, or 'place of the spears', and it's home to unique species of frog, skink and gecko.

Green Island

Green Island's long, dog-legged jetty heaves under the weight of boatloads of day trippers who depart by midafternoon, leaving the island a picture-postcard ghost town for resort guests. This beautiful coral cay is only 45 minutes from Cairns and has a rainforest interior with interpretive walks, a fringing white-sand beach and snorkelling just offshore. You can walk around the island in about 30 minutes.

The island and its surrounding waters are protected by their national- and marine-park status. **Marineland Melanesia** (07-4051 4032; www.marinelandgreenisland.com.au; adult/child $18/8) has an aquarium with fish, turtles, stingrays and crocodiles, as well as a collection of Melanesian artefacts.

Luxurious **Green Island Resort** (07-4031 3300, 1800 673 366; www.greenislandresort.com.au; ste $570-670; ❄@≋) has large, tasteful timber-clad rooms, and bookings include breakfast, sunset drinks, guided walks and free snorkle equipment and kayak hire. Island transfers are included. It's partially open to day trippers (using a separate pool), so even if you're not staying you can enjoy the restaurants, bars, ice-cream parlour and water-sports facilities.

Great Adventures (07-4044 9944; www.greatadventures.com.au; 1 Spence St, Cairns; adult/child $79/37.50) and **Big Cat** (07-4051 0444; www.greenisland.com.au; adult/child from $79/37.50) run day trips, with optional glass-bottomed boat and semisubmersible tours.

Alternatively, sail to the island aboard **Ocean Free** (07-4052 1111; www.oceanfree.com.au; adult/child from $140/95), spending most of the day offshore at Pinnacle Reef, with a short stop on the island.

Fitzroy Island

A steep mountaintop rising from the sea, Fitzroy Island has coral-strewn beaches, woodlands and walking tracks, and Australia's last staffed lighthouse. The most popular snorkelling spot is around the rocks at **Nudey Beach** (1.2km from the resort), which, despite its name, is not clothing-optional, so bring your togs.

You can pitch a tent at the **Fitzroy Island Camping Ground** (07-4044 6700; camp sites $33), run by Cairns Regional Council. It has showers, toilets and barbecues; advance bookings are essential.

Refurbished accommodation at the **Fitzroy Island Resort** (07-4044 6700; www.fitzroyisland.com; studios $195, cabins $369, 1 & 2 bedroom ste $350-515; ❄≋) ranges from studios and beachfront cabins through to two-bedroom apartments. Its restaurant, bar and kiosk are open to day trippers.

Raging Thunder (www.ragingthunder.com.au) runs one trip a day from Cairns (departing 8.30am, adult/child $60/30).

Frankland Islands

If the idea of hanging out on one of five uninhabited coral-fringed islands with excellent snorkelling and stunning white sandy beaches appeals – and if not, why not? – cruise out to the Frankland Group National Park.

Camping is available on High or Russell Islands, which both feature rainforest areas – contact **Queensland National Parks** (☎13 74 68; www.nprsr.qld.gov.au; permits $5.45) for advance reservations and – in case you were getting any ideas about dropping out of life for a while – seasonal restrictions.

Frankland Islands Cruise & Dive (☎07-4031 6300; www.franklandislands.com.au; adult/child from $149/79) runs excellent day trips, which include a cruise down the Mulgrave River, snorkelling gear and lunch. Guided snorkelling tours with a marine biologist and diving packages are also offered. Transfers for campers to/from Russell Island are available. Boats depart from Deeral; transfers from Cairns and the northern beaches cost $16 per person.

You'll need to organise your own boat or charter to reach High Island.

Cairns' Northern Beaches

Since Cairns doesn't have a beach, locals and tourists head offshore to the islands or travel slightly north in search of golden sands. Most turn-offs from the Captain Cook Hwy lead to small communities taking advantage of an easy, relaxed seaside lifestyle. There's a distinctive beach-holiday vibe and each community has its own character: Yorkeys is popular with sailors, Trinity with families; Palm Cove is a swanky honeymoon haven. Only Ellis Beach and Palm Cove have camp sites.

Sunbus travels to the beaches throughout the week.

Holloways Beach

The Coral Sea meets a rough ribbon of sand at quiet Holloways Beach. It's a mostly residential area, with beachside homes making way for a handful of tourist developments.

Pacific Sands (☎07-4055 0277; www.pacificsandscairns.com; 1-19 Poinciana St; d $109-145; ❄📶🏊) is a complex of bright self-contained two-bedroom apartments stretching one block back from the beach.

At **Cairns Beach Resort** (☎07-4037 0400, 1800 150 208; www.cairnsbeachresort.com.au; 129 Oleander St; d $185-230; ❄@🏊) there's a flash tropical ambience to the large blocks of one-bedroom beachfront apartments.

The breezy cafe, **Strait on the Beach** (100 Oleander St; mains $15-20; ⏰7.30am-8.30pm daily), has a chunky timber deck overlooking the beach – perfect for reading the paper over coffee or breakfast.

Yorkeys Knob

The most appealing of Cairns' northern beaches, Yorkeys is a sprawling, low-key settlement on a white-sand beach. In the crescent-shaped Half Moon Bay is the marina, supporting 200 bobbing boats.

Kite Rite (☎07-4055 7918; www.kiterite.com.au; Shop 9, 471 Varley St; per hr $80) offers stand-up paddleboard, kite- and windsurfing instruction, including gear hire, and a two-day certificate course ($499).

A block or so back from the beach, **Villa Marine** (☎07-4055 7158; www.villamarine.com.au; 8 Rutherford St; d $99-139; ❄📶🏊) is the best-value spot in Yorkeys. Friendly owner Peter makes you feel at home in the retro-style, single-storey self-contained apartments arranged around a pool.

Yorkeys Knob Boating Club (☎07-4055 7711; www.ykbc.com.au; 25-29 Buckley St; mains $17-28; ⏰noon-3pm, 6-9pm daily, 8-10am Sat & Sun; 🖉), a diamond find, serves up seafood and faves such as burgers and steaks. Go for the cod if it's on the menu, or the cooked-to-perfection calamari, order a schooner (or two – there's a local courtesy bus) and take a seat on the deck and dream about sailing away on one of the luxury yachts moored out the front.

Trinity Beach & Around

High-rise developments detract from Trinity Beach's long stretch of sheltered white sand, but holidaymakers love it – turning their backs to the buildings and focusing on what is one of Cairns' prettiest northern beaches. Accommodation is plentiful along the beachfront.

Self-contained apartments are just footsteps from the beach at **Castaways** (☎07-4057 6699; www.castawaystrinitybeach.com.au; cnr Trinity Beach Rd & Moore St; 1-/2-bedroom apt $110/135; ❄🏊), which has three pools, spas, tropical gardens and good stand-by rates.

L'Unico Trattoria (☑07-4057 8855; www.lunico.com.au; mains $16-44; ☺noon-late daily; ☑), opening to a wrap-around wooden deck, serves stylish Italian cuisine, including veal with sweet-potato mash, homemade four-cheese gnocchi and wood-fired pizzas, along with specials such as Moreton Bay bugs cooked with wine and garlic. It has a beachside location, and a stellar wine list.

Clifton Beach

Local and leisurely, Clifton Beach has a good balance of residential and holiday accommodation and services. You can walk north along the beach about 2km to Palm Cove from here.

Clifton Palms (☑07-4055 3839; www.cliftonpalms.com.au; 35-41 Upolu Esplanade; 1/2-bedroom apt $90/145; ❄@☀) has freestanding single-storey apartments backed by a curtain of green hills, with a big poolside barbecue area.

Opposite Clifton Palms, **Clifton Capers Bar & Grill** (☑07-4059 2311; www.cliftoncapers.com; 14 Clifton Rd; mains $18-38; ☺3pm-late Tue-Fri, 11.30am-late Sat & Sun) is highly rated among locals and has a range of pastas, pizzas and seafood. It's a pleasant, relaxed setting, and there's live music on Thurdays and Sundays.

Palm Cove

More intimate than Port Douglas and much more upmarket than its southern neighbours, Palm Cove is essentially one big promenade along Williams Esplanade, with a stretch of coarse white-sand beach and top-notch restaurants luring sun lovers out of their luxury resorts. Sir Elton John reportedly owns a house/recording studio in the headlands here.

Beach strolls, shopping and leisurely swims will be your chief activities here, but there's no excuse for not getting out on the water. **Palm Cove Watersports** (☑0402 861 011; www.palmcovewatersports.com; kayak hire per hour $33) organises 1½-hour early-morning sea-kayaking trips ($53) and half-day paddles to Double Island (adult/child $93/73), offshore from Palm Cove.

Just west of Palm Cove, the **Cairns Tropical Zoo** (☑07-4055 3669; www.cairnstropicalzoo.com.au; Captain Cook Hwy; adult/child $33/16.50, Cairns Night Zoo adult/child $97/48.50; ☺8.30am-4pm daily) offers an up-close wildlife experience with crocodiles and snakes, koala photo sessions and kangaroo feeding. Transfers are available from Palm Cove, Port Douglas and Cairns and the northern beaches.

Most of Palm Cove's accommodation has a minimum stay of two nights. The **Palm Cove Camping Ground** (☑07-4055 3824; 149 Williams Esplanade; unpowered/powered sites $19/27) is a council-run beachfront camping ground near the jetty, with barbecue area and laundry. There are no cabins, but it's the only way to do Palm Cove on the cheap!

The bright self-contained apartments at **Silvester Palms** (☑07-4055 3831; www.silvesterpalms.com.au; 32 Veivers Rd; 1-/2-/3-bedroom apt $110/135/195; ❄☀☀) are an affordable alternative to Palm Cove's city-sized resorts, and good for families.

Once the private residence of an army brigadier, the **Reef House Resort & Spa** (☑07-4080 2600; www.reefhouse.com.au; 99 Williams Esplanade; d from $279; ❄@☀☀) is more intimate and understated than most of Palm Cove's resorts. Whitewashed walls, wicker furniture and big beds romantically draped in muslin all add to the air of refinement. The Brigadier's Bar works on a quaint honesty system; complimentary punch is served by candlelight at twilight. The inhouse restaurant and spa are both well-regarded. Off-season rates offer good value.

Step through the large lobby at **Peppers Beach Club & Spa** (☑1300 987 600, 07-5665 4426; www.peppers.com.au; 123 Williams Esplanade; d from $175; ❄@☀☀) and into a wonder world of swimming pools – there's the sand-edged lagoon pool and the leafy rainforest pool and swim-up bar, plus tennis courts and spa treatments. Even the standard rooms have private balcony spas, and the penthouse suites (from $549) have their own rooftop pool. The top-notch service exceeds expectations.

The charming **Melaleuca Resort** (☑1800 629 698; www.melaleucaresort.com.au; 85-93 Williams Esplanade; d $195-250; ❄☀) has 24 one-bedroom apartments, all with kitchens, balconies and laundry facilities.

Palm Cove has some fine restaurants and cafes strung along the esplanade. All of the resort hotels have swish dining options open to nonguests.

Join hipsters as they down pints at **The Rising Sun** (☑07-4059 0889; 95 Williams Esplanade; dishes $16-36, drinks from $6; ☺11am-midnight daily), a sassy, breezy beachfront bar/bistro. If you get too hammered, stumble through to the attached Sarayi boutique hotel to sleep it off.

The **Surf Club Palm Cove** (☎07-4059 1244; 135 Williams Esplanade; meals $14-30; ⏲6pm-late) is a great local for a drink in the sunny garden bar. Bargain-priced seafood plus decent kids' meals.

Apres Beach Bar & Grill (☎07-4059 2000; www.apresbeachbar.com.au; 119 Williams Esplanade; mains $23-39; ⏲7.30am-late daily) is decked out with a zany interior of bric-a-brac hanging from the ceiling. Regular live music and karaoke nights keep the drinkers entertained.

Award-winning **Nu Nu** (☎07-4059 1880; www.nunu.com.au; 123 Williams Esplanade; mains $31-47; ⏲11am-late Mon-Fri, 8.30am-late Sat & Sun) has one of the highest profiles on the coast, so you'll need to book ahead to dine in its designer setting. The modern Australian dishes combine the best of Asian and Mediterranean cuisine. Dishes such as the red curry barramundi and mushroom-poached Cape Grim tenderloin will induce indecision and the tasting menus (from $95) are good value.

A rustic beach house near the jetty is the setting for zingy Asian dining at **Beach Almond** (☎07-4059 1908; www.beachalmond.com; 145 Williams Esplanade; mains $28-59; ⏲11am-3pm Sat & Sun, 6-10pm daily). Black-pepper prawns, ginger pork belly, Singaporean mud crab and Balinese barra are among the fragrant, freshly prepared innovations. Live jazz on Sundays helps ease the wallet-busting prices.

The two-storey, ice cream–coloured **Paradise Village Shopping Centre** (113 Williams Esplanade) has a post office (with internet access for $4 an hour), a small supermarket and a newsagent.

Ellis Beach

Ellis Beach is the last of the northern beaches and the closest to the highway, which runs right past it. The long, sheltered bay is a stunner, with a palm-fringed, patrolled swimming beach and stinger net in summer. This is where the coastal drive to Port Douglas really gets interesting.

At **Hartley's Crocodile Adventures** (☎07-4055 3576; www.crocodileadventures.com; adult/child $33/17.50; ⏲8.30am-5pm daily), daily events include tours of the croc farm, along with feedings, 'crocodile attack' shows, and boat cruises on its lagoon.

Ellis Beach Oceanfront Bungalows (☎1800 637 036, 07-4055 3538; www.ellisbeach.com; Captain Cook Hwy; unpowered sites $32, powered sites $35-46, cabins without bathroom $95-115, bungalows $155-210; ❄@≋) is a palm-shaded beachfront paradise with camp sites, cabins and contemporary bungalows that enjoy widescreen ocean TV.

Across the road from the Bungalows, **Ellis Beach Bar 'n' Grill** (Captain Cook Hwy; mains $15-28; ⏲8am-8pm daily) has good food, live music some Sunday afternoons and, best of all, pinball. If you don't bring your own food, it's the only place to eat in the area.

ATHERTON TABLELAND

Waterfalls, lush green pastures complete with well-fed dairy cows and patches of remnant rainforest make up the tablelands, though the bordering areas are dramatically different; expect dry, harsh outback and much thinner cattle. In some areas the altitude reaches more than 1000m, making this area one of the most pleasant to travel around – weather-wise. Plenty of people self-drive around the area, though since most towns are close together, bike tours are popular.

ℹ Getting There & Around

There are bus services to the main towns from Cairns (generally three services on weekdays, two on Saturday and one on Sunday), but not to the smaller towns or all the interesting areas *around* the towns, so it's worth hiring your own wheels.

Trans North (p440) has regular bus services connecting Cairns with the tableland, departing from Cairns Central Rail Station and running to Kuranda ($8, 30 minutes), Mareeba ($16.80, one hour), Atherton ($22, 1¾ hours) and Herberton ($28, two hours).

John's Kuranda Bus (☎0418 772 953) runs a service between Cairns and Kuranda two to five times daily ($5, 30 minutes).

Kerry's (☎0427 841 483) serves Ravenshoe ($33, 2½ hours). John's and Kerry's buses depart from Cairns' Lake St Transit Centre.

Kuranda

POP 3000

Kuranda is a hop, skip and jump – or make that a historic train journey, sky-rail adventure or winding bus trip – from Cairns. The village itself is sprawling sets of markets nestled in a spectacular tropical-rainforest setting where you'll find everything from made-in-China Aboriginal art to emu oil. The locals are a friendly bunch, well prepared for the hordes of tourists that arrive in the morning and depart with full bellies, bags and memory cards at almost precisely 3.30pm. There's little reason to stay overnight, as this is really a day-trippers' domain.

Sights & Activities

There are several signed **walks** in the markets, and a short walking track (the Jumrum Walk) through **Jumrum Creek Conservation Park** (off Barron Falls Rd) leads you to a big population of fruit bats.

Further south, Barron Falls Rd divides: the left fork will take you to a wheelchair-accessible **lookout** over the Barron Falls, while the right fork becomes the Jungle Walk section of the trail and leads down to the Barron River. From there, the River Walk leads back up to the Scenic Railway station and back into town.

Kuranda Original Rainforest Markets MARKET
(www.kurandaoriginalrainforestmarket.com.au; Therwine St; 9am-3pm) With revamped boardwalks terraced in the rainforest and wafting incense, the original markets first opened in 1978 and are still the best place to pick up hemp products, handicraft, and sample local produce such as honey and fruit wines.

Heritage Markets MARKET
(www.kurandamarkets.com.au; Rob Veivers Dr; 9am-3pm) Across the road from the original markets, the heritage markets overflow with souvenirs and crafts such as ceramics, emu oil, jewellery, clothing, secondhand books and that kangaroo scrotum bottle opener you've always wanted.

Rainforestation ZOO
(07-4085 5008; www.rainforest.com.au; Kennedy Hwy; adult/child $40/21; 9am-4pm) An enormous tourist park east of town with a wildlife section, river cruises and an Aboriginal show.

Shambala Animal Kingdom ZOO
(07-4093 7777; www.shambalaanimalkingdom.com.au; Kennedy Hwy; adult/child $28/14, morning feeding sessions $50/30; 9am-4.30pm daily) Spot safari animals and catch morning animal-feeding sessions with lions; 9km west of Kuranda.

Kuranda Koala Gardens ANIMAL SANCTUARY
(07-4093 9953; www.koalagardens.com; Heritage Markets, Rob Veivers Dr; adult/child $16.50/8.25; 9.45am-4pm daily) Check out native Aussie animals such as koalas, wallabies, wombats and reptiles galore.

Australian Butterfly Sanctuary ANIMAL SANCTUARY
(07-4093 7575; www.australianbutterflies.com; 8 Rob Veivers Dr; adult/child $18/9; 9.45am-4pm daily) Flighty, pretty things. Half-hour tours available.

Birdworld ANIMAL SANCTUARY
(07-4093 9188; www.birdworldkuranda.com; Heritage Markets, Rob Veivers Dr; adult/child $16.50/8.25; 9am-4pm) In the Heritage Markets; home to 80 bird species.

Australian Venom Zoo ZOO
(07-4093 8905; www.tarantulas.com.au; 8 Coondoo St; adult/child $16/10; 10am-4pm daily) For lovers of reptiles and creepy crawlies.

Kuranda Riverboat CRUISE
(07-4093 7476; adult/child $15/7; hourly 10.45am-2.30pm) Behind the train station. Hop aboard for a 45-minute calm-water cruise along the Barron River.

Sleeping & Eating

Kuranda Rainforest Park CAMPGROUND $
(07-4093 7316; www.kurandarainforestpark.com.au; 88 Kuranda Heights Rd; unpowered/powered sites $28/30, s/d without bathroom $30/60, cabins $95-110;) This excellent, well-tended park lives up to its name with grassy camping sites enveloped in rainforest. The basic but cosy private 'backpacker rooms' open to a tin-roofed timber deck, cabins come with poolside or garden views, and there's an on-site restaurant (mains $14 to $36, open 6pm to 10pm Wednesday to Sunday). It's a 10-minute walk from town via a forest trail.

Kuranda Hotel Motel MOTEL $$
(07-4093 7206; www.kurandahotel.com.au; cnr Coondoo & Arara Sts; d $120;) Locally known as the 'bottom pub', the back of the Kuranda Hotel Motel has spacious '70s-style motel rooms with exposed brick and tinted crinkle-cut glass. The pub is open for lunch daily and dinner Thursday to Saturday.

★ **Petit Cafe** CREPERIE $
(www.petitcafekuranda.com; Shop 35, Kuranda Original Rainforest Markets; crepes $10-17) Tucked at the back of the original markets, *le* French

Kuranda

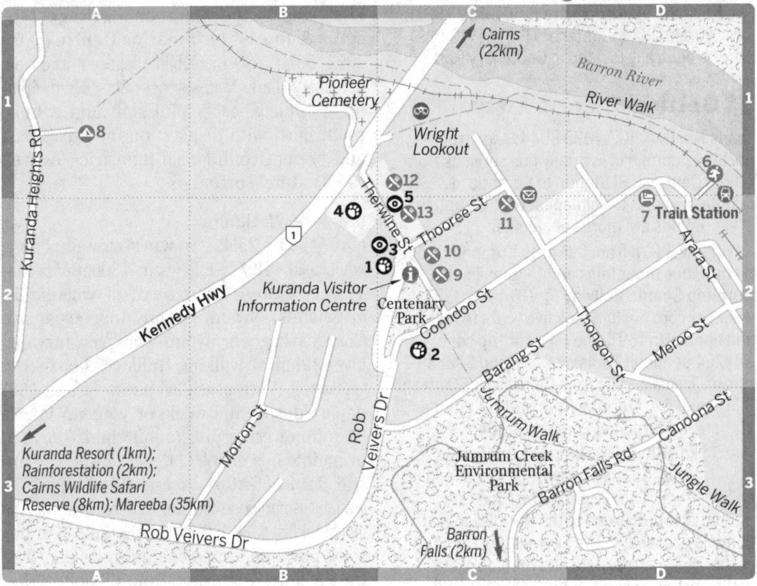

Kuranda

Sights

1 Australian Butterfly Sanctuary C2
2 Australian Venom Zoo C2
Birdworld .... (see 3)
3 Heritage Markets C2
4 Kuranda Koala Gardens B2
5 Kuranda Original Rainforest Markets C2

Activities, Courses & Tours

6 Kuranda Riverboat D1

Sleeping

7 Kuranda Hotel Motel D2
8 Kuranda Rainforest Park A1

Eating

9 Annabel's Pantry C2
10 German Tucker C2
11 Kuranda Coffee Republic C2
12 Petit Cafe C1
13 Sweet Leaf Living Foods C2

chef Aurelien Breguet whips up a mouth-watering range of crepes with savoury or sweet fillings. Fresh produce and winning combinations such as macadamia pesto and feta cheese make this *the* only place to eat if you're short on time.

Kuranda Coffee Republic CAFE $
(10 Thongon St; coffees $3.50-5.50; ⌚8am-4pm Mon-Fri, 9am-4pm Sat & Sun) Food is basically limited to biscotti but have a chat with locals over your latte at this popular coffee shop.

Sweet Leaf Living Foods ORGANIC, VEGAN $
(Shop 39, Kuranda Original Rainforest Markets; dishes $9.50-12.50; ⌚10am-3pm Wed-Sun; ✎) Organic vegan juices, wraps and salads to sate your appetite while the hippie owner regales you with little-known facts about coconut trees in Australia.

German Tucker GERMAN, AUSTRALIAN $
(Therwine St; dishes $6-16, beers from $6; ⌚10am-2.30pm daily) Emu, crocodile or kangaroo sausages with sauerkraut? German Tucker serves extreme Australiana/traditional German fare and German beer.

Annabel's Pantry BAKERY $
(Therwine St; pies $4.50-5; ⌚10am-3pm daily; ✎) With around 25 pie varieties, including kangaroo and spinach-and-feta rolls, Annabel's is great for lunch on a budget.

Information

The **Kuranda visitor centre** (07-4093 9311; www.kuranda.org; Centenary Park; 10am-4pm) is centrally located in Centenary Park.

Getting There & Away

Trans North (07-4095 8644; www.transnorthbus.com) has five daily bus services from Cairns Central Rail Station to Kuranda ($8, 30 minutes). This is the cheapest way, though the other options are more spectacular.

Winding 34km from Cairns to Kuranda through picturesque mountains and 15 tunnels, the **Kuranda Scenic Railway** (07-4036 9333; www.ksr.com.au) line took five years to build and opened in 1891. The 1¾-hour trip costs $48/24 per adult/child one way, and $72/36 return. Trains depart from Cairns at 8.30am and 9.30am daily, returning from pretty Kuranda station on Arara St at 2pm and 3.30pm.

At 7.5km, **Skyrail Rainforest Cableway** (07-4038 1555; www.skyrail.com.au; adult/child one way $45/22.50, return $68/34; 9am-5.15pm) is one of the world's longest gondola cableways. The Skyrail runs from the corner of Kemerunga Rd and the Cook Hwy in the northern Cairns suburb of Smithfield (15 minutes' drive north of Cairns) to Kuranda (Arara St), taking 90 minutes. It includes two stops along the way with boardwalks and interpretive panels. The last departure from Cairns and Kuranda is at 3.30pm; transfers are available to/from the Cairns departure terminal. Combination Scenic Railway and Skyrail deals are available. As space is limited, only day packs are allowed on board; advance bookings are recommended.

Mareeba

POP 10,200

At the centre of industrious cattle, coffee and sugar enterprises, Mareeba is essentially an administrative and supply town for the northern tableland and parts of Cape York Peninsula. The main street boasts some quaint old facades (it almost passes for a midwest American town), and the region's natural beauty is typified by the expansive wetlands to the north. Mareeba is more desert than tableland but has some wonderful attractions nearby. If you're around in mid-July, don the RM Williams boots and be sure to see the **Mareeba Rodeo** (www.mareebarodeo.com.au) at Kerribee Park.

There's plenty of seasonal work, with mango season from January to March and avocado work from February to March. Check out the QITE website (www.qite.com.au).

Sights & Activities

First stop is the **Mareeba Heritage Museum & Tourist Information Centre** (07-4092 5674; www.mareebaheritagecentre.com.au; Centenary Park, 345 Byrnes St; 8am-4pm) FREE, which has helpful staff and a huge room filled with displays on the area's past and present commercial industries, as well as its natural surrounds.

Mareeba Wetlands PARK

(07-4093 2514; www.mareebawetlands.org; adult/child $15/7.50; 9am-4.30pm Apr-Jan) This is a 20-sq-km reserve of woodlands, grasslands, swamps and the expansive Clancy's Lagoon, a bird-watchers' nirvana. Over 12km of walking trails criss-cross the wetlands. Various safari tours (from $38) depart during the week, or you can take a 30-minute eco-cruise (adult/child $15/7.50) or paddle in a canoe ($15 per hour). The on-site **Jabiru Safari Lodge** (07-4093 2514; ww.jabirusafarilodge.com.au; cabins per person incl breakfast $128-150, all inclusive $198-229) has solar-powered tented cabins and a spa. Take the Pickford Rd turn-off from Biboohra, 7km north of Mareeba.

Granite Gorge Nature Park PARK

(07-4093 2259; www.granitegorge.com.au; adult/child $7.50/2) Granite Gorge Nature Park is a privately owned park with huge granite boulders, rock wallabies, walking tracks and waterfalls tumbling into a croc-free swimming hole. There are picnic areas, a campground (unpowered/powered sites per person including park entry $12/14) and self-contained cabins ($95). Granite Gorge is 12km southwest of Mareeba along Chewko Rd, from where the turn-off is signposted to your right.

Mt Uncle Distillery DISTILLERY

(07-4086 8008; www.mtuncle.com; 1819 Chewko Rd, Walkamin; 10am-4.30pm daily) Mt Uncle Distillery produces whisky, as well as rum, honey vodka and seasonal liqueurs (tastings $10). Don't miss a meal at its understated **Bridges Cafe** (mains $10-19), hand-built by the owners from the timber of a former local bridge. The wood-fired pizzas are delicious. It's signposted along Chewko Rd, 15.5km south of Mareeba.

Sleeping & Eating

Kerribee Park Camping Grounds CAMPGROUND $

(07-4092 1654; www.mareebarodeo.com.au; Mareeba Rodeo Grounds, 614 Dimbulah Rd; unpowered/powered sites $10/14) Cheap camping but no shade.

Jackaroo Motel MOTEL $$
(07-4092 2677; www.jackaroomotel.com; 340 Byrnes St; d $130;) Mareeba's most upmarket motel has a saltwater swimming pool and a barbecue area.

Mareeba Lodge MOTEL $$
(07-4092 2266; www.mareebalodge.com.au; 21 Byrnes St; s $90-100, d $100-110;) Friendly motel, situated in a central location.

Ant Hill Hotel & Steakhouse STEAKHOUSE $$
(07-4092 2147; 79 Byrnes St; mains $15-30; lunch & dinner) At this pub in the town centre you'll find tasty specials with all the classics – barra, burgers and steak, and a bargain bar menu (mains $10).

Chillagoe

POP 350

Even on a day trip from Cairns, the charismatic former gold-rush town of Chillagoe, about 140km west of Mareeba, can fulfil any romantic notion you may have of the outback – but owing to the distance involved in travelling here, an overnight stay is preferable.

Chillagoe's excellent visitor centre, the **Hub** (07-4094 7111; www.chillagoehub.com.au; Queen St; 8.30am-5pm Mon-Fri, 8am-3.30pm Sat & Sun), has interesting historical displays. Knowledgeable staff can direct you to **Indigenous rock-art sites**, the local **swimming hole**, the old **smelter site**, a hodge-podge little **history museum** with a piano played during silent movies, and an eccentric local with a cool old **Ford collection**. It also books ranger-guided tours of Chillagoe's amazing, must-see **limestone caves** (adult/child $31/16.50). Three of the 500-plus caves can be visited: **Donna** (9am), **Trezkin** (11am) and **Royal Arch** (1.30pm). There are several other caves you can self-explore but bring a torch/headlamp and wear sturdy shoes.

The annual **Chillagoe Rodeo** (www.chillagoerodeo.com.au) takes place in May.

Rustic-on-the-outside, modern-on-the-inside miners shacks make up **Chillagoe Cabins** (07-4094 7206; www.chillagoe.com; Queen St; s/d $108/140;), where the owner has a small wildlife-rescue menagerie and offers town tours (from $20). There's a camp kitchen and barbecue, or you can order home-cooked meals. Chillagoe's former post office is now the **Chillagoe Guesthouse** (07-4222 1135; www.chillagoeguesthouse.com.au; 16-18 Queen St; d $120-140, units $140-300;). Rates include a brekkie hamper and free wi-fi.

The **Chillagoe Bus Service** (07-4094 7155; adult/child $38/29) departs from Chillagoe on Monday, Wednesday and Friday, returning from Mareeba on the same days. **Billy Tea Bush Safaris** (www.billytea.com.au; tours adult/child $195/140) runs day tours from Cairns.

Atherton

POP 7300

Atherton, the 'capital' of the tableland, is a farming town with little to offer travellers but a rest in the journey, or a chance to get their hands and shoes dirty picking fruit and vegetables year-round. **The Atherton Tableland Information Centre** (07-4096 7405; www.athertontablelands.com.au; cnr Main & Silo Rds) has useful information, including self-drive itineraries, Australia-wide booking facilities and seasonal work updates.

As you approach Atherton from Herberton in the southwest, you see the **Hou Wang Temple** (www.houwang.org.au; 86 Herberton Rd; adult/child $10/5; 11am-4pm Wed-Sun), which is testament to the Chinese migrants who flocked to the area to search for gold in the late 1800s. It's the only Chinese temple in Australia built of corrugated iron and is on the site of Atherton's former Chinatown.

The **Crystal Caves** (07-4091 2365; www.crystalcaves.com.au; 69 Main St; adult/child $23/15; 8.30am-5pm Mon-Fri, to 4pm Sat, 10am-4pm Sun, closed Feb) is a mineralogical museum in an artificial grotto that winds for a block under Atherton's streets. It houses rose-quartz boulders, dazzling blue topaz and assorted fossils. Don a hard hat and check out the pièce de résistance – the world's largest amethyst geode, a 3.25m, 2.7-tonne giant excavated from Uruguay.

The **Barron Valley Hotel** (07-4091 1222; www.bvhotel.com.au; 53 Main St; s/d without bathroom $40/60, with bathroom $60/85;) is a heritage-listed art-deco beauty, with tidy rooms popular with long-term guests, and a restaurant serving hearty meals (mains $18 to $35).

Perched on Hallorans Hill, the **Atherton Blue Gum B&B** (07-4091 5149; www.athertonbluegum.com; 36 Twelfth Ave; d $130-180;)

has superb views from the verandah. Rooms have pine panelling and big windows, and there's a heated pool and spa. There's a newer sister property up the road.

Woodlands Tourist Park (07-4091 1407; www.woodlandscp.com.au; 141 Herberton Rd; unpowered/powered sites $27/35, cabins $90-140;) is a favourite with families thanks to its waterfall pool and playground. It also has refurbished miners-quarters rooms with polished floorboards, and there are shared cooking facilities and free wi-fi. The park is 1.5km south of the centre.

Lake Tinaroo & Around

Lake Tinaroo is a mecca for the Aussie who loves nothing but setting up the tent, opening up the esky and planning for a day's fishing. The enormous artificial lake and dam were originally created for the Barron River hydroelectric power scheme, and drowned trees still poke their bones out of the water. **Tinaroo Falls**, at the northwestern corner of the lake, is the main settlement.

Barramundi fishing is legendary in the croc-free artificial lake and is permitted year-round. Fishing permits (per week/year $7.45/37, children free) covering all of Queensland's dams are readily available from local businesses and accommodation places, or order online at **Queensland's Department of Primary Industries** (www.dpi.qld.gov.au/fishweb). Head out for a fish or simply a sunset cruise with a glass of wine aboard the super-comfy 'floating lounge room' skippered by **Lake Tinaroo Cruises** (0457 033 016; www.laketinaroocruises.com.au; 2/4hr boat charters $200/300). Rates are for the whole boat (up to 12 people).

The **Barra Bash** (www.tinaroobarrabash.com.au) fishing competition is held annually during October around the full moon; it's a great event attracting loads of people.

The **Danbulla Forest Drive** winds its way through rainforest and softwood plantations along the north side of the lake. It's 28km of unsealed but well-maintained road passing a number of picnic areas and attractions, including pretty **Lake Euramoo** and the **Cathedral Fig** – a gigantic strangler fig tree shouldering epiphytes nestling in its branches. The tree is accessed by a boardwalk and signposted along a sealed road off the Gilles Hwy. There are five **Queensland Parks campgrounds** (13 74 68; www.nprsr.qld.gov.au; permits $5.45) in the Danbulla State Forest. All have water, barbecues and toilets; advance bookings are essential.

In Tinaroo Falls, the **Discovery Lake Tinaroo Holiday Park** (07-4095 8232; www.discoveryholidayparks.com.au; 3 Tinaroo Falls Dam Rd; unpowered/powered sites $27/31, cabins $89-129;) is a modern, well-equipped and shady camping ground with fuel, a small shop and an on-site cafe (mains $10.50 to $17). It also rents out tinnies ($90 per half-day) and canoes ($10 per hour).

Yungaburra

POP 1150

Only 12km from Atherton is this friendly town packed with charming cafes, excellent restaurants, day spas and some of the best accommodation in the region. The locals and architecture give this town its quaint village atmosphere, and it's the ideal spot to hang your backpack and establish a base for the surrounding area. **Yungaburra Information Centre** (07-4095 2416; www.yungaburra.com; 16 Cedar St) doles out town and regional info.

The **Tablelands Folk Festival** (http://tff.fnqnet.org/festival; tickets $55, camping $22.50) is a fabulous weekend-long community event held in Yungaburra and Herberton every October. It features music, workshops, performances and a market. The **Yungaburra Markets** (www.yungaburramarkets.com; Gillies Hwy; 7.30am-12.30pm) are held in town on the fourth Saturday of every month; at this time the town is besieged by avid craft and food shoppers. About 3km out of town, the magnificent 500-year-old **Curtain Fig** is a must-see. Looking like a *Lord of the Rings* prop, it has aerial roots that hang down to create a feathery curtain.

Yungaburra has two **platypus-viewing platforms** on Peterson Creek – one by the bridge on the Gillies Hwy and another at a spot known as Allumbah Pocket (the town's original name) further west. The two are joined by a 2km **walking trail** along the creek, which continues east to Railway Bridge.

On the Wallaby (07-4095 2031; www.onthewallaby.com; 34 Eacham Rd; tours from $99, night canoeing $30) runs excellent half-day bike and canoe tours – including wildlife spotting while night canoeing. Nonguests are welcome. **Tableland Adventure Guides** (0448 517 979; www.tablelandadventureguides.com.au; half-day tours min 2 people from $95) runs guided bike tours along tracks and rail trails, kayaking on Lake Tinaroo and hiking in World Heritage rainforest.

Sleeping

On the Wallaby HOSTEL $

(07-4095 2031; www.onthewallaby.com; 34 Eacham Rd; camping $10, dm/d shared bathroom $24/55; @) With handmade timber furniture and mosaics, and spotless rooms (without TV), it's easy to feel at home here. Nature-based tours depart daily; tour packages and transfers ($30 one way) are available from Cairns.

Kookaburra Lodge MOTEL $

(07-4095 3222; www.kookaburra-lodge.com; cnr Oak St & Eacham Rd; s/d $80/90;) Stylish little rooms opening out to restful tropical gardens.

Williams Lodge B&B $$$

(07-4095 3449; www.williamslodge.com; Cedar St; d $170-275; @) Built in 1911 and still owned and run by the Williams family, all of the rooms in this heritage Queenslander open onto the verandah, including enormous suites fitted with original period furniture and four-poster beds (some with spa baths). Grand touches include a pianola lounge, a wine bar and a billiard table. Under 12s aren't allowed.

Foxwell Park B&B $$$

(07-4096 6183; www.foxwellpark.com.au; Foxwell Rd; r $200-250; @) In rolling countryside 7km southwest of Yungaburra, Foxwell's beautifully restored pair of century-old timber buildings have original tiles and pressed-tin ceilings. Suites open onto deep, private verandahs overlooking the 24-hectare estate. Excellent French-inspired restaurant (mains $25 to $35; open dinner Wednesday to Sunday, nightly for guests).

Mt Quincan Crater Retreat CABIN $$$

(07-4095 2255; www.mtquincan.com.au; Peeramon Rd; d $245-320;) In secluded rainforest, these luxurious pole cabins and tree houses have been built for sheer countryside indulgence, with double spas, indoor and outdoor showers, wood fires and stupendous views. Children aren't permitted. It's 3km south of town; follow the road to Peeramon to the signposted turn-off.

Eating & Drinking

Whistlestop Cafe CAFE $

(07-4095 3913; 36 Cedar St; mains $9-15; 9.30am-3.30pm Mon-Fri, 8am-3pm Sat, 8am-noon Sun;) This garden-set cafe serves breakfast, rice slices and vegie lasagne, but leave room for the souffle-style Tuscany chocolate cake.

★ **Flynn's** MEDITERRANEAN $$

(07-4095 2235; 17 Eacham Rd; mains lunch $6-19, dinner $30, 3-course menus $50; 11am-2.30pm & 5.30-10.30pm Fri-Tue) Between ducking outside to pick his own vegies and running the whole place almost single-handedly, Kiwi culinary maestro Liam has managed to put Yungaburra on the foodie map. The menu changes daily, but expect a mix of Italian, French and Mediterranean dishes such as duck liver cognac pâté and fish of the day. Lunch is simpler but just as good.

Nick's Restaurant SWISS, ITALIAN $$

(07-4095 9330; www.nicksrestaurant.com.au; 33 Gillies Hwy; mains $16.50-36.50; 11.30am-3pm Sat & Sun, 5.30-11pm Tue-Sun;) This Swiss chalet-style number makes for a fun night out, with costumed staff, beer steins, a piano-accordion serenade and possibly some impromptu yodelling. Food spans schnitzels to bratwurst and pasta, plus several vegetarian options. Nick also owns the **pizzeria** next door.

Lake Eacham Hotel PUB

(07-4095 3515; 6-8 Kehoe Pl; bar 11am-11pm) Better known as the 'Yungaburra Pub', down a pint at this local and admire the swirling wooden staircase of this grand old hotel.

Crater Lakes National Park & Around

Part of the Wet Tropics World Heritage Area, the two mirror-like crater lakes of Lake Eacham and Lake Barrine are both croc-free and nestled among rainforest easily reached by sealed roads off the Gillies Hwy. Camping is not permitted.

The larger of the two lakes, **Lake Barrine** is cloaked in thick old-growth rainforest; a 5km walking track around its edge takes about 1½ hours. The **Lake Barrine Rainforest Tea House** (07-4095 3847; www.lakebarrine.com.au; Gillies Hwy; mains $7.50-18; 8am-3pm daily) sits out over the lakefront. Upstairs you'll feel like you're aboard a boat as you take Devonshire tea or order a meal. To actually be aboard a boat, visit the booking desk downstairs for 45-minute **lake cruises** (adult/child $16/8; 9.30am, 11.30am, 1.30pm). A 100m stroll away are two enormous, neck-tilting, 1000-year-old kauri pines.

The crystal-clear waters of **Lake Eacham** are ideal for swimming and spotting turtles; there are sheltered lakeside picnic areas, a swimming pontoon and a boat ramp. The 3km lake-circuit track is an easy walk and takes less than an hour. Stop in at the **Rainforest Display Centre** (McLeish Rd; ⌚9am-1pm Mon, Wed & Fri) at the ranger station for information on the area.

The pretty **Lake Eacham Caravan Park** (☎07-4095 3730; www.lakeeachamtouristpark.com; Lakes Dr; unpowered/powered sites $19/25, cabins $90-110; @), 1km down the Malanda road from Lake Eacham, has cosy cabins and its cafe serves breakfast, light lunches and tea.

Crater Lakes Rainforest Cottages (☎07-4095 2322; www.craterlakes.com.au; Lot 17, Eacham Cl, Lake Eacham; d $240; ❄@) has four individually themed timber cottages. Ideally spaced in its own private patch of rainforest, each is a romantic hideaway filled with candles, fresh flowers, and logs for the wood stoves, with spa baths, fully fitted kitchens and breakfast hampers with bacon, eggs and chocolates, plus fruit to feed the birds. There's no minimum stay, but you probably won't want to leave. The cottages are off Lakes Dr.

Rose Gums (☎07-4096 8360; www.rosegums.com.au; Land Rd, Butcher's Creek; d $297 & $342) offers totally private, eco-friendly treetop pads that are fitted out with spas, wood-burning heaters and king-size beds. All come with breakfast hampers, kitchens and barbecues, but you can also dine on Mediterranean cuisine at the on-site restaurant (mains $35, open 5.30pm to 10pm). Minimum stay is two nights.

Malanda & Around

POP 2050

Forming the eastern part of the Atherton–Yungaburra–Malanda triangle is this little town 15km south of Lake Eacham. Its claim to fame is that it has the nation's longest continually running picture theatre, the **Majestic** (established 1927), but locals are still mightily proud that Australian cricketer Don Bradman played cricket here.

Guided rainforest walks (per person $15), led by members of the Ngadjonji community, can be organised through Malanda's **visitor centre** (☎07-4095 1234; www.malandafalls.com) at the **Malanda Dairy Centre** (☎07-4095 1234; www.malandadairycentre.com; 8 James St; tours adult/child $11/7; ⌚10am & 11am Mon-Fri). The dairy centre offers 40-minute factory tours including a cheese platter or milkshake. Its licensed **cafe** (mains $14-28; ✎) is the best place to eat in town.

Along the Atherton road, on the outskirts of town, are **Malanda Falls**, home to saw-shelled turtles and red-legged pademelons. Right next to Malanda Falls, **Malanda Falls Caravan Park** (☎07-4096 5314; www.malandafalls.com.au; 38 Park Ave; unpowered/powered sites $18/22, cabins $75-85) has tidy cabins and camp sites within earshot of the flowing falls. Kids will love the on-site animal pen.

On the Millaa Millaa Rd, 10km from Malanda, is the tiny village of **Tarzali**, which offers some accommodation options including the lovely **Tarzali Pewtermill B&B** (☎07-4094 1122; www.tarzalipewtermill.com; 52 Sheehan Rd, Tarzali; d $95-110; ❄). **Tarzali Lakes Fishing Park** (☎07-4097 2713; www.tarzalilakes.com; Millaa Millaa Rd, Tarzali; fishing 2hr/day $20/40; ⌚10am-4pm Thu-Tue) has artificial lakes stocked with jade perch and barramundi; you can fish or just buy your 'catch' and other food smoked on-site at the cafe (mains $10.50 to $36). There's plenty of bird life here, plus self-guided platypus-spotting tours ($5).

The superbly designed all-timber pole houses of the **Canopy** (☎07-4096 5364; www.canopytreehouses.com.au; Hogan Rd, Tarzali, via Malanda; d $229-349; 📶) 🍃 are set amid a pristine patch of old-growth rainforest. There's a minimum two-night stay. Surrounded by forest on the Johnstone River, **Rivers Edge Rainforest Retreat** (☎07-4095 2369; www.riversedgeretreat.com.au; d from $298; ❄@) has two secluded luxury timber lodges with lavish touches like a sliding-glass wall in the spa bathroom and a wood fire. It's a minimum two-night stay.

Travellers Rest (☎07-4096 6077; 1720 Millaa Millaa Rd, Tarzali; s/d without bathroom incl breakfast $60/95), an English-style country farmhouse 5km south of Malanda, is a cosy budget place with a billiard room, a formal dining room and fresh, floral rooms. Book ahead for Saturday's murder-mystery nights.

Millaa Millaa & the Waterfall Circuit

Why stop at one waterfall when you can visit four (!) along this 16km 'waterfall circuit' near Millaa Millaa, 24km south of Malanda? Start by taking Theresa Creek Rd, 1km east of Millaa Millaa on Palmerston Hwy. **Millaa Millaa Falls**, the largest, has a swimming hole, change rooms and a grassy picnic spot. Continuing round the circuit, you reach **Zillie Falls**, where you can watch Teresa Creek falling into the abyss. Step down past fern fronds to the rocky **Ellinjaa Falls** before returning to the Palmerston Hwy, just 2.5km out of Millaa Millaa. A further 5.5km down the Palmerston Hwy there's a turn-off to **Mungalli Falls**, 5km off the highway.

At the country-style **Mungalli Creek Dairy** (☎07-4097 2232; www.mungallicreekdairy.com.au; 251 Brooks Rd; meals $18; ⏰10am-4pm, closed Feb), 3km off Palmerston Hwy, you can sample cheeses and creamy yoghurts or order cooked dishes like three-cheese pie followed by a sinfully rich Sicilian cheesecake.

A little further along the Palmerston Hwy from Mungalli Creek Dairy is the Mamu Rainforest Canopy Walkway (p412).

At the **Falls Teahouse** (☎07-4097 2237; www.fallsteahouse.com.au; Palmerston Hwy; s/d incl breakfast $65/120; ⏰10am-5pm daily), you can sit next to the pot-belly stove, or on the back verandah overlooking rolling farmland to tuck into dishes such as pan-fried barra and local beef pies (meals $7 to $23). The three guest rooms are individually decorated with period furniture. It's at the intersection of the Millaa Millaa Falls turn-off.

Herberton

POP 2164

Herberton is a lovely town dotted with jacaranda trees and perched on a hilly area abutting the outback. Wonderful heritage buildings line the main street, which leads to the riverside site of a former tin mine. Herberton's star attraction is the **Herberton Historic Village** (☎07-4097 2002; www.herbertonhistoricvillage.com.au; 6 Broadway; adult/child $25/12; ⏰9am-5pm, last entry 3.30pm), a collection of 50 original buildings dating back as far as 1870 that have been moved here from various locales, restored and filled with some fascinating historic exhibits. Highlights include a pub, a blacksmith's workshop, Ada's frock salon, a school house and a grocery store.

Situated on the site of an old tin mine, the **Herberton Mining Museum & Information Centre** (☎07-4096 3473; www.herbertonvisitorcentre.com.au; 1 Jacks Rd, Great Northern Mining Centre; museum adult/child $5/3; ⏰9am-4pm) has an informative display on the region's mining history and geology, including a gallery of minerals. It's the starting point for a number of **historic walking trails** (from 1km to 12km) and stocks trail maps.

The best place to eat in town is the laid-back **Jacaranda Coffee Lounge** (☎07-4096 2177; 52 Grace St; dishes $6-18; ⏰9.30am-7.30pm Tue-Fri) where you can chow down on fish burgers, steak sandwiches and even Asian-style dishes.

Accommodation is limited; try Herberton's original post office, which is now the **Herberton Heritage Cottage B&B** (☎0427 962 670; www.herbertonheritagecottage.com.au; 2 Perkins St; r $155; ❄). The two heritage-style rooms incorporate mod cons like spas and DVD players.

Mt Hypipamee National Park

Between Atherton and Ravenshoe, the Kennedy Hwy passes the eerie, and hard to pronounce, **Mt Hypipamee crater**, which could be a scene from a sci-fi film and certainly adds some vertigo to the itinerary. It's a scenic 700m (return) walk from the picnic area, past **Dinner Falls**, to this narrow, 138m-deep crater with its moody-looking lake far below.

Ravenshoe

POP 1442

Ravenshoe (pronounced *hoe*, not *shoe*) is home to 'Queensland's Highest Pub': **Hotel Tully Falls** stands proudly at the tip of this town at the grand altitude of 930m. **Ravenshoe Visitor Centre** (☎07-4097 7700; www.ravenshoevisitorcentre.com.au; 24 Moore St; ⏰9am-4pm daily) has helpful staff and is home to the **Nganyaji Interpretive Centre**, which explains the Jirrbal people's traditional lifestyle. Six kilometres northeast are 20 **wind turbines** that comprise the Windy Hill Wind Farm, fascinating when viewed up close.

Nearby waterfalls (no swimming) include **Little Millstream Falls**, 3km south of Ravenshoe; and **Tully Falls**, around 20km further south on the Tully Falls Rd (which doesn't go through to Tully). The 13m-high **Millstream Falls** (signposted off the Savannah Way towards Innot Hot Springs, from where it's 1km to the car park) are said to be the widest in Australia in flood.

Off the Kennedy Hwy, down a 4.5km unsealed road, **Possum Valley B&B** (07-4097 8177; www.bnbnq.com.au/possumvalley; Evelyn Central, via Ravenshoe; s/d $60/75) consists of two cottages clinging to the fringe of World Heritage–listed rainforest. The B&B uses solar and hydroelectricity and tank water.

PORT DOUGLAS TO COOKTOWN

Port Douglas

POP 3205

Port Douglas (or just 'Port') is the flashy playground of tropical northern Queensland. For those looking to escape Cairns' bustling traveller scene, Port Douglas is more sophisticated and more intimate. It also has a beautiful white-sand beach right on its doorstep, and the Great Barrier Reef is less than an hour offshore.

Accommodation options are spread all over the region, and the larger resorts spread themselves along the 6km-long Port Douglas Rd that links Captain Cook Hwy with the town centre. Busy, centre-of-town Macrossan St links the jetty and pier with Four Mile Beach on Trinity Bay.

Sights & Activities

On a sunny, calm day, Four Mile Beach will take your breath away. It is sand and palm trees for as far as you can see – head up to **Flagstaff Hill** (Island Point Rd) lookout for a great view.

At the Cooktown Hwy turn-off, **Wildlife Habitat Port Douglas** (07-4099 3235; www.wildlifehabitat.com.au; Port Douglas Rd; adult/child $32/16; 8am-5pm) endeavours to keep and showcase native animals, such as tree kangaroos, in enclosures that closely mimic their natural environment. It's located at the entrance to Port Douglas, off Captain Cook Hwy, about 6km from the town centre.

On Sunday the grassy foreshore of Anzac Park spills over with the excellent **Port Douglas Markets** (end of Macrossan St; 8am-1.30pm Sun). You'll find stalls selling arts, crafts and jewellery, local tropical fruits, food stalls and even massage tents.

The **Port Douglas Yacht Club** (07-4099 4386; www.portdouglasyachtclub.com.au; 1 Spinnaker Cl) offers free sailing with club members every Wednesday afternoon. It's a great way to get out on the water and meet some locals.

Several companies offer PADI open-water certification as well as advanced dive certificates, including **Blue Dive** (0427 983 907; www.bluedive.com.au; 4-5 day open-water courses from $750). For one-on-one instruction, learn with **Tech Dive Academy** (07-3040 1699; www.tech-dive-academy.com; 4-day open-water courses from $1090).

Port Douglas Boat Hire BOATING
(07-4099 6277; Berth C1, Marina Mirage; per hr $33-43) Rents a range of boats, including dinghies ($33 per hour) and canopied, family-friendly pontoon boats ($43 per hour) to take on the inlet. Fishing gear available.

St Mary's by the Sea CHURCH
(6 Dixie St) FREE Worth a peek inside, this white timber church was built in 1911 and relocated to its seaside position in 1989.

Wind Swell WATERSPORTS
(0427 498 042; www.windswell.com.au; from $149) Offers kite surfing, paddle boarding and wakeboarding for everyone from beginners to high flyers.

Tours

The unrelenting surge of visitors to the reef off Port Douglas has impacted on its general condition, and although you'll still see colourful corals and marine life, it has become patchy in parts. Tours typically make two to three stops on the outer and ribbon reefs, including St Crispins, Agincourt, Chinaman and Tongue Reefs. Trip prices generally include reef tax, snorkelling and transfers from your accommodation, plus lunch and refreshments. Add around $250 for an introductory dive. Certified divers will pay around $250 for two dives with all gear included.

Several operators offer cruises to Low Isles, a coral cay surrounded by a lagoon and topped by a lighthouse. The cay offers good snorkelling and the chance to see turtle-nesting grounds. Trips leave from Marina Mirage.

There are numerous outfits running day trips to Cape Tribulation, some via Mossman Gorge. Many of the tours out of Cairns also do pick-ups from Port Douglas.

BTS Tours GUIDED TOUR
(07-4099 5665; www.btstours.com.au; 49 Macrossan St; Daintree adult/child $150/115, Mossman Gorge $48/26) Tours to the Daintree Rainforest and Cape Trib, including canoeing. Also to Mossman Gorge.

Port Douglas

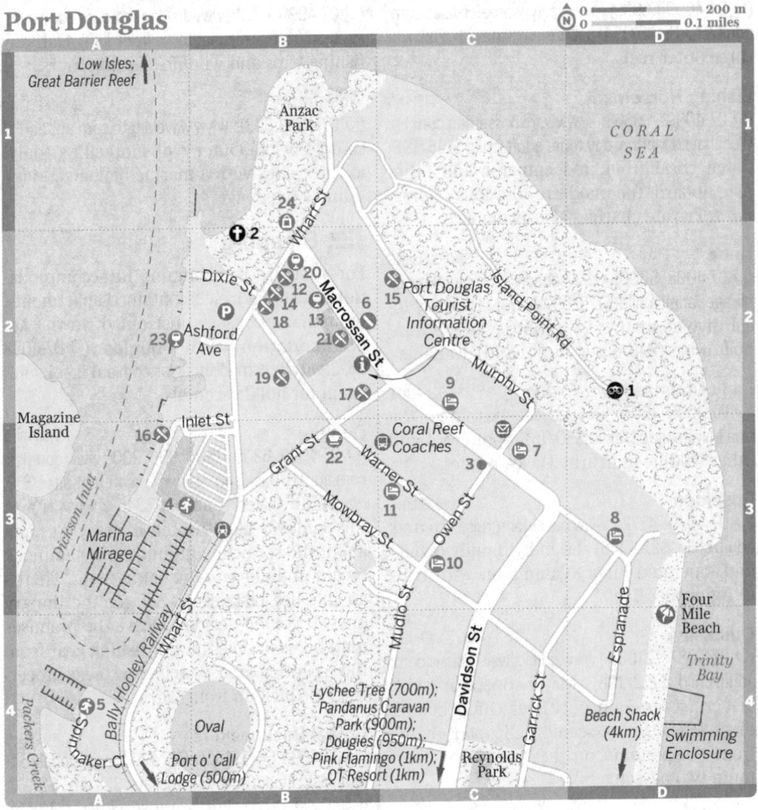

Port Douglas

Sights
1 Flagstaff Hill D2
2 St Mary's by the Sea B2

Activities, Courses & Tours
3 BTS Tours C3
4 Port Douglas Boat Hire A3
5 Port Douglas Yacht Club A4
6 Tech Dive Academy B2

Sleeping
7 Accommodation Port Douglas C3
8 By the Sea Port Douglas D3
9 Global Backpackers C2
10 Hibiscus Gardens C3
11 ParrotFish Lodge C3

Eating
12 2 Fish B2
13 Coles Supermarket B2
14 Harrisons Restaurant B2
15 Nautilus C2
16 On the Inlet A3
17 Original Mocka's Pies B2
18 Salsa Bar & Grill B2
19 Seafood House B2

Drinking & Nightlife
20 Court House Hotel B2
21 Iron Bar B2
22 Origin Espresso B3
Port Douglas Yacht Club .... (see 5)
23 Tin Shed A2

Shopping
24 Port Douglas Markets B1

Calypso
SNORKELLING

(☑07-4099 6999; www.calypsoreefcruises.com; adult/child $195/154) Large catamaran visiting three outer reefs.

Fishing Norseman
FISHING

(☑07-4099 6668; www.mvnorseman.com.au; Closehaven Marina; day tours adult/child $215/195) Catch coral trout, red emperor and other fish aboard the modern 18m-long *Norseman*. Private charters also available.

Haba
SNORKELLING

(☑07-4098 5000; www.habadive.com.au; Marina Mirage; adult/child $175/99) Long-standing local dive company; 25-minute glass-bottom-boat tours ($16/8 per adult/child) available.

Lady Douglas River Cruise
CRUISE

(☑07-4099 1603; www.ladydouglas.com.au; Marina Mirage; adult/child $30/15) Spot crocs and other wildlife at nearby Dickson Inlet.

Poseidon
SNORKELLING

(☑07-4099 4772; www.poseidon-cruises.com.au; adult/child $210/145) Friendly family-owned and -operated luxury catamaran with trips to Agincourt Reef.

Quicksilver
CRUISE

(☑07-4087 2100; www.quicksilver-cruises.com; adult/child $212/106) Major operator with fast cruises to Agincourt Reef. Offers helmet dives ($142), plus scenic helicopter flights from the pontoon on the reef ($148, minimum two passengers).

Reef & Rainforest Connections
ECOTOUR

(☑07-4035 5566; www.reefandrainforest.com.au; adult/child from $163/105) 🍃 A range of day ecotours, including Cape Trib and Bloomfield Falls, Kuranda and Mossman Gorge.

Sail Tallarook
SAILING

(☑07-4099 4070; www.sailtallarook.com.au; adult/child half-day sail $99/75) Historic 90ft yacht sailing to the Low Isles. Sunset cruises include cheese platters; BYO drinks.

Sailaway
SAILING, SNORKELLING

(☑07-4099 4772; www.sailawayportdouglas.com; adult/child $205/125) Popular sailing and snorkelling trip to the Low Isles that's great for families. Also offers 90-minute twilight sails ($50) off the Port Douglas coast.

Synergy
SAILING, SNORKELLING

(☑07-4084 2800; www.synergyreef.com.au; adult/child $275/205) With a maximum of just 12 passengers, the *Synergy* sails to the outer reefs.

Tropical Fishing & Eco Tours
FISHING, TOUR

(☑07-4099 4272; www.fishingecotours.com; fishing trips from $90; inlet tours from $30) Half-day fishing trips and wildlife-spotting tours.

Wavelength
SNORKELLING

(☑07-4099 5031; www.wavelength.com.au; adult/child $225/165) Outer reef snorkelling (only) at three sites with a marine biologist. Maximum 30 passengers.

🛏 Sleeping

Port Douglas is swimming in accommodation, most of it in self-contained apartments, or upmarket resorts just out of town. **Accommodation Port Douglas** (☑07-4098 5522; www.accomportdouglas.com.au) is a useful agent for holiday rentals.

Dougies
HOSTEL $

(☑07-4099 6200, 1800 996 200; www.dougies.com.au; 111 Davidson St; per person tent sites $13, dm $26, d shared bathroom $34; ❄@🛜☀) At this laid-way-back hostel, it's easy to hang about the sprawling grounds in a hammock by day and move to the bar at night. There's an inhouse restaurant, Zai, for the hungry ones. If you do decide to leave the premises for a bit, rent bikes and/or fishing gear from the reception area, which also stocks groceries. Free pick-up from Cairns.

Global Backpackers
HOSTEL $

(☑07-4099 5641, 1800 682 647; www.globalportdouglas.com.au; 38 Macrossan St; dm $27-32, d $80; ❄@🛜) Port's most central hostel doesn't have a pool, but it's bang in the middle of Macrossan St above the Rattle n Hum restaurant-bar. Modern rooms are decked out in sleek dark-brown tones, doubles all have bathroom, and the kitchen and common room open onto a big balcony.

ParrotFish Lodge
HOSTEL $

(☑1800 995 011, 07-4099 5011; www.parrotfishlodge.com; 37-39 Warner St; dm $25-33, d with/without bathroom $80/70; ❄@☀) Energetic backpackers place with extreme beach decor and lots of freebies, including breakfast and pick-ups from Cairns.

Pandanus Caravan Park
CAMPGROUND $

(☑07-4099 4034; www.pandanuscp.com.au; 97-107 Davidson St; unpowered/powered sites $35/42, cabins $80-90, units $105; ❄@🛜☀) Five minutes' stroll from the beach, this large, shady park has a good range of cabins and free gas barbecues.

Port o' Call Lodge
HOSTEL **$**

(☑ 07-4099 5422; www.portocall.com.au; cnr Port St & Craven Cl; dm $38, d $110-129; ❀ @ 🛜 🏊) 🔹 Low-key solar- and wind-powered, YHA-associated hostel with a good-value bistro (mains $17 to $26).

Pink Flamingo
BOUTIQUE HOTEL **$$**

(☑ 07-4099 6622; www.pinkflamingo.com.au; 115 Davidson St; r $125 & 185; ❀ @ 🛜 🏊) Flamboyant fuchsia-, purple- and orange-painted rooms opening to private walled courtyards (with hammocks, outdoor baths and outdoor showers) and a groovy mirror-balled alfresco bar make the Pink Flamingo a fun place. Outdoor movie nights, a gym and bike rental are also offered. Gay-owned, gay-friendly and all-welcoming (except for kids).

By the Sea Port Douglas
APARTMENT **$$**

(☑ 07-4099 5387; www.bytheseaportdouglas.com. au; 72 Macrossan St; d from $185; ❀ @ 🛜 🏊) Close to the beach and town centre, the 12 self-contained rooms here are spread over three levels – the upper rooms have 'filtered' views through the palm trees to the beach. Rooms are self-contained and renovated in neutral hues. Cheap online rates.

★ QT Resort
RESORT **$$$**

(☑ 07-4099 8900; www.qtportdouglas.com.au; 87-109 Port Douglas Rd; d $240-260, villa $290-410; ❀ @ 🛜 🏊) Port's newest resort is also its hippest with its cool mod decor and DJ-spinning lounge beats in the cocktail bar. The inhouse restaurant, Bazaar, serves up a quality buffet spread and staff are all smiles as they lead you to your stylish rooms complete with flat-screen TVs and plush beds. QT also hosts Moonlight Cinema. Competitive online packages.

Sea Temple Resort & Spa
RESORT **$$$**

(☑ 07-4084 3500, 1800 833 762; www.mirvachotels.com.au; Mitre St; d from $300; ❀ @ 🛜 🏊) Port Douglas' most luxurious five-star and its championship links golf course are set in lush tropical gardens near the southern end of Four Mile Beach. Rooms range from slick spa studios to the opulent 'swim out' penthouse with direct access to the enormous lagoon pool. Rooms start at $199 online.

Hibiscus Gardens
RESORT **$$$**

(☑ 1800 995 995; www.hibiscusportdouglas.com. au; 22 Owen St; d $145-385; ❀ @ 🏊) Balinese influences of teak furnishings and fixtures, bi-fold doors and plantation shutters – as well as the occasional Buddha – give this stylish

resort an exotic ambience. The in-house day spa, specialising in indigenous healing techniques and products, is a great place to be pampered.

✖️ Eating

Original Mocka's Pies
TAKEAWAY **$**

(☑ 07-4099 5295; 9 Grant St; pies $4.50-6; ⊙ 8am-4pm) An institution serving amazing Aussie pies filled with exotic ingredients such as crocodile and kangaroo. The steak pie is oozing with chunks of tender, slow-cooked Black Angus.

Four Mile Seafood & Takeaway
SEAFOOD, BURGERS **$**

(Four Mile Beach Plaza, Barrier St, Four Mile Beach; dishes $8-15; ⊙ 9am-8pm Mon-Sat, 11am-8pm Sun) Whips up fish and chips and tasty burgers.

Salsa Bar & Grill
MODERN AUSTRALIAN **$$**

(☑ 07-4099 4922; www.salsaportdouglas.com.au; 26 Wharf St; mains $20-37; ⊙ 11.30am-3pm & 5.30-10.30pm; 🅿) In a white Queenslander, Salsa is a stayer on Port's often fickle scene. Try the Cajun jambalaya (rice with prawns, yabbies, squid, crocodile sausage and smoked chicken) or the kangaroo loin with sweet potato pie.

On the Inlet
SEAFOOD **$$**

(☑ 07-4099 5255; www.portdouglasseafood.com; 3 Inlet St; mains $24-40; ⊙ 11.30am-10pm) At this restaurant jutting out over Dickson Inlet, tables are spread out along an atmospheric deck where you can await the daily 5pm arrival of George the 250kg grouper, who comes to feed. Take up the bucket-of-prawns-and-a-drink deal for $18 from 3.30pm to 5.30pm, or choose your own crayfish and mud crabs from the live tank.

Beach Shack
MODERN AUSTRALIAN **$$**

(☑ 07-4099 1100; www.the-beach-shack.com.au; 29 Barrier St, Four Mile Beach; mains $23-34; ⊙ 11.30am-3pm & 5.30-10pm; 🅿) There'd be an outcry if this locals' favourite took its macadamia-crumbed eggplant (with grilled and roasted veggies, goat's cheese and wild rocket) off the menu. The unique setting, a lantern-lit garden with sand underfoot, lures diners to the southern end of Four Mile Beach. Good reef fish, pizzas and blackboard specials, too.

★ Harrisons Restaurant
MODERN AUSTRALIAN **$$$**

(☑ 07-4099 4011; www.harrisonsrestaurant.com.au; 22 Wharf St; mains $38-56, 4-/6-course $75/100)

Marco-Pierre-White–trained chef and owner Spencer Patrick whips up culinary gems that stand toe-to-toe with Australia's best. Fresh locally sourced produce is turned into dishes such as rabbit croquettes with goats curd fondant and Angus rib-eye *steak frites* served with melt-in-your-mouth bone marrow. The degustation menu is a bargain. Possibly the only place in Port where diners bother swapping their thongs for shoes.

Nautilus MODERN AUSTRALIAN **$$$**
(☎07-4099 5330; www.nautilus-restaurant.com.au; 17 Murphy St; mains $33-50; ⊙dinner) Once you make it up a steep hill, you'll find intimate white-clothed tables amid tall palms at this decades-old fine-dining institution. The menu spans seafood and steaks including dishes such as mud crab cooked in yellow coconut and kaffir lime. The *pièce de résistance* is the seven-course chef's tasting menu ($115; $170 with paired wines). Children under eight aren't accepted.

2 Fish SEAFOOD **$$$**
(☎07-4099 6350; www.2fishrestaurant.com.au; 7/20 Wharf St; mains $29-40; ⊙11.30am-3pm & 5.30-10pm) 2 Fish offers a seafood extravaganza: more than 15 types of fish, from coral trout to red emperor and wild barramundi, are prepared in a variety of innovative ways, or go for the decadent seafood platter for two ($160).

Self-Catering

Stock up on supplies at the large **Coles Supermarket** (11 Macrossan St) in the Port Village shopping centre. For locally caught seafood, including prawns, mud crabs and a big range of fish, head to **Seafood House** (11 Warner St; seafood platters from $45; ⊙9.30am-5pm).

Drinking & Nightlife

Drinking and dining go hand in hand in Port Douglas. Even before the cutlery is packed away, many restaurants become inviting places for a drink.

Tin Shed LICENSED CLUB
(www.thetinshed-portdouglas.com.au; 7 Ashford Ave; drinks from $4; ⊙10am-10pm) Port Douglas' Combined Services Club is a locals' secret. This is a rare find: bargain dining on the waterfront, and even the drinks are cheap. Sign in, line up and grab a table on the river- or shore-fronting deck.

Origin Espresso COFFEE SHOP
(☎07-4099 4586; cnr Grant & Warner Sts; coffee $3.50-4; ⊙8am-4pm daily) Origin, with its silk-smooth lattes and complex espressos, is the only place worth getting coffee in Port.

Iron Bar PUB
(☎07-4099 4776; www.ironbarportdouglas.com.au; 5 Macrossan St; mains $15-30; ⊙11am-3am) A bit of wacky outback-shearing-shed decor never goes astray in Queensland. It's well done – all rustic iron and distressed timber. After polishing off your aged steaks, grab a beer and head upstairs for a flutter on the cane-toad races ($5).

Court House Hotel PUB
(☎07-4099 5181; www.courthouseportdouglas.com.au; cnr Macrossan & Wharf Sts; ⊙11am-late) Commanding a prime corner location, the 'Courty' is a lively local, with cover bands on weekends.

Port Douglas Yacht Club LICENSED CLUB
(www.portdouglasyachtclub.com.au; 1 Spinnaker Cl; ⊙bar 4-10pm Mon-Fri, noon-10pm Sat & Sun) Another local favourite, with a spirited nautical atmosphere. Inexpensive meals are served nightly.

☆ Entertainment

Moonlight Cinema CINEMA
(www.moonlight.com.au; 87-109 Port Douglas Rd, QT Resort, Port Douglas; tickets adult/child $16/12; ⊙Jun-Oct) Bring a picnic or hire a bean bag for twilight outdoor movie screenings.

ℹ Information

The **Port Douglas Tourist Information Centre** (☎07-4099 4540; www.tourismportdouglas.com.au; 50 Macrossan St; ⊙8am-6.30pm) has maps and makes tour bookings.

ℹ Getting There & Away

Sun Palm (☎07-4087 2900; www.sunpalmtransport.com) has frequent daily services between Port Douglas and Cairns ($35, 1½ hours) via the northern beaches and the airport, and up the coast to Mossman ($10, 20 minutes), Daintree Village and the ferry ($20, one hour), and Cape Tribulation ($48, three hours).

Airport Connections (☎07-4099 5950; www.tnqshuttle.com; adult/child $36/18; ⊙btwn 3am & 5pm) runs a shuttle-bus service ($36, four daily) between Port Douglas, Cairns' northern beaches and Cairns Airport, continuing on to Cairns CBD.

Country Road Coachlines (☎07-4069 5446; www.countryroadcoachlines.com.au) has a bus service between Port Douglas and Cooktown on the coastal route via Cape Tribulation three times a week ($70), weather permitting.

Getting Around

BICYCLE

Port Douglas Bike Hire (07-4099 5799; www.portdouglasbikehire.com.au; cnr Wharf & Warner Sts; per day $19) has a huge range of bikes for hire and offers advice on cycling routes.

BUS

Sun Palm runs in a continuous loop every half-hour (from 7am to midnight) from Wildlife Habitat Port Douglas to the Marina Mirage, stopping regularly en route. Flag down the driver at marked bus stops.

CAR & MOTORCYCLE

Port Douglas has plenty of small, local car-hire companies as well as major international chains, such as **Budget** (07-4099 5702; www.budget.com.au; 2/11 Warner St) and **Thrifty** (07-4099 5555; www.thrifty.com.au; 50 Macrossan St). It's just about the last place before Cooktown where you can hire a 4WD. Expect to pay around $65 a day for a small car and $130 a day for a 4WD, plus insurance.

TAXI

Port Douglas Taxis (13 10 08) offers 24-hour service.

Mossman

POP 1733

Mossman is an unassuming town criss-crossed with cane-train tracks and featuring the wonderful **Mossman Gorge** (07-4099 7000; www.mossmangorge.com.au; Mossman Gorge Centre; shuttle bus adult/child $5/2.50; 8am-6.30pm), which draws in tourists by the van-load. There's a great 2.4km walk there, and swimming is possible, but be aware of the danger of swimming after heavy rain.

To truly appreciate the gorge's cultural significance, book one of the 1½-hour Indigenous-guided **Kuku-Yalanji Dreamtime Walks** (www.yalanji.com.au; adult/child $50/25; 9am, 11am, & 3pm) through the **Mossman Gorge Centre**. This is the slick new gateway to the gorge, complete with an art gallery, retail section and an inhouse restaurant that serves bush tucker.

The Indigenous-run **Janbal Gallery** (07-4098 3917; www.janbalgallery.com.au; 5 Johnston Rd; 10am-5pm Tue-Sat) is a great place to browse or buy impressive artwork.

The rooms at **Mossman Gorge B&B** (07-4098 2497; www.bnbnq.com.au/mossgorge; Lot 15, Gorge View Cres; r $130-150) have dark timber floors, feature walls and antiques. The guest spaces are cosy, and the views and bird life are mesmerising. Breakfast is included. Up the road, the **Papillon** (07-4098 2760; www.papillonstays.com.au; 36 Coral Sea Dr, Mossman; r from $130;) is Mossman's best accommodation. It's a fabulous B&B complete with a pool, split-level living and modern, comfortable rooms.

Run by a talented French-Australian team, **Mojo's** (07-4098 1202; www.mojosbarandgrill.com.au; 41 Front St; mains $20-29; 11.30am-2pm Mon-Fri, 6pm-late Mon-Sat;) serves exquisite fusion fare such as gnocchi with blue cheese and caramelised pear, king crab and sweet corn risotto, pork belly spring rolls, and steaks and chops.

BTS (07-4099 5665; www.portdouglasbus.com; 49 Macrossan St, Port Douglas) has return shuttles from Port Douglas to Mossman Gorge (adult/child $22/15, 8.15am and 12.15pm) and also runs day trips to the gorge. **Coral Reef Coaches** (07-4098 2800; www.coralreefcoaches.com.au) runs coaches from Cairns (adult/child $40/20). Book ahead.

Daintree Village

POP 146

Surprisingly, given its tropical-rainforest surrounds, Daintree Village is not tree-covered; cattle farms operate in large clearings next to the Daintree River. Most folk come here to see crocodiles, and there are several small operators who will take you on croc-spotting boat tours. Otherwise, there's little more on offer.

Tours

Bruce Belcher's Daintree CRUISE
(07-4098 7717; www.daintreerivercruises.com; 1hr cruises adult/child $25/10) One-hour river cruises on a covered boat.

Daintree Argo Rainforest Tours TOUR
(0409 627 434; www.daintreeadventuretours.com.au; Upper Daintree Rd; 1hr tours $45) Rainforest and cattle-country tours aboard an open-topped amphibious vehicle.

Daintree River Wild Watch CRUISE
(07-4098 7068; www.daintreeriverwildwatch.com.au; 2hr cruises adult/child $55/35) Informative sunrise birdwatching cruises and sunset photography nature cruises.

DAINTREE NATIONAL PARK: THEN & NOW

The greater Daintree rainforest is protected as part of Daintree National Park. The area has a controversial history: despite conservationist blockades, in 1983 the Bloomfield Track was bulldozed through lowland rainforest from Cape Tribulation to the Bloomfield River, and the ensuing international publicity indirectly led the federal government to nominate Queensland's wet tropical rainforests for World Heritage listing. The move drew objections from the Queensland timber industry and the state government, but in 1988 the area was inscribed on the World Heritage list, resulting in a total ban on commercial logging within its boundaries.

World Heritage listing doesn't affect land ownership rights or control, and since the 1990s efforts have been made by the Queensland government and conservation agencies to buy back and rehabilitate freehold properties, add them to the Daintree National Park and install visitor-interpretation facilities. Sealing the road to Cape Tribulation in 2002 opened the area to rapid settlement, triggering the buy-back of hundreds more properties. Coupled with development controls, these efforts are now bearing fruit in the form of forest regeneration. Check out **Rainforest Rescue** (www.rainforestrescue.org.au) for more information.

Biodiversity

Far North Queensland's wet tropics area has amazing pockets of biodiversity. The Wet Tropics World Heritage Area stretches from Townsville to Cooktown and covers 894,420 hectares of coastal zones and hinterland, diverse swamp and mangrove-forest habitats, eucalypt woodlands and tropical rainforest. It covers only 0.01% of Australia's surface area, but has 36% of all the mammal species, 50% of the bird species, around 60% of the butterfly species and 65% of the fern species.

Sleeping & Eating

Daintree Riverview CAMPGROUND $
(☎0409 627 434; www.daintreeriverview.com; Stewart St; unpowered/powered sites $10/30, cabins $99-110) Riverside camping and good-value cabins.

Red Mill House B&B $$$
(☎07-4098 6233; www.redmillhouse.com.au; 11 Stewart St; s/d $160/220; ❄@≋) The large verandah overlooking the rainforest garden is a prime spot to observe the resident bird life. There are four well-appointed rooms, a large communal lounge and library, and a two-bedroom family unit (from $270). Guided birding walks are available on request.

Croc Eye Cafe CAFE $$
(☎07-4098 6229; www.croceyecafe.com; 3 Stewart St; mains $17-40; ⊙8am-3pm) Serves fish and chips, burgers and, of course, crocodile dishes such as spaghetti and *san choi bao*.

Around Cape Tribulation

Rainforest, beaches, cassowaries, bats and some fairly hard-core driving are features of this intriguing area where tropical rainforest meets the sea. It's only accessible via cable ferry (or 4WD from Cooktown) and, adding to its mystery, it's where rainforest retreat-style accommodation regularly gets taken over by the surrounding greenery, and the sun is rarely seen through thick foliage.

About 11km before Daintree Village and 24km north of Mossman is the turn-off to the **Daintree River cable ferry** (car/motorcycle/bicycle & pedestrian one way $13/6/1; ⊙6am-midnight), which runs every 15 minutes or so and takes two minutes to cross the river into the Cape Tribulation area. It's then another 34km by sealed road to Cape Tribulation.

Part of the Wet Tropics World Heritage Area, the region from Daintree River north to Cape Tribulation is famed for its ancient rainforest and the rugged mountains of **Thornton Peak** (1375m) and **Mt Sorrow** (770m).

Electricity is powered by generators and solar energy in this area and few places have air-con. Cape Trib is a popular day trip from Port Douglas and Cairns though tourism has slowed in recent years. Still, it's worth booking ahead during peak season.

You can get fuel and some supplies at **Rainforest Village** (☎07-4098 9015; www.rainforestvillage.com.au; Cape Tribulation Rd; ⊙7am-7pm), 16km from the ferry.

Cape Kimberley to Noah Beach charts a route from the Daintree River to Cape Tribulation.

Cape Kimberley

About 3km beyond the Daintree River crossing, a 5km unsealed road leads to Cape Kimberley Beach, a beautiful quiet beach with Snapper Island just offshore. The island is national park, with a fringing reef. Access is by private boat; **Crocodylus Village** (www.crocodyluscapetrib.com) runs two-day sea-kayaking tours here ($299; Monday, Wednesday and Friday). You'll need to obtain a permit for the **camp site** (13 74 68; www.nprsr.qld.gov.au; permits $5.45) on the southwest side of Snapper Island, where there's a toilet and picnic tables. Take a fuel stove, as fires are not permitted.

Cow Bay

There's a footpath from the main road to beautiful Cow Bay, where you'll find rainforest logs wedged into the coral-filled sand. It's a popular fishing spot, too.

Before the turn-off to the Jindalba Boardwalk is the **Walu Wugirriga (Alexandra Range) lookout**, which offers marvellous views over the Alexandra Range and Snapper Island.

The **aerial walkway** at the **Daintree Discovery Centre** (07-4098 9171; www.daintree-rec.com.au; Tulip Oak Rd; adult/child with 7-day re-entry $32/16; 8.30am-5pm) takes you high into the forest canopy. There are a few short interpretive walks and a small theatre running films on cassowaries, crocodiles, conservation and climate change. The (included) audio guide offers an excellent Indigenous tour.

Just past the centre, the **Jindalba Boardwalk** snakes a 700m and 2.7km circuit through the rainforest.

Cow Bay Horse Rides (07-4098 9202; www.cowbayhorserides.com.au; 1507 Cape Tribulation Rd; 1/2hr rides $65/120) runs very personalised rides – from one to four people – on its forested property.

Of course, Cow Bay's real highlight lies at the end of the road, where the beautiful white-sand **Cow Bay Beach** rivals any coastal paradise.

The laid-back **Epiphyte B&B** (07-4098 9039; www.rainforestbb.com; 22 Silkwood Rd; s/d/cabins incl breakfast $70/85/140) is set on a lush 6-hectare property with individually styled rooms of varying sizes but all with their own verandah. Even better is the spacious, super-private cabin with a patio, kitchenette and sunken bathroom.

Along the sealed Buchanan Creek Rd (often called Cow Bay Rd), ultra-basic green canvas safari-style huts merge with the surrounding foliage at the YHA-associated **Crocodylus Village** (07-4098 9166; www.crocodyluscapetrib.com; Buchanan Creek Rd; dm $25 d $70-85;). If you prefer solid walls, go for the four- to six-bed dorms or private rooms. Its bar and restaurant (mains $15, open 8am to 10am and 6pm to 9pm) are both open to the public, as are activities including half-day kayaking trips ($79) and adventurous two-day sea-kayaking tours to Snapper Island.

At **Daintree Rainforest Bungalows** (07-4098 9229; www.daintreerainforestbungalows.com; Lot 40, Spurwood Rd; d $110), the free-standing wooden cabins are simple but stylish, with violet- and lilac-toned fabrics, covered decks overlooking the rainforest and a kitchenette area complete with a camping stove. Two nights' minimum stay.

Set back from the main road amid rainforest, the **Daintree Rainforest Retreat Motel** (07-4098 9101; www.daintreeretreat.com.au; 1473 Cape Tribulation Rd; r $145-240, cabin $470;) is done out in striking tropical colour schemes and glossy woodwork. Some rooms have kitchenettes and the four-bedroom pole cabin has a beach-facing spa.

If you're craving a counter meal and glass of beer, the **Cow Bay Hotel** (07-4098 9011; Cape Tribulation Rd; mains $12-25; 11am-3pm & 6-9.30pm), adjacent to the turn-off to the beach, is the only real pub in the whole Daintree region. Takeaway alcohol is available, and there's an adjacent block of basic motel-style rooms (single/double $77/99).

Cow Bay to Cooper Creek

This section of road is an easy, winding drive with several worthwhile stops en route to Cooper Creek. The **Daintree Ice Cream Company** (07-4098 9114; Lot 100, Cape Tribulation Rd; ice creams $6; 11am-5pm) serves up four scoops of exotic flavours that change daily. You might choose from wattleseed, black sapote, macadamia, mango, coconut or jackfruit – they're all delicious. Work it off on a 20-minute self-guided orchard walk.

The family-friendly **Lync-Haven Rainforest Retreat** (07-4098 9155; www.lynchaven.com.au; Lot 44, Cape Tribulation Rd; unpowered/powered sites $14/32, d $99-160;) is set on a

Cape Tribulation Area

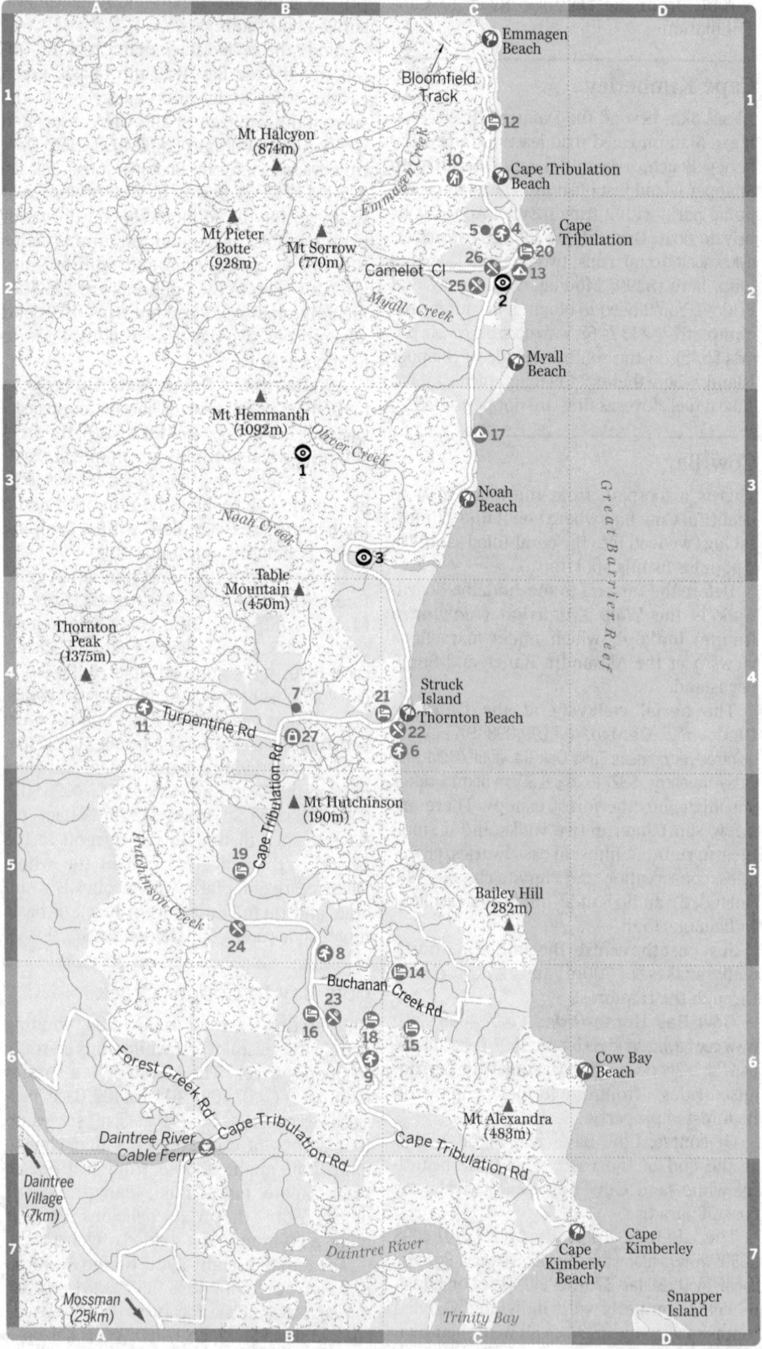
0 5 km
0 2.5 miles
Emmagen Beach
Bloomfield Track
12
Mt Halcyon (874m)
Emmagen Creek
10
Cape Tribulation Beach
Mt Pieter Botte (928m)
Mt Sorrow (770m)
5
4
Cape Tribulation
20
26
13
Camelot Cl
25
2
Myall Creek
Myall Beach
Mt Hemmanth (1092m)
Oliver Creek
17
1
Noah Beach
Great Barrier Reef
Noah Creek
3
Table Mountain (450m)
Thornton Peak (1375m)
Struck Island
7
21
Thornton Beach
11
Turpentine Rd
27
22
6
Cape Tribulation Rd
Mt Hutchinson (190m)
Hutchinson Creek
19
Bailey Hill (282m)
24
8
14
Buchanan Creek Rd
23
16
18
15
9
Cow Bay Beach
Forest Creek Rd
Mt Alexandra (483m)
Daintree River Cable Ferry
Cape Tribulation Rd
Cape Tribulation Rd
Daintree Village (7km)
Cape Kimberly Beach
Cape Kimberley
Daintree River
Mossman (25km)
Trinity Bay
Snapper Island

Cape Tribulation Area

Sights

1 Daintree Rainforest......B3
2 Dubuji Boardwalk......C2
3 Marrdja Botanical walk......B3

Activities, Courses & Tours

4 Bat House......C2
5 Cape Trib Exotic Fruit Farm......C2
6 Cape Tribulation Wilderness Cruises......C4
7 Cooper Creek Wilderness......B4
8 Cow Bay Horse Rides......B5
9 Daintree Discovery Centre......B6
Mason's Tours......(see 25)
10 Mt Sorrow Ridge Walk......C1
11 Prema Shanti......A4

Sleeping

12 Cape Trib Beach House......C1
Cape Trib Exotic Fruit Farm Cabins......(see 5)
13 Cape Tribulation Camping......C2
14 Crocodylus Village......C6
15 Daintree Rainforest Bungalows......C6
16 Daintree Rainforest Retreat Motel......B6
17 DERM Campground......C3
18 Epiphyte B&B......B6
19 Lync-Haven Rainforest Retreat......B5
20 PK's Jungle Village......C2
21 Thornton Beach Bungalows......C4

Eating

22 Cafe on Sea......C4
23 Cow Bay Hotel......B6
24 Daintree Ice Cream Company......B5
IGA Supermarket......(see 20)
Jungle Bar......(see 20)
25 Mason's Store & Cafe......C2
26 Whet Restaurant & Cinema......C2

Shopping

27 Rainforest Village......B4

16-hectare property on the main road about 5km north of Cow Bay, with walking trails, hand-reared kangaroos and resident croc Boris. Its restaurant (mains $14 to $28, open 8am to 10pm) serves robust steaks, burgers, pasta and fish, and there are outdoor evening movie screenings.

Cooper Creek

A smattering of sights nestles in the bend of Cooper Creek at the base of dramatic Thornton Peak.

Just south of the creek itself, **Rainforest Village** (07-4098 9015; www.rainforestvillage.com.au; 7am-7pm) sells groceries, ice and fuel, and has a small **campground** (unpowered/powered sites $24/32).

Book ahead for a walk with **Cooper Creek Wilderness** (07-4098 9126; www.ccwild.com; Cape Tribulation Rd; guided walks $55-240). After a walk through the Daintree rainforest, you'll take a dip in Cooper Creek. Night walks and full-day tours are also available.

Cape Tribulation Wilderness Cruises (0457 731 000; www.capetribcruises.com; Cape Tribulation Rd; adult/child $30/20) has day and night mangrove cruises down Cooper Creek in search of crocs.

Prema Shanti (07-4098 9006; www.premashanti.com; Turpentine Rd; classes per hr $18) is a peaceful yoga retreat with drop-in yoga and meditation classes (by reservation) and massage treatments available.

Thornton Beach

A sliver of vegetation separates Cape Tribulation Rd from magnificent crescent-shaped Thornton Beach. There's a small, rocky offshore island, and opportunities for snorkelling. Best of all is the licensed **Cafe on Sea** (07-4098 9118; Cape Tribulation Rd; mains $12-25; 9am-4pm), only a towel-length back from the beach.

Directly across the road, **Thornton Beach Bungalows** (07-4098 9179; www.thorntonbeach.com; Cape Tribulation Rd; cabins/houses $85/250) has two petite cabins, plus a beach house sleeping four (two-night minimum).

Noah Beach & Around

Marrdja Botanical Walk is a beautiful 1.2km (45-minute) interpretive boardwalk that follows the creek through a section of rainforest packed with fan palms and past mangroves to a lookout over Noah Creek. Wear insect repellent to beat the midges.

Noah Valley Mountain Treks (07-4098 9292; noahvalleymountaintreks@activ8.net.au; half-day/night treks $60/40) guide enviro-oriented, challenging treks through the Noah Valley.

The **Noah Beach Campground** (13 74 68; www.nprsr.qld.gov.au; Cape Tribulation Rd; per person $5.45) has 15 sites set 100m back from the beach beneath red-trunked trees. There are toilets but no showers. Watch out for crocs.

Cape Tribulation

The Indigenous Kuku-yalanji people called the area Kulki, but the name Cape Tribulation was given by Captain Cook after his ship ran aground on Endeavour Reef. This little piece of paradise retains a frontier quality, with low-key development, road signs alerting drivers to cassowary crossings, and crocodile warnings that make beach strolls that little bit less relaxing.

The rainforest tumbles down to two magnificent, white-sand beaches – Myall and Cape Trib – separated by a knobby cape. The village of Cape Tribulation marks the end of the road, literally, and the beginning of the 4WD-only coastal route along the Bloomfield Track towards Cooktown and beyond.

Serious, fit walkers should lace up early for the **Mt Sorrow Ridge Walk** (7km, five to six hours return, start no later than 10am); it's strenuous but worth it. The start of the marked trail is about 150m north of the Kulki picnic area car park, on your left. For the less hardcore, head to **Myall Beach** where you can do the 1.2km **Dubuji Boardwalk** through a mangrove swamp.

◉ Sights & Activities

Jungle Surfing ZIPLINE, HIKING
(☑07-4098 0043; www.junglesurfing.com.au; zipline $90, night walks $40; ◷ night walks 7.30pm) Jungle Surfing is an exhilarating zipline (flying fox) through the rainforest canopy, stopping at five tree platforms. It also runs guided **forest night walks**. Rates include pick-ups throughout Cape Trib.

Bat House WILDLIFE WATCHING
(☑07-4098 0063; www.austrop.org.au; Cape Tribulation Rd; admission $4; ◷ 10.30am-3.30pm Tue-Sun) Volunteers from Austrop, a local conservation organisation, run the Bat House, a nursery for the flying fox.

Ocean Safari SNORKELLING
(☑07-4098 0006; www.oceansafari.com.au; adult/child $119/76; ◷ 9am & 1pm) Ocean Safari leads small groups (25 people maximum) on snorkelling cruises to the Great Barrier Reef, just half an hour offshore. Free pick-up from your Cape Trib accommodation.

Cape Trib Horse Rides HORSE RIDING
(☑07-4098 0030; www.capetribhorserides.com.au; per person $89; ◷ 8am & 2.30pm) Leisurely rides along the beach. Free pick-up from your accommodation.

☞ Tours

Paddle Trek Kayak Tours KAYAKING
(☑07-4098 0043; www.capetribpaddletrek.com.au; kayak hire per hour $16-55, trips from $69) Guided kayaking trips and kayak hire. Free pick-up from your accommodation.

D'Arcy of the Daintree DRIVING TOUR
(☑07-4098 9180; www.darcyofdaintree.com.au; tours adult/child from $119/80) Entertaining 4WD trips up the Bloomfield Track to Wujal Wujal Waterfalls and as far as Cooktown and down Cape Tribulation Rd. Free pick-ups from Cape Trib and Cow Bay.

Mason's Tours WALKING, TOUR
(☑07-4098 0070; www.masonstours.com.au; Mason's Store, Cape Tribulation Rd; tours $300-1250) Lawrence Mason conducts interpretive walks lasting two hours to a full day. Also runs 4WD tours up the Bloomfield Track to Cooktown. Advance booking necessary.

Cape Trib Exotic Fruit Farm TOUR
(☑07-4098 0057; www.capetrib.com.au; Lot 5, Nicole Dr; tour $25; ◷ 2pm) Bookings are essential for 90-minute tours and tastings at the magnificent tropical orchards of Cape Trib Exotic Fruit Farm.

⊨ Sleeping & Eating

Restaurants at Cape Trib's accommodation are all open to nonguests.

Cape Trib Beach House HOSTEL $
(☑07-4098 0030; www.capetribbeach.com.au; dm $26-32, d $75, cabins $130-180; ❋@☎☒) The rainforest huts at this low-key beachfront property are home to dorms through to timber cabins. There's a tidy communal kitchen as well as an open-deck licensed **restaurant** (mains $7-34, open 8am-10.30pm) with cheap drinks. Bike hire (per day $20) is available.

PK's Jungle Village HOSTEL $
(☑07-4098 0040; www.pksjunglevillage.com; Cape Tribulation Rd; unpowered sites per person $15, dm $25-28, d $95 & $125; ❋@☎☒) From this longstanding backpacker hub you can reach Myall Beach by boardwalk. Its **Jungle Bar** (mains $15-25; ◷ restaurant lunch & dinner, bar noon-midnight) is the entertainment epicentre of Cape Trib.

Cape Tribulation Camping CAMPGROUND $
(☑07-4098 0077; www.capetribcamping.com.au; Cape Tribulation Rd; unpowered & powered sites for 2 $40, safari huts s/d $45/70; @) Sociable

beachfront spot with a nightly communal fire and friendly managers and kayak hire (per day $60 to $70). The Sand Bar (open 11am to 8.30pm) serves drinks and delish wood-fired pizzas (pizzas $14 to $24).

★ Cape Trib Exotic Fruit Farm Cabins CABIN $$
(☎07-4098 0057; www.capetrib.com.au; Lot 5, Nicole Dr; d $185) Amid the orchards of Cape Trib Exotic Fruit Farm, this pair of timber pole cabins have exposed timber floors, ceilings and huge decks, and are equipped with electric Eskies. Rates include breakfast hampers filled with tropical fruit from the farm. Minimum stay is two nights. Book in advance!

Rainforest Hideaway B&B $$
(☎07-4098 0108; www.rainforesthideaway.com; 19 Camelot Cl; d $130-140) You know you're at Queenland's quirkiest digs when you turn into the property and find two massive Easter Island heads staring back at you. This colourful B&B has been single-handedly built by its owner, artist and sculptor 'Dutch Rob' – even the furniture and beds are handmade. Room 1092 has an open shower/toilet facing the rainforest! A beautiful sculpture trail winds through the property; rates include breakfast.

Mason's Store & Cafe CAFE, SELF-CATERING $
(Cape Tribulation Rd; mains $15; ⏲10am-4pm Sun-Thu, 10am-7pm Fri & Sat) Laid-back cafe dishing up crocodile, emu and roo burgers with buffalo and camel to be added to the menu! The store sells limited groceries, souvenirs and takeaway alcohol. Bring a towel as there's a swimming hole behind the store (by donation).

IGA Supermarket SUPERMARKET $
(☎07-4098 0015; PK's Jungle Village; ⏲8am-6pm) The Daintree's largest supermarket.

Whet Restaurant & Cinema AUSTRALIAN, INDIAN $$
(☎07-4098 0007; www.whet.net.au; 1 Cape Tribulation Rd; mains $21.50-33, movies $10; ⏲11.30am-3pm & 5.30-9.30pm) Serves a decent range of delectable modern Australian dishes including wild-caught barra steamed in ginger. For something a bit more fiery, you should visit on Friday nights for Indian food (mains $16 to $18). Whet is also the only place around where you can get a meal much after 8pm. Movie screenings ($10) are at 2pm, 4pm and 8pm.

ℹ Getting There & Away

Country Road Coach Lines (☎07-4045 2794; www.countryroadcoachlines.com.au) travels the coastal route from Cairns to Cooktown via Cape Tribulation (adult/child $49/24.50) on Monday, Wednesday and Friday (departing from Cairns at 7am) and departs from Cape Tribulation for Cairns at 10.10am on Tuesday, Thursday and Saturday.

North to Cooktown

Aside from flying in, there are two routes to Cooktown from the south: the coastal route from Cape Tribulation via the 4WD-only **Bloomfield Track**, and the inland route, which is sealed all the way via the Peninsula and Cooktown Developmental Rds.

The Bloomfield Track is one of the frontier roads of Australia, and it wasn't until 1983, when it was controversially bulldozed through the Daintree, that people could actually drive from Cooktown to Cape Tribulation via the coast. There are reasons why it's 4WD only: it's unsealed, there are flooded creek crossings and very steep and slippery hills, and it's usually impossible to use during the Wet. Check road conditions at Mason's Store & Cafe before heading off.

Thirty kilometres north of Cape Tribulation and a must-see along the way is **Bloomfield Falls**, aka Wujal Wujal Falls (after crossing the Bloomfield River turn left). Crocs inhabit the river and the site is significant to the Indigenous Wujal Wujal community located just north of the river. Wujal Wujal residents, the **Walker family** (☎07-4040 7500; www.bamaway.com.au; adult/child $25/12.50; ⏲by reservation), run highly recommended half-hour walking tours of the falls and surrounding forest.

North from Wujal Wujal the track heads for 46km through the tiny settlements of **Ayton (Bloomfield)**, **Rossville** (a former hippie commune with a market every second Saturday morning) and **Helenvale** to meet the sealed Cooktown Developmental Rd, 28km south of Cooktown.

The **Lion's Den Hotel** (☎07-4060 3911; www.lionsdenhotel.com.au; 398 Shiptons Flat Rd, Helenvale; unpowered/powered sites $10/26, s/d $45/65, d safari tents $80; ❄🏊) is a well-known watering hole that has graffiti-covered corrugated-iron walls and a slab-timber bar. You can pitch your own tent or sleep in an above-ground safari-style tent. You'll find good pub grub (mains $12 to $23, open noon to 2.30pm and 6pm to 7.30pm) and fuel is available.

Cooktown

POP 2339

At the southeastern edge of Cape York Peninsula, Cooktown is a small place with a big history: for thousands of years Waymbuurr was the place the local Guugu Yimithirr and Kuku Yalanji people used as a meeting ground, and it was here that on 17 June 1770, Lieutenant (later Captain) Cook beached the *Endeavour*. The *Endeavour* had earlier struck a reef offshore from Cape Tribulation, and Cook and his crew spent 48 days here while they repaired the damage – making it the site of Australia's first, albeit transient, non-Indigenous settlement.

Cooktown is also a hot spot for anglers who come here hoping to hook a giant barramundi or 10. Work is often available on banana plantations.

Sights & Activities

Cooktown hibernates from November to April, and many attractions and tours close or have reduced hours.

James Cook Museum MUSEUM
(☎07-4069 5386; cnr Helen & Furneaux Sts; adult/child $10/3; ⏲9.30am-4pm) Housed in the imposing 1880s St Mary's Convent, this museum explores Cooktown's intriguing past. From a traditional outrigger canoe to the *Endeavour's* massive anchor, there's a host of interesting displays.

Grassy Hill LOOKOUT
(162m) Has an unused lighthouse and spectacular 360-degree views – especially worthwhile at sunrise. There's a snaking road to the top, or a very steep 20-minute walk up. Cook climbed this hill looking for a passage out through the reefs. Another walking trail (800m one way, 25 minutes) leads from the summit down to the beach at Cherry Tree Bay. Located at the northern end of town.

Nature's Powerhouse INTERPRETIVE CENTRE
(☎07-4069 6004; www.naturespowerhouse.com.au; off Walker St; admission by donation; ⏲9am-5pm) Nature's Powerhouse is an environmental interpretive centre that is home to two excellent galleries: the **Charlie Tanner Gallery**, with pickled and preserved creepy-crawly exhibits; and the **Vera Scarth-Johnson Gallery**, displaying botanical illustrations of the region's native plants.

Cooktown Botanic Gardens GARDEN
(off Walker St; ⏲24hr) FREE Cooktown's 62-hectare Botanic Gardens is filled with native and exotic tropical plants, including rare orchids. The gardens are among Australia's oldest and most magnificent. Located behind Nature's Powerhouse.

Bicentennial Park PARK
Bicentennial Park is home to the much-photographed bronze **Captain Cook statue**. Nearby, the **Milbi Wall** (Story Wall) is a 12m-long mosaic depicting the local Gungarde (Guugu Yimithirr) Indigenous people's stories of creation and European contact, as well as scenes from WWII and recent attempts at reconciliation.

Cooktown Reef Charters FISHING, SNORKELLING
(☎07-4069 5396; www.reefcharters.com.au; from $240 per person) Game-fishing day trips with the option of snorkelling.

Gone Fishing FISHING, TOUR
(☎07-4069 5980; www.fishingcooktown.com; fishing half-/full day $115/230, wildlife tour $60) River-fishing tours plus two-hour wildlife-spotting cruises.

Tours

Tours operate regularly out of Cooktown from May to October, with scaled-back schedules from November to April.

★**Guurrbi Tours** INDIGENOUS CULTURE
(☎07-4069 6043; www.guurrbitours.com; tours 2/4hr $85/120, self-drive $65/95; ⏲Mon-Sat) Nugalwarra family elder Willie Gordon runs revelatory tours that use the physical landscape to describe the spiritual landscape, providing a powerful insight into Aboriginal culture and lore. Cooktown pick-ups are from your accommodation; self-drivers meet near the Hopevale Aboriginal Community. Book in advance.

Maaramaka Walkabout Tours INDIGENOUS CULTURE
(☎07-4060 9389; irenehammett@hotmail.com; tours 1/2hr $84/42) Aboriginal cultural stories, rainforest walks, bush tucker and tea in a gorgeous setting near Hopevale; call for arrangements.

Festivals & Events

Cooktown Discovery Festival HISTORICAL
(www.cooktowndiscoveryfestival.com.au; ⏲early Jun) Held over the Queen's Birthday weekend (early June) to commemorate Captain Cook's landing in 1770 with a costumed re-enactment and fancy dress grand parade, as

well as indigenous workshops and a traditional corroboree.

Sleeping

Cooktown Holiday Park CAMPGROUND $
(07-4069 5417; www.cooktownholidaypark.com.au; 31-41 Charlotte St; powered sites $44, cabins without bathroom $100, motel units from $130, cabins with bathroom $140-160;) Cooktown's best-equipped caravan park, with cabins, a camp kitchen and a big saltwater pool.

Endeavour Falls Tourist Park CAMPGROUND $
(07-4069 5431; www.endeavourfallstouristpark.com.au; Endeavour Valley Rd; unpowered/powered sites $24/28, cabins $115;) Situated 32km northwest on the road to Hopevale (15km unsealed), this well-run, peaceful park backs onto the Garden of Eden–like Endeavour Falls (with a resident croc – don't swim!). Its well-stocked shop serves takeaways ($6.50 to $13.50) and has fuel.

Pam's Place Hostel & Cooktown Motel HOSTEL, MOTEL $
(07-4069 5166; www.cooktownhostel.com; cnr Charlotte & Boundary Sts; dm/s/d $27.50/55/60, motel d $100;) Cooktown's YHA-associated hostel is uninspired but rooms are clean and functional and it's probably the cheapest place to stay in town. The managers can help find harvest work.

★**Hillcrest Guest House** B&B $$
(07-4069 6308; 130 Hope St; r with shared bathroom $75-90, motel/self-contained r $110/135;) Housed in an 1880s Queenslander, all the rooms at this B&B are comfortable, charming and spotless but it's the swimming pool, the very first built in Cooktown, that is the main draw. You can treat yourself to a breakfast spread (real coffee!) in the shared kitchen after a morning dip. Motel rooms are situated beside a patch of grass where shy wallabies come out in the evenings to feed.

Milkwood Lodge CABIN $$
(07-4069 5007; www.milkwoodlodge.com; Annan Rd; d $140;) In a patch of rainforest 2.5km south of town, these six split-level cabins are beautifully designed with bushland views from private balconies.

Alkoomie Cattle Station Mountain Retreat FARM STAY $$
(07-4069 5463; www.alkoomie.com.au; Alkoomie Station; tents $80, self-contained units $100, d incl meals $199-225;) You'll need a 4WD to reach this 18,000-hectare working cattle station, 45km west of Cooktown. Activities include horse riding, feeding farm animals, swimming below waterfalls and nightly stargazing, plus day tours.

Seaview Motel MOTEL $$
(07-4069 5377; www.cooktownseaviewmotel.com.au; 178 Charlotte St; d $99-175, townhouses $235;) Awesomely located opposite the wharf, with a large variety of rooms (including townhouses and some with private balconies). Rates include continental breakfast.

Sovereign Resort Hotel HOTEL $$$
(07-4043 0500; www.sovereign-resort.com.au; cnr Charlotte & Green Sts; d $180-220, tr & q $210-280;) Cooktown's priciest digs are right on the main street, with a warren of breezy, slightly dated tropical-style rooms with wooden-slat blinds and tile floors.

Eating & Drinking

Gill'd & Gutt'd FISH & CHIPS $
(07-4069 5863; Fisherman's Wharf, Webber Esplanade; mains $7-12; 11.30am-9pm) Fish and chips the way it should be – fresh and right on the waterside wharf.

The Italian ITALIAN $
(07-4069 6338; Charlotte St; mains $13-22; 5-9.30pm Mon-Sat) Popular Italian restaurant serving old-school Aussie-style pizzas in a bustling environment. Takeaways available.

Cornett's IGA SUPERMARKET $
(cnr Helen & Hogg Sts; 8am-7pm Mon-Fri, 8am-6pm Sat, 9am-5pm Sun) Groceries.

Balcony Restaurant MODERN AUSTRALIAN $$
(07-4069 5400; Sovereign Resort, cnr Charlotte & Green Sts; mains $25-33; 7-9.30am & 6-10pm) Upstairs, the Sovereign Resort's formal Balcony Restaurant serves French-inspired Mod Oz cuisine like confit of duck with sweet potato puree or pistachio-crusted rack of lamb (along with seafood, of course). The **Cafe-Bar** (mains $11-23; 11am-8pm;) has reasonably priced seafood, pizzas and BLTs, as well as pool tables and free internet.

Cooktown Bowls Club LICENSED CLUB $$
(07-4069 5819; Charlotte St; mains $15-25; 11.30am-2.30pm Wed-Fri, 5.30-10pm daily;) Have a huge bistro meal before joining in social bowls on Wednesday and Saturday afternoon and barefoot bowls on Wednesday evening.

Restaurant 1770 MODERN AUSTRALIAN **$$$**
(☎07-4069 5440; 7 Webber Esplanade; breakfast $19, lunch & dinner mains $30-39; ⏰7.30-9.30am, 11.30am-2pm & 6-9.30pm Tue-Sat; ✎) Opening onto a romantic waterside deck right next to the wharf, fresh fish – such as beer-battered barra and coral trout – takes top billing, but save space for mouth-watering desserts.

Cooktown Hotel PUB
(☎07-4069 5308; www.cooktownhotel.com; 96 Charlotte St; ⏰10am-midnight) The double-storey timber 'Top Pub' is a local landmark at the top (southern) end of Charlotte St. Plenty of character, plenty of locals and a side beer garden to sit with a beer, pizza and pub grub.

ℹ Information

Check www.cooktownandcapeyork.com for information on the town and surrounding areas.

Cooktown Travel Centre (☎07-4069 5446; 113 Charlotte St) Information and bookings for tours, transport and accommodation.

Nature's Powerhouse (☎07-4069 6004; www.naturespowerhouse.com.au; Walker St; ⏰9am-5pm) Has brochures outlining some of the area's excellent walking trails, including a walk to the Coral Sea beaches at Finch Bay (25 minutes) and Cherry Tree Bay (one hour).

ℹ Getting There & Around

Cooktown's airfield is 10km west of town along McIvor Rd. **Hinterland Aviation** (☎07-4035 9323; www.hinterlandaviation.com.au) has one to four flights daily except Sunday to/from Cairns (one way $410, 40 minutes).

Country Road Coachlines (☎07-4045 2794; www.countryroadcoachlines.com.au) runs a daily bus service between Cairns and Cooktown ($79) on either the coastal route (Bloomfield Track, via Port Douglas) or inland route (via Mareeba), depending on the day of departure and the condition of the track.

For a **taxi** call ☎07-4069 5387.

Lizard Island

The spectacular islands of the Lizard group are clustered just 27km off the coast about 100km from Cooktown. Jigurru (Lizard Island), a sacred place for the Dingaal Indigenous people, has dry, rocky and mountainous terrain for bushwalking, glistening white swimming beaches, and a relatively untouched fringing reef for snorkelling and diving. Apart from the ground where the luxury resort stands, the entire island is national park, so it's open to anyone who makes the effort to get here.

There are good dives right off the island, and the outer Barrier Reef is less than 20km away, including two of Australia's best-known dive sites – Cod Hole and Pixie Bommie. Lizard Island Resort offers a full range of diving facilities to its guests. Some live-aboard tours from Cairns dive the Cod Hole.

There are great walks through country that switches from mangrove to rainforest to dry and rocky in mere minutes, including a superb hike up to **Cook's Look** (368m); allow three hours return. The trail starts from the northern end of Watson's Bay near the camp site.

Accommodation options are camping or a five-star luxury resort. **Lizard Island Resort** (☎1300 863 248; www.lizardisland.com.au; Anchor Bay; d from $1444; ❄@📶🏊) has luxurious villas, spa treatments and a top restaurant. Kids aren't allowed. The **camping ground** (per person $5.45) is a 10-minute walk from the resort, at the northern end of Watson's Bay. You'll need a permit from **Queensland Parks** (☎13 74 68; www.nprsr.qld.gov.au), and it's worth checking that the water pump, toilets and gas barbecues are working. Campers must be self-sufficient, though the resort's bar is accessible if you're after a drink.

Book through the resort for all air transfers to/from Cairns (return $590). Flight time is one hour. **Daintree Air Services** (☎1800 246 206, 07-4034 9400; www.daintreeair.com.au) has full-day tours from Cairns at 8am (from $750). The trip includes lunch, snorkelling gear, transfers and a local guide.

GULF SAVANNAH

The world has a different tint out here: the east coast's green cloud-tipped mountains and sugarcane fields give way to a flat, red dust-coated landscape of sweeping grass plains, scrubby forest and mangroves engraved by an intricate network of seasonal rivers and croc-filled tidal creeks that drain into the Gulf of Carpentaria. The fishing here is legendary, particularly for barramundi (barra season runs from mid-January to the end of September).

Most of this area is on – or just off – the epic Savannah Way, which stretches right across the north of the country from Cairns to Broome. Stop by rusting roadhouses and

HOPE ISLANDS

Adventurous souls can play Robinson Crusoe out on the Hope Islands National Park, with just you and nature (and the odd passing boat). **East Hope** and **West Hope** islands are sand cays about 10km offshore from the mainland, 37km southeast of Cooktown. Both are national parks, which protects the hardy mangroves and shrub vegetation. West Hope is an important nesting site for pied imperial pigeons – access is not permitted during nesting from 1 September to 31 March. Snorkelling is excellent around both islands but best on the leeward margin of the East Hope Island reef; beware of strong currents. East Hope Island has three **camp sites** (camping per person $5.45) with toilets, tables and fire places. Permits are required and there's a seven-day limit; contact **Queensland Parks** (13 74 68; www.nprsr.qld.gov.au). Take drinking water, food and a fuel stove.

Getting here isn't cheap. Contact **Bloomfield River Water Sports** (07-4060 8252; flyingfox@animalaware.net; Cnr West & First St, Ayton; $180 per person) for travel information and to arrange return boat transfers to Hope Islands National Park.

you'll meet folk with stories to tell, and not many people to tell them to (mobile-phone service is nonexistent in some places). And you don't even need a 4WD to explore most of it – just a sense of adventure.

Information

Check www.gulf-savannah.com.au and www.savannahway.com.au for info.

Getting There & Around

AIR

Skytrans (1300 759 872; www.skytrans.com.au) flies several times a week between Cairns and Normanton (from $190) and Burketown (from $200), and between Mt Isa and Burketown (from $190).

BUS

Trans North (07-4096 8644; www.transnorthbus.com) has a service from Cairns to Karumba ($148, 11 hours) three times a week, departing from Cairns Monday, Wednesday and Friday, stopping at the Undara turn-off ($65, five hours), Georgetown ($84, 6½ hours), Croydon ($107, 8½ hours) and Normanton ($143, 10½ hours). The return service runs Tuesday, Thursday and Saturday.

No buses link Normanton with Mt Isa or Burketown.

CAR & MOTORCYCLE

The sealed Gulf Developmental Rd (Savannah Way, Rte 1) runs from Cairns to Normanton. From here you can continue on bitumen up to Karumba, or continue on the gravel Gulf Track to Burketown and beyond to the Northern Territory (NT) border.

Heading south from Burketown the unsealed road to Camooweal runs via Gregory Downs and Boodjamulla (Lawn Hill) National Park, while the Nardoo–Burketown Rd cuts across to meet the Burke Developmental Rd at the Burke & Wills Roadhouse. Many sealed roads are single-file.

TRAIN

The historic **Savannahlander** (1800 793 848, 07-4053 6848; www.savannahlander.com.au; one way/return $227/381), aka the 'Silver Bullet', chugs along a traditional mining route from Cairns to Forsayth and back, departing from Cairns on Wednesday at 6.30am and returning on Saturday at 6.40pm. A range of tours (including side trips to Chillagoe, Undara and Cobbold Gorge) and accommodation can be booked online.

The snub-nosed **Gulflander** (07-4745 1391; www.gulflander.com.au; one way/return $67/111) runs once weekly in each direction between Normanton and Croydon on the 1891 gold-to-port railway line alongside the Gulf Developmental Rd. It leaves Normanton on Wednesday at 8.30am, and leaves Croydon on Thursday at 8.30am.

TOURS

Several operators run tours from Cairns, including **Wilderness Challenge** (07-4035 4488, 1800 354 486; www.wilderness-challenge.com.au; 9-day accommodated tours from $3195, 11-day camping safaris from $3195).

The Savannah Way

Undara Volcanic National Park

About 190,000 years ago, the Undara shield volcano erupted, sending molten lava coursing through the surrounding landscape. While the surface of the lava cooled and hardened, hot lava continued to race through the centre of the flows, eventually leaving the world's longest continuous (though fragmented) lava tubes.

All up there are over 160km of tubes, but only a fraction can be visited, on guided tours only. Most are operated by **Undara Experience** (07-4097 1900, 1800 990 992; www.undara.com.au; 2-4hr tours $50-90). Tours only run in the Dry. Overnight tours run from Cairns; **Bedrock Village Caravan Park & Tours** (07-4062 3193; www.bedrockvillage.com.au; full day adult/child $124/62, half-day $76/38) has tours from Mt Surprise.

The closest accommodation to the tubes and national park is at the resort-like **Undara Experience** (1800 990 992; www.undara.com.au; unpowered/powered sites $11/16, d swag tents $42, d cabins $194, s carriages without bathroom $79, d carriages with/without bathroom $179/158;), which has atmospheric vintage railway carriages converted into comfy rooms (some with bathroom). Facilities include barbecues and campfire entertainment. There's also a campfire bush breakfast (adult/child $25/12.50) and a bistro (lunch buffet adult/child $25/12.50, dinner mains $18 to $34). Meals need to be booked in advance.

The turn-off to Undara is 81km southwest of Innot Hot Springs, from where it's a sealed 15km.

Undara to Croydon

Back on the Gulf Developmental Rd, 39km past the Undara turn-off, the 'jewel of a town' **Mt Surprise** (population 306) lives up to its moniker, with gem collections, snake collections, even a miniature horse collection. It's a good base for fossicking in the nearby gemfields – Pete and Pam at **Mt Surprise Gems** (07-4062 3055; www.thegemden.com.au; Garland St) run **fossicking tours** (half-day incl transport/self-drive $76/60; Apr-Sep), rent out tools (per day $25) and can issue licences (per month $6.85, Queensland-wide).

At **Planet Earth Adventures** (07-4062 3127; p.e.a.@bigpond.com.au; unpowered/powered sites per person $10/17, dishes $5-12), Russell Dennis has a **snake museum** (gold coin donation) where you can see deadly taipans and king browns, and **free snake shows** (10am Sunday), including snake-bite education. The snake show can be seen at other times by arrangement for $10. Besides offering a basic campsite, it also has a cafe serving simple fare such as coffee, burgers and sandwiches.

Shaded **Mt Surprise Tourist Van Park, Motel & BP Roadhouse** (07-4062 3153, 1800 447 982; 23 Garland St; unpowered/powered sites $17/24, cabins $55-89;) has a miniature horse stud and a BYO cafe (mains $5 to $19, open 7am to 7pm) serving sandwiches, burgers and the like. Excellent **Bedrock Village Caravan Park & Tours** (07-4062 3193; www.bedrockvillage.com.au; Garnet St; unpowered/powered sites $20/28, cabins $90-112) has cabins with bathrooms and meals on request. Pizza nights and local tours complete the experience.

About 32km west, the partly sealed **Explorers' Loop** (check road conditions) takes you on a 150km loop through old goldmining towns. At **Einasleigh**, have a drink at the only pub and check out the publican's amazing miniature dollhouse collection before strolling across to the gorge. Continue past **Forsayth** to the private spring-fed oasis of **Cobbold Gorge**. **Cobbold Gorge Village** (07-4062 5470, 1800 669 922; www.cobboldgorge.com.au; sites unpowered/powered/with bathroom $12/34/49, cabins $90-112; Apr-Oct;) runs three-hour bushwalking **tours** (adult/child $75/37.50; Apr-Oct) that culminate with a boat cruise through the stunning gorge. Look for crocs basking on the rocks. The infinity pool with a swim-up bar (!) at the village is a welcome find in the middle of the dry surroundings. Meals (dinner mains $25) and all-day snacks $7-12 are available.

Cobbold Gorge tours can pick up in **Georgetown** (population 244), the endpoint of the loop, back on the Savannah Way. There's not much here, bar a resident monitor lizard, a free swimming pool, and the flash **Terrestrial Centre** (07-4062 1485; 8am-5pm May-Sep, 8.30am-4.30pm Mon-Fri Oct-May), home to a **visitor centre** and the shimmering, 4500-strong **Ted Elliot Mineral Collection** (adult/child $11/9).

Croydon

POP 313

Incredibly, little Croydon was once the biggest town in the Gulf. Gold was discovered in Croydon in 1885, but by the end of WWI it had run out and the place became little more than a ghost town.

Croydon's **visitor information centre** (07-4745 6125; Samwell St; 9am-4.30pm daily Apr-Oct, Mon-Fri Nov-Mar) screens well-produced historical videos, and has details of the remaining historic town buildings and barramundi-stocked Lake Belmore, 4km north of the centre.

The **Club Hotel** (07-4745 6184; cnr Brown & Sircom Sts; mains $20-30; lunch & dinner;), built in 1887, is the only pub left from the mining heyday, serving up huge meals, ice-cold beer, and sunset views from the verandah.

At the **Croydon General Store** (07-4745 6163; Sircom St; 7am-7pm Mon-Fri, 9am-7.30pm Sat & Sun) the sign declares this the 'oldest store in Australia, established 1894'. While we didn't test the veracity of its claim, the interior is definitely a throwback to ye olde days: wooden floorboards and a small collection of historical curios worth checking out.

Campers can pitch up at **Croydon Caravan Park** (07-4745 6238; caravanpark@croydon.qld.gov.au; cnr Brown & Alldridge Sts; unpowered/powered sites $15/30, cabins $95;).

Normanton

POP 1469

The port for Croydon's gold rush, Normanton essentially consists of one long main street these days. The Norman River produces whopping barramundi; every Easter the **Barra Bash** lures big crowds, as do the **Normanton Rodeo & Show** (mid-June) and the **Normanton Races** (September).

Local info is available from the **visitor information & heritage centre** (07-4745 1065; www.carpentaria.qld.gov.au; cnr Caroline & Landsborough Sts; 9am-4pm Mon-Fri, to noon Sat) and from Normanton's Victorian-era **train station**.

For a room to snooze in and an artesian spa to soak in, try the friendly **Normanton Tourist Park** (07-4745 1323; www.normantontouristpark.com.au; 14 Brown St; unpowered/powered sites $24/32, cabins with/without bathroom $100/65;) located in a shady setting.

Karumba

POP 587

Ay Karumba! When the fish are biting and the sun sinks into the Gulf in a fiery ball of burnt ochre, this is a little piece of outback paradise. Even if you don't like fishing, it's the only town accessible by sealed road on the entire Gulf coast.

The actual town is on the Norman River, while Karumba Point – the best place to stay – is about 6km away by road on the beach. Karumba's **visitor information centre** (07-4745 9582; www.carpentaria.qld.gov.au; Walker St, Karumba Town; 9.30am-1pm & 2-4.30pm Mon-Fri, 9am-noon Sat, noon-3pm Sun Apr-Oct, 9.30am-2.30pm Tue-Fri Nov-Mar) has details of fishing charters, and barra-breeding hatchery tours.

Karumba Point Sunset Caravan Park (07-4745 9277; www.sunsetcp.com.au; 53 Palmer St, Karumba Point; unpowered/powered sites $33/40, cabins without bathroom $101, en suite villas $121;) has spotless amenities. Breezy, stylish **End of the Road Motel** (07-4745 9599; www.endoftheroadmotel.com.au; 26 Palmer St, Karumba Point; d $145-190;) is next door to the **Sunset Tavern** (07-4745 9183; The Esplanade, Karumba Point; mains $15-30; 10am-midnight) – *the* place to take in those glorious sunsets, ice-cold beer in hand. **Ash's Holiday Units** (07-4745 9132; www.ashsholidayunits.com.au; 21 Palmer St; s/d $90/95;) are self-contained with a cafe serving great fish and chips.

Normanton to Cloncurry

The sealed 378km of road between Normanton and Cloncurry is mostly single file, and floodway signs give you an idea of what it's like during the Wet: wet. The flat dry-grass country slowly morphs into small rises and forests of termite hills.

Everyone stops at the **Burke & Wills Roadhouse** (07-4742 5909; unpowered/powered sites $20/25, d $75; 5.30am-midnight, restaurant till 9pm;) to down a cold drink among noisy apostle birds. Fuel is available.

The **Quamby Hotel** (07-4742 5952; Matilda Hwy; s/d $50/70, mains $15-25; dinner 6-9pm;) is 135km from the Roadhouse and 43km north of Cloncurry. Camping's available on request, but there's no fuel.

Normanton to Northern Territory

At the start of the unsealed, dusty stretch from Normanton to the NT, stop by eerie **Burke & Wills Camp 119**, the northernmost camp of the ill-equipped explorers' wretched 1861 expedition – they came within just 5km of reaching the gulf. The camp is signposted 37km west of Normanton.

Besides legendary fishing, isolated **Burketown** (population 202) is the best place in the world to witness the extraordinary 'morning glory' phenomenon (p464).

Burketown Pub (☎07-4745 5104; www.burketownpub.com; Beames St; s/d $65/85, units $100-140; ❄), the heart and soul of Burketown, was originally built as the local customs house in the late 1860s and was recently rebuilt after a fire. Swap stories with locals and travellers in the beer garden, or over a meal (mains $9 to $30, open 11am to 2pm and 6pm to 9pm). Nearby, **Burketown Caravan Park** (☎07-4745 5118; www.burketowncaravanpark.net.au; Sloman St; powered sites $30, d & cabins without bathroom $70-90, cabins with bathroom $120; ❄) has a **takeaway van** (mains $9-25; ⊙noon-2pm & 6-9pm) dishing up *Ben Hur*-sized brekkies and two-handed barra burgers.

The only fuel stop for the 486km run between Burketown and Borroloola (NT) is the **Doomadgee Aboriginal Community** (☎07-4745 8188). You're welcome to buy fuel and supplies here; village access is subject to council permission, and alcohol is restricted.

It's another 80km of Melaleuca scrub to **Hell's Gate Roadhouse** (☎07-4745 8258; unpowered sites $20), 50km from the NT border. It has fuel, camping (no power) and snacks (ie pies), but it's cash only.

Burketown to Camooweal

The 334km unsealed road from Burketown to Gregory Downs is the most direct route to beautiful Boodjamulla (Lawn Hill) National Park. For 2WDs, the easiest route to Gregory Downs is the sealed road from the Burke & Wills Roadhouse.

MORNING GLORY

Between approximately August and November, Burketown becomes the home of intrepid cloud-surfers, when 'morning glory' clouds frequently (but unpredictably) roll in. A rare meteorological phenomenon, these tubular clouds come in wave-like sets of up to eight. Each can be up to 1000km long by 2km high, and travel at speeds of up to 60km per hour. As the sun rises, gliders head up in the hope of catching one; ask around and chances are someone will take you along for the ride. For a close-up look at the clouds aboard a light plane, contact Gulf-wide charter company **Savannah Aviation** (☎07-4745 5177; www.savannah-aviation.com; per hr for up to 4 people $650).

The park entrance is 100km west of **Gregory Downs** (population 40) on the pretty Gregory River. Fuel is available at the **Gregory Downs Hotel** (☎07-4748 5566; camp sites per person $15, d motel units $100; ❄), a laid-back spot to quench your thirst and tuck into decent pub meals (mains $10 to $25, open noon to 2pm daily and 6pm to 9pm Monday to Saturday).

Boodjamulla (Lawn Hill) National Park

A series of deep flame-red sandstone gorges, fed by spring water and lined with palms, provides a haven for wildlife at this outback oasis. The Waanyi Aboriginal people have inhabited the area for some 30,000 years, and paintings abound. Book ahead for all accommodation.

In the southern part of the park is the World Heritage–listed **Riversleigh fossil field** (adult/child $12/7.50), with a small **campground** (☎13 74 68; www.nprsr.qld.gov.au; per person $5.45; ⊙Mar-Oct). The fossils include everything from giant snakes and carnivorous kangaroos to pocket-sized koalas.

Some 20km of walking tracks fan out around Lawn Hill Gorge, while the emerald-green waters are idyllic for a swim or a paddle in a canoe with the red cliffs towering above.

The main hub is **Adel's Grove** (☎07-4748 5502; www.adelsgrove.com.au; unpowered sites/permanent tents/d $34/100/130; ⊙camping year-round, other accommodation & facilities Easter-late Oct), 10km east of the park entrance. It's a mini-resort with an on-site bar and **restaurant** (breakfast $12.50, lunch mains $10-15, 2-course dinner $30). Fuel, food packs and basic groceries are available, as well as fascinating Riversleigh fossil field tours ($75 for a half-day tour), and canoe hire (from $20 per hour).

CAPE YORK PENINSULA

Rugged and remote Cape York Peninsula has one of the wildest tropical environments on the planet. The Great Dividing Range forms the spine of the cape, with tropical rainforests and palm-fringed beaches on its eastern flanks and sweeping savannah woodlands, eucalypt forests and coastal mangroves on its west. This untamed landscape undergoes an amazing transformation each year when the torrential rains and flooded rivers of the monsoonal 'wet season' form vast wetlands that isolate the region.

The overland pilgrimage to the tip of Australia is one of the greatest 4WD routes on the continent, an exhilarating trek into Australia's last great frontier. The challenge of rough corrugated roads, difficult creek crossings and croc-infested rivers is part of the adventure, the cape's rich bird life and untouched wilderness its reward.

Avoid the wet season (November to March), when heavy rains can close roads for lengthy periods. The best time to visit is early in the dry season, generally from the beginning of June, when days are warm and evenings are cool.

Tours

Tour operators run trips to the cape – mainly from Cairns, some from Cooktown. Most tours range from six to 14 days and take five to 20 passengers. Tours generally run between April and October, but dates may be affected by an early or late wet season. Places visited include Laura, Split Rock gallery, Lakefield National Park, Coen, Weipa, the Eliot River System (including Twin Falls), Bamaga, Somerset and Cape York; Thursday and Horn Islands are usually an optional extra. Many operators offer different combinations of land, air and sea travel, and camping or motel-style accommodation. Prices include meals, accommodation, and transfers from Cairns.

Heritage Tours TOUR
(☎1800 77 55 33, 07-4054 7750; www.heritagetours.com.au; 7-day fly/drive tours from $2199; ⊙May-Oct) Big range of tours, including fly/drive, cruise and overland with camping or accommodation options.

Wilderness Challenge TOUR
(☎1800 354 486, 07-4035 8888; www.wildernesschallenge.com.au; 7-day camping tours $2095, 7-day accommodated fly/drive tours $3195; ⊙May-Oct) Informative guides and a range of fly/drive/cruise and camping and accommodation options ranging from five to 12 days.

Oz Tours Safaris TOUR
(☎1800 079 006; www.oztours.com.au; 7-day fly/drive camping tours from $1995, 16-day overland tours from $3500) Numerous tours, air/sea/overland options, and camping or motel options ranging from seven to 16 days.

Cape York Motorcycle Adventures MOTORCYCLING, TOUR
(☎07-4059 0220; www.capeyorkmotorcycles.com.au; 8-day tours $5445) This all-inclusive motorcycle tour is from Cairns to the Tip, passing through Cape Trib and other places.

Aurukun Wetland Charters CULTURAL TOUR
(☎07-4058 1441; www.aurukunwetlandcharters.com; 3-5 day tours from $750 per day) In the remote western cape south of Weipa, this cultural and wildlife tour is led by Indigenous guides from the Aurukun community. Accommodation is aboard the MV *Pikkuw* (maximum eight passengers). These wetlands are exceptional for birdwatching.

Information & Permits

The foremost consideration of a cape trip is good preparation. Carry spares, tools and equipment, and check **RACQ road reports** (☎13 19 40; www.racq.com.au). Water can be scarce along the main track, and roadhouses stock only basic food supplies.

North of the Dulhunty River, **permits** (☎13 74 68; www.nprsr.qld.gov.au; permits $5.45) are required to camp on Aboriginal land – basically all the land north of the river. The Injinoo people are the traditional custodians of much of this land and the Injinoo Aboriginal Community, which runs the ferry across the Jardine River, includes a camping permit in the ferry fee.

Travelling across Aboriginal land elsewhere on the cape may require an additional permit, which you can obtain by contacting the relevant community council. See the Cape York Sustainable Futures website (www.cypda.com.au) for details. Permits can take up to six weeks.

Be aware that mobile-phone coverage is sporadic and Telstra-network only.

ALCOHOL RESTRICTIONS

On the way up to the cape you'll see signs warning of alcohol restrictions, which apply to all visitors. In some communities alcohol is banned completely and cannot be carried in. In the Northern Peninsula Area (north of the Jardine River) you can carry a maximum of 11.25L of beer (or 9L of premixed spirits) and 2L of wine per vehicle (not per person). Fines for breaking the restrictions are huge – up to $41,250. For up-to-date information see www.datsima.qld.gov.au.

MAPS & BOOKS

The Hema maps *Cape York & Lakefield National Park* and the RACQ maps *Cairns/Cooktown/Townsville* and *Cape York Peninsula* are the best. Ron and Viv Moon's *Cape York – an Adventurer's Guide* is a comprehensive guide for 4WD and camping enthusiasts.

Cape York Peninsula

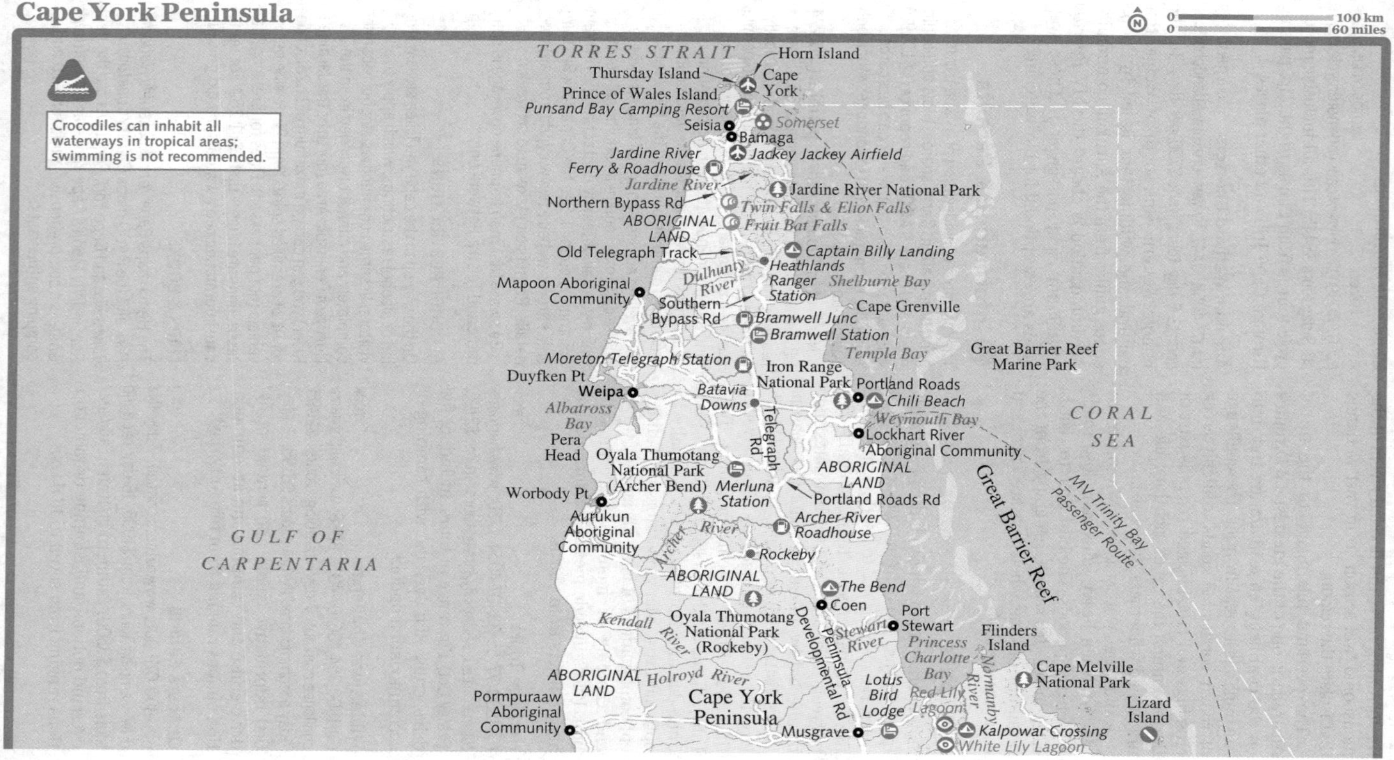
0 100 km
0 60 miles
Crocodiles can inhabit all waterways in tropical areas; swimming is not recommended.
TORRES STRAIT
Horn Island
Thursday Island
Cape York
Prince of Wales Island
Punsand Bay Camping Resort
Somerset
Seisia
Bamaga
Jackey Jackey Airfield
Jardine River Ferry & Roadhouse
Jardine River
Jardine River National Park
Northern Bypass Rd
Twin Falls & Eliot Falls
Fruit Bat Falls
ABORIGINAL LAND
Old Telegraph Track
Captain Billy Landing
Heathlands Ranger Station
Dulhunty River
Shelburne Bay
Mapoon Aboriginal Community
Southern Bypass Rd
Cape Grenville
Bramwell Junc
Bramwell Station
Templa Bay
Great Barrier Reef Marine Park
Moreton Telegraph Station
Iron Range National Park
Duyfken Pt
Weipa
Portland Roads
Chili Beach
Batavia Downs
Albatross Bay
Weymouth Bay
Telegraph Rd
CORAL SEA
Lockhart River Aboriginal Community
Pera Head
Oyala Thumotang National Park (Archer Bend)
Merluna Station
ABORIGINAL LAND
Portland Roads Rd
Worbody Pt
Aurukun Aboriginal Community
Archer River
Archer River Roadhouse
Great Barrier Reef
MV Trinity Bay Passenger Route
GULF OF CARPENTARIA
Rockeby
ABORIGINAL LAND
The Bend
Coen
Port Stewart
Kendall River
Oyala Thumotang National Park (Rockeby)
Peninsula Developmental Rd
Stewart River
Princess Charlotte Bay
Flinders Island
Normanby River
Cape Melville National Park
ABORIGINAL LAND
Holroyd River
Cape York Peninsula
Lotus Bird Lodge
Red Lily Lagoon
Pormpuraaw Aboriginal Community
Musgrave
Kalpowar Crossing
White Lily Lagoon
Lizard Island

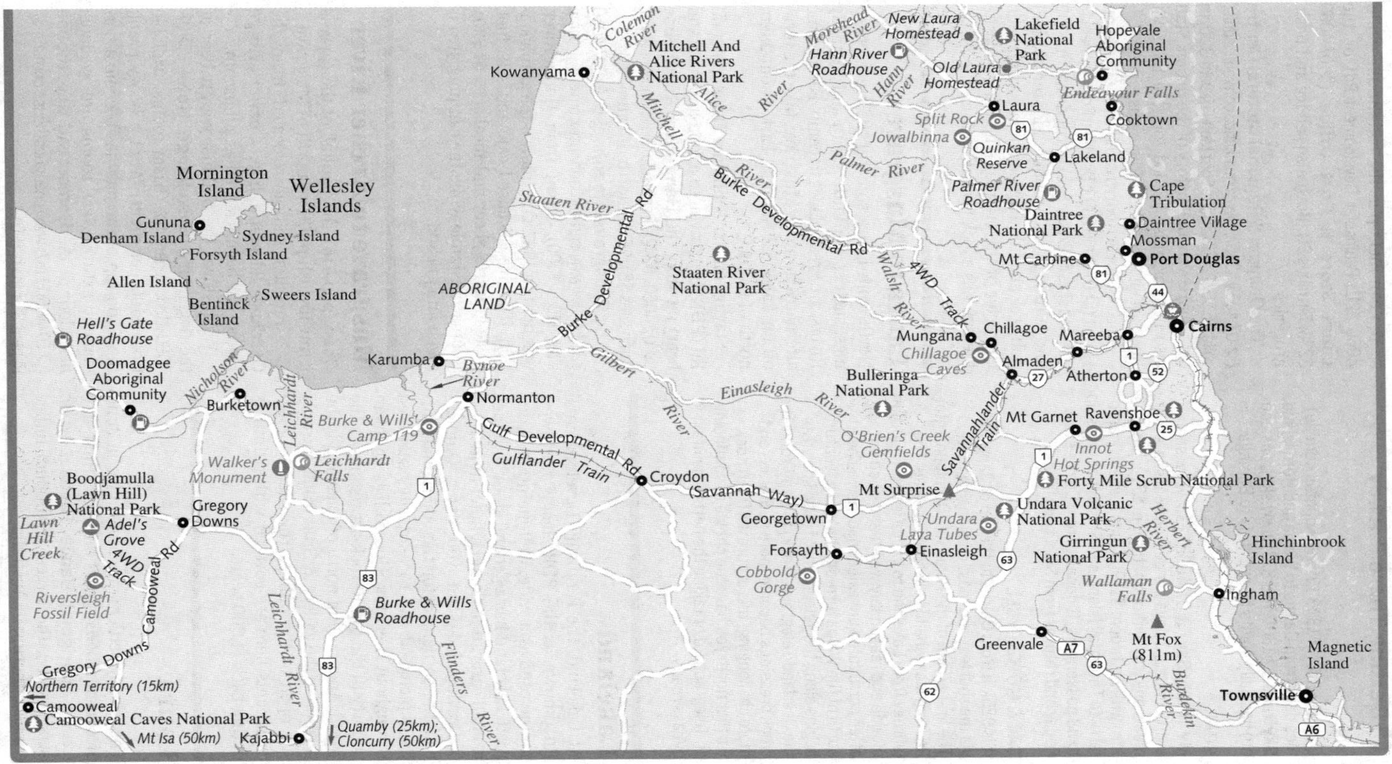
Coleman River
Mitchell And Alice Rivers National Park
Kowanyama
Morehead River
New Laura Homestead
Hann River Roadhouse
Lakefield National Park
Hopevale Aboriginal Community
Old Laura Homestead
Hann River
Endeavour Falls
Alice River
Mitchell River
Laura
Cooktown
Split Rock
Jowalbinna
Quinkan Reserve
Lakeland
Palmer River
Mornington Island
Wellesley Islands
Gununa
Denham Island
Sydney Island
Forsyth Island
Allen Island
Bentinck Island
Sweers Island
Staaten River
Burke Developmental Rd
Palmer River Roadhouse
Cape Tribulation
Daintree National Park
Daintree Village
Mossman
Mt Carbine
Port Douglas
Staaten River National Park
Walsh River
4WD Track
ABORIGINAL LAND
Hell's Gate Roadhouse
Doomadgee Aboriginal Community
Nicholson River
Burketown
Leichhardt River
Karumba
Bynoe River
Normanton
Gilbert River
Chillagoe
Mungana
Chillagoe Caves
Mareeba
Cairns
Almaden
Atherton
Bulleringa National Park
Einasleigh River
Burke & Wills Camp 119
Walker's Monument
Leichhardt Falls
Gulf Developmental Rd
Gulflander Train
Croydon
(Savannah Way)
O'Brien's Creek Gemfields
Savannahlander Train
Mt Garnet
Ravenshoe
Innot Hot Springs
Forty Mile Scrub National Park
Mt Surprise
Boodjamulla (Lawn Hill) National Park
Gregory Downs
Lawn Hill Creek
Adel's Grove
4WD Track
Camooweal Rd
Georgetown
Undara Volcanic National Park
Undara Lava Tubes
Herbert River
Girringun National Park
Hinchinbrook Island
Forsayth
Einasleigh
Cobbold Gorge
Riversleigh Fossil Field
Burke & Wills Roadhouse
Wallaman Falls
Ingham
Leichhardt River
Flinders River
Greenvale
Mt Fox (811m)
Gregory Downs
Northern Territory (15km)
Camooweal
Camooweal Caves National Park
Mt Isa (50km)
Kajabbi
Quamby (25km); Cloncurry (50km)
Burdekin River
Magnetic Island
Townsville
1
25
27
44
52
62
63
81
83
A6
A7

Getting There & Away

AIR

QantasLink (13 13 13; www.qantas.com.au) flies daily from Cairns to Weipa and Horn Island.

Skytrans (1300 759 872; www.skytrans.com.au) has daily flights from Cairns to Bamaga.

BOAT

MV Trinity Bay (07-4035 1234; www.seaswift.com.au; 2 days per person twin share incl meals one way without bathroom $710, 5-day return with bathroom $1590) runs a weekly cargo ferry to Thursday Island and Seisia that takes up to 38 passengers. It departs from Cairns every Friday and returns from Seisia on Monday.

CAR & MOTORCYCLE

It is 925km from Cairns to the top of Cape York via the shortest and most challenging route. The first 175km of the Peninsula Developmental Rd from Mareeba to Lakeland is sealed. The journey from Lakeland to Weipa is nearly 600km of wide and reasonably well-maintained but often corrugated unsealed road. As you head north of the Weipa turn-off, the real adventure begins along the Telegraph Rd (also known as the Overland Telegraph Track) to Cape York. The creek crossings become more numerous and more challenging: this is pure 4WD territory. Further north you have the choice of continuing on Telegraph Rd or taking the better-maintained bypass roads.

Lakeland

At Lakeland, the Peninsula Developmental Rd (known as the PDR) heads northwest up the cape as a wide, well-maintained dirt road. Lakeland has a general store with fuel, a small caravan park and a hotel-motel.

Leaving Lakeland you enter Quinkan country, so named for the Aboriginal spirits depicted at the rock-art sites scattered throughout this area. Unesco lists Quinkan country in the top 10 rock-art regions in the world. About 50km north of Lakeland is the turn-off to the gallery at **Split Rock**, the only site open to the public. The sandstone escarpments here are covered with paintings dating back 14,000 years.

Laura

POP 120

This sleepy settlement comes alive in June of odd-numbered years with the three-day **Laura Aboriginal Dance Festival** (www.laurafestival.tv), the largest traditional Indigenous gathering in Australia.

You can fuel up at the **roadhouse** (07-4060 2211; Peninsular Development Rd) or the **Laura Store & Post Office** (07-4060 3238; Terminus St). Both also sell ice and basic groceries.

The **Quinkan & Regional Cultural Centre** (07-4060 3457; www.quinkancc.com.au; adult/child $5.50/2; 8.30am-5pm Mon-Fri, 9am-3.30pm Sat & Sun) covers the history of the region. Staff also help organise guided tours of the Split Rock art sites with an Indigenous guide.

The historic, corrugated-iron **Quinkan Hotel** (07-4060 3393; Deighton Rd; unpowered/powered sites $23/30, r $75) burnt down in 2002 and although the rebuilt and refurbished pub is clean and functional it lacks the rustic character of the original. The park opposite the pub has a lock-up dating from the 1880s.

Laura to Musgrave

North from Laura some of the creek crossings, such as the Little Laura and Kennedy Rivers, are great places to camp. For a scenic alternative route to Musgrave, take the turn-off for Lakefield National Park, about 28km north of Laura.

Staying on the Peninsula Developmental Rd (PDR) brings you to a food-and-fuel (and beer) pit stop, the **Hann River Roadhouse** (07-4060 3242; Peninsula Developmental Rd; camp sites $8), 76km north of Laura.

The **Musgrave Roadhouse** (07-4060 3229; www.musgraveroadhouse.com.au; camp sites $10, r $100), 80km from Hann River, was built in 1887. Originally a telegraph station, it's now a licensed cafe and sells fuel, basic groceries, beer and meals ($5 to $30). Rooms are simple while the camping area is green and grassed.

Musgrave to Archer River

Coen (pop 416), the 'capital' of the cape, is a tiny township 108km north of Musgrave.

A repeater station relocated from the Overland Telegraph line, **Coen Heritage House** has been restored as a museum.

Wash down the bulldust with a beer at the legendary **S'Exchange Hotel** (07-4060 1133; Regent St) (basic rooms available from $100 per night). After a boozy prank the 'S' on top of the pub has become a permanent fixture. Neat rooms are available next door at the **Homestead Guesthouse** (07-4060 1157; www.coenguesthouse.com.au; 37 Regent St; r from $90).

A picturesque riverside spot for campers is at the **Bend**, about 5km north of Coen. Twenty-five kilometres north is the turn-off to the remote **Mungkan Kandju National Park**.

There are plenty of shady and pleasant camping locations along the river, but if you're wanting to observe life on a working cattle station, **Merluna Station** (☎07-4060 3209; www.merlunastation.com.au; unpowered sites $13, cabins $130-150, s/d without bathroom $80/100; ❄), about 80km northwest of the Archer River Roadhouse, has accommodation in converted workers quarters.

The **Archer River Roadhouse** (☎07-4060 3266; archerriverroadhouse@bigpond.com; unpowered sites adult/child $10/5, r $68; ⏰7.30am-10pm; ❄), 66km north of Coen, is the last fuel stop before Bramwell Junction (170km north on Telegraph Rd) or Weipa (197km west on the PDR). Campsites and simple rooms are also available here. After a meal, look for the memorial dedicated to Toots, a tough-talking female truck driver and a Cape York legend.

Weipa

POP 3344

Weipa, the largest town on the cape, is the site of the world's largest bauxite mine (the ore from which aluminium is processed), but for most visitors Weipa is a fishing town, renowned for barramundi. All of Weipa's accommodation can book various tours and fishing charters.

The **Weipa Caravan Park & Camping Ground** (☎07-4069 7871; www.campweipa.com; unpowered/powered sites $30/35, cabins without bathroom $50-100, with bathroom $120-140, lodge r $165-180; ❄@≋) has a shady spot on the waterfront, and operates as the town's informal tourist office, organising mine and fishing tours. It's walking distance to the local supermarket and shops. It offers a town and mine tour (adult/child $40/12) to see the mind-boggling extent of the mining operation – 22,000 tons of bauxite are mined every 24 hours and promptly sent onto waiting ships in the harbour.

Weipa Air (☎07-4069 7807) has scenic and charter flights over the coast and Cape York.

Archer River to Bramwell Junction

Roughly 36km north of the Archer River Roadhouse, a turn-off leads 135km through the **Iron Range National Park** to the tiny coastal settlement of Portland Roads. This park has Australia's largest area of lowland rainforest, with animals that are found no

WORTH A TRIP

LAKEFIELD NATIONAL PARK

Lakefield National Park, Queensland's second-largest national park, is renowned for its vast river systems, spectacular wetlands and prolific bird life. Covering more than 537,000 hectares, the park encompasses a rich and diverse landscape across the flood plains of the Normanby, Kennedy, Bizant, Morehead and Hann Rivers. This extensive river system drains into Princess Charlotte Bay on the park's northern perimeter.

Old Laura Homestead, near the junction with the Battle Camp Rd from Cooktown, was built soon after the 1874 Palmer River gold rush. The **ranger station** (☎07-4060 3260) is located at New Laura, about 25km north of the junction.

The best camping facilities (with toilets and showers) are at **Kalpowar Crossing** (per person $5.45) beside the Laura River. Book permits online via **Queensland Parks** (☎13 74 68; www.nprsr.qld.gov.au; permits $5.45).

The picturesque **Red Lily Lagoon** and **White Lily Lagoon**, about 8km north of the Lakefield ranger base, attract masses of bird life, including jabirus, brolgas and magpie geese. The red lotus lilies at Red Lily Lagoon are best appreciated in the morning when the blossoms are in full bloom.

Soon after Hann Crossing the flat, treeless landscape of Nifold Plain stretches from horizon to horizon, its spectacular monotony broken only by sweeping grasslands and giant termite mounds.

About 26km before Musgrave, **Lotus Bird Lodge** (☎07-4060 3400; www.lotusbird.com.au; Marina Plains Rd; s/d incl meals $440/600 ; ⏰May-Nov only; ≋), a favourite with birdwatchers, has comfortable timber cabins overlooking an idyllic lagoon.

further south in Australia. A popular camp site is **Chili Beach**, south of Portland Roads. Otherwise, to savour a little luxury in the wilderness, stay in **Portland House** (07-4060 7193; www.portlandhouse.com.au; per person $85), a self-contained beachside cottage.

From Archer River, the Peninsula Developmental Rd continues towards Weipa, but after 48km the **Telegraph Road** branches off north for a rough and bumpy 22km stretch to the **Wenlock River** crossing. Note the sign in the tree at the crossing, which marks floodwaters of 14.3m.

On the northern bank of the Wenlock, **Moreton Telegraph Station** (07-4060 3360; www.moretonstation.com.au; unpowered sites per person $10, safari tents s/d $158/194, cabins s/d $243/298), formerly a station on the Overland Telegraph Line, has a safari camp set-up. You can buy fuel, meals and beer, and perform basic workshop repairs.

Bramwell Junction Roadhouse (07-4060 3230; unpowered sites per person $12) marks the junction of the new Southern Bypass Rd and the historic Old Telegraph Track. This is the last fuel and supplies stop before the Jardine River Ferry (only open from 8am to 5pm). Fifteen kilometres before the roadhouse is the turn-off to Australia's most northern cattle station, **Bramwell Station** (07-4060 3300; bramwelltouristpark@harboursat.com.au; camping per person $10), which offers basic accommodation, camping and meals.

Bramwell Junction to Jardine River

After Bramwell Junction there are two routes to the Jardine River ferry. The longer route on the graded and reasonably well-maintained Southern and Northern Bypass Rds is quicker and avoids most of the creeks and rivers between the Wenlock and Jardine Rivers.

The more direct but more challenging route down the **Old Telegraph Track** (commonly called the OTT or 'the Track') is where the real Cape York adventure begins.

The OTT follows the remnants of the Overland Telegraph Line, which was constructed during the 1880s to allow communications from Cairns to the cape via a series of repeater stations and an underwater cable link to Thursday Island. The OTT is a serious 4WD experience with deep corrugations, powdery sand and difficult creek crossings (especially the **Dulhunty River** crossing).

A road leaves the OTT 2km north of the Dulhunty and heads for **Heathlands Ranger Station** (07-4060 3241), looping past the difficult Gunshot Creek crossing. Back on the OTT, the road becomes sandy for a stretch before joining the Southern Bypass Rd.

After 9km, the Northern Bypass Rd heads west to the Jardine River ferry crossing, but if you continue another 3km you reach the turn-off to **Fruit Bat Falls**. Another 7km on the OTT takes you to the turn-off for **Twin Falls & Eliot Falls**. The falls and the deep emerald-green swimming holes here are spectacular, and worth a long visit. The **camping ground** (per person $5.45) is the most popular site on the trip north.

The old vehicular crossing of the Jardine River on the OTT is closed. The only access to the Jardine River ferry is on the Northern Bypass Rd.

Jardine River

The Jardine River is Queensland's largest perennial river, spilling more fresh water into the sea than any other river in Australia. The **Jardine River Ferry & Roadhouse** (07-4069 1369; unpowered sites per person $5; 8am-5pm), run by the Injinoo Community Council, sells fuel and operates a ferry during the dry season ($88 return, plus $11 for trailers). The fee includes a permit for bush camping between the Dulhunty and Jardine Rivers, and in designated areas north of the Jardine.

Stretching east to the coast from the main track is the impenetrable country of **Jardine River National Park**. It includes the headwaters of the Jardine and Escape Rivers, where explorer Edmund Kennedy was killed by Aborigines in 1848.

Northern Peninsula Area

Everything north of the Jardine River is known as the Northern Peninsula Area (NPA to the locals).

Bamaga & Seisia

The first settlement, 45km north of the Jardine River, is **Bamaga** (population 1046), home to Cape York Peninsula's largest Torres Strait Islander community. There's a small shopping centre, a bottle shop, a hospital and an airstrip.

Five kilometres northwest of Bamaga, **Seisia** (population 204) overlooks the Torres Strait and is a great base from which to explore the tip.

Cape York Adventures (07-4069 3302; www.capeyorkadventures.com.au; boat charter per day from $800, 5-7 day tours from $3500) offers half- and full-day fishing trips and sunset cruises, as well as tours from Cairns up to Bamaga.

Seisia Holiday Park (07-4069 3243; unpowered/powered sites per person $12/15, lodge s/d $80/120, cottages $180-240, villas $210-240;), next to Seisia's wharf, is a popular campground with good facilities and a restaurant (meals from $15). The park is also a booking agent for scenic flights, 4WD tours and the ferry to Thursday Island.

The **Loyalty Beach Campground & Fishing Lodge** (07-4069 3372; www.loyalty-beach.com; unpowered/powered sites $12/28, lodge s/d $125/150, beach lodge $260), on the beachfront 3km from the wharf, is quieter than the holiday park. Meals are served up at night and management can help with tour bookings and fishing charters.

Peddells Ferry Service (07-4069 1551; www.peddellsferry.com.au; adult/child $56/28; 8am & 4pm Mon-Sat Jun-Sep, Mon, Wed & Fri Oct-May) runs regular ferries from Seisia jetty to Thursday Island.

The Tip

From Bamaga the road north passes Lockerbie Homestead. The **Croc Tent** (07-4069 3210; www.croctent.com.au; 7.30am-6pm), across the road, sells souvenirs and provides an unofficial tourist information service. The road then passes through the northernmost rainforest in Australia, **Lockerbie Scrub**, before reaching a Y-junction.

The track right leads to the pretty foreshore of **Somerset** with a campground. The left track leads 10km down the road to the now defunct Pajinka Wilderness Lodge. A 1km walk through the forest and along the beach (over the headland if the tide's in) takes you to **Cape York**, the northernmost tip of Australia.

On the western side of the tip, the scenic **Punsand Bay Camping Resort** (07-4069 1722; www.punsand.com.au; unpowered/powered sites per person $10/15, tents $140-200, air-con cabins $220;) is a remote haven in the wilderness. A dip in the pool, or a cold beer in the breezy restaurant, tops off the tip experience.

Thursday Island & Torres Strait Islands

Australia's most northern frontier consists of more than 100 islands stretching like stepping stones for 150km from the top of Cape York Peninsula to Papua New Guinea. The islands vary from the rocky, northern extensions of the Great Dividing Range to small coral cays and rainforested volcanic mountains.

Torres Strait Islanders came from Melanesia and Polynesia about 2000 years ago, establishing a unique culture different from those of Papua New Guinea and the Australian Aboriginal people.

Although **Prince of Wales Island** is the largest of the group, the administrative capital is tiny **Thursday Island** (it's only 3 sq km), 30km off the cape. Although lacking its own freshwater supply, Thursday Island (population 2610) was selected for its deep harbour, sheltered port and proximity to major shipping channels. One of 17 inhabited islands in the strait, TI (as it's locally known) was once a major pearling centre, and the legacy of that industry has resulted in a cultural mix of Asians, Europeans and Islanders.

Horn Island (population 539) is the air-and-ferry transport hub for the region with connecting ferries to TI. **Erub** (Darnley Island as it is also known) is in the eastern group. It's another important island as it has come into the spotlight as a campaigner for equal recognition of Torres Strait Islanders' rights.

Regular ferry services connect Seisia with Thursday and Horn Islands. To visit other inhabited Torres Strait Islands requires permission from the island's council; contact the **Torres Strait Regional Council** (07-4048 6200; www.tsirc.qld.gov.au; Torres Strait Haus, 46 Victoria Pde, Thursday Island)

Sights & Activities

On Thursday Island, the **Gab Titui Cultural Centre** (07-4069 0888; www.gabtitui.com.au; cnr Victoria Pde & Blackall St; admission $6; 10am-5.30pm Mon-Sat, by apt Sun) houses a modern gallery displaying the people's history of the Torres Strait; it also hosts cultural events and exhibitions by local artists, and has a popular outdoor cafe, Ilan.

TI's pearling heyday resulted in fatalities from decompression sickness. The **Japanese Pearl Divers Memorial** at the cemetery presides over the many Japanese divers buried here. TI's war history can be experienced with a visit to **Green Hill Fort**, which was built in 1893 in response to fears of a Russian invasion. The **Torres Strait Museum**, in the fort, displays war paraphernalia and local artefacts. The fort and museum can be visited through a bus tour run by Peddells.

The **All Souls Quetta Memorial Church** was built in 1893 in memory of the 134 lives that were lost when the *Quetta* struck an uncharted reef and sank within three minutes. Inside the church is memorabilia from a number of shipwrecks, including a coral-encrusted porthole recovered from the *Quetta* in 1906.

The **Heritage Museum & Art Gallery** (☎07-4069 2222; www.torresstrait.com.au; Horn Island; adult/child $7/4) at the Gateway Torres Strait Resort on Horn Island is a good source of information on the region's WWII history.

Tours

Peddells Ferry Island Tourist Bureau BUS, TOUR
(☎07-4069 1551; www.peddellsferry.com.au; adult/child $31/16; ⏲8.30am-5pm) Ninety-minute bus tours of TI, taking in all the major tourist sites. Also runs Cape York 4WD day trips and Horn Island WWII tours.

Tony's Island Adventures FISHING, TOUR
(☎07-4069 1965; www.tonysislandadventures.com.au; 10 Pearl St, Thursday Island) Offers fishing trips and tours of various Torres Strait Islands, including Friday, Hammond and Goodes Islands.

Sleeping & Eating

Gateway Torres Strait Resort HOTEL $$
(☎07-4069 2222; www.torresstrait.com.au; 24 Outie St, Horn Island; r from $180; ❄@≋) This place has passable rooms and self-contained units. The resort houses a museum as well as a restaurant that offers buffet dinners and lunches during the dry season. It's a five-minute walk from the Horn Island wharf.

Grand Hotel HOTEL $$$
(☎07-4069 1557; www.grandhotelti.com.au; 6 Victoria Pde, Thursday Island; s $200-210, d $235-260; ❄@) On a hill behind the TI wharf, the Grand has modern rooms with ocean and mountain views. The restaurant (mains $15 to $30, open dinner Monday to Saturday) has a balcony with sweeping views. Rates include breakfast.

Thursday Island Motel MOTEL $$$
(☎07-4069 1569; cnr Jardine & Douglas Sts, Thursday Island; s/d incl breakfast $200/215; ❄@) These comfortable motel units, connected to the back of the Federal Hotel, are a good choice.

Torres Strait Hotel PUB $$
(☎07-4609 1141; cnr Normaby & Douglas St, Thursday Island; dishes $12-28) Claim bragging rights by chowing down on a saucy crayfish pie at 'Australia's Northernmost Pub'.

Getting There & Around

QantasLink (☎13 13 13; www.qantas.com.au) flies daily from Cairns to Horn Island. **West Wing Aviation** (www.westwing.com.au) connects Horn Island to other islands.

Peddells Ferry Service (☎07-4069 1551; www.peddellsferry.com.au; Engineers Jetty) Runs regular services between Seisia and Thursday Island. From June to September it has two daily services from Monday to Saturday (adult/child $56/28 one way, 70 minutes), and from October to May it operates only on Monday, Wednesday and Friday. The ferry departs from Thursday Island for Seisia at 6.30am and 2.30pm, and Seisia for Thursday Island at 8am and 4pm.

McDonald Charter Boats (☎1300 664 875; www.tiferry.com.au) Runs ferries between TI and Horn Island roughly hourly between 6.10am and 6.30pm (adult/child $24/12 one way, 15 minutes), as well as a water-taxi service between other Torres Strait Islands. McDonald also operates a bus service to and from Horn Island Airport.

Rebel Marine (☎07-4069 1586; www.rebeltours.com.au) Operates a water taxi between Thursday Island and Horn Island Airport, connecting with all QantasLink flights ($20 one way).

Melbourne & Victoria

Includes ➡

Best Regional Dining

- ➡ Koonwarra Store (p606)
- ➡ Lake House (p584)
- ➡ Royal Mail Hotel (p555)
- ➡ Stefano's Restaurant (p561)

Best Places to Stay

- ➡ Ovolo (p502)
- ➡ Art Series (Cullen) (p504)
- ➡ YHA Eco Beach (p543)
- ➡ Theatre Royal Back Stage (p580)

Why Go?

Melbourne, Australia's second-largest city, is the state's urban hub and the nation's artistic centre. Here, culture junkies and culinary perfectionists feast on art, music, theatre, cinema and cuisine for every budget.

Scalloping its way around coves, beaches and cliffs to the west, the Great Ocean Road is great indeed. Wild surf pounds the shoreline and enigmatic coastal towns mingle with lush national parks.

In the High Country, brilliant autumn colours segue into snowfields and back again to sleepy summer towns, haunted by pale gums. Skis get a workout in winter, and cycling, horse riding and cheeky weekends are the mainstays of summer.

If wild landscapes are your weakness, head to the Grampians National Park, sprawled amid the dry plains of the Western District. Australia's southernmost mainland tip is the spiritually reviving Wilsons Promontory National Park.

When to Go

Melbourne

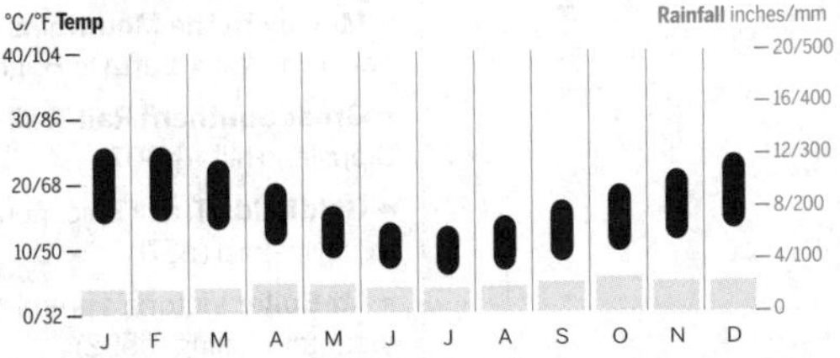

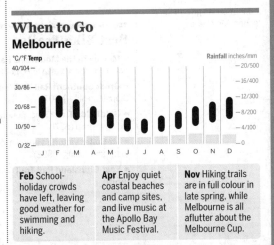

Feb School-holiday crowds have left, leaving good weather for swimming and hiking.

Apr Enjoy quiet coastal beaches and camp sites, and live music at the Apollo Bay Music Festival.

Nov Hiking trails are in full colour in late spring, while Melbourne is all aflutter about the Melbourne Cup.

TOP TIPS

- Head to the wharf in seaside towns and buy fresh seafood straight off the boat.
- **Half Tix** (www.halftixmelbourne.com) sells cheap tickets for day trips from Melbourne (think wineries or penguins) and Melbourne theatre performances.

Fast Facts

- Population: 5,6 million
- Area: 227,500 sq km
- Coastline: 2000km
- Number of wineries: 850

Advance Planning

- Avoid the coast from Christmas until late January and during Easter; school holidays equate to packed beaches, booked-out accommodation and restricted access to popular hiking trails. See www.education.vic.gov.au for school term dates.

Great Ocean Road

This is one of the most popular touring routes in Australia and, blow us down with a limestone outcrop, it's worth the hype. Take plenty of time – at least a week – to get the best from this region.

Start in the surfing mecca of Torquay by checking out the waves at Bells Beach, then head to family-friendly Anglesea to see kangaroos grazing on the golf course. Aireys Inlet is next: tour the lighthouse then plan an overnight stay in the resort town of Lorne. Break up the sea views with a detour up into the rainforests of the Otway Ranges. Back on the Great Ocean Road, head to the fishing village of Apollo Bay for a day or two. It's quite a stretch to Port Campbell National Park and its famed Twelve Apostles; take the time to count them and spend a night in Port Campbell to get a feel for the area. Look for whales off Warrnambool's coast then continue west to quaint, and very Irish, Port Fairy. If there's time, head to tiny Cape Bridgewater to meet its seal population.

DON'T MISS

Who can resist the nightly parade of cute little penguins waddling out of the ocean and into their sandy burrows at Phillip Island? Not the three-million-plus tourists who visit annually, that's for sure. This little island in Western Port Bay also has fabulous surf beaches, a moto-GP circuit and wildlife parks.

For sheer natural beauty, Wilsons Promontory has it all. Jutting into Bass Strait, this national park is isolated but accessible, boasting sublime ocean beaches and some of the best wilderness hiking in the state. To take advantage of its well-maintained network of trails and bush camping areas, you just need to grab a map, strap on a pack and disappear into the wilds.

Best Bike Trails

- **Murray to the Mountains Rail Trail** Scenic High Country ride from Wangaratta to Bright (p597)
- **Great Southern Rail Trail** Ride through the South Gippsland hills (p607)
- **Goldfields Track** Epic mountain-biking trail from Ballarat to Daylesford (p578)
- **Mt Buller** Victoria's premier downhill and cross-country mountain-biking (p592)
- **East Gippsland Rail Trail** Cycling trail in Victoria's far east (p610)

History

In 1803 a party of convicts, soldiers and settlers arrived at Sorrento (on the southern edge of Port Phillip Bay), but the settlement was soon abandoned. The first permanent European settlement in Victoria was established in 1834 at Portland (in the Western District) by the Henty family from Van Diemen's Land (Tasmania), some 46 years after Sydney was colonised. In 1851 Victoria won separation from New South Wales, and in that same year the rich Victorian goldfields were discovered, attracting immigrants from around the world. Towns such as Beechworth and Ballarat boomed during the gold rush, and are veritable museum pieces today. Melbourne was founded in 1835 by enterprising Tasmanians and it retains much Victorian-era charm and gold-boom 1880s architecture to this day.

The latter half of the 20th century saw a huge influx of immigrants into Victoria, particularly Melbourne, and the city is now widely regarded as Australia's most multicultural city. It has one of the largest Greek populations per capita in the world and is heavily influenced by Italian, Eastern European and Southeast Asian cultures.

The 1990s and 21st century have seen a period of ferocious development – a process that continues today – and the face of the CBD has changed and spread markedly with the building of Docklands and the construction of architectural landmarks such as Federation Square.

Indigenous Victoria

Aboriginal people have lived in Victoria for an estimated 40,000 years. They lived in some 38 different dialect groups that spoke 10 separate languages. These groups were further divided into clans and subclans, each with its own customs and laws, and each claiming ownership of a distinct area of land. Before British colonisation, the Yarra Valley region was occupied by members of the Woiworung clan of the Kulin Nation, known as the Wurundjeri.

As many as 100,000 Aboriginal people lived in Victoria before Europeans arrived; by 1860 there were as few as 2000 left alive. Today around 27,000 Koories (Aboriginal people from southeastern Australia) live in Victoria, and more than half live in Melbourne.

There has been a strong movement to revive Aboriginal culture in Victoria and cultural centres exist around the state, including the excellent Brambuk Cultural Centre and Gariwerd Dreaming Theatre, both in Halls Gap in the Grampians National Park. Run by local Koorie communities, these centres provide insights into Koorie history, culture, art, music and dance, and provide tours to local rock-art sites.

In Bairnsdale, the Krowathunkoolong Keeping Place is a Koorie cultural centre that explores Kurnai daily life before and after white settlement.

Based in Mildura, Harry Nanya's Graham Clarke provides acclaimed tours into Lake Mungo National Park, with excellent commentary about the traditional occupants of the land.

In Melbourne, the Ian Potter Centre: NGV Australia has a renowned collection of Aboriginal and Torres Strait Islander art, while the Aboriginal Heritage Walk takes you through the story of the Boonwurrung and Woiworung peoples, on whose ancestral grounds the Royal Botanic Gardens now sit.

Melbourne itself is divided between the Wurundjeri and the Boonwurrung peoples, and both groups are represented by female elders – Aunty Joy Murphy and Aunty Carolyn Briggs.

For more information about the history of Victoria's indigenous people, visit the Koorie Heritage Trust Cultural Centre or the interesting and comprehensive Bunjilaka Indigenous centre at Melbourne Museum.

A 'Welcome to Country' ceremony – which can vary from a speech to a traditional dance or a smoking ceremony – by an Aboriginal community member is now common protocol across the state and these are performed at a diverse range of functions. An 'Acknowledgement Ceremony' is common at forums, whereby the first speaker pays recognition and respect to the traditional owners of the land. Similarly, a gum-leaf ceremony is common at dinners and events.

The website of **Visit Victoria** (www.visitvictoria.com) has an excellent link to Aboriginal culture, heritage, history and sites in Victoria. Another good resource is **Aboriginal Tourism Victoria** (www.aboriginaltourismvictoria.com.au).

Aboriginal Melbourne: The Lost Land of the Kulin People by Gary Presland (rereleased 2001), and *Aboriginal Victorians: A History Since 1800* by Richard Broome (2005), also give valuable insight into the culture and life of the region's original inhabitants.

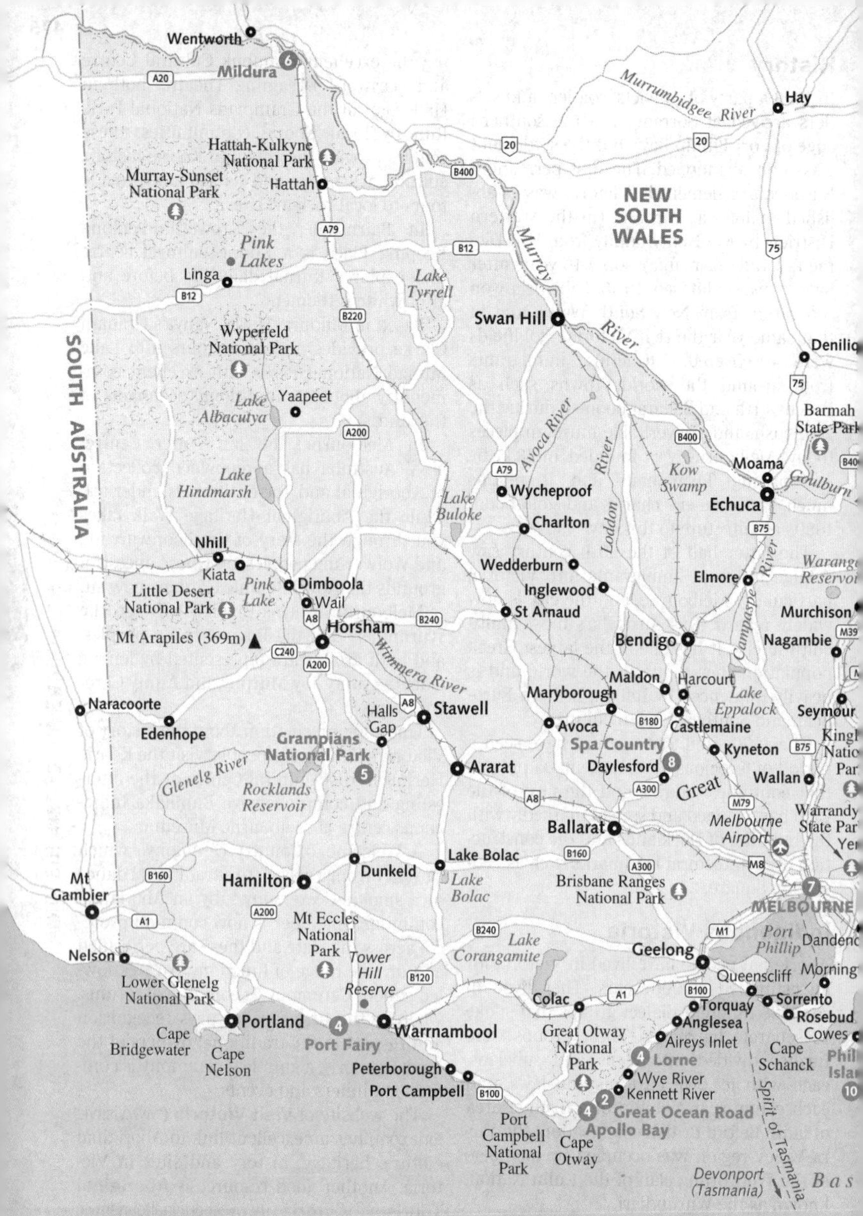

Melbourne & Victoria Highlights

1 Get exquisitely lost in the wilderness of **Croajingolong National Park** (p616)

2 Curl your way around the magical twists of the **Great Ocean Road** (p535) all the way to Port Campbell National Park

3 Revel down the ski slopes of the **High Country** (p587)

4 Make merry at music festivals in **Apollo Bay** (p542), **Lorne** (p541) and **Port Fairy** (p548)

5 Experience breathtaking hikes and Aboriginal culture in the **Grampians National Park** (p551)

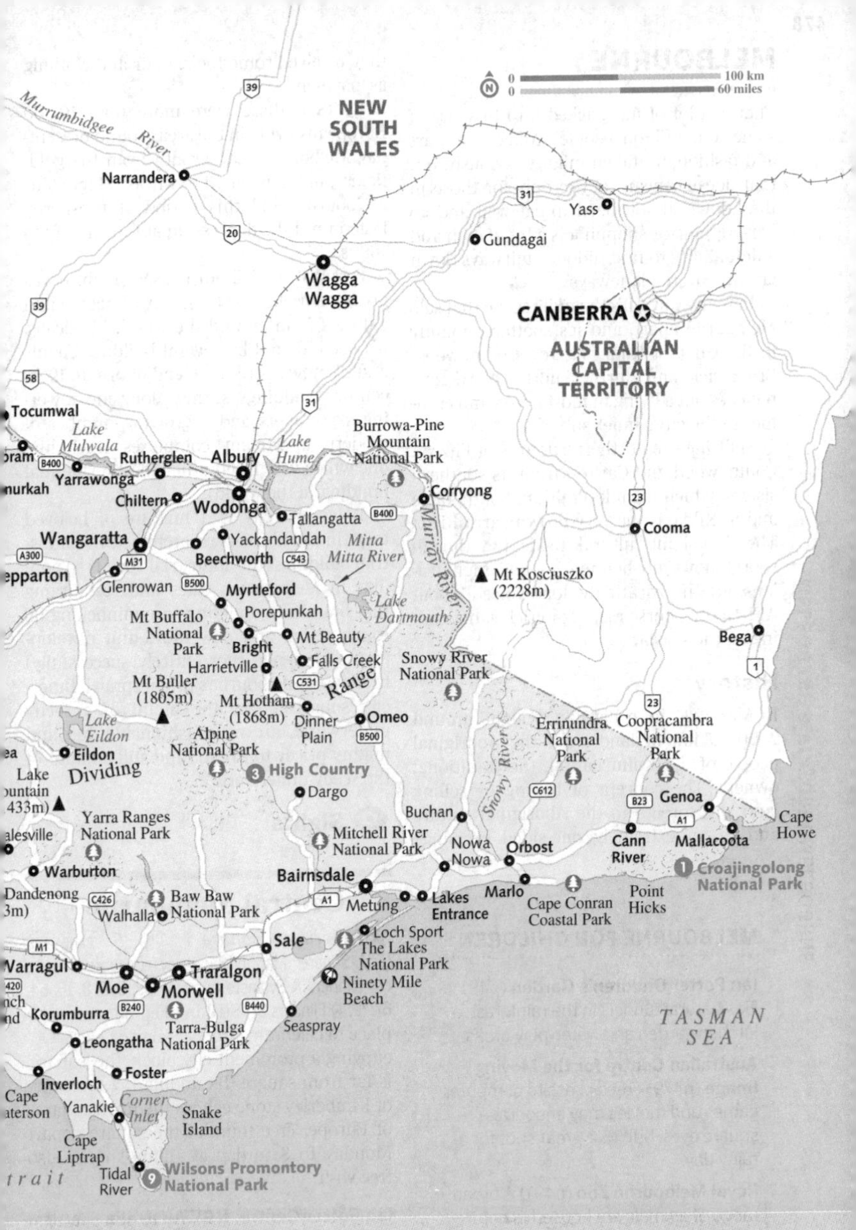

6 Meander the Murray on a paddle steamer in **Mildura** (p557)

7 Hit the funky suburbs of Melbourne and get low-key and groovy in **Fitzroy** (p488), sun-kissed in **St Kilda** (p493) and styled up in **South Yarra** (p491)

8 Soak in the mineral springs of **spa country** (p582), just a 1½-hour drive from the city

9 Go hiking at **Wilsons Promontory National Park** (p607)

10 Watch penguins parading home at **Phillip Island** (p531)

MELBOURNE

POP 4 MILLION

There's a lot of fun packed into this city of some four million people. Coffee, food, art and fashion are taken mighty seriously, but that doesn't mean they're only for those in the know; all you need to eat well and go bar-hopping or shopping is a bit of cash and a deft ability to find hidden stairways down graffiti-covered laneways.

In many ways, it's the indie scene that sets Melbourne apart, and it's spottable mainly in the CBD, St Kilda, Fitzroy, Collingwood, Brunswick and, further north, Northcote, but ekes out a living in most nooks and crannies in the city's inner suburbs.

Splitting the northern suburbs of Fitzroy, Collingwood and Carlton from its southern sisters, which include Prahran, South Yarra and St Kilda, is the very brown Yarra River. There's a slight cultural divide, too, though sport knows no boundaries and Melburnians are intoxicatingly loud-voiced about AFL (footy), horse racing or cricket, depending on the season.

History

In May 1835 John Batman 'bought' around 2400 sq km of land from the Aboriginal people of the Kulin nation, the traditional owners. The concept of buying or selling land was foreign to the Aboriginal culture and in an extremely one-sided exchange they received some tools, flour and clothing as 'payment'.

By 1840 there were more than 10,000 Europeans living in the area around present-day Melbourne. The wealth from the goldfields built this city, known as 'Marvellous Melbourne', and this period of prosperity lasted until the depression at the end of the 1880s.

Post-WWII, Melbourne's social fabric was greatly enriched by an influx of people and cultures from around the world. Physically, it's been altered by several building booms and it's now a striking blend of ornate 19th-century buildings sitting alongside towering skyscrapers and a growing number of modern apartment complexes (including one which was, briefly, the tallest residential building in the world).

Today the city is a mixture of beloved towering gold-rush-era architecture, industrial buildings (the 'industrial' look is so popular in Melbourne's cafes and restaurants that brand-new buildings are mimicking its rough style), and new multi-unit developments, designed (not entirely successfully) to stave off Melbourne's urban sprawl. Inner-city suburbs, once the haunt of a seedy underworld, are now fashionable, hip and mighty pricey to live in (and still a haunt of the seedy underworld).

MELBOURNE FOR CHILDREN

Ian Potter Children's Garden (p491) Has natural tunnels in the rainforest, a kitchen garden and water-play areas.

Australian Centre for the Moving Image (p479) Free access to computer games and movies may encourage square eyes, but it's a great spot for a rainy day.

Royal Melbourne Zoo (p491) A broad range of animals are housed in nature-like enclosures.

National Sports Museum (p487) Just walking in will get your junior champion's heart rate up.

Melbourne Museum (p490) The Children's Gallery has hands-on exhibits that make kids squeal.

Sights

Central Melbourne

★Federation Square LANDMARK
(Fed Square; Map p484; www.fedsquare.com.au; cnr Flinders & Swanston Sts; 1, 3, 5, 6, 8, 16, 64, 67, 72, Flinders St) Striking Fed Square is the place to celebrate, protest, relax or party. Occupying a prominent city block, the 'square' is far from square. Its undulating forecourt of Kimberley stone echoes the town squares of Europe. Free tours of the square depart Monday to Saturday at 11am. There's also free wi-fi.

Ian Potter Centre: NGV Australia GALLERY
(Map p484; 03-8662 1555; www.ngv.vic.gov.au; Federation Sq; exhibition costs vary; 10am-5pm Tue-Sun; 1, 3, 5, 6, 8, 16, 64, 67, 72, Flinders St) FREE This houses a collection of Australian paintings, decorative arts, photography, prints, drawings, sculpture, fashion, textiles and jewellery. The gallery's indigenous collection dominates the ground floor and

MELBOURNE IN...

Two Days

Join a walking tour to see Melbourne's street art, then enjoy lunch at **Cumulus Inc** in art-gallery-lined Flinders Lane. Soak up the view and a local brew from a rooftop bar until it's time to join an evening kayaking tour of the Yarra River. Day two, shop your way to the **Queen Victoria Market**. Take your bites to eat to **Flagstaff Gardens** before catching a tram to **St Kilda**, where you can take sunset photos and stroll along the beach and pier. Check out the little penguins at the St Kilda breakwater before propping up a bar in lively **Acland St** for the evening.

One Week

Check out **NGV Australia** and **ACMI** before heading to **Fitzroy** and **Collingwood**. Shop along **Gertrude St** and feast at Cumulus Inc's sibling **Cutler & Co**. You're close to the **Melbourne Museum**, so spend a couple of hours there then revive with a **Lygon St** coffee. Back in the CBD, dine on dumplings at **HuTong Dumpling Bar** in Chinatown, or at **Flower Drum** across the lane. Spend the next day clothes shopping in busy **Prahran** and **South Yarra**. In winter, catch a footy game at the **MCG** before going low-fi at one of the city's laneway bars. Get some rooftop time at Fitzroy's **Naked for Satan** then see live music at the **Northcote Social Club** in Northcote or **Corner Hotel** in Richmond.

seeks to challenge ideas of the 'authentic'. The contemporary exhibits upstairs are well worth checking out.

Australian Centre for the Moving Image MUSEUM
(ACMI; Map p484; ☎03-8663 2200; www.acmi.net.au; Federation Sq; ⏰10am-6pm; 🚋1, 3, 5, 6, 8, 16, 64, 67, 72, 🚆Flinders St) FREE ACMI educates, enthrals and entertains in equal parts, and has enough games and movies on call for days, or even months, of screen time. *Screenworld* is an exhibition that celebrates the work of mostly Australian cinema and TV, and upstairs the Australian Mediatheque is set aside for the viewing of programs from the National Film and Sound Archive and ACMI.

Birrarung Marr PARK
(Map p484; btwn Federation Sq & the Yarra River; 🚋1, 3, 5, 6, 8, 16, 64, 67, 72, 🚆Flinders St) Featuring grassy knolls, river promenades and a thoughtful planting of indigenous flora, Birrarung Marr also houses the sculptural and musical **Federation Bells** (http://federationbells.com.au), which ring according to a varying schedule.

★**Hosier Lane** STREET
(Map p484; Hosier Lane; 🚋75, 70) This lane is Melbourne's best-known canvas for street art, and its cobbled length draws camera-wielding crowds. Pieces change almost daily, and reach for the sky. Keep an eye down low, too; you might even find oddities like a cement gun.

Young & Jackson's HISTORIC BUILDING
(Map p484; www.youngandjacksons.com.au; cnr Flinders & Swanston Sts; 🚌Tourist Shuttle, 🚋City Circle, 1, 3, 5, 6, 8, 16, 64, 67, 72, 🚆Flinders St) This pub is known more for its painting of pre-pubescent *Chloe* than beer. Painted by Jules Joseph Lefebvre, naked *Chloe* was a hit at the Paris Salon of 1875. It caused an outcry in pursed-lipped provincial Melbourne, and was removed from the National Gallery of Victoria. Bought by a publican, *Chloe* continues to enthral at Young & Jackson's.

Block Arcade HISTORIC BUILDING
(Map p484; www.theblockarcade.com.au; 282 Collins St; 🚋109) This arcade was built in 1891 and features etched-glass ceilings and amazing mosaic floors. Doing 'the Block' (walking around the block) was a popular pastime in 19th-century Melbourne, as it was the place to shop and be seen. **Hopetoun Tea Rooms** (Map p484; ☎03-9650 2777; www.hopetountearooms.com.au; 282 Collins St; dishes $13-21; ⏰8am-5pm) are as famous for their queue as their pavlova.

Royal Arcade HISTORIC BUILDING
(Map p484; www.royalarcade.com.au; 335 Bourke St Mall; 🚋86, 96) This Parisian-style arcade was built between 1869 and 1870 and is Melbourne's oldest; the upper walls retain much of the original 19th-century detail. The black-and-white chequered path leads to the

Melbourne

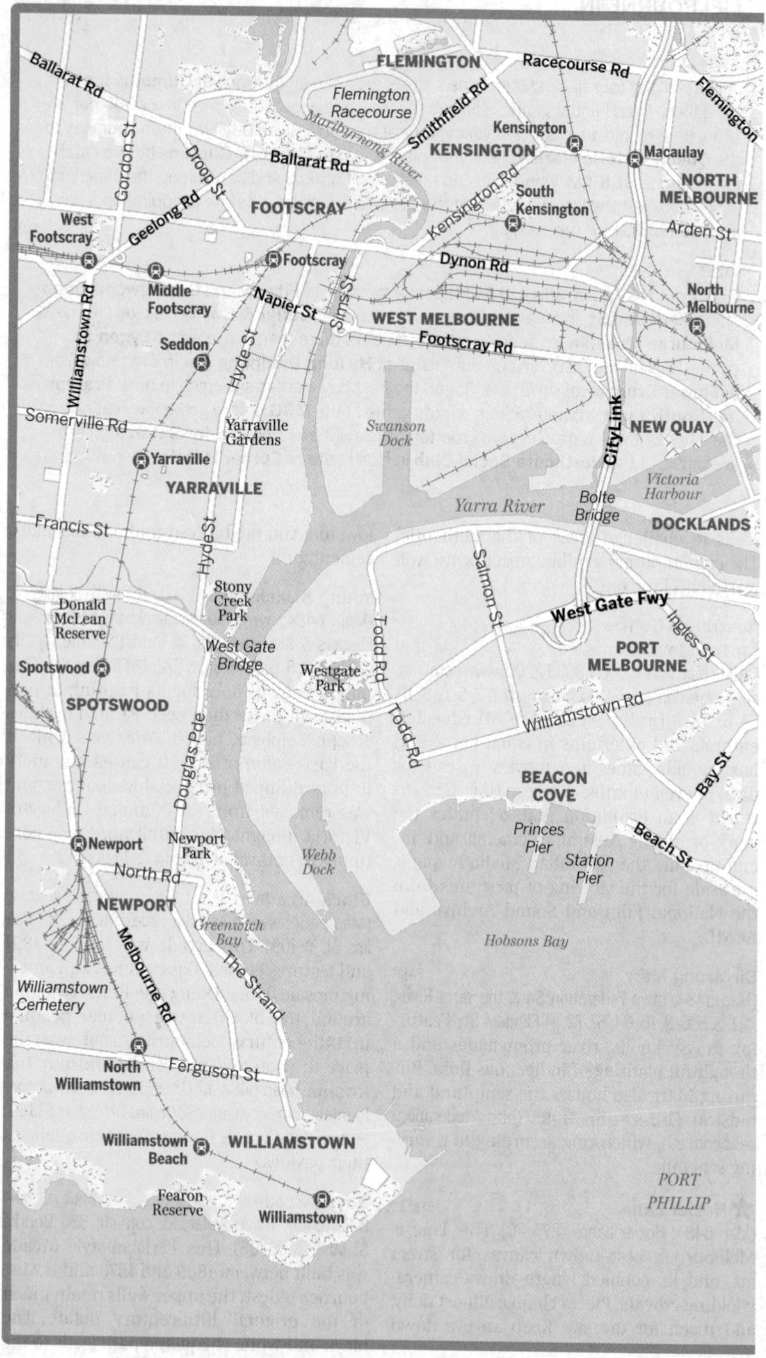
FLEMINGTON
Racecourse Rd
Ballarat Rd
Flemington Racecourse
Maribyrnong River
Smithfield Rd
Flemington
Kensington
KENSINGTON
Macaulay
NORTH MELBOURNE
Gordon St
Droop St
Ballarat Rd
Geelong Rd
FOOTSCRAY
Kensington Rd
South Kensington
Arden St
West Footscray
Footscray
Dynon Rd
Middle Footscray
Napier St
Sims St
North Melbourne
WEST MELBOURNE
Williamstown Rd
Seddon
Hyde St
Footscray Rd
Somerville Rd
Yarraville Gardens
Swanson Dock
CityLink
NEW QUAY
Yarraville
YARRAVILLE
Victoria Harbour
Yarra River
Bolte Bridge
DOCKLANDS
Francis St
Hyde St
Salmon St
Stony Creek Park
Donald McLean Reserve
West Gate Fwy
Todd Rd
Ingles St
West Gate Bridge
PORT MELBOURNE
Spotswood
Westgate Park
SPOTSWOOD
Williamstown Rd
Todd Rd
Douglas Pde
BEACON COVE
Bay St
Princes Pier
Newport
Newport Park
Webb Dock
Beach St
Station Pier
North Rd
NEWPORT
Greenwich Bay
Hobsons Bay
Melbourne Rd
The Strand
Williamstown Cemetery
North Williamstown
Ferguson St
Williamstown Beach
WILLIAMSTOWN
PORT PHILLIP
Fearon Reserve
Williamstown

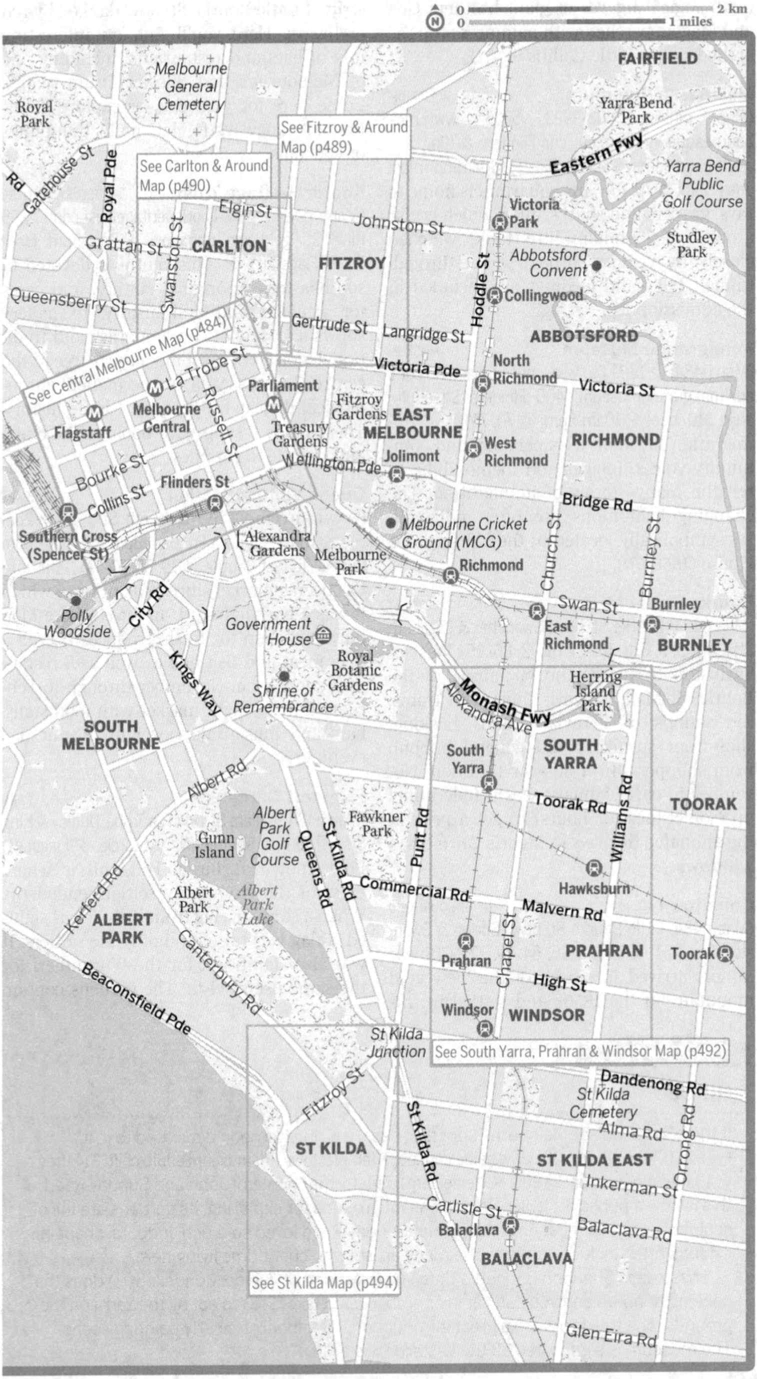
0 2 km
0 1 miles
N
FAIRFIELD
Yarra Bend Park
Eastern Fwy
Yarra Bend Public Golf Course
Studley Park
Melbourne General Cemetery
Royal Park
See Fitzroy & Around Map (p489)
See Carlton & Around Map (p490)
Gatehouse St
Rd
Royal Pde
Elgin St
Johnston St
Victoria Park
Grattan St
Swanston St
CARLTON
FITZROY
Hoddle St
Abbotsford Convent
Collingwood
Queensberry St
Gertrude St
Langridge St
ABBOTSFORD
See Central Melbourne Map (p484)
La Trobe St
Victoria Pde
North Richmond
Victoria St
Parliament
Flagstaff
Melbourne Central
Russell St
Fitzroy Gardens
EAST MELBOURNE
Treasury Gardens
West Richmond
RICHMOND
Wellington Pde
Jolimont
Bourke St
Collins St
Flinders St
Bridge Rd
Southern Cross (Spencer St)
Alexandra Gardens
Melbourne Park
Melbourne Cricket Ground (MCG)
Richmond
Church St
Burnley St
Polly Woodside
City Rd
Swan St
Burnley
Government House
East Richmond
BURNLEY
Kings Way
Royal Botanic Gardens
Shrine of Remembrance
Herring Island Park
Monash Fwy
Alexandra Ave
SOUTH MELBOURNE
South Yarra
SOUTH YARRA
Toorak Rd
TOORAK
Williams Rd
Albert Rd
Albert Park Golf Course
Fawkner Park
Gunn Island
St Kilda Rd
Queens Rd
Punt Rd
Hawksburn
Kerferd Rd
Albert Park
Albert Park Lake
Commercial Rd
Malvern Rd
ALBERT PARK
Chapel St
PRAHRAN
Toorak
Prahran
High St
Canterbury Rd
Beaconsfield Pde
Windsor
WINDSOR
St Kilda Junction
See South Yarra, Prahran & Windsor Map (p492)
Dandenong Rd
St Kilda Cemetery
Fitzroy St
Alma Rd
Orrong Rd
ST KILDA
ST KILDA EAST
Inkerman St
Carlisle St
Balaclava
Balaclava Rd
BALACLAVA
See St Kilda Map (p494)
Glen Eira Rd

mythological figures of giant brothers Gog and Magog, perched with hammers atop the arched exit to Little Collins St.

Melbourne Aquarium AQUARIUM
(Map p484; ☎03-9923 5925; www.melbourneaquarium.com.au; cnr Flinders & King Sts; adult/child/family $35/22/92; ⏰9.30am-6pm, last entry 5pm; 🚊70, 75) This aquarium is home to rays, gropers and sharks, all of which cruise around a 2.2-million-litre tank, watched closely by visitors through a see-through tunnel. Talks and feedings are included in the admission fee.

Immigration Museum MUSEUM
(Map p484; ☎13 11 02; www.museumvictoria.com.au/immigrationmuseum; 400 Flinders St; adult/child $10/free; ⏰10am-5pm; 🚊70, 75) The Immigration Museum uses personal and community voices, images and memorabilia to tell the many stories of immigration. The changing exhibitions are often poignant. It's symbolically located in the old Customs House (1858–70).

Bourke Street Mall STREET
(Map p484; Bourke St, btwn Swanston & Elizabeth Sts; 🚊1, 3, 5, 6, 8, 16, 64, 67, 72, 86, 96) West of Swanston St marks the beginning of the Bourke St Mall, which is thick with trams, the sounds of Peruvian bands busking, shop-front spruikers and general hubbub from shoppers. In a 60-year tradition, November to early January sees people lining up (sometimes for hours) to get a peek at the animated displays in **Myer's Christmas windows**.

Chinatown NEIGHBOURHOOD
(Map p484; Little Bourke St, btwn Spring & Swanston Sts; 🚊1, 3, 5, 6, 8, 16, 64, 67, 72) Chinese miners arrived in search of the 'new gold mountain' in the 1850s and settled in this strip of Little Bourke St, now flanked by red archways. Here you'll find an interesting mix of bars and restaurants, including one of Melbourne's best, Flower Drum (p507). Come here for yum cha, or explore its attendant laneways for late-night dumplings or cocktails.

Koorie Heritage Trust CULTURAL CENTRE
(Map p484; www.kooriehеritagetrust.com; 295 King St; gold-coin donation; ⏰9am-5pm Mon-Fri; 🚆Flagstaff) 🍃 This centre is devoted to southeastern Aboriginal culture, and cares for artefacts and oral history. Its gallery shows a variety of contemporary and traditional work. There's a model scar tree at the centre's heart, as well as a permanent chronological display of Victorian Koorie history. There's also a shop with books, CDs, crafts and bush-food supplies.

Queen Victoria Market MARKET
(www.qvm.com.au; 513 Elizabeth St; ⏰6am-2pm Tue & Thu, 6am-5pm Fri, 6am-3pm Sat, 9am-4pm Sun; 🚌Tourist Shuttle, 🚊19, 55, 57, 59) This site has been a market since 1878, prior to which it was a burial ground, and it is where Melburnians shop for fresh produce. There's a deli, meat and fish hall as well as a restaurant zone. From November through to February a lively night market with food stalls, bars and music takes over on Wednesday evenings.

Flagstaff Gardens PARK
(Map p484; William St, btwn La Trobe, Dudley & King Sts; 🚌Tourist Shuttle, 🚊City Circle, 🚆Flagstaff) First known as Burial Hill, this is where most of the city's early settlers ended up. When a ship arriving from Britain was sighted, a flag was raised to notify the settlers. It was also significant for the Wurundjeri for the same useful vista. The gardens contain

WORTH A TRIP

HEIDE

If there's one out-of-Melbourne spot that deserves an afternoon dedicated to it, it's **Heide** (☎03-9850 1500; www.heide.com.au; 7 Templestowe Rd; museum adult/child $14/free; ⏰10am-5pm Tue-Sun; 🚌903, 🚆Heidelberg). The former home of John and Sunday Reed, this is now a public art gallery with pleasant grounds for exploring. Its gardens are full of sculptures and the kitchen gardens that Sunday Reed loved so much. Indoors, changing exhibits often include works by the many artists who spent time living here.

These days Shannon Bennett's Cafe Vue (offspring of Vue de Monde; p507) does the cooking honours and you can eat in or grab a lunch box ($18) to eat by the Yarra on the grounds. The free tours are a great introduction to Melbourne's early painting scene. The museum is signposted off the Eastern Fwy.

Moreton Bay figs and spotted, sugar and river red gums.

State Library of Victoria LIBRARY
(Map p484; ☎03-8664 7000; www.slv.vic.gov.au; 328 Swanston St; ⊙10am-9pm Mon-Thu, to 6pm Fri-Sun; 1, 3, 5, 6, 8, 16, 64, 67, 72, Melbourne Central) On the library's opening in 1856, people entering were required to sign in, be over 14 years old and have clean hands. Today you just have to leave your bags in the locker room ($2 to $3 for four hours) and maintain some shush. The stunning octagonal **La Trobe Reading Room** was completed in 1913. Don't miss seeing Ned Kelly's armour.

Parliament House HISTORIC BUILDING
(Map p484; ☎03-9651 8568; www.parliament.vic.gov.au; Spring St; ⊙tours 9.30am, 10.30am, 11.30am, 1.30pm, 2.30pm, 3.45pm Mon-Fri; City Circle, 86, 96, Parliament) FREE The grand steps of Victoria's parliament (c 1856) are often dotted with brides smiling for the camera or placard-holding protesters doing the opposite. Inside, the ornamental plasterwork, stencilling and gilt are full of gold-rush-era pride and optimism. Though they've never been used, gun slits are visible just below the roof. Free half-hour tours are held when parliament is in recess.

Old Melbourne Gaol HISTORIC BUILDING
(Map p484; ☎03-8663 7228; www.oldmelbournegaol.com.au; Russell St; adult/child/family $25/14/55; ⊙9.30am-5pm; City Circle) This forbidding monument to 19th-century justice is now a museum. It was built of bluestone in 1841, and was a prison until 1929. The bleak cells display casts of the heads of some who were hanged here, a chilling 'by-product' of the era's obsession with phrenology. Bushranger Ned Kelly heard the clang of the trap here in 1880.

Southbank & Docklands

Southbank, once a gritty industrial site, sits directly across the Yarra from Flinders St. Behind Southgate's shopping mall is the city's major arts precinct including the NGV International and Arts Centre Melbourne. Back down by the river, the promenade stretches to the Crown Casino & Entertainment Complex, a self-proclaimed 'world of entertainment', pulling in visitors 24/7. To the city's west lies Docklands.

DON'T MISS

FOOTSCRAY

Head west beyond the city's remaining working docklands and uncover Footscray, home of the headquarters of Lonely Planet. Almost half of Footscray's population was born overseas, the majority in Vietnam, Africa, China, Italy and Greece. **Footscray Market** (cnr Hopkins & Leeds St; ⊙7am-4pm Tue, Wed & Sat, to 6pm Thu, to 8pm Fri; Footscray), right next to the Footscray train station, is testament to the area's diversity. And you can't go past Vietnamese *pho* (noodle soup) at **Hung Vuong** (☎03-9689 6002; 128 Hopkins St; mains $9; 402, Footscray).

Arts Centre Melbourne ARTS CENTRE
(Map p484; www.theartscentre.com.au; 100 St Kilda Rd; Tourist Shuttle, 1, 3, 5, 6, 8, 16, 64, 67, 72, Flinders St) Arts Centre Melbourne is made up of two separate buildings: **Hamer Hall** formerly the Melbourne Concert Hall, and the **theatres building** (under the spire). The **Famous Spiegeltent**, a Belgian mirror tent, stages cabaret, music and comedy from February to April. Explore the free galleries **Gallery 1** and **St Kilda Road Foyer Gallery** and the weekly **makers market** (Sundays from 10am to 4pm).

NGV International GALLERY
(☎03-8662 1555; www.ngv.vic.gov.au; 180 St Kilda Rd; exhibition costs vary; ⊙10am-5pm Wed-Mon; Tourist Shuttle, 1, 3, 5, 6, 8, 16, 64, 67, 72) FREE Beyond the water wall you'll find international art that runs from the ancient to the contemporary. Completed in 1967, the original NGV building – Roy Grounds' 'cranky icon' – was one of Australia's most controversial but ultimately respected modernist masterpieces. Don't miss a gaze up at the Great Hall's stained-glass ceiling.

Eureka Skydeck LOOKOUT
(Map p484; www.eurekaskydeck.com.au; 7 Riverside Quay; adult/child/family $19/10/42, The Edge extra $12/8/29; ⊙10am-10pm, last entry 9.30pm; Tourist Shuttle) Eureka Tower, built in 2006, has 92 storeys. Take a wild elevator ride to almost the top and you'll do 88 floors in 38 seconds. 'The Edge' – not a member of U2, but a slightly sadistic glass cube – propels you out of the building.

Central Melbourne

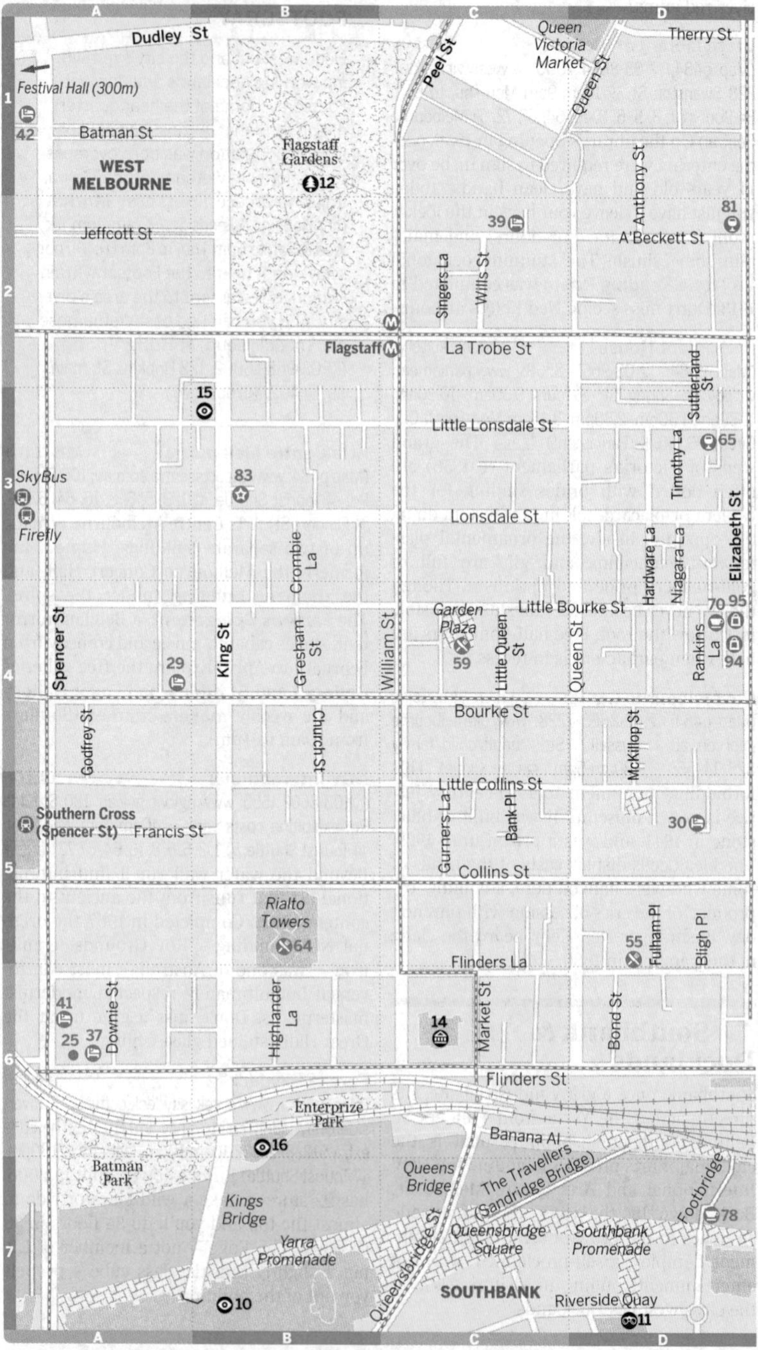

MELBOURNE & VICTORIA MELBOURNE

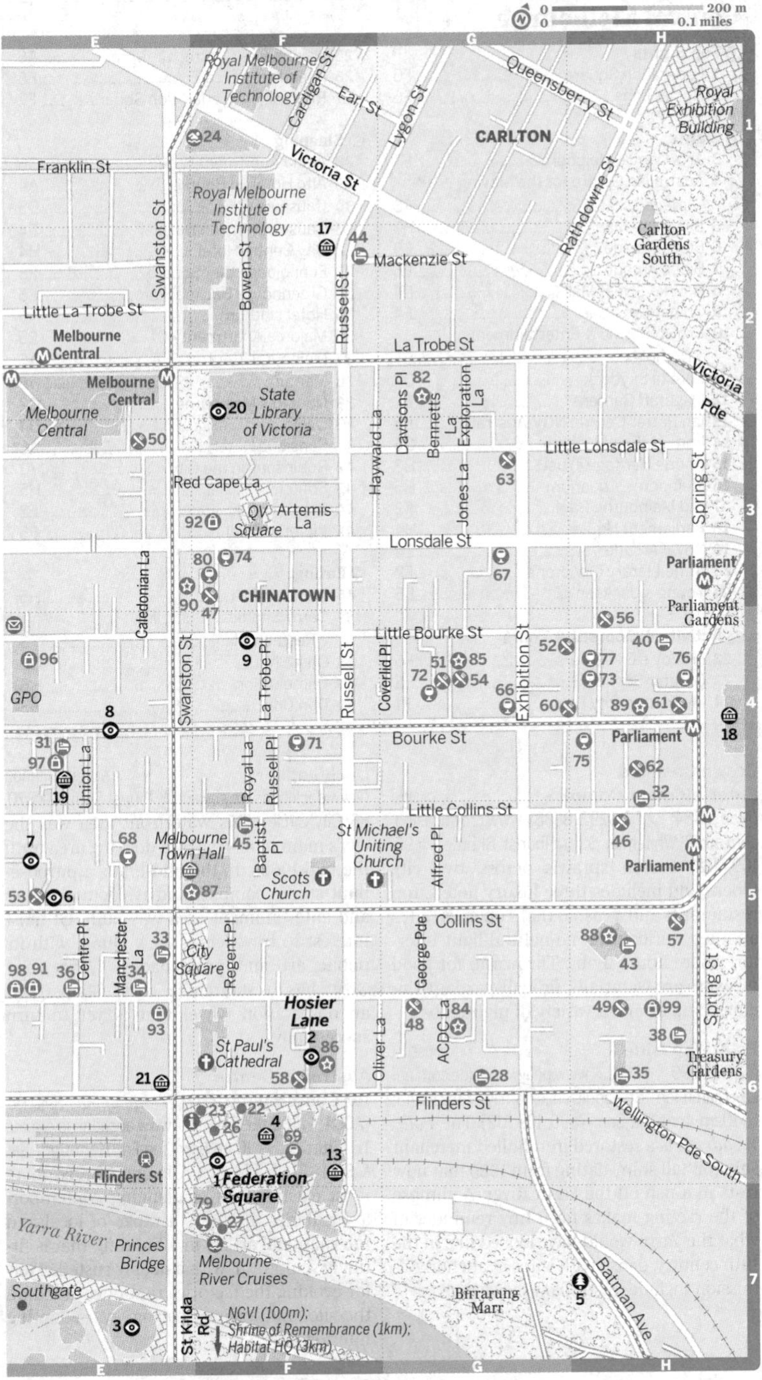

0 200 m
0 0.1 miles
E
F
G
H
Royal Melbourne Institute of Technology
Cardigan St
Earl St
Lygon St
Queensberry St
Royal Exhibition Building
CARLTON
24
Victoria St
Franklin St
Royal Melbourne Institute of Technology
Swanston St
Bowen St
17
44
Mackenzie St
Rathdowne St
Carlton Gardens South
Little La Trobe St
Melbourne Central
RussellSt
La Trobe St
Victoria Pde
Melbourne Central
Melbourne Central
20
State Library of Victoria
50
Davisons Pl
82
Hayward La
Bennetts La
Exploration La
Little Lonsdale St
Red Cape La
63
Jones La
Spring St
92
QV Square
Artemis La
Lonsdale St
80
74
67
Parliament
Caledonian La
90
47
CHINATOWN
56
Parliament Gardens
Little Bourke St
9
40
96
52
77
Swanston St
La Trobe Pl
Russell St
Coverlid Pl
51
85
76
72
54
73
Exhibition St
66
GPO
8
60
89
61
18
31
Bourke St
71
Parliament
97
75
19
Union La
Royal La
Russell Pl
62
32
Little Collins St
7
68
Melbourne Town Hall
45
Baptist Pl
St Michael's Uniting Church
Alfred Pl
46
Parliament
53
6
87
Scots Church
Collins St
George Pde
57
88
Centre Pl
Manchester La
33
City Square
Regent Pl
43
98
91
36
34
Spring St
Hosier Lane
49
99
93
84
48
2
ACDC La
38
St Paul's Cathedral
86
Oliver La
Treasury Gardens
21
58
28
35
Flinders St
Wellington Pde South
23
22
26
4
69
13
Flinders St
1 Federation Square
79
27
Yarra River
Princes Bridge
Melbourne River Cruises
Batman Ave
Southgate
Birrarung Marr
5
3
St Kilda Rd
NGVI (100m); Shrine of Remembrance (1km); Habitat HQ (3km)
1
2
3
4
5
6
7

Central Melbourne

Crown Casino & Entertainment Complex CASINO
(Map p484; ☎03-9292 8888; www.crowncasino.com.au; 8 Whiteman St; Tourist Shuttle, 96, 109, 112) Crown sprawls across two city blocks and includes three luxury hotels, top restaurants and a casino that's open 24/7. It's another world in its no-natural-light interior, where hours fly by. Thrown in for good measure are waterfalls, fireballs, a giant cinema complex and a variety of nightclubs.

Polly Woodside MUSEUM
(☎03-9699 9760; www.pollywoodside.com.au; 2a Clarendon St; adult/child/family $16/10/43; 10am-4pm Thu-Sun; 96, 109, 112) The *Polly Woodside* is a restored iron-hulled merchant ship (or 'tall ship') dating from 1885 that now rests in a pen off the Yarra River. A glimpse of the rigging makes for a tiny reminder of what the Yarra would have looked like in the 19th century, dense with ships at anchor. Admission includes a stroll on the ship.

Docklands NEIGHBOURHOOD
(www.docklands.vic.gov.au; Tourist Shuttle, 70, 86, City Circle) This waterfront area was the city's main industrial and docking area until the mid-1960s. In the mid-1990s a purpose-built studio complex and residential, retail and entertainment area was built. Of most interest to travellers is **New Quay**, with its public art and promenades. **Waterfront City** has restaurants, bars, shops and an observation wheel that is yet to turn successfully.

Australian Centre for Contemporary Art GALLERY
(ACCA; ☎03-9697 9999; www.accaonline.org.au; 111 Sturt St; 10am-5pm Tue-Fri, 11am-6pm Sat & Sun; 1) FREE ACCA is one of Australia's most exciting and challenging contemporary galleries. It shows a range of local and international artists in a building that is fittingly sculptural, with a deeply rusted exterior evoking the factories that once stood on the site, and a slick, soaring, ever-adapting interior.

51 Flower Drum ... G4
52 Gingerboy ... G4
53 Hopetoun Tea Rooms ... E5
54 HuTong Dumpling Bar ... G4
55 Huxtaburger ... D5
56 Longrain ... H4
57 Mamasita ... H5
58 MoVida ... F6
59 Movida Aqui ... C4
Movida Next Door ... (see 58)
60 Pellegrini's Espresso Bar ... G4
61 Red Pepper ... H4
62 The Waiters Restaurant ... H4
63 Trunk ... G3
64 Vue de Monde ... B5

Drinking & Nightlife
65 1000£Bend ... D3
66 1806 ... G4
67 Aylesbury ... G3
68 Bar Americano ... E5
69 Beer DeLuxe ... F6
70 Brother Baba Budan ... D4
71 Carlton Hotel ... F4
72 Croft Institute ... G4
73 Double Happiness ... H4
74 Ferdydurke ... F3
Lui Bar ... (see 64)
75 Madame Brussels ... H4
76 Melbourne Supper Club ... H4
77 New Gold Mountain ... H4
78 Ponyfish Island ... D7
79 Riverland ... F7
80 Section 8 ... F3
Siglo ... (see 76)
81 Workshop ... D2

Entertainment
82 Bennetts Lane ... G2
83 Brown Alley ... B3
84 Cherry ... G6
85 Ding Dong Lounge ... G4
86 Forum Theatre ... F6
87 Half Tix Melbourne ... E5
Hamer Hall ... (see 3)
88 Kino Cinemas ... H5
89 Palace Theatre ... H4
90 Rooftop Cinema ... E3
Toff in Town ... (see 90)

Shopping
91 Aesop ... E5
92 Aesop ... F3
93 Alice Euphemia ... E6
94 Captains of Industry ... D4
95 Crumpler ... D4
96 Fat ... E4
97 Hunter Gatherer ... E4
98 Polyester Records ... E5
99 Shop ... H6

Melbourne Recital Centre ARTS CENTRE
(03-9699 3333; www.melbournerecital.com.au; cnr Southbank Blvd & Sturt St; Tourist Shuttle, 1) This award-winning (for its acoustics) building may look like a framed piece of giant honeycomb, but it is actually the home (or hive) of the Melbourne Chamber Orchestra and lots of small ensembles. From Flinders St Station cross the Yarra and turn right at Southbank Blvd.

East Melbourne & Richmond

East Melbourne's sedate wide streets are lined with grand double-fronted Victorian terraces and Italianate mansions. It's also home to the mighty Melbourne Cricket Ground (MCG). On the other side of perpetually clogged Punt Rd/Hoddle St is the suburb of Richmond, which houses a vibrant stretch of Vietnamese restaurants along Victoria St, clothing outlets along Bridge Rd and some good drinking spots along Church St.

Melbourne Cricket Ground STADIUM
(MCG; 03-9657 8888; www.mcg.org.au; Brunton Ave; tour adult/child/family $20/10/50; 10am-3pm; Tourist Shuttle, 48, 75, Jolimont) For many Australians the 'G' is considered hallowed ground. In 1858 the first game of Aussie Rules football was played here, and in 1877 it was the venue for the first Test cricket match between Australia and England. Tours get you right out onto the ground. Pedestrian access from the CBD is via William Barak bridge.

The MCG was the central stadium for the 1956 Melbourne Olympics and the 2006 Commonwealth Games.

National Sports Museum MUSEUM
(NSM; 03-9657 8879; www.nsm.org.au; Brunton Ave; adult/child/family $20/10/50; 10am-5pm) See Cathy Freeman's famous Sydney Olympics running suit and more of Australia's sporting memorabilia. The interactive gallery is a hit with kids, as they get to handball a footy and shoot hoops. There's a discount if you buy an MCG tour and NSM entry together.

Fitzroy Gardens PARK
(Wellington Pde, btwn Lansdowne & Albert Sts; Tourist Shuttle, 75, Jolimont) The city drops away suddenly just east of Spring St, giving way to Melbourne's beautiful backyard, the Treasury and Fitzroy Gardens, whose stately avenues are lined with English elms, flower beds, expansive lawns, strange fountains, a photogenic observatory and a creek.

Cooks' Cottage HISTORIC BUILDING
(03-9419 5766; www.cookscottage.com.au; adult/child/family $5/2.50/13.50; 9am-5pm) This' Yorkshire cottage (c 1755) built by the parents of Captain James Cook was shipped in 253 packing cases and reconstructed in 1934. Nearby is Ola Cohn's kookily carved **Fairies' Tree**. In 1932 the 300-year-old stump was embellished with fairies, kangaroos, emus and possums. The Fitzroy Gardens' **Scarred Tree** (now a stump) was once stripped of a piece of its bark to make a canoe by Aboriginal people.

Fitzroy & Around

Fitzroy, Melbourne's first suburb, had a reputation for vice and squalor. Today it's a gentrified version of its old self; a mix of housing-commission towers, fancy restaurants, cafes and boutique shops. Gertrude St, where once grannies feared to tread, is Melbourne's street of the moment. Smith St has some rough edges, though talk turns more to its smart restaurants rather than its down-and-out days of old. It's been a social spot for indigenous people for centuries, and still is.

When evening sets on Northcote's High St, it hums to the sound of food trucks on Ruckers Hill and a thousand Converse One Stars hitting the pavement in search of fun.

Centre for Contemporary Photography GALLERY
(CCP; Map p489; 03-9417 1549; www.ccp.org.au; 404 George St; 11am-6pm Wed-Fri, noon-5pm Sat & Sun; 86) FREE This not-for-profit centre has a changing schedule of modern photographic exhibitions across four galleries. It's worth passing by after dark to see the night projection window.

Abbotsford Convent HISTORIC SITE
(03-9415 3600; www.abbotsfordconvent.com.au; 1 St Heliers St; 7.30am-10pm; 200, 201, 207, Collingwood) FREE The convent, which dates back to 1861, is spread over 7 hectares of riverside land 4km from the CBD. The nuns have been replaced with a rambling collection of creative studios and community offices. The **Convent Bakery** supplies impromptu picnic provisions, and Shadow Electric (p516) provides beverages and open-air cinema over summer. Most weekends see market action, too.

Yarra Bend Park PARK
(www.parkweb.vic.gov.au; 200, 201, 207, Victoria Park) About 4km northeast of the CBD is Yarra Bend Park, a popular recreational spot

Fitzroy & Around

Sights
1 Centre for Contemporary Photography C3

Activities, Courses & Tours
2 Fitzroy Swimming Pool C1

Sleeping
3 Brooklyn Arts Hotel C7
4 Home@The Mansion A7
5 Nunnery A5
6 Tyrian Serviced Apartments B3

Eating
7 Babka Bakery Cafe B2
8 Birdman Eating C6
9 Charcoal Lane B6
10 Commoner B3
11 Cutler & Co A6
12 Huxtaburger D6
13 Marios B3
14 Vegie Bar B2

Drinking & Nightlife
15 De Clieu Cafe C6
16 Little Creatures Dining Hall B4
17 Naked for Satan B3
18 Napier Hotel C4
19 Polly B2
20 Proud Mary D5
21 The Standard A4

Shopping
22 Aesop D6
23 Crumpler D6
24 Fat B4
25 Hunter Gatherer B3
26 Polyester Records B2
27 Rose Street Artists' Market B2
28 SpaceCraft C6
29 Third Drawer Down C6

Fitzroy & Around

where the Yarra flows through bushland. Cockatoos screech and grey-headed flying foxes roost in the trees, yet it's only minutes from offices. Boathouse Rd houses the 1860s Studley Park Boathouse (p496), which has a kiosk and restaurant, BBQs, ducks, and boats and canoes for hire.

Carlton & Around

Lygon St reaches out through leafy North Carlton to booming Brunswick. Here you'll find a vibrant mix of students, long-established families, renovators and newly arrived migrants. The central Brunswick artery, Sydney Rd, is perpetually clogged with traffic and packed with Middle Eastern restaurants and grocers. Lygon St down East Brunswick way just keeps getting more fashionable, with a growing cluster of restaurants, breweries and bars.

★**Melbourne Museum** MUSEUM

(Map p490; ☎13 11 02; www.museumvictoria.com.au; 11 Nicholson St; adult/child & student $10/free, exhibitions extra; ⏰10am-5pm; Tourist Shuttle, City Circle, 86, 96, Parliament) This modern museum mixes old-style object displays with themed interactive areas. It provides a grand sweep of Victoria's natural and cultural histories: walk through the reconstructed laneway lives of the 1800s or become immersed in the legend of champion racehorse Phar Lap. Bunjilaka, on the ground floor, presents indigenous stories and history told through objects and Aboriginal voices.

Royal Exhibition Building HISTORIC BUILDING

(Map p490; ☎13 11 02; www.museumvictoria.com.au/reb; Nicholson St; tours adult/child $5/3.50; Tourist Shuttle, City Circle, 86, 96, Parliament) Built for the International Exhibition in 1880, and winning Unesco World Heritage status in 2004, this Victorian edifice symbolises the glory days of the Industrial

Carlton & Around

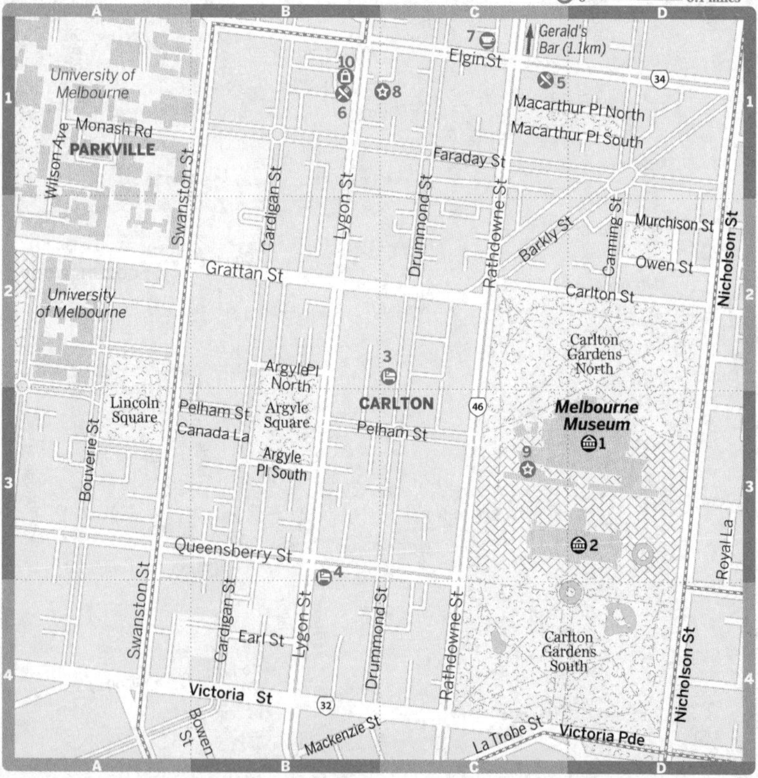

Revolution, Empire and 19th-century Melbourne's economic supremacy. Australia's first parliament was held here in 1901; these days it's often home to food, hot-rod and design shows. Tours depart Melbourne Museum most days at 2pm.

Royal Melbourne Zoo ZOO
(03-9285 9300; www.zoo.org.au; Elliott Ave; adult/child $26.10/13; 9am-5pm; 505, 55, Royal Park) This large zoo's theme is 'fighting extinction', and there are plenty of conservation messages on the lush grounds. The elephant enclosure is a standout, as is the hothouse full of butterflies. Native animals are in natural bush settings, and there's a platypus aquarium. Zoo Twilights bring live music to the zoo as the sun goes down from late January to March.

South Yarra, Prahran & Windsor

This neighbourhood is synonymous with glitz and glamour; it might be south but it's commonly referred to as the 'right' side of the river (on which plots of land were historically larger).

Chapel St's South Yarra strip has fashion and designer attitude, with a parade of doof-doof cars building to an evening crescendo. Factories have made way for apartments in the Claremont St precinct, and it's now bursting with vibrant restaurants, cafes and hotels. Prahran and Windsor are gutsy spots with good restaurants, bars and some refreshingly eclectic businesses. Commercial Rd houses the Prahran Market, where locals shop for fruit, veg and upmarket deli delights.

Hawksburn Village, up the Malvern Rd hill, and High St Armadale make for stylish boutique clothes shopping.

Royal Botanic Gardens GARDENS
(www.rbg.vic.gov.au; 7.30am-sunset; Tourist Shuttle, 8) FREE These beautiful gardens feature a global selection of plants and a surprising amount of wildlife, including waterfowl, ducks, swans, child-scaring eels, cockatoos and possums. Kids love the nature-based **Ian Potter Children's Garden** (Children's Garden open Wed-Sun, closed school term 3). Around the gardens is the **Tan**, a 4km-long former horse-exercising track, now used to exercise joggers. Summer sees the gardens play host to the Moonlight Cinema (p516).

Shrine of Remembrance MONUMENT
(www.shrine.org.au; Birdwood Ave; 10am-5pm; Tourist Shuttle, 3, 5, 6, 8, 16, 64, 67, 72) FREE Up from St Kilda Rd is the massive Shrine of Remembrance, built as a memorial to Victorians killed in WWI. Tens of thousands attend the annual moving Anzac Day (25 April) dawn service. Inside, the architecturally designed visitor centre is a sombre tribute to lives lost. From the CBD, follow Swanston St along to St Kilda Rd.

Governor La Trobe's Cottage & Government House HISTORIC BUILDING
(03-8663 7260; www.nationaltrust.org.au; Kings Domain; tours adult/child $20/10; Tourist Shuttle) East of the Shrine is **Governor La Trobe's Cottage** (cnr Birdwood Ave & Dallas Brooks Dve; www.nationaltrust.org.au; adult/child $5/3; 2pm-4pm Sun Oct-Apr; Tourist Shuttle), the original government house building that was sent out in prefabricated form from England in 1840. In stark contrast is the Italianate pile of **Government House** (03-8663 7260; www.nationaltrust.org.au; Government House Dr; Tourist Shuttle). This replica of Queen Victoria's Isle of Wight palace has been home to all serving Victorian governors since 1872. Tours visit both houses on Mondays and Thursdays.

Herring Island Park PARK
(Map p492; http://home.vicnet.net.au/~herring; Alexander Ave; 8, 78, Burnley) It's hard to

Carlton & Around

Top Sights
1 Melbourne Museum D3

Sights
2 Royal Exhibition Building D3

Sleeping
3 169 Drummond C2
4 Downtowner on Lygon B3

Eating
5 Abla's C1
6 Tiamo B1

Drinking & Nightlife
7 Campos C1

Entertainment
8 Cinema Nova C1
9 Imax C3

Shopping
10 Readings B1

South Yarra, Prahran & Windsor

South Yarra, Prahran & Windsor

believe, amid the sculptures and bush, that this teeny island in the Yarra River was once a dumping ground. It's not easy to get to but once you get there, enjoy a picnic or BBQ in the recreated pre-1835 landscape. There's an infrequent **Parks Victoria punt** (Map p492; 13 19 63; per person $2; 11.30am-5pm Sat & Sun Dec-Mar) from Alexander Ave), .

Prahran Market MARKET

(Map p492; www.prahranmarket.com.au; 163 Commercial Rd; 7am-5pm Tue, Thu & Sat, to 7pm Fri, 10am-3pm Sun; 72, 78, Prahran) The Prahran Market has been an institution since it opened in 1864 and is one of the finest produce markets in the city. As well as fresh offerings, an upmarket selection of stalls serves coffee, chocolates and fine food.

St Kilda & Around

Come to St Kilda for its briny breezes, seaside walking/running/roller-blading/cycling path, seedy history and a good old bit of people-watching.

St Kilda's palm trees, bay vistas and pink-stained sunsets are heartbreakingly beautiful. On weekends, the volume is turned up, traffic crawls and a street-party atmosphere sets in. Cake-shop-clad Acland St's western strip is pleasantly leafy and nostalgically residential. Many long-time locals have turned to Carlisle St's eastern reach, which is traditionally a devout Jewish neighbourhood but is now also known for its wine bars, beer bars and all-day breakfast cafes.

Luna Park AMUSEMENT PARK

(Map p494; 03-9525 5033; www.lunapark.com.au; 18 Lower Esplanade; adult/child single-ride ticket $10/8, unlimited-ride ticket $46/36; 16, 96) It opened a century ago and still retains the feel of an old-style amusement park with creepy Mr Moon's gaping mouth swallowing you up whole on entering. There's a heritage-listed scenic railway and the full complement of gut-churning modern rides. For grown-ups, the noise and lack of greenery or shade can pall all too quickly. Check the website for opening hours.

St Kilda Foreshore BEACH

(Map p494; Jacka Blvd; 16, 96) Despite palm-fringed promenades, a parkland strand and a long stretch of sand, don't expect Bondi or Noosa. St Kilda's seaside appeal is more Brighton, England, than *Baywatch,* despite 30-odd years of glitzy development. And that's the way Melburnians like it; a certain depth of character and an all-weather charm, with wild days on the bay providing for spectacular cloudscapes and terse little waves, as well as the more predictable sparkling blue of summer.

St Kilda Pier PIER

(Map p494; Jacka Blvd; 16, 96) The breakwater at the end of the pier was built in the 1950s and houses a colony of more than 1000 little penguins. Visit the penguins at sunset (volunteers are on hand to point them out), or see them from a prime location on a stand-up paddleboarding trip (p497). If you're

St Kilda

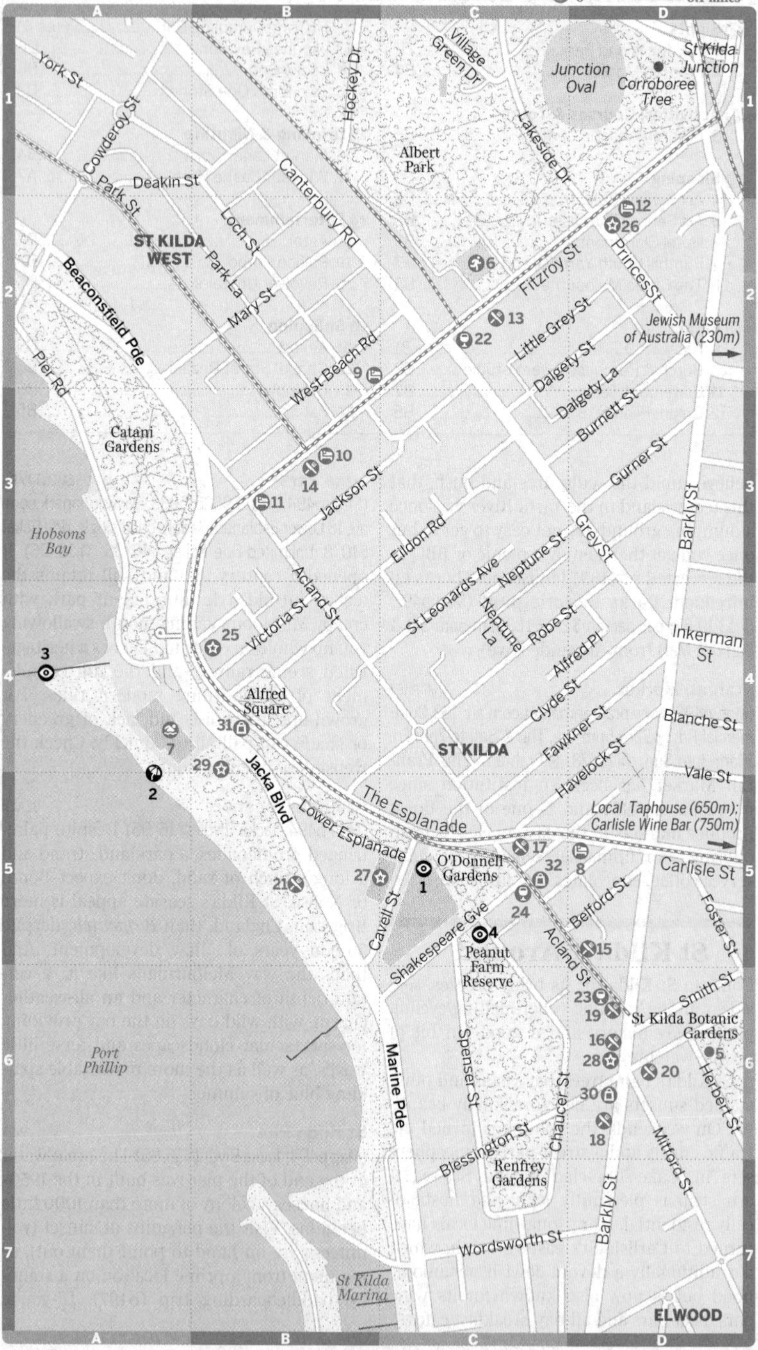
0 200 m
0 0.1 miles
York St
Cowderoy St
Park St
Deakin St
Loch St
ST KILDA WEST
Park La
Mary St
Canterbury Rd
Hockey Dr
Village Green Dr
Albert Park
Junction Oval
Corroboree Tree
St Kilda Junction
Lakeside Dr
Princes St
Fitzroy St
Little Grey St
Dalgety St
Dalgety La
Burnett St
Gurner St
Jewish Museum of Australia (230m)
West Beach Rd
Beaconsfield Pde
Pier Rd
Catani Gardens
Hobsons Bay
Jackson St
Eildon Rd
Acland St
Victoria St
St Leonards Ave
Neptune St
Neptune La
Grey St
Barkly St
Robe St
Alfred Pl
Inkerman St
Clyde St
Fawkner St
Havelock St
Blanche St
Vale St
Alfred Square
ST KILDA
Jacka Blvd
The Esplanade
Lower Esplanade
Local Taphouse (650m); Carlisle Wine Bar (750m)
Carlisle St
O'Donnell Gardens
Cavell St
Shakespeare Gve
Peanut Farm Reserve
Belford St
Foster St
Smith St
St Kilda Botanic Gardens
Herbert St
Port Phillip
Marine Pde
Spenser St
Chaucer St
Mitford St
Blessington St
Renfrey Gardens
Wordsworth St
St Kilda Marina
ELWOOD

St Kilda

Sights
1 Luna Park C5
2 St Kilda Foreshore A5
3 St Kilda Pier A4
4 Veg Out Community Gardens C5

Activities, Courses & Tours
Kite Republic .... (see 7)
5 Port Phillip Eco Centre D6
6 St Kilda Bowling Club C2
7 St Kilda Sea Baths A4
Stand Up Paddle Boarding .... (see 7)
Sunset Eco Penguin Tour .... (see 7)

Sleeping
8 Base D5
9 Hotel Tolarno B2
10 Hotel Urban B3
11 Prince B3
12 Ritz D2

Eating
13 Banff C2
14 Cafe di Stasio B3
15 Cicciolina D5
16 Claypots D6
17 Galleon Cafe C5
18 I Carusi II D6
19 La Roche D6
20 Lentil as Anything D6
Radio Mexico .... (see 17)
21 Stokehouse Cafe B5

Drinking & Nightlife
22 George Public Bar C2
23 Veludo D6
24 Vineyard C5

Entertainment
25 Esplanade Hotel B4
26 Official Neighbours Trivia Night D2
27 Palais Theatre C5
28 Pure Pop Records D6
29 St Kilda Open Air Cinema B4

Shopping
30 Dot Herbey D6
31 Esplanade Market B4
32 Hunter Gatherer C5
Readings .... (see 15)

photographing the blue bundles don't use your flash.

Veg Out Community Gardens GARDENS
(Map p494; www.vegout.asn.au; cnr Shakespeare Grove & Chaucer St; farmers market 8.30am-1pm 1st Sat of month) Tucked off Acland St near Luna Park is this bright and colourful community-run garden. Locals work on their own plots, but it's truly a communal vibe. Buy up big on farmers market days or lend a helping hand on the first Sunday of the month.

Jewish Museum of Australia MUSEUM
(03-9834 3600; www.jewishmuseum.com.au; 26 Alma Rd; adult/child/family $10/5/20; 10am-4pm Tue-Thu, 10am-5pm Sun; 3, 67) Interactive displays tell the history of Australia's Jewish community from the earliest days of European settlement, while permanent exhibitions celebrate Judaism's rich cycle of festivals and holy days. Follow St Kilda Rd from St Kilda Junction then turn left at Alma Rd.

South Melbourne, Port Melbourne & Albert Park

Head to South Melbourne for its large fresh-food market, homeware shops and top cafes (seems there's a coffee competition going on). Albert Park Lake is the place for sporting and relaxation pursuits, but it also manages to squeeze in an annual Grand Prix. Albert Park and nearby Middle Park both have refined, genteel town centres. At nearby Port Melbourne is Station Pier, the passenger terminal for the ferry service between Melbourne and Tasmania.

South Melbourne Market MARKET
(www.southmelbournemarket.com.au; cnr Coventry & Cecil Sts; 8am-4pm Wed, Sat & Sun, to 5pm Fri; 96) The market's labyrinthine interior is packed to overflowing with an eccentric collection of stalls selling everything from carpets to *bok choy* (Chinese greens). Its hangover-relieving dim sims are famous and sold at various cafes around Melbourne (as 'South Melbourne Market Dim Sims' no less!). Don't miss a coffee from **Clement** (www.clementcoffee.com; Stall 89, 116-136 Cecil St; 7.30am-4.30pm).

Albert Park Lake LAKE
(btwn Queens Rd, Fitzroy St, Aughtie Dr & Albert Rd; 96) Elegant black swans give their inimitable bottoms-up salute as you circumnavigate the 5km perimeter of this artificial lake. Jogging, cycling, walking or clamouring over play equipment is the appropriate

human equivalent. Lakeside Dr was an international motor-racing circuit in the 1950s, and since 1996 the revamped track has been the venue for the Australian Formula One Grand Prix (p500) each March.

Station Pier LANDMARK

(www.portofmelbourne.com; 🚊109) Station Pier is Melbourne's main sea passenger terminal, and is where the *Spirit of Tasmania*, cruise ships and navy vessels dock. In operation since 1854, it has sentimental associations for many migrants who arrived by ship in the 1950s and 1960s, and for servicemen and women who used it during WWII. A gaggle of flash-looking restaurants struggle for business near the marina.

Activities

In summer, hit the sand at one of the city's metropolitan beaches. St Kilda, Middle Park and Port Melbourne are popular patches, with suburban beaches at Brighton (with its photogenic bathing boxes) and Sandringham also pulling a crowd. Public pools are also well loved.

Cycling maps are available from the Melbourne Visitor Information Centre at Federation Sq and **Bicycle Victoria** (www.bicyclenetwork.com.au). You won't be alone on the roads; peddlers range from slow cyclists in high heels to speedy commuters. Wearing a helmet while cycling is compulsory in Australia (with a $176 fine if you get caught without one on your head). Borrow a bike from the public scheme, a private scheme or a vintage scheme.

Formerly the domain of senior citizens wearing starched white uniforms, bowling clubs are now inundated by younger types: barefoot, with a beer in one hand and a bowl in the other.

Studley Park Boathouse CANOEING

(☎03-9853 1828; www.studleyparkboathouse.com.au; 1 Boathouse Rd, Kew) Pack a picnic then hire a two-person canoe or kayak from the boathouse ($36 for the first hour).

Humble Vintage BICYCLE RENTAL

(☎0432 032 450; www.thehumblevintage.com) Get yourself a set of special wheels from this collection of retro racers, city bikes and

THE SPORTING LIFE

Cynics snicker that sport is the sum of Victoria's culture, although they're hard to hear above all that cheering, theme-song singing and applause. Victorians do take the shared spectacle of the playing field very seriously. It's undeniably the state's most dominant expression of common beliefs and behaviour, and brings people from all backgrounds together. It's also a lot of fun: sporting events are followed with such fervour that the crowd is often a spectacle in itself.

The Events

Melbourne is the birthplace of Australian Rules football and hosts a disproportionate number of international sporting events, including the Australian Open (tennis), Australian Formula One Grand Prix and Melbourne Cup (horse racing). The city's arenas, tracks, grounds and courts are regarded as the world's best-developed and well-situated cluster of facilities. Still more major events that Victoria is home to include the Rip Curl Pro (aka the Bells Beach Surf Classic), the Australian Motorcycle Grand Prix on Phillip Island, the Stawell Gift and numerous country horse races, including the atmospheric Hanging Rock meet.

The Footy

Underneath the cultured chat and designer threads of your typical Melburnian, you'll find a heart that truly belongs to one thing: the footy. Understanding the basics of Australian Rules Football is definitely a way to get a local engaged in conversation, especially during the winter season. Melbourne is the national centre for the Australian Football League (AFL); all but nine of its 18 clubs are based here.

During the footy season (March to September), the vast majority of Victorians become obsessed, entering tipping competitions at work, discussing groin injuries and suspensions over the water cooler, and devouring the huge chunks of the daily newspapers devoted to mighty victories, devastating losses and the latest bad-boy behaviour (on and off the field).

DON'T MISS

WILLIAMSTOWN

Williamstown is a yacht-filled gem just a short boat ride (or drive or train ride) from Melbourne's CBD. It has stunning views of Melbourne, and a bunch of touristy shops along its esplanade. The park by the marina is made for picnics or takeaway fish 'n' chips.

Gem Pier is where passenger ferries dock to drop off and collect those who visit Williamstown by boat. It's a fitting way to arrive, given the area's maritime ambience. **Williamstown Ferries** (☎03-9517 9444; www.williamstownferries.com.au; one-way Williamstown-CBD adult/child $15/7.50) plies Hobsons Bay daily, stopping at Southgate and visiting a number of sites along the way, including Docklands. **Melbourne River Cruises** (Map p484; ☎03-8610 2600; www.melbcruises.com.au; one-way Williamstown-CBD adult/child $22/11) also docks at Gem Pier, travelling up the Yarra River to Southgate. Pick up a timetable from the very useful visitor centre in Williamstown or at Federation Sq, or contact the companies directly; bookings are advised.

women's bikes. Rates are $30 per day, or $80 per week, and include lock, helmet and a terrific map. Bikes can be picked up from St Kilda, Fitzroy and the CBD.

Rentabike @ Federation Square BICYCLE RENTAL, BICYCLE TOUR
(Map p484; ☎0417 339 203; www.rentabike.net.au; Federation Sq; bike hire 1hr/day/week $15/35/100; Flinders St) Rents out bikes including child seats and 'tagalongs'. Also runs bike tours.

North Fitzroy Bowls LAWN BOWLS
(☎03-9481 3137; www.barefootbowling.com.au; 578 Brunswick St; 112) There's maximum hipster enjoyment to be had here, with lights for night bowls, green-side barbecues and cheap beer. Phone to make a booking and for opening times. From Fitzroy, continue north along Brunswick St and cross Alexander Pde – it's on your right.

St Kilda Bowling Club LAWN BOWLS
(Map p494; ☎03-9534 5229; www.stkildabowlingclub.com.au; 66 Fitzroy St; noon-sunset Tue-Sun; 16, 96) The only dress code at this popular bowling club is shoes off. So join the many others who de-shoe to enjoy an $8 pint of beer and a bowl in the great outdoors. Games are $20 per person.

Stand Up Paddle Boarding STAND-UP PADDLEBOARDING
(Map p494; ☎0416 184 994; www.supb.com.au; St Kilda Sea Baths, 10-18 Jacka Blvd; per hour $25; 96) Hire SUP equipment and explore the bay off St Kilda Beach.

Kite Republic KITESURFING
(Map p494; ☎0418 583 233; www.kiterepublic.com.au; St Kilda Sea Baths, 10-18 Jacka Blvd; from $50; 96) When the winds pick up, Port Phillip Bay at St Kilda is filled with kitesurfers. Kite Republic will get you up there with them.

Fitzroy Swimming Pool SWIMMING
(Map p489; ☎03-9205 5180; 160 Alexandra Pde; adult/child $5/3; 11, 112) Between laps, locals love catching a few rays up in the bleachers or on the lawn. The pool's Italian 'Aqua Profonda' sign was painted in 1953 – an initiative of the pool's manager who frequently had to rescue migrant children who couldn't read the English signs. The sign is heritage listed (misspelled and all – it should be 'Acqua').

Melbourne City Baths SWIMMING
(Map p484; ☎03-9663 5888; 420 Swanston St; adult/child $6/3; 6am-10pm Mon-Thu, 6am-8pm Fri, 8am-6pm Sat & Sun; Melbourne Central) The City Baths first opened in 1860 and were intended to stop people bathing in the seriously polluted Yarra River. Enjoy a swim in the beautiful 1903 heritage-listed building.

Prahran Aquatic Centre SWIMMING
(Map p492; ☎03-8290 7140; 41 Essex St; adult/child $5.50/3; 72, 78, Prahran) This glam 50m heated outdoor pool is surrounded by a stretch of lawn and has a deck with sunbeds. The on-site cafe is a must for the locals who can't do without their latte, semi-naked or not.

Tours

Aboriginal Heritage Walk INDIGENOUS TOUR
(☎03-9252 2300; www.rbg.vic.gov.au; Royal Botanic Gardens, Birdwood Ave, South Yarra; adult/child $25/10; 11am Tue-Fri & 1st Sun of the month; Tourist Shuttle, 8) The Royal Botanic Gardens are on a traditional camping and meeting place of the area's original owners, and this tour takes you through

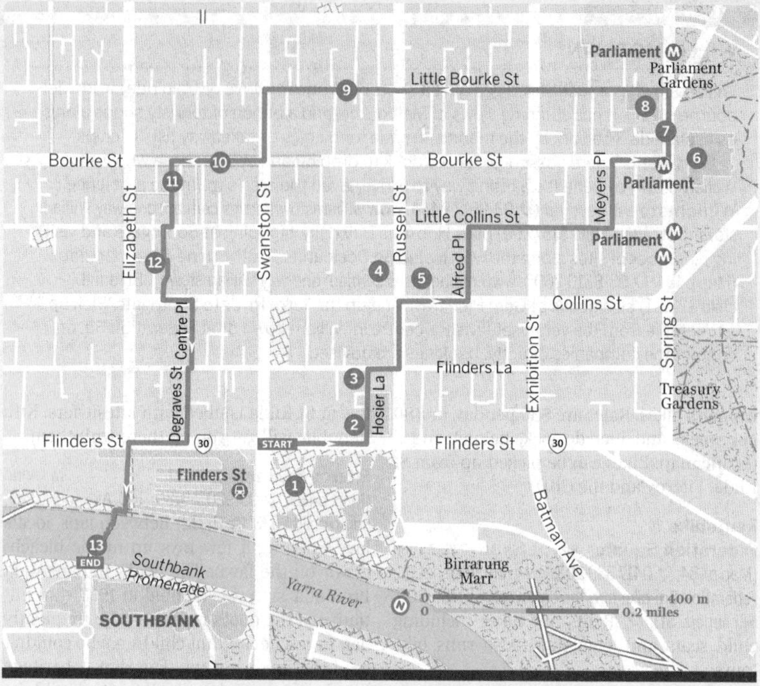

City Walk Melbourne CBD

START FEDERATION SQUARE
FINISH PONYFISH ISLAND
LENGTH 3.5KM; 2½ HOURS

Melbourne's CBD is a warren of beautiful alleys and laneways, some cobblestone, some bluestone, and all laden with character.

Start your foray into them at an obvious point – 1 **Federation Square** (p478). Head east along Flinders St and then turn left onto 2 **Hosier Lane** (p479). Depending on the existence of hunger pangs you could pop into 3 **MoVida** (p505) for a scrummy round of tapas, or keep moving. Turn right at Flinders Lane, left onto Russell St and then right onto Collins St. Stop to admire 4 **Scots Church** and 5 **St Michael's Uniting Church** and make your way east along the 'Paris' end of Collins St.

Find respite from the main strip and take a left onto Alfred Pl, which leads to Little Collins St. Turn right and continue along Little Collins St, turning left onto Meyers Pl. Turn right onto Bourke St and you'll hit the eastern border of the CBD, where 6 **Parliament House** (p483) strikes a pose. Check it out from rooftop bar 7 **Siglo** (p513).

Continue left on Spring St and left again onto Little Bourke St, past the 8 **Princess Theatre**. Head down Little Bourke St into the heart of 9 **Chinatown** (p482).

Turn left at Swanston St and then right on Bourke St to amble through 10 **Bourke Street Mall** (p482). Ogle at the shops and people and then potter through the glorious old 11 **Royal Arcade** (p479). Dog-leg from Little Collins into 12 **Block Arcade** (p479). Cross Collins St and head down Centre Pl and Degraves St for shoulder-to-shoulder cafes and boutiques.

Cross Flinders St via the pedestrian tunnel beneath the railway tracks to reach the Yarra River. Find the footbridge and head down the steps midway to 13 **Ponyfish Island** (p513). Finish up here with a well-earned beer.

their story – from songlines to plant lore, all in 90 minutes.

City Circle Trams TRAM TOUR
(1800 800 007; www.ptv.vic.gov.au; 35) FREE Free W-class trams that trundle around the city perimeter (and into the depths of Docklands) from 9am to 6pm daily.

Freddy's Bike Tours BIKE TOUR
(Map p484; 0431 610 431; www.freddysbiketours.com.au; Federation Sq; tours $39; departs 10.30am) Explore Melbourne's highlights in small groups on fire-engine-red bicycles. It's a blister-free way to get orientated. If you like the bike you can buy it.

Greeter Service WALKING TOUR
(Map p484; 03-9658 9658; Melbourne Visitor Centre, Federation Sq) FREE This free two-hour 'orientation tour' departs Fed Square daily at 9.30am (bookings required) and is run by volunteer 'greeters' who are keen to share their knowledge. It's aimed at giving visitors to Melbourne a good understanding of the layout and sights of Melbourne.

Hidden Secrets Tours WALKING TOUR
(03-9663 3358; www.hiddensecretstours.com; tours $70-195) Offers a variety of walking tours covering lanes and arcades, wine, architecture, coffee and cafes, and vintage Melbourne.

Kayak Melbourne KAYAK TOURS
(0418 106 427; www.kayakmelbourne.com.au; tours $99; 11, 31, 48) FREE Kent takes you past Melbourne city's newest developments and you'll get explanations about the older ones, too. Moonlight tours are most evocative and include a fish 'n' chips dinner; they depart from North Wharf Rd, Shed 2, Victoria Harbour.

Melbourne By Foot WALKING TOUR
(0418 394 000; www.melbournebyfoot.com; tours $35) Take a couple of hours out with Dave and experience a mellow, informative walking tour that covers street-art and politics, and gives great insights into Melbourne's history and diversity. Dave also runs evening beer tours ($80). Highly recommended.

Melbourne City Tourist Shuttle BUS TOUR
(Tourist Shuttle; www.thatsmelbourne.com.au; 9.30am-4.30pm) FREE This free hop-on hop-off tourist shuttle takes about 90 minutes to make its 13 stops around Melbourne and its inner suburbs. Stops include Lygon St, Queen Victoria Market, Docklands, Melbourne Museum, the MCG and the Shrine of Remembrance.

Melbourne Street Art Tours ART TOUR
(03-9328 5556; www.melbournestreettours.com; tours $69; Tue, Thur & Sat) Three-hour tours exploring the street-art side of Melbourne, a drink included. The tour guides are themselves street artists, so you'll get a good insight into this popular art.

Peek Tours Free Tour WALKING TOUR
(Map p484; www.peektours.com.au; Federation Sq; tips based; Flinders St) These new-to-Melbourne free tours are actually tips based; you tip your guide after the three-hour walk. Expect basic tours with an occasionally negative dig at Melbourne (perhaps because Peek Tours originated in Sydney?).

Port Phillip Eco Centre WALKING TOUR
(Map p494; 03-9534 0670; www.ecocentre.com; 55a Blessington St, St Kilda) FREE In summer, the centre runs popular free coastal sunset walks showing the diverse environment of the St Kilda seafront.

Sunset Eco Penguin Tour STAND-UP PADDLEBOARDING
(Map p494; 0416 184 994; www.supb.com.au; tours $130; 96) See St Kilda's penguin colony from the water while you navigate your paddleboard standing up (cost includes a lesson and wetsuit hire).

Festivals & Events

Melbourne isn't fussy about when it gets festive. Winter's chills or summer's swelter are no excuse, with Melburnians joining like-minded types at outdoor festivals, cinemas, performance spaces or sporting venues year-round.

Australian Open TENNIS
(www.australianopen.com; National Tennis Centre) The world's top tennis players and huge, merry-making crowds descend in January for Australia's Grand Slam tennis championship.

Midsumma Festival GAY, LESBIAN
(www.midsumma.org.au) Melbourne's annual gay and lesbian arts festival features more than 100 events from mid-January to mid-February, with a Pride March finale.

Big Day Out MUSIC
(www.bigdayout.com; Flemington Racecourse; tickets $165) The national rock-fest comes to town each Australia Day (26 January).

Chinese New Year CULTURAL
(www.chinatownmelbourne.com.au; Little Bourke St) Melbourne has celebrated the lunar new year every February since Little Bourke St became Chinatown in the 1860s.

St Kilda Festival MUSIC
(www.stkildafestival.com.au; Acland & Fitzroy Sts) FREE This week-long festival ends in a suburb-wide street party on the second Sunday of February.

St Jerome's Laneway Festival MUSIC
(www.lanewayfestival.com.au; Footscray Community Arts Centre, 45 Moreland Rd) Iconic indie festival held each February, featuring local and international music artists, which has exploded from its initial CBD laneway locale to riverside Footscray.

Sustainable Living Festival ENVIRONMENT
(www.festival.slf.org.au) Focusing on green living, this festival takes over Federation Sq in February with plenty of stalls. Check the website for other activities.

Melbourne Bikefest BIKE
(www.melbournebikefest.com.au) Bikefest hits Melbourne's streets annually from mid-February to mid-March; events include markets, picnics and bike rides.

Melbourne Fashion Festival FASHION
(www.mff.com.au; Mar) This style-fest held in March features salon shows and parades showcasing new creations of established designers.

Melbourne Food & Wine Festival FOOD
(www.melbournefoodandwine.com.au) Market tours, wine tastings, cooking classes and presentations by celeb chefs take place at venues across the city (and state) for two weeks in March.

Moomba FESTIVAL
(www.thatsmelbourne.com.au; Alexandra Gardens) A waterside festival famous locally for its wacky Birdman Rally, where competitors launch themselves into the Yarra River in homemade flying machines. Also has local music, fireworks and carnival rides. Held over the Labour Day long weekend in March.

Australian Formula One Grand Prix CAR RACING
(1800 100 030; www.grandprix.com.au; Albert Park; tickets from $55) The 5.3km street circuit around the normally tranquil Albert Park Lake (p495) is known for its smooth, fast surface. The buzz, both on the streets and in your ears, takes over Melbourne for four days of rev-head action each March.

Melbourne International Comedy Festival COMEDY
(www.comedyfestival.com.au; Melbourne Town Hall) An enormous range of local and international comic talent hits town for four weeks of laughs from late March to late April.

JUST FOR NEIGHBOURS FANS

Love *Neighbours*? A visit to Melbourne would not be complete without a trip to the legendary Ramsay St. Pin Oak Ct in Vermont South is the suburban street that has been the home of the show for nearly 30 years.

The **Official Neighbours Tour** (03-9629 5866; www.neighbourstour.com.au) is approved by the show's producers and the residents of Pin Oak Ct. If you're lucky, you might see it being filmed and grab a photo and autograph. Two tours are available: the $50 tour runs twice daily Monday to Friday and visits Ramsay St, plus you get the chance to meet a *Neighbours* actor. The second, more comprehensive tour, costs $68 and visits the street and the outside studio sets of the Lassiters' complex, Carpenter Mechanics and Charlie's Bar. This tour runs on weekends and over the Christmas holidays. Official merchandise is available on the tours and from the **Neighbours Centre** (Map p484; 570 Flinders St).

If you want to make the pilgrimage yourself, look up Melway map 62 (Ref E8) or, if you don't have wheels, take the train to Glen Waverley station and bus 888 or 889 north; get off at Vision Dr near Burwood Hwy. Tram 75 from Flinders St will take you all the way to the corner of Burwood Hwy and Springvale Rd; a short walk south takes you to Weeden Dr, and Pin Oak Ct is third on the left.

The **Official Neighbours Trivia Night** (Map p494; bookings 03-9629 5866; www.neighboursnight.com.au; Elephant & Wheelbarrow, 169 Fitzroy St; tickets $40) is held every Monday night, and you can meet and have photos taken with *Neighbours* actors. It includes a one-hour concert by Waiting Room, featuring Alan Fletcher (aka Dr Karl Kennedy).

Good Beer Week BEER
(www.goodbeerweek.com.au) Melbourne celebrates its plethora of local breweries (and international brews) during this week-long festival in May.

Great Australasian Beer SpecTAPular BEER
(www.gabsfestival.com.au) More than 60 breweries turn up to show off their best brews over this all-weekend event in May.

Melbourne Jazz JAZZ
(www.melbournejazz.com) International jazz cats head to town in June and join locals for gigs at venues including Bennetts Lane, Federation Sq and Melbourne Recital Centre.

Melbourne International Film Festival FILM
(MIFF; www.melbournefilmfestival.com.au) Midwinter movie love-in bringing out black-skivvy-wearing cinephiles in droves. Held over three weeks from late July to mid-August.

Melbourne Writers Festival LITERATURE
(www.mwf.com.au) Yes, Melbourne is a Unesco 'city of literature', and it's proud of its writers and, indeed, readers. Beginning in the last week of August, the Writers Festival features forums and events at various venues including the **Wheeler Centre** (03-9094 7800; www.wheelercentre.com; 176 Little Lonsdale St).

AFL Grand Final FOOTBALL
(www.afl.com.au; MCG) It's easier to kick a goal from the boundary line than to pick up random tickets to the Grand Final, traditionally held on the last Saturday in September, but it's not hard to get your share of finals fever anywhere in Melbourne (particularly at pubs).

Melbourne Fringe Festival ARTS
(www.melbournefringe.com.au) The Fringe showcases experimental theatre, music and visual arts from late September to early October.

Melbourne International Arts Festival ARTS
(www.melbournefestival.com.au) Held at various venues around the city in October, this festival features a thought-provoking program of Australian and international theatre, opera, dance, visual art and music.

Melbourne Cup HORSE RACING
(www.springracingcarnival.com.au) Culminating in the prestigious Melbourne Cup, the Spring Racing Carnival is as much a social event as a sporting one. Cup Day, held on the first Tuesday in November, is a public holiday in Melbourne.

Boxing Day Test CRICKET
(www.mcg.org.au; MCG) Boxing Day (26 December) is day one of Melbourne's annually scheduled international Test match, drawing out the cricket fans. Expect some shenanigans from Bay 13.

WORTH A TRIP

SAFARI FUN!

Werribee Open Range Zoo (1300 966 784; www.zoo.org.au; K Rd; adult/child $26.10/13; 9am-5pm, last entry 3.30pm) is a 225-hectare African-safari-style experience about 30 minutes southwest of Melbourne. Meerkats greet you at the entrance and admission includes a safari tour (on an open-windowed bus). You'll see plenty of ostriches, bison, Mongolian wild horses, hippos, rhinos, zebras and giraffes grazing on the savannah.

Sleeping

Stay in the CBD for good access to the main sights, or spread your wings and get to know an inner-city suburb like funky Fitzroy, seaside St Kilda or smart South Yarra.

Central Melbourne

Melbourne Central YHA HOSTEL $
(Map p484; 03-9621 2523; www.yha.com.au; 562 Flinders St; dm/d $34/100; ; 70) This heritage building has been transformed by the YHA. Expect handsome rooms, two kitchens, a great rooftop area and, for something unique, choose one of the two rooftop doubles.

Greenhouse Backpacker HOSTEL $
(Map p484; 03-9639 6400; www.greenhousebackpacker.com.au; 6/228 Flinders Lane; dm/s/d incl breakfast $35/80/90; ; Flinders St) Greenhouse has a fun vibe and is extremely well run – it knows what keeps backpackers content. Freebies include internet access, rooftop BBQs, luggage storage and city walks. It's kept clean and staff are helpful. There's double-bed bunks for couples in the mixed dorms as well as single-sex dorms.

City Centre Hotel HOTEL $
(Map p484; 03-9654 5401; www.citycentrebudgethotel.com.au; 22 Little Collins St; s/d/f $75/92/140;

@ 🛜; (ℝ Parliament) While nothing quite matches, including the colour scheme, this 38-room hotel is cheap. It's located at the city's prettier end, down a 'Little' street, up some stairs, and inside an unassuming building. All rooms share bathrooms but they are light-filled with working windows. There's also free wi-fi and a laundry.

★ Ovolo
BOUTIQUE HOTEL $$

(Map p484; ☑ 03-8692 0777; www.ovologroup.com; 19 Little Bourke St; r incl breakfast $195; P 🛜; 🚃 96, ℝ Parliament) Shh, don't tell everyone, but there's a free minibar in each room, and a free daily happy hour. Wait, tell everyone, because this new boutique hotel is friendly, fun and one of Melbourne's best. Rooms are light-filled and edgy, with interesting views.

Urban Central Backpackers
HOSTEL $$

(☑ 03-9639 3700, 1800 631 288; www.urbancentral.com.au; 334 City Rd; dm/d/f incl breakfast from $31/125/155; ✳@🛜; 🚃 55, 112) Housed in a functional grey block monolith, this hostel is surprisingly warm, colourful and bright on the inside. Dorms are neat and tidy, there's a great (cheap) bar downstairs and rap-jumping off the roof ($79 for three jumps). Staff are friendly and helpful.

Nomad's Melbourne
HOSTEL $$

(Map p484; ☑ 03-9328 4383; www.nomadshostels.com; 198 A'Beckett St; dm $20-36, d $120; P ✳🛜; ℝ Flagstaff) This hostel boasts a mix of four- to 14-bed dorms (groups can take hold of a four-bed dorm with en suite). There's a rooftop area with BBQ, a bar, and plenty of gloss (especially in the girls-only 'Princess Wing').

Space Hotel
HOSTEL $$

(Map p484; ☑ 1800 670 611, 03-9662 3888; 380 Russell St; dm/d $35/105; @🛜; 🚃 24, 30) The CCTV cameras keeping an eye on the hallways give some idea of the high-tech ways of this hostel. There's a spa on the roof, huge kitchens and even a small cinema to keep you busy, and the downstairs bar certainly gets rowdy. It's ideal if you're looking for a clean and secure place to sleep.

Econolodge City Square
HOTEL $$

(Map p484; ☑ 03-9654 7011; www.citysquaremotel.com.au; 67 Swanston St; incl breakfast s $90-100, d $125-145; P ✳🛜; ℝ Flinders St) The foyer is not much, but the rooms are dirt cheap and the staff charming. Windows are double-glazed to dull the sound of tram bells, and there's bread, butter and Vegemite in the room for breakfast.

Pensione Hotel
HOTEL $$

(Map p484; ☑ 03-9621 3333; www.pensione.com.au; 16 Spencer St; r $125; P ✳@🛜; 🚃 96, 109, 112) The Pensione isn't being cute christening some rooms 'petit double' – they're squeezy – but what you don't get in size is more than made up for in spot-on style and super-reasonable rates. Rooms close to the neighbouring backpackers get a 'sweet dreams' pack.

Alto Hotel on Bourke
HOTEL $$

(Map p484; ☑ 03-8608 5500; www.altohotel.com.au; 636 Bourke St; r from $140; P ✳@🛜; 🚃 86, 96) ✎ This environment-minded hotel runs on 100% green power and has water-saving showers, double-glazed windows that open, its own beehive and in-room recycling. Rooms are also well equipped, light and neutrally decorated.

Adina Apartment Hotel
SERVICED APARTMENTS $$

(Map p484; ☑ 03-8663 0000; www.adinahotels.com.au; 88 Flinders St; apt from $165; P ✳🛜; 🚃 City Circle, 70, 75) These cool monochromatic apartments are extra large and luxurious. Ask for one at the front for amazing parkland views or get glimpses into Melbourne's lanes from the giant timber-floored studios. All have full kitchens.

Mercure
HOTEL $$

(Map p484; ☑ 03-9205 9999; www.accorhotels.com.au; 13 Spring St; r from $189; P ✳@🛜⛉) Friendly staff and a perfect 2pm checkout on Sundays add sparkle to the recently renovated rooms. Bathrooms shine and each room has a Melbourne scene taking up a wall. Go for a pricier one with sweet Treasury Gardens views.

Robinsons in the City
BOUTIQUE HOTEL $$

(Map p484; ☑ 03-9329 2552; www.ritc.com.au; 405 Spencer St; r incl breakfast from $165; P ✳🛜; 🚃 75, 96) Robinsons is a gem with six large rooms and warm service. The building is a former bakery, dating from 1850, but it's been given a modern, eclectic look. Most rooms have their own bathroom in the hall.

Causeway Inn on the Mall
HOTEL $$

(Map p484; ☑ 03-9650 0688; www.causeway.com.au; 327 Bourke St Mall; r incl breakfast $153; ✳@🛜; 🚃 86, 96) The Causeway Inn is always busy and often full. Bonuses include helpful staff and daily paper, and a location bang in the middle of the city. The hotel entrance is actually in the Causeway.

Victoria Hotel HOTEL $$
(Map p484; ☎03-9669 0000; www.victoriahotel.com.au; 215 Little Collins St; s $99-110 d $125-145; P ❄ @ 📶 🏊) The original Vic opened its doors in 1880 but don't worry, the plumbing has been updated since then. There are around 400 rooms here, and all differ slightly. The Heritage rooms are reasonably upmarket, and the rest are in a process of renewal. Facilities include a plunge pool.

Causeway 353 HOTEL $$
(Map p484; ☎03-9668 1888; www.causeway.com.au; 353 Little Collins St; r incl breakfast from $164; P ❄ @ 📶; 🚋86, 96) Who needs a view when you've got a laneway location? You will be more than relaxed after spending a night in simple, stylish rooms, which feature long and dark timber bedheads, king-sized beds and smart leather furniture.

Majorca Apartment 401 SERVICED APARTMENT $$$
(Map p484; ☎03-9428 8104; www.apartment401.com.au; Majorca Building, 258 Flinders Lane; apt from $250; ❄ 📶; 🚆Flinders St) This is the ultimate in like-a-local living. This single apartment is in one of the city's loveliest art-deco buildings and has a balcony watching over a bustling vortex of laneways. Expect replica vintage furniture, timber floorboards and huge windows. There's a two-night minimum stay.

Crown Metropol HOTEL $$$
(☎03-9292 6211; www.crownhotels.com.au; 8 Whiteman St; r from $295; 🏊; 🚋96, 109, 112) Guests here have access to the most extraordinary infinity pool in Melbourne. Yes, you too can be swimming laps 27 levels up while visually plotting the schedule for your day ahead. The beautifully appointed luxe twin rooms are the cheapest on offer and sleep four.

Sofitel HOTEL $$$
(Map p484; ☎03-96530000; www.sofitelmelbourne.com.au; 25 Collins St; r from $270; P ❄ @ 📶 🏊; 🚋11, 48, 109, 112, 🚆Parliament) Guest rooms at the Sofitel start on the 36th floor, so you are guaranteed views that will make you giddy. The rooms have timber features, including clever blockout shutters, and plenty of marble. No35 is an excellent restaurant on level (you guessed it) 35.

Hotel Lindrum BOUTIQUE HOTEL $$$
(MGallery Accor; Map p484; ☎03-9668 1111; www.hotellindrum.com.au; 26 Flinders St; r from $245; P ❄ 📶; 🚋70, 75) This attractive hotel was once the pool hall of the legendary and literally unbeatable Walter Lindrum. It's one of Melbourne's most interesting boutique hotels, but spring for a deluxe room so you will snare either arch or bay windows and marvellous views of Melbourne. And, yes, there's a pool table.

Fitzroy & Around

Home@The Mansion HOSTEL $
(Map p489; ☎03-9663 4212; www.homemansion.com.au; 80 Victoria Pde, East Melbourne; dm $29-34, d $90; @ 📶; 🚋City Circle, 30, 96, 🚆Parliament) This grand-looking heritage building houses 92 dorm beds and a couple of doubles, all of which are light and bright and have lovely high ceilings. There are two small areas for Playstation and TV-watching, a courtyard out the front and a sunny kitchen.

Collingwood Backpackers HOSTEL $
(☎0420 804 208; www.collingwoodbackpackers.com; 137-139 Johnston St, Collingwood; dm $28; P @ 📶; 🚌200, 201, 207, 🚋86, 🚆Victoria Park) Going against the high-tech, high-gloss grain of some hostels is Collingwood Backpackers. Call ahead to book your room (walk-ins are discouraged) and expect a smoky, friendly, sharehouse kind of atmosphere. Rooms have wi-fi access and, like owner Paul, plenty of, ahem, character. To find it follow Johnston St east of Smith St.

Nunnery HOSTEL $$
(Map p489; ☎03-9419 8637; www.nunnery.com.au; 116 Nicholson St, Fitzroy; dm incl breakfast $32, s/d $90/120; @ 📶; 🚋96) The Nunnery oozes atmosphere, with sweeping staircases and many original features; the walls are dripping with religious works of art and ornate stained-glass windows. You'll be giving thanks for the big comfortable lounges and communal areas.

Brooklyn Arts Hotel B&B $$
(Map p489; ☎03-9419 9328; www.brooklynartshotel.com.au; 50 George St, Fitzroy; s/d incl breakfast $95/135; 📶; 🚋86) There are seven very different rooms in this rustic B&B. Owner Maggie has put the call out for artistic people and they've responded by staying, so expect lively conversation over the continental breakfast. Rooms are clean (but certainly not sterile!), colourful and beautifully decorated; one even houses a piano.

Tyrian Serviced Apartments SERVICED APARTMENT $$
(Map p489; ☎03-9415 1900; www.tyrian.com.au; 91 Johnston St, Fitzroy; r from $200; P❄📶; 🚋112) These spacious, self-contained modern apartments have a certain Fitzroy celeb vibe, which you'll feel from the moment you walk down the dimmed hallway to reception. Big couches, flat-screen TVs and private balconies add to the appeal.

Carlton

Downtowner on Lygon HOTEL $$
(Map p490; ☎03-9663 5555; www.downtowner.com.au; 66 Lygon St; r from $174; P❄@📶🏊; 🚋1, 8) The Downtowner is a surprising complex of different-sized rooms, including joining rooms perfect for families and other groups. Ask for a light-bathed room if you can. It's perfectly placed between the CBD and Lygon St restaurants.

169 Drummond B&B $$
(Map p490; ☎03-9663 3081; www.169drummond.com.au; 169 Drummond St; d incl breakfast $135-145; 🚋1, 8) A privately owned and very friendly guesthouse with en suite rooms in a renovated, 19th-century terrace. In the inner north, just one block from vibrant Lygon St.

South Yarra, Prahran & Windsor

Hotel Claremont GUESTHOUSE $
(Map p492; ☎03-9826 8000; www.hotelclaremont.com; 189 Toorak Rd, South Yarra; dm/d incl breakfast $42/89; @📶; 🚋8, 🚆South Yarra) In a large heritage building dating from 1886, the Claremont is good value, with comfortable rooms, high ceilings and shared bathrooms. Don't expect fancy decor: it's simply a clean, welcoming cheapie.

★**Art Series (Cullen)** BOUTIQUE HOTEL $$
(Map p492; ☎03-9098 1555; www.artserieshotels.com.au/cullen; 164 Commercial Rd, Prahran; r from $189; ❄@📶; 🚋72, 78, 79, 🚆Prahran) Expect visions of Ned Kelly shooting you from the glam opaque room/bathroom dividers in this lively hotel resplendent in the works of recently departed Sydney artist Adam Cullen. Borrow the 'Cullen Car' ($55 per day) or Kronan bike ($5 per hour) and let the whole of Melbourne know where you're staying.

Punthill South Yarra Grand APARTMENT $$
(Map p492; ☎1300 731 299; www.punthill.com.au; 7 Yarra St, South Yarra; r from $180; P❄📶; 🚋8,78, 🚆South Yarra) It's the little things, like a blackboard and chalk in the kitchen for messages, and chocolates by the bed, that make this modern apartment hotel ooze friendliness. All rooms have a laundry, balcony and a tin dog chilling out on fake grass. Right in the hub of the Claremont district.

Art Series (The Olsen) BOUTIQUE HOTEL $$
(Map p492; ☎03-9040 1222; www.artserieshotels.com.au/olsen; 637 Chapel St, South Yarra; r from $200; P❄📶🏊; 🚋8, 78, 🚆South Yarra) Artist John Olsen is the muse for this still-shiny hotel on the Yarra River end of Chapel St. International celebs stay here, and we think we know why: attentive staff, a glam foyer and the art-rich open-plan rooms have everything you need (including a small kitchen). Oh, and the hotel pool juts out over Chapel St. It's a must-stay.

The Como Melbourne HOTEL $$$
(MGallery Collection; Map p492; ☎03-9825 2222; www.mirvachotels.com; 630 Chapel St, South Yarra; r from $275; P❄@📶🏊; 🚋8, 78, 🚆South Yarra) From its pink foyer with water features, to rooms with almost-floor-to-ceiling mirrors and grand bathrooms, MGallery screams five star. It's certainly got great service, and plenty of style.

St Kilda & Around

St Kilda is a budget-traveller enclave, but there are some stylish options a short walk from the beach, too.

Ritz HOSTEL $
(Map p494; ☎03-9525 3501; www.ritzbackpackers.com; 169 Fitzroy St, St Kilda; dm/d incl breakfast $26/80; 📶; 🚋3a, 16, 79) Above a corner pub renowned for hosting the popular *Neighbours* trivia nights, the Ritz has an excellent location, opposite an inner-city lake and park, and is only a five-minute walk from St Kilda's heart. It can get noisy when live music is cranking downstairs on weekends.

Habitat HQ HOSTEL $
(☎1800 202 500, 03-9537 3777; www.habitathq.com.au; 333 St Kilda Rd, St Kilda; dm incl breakfast from $32, d $89-99; P❄@📶; 🚋3, 67, 79) This hostel has it all: open-plan communal spaces, a beer garden, a travel agent and a pool table for starters. Fun, busy and well run, though rooms could do with a good scrub.

It's on St Kilda Rd, between Inkerman and Carlisle Sts.

Base HOSTEL **$$**
(Map p494; ☎03-8598 6200; www.stayatbase.com; 17 Carlisle St, St Kilda; dm/r $30/115; P❄@📶; 🚋3a, 16, 79, 96) Fun-filled Base has streamlined dorms, each with en suite, or slick doubles. There's a 'sanctuary' for female travellers, where tea and coffee is delivered free on weekend mornings, maybe to make up for the weekly free champagne 'for ladies'. Live music nights keep the good-time vibe happening.

Hotel Tolarno HOTEL **$$**
(Map p494; ☎03-9537 0200; www.hoteltolarno.com.au; 42 Fitzroy St, St Kilda; r from $155; ❄@📶; 🚋3a, 16, 96, 112) This is an art hotel, pure and simple. The owner acquires new paintings annually, and even the location was once Georges Mora's seminal gallery Tolarno. The restaurant downstairs bears the name of his artist wife, Mirka. Every room is different; expect bright colours and eclectic furniture.

Hotel Urban HOTEL **$$**
(Map p494; ☎03-8530 8888; www.urbanstkilda.com.au; 35-37 Fitzroy St, St Kilda; r from $165; P❄@📶🏊; 🚋16, 79, 96, 112) Rooms at Hotel Urban use a lot of blond wood and white to maximise space, and are simple, light and calming. Two rooms are circular with free-standing in-room spas. Guests get free access to the St Kilda Sea Baths.

Prince HOTEL **$$**
(Map p494; ☎03-9536 1111; www.theprince.com.au; 2 Acland St, St Kilda; r incl breakfast from $169; P❄@📶🏊; 🚋3a, 16, 96, 112) The Prince has a suitably dramatic lobby and the rooms are an interesting mix of the original pub's proportions, natural materials and a pared-back aesthetic. Larger rooms and suites feature some key pieces of vintage modernist furniture.

Middle Park Hotel PUB **$$**
(☎03-9690 1958; www.middleparkhotel.com.au; 102 Canterbury Rd, Middle Park; r incl breakfast from $160; ❄@📶; 🚋96) When you're given an x-rated 'intimacy' pack ($70), you might be wondering what kind of hotel you've booked yourself into, but relax. Rooms are luxurious and modern – expect iPod docks and rain showerheads at the top of the wooden staircase. There's a modern pub and restaurant downstairs, and the cooked gourmet breakfast is a treat.

Art Series (Blackman) BOUTIQUE HOTEL **$$$**
(☎1800 278 468, 03-9039 1444; www.artserieshotels.com.au/blackman; 452 St Kilda Rd, Melbourne; r from $239; ❄📶; 🚋3, 5, 6, 8, 16, 64, 67, 72) This Art Series hotel may not have one single original Blackman painting (though it does have loads of prints and room decals), but it boasts superb views (aim for a corner suite for views of Albert Park Lake and the city skyline), luxurious beds and blackout curtains for a sleep-in. Aimed at corporates, but suits the splurger, too.

Eating

Central Melbourne

Don Don JAPANESE **$**
(Map p484; 198 Little Lonsdale St; mains $6-8; ⏰11am-3.30pm Mon-Fri; 🚋City Circle, 🚆Melbourne Central) There's plenty of space at the new Don Don, though it fills fast. Grab a takeaway container filled with hot and tasty Japanese food and join the masses eating it on the State Library's lawns.

Red Pepper INDIAN **$**
(Map p484; 14-16 Bourke St; mains $10-13; ⏰9am-2.30am; 🚋86, 96, 🚆Parliament) It's mighty rare to get a decent meal for under $10, but it's possible here. The local Indian community knows it's good, coming for the fresh naan and daal. The mango lassis are delicious and it's almost always open.

Camy Shanghai Dumpling Restaurant CHINESE **$**
(Map p484; 23-25 Tattersalls Lane; dishes $6.50; ⏰11.30am-10pm) There's nothing fancy here: pour your own plastic cup of overboiled tea from the urn, then try a variety of dumplings with some greens. Put up with the dismal service and you've found one of the last places in town you can fill up for under $10.

★**MoVida** SPANISH **$$**
(Map p484; ☎03-9663 3038; www.movida.com.au; 1 Hosier Lane; tapas $4-6, raciones $10-24; ⏰noon-late; 🚋70, 75, 🚆Flinders St) Finished looking at the surrounding street art? Now line up along the bar, cluster around little window tables or, if you've booked, take a table in the dining area. **MoVida Next Door** (Map p484; cnr Flinders St & Hosier Lane; ⏰5pm-late Tue-Thu, noon-midnight Fri & Sat, 2pm-9pm Sun) is the perfect place for tapas, while in the lawyer end of town is the larger **MoVida Aqui** (Map p484; 1st fl, 500 Bourke St; ⏰noon-late Mon-Fri, 6pm-late

Sat), also home to a lovely terrace that houses lively Paco's Tacos ($6 tacos).

Mamasita MEXICAN $$
(Map p484; ☎03-9650 3821; www.mamasita.com.au; Level 1, 11 Collins St; mains $15-28; ⏰noon-12pm Mon-Thu, to 2am Fri & Sat, to 10pm Sun; 🚋City Circle, 11, 31, 48, 109, 112) You see a line snaking along Collins St at 7pm and wonder if it's worth it. Mamasita has been making Melburnians wait for years now, and the lines only get longer so, in short, yes! There are 180 types of tequila, and the two-bite *tostaditas* are piled high with delicious ingredients like prawn or pork shoulder. Don't miss the chargrilled corn.

Cumulus Inc MODERN AUSTRALIAN $$
(Map p484; www.cumulusinc.com.au; 45 Flinders Lane; mains $21-38; ⏰7am-11pm Mon-Fri, 8am-11pm Sat & Sun; 🚋City Circle) Watch Melburnians mope into their smartphones at this reasonably priced and very cool restaurant. The focus is on beautiful produce and simple but artful cooking, and its $16 breakfast (including sublime coffee) is better than anything a hotel can muster up.

Chin Chin THAI $$
(Map p484; ☎03-8663 2000; www.chinchinrestaurant.com.au; 125 Flinders Lane; mains $19-33; ⏰11am-late) Spunky Thai dining thrives in this busied-up shell of an old building on Flinders Lane. The menu is long, curries are madly tasty and everything on the plates is bright and fresh, with ribbons of flavour ticking the right palate boxes. No bookings, but GoGo Bar downstairs will have you till there's space.

HuTong Dumpling Bar CHINESE $$
(Map p484; www.hutong.com.au; 14-16 Market Lane; mains $15-22; ⏰11.30am-3pm & 5.30-10.30pm) HuTong's windows face out on the famed Flower Drum, and its reputation for divine *xiao long bao* (soupy dumplings) means getting a lunchtime seat anywhere in this three-level building is just as hard. Downstairs, watch chefs make the delicate dumplings, then hope they don't watch you making a mess eating them. There's also a branch in **Prahran** (Map p492; 162 Commercial Rd).

Bar Lourinhã TAPAS $$
(Map p484; ☎03-9663 7890; www.barlourinha.com.au; 37 Little Collins St; tapas $12-24; ⏰noon-11pm Mon-Thu, noon-1am Fri, 4pm-1am Sat; 🚉Parliament) Matt McConnell's northern Spanish-Portuguese specialities have the swagger and honesty of an Iberian shepherd, but with a metropolitan touch. Start light with the zingy kingfish pancetta and finish with the house-made chorizo or baked *morcilla* (blood sausage).

Trunk AMERICAN, ITALIAN $$
(The Diner; Map p484; ☎03-9663 7994; www.trunktown.com.au; 275 Exhibition St; mains $18-26; ⏰7.30am-4pm) Trunk's American-styled

NO RESERVATIONS

A recent trend in Melbourne's fine-dining scene has many of the city's hottest restaurants taking the innovative approach of a 'no bookings' policy. The move has received its share of love and criticism but is mostly aimed at delivering more flexibility and spontaneity. For visitors to Melbourne, testing its culinary credentials will be high on the to-do list, but just be aware you'll be playing the waiting game at some of the best spots. But, of course, good things come to those who wait.

Longrain (p507) was one of the first restaurants to adopt communal dining with group-only bookings. 'Reservations are too tricky and don't work with the kind of atmosphere we are trying to create', it explains. The downside is you can expect to wait up to 1½ hours so get there around 6pm to avoid a lengthy wait, or you can start off with drinks and starters in the cocktail bar. Cumulus Inc (p506) tells us it regards itself 'not so much as a restaurant but as an eating house and bar' by opening all day with no bookings, so diners can show up any time.

Chin Chin (above) is another city eatery with a buzzing atmosphere thanks to its no-reservation policy. The attached GoGo Bar downstairs is a clever way around this, where you can sip while you wait. The consistent popularity of MoVida Next Door (p505) and Mamasita (p506) means dinner waits are almost guaranteed but diners are well rewarded. And, thankfully, most places will take your mobile number and call once a spot has opened so you're not awkwardly hanging around waiting.

Kate Morgan

diner – it's very much burgers and dogs – has a busy, fun feel to it. Next door a former synagogue makes a classy Italian option for dinner or drinks.

The Waiters Restaurant ITALIAN **$$**

(Map p484; ☎03-9650 1508; 1st fl, 20 Meyers Pl; mains $15-24; ⏰noon-2.30pm Mon-Fri & 6pm-late Mon-Sat; Ⓡ Parliament) Down a laneway and up some stairs, this restaurant has an interior that will make you feel like you stepped into another era. Opened in 1947, it still bears '50s drapes, wood panelling and Laminex tables. Once a place for Italian and Spanish waiters to unwind after work, it now lets everyone enjoy its hearty plates of red-sauce pasta and daily specials.

Pellegrini's Espresso Bar ITALIAN, CAFE **$$**

(Map p484; ☎03-9662 1885; 66 Bourke St; mains $16-18; ⏰8am-11.30pm Mon-Sat, noon-8pm Sun) The iconic Italian equivalent of a classic 1950s diner, Pellegrini's has remained genuinely unchanged for decades. Pick and mix from the variety of pastas and sauces and enjoy the jovial atmosphere. In summer, finish with a ladle of $3 watermelon granita.

Longrain THAI **$$**

(Map p484; ☎03-9671 3151; www.longrain.com; 44 Little Bourke St; mains $25-40; ⏰noon-3pm Fri & dinner 6pm-late Mon-Thu, from 5.30pm Fri-Sun; Ⓡ Parliament) Perfectly balanced Thai food served in a dining hall and adjacent noisy bar. No bookings, so you'll be encouraged to have a drink to stop your mouth watering while you wait.

Gingerboy ASIAN **$$$**

(Map p484; ☎03-9662 4200; www.gingerboy.com.au; 27-29 Crossley St; shared dishes $32-50; ⏰noon-2.30pm & 5.30pm-late Mon-Fri, dinner only Sat; 🚋86, 96) Brave the aggressively trendy surrounds and weekend party scene, as talented Teague Ezard does a fine turn in flash hawker cooking. Flavours pop in dishes such as red duck leg curry and crispy chilli salt cuttlefish. Bookings are required.

Flower Drum CHINESE **$$$**

(Map p484; ☎03-9662 3655; www.flower-drum.com; 17 Market Lane; mains $35-55; ⏰noon-3pm & 6-11pm Mon-Sat, 6-10.30pm Sun) The Flower Drum continues to be Melbourne's most celebrated Chinese restaurant. The finest, freshest produce prepared with absolute attention to detail keeps this Chinatown institution booked out for weeks in advance. The sumptuous but ostensibly simple Cantonese food is delivered with the slick service you'd expect in such elegant surrounds.

Vue de Monde FRENCH, MODERN AUSTRALIAN **$$$**

(Map p484; ☎03-9691 3888; www.vuedemonde.com.au; Rialto, 525 Collins St; degustation $200-250; ⏰reservations from noon-2pm Tue-Fri & Sun, 6-9.15pm Mon-Sat; 🚋11, 31, 48, 109, 112, Ⓡ Southern Cross) Melbourne's favoured spot for occasion dining has extraordinary views from the 55th floor of the Rialto. Expect fantastic French cuisine thanks to visionary Shannon Bennett; designwise, there's plenty of kangaroo fur and locally made bespoke furniture. Book ahead. If you can't get in, at least venture up for a fabulous cocktail from the Lui Bar (p511).

North Melbourne

Auction Rooms CAFE **$**

(107 Errol St; mains $8-19; ⏰7am-5pm Mon-Wed & Sun, to 10pm Thu-Sat; 🚋57) This insanely busy cafe serves up Small Batch coffee and inventive mains, though sometimes you may wonder if it's still operating as an auction room (everyone just seems so...polished). From Queen Victoria Market head west along Victoria St, then take a right at Errol St.

Courthouse Hotel PUB **$$**

(☎03-9329 5394; www.thecourthouse.net.au; 86 Errol St; mains $22-37; ⏰noon-3pm & 6-10pm Mon-Sat; 🚋57) This corner pub has managed to retain the comfort and familiarity of a local while taking food, both in its public bar and its more formal dining spaces, very seriously. Enjoy mains like rare roasted and cured kangaroo or choose from its simpler (and cheaper) bar menu.

Richmond

If you love Vietnamese food, don't miss Richmond's Victoria St (the east end of Collingwood and Fitzroy's Victoria Pde).

Pacific Seafood BBQ House CHINESE **$$**

(☎03-9427 8225; 240 Victoria St; mains $15-25; ⏰10.30am-10.30pm; 🚋24, 31, 109, Ⓡ North Richmond) Seafood in tanks and script-only menus on coloured craft paper make for an authentic, fast and fabulous dining experience. Tank-fresh fish is done simply, perhaps steamed with ginger and greens, and washed down with Chinese beer. Book, or be ready to queue.

Richmond Hill Cafe & Larder CAFE $$
(☎03-9421 2808; www.rhcl.com.au; 48-50 Bridge Rd; lunch $12-26; ⊙8.30am-5pm; 🚊75, 🚆West Richmond) Once the domain of well-known cook Stephanie Alexander, it still boasts its lovely cheese room and simple, comforting food like cheesy toast. There are breakfast cocktails for the brave and it is quite un-hipsterfied. Wellington Pde in the CBD becomes Bridge Rd.

Baby PIZZA $$
(Map p492; ☎03-9421 4599; www.babypizza.com.au; 631-633 Church St; mains $17; ⊙7am-11pm; 🚊70, 78, 🚆East Richmond) Ignore the porno light feature (you won't notice it if you dine by day) and get into the food and vibe. Delicious pizza, the occasional Aussie TV star and many, many trendy folk. It's busy, bold and run by restaurant king Christopher Lucas (Chin Chin), so it's quite brilliant. Even for a pizza joint.

Fitzroy & Around

Huxtaburger BURGERS $
(Map p489; ☎03-9417 6328; www.huxtaburger.com.au; 106 Smith St, Collingwood; burgers from $8.50; ⊙11.30am-10pm Mon-Thu & Sun, to 11pm Fri & Sat; 🚊86) Set up just like the Australian fish 'n' chip shop of old, Huxtaburger is a one-stop burger shop. Fries come crinklecut and seats come roadside. There's also a branch in the **city** (Map p484; Fulham Pl, off Flinders Lane; ⊙11.30am-10pm Mon-Sat).

Vegie Bar VEGETARIAN $
(Map p489; www.vegiebar.com.au; 380 Brunswick St, Fitzroy; mains $14-16; ⊙11am-late Mon-Fri, from 9am Sat & Sun; 🖉; 🚊112) Tasty vegetarian curries, burgers, raw foods and seasonal broths can be eaten outside along fab Brunswick St itself, or in the cavernous, shared-table space inside.

Babka Bakery Cafe BAKERY, CAFE $
(Map p489; 358 Brunswick St, Fitzroy; mains $10-16; ⊙7am-7pm Tue-Sun; 🚊112) Russian flavours infuse the lovingly prepared breakfast and lunch dishes, and the heady aroma of cinnamon and freshly baked bread makes even just a coffee worth queuing for. Cakes are notable and can be taken away whole.

Moroccan Soup Bar NORTH AFRICAN, VEGETARIAN $$
(☎03-9482 4240; 183 St Georges Rd, Fitzroy North; banquet $20; ⊙6pm-10pm Tue-Sun; 🖉; 🚊112) Prepare to queue before being seated by Hana, who'll recite the menu. Best bet is the banquet, which, for three courses, is great value. The sublime chickpea bake has locals queuing with their own pots and containers to nab some takeaway. From Fitzroy, continue north along Brunswick St and cross Alexander Pde.

Charcoal Lane MODERN AUSTRALIAN $$
(Map p489; ☎03-9418 3400; www.charcoallane.com.au; 136 Gertrude St, Fitzroy; mains $27-35; ⊙noon-3pm & 6-9pm Tue-Sat; 🚊86) 🍃 This training restaurant for Aboriginal and disadvantaged young people is one of the best places to try native flora and fauna; menu items include wallaby tartare and tanami spiced kangaroo.

Marios CAFE $$
(Map p489; 303 Brunswick St, Fitzroy; mains $17-30; ⊙7am-9.30pm; 🚊112) Mooching at Marios is on the Melbourne 101 curriculum. Breakfasts are big and served all day, the service is swift and the coffee is old-school strong.

Commoner MODERN BRITISH $$
(Map p489; ☎03-9415 6876; www.thecommoner.com.au; 122 Johnston St, Fitzroy; mains $13-30; ⊙noon-3pm Fri-Sun, 6pm-late Wed-Sun; 🚊112) If you need to be convinced of this off-strip restaurant's serious intent, the Sunday wood-grilled meats should do it. There's the billiant five-course 'feed me' menu, too. Take a breather in the upstairs bar.

Birdman Eating TAPAS $$
(Map p489; ☎03-9416 4747; www.birdmaneating.com.au; 238 Gertrude St, Fitzroy; mains $12-18; ⊙7am-6pm; 🚊86) Popular? You bet. It is named after the infamous Birdman Rally held during Melbourne's Moomba festival, and you'll be glad you don't have to hurl yourself off a bridge to sit pretty on Gertrude St and eat Welsh rarebit or dip into leek pâté.

Cutler & Co MODERN AUSTRALIAN $$$
(Map p489; ☎03-9419 4888; www.cutlerandco.com.au; 55 Gertrude St, Fitzroy; mains $39-47; ⊙noon-late Fri & Sun, 6pm-late Mon-Thu; 🚊86) This is Andrew McConnell's fine dining restaurant, and though its decor might be a little over the top, its attentive, informed staff and joy-inducing meals have quickly made this one of Melbourne's best.

Carlton & Around

Avoid Carlton's Lygon St spruikers and keep travelling north past Grattan St; some of

Melbourne's loveliest cafes and restaurants lie here and beyond. Don't miss the East Brunswick end of Lygon St for interesting eats.

Tiamo ITALIAN $

(Map p490; 303 Lygon St, Carlton; mains $9-24; 7am-10.30pm Mon-Sat, to 10pm Sun; Tourist Shuttle) When you've had enough of pressed, siphoned, pour-over filtered and plunged coffee, head here to one of Lygon St's original Italian cafe-restaurants. There's laughter and the relaxed *joie de vivre* only a time-worn restaurant can have.

Abla's LEBANESE $$

(Map p490; 03-9347 0006; www.ablas.com.au; 109 Elgin St, Carlton; mains $27; noon-3pm Thu & Fri, 6-11pm Mon-Sat; 205, 1, 8, 96) The kitchen is steered by Abla Amad, whose authentic, flavour-packed food has been feeding customers since 1979. Bring a bottle of your favourite plonk and enjoy the $60 compulsory banquet on Friday and Saturday nights.

Rumi MIDDLE EASTERN $$

(03-9388 8255; 116 Lygon St, East Brunswick; mains $17-23; 6-10pm; 1, 8) A fabulously well-considered place that serves up a mix of traditional Lebanese cooking and contemporary interpretations of old Persian dishes. The *sigara boregi* (cheese and pine-nut pastries) are a local institution and tasty mains like slow-cooked lamb are balanced with an interesting selection of vegetable dishes. From Carlton, continue north along Lygon St into East Brunswick.

Hellenic Republic GREEK $$

(03-9381 1222; www.hellenicrepublic.com.au; 434 Lygon St, East Brunswick; mains $16-30; noon-4pm Fri, 11am-4pm Sat & Sun, 5.30pm-late Mon-Sun; 1, 8) The Iron Bark grill at George Calombaris' restaurant works overtime grilling up pitta, tiger prawns, local snapper and luscious lamb. Follow Lygon St north from Carlton – it's in East Brunswick.

Bar Idda ITALIAN $$

(03-9380 5339; www.baridda.com.au; 132 Lygon St, East Brunwsick; mains $15-21; 6pm-late Mon-Sat; 1, 8) The diner-style table coverings give little clue to the tasty morsels this Sicilian restaurant serves. Try the 18-hour red wine lamb or vegetarian layered eggplant. Follow Lygon St north from Carlton.

South Yarra, Prahran & Windsor

Burch & Purchese Sweet Studio SWEETS $

(Map p492; 03-9827 7060; www.burchandpurchese.com; 647 Chapel St, South Yarra; from $3; 10am-6.30pm; 78) Pity the folk who work near here – they have to pass this simply incredible sweet shop daily. Oh the temptation. Our pick? Salted-caramel anything.

Lucky Coq PIZZA $

(Map p492; www.luckycoq.com.au; 179 Chapel St, Windsor; mains $4; noon-3am; 6, 78, Prahran) Bargain pizzas and plenty of late-night DJ action make this a good start or end to a Chapel St eve. Dress code is no suits or jackets (yay!).

Two Birds One Stone CAFE $$

(Map p492; 03-9827 1228; www.twobirdsonestonecafe.com.au; 12 Claremont St, South Yarra; mains $15-19; 7am-4pm Mon-Fri, from 8am Sat & Sun; 8, 78, South Yarra) This nouveau industrial cafe in buzzing Claremont St serves

FOOD TRUCKS

Melbourne's long had an association with food vans; a game of suburban footy isn't complete without greasy vans dishing out hot jam doughnuts, hot meat pies and hot chips to freezing fans, and what would a trip to the beach be without an ice-cream van playing its tune? So you could say we've been there done that. But getting quality food from a van is a different matter. Perhaps appealing to our love of 'pop-up' shops and bars (outlets that 'pop up' in a space then disappear once the hype has died), fabulous food trucks have begun plying the streets of Melbourne. Each day the different trucks use Twitter and Facebook to let their followers and friends know where they will be, and dutiful, hungry folk respond by turning up street-side for a meal. Favourite Melbourne food trucks to chase down include Taco Truck (@tacotruckmelb), Gumbo Kitchen (serving New Orleans–style food; @GumboKitchen) and Beatbox Kitchen (serving gourmet burgers and fries to beats; @beatboxkitchen). They're more often than not found parkside on the northside, with one of the most picturesque spots they pull up at being Ruckers Hill, Northcote.

almost perfect coffee and unusual cafe fare including king whiting pide and twice-cooked marmalade French toast.

Colonel Tan's THAI $$

(Map p492; www.coloneltans.com.au; 229 Chapel St, Prahran; mains $16; ⌚5-11pm Tue-Thu & Sat, noon-11pm Fri; 78, Prahran) Lamps hang upside down alongside chandeliers in this share-house style restaurant, yet you'll still barely be able to see the one-page menu or your food. It morphs into a disco come weekends, but get in while the food's hot; this is Thai done beautifully.

Claremont Tonic ASIAN $$

(Map p492; 03-9827 0399; www.claremont-tonic.com.au; 15a Claremont St, South Yarra; mains $18-38; ⌚noon-2.30pm & 6pm-late Tue-Fri, from 6.30pm Sat; 78, South Yarra) Get your fix of South Yarra Fried Chicken here, or try a super juice at the expansive bar. The rock 'n' roll attitude of staff is maybe a little too much, but the Asian dishes are worth the scowl.

Jacques Reymond MODERN AUSTRALIAN $$$

(Map p492; 03-9525 2178; www.jacquesreymond.com.au; 78 Williams Rd, Prahran; degustation menu from $140; ⌚noon-1.30pm Thu & Fri, 6.30-9pm Tue-Sat; 6) Reymond was a local pioneer of degustation dining. There's an innovative vegetarian version. Expect a French-influenced, Asian-accented menu with lovely details including house-churned butter.

St Kilda & Around

Lentil as Anything VEGETARIAN $

(Map p494; www.lentilasanything.com; 41 Blessington St, St Kilda; prices at customers' discretion; ⌚11am-9pm; ; 16, 96) Choose from the always-organic, no-meat menu and pay what you can afford. This unique not-for-profit operation provides training and educational opportunities for marginalised people. There's another branch at the **Abbotsford Convent** (1 St Heliers St).

Banff PIZZA $

(Map p494; www.banffstkilda.com; 145 Fitzroy St, St Kilda; mains $9; ⌚8am-10pm; 3a, 16) It's not just the daily 3pm to 6pm happy 'hour' (or three) that keeps Banff's Fitzroy St–fronting chairs occupied: it's also the $9 pizzas ($6 for lunch).

Galleon Cafe CAFE $

(Map p494; 9 Carlisle St, St Kilda; mains $10; ⌚7am-5pm; 3a, 16, 79) Friendly folk, a decent amount of elbow room and low-key music make this a cheery place to down a coffee and lunch in busy St Kilda. At night, hit **Radio Mexico** (Map p494; 03-9534 9990; www.radiomexico.com.au; 11-13 Carlisle St) next door.

Batch Espresso CAFE $

(320 Carlisle St, Balaclava; mains $16; ⌚9am-5pm; 3, 3a, 16, Balaclava) Its walls are decorated with bric-a-brac donated by locals who love the Aussie cooking with a retro bent. Good luck getting a seat during the weekend-only all-day brunches. Carlisle St runs east off St Kilda Rd.

Mart 130 CAFE $

(03-9690 8831; 107 Canterbury Rd, Middle Park; dishes $6-20; ⌚7.30am-5pm; 96) Where the light-rail trams now run was once a fully fledged railway line with a string of Federation-style stations. Mart 130 serves up corn fritters and bircher in one of these stations, overlooking the park. Weekends are busy.

La Roche PUB $

(Map p494; 03-9534 1472; www.laroche.net.au; 185 Acland St, St Kilda; mains $13; ⌚8am-1am; 96) Feed yourself with gigantic servings for less than $15 at this backpackers' fave. You can't go wrong.

Cicciolina MEDITERRANEAN $$

(Map p494; www.cicciolinastkilda.com.au; 130 Acland St, St Kilda; mains $19-40; ⌚lunch & dinner; 16, 96) This warm room of dark wood, subdued lighting and pencil sketches is a St Kilda institution. The inspired mod-Med menu is smart and generous, and the service warm. It doesn't take bookings; eat early or while away your wait in the moody little back bar. The sister restaurant, **Ilona Staller** (03-9534 0488; www.ilonastaller.com.au; 282 Carlisle St; mains $38-41; ⌚noon-late; 3, 16, Balaclava), is nearby.

Stokehouse Cafe ITALIAN $$

(Map p494; 03-9525 5445; www.stokehouse.com.au; 30 Jacka Blvd, St Kilda; shared plates $6-25; ⌚noon-late Tue-Fri, 7.30am-late Sat-Mon; 3a, 16, 96) It's hard to beat this iconic Melbourne restaurant's beachfront position, and renovations have turned the cafe downstairs into a modern share-plate style cafe. Upstairs is dedicated to fine diners, with mains around $36.

Claypots SEAFOOD $$

(Map p494; 03-9534 1282; 213 Barkly St, St Kilda; mains $25-35; ⌚noon-3pm & 6pm-1am; 96) A local favourite, Claypots serves up seafood in its namesake. Get in early to both get a seat and ensure the good stuff is still available, as hot items go fast.

I Carusi II PIZZA $$
(Map p494; ☎03-9593 6033; 231 Barkly St, St Kilda; pizza $16-21; ⏱6-11pm; 🚋16, 96) Located beyond the Acland St chaos in a nostalgic corner shop, I Carusi pizzas have a particularly tasty dough and follow the less-is-more tenet, with top-quality mozza, pecorino and a small range of other toppings. Bookings advised, and don't miss the upstairs bar.

★**Attica** MODERN $$$
(☎03-9530 0111; www.attica.com.au; 74 Glen Eira Rd, Ripponlea; 8-course tasting menu $175; ⏱6.30pm-late Tue-Sat; 🚋67, 🚆Ripponlea) Staking its claim to fame by being the only Melbourne restaurant to regularly make it onto San Pellegrino's Best Restaurant list, Attica is a suburban restaurant that serves Ben Shewry's creative dishes degustation-style. Expect small portions of texture-oriented delight, like potatoes cooked in earth. To get here, follow Brighton Rd south to Glen Eira Rd.

Cafe di Stasio ITALIAN $$$
(Map p494; ☎03-9525 3999; www.distasio.com.au; 31a Fitzroy St, St Kilda; mains $26-43; ⏱noon-3pm & 6-11pm; 🚋16, 96, 112) Capricious white-jacketed waiters, a tenebrous Bill Henson photograph and a jazz soundtrack set the mood. The $35 daily lunch special is a winner, as is the neighbouring bar, with its marble 'altar'.

Drinking & Nightlife

Melbourne's bars are legendary, and from laneway hideaways to brassy corner establishments, it's easy to quickly locate a 'local' that will please the senses and drinking palate.

Central Melbourne

★**Bar Americano** COCKTAIL BAR
(Map p484; www.baramericano.com; 20 Pesgrave Pl, off Howey Pl; ⏱8.30am-1am) Bring your cash and throw it away on some of the most bespoke cocktails around. This is a petite hideaway with authentic class.

Lui Bar COCKTAIL BAR
(Map p484; www.vuedemonde.com.au; Level 55, Rialto, 525 Collins Street; ⏱5.30pm-midnight Mon, noon-midnight Tue-Fri, 5.30pm-late Sat, noon-evening Sun) Set high on level 55 of the Rialto is this *tres* fancy bar with a very sophisticated air. Cocktails come from 'yesterday' or 'tomorrow' and snacks include chickpea fries and apple and cinnamon doughnuts. An experience (dress nicely). Live music Sundays.

Carlton Hotel BAR
(Map p484; www.thecarlton.com.au; 193 Bourke St; ⏱4pm-late) OTT Melbourne rococo gets another workout here (think giraffe heads leering over a glittery black room) and never fails to raise a smile. Check out the rooftop Palmz if you're looking for some Miami-flavoured vice or just a great view.

Madame Brussels BAR
(Map p484; www.madamebrussels.com; Level 3, 59-63 Bourke St; ⏱noon-1am) Head here if you've had it with Melbourne-moody and all that dark wood. Although named for a famous 19th-century madam, it feels like a camp '60s rabbit hole you've fallen into, with much AstroTurfery and staff dressed *à la* the country club.

Brother Baba Budan CAFE
(Map p484; www.evenseeds.com.au; 359 Little Bourke St; ⏱7am-6pm Mon-Fri, 8am-5pm Sat, 9am-5pm Sun; 🚋19, 57, 59) Chairs hang from the roof, perhaps making it known that it's best to get your Seven Seeds coffee takeaway.

1000£Bend BAR
(Map p484; www.thousandpoundbend.com.au; 361 Little Lonsdale St; ⏱8.30am-11.30pm Mon-Wed, to 1am Thu-Sat; 📶) Breakfast, lunch, dinner and cruisy folk using the free wi-fi – that's not all at this mega warehouse of entertainment. It's also a whopping great venue for art shows and plays.

PERFECT CAFFEINE HITS

There's a reason Melbourne's coffee is so celebrated (by its residents, at least): much of it is roasted here. Matt Holden, editor of the *Age Good Cafe Guide* has sampled the brown stuff at more than 150 cafes. Here are some of his favourite roasters, and where you can find their brews.

- **Seven Seeds** De Clieu Cafe (p514), Brother Baba Budan (p511)
- **Padre** Brunswick East Project (p515)
- **Market Lane** (p513)
- **Small Batch** Auction Rooms (p507)

Riverland BAR
(Map p484; ☎03-9662 1771; www.riverlandbar.com; Vaults 1-9 Federation Wharf, under Princes Bridge; ⊙10am-late; 🚉Flinders St) This bluestone beauty sits by the water below Princes Bridge and keeps things simple with good wine, four beers on tap and bar snacks.

Section 8 BAR
(Map p484; www.section8.com.au; 27-29 Tattersalls Lane; ⊙10am-late Mon-Fri, noon-late Sat & Sun) The latest in bar-in-a-carpark entertainment. Come and sink a local Mountain Goat beer with the after-work crowd, who make do with shipping pallets for decor. **Ferdydurke** (Map p484; ☎03-9639 3750; www.ferdydurke.com.au; Levels 1 & 2, 31 Tattersalls Lane, corner Lonsdale St; ⊙noon–1am) is a neighbouring rooftop bar run by the same wacky folk.

Beer DeLuxe BAR
(Map p484; www.beerdeluxe.com.au; Federation Sq, Flinders St; ⊙11am-11pm Sun-Wed, to late Thu-Sat; 🚌Tourist Shuttle, 🚋City Circle, 🚉Flinders St) There are 14 beers on tap at this very central location, and staff will help you decide which one to try.

Double Happiness BAR
(Map p484; ☎03-9650 4488; www.double-happiness.org; 21 Liverpool St; ⊙4pm-1am Mon-Wed, 4pm-3am Thu & Fri, 6pm-3am Sat, 6pm-1am Sun ; 🚋86, 96, 🚉Parliament) This stylish hole in the wall doesn't just do Chinese-themed decor, it also offers Chinese and Vietnamese beers. Try a Beer Hanoi (rice lager) or Great Leap Forward cocktail.

New Gold Mountain BAR
(Map p484; ☎03-9650 8859; www.newgoldmountain.org; Level 1, 21 Liverpool St; ⊙6pm-late Tue-Thu, to 5am Fri & Sat; 🚋86, 96, 🚉Parliament) Unsignposted New Gold Mountain's intense chinoiserie interior comes as a shock. Two upstairs floors are filled with tiny screen-shielded corners, with decoration so delight-

OPEN-AIR DRINKING

Melbourne may be home to some of the coolest bars hidden down city laneways, but when the summer sun beats down and daylight savings is on our side, it's time for some fresh air and natural light. Whether it's riding an elevator to a secret rooftop or chugging jugs of ale at a beer garden, here are some of our favourite open-air drinking spots.

Rooftop Bars

Madame Brussels (p511), with her garden-party vibe, overlooking Bourke St, is a winning spot to enjoy a jug of homemade Pimms, while up the road, backpackers and city 'suits' mingle at the tropical-themed Palmz at the Carlton Hotel (p511). Stylish newcomer **Aylesbury** (Map p484; ☎03-9077 0451; 103 Lonsdale St; ⊙noon-late) is accessed by a lift to a sophisticated terrace with a stunning vista of the spires of St Patrick's Cathedral. Rooftop Bar (p516) attracts a hip crowd wolfing down burgers and cocktails while catching flicks at its open-air cinema, and iconic Siglo's (p513) terrace comes with Parisian flair, wafting cigar smoke and serious drinks.

Our pick for inner-city views is the new rooftop bar at Naked for Satan (p513): a wrap-around decked balcony with bright deckchairs looking over Fitzroy's cute tin-roof cottages, smokestacks and historic buildings, and further beyond to the glinting CBD high-rises – a beautiful sight at dusk.

Outdoor Bars & Beer Gardens

For a backyard pub atmosphere you can't go past the leafy beer garden of Fitzroy faithful **The Standard** (Map p489; ☎03-9419 4793; 293 Fitzroy St; ⊙3-11pm Mon & Tue, noon-11pm Wed-Sat, noon-9pm Sun; 🚋96, 112) or way across the river at Tiki-themed Windsor Castle (p513). The bluestone of Riverland (p512) sits pretty on the banks of the Yarra, while **Boatbuilders Yard** (☎03-9686 5088; 23 South Wharf Promenade; ⊙7am-late) occupies a slice of South Wharf, next to the historic *Polly Woodside* ship, where deckchairs sit riverside under umbrellas on synthetic turf, and bocce hire is free. Other worthy mentions are Brunswick favourite **The Retreat** (☎03-9380 4090; 280 Sydney Rd; ⊙noon-late; 🚋19, 🚉Brunswick), and Ponyfish Island (p513), for its commanding location under a footbridge in the middle of the Yarra.

Kate Morgan

fully relentless you feel as if you're trapped in an art-house dream sequence.

Melbourne Supper Club BAR

(Map p484; ☎03-9654 6300; Level 1, 161 Spring St; ⌚5pm-4am Sun-Thu, to 6am Fri & Sat; 🚊95, 96, 🚆Parliament) The oh-so-sophisticated Supper Club is open very late and is a favoured after-work spot for performers and hospitality types. Cosy into a Chesterfield, browse the encyclopaedic wine menu and relax; the sommeliers will cater to any liquid desire. Upstairs rooftop bar **Siglo** (Map p484; ☎03-9654 6300; Level 2, 161 Spring St; ⌚5pm-3am) is stunning. Its retractable roof suits Melbourne, and the Parliament House views remind one of Europe.

Ponyfish Island CAFE, BAR

(Map p484; www.ponyfish.com.au; under Yarra Pedestrian Bridge; ⌚8am-1am) What's that secretly poised under a bridge arcing over the brown Yarra River? A private swimmers club? Nup. Look for the fixed-gear bikes chained up mid-bridge and head down the steps to Melbourne's most unusual snack and drinking spot. There's Bulmers on tap and draught beer which, this being an open-air bar, is not the only draught you'll get.

1806 COCKTAIL BAR

(Map p484; www.1806.com.au; 169 Exhibition St; ⌚5pm-2am Mon-Thu, to 5am Fri & Sat, 7pm-2am Sun) This rather mainstream cocktail bar doesn't pack up its stirrers until the wee hours. Not only does it serve a long list of cocktails (you can buy the book), it also runs sessions designed to bring out the mixologist in you ($145).

Workshop BAR

(Map p484; www.theworkshopbar.com.au; 413 Elizabeth St; ⌚10am-late Mon-Fri, 1pm-late Sat & Sun; 🚊19, 57, 59, 🚆Melbourne Central) This industrial bar offers healthy lunches early and live music or DJs playing late. At any time there's perfect Elizabeth St–gazing from the outdoor area.

Croft Institute BAR

(Map p484; ☎03-9671 4399; www.thecroftinstitute.com; 21-25 Croft Alley; ⌚5pm-1am Mon-Thu, 8pm-3am Fri & Sat) Located in a laneway off a laneway, the lab-themed Croft is a test of drinkers' determination. Prescribe yourself a beaker of house-distilled vodka in the downstairs laboratory. There's a $10 cover charge on Friday and Saturday nights.

Alumbra CLUB

(www.alumbra.com.au; 161 Harbour Esplanade, Shed 9, Central Pier; ⌚6pm-late Thu, 4pm-3am Fri & Sat, 4pm-1am Sun; 🚊Tourist Shuttle, 🚊70, City Circle) Great music and a stunning location will impress – even if the Bali-meets-Morocco follies of the decorator don't.

Brown Alley CLUB

(Colonial Hotel; Map p484; ☎03-9670 8599; www.brownalley.com; 585 Lonsdale St; ⌚9pm-late Thu-Sun; 🚆Flagstaff) This historic pub hides away four fully fledged nightclubs with a 24-hour licence. It's enormous, with distinct rooms that can fit up to 1000 people.

Richmond, Prahran & Windsor

Windsor Castle Hotel PUB

(Map p492; 89 Albert St, Windsor; 🚊5, 64, 🚆Windsor) Cosy nooks, sunken pits, fireplaces (or, in summer, a very popular beer garden) and yummo pub meals make this off-the-main-drag pub an attractive option.

Mountain Goat Brewery BREWERY

(www.goatbeer.com.au; cnr North & Clark Sts, Richmond; ⌚from 5pm Wed & Fri only; 🚊48, 75, 🚆Burnley) This local microbrewery is set in a massive beer-producing warehouse. Enjoy its range of beers while nibbling on pizza, or join a free brewery tour on Wednesday night. To find it head down Richmond's Bridge Rd, turn left at Burnley St and right at North St.

Market Lane CAFE

(Map p492; ☎03-9804 7434; www.marketlane.com.au; Shop 13, Prahran Market, 163 Commercial Rd; ⌚7am-5pm Tue, Thu-Sat, to 4pm Wed, 8am-5pm Sun; 🚊72, 78, 🚆Prahran) Enjoy the freshly roasted beans among the market hubbub, or join the free cupping (tasting) session at 10am on Fridays and Saturdays.

Revolver Upstairs CLUB

(Map p492; www.revolverupstairs.com.au; 229 Chapel St, Prahran; ⌚noon-4am Mon-Fri, 24hr Sat-Mon; 🚊6, 🚆Prahran) Rowdy Revolver can feel like an enormous version of your own lounge room, but with 54 hours of nonstop music starting late Saturday night and ending Monday morning, you're probably glad it's not.

Fitzroy & Around

★**Naked for Satan** BAR

(Map p489; ☎03-9416 2238; www.nakedforsatan.com.au; 285 Brunswick St, Fitzroy; ⌚noon-12am Sun-Thu, noon-1am Fri & Sat; 🚊112) Vibrant, loud and reviving an apparent Brunswick St legend (a

DON'T MISS

TO BEER, OR NOT TO BEER

Australia's beer scene is undergoing a revolution. It's not about the old-school brands but a new wave of craft beer. New microbreweries are popping up from coast to coast every month alongside beer bars and bottle shops specialising in the latest brews.

Nowhere has the revolution taken hold like Melbourne, where even high-end restaurants are adding local and international craft beers to their menus. Home to the two biggest events in the Australian beer calendar – Good Beer Week (p501) and the Great Australasian Beer SpecTAPular (p501) – its vibrant beer scene is even garnering international attention.

Three Breweries

- **Mountain Goat Brewery** (p513)
- **Temple Brewery & Brasserie** (p515)
- **Matilda Bay Brewery** (03-9673 4545; 89 Bertie St, Port Melbourne; noon-9pm Tue-Thu, to 11pm Fri & Sat)

Three Bars with Great Beer

- **Great Northern Hotel** (p515)
- **The Local Taphouse** (www.thelocal.com.au; 184 Carlisle St, St Kilda; noon-late; 16, 78, Balaclava)
- **Slow Beer** (03-9421 3838; 468 Bridge Rd, Richmond; noon-9pm; 48, 75)

Three Brews to Try

- **Mountain Goat Hightail**
- **Temple Saison**
- **Moon Dog Love Tap**

James Smith is the author of craftypint.com, an online guide to beery goings-on in Melbourne

man nicknamed Satan who would get down and dirty, naked because of the heat, in an illegal vodka distillery under the shop), this place packs a punch both with its popular *pintxos* (bite-sized sandwiches; $1 to $2) and cleverly named beverages. Its stunning, sprawling rooftop bar is outstanding.

Proud Mary CAFE
(Map p489; 03-9417 5930; 172 Oxford St, Collingwood; 7.30am-4pm Mon-Fri, 8.30am-4pm Sat & Sun; 86) Known for its silky-smooth coffee, this corner-situated industrial cafe also has a decent breakfast and lunch menu (think house-smoked salmon). Queues can be dramatically long.

Napier Hotel PUB
(Map p489; 03-9419 4240; www.thenapierhotel.com; 210 Napier St, Fitzroy; 3-11pm Mon-Thu, 1pm-1am Fri & Sat, 1-11pm Sun; 112, 86) The Napier has stood on this corner for over a century and many pots have been pulled as the face of the neighbourhood changed. It's still a great spot for pub grub.

De Clieu Cafe CAFE
(Map p489; 187 Gertrude St, Fitzroy; 7am-6.30pm Mon-Sat, 8am-6.30pm Sun; 86) De Clieu (pronounced clue) is a delightful industrial cafe with polished concrete floors, a short menu and a tall sense of humour. Pull up a window sill and watch Fitzroy go past.

Little Creatures Dining Hall BEER HALL
(Map p489; www.littlecreatures.com.au; 222 Brunswick St, Fitzroy; 8am-late; ; 112) With free community bikes for customers, complimentary wi-fi and a daytime kid-friendly groove, this vast drinking hall is the perfect place to spend up big on pizzas ($18) and enjoy local wine and beer.

Polly COCKTAIL BAR
(Map p489; 03-9417 0880; 401 Brunswick St, Fitzroy; 5pm-1am Sun-Wed, 5pm-late Thu, 5pm-3am

Fri-Sat;) Polly is a quiet place that melds a luxe sensibility and slick service with lots of ornate carved wood and plush velvet. Ease yourself into a lounge and peruse the extensive drinks list – you're not going anywhere in a hurry. Each night there are a couple of $14 cocktail specials.

Carlton & Around

Campos CAFE

(Map p490; 03-9347 7445; www.camposcoffee.com; 144 Elgin St, Carlton; 7am-4pm Mon-Sat; Tourist Shuttle, 250, 251, 253) Sydney coffee fave Campos has taken on Little Italy in Carlton and is winning in a big way. Coffee here is wonderful, and the long shared tables are a great spot to taste some of the yummy lunches and delectable cakes.

Gerald's Bar WINE BAR

(386 Rathdowne St, North Carlton; 5-11pm Mon-Sat; 253, 1, 8) Wine by the glass is democratically selected at Gerald's and they spin some fine vintage vinyl from behind the curved wooden bar. If you get hungry, there are delightfully fresh morsels to sink your teeth into (it owns the neighbouring butcher and fruit-and-veg shop too).

Brunswick East Project CAFE

(03-9381 1881; www.padrecoffee.com.au; 438 Lygon St, East Brunswick; 7am-4pm Mon-Sat, 8am-4pm Sun; 1, 8) One of its best-selling coffee blends is called 'Daddy's Girl', and there's also a 'Hey Buddy!' blend, so full kudos for names. This is the home of Padre coffee, and it's a funky spot to drink it (and eat) too. There are also branches at South Melbourne Market (p495) and Queen Victoria Market (p482).

Temple Brewery BREWERY

(03-9380 8999; www.templebrewing.com.au; 122 Weston St, East Brunswick; 5.30-11pm Wed & Thu, noon-11pm Fri & Sat, noon-9pm Sun; 1, 8) Try a seasonal craft brew (there are eight on tap) at this very classy brewery with a brasserie, or try five for $19. Don't miss a taste of Saison.

Great Northern Hotel BAR

(03-9380 9569; www.gnh.net.au; 644 Rathdowne St, North Carlton; 11am-1am Tue-Sat, 11am-11pm Sun; 253, 1, 8) Sure, Carlton Draught's on tap at the Great Northern (it is in Carlton, after all) but this large corner pub has 16 other locals on tap, too. Venture past the front bar and into the sprawling palm-fringed beer garden to dig into one of the $12 meal specials.

St Kilda & Around

Carlisle Wine Bar WINE BAR

(03-9531 3222; www.carlislewinebar.com.au; 137 Carlisle St, Balaclava; 3pm-1am Mon-Fr, 11am-1am Sat & Sun; 3, 16, Balaclava) Locals love this often-rowdy, wine-worshipping former butcher's shop. The staff will treat you like a regular and find you a glass of something special, or effortlessly throw together a cocktail amid the weekend rush. Carlisle St runs east off St Kilda Rd.

George Public Bar BAR

(Map p494; www.georgepublicbar.com.au; Basement, 127 Fitzroy St, St Kilda; 96, 16) There are five bars within this building. Behind the Edwardian arched windows of the George Hotel is the Melbourne Wine Room and a large front bar that keeps the after-work crowd happy. In the bowels of the building is the George Public Bar, once referred to as the Snakepit but wearing a classier skin now.

Veludo BAR

(Map p494; www.veludo.com.au; 175 Acland St, St Kilda; 4pm-2am Wed & Thu, noon-3am Fri-Sun; 96) It's big, it's brassy and it's got a rooftop bar. Veludo's relatively late closing means that most St Kilda–ites have ducked in here after everything else has shut. Upstairs has live music most nights.

Vineyard BAR

(Map p494; www.thevineyard.com.au; 71a Acland St, St Kilda; 3a, 16, 96) The perfect corner position and a courtyard barbie attract crowds of backpackers and scantily clad young locals who enjoy themselves so much as to drown out the neighbouring scenic railway.

☆ Entertainment

Cinemas

Cinema multiplexes are spread throughout Melbourne city, and there are quite a few treasured independent cinemas in both the CBD and surrounding suburbs. Grab a choc-top (ice cream dipped in chocolate) and check one out.

Astor CINEMA

(Map p492; 03-9510 1414; www.astortheatre.net.au; cnr Chapel St & Dandenong Rd, St Kilda; adult/child $15/13; 5, 64, 78, Windsor) This place holds not-to-be-missed art deco nostalgia,

GAY & LESBIAN MELBOURNE

These days, Melbourne's gay and lesbian community is well and truly integrated into the general populace. Here are some highlights:

- **Midsumma Festival** (p499) has a diverse program with around 150 cultural, community and sporting events.
- **MCV** (http://gaynewsnetwork.com.au) is a free weekly newspaper, and is online.
- Gay and lesbian community radio station **JOY 94.9 FM** (www.joy.org.au) is another important resource for visitors and locals.
- Gay men are particularly welcomed at the **Peel Hotel** (☎03-9419 4762; www.thepeel.com.au; 113 Wellington St, Collingwood; ⏲9pm-dawn Thu-Sat; 🚋86) nightclub, and **169 Drummond** (p504) has been offering gay-friendly accommodation for two decades.

with double features every night of old and recent classics. Wicked Wednesday tickets are $10.

Cinema Nova CINEMA
(Map p490; www.cinemanova.com.au; 380 Lygon St, Carlton; adult/child $18/11; 🚌Tourist Shuttle, 🚋1, 8) Nova has current film releases. On Mondays, tickets are a measly $6 before 4pm, $9 after.

Kino Cinemas CINEMA
(Map p484; ☎03-9650 2100; www.palacecinemas.com.au; Collins Pl, 45 Collins St; adult/child $19.50/14.50; 🚋11, 31, 48, 109, 112) This licensed CBD cinema specialises in quality art-house releases. It's close to great bars, too, for after-flick drinks.

Imax CINEMA
(Map p490; ☎03-9663 5454; www.imaxmelbourne.com.au; Melbourne Museum, Carlton Gardens; adult/child $18/13.50; 🚌Tourist Shuttle, 🚋86, 96) Within the same complex as the Melbourne Museum, this theatre screens films in super-wide 70mm format.

Palace Como CINEMA
(Map p492; ☎03-9827 7533; www.palacecinemas.com.au; Como Centre, cnr Toorak Rd & Chapel St, South Yarra; adult/child $19/13.50; 🚋8, 78, 🚆South Yarra) Glamorous cinema that hosts film festivals and has fab Monday and Friday deals (from 6pm cocktails and tapas are half-price). Tickets are $12.50 on Tuesdays.

Outdoor Cinemas

Outdoor cinemas are popular in summer; check websites for seasonal opening dates and program details. Movies are often old-time faves, but new releases also get a showing. Tickets are usually $20 and can sell out quickly.

St Kilda Open Air Cinema CINEMA
(Map p494; www.openaircinemas.com.au; South Beach Reserve, Jacka Blvd, St Kilda; 🚋79, 96) There's often live pre-movie music and, of course, salty sea air to inhale.

Rooftop Cinema CINEMA
(Map p484; www.rooftopcinema.com.au; Level 6, Curtin House, 252 Swanston St) Here we have amazing city views, an ABD (all day burger) stall to keep you fed and a bar to keep you watered.

Moonlight Cinema CINEMA
(www.moonlight.com.au; Gate D, Royal Botanic Gardens, Birdwood Ave) Bring along a rug, pillow and moonlight supper, and set up an outdoor living room in the middle of the gardens.

Shadow Electric CINEMA
(www.shadowelectric.com.au; Abbotsford Convent, 1 St Heliers St, Abbotsford; 🚌200, 201, 207, 🚆Collingwood) An outdoor cinema in what was an old convent. Loads of pop-up-shop cred.

Theatre

There is no distinct theatre district in Melbourne; individual companies and theatres are spread across town. Try **Half Tix Melbourne** (Map p484; www.halftixmelbourne.com; Melbourne Town Hall, 90-120 Swanston St; ⏲10am-2pm Mon, 11am-6pm Tue-Fri, 10am-4pm Sat; 🚆Flinders St) for cheap tickets: you need to front up at the Half Tix office in person on the day (or, for Sunday performances, on Saturday) with cash.

Malthouse Theatre THEATRE
(☎03-9685 5111; www.malthousetheatre.com.au; 113 Sturt St, Southbank; 🚋1) The Malthouse Theatre Company produces theatre that makes you sit on the edge of your seat. From Flinders St Station walk across Princes Bridge and along St Kilda Rd. Turn right at Grant St then left to Sturt St.

Melbourne Theatre Company THEATRE
(MTC; ☎03-8688 0800; www.mtc.com.au; 140 Southbank Blvd, Southbank; 🚊1) Melbourne's oldest theatrical company creates 15 productions annually, ranging from contemporary and modern (including many new Australian works) to Shakespeare and other classics.

Live Music

Northcote Social Club LIVE MUSIC
(☎03-9489 3917; www.northcotesocialclub.com; 301 High St, Northcote; ⏲4pm-late Mon, noon-late Tue-Thu & Sun, noon-3am Fri & Sat; 🚊86, 🚆Northcote) This awesome live-music venue sees plenty of big and little stars from abroad and home. If you're just after a drink, the front bar buzzes, or there's a large deck out the back for lazy afternoons. A perfect, and well-loved, local. Head north along Hoddle St to reach High St.

Corner Hotel LIVE MUSIC
(☎03-9427 9198; www.cornerhotel.com; 57 Swan St, Richmond; ⏲4pm-late Tue & Wed, noon-late Thur-Sun; 🚊70, 🚆Richmond) This midsized venue has seen plenty of loud and live action over the years. If your ears need a break, check out the huge rooftop bar with city skyline glimpses. The crowd upstairs is often more suburban than the music fans below. Wednesday night trivia (from 7.30pm, bookings ☎03-9427 7300) has a cult following.

Bennetts Lane LIVE MUSIC
(Map p484; www.bennettslane.com; 25 Bennetts Lane; tickets from $15; ⏲9pm-late) Bennetts Lane has long been the boiler room of Melbourne jazz. It attracts the cream of local and international talent and an audience that knows when it's time to applaud a solo. Beyond the cosy front bar, there's another space reserved for big gigs.

Ding Dong Lounge LIVE MUSIC
(Map p484; www.dingdonglounge.com.au; 18 Market Lane; ⏲7pm-late Wed-Sat) Ding Dong walks the live-music walk and is a great place to see a smaller touring act or catch local bands. There's indie music on Friday nights and a disco till dawn on Saturday nights.

Esplanade Hotel LIVE MUSIC
(Map p494; ☎03-9534 0211; www.espy.com.au; 11 The Esplanade, St Kilda; ⏲noon-1am Mon-Wed & Sun, noon-3am Thu & Fri, 8am-3am Sat; 🚊96, 16) Rock pigs rejoice. The Espy remains gloriously shabby and welcoming to all. Bands play most nights in a variety of rooms, including the front bar, and there's a

HEADLINE ACTS

When the rock gods (or more commonly pop, R&B and hip-hop stars) roll into town and are too big for Melbourne's beloved medium-sized venues such as the Corner Hotel or the Northcote Social Club, they are likely to play at one of the following venues:

Festival Hall (www.festivalhall.com.au; 300 Dudley St; 🚊24, 30, 34, 70) This old boxing stadium is a fave for live-music acts.

Palace Theatre (Map p484; www.palace.com.au; 20-30 Bourke St) Features acts ranging from reggae masters to indie darlings.

Forum Theatre (Map p484; ☎tickets 13 61 00; www.marrinertheatres.com.au; 150-152 Flinders St; 🚆Flinders St) One of the city's most atmospheric live-music venues, it does double duty as a cinema during the Melbourne Film Festival. The Arabic-inspired exterior houses an equally interesting interior, with the southern sky rendered on its domed ceiling.

Hamer Hall (p483) The redevelopment is complete and this concert hall is a beautiful central venue.

Palais Theatre (Map p494; ☎03-9525 3240, tickets 13 61 00; www.palaistheatre.net.au; Lower Esplanade, St Kilda) Standing gracefully next to Luna Park, the Palais is a St Kilda icon. Not only is it a beautiful old space, but it also stages some pretty special performances.

Rod Laver Arena (www.mopt.com.au; Batman Ave; 🚊70) A giant, versatile space used for headline concerts (from the Eagles to Chemical Brothers) and the Australian Open tennis, with a huge sunroof. Not the most atmospheric of venues, but then it's all about the spectacle. Ditto for the nearby **Hisense Arena** (Melbourne Park).

Sidney Myer Music Bowl (www.theartscentre.net.au) This beautiful amphitheatre in the Kings Domain gardens is used for a variety of outdoor events, from the New Year's Day rave **Summerdayze** to performances by the Melbourne Symphony Orchestra.

spruced-up diner-like kitchen along the side. And for the price of a pot of beer you get front-row seats for the pink-stained St Kilda sunset.

Pure Pop Records LIVE MUSIC
(Map p494; ☎03-9525 5066; www.purepop.com.au; 221 Barkly St, St Kilda; 96) What do you do when faced with noise complaints? The owner of this independent record store has had plenty of innovative ideas, including a 'buy a brick' scheme designed to help soundproof this little venue. Bands play on Saturday and Sunday arvos, and entry is usually free.

Toff in Town LIVE MUSIC
(Map p484; ☎03-9639 8770; www.thetoffintown.com; Level 2, Curtin House, 252 Swanston St; 5pm-late Sun-Thu, 3pm-late Fri) An atmospheric venue well suited to cabaret, but that also works for intimate gigs by indie bands and DJs. Head down the stairs for Cookie and up to the view-filled open-air Rooftop Bar.

Tote LIVE MUSIC
(www.thetotehotel.com; cnr Johnston & Wellington Sts, Collingwood; 4pm-late Tue-Sun; 86) The Tote's closure in 2010 brought Melbourne to a stop. People protested on the CBD streets against the liquor-licensing laws that were blamed for the closure, and there were howls of displeasure on the airwaves. The punters won, laws changed and the Tote reopened to continue its tradition of live bands playing dirty rock.

Cherry LIVE MUSIC
(Map p484; www.cherrybar.com.au; AC/DC Lane; 6pm-midnight Mon & Tue, 5pm-3am Wed, 5pm-5am Thu-Sat, 1pm-midnight Sun) This rock 'n' roll refuge has local acts till 11.30pm, when a DJ takes over. Secret performances are popular, especially when well-known bands are in town. There's often a queue, but once inside, a relaxed, slightly anarchic spirit prevails.

Dance

Australian Ballet BALLET
(☎1300 369 741; www.australianballet.com.au; 2 Kavanagh St, Southbank) Based in Melbourne and now over 40 years old, the Australian Ballet performs traditional and new works at the Arts Centre Melbourne.

Chunky Move DANCE
(www.chunkymove.com; 111 Sturt St, Southbank) Melbourne-based Chunky Move perform 'genre-defying' dance around the world and, when at home, at the CUB Malthouse.

Shopping

Central Melbourne

Captains of Industry CLOTHING
(Map p484; ☎03-9670 4405; www.captainsofindustry.com.au; Level 1, 2 Somerset Pl; 8am-9pm Mon-Thu, 8am-11pm Fri; 19, 57, 59) Where can you get a haircut, and a bespoke suit and pair of shoes made in the one place? Here. The hard-working folk at Captains also offer homey breakfasts, thoughtful lunches and beery dinners. To work!

Shop CRAFT, DESIGN
(Craft Victoria; Map p484; www.craft.org.au; 31 Flinders Lane; 10am-5pm Mon-Sat; 70, 75, City Circle) The retail arm of Craft Victoria, Shop showcases the handmade. Its range of jewellery, textiles, accessories, glass and ceramics bridges the art/craft divide and makes for some wonderful mementos of Melbourne. It has three vibrant gallery spaces.

Alice Euphemia FASHION, JEWELLERY
(Map p484; Shop 6, Cathedral Arcade, Nicholas Building, 37 Swanston St; 10am-6pm Mon-Sat & noon-5pm Sun; Flinders St) Art-school cheek abounds in the labels sold here and the jewellery similarly sways between the shocking and exquisitely pretty. Everything is Australian made.

Aesop BEAUTY
This home-grown skincare company specialises in products made from simple ingredients in simple packaging. The range is wide and based on botanical extracts. With branches in **QV** (Map p484; 35 Albert Coates Lane), **Flinders Lane** (Map p484; 268 Flinders Lane), **Fitzroy** (Map p489; 242 Gertrude St) and **Prahran** (Map p492; 143 Greville St).

Fitzroy

Third Drawer Down DESIGN
(Map p489; www.thirddrawerdown.com; 93 George St; 11am-5pm Mon-Sat; 86) This seller-of-great-things makes life beautifully unusual by stocking everything from sesame-seed grinders to beer-o'clock beach towels and 'come in, we're closed' signs.

MELBOURNE'S BEST MARKETS

Rose Street Artists' Market (Map p489; www.rosestmarket.com.au; 60 Rose St, Fitzroy; 11am-5pm Sat; 112) One of Melbourne's best and most popular art-and-craft markets, just a short stroll from Brunswick St.

Camberwell Sunday Market (www.sundaymarket.com.au; Station St, behind cnr of Burke & Riversdale Rds, Camberwell; gold coin donation; 7am-12.30pm Sundays; 70, 75, Camberwell) This is where Melburnians come to offload their unwanted items and antique hunters come to find them.

Esplanade Market (Map p494; www.esplanademarket.com; btwn Cavell & Fitzroy Sts, St Kilda; 10am-5pm Sun; 96) Fancy shopping with a seaside backdrop? A kilometre of trestle tables joined end to end carry individually crafted products from toys to organic soaps to large metal sculptures of fishy creatures.

Queen Victoria Market (p482) Don't miss this 130-year old market with its meat hall, deli and expansive fruit and vegie sections. On Wednesdays during summer it also plays host to a lively and musical night market (from 5.30pm to 10pm).

Crumpler ACCESSORIES
(Map p489; 03-9417 5338; www.crumpler.com.au; 87 Smith St, cnr Gertrude St; 10am-6pm; 86) Crumpler's bike-courier bags started it all and its durable, practical designs can now be found around the world. It makes bags for cameras, laptops and iPods as well as its original messenger style. Also branches in the **CBD** (Map p484; 03-9600 3799; 355 Little Bourke St; 10am-6pm, until 8pm Fri) and **Prahran** (Map p492; 03-9529 7837; 182 Chapel St; 10am-6pm, until 8pm Fri).

SpaceCraft HOMEWARES, FASHION
(Map p489; www.spacecraftaustralia.com; 255 Gertrude St; 11am-6pm Mon-Fri, 10am-6pm Sat, 11am-5pm Sun) An excellent place to find a made-in-Melbourne souvenir that won't end up at the back of the cupboard. Textile artist Stewart Russell's botanical and architectural designs adorn everything from stools to socks to single-bed doonas.

Polyester Records MUSIC
(Map p489; 387 Brunswick St; 10am-9pm; 112) This great record store has been selling Melburnians independent music from around the world for decades, and also sells tickets for gigs. There's also a branch in the **CBD** (Map p484; 288 Flinders Lane).

Carlton

Readings BOOKS
(Map p490; www.readings.com.au; 309 Lygon St; Tourist Shuttle, 16) A potter around this defiantly prospering indie bookshop can occupy an entire afternoon if you're so inclined. There's a dangerously loaded (and good-value) specials table, switched-on staff and everyone from Lacan to *Charlie and Lola* on the shelves. Also in **St Kilda** (Map p494; 03-9525 3852; 112 Acland St; 96) and elsewhere.

South Yarra, Prahran & Windsor

Chapel Street Bazaar VINTAGE
(Map p492; 03-9521 3174; 217-223 Chapel St, Prahran; 10am-6pm; 78, Prahran) Calling this a 'permanent undercover collection of market stalls' won't give you any clue to what's tucked away here. This old arcade is a retro-obsessive riot. It doesn't matter if kitchen canisters or Noddy egg cups are your thing, you'll find it here.

Fat FASHION, ACCESSORIES
(Map p492; www.fat4.com; 272 Chapel St, Prahran; 78, Prahran) The Fat girls' empire has changed the way Melbourne dresses, catapulting a fresh generation of designers into the city's consciousness, including locals P.A.M and Kloke. Other branches are in the **CBD** (Map p484; GPO, 350 Bourke St) and **Fitzroy** (Map p489; 209 Brunswick St).

St Kilda

Dot Herbey FASHION, ACCESSORIES
(Map p494; www.dotandherbey.com; 229 Barkly St) Grandma Dot and Grandpa Herb smile down upon this tiny corner boutique from a mural-sized photo, right at home among the Japanese fabrics and Italian silks.

Hunter Gatherer
FASHION

(Map p494; 82a Acland St; 🚇96) This op shop features the most retro of welfare organisation Brotherhood of St Laurence's 26-odd op shops. Branches include **Fitzroy** (Map p489; 274 Brunswick St; ⊙10.15am-5.45pm, until 8pm Fri) and the **CBD** (Map p484; Royal Arcade).

ℹ Information

DANGERS & ANNOYANCES

There are occasional reports of alcohol-fuelled violence in some parts of Melbourne's CBD, in particular King St.

Riding a bicycle without a helmet is against the law; police can fine you $176 for the offence. Helmets ($5 with a $3 refund on return) are available from 7Eleven stores.

Some parking spots become Clearways during peak hour; check signage carefully as fines and vehicle recovery can cost $400.

EMERGENCY

For police, ambulance or fire emergencies dial ☑ 000.

Centre Against Sexual Assault (CASA; ☑1800 806 292)

Poisons Information Centre (☑13 11 26)

Translating & Interpreting Service (☑13 14 50) Available 24 hours.

INTERNET ACCESS

Wi-fi is available free at CBD spots including Federation Sq. Hotels often charge between $3 and $20 per hour for wi-fi. If you don't have a laptop or smartphone, there are plenty of internet cafes around Melbourne (from $2 per hour).

MEDIA

The *Age* (www.theage.com.au) covers local, national and international news, as does the *Herald Sun* (www.heraldsun.com.au). The *Broadsheet* (www.broadsheet.com.au) is available from cafes.

Music is covered in free street magazines *Beat* (www.beat.com.au) and *Inpress*.

MEDICAL SERVICES

Mulqueeny Midnight Pharmacy (☑03-9510 3977; cnr Williams Rd & High St, Windsor; ⊙8am-midnight; 🚇6)

Royal Melbourne Hospital (☑03-9342 7000; www.rmh.mh.org.au; cnr Grattan St & Royal Pde; 🚇19, 59) The most central public hospital with an emergency department.

Tambassis Pharmacy (☑03-9387 8830; cnr Sydney & Brunswick Rds; ⊙8am-midnight; 🚇19)

Travel Doctor (TVMC; ☑03-9935 8100; www.traveldoctor.com.au; Level 2, 393 Little Bourke St) Specialises in vaccinations.

MONEY

There are ATMs throughout Melbourne. Bigger hotels offer a currency exchange service, as do most banks during business hours, and there's a bunch of exchange offices on Swanston St.

POST

Melbourne GPO (Map p484; ☑13 13 18; www.auspost.com.au; 250 Elizabeth St, cnr Little Bourke St; ⊙8.30am-5.30pm Mon-Fri, 9am-5pm Sat)

TOURIST INFORMATION

Melbourne Visitor Centre (MVC; Map p484; ☑03-9658 9658; Federation Sq; ⊙9am-6pm; 🛜) Comprehensive tourist information including excellent resources for mobility-impaired travellers.

USEFUL WEBSITES

Lonely Planet (lonelyplanet.com/melbourne) Useful links and city info.

That's Melbourne (www.thatsmelbourne.com.au) Downloadable maps, info and podcasts from the City of Melbourne.

Three Thousand (www.threethousand.com.au) A weekly round-up of (groovy) local goings on.

Visit Victoria (www.visitvictoria.com.au) Highlights events in Melbourne and Victoria.

ℹ Getting There & Away

AIR

Two airports serve Melbourne: **Avalon** (☑1800 282 566, 03-5227 9100; www.avalonairport.com.au) and **Tullamarine** (☑03-9297 1600; www.melbourneairport.com.au), though at present only **Jetstar** (☑13 15 38; www.jetstar.com) operates from Avalon. Tullamarine Airport also has some Jetstar flights, in addition to domestic and international flights offered by **Tiger** (☑03-9034 3733; www.tigerairways.com), **Qantas** (☑13 67 89; www.virginaustralia.com), **Virgin Australia** (☑13 13 13; www.qantas.com) and other carriers. **Sharp Airlines** (☑1300 556 694; www.sharpairlines.com) has services from Melbourne to Portland and Hamilton in regional Victoria, from smaller Essendon Airport.

Tullamarine Airport has a **left-luggage facility** (Terminal 2, International Arrivals, Ground Fl; per 24 hr $15; ⊙5.30am-12.30am).

BOAT

Spirit of Tasmania (☑1800 634 906; www.spiritoftasmania.com.au) The *Spirit of Tasmania* crosses Bass Strait from Melbourne to Devonport, Tasmania, at least nightly; there are also day sailings during peak season. It takes 11 hours and departs from Station Pier, Port Melbourne.

BUS

Southern Cross Station (www.southerncrossstation.net.au, Spencer St) This is the main terminal for interstate bus services. There is a left luggage facility here ($12 per 24 hours).

Firefly (Map p484; ☎1300 730 740; www.fireflyexpress.com.au) Servicing Adelaide and Sydney.

Greyhound (☎1300 473 946; www.greyhound.com.au) Australia-wide.

V/Line (☎1800 800 007; www.vline.com.au; Southern Cross Station) Around Victoria.

TRAIN

Interstate trains arrive and depart from **Southern Cross Station** (www.southerncrossstation.net.au, Spencer St).

Getting Around

TO/FROM THE AIRPORT

Tullamarine Airport

There are no trains or trams to Tullamarine Airport.

The cheapest way to get to Tullamarine is to catch the train to Broadmeadows, then bus 901 to the airport. It's around $6 with a myki card (but takes a minimum of 40 minutes).

Taxis charge from $45 for the trip to Melbourne's CBD, or you can catch **SkyBus** (Map p484; ☎03-9335 2811; www.skybus.com.au; adult/child one-way $17/7; Ⓡ Southern Cross Station), a 20-minute express bus service to/from Southern Cross Station.

Part of the main route into Melbourne from Tullamarine Airport is a toll road run by **CityLink** (☎13 26 29; www.citylink.com.au). If you're making your own way there, you'll need to buy a Tulla Pass ($5.15) online or over the phone. If you have more time and less money, take the exit ramp at Bell St then head up Nicholson St to the CBD.

Avalon Airport

Avalon Airport Transfers (☎03-9689 7999; www.sitacoaches.com.au; Southern Cross Station; one-way $22) Avalon Airport Transfers meet Jetstar flights into and out of Avalon. It departs from Southern Cross Station taking approximately 50 minutes; check website for times. No booking required.

BICYCLE

Melbourne Bike Share (☎1300 711 590; www.melbournebikeshare.com.au) Melbourne Bike Share began in 2010 and has had a slow start, mainly blamed on Victoria's compulsory helmet laws. Subsidised safety helmets are now available at 7Eleven stores around the CBD ($5 with a $3 refund on return). Daily ($2.70) and weekly ($8) subscriptions require a credit card and $50 security deposit. Each first half-hour of hire is free.

CAR & MOTORCYCLE

Car Hire

Avis (☎13 63 33; www.avis.com.au)

Budget (☎13 27 27; www.budget.com.au)

Europcar (☎1300 131 390; www.europcar.com.au)

Hertz (☎13 30 39; www.hertz.com.au)

Rent a Bomb (☎13 15 53; www.rentabomb.com.au)

Thrifty (☎1300 367 227; www.thrifty.com.au)

Car Sharing

Car-sharing companies that operate in Melbourne include **Green Share Car** (☎1300 575 878; www.greensharecar.com.au), **Go Get** (☎1300 769 389; www.goget.com.au) and **Flexi Car** (☎1300 363 780; www.flexicar.com.au). You rent the cars by the hour or the day, and the price includes petrol. They vary on joining fees (between $25 and $40) and how they charge (per hour and per kilometre). The cars are parked in and around the CBD in designated 'car share' car parks. Car sharing costs around $15 per hour depending on the plan you choose.

Parking

Parking inspectors are particularly vigilant in the CBD; most of the street parking is metered and if you overstay you'll probably be fined (between $70 and $141). Also keep an eye out for parking spots that become Clearway zones during peak hour; your car may be towed and will cost $400 to retrieve. There are plenty of parking garages in the city; those run by the City of Melbourne usually have the best rates ($10 for two hours). Motorcyclists are allowed to park on the footpath.

Toll Roads

Car drivers will need to purchase a pass if they are planning on using one of the two toll roads (CityLink or EastLink, which runs from Ringwood to near Frankston). Motorcycles travel free on CityLink.

HOOK TURNS

Striking fear into all non-locals is Melbourne's 'hook turn' (though it's easy once you get the hang of it). Basically, many of the city's intersections require you to make a right-hand turn from the left lane so you don't block oncoming trams. When you see a 'Right Turn from Left Only' sign, often hanging from tram lines, get in the left lane and wait with your right indicator on; when the light turns green in the street you want to turn into, hook right and complete your turn.

WORTH A TRIP

MACEDON RANGES & HANGING ROCK

A short detour off the Calder Fwy (Rte M79), less than an hour north of Melbourne, the Macedon Ranges is a beautiful area of low mountains, native forest and wineries. It covers the towns of Gisborne, Woodend, Lancefield, Romsey, Kyneton and the legendary Hanging Rock.

Mt Macedon is a 1010m-high extinct volcano with numerous walking tracks. The scenic route up Mt Macedon Rd takes you past mansions with beautiful gardens. At the summit is a cafe, viewpoints and a 21m-high memorial cross.

Beyond the summit turn-off, the road heads to quaint **Woodend**, or take the signed road on the right to **Hanging Rock** (www.visitmacedonranges.com; per vehicle $10; ⏲9am-5pm), sacred site of the Wurundjeri people. The rock was a refuge for bushrangers, but attained fame with Joan Lindsay's novel *Picnic at Hanging Rock* (and the subsequent film directed by Peter Weir), about the mysterious disappearance of a group of schoolgirls. In Woodend, easily reached by V/Line train from Melbourne, the excellent **Holgate Brewhouse** (☎03-5427 2510; www.holgatebrewhouse.com; 79 High St; d $135-185; mains $19-29; ⏲noon-late) is a cracking brewery-pub producing a range of hand-pumped European-style ales and lagers on-site. The kitchen serves hearty Mod Oz bistro food.

Further north, **Kyneton** was an early coach stop between Melbourne and the goldfields, and today its historic Piper St precinct is lined with old bluestone buildings, antique shops and fabulous cafes and restaurants.

Citylink (☎13 26 29; www.citylink.com.au)
Eastlink (☎13 54 65; www.citylink.com.au)

PUBLIC TRANSPORT

Flinders St Station is the main train station connecting the city and suburbs. The City Loop runs under the city, linking the four corners of town.

An extensive network of tram lines covers every corner of the city, running north–south and east–west along most major roads. Trams run roughly every 10 minutes Monday to Friday, every 10 to 15 minutes on Saturday, and every 20 minutes on Sunday. Check **Public Transport Victoria** (PTV; ☎1800 800 007; www.ptv.vic.gov.au; Southern Cross Station, Spencer St; 🚉Southern Cross) for more information. Also worth considering is the free City Circle (p499) tram, which loops around town, and the Melbourne City Tourist Shuttle (p499) bus.

Melbourne's buses, trams and trains use **myki** (www.myki.com.au), which is a 'touch on, touch off' card. You must purchase a plastic myki card ($6) and put credit on it before you travel, which can be problematic for travellers. Some hostels are collecting myki cards from travellers who leave Melbourne, but it's best to buy a myki Visitor Pack ($14) at the airport, Skybus terminal or the PTV Hub at Southern Cross Station on arrival.

The myki card can be topped up at 7Eleven stores, machines at most train stations and at some CBD tram stops (online top-ups can take 24 hours to process). Fines for not travelling with a valid myki are $207 and ticket inspectors are vigilant and unforgiving.

Costs for zone 1, which is all that most travellers will need: two-hour $3.50, daily $7.

TAXI

Taxis are metered and need an estimated prepaid fare when hailed between 10pm and 5am. You may need to pay more or get a refund depending on the final fare. Toll charges are added to fares. A small tip is usual but not compulsory.

QUEENSCLIFF & THE BELLARINE PENINSULA

New wineries flank the hillsides of the Bellarine Peninsula, but visitors have been coming here for its seaside village ambience for centuries. The Bellarine almost forms a connection with the Mornington Peninsula – there's only a 3.5km-wide stretch of water between Point Nepean on the Mornington Peninsula and the Bellarine's Point Lonsdale. Besides watching ships being navigated through that stretch, pastimes include trying gourmet food, relaxing on (or diving or snorkelling off) beaches, and meandering around affluent villages.

Accommodation prices soar from Christmas to the end of January, and some caravan parks even have minimum-stay requirements. Weekends, even in the depths of winter, also see prices rise.

Getting There & Away

BUS

McHarry's Buslines (☎03-5223 2111; www.mcharrys.com.au) McHarry's Buslines connects Geelong with most peninsula towns, such as Barwon Heads (30 minutes), Ocean Grove (45 minutes), Portarlington (45 minutes), Queenscliff (one hour) and Point Lonsdale (55 minutes). A two-hour myki is $3.50; full-day is $7.

CAR & MOTORCYCLE

From Melbourne the Bellarine Peninsula is easily accessible via the Princess Fwy (M1) to Geelong. Rather than taking the Geelong bypass, head through Geelong to the Bellarine Hwy (route 91).

FERRY

Queenscliff Sorrento Ferry (☎03-5258 3244; www.searoad.com.au; one-way foot passenger adult/child $10/8, 2 adults & car $69; ⏲hourly 7am-6pm) This car and passenger ferry runs between Queenscliff and Sorrento.

Queenscliff

POP 1420

Historic Queenscliff is a lovely spot, popular with day-tripping and overnighting Melburnians who come for fine food and wine, boutique shopping and leisurely walks along the beach. The views across the Port Phillip

Around Melbourne

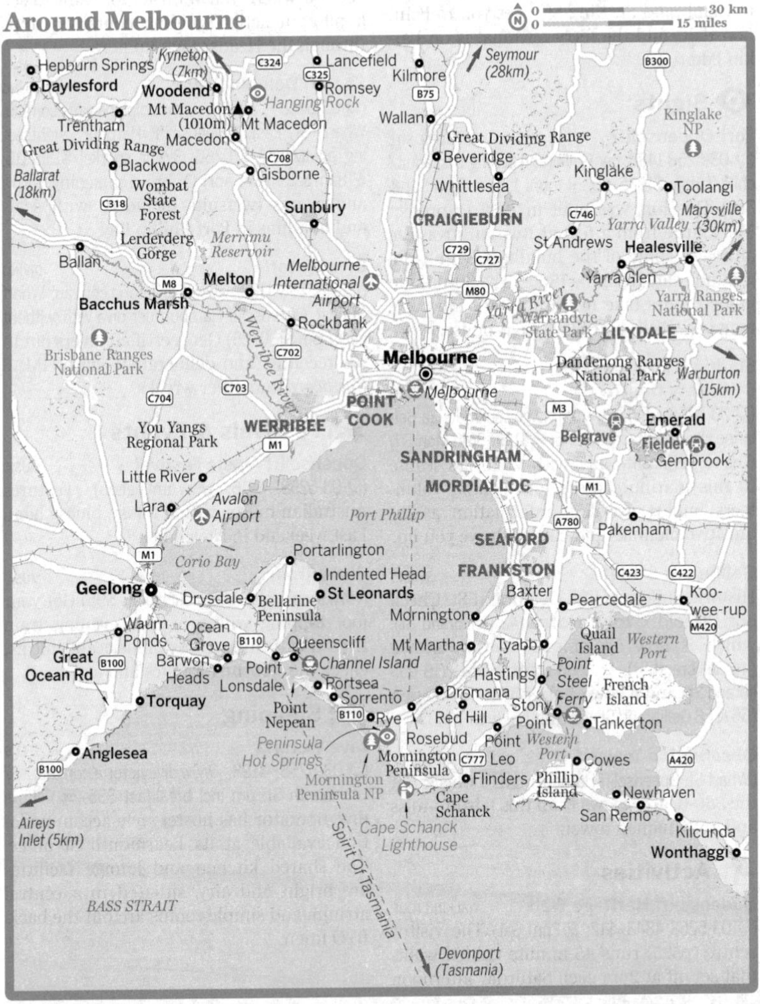

Heads and Bass Strait are glorious, and a new observation tower by the ferry terminal shows off the town and surrounds beautifully.

Queenscliff was established for the pilots who, to this day, steer ships through the treacherous Port Phillip Heads. Known as 'the Rip', this is one of the most dangerous seaways in the world. In the 1850s Queenscliff was a favoured settlement for diggers who'd struck it rich on the goldfields, and wealthy Melburnians and the Western District's squattocracy flocked to the town. Extravagant hotels and guesthouses from the era still operate today, giving Queenscliff a historic charm and grandness.

The main drag, Hesse St, runs parallel to Gellibrand St. King St takes you to Point Lonsdale, and the ferry terminal is on Larkin Pde.

Sights

Fort Queenscliff HISTORIC SITE
(03-5258 1488; cnr Gellibrand & King Sts; adult/child/family $10/5/25; tours 1pm & 3pm Sat & Sun) This fort was built in 1882 to protect Melbourne from a feared Russian invasion, although some of the buildings within the grounds date from the 1860s. The 90-minute guided tours take in the military museum, magazine, cells and Black Lighthouse.

Marine & Freshwater Discovery Centre AQUARIUM
(03-5258 3344; www.dpi.vic.gov.au/mdc; 2a Bellarine Hwy; adult/child $8/5; 11am-3pm Mon-Fri) Get to grips, literally, with Victoria's sealife in this marine centre's touch tank. Volunteers impart excellent information as inquisitive blennies and cuttlefish eye you up.

Gellibrand Street STREET
Historic buildings line Gellibrand St. Check out the old **Ozone Hotel** (42 Gellibrand St), which is now apartments, **Lathamstowe** (44 Gellibrand St), **Queenscliff Hotel** (16 Gellibrand St) and a row of old **pilots' cottages** (66 & 68 Gellibrand St) dating back to 1853.

Observation Tower LANDMARK
(Wharf St, Queenscliff Harbour) FREE Check out the 360-degree views from this hard-to-miss and aptly named tower.

Activities

Queenscliff Heritage Walk WALKING TOUR
(03-5258 4843; $12; 2pm Sat) The visitor centre (p525) runs 45-minute guided walks that set off at 2pm each Saturday afternoon or by appointment; the price also includes afternoon tea.

Bellarine Peninsula Railway TRAIN
(03-5258 2069; www.bpr.org.au; Queenscliff train station; return adult/child/family $30/20/70; departs 11.15am, 1.15pm & 2.45pm Sun year-round, plus Tue during school holidays) Run by a group of cheerful volunteer steam-train tragics, with beautiful trains plying the 1¾-hour return journey to Drysdale.

South Bay Eco Adventures ADVENTURE TOUR
(03-5258 4019; www.southbayecoadventures.com; Wharf St East, Queenscliff Harbour; DiscoveryTtour adult/child $65/35) These tours get you where you want to go. Want to see a pilot in action guiding container ships through the Heads? Sign up here.

Sea-All Dolphin Swims SNORKELLING
(03-5258 3889; www.dolphinswims.com.au; Wharf St East, Queenscliff Harbour; sightseeing adult/child $70/60, 3½-hr snorkel $135/115; 8am & 1pm Oct-Apr) Offers sightseeing tours and swims (wetsuits included) with seals and dolphins in Port Phillip Bay.

Dive Victoria DIVING
(03-5258 1188; www.divevictoria.com.au; Wharf St East, Queenscliff Harbour; per dive with/without gear from $130/65) Gets certified divers out to see recently (and deliberately) sunk HMAS *Canberra* and other wrecks.

Festivals & Events

Queenscliff Music Festival MUSIC
(03-5258 4816; www.qmf.net.au) Features Australian musos with a folksy, bluesy bent. Last weekend in November.

Blues Train MUSIC
(www.thebluestrain.com.au; tickets $95) Get your foot tapping with irregular evening train trips that feature rootsy music and meals; check the website for dates and artists.

Sleeping

Dive Victoria HOSTEL $
(03-5258 4188; www.divevictoria.com.au; 37 Learmonth St; dm incl breakfast $35;) This dive operator has hostel-style accommodation available at its Learmonth St office. The shared kitchen and lounge facilities are bright and airy, situated in a central atrium, and simple rooms are out the back. BYO linen.

Queenscliff Inn HOTEL $
(☎03-5258 4600; www.queenscliffinn.com; 59 Hesse St; d/f without bathroom $90/140) This Edwardian inn has simple but sweet period-style rooms. There's a common area and a good restaurant on-site, as well as a self-catering kitchen.

Queenscliff Tourist Parks CAMPGROUND, CABINS $$
(☎03-5258 1765; www.touristparks.queenscliffe.vic.gov.au; 134 Hesse St; powered sites/cabins $32-52/124) This friendly council-run camping ground around Queenscliff's footy field is five minutes' walk from town and almost on the beach.

Athelstane House BOUTIQUE HOTEL $$
(☎03-5258 1024; www.athelstane.com.au; 4 Hobson St; r incl breakfast $175; 📶) Athelstane House has smart and comfortable rooms in a beautifully kept historical building. All rooms come with spas and balcony rooms are spacious. The on-site restaurant and bar will keep you well fed and watered.

Vue Grand HOTEL $$$
(☎03-5258 1544; www.vuegrand.com.au; 46 Hesse Street; traditional $200, turret incl breakfast from $400) The Vue's traditional rooms are nothing on its turret suite (boasting 360-degree views) and bay-view rooms (with freestanding bath-tubs in the lounge), but prices differ by hundreds. If you can't get the turret room, the turret-level rooftop bar is a fine spot for a beverage or two on a sunny day.

Eating & Drinking

Café Gusto CAFE $
(☎03-5258 3604; 25 Hesse St; mains $15; ⏲8.30am-4pm) This popular Queenscliff eatery is great for breakfast and has a spacious garden out the back. It uses lots of local produce and makes everything from the relishes to the baked beans on-site.

Lix CAFE $
(Shop 6, 4 Wharf St, Queenscliff Harbour; meals $5.50; ⏲7.30am-5pm) This new waterside cafe serves up simple toasted sandwiches, moreish smoothies and coffee.

Vue Street Bar PIZZERIA $$
(46 Hesse St; mains $17; ⏲11.30am-8pm Wed-Sat noon-5pm Sun) Sit and watch Queenscliff wander by, a local beer in one hand and slice of pizza in the other. Terrific meals, great ambience.

The Lounge @ Salt COCKTAIL BAR
(☎03-5258 3988; www.salt-art.com.au; 33-35 Hesse St; ⏲noon-early evening Sat & Sun) This glamorous bar has quality retro furniture, sea views from the balcony and art on its walls. Relax with a refreshing cocktail or glass of local *vino*.

Information

Queenscliff Visitor Centre (☎03-5258 4843; www.queenscliffe.vic.gov.au; 55 Hesse St; ⏲9am-5pm) Internet access is offered for $6 per hour (also available next door at the library).

Point Lonsdale

POP 2500

Sights & Activities

Point Lonsdale, 5km southwest of Queenscliff, is a laid-back community with cafes and an operational 1902 **lighthouse**. From the foreshore car park you can walk to the **Rip View lookout** to watch ships entering the Rip, to **Point Lonsdale Pier** and to the lighthouse. There's good **surf** off the rocky beach below the car park.

Below the lighthouse is **Buckley's Cave**, where William Buckley lived with indigenous people for 32 years after he escaped the Sorrento convict settlement.

Sleeping & Eating

Point Lonsdale Guest House GUESTHOUSE $$
(☎03-5258 1142; www.pointlonsdaleguesthouse.com.au; 31 Point Lonsdale Rd; r $110-250; 📶🏊) The huge range of rooms in this former Terminus House (1884) range from basic motel rooms to the lavish Bollinger room. Lighthouse views come at a premium. There's a communal kitchen, tennis court and BBQ facilities.

Grow Naturally CAFE $
(59 Point Lonsdale Rd; mains $10-19; ⏲9am-3pm Wed-Sun) Serving up healthy meals cheaply isn't necessarily easy, but this small cafe succeeds.

Kelp MODERN AUSTRALIAN $$
(67 Point Lonsdale Rd; mains $18-42; ⏲8am-9pm) This modern cafe-restaurant offers breakfasts and lunchtime pita-bread wraps and salads, while on the premium-priced dinner menu you will find venison and squid ink linguine.

Barwon Heads

POP 3600

At the mouth of the broad Barwon River, Barwon Heads is a haven of sheltered beaches, surf shops, tidal river flats and holiday-makers.

Sights

Beaches BEACH

Feisty **Thirteenth Beach**, 2km west of town, is popular with surfers. There are short walks around the headland and the **Bluff** with panoramic sea vistas, and **scuba-diving** spots under the rocky ledges below.

Jirrahlinga Koala & Wildlife Sanctuary WILDLIFE RESERVE

(03-5254 2484; www.jirrahlinga.com.au; Taits Rd; adult/child $18/10) This koala sanctuary looks after injured koalas in its on-site hospital and also houses sleepy wombats and reptiles.

Sleeping

Barwon Heads Caravan Park CAMPGROUND $

(03-5254 1115; www.barwoncoast.com.au; Ewing Blyth Dr; unpowered/powered sites $41/55, d/f cabins $95/155, beach house $275) Right on the Barwon River, this park has fancy beach houses as well as tea-tree-shaded sites, tennis courts and playgrounds. Prices are much cheaper off-peak.

Seahaven Village APARTMENT $$

(03-5254 1066; www.seahavenvillage.com.au; 3 Geelong Rd; d $145-295;) Seahaven is a cute cluster of self-contained studios and cottages that offer great facilities, such as electric blankets, open fires, full kitchens and entertainment systems.

Eating

Starfish Bakery BAKERY $

(78 Hitchcock St; meals $7-10; 7am-4pm Wed-Mon) This relaxed, colourful bakery-cafe makes its own pastries and bread. It also offers takeaway meals ($14) that are excellent for campers.

Little Tuckles CAFE $

(0458 910 244; 1 Flinders Pde; mains $9; 6.30am-2pm) Tucked to the side of the beachside roundabout is this cute and cheerful little cafe. The coffee's great and there are plenty of takeaway treats, or stay and catch some sun in the courtyard.

At the Heads MODERN AUSTRALIAN $$

(03-5254 1277; www.attheheads.com.au; Jetty Rd; meals $26-32; 8am-9pm) Built on stilts over the mouth of the river, this light, airy cafe-restaurant has huge breakfasts, local fare and the most amazing views. Its bustling family ambience makes it a fun daytime locale.

THE YARRA VALLEY

An hour northeast of Melbourne, the Yarra Valley is one of Victoria's premier wine regions, with surrounding national parks that are superb for walking and cycling. Healesville and Yarra Glen are the main towns in the Yarra Valley; both are central to many of the wineries.

There's some good walking in national parks in the area, including Warrandyte State Park, Yarra Ranges National Park and Kinglake National Park.

Activities

One-hour dawn balloon flights with the following operators include champagne breakfast and cost from $250 to $315: **Balloon Sunrise** (03-9005 2212; www.hotairballooning.com.au); **Global Ballooning** (1800 627 661; www.globalballooning.com.au); **Go Wild Ballooning** (03-9739 0772; www.gowildballooning.com.au).

Tours

Eco Adventure Tours CULTURAL TOUR

(03-5962 5115; www.ecoadventuretours.com.au; walks from $25) Offers nocturnal wildlife-spotting and cultural walks in the Healesville, Toolangi and Dandenongs area.

Yarra Valley Winery Tours WINE

(1300 496 105; www.yarravalleywinerytours.com.au; tours from $105) Daily tours taking in four or five wineries.

Information

Yarra Valley Visitor Centre (03-5962 2600; www.visityarravalley.com.au; Harker St, Healesville; 9am-5pm) Just off the highway in Healesville, this tourist office has helpful staff.

Getting There & Away

Suburban trains go as far as Lilydale (zone 1 and 2 myki ticket). **McKenzie's Bus Lines** (03-5962 5088; www.mckenzies.com.au) runs route 684 from Melbourne to Healesville (1½ hours) and Marysville (2 hours) daily. Routes 685 and 686 stop at Healesville Sanctuary.

Healesville

POP 7900

Pretty little Healesville is the main base for the Yarra Valley wineries and Yarra Ranges forest drive, and is the gateway north to the High Country. It is the 'capital' of the Lower Yarra Valley.

Sights

Healesville Sanctuary WILDLIFE SANCTUARY
(03-5957 2800; www.zoo.org.au; Badger Creek Rd; adult/child/family $26/13/60; 9am-5pm; 685, 686) This wildlife park is full of kangaroos, dingoes, lyrebirds, Tasmanian devils, bats, koalas, eagles, snakes and lizards. The Platypus House displays these shy underwater creatures and has platypus shows (11.30am and 2pm). Birds of Prey presentations (noon and 2.30pm) feature wedge-tailed eagles and owls soaring through the air.

Sleeping & Eating

Healesville is the main accommodation centre for the region, though there are B&Bs scattered around the valley. Some wineries also have accommodation.

Badger Creek Holiday Park CAMPGROUND $$
(03-5962 4328; www.badgercreekholidays.com.au; 419 Don Rd; powered sites $43, cabins $132-220;) The creekside location is lovely and this BIG4 park is well kitted out with facilities such as an adventure playground, games room, camp kitchen, pool and tennis courts.

Healesville Hotel HOTEL $$
(03-5962 4002; www.yarravalleyharvest.com.au; 256 Maroondah Hwy; d Mon-Thu $110, Fri & Sun $130, Sat incl dinner $325;) An iconic Healesville landmark, this restored 1910 hotel offers beautiful rooms situated upstairs (ask for one that has verandah access) with pressed-tin ceilings and shared bathrooms. On weekends the restaurant has a set menu on offer, which will set you back at least $55.

Giant Steps & Innocent Bystander TAPAS, PIZZA $$
(1800 661 624; www.innocentbystander.com.au; 336 Maroondah Hwy; mains $20-45; 10am-10pm, from 8am Sat & Sun;) The industrial-sized Giant Steps & Innocent Bystander just out of town is a buzzing restaurant, winery and cellar door – a great place for a lunch

YARRA VALLEY WINERIES

The Yarra Valley has more than 80 wineries and 50 cellar doors scattered around its rolling hills – the first vines were planted at Yering Station in 1838. The region produces cool-climate, food-friendly drops such as chardonnay and pinot noir.

Beer and cider have a long history in the region too; pick up the Yarra Valley Cider & Ale Trail (www.ciderandaletrail.com.au) brochure at venues. Some top Yarra Valley wineries with cellar door sales and tastings include:

Domain Chandon (03-9738 9200; www.chandon.com.au; 727 Maroondah Hwy; 10.30am-4.30pm) This slick operation is worth a visit for the free guided tours (11am, 1pm and 3pm). Tastings $5.

Rochford (03-5962 2119; www.rochfordwines.com; 878 Maroondah Hwy; 9am-5pm) Rochford is best known for its winery concerts.

Sticks (03-9730 1022; www.sticks.com.au; 179 Glenview Rd; 10am-5pm) Small energetic winery with Sunday Sessions rocking the vines with live music.

TarraWarra Estate (03-5957 3510; www.tarrawarra.com.au; 311 Healesville–Yarra Glen Rd; Art gallery admission $5; 11am-5pm) TarraWarra has a striking and modern art gallery showing wonderful exhibitions. Refuel at the neighbouring bistro and cellar door. Tastings $4.

Yering Farm Wines (03-9739 0461; www.yeringfarmwines.com; St Huberts Rd; 10am-5pm) A rustic and friendly little cellar door in an old hay shed with lovely views.

Yering Station (03-9730 0100; www.yering.com; 38 Melba Hwy; 10am-5pm Mon-Fri, 10am-6pm Sat & Sun) Taste wines in the original 1859 winery and walk through the lovely grounds to the modern fine-dining restaurant.

of tapas, pizza or a cheese platter, a lazy afternoon drink or a spot of wine and cheese tasting. Head across the car park to White Rabbit Brewery for a beer.

Marysville & Lake Mountain

Marysville was at the epicentre of the tragic 2009 bushfires. Most of the town's buildings were destroyed and 34 people lost their lives, but the community is rebuilding, and this beautiful setting is the main base for the cross-country ski fields at Lake Mountain.

Sights & Activities

Bruno's Art & Sculptures Garden GALLERY
(03-5963 3513; 51 Falls Rd; adult/child $10/5; garden 10am-5pm daily, gallery 10am-5pm Sat & Sun) Bruno's Art & Sculptures Garden was badly damaged in the 2009 fires but more than 100 of the terracotta sculptures have been repaired, and Bruno is busy creating more. A delightful setting full of regeneration.

Steavenson Falls WATERFALL
(until 11pm) This 84m waterfall is vastly different today than when it was a stream of water running through charred surrounds in 2009. The infrastructure has been rebuilt and it has excellent accessibility and facilities for visitors. It is floodlit each evening until 11pm.

Lake Mountain Resort SKIING
(03-5957 7222; www.lakemountainresort.com.au; Snowy Rd; 8am-4.30pm Mon-Fri Oct-May, until 6.30pm Jun-Sep) Lake Mountain (1433m) is the premier cross-country ski resort in Australia, with 37km of trails and several toboggan runs. There's an imposing new cafe and separate ski-hire centre. In summer there are marked hiking and mountain-biking trails, however the cafe is closed.

Sleeping

Marysville Caravan & Holiday Park CAMPGROUND, CABINS $$
(03-5963 3247; www.marysvillecaravanpark.com.au; 1130 Buxton Rd; powered sites $33, cabins from $105) This little park straddles a lovely creek (ideal for cooling off in) and features towering gums that survived the bushfire. It's a short walk into town.

Information

Marysville Visitor Information Centre (03-5963 4567; www.marysvilletourism.com; 5 Murchison St; 9am-5pm Mon-Fri, 10am-4pm Sat & Sun) Plenty of information as well as local crafts and souvenirs for sale.

THE DANDENONGS

On a clear day, the Dandenong Ranges and their highest peak, Mt Dandenong (633m), can be seen from Melbourne. The landscape is a patchwork of exotics and natives with a lush understorey of tree ferns – it's the most accessible bushwalking in Melbourne's backyard, and the quaint towns of Olinda, Sassafras and Emerald make a nice escape.

BLACK SATURDAY

On 7 February 2009, parts of Victoria were engulfed in a deadly firestorm that became known as Black Saturday. Fuelled by extreme temperatures, tinder-dry conditions and strong winds, the ferocity and speed of the fires took residents and authorities by surprise. The worst hit area was the Yarra Ranges northeast of Melbourne, where within a few devastating hours the tiny bush towns of Marysville, Kinglake, Strathewen, Flowerdale and Narbethong were engulfed. Marysville and Kinglake were virtually razed and the fires hit so quickly that many residents had no chance of escape. Many fire victims died in their homes or trapped in their cars while trying to escape, some blocked by fallen trees across the roads.

The statistics tell a tragic tale: 173 people dead, more than 2000 homes destroyed, an estimated 7500 people left homeless, and more than 4500 sq km burned out. What followed from the shell-shocked state and nation was a huge outpouring of grief, humanitarian aid and charity, while the government established a royal commission into the events and future fire safety and warning strategies. Today, the towns of Marysville, Kinglake and other fire-affected communities are courageously rebuilding and welcoming the return of tourists, while the blackened bushland and forests are regenerating as nature intended.

WORTH A TRIP

ST ANDREWS

Sleepily ensconsed in the hills 35km north of Melbourne, this little village is best known for the weekly **St Andrews Market** (8am-2pm Sat). Every Saturday morning the scent of eucalypt competes with incense, and the bird life with guitar strumming as a hippy crowd comes to mingle and buy handmade crafts, knitwear and jewellery, fresh produce and secondhand goods. Enjoy a shiatsu massage or sip chai in the chai tent while buskers create the soundtrack.

Sights & Activities

Puffing Billy TRAIN
(03-9754 6800; www.puffingbilly.com.au; Old Monbulk Rd; return adult/child/family $59/30/120) Puffing Billy is an immensely popular steam train that snakes through lush fern gullies and bush. There are up to six departures between Belgrave and Gembrook daily during holidays, and four on other days.

Trees Adventure ADVENTURE SPORTS
(03-9752 5354; www.treesadventure.com.au; Glen Harrow Gardens, Old Monbulk Rd; 2hr session adult/child $39/33; 11am-5pm Mon-Fri, 9am-5pm Sat & Sun; Belgrave) Past Puffing Billy, Trees Adventure is a blast of tree-climbs, flying foxes and obstacle courses in a stunning patch of old-growth forest that boasts sequoia, mountain ash and Japanese oak trees.

Dandenong Ranges National Park PARK
(Upper Ferntree Gully, Belgrave) This park is made up of the four largest areas of remaining forest in the Dandenongs. The Ferntree Gully area has several short walks, including the popular **1000 Steps/Kokoda Track Memorial Walk** up to One Tree Hill picnic ground (two hours return), which commemorates Australian WWII servicewomen and men who served in New Guinea. **Sherbrooke Forest** has a towering cover of mountain ash trees. Reach the start of its eastern forest walk (7km), just 1km or so from Belgrave station.

SkyHigh Mt Dandenong VIEWPOINT
(03-9751 0443; www.skyhighmtdandenong.com.au; Observatory Rd; vehicle entry $5; 8am-11pm; 688) Drive or catch the bus up to this restaurant, cafe and maze for amazing views over Melbourne and Port Phillip Bay from the highest point in the Dandenongs.

Information

Dandenong Ranges & Knox Visitor Information Centre (03-9758 7522; www.experiencethedandenongs.com.au; 1211 Burwood Hwy; 9am-5pm; Upper Ferntree Gully) The visitor information centre is outside Upper Ferntree Gully train station.

Getting There & Away

Trains run on the Belgrave line to the foothills of the Dandenongs (zone 1 and 2 myki). From Upper Ferntree Gully train station it's a 10-minute walk to the start of the Ferntree Gully section of the national park.

MORNINGTON PENINSULA

The Mornington Peninsula – the boot-shaped bit of land between Port Phillip Bay and Western Port Bay – has been Melbourne's summer playground since the 1870s, when paddle steamers ran down to Portsea. Today, the calm 'front beaches' on the Port Phillip Bay side are still a big magnet for family holidays at towns such as Mornington, Rosebud, Dromana, Rye, Blairgowrie and Sorrento. The rugged ocean 'back beaches' facing Bass Strait offer challenging surfing and stunning walks along the coastal strip, part of Mornington Peninsula National Park.

Don't overlook a trip to the peninsula's interior, where lovely stands of native bushland are interspersed with vineyards and orchards – foodies love this region, where a winery lunch is a real highlight.

Tours

Bunyip Tours (p545) runs Mornington Peninsula Explorer bus tours that depart Melbourne. Choices include dolphins and seals; dive, snorkel, kayak; or Peninsula Hot Springs and strawberries.

APT BUS
(1300 655 965; www.australiasightseeing.com; tours from adult/child $177/89) Day trips heading from Melbourne to the Mornington Peninsula; choose from wineries or strawberry picking. Includes lunch.

Information

Peninsula Visitor Information Centre (☎03-5987 3078, 1800 804 009; www.visitmorningtonpeninsula.org; 359b Nepean Hwy, Dromana; ⏱9am-5pm) Can book accommodation and tours.

Getting There & Around

Metro trains run from Flinders St Station (zone 1) to Frankston Station (zone 2). **Portsea Passenger Service** (☎03-5986 5666; www.ptv.vic.gov.au) bus 788 runs from Frankston to Portsea ($2.30, 1½ hours) via Mornington, Dromana and Sorrento. This is one of the few routes where you can buy a short-term myki ticket on board.

Queenscliff Sorrento Ferry (p523) links the Bellarine Peninsula with the Mornington Peninsula. Inter Island Ferries (p535) runs between Stony Point and Cowes (Phillip Island) via French Island.

Sorrento & Portsea

POP 2000

Historic Sorrento is the standout town on the Mornington Peninsula for its beautiful limestone buildings, ocean and bay beaches and buzzing seaside summer atmosphere. This was the site of Victoria's first official European settlement, established by an expedition of convicts, marines, civil officers and free settlers that arrived from England in 1803.

Only 4km further west, tiny Portsea also has good back beaches, and diving and watersports operators.

Sights & Activities

Grand 19th-century buildings include the **Hotel Sorrento** (☎03-5984 2206; www.hotelsorrento.com.au; 5-15 Hotham Rd; motel r $195-280, apt $220-320), **Continental Hotel** (☎03-5984 2201; www.continentalhotel.com.au; 1-21 Ocean Beach Rd) and Koonya; built in 1871, 1875 and 1878 respectively.

There are plenty of swimming and walking opportunities along Sorrento's sandy beaches and bluffs. At low tide, the rock pool at the back beach is a safe spot for adults and children to swim and snorkel, and the surf beach here is patrolled in summer. The ferry to Queenscliff departs daily for the short trip across the heads.

Moonraker Charters DOLPHIN TOUR
(☎03-5984 4211; www.moonrakercharters.com.au; 7 George St, Sorrento; adult/child sightseeing $55/45, dolphin & seal swimming $125/115) Operates three-hour dolphin- and seal-swimming tours from Sorrento Pier.

Polperro Dolphin Swims DOLPHIN TOUR
(☎03-5988 8437; www.polperro.com.au; adult/child sightseeing $55/35, dolphin & seal swimming $125) Morning and afternoon dolphin- and seal-swimming tours from Sorrento Pier.

Bay Play DIVING, WATER SPORTS
(☎03-5984 0888; www.bayplay.com.au; 3755 Pt Nepean Rd, Portsea) Diving trips, dolphin swims, sea-kayaking tours (adult/child $99/88) and snorkelling to the local sea dragon colony.

Dive Victoria DIVING, SNORKELLING
(☎03-5984 3155; www.divevictoria.com.au; 3752 Point Nepean Rd, Portsea; snorkelling $85, s/d dive with gear $130/210) Diving and snorkelling trips.

Sleeping

Prices rise with the temperature from mid-December to the end of January, and during Easter and school holidays, when places routinely book out.

Sorrento Foreshore Camping Ground CAMPGROUND $
(☎03-5950 1011; Nepean Hwy; unpowered/powered sites $40/45; ⏱Nov-May) Hilly, bushclad sites between the bay beach and the main road into Sorrento.

Sorrento Beach House YHA HOSTEL $$
(☎03-5984 4323; www.sorrento-beachhouse.com; 3 Miranda St; dm/d $45/120) This purpose-built hostel in a quiet but central location maintains a relaxed atmosphere. The back deck and garden are great places to catch up with other travellers.

DON'T MISS

PENINSULA HOT SPRINGS

Peninsula Hot Springs (☎03-5950 8777; www.peninsulahotsprings.com; Springs Lane, Rye; bathhouse adult/child Tue-Thu $25/15, Fri-Mon $30/20) Peninsula Hot Springs is a large, luxurious complex that utilises hot, mineral-rich waters pumped from deep underground. Spend a day resting in the different outdoor pools and hammam in its more than 16 areas. Private spa, bathing and massage treatments are also available.

Carmel of Sorrento GUESTHOUSE $$
(☎03-5984 3512; www.carmelofsorrento.com.au; 142 Ocean Beach Rd; d $150-220, apt from $220) This lovely old limestone house right in the centre of Sorrento has been tastefully restored in period style and neatly marries the town's history with contemporary comfort.

Eating & Drinking

The Baths FISH & CHIPS $
(☎03-5984 1500; www.thebaths.com.au; 3278 Point Nepean Rd; mains $10; ⊙noon-8pm) Forget the restaurant and enjoy the popular takeaway fish and chippery at the front.

Smokehouse PIZZA $$
(☎03-5984 1246; 182 Ocean Beach Rd; mains $20-38; ⊙6-9pm) Gourmet pizzas and pastas are the speciality at this local family favourite. Innovative toppings and the aromas wafting from the wood-fired oven are a winner.

The Sisters CAFE $$
(151 Ocean Beach Rd; mains $16) Settle yourself between the vegie gardens and enjoy delish coffee and treats like local field mushrooms.

Portsea Hotel BISTRO $$
(☎03-5984 2213; www.portseahotel.com.au; Point Nepean Rd, Portsea; mains $26-32) This iconic sprawling pub is Portsea's pulse, with a great lawn and terrace area looking over the bay. There's an excellent bistro and old-style accommodation that increases in price based on sea views and season.

Information

Sorrento Visitor Centre (☎03-5984 5678; 2 St Aubins Way; ⊙10am-4pm) The small visitor centre is on the main drag in town.

Point Nepean & Mornington Peninsula National Parks

The peninsula's tip is marked by the scenic **Point Nepean National Park** (www.parkweb.vic.gov.au; Point Nepean Rd), originally a quarantine station and army base. There are long stretches of traffic-free road for excellent cycling, and walking trails leading to beaches. You can hire bikes at the Point Nepean visitor centre ($25 per day) or take the shuttle (adult/child return $10/7.50), a hop-on, hop-off bus service.

Mornington Peninsula National Park (www.parkweb.vic.gov.au) covers the dramatic sliver of coastline between Portsea and Cape Schanck, where rugged ocean beaches are framed by cliffs and bluffs. You can hike the Coastal Walk all the way from London Bridge at Portsea to Cape Schanck (30km) along a marked trail.

Built in 1859, **Cape Schanck Lighthouse** (☎03-5988 6184; www.capeschancklighthouse.com.au; 420 Cape Schanck Rd; museum only adult/child/family $13.50/9.50/37, museum & lighthouse $16.50/10.50/44; ⊙10.30am-4pm) is a photogenic working lighthouse, with a kiosk, museum, information centre and regular guided tours. You can stay at **Cape Schanck B&B** (☎1300 885 259; www.capeschancklighthouse.com.au; 420 Cape Schanck Rd; d from $150) in the limestone keeper's cottage.

PHILLIP ISLAND

POP 9400

Famous for the Penguin Parade and Grand Prix racing circuit, Phillip Island is a spectacular natural environment, attracting a curious mix of surfers, petrolheads and international tourists making a beeline for those little penguins.

At its heart, 100-sq-km Phillip Island is still a farming community, but along with the penguins and people, it's also home to a large seal colony and a koala colony. The rugged south coast has some fabulous surf beaches and the summer swell of tourists means there's a swag of family attractions, plenty of accommodation and cruisy cafes dotted around the island. Visit in winter and you'll find a very quiet place where the local population of farmers, surfers and hippies go about their business. The island

BIRDS & WILDLIFE

Mutton birds, also known as short-tailed shearwaters, colonise the dunes around Cape Woolamai from late September to April. Your best chance of seeing them is at the Penguin Parade as they fly in at dusk, or at the rookeries at Woolamai Beach.

There's a wide variety of other water birds around, including pelicans. Watch them being fed on the mainland at the San Remo Fisherman's Co-Op (11.30am/noon daily). They're also in the swampland at Rhyll Inlet and Rhyll Wetland.

Phillip Island

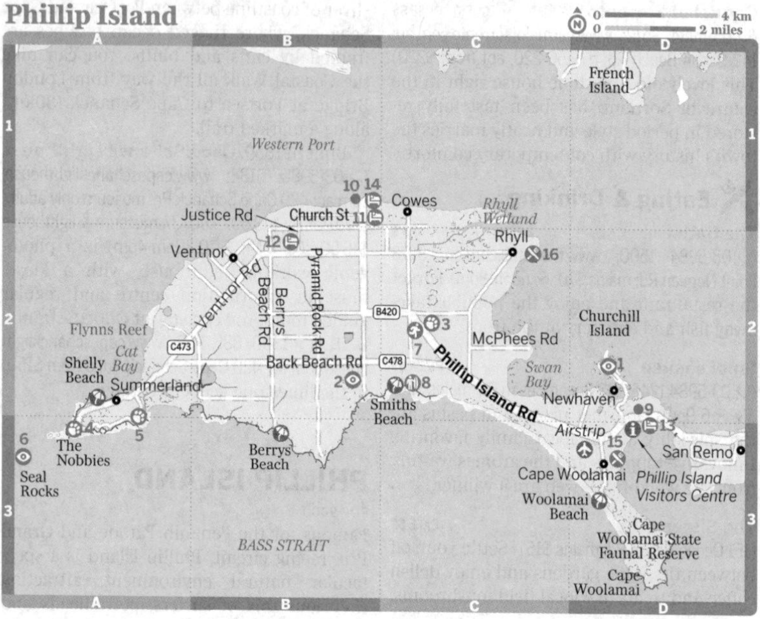

was originally settled by the Boonwurrung/Bunurong people, who thrived on a diet of seafood and short-tailed shearwaters.

Sights & Activities

Phillip Island Nature Parks

The nature parks comprise three of the island's biggest attractions: the **Penguin Parade** (☎03-5951 2800; www.penguins.org.au; Summerland Beach, 1810 Phillip Island Rd, Cowes; adult/child/family $22/11/55; ⏱10am-dusk, penguins arrive at sunset); **Koala Conservation Centre** (☎03-5951 2800; www.penguins.org.au; adult/child/family $11/5.50/27.50; ⏱10am-5pm, extended hours in summer), with elevated boardwalks; and **Churchill Island** (☎03-5956 7214; www.penguins.org.au; Phillip Island Rd, Newhaven; adult/child/family $11/5.50/27.50; ⏱10am-5pm), a working farm, where Victoria's first crops were planted. Today it features historic displays, including butter churning and blacksmithing.

If you're keen on all three attractions, buy the **Three Parks Pass** (www.penguins.org.au; adult/child/family $38/19/94), which is valid for six months (you can only visit the Penguin Parade once though) and is available online and at venues in Phillip Island.

Most people come for the little penguins, the smallest of their kind in the world. The penguin complex includes two concrete amphitheatres that hold up to 3800 spectators, who visit to see the little fellas waddle from the sea to their land-based nests just after sunset. Penguin numbers swell in summer, after breeding, but they parade year-round. You get a closer view from the boardwalks as they search for their burrows and mates. There are a variety of specialised tours, which offer ranger accompaniment or seeing the penguins from the vantage of a Skybox (an elevated platform). Book well in advance in summer and always wear warm clothing.

Seal Rocks & the Nobbies

The extreme southwestern tip of Phillip Island leads to the Nobbies. Beyond them is Seal Rocks, inhabited by Australia's largest colony of Australian fur seals. The **Nobbies Centre** (☎03-5951 2852; www.penguins.org.au; ⏱11am until one hour before sunset) FREE houses an interesting interpretive display with interactive panels and games. You can see the 10,000 to 20,000 Australian fur seals if you pay $5 (for four minutes) to remotely control a video camera that watches over Seal Rocks. The best way to see them is on a Wildlife Coast Cruise.

Phillip Island

Sights

Activities, Courses & Tours

Sleeping

Eating

Motor Racing Circuit

Even when the motorbikes aren't racing, petrolheads love the **Grand Prix Motor Racing Circuit** (03-5952 9400), which holds the Australian Motorcycle Grand Prix each October. The **visitor centre** (03-5952 9400; www.phillipislandcircuit.com.au; Back Beach Rd; 9.30am-5pm) runs 45-minute **guided circuit tours** (adult/child/family $19/10/44; tours 11am & 2pm), which include access to the History of Motorsport Display. You can also cut laps of the track in hotted-up V8s ($195, booking essential).

Beaches & Surfing

Ocean beaches on the south side of the island include **Woolamai**, a popular surf beach with dangerous rips and currents. The surf at **Smiths Beach** is more family-friendly, though it gets busy on summer weekends. Both beaches are patrolled in summer. There are calm, sheltered beaches at Cowes.

Island Surfboards SURFING
(www.islandsurfboards.com.au; lessons $60, surfboard hire per hr/day $13/40) Located at **Smiths Beach** (03-5952 3443; 65 Smiths Beach Rd) and **Cowes** (03-5952 2578; 147 Thompson Ave), Island Surfboards can start your wax-head career with wetsuit hire and lessons for all skill levels.

Out There SURFING
(03-5956 6450; www.outthere.net.au) Surfing lessons ($60) and surfboard hire ($35 per day).

Other Attractions

Phillip Island Chocolate Factory FOOD TOUR
(03-5956 6600; www.phillipislandchocolatefactory.com.au; 930 Phillip Island Rd; tours adult/child/family $15/10/45; 9am-6pm) As well as wall-to-wall made-in-Belgium chocolate, there's a walk-through tour of the chocolate-making process, including a remarkable gallery of chocolate sculptures, from a replica of Michelangelo's *David* to an entire model chocolate village! Naturally, you can buy chocolate penguins.

Amaze'n Things AMUSEMENT PARK
(03-5952 2283; www.amazenthings.com.au; 1805 Phillip Island Rd; adult/child/family $33/23/99; 9am-6pm, last admission 4pm) With an illusion maze, minigolf, puzzle island and lots of activities, this whacky fun park is great for kids, but gets the adults in too.

Tours

Go West DAY TOUR
(1300 736 551; www.gowest.com.au; 1-day tour $130) Tour from Melbourne that includes food tastings, entry fees and iPod commentary in several languages. It visits several island attractions, including the Penguin Parade.

Wildlife Coast Cruises BOAT TOUR
(03-5952 3501; www.wildlifecoastcruises.com.au; Rotunda Bldg, Cowes Jetty; seal-watching adult/child $70/48) A variety of cruises from Cowes including a daily two-hour seal-watching cruise. From October to April join a twilight cruise (adult/child $35/25) or half-day cruise to French Island (adult/child $75/55).

Festivals & Events

Pyramid Rock Festival MUSIC
(www.thepyramidrockfestival.com; 3-day pass from $314) This four-day music festival coincides with New Year festivities and features some of the best Aussie bands.

Australian Motorcycle Grand Prix MOTORCYCLE RACING
(www.motogp.com.au) The island's biggest event – three days of speedy bike action in October.

Sleeping

Phillip Island's prices peak during motor races, Christmas, Easter and school holidays, so book as far ahead as possible. Most of the accommodation is in and around Cowes.

Chill House Backpackers HOSTEL $
(0431 413 275; www.chillhouse.com.au; 8 Watchorn Rd, Cowes; dm/d $35/80;) Cosy, welcoming, relaxed and well equipped, Chill House is down a side street off Settlement Rd, close to the town centre.

The Island Accommodation YHA HOSTEL $$
(03-5956 6123; www.theislandaccommodation.com.au; 10-12 Phillip Island Rd; dm/d $30/155; @) This large purpose-built backpackers has huge identical living areas on each floor, complete with table-tennis tables and cosy fireplaces for winter. Its rooftop deck has terrific views and its eco-credentials are excellent. Cheapest dorms sleep 12 and doubles are motel-standard.

Surf & Circuit Accommodation APARTMENT $$
(03-5952 1300; www.surfandcircuit.com; 113 Justice Rd; apt $135-380;) Ideal for families or groups, these eight spacious, modern and comfortable two- and three-bedroom units accommodate up to six and 10 people. They have kitchens and lounges with plasma TVs and patios, and some have spas.

Waves Apartments APARTMENT $$
(03-5952 1351; www.thewaves.com.au; 1 Esplanade, Cowes; d/tr/q from $180/220/240;) Some of these slick apartments overlook Cowes main beach so you can't beat the balcony views if you go for a beachfront unit. The modern self-contained apartments come with spa and balcony or patio.

Eating & Drinking

Most of the eateries are in Cowes – the Esplanade and Thompson Ave are crowded with fish-and-chip shops, cafes and takeaways – but there are a few more gems scattered around the island.

Cowes

Madcowes CAFE, DELI $
(03-5952 2560; 17 The Esplanade; mains $9-19; 7am-4pm) This excellent cafe looks out to the main beach. Try the hotcakes or the grazing platter and enjoy one of the most popular cafes in town.

Cowes Tandoori Indian Restaurant INDIAN $
(03-5952 3896; 134 Thompson Ave; mains $14-16; 6-10pm Tue-Sun) It may not win in the ambience stakes, but grab a takeaway dish like garlic chilli prawn curry and eat it on the beach.

Infused MODERN AUSTRALIAN $$
(03-5952 2655; www.infused.com.au; 115 Thompson Ave; mains $28-42; 9am-late Wed-Mon) Infused's groovy mix of timber, stone and lime-green decor makes a relaxed place to enjoy a beautifully presented lunch or dinner, or just a late-night cocktail. The eclectic Mod Oz menu is strong on seafood and moves from freshly shucked oysters to grain-fed Scotch fillet.

Cape Woolamai

White Salt FISH & CHIPS $
(03-5956 6336; 7 Vista Pl; fish from $5, meal packs from $15; noon-8pm Thu-Tue, from 4.30pm Wed) White Salt serves the best fish and chips on the island – select fish fillets and hand-cut chunky chips, tempura vegetables and delicious souvlakis.

Curry Leaf INDIAN $
(03-5956 6772; 9 Vista Pl; mains $12-25; noon-8pm Wed-Mon;) This cheery Indian restaurant and takeaway is popular for its ready-made curries.

Rhyll

Foreshore Bar & Restaurant PUB $$
(03-5956 9520; www.theforeshore.com.au; 11 Beach Rd; mains $24-35; 11am-late) The water views from the timber deck of the classy village pub and restaurant complement your lunchtime fish and chips (go deluxe) or bowl of mussels.

Information

Phillip Island Visitor Centre (1300 366 422; www.visitphillipisland.com; 9am-5pm, till 6pm school holidays) The main visitor centre for the island is on the main road in **Newhaven** (895 Phillip Island Tourist Rd), and there's a smaller centre at **Cowes** (cnr Thompson & Church Sts).

Waterfront Internet Service (03-5952 3312; http://waterfront.net.au; Shop 1/130 Thompson Ave, Cowes; per hr $8; 9am-5pm Mon-Fri, 10am-1pm Sat;) Internet access.

Getting There & Away

By car, Phillip Island is accessed from the mainland across the bridge at San Remo. From Melbourne take the Monash Fwy (M1) and exit at Pakenham, joining the South Gippsland Hwy at Koo Wee Rup.

V/Line (☎1800 800 007; www.vline.com.au) V/Line has train services from Melbourne's Southern Cross Station to Dandenong Station or Koo Wee Rup connecting to a bus to Cowes ($12.40, 2½ to 3½ hours). There are no direct services.

Inter Island Ferries (☎03-9585 5730; www.interislandferries.com.au; return adult/child/bike $24/12/8) Inter Island Ferries runs between Stony Point, on the Mornington Peninsula, and Cowes via French Island (45 minutes). There are two sailings on Monday and Wednesday, and three on all other days.

Getting Around

Island E-bike Hire (☎0457 281 965; 142 Caltex, Thompson Ave, Cowes; per hr/day $20/50) Hire an electric bike and zoom around the whole island. Includes helmets.

Oz Bikes (☎0401 863 622; Waves, 1 The Esplanade, Cowes; per hr/day $25/35) Plenty of bikes for hire here.

GREAT OCEAN ROAD

The Great Ocean Road (B100) is one of Australia's most famous road-touring routes. It takes travellers past world-class surfing breaks, through pockets of rainforest and calm seaside towns, and under koala-filled tree canopies. It shows off heathlands, dairy farms and sheer limestone cliffs and gets you up close and personal with the dangerous crashing surf of the Southern Ocean. Walk it, drive it, enjoy it.

Geelong

POP 173,000

Geelong is a confident town proud of its two icons: Geelong football team (aka the Cats) and the Ford Motor Company. The Cats have had a fair run in the AFL recently, winning the Grand Final in 2007 (for the first time in 44 years) and again in 2009 and 2011. Australia's automobile industry is in decline, but Ford, Geelong's other blue-and-white icon, continues its local presence.

The Wathaurong people – the original inhabitants of Geelong – called the area Jillong. Geelong's bypass means travellers can skip the city and head straight to the Great Ocean Road, but there are actually plenty of reasons to stop.

Sights & Activities

Wander Geelong's terrific **waterfront**, and locate Jan Mitchell's 100-plus **painted bollards**. At **Eastern Beach**, stop for a splash about at the rejuvenated (and free) art-deco **bathing pavilion**.

Geelong Art Gallery GALLERY
(www.geelonggallery.org.au; Little Malop St; ⏲9.30am-5pm Mon-Fri, 10am-5pm Sat & Sun) FREE This gallery houses more than 4000 works. Its Australian collection is strong and includes Frederick McCubbin's 1890 *A Bush Burial*, and *View of Geelong*, by Eugene von Guérard.

GREAT OCEAN ROAD DISTANCES & TIMES

JOURNEY	DISTANCE	TIME
Melbourne to Geelong	75km	1hr
Geelong to Torquay	21km	15min
Torquay to Anglesea	21km	15min
Anglesea to Aireys Inlet	10km	10min
Aireys Inlet to Lorne	22km	15min
Lorne to Apollo Bay	45km	1hr
Apollo Bay to Port Campbell	88km	70min
Port Campbell to Warrnambool	66km	1hr
Warrnambool to Port Fairy	28km	20min
Port Fairy to Portland	72km	1hr
Portland to Melbourne	440km	6½hr

Great Ocean Road & Southwest Coast

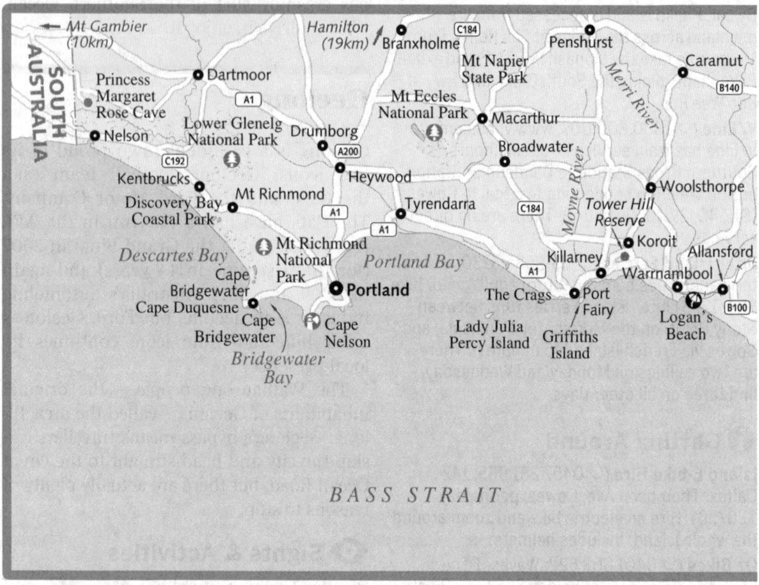

National Wool Museum MUSEUM
(www.nwm.vic.gov.au; 26 Moorabool St; adult/child/family $7.50/4/25; ⌚9.30am-5pm Mon-Fri, 10am-5pm Sat & Sun) This museum showcases the history, politics and heritage of wool production in a lovely 1872 bluestone building.

Geelong Helicopters SCENIC FLIGHTS
(☎0422 515 151; www.geelonghelicopters.com.au; adult/child $45/35) Check out Bells Beach from the air. Operates from the waterfront.

WSUP STAND-UP PADDLEBOARDING
(☎0439 113 457; www.wsup.com.au; Eastern Beach; group lessons $50) Enjoy Eastern Beach (among the boats) by stand-up paddleboard.

Bay City Seaplanes SCENIC FLIGHTS
(☎0438 840 205; www.baycityseaplanes.com.au; flights per person from $35) Swirl around the Aireys Inlet lighthouse on a scenic flight. Operates from Geelong waterfront.

Sleeping

Irish Murphy's Geelong Hostel HOSTEL $
(☎03-5221 4335; www.irishmurphysgeelong.com.au; 30 Aberdeen St; dm/s/d $50/60/80; wi-fi) This is a great, if pricey, hostel for backpackers to lay their hats. This Irish pub has swished itself up and put 18 beds into a bunch of rooms upstairs. Expect high ceilings, lovely linen and new carpets. The corner TV lounge is bright and the setup is just five minutes' walk from Geelong Station. Shared bathroom.

Gatehouse on Ryrie GUESTHOUSE $$
(☎0417 545 196; www.gatehouseonryrie.com.au; 83 Yarra St; d incl breakfast $100-130; @ wi-fi) This large and well-kept B&B was built in 1897. Rooms are spacious with shared bathrooms and there's a communal kitchen and lounge area.

Eating

Fuel CAFE $
(Shed 2, Gore Pl; mains $10; ⌚7.30am-4pm Mon-Fri) With excellent Campos coffee, and about 1000 smiles per minute from staff, this is a welcoming cafe oozing a mix of industrial and cycling chic.

Go! CAFE $
(www.cafego.com.au; 37 Bellarine St; mains from $10; ⌚7am-4pm Mon-Fri, 8am-4pm Sat) Go! is a fun cafe that serves great food in a riot of colour and amusement. The covered courtyard out the back is huge and welcoming, and staff could not be sweeter.

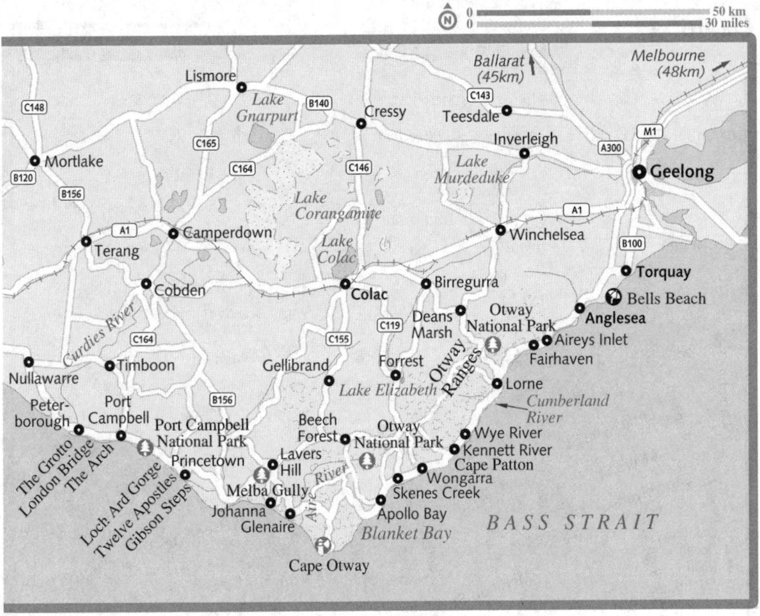

Edge Geelong PUB $$
(www.edgegeelong.com.au; 6-8 Eastern Beach Rd; mains $15; ⏲9am-11pm Mon-Thu, 9am-1am Fri, 8am-1am Sat, 8am-11pm Sun) Serves hearty portions of pub staples, including chicken parma and porterhouse steak, and delves into tapas. Next to a park, has great views, and is friendly and loved by locals.

Le Parisien FRENCH $$$
(☎03-5229 3110; www.leparisien.com.au; 15 Eastern Beach Rd; mains $40-45; ⏲11am-9.30pm) Feast on classic French cuisine *à l'Australienne* (try the kangaroo fillet) at this ever-popular restaurant right on the water.

Drinking

CQ COCKTAIL BAR
(Level 1, Cunningham Pier, 10 Western Beach Foreshore Rd; ⏲noon-late Thu-Sun) Climb the sweeping steps to CQ, and check out its smart fit-out, and cocktail and 'bites' menus.

Information

Geelong Otway Tourism Visitor Information Centre (www.visitgreatoceanroad.org.au; Princes Hwy; ⏲9am-5pm) Helpful info about everything Geelong. Located at the service station in Little River, about 25km northeast. Also located at the National Wool Museum and on the waterfront.

Getting There & Away

AIR

Jetstar (☎13 15 38; www.jetstar.com) flies domestic routes from nearby Avalon Airport.

BUS

Avalon Airport Shuttle (☎03-5278 8788; www.avalonairportshuttle.com.au) The shuttle meets flights at Avalon Airport and travels to Geelong ($17, 35 minutes), Bellarine and the Great Ocean Road (from $30).

Gull Airport Service (☎03-5222 4966; www.gull.com.au; 45 McKillop St) Operates 12 to 15 services a day between Geelong and Melbourne's Tullamarine Airport ($30, 1¼ hours).

V/Line (☎1800 800 007; www.vline.com.au) V/Line buses run from Geelong to Apollo Bay ($16.40, 2½ hours, two to four daily) via Torquay ($3.60, 30 minutes) and Lorne ($10, 1½ hours). On Monday, Wednesday and Friday a bus continues to Port Campbell ($28.60, 4½ hours) and Warrnambool ($32.20, six hours).

CAR

The 25km Geelong Ring Rd runs from Corio to Waurn Ponds, bypassing Geelong entirely. To get to the city, stay on the Princes Hwy (M1).

TRAIN

V/Line (☎1800 800 007; www.vline.com.au) runs from **Geelong Train Station** (☎03-5226

Geelong

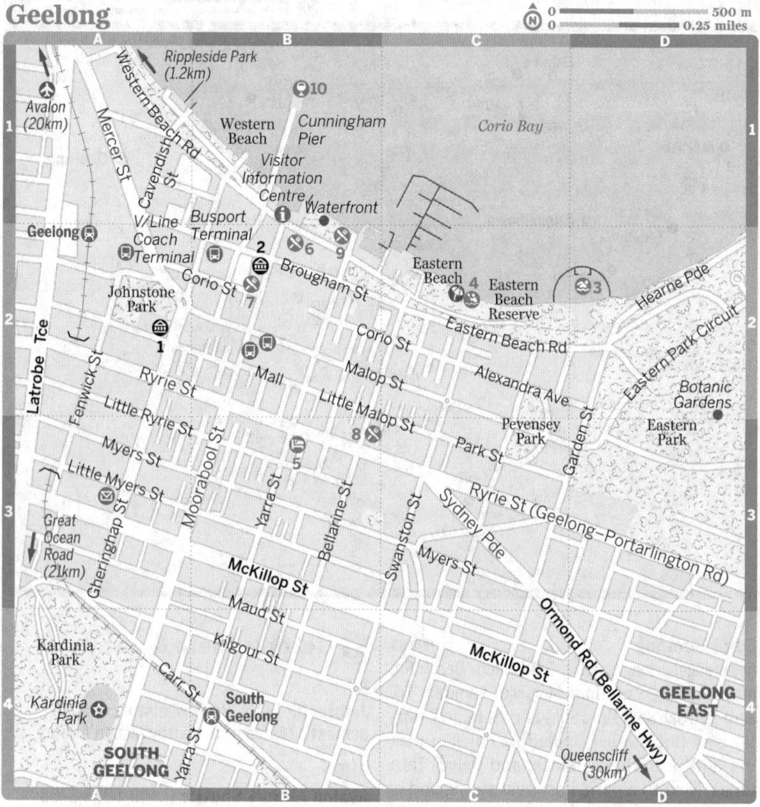

Geelong

Sights
1 Geelong Art Gallery A2
2 National Wool Museum B2

Activities, Courses & Tours
3 Bathing Pavilion D2
4 WSUP C2

Sleeping
5 Gatehouse on Ryrie B3

Eating
6 Edge Geelong B2
7 Fuel B2
8 Go! B3
9 Le Parisien B2

Drinking & Nightlife
10 CQ B1

6525; Gordon Ave) to Melbourne's Southern Cross Station ($11, one hour, frequently). Trains also head to Warrnambool ($22.20, 2½ hours, three daily).

Torquay

POP 13,600

In the 1960s and '70s, Torquay was just another sleepy seaside town. Back then surfing in Australia was a decidedly counter-cultural pursuit, and its devotees were crusty hippy drop-outs living in clapped-out Kombis, smoking pot and making off with your daughters. Since then surfing has become unabashedly mainstream, a huge transglobal business. The town's proximity to world-famous Bells Beach and status as home of two iconic surf brands – Ripcurl and Quiksilver, both initially wetsuit makers –

ensures Torquay is the undisputed capital of Australian surfing.

Sights & Activities

Surf World Museum
MUSEUM

(www.surfworld.com.au; Surf City Plaza, Beach Rd; adult/child/family $10/6/20; ⊙9am-5pm) Embedded at the rear of the Surf City Plaza is this homage to Australian surfing, with shifting exhibits, a theatre and displays of old photos and rare and unique surfboards.

Spring Creek Horse Rides
HORSE RIDING

(✔03-5266 1541; www.springcreekhorserides.com.au; 245 Portheath Rd; 1/2hr rides $45/65) Guided horse rides through Spring Creek Valley.

Go Ride a Wave
SURFING

(✔1300 132 441; www.gorideawave.com.au; 1/15 Bell St; 2hr lessons incl hire $65; ⊙9am-5pm summer) Hires surfing gear, sells secondhand equipment and offers lessons (cheaper when booked in advance).

Westcoast Surf School
SURFING

(✔03-5261 2241; www.westcoastsurfschool.com; 2hr lessons $55; ⊙9am-5pm summer) Runs beginner lessons each weekend from November until Easter.

Torquay Surfing Academy
SURFING

(✔03-5261 2022; www.torquaysurf.com.au; 34a Bell St; 2hr lessons $60; ⊙9am-5pm) Surf school offering travellers' surf passes for $99 (inclues two-hour surf lesson and four-hour board hire) and return packages from Melbourne for $149.

Sleeping

Home @ Bells Beach
HOSTEL $

(✔03-5261 4029; www.homehostels.com.au; 51-53 Surfcoast Hwy; dm/d $28/90; @🛜) Refurbished and given a new life by the @home crew, this budget option is on the highway and has shared facilities and surfboard hire. Reception staff go surfing from 2pm to 5pm.

Torquay Foreshore Caravan Park
CAMPGROUND, CABINS $

(✔03-52612496; www.torquaycaravanpark.com.au; powered sites $31-65, d cabins $75-275) Just behind Back Beach but close to town is the largest camping ground on the Surf Coast. Facilities include a camp kitchen and recreation room. Pricey luxury cabins offer sea views.

Beachside Accommodation Torquay
APARTMENT $$

(✔03-5261 5258; www.beachsideaccommodation torquay.com.au; 24 Felix Cres; d $100; ❄🛜) Clean, compact and just two minutes from Fishermans Beach, these two units are great value and ideal for a few days' stay.

Bellbrae Harvest
APARTMENT $$$

(✔0438 662 090; www.bellbraeharvest.com.au; 45 Portreath Rd; d $200; ❄) Far from the madding crowd, here are three separate (and stunning) split-level apartments looking onto a dam. Expect rainwater shower heads, kitchenettes, huge flat-screen TVs and lots and lots of peace.

Eating

Cafe Moby
CAFE $

(41 The Esplanade; mains $9-19; ⊙7am-3pm) This old weatherboard on the Esplanade harks back to a time when Torquay was simple. Enjoy the home-baked goodies; it's like living in a sharehouse with a pastry chef.

Scorched
MODERN AUSTRALIAN $$

(✔03-5261 6142; www.scorched.com.au; 17 The Esplanade; mains $26-36; ⊙3-9pm Mon-Thu, 10.30am-9pm Fri-Sun Dec & Jan, 3-9pm Wed-Thu, 10.30am-9pm Fri & Sat, 10.30am-3pm Sun Feb-Nov) This restaurant overlooks the waterfront and has windows that open right up to let the sea breeze in. It's about seasonal food served tapas-style here, so make a reservation and try the grazing plate.

Shopping

Quick Stop Shop
CLOTHING

(17 Baines Crt; ⊙9am-5.30pm) This is the spot to buy Quiksilver cheapies.

Baines Beach Surf Seconds
CLOTHING

(16 Baines Crt; ⊙9am-5.30pm) Head to Baines for RipCurl bargains.

Information

Torquay Visitor Information Centre (www.greatoceanroad.org; Surf City Plaza, Beach Rd; ⊙9am-5pm) Torquay has a well-resourced tourist office next to the Surf World Museum.

Getting There & Away

McHarry's Buslines (✔03-5223 2111; www.mcharrys.com.au) runs buses almost hourly between 7am and 9pm from Geelong Station to Torquay ($3.60, 30 minutes). **V/Line** (✔1800 800 007; www.vline.com.au) has four buses daily from Geelong to Torquay (two on weekends).

If you're driving, Torquay is 15 minutes south of Geelong on the B100.

Torquay to Anglesea

About 7km from Torquay is **Bells Beach** along the Great Ocean Road. The powerful point break at Bells is part of international surfing folklore (it's here, in name only, that Keanu Reeves and Patrick Swayze had their ultimate showdown in the film *Point Break*). It's notoriously inconsistent, but when the long right-hander is working it's one of the longest rides in the country. Since 1973, Bells has hosted the **Rip Curl Pro** (www.aspworldtour.com) every Easter – *the* glamour event on the world-championship ASP World Tour. The Rip Curl Pro regularly decamps to Johanna, two hours west, when fickle Bells isn't working.

Nine kilometres southwest of Torquay is the turn-off to spectacular **Point Addis** (3km after the turn-off). It's a vast sweep of pristine 'clothing optional' beach that attracts surfers, hang-gliders and swimmers. At Point Addis there's a signposted **Koorie Cultural Walk**, a 1km circuit trail to the beach through the **Ironbark Basin** nature reserve.

The **Surf Coast Walk** (www.visitgreatoceanroad.org.au/surfcoastwalk) takes walkers along coastlines and through the hinterland from Point Impossible to Fairhaven and can be done in stages – the full route is 44km. Pick up the *Surf Coast Walk* map from visitor centres.

Anglesea

POP 2500

Anglesea's **Main Beach** is the ideal spot to learn to surf, while sheltered **Point Roadknight Beach** is good for kiddies. Check out the resident kangaroo population at the town's golf course (up Noble St), or hire a paddle boat and cruise up the Anglesea River.

Activities

Go Ride A Wave SURFING
(☎1300 132 441; www.gorideawave.com.au; 143b Great Ocean Rd; ⏲9am-5pm) Rents out kayaks and surfboards and runs two-hour surfing lessons (from $65).

Sleeping

Anglesea Backpackers HOSTEL $$
(☎03-5263 2664; www.angleseabackpackers.com; 40 Noble St; dm/d/family $35/115/150) This compact, clean and bright backpackers has one dorm room, a double, and a family room. From town, head over the bridge and take the first right.

Rivergums B&B B&B $$
(☎03-5263 3066; www.anglesearivergums.com.au; 10 Bingley Pde; d $100-160; ❄) Opposite the river, this B&B offers either a self-contained bungalow or a private river-facing room with kitchenette adjoining the house. Both are spacious and impeccably clean.

Eating

Red Till CAFE $
(143a Great Ocean Rd; ⏲7am-4pm daily Dec & Jan, Sat-Mon & Thur Feb-Nov; 📶) This cafe, on the outskirts of town, does coffee and retro decor as good as its Melbourne peers do – only the pace of life is different. It's known for its vegetarian breakfasts. Check out its beachside kiosk at Point Roadknight over summer.

Locanda Del Mare ITALIAN $$
(5 Diggers Pde; mains $20-28; ⏲6-8.30pm daily Dec & Jan, closed Wed Feb-Nov) This authentic Italian restaurant hidden behind Anglesea's petrol station gets rave reviews, especially for its wonderful desserts.

Information

Anglesea Visitor Information Centre (Anglesea River Bank, Great Ocean Rd; ⏲9am-5pm) Get your information then cook up some sausages in the adjacent BBQ area.

Getting There & Away

V/Line (☎1800 800 007; www.vline.com.au) has services linking Anglesea with Geelong and the Great Ocean Road.

The Geelong bypass has reduced the time it takes to drive from Melbourne to Anglesea to around 75 minutes.

HARD YAKKA

The first sections of the Great Ocean Road were constructed by hand (using picks, shovels and crowbars) by returned WWI soldiers. Work began in September 1919 and the road between Anglesea and Apollo Bay was completed in 1932.

Aireys Inlet

POP 700

You've got to love a town where the locals pitched in and reclaimed the pub as their own. Not only that, Aireys Inlet is home to a **lighthouse** (c 1891) and glorious stretches of beach, including horse-friendly **Fairhaven** and hang-glider hot spot **Moggs Creek**.

Sights & ctivities

Blazing Saddles HORSE RIDING
(03-5289 7322; www.blazingsaddlestrailrides.com; Lot 1 Bimbadeen Dr; 1¼/2½hr rides $45/95) Hop on a horse and head into the bush or along the stunning beach (or both).

Split Point Lighthouse Tours LIGHTHOUSE
(1800 174 045; www.splitpointlighthouse.com.au; adult/child $12/7; 10am-4pm Jan, 11am-2pm Feb-Dec) Head up 34m-high Split Point Lighthouse and take in the views on a guided 45-minute tour.

Sleeping

Cimarron B&B B&B $$
(03-5289 7044; www.cimarron.com.au; 105 Gilbert St; d incl breakfast $150-175;) This house was built in 1979 from local timbers using only wooden pegs and shiplap joins, and is an idyllic getaway for traditional B&B seekers. Choose from a loft-style double with vaulted timber ceilings and Point Roadknight views, or the cosy downstairs apartment. Out back, it's all state park and wildlife. Gay-friendly, but no kids.

Lightkeepers Inn MOTEL $$
(03-5289 6666; www.lightkeepersinn.com.au; 64 Great Ocean Rd; d $110;) Expect clean motel rooms with extra thick walls for peace and quiet. Trevor runs the place and has an excellent knowledge of local walks and mountain-biking opportunities.

Eating

A La Grecque GREEK $$
(03-5289 6922; www.alagrecque.com.au; 60 Great Ocean Rd; mains $28-38; 9-11.30am, 12.30-2.30pm & 6-10pm daily Dec-Mar, Wed-Sun Apr-Nov, closed Jun-Aug) This modern Greek taverna is outstanding and serves meze including cured kingfish with apple, celery and a lime dressing, and mains like chargrilled cuttlefish. The verandah is an ideal spot to lunch mid-drive.

Lorne

POP 1400

Lorne has an incredible natural beauty; tall gum trees line its hilly streets and Loutit Bay gleams irresistibly. Lorne gets busy; in summer you'll be competing with day-trippers for restaurant seats and boutique bargains but, thronged with tourists or not, Lorne is a lovely place to hang out.

Sights & Activities

Qdos Art Gallery GALLERY
(03-5289 1989; www.qdosarts.com; 35 Allenvale Rd; 8.30am-6pm daily Dec & Jan, 9am-5.30pm Thu-Mon Feb-Nov) FREE Qdos, tucked in the hills behind Lorne, always has something arty in its galleries, and sculptures dot its Aussie bush landscape. Its cafe fare is nothing but delicious, and you can stay the night in one of the luxury Zen treehouses ($225 per night, two-night minimum, no kids).

Erskine Falls WATERFALL
Head out of town to see this lovely waterfall. It's an easy walk to the viewing platform or 250 (often slippery) steps down to its base, from which you can explore further or head back on up.

Festivals & Events

Falls Festival MUSIC
(www.fallsfestival.com; tickets $310-410) A four-day knees-up over New Year's on a farm out of town featuring a top line-up of rock and indie groups. Tickets include camping.

Sleeping

There's often a minimum two-night stay on weekends in Lorne, and high-season rates can be nearly double winter prices. For other options, ask at the visitor centre.

Great Ocean Road Backpackers HOSTEL $
(03-5289 1070; 10 Erskine Ave; dm/d $35/90;) Tucked away in the bush among the cockatoos and koalas is this two-storey timber lodge with simple dorms and doubles. There's a pleasant deck and small kitchen.

Lorne Foreshore Caravan Park CAMPGROUND $
(1300 364 797; www.lornecaravanpark.com.au; 2 Great Ocean Rd; powered sites $32-60, cabins from $70) Book here for Lorne's five caravan parks. Erskine River Park is the prettiest; on the left-hand side as you enter Lorne, just

before the bridge. Book well ahead for peak-season stays.

Chapel COTTAGES $$$
(☎03-5289 2622; thechapellorne@bigpond.com; 45 Richardson Blvd; d $200; ❄) Outstanding – this contemporary two-level bungalow has tasteful Asian furnishings, splashes of colour and bay windows (without curtains) that open into the forest. It's secluded and romantic.

Allenvale Cottages COTTAGES $$$
(☎03-5289 1450; www.allenvale.com.au; 150 Allenvale Rd; d from $215) These four self-contained early-1900s timber cottages each sleep four (or more), and have been luxuriously restored. They're 2km northwest of Lorne, arrayed among shady trees and green lawns, complete with bridge, babbling brook and clucking chickens. Ideal for families.

Eating

Bottle of Milk BURGERS $
(www.thebottleofmilk.com; 52 Mountjoy Pde; burgers from $8.50; ⏲6.30am-9pm daily high season, 8am-3pm Mon-Fri & 8am-8pm Sat & Sun low season) Sit back on one of the old-school chairs at this cool version of a diner, and tuck into a classic burger stacked with fresh ingredients. Check out Pizza Pizza by the river (it's run by the same clever folk).

Mexican Republic MEXICAN $
(☎03-5289 1686; 1a Grove Rd; large plates $12-14; ⏲noon-9pm high season, call for low season hours) Mexican isn't only a Melbourne phenomenon; Lorne welcomed a brand new Mexican restaurant in 2012. Tostaditas come with pork shoulder or pumpkin; large plates offer marinated chicken burritos or black bean quesadillas. Wine here is served in a latte glass.

Information

Lorne Visitor Centre (☎1300 891 152; www.visitsurfcoast.com.au; 15 Mountjoy Pde; ⏲9am-5pm) Stacks of information, helpful staff and an accommodation booking service.

Cumberland River

Just 7km southwest of Lorne is Cumberland River. There's nothing much here – no shops or houses – other than the wonderful **Cumberland River Holiday Park** (☎03-5289 1790; www.cumberlandriver.com.au; Great Ocean Rd; unpowered sites $37, en-suite cabins from $95). This splendidly located bushy camping ground is next to a lovely river and high craggy cliffs that rise on the far side.

Wye River

POP 230

The Great Ocean Road snakes spectacularly around the cliff-side from Cumberland River before reaching this little town with big ideas.

Wye River Foreshore Camping Reserve CAMPGROUND $
(☎03-5289 0412; sites $30; ⏲Nov-Apr) This camping site offers powered beachside sites during summer and has laid-back appeal.

★**Wye General** CAFE $$
(www.thewyegeneral.com; 35 Great Ocean Rd; dinner $15-26; ⏲8am-10pm) There's nothing general about this terrific cafe and shop. From inhouse pastries to take-home meals ($11 to $15), this smart indoor-outdoor joint has polished concrete floors, timber features and an impressive confidence.

Kennett River

About 5km along from Wye River is Kennett River, which has some truly great **koala spotting**. In town, just behind the caravan park, walk 200m up Grey River Rd and you'll see bundles of sleepy koalas clinging to the branches. *Ooh aah!* **Glow worms** light up the same stretch at night (take a torch).

Kennett River Holiday Park CAMPGROUND, CABINS $
(☎1300 664 417, 03-5289 0272; www.kennettriver.com; unpowered/powered sites $50/55, cabins from $95; @📶) This friendly holiday park has free wireless internet, free BBQs and plenty of koalas. Rates are 40% cheaper off-peak.

Apollo Bay

POP 1100

Apollo Bay is synonymous with music festivals, the Otways and lovely beaches. Majestic rolling hills provide a postcard backdrop to the town, while broad, white-sand beaches dominate the foreground. It's an ideal base for exploring magical Cape Otway and Otway National Park.

Sights & Activities

Community Market MARKET
(www.apollobay.com/market_place; 9am-1pm Sat) This market is held along the main strip and is the perfect spot for picking up local apples, locally made souvenirs and just-what-you've-always-wanted table lamps made from tree stumps.

Apollo Bay Sea Kayaking KAYAKING
(0405 495 909; www.apollobaysurfkayak.com.au; 2hr tours $65) Head out from Marengo beach to an Australian fur seal colony on a two-seated kayak. Not recommended for under 12s.

Apollo Bay Fishing & Adventure Tours SCENIC TOURS
(03-5237 7888; www.apollobayfishing.com.au; 4hr trips adult/child $110/90) Reel in the big'uns on a four-hour adventure or go for a one-hour seal encounter ($35).

Otway Expeditions ADVENTURE SPORTS
(03-5237 6341; http://otwayexpeditions.tripod.com; argo rides/mountain bike tours $45/65) Take a dual-suspension bike through the Otways or on 15 purpose-built tracks (minimum five people), or go nuts in an amphibious all-terrain 8x8 argo buggy. See iRide Apollo Bay on Facebook.

Festivals & Events

Apollo Bay Music Festival MUSIC
(03-5237 6761; www.apollobaymusicfestival.com; weekend pass $125, under 15 free) Held over a weekend in early April this three-day festival features classical, folk, blues, jazz, rock and some edgy contemporary sounds too. The town truly comes alive.

Sleeping

There are 11 camp sites in the Western Otways, run by **Parks Victoria** (13 19 63; www.parkweb.vic.gov.au) Some have facilities, some have none; best of all, they're free. The closest to Apollo Bay is Beauchamp Falls, inland towards Beech Forest.

★ **YHA Eco Beach** HOSTEL $
(03-5237 7899; 5 Pascoe St; dm $35-42, d $85-102, f $100-122; @) Even if you're not on a budget, this three-million-dollar, architect-designed hostel is an outstanding place to stay. Its eco-credentials are too many to list here, but it's a wonderful piece of architecture with great lounge areas, kitchens, TV rooms, an internet lounge and a rooftop terrace.

> DON'T MISS
>
> ### WALKING THE GREAT OCEAN ROAD
>
> The multiday **Great Ocean Walk** (www.greatoceanwalk.com.au) starts at Apollo Bay and runs all the way to the Twelve Apostles – you can do shorter walks, or the whole 104km trek over eight days. Designated camp sites ($25 per site) are spread along the walk; pre-book through **Parks Victoria** (13 19 63; wwww.parkweb.vic.gov.au) two weeks in advance. It's possible to start at one point and arrange a pick-up at another (there are few public transport options): **Walk 91** (03-5237 1189; www.walk91.com.au) arranges transport, equipment hire and can take your backpack to your destination for you; **GOR Shuttle** (03-5237 9278, 0428 379 278) is a recommended shuttle service for luggage and walkers – they'll pick you up when your walking's done.

Surfside Backpackers HOSTEL $
(03-5237 7263; www.surfsidebackpacker.com; cnr Great Ocean Rd & Gambier St; dm $23-30, d $65;) Awesome water views, rooms with character and updates where it counts (a new kitchen, for example) make this homey backpackers worth considering.

Nelson's Perch B&B B&B $$
(03-5237 7176; www.nelsonsperch.com; 54 Nelson St; d incl breakfast $185; @) Nelson's looks fresher than some of the town's weary B&Bs, though it's not close to the bay. There are three smart rooms, each with a courtyard.

Eating

Apollo Bay Fishermen's Co-op SEAFOOD $
(Breakwater Rd; 11am-7pm) Sells fresh fish and seafood from the wharf as well as uber-fresh fish and chips.

Wickens Provedore & Deli CAFE $
(137 Great Ocean Rd; $7-12; 8am-5pm Dec-Jan, closed Tue Feb-Nov;) How do you like your coffee? Here you can choose from cold drip Chemex or, well, your standard (but the beans will still be interesting). It's Melbourne, albeit with a more sun-bleached clientele. Great food menu, too.

Chris's Beacon Point Restaurant GREEK $$
(☎03-5237 6411; www.chriss.com.au; 280 Skenes Creek Rd; mains $30-48; ⏲noon-2pm Sat & Sun, from 6pm daily) A hilltop fine-dining sanctuary with breathtaking views over Bass Strait and Apollo Bay, 6km away. It's a beautifully designed restaurant serving up fresh seafood with a Greek spin.

La Bimba MODERN AUSTRALIAN $$$
(☎03-5237 7411; 125 Great Ocean Rd; mains $36-42; ⏲8am-3.30pm & 6-10pm) This upstairs Mod Oz restaurant is outstanding – definitely worth the splurge. It's a warm, relaxed smart-casual place with views, friendly service and a good wine list.

Information

Great Ocean Road Visitor Centre (☎1300 689 297; 100 Great Ocean Rd; ⏲9am-5pm) Sells discount tickets and pins up accommodation vacancy sheets for those who arrive after hours.

Around Apollo Bay

Seventeen kilometres past Apollo Bay is **Maits Rest Rainforest Boardwalk**, an easy 20-minute rainforest-gully walk. Inland, 5km from Beech Forest, is the **Otway Fly** (☎03-5235 9200; www.otwayfly.com; Phillips Track; adult/child/family $24/9.50/55; ⏲9am-5pm, last entry 4pm). Do the 25m-high tree-top walk or add abseiling or a 3½ hour zip-line tour (adult/child $104/75) to the mix. The views of the forest canopy are especially good from the 47m-high lookout tower.

Cape Otway

Cape Otway is the second-most southerly point of mainland Australia (after Wilsons Promontory) and one of the wettest parts of the state. This coastline is particularly beautiful, rugged and dangerous. More than 200 ships came to grief between Cape Otway and Port Fairy between the 1830s and 1930s, which led to its 'Shipwreck Coast' moniker. At the end of Lighthouse Rd is Australia's oldest lighthouse, the **Cape Otway Lightstation** (☎03-5237 9240; www.lightstation.com; Lighthouse Rd; adult/child/family $19/8/47; ⏲9am-5pm), dating back to 1848. You can't see anything from the car park, and an entry fee is required to view the lighthouse. Inside you'll find a cafe, an art gallery, roaming actors and a haunted lightkeeper's house.

Blanket Bay CAMPGROUND $
(☎13 19 63; www.parkweb.vic.gov.au; sites high season # Easter $14, low season free) Blanket Bay is serene (depending on your neighbours) and the nearby beach is beautiful. This spot is so popular that from Christmas to late January sites must be won by ballot (held in October).

Bimbi Park CAMPGROUND, CABINS $
(☎03-5237 9246; www.bimbipark.com.au; Manna Gum Dr; unpowered/powered sites $30/35, cabins $60-185; 📶) Down a dirt road 3km from the lighthouse is this pleasant accommodation spot. Pitch your tent or stay in one of the fancy (or not-so-fancy) cabins. There's a climbing tower ($15 per hour) and horse rides ($55 per hour).

Great Ocean Ecolodge ECO-LODGE $$$
(☎03-5237 9297; www.greatoceanecolodge.com; 635 Lighthouse Rd; s/d incl breakfast from $260/380) 🍃 Love Australia's iconic animals? Book a room here and you might find a young koala resting in reception. The attached Conservation Ecology Centre rescues and rehabilitates wildlife. The rooms are luxurious post-and-beam creations and the mud-brick lodge is solar-powered. Rates (which help fund the centre) include an evening walking tour and eco-activities.

Lighthouse Keeper's Residence B&B $$$
(Cape Otway Lightstation; www.lightstation.com; Lighthouse Rd; d from $255) Options at this windswept spot include booking the whole Head Lightkeeper's House (sleeps 16), or the smaller Manager's B&B (sleeps two). Rooms are showing their age. Camp your van here overnight for $25.

Cape Otway to Port Campbell National Park

After Cape Otway, the Great Ocean Road levels out and enters the fertile Horden Vale flats, returning briefly to the coast at tiny **Glenaire**. Then the road returns inland and begins the climb up to **Lavers Hill**. On overcast or rainy days the hills here can be seriously fog-bound, and the twists and turns can be challenging when you can't see the end of your car bonnet.

Six kilometres north of Glenaire, a 5km detour goes down Red Johanna Rd winding through rolling hills and past grazing cows to the wild thrashing surf of **Johanna Beach** (forget swimming). The world-famous Rip Curl Pro surfing competition relocates here when Bells Beach isn't working.

Camping Ground CAMPGROUND
(Parks Victoria; ☎13 19 63; www.parkweb.vic.gov.au) FREE This Johanna campground is on a protected grassy area between the dunes and the rolling hills. Book ahead, but there are no fees due or permits required. There's an ablutions facility, but fires are banned and you'll need to bring in your own drinking water.

Boomerangs APARTMENT $$$
(☎03-5237 4213; www.theboomerangs.com; cnr Great Ocean & Red Johanna Rds; d from $230;) These boomerang-shaped cabins have vaulted ceilings, jarrah floorboards, leadlighting, spas and commanding views of the Johanna Valley. The on-site owners are lovely.

Port Campbell National Park

The road levels out after leaving the Otways and enters narrow, relatively flat scrubby escarpment lands that fall away to sheer, 70m cliffs along the coast between Princetown and Peterborough – a distinct change of scene. This is Port Campbell National Park, home to the Twelve Apostles – the most famous and photographed stretch of the Great Ocean Road. For eons, waves and tides have crashed against the soft limestone rock, eroding, undercutting and carving out a fascinating series of rock stacks, gorges, arches and blowholes.

The **Gibson Steps**, hacked by hand into the cliffs in the 19th century by local landowner Hugh Gibson (and more recently replaced by concrete steps), lead down to feral **Gibson Beach**, an essential stop. This beach, and others along this stretch of coast, is not suitable for swimming because of strong currents and undertows – you can walk along the beach, but be careful not to be stranded by high tides or nasty waves.

The lonely **Twelve Apostles** are rocky stacks that have been abandoned in the ocean by retreating headland. Today, only seven Apostles can be seen from the viewing platforms. The understated roadside **lookout** (Great Ocean Rd; ⌚9am-5pm), 6km past Princetown, has public toilets and a cafe. Helicopters zoom around the Twelve Apostles, giving passengers an amazing view of the rocks. **12 Apostles Helicopters** (☎03-5598 8283; www.12apostleshelicopters.com.au) is just behind the car park at the lookout and offers a 10-minute tour covering the Twelve Apostles, Loch Ard Gorge, Sentinel Rock and Port Campbell for $145 per person (including a DVD).

Nearby **Loch Ard Gorge** is where the Shipwreck Coast's most famous and haunting tale, in which two young survivors of the wrecked iron clipper *Loch Ard* made it to shore, unfolded.

Port Campbell

POP 600

This small, windswept town is poised on a dramatic, natural bay, eroded from the surrounding limestone cliffs, and almost perfectly rectangular in shape. It's a friendly place with some great bargain accommodation options, and makes an ideal spot for debriefing after the Twelve Apostles. The tiny bay has a lovely sandy beach, the only safe place for swimming along this tempestuous coast.

Sights & Activities

There is stunning **diving** in the kelp forests, canyons and tunnels of the **Arches Marine Sanctuary** and to the **Loch Ard wreck**. There are shore dives from **Wild Dog Cove** and **Crofts Bay**. A 4.7km **Discovery Walk**, with signage, gives an introduction to the area's natural and historical features. It's just out of town on the way to Warrnambool.

Tours

Most tours depart Melbourne and cover the Great Ocean Road in a day, including Great Ocean Road 'Classic' or 'Sunset' tours run by **Bunyip Tours** (☎1300 286 947; www.bunyiptours.com).

Port Campbell Touring Company TOUR
(☎03-5598 6424; www.portcampbelltouring.com.au; half-day tours $85) Runs evening and day tours from Port Campbell and two to three day tours from Melbourne.

Port Campbell Boat Charters FISHING
(☎03-5598 6411; www.portcampbellboatcharters.com.au; from $50) Runs diving, scenic and fishing tours.

Adventure Tours TOUR
(☎1800 068 886; www.adventuretours.com.au; $130) Day trips from Melbourne along the

Great Ocean Road to the Twelve Apostles (and back).

Autopia Tours TOUR
(☎03-9391 0261; www.autopiatours.com.au; tours $125) One day along the Great Ocean Road, with dinner (not included) in Colac.

Go West Tours TOUR
(☎1300 736 551; www.gowest.com.au; tousr $120) Full-day tour exploring the Great Ocean Road with lunch and wi-fi included.

Otway Discovery Tour TOUR
(☎03-9629 5844; www.greatoceanroadtour.com.au; tours $95) A cheap Great Ocean Road tour that includes Bells Beach and the Twelve Apostles.

Ride Tours TOUR
(☎1800 605 120; www.ridetours.com.au; tours $195) Two-day, one-night trips along the Great Ocean Road. Includes breakfast, dinner and accommodation.

Sleeping & Eating

Port Campbell Guesthouse GUESTHOUSE $
(☎0407 696 559; www.portcampbellguesthouse.com.au; 54 Lord St; s/d incl breakfast $40/70; ❄@) It's great to find a home away from home, and this property close to town has a cosy house with four bedrooms out back and a separate motel-style 'flashpackers' section up front. Clean and friendly.

Port Campbell Hostel HOSTEL $
(☎03-5598 6305; www.portcampbellhostel.com.au; 18 Tregea St; dm/d $25/72; @📶) This purpose-built double-storey backpackers has rooms with western views, a huge shared kitchen and an even bigger lounge-bar area. It's big on recycling and the toilets are ecofriendly, too. Hang out in the lounge and read the day's papers or get involved with a Mills & Boon.

12 Rocks Cafe Bar CAFE $$
(19 Lord St; mains $20-30; ⏲8.30am-11pm) Watch flotsam wash up on the beach from this busy place, which has the best beachfront views. Try a local Otways beer with a pasta or seafood main, or just duck in for a coffee.

Waves Restaurant MODERN AUSTRALIA, CAFE $$
(www.wavesportcampbell.com.au; 29 Lord St; mains $30; ⏲8am-8pm) Not a place to go if you're in a hurry, but the menu ranges from scones and jam in the afternoon to a seafood platter for two in the evening.

Information

Port Campbell Visitor Centre (☎1300 137 255; www.visit12apostles.com.au; 26 Morris St; ⏲9am-5pm) Stacks of regional and accommodation information and interesting shipwreck displays – the anchor from the *Loch Ard*, salvaged in 1978, is out the front.

Getting There & Away

V/Line (☎1800 800 007; www.vline.com.au) trains depart Southern Cross Station in Melbourne 9am Monday, Wednesday and Friday; change to a bus in Geelong for Port Campbell ($33, 6½ hours).

Port Campbell to Warrnambool

The Great Ocean Road continues west of Port Campbell passing more rock stacks. The next one is the **Arch**, offshore from Point Hesse.

Nearby is **London Bridge**...fallen down! Now sometimes called London Arch, it was

THE WRECK OF THE LOCH ARD

The Victorian coastline between Cape Otway and Port Fairy was a notoriously treacherous stretch of water in the days of sailing ships, due to hidden reefs and frequent heavy fog. Over 40 years more than 80 vessels came to grief on this 120km stretch.

The most famous wreck was that of the iron-hulled clipper *Loch Ard*, which foundered off Mutton Bird Island at 4am on the final night of its long voyage from England in 1878. Of 37 crew and 19 passengers on board, only two survived. Eva Carmichael, a nonswimmer, clung to wreckage and was washed into a gorge, where apprentice officer Tom Pearce rescued her. Tom heroically climbed the sheer cliff and raised the alarm but no other survivors were found. Eva and Tom were both 19 years old, leading to speculation in the press about a romance, but nothing actually happened – they never saw each other again and Eva soon returned to Ireland (this time, perhaps not surprisingly) via steamship.

HOW MANY APOSTLES?

The Twelve Apostles are not 12 in number, and, from all records, never have been. From the viewing platform you can clearly count seven Apostles, though are there some obscure others over there? We consulted widely with Parks Victoria officers, tourist office staff and the cleaner at the lookout, but it's still not clear. Locals tend to say 'It depends where you look from', which, really, is true.

The Apostles are called 'stacks' in geologic lingo, and the rock formations were originally called the Sow and Piglets. Someone in the '60s (nobody can recall who) thought they might attract some tourists with a more venerable name, so they were renamed 'the Apostles'. Since apostles tend to come by the dozen, the number 12 was added sometime later. The two stacks on the eastern (Otway) side of the viewing platform are not technically Apostles – they're Gog and Magog (picking up on the religious nomenclature yet?).

So there aren't 12 stacks; in a boat or helicopter you might count 11. The soft limestone cliffs are dynamic and changeable, constantly eroded by the unceasing waves – one 70m-high stack collapsed into the sea in July 2005 and the Island Archway lost its archway in June 2009. If you look carefully at how the waves lick around the pointy part of the cliff base, you can see a new Apostle being born. The labour lasts many thousands of years.

once a double-arched rock platform linked to the mainland. Visitors could walk out across a narrow natural bridge to the huge rock formation. In January 1990 the bridge collapsed, leaving two terrified tourists marooned on the world's newest island – they were eventually rescued by helicopter. Nearby is the **Grotto**.

The **Bay of Islands** is 8km west of tiny **Peterborough**, where a short walk from the car park takes you to magnificent lookout points.

You can't help but notice the acres and acres of farming land here, and if you're driving keep an eye out for milk trucks pulling slowly into and out of farms. Tacky but fun **Cheese World** (www.cheeseworld.com.au; Great Ocean Rd; ⏲9.30am-4.30pm Mon-Fri, 9am-3pm Sat & 10am-3pm Sun) is opposite the area's main dairy factory, and has a museum, restaurant, cheese cellar and tasty $5 milkshakes. It's 12km before Warrnambool.

The Great Ocean Road ends near here where it meets the Princess Hwy, which continues through the traditional lands of the Gunditjmara people into South Australia.

Warrnambool

POP 32,500

Warrnambool was originally a whaling and sealing station – now it's booming as a major regional commercial and whale-watching centre. Its historic buildings, waterways and tree-lined streets are attractive, especially by the waterfront, and there's a large student population who attend the Warrnambool campus of Deakin University.

Sights & Activities

Flagstaff Hill Maritime Village REPLICA VILLAGE
(☎03-5559 4600; www.flagstaffhill.com; Merri St; adult/child/family $16/7/39; ⏲9am-5pm) This major tourist attraction is modelled on an early Australian coastal port. See the cannon and fortifications, built in 1887 to withstand the perceived threat of Russian invasion, and **Shipwrecked** (adult/child/family $26/14/6), an engaging evening sound-and-laser show of the *Loch Ard*'s plunge.

Logan's Beach Whale-Watching Platform WHALE WATCHING
Southern right whales come to mate and nurse their bubs in the waters off Logan's Beach from July to September, breaching and fluking off the platform. It's a major tourist drawcard, but sightings are not guaranteed. The information centre knows what's going on whale-wise, so give them a call to find out if there are whales around.

Warrnambool Art Gallery GALLERY
(www.warrnambool.vic.gov.au; 165 Timor St; ⏲10am-5pm Mon-Fri, noon-5pm Sat & Sun) FREE The permanent Australian collection includes such notable painters as James Gleeson, Robert Dowling and Eugene von Guérard.

Rundell's Mahogany Trail Rides HORSE RIDING
(☎0408 589 546; www.rundellshorseriding.com.au; 2hr beach rides $70) Get to know some of Warrnambool's quiet beach spots by horseback.

Sleeping

Warrnambool Beach Backpackers HOSTEL $
(☎03-5562 4874; www.beachbackpackers.com.au; 17 Stanley St; dm/d $26/80; P @) Close to the sea, through the jail door, this former museum has a huge living area with a bar, internet access, kitchen and free pick-up. Borrow a surfboard ($20) or bike ($15) and explore.

Atwood Motor Inn MOTEL $
(☎03-5562 7144; www.atwoodmotorinn.com.au; 8 Spence St; d from $95; P) Expect spacious motel-style rooms with flat-screen TVs and bathrooms big enough to wash a (small) whale in. The standard doubles are the smallest, but are still comfortable.

Hotel Warrnambool PUB $$
(☎03-5562 2377; www.hotelwarrnambool.com.au; cnr Koroit & Kepler Sts; d with/without bathroom $140/110; P) Recent renovations in this historic 1894 pub have done wonders for the rooms, which have plasma TVs and access to a kitchenette and lounge. Some have bathrooms and balconies. Downstairs is one of the busiest pub-eateries in town.

Eating & Drinking

Wyton Eating House CAFE $
(www.wytonevents.com; 91 Kepler St; mains $12; 9am-6.30pm Mon-Sat) Just to confuse you, there are two cafes sharing a name on this street. Both have great food and excellent coffee; Wyton Eating House at No 91 has healthy salads and pastas that you can take away, while up the road Wyton Cellars at No 127 has delectable raspberry and white chocolate muffins.

Warrnambool Bowls Club PUB $
(☎03-5561 4586; www.warrnamboolbowls.com.au; 75 Timor St; mains $10; 11.30am-2pm daily plus 5.30-7.30pm Tue & Wed, 6-8pm Thu-Mon) Even if you're not wearing bowling whites you can dine at Warrnambool's busy lawn bowls club. Here a glass of decent wine costs less than $5 and specials will set you back $10. You're unlikely to be the oldest one in the room. Bookings advised.

Fishtales Café CAFE $
(☎03-5561 2957; 63 Liebig St; mains $7-16; 7am-9pm) A cheery cafe serving burgers, fish and chips and vegetarian specials, with a sunny courtyard out the back.

Information

Warrnambool Visitor Centre (☎1800 637 725; www.visitwarrnambool.com.au; Merri St; 9am-5pm) Located in the Flagstaff Hill complex, this visitor centre produces a useful travel map and has bicycle hire ($30 per day).

Getting There & Away

V/Line (☎1800 800 007; www.vline.com.au; Merri St) trains depart Melbourne's Southern Cross Station for Geelong, from where you can take a bus along the Great Ocean Road to Warrnambool ($31, eight hours). A direct V/Line train links Warrnambool to Melbourne ($31, 3½ hours, three daily).

There are regular V/Line buses from Warrnambool to Port Fairy ($4.20, 25 minutes) and four continue to Portland ($11, 1½ hours). There's a bus on Monday, Wednesday and Friday to Apollo Bay ($19, 3½ hours). A bus from Warrnambool to Halls Gap ($25, 2 hours), in the Grampians, departs Warrnambool 7.45am on Tuesday and Friday and 8.15am on Sunday.

Tower Hill Reserve

Tower Hill, 15km west of Warrnambool, is a vast caldera born in a volcanic eruption 35,000 years ago. Aboriginal artefacts unearthed in the volcanic ash show that indigenous people lived in the area at the time. It's one of the few places where you'll spot wild emus, kangaroos and koalas hanging out together.

There are excellent day walks, including the steep 30-minute **Peak Climb** with spectacular 360-degree views.

Tower Hill Reserve Visitors Centre TOURIST INFORMATION
(☎03-5561 5315; 10am-4pm) This info centre run by the Worn Gundidj Aboriginal Cooperative is a lovely spot to learn about the area's pre-settlement history and buy souvenirs. See a copy of Eugene von Guérard's painting of Tower Hill in 1855 (the real one's in Warrnambool Art Gallery).

Port Fairy

POP 3100

This seaside township at the mouth of the Moyne River was settled in 1835, and the first arrivals were whalers and sealers. Port Fairy still has a large fishing fleet and a relaxed, salty feel, with its old bluestone and sandstone buildings, whitewashed cottages, colourful fishing boats and tree-lined streets. The town is very much a luxury tourist destination and is home to art galleries, antique shops and boutiques.

⊙ Sights & Activities

The visitor centre has brochures and maps that show the popular **Shipwreck Walk** and **History Walk**. On **Battery Hill** there's a lookout point, and cannons and fortifications that were positioned here in the 1860s. Below there's a lovely one-hour walk around **Griffiths Island**, where the Moyne River empties into the sea. The island is connected to the mainland by a footbridge, and is home to a protected **mutton-bird colony** (they descend on the town each October and stay until April) and a modest **lighthouse**.

✦ Festivals & Events

Port Fairy Folk Festival　　MUSIC
(www.portfairyfolkfestival.com; adult/child 13-17 $235/80) Australia's premier folk-music festival is held on the Labour Day long weekend in early March. Book accommodation early.

⊨ Sleeping

Port Fairy YHA　　HOSTEL $
(☑ 03-5568 2468; www.portfairyhostel.com.au; 8 Cox St; dm $26-30, d/f/2-bed apt from $80/130/250; @ 🛜) In the rambling 1844 (former) home of merchant William Rutledge, this friendly and well-run hostel (the oldest in Australia) has a large kitchen, a pool table and free cable TV.

Pelican Waters　　CABINS $$
(☑ 03-5568 1002; www.pelicanwatersportfairy.com.au; 34 Regent St; cabins & carriages from $100; ❄) Why stay in a hotel when you can sleep in a train? This beautifully presented property has cabins as well as two two-bedroom converted Melbourne train carriages.

Daisies by the Sea B&B　　B&B $$
(☑ 03-5568 2355; www.port-fairy.com/daisiesbythesea; 222 Griffiths St; d incl breakfast from $160; ❄🛜) Nod off to the sound of the crashing waves just 50m from your door in these two cosy beachfront suites, 1.5km from town.

✕ Eating

Rebecca's Cafe　　CAFE $
(70-72 Sackville St; mains $9-16; ⊙7am-6pm) Excellent for breakfast and light lunches, Rebecca's has interesting items on the menu including rich wild-rice porridge topped with rhubarb, as well as the usual cakes, muffins, slices, scones and biscuits.

Merrijig Inn　　MEDITERRANEAN $$$
(☑ 03-5568 2324; www.merrijiginn.com; cnr Campbell & Gipps Sts; mains $30-38; ⊙6-9pm Thu-Mon) Seasonal is the key to dining here; the friendly owners have a lovely kitchen garden and you'll no doubt be eating something from that. The front bar (c 1842) opens daily at 4pm, and you can really settle in if you've booked an upstairs attic room ($140, including breakfast).

Stag　　MODERN AUSTRALIAN $$$
(☑ 03-5568 3229; 22 Sackville St; mains $32-38; ⊙6-10pm Tue-Sat) Sometimes seafood done simply is all you want in a fishing town, and the Stag does it beautifully. Here it's served in a smart atmosphere, with attentive service and a long wine list.

MELBOURNE & VICTORIA PORT FAIRY

CAPE BRIDGEWATER

Cape Bridgewater is a 21km detour off the Portland–Nelson Rd. The stunning 4km arc of **Bridgewater Bay** is perhaps one of Australia's finest stretches of white-sand surf beach, backed by pristine dunes. The windy farm-lined road continues to **Cape Duquesne** where walking tracks lead to a **blowhole** and the **Petrified Forest** on the cliff-top. A longer two-hour return walk takes you to a **seal colony** where you can see dozens of fur seals sunning themselves on the rocks.

Stay at friendly **Sea View Lodge B&B** (☑ 03-5526 7276; Bridgewater Rd; s/d incl breakfast $110/140; 🛜), or **Cape Bridgewater Coastal Camp** (☑ 03-5526 7247; www.capebridgewatercoastalcamp.com.au; Blowhole Rd; unpowered sites/dm/houses $20/30/150), which has sparkling dorms, self-contained houses and a huge camp kitchen. The camp also runs fun **Seals by Sea tours** (☑ 03-5526 7247; adult/child $35/20).

Information

Port Fairy Visitor Centre (03-5568 2682; www.visitportfairy-moyneshire.com.au; Bank St; 9am-5pm) Can recharge your mobile phone's battery while providing spot-on information.

Getting There & Away

V/Line (1800 800 007; www.vline.com.au) buses connect to Portland ($7.80, one hour), Warrnambool ($4.20, 25 minutes) and, on Tuesday, Friday and Sunday, Halls Gap ($25, two hours).

Port Fairy is 20 minutes west of Warrnambool on the A1.

Portland

POP 9800

There's a charm to largish Portland; it has historic houses, a bunch of ghost stories and is a short distance from a lovely lighthouse. It's also the start and end of the **Great South West Walk**. Portland was Victoria's first European settlement, and became a whaling and sealing base in the early 1800s. Blessed Mary MacKillop, Australia's first saint, arrived here from Melbourne in 1862 and founded Australia's first religious order.

Sleeping & Eating

Portland Holiday Village CAMPGROUND $
(03-5523 7567; www.holidayvillage.com.au; 37 Percy St; unpowered/powered sites from $20/40, cabins from $85;) This central caravan park has decent facilities including a large camp kitchen. The cheaper cabins have shared bathrooms.

GREAT SOUTH WEST WALK

This 250km signposted loop begins and ends at Portland's information centre, and takes in some of the southwest's most stunning natural scenery, from the remote, blustery coast, through the river system of the Lower Glenelg National Park and back through the hinterland to Portland. The whole loop would take at least 10 days, but it can be done in sections. Maps are available from the Portland visitor centre and the Parks Victoria and visitor centre in Nelson. Also check out the walk's own website www.greatsouthwestwalk.com.

★ **Annesley House** BOUTIQUE HOTEL $$
(0429 852 235; www.annesleyhouse.com.au; 60 Julia St; d from $145;) This recently restored former doctor's mansion (c 1878) has six very different self-contained rooms, some featuring clawfoot baths and lovely views. All feature a unique sense of style. Highly recommended.

Deegan Seafoods FISH & CHIPS $
(106 Percy St; mains $10; 11am-8pm Mon-Fri) This fish-and-chip shop serves up some of the freshest fish in Victoria.

Information

Portland Visitor Centre (1800 035 567; www.glenelg.vic.gov.au; Lee Breakwater Rd; 9am-5pm) In the impressive-looking Maritime Discovery Centre.

Getting There & Away

V/Line (1800 800 007; www.vline.com.au) buses connect Portland with Port Fairy three times daily and once on Sunday ($7.80, 55 minutes), and also with Warrnambool ($11, 1½ hours).

Nelson

POP 230

Tiny Nelson is the last vestige of civilisation before the South Australian border – with just a general store, pub and handful of accommodation places. It's a popular holiday and fishing spot at the mouth of the **Glenelg River**, which flows through **Lower Glenelg National Park**. Note that Nelson uses South Australia's 08 telephone area code. Why? We dunno!

Sights & Activities

Nelson Boat & Canoe Hire BOATING
(08-8738 4048; www.nelsonboatandcanoehire.com.au) This outfit can rig you up for serious river-camping expeditions – canoe hire costs from $65 a day. It also has paddle boats for hire for $20 for 30 minutes.

Glenelg River Cruises CRUISE
(08-8738 4191; cruises adult/child $30/10) Cruises depart Nelson daily (except Thursday and Monday) at 1pm for a leisurely 3½-hour cruise to the **Princess Margaret Rose Cave** (08-8738 4171; www.princessmargaretrosecave.com; adult/child/family $16/10/37). If you travel to the cave on your own, you'll find it about 17km from Nelson, towards the border.

Sleeping & Eating

There are nine **camp sites** between Nelson and Dartmoor along the Glenelg River that are popular with canoeists but are also accessible by road. They have rain-fed water tanks, toilets and fire places (BYO firewood). Forest Camp South is the nicest, right on the river, rich in bird life and easily accessible from the Portland–Nelson Rd. Camping permits are issued by Parks Victoria in Nelson or online.

Nelson Hotel PUB $
(08-8738 4011; www.nelsonhotel.com.au; Kellett St; d/apt incl breakfast from $60/110, mains $17-30; noon-2pm & 6-8.30pm;) This hotel has a dusty stuffed pelican above the bar and plenty of fried food on the menu. The quarters are plain but adequate with shared facilities, and the attached studio is fine for a night.

Information

Parks Victoria & Nelson Visitor Centre
(08-8738 4051; http://parkweb.vic.gov.au; 9am-5pm) Just before the Glenelg River bridge.

GRAMPIANS & THE WESTERN DISTRICTS

Western Victoria is a large expanse of wheat fields, grain silos, rolling farmland and sheep properties known as the Wimmera (west) and the Mallee (northwest), separated by the Western Hwy (Rte A8), the main inland route between Melbourne and Adelaide. In the far northwest, large swathes of this land are given over to desert national parks. You'll also find outliers of the Great Dividing Range – the star attraction out here is the Grampians National Park, while further west Mt Arapiles State Park is one of Australia's most famous rock-climbing venues, and the Little Desert National Park is a good spot for hiking and camping.

Getting There & Away

The *Overland*, the Melbourne–Adelaide train, runs through the Wimmera, stopping at Ararat, Stawell, Horsham and Dimboola, three times a week. **V/Line** (13 61 96; www.vline.com.au) has train and bus services between Melbourne and major towns.

Firefly Express (1300 730 740; www.fireflyexpress.com.au) and **Greyhound Australia** (1300 473 946; www.greyhound.com.au) also pass through Horsham daily on their Melbourne–Adelaide run. From Horsham you can take a bus north to Mildura and south to Hamilton and Portland.

DON'T MISS

CAPE NELSON LIGHTHOUSE

Cape Nelson Lighthouse is a wonderful spot for a flash bite to eat and some stunning views. **Isabella's Cafe** (03-5523 5119; 10am-4pm) takes pride of place at its blustering base and offers excellent deli-style food within its thick bluestone walls. **Lighthouse tours** (adult/child $15/10; 10am & 2pm) get you high up, while those wanting to stay a while can book a self-contained **Assistant Lighthouse Keepers' Cottage** (www.capenelsonlighthouse.com.au; d from $180).

Grampians National Park

The Grampians (known as Gariwerd to local Koories) is a paradise for bushwalkers and rockclimbers and is one of Victoria's most outstanding natural features. The rich diversity of flora and fauna, unique sandstone rock formations, Aboriginal rock art and accessible walking trails offer something for everyone. The hills are at their best in spring, when wildflowers carpet the ranges.

Sealed access roads in the park run from Halls Gap south to Dunkeld and northwest through the park to the Wartook Valley and Horsham. Off these roads are side trips to some of the park's most notable sights such as **McKenzies Falls**, **Reed Lookout** for walks to the Balconies, **Boroka Lookout** and the **Zumstein Picnic Area**.

Close to Halls Gap, the **Wonderland Range** has some spectacular and accessible scenery. There are scenic drives and walks, from an easy stroll to Venus Bath (30 minutes) to a walk up to the Pinnacles Lookout (five hours). Walking tracks start from Halls Gap, and the Wonderland and Sundial car parks.

Like many parts of Victoria, the Grampians have been affected by both fires and floods in recent years – check with Parks Victoria about track conditions.

Sleeping

Parks Victoria maintains 11 **camp sites** (site per vehicle or 6 people $17.60) throughout the

The Grampians (Gariwerd)

0 10 km
0 5 miles

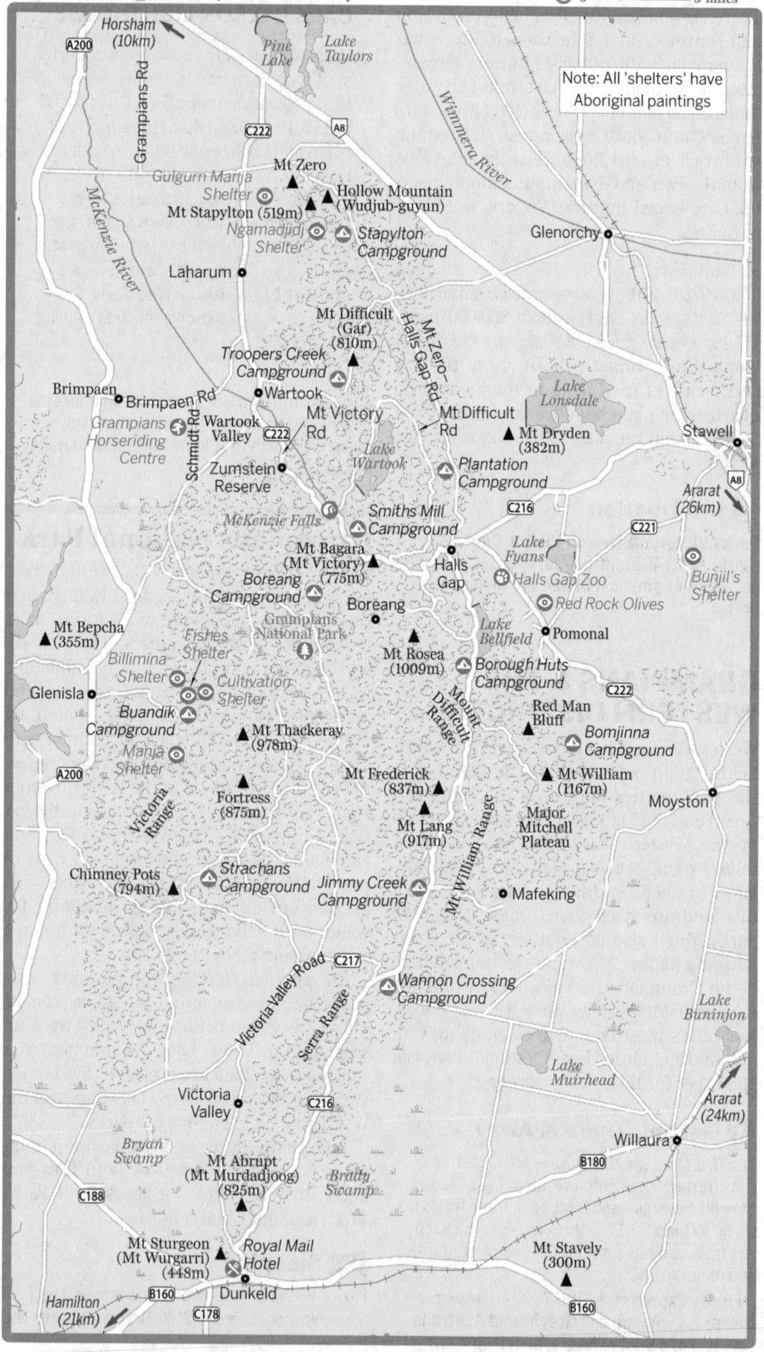
Horsham (10km)
A200
Grampians Rd
Pine Lake
Lake Taylors
Note: All 'shelters' have Aboriginal paintings
Wimmera River
C222
A8
Mt Zero
Gulgurn Manja Shelter
Hollow Mountain (Wudjub-guyun)
Mt Stapylton (519m)
McKenzie River
Ngamadjidj Shelter
Stapylton Campground
Glenorchy
Laharum
Mt Difficult (Gar) (810m)
Mt Zero–Halls Gap Rd
Troopers Creek Campground
Lake Lonsdale
Brimpaen
Brimpaen Rd
Wartook
Grampians Horseriding Centre
Schmidt Rd
Wartook Valley
C222
Mt Victory Rd
Mt Difficult Rd
Mt Dryden (382m)
Stawell
Lake Wartook
Zumstein Reserve
Plantation Campground
A8
Ararat (26km)
C216
McKenzie Falls
Smiths Mill Campground
C221
Lake Fyans
Mt Bagara (Mt Victory) (775m)
Halls Gap
Halls Gap Zoo
Bunjil's Shelter
Boreang Campground
Red Rock Olives
Boreang
Mt Bepcha (355m)
Fishes Shelter
Grampians National Park
Lake Bellfield
Pomonal
Mt Rosea (1009m)
Billimina Shelter
Borough Huts Campground
Glenisla
Cultivation Shelter
Mount Difficult Range
C222
Buandik Campground
Red Man Bluff
Mt Thackeray (978m)
Bomjinna Campground
Manja Shelter
A200
Mt Frederick (837m)
Mt William (1167m)
Fortress (875m)
Moyston
Victoria Range
Mt Lang (917m)
Major Mitchell Plateau
Mt William Range
Chimney Pots (794m)
Strachans Campground
Jimmy Creek Campground
Mafeking
Victoria Valley Road
C217
Wannon Crossing Campground
Serra Range
Lake Buninjon
Lake Muirhead
Ararat (24km)
Victoria Valley
C216
Willaura
Bryan Swamp
Mt Abrupt (Mt Murdadjoog) (825m)
Brady Swamp
B180
C188
Mt Sturgeon (Mt Wurgarri) (448m)
Royal Mail Hotel
Mt Stavely (300m)
Dunkeld
Hamilton (21km)
B160
C178
B160

park, with toilets, picnic tables and fireplaces (BYO drinking water). Permits are required; you can register and pay at the office of the Brambuk Cultural Centre in Halls Gap. Our favourite sites are Smiths Mill, near MacKenzies Falls, and Stapylton, the northern section.

Information

Halls Gap Visitor Centre (1800 065 599; www.grampianstravel.com.au; Grampians Rd; 9am-5pm) Helpful staff can book tours, accommodation and activities.

Parks Victoria (13 19 63, 03-5361 4000; www.parkweb.vic.gov.au) In the same complex as the Brambuk Cultural Centre, with maps and brochures, camping permits and fishing licences.

Getting There & Away

V/Line (13 61 96; www.vline.com.au) has a daily train/coach service from Melbourne to Halls Gap ($30.10, four to five hours), with changes required at Ballarat and/or Stawell. There are three buses a day Monday to Friday and one on Saturday and Sunday between Halls Gap and Stawell ($6.30, 35 minutes).

Christians Bus Company runs a service between Ararat and Warrnambool on Tuesday, Friday and Sunday, stopping at Halls Gap, Dunkeld, Hamilton and Port Fairy.

ROCK ART

Traditional Aboriginal owners have been occupying Gariwerd for more than 20,000 years and it is the most accessible place in Victoria to see indigenous rock art. Sites include **Bunjil's Shelter**, near Stawell, one of Victoria's most sacred indigenous sites and best seen on a guided tour from the Brambuk Cultural Centre (adult/child $50/30). Rock-art sites in the west of the park are the **Manja Shelter** (Cave of Hands), reached from the Harrop Track car park, and the **Billimina Shelter**, near the Buandik campground. In the north is the **Ngamadjidj Shelter**, reached from the Stapylton campground.

Halls Gap

POP 305

Spread out below the craggy Wonderland Range, Halls Gap is a pretty little one-street town – sleepy in winter but mighty busy during holidays. This is the main accommodation base and easiest access for the best of the Grampians. Here kangaroos graze on front lawns and the air is thick with the songs of kookaburras and parrots. The main street through town has a neat little knot of shops, a supermarket, adventure activity offices, restaurants and cafes.

This is the place to organise adventure activities like rock climbing, hiking, biking, and kayaking on Lake Bellfield or Lake Wartook.

Annual events include the **Grampians Jazz Festival** in February, and the **Halls Gap Film Festival** in November.

Sights & Activities

★**Brambuk Cultural Centre** CULTURAL CENTRE
(03-5361 4000; www.brambuk.com.au; Grampians Tourist Rd; 9am-5pm) FREE Your first stop should be this superb cultural centre, 2.5km south of Halls Gap. The building itself is a striking design that combines timeless Aboriginal motifs with contemporary design and building materials. Run by five Koorie communities in conjunction with Parks Victoria, the centre offers insights into local culture and history through Koorie stories, art, music, dance, weapons, tools and photographs. The **Gariwerd Dreaming Theatre** (adult/child/family $5/3/12) shows hourly films explaining Dreaming stories of Gariwerd and the creation story of Bunjil. Three-hour cultural and **rock-art tours** can be booked here.

The complex includes the Parks Victoria office, a souvenir shop and **Brambuk Bushfoods Café** (meals $11-26; 9am-4pm), with a lovely deck overlooking the gardens.

Halls Gap Zoo ZOO
(5356 4668; www.hallsgapzoo.com.au; adult/child/family $18/9/45; 10am-5pm Wed-Mon) Get up close to Australian native animals such as wallabies, grey kangaroos, quolls and wombats, but also exotic critters like meerkats, spider monkeys, bison and tamarin. There are breeding and conservation programs, and various 'meet the animals'-type encounters at an extra charge – the website has timings.

Tours

Absolute Outdoors ADVENTURE
(03-5356 4556; www.absoluteoutdoors.com.au; 105 Main Rd) Rock climbing, abseiling, moun-

tain-biking, canoeing and guided nature walks from $60. Mountain-bike hire costs $10/25/40 per hour/half-/full day.

Eco Platypus Tours DAY TRIP
(☎1800 819 091; www.ecoplatypustours.com; tours $99) Full-day bus tour from Melbourne visiting the main sights in the northern Grampians.

Fitopia ADVENTURE
(☎0408 838 950; www.grampiansactivitytours.com.au) Hires kayaks, catamarans and mountain bikes but the cool money is on the 'blo-kart' and dirt buggy adventures.

Grampians Horseriding Adventures HORSE RIDING
(☎03-5383 9255; www.grampianshorseriding.com.au; 430 Schmidt Rd, Wartook Valley; 2½hr rides $100; ⏲10am & 2pm) Horse-riding adventures around a grand property with sweeping views.

Grampians Mountain Adventure Company ADVENTURE
(GMAC; ☎0427 747 047; www.grampiansadventure.com.au; half-/full day from $95/145) Specialises in rock-climbing and abseiling adventures.

Grampians Personalised Tours & Adventures ADVENTURE
(☎0429 954 686, 03-5356 4654; www.grampianstours.com) Offers a range of 4WD tours (half/full day from $79/149), guided bushwalks, night walks ($20) and scenic flights over the ranges (three/five people $170/280).

Hangin' Out ROCK CLIMBING
(☎03-5356 4535, 0407 684 831; www.hanginout.com.au; 4hr/full day rock climbing $75/130) Get started with a four-hour introductory session.

Sleeping

★**Grampians YHA Eco-Hostel** HOSTEL $
(☎03-5356 4544; www.yha.com.au; cnr Grampians Tourist Rd & Buckler St; dm/d $34/89; @) This architecturally designed and eco-friendly hostel utilises solar power and rainwater tanks and makes the most of light and space. It's beautifully equipped with a spacious lounge with open fire, MasterChef-quality kitchen and spotless rooms.

Brambuk Backpackers HOSTEL $
(☎03-5356 4250; www.brambuk.com.au; Grampians Tourist Rd; dm/d $28/68; @ wi-fi) Across from the cultural centre, this friendly Aboriginal-owned and -run hostel gives you a calming sense of place with a relaxed feel and craggy views from the lounge windows.

Tim's Place HOSTEL $
(☎03-5356 4288; www.timsplace.com.au; 44 Grampians Rd; dm/s/d $27/55/70, apt from $90; @ wi-fi) Friendly, spotless backpackers with homely eco-feel; free mountain bikes, wi-fi and herb garden.

Halls Gap Caravan Park CAMPGROUND $
(☎03-5356 4251; www.hallsgapcaravanpark.com.au; Grampians Rd; unpowered/powered sites from $27/34, cabins $85-150; ❄) Camping and cabins right in the town centre.

D'Altons Resort COTTAGES $$
(☎03-5356 4666; www.daltonsresort.com.au; 48 Glen St; studio/deluxe/family cottages from $110/125/160; ❄ wi-fi) These lovely timber cottages, with cosy lounge chairs, cute verandahs and log fires, spread up the hill back from the main road. Deluxe rooms come with spa. Great value.

Pinnacle Holiday Lodge MOTEL $$
(☎03-5356 4249; www.pinnacleholiday.com.au; 21-45 Heath St; 1-/2-bedroom unit $112-167, d with spa $140-175; ❄ pool) This well-kept and central property behind the Stony Creek shops is a cut above most of Halls Gap's motels. The spacious grounds have a real bucolic feel and have barbecue areas, an indoor pool and tennis courts.

Mountain Grand Guesthouse GUESTHOUSE $$
(☎03-5356 4232; www.mountaingrand.com.au; Grampians Tourist Rd; s/d incl breakfast $146/166; ❄ wi-fi) This gracious, old-fashioned timber guesthouse prides itself on being a traditional lodge where you can take a pre-dinner port in one of the lounge areas and mingle with other guests. The rooms are small but clean.

Eating

Halls Gap's small selection of eateries (and supermarket) are mostly along Grampians Tourist Rd and the boardwalk beside pretty Stony Creek, where the bakery makes sublime vanilla slices, and the Pink Panther Café does good pizzas. In the Smugglers Hearth souvenir shop you'll find delicious homemade fudge from the Grampians Fudge Factory.

Livefast Lifestyle Cafe CAFE $
(www.livefast.com.au; Shop 5 Stony Creek Stores; light meals $8-16, mains $24-28; ⏲7am-5pm,

7am-late Wed-Sun) Good strong coffee, sunny atmosphere and energetic staff are the hallmarks of this cafe, where you can get an early breakfast, fat focaccia for lunch, or call in for a glass of Grampians wine with some live music in the evening.

Kookaburra Restaurant MODERN AUSTRALIAN **$$**
(☎03-5356 4222; www.kookaburrabarbistro.com.au; 125-127 Grampians Rd; mains $24-34; ⏰from 6pm Tue-Sun, also noon-3pm Sun) This Halls Gap institution is renowned for its crispy-skin duck, Aussie dishes like barramundi and kangaroo fillet, and the tavern-style bar. There's a good-value 'eat early' deal if you order by 6.30pm.

Halls Gap Hotel PUB **$$**
(☎03-5356 4566; www.hallsgaphotel.com.au; 2262 Grampians Rd; mains $15-32; ⏰noon-2pm Wed-Sun, from 6pm daily) For generous no-nonsense bistro food and pizzas, you can't beat the local pub, about 2km north of town. With views of the Grampians, it's a social place for a beer after a day's bushwalking.

Dunkeld

The southern access to the Grampians, Dunkeld is a sleepy little town in the shadows of dramatic **Mt Abrupt** and **Mt Sturgeon**, both of which you can hike. Its **visitor centre** (☎03-5577 2558; www.visitsoutherngrampians.com.au; Parker St) has useful information.

The **Royal Mail Hotel** (☎03-5577 2241; www.royalmail.com.au; Parker St; bar meals $18-34, restaurant menu $180; ⏰bar & bistro noon-2pm & 6-9pm, restaurant from 6pm Wed-Sun) is a historic pub transformed into a stylish modern hotel with a fine bar, bistro and one of Victoria's top restaurants.

In November, the **Dunkeld Cup** is a fun country race meeting.

Horsham

POP 15,260

The major town to the northwest of the Grampians, and the capital of the Wimmera region, Horsham has good transport connections and makes a convenient base for exploring the surrounding national parks and Mt Arapiles.

Horsham Regional Art Gallery GALLERY
(☎03-5362 2888; www.horshamartgallery.com.au; 21 Roberts Ave; gold coin donation; ⏰10am-5pm Tue-Fri, 1-4.30pm Sat & Sun) Houses the Mack Jost Collection of significant Australian artists, including works by Rupert Bunny, Sir Sidney Nolan, John Olsen and Charles Blackman.

Grampians & Horsham Visitor Centre TOURIST INFORMATION
(☎03-5382 1832; www.visithorsham.com.au; 20 O'Callaghan's Pde; ⏰9am-5pm) Has information on accommodation and the surrounding areas.

Mt Arapiles State Park

Mt Arapiles, a sandstone lump rising from the otherwise flat Wimmera plains 37km west of Horsham, is Victoria's premier rock-climbing destination. At 369m it's not a very big mountain, but with more than 3000 routes to scale, it attracts salivating climbers from around the world. In the tiny nearby town of Natimuk (12km east), a community of avid climbers has set up shop to service visitors, and the town has also developed into something of a centre for artists.

Even if you're not into climbing, you can drive or walk (1.7km from Centenary Park) to the summit for sensational views over the plains.

Activities

Arapiles Mountain Shop ROCK CLIMBING
(☎03-5387 1529; 67 Main St) Sells and hires climbing equipment.

Arapiles Climbing Guides ROCK CLIMBING
(☎03-5384 0376; www.arapiles.com.au; Natimuk) Professional instructors and guides.

Natimuk Climbing Company ROCK CLIMBING
(☎03-5387 1329; www.climbco.com.au; 6 Jory St) Advanced courses and guide hire.

Sleeping & Eating

Pines Camping Ground CAMPGROUND **$**
(Centenary Park; camp sites $4) Most climbers head for this popular site at the base of the mountain, which is 2km in from the park entrance. There's bore water but no showers.

National Hotel HOTEL **$**
(☎03-5387 1300; 65 Main St; d $65-75) The pub in Natimuk has tidy cabins at the back and pub rooms upstairs, plus counter meals.

Little Desert National Park

Of all western Victoria's desert national parks, this is among the most accessible, though its rich diversity of plants and wildflowers belies the 'desert' tag. Two sealed roads between the Western and Wimmera Hwys pass through the park, or you can take the well-maintained gravel road from Dimboola. The park's best-known resident is the mallee fowl.

For a brief introduction to the park there are several well-signposted walks: south of Dimboola is the **Pomponderoo Hill Nature Walk**, south of Nhill is the **Stringybark Nature Walk** and south of Kiata is the **Sanctuary Nature Walk**.

Sleeping

There are national park **camping grounds** (camp sites $17.60) in the eastern block at Horseshoe Bend and Ackle Bend, both on the Wimmera River south of Dimboola, and south of Kiata.

★Little Desert Nature Lodge CAMPGROUND, RESORT $
(03-5391 5232; www.littledesertlodge.com.au; camp sites $25, bunkhouse d $44, B&B s/d $115/125;) On the northern edge of the desert 16km south of Nhill, this bush retreat is a superb base for exploring the park, with a spacious camping ground, bunkhouse, comfortable en-suite motel-style rooms and a restaurant. A key attraction is the tour of the mallee-fowl aviary ($30), where you can see these rare birds in a breeding program,

OFF THE BEATEN TRACK

THE MALLEE

Victoria's emptiest corner, the vast Mallee, takes its name from the mallee scrub that once covered the region. Mallee gums are canny desert survivors – 1000-year-old root systems are not uncommon – and for the indigenous people the region yielded plentiful food. The sky seems vast as you drive through this dead-flat semi-arid region – you don't have to visit central Australia to get a taste of the outback!

The farmers of this district have done it hard during years of drought, with the northern area dependent on the Murray River for water supply. Rains came in 2010–11, rejuvenating the Wimmera River to the south and in turn filling Lake Hindmarsh. National parks in this region are remote, wild and in many areas only accessible by 4WD. Plan ahead: avoid travel in summer, carry plenty of water, don't rely on GPS or a phone signal and seek advice from **Parks Victoria** (13 19 63; www.parkweb.vic.gov.au).

Wyperfeld National Park

Wyperfeld is a vast but accessible park of river red gum, mallee scrub, sand plains and, in the spring, a carpet of native wildflowers. A sealed road from the southern park entrance near **Yaapeet** leads to the visitor centre at **Wonga Campground** (camp sites $17.60), with pit toilets, picnic tables and fireplaces. **Casuarina Campground** (sites free) in the north is reached via a gravel road off the Patchewollock–Baring Rd.

Murray-Sunset National Park

This 6630-sq-km park is arid and much of it is hard to reach. An unsealed road leads from **Linga** on the Mallee Hwy up to the **Pink Lakes** at the southern edge of the park, where there's a basic camping ground. Beyond this you must have a 4WD. The **Shearer's Quarters** (03-5028 1218; dm $61) has basic group accommodation on the park's western side, sleeping up to 14 people.

Hattah-Kulkyne National Park

Hattah-Kulkyne National Park is more accessible and has some fertile riverside areas, lined with red gum, black box, wattles and bottlebrush. The **Hattah Lakes** system fills when the Murray floods and is a great spot for birdwatching and bushwalking.

The access road is at **Hattah**, 70km south of Mildura on the Calder Hwy. The visitor information centre is 5km into the park. There are camp sites ($17.60) at Lake Hattah and Lake Mournpoul, but limited water. Camping is also possible anywhere along the Murray River frontage.

the mallee-fowl sanctuary tour ($130), and the Nocturnal Wildlife Encounter ($30). All tour prices cover two people.

Information

Little Desert Park Office (☎13 19 63; www.parkweb.vic.gov.au; Nursery Rd) Off the Western Hwy south of Dimboola.

Dimboola

On the now-flowing Wimmera River, Dimboola is a classic country town made famous by Jack Hibberd's play *Dimboola*, and the subsequent 1979 John Duigan film of the same name, about a country wedding. The Little Desert National Park entrance is about 4km south of town on what starts out as a sealed road, but from then on becomes gravel.

Dimboola has a caravan park, and budget rooms at the **Victoria Hotel** (☎03-5389 1630; 32 Wimmera St; s/d $35/60).

Riverside Host Farm CABINS $
(☎03-5389 1550; 150 Riverside Rd; sites $25, cabins d $88; ❄) This friendly working farm on a bend in the Wimmera River is a lovely place to stay, with cosy self-contained cabins, camp sites and a rustic open-sided camp kitchen-lounge area with pot-belly stove. Hire canoes or help out with farm activities.

Nhill

Nhill is the main base for the northern entrance to Little Desert National Park and Kiata campground.

Hindmarsh Visitor Centre TOURIST INFORMATION
(☎03-5391 3086; www.hindmarsh.vic.gov.au; Victoria St; ⏰9am-5pm) Information on the park, local sights and accommodation.

MURRAY RIVER

State border, irrigation lifeline and recreational magnet for waterskiers, canoeists, campers and golfers, the mighty Murray is Australia's longest and most important inland waterway. It's a stirring place of paddle steamers and houseboat holidays, wineries and orchards, bush camping, fishing, balmy weather and red gum forests.

The river flows almost 2400km from the Snowy Mountains to Encounter Bay in South Australia, supplying vital irrigation for orchards, vineyards and farms. Some of Australia's earliest explorers travelled along the river, and long before roads and railways crossed the land, the Murray's paddle steamers carried supplies to and from remote sheep stations – you can still cruise on paddle steamers at Mildura, Swan Hill and Echuca. Get off the Murray Valley Hwy along the frequent tracks (often marked 'River access') that lead you to the banks for camping and fishing among magnificent red-gum forests.

Mildura

POP 31,360

Sunny Mildura is a real riviera oasis town – it's as isolated as anywhere you'll find in Victoria, but after driving for hours past parched farmlands, you're greeted by miles of fertile vineyards and citrus orchards and a prosperous riverside city centre. Backpackers flock here for the abundant year-round fruit-picking and agricultural work.

The town developed in the late 1880s when William Chaffey pioneered the irrigation system, and today it's a thriving tourist town with lush golf courses, art-deco buildings, river cruises and as much sunshine as anywhere in the state. The Murray River is the central attraction, but there's plenty to do in the region, including checking out the fine culinary scene on Langtree Ave.

Sights & Activities

Mildura owes much to the Chaffey brothers and their innovative irrigation systems. Pick up a copy of *The Chaffey Trail* from the visitor centre and follow their story. Emerging from the Chaffey vision were the **Mildura Wharf**, now a mooring for paddle boats, the **weir** and the **lock**, which is operated at 11am, 12.30pm, 2pm and 3.30pm, and the **Old Psyche Bend pump station** at Kings Billabong, 8km southeast of town.

Rio Vista & Mildura Arts Centre HISTORIC BUILDING
(☎03-5018 8330; www.milduraartscentre.com.au; 199 Cureton Ave; ⏰10am-5pm) FREE Chaffey's grand homestead, the historic Queen Anne-style Rio Vista, has been beautifully preserved and restored with each room set up as a series of historical displays depicting colonial life in the 19th century.

In the same complex, the Mildura Arts Centre reopened in 2012 after a major up-

Murray River

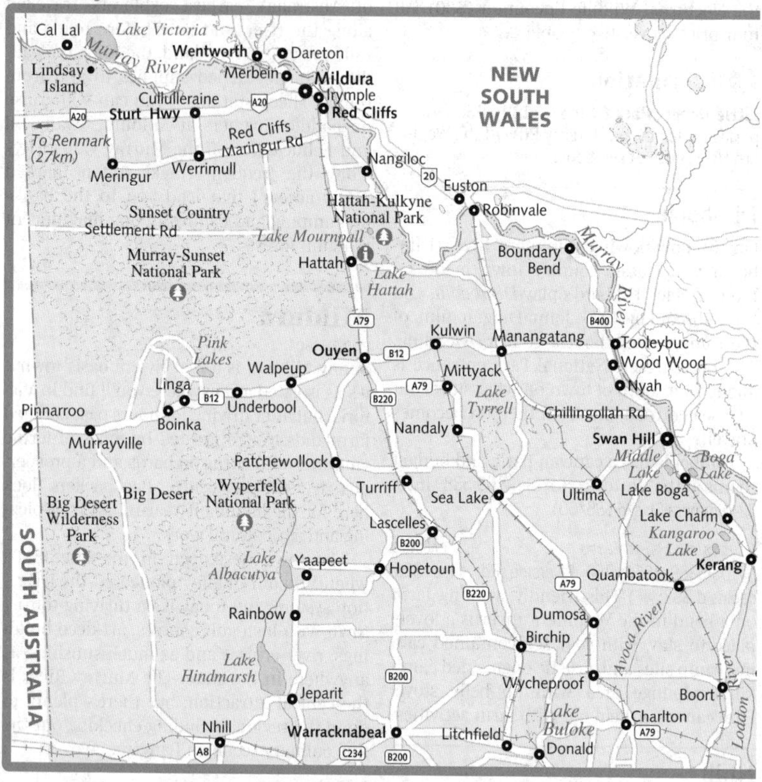

grade. As well as a number of galleries housing permanent and changing exhibitions, there's a state-of-the-art theatre for performing arts, and a cafe.

Old Mildura Homestead HISTORIC SITE
(Cureton Ave; admission by donation; ⏲9am-6pm) Along the river this cottage was the first home of William B Chaffey. The heritage park here contains a few other historic log buildings and has picnic and barbecue facilities.

Apex Beach BEACH
About 3km northwest of the centre is this sandy beach on the Murray, a popular swimming and picnic spot. Kayaks and canoes can be hired from the caravan park (from $30).

Mildura Waves SWIMMING
(☎03-5023 3747; www.milduawaves.com.au; cnr Deakin Ave & 12th St; adult/child from $5.75/3.25; ⏲6am-9pm Mon-Thu, to 7pm Fri, 8am-6pm Sat & Sun) Excellent swimming complex with an artificial wave pool and high diving board.

Tours

Paddle boats depart from the Mildura Wharf. For bookings call ☎03-5023 2200, or go to www.paddlesteamers.com.au.

PS Melbourne CRUISE
(2hr cruise adult/child $27/12; ⏲10.50am & 1.50pm) One of the original paddle steamers, and the only one still driven by steam power. In the off-season this cruise is aboard the PV *Rothbury* on Friday and Saturday.

PV Rothbury CRUISE
(winery cruise adult/child $62/30, lunch cruise $29/13) The fastest of the riverboats. It offers a winery cruise on Thursday, visiting Trentham Winery Estate and with a BBQ lunch at Kings Billabong, and on Tuesday there's a lunch cruise to Gol Gol Hotel.

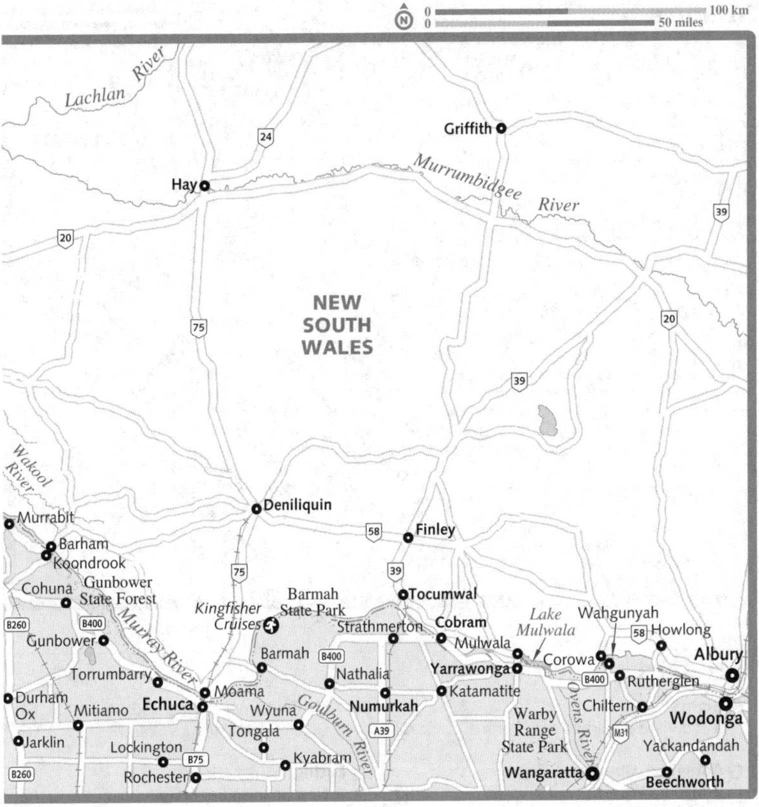

PV Mundoo CRUISE
(dinner cruise adult/child $62/30) Evening dinner cruise every Thursday from 7pm.

Harry Nanya Tours CULTURE
(☎03-5027 2076; www.harrynanyatours.com.au; tours adult/child $180/110, tag along $90/45) Indigenous guide Graham Clarke keeps you enchanted with Dreaming stories and his deep knowledge and understanding of the Mungo region (p232).

Moontongue Eco-Adventures KAYAKING
(☎0427 898 317; www.moontongue.com.au; kayak tours $25-50) A sunset kayaking trip is a great way to see the river and its wildlife.

Wild Side Outdoors ADVENTURE
(☎0428 242 852, 03-5024 3721; www.wildsideoutdoors.com.au) Ecofriendly outfit offering a sunset kayaking tour at Kings Billabong (adult/child $35/15), and canoe/kayak/mountain-bike hire (per hour $30/20/20).

Mildura Ballooning SCENIC FLIGHTS
(☎03-5024 6848; www.milduraballooning.com.au; adult/child $295/195; ⊙dawn) Enjoy the sunrise from the air with a one-hour dawn balloon flight over the wonderful patchwork of vineyards, orchards and the Murray.

Festivals & Events

Mildura Wentworth Arts Festival ARTS
(www.artsmildura.com.au/mwaf) Magical concerts by the river; held in February/March.

Mildura Country Music Festival MUSIC
(www.milduracountrymusic.com.au) Ten days of free concerts in late September/early October.

Mildura Jazz, Food & Wine Festival MUSIC
(www.artsmildura.com.au/jazz) Traditional bands, great food, good wine; held in October or November.

Mildura

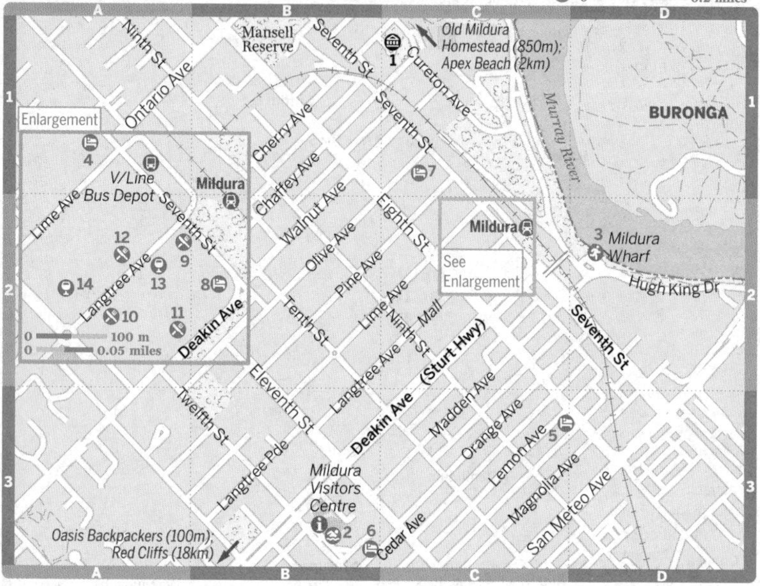

Mildura

Sights

1 Rio Vista & Mildura Arts Centre C1

Activities, Courses & Tours

2 Mildura Waves B3
3 PS Melbourne D2
PV Mundoo............ (see 3)
PV Rothbury............ (see 3)

Sleeping

4 7th Street Motel............A1
5 Mildura City Backpackers............ C3
6 Mildura International Backpackers B3
7 Misty's Manor & Ditto Daddy's C1
8 Quality Hotel Mildura Grand............B2

Eating

9 New Spanish Bar & Grill............A2
Pizza Café at the Grand .... (see 9)
10 Restaurant Rendezvous A2
11 Stefano's Café Bakery A2
Stefano's Restaurant............ (see 8)
12 Thai-riffic............A2

Drinking & Nightlife

13 Mildura Brewery............A2
14 Sandbar A2

Sleeping

Mildura has a dozen or so hostels and budget guesthouses (most geared towards backpackers looking for seasonal work), as well as plenty of caravan parks, motels, hotels – and houseboats. Staying on a houseboat is bliss and the Mildura region has more than a dozen companies that hire houseboats ranging from two to 12 berths and from modest to luxurious.

Apex RiverBeach Holiday Park CAMPGROUND $
(☎03-5023 6879; www.apexriverbeach.com.au; Cureton Ave; unpowered/powered sites $33/38, cabins $85-125; ❄📶) Thanks to a fantastic location on sandy Apex Beach, this bush park is always popular.

Mildura City Backpackers HOSTEL $
(☎03-5022 7922; www.milduracitybackpackers.com.au; 50 Lemon Ave; dm per night/week $22/140, d $55/330) In a heritage weatherboard house, this working hostel has a welcoming feel.

Oasis Backpackers HOSTEL $
(☎0401 344 251, 03-5022 8200; www.milduraoasisbackpackers.com.au; 230-232 Deakin Ave; dm/d

per week $150/320; ❄@📶🏊) Oasis is Mildura's best equipped but rowdiest backpacker hostel, with a great pool and patio bar area. Still, it's aimed squarely at workers, with a minimum one-week stay. The owners can organise seasonal work, though it's not guaranteed.

Mildura International Backpackers HOSTEL $
(☎0408 210 132; www.mildurabackpackers.com.au; 5 Cedar Ave; dm per night/week $25/129; ❄@📶) Basic but friendly house where the rooms have two or four beds (not bunks) and the owners will help you find work.

7th Street Motel MOTEL $
(☎03-5021 1888; www.7thstreetmotelmildura.com.au; 153 Seventh St; s/d/f from $90/95/130; ❄📶🏊) Brilliant location and a warm welcome make this one of Mildura's better-value motels. Decor is old-school, but it's well equipped.

Acacia Holiday Apartments APARTMENT $
(☎03-5023 3855; www.acaciaapartments.com.au; 761 Fifteenth St; d cabins $80-110, 1-/2-/3-bedroom apt from $110/120/160; ❄@📶🏊) Southwest of the centre, these budget cabins and spacious self-contained units offer outstanding value, with discounts for extended stays.

★**Quality Hotel Mildura Grand** HOTEL $$
(☎1800 034 228, 03-5023 0511; www.qualityhotelmilduragrand.com.au; Seventh St; s/d/ste incl breakfast from $80/145/180; ❄📶🏊) The standard rooms at the Grand aren't the most luxurious in town, but staying at this landmark hotel gives you the feeling of being part of something special. Many rooms open onto a delightful courtyard garden, and there's a gym, pool and spa.

Misty's Manor & Ditto Daddy's APARTMENT $$
(☎0419 840 451; www.couplesretreatsmildura.com.au; 16 Olive Ave; d $165-185; ❄📶) These two 'couples only' apartments are spectacular in their design and decoration – an unlikely mix of corrugated iron, stone and recycled timber, with fanciful colour schemes.

Mildura Houseboats HOUSEBOAT $$$
(☎1800 800 842, 03-5024 7770; www.mildurahouseboats.com.au; 3 nights $550-1600) Along with sister company Willandra Houseboats, this family-run outfit has a big range of houseboats.

Eating

Mildura's cafe and restaurant precinct runs along Langtree Ave (otherwise known as 'Feast Street') and around the block dominated by the Grand Hotel. Italian raconteur Stefano de Pieri perhaps single-handedly stamped the town on the foodie map, but others are jumping onboard.

If the budget is tight, look out for cheap meal deals at pubs like the Settlers Tavern.

Stefano's Café Bakery CAFE $
(☎03-5021 3627; 27 Deakin Ave; meals $10-23; ⏲7.30am-4pm Mon-Fri, 7.30am-3pm Sat, 8am-2pm Sun) Fresh bread baked daily, Calabrese eggs, pastries and, of course, good coffee – Stefano's casual daytime cafe and bakery keeps things fresh and simple, with outdoor tables under vine-covered shade. Also a food store, gallery and wine cellar door.

Pizza Café at the Grand PIZZA $
(☎03-5022 2223; www.pizzacafe.com.au; 18 Langtree Ave; pizza & pasta $13-19; ⏲11am-11pm Mon-Thu, 11am-11.30pm Sat, 11.30am-11pm Sun) For simple, inexpensive Italian – with all the atmosphere of the Grand Hotel dining strip – Pizza Café is perfect. The wood-fired pizzas hit the spot but there's also a supporting cast of salads, pastas and chicken dishes.

Thai-riffic THAI $$
(☎03-5021 5225; www.thai-riffic.com.au; 35 Langtree Ave; mains $14-23; ⏲noon-2pm Thu & Fri, 6-11pm Mon-Sat) Soothing decor, sharp service and authentic Thai cuisine makes this a popular Asian experience on Feast Street. The chefs are happy to turn up the heat if you like it spicy.

Restaurant Rendezvous FRENCH $$
(☎03-5023 1571; www.rendezvousmildura.com.au; 34 Langtree Ave; mains $18-39; ⏲noon-4pm Mon-Fri, 6pm-late Mon-Sat) Though almost swallowed up by the Grand, this long-running place has a warm, casual atmosphere that complements the perfectly prepared Mediterranean-style seafood, grills, pastas and crepes.

★**Stefano's Restaurant** ITALIAN $$$
(☎03-5023 0511; Quality Hotel Mildura Grand, Seventh St; set menu $110; ⏲noon-3pm Fri-Sat, from 6pm Mon-Sat,) Descend into the former underground wine cellar at the Grand Hotel to see Stefano work his magic with the ever-changing six- to eight-course Italian degustation. It's an intimate, candle-lit experience and very popular – book well in advance. On

Friday and Saturday there's a two- or three-course lunch menu.

New Spanish Bar & Grill STEAKHOUSE $$$
(☎03-5021 2377; www.seasonsmildura.com.au; cnr Langtree Ave & Seventh St; mains $29-39; ⊙from 6pm Tue-Sun) This carnivore's delight specialises in top-quality steaks and barbecue food, including kangaroo and Mallee T-bone.

Drinking & Entertainment

Mildura has a compact but lively nightlife scene, buoyed by an ever-changing crew of backpackers and itinerant fruit pickers.

★**Mildura Brewery** BREWERY
(☎03-5022 2988; 20 Langtree Ave; ⊙noon-late) Set in the former Astor cinema, this is Mildura's trendiest drinking spot. Shiny stainless-steel vats, pipes and brewing equipment make a great backdrop to the stylish art-deco lounge, and the beers brewed here – honey wheat beer and Mallee Bull among them – are superb. Good food, too.

Sandbar LIVE MUSIC
(☎03-5021 2181; www.thesandbar.com.au; cnr Langtree Ave & Eighth St; ⊙noon-late Tue-Sun) On a balmy evening locals flock to the fabulous beer garden at the back of this lounge bar in a corner art-deco former bank building. Local, national, original and mainstream bands play in the front bar Thursday to Sunday nights.

Information

Mildura Visitor Centre (☎03-5018 8380, 1800 039 043; www.visitmildura.com.au; cnr Deakin Ave & 12th St; ⊙9am-5.30pm Mon-Fri, to 5pm Sat & Sun) In the Alfred Deakin Centre. There's a free accommodation-booking service, interesting displays, a cafe and helpful staff who book tours and activities. Free internet access in the library next door.

SEASONAL WORK

Mildura is king of the casual fruit-picking industry in northwest Victoria. Harvest season runs from January through March, but casual work on farms and orchards is available year-round. Some farmers allow camping but often you'll need to stay in town, so transport may be necessary. Backpacker hostels in Mildura can help line up work and arrange transport (usually for a fee).

Madec Harvest Labour Office (☎03-5021 3472; www.madec.edu.au; 126-130 Deakin Ave) has comprehensive listings of fruit-picking work.

Getting There & Away

AIR

Regional Express Airlines (Rex; ☎13 17 13; www.regionalexpress.com.au), **Qantas** (☎13 13 13; www.qantas.com.au) and **Virgin Australia** (☎13 67 89; www.virginaustralia.com) all fly between Mildura and Melbourne daily. Rex also flies daily to Adelaide, Sydney and Broken Hill.

BUS & TRAIN

Long-distance buses operate from a depot at the train station on Seventh St, but there are currently no passenger trains to or from Mildura.

V/Line (☎1800 800 007; www.vline.com.au) Train/bus service to/from Melbourne via Bendigo or Swan Hill ($41.40, 7½ hours, three daily). V/Line's Murraylink is a daily bus service connecting the towns along the Murray from Mildura: Swan Hill ($24.90, three hours, three daily), Echuca ($34.10, six hours, via Kerang, one daily) and Albury-Wodonga ($42.50, 10 hours, one daily).

Greyhound Australia (☎1300 473 946; www.greyhound.com.au) Buses stop at Mildura on Monday, Wednesday, Thursday and Friday on the route between Adelaide ($80, 5½ hours) and Sydney ($183, 18 hours).

Swan Hill

POP 9900

Swan Hill is a relaxing riverside community without the tourist hype of Mildura or Echuca, but which still boasts a few sights, such as Australia's oldest recreated pioneer museum. It was named by intrepid explorer Major Thomas Mitchell in 1836, after he was kept awake by swans in the nearby lagoon. Today it's an important regional centre surrounded by irrigated farmlands. Fruit pickers can find work on farms about 25km northwest of Swan Hill around Nyah.

Sights & Activities

Pioneer Settlement HISTORIC VILLAGE
(☎03-5036 2410; www.pioneersettlement.com.au; Horseshoe Bend; adult/child/family $26/20/70; ⊙9.30am-4pm) Swan Hill's major attraction is an enjoyable re-creation of a riverside port town. The dusty old-time streets feature shops, an old school and church, vintage car rides, an Aboriginal keeping place and the fascinating Kaiser Stereoscope. Volunteers in period costume enhance the illusion.

The paddle steamer PS *Pyap* makes one-hour **cruises** (adult/child $19.50/14) along the Murray at 2.30pm daily with an additional cruise at 10.30am on weekends and holidays. Every night at dusk a 45-minute **sound-and-light show** (adult/child $19.50/14) brings the historic old town to life. The cruise and show can be combined with admission at a discount.

Swan Hill Regional Art Gallery GALLERY
(☎03-5036 2430; www.swanhillart.com; Horseshoe Bend; admission by donation; ⌚10am-5pm Tue-Sun) Near the Pioneer Settlement, this gallery exhibits the works of contemporary artists.

Sleeping & Eating

Most backpackers looking for fruit-picking work head out to the small communities of Nyah and Nyah West, which has a couple of backpacker hostels. There's also free riverside camping at the Nyah Recreation Reserve.

In Swan Hill, ask at the visitor centre about local homestays. For cheap counter meals Swan Hill has a couple of pubs, as well as the Swan Hill Club.

Riverside Caravan Park CAMPGROUND $
(☎1800 101 012, 03-5032 1494; http://riverside-swanhill-holiday-park.vic.big4.com.au; 1 Monash Dr; unpowered/powered sites from $31/35, cabins $105-160) On the banks of the Murray and close to the Pioneer Settlement, this park enjoys a fabulous central location.

Travellers Rest Motor Inn MOTEL $$
(☎03-5032 9644; www.bestwestern.com.au/travellersrest; 110 Curlewis St; d $145; ❄📶🏊) Right in the middle of town, this modern well-appointed motel sits in the shade of the famous Burke and Wills Tree.

Jilarty Gelato Bar ICE CREAM $
(☎03-5033 0042; 233 Campbell St; ⌚8am-5.30pm Mon-Sat, 10am-4pm Sun) Specialises in gelati with local fruit flavours, along with great coffee and Spanish churros.

★ **Java Spice** THAI $$
(☎03-5033 0511; www.javaspice.com.au; 17 Beveridge St; mains $19-32; ⌚noon-2pm Fri & Sun, from 6pm Tue-Sun; 🌿) Dining under open-sided thatched and teak wood huts in a tropical garden, you'll think you've been transported to Southeast Asia. The authentic cuisine is predominantly Thai, with some Malaysian and Indonesian influences mixed in.

Spoons Riverside Café MODERN AUSTRALIAN $$
(☎03-5032 2601; www.spoonsriverside.com.au; Horseshoe Bend; mains lunch $9.50-17, dinner $26-34; ⌚8am-5pm Sun-Wed, 8am-11pm Thu-Sat) Great location with a big timber deck overlooking the Little Murray River and Pioneer Settlement. As well as lunchtime sandwiches and an evening menu including dishes such as risotto or crispy duck, there's a provedore deli selling fresh produce and gourmet hampers.

Information

Swan Hill Region Information Centre (☎03-5032 3033, 1800 625 373; www.swanhillonline.com; cnr McCrae & Curlewis Sts) The visitor centre has maps, loads of tourist brochures and internet access.

Getting There & Away

Swan Hill is on the Murray Valley Hwy, 218km from Mildura and 156km from Echuca. **V/Line** (☎1800 800 007; www.vline.com.au) has two direct trains between Melbourne and Swan Hill ($35.80, 4½ hours), and some train/coach services with a change at Bendigo. There are daily V/Line coaches to Mildura ($26.60, three hours) and Echuca ($16.40, 2½ hours).

Echuca

POP 12,613

Echuca is the paddle-steamer capital of Victoria and a classic Murray River town, bursting with history, nostalgia and, of course, river boats. The Aboriginal name translates as 'meeting of the waters', as it's here that three great rivers meet – the Goulburn, Campaspe and Murray. The highlight is unquestionably the historic port area and the rivers themselves; while it might feel a bit touristy, the town glows with an upbeat atmosphere and some fabulous restaurants and bars.

Echuca was founded in 1853 by ex-convict Harry Hopwood. At the peak of the river-boat era there were more than 100 paddle steamers plying the waters between Echuca and outback sheep stations. The Melbourne–Echuca railway line opened in 1864 and within a decade, the boom years of the river-boat trade had ended.

Sights

Even if you don't take in the wharf, you can wander down the pedestrian Murray Esplanade, lined with historic buildings, restaurants and a blacksmith and woodturning shop.

Echuca

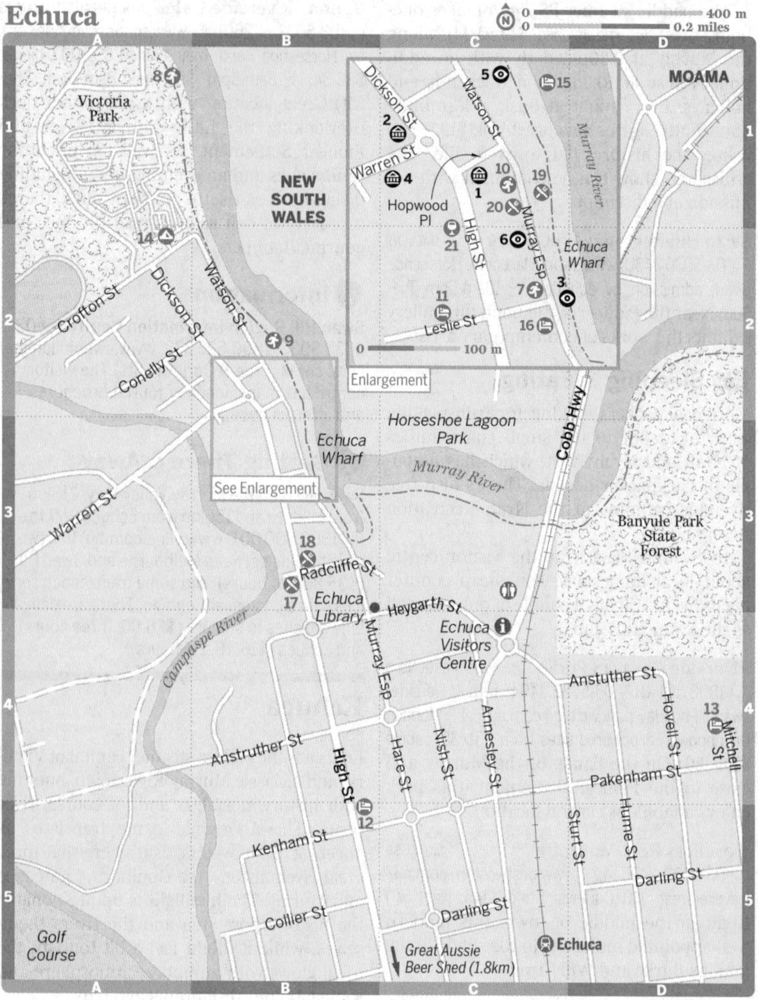

Taste local wines and food at the 1884 **Customs House** (☎03-5482 5209; www.thecustomshouseechuca.com.au; 2 Leslie St; ⏱9.30am-5.30pm), and at **St Anne's** (☎03-5480 6955; www.stanneswinery.com.au; 53 Murray Esplanade; ⏱10am-6pm), where the giant port barrels will inspire you to taste the range of ports aged in bourbon and rum barrels.

Historic Port of Echuca HISTORIC SITE
(☎03-5482 4248; www.portofechuca.org.au; cnr Leslie St & Murray Esplanade; Wharf Walk passport adult/child/family $12.45/8.50/37.70, with paddle-boat cruise $29/15/77; ⏱9am-5pm, guided tours 11.15am) Echuca's star attraction is the old port area, where paddle steamers dock and you really feel transported back to the heyday of the river. It's not a theme park – everything here is original.

In the wharf's cargo shed, dioramas depict life on the river boats and restored historic **paddle steamers** are moored alongside the wharf. Across the road at the **Star Hotel** (1867) you can escape through the underground tunnel that helped drinkers avoid the police when the pub was a 'sly grog shop'.

Echuca

Sights

1 Bridge Hotel C1
2 Echuca Historical Museum C1
3 Historic Port of Echuca C2
4 National Holden Museum C1
5 Riverboat Dock C1
6 Sharp's Magic Movie House & Penny Arcade C2

Activities, Courses & Tours

7 Customs House C2
8 Echuca Boat & Canoe Hire A1
9 PS Emmylou B2
10 St Anne's C1

Sleeping

11 Campaspe Lodge C2
12 Echuca Backpackers B5
13 Echuca Gardens D4
14 Echuca Holiday Park A2
15 Rich River Houseboats C1
16 Steampacket B&B C2

Eating

17 Beechworth Bakery B3
18 Ceres B3
19 Oscar W's Wharfside C1
20 Star Hotel & Wine Bar C1

Drinking & Nightlife

21 Shamrock Hotel C2

At the **Bridge Hotel** (1 Hopwood Pl), built by Harry Hopwood in 1859, your ticket admits you to a historic upstairs recreation of a 19th-century home. Downstairs the Bridge is a pub and restaurant.

Sharp's Magic Movie House & Penny Arcade CINEMA
(☎03-5482 2361; 43 Murray Esplanade; adult/child/family $15/10/45; ⏰9am-5pm) Authentic penny-arcade machines and free fudge tasting. The movie house shows old movies.

Echuca Historical Museum MUSEUM
(☎03-5480 1325; www.echucahistoricalsociety.org.au; 1 Dickson St; adult/child $5/1; ⏰11am-3pm) In the old police station is this museum; classified by the National Trust.

National Holden Museum MUSEUM
(☎03-5480 2033; www.holdenmuseum.com.au; 7 Warren St; adult/child/family $7/3/16; ⏰9am-5pm) Car buffs should check out this museum, dedicated to Australia's four-wheeled icon. There are more than 40 beautifully restored Holdens, from FJ to Monaro.

Great Aussie Beer Shed MUSEUM
(☎03-5480 6904; www.greataussiebeershed.com.au; 377 Mary Ann Rd; adult/child/family $9.50/3.50/19; ⏰9am-5pm Sat, Sun & holidays) Wall-to-wall shrine of beer cans and Aussie memorabilia in a huge shed. It's the result of 30 years of collecting – one even dates back to Federation. The owner will spin a few yarns.

Activities & Tours

A paddle-steamer cruise along the Murray is pretty much obligatory here, and at least five boats have daily cruises, some offering lunch and winery cruises. Head down to the wharf and check out the sailing times or see www.echucapaddlesteamers.net.au or www.emmylou.com.au.

PS *Alexander Arbuthnot,* PS *Canberra,* PS *Pevensey* and *Pride of the Murray* are all in regular service, and one-hour cruises cost around $23/10 per adult/child. **MV Mary Ann** (☎03-5480 2200; www.maryann.com.au) isn't a traditional paddle steamer, but a cruising restaurant offering lunch and dinner cruises.

PS Emmylou CRUISE
(☎03-5482 5244; www.emmylou.com.au; 1½hr cruise adult/child $33/15, 3hr dinner cruise $125/55) Locally built paddle steamer driven by an original 1906 engine, with the added luxury of an onboard restaurant.

Echuca Moama Wine Tours WINE
(☎1300 798 822; www.echucamoamawinetours.com.au; tours from $85) Includes paddle-steamer cruise, lunch and visits to four wineries.

Echuca Boat & Canoe Hire BOAT HIRE
(☎03-5480 6208; www.echucaboatcanoehire.com; Victoria Park Boat Ramp) Hires out tinnies (per one/two hours $40/65), 'barbie boats' (10 people $100/150), kayaks ($16/26) and canoes ($20/30). Self-guided 'campanoeing' trips are also available, where you can arrange to be dropped upstream and canoe back.

Festivals & Events

Riverboats Music Festival MUSIC
(www.riverboatsmusic.com.au) Contemporary Aussie music festival beside the Murray; third weekend in February.

WORTH A TRIP

BARMAH NATIONAL PARK

About 40km northeast of Echuca (via the Cobb Hwy in NSW), Barmah is a significant wetlands area of the Murray River floodplain. It's the largest remaining red-gum forest in Australia, and the swampy understorey usually floods, creating a wonderful breeding area for many species of fish and birds.

The park entry is about 5km north of the tiny town of Barmah (turn at the pub). From the day-use area, **Kingfisher Cruises** (☎03-5855 2855; www.kingfishercruises.com.au; adult/child/family $32/21/98; ⏰10.30am Sun, Mon, Wed, Thu & Sat) takes you out in a flat-bottom boat for an informative two-hour cruise.

You can camp free in the park, or at the Barmah Lakes camping area, which has tables, barbecue areas and pit toilets.

Echuca-Moama Winter Blues Festival MUSIC
(www.winterblues.com.au) Echuca's premier winter festival in late July features local and nationally renowned blues artists.

Sleeping

About 7km east of town, **Christies Beach** is a free camping area on the banks of the Murray. There are pit toilets, but bring water and firewood.

Hiring a houseboat is a great way to experience river life, and Echuca-Moama has plenty of them. Fully-equipped boats sleep from four to 12 people. Rates vary wildly according to size and season – four nights midweek in the low season will cost from $1200 to $2600 depending on the boat. Weekends and high season are at least double. The visitor centre has details and a booking service.

Note that many other accommodation places also charge a premium from Friday to Sunday.

Echuca Gardens HOSTEL, GUESTHOUSE $
(☎03-5480 6522; www.echucagardens.com; 103 Mitchell St; dm $30, wagon $80-150, guesthouse $110-180; @) Run by inveterate traveller Kym, this thoroughly enjoyable place is part YHA hostel and part guesthouse, all set in beautiful gardens with ponds, statues, chooks and fruit trees. The cute 'gypsy wagons' in the garden offer unique accommodation.

Echuca Backpackers HOSTEL $
(☎03-5480 7866; www.backpackersechuca.com.au; 410-424 High St; dm $25, s/d with bathroom $55/60; ❄@) In a former school building on Echuca's main street, this busy hostel is clean and well equipped, and the staff can help you find work.

Echuca Holiday Park CAMPGROUND $
(☎03-5482 2157; www.echucacaravanpark.com.au; 51 Crofton St; unpowered/powered sites $32/35, cabins $95-175; ❄📶🏊) Beside the river just a short walk from town, this park is pretty cramped but the facilities are good.

Steampacket B&B B&B $$
(☎03-5482 3411; www.steampacketinn.com.au; cnr Murray Esplanade & Leslie St; d incl breakfast $155-205; ❄) Staying in the old port area is all part of the Echuca experience and this 19th-century National Trust–classified B&B offers genteel rooms with old-fashioned charm, linen and lace, and brass bedsteads (but air-con and flat-screen TVs too).

Campaspe Lodge MOTEL $$
(☎03-5482 1087; www.echucahotel.com; 567-571 High St; d weekdays/weekends from $95/125; ❄📶) Behind the Echuca Hotel, this group of motel units is great value, with private verandahs and big windows to take in the view of the Campaspe River. There are budget rooms in the pub itself for $40 per person.

Rich River Houseboats HOUSEBOAT
(☎03-5480 2444; www.richriverhouseboats.com.au; Riverboat Dock; 4 nights from $1200) Right in town, with a range of beautiful boats. Good off-season deals.

Eating & Drinking

Conveniently, the port area and the top end of High St have some excellent restaurants and cafes. Supermarkets, pubs and takeaways can be found in the town centre around Hare St.

Beechworth Bakery BAKERY $
(☎1300 233 784; 513 High St; meals $5-12; ⏰6am-6pm) In a magnificent old building with wraparound balcony and a deck overlooking the Campaspe River, this cheerful bakery whips up fresh breads, pies, cakes and sandwiches.

★**Oscar W's Wharfside** MOD AUSTRALIAN $$
(☎03-5482 5133; www.oscarws.com.au; 101 Murray Esplanade; mains lunch $12-24, dinner $22-44; ⏲11am-late) The glorious location in the old port area with a terrace overlooking the Murray is unbeatable. Oscar's delivers with its food and service. Lunch on the Deck Bar is largely small plates with Mediterranean flavours, while dinner in the Red Gum Grill includes quail, kangaroo and big steaks.

Star Hotel & Wine Bar BAR, BISTRO $$
(☎03-5480 1181; www.starhotelechuca.com.au; 45 Murray Esplanade; mains $12-26; ⏲8am-2pm, till late Wed-Sun) The historic 'Star Bar' in the port area is still one of the liveliest places in town for a meal or drink, especially on weekends when live music plays. Full cooked breakfasts and reasonably priced meals of calamari, chicken parma and wood-fired pizza are available.

Ceres EUROPEAN $$
(☎03-5482 5599; www.ceresechuca.com.au; 554 High St; mains lunch $19-25, dinner $25-35; ⏲10am-late Mon-Fri, 9am-late Sat & Sun) One of Echuca's finest restaurants in recent years, Ceres has moved its Mediterranean magic from the grand old flour mill to a more touristy High St location – a bright and busy two-storey place with 1st-floor balcony and tables on the footpath.

Shamrock Hotel PUB
(☎03-5482 1058; www.shamrockhotel.com.au; 583 High St) The popular and friendly Shamrock is the place for Guinness, live music on weekends and cheap pub food.

ℹ Information

Echuca Visitor Centre (☎1800 804 446; www.echucamoama.com; 2 Heygarth St; ⏲9am-5pm) In the old pump station, the visitor centre has helpful staff, an accommodation booking service and internet access.

ℹ Getting There & Away

V/Line (☎1800 800 007; www.vline.com.au); has one direct Melbourne–Echuca train on weekdays and two on weekends (return $23, 3½ hours); there are another six train/bus services daily, with changes at Bendigo, Murchison or Shepparton.

Rutherglen

POP 2125

Rutherglen has bags of history with some marvellous gold-rush-era buildings gracing the town (gold was discovered here in 1860), but today it's red wine that pumps through the region's veins – this is undoubtedly one of northern Victoria's finest wine-growing districts. In town you can dine at some excellent cafes and restaurants, browse antique and bric-a-brac shops, or head out and cycle some of the miles of flat trails. If you're looking for the river, it's about 10km northwest at the tiny Murray town of **Wahgunyah**, conveniently linked to Rutherglen by a cycle path.

Southeast of Rutherglen, about 20km, is **Chiltern**, a charming gold-rush town established in 1851 and worth a visit for its historic 19th-century buildings.

Four local wineries (Pfeiffer, Cofield, Campbell and Rutherglen Estates) offer

RUTHERGLEN REDS

Rutherglen's wineries produce superb fortifieds (port, muscat and tokay) and some potent durif and shiraz – among the biggest, baddest and strongest reds. See www.winemakers.com.au for more information. Some of the best:

➡ **All Saints** (☎02-6035 2222; www.allsaintswine.com.au; All Saints Rd, Wahgunyah; ⏲9am-5.30pm Mon-Sat, 10am-5.30pm Sun) Fairy-tale castle, restaurant and cheese tasting.

➡ **Cofield** (☎02-6033 3798; www.cofieldwines.com.au; Distillery Rd, Wahgunyah; ⏲9am-5pm Mon-Sat, 10am-5pm Sun) Small family operation and the excellent Pickled Sisters Cafe.

➡ **Morris** (☎02-6026 7303; www.morriswines.com.au; Mia Mia Rd, Rutherglen; ⏲9am-5pm Mon-Sat, 10am-5pm Sun) Famous for its fortified wines, Morris has been around for more than 150 years.

➡ **Pfeiffer** (☎02-6033 2805; www.pfeifferwinesrutherglen.com.au; 167 Distillery Rd, Wahgunyah; ⏲9am-5pm Mon-Fri, 10am-5pm Sun) Situated on picturesque Sunday Creek.

➡ **Rutherglen Estates** (☎02-6032 8516; www.rutherglenestates.com.au; Tuileries Complex, Drummond St, Rutherglen; ⏲10am-6pm) Closest cellar door to town.

➡ **Vintara** (☎0447 327 517; www.vintara.com.au; Fraser Rd, Rutherglen; ⏲10am-5pm) Boutique winery and restaurant.

THE MAN FROM SNOWY RIVER

You might have seen the film and read Banjo Paterson's famous poem, but out at **Corryong**, 120km east of Wodonga and close to the source of the Murray River, they live the legend. Corryong is a pretty township surrounded by alpine country – a natural playground for trout fishing, canoeing, cycling and bushwalking – and some say the home of Jack Riley, a stockman thought to have been the inspiration for Paterson's *The Man from Snowy River*.

The **Man From Snowy River Museum** (☎03-6076 2600; www.manfromsnowyriver-museum.com; 103 Hanson St; adult/child $4/1; ⏰10am-4pm Sep-May, 11am-3pm Jun-Aug) tells the story of Jack Riley.

The **Corryong visitor centre** (☎03-6076 2277; 50 Hanson St; ⏰9am-5pm) has info on the region, including **Jack Riley's Grave** (Corryong Cemetery), inscribed with the words, 'In memory of the Man from Snowy River, Jack Riley, buried here 16th July 1914'.

The **Man From Snowy River Bush Festival** (www.bushfestival.com.au) is four days of whip-cracking, horse riding and yarn-spinning fun in March/April.

free 'Behind the Scenes' **winery tours** on a rotating basis from Monday to Thursday at 2pm, which take you into the world of the winemaking process. Advanced bookings through the visitor centre are essential.

Rutherglen Wine Experience WINE
(☎1800 622 871; www.rutherglenvic.com; 57 Main St; ⏰9am-5pm) Rutherglen Wine Experience combines the visitor information centre with a cafe and wine-tasting room. Hire bikes for winery touring ($25/35 per half-/full day) or pick up the heritage-walks brochure. It can also provide information about Rutherglen's busy calendar of wine and food events, including **Tastes of Rutherglen** (March) and **Winery Walkabout** (June), and local winery tours.

Sleeping

Victoria Hotel PUB $
(☎02-6032 8610; www.victoriahotelrutherglen.com.au; 90 Main St; d without bathroom $70-90, with bathroom $100-130; ❄) This beautiful National Trust–classified pub has history, great bistro food and some inviting accommodation – the spruced-up front rooms have en-suites and views over Main St, with access to the wide, lace-trimmed balcony. Most other rooms are neat pub-style with shared bathrooms.

Rutherglen Caravan & Tourist Park CAMPGROUND $
(☎02-6032 8577; www.rutherglentouristpark.com; 72 Murray St; unpowered/powered sites $25/32, cabins $88-125; ❄) This neat little park sits on the banks of tiny Lake King, close to the golf course, swimming pool and town centre.

Motel Woongarra MOTEL $$
(☎02-6032 9588; www.motelwoongarra.com.au; cnr Main & Drummond Sts; d/f $105/140; ❄📶🏊) Close to the centre of town, Woongarra has spacious, neat rooms. The friendly owners run limousine winery tours.

★**Tuileries** BOUTIQUE HOTEL $$
(☎02-6032 9033; www.tuileriesrutherglen.com.au; 13 Drummond St; d incl breakfast $199, with dinner $299; ❄📶🏊) All rooms are individually decorated in bright contemporary tones at this luxurious place next to the Jolimont Cellars. There's a guest lounge, tennis court, pool and an outstanding restaurant and cafe.

Eating

Main St is lined with quality cafes, restaurants, pubs and takeaway places – the Vic is the pick of the pubs in town, while the Star Hotel has an attached Chinese restaurant. A number of wineries also have quality restaurants, including All Saints, Cofield and Vintara.

Parkers Pies BAKERY $
(☎02-6032 9605; 86-88 Main St; pies $5-7; ⏰8am-4.30pm Mon-Fri, 8am-5pm Sat, 9am-4pm Sun) If you think a pie is a pie, this award-winning local institution might change your mind. Try the gourmet pastries – emu, venison, crocodile, buffalo and curry.

Tuileries Restaurant & Cafe MEDITERRANEAN $$
(☎02-6032 9033; www.tuileriesrutherglen.com.au; 13 Drummond St; mains lunch $12.90, dinner $23-35; ⏰noon-late) Tuileries has two outstanding choices: the super courtyard cafe where everything from gnocchi to nasi goreng is

conveniently priced at $12.90 for lunch and $23.90 at dinner; and the stylish Mod Oz restaurant open in the evenings. Rutherglen's best.

Getting There & Away

V/Line (1800 800 007; www.vline.com.au) has a train/coach service between Melbourne and Rutherglen with a change at Wangaratta ($31, 3½ hours, eight weekly). During festivals, bus transport to wineries can be organised through the visitor centre.

The daily Murraylink bus connecting Wodonga with Mildura stops at Rutherglen. The bus stop is at the western end of Main St.

Wodonga

POP 16,500

The border town of Wodonga is separated from its twin, Albury (p225), by the Murray River. Although a busy little town with a lake formed off Wodonga Creek, most of the attractions and the best of the accommodation are on the NSW side in Albury.

Across the causeway, the **Wodonga visitor information centre** (1300 796 222; www.alburywodongaaustralia.com.au; Gateway Village, Hume Hwy; 9am-5pm) has info about Victoria and NSW. This is the start of the **High Country Rail Trail** (www.highcountryrailtrail.org.au), a gravel cycling/walking path that skirts around the southern end of Lake Hume to Old Tallangatta.

For 24 years from the end of WWII, **Bonegilla**, 10km east of Wodonga, was Australia's first migrant reception centre, providing accommodation and training for some 320,000 migrants. At the **Bonegilla Migrant Experience** (02-6020 6912; www.bonegilla.org.au; Bonegilla Rd; admission free, group tours by appointment $5; 10am-4pm) you can visit some of the preserved buildings of Block 19 and see photos and historical references.

GOLDFIELDS

The central Victoria region was literally built on gold. The discovery of alluvial gold near Ballarat in 1851 transformed it from a colonial backwater of pastoralists and convicts into the richest and most prosperous part of the colonies. From those heady days came major regional towns such as Bendigo, Ballarat and Castlemaine, which still boast impressive Victorian-era buildings. Smaller towns such as Kyneton, Maldon and Maryborough make the most of their historic past, while Daylesford and Hepburn Springs are popular for their liquid gold – abundant mineral springs and the spa centres that have grown around them.

Ballarat

POP 86,000

Victoria's largest inland city, Ballarat is famous as the site of the Eureka Rebellion, a 19th-century battle between miners and authorities. Today the city's gold-rush legacy can be seen in its superb Victorian architecture and at the immensely popular Sovereign Hill gold-mining village. Rug up if you visit in winter – Ballarat is notoriously cold.

The area around Ballarat was known to the local Koories as 'Ballaarat', meaning 'resting place'. Around 25 pre-European clans identify themselves collectively as Wathaurong people. European pastoralists arrived in 1837 and the discovery of gold at nearby Buninyong in 1851 saw thousands of diggers flock to the area. After alluvial goldfields were played out, deep shaft mines were sunk, striking incredibly rich quartz reefs that were worked until the end of WWI.

Sights & Activities

The main drag, impressive **Sturt St**, with its island gardens, had to be three chains wide (60m) to allow for the turning circle of bullock wagons.

Running north–south, **Lydiard St** is one of Australia's finest streetscapes for Victorian-era architecture. Impressive buildings include Her Majesty's Theatre (p574; 1875), Craig's Royal Hotel (1853), George Hotel (p573; 1854), the art gallery (1890) and the Mining Exchange (p572; 888).

Ballarat's state of the art Museum of Australian Democracy at Eureka (p572) opened in 2013.

★ **Sovereign Hill** HISTORIC VILLAGE
(03-53371100; www.sovereignhill.com.au; Bradshaw St; adult/student/child/family $45/36/20.50/113; 10am-5pm) You'll need to set aside at least half a day to get the most out of this fascinating re-creation of an 1860s gold-mining township. The site was mined in the gold-rush era and much of the equipment, and the mine shaft, is original. The main street

Ballarat

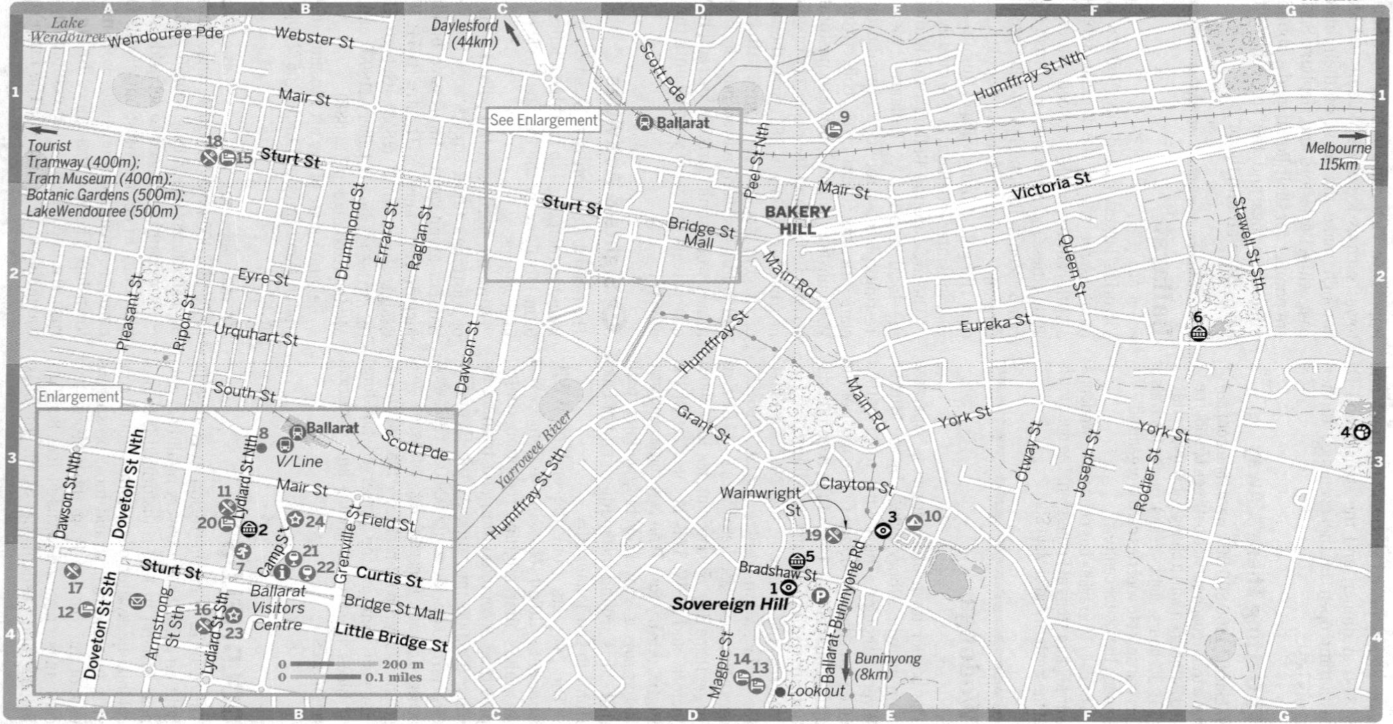
Lake Wendouree
Wendouree Pde
Webster St
Daylesford (44km)
Mair St
Tourist Tramway (400m); Tram Museum (400m); Botanic Gardens (500m); LakeWendouree (500m)
Sturt St
Drummond St
Errard St
Raglan St
Eyre St
Pleasant St
Ripon St
Urquhart St
South St
Dawson St
See Enlargement
Ballarat
Bridge St Mall
Scott Pde
Peel St Nth
BAKERY HILL
Main Rd
Humffray St
Grant St
Yarrowee River
Humffray St Sth
Humffray St Nth
Victoria St
Melbourne 115km
Stawell St Sth
Queen St
Eureka St
York St
Otway St
Joseph St
Rodier St
Clayton St
Wainwright St
Bradshaw St
Sovereign Hill
Ballarat-Buninyong Rd
Buninyong (8km)
Magpie St
Lookout
Enlargement
Dawson St Nth
Doveton St Nth
Doveton St Sth
Lydiard St Nth
Lydiard St Sth
V/Line
Camp St
Grenville St
Field St
Curtis St
Ballarat Visitors Centre
Little Bridge St
Armstrong St Sth
1
2
3
4
5
6
7
8
9
10
11
12
13
14
15
16
17
18
19
20
21
22
23
24
A
B
C
D
E
F
G
0
1 km
0.5 miles
200 m
0.1 miles

Ballarat

Top Sights

1 Sovereign Hill D4

Sights

2 Art Gallery of Ballarat B3
3 BADAC Cultural Education Centre E3
4 Ballarat Wildlife Park G3
5 Gold Museum E4
6 Museum of Australian Democracy at Eureka G2

Activities, Courses & Tours

7 Gold Shop B4
8 Welcome Nugget B3

Sleeping

9 Ballarat Backpackers Hostel E1
10 Ballarat Goldfields Holiday Park E3
Craig's Royal Hotel .... (see 16)
11 George Hotel B3
12 Oscar's A4
13 Sovereign Hill Lodge D4
14 Sovereign Hill YHA D4
15 Western Hotel B1

Eating

16 Craig's Royal Hotel B4
17 L'Espresso A4
18 Olive Grove B1
19 Restaurante Da Uday E3
20 The Lane B3

Drinking & Nightlife

21 Haida B4
22 Irish Murphy's B4

Entertainment

23 Her Majesty's Theatre B4
24 Karova Lounge B3

is a living history museum with folks performing their chores dressed in period costume and interacting with visitors. An old-time lolly shop, gold panning, a gold pour and street theatre offer a flavour of the times. Most activities inside are free except for the **underground mine tour** (adult/child $7.50/4) and **coach rides** ($5.50/4). If you have time, ask about about having your ticket validated for two days (free) and spread out your visit. Sovereign Hill opens again at night for the impressive sound-and-light show **Blood on the Southern Cross** (03-5337 1199; adult/student/child/family $55/44/29.50/148.50, combined with Sovereign Hill ticket $100/80/50/261.50), a dramatic simulation of the Eureka Stockade battle. There are two shows nightly but times vary so check in advance; bookings are essential.

Your ticket gets you into the nearby **Gold Museum** (Bradshaw St; adult/child $10.80/5.70; 9.30am-5.30pm), which sits on a mullock heap from an old mine. There are imaginative displays and samples from all the old mining areas, as well as gold nuggets, coins and a display on the Eureka Rebellion.

Art Gallery of Ballarat — GALLERY

(03-5320 5858; www.balgal.com; 40 Lydiard St Nth; 10am-5pm) FREE The oldest provincial gallery in Australia, this 1890 architectural gem houses a wonderful collection of early colonial paintings, works from noted Australian artists and contemporary works. Free iPod tours are available and there are free guided tours at 2pm Wednesday to Sunday.

Lake Wendouree — LAKE

Lake Wendouree is a natural focal point for the town, encircled by a walking path with old boat sheds, playgrounds and picnic spots.

Botanic Gardens — GARDENS

(Wendouree Pde; sunrise-sunset) On the western side of the lake are Ballarat's beautiful and serene gardens, first planted in 1858. Stroll through the 40 hectares of immaculately maintained rose gardens, wide lawns and colourful conservatory. There's a visitor centre in the glass Robert Clark Conservatory (open 9am to 5pm).

Ballarat Tramway Museum — MUSEUM

(03-5334 1580; www.btm.org.au; rides adult/child $4/2; 12.30-5pm Sat & Sun, daily during holidays) The tram operates on a short section of tramline around Lake Wendouree, departing from the Tramway Museum, which has a collection of trams, photographs and memorabilia. Horse-drawn trams started running in the city in 1887, later replaced by electric trams, which ran until 1971.

BADAC Cultural Education Centre — CULTURAL CENTRE

(03-5332 2755; www.badac.net.au; 407 Main Rd; 9am-5pm Mon-Fri) FREE This excellent cultural centre has a 'Living History' museum and displays about the local Wathaurong people, Koorie history and art. Enthusiastic staff offer free tours and there's a cafe.

THE EUREKA REBELLION

Life on the goldfields was a great leveller, erasing social distinctions as doctors, merchants, ex-convicts and labourers toiled side by side in the mud. But as the easily won gold began to run out, the diggers recognised the inequalities between themselves, the privileged few who held land, and the government.

The limited size of claims and the inconvenience of licence hunts, coupled with police brutality and taxation without political representation, fired the unrest that led to the Eureka Rebellion.

In September 1854, Governor Hotham ordered the hated licence hunts to be carried out twice weekly. The following month a miner was murdered near a Ballarat hotel after an argument with the owner, James Bentley. Bentley was found not guilty by a magistrate (and business associate), and a group of miners rioted and burned his hotel. Bentley was retried and found guilty, but the rioting miners were also jailed, which fuelled their distrust of authority.

Creating the Ballarat Reform League, the diggers called for the abolition of licence fees, the right of miners to vote, and increased opportunities to purchase land.

On 29 November 1854 about 800 miners, led by Irishman Peter Lalor, burnt their licences at a mass meeting and built a stockade at Eureka, where they prepared to fight for their rights.

On 3 December the government ordered troopers to attack the stockade. There were only 150 diggers within the barricades at the time and the fight lasted only 20 minutes, leaving 30 miners and five troopers dead.

The short-lived rebellion was ultimately successful. The miners won the sympathy of Victorians, and the government chose to acquit the leaders of the charge of high treason. The licence fee was abolished and a miner's right, costing £1 a year, gave the right to search for gold and to fence in, cultivate and build a dwelling on a moderate-sized piece of land – and to vote. The rebel leader Peter Lalor became a member of parliament some years later.

The new **Museum of Australian Democracy at Eureka** (MADE; ☎1800 287 113; www.made.org) occupies the site of the original stockade and includes an interpretive centre and the treasured remains of the original Eureka flag.

Kryal Castle THEME PARK
(☎03-5334 7388; www.kryalcastle.com.au; 121 Forbes Rd, Leigh Creek; adult/child/family $28.50/17/79; ⏲10am-5pm) This fanciful replica medieval castle, originally built in 1972, reopened in 2013 as an ambitious theme park with dragon's lair, knights on horseback in jousting shows, dungeons and a wizard world. Great for families and Harry Potter fans! It's 8km east of Ballarat.

Ballarat Wildlife Park ZOO
(☎03-5333 5933; www.wildlifepark.com.au; cnr York & Fussell Sts; adult/child/family $25/15/70; ⏲9am-5.30pm, tour 11am) A fun zoo with mostly native animals, reptiles and a few exotics. Daily shows feature snakes, koalas, wombats and crocodiles.

Ballarat Bird World AVIARY
(☎03-5341 3843; www.ballaratbirdworld.com.au; 408 Eddy Ave, Mt Helen; adult/child/family $10/6/30; ⏲10am-5pm) Boasts 40 species of birds hanging out in a peaceful garden aviary south of town, with walkways, ponds and waterfalls.

Gold Shop EQUIPMENT HIRE
(☎03-5333 4242; www.thegoldshop.com.au; 8a Lydiard St Nth; ⏲10am-5pm Mon-Sat) Hopeful prospectors can pick up miners' rights, rent metal detectors and see real nuggets at the old Mining Exchange building.

Tours

Eerie Tours GHOST
(☎1300 856 668; www.eerietours.com.au; adult/child/family $25/15/65) Relive the ghoulish parts of Ballarat's past with a night-time ghost tour or cemetery tour.

Welcome Nugget BICYCLE
(☎0423 268 618; www.ballarat.com/ballaratonabike; 128 Lydiard St Nth; 3-/8-hour bike hire $13/18) Bike tours and hire.

Festivals & Events

Summer Sundays is a series of free concerts in the botanic gardens every Sunday evening in January.

Ballarat Beer Festival FOOD, DRINK
(www.ballaratbeerfestival.com.au) Sample a range of beer, cider and food at the city oval in January.

Begonia Festival STREET FESTIVAL
(www.ballaratbegoniafestival.com) Ballarat's biggest festival, on the Labour Day long weekend in March, features a street parade, free concerts at Lake Wendouree and open gardens.

Sleeping

Ballarat's grand old hotels, B&Bs and cottages all offer gracious accommodation, and there are many motels, a couple of pub-style hostels and caravan parks.

Sovereign Hill YHA HOSTEL $
(☎03-5337 1159; ballarat@yha.com.au; Magpie St; dm/s/d $35/49/68) This cute but very compact YHA cottage in the Sovereign Hill Lodge complex has just four rooms around a central kitchen/dining area.

Western Hotel PUB $
(☎03-5332 2218; www.westernhotel.com.au; 1221 Sturt St; dm/s/d $35/45/70) The simple upstairs pub rooms here are good value ($10 cheaper if you bring your own linen). Shared kitchen.

Ballarat Backpackers Hostel HOSTEL $
(☎0427 440 661; www.ballarat.com/easternstation/index.htm; 81 Humffray St Nth; s/d/f $40/65/90) In the old Eastern Station Hotel, this refurbished guesthouse is also a pub with occasional live music (might get noisy on weekends). Close to the train line.

Ballarat Goldfields Holiday Park CAMPGROUND $
(☎03-5332 7888; www.ballaratgoldfields.com.au; 108 Clayton St; powered sites $37, cabins $77-113;) Close to Sovereign Hill, with a family holiday atmosphere. Some cabins are like miners' cottages.

George Hotel HOTEL $$
(☎03-5333 4866; www.georgehotelballarat.com.au; 27 Lydiard St Nth; d/f/ste from $135/215/260;) This grand old pub has seen bags of history since it was first built in 1852. It's right in the thick of things on Lydiard St and the refurbished rooms are tasteful and comfortable.

Sovereign Hill Lodge HISTORIC HOTEL $$
(☎03-5337 1159; www.sovereignhill.com.au; Magpie St; s $150, d from $170;) Up behind Sovereign Hill is a range of accommodation. Within the 1850s village itself, **Steinfeld's** (s/d $150/170) is the top pick – six elegant heritage rooms and a common lounge overlooking the old township.The **Governor's Rooms** (d with/without spa $235/200) feature stylish heritage rooms around a cosy guest lounge with fireplace and bar.

Oscar's BOUTIQUE HOTEL $$
(☎03-5331 1451; www.oscarshotel.com.au; 18 Doveton St; d $150-200, spa room $225;) The 13 rooms in this attractive art-deco hotel have been tastefully refurbished to include double showers and spas (watch a flat-screen TV from your spa). There's a good restaurant downstairs.

Eating

Ballarat offers plenty of dining options around Sturt and Lydiard Sts and there's a nice cafe strip on the Sturt St '400 Block' between Dawson and Doveton Sts. For cheap eats, Bakery Hill – once the centre of goldfields activity – has a string of Indian, Japanese and fast-food restaurants.

L'Espresso ITALIAN $
(☎03-5333 1789; 417 Sturt St; mains $11-20; 7.30am-6pm Sun-Thu, to 11pm Fri & Sat) A mainstay on Ballarat's cafe scene, this trendy and very busy Italian-style place doubles as a record shop – choose from the whopping jazz, blues and world-music CD selection while you wait for your espresso, falafel or risotto.

★ **The Lane** CAFE, PIZZERIA $$
(☎03-5333 4866; 27 Lydiard St Nth; pizza $16-23, mains $20-36; 7am-late) The laneway running beside the George Hotel buzzes with all-day diners in one form or another. At the front is a bright cafe with breakfast and light meals and a bar; at the back is a great little pizzeria which doubles as an à la carte restaurant in the evenings.

Olive Grove DELI, CAFE $$
(☎03-5331 4455; 1303 Sturt St; dishes $12-24; 8am-4pm;) The Olive Grove brings in locals lingering over coffee, gourmet baguettes or bagels, or browsing the deli delights of cakes, cold meats and cheeses.

Restaurante Da Uday INTERNATIONAL $$
(☎03-5331 6655; www.dauday.com; 7 Wainwright St; mains $18-26, pizza $10-18; ⊙noon-2pm & 5.30pm-late Tue-Sun) This little restaurant near Sovereign Hill serves up excellent and authentic Indian, Thai and Italian – each with their own menu – in a cosy weatherboard cottage or flower-filled garden. The $15 lunch deal is good value.

Craig's Royal Hotel MODERN AUSTRALIAN $$$
(☎03-5331 1377; www.craigsroyal.com.au; 10 Lydiard St Sth; mains $28-35; ⊙7am-10pm) Even if you can't afford to stay here, you can experience some royal treatment with a cocktail in historic Craig's Bar, or coffee in Craig's Café & Larder. For fine dining, the Gallery Bistro is a sumptuous atrium dining room serving Modern Australian and French-inspired cuisine. Every Sunday at 3.30pm High Tea is served at the hotel ($59.50).

Drinking & Entertainment

With a large student population, Ballarat has lively nightlife. There are some fine old pubs around town, but most of the entertainment is centred on Lydiard St and the nearby Camp St precinct.

Irish Murphy's PUB
(☎03-5331 4091; www.murphysballarat.com.au; 36 Sturt St; mains $18-30; ⊙11am-11pm, till 3am Wed-Sun) The Guinness flows freely at this atmospheric Irish pub. It's a welcoming place and the live music draws people of all ages. Lunch and dinner daily.

Haida LOUNGE
(☎03-5331 5346; www.haidabar.com; 12 Camp St; ⊙5pm-late Wed-Sun) Haida is a loungy two-level bar where you can relax with a cocktail by the open fire or chill out to DJs and live music downstairs.

Karova Lounge LIVE MUSIC
(☎03-5332 9122; www.karovalounge.com; cnr Field & Camp Sts; ⊙9pm-late Wed-Sat) Ballarat's best live-music venue showcases local and touring bands in grungy, industrial style.

Her Majesty's Theatre THEATRE
(☎03-5333 5888; www.hermaj.com; 17 Lydiard St Sth) Ballarat's main venue for the performing arts since 1875, 'Her Maj' is in a wonderful Victorian-era building and features theatre, live music, comedy shows and local productions.

Shopping

Trash & Trivia Market MARKET
(Creswick Rd; ⊙8am-1pm Sun) At the Ballarat Showgrounds, 2km north of the city centre just off the Midland Hwy.

Information

Ballarat Visitor Centre (☎1800 446 633, 03-5320 5741; www.visitballarat.com.au; cnr Camp & Sturt Sts; ⊙9am-5pm) The excellent visitor centre should be in its new (and final) location by the time you read this. Ask about the Ballarat Pass, which gives discounted admission to Sovereign Hill, Kryal Castle and Ballarat Wildlife Park.

Getting There & Away

BUS

Greyhound Australia (☎1300 473 946; www.greyhound.com.au) buses between Adelaide and Melbourne stop in Ballarat if you ask the driver (departs Adelaide 8.15pm, adult $86, 7½ hours).

Airport Shuttle Bus (☎03-5333 4181; www.airportshuttlebus.com.au) goes direct from Melbourne's Tullamarine Airport to Ballarat train station (adult/child $32/17, 1½ hours, 10 daily, seven on weekends).

There are also regular **V/Line** (☎1800 800 077; www.vline.com.au) buses to regional centres like Bendigo, Castlemaine, Geelong and Ararat.

TRAIN

V/Line (☎1800 800 007; www.vline.com.au) has frequent direct trains between Melbourne (Southern Cross Station) and Ballarat ($17.80, 1½ hours, 13 to 17 daily).

Bendigo

POP 82,800

You don't have to look far to find evidence of Bendigo's heritage – it's in the magnificent Shamrock Hotel, the Central Deborah Goldmine and the Chinese dragons that awaken for the Easter Festival.

Gold was discovered at nearby Ravenswood in 1851, and during the boom years between the 1860s and 1880s, mining companies poured money into the town, resulting in the Victorian architecture that graces Bendigo's streets today. By the 1860s, diggers were no longer tripping over surface nuggets, and so deep mining began. Local legend has it that you can walk underground from one side of the town to the other. These days Bendigo is a prosperous provincial centre with fine public gardens, a lively cafe and restaurant scene, and one of Victoria's best regional art galleries.

Bendigo is the centre of an excellent **wine region** that stretches south to Harcourt. See www.bendigowine.org.au, or ask for a touring map from the visitor centre.

Sights

If you plan on seeing the main sights, the **Bendigo Experience Pass** (adult/child/family $50/26.50/128) is good value. Ask at the visitor centre.

★ **Central Deborah Goldmine** HISTORIC SITE
(☎ 03-5443 8322; www.central-deborah.com; 76 Violet St; adult/child/family mine experience $28.50/15/78.50; ⏲ 9.30am-5pm) For a very deep experience, descend into this 500m-deep mine with a geologist. It has been worked on 17 levels, and about 1000kg of gold has been removed. After donning hard hats and lights, you're taken 61m down the shaft to inspect the operations, complete with drilling demonstrations. More adventurous types can try the underground adventure ($75/45/190), which goes to the third level, with an underground lunch. On the surface is an interpretive centre, poppet head and engine room. You can do a self-guided surface tour ($14/7/38).

Bendigo Talking Tram TRAM
(☎ 03-5442 2821; www.bendigotramways.com; adult/child/family $16/10/47, valid 2 days; ⏲ 10am-5pm) For an interesting tour of the city, hop aboard one of the restored vintage 'talking' trams. The hop-on, hop-off trip runs from the Central Deborah Mine to the **Tramways Museum** (1 Tramways Rd; admission free with tram ticket; ⏲ 10am-5pm) every half-hour, making half a dozen stops.

★ **Golden Dragon Museum & Gardens** MUSEUM
(☎ 03-5441 5044; www.goldendragonmuseum.org; 1-11 Bridge St; adult/child/family $11/6/28; ⏲ 9.30am-5pm) Bendigo's obvious Chinese heritage sets it apart from other goldfields towns, and this fantastic museum and garden is the place to experience it. Walk through a huge wooden door into an awesome chamber filled with dragons, including the Imperial Dragons Old Loong (the oldest in the world) and Sun Loong (the longest in the world, at over 100m). Outside, the Yin Yuan (Garden of Joy) classical Chinese gardens are a tranquil little haven with bridges, water features and ornamental shrubs.

Bendigo Art Gallery GALLERY
(☎ 03-5434 6088; www.bendigoartgallery.com.au; 42 View St; admission by donation; ⏲ 10am-5pm, tours 2pm) The permanent collection includes outstanding colonial and contemporary Australian art, such as work by Charles Blackman, Fred Williams, Rupert Bunny and Lloyd Rees; the annual temporary exhibitions are cutting edge. The Gallery Café overlooks Rosalind Park.

Sacred Heart Cathedral CHURCH
(cnr Wattle & High Sts) You can't miss the soaring steeple of this wonderful cathedral. Inside, beneath the high vaulted ceiling, there's a magnificently carved bishop's chair, some beautiful stained-glass windows, and wooden angels jutting out of the ceiling arches.

Joss House Temple TEMPLE
(☎ 03-5443 8255; www.bendigojosshouse.com; Finn St; adult/child/family $5.50/3.50/11; ⏲ 11am-4pm) Painted red, the traditional colour for strength, this is the only remaining practising joss house in central Victoria. It's 2km northwest of the centre and on the tram route.

Rosalind Park PARK
(cnr View St & Pall Mall) In the city centre, this lovely green space has lawns, big old trees, fernery and the fabulous **Cascades Fountain**. Climb to the top of the hilltop poppet-head **lookout tower** for sensational 360-degree views or wander through the **Conservatory Gardens**.

Lake Weeroona LAKE
(cnr Nolan & Napier Sts) Bendigo's little lake, 1.5km northeast of the centre, is a favourite spot for boating, kayaking or just walking around the path that encircles it.

Bendigo Pottery POTTERY
(☎ 03-5448 4404; www.bendigopottery.com.au; 146 Midland Hwy; ⏲ 9am-5pm) FREE Australia's oldest pottery works, the Bendigo Pottery was founded in 1857 and is classified by the National Trust. You can learn to throw a pot ($12 per half-hour lesson) or check out the attached **museum** (adult/child $8/4). It's 7km northeast of the centre.

White Hills Botanic Gardens GARDENS
These gardens, 2km north of town, feature many exotic and rare plant species, a small fauna park, an aviary and barbecue facilities.

Bendigo

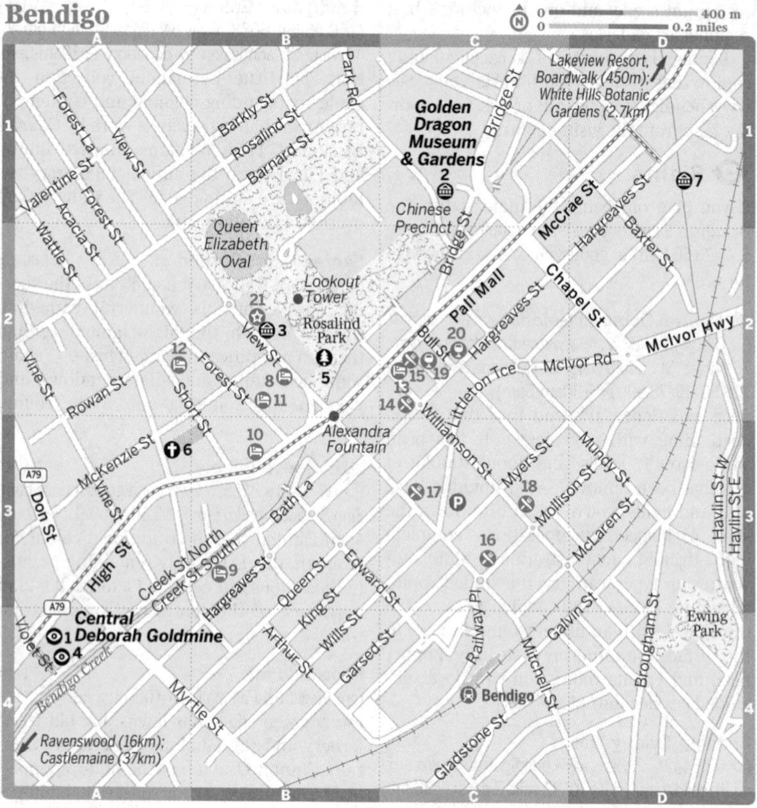

Activities

The **O'Keefe Rail Trail**, a hike-or-bike trail, starts on the Midland Hwy near the northeast corner of Lake Weroona and meanders for 19km to Axedale.

Ironbark Horse Trail Rides HORSE RIDING
(03-5436 1565; www.bwc.com.au/ironbark; Watson St; 1hr/2hr rides $40/70; 8.30am-5pm Mon-Sat) Organises various horse rides including the Great Australian Pub Ride to Allies Hotel in Myers Flat (with lunch $100). Self-contained bush cabins are also available.

Bendigo Gold World PROSPECTING
(03-5448 4140; www.bendigogold.com.au; Watson St; half-/full-day tours $280/380; 8.30am-5pm Mon-Sat) Located in the Ironbark complex, Bendigo Gold World operates fossicking and detecting tours, and hires out prospecting equipment.

Festivals & Events

Easter Festival CARNIVAL
Bendigo's major festival has been running continuously since 1871 and attracts thousands with its carnival atmosphere and colourful and noisy procession of Chinese dragons, led by Sun Loong, the world's longest imperial dragon.

Bendigo Cup HORSE RACING
(www.racingvictoria.net.au/vcrc/bendigo) Part of the Spring Racing Carnival; held in November.

Sleeping

Several accommodation services offer lovely maisonettes, townhouses, suites and apartments in the heart of the city: try **Allawah Bendigo** (03-5441 7003; www.allawahbendigo.com; 45 View St) and **Bendigo Holiday Accommodation** (03-5443 7870; www.bendigoholidayaccommodation.com; 20 High St).

Bendigo

Bendigo Backpackers HOSTEL $
(☎03-5443 7680; www.bendigobackpackers.com.au; 33 Creek St Sth; dm/d/f $30/70/100; ❄) This small, homey hostel flies the budget flag for Bendigo. It's in a weatherboard cottage in a great central location.

Central City Caravan Park CAMPGROUND $$
(☎1800 500 475, 03-5443 6937; www.centralcitycaravanpark.com.au; 362 High St, Golden Square; unpowered/powered sites $32/40, cabins $100-185; ❄≋) The closest park to the city centre has shady sites, a camp kitchen and en suite cabins.

★ **Shamrock Hotel** HOTEL $$
(☎03-5443 0333; www.hotelshamrock.com.au; cnr Pall Mall & Williamson St; d $140-195, ste $245) One of Bendigo's historic icons, the Shamrock is a stunning Victorian building with stained glass, original paintings, fancy columns and a *Gone with the Wind*–style staircase. The refurbished upstairs rooms range from small standard rooms to spacious deluxe and spa suites.

Flynn's Place BOUTIQUE HOTEL $$
(☎03-5444 0001; www.flynnsplace.com.au; 104 Short St; d $165-195; ❄☎) The two modern self-contained apartments at Flynn's are sleekly fitted out and furnished in a historic building, with queen beds, widescreen TVs, DVDs, sound systems and free wi-fi. Good location.

City Centre Motel MOTEL $$
(☎03-5443 2077; www.citycentremotel.com.au; 26 Forest St; s/d from $80/115, weekends d $130) One of Bendigo's most central motels – a block from the art gallery. The cheaper rooms are a little dated but very good value.

Lakeview Resort MOTEL $$
(☎03-5445 5300; www.lakeviewresort.com.au; 286 Napier St; d/f incl breakfast $150/200; ❄☎≋) You've got Lake Weeroona across the road, spacious units around the central courtyard, shaded pool, piazza, and Quills, a fine-dining restaurant with an excellent reputation.

✕ Eating

Bendigo has an excellent range of cafes, pubs (including the Shamrock) and restaurants, most in the convenient block bounded by Pall Mall, Bull St, Hargreaves St and Mitchell St.

Piyawat Thai THAI $
(☎03-5444 4450; 136 Mollison St; mains $12-18; ⊙6-11pm Tue-Sun; ✎) Tucked away in a cosy house a couple of blocks south of the centre, this authentic Thai restaurant serves fabulously fragrant curries, noodles and stir-fries at affordable prices.

Toi Shan CHINESE $
(☎03-5443 5811; 67 Mitchell St; mains $12-19, buffet $12.50-15.50; ⊙noon-2.30pm & 5-10pm) With cheap and cheerful Chinese, Toi Shan has been around since the gold rush. You can fill up with the lunchtime smorgasbord on weekdays and at dinner Friday and Sunday.

Gillies PIES $
(Hargreaves St Mall; pies from $4; ⊙9am-5.30pm Sat-Thu, till 9pm Friday) The pie window on the corner of the mall here is a Bendigo institution.

OFF THE BEATEN TRACK

GOLDFIELDS TRACK

Following routes once taken by miners and gold seekers, this 210km hiking and mountain-biking trail links central Victoria's main gold-rush towns. The trail is divided into three sections. At the southern end, the 90km Wallaby Track starts at Ballarat (or a few kilometres south at Mt Buninyong) and runs via Creswick to Daylesford. From there the Dry Diggings Track continues north for 62km to Castlemaine, then the Leanganook Track takes you the final 58km to Bendigo. The whole trail is well signposted, passing forest and bushland and can be walked or ridden in shorter stages. See www.goldfieldstrack.com.au for trail maps and information.

★GPO MEDITERRANEAN $$

(03-5443 4343; www.gpobendigo.com.au; 60-64 Pall Mall; tapas $7-16, mains $17-29; 11am-late;) The food and atmosphere at the GPO is superb and rated highly by locals. There's an emphasis on Mediterranean-style dining with share tapas plates, innovative pizzas, cheese and charcuterie, plus a great drinks list.

Wine Bank WINE BAR $$

(03-5444 4655; www.winebankonview.com; 45 View St; mains $13-38; 7.30am-11pm Mon-Thu, 7.30am-1am Fri, 8.30am-1am Sat, 8.30am-4pm Sun) Wine bottles line the walls in this former 1876 bank building. It's both a wine shop and bar specialising in central Victorian wines, and an atmospheric Italian-style cafe serving breakfast, tapas and platters.

Barzurk CAFE, BAR $$

(03-5442 4032; 66 Pall Mall; tapas $7-13, mains $16-23; 11am-late Wed-Mon) A trendy but casual streetside cafe-bar with pressed-tin ceilings and a courtyard out the back. The menu includes tapas, pasta, risotto and gourmet pizza.

Woodhouse STEAKHOUSE, PIZZERIA $$

(03-5443 8671; www.thewoodhouse.com.au; 101 Williamson St; pizza $13-20, mains $20-60; noon-2.30pm Thu-Fri, 5.30pm-late Mon-Sat) With its red-gum chargrill, Woodhouse is Bendigo's fanciest steak joint with cuts like wagyu grain-fed for 600 days, and also more humble (but still gourmet) wood-fired pizzas. Good for a splurge.

Boardwalk CAFE $$

(03-5443 9855; www.theboardwalkbendigo.com.au; Nolan St; mains $16-30; 7.30am-5pm Mon-Fri, 8am-5pm Sat & Sun) Grab a table on the alfresco deck overlooking Lake Weeroona on a fine day and you can't help but like this place. It's a popular breakfast spot after a jog around the lake.

Bendigo Ninesevensix TRAM RESTAURANT $$$

(03-5444 4655; www.bendigoninesevensix.com.au; set menu $98; dinner Sat) Every Saturday night a 1952 Melbourne W-class tram becomes a rolling restaurant, with a set menu including three courses and free drinks – a great way to see the city.

Drinking & Entertainment

Bendigo has a lively night life – some clubs are open as late as 5am, but all have a 2am lockout. The main nightlife zone is Bull St and along Pall Mall; uni nights are Tuesday and Thursday.

Metro & Pugg Mahones PUB

(03-5443 4916; 224 Hargreaves St; 10.30am-late Mon-Sat) With Guinness (and many other beers) on tap, Puggs has a thickly welcoming atmosphere, not unreasonable doorstaff, beer garden and balcony, while the adjoining Metro has live music every Friday and Saturday night till 3am.

★Dispensary Enoteca COCKTAIL BAR

(03-5444 5885; www.thedispensaryenoteca.com; 9 Chancery Lane; 11.30am-late Tue-Sat, 11.30am-4pm Sun & Mon) Hidden down tiny Chancery Lane, the Dispensary serves food throughout the day, but it's also a trendy little cocktail bar with a mind-boggling selection of beers, spirits, wines, cocktails and cigars.

Capital THEATRE

(03-5434 6100; www.bendigo.vic.gov.au; 50 View St) The beautifully restored Capital Theatre is the main venue for the performing arts, with hundreds of performances and exhibitions each year.

Star Theatre CINEMA

(03-5446 2025; www.starcinema.org.au; Eaglehawk Town Hall, 1 Peg Leg Rd; adult/child $14/10; from 1.30pm) Watch a flick with a beer or wine in decadent armchair comfort at this classic cinema, 6km northeast of the city centre.

Information

Bendigo Visitor Centre (☎03-5434 6060, 1800 813 153; www.bendigotourism.com; 51-67 Pall Mall; ⏰9am-5pm) In the historic former post office is this free accommodation and tour booking service. Also here is the free Post Office Gallery.

Goldfields Library (☎03-5449 2700; 96-98 Pall Mall; ⏰9am-6pm Mon-Fri, 10am-1pm Sat) Free internet access (one hour limit).

Getting There & Away

V/Line (☎1800 800 007; www.vline.com.au) has frequent trains between Melbourne and Bendigo ($19, two hours, 18 to 20 daily) via Kyneton and Castlemaine. V/Line buses also depart from the train station and will get you to regional centres like Ballarat ($14.80, two hours), Daylesford ($7.80, 1½ hours), Shepparton ($8.80, 1¾ hours) and Echuca ($5.40, 1¼ hours).

Bendigo Airport Service (☎03-5444 3939; www.bendigoairportservice.com.au; adult one-way/return $39/74, child $15/30) Buses direct between Melbourne's Tullamarine Airport and Bendigo train station (two hours, seven daily). Bookings essential.

Castlemaine

POP 9125

Castlemaine is a thoroughly enjoyable working-class town where a growing community of artists, writers and tree-changers live amid some inspiring gold-rush architecture and gardens. Even after the gold ran out, the town kept its reputation for industry and innovation – this was the birthplace of the Castlemaine XXXX beer-brewing company (now based in Queensland – the original brewery on Elizabeth St is today an antique complex) and Castlemaine Rock, a hard-boiled sweet lovingly produced by the Barnes family since 1853. It's also the 'Street Rod Centre of Australia', where hot-rods have been built and shown off since 1962.

After gold was discovered at Specimen Gully in 1851, the Mt Alexander Diggings attracted some 30,000 diggers and Castlemaine became the thriving marketplace for the goldfields. The town's importance waned as the surface gold was exhausted by the 1860s but, fortunately, the centre of town was well established by then and remains relatively intact.

Castlemaine hosts the biennial **State Festival** (www.castlemainefestival.com.au), in March/April of odd-numbered years, one of Victoria's leading arts events.

Sights & Activities

Castlemaine Art Gallery & Historical Museum GALLERY, MUSEM
(☎03-5472 2292; www.castlemainegallery.com; 14 Lyttleton St; adult/student/child $4/2/free; ⏰10am-5pm Mon-Fri, noon-5pm Sat & Sun) The impressive gallery, in a superb art-deco building, has a collection of colonial and contemporary Australian art including works by Frederick McCubbin, Arthur Streeton, Tom Roberts and Russell Drysdale; downstairs is a local history museum.

Castlemaine Botanic Gardens GARDENS
Enjoy a stroll in the expansive gardens, just north of the town centre.

Buda MUSEUM
(☎03-5472 1032; www.budacastlemaine.org; 42 Hunter St; adult/child/family $11/5/26; ⏰noon-5pm Wed-Sat, 10am-5pm Sun) Dating from 1861, Buda was home to Hungarian silversmith Ernest Leviny and his descendants for 120 years. The family's art and craft collections and personal belongings are on display, and the home is surrounded by a lovely garden.

Restorers Barn ANTIQUES
(☎03-5470 5667; www.restorersbarn.com.au; 129-133 Mostyn St; ⏰10am-5.30pm Mon-Fri, 10am-4pm Sat & Sun) Collectors love the barn, a big shed in town dripping with interesting bric-a-brac, collectables and tools.

Harcourt Region WINE
About 10km northwest of Castlemaine is Harcourt, known as Victoria's 'apple centre', though in recent years it has also developed as an excellent mini wine region – the tourist office can provide a map and a list of cellar doors. Apples and grapes are combined at **Bress** (☎03-5474 2262; www.bress.com.au; 3894 Calder Hwy; ⏰11am-5pm Sat & Sun), an excellent winery and cidery.

Sleeping

The free **Mt Alexander accommodation booking service** (☎1800 171 888; www.maldoncastlemaine.com) covers Castlemaine, Maldon and surrounds.

Castlemaine Gardens Caravan Park CAMPGROUND $
(☎03-5472 1125; castlemaine-gardens-caravan-park.vic.big4.com.au; Doran Ave; unpowered/powered sites $31/36, cabins $85-135) Nicely located next to the Botanic Gardens and public swimming pool.

DON'T MISS

GOLDFIELDS RAILWAY

It's a nostalgic journey aboard the beautifully restored steam trains of the **Victorian Goldfields Railway** (☎03-5470 6658; www.vgr.com.au; adult/child/family single $25/10/55, return $35/15/75; ⏲from Maldon 10.30am & 2.30pm Wed, Sat & Sun). The train runs along the original line between Maldon and Castlemaine through the Muckleford forest, passing over some lovely old trestle bridges. For a little extra, go 1st class (adult/child/family $45/25/100) in an oak-lined viewing carriage. The one-way trip takes only 45 minutes, or two hours return.

Midland Private Hotel GUESTHOUSE $$
(☎0487 198 931; www.themidland.com.au; 2 Templeton St; d $150) Opposite the train station, this lace-decked 1879 hotel is mostly original so the rooms are old-fashioned and a bit small but it has plenty of charm, from the art-deco entrance to the magnificent guest lounge and attached Maurocco Bar.

Colonial Motel MOTEL $$
(☎03-5472 4000; www.castlemainemotel.com.au; 252 Barker St; s/d $115/125, spa unit $155, apt $195; ❄📶) Conveniently central and the best of Castlemaine's motels, the Colonial has modern rooms (some with spa) and high-ceilinged apartments in a beautifully converted school building.

★**Theatre Royal Back Stage** BOUTIQUE HOTEL $$$
(☎03-5472 1196; www.theatreroyal.info; 30 Hargreaves St; d incl breakfast $220-240; ❄📶) It's a unique experience staying backstage in this 1854 theatre. The two suites are compact, but beautifully decorated with period furniture and cinema memorabilia, and are literally right behind the velvet curtain – the rate includes admission to all movies screened during your stay.

Eating

Castlemaine's foodie scene has developed into one of central Victoria's best. Mostyn and Barker Sts are the best places to start.

Taste of the Orient CHINESE $
(☎03-5470 5465; www.tasteoftheorient.com.au; 223 Barker St; yum cha $2.50-10; ⏲11am-8.30pm Thu-Sat, 11am-3pm Sun) The tasty dim sum dishes practically walk out the door at this simple yum cha joint run by a Hong Kong chef.

Saffs Cafe CAFE $
(☎03-5470 6722; 64 Mostyn St; mains $8-22; ⏲8am-5pm, till late Wed-Sun) A local favourite, Saffs is a bright, friendly place with good coffee, cake, brilliant breakfasts, local artwork on the walls and a rear courtyard.

Apple Annie's BAKERY, CAFE $
(☎03-5472 5311; www.appleannies.com.au; 31 Templeton St; mains $5-17; ⏲8am-5pm Wed-Sat, 8am-3pm Sun) For fresh bread, mouth-watering cakes and hand-rolled croissants, it's hard to beat this country-style cafe and bakery with a bright courtyard out back.

Good Table EUROPEAN $$
(☎03-5472 4400; www.thegoodtable.com.au; 233 Barker St; mains $14-37; ⏲noon-2pm Thu-Sun, from 6pm daily) There have been numerous incarnations of this lovely corner hotel, but the Good Table does it in style with a thoughtful European-influenced menu and the uber-cool Hickster bar on the upstairs balcony. Menus change seasonally – Monday to Wednesday evenings are a bargain with two/three courses for $25/30.

Public Inn MODERN AUSTRALIAN $$$
(☎03-5472 3568; www.publicinn.com.au; 165 Barker St; mains $29-38; ⏲noon-3pm & 6pm-late) The former Criterion Hotel has been brilliantly transformed into a slick bar and restaurant that wouldn't look out of place in Manhattan with its plush tones and Chesterfield couches. Food is high-end 'gastropub' – there's a two-course lunch menu for $39. Check out the 'barrel wall', where local wines are dispensed.

☆ Entertainment

Theatre Royal CINEMA
(☎03-5472 1196; www.theatreroyal.info; 28 Hargreaves St; adult/child $15/12) Catch a movie or live show at Australia's longest continuously running theatre. Gold-class armchairs cost $5 extra. Session times on the website. There's Sunday afternoon live music in the courtyard out back.

Information

Castlemaine Visitor Centre (☎03-5471 1795; www.maldoncastlemaine.com; Mostyn St; ⏲9am-5pm) It's in the magnificent old

Castlemaine Market, the town's original market building fronted with a classical Roman-basilica facade topped with a statue of Ceres, the Roman goddess of the harvest. There's also a changing gallery, audiovisual displays and bike hire (half-/full day $20/30).

Getting There & Away

Castlemaine is on the main Melbourne–Swan Hill railway line: **V/Line** (1800 800 007; www.vline.com.au) trains run hourly between Melbourne and Castlemaine ($13.80, 1½ hours, 18 daily) via Woodend and Kyneton, and continue to Bendigo ($4.20, 25 minutes). The railway station is on Kennedy St, one block west of the town centre.

Maldon

POP 1236

Maldon is a well-preserved relic of the gold-rush era, with many fine buildings constructed from local stone. The population is a scant reminder of the 20,000 who used to work the local goldfields, but this is still a living, working town – busy with tourists on weekends but reverting to its sleepy self during the week.

The town centre consists of High St and Main St, lined with antique shops, cafes, old toy shops, lolly shops, bookshops and the two remaining pubs – the Maldon and Kangaroo Hotels.

Folk-music fans will enjoy the annual **Maldon Folk Festival** (www.maldonfolkfestival.com; tickets 1/2 days $60/110), held in early November.

Sights & Activities

Take the 3km drive or walk up **Mt Tarrengower** for panoramic views from the poppet-head lookout. Remnants of Maldon's mining past can be seen on short walks around town: the 24m-high **Beehive Chimney** is just east of main street, and south of town is the old **North British Mine**, where interpretive boards tell the story of what was once one of the world's richest mines.

Carman's Tunnel HISTORIC SITE
(03-5475 2656; off Parkin's Reef Rd; adult/child $7.50/2.50; tours 1.30pm, 2.30pm & 3.30pm Sat & Sun, daily during school holidays) A 570m-long mine tunnel, excavated in the 1880s, that took two years to dig yet produced only $300 worth of gold. Now you can descend with a guide for a 45-minute candlelight tour.

Sleeping & Eating

Butts Reserve Camp Site CAMPGROUND
(Mt Tarrengower Rd) FREE Has toilets and picnic tables. From High St, head west along Franklin St and follow the signs to Mt Tarrengower.

Maldon Holiday Cottages COTTAGES $
(03-5475 2927; smarsden@tadaust.org.au; 28 Sells Lane; d $80) These three cottages provide simple but comfortable budget accommodation, each with kitchen facilities and separate living room with TV and DVD.

Gold Exchange Cafe CAFE $
(44 Main St; meals $7-14; 9am-5pm Wed-Sun) This tiny licensed cafe with retro furniture does good coffee, salads, pies and yabbie burgers.

Penny School Gallery & Cafe CAFE, GALLERY $
(03-5475 1911; www.pennyschoolgallery.com.au; 11 Church St; lunch $11-16.50; 11am-5pm Wed-Sun, 11am-10pm Fri & Sat) In a lovely heritage building away from the Main St bustle, this light-filled cafe-restaurant-gallery features changing exhibitions. It's a great spot for a Mod Oz lunch or coffee and cake.

Information

Maldon Visitor Centre (03-5475 2569; www.maldoncastlemaine.com; 95 High St; 9am-5pm) Pick up the *Information Guide* and *Historic Town Walk* brochures.

Getting There & Away

Castlemaine Bus Lines (03-5472 1455) runs three buses daily between Castlemaine and Maldon, connecting with trains to and from Melbourne.

Daylesford & Hepburn Springs

POP 3265

Set among the idyllic hills, lakes and forests of the central highlands, Daylesford and Hepburn Springs form the 'spa centre of Victoria', and have developed into quite the bohemian weekend getaway, though the area's mineral springs have been attracting fashionable Melburnians since the 1870s. Even if you don't indulge in a spa treatment, there are lots of great walks, a fabulous foodie scene and an arty, alternative vibe – the local population is an interesting blend of hippies and old-timers, and there's a thriving gay and lesbian scene here.

PAMPERING SOAKS

The Daylesford and Hepburn Springs region is well known for its rejuvenating mineral spa treatments. Along with a soak or facial, you can fork out plenty of money for herbal treatments, massages and mud packs.

➡ **Daylesford Day Spa** (03-5348 2331; www.daylesforddayspa.com.au; 25 Albert St, Daylesford) Start with a vitamin-rich mud body mask and steam in a body-care cocoon, before a scalp massage and Vichy shower.

➡ **Endota Spa** (03-5348 1169; www.endotadayspa.com.au/daylesford; cnr Vincent St & Central Springs Rd, Daylesford) Hot stones and Hawaiian lomi lomi massage.

➡ **Massage Healing Centre** (03-5348 1099; www.massagehealing.com.au; 5/11 Howe St, Daylesford) For a modest, down-to-earth alternative to the glitz-and-glam spa resorts.

➡ **Mineral Spa at Peppers** (03-5348 2100; www.mineralspa.com.au; Springs Retreat; 124 Main Rd, Hepburn Springs) Have an algae gel wrap, based on an ancient Chinese treatment, then move into the lavender steam room, or take a soft pack float.

➡ **Salus** (03-5348 3329; www.lakehouse.com.au; Lake House, King St, Daylesford) The pampering starts as you walk through a small rainforest to your exotic jasmine-flower bath in a cedar-lined treehouse overlooking the lake.

➡ **Shizuka Ryokan** (03-5348 2030; www.shizuka.com.au; 7 Lakeside Dr, Hepburn Springs) Shiatsu massage, geisha facials and spa treatments with natural sea salts and seaweed extracts, ginseng and green tea at this Japanese-style country spa retreat.

Daylesford is the main centre, with most of the action on Vincent St. Continue north for 3km to reach the charming hamlet of Hepburn Springs. The best places to fill your bottles with mineral spring water are at the Hepburn Springs Reserve and around Lake Daylesford.

Sights & Activities

Boats and canoes can be hired at **Lake Daylesford**, though the popular Boathouse Cafe burned down in 2012. The lake is also ringed by marked walking trails. Or head out to **Jubilee Lake**, a popular local swimming hole about 3km southeast of town.

★ **Hepburn Bathhouse & Spa** SPA
(03-5321 6000; www.hepburnbathhouse.com; Mineral Springs Reserve, Hepburn Springs; 9am-6.30pm) The historic Hepburn Bathhouse & Spa is all spruced up and specialises in relaxation baths and hydrotherapy treatments using mineral water pumped from ancient underground cavities. Two-hour entry to the public pool and spa costs $25 ($37 Friday to Monday), while private spas start at $70. Around the spa are picnic areas and several **mineral springs** where you can fill your own bottles from pumps, as well as the historic **Pavilion Cafe**. There are some good **walking trails**; pick up maps and guides from the visitor centre.

Convent Gallery GALLERY
(03-5348 3211; www.theconvent.com.au; 7 Daly St, Daylesford; admission $5; 10am-4pm) This magnificent 19th-century convent has been converted into an art gallery with changing exhibitions, a cafe and the Altar Bar.

Daylesford Spa Country Railway TOURIST TRAIN
(0421 780 100; www.dscr.com.au; Daylesford train station; adult/child/family $10/8/25; 10am-2.30pm Sun) Operates one-hour rides every Sunday on restored rail motors.

Wombat Hill Botanic Gardens GARDENS
(Central Springs Rd, Daylesford) These beautiful gardens are worth a stroll for the many oaks, pine and cypress trees, and a new cafe.

Daylesford Sunday Market MARKET
(8am-3pm Sun) Flea market at the train station every Sunday.

Chocolate Mill FOOD
(03-5476 4208; www.chocmill.com.au; 5451 Midland Hwy, Mt Franklin; 10am-4.45pm, tour at 11am & 2pm) This place is worth the 10-minute drive from Daylesford for its fine chocolate and cafe. You can watch the Belgian chocolates being made by hand at the free demos.

Mill Markets MARKET
(03-5348 4332; www.millmarkets.com.au; 105 Central Springs Rd, Daylesford; 10am-6pm) You

could just about fit a Boeing 747 in the enormous Mill Markets, which house a mind-boggling collection of furniture, collectables, antiques, books and retro fashions.

Festivals & Events

ChillOut Festival GAY, LESBIAN
(www.chilloutfestival.com.au) Held over the Labour Day long weekend in March, this gay and lesbian pride festival is Daylesford's biggest and most colourful annual event, attracting thousands of people for street parades, music and dance parties.

Swiss Italian Festa ITALIAN
(www.swissitalianfesta.com) Held in late October, this festival draws on the region's European roots with literary events, music, food, wine and art.

Sleeping

Even with 5000 beds in the region, accommodation fills up fast during holidays – most places charge more on weekends and stipulate a two-night stay. You can camp for free at **Mt Franklin**, an extinct volcano 10km north of Daylesford. Bookings for the region's charming guesthouses, cottages and B&Bs can be made through agencies in Daylesford: try **Daylesford Cottage Directory** (03-5348 1255; www.cottagedirectory.com.au; 16 Hepburn Rd), **Daylesford Getaways** (03-5348 4422; www.dayget.com.au; 14 Vincent St) and **Escapes Daylesford** (03-5348 1448; www.dabs.com.au; 94 Vincent St).

Daylesford

Jubilee Lake Holiday Park CAMPGROUND $
(1800 686 376, 03-5348 2186; www.jubileelake.com.au; 151 Kale Rd; unpowered/powered sites $21/30, cabins $75-160;) Set in bushland on the edge of pretty Jubilee Lake, this friendly place is run by a community cooperative and is the best park in the region. Canoe hire available.

Daylesford Central Motor Inn MOTEL $$
(03-5348 2029; www.daylesfordcentralmotorinn.com; 54 Albert St; d/f from $110/160, with spa $150;) An easy stroll from the town centre, this is a standard but comfortable motel.

Balconies B&B $$
(03-5348 1322; www.balconiesdaylesford.com.au; 35 Perrins St; B&B from $160;) The nine rooms at this luxury B&B offer country-style chic surrounded by lovely gardens.

★ **Lake House** BOUTIQUE HOTEL $$$
(03-5348 3329; www.lakehouse.com.au; King St; d incl breakfast from $550;) You can't talk about Daylesford without waxing on about the Lake House, a superb family-run property overlooking Lake Daylesford. Set in rambling gardens with bridges and waterfalls, the 33 rooms are split into spacious waterfront rooms with balcony decks, and lodge rooms with private courtyards. Off-season midweek specials can make it affordable.

Hepburn Springs

Continental House GUESTHOUSE $
(03-5348 2005; www.hepburnretreatcentre.com.au; 9 Lone Pine Ave; s/d $55/90, cottage $100/130) Also called the Hepburn Retreat Centre, this rambling, timber guesthouse is a 'vegan sanctuary', a little slice of alternative-lifestyle budget heaven and yoga retreat. There are basic rooms in the house, cottages in the garden, a laid-back vibe, yoga classes and vegan cooking courses.

Mooltan Guesthouse GUESTHOUSE $$
(03-5348 3555; www.mooltan.com.au; 129 Main Rd; s/d midweek from $80/100, weekend from $100/130) Behind a well-clipped hedge, this inviting Edwardian country home has large lounge rooms, a billiard table and tennis court. Bedrooms open onto a broad verandah overlooking the Mineral Springs Reserve. The cheapest rooms have shared facilities.

Shizuka Ryokan GUESTHOUSE $$$
(03-5348 2030; www.shizuka.com.au; 7 Lakeside Dr; d $280-380) Inspired by traditional places of renewal and rejuvenation in Japan, this traditional minimalist getaway has six rooms with private Japanese gardens, tatami matting and plenty of green tea. Discounts for multiple nights and spa packages.

Eating & Drinking

These two towns are walk-in gourmet treats. Every second business on Vincent St in Daylesford is a cafe or foodstore and there's a buzzing atmosphere here on weekends.

Daylesford

Cliffy's Emporium DELI, CAFE $
(03-5348 3279; www.cliffys.com.au; 30 Raglan St; mains $10-25; 9am-5pm daily, till late Sat;) Behind the vine-covered verandah of this local institution is an old-world shop crammed with organic vegies, cheese, preserves and

the spicy aromas of fruit chutneys and roasting coffee. Occupying a narrow side section, the busy cafe is perfect for breakfast, pies and baguettes.

★ Breakfast & Beer CAFE, BAR $$
(☎03-5348 1778; www.breakfastandbeer.com.au; 117 Vincent St; mains $12-30; ⏲8am-11pm Wed-Sun) Straight out of the backstreets of Bruges, this inspired European-style cafe stocks fine local and imported beer, and a boutique menu strong on local produce, including innovative breakfast/brunch fare.

Koukla Café PIZZA $$
(☎03-5348 2363; www.frangosandfrangos.com; 82 Vincent St; pizzas $21; ⏲7.30am-late) Part of Frangos and Frangos, this moody European-style corner cafe is a great place for coffee on the couch or sourdough wood-fired pizza for lunch or dinner. Next door is the equally cool Jimmy's Bar.

Lake House MODERN AUSTRALIAN $$$
(☎03-5348 3329; www.lakehouse.com.au; King St; mains $36-40; ⏲noon-2.30pm & 6-9.30pm) The Lake House has long been regarded as Daylesford's top dining experience and it doesn't disappoint, with stylish purple high-back furniture, picture windows showing off Lake Daylesford, a superb seasonal menu, award-winning wine list and impressive service. Tasting menus from $80.

Kazuki's JAPANESE $$$
(☎03-5348 1218; www.kazukis.com.au; 1 Camp St; 2-/3-courses $60/75, tasting menu 5-/6-courses $80/100; ⏲noon-2pm Fri-Mon, 6pm-late Thu-Tue) This fusion of Japanese and French cuisine with local produce brings an unexpected twist to Daylesford's dining scene. The two-room restaurant, incorporating a wine and sake bar, is intimate, with a nice alfresco courtyard at the side. There's a banquet lunch for $65.

Perfect Drop WINE BAR
(☎03-5348 3373; www.aperfectdrop.com; 5 Howe St; ⏲5pm-late Mon-Fri, from noon Sat & Sun) This sweet little wine bar and restaurant really is the place for a perfect drop, with local wines a speciality. It has a relaxed, loungy feel for drinking and chatting, and lots of share plates.

Hepburn Springs

Red Star Café CAFE $$
(☎03-5348 2297; www.theredstar.com.au; 115 Main Rd; mains $10-22; ⏲8am-4pm) The weatherboard shopfront is like someone's home, with loungy couches, bookshelves, great music, a garden out the back and a funky local vibe.

Old Hepburn Hotel PUB
(☎03-5348 2207; www.oldhepburnhotel.com.au; 236 Main Rd; ⏲4pm-midnight Mon-Tue, noon-midnight Wed-Thu, noon-1am Fri-Sat, noon-11pm Sun) For a classic Aussie pub experience and live music. Bands play most weekends.

Information

Daylesford Visitor Centre (☎1800 454 891, 03-5321 6123; www.visitdaylesford.com; 98 Vincent St; ⏲9am-5pm) A cheery place, with stacks of information.

Getting There & Around

Daily **V/Line** (☎1800 800 007; www.vline.com.au) services connect Melbourne by train to Woodend then bus to Daylesford ($11, two hours). Weekday V/Line buses run from Daylesford to Ballarat ($7.80, one hour), Castlemaine ($4.20, 35 minutes) and Bendigo ($7.80, 1½ hours). The bus stop is on Bridport St opposite the fire station.

GOULBURN VALLEY & HUME HIGHWAY REGION

The Hume Hwy (M31) is the multilane link between Melbourne and Sydney via Albury Wodonga. Most travellers put their foot down as they bypass all the towns, but there are a few hidden attractions just off the freeway – including 'Kelly Country', places associated with the legend of bushranger Ned Kelly. To the east are the foothills of Victoria's High Country: get off at Seymour for Mansfield and Mt Buller, or Wangaratta for Mt Hotham and Falls Creek.

West of the Hume is the Goulburn Valley, Victoria's fruit bowl and a popular area for seasonal work. The valley's other main crop is wine, and several wineries are worth a visit, notably the impressive Tahbilk and Mitchelton wineries near Nagambie.

Activities

River Country Adventours CANOEING
(☎03-5852 2736; www.adventours.com.au; half-/full-day hire $55/85, safari $229) Runs canoe and camping safaris on the Goulburn and Murray Rivers from Seymour, Shepparton, Wyuna, Nagambie and other sites.

Shepparton

POP 42,740

Laid-back, multicultural 'Shepp' is the capital of the Goulburn Valley, where the Goulburn and Broken Rivers meet. This is the heart of a rich farming and fruit-growing region so it's popular with travellers looking for fruit-picking work. Look out for the extraordinarily colourful 'Mooving Art' cows dotted around town – such ironic rural art.

Sights & Activities

Shepparton Art Museum GALLERY
(03-5832 9861; www.sheppartonartmuseum.com.au; Eastbank Centre, 70 Welsford St; 10am-4pm) FREE Has a fine permanent collection of paintings, ceramics and contemporary Australian art.

Bangerang Cultural Centre CULTURAL CENTRE
(03-5831 1020; www.bangerang.org.au; 1 Evergreen Way; 9am-4pm Mon-Fri) FREE An indigenous gallery, museum and keeping place, this is well worth a visit for its unique collection of Koorie art and artefacts.

Sleeping & Eating

Shepparton Backpackers HOSTEL $
(03-5831 6556; www.sheppartonbackpackers.com.au; 139 Numurkah Rd; dm/d from $25/85, dm per week $135; @) Tucked away behind a car wash 3km north of town, this well-equipped hostel is the place to stay if you're looking for agricultural work in the region.

Victoria Lake Holiday Park CAMPGROUND $
(03-5821 5431; www.viclakeholidaypark.com.au; 536 Wyndham St; unpowered/powered sites $27/32, cabins $100-140;) Beside Victoria Park Lake, this friendly park has plenty of grass and shade, bicycle paths and good facilities.

Cellar 47 ITALIAN $$
(03-5831 1882; www.cellar47.com; 170 High St; mains $16-32; lunch & dinner Mon-Sat) With its sleek black-and-glass bar and gourmet wood-fired pizzas, this is a long-standing local favourite.

Information

Shepparton Visitor Centre (03-5831 4400, 1800 808 839; www.discovershepparton.com.au; Wyndham St; 9am-5pm) At the southern end of Victoria Park Lake.

SEASONAL WORK

There's harvesting or pruning work virtually year-round in the Shepparton-Mooroopna area and it's well set up for travellers. The main season is January to May (apples, peaches and pears) and there's pruning work available from May to August.

CVGT (1300 724 788; www.cvgt.com.au; cnr Welsford & Sobraon Sts) runs a harvest hotline and has comprehensive listings of fruit-picking work. Backpacker hostels in Shepparton and Mooroopna can help with finding work.

Getting There & Away

Shepparton train station is on Purcell St close to the town centre. There are daily **V/Line** (1800 800 007; www.vline.com.au) trains and buses to/from Melbourne ($20, 2½ hours, three daily).

Nagambie

POP 1550

On the shores of pretty **Lake Nagambie**, created by the construction of the Goulburn Weir back in 1887, Nagambie is a popular base for water sports and skydiving.

Two excellent wineries are just south of town: **Mitchelton Wines** (03-5736 2222; www.mitchelton.com.au; 470 Mitchellstown Rd; 10am-5pm), with a restaurant and award-winning shiraz, and **Tahbilk Winery** (03-5794 2555; www.tahbilk.com.au; 254 O'Neils Rd; 9am-5pm Mon-Fri, 10am-5pm Sat & Sun). Tahbilk opens onto the **Wetlands & Wildlife Reserve** (admission gold coin donation, cruise $5; 11am-4pm Mon-Fri, 10am-4.30pm Sat & Sun), with boardwalks or boat tours through a natural area rich in bird life. Entry is via the excellent Tahbilk Cafe.

Skydive Nagambie SKYDIVING
(03-5794 2626, 1800 266 500; www.skydivenagambie.com; 52 Kettles Rd) Offers tandem dives ($399) from 14,000ft or learn-to-skydive courses.

Information

Nagambie Visitor Information Centre (1800 444 647, 03-5794 1471; www.nagambielakesandstrathbogieranges.com.au; 3/317 High St; 9am-5pm) Staff are passionate about their lake, their town and their region.

Glenrowan

POP 300

Ned Kelly's legendary bushranging exploits came to their bloody end here in 1880. The story of Ned and his gang has become an industry in this one-street town – a short detour off the main highway – and you can't drive through Glenrowan without being confronted by the legend and his souvenirs, including a 2m-high armour-clad statue. The main sites of the historic capture are signposted, so pick up a walking map and follow the trail.

At the Glenrowan Tourist Centre, **Ned Kelly's Last Stand** (03-5766 2367; www.glenrowantouristcentre.com.au; 41 Gladstone St; adult/child/family $27/20/70; 9.30am-4.30pm, shows every 30min) is an animated theatre – Ned's story is told in a series of rooms by a cast of clunky but surprisingly lifelike animatronic characters, culminating in a smoky shoot-out and Ned's hanging.

Nearby, behind Kate's Cottage, a **museum** (03-5766 2448; 35 Gladstone St; adult/child $6/1; 9am-5.30pm) holds Kelly memorabilia and artefacts gathered from all over the district, and a replica of the Kelly home.

Glenrowan has several country-style cafes, motels, and the local pub, as well as a small wine region.

Wangaratta

POP 17,380

Wangaratta (just plain old 'Wang' to the locals) is a busy commercial centre along the Hume Hwy and is the turn-off for the ski fields along the Great Alpine Road and for the Rutherglen wine region. The name means 'resting place of the cormorants' and the town sits neatly at the junction of the Ovens and King Rivers. The main claim to fame here is the almost-world-famous **Wangaratta Jazz & Blues** (box office 03-5722 8199; www.wangarattajazz.com), a four-day jazz extravaganza in early November.

Sights & Activities

At the **Wangaratta Cemetery** you'll find the grave of notorious bushranger Dan 'Mad Dog' Morgan. It contains most of Morgan's

THE KELLY GANG

Bushranger and outlaw he may have been, but Ned Kelly is probably Australia's greatest folk hero and a symbol of the Australian rebel character.

Born in Beveridge in 1855 to Irish parents (his father an ex-convict), Ned was first arrested when he was 14 and spent the next 10 years in and out of jails, including Beechworth Gaol. In 1878 a warrant was issued for his arrest for stealing horses, so he and his brother Dan went into hiding. Their mother and two friends were arrested, sentenced and imprisoned for aiding and abetting.

Ned and Dan were joined in their hideout in the Wombat Ranges, near Mansfield, by Steve Hart and Joe Byrne. Four policemen – Kennedy, Lonigan, Scanlon and McIntyre – came looking for them, and, in a shoot-out at Stringybark Creek, Ned killed Kennedy, Lonigan and Scanlon. McIntyre escaped to Mansfield and raised the alarm.

The government put up a £500 reward for any of the gang members, dead or alive. In December 1878 the gang held up the National Bank at Euroa, and got away with £2000. Then, in February 1879, they took over the police station at Jerilderie, locked the two policemen in the cells, and robbed the Bank of New South Wales wearing the policemen's uniforms. By this time the reward was £2000 per head.

On 27 June 1880, the gang held 60 people captive in a hotel in Glenrowan. A trainload of police and trackers was sent from Melbourne. Surrounded, the gang holed up in the hotel and returned fire for hours, while famously wearing heavy armour made from ploughshares. Ned was shot in the legs and captured, and Dan Kelly, Joe Byrne and Steve Hart, along with several of their hostages, were killed.

Ned Kelly was brought to Melbourne, tried, then hanged on 11 November 1880. He met his end bravely; his last words are famously quoted as, 'Such is life'.

His death mask, armour and the gallows on which he died are on display in the Old Melbourne Gaol (p483).

In a final chapter in 2013, Kelly's remains were again laid to rest at Greta cemetery near Wangaratta.

remains: his head was taken to Melbourne for a study of the criminal mind, and his scrotum was supposedly fashioned into a tobacco pouch.

Wangaratta is the start of the Murray to Mountains Rail Trail (p597), which runs east via Beechworth to Bright.

Sleeping & Eating

Wangaratta has a decent range of typical motels, which can be booked online at www.visitwangaratta.com.au.

Painters Island Caravan Park CAMPGROUND $
(☎03-5721 3380; www.paintersislandcaravanpark.com.au; Pinkerton Cres; unpowered/powered sites from $30, cabins $80-150;) On the banks of the Ovens River but close to the town centre, this impressive park has a playground, camp kitchen and a good range of cabins.

Hermitage Motor Inn MOTEL $$
(☎03-5721 7444; www.hermitagemotorinn.com.au; cnr Cusack & Mackay Sts; d/f from $110/150;) Close to the town centre, the Hermitage is the pick of Wang's motels, with spacious rooms, contemporary decor, free wi-fi and a pool.

Cafe Derailleur CAFE $
(☎03-5722 9589; www.cafederailleur.com.au; 38 Norton St; dishes $8.50-16.50; 7am-4pm Mon-Fri, 7am-2pm Sat) Opposite the train station, this retro cafe is popular with cyclists and locals alike for heart-starting organic coffee and gourmet breakfast and lunch concoctions.

Vine Hotel PUB $
(☎03-5721 2605; www.thevinehotel.net.au; 27 Detour Rd; mains $13-24; noon-2pm daily, 6-8pm Mon-Sat) Ned Kelly and his gang used to hang out here, about 3km north of town. These days the food is better and you're less likely to get shot. Go underground to the small museum and cellars.

Rinaldo's Casa Cucina ITALIAN $$
(☎03-5721 8800; www.rinaldos.com.au; 8-10 Tone Rd; mains $19-33; noon-2pm Fri & Sat, 6-10pm Tue-Sat) Rinaldo's industrial-sized dining room features fresh pasta dishes and modern Mediterranean versions of steak and seafood prepared under local chef Adam Pizzini. Ask about cooking classes.

Information

Wangaratta Visitor Centre (☎03-5721 5711, 1800 801 065; www.visitwangaratta.com.au; 104 Murphy St; 9am-5pm) The helpful tourist office has audiovisual displays and videos depicting local rail trails and snippets from the annual Wangaratta Jazz & Blues Festival.

Getting There & Away

Wangaratta train station is just west of the town centre on Norton St. There are three direct intercity **V/Line** (☎1800 800 007; www.vline.com.au) trains daily from Melbourne ($26.60, 2¾ hours) continuing to Albury. There's one V/Line bus daily from Wangaratta to Rutherglen ($4.20, 35 minutes) and Bright ($8.80, 2½ hours).

HIGH COUNTRY

Victoria is blessed with the spectacular High Country, which peaks between the Snowy Mountains and Alpine National Park in the state's northeast. This is one of Australia's favourite year-round mountain playgrounds, attracting skiers and snowboarders in winter, and bushwalkers and mountain-bikers in summer.

There are plenty of activities on offer, but it's the ski resorts that really pull the crowds for the brief 'white season'. Skiers and snowboarders flock to Mt Buller, Mt Hotham and Falls Creek in particular, all of which have good on-mountain infrastructure, accommodation, restaurants and nightlife. The ski season officially launches, with or without snow, on the Queen's Birthday long weekend in June and runs until mid-September. The best deals are to be found in June and September (low season), with July and August (high season) the busiest and most expensive time. If you need to ski on a budget, visit midweek or stay in one of the gateway towns and bus up the mountain.

For the even less cashed-up, the 'green season' – anywhere from November to May – offers plenty of adrenalin, with alpine trekking, horse riding, canoeing, abseiling and mountain biking, or more restful but oh-so-enjoyable pursuits such as touring the wineries and gourmet regions of Milawa, King Valley, Bright and historic Beechworth.

Lake Eildon National Park

Lake Eildon National Park protects 277 sq km of bushland surrounding the massive namesake lake that was created by damming the Goulburn River in the 1950s. The little one-pub town of **Eildon** (pop 730) is

High Country

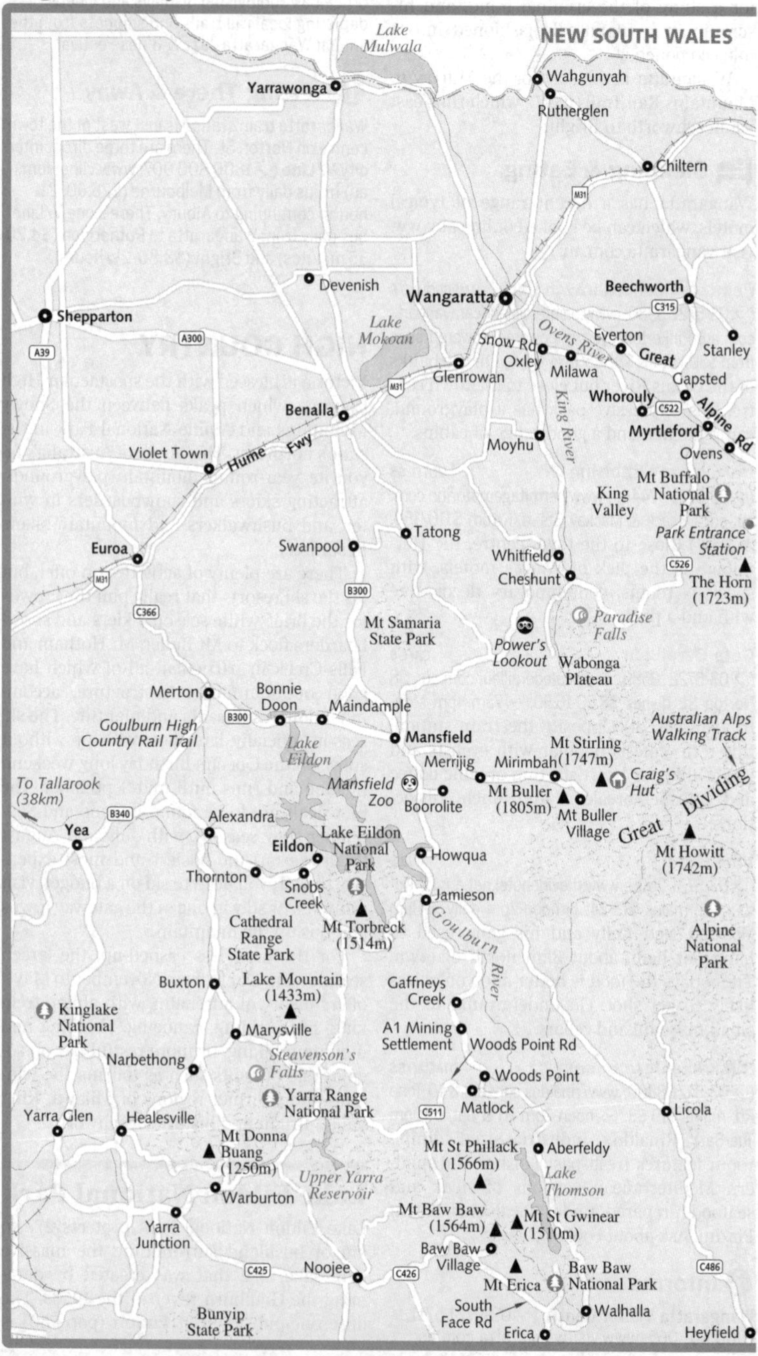
NEW SOUTH WALES
Lake Mulwala
Yarrawonga
Wahgunyah
Rutherglen
Chiltern
M31
Devenish
Wangaratta
Beechworth
C315
Shepparton
A300
A39
Lake Mokoan
Snow Rd
Oxley
Ovens River
Everton
Great
Stanley
Milawa
Glenrowan
Gapsted
M31
Benalla
Whorouly
C522
Alpine Rd
Myrtleford
Ovens
Hume Fwy
Violet Town
Moyhu
King River
Mt Buffalo National Park
King Valley
Park Entrance Station
Tatong
Swanpool
Euroa
Whitfield
Cheshunt
C526
The Horn (1723m)
M31
B300
C366
Paradise Falls
Mt Samaria State Park
Power's Lookout
Wabonga Plateau
Merton
Bonnie Doon
Maindample
B300
Goulburn High Country Rail Trail
Lake Eildon
Mansfield
Australian Alps Walking Track
Mt Stirling (1747m)
Merrijig
Mirimbah
Craig's Hut
To Tallarook (38km)
Mansfield Zoo
Boorolite
Mt Buller (1805m)
Mt Buller Village
Great Dividing
B340
Yea
Alexandra
Lake Eildon National Park
Eildon
Mt Howitt (1742m)
Howqua
Thornton
Snobs Creek
Jamieson
Mt Torbreck (1514m)
Goulburn River
Alpine National Park
Cathedral Range State Park
Buxton
Lake Mountain (1433m)
Gaffneys Creek
Kinglake National Park
Marysville
A1 Mining Settlement
Woods Point Rd
Narbethong
Steavenson's Falls
Woods Point
Yarra Range National Park
Matlock
C511
Licola
Yarra Glen
Healesville
Mt Donna Buang (1250m)
Mt St Phillack (1566m)
Aberfeldy
Lake Thomson
Upper Yarra Reservoir
Warburton
Mt Baw Baw (1564m)
Mt St Gwinear (1510m)
Yarra Junction
Baw Baw Village
C425
Noojee
C426
Mt Erica
Baw Baw National Park
C486
South Face Rd
Walhalla
Bunyip State Park
Erica
Heyfield

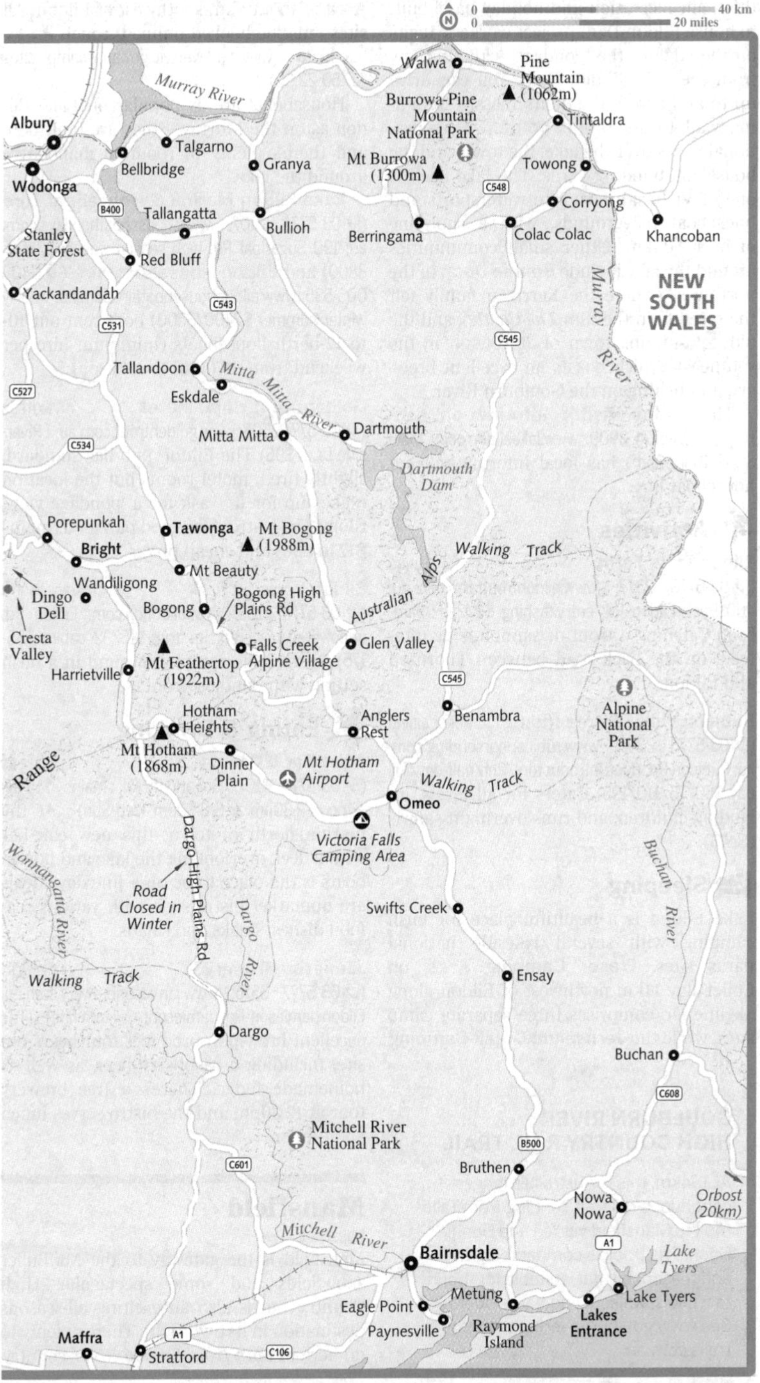
0
40 km
0
20 miles
Murray River
Albury
Wodonga
Talgarno
Bellbridge
Granya
Walwa
Pine Mountain (1062m)
Burrowa-Pine Mountain National Park
Mt Burrowa (1300m)
Tintaldra
Towong
Corryong
Khancoban
Colac Colac
Berringama
Bullioh
Tallangatta
B400
C548
Stanley State Forest
Red Bluff
Yackandandah
C543
C531
C527
C545
NEW SOUTH WALES
Murray River
Tallandoon
Eskdale
Mitta Mitta River
Mitta Mitta
Dartmouth
Dartmouth Dam
C534
Porepunkah
Tawonga
Mt Bogong (1988m)
Bright
Mt Beauty
Wandiligong
Dingo Dell
Cresta Valley
Bogong
Bogong High Plains Rd
Australian Alps Walking Track
Falls Creek Alpine Village
Glen Valley
Mt Feathertop (1922m)
Harrietville
C545
Benambra
Alpine National Park
Hotham Heights
Mt Hotham (1868m)
Anglers Rest
Dinner Plain
Mt Hotham Airport
Range
Walking Track
Omeo
Victoria Falls Camping Area
Wonnangatta River
Dargo High Plains Rd
Road Closed in Winter
Dargo River
Buchan River
Swifts Creek
Walking Track
Ensay
Dargo
Buchan
C608
Mitchell River National Park
C601
B500
Bruthen
Nowa Nowa
Orbost (20km)
A1
Mitchell River
Bairnsdale
Lake Tyers
Lake Tyers
Metung
Eagle Point
Lakes Entrance
Paynesville
Raymond Island
Maffra
A1
Stratford
C106

the main recreation and holiday base, built to house Eildon Dam project workers. It sits on the edge of the 'pondage' – the outflow from the Lake Eildon Dam. You can drive up to and across the dam's massive retaining wall to a **lookout point**, with sensational views over the lake, the town, and the houseboat-building yards. The lake itself is one of Victoria's favourite watersports and houseboat playgrounds, with a shoreline of over 500km. Other small communities around the lake include **Bonnie Doon** in the northwest (where the Kerrigan family felt the serenity in the film *The Castle*), and the old gold-mining town of **Jamieson** in the southeast, which boasts an excellent brewery, and fishing on the Goulburn River.

The **Eildon visitor information centre** (☎03-5774 2909; www.lakeeildon.com; Main St; ⏲10am-2pm) has local information and houseboat hire.

Activities

Eildon Trout Farm FISHING
(☎03-5773 2377; www.eildontroutfarm.com.au; 460 Back Eildon Rd; entry/fishing $2/2; ⏲9am-5pm) Catching a trout or salmon is guaranteed, on the back road between Thornton and Eildon.

Rubicon Valley Horse-Riding HORSE RIDING
(☎03-5773 2292; www.rubiconhorseriding.com.au; Rubicon Rd; rides introductory/2hr/half-day/full day $50/75/110/195) Caters for all levels, including children, and runs overnight safaris ($475).

Sleeping

Lake Eildon is a beautiful place for bush camping with several lakeside national parks sites. **Fraser Camping Area**, on Coller Bay 14km northwest of Eildon along Skyline Dr, comprises three separate camp sites, while the **Jerusalum Creek Camping Area** is about 8km southwest of Eildon. All sites must be booked online through **Parks Victoria** (www.parkweb.vic.gov.au; camp sites $17.50-22.50).

Houseboats are as popular on Lake Eildon as on the Murray – they are built here and there's plenty of room to manoeuvre around the lake.

Lake Eildon Marina & Houseboat Hire (☎03-5774 2107; www.houseboatholidays.com.au; 190 Sugarloaf Rd; high season weekly $2500-3800) and **Eildon Houseboat Hire** (☎0408 005 535; www.eildonhouseboathire.com.au; weekly winter/summer $2400/3500) both rent out 10- to 12-berth houseboats (minimum hire per weekend from $1700 in low season).

Golden Trout Hotel Motel MOTEL $
(☎03-5774 2508; www.goldentrout.com.au; 1 Riverside Dr; d $95) The Eildon pub has standard, slightly tired, motel rooms but the location makes up for it – ask for a 'pondage view' room. The bistro does good pub food (mains $17 to $30) and cheap pizzas.

Eildon Caravan Park CAMPGROUND $
(☎03-5774 2105; www.eildoncp.com; Eildon Rd; unpowered/powered site from $15/32, cabins $85-175) Rustic little camping ground in a bush setting with pondage frontage.

Eating & Drinking

Aqua Bar & Cafe CAFE $$
(☎03-5774 2107; Sugarloaf Rd; mains $15-27; ⏲noon-2.30pm & 6-8.30pm Wed-Sun) At the marina north of town, this new cafe-bar with a deck overlooking the lake and houseboats is the place to be on a fine day. Meals are upmarket bistro-style with various seafood dishes, steaks and salads.

Jamieson Brewery BREWERY
(☎03-5777 0515; www.jamiesonbrewery.com.au; Eildon-Jamieson Rd, Jamieson; ⏲11am-late) This excellent brew-pub produces four beers on-site, including a raspberry beer, as well as homemade fudge. There's a free brewery tour at 12.30pm and the bistro serves lunch and dinner.

GOULBURN RIVER HIGH COUNTRY RAIL TRAIL

At 134km, this is Australia's longest continuous rail trail, running from Tallarook to Mansfield via Yea and Bonnie Doon. The track is compacted gravel and reasonably flat, suitable for mountain bikes, walkers and horse riders. See www.goulburnriverhighcountryrailtrails.com.au.

Mansfield

POP 3070

Mansfield is the gateway to the Mt Buller snowfields and some spectacular High Country, but is also an exciting all-seasons destination in its own right. There's plenty to do here in *Man from Snowy River* country,

HORSING AROUND

The hills around Mansfield are *Man from Snowy River* country, the best place in Victoria to saddle up for a trail ride.

➡ **Hidden Trails** (☎03-5776 9867; www.hiddentrails.com.au; 462 Bunstons Rd, Tolmie; 1/2/3hr $50/70/100) Daily rides and extended High Country treks.

➡ **High Country Horses** (☎03-5777 5590; www.highcountryhorses.com.au; Mt Buller Rd; 2hr/half-day rides $90/120, overnight from $550; ⊙Oct-May) Based at Merrijig on the way to Mt Buller; offers anything from a short trot to overnight treks to Craig's Hut, Howqua River and Mt Stirling.

➡ **Lovick's** (☎03-5777 5150; www.lovicks.com.au; Merrijig; weekend rides $470) One of the original horse-riding outfits; Charlie Lovick was Master of Horse for the 1982 film *Man from Snowy River*. Specialises in extended rides.

➡ **McCormacks Mountain Valley Trail Rides** (☎03-5777 5542; www.mountainvalleytrailrides.com.au; 43 McCormack's Rd, Merrijig; day ride from $240, overnight from $550; ⊙Oct-May) Experienced locals take you into the King Valley and High Country, including a four-day adventure for $1000.

➡ **Watson's Mountain Country Trail Rides** (☎03-5777 3552; www.watsonstrailrides.com.au; Three Chains Rd; 1/2hr $40/80, 1-/2-day rides from $200/555) A peaceful property southeast of Mansfield where children can learn with pony rides or short trail rides, or you can take off on overnight catered rides.

with horse riding and mountain biking popular in summer, and a buzzing atmosphere in winter when the snow bunnies hit town.

Sights & Activities

Mansfield Zoo ZOO
(☎03-5777 3576; www.mansfieldzoo.com.au; 1064 Mansfield Woods Point Rd; adult/child/family $15/8/44; ⊙10am-5.30pm, till 6.30pm in summer) A surprisingly good wildlife park with lots of native fauna and some exotics such as a pair of white lions. You can sleep in the paddocks in a swag (adult/child $65/45, including zoo entry for two days) and wake to the dawn wildlife chorus.

Mansfield Cemetery CEMETERY
The graves of the three Mansfield police officers killed by Ned Kelly and his gang in 1878 at Stringybark Creek rest in this cemetery at the end of Highett St.

All Terrain Cycles MOUNTAIN BIKING
(☎03-5775 2724; www.allterraincycles.com.au; 58 High St) Hires out top-quality mountain bikes, rail trail bikes and safety equipment, from $45 per day to $125 for the top downhill bikes. Also runs guided tours.

Outdoor Pleasure ADVENTURE
(☎03-5775 2826; www.outdoorpleasure.com.au; 52 High St) Hires out kayaks (from $60) and stand-up paddleboards ($70).

Sleeping

Mansfield Holiday Park CAMPGROUND $
(☎03-5775 1383; www.mansfieldholidaypark.com.au; Mt Buller Rd; unpowered/powered sites from $28/32, cabins $70-120; 🏊) On the edge of town, this is a spacious caravan park with a pool, minigolf, camp kitchen and comfortable cabins.

Mansfield Travellers Lodge HOSTEL, MOTEL $$
(☎03-5775 1800; www.mansfieldtravellerslodge.com.au; 116 High St; dm $25, s/d/f from $95/110/180; ❄) This is a long-time favourite with backpackers and families. The spacious dorms are in a restored heritage building with kitchen, while the motel section features spacious one- and two-bedroom units.

Banjo's Accommodation CABINS $$
(☎03-5775 2335; www.banjosmansfield.com.au; cnr Mt Buller Rd & Greenvale Lane; d/q $120/180; 🏊) These family- and backpacker-friendly self-contained units on the edge of town can sleep up to five people in the studios and six in the two-bedroom units. They're modern and spacious and the expansive grounds are perfect for letting kids run around.

Highton Manor BOUTIQUE B&B $$
(☎03-5775 2700; www.hightonmanor.com.au; 140 Highton Lane; d stable/manor/tower incl breakfast $130/$225/365; 🏊) Built in 1896 for Francis Highett, who sang with Dame Nellie Melba,

this stately two-storey manor has style and romance but doesn't take itself too seriously. Has modern rooms in converted stables, and lavish period rooms in the main house.

Eating & Drinking

There's a farmers market at the Mansfield Primary School on the fourth Saturday of each month.

★ Mansfield Regional Produce Store CAFE $
(03-5779 1404; www.theproducestore.com.au; 68 High St; mains $12-18; 9am-5pm Tue-Sun, dinner Fri;) The best spot in town for coffee or a light lunch, this rustic store stocks an array of local produce, wines and fresh-baked artisan breads.

Deck on High MODERN AUSTRALIAN $$
(03-5775 1144; www.thedeckonhigh.com.au; 13-15 High St; mains $25-36; 11am-late Mon & Wed-Fri, 10am-late Sat & Sun) A sophisticated but relaxed bar-restaurant, the Deck offers a Mod Oz and international menu of tapas-style plates and mains of pork belly, roast duck or Singapore squid. The bar or terrace are great places for a drink.

Mansfield Hotel PUB $$
(03-5775 2101; www.mansfieldhotel.com.au; 86 High St; mains $18-32; noon-2pm & 6-9pm) Newly renovated after a 2010 fire, the Mansfield has a huge dining room and extensive bistro menu and pizzas to go with it. Pull up a couch by the fireplace in winter or eat out in the sunny beer terrace in summer.

Old Fire Station Restaurant INTERNATIONAL $$
(03-5779 1600; www.oldfirestation.net.au; 28 Highett St; mains $19-39; 4-11pm Wed-Sun) Enter the bright red doors to this cosy bistro in the renovated old fire station or sit out on the shaded terrace. The speciality here is steak but there's a good range of European-influenced pasta and chicken dishes and local wines.

Entertainment

★ Mansfield Armchair Cinemas CINEMA
(03-5775 2049; www.the-mac.com.au; 1 Chenery St; adult/child from $16.50/12.50; Tue, Wed & Fri-Sun) This cool community-run twin cinema employs local students and shows mainstream movies in digital. Pay a little extra for a 'gold class' armchair or a giant beanbag.

Information

Mansfield & Mt Buller High Country Visitor Centre (1800 039 049; www.mansfield-mt-buller.com.au; Maroondah Hwy; 9am-5pm) Next to the old railway station; check out the felt mural on display.

Getting There & Away

V/Line (1800 800 007; www.vline.com.au) buses run twice daily (once Sunday) from Melbourne ($24.60, three hours). **Mansfield–Mt Buller Bus Lines** (03-5775 2606; www.mmbl.com.au) runs at least seven buses daily during the ski season from Mansfield to Mt Buller (adult/child return $56/39).

Mt Buller

ELEV 1805M

Victoria's busiest ski resort, Buller buzzes all winter long. It's also developing into a popular summer choice for mountain bikers and hikers, with a range of cross-country and downhill trails. The extensive lift network includes the Northside Express chairlift that begins in the day car park and

BIKING MT BULLER

Mt Buller has become one of the great summer mountain-biking destinations in Australia, with a network of trails around the summit, and exhilarating downhill tracks. From 26 December to the end of January, the Northside Express chairlift operates on weekends (all-day lift and trails access $58). If you're not biking you can still ride the chairlift all day (adult/child $18/13).

Over the same period a shuttle bus runs Thursday to Sunday from the **Mirimbah Store** (03-5777 5529; www.mirimbah.com.au; per ride $13, daily $30; 8am-4pm Thu-Sun Sep-May, daily in winter) at the base of the mountain, to the summit car park, from where you can ride all the way back down on a number of trails. The most popular is the 1½-hour **Delatite River Trail**, with 13 river crossings, but there are dozens more downhill and cross-country trails. The owners of the Mirimbah Store (which, incidentally, is also a fabulous year-round cafe) are experienced riders and a mine of information on the trails.

drops you off in the middle of the ski runs. Cross-country trails link Mt Buller with **Mt Stirling**. For nonskiers there's tobogganing and snowshoeing. **Ducks & Drakes** (www.ducksanddrakes.net; tours $45-55) runs 1½-hour guided snowshoeing tours from the clock tower, including equipment and hot chocolate.

Sleeping

High Country Reservations (1800 039 049; www.mansfieldmtbuller.com.au) and **Mt Buller Alpine Reservations** (03-5777 6633; www.mtbullerreservations.com.au) book lodge accommodation.

YHA Mt Buller HOSTEL $
(03-5777 6181; www3.yha.com.au/hostels/vic/ski-region/mount-buller; The Ave; dm $60-70) Buller's winter-only YHA was being rebuilt at the time of writing, so expect brand-new facilities.

Mt Buller Chalet CHALET $$$
(03-5777 6566; www.mtbullerchalet.com.au; Summit Rd; d incl breakfast summer/winter from $215/530;) Open year-round, the chalet offers a sweet range of suites, a library with billiard table, well-regarded eateries, an impressive sports centre and heated pool. Inside is the casual Apres Bar and the fine-dining Black Cockatoo restaurant. The Chalet also operates nearby **Buller Backpackers** (www.bullerbackpackers.com.au; dm $55).

Hotel Enzian CHALET $$$
(03-5777 6924; www.hotelenzian.com.au; 69 Chamois Rd; r from $270) Year-round Enzian has a good range of lodge rooms and apartments.

Eating & Drinking

There's a licensed supermarket in the village centre and various cafes and fast-food eateries around the village.

Pension Grimus AUSTRIAN $$
(03-5777 6396; www.pensiongrimus.com.au; Breathtaker Rd; mains $25-40; dinner daily, lunch Sat & Sun) One of Buller's originals; the Austrian-style food at the Kaptan's Restaurant, impromptu music and pumping bar will give you a warm, fuzzy feeling after a day on the slopes.

Kooroora Hotel PUB
(03-5777 6050; Village Sq; till 3am in winter) Rocks hard and late during the ski season, and the popular Hoohah Kitchen serves good bistro meals (8am to 10pm).

CRAIG'S HUT

Cattledrivers built mountain huts for shelter throughout the High Country from the 1850s, but it's ironic that the best known is a more recent creation. Craig's Hut, on Mt Stirling, was built in 1981 for the film *The Man from Snowy River* and became something of a popular pilgrimage for hikers. It burned down in the 2006 bushfires but was rebuilt in 2007. Today you can drive most of the way to the hut (the last 2km is on foot) or you can walk there from Mt Buller. The views are superb.

Information

Mt Buller Resort Management Board (03-5777 6077; www.mtbuller.com.au; Community Centre, Summit Rd; 8.30am-5pm) There's an information desk in the village centre. Entrance fees to the Horse Hill day car park in winter are $37 per car. Lift tickets cost $108/59 per adult/child. Combined lift-and-lesson packages start at $156/140.

Getting There & Around

Mansfield-Mt Buller Buslines (03-5775 2606; www.mmbl.com.au) runs a winter service from Melbourne on Wednesday, Friday and Sunday (adult/child return $180/140) or from Mansfield daily ($56/39), and charter services in summer.

Ski-season car parking is below the village; a 4WD taxi service transports people to their village accommodation.

King Valley & the Snow Road

In the foothills of the Alpine National Park, the King Valley is a prosperous but relatively unheralded wine region noted for its Italian varietals and cool-climate wines such as sangiovese, barbera, sparkling prosecco, and pinot grigio. The valley extends south along the King River, through the tiny towns of Mohyu, Whitfield and Cheshunt – in keeping with local tourism taglines the road between Oxley and Whitfield is sometimes known as the 'Prosecco Road'.

Among the best wineries are **Dal Zotto Estate** (03-5729 8321; www.dalzotto.com.au; Main Rd, Whitfield; 10am-5pm), with the fine Trattoria restaurant, and **Pizzini** (03-5729 8278; www.pizzini.com.au; 175 King Valley Rd,

Whitfield; 10am-5pm), with a B&B and cooking school. For more information check out www.winesofthekingvalley.com.au.

The King Valley can be reached off the Hume Hwy, Snow Road or on the scenic mountain drive from Mansfield, which passes the superb **Power's Lookout**.

Milawa Gourmet Region

In-the-know travellers heading for the mountains bypass the first section of the Great Alpine Road between Wangaratta and Myrtleford and take the 'Snow Road' instead, where the **Milawa Gourmet Region** (www.milawagourmet.com) is the place to indulge your tastebuds.

First up is Oxley, where the **King River Cafe** (03-5727 3461; www.kingrivercafe.com.au; Snow Rd; mains $11-30; 10am-late Wed-Sun, 10am-3pm Mon) is a cool stop for scrumptious dishes, good coffee and local wines.

About 5km further, the main street of Milawa boasts **Milawa Mustard** (03-5727 3202; www.milawamustards.com.au; The Cross Roads; 10am-5pm), which offers tastings of its handmade seeded mustards, herbed vinegars and preserves; the **Olive Shop** (03-5727 3887; www.theoliveshop.com.au; 1605 Snow Rd; 10am-5pm), with oils and tapenades for sampling; and **Walkabout Honey** (03-5727 3468; Snow Rd; 10am-5pm), where you can sample a range of honeys.

Next stop is the region's best-known winery, **Brown Brothers** (03-5720 5500; www.brownbrothers.com.au; Bobbinawarrah Rd, Milawa; 9am-5pm). The winery's first vintage was in 1889, and it has remained in the hands of the same family ever since. As well as the tasting room, there's the superb Epicurean Centre restaurant, a gorgeous garden, kids' play equipment, and picnic and barbecue facilities.

Back on the highway, **Snow Road Produce** (03-5727 3688; www.snowroadproduce.com; 1604 Snow Rd; light meals $5.50-10.50; 7am-6pm Mon-Thu, 7am-10pm Fri-Sun) is a chic, modern cafe and produce store stocking local wine and beers and serving hot breakfast, open sandwiches and cheese platters.

About 2km north, **Milawa Cheese Company** (03-5727 3589; www.milawacheese.com.au; Factory Rd; 9am-5pm, meals 9.30am-3pm) excels at soft farmhouse brie (from goat or cow) and pungent washed-rind cheeses. There's a bakery here and an excellent restaurant where the speciality is a variety of pizzas using Milawa cheese.

Just off the Snow Road on the Ovens River flood plain is the little farming community of Whorouly, which has the **2 Cooks Cafe** (03-5783 6110; www.the2cookscafe.com.au; 577 Whorouly Rd; dishes $12.50-17.50; 9am-5pm Fri-Mon, dinner Fri), a sweet cafe and deli where the namesake cooks make their own sauces and jams, as well as serving good coffee and innovative meals like wagyu bangers and mash. Nearby is the **Whorouly Hotel** (03-5727 1424; 542 Whorouly Rd; mains $8-25; from 6pm Wed, Fri & Sat), a friendly country pub where you can get a hearty bistro meal. It's a mere 5km detour from the popular Murray to Mountains Rail Trail.

Beechworth

POP 2790

Beechworth's historic honey-coloured granite buildings and wonderful gourmet offerings make this one of northeast Victoria's most enjoyable old-time towns. It's listed by the National Trust as one of Victoria's two 'notable' towns (the other is Maldon), and you'll soon see why: this living legacy of the gold-rush era will take you back to the days of miners and bushrangers.

Sights & Activites

Down near pretty **Lake Sambell** you'll find the **Chinese Gardens**, a tribute to the Chinese gold miners.

The visitor centre runs two-hour **walking tours** (adult/child/family $10/7.50/25; 10.15am & 1.15pm) covering the gold rush and Ned Kelly connections.

As well as being on the Murray to Mountains Rail Trail, Beechworth has a dedicated **mountain-bike park**, about 1.5km northeast of the town centre off Alma Rd. Pick up a map at the visitor centre.

Historic & Cultural Precinct HISTORIC SITE
(1300 366 321; ticket for all sites plus 2 guided tours adult/child/family $25/15/50; 9am-5pm) Beechworth's main attraction is the group of well-preserved buildings that make up the Historic & Cultural Precinct, which can all be visited with the combined 'Golden Ticket'. First is the **Town Hall** (Ford St), where you'll find the visitor centre and the free Echoes of History audiovisual show. At the back is the cell that held bushranger Harry Power. Across the road is the **Beechworth Court-**

WORTH A TRIP

YACKANDANDAH

An old gold-mining town nestled in beautiful hills and valleys east of Beechworth, 'Yack' (pop 950), as it's universally known, is original enough to be classified by the National Trust. You might recognise it as the setting for the 2004 film *Strange Bedfellows*, starring Paul Hogan and Michael Caton.

Today many of the historic shops in the main street contain galleries, antiques, vintage clothing and curios: **A Bear's Old Wares** (☎02-6027 1114; www.abearsoldwares.com; 12 High St; ⊙9am-5.30pm) is a fascinating shop crammed with Buddhist and Hindu idols, prayer flags, Tibetan jewellery and wall hangings.

Karr's Reef Goldmine (☎0408 975 991; tours adult/child $25/20; ⊙10am, 1pm & 4pm Sat & Sun) is an old mine dating from 1857. On the 1½-hour guided tours you don a hard hat and descend into the original tunnels to learn a bit about the mine's history.

The biggest event of the year is the **Yackandandah Folk Festival** (www.folkfestival.yackandandah.com), with three days of music, parades, workshops and fun at venues around town in mid- to late March.

Yackandandah visitor centre (☎02-6027 1988; www.uniqueyackandandah.com.au; 27 High St; ⊙9am-5pm) is in the old post office. Pick up the free *A Walk in High Street* brochure.

house (adult/child/family $8/5/16; ⊙9.30am-5pm), where the trials of many key historical figures took place, including Ned Kelly and his mother, whose cells can still be seen. Send a telegram from the **Telegraph Station**, the original Morse-code office. Other buildings in this precinct include the **Sub-Treasury**, **Chinese Protector's Office** and **Gold Warden's office**. Walk through to Loch St to the **Burke Museum** (adult/child/family $8/5/16; ⊙10am-5pm), established as a memorial to the explorer Robert O'Hara Burke, who was Beechworth's superintendent of police before he set off on his fateful trek north with William Wills.

Beechworth Gaol Unlocked MUSEUM
(☎1300 774 766; www.beechworthgaol.com.au; cnr Ford & William Sts; tour adult/child/family from $22.50/17.50/75; ⊙tours 11am, 1pm & 3pm) The Beechworth Gaol released its last prisoners in 2006 but now it's open for spooky guided tours which take in the cells of former residents Ned Kelly and Harry Power, the guard towers and the gallows. Book ahead.

Beechworth Honey Experience FOOD
(☎03-5728 1432; www.beechworthhoney.com.au; cnr Ford & Church Sts; ⊙9am-5pm) FREE Beechworth Honey Experience takes you into the fascinating world of honey and bees with a self-guided audiovisual tour, live hive and honey tastings.

Beechworth Ghost Tours GHOST
(☎0447 432 816; www.beechworthghosttours.com; asylum tour adult/child/family $30/15/85, murder tour $25/15/75; ⊙from 8pm) Beechworth's spooky past comes to life in these popular walking tours at a former lunatic asylum and the sites of murders. Book ahead if you can.

Tours

Stick & Stones Adventures OUTDOORS
(☎02-6027 1483; www.sticksandstonesadventures.com.au; adult/child $120/85; ⊙tours Thu-Sun) This outfit specialises in food, wine and adventure trips. The 'Day in the Wild' tour on Sunday covers bush survival, including fire-making and collecting bush tucker.

Sleeping

Beechworth is well endowed with cottages and heritage B&Bs; check out www.beechworth.com/accommodation.

Old Priory GUESTHOUSE $
(☎03-5728 1024; www.oldpriory.com.au; 8 Priory Lane; dm/s/d $45/65/95, cottages $140) This historic convent is a charming old place that's often used by school groups, but it's the best budget choice in Beechworth.

Lake Sambell Caravan Park CAMPGROUND $
(☎03-5728 1421; www.caravanparkbeechworth.com.au; Peach Dr; unpowered/powered sites $26/32, cabins $90-135; ❄📶) This shady park next to pretty Lake Sambell has cool facilities

including a camp kitchen, a playground and bike and kayak hire.

Armour Motor Inn MOTEL $$
(03-5728 1466; www.armourmotorinn.com.au; 1 Camp St; s/d/f $110/120/150;) Good value and very central motel.

Freeman on Ford B&B $$$
(03-5728 2371; www.freemanonford.com.au; 97 Ford St; s/d incl breakfast from $255/275;) In the 1876 Oriental Bank, this glorious place offers Victorian luxury, right in the centre of town.

Eating & Drinking

For a town of its size, Beechworth has some fantastic feasting, from provedores and pantries stocking fresh local produce to serious fine-dining restaurants in historic buildings.

★**Bridge Road Brewers** BREWERY, PIZZERIA $
(03-5728 2703; www.bridgeroadbrewers.com.au; Ford St; pizza $12-21; 11am-5pm Mon-Sat, 11am-11pm Sun) Hiding behind the imposing Tanswells Commercial Hotel, Beechworth's gem of a microbrewery produces some excellent beers. It serves fresh-baked pretzels and super house-made Italian pizzas for lunch Wednesday to Sunday and dinner Sunday – try the apple and blue cheese.

Beechworth Bakery BAKERY $
(1300 233 784; 27 Camp St; light meals $3-10; 6am-7pm) Popular with locals and tourists, but you won't have trouble finding a seat in this barn-sized original in a well-known bakery chain. Good for pies and pastries, cakes, sandwiches and the signature beesting.

Provenance MODERN AUSTRALIAN $$$
(03-5728 1786; www.theprovenance.com.au; 86 Ford St; mains $25-37, degustation menu $100; 6.30pm-late Wed-Sun) In an 1856 bank building, Provenance is elegant but contemporary fine dining. The innovative menu features dishes such as Milawa duck breast, and some inspiring vegetarian choices.

Information

Beechworth Visitor Centre (1300 366 321; www.beechworthonline.com.au; 103 Ford St; 9am-5pm) In the old town hall building, this efficient office has an accommodation and activity booking service. Ask about the Golden Ticket which gives admission to the historic precinct and two guided walking tours (valid two days).

Getting There & Away

Beechworth is just off the Great Alpine Road, 36km east of Wangaratta. **V/Line** (1800 800 007; www.vline.com.au) runs a train/bus service between Melbourne and Beechworth with a change at Wangaratta ($31, 3½ hours, four daily). There are direct buses from Wangaratta ($4.40, 35 minutes, five daily) and Bright ($4.20, 50 minutes, two daily). Each of these services only runs once on weekends.

Myrtleford

POP 2710

Along the Great Alpine Road near the foothills of Mt Buffalo, Myrtleford is yet another 'Gateway to the Alps', and a worthwhile stop if you're heading to the snowfields or exploring the gourmet region. **Myrtleford visitor centre** (03-5755 0514; www.visitmyrtleford.com; 38 Myrtle St; 9am-5pm) has information and a booking service. If you're looking to jump on the rail trail here, **Myrtleford Cycle Centre** (03-5752 1511; www.myrtlefordcycle.com; 59 Clyde St; per day/weekend $25/45; 9am-5.30pm Tue-Sat, 10am-2pm Sun) rents bikes.

Butter Factory CAFE $
(03-5752 2300; www.thebutterfactory.com.au; Great Alpine Rd; meals $6.50-18.50; 8.30am-5pm Thu-Tue;) This excellent cafe and produce store is indeed in an old butter factory, and you can see butter being churned here most days or take a tour ($5) of the process on at 11am Thursday. The produce store stocks a wide range of local jams, sauces, honey and pickles, while the cafe is a special place for an organic breakfast or lunch of platters, burgers and other light meals.

Mt Buffalo National Park

ELEV 1500M

Beautiful Mt Buffalo is an easily accessible year-round destination – in winter it's a tiny family-friendly resort for cross-country skiing and tobogganing, and in summer it's a brilliant spot for bushwalking, mountain biking and rock climbing. Fit road cyclists regularly pedal to the summit and freewheel back down.

It was named in 1824 by the explorers Hume and Hovell on their trek from Sydney to Port Phillip, and declared a national park in 1898. The main access road is out of Porepunkah, between Myrtleford and Bright.

First stop is the **Gorge Day Visitor Area**, where short walks lead to granite outcrops and lookout points with stunning mountain and valley views. The **Big Walk**, an 11km, five-hour ascent of the mountain from Eurobin Creek Picnic Area, finishes here (though it's easier to start here and walk down). There's also an easy walking track to **Lake Catani**, a good spot for summer swimming, canoeing and picnicking.

The road contines past Dingo Dell and Cresta Valley to just below the summit of the **Horn** (1723m), the highest point on the massif. It's a stiff walk from the car park to the top for unbeatable 360-degree views of the High Country.

Activities

There are 14km of groomed **cross-country ski trails** starting out from the Cresta Valley car park. In summer Mt Buffalo is a **hang-gliding** paradise, and the near-vertical walls of the Gorge provide some of Australia's most challenging **rock climbing**. Kayaks (from $30/50 per half-/full-day) can be hired through the year-round Dingo Dell Cafe.

Adventure Guides Australia OUTDOORS
(☎0419 280 614; www.visitmountbuffalo.com.au) This experienced and established operator has the mountain covered with abseiling and rock climbing (from $88) and caving through an underground river system (from $120). It also runs a cross-country ski school in winter.

Eagle School of Microlighting MICROLIGHTING
(☎03-5750 1174; www.eagleschool.com.au; flights $70-300) Exhilarating tandem flights over Mt Buffalo region.

Sleeping

The grand, century-old **Mt Buffalo Chalet**, overlooking the Gorge area, closed in 2007 and is in the hands of Parks Victoria, who are still looking for a plan to bring it back to its former glory.

Lake Catani Campground (camp sites per person $28; ⊙Nov-Apr) is a popular summer campground with toilets and showers. Book through **Parks Victoria** (☎13 19 63; www.parkweb.vic.gov.au).

Bright

POP 2165

Famous for its glorious autumn colours, Bright is a popular year-round destination in the foothills of the Alps and a gateway to Mt Hotham and Falls Creek. Skiers make a beeline through Bright in winter, but it's a lovely all-season base for exploring the Alpine National Park, paragliding, fishing and kayaking on local rivers, bushwalking and exploring the region's wineries. Plentiful accommodation and some smart restaurants and cafes complete the picture.

MURRAY TO THE MOUNTAINS RAIL TRAIL

The **Murray to the Mountains Rail Trail** (www.murraytomountains.com.au) is one of the High Country's best walking/cycling trails for families or casual riders – it's sealed and relatively flat for much of the way and passes through spectacular rural scenery of farms, forest and vineyards. The 94km trail runs from Wangaratta to Bright via Beechworth, Myrtleford and Porepunkah. You can hire bikes in Bright and Myrtleford or call **Riding High Cycling Tours** (☎03-5725 1343, 0402 858 268; www.ridinghigh.com.au; bike hire per day $30) who will deliver a hire bike to you. They also offer cycling tours and transfers.

Sights & Activities

Walking trails around Bright include the 3km riverside **Canyon Walk**, 4km **Cherry Walk** and a 6km track to **Wandiligong** that follows Morses Creek.

There are good wineries around Bright, the standout being **Boynton's Feathertop** (☎03-5756 2356; www.boynton.com.au; 6619 Great Alpine Rd, Porepunkah; ⊙10am-5pm) at Porepunkah, with an alfresco lunch restaurant, deli with local cheeses and produce, a brewery and great views from the elevated terrace. For something different, you can sample a range of liqueurs, schnapps and fruit brandy distilled on-site at **Great Alpine Liqueurs** (☎03-5755 1002; www.greatalpineliqueurs.com.au; 36 Churchill Ave; ⊙10am-4.30pm Fri-Mon, daily during holidays).

The Murray to Mountains Rail Trail starts (or ends) behind the old train station. Bikes, tandems and baby trailers can be rented from **Cyclepath** (☎03-5750 1442; www.cyclepath.com.au; 74 Gavan St; per hr from $20, half-/full-day from $24/32, mountain/road bikes $44/60).

Bright is a base for all sorts of adventure activities – paragliding enthusiasts catch the thermals from nearby Mystic Mountain.

Active Flight PARAGLIDING
(☎0428 854 455; www.activeflight.com.au) Introductory paragliding course (from $245) or tandem flights ($130 to $220).

Alpine Paragliding PARAGLIDING
(☎0428 352 048; www.alpineparagliding. com; 100 Gavan St; ⊙Oct-Jun) Tandem flights from Mystic ($130 to $250) and two-day courses ($500).

Bright Microflights MICROLIGHTING
(☎03-5750 1555; brightmicroflights@swiftdsl.com.au; Buckland Valley Rd, Porepunkah) Takes you on powered hang-glider flights over Porepunkah ($70), Mt Buffalo ($125) or both ($155).

Tours

Bright Limousines WINE
(☎03-5755 1144; www.brightlimousines.com.au; from $75) Visit wineries or country pubs in style with these stretch-limo tours.

Festivals & Events

Bright Autumn Festival STREET FESTIVAL
(www.brightautumnfestival.org.au) Open gardens and a popular gala day; held April or May.

Bright Spring Festival STREET FESTIVAL
(www.brightspringfestival.com.au) Celebrate all things Bright and beautiful. Runs over two weeks in late October/early November, culminating on the Melbourne Cup weekend.

Sleeping

There's an abundance of accommodation, but rooms are scarce and pricey during Christmas and Easter holiday seasons and festivals.

Bright Backpackers Outdoor Inn CAMPGROUND $
(☎0418 528 631, 03-5755 1154; www.brightbackpackers.com.au; 106 Coronation Dr; unpowered/powered sites from $16/18, s/d cabins $33/55;) This basic but laid-back park at the foot of Mystic Mountain is popular with paragliders and is the cheapest place in town.

Bright Velo HOTEL $$
(☎03-57551074; www.brightvelo.mobi; 2 Ireland St; d from $100, apt & heritage B&B $150-170) A range of good-value accommodation aimed at (but not exclusive to) cyclists, with bike racks, storage, local advice and a great cafe. Accommodation includes simple motel rooms, two-bedroom units sleeping up to five people, and B&B in the heritage rooms of the former Oriental Hotel.

Coach House Inn MOTEL $$
(☎1800 813 992; www.coachhousebright.com.au; 100GavanSt;s/d$85/105,moteld/tr/f$125/145/165;) Central place with simple but good-value rooms and self-contained motel-style units sleeping from two to six people.

Elm Lodge Motel MOTEL $$
(☎03-5755 1144; www.elmlodge.com.au; 2 Wood St; d $120-150, spa cottage $160;) This slightly quirky set of burgundy and pine units has rooms for all budgets, from a studio cheapie to spacious two-bedroom self-contained apartments with polished floorboards, and spa rooms.

Odd Frog BOUTIQUE HOTEL $$
(☎0418 362 791; www.theoddfrog.com; 3 McFadyens Ln; d $150-195, q $250) In a bush setting a short walk south of town, these contemporary, ecofriendly studios feature light, breezy spaces, fabulous outdoor decks with a telescope for star-gazing, and spas. The bush-design features clever use of the hilly site, with sculptural steel-frame foundations and flying balconies.

Eating & Drinking

Ireland St has cafes, takeaways and the Alpine Hotel, and there's good dining along Gavan St, the highway through town.

Cafe Velo CAFE $
(☎03-5755 1074; 2 Ireland St; dishes $6-15; ⊙7.30am-4pm) This supercool retro bike-themed cafe serves arguably the town's best coffee, tasty breakfasts and vegie dishes. Run by former champion road cyclist, Wayne Hildred, this is the place to come for advice and refreshments if you're on two wheels.

Pepperleaf Bushtucker Restaurant MODERN AUSTRALIAN $$
(☎03-5755 1537; 2a Anderson St; tapas from $6, mains $18-27; ⊙noon-2pm & 6pm-late Thu-Tue, breakfast weekends) Pepperleaf specialises in using 'native' ingredients including wattleseed, quandong, wild limes and lemon myrtle with game meats such as crocodile, emu and kangaroo to create innovative 'indigenous' dishes.

Thirteen Steps WINE BAR $$
(☎03-5750 1313; www.thirteensteps.com.au; 14 Barnard St; mains $15-22; ⊙5-11pm Thu-Mon) De-

scend into the cellar at this intimate wine bar and feast on Harrietville smoked trout and zucchini fritters. Good for a romantic drink.

Simone's Restaurant ITALIAN $$$
(☎03-5755 2266; www.simonesbright.com.au; 98 Gavan St; mains $32-37; ⏰from 6.30pm Tue-Sat) For 20 years owner-chef Patrizia Simone has been serving outstanding Italian food, with a focus on local ingredients and seasonal produce, in the rustic dining room of this heritage-listed house. Bookings essential. Patrizia has also started a cooking school with regular classes on Friday, Saturday or Sunday ($150 to $180).

★**Bright Brewery** BREWERY
(☎03-5755 1301; www.brightbrewery.com.au; 121 Gavan St; ⏰noon-10pm; 📶) This expanding boutique brewery produces a quality range of beers and beer-friendly food like pizza, kransky and nachos, and the latest addition is a well-regarded restaurant. There's a guided tour and tasting on Friday at 3pm ($18), live music on Sunday, and you can learn to be a brewer for a day ($360).

ℹ Information

Alpine Visitor Information Centre (☎03-5755 0584, 1800 111 885; www.greatalpinevalleys.com.au; 119 Gavan St) Has a busy accommodation booking service, Parks Victoria information and the attached Riverdeck Café. Internet access.

ℹ Getting There & Away

V/Line (☎1800 800 007; www.vline.com.au) runs train/coach services from Melbourne ($32.20, 4½ hours, two daily) with a change at Wangaratta ($8.80, 1½ hours). During the ski season the **Snowball Express** (☎1300 656 546; www.snowballexpress.com.au) operates from Melbourne to Bright (return $130), continuing up to Mt Hotham (return $50, 1½ hours).

Mt Beauty & the Kiewa Valley

POP 1655

No, it's not a mountain, but it is beautiful. Huddled at the foot of Mt Bogong (Victoria's highest mountain) on the Kiewa River, Mt Beauty and its twin villages of Tawonga and Tawonga South are the gateways to Falls Creek ski resort. The drive from Bright has some lovely alpine views, particularly from Tawonga Gap Lookout. A scenic loop drive runs via the **Happy Valley Tourist Road** from Ovens to Mt Beauty.

The **Mt Beauty Music Festival** (www.musicmuster.org.au) brings together folk, blues and country musicians in April.

Sights & Activities

The 2km **Tree Fern Walk** and the longer **Peppermint Walk** both start from Mountain Creek picnic and camping ground, on Mountain Creek Rd, off the Kiewa Valley Hwy. About 1km from Bogong Village (towards Falls Creek), the 1.5km return **Fainter Falls Walk** takes you to a pretty cascade.

There's an interesting visitor information centre at the **Bogong Power Station** (☎03-5754 3318; Bogong High Plains Rd; ⏰11am-3pm Sun & Mon) FREE, a working hydroelectric plant about 20km from Mt Beauty.

Bogong Horseback Adventures HORSE RIDING
(☎03-5754 4849; www.bogonghorse.com.au; Mountain Creek Rd, Tawonga; 2/3hr $90/110, full-day with lunch $220) Horse riders can experience this beautiful area with Bogong Horseback Adventures; also organises packhorse tours from five to seven days.

Rocky Valley Bikes OUTDOORS
(☎03-5754 1118; www.rockyvalley.com.au; Kiewa Valley Hwy) Hires mountain and cross-country bikes from $35/50 per half-/full day, and snowsports equipment and chains in the white season.

Sleeping

There's camping along the Kiewa River and several motels along the highway.

Mount Beauty Holiday Centre CAMPGROUND $
(☎03-5754 4396; www.holidaycentre.com.au; Kiewa Valley Hwy; unpowered/powered sites $28/33, cabins & yurts $100-150; ❄📶) This family caravan park close to the town centre has river frontage, games, a drying room and an interesting range of cabins, including hexagonal 'yurts'.

Dreamers APARTMENT $$$
(☎03-5754 1222; www.dreamersmtbeauty.com.au; Kiewa Valley Hwy; d $200-490; 📶) 🍃 Each of Dreamer's stunning self-contained eco apartments offers something special and architecturally unique. Sunken lounges, open fireplaces, loft bedrooms and balcony spas are some of the highlights. Great views, a cafe and a pretty lagoon complete a dreamily romantic experience.

Eating & Drinking

Flour + Water PIZZERIA $
(☎ 03-5754 4449; www.flourpluswater.com; 171 Kiewa Valley Hwy, Tawonga South; pizza $10-15, mains $25; ⏲ 5pm-late winter & school holidays) Fine pizzas, including exotic types like sweet chilli Thai, are the trademark at this casual but charismatic little eatery just outside town.

Å Skafferi SWEDISH $
(☎ 03-5754 4544; 84 Bogong High Plains Rd, Mt Beauty; meals $6-18; ⏲ 8am-4pm Thu-Mon) This cool Swedish pantry and foodstore is part of the Svärmisk spa complex – lunch on Swedish meatballs or the sampler of herring and *knackebrod* (crisp bread).

Roi's Diner Restaurant ITALIAN $$
(☎ 03-5754 4495; 177 Kiewa Valley Hwy, Tawonga; mains $27-35; ⏲ Thu-Sun 6.30-9.30pm) An unassuming timber shack on the highway at Tawonga, 5km from Mt Beauty, Roi's is an award-winning restaurant, specialising in exceptional modern Italian cuisine like roast pickled pork loin chop.

Sweetwater Brewing Company BREWERY
(☎ 03-5754 1881; www.sweetwaterbrewing.com.au; 211 Kiewa Valley Hwy, Tawonga South; ⏲ 1-6pm Fri-Sun) Boutique brewery producing five very drinkable beers.

Information

Mt Beauty Visitor Centre (☎ 03-5755 0596, 1800 111 885; www.greatalpinevalleys.com.au; 31 Bogong High Plains Rd) Has an accommodation-booking service and displays on the history and nature of the region.

Getting There & Away

V/Line (☎ 1800 800 007; www.vline.com.au) operates a train/bus/taxi service from Melbourne to Mt Beauty ($36.40, 5½ hours), via Seymour and Bright, from Monday to Friday. The taxi service runs from Bright to Mt Beauty weekdays at 4.40pm ($5.40, 45 minutes). In winter, **Falls Creek Coach Service** (☎ 03-5754 4024; www.fallscreekcoachservice.com.au) operates direct daily buses to Mt Beauty from Melbourne (one-way/return $86/134) and Albury ($34/53), both continuing to Falls Creek ($37/58).

Falls Creek

ELEV 1780M

Victoria's glitzy, fashion-conscious resort, Falls Creek combines a picturesque alpine setting with impressive skiing and infamous après-ski entertainment. Skiing is spread over two main areas – the Village Bowl and Sun Valley – with 19 lifts, a vertical drop of 267m and Australia's longest beginner run at **Wombat's Ramble**.

It's not all snow sports though, and Falls has a great summer program, which includes hiking and horse riding. **Mountain biking** is gaining popularity here in the green season, with developing downhill and cross-country trails.

Sleeping

In winter the lodges at Falls are truly ski-in, ski-out. Accommodation can be booked via **Falls Creek Central Reservations** (☎ 1800 033 079; www.fallscreek.com.au/centralreservations).

Alpha Lodge LODGE $
(☎ 5758 3488; www.alphaskilodge.com.au; dm summer/winter from $30/109) A spacious affordable lodge set-up with a sauna, a large lounge with panoramic views and a communal kitchen.

Viking Alpine Lodge LODGE $$
(☎ 03-5758 3247; 13 Parallel St; d/q summer from $110/200, ski season from $320/500) Viking offers good-value accommodation all year with excellent communal facilities including lounge, kitchen and great views.

Quay West Resort & Spa HOTEL $$$
(☎ 03-5732 8000, 1800 630 882; www.quaywestfallscreek.com.au; 17 Bogong High Plains Rd; 1-bedroom apt summer/winter from $225/600) Dominating Falls Creek village, this resort has luxurious self-contained apartments with super views, as well as a day spa and the Alta restaurant. Open year-round.

Eating & Drinking

Quality kiosks, cafes and restaurants abound and there's a supermarket with a bottle shop for self-caterers.

Cafe Milch WINE BAR $
(☎ 0408 465 939; 50 Schuss St; mains $12-24; ⏲ 8am-11pm) The hip place to see and be seen, this cafe-bar offers Mod Oz food, a blazing fire and a good wine list.

Three Blue Ducks CAFE $$
(☎ 03-5758 3863; www.huski.com.au; 3 Sitzmark St; mains $16-30; ⏲ 7.30am-11pm) At Huski apartments this slick new cafe and produce store brings the successful Sydney venture to the mountains.

Man Hotel PUB
(☎03-5758 3362; www.themanfallscreek.com; 20 Slalom St; ⏲4pm-late) 'The Man' hotel has been around forever, is open all year and is the heart of Falls' nightlife. In winter it fires up as a club, cocktail bar and live-music venue featuring popular Aussie bands.

ℹ Information

Ski-season daily resort entry is $39.50 per car. One-day lift tickets cost $106/90/53 per adult/student/child, with discounts available for two or more days. Combined lift-and-lesson packages cost $160/136/109. Lift tickets also cover Mt Hotham. An accommodation transfer service for luggage ($33 return) operates between the village terminal and the lodges. Car parking for day visitors is at the base of the village, next to the ski lifts.

Falls Creek Resort Management (☎03-5758 1200; www.fallscreek.com.au; 1 Slalom St; ⏲winter 8.30am-5pm, summer 9am-5pm Mon-Fri, 10am-3pm Sat & Sun) Visitor information and useful maps and guides to ski trails and summer hiking.

ℹ Getting There & Around

Falls Creek is 375km from Melbourne, a 4½-hour drive. During the winter, **Falls Creek Coach Service** (☎03-5754 4024; www.fallscreek-coachservice.com.au) operates four times a week between Falls Creek and Melbourne (one-way/return $105/170) and also runs services to and from Albury ($60/95) and Mt Beauty ($37/58). There's a reduced service over summer.

If you want to ski Mt Hotham for the day, jump on the HeliLink for $125 return if you have a valid lift ticket.

Harrietville

POP 234

Harrietville, a pretty little town nestled on the Ovens River below Mt Feathertop, is the last stop before the start of the winding road up to Mt Hotham. The village is the starting and finishing point for various **alpine walking tracks**, including the popular Mt Feathertop walk, Razorback Ridge and Dargo High Plains walks. You can hire bikes ($50 per day) from Snowline Hotel, which also runs mountain-bike tours and mountain transfers for hikers.

In late November the annual **Blue Grass Festival** (www.harrietvillebluegrass.com.au) takes over the town.

Snowline Hotel MOTEL $$
(☎03-5759 2524; www.snowlinehotel.com.au; Great Alpine Rd; d from $115) The Snowline has been operating for over 100 years, and offers inexpensive off-mountain accommodation in comfortable motel rooms. The pub bistro (mains $20 to $30) has a loyal following, especially for its chicken parma, Harrietville trout and Tasmanian Angus steak.

★**Shady Brook Cottages** COTTAGES $$
(☎03-5759 2741; www.shadybrook.com.au; Mountain View Walk; 1-/2-bed cottage from $130/165; ❄@) A magnificent garden envelopes this lovely, peaceful group of romantic self-contained country-style cottages. Two come with spa and all have balconies and mod cons.

Mt Hotham & Dinner Plain

ELEV 1868M

Serious hikers, skiers and snowboarders make tracks for Mt Hotham, with some of the best and most challenging downhill runs in the country – 320 hectares of downhill runs, with a vertical drop of 428m and about 80% of the ski trails intermediate or advanced black diamond runs. Over at **Dinner Plain**, 10km from Hotham village and linked by a free shuttle, there are excellent cross-country trails around the village, including the **Hotham–Dinner Plain Ski Trail**.

From November to May, Hotham and Dinner Plain boast some stunning alpine trails for hiking and mountain biking. The most popular is the 22km return trip to **Mt Feathertop** (1922m) via Razorback Ridge. At Dinner Plain, **Adventures with Altitude** (☎03-5159 6608; www.adventureswithaltitude.com.au; bike hire per hr/half-/full day $18/35/50) provides mountain-biking gear and trail maps. Guided mountain-bike tours start at $70/180 for one/two days and it also organises guided bushwalks and horse riding.

Sleeping

Ski-season accommodation generally has a minimum two-night stay. Booking agencies:

Dinner Plain Accommodation (☎1800 444 066; www.accommdinnerplain.com.au; Big Muster Dr)

Dinner Plain Central Reservations (☎1800 670 019; www.dinnerplain.com; Big Muster Dr)

Mt Hotham Accommodation Service (☎1800 032 061; www.mthothamaccommodation.com.au)

Mt Hotham Central Reservations (☎1800 657 547; www.skicom.com.au)

Leeton Lodge LODGE $
(☎03-5759 3283; www.leetonlodge.com; Dargo Ct, Mt Hotham; dm summer $40, winter $60-80) Classic family ski-club lodge with 30 beds, cooking facilities and good views. Open year-round.

General Lodge LODGE $$
(☎03-5759 3523; www.thegeneral.com.au; Great Alpine Rd, Mt Hotham; apt $150) Behind the General are these fully self-contained apartments, with lounge and kitchen and views from the balcony.

Currawong Lodge LODGE $$
(☎1800 635 589, 03-5159 6452; www.currawonglodge.com.au; Big Muster Dr, Dinner Plain; summer s/d $80/130, ski season 2-night minimum d $210) Currawong Lodge welcomes you with a huge communal lounge-and-kitchen area with a monster open fireplace, TV, DVD and stereo. At this price you can ski with a conscience.

Arlberg Resort APARTMENT $$$
(☎03-5986 8200; www.arlberghotham.com.au; Mt Hotham; 2-night minimum d from $430-830;)

ALPINE HIGHWAYS

If you want to feel like you're cruising on the roof of Victoria, the High Country has three great 'highways' that will take you up and over the mountains and down to the Gippsland coast. All three link up with Omeo and become the Great Alpine Road down to Bairnsdale. They are a joy for car or motorcycle touring, or for an increasing number of hard-core cyclists.

Great Alpine Road

The High Country version of the Great Ocean Road, this much-loved 308km route starts at Wangaratta and follows the Ovens Valley through Myrtleford, Bright and Harrietville before passing over Mt Hotham and Dinner Plain then descending to Omeo and all the way down to Bairnsdale in East Gippsland. It's Australia's highest year-round-accessible sealed road. The section from Omeo southeast to Bruthen is particularly scenic, following the valley of the Tambo River and passing farmland, vineyards and the pretty communities of Swifts Creek and Ensay. At Bruthen you can finish the trip with a beer and a bite at the **Bullant Brewery** (☎03-5157 5307; www.bullantbrewery.com; 46 Main St; meals $16-28; 11am-5pm Wed, Thu, Sun, 11am-10pm Fri & Sat), a boutique backcountry brewer serving up meals of pizzas and gourmet burgers.

Omeo Highway

Stretching almost 300km from the Murray River to the coast, the Omeo Hwy takes in some of Victoria's most scenic and diverse countryside. The highway is unsealed in sections (between Mitta Mitta and Glen Willis), and snow often makes it difficult or impossible to pass in winter.

At Anglers Rest, beside the Cobungra River, **Blue Duck Inn** (☎03-5159 7220; www.blueduckinn.com.au; Omeo Hwy; mains $18-27, cabins $130-150; meals noon-2pm & 6-8pm Wed-Sun) is popular with anglers, motorcyclists, kayakers and bushwalkers for its hearty meals and barbecue area by the river. The two-bedroom self-contained cabins here are very cosy. There are also two free **camping areas** just off the highway.

About 30km south of Anglers Rest, you reach Omeo and join up with the Great Alpine Road.

Bogong High Plains Road

In 2009, the Bogong High Plains Rd was finally sealed all the way from Falls Creek to the Omeo Hwy, creating another fabulous summer tourist route (generally passable November to April). The journey starts at Mt Beauty and climbs up through Bogong village to Falls Creek ski resort. From there it skirts Rocky Valley Lake and winds 35km to join the Omeo Hwy about 11km north of Anglers Rest. The result is a superb alpine loop from Bright, over Mt Hotham via Omeo to Falls Creek, down to Mt Beauty and back to Bright – a distance of about 250km. Look out for signs pointing to historic mountain huts, including **Wallace Hut**, just off the road past Falls Creek.

The largest resort on the mountain, the Arlberg has a big range of apartments and motel-style rooms, plus restaurants, bars, ski hire and a heated pool. Ski season only.

Rundell's Alpine Lodge LODGE $$$
(☎03-5159 6422; www.rundells.com.au; Big Muster Dr, Dinner Plain; summer d from $200, ski season 2-night minimum $350;) This sprawling complex is a well-run hotel with all the comforts – spa, sauna and restaurant-bar.

Eating & Drinking

In winter, there are plenty of great eating choices here. In summer a couple of places serve meals and there's a small supermarket. Good places for an après-ski drink include Jack Frost, Avalanche Bar and **Swindlers** (☎03-5759 4421; mains $16-40; breakfast, lunch & dinner).

General PUB $
(☎03-5759 3523; Great Alpine Rd, Mt Hotham; meals $10-30; lunch & dinner) The ever-reliable 'Gen' is open all year and is a popular watering hole with a menu of pizzas, good bistro meals and internet.

Dinner Plain Hotel PUB $$
(☎03-5159 6462; www.dinnerplainhotel.com.au; Dinner Plain; mains $10-28; noon-2pm & 6-9pm) The barn-sized local pub is the social hub of Dinner Plain and a friendly place to hang out year-round, with roaring open fires and a bistro serving good pub grub and pizzas.

Information

The ski-season admission fee is $35 per car per day, and $12 for bus passengers (this may be included in your fare). Lift tickets (peak) per adult/student/child cost $102/87/51. Lift tickets also cover Falls Creek.

Dinner Plain Visitor Centre (☎1300 734 365; www.visitdinnerplain.com) Get information in the village centre.

Mt Hotham Alpine Resort Management Board (☎03-5759 3550; www.mthotham.com.au) At the village administration centre. Collect a range of brochures with maps for short, eco, heritage and village walks.

Getting There & Around

AIR

Mt Hotham Airport services Hotham Heights and Dinner Plain, but its only current commercial flights are run in winter by QantasLink from Sydney (from $189); it also serves charter flights.

BUS

During the ski season, **Snowball Express** (☎03-9370 9055, 1800 659 009; www.snowballexpress.com.au) has daily buses from Melbourne to Mt Hotham ($180 return, six hours), via Wangaratta, Myrtleford, Bright and Harrietville. **O'Connell's Bus Lines** (☎0428 591 377; www.omeobus.com.au) operates a daily 'Alps Link' service between Omeo and Mt Hotham ($4.40), continuing to Bright ($5.60).

SHUTTLE

A free shuttle runs frequently around the resort from 7am to 3am; a separate shuttle service also operates to Dinner Plain.

Omeo

POP 270

High in the hills between the Alpine National Park and Gippsland, historic Omeo comes as a bit of a surprise after the winding drive up from the coast or down from the mountains. This is the back road to Mt Hotham and the main town on the eastern section of the Great Alpine Road. In the gold-rush days of the 1850s, Omeo was home to the wildest and most remote goldfields in the state. It attracted many Chinese diggers whose legacy you can see on the **Oriental Claims Walk**. Today, you can't help but stay a while to wander the steep main street and breathe the crisp mountain air.

Learn a bit about Omeo's gold-rush past in the **Historic Park & Museum** (Great Alpine Rd; 10am-2pm), which includes the courthouse, log jail (1858) and police residence.

Sleeping & Eating

There's free camping at Victoria Falls, 18km west of Omeo. In town, there's a bakery, a couple of cafes and takeaway shops.

Omeo Caravan Park CAMPGROUND $
(☎03-5159 1351; www.omeocaravanpark.com.au; Old Omeo Hwy; unpowered/powered sites $28/32, cabins from $100) In a pretty valley alongside the Livingstone Creek about 2km from town, this park has spacious, grassy sites.

Golden Age Hotel HOTEL $$
(☎03-5159 1344; www.goldenageomeo.com.au; Day Ave; s/d from $50/80, d with spa $157) This beautiful art-deco corner pub dominates Omeo's main street. Upstairs are simple but elegant pub rooms, some with en suite and spa. The welcoming restaurant (mains $16 to $29) serves plates piled high with reliable fare of steaks, salads and gourmet pizzas.

Snug as a Bug Motel MOTEL $$
(☎03-5159 1311; www.motelomeo.com.au; 188 Great Alpine Rd; d/f from $100/180) Has a range of accommodation in lovely historic country-style buildings. As well as the main guesthouse, there are family-size motel rooms and a cute self-contained cottage.

Information

Omeo Visitor Information Centre (☎03-5159 1679; www.omeoregion.com.au; 152 Day Ave; ⊙10am-3pm Tue-Sun)

Getting There & Away

Omeo Bus Lines (☎0427 017 732) has one bus on weekdays between Omeo and Bairnsdale ($18, two hours). **O'Connell's Bus Lines** (☎0428 591 377; www.omeobus.com.au) operates a daily summer 'Alps Link' service between Omeo and Bright ($10.40) via Mt Hotham and Dinner Plain on Monday, Wednesday and Friday. A winter service to Dinner Plain and Mt Hotham operates on Sunday, Wednesday and Friday.

GIPPSLAND

It might not be as well known as the Great Ocean Road to the west, but Victoria's southeast coast easily boasts the state's best beaches, along with impossibly pretty lakeside villages and Victoria's finest coastal national parks, typified by the glorious Wilsons Promontory. While most travellers head for the coast between Phillip Island and Mallacoota – the cool route between Melbourne and Sydney – Gippsland also encompasses a vast inland area of farmland, power stations, High Country foothills and forest wilderness.

West Gippsland & the Latrobe Valley

The Princes Hwy follows the power lines past dairy country to the source in the Latrobe Valley. The working-class region between Moe and Traralgon contains one of

Gippsland

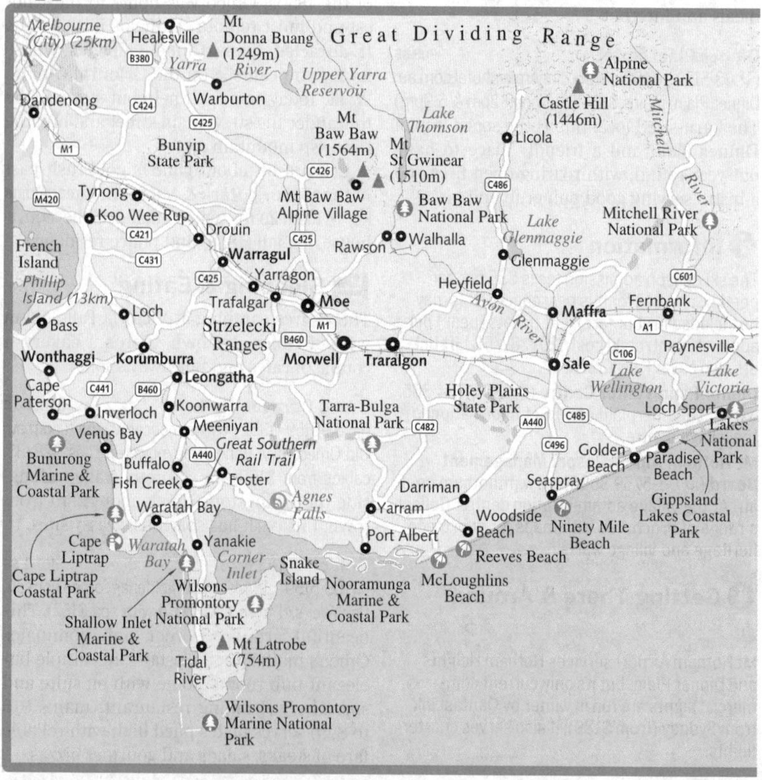

the world's largest deposits of brown coal, which is consumed by massive power stations at Yallourn, Morwell, Hazelwood and Loy Yang; together they produce up to 85% of Victoria's electricity.

Mt Baw Baw

ELEV 1564M

High in the Baw Baw National Park, this is Victoria's smallest (and cheapest) downhill resort – a relaxed option for beginners – and a fine destination for summer bushwalking.

Activities

Mt Baw Baw Alpine Resort Management Board (☎03-5165 1136; www.mountbawbaw.com.au) provides tourist information and accommodation bookings. Several ski-hire places operate during the season, including **Mt Baw Baw Ski Hire** (☎03-5165 1120; www.bawbawskihire.com.au). Ski-season admission fees are $30/35 weekdays/weekends per car for the day car park. The ski lifts operate only if there is snow; day tickets cost $67/47 per adult/child on weekdays and $72/52 on weekends. During summer admission is free.

Baw Baw has some challenging downhill and cross-country mountain-biking trails. The **Downhill Track** has a 300m vertical drop and is open daily from December to April. A shuttle bus ($10) runs half-hourly if there are enough riders. **Adventure Hub** (☎03-5165 1136; bike hire 2/4/8hr $28/45/70), in the village, hires out mountains bikes and can provide trail maps for cross-country routes.

Sleeping & Eating

There's an **accommodation booking service** (☎1300 651 136).

Alpine Hotel HOTEL $$
(☎03-5165 1136; Currawong Rd; dm/d from $30/110) Good-value year-round motel and

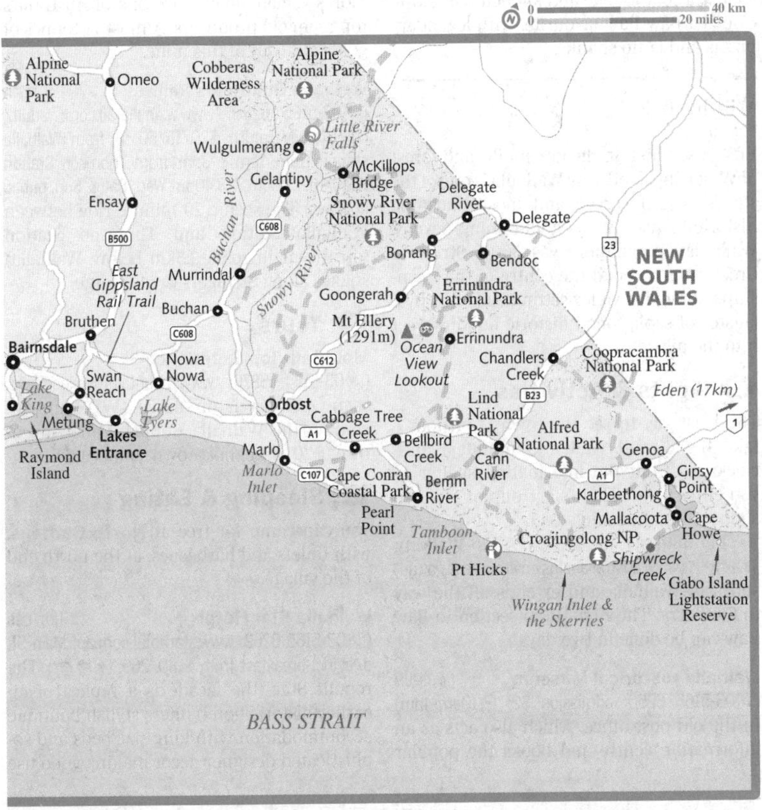

WORTH A TRIP

KOONWARRA

But a blip on the South Gippsland Hwy, Koonwarra has made a name for itself thanks to a fine food store, organic cooking school, day spa and some boutique wineries.

Koonwarra Store (☎03-5664 2285; cnr South Gippsland Hwy & Koala Dr; mains $14-22; ⏲8.30am-5.30pm) Local produce and wines are on sale in this renovated timber building. Alongside the deli and food store, the renowned cafe serves simple food with flair. Outside is a lovely shaded garden, and there's a farmers market, gallery and craft emporium attached.

Milly & Romeo's Artisan Bakery & Cooking School (☎03-5664 2211; Koala Dr; ⏲9am-4pm Thu-Sun) This cool cafe and bakery is also a popular cooking school with short courses in making cakes, bread, traditional pastries and pasta.

backpacker accommodation (BYO linen for dorms) above the pub.

Kelly's Lodge B&B $$
(☎03-5165 1129; www.kellyslodge.com.au; 11 Frosti Lane; r summer/winter from $120/370) This long-running and super-friendly place is in the centre of everything, with four comfortable rooms, a cosy lounge and kitchen. The ski-in cafe is a Baw Baw favourite, with legendary pizzas and lamb shanks.

Walhalla

POP 20

Ensconsed high in the green hills and forest of West Gippsland, tiny Walhalla is one of the state's best-preserved and most charming historic towns – in its gold-mining heyday, Walhalla's population was 5000. Stringers Creek runs through the centre of the township – an idyllic valley setting encircled by a cluster of sepia-toned historic buildings set into the hillsides.

Sights & Activities

The best way to see the town is on foot – take the **circuit walk** (45 minutes) anticlockwise from the information shelter as you enter town. There's a group of restored shops along the main street.

The 680km **Australian Alps Walking Track** (www.australianalps.environment.gov.au) starts in Walhalla and extends all the way to Canberra. The first 40km section to Baw Baw can be done in two days.

Walhalla Historical Museum MUSEUM
(☎03-5165 6250; admission $2; ⏲10am-4pm) In the old post office, which also acts as an information centre and books the popular two-hour **ghost tours** (www.walhallaghosttour.info; adult/child $25/18) on Saturday nights.

Long Tunnel Extended Gold Mine MINE
(☎03-5165 6259; off Walhalla-Beardmore Rd; adult/child/family $19.50/13.50/49.50; ⏲1.30pm daily, plus noon & 3pm Sat, Sun & holidays) Relive the mining past with a guided tour that explores Cohens Reef, once one of Australia's top reef-gold producers. Almost 14 tonnes of gold came out of this mine.

Walhalla Goldfields Railway TRAIN
(☎03-5165 6280; www.walhallarail.com; adult/child/family return $20/15/50; ⏲from Walhalla station 11am, 1pm & 3pm, from Thomson Station 11.40am, 1.40pm & 3.40pm Wed, Sat & Sun, public holidays) The scenic 20-minute ride between Walhalla Station and Thomson Station (on the main road, 3.5km before Walhalla) snakes along Stringers Creek Gorge.

Tours

Mountain Top Experience 4WD
(☎03-5134 6876; www.mountaintopexperience.com) Operates nature-based 4WD tours, including the Walhalla Copper Mine Adventure ($20) and ghost-town tours ($25).

Sleeping & Eating

You can camp for free at **North Gardens**, with toilets and barbecues, at the north end of the village.

Walhalla Star Hotel HOTEL $$
(☎03-5165 6262; www.starhotel.com.au; Main St; d/tr incl breakfast from $180/269; ❄@📶) The rebuilt Star (the facade is a replica of an earlier historic hotel) offers stylish boutique accommodation with king-size beds and sophisticated designer decor making good use

of local materials such as corrugated-iron water tanks. Excellent restaurant.

Walhalla Lodge Hotel PUB $$
(☎03-5165 6226; Main St; mains $17-25; ⏲noon-2pm & 6-9pm Wed-Mon) The Wally Pub is a cosy, one-room pub decked out with prints of old Walhalla and serving good-value counter meals.

Korumburra to Fish Creek

South Gippsland has plenty of gems along the coast between Inverloch and Wilsons Promontory – Cape Paterson, Venus Bay, Cape Liptrap Coastal Park and Waratah Bay are all worth DIY exploration. Inland, the South Gippsland Hwy passes through the beautiful 'blue' rounded hills of the Strzelecki Ranges, past farming communities and trendy villages like Koonwarra and Fish Creek. The 49km Great Southern Rail Trail cycle/walking path meanders through bushland between Leongatha and Foster.

The first sizeable town along the South Gippsland Hwy is Korumburra, hugging the edge of the Strzelecki Ranges. **Prom Country Information Centre** (☎03-5655 2233, 1800 630 704; www.visitpromcountry.com.au; South Gippsland Hwy) is on the way out of town next to **Coal Creek** (☎03-5655 1811; www.coalcreekvillage.com.au; ⏲10am-4.30pm Thu-Mon, daily during school holidays) FREE, an interesting re-creation of a 19th-century mining town.

Volunteers operate the **South Gippsland Railway** (☎1800 442 211, 03-5658 1111; www.sgr.org.au; adult/child/family return $26/17/86), which runs heritage diesel trains along scenic tracks from Korumburra to Leongatha and Nyora on Sundays and public holidays.

Off the South Gippsland Hwy towards Wilsons Prom, **Fish Creek** is an arty little community with craft studios, bookshops, galleries, some good cafes and the popular Fishy Pub. It's on the Great Southern Rail Trail.

Wilsons Promontory National Park

'The Prom', as it's affectionately known, is one of the most popular national parks in Australia and our favourite coastal park. The bushland and coastal scenery here is out of this world and the hiking and camping opportunities are exceptional.

Wilsons Promontory is an important area for the Kurnai and Boonwurrung peoples, and middens have been found in many places, including Cotters and Darby Beaches, and Oberon Bay. The southernmost part of mainland Australia, the Prom once formed a land bridge that allowed people to walk to Tasmania.

Tidal River, 30km from the park entry, is the hub, and home to the Parks Victoria office, a general store, a cafe and accommodation. The wildlife around Tidal River is remarkably tame: kookaburras and rosellas lurk expectantly (resist the urge to feed them), and wombats nonchalantly waddle out of the undergrowth.

Although there's a staffed **entry station** (⏲9am-sunset), where you receive a ticket, entry is free. There's no fuel available at Tidal River.

Activities

There are more than 80km of marked **walking trails** here, taking you through forests, marshes, valleys of tree ferns, low granite mountains and along beaches backed by sand dunes. Even nonwalkers can enjoy much of the park's beauty, with car park access off the Tidal River road leading to gorgeous beaches and lookouts.

Swimming is safe from the beautiful beaches at **Norman Bay** (Tidal River) and around the headland at **Squeaky Beach** – the ultra-fine quartz sand here really does sing beneath your feet!

If you're travelling light, you can hire camping equipment, including tents, stoves, sleeping bags and backpacks, from **Wilsons Prom Hiking Hire** (☎0400 377 993; www.wilsonspromhikinghire.com.au; 3670 Prom Rd, Yanakie).

First Track Adventures ADVENTURE TOUR
(☎03-5634 2761; www.firsttrack.com.au) This Gippsland-based company organises customised bushwalking, canoeing and abseiling trips to the Prom for individuals and groups. Prices vary with group size and activity.

Tours

Bunyip Tours BUS TOUR
(☎1300 286 947; www.bunyiptours.com; from $120; ⏲Wed & Sun) One-day guided tour to the Prom from Melbourne, with several hours of bushwalking and the option of staying on another two days to explore by yourself.

Wilsons Promontory National Park

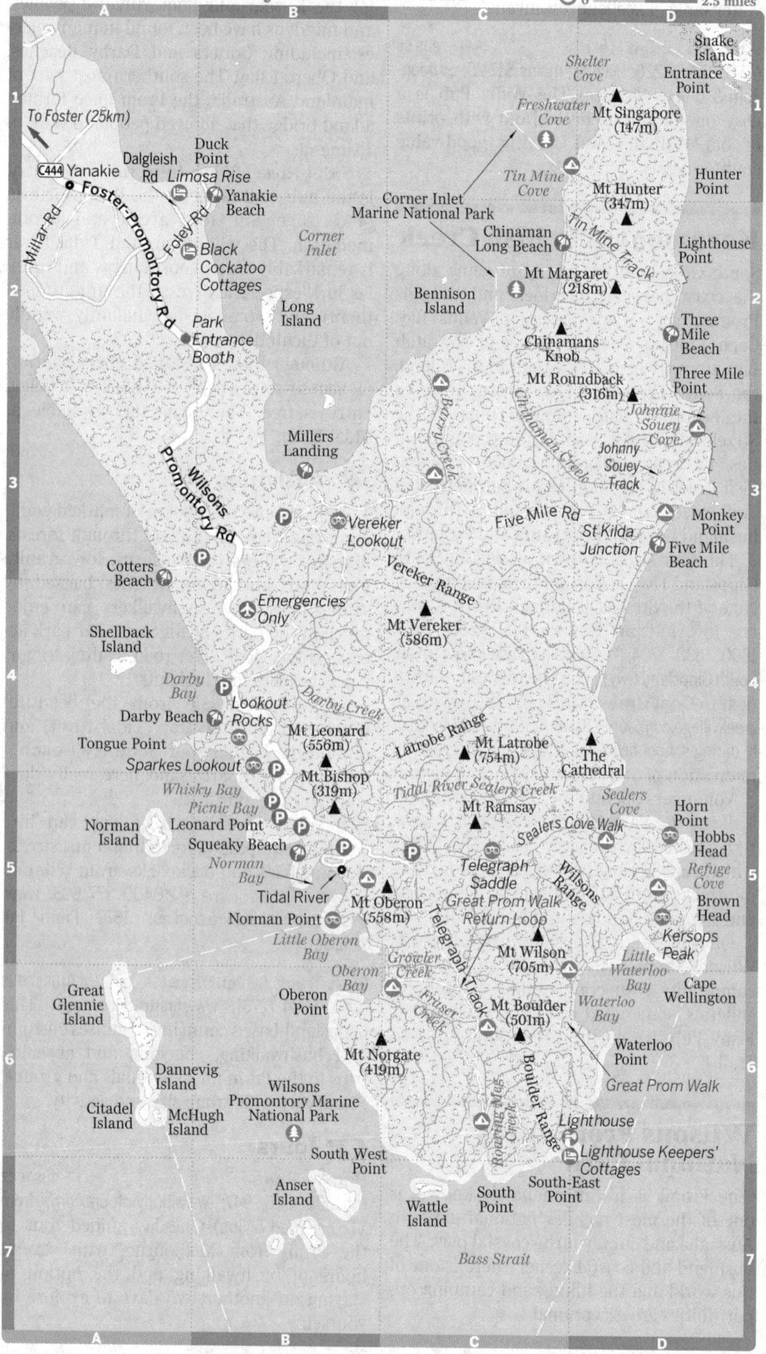

Sleeping

The main accommodation base is at Tidal River, but there are 11 bush-camping (outstation) areas around the Prom, all with pit or compost toilets, but no other facilities; carry in your own drinking water. Overnight hikers need camping permits (adult/child per night $10/5), which must be booked ahead through Parks Victoria.

Tidal River

Situated on Norman Bay, and a short walk to a stunning beach, Tidal River is justifiably popular. Book ahead through Parks Victoria for weekends and holidays. For the Christmas school-holiday period there's a ballot for sites (apply online by 31 July).

Accommodation includes **camp sites** (unpowered sites per car & three people $33, powered sites per vehicle & up to eight people $55); **huts** (4-/6-bed $80/121); **cabins** (d $207, extra adult $28); luxury **safari tents** (d $302, extra person $22); and the isolated **Lighthouse Keepers' Cottage** (8-bed cottage $90-100, 20-bed $120-134) at the southern tip of the Prom.

Yanakie & Foster

Prom Coast Backpackers HOSTEL $
(☎0427 875 735; www.promcoastyha.com.au; 40 Station Rd; dm/d/f from $30/70/90; @) This comfy little 10-bed YHA cottage in Foster is the closest backpacker hostel to the park. If you're lucky you may be able to hitch a lift to the Prom from here.

Black Cockatoo Cottages COTTAGES $$
(☎03-5687 1306; www.blackcockatoo.com; 60 Foley Rd; d $160, six-person house $180) You can take in glorious views of the national park without leaving your very comfortable bed in these stylish, black-timber cottages. There are three modern cottages and a three-bedroom house.

Eating

Tidal River General Store & Café CAFE $
(mains $5-22; ⏲9am-5pm Sun-Fri, 9am-6pm Sat) The store stocks grocery items and some camping equipment, but if you're hiking or staying a while it's cheaper to stock up in Foster. The attached cafe serves takeaway food such as pies and sandwiches, as well as breakfast, light lunches and bistro-style meals on weekends and holidays.

Information

Parks Victoria (☎13 19 63; www.parkweb.vic.gov.au; ⏲8.30am-4.30pm) The helpful visitor centre books all park accommodation, including permits for camping away from Tidal River.

Getting There & Away

The Prom is best reached with your own wheels or on a tour. At the time of research there was no public transport to Tidal River but you can get a **V/Line** (☎11800 800 007) bus from Melbourne to Foster ($19.80, three hours) or Fish Creek ($17.60, 2½ hours) and try to hitch a lift from there.

TOP FIVE PROM WALKS

Great Prom Walk This is the most popular long-distance hike, a moderate 45km circuit across to Sealers Cove from Tidal River, down to Refuge Cove, Waterloo Bay, the lighthouse and back to Tidal River via Oberon Bay. Allow three days, and coordinate your walks with tide times, as creek crossings can be hazardous.

Sealers Cove Walk The best overnight hike, this two-day walk starts at Telegraph Saddle and heads down Telegraph Track to stay overnight at beautiful Little Waterloo Bay (12km, 4½ hours). The next day walk on to Sealers Cove via Refuge Cove and return to Telegraph Saddle (24km, 7½ hours).

Lilly Pilly Gully Nature Walk An easy 5km (two-hour) walk through heathland and eucalypt forests, with lots of wildlife. Start at the car park or from Tidal River.

Mt Oberon Summit This moderate-to-hard 7km (2½-hour) walk is an ideal introduction to the Prom, with panoramic views from the summit. The free Mt Oberon shuttle bus can take you to the Telegraph Saddle car park and back.

Squeaky Beach Nature Walk Another easy 5km return stroll from Tidal River through coastal tea trees and banksias to a sensational white-sand beach. Take the Tidal Overlook detour for superb views over Tidal River and Squeaky Beach.

Gippsland Lakes

The sublime Gippsland Lakes comprise the largest inland waterway system in Australia. There are three main lakes that interconnect: Lake King, Lake Victoria and Lake Wellington, which are actually lagoons, separated from the ocean by a narrow strip of sand dunes known as Ninety Mile Beach. The dunes were artificially breached at Lakes Entrance in 1889 to allow ocean-going fishing boats to shelter in the placid waters. The Lakes National Park protects 2400 hectares of native habitat.

Sale

POP 12,770

Gateway to the Gippsland Lakes, Sale has plenty of accommodation, shops, restaurants and pubs, making it a reasonable town-sized base for exploring Ninety Mile Beach, around 35km south.

The **Sale Wetlands Walk** (4km, 1½ hours) is a pleasant wander around Lake Gutheridge and adjoining wetlands, and incorporates an **Indigenous Art Trail** commemorating the importance of the wetlands to the local Gunai/Kurnai population. **Sale Common**, a 300-hectare wildlife refuge with bird hides, an observatory, a waterhole, boardwalks and other walking tracks is part of an internationally recognised wetlands system.

Information

Wellington Visitor Information Centre (03-5144 1108; www.tourismwellington.com.au; 8 Foster St; 9am-5pm) Internet facilities and a free accommodation booking service.

MAFFRA

About 18km north of Sale, Maffra is a busy little community surrounded by dairy farmland. This area can be of particular interest to travellers looking for casual agricultural work. **Cambrai Hostel** (03-5147 1600; www.maffra.net.au/hostel; 117 Johnson St; dm per night/week $28/160; @) is a part-pub-part-backpackers joint geared up for working travellers – the owner can hook you up with local farmers. It's a lot of fun and Gippsland's busiest backpacker hostel.

Ninety Mile Beach

Isolated Ninety Mile Beach is a narrow strip of sand backed by dunes and lagoons that stretches unbroken for more-or-less 90 miles (150km) from near McLoughlins Beach to the channel at Lakes Entrance – arguably Australia's longest uninterrupted beach. The area is great for surf-fishing, camping and long beach walks, though the crashing surf can be dangerous for swimming, except where patrolled at Seaspray and Lakes Entrance.

On the road between Seaspray and Golden Beach are free **camp sites**, nestled back from the beach and shaded by tea tree – it's hard to get a spot over summer holidays, but at other times it's supremely peaceful. Some sites have barbecues and pit toilets, but you need to bring your own water and firewood. Hot showers are available at **Golden Beach** ($2).

Loch Sport (pop 780) is a small, bushy town sprawling along a narrow spit of land with a lake on one side and the ocean on the other. There are some good swimming areas here for children, along with a pub and marina.

A spit of land surrounded by lakes and ocean, **Lakes National Park** covers 2390 hectares of coastal bushland and is reached by road from Loch Sport, or by boat from Paynesville (5km). The Parks Victoria office is at the park entrance near Loch Sport. The only camping in the park is at Emu Bight.

Bairnsdale

POP 11,820

Bairnsdale is East Gippsland's commercial hub and the turn-off for the Great Alpine Road to Omeo or south to Paynesville and Raymond Island.

Sights & Activities

On the edge of town, the **MacLeod Morass Boardwalk** is a wetland reserve with walking tracks and bird hides.

The **East Gippsland Rail Trail** (www.eastgippslandrailtrail.com) is Gippsland's longest bike and walking track, which leads 97km east to Orbost, via Bruthen and Nowa Nowa, or you can detour through state forest to Lakes Entrance. Orbost-based **Snowy River Cycling** (0428 556 088; www.snowyrivercycling.com.au) can organise self-guided rail trail tours with bike hire ($35) and transfers from Bairnsdale or Orbost.

About 16km south of Bairnsdale, the little lake town of **Paynesville** is worth a trip to take the free flat-bottom ferry across to **Raymond Island**, known for its large colony of koalas.

Krowathunkoolong Keeping Place CULTURAL CENTRE
(03-5152 1891; 37-53 Dalmahoy St; adult/child $3.50/2.50; 9am-5pm Mon-Fri) Krowathunkoolong Keeping Place, behind the train station, is a Koorie cultural centre that explores Kurnai daily life before and after white settlement.

Sleeping & Eating

Grand Terminus Hotel PUB $
(03-5152 4040; www.grandterminus.com.au; 98 MacLeod St; s/d/tr $65/75/130, mains $12-28) This grand old corner pub with wraparound corner balcony has good-value en suite rooms upstairs, while the above-average bistro serves up meals of osso bucco and chicken parma.

River Grill MODERN AUSTRALIAN $$
(03-5153 1421; 2 Wood St; mains $23-38; noon-2pm & 7pm-late Mon-Sat) Bairnsdale's best restaurant offers contemporary food with a Mediterranean touch.

Information

Bairnsdale Visitor Centre (03-5152 3444, 1800 637 060; www.discovereastgippsland.com.au; 240 Main St; 9am-5pm) Next to St Mary's Church; free accommodation booking service.

Metung

POP 1010

Curling around Bancroft Bay, tiny Metung is one of the prettiest towns on the Gippsland Lakes. Besotted locals call it the Gippsland Riviera, and with its absolute waterfront location, gleaming marina and unhurried charm it does feel like a yachties' playground. It's all about getting out on the water here.

Sights & Activities

At the visitor centre, **Slipway Boat Hire** (03-5156 2969) has small motor boats for hire from $55 for an hour to $165 for the day.

At high noon it's quite a sight to see pelicans fly in like dive bombers for fish issued outside the Metung Hotel.

Director CRUISE
(03-5156 2628; www.thedirector.com.au; 2½hr cruise adult/child/family $45/10/105; 3pm Tue, Thu & Sat) Afternoon cruises with drinks and local cheeses included. Also hires out small **boats** (1/2/3hr, $80/100/120) and **kayaks** (1/2hr $25/45).

Riviera Nautic BOAT HIRE
(03-5156 2243; www.rivieranautic.com.au; 185 Metung Rd; yachts & cruisers for 3 days from $1089) Riviera Nautic hires out boats and yachts for cruising, fishing and sailing on the Gippsland Lakes.

Sleeping & Eating

Accommodation is available through **Metung Accommodation** (Slipway Villas; 03-5156 2861; www.metungaccommodation.com.au). The nearest camping is at Swan Reach, 10km north.

Metung Holiday Villas CABINS $$
(03-5156 2306; www.metungholidayvillas.com; cnr Mairburn & Stirling Rds; cabins $150-250;) This minivillage of semi-luxury cabins is one of the best deals in Metung, with bargain online rates.

★**Metung Galley** CAFE $$
(03-5156 2330; www.themetunggalley.com.au; 50 Metung Rd; lunch $16-24, dinner $20-35; 7am-late) City style meets local produce and seaside charm at this super-chic, innovative cafe-restaurant and wine bar. The Galley offers great coffee, tapas plates and quality dishes like local seafood and Gippsland lamb. There's even a takeaway fish-and-chip window.

Metung Hotel PUB $$
(03-5156 2206; www.metunghotel.com.au; 1 Kurnai Ave; mains $14-33; lunch & dinner) You can't beat the location overlooking Metung Wharf, and the big windows and outdoor timber decking make the most of the water views. The hotel also has basic double rooms with shared bathroom for $85.

Information

Metung Visitor Centre (03-5156 2969; www.metungtourism.com.au; 3/50 Metung Rd; 9am-5pm) Accommodation booking and boat-hire services.

Lakes Entrance

POP 5965

Lakes Entrance is a scenic beauty, with the shallow Cunninghame Arm waterway separating town and the fishing boats from the crashing ocean beaches and Bass Strait. It's an undeniably gorgeous location, but in holiday season Lakes is a packed-out tourist town with a graceless strip of motels, caravan parks, minigolf courses and souvenir shops lining the Esplanade. Visit out of season, and it's very quiet: on a sunny day, the bobbing fishing boats, fresh seafood, endless beaches, pelicans and cruises through the inlets will easily win you over.

◉ Sights & Activities

A long **footbridge** crosses the Cunninghame Arm inlet just east of the town centre to the ocean and Ninety Mile Beach. From December to Easter, paddle boats, canoes and sailboats can be hired by the footbridge on the ocean side.

For exploring the lakes, three operators along Marine Pde (on the backside of the town centre) offer **boat hire** (per 1/4/8hr $40/90/150); no licence required.

On the Princes Hwy on the western side of town, **Kalimna Lookout** is a popular viewing spot, with coin-operated binoculars. For an even better view of the ocean and inlet, take the road directly opposite to **Jemmy's Point Lookout**.

Surf Shack   SURFING
(☑03-5155 4933; www.surfshack.com.au; 507 The Esplanade; 2hr lesson $50) Surf shop running surfing lessons (gear provided) and tours out to Cape Conran.

⌖ Tours

Lonsdale Cruises   CRUISE
(☑03-9013 8363; Post Office Jetty; 3hr cruise adult/child/family $50/25/120; ⊘1pm) ◢ Scenic eco cruises out to Metung and Lake King.

Peels Lake Cruises   CRUISE
(☑0409 946 292; Post Office Jetty; 4hr Metung lunch cruise adult/child $50/14; ⊘11am Tue-Sun) Lunch cruises aboard the *Stormbird* to Metung at 11am; on Wednesday and Saturday the lunch cruise goes to Wyanga Park Winery ($55).

Sea Safari   CRUISE
(☑0458 511 438; www.lakes-explorer.com.au; Post Office Jetty; 1/2hr cruise $15/25) ◢ These safaris aboard the Lakes Explorer have a focus on research and marine ecology.

🛏 Sleeping

Lakes Entrance has stacks of accommodation, much of it your typical motels, holiday apartments and caravan parks, squeezed cheek-by-jowl along the Esplanade. Prices more than double during holiday periods, but there are good discounts available out of season.

Riviera Backpackers YHA   HOSTEL $
(☑03-5155 2444; www.yha.com.au; 660-71 The Esplanade; dm/d $25/50; @ ⧉ ⊠) This well-located YHA has clean rooms in old-style brick units, each with two or three bedrooms and an en suite. There's a big communal kitchen and kayak hire.

Eastern Beach Tourist Park   CAMPGROUND $
(☑03-5155 1581; www.easternbeach.com.au; 42 Eastern Beach Rd; unpowered/powered sites $31/35, cabins $140-190; @ ⧉) Most caravan parks in Lakes pack 'em in, but this one has space, grassy sites and a great location away from the hubbub of town back from Eastern Beach.

Killara   APARTMENT $
(☑03-5155 1220; 4 Long St; d from $75; ✳) These self-contained two-bedroom units are basic but a bargain. In a quiet location near Eastern Beach.

Lazy Acre Log Cabins   CABINS $
(☑03-5155 1323; www.lazyacre.com; 35 Roadknight St; d $89-118; ⧉ ⊠) Cute self-contained timber cabins a block back from the Esplanade, shaded with old gum trees. Excellent value outside the holiday season.

Kalimna Woods   COTTAGES $$
(☑03-5155 1957; www.kalimnawoods.com.au; Kalimna Jetty Rd; d $130, with spa $170; ✳) Retreat 2km from the town centre to Kalimna Woods, where cosy self-contained cottages with log fires are set in a large rainforest and bush garden, complete with friendly resident possums and birds.

🍴 Eating & Drinking

With the largest fishing fleet in Victoria, Lakes Entrance is the perfect place to indulge in fresh seafood. You can sometimes buy shellfish (prawns, bugs etc) straight from local boats or try the fresh fish counter at Ferryman's.

Six Sisters & A Pigeon CAFE $
(☎03-5155 1144; 567 The Esplanade; meals $9-18; ⏲7am-3pm Tue-Sun; ✎) The name alone should guide you to this quirky licensed cafe on the Esplanade opposite the footbridge. Good coffee, all-day breakfasts – Mexican eggs, French toast or Spanish omelette – and lunches of focaccias and baguettes.

★**Ferryman's Seafood Cafe** SEAFOOD $$
(☎03-5155 3000; www.ferrymans.com.au; Middle Harbour, The Esplanade; mains $13-31; ⏲10am-late, seafood sales 8.30am-5pm) It's hard to beat the ambience of dining on the deck of this floating cafe-restaurant, which will fill you to the gills with seafood, including good ol' fish and chips. Downstairs is fresh seafood sales.

Miriam's Restaurant STEAKHOUSE, SEAFOOD $$
(☎03-5155 3999; www.miriamsrestaurant.com.au; cnr The Esplanade & Bulmer St; mains $20-38; ⏲6pm-late) The upstairs dining room at Miriam's overlooks the Esplanade, and the Gippsland steaks, seafood dishes and casual cocktail-bar atmosphere are excellent.

Floating Dragon CHINESE $$
(☎03-5155 1400; www.floatingdragon.com.au; 160 The Esplanade; mains $25-39; ⏲6pm-late Tue-Sun, noon-2pm Sun) This floating restaurant dishes up high-end Cantonese cuisine with soothing views through the floor-to-ceiling windows. The best deal is yum cha for Sunday lunch.

Waterwheel Beach Tavern PUB $$
(☎03-5156 5855; www.waterwheelbeachtavern.com; 577 Beach Rd; mains $18-34; ⏲noon-2pm & 6-8pm) It's worth the trip out to Lake Tyers, 10 minutes' drive from Lakes Entrance, for a beer at this beachside pub. The setting is superb and the bistro food is hearty pub classics.

Information

Lakes Entrance Visitor Centre (☎03-5155 1966, 1800 637 060; www.discovereastgippsland.com.au; cnr Princes Hwy & Marine Pde; ⏲9am-5pm) Free accommodation and tour booking service. Also check out www.lakesentrance.com.

Getting There & Away

V/Line (☎1800 800 007; www.vline.com.au) runs a train/bus service from Melbourne to Lakes Entrance via Bairnsdale ($34.20, 4½ hours, three daily).

East Gippsland & the Wilderness Coast

Beyond the Gippsland Lakes stretches a wilderness area of spectacular coastal national parks and old-growth forest. Much of this region wasn't cleared for agriculture and contains some of the most remote and pristine national parks in the state, making logging in these ancient forests a hot issue. This is a supreme place for camping, hiking and taking it slowly.

Buchan

POP 385

Leaving the coast, you'll find Buchan, a beautiful town in the foothills of the Snowy Mountains about 56km north of Lakes Entrance, famous for its intricate limestone cave system, which has been open to visitors since 1913.

Tours

Guided tours, alternating between **Royal Cave** and **Fairy Cave**, are run by **Parks Victoria** (☎13 19 63; www.parks.vic.gov.au; tours adult/child/family $18/10.50/49.80, two caves $27/15.60/74.40; ⏲10am, 11.15am, 1pm, 2.15pm & 3.30pm). Combined cave tours are slightly cheaper. The rangers also offer hard-hat guided tours to **Federal Cave** during the high season.

Sleeping

Buchan Caves Reserve CAMPGROUND $
(☎13 19 63; www.parks.vic.gov.au; unpowered/powered sites $23/30, cabins $87, wilderness retreats $165; ⛟) You can stay right by the caves at this serene camping ground, edged by state forest and walking trails.

Buchan Lodge HOSTEL $
(☎03-5155 9421; www.buchanlodge.com.au; 9 Saleyard Rd; dm $25) A short walk from the town centre, this welcoming pine-log backpackers has a great feel, large dorms and a well-equipped kitchen. It's great for lounging about and taking in the country views.

Getting There & Away

Buchan Bus 'n' Freight (☎03-5155 0356) operates a service on Wednesday and Friday from Bairnsdale to Buchan ($20, 1½ hours), linking with the train from Melbourne. At other times you'll need your own transport.

OFF THE BEATEN TRACK

SNOWY RIVER & ERRINUNDRA NATIONAL PARKS

The Snowy River and Errinundra national parks, located north of Orbost, occupy a large chunk of Victoria's eastern corner between the alpine country and the Princes Hwy. These two isolated wilderness parks are linked in the north by the partially unsealed MacKillops Rd, making it possible to do a superb driving loop from Orbost via Buchan. In dry weather it's passable with conventional vehicles but check road conditions with Parks Victoria – some of the dirt roads in Errinundra are impassable in winter and a narrow single-car-width section near MacKillops Bridge means it's unsuitable for caravans or trailers.

Snowy River National Park

Northeast of Buchan, this is one of Victoria's most isolated and spectacular national parks, dominated by deep gorges carved through limestone and sandstone by the Snowy River on its route from the Snowy Mountains in NSW to its mouth at Marlo. The entire park is a smorgasbord of unspoiled, superb bush and mountain scenery, ranging from alpine woodlands and eucalypt forests to rainforests.

On the west side of the park, the views from the well-signposted cliff-top lookouts over **Little River Falls** and **Little River Gorge**, Victoria's deepest gorge, are awesome. From there it's about 20km to **McKillops Bridge**, a huge bridge spanning the Snowy River, making it possible (if a little scary) to drive across to Errinundra National Park. In the south of the park, **Raymond Falls** can easily be reached from Orbost via Moresford Rd.

There's free camping at six basic sites around the park, but the main site is McKillops Bridge, with toilets and fireplaces.

Karoonda Park (☎03-5155 0220; www.karoondapark.com; 3558 Gelantipy Rd; s/d/tr $50/70/90, cabins per 6 people $115; ❄@☒), 40km north of Buchan, is a working sheep and cattle property with comfortable backpacker and cabin digs, adventure tours and farm activities.

Errinundra National Park

Errinundra National Park contains Victoria's largest cool-temperate rainforest, but the forests surrounding the park are a constant battleground between loggers and environmentalists who are trying to protect old-growth forests.

The national park covers an area of 256 sq km and has three granite outcrops that extend into the cloud, resulting in high rainfall, deep, fertile soils and a network of creeks and rivers that flow north, south and east. You can explore the park by a combination of scenic drives, and short and medium-length walks. **Mt Ellery** has spectacular views; **Errinundra Saddle** has a rainforest boardwalk; and from **Ocean View Lookout** there are stunning views down the Goolengook River as far as Bemm River.

Frosty Hollow Camp Site (sites free) is the only camping area within the national park, on the eastern side. There are also free camping areas on the park's edges – at Ellery Creek in Goongerah, and at Delegate River.

Jacarri (☎03-5154 0145; www.eastgippsland.net.au/jacarri; cnr Bonang Hwy & Ellery Creek Track, Goongerah; d/f $90/100) is a neat two bedroom eco-cottage located on the organic farm of conservationist Jill Redwood.

Tours

Gippsland High Country Tours (☎03-5157 5556; www.gippslandhighcountrytours.com.au) An ecotourism award winner running easy, moderate and challenging four- to seven-day hikes in Errinundra, Snowy River and Croajingolong National Parks.

Snowy River Expeditions (☎03-5155 0220; www.karoondapark.com/sre; Karoonda Park; tours per day $85-150) This established company based at Karoonda Park runs adventure tours including one-, two- or four-day rafting trips on the Snowy, and half- or full-day abseiling or caving trips.

Orbost & Marlo

POP 2145

Most travellers whizz through Orbost, as the Princes Hwy bypasses the town centre, but this is a major East Gippsland junction: the Bonang Rd heads north towards the Snowy River and Errinundra National Parks, and Marlo Rd follows the Snowy River south to Marlo and continues along the coast to Cape Conran. It's a good place to refuel and stock up on supplies.

Just 15km south of Orbost, Marlo is a sleepy beach town with an undeniably pretty outlook at the mouth of the Snowy River. Aside from the gorgeous coast, the main attraction here is the **PS Curlip** (☎0411 395 903; www.paddlesteamercurlip.com.au; adult/child/family $25/15/60), a replica of an 1890 paddle steamer that once chugged up the Snowy River to Orbost. It's run on a volunteer basis so usually only sails during busy holiday periods but check the website or call for the schedule. You can buy tickets at the general store in town.

Orbost Visitor Information Centre TOURIST INFORMATION
(☎03-5154 2424; cnr Nicholson & Clarke Sts; ⏲9am-5pm) The helpful visitor centre is in the historic 1872 Slab Hut.

Cape Conran Coastal Park

This blissfully wild but easily accessible part of the coast is one of Gippsland's most beautiful, with long stretches of remote white-sand beaches. The 19km coastal route from Marlo to Cape Conran is particularly pretty, bordered by banksia trees, grass plains, sand dunes and the ocean.

Cabbage Tree Palms, a short detour off the road between Cape Conran and the Princes Hwy, is Victoria's only stand of native palms – a tiny rainforest oasis.

Parks Victoria runs three excellent **accommodation** (☎03-5154 8438; www.conran.net.au; camp sites $26.80, cabins up to 4 people $147, lodge $291, safari tents $165) options, including foreshore camp sites, cabins and safari tents.

Mallacoota

POP 1030

Far-flung Mallacoota is a real gem – Victoria's most easterly town but an easy detour if you're heading along the coastal route between Melbourne and Sydney. It's snuggled on the vast Mallacoota Inlet and surrounded by the bushland and beachside dunes of wild and beautiful Croajingolong National Park. Those prepared to come this far are treated to long empty ocean surf beaches, tidal river mouths and swimming, fishing and boating on the inlet.

Sights & Activities

There are some good walks from town, including the 4km boardwalk stroll around the inlet to Karbeethong. The nearest surf beaches are a short walk south of town at **Bastion Point** and further round at **Betka Beach**.

One of the best ways to experience the beauty of Mallacoota and its estuarine waters is by boat. **Mallacoota Hire Boats** (☎0438 447 558; Main Wharf, cnr Allan & Buckland Drs; motor boats per 2/4/6hr $60/100/140) is centrally located and hires out small motor boats and fishing gear. Call **Mallacoota Equipment Hire** (☎0488 329 611; www.mallacootahire.com) to rent bikes (from $10) and kayaks (from $15).

On Gabo Island, 14km offshore from Mallacoota, the windswept 154-hectare **Gabo Island Lightstation Reserve** is home to sea birds and one of the world's largest colonies of little penguins – far outnumbering those at Phillip Island. The island has an operating **lighthouse**, built in 1862, which is the tallest in the southern hemisphere, and you can stay in the old keepers' cottages; contact **Parks Victoria** (www.parkweb.vic.gov.au).

Tours

MV Loch-Ard CRUISE
(☎03-5158 0764; Main Wharf; adult/child 2hr cruise $30/12) Runs several inlet cruises from the Main Wharf.

Porkie Bess CRUISE, FISHING
(☎0408 408 094; 2hr cruise $30, fishing trip $60) A 1940s wooden boat offering fishing trips and cruises around the lakes, and ferry services for hikers ($20 per person, minimum four). Departs Karbeethong Jetty.

Wilderness Coast Ocean Charters ISLAND
(☎0417 398 068, 03-5158 0701) Runs trips to Gabo Island ($60 per person return day trip; $60 each way if you stay overnight).

Sleeping

Mallacoota has lots of holiday accommodation but during the Easter and Christmas school holidays you'll need to book well ahead and pay a premium.

★Adobe Mudbrick Flats APARTMENT $
(☎0409 580 0329, 03-5158 0329; www.adobe-holidayflats.com.au; 17 Karbeethong Ave; d $75, q $90-110) A labour of love by Margaret and Peter Kurz, these unique mud-brick flats in Karbeethong, a few kilometres north of Mallacoota, are something special. With an emphasis on recycling and eco-friendliness, the array of whimsical apartments are comfortable and great value. There's lots of wildlife around and you can rent kayaks.

★Mallacoota Foreshore Holiday Park CAMPGROUND $
(☎03-5158 0300; www.mallacootaholidaypark.com.au; cnr Allan Dr & Maurice Ave; unpowered sites $20-29, powered sites $26-38;) Curling around the Mallacoota Inlet, the grassy sites here are serious waterfront and morph into one of Victoria's most sociable and scenic caravan parks. No cabins, but it's the best of Mallacoota's numerous parks for campers.

Karbeethong Lodge GUESTHOUSE $$
(☎03-5158 0411; www.karbeethonglodge.com.au; 16 Schnapper Point Dr; d $110-220) It's hard not to be overcome by a sense of serenity as you rest on the broad verandahs of this early 1900s timber guesthouse, with uninterrupted views over Mallacoota Inlet.

Mallacoota Wilderness Houseboats HOUSEBOAT $$$
(☎0409 924 016; www.mallacootawilderness-houseboats.com.au; Karbeethong Jetty; 4 nights midweek from $1050, weekly $1650) These six-berth houseboats are not super-luxurious but there is no better way to explore Mallacoota's waterways.

Eating

★Lucy's ASIAN $
(☎03-5158 0666; 64 Maurice Ave; dishes $10-22; 8am-8pm) Lucy's is a real find out here – famous for the delicious and great-value homemade rice noodles with chicken, prawn or abalone, and tasty homemade dumplings.

Croajingolong Cafe CAFE $
(☎03-5158 0098; Shop 3, 14 Allan Dr; mains $6-14; 8.30am-4pm Tue-Sun;) Overlooking the inlet, this is the place to enjoy a coffee, baguette or pancake breakfast.

Mallacoota Hotel PUB $$
(☎03-5158 0455; www.mallacootahotel.com.au; 51-55 Maurice Ave; mains $17-32; noon-2pm & 6-8pm) The local pub bistro serves hearty meals from its varied menu. Bands play regularly in the summer. There's a good-value **motel** (s/d $80/100) attached.

Information

Mallacoota Visitor Centre (☎03-5158 0800; www.visitmallacoota.com.au; Main Wharf, cnr Allan & Buckland Dr; 10am-4pm) The quirky painted visitor booth down by the wharf is operated by friendly volunteers, so operating hours are erratic.

Getting There & Away

Mallacoota is 23km southeast of Genoa. From Melbourne, take the V/Line (☎1800 800 007;www.vline.com.au) train/bus combination to Genoa ($41.40, 7½ hours, one daily) via Bairnsdale. **Mallacoota–Genoa Bus Service** (☎1800 800 007) meets the V/Line coach on Monday, Thursday and Friday, plus Sunday during school holidays, and runs to Mallacoota ($3.50, 30 minutes).

Croajingolong National Park

Croajingolong is one of Australia's finest coastal wilderness national parks, recognised with its listing as a World Biosphere Reserve by Unesco. For remote camping, bushwalking, fishing, swimming and surfing, this one is hard to beat, with unspoiled beaches, inlets, estuaries and forests. The park covers 875 sq km, stretching for about 100km from Bemm River to the NSW border. The five inlets – **Sydenham**, **Tamboon**, **Mueller**, **Wingan** and **Mallacoota** – are popular canoeing and fishing spots.

Point Hicks was the first part of Australia to be spotted by Captain Cook and the *Endeavour* crew in 1770, and was named after his first Lieutenant, Zachary Hicks. There's a **lighthouse** here, open for tours from Friday to Monday at 1pm, and accommodation in the old cottages. You can still see remains of the SS *Saros*, which ran ashore in 1937.

Sleeping

There are four designated camp sites: Wingan Inlet and Shipwreck Creek can be booked through **Parks Victoria** (☎13 19 63; www.parkweb.vic.gov.au; camp sites $20); Thurra River and Mueller Inlet through Point Hicks Lighthouse. During Christmas school holidays sites are only available by a ballot.

Point Hicks Lighthouse COTTAGES $$
(☎03-5158 4268, 03-5156 0432; www.pointhicks.com.au; bungalow $120, cottage $330) This remote lighthouse has two comfortable, heritage-listed cottages, and one double bungalow. The cottages sleep six people and have sensational ocean views and wood fires.

Getting There & Away

Access roads of varying quality lead into the park from the Princes Hwy. Apart from the Genoa–Mallacoota Rd and about 17km of road from Cann River to Tamboon, all roads are unsealed and can be very rough in winter, so check road conditions with Parks Victoria before venturing on, especially during or after rain. **Bemm River**, a popular fishing haunt on the west side of Sydenham Inlet, is accessible by sealed road.

Tasmania

Includes ➡

Best Places to Eat

- Pigeon Hole (p639)
- Garagistes (p638)
- Stillwater (p675)
- Red Velvet Lounge (p650)
- Cable Station Restaurant (p694)

Best Places to Stay

- Astor Private Hotel (p636)
- All Angels Church House (p649)
- Freycinet Eco Retreat (p664)
- Two Four Two (p674)
- @VDL (p694)

Why Go?

Dazzlin' Tassie is brilliant, beautiful and accessible. It's compact enough to 'do' in a few weeks and layered enough to keep bringing you back. Look forward to exquisite beaches, jagged mountain ranges, rarefied alpine plateaus, plentiful wildlife and vast tracts of virgin wilderness, much of it within a World Heritage area. Tasmania produces superb gourmet food and wine, and a flourishing arts scene and urban cool highlight its positive and vibrant future.

Tasmania's past incorporates an often tragic Aboriginal and convict history, much of it vital to understanding the story of Australia itself. Tasmania's pioneering heritage is showcased throughout the island, often against the backdrop of some of Australia's most impressive colonial architecture.

For the outdoors buff, Tassie's bushwalking, cycling, rafting and kayaking opportunities rank among the best on the planet. Tasmania is still Australia, but bewitchingly, just that little bit different.

When to Go

Hobart

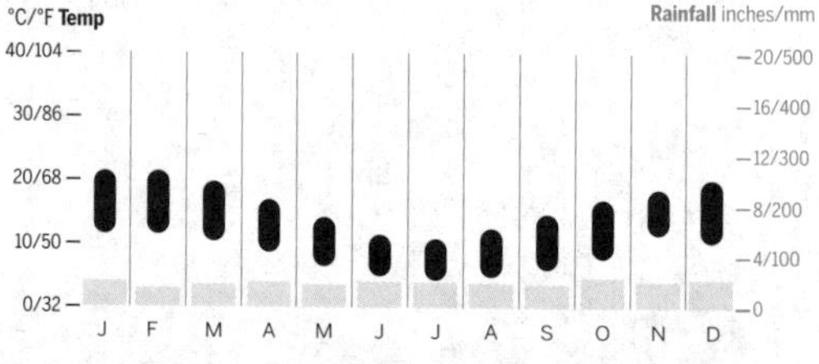

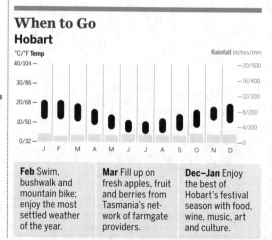

Feb Swim, bushwalk and mountain bike; enjoy the most settled weather of the year.

Mar Fill up on fresh apples, fruit and berries from Tasmania's network of farmgate providers.

Dec–Jan Enjoy the best of Hobart's festival season with food, wine, music, art and culture.

History

There were perhaps 10,000 indigenous Australians living on Tasmania when Dutchman Abel Janszoon Tasman became the first European to sight the island. His ships first came upon the island's northwest coast on 24 November 1642 and then skirted around the southern and southeastern coastlines. He named the island Van Diemen's Land after the Dutch East Indies' governor. Since Tasman's voyages yielded nothing of value for the Dutch East India Company, European contact with the island ceased for more than another century until the British arrived at Sydney Cove in 1788 – Van Diemen's Land would become a convenient pit stop en route to New South Wales. In 1798 Matthew Flinders circumnavigated Van Diemen's Land, proving it was an island. In 1803 Risdon Cove, on the Derwent River, became the site of Australia's second British colony. The settlement moved a year later to the present site of Hobart, where fresh water ran plentifully off Mt Wellington.

Convicts accompanied the first settlers as labourers, but the grim penal settlements weren't built until later: on Sarah Island in Macquarie Harbour in 1822, on Maria Island in 1825 and at Port Arthur in 1830. In subsequent decades Van Diemen's Land became infamous for the most apocalyptic punishments and deprivations exacted on convicts anywhere in the British colonies – the most fearsome, terrible of destinations. By the 1850s every second islander was a convict and Van Diemen's Land had whole industries exploiting the misery of convict labour. Hobart Town and Launceston festered with disease, prostitution and drunken lawlessness.

In 1856 the 'social experiment' of convict transportation to Van Diemen's Land was abolished. In an effort to escape the stigma of its horrendous penal reputation, Van Diemen's Land renamed itself Tasmania, after the Dutchman. By this time, however, the island's Aboriginal peoples had been practically annihilated by a mixture of concerted ethnic cleansing, disease, forced labour, and ultimately doomed resettlement and assimilation schemes.

The 1870s and '80s saw prospectors arrive after gold was discovered, and the state's rugged and remote west was opened up by miners and timber workers seeking Huon pine, myrtle and sassafras. So began the exploitation of Tasmania's natural resources. In the 1960s and '70s conservationists fought unsuccessfully to stop the hydroelectric flooding of Lake Pedder. In the 1980s the issue flared again; this time the fledgling pro-environment movement successfully campaigned against flooding the Franklin River for similar purposes. Leaders in these campaigns were instrumental in forming the United Tasmania Group in 1972, regarded as the world's first Green political party. The Australian Greens party has since become a force in Australian federal politics.

The long-running debate between pro-logging groups, pro-pulp mill corporations and conservationists keen to protect Tasmania's old-growth forests and wild heritage continues. In 2012, a 'peace deal' was ratified, the culmination of years of discussions between the forest industry, timber workers and conservation groups. The agreement includes a moratorium on the logging of high-conservation-value forests, but remains a contentious and sometimes divisive agreement steeped in compromise.

In early 2013 approval was granted by the Tasmanian state government for mining in the remote Tarkine wilderness area in the state's northwest. The decision has created Tasmania's latest battleground in the ongoing conflict between environmental and industrial concerns, and is more evidence of the delicate balancing act of generating jobs and preserving Tassie's wilderness heritage.

Indigenous Tasmania

The treatment of Tasmania's indigenous peoples by early European settlers is a tragic and shameful story. Isolated from the Australian mainland by rising sea levels 10,000 years ago, the island's Aboriginal peoples developed a distinct, sustainable, seasonal culture of hunting, fishing and gathering.

When European pastoralists arrived, they fenced off sections of fertile land for farming. Indigenous Australians lost more and more of their rightful hunting grounds, and battles erupted between blacks and whites – resulting in the so-called Black Wars. Lieutenant-Governor George Arthur declared martial law in 1828 and Aboriginal tribes were systematically murdered, incarcerated or forced at gunpoint from districts settled by whites. Many more succumbed to European diseases.

An attempt to resettle Tasmania's remaining Aboriginal peoples to Flinders Island – to 'civilise' and Christianise them – occurred

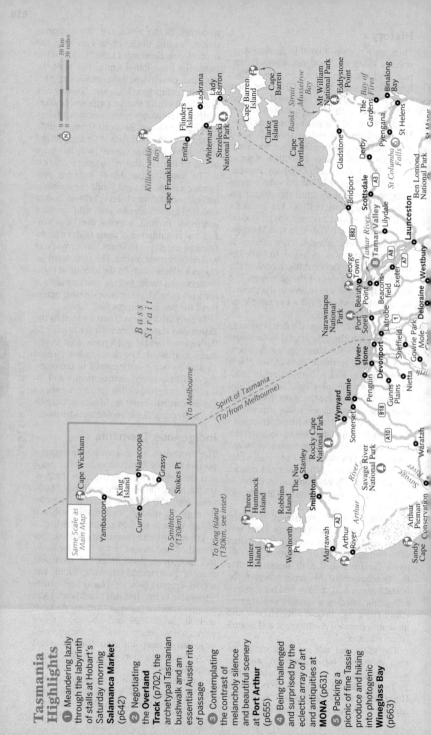

Tasmania Highlights

1 Meandering lazily through the labyrinth of stalls at Hobart's Saturday morning **Salamanca Market** (p642)

2 Negotiating the **Overland Track** (p702), the archetypal Tasmanian bushwalk and an essential Aussie rite of passage

3 Contemplating the contrast of melancholy silence and beautiful scenery at **Port Arthur** (p655)

4 Being challenged and surprised by the eclectic array of art and antiquities at **MONA** (p631)

5 Packing a picnic of fine Tassie produce and hiking into photogenic **Wineglass Bay** (p663)

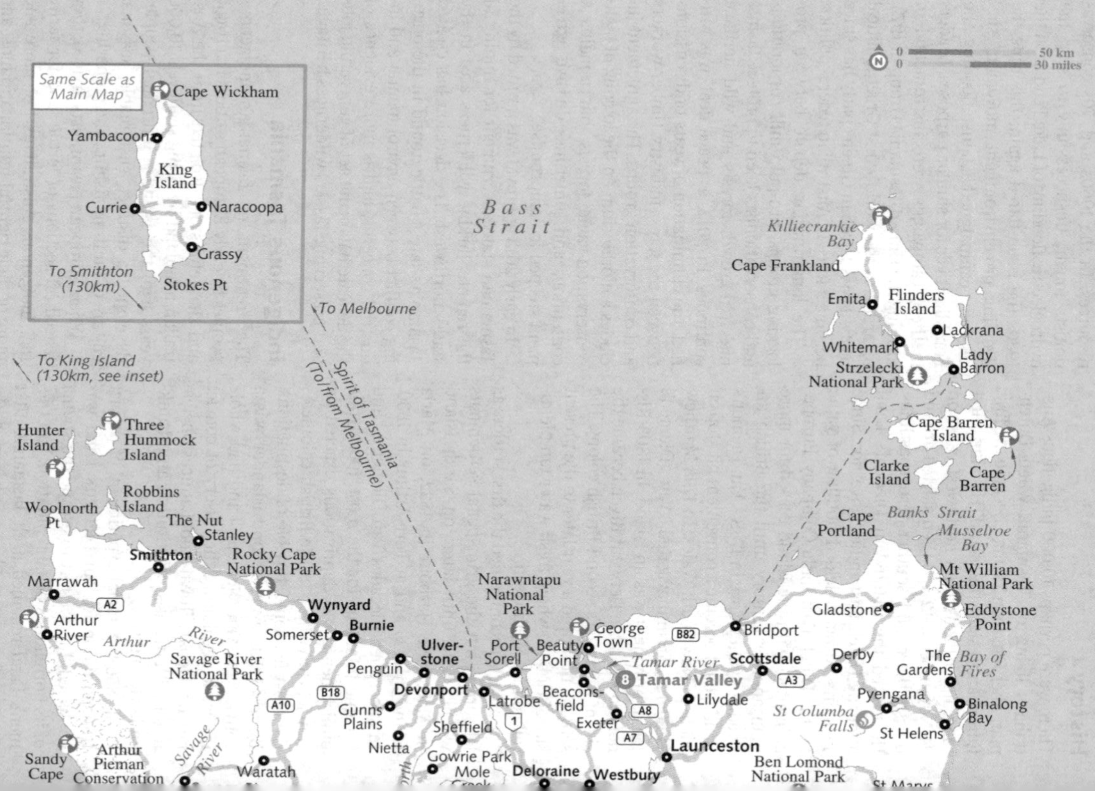

6 Bumping and bouncing into the Southern Ocean on a boat cruise from **Bruny Island** (p647)

7 Sea kayaking on the still, crystalline waters of **Bathurst Harbour** (p646)

8 Taking the foot off the travel accelerator with a lazy, lingering lunch in the **Tamar Valley** (p677) wine region

DON'T MISS

ADRENALIN-FUELLED TASMANIA

Tasmania definitely punches above its weight if you're looking to get your adrenalin pumping, almost always with the backdrop of some of Australia's finest wilderness scenery:

- Mountain biking helter skelter down the imposing hulk of Hobart's Mt Wellington
- Rafting the impetuous rapids of the Franklin River
- Abseiling 140m down the sheer concrete monolith that is Gordon Dam
- Whizzing through the forest canopy on a cable hang glider in the Tahune Forest
- Sea kayaking around the misty coves and isolated bays of Bathurst Harbour

between 1829 and 1834, but most died of despair, poor food or respiratory disease. Of the 135 taken to the island, only 47 survived to be transferred to another settlement at Oyster Cove in Tasmania's south in 1847. Within 32 years the entire Aboriginal population at Oyster Cove had perished.

European sealers had been working in Bass Strait since 1798 and, although they occasionally raided tribes along the coast, their contact with Aboriginal people was mainly based on trade. Aboriginal women were also traded and many sealers settled on Bass Strait islands with these women and had families.

There's a simple memorial on Bruny Island to Truganini, who was said to be the last true indigenous Tasmanian. Truganini died in her 70s in Hobart in 1876 (she was, in fact, outlived by two women of unmixed ancestry). Her sad life and death was reported at the time as 'the end of the native problem' and her skeleton was displayed in the Hobart museum, but she's since become a symbol of the horror of the attempted genocide of Tasmania's indigenous peoples.

By 1847 an Aboriginal community, with a lifestyle based on both Aboriginal and European ways, had emerged on Flinders and other islands in the Furneaux Group. Although the last Tasmanian Aboriginal peoples died in the 19th century, the strength of the community helped save the race from oblivion. Today, thousands of descendants of this community live in Tasmania.

Tasmania's indigenous peoples continue to claim rights to land and compensation for past injustices. Acknowledgment of the treatment meted out to Aboriginal peoples by Europeans has resulted in the recognition of native titles to land. In 1995 the Tasmanian government returned 12 sites to the Tasmanian Aboriginal community, including Oyster Cove, Kutikina Cave and Steep Island. Wybalenna was added to this list in 1999, and areas of Cape Barren and Clarke Islands in 2005.

National Parks

Tasmania has a greater percentage of land protected as national parks and reserves than any other Australian state, and activities include hiking, canoeing and kayaking, caving, swimming and surfing. Tasmania has 19 national parks totalling more than 1.4 million hectares – nearly 21% of the island's land area.

In 1982 Tasmania's four largest national parks (Southwest, Franklin-Gordon Wild Rivers, Cradle Mountain-Lake St Clair and Walls of Jerusalem) and much of the Central Plateau were placed on the Unesco World Heritage list. This listing acknowledges the combined region as one of the planet's last great temperate wilderness areas.

An entry fee is charged for all of Tasmania's national parks. Passes are available at most park entrances, many visitor information centres, the *Spirit of Tasmania* ferries and at the state-wide offices of **Service Tasmania** (☎1300 135 513; www.service.tas.gov.au).

A 24-hour pass to any number of parks costs $24 per car (including up to eight passengers) or $12 per individual (arriving by bus, or for bushwalkers, cyclists and motorcyclists). The best value for most travellers is the eight-week pass ($30/60 per person/vehicle).

See the Parks & Wildlife Service (p643) website. From around mid-December to mid-February rangers run free family-friendly activities at major parks.

Activities

See the following websites.

Parks & Wildlife Service INFORMATION
(www.parks.tas.gov.au) Click on 'Recreation'.

Tourism Tasmania INFORMATION
(www.discovertasmania.com) Click on 'Activities & Attractions'.

Bushwalking

Tasmania's Overland Track – six days and 65km through the sublime Cradle Mountain-Lake St Clair National Park – is Australia's most famous bushwalk and widely ranked among the world's top 10 walks. Another epic bushwalk is the six- to eight-day, 85km South Coast Track.

Lonely Planet's *Walking in Australia* has info on some of Tasmania's best (longer) walks. Some of Tassie's wilderness areas can be experienced on much shorter walks: Parks & Wildlife Service's *60 Great Short Walks* brochure lists the state's best short walks from 10-minute strolls to day-long hikes. Check the Parks & Wildlife Service website for more information.

On long walks remember that in any Tasmanian season a beautiful day can quickly turn ugly, so warm clothing, waterproof gear, a tent, map and compass are essential. **Tasmap** (www.tasmap.tas.gov.au) produces excellent maps online or from visitor information centres. In Hobart you'll find maps at **Service Tasmania** (Map p632; ☎1300 135 513; www.service.tas.gov.au; 134 Macquarie St; ⏲8.15am-5pm Mon-Fri) and the Tasmanian Map Centre (p642).

Fishing

See www.ifs.tas.gov.au for information on fishing in Tasmania.

Tasmania's Lake Country on the Central Plateau features glacial lakes, crystal-clear streams and world-class trout fishing. Operators can organise guides, lessons or fishing trips – see **Trout Guides & Lodges Tasmania** (www.troutguidestasmania.com.au).

On the east coast charter fishing is big business.

Rafting & Sea Kayaking

The Franklin River is famous for full-bore white-water rafting and the Parks & Wildlife website has good information on this activity. Other rivers offering rapids thrills include the Derwent (upstream from Hobart), the Picton (southwest of Hobart) and the Mersey in the north.

Sea-kayaking centres include Kettering southeast of Hobart, Bruny Island and the southwest coast; and Coles Bay on the Freycinet Peninsula.

Sailing

Studded with inlets and harbours, the D'Entrecasteaux Channel and Huon River south of Hobart are excellent for sailing. For casual berths in Hobart, contact the **Royal Yacht Club of Tasmania** (☎03-6223 4599; www.ryct.org.au) in Sandy Bay.

Scuba Diving

Despite the chilly water there are some excellent diving opportunities, particularly on the east coast. A great artificial site was created by the scuttling of the *Troy D* in 2007 off the west coast of Maria Island – see www.troyd.com.au. Rocky Cape on the north coast offers marine life aplenty, while shipwrecks abound around King and Flinders Islands.

Tasmanian diving courses are cheaper than on the mainland. Contact operators at the Bay of Fires, Eaglehawk Neck, Bicheno and King Island.

Surfing

Tasmania has brilliant surfing spots with river mouths, and point and reef breaks, and a full-length wetsuit is essential. Close to Hobart, the most reliable spots are Clifton Beach and Goats Beach (unsigned) en route to South Arm. The southern beaches on Bruny Island, particularly Whalebone Point in Cloudy Bay, offer consistent swell. The east coast from Bicheno north to St Helens has solid beach breaks when conditions are working. At Marrawah on the west coast the waves are often towering. Shipstern Bluff is about a two-hour walk into the Tasman National Park on the Tasman Peninsula south of Port Arthur around Raoul Bay, and is allegedly Australia's heaviest wave.

See www.tassiesurf.com.

Swimming

The north and east coasts of Tasmania offer countless sheltered, white-sand beaches, but the water is quite cold. Beautiful swimming beaches include Wineglass Bay, Bay of Fires, (watch for rips), Binalong Bay outside St Helens, Boat Harbour Beach and Penguin Beach.

Wine Regions

Since the mid-1950s Tasmania has gained international recognition for producing quality wines, characterised by their full, fruity flavour, along with the high acidity expected of cool, temperate wine regions. Today vineyards across the state are producing award-winning pinot noirs, rieslings and chardonnays, and Tassie wineries are growing grapes for many of the top Australian sparkling wine brands.

Tasmania can be split into two main wine-growing regions: the north and east around Launceston (the Tamar Valley) and Bicheno, and the south around Hobart (the Coal River Valley).

Tours

Most trips depart from Hobart, but some depart from Launceston or Devonport.

Herbaceous Tours FOOD, WINE
(0416 970 699; www.herbaceoustours.com.au; per person $55-130) Specialist food and wine tours including Hobart, the Coal River Valley wine region, Bruny Island and the Huon Valley.

Jump Tours BACKPACKER
(0422 130 630; www.jumptours.com) Youth- and backpacker-oriented tours of Tasmania from two to five days. Also available is a one-day departure to Port Arthur taking in spectacular Tasman Peninsula scenery.

Tarkine Trails BUSHWALKING
(0405 255 537; www.tarkinetrails.com.au) Guided walks in the Tarkine wilderness and on the Overland Track. Accommodation is either in tents (some luxury options) or comfortable wilderness retreats.

TASafari 4WD
(0417 002 508, 1300 882 415; www.tasafari.com.au) Eco-certified 4WD camping tours from four to 14 days.

Tasmanian Expeditions OUTDOOR ACTIVITIES
(1300 666 856, 03-6339 3999; www.tasmanianexpeditions.com.au) Activity-based tours including bushwalking, cabin-based walks, canyoning, rafting, rock climbing, cycling and sea kayaking.

Tours Tasmania BACKPACKER
(1800 777 103; www.tourstas.com.au) Small-group, backpacker-oriented full-day trips from Hobart to Wineglass Bay, Mt Field National Park, Port Arthur and the Huon Valley. Also departures from Launceston to Cradle Mountain and the east coast.

Under Down Under BACKPACKER
(1800 064 726; www.underdownunder.com.au) Backpacker-friendly trips, including three- to nine-day tours of the east coast, west coast and the Tarkine wilderness.

Seasonal Work

Casual work can usually be found during summer in the major tourist centres, mainly working in tourism, hospitality, labouring, gardening or farming. Seasonal fruit-picking is hard work and pay is proportional to the quantity and quality of fruit picked. Harvest is from December to April in the Huon and Tamar Valleys. Grape-picking jobs are sometimes available in late autumn and early winter, as some wineries still hand-pick their crops.

Information

Tourism Tasmania (1300 827 743, 03-6230 8235; www.discovertasmania.com) provides loads of travel information.

Most major towns have information centres containing state-wide listings of accommodation, events, public transport and activities.

The following are useful information sources:

Parks & Wildlife Service (www.parks.tas.gov.au) Walks, camp sites, activities and facilities in the state's national parks and reserves.

Royal Automobile Club of Tasmania (RACT; 13 27 22; www.ract.com.au) Roadside automotive assistance, road weather updates and travel information.

Getting There & Away

Tasmania's quarantine service rigorously protects the state's disease-free agriculture – all visitors (including those from mainland Australia) must dispose of all plants, fruits and vegetables prior to or upon arrival.

If you're travelling in a group or with family and want to take a vehicle to Tasmania, the cheapest option is to combine low-cost airline tickets for the bulk of the group, and car and driver-only passage on the ferry from Melbourne.

AIR

There are no direct international flights to/from Tasmania. The following airlines fly between Tasmania and mainland Australia:

Jetstar (13 15 38; www.jetstar.com.au) Direct flights from Melbourne and Sydney to Hobart and Launceston.

Qantas (13 13 13; www.qantas.com.au) Direct flights from Sydney, Brisbane and Melbourne to Launceston and Hobart. QantasLink (the regional subsidiary) flies between Melbourne and Devonport.

Regional Express (13 17 13; www.regionalexpress.com.au) Flies from Melbourne to Burnie/Wynyard and King Island.

Sharp Airlines (1300 556 694; www.sharpairlines.com) Flights from Launceston and Melbourne (Essendon airport) to Flinders Island. Also flies from Burnie/Wynyard to King Island.

Tiger Airways (☎03-9999 2888; www.tigerairways.com.au) Flies from Melbourne to Hobart.

Virgin Australia (☎13 67 89; www.virgin-australia.com) Direct flights from Melbourne, Sydney, Brisbane, Canberra and Adelaide to Hobart, and from Melbourne, Brisbane, Perth and Sydney to Launceston.

BOAT

The **Spirit of Tasmania** (☎1800 634 906, 03-6421 7209; www.spiritoftasmania.com.au) operates two car and passenger ferries that cruise nightly between Melbourne and Devonport in both directions, usually departing at 7.30pm and taking about 10 hours shore to shore. Additional daytime sailings are scheduled during peak and shoulder seasons. Fares vary for travel in peak (mid-December to late January), shoulder (late January to April, and September to mid-December) and off-peak (May to August) seasons. There's a range of cabin and seat options, and child, student, pensioner and senior discounts apply. Some cabins are wheelchair-accessible.

The Devonport terminal is on the Esplanade in East Devonport, and the Melbourne terminal is at Station Pier in Port Melbourne. Indicative one-way adult fares are as follows, but actual fares fluctuate based on demand and day of travel availability.

FARE TYPE	OFF PEAK	PEAK
Ocean-view recliner seat	$99	$128
Shared 4-berth cabin	$61	$132
Twin cabin	$94	$165
Deluxe Cabin	$329	$358
Standard vehicles & campervans (up to 5.3m)	$79	$89
Motorbikes	$64	$64
Bicycles	$6	$6

Getting Around

AIR

Air travel within Tasmania is uncommon, but bushwalkers sometimes use light air services to/from the southwest. **Par Avion** (☎03-6248 5390; www.paravion.com.au) fly between Hobart and remote Melaleuca (one-way/return $205/400).

BICYCLE

Tassie is a good size for exploring by bicycle. Some areas are pretty hilly and the weather can be unpredictable, but the routes are scenic and the towns aren't too far apart. Cycling between Hobart and Launceston via either coast (the east coast is a cycling favourite) usually takes 10 to 14 days. For a full 'Lap of the Map', allow 18 to 28 days.

See **Bicycle Tasmania** (www.biketas.org.au) for more information.

BUS

Redline Coaches (☎1300 360 000; www.tasredline.com.au) and **Tassielink** (☎1300 300 520, 03-6235 7300; www.tassielink.com.au) cover most of the state, running along most major highways year-round (weekend services are less frequent). Redline services the Midland Hwy between Hobart and Launceston, the north coast between Launceston and Smithton, north from Launceston to George Town, and to the east coast. Tassielink runs from both Hobart and Launceston to the west and to the east coast, from Hobart to Port Arthur, and south from Hobart down to the Huon Valley. Redline's Main Road Express connects Bass Strait ferry arrivals/departures in Devonport to Launceston, Hobart and Burnie.

Additionally, **Metro Tasmania** (☎13 22 01; www.metrotas.com.au) runs regular services south from Hobart as far as Woodbridge and Cygnet, and north to Richmond and New Norfolk. Smaller operators service important tourist routes – see relevant sections for details.

A one-way trip between Devonport and Launceston is around $23 and takes 1½ hours, Hobart to Launceston is $33 (2½ hours) and Hobart to Devonport is $56 (four hours).

CAR, CAMPERVAN & MOTORCYCLE

Tassie is ideal for travelling by road as distances are relatively short, and driving conditions are generally good. You can bring vehicles across on the ferry, but renting may be cheaper, particularly for shorter trips, and rates are usually more affordable than on the mainland. If you're renting, always ask about the company's policy on driving on unsealed roads as some of Tasmania's natural attractions are reached by dirt road. Check carefully as you may void your insurance on unsealed roads.

Watch out for wildlife and avoid driving between dusk and dawn when critters are active (roadkill is ubiquitous). One-lane bridges on country roads and log trucks speeding around sharp corners also demand caution. In cold weather be wary of 'black ice' on shady mountain passes.

Big international car rental companies have booking desks at airports and in major towns, with standard rates for small-car hire from $50 to $80 per day in summer high season. Book well in advance, for a week's hire or more, and rates can fall dramatically, especially outside high season. Compare rental deals on **Vroom Vroom Vroom** (www.vroomvroomvroom.com.au).

Small local firms rent older cars for as little as $40 a day, depending on the season and rental length. They'll often ask for a bond of $300 or more.

TASMANIA – TASTE THE DIFFERENCE

Kick off your exploration of Tassie's great food and wine scene in Hobart. Also read Graeme Phillip's **A Guide to Tasting Tasmania** (www.tastingtasmania.com), updated annually and available online or from Fullers (p642) bookshop.

➡ Pick your own berries at the Sorell Fruit Farm (p654)

➡ Slurp oysters fresh from the Freycinet Marine Farm (p664) or at Get Shucked (p648) on Bruny Island

➡ Attend a Tasmanian food and wine festival – get salivating for The Taste (p634) or Savour Tasmania (p635) in Hobart, or Festivale (p673) in Launceston

➡ Sample local and sustainable produce at a farmers market, either at Hobart's Tas Farm Gate (p637) market or Harvest (p676) in Launceston

➡ Explore Hobart with Gourmania (p633), or venture further with Herbaceous Tours (p624), Bruny Island Safaris (p648) or the Long Lunch Tour Co (p663)

Well-surfaced scenic roads and relatively light traffic make motorcycling in Tasmania fantastic. Contact **Tasmanian Motorcycle Hire** (☎0418 365 210; www.tasmotorcyclehire.com.au).

With loads of camping grounds and free-camping areas, Tassie is *the* place for a campervanning holiday. They're economical too (from around $90 per day).

Lo-Cost Auto Rent (www.locostautorent.com) Hobart (☎03-6231 0550; 94 Harrington St) Launceston (☎03-6391 9182; 7 Brisbane St)

Selective Car Rentals (☎1800 300 102, 03-6234 3311; www.selectivecarrentals.com.au; 47 Bathurst St, Hobart) Offices also in Launceston and Devonport.

Britz (☎1800 331 454; www.britz.com.au) Rents campervans and 4WDs.

Campervan Hire Tasmania (☎03-6391 9357; www.campervanhiretasmania.com)

Maui (☎1300 363 800; www.maui.com.au)

Tasmanian Campervan Hire (☎1800 807 119; www.tascamper.com)

Tasmanian Campervan Rentals (☎03-6248 1867; www.tasmaniacampervanrentals.com.au)

Tasmanian Motor Shacks (☎03-6248 4418; www.tassiemotorshacks.com.au)

Cheap Motorhome Hire (www.cheaptasmaniamotorhomehire.com.au)

Fetch (www.fetchcampervanhire.com.au)

Getabout Oz (www.getaboutoz.com)

HOBART

POP 212,000

Australia's second-oldest city and southernmost capital lies at the foothills of Mt Wellington on the banks of the Derwent River. Hobart's waterfront areas around Sullivans Cove – Macquarie Wharf, Constitution Dock, Salamanca Place and Battery Point – are simply gorgeous with their neat Georgian buildings and the towering bulk of Mt Wellington behind. The town's rich colonial heritage and natural charms are accented by a spirited, rootsy atmosphere: festivals, superb restaurants and hip urban bars abound. Hobartians are super-relaxed, very friendly and have none of the haughtiness of the Melbourne and Sydney gentry. On summer afternoons the sea breeze blows and yachts tack across the river. On winter mornings the pea-soup 'Bridgewater Jerry' fog lifts to reveal the snow-capped summit of the mountain. In recent years, Hobart's emerging food scene and the stellar attractions of MONA (Museum of Old & New Art) have seen the city attain a significant international reputation.

History

The seminomadic Mouheneer people were the original inhabitants of the area. Risdon Cove on the Derwent River's eastern shore was the first European settlement in 1803, but just a year later the settlers decamped to the site of present-day Hobart.

Britain's jails were overflowing with criminals in the 1820s, and so tens of thousands of convicts were chained together into rotting hulks and transported to Hobart Town to serve their sentences in vile conditions. By the 1850s Hobart was rife with sailors, soldiers, whalers, ratbags and prostitutes shamelessly boozing, brawling and bonking in and around countless harbourside taverns.

The city has only ever partially sobered up, and anytime is beer-o'clock at legendary pub Knopwood's. Skeletons rattle in closets, but Hobart's relaxed vibe make it easy to forget they're there.

Sights

All places of interest in central and waterfront Hobart are in easy walking distance of each other.

Salamanca Place, an impressive row of sandstone Georgian warehouses, lines the southern fringe of Sullivans Cove, the city's harbour and social epicentre. Just south of Salamanca Place is Battery Point, Hobart's increasingly gentrified early colonial district.

Ascend Mt Wellington for superb views of the city.

SYDNEY TO HOBART YACHT RACE

Arguably the world's greatest and most treacherous open-ocean yacht race, the Sydney to Hobart Yacht Race (p634) winds up at Hobart's Constitution Dock every New Year's Eve. As the storm-battered maxis limp across the finish line, champagne corks pop and weary sailors turn the town upside down. On New Year's Day, find a sunny spot by the harbour, munch some lunch from The Taste (p634) food festival and count the spinnakers on the river.

Waterfront & Salamanca Place

Salamanca Place HISTORIC AREA

(Map p632) This picturesque row of four-storey sandstone warehouses on Sullivans Cove is Australia's best-preserved historic urban precinct. Salamanca Place was the hub of old Hobart Town's trade and commerce, but by the mid-20th century many of these 1830s whaling-era buildings had become decrepit ruins. The 1970s saw the dawning of Tasmania's sense of 'heritage', which helped to reinvigorate the warehouses as restaurants, cafes, bars and shops.

The **Salamanca Arts Centre** (Map p632; 03-6234 8414; www.salarts.org.au; 77 Salamanca Pl; shops & galleries 9am-6pm) occupies seven Salamanca warehouses and is home to many galleries, studios, performing arts venues and public spaces.

To reach Salamanca Place from Battery Point, descend the well-weathered **Kelly's Steps**.

Waterfront HISTORIC AREA

Centred on **Victoria Dock** (a working fishing harbour) and **Constitution Dock** (chock-full of floating takeaway-seafood punts), Hobart's waterfront is a brilliant place to explore.

Celebrations surrounding the finish of the annual Sydney to Hobart Yacht Race revolve around Constitution Dock at New Year's. The fabulous food festival, The Taste, is also in full swing around this time.

Hunter Street has a row of fine Georgian warehouses, most of which comprised the old Henry Jones IXL jam factory. It's occupied these days by the Art School division of the University of Tasmania and the über-swish Henry Jones Art Hotel and its affiliated restaurants and galleries.

★ **Tasmanian Museum & Art Gallery** MUSEUM

(Map p632; www.tmag.tas.gov.au; 40 Macquarie St; 10am-5pm) FREE Reopened in early 2013 after a $30 million redevelopment, this superb museum includes the Commissariat Store (1808; the state's oldest building), colonial relics and art, and excellent Aboriginal displays. There are free guided tours at 2.30pm from Wednesday to Sunday. Take in the Islands to Ice: Antarctica exhibition before recharging in the museum's cafe.

Lark Distillery DISTILLERY

(Map p632; 03-6231 9088; www.larkdistillery.com.au; 14 Davey St; tours per person $15, whisky tours one/two days from $215/395; 10am-7pm Sun-Wed, 10am-8pm Thu & Sat, 10am-late Fri) Lark Distillery produces fruit liqueurs (free tastings) and single malt whisky ($2.50 per tasting). Distillery tours happen at 2.30pm Monday to Saturday. You can also get bar snacks and there's live blues and folk music on most Friday and Saturday nights. Lark Distillery also runs **whisky tours**, exploring Tasmania's emerging whisky scene.

Battery Point, Sandy Bay & South Hobart

Battery Point HISTORIC AREA

(Map p628; www.batterypoint.net) An empty rum bottle's throw from the once notorious Sullivans Cove waterfront is a nest of tiny 19th-century cottages and laneways. The old maritime village of Battery Point takes its

Hobart

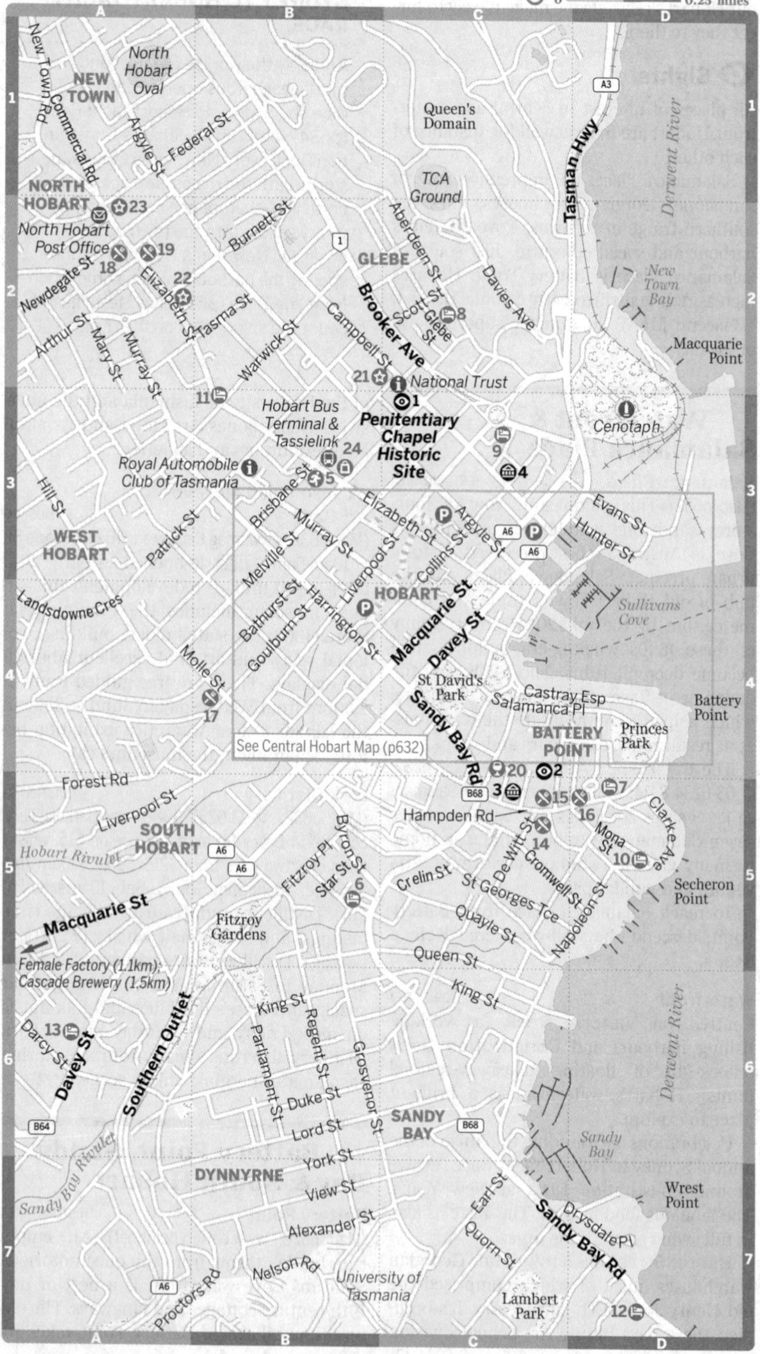

TASMANIA HOBART

Hobart

Top Sights
1 Penitentiary Chapel Historic Site ... C3

Sights
2 Battery Point ... C4
3 Narryna Heritage Museum ... C5
4 Theatre Royal ... C3

Activities, Courses & Tours
5 Art Bikes ... B3

Sleeping
6 Apartments on Star ... B5
7 Battery Point Boutique Accommodation ... D5
8 Corinda's Cottages ... C2
9 Fountainside ... C3
10 Grand Vue Private Hotel ... D5
11 Lodge on Elizabeth ... B3
12 Motel 429 ... D7
13 The Islington ... A6

Eating
14 Environs ... C5
15 Jackman & McRoss ... C5
16 Jam Jar Lounge ... D5
17 Pigeon Hole ... B4
18 Raincheck Lounge ... A2
19 Sweet Envy ... A2

Drinking & Nightlife
20 Preachers ... C4

Entertainment
21 Brisbane Hotel ... B2
22 Republic Bar & Café ... A2
23 State Cinema ... A2

Shopping
24 Tas Farm Gate Market ... B3

name from the 1818 gun battery that stood on the promontory.

Battery Point's liquored-up ale houses on **Hampden Road** have been refitted as cafes and restaurants, and now cater to a less raucous clientele. Stumble up Kelly's Steps from Salamanca Place and dogleg into **South Street** where red lights once burned night and day. Spin around the picturesque **Arthur Circus**, check out **St George's Anglican Church** on Cromwell St, or shamble down **Napoleon Street** to the waterfront. For a fortifying ale, duck into the salty 1846 **Shipwrights Arms Hotel** on Trumpeter St.

Narryna Heritage Museum MUSEUM
(Map p628; ☎03-6234 2791; www.narryna.com.au; 103 Hampden Rd; adult/child $10/4; ⏰10.30am-5pm Mon-Fri, 12.30-5pm Sat-Sun) This stately Georgian sandstone-fronted mansion (1836) is set in established grounds and contains a treasure trove of domestic colonial artefacts.

Female Factory HISTORIC SITE
(☎03-6233 6656; www.cascadefemalefactory.wordpress.com; 16 Degraves St; Heritage tour adult/concession/family $15/10/40, 'Her Story' dramatisation adult/concession/family $20/12.50/60; ⏰9.30am-4pm) Finally being recognised as an important historic site (one in four convicts transported to Van Diemen's Land was a woman), this was where Hobart's female convicts were incarcerated. Major archaeological work is ongoing, and two 45-minute tours are available – a Heritage guided tour taking in the whole site, and 'Her Story', a dramatisation of the harsh life in the Female Factory. Bookings are essential; see online or phone to confirm the latest tour schedule.

It's not far from the Cascade Brewery, so combine both for a fascinating afternoon. Take bus 43, 44, 46 or 49 and alight at stop 16.

Cadbury Chocolate Factory LANDMARK
(☎1800 627 367; www.cadbury.com.au; Cadbury Rd; adult/child/family $7.50/4/17.5; ⏰8.30am-3.30pm Mon-Fri except public holidays) A must for sweet-tooths is the Cadbury Chocolate Factory, 15km north of the city centre. Enjoy samples and invest in low-priced choc products.

Some companies offer day trips and river cruises incorporating the Cadbury tour, or book directly with Cadbury by phone or online and make your own way here on bus 37, 38 or 39 to Claremont from stop E on Elizabeth St.

Mt Wellington PARK
(www.wellingtonpark.org.au) Cloaked in winter snow, Mt Wellington peaks at 1270m, towering above Hobart. The citizens find reassurance in its constant, solid presence, while outdoors types hike and bike on its leafy flanks. And the view from the top is unbelievable! Don't be deterred it's overcast – often the peak rises above cloud level and looks out over a magic carpet of cotton-topped clouds.

Hacked out of the mountainside during the Great Depression, the 22km road to the top winds up from the city through thick temperate forest, opening out to lunar rockscapes at the summit. If you don't have wheels, local buses 48 and 49 stop at Fern Tree halfway up the hill, from where it's a five- to six-hour return walk to the top via Fern Glade Track, Radfords Track, Pinnacle Track, then the steep Zig Zag Track. The Organ Pipes walk from the Chalet (en route to the summit) is a flat track below these amazing cliffs. Pick up the *Mt Wellington Walks* map ($4.10 from the visitor centre) or download PDF maps at www.wellingtonpark.com.au.

Some bus-tour companies include Mt Wellington in their itineraries. Another option is the **Mt Wellington Shuttle Bus Service** (☎0408 341 804; per person return $25), departing the visitor centre at 10.15am and 1.30pm daily.

You can also bomb down the slopes on a mountain bike with **Mt Wellington Descent** (☎1800 064 726; www.underdownunder.com.au; adult/child $75/65). Kick off with a van ride to the summit, followed by more than 21km of downhill cruising (mostly on sealed roads, but with off-road options). Tours depart at 10am and 1pm daily, with an additional 4pm departure in January and February.

Cascade Brewery BREWERY
(☎03-6224 1117; www.cascadebrewery.com.au; 140 Cascade Rd; 2hr tours adult/student $22/17, 1hr heritage tours adult/child/family $15/12/42; ⏲brewery tours hourly 10-2pm, heritage tours 12.30pm & 2.30pm Mon-Fri) Around a bend in South Hobart, standing in startling Gothic isolation, is Australia's oldest brewery. Cascade was established in 1832 next to the clean-running Hobart Rivulet, and is still pumping out beer and soft drinks today. Tours involve plenty of stair climbing, with tastings at the end. You'll need to be at least 18, and wear flat, enclosed shoes and long trousers (no shorts or skirts). You can take a tour on weekends, but none of the machinery will be operating. A full-of-history one-hour wander around Cascade's lovely gardens is also on offer for visitors of all ages. Online or phone bookings are essential. Take bus 43, 44, 46 or 49 from Elizabeth St at Franklin Sq and alight at stop 18.

City Centre

★ Penitentiary Chapel Historic Site HISTORIC SITE
(Map p628; www.penitentiarychapel.com; cnr Brisbane & Campbell Sts; tours adult/child/family $10/8/20; ⏲tours 10am, 11.30am, 1pm & 2.30pm Sun-Fri, 1pm & 2.30pm Sat) Ruminating over the court rooms, cells and gallows here, writer TG Ford mused, 'As the Devil was going through Hobart Gaol, he saw a solitary cell; and the Devil was pleased for it gave him a hint, for improving the prisons in hell.' Take the excellent National Trust-run tour or the one-hour Penitentiary Chapel Ghost Tour (p634), held on Monday and Friday nights (bookings essential).

Parliament House HISTORIC BUILDING
(Map p632; www.parliament.tas.gov.au; Salamanca Pl; 45min tours free; ⏲tours 10am & 2pm Mon-Fri except when parliament sits) Presiding over an oak-studded park adjacent to Salamanca Place is Tasmania's sandstone Parliament House, completed in 1840 and originally used as a customs house.

HOBART IN...

Two Days

Get your head into history mode with a stroll around **Battery Point** – a leisurely brunch at **Environs** will sustain your afternoon exploration of nearby **Salamanca Place**. It's definitely worth taking a guided walking tour of this area. Explore Hobart's maritime heritage at the **Maritime Museum of Tasmania** before a promenade along the Sullivans Cove waterfront and a seafood dinner at **Blue Eye**. Kick on with Tassie craft beer at the funky **Preachers**, or a single malt at the **Nant Whisky Cellar & Bar**.

On day two recuperate over a big breakfast at **Machine Laundry Café** then blow out the cobwebs with a mountain bike ride down **Mt Wellington**. Spend the afternoon at the challenging **MONA** (Museum of Old & New Art), before dinner, drinks and live music at **Republic Bar & Café**, North Hobart's happening hub.

Theatre Royal HISTORIC BUILDING
(Map p628; www.theatreroyal.com.au; 29 Campbell St; 1hr tours adult/child $12/10; ⌚ tours 11am Mon, Wed & Fri) Take a backstage tour of Hobart's most prestigious theatre. Built in 1837, it's actually Australia's oldest continuously operating theatre.

Maritime Museum of Tasmania MUSEUM
(Map p632; www.maritimetas.org; 16 Argyle St; adult/child $7/5; ⌚ 9am-5pm) The excellent Maritime Museum of Tasmania has a fascinating collection of photos, paintings, models and relics.

Town Hall HISTORIC BUILDING
(Map p632; 50 Macquarie St) Built in 1864, and inspired by the Palazzo Farnese in Rome.

St David's Cathedral CHURCH
(Map p632; cnr Murray & Macquarie Sts) Built in 1868, and regarded as one of the finest works outside of Britain by leading Victorian architect, George Bodley.

North & West Hobart

★**MONA** GALLERY
(☎ 03-6277 9900; www.mona.net.au; 655 Main Rd, Berriedale; adult/concession/child under 18 $20/18/free; ⌚ 10am-6pm Wed-Mon, also open Tue in Jan) Fast becoming Tasmania's biggest attraction is MONA, the $75 million Museum of Old & New Art, which owner David Walsh describes as 'a subversive adult Disneyland'. The extraordinary installation is arrayed across three underground levels concealed inside a sheer rock face. Ancient antiquities are showcased next to more recent works by Sir Sidney Nolan and British *enfant terrible*, Damien Hirst.

To get to MONA catch a fast ferry or bus from the **MONA Brooke St Ferry Terminal** (Map p632; 30 minutes, per person return $20). Another option is to a rent a bicycle at the terminal (per person $20), and cycle 12km to MONA on Hobart's Inter-City cycleway along the Derwent River. You can then catch the bus or ferry back to Hobart.

Moorilla Estate WINERY, BREWERY
(☎ 03-6277 9900; www.mona.net.au; 655 Main Rd, Berriedale; tastings free, lunch mains $27-35, dinner degustation menu $75-175; ⌚ 10am-5pm, The Source noon-2.30pm Wed-Mon, from 6.30pm Wed-Sat) Twelve kilometres north of Hobart's centre, Moorilla occupies a saucepan-shaped peninsula jutting into the Derwent River. Founded in the 1950s, Moorilla plays a prominent and gregarious role in Hobart society. Stop by for wine and 'Moo Brew' beer tastings, have lunch or dinner at the outstanding restaurant **The Source**, or catch a summer concert on the lawns. MONA shares the same dramatic location.

Activities

Cycling

The *Hobart Bike Map* ($4 from the visitor centre), details cycle paths and road routes.

Art Bikes CYCLING
(Map p628; www.artbikes.com.au; 146 Elizabeth St, Arts Tasmania; ⌚ Arts Tasmania 9am-4.30pm Mon-Fri, TMAG 10am-4.30pm Mon-Sun) Excellent free service with modern European-styled bikes. Pick them up either from **Arts Tasmania**, or at the Tasmanian Museum & Art Gallery (TMAG; p627) near the waterfront. You'll need photo ID and a credit card.

Hobart Bike Hire CYCLING
(Map p632; ☎ 0447 556 189; www.hobartbikehire.com.au; Macquarie Wharf No 1, Franklin Wharf; from $15/20/30 per hour/day/24 hours) Centrally-located on Hobart's waterfront with lots of ideas for self-guided tours around the city or along the Derwent River. Electric bikes are also available, and maps and helmets are included.

Tall Ship Sailing

Lady Nelson SAILING
(Map p632; ☎ 03-6234 3348; www.ladynelson.org.au; adult/child $25/10; ⌚ 11am, 1pm, 3pm Sat-Sun Oct-Mar, no 3pm sailing Apr-Sep) Trips on a replica of the surprisingly compact brig the Lady Nelson, one of the first colonial ships to sail to Tasmania. Longer overnight trips are also on offer.

Windeward Bound SAILING
(Map p632; ☎ 03-6224 7965, 0418 120 399; www.windewardbound.com; 3hr sail incl lunch adult/child $75/35; ⌚ Thu-Sun) An elegant replica tall ship with lots of opportunity to get involved with the sailing. Also runs occasional eight-day voyages around Port Davey and Recherche Bay.

Tours

Captain Fell's Historic Ferries CRUISES
(Map p632; ☎ 03-6223 5893; www.captainfellshistoricferries.com.au) Good-value lunch (from $30 per adult) and dinner ($45) cruises on cute old ferries, and longer day cruises on a more modern boat to Bruny Island

Central Hobart

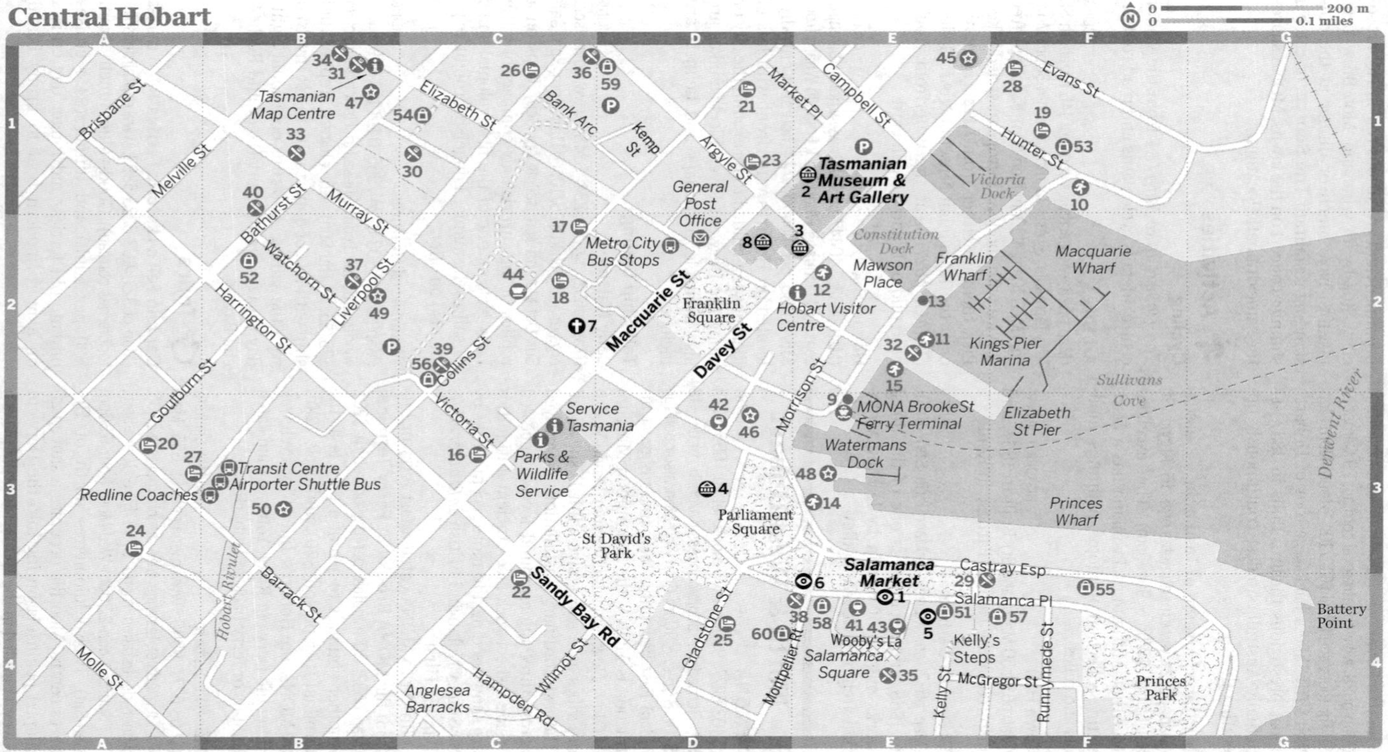

Central Hobart

Top Sights		
1	Salamanca Market	E4
2	Tasmanian Museum & Art Gallery	E1
Sights		
3	Maritime Museum of Tasmania	E2
4	Parliament House	D3
5	Salamanca Arts Centre	E4
6	Salamanca Place	E4
7	St David's Cathedral	C2
8	Town Hall	D2
Activities, Courses & Tours		
9	Captain Fell's Historic Ferries	E3
10	Hobart Bike Hire	F1
11	Lady Nelson	E2
12	Lark Distillery	E2
13	Tasman Island Cruises	E2
14	Wild Thing	E3
15	Windeward Bound	E2
Sleeping		
16	Astor Private Hotel	C3
17	Central Café Bar	C2
18	Central City Backpackers	C2
19	Henry Jones Art Hotel	F1
20	Hobart Hostel	A3
21	Hotel Collins	D1
22	Mantra One	C4
23	Montgomery's Private Hotel & YHA	D1
24	Pickled Frog	A3
25	Salamanca Inn	D4
26	Tassie Backpackers	C1
27	Transit Centre Backpackers	A3
28	Zero Davey	F1
Eating		
29	Blue Eye	E4
30	Criterion Street Café	C1
31	ethos eat drink	B1
32	Fish Frenzy	E2
33	Garagistes	B1
34	Ivory Cafe	B1
35	Machine Laundry Café	E4
36	Pilgrim Coffee	C1
37	R. Takagi Sushi	B2
38	Retro Café	E4
39	Sawak	C2
40	Sidecar	B1
	Tricycle Café Bar	(see 5)
Drinking & Nightlife		
	Barcelona	(see 58)
	IXL Long Bar	(see 19)
41	Jack Greene	E4
	Knopwood's Retreat	(see 58)
42	Lower House	D3
43	Nant Whisky Cellar & Bar	E4
44	Yellow Bernard	C2
Entertainment		
45	Federation Concert Hall	E1
46	Mobius	D3
47	New Sydney Hotel	B1
48	Observatory	E3
	Syrup	(see 58)
49	The Grand Poobah	B2
50	Village Cinemas	B3
Shopping		
51	A Common Ground	E4
52	Antiques to Retro	B2
53	Art Mob	F1
54	Cool Wine	C1
55	Despard Gallery	F4
56	Fullers Bookshop	C2
57	Handmark Gallery	F4
58	Salamanca Fresh Fruit Market	E4
59	Woolworths	D1
60	Wursthaus	D4

(Saturday and Sunday only). Also runs coach or double-decker bus sightseeing trips around town and to Mt Wellington, the Cadbury Chocolate Factory and Richmond.

Gourmania FOOD
(☎0419 180 113; www.gourmaniafoodtours.com.au; per person from $95) Former pastry chef and proud sixth-generation Tasmanian Mary McNeill conducts flavour-filled walking tours around Salamanca and central Hobart with plenty of opportunities to try local foods and chat to restaurant, cafe and shop owners. Take a tour when you first arrive in town, and you'll discover the best places to return to later in your stay.

Gray Line SIGHTSEEING
(☎1300 858 687; www.grayline.com.au) City coach tours (adult/child from $44/22) and visits to MONA (adult/child from $87/43.50) plus destinations including Mt Wellington, Richmond and the Bonorong Wildlife Centre (p644).

Ghost Tours of Hobart & Battery Point HISTORICAL
(☎0439 335 696; www.ghosttoursofhobart.com.au; adult/child $25/15) Two-hour walking tours oozing ectoplasmic tall tales departing from The Bakehouse in Salamanca Sq at dusk. Bookings essential.

DON'T MISS

HOBART'S WELL-PRESERVED OLD BUILDINGS

Hobart's cache of amazingly well-preserved old buildings makes it exceptional among Australian cities. There are more than 90 buildings classified by the National Trust here – 60 of these are on Macquarie and Davey Sts. The intersection of Macquarie and Murray Sts features a gorgeous sandstone edifice on each corner. For detailed information contact the **National Trust** (Map p628; ☎03-6223 5200; www.nationaltrust.org.au; cnr Brisbane & Campbell Sts; ⏰9am-1pm Mon-Fri), or pick up the Hobart's Historic Places brochure from the visitor centre.

Hobart Historic Tours HISTORICAL
(☎03-6227 9029, 03-6224 2556; www.hobarthistorictours.com.au; adult/child/family $30/14/75; ⏰Oct-Apr, groups only from May-Sep) Highly informative 90-minute walking tours of Hobart (3pm Tuesday, Thursday, Saturday and 9.30am Sunday) and historic Battery Point (3pm Saturday). Also available is an Old Hobart Pub Tour (5pm Thursday-Saturday) taking in waterfront watering holes, but not recommended for childen. Book at the Hobart visitor centre (p643).

Louisa's Walk HISTORICAL
(☎03-6229 8959, 0437 276 417; www.livehistoryhobart.com.au; 1½ hr tour adult/child $35/17.50) Engaging tours of Hobart's female convict heritage at the Female Factory interpreted through 'strolling theatre'. Tours depart the Female Factory (p629) at 11am.

Penitentiary Chapel Ghost Tour HISTORICAL
(☎03-6231 0911; www.hobartghosts.com; adult/child/family $15/10/40; ⏰8.30pm Mon & Fri) Historic hauntings at Hobart's old gaol. Bookings essential.

Red Decker SIGHTSEEING
(☎03-6236 9116; www.reddecker.com.au) Commentated sightseeing on an old London double-decker bus. Buy a 20-stop, hop-on-hop-off pass (adult/child/concession $30/16/25), or do the tour as a 90-minute loop. Pay a bit more and add a Cascade Brewery tour or include Mt Wellington or the Cadbury Chocolate Factory into the mix. All passes are valid for three days.

Sullivans Coves Walks HISTORICAL
(☎03-6245 1208; www.sullivanscovewalks.com.au; adult/child $20/12.50; ⏰Mon-Sat) Hobart's maritime history comes alive on these interesting walking tours.

Tasman Island Cruises CRUISES
(Map p632; ☎03-6250 2200; www.tasmancruises.com.au; full-day tour adult/child $180/125) Take a bus to Port Arthur for a three-hour eco-cruise around Tasman Island, or meet the boat at the departure point (adult/child $110/65) with your own transport. Other options incorporate a visit to Port Arthur Historic Site (p655) or the Tasmanian Devil Conservation Park (p654). Day trips for Bruny Island cruises are also possible from Hobart with the same company.

Wild Thing JET-BOATING
(Map p632; ☎1300 137 919; www.wildthingadventures.com.au) A speedy red boat churning up the froth around the Derwent River ($39).

Festivals & Events

Hobart Summer Festival ART, MUSIC
Hobart's premier festival, focused on the waterfront: two weeks of theatre, kids' activities, concerts, buskers, New Year's Eve shenanigans and The Taste festival.

Sydney to Hobart Yacht Race SAILING
(www.rolexsydneyhobart.com) Yachts competing in this annual race start arriving in Hobart around 29 December.

The Taste FOOD, WINE
(www.tastefestival.com.au) On either side of New Year's Eve, this week-long harbour-side event celebrates Tassie's gastronomic prowess. The seafood, wines, beer and cheeses are predictably fabulous, or branch out into mushrooms, truffles and raspberries. Stalls are a who's who of the Hobart restaurant scene.

MONA FOMA CULTURAL
(www.mofo.net.au) January's wonderfully eclectic array of music, arts and culture with high profile and respected names like John Cale, Nick Cave and David Byrne. A corresponding winter festival dubbed **Dark MOFO** kicked off in June 2013.

Australian Wooden Boat Festival HERITAGE
(www.australianwoodenboatfestival.com.au) Biennial event in mid-February (odd-numbered years) to coincide with the Royal Hobart Regatta. The festival showcases Tasmania's boat-building heritage and maritime traditions.

Royal Hobart Regatta SAILING
(www.royalhobartregatta.com) Three days of aquatic yacht-watching and mayhem on the Derwent River. Annually in mid-February, so it coincides with the Australian Wooden Boat Festival every second year.

Ten Days on the Island CULTURAL
(www.tendaysontheisland.com) Tasmania's premier cultural festival – a biennial event (odd-numbered years, usually mid to late March), celebrating arts, music and culture at state-wide venues.

Lumina CULTURAL
(www.lumina.discovertasmania.com) Tasmania's newest festival with winter events including late May's **Savour Tasmania** (www.savourtasmania.com) food festival and July's **Festival of Voices** (www.festivalofvoices.com).

Tasmanian Beerfest BEER
(www.tasmanianbeerfest.com.au) November's opportunity to sample more than 200 beers and ciders from around Australia and the world.

Falls Festival MUSIC
(www.fallsfestival.com.au) Three days from December 29 to January 1 of live Oz and international tunes with an alternative bent. Held at Marion Bay, an hour south of Hobart.

Sleeping

The pumping-est areas to stay are the Sullivans Cove waterfront and Salamanca Place, though prices here are higher and vacancy rates low. The CBD has less ambience, and most of the backpacker hostels and pubs with accommodation are here.

To the north is North Hobart with a range of apartments, B&Bs and good restaurants. Accommodation in waterside Sandy Bay is surprisingly well priced, but it's a fair hike from town.

Top-end Hobart accommodation can be quite reasonable. A budget of around $230 will stretch to designer hotels, historic guesthouses and modern waterside apartments.

City Centre

Hobart Hostel HOSTEL $
(Map p632; ☎1300 252 192; www.hobarthostel.com; cnr Goulburn & Barrack Sts; dm $26-29, d/tw/tr from $80; @ 📶) In a former pub, Hobart Hostel offers clean, colourful and spotless dorms, with good value twins and doubles upstairs. The friendly owners were planning a greater focus on accommodation for couples when we visited. Welcome to one of Hobart's best hostels.

Pickled Frog HOSTEL $
(Map p632; ☎03-6234 7977; www.thepickledfrog.com; 281 Liverpool St; dm $24-28, s/d $62/67; @ 📶) This ramshackle hostel fills an old pub on the CBD fringe with party vibes. Cheap beer, big-screen TVs, pool table, slightly homesick backpackers checking out Facebook and Twitter – you get the picture.

Tassie Backpackers HOSTEL $
(Map p632; ☎03-6234 4981; www.tassiebackpackers.com; 67 Liverpool St, Brunswick Hotel; dm $21-27, s/d/tw $55/69/69; 📶) This hostel above the Brunswick Hotel has plenty of shared spaces including a kitchen and laundry, and downstairs there's a colourful outdoor area

HOBART FOR CHILDREN

Parents won't break the bank keeping the troops entertained in Hobart. The free Friday-night music in the courtyard at the Salamanca Arts Centre is a family-friendly affair, while the street performers, buskers and visual smorgasbord of Saturday's Salamanca Market captivate kids of all ages. There's always something interesting going on around the waterfront, and you can feed the whole family on a budget at the floating fish punts on Constitution Dock.

Rainy-day attractions include the Tasmanian Museum & Art Gallery, the Maritime Museum of Tasmania and the Cadbury Chocolate Factory.

Take a boat cruise on the Derwent River; assail the heights of Mt Wellington or Mt Nelson; rent a bike and explore the cycling paths; pack the teens into the Kombi and go surfing at Clifton Beach. The minute you head out of town the child-friendly options increase, with an abundance of animal parks, beaches, caves, nature walks and mazes to explore; see the Around Hobart section.

If you're needing a romantic dinner date just for two, contact the **Mobile Nanny Service** (☎0437 504 064; www.mobilenannyservice.com.au).

with funky murals. The Brunswick's also had a recent makeover, and it serves decent pub food.

Central City Backpackers HOSTEL $
(Map p632; ☎1800 811 507; www.centralcityhobart.com; 138 Collins St; dm $21-27, s/d $55/69; @ wi-fi) Centrally located, this maze-like hostel has loads of communal space, a great kitchen, OK rooms and friendly staff.

Transit Centre Backpackers HOSTEL $
(Map p632; ☎03-6231 2400; www.transitbackpackers.com; 251 Liverpool St; dm $19-27, tw/d from $56/65; @) This friendly spot has a huge communal area, strewn with shared couches, bookshelves and a kitchen and laundry. The helpful owners are a mine of information on what to do around town, and a statewide bus stop is conveniently located just over the road.

Montgomery's Private Hotel & YHA HOSTEL $
(Map p632; ☎03-6231 2660; www.montgomerys.com.au; 9 Argyle St; dm $28-30, s & d with/without bathroom from $98/88; @) Attached to Montgomery's pub, this centrally located YHA has dorms of all sizes, en suite singles and doubles, and family rooms. Look forward to karaoke downstairs on Friday and Saturday nights.

★ **Astor Private Hotel** HOTEL $$
(Map p632; ☎03-6234 6611; www.astorprivatehotel.com.au; 157 Macquarie St; s from $77, d $93-140; wi-fi) A rambling, 1920s charmer, the Astor features stained-glass windows, old furniture, ceiling roses and the irrepressible Tildy at the helm. Older-style rooms have shared facilities, and newer en suite rooms are also excellent value. Breakfast included.

Fountainside HOTEL $$
(Map p628; ☎03-6213 2999; www.fountainside.com.au; 40 Brooker Ave; d from $173; wi-fi) Venture past the old-school 1980s reception and exterior to discover rooms that are surprisingly modern and spacious. The building hugs a busy roundabout, but well-insulated windows combat most traffic noise.

Central Café Bar HOTEL $$
(Map p632; ☎03-6234 4419; www.centralcafebar.com; 73 Collins St; d & tw $125; wi-fi) Downstairs is a classic Aussie pub with gaming machines and big-screen sport, but upstairs are surprisingly modern double rooms with flat-screen TVs and designer furniture.

Mantra One APARTMENT $$
(Map p632; ☎03-6221 6000; www.mantraone-sandybayroad.com.au; 1 Sandy Bay Rd; d from $141; wi-fi) These spacious and stylish loft apartments in a restored heritage building are a short stroll from the restaurants of Salamanca and Battery Point. Ask for a room on the building's southern side to negate occasional road noise from busy Davey St.

Hotel Collins HOTEL $$$
(Map p632; ☎03-6226 1111; www.hotelcollins.com.au; 58 Collins St; d $225-253, apt $335-485; wi-fi) A youthful energy at reception flows through to spacious rooms and apartments, many with sterling views of Mt Wellington's imposing bulk. Downstairs is the relaxed Fifty8 cafe and bar.

Waterfront & Salamanca Place

Henry Jones Art Hotel BOUTIQUE HOTEL $$$
(Map p632; ☎03-6210 7700; www.thehenryjones.com; 25 Hunter St; d $255-399; @ wi-fi) Located on the waterfront in a restored jam factory, the snazzy HJ is a beacon of sophistication in sometimes-sleepy Hobart. Modern art enlivens the walls, while facilities and downstairs distractions (bar, restaurant, cafe) are world class. The hotel also makes smart use of recycled materials.

Zero Davey APARTMENT $$$
(Map p632; ☎1300 733 422; www.escapesresorts.com.au; 15 Hunter St; apt from $280; air-con wi-fi) Modern, funky, recently redecorated, apartments on the edge of Hobart's interesting harbourfront precinct. Try and secure one with a balcony for views of Hobart's raffish fishing fleet. Check online for good discounts.

Salamanca Inn APARTMENT $$$
(Map p632; ☎1800 030 944, 03-6223 3300; www.salamancainn.com.au; 10 Gladstone St; apts from $280) Located just a short downhill stroll to the heritage precinct's galleries, craft shops, cafes, bars and restaurants, the Salamanca Inn has good-value two-bedroom apartments that are perfect for travelling families.

North & West Hobart

Lodge on Elizabeth B&B $$
(Map p628; ☎03-6231 3830; www.thelodge.com.au; 249 Elizabeth St; r incl breakfast from $130-150, self-contained cottage $195; @) Built in 1829, this old-timer has been a school house, a

boarding house and a halfway house, but now opens its doors as a value-for-money guesthouse. Rooms are dotted with antiques, and all have en suites. A self-contained cottage (two night minimum stay) overlooks a courtyard at the rear of the property.

The Islington BOUTIQUE HOTEL **$$$**
(Map p628; ☎03-6220 2123; www.islingtonhotel.com; 321 Davey St; d $395-595; 🛜) One of Hobart's best, the Islington effortlessly combines a heritage building with interesting antique furniture, contemporary art and a glorious garden. Service is attentive but understated, and breakfast is served in an expansive conservatory.

Corinda's Cottages B&B **$$$**
(Map p628; ☎03-6234 1590; www.corindascottages.com.au; 17 Glebe St; d incl breakfast $250-300; @🛜) Gorgeous Corinda, a renovated Victorian mansion with meticulously maintained parterre gardens, sits high on the Glebe hillside a short (steep!) walk from town. Three self-contained cottages provide contemporary comforts, and breakfast is DIY gourmet (eggs, muffins, fresh coffee etc).

Battery Point, Sandy Bay & South Hobart

Battery Point Boutique Accommodation APARTMENT **$$**
(Map p628; ☎03-6224 2244; www.batterypointaccommodation.com.au; 27-29 Hampden Rd; d $175, extra person $35; 🛜) Colonial midrange apartments set in a block of four salmon-coloured serviced apartments (sleeping three, with full kitchens) in Battery Point's heart.

Motel 429 MOTEL **$$**
(Map p628; ☎03-6225 2511; www.motel429.com.au; 429 Sandy Bay Rd; d $135-200; @🛜) Not far from the casino, some of the rooms in this motel have a sleek designer sheen. Standard rooms are more functional, but still good value. The staff are friendly, and the restaurants of Sandy Bay are just a short drive away.

Apartments on Star APARTMENTS **$$$**
(Map p628; ☎03-6225 4799; www.apartmentsonstar.com.au; 22 Star St, Sandy Bay; apt $185-230; 🛜) This block of 1970s flats in Sandy Bay is now four thoroughly 21st-century apartments with Sandy Bay's good restaurant scene just down the hill. That's if you can pull yourself away from rustling up something special in the designer kitchens and enjoying a Tassie wine with maritime views.

Grand Vue Private Hotel B&B **$$$**
(Map p628; ☎03-6223 8216; www.grande-vue-hotel.com; 8 Mona St, Battery Point; d $225-250; 🛜) The 'vues' from this lovingly restored brick mansion take in the sweep of Sandy Bay and the Wrest Point casino. Sleek and modern bathrooms and superfriendly service lift Grande Vue above other similar, nearby accommodation. Breakfast ($12.50) includes still-warm freshly-baked goodies from Jackman & McRoss bakery.

Outside the City

Barilla Holiday Park CAMPGROUND **$$**
(☎1800 465 453; www.barilla.com.au; 75 Richmond Rd; unpowered/powered sites $30/37, cabins & units $80-158; @🛜) A decent option for those with wheels, Barilla is midway between Hobart (12km) and Richmond (14km). It's close to the airport, the Coal River Valley wineries, and a couple of good wildlife parks around Richmond. Mini-golf and an onsite pizza restaurant should keep the kids happy.

Hobart Cabins & Cottages CABIN **$$**
(☎03-6272 7115; www.hobartcabinscottages.com.au; 19 Goodwood Rd; cabins & cottages $120-130, 3-bedroom house per d $200; 🛜) About 8km north of the centre, with a range of cottages and cabins, and a three-bedroom house sleeping up to 10.

Eating

Downtown Hobart proffers some good brunch and lunch venues, and a few recent openings are now providing dinner.

Salamanca Place has excellent cafes and restaurants, and is especially busy during Saturday's market festivities. Battery Point's Hampden Road cafes are always worth a look, while Elizabeth St in North Hobart has a diverse collection of cosmopolitan cafes and ethnic restaurants.

For Hobart's best pub food, head to the New Sydney Hotel or the Republic Bar & Café.

The most central self-catering option is Woolworths (p642) supermarket. Hobart's **Tas Farm Gate** (Map p628; www.tasfarmgate.com.au; cnr Melville & Elizabeth Sts; ⏲9am-1pm Sun) market takes place weekly, and Wursthaus (p642) and A Common Ground (p642) both have fine selections of picnic-ready Tasmanian produce.

City Centre

R. Takagi Sushi JAPANESE $

(Map p632; 155 Liverpool St; sushi $7-10; 10.30am-5.50pm Mon-Fri, to 4pm Sat, 11.30am-2.30pm Sun) Hobart's best sushi spot makes the most of Tasmania's great seafood. Udon noodles and miso also feature at this sleek, compact eatery that's a favourite of central Hobart desk jockeys.

Pilgrim Coffee CAFE $

(Map p632; 48 Argyle St; snacks & light meals $6-12; 6am-4.30pm Mon-Fri) With exposed bricks, timber beams and distressed walls, Pilgrim is one of Hobart's funkiest cafes. Interesting wraps and panini are combined with expertly prepared coffee, and you'll probably fall into conversation with the friendly locals on the big shared tables.

Sawak MALAYSIAN $

(Map p632; 131 Collins St; mains $8-13; 11am-3pm & 5-9pm Mon-Sat) Pop into the bustling Sawak for a well-priced fix of spicy Malaysian food. It's popular with Asian students from the University of Tasmania, crowding in for an authentic taste of home with classic dishes like prawn *laksa* (spicy noodle soup) and *char kway teow* (stir-fried flat noodles).

Ivory Cafe THAI $$

(Map p632; 03-6231 6808; 112 Elizabeth St; mains $12-20; 11.30am-3pm Mon-Sat, 5-9pm Tue-Sat) Hobart's most popular Asian restaurant is also one the city's smallest eateries, and loyal regulars return for well-prepared versions of all your Thai favourites. If you're dining solo, sit at the front window looking out onto Elizabeth St's occasional bustle.

Criterion Street Café CAFE $$

(Map p632; 10 Criterion St; mains $12-18; 7am-4pm Mon-Sat) Criterion Street Café effortlessly keeps both breakfast and lunch fans happy, and caffeine fiends buzzing through the day. Try the cinnamon porridge with rhubarb, or the chilli and green corn fritters.

Sidecar TAPAS $$

(Map p632; 129 Bathurst St; small plates $10-18; 5pm-late daily, lunch from noon Fri) Originally set up for diners waiting for a table at nearby Garagistes, the sleek and industrial Sidecar is now one of Hobart's best small bars in its own right. Conversation comes naturally at the shared zinc counter, further enhanced by an excellent wine and beer list and small plates including charcuterie, spicy pigs ears and wagyu hot dogs.

★ **Garagistes** MODERN AUSTRALIAN $$$

(Map p632; 03-6231 0558; www.garagistes.com.au; 103 Murray St; shared plates $19-36; from 6pm Wed-Thu, from 5pm Fri-Sat) Garagistes delivers innovative shared plates in a simple, yet dramatic, space. Owner Luke Burgess continually pushes the culinary envelope with an ever-changing menu inspired by local produce from around the state. Highlights could include marinated calamari, striped trumpeter fish or slow-cooked wagyu beef. There's no reservations, and waiting diners are sometimes asked to relax with a drink at the nearby Sidecar.

ethos eat drink MODERN AUSTRALIAN $$$

(Map p632; 03-6231 1165; www.ethoseatdrink.com; 100 Elizabeth St; noon-2.30pm & 6pm-late Tue-Sat, 9am-noon Sat & 9am-2pm Sun) Hidden away in a brick courtyard, ethos rigourously supports local farmers and producers. The menu is very seasonal, with selected ingredients prepared to showcase whatever is especially fresh. Options include a $65 chef's selection of small tasting plates and a smaller $35 lunch option. Bookings essential.

Waterfront & Salamanca Place

Head to Wursthaus (p642) for deli produce or the **Salamanca Fresh Fruit Market** (Map p632; 41 Salamanca Pl) for fruit and groceries.

Retro Café CAFE $$

(Map p632; 31 Salamanca Pl; mains $12-21; 8am-5pm) Funky Retro is ground zero for Saturday brunch among the market stalls. Masterful breakfasts, bagels, salads and burgers interweave with laughing staff, chilled-out jazz and the rattle and hum of the coffee machine.

Machine Laundry Café CAFE $$

(Map p632; 12 Salamanca Sq; mains $10-18; 7.30am-5pm Mon-Fri, 8.30am-4pm Sat-Sun) Hypnotise yourself watching the tumble dryers spin at this bright, retro-style cafe, where you can wash your dirty clothes while discreetly adding fresh juice, soup or coffee stains to your clean ones. We're big fans of the chilli-infused roti wrap for breakfast.

Tricycle Café Bar CAFE $$

(Map p632; 71 Salamanca Pl; mains $10-20; 8am-3pm Mon-Sat) This cosy, red-painted nook near the Salamanca Arts Centre serves up a range of cafe classics (BLTs, toasties, free-range scrambled eggs, salads and fair trade coffee). Sip wine by the glass from the mirror-backed bar.

Blue Eye SEAFOOD $$
(Map p632; ☎03-6223 5297; www.fishfish.com.au; 1 Castray Esplanade; small plates $11-16, mains $22-35; ⊙noon-3pm Tue-Sat, from 5pm Mon-Sat) Standouts include chargrilled salmon, chilli salt squid, and terrific Tasmanian scallops. Kick off with a starter of Bruny Island oysters or salmon sashimi, fresh from the Huon Valley. Moo Brew beer is on tap, and Tasmanian craft beers and wines complete a tasty picture.

Fish Frenzy SEAFOOD $$
(Map p632; www.fishfrenzy.com.au; Elizabeth St Pier; meals $12-25; ⊙11am-9pm) A casual, waterside spot brimming with fish and chips, fishy salads (salt and pepper calamari, warm octopus) and fish burgers. The eponymous 'Fish Frenzy' ($17) delivers a little bit of everything. No bookings, and please don't feed the seagulls.

Battery Point, Sandy Bay & South Hobart

Jackman & McRoss BAKERY $
(Map p628; 57-59 Hampden Rd, Battery Point; meals $8-13; ⊙7am-5pm) Be sure to swing by this conversational, neighbourhood bakery-cafe, even if it's just to gawk at the display cabinet full of delectable pies, tarts, baguettes and pastries. Early morning cake and coffee may evolve into quiche or soup for lunch.

Environs CAFE $$
(Map p628; www.environs.biz; 38 Waterloo Crescent; mains $8-20; ⊙7.30am-4pm Mon-Sat, 8am-4pm Sun) Hip and friendly service combined with modern decor and a garden area. It's a top spot for a leisurely breakfast before a walk around Battery Point - try the field mushrooms with parmesan - and Tasmanian wines and beers partner with lunch options including duck and orange risotto and a wagyu beef burger.

Jam Jar Lounge CAFE $$
(Map p628; www.jamjarlounge.com; 45 Hampden Rd; mains $10-22; ⊙7.30am-4pm Wed-Thu, 7.30am-10pm Fri, 8am-4pm Sat-Sun; 📶) Art deco style infuses a 19th-century cottage at this friendly combination of cafe and bistro. Break up your exploration of Battery Point with excellent cakes, coffee and counter food, and on Friday nights, the big shared tables are awash with locals tucking into Asian- and Med-inspired tapas ($9-15).

North & West Hobart

★Pigeon Hole CAFE $
(Map p628; 93 Goulburn St; mains $10-13; ⊙8am-4.30pm Mon-Sat) This funky, friendly cafe is the kind of place every inner-city neighbourhood should have. The freshly baked panini are the best you'll have, and the foodie owners always concoct innovative spins on traditional cafe fare. Try the baked eggs *en cocotte* with serrano ham for a lazy brunch.

Sweet Envy CAFE $
(Map p628; www.sweetenvy.com; 341 Elizabeth St, North Hobart; snacks & cakes $5-10; ⊙8.30am-6pm Tue-Fri, to 5pm Sat) A delicate diversion along North Sydney's restaurant strip, Sweet Envy conjures up gossamer-light macarons, madeleines and cupcakes. Gourmet pies and sausage rolls (try the lamb and harissa) and fantastic ice creams and sorbets are made right on the premises.

Raincheck Lounge CAFE $$
(Map p628; 392 Elizabeth St, North Hobart; tapas $8-15, mains $12-28; ⊙7.30am-10pm Mon-Fri, from 8.30am Sat-Sun) Raincheck's Moroccan-styled room and sidewalk tables see punters sipping coffee, reconstituting over big breakfasts and conversing over tasty treats like venison and mushroom pie. Mix and match tapas, or ask about the good value 'Chef's Table' ($65 for four courses for two people) for dinner from Wednesday to Saturday.

Drinking & Nightlife

Great pubs and bars abound around Salamanca Place and the waterfront. North Hobart also has a good selection of pubs and bars.

See also the New Sydney Hotel, Republic Bar & Café and Lark Distillery.

Preachers CRAFT BEER
(Map p628; 5 Knopwood St; ⊙noon-midnight Mon-Sat, to 8.30pm Sun) Grab a seat on the retro sofas inside, or adjourn to the ramshackle garden bar. Both spots are perfect locations to sample lots of different Australian craft beers with a cross-section of Hobart hipsters and students. Tassie micro-breweries are particularly well supported, and a steady

flow of $15 burgers and $12 bar snacks keeps a younger indie crowd satisfied.

Knopwood's Retreat PUB
(Map p632; www.knopwoods.com; 39 Salamanca Pl; ⏲10am-late) Adhere to the 'when in Rome' dictum and head for Knoppies, Hobart's best pub, which has been serving ales to seagoing types since the convict era. For most of the week it's a cosy watering hole with an open fire and pretty good food. On Friday nights the city workers swarm and the crowd spills across the street.

Nant Whisky Cellar & Bar BAR
(Map p632; www.nantdistillery.com.au; Wooby's Lane; ⏲3pm-midnight Wed-Thu, noon-midnight Fri-Sun) Squeeze into this compact bar with a superb heritage ambience – it takes just 36 people – and discover how well whisky from the Nant Distillery in Tasmania's Midlands compares to other peaty and smokey drops from around the world. Local art is on display, and Nant's range of whisky can be partnered with Tasmanian artisan foods.

Yellow Bernard CAFE
(Map p632; www.yellowbernard.com; 109 Collins St; ⏲7am-4pm Mon-Fri) With a global selection of interesting blends, they take their coffee *very* seriously at Yellow Bernard. We also think their chai – made with honey and their own spice blend – is a perfect way to recharge while exploring Hobart's CBD.

Barcelona BAR
(Map p632; www.barcelonahobart.com; Salamanca Sq; ⏲11am-late) Lots of different beers on tap, a slick wine list and well-priced bistro-style food make this one of Salamanca's most versatile drinking spots. The outdoor tables are perfect for people-watching Salamanca Square–style, and it's very popular with a younger crowd.

Jack Greene CRAFT BEER
(Map p632; www.facebook.com/jackgreenebar; 47-48 Salamanca Place; burgers $18-20; ⏲11am-late) Service can be a little *too* casual, and the gourmet burgers are a bit expensive, but the always-busy Jack Greene is a worthwhile stop if you're a travelling beer fan. Lots of different bottled brews fill the fridges, and there's an ever-changing mix of sixteen beers on tap from around Australia and New Zealand.

IXL Long Bar BAR
(Map p632; 25 Hunter St; ⏲5-10.30pm Mon-Thu, 3-10.30pm Sat, 5-9pm Sun) Prop yourself at the glowing bar at the Henry Jones Art Hotel and check out Hobart's fashionistas over cocktails. If there are no spare stools at the

DON'T MISS

BREWING UP A TASSIE STORM

The Tasmanian craft brewing scene kicked off with Moorilla Estate's Moo Brew – advertising slogan 'Not suitable for bogans' – but now includes breweries in other areas of Tasmania.

The most consistent places to try Tassie's craft beers on tap in Hobart are Preachers (p639), the New Sydney Hotel (p641), and Jack Greene (p640). Try and time a Hobart visit with November's Tasmanian Beerfest (p635).

Keep an eye out for the following:

➡ **Moo Brew's** (www.moobrew.com.au) standout beers include a zingy hefeweizen and a hoppy pilsner. Try the beer on tap at Hobart's Lark Distillery or the IXL Long Bar at the Henry Jones Art Hotel. A tasty recent addition to the Moo Brew range is Belgo, a hoppy Belgian-influenced pale ale.

➡ **Seven Sheds** (www.sevensheds.com) specialises in a malty Kentish ale, and also produces regular seasonal brews and honey-infused mead. Hobart's New Sydney Hotel usually has Seven Sheds on tap.

➡ The **Ironhouse Brewery's** (www.ironhouse.com.au) beers include a pale ale and a Czech-style pilsner. Try them both at Blue Eye (p639) in Salamanca.

➡ **Two Metre Tall** (www.2mt.com.au) makes real ale and ciders, with ingredients sourced locally from its farm in the Derwent Valley. Try them with seafood at Blue Eye.

➡ **Van Dieman Brewing** (www.vandiemanbrewing.com.au) produces seven beers including the Jacob's Ladder English-style amber ale. Van Dieman's beers are often on tap at Preachers.

not-so-long bar, flop onto the leather couches in the lobby.

Lower House BAR

(Map p632; 9-11 Murray St, basement; ⏲noon-late Mon-Sat) Across the road from Parliament House is this hip basement bar, keeping escapee MPs lubricated with top-shelf whiskies, cocktails and a massive wine list. Mature crowd and occasional DJs.

Observatory CLUB

(Map p632; www.observatorybar.com.au; Murray St Pier, L1; ⏲3pm-late Wed-Sun) Sip a 'Big O' cocktail as you swan between loungy nooks. DJs kick in on Friday and Saturday, and don't dress down as the bouncers are quite choosy.

Syrup CLUB

(Map p632; 39 Salamanca Pl; admission varies; ⏲9pm-late Thu-Sat) Over two floors above Knopwood's Retreat, this is an ace place for late-night drinks and DJs playing to the techno/house crowd.

Mobius CLUB

(Map p632; www.facebook.com/mobius.bar; 7 Despard St; admission varies; ⏲9pm-late Thu-Sat) A pumping, clubby dungeon meets cool lounge bar behind the main waterfront area. Occasional name DJs.

☆ Entertainment

The *Mercury* newspaper lists Hobart's entertainment options in its Thursday edition. The free monthly *Sauce* entertainment rag provides detailed arts listings. Also see www.thedwarf.com.au. The Lark Distillery also has live music on Friday and Saturday.

Republic Bar & Café LIVE MUSIC

(Map p628; www.republicbar.com; 299 Elizabeth St) The art-deco Republic is the number-one live-music pub in town, and often showcases up-and-coming international bands. With loads of different beers and excellent food, it's the kind of place you'd love to call your local.

New Sydney Hotel LIVE MUSIC

(Map p632; www.newsydneyhotel.com.au; 87 Bathurst St) Low-key folk, jazz, blues and comedy playing Tuesday to Sunday nights (usually free). See the website for gig listings. Good pub food is complemented by an ever-changing selection of Tassie craft beers.

The Grand Poobah LIVE MUSIC

(Map p632; www.facebook.com/thegrandpoobahbar; 142 Liverpool St; ⏲7.30-10.30pm Mon, 7pm-late Tue, 9pm-late Fri-Sat, noon-10pm Sun) This hip and bohemian bar also doubles as a live venue with everything from live bands to DJs, dance and comedy.

> DON'T MISS
>
> **FRIDAY NIGHT FANDANGO**
>
> Some of Hobart's best live music airs every Friday year-round from 5.30pm to 7.30pm at the Salamanca Arts Centre (p627) courtyard, just off Wooby's Lane. It's a free community event that started around 2000, with the adopted name 'Rektango', borrowed from a band that sometimes plays here. Acts vary from month to month – expect anything from African beats to rockabilly, folk or gypsy-Latino. Drinks essential (sangria in summer, mulled wine in winter); dancing optional.

Brisbane Hotel LIVE MUSIC

(Map p628; www.facebook.com/thebrisbanehotelhobart; 3 Brisbane St) This progressive live-music venue features the original, offbeat and uncommercial, including punk, metal, hip-hop and singer-songwriters.

Federation Concert Hall CONCERT HALL

(Map p632; ☎1800 001 190; www.tso.com.au; 1 Davey St; ⏲box office 9am-5pm Mon-Fri) This concert hall showcases the Tasmanian Symphony Orchestra.

State Cinema CINEMA

(Map p628; ☎03-6234 6318; www.statecinema.com.au; 375 Elizabeth St) The State shows independent and art-house flicks from local and international filmmakers. There's a great cafe and bar onsite, and an excellent bookstore just next door. During summer, films are occasionally screened in the open-air Rooftop Cinema.

Village Cinemas CINEMA

(Map p632; ☎1300 555 400; www.villagecinemas.com.au; 181 Collins St) An inner-city multiplex screening mainstream releases. Cheap-arse Tuesday tickets are $11.50.

Shopping

Head to Salamanca Place for shops and galleries stocking Huon pine knick-knacks, hand-knitted beanies, local cheeses, sauces, jams, fudge and other assorted edibles.

On Elizabeth St between Melville St and Bathurst St are stores selling outdoor apparel and equipment.

A Common Ground FOOD & DRINK
(Map p632; www.acommonground.com.au; 77 Salamanca Place, Shop 3, Salamanca Arts Centre; 10am-4pm Mon-Fri, 8.30am-3pm Sat) Bruny Island cheese, Tasmanian smallgoods and Seven Sheds beer are all among the local artisan produce squeezed into this tiny store in Salamanca.

Antiques to Retro ANTIQUES
(Map p632; 03-6236 9422; www.antiquestoretro.com.au; 128 Bathurst St; 10am-5pm Mon-Fri, 10am-4pm Sat-Sun) A browse-worthy selection of antiques.

Art Mob ARTS & CRAFTS
(Map p632; 03-6236 9200; www.artmob.com.au; 29 Hunter St; 10am-late) Indigenous fine art and jewellery with an emphasis on the work of Tasmanian Aboriginal artists.

Cool Wine WINE
(Map p632; www.coolwine.com.au; Criterion St, Shop 8, Mid City Arcade; 9.30am-6.30pm Mon-Sat) Tasmanian fine wine and craft beers.

Despard Gallery ARTS & CRAFTS
(Map p632; 03-6223 8266; www.despard-gallery.com.au; 15 Castray Esplanade; 10.30am-5pm Mon-Sat, 11am-4pm Sun) Contemporary Tasmanian arts.

Fullers Bookshop BOOKS
(Map p632; 03-6234 3800; www.fullersbookshop.com.au; 131 Collins St; 8.30am-6pm Mon-Fri, 9am-5pm Sat, 10am-4pm Sun) Literature and travel guides, including many Tasmanian titles. There's also a good cafe here.

DON'T MISS

SALAMANCA MARKET

Colourful bohemian types and craftspeople have been selling their wares at **Salamanca Market** (Map p632; 8.30am-3pm Sat) on Saturday mornings since 1972. They come from all over the state's southern reaches with their fresh produce, secondhand clothes and books, tacky tourist souvenirs, CDs, cheap sunglasses, antiques and bric-a-brac. See www.salamanca.com.au for what's available at the market, and get planning to maximise your time in this labyrinth of gourmet produce, buskers, ethnic food, and arts and crafts.

Handmark Gallery ARTS & CRAFTS
(Map p632; 03-6223 7895; www.handmarkgallery.com; 77 Salamanca Pl; 10am-6pm) Local ceramics, glass, wood, jewellery and textiles, plus paintings and sculpture.

Woolworths SUPERMARKET
(Map p632; 42 Argyle St, Wellington Centre; 7am-10pm) Centrally-located supermarket.

Wursthaus FOOD
(Map p632; www.wursthaus.com.au; 1 Montpelier Retreat; 8am-6pm Mon-Fri, 9am to 5pm Sat-Sun) Fine-food showcase selling speciality smallgoods, cheeses, breads, wines and pre-prepared meals. They're big supporters of Tasmanian produce.

Information

EMERGENCY

Hobart Police Station (03-6230 2111; www.police.tas.gov.au; 43 Liverpool St; 24hr)

Police, Fire & Ambulance (000)

INTERNET ACCESS

Expect to pay around $6 per hour at internet cafes.

Drifters Internet Café (Salamanca Pl, Shop 9/33; 9am-6.30pm) Printing and scanning available.

INTERNET RESOURCES

Hobart City (www.hobartcity.com.au) City council website.

Rita's Bite (www.pc-rita.blogspot.com) Food blog covering the Hobart eating-out scene.

The Dwarf (www.thedwarf.com.au) Online gig guide.

MAPS

The visitor centre supplies basic city maps. For more comprehensive coverage try the *Hobart & Surrounds Street Directory* or the UBD *Tasmania Country Road Atlas* available at larger newsagents and bookshops. Travellers with disabilities should check out the useful *Hobart CBD Mobility Map* from the visitor centre.

Royal Automobile Club of Tasmania (RACT; Map p628; 13 27 22; www.ract.com.au; cnr Murray & Patrick Sts; 8.45am-5pm Mon-Fri) Driving-specific information.

Tasmanian Map Centre (Map p632; 03-6231 9043; www.map-centre.com.au; 100 Elizabeth St; 9.30am-5.30pm Mon-Fri, 10.30am-2.30pm Sat) Good for bushwalking maps.

MEDIA

Hobart's long-running newspaper the *Mercury* (aka 'the Mockery') is handy for discovering what's on where. The Thursday edition lists entertainment options. Online see www.themercury.com.au.

In hipper shops, bars and cafes – like Yellow Bernard (p640) and the bookshop at the State Cinema (p641) in North Hobart – pick up a copy of *We Are Hobart*, an excellent giveaway map showcasing cool eating, drinking and shopping locations around town.

MEDICAL SERVICES

Australian Dental Association Emergency Service (☎03-6248 1546) Advice for dental emergencies.

Chemist on Collins (93 Collins St) Centrally-located in the CBD.

City Doctors & Travel Clinic (☎03-6231 3003; www.citydoctors.com.au; 93 Collins St) A standard consultation is $72.

Royal Hobart Hospital (☎03-6222 8423; www.dhhs.tas.gov.au; 48 Liverpool St; ⏲24hr) Argyle St emergency entry.

Salamanca Medical Centre (☎03-6223 8181; 5a Gladstone St; ⏲8.30am-6pm Mon-Fri, 10am-3pm Sat, noon-3pm Sun) Centrally-located in Salamanca.

MONEY

Banks and ATMs are around Elizabeth Street Mall.

POST

General Post Office (GPO; Map p632; cnr Elizabeth & Macquarie Sts) Located in a grand heritage building.

TOURIST INFORMATION

Hobart Visitor Centre (Map p632; ☎1800 990 440; www.hobarttravelcentre.com.au; cnr Davey & Elizabeth Sts; ⏲8.30am-5.30pm Mon-Fri, 9am-5pm Sat-Sun) Information and statewide tour and accommodation bookings.

Parks & Wildlife Service (Map p632; ☎1300 135 513; www.parks.tas.gov.au; 134 Macquarie St; ⏲9am-5pm Mon-Fri) Information for bushwalking and all national parks.

Getting There & Away

AIR

See p624 for details of domestic airlines flying to Hobart.

BUS

There are two main intrastate bus companies operating to/from Hobart. Check online for timetable/fare information or ask at the Hobart Visitor Centre.

Redline Coaches (Map p632; ☎1300 360 000; www.redlinecoaches.com.au; 230 Liverpool St) Operates from the Transit Centre.

Tassielink (☎1300 300 520; www.tassielink.com.au; 64 Brisbane St) Operates from the Hobart Bus Terminal.

Getting Around

TO/FROM THE AIRPORT

Hobart Airport (☎03-6216 1600; www.hobartairpt.com.au) is at Cambridge, 16km east of town. The **Airporter Shuttle Bus** (Map p632; ☎1300 385 511; www.redlinecoaches.com.au; one way/return $17/30) scoots between the Transit Centre and the airport (via various city pick-up points), connecting with all flights. Bookings essential.

A taxi between the airport and the city centre will cost around $42 between 6am and 8pm weekdays, and around $50 at other times.

BICYCLE

See p625 for companies hiring bicycles in Hobart.

BUS

Metro Tasmania (☎13 22 01; www.metrotas.com.au) operates the local bus network, which is reliable but infrequent outside of business hours. The **Metro Shop** (⏲8.30am-5.30pm Mon-Fri), inside the General Post Office on the corner of Elizabeth and Macquarie Sts, handles ticketing and enquiries. Most buses depart from this section of Elizabeth St, or from nearby Franklin Sq.

One-way fares vary with distances ('sections') travelled (from $2.80 to $6). For $5 you can buy an unlimited-travel Day Rover ticket, valid after 9am Monday to Friday, and all day Saturday, Sunday and public holidays. Buy one-way tickets from the driver (exact change required) or ticket agents (newsagents and most post offices); day passes are only available from ticket agents. If you're in town for an extended period, look at buying a Greencard ($10), which provides discounts of around 20% on normal tickets.

CAR

Timed, metered parking predominates in the CBD and tourist areas like Salamanca and the waterfront.

The big car rental firms have airport desks. Cheaper local firms with city offices offer daily rental rates starting at around $40.

TAXI

City Cabs (☎13 10 08)

Maxi-Taxi Services (☎13 32 22; www.hobartmaxitaxi.com.au) Includes wheelchair-accessible vehicles.

AROUND HOBART

Riverside communities, historic towns, pretty pasturelands and stands of native bush are all just a few minutes' drive beyond the Hobart city limits. The ghosts of Tasmania's convict past drag their leg-irons in historic Richmond, while wilderness, wildlife, waterfalls and great short walks at Mt Field National Park make a terrific day trip from the capital.

Richmond

POP 880

Straddling the Coal River 27km northeast of Hobart, historic Richmond was once a strategic military post and convict station on the road to Port Arthur. Riddled with 19th-century buildings, it's arguably Tasmania's premier historic town.

Rowboats and bicycles can be hired from the **Richmond Park Boat House** (☎03-6260 1099; www.richmondparkboathouse.com.au; 56 Bridge St, Millers Cottage; rowboats from $25 per 30 minutes; ⏲10am-4pm) to explore the town, and decent wildlife parks and the nearby Coal River Valley wine region provide more contemporary distractions.

See www.richmondvillage.com.au.

Sights & Activities

Richmond Bridge LANDMARK
(Wellington St) This chunky but elegant bridge still funnels traffic across the Coal River, and is the town's proud centrepiece. Built by convicts in 1823, making it the oldest road bridge in Australia, it's purportedly haunted by the 'Flagellator of Richmond', George Grover, who died here in 1832.

Richmond Gaol HISTORIC BUILDING
(www.richmondgaol.com.au; 37 Bathurst St; adult/child $8/4; ⏲9am-5pm) The northern wing of the remarkably well-preserved gaol was built in 1825, five years before the penitentiary at Port Arthur. Like Port Arthur, fascinating historic insights abound, but the mood is pretty sombre.

Old Hobart Town Historic Model Village HISTORIC PARK
(www.oldhoberttown.com; 21a Bridge St; adult/child/family $14/3.50/30; ⏲9am-5pm) This painstaking re-creation of Hobart Town in the 1820s was built from the city's original plans. The kids will love it.

ZooDoo Wildlife Fun Park WILDLIFE RESERVE
(www.zoodoo.com.au; 620 Middle Tea Tree Rd; adult/child $22/12; ⏲9am-5pm) ZooDoo, 6km west of Richmond on the road to Brighton, has 'safari bus' rides, playgrounds, picnic areas and half of Dr Dolittle's Facebook friends including lions, tigers, llamas, Tasmanian devils and wallabies.

Bonorong Wildlife Centre WILDLIFE RESERVE
(www.bonorong.com.au; 593 Briggs Rd; adult/child/family $24/10/60; ⏲9am-5pm) Some 17km west of Richmond, 'Bonorong' derives from an Aboriginal word meaning 'native companion'. Look forward to Tasmanian devils, koalas, wombats, echidnas and quolls. The emphasis here is on conservation, education and the rehabilitation of injured animals. Special 'night feeding tours' (adult/child $149/49) are also available. These tours get you up close and personal with Bonorong's menagerie, and bookings are essential.

St John's Church CHURCH
(Wellington St) The first Roman Catholic church in Australia was built in 1836.

St Luke's Church of England CHURCH
(Edward St) Completed in 1834.

Courthouse HISTORIC BUILDING
(Forth St) Built in 1825.

Old Post Office HISTORIC BUILDING
(Bridge St) From 1826.

Richmond Arms Hotel HISTORIC BUILDING
(Bridge St) Serving cold ones since 1888.

Sleeping & Eating

Daisy Bank Cottages COTTAGE $$
(☎03-6260 2390; www.daisybankcottages.com; Daisy Bank, off Middle Tea Tree Rd; d $160-170) This place is a rural delight with two spotless, self-contained units (one with spa) in a converted 1840s sandstone barn. There are loft bedrooms, views of the Richmond rooftops, and plenty of farm-oriented distractions for the kids.

Richmond Cottages COTTAGE $$
(☎03-6260 2561; www.richmondcottages.com; 12 Bridge St; d from $150) On offer are two independent abodes. Ivy Cottage is a family-friendly, three-bedroom home (complete with claw-foot bath), and behind it The Stables is a rustic one-bedroom cottage with spa.

WORTH A TRIP

WINE TOURING IN THE COAL RIVER VALLEY

Richmond is also the centre of the Coal River Valley wine region. Some operations include gourmet restaurants, while others are small family-owned vineyards only open by appointment. See winesouth.com.au.

Meadowbank Estate (☎03-6248 4484; www.meadowbankwines.com.au; 699 Richmond Rd, Cambridge; mains $35; ⏲tasting 10am-5pm, lunch noon-3pm) Meadowbank's acclaimed restaurant serves lunch daily, along with award-winning pinot gris, sauvignon blanc and pinot noir. Don't miss *Flawed History*, an in-floor jigsaw by local artist Tom Samek. Restaurant bookings are recommended, especially on weekends.

Puddleduck Vineyard (www.puddleduckvineyard.com.au; 992 Richmond Rd, Richmond; ⏲10am-5pm) Small family-run vineyard producing just 1000 cases per year. Riesling, merlot, chardonnay and 'Bubbleduck' sparkling white. Cheese platters ($18) are for sale, or fire up their barbecues and cook your own steak and sausages.

Richmond Arms Hotel HOTEL, PUB **$$**
(☎03-6260 2109; www.richmondarmshotel.com.au; 42 Bridge St; d from $110) The grand old Richmond pub has four good-quality motel-style units in the adjacent former stables. On-site there's the dual attraction of the cosy dining room (mains $20-27, open lunch and dinner) and a sunny garden bar. Coal River Valley wines are available.

Ashmore on Bridge Street CAFE **$$**
(☎03-6260 2238; www.ashmoreonbridge.com.au; 34 Bridge St; mains $11-21; ⏲9am-4pm daily, dinner from 6pm Tue-Wed) Order up a big breakfast, French toast or eggs Florentine with Richmond's best coffee, or snappy lunches including salmon fettucine or Moroccan spiced chicken. Bookings are essential for Ashmore's Tuesday and Wednesday night dinners.

Anton's PIZZA **$$**
(42a Bridge St; mains $17-26; ⏲10am-2.30pm Mon-Thu, 10am-9pm Fri-Sat, 11am-7pm Sun) Next to the Richmond Arms Hotel, this small shop churns out first-class pizzas, plus pasta, antipasto, salads, desserts and gelati.

Getting There & Away

Tassielink (☎1300 653 633; www.tassielink.com.au) runs from the **Hobart Bus Terminal** (64 Brisbane St) Monday to Friday at 8am, 8.30am, 10.30am, 12.30pm and 2.30pm (45 minutes, one way $7.20). On Saturday buses leave Hobart at 8.30am and 2.55pm.

The **Richmond Tourist Bus** (☎0408 341 804; www.hobartshuttlebus.com; adult/child return $30/20; ⏲9am & 12.20pm) runs a twice-daily service from Hobart, with three hours to explore Richmond before returning. Call for bookings and pick-up locations. Fares include entry to Richmond Gaol.

Mt Field National Park

Declared a national park in 1916, Mt Field is famed for its spectacular mountain scenery, alpine moorlands and lakes, rainforest, waterfalls and abundant wildlife. It's 80km northwest of Hobart and makes a terrific day trip.

The park's **visitor information centre** (☎03-6288 1149; www.parks.tas.gov.au; 66 Lake Dobson Rd; ⏲8.30am-5pm Nov-Apr, 9am-4pm May-Oct) houses a cafe and displays on the park's origins, and provides information on walks. Day-use facilities include barbecues, shelters and a playground.

Sights & Activities

Russells Falls WALKING
Don't miss the magnificently tiered, 45m-high Russell Falls, an easy 20-minute return amble from behind the visitor information centre. The path is suitable for prams and wheelchairs. There are also easy walks to **Lady Barron Falls** and **Horseshoe Falls**, and longer bushwalks.

Mt Mawson SKIING
(☎recorded message service 03-6288 1166) Skiing at Mt Mawson is sometimes an option, when nature sees fit to deposit snow (infrequently in recent years). Snow reports are available online at www.ski.com.au, or via a recorded message service.

Sleeping & Eating

Self-caterers need to buy supplies before arriving at Mt Field National Park. There is also good accommodation at Westerway, about 7km from the park entrance.

Lake Dobson Cabins CABIN $
(☎03-6288 1149; www.parks.tas.gov.au; Lake Dobson Rd; cabins up to 6 people $45) These three simple, six-bed cabins are 14km inside the park. All are equipped with mattresses, cold water, wood stove and firewood (there's no power), and have a communal toilet block. Bring your own gas lamps and cookers, plus cooking utensils.

National Park Campground CAMPGROUND $
(☎03-6288 1149; www.parks.tas.gov.au; unpowered/powered sites $16/20) Self-registration campground with adequate facilities (toilets, showers, laundry and free barbecues) just inside the park gates. Bookings not required. Site prices are additional to national park entry fees.

Duffy's Country Accommodation COTTAGE $$
(☎03-6288 1373; www.duffyscountry.com; 49 Clark's Rd; d $125-135, extra adult/child $25/15; @) Overlooking a field of raspberry canes are two immaculate self-contained cabins, one a studio-style cabin for couples, the other a two-bedroom relocated rangers' hut from Mt Field National Park. Breakfast provisions are provided including toast, eggs and homemade raspberry jam.

Platypus Playground COTTAGE $$
(☎0413 833 700; www.riverside-cottage.com; 1658 Gordon River Rd; d $165) You can't miss this cute, red riverside cottage at Westerway, offering eco-friendly accommodation. Winning features include an outdoor deck over the river and the chance to spot a platypus or hook a trout.

Getting There & Away

The drive to Mt Field through the Derwent River Valley and Bushy Park is an absolute stunner with river rapids, hop fields, rows of poplars and hawthorn hedgerows. Some Hobart-based tour operators offer Mt Field day trips.

THE SOUTHEAST

The southeast offers rolling hills and valleys, riverside towns, and quiet harbours and inlets. It's a gentle collection of agrarian communities producing cherries, apricots, Atlantic salmon and cool-climate wines. The fruit-filled hillsides of the Huon Valley give way to the sparkling inlets of the D'Entrecasteaux Channel. Bruny Island waits enticingly offshore, and the Hartz Mountains National Park is not far inland.

See www.huontrail.org.au.

Getting There & Around

The southeast has three distinct areas: the peninsula, including Kettering and Cygnet; Bruny Island; and the Huon Hwy coastal strip linking Huonville with Cockle Creek.

Metro Tasmania (☎13 22 01; www.metrotas.com.au) runs several weekday buses from Hobart south to Kettering ($7.50, 50 minutes) and Woodbridge ($9.70, one hour). A bus from Hobart also runs once each weekday to Snug, then inland across to Cygnet ($11.50, one hour).

Tassielink (☎1300 300 520; www.tassielink.com.au) buses service the Huon Hwy from Hobart through Huonville ($9.90, one hour) several times a day (once on Saturday and Sunday), with some continuing to Geeveston ($13, 1½ hours) and Dover ($20, 1¾ hours, not Sunday).

Kettering

POP 400

Sleepy Kettering is a launching place for sea kayakers exploring the D'Entrecasteaux Channel, but most people just blow through to board the Bruny Island ferry.

The Bruny D'Entrecasteaux Visitor Centre (p649) next to the ferry terminal books accommodation on Bruny Island.

Activities

Roaring 40s Ocean Kayaking KAYAKING
(☎03-6267 5000; www.roaring40skayaking.com.au; Ferry Rd, Oyster Cove Marina; closed Aug-Sep) This company offers gear rental to kayakers, and organises kayaking trips for all levels of experience. A half-day paddle around Oyster Cove costs $95; a full day on the D'Entrecasteaux Channel costs $165, including lunch and return transport from Hobart. A full day around the Tasman Peninsula costs $275 including transport from Hobart. Check the website for other weekend paddles around the Hobart and southeastern Tasmania region. Extended three- and seven-day trips around the Tasman Peninsula and the southwest including Bathurst Harbour are also available.

Sleeping & Eating

Herons Rise Vineyard COTTAGE $$
(☎03-6267 4339; www.heronsrise.com.au; 1000 Saddle Rd; d without/with breakfast $125/140, extra

The Southeast

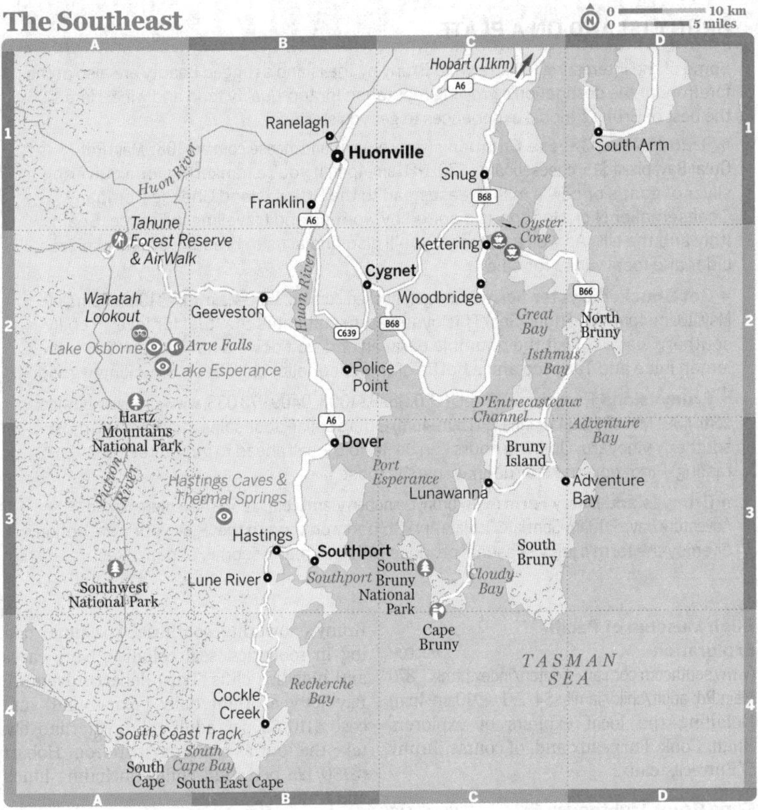

person $30) Just north of town, Herons Rise has three upmarket, self-contained cottages set in lush surroundings among the vines. Dinners are available by arrangement (per person $42.50).

Bruny Island

POP 600

Bruny Island is almost two islands joined by a narrow, sandy isthmus called the Neck. Famous for its wildlife (fairy penguins, echidnas, mutton birds, albino wallabies) it's a sparsely populated and undeveloped retreat, soaked in ocean rains in the south, and dry and scrubby in the north. It was named after French explorer Bruny D'Entrecasteaux.

You need a few days to appreciate Bruny's isolated coastal communities, swimming and surf beaches, and the forests and walking tracks within the **South Bruny National Park** (www.parks.tas.gov.au) – don't try to cram it into a day trip, especially on holiday weekends when there are long waits for the ferry.

Accommodation is in self-contained cottages and guesthouses, and a car or bicycle is essential for getting around. Supplies are available at the well-stocked Adventure Bay general store and a small shop at Alonnah. Note that some island roads are unsealed, and not all car rental companies are cool with this concept.

Sights & Activities

Bruny Island Neck Game Reserve WILDLIFE RESERVE

Climb the 273 steps up to the lookout at the **Hummock** at the Bruny Island Neck Game Reserve. All around are the rookeries of mutton birds and little penguins that nest in the dunes – the penguins can be seen emerging from the sea at dusk. This is also the site of the **Truganini Memorial**, providing another moment of reflection on Tasmania's grim history.

BRUNY ISLAND ON A PLATE

Some of the interesting folk drawn to Bruny by the island's rugged beauty are also at the forefront of the destination's growing reputation for top-quality food and wine. Here's the best of Bruny's foodie experiences to get you started:

➡ **Bruny Island Cheese Company** (www.brunyislandcheese.com.au; 1087 Main Rd, Great Bay; pizza $15, cheeseboards $30; ⏲11am-4pm) If you're hankering for a quivering sliver of goat's or cow's milk cheese head to the Bruny Island Cheese Company. Cheesemaker Nick Haddow is inspired by working and travelling in France, Spain, Italy and the UK. As well as cheese, you'll also find artisan bread, woodfired pizzas, cider and local wines for sale.

➡ **Get Shucked Oyster Farm** (www.getshucked.com.au; 1650 Main Rd; ⏲10am-5pm Oct-May, 10am-4pm Mon-Fri Jun-Sep) This oyster farm cultivates the 'fuel for love' in chilly southern waters. Visit their humble caravan and wolf down a half-dozen ($8) with lemon juice and Tabasco and a bottle of (nonalcoholic) chilli beer. Shuckingly good.

➡ **Bruny Island Premium Wines** (☎03-6293 1008, 0409 973 033; www.brunyislandwine.com; 4391 Main Rd, Lunawanna; ⏲11am-4pm) Offers cellar-door sales at Australia's most southerly vineyard. Opening hours can be flexible – call ahead to guarantee your tasting. Pinot noir and chardonnay rule the roost.

➡ **Bruny Island Berry Farm** (www.brunyislandberryfarm.com.au; 562 Adventure Bay Rd, Adventure Bay; ⏲10am-5pm late Oct-late Apr) Go berry crazy with the 'Pick your own' option, or enjoy the farm's juicy seasonal produce with ice cream, scones or pancakes.

Bligh Museum of Pacific Exploration MUSEUM
(www.southcom.com.au/~jontan/index.html; 876 Main Rd; adult/child/family $4/2/1; ⏲10am-4pm) Detailing the local exploits of explorers Bligh, Cook, Furneaux and, of course, Bruny D'Entrecasteaux.

Cape Bruny Lighthouse MONUMENT
(☎03-6298 3114; www.brunyisland.net.au/Cape_Bruny/Lightstation/lighthouse.html; tours adult/child $5/2; ⏲reserve 10am-4pm) Also worth visiting is this 1836 lighthouse on South Bruny. Take a tour (one day's advance booking required) or wander the surrounding **reserve**, with expansive views from the rugged cape headland over mainland Tasmania's southernmost reaches.

Art at the Point GALLERY
(☎03-6260 6424; www.artatthepoint.com.au; Dennes Pt; ⏲10am-4pm Fri-Sun, Sep-Apr, reduced hours in winter) Excellent gallery showcasing Tasmanian and Bruny Island artists. Check the website for regular special exhibitions. The gallery shares a modern building with the Jetty Cafe (p649) on Dennes Point.

Tours

Bruny Island Cruises BOAT CRUISE
(☎03-6293 1465; www.brunycruises.com.au) Operates sensational three-hour tours of Bruny's towering southeast coastline, taking in rookeries, seal colonies, bays, caves and high sea cliffs. Trips depart Adventure Bay jetty at 11am daily (year-round) and cost $110/65 per adult/child. Alternatively, take the tour as a full-day trip from Hobart ($180/125 per adult/child), including lunch and transfers.

Inala Nature Tours WALKING, 4WD
(☎03-6293 1217; www.inalabruny.com.au; 320 Cloudy Bay Rd) Inala runs highly regarded personalised walking and 4WD tours of the island (from half a day to three days), focused on flora and fauna. The tour leader is a botanist, zoologist and conservationist, and her 250-hectare property is home to almost 140 bird species.

Bruny Island Safaris TOUR
(☎0437 499 795; www.brunyislandsafaris.com.au; per person $140) Full-day tours departing Hobart and taking in Bruny's history and landscapes. Look forward to opportunities to sample the island's culinary bounty.

Sleeping

Self-contained cottages abound on Bruny Island, most suitable for mid-sized groups and offering economical one-week rates.

Bookings are essential as owners/managers and their keys aren't always easily located – the **Bruny D'Entrecasteaux Visitor Centre** (☎03-6267 4494; www.brunyislandaccommodationandtours.com; 81 Ferry Rd; ⊙9am-5pm) is a good starting point. Also see www.brunyisland.com for accommodation listings.

If you have a vehicle and a tent, the cheapest island accommodation is the free bush camping grounds. Camping on Bruny is restricted to sites within South Bruny National Park (national park passes required), at Jetty Beach – a beautiful sheltered cove 3km north of the lighthouse – and at Cloudy Bay. There's also a camp site outside the national park at Neck Beach, at the southern end of the Neck. All sites have pit toilets and fireplaces; BYO firewood and water.

Captain James Cook Memorial Caravan Park CAMPGROUND **$$**
(☎03-6293 1128; www.capcookolkid.com.au; 786 Main Rd; unpowered/powered sites $5/28, on-site vans $44-55, cabins $140;) Right by the beach, this grandly named park could do with a few trees, but has decent facilities including some swish new one-bedroom cabins with private decks. Fishing charters are also available.

Explorers' Cottages MOTEL **$$**
(☎03-6293 1271; www.brunyisland.com; 20 Lighthouse Rd, Lunawanna; d $205) Just south of Lunawanna en route to the lighthouse, these bright, beachy, independent cottages sleep four with lounge areas, log fires, and outdoor decks.

★**All Angels Church House** RENTAL HOUSE **$$$**
(☎03-6293 1271; www.brunyisland.com; 4561 Bruny Island Main Rd; d $235) Your prayers have been answered with this restored church, now rental accommodation with three bedrooms, and a high-ceilinged open-plan lounge. Fire up the barbecue in the sheltered garden, eat alfresco on the picnic table, or dine inside on the huge shared table.

Eating

Pick up provisions and takeaways at the island's general stores. Don't miss the beaut gourmet pies and baking from the tiny kiosk at the ferry departure point.

Hotel Bruny PUB **$$**
(www.hotelbruny.com; Main Rd; mains $21-29; ⊙lunch & dinner;) A recent makeover has really reinvigorated this classic Aussie pub. Look forward to excellent seafood – including local oysters served five ways – and top notch mains like grilled Atlantic salmon (also from Bruny). The beer and wine selection showcases the best of Tasmania, and there's free wi-fi. A couple of recently renovated adjacent motel units (d $129) are good value.

Bruny Island Smoke House CAFE **$$**
(☎03-6260 6344; www.brunyislandsmokehouse.com.au; 360 Lennon Rd; ⊙lunch & dinner daily Nov-Easter, to 5pm Thu-Sat other times of year) Managed with pizzazz, 'BISH' is a winner – smoked fish and meats, beer, wine, decent coffee and astounding views from the deck. The shared platters are great value for groups. Drop by after you get off the ferry to confirm opening hours.

Jetty Café at the Point CAFE **$$**
(☎03-6260 6245; www.jettycafebrunyisland.com; Dennes Pt; lunch $15-20, dinner $28-30; ⊙10am-9pm Thu-Sun) Part cafe-restaurant, and part providore, Dennes Point's stylish Jetty Café is a great addition to Bruny's dining scene. Seasonal menus including local salmon, lamb, wallaby and oysters go well with Tassie wines and beers. Phone ahead as opening hours vary seasonally. The same building also houses the Art at the Point (p648) gallery.

Hothouse Café CAFE **$$**
(☎03-6293 1131; 46 Adventure Bay Rd; lunch $16-18, dinner $28-30; ⊙daily from 10am, dinner by arrangement;) This cafe at Morella Island Retreat has ocean views and a menu of interesting snacks and mains including gourmet burgers and vegetarian and salmon wraps. Bookings are essential for dinner.

Getting There & Around

Access to the island is via **car ferry** (☎03-6272 3277) from Kettering across to Roberts Point on the north of the island. There are at least 10 services daily, taking 20 minutes one way. The first ferry from Kettering is at 6.35am (7.45am Sunday), the last at 6.30pm (7.30pm Friday). The first ferry from Bruny is at 7am (8.25am Sunday), the last at 7pm (7.50pm Friday). The timetable may vary, so double-check departure times. Return fares: cars $30 ($35 on public holidays and public holiday weekends), motorcycles $5, bicycles $5 and foot passengers free.

Note that around summer weekends and Christmas and Easter, there are often queues to access the ferry, despite the addition of more sailings. At these times it's not worth considering Bruny Island as a day trip as you're likely to spend a significant amount of time waiting to catch the ferry from either end.

Metro Tasmania (☎13 22 01; www.metrotas.com.au) runs mainly weekday-only buses from Hobart to Kettering, stopping on request at the Kettering ferry terminal. On Saturday morning there is only one morning and one afternoon bus departing Hobart. The ferry terminal on Bruny is a long way from anywhere – BYO transport.

Cygnet

POP 840

Bruny D'Entrecasteaux originally named this little rural neighbourhood Port de Cygne Noir (Port of the Black Swan) because of the swans that proliferate on the bay. Youthfully reincarnated as Cygnet (baby swan), the town has evolved into an artsy enclave while still functioning as a major centre for regional fruit production. A couple of excellent eateries make it worth a visit.

The ever-popular **Cygnet Folk Festival** (www.cygnetfolkfestival.org) is three days of words, music and dance in January. The warmer months also provide abundant fruit-picking work for backpackers.

Sleeping & Eating

Commercial Hotel PUB $

(☎03-6295 1296; 2 Mary St; s/d without bathroom $65/85) Upstairs at the rambling old Commercial are decent pub rooms, all redecorated with flat-screen TVs, fridges and new beds. Downstairs, laconic locals occupy the bar and dive into robust seafood spreads.

Cherryview COTTAGE $$

(☎03-6295 0569; www.cherryview.com.au; 90 Supplice Rd; d $160) This self-contained cottage on 10 quiet hectares is decked out with cosy wooden furniture and enjoys misty morning views over nearby cherry orchards. Oriental rugs, wooden floors and a king-size bed make it ideal for a romantic getaway.

Old Bank B&B B&B $$$

(☎03-6295 0769; www.oldbank.com.au; 20 Mary St; d incl breakfast $225-250; wi-fi) Cygnet's grand and stately former bank is now the town's best accommodation with three spacious bedrooms dripping in natural wood, Oriental carpets, and king-size beds with luxury linen. The bathrooms are especially lovely with gleaming Art Deco touches and wooden vanities crafted from recycled timber. Downstairs, breakfast and early evening drinks are served in the Orangery, a modern conservatory.

Lotus Eaters Café CAFE $

(10 Mary St; light meals $10-17; ⏲9am-4pm Thu-Mon) This excellent cafe has a rigorous focus on everything seasonal, organic, free-range and local. Have a cup of warming chai with one of their ever-changing freshly-baked cakes.

★ **Red Velvet Lounge** CAFE $$$

(☎03-6295 0466; www.theredvelvetlounge.com.au; 24 Mary St; breakfast & lunch $9-29, four-course dinner $65; ⏲9am-5pm daily, dinner from 6pm Fri-Sat) This funky restaurant and coffeehouse serves deliciously healthy meals showcasing local Huon Valley produce. Breakfast and lunch are both leisurely affairs, and on Friday and Saturday evenings (bookings essential), four-course dinners showcase dishes like zucchini flowers stuffed with goat curd or wood-roasted free-range chicken. Definitely worth the 40-minute drive from Hobart.

Huonville & Around

Huonville (population 1940), on the banks of the Huon River, is the biggest town south of Hobart and sits in a region of pretty hillside orchards and riverfront villages. The town was traditionally the centre of Tasmania's prodigious apple-growing industry, and now the region's farmers have diversified into viticulture, cherries, berries and stone fruit. Just down the road, pretty riverside **Franklin** has good eateries.

The **Huon Valley Visitor Centre** (☎03-6264 0326; www.huontrail.org.au; 2273 Huon Hwy; ⏲9am-5pm Oct-Mar, 10am-4pm Apr-Sep) is on the way into town coming from Hobart.

Sights & Activities

Huon Apple & Heritage Museum MUSEUM

(☎03-6266 4345; www.applemuseum.huonvalley.biz; 2064 Main Rd; adult/child $5.50/3; ⏲8.30am-5.30pm) At Grove, 6km north of Huonville, with displays on almost 400 varieties of apples and 19th-century orchard life.

Huon Jet JET-BOATING

(☎03-6264 1838; www.huonjet.com; adult/child $75/52; ⏲9am-5pm) A 35-minute, heart-in-your-mouth jet-boat ride. Boats leave from by the river on the road south to Cygnet.

Sleeping & Eating

Huon Bush Retreats CABIN $$
(03-6264 2233; www.huonbushretreats.com; 300 Browns Rd; d tepees $145, d cabins from $295, tent & campervan sites $30) This wildlife-friendly retreat is on a habitat reserve on Mt Misery. On-site are modern, self-contained cabins, a larger disabled-access cabin, luxury tepees, tent and campervan sites, plus walking tracks and barbecue shelters.

DS Coffee House & Internet Lounge CAFE $
(34 Main Rd, Huonville; light meals $8-15; 7.30am-5pm Mon-Fri, 9am-4.30pm Sat-Sun;) This funky collection of retro furniture feels like your first student flat at university. It's also a handy internet lounge with PCs for hire and wi-fi on offer. On Friday evenings there are special 'curry nights'.

Franklin Woodfired Pizza PIZZA $$
(Huon Hwy, Franklin; pizzas $12-18; 5-9pm Thu-Sun) This tiny tin shack bakes fantastic take-away pizzas inside a kooky corrugated-iron oven. Try the one with salmon and capers.

Petty Sessions CAFE $$
(03-6266 3488; www.pettysessions.com.au; 3445 Huon Hwy, Franklin; lunch $12-24, dinner $24-35; 10am-4pm & 6-8.30pm) A picket fence and picture-perfect gardens enshroud this likeable cafe inside an 1860 courthouse in Franklin. Head for the deck and try local produce like renowned Huon Valley mushrooms and Huon River salmon. Local southern Tasmanian wines also feature.

Geeveston & Around

Trying hard to shake its reputation as a redneck logging town, Geeveston (population 760) now pitches itself as a tourist centre for Tassie's deep south, with good accommodation and eateries close to the Hartz Mountains and Tahune Forest AirWalk and Eagle Glide.

Sights & Activities

Tahune Forest AirWalk WALKING
(1300 720 507; www.adventureforests.com.au; adult/child $25/13; 9am-5pm Nov-Mar, 10am-4pm Sep-Apr) Tahune Forest, 29km west of Geeveston, has 600m of steel wheelchair-accessible walkways suspended 20m above the forest floor. There are also walking trails, and a 6km mountain bike track prescribes the surrounding forest. Bring your own bike or hire one onsite ($25 for two hours).

Tahune Eagle Glide HANG-GLIDING
(1300 720 507; www.adventureforests.com.au; one/two crossings $13.50/25; 9am-5pm Nov-Mar, 10am-4pm Sep-Apr) Assess the Tahune Forest from incredible heights. Wannabe eagles are strapped into a hang-glider, which in turn is latched to a 220m cable 30m above the Huon River and forest.

Sleeping & Eating

Cambridge House B&B $$
(03-6297 1561; www.cambridgehouse.com.au; cnr School Rd & Huon Hwy; d with shared facilities $115, d with bathroom $140) A photogenic 1930s B&B offering upstairs accommodation in three bedrooms with shared facilities (ideal for families), or a downstairs en suite room. Baltic pine ceilings and the timber staircase are wonders. Check out the friendly platypus at the bottom of the garden.

Masaaki's Sushi JAPANESE $$
(20b Church St; sushi $10-20; 11.30am-6.30pm Fri-Sat) Tasmania's best sushi – including fresh wasabi – is actually found in sleepy Geeveston. Note the limited opening hours, but also know you'll find Masaaki and his excellent food at Hobart's weekly Tas Farm Gate Market (p637) on a Sunday morning.

Contented Bear CAFE $$
(6 Church St; snacks and light meals $8-20; 10am-2pm;) Try a homemade scallop mornay pie for lunch or enjoy a Devonshire tea with homemade scones. Caution: must like teddy bears.

Hartz Mountains National Park

The wilderness of this **park** (www.parks.tas.gov.au), part of Tasmania's World Heritage Area, is only 84km from Hobart – easy striking distance for day-trippers and weekend walkers. The park is renowned for its jagged peaks, glacial tarns, gorges, alpine moorlands and dense rainforest. Rapid weather changes are common, and even day walkers should bring waterproofs and warm layered clothing.

There are some great hikes and isolated viewpoints in the park. **Waratah Lookout**, 24km from Geeveston, is an easy five-minute shuffle from the road. Other well-surfaced short walks include **Arve Falls** (20 minutes return) and **Lake Osborne** (40 minutes return). The steeper **Lake Esperance** walk (about two hours return) takes you through sublime high country.

There are basic day facilities within the park – toilets, shelters, picnic tables, barbecues – but camping is not allowed. Collect a *Hartz Mountains National Park* brochure from the Geeveston or Huonville visitor information centres.

Dover & Around

Dover (population 465) is a chilled-out base for exploring the far south. In the 19th century Dover was a timber-milling town, but nowadays fish farms harvest Atlantic salmon for export throughout Asia. This is Tasmania's last vestige of civilisation for travellers heading south, and the place to stock up on fuel and supplies. On the road from Geeveston, take the pretty detour around Police Point, which provides superb views over the lower Huon River and D'Entrecasteaux Channel with its salmon farms and watercraft.

See www.farsouthtasmania.com.

🛏 Sleeping & Eating

Far South Wilderness Lodge & Backpackers   CABIN $
(☑ 03-6298 1922; www.farsouthwilderness.com.au; Narrows Rd; d $80) ◗ On the Esperance River 5km south of Dover, Far South provides some of Tasmania's best budget accommodation, with a bushy waterfront setting, a cosy lounge piled high with *National Geographic* mags, quality accommodation and a strong environmental focus. Mountain bikes can be rented ($15 per day), and accommodation includes double rooms and cabins ($75) sleeping up to six.

Dover Beachside Tourist Park   CAMPGROUND $
(☑ 03-6298 1301; www.dovercaravanpark.com.au; 27 Kent Beach Rd; unpowered/powered sites $22.50/32.50, cabins from $95; ☎) Opposite a sandy beach, this proudly maintained park features grassy expanses, spotless cabins and a bookshelf full of beachy, trashy novels.

Jetty House   B&B $$
(☑ 03-6298 3139; www.southportjettyhouse.com; Main Rd; s/d incl breakfast $120/160, extra person $25; ☎) ◗ Around 10km south of Dover at Southport, this rambling, verandah-encircled and family-run homestead was built in 1875. Rates include a full cooked breakfast and afternoon tea. Dinner is by arrangement. Minimum two nights stay, and

an ideal treat before or after negotiating the Southwest Track.

Post Office 6985   SEAFOOD, PIZZA $$
(☑ 03-6298 1905; Main Rd; mains $15-30; ⊙ 10am-8pm Wed-Sun, pizza from 3pm Thu-Sat) This is a surprise... Leonard Cohen and alt-country on the stereo, cool decor and lots of up-to-date music and food magazines. The menu features local seafood, wood-fired pizzas and tasty gourmet pies and burgers.

St Imre   WINERY $$
(☑ 03-6298 1781; www.stimrevineyard.com.au; 6900 Huon Hwy; ⊙ tastings 10am-5pm Sat-Sun, dinner Fri) ◗ Specialising in pinot noir, chardonnay and the robust and rustic 'Tiger Blood', this hillside vineyard also offers three-course dinners ($45) on Friday nights, usually reflecting the owners' Hungarian heritage. Booking ahead is essential by the Thursday prior.

Hastings Caves & Thermal Springs

The Hastings Caves & Thermal Springs facility, signposted inland from the Huon Hwy, is 21km south of Dover. The only way to explore the caves is via guided tour; buy tickets at the **Hastings visitor information centre** (☑ 03-6298 3209; www.parks.tas.gov.au; adult/child $24/12; ⊙ 10.30am-3.30pm Feb-Christmas Eve, 9am-5pm Boxing Day to Jan). Tours leave at 11.30am, 12.30pm, 2.15pm and 3.15pm with additional tours through January.

Admission includes a 45-minute tour of the amazing dolomite **Newdegate Cave**, plus entry to the **thermal swimming pool** behind the visitor information centre, filled with 28°C (supposedly) water from thermal springs (pool-only admission adult/child $5/2.50).

Cockle Creek

Australia's most southerly drive is a 19km corrugated-gravel stretch from **Ida Bay** past the gentle waves of **Recherche Bay** to Cockle Creek. A grand grid of streets was once planned for Cockle Creek, but dwindling coal seams and whale numbers poured cold water on that idea. There's free camping along the Recherche Bay foreshore, or pitch your tent just within Southwest National Park (national park fees apply). You can walk to windy **Whale Head** and onto the **South East Cape**.

The Cockle Creek area features craggy, clouded mountains, brilliant long beaches: perfect for camping and bushwalking. The challenging **South Coast Track** starts (or ends) here, taking you through to Melaleuca in the Southwest National Park. Combined with the **Port Davey Track** you can walk all the way to Port Davey in the southwest. Contact **Evans Coaches** (☎03-6297 1335; www.evanscoaches.com.au) for transport to trailheads.

TASMAN PENINSULA

Port Arthur Historic Site is the Tasman Peninsula's centre of activity, but the area also offers 300m-high sea cliffs, empty surf beaches, and stunning bushwalks through thickly wooded forests and isolated coastlines. Much of the area constitutes the Tasman National Park (p654).

In January 2013, devastating bushfires swept through parts of the Tasman Peninsula, destroying more than 100 homes and businesses, especially in the riverside town of Dunalley. Fortunately there was no human loss of life.

See www.tasmanregion.com.au and www.portarthur.org.au.

Tours

Gray Line SIGHTSEEING
(☎1300 858 687; www.grayline.com.au; full-day tour adult/child from $108/54) Coach tours ex-Hobart, including a harbour cruise around the Isle of the Dead, Port Arthur admission and guided tour, and pit stops at Tasman Arch and the Devils' Kitchen.

Navigators SIGHTSEEING
(☎03-6223 1914; www.navigators.net.au; Brooke St Pier; full-day tour from adult/child $159/128; ⏱Wed, Fri & Sat Oct-May) Cruises from Hobart to Port Arthur, returning on a coach. Includes

Tasman Peninsula

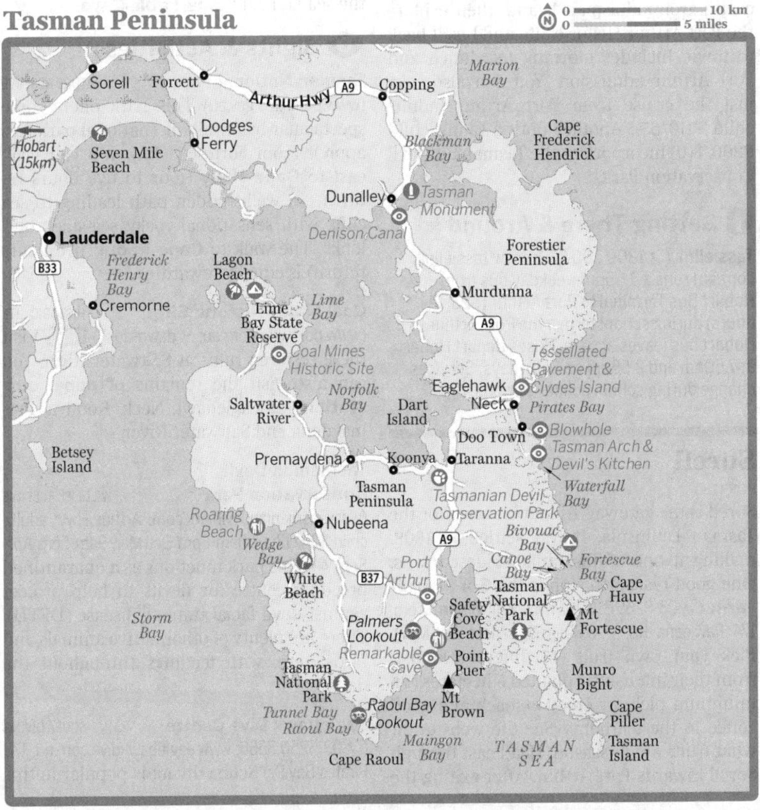

entrance to the historic site, guided tour and morning tea. Also offer cruises around Tasman Island from Port Arthur.

Roaring 40s Ocean Kayaking KAYAKING
(☎03-6267 5000; www.roaring40stours.com.au; 1-/3-day tour $275/1250) Based in Kettering, Roaring 40s also conducts epic sea-kayaking tours around the Tasman Peninsula, paddling past the monumental coastline. Prices include equipment, meals, accommodation and transfers from Hobart.

Tours Tasmania SIGHTSEEING
(☎1800 777 103; www.tourstas.com.au; full-day tours $110-120; ⏰Tue, Wed, Fri & Sat) Small-group backpacker-focused day trips including Port Arthur and the Tasmanian Devil Conservation Park, and Port Arthur combined with Remarkable Cave and Tasman Arch.

Tasman Island Cruises WILDLIFE
(☎03-6250 2200; www.tasmancruises.com.au; full-day tour from adult/child $210/140) Take a bus to Port Arthur for a three-hour eco-cruise around Tasman Island, then explore the Port Arthur Historic Site and bus it back to town. Includes morning tea, lunch and Port Arthur admission. You can also take just the cruise from Port Arthur (adult/child $110/65). Another option (adult/child $200/140) incorporates the Tasmanian Devil Conservation Park.

Getting There & Around

Tassielink (☎1300 300 520; www.tassielink.com.au) runs a 3.55pm weekday bus from Hobart Bus Terminal to Port Arthur ($23, 2¼ hours) during school terms; the Port Arthur to Hobart bus leaves at 6am. Buses depart Hobart at 7.50am and 2.55pm on Saturdays. Services change during school holiday periods.

Sorell

POP 1730

Sorell is the gateway T-junction town for the Tasman Peninsula. It was settled in 1808, making it one of Tasmania's oldest towns. One good reason to stop is the **Sorell Fruit Farm** (☎03-6265 3100; www.sorellfruitfarm.com; 174 Pawleena Rd; ⏰8.30am-5pm late Oct-May). Pick your own fruit (15 different kinds!) from their intensively planted 5 hectares ($6 minimum pick) or enjoy a snack and good coffee in the tearooms. See the website for what fruits are in season. Head east through Sorell towards Port Arthur. After exiting the town you'll see Pawleena Rd signposted on your left.

Eaglehawk Neck to Port Arthur

Most tourists associate the Tasman Peninsula only with Port Arthur, but there are many attractions down this way. Buy *Peninsula Tracks* by Peter and Shirley Storey ($18) for track notes on 35 walks in the area. The *Convict Trail* booklet, available from visitor information centres, covers the peninsula's historic sites.

Approach Eaglehawk Neck from the north, then turn east onto Pirates Bay Dr for the **lookout** – the Pirates Bay views extending to the rugged coastline beyond are truly incredible. Also clearly signposted around Eaglehawk Neck are some bizarre and precipitous coastal formations: **Tessellated Pavement**, the **Blowhole**, **Tasman Arch** and **Waterfall Bay**. South of Port Arthur is the sea-gouged **Remarkable Cave**.

Sights & Activities

Tasman National Park NATURE RESERVE
(www.parks.tas.gov.au) This park offers some spectacular bushwalking (national park fees apply). From Fortescue Bay, you can walk east to **Cape Hauy** (four to five hours return) – a well-trodden path leading to sea cliffs with sensational rocky sea-stack outlooks. The walk to **Cape Raoul** (five hours return) is equally rewarding.

Coal Mines Historic Site HISTORIC SITE
(www.portarthur.org.au; ⏰dawn-dusk) FREE Visit these restored ruins at Saltwater River. You can also visit the remains of **penal outstations** at Eaglehawk Neck, Koonya, Premaydena and Saltwater River.

Tasmanian Devil Conservation Park WILDLIFE RESERVE
(www.tasmaniandevilpark.com; Arthur Hwy; adult/child $24/13; ⏰9am-6pm Oct-Mar, 9am-5pm Apr-Sep) This park functions as a quarantined breeding centre for devils to help protect against devil facial tumour disease (DFTD). There are plenty of other native animals and birds here, with feedings throughout the day.

Eaglehawk Dive Centre SCUBA DIVING
(☎03-6250 3566; www.eaglehawkdive.com.au; 178 Pirates Bay Dr) Scuba diving is popular in this area.

TIGERS & DEVILS

There are two endings to the story of the Tasmanian tiger (*Thylacinus cynocephalus*, or thylacine). The thylacine – a striped, nocturnal, dog-like predator – was once widespread in Tasmania (and also roamed mainland Australia and New Guinea until about 2000 years ago). Conventional wisdom says that it was hunted to extinction in the 19th and early 20th centuries, and that the last-known specimen died in Hobart Zoo in 1936. Despite hundreds of alleged sightings since, no specimen, living or dead, has been confirmed. The second version of the story is that the shy, illusive tigers still exist in the wilds of Tasmania. Scientists scoff at such suggestions, but Tasmanian folklore seems reluctant to let go of this tantalising possibility. David Owen's *Thylacine* examines this phenomenon and traces the animal's demise, and in the 2011 film *The Hunter*, Willem Dafoe features as a man searching for the last thylacine in Tasmania.

The rambunctious Tasmanian devil *(Sarcophilus harrisii)* is definitely still alive, but devil facial tumour disease (DFTD, a communicable cancer) infects up to 75% of the wild population (the real beast looks nothing like the Warner Bros cartoon). Quarantined populations have been established around the state, but efforts to find a cure have been depressingly fruitless. In the meantime, you can check them out at wildlife parks around the state, and get up-to-date information on ongoing efforts to control the impact of DFTD.

Sleeping

Taranna Cottages & Campervan Park CABIN $

(☎03-6250 3436; www.tarannacottages.com.au; cnr Arthur Highway & Nubeena Rd; d $95, extra adult/child $20/10, unpowered sites $20) Perhaps the best-value accommodation on the peninsula, this enterprise at the southern end of Taranna features three neat-as-a-pin self-contained apple pickers' cottages. They exude basic, rustic charm in a quiet bush setting and have open fires. Breakfast provisions (free-range eggs, homemade jams) are a few dollars extra. There's also parking for self-contained campervans.

Norfolk Bay Convict Station B&B $$

(☎03-6250 3487; www.convictstation.com; 5862 Arthur Hwy; d incl breakfast $160-180) Built in 1838 and once the railway's port terminus and an old pub, this gorgeous place is now a top-quality waterfront B&B. Eclectic rooms come with homemade buffet breakfasts and complimentary port. Fishing gear and a dinghy are for hire.

Port Arthur

POP 300

In 1830 Lieutenant-Governor George Arthur chose the Tasman Peninsula to confine prisoners who had committed further crimes in the colony. A 'natural penitentiary', the peninsula is connected to the mainland by a strip of land less than 100m wide – Eaglehawk Neck. To deter escape, ferocious guard dogs were chained across the isthmus.

From 1830 to 1877, 12,500 convicts did hard, brutal prison time at Port Arthur. Port Arthur became the hub of a network of penal stations on the peninsula, its fine buildings sustaining thriving convict-labour industries, including timber milling, shipbuilding, coal mining, shoemaking, and brick and nail production.

Australia's first railway literally 'ran' the 7km between Norfolk Bay and Long Bay: convicts pushed the carriages along the tracks. A semaphore telegraph system allowed instant communication between Port Arthur, other peninsula outstations and Hobart. Convict farms provided fresh vegetables, a boys' prison was built at Point Puer to reform and educate juvenile convicts, and a church was erected.

Although Port Arthur is a hugely popular tourist site – over 300,000 visitors annually – it remains a sombre, confronting and haunting place. What makes it all the more poignant is the scale of the penal settlement and its genuine beauty. The stonemasonry work, gothic architecture, lawns and gardens are all exquisite.

Sights & Activities

Port Arthur Historic Site HISTORIC SITE

(☎03-6251 2310, Historic Ghost Tour 1800 659 101; www.portarthur.org.au; Arthur Hwy; adult/child from $32/16, Historic Ghost Tour adult/child $25/15);

DON'T ASK – THE PORT ARTHUR MASSACRE

Staff at the Port Arthur Historic Site won't speak of the 1996 massacre. Many lost relatives and colleagues, and Martin Bryant's name will not be spoken. On the morning of Sunday 28 April, 28-year-old Bryant drove from Hobart with a sports bag of semiautomatic weapons. Over the course of the late morning and afternoon he murdered 35 people and injured 37 more in and around the Port Arthur Historic Site. He took a hostage into a local guesthouse and held off police for a further 18 hours, killing the hostage and setting the guesthouse on fire before surrendering to police. He remains imprisoned north of Hobart, having received 35 life sentences. The Port Arthur Massacre is one of the world's worst killing sprees in a single event. The incident precipitated Australia's strict gun-control laws.

tours & buildings 9am-5pm, grounds 8.30am-dusk) The visitor centre here includes a cafe and restaurant. Downstairs is an interpretation gallery, where you can follow the convicts' journey from England to Tasmania.

Guided tours (included in admission) leave regularly from the visitor centre. You can visit all the restored buildings, including the Old Asylum (now a museum and cafe) and the Model Prison. Admission tickets, valid for two consecutive days, also entitle you to a short harbour cruise circumnavigating (but not stopping at) the **Isle of the Dead**. For an additional $15/8 per adult/child, you can visit the island on 40-minute guided tours – count headstones and listen to some stories. You can also tour to **Point Puer** boys' prison for the same additional prices.

Extremely popular is the 90-minute, lantern-lit **Historic Ghost Tour**, which leaves from the visitor centre nightly at dusk. Bookings are essential, and many visitors buy an **After Dark Pass** ($68) which combines the ghost tour with dinner at Felon's Bistro.

Sleeping

Port Arthur Holiday Park CAMPGROUND $

(03-6250 2340; www.portarthurhp.com.au; Garden Point Rd; dm $20, unpowered sites $25, powered sites $29-37, cabins $115-130;) Spaciously sloping with plenty of greenery, this well-facilitated park (including camp kitchen, wood BBQs and shop) is 2km before Port Arthur, not far from a sheltered beach. Port Arthur's only budget option.

Sea Change Safety Cove B&B $$$

(03-6250 2719; www.safetycove.com; 425 Safety Cove Rd; d $180-240) This guesthouse has fantastic views including misty cliffs and sea-wracked beaches. It's 4km south of Port Arthur, just off the sandy sweep of Safety Cove Beach. There's a beaut communal deck, a couple of B&B rooms inside the house, plus a large independent unit sleeping five.

Stewarts Bay Lodge RESORT $$$

(03-6250 2888; www.stewartsbaylodge.com.au; 6955 Arthur Hwy; d $173-390; @) Arrayed around a gorgeous hidden cove, Stewarts Bay Lodge combines older, more rustic units with newer deluxe accommodation. Modern kitchens are great for making the most of good local produce, but you'll also want to dine at the sleek Taylor's Restaurant.

Eating

Eucalypt CAFE $$

(6962 Arthur Hwy; mains $13-18; 8am-5pm) A versatile spot near the turn-off to Port Arthur, Eucalypt does robust breakfasts, the area's best coffee, and hearty lunches including scallop pot pie. It also functions as a providore selling local produce and crafts.

Felons Bistro MODERN AUSTRALIAN $$

(1800 659 101; mains $23-32; from 5pm) In the Port Arthur visitor centre, Felons is a worthy choice before you head off on the Historic Ghost Tour. Upmarket, creative dinners with a steak and seafood bias including tuna and salmon reinforce their catchy slogan: 'Dine with Conviction'. Reservations advised.

Taylor's Restaurant MODERN AUSTRALIAN $$$

(03-6250 2771; 6955 Arthur Hwy, Stewarts Bay Lodge; lunch $18-21 & dinner $28-38; noon-late;) Taylor's showcases Tasmanian produce with Macquarie harbour trout, Cape Grim steak, and venison from nearby Doo Town. Definitely worth a detour if you're overnighting anywhere on the peninsula. Bookings recommended in summer.

THE MIDLANDS

Tasmania's Midlands are the very antithesis of the forested wilderness areas the island is famous for. The early settlers comprehensively cleared this area for sheep and cattle grazing, and planted willows, poplars and hawthorn hedgerows around their settlements and along the fertile river valleys. The Midlands' baked, straw-coloured plains and hillsides, and grand Georgian mansions feel distinctly English.

The Midlands' agricultural potential fuelled Tasmania's settlement – coach stations, garrison towns, stone villages and pastoral properties sprang up as convict gangs hammered out the road between Hobart and Launceston.

The upgrading of Tasmania's main north–south road – the Midland Hwy (aka Heritage Highway) – bypassed many old towns along the old route. Pull off the highway to Ross and Oatlands to explore the Georgian main streets, antique shops and some of Australia's best-preserved colonial architecture.

See www.southernmidlands.tas.gov.au and www.northernmidlands.tas.gov.au.

Getting There & Around

Redline Coaches (1300 360 000; www.tasredline.com.au) powers along the Midland Hwy several times daily; you can jump off at any of the main towns except on express services. The Hobart to Launceston fare is $39.70 (about 2½ hours). One-way from Hobart/Launceston to Oatlands costs $20.60/23.50; to Ross it's $29.30/13.30 and to Campbell Town it's $29.30/13.30.

Oatlands

POP 540

Established as a garrison town in 1832, Oatlands serves a thriving tourist trade, but remains stately and restrained about it. Surveyors proposed 80km of streets for the little town that today contains Australia's largest collection of Georgian architecture and many splendid early dry-stone walls. On the impressive main street alone there are 87 historic buildings, some now housing galleries and craft stores.

Oatlands visitor centre (03-6254 1212; www.heritagehighwaytasmania.com.au; Mill Lane; guided tours adult/child/family $12/8/25; 9am-5pm) proffers general info and handles accommodation bookings. Located near Callington Mill, it runs regular guided tours of the town's attractions (adult/child/family $12/8/25, minimum four people), and has excellent maps and brochures for independent exploration.

Sights

Callington Mill LANDMARK
(www.callingtonmill.com.au; Mill Lane; Miller's Way tours adult/child/family $12/8/25; 9am-5pm) Visible throughout the town, Callington Mill was built in 1837 and ground flour until 1891. After years of neglect it was fully restored and reopened in 2010. It's a fascinating piece of engineering, all fully explained on guided tours. The mill is also back to producing high-grade, organic flour, used extensively across the road at the Companion Bakery.

History Room MUSEUM
(9am-5pm) FREE This is an old garage full of photos, relics and old knick-knacks. While you're here, pick up the free handouts *Welcome to Historic Oatlands*, which includes self-guided town tour directions. Hours can be flexible.

Sleeping & Eating

There's free camping for caravans and campervans in the picnic area beside Lake Dulverton at the northern end of the Esplanade.

Oatlands Lodge B&B $$
(03-6254 1444; oatlandslodge@bigpond.com; 92 High St; s/d incl breakfast $100/130) Warm and inviting in two-storey, hen-pecked sandstone splendour, Oatlands Lodge is the cream of the town's accommodation. Rates include a huge breakfast spread and lots of conversation with the friendly owners.

Companion Bakery BAKERY $
(www.companionbakery.com.au; 106 High St; snacks & light meals $6-15; 9am-4pm Wed-Sun) Wood-fired. Organic. Seriously good coffee. What's not to like about the Companion Bakery? As well as Tasmania's best sourdough sandwiches, other sustenance before or after exploring Oatlands' heritage vibe includes Moroccan lamb rolls, good pastries and quiche.

Ross

POP 270

Another tidy Midlands town is Ross, 120km north of Hobart. Established in 1812 as a garrison town to protect Hobart–Launceston travellers from bushrangers, it quickly became an important coach staging post. Tree-lined streets are wrapped in colonial charm and history.

The **crossroads** in the middle of town leads you in one of four directions: temptation (represented by the Man O'Ross Hotel), salvation (the Catholic church), recreation (the town hall) and damnation (the old jail).

Sights & Activities

Some notable historic edifices in Ross include the 1832 **Scotch Thistle Inn** (Church St), now a private residence; the 1830 **barracks** (Bridge St), restored by the National Trust and also a private residence; the 1885 **Uniting Church** (Church St); the 1868 **St John's Anglican Church** (cnr Church & Badajos Sts); and the still-operating 1896 **post office** (26 Church St).

Tasmanian Wool Centre MUSEUM
(www.taswoolcentre.com.au) Sells garments, scarves and beanies made from super-fine merino wool. The **Ross visitor information centre** (☎03-6381 5466; www.visitross.com.au; Church St; ⏰9am-5pm) is located here.

Ross Bridge MONUMENT
The impressive Ross Bridge (1836) is the third-oldest bridge in Australia. The bridge is floodlit at night and light reflecting from the water makes eerie shifting shadows on the 186 carvings that decorate the arches.

Ross Female Factory MUSEUM
(⏰9am-5pm) FREE Off Bond St, the Ross Female Factory was one of only four female convict prisons in the colony. One building is still standing, and archaeological excavations are under way. Descriptive signs and poignant personal stories provide insights into the prisoners' lives.

Sleeping & Eating

Ross Caravan Park CAMPGROUND $
(☎03-6381 5224; www.rossmotel.com.au; Bridge St; unpowered/powered sites $24/28, cabin $60; 📶) As well as camping, the utilitarian, barracks-style cabins sleep two to four people, have cooking facilities and offer the cheapest accommodation in town. Bathrooms are shared, and you'll need your own linen. Reception is at the Ross Motel.

Stone Cottage COTTAGE $
(☎03-6381 5444; skummreow@hotmail.com; Church St; d $90, extra adult/child $20/10) One of the town's best options for families, with a truckload of kids' toys and DVDs, and an expansive garden with well-established fruit trees. The country kitchen with a long wooden table is just perfect for lazy lunches and dinners. Enquire at the Ross post office.

Country Style Cabin COTTAGE $
(☎03-6381 5453; www.rossaccommodationcabin.com.au; 13-17 Bridge St; d incl breakfast $99) Enjoying a rural outlook with sheep as close neighbours, this modern wood-lined cottage has an open-plan lounge with a flat-screen TV and loads of magazines.

Ross Motel MOTEL $$
(☎03-6381 5224; www.rossmotel.com.au; 2 High St; d incl breakfast $135; 📶) Ross Motel offers spic-and-span Georgian-style cottage units, each with microwave, fridge, TV and DVD (prices include breakfast provisions). Family units sleep four.

Bakery 31 CAFE $
(31 Church St; light meals $5-10; ⏰7am-5pm) This jack-of-all-trades store has an olden-days vibe, an open fire and a fuss-free menu of breakfast, soups, homemade cakes and sandwiches. The scallop pies are renowned around all of Tasmania.

Man O'Ross Hotel PUB $$
(35 Church St; mains $18-24; ⏰noon-9pm; 📶) The town's heritage pub offers a surprisingly diverse menu including goodies like Tasmanian salt-crusted lamb and robust Sri Lankan curries. The shady garden bar is the place to be on a summer afternoon.

Campbell Town

POP 770

Campbell Town, 12km north of Ross, was established as yet another garrison settlement. Unlike Oatlands and Ross, the Midland Hwy still trucks right through town.

The first white settlers here were Irish timber-workers who spoke Gaelic and had a particularly debauched reputation.

Rows of **red bricks** set into the High St footpath detail the crimes, sentences and arrival dates of convicts like Ephram Brain and English Corney, sent to Van Diemen's

Land for crimes as various as stealing potatoes, bigamy and murder.

The bridge across the Elizabeth River was completed in 1838, making it almost as old as the Ross Bridge. Locals call it the **Red Bridge** because it was convict-built from more than 1.5 million red bricks baked on-site.

See www.campbelltowntasmania.com.

Sleeping & Eating

Fox Hunters Return B&B $$
(03-6381 1602; www.foxhunters.com.au; 132 High St; d $139-159;) Built with convict labour in 1833 as a coaching inn, the Fox Hunters Return now offers spacious rooms, each with private bathroom and lounge area. The cellar under the main building housed convicts during the construction of the neighbouring Red Bridge. Now it's the 'Book Cellar', specialising in heritage homes and books on Tasmania. It's open daily 10am to 4pm, or by arrangement.

Red Bridge Café & Providore CAFE $
(www.redbridgecafe.com.au; 137 High St; light meals $10-15; 7.30am-5pm;) This former brewery now incorporates a huge dining room with shared wooden tables. Great home-style-baking, interesting sandwiches and gourmet pies make the Red Bridge an essential stop heading north or south. The cafe's providore is packed with the best of Tasmanian food, wine and beer.

Zeps CAFE $$
(03-6381 1344; 92 High St; meals $15-27; 7am-4pm Sun-Mon, 7am-8pm Tue-Sat) Another top refuelling spot is the hyperactive Zeps, serving brekky, panini, pasta, gourmet pies and good coffee throughout the day, plus pizza and more substantial mains in the evening. It's a handy dinner destination if you're staying in Ross and have already eaten at the pub.

EAST COAST

Tasmania's laid-back east coast is drop-dead gorgeous. Hardy types will find superb opportunities for swimming in clean, clear water, while the rest can enjoy walking barefoot along the white-sand beaches. Mild, sunny days lure summer holidaymakers from Hobart, while mainlanders in campervans explore the east coast's squeaky beaches and fishing towns. Wineglass Bay and the pink granite peaks of Freycinet National Park are justifiably world-famous.

See www.tasmaniaseastcoast.com.au.

Getting There & Around

BICYCLE

The Tasman Hwy along the east coast, Tasmania's most popular cycle-touring route, is wonderfully varied. The route takes you through pretty seaside towns, forests and plenty of places to swim. Traffic is usually light, and the hills aren't too steep, particularly the section from Chain of Lagoons to Falmouth (east of St Marys).

BUS

Tassielink (1300 300 520; www.tassielink.com.au) provides east-coast services from Hobart, running at least three times per week.

JOURNEY	PRICE ($)	DURATION (HR)
Hobart–Bicheno	36	3
Hobart–Coles Bay turn-off	34	2¾
Hobart–Orford	16	1¼
Hobart–St Helens	51	4
Hobart–Swansea	29	2¼
Hobart–Triabunna	20	1½

Bicheno Coach Service (03-6257 0293; www.freycinetconnections.com.au) runs between Bicheno, Coles Bay and Freycinet National Park, connecting with east-coast Tassielink coaches at the Coles Bay turn-off. Booking ahead is required for these services.

JOURNEY	PRICE ($)	DURATION (MIN)
Bicheno–Coles Bay	9	35
Coles Bay–Freycinet NP	5	10
Coles Bay turn-off–Coles Bay	9	25
Coles Bay turn-off–Freycinet NP	11	35

Calow's Coaches (03-6372 5166; www.calowscoaches.com.au) provides services linking Bicheno, St Helens and Launceston. Buses between Bicheno and St Helens travel via St Marys. Note that prebooking is necessary for some services; check the website. Some buses link with Tassielink and Redline for onward travel south to Hobart.

East Coast

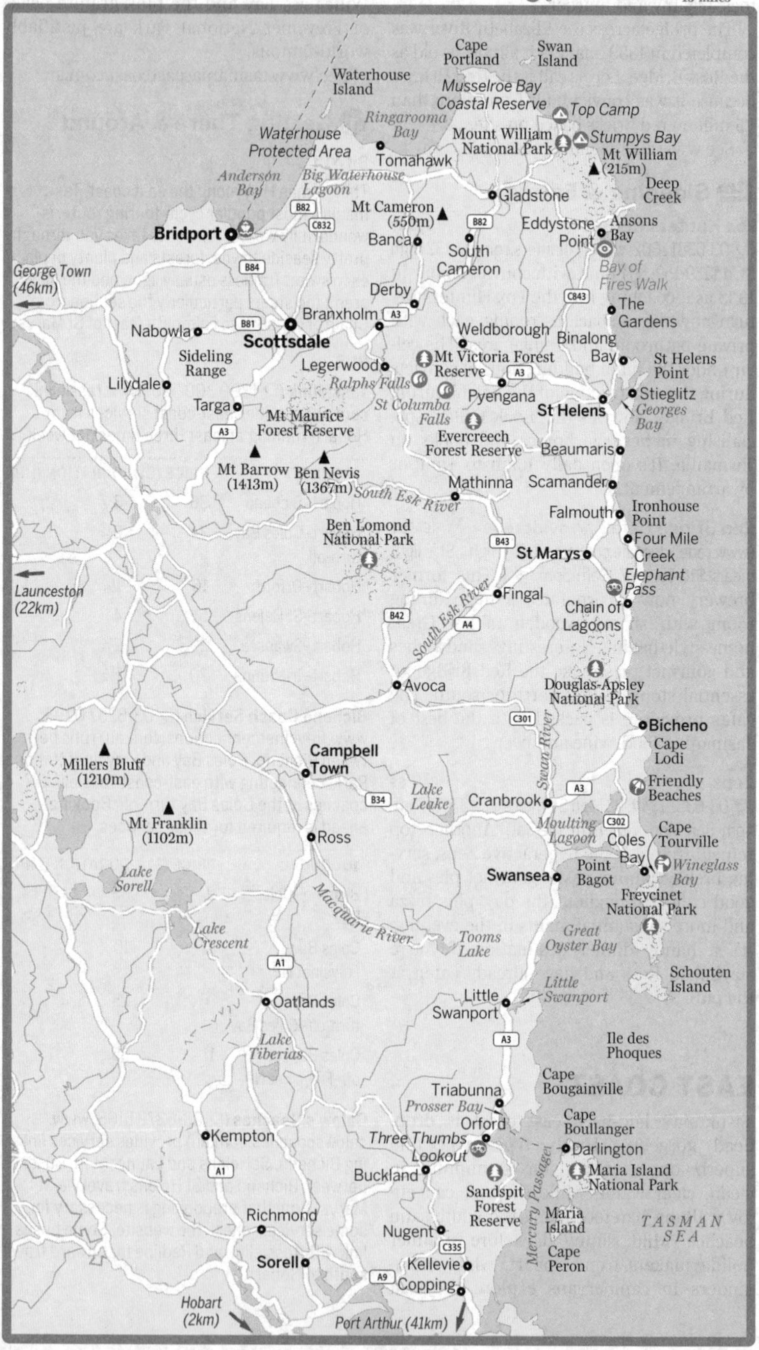
0 30 km
0 15 miles
Cape Portland
Swan Island
Waterhouse Island
Musselroe Bay Coastal Reserve
Top Camp
Ringarooma Bay
Waterhouse Protected Area
Tomahawk
Mount William National Park
Stumpys Bay
Mt William (215m)
Anderson Bay
Big Waterhouse Lagoon
Gladstone
Deep Creek
Mt Cameron (550m)
Eddystone Point
Ansons Bay
Bridport
Banca
South Cameron
Bay of Fires Walk
George Town (46km)
Derby
The Gardens
Branxholm
Nabowla
Scottsdale
Weldborough
Binalong Bay
Sideling Range
Mt Victoria Forest Reserve
St Helens Point
Legerwood
Lilydale
Ralphs Falls
Pyengana
Stieglitz
Targa
St Columba Falls
St Helens
Georges Bay
Mt Maurice Forest Reserve
Evercreech Forest Reserve
Beaumaris
Mt Barrow (1413m)
Ben Nevis (1367m)
Mathinna
Scamander
South Esk River
Falmouth
Ironhouse Point
Ben Lomond National Park
Four Mile Creek
St Marys
Elephant Pass
Launceston (22km)
Fingal
Chain of Lagoons
South Esk River
Avoca
Douglas-Apsley National Park
Bicheno
Cape Lodi
Millers Bluff (1210m)
Campbell Town
Swan River
Friendly Beaches
Lake Leake
Cranbrook
Mt Franklin (1102m)
Moulting Lagoon
Cape Tourville
Ross
Coles Bay
Wineglass Bay
Point Bagot
Lake Sorell
Swansea
Freycinet National Park
Macquarie River
Lake Crescent
Tooms Lake
Great Oyster Bay
Schouten Island
Little Swanport
Oatlands
Little Swanport
Ile des Phoques
Lake Tiberias
Cape Bougainville
Triabunna
Prosser Bay
Cape Boullanger
Orford
Kempton
Three Thumbs Lookout
Darlington
Maria Island National Park
Buckland
Sandspit Forest Reserve
Mercury Passage
Maria Island
TASMAN SEA
Richmond
Nugent
Cape Peron
Sorell
Kellevie
Copping
Hobart (2km)
Port Arthur (41km)
B82
C832
B84
B81
A3
B43
B42
A4
C301
C843
A3
C302
B34
A1
A9
C335

JOURNEY	PRICE ($)	DURATION (HR)
St Helens–Launceston	$31.60	2½
Bicheno–Launceston	33.20	3
Bicheno–St Helens	$13.20	1

Triabunna & Maria Island National Park

About 8km north of Orford is Triabunna (population 800), the departure point for ferries to Maria Island National Park. Book and buy ferry tickets and national park passes at the **Triabunna visitor information centre** (☎03-6257 4772; cnr Charles St & The Esplanade; ⊙9am-5pm, closed for lunch 12.30-1.30pm).

A few kilometres offshore, car-free **Maria Island** (www.parks.tas.gov.au; day admission per person $12) was declared a national park in 1972. Its mixed history provides some interesting convict and industrial ruins among some exquisite natural features: forests, fern gullies, fossil-studded sandstone and limestone cliffs, and empty beaches. Maria is popular with bushwalkers, mountain bikers and birdwatchers, and snorkellers and divers are in for a treat. National park fees apply; island info is available at the visitors reception area in the old Commissariat Store near the ferry pier.

From 1825 to 1832 **Darlington** was Tasmania's second penal colony (the first was Sarah Island near Strahan). The remains of the convict village are well preserved and easy to explore.

The **Maria Island Walk** (☎03-6234 2999; www.mariaislandwalk.com.au; per person $2250) is a four-day guided walk of the island, with the emphasis on nature, history and minimal-impact walking. Trips run from October to April and include transfers from Hobart to the island, meals and accommodation.

Don't miss walks to the top of **Bishop & Clerk** (four hours return), the **Fossil Cliffs** (two hours return) and **Painted Cliffs** (2½ hours return).

The cells in Darlington's old **Penitentiary** (☎03-6257 1420; maria.island@parks.tas.gov.au; dm/d/6-bed unit $15/44/84) have been converted into very basic, unpowered bunkhouses (bring gas lamps, utensils and cookers). Book well ahead. Hot showers are available.

Sleeping & Eating

Bookings aren't required for Maria's **camping grounds** (unpowered sites $13) at Darlington, French's Farm and Encampment Cove. Only the Darlington site has cooking facilities (gas barbecues); fires are permitted in designated fireplaces but are often banned during summer.

There are no shops on the island so BYO supplies.

Triabunna Cabin & Caravan Park CAMPGROUND $
(☎03-6257 3575; www.mariagateway.com; 4 Vicary St; unpowered/powered sites $25/28, on-site vans $70, cabins $120-130; 📶) A neat, compact caravan park with decent facilities and a backpacker dorm.

Tandara Motor Inn MOTEL $$
(☎03-6257 3333; Tasman Hwy; d $135) Triabunna's best place to stay, with bright, recently refurbished motel rooms and free use of the on-site tennis courts.

Getting There & Away

The **Maria Island Ferry** (☎0419 746 668; www.mariaislandferry.com.au; adult/child return $35/25, bikes $10; ⊙9.30am & 3.30pm daily Dec-Apr, 10.30am & 3pm Mon, Wed, Fri, Sun May-Nov) operates from the marina near the Triabunna visitor information centre.

Another ferry option is with **East Coast Cruises** (☎03-6257 1300; www.eastcoastcruises.com.au; adult/child return $35/25, bikes $10; ⊙9am & 10.30am daily Dec-Apr, reduced service May-Nov). East Coast also offer a one-day boat tour including a three-hour cruise around the island, a walk on the island, national park entry and snacks. Bus transfers (one-way/return $25/40) are also available from Hobart.

Swansea

POP 560

Founded in 1820, Swansea sits on the western sheltered shores of beautiful Great Oyster Bay with magnificent views over the Freycinet Peninsula. Once another sleepy seaside village, Swansea's rise has coincided with Tasmania's tourism boom and today offers good B&B accommodation and restaurants and an interesting museum. You're also in striking distance of some good east coast vineyards.

Sights

Historic Buildings HISTORIC BUILDING
There are many still-functioning historic buildings, including the 1860 **Council Chambers** (Noyes St), the 1871 **Anglican Church** (Noyes St) and the redbrick 1838 **Morris' General Store** (13 Franklin St).

Bark Mill Museum Swansea MUSEUM
(www.barkmilltavern.com.au; 96 Tasman Hwy; adult/child $10/6; 9am-4pm) This excellent museum features working models of black-wattle bark processing equipment used in tanning leather, and displays on Swansea's early history, from French exploration to agriculture and industry.

Heritage Centre MUSEUM
(03-6256 5072; 22 Franklin St; 10am-4pm) FREE Reopened in 2012 with informative local history exhibits. Also houses Swansea's **visitor information centre** (9am to 5pm).

Spring Vale Vineyards WINERY
(www.springvalewines.com; 130 Spring Vale Rd; 11am-4pm) This vineyard is at Cranbrook, about 15km north of Swansea. The cellar door is housed in an 1842 stables. Try their wonderful pinot gris, one of Tassie's hottest wines.

Coombend Estate WINERY
(www.coombend.com.au; off Tasman Hwy; Wed-Sun 10am-5pm) Just past the Great Oyster Bay lookout, with 3000 acres of vines, Coombend Estate is Tasmania's largest vineyard. There are tastings and cellar door sales and you can also try and buy their olive oil.

Milton Vineyard WINERY
(www.miltonvineyard.com.au; off Tasman Hwy; 10am-5pm) Milton is 13km north of Swansea, and has tastings in an attractive pavilion overlooking a lake and the vineyards. You can buy one of their cheese platters or picnic by the lake. Try the sparkling rose.

Sleeping

Swansea Backpackers HOSTEL $$
(03-6257 8650; www.swanseabackpackers.com.au; 98 Tasman Hwy; camping $15, dm $31-37, d $87, f $150;) The backpackers next door to the Swansea Bark Mill has smart and spacious public areas and a shiny stainless-steel kitchen. The rooms surround a shady deck and are clean and peaceful.

Redcliffe House B&B $$
(03-6257 8557; www.redcliffehouse.com.au; 13569 Tasman Hwy; d $150-180;) This restored heritage farmhouse, built in 1835, is just north of town. The rooms are beautifully decorated and a guest lounge is equipped with books and a decanter of port. There's also a self-contained apartment with breakfast provisions supplied.

Wagner's Cottages COTTAGE $$$
(03-6257 8494; www.wagnerscottages.com; Tasman Hwy; d $180-270) Wagner's has four stone cottages set in lush gardens one kilometre south of town. Each has a deep spa bath, and there are open fires, fresh flowers, a DVD library and complimentary port. Our favourite is the eponymous Wagner's Cottage, a spacious two-storey 1850s stone edifice with a wonderfully-private garden.

Eating

Onyx CAFE $
(26 Franklin St; snacks & light meals $9-15; 9.30am-4pm;) This cosy bricklined cafe also includes an excellent providore with local wines, gourmet sauces and other picnic-ready goodies. Friendly service and the best coffee in town are combined with tasty wraps, quiche and soups.

Kate's Berry Farm CAFE $
(www.katesberryfarm.com; 12 Addison St, off Tasman Hwy; teas & snacks $10-13; 9.30am-4.30pm) Kate's farm, about 3km south of Swansea, has become an essential stop for east-coast tourers. It sells homemade jams, wines, sauces, and has a nice cafe serving berry-good afternoon teas and hearty savoury pot pies.

Banc MODERN AUSTRALIAN $$
(03-6257 8896; www.thebancrestaurant.com.au; cnr Franklin & Maria Sts; mains $24-32; from 5.30pm) New owners have installed a cosy outdoor area – complete with a wood-fired pizza oven – and are now focusing on dinners with a Mediterranean or Asian spin and lots of good local seafood.

Swansea Bark Mill Tavern & Bakery PUB $$
(www.barkmilltavern.com.au; 96 Tasman Hwy; mains $12-32, pizza $15-23; bakery 6am-4pm, tavern noon-2pm & 5.30-8pm) There are two good dining options at the Swansea Bark Mill. The bakery does cooked breakfasts until 11am, and the tavern offers great pub fare, excellent wood-fired pizzas and takeaways.

Piermont Restaurant MODERN AUSTRALIAN $$$
(☎03-6257 8131; www.piermont.com.au; Tasman Hwy; mains $32-40; ⏲from 6pm Thu-Tue, closed Aug) Piermont has gorgeous vistas over Great Oyster Bay, and this much-awarded restaurant works magic with all that's local and fresh. As well as an innovative à la carte menu, there's also a fabulous five-course degustation menu ($100 with wine, $75 without).

Coles Bay & Freycinet National Park

The spectacular 485m-high pink-orange granite outcrops known as the Hazards dominate the tiny town of Coles Bay (population 473). Brilliant Freycinet Peninsula (pronounced *fray*-sin-ay) is one of Tasmania's principal tourism drawcards, and Coles Bay exists as the gateway and service town for its national park. The peninsula's sublime white-sand beaches, secluded coves, rocky cliffs and outstanding bushwalks make it an essential visit on any east coast itinerary. Note that everything in Coles Bay is expensive, and the town is geared towards tourism.

See www.freycinetcolesbay.com.

Sights & Activities

Freycinet National Park NATURE RESERVE
(www.parks.tas.gov.au) Sheathed in coastal heaths, orchids and wildflowers, Freycinet incorporates Freycinet Peninsula, people-free Schouten Island and the lesser-known Friendly Beaches north of Coles Bay. Black cockatoos, yellow wattlebirds, honeyeaters and Bennett's wallabies flap and bounce between the bushes. Long hikes include the two-day, 31km peninsula circuit, and shorter tracks include the up-and-over saddle climb to **Wineglass Bay**. Ascend the saddle as far as **Wineglass Bay Lookout** (one to 1½ hours return, 600 steps each way) or continue down the other side to the beach (2½ to three hours return). Alternatively, the 500m wheelchair-friendly boardwalk at **Cape Tourville** affords sweeping coastal panoramas and a less-strenuous glimpse of Wineglass Bay. On longer walks, sign in (and out) at the registration booth at the car park; national park fees apply.

Coles Bay Gear Hire WATER SPORTS
(☎0419 255 604; Garnett Ave boat ramp) Hires dinghies with outboards and all safety equipment ($100/120 per two/three hours). Also rents fishing equipment (with boats or without) and can advise on good shore-based fishing spots. The friendly owner even guts and fillets your fish for you when you return. Snorkelling equipment and Canadian canoes ($55/65 per two/three hours for two people) are also available for hire.

Tours

Freycinet Adventures KAYAKING
(☎03-6257 0500; www.freycinetadventures.com.au; 2 Freycinet Dr) Freycinet Adventures offers three-hour tours ($95) twice daily (morning and twilight – times vary seasonally) that allow you to get a glimpse of the peninsula from the water. Kayak hire is available for experienced paddlers ($55 per person per day).

Freycinet Experience GUIDED WALK
(☎03-6223 7565, 1800 506 003; www.freycinet.com.au; ⏲Nov-May) Freycinet Experience offers a four-day, 37km, fully catered traverse of the entire peninsula ($2275). Walkers return each evening to the secluded and environmentally sensitive Friendly Beaches Lodge to enjoy gourmet meals and local wine.

All4Adventure QUAD BIKING
(☎03-6257 0018; www.all4adventure.com.au; Coles Bay Esplanade; two-hour tours adult/child $129/79, half-day tours adult/child $219/119) Get off the beaten track into more remote areas of the national park. Two-hour quad bike tours (with 30 minutes' training beforehand) depart daily at 1pm and 4.30pm (the latter only from November to March). Half-day tours to the Friendly Beaches and lovely Bluestone Bay depart at 8am. A driver's licence is essential, and tours are restricted to children five years and older.

Wineglass Bay Cruises CRUISES
(☎03-6257 0355; www.freycinetseacharters.com; depart jetty on the Esplanade; adult/child $110/75; ⏲Sep-May) Four-hour cruises to Wineglass Bay including champagne, oysters and nibbles. Look forward to dolphins, sea eagles, seals, penguins and perhaps migrating whales in the right season. Departure times vary through the year (9am midsummer and 10am shoulder season). Book several days in advance.

Long Lunch Tour Co FOOD
(☎0409 225 841; www.longlunchtourco.com.au) Foodie Brad Bowden arranges gastronomic

adventures of the east coast. Combine top wines, tempting morsels, oysters and berries ($130), take an afternoon wine-and-nibbles tour ($99), or travel all the way from Hobart stopping to wine and dine along the way ($220).

Sleeping

Accommodation is at a premium at Christmas, January and Easter, so book well ahead. Expect higher prices than in other parts of the state.

Richardsons Beach CAMPGROUND $
(☎ visitor centre 03-6256 7000; www.parks.tas.gov.au; unpowered sites for 2/family $13/16, extra adult/child $5/2.50, powered sites $16/22, extra adult/child $7/3.50) There are pretty beachside camping spots with toilets and running water all along Richardsons Beach. Between December and until after Easter allocation of sites is by a ballot system. Download the application form on the **national parks** website or by calling the **visitor centre**. Applications must be submitted by 31 July. There's sometimes the odd tent spot left over, so it's worth calling to see if they can squeeze you in. Outside the ballot period, bookings can be made in advance at the visitor centre. National park entry fees apply.

There's superb walk-in free camping (national park fees apply) at **Wineglass Bay** (1½ hours from the car park), **Hazards Beach** (three hours), **Cooks Beach** (4½ hours) and **Bryans Beach** (5½ hours). BYO drinking water and note the park is a fuel-stove only area.

Iluka Holiday Centre CAMPGROUND $
(☎ 1800 786 512, 03-6257 0115; www.iluka-holidaycentre.tas.big4.com.au; Coles Bay Esplanade; unpowered/powered sites $30/40, cabins & units d $110-180; wi-fi) Iluka is a big friendly park that's a favourite with local holidaymakers, so book ahead. Iluka Backpackers has six four-bed dorms ($30 per person) and just one double ($72). Discounts for YHA members.

Freycinet Rentals RENTAL HOUSE $$
(☎ 03-6257 0320; www.freycinetrentals.com; 5 Garnet Ave; cottages $150-230) This is your hub for renting holiday cottages and beach 'shacks' in and around Coles Bay. Prices vary considerably from summer to winter and minimum stays apply for long weekends and Christmas holidays.

Hubie's Hideaway RENTAL HOUSE $$
(☎ 03-6257 0344, 0427 570 344; www.nauticabutnice.com.au/hubies-hideaway; 33 Coles Bay Esplanade; d $150, extra adult/child $20/10) At this cute timber cabin, you'll fall asleep to the sound of the sea. It's close to the shops and bakery and sleeps up to seven.

Edge of the Bay RESORT $$$
(www.edgeofthebay.com.au; 2308 Main Rd; d & ste $218-298, cottage d $185-270, extra person $30; wi-fi) This peaceful, small resort is right on the beach, 4km north of Coles Bay. It has smartly decorated waterside suites, and cottages sleeping up to five. There are mountain bikes, dinghies and two artificial grass tennis courts for guests' use. There's also an excellent restaurant on site.

★ **Freycinet Eco Retreat** APARTMENT $$$
(☎ 0408 504 414, 03-6257 0300; www.mtpaul.com; d $220-360, minimum 2-night stay) To really get away from it all at Freycinet, retreat up to Mount Paul and stay at these carefully crafted eco-lodges with only wildlife for neighbours. Both lodges have superb bush and ocean views, and are spacious, airy and trimmed with lots of natural wood. Also available is the more rustic Saltwater Shack, a cosy retro cottage in a wonderfully private forested location.

Eagle Peaks APARTMENT $$$
(☎ 03-6257 0444; www.eaglepeaks.com.au; 11-13 Oyster Bay Crt; d $245-395) There are two beautiful timber and rammed-earth studios here, just south of Coles Bay. Each unit has its own kitchenette, timber deck and comfortable king-sized beds. Also rents the immaculate Beachouse (double $235 to $370, extra adult $40), sleeping four.

Eating

Freycinet Bakery & Café BAKERY $
(Coles Bay Esplanade, Shop 2; snacks and light meals $4-15; ⏲ 8am-4pm) Pick up pies, cakes and sandwiches here or enjoy a lazy all-day breakfast outside.

Tombolo CAFE, PIZZA $$
(6 Garnet Ave; mains $16-22; ⏲ 8.30am-4pm Tue, 8.30am-8pm Wed-Sun) Local wines and seafood, wood-fired pizzas and the best coffee in town, all served on a spacious deck with maritime views.

Freycinet Marine Farm SEAFOOD $$
(www.freycinetmarinefarm.com; 1784 Coles Bay Rd; plates $14-25; ⏲ 9am-5pm daily Sep-May, honesty

system Jun-Aug) Just off the Coles Bay road is Freycinet Marine Farm, which grows huge, succulent oysters in the tidal waters of Moulting Lagoon. Try freshly shucked oysters ($15 a dozen), mussels, rock lobsters and abalone. BYO wine or beer (or buy here) and enjoy a seafood picnic. In winter, put your money in the box and help yourself from the fridge.

Iluka Tavern PUB $$
(Coles Bay Esplanade; mains $22-28; ⏲11am-10pm; 📶) This popular, friendly pub gets packed with tourists and locals. Among the reef 'n' beef and chicken parmigiana, you'll also find pork belly with sweet potato and seafood marinara. There's a good kids' menu, too.

Edge MODERN AUSTRALIAN $$$
(☎03-6257 0102; www.edgeofthebay.com.au; 2308 Main Rd; mains $28-34; ⏲from 6pm; ✎) Get to the Edge of the Bay Resort early to enjoy the water views. The chefs serve up fresh east coast produce and plenty of ocean-fresh bounty. Try the seafood with squid ink pasta, or the market fish with caramelised fennell and a caper and anchovy mash. There are also meaty and vegetarian options.

Information

At the park entrance is the **Freycinet National Park Visitor Centre** (☎03-6256 7000; www.parks.tas.gov.au; Freycinet Dr; ⏲8am-5pm Nov-Apr, 9am-4pm May-Oct) – pay your park fees or catch free ranger-led activities in summer.

In Coles Bay itself, **Coles Bay Trading** (☎03-6257 0109; 1 Garnet Ave; ⏲8am-6pm Mar-Nov, 7am-7pm Dec-Feb) is a general store with a post office, ATM and cafe. Freycinet Adventures (p663) hires out essential camping equipment and also runs water taxis to Hazards Beach, Cooks Beach or Schouten Island.

Getting There & Away

Bicheno Coach Service (p659) runs between Bicheno, Coles Bay and Freycinet National Park, connecting with east-coast Redline and Tassielink coaches at the Coles Bay turn-off.

Bicheno

POP 640

Unlike Swansea and Coles Bay, Bicheno is still a functioning fishing port. With brilliant ocean views and lovely beaches, it's madly popular with holidaymakers, but Bicheno never sold its soul and remains rough-edged and unwashed. A busy fishing fleet still comes home to harbour in the Gulch with pots of lobsters and scaly loot. Food and accommodation prices in Bicheno are more realistic after Freycinet.

The **Bicheno visitor information centre** (☎03-6375 1500; 41b Foster St; ⏲10am-4pm Mon-Fri, 10am-noon Sat, noon-4pm Sun) assists with information and accommodation.

Sights & Activities

Douglas-Apsley National Park NATURE RESERVE
(☎03-6256 7000; www.parks.tas.gov.au) Five kilometres north of Bicheno is the turn-off to Douglas-Apsley National Park, protecting undisturbed dry eucalypt forest, waterfalls, gorges and an abundance of birds and animals. Walk to the swimming hole at **Apsley Gorge** (two to three hours return) or to the **Apsley River Waterhole** (15 minutes return). There's basic, walk-in bush camping here, too (free, but national park fees apply).

East Coast Natureworld NATURE RESERVE
(☎03-6375 1311; www.natureworld.com.au; adult/child/family $22.50/10.50/56; ⏲9am-5pm) This is 7km north of Bicheno and is one of Tasmania's best nature parks. Highlights include a walk-through aviary and seething snake pits. Also look out for Tasmanian devils and plenty of free-roaming native animals. Check the website for feeding times; Tassie devils chow down at 10am, 12.30pm and 3.30pm.

Bicheno Dive Centre SCUBA DIVING
(☎03-6375 1138; www.bichenodive.com.au; 2 Scuba Crt; ⏲9am-5pm) Hires diving equipment and organises underwater adventures. Explore the submarine caves and rock formations at **Governor Island Marine Reserve** near the Gulch.

Foreshore Footway WALKING
This 3km footway extends south from **Redbill Beach**, which has solid sandy breaks, to **Peggys Point**, the **Gulch** and along to the **Blowhole**, returning along footpaths with panoramic town views. **Whalers Hill** is the lookout from where whales were spotted in the old days. If the tide is low, you can wade over a sandy isthmus to **Diamond Island** at the northern end of Redbill Beach. Keep an eye on the tide though, so you don't get stuck on the island.

Tours

Bicheno Penguin Tours BIRDWATCHING
(03-6375 1333; www.bichenopenguintours.com.au; adult/child $25/15; dusk nightly) This outfit runs informative one-hour tours of the fairy penguin rookery at the northern end of Redbill Beach. Tours depart the surf shop in the town centre near Passini's and bookings are essential.

Bicheno Glass Bottom Boat BOAT
(03-6375 1294; the Gulch; tours adult/child $20/5; 10am, noon & 2pm) Take the 40-minute coastal tour, with lots of info provided on the underwater world.

Sleeping & Eating

Bicheno Backpackers HOSTEL $
(03-6375 1651; www.bichenobackpackers.com; 11 Morrison St; dm $27-29, d/tr $75/100) This friendly backpackers stretches across two mural-painted buildings. The double rooms are quite plush (the sea-view one's the pick) and for hire are bikes, kayaks, surfboards, boogie boards and fishing rods.

Bicheno East Coast Holiday Park CAMPGROUND $
(03-6375 1999; www.bichenoholidaypark.com.au; 4 Champ St; powered sites $33, d unit $105, d cabin $138, park cottage $165;) This neat, friendly park has plenty of green grass and is centrally located with a BBQ, camp kitchen, laundry facilities and kids' playground. It also allows showers for non-stayers ($5).

Bicheno by the Bay CABIN $$
(03-6375 1171; www.bichenobythebay.com.au; cnr Foster & Fraser Sts; 1-bedroom unit $150-190, 2-bedroom unit $180-230, motel d $110-160;) There are 20 cabins in a bushland setting here, some with sea views. Facilities include an outdoor heated pool, a tennis court and kids' playground. More modern motel rooms – completed in 2010 – are also good value.

Windows on Bicheno B&B $$$
(03-6375 2010; www.windowsonbicheno.com.au; 13 James St; d $250-350) This fantastic B&B has just two luxurious, stylish suites, furnished and managed with absolute attention to detail. Spot whales from the balcony, relax on the comfy leather sofas, or wallow in your deep spa bath for two.

Blue Edge Bakery BAKERY $
(55 Burgess St; meals $5-15; 6am-4pm) Blue Edge does good sandwiches, pies, cakes and salads. Pick up freshly made breads, or tuck into a chicken and camembert pie.

Passini's ITALIAN $$
(03-6375 1076; 70 Burgess St; mains $15-30; 9am-late Mon-Sat, 9am-2pm Sun) Passini's includes antipasto plates, focaccia and lasagne, and pretty good wood-fired pizza. Service can be a little haphazard, especially during the height of summer, but there's good gourmet providore and a handy takeaway menu.

Sea Life Centre Restaurant SEAFOOD $$
(www.sealifecentre.com.au; 1 Tasman Hwy; mains $24-35; 10am-9pm;) Settle in for views over the startlingly blue waters of the Gulch. The crayfish and seafood chowder are especially recommended by locals, and new management has revamped the menus with offerings including Tasmanian salmon and a Thai seafood curry.

Sir Loin Breier DELI $$
(57 Burgess St; 9am-5pm Mon-Sat) This superior butcher's shop overflows with cooked local crayfish, smoked trout, oysters, gourmet pies, cheeses and smoked quail sausages. Stock up for picnics.

St Marys

POP 520

Most of the tourist traffic bypasses St Marys, but the beautiful drive up the mountains from the coast is definitely worthwhile. Just 10km from the coast, St Marys is 600m above sea level near the St Nicholas Range. It's an unpretentious little town with weatherboard cottages, a pub and a post office.

Sleeping & Eating

Mariton House B&B $$
(03-6372 2059; www.maritonhouse.com; 1 Irishtown Rd; d/tw $105-125) Just off the A4 Esk Hwy from St Marys Pass, Mariton House has charming B&B accommodation in a historic country home built in the 1880s. Guests 12 years and over can also take part in horse-riding excursions ($60/90 per one/two persons for a 90 minute to two-hour trail ride), and rides along nearby east coast beaches can also be arranged.

Purple Possum Wholefoods CAFE $
(www.purplepossum.com.au; 5 Story St; light meals $7.50-15; 9am-4.30pm Mon-Sat;) An un-

expected and welcome find, this place has homemade soups, vegetarian wraps, and fabulous coffee and cakes. Don't miss the rhubarb cake.

Mt Elephant Fudge CAFE $
(7 Story St; from $3; ⊙10am-5pm Wed-Sun) This sweet spot serves up fudge in 10 different flavours, handmade chocolates, Belgian hot chocolate, smoothies, sundaes and delicious cheesecake.

THE NORTHEAST

The northeast gets relatively few travellers, giving the region a more undeveloped and wild feeling than the rest of the east coast. Pretty seaside St Helens is the main centre and a good base for exploring the wildlife-rich national park, waterfalls and miles of empty coastline. Fishing opportunities abound, with a corresponding array of good seafood eateries.

See www.northeasttasmania.com.au.

Getting There & Around

Tassielink (☎1300 300 520; www.tassielink.com.au) has services between Hobart and Bicheno ($50.50, four hours) connecting with Calow's Coaches (p659) for travel up the east coast. From Launceston, **Sainty's** (☎0437 469 186; www.saintysnortheastbusservice.com.au) run services to Derby.

St Helens

POP 2050

Sprawling around picturesque Georges Bay, St Helens was established as a whaling town in 1830 and soon after 'swanners' came to harvest the downy under-feathers of the bay's black swans. It's long been an important fishing port and today is home to Tasmania's largest fishing fleet.

About 26km west of St Helens, turn off to tiny **Pyengana** and the feathery 90m-high **St Columba Falls**, the state's highest. Further on is **Derby**, an old tin-mining town with B&Bs, galleries and pubs. Derby's recently-opened **Tin Dragon Interpretation Centre** (www.trailofthetindragon.com; Main St; adult/child $12/6; ⊙10am-4pm) tells the fascinating story of Derby's thriving past as a mining hub.

Sights & Activities

Big-game fishing charters in St Helens include **Professional Charters** (☎0419 383 362, 03-6376 3083; www.gamefish.net.au) and **Gone Fishing Charters** (☎03-6376 1553, 0419 353 041; www.breamfishing.com.au).

St Helens History & Visitor Information Centre MUSEUM
(☎03-6376 1744; 61 Cecilia St; admission by donation; ⊙9am-5pm) Memorabilia and photographs of old St Helens.

East Lines WATER SPORTS
(☎03-6376 1720; http://eastlines.wordpress.com; 28 Cecilia St) Hires surfboards, wetsuits, snorkelling gear, fishing rods and bicycles. For diving, contact **Bay of Fires Dive** (☎03-6376 8335, 0419 372 342; www.bayoffiresdive.com.au; 291 Gardens Rd) at Binalong Bay.

Beaches

There are good swimming beaches at **Binalong Bay** (11km north on Binalong Bay Rd), **Jeanneret Beach** and **Sloop Rock** (15km north; take Binalong Bay Rd then The Gardens turn-off for both), **Stieglitz** (7km east on St Helens Point), and at **St Helens Point** and **Humbug Point**. Also on St Helens Point are the wind-weathered **Peron Dunes** (8km east).

Sleeping

There are free camping sites north of St Helens at Humbug Point Nature Recreation Area. The turn-off is 7km out of town, en route to Binalong Bay. The camping area is a further 5km through the reserve, at Dora Point.

St Helens Caravan Park CARAVAN PARK $
(☎03-6376 1290; www.sthelenscp.com.au; 2 Penelope St; unpowered sites d $28-38, powered $30-40, cabins & villas d $80-200, extra person $15; @ 📶) With good, clean facilities, this park is 1km south of the town centre.

St Helens Backpackers HOSTEL $
(☎03-6376 2017; www.sthelensbackpackers.com.au; 9 Cecilia St; dm $30, d $65-80) This hostel is spic-and-span, peaceful and spacious. The 'flashpacker' section has dorms and doubles with fancy bathrooms. Chill out on the spacious deck and BBQ the night away. Bike hire is $20 per day, and camping trips to the Bay of Fires can also be arranged.

Kellraine Units APARTMENT $
(☎03-6376 1169; www.kellraineunits.com.au; 72 Tully St; d $85, extra adult/child $40/20) On the

way out of town to the north, these clean, self-contained units (one with wheelchair access) are good value.

Bay of Fires Character Cottages RENTAL HOUSE $$$
(☎03-6376 8262; www.bayoffirescottages.com.au; 64-74 Main Rd; d $180-270) Up at Binalong Bay, these eight colourful, modern one- to three-bedroom cottages are beautifully appointed with kitchens, laundries and barbecues. Best of all are the million-dollar views from the private balconies.

Eating & Drinking

Salty Seas SEAFOOD $
(18 Medeas Cove Esplanade; ⏲10am-5pm Mon-Fri, 10am-2pm Sat) Crayfish are the speciality here – choose them out of the tanks – but there are also oysters, mussels and fish fresh. Feast on their deck overlooking a bird sanctuary. Prices vary according to market demand, but it's all extremely fresh and good value.

Blue Shed Restaurant SEAFOOD $$$
(☎03-6376 1170; www.blueshedrestaurant.com.au; Marina Pde; mains $34-38; ⏲restaurant from 6pm, takeaways 11.30am-2.30pm & 5-7.30pm) Welcome to the best seafood restaurant in St Helens, complete with excellent views of the town's compact fishing harbour. Start with the crispy squid with chilli spice salt, then opt for grilled ocean trout or rock lobster with herb and mascarpone butter. It also does seafood takeaways.

Binalong Bay Cafe MODERN AUSTRALIAN $$$
(☎03-6376 8116; 64a Main Rd, Binalong Bay; breakfast & lunch $12-24, dinner $30-38; ⏲9am-8pm) With Bay of Fires views, the Binalong Bay Cafe has one of the best locations in Tasmania. Thankfully, the food is also well up to scratch with interesting and vibrant spins on classic dishes. We especially enjoyed a lazy brunch of the sand crab omelette with Asian slaw and chilli jam. It's a 15-minute drive from St Helens.

Crossroads BAR
(www.crossroadswinebar.com.au; 5/34 Quail St; ⏲3pm-late daily in summer, Tue-Sun in winter; 📶) This welcoming bar is one of the east coast's only regular live music venues with blues, country and rock gigs most Friday nights. On other evenings, music-loving owners Steve and Jan usually fire up music DVDs to complement a few cold ones, and the TV is a guaranteed sports-free zone.

Bay of Fires

Binalong Bay Rd heads northeast from St Helens over a low tidal swamp before it makes its way to lovely Binalong Bay. This is the only permanent community at the Bay of Fires, but it's just a clutch of holiday houses, the excellent Binalong Bay Cafe, and underwater adventure opportunities with Bay of Fires Dive (p667). To get to the Bay of Fires proper, follow the road towards the ramshackle shack-town of **The Gardens**. The Bay of Fires' northern end is reached via the C843, the road to the Ansons Bay settlement and Mt William National Park.

The Bay of Fires is exquisite – powder-white sands and cerulean-blue water is backed by scrubby bush and lagoons. Despite the proliferation of signature bright-orange lichen on the rocky points and headlands, the early explorers named the bay after seeing Aboriginal fires along the shore. Ocean beaches offer reliable surfing but potentially dangerous swimming – beware of rips and currents. The lagoons offer safe swimming.

For a deluxe wilderness experience, the **Bay of Fires Walk** (☎03-6392 2211; www.bayoffires.com.au; from $2125; ⏲Oct-May) is a fully catered four-day walk from Boulder Point south to Ansons Bay. Accommodation includes two nights at the company's magnificent ecofriendly **Bay of Fires Lodge** (☎03-6392 2211; www.bayoffireslodge.com.au).

There are wonderful free camping spots along the bay, mostly without toilets or fresh water. There are good options immediately north of Binalong Bay, accessed by road from St Helens (take the turn-off to The Gardens). In the northern reaches, there are beachfront sites at Policemans Point, reached by a turn-off before Ansons Bay.

Mt William National Park

The isolated **Mt William National Park** (www.parks.gov.tas.au) features long sandy beaches, low ridges and coastal heathlands. Visit during spring or early summer for blooming wildflowers. The highest point, Mt William (1½-hour return walk), stands only 216m tall, but offers great views. The area was declared a national park in 1973, primarily to protect Tasmania's remaining Forester (eastern grey) kangaroos that were nearly wiped out by disease in the 1950s and '60s. Activities include birdwatching and wildlife-spotting, fishing, swimming, surfing and diving.

At Eddystone Point is the impressive **Eddystone Lighthouse**, built from granite blocks in the 1890s. A small picnic spot here overlooks a beach with red granite outcrops. You can also camp at **Stumpys Bay** and **Musselroe Top Camp**. The park is well off the main roads, accessible from the north or south. The northern end is 17km from Gladstone; the southern end around 60km from St Helens. Try to avoid driving here at night when animals are bounding about.

Pipers River Region

The reason to visit this region is the wonderful vineyards.

Sights & Activities

Pipers Brook WINERY
(☎03-6382 7527; www.kreglingerwineestates.com; 1216 Pipers Brook Rd; Winery Café $14-25; ⏲10am-5pm, Winery Café 10am-2pm) This is the region's most famous vineyard, where you can try Pipers Brook, Ninth Island and Krieglinger wines in an architecturally innovative building that also houses the **Winery Café**.

Jansz Wine Room WINERY
(☎03-6382 7066; www.jansztas.com; 1216b Pipers Brook Rd; ⏲10am-4.30pm) Learn all about *'méthode Tasmanoise'*, taste damn fine sparkling wine, and take in the views with a cheese platter on the lakeside terrace.

Bay of Fires Wines WINERY
(☎03-6382 7622; www.bayoffireswines.com.au; 40 Baxters Rd; ⏲10am-5pm, 11am-4pm Jun-Aug) Around 15km south of Pipers River, Bay of Fires Wines is the home of prestigious Arras Sparkling and excellent examples of riesling, pinot noir and pinot gris.

Delamere WINERY
(☎03-6382 7190; www.delamerevineyards.com.au; 4238 Bridport Rd, or B82 Hwy, Pipers Brook; ⏲10am-5pm) Superb chardonnay and pinot noir wines.

LAUNCESTON

POP 71,400

Tasmania's second-largest city is an unhurried and easygoing place, and while Hobart is more cosmopolitan, Launceston is very likeable with a remarkable stock of Victorian, Federation, Edwardian and art deco architecture.

Launceston's beginnings, however, were anything but refined. When the Reverend Horton visited in 1822, he wrote to his superiors: 'The wickedness of the people of Launceston exceeds all description. If you could witness the ignorance, blasphemy, drunkenness, adultery and vice of every description, you would use every effort to send them more missionaries.' Launceston seems to be still emerging from its colonial-outpost roots, and buffing off some rough edges along the way, but transforming itself into a glorious historic town with a glam all of its own. The University of Tasmania is here and the many excellent restaurants, galleries and cultural and sporting institutions testify to modern 'Lonnie's' more cosmopolitan outlook.

The city grid is around Brisbane St Mall, which runs between Charles and St John Sts. Flanking the old seaport are a string of trendy eateries and a hotel. West of the city is Cataract Gorge, a rugged ravine that's one of the city's major tourist drawcards. Charles St south of the CBD is the groovy, caffeinated, bohemian strip with good restaurants and cafes.

See www.visitlauncestontamar.com.au.

Sights & Activities

★**Cataract Gorge** PARK
(Map p670; www.launcestoncataractgorge.com.au; swimming pool admission free, chairlift one-way adult/child $12/8, return $15/10; ⏲9am-dusk, swimming pool Nov-Mar, chairlift 9am-dusk) A 10-minute walk west of the city is the fabulous Cataract Gorge. Surrounded by a wildlife reserve, near-vertical basalt cliffs crowd the banks of the South Esk River as it enters the Tamar. During the day, teens plunge into the river and rock-climbers defy gravity; at night the floodlit cliffs take on a shifty, shadow-strewn countenance.

Walking tracks on either side of the gorge lead from Kings Bridge up to **First Basin**, where there's a **swimming pool**, picnic grounds, a quality restaurant with resident peacocks, and trails leading to vista-packed lookouts. Both a suspension bridge and a **chairlift** sail across First Basin. A walking track (about 45 minutes one way) leads further up the gorge to **Second Basin** and the old Duck Reach power station. On hot summer days the gorge and swimming pool take on a beach-like scene.

Launceston

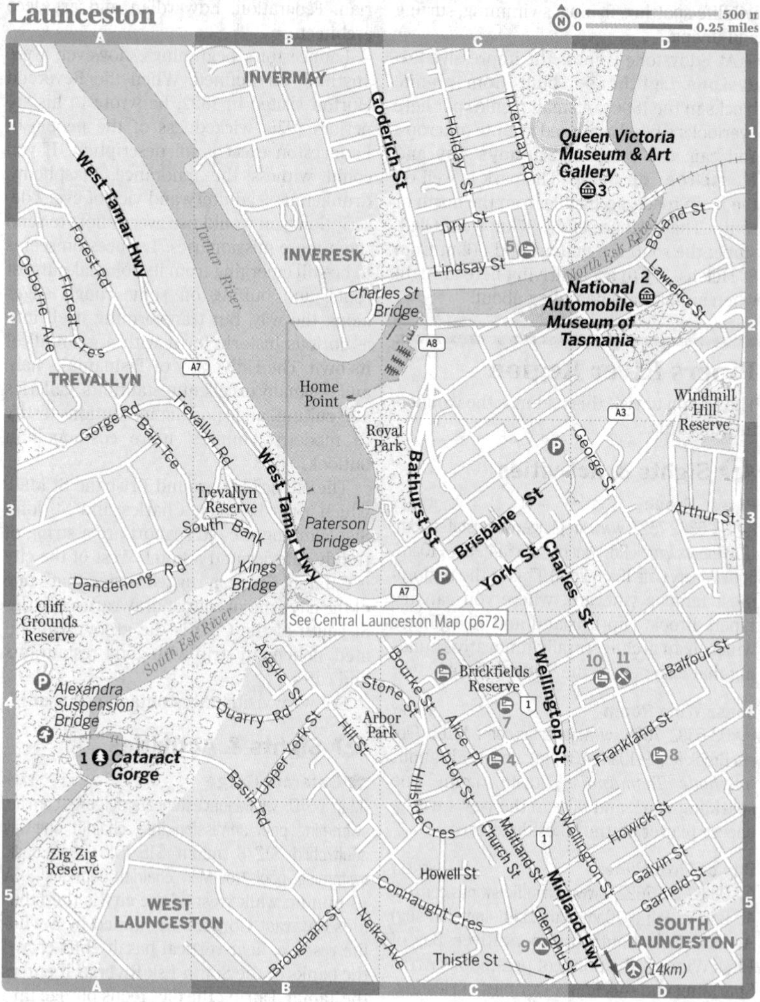

★ Queen Victoria Museum & Art Gallery MUSEUM

(Map p672; ☎03-6323 3777; www.qvmag.tas.gov.au; Planetarium adult/child $5/3; ⏲10am-5pm, Planetarium shows 2pm & 4pm Tue-Fri, 2pm & 3pm Sat) **FREE** Launceston's wonderful museum is across two sites. The stylishly renovated industrial warehouses at **Inveresk Railyards** (Map p672; 2 Invermay Rd; ⏲10am-5pm) contain natural and social history and technology-focused collections, and host touring exhibitions (entrance fee). Inveresk Railyards is also home to Launceston's **Planetarium**, which hosts a changing series of shows explaining the wonders of the universe.

The museum's 1890s **Royal Park** (Map p670; 2 Wellington St, Royal Park; ⏲10am-5pm, free guided tours 11am & 2pm Sun) building was recently renovated to reveal its original Victorian architectural glory, and the location's **QVMAG Art Gallery** now houses collections of colonial painting and decorative arts.

★ National Automobile Museum of Tasmania MUSEUM

(Map p670; www.namt.com.au; 86 Cimitiere St; adult/child $11.75/6.50; ⏲9am-5pm Sep-May,

Launceston

Top Sights
1 Cataract Gorge.......A4
2 National Automobile Museum of Tasmania.......D2
3 Queen Victoria Museum & Art Gallery.......D1

Sleeping
4 Alice's Cottages & Spa Hideaways.......C4
5 Arthouse Backpacker Hostel.......C2
6 Auldington.......C4
7 Launceston Backpackers.......C4
8 The Charles.......D4
9 Treasure Island Caravan Park.......C5
10 Two Four Two.......D4

Eating
Blue Café Bar.......(see 3)
11 Burger Got Soul.......D4
Caffe Mondello.......(see 10)

10am-4pm Jun-Aug) Petrol-heads get all revved up over the displays here, one of Australia's best presentations of classic and historic cars and motorbikes. The '69 Corvette Stingray will burn tyre tracks into your retinas.

Franklin House HISTORIC BUILDING
(www.nationaltrusttas.org.au; 413 Hobart Rd; adult/child $10/free; 9am-5pm Mon-Sat, noon-4pm Sun) Just south of the city, Franklin House is one of Launceston's most attractive Georgian homes. Built in 1838, it's now beautifully restored, furnished and managed by the National Trust. Franklin Village–bound Metro buses 40 and 50 from the city stop here.

Design Centre of Tasmania GALLERY
(Map p672; www.designcentre.com.au; cnr Brisbane & Tamar Sts; Wood Design Collection adult/child $5/free; 9.30am-5.30pm Mon-Fri, 10am-4pm Sat summer) On the fringes of City Park, the excellent **Wood Design Collection** showcases local creations in wood, with more sassafras, Huon pine and myrtle than you can shake a stick at. There's also top-notch craftwork for sale – great for classy Tassie gifts.

City Park PARK
(Map p672; www.launceston.tas.gov.au; Japanese macaques 8am-4pm Apr-Sep, to 4.30pm Oct-Mar) Wonderful, green City Park has enormous oaks and plane trees, an elegant fountain, a conservatory with changing plant displays, a Victorian bandstand and a playground and mini train for kids. A glass-walled enclosure of **Japanese macaques** was a gift from Japanese sister city Ikeda.

Tamar Island Wetlands NATURE RESERVE
(West Tamar Hwy; adult/child $3/2; 10am-4pm Apr-Sep, 9am-5pm Oct-Mar) A 10-minute drive north of the city, there's a 2km wheelchair-friendly boardwalk through this wetland reserve teeming with bird life. The island has BBQs and is perfect for picnicking, and there's an excellent interpretation centre so you can identify which avian species you're spying on.

Boag's Centre for Beer Lovers BREWERY
(Map p672; 03-6332 6300; www.boags.com.au; 39 William St; per person $30; tours 9.30am, 11.30am, 1.30pm, 3pm, 5pm, reduced in winter) Boag's beer – northern Tasmania's favourite – has been brewed on William St since 1881. Explore the brewery, and taste the beers, on a brewery tour.

Tours

Launceston City Ghost Tours WALKING
(0421 819 373; www.launcestoncityghosttours.com; adult/child $25/15; departs at dusk) Spooky 90-minute tours around the city's back alleys and lanes with theatrical guides, departing from the Royal Oak Hotel. Bookings are essential.

Launceston Historic Walks WALKING
(Map p672; 03-6336 2213; per person $15; 4pm Mon, 10am Tue-Sat) Get your historical bearings with a 1½-hour walking journey through the Georgian, Victorian and modern architecture of the city. Walks start at the 1842 Gallery on the corner of St John and Cimitere Sts. You can also book there.

Mountain Bike Tasmania MOUNTAIN BIKING
(0447 712 638; www.mountainbiketasmania.com.au) Guided rides with transport, equipment and lunch/snacks provided. Rides include a Ben Lomond Descent ($225), negotiating the Trevallyn Reserve near Launceston ($120), and a morning exploring Launceston's Riverside Trails ($100).

Tamar River Cruises RIVER CRUISES
(Map p672; 03-6334 9900; www.tamarrivercruises.com.au; Home Point Pde) Fifty-minute Cataract Gorge cruises (adult/child $25/12), plus

Central Launceston

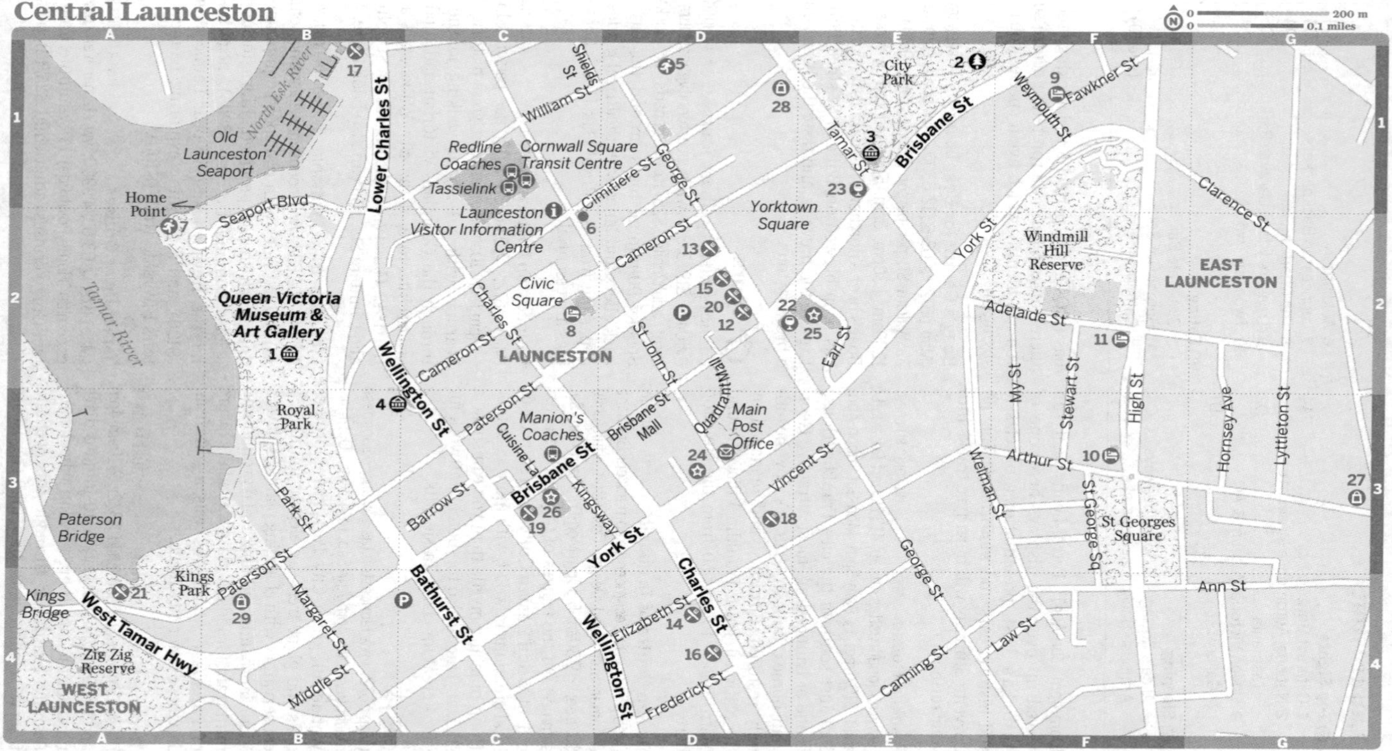

Central Launceston

Top Sights
1 Queen Victoria Museum & Art Gallery ... B2

Sights
2 City Park ... E1
3 Design Centre of Tasmania ... E1
4 QVMAG Museum ... B3

Activities, Courses & Tours
5 Boag's Centre for Beer Lovers ... D1
6 Launceston Historic Walks ... C2
7 Tamar River Cruises ... A2

Sleeping
8 Airlie on the Square ... C2
9 Areca Boutique Hotel ... F1
10 Ashton Gate ... F3
11 Kurrajong House ... F2

Eating
12 Alchemy Bar & Restaurant ... D2
13 Black Cow ... D2
14 Buddha ... D4
15 Cocobean Chocolate ... D2
16 Fresh ... D4
17 La Mezcla ... B1
18 Milkbar ... D3
19 Monty's Food Hall ... C3
20 Pierre's ... D2
21 Stillwater ... A4

Drinking & Nightlife
22 Dickens Cider House ... D2
23 Royal Oak Hotel ... E1

Entertainment
24 Hotel New York ... D3
25 Princess Theatre ... E2
26 Village Cinemas ... C3

Shopping
27 Alps & Amici ... G3
28 Harvest ... D1
Mill Providore + Gallery ... (see 21)
29 Pinot Shop ... B4

longer lunch, afternoon and dinner cruises exploring the Tamar River.

Festivals & Events

Festivale FOOD, CULTURE
(www.festivale.com.au) Three days in early to mid-February devoted to eating, drinking, arts and entertainment, staged in City Park.

Three Peaks Race SPORTS
(www.threepeaks.org.au) Over the four days of Easter, teams sail from Beauty Point (north of Launceston) to Hobart, pausing for runners to scale three mountains along the way. A detour northeast to Flinders Island always makes things really interesting.

Royal Launceston Show AGRICULTURAL SHOW
(www.launcestonshowground.com.au) Old hands display their herds at this show held in October.

Sleeping

Arthouse Backpacker Hostel HOSTEL $
(Map p670; 03-6333 0222, 1800 041 135; www.arthousehostel.com.au; 20 Lindsay St; 4-/6-/8-bed dm $27/25/23, s/d $55/65;) The Arthouse has spacious, airy dorms with a wide upstairs verandah and a BBQ-ready courtyard. Hire bikes or camping equipment. It's also set up for disabled travellers.

Launceston Backpackers HOSTEL $
(Map p670; 03-6334 2327; www.launcestonbackpackers.com.au; 103 Canning St; dm $24, tw/tr $28/25, s $52, d with/without bathroom $67/58;) This backpackers is in a leafy location overlooking Brickfields Reserve, but it's not Tassie's most inspiring hostel. Rooms are clean and airy though, and the staff are friendly and helpful.

Treasure Island Caravan Park CAMPGROUND $
(Map p670; 03-6344 2600; www.treasureisland-tasmania.com.au; 94 Glen Dhu St; unpowered sites s/d $20/20, powered $32, on-site vans $60, cabins $90-100) Just 2.5km from the city, there are camping and caravan spots here. Facilities include a kids playground, campers kitchen and laundry.

Kurrajong House B&B $$
(Map p672; 03-6331 6655; www.kurrajonghouse.com.au; cnr High & Adelaide Sts; d $145-200;) Rooms are quite sophisticated and adults-only; kids under 16 will need to stay at home. Outside there's a scented rose garden and a tranquil courtyard. Hearty cooked breakfasts are served in the conservatory.

Areca Boutique Hotel BOUTIQUE HOTEL $$
(Map p672; ☎03-6331 2082; www.arecalaunceston.com.au; 12 York St; d $125; ❄📶) The occasional Asian-tinge to the interior decor is slightly incongruous in heritage Launceston, but this excellent value new opening certainly has spic-and-span and spacious rooms, and is just a short (uphill) walk from the centre of town. A continental buffet breakfast is included.

Alice's Cottages & Spa Hideaways BOUTIQUE HOTEL $$
(Map p670; ☎03-6334 2231; www.alicescottages.com.au; 129 Balfour St; d $170-230) Alice's offers several sumptuously decorated B&B cottages, including 'Camelot' and 'The Boudoir', where it's all spas, four-post beds, open fires and self-contained privacy.

Airlie on the Square B&B $$
(Map p672; ☎03-6334 0577; www.airlielodge.com.au; Civic Sq; s $110, d $130-150; 📶) Airlie is housed in the last of the beautiful old buildings on Civic Sq – the others were demolished to make way for 1970s and '80s concrete. Wonderfully peaceful Airlie has been thoughtfully decorated and the friendly owner serves scrumptious breakfasts.

Ashton Gate B&B $$
(Map p672; ☎03-6331 6180; www.ashtongate.com.au; 32 High St; d $160-200, cottage $200; 📶) This thoroughly welcoming Victorian B&B exudes a sense of home, and each en suite room is stylishly decorated with immaculate period taste. There's also a self-contained cottage in the Old Servants Quarters.

★ **Two Four Two** APARTMENT $$$
(Map p670; ☎03-6331 9242; www.twofourtwo.com.au; 242 Charles St; d incl breakfast $220-250; 📶) Alan the furniture maker has channelled his craft into four independent townhouses, each with blackwood, myrtle or Tasmanian oak detailing. Flat-screen TVs, stainless-steel kitchens, coffee machines and spa baths complete the Lonnie luxe experience.

The Charles HOTEL $$$
(Map p670; ☎03-6337 4100; www.hotelcharles.com.au; 287 Charles St; d from $220; 📶) Launceston's hippest hotel was once a dreary hospital. It's all light and bright now with snappy decor, switched-on service and a stylish restaurant (meals $15 to $35, open breakfast, lunch and dinner). The cheaper rooms are a squeeze – pay a bit extra for a more spacious studio.

Auldington HOTEL $$$
(Map p670; ☎03-6331 2050; www.auldington.com.au; 110 Frederick St; d from $230; 📶) This small private hotel has a historic exterior complete with lacy wrought-iron balconies which belies the funky, modern fit-out inside. It's located in a quiet spot in town.

✗ Eating

Milkbar CAFE $
(Map p672; www.themilkbarcafeworkshop.blogspot.com; 139 St John St; snacks & light meals $5-10; ⏲8am-4.30pm Mon-Fri) 🍃 Effortlessly combining 1960s retro cool and 21st-century hipster chic, Milkbar does excellent coffee, huge milkshakes – the chai-flavoured one is virtually a liquid meal in itself – and home-style baking and sandwiches. Much of the menu is local and sustainable, and don't miss the shop out the back showcasing vintage-inspired crafts.

Cocobean Chocolate CAFE $
(Map p672; www.cocobeanchocolate.com.au; 82 George St; chocolate snacks $3-9.50; ⏲9am-5pm Mon-Fri, 9.30am-2pm Sat) Chocolate-themed tasting plates, ice cream and handmade cookies all feature, and the coffee and hot chocolate (of course) are also delicious. Try the white hot chocolate for something different.

Burger Got Soul BURGERS $
(Map p670; www.burgergotsoul.com; 243 Charles St; burgers $10.50-16.90; ⏲11am-9pm; 📶🖊) Best burgers in Launceston, served in a funky atmosphere. It's healthy too: good, lean meat, the freshest bread and crunchy salads. There are Soul Veggie Burgers for non meat-eaters. Free wi-fi.

Monty's Food Hall ASIAN $
(Map p672; cnr Brisbane & Wellington sts; mains $10-15; ⏲10am-9.30pm) Good value ethnic eats including Thai, Indian and Japanese.

Fresh CAFE $$
(Map p672; www.freshoncharles.com.au; 178 Charles St; mains $10-22, shared plates $35-65; ⏲8.30am-3pm Mon-Thu & Sat, 8.30-late Fri; 📶🖊) 🍃 Retro-arty Fresh offers an all-vegetarian/vegan menu that's both deliciously tempting and environmentally aware. It does energising breakfasts, linger-over lunches, and coffees and cakes in between. Pop in for dinner on a Friday night, share a few Aussie craft beers, and ask if there are any gigs coming up.

Blue Café Bar CAFE $$
(Map p670; www.bluecafebar.com.au; Inveresk Rail-yards; mains $15-30; ⊙8am-4pm Sun-Thu, 8am-late Fri-Sat) This stylish eatery serves awesome coffee and scrumptious local/organic produce to an arty, young crowd. Pop in for prosciutto and herb croquettes for breakfast, and come back for dinner (weekends only) of pork belly with spanner crab and Asian slaw. Look forward to an interesting beer and wine list, too.

Buddha THAI $$
(Map p672; ☎03-6334 1122; 168 Charles St; mains $16-20; ⊙10am-late Tue-Sun) Popular Thai restaurant with outside seating looking out onto leafy Princes Square. Dinner on Friday and Saturday nights is very popular and booking ahead is recommended.

La Mezcla SPANISH, TAPAS $$
(Map p672; ☎03-6331 0557; www.lamezcla.com.au; 31 Seaport Blvd; tapas $7, mains $18-24; ⊙11am-late Mon-Fri, 8am-late Sat-Sun) Spanish style comes to Launceston at La Mezcla with well-priced and authentic tapas served in a spacious room with a waterfront location. A good wine list and a surprising range of interesting bottled beers may see you lingering on the leather couches for longer than you planned.

Pierre's FRENCH $$
(Map p672; ☎03-6331 6835; www.pierres.net.au; 88 George St; lunch $18-25, dinner $20-35; ⊙8am-late Tue-Sat) Coolly done up in dark leather with low lighting, Pierre's offers Gallic classics like steak tartare and fries, grilled quail and confit duck. Stylish, relaxed and welcoming.

Caffe Mondello CAFE $$
(Map p670; 242 Charles St; mains $13-20; ⊙7am-4.30pm Tue-Sun) A relatively new arrival to Launceston's Charles St cafe strip, the chic Caffe Mondello serves up all-day breakfasts and lunchtime pizzas; the prawn one is particularly tasty. Nab an outdoor table and relax with one of the city's best espressos.

Alchemy Bar & Restaurant BAR, TAPAS $$
(Map p672; 90 George St; tapas $6-12, mains $15-30; ⊙11am-late) One of Lonnie's oldest pubs is now a sleek bar with thoroughly 21st-century attractions including live bands, DJs, craft beer and tapas. The sidewalk tables are perfect on a warm summer's evening, and inside lots of nooks, crannies and shared tables create a buzzing ambience. Bar food includes salt and pepper squid and mini-burgers, and $12 lunches are a good value.

★Stillwater MODERN AUSTRALIAN $$$
(Map p672; ☎03-6331 4153; www.stillwater.net.au; 2 Bridge Rd, Ritchie's Mill; breakfast $8-23, lunch $21-31, dinner $42-44; ⊙8.30am-3pm daily, 6pm-late Tue-Sat;) Set in the stylishly renovated 1840s Ritchie's Flour Mill beside the Tamar, Stillwater does laid-back breakfasts, relaxed lunches – and then puts on the Ritz for dinner. There are delectable seafood, meaty and vegetarian mains, and the emphasis is on locally sourced produce. For the full Stillwater experience, try the six-course tasting menu (with/without wine matches $125/185).

Black Cow STEAKHOUSE $$$
(Map p672; ☎03-6331 9333; www.blackcowbistro.com.au; 70 George St; dinner mains $30-43; ⊙5.30pm-late) This high-class bistro/steakhouse specialises in Tasmanian free-range, grass-fed beef. They offer six different melt-in-the-mouth cuts and is Tassie's best steakhouse. Try the tender eye fillet with Black Cow butter or the very special truffle Bernaise sauce. Book ahead.

Drinking & Entertainment

Dickens Cider House BAR
(Map p672; www.facebook.com/DickensCiderhouse; 63a Brisbane St; ⊙from 5pm Thu-Fri, from noon Sat-Sun) Crisp and refreshing apple and pear ciders are served on tap at this cosy bar combining modern decor with rustic wood panelling straight from an apple packing shed. Sampling before buying is definitely encouraged by the friendly bar staff, and Tamar Valley wines and Tasmanian beers are tasty backup options.

Royal Oak Hotel PUB
(Map p672; 14 Brisbane St; ⊙11am-late) Hands-down Launceston's best pub – grungy, friendly and convivial – with stacks of beers on tap, open mic nights and regular gigs from local and touring Aussie mainland acts. Decent pub meals and a kids' menu.

Hotel New York PUB
(Map p672; www.hotelnewyork.net.au; 122 York St; ⊙3pm-midnight Mon-Wed, 2pm-5.30am Thu-Sat) This pub hosts a steady stream of local and interstate acoustic and full-blown rock acts, plus DJs in Reality nightclub out the back (Thursday to Saturday from 11pm).

Princess Theatre THEATRE
(Map p672; ☎03-6323 3666; www.theatrenorth.com.au; 57 Brisbane St) Built in 1911 and incorporating the smaller Earl Arts Centre, the Princess stages an eclectic mix of local and mainland drama, dance and comedy acts.

Village Cinemas CINEMA
(Map p672; ☎1300 555 400; www.villagecinemas.com.au; 163 Brisbane St; tickets adult/child $16.50/12) Screens mainstream Hollywood fodder. On Tuesday all sessions cost $11.50.

Shopping

Harvest MARKET
(Map p672; www.harvestmarket.org.au; Cimitiere St carpark, opposite Albert Hall; ⊙8.30am-12.30pm Sat) Excellent weekly gathering of sustainable and organic suppliers from around northern and western Tasmania. Wine, craft beer, artisan bakers, cheese and salmon all feature, and fruit and veg are also for sale.

Alps & Amici FOOD
(Map p672; www.alpsandamici.com; cnr Abbott & Arthur Sts; ⊙7.30am-6.30pm Mon-Fri, 8am-2pm Sun) Esteemed chef Daniel Alps runs this smart providore where you can buy his restaurant-quality meals to take away, classy cakes, cheeses, meats and seafood, the freshest fruit and veg, and Tasmanian beer and wine.

Mill Providore + Gallery FOOD
(Map p672; www.millprovidore.com.au; 2 Bridge Rd; ⊙8.30am-5pm Mon-Fri, 9am-4pm Sat-Sun) Above Stillwater Restaurant in the Ritchie's Mill complex, you'll find this treasure-trove of everything for the home, kitchen, stomach and soul. There's a brilliant delicatessen and chocolatier for picnic goodies.

Pinot Shop WINE
(Map p672; www.pinotshop.com; 135 Paterson St; ⊙10am-6pm Mon-Thu, 10am-7pm Sat-Sun) This boutique bottle-o specialises in pinot noirs and fine wines – particularly of the Tasmanian variety. It also does premium international and 'big-island' vintages.

Information

Banks and ATMs are located on St John and Brisbane Sts near the mall. There are post offices on St John and Cameron Sts.

Launceston Visitor Information Centre
(Map p672; ☎1800 651 827; www.visitlauncestontamar.com.au; cnr St John & Cimitiere Sts; ⊙9am-5pm Mon-Fri, 9am-1pm Sat-Sun) Statewide accommodation, tour and transport bookings.

Getting There & Away

AIR

See p624 for details of domestic airlines flying to Hobart.

BUS

Redline Coaches (Map p672; ☎1300 360 000; www.tasredline.com.au) and **Tassielink** (Map p672; ☎1300 300 520; www.tassielink.com.au) depart Launceston from the **Cornwall Square Transit Centre** (Map p672; cnr St John & Cimitiere Sts), just behind the visitor information centre. **Manion's Coaches** (Map p672; ☎03-6383 1221; www.manionscoaches.com.au; 168 Brisbane St) has services that run from Launceston up the West Tamar Valley.

Redline: Main fares and routes:

JOURNEY	PRICE ($)	DURATION (HR)
Launceston–Burnie	38	2¼
Launceston–Deloraine	14	¾
Launceston–Devonport	24	1½
Launceston–George Town	12	¾
Launceston–Hobart	40	2½
Launceston–Stanley	58	4

Tassielink: Main fares and routes:

JOURNEY	PRICE ($)	DURATION (HR)
Launceston–Bicheno (links with Calow's)	34	2½
Launceston–Cradle Mountain	59	3
Launceston–Devonport (meeting ferries)	24	1¼
Launceston–Hobart	34	2½
Launceston–Queenstown	72	6
Launceston–Sheffield	30	2
Launceston–Strahan	82	8¾

Getting Around

TO/FROM THE AIRPORT

Launceston Airport is 15km south of town. **The Airporter** (03-6343 6677; adult/child $15/8) is a door-to-door airport shuttle bus. A taxi to/from the city costs about $45.

BICYCLE

Arthouse Backpacker Hostel (p673) rents out bikes.

BUS

Metro (13 22 01; www.metrotas.com.au) has a Day Rover pass ($5) for unlimited travel after 9am. Buses depart from the two blocks of St John St between Paterson and York Sts. Many routes don't operate in the evening or on Sunday.

There's also a free Tiger Bus that links Inveresk to Princes Park and Windmill Hill Monday to Friday between 10am and 3.30pm.

CAR

The big-name rental companies have either Launceston Airport or city offices. Smaller operators have cars from around $40 per day: **Lo-Cost Auto Rent** (1300 883 739; www.rentforless.com.au; 80 Tamar St)

AROUND LAUNCESTON

Tamar Valley

The broad Tamar River flows north 64km from Launceston and empties into Bass Strait. Along its flanks are orchards, forests, pastures and vineyards.

The **Tamar Visitor Information Centre** (1800 637 989, 03-6394 4454; www.tamarvalley.com.au; Main Rd, Exeter; 8.30am-5pm) is in Exeter in the West Tamar Valley.

This is Tasmania's key wine-producing area, and the premium wines created here have achieved international recognition. See **Tamar Valley Wine Route** (www.tamarvalleywines.com.au) for touring information.

Getting There & Around

For cyclists, the ride north along the Tamar River is a gem.

On weekdays **Manion's Coaches** (03-6383 1221; www.manionscoaches.com.au; 72 Shaw St, Beaconsfield) services the West Tamar Valley from Launceston.

Lees Coaches (03-6334 7979; www.leescoaches.com) services the East Tamar Valley from Launceston's Cornwall Square Transit Centre.

Rosevears

POP 270

This pretty little riverside hamlet is on a side road off the West Tamar Hwy. With some super wineries in the area, this is wine-buff heaven.

Call into **Ninth Island Vineyard Strathlynn** (www.kreglingerwineestates.com; 95 Rosevears Dr; cellar door 10am-5pm), an outlet for Pipers Brook Vineyard. Back on the main road, follow the signs for wine tasting at **Rosevears Estate** (03-6330 1800; www.rosevears.com.au; 1a Waldhorn Dr; cellar door 10am-5pm), where there is also plush self-contained accommodation (1- & 2-bedroom cottages $150-250).

Built in 1831 **Rosevears Waterfront Tavern** (www.rosevearstavern.com.au; 215 Rosevears Dr; mains $20-25; lunch & dinner) offers pub-grub favourites including chicken parmigiana, and more sophisticated fare including pork belly and marinated roasted quail. The river views are superb, the beer terrace lovely, and the bas-relief murals bizarre. Pizzas ($18-23) range from Tuscan to Mexican, and there's live music most Sunday afternoons from around 2.30pm.

Beauty Point & Around

POP 1500

At Beauty Point is the coo-inducing **Seahorse World** (03-6383 4111; www.seahorseworld.com.au; Inspection Head Wharf; adult/child $20/9; 9.30am-4.30pm Sep-Apr, 10am-3pm May-Aug), where the cute sea horses are hatched and raised to supply aquariums worldwide. Next door is **Platypus House** (03-6383 4884; www.platypushouse.com.au; Inspection Head Wharf; adult/child $20/9; 9.30am-3.30pm), a wildlife centre with platypuses and echidnas.

South of Beauty Point is **Beaconsfield**, the gold-mining town that made world news after a mine collapse and rescue in April 2006. The **Beaconsfield Mine & Heritage Museum** (www.beaconsfieldheritage.com.au; West St; adult/child $11/4; 9.30am-4.30pm) details mining history through interactive exhibits.

Visit all of the above attractions with a **Triple Pass** (adult/family $43/115) from the Tamar visitor information centre (p677) in Exeter.

Around Launceston

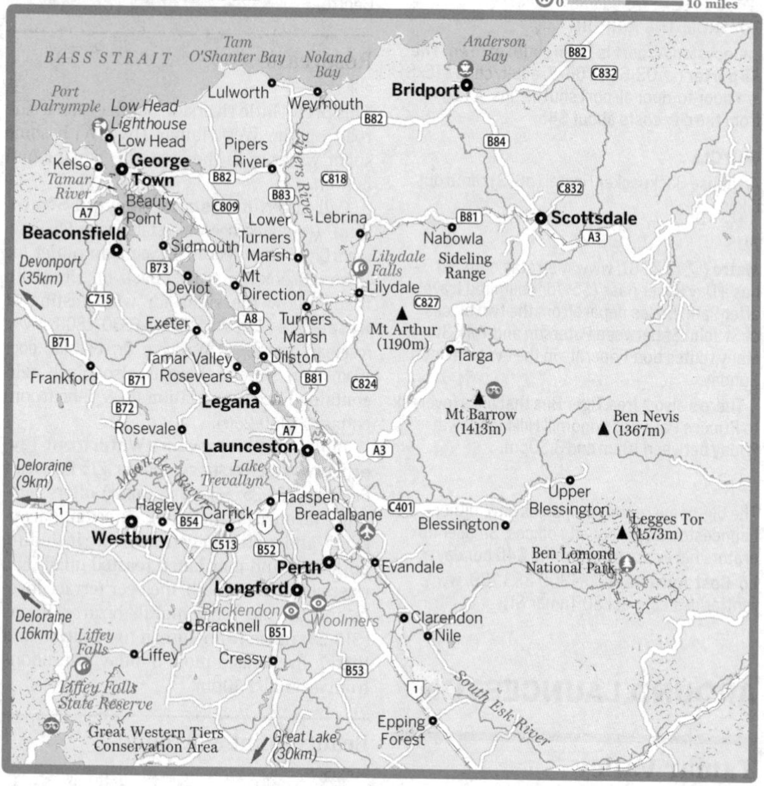

Beauty Point Tourist Park CAMPGROUND $
(☎03-6383 4536; www.beautypointtouristpark.com.au; 36 West Arm Rd, Beauty Point; powered sites $30, on-site vans d $99, cabins $99-149; 📶) Sheltered camping on the waterfront and a range of vans and cabins.

Tamar Cove MOTEL $$
(☎03-6383 4375; www.tamarcove.com; 4421 Main Rd, Beauty Point; d $119-139, mains $15-30; 📶🏊) Tamar Cove has a stylish motel and terrific restaurant. Try the renowned seafood chowder or the local scallops. Lunches start at $12 if you're out and about exploring the Tamar Valley and find yourself in need of a good value meal.

George Town

POP 4270

Historic George Town, on the eastern lip of the Tamar River mouth, is Australia's third-oldest settlement (after Sydney and Hobart). George Town was established in 1804 by Lieutenant Colonel Paterson to guard against the French who were reconnoitring the area. Sadly, little remains of the original township (now defined by an aluminium smelter). The **visitor information centre** (☎03-6382 1700; www.provincialtamar.com.au; Main Rd; ⏲9am-5pm) rents bicycles to explore George Town and nearby Low Head.

Ask about Heritage Trail maps taking in the town's two centuries of history, including the **Bass & Flinders Centre** (8 Elizabeth St; adult/child/family $10/4/24), an excellent local museum with a replica of the *Norfolk*, the compact craft that Bass and Flinders used for their 1897 circumnavigation of Van Diemen's Land.

Pier Hotel HOTEL $$
(☎03-6382 1300; www.pierhotel.com.au; 5 Elizabeth St; d $160-230, bistro mains $20-33; 📶) The Pier Hotel offers self-contained villas (sleeping four), spotless motel rooms and a beery

bistro with outdoor riverfront seating and a decent menu.

Low Head

POP 465

Low Head, sitting on a sandy spit, is north of George Town and virtually contiguous with it. It's much more attractive than George Town – a beachy holiday town centred on the **Low Head Historic Precinct**.

Helping ships navigate into the Tamar, **Low Head Pilot Station** is Australia's oldest (1805) and houses an interesting **maritime museum** (☎03-6382 2826; Low Head Rd; adult/child $5/3; ⊙10am-4pm) cluttered with historical items and displays. There's also heritage accommodation here in the 1860s **Pilot's Row** (☎03-6382 2826; bookings@lowheadpilotstation.com; Low Head Rd; d from $150-230) with nine separate colonial cottages available for rent.

On Low Head itself, the view from the 1888 **lighthouse** is a winner. Penguins return to their burrows here every night, and can be viewed with **Low Head Penguin Tours** (☎0418 361 860; http://penguintours.lowhead.com; adult/child $18/10; ⊙dusk). There's good surf at **East Beach** on Bass Strait, and safe swimming in the river.

Low Head Tourist Park CAMPGROUND **$**
(☎03-6382 1573; www.lowheadtouristpark.com.au; 136 Low Head Rd; unpowered/powered sites $18/32, dm $25, cabins $96-100, cottages $120-130) Comfortable timber-lined cabins as well as caravan and camping spots – river and water views included.

Longford & Around

Longford (population 3030), a National Trust-classified town 27km south of Launceston, hosted the 1965 Australian Grand Prix. You wouldn't think it now – the cars are gone – but the area is noted for its historic estates.

Unesco World Heritage-listed **Woolmers** (☎03-6391 2230; www.woolmers.com.au; Woolmers Lane, Longford; admission $14/5, tours adult/child/family from $20/7/45; ⊙10am-4pm, tours 11.15am, 12.30pm & 2pm) was built in 1819 and features a 2-hectare rose garden and buildings full of antiques.

Nearby is **Brickendon** (☎03-6391 1383; www.brickendon.com.au; Woolmers Lane, Longford; adult/child $12/4.50, cottages d $130-190; ⊙9.30am-5pm Oct-May, to 4pm Jun-Sep), a more modest estate dating from 1824, with heritage gardens and a still-functioning farm village. Both Woolmers and Brickendon offer self-contained accommodation in restored colonial-era cottages.

Around 10km west of Longford is the gorgeous **Liffey Valley**. It's well worth a short detour to explore the **Liffey Falls State Reserve**.

Grand, government-owned 1819 **Entally Estate** (www.entally.com.au; Old Bass Hwy, Hadspen; adult/child $10/8; ⊙10am-4pm), set in beautiful grounds, is the highlight of **Hadspen**, 15km north of Longford.

Sleeping & Eating

Racecourse Inn INN **$$**
(☎03-6391 2352; www.racecourseinn.com; 114 Marlborough St; s $140-170, d $160-200; 📶) A welcoming restored Georgian inn with antique-decorated rooms, and guests can dine in the restaurant.

Red Feather Inn BOUTIQUE HOTEL **$$$**
(☎03-6393 6506; www.redfeatherinn.com.au; 42 Main St; d incl breakfast $250-350) One of Tasmania's best boutique hotels. You can eat dinner here if you stay (three courses, $85 per person). Private classes can be arranged on request in the on-site cooking school, or you can join one of their regular courses.

JJ's Bakery & Old Mill Café CAFE **$$**
(52 Wellington St; mains $12-20; ⊙7am-5.30pm Mon-Fri, to 5pm Sat & Sun) In the Old Emerald flour mill, this place turns out pizzas and splendid baked goods.

Evandale

POP 1060

Of all Tasmania's historic towns, immaculately preserved Evandale is one of the best. It's around 20km south of Launceston in the South Esk Valley. The **Evandale Market** (www.evandaletasmania.com; ⊙8am-1.30pm) happens every Sunday, and the **visitor information centre** (☎03-6391 8128; www.evandaletasmania.com; 18 High St; ⊙9am-5pm Oct-Apr, 10am-4pm May-Sep) has brochures on walking tours to explore the town's architectural heritage.

The highlight of the annual **Evandale Village Fair & National Penny Farthing Championships** (www.evandalevillagefair.com; adult/child $7/free; ⊙Feb) is the Penny Farthing races, cheered on by townsfolk in historic dress.

Around 11km south of Evandale, is the National Trust-listed **Clarendon Homestead** (☎03-6398 6220; www.nationaltrusttas.org.au; 234 Clarendon Station Rd; adult/child $10/free; ⏰10am-4pm Sep-Jun), a grand neoclassical mansion (1838) surrounded by impressive parklands.

Sleeping & Eating

Wesleyan Chapel RENTAL HOUSE $$
(☎03-6331 9337; www.windmillhilllodge.com.au; 28 Russell St; d incl breakfast $130-140) Built in 1836, tiny Wesleyan has a chequered past but is now stylish accommodation for two.

Ingleside Bakery Café CAFE $$
(4 Russell St; mains $10-19; ⏰8.30am-5pm) Serves all-day breakfasts and light lunches amid local art and antiques. There's also an excellent providore with lots of rustic country-style produce, Tasmanian wines, and beer from Evandale's very own Van Dieman Brewing.

Ben Lomond National Park

Tassie's most reliable snow sports centre is this 165-sq-km **park** (www.parks.tas.gov.au), 55km southeast of Launceston. Bushwalkers traipse through when the snow melts, swooning over alpine wildflowers during spring and summer.

See www.skibenlomond.com.au; national park fees apply.

Sleeping & Eating

Creek Inn PUB $$
(☎03-6390 6199; d winter $200) Stay at Tasmania's highest-altitude pub during the ski season. There's a fully licensed restaurant and, during ski season (July to September), a kiosk and ski shop. Lift tickets cost adult/child $55/230 per day; ski hire (including lift ticket and a ski lesson) is adult/child $120/85.

Getting There & Away

During the ski season, Tasmanian Expeditions run a bus ($45 return) up to the ski fields from Launceston. The bus leaves at 8am outside the Launceston Visitor Information Centre (p676), and can also be picked up at the base of the mountain ($15 return). Pre-book for Launceston departures only on 1300 666 856.

Outside the ski season, driving is your only option. The route up to the alpine village includes Jacob's Ladder, a ludicrously steep ascent on an unsealed hairpin-bend road – fit snow chains on tyres in winter.

THE NORTH

Tasmania's North is a region of populated seaside towns and the vast open reaches and hillside communities of the Great Western Tiers. Much of this area is extensively cultivated – rust-coloured, iron-rich soils and verdant pastures extend north and west of Launceston – but there are also important stands of forest, glacial valleys, dolerite peaks and mighty rivers. Get off the main highway and explore the quiet minor roads and towns.

Getting There & Around

Redline Coaches (☎1300 360 000; www.tasredline.com.au) has several northern services daily.

JOURNEY	PRICE ($)	DURATION (HR)
Launceston–Burnie	38	2¾
Launceston–Deloraine	14	¾
Launceston–Devonport	24	1½
Launceston–Penguin	35	2¼
Launceston–Ulverstone	30	2

Tassielink (☎1300 300 520; www.tassielink.com.au) runs the daily Main Road Express to meet the Bass Strait ferry. The early morning express bus runs from Devonport to Launceston and Hobart. The bus returns in the opposite direction in the afternoon to meet evening boat departures. Typical one-way fares are:

JOURNEY	PRICE ($)	DURATION (HR)
Devonport–Cradle Mountain	41	1½
Devonport–Hobart	57	4¼
Devonport–Launceston	24	1¼
Devonport–Sheffield	5	½
Devonport–Strahan	64	7¼

Devonport

POP 24,300

Tasmania's third-largest city, Devonport is less interesting than Hobart and Launceston, but a couple of recently opened cafes and restaurants have added a more cosmopolitan sheen. The *Spirit of Tasmania* Bass Strait ferry arrives from Melbourne every morning (and evening in summer).

Sights & Activities

Mersey Bluff LANDMARK

Lighthouse-topped Mersey Bluff is the most striking feature of Devonport. The red-and-white-striped lighthouse was built in 1889 to aid navigation into the expanding port, which still handles agricultural produce from northern Tasmania.

Tiagarra MUSEUM

(03-6426 1004; michelle@sixriverscorporation.com.au; Bluff Rd; adult/child $10/5) The absorbing displays here tell the story of Aboriginal culture in Tasmania from the time humans first crossed over the land bridge that's now under Bass Strait. There's a soberingly frank assessment of the decimation of Aboriginal society and culture at the time of European invasion. Opening hours vary, so interested travellers are requsted to contact the Six Rivers Aboriginal Corporation before visiting.

House of Anvers CHOCOLATE FACTORY

(www.anvers-chocolate.com.au; 9025 Bass Hwy; 7am-7pm) House of Anvers is both a chocolate factory and a museum of chocolate. Look forward to fudges, truffles and amazing chocolate-orange slices. Come for a *pain au chocolat* (croissant filled with chocolate) washed down with a superb hot chocolate. It's 8km southeast of town on the Bass Hwy.

Bass Strait Maritime Centre MUSEUM

(6 Gloucester Ave; adult/child $5/2; 10am-4.30pm Oct-Mar, closes 4pm Apr-Sep) This museum is in the former harbour-master's residence (c 1920) and pilot station near the Devonport foreshore. The centre reopened in early 2013 with pride of place going to the *Julie Burgess*, a restored ketch that saw plenty of action on Bass Strait. Other exhibits include model boats across the years, and an interpretive centre and viewing platform complete an interesting attraction.

Don River Railway MUSEUM

(www.donriverrailway.com.au; Forth Main Rd; adult/child/family $17/12/38; 9am-5pm) This railway is 4km west of town, just off the Bass Hwy. The entry price includes a half-hour ride in a diesel train (between 10am and 4pm), and you can hop on the puffing steam train on Sundays and public holidays.

Devonport Regional Gallery GALLERY

(www.devonportgallery.com; 45-47 Stewart St; 10am-5pm Mon-Fri, noon-5pm Sat, 1-5pm Sun) This excellent gallery houses predominantly 20th-century Tasmanian paintings, contemporary art by local and mainland artists, plus ceramics and glasswork.

Murray's Day Out DRIVING TOUR

(03-6424 5250; www.murraysdayout.com.au; day trips per person from $150) Proud and passionate Tasmanian Murray offers 'service with humour' in his comfortable van (seating up to seven). Go all the way west to Marrawah, drop in on Cradle Mountain or just tool around the back lanes near Devonport.

Sleeping

Mersey Bluff Caravan Park CAMPGROUND $

(03-6424 8655; www.merseybluff.com.au; 41 Bluff Rd; unpowered/powered sites d $12/32, on-site vans d $65-90) In a seaside setting on Mersey Bluff, this pleasantly treed park is just steps from the beach. There's a campers kitchen and BBQ facilities.

Tasman Backpackers HOSTEL $

(03-6423 2335; www.tasmanbackpackers.com.au; 114 Tasman St; dm $20-25, tw/d $50/52;) This hostel was once a sprawling nurses quarters but it's now a friendly place to stay with an international feel. It offers free ferry/bus station pick-ups, and can arrange fruit-picking jobs.

Barclay Motor Inn MOTEL $$

(03-6424 4722; www.barclaymotorinn.com.au; 112 North Fenton St; d $140-180;) This may not be your most architecturally rewarding stay in Tasmania but the welcome is friendly and the well-priced rooms are spic-and-span. Amenities include a swimming pool and tennis court.

Eating

★**Laneway** CAFE $$

(www.lane-way.com.au; 2/38 Steele St; mains $10-20; 7.30am-4pm) Filling a former bakery, we reckon Laneway is one of Tassie's best cafes. Hip waitstaff deliver robust brekkies including smashed avocado with poached eggs and pancetta, and the sunny heritage space also functions as a deli showcasing local beer, wine and artisan produce. Evening events with special dinner menus are sometimes scheduled, so pop by to see what's on.

Drift MODERN AUSTRALIAN **$$**
(www.drift.au.com; 41 Bluff Rd; tapas $10-16, mains $24-30; ⌚10am-late) Devonport's most bustling restaurant is in the modern building housing the Devonport Surf Club. Order a burger ($8 to $16) from the casual, alfresco window, or sample interesting tapas and bigger meals inside the stylish interior. Menu highlights include salt and pepper octopus and duck tacos, and there's a big focus on organic, free range and local.

Tapas Lounge Bar BAR, CAFE **$$**
(www.tapasloungebar.com; 97a Rooke St Mall; tapas $9.50-12.50, mains $17-22; ⌚4pm-late Wed-Sun, food from 6.30pm) Upstairs in the Rooke St Mall and decked out in black leather, this place has funky music, and the tapas-style menu also has shared platters ($30 to $60) and options for kids. After 9pm it morphs into a bar with live music from Thursday to Sunday.

The Wagyu Pie Company CAFE **$$**
(www.wagyupiecompany.com.au; 11 Oldaker St; snacks & light meals $10-18; ⌚7am-4pm Sun-Thu, 7am-9pm Fri-Sat) Decent range of pies, pizza and sandwiches, and bigger meals ($17 to $26) on Friday and Saturday nights.

Drinking & Entertainment

Central at the Formby BAR
(82 Formby Rd; ⌚2pm-late) Devonport's best bar is all bohemian chic with leather sofas and laid-back cool, and they fold the concertina windows open onto the river on warm nights. There are live bands Friday and Saturday; Sunday afternoons see acoustic sessions and a more sophisticated crowd.

Information

Devonport Visitor Information Centre (☎03-6424 4466, 1800 649 514; www.devonporttasmania.travel; 92 Formby Rd; ⌚7.30am-5pm) Across the river from the ferry terminal, it opens to meet ferry arrivals. Free baggage storage is available.

Online Access Centre (21 Oldaker St; ⌚9.30am-5.30pm Mon-Thu, 9.30am-7pm Fri, 9.30am-1.30pm Sat, 11am-5pm Sun) Internet access at the library.

Getting There & Away

AIR

QantasLink (☎13 13 13; www.qantas.com.au) Regular flights to Melbourne.

BOAT

Spirit of Tasmania (☎1800 634 906; www.spiritoftasmania.com.au; ⌚Customer Contact Centre 8am-8.30pm Mon-Sat, 9am-8pm Sun) Ferries sail between Station Pier in Melbourne and the ferry terminal on the Esplanade in East Devonport.

BUS

Redline Coaches (☎1300 360 000; www.tasredline.com.au) and **Tassielink** (☎1300 300 520; www.tassielink.com.au) run services between Launceston and Devonport. Tassielink also runs from Devonport to Cradle Mountain, continuing to the west coast (Zeehan, Strahan, Queenstown etc).

The Redline Coaches stop at Edward St and the ferry terminal. Tassielink coaches stop outside the Devonport Visitor Information Centre and the ferry terminal.

Getting Around

Devonport Airport is 5km east of town. A **shuttle bus** (☎1300 659 878; per person $15) runs between the airport and ferry terminals, the visitor information centre and city accommodation; bookings are essential. A **taxi** (☎03-6424 1431) to/from the airport costs about $25.

A cross-Mersey ferry operates between a pontoon near the post office and the *Spirit of Tasmania* terminal. It runs on demand from 7.30am to 6pm Monday to Saturday ($2.50 one-way).

For car rental:

Europcar (☎03-6427 0888; www.europcar.com.au) Located at the ferry terminal.

Thrifty (☎1800 030 730, 03-6427 9119; www.thrifty.com.au) Services at the ferry terminal.

Deloraine

POP 2240

Deloraine, at the foot of the Great Western Tiers, is an artsy rural town of fine Georgian and Victorian buildings set on the tumbling hills around the handsome Meander River. Public sculptures and huge European trees are a feature of the main street, as are Deloraine's groovy eateries, galleries and interesting bric-a-brac stores. The annual four-day **Tasmanian Craft Fair** (www.tascraftfair.com.au; ⌚late Oct-early Nov) sees visitors book out accommodation from Launceston to Devonport for the festivities.

Great Western Tiers visitor information centre (☎03-6362 5280; www.greatwesterntiers.net.au; 98 Emu Bay Rd; ⏲9am-5pm) handles accommodation bookings, and advises on many excellent walks in the area. Mountain bikes are also available to rent (per hour/day/week $10/25/140), and the centre can provide a map detailing four wonderful rides of one- to two-days in the surrounding area. Pre-departure, check out the Great Western Tiers website for maps and podcasts outlining each of the rides.

Sights & Activities

Deloraine Folk Museum & YARNS: Artwork in Silk MUSEUM
(98 Emu Bay Rd; adult/child $8/2; ⏲9.30am-4pm) The museum's centrepiece is an exquisite four-panel, quilted and appliquéd depiction of the Meander Valley through a year of seasonal change. Each of the four panels entailed 2500 hours of labour and the whole project took three years to complete. It's now housed in a purpose-built auditorium, where you can witness a fascinating presentation explaining the work. A recent addition is an exhibition on Deloraine's time as a probation station from 1843 to 1847.

41° South Aquaculture SALMON FARM
(www.41southtasmania.com; 323 Montana Rd; snacks & light meals $8-12; ⏲9am-4pm) Stop by for smoked salmon, which you can taste (free) and buy in the tasting room, or try the signature salmon burger in the attached cafe. Self-guided tours of the interesting operation cost adult/child/family $10/7/25. Ginseng- and honey-infused products are also available. It's 6km out of town towards Mole Creek (signed down Montana Rd).

Ashgrove Farm Cheese CHEESE FACTORY
(www.ashgrovecheese.com.au; 6173 Bass Hwy; ⏲7.30am-6pm Oct-Apr, 7.30am-5pm May-Sep) Journey 15km north of Deloraine to find this award-winning cheese factory. You can watch the cheeses being made and then sample the fine results in their tasting room/providore.

Sleeping & Eating

Deloraine Apex Caravan Park CAMPGROUND $
(☎03-6362 2345; West Pde; unpowered/powered sites d $25/30) This simple camp spot is at the bottom of the main street by the Meander River. Don't be alarmed if an almighty thundering disturbs your slumber here: the train tracks are adjacent.

Bluestone Grainstore B&B $$
(☎03-63624722;www.bluestonegrainstore.com.au; 14 Parsonage St; d $155-170;) A 150-year-old warehouse has been renovated with great style here: think whitewashed stone walls, crisp linen, leather bedheads and deep oval bathtubs. There's even a mini movie theatre and films to choose from. Breakfasts showcase organic local produce.

Tierview Twin Cottages COTTAGE $$
(☎03-6362 2377; 125 Emu Bay Rd; cottage d $120-140) Just off the main street, these cottages offer comfortable independent accommodation. One has an open fire, the other a spa bathroom.

Deloraine Deli DELI, CAFE $$
(36 Emu Bay Rd; mains $10-20; ⏲8.30am-5pm Mon-Sat) A fine place for late-morning baguettes, bagels and focaccia, with a variety of tasty fillings. Its coffee is pungently superb, and it does dairy- and gluten-free meals, too.

Restaurant Red ITALIAN $$$
(☎03-6362 3669; 81 Emu Bay Rd; mains $25-38, pizza $18-32; ⏲noon-10pm) Set in the 1886 Bank of Australia building, this place looks classy, smells amazing, and the food tastes sublime. It's fantastic Italian-inspired fare: from wood-fired pizza to saltimbocca and veal scallopini, with a well-chosen wine list to match.

Mole Creek

POP 220

Mole Creek, about 25km west of Deloraine, is an unflattering name for this tiny creek-plains town at the feet of the towering cracks of the Great Western Tiers. The environs are packed with attractions (it's a favourite area for cavers and bushwalkers) and the town makes a great base for exploring the Great Western Tiers and the national parks of the Walls of Jerusalem and Cradle Mountain (the B12 road through Mole Creek is an interesting alternative route to Cradle Mountain).

For more information see www.molecreek.info.

Sights & Activities

Mole Creek Karst National Park NATURE RESERVE
(www.parks.tas.gov.au) Around Mole Creek (once overrun with thylacines) are limestone

caves in the leatherwood honey apiaries and this fantastic wildlife park.

Marakoopa Cave CAVE
A wet cave 15km from Mole Creek, Marakoopa features underground streams and glow-worms. **King Solomons Cave**, a dry cave with light-reflecting calcite crystals, has fewer steps. Each cave costs $19/9.50 per adult/child; tour times are displayed on access roads, or call the **Mole Creek Caves Ticket Office** (☎03-6363 5182; www.molecreek.info; 330 Mayberry Rd, Mayberry). Wear warm clothes – cave temperatures average 9°C.

R Stephens HONEY FACTORY
(www.leatherwoodhoney.com.au; 25 Pioneer Dr; 9am-4pm Mon-Fri Jan-Apr) The leatherwood tree only grows in damp, western Tasmania, and honey from its flowers is delicious. Tasmanian kids grow up studying the weird bee on the honey labels from the R Stephens honey factory. Factory tours are not available, but you can still taste and purchase the sticky stuff.

Trowunna Wildlife Park WILDLIFE RESERVE
(www.trowunna.com.au; adult/child/family $20/10/50; 9am-5pm, guided tours 11am, 1pm, 3pm) About 5km east of Mole Creek on the B12 road is this first-rate park, specialising in Tasmanian devils and wombats.

Honey Farm FARM
(www.thehoneyfarm.com.au; 39 Sorell St; 9am-5pm Sun-Fri) At nearby Chudleigh there's a honey farm and shop with free honey tastings and an interactive beehive. Honey-infused cosmetics and skincare products are for sale, and the many different honey-flavoured ice creams are also worth a stop.

Devils Gullet LANDMARK
The gravel Lake Mackenzie road ascends into the alpine reaches of the Western Tiers plateau – take warm clothes year-round and watch for sudden weather changes. Follow this road to Devils Gullet, where there's about a 40-minute return walk leading to a heart-in-mouth platform bolted to the top of a dramatic gorge.

Wild Cave Tours CAVE TOURS
(☎03-6367 8142; www.wildcavetours.com; 165 Fernlea Rd) Offers half-/full-day adventures in the area's other caves for $95/190, including caving gear.

Sleeping & Eating

Mole Creek Caravan Park CAMPGROUND $
(☎03-6363 1150; www.molecreek.net.au; cnr Mole Creek & Union Bridge Rds; unpowered/powered sites $20/25, cabins $75;) This is a thin sliver of a park about 4km west of town beside Sassafras Stream, at the turn-off to the caves and Cradle Mountain.

Mole Creek Hotel HOTEL, PUB $
(☎03-6363 1102; www.molecreekhotel.com; Main Rd; s/d $55/90) A classic small-town pub with bright upstairs rooms. The Tiger Bar (mains $17 to $28) is a thylacine shrine wallpapered with old newspaper clippings and serves hearty pub standards. Try the Tassie Tiger Dark Ale, brewed especially for the pub.

★**Mole Creek Guest House & Cafe** B&B $$
(☎03-6363 1399; www.molecreekgh.com.au; 100 Pioneer Dr; s $115-145, d $130-175; @) There are beautifully renovated and spacious rooms here, including a cosy private cinema packed with good DVDs. Downstairs the restaurant serves everything from hearty breakfasts and lunches ($13 to $18), to steak or grilled ocean salmon for dinner (mains $16 to $32). A few interesting vegetarian options punctuate the menu, and the property's beautiful gardens include a meandering creek complete with platypuses.

Walls of Jerusalem National Park

This isolated Central Plateau **national park** (www.parks.tas.gov.au), part of the Tasmanian Wilderness World Heritage Area, features glacial lakes and valleys, alpine flora and the rugged dolerite Mt Jerusalem (1459m). It's a favourite of experienced bushwalkers with a lust for challenging, remote hiking. The most popular walk here is the full-day trek to the 'Walls'; you can also camp in the park. National park fees apply.

For a guided walk, Tasmanian Expeditions (p624) operates a six-day Walls trip for $1545.

Access to the Walls is from Sheffield or Mole Creek. From Mole Creek take the B12 west, the C138 south then the C171 (Mersey Forest Rd) to Lake Rowallan; remain on this road, following the C171 and/or Walls of Jerusalem signs to the start of the track. Pick up the *Walls of Jerusalem Map* ($10.50) from Mole Creek Caves Ticket Office.

Sheffield & Around

POP 1030

Sheffield was settled in 1859, but by the 1980s it was a failing rural town. Then some bright spark suggested they paint large murals on Sheffield's public walls to attract tourists, and the town's fortunes began to change. These days there are more than 50 murals and Sheffield has its own annual painting festival, **Muralfest** (www.muralfest.com.au; late Mar-early Apr).

The **Kentish visitor information centre** (03-6491 1036; www.sheffieldcradleinfo.com.au; 5 Pioneer Cres; 9am-5pm) has mural maps and audio tours, and regional information.

The scenery around Sheffield is lovely with hulking **Mt Roland** (1234m) rising above farmlands, forests and fish-filled rivers. Nearby is deep **Lake Barrington**, an international rowing venue.

Tasmazia (www.tasmazia.com.au; 500 Staverton Rd; adult/child $20/10; 10am-4pm Apr-Nov, 9am-5pm Dec-Mar), at the Lake Barrington turn-off, combines leafy mazes, the cheesy-as-hell Lower Crackpot model village, a lavender patch and pancake parlour.

Sleeping & Eating

Sheffield Cabins CABIN $
(03-6491 2176; www.sheffieldcabins.com.au; 1 Pioneer Cres; d $100-105, extra adult/child $15/10) These simple clean, self-contained cabins are close to the visitor centre and are excellent value.

Glencoe Rural Retreat B&B $$
(03-6492 3267; www.glencoeruralretreat.com.au; 1468 Sheffield Rd; d $175;) Just north of Sheffield at Barrington, this property is owned by celebrated French chef Remi Bancal. Stay in the romantic rooms (no kids under 12) and enjoy a three-course dinner ($65) – available by prior arrangement. There's also a cafe open to the public (mains $25, open for lunch Wednesday to Friday and Sunday) offering French-Creole cooking.

Skwiz Café Gallery CAFE $
(www.fridaynitemusic.org; 63 Main St; mains $8-15; 8am-4pm) This friendly, arty cafe has Sheffield's best coffee. With its retro decor and funky music, it's a great place to hang out, have a slap-up breakfast, lazy lunch, or coffees and cakes in between. Look forward to live blues and roots music on Friday nights.

King Island

A skinny sliver of land 64km long and 27km wide, population 1700, King Island (or KI as locals call it) is a laid-back place where everyone knows everyone. The island's green pastures famously produce a rich dairy bounty, and its surrounding seas supply fabulously fresh seafood. Locals dry kelp to extract its goodies and tend lighthouses, four of which guard the rocky coastline. King Island also has consistently good surf. At the time of writing, the island's residents were considering a proposal to construct a $2 billion wind farm comprising 200 turbines, a significant investment for the remote island.

Sights

King Island Dairy DAIRY
(03-6462 0947; www.kidairy.com.au; North Rd; noon-4pm Sun-Fri) King Island Dairy's Fromagerie is 8km north of Currie (just beyond the airport). Taste their award-winning bries, cheddars and feisty blues and then stock up in their shop.

Lighthouses & Shipwrecks HISTORIC SITES
Drive right up to the tallest lighthouse in the southern hemisphere at **Cape Wickham**. This 48m tower was built in 1861 after several ships had been wrecked on the island's treacherous coastline. The **Currie Lighthouse** (0439 705 610; adult/child $15/7.50; tours 3.30pm Wed & Sat) was built in 1880, and there are more lighthouses at **Stokes Point** and **Naracoopa**. For information on lightkeeping and shipwrecks visit the **King Island Museum** (Lighthouse St, Currie; adult/child $5/1; 2-4pm, closed Jul & Aug).

Activities

Surfing is brilliant in the cool, clear waters here: *Surfing Life* magazine has voted the break at Martha Lavinia as one of the top 10 waves in the world.

Surf and freshwater **fishing** almost guarantee a good catch, and you can **swim** at many of the island's unpopulated beaches (though beware of rips and currents) and freshwater lagoons. Bring your own gear for the legendary **snorkelling** and **diving** here: there's crayfish and abalone to catch if you have a licence.

For **bushwalking**, go independently or take a guided walk with **King Island Rambles** (0439 705 610; www.kingislandrambles.wordpress.com; adult/child/family $30/10/70;

⏲ platypus tours 8-9.30am Sat & Tue). Activities with King Island Rambles also include platypus viewings and guided drives around the island (per person $115). Horseriding is also available on KI.

Spotting **wildlife** is easy on KI. There are rufus and Bennett's wallabies, pademelons, snakes, echidnas, platypus, and you may even glimpse some seals. The island has 78 bird species, and on summer evenings little penguins come ashore around the Grassy breakwater.

Sleeping

Bass Cabins & Campground CAMPGROUND $
(☎03-6462 1168; 5 Fraser Rd; camp site per person $12, cabin d $120) There are a few camp spots here with bathroom facilities adjacent and a couple of two-bedroom cabins. It's 1.5km from the centre of Currie.

Portside Links APARTMENTS, B&B $$
(☎03-6461 1134; www.portsidelinks.com.au; Grassy Harbour Rd; apt d $170) Two beautiful apartments and B&B accommodation close to the beach. There's also the added attraction of an art gallery and cafe (open 10am to 4pm Sunday and Tuesday).

Naracoopa Holiday Units COTTAGES $$
(☎03-6461 1326; www.naracoopaholidayunits.com.au; 125 The Esplanade; d $130-140, extra adult/child $25/15) Bright, clean and peaceful cottages on Sea Elephant Bay. The owners are a mine of island information and can arrange car hire.

Eating

Must-tries include KI cheese and dairy products, but also crayfish in season (November to August), oysters, crabs, grass-fed beef, free-range pork and game.

Harbour Road Cafe CAFE $
(24 Edward St, Currie; snacks $4-10; ⏲9am-5pm Mon-Fri, 10am-5pm Sat-Sun) This raffish combo of cafe, florist and gift shop is King Island's funkiest cafe. Regular quiche and soup specials combine with freshly-baked scones daubed with jam and luscious King Island whipped cream. Focaccia sandwiches, wine and beer are also available.

Renae's Cafe CAFE $$
(28 Edward St, Currie; snacks & light meals $10-22; ⏲8.30am-4pm Tue-Sat, 8.30am-1pm Sun; 📶) Good coffee and hearty cooked brekkies (weekends only).

Kings Cuisine at Bold Head Brasserie MODERN AUSTRALIAN $$
(☎03-6461 1003; www.kingscuisine.com.au; 10 Main Rd, Grassy; mains $24-28; ⏲noon-2pm Thu-Sun, from 6pm Wed-Mon) Fine dining with innovative use of local King Island produce. Booking ahead is recommended.

Boomerang by the Sea MODERN AUSTRALIAN $$$
(☎03-6462 1288; www.boomerangbythesea.com.au; Golf Club Rd; mains $26-40; ⏲dinner from 6pm Mon-Sat) Excellent menu that's big on seafood, and has fantastic views.

Information

King Island Tourism (☎03-6462 1355, 1800 645 014; www.kingisland.org.au; 5 George St, Currie) Ask about the *King Island Grazing Trails* map, detailing historical, natural and cultural walks around the island. King Island Tourism's website is an excellent pre-trip planning resource.

Online Access Centre (5 George St) Wi-fi access is also available at Renae's Cafe.

Getting There & Away

King Island Airlines (☎03-9580 3777; www.kingislandair.com.au) Melbourne Moorabbin–King Island (one-way $210).

Regional Express (☎13 17 13; www.regionalexpress.com.au) Melbourne Tullamarine–King Island (one-way from $160).

Sharp Airlines (☎1300 556 694; www.sharpairlines.com) Launceston–King Island (one-way from $261) and Burnie/Wynyard–King Island (one-way from $200).

Getting Around

King Island Car Rental (☎1800 777 282, 03-6462 1282; kicars2@bigpond.com; 2 Meech St) Per day from around $80.

P&A Car Rental (☎03-6462 1603; 1 Netherby Rd) Per day from around $80.

Ulverstone & Around

Unhurried Ulverstone (population 9800) has a relaxed, uncommercial atmosphere at the mouth of the Leven River. The town became an important commercial port with the coming of the railway in 1890, but a decade later the rail was extended to Burnie and with it went the shipping activity. Today it's home to a few fishing boats, retirees, some gracious old buildings and quite a ridiculous clock tower. The **Ulverstone visitor information centre** (☎03-6425 2839; www.centralcoast.tas.gov.au; 13 Alexandra Rd; ⌚9am-5pm Sep-May, 10am-4pm Jun-Aug) is a much classier piece of architecture. A few good eateries make it a worthy lunch stop as well.

Sights & Activities

Gunns Plains Caves CAVE
(☎03-6429 1388; www.gunnsplainscaves.com.au; adult/child $12/6; ⌚10am-4pm) The B17 road does a worthwhile loop from the A1 coast highway, and goes to Gunns Plains, 25km south of Ulverstone. Take a guided tour of the 'shawl' formations here.

Wings Wildlife Park WILDLIFE RESERVE
(www.wingswildlife.com.au; 137 Winduss St; adult/child $20/10; ⌚10am-4pm) Also at Gunns Plains is this family-oriented place with farm and native animals, including reptiles, birds of prey and a bossy rooster.

Leven Canyon Lookout LANDMARK
South of Gunns Plains, the Leven River stutters through a 274m-deep gorge. Follow the 41km road from Ulverstone through Nietta to the jaw-dropping Leven Canyon Lookout. A 20-minute return track leads to a gorge-top viewing platform.

Discover the Leven River Cruises CRUISE
(☎0400 130 258; www.discovertheleven.com; adult/child $55/25) Two hour cruises exploring the history, flora and fauna of the Leven River. Longer five hour cruises including a meal are also available (adult/child $98/50).

Sleeping & Eating

Big 4 Ulverstone Holiday Park CAMPGROUND $
(☎1800 008 028, 03-6425 2624; www.big4ulverstone.com.au; 57 Water St; unpowered/powered sites $35/38, cabins from $110, units $126-179; @☎) Set in grassy surroundings just behind East Beach, this park has good facilities, including a campers kitchen and playgrounds.

Ulverstone River Retreat APARTMENT $$
(☎03-6425 2999; www.ulverstoneriverretreat.com.au; 37 Lobster Creek Rd; d $130-165, extra person $25) Watch kingfishers from your front deck, fish and kayak the river, or just soak up the birdsong and peace. This gorgeous riverside spot offers a smart upstairs apartment and a separate villa, both with decks out front and BBQ facilities.

thirtythree cups CAFE $
(31 King Edward St; breakfast $8.50-12.50, lunch $14.50-16.50; ⌚9am-4pm Mon-Fri, 8am-2pm Sat) Ulverstone's stab at a cosmopolitan laneway cafe has a hip retro vibe and features innovative salads and healthy Med- and Asian-inspired lunches. The excellent coffee goes well with homestyle baking including cupcakes and macarons, and organic and gluten-free options abound.

Deli Central CAFE $$
(48b Victoria St; meals $10-18; ⌚8am-4pm Mon-Thu, 8am-late Fri, 8am-5pm Sat-Sun) Look forward to wonderful breakfasts of chewy French sourdough with poached free-range eggs and homemade relish, or roast pumpkin and caramelised-onion tart for lunch. Stock up for picnics at their impressive deli counter, and pop in for their special tapas menu on Friday nights.

Pier 01 MODERN AUSTRALIAN $$
(www.pier01.com.au; 3 Wharf Rd; lunch $16-23, dinner $28-36; ⌚noon-late Mon-Fri, 8am-late Sat-Sun) This cavernous bar, cafe and restaurant is part of Ulverstone's flash new riverside precinct. Secure an outdoor table and tuck into good value tasting platters ($22.50) or mains including ocean trout and Cape Grim steaks. Interesting burgers and salads feature at lunch, and there's occasional live music on Sunday afternoon from 4pm.

Pedro's the Restaurant SEAFOOD $$$
(www.pedrostherestaurant.com.au; Wharf Rd; lunch $10-18, dinner $29-38; ⌚noon-late) Grab a riverside table and savour tastes of the sea at sunset. The paradise seafood platter for two ($135) is the most popular offering here. There's also **Pedro's Takeaway** (mains $5-14; ⌚11am-7pm) for fish and chips, next door.

Penguin

POP 3050

This quaint little seaside village – complete with a huge concrete penguin on the foreshore and penguin-shaped rubbish bins – lures tourists with its fantastic beaches.

Driving from Ulverstone, take the old Bass Hwy along the coast. As you approach Penguin, the countryside takes on a gentrified, rural feel with cottage gardens, a narrow-gauge railway track and beaches.

Every Sunday off Arnold St the popular undercover **Penguin Market** (⌚9am-3.30pm) takes place. There are some browse-worthy stalls here selling local produce, art and crafts, gifts and collectables. Check out the Penguin **visitor information centre** (☎03-6437 1421; 78 Main Rd; ⊙9am-4pm).

Sleeping & Eating

The Madsen BOUTIQUE HOTEL **$$$**
(☎03-6437 2588; www.themadsen.com; 64 Main St; d $160-300; @☎) Penguin's best place to stay is this stylish hotel, where the top rate will score you the spacious front room (a former banking chamber), with Bass Strait sea views.

Renaessance CAFE **$**
(95 Main Rd; breakfast $6-10, lunch $10-15; ⊙9am-5pm Mon-Sat, 10am-4pm Sun) Penguin's best cafe is the most sophisticated place for many a mile, with a pristine white interior giving way to a sun-drenched, brick-lined conservatory. Hip service delivers fine coffee and cake, and tasting platters featuring salmon and pâté are partenered with a concise beer and wine list.

Wild Café Restaurant MODERN AUSTRALIAN **$$**
(☎03-6437 2000; 87 Main Rd; lunch $15-22, dinner $29-32; ⊙noon-late Wed-Sun) This is one of the best restaurants on the northwest coast. Gaze over the water while you enjoy top-notch contemporary Aussie cuisine. Try the Thai-inspired char-grilled calamari, or other Asian-influenced dishes including pork belly. Just try not to get too surprised by the occasional passing freight train.

THE NORTHWEST

Tassie's Northwest is lashed by Roaring Forties winds and in excess of 2m of rain each year, and boasts coastal heathlands, wetlands and dense temperate rainforests unchanged from Gondwana times. Communities here are either isolated rural outposts or tricked-up tourist traps. The further west you get, the fewer fellow travellers you'll encounter until you reach the woolly wilds of Tasmania's northwest tip, a region of writhing ocean beaches and tiny communities with no landfall until South America.

Getting There & Around

AIR

Regional Express (☎13 17 13; www.regional-express.com.au) Melbourne–Burnie/Wynyard (one-way from $149).

BUS

There are no public transport services to Marrawah or Arthur River, but **Redline Coaches** (☎1300 360 000; www.tasredline.com.au) services the Northwest's larger towns:

JOURNEY	PRICE ($)	DURATION (MIN)
Burnie–Boat Harbour	10	30
Burnie–Smithton	23	90
Burnie–Stanley	20	60
Burnie–Wynyard	8	20
Launceston–Burnie	38	160

From Monday to Saturday **Metro** (☎03-6431 3822; www.metrotas.com.au) has regular buses from Burnie to Penguin, Ulverstone and Wynyard (all $5.60 one-way), departing from Cattley St.

CAR & MOTORCYCLE

The main north-to-west-coast route is the Murchison Hwy (A10) from Somerset west of Burnie, running through to Queenstown. The Western Explorer is the inland road from Smithton through the Tarkine wilderness area to the west coast, including a difficult 50km section between Arthur River and Corinna. Promoted as a tourist route, the road is OK for non-4WD vehicles, but it's remote, potholed and mostly unsealed – think twice in bad weather or after dark. Fill up your tank in Marrawah in the north or Zeehan in the south, as there's no petrol in between. The **Arthur River Parks & Wildlife Service** (☎03-6457 1225; www.parks.tas.gov.au) provides road condition updates.

At Corinna there's a vehicle ferry across the Pieman River, from where you continue to Zeehan and the rest of the west.

Burnie

POP 19,060

Built on Emu Bay, Burnie is Tasmania's fourth-largest city. It's a deepwater port and shipping is a lynchpin of the economy. Burnie was long home to a huge paper mill (it closed in 2010), and manufacturing and agricultural-services industries also feature. However a beachy vibe and emerging arty and environmental scenes provide balance, and the coastal highway east and west of the city is an often spectacular drive. Burnie also has an enviable stock of art deco architecture.

Sights & Activities

Makers Workshop MUSEUM

(☎03-6430 5831; www.discoverburnie.net; 2 Bass Hwy; Creative Paper tours adult/child $15/8; ⏲9am-5pm) Part museum, part arts centre, this dramatic structure dominates the Western end of Burnie's main beach. Come here for **tourist information**, but also to get acquainted with this city's creative heart. You'll notice the life-sized **paper people** in odd corners of the workshop's cavernous contemporary interior. These are the work of **Creative Paper**, Burnie's handmade paper producers. Look out for the **makers' studios** stationed throughout the arts centre where you can watch local artisans at work. There's also a good cafe and providore with beach views and a cheese-tasting facility.

Burnie Regional Art Gallery GALLERY

(www.burniearts.net; Wilmot St, Burnie Arts & Function Centre; ⏲10am-4.30pm Mon-Fri, 1.30-4.30pm Sat & Sun) FREE This art gallery has excellent exhibitions of contemporary Tasmanian artworks, including fine prints by some of Australia's most prominent artists.

Penguin Observation Centre WILDLIFE WATCHING

A boardwalk on Burnie's foreshore leads from Hilder Pde to the western end of West Beach. Take a free **Penguin Interpretation Tour** (☎0437 436 803; ⏲sunset Oct-Feb) about one hour after dusk as the penguins emerge from the sea and waddle back to their burrows. Volunteer wildlife guides talk about the penguins' habits.

Hellyers Road Whisky Distillery DISTILLERY

(☎03-6433 0439; www.hellyersroaddistillery.com.au; 153 Old Surrey Rd; tours adult/child under 16 $14/free; ⏲10am-4.30pm) Hellyers Rd is recognised as the home of some of Australia's finest whiskies. Tour the distillery at 10.30am or 2pm to understand the craft behind Hellyers' golden single malt, and afterwards sample whisky, whisky cream and Southern Lights vodka. The on-site cafe serves snacks and lunches.

Sleeping

Burnie Oceanview CAMPGROUND $

(☎03-6431 1925; www.burniebeachaccommodation.com.au; 253 Bass Hwy; unpowered/powered sites d $24/29.50, dm $25, on-site vans d $55, cabins & units d $92-139; @ ≋) Located 4km west of the city centre, this park has backpacker rooms, grassy camping sites, vans with kitchenettes, and cabins.

Seabreeze Cottages RENTAL HOUSE $$

(☎0439 353 491; www.seabreezecottages.com.au; s/d from $160/175) These chic and modern cottages are just west of the city centre. There's the cool, contemporary **Beach House** (243 Bass Hwy, Cooee) just a stroll across the road from the beach, and cute **Number Six** (6 Mollison St), both a 10-minute walk to town.

Duck House COTTAGE $$

(☎03-6431 1712; www.duckhousecottage.com.au; 26 Queen St; s/d $120/160, extra adult/child $30/20) Salvation Army stalwarts Bill and Winifred Duck lived here for 30 years, and have been immortalised in this charming little two-bedroom cottage. Next door is **Mrs Philpott's** (26 Queen St), sleeping up to seven, with lead-lighting, a claw-foot bath and brass bedsteads for the same rates.

Ikon Hotel BOUTIQUE HOTEL $$$

(☎03-6432 4566; www.ikonhotel.com.au; 22 Mount St; d $220; ❄) Boutique hotel chic comes to Burnie at the centrally-located Ikon Hotel. The building's heritage exterior is complemented by sleek and spacious modern suites with leather furniture and compact kitchenettes. Interesting modern and retro art punctuates the walls, the bathrooms are huge, and the rooms are bright and airy.

Eating & Drinking

Another Mother CAFE $

(14 Cattley St; mains $9-15; ⏲7am-4pm Tue-Sat;) With bright red walls, eclectic furniture and local photography, this eatery offers wholesome predominantly vegetarian (and some meaty) dishes crafted from local produce – organic where possible. Its sister establishment is **Hot Mother Lounge** (70 Wilson St; ⏲7am-3pm Mon-Fri), serving equally good wraps and soups.

Rienos CAFE, BAR $

(☎03-6432 4575; 12 Cattley St; snacks & light meals $10-15; ⏲10am-late) An amazing aroma of garlic greets you as you walk through the door of this tapas and wine bar. It does soups, salads, bruschettas and fine antipasto platters with an emphasis on laid back and shared eating. When it's busy, this one of a few places in Burnie where you can order until late.

The Northwest

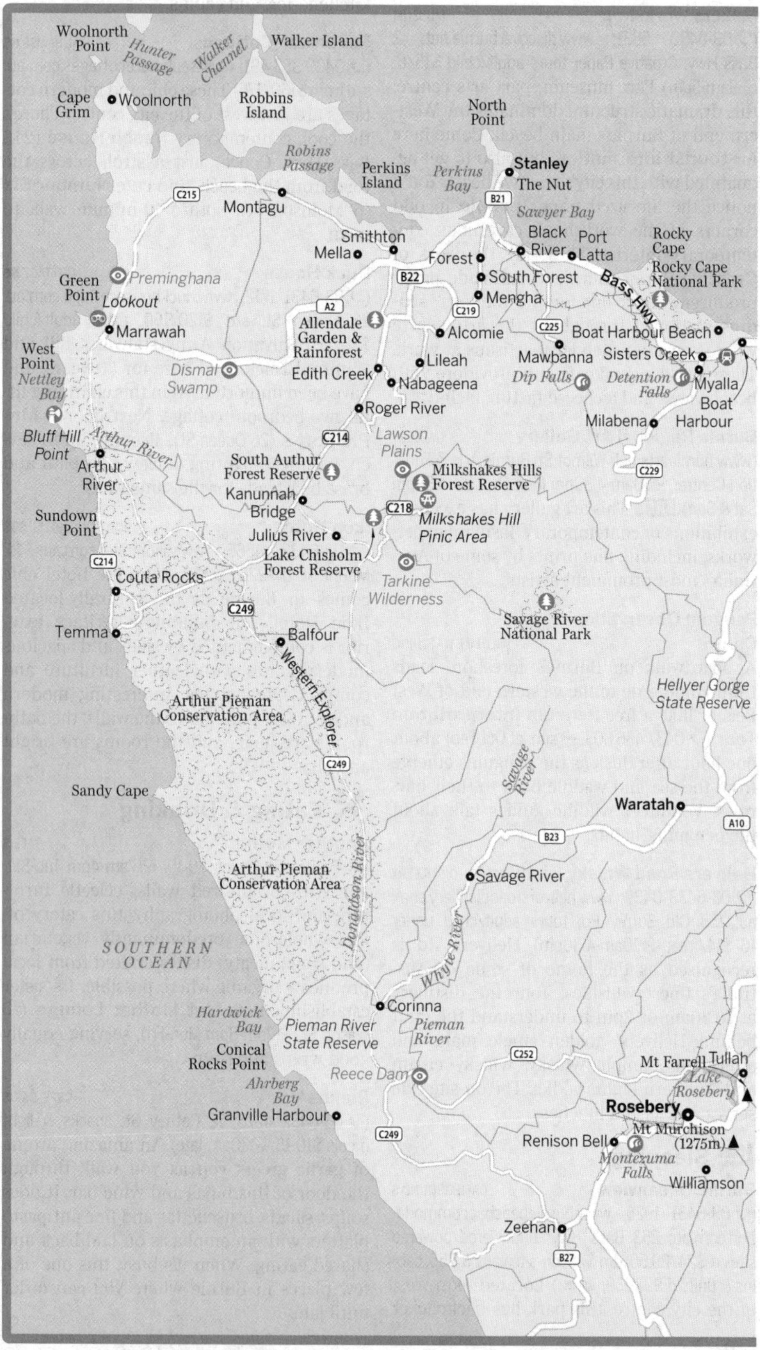
Woolnorth Point
Hunter Passage
Walker Channel
Walker Island
Cape Grim
Woolnorth
Robbins Island
North Point
Robins Passage
Perkins Island
Perkins Bay
Stanley
The Nut
C215
Montagu
B21
Sawyer Bay
Smithton
Mella
Black River
Port Latta
Rocky Cape
Forest
South Forest
Rocky Cape National Park
Green Point
Preminghana
B22
Bass Hwy
Mengha
Lookout
A2
C219
Marrawah
Allendale Garden & Rainforest
Alcomie
C225
Boat Harbour Beach
West Point
Mawbanna
Sisters Creek
Nettley Bay
Dismal Swamp
Lileah
Edith Creek
Dip Falls
Detention Falls
Myalla
Nabageena
Boat Harbour
Roger River
Milabena
Bluff Hill Point
Arthur River
Lawson Plains
C214
Arthur River
South Authur Forest Reserve
Milkshakes Hills Forest Reserve
C229
Kanunnah Bridge
C218
Milkshakes Hill Pinic Area
Sundown Point
Julius River
Lake Chisholm Forest Reserve
C214
Tarkine Wilderness
Couta Rocks
C249
Savage River National Park
Temma
Balfour
Western Explorer
Hellyer Gorge State Reserve
Arthur Pieman Conservation Area
C249
Savage River
Sandy Cape
Waratah
A10
B23
Savage River
Arthur Pieman Conservation Area
Donaldson River
Whyte River
SOUTHERN OCEAN
Corinna
Hardwick Bay
Pieman River State Reserve
Pieman River
Conical Rocks Point
C252
Mt Farrell
Tullah
Reece Dam
Lake Rosebery
Ahrberg Bay
Rosebery
Granville Harbour
Mt Murchison (1275m)
C249
Renison Bell
Montezuma Falls
Williamson
Zeehan
B27

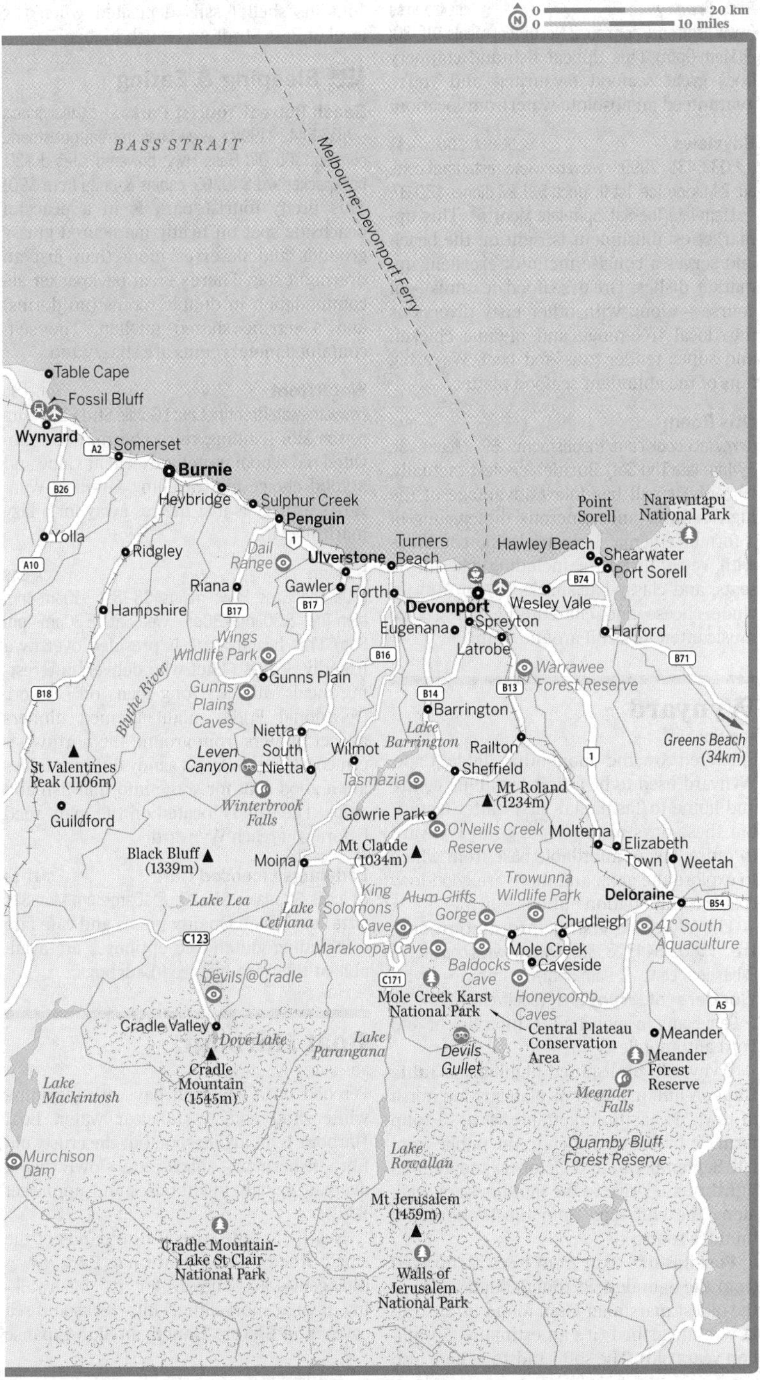
0 20 km
0 10 miles
BASS STRAIT
Melbourne-Devonport Ferry
Table Cape
Fossil Bluff
Wynyard
A2
Somerset
Burnie
B26
Heybridge
Sulphur Creek
Penguin
Yolla
Ridgley
A10
Dail Range
Ulverstone
Turners Beach
Hawley Beach
Point Sorell
Narawntapu National Park
Shearwater
Port Sorell
B74
Riana
Gawler
Forth
Devonport
Wesley Vale
Hampshire
B17
Spreyton
Eugenana
Latrobe
Harford
Wings Wildlife Park
B16
Warrawee Forest Reserve
B71
Gunns Plain
Gunns Plains Caves
Blythe River
B18
B14
B13
Barrington
Lake Barrington
Nietta
South Nietta
Wilmot
Railton
Greens Beach (34km)
Leven Canyon
Tasmazia
Sheffield
St Valentines Peak (1106m)
Winterbrook Falls
Mt Roland (1234m)
Guildford
Gowrie Park
O'Neills Creek Reserve
Moltema
Elizabeth Town
Weetah
Black Bluff (1339m)
Moina
Mt Claude (1034m)
Trowunna Wildlife Park
Deloraine
B54
Lake Lea
King Solomons Cave
Alum Cliffs Gorge
Chudleigh
41° South Aquaculture
Lake Cethana
C123
Marakoopa Cave
Mole Creek
Baldocks Cave
Caveside
Devils @Cradle
C171
Mole Creek Karst National Park
Honeycomb Caves
A5
Cradle Valley
Dove Lake
Lake Parangana
Central Plateau Conservation Area
Meander
Cradle Mountain (1545m)
Devils Gullet
Meander Forest Reserve
Lake Mackintosh
Meander Falls
Murchison Dam
Lake Rowallan
Quamby Bluff Forest Reserve
Mt Jerusalem (1459m)
Cradle Mountain-Lake St Clair National Park
Walls of Jerusalem National Park

Fish Frenzy SEAFOOD $$
(www.fishfrenzy.com.au; 2 North Tce; meals $12-30; ⏰11am-9pm) This upbeat fish and chippery does great seafood favourites, and you're guaranteed an absolute waterfront location.

Bayviews MODERN AUSTRALIAN $$
(☎03-6431 7999; www.bayviewsrestaurant.com.au; 2 Marine Tce, 1st fl; lunch $21-27, dinner $30-37; ⏰11am-late Tue-Sat, 5pm-late Mon) This upmarket establishment is right on the beach and serves a concise menu of excellent upmarket dishes. Great seafood features – of course – along with other tasty diversions into local free-range and organic chicken and super tender grass-fed beef. We're big fans of the abundant seafood platter.

Otis Room BAR
(www.facebook.com/theotisroom; 69 Mount St; ⏰4pm-late Thu-Sat) Burnie's coolest (actually, it's only) small bar takes advantage of the high ceilings and generous dimensions of a former cinema. Industrial chic combines with retro furniture including old movie seats, and classy bar snacks ($7 to $16) include cheese and charcuterie plates. Live music often kicks off around 8pm.

Wynyard

POP 4810

Sheltered by the monolithic Table Cape, Wynyard used to be a timber-milling centre and home to Tasmania's first butter factory, but these days most people go to Wynyard to retire. It's an affordable base from which to explore the area, and there are good low-cost accommodation options.

The **Wynyard visitor information centre** (☎03-6443 8330; www.wowtas.com.au; 8 Exhibition Link; ⏰9am-5pm) combines with **Wonders of Wynyard** (adult/child $8/4.50; ⏰9am-5pm), a polished exhibition of old Ford automobiles.

Wynyard's undisputed highlight is **Table Cape**. A hulking igneous plateau 4km north of town, it has unforgettable views, a tulip farm (in bloom and open to the public from late September to mid-October) and an 1888 **lighthouse**. Drive to the lighthouse or walk along the cliff tops from the **lookout** (30 minutes return).

Fossil Bluff, 3km from town signposted from the Saunders St roundabout, is where the oldest marsupial fossil found in Australia was unearthed (it's an estimated 20 million years old). The soft sandstone here also contains shell fossils deposited when the level of Bass Strait was much higher.

Sleeping & Eating

Beach Retreat Tourist Park CAMPGROUND $
(☎03-6442 1998; www.beachretreattouristpark.com.au; 30b Old Bass Hwy; powered sites d $30, backpacker s/d $40/65, cabins & units from $90) This pretty tourist park is in a peaceful beachside spot on neatly manicured grassy grounds and deserves more than just an overnight stay. There's great backpacker accommodation in double rooms (no dorms) and a terrific shared kitchen. The self-contained motel rooms are snazzy, too.

Waterfront MOTEL $$
(www.thewaterfront.net.au; 1 Goldie St; d $125, extra person $15) Exuding retro charm, this renovated old school motel is excellent value and a good choice for travelling families. Wynyard's estuary is just metres away for a lazy maritime vibe.

Splash CAFE $$
(30a Old Bass Hwy; mains $8-18; ⏰10am-4pm Mon-Tue, 8.30am-8.30pm Wed-Sat, 8.30am-4pm Sun) This beachy cafe is presided over by a friendly Scottish chef who delivers interesting meals with a strong focus on seafood. Occasional Friday night themed dinners attract punters from around the northwestern coast, and Splash's sandy outdoor tables are a good spot for some informal fish and chips. The cafe is located on the main road before you reach Wynyard.

Ladybugs Licensed Café CAFE $$
(8 Inglis St; mains $16-20; ⏰10am-8pm Mon-Sat, pizza from 5-8pm) Quality pizzas and cafe fare – including gluten-free options – are available at the retro-inspired Ladybugs.

Boat Harbour

POP 140

Perched on a beautiful bay with gleaming white sand and crystal-clear water, Boat Harbour is an idyllic spot, but the crusty old fibro fishermen's shacks are slowly being overrun by ugly townhouses and upmarket B&Bs.

Nearby are the coastal heathlands of the small **Rocky Cape National Park** (www.parks.gov.tas.au), known for its bushwalking, diving, snorkelling, shipwrecks and sea caves; and **Sisters Beach**, an 8km expanse of bleached sand with safe swimming, good fishing, a boat ramp and a general store.

Boat Harbour Beach House RENTAL HOUSE $$$
(☑ 03-6445 0913; www.boatharbourbeachhouse. com; d $200-220) Boat Harbour Beach House is actually two independent, multi-bedroom beachhouses: **The Waterfront** (314 The Esplanade) and **The Water's Edge** (320 The Esplanade). Both are beautifully renovated, with outdoor decks and barbecues.

Harvest & Cater CAFE $$
(1 Port Rd; mains $15-30; ⊙ from 8.30am) Next to the surf club, the recently-opened Harvest & Cater does excellent burgers and Asian-inspired salads, and there's live acoustic music on summer Sundays from 5pm. Saturday is open mic night, if you're inspired to perform by Boat Harbour's gorgeous crescent-shaped beach.

Stanley

POP 550

Europeans established Stanley back in 1826, well before any other northwest settlements, and for a long time it was only accessible by sea. The Peerapper people were the original inhabitants of Stanley's little isthmus and peninsula, and back then the extraordinary bulbous Circular Head (better known as The Nut) was covered in forest. Buffeted by cold ocean winds, Stanley lives for two things: fishing (particularly crayfish) and tourism. Every second house is a 'heritage B&B', and there are several good eateries here.

◎ Sights & Activities

The Nut LANDMARK
(chairlift adult/child $12/10; ⊙ chairlift 9.30am-5pm Oct-May, 10am-4pm Jun-Sep) This striking 152m-high volcanic rock formation can be seen for many kilometres around Stanley. It's a steep 20-minute climb to the top. The best lookout is a five-minute walk to the south of the **chairlift**, and you can also take a 35-minute walk (2km) on a path around the top. In summer you can wait to view short-tailed shearwaters (also called mutton birds) returning at dusk after a day's fishing.

Seaquarium AQUARIUM
(Fisherman's Dock; adult/child $12/6; ⊙ 10am-4pm) Providing a great display of marine life, Seaquarium is a fun and educational place to bring the kids. A highlight is the touchy-feely tank.

Highfield HISTORIC BUILDING
(www.historic-highfield.com.au; Green Hills Rd; adult/child $10/5; ⊙ 10am-4pm) This homestead 2km north of town was built in 1835 for the chief agent of the Van Diemen's Land Company. It's a rare example of domestic architecture of the Regency period in Tasmania. Tour the house and the stables, grain stores, workers' cottages and chapel.

Van Diemen's Land Company Store HISTORIC BUILDING
(16 Wharf Rd) This bluestone warehouse on the seafront dates from 1844, and while it once held bales of wool for export, it now houses an exclusive boutique hotel, @VDL.

Tarkine Forest Adventures ADVENTURE CENTRE
(☑ 1300 720 507; www.adventureforests.com.au; adult/child $20/10; ⊙ 9am-5pm Nov-Mar, 10am-4pm Apr-Oct) Fifty-four kilometres southwest of Smithton is this forest adventure centre, formerly known as Dismal Swamp. There's a 110m-long slide that provides a thrilling descent into a blackwood-forested sinkhole: sliders must be over eight years old and at least 90cm tall. There's also a cafe, an interpretation centre and forest floor boardwalks.

☞ Tours

Stanley Seal Cruises WILDLIFE WATCHING
(☑ 03-6458 1294, 0419 550 134; www.stanleysealcruises.com.au; Fisherman's Dock; adult/child/ under 5 $49/17/5) Provides 75-minute cruises to see up to 500 Australian fur seals sunning themselves on Bull Rock. Departures are at 10am and 3pm from October to April, and at 10am in May, June and September, sea conditions permitting.

⨭ Sleeping

Stanley Cabin & Tourist Park CAMPGROUND $
(☑ 03-6458 1266; www.stanleycabinpark.com.au; Wharf Rd; unpowered sites d $25, powered sites d $27, dm $26, cabins d $85-110; 🛜) This spectacularly sited spot has waterfront camp sites, neat cabins and a backpackers hostel comprising six twin rooms.

Stanley Hotel HOTEL $
(☑ 1800 222 397, 03-6458 1161; www.stanleytasmania.com.au; 19 Church St; s/d with shared facilities $50/70, d with bathroom $140) This hotel's brightly painted rooms are a great option in sleepy Stanley. Sit out on the upstairs verandah and look down on the Stanley streetscape. Also runs six self-catering **Abbeys**

Cottages (d $180-220), and the downstairs bistro is highly regarded.

Cable Station Restaurant & Accommodation BOUTIQUE HOTEL $$$
(☎03-6458 1312; www.oldcablestation.com.au; 435 Greenhills Rd, West Beach; d $155-300) Having maintained a telephonic link with the mainland for over 30 years from 1935, this place now upholds a sophisticated guesthouse. Comprising private en suite accommodation (one with a spa) and a self-contained cottage (sleeping up to four), this option offers sea views, seclusion and peace. There's also an excellent on-site restaurant.

★@VDL BOUTIQUE HOTEL $$$
(☎0437 070 222, 03-6458 2032; www.atvdl-stanley.com.au; 16 Wharf Rd; d $250-350; 📶) This former 1840s bluestone warehouse is now a boutique hotel with two suites and a loft apartment. Everything is top class from the bedding to the artworks. Also on offer is @The Base (32 Alexander Tce; d $135-165), a nearby heritage house divided into two similarly stylish suites. At the time of writing, an additional designer loft was being added to this property.

Eating

Hursey Seafoods SEAFOOD $
(2 Alexander Tce; mains $8-15; ⏰9am-6pm) Hursey's is awash with tanks of live sea creatures – fish, crayfish, crabs and eels – for the freshest of (uncooked) seafood takeaways. Choose your own for self-catering or pick up a cooked crayfish.

Julie & Patricks Cafe SEAFOOD $$
(Alexander Tce; mains $12-29; ⏰11.30am-10pm) This is the best place in Stanley for fresh crayfish, served natural or mornay ($70 to $170), and they also do prawns, scallops, calamari and platters to share. Downstairs takeaways are also great.

Stanley's on the Bay MODERN AUSTRALIAN $$$
(☎03-6458 1404; 15 Wharf Rd; mains $22-39; ⏰from 6pm Mon-Sat Sep-Jun) Set inside the historic Ford's Store at Stanley Village, this fine-dining establishment specialises in steak and seafood. The wonderful seafood platter for two ($100) overflows with local scallops, oysters, fish, octopus and salmon.

★Cable Station Restaurant MODERN AUSTRALIAN $$$
(☎03-6458 1312; www.oldcablestation.com.au; 435 Greenhills Rd, West Beach; two-course lunch $35, two-/three-course dinner $55/65) This is a truly sophisticated dining option offering fine food in the salubrious surrounds of the Cable Station. Don't miss the wood oven roasted Stanley Crayfish (it needs to be pre-ordered) or the delectable Black River lamb. The char-grilled octopus and basil pesto is also world famous in Tasmania. For a more casual spin on the Cable Station experience, check out their food truck that's a regular visitor to Launceston's Harvest (p676) farmers' market on Saturday mornings.

Xanders MODERN AUSTRALIAN $$$
(☎03-6458 1111; 25 Church St; mains $36-40; ⏰from 6pm Wed-Sun) Stanley's flashest fine-dining restaurant is set in an old house on the main street with views back and front. The menu here has an accent on fish and seafood, but also serves the area's best beef, and specials like duck. There's a good kids menu, too.

Information

Stanley Visitor Information Centre (☎1300 138 229, 03-6458 1330; www.stanley.com.au; 45 Main Rd; ⏰9am-5pm Mon-Fri, 10am-4pm Sat-Sun) Located on your left as you enter town.

Marrawah

POP 370

At Marrawah, with its open pastureland punctuated by stands of old conifers, the wild Southern Ocean occasionally coughs up pieces of ships wrecked off the rugged coast. The area's beaches and rocky outcrops are hauntingly beautiful, particularly at dusk, and the seas and surf are often monstrous.

Geoff King from **King's Run Wildlife Tours** (☎03-6457 1191; www.kingsrun.com.au; per person $100-125) runs evening trips to a remote fishing shack on his 330-hectare property to watch Tasmanian devils tuck into roadkill. It's a special experience and definitely worth travelling here for.

In the township, the **Marrawah Tavern** (☎03-6457 1102; Comeback Rd; mains $15-33; ⏰noon-10pm Mon-Wed, to midnight Thu-Sat, to 9pm Sun) serves counter meals but doesn't have accommodation. There's a free but very basic (and windy!) camping area with toilets and a cold shower by the beach at Green Point, 2km from Marrawah.

The compact, blue-and-pine **Marrawah Beach House** (☎03-6457 1285; d from $160, extra person $25) has amazing views across the beach to oblivion. Fully self-contained, it sleeps four.

Arthur River

POP 120

Fifteen kilometres south of Marrawah is Arthur River, an isolated bevy of fibro fishing shacks and holiday houses. Breezy and briny **Gardiner Point**, signposted off the main road south of the old timber bridge, has been christened the 'Edge of the World'. From here you can drive 110km south to Corinna on the West Coast via the Western Explorer road.

Activities

Arthur River Canoe & Boat Hire BOATING
(☎03-6457 1312; 1429 Arthur River Rd; ⏰9am-5pm) Hires out motorboats ($30/180 per hour/day), canoes ($18/80) and kayaks ($14/60). You can take the canoes upriver and camp for as long as you like. Waterproof drums are provided; BYO everything else. Note that a 'day' is classed as eight hours.

Tours

Arthur River Cruises SCENIC CRUISE
(☎03-6457 1158; www.arthurrivercruises.com; adult/child $95/35; ⏰10am-3pm Sep-May) If you're not into fishing, take a scenic cruise on the Arthur River, cruising upriver to the confluence of the Arthur and Frankland Rivers for a barbecue and a rainforest walk. Children under six years are allowed on this cruise and are free.

AR Reflections River Cruises CRUISE
(☎03-6457 1288; www.arthurriver.com.au; adult/child $95/48; ⏰10.15am-4.15pm) An excellent Arthur River cruise, here passengers get a guided rainforest walk and a gourmet lunch. Sorry, but children under six years of age aren't allowed.

Sleeping & Eating

There is decent self-catering accommodation in Arthur River, but no eateries (only two takeaway stores). Pitch a tent at Manuka, Peppermint or Prickly Wattle **camping grounds** (sites $13) around Arthur River; self-register at the **Arthur River Parks & Wildlife Service** (☎03-6457 1225; www.parks.tas.gov.au; ⏰24hr registration booth) on the main street.

Arthur River Caravan Park CARAVAN PARK $
(☎03-6457 1212; www.arthurrivercabinpark.com; 1239 Arthur River Rd; unpowered/powered sites $25/28, cabins $90-105) Just north of town, this park has old and new cabins, and plenty of wildlife passing through.

Arthur River Holiday Units MOTEL $$
(☎03-6457 1288; www.arthurriver.com.au; 2 Gardiner St; d $120, extra person $30) Has several comfortable (if a little dated) riverside units ranging from one to three bedrooms.

THE WEST

Primeval, tempestuous and elemental – this region of Tasmania is unlike anywhere else in Australia. Towering, jagged mountain ranges, button-grass-covered alpine plateaus, raging tannin-stained rivers, dense impenetrable rainforest and unyielding rain. Humans never tamed this western wilderness and today much of the region comprises Tasmania's World Heritage Area. Tourist-centric Strahan aside, the few towns and settlements here are rough and primitive, weathered and hardened by wilderness.

Prior to 1932, when the Hobart–Queenstown road was built, the only way into the area was by sea, through the dangerous Hells Gates into Strahan's Macquarie Harbour. European settlement brought convicts, soldiers, loggers, prospectors, railway gangs and fishermen to the area. In the 20th century, outdoor adventurers, naturalists and environmental crusaders were lured into the wilderness. The proposed damming of the Franklin and Lower Gordon Rivers in the 1980s sparked the greatest environmental debate in Australian history, and fostered an ecotourism boom around Strahan.

See www.westernwilderness.com.au.

Getting There & Around

Tassielink (☎1300 300 520; www.tassielink.com.au) buses run from Hobart to the west coast five times per week. The duration of the Strahan journey varies with Queenstown stopover times.

JOURNEY	PRICE ($)	DURATION (HR)
Hobart–Bronte Junction	37	2¼
Hobart–Derwent Bridge	44	3¼
Hobart–Lake St Clair	51	2¾
Hobart–Queenstown	65	5
Hobart–Strahan	75	6-8¾

From Launceston, Tassielink buses run three times per week:

JOURNEY	PRICE ($)	DURATION (HR)
Launceston–Cradle Mountain	59	3
Launceston–Devonport	24	1¼ (meeting ferries)
Launceston–Gowrie Park	40	2¼
Launceston–Queenstown	72	6
Launceston–Sheffield	30	2
Launceston–Strahan	82	8¾
Launceston–Zeehan	62	5½

Drivers heading north along the rugged Western Explorer road should fill up at Zeehan or Waratah; there's no fuel at Corinna or Arthur River, only at distant Marrawah.

Corinna

POP 5

Tiny, peaceful Corinna, on the northern bank of the Pieman River, was once a thriving gold-mining settlement of more than 2500 people, but nowadays the whole town is run as an isolated tourist resort with a strong environmentalist focus. The ambitious owners have renovated the old pub and built 14 self-contained, solar-powered **cabins** (☎03-6446 1170; www.corinna.com.au; backpackers s/d $50/90, cottages d $150-220, houses sleeping 4 $250; extra person $25) on the hillside. Note this is the only place to stay and eat here.

Pieman River Cruises (☎03-6446 1170; adult/child $90/51; ⏲10am-2.30pm) operates from here – a laid-back, rustic alternative to Strahan's crowded, mass-produced Gordon River cruises. Four-hour cruises on the *Arcadia II* pass an impressive gorge and forests of eucalypts, ferns and Huon pines en route to Pieman Heads, where you can rummage around the log-strewn beaches. Bookings are essential. Also on offer are **canoe and kayak** paddles on the Pieman (half/full day $40/80), **fishing** (rod hire half/full day $10/20) and boat trips on the smaller and more nimble *Seawater* to **Lovers' Falls** (adult/child $50/25) where you can be dropped with a picnic hamper.

The *Fatman* **ferry** (motorcycles & bicycles/standard vehicle/caravan $10/20/25; ⏲9am-5pm Apr-Sep, to 7pm Oct-Mar) crosses the Pieman on demand (the only way across the river).

Queenstown

POP 3400

The extraordinary Lyell Hwy winds down from the mountains into Queenstown through a surreal moonscape of eroded gullies and bare hillsides. This is the legacy of environmentally destructive mining. Mining activities and sulphur emissions are now controlled, and greenery is springing up on the slopes. Ironically, some locals want to keep the green away, believing the bald hills and gravel football field attract the tourists.

Although Queenstown is now getting in on the tourism trend, it's still got that authentic, rough-and-ready pioneer town feel. You can spot miners in boilersuits wandering the streets and there's a rich social and industrial history that still feels alive.

The town's biggest (and priciest) attraction is the West Coast Wilderness Railway, a restored line traversing the pristine wilderness between Queenstown and Strahan. Note that in April 2013 the railway's former private operators discontinued the service, it was hoped the service would recommence around September 2013 for the summer of 2013/1014. See the boxed text (p698) for more information.

⊙ Sights

Eric Thomas Galley Museum MUSEUM
(☎03-6471 1483; 1 Driffield St; adult/child/family $6/4/13; ⏲9.30am-5pm Mon-Fri, 12.30-5pm Sat & Sun Oct-April, reduced winter hours) This museum started life as the Imperial Hotel in 1898. Inside are diverting displays of old photographs with idiosyncratic captions. It doubles as the Queenstown visitor information centre.

LARQ Gallery GALLERY
(☎03-6471 2805; www.landscapeartresearchqueenstown.wordpress.com; 8 Hunter St; ⏲2pm-6pm Tues-Sat mid-Jan–mid-Jun) FREE Run by internationally renowned Tasmanian artist Raymond Arnold, Landscape Art Research Queenstown is a wonderful gallery that runs exhibitions by local and visiting artists and community workshops in printmaking and painting. Its mission is to nurture a breed of art that's inspired by the powerful natural landscapes of the west coast. It's an excellent institution and definitely worth visiting.

Spion Kop Lookout LANDMARK

For top-of-the-town views, follow Hunter St uphill, turn left onto Bowes St, then a sharp left onto Latrobe St to a small car park. From here a short, steep track ascends Spion Kop Lookout.

Tours

Mt Lyell Mine Tours MINE

(☎0407 049 612; tours $80; ⏲10am & 2pm) The abandoned open-cut mine **Iron Blow** can be seen from a lookout off the Lyell Hwy, while mining continues deep beneath the massive West Lyell crater. Take a two-hour tour with this outfit. Minimum age is 14; bookings are essential.

Sleeping

Empire Hotel HOTEL $

(☎03-6471 1699; 2 Orr St; s $30, d with/without bathroom $80/60) The rooms here aren't as magnificent as the imposing blackwood staircase that's a National Trust-listed treasure, but they are relatively clean and tended by friendly staff. There are great meals served in the dining room.

Queenstown Cabin & Tourist Park CAMPGROUND $

(☎03-6471 1332; www.westcoastcabins.com.au; 17 Grafton St; unpowered/powered sites $5/28, on-site vans d $70, d cabins $80-100) This basic park is set on gravel, but it does have a small grassy camping area.

Mt Lyell Anchorage B&B $$

(☎03-6471 1900; www.mtlyellanchorage.com; 17 Cutten St; s $80-130, d $130-160) This 1890s weatherboard home has been completely transformed into a wonderful little guesthouse with quality beds, linen and luxuriously deep carpets. There are also two self-contained apartments ($150 for up to four people, $200 for up to six). Breakfast provisions included for all.

Penghana B&B $$$

(☎03-6471 2560; www.penghana.com.au; 32 Esplanade; s $150, d from $145, ste $280; 📶) This National Trust-listed mansion (1898) is on a hill above town amid a beautiful garden. The house includes a billiards room and a grand dining room for enjoying hearty breakfasts and evening meals by arrangement.

Eating & Drinking

Café Serenade CAFE $$

(40 Orr St; mains $11-18; ⏲8.30am-4pm; 🌿) Look forward to yummy soups, sourdough toasted sandwiches, salads and good vegetarian options, as well as hearty roasts and curries. Also does gluten-free and dairy-free sweet treats, and the coffee is excellent.

Empire Hotel PUB $$

(☎03-6471 1699; 2 Orr St; mains $15-28; ⏲11am-10pm, lunch noon-2pm, dinner 5.30-8pm) This old miners pub has survived the ages and includes an atmospheric heritage dining room serving a changing menu of hearty pub standards, including roasts, pastas, and fine steaks and ribs. Craft beers from Tasmania's Seven Sheds Brewery are often on tap.

Entertainment

Paragon Theatre CINEMA

(www.theparagon.com.au; 1 McNamara St; snacks & tapas $6-14; ⏲screenings 8pm Fri & 2pm, 4.30pm, 8pm Sat) This refurbished art deco theatre screens Hollywood flicks on Friday and Saturday, and the attached cafe and wine bar opens at the same time for coffee, beer and wine, and shared platters of cheese and salami.

Strahan

POP 700

Strahan, 40km southwest of Queenstown on the Macquarie Harbour, is the only vestige of civilisation on Tasmania's wild west coast. Visitors come in droves seeking a taste of Tasmania's famous wilderness, whether by seaplane, a Gordon River cruise or the Wilderness Railway.

Macquarie Harbour was discovered in the early 1800s by sailors searching for Huon pine. The area was inaccessible by land and proved difficult to reach by sea – dubious assets that prompted the establishment of a brutal penal colony on Sarah Island in 1821. In the middle of Macquarie Harbour, Sarah Island isolated the colony's worst convicts, their muscle used to harvest Huon pine nearby. Convicts worked 12 hours a day, often in leg irons, felling pines and rafting them back to the island's sawpits where they were used to build superb ships. In 1834, after the establishment of the Port Arthur penal settlement, Sarah Island was abandoned.

DON'T MISS

WEST COAST WILDERNESS RAILWAY

The old railway from Queenstown to Strahan was a remarkable engineering feat. Built to transport copper from Queenstown's Mt Lyell mine to the Macquarie Harbour port at Strahan, it passes through dense forest, crosses wild rivers via 40 bridges, and stops at old stations on its route. The rack-and-pinion line opened in 1896, utilising the Abt system (involving a third, toothed, lock-on rail) to allow fully loaded mining carriages to tackle steep 1:16 gradients.

After closing in 1963 the railway fell into disrepair, but was magnificently restored to reopen as a tourist attraction in 2002. Unfortunately because of the cost of ongoing track maintenance, in April 2013 private operators the Federal Group ceased operating the four-hour journey between Strahan and Queenstown.

Because of the importance to the local West Coast and broader Tasmanian tourism industries, state and federal governments in Hobart and Canberra stepped up with a $6 million four-year package to support essential track maintenance and capital improvements through the winter of 2013. At the time of writing, new private operators were being sought, and it was hoped the service would recommence in time for the 2013/2014 summer tourist season. For the latest information, enquire at the tourist information centres in Hobart, Launceston, Queenstown or Strahan, or check www.westcoastwildernessrailway.com.au, www.discovertasmania.com or www.westernwilderness.com.au. In Queenstown, the station is on Driffield St, opposite the Empire Hotel.

Today, Strahan's harbourside main street is undeniably attractive, but the town's robust focus on tourism can make it slightly overcommercialised.

It can snow here in summer or blow a blizzard on a whim, so pack winter-weight and waterproof clothing.

For information see www.destinationstrahan.com.au; www.strahanvillage.com.au and www.strahantasmania.com.

Sights & Activities

West Coast Reflections MUSEUM
(Esplanade; 10am-6pm summer, noon-5pm winter) The museum section of the Strahan visitor centre offers a creative and thought-provoking display on the history of the west coast, with a refreshingly blunt appraisal of the region's environmental disappointments and achievements.

Beaches WALKING, BIRDWATCHING
Some attractions in Strahan include the storm-battered, 33km-long **Ocean Beach**, 6km from town. The rips rip and the undertows tow – swimming isn't recommended, but visiting at sunset is. From October to April the Ocean Beach dunes become a **mutton-bird rookery**, the birds returning from winter migration. Ask at the visitor information centre about ranger-run tours in January and February. **West Strahan Beach**, closer to town, has a gently sloping sandy bottom that's OK for swimming. About 14km along the road from Strahan to Zeehan are the spectacular **Henty Dunes**, impressive 30m-high sand mountains.

The Ship That Never Was THEATRE
(Esplanade; adult/child $20/10; 5.30pm Sep-May, box office opens at 5pm) This unmissable play tells the story of convicts who escaped from Sarah Island in 1834 by hijacking a ship they were building and sailing it all the way to Chile. It's great fun for all age groups, and there's lots of crowd participation. Don't be shy. Despite more than 5000 performances, it's always an energetic and entertaining experience.

Tours

Cruises up the Gordon River cross vast Macquarie Harbour to Hells Gates and the entrance to the Southern Ocean, before visiting Sarah Island, the site of Van Diemen's Land most infamously cruel penal colony. After lunch, boats continue up the river for a rainforest walk at Heritage Landing.

Also on offer in Strahan are scenic flights, 4WD tours, quad biking, kayaking, and sand-boarding down the towering Henty Dunes.

Gordon River Cruises CRUISE
(1800 628 288, 03-6225 7016; www.puretasmania.com.au; The Esplanade) Offers 5½-hour cruises departing at 8.30am daily, and also at 2.45pm over summer. Cost depends on

where you sit. Standard seats with an excellent buffet lunch cost from $105/42 per adult/child. You can pay more for window-recliner seats, but the windows fog up and people wander around anyway, and they're not worth the extra money. Or you can pay $220 (all tickets) for the Captain's Premier Upper Deck with a buffet lunch and all beverages included.

World Heritage Cruises CRUISE
(☎03-6471 7174; www.worldheritagecruises.com.au; The Esplanade) Take a 5¾-hour morning or afternoon cruise (January only) on the Gordon River, costing per adult/child $105/50 including a fine buffet lunch, or pay $130/75 for premium window seats. You can buy a Gold Pass ticket (adult/child $150/80) including a glass of wine, *Story of Sarah Island* booklet and premium window seats.

Wild Rivers Jet JET-BOATING
(☎03-6471 7396; www.wildriversjet.com.au; The Esplanade) Fifty-minute jet-boat rides on the hour from 9am to 4pm up the King River's rainforest-lined gorges. The experience costs $68/40 per adult/child. Minimum two people; bookings recommended.

West Coast Yacht Charters SAILING
(☎03-6471 7422; www.westcoastyachtcharters.com.au; The Esplanade) Overnight Gordon River sightseeing cruises onboard the 60ft steel ketch *Stormbreaker*. The boat carries just 10 passengers, making it a much more intimate experience. One night, including a visit to Sarah Island and all meals, costs $350/175 per adult/child. Also available are three-hour fishing and kayaking trips ($90/70) including a crayfish lunch. If crayfish is out of season, the cost is $70/45. Overnight cruises taking in the upper reaches of the Gordon cost $280/140 per adult/child.

Strahan Seaplanes & Helicopters SCENIC FLIGHTS
(☎03-6471 7718; www.adventureflights.com.au; ⏲mid-Sep-May) Seaplane and helicopter flights over the region. Seaplane options include 80-minute flights over Frenchmans Cap, the Franklin and Gordon Rivers, and Sarah Island (per adult/child $245/150), and 65-minute flights over the Cradle Mountain region ($300/170). A 60-minute helicopter flight over the Teepookana Forest Reserve costs $245/150, and a quick 15 minutes over Hells Gates and Macquarie Harbour costs $130/70.

Sleeping

Discovery Holiday Parks Strahan CARAVAN PARK $
(☎03-6471 7239; www.discoveryholidayparks.com.au; cnr Andrew & Innes Sts; unpowered sites d $20-35, powered sites $30-45, cabins $135-145; @) Right on Strahan's West Beach, this neat and friendly park has good facilities including a camp kitchen, BBQs and a kids' playground.

Strahan Backpackers HOSTEL $
(☎03-6471 7255; www.strahanbackpackers.com.au; 43 Harvey St; unpowered sites d $20, dm $27-30, d from $65, cabins from $75; @ ᯤ) In an attractive bush setting 15 minutes' walk from the town centre are these plain bunks and doubles, and cute, A-frame cabins. Discounts apply for YHA members.

Strahan Bungalows APARTMENT $$
(☎03-6471 7268; www.strahanbungalows.com.au; cnr Andrew & Harvey Sts; d $90-170, extra person $30) Decorated with a nautical theme, these award-winning self-contained bungalows are bright, light and friendly. It's close to the beach, and less than 15 minutes' walk from the centre of town.

The Crays COTTAGE $$
(☎03-6471 7422, 0419 300 994; www.thecraysaccommodation.com; 11 Innes St & 59 Esplanade; d $180-220) The Crays has two self-contained units on Innes St and six bright, new, roomy architect-designed cottages on the Esplanade opposite Risby Cove. There are reduced prices for cruises on the yacht *Stormbreaker* with West Coast Yacht Charters.

West Coast Yacht Charters YACHT B&B $
(☎03-6471 7422, 0419 300 994; www.westcoastyachtcharters.com.au; The Esplanade; d $100, dm adult/child $50/25) If you're hankering to sleep in a floating bunk on a wharf-moored yacht, then this is a great option. Because the yacht is used for charters, it has late check-in and early check-out (be prepared to check in after 5pm and disembark before 9am). The yacht isn't moored every night, so book ahead. Prices include continental breakfast.

Ormiston House B&B $$$
(☎03-6471 7077; www.ormistonhouse.com.au; The Esplanade; d $200-270) This stunning 1899 mansion was built by Frederick Ormiston, Strahan's founder, and offers stately yet relaxed B&B accommodation in five antique-filled rooms. Well-tended gardens and a

friendly welcome add to a top place to stay after exploring the rugged hinterland.

Eating

Schwoch Seafoods SEAFOOD $$
(The Esplanade; seafoood $10-15, pizza $18-26; noon-8pm Mon-Sat, 5-8pm Sun) The best fish and chips in town – grilled or battered and briny fresh. Crayfish is sometimes available, and there' are also good burgers and pizzas. Eat in or take away, and don't feed the squawking squadrons of seagulls.

Risby Cove MODERN AUSTRALIAN $$
(03-6471 7572; www.risbycove.com.au; The Esplanade; mains $23-36; breakfast & lunch, dinner from 6pm) People come from all over to dine at the Cove. The menu features fancy dishes like blue eye trevalla with a wasabi souffle or twice-cooked duck with shitake mushrooms. Tassie scallops and Bruny Island oysters usually feature, and there is always fresh Macquarie Harbour ocean trout. Bookings recommended, especially during summer.

Regatta Point Tavern PUB $$
(The Esplanade; mains $20-38; noon-10pm, meals noon-2pm & 6-8pm) Eat with the locals 2km around the bay from Strahan's centre. -There are the usual steaks and burgers as well as good fresh fish. Check out the crayfish mornay – in season – if you're after something fancy. There's also a decent kids' menu.

Information

Parks & Wildlife Service (03-6471 7122; www.parks.tas.gov.au; The Esplanade; 9am-5pm Mon-Fri) In the old Customs House – also houses the post office, online access centre and an ATM.

West Coast Visitor Information Centre (03-6472 6800; www.westcoast.tas.gov.au; The Esplanade; 10am-6.30pm Dec-Mar, to 6pm Apr-Nov) Includes the West Coast Reflections museum.

Franklin-Gordon Wild Rivers National Park

Saved from hydroelectric immersion in the 1980s, this World Heritage-listed **national park** (www.parks.tas.gov.au) embraces the catchment areas of the Franklin and Olga Rivers and part of the Gordon River – all exceptional rafting, bushwalking and climbing areas. The park's snow-capped summit

RAFTING THE FRANKLIN

Rafting the churning waters of the Franklin River is thrillingly hazardous; for the inexperienced, tour companies offer complete rafting packages. Whether you go with an independent group or a tour operator, you should contact the park rangers at the **Queenstown Parks & Wildlife Service** (03-6471 2511; Penghana Rd) or the **Lake St Clair visitor information centre** (03-6289 1172; Cynthia Bay) for current information on permits, weather, regulations and environmental considerations. See also detailed 'Franklin River Rafting Notes' at www.parks.tas.gov.au.

Expeditions should register at the booth at the junction of the Lyell Hwy and the Collingwood River, 49km west of Derwent Bridge. Rafting the length of the river, starting at Collingwood River and ending at Sir John Falls, takes between eight and 14 days. It's also possible to do shorter trips. From the exit point, you can be picked up by a Strahan Seaplanes & Helicopters (p699) seaplane or by **West Coast Yacht Charters** (0419 300 994, 03-6471 7422; www.tasadventures.com) *Stormbreaker* for the trip back to Strahan. Or you can paddle 22km further downriver to meet a Gordon River cruise boat at Heritage Landing.

Tours run mainly from December to March. There are a few tour companies with complete rafting packages (departing Hobart).

- **Rafting Tasmania** (03-6239 1080; www.raftingtasmania.com) Five-/seven-/10-day trips costing $1750/2100/2700.
- **Tasmanian Expeditions** (1300 666 856; www.tasmanianexpeditions.com.au) Nine-day trips for $2595. An 11-day expedition ($2795) includes a climb to the summit of Frenchmans Cap.
- **Water By Nature** (1800 111 142, 0408 242 941; www.franklinrivertasmania.com) Five-/seven-/10-day trips for $1940/2240/2790.

is **Frenchmans Cap** (1443m; a challenging three- to five-day walk). The park also boasts a number of unique plant species and the major indigenous Australian archaeological site at **Kutikina Cave**.

Much of the park consists of deep river gorges and impenetrable rainforest, but the Lyell Hwy traverses its northern end. There are a handful of short walks starting from the highway, including hikes to **Nelson Falls** (20 minutes return) and **Donaghys Hill** (40 minutes return), from where you can see the Franklin River and the sky-high white quartzite dome of Frenchmans Cap.

Cradle Mountain-Lake St Clair National Park

Tasmania is world famous for the stunning 168,000-hectare World Heritage area of **Cradle Mountain-Lake St Clair**. Mountain peaks, dank gorges, pristine lakes, tarns and wild moorlands extend triumphantly from the Great Western Tiers in the north to Derwent Bridge on the Lyell Hwy in the south. It was one of Australia's most heavily glaciated areas, and includes Mt Ossa (1617m) – Tasmania's highest peak – and Lake St Clair, Australia's deepest natural freshwater lake (167m).

The preservation of this region as a **national park** (www.parks.tas.gov.au) is due in part to Austrian immigrant Gustav Weindorfer. In 1912 he built a chalet out of King Billy pine, called it Waldheim (German for 'Forest Home') and, from 1916, lived there permanently. Today the site of his chalet at the northern end of the park retains the name Waldheim.

There are fabulous day walks at both Cradle Valley in the north and Cynthia Bay (Lake St Clair) in the south, but it's the outstanding 80.5km Overland Track between the two that has turned this park into a bushwalkers' mecca.

Sights & Activities

Bushwalking is the primary lure of this national park. Aside from the Overland Track there are dozens of short walks here. For Cradle Valley visitors, behind the Cradle Mountain visitor information centre there is an easy but first-rate 20-minute circular boardwalk through the adjacent rainforest, called the **Pencil Pine Falls & Rainforest Walk**, suitable for wheelchairs and prams. Nearby is another trail leading to **Knyvet Falls** (about 45 minutes return), as well as the **Enchanted Walk** alongside Pencil Pine Creek (20 minutes return), and the **King Billy Walk** (about one hour return). The **Cradle Valley Walk** (2½ hours one way) is an 8.5km-long boardwalk linking the Cradle Mountain visitor information centre and Dove Lake. The **Dove Lake Walk** is a 6km lap of the lake, which takes around two hours.

Devils @Cradle WILDLIFE RESERVE
(☎03-6492 1491; www.devilsatcradle.com; 3950 Cradle Mountain Rd; adult/child/family $16/10/40-55; ⏲daytime hours 10am-4pm, night tours also available) This excellent park is the place to have close encounters with Tasmanian devils. Here you can watch these fascinating creatures and learn about the facial tumour disease that's threatening their survival. The mainly nocturnal animals are observed most spectacularly at feeding times (5.30pm, also 8.30pm during daylight savings only). Entry fees for the night feeding tours are: adult/concession/child/family $27.50/15/15/65-87.50.

Larmairremener tabelti CULTURAL WALK
At Cynthia Bay, this Aboriginal culture walk winds through the lands of the Larmairremener, the indigenous people of the region. The walk (about one hour return) starts at the visitor information centre. Another way to do some walking here is to catch the ferry service to either **Echo Point Hut** or **Narcissus Hut** and walk back to Cynthia Bay along the lakeshore. From Echo Point it's four to five hours' walk back; from Narcissus it's five to six hours.

Tours

Almost every tour operator offers day trips or longer tours to the area (including guided walks along the Overland Track).

Cradle Country Adventures HORSE RIDING
(☎1300 656 069; www.cradleadventures.com.au) Half-day, full-day and multiday horse riding trips are available (two-hour trip $95, full day from $220). Running just outside the World Heritage areas, quad bike tours are also available (www.cradlemountainquadbikes.com.au; two-hour trip $129).

Cradle Mountain Canyons CANYONING
(☎1300 032 384; www.cradlemountaincanyons.com.au; adult/child $100/80; ⏲departures at 8.30pm and 1.30pm) Scramble, abseil and climb down a procession of pools and waterfalls

while wearing a snug-fitting wetsuit. Choose between the Lost World Canyon (for beginners) or the Dove Canyon (for more advanced canyoning), and see the region's extreme beauty up close and personal. Cradle Mountain Canyon's office is located adjacent to the Cradle Mountain visitor information centre.

Cradle Mountain Helicopters FLIGHTSEEING
(☎03-6492 1132; www.adventureflights.com.au; Cradle Mountain Rd; ⊙flights late Sep-Jun) Thirty-minute flights cost $245/150 per adult/child.

Cradle Mountain Huts BUSHWALKING
(☎03-6392 2211; www.cradlehuts.com.au; from $2850; ⊙Oct-May) A six-day/five-night, guided walk along the Overland Track staying in private huts with others carrying your pack.

Tasmanian Expeditions BUSHWALKING
(☎1300 666 856; www.tasmanianexpeditions.com.au; ⊙Nov-Apr) Six-day/five-night Overland Track trip for $1995 and a six-day Cradle Mountain/Walls of Jerusalem walk for $1545.

THE OVERLAND TRACK

Australia's most famous trek is usually tackled as a six-day, five-night epic 65km walk between Cradle Valley in the north and Lake St Clair in the south. The scenery is breathtaking and takes in some of Tasmania's highest peaks, through tall eucalypt forests bursting with wildlife, and across exposed alpine moors and buttongrass valleys of unsurpassed beauty.

The Overland Track is at its most picturesque in the summer months when the alpine wildflowers are blooming. This December-to-April period has more daylight hours and warmer temperatures, but there are fewer walkers in the spring and autumn months. Only very experienced walkers should tackle the track in winter. All walkers must register the start and finish of their walk at either end of the track.

In 1953 fewer than 1000 people walked the Overland Track, but by 2004 the trail was being pounded by 9000 hikers annually. To preserve the area's delicate ecology and avoid environmental degradation and overcrowding, some changes to walking conditions have been introduced:

- There's a booking system in place from 1 October to 31 May and a maximum number of walkers per day. Bookings for the season open on 1 July.
- There are track fees of $200/160 per adult/child aged 5-17 and concession, to cover costs of sustainable track management (these apply from October to May only). National park fees are not included in these costs.
- The compulsory walking direction from October to May is north to south.

Departing Cradle Valley, walkers sometimes start at Dove Lake, but the recommended route begins at Ronny Creek, around 5km from the Cradle Mountain visitor information centre. There are many secondary paths off the main track, scaling mountains like Mt Ossa and detouring to lakes, waterfalls and valleys, so the length of time you spend on the track is only limited by the amount of supplies you can carry.

Once you reach Narcissus Hut at the northern end of Lake St Clair, you can walk around the lake's edge to Cynthia Bay (a five- to six-hour walk) or take the ferry run by Lake St Clair Wilderness Resort. To guarantee a seat, you must book the ferry before you start walking, then when you get to Narcissus Hut, use the radio to confirm your booking.

You can bunk down in the excellent huts along the track, but in summer they're full of snoring hikers and smelly socks. To preserve your sanity, bring a tent and pitch it on the established timber platforms around each hut. Campfires are banned, so fuel stoves are essential. There's plenty of clean drinking water available along the way, but boil anything you have doubts about.

Book your walk online at www.overlandtrack.com.au, where there's stacks of info and where you can order *The Overland Track – One Walk, Many Journeys* booklet detailing track sections, flora and fauna. It comes packaged for $34.95 with the 1:100,000 Lake St Clair Map & Notes and a nifty pack swing tag. Visitor information centres also sell the booklet and map. Lonely Planet's *Walking in Australia* guide also has detailed walk descriptions.

Sleeping & Eating

Cradle Valley

Self-caterers should stock up before heading to Cradle Valley; minimal supplies are sold at the Cradle Mountain Cafe, Discovery Holiday Parks shop and Cradle Mountain Lodge. There is an ATM at the cafe in the Cradle Mountain visitor information centre.

Discovery Holiday Parks Cradle Mountain CAMPGROUND $
(☎03-6492 1395; www.discoveryholidayparks.com.au; Cradle Mountain Rd; unpowered/powered sites d $35/49, dm $32, cabins from $99, cottages from $149; @ 🛜) This bushland complex is 2.5km from the national park. It has well-separated sites, a YHA-affiliated hostel, a camp kitchen and laundry and self-contained cabins.

★**Cradle Mountain Highlanders Cottages** COTTAGE $$
(☎03-6492 1116; www.cradlehighlander.com.au; Cradle Mountain Rd; d $120-210, extra adult/child $30/20) These immaculate timber cottages all have wood or gas fires and queen-sized beds. Three cabins include a spa, and the surrounding bush is filled with curious wildlife. Welcome to one of the best places to stay at Cradle Mountain.

Cradle Mountain Wilderness Village CABIN $$$
(☎03-6492 1500; www.cradlevillage.com.au; Cradle Mountain Rd; d $220-360; @) Quite luxurious chalets and cabins are set peacefully in eucalypt groves, and if you can score a last minute online discount for one of the new Premium chalets, you're guaranteed a very comfortable night.

Cradle Mountain Lodge RESORT $$$
(☎03-6492 2103, 1300 806 192; www.cradlemountainlodge.com.au; Cradle Mountain Rd; d $400-840, extra adult $72; @) This stone-and-timber resort near the national park entrance has nearly 100 cabins surrounding the main lodge. There's good eating at the house restaurants – the fine-dining **Highland** (two/three courses $59/69, five course degustation $90; ⏰breakfast, lunch & dinner) and the laid-back **Tavern** (mains $16-26; ⏰11.30am-late) There's also a spa retreat, and lots of outdoor activities and guided walks are also open to outside guests. Check online for good discounts and phone to ask what activities are planned.

DON'T MISS

WALL IN THE WILDERNESS

On your journey between Derwent Bridge and Bronte Park, don't miss **The Wall** (www.thewalltasmania.com; adult/child $10/6; ⏰9am-5pm Sep-April, 9am-4pm May-Aug). This creation is a work of art in progress. Wood sculptor Greg Duncan is carving a panorama in wood panels depicting the history of the Tasmanian highlands. The scale is incredible: when it's finished the scene will be 100m long, and will take an estimated ten years to complete. Though the tableau is large-scale, it's carved with breathtaking skill and detail: from the veins in the workers' hands, to the creases in their shirts, to the hair of their beards. The Wall is 2km east of Derwent Bridge.

Cynthia Bay & Derwent Bridge

Lake St Clair Lodge CAMPGROUND $
(☎03-6289 1137; www.lakestclairlodge.com.au; unpowered/powered sites d $25/35, dm/d $40/110, d cottages & studios $190-330) This lakeside accommodation hub is bookended by Lake St Clair and serrated mountain peaks. There are lots of walking opportunities and plentiful wildlife. Ongoing improvements include a new campers' kitchen and extremely comfortable suites with kitchenettes, cosy fireplaces and balconies. New spa-studios might be just what you need after the rigours of the Overland Track.

Derwent Bridge Wilderness Hotel HOTEL, PUB $$
(☎03-6289 1144; www.derwentbridgewildernesshotel.com.au; Lyell Hwy; dm $30, linen $5, d with/without bathroom $140/120) This is a brilliant spot on a freezing day with roaring log fires, cold beers and heartily excellent pub meals. The accommodation is simple but comfortable, and the bar has a soaring, timber-beamed ceiling, a pool table, jukebox and easy-going vibe. If you've just finished the Overland Track, the 'King Billy' porterhouse steak is the recommended celebration.

Derwent Bridge Chalets & Studios COTTAGE $$$
(☎03-6289 1000; www.derwent-bridge.com; Lyell Hwy; d $175-245, extra adult/child $40/25; @)

Just 5km from Lake St Clair (500m east of the turn-off) this place has one-, two- and three-bedroom independent cabins and studios, some with spa but all with full kitchen and laundry facilities. Local wildlife comes visiting at dusk.

Hungry Wombat Café CAFE $
(Lyell Hwy; mains $6-15; ⏲8am-6pm summer, 9am-5pm winter) This friendly cafe serves big breakfasts, and loads of homemade soups, fish and chips and snacks to get you through an active day. There's also a small grocery section.

ℹ Information

All walking tracks in the park are signposted, well defined and easy to follow, but it's prudent to carry a map – pick one up at park visitor information centres.

CRADLE VALLEY

Cradle Mountain visitor information centre (☎03-6492 1110; www.parks.tas.gov.au; Cradle Mountain Rd; ⏲8am-5pm, reduced hours in winter) provides extensive bushwalking information (including national park and Overland Track passes and registration), and informative flora, fauna and park history displays.

Just inside the park boundary is the **Rangers Station interpretation centre** (⏲9am-5pm during daylight saving, 9.30am-4pm in winter). A compact auditorium screens videos on the natural history of Cradle Mountain and the tracks in the area. There are also Aboriginal cultural displays here.

Regardless of season, be prepared for cold, wet weather around Cradle Valley. On average it rains here seven days out of 10, and is cloudy eight days in 10. The sun shines all day only one day in 10, and it snows on 54 days each year.

LAKE ST CLAIR

Occupying one wing of a large building at Cynthia Bay on the park's southern boundary is the **Lake St Clair visitor information centre** (☎03-6289 1172; www.parks.tas.gov.au; Cynthia Bay; ⏲8am-5pm), providing rock-solid walking advice, national park passes and displays.

At the adjacent, separately run Lake St Clair Lodge, you can book a range of accommodation or a seat on a ferry or lake cruise.

ℹ Getting There & Away

Tassielink (☎1300 300 520; www.tassielink.com.au) buses service both Cradle Mountain and Lake St Clair.

Contact **Saintys** (☎03-6334 6456; www.saintyscoaches.com.au) regarding on-demand services from Devonport to Cradle Mountain, Launceston to Cradle Mountain, and Devonport or Launceston to Lake St Clair.

Ask around at bushwalking shops or hostels and you might get lucky with cheaper, shared transport.

ℹ Getting Around

CRADLE VALLEY

To avoid overcrowding on the narrow road into Cradle Mountain and gridlock at the Dove Lake car park, there's now a shuttle bus into the park. Buses run every 10 to 20 minutes between about 8am and 8pm in summer (reduced hours in winter) from the Cradle Mountain Transit Centre (by the visitor centre) where you park your car. The fare is included in a valid parks pass. Buses stop at the Rangers Station interpretation centre, Snake Hill, Ronny Creek and Dove Lake.

KEEPING SAFE – BLIZZARDS & HYPOTHERMIA

Blizzards can occur in Tasmania's mountains at any time of year. Bushwalkers need to be prepared for such freezing eventualities, particularly in remote areas. Take warm clothing such as thermals and jackets, plus windproof and waterproof garments. Carry a high-quality tent suitable for snow camping and enough food for two extra days, in case you get held up by bad weather.

Hypothermia is a significant risk, especially during the winter months in southern parts of Australia – and especially in Tasmania. Strong winds produce a high chill factor that can result in hypothermia even in moderately cool temperatures. Early signs include the inability to perform fine movements (such as doing up buttons), shivering and a bad case of the 'umbles' (fumbles, mumbles, grumbles and stumbles). The key elements of treatment include moving out of the cold, changing out of any wet clothing into dry clothes with wind- and waterproof layers, adding insulation and providing fuel (water and carbohydrates) to allow shivering, which builds the internal temperature. In severe hypothermia, shivering actually stops: this is a medical emergency requiring rapid evacuation in addition to the above measures.

CYNTHIA BAY & DERWENT BRIDGE

Lake St Clair Lodge (☎03-6289 1137; www.lakestclairlodge.com.au) operates bushwalkers' ferry trips to and from Narcissus Hut at the northern end of Lake St Clair (30 to 40 minutes). The one-way fare is adult/child $40/20. The boat departs Cynthia Bay three times daily (9am, 12.30pm and 3pm) October to early May (or on demand, minimum six people) stopping at Narcissus Hut about 30 minutes later. If you're using the ferry service at the end of your Overland Track hike, for which bookings are essential, you *must* radio the ferry operator when you arrive at Narcissus to reconfirm your booking.

Saintys (p704) runs an on-demand service that must be pre-booked between Cynthia Bay/Lake St Clair and Derwent Bridge. The distance is 5km.

Flinders Island

Flinders Island and the other 51 islands of the Furneaux Group are all that remains of the land bridge that connected Tasmania with mainland Australia 10,000 years ago. Between 1829 and 1834, 135 indigenous peoples from Flinders Island were transported to Wybalenna to be 'civilised and educated'. After 14 years, only 47 survived. Today, Flinders is a rural and fishing community of 900. Activities include bushwalking, wildlife spotting, fishing, kayaking, snorkelling and diving, and there's an emerging organic food scene.

Sights

Wybalenna Historic Site HISTORIC SITE

A few piles of bricks, the chapel and cemetery are all that remains of this settlement that once 'cared for' Aboriginal people. Eighty-seven people died here from poor food, disease and despair.

Furneaux Museum MUSEUM

(8 Fowlers Rd; adult/child $4/free; ⏲1-5pm daily late Dec-Jan, 1-4pm Sat & Sun Feb-Nov) Nearby at Emita is the engrossing Furneaux Museum, housing a variety of Aboriginal artefacts (including beautiful shell necklaces), sealing and shipwreck relics, and a display on the seasonal mutton-birding industry.

Sleeping

Flinders Island Cabin Park CARAVAN PARK $

(☎03-6359 2188; www.flindersislandcp.com.au; 1 Bluff Rd; campsites for 2 $14, cabin s $35, d $60-95, extra person $15) Close to the airport, this park is about 4km north of Whitemark. Eight family-sized, quality cabins are on offer, some with private bathroom and all with cooker and TV. The friendly owner also has cars ($66 per day) and bikes ($25 per day) for rent.

Vistas on Trousers Point LODGE $$

(☎03-6359 4586; www.vistasontrouserspoint.com.au; 855 Trousers Point Rd; d $155-185) Each of the rooms in this comfortable lodge is uniquely decorated, often with an Indian or Asian ambience. Jump on a mountain bike to explore the surrounding area, before relaxing in the outdoor spa and looking forward to another top-notch meal in the lodge's Chappells restaurant. Well-travelled owners Ken and Carolyn can also kit you out with hiking, snorkelling and fishing gear.

Eating

Flinders is known for fresh seafood, lamb and game, and organic vegetables.

Freckles Cafe CAFE $

(7 Lagoon Rd, Whitemark; snacks & light meals $10-14; ⏲7am-5.30pm Mon-Fri) Decent coffee, wraps and sandwiches in bustling downtown Whitemark.

Shearwater Restaurant PUB $$

(Furneaux Tavern, Franklin Pde, Lady Barron; mains $15-33; ⏲noon-1.30pm & 6-7.30pm) Excellent bistro food, but closes early. Ask the owners about opening hours for their Unavele Vineyard. Their sauvignon blanc, chardonnay and riesling are usually on the wine list at Shearwater.

Chappells Restaurant at Vistas MODERN AUSTRALIAN $$$

(☎03-6359 4586; www.vistasintrouserspoint.com.au; 855 Trousers Point Rd; mains $32-37; ⏲6pm-late Thu-Sun, noon-2.30pm Sat-Sun) Fine dining with views at Vistas on Trousers Point. Lots of local seafood and organic Flinders Island vegetables are usually featured, and the laidback ambience is more like dining at the house of some good friends. Bookings essential.

Information

There are no ATMs, but most businesses have Eftpos facilities for cash withdrawals.

Online Access Centre (☎03-6359 2151; 2 Davies St, Whitemark; ⏲5-7pm Mon-Tue, 10am-1pm & 2-5pm Wed-Fri) At the library.

Service Tasmania (☎03-6359 2201; 2 Lagoon Rd, Whitemark; ⏲10am-4pm Mon-Fri) Walking track advice and national park passes.

The Southwest

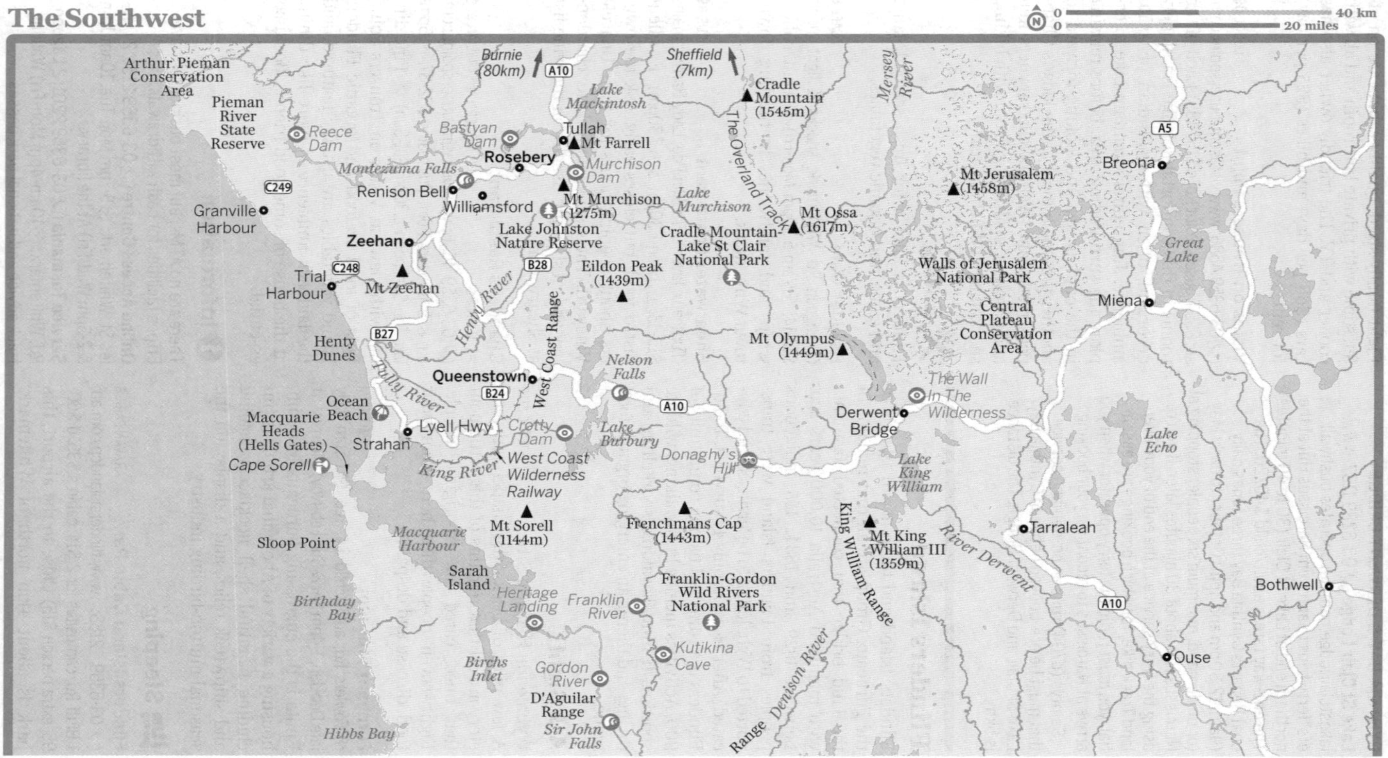

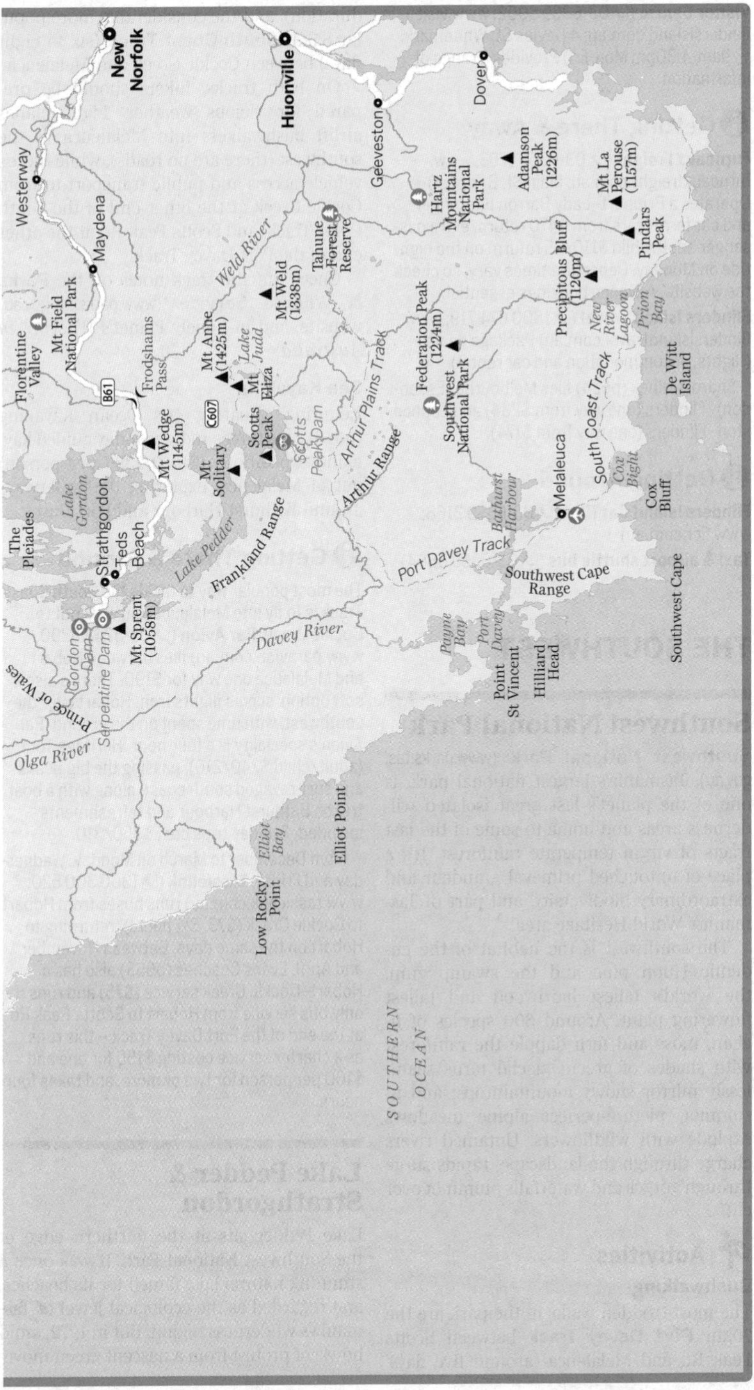
New Norfolk
Huonville
Dover
Geeveston
Westerway
Maydena
Florentine Valley
Mt Field National Park
Weld River
Tahune Forest Reserve
Hartz Mountains National Park
Adamson Peak (1226m)
Mt La Perouse (1157m)
Pindars Peak
Precipitous Bluff (1120m)
Mt Weld (1338m)
Frodshams Pass
B61
Mt Anne (1425m)
Lake Judd
Mt Eliza
C607
Federation Peak (1224m)
Arthur Plains Track
New River Lagoon
Prion Bay
De Witt Island
South Coast Track
Southwest National Park
Mt Wedge (1145m)
Scotts Peak
Scotts Peak Dam
Mt Solitary
Arthur Range
Lake Gordon
The Pleiades
Strathgordon
Teds Beach
Lake Pedder
Frankland Range
Bathurst Harbour
Melaleuca
Cox Bight
Cox Bluff
Port Davey Track
Southwest Cape Range
Southwest Cape
Gordon Dam
Serpentine Dam
Mt Sprent (1058m)
Davey River
Prince of Wales
Olga River
Payne Bay
Port Davey
Point St Vincent
Hilliard Head
Elliot Bay
Elliot Point
Low Rocky Point
SOUTHERN OCEAN

Visitor Centre (☎ 03-6359 5002; www.visitflindersisland.com.au; 4 Davies St, Whitemark; ⏲ 9am-4.30pm Mon-Fri) Provides a range of information.

Getting There & Away

Furneaux Freight (☎ 03-6356 1753; www.furneauxfreight.com.au; Main St, Bridport) Operates a Bridport–Lady Barron passenger and car ferry (cars from $470 return, extra passenger adult/child $110/65 return) on the high tide on Monday. Departure times vary, so check the website. Advance bookings essential.

Flinders Island Travel (☎ 1800 674 719; www.flindersislandtravel.com.au) Package deals (flights, accommodation and car rental).

Sharp Airlines (p624) flies Melbourne (Essendon)–Flinders (one way from $234) and Launceston–Flinders (one way from $174).

Getting Around

Flinders Island Car Hire (☎ 03-6359 2168; www.ficr.com.au)

Taxi & airport shuttle bus (☎ 03-6359 3664)

THE SOUTHWEST

Southwest National Park

Southwest National Park (www.parks.tas.gov.au), Tasmania's largest national park, is one of the planet's last great isolated wilderness areas and home to some of the last tracts of virgin temperate rainforest. It's a place of untouched primeval grandeur and extraordinary biodiversity, and part of Tasmania's World Heritage area.

The southwest is the habitat of the endemic Huon pine and the swamp gum, the world's tallest hardwood and tallest flowering plant. Around 300 species of lichen, moss and fern dapple the rainforest with shades of green; glacial tarns seamlessly mirror snowy mountaintops; and in summer, picture-perfect alpine meadows explode with wildflowers. Untamed rivers charge through the landscape, rapids surge through gorges and waterfalls plummet over cliffs.

Activities

Bushwalking

The most-trodden walks in the park are the 70km **Port Davey Track** between Scotts Peak Rd and Melaleuca (around five days' duration), and the considerably more popular 85km **South Coast Track** (six to eight days) between Cockle Creek and Melaleuca.

On both tracks, hikers should be prepared for vicious weather. Light planes airlift bushwalkers into Melaleuca in the southwest (there are no roads), while there's vehicle access and public transport to/from Cockle Creek at the other end of the South Coast Track, and Scotts Peak Rd at the other end of the Port Davey Track.

Check out the track notes on the **Parks & Wildlife Service** (www.parks.tas.gov.au) website, and in Lonely Planet's *Walking in Australia.*

Sea Kayaking

Kettering's Roaring 40s Ocean Kayaking (p646) runs three- and seven-day guided kayaking expeditions ($1650/2395 per person) out of Melaleuca, exploring the waterways around Bathurst Harbour and Port Davey.

Getting There & Around

The most popular way to tackle the South Coast Track is to fly into Melaleuca and walk out to Cockle Creek. **Par Avion** (☎ 03-6248 5390; www.paravion.com.au) flies between Hobart and Melaleuca one way for $190. There's also a soft option: scenic flights from Hobart over the southwest, with time spent on the ground. Par Avion's speciality is a four-hour 'Heritage Tour' (adult/child $240/210), passing the big peaks and surf-ravaged south coast, along with a boat trip on Bathurst Harbour and refreshments included. Full-day trips cost $350/310.

From December to March on Monday, Wednesday and Friday, **Tassielink** (☎ 1300 300 520; www.tassielink.com.au) runs buses from Hobart to Cockle Creek ($73, 3½ hours), returning to Hobart on the same days. Between November and April, Evans Coaches (p653) also has a Hobart–Cockle Creek service ($75) and runs the only bus service from Hobart to Scotts Peak Rd at the end of the Port Davey Track – this runs as a charter service costing $150 for one and $100 per person for two or more, and takes four hours.

Lake Pedder & Strathgordon

Lake Pedder sits at the northern edge of the Southwest National Park. It was once a stunning natural lake famed for its beaches, and regarded as the ecological jewel of Tasmania's wilderness region. But in 1972, amid howls of protest from a nascent green movement, it was flooded to become part of the Gordon River power development.

Tiny **Strathgordon** (population 30) was built to service employees during construction of the Gordon River Power Scheme. On a clear day (about one in five!), the drive here from Mt Field is bedazzling – bleak peaks, empty buttongrass plains and rippling lakes. About 12km west of Strathgordon is the **Gordon Dam Lookout** and **visitor information centre** (Gordon River Rd; 9am-6.30pm), poised above the 140m-high Gordon Dam and providing info on the scheme.

You can't go inside the underground power station any more, but you can plunge over the edge of the dam wall by spending a day with Hobart-based **Aardvark Adventures** (03-6273 7722, 0458 127 711; www.aardvarkadventures.com.au), which organises abseiling trips here ($210, suitable for beginners, minimum two people). It's the highest commercial abseil in the world. Trips depart from Hobart.

Adelaide & South Australia

Includes ➜

Off The Beaten Track

- ➜ Port Lincoln (p788)
- ➜ Oodnadatta Track (p805)
- ➜ Melrose (p794)
- ➜ Burra (p783)

Best Places to Stay

- ➜ Port Elliot Beach House YHA (p88)
- ➜ Stirling Hotel (p743)
- ➜ Wilpena Pound Resort (p798)
- ➜ Marion Bay Motel (p785)
- ➜ Largs Pier Hotel (p727)

Why Go?

Escape the east-coast frenzy in relaxed South Australia (SA). The driest state on the driest continent, SA beats the heat by celebrating life's finer things: fine landscapes, fine festivals, fine food and (...OK, forget the other three) fine wine.

Adelaide is a chilled-out, gracious city offering world-class festivals, restaurants, pubs and a hedonistic arts scene. A day trip away, McLaren Vale and the Barossa and Clare Valleys are long-established wine regions. Further afield are the watery wilds of the Limestone Coast, and the Murray River, curling Mississippi-like towards the sea. Kangaroo Island's wildlife, forests and seafood await just offshore.

To the west, Yorke Peninsula and Eyre Peninsula are off the beaten track: both beachy, slow-paced detours. Wheeling into the Flinders Ranges, wheat fields give way to arid cattle stations beneath ochre-coloured peaks. Further north, eccentric outback towns such as Woomera and Coober Pedy emerge from the dead-flat desert haze.

When to Go

Adelaide

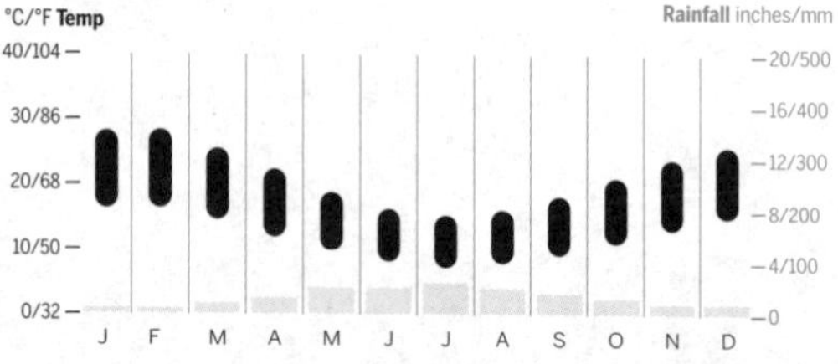

Feb–Mar Adelaide's festival season hits its straps: Fringe and WOMADelaide are highlights.

Apr–May Low autumn sunsets and russet-red grapevines: harvest is in the air.

Sep Football finals time: yell yourself silly in the stands, beer and pie in hand(s).

History

South Australia was declared a province on 28 December 1836, when the first British colonists landed at Holdfast Bay (current-day Glenelg). The first governor, Captain John Hindmarsh, named the state capital Adelaide, after the wife of the British monarch, William IV. While the eastern states struggled with the stigma of convict society, SA's colonists were free citizens – a fact to which many South Australians will happily draw your attention.

The founders based the colony on a utopian 19th-century ideal of social engineering. Land was sold at set prices by the British government to help establish mainly young, skilled married couples; the concept was that equal numbers of men and women, free from religious and political persecution, would create an egalitarian new order.

Between 1838 and 1841, 800 German farmers and artisans (many persecuted Lutherans from Prussia) arrived and settled Hahndorf in the Adelaide Hills – now the best preserved German village in the state. Many more followed over the next decade, bringing vine cuttings with them – SA's famous vineyards began to take root.

The young colony's early progress was slow – only British government funds saved it from bankruptcy – but it became self-supporting by the mid-1840s and self-governing by 1856. Following the successful crossing of the continent by local explorers, SA won the contract to lay the Overland Telegraph from Port Augusta to Darwin, connecting Australia to the world by telegram (1872) and, later, telephone. Following a long recession in the late 19th century, the government became the first to introduce income tax – a fact to which South Australians are hesitant to draw your attention…

SA has maintained its socially progressive creed: trade unions were legalised in 1876; women were permitted to stand for parliament in 1894; and the state was one of the first places in the world to give women the vote, and the first state in Australia to outlaw racial and gender discrimination, legalise abortion and decriminalise gay sex.

Indigenous Adelaide & South Australia

SA offers up some great opportunities to learn about Aboriginal cultures and beliefs. Some of the best include the indigenous-run Bookabee Tours (p715) of Adelaide and the Flinders Ranges, Yorke Peninsula cultural tours run by Adjahdura Land (p783), and Adelaide's Tandanya National Aboriginal Cultural Institute (p719). Also in Adelaide is the Australian Aboriginal Cultures Gallery in the South Australian Museum (p717).

SA's best-known Aboriginal language is Pitjantjatjara (also known as Pitjantjara), which is spoken throughout the Anangu-Pitjantjarjara Aboriginal Lands of northern SA, down almost to the Great Australian Bight. The traditional language of the Adelaide area is Kaurna. Many Kaurna-derived place names have survived around the city: Aldinga comes from *Ngultingga,* Onkaparinga from *Ngangkiparringga,* and Noarlunga from *Nurlungga.* The Adelaide Hills region is Peramangk country.

The Coorong, in Ngarrindjeri country, is a complex series of dunes and salt pans separated from the sea by the long, thin Younghusband Peninsula. It takes its name from the Ngarrindjeri word *kurangh,* meaning 'long neck'. According to the Ngarrindjeri, their Dreaming ancestor, Ngurundjeri, created the Coorong and the Murray River.

The iconic Ikara (Wilpena Pound), a natural basin in Flinders Ranges National Park, is sacred to the Adnyamathanha people, who have lived in the area for more than 15,000 years. Dreaming stories tell of two *akurra* (giant snakes) who coiled around Ikara during an initiation ceremony, creating a whirlwind and devouring the participants. The snakes were so full after their feast they couldn't move, and willed themselves to die, thus creating the landmark.

In 1966, SA became the first state to grant Aboriginal people title to their land. In the early 1980s most of the land west of the Stuart Hwy and north of the railway to Perth was transferred to Aboriginal ownership. Cultural clashes still sometimes occur, however, exemplified by the politically and culturally divisive Hindmarsh Bridge controversy in the 1990s, which pitted Aboriginal beliefs against development.

National Parks

Around 22% of SA's land area is under some form of official conservation management, including national parks, recreation parks, conservation parks and wildlife reserves. The **Department of Environment, Water & Natural Resources** (DEWNR; www.environment.sa.gov.au) manages the state's conservation areas and sells park passes and camping

Adelaide & South Australia Highlights

1. Sniff out the ripest cheese, fullest fruit and strongest coffee at Adelaide's **Central Market** (p55).
2. Swirl, nose and quaff your way through **McLaren Vale** (p744), our favourite SA wine region.
3. Trundle past pelicans, dunes and lagoons in **Coorong National Park** (p761).
4. Listen to the seals snort on **Kangaroo Island** (p752).
5. Hike up to the lofty, desolate rim of **Ikara (Wilpena Pound**; p797) in the Flinders Ranges National Park.
6. Catch a cricket match or some AFL football at the redesigned **Adelaide Oval** (p718).
7. Noodle for opals in the moonscape mullock at **Coober Pedy** (p801).
8. Slurp down a dozen briny oysters at **Coffin Bay** (p790).
9. Scout for passing whales off **Victor Harbor** (p748) or **Head of Bight** (p792) west of Ceduna.

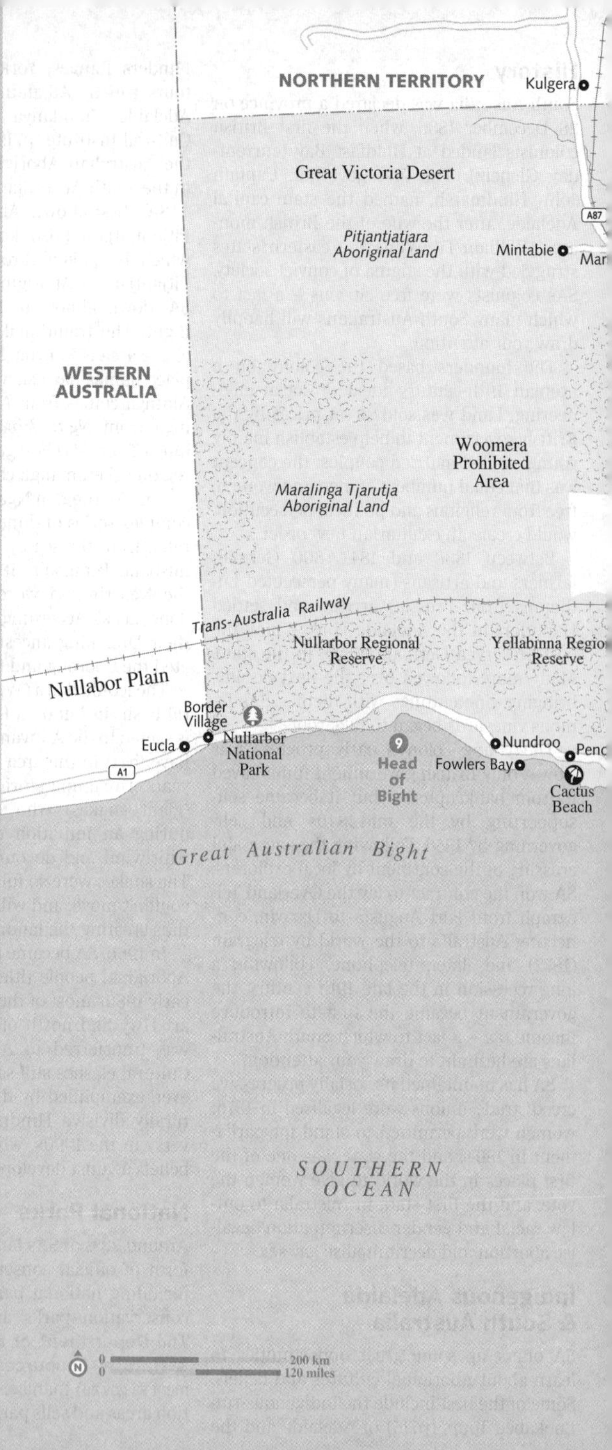

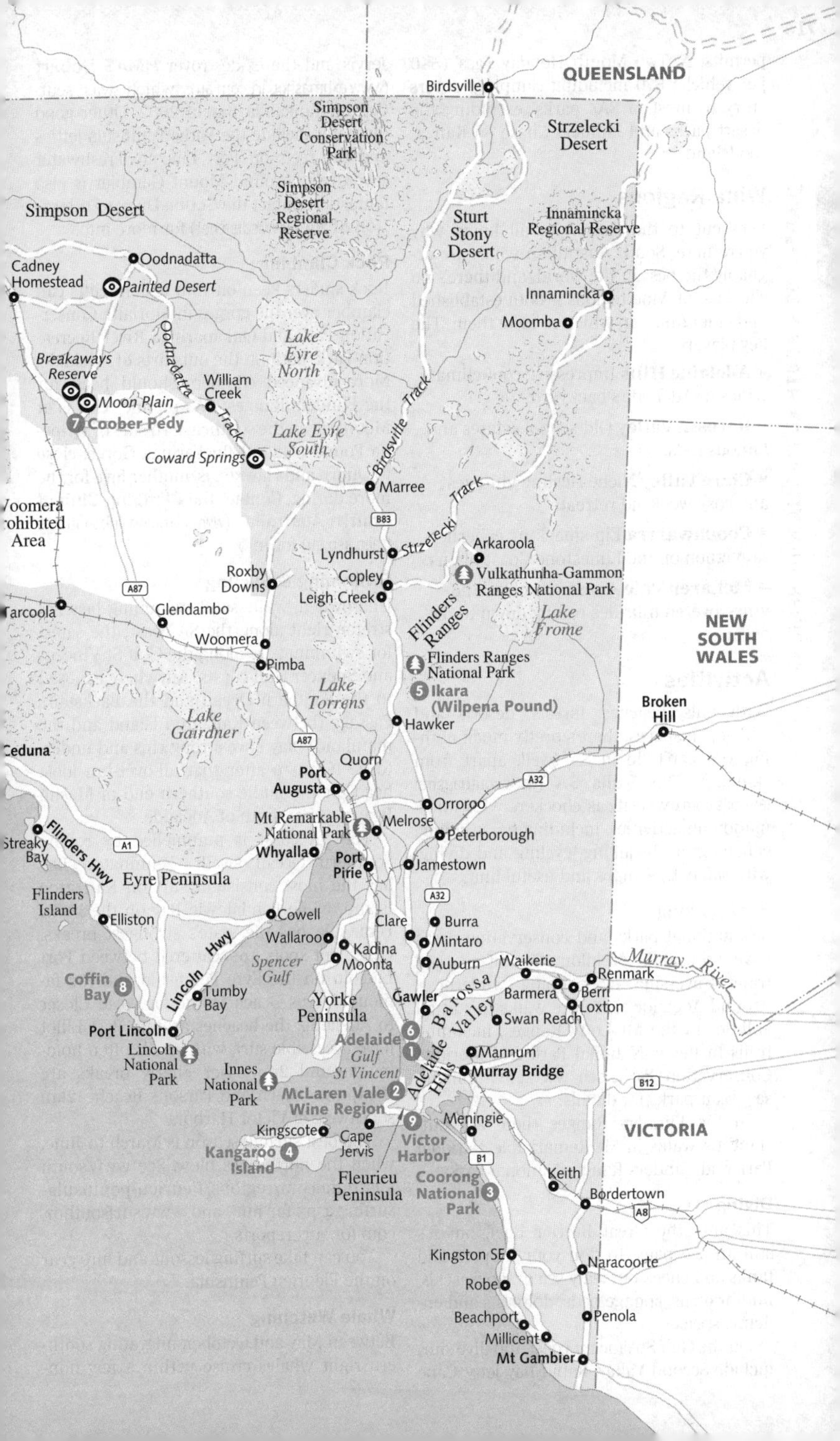
QUEENSLAND
Birdsville
Simpson Desert Conservation Park
Strzelecki Desert
Simpson Desert Regional Reserve
Simpson Desert
Sturt Stony Desert
Innamincka Regional Reserve
Oodnadatta
Cadney Homestead
Painted Desert
Innamincka
Moomba
Oodnadatta Track
Lake Eyre North
Breakaways Reserve
William Creek
Moon Plain
7 Coober Pedy
Lake Eyre South
Birdsville Track
Coward Springs
Marree
Strzelecki Track
B83
Woomera Prohibited Area
Arkaroola
Lyndhurst
Roxby Downs
Copley
Vulkathunha-Gammon Ranges National Park
Leigh Creek
A87
Flinders Ranges
Lake Frome
Tarcoola
Glendambo
NEW SOUTH WALES
Woomera
Flinders Ranges National Park
Pimba
5 Ikara (Wilpena Pound)
Lake Torrens
Lake Gairdner
Broken Hill
Hawker
Ceduna
A87
Quorn
Port Augusta
A32
Orroroo
Mt Remarkable National Park
Melrose
Streaky Bay
Flinders Hwy
Peterborough
A1
Whyalla
Port Pirie
Jamestown
Eyre Peninsula
Flinders Island
A32
Elliston
Cowell
Clare
Burra
Wallaroo
Mintaro
Lincoln Hwy
Kadina
Spencer Gulf
Moonta
Auburn
Waikerie
Murray River
Renmark
Coffin Bay 8
Barossa Valley
Barmera
Berri
Tumby Bay
Yorke Peninsula
Gawler
Loxton
Swan Reach
Port Lincoln
6 Adelaide
1
Gulf St Vincent
Mannum
Lincoln National Park
Adelaide Hills
Murray Bridge
Innes National Park
B12
McLaren Vale 2 Wine Region
9 Victor Harbor
Meningie
Kingscote
Cape Jervis
VICTORIA
Kangaroo 4 Island
B1
Keith
Fleurieu Peninsula
Coorong National 3 Park
Bordertown
A8
Kingston SE
Naracoorte
Robe
Beachport
Penola
Millicent
Mt Gambier

permits. A 'Two Month Holiday Pass' ($40 per vehicle; $70 including camping) covers entry to most of SA's parks, excluding the desert parks and Flinders Chase on Kangaroo Island.

Wine Regions

Let's cut to the chase: we all know why you're here. South Australian wines are arguably the best in the world, and there's no shortage of wine regions – both established and emerging – in which to taste them. The key players:

➡ **Adelaide Hills** Impressive cool-climate wines in Adelaide's backyard.

➡ **Barossa Valley** Old-school estates and famous reds.

➡ **Clare Valley** Niche riesling vintages and cosy weekend retreats.

➡ **Coonawarrra** Lip-smacking cabernet sauvignon on the Limestone Coast plains.

➡ **McLaren Vale** Awesome shiraz and vine-covered hillsides rolling down to the ocean.

Activities

With hills, beaches, forests, deserts and wide-open spaces, there's pretty much nothing you can't do in SA (well, apart from skiing...). The **Trails SA** (www.southaustraliantrails.com) website is chockers with information on activities, including horse riding, canoeing, bushwalking, cycling and diving, with safety tips, maps and useful links.

Bushwalking

SA's national parks and conservation areas have thousands of kilometres of marked trails traversing eye-popping wilderness. Around Adelaide there are walks to suit all abilities in the Mt Lofty Ranges, including trails in Belair National Park and Morialta Conservation Park; see www.environment.sa.gov.au/parks for details.

In the Flinders Ranges there are outstanding walks in Mt Remarkable National Park and Flinders Ranges National Park.

Diving

This ain't the Great Barrier Reef, but it's still an ace place to don your flippers and tanks and check out leafy sea dragons, seals, nudibranchs, sponge beds, dolphins and endemic species.

Off the Gulf St Vincent coast, top dive sites include Second Valley, Rapid Bay jetty, Cape Jervis and the ex-destroyer **HMAS Hobart** (www.exhmashobart.com.au), which was scuttled off Yankalilla Bay in 2002. Other good dive sites include the Yorke Peninsula jetties and the reefs off Port Lincoln. Freshwater cave diving around Mount Gambier is also fantastic. Contact the **Scuba Divers Federation of SA** (www.sdfsa.net) for more info.

Rock Climbing

Rock spiders keen on 10m to 15m cliffs can clamber over the gorges in Morialta Conservation Park and Onkaparinga River Recreation Park, both on the outskirts of Adelaide. More-advanced climbers should head for the Flinders Ranges: SA's premier cliff is at Moonarie on the southeastern side of Wilpena Pound – 120m! Buckaringa Gorge, close to Quorn and Hawker, is another fave for the more daring. Contact the **Climbing Club of South Australia** (www.climbingclubsouthaustralia.asn.au) for info.

Swimming & Surfing

Uncrowded, white-sand swimming beaches stretch right along the SA coast; the safest for swimming are along the Gulf St Vincent and Spencer Gulf coasts. Anywhere exposed to the Southern Ocean and the Backstairs Passage (between Kangaroo Island and the mainland) may have strong rips and undertows. If you're after that all-over-tan look, head for the nudie southern end of Maslin Beach, 40km south of Adelaide.

The SA coast is pummelled by rolling Southern Ocean swells. Pennington Bay has the most consistent surf on Kangaroo Island, while Pondalowie Bay on the Yorke Peninsula has the state's strongest breaks. Other hot spots are scattered between Port Lincoln on the Eyre Peninsula and the famous Cactus Beach in the far west. Closer to Adelaide, the beaches around Port Elliot have accessible surf, with swells often holding around 2m; other gnarly breaks are Waitpinga Beach and Parsons Beach, 12km southwest of Victor Harbor.

The best surfing season is March to June, when the northerlies blow. See www.southaustralia.com/regions/fleurieu-peninsula-surfing.aspx for info, and www.surfsouthoz.com for surf reports.

You can take surfing lessons and hire gear on the Fleurieu Peninsula.

Whale Watching

Between May and October, migrating southern right whales cruise within a few hundred metres of SA shores as they head to/from their Great Australian Bight breeding grounds. Once prolific, southern right whales suffered unrestrained slaughter during the 19th century, which reduced the whale population from 100,000 to just a few hundred by 1935. Although an endangered species, they are fighting back and the population worldwide may now be as high as 7000.

Key spots for whale watching include Victor Harbor and Head of Bight beyond Ceduna on the far west coast.

To find out about current whale action call the **Whale Information Hotline** (☎1900 942 537), or contact the South Australian Whale Centre in Victor Harbor.

Tours

Whatever your persuasion or destination, there's probably a SA tour to suit you. There are plenty of tours in and around Adelaide, including day trips to the Adelaide Hills, Fleurieu Peninsula, Murray River and the Barossa and Clare Valleys.

Further afield, outback tours usually include the Flinders Ranges and Coober Pedy, some continuing north to Alice Springs and Uluru in the Northern Territory. Some of the prime movers:

Adventure Tours WILDERNESS
(☎08-8132 8230, 1800 068 886; www.adventuretours.com.au) Wide range of bus tours around SA and interstate, including trips from Adelaide to Alice Springs and Uluru, Darwin and Kakadu National Park, Kangaroo Island and the Great Ocean Road. Seven days Adelaide to Alice costs $1020; 14 days Adelaide to Darwin is $2113.50.

Bookabee Tours INDIGENOUS
(☎08-8235 9954; www.bookabee.com.au) Indigenous-run cultural tours to the Flinders Ranges. Two-/three-/four-/five-day tours cost $995/1520/2025/2500.

Earth Adventure KAYAKING
(☎08-8165 2024; www.earthadventure.com.au) Short and long kayaking and canoeing trips around SA waters, from the Port River at Port Adelaide to the Murray River, Kangaroo Island and Coffin Bay.

Groovy Grape GUIDED TOUR
(☎1800 661 177; www.groovygrape.com.au) Small-group tours including a three-day trip from Melbourne to Adelaide via the Great Ocean Road ($425), and seven days from Adelaide to Alice Springs via the Flinders Ranges, Coober Pedy and Uluru ($975). Includes meals, camping and national park entry fees. Kangaroo Island and Barossa Valley tours also available.

Heading Bush WILDERNESS
(☎1800 639 933; www.headingbush.com) Rugged, small-group, 10-day Adelaide to Alice Springs expeditions are $1995 all inclusive. Stops include the Flinders Ranges, Coober Pedy, Simpson Desert, Aboriginal communities, Uluru and West MacDonnell Ranges. Yorke Peninsula and dedicated Flinders Ranges tours also available.

Swagabout Tours WILDERNESS
(☎0408 845 378; www.swagabouttours.com.au) Dependable small-group tours with the option of staying in hotels or camping under the stars. The all-inclusive five- to 10-day Adelaide–Alice Springs trips (per day camping/hotels around $300/500) take in the Clare Valley, Flinders Ranges, Oodnadatta Track, Dalhousie Springs and Uluru. Also runs dedicated trips to the Clare Valley, Kangaroo Island and Eyre Peninsula.

Information

South Australian Visitor Information Centre (Map p718; ☎1300 764 227; www.southaustralia.com; 108 North Tce, Adelaide; ⌚9am-5pm Mon-Fri, 9am-2pm Sat, 10am-3pm Sun) Abundantly stocked with info (including fab regional booklets) on Adelaide and SA.

Department of Environment, Water & Natural Resources (DEWNR; Map p718; ☎08-8124 4972; www.environment.sa.gov.au; Level 1, 100 Pirie St, Adelaide; ⌚9am-5pm Mon-Fri) Maps and parks information.

Royal Automobile Association of South Australia (RAA; Map p718; ☎08-8202 4600; www.raa.net; 41 Hindmarsh Sq, Adelaide; ⌚8.30am-5pm Mon-Fri, 9am-noon Sat) Auto advice and plenty of maps.

Getting There & Around

AIR

International, interstate and regional flights service Adelaide Airport (p739), 7km west of the city centre. The usual car-rental suspects all have desks here. Major airlines include:

Jetstar (www.jetstar.com.au) Direct flights between Adelaide and Perth, Darwin, Cairns, Brisbane, Sydney and Melbourne.

Qantas (www.qantas.com.au) Direct flights between Adelaide and Perth, Alice Springs, Darwin, Cairns, Brisbane, Sydney, Canberra and Melbourne.

TAKE THE LONG WAY HOME

South Australia has three epic long-distance trails for hiking and cycling:

Heysen Trail (www.heysentrail.asn.au) Australia's longest walking trail: 1200km between Cape Jervis on the Fleurieu Peninsula and Parachilna Gorge in the Flinders Ranges. Access points along the way make it ideal for half- and full-day walks. Note that due to fire restrictions, some sections of the trail are closed between December and April.

Kidman Trail (www.kidmantrail.org.au) A 10-section cycling and walking trail between Willunga on the Fleurieu Peninsula and Kapunda north of the Barossa Valley.

Mawson Trail (www.southaustraliantrails.com) A 900km bike trail between Adelaide and Blinman in the Flinders Ranges, via the Adelaide Hills and Clare Valley.

Regional Express (Rex; www.regionalexpress.com.au) Flies from Adelaide to regional centres around SA, including Kingscote (from $110, 35 minutes), Coober Pedy (from $235, two hours), Ceduna (from $180, 1½ hours), Mount Gambier (from $200, 1¼ hours), Port Lincoln (from $100, 50 minutes) and Whyalla ($135, 50 minutes).

Tiger Airways (www.tigerairways.com.au) Direct flights between Adelaide and Melbourne.

Virgin Australia (www.virginaustralia.com) Direct flights between Adelaide and Perth, Brisbane, Sydney, Canberra and Melbourne.

BUS

Buses are usually the cheapest way of getting from A to B in SA, and the bus companies have more comprehensive networks than the rail system. Adelaide Central Bus Station (p739) has ticket offices and terminals for all major interstate and statewide services. For online bus timetables see the **Bus SA** (www.bussa.com.au) website.

The major long-haul operators:

Firefly Express (☎1300 730 740; www.fireflyexpress.com.au) Buses between Adelaide and Melbourne (from $65, 11 hours), continuing to Sydney.

Greyhound Australia (☎1300 473 946; www.greyhound.com.au) Services between Adelaide and Melbourne (from $56, 11 hours) continuing to Sydney; and Adelaide and Alice Springs (from $190, 20 hours) continuing to Darwin.

Premier Stateliner (☎08-8415 5555; www.premierstateliner.com.au) State-wide bus services.

V/Line (☎1800 800 007; www.vline.com.au) Bus and bus/train services between Adelaide and Melbourne (from $50, 12 hours).

CAR & MOTORCYCLE

If you're driving between Adelaide and Melbourne, make sure you go via the Great Ocean Road (www.visitvictoria.com) between Torquay and Warrnambool in Victoria – one of the best coastal drives in the world, with awesome views and more twists and turns than a Hitchcock plot.

To hitch a ride (sharing petrol costs) or buy a secondhand car, check out hostel noticeboards.

The Great Ocean Road route is considerably longer than the inland route via Horsham (around 960km and 12 hours versus 730km and eight hours), but it's worth it.

TRAIN

Interstate trains run by **Great Southern Rail** (☎13 21 47; www.gsr.com.au) grind into the Adelaide Parklands Terminal (p739), 1km southwest of the city centre. The following trains depart from Adelaide regularly:

The Ghan To Alice Springs (seat/sleeper $431/1190, 19 hours)

The Ghan To Darwin ($842/2290, 47 hours)

The Indian Pacific To Perth ($553/1750, 39 hours)

The Indian Pacific To Sydney ($375/850, 25 hours)

The Overland To Melbourne (from $116, 11 hours)

ADELAIDE

POP 1.29 MILLION

Sophisticated, cultured, neat casual – this is the self-image Adelaide projects, a nod to the days of free colonisation without the 'penal colony' taint. Adelaidians may remind you of their convict-free status, but the city's stuffy, affluent origins did more to inhibit development than promote it. Bogged down in the old-school doldrums and painfully short on charisma, this was a pious, introspective place.

But these days things are different. Multicultural flavours infuse Adelaide's restaurants; there's a pumping pub, arts and live-music scene; and the city's festival calendar has vanquished dull Saturday nights. And, of course, there's the local wine. Residents flush with hedonism at the prospect of a punchy McLaren Vale shiraz or summer-scented Clare riesling.

That said, a subtle conservatism remains. 'What school did you go to?' is a common salvo from those unsure of your place in the social hierarchy, while countercultural urges bubble up through Adelaide's countless sex shops, kung-fu dojos and huge bottle shops.

Just down the tram tracks is beachy Glenelg, Adelaide with its guard down and boardshorts up; and Port Adelaide, a historic enclave slowly developing into SA's version of Fremantle. Inland, Adelaide's winking plains rise to the Adelaide Hills, just 12 minutes up the freeway. The Hills' gorgeous valley folds, old-fangled towns and cool-climate vineyards are all close at hand.

Sights

Central & North Adelaide

★**Central Market** MARKET
(Map p718; www.adelaidecentralmarket.com.au; Gouger St; 7am-5.30pm Tue, 9am-5.30pm Wed & Thu, 7am-9pm Fri, 7am-3pm Sat) Satisfy both obvious and obscure culinary cravings at the 250-odd stalls in Adelaide's superb Central Market. A sliver of salami from the Mettwurst Shop, a sliver of English stilton from the Smelly Cheese Shop, a tub of blueberry yoghurt from the Yoghurt Shop – you name it, it's here. Good luck making it out without eating anything. Adelaide's Chinatown is right next door.

★**Art Gallery of South Australia** GALLERY
(Map p718; www.artgallery.sa.gov.au; North Tce; 10am-5pm) FREE Spend a few hushed hours in the vaulted, parquetry-floored gallery that represents the big names in Australian art. Permanent exhibitions include Australian, modern Australian, contemporary Aboriginal, Asian, Islamic and European art (19 bronze Rodins!). Progressive temporary exhibitions occupy the basement. Free guided tours (11am and 2pm daily) and lunchtime talks (12.30pm daily).

★**South Australian Museum** MUSEUM
(Map p718; www.samuseum.sa.gov.au; North Tce; 10am-5pm) FREE Digs into Australia's natural history with special exhibits on whales and Antarctic explorer Sir Douglas Mawson, and an Aboriginal Cultures Gallery displaying artefacts of the Ngarrindjeri people of the Coorong and lower Murray. The giant squid is the undisputed highlight of the free tours (11am weekdays, 2pm and 3pm weekends). There's a cool cafe here too.

Adelaide Zoo ZOO
(Map p728; www.zoossa.com.au; Frome Rd; adult/child/family $31.50/18/85; 9.30am-5pm) Around 1800 exotic and native mammals, birds and reptiles roar, growl and screech at Adelaide's wonderful zoo, which opened in 1883. There are free **walking tours** half-hourly (plus a slew of longer and overnight tours focusing on specific environments and

ADELAIDE IN...

Two Days

If you're here at Festival, WOMADelaide or Fringe time, lap it up. Otherwise, kick-start your day at the **Central Market** (p55) then wander through the **Adelaide Botanic Garden** (p718), finishing up at the **National Wine Centre** (p718). After a few bohemian beers at the **Exeter** (p734) hotel, have a ritzy dinner on Rundle St. Next day, visit the **South Australian Museum** (p717) and then see if the Bradman Collection Museum at the **Adelaide Oval** (p718) has reopened. Check out **Tandanya National Aboriginal Cultural Institute** (p719) before riding the tram to Glenelg for a swim and fish and chips on the sand.

Four Days

Follow the two-day itinerary – perhaps slotting in the **Art Gallery of South Australia** (p717) and **Jam Factory Contemporary Craft & Design Centre** (p721) – then pack a picnic basket of Central Market produce and take a day trip out to the nearby Adelaide Hills, McLaren Vale or Barossa Valley wine regions. Next day, truck out to the museums and historic pubs of Port Adelaide, then catch a band at the **Grace Emily Hotel** (p734) back in the city, before dinner on Gouger St.

Central Adelaide

species), feeding sessions and a children's zoo. Until Wang Wang and Funi – Australia's only giant pandas – arrived in 2009 (pandemonium!), the major drawcard was the Southeast Asian rainforest exhibit.

You can take a river cruise to the zoo from the Festival Centre on Popeye (p722).

National Wine Centre of Australia WINERY
(Map p728; www.wineaustralia.com.au; cnr Botanic & Hackney Rds; 9am-5pm) FREE Check out the free self-guided, interactive **Wine Discovery Journey** exhibition, paired with tastings of Australian wines (from $10), at this very sexy wine centre (actually a research facility for the University of Adelaide, more than a visitor centre per se). You will gain an insight into the issues winemakers contend with, and even have your own virtual vintage rated. Free 30-minute tours run at 11.30am daily. Friday-evening 'uncorked' drinks happen at 4.30pm, and here's a cool cafe here too.

Adelaide Botanic Garden GARDENS
(Map p728; www.botanicgardens.sa.gov.au; North Tce; 7.15am-sunset Mon-Fri, from 9am Sat & Sun, Bicentennial Conservatory 10am-4pm) FREE Meander, jog or chew through your trashy airport novel in these lush city-fringe gardens. Highlights include a restored 1877 palm house, the waterlily pavilion (housing the gigantic *Victoria amazonica*), a cycad collection and the fabulous steel-and-glass arc of the **Bicentennial Conservatory**, which re-creates a tropical rainforest. Free 1½-hour guided walks depart from the Schomburgk Pavilion at 10.30am daily.

Adelaide Oval LANDMARK
(Map p728; 08-8300 3800; www.cricketsa.com.au; King William Rd, North Adelaide; tour adult/child $10/5; tour 10am Mon-Fri) Hailed as the world's prettiest cricket ground, the Adelaide Oval hosts interstate and international cricket matches in summer, plus South Australian National Football League

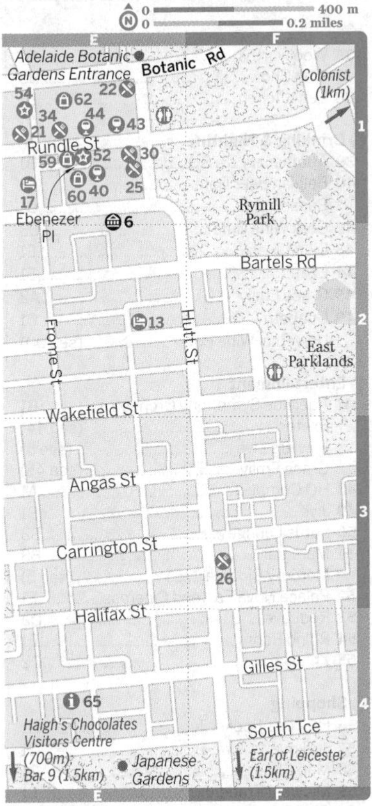

(SANFL) football games in winter. A wholesale redevelopment is underway (www.adelaideovalredevelopment.com.au), which will boost seating capacity to 50,000 and bring national Australian Football League (AFL) games here. A bronze **statue of 'the Don'** (Sir Donald Bradman) cracks a cover drive out the front. When there are no games happening you can take a two-hour **tour**, departing from the northern gates on Pennington Tce. Call or check the website for tour details. Note that the **Bradman Collection Museum** is on ice until the redevelopment is complete.

Tandanya National Aboriginal Cultural Institute GALLERY

(Map p718; ☎08-8224 3200; www.tandanya.com.au; 253 Grenfell St; ⏲10am-5pm) Tandanya offers an insight into the culture of the local Kaurna people, whose territory extends south to Cape Jervis and north to Port Wakefield. Inside the cultural institute there are interactive displays on living with the land, as well as galleries, gifts and a cafe. There are didgeridoo or Torres Strait Islander **cultural performances** (adult/child $5/3, ⏲noon Tue-Sun), pre-booked group **tours** (tours $5-10), plus indigenous short-film and documentary screenings in the theatre.

Migration Museum MUSEUM

(Map p728; www.migrationmuseum.com.au; 82 Kintore Ave; ⏲10am-5pm Mon-Fri, 1-5pm Sat & Sun) This engaging social-history museum tells the story of the many migrants who have made SA their home. The museum has info on 100-plus nationalities (as opposed to individuals) in its database, along with some poignant personal stories. Occupies the site of a former Aboriginal boarding school and destitute asylum.

West Terrace Cemetery CEMETERY

(Map p718; www.aca.sa.gov.au; West Tce; ⏲6.30am-6pm Nov-Apr, 6.30am-8.30pm May-Oct) FREE Driven-by and overlooked by most Adelaidians, this amazing old cemetery (established in 1837, and now with 150,000 residents) makes a serene and fascinating detour. The 2km self-guided **Heritage Highlights Interpretive Trail** meanders past 29 key sites; collect collect a brochure at the West Tce entrance.

Adelaide Gaol MUSEUM

(Map p728; ☎08-8231 4062; www.adelaidegaol.org.au; 18 Gaol Rd, Thebarton; adult/child/family $13/8/32, with guided tour $17/11/48, ghost tours $28; ⏲10am-5pm Sun-Fri, last entry 3.30pm, guided tours 11am, noon & 1pm Sun, ghost tours sunset Thu-Sat) Only decommissioned in 1988, this old lock-up has a grim vibe, but its displays of homemade bongs, weapons and escape devices are amazing. Commentary tapes are available for self-guided tours (included in the admission price). Bookings are required for **guided tours** and adults-only **ghost tours**.

Haigh's Chocolates Visitors Centre TOUR

(Map p732; ☎08-8372 7070; www.haighschocolates.com; 154 Greenhill Rd, Parkside; ⏲8.30am-5.30pm Mon-Fri, 9am-5pm Sat, tours 11am, 1pm & 2pm Mon-Sat) FREE If you've got a chocolate problem, get guilty at this iconic factory. Free **tours** take you through the chocolate life-cycle from cacao nut to hand-dipped truffle (with samples if you're good). Tour bookings essential.

Central Adelaide

Top Sights
1 Art Gallery of South Australia D1
2 Central Market C3
3 South Australian Museum D1

Sights
Australian Experimental Art Foundation .... (see 5)
4 Gilles Street Market D4
5 Jam Factory Contemporary Craft & Design Centre B1
6 Tandanya National Aboriginal Cultural Institute E1
7 West Terrace Cemetery A4

Activities, Courses & Tours
8 Bicycle SA B2

Sleeping
9 Adelaide Backpackers Inn D3
10 Adelaide Central YHA B2
11 Adelaide City Park Motel D4
12 Backpack Oz D2
13 Clarion Hotel Soho E2
14 Hostel 109 .... D3
15 Hotel Metropolitan C3
16 Hotel Richmond D1
17 Majestic Roof Garden Hotel E1
18 My Place A2
19 Quest on Sturt C4
20 Shakespeare International Backpackers B2

Eating
21 Amalfi Pizzeria Ristorante E1
22 Botanic Café E1
Central Market .... (see 2)
23 Edinburgh Castle A2
24 Evergreen B3
25 Galaxy Lartay E1
26 Good Life F3
27 Hotel Wright Street C3
28 Jasmin Indian Restaurant D1
29 Jerusalem Sheshkabab House B1
30 Lemongrass Thai Bistro E1
Lucia's Pizza & Spaghetti Bar .... (see 2)
31 Mesa Lunga B3
32 Press C2
33 Prince Albert A3
Sosta .... (see 30)
34 Vego & Lovin' It E1
35 Village Indian B3
36 Woolworths D1
37 Ying Chow B3
38 Zen Kitchen D1

Drinking & Nightlife
39 Apothecary 1878 .... B1
40 Belgian Beer Café E1
41 Casablabla C1
42 Cork Wine Cafe C3
43 Distill E1
44 Exeter E1
45 Grace Emily A2
46 Udaberri C1
Universal Wine Bar .... (see 30)

Entertainment
47 Adelaide Symphony Orchestra B1
Exeter .... (see 44)
Fowlers Live .... (see 5)
Grace Emily .... (see 45)
48 HQ Complex A1
49 Jive B1
50 Lotus Lounge B3
51 Mars Bar B3
Mercury Cinema .... (see 5)
52 Palace Nova Eastend Cinemas E1
53 RedLove D2
54 Rhino Room E1
55 Zhivago C2

Shopping
56 Imprints Booksellers B1
57 Jurlique C1
58 Map Shop C1
59 Midwest Trader E1
60 Old Midwest E1
61 T'Arts D1
62 Title E1
Urban Cow Studio .... (see 54)

Information
63 Adelaide Visitor Information Centre Rundle Mall C1
64 Department of Environment, Water & Natural Resources D2
65 Disability Information & Resource Centre E4
66 Royal Automobile Association of South Australia D2
67 South Australian Visitor Information Centre B1
68 Women's Information Service D2

Adelaide Parklands GARDENS

The city and ritzy North Adelaide are surrounded by a broad band of parklands. Colonel William Light, Adelaide's controversial planner, came up with the concept, which has been both a blessing and a curse for the city. Pros: heaps of green space, clean air and sports grounds for the kids. Cons: bone-dry in summer, perverts loitering and a sense that the city is cut off from its suburbs.

Don't miss the **Japanese Gardens** on South Tce and the **statue of Colonel William Light** overlooking the gleaming city office towers from Montefiore Hill.

Gilles Street Market MARKET
(Map p718; www.gillesstreetmarket.com.au; 91 Gilles St, Gilles Street Primary School; ⏲10am-4pm 3rd Sun of the month) Kids' clothes, fashion, arts, crafts and hubbub take over an East End school grounds. Open twice-monthly during summer.

Jam Factory Contemporary Craft & Design Centre GALLERY
(Map p718; www.jamfactory.com.au; 19 Morphett St; ⏲10am-5pm Mon-Sat, from 1pm Sun) FREE Quality contemporary local arts and crafts, plus workshops and a hell-hot glass-blowing studio (watch from the balcony above) turning out gorgeous glass.

Australian Experimental Art Foundation GALLERY
(AEAF; Map p718; www.aeaf.org.au; cnr Morphett St & North Tce, Lion Arts Centre; ⏲11am-5pm Tue-Fri, from 2pm Sat) FREE A focus on innovation, with a hip bookshop specialising in film, architecture, culture and design.

Inner Suburbs

Coopers Brewery BREWERY
(Map p732; ☎08-8440 1800; www.coopers.com.au; 461 South Rd, Regency Park; 1½hr tours per person $22; ⏲tours 1pm Tue-Fri) You can't possibly come to Adelaide without entertaining thoughts of touring Coopers Brewery. Tours take you through the brewhouse, bottling hall and history museum, where you can get stuck into samples of stouts, ales and lagers (some of which are carbon neutral). Bookings required; minimum age 18. The brewery is in the northern suburbs – grab a cab, or walk 1km from Islington train station.

Penfolds Magill Estate Winery WINERY
(Map p732; ☎08-8301 5569; www.penfolds.com.au; 78 Penfolds Rd, Magill; tastings free-$50; ⏲10am-5pm) This 100-year-old winery is home to Australia's best-known wine – the legendary Grange. Taste the product at the cellar door, dine at the restaurant, take the **Heritage Tour** ($15), or steel your wallet for the **Great Grange Tour** ($150). Tour bookings are essential.

Glenelg

Glenelg, or 'the Bay' – the site of SA's colonial landing – is Adelaide at its most 'LA'. Glenelg's beach faces towards the west, and as the sun sinks into the sea, the pubs and bars burgeon with surfies, backpackers and sun-damaged sexagenarians. The tram rumbles in from the city, past the Jetty Rd shopping strip to the alfresco cafes around Moseley Sq.

Take the tram to Glenelg from the city or bus 167, 168 or 190.

Glenelg Visitor Information Centre TOURIST INFORMATION
(☎08-8294 5833; www.glenelgsa.com.au; Shop 22, Marina Pier, Holdfast Shores, Glenelg; ⏲9am-4.30pm Mon-Fri, 10am-3pm Sat, 10am-2pm Sun) The visitor centre has the local low-down, incuding info on local diving and sailing opportunities.

Bay Discovery Centre MUSEUM
(Map p732; www.baydiscovery.com.au; Moseley Sq, Town Hall; admission gold coin donation; ⏲10am-5pm summer, 10am-4pm winter) This low-key museum in Glenelg's 1887 Town Hall building depicts the social history of Glenelg from colonisation to today, and addresses the plight of the local Kaurna people, who lost both their land and voice. Don't miss the relics dredged up from the original pier, and the spooky old sideshow machines.

Port Adelaide

Bogged in boganity for decades, Port Adelaide – 15km northwest of the city – is in the midst of gentrification, morphing its warehouses into art spaces and museums, and its brawl-house pubs into boutique beer emporia. Things are (slowly) on the up!

Adelaide's solitary tram line is rumoured to be extending to Port Adelaide at some stage. Until then, bus 150 will get you here from North Tce, or you can take the train.

Port Adelaide Visitor Information Centre TOURIST INFORMATION
(☎08-8405 6560, 1800 629 888; www.portenf.sa.gov.au; 66 Commercial Rd; Port Walks gold coin donation; ⏲9am-5pm, Port Walks 2pm Thu & Sun; 📶) This helpful visitor centre books guided **Port Walks** around the heritage area, and stocks brochures on self-guided history and heritage-pub walks, plus the enticements of neighbouring Semaphore. Activities include dolphin cruises and kayaking.

South Australian Maritime Museum MUSEUM
(Map p732; www.samaritimemuseum.com.au; 126 Lipson St; adult/child/family $10/5/25; ⏲10am-5pm daily, lighthouse 10am-2pm Sun-Fri) This salty cache is the oldest of its kind in Australia. Highlights include the iconic Port Adelaide Lighthouse ($1 on its own, or included in museum admission), busty figureheads made everywhere from Londonderry to Quebec, shipwreck and explorer displays, and a computer register of early migrants.

National Railway Museum MUSEUM
(Map p732; www.natrailmuseum.org.au; Lipson St Sth; adult/child/family $12/6/32; ⏲10am-5pm) Trainspotters rejoice! A delightfully nerdy museum crammed with railway memorabilia. The bookshop stocks as much *Thomas the Tank Engine* merch as you can handle.

South Australian Aviation Museum MUSEUM
(Map p732; www.saam.org.au; 66 Lipson St; adult/child/family $9/4.50/22; ⏲10.30am-4.30pm) This collection of retired old birds (and rockets from Woomera) roosts in an old hangar in the Port Adelaide back streets.

Fishermen's Wharf Market MARKET
(Map p732; www.fishermenswharfmarkets.com.au; Black Diamond Sq; ⏲9am-5pm Sun) If you're visiting the Port on a Sunday, this waterside, two-level indoor market has antiques, bric-a-brac and crappy collectables.

Activities

Cycling & Walking

Adelaide is pancake flat – perfect for cycling and walking (if it's not too hot!). You can take your bike on trains any time, but not buses. **Trails SA** (www.southaustraliantrails.com) offers loads of cycling- and hiking-trail info: pick up its *40 Great South Australian Short Walks* brochure.

There are free guided walks in the Adelaide Botanic Gardens, plus self-guided city walks detailed in brochures from the South Australian Visitor & Travel Centre. The riverside **Linear Park Trail** is a 40km walking/cycling path running from Glenelg to the foot of the Adelaide Hills, mainly along the River Torrens. Another popular hiking trail is the steep **Waterfall Gully Track** (three hours return) up to Mt Lofty Summit and back.

Eagle Mountain Bike Park PARK
(Map p732; www.bikesa.asn.au; Mt Barker Rd, Leawood Gardens; ⏲dawn-dusk) FREE Mountain bikers should check out the Eagle Mountain Bike Park in the Adelaide Hills, which has 21km of trails. Check the website for directions.

Bicycle SA BICYCLE HIRE
(Map p718; ☎08-8168 9999; www.bikesa.asn.au; 111 Franklin St; ⏲9am-5pm) Free 'Adelaide City Bikes' (bring your driver's licence or passport), plus cycling maps and advice.

Bikeabout CYCLING TOURS
(☎0413 525 733; www.bikeabout.com.au) Barnstorming one-day 'Radelaide' mountain-bike sessions (from $130), plus mountain-bike hire (from $30 per day) and tours through the Barossa Valley, McLaren Vale and Clare Valley wine regions.

Escapegoat CYCLING TOURS
(☎08-8121 8112; www.escapegoat.com.au) Ride from the 710m Mt Lofty Summit down to Adelaide ($90), or take a day trip through McLaren Vale by bike ($120). Flinders Ranges bike trips also available.

Glenelg Bicycle Hire BICYCLE HIRE
(Map p732; ☎08-8376 1934; www.glenelgbicyclehire.com.au; 71 Broadway, Norfolk Motor Inn, Glenelg South) Cruise 'The Bay' on a mountain bike (per day $40) or tandem (per day $65).

Linear Park Hire BICYCLE HIRE
(Map p728; ☎0400 596 065; Elder Park; bikes per day $30; ⏲9am-5pm) Bike hire, with helmets and locks.

Water Activities

Adelaide gets *reeeeally* hot in summer. Hit the beach at Glenelg, or try any other activity that gets you out on the water. For more options, check out **Popeye** (Map p728; www.thepopeye.com.au; return adult/child $12/6, one-way $4/2; ⏲10am-4pm) river cruises and Captain Jolley's Paddle Boats (p723).

Adelaide Aquatic Centre SWIMMING
(Map p728; www.cityofadelaide.com.au; Jeffcott Rd, North Adelaide; casual swim adult/child/family $7.50/6/21; ⏲6am-9pm Mon-Fri, 7am-7pm Sat & Sun) The closest pool to the city, with indoor swimming and diving pools, and the usual gym, sauna and spa stuff.

Adventure Kayaking SA KAYAKING
(☎08-8295 8812; www.adventurekayak.com.au; tours per adult/child from $50/25, kayak hire per

ADELAIDE FOR CHILDREN

The free monthly paper **Adelaide's Child** (www.adelaideschild.com.au), available at cafes and libraries, is largely advertorial but contains comprehensive events listings. *Adelaide for Kids: A Guide for Parents*, by James Muecke, has comprehensive details and is available at bookshops.

There are few kids who won't love the **tram ride** from the city down to Glenelg (kids under five ride for free!). You may have trouble getting them off the tram – the lure of a splash in the shallows at the **beach** followed by some fish and chips on the lawn should do the trick.

During school holidays, the South Australian Museum (p717), **State Library of South Australia** (08-8207 7250; www.slsa.sa.gov.au; cnr North Tce & Kintore Ave, 1st fl; 10am-8pm Mon-Wed & Fri, to 6pm Thu & Fri, to 5pm Sat & Sun), Art Gallery of South Australia (p717), Adelaide Zoo (p717) and Adelaide Botanic Garden (p718) run inspired kid- and family-oriented programs with accessible and interactive general displays. The Art Gallery also runs a **START at the Gallery** kids' program (tours, music, activities) from noon to 3pm on the first Sunday of the month.

Down on the River Torrens, **Captain Jolley's Paddle Boats** (Map p728; www.captainjolleyspaddleboats.com; Elder Park; hire per 30min $15; 9.30am-6pm daily summer, 10am-4pm Sat & Sun winter) make a satisfying splash.

Live out the kids' (or perhaps your own) *Charlie and the Chocolate Factory* fantasies on a tour at Haigh's Chocolates Visitors Centre (p719). Not the best for young diets, perhaps, but the chocolates sure are Wonka-worthy.

In Port Adelaide, you can check out the Maritime Museum (p722), National Railway Museum (p722) or South Australian Aviation Museum (p722), or set sail on a **dolphin-spotting cruise**.

Dial-An-Angel (08-8267 3700, 1300 721 111; www.dialanangel.com.au) provides nannies and babysitters to all areas.

3hr adult/child $45/30) Family-friendly guided kayak tours around the Port River estuary (dolphins, mangroves, shipwrecks). Also offers kayak hire.

Temptation Sailing DOLPHIN WATCHING
(Map p732; 0412 811 838; www.dolphinboat.com.au; Holdfast Shores Marina, Glenelg; 3½hr dolphin watch/swim $68/98) Eco-accredited catamaran cruises to watch or swim with dolphins. There are twilight and 1½-hour day cruises too.

Dolphin Explorer Cruises DOLPHIN WATCHING
(Map p732; 08-8447 2366; www.dolphinexplorer.com.au; Commercial Rd, Port Adelaide; 2hr cruises from adult/child $10/6; daily) Cruises depart from Port Adelaide's Fishermen's Wharf to ogle the local bottlenose dolphins. Lots of cruise-and-dine options also available.

Adelaide Scuba DIVING
(Map p732; 08-8294 7744; www.adelaidescuba.com.au; Patawalonga Frontage, Glenelg North; 9am-5.30pm Mon-Fri, 8am-5pm Sat & Sun) Hires out snorkelling gear (per day $30) and runs local dives (single/double dive $65/130).

Adelaide Gondola BOATING
(Map p728; 08-8358 1800; www.adelaidegondola.com.au; War Memorial Dr, North Adelaide; 4 people per 40 min $110) Maybe if you squint...no, it still doesn't look like Venice. But cruising the River Torrens may still float your boat. You can even order a bottle of wine!

Tours

A great way to see Adelaide is to circle around the main sights on the **free city buses** (see p739). Beyond the city, day tours cover the Adelaide Hills, Fleurieu Peninsula, Barossa Valley and Clare Valley. Note that one-day trips to the Flinders Ranges and Kangaroo Island tend to be rushed and not great value for money.

Adelaide's Top Food & Wine Tours FOOD & WINE
(08-8386 0888; www.topfoodandwinetours.com.au) Uncovers SA's gastronomic soul with dawn ($65 including breakfast) and morning ($50) tours of the buzzing Central Market where stallholders introduce their produce. Adelaide Hills, McLaren Vale, Barossa and Clare Valley tours also available.

LOCAL KNOWLEDGE

ADELAIDE ARTS & FESTIVALS

Emma Fey, Development Manager at the Art Gallery of South Australia, filled us in on some highlights of Adelaide's festival calender and arts scene.

Festival Season

The Adelaide Festival, the Fringe Festival, Adelaide Writers' Week and the Clipsal 500 (V8 race) all happen around February/March. Energy breeds energy: everyone is out and about and the weather's good. I can't think of anywhere else where you can see alternative Fringe-dwellers next to racing enthusiasts. The people-watching is great!

Art in the City

The Art Gallery of South Australia is in the middle of the North Tce precinct (next to the museum, the university, between the city and the river). The gallery has recently refurbished and rehung its Elder and Melrose wings, and is engaging a wider audience – especially young people and children with a new dedicated art-making space called 'The Studio'. There are also contemporary art spaces popping up in little laneways around the precinct.

Best Free Events

All sorts of amazing free events appear around the city, especially during the Adelaide Festival. Guerilla street art teamed with pop-up dining experiences, the sensational Adelaide Festival Club Barrio (late-night club) and the Art Gallery of SA's free daily programs.

Bookabee Tours INDIGENOUS
(☎08-8235 9954; www.bookabee.com.au) Indigenous-run half-/full-day city tours ($105/205) focusing on bush foods in the Adelaide Botanic Gardens, Tandanya National Aboriginal Cultural Institute and the South Australian Museum. A great insight into Kaurna culture. Longer outback tours also available.

Adelaide Sightseeing GUIDED TOUR
(☎1300 769 762; www.adelaidesightseeing.com.au) Runs a city highlights tour ($62) including North Tce, Glenelg, Haigh's Chocolates and the Adelaide Oval (among other sights). Central Market, Barossa Valley, McLaren Vale, Adelaide Hills and Kangaroo Island tours also available (among other destinations).

Enjoy Adelaide GUIDED TOUR
(☎08-8332 1401; www.enjoyadelaide.com.au) Half-day city highlights tour ($45) with diversions to Mt Lofty Summit and Hahndorf. Barossa Valley tours also available.

Integrity Tours GUIDED TOUR
(☎0402 120 361, 08-8382 9755; www.integritytoursandcharter.com.au) Adelaide city-lights evening tours ($64), plus half-/full-day tours to the Adelaide Hills (from $59/89) and full-day McLaren Vale/Fleurieu Peninsula explorations (from $89).

Gray Line GUIDED TOUR
(☎1300 858 687; www.grayline.com.au) Half-day city tours with a river cruise ($86) or tram ride and seaside lunch at Glenelg ($93). Adelaide Zoo and Adelaide Hills add-ons also available.

Festivals & Events

Tour Down Under CYCLING
(www.tourdownunder.com.au) The world's best cyclists sweating in their lycra: six races through SA towns, with the grand finale in Adelaide in January.

Adelaide Fringe ARTS
(www.adelaidefringe.com.au) This annual independent arts festival in February and March is second only to the Edinburgh Fringe. Funky, unpredictable and downright hilarious.

Adelaide Festival ARTS
(www.adelaidefestival.com.au) Top-flight international and Australian dance, drama, opera, literature and theatre performances in March. Don't miss the Northern Lights along North Tce – old sandstone buildings ablaze with lights – and the Barrio late-night club.

Clipsal 500 MOTORSPORT
(www.clipsal500.com.au) Rev-heads flail their mullets as Adelaide's streets become a four-day Holden versus Ford racing track in March.

WOMADelaide MUSIC

(www.womadelaide.com.au) One of the world's best live-music events, with more than 300 musicians and performers from around the globe. In March.

Adelaide Cabaret Festival CABARET

(www.adelaidecabaretfestival.com) The only one of its kind in the country. Held in June.

South Australian Living Artists Festival ARTS

(SALA; www.salafestival.com.au) Progressive exhibitions and displays across town in August (expired artists not allowed).

Adelaide Guitar Festival MUSIC

(www.adelaideguitarfestival.com.au) Annual axe-fest with a whole lotta rock, classical, country, blues and jazz. In August.

City to Bay FUN RUN

(www.city-bay.org.au) In September, the annual 12km fun run from the city to Glenelg; much sweat and cardiac duress.

Royal Adelaide Show AGRICULTURAL

(www.theshow.com.au) The agricultural, the horticultural and plenty of showbags. In September.

OzAsia Festival CULTURAL

(www.ozasiafestival.com.au) Food, arts, conversation, music and the mesmerising Moon Lantern Festival. In September.

SANFL Grand Final FOOTBALL

(www.sanfl.com.au) September is the zenith of the local Aussie Rules football season.

Christmas Pageant CULTURAL

(www.cupageant.com.au) An Adelaide institution for 70-plus years – kitschy floats, bands and marching troupes occupy city streets for a day in November.

Feast Festival GAY & LESBIAN

(www.feast.org.au) Three weeks in November in Adelaide, with a carnival, theatre, dialogue and dance.

Sleeping

Most of Adelaide's budget accommodation is in the city centre, but in a town this easy to navigate, staying outside the CBD is viable. North Adelaide is under the flight path, but it's otherwise low-key. For beachside accommodation, try Glenelg. 'Motel Alley' is along Glen Osmond Rd, the main southeast city access road. See www.bandbfsa.com.au for B&B listings.

Central Adelaide

My Place HOSTEL $

(Map p718; ☎08-8221 5299; www.adelaidehostel.com.au; 257 Waymouth St; dm/d incl breakfast from $26/68; P ❄ @ 🛜) The antithesis of the big formal operations, My Place has a welcoming, personal vibe and is just a stumble from the Grace Emily, arguably Adelaide's best pub! There's a cosy TV room, barbecue terrace above the street, beach-bus in summer, and regular pizza and pub nights – great for solo travellers.

Adelaide Central YHA HOSTEL $

(Map p718; ☎08-8414 3010; www.yha.com.au; 135 Waymouth St; dm from $29, d without/with bathroom from $79/95; P ❄ @ 🛜) The YHA isn't known for its gregariousness, but you'll get plenty of sleep in the spacious and comfortable rooms here. This is a seriously schmick hostel with great security, roomy kitchen and lounge area and immaculate bathrooms. A real step up from the average backpackers around town. Parking $10 per day.

Majestic Roof Garden Hotel HOTEL $$$

(Map p718; ☎08-8100 4400; www.majestichotels.com.au; 55 Frome St; d from $200; P ❄ @ 🛜) Everything looks new in this Japanese-themed place – a speck of dirt would feel lonely. Book a room facing Frome St for a balcony and the best views, or take a bottle of wine up to the rooftop garden to watch the sunset. Good walk-in and last-minute rates; parking from $18 per day.

Hotel Metropolitan HOTEL $

(Map p718; ☎08-8231 5471; www.hotelmetro.com.au; 46 Grote St; s/tw/d from $55/85/90) Knocked up in 1883, the Metropolitan pub is still looking pretty. Its 26 rooms upstairs feature stripy linen, high ceilings, little flat-screen TVs and various bedding configurations. 'It used to be quite an experience staying here...' says the barman, raising his eyebrows. We're not sure what he meant, but these days you can expect a decent budget sleep in a beaut city location. Shared bathrooms.

Hotel Richmond HOTEL $$

(Map p718; ☎08-8215 4444; www.hotelrichmond.com.au; 128 Rundle Mall; d from $165; P ❄ 🛜) This opulent hotel in a grand 1920s building in the middle of Rundle Mall has mod-minimalist rooms with king-sized beds, marble bathrooms and American oak and Italian furnishings. Oh, and that hotel rarity – opening windows. Rates include breakfast, movies and papers. Parking from $16 per day.

Clarion Hotel Soho HOTEL $$
(Map p718; ☎08-8412 5600; www.clarionhotelsoho.com.au; 264 Flinders St; d $145-590; P ❄ 📶 🏊) Attempting to conjure up the vibe of London's Soho district, these 30 very plush suites (some with spas, most with balconies) are complemented by sumptuous linen, 24-hour room service, iPod docks, Italian marble bathrooms, jet pool and a fab restaurant. Rates take a tumble midweek. Parking is available from $15.

Hostel 109 HOSTEL $
(Map p718; ☎08-8223 1771, 1800 099 318; www.hostel109.com; 109 Carrington St; dm/s/d/tr $30/60/80/99; ❄ @ 📶) A small, well-run hostel in a quiet corner of town, with a couple of little balconies over the street and a cosy kitchen/communal area. Spotlessly clean and super-friendly, with lockers, travel info, good security and gas cooking. The only negative: rooms open onto light wells rather than the outside world.

Quest on Sturt APARTMENTS $$$
(Map p718; ☎08-8416 4200; www.questapartments.com.au; 14 Sturt St; 1-/2-/3-bed apt from $200/210/250; P ❄ 📶) Almost a mini-suburb within the CBD, this tight enclave of two-storey, multicoloured apartments wins point for location (utterly central), security and privacy. Various online deals include breakfast, free internet, free parking, a bottle of wine etc. Good for urbanite families.

Backpack Oz HOSTEL $
(Map p718; ☎1800 633 307, 08-8223 3551; www.backpackoz.com.au; cnr Wakefield & Pulteney Sts; dm/s/d from $25/55/65; ❄ @ 📶) It doesn't look like much externally, but this converted pub (the old Orient Hotel) strikes the right balance between party and placid. There are spacious dorms and an additional no-frills guesthouse over the road (good for couples), and guests can still get a coldie and shoot some pool in the bar. Communal area; free barbecue on Wednesday.

Adelaide City Park Motel MOTEL $$
(Map p718; ☎08-8223 1444; www.citypark.com.au; 471 Pulteney St; d without/with bathroom from $99/120, tr/f from $160/210; P ❄ 📶) Immaculate bathrooms, leather lounges, winsome French prints and an easy walk to the Hutt St restaurants. Free parking, DVDs and wireless internet, too. Ask about the apartments on the way to Glenelg (one- and two-bedroom units $175 to $225).

Adelaide Backpackers Inn HOSTEL $
(Map p718; ☎1800 099 318, 08-8223 6635; www.abpi.com.au; 112 Carrington St; dm/s/d/tr $27/60/70/99; ❄ @ 📶) A relaxed and surprisingly decent place filling out an 1841 pub (the ol' Horse & Jockey) that's had a recent facelift (new bathrooms, fridges, carpets, washing machines, snappy paint colours etc). Handy to Hutt and Rundle Sts.

Shakespeare International Backpackers HOSTEL $
(Map p718; ☎1800 556 889, 08-8231 7655; www.shakeys.com.au; 123 Waymouth St; dm/s/d from $26/80/80; ❄ @ 📶) Rambling through an old downtown pub (1879), laid-back Shakeys has friendly staff, a serious stainless-steel kitchen, free linen and a balcony over the street (look down on the suits and count your blessings). There was a new bar/travel desk being built downstairs when we visited.

North Adelaide

Greenways Apartments APARTMENTS $$
(Map p728; ☎08-8267 5903; www.greenwaysapartments.com; 41-45 King William Rd, North Adelaide; 1-/2-/3-bedroom apt $120/150/190; P ❄ 📶) These 1938 apartments ain't flash (floral tiles and rude 1970s laminates), but if you have a pathological hatred of 21st-century open-plan 'lifestyles', then Greenways is for you! And where else can you stay in clean, perfectly operational apartments so close to town at these rates? A must for cricket fans, the Adelaide Oval is a lofted hook shot away – book early for Test matches.

Minima Hotel HOTEL $$
(Map p728; ☎08-8334 7766; www.majestichotels.com.au; 146 Melbourne St, North Adelaide; d from $100; P ❄ @) A spaceship has landed in ye olde North Adelaide! Just a few years old, Minima offers compact but super-stylish rooms in a winning Melbourne St location. Check-in is DIY – use the touch screen in the lobby. Limited parking $9.50 per night.

Princes Lodge Motel MOTEL $
(Map p728; ☎08-8267 5566; www.princeslodge.com.au; 73 LeFevre Tce, North Adelaide; s/d/f incl breakfast from $65/85/145; P ❄ 📶) In a grand 1913 house overlooking the parklands, this friendly, eclectic lodge has high ceilings, new TVs and a certain faded grandeur. Close to the chichi North Adelaide restaurants and within walking distance of the city. Great value with heaps of character. The budget

rooms in the old coachhouse out the back are a steal.

Tynte Street Apartments APARTMENTS $$
(Map p728; ☎08-8334 7783; www.majestichotels.com.au; 82 Tynte St, North Adelaide; d/1-bedroom apt from $125/175, extra adult $20; P ❄ ☁) These post-modern, red-brick, self-contained apartments on a tree-lined street near the O'Connell St cafes and pubs, sleeping three. Check-in is 1km away at 9 Jerningham St. Free parking to boot.

O'Connell Inn MOTEL $$
(Map p728; ☎08-8239 0766; www.oconnellinn.com.au; 197 O'Connell St, North Adelaide; d from $150; P ❄ ☁) It's absurdly difficult to find a decent motel in Adelaide (most are mired in the '90s'), but this one makes a reasonable fist of the the new century. It's smallish, friendly, affordable and in a beaut location – handy for forays north to the Barossa, Clare, Flinders etc.

Inner Suburbs

Levi Park Caravan Park CARAVAN PARK $
(Map p732; ☎08-8344 2209; www.levipark.com.au; 1a Harris Rd, Vale Park; unpowered/powered sites from $33/35, cabins/apt from $102/145; ❄ @ ☁) This leafy, grassy Torrens-side park is 5km from town and loaded with facilities, including tennis courts and a palm-fringed cricket oval. Apartments are in the restored Vale House, purportedly Adelaide's oldest residence!

Adelaide Caravan Park CARAVAN PARK $
(Map p728; ☎08-8363 1566; www.adelaidecaravanpark.com.au; 46 Richmond St, Hackney; powered sites $36-40, cabins & units $119-166; ❄ @ ☁ ≋) A compact, no-frills park on the River Torrens, rather surprisingly slotted in on a quiet street 2km northeast of the city centre. Clean and well run, with a bit of green grass if it's not too far into summer.

Glenelg & Beach Suburbs

Glenelg Holiday & Corporate Letting (☎0417 083 634, 08-8376 1934; www.glenelgholiday.com.au; ❄) and **Glenelg Letting Agency** (Map p732; ☎08-8294 9666; www.baybeachfront.com.au; ❄) offer self-contained beachside apartments in Glenelg from around $140 per night.

★**Largs Pier Hotel** HOTEL $$
(Map p732; ☎08-8449 5666; www.largspierhotel.com.au; 198 Esplanade, Largs Bay; d/apt from $159/199; P) Wow, what a surprise! In the otherwise subdued beach suburb of Largs Bay, 5km north of Port Adelaide, is this 130-year-old, three-storey wedding-cake hotel. A bucket of money has been poured into it over recent years, and it's looking great: sky-high ceilings, big beds, taupe-and-chocolate colours and beach views. There's also a low-slung wing of motel rooms off to one side, and apartments across the street.

Glenelg Beach Hostel HOSTEL $
(Map p732; ☎08-8376 0007, 1800 359 181; www.glenelgbeachhostel.com.au; 1-7 Moseley St, Glenelg; dm/s/d/f from $25/60/70/110; @ ☁) A couple of streets back from the beach, this beaut old terrace (1879) is Adelaide's budget golden child. Fan-cooled rooms maintain period details and are bunk-free. There's cold Coopers in the basement bar (live music on weekends), open fireplaces, lofty ceilings, girls-only dorms and a courtyard garden. Book *waaay* in advance in summer.

Seawall Apartments APARTMENTS $$$
(Map p732; ☎08-8295 1197; www.seawallapartments.com.au; 21-25 South Esplanade, Glenelg; 1-/2-/3-/4-bed apts from $200/270/380/430; P ❄ ☁) Readers recommend this renovated row of old houses, a five-minute wander along the sea wall from Mosely Sq in Glenelg. They really didn't need a gimmick – the location seals the deal – but the facades are festooned with kitsch nautical paraphernalia (nets, boats, oars, shark jaws...). Inside the apartments are roomy, contemporary and immaculate.

Adelaide Shores CARAVAN PARK $
(Map p732; ☎08-8355 7320, 1800 444 567; www.adelaideshores.com.au; 1 Military Rd, West Beach; powered sites $36-57, 1-/2-bed cabins from $87/134; P ❄ @ ≋) Hunkered-down behind the West Beach dunes with a walking/cycling track extending to Glenelg (3.4km) in one direction and Henley Beach (3.5km) in the other, this is a choice spot in summer. There are lush sites, glistening amenities and passing dolphins.

Stamford Grand Hotel HOTEL $$$
(Map p732; ☎08-8376 1222; www.stamford.com.au; Moseley Sq, Glenelg; d city/ocean views from $200/250; P ❄ @ ☁ ≋) The first Glenelg edifice to scrape the sky with any real authority, this plush, pink-hued hotel overlooks

North Adelaide

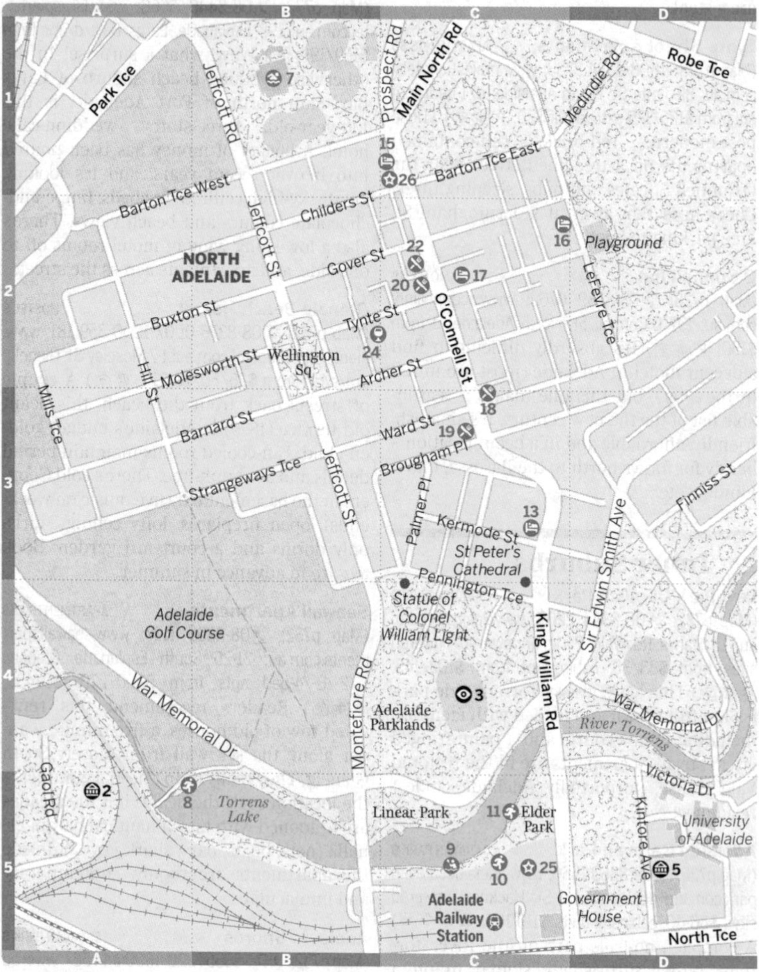

Gulf St Vincent. Dinner, bed and breakfast packages are decent value; good off-season rates. Just sidestep the faux gold-leaf embellishments and chesterfields in the lobby. Parking from $15.

Eating

Foodies flock to West End hot spots like Gouger St (pronounced 'Goo-jer'), Chinatown and food-filled Central Market. There are some great pubs here too. Artsy, alternative Hindley St – Adelaide's dirty little secret – has a smattering of good eateries. In the East End, Rundle St and Hutt St offer al-fresco cafes and people-watching. North Adelaide's Melbourne and O'Connell Sts have a healthy spread of bistros, provedores and pubs.

West End

Press MODERN AUSTRALIAN $$$

(Map p718; ☎08-8211 8048; www.pressfoodandwine.com.au; 40 Waymouth St; mains $16-46; ⊙noon-9pm Mon-Sat) The best of an emerging strip of restaurants on office-heavy Waymouth St. Super-stylish (brick, glass, lemon-coloured chairs) and not afraid of offal

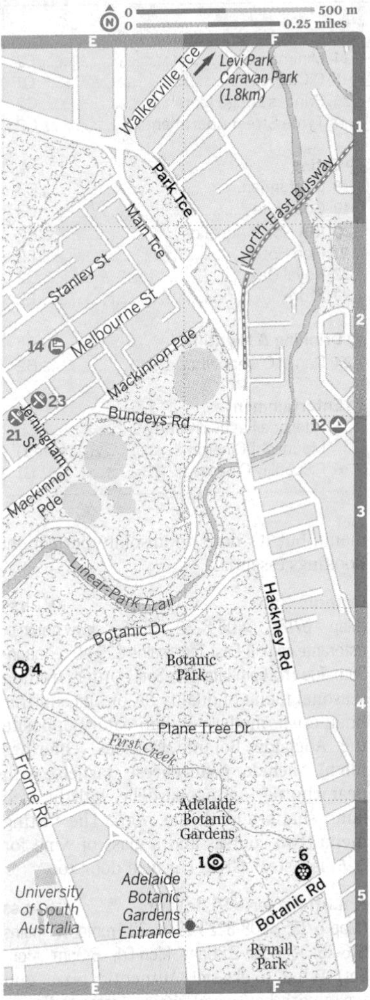

(pan-fried lamb's brains, grilled calf's tongue) or things raw (beef carpaccio, gravlax salmon) and confit (duck leg, onion, olives). Try the house-made spicy beef sausages, or the tasting menu ($68 per person).

Mesa Lunga MEDITERRANEAN **$$**
(Map p718; ☎08-8410 7617; www.mesalunga.com; cnr Gouger & Morphett Sts; tapas $4-14, mains $16-28; ⏲noon-3pm Fri, noon-late Sun, 6pm-late Tue-Sat) In a fishbowl corner room with a sexy dark-wood wine wall, sassy Mesa Lunga serves tapas and quality pizzas. Order some *gamba* (black-salted prawn and chorizo in pastry) and anchovies stuffed with Manzanillo olives, washed down with some sparkling sangria. Magic.

Lucia's Pizza & Spaghetti Bar ITALIAN **$**
(Map p718; www.lucias.com.au; 2 Western Mall, Central Market; meals $8-13; ⏲7am-4pm Mon-Thu & Sat, to 9pm Fri) This little slice of Italy has been around since Lucia was a lot younger. All her pasta, sauces and pizzas are authentically homemade – perfection any time of day. If you like what you're eating, you can buy fresh pasta next door at Lucia's Fine Foods.

Village Indian INDIAN **$$**
(Map p718; ☎08-8212 2536; www.thevillagerestaurant.com.au; 125 Gouger St; mains $14-29; ⏲noon-2.30pm Tue-Fri, 5.30-9pm Tue-Sun; ✎) Taking on Jasmin for bragging rights as Adelaide's best Indian restaurant, the Village (all smooth service, nice knives and balloon-like wine glasses) offers some unusual subcontinental offerings. Try the Kashmiri Goat Yakhni (simmered in yoghurt, aniseed and cardamon) or Moreton Bay Bug masala. Busy Gouger St location.

Evergreen CHINESE **$**
(Map p718; ☎08-8212 1686; 31 Moonta St; yum cha $5-19; ⏲11am-3pm Mon-Sat, 5pm-late Mon-Sun; ✎) A few steps away from the Gouger St fray, Chinatown's Evergreen has rapidly earned a rep for great yum cha. There are a staggering 182 items on the menu (everything from eggplant hotpot to stir-fried ginger scallops), plus a passable wine list and paper tablecloths so you can get messy.

Jerusalem Sheshkabab House MIDDLE EASTERN **$**
(Map p718; ☎08-8212 6185; 131 Hindley St; mains $10-15; ⏲11.30am-2.30pm & 5.30-10pm Tue-Sat, 4-10pm Sun; ✎) A skinny Hindley St room that's been here forever, serving magnificent Middle Eastern and Lebanese delights: falafels, hummus, tabouleh, tahini and (of course) sheshkababs.

Ying Chow CHINESE **$$**
(Map p718; 114 Gouger St; mains $11-17; ⏲noon-2.45pm Fri, 5pm-12.45am daily) This fluoro-lit, bossy-staffed eatery is a culinary gem, serving cuisine styled from the Guangzhou region, such as 'BBC' (bean curd, broad beans and Chinese chutney) and steamed duck with salty sauce. It gets packed – with queues out the door (no bookings) – but it's worth the wait.

North Adelaide

East End

★ Galaxy Lartay CAFE $

(Map p718; 31 East Tce; mains $7-15; noon-4pm Tue-Sun;) In a lovely old red-brick East End shopfront, our new favourite Adelaide cafe keeps sketchy opening hours – but don't let that stop you from wandering by to see if they're open. The vibe is arty, hippie, retro and communal: expect big servings of tarts, quiches, curries and pies, plus creative juices, lassis and solid coffee. And you can get a beer here too!

Zen Kitchen VIETNAMESE $

(Map p718; www.zenkitchen.com.au; Unit 7, Tenancy 2, Renaissance Arc; mains $6-14; 11am-4pm Mon-Thu, to 8pm Fri, to 3pm Sat) Superb, freshly constructed cold rolls, *pho* soups and super-crunchy barbecue pork bread rolls, eat-in or take away. Wash it all down with a cold coconut milk or a teeth-grindingly strong Vietnamese coffee with sugary condensed milk. Authentic, affordable and absolutely delicious.

Jasmin Indian Restaurant INDIAN $$

(Map p718; 08-8223 7837; www.jasmin.com.au; 31 Hindmarsh Sq, basement; mains $26-29; noon-2.30pm Thu & Fri, 5.30-9pm Tue-Sat) Magical North Indian curries and consummately professional staff (they might remember your name from when you ate here in 2006). There's nothing too surprising about the menu, but it's done to absolute perfection. Bookings essential.

Botanic Café ITALIAN $$

(Map p718; 08-8232 0626; www.botanic-ristorante.com; 4 East Tce; mains $25-40; noon-3pm Tue-Fri, 6pm-late Thu-Sat) Order from a seasonal menu of quality SA produce in this linen-crisp, modern Italian eatery opposite the Adelaide Botanic Gardens. Offerings might include goats-cheese tartlets with pear chutney, or pappardelle with braised lamb shank and thyme *ragu*. The tasting menu (two courses and a glass of wine for $25) is a steal. Great bar next door, too.

Amalfi Pizzeria Ristorante ITALIAN $$

(Map p718; 08-8223 1948; 29 Frome St; mains $16-26; noon-2.30pm Mon-Fri, 6-9pm Mon-Sat) What a classic! Authentic pizza and pasta with bentwood chairs, terrazzo floors, specials scribbled on a chalkboard, sleep-defeating coffee and imagined Mafioso mutterings in the back room.

Sosta ARGENTINEAN $$$

(Map p718; 08-8232 6799; www.sostaargentiniankitchen.com.au; 291 Rundle St; tapas $16-26, mains $33-45; noon-2.30pm Mon-Fri, 6-9.30pm daily) Beef, lamb, pork, chicken, fish…vegetarians run for the hills! Sosta's aged 1kg T-bone steaks are legendary. With crisp white tablecloths and blood-brown floorboards, it's an elegant place to launch your nocturnal East End foray.

Vego & Lovin' It VEGETARIAN $
(Map p718; 240 Rundle St, Level 1; meals $7-13; ⏲10am-3pm Mon-Fri; ✎) Get your weekly vitamin dose disguised in a scrumptious vegie burger, wrap or focaccia at this artsy upstairs kitchen. Dreadlocked urban renegades order 'extra alfalfa but no hummus'. Has the cool mosaic sign been fixed yet?

Lemongrass Thai Bistro THAI $$
(Map p718; ☎08-8223 6627; www.lemongrassthaibistro.com.au; 289 Rundle St; mains $16-26; ⏲11.30am-3pm Mon-Fri, 5pm-late daily; ✎) Affordable, breezy Thai joint right in the Rundle St mix. Mango and coconut chicken, red curry beef (or kangaroo!), clattering chairs and chilli chatter.

North Adelaide

Store CAFE, BISTRO $$
(Map p728; ☎08-8361 6999; www.thestore.com.au; 157 Melbourne St; breakfast $8-19, mains $15-28; ⏲7am-3pm daily, 5.30-9pm Thu-Sun; ✎) Some much-needed hipness in stuffy North Adelaide, Store is a combo of casual Parisian bistro and jazzy cafe. The decor is retro-kitsch (Art Nouveau posters, stag horns, Tretchikoff prints), while on your plate you can expect rapid-fire pastas, risottos, burgers and classy fish, chicken and beef dishes, none of which will break the bank. Impressive wine list, too.

d'Artagnan BISTRO $$$
(Map p728; ☎08-8267 6688; www.dartagnan.net.au; 26 O'Connell St; mains $34-42; ⏲6pm-midnight Tue-Sat) Looking like a transplanted tavern from the era of King Louis XIII (all moody mirrors, velvet, dark wood, candles and chandeliers), d'Artagnan is bravely pushing the boundaries of the Adelaide dining experience (places you can eat after 9pm are almost unheard of). Expect meaty mains cooked with Franco flair. No sign of the other musketeers...

Royal Oak PUB $$
(Map p728; ☎08-8267 2488; www.royaloakhotel.com.au; 123 O'Connell St; mains $12-34; ⏲8am-noon Sat & Sun, noon-3pm & 6-9.30pm daily) Winning pub grub at this enduring (and endearing) local: steak sangers, vegie lasagne, lamb-shank pie, eggs Florentine and French toast with maple syrup (not all at once). Quirky retro vibe; live jazz/indie-rock Tuesday, Wednesday, Friday and Sunday.

Lion Hotel PUB $$$
(Map p728; ☎08-8367 0222; www.thelionhotel.com; 161 Melbourne St; mains $30-40; ⏲noon-3pm Mon-Fri & Sun, 6-10pm Mon-Sat) Off to one side of this upmarket boozer (all big screens, beer terraces and business types) is a sassy restaurant with a cool retro interior and romantic vibes. Hot off the menu are luscious Coorong Angus steaks, market fish and corn-fed chicken breasts, served with very un-pubby professionalism. Breakfast next door in the bar (mains $10 to $26).

Inner Suburbs

Bar 9 CAFE $
(Map p732; ☎08-8373 1108; www.bar9.com.au; 96 Glen Osmond Rd, Parkside; mains $11-17; ⏲7.30am-4pm Mon-Fri, 8.30am-2pm Sat & Sun) If you're serious about coffee, this bean barn – a short

WEST END PUB GRUB

Wander the West End backstreets for some great-value pub food.

Edinburgh Castle (Map p56; ☎08-8231 1435; www.edinburghcastlehotel.com; 233 Currie St; mains from $10; ⏲noon-2pm & 6-8pm Tue-Sun; ✎) Super cheap $10 menu (the students love it) featuring schnitzels, burgers, vegie lasagne, and beer-battered whiting. Live original bands most nights.

Prince Albert (Map p718; ☎08-8212 7912; www.princealberthotel.com.au; 254 Wright St; mains $10-20; ⏲noon-2.30pm & 6-8.30pm) Cheap pub grub that looms large: steaks, rissoles, burgers, hanging-off-the-plate schnitzels and signature West End sausages. Below-the-belt body piercings not a prerequisite.

Hotel Wright Street (Map p718; ☎08-8211 8000; www.hotelwrightstreet.com.au; 88 Wright St; mains $17-28; ⏲8am-noon Sat & Sun, noon-3pm & 5.30-9pm daily) Mod-industrial renovations, cruising gay guys, makeup-caked cougars and kooky DJs. Oh yeah, and great fish and chips, steaks and schnitzels too.

Greater Adelaide

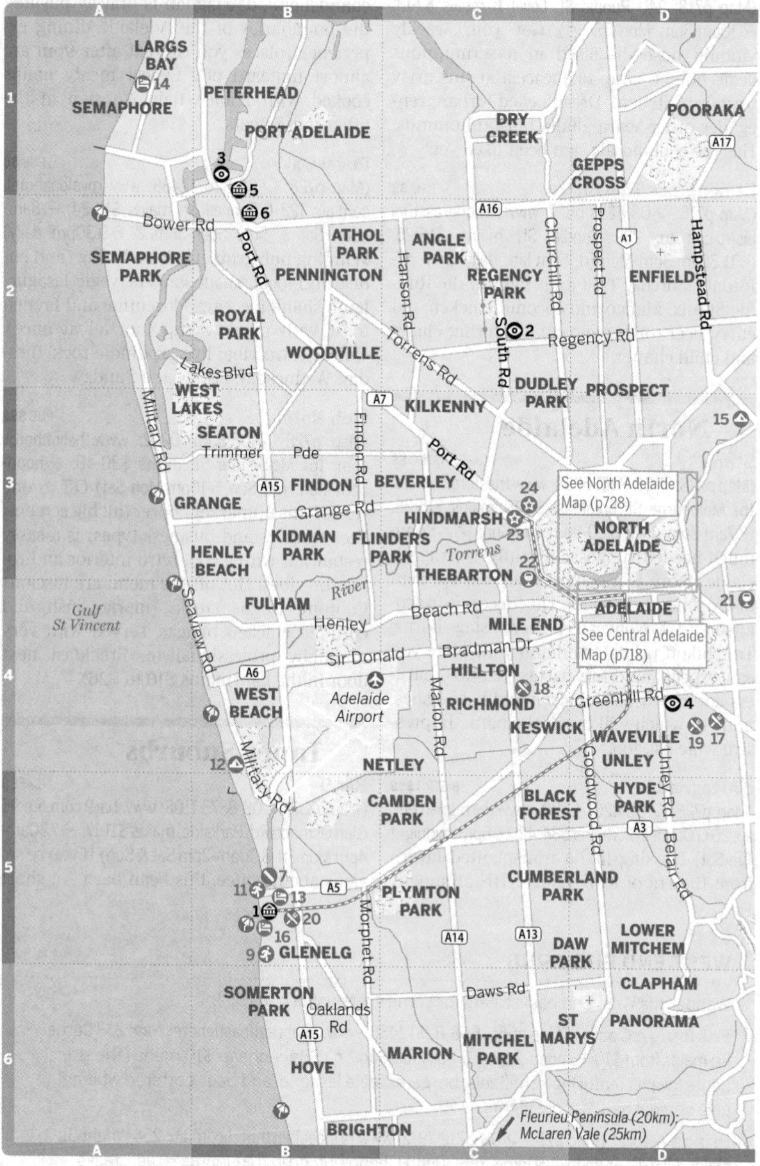

hop southeast of the city centre – is for you. Food is almost secondary here: the hipster, cardigan-wearing customers are too busy discussing the coffee specials board to eat. But if you are hungry, Bar 9 does a mean bacon-and-eggs, vanilla bircher muesli and creamy mushrooms on toast.

Earl of Leicester PUB **$$**

(Map p732; ☎08-8271 5700; www.earl.com.au; 85 Leicester St, Parkside; mains $17-34; ⊙noon-3pm & 6-9pm) Hidden in the suburban Parkside backstreets is this atmospheric old bluestone pub (1886), serving a winning combo of crafty beers and huge schnitzels. The

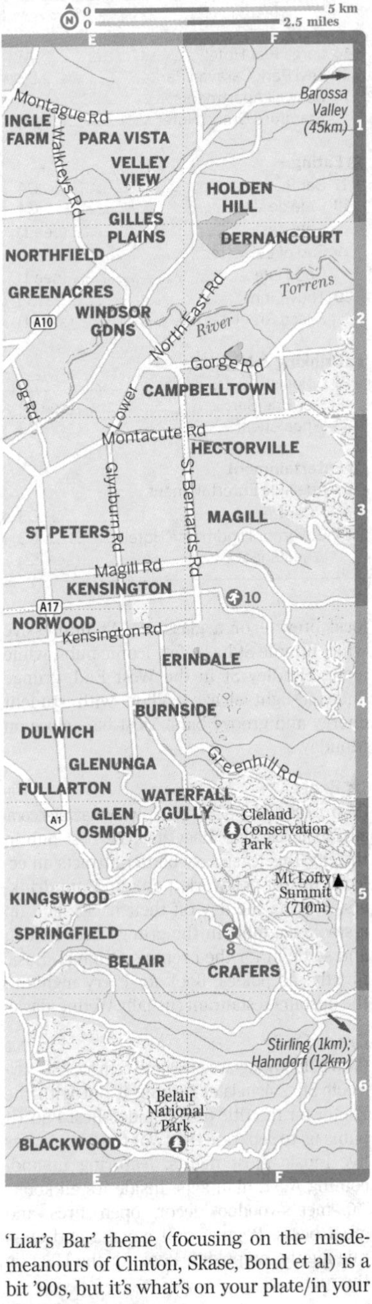

'Liar's Bar' theme (focusing on the misdemeanours of Clinton, Skase, Bond et al) is a bit '90s, but it's what's on your plate/in your glass that counts.

Café de Vili's FAST FOOD **$**
(Map p732; www.vilis.com; 2-14 Manchester St, Mile End Sth; meals $3-14; ⏲24hr) Vili's pies are a South Australian institution. Next to its factory, just west of the West End, is this all-night diner, serving equally iconic 'pie floaters' (a meat pie floating in pea soup, topped with mashed potato, gravy and sauce – outstanding!), plus sausage rolls, pasties, burgers, pancakes, cooked breakfasts, custard tarts, donuts...

Glenelg

Cafe Zest CAFE **$**
(Map p732; ☎08-8295 3599; www.zestcafegallery.com.au; 2a Sussex St; meals $5-20; ⏲7.30am-5.30pm; ✎) This cafe-gallery fills a tiny crack between buildings, but its laid-back vibe and brilliant breakfasts more than compensate for any shortcomings in size. Baguettes and bagels are crammed with creative combos, or you can banish your hangover with some 'Zesty Eggs': on buttered toast with seeded mustard, orange zest cream and smoked salmon. Great coffee, arty staff, and vegetarian specials too.

Good Life PIZZERIA **$$**
(Map p732; ☎08-8376 5900; www.goodlifepizza.com; cnr Jetty Rd & Moseley St, Level 1; pizzas $14-39; ⏲noon-2.30pm Tue-Fri & Sun, 6pm-late daily; ✎) 🍃 At this brilliant organic pizzeria above the Jetty Rd tram-scape, thin crusts are stacked with tasty toppings like free-range roast duck, Spencer Gulf 'monster' prawns and spicy Angaston salami. *Ahhh, life is good...* Also has a branch in the **city** (Map p718; ☎08-8223 2618; 170 Hutt St; ⏲noon-2.30pm Mon-Fri, 6pm-late daily; ✎) 🍃 and **North Adelaide** (Map p728; ☎08-8267 3431; Shop 5, 11 O'Connell St, North Adelaide; ⏲noon-2.30pm Tue-Fri, 6pm-late daily; ✎) 🍃.

Thuy-Linh VIETNAMESE **$$**
(Map p732; ☎08-8295 5746; 168c Jetty Rd; mains $15-19, banquets per person from $24; ⏲11.30am-2.30pm Tue-Fri, 5-10pm Tue-Sun) Astonishingly unpretentious Vietnamese/Chinese eatery at the city end of Jetty Rd. Don't expect too much from the interior design – just super-attentive service and a swathe of fresh seafood, meat and noodle delights.

Zucca Greek Mezze GREEK **$$$**
(Map p732; ☎08-8376 8222; www.zucca.com.au; Shop 5, Marina Pier, Holdfast Shores; mezze $5-21, mains $32-45; ⏲noon-3pm & 6pm-late) Spartan

Greater Adelaide

Sights
1 Bay Discovery Centre B5
2 Coopers Brewery C2
3 Fishermen's Wharf Market B1
4 Haigh's Chocolates Visitors Centre D4
5 National Railway Museum B1
6 South Australian Aviation Museum B2
South Australian Maritime Museum .... (see 3)

Activities, Courses & Tours
7 Adelaide Scuba B5
Dolphin Explorer Cruises .... (see 3)
8 Eagle Mountain Bike Park F5
9 Glenelg Bicycle Hire B5
10 Penfolds Magill Estate Winery F3
11 Temptation Sailing B5

Sleeping
12 Adelaide Shores B4
Glenelg Beach Hostel .... (see 1)
13 Glenelg Letting Agency B5
14 Largs Pier Hotel A1
15 Levi Park Caravan Park D3
16 Seawall Apartments B5
Stamford Grand Hotel .... (see 1)

Eating
17 Bar 9 .... D4
18 Café de Vili's C4
Cafe Zest .... (see 1)
19 Earl of Leicester D4
Good Life .... (see 1)
20 Thuy-Linh B5
Zucca Greek Mezze .... (see 11)

Drinking & Nightlife
21 Colonist D4
Pier One Bar .... (see 11)
22 Wheatsheaf C3

Entertainment
23 Adelaide Entertainment Centre C3
24 Governor Hindmarsh Hotel C3
Wheatsheaf .... (see 22)

linen, marina views, super service and a contemporary menu of tapas-style mezze plates – you wouldn't find anything this classy on Santorini. The grilled Cyprian haloumi with sweetened raisins and salty pistachio crumble are sublime.

Self-Catering

Central Market MARKET $
(Map p718; www.adelaidecentralmarket.com.au; Gouger St; 7am-5.30pm Tue, 9am-5.30pm Wed & Thu, 7am-9pm Fri, 7am-3pm Sat) This place is an exercise in sensory bombardment: a barrage of smells, colours and yodelling stallholders selling fresh vegetables, breads, cheeses, seafood and gourmet produce. There are cafes, hectic food courts and a supermarket here as well.

IGA North Adelaide SUPERMARKET $
(Map p728; www.iga.net.au; 113 O'Connell St, North Adelaide; 8am-10pm) Look for the nifty deli/butcher counter out the front.

Woolworths SUPERMARKET $
(Map p718; www.woolworths.com.au; 80 Rundle Mall; 7am-9pm Mon-Fri, 7am-5pm Sat, 11am-5pm Sun)

Drinking & Nightlife

Pubs & Bars

For a true Adelaide experience, head for the bar and order a schooner of Coopers – the local brew – or a glass of SA's impressive wine. Rundle St has a few iconic pubs, while along Hindley St in the West End, grunge and red-light sleaze collide with student energy and groovy bars. Most bars close on Monday.

★ **Exeter** PUB
(Map p718; 08-8223 2623; www.theexeter.com.au; 246 Rundle St; 11am-late) The best pub in the city, this legendary boozer attracts an eclectic mix of postwork, punk and uni drinkers, shaking the day off their backs. Pull up a stool or a table in the grungy beer garden and settle in for the evening. Original music nightly; no pokies. Book for curry nights in the upstairs restaurant (usually Wednesdays).

Grace Emily PUB
(Map p718; www.graceemilyhotel.com.au; 232 Waymouth St; 4pm-late) Duking it out with the Exeter for the title of 'Adelaide's Best Pub' (it pains us to separate the two) the 'Gracie' has live music most nights, featuring up-and-coming Australian acts. Inside it's all kooky '50s-meets-voodoo decor, open fires and great beers. Regular cult cinema and open mic nights; no pokies. Look for the UFO on the roof.

Wheatsheaf PUB
(Map p732; www.wheatsheafhotel.com.au; 39 George St, Thebarton; 11am-midnight Mon-Fri,

noon-midnight Sat, noon-9pm Sun;) A hidden gem under the flight path in industrial Thebarton, with an artsy crowd of students, jazz musos, lesbians, punks and rockers. Tidy beer garden, live music, open fires and rumours of a new kitchen opening soon. Great beer list.

Cork Wine Cafe WINE BAR

(Map p718; www.facebook.com/corkwinecafe; 61a Gouger St; 4pm-midnight Mon-Thu, 3pm-1am Fri & Sat, 4pm-10pm Sun;) A down-sized Frenchie hole-in-the-wall wine bar, unexpected among the fluoro-lit Chinese restaurants along this stretch of Gouger St. Well-worn floorboards, bentwood chairs, absinthe posters...perfect for a quick vino before dinner (see fluoro-lit Chinese restaurants, above).

Udaberri BAR

(Map p718; www.udaberri.com.au; 11-13 Leigh St; 4pm-late Tue-Thu, 3pm-late Fri, 6pm-late Sat) Taking a leaf out of the Melbourne book on laneway boozing, Udaberri is a little hole-in-the-wall bar on compact Leigh St, serving Spanish wines by the glass, a few good beers on tap and pintxos (Basque bar snacks) like oysters, cheeses, *jamon* and tortillas. Why aren't there more bars like this in Adelaide?

Casablabla BAR

(Map p718; www.casablabla.com; 12 Leigh St; 4pm-late Tue-Fri, 6pm-late Sat) Billing itself as a 'multicultural tapas lounge bar', Casablabla covers a lot of bases but does it well. The atmosphere is eclectic: exotic art (a bit of Morocco, a bit of Bali, a bit of Brazil), hookah pipes, fish tanks, burnt-orange walls... Sip cocktails in the middle of it all and tune in to reggae, funk, soul and jazz.

Belgian Beer Café THEME BAR

(Map p718; www.oostende.com.au; 27-29 Ebenezer Pl; 11am-midnight Sun-Thu, 11am-2am Fri & Sat) There's shiny brass, sexy staff, much presluicing of glasses and somewhere upwards of 26 imported Belgian superbrews (we lost count...). Order some *moules-frites* to go with your *weiss* beer. Off Rundle St.

Apothecary 1878 WINE BAR

(Map p718; www.theapothecary1878.com.au; 118 Hindley St; 5pm-late Tue-Sat) Classy coffee and wine at this gorgeous chemist-turned-bar. Medicine cabinets, bentwood chairs and Parisian marble-topped tables. Perfect first-date territory.

Colonist PUB

(Map p732; www.colonist.com.au; 44 The Parade, Norwood; 9am-late) Funky countercultural boozing on Norwood's otherwise mainstream Parade. Wonderfully well-worn, and bedecked in Gustav Klimt–style murals. Packed after Norwood FC (Aussie Rules football) games empty out from the ground across the road.

Universal Wine Bar WINE BAR

(Map p718; www.universalwinebar.com.au; 285 Rundle St; noon-late) A snappy crowd clocks in to this stalwart bar to select from 400-plus South Australian and international wines, and a menu (mains $19 to $36) packed with SA produce. 'The scene is very Italian', says the barman.

Daniel O'Connell PUB

(Map p728; www.danieloconnell.com.au; 165 Tynte St, North Adelaide; 11am-midnight) An 1881 Irish pub without a whiff of kitsch Celtic cash-in: just great Guinness, open fires, acoustic music and a house-sized pepper tree in the beer garden (166 years old and counting).

Distill COCKTAIL BAR

(Map p718; www.distillhealth.com.au; 286 Rundle St; noon-2.30am Tue, Wed, Fri & Sun, 5pm-late Thu & Sat) Super-sassy Rundle St bar with a tight dress code (to the nines) and a kickin' organic cocktail list. Cheese boards and pizzas are available, but no-one here looks like they eat anything with any regularity.

Pier One Bar BAR

(Map p732; www.glenelgpier.com.au; 18 Holdfast Promenade, Glenelg; noon-midnight Mon-Thu, noon-2am Fri, 11am-2am Sat & Sun) A cavernous mainstream sports bar with voyeuristic beach views and fold-back windows for when the sea breeze drops. As many screens as staff (a lot of each), and raucous Sunday sessions.

PINT OF COOPERS PLEASE!

Things can get confusing at the bar in Adelaide. Aside from 200ml (7oz) 'butchers' – the choice of old men in dim, sticky-carpet pubs – there are three main beer sizes: 285ml (10oz) 'schooners' (pots or middies elsewhere in Australia), 425ml (15oz) 'pints' (schooners elsewhere) and 568ml (20oz) 'imperial pints' (traditional English pints). Now, go forth and order with confidence!

Clubs

Online, check out www.onion.com.au. Cover charges can be anything from free to $15, depending on the night. Most clubs close Monday to Wednesday.

Zhivago CLUB

(Map p718; www.zhivago.com.au; 54 Currie St; 9pm-late Fri-Sun) At the pick of the West End clubs (there are quite a few of 'em – some are a bit moron-prone), Zhivago's DJs pump out everything from reggae and dub to quality house. Popular with the 18 to 25 dawn patrol.

RedLove CLUB

(Map p718; www.redlove.com.au; Level 1, 170 Pulteney St; 4pm-late Fri, 9pm-late Sat) This cool upstairs club used to be a pool hall (lots of elbow room). Spinning old-school RnB, funk and house to a 25-to-35 kinda crowd (old enough to remember the '90s, young enough not to have to hurry home to the babysitter).

Lotus Lounge CLUB

(Map p718; www.lotuslounge.net.au; 268 Morphett St; 6pm-late Tue-Sat) We like the signage here – a very minimal fluoro martini glass with a flashing olive. Inside it's a glam lounge with cocktails, quality beers and Adelaide dolls cuttin' the rug. Expect queues around the corner on Saturday nights.

HQ Complex CLUB

(Map p718; www.hqcomplex.com.au; 1 North Tce; 8pm-late Wed & Sat) Adelaide's biggest club fills five big rooms with shimmering sound and light. Night-time is the right time on Saturdays – the biggest (and trashiest) club night in town. Retro Wednesdays.

Mars Bar CLUB

(Map p718; www.themarsbar.com.au; 120 Gouger St; 9pm-late Thu-Sat) The lynchpin of Adelaide's nocturnal gay and lesbian scene, always-busy Mars Bar features glitzy decor, flashy clientele and OTT drag shows.

☆ Entertainment

Artsy Adelaide has a rich cultural life that stacks up favourably with much larger cities. For big-ticket event bookings:

BASS (13 12 46; www.bass.net.au)

Moshtix (1300 438 849; www.moshtix.com.au)

Venue Tix (08-8225 8888; www.venuetix.com.au)

Adelaide Now (www.adelaidenow.com.au) City-wide events, cinema and gallery details.

Adelaide Review (www.adelaidereview.com.au) Theatre and gallery listings.

Adelaide Theatre Guide (www.theatreguide.com.au) Booking details, venues and reviews for comedy, drama and musicals.

Music SA (www.musicsa.com.au) All-genre online musical listings.

Live Music

With serious musical pedigree (from Cold Chisel to Bon Scott and the Audreys), Adelaide knows how to kick out the jams! The free street-press papers *Rip It Up* (www.ripitup.com.au) and *dB* (www.dbmagazine.com.au) – available from record shops, pubs and cafes – have band and DJ listings and reviews. Cover charges vary with acts.

★ **Governor Hindmarsh Hotel** LIVE MUSIC

(Map p732; www.thegov.com.au; 59 Port Rd, Hindmarsh; 11am-late) Ground Zero for live music in Adelaide, 'The Gov' hosts some legendary local and international acts. The odd Irish band fiddles around in the bar, while the main venue features rock, folk, jazz, blues, salsa, reggae and dance. A huge place with an inexplicably personal vibe. Good food, too.

Grace Emily LIVE MUSIC

(Map p718; www.graceemilyhotel.com.au; 232 Waymouth St) West End alt-rock, country and acoustic, plus open-mic nights. Are the Bastard Sons of Ruination playing tonight?

Jive LIVE MUSIC

(Map p718; www.jivevenue.com; 181 Hindley St; varies) In a converted theatre, Jive caters to an off-beat crowd of student types who like their tunes funky, left-field and removed from the mainstream. A sunken dance floor = great views from the bar!

Wheatsheaf LIVE MUSIC

(Map p732; www.wheatsheafhotel.com.au; 39 George St, Thebarton; 11am-midnight Mon-Fri, noon-midnight Sat, noon-9pm Sun) Eclectic offerings (acoustic, blues, country...and a brilliant beer list) in the semi-industrial Thebarton wastelands. Don't let the flightpath sonics put you off.

Exeter LIVE MUSIC
(Map p718; www.theexeter.com.au; 246 Rundle St; ⏲11am-late) The East End's rockin' soul: original indie bands, electronica and acoustic in the undercover beer garden.

Fowlers Live LIVE MUSIC
(Map p718; www.fowlerslive.com.au; 68 North Tce; ⏲varies) Inside the former Fowler Flour Factory, this 500-capacity venue is a devilish temple of hard rock, punk and metal.

Jazz Adelaide LIVE MUSIC
(www.jazz.adelaide.onau.net) Finger-snappin' za-bah-dee-dah.

Adelaide Symphony Orchestra ORCHESTRA
(Map p718; www.aso.com.au) Online listings for the estimable ASO.

Cinemas

Check out www.my247.com.au/adelaide/cinemas for movie listings. Tickets generally cost around adult/child $19/13 (cheaper on Tuesdays).

Palace Nova Eastend Cinemas CINEMA
(Map p718; ☎08-8232 3434; www.palacenova.com; 250 & 251 Rundle St; ⏲10am-midnight) Facing-off across Rundle St, both these cinema complexes screen 'sophisticated cinema': new-release art-house, foreign-language and independent films as well as some mainstream flicks. Fully licensed, too.

Moonlight Cinema CINEMA
(Map p728; ☎1300 551 908; www.moonlight.com.au; Botanic Gardens; ⏲mid-Dec–mid-Feb) In summer, pack a picnic and mosquito repellent, and spread out on the lawn to watch old and new classics under the stars. 'Gold Grass' tickets secure you a prime-viewing beanbag and cost a little more.

Piccadilly Cinema CINEMA
(Map p728; ☎08-8267 1500; www.wallis.com.au; 181 O'Connell St, North Adelaide) A beaut old art-deco cinema on the main North Adelaide strip, with a sexily curved street frontage and chevron-shaped windows spangled across the facade. It screens mostly mainstream releases.

Mercury Cinema CINEMA
(Map p718; ☎08-8410 0979; www.mercurycinema.org.au; 13 Morphett St, Lion Arts Centre) The Mercury screens art-house releases, and is home to the Adelaide Cinémathèque (classic, cult and experimental flicks).

Theatre & Comedy

Adelaide Festival Centre PERFORMING ARTS
(Map p728; www.adelaidefestivalcentre.com.au; King William Rd; ⏲varies) The hub of performing arts in SA, this crystalline white Festival Centre opened in June 1973, four proud months before the Sydney Opera House! The **State Theatre Company** (www.statetheatrecompany.com.au) is based here.

Adelaide Entertainment Centre CONCERT VENUE
(Map p732; www.theaec.net; 98 Port Rd, Hindmarsh; ⏲varies) Around 12,000 bums on seats for everyone from the Wiggles to Stevie Wonder.

Rhino Room COMEDY
(Map p718; www.rhinoroom.com.au; 13 Frome St; ⏲7.30pm-late Mon, Thu & Fri) Live stand-up acts from around Australia and overseas on Thursday and Friday nights, plus open-mic comedy on Mondays.

Sport

As most Australian cities do, Adelaide hangs its hat on the successes of its sporting teams. In the **Australian Football League** (AFL; www.afl.com.au), the Adelaide Crows and Port Adelaide Power have sporadic success (and will be playing at the Adelaide Oval from 2014). Suburban Adelaide teams compete in the **South Australian National Football League** (SANFL; www.sanfl.com.au). The football season runs from March to September.

In the **National Basketball League** (NBL; www.nbl.com.au), the Adelaide 36ers have been a force for decades. In soccer's **A League** (www.a-league.com.au), Adelaide United are usually competitive. In summer, under the auspices of **Cricket SA** (www.cricketsa.com.au), the Redbacks play one-day and multiday state matches at the Adelaide Oval. The Redbacks re-brand as the Adelaide Strikers in the national **T20 Big Bash** (www.bigbash.com.au) competition.

Shopping

Shops and department stores (Myer, David Jones et al) line Rundle Mall. The beautiful old arcades running between the mall and Grenfell St retain their original splendour, and house eclectic little shops. Rundle St and the surrounding lanes are home to boutique and retro clothing shops.

★**Title** BOOKS, MUSIC
(Map p718; www.titlespace.com; 2/15 Vaughan Pl; ⏲10am-6pm Mon-Thu & Sat, 10am-9pm Fri,

11am-5pm Sun) Lefty, arty and subversive in the best possible way, Title is the place to find that elusive Miles Davis disc or Charles Bukowski poetry compilation.

Imprints Booksellers BOOKS
(Map p718; www.imprints.com.au; 107 Hindley St; ⌚9am-6pm Mon & Tue, 9am-9pm Wed-Fri, 9am-5pm Sat, 11am-5pm Sun) The best bookshop in Adelaide in the worst location (in the thick of the Hindley St strip-club fray)? Jazz, floorboards, Persian rugs and occasional live readings and book launches.

Midwest Trader CLOTHING, ACCESSORIES
(Map p718; www.midwesttrader.com.au; Shop 1 & 2 Ebenezer Pl; ⌚10am-6pm Mon-Thu & Sat, 10am-9pm Fri, noon-5pm Sun) Stocks a toothy range of punk, rock, skate and rockabilly gear. Its sister store **Old Midwest** (Map p718; www.midwesttrader.com.au/old-midwest; 7 Ebeneezer Pl; ⌚10am-6pm Mon-Thu & Sat, 10am-9pm Fri, noon-5pm Sun) across the street sells awesome American vintage.

Urban Cow Studio DESIGN
(Map p718; www.urbancow.com.au; 11 Frome St; ⌚10am-6pm Mon-Thu, 10am-9pm Fri, 10am-5pm Sat, noon-5pm Sun) The catch cry here is 'Handmade in Adelaide' – a brilliant assortment of paintings, jewellery, glassware, ceramics and textiles, plus there's a gallery upstairs. Their 'Heaps Good' T-shirts are appropriately pro-SA on a hot summer's afternoon.

Jurlique COSMETICS
(Map p718; www.jurlique.com.au; Shop 2Ga, 50 Rundle Mall Plaza, Rundle Mall; ⌚9am-6pm Mon-Thu, 9am-9pm Fri, 9am-5pm Sat, 11am-5pm Sun) An international success story, SA's own Jurlique sells fragrant skincare products (some Rosewater Balancing Mist, anyone?) that are pricey but worth every cent.

T'Arts DESIGN
(Map p718; www.tartscollective.com.au; 10g Gays Arcade, Adelaide Arcade, Rundle Mall; ⌚10am-5pm Mon-Sat) Textiles, jewellery, bags, cards and canvasses from a 35-member local arts co-op. Meet the artists in-store.

Map Shop MAPS
(Map p718; www.mapshop.net.au; 6-10 Peel St; ⌚9.30am-5pm Mon-Fri, 9am-12.30pm Sat) Maps, charts and guides for walking, hiking and touring, plus GPS sales and advice.

ℹ Information

EMERGENCY

Ambulance (☎emergency 000, nonemergency 1300 881 700; www.saambulance.com.au)

Fire (☎emergency 000, nonemergency 08-8204 3600; www.mfs.sa.gov.au)

Lifeline (☎13 11 14; www.lifeline.org.au; ⌚24hr) Crisis support.

Police (☎emergency 000, nonemergency 13 14 44; www.sapolice.sa.gov.au)

RAA Emergency Roadside Assistance (☎13 11 11; www.raa.net)

INTERNET ACCESS

Arena Internet Café (264 Rundle St, Level 1; ⌚11am-midnight Mon-Thu, 10am-late Fri-Sun)

Internet Coffee (53 Hindley St; ⌚7am-8pm Mon-Fri, 8am-7pm Sat, open later Dec-Feb)

MEDIA

Adelaide's daily tabloid is the parochial *Advertiser,* though the *Age, Australian* and *Financial Review* are also widely available.

Adelaide Review (www.adelaidereview.com.au) Highbrow articles, culture and arts. Free fortnightly.

Blaze (www.gaynewsnetwork.com.au) Gay-and-lesbian street press.

dB (www.dbmagazine.com.au) Local street press; loaded with music info.

Rip it Up (www.ripitup.com.au) Rival street press to dB; buckets of music info.

MEDICAL SERVICES

Emergency Dental Service (☎08-8222 8222; www.sadental.sa.gov.au)

Midnight Pharmacy (13 West Tce; ⌚7am-midnight Mon-Sat, 9am-midnight Sun)

Royal Adelaide Hospital (☎08-8222 4000; www.rah.sa.gov.au; 275 North Tce; ⌚24hr) Emergency department (not for blisters!) and STD clinic.

Women's & Children's Hospital (☎08-8161 7000; www.cywhs.sa.gov.au; 72 King William Rd, North Adelaide; ⌚24hr) Emergency and sexual-assault services.

MONEY

American Express (www.americanexpress.com; Citi Centre Arcade, Rundle Mall; ⌚9am-5pm Mon-Fri, to noon Sat) Foreign currency exchange.

Travelex (www.travelex.com.au; Beehive Corner, Rundle Mall; ⌚9am-5.30pm Mon-Fri, to 5pm Sat) Foreign currency exchange.

POST

Adelaide General Post Office (GPO; www.auspost.com.au; 141 King William St; ⌚8.30am-5.30pm Mon-Fri)

Post Office (www.auspost.com.au; 61 North Tce; ⌚9am-5pm Mon-Fri)

TOURIST INFORMATION

The South Australian Visitor Information Centre (p715) is a valuable resource.

Adelaide Visitor Information Centre Rundle Mall (Map p718; ☎08-8203 7611; www.southaustralia.com; Rundle Mall; ⌚10am-5pm Mon-Fri, 10am-4pm Sat & Sun) Adelaide-specific information, and free city-centre walking tours at 9.30am Monday to Friday. At the King William St end of the mall.

Disability Information & Resource Centre (DIRC; Map p718; ☎08-8236 0555, 1300 305 558; www.dircsa.org.au; 195 Gilles St; ⌚9am-5pm Mon-Fri) Info on accommodation, venues and travel for people with disabilities.

Women's Information Service (Map p718; ☎08-8303 0590, 1800 188 158; www.wis.sa.gov.au; Ground Fl, 91-97 Grenfell St, Chesser House; ⌚10am-4pm Mon, Tue, Thu & Fri)

Getting There & Away

AIR

Adelaide Airport (ADL; ☎08-8308 9211; www.aal.com.au; 1 James Schofield Dr, Adelaide Airport) is connected by regular flights to most Australian capitals and many regional centres. See Getting There & Around (p715) for airline info.

BUS

Adelaide Central Bus Station (www.sa.gov.au; 85 Franklin St; ⌚6am-9.30pm) has ticket offices and terminals for all major interstate and statewide services. See Getting There & Around (p716) for more info.

CAR & MOTORCYCLE

The major international car-rental companies have offices at Adelaide Airport and in the city. Note that some companies don't allow vehicles to be taken to Kangaroo Island. Local operators include:

Acacia Car Rentals (www.acaciacarrentals.com.au; 91 Sir Donald Bradman Dr, Hilton; ⌚8am-5pm Mon-Fri, 8am-noon Sat) Cheap rentals for travel within a 100km radius of Adelaide; scooter hire available.

Access Rent-a-Car (www.accessrentacar.com; 464 Port Rd, West Hindmarsh; ⌚8am-6pm Mon-Fri, 8am-noon Sat & Sun) Kangaroo Island travel permitted.

Cut Price Car & Truck Rentals (www.cutprice.com.au; cnr Sir Donald Bradman Dr & South Rd, Mile End; ⌚7.30am-5pm Mon-Fri, 8am-3pm Sat & Sun) 4WD hire available.

Koala Car Rentals (www.koalarentals.com.au; 41 Sir Donald Bradman Dr, Mile End; ⌚7.30am-5pm Mon-Fri, 8am-3pm Sat & Sun)

TRAIN

Adelaide's interstate train terminal is **Adelaide Parklands Terminal** (www.gsr.com.au; Railway Tce, Keswick; ⌚6am-1.30pm Mon, Wed & Fri, 7am-6.30pm Tue, 9am-7pm Thu, 5.15-6.30pm Sat, 8.30am-7pm Sun), 1km southwest of the city centre. See Getting There & Around (p716) for details.

Getting Around

TO/FROM THE AIRPORT & TRAIN STATION

Pre-booked private **SkyLink** (☎1300 383 783; www.skylinkadelaide.com) minibuses connect the airport and the train station with the city (one-way $10; 6am to 11.30pm). Public Adelaide Metro JetBuses (p739) ply the same route ($3 to $5; 5am to 11pm).

Taxis charge around $25 into the city (15 minutes). Many hostels will pick you up and drop you off if you're staying with them.

BICYCLE

With a valid passport or driver's licence you can borrow an 'Adelaide City Bike' (for free!) from **Bicycle SA** (☎08-8168 9999; www.bikesa.asn.au; 111 Franklin St; ⌚9am-5pm). Helmet and lock provided.

Down at the beach, hire a bike from **Glenelg Bicycle Hire** (☎08-8376 1934; www.glenelgbicyclehire.com.au; 71 Broadway, Norfolk Motor Inn, Glenelg South; per day $40; ⌚9am-5pm).

PUBLIC TRANSPORT

Adelaide Metro (☎1300 311 108; www.adelaidemetro.com.au; cnr King William & Currie Sts; ⌚8am-6pm Mon-Fri, 9am-5pm Sat, 11am-4pm Sun) provides timetables and sells tickets for Adelaide's integrated bus, train and tram network.

Tickets can also be purchased on board, at staffed train stations and in delis and news agents. Ticket types include day trip ($9.10), two-hour peak ($4.90) and two-hour off-peak ($3) tickets. Peak travel time is before 9am and after 3pm. Kids under five ride free!

Bus

Adelaide's buses are clean and reliable. Most services start around 6am and run until midnight. Additional services:

99C City Loop Bus (www.adelaidemetro.com.au; ⌚8.30am-9.30pm Mon-Fri, 9am-5.30pm Sat, 10am-5.30pm Sun) Adelaide Metro's free 99C City Loop Bus runs clockwise and anticlockwise around the CBD fringe from Adelaide Train Station on North Tce, passing the Central Market en route. Every 20 minutes weekdays; every 30 minutes Friday night and weekends.

Adelaide Connector Bus (www.cityofadelaide.com.au; ⌚8am-6pm Mon-Thu, 8am-9pm Fri, 10am-5pm Sat & Sun) Adelaide City Council runs this free service, looping around the CBD and North Adelaide. There are two hourly services – Blue and Red – plying the same route in opposite directions. Key stops include the Adelaide Zoo, Rundle Mall, Hutt St, Central Market, Hindley St, North Tce and O'Connell St.

After Midnight Buses (www.adelaidemetro.com.au; ⏲midnight-5am Sat) Adelaide Metro's After Midnight buses run select standard routes but have an 'N' preceding the route number on their displays. Standard ticket prices apply.

Train

Adelaide's hokey old diesel trains depart from **Adelaide Railway Station** (North Tce), plying five suburban routes (Belair, Gawler, Grange, Noarlunga and Outer Harbour). Trains generally run between 6am and midnight (some services start at 4.30am).

Tram

Adelaide state-of-the-art trams rumble to/from Moseley Sq in Glenelg, through Victoria Sq in the city and along North Tce to the Adelaide Entertainment Centre. Trams run approximately every seven or eight minutes on weekdays (every 15 minutes on weekends) from 6am to midnight daily. Standard ticket prices apply, but the section between South Tce and the Adelaide Entertainment Centre is free.

TAXI

Adelaide Independent Taxis (☎13 22 11, wheelchair-access cabs 1300 360 940; www.aitaxis.com.au)

Adelaide Transport (☎08-8212 1861; www.adelaidetransport.com.au) Minibus taxis for four or more people.

Suburban Taxis (☎13 10 08; www.suburbantaxis.com.au)

Yellow Cabs (☎13 22 27; www.yellowcabgroup.com.au)

ADELAIDE HILLS

When the Adelaide plains are desert-hot in the summer months, the Adelaide Hills (technically the Mt Lofty Ranges) are always a few degrees cooler, with crisp air, woodland shade and labyrinthine valleys. Early colonists built stately summer houses around Stirling and Aldgate, and German settlers escaping religious persecution also arrived, infusing towns such as Hahndorf and Lobethal with European values and architecture.

The Hills make a brilliant day trip from Adelaide: hop from town to town (all with at least one pub), passing carts of fresh produce for sale, stone cottages, olive groves and wineries along the way.

Online, go to www.visitadelaidehills.com.au, and www.adelaidehillswine.com.au for cellar-door listings.

Getting There & Around

Adelaide Metro (www.adelaidemetro.com.au) runs buses between the city and most Hills towns. The 864 and 864F city–Mt Barker buses stop at Stirling, Aldgate and Hahndorf. The 823 runs from Crafers to Mt Lofty Summit and Cleland Wildlife Park; the 830F runs from the city to Oakbank, Woodside and Lobethal.

Alternatively, there are a few good Hills day-tour options departing Adelaide (see p723).

Hahndorf

POP 1810

Like the Rocks in Sydney, and Richmond near Hobart, Hahndorf is a 'ye olde worlde' colonial enclave that trades ruthlessly on its history: it's something of a kitsch parody of itself.

That said, Hahndorf is undeniably pretty, with Teutonic sandstone architecture, European trees, and flowers overflowing from half wine barrels. And it *is* interesting: Australia's oldest surviving German settlement (1839), founded by 50 Lutheran families fleeing religious persecution in Prussia. Hahndorf was placed under martial law during WWI, and its name changed to 'Ambleside' (renamed Hahndorf in 1935). It's also slowly becoming less kitsch and more cool: there are a few good cafes here now, and on a sunny day the main street is positively lively.

Sights & Activities

Hahndorf Academy & Heritage Museum MUSEUM
(www.hahndorfacademy.org.au; 68 Main St, Hahndorf; ⏲10am-5pm; 👪) The 1857 building houses an art gallery with rotating exhibitions and original sketches by Sir Hans Heysen, the famed landscape artist and Hahndorf homeboy (ask about tours of his nearby former studio, The Cedars). The museum depicts the lives of early German settlers, with churchy paraphernalia, dour dresses and farm equipment. The Adelaide Hills Visitor Information Centre (p742) is here too.

Hahndorf Walking Tours WALKING TOUR
(☎0477 288 011; hahndorfwalkingtours@gmail.com; per person from $10; ⏲10am Sat & 2pm Sun,

Adelaide Hills

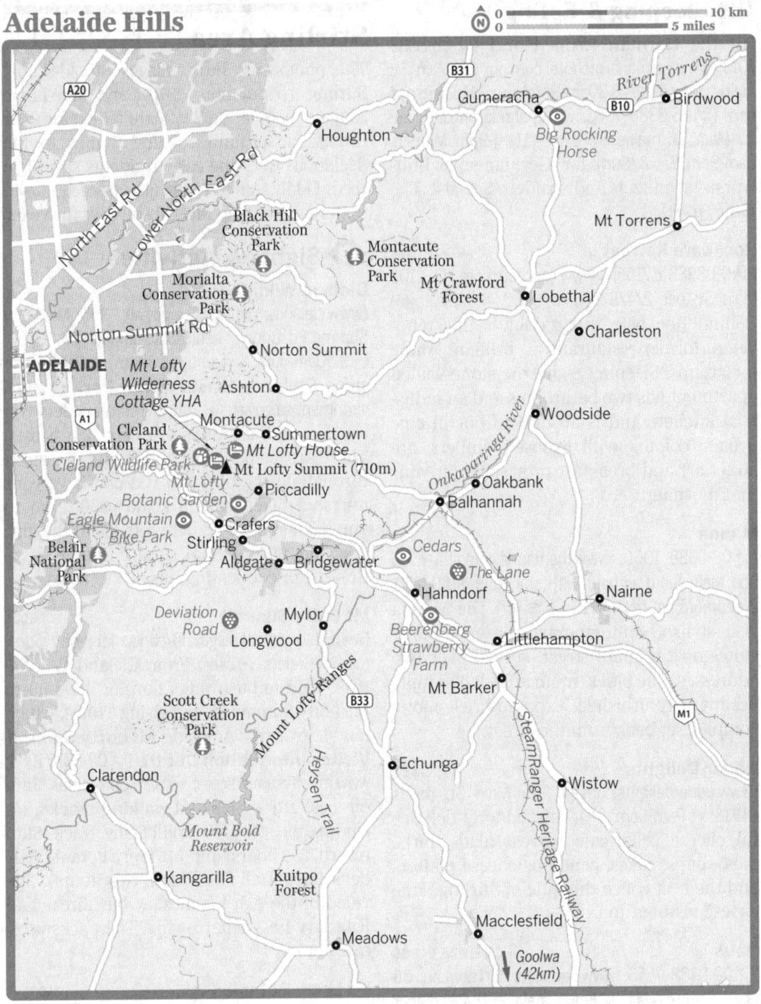

extra tours Oct-Apr) Departing the Hahndorf Academy, these 90-minute, 2km history-soaked walks are a great way to get a feel for the old town. Bookings essential.

The Lane WINERY

(☎08-8388 1250; www.thelane.com.au; Ravenswood Lane, Hahndorf; ⏰10am-4pm Mon-Thu, 10am-5pm Fri-Sun) Wow! What a cool building, and what a setting! Camera-conducive views and contemporary varietals (viognier, pinot grigio, pinot gris), plus an outstanding restaurant (book for lunch).

Beerenberg Strawberry Farm STRAWBERRY FARM

(☎08-8388 7272; www.beerenberg.com.au; Mount Barker Rd, Hahndorf; strawberry picking per adult/child $3/free, strawberries per kg from $9.50; ⏰9am-5pm, last entry 4.15pm) Pick your own strawberries between November and May from this famous, family-run farm, also big-noted for its plethora of jams, chutneys and sauces.

🛏 Sleeping & Eating

Hit the **German Arms Hotel** (☑08-8388 7013; www.germanarmshotel.com.au; 69 Main St; mains $16-29; ⊙8.30am-9pm) or **Hahndorf Inn** (☑08-8388 7063; www.hahndorfinn.com.au; 35 Main St; mains $17-32; ⊙11am-9pm Mon-Fri, 8am-9pm Sat & Sun) for German-style bratwursts, schnitzels and strudels. See also The Lane (p741).

Rockbare Retreat   APARTMENT $$$
(☑08-8388 7155; www.rockbare.com.au; 102 Main St; per 2/4/8 people $400/400/520; ✲) Behind Rockbare cellar door is this renovated former-restaurant – brilliant value for groups. Sleeping eight, the stone-walled apartment has two bathrooms and an industrial kitchen, and is all decked out in chic urbane colours with exposed timbers, abstract art and breakfast provisions for your first morning.

Manna   MOTEL $$
(☑08-8388 1000; www.themanna.com.au; 25 & 35a Main St; d without/with spa from $160/220, 2-bedroom apt from $220; ✲🐾🖵) The Manna is a stylish, contemporary maze of motel suites on the main street, spread over two addresses. The older (more affordable) units occupy a refurbished, exposed-brick motel complex set back from the street.

Udder Delights   CAFE $
(www.udderdelights.com.au; 91a Main St; meals $11-18; ⊙9am-5pm; 🐾) This udderly delightful cheese cellar/cafe serves salads, tarts, pies, soups, cakes, generous cheese platters and the best coffee this side of Stirling. Free cheese tastings, too.

Haus   CAFE, WINE BAR $$
(☑08-8388 7555; www.haushahndorf.com.au; 38 Main St; breakfast & lunch mains $13-28, dinner $25-33; ⊙7.30am-11pm) Haus brings some urban hip to the Hills. Rustic-style pizzas are laden with local smallgoods, and the wine list is huge (lots of Hills drops). Also on offer are baguettes, pasta, burgers, salads and quiches. Good coffee, too.

ℹ Information

Adelaide Hills Visitor Information Centre
(☑08-8388 1185, 1800 353 323; www.visit adelaidehills.com.au; 68 Main St; ⊙9am-5pm Mon-Fri, 10am-4pm Sat & Sun) The usual barrage of brochures, plus accommodation bookings and internet access. Pick up its *Short Winery Trail* map if you're thirsty.

Stirling Area

The photogenic little villages of old-school Stirling (population 2870) and one-horse Aldgate (population 3350) are famed for their bedazzling autumn colours, thanks to the deciduous trees the early residents saw fit to seed. Oddly, Aldgate has also been home to both Bon Scott and Mel Gibson over the years.

◉ Sights & Activities

Cleland Wildlife Park   ZOO
(www.clelandwildlifepark.sa.gov.au; 365 Mt Lofty Summit Rd, Crafers; adult/child/family $20/10/50; ⊙9.30am-5pm, last entry 4.30pm) Within the steep **Cleland Conservation Park** (www.en vironment.sa.gov.au; ⊙24hr), this place lets you interact with all kinds of Australian beasts. There are keeper talks and feeding sessions throughout the day, and you can have your mugshot taken with a koala ($30, 2pm to 4pm). There's a cafe here too. From the city, take bus 864 or 864F from Grenfell St to Crafers for connecting bus 823 to the park.

Mt Lofty Summit   LOOKOUT
(www.environment.sa.gov.au/parks; Mt Lofty Summit Rd, Crafers; ⊙24hr) From Cleland Wildlife Park you can bushwalk (2km) or drive up to Mt Lofty Summit (a surprising 710m), which has views across Adelaide. **Mt Lofty Summit Visitor Information Centre** (☑08-8370 1054; www.mtloftysummit.com; ⊙9am-5pm) has info on local attractions and **walking tracks**, including the steep Waterfall Gully Track (8km return, 2½ hours) and Mt Lofty Botanic Gardens Loop Trail (7km loop, two hours). The video of the Ash Wednesday bushfires of 16 February 1983 is harrowing. There's a snazzy cafe here.

Mt Lofty Botanic Garden   GARDENS
(www.botanicgardens.sa.gov.au; gates on Mawson Dr & Lampert Rd, Crafers; ⊙8.30am-4pm Mon-Fri, 10am-5pm Sat & Sun) FREE From Mt Lofty, truck south 1.5km to the cool-climate slopes of the botanic garden. Nature trails wind past a lake, exotic temperate plants, native stringybark forest and bodacious rhododendron blooms. Free guided walks depart the Lampert Rd car park at 10.30am on Thursdays from September to October and March to May.

Deviation Road   WINERY
(www.deviationroad.com; 214 Scott Creek Rd, Longwood; ⊙10am-5pm) Nothing deviant about the wines here: sublime pinot noir, substantial shiraz, zingy pinot gris and a very decent

bubbly, too. Grab a cheese platter and wind down in the afternoon in the sun.

Stirling Markets MARKET
(www.stirlingmarket.com.au; Druids Ave, Stirling; ⏲10am-4pm 4th Sun of the month) This lively market takes over oak-lined Druids Ave in Stirling: much plant-life, busking, pies, cakes and Hills knick-knackery (not many druids...).

Sleeping & Eating

Mt Lofty House HISTORIC HOTEL $$$
(☎08-8339 6777; www.mtloftyhouse.com.au; 74 Summit Rd, Crafers; d from $229;) Proprietarily poised above Mt Lofty Botanic Garden (*awesome* views), this 1850s baronial mansion has lavish heritage rooms and garden suites, plus an upmarket restaurant (also with killer views). The perfect honeymooner or dirty weekender.

Mt Lofty Wilderness Cottage YHA CABIN $$
(☎08-8414 3000; www.yha.com.au; Mt Lofty Summit Rd, Crafers; per night $140) A short detour off the road on the steep flanks of Mt Lofty, this 1880 stone cottage was originally a shepherd's hut. Today it's a basic, self-contained, two-bedroom cabin sleeping eight, with peek-a-boo views of Adelaide through the eucalypts. Minuimun two-night stay.

★**Stirling Hotel** PUB, BOUTIQUE HOTEL $$
(☎08-8339 2345; www.stirlinghotel.com.au; 52 Mt Barker Rd, Stirling; mains $16-38; ⏲noon-3pm & 6-9pm Mon-Fri, 8am-9pm Sat & Sun) The owners spent so much money tarting up this gorgeous old dame, it's a wonder they can pay the staff. A runaway success, the free-flowing bistro (classy pub grub) and romantic restaurant (upmarket regional cuisine) are always packed.

Upstairs are five elegant, contemporary suites (doubles from $220), three of which have open fireplaces (for winter) and breezy balconies (for summer). All have flat-screen TVs, quality linen and luxe bathrooms you'll actually want to spend time in.

Organic Market & Café CAFE $
(www.organicmarket.com.au; 5 Druids Ave, Stirling; meals $8-18; ⏲8.30am-5pm;) Rejecting Stirling's pompous tendencies, hirsute Hills types flock to this vibrant, hippie cafe. It's the busiest spot in town – and rightly so. The food's delicious and everything's made with love. Gorge on bruschetta, plump savoury muffins, great coffee and wicked Portuguese custard tarts.

Oakbank & Woodside

Strung-out Oakbank (population 450), lives for the annual **Oakbank Easter Racing Carnival** (www.oakbankracingclub.com.au), said to be the greatest picnic race meeting in the world. It's a two-day festival of equine splendour, risqué dresses and 18-year-olds who can't hold their liquor.

Agricultural Woodside (population 1830) has a few enticements for galloping gourmands. **Woodside Cheese Wrights** (www.woodsidecheese.com.au; 22 Henry St, Woodside; tastings free, cheeses from $4; ⏲10am-4pm) is a passionate and unpretentious gem producing classic, artisan and experimental cheeses (soft styles a speciality) from locally grazing sheep and cows. Stock up on rocky road, scorched almonds and appallingly realistic chocolate cow pats at **Melba's Chocolate & Confectionery Factory** (www.melbaschocolates.com; 22 Henry St, Woodside; tastings free, chocolates from $2; ⏲9am-4.30pm).

Gumeracha, Birdwood & Lobethal

A scenic drive from Adelaide to Birdwood leads through the Torrens River Gorge to Gumeracha (population 400), a hardy hillside town with a pub at the bottom (making it hard to roll home). The main lure here is climbing the 18.3m-high **Big Rocking Horse** (www.thetoyfactory.com.au; Birdwood Rd, Gumeracha; admission $2; ⏲9am-5pm), which doesn't actually rock, but is unusually tasteful as far as Australia's 'big' tourist attractions go.

Behind an impressive 1852 flour mill in Birdwood (population 1130), the **National Motor Museum** (☎08-8568 4000; www.history.sa.gov.au; Shannon St, Birdwood; adult/child/family $12/5/30; ⏲9am-5pm) has a collection of immaculate vintage and classic cars (check out the DeLorean!) and motorcycles. The museum marks the finishing line for September's **Bay to Birdwood** (www.baytobirdwood.com.au): a convoy of classic cars chugging up from the city.

Nearby is Lobethal (population 1660), established by Lutheran Pastor Fritzsche and his followers in 1842. Like Hahndorf, Lobethal was renamed during WWI and 'Tweedale' was the rather unfortunate choice. It hits its straps during the **Lights of Lobethal** (www.lightsoflobethal.com.au) Christmas festival in December. Repair to the **Lobethal Bierhaus** (☎08-8389 5570; www.bierhaus.com.au; 3a Main St, Lobethal; ⌚noon-10pm Fri & Sat, noon-6pm Sun) for some serious microbrewed concoctions.

FLEURIEU PENINSULA

Patterned with vineyards, olive groves and almond plantations running down to the sea, the Fleurieu (pronounced *floo*-ree-oh) is Adelaide's weekend playground. The McLaren Vale Wine Region is booming, producing gutsy reds (salubrious shiraz) to rival those from the Barossa Valley (actually, we think McLaren Vale wins hands down). Further east, the Fleurieu's Encounter Coast is an engaging mix of surf beaches, historic towns and whales cavorting offshore.

Online, see www.fleurieupeninsula.com.au.

McLaren Vale

POP 2910

Flanked by the wheat-coloured Willunga Scarp and encircled by vines, McLaren Vale is just 40 minutes south of Adelaide. Servicing the wine industry, it's an energetic, utilitarian town that's not much to look at, but has some great eateries.

Sights & Activities

Most people come to McLaren Vale to cruise the **wineries**. You could spend days doing nothing else!

It seems like most of Adelaide gets tizzied-up and buses down to the annual **Sea & Vines Festival** (www.southaustralia.com/info.aspx?id=9001064) over the June long weekend. Local wineries cook up seafood, splash wine around and host live bands.

Shiraz Trail CYCLING

An up-tempo way to get the McLaren Vale vibe is to explore this 8km walking/cycling track, running along an old railway line between McLaren Vale and Willunga. Hire a bike from **Oxygen Cycles** (☎08-8323 7345; www.oxygencycles.com; 143 Main Rd; bike hire per half/full day $15/40; ⌚10am-6pm Tue-Fri, 9am-5pm Sat, 11am-4pm Sun); ask the visitor information centre for a map.

Tours

You can also organise McLaren Vale tours departing Adelaide (see p723).

Bums on Seats GUIDED TOUR

(☎0438 808 253; www.bumsonseats.com.au; per person from $75) McLaren Vale and Fleurieu day tours for small groups.

Chook's Little Winery Tours GUIDED TOUR

(☎0414 922 200; www.chookslittlewinerytours.com.au; per person from $90) Small-group tours visiting some of the lesser-known boutique McLaren Vale wineries.

McLaren Vale Tours GUIDED TOUR

(☎0414 784 666; www.mclarenvaletours.com.au) Customised, locally-run tours around McLaren Vale and the Fleurieu; call for prices.

WORTH A TRIP

CURRENCY CREEK & LANGHORNE CREEK WINERIES

Once slated as the capital of SA, Currency Creek, 10km north of Goolwa, is now content with producing award-winning wines. **Currency Creek Winery** (☎08-8555 4069; www.currencycreekwinery.com.au; Winery Rd, Currency Creek; ⌚10am-5pm) has 160 acres under vine (brilliant cabernet sauvignon) plus a fab restaurant (mains $18 to $32, open noon to 3pm Thursday to Sunday and 6pm to 9pm Friday and Saturday). Bookings advised.

Further north, 16km east of Strathalbyn, Langhorne Creek is one of Australia's oldest wine-growing regions (www.langhornewine.com.au), producing shiraz, cabernet sauvignon and chardonnay. A couple of the 20-plus wineries here:

➡ **Bleasdale Winery** (www.bleasdale.com.au; Wellington Rd, Langhorne Creek; ⌚10am-5pm) The district's first winery, with a large range, historic cellars and an old redgum lever press.

➡ **Bremerton** (www.bremerton.com.au; Strathalbyn Rd, Langhorne Creek; ⌚10am-5pm) Run by two sisters, Bremerton is an innovative operator in an old-school region. Top chardonnay and shiraz.

Fleurieu Peninsula

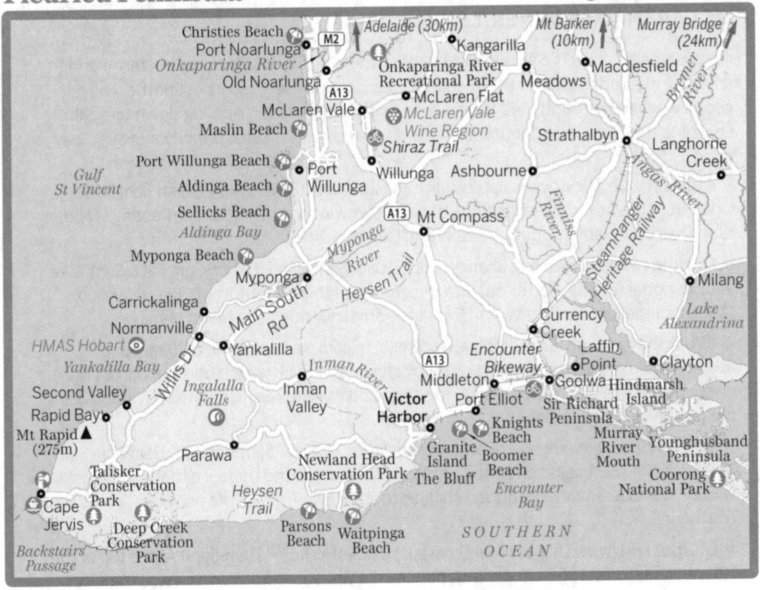

Wine Diva Tours GUIDED TOUR
(☎08-8323 9806; www.winedivatours.com.au; per person from $150) Upmarket half- or full-day wine tours in Mercedes-driven comfort.

Sleeping & Eating

You can also eat at some of McLaren Vale's cellar doors; see the McLaren Vale Wineries boxed text (p746).

Red Poles B&B $$
(☎08-8323 8994; www.redpoles.com.au; 190 McMurtrie Rd; d without/with bathroom $115/125; ❄📶) Nooked away in a bushy enclave, eccentric Red Poles is a great place to stay (and eat!). Aim for the rustic en-suite room – it's bigger than its two counterparts. Order up a saltbush lamb salad (mains $27 to $33, serving noon to 3pm Wednesday to Friday, from 9.30am Saturday and Sunday), and check out some local artwork while you wait. Live music Sunday afternoons.

McLaren Vale Lakeside Caravan Park CARAVAN PARK $
(☎08-8323 9255; www.mclarenvale.net; 48 Field St; unpowered/powered/en-suite sites $29/34/44, cabins $115-135; ❄🏊) A short walk from town, this park by an artificial lake (any water this summer?) is as affordable as McLaren Vale accommodation gets. There's a camp kitchen, pool, spa, tennis court and trashy book exchange. Good winter rates. The Shiraz Trail runs right past.

McLaren Vale Motel & Apartments MOTEL, APARTMENT $$
(☎08-8323 8265, 1800 631 817; www.mclarenvalemotel.com.au; cnr Main Rd & Caffrey St; s/d/f/apt from $120/145/150/250; ❄@📶🏊) A digestive walk from main-street restaurants, this cheery motel has been around since the '80s but is still in good shape. There are solid doubles, new studio apartments and family suites, plus a pool fringed by scruffy-looking palms.

Vale Inn MODERN AUSTRALIAN $$
(☎08-8323 8769; www.mvbeer.com; 190 McMurtrie Rd; mains $16-28; ⏲10am-6pm Mon, Thu & Sun, 10am-9pm Fri & Sat) This old vine-covered inn has been reborn as a beery bar/bistro. McLaren Vale Beer Co is based here: don't leave without trying its much-awarded Vale Ale, or the meaty Vale Dark or smooth Vale IPA. Food-wise it's zingy pizzas (try the duck, Spanish onion and brie), curries, steaks and seafood.

Blessed Cheese CAFE $
(www.blessedcheese.com.au; 150 Main Rd; mains $7-21; ⏲8am-4.30pm Mon-Thu, 8am-5pm

DON'T MISS

MCLAREN VALE WINERIES

If the Barossa Valley is SA wine's old-school, then McLaren Vale is the upstart teenager smoking cigarettes behind the shed and stealing nips from dad's port bottle. The gorgeous vineyards around here have a Tuscan haze in summer, rippling down to a calm coastline that's similarly Ligurian. This is shiraz country – solid, punchy and seriously good.

➡ **Alpha Box & Dice** (www.alphaboxdice.com.au; Lot 50 Olivers Rd; ⏲10am-5pm Fri-Sun) One out of the box, this refreshing little gambler wins top billing for interesting blends, funky retro furnishings, quirky labels and laid-back staff.

➡ **Coriole** (www.coriole.com; Chaffeys Rd; ⏲10am-5pm Mon-Fri, 11am-5pm Sat & Sun) Take your regional tasting platter out into the garden of this beautiful cottage cellar door (1860), made lovelier by a swill of Redstone shiraz or flagship chenin blanc.

➡ **d'Arenberg** (☎08-8329 4888; www.darenberg.com.au; Osborn Rd; ⏲10am-5pm) 'd'Arry's' relaxes atop a hillside and enjoys fine views. The wine labels are part of the character of this place: the Dead Arm shiraz and the Broken Fishplate sauvignon blanc are our faves. Book for lunch.

➡ **Wirra Wirra** (www.wirrawirra.com; McMurtrie Rd; ⏲10am-5pm Mon-Sat, 11am-5pm Sun) This barnlike 1894 cellar door has a grassy picnic area, and there's a roaring fire inside in winter. Sample reasonably priced stickies (dessert wines) and the popular Church Block red blend.

➡ **Chapel Hill** (www.chapelhillwine.com.au; 1 Chapel Hill Rd; ⏲11am-5pm) At the top of the hill is this restored 1865 chapel with panoramic vineyard and ocean views. The Vicar shiraz will banish your piety.

Fri-Sun) This blessed cafe cranks out great coffee, croissants, wraps, salads, tarts, burgers, cheese platters, murderous cakes and funky sausage rolls. The menu changes every couple of days, always with an emphasis on local produce. The aromas emanating from the cheese counter are deliciously stinky.

Barn MODERN AUSTRALIAN **$$**
(☎08-8323 8618; www.thebarnbistro.com.au; tapas $6-16, mains $26-36) Retro-mod prints and furniture adorn this 1840s cottage bistro, which quadruples-up as a cellar door, art gallery and wine bar. Mains are fishy and meaty, done with contemporary flair, or settle in for some tapas and a glass or two of good local stuff.

☆ Entertainment

Black Cockatoo Arthouse CINEMA, LIVE MUSIC
(☎08-8323 9294; www.blackcockatooarthouse.blogspot.com; 1 Park St; admission free-$15; ⏲varies) In a nondescript warehouse behind the police station, Black Cockatoo Arthouse is an independent, nonprofit art space with cinema, live music, DJs and exhibitions.

ℹ Information

McLaren Vale & Fleurieu Visitor Information Centre (☎08-8323 9944; www.mclarenvale.info; 796 Main Rd; ⏲9am-5pm Mon-Fri, 10am-4pm Sat & Sun) At the northern end of McLaren Vale. Winery info, plus accommodation assistance and Sealink bus/ferry bookings for Kangaroo Island.

ℹ Getting There & Away

Regular **Adelaide Metro** (www.adelaidemetro.com.au) suburban trains run between Adelaide and Noarlunga (one hour). From here, buses 751 and 753 run to McLaren Vale and Willunga (45 minutes). Regular Adelaide Metro ticket prices apply.

Willunga

POP 2260

A one-horse town with three pubs (a winning combo!), artsy Willunga took off in 1840 when high-quality slate was discovered nearby and exported across Australia. Today, the town's early buildings along sloping High St are occupied by gourmet eateries and galleries. The Kidman Trail (p716) kicks off here.

Sights & Activities

Willunga Farmers Market MARKET
(www.willungafarmersmarket.com; Willunga Town Sq; 8am-12.30pm Sat) Heavy on the organic, the bespoke and the locally-sourced, Willunga Farmers Market is on Saturday mornings on the corner of High St and Main Rd.

Willunga Slate Museum MUSEUM
(www.nationaltrust.org.au/sa/willunga-slatemuseum; 61 High St; adult/child $5/free; 1-4pm Tue, Sat & Sun) At the top end of Willunga's ascending high street is this cluster of old stone buildings, which at various times have housed a police station, a courthouse, a prison and a boys school. These days the emphasis is on Willunga's slate-mining history and the Cornish miners who did all the dirty work.

Sleeping & Eating

Willunga House B&B B&B $$$
(08-8556 2467; www.willungahouse.com.au; 1 St Peters Tce; d incl breakfast $210-280;) If you're looking for a real treat, this graceful, two-storey 1850 mansion off the main street is for you: Baltic-pine floorboards, Italian cherry-wood beds, open fires, indigenous art and a swimming pool. Breakfast is a feast of organic muesli, fruit salad and poached pears, followed by cooked delights.

Russell's Pizza PIZZA $$
(08-8556 2571; 13 High St; pizzas from $24; 6-9pm Fri & Sat) It may look like a ramshackle chicken coop, but Russell's is the place to be on weekends for sensational wood-fired pizza. No-one minds the wait for a meal (which could be an hour) – it's all about the atmosphere. It's super popular, so book way ahead.

Fino MODERN AUSTRALIAN $$
(08-8556 4488; www.fino.net.au; 8 Hill St; mains $18-48; noon-3pm Tue-Sun, 6.30-9pm Fri & Sat) A regular on 'Australia's Top 100 Restaurants' lists and with a cabinet full of regional awards for both food and wine, Fino is fine indeed. It's a low-key conversion of a slate-floored stone cottage, with a small, simple menu of small, simple dishes, sourced locally as much as possible. The Berkshire pork shoulder with coleslaw is a winner.

Information

Willunga Environment Centre (08-8556 4188; www.willungaenviro.org.au; 18 High St; 10am-3pm Mon-Fri, 9am-1pm Sat) Basic tourist info and details on local flora and fauna.

Gulf St Vincent Beaches

There are some ace swimming beaches (but no surf) along the Gulf St Vincent coastline, extending from suburban **Christies Beach** onto **Maslin Beach**, the southern end of which is a nudist and a gay hang-out. Maslin is 45 minutes from Adelaide by car – just far enough to escape the sprawling shopping centres and new housing developments trickling south from the city.

Port Willunga is home to the eternally busy, cliff-top seafood shack the **Star of Greece** (08-8557 7420; www.starofgreececafe.com.au; 1 The Esplanade, Port Willunga; mains $28-34; noon-3pm Wed-Sun, 5.30pm-9pm Fri & Sat), named after a shipwreck: funky decor, great staff and a sunny outdoor patio. We asked the waiter where the whiting was caught: he looked out across the bay and said, 'See that boat out there?'. There's a takeaway kiosk too (snacks $5 to $10, open 10am to 3pm).

On the highway above **Sellicks Beach** is a classily renovated 1858 pub, the **Victory Hotel** (08-8556 3083; www.victoryhotel.com.au; Main South Rd, Sellicks Beach; mains $17-34; noon-3pm & 6-9pm). There are awesome views of the silvery gulf, a cheery, laid-back vibe and a beaut beer garden. Factor in inspired meals, an impressive cellar and wines by the glass and you'll be feeling victorious. Three B&B cabins too (doubles from $150).

Keep on trucking south to cute little **Yankalilla**, which has the regional **Yankalilla Bay Visitor Information Centre** (08-8558 0240; www.yankalilla.sa.gov.au; 163 Main South Rd, Yankalilla; 9am-5pm Mon-Fri, 10am-4pm Sat & Sun). There's a small local history **museum** (adult/child $3/1) out the back (look for the radar antenna from the scuttled *HMAS Hobart*, now a nearby dive site offshore). Also in 'Yank' is quirky **Lilla's Cafe** (08-8558 2525; www.lillascafe.com.au; 163 Main South Rd, Yankalilla; mains $15-25; 8.30am-4pm Sun-Tue & Thu, 8.30am-9pm Fri & Sat) – perfect for coffee and cake or generous wood-fired pizzas on Friday and Saturday nights. Jenny the donkey will finish off anything you can't eat.

About 60km south of Adelaide is **Carrickalinga**, which has a gorgeous arc of white sandy beach: it's a very chilled spot with no shops. For supplies and accommodation, head to neighbouring **Normanville**, which has a rambling pub, a supermarket, a couple of caravan parks and the **Jetty Food Store** (08-8558 2537; www.jettyfoodstore.com; 48a Main Rd; meals $8-16; 7.30am-5.30pm). The motto here is 'Coastal food hunted and gathered for you'. Grab an organic coffee, a dozen Kangaroo Island oysters, some locally caught fish and chips, or raid the fridge for gourmet cheeses, dips and olives. About 10km out of Normanville along Hay Flat Rd are the picturesque little **Ingalalla Falls** (follow the signs from the Yankalilla side of town).

There's not much at **Cape Jervis**, 107km from Adelaide, other than the Kangaroo Island ferry terminal, and the start point for the Heysen Trail (p716). Nearby, **Deep Creek Conservation Park** (www.environment.sa.gov.au; per car $10) has sweeping coastal views, a wicked waterfall, man-size yakkas (*Xanthorrhoea semiplana tateana*), sandy beaches, kangaroos, kookaburras and bush camping areas (per car from $13).

Off the road to Deep Creek Conservation Park are the curved roofs of the superb **Ridgetop Retreats** (☎08-8598 4169; www.southernoceanretreats.com.au; d $245): three corrugated-iron-clad, self-contained luxury units in the bush, with wood heaters, leather lounges and stainless-steel benchtops.

Victor Harbor

POP 11,500

The biggest town on the Encounter Coast is Victor Harbor (yes, that's the correct spelling: blame one of SA's poorly schooled early Surveyor Generals). It's a raggedy, brawling holiday destination with three huge pubs and migrating whales offshore. In November the grassy foreshore runs rampant with teenage school-leavers blowing off hormones at the **Schoolies Festival** (www.schooliesfestival.com.au).

Sights & Activities

South Australian Whale Centre MUSEUM
(☎08-8551 0750; www.sawhalecentre.com; 2 Railway Tce; adult/child/family $8/4/20; ⏲10.30am-5pm) Victor Harbor is on the migratory path of southern right whales (May to October). The multilevel South Australian Whale Centre has impressive whale displays (including a big stinky skull) and can give you the low-down on where to see them. Not whale season? Check out the big mammals in the new 3D-cinema.

Horse-drawn Tram TRAM
(www.horsedrawntram.com.au; return adult/child/family $8/6/22; ⏲hourly 10am-4pm) Just offshore is the boulder-strewn **Granite Island**, connected to the mainland by a 632m causeway built in 1875. You can walk to the island, but it's more fun to take the 1894 double-decker tram pulled by a big clydesdale. Tickets available from the driver or visitor information centre.

Encounter Bikeway CYCLING
(www.tourismvictorharbor.com.au/walks_trails.html) The much-wheeled Encounter Bikeway extends 30km from Victor Harbor to Laffin Point beyond Goolwa. The visitors centre stocks maps; hire a bike from **Victor Harbor Cycle Skate Bay Rubber** (☎08-8552 1417; www.victorharborcycles.com; 73 Victoria St; bike hire per 4/8 hr $30/40; ⏲9am-5pm Mon & Wed-Fri, 10am-3pm Sat & Sun).

Big Duck BOAT TOUR
(☎0405 125 312; www.thebigduck.com.au; 30min tours adult/child/family $35/25/110, 1hr $55/45/180) Do a lap of Granite Island and check out seals, dolphins and whales (but sadly not many penguins these days) on the rigid inflatable Big Duck boat. Call for times and bookings.

Encounter Coast Discovery Centre MUSEUM
(www.nationaltrust.org.au/sa; 2 Flinders Pde; adult/child/family $5/3/13; ⏲1-4pm) Inside Victor's 1866 Customs House on the foreshore, this National Trust museum has interesting local-history displays from pre-European times to around 1900: whaling, railways, shipping and local Aboriginal culture. Good for a rainy day.

Sleeping & Eating

Anchorage GUESTHOUSE $$
(☎08-8552 5970; www.anchorageseafronthotel.com; 21 Flinders Pde; s/d/apt from $55/100/250; @) This grand old seafront guesthouse is the pick of the local crop. Immaculately maintained, great-value rooms open off long corridors. Most rooms face the beach, and some have a balcony (you'd pay through the nose for this in Sydney!). The cheapest rooms are view-free and share bathrooms. The cafe-bar downstairs is a winner.

Victor Harbor Holiday & Cabin Park CARAVAN PARK $
(☎08-8552 1949; www.victorharborholiday.com.au; 19 Bay Rd; unpowered/powered sites $30/36, vans/cabins from $52/85; ❄@📶) The friendliest operation in town, with tidy facilities, free barbecues and a rambling grassed area to pitch a tent on. Runs rings around Victor's other caravan parks.

Nino's CAFE **$$**
(☎08-8552 3501; www.ninoscafe.com.au; 17 Albert Pl; mains $15-33; ⏰10am-10pm Mon-Thu, 10am-midnight Fri-Sun) Nino's cafe has been here since 1974, but it manages to put a contemporary sheen on downtown VH. Hip young staff and a mod interior set the scene for gourmet pizzas, pasta, salads, risottos and meaty Italian mains. Good coffee, cakes and takeaways, too.

Anchorage Cafe MODERN AUSTRALIAN **$$**
(☎08-8552 5970; www.anchorageseafronthotel.com; 21 Flinders Pde; tapas $7-14, mains $16-35; ⏰8-11am, noon-2.30pm & 5.30-8.30pm) This salty sea cave at the Anchorage hotel has an old whaling boat for a bar and a Med/Mod Oz menu (baguettes, pizzas, souvlaki) peppered with plenty of seafood. There's great coffee, tapas and cakes, plus Euro beers and a breezy terrace on which to drink them.

Information

Victor Harbor Visitor Information Centre
(☎1800 557 094, 08-8551 0777; www.tourismvictorharbor.com.au; Foreshore; ⏰9am-5pm) Handles tour and accommodation bookings. Stocks the *Beaches on the South Coast* brochure if you feel like a swim, and the *Old Port Victor* history walk brochure.

Getting There & Away

BUS

Premier Stateliner (www.premierstateliner.com.au) runs buses to Victor Harbor from Adelaide ($22, 1¾ hours, one to three daily) continuing to Goolwa.

TRAIN

On the first and third Sundays from June to November inclusive, **SteamRanger Heritage Railway** (☎1300 655 991; www.steamranger.org.au) operates the *Southern Encounter* (adult/child return $69/36) tourist train from Mt Barker in the Adelaide Hills to Victor Harbor via Strathalbyn, Goolwa and Port Elliot. The *Cockle Train* (adult/child return $28/14) runs along the Encounter Coast between Victor Harbor and Goolwa via Port Elliot every Sunday and Wednesday, and daily during school holidays.

Port Elliot

POP 3100

About 8km east of Victor Harbor, historic (and today, rather affluent) Port Elliot is set back from **Horseshoe Bay**, an orange-sand arc with gentle surf and good swimming. Norfolk Island pines reach for the sky, and there are whale-spotting updates posted on the pub wall. If there are whales around, wander out to **Freemans Knob** lookout at the end of the Strand and peer through the free telescope.

OFF THE BEATEN TRACK

RAPID BAY

About 15km south of Normanville, follow the signs past bald hills and farmhouse ruins to Rapid Bay. In the 1950s this was a boomtown, the local limestone quarry shipping 60,000 tonnes of lime per month from the enormous jetty. Production ceased in 1981; since then Rapid Bay has assumed a gothic, ghost-town atmosphere. Empty '50s villas and workers' quarters line the streets, and the local shop (closed) has signs advertising soft drinks they don't make anymore. The jetty (recently rebuilt; www.rapidbayjetty.org) has become a popular fishing and diving site.

Rapid Bay was also the site of Adelaide founder Colonel William Light's first landing in SA in 1836, in his ship the *Rapid*. There's a stone down by the shore with 'WL 1836' carved into it.

Activities

Commodore Point, at the eastern end of Horseshoe Bay, and nearby **Boomer Beach** and **Knights Beach** have reliable waves for experienced surfers. The beach at otherwise missable **Middleton**, the next town towards Goolwa, also has solid breaks. You can learn to surf (around $40 for a two-hour lesson, including gear) with **South Coast Surf Academy** (☎0414 341 545; www.danosurf.com.au) and **Surf & Sun** (☎1800 786 386; www.surfandsun.com.au).

History buffs should look for the *Walk Into History at Port Elliot* pamphlet (try Goolwa Visitor Information Centre (p752)) detailing a couple of history walks around town.

Big Surf Australia SURFING
(☎08-8554 2399; info@bigsurfaustralia.com; 24 Goolwa Rd, Middleton; surfboards/bodyboards/wetsuits per day $30/20/15; ⏰9am-5pm) For surf-gear hire, check out Big Surf Australia in Middleton.

Port Elliot Bike & Leisure Hire BICYCLE HIRE
(☎0448 370 007; www.portelliotbikeleisurehire.myob.net; 85-87 Hill St; per day $40) Pick up a mountain bike and hit the Encounter Bikeway (p748), running through Port Elliot to Goolwa (15km east) and Victor Harbor (7km west).

Sleeping & Eating

★**Port Elliot Beach House YHA** HOSTEL $
(☎08-8554 1885; www.yha.com.au; 13 The Strand; dm/d/f from $28/90/125; ❄@) Built in 1910 (the old Arcadia Hotel), this sandstone beauty has sweeping views across the Port Elliot coastline. If you can drag your eyes away from the view, you'll find polished floorboards and contemporary colours splashed around. It's a classy fit-out, and the only backpackers on the Fleurieu Peninsula. Surf lessons are almost mandatory, and the Flying Fish Cafe is 200m away.

Port Elliot Holiday Park CARAVAN PARK $
(☎08-8554 2134; www.portelliotholidaypark.com.au; Port Elliot Rd; powered sites/cabins/units/cottages from $33/90/115/150; ❄@) In an unbeatable position behind the Horseshoe Bay dunes (it can be a touch windy), this 5-hectare park, with lush grass and healthy-looking trees has all the requisite facilities, including a shiny camp kitchen and all-weather barbecue area. Prices plummet in winter.

Royal Family Hotel PUB $
(☎08-8554 2219; www.royalfamilyhotel.com.au; 32 North Tce; s/d $50/65) It's doubtful that Prince Chuck has ever stayed here, but if he did he'd find surprisingly decent pub rooms with clean shared bathrooms, a TV lounge and balcony over the main street. Downstairs the bistro serves counter meals fit for a king (mains $16 to $30, serving noon to 2pm and 6pm to 8pm).

Flying Fish Cafe MODERN AUSTRALIAN $$
(☎08-8554 3504; www.flyingfishcafe.com.au; 1 The Foreshore; takeaways $10-15, mains $20-40; ⏲9-11am Sat & Sun, noon-3pm daily, 6-9pm Fri & Sat) Sit down for lunch and you'll find yourself here all day – the views of Horseshoe Bay are sublime. Otherwise grab some quality takeaway of Coopers-battered flathead and chips and head back to the sand. At night things get a little classier, with à-la-carte mains that focus on independent SA producers.

Cockles on North CAFE, MODERN AUSTRALIAN $
(☎08-8554 3187; www.cocklescafe.com.au; 4/33 North Tce; mains $10-19; ⏲7.30am-4pm; 📶) A bright, breezy, open-sided foodie haunt with a huge deck overlooking the main strip. Expect good coffee, all-day breakfasts, snazzy desserts and mains such as felafels, corn fritters with avocado and smoked salmon, and king-prawn pasta.

Getting There & Away

Premier Stateliner (www.premierstateliner.com.au) has daily bus services between Adelaide and Port Elliot ($22, two hours, one to three daily), via Victor Harbor and continuing to Goolwa.

Goolwa

POP 6500

Much more low-key and elegant than kissing-cousin Victor Harbor, Goolwa is an unassuming town where the rejuvenated Murray River empties into the sea. Beyond the dunes is a fantastic beach with ranks of breakers rolling in from the ocean, same as it ever was... The **South Australian Wooden Boat Festival** (www.woodenboatfestival.com.au) attracts boating enthusiasts here in February in odd-numbered years.

BUILDING BRIDGES (NOT...)

First proposed in 1988, construction of the Hindmarsh Island Bridge at Goolwa was opposed by Ngarrindjeri women who had concerns about the spiritual and cultural significance of the site. A series of court battles ensued, pitting Aboriginal beliefs against development, culminating in a royal commission (1995) that ruled that the claims of Aboriginal 'secret women's business' were fabricated. Further court appeals were launched, and in August 2001 the Federal Court overturned the royal commission, finding the Ngarrindjeri claims to be legitimate. Unfortunately, this vindication came five months after the bridge was officially opened. The decade-long furore was a step backwards for reconciliation; the bridge remains a source of contention.

Sights & Activities

At **Goolwa Beach** a boardwalk traverses the dunes looking out at the barrelling surf: **Goolwa Barrells** (08-8555 5422; www.barrellsurf.com.au; 10c Cadell St; hire per day longboard/bodyboard/wetsuit $25/10/15; 9.30am-5.30pm) has surfboard hire. You can learn to surf with **Ocean Living Surf School** (0487 921 232; www.olsurfschool.com.au; 2/4hr lesson $35/65).

The coastal **Encounter Bikeway** (www.tourismvictorharbor.com.au/walks_trails.html) runs for 30km between Goolwa and Victor Harbor (maps available at the Goolwa visitor centre).

Steam Exchange Brewery BREWERY
(08-8555 3406; www.steamexchange.com.au; Goolwa Wharf; tastings $3; 10am-5pm Wed-Sun) Down on the wharf, the Steam Exchange Brewery is a locally-run brewery, turning out manly stouts and ales. Sip a Southerly Buster Dark Ale and look out over the rippling river. Is the whiskey distillery up-and-running yet? Small tasting fee; group tours by arrangement.

Canoe the Coorong CANOEING
(0424 826 008; www.canoethecoorong.com; adult/child $135/85) Full-day paddles around the Coorong and Murray River mouth departing Goolwa. Includes lunch and a bush-tucker walk through the dunes.

Spirit of the Coorong CRUISE
(08-8555 2203, 1800 442 203; www.coorongcruises.com.au; Goolwa Wharf) Spirit of the Coorong runs eco-cruises on the Murray and into the Coorong National Park, including lunch and guided walks. The four-hour Coorong Discovery Cruise (adult/child $84/62) runs on Thursdays all year, plus Mondays from October to May. The six-hour Coorong Adventure Cruise ($98/67) runs on Sundays all year, plus Wednesdays from October to May. There's also a two-hour Murray Mouth Cruise ($35/18) on Saturdays from October to April. Bookings essential.

Goolwa Riverboat Centre CRUISE
(08-8555 2108, 1300 466 592; www.oscar-w.info; Goolwa Wharf; adult/child/family $20/8/48; varies) Check out the Murray River on a one-hour paddle-steamer ride aboard the 130-year-old *Oscar W*. It's hard to imagine now, but in 1875 there were 127 riverboats plying the river between here and NSW! Call for times and bookings.

Sleeping

Holiday rentals in and around Goolwa are managed by **LJ Hooker** (08-8555 1785; www.ljh.com.au/goolwa; 25 Cadell St) and the **Professionals** (08-8555 2122; www.goolwaprofessionals.com.au; 1 Cadell St), both of whom have houses for as little as $80 per night (though most are around $130) and good weekly rates.

Australasian BOUTIQUE HOTEL $$$
(08-8555 1088; www.australasian1858.com; 1 Porter St; d incl breakfast from $325;) This gorgeous 1858 stone hotel at the head of Goolwa's main street has been reborn as a sassy B&B, with a sequence of Japanese-inspired decks and glazed extensions and an upmarket dining room. The five plush suites all have views, and the breakfast will make you want to wake up here again. Two-night minimum.

Jackling Cottage B&B B&B $$
(08-8555 3489; www.goolwaheritagecottages.com; 18 Oliver St; B&B d from $195, holiday rental 2 nights $330;) A lovely old 1860s cottage on a nondescript Goolwa backstreet (just ignore the petrol station across the road), surrounded by rambling roses and limestone walls. Two bedrooms, sleeping four – good for families or a couple of couples looking for a low-key weekend by the sea. A short stroll to the main drag. Also available as a holiday rental (no breakfast).

Eating

Café Lime CAFE $
(1/11 Goolwa Tce; meals $10-21; 9am-3pm) Pick up heat-and-eat gourmet dinners or a takeaway cone of salt-and-pepper squid with lime-salted fries. If you feel like lingering, nab a table for beer-battered Coorong mullet (not a description of a haircut at the pub), baguettes, curries, soups and pasta. Espresso perfecto.

Hector's CAFE, MODERN AUSTRALIAN $$
(08-8555 5885; www.hectorsonthewharf.com; Goolwa Wharf; mains $10-32; 9am-3pm daily, 6pm-late Fri & Sat) Right on the Murray under the span of the Hindmarsh Island Bridge, eating at Hector's (festooned with fishing rods) is like hanging out in your mate's boathouse. Seafood chowder and spinach-and-fetta pie are sweetly complemented by jazzy tunes and local wines. There's good coffee, too.

Information

Goolwa Visitor Information Centre (☎1300 466 592; www.visitalexandrina.com; 4 Goolwa Tce; ⏰9am-5pm Mon-Fri, 10am-4pm Sat & Sun) Inside an 1857 post office, with detailed local info (including accommodation).

Getting There & Away

Premier Stateliner (www.premierstateliner.com.au) runs buses daily between Adelaide and Goolwa ($22, two hours, one to three daily).

See p749 for info on tourist steam trains running between Goolwa, Victor Harbor and the Adelaide Hills.

KANGAROO ISLAND

From Cape Jervis, car ferries chug across the swells of the Backstairs Passage to Kangaroo Island (KI). Long devoid of tourist trappings, the island these days is a booming destination for wilderness and wildlife fans – it's a veritable zoo of seals, birds, dolphins, echidnas and (of course) kangaroos. Still, the island remains rurally paced and underdeveloped – the kind of place where kids ride bikes to school and farmers advertise for wives on noticeboards. Island produce is a highlight.

See www.tourkangarooisland.com.au.

History

Many KI place names are French, attributable to Gallic explorer Nicholas Baudin who surveyed the coast in 1802 and 1803. Baudin's English rival, Matthew Flinders, named the island in 1802 after his crew feasted on kangaroo meat here. By this stage the island was uninhabited, but archaeologists think indigenous Australians lived here as recently as 2000 years ago. Why they deserted KI is a matter of conjecture, though the answer is hinted at in the indigenous name for KI: 'Karta', or 'Land of the Dead'. In the early 1800s an indigenous presence (albeit a tragically displaced one) was re-established on KI when whalers and sealers abducted Aboriginal women from Tasmania and brought them here.

Activities

The safest **swimming** is along the north coast, where the water is warmer and there are fewer rips than down south. Try Emu Bay, Stokes Bay, Snelling Beach or Western River Cove.

For **surfing**, hit the uncrowded swells along the south coast. Pennington Bay has strong, reliable breaks; Vivonne Bay and Hanson Bay in the southwest also serve up some tasty waves. Pick up the *Kangaroo Island Surfing Guide* brochure from visitor information centres.

There's plenty to see under your own steam on KI. Check out www.tourkangarooisland.com.au/wildlife/walks.aspx for info on **bushwalks** from 1km to 18km.

The waters around KI are home to 230 species of fish, plus coral and around 60 shipwrecks – great **snorkelling** and **diving**! **Kangaroo Island Dive & Adventures** (☎08-8553 3196; www.kangarooislanddiveandadventures.com.au; guided shore/boat dives from $195/320, snorkelling/diving equipment hire from $45/120) runs diving trips and offers gear hire.

Skidding down the dunes at **Little Sahara** is great fun. **Kangaroo Island Outdoor Action** (☎08-8559 4296; www.kioutdooraction.com.au; Jetty Rd, Vivonne Bay) rents out sandboards/toboggans ($29/39 per day), plus single/double kayaks ($39/69 for four hours).

There's plenty of good **fishing** around the island, including jetties at Kingscote, Penneshaw, Emu Bay and Vivonne Bay. Fishing charter tours (half-/full day from $100/200) include tackle and refreshments, and you keep what you catch. Try **Kangaroo Island Fishing Adventures** (☎08-8559 3232; www.kangarooislandadventures.com.au).

Tours

See also Tours on p715. Stay at least one night on the island if you can (one-day tours are hectic). A few operators:

Surf & Sun WILDLIFE
(☎1800 786 386; www.surfandsun.com.au) Two-day all-inclusive tours ex-Adelaide/KI ($445/309), with a strong focus on wildlife and activities.

Kangaroo Island Adventure Tours GUIDED TOUR
(☎08-8202 8678; www.kiadventuretours.com.au) Two-day, all-inclusive tours ex-Adelaide ($389) with a backpacker bent and plenty of activities.

Kangaroo Island Marine Tours WILDLIFE
(☎0427 315 286; www.kimarineadventures.com) Ninety-minute boat tours ($82.50) and longer half-day jaunts ($165), which include

ALL CREATURES GREAT & SMALL

You bump into a lot of wildlife on KI (sometimes literally). Kangaroos, wallabies, bandicoots and possums come out at night, especially in wilderness areas such as Flinders Chase National Park. Koalas and the platypus were introduced to Flinders Chase in the 1920s when it was feared they would become extinct on the mainland. Echidnas mooch around in the undergrowth, while goannas and tiger snakes keep KI suitably scaly.

Of the island's 267 bird species, several are rare or endangered. One species – the dwarf emu – has gone the way of the dodo. Glossy black cockatoos may soon follow it out the door due to habitat depletion.

Offshore, dolphins and southern right whales are often seen cavorting in the waves, and there are colonies of little penguins, New Zealand fur seals and Australian sea lions here too.

swimming with dolphins, visiting seal colonies and access to remote areas of KI.

Cruising Kangaroo Island KAYAKING
(☎0439 507 018; www.cruisingkangarooisland.com; ⊙Oct-Apr) Two- to three-hour kayak paddles around choice KI coastal spots, from $80 per person.

Alkirna Nocturnal Tours WILDLIFE
(☎08-8553 7464; www.alkirna.com.au; ⊙Mar-Jan) Nightly two-hour, naturalist-led tours (adult/child $60/40) viewing nocturnal critters around American River.

Sealink SIGHTSEEING
(☎13 13 01; www.sealink.com.au) The ferry company runs a range of KI-highlight coach tours departing Adelaide (one/two days from $248/516). 4WD tours also available.

Sleeping

KI accommodation is expensive, adding insult to your wallet's injury after the pricey ferry ride. Self-contained cottages, B&Bs and beach houses charge from $150 per night per double (usually two-night minimum stay). There are some great camp sites around the island though, plus a few midrange motels. Quality caravan parks and hostels are scarce. Accommodation booking services include:

Gateway Visitor Information Centre ACCOMMODATION SERVICES
(☎1800 811 080; www.tourkangarooisland.com.au/accommodation)

Kangaroo Island Holiday Accommodation ACCOMMODATION SERVICES
(☎08 8553 9007; www.kangarooislandholidayaccommodation.com.au)

Sealink ACCOMMODATION SERVICES
(☎13 13 01; www.sealink.com.au/kangaroo-island-accommodation)

Information

The main Gateway Visitor Information Centre (p756) is in Penneshaw. There are ATMs in Kingscote and Penneshaw. **Kangaroo Island Hospital** (☎08-8553 4200; www.countryhealthsa.sa.gov.au; The Esplanade; ⊙24hr) is in Kingscote. Island mobile phone reception is patchy outside the main towns (best with Telstra). There are supermarkets at Penneshaw and Kingscote, and a general store at American River.

Kangaroo Island Pass (www.environment.sa.gov.au; adult/child/family $68/42/185) Covers all park and conservation area entry fees, and ranger-guided tours at Seal Bay, Kelly Hill Caves, Cape Borda and Cape Willoughby. Passes available online or at most sights.

Getting There & Away

AIR

Regional Express (Rex; www.regionalexpress.com.au) flies daily between Adelaide and Kingscote (return from $220).

BUS

Sealink operates a morning and afternoon bus service between Adelaide Central Bus Station and Cape Jervis (return adult/child $50/26, 2¼ hours one way).

FERRY

Sealink (☎13 13 01; www.sealink.com.au) operates a car ferry between Cape Jervis and Penneshaw on KI, with at least three ferries each way daily (return adult/child from $96/48, bicycles/motorcycles/cars $22/58/280, 45 minutes one way). One driver is included with the vehicle price (cars only, not bikes).

Kangaroo Island

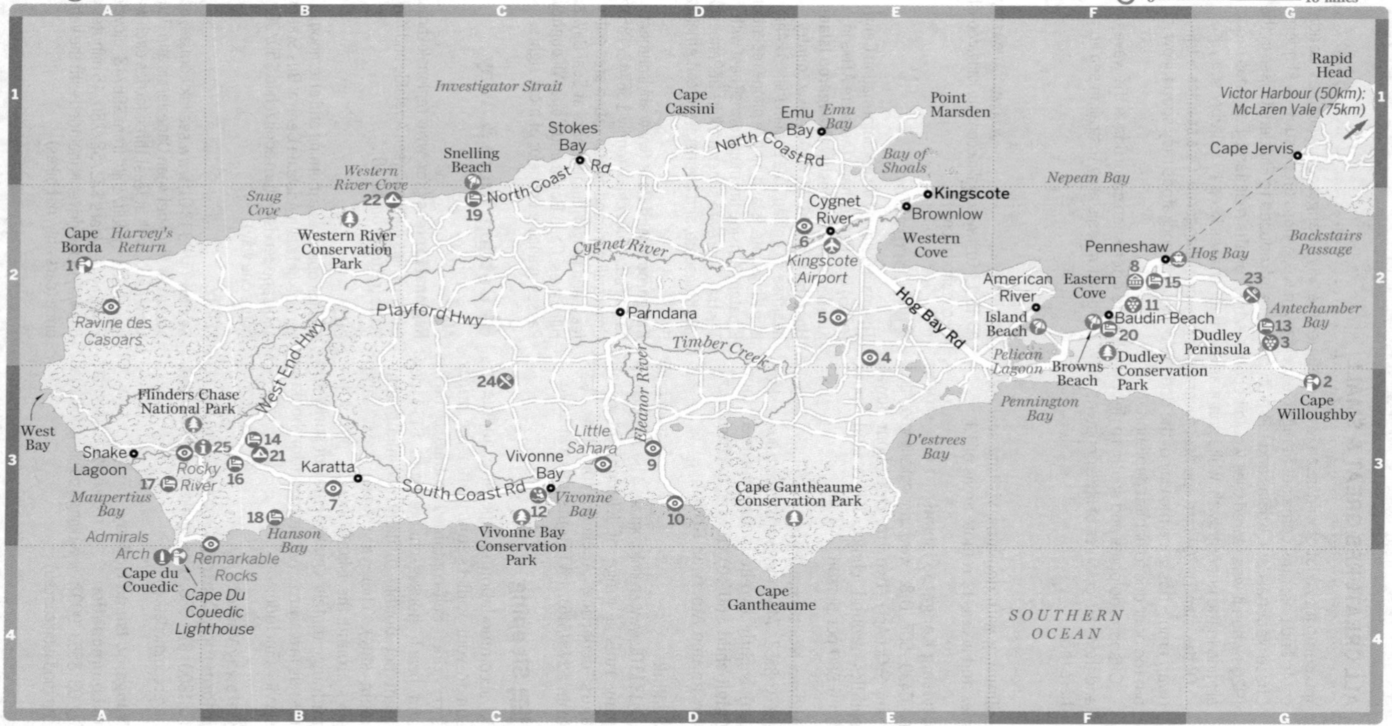

Kangaroo Island

Sights

1	Cape Borda Lightstation	A2
2	Cape Willoughby Lightstation	G3
3	Chapman River Wines	G2
4	Clifford's Honey Farm	E2
5	Emu Ridge Farm Eucalyptus Distillery	E2
6	Island Pure Sheep Dairy	E2
7	Kelly Hill Conservation Park	B3
8	Penneshaw Maritime & Folk Museum	F2
9	Raptor Domain	D3
10	Seal Bay Conservation Park	D3
11	Sunset Winery	F2

Activities, Courses & Tours

12	Kangaroo Island Outdoor Action	C3

Sleeping

13	Antechamber Bay Ecocabins	G2
14	Flinders Chase Farm	B3
15	Gateway Visitor Information Centre	F2
16	Kangaroo Island Wilderness Retreat	B3
17	Rocky River	A3
18	Southern Ocean Lodge	B3
19	Stone House	C2
20	Wallaby Beach House	F2
21	Western Kangaroo Island Caravan Park	B3
22	Western River Cove Campsite	B2

Eating

23	Dudley Cellar Door	G2
24	Marron Café	C3

Information

25	Flinders Chase Visitor Information Centre	B3
	Gateway Visitor Information Centre	(see 15)

Getting Around

There's no public transport anywhere on the island: take a tour or bring or hire some wheels. The island's main roads are sealed, but the rest are gravel, including those to Cape Willoughby, Cape Borda and the North Coast Rd (take it slowly, especially at night). There's petrol at Kingscote, Penneshaw, American River, Parndana and Vivonne Bay.

TO/FROM THE AIRPORT

Kingscote Airport is 14km from Kingscote. **Kangaroo Island Transfers** (☎0427 887 575; www.kitransfers.com.au) connects the airport with Kingscote (per person $20, minimum two people), American River ($30) and Penneshaw ($40). Solo travellers pay double (eg Kingscote $40). Bookings essential.

TO/FROM THE FERRY

Sealink (p753) runs a twice-daily shuttle between Penneshaw and American River (adult/child $14/7, 30 minutes) and Kingscote ($17/9, one hour). Bookings essential.

CAR HIRE

Not all Adelaide car-rental companies will let you take their vehicles onto KI. **Budget** (www.budgetki.com) and **Hertz** (www.hertz.com.au) supply cars to Penneshaw, Kingscote and Kingscote Airport.

Penneshaw & Dudley Peninsula

Looking across Backstairs Passage to the Fleurieu Peninsula, Penneshaw (population 300), on the north shore of the Dudley Peninsula, is the ferry arrival point. The passing tourist trade lends a certain transience to the businesses here, but the pub, hostel and general store remain authentically grounded. As do the resident little penguins. En route to American River, Pennington Bay has consistent surf.

Sights & Activities

Penneshaw Penguin Centre ECOTOUR
(☎08-8553 1103; www.southaustralia.com/9005545.aspx; cnr Middle Tce & Bay Tce, Penneshaw; adult/child/family $13/10/35; ⏲6-9.30pm Mar-Jan) On the foreshore near the ferry terminal, this centre provides an unobtrusive view of the little local waddlers that nest here. Tours are included in admission; book ahead. Kids under seven free.

Chapman River Wines WINERY
(www.goodfoodkangarooisland.com/wine/chapmanriverwines.asp; off Cape Willoughby Rd, Antechamber Bay; ⏲11am-4.30pm Thu-Mon Sep-Jun) Occupying a converted aircraft hangar, this

eccentric winery makes a mean merlot. The interior is festooned with art and quirky bits of salvage from churches, pubs and homesteads around SA. Good coffee, too.

Penneshaw Maritime & Folk Museum MUSEUM
(www.nationaltrustsa.org.au; 52 Howard Dr, Penneshaw; adult/child/family $3/2/7; ⏲3-5pm Wed-Sun Sep-May) Displays artefacts from local shipwrecks and early settlement (check out those girthsome millstones!), plus endearingly geeky models of Flinders' *Investigator* and Baudin's *Geographe*.

Cape Willoughby Lightstation LIGHTHOUSE
(www.environment.sa.gov.au; Cape Willoughby Rd; tours adult/child/family $14.50/9/38; ⏲tours 11.30am, 12.30pm, 2pm, 3pm & 4pm) About 28km southeast of Penneshaw (unsealed road), this lighthouse first shone in 1852 and is now used as a weather station. Lots of shipwreck info, plus basic cottage accommodation (doubles from $170; book through the DEWNR).

Kangaroo Island Farmers Market MARKET
(www.goodfoodkangarooisland.com/tastingki/farmersmarket.asp; Lloyd Collins Reserve, Frenchmans Tce, Penneshaw; ⏲9am-1pm 1st Sun of the month) Baked goods, chutneys, seafood, olive oil, honey, eggs, cheese, yoghurt...and of course wine! Sealink (p753) sometimes offers dedicated passenger-only return tickets from the mainland if you'd just like to visit the market for the day.

Sunset Winery WINERY
(www.sunset-wines.com.au; Penneshaw–Kingscote Rd; ⏲11am-5pm) Wow, what a view! If you can make it up the steep driveway, Sunset has brilliant sauvignon blanc and sparkling shiraz, and serves savoury platters to go with the panorama.

Sleeping & Eating

Antechamber Bay Ecocabins CABINS $$
(☎08-8553 1557; www.kiecocabins.com; 142 Creek Bay Rd, Antechamber Bay; d from $140, extra adult/child $10/free) Off Cape Willoughby Rd, these two eight-bed cabins are run by a couple of IT industry runaways. On 22 hectares behind the dunes, the cabins are rudimentary but perfectly comfortable, with roofless showers, self-composting toilets, and solar power and hot water. Kayaks and fishing gear available.

Kangaroo Island YHA HOSTEL $
(☎08-8553 1344; www.yha.com.au; 33 Middle Tce, Penneshaw; dm $35, d without/with bathroom $75/110, f $220;) Occupying an old '60s motel with faux-brick cladding, the island YHA has spacious, freshly painted rooms, mostly with en-suite bathrooms. There's a sunny communal kitchen, little lounge and laundry, and penguins at the bottom of the garden.

Wallaby Beach House RENTAL HOUSE $$
(☎08-8362 5293; www.wallabybeachhouse.com.au; Browns Beach; d from $180, extra person $25;) A secluded, self-contained three-bedroom beach house, 13km west of Penneshaw on unpeopled Browns Beach. Simple but stylish decor, with broad sunset views and passing seals, dolphins and penguins to keep you company. Sleeps six.

★**Dudley Cellar Door** CAFE $$
(☎08-8553 1567; www.dudleywines.com.au; 1153 Cape Willoughby Rd, Cuttlefish Bay; mains $25-28; ⏲10am-5pm) KI's pioneering winery has a new cellar door, 12km east of Penneshaw. It's a fancy corrugated iron shed, with astonishing views back to the mainland and serving superb pizzas (try the King George whiting version), oysters and buckets of prawns – just perfect with a bottle of chardonnay on the deck.

Fish SEAFOOD $
(☎0439 803 843; www.2birds1squid.com; 43 North Tce, Penneshaw; mains $13-18; ⏲dinner mid-Oct–May) Takeaway fish and chips like you ain't never had before – grilled, beer-battered or crumbed whiting and garfish – plus giant KI scallops, marron, lobster medallions, prawns and oysters. Dunk them in an array of excellent homemade sauces.

Information

Gateway Visitor Information Centre (☎08-8553 1185; www.tourkangarooisland.com.au; Howard Dr; ⏲9am-5pm Mon-Fri, 10am-4pm Sat & Sun;) Just outside Penneshaw on the road to Kingscote, this centre is stocked with brochures and maps. Also books accommodation and sells park entry tickets and the Kangaroo Island Pass.

American River

POP 230

Between Penneshaw and Kingscote on the way to nowhere in particular, American River squats redundantly by the glassy Pelican

Lagoon. The town was named after a crew of American sealers who built a trading schooner here in 1804. There's no such industriousness here today, just a general store and plenty of pelicans.

From the end of Scenic Dr, a **coastal walk** (2km one way) passes through natural scrub, sugar gums and she-oak en route to some old fish-cannery ruins.

Sleeping & Eating

All Seasons Kangaroo Island Lodge MOTEL $$
(☎08-8553 7053, 1800 355 581; www.kilodge.com.au; Lot 2, Scenic Dr, American River; d incl breakfast $149-279; ❄@🛜≋) Up-to-scratch motel suites overlooking either the pool or lagoon (the rammed-earth wing has the best rooms). The restaurant plates up plenty of local seafood (mains $20 to $30, serving 7.30am to 9am and 6pm to 8pm).

Island Coastal Units MOTEL, CABINS $$
(☎08-8553 7010; www.kangarooislandcoastalunits.com.au; Tangara Dr, American River; units/cabins from $110/120, extra person $20) A low row of basic one- and two-bedroom motel-style units among trees opposite the foreshore, plus four beautiful self-contained cabins with solar hot water, gas cooktops and air-con (pay the extra $10!).

American River Campsite CAMPGROUND $
(☎08-8553 4500; www.kangarooisland.sa.gov.au; Tangara Dr, American River; unpowered sites per 2 people $15, extra person $5) Shady, council-run camping beside the lagoon, with fire pits, showers and toilets. You will need to pay via self-registration.

Oyster Farm Shop SEAFOOD $
(☎08-8553 7122; www.goodfoodkangarooisland.com/food/kio_shop.asp; Tangara Dr; meals $8.50-21; ⊙11am-3pm Mon-Fri) Operated by a local oyster farm, this little shack acts as an outlet for sustainable seafood producers from all over the island. Oysters, marron, abalone, King George whiting...even barramundi, cooked into meals or takeaway uncooked. A dozen fresh unshucked oysters are a paltry $8.50.

American River General Store SELF-CATERING
(☎08-8553 7015; Scenic Dr; ⊙7.30am-6pm) Packed to the northern hemisphere with provisions, bait and tackle, plus there's an amazing hardware 'cupboard', petrol and a bottle shop.

Kingscote

POP 1700

Snoozy seaside Kingscote (pronounced 'kings-coat') is the main settlement on KI, and the hub of island life. It's a photogenic town with swaying Norfolk Island pines, a couple of pubs and some decent eateries.

Sights & Activities

Kangaroo Island Penguin Centre ECOTOUR
(www.kipenguincentre.com.au; Kingscote Wharf; adult/child/family $17/6/40, pelican feeding adult/child $5/3; ⊙tours 8.30pm & 9.30pm Oct-Jan & Mar, 7.30pm & 8.30pm Apr-Oct, closed Feb, pelican feeding 5pm) Runs one-hour tours of its saltwater aquariums and the local penguin colony, plus some stargazing if the sky is clear. It also runs informative (and comical) **pelican feeding** sessions at the adjacent wharf.

Hope Cottage Museum MUSEUM
(www.hopecottagemuseum.com; Centenary Ave; adult/child $6/2; ⊙1-4pm daily Sep-Jul, Sat only Aug) Built on the hill in 1857, this cottage is now a fastidiously maintained National Trust museum decked out in period style, with a reconstructed lighthouse, an amazing old quilt, a tiny walled rose garden and KI's first piano.

Kangaroo Island Spirits DISTILLERY
(KIS; www.kispirits.com.au; 856 Playford Hwy, Cygnet River; tastings free, bottles from $35; ⊙11am-5pm Wed-Sun, daily during school holidays) This fiesty little moonshiner makes small-batch gin with KI native juniper berries, plus vodka, brandy and liqueurs (try the honey and walnut version, using organic KI honey).

Island Beehive APIARY
(www.island-beehive.com.au; 1 Acacia Dr, Kingscote; tours adult/child/family $4.50/3/13; ⊙9am-5pm, group tours every 30min 9.30am-4pm) Runs factory tours where you can study up on passive, hard-working Ligurian bees and beekeeping, then stock up on by-products (bee-products?), including delicious organic honey and honeycomb ice cream. Tours for groups.

Island Pure Sheep Dairy DAIRY
(www.islandpure.com.au; 127 Gum Creek Rd, Cygnet River; tours adult/child/family $6.50/5.50/22; ⊙noon-4pm) Near Cygnet River, 12km from Kingscote, this dairy features 1500 sheep lining up to be milked (around 2pm daily). Take a tour of the factory, which includes

yoghurt and cheese tastings (the haloumi is magic).

Kingscote Tidal Pool SWIMMING
(www.kangarooisland.sa.gov.au/page.aspx?u=222; Chapman Tce; daylight hours) FREE Kingscote beaches are lousy for swimming: locals usually head 18km northwest to Emu Bay, or to this 50m tidal swimming pool, which has a couple of pontoons and grassy banks to sun yourself on.

Sleeping & Eating

Aurora Ozone Hotel HOTEL $$
(08-8553 2011, 1800 083 133; www.aurora resorts.com.au; cnr Commercial St & Kingscote Tce; d pub/motel from $129/165, 1-/2-/3-bed apt from $190/340/540;) Opposite the foreshore with killer views, the 100-year-old Ozone pub has quality pub rooms upstairs, motel rooms, and stylish deluxe apartments in a new wing across the street. The eternally busy bistro (mains $20 to $48) serves meaty grills and seafood, and you can pickle yourself on KI wines at the bar.

Kangaroo Island Central Backpackers HOSTEL $
(08-8553 2787; www.kicentralbackpackers.com; 19 Murray St, Kingscote; dm/d from $25/60;) Just a couple of blocks from Kingscote's main strip, this small, innocuous hostel is clean and affordable, and has a cosy lounge, lush lawns and a beaut en-suite double cabin out the back. It feels like staying at someone's house – good or bad, depending on how sociable you're feeling.

Seaview Motel MOTEL, GUESTHOUSE $$
(08-8553 2030; www.seaview.net.au; 51 Chapman Tce, Kingscote; guesthouse s/d $90/100, motel $146/156, extra adult/child $25/15;) It seems like this place is always full – surely a good sign! Choose from older-style 1924 guesthouse rooms with shared facilities (no air-con), or refurbished 1980s motel rooms. Family-owned, and quite affordable by KI standards.

Kingscote Nepean Bay Tourist Park CARAVAN PARK $
(08-8553 2394; www.kingscotetouristpark.com.au; cnr First & Third Sts, Brownlow; unpowered/powered sites $32/38, cabins/units from $90/135;) You'll find the standard gamut of caravan park delights behind the dunes in Brownlow, 3km southwest of Kingscote. You can walk back to Kingscote via a coastal walking trail. Better for camping than cabins.

Yellow Ash 'n' Chili MEXICAN $$
(59 Dauncy St, Kingscote; mains $16-22; 10am-3pm & 6-8pm Tue-Sat, 10am-3pm Sun) Making a chilli-coloured splash on the KI foodie scene, this casual, brightly painted bungalow on Kingscote's main drag is run by a Californian who knows a thing or two about Mexican food. Expect simple but delicious tostadas, quesadillas, enchiladas etc, made with home-grown tomatoes and chillis and organic flour. Love the 'Day of the Dead' mural.

Kangaroo Island Fresh Seafoods SEAFOOD $
(www.goodfoodkangarooisland.com/eatingout/kifreshseafood.asp; 26 Telegraph Rd, Kingscote; meals $8-16; 8am-8pm Mon-Sat) This unassuming place attached to a petrol station has some of the best seafood you're ever likely to taste. A dozen fat oysters go for around a dollar each, then there are all manner of cooked and fresh KI seafood packs and combos. Superb!

Bella ITALIAN $$
(08-8553 0400; www.restaurantbella.com.au; 54 Dauncey St, Kingscote; pizzas $14-39, mains $26-32; 9am-late Mon-Fri, 10am-late Sat, 11am-late Sun) Sit inside or sidewalk al fresco at Bella, a cheery Italian cafe/restaurant/pizza bar. Pizzas start at 11.30am (eat in or takeaway); dinner is à la carte, featuring American River oysters, Spencer Gulf king prawns, local roo and whiting.

Information

Natural Resources Centre (Department of Environment, Water & Natural Resources; 08-8553 4444, accommodation bookings 08-8553 4410; www.environment.sa.gov.au; 37 Dauncey St, Kingscote; 9am-5pm Mon-Fri) Sells the Kangaroo Island Pass and has info on national parks.

North Coast Road

Exquisite beaches (calmer than the south coast), bushland and undulating pastures dapple the North Coast Rd, running from Kingscote along the coast to the Playford Hwy 85km west (the bitumen expires at Emu Bay). There's not a whole lot to do here other than swan around on the beach – sounds good!

About 18km from Kingscote, **Emu Bay** is a holiday hamlet with a 5km-long, white-sand beach flanked by dunes – one of KI's best swimming spots. Around 36km further west, **Stokes Bay** has a penguin rookery and broad rock pool you access by scrambling through a 20m tunnel in the cliffs at the bay's eastern end (mind your head!). Beware the rip outside the pool.

The view as you look back over **Snelling Beach** from atop Constitution Hill is awesome! Continue 7km west and you'll hit the turn-off to **Western River Cove**, where a small beach is crowded in by sombre basalt cliffs. The ridge-top road in is utterly scenic (and steep).

Sleeping & Eating

Western River Cove Campsite CAMPGROUND $
(www.kangarooisland.sa.gov.au; unpowered sites per 2 people $15, extra person $5) This self-registration camp site is just a short walk from the beach and a footbridge over the river (it's so tempting to dangle a line). There's a toilet block and a barbecue hut but no showers.

Emu Bay Holiday Homes CABINS, RENTAL HOUSE $
(08-8553 5241; www.emubaysuperviews.com.au; 21 Bayview Rd, Emu Bay; cabins $90, holiday homes $115-145, extra person $20;) Great-value (if a little frilly) cabins and holiday homes in a large flower-filled garden on the hill above Emu Bay beach (great views!). The self-contained cabins (caravan-park cabins with a facelift, sans air-con) sleep four or six; the holiday homes sleep six or 10.

Stone House RENTAL HOUSE $$$
(www.life-time.com.au; North Coast Rd, Snelling Beach; d from $410;) It's pricey, but it's worth it: a gorgeous self-contained stone-and-timber house on the hillside above beautiful Snelling Beach (actually, it's not that pricey if there's a few of you: from $460 for six people in three bedrooms). Floor-to-ceiling windows, quirky artworks, a couple of decks and daisy-studded lawns.

Rockpool Café CAFE $$
(08-8559 2277; North Coast Rd, Stokes Bay; mains $15-27; 11am-5pm Tue-Sun, daily during school holidays) Don't worry about sandy feet at this casual, al fresco joint in Stokes Bay. 'What's the house special?', we asked. 'Whatever I feel like doin'!', said the chef (usually seafood, washed down with local wines and decent espresso).

South Coast Road

The south coast is rough and wave-swept compared with the north.

Sights & Activities

Seal Bay Conservation Park NATURE RESERVE
(08-8553 4460; www.environment.sa.gov.au/sealbay; Seal Bay Rd; self-guided tours adult/child/family $15/9/40, guided $32/18/80, twilight $60/36/165; tours 9am-4.15pm year-round, extra tours Dec-Feb) 'Observation, not interaction' is the mentality. Guided tours stroll along the beach (or boardwalk on self-guided tours) to a colony of (mostly sleeping) Australian sea lions. Twilight tours December and January. Bookings advised.

Clifford's Honey Farm APIARY
(www.cliffordshoney.com.au; 1157 Elsegood Rd, Haines; 9am-5pm) It's almost worth swimming the Backstairs Passage for the honey ice cream (sourced from a colony of rare Ligurian bees) at this charming, uncommercial farm. A bit off the tourist radar (again, charming).

Kelly Hill Conservation Park NATURE RESERVE
(08-8553 4464; www.environment.sa.gov.au; South Coast Rd; tours adult/child/family $15/9/40, caving $65/39/176; tours 10.30am, then hourly 11.15am-4.15pm) This series of dry limestone caves was 'discovered' in the 1880s by a horse named Kelly, who fell into them through a hole. Take the standard **show cave tour**, or add on an **adventure caving tour** (following the 2.15pm standard tour; bookings essential). The **Hanson Bay Walk** (9km one way) runs from the caves through mallee scrub and past freshwater wetlands.

Emu Ridge Farm Eucalyptus Distillery DISTILLERY, GALLERY
(www.emuridge.com.au; 691 Willsons Rd, MacGillivary; admission free, self-guided tours adult/child $4.50/2; 9am-2pm) A detour off Hog Bay or Birchmore roads takes you past this self-sufficient operation (all solar-, steam- and wind-powered) extracting eucalyptus oil from Kangaroo Island's narrow-leaf mallee. The attached craft gallery sells eucalyptus-oil products.

Raptor Domain AVIARY
(www.kangarooislandbirdsofprey.com.au; cnr South Coast Rd & Seal Bay Rd; birds of prey adult/child/family $15/10/45, reptiles $10/8/32; 10.30am-4pm) Check out some KI wedge-tailed eagles,

barn owls and kookaburras at a one-hour birds-of-prey display (11.30am and 2.30pm), or go scaly at a one-hour lizards and snakes show (1pm).

🛏 Sleeping & Eating

Flinders Chase Farm HOSTEL, CABINS $$
(☑ 08-8559 7223; www.flinderschasefarm.com.au; 1561 West End Hwy; dm/cabins $25/70, d & tw with bathroom $110) A working farm with charm, a short drive from Flinders Chase National Park. Accommodation includes immaculate dorms, a couple of cosy cabins and en-suite rooms in a lodge. There's also a terrific camp kitchen, fire pits and 'tropical' outdoor showers.

Western Kangaroo
Island Caravan Park CAMPGROUND $
(☑ 08-8559 7201; www.westernki.com.au; 7928 South Coast Rd, Flinders Chase; unpowered/powered sites $22/28, cabins $110-190; ❄) A few minutes' drive east of Flinders Chase National Park, this friendly park has shady gums and resident roos. Check out the koala and lagoon walks, and the phone booth inside an old bakery truck. The shop sells groceries, homemade heat-and-eats and (for guests only) beer and wine.

Kangaroo Island
Wilderness Retreat HOTEL, RESORT $$
(☑ 08-8559 7275; www.kiwr.com; Lot 1, South Coast Rd, Flinders Chase; d $176-360; ❄ @ 🕸) A low-key, log-cabin-style resort on the Flinders Chase doorstep with resident grazing wallabies. Accommodation ranges from basic motel-style rooms to flashy spa suites. There's a petrol pump, a bar and a restaurant here too, serving breakfast (mains $17 to $25, 7.30am to 9.30am) and dinner (mains $28 to $35, 6pm to 8.30pm).

Marron Café MODERN AUSTRALIAN $$
(☑ 08-8559 4114; www.andermel.com.au/cafe.htm; 804 Harriet Rd, Central Kangaroo Island; mains $16-38; ⊙ 11am-4.30pm) Around 15km north of Vivonne Bay you can check out marron in breeding tanks, then eat some! It's a subtle taste, not necessarily enhanced by the heavy sauces issued by the kitchen. There are steak and chicken dishes, for the crustacean-shy. Last orders 4pm.

Flinders Chase National Park

Occupying the western end of the island, Flinders Chase National Park is one of SA's top national parks. Much of the park is mallee scrub, but there are some beautiful, tall sugar-gum forests, particularly around Rocky River and the Ravine des Casoars, 5km south of Cape Borda.

⊙ Sights & Activities

Once a farm, **Rocky River** is a rampant hotbed of wildlife, with kangaroos, wallabies and Cape Barren geese competing for your affections. A slew of good walks launch from behind the visitors centre, including the **Rocky River Hike** on which you might spy a platypus (9km loop, three hours).

From Rocky River, a road runs south to a remote 1906 **lighthouse** atop wild Cape du Couedic. A boardwalk weaves down to **Admirals Arch**, a huge archway ground out by heavy seas, and passes a colony of New Zealand fur seals (sweet smelling they ain't...).

At Kirkpatrick Point, a few kilometres east of Cape du Couedic, the much photographed **Remarkable Rocks** are a cluster of hefty, weather-gouged granite boulders atop a rocky dome that arcs 75m down to the ocean.

On the northwestern corner of the island, the 1858 **Cape Borda Lightstation** (☑ 08-8553 4465; www.environment.sa.gov.au/parks; admission free, tours adult/child/family $14.50/9/38; ⊙ 9am-5pm, tours 11am, 12.30pm & 2pm) stands

---

SOUTHERN OCEAN LODGE

Millionaires, start your engines! The shining star in the SA tourism galaxy is **Southern Ocean Lodge** (☑ 08-9918 4355; www.southernoceanlodge.com.au; Hanson Bay; d per night from $1980; ❄ @ 🕸) , a sexy, low-profile snake tracing the Hanson Bay cliff-top – a real exercise in exclusivity. There's a two-night minimum stay; you get airport transfers, all meals and drinks and guided tours of KI.

If you want a sticky-beak, don't expect to see anything from the road: all you'll find is a steely set of gates and an unreceptive intercom: privacy is what guests are paying for here (Hey, wasn't that Teri Hatcher in that 4WD?). But you can catch a sneaky glimpse from Hanson Bay beach.

tall above the rippling iron surface of the Southern Ocean. There are walks here from 1.5km to 9km, and extra tours at 3.15pm and 4pm during summer holidays.

At nearby Harvey's Return a **cemetery** speaks poignant volumes about the reality of isolation in the early days. From here you can drive to **Ravine des Casoars** (literally 'Ravine of the Cassowaries', referring to the now-extinct dwarf emus seen here by Baudin's expedition). The challenging **Ravine des Casoars Hike** (7km return, three hours) tracks through the ravine to the coast

Sleeping & Eating

There are campgrounds at **Rocky River** (per person/car $9/27), **Snake Lagoon** (per person/car $7/13), **West Bay** (per person/car $7/13) and **Harvey's Return** (per person/car $7/13); book through the **Department of Environment, Water & Natural Resources** (DEWNR; ☎08-8553 4490; flinderschase@sa.gov.au).

There's also refurbished cottage accommodation at Rocky River – the budget **Postmans Cottage** (d $70) and family-friendly **Mays Homestead** (d $133) – and lightkeepers' cottages at **Cape du Couedic** and **Cape Borda** (basic huts to stone cottages, d $22-170). Book through the **Department of Environment, Water & Natural Resources** (☎08-8553 4410; kiparksaccom@sa.gov.au).

On the food front, the only option here if you're not self-catering is the **Chase Cafe** (☎08-8559 7339; www.thechasecafe.com.au; Flinders Chase Visitor Information Centre; meals $9-27; ⊙9am-3.30pm) at the visitors centre, serving burgers, wraps, soup, coffee, and wines by the glass.

Information

Flinders Chase Visitor Information Centre (☎08-8559 7235; www.environment.sa.gov.au/parks; South Coast Rd, Flinders Chase; ⊙9am-5pm) Info, maps and camping/accommodation bookings, plus a cafe and displays on island ecology.

LIMESTONE COAST

The Limestone Coast – strung-out along southeastern SA between the flat, olive span of the lower Murray River and the Victorian border – is a curiously engaging place. On the highways you can blow across these flatlands in under a day, no sweat, but around here the delight is in the detail. Detour off-road to check out the area's lagoons, surf beaches and sequestered bays. Also on offer are wine regions, photogenic fishing ports and snoozy agricultural towns. And what's *below* the road is even more amazing: a bizarre subterranean landscape of limestone caves, sinkholes and bottomless crater lakes.

Online, see www.thelimestonecoast.com.

Getting There & Away

The Dukes Hwy (Rte A8) is the most direct route between Adelaide and Melbourne (729km), but the coastal Princes Hwy (Rte B1; about 900km) adjacent to the Coorong National Park is definitely more scenic.

AIR

Regional Express (Rex; www.regionalexpress.com.au) flies daily between Adelaide and Mount Gambier (one way from $160).

BUS

Premier Stateliner (www.premierstateliner.com.au) runs two bus routes – coastal and inland – between Adelaide and Mount Gambier ($73, seven hours). From Adelaide along the coast (Tuesday, Thursday, Friday and Sunday) via the Coorong you can stop at Meningie ($36, two hours), Robe ($64, 4½ hours) and Beachport ($68, 5¼ hours). The inland bus runs daily via Naracoorte ($71, five hours) and Penola ($70, 5¾ hours).

Coorong National Park

The amazing **Coorong National Park** (www.environment.sa.gov.au) is a fecund lagoon landscape curving along the coast for 145km from Lake Alexandrina towards Kingston SE. A complex series of soaks and salt pans, it's separated from the sea by the chunky dunes of the **Younghusband Peninsula**. More than 200 species of waterbirds live here. *Storm Boy*, an endearing film about a young boy's friendship with a pelican (based on the novel by Colin Thiele), was filmed here.

In the 1800s the bountiful resources of the Coorong supported a large Ngarrindjeri population. The Ngarrindjeri are still closely connected to the Coorong, and many still live here.

At the edge of the Coorong on **Lake Albert** (a large arm of Lake Alexandrina), **Meningie** (population 900) was established as a minor port in 1866. These 'lower lakes' have returned to life recently, in the wake of the 2011 Murray River floods. Prior to this, the lakes were shrinking rapidly, and the entire Coorong ecosystem was under threat through salination and species decline. A momentary reprieve from climate change? Time will tell...

The Princes Hwy scuttles through the park, but you can't see much from the road. Instead, take the 13km, unsealed **Coorong Scenic Drive**. Signed as Seven Mile Rd, it starts 10km southwest of Meningie off the Narrung Rd, and takes you right into the landscape, with its stinky lagoons, sea mists, fishing shanties, pelicans and wild emus. The road rejoins the Princes Hwy, 10km south of Meningie.

It looks a little shabby, but **Camp Coorong** (☎08-8575 1557; www.ngarrindjeri.net; Princes Hwy; museum admission per car $5; ⏰vary) – run by the Ngarrindjeri Lands and Progress Association and 10km south of Meningie – has a museum and is a great place to learn about Ngarrindjeri culture. Call ahead to make sure it's open.

With a 4WD you can access **Ninety Mile Beach**, a well-known surf-fishing spot. The easiest ocean access point is 3km off the Princes Hwy at 42 Mile Crossing, 19km south of Salt Creek.

On the southern fringe of the Coorong is **Kingston SE** (www.kingstonse.com.au) with a population of 2230. The town is a hotbed of crayfishing, and hosts the weeklong **Lobsterfest** in May. One of Australia's 'big' tourist attractions, the anatomically correct Larry the Lobster is a famed resident.

For a watery perspective, try Spirit of the Coorong (p751) in Goolwa, which runs ecocruises into the national park, including lunch and a guided walk. Adelaide bus connections available.

Sleeping & Eating

There are 11 bush **camp sites** (www.environment.sa.gov.au; per person/car $7/13) in the park, but you need a permit from the DEWNR, available from the Meningie visitor information centre or the Meningie petrol station. There are also 'honesty boxes' at some of the larger campgrounds.

★**Dalton on the Lake** B&B $$

(☎08-8575 1162, 0428 737 161; admason@lm.net.au; 30 Narrung Rd, Meningie; d from $130; ❄) Generous in spirit and unfailingly clean, this lakeside B&B goes to great lengths to ensure your stay is comfortable. There'll be fresh bread baking when you arrive, jars of homemade biscuits, and bountiful bacon and eggs for breakfast. There's a modern self-contained studio off to one side, or a renovated stone cottage – book either, or both.

Lake Albert Caravan Park CARAVAN PARK $

(☎08-8575 1411; www.lakealbertcaravanpark.com.au; 25 Narrung Rd, Meningie; unpowered/powered sites from $23/30, cabins without/with bathroom from $70/95; ❄📶) A breezy park with a beaut aspect overlooking pelican-prone Lake Albert (the best camp sites are absolute lakefront). The four deluxe two-bedroom cabins ($150) are the pick of the cabins.

Coorong Wilderness Lodge CAMPGROUND, CABINS $$

(☎08-8575 6001; www.coorongwildernesslodge.com; off Princes Hwy; unpowered/powered sites $15/30, dm/d/cabins, $40/90/200; ❄) At isolated Hack Point, 25km south of Meningie, this fish-shaped conference centre is run by a local Ngarrindjeri family. The bunkhouse and camp sites here are a bit ordinary, but the new kitchen-cabins are lovely. You can also book a bush-tucker walk ($30) or hire a kayak (half-/full day $40/60).

Cheese Factory Restaurant PUB $$

(☎08-8575 1914; www.meningie.com.au; 3 Fiebig Rd, Meningie; mains $19-28; ⏰noon-2pm Tue-Sun, 5.30-late Wed & Sun) In a converted cheese factory (you might have guessed), this outfit gives the Meningie pub a run for its money. Lean on the front bar with the locals, or munch into steaks, lasagne, mixed grills, Coorong mullet or a Coorong burger (with mullet!) in the cavernous dining room. The very lo-fi **Meningie Cheese Factory Museum** (www.meningiecheesefactorymuseum.com; admission $3; ⏰11am-5pm) is here too (butter churns, old typewriters, domestic knick-knackery)

Information

Meningie Visitor Information Centre (☎08-8575 1770; www.meningie.com.au; 14 Princes Hwy; ⏰10am-4.30pm) Coorong camping permits and local info.

Robe

POP 1130

Robe is a cherubic little fishing port that's become a holiday hot spot for Adelaidians and Melburnians alike. The sign saying 'Drain L Outlet' as you roll into town doesn't promise much, but along the main street you'll find quality eateries and boundless accommodation, and there are some magic beaches and lakes around town. Over Christmas and Easter, Robe is packed to the heavens – book *waaay* in advance.

Sights & Activities

Heritage-listed buildings dating from the late 1840s to 1870s litter the streets of Robe, including the upstanding little 1863 **Customs House** (www.nationaltrustsa.org.au; Royal Circus; adult/child $2/50¢; 2-4pm Tue & Sat Feb-Dec, 2-4pm Mon-Sat Jan), now a nautical museum.

Little Dip Conservation Park (www.environment.sa.gov.au) runs along the coast for about 13km south of town. It features a variety of habitats including lakes, wetlands and dunes, and some beaut beaches, Aboriginal middens, walks and camping spots (per person/car $7/13). Access is via Nora Creina Rd.

The small town beach has safe swimming, while **Long Beach** (2km from town), is good for surfing, sailboarding and lazy days (safe swimming in some sections – ask at the visitors centre). **Steve's Place** (08-8768 2094; stevesplace66@internode.on.net; 26 Victoria St; 9.30am-5pm Mon-Fri, 9am-1pm Sat, 10am-1pm Sun) rents out boards/bodyboards/wetsuits (per day $40/20/20), and is also the best place for info on the annual **Robe Easter Classic** in April, SA's longest-running surf comp (since 1968).

Sleeping

Local rental agents with properties from as low as $80 per night in the off season include **Happyshack** (0403 578 382, 08-8768 2341; www.happyshack.com.au), **SAL Real Estate** (08-8768 2737; www.salrealestate.com.au; 25 Victoria St) and **Robe Lifestyle** (1300 760 629; www.robelifestyle.com.au).

Caledonian Inn HOTEL **$$**
(08-8768 2029; www.caledonian.net.au; 1 Victoria St; pub/cottage/villa d from $85/185/500;) This historic inn has it all under one roof (actually, several roofs). The half-dozen pub rooms upstairs share bathroom facilities but are bright and cosy, while the split-level, self-contained units – all rattan and white-painted wood – are sandwiched between the pub and beach. The plush villa sleeps eight. The pub grub is good, too (mains $18 to $36, serving noon to 2pm and 6pm to 8pm).

Grey Masts B&B **$$$**
(0411 627 146; www.greymasts.com.au; cnr Victoria & Smillie Sts; d from $200) A lovely, L-shaped, low-ceilinged 1850s stone cottage behind the local bookshop. The two bedrooms sleep four, and there's a compact kitchen, welcoming lounge and flower-filled garden. The Savage family (Mr and Mrs Savage and their 12 sons!) once lived here.

Lakeside Tourist Park CARAVAN PARK **$**
(08-8768 2193; www.lakesiderobe.com.au; 24 Main Rd; unpowered/powered sites from $32/34, cabins/villas from $66/95;) Right on Lake Fellmongery (a 'fellmonger' is a wool washer, don't you know), this abstractly laid-out, rather boutique park has heritage-listed pine trees, plenty of grass, basic cabins and flashy villas.

Robe Lakeview Motel & Apartments MOTEL **$$**
(08-8768 2100; www.robelakeviewmotel.com.au; 2 Lakeside Tce; d/2-bedroom apt from $110/225, extra person $15;) Overlooking the water-skiing mecca Lake Fellmongery, the keenly managed Lake View is Robe's best motel. The decor is on the improve (slowly banishing the '90s), the rooms are roomy and immaculately clean, and the barbecue area pumps during summer.

Eating

Union Cafe CAFE **$**
(08-8768 2627; 4/17-19 Victoria St; mains $9-19; 8am-4pm;) Robe's best coffee is at this curiously angled corner cafe with polished-glass fragments in the floor and improvised chandeliers on the ceiling. Unionise your hangover with big breakfasts (berry pancakes with bacon and maple syrup), stir-fries, pastas and risottos.

Vic Street Pizzeria PIZZA **$$**
(08-8768 2081; www.vicstreet.com.au; 6 Victoria St; mains $10-21; 11am-9pm) Vic Street is a high-energy, all-day cafe, serving good coffee and gourmet pizzas (we can recommend the 'Humdinger': ham, salami, chicken, red onion, olives, capsicum and pineapple). Mod-Asian interior touches, cool tunes on the stereo and local wines, too.

Robe Providore CAFE **$**
(08-8768 2891; 4 Victoria St; mains $13-18; 8am-late) A bit of 'big city' comes to Robe at this polished concrete-and-white eatery, serving good coffee, big breakfasts (eggs benedict, house-baked pastries), considered lunches (calamari salad) and wood-oven pizzas at night (try the pork-and-fennel sausage version). There are communal tables and bench seats.

Information

Robe Visitor Information Centre (☎08-8768 2465, 1300 367 144; www.robe.com.au; Mundy Tce, Public Library; ⏰9am-5pm Mon-Fri, 10am-4pm Sat & Sun; 📶) Displays, brochures and free internet. Look for *Scenic Drive, Heritage Drive* and *A Walk Through History* pamphlets.

Beachport

POP 350

'See and be seen: headlights 24 hours!' say billboards on the way into Beachport. A town that's desperate to be noticed? A plaintive cry for attention? We like it the way it is: low-key and beachy, with aquamarine surf, the famous 800m-long jetty, staunch stone buildings and rows of Norfolk Island pines. Forget about being seen – your time here will be perfectly anonymous.

Sights & Activities

Old Wool & Grain Store Museum MUSEUM
(☎08-8735 8029; www.nationaltrust.org.au/sa; 5 Railway Tce; adult/child/family $5/2/10; ⏰10am-4pm) In a National Trust building on the main street. Inside are relics from Beachport's whaling and shipping days, rooms decked out in 1870s style and a new display on the local Buandi people.

Beachport Conservation Park NATURE RESERVE
(www.environment.sa.gov.au) There are some great walking tracks in the 710-hectare park, sandwiched between the coast and Lake George 2km north of town. Aboriginal middens, sheltered coves, lagoons and bush camping (per person/car $7/13).

Pool of Siloam SWIMMING
(Bowman Scenic Dr) In the dunes on the western outskirts of town, the pool is great for swimming; the water is seven times saltier than the ocean. Ask at the vistor information centre for directions.

Sleeping & Eating

Bompas HOTEL, CAFE $
(☎08-8735 8333; www.bompas.com.au; 3 Railway Tce; d without/with bathroom from $100/125; 📶) In what was Beachport's first pub, Bompas is an all-in-one small hotel and licensed restaurant-cafe. Rooms upstairs are generously sized and strewn with modern art (shoot for room No 3 – more expensive, but worth it for the million-dollar views and deep balcony). Menu offerings downstairs (mains $9 to $23, serving noon to 2pm and 6pm to 8pm, plus breakfast on weekends) include curries, schnitzels and pies, with local and imported beers.

Southern Ocean Tourist Park CARAVAN PARK $
(☎08-8735 8153; sotp@bigpond.net.au; Somerville St; unpowered/powered sites $26/30, cabins from $105; ❄) This well-pruned, shady park is nooked into the base of a hill in the town centre. Facilities include a laundry, covered barbecues, crayfish cookers and a great little playground. The new kitchen cabins on the hilltop are lovely.

Information

Beachport Visitor Information Centre (☎08-8735 8029; www.wattlerange.sa.gov.au; Millicent Rd; ⏰9am-5pm Mon-Fri, 10am-4pm Sat & Sun) Info-packed, on the road into town. Look for the *Beachport's Bowman Scenic Drive* brochure.

Mount Gambier

POP 24,900

Strung out along the flatlands below an extinct volcano, Mount Gambier is the Limestone Coast's major town and service hub. 'The Mount' sometimes seems a little short on urban virtues, but it's not what's above the streets that makes Mount Gambier special – it's the deep Blue Lake and caves that worm their way though the limestone beneath the town. Amazing!

Sights & Activities

Blue Lake LAKE
(John Watson Dr; ⏰24hr) FREE Mount Gambier's big-ticket item is the luminous, 75m-deep lake, which turns an insane hue of blue during summer. Perplexed scientists think it has to do with calcite crystals suspended in the water, which form at a faster rate during the warmer months. Consequently, if you visit between April and November, the lake will look much like any other – a steely grey.

Acquifer Tours (☎08-8723 1199; www.aquifer tours.com; cnr Bay Rd & John Watson Dr; adult/child/family $9/4/25; ⏰tours 9am-5pm Nov-Jan, 9am-2pm Feb-May & Sep-Oct, 9am-noon Jun-Aug) runs hourly tours, taking you down near the lake shore in a glass-panelled lift.

Riddoch Art Gallery GALLERY
(www.riddochartgallery.org.au; 1 Bay Rd; ⏰10am-5pm Mon-Fri, 11am-3pm Sat & Sun) FREE If the lake isn't blue, don't feel blue – cheer yourself

OFF THE BEATEN TRACK

PORT MACDONNELL

Around 30km south of Mount Gambier, snoozy crayfishing Port MacDonnell (population 700) is SA's southernmost town. It was once the second-busiest port in the state, which explains the handsome 1863 **Customs House** (☎08-8738 2475, 0418 854 595; www.thecustomshouse.com.au; 3 Charles St, Port MacDonnell; d from $260), now a B&B.

Around 40 ships have sunk along the coast near here since 1844. The **Port MacDonnell & District Maritime Museum** (www.dcgrant.sa.gov.au/page.aspx?u=449; 5-7 Charles St, Port MacDonnell; adult/child $5/3; ⏲9am-5pm Mon-Thu, 9am-8pm Fri, 10am-4pm Sat & Sun) is a barnacle-encrusted trove of artefacts recovered from the shipwrecks.

up at one of Australia's best regional galleries. There are three galleries (touring and permanent exhibitions, contemporary installations, community displays), plus heritage exhibits and a cinema screening local history flicks. Free tours 11am Thursday.

Cave Gardens CAVE
(cnr Bay Rd & Watson Tce; ⏲24hr) FREE A 50m-deep sinkhole right in the middle of town, with the odd suicidal shopping trolley at the bottom. You can walk down into it, and watch the nightly Sound & Light Show (8pm) telling local Aboriginal Dreaming stories.

Engelbrecht Cave CAVE
(☎08-8723 5552; www.mtgambiersa.com.au/attractions/engelbrecht-cave; Jubilee Hwy W, off Chute St; tours adult/child/family $12/8/34; ⏲tours hourly 9am-4pm, to 3pm winter) A meandering cave system running beneath Jubilee Hwy and 19 local houses! Tours last 45 minutes and take you down to an underground lake (call for cave-diving info). There's also a cafe here.

Umpherston Sinkhole CAVE
(☎0429 349 328; 2160 Jubilee Hwy E; admission free, guided tours adult/child/family $9/4/20, self-guided tours adult/child $5/free; ⏲24hr, tours 9am-9pm summer, 10am-4pm winter) FREE Once 'a pleasant resort in the heat of summer' on James Umpherston's long since subdivided estate. It's free to check it out, or you can take a self-guided or guided tour.

Sleeping

Park Hotel PUB $$
(☎08-8725 2430; www.parkhotel.net.au; 163 Commercial St W; d from $140; ❄📶) In Mount Gambier's western wastelands, this old corner pub has spent a fortune renovating its three upstairs rooms. Polished timber floors, double glazing, marble bathrooms and coffee-and-cream colour schemes – a really slick product.

Colhurst House B&B $$
(☎08-8723 1309; www.colhursthouse.com.au; 3 Colhurst Pl; d incl breakfast from $170; ❄) Most locals don't know about Colhurst – it's up a laneway off a sidestreet (Wyatt St) and you can't really see it from downtown Mt G. It's an 1878 mansion built by Welsh migrants, and manages to be old-fashioned without being twee. There's a wrap-around balcony upstairs with great views over the rooftops. Cooked breakfasts, too.

Old Mount Gambier Gaol HOSTEL $
(☎08-8723 0032; www.hmgetaway.com.au; 25 Margaret St; dm/tw/d from $26/60/80; 📶) If you can forget that this place was a prison until 1995 (either that or embrace the fact), these refurbished old buildings make for an atmospheric and affordable stay. There's a regulation backpacker dorm in one building, or you can up the spooky stakes and sleep in a former cell. There's a bar with occasional live bands.

Blue Lake Holiday Park CARAVAN PARK $
(☎08-8725 9856, 1800 676 028; www.bluelake.com.au; Bay Rd; unpowered/powered sites from $31/36, cabins/units/bungalows from $98/120/180; ❄@📶🏊) Adjacent to the Blue Lake, a golf course and walking and cycling tracks, this amiable park has some natty grey-and-white cabins and well-weeded lawns. There are also spiffy contemporary, self-contained 'retreats' (from $200) that sleep four.

Eating

Yoeys CAFE $
(www.yoeys.com.au; 32 James St; items $5-14; ⏲8.30am-5.30pm Mon-Fri, 8.30am-1.30pm Sat) What a find! A gourmet cafe-providore with shelves full of cakes, muffins, breads, chocolates, pasta and gourmet foodie hampers; a fabulous cheese fridge (rustic Italian goats' cheese anyone?); and the best coffee in town. Soups, pies and pasties, too.

Bullfrogs MODERN AUSTRALIAN $$
(08-8723 3933; www.bullfrogs.com.au; 7 Percy St; mains $11-32; 11am-late) Spread over three floors of a fabulous old stone mill building, this is the place for beef and lamb grills, boutique beers, Coonawarra wines, cocktails, trusty coffee and occasional acoustic troubadours. Hard to beat.

Banana Tree Cafe & Terrace THAI $$
(08-8723 9393; www.bananatree.com.au; 53 Gray St; mains $16-33; 11am-2pm & 6-9pm) Authentic Thai in Mount Gambier! Colourful and appropriately tacky (faux rattan, chandeliers, commercial FM), backstreet Banana Tree serves chilli-laden dishes like beef-and-basil stir-fry and a smokin' green chicken curry.

Jens Town Hall Hotel PUB $$
(08-8725 1671; 40 Commercial St E; mains $15-29; noon-2pm & 6-8pm) The most palatable place for a beer in the Mount (there are a lot of rambling old pubs here), the 1884 Jens has a vast dining room plating up equally large steaks, mixed grills, pastas, seafood and a damn fine lasagne. There are $12 lunch specials.

Information

Mount Gambier Visitor Information Centre (08-8724 9750, 1800 087 187; www.mountgambiertourism.com.au; 35 Jubilee Hwy E; 9am-5pm) Has details on local sights, activities, transport and accommodation. **Lady Nelson Discovery Centre** (adult/child $2/1) is here too, featuring a replica of the historic brig *Lady Nelson*.

PENOLA & THE COONAWARRA WINE REGION

A rural town on the way up (what a rarity!), Penola (population 1670) is the kind of place where you walk down the main street and three people say 'Hello!' to you before you reach the pub. The town is famous for two things: first, for its association with the Sisters of St Joseph of the Sacred Heart, co-founded in 1867 by Australia's first saint, Mary MacKillop; and secondly, for being smack bang in the middle of the Coonawarra Wine Region.

Sights & Activities

Mary MacKillop Interpretive Centre MUSEUM
(www.mackilloppenola.org.au; cnr Portland St & Petticoat La; adult/child $5/free; 10am-4pm) The centre occupies a jaunty building with a gregarious entrance pergola (perhaps not as modest as Saint Mary might have liked!). There's oodles of info on Australia's first saint here, plus the Woods MacKillop Schoolhouse, the first school in Australia for children from lower socioeconomic backgrounds.

John Riddoch Centre MUSEUM
(www.wattlerange.sa.gov.au/tourism; 27 Arthur St; 9am-5pm Mon-Fri, 10am-4pm Sat & Sun) FREE In the visitor centre building, this museum casts a web over local history back to the 1850s, covering the local Pinejunga people and original Penola pastoralist Riddoch, who 'never gave in to misfortune' and was 'steady and persistent'. Closed for a refurbishment when we revisited.

Petticoat Lane STREET
One of Penola's first streets. Most of the original buildings have been razed, but there are still a few old timber-slab houses, redgum kerbs and gnarly trees to see.

Sleeping & Eating

See www.coonawarradiscovery.com for B&B listings. Many local Coonawarra wineries also have restaurants.

Must@Coonawarra MOTEL $$
(08-8737 3444; www.mustatcoonawarra.com.au; 126 Church St; r from $165;) On the way up the winery strip, plush Must is a newish option with jaunty roof curves reminiscent of a certain opera venue in Sydney. Accommodation ranges from studios to apartments, with sustainable features aplenty: rain-water showers, double glazing and insulation, solar hot water, natural cleaning products etc. Bike hire costs $20 per day.

Heyward's Royal Oak Hotel PUB $
(08-8737 2322; www.heywardshotel.com.au; 31 Church St; s $55, d & tw $88) The Royal Oak – a lace-trimmed, main-street megalith built in 1872 – is Penola's community hub. The rooms upstairs are a bit tatty and share bathrooms, but they're good bang for your buck. Downstairs the huge tartan-carpeted dining room (mains $20 to $33, open 11.30am to 2pm and 6pm to 8pm) serves classy pub food (roo fillets with pepper crust and cabernet glaze) and schnitzels as big as your head. There's a summery beer garden, too.

Georgie's Cottage B&B $$
(☎08-8737 3540; www.georgiescottage.com; 1 Riddoch St; d from $185; ❄) Feeling romantic? A short stroll from town on the road to Millicent, Georgie's is a cute little stone cottage fronted by blooming roses and hollyhocks. Gourmet provisions include chocolates and wine, which you may or may not feel like cracking into for breakfast.

Pipers of Penola MODERN AUSTRALIAN $$$
(☎08-8737 3999; www.pipersofpenola.com.au; 58 Riddoch St; mains $30-37; ⏲6-9pm Tue-Sat) A classy, intimate dining room tastefully constructed inside an old Methodist church, with friendly staff and seasonal fare. The menu is studded with words like 'galette', 'kromeski' and 'rotollo' – seriously gourmet indicators! The prices are getting up there, but quality is too. Superb wine list with lots of locals.

diVine CAFE $
(☎08-8737 2122; www.penola.org/divine.htm; 39 Church St; mains $10-19; ⏲9am-5pm) A bright, mod cafe serving baguettes, all-day breakfasts, great coffee and internationally inspired lunches (try the steamed Chinese pork buns). Nattering Penolans chew muffins and local cheeses, discussing the nuances of various vintages.

Information

Penola Visitor Information Centre (☎08-8737 2855, 1300 045 373; www.wattlerange.sa.gov.au/tourism; 27 Arthur St; ⏲9am-5pm Mon-Fri, 10am-4pm Sat & Sun) Services the Coonawarra region, with info about local cycling routes and winery tours. The John Riddoch Centre is also here. Pick up the *Penola Cycle Trails* and *Walk With History* brochures.

NARACOORTE CAVES NATIONAL PARK

About 10km southeast of Naracoorte township, off the Penola road, is the only World Heritage–listed site in SA. The discovery of an ancient fossilised marsupial in these limestone caves raised palaeontological eyebrows around the world, and featured in the BBC's David Attenborough series *Life on Earth*.

The park visitor centre doubles as the impressive **Wonambi Fossil Centre** (☎08-8762 2340; www.environment.sa.gov.au/naracoorte; Hynam-Caves Rd; adult/child/family $13/8/36; ⏲9am-5pm) – a re-creation of the rainforest that covered this area 200,000 years ago. Follow a ramp down past grunting, life-sized reconstructions of extinct

DON'T MISS

COONAWARRA WINERIES

When it comes to spicy cabernet sauvignon, it's just plain foolish to dispute the virtues of the Coonawarra Wine Region (www.coonawarra.org). The *terra rossa* (red earth) soils here also produce irresistible shiraz and chardonnay. Five of the best:

➡ **Zema Estate** (www.zema.com.au; Riddoch Hwy; ⏲9am-5pm) A steadfast, traditional winery started by the Zema family in the early '80s. It's a low-key affair with a handmade vibe infusing the shiraz and cab sav.

➡ **Rymill Coonawarra** (www.rymill.com.au; Riddoch Hwy; ⏲10am-5pm) Rymill rocks the local boat by turning out some of the best sauvignon blanc you'll ever taste. The cellar door is fronted by a statue of two duelling steeds – appropriately rebellious.

➡ **Majella Wines** (www.majellawines.com.au; Lynn Rd; ⏲10am-4.30pm) The family that runs Majella are fourth-generation Coonawarrans, so they know a thing or two about gutsy reds.

➡ **Balnaves of Coonawarra** (www.balnaves.com.au; Riddoch Hwy; ⏲9am-5pm Mon-Fri, noon-5pm Sat & Sun) The tasting notes here ooze florid wine speak (dark seaweed, anyone?), but even if your nosing skills aren't that subtle, you'll enjoy the cab sav and chardonnay.

➡ **Wynns Coonawarra Estate** (www.wynns.com.au; 2 Memorial Dr; ⏲10am-5pm) The oldest Coonawarra winery, Wynns' cellar door dates from 1896 and was built by Penola pioneer John Riddoch. Top-quality shiraz, fragrant riesling and golden chardonnay are the mainstays.

animals, including a marsupial lion, a giant echidna, *Diprotodon australis* (koala meets grizzly bear), and *Megalania prisca* – 500kg of bad-ass goanna.

The 26 limestone caves here, including **Alexandra Cave, Cathedral Cave** and **Victoria Fossil Cave**, have bizarre formations of stalactites and stalagmites. Prospective Bruce Waynes should check out the **Bat Cave**, from which thousands of endangered southern bentwing bats exit en masse at dusk during summer. You can see the **Wet Cave** by self-guided tour (adult/child/family $9/5.50/25), but the others require ranger-guided tours. Single-cave tours start at adult/child/family $20/12/55. There's also budget accommodation here at **Wirreanda Bunkhouse** (☎08-8762 2340; www.environment.sa.gov.au/naracoorte; dm/powered sites from $22/25), which is often full of school kids but can be booked by travellers.

For more local info and tips on places to stay, contact **Naracoorte Visitor Information Centre** (☎08-8762 1399; www.naracoortelucindale.com; 36 MacDonnell St; ⏲9am-5pm Mon-Fri, 10am-4pm Sat & Sun) in Naracoorte.

MURRAY RIVER

On the lowest gradient of any Australian river, the slow-flowing Murray hooks through 650 South Australian kilometres. Tamed by weirs and locks, the Murray irrigates the fruit trees and vines of the sandy Riverland district to the north, and winds through the dairy country of the Murraylands district to the south. Raucous flocks of white corellas and pink galahs launch from cliffs and river red gums and dart across lush vineyards and orchards.

Prior to European colonisation, the Murray was home to Meru communities. Then came shallow-draught paddle steamers, carrying wool, wheat and supplies from Murray Bridge as far as central Queensland along the Darling River. With the advent of railways, river transport declined. These days, waterskiers, jet skis and houseboats crowd out the river, especially during summer. If your concept of riverine serenity doesn't include the roar of V8 inboards, then avoid the major towns and caravan parks during holidays and weekends.

Online, see www.themurrayriver.com.

Sights & Activities

Houseboating is big business on the Murray. Meandering along the river is great fun – you just need to be over 18 with a current driving licence. Boats depart from most riverside towns; book ahead, especially between October and April.

The **Houseboat Hirers Association** (☎08-8231 8466, 1300 665 122; www.houseboatbookings.com) website has pictures of each boat and can make bookings on your behalf. For a three-night weekend, expect to pay anywhere from $670 for two people to $2700 for a luxury 10-bed boat. Most boats sleep at least two couples and there's generally a bond involved (starting at $200). Many provide linen – just bring food and fine wine. See also SA Tourism's *Houseboat Holidays* booklet for detailed houseboat listings.

Getting There & Away

LinkSA (www.linksa.com.au) runs several daily bus services between Adelaide and Murray Bridge ($20, 1¼ hours), plus Adelaide to Mannum ($27, 2½ hours) from Monday to Friday (which involves a bus change at Mt Barker in the Adelaide Hills). **Premier Stateliner** (www.premierstateliner.com.au) runs daily Riverland buses from Adelaide, stopping in Waikerie ($42, 2½ hours), Barmera ($52, 3¼ hours), Berri ($52, 3½ hours) and Renmark ($52, four hours). Buses stop at Loxton ($52, 3¾ hours) daily, except Saturday.

ROLLIN' ON THE RIVER

Until 2011, Old Man Murray was in dire straits, degraded by drought, salinisation, evaporation, upstream irrigation and the demands of servicing SA's domestic water requirements. Ecosystems were awry and many farmers faced bankruptcy. Debate raged over solutions: federal control of the Murray-Darling Basin? Stiffer quotas for upstream irrigators? A weir at Wellington? Opening the Goolwa barrages and letting salt water flood the lower lakes? Things were grim.

In 2011 the drought broke: flooding upstream in Queensland, New South Wales and Victoria and rains delivered by Tropical Cyclone Yasi got things flowing, purging the backlog of silt and salt, and filling wetlands with life. But what about the future? See www.savethemurray.com for the latest ideas on how to keep Old Man Murray a-flowin'.

Murray Bridge

POP 18,370

SA's largest river town is a rambling regional hub (the fifth-biggest town in SA) with lots of old pubs but an underutilised riverfront, a huge prison and not a great deal of charm.

Sights

Murray Bridge Regional Gallery GALLERY
(www.murraybridgegallery.com.au; 27 6th St; ⊙10am-4pm Tue-Sat, 11am-4pm Sun) FREE This is the town's cultural epicentre and houses touring and local exhibitions: painting, ceramics, glasswear, jewellery and prints.

Monarto Zoo ZOO
(www.monartozoo.com.au; Princes Hwy, Monarto; adult/child/family $31.50/18/85; ⊙9.30am-5pm, last entry 3pm) About 14km west of town, the excellent open-range zoo is home to Australian and African beasts including cheetahs, rhinos and giraffes (and the cute offspring thereof). A hop-on/hop-off bus tour is included in the price; keeper talks happen throughout the day.

Captain Proud Paddle Boat Cruises CRUISE
(☎0466 304 092; www.captainproud.com.au; Wharf Rd; 1/2/3hr cruises $25/45/49) River cruises from one-hour sightseeing to longer jaunts with lunch, high tea or drinks and cheese platters. Call for times and bookings.

Sleeping

Adelaide Road Motor Lodge MOTEL $
(☎08-8532 1144; www.adelaiderdmotorlodge.com; 212 Adelaide Rd; d from $80, tr & q $130-215;) If you're stuck for a bed here, your best bet is probably this funky '60s number with a 21st-century facelift – one of several motels on the road in from the Murray Bridge–Adelaide freeway.

Information

Murray Bridge Visitor Information Centre
(☎1800 442 784, 08-8339 1142; www.murraybridge.sa.gov.au; 3 South Tce; ⊙9am-5pm) Stocks the *Murray Bridge Accommodation Guide* and *Eating Out in Murray Bridge* brochures, and has info on river-cruise operators.

Mannum to Waikerie

Clinging to a narrow strip of riverbank 84km east of Adelaide, improbably cute Mannum (population 6750) is the unofficial houseboat capital of the world! The *Mary Ann,* Australia's first riverboat, was knocked together here in 1853 and made the first paddle-steamer trip up the Murray. The Mannum visitor information centre incorporates the **Mannum Dock Museum of River History** (www.psmarion.com; 6 Randell St, Mannum; adult/child $7.50/3.50), featuring info on local Ngarrindjeri Aboriginal communities, an 1876 dry dock and the restored 1897 paddle steamer *PS Marion,* on which you can occasionally chug around the river.

Breeze Holiday Hire (☎0438 802 668; www.murrayriver.com.au/breeze-holiday-hire-1052) hires out canoes and kayaks (per day $75), dinghies with outboards (per day $95) and fishing gear (per day $15), and can get you waterskiing too.

From Mannum to Swan Reach, the eastern riverside road often tracks a fair way east of the river, but various lookouts en route help you scan the scene. Around 9km south of Swan Reach, the Murray takes a tight meander called **Big Bend**, a sweeping river curve with pock-marked, ochre-coloured cliffs.

Sedentary old Swan Reach (population 850), 70km southwest of Waikerie, is a bit of a misnomer: an old pub and plenty of pelicans but not many swans.

A citrus-growing centre oddly festooned with TV antennas, Waikerie (population 4630) takes its name from the Aboriginal phrase for 'anything that flies'. There's plenty of bird life around here, with 180 species recorded at **Gluepot Reserve** (☎08-8892 9600; www.riverland.net.au/gluepot; Gluepot Rd; cars per day/overnight $5/10; ⊙8am-6pm), a mallee scrub area 64km north of Waikerie (off Lunn Rd) and part of Unesco's Bookmark Biosphere Reserve. Before you head off, check with Waikerie's Shell service station on Peake Tce to see if you'll need a gate key.

Tours

Jester Cruises CRUISE
(☎0419 909 116, 08-8569 2330; www.jestercruises.com.au; 1¾/2½hr tours $30/60) Cruise up and down the river from Mannum on the 40-seat Jester, running most days.

Proud Mary CRUISE
(☎08-8406 444; www.proudmary.com.au; 1½hr tour adult/child $55/40) Lunch cruises on a big boat on the big river, departing from Mannum. Brush up on your Creedence Clearwater Revival lyrics.

Sleeping & Eating

Mannum Motel MOTEL $$
(08-8569 1808; www.mannummotel.com.au; 76 Cliff St, Mannum; d/f from $130/150;) This unobtrusive brown-brick '80s number squats on a rise above the ferry crossing at Mannum. Some of the larger units have kitchenettes if you don't fancy the in-house bistro or a trip to the pub for dinner.

Mannum Caravan Park CARAVAN PARK $
(08-8569 1402; www.mannumcaravanpark.com.au; Purnong Rd, Mannum; unpowered/powered sites $25/29, cabins/villas from $64/120;) A clean-cut caravan park right on the river next to the Mannum ferry crossing. Ducks and water hens patrol the lawns, and there's a pool table in the games room if it's raining. Lots of shade-giving gums.

Waikerie Hotel Motel HOTEL-MOTEL $
(08-8541 2999; www.waikeriehotel.com; 2 McCoy St, Waikerie; d $79-139;) Waikerie's main-street pub has clean, affordable hotel rooms (all with bathroom, rather unusually) and updated motel rooms out the back. The oldest part of the pub burnt down in 2012, two days shy of its 100th birthday! The bistro does pub-grub classics (mains $16 to $35, serving noon to 2pm and 6pm to 8pm).

Murray River Queen RIVERBOAT $
(08-8541 2651; www.murrayriverqueen.com.au; Leonard Norman Dr, Waikerie; dm $30, d without/with bathroom from $55/90) When it's not cruising the Murray, this 1974 paddleboat berths at Waikerie and offers basic bunkrooms (a tad shabby and dim but undeniably novel) and more upmarket doubles. The onboard cafe is good for a light lunch (items $6 to $15, open 8.30am to 4pm Wednesday to Sunday). It's managed by the local caravan park.

Pretoria Hotel PUB $$
(08-8569 1109; www.pretoriahotel.com.au; 50 Randell St, Mannum; mains $16-28; noon-2pm & 6-8pm) The family-friendly Pretoria (built 1900) has a vast bistro and deck fronting the river, and plates up big steaks, roo fillets and parmas plus Asian salads and good seafood. When the 1956 flood swamped the town they kept pouring beer from the 1st-floor balcony!

DON'T PAY THE FERRYMAN

As the Murray curls abstractly across eastern SA, roads (on far more linear trajectories) invariably bump into it. Dating back to the late 19th century, a culture of free, 24-hour, winch-driven ferries has evolved to shunt vehicles across the water. Your car is guided onto the punts by burly, bearded, fluoro-clad ferrymen, who lock safety gates into position then shunt you across to the other side. There are 11 ferries in operation, the most useful of which are those at Mannum, Swan Reach and Waikerie. Turn off your headlights if you're waiting for the ferry at night so you don't bedazzle the approaching skipper.

Information

Mannum Visitor Information Centre (08-8569 1303, 1300 626 686; www.psmarion.com; 6 Randell St, Mannum; 9am-5pm Mon-Fri, 10am-4pm Sat & Sun) Cruise and houseboat bookings, *Mannum Historic Walks* brochures and the **Museum of River History**.

Barmera & Around

On the shallow shores of Lake Bonney (upon which world land-speed record-holder Donald Campbell unsuccessfully attempted to break his water-speed record in 1964), snoozy Barmera (population 4290) was once a key town on the overland stock route from NSW. These days the local passion for both kinds of music (country *and* western) lends a simple optimism to proceedings. Kingston-On-Murray (population 260; aka Kingston OM) is a tiny town en route to Waikerie.

Sights & Activities

The once ephemeral **Lake Bonney** has been transformed into a permanent lake ringed by large, drowned red gums, whose stark branches are often festooned with birds. If you're feeling uninhibited, there's a nudist beach at **Pelican Point Holiday Park** (www.riverland.net.au/pelicanpoint) on the lake's western shore.

There are wildlife reserves with walking trails and camping (per car $7) at Moorook on the road to Loxton, and Loch Luna across the river from Kingston-On-Murray. Loch Luna backs onto the Overland Corner Hotel. Both reserves have nature trails and are prime spots for birdwatching and canoeing. Self-register camping permits are available at reserve entrances.

There are also walking trails at the Overland Corner Hotel.

★ Banrock Station Wine & Wetland Centre WINERY
(www.banrockstation.com.au; Holmes Rd, Kingston OM; ⏲9am-4pm Mon-Fri, 9am-5pm Sat & Sun) Overlooking regenerated, feral-proofed wetlands off the Sturt Hwy at Kingston OM, carbon-neutral Banrock Station Wine & Wetland Centre is a stylish, rammed-earth wine-tasting centre (love the tempranillo) and jazzy lunchtime restaurant (mains $17 to $25 – try the cumquat-glazed pork), using ingredients sourced locally. There are three wetland walks here: 2.5km and 4.5km ($3), and 8km ($5).

Rocky's Hall of Fame Pioneers Museum MUSEUM
(www.murrayriver.com.au/barmera/rockys-hall-of-fame-pioneers-museum; 4 Pascoe Tce, Barmera; adult/child $2/1; ⏲10am-noon & 1-3pm Wed-Mon) Country music is a big deal in Barmera, with the **South Australian Country Music Festival & Awards** (www.riverlandcountrymusic.com) happening here in June, and Rocky's Museum blaring sincere rural twangings down the main street from outdoor speakers. Don't miss the 35m Botanical Garden Guitar out the back, inlaid with the handprints of 160 country musos: from Slim Dusty to Kasey Chambers and everyone in between.

Sleeping & Eating

Discovery Holiday Parks Lake Bonney CARAVAN PARK $
(☎08-8588 2234; www.discoveryholidayparks.com.au; Lakeside Ave, Barmera; unpowered/powered sites from $22/29, cabins from $94; ❄📶🏊) This keenly managed lakeside park has small beaches (safe swimming), electric barbecues, camp kitchen, laundry and plenty of room for kids to run amok. Plenty of trees; waterfront camp sites.

Barmera Lake Resort Motel MOTEL $
(☎08-8588 2555; www.barmeralakeresortmotel.com.au; Lakeside Dr, Barmera; d $90-145, f from $185; ❄🏊) Right across the road from the lake, this good-value motel has a barbecue, pool, laundry and tennis court. Rooms are nothing flash, but immaculate; most have lake views.

Overland Corner Hotel PUB $$
(☎08-8588 7021; www.murrayriver.com.au/overland-corner; Old Coach Rd; mains $16-28; ⏲noon-2pm Tue-Sun, 6-8pm Thu-Sat) Off the Morgan Rd, 19km northwest of Barmera, this moody 1859 boozer is named after a Murray River bend where drovers used to camp. The pub walls ooze character and the meals are drover sized, plus there's a museum, a resident ghost and a beaut beer garden. An 8km self-guided **Overland Corner Walking Trail** leads to the river; pick up a brochure at the pub or Barmera visitor information centre.

Information

Barmera Visitor Information Centre (☎08-8588 2289, 1300 768 468; www.barmeratourism.com.au; Barwell Ave, Barmera; ⏲9am-5pm Mon-Fri, 10am-2pm Sat & Sun) Help with transport and accommodation bookings. Pick up the *Historic Overland Corner* walking trail brochure.

Loxton

POP 4100

Sitting above a broad loop of the slow-roaming Murray, Loxton proclaims itself the 'Garden City of the Riverland'. The vibe here is low-key, agricultural and untouristy, with more tyre distributors, hardware shops and irrigation supply outlets than anything else.

Sights & Activities

From Loxton you can canoe across to Katarapko Creek and the Katarapko Game Reserve in the **Murray River National Park** (www.environment.sa.gov.au); hire canoes from Loxton Riverfront Caravan Park.

Tree of Knowledge LANDMARK
Down by the river near the caravan park, the Tree of Knowledge is marked with flood levels from previous years. The bumper flows of 1931, '73, '74 and '75 and 2011 were totally outclassed by the flood-to-end-all-floods of 1956, marked about 4m up the trunk.

Loxton Historical Village MUSEUM
(www.loxtonhistoricalvillage.com.au; Allen Hosking Dr; adult/child/family $12/6/30; ⏲10am-4pm Mon-Fri, to 5pm Sat & Sun) The mildly kitsch (but nonetheless interesting) Loxton Historical Village is a re-created time warp of 45 dusty, rusty old buildings with costumed staff.

Sleeping & Eating

Harvest Trail Lodge HOSTEL $
(08-8584 5646; www.harvesttrail.com; 1 Kokoda Tce; dm per night/week $45/125;) Inside a converted '60s waterworks office are four-bed dorms with TVs and fridges, and a barbecue balcony to boot. Staff will find you fruit-picking work, and shunt you to and from jobs.

Loxton Hotel HOTEL-MOTEL $$
(08-8584 7266, 1800 656 686; www.loxtonhotel.com.au; 45 East Tce; hotel s/d from $80/105, motel from $120/135;) With all profits siphoned back into the Loxton community, this large complex offers immaculate rooms with tasty weekend packages. The original pub dates from 1908, but it has been relentlessly extended. Bistro meals are available for breakfast, lunch and dinner (mains $17 to $28).

Loxton Riverfront Caravan Park CARAVAN PARK $
(08-8584 7862, 1800 887 733; www.lrcp.com.au; Sophie Edington Dr; unpowered/powered sites from $22/32, cabins without/with bathroom from $62/75;) Situated on the gum-studded Habels Bend, about 2km from town, this affable riverside caravan park bills itself as 'The Quiet One'. You can hire a canoe (per hour/day $11/55), and there's a free nine-hole golf course (usually sandy, occasionally flooded).

Information

Loxton Visitor Information Centre (08-8584 8071, 1300 869 990; www.loxtontourism.com.au; Bookpurnong Tce, Loxton Roundabout; 9am-5pm Mon-Fri, 9am-4pm Sat, 10am-4pm Sun) A friendly place for accommodation, transport and national-park info, plus a small art gallery. Look for the *Historic Walks of Loxton* brochure.

Berri

POP 7440

The name Berri derives from the Aboriginal term *berri berri*, meaning 'big bend in the river', and it was once a busy refuelling stop for wood-burning paddle steamers. These days Berri plays its role as an affluent regional hub for both state government and agricultural casual-labour agencies, and is one of the better places to chase down casual harvest jobs.

Sights & Activities

Road access to the scenic Katarapko Creek section of the **Murray River National Park** (www.environment.sa.gov.au) is off the Stuart Hwy between Berri and Barmera. This is a beaut spot for bush camping (per car $7), canoeing and birdwatching.

Riverland Farmers Market MARKET
(www.riverlandfarmersmarket.org.au; Crawford Tce, Senior Citizens Hall; 7.30-11.30am Sat) All the good stuff that grows around here in one place. A bacon-and-egg roll and some freshly squeezed orange juice will right your rudder.

A Special Place for Jimmy James GARDENS
(Riverview Dr; 24hr) A short amble from the visitor centre, A Special Place for Jimmy James is a living riverbank memorial to the Aboriginal tracker who could 'read the bush like a newspaper'. Whimsical tracks and traces are scattered around granite boulders.

River Lands Gallery GALLERY
(www.countryarts.org.au; 23 Wilson St; 10am-4pm Mon-Fri) As the murals and totem poles around the base of Berri Bridge attest, Berri is an artsy kinda town. This gallery displays local, indigenous and travelling painting, sculpture, weaving and digital media exhibitions.

BMS Tours CRUISE
(0408 282 300; www.houseboatadventure.com.au/BMStours.php; tours from $60;) Murray tours from Berri on an Everglades-style airboat called *Elka*.

Sleeping & Eating

Berri Backpackers HOSTEL $
(08-8582 3144; www.berribackpackers.com.au; 1081 Old Sturt Hwy; dm per night/week $25/160;) On the Barmera side of town, this eclectic hostel is destination *numero uno* for work-seeking travellers, who chill out after a hard day's manual toil in quirky new-age surrounds. Rooms range from messy dorms to doubles, share houses, a tepee and a yurt – all for the same price. The managers can hook you up with harvest work (call in advance).

Berri Resort Hotel HOTEL-MOTEL $$
(08-8582 1411, 1800 088 226; www.berriresorthotel.com; Riverview Dr; hotel s & tw $75, motel d $155-175;) This mustard-and-maroon monolith across the road from the

river has hotel rooms (shared bathrooms) and a wing of spacious en-suite motel rooms. The cavernous bistro serves upmarket pub grub (mains $10 to $33, open for breakfast, lunch and dinner). A slick operation, albeit a bit Vegas.

Sprouts Café CAFE $
(08-8582 1228; www.sproutscafe.com.au; 28 Wilson St; mains $6-14; 8.30am-4pm Mon-Fri, 9.30am-1pm Sat) A cheery new cafe on the hill a few blocks back from the river, with a natty lime-green colour scheme. Serves soups, quiches, burgers, curries, wraps and good coffee. There are homemade cakes and scones, too.

Information

Berri Visitor Information Centre (1300 768 582, 08-8582 5511; www.berribarmera.sa.gov.au; Riverview Dr; 9am-5pm Mon-Fri, 9am-2pm Sat, 10am-2pm Sun) Right by the river, with brochures, internet, maps, waterproof canoeing guides ($10) and cluey staff.

Renmark

POP 9870

Renmark is the first major river town across from the Victorian border, about 254km from Adelaide. It's not a pumping tourist destination by any means, but has a relaxed vibe and grassy waterfront, where you can pick up a houseboat. This is the hub of the Riverland wine region: lurid signs on the roads into town scream 'Buy 6 Get 1 Free!' and 'Bulk port $4/litre!'.

Sights & Activities

Riverland Leisure Canoe Tours CANOEING
(08-8595 5399; www.riverlandcanoes.com.au; half-/full-day tours $75/120) Slow-paced guided canoe tours on the Murray, departing Paringa across the river from Renmark. Canoe/kayak hire (per day $65/55) and evening and moonlight tours also available.

Chowilla Game Reserve NATURE RESERVE
(www.environment.sa.gov.au) Upstream from town, Chowilla Game Reserve is great for bush camping (per car $7), canoeing and bushwalking. Access is along the north bank from Renmark or along the south bank from Paringa. For more info, contact the **Department of Environment, Water & Natural Resources** (DEWNR; 08-8595 2111; 28 Vaughan Tce, Berri) in Berri.

Sleeping & Eating

Renmark Hotel HOTEL-MOTEL $$
(08-8586 6755, 1800 736 627; www.renmarkhotel.com.au; Murray Ave; hotel/motel d from $90/110;) What a beauty! The sexy art-deco curves of Renmark's humongous pub are looking good these days, thanks to a $3.5-million overhaul. Choose from older-style hotel rooms and upmarket motel rooms. On a sultry evening it's hard to beat a cold beer and some grilled barramundi on the balcony at Nanya Bistro (mains $18 to $28, serving from noon to 2.30pm and 5.30pm to 9pm).

Renmark Riverfront Caravan Park CARAVAN PARK $
(08-8586 6315, 1300 664 612; www.big4renmark.com.au; Sturt Hwy; unpowered/powered sites from $30/35, cabins $72-285;) Highlights of this spiffy riverfront park, 1km east of town, include a camp kitchen, canoe (single/double per hour $10/15), paddleboats (per hour $20) and absolute waterfront cabins and powered sites. The newish corrugated-iron cabins are top notch, and look a little 'Riviera' surrounded by scraggly palms. The waterskiing fraternity swarms here during holidays.

Information

Renmark Paringa Visitor Information Centre (08-8586 6704, 1300 661 704; www.visitrenmark.com; 84 Murray Ave; 9am-5pm Mon-Fri, 9am-4pm Sat, 10am-4pm Sun) All the

RIVERLAND FRUIT PICKING

The fruit- and grape-growing centres of Berri, Barmera, Waikerie, Loxton and Renmark are always seeking harvest workers. Work is seasonal but there's usually something that needs picking (stonefruit, oranges, grapes, apples...), except for mid-September to mid-October and mid-April to mid-May when things get a bit quiet. If you have a valid working visa and don't mind sweating it out in the fields, ask the local backpacker hostels about work. Also try **MADEC Jobs Australia Berri Harvest Labour Office** (1800 062 332; www.madec.edu.au; 3 Riverview Dr) and **National Harvest Information Service** (1800 062 332; www.jobsearch.gov.au/harvesttrail).

usual brochures and info, plus an interpretive centre and the recommissioned 1911 paddle steamer *PS Industry* (gold-coin donation). Rumoured to be relocating – call them if they're not where they're supposed to be.

BAROSSA VALLEY

With hot, dry summers and cool, moderate winters, the Barossa is one of the world's great wine regions – an absolute must for anyone with even the slightest interest in a good drop. It's a compact valley – just 25km long – yet it manages to produce 21% of Australia's wine, and makes a no-fuss day trip from Adelaide, 65km to the southwest.

The local towns have a distinctly German heritage, dating back to 1842. Fleeing religious persecution in Prussia and Silesia, settlers (bringing their vine cuttings with them) created a Lutheran heartland where German traditions persist today. The physical remnants of colonisation – gothic church steeples and stone cottages – are everywhere. Cultural legacies of the early days include a dubious passion for oom-pah bands, and an appetite for wurst, pretzels and sauerkraut.

Online, see www.barossa.com.

Tours

Wine-flavoured day tours departing from Adelaide or locally are bountiful. The Barossa visitor information centre makes bookings. Just a few of the many tours available:

Barossa Epicurean Tours FOOD & WINE
(☎08-8564 2191; www.barossatours.com.au; full-/half-day tours $100/70) Good-value, small-group tours visiting the wineries of your choice and Mengler Hill Lookout.

Barossa Classic Cycle Tours CYCLING
(☎0427 000 957; www.bccycletours.com.au; tours per person per day from $260) One- and two-day cycling tours of the valley, covering about 30km per day. Cheaper rates for bigger groups.

Barossa Wine Lovers Tours WINE
(☎08-8270 5500; www.wineloverstours.com.au; tours incl lunch from $70) Minibus or car tours to wineries, lookouts, shops and heritage buildings…a good blend.

Barossa Experience Tours SIGHTSEEING
(☎08-8563 3248; www.barossavalleytours.com; half-/full-day tours from $85/120) Local small-group operator whisking you around the major sites. The Food & Wine Experience ($240) includes lunch, cheese tastings and a glass of wine.

Balloon Adventures BALLOONING
(☎08-8389 3195; www.balloonadventures.com.au; flights adult/child $300/195) Fly the Barossa sky in a hot-air balloon. One-hour flights depart Tanunda and include a champagne breakfast.

Festivals & Events

Barossa under the Stars MUSIC
(www.barossaunderthestars.com.au) Wine-slurping picnickers watch easy-listening crooners such as Chris Isaak and Sting in January.

Barossa Vintage Festival FOOD & WINE
(www.barossavintagefestival.com.au) This week-long festival has music, maypole dancing, tug-of-war contests etc; around Easter in odd-numbered years.

Barossa Gourmet Weekend FOOD & WINE
(www.barossagourmetweekend.com.au) Fab food matched with winning wines at select wineries; happens in late winter or early spring.

A Day on the Green MUSIC
(www.adayonthegreen.com.au) A mature-age moshpit at Peter Lehmann Wines, with acts such as Simply Red and Diana Krall. Held in December.

Getting There & Around

BUS & TRAIN

Adelaide Metro (www.adelaidemetro.com.au) runs daily trains to Gawler ($4.90, one hour), from where **LinkSA** (www.linksa.com.au) buses run to Tanunda ($9.50, 45 minutes), Nuriootpa ($12, one hour) and Angaston ($14.50, 1¼ hours).

TAXI

Barossa Taxis (☎0411 150 850) Taxis for up to nine people; 24-hour service.

Tanunda

POP 4690

At the centre of the valley both geographically and socially, Tanunda is the Barossa's main tourist town. Tanunda manages to morph the practicality of Nuriootpa with the charm of Angaston without a sniff of self-importance. The wineries are what you're here for – sip, sip, sip!

Barossa Valley

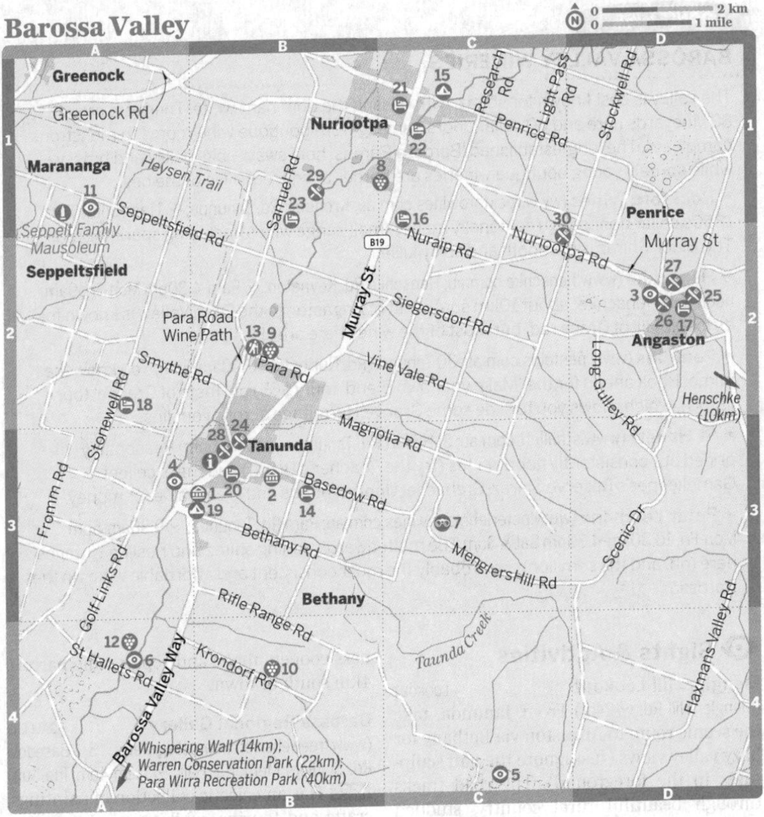

Barossa Valley

Sights

Barossa Farmers Market .... (see 30)
1 Barossa Museum B3
2 Barossa Regional Gallery B3
3 Barossa Valley Cheese Company D2
4 Goat Square A3
5 Kaiserstuhl Conservation Park C4
6 Keg Factory A4
7 Mengler Hill Lookout C3
8 Penfolds C1
9 Peter Lehmann Wines B2
10 Rockford Wines B4
11 Seppeltsfield Road A1
12 St Hallett A4

Activities, Courses & Tours

13 Para Road Wine Path B2

Sleeping

14 Barossa Backpackers B3
15 Barossa Valley Tourist Park C1
16 Doubles d'Vine C1
17 Marble Lodge D2
18 Stonewell Cottages A2
19 Tanunda Caravan & Tourist Park B3
20 Tanunda Hotel B3
21 Vine Court C1
22 Vine Inn C1
23 Whistler Farm B1

Eating

24 1918 Bistro & Grill B3
25 Angas Park D2
26 Angaston Hotel D2
27 Blond Coffee D2
Die Barossa Wurst Haus Bakery .... (see 28)
28 Ferment Asian B3
29 Maggie Beer's Farm Shop B1
30 Vintners Bar & Grill C2

DON'T MISS

BAROSSA VALLEY WINERIES

The valley is best known for shiraz, with riesling the dominant white. There are around 80 vineyards here and 60 cellar doors, ranging from boutique wine rooms to monstrous complexes. The long-established 'Barossa Barons' hold sway – big, ballsy and brassy – while spritely young boutique wineries are harder to sniff out. Five of the best:

➡ **Rockford Wines** (www.rockfordwines.com.au; Krondorf Rd, Tanunda; ⏲11am-5pm) This 1850s cellar door sells traditionally made, small-range wines, including sparkling reds. The Black Shiraz is a smooth and spicy killer.

➡ **Henschke** (www.henschke.com.au; Henschke Rd, Keyneton; ⏲9am-4.30pm Mon-Fri, 9am-noon Sat) Henschke, about 10km southeast of Angaston in the Eden Valley, is known for its iconic Hill of Grace red, but most of the wines here are classics.

➡ **Penfolds** (www.penfolds.com.au; 30 Tanunda Rd, Nuriootpa; ⏲10am-5pm) You know the name. Book ahead for the 'Make your own Blend' tour ($65) or 'Taste of Grange' tour ($150), which allows you to slide some Grange Hermitage across your lips.

➡ **St Hallett** (www.sthallett.com.au; St Hallett Rd, Tanunda; ⏲10am-5pm) Reasonably priced but consistently good whites (try the Poacher's Blend) and the excellent Gamekeeper's Reserve Shiraz-Grenache. Unpretentious and great value for money.

➡ **Peter Lehmann** (www.peterlehmannwines.com.au; Para Rd, Tanunda; ⏲9.30am-5pm Mon-Fri, 10.30am-4.30pm Sat & Sun) The multi-award-winning shiraz and riesling vintages here (oh, and the semillon) are probably the most consistent and affordable wines in the Barossa.

Sights & Activities

Mengler Hill Lookout LOOKOUT
(Mengler Hill Rd; ⏲24hr) From Tanunda, take the scenic route to Angaston via Bethany for hazy valley views (just ignore the naff sculptures in the foreground). The road tracks through beautiful rural country, studded with huge eucalypts.

Barossa Museum MUSEUM
(www.barossamuseum.com.au; 47 Murray St; adult/child $2/1; ⏲10am-5.30pm Tue-Fri, 9am-12.30pm Sat) Inside this 1856 post office building are displays of bone-handled cutlery, butter-making gear, photos of top-hatted locals, a re-created colonial bedroom and an amazing map of Germany pinpointing the homelands of Barossa settlers. The indigenous coverage could use a little help. Access via the bike-repair shop out the front.

Goat Square HISTORIC SITE
(John St) Tanunda is flush with historic buildings, including the cottages around this square, on John St. This was the *ziegenmarkt,* a meeting and market place, laid out in 1842 as Tanunda's original town centre.

Keg Factory FACTORY TOURS
(www.thekegfactory.com.au; Lot 10, St Hallett Rd; ⏲10am-4pm) FREE Watch honest-to-goodness coopers make and repair wine barrels, 4km south of town.

Barossa Regional Gallery GALLERY
(www.freewebs.com/barossagallery; 3 Basedow Rd, Soldiers Memorial Hall; ⏲11am-4pm Tue-Sun) FREE Has an eclectic collection of paintings, crafts and touring exhibitions, plus an impressive set of organ pipes at the back of the room.

Whispering Wall INDUSTRIAL
(off Yettie Rd; ⏲24hr) About 7km southwest of Lyndoch, itself 13km south of Tanunda, the Barossa Reservoir dam is better known as the Whispering Wall. The huge concrete curve has amazing acoustics: whispers at one end of the wall can be heard clearly 150m away at the other. The perfect spot to propose?

Sleeping

Tanunda Hotel PUB $
(☎08-8563 2030; www.tanundahotel.com.au; 51 Murray St; d without/with bathroom $70/80, apt from $200; ❄) This boisterous ol' 1846 pub in the town centre is a real community hub. Pub rooms upstairs are good value and clean; out the back are nine ritzy mauve-coloured apartments. Downstairs, Duran Duran wails on the jukebox and schnitzels

fall off the edges of plates (mains $17 to $28, serving noon to 2pm and 6pm to 8pm).

Barossa Backpackers HOSTEL $

(☎08-8563 0198; www.barossabackpackers.com.au; 9 Basedow Rd; unpowered sites/dm/d from $20/27/80; @ 📶) At last, a backpackers in the Barossa! Occupying a converted, U-shaped winery office building 500m from Tanunda's main street, it's a clean and ship-shape affair (if still a little office-like and spartan). Management can help you find picking/pruning work. Bike hire is $20 per day.

Stonewell Cottages B&B $$$

(☎0417 848 977; www.stonewellcottages.com.au; Stonewell Rd; cottages d incl breakfast from $355; ❄) These romantic, waterfront spa retreats are surrounded by vines and offer unbeatable privacy, comfort and serenity. Pet ducks waddle around rusty old ploughs as waterbirds splash down in the reservoir. Pricey, but worth it (cheaper for online bookings).

Tanunda Caravan & Tourist Park CARAVAN PARK $

(☎08-8563 2784; www.tanundacaravantouristpark.com.au; Barossa Valley Way; unpowered/powered sites from $33/36, cabins without/with bathroom from $77/108, villas from $285; ❄ @ 📶 🏊) This spacious park is dotted with mature trees offering a little shade for your hangover. Facilities include a playground, barbecues, laundry and bike hire for guests (per day $30). The flashy new villas sleep up to six and have a two-night minimum stay.

Eating

Ferment Asian SOUTHEAST ASIAN $$

(☎08-8563 0765; www.fermentasian.com.au; 90 Murray St; mains $22-26; ⏲noon-2.30pm Tue-Sun, 6pm-9.30pm Wed-Sat) Having recently featured in the *Weekend Australian* magazine's 'Top 50 Restaurants' listings, Ferment is hot property right now. What sounds exotic is actually refreshingly simple: *goi bo den* = grilled Barossa Angus beef with herb salad; *ca ri vit* = red duck curry with lychees and pineapple. Modern Vietnamese in a lovely old stone villa.

Die Barossa Wurst Haus Bakery BAKERY $

(86a Murray St; meals $4-18; ⏲7am-4pm) This fast-not-flashy bakery serves *mettwurst* (Bavarian sausage) rolls, cheeses, pies, cakes, strudel and all-day breakfasts. It's hard to go past a trad German roll with kransky sausage, sauerkraut, cheese and mustard. An emasculating display of phallic wursts dangles above the counter.

1918 Bistro & Grill MODERN AUSTRALIAN $$

(☎08-8563 0405; www.1918.com.au; 94 Murray St; mains $27-35; ⏲noon-2.30pm & 6.30-9pm) This enduring restaurant occupies a lovely old villa, set back from the street beneath a massive Norfolk Island pine. It's a sassy affair serving adventurous mains such as pork belly confit with braised cabbage and black-pudding crumble. Book a verandah table.

Information

Barossa Visitor Information Centre (☎08-8563 0600, 1300 852 982; www.barossa.com; 66-68 Murray St, Tanunda; ⏲9am-5pm Mon-Fri, 10am-4pm Sat & Sun; 📶) The lowdown on the valley, plus internet, bike hire and accommodation and tour bookings. Stocks the *A Town Walk of Tanunda* brochure.

Nuriootpa

POP 5030

Along an endless main street at the northern end of the valley, Nuriootpa is the Barossa's commercial centre. It's not as endearing as Tanunda or Angaston, but has a certain agrarian appeal. Lutheran spirit runs deep in Nuri: a sign says, 'God has invested in you – are you showing any interest?'

Sights & Activities

Seppeltsfield Road STREET

(www.seppeltsfieldroad.com) An incongruous avenue of huge palm trees meandering through the vineyards behind Nuri. Beyond Marananga the palm rows veer off the roadside and track up a hill to the Seppelt Family Mausoleum – a Grecian shrine fronted by chunky Doric columns.

Para Road Wine Path WALKING, CYCLING

(www.pararoadwinepath.com.au) Between Nuriootpa and Tanunda – a short-and-sweet walking/cycling trail passing four wineries.

Sleeping & Eating

Doubles d'Vine COTTAGE $

(☎08-8562 2260; www.doublesdvine.com.au; cnr Nuraip Rd & Barossa Valley Way; lodge/cottage d $80/90; ❄ 📶 🏊) Affordable accommodation 1.5km south of Nuri, this is a self-contained cottage and separate 'lodge' (a renovated apricot shed) with two en-suite doubles and shared lounge and kitchen. Both have wood heaters, barbecues and access to the pool.

Reduced rates for two nights or more; bike hire for guests is $25 per day.

Whistler Farm B&B $$
(☎ 0415 139 758; www.whistlerfarm.com.au; 616 Samuel Rd; d incl breakfast $195; ❄ 📶) Surrounded by vineyards and native shrubs, this farmhouse B&B has a private guest wing with exposed timber beams, separate guest entry and two country-style rooms. Snooze on the wide verandah and contemplate a day's successful (or imminent) wine touring.

Barossa Valley Tourist Park CARAVAN PARK $
(☎ 08-8562 1404; www.barossatouristpark.com.au; Penrice Rd; unpowered/powered sites from $29/34, cabins without/with bathroom from $59/72; ❄ @ 📶) There are at least six different kinds of cabin at this shady park, lined with pine trees next to the Nuriootpa football oval (go Tigers!). All cabins have TVs, fridges, cooking facilities and small balconies. Check out the 1930 Dodge 'House on Wheels' out the front – the seminal caravan?

Vine Inn MOTEL $$
(☎ 08-8562 2133; www.vineinn.com.au; 14 Murray St; s/d/1-/2-bedroom from $95/105/155/210; ❄ 📶 🏊) Regulation motel with swimming pool. The pub bistro (mains $15 to $30, serving 7am to 9am, noon to 2.30pm and 6pm to 8pm) serves pub grub amid bright lights, palms and pokies. Tandem business with **Vine Court** (49 Murray St; ❄ 📶) motel further up Murray St (same prices).

Maggie Beer's Farm Shop DELI $
(www.maggiebeer.com.au; 50 Pheasant Farm Rd; items $5-20; ⏲ 10.30am-5pm) Celebrity SA gourmand Maggie has been hugely successful with her range of condiments, preserves and pâtés (and TV appearances!). The vibe here isn't as relaxed as it used to be, but stop by for some gourmet tastings, an ice cream, cooking demo or a hamper of delicious bites. Off Samuel Rd.

Angaston

POP 1870

Photo-worthy Angaston was named after George Fife Angas, a pioneering Barossa pastoralist. An agricultural vibe persists, as there are relatively few wineries on the town doorstep: cows graze in paddocks down the ends of streets, and there's a vague whiff of fertiliser in the air. Along the main drag are two pubs, some terrific eateries and a few B&Bs in old stone cottages (check for double glazing and ghosts – we had a sleepless night!).

Sights

Barossa Valley Cheese Company CHEESE WRIGHT
(www.barossacheese.com.au; 67b Murray St; ⏲ 10am-5pm Mon-Fri, 10am-4pm Sat, 11am-3pm

OFF THE BEATEN TRACK

BAROSSA REGIONAL PARKS

For a little grape-free time away from the vines, you can't beat the Barossa's regional parks, with walking tracks for everyone from Sunday strollers to hardcore bushwalkers. The Barossa visitor information centre (p115) can help with maps and directions.

Kaiserstuhl Conservation Park (☎ 08-8280 7048; www.environment.sa.gov.au; Tanunda Creek Rd, Angaston; ⏲ daylight hours) Known for excellent walks, 390-hectare Kaiserstuhl is en route from Mengler Hill to Angaston. The Stringybark Loop Trail (2.4km) and Wallowa Loop Trail (6.5km) start at the entrance, and there are fantastic views from atop the Barossa Ranges. Look for Nankeen kestrels and western grey roos.

Para Wirra Recreation Park (☎ 08-8280 7048; www.environment.sa.gov.au; Humbug Scrub Rd, One Tree Hill; per person/car $4/10; ⏲ 8am-sunset) In the northern Mt Lofty Ranges, a 45km hook south of Tanunda – 1417 hectares of walking tracks, scenic drives, barbecues and tennis courts. Emus search hopefully around picnic areas; western grey roos graze in the dusk.

Warren Conservation Park (☎ 08-8280 7048; www.environment.sa.gov.au; Watts Gully Rd, Kersbrook; ⏲ daylight hours) FREE Near Para Wirra – 363 tranquil hectares of wattles, banksias and spring heaths, plus pink, blue and statuesque river red gums. Steep tracks for experienced hikers.

Sun) The Barossa Valley Cheese Company is a fabulously stinky room, selling handmade cheeses from local cows and goats. Tastings are free, but it's unlikely you'll leave without buying a wedge of the Washington Washed Rind.

Barossa Farmers Market MARKET
(www.barossafarmersmarket.com; cnr Stockwell & Nuriootpa Rds; 7.30-11.30am Sat) Happens near Vintners Bar & Grill every Saturday. Expect hearty Germanic offerings and lots of local produce.

Sleeping & Eating

Marble Lodge B&B $$
(08-8564 2478; www.marblelodge.com.au; 21 Dean St; d from $185;) A grandiose 1915 Federation-style villa on the hill behind the town, built from local pink and white granite. Accommodation in two plush suites behind the house (high-colonial or high-kitsch, depending on your world view). Breakfast is served in the main house.

Angaston Hotel PUB $$
(08-8564 2428; www.plushgroup.com/angaston.html; 59 Murray St; mains $13-24; noon-2pm & 6-8pm) The better looking of the town's two pubs, the friendly 1846 Angaston serves Barossa wines and the cheapest steaks this side of Argentina. Just try to ignore the *Triumph of Silenus* mural on the dining room wall ('Oh it's hideous!' says the barmaid). There's basic shared-bathroom pub accommodation upstairs (single/double $50/70).

Blond Coffee CAFE $
(www.blondcoffee.com.au; 60 Murray St; mains $8-22; 7.30am-5.30pm Mon-Fri, 8.30am-5.30pm Sat, 9am-5.30pm Sun) An elegant, breezy room with huge windows facing the main street, Blond serves nutty coffee and all-day cafe fare, including awesome pumpkin, capsicum and fetta muffins. There's also a wall full of local produce (vinegar, olive oil, biscuits and confectionery). Fake-blonde botoxed tourists share the window seats with down-to-earth regulars.

Vintners Bar & Grill MODERN AUSTRALIAN $$
(08-8564 2488; www.vintners.com.au; cnr Stockwell & Nuriootpa Rds; mains $18-39; noon-2.30pm daily, 6.30-9pm Mon-Sat) One of the Barossa's landmark restaurants, Vintners stresses simple elegance in both food and atmosphere. The dining room has an open fire, vineyard views and bolts of crisp white linen; menus concentrate on local produce (pray the duck-leg curry is on the menu when you visit).

Angas Park DELI $
(www.angaspark.com.au; 3 Murray St; 9am-5pm Mon-Sat, 10am-5pm Sun) At the top end of the main street, Angas Park is an iconic SA company (recognise the little yellow bags?), selling mostly Australian-grown dried fruits, chocolates and nuts: brilliant for a picnic pick-me-up.

CLARE VALLEY

Take a couple of days to check out the Clare Valley, two hours north of Adelaide. At the centre of the fertile Mid-North agricultural district, the skinny valley produces world-class rieslings and reds. This is gorgeous countryside, with open skies, rounded hills, stands of large gums and wind rippling over wheat fields. Towns here date from the 1840s, many built to service the Burra copper mines.

Tours

Clare Valley tours also depart from Adelaide; see p723.

Clare Valley Experiences SIGHTSEEING
(08-8842 1880; www.clarevalleyexperiences.com; tours from $75) 'Grape Express' half-day Clare tours and Riesling Trail rides; good rates for groups.

Clare Valley Tours SIGHTSEEING
(0418 832 812, 08-8843 8066; www.cvtours.com.au; 4/6hr tours $86/100) Minibus tours taking in the Clare wineries, Martindale Hall and Burra.

Swagabout Tours SIGHTSEEING
(0408 845 378; www.swagabouttours.com.au) Dependable, small-group full-day Clare Valley day trips (from $150).

Festivals & Events

A Day on the Green MUSIC
(www.adayonthegreen.com.au) The Barossa's favourite festival comes to the Clare Valley in February. Lionel Ritchie, Crowded House, Daryl Braithwaite...

Clare Valley Gourmet Weekend FOOD & WINE
(www.clarevalleywinemakers.com.au/gourmet.php) A frenzy of wine, food and music in May.

THE RIESLING TRAIL

Following the course of a disused railway line between Auburn and Clare, the fabulous Riesling Trail is 24km of wines, wheels and wonderment. It's primarily a cycling trail, but the gentle gradient means you can walk or push a pram along it just as easily. It's a two-hour dash end to end on a bike, but why hurry? There are three loop track detours and extensions to explore, and dozens of cellar doors to tempt you along the way.

For bike hire, check out Clare Valley Cycle Hire (p120) or Riesling Trail Bike Hire in Clare, or Cogwebs (p780) in Auburn.

Clare Show   AGRICULTURAL

(www.sacountryshows.com) The largest one-day show in SA, held in October.

ℹ Getting There & Around

BICYCLE

In Auburn and Clare you can hire a bike to pelt around the wineries. Rates are around $25/40 per half-/full day.

BUS

Yorke Peninsula Coaches (☑08-8821 2755; www.ypcoaches.com.au) Adelaide to Auburn ($28, 2¼ hours) and Clare ($36, 2¾ hours), running Tuesday to Thursday and Sunday. Extends to Burra ($36, 3¼ hours) on Thursday.

TAXI

Clare Valley Taxi Service (☑0419 847 900) Drop-off/pick-up anywhere along the Riesling Trail.

Auburn

POP 320

Sleepy, 1849 Auburn – the Clare Valley's southernmost village – is a leave-the-back-door-open-and-the-keys-in-the-ignition kinda town, with a time-warp vibe that makes you feel like you're in an old black-and-white photograph. The streets are defined by beautifully preserved, hand-built stone buildings; cottage gardens overflow with untidy blooms. Don't forget to pick up a copy of the *Walk with History at Auburn* brochure from the Clare Valley visitor information centre.

Now on the main route to the valley's wineries, Auburn initially serviced bullockies and South American muleteers whose wagons – up to 100 a day – trundled between Burra's copper mines and Port Wakefield.

The brilliant 25km **Riesling Trail** starts (or ends) at the restored Auburn Train Station. **Cogwebs** (☑0400 290 687, 08-8849 2380; www.cogwebs.com.au; 30 Main North Rd; bike hire per half-/full day $25/40, tandems $35/65; ◷8.30am-6pm Thu-Tue) has bike hire.

🛏 Sleeping & Eating

Auburn Shiraz Motel   MOTEL **$**

(☑08-8849 2125; www.auburnshirazmotel.com.au; Main North Rd; s/d/tr from $80/90/120; ❄🐕🗬) This small motel on the Adelaide side of town has been proudly renovated with shiraz-coloured render and cabernet-coloured doors. There are nine bright units and friendly hosts. Bike hire $40 per day.

Rising Sun Hotel   PUB **$$**

(☑08-8849 2015; www.therisingsunhotel.com.au; 19 Main North Rd; mains $16-35; ◷noon-2pm & 6-8pm; 🗬) This classic 1850 pub has a huge rep for its atmosphere, food and accommodation. The pub food is unpretentious (but unremarkable), with plenty of local wines to try. Accommodation takes the form of en-suite pub rooms and cottage mews rooms out the back (doubles from $90 and $125 respectively).

Cygnets at Auburn   CAFE **$**

(☑08-8849 2030; www.cygnetsatauburn.com.au; Main North Rd; mains $10-20; ◷9.30am-4pm Fri-Mon) This gourmet cafe serves and stocks local produce, and has the best coffee in town. The scones with homemade raspberry jam steal the show ('Oh, so light!' says one happy customer). There's also cottage B&B accommodation out the back in the 1860 stables (doubles from $125).

Mintaro

POP 230

Heritage-listed Mintaro (founded 1849) is a lovely stone village that could have been lifted out of the Cotswolds and plonked into the Australian bush. There are very few architectural intrusions from the 1900s – the whole place seems to have been largely left to its own devices. A fact for your next trivia night: Mintaro slate is used internationally in the manufacture of billiard tables. Pick up the *Historic Mintaro* pamphlet around the valley.

Sights

Martindale Hall HISTORIC BUILDING
(☎08-8843 9088; www.martindalehall.com; 1 Manoora Rd; adult/child $10/2.50; 11am-4pm Mon-Fri, noon-4pm Sat & Sun) Martindale Hall is an astonishing 1880 manor 3km from Mintaro. Built for young pastoralist Edmund Bowman Jnr, who subsequently partied away the family fortune (OK, so drought and plummeting wool prices played a part... but it was mostly the partying), the manor features original furnishings, a magnificent blackwood staircase, Mintaro-slate billiard table and an opulent, museum-like smoking room. The hall starred as Appleyard College in the 1975 Peter Weir film *Picnic at Hanging Rock*. B&B and DB&B accommodation packages allow you to spend a spooky night here ($120 and $250 respectively). *Mirandaaa...*

Mintaro Maze MAZE
(www.mintaromaze.com; Jacka Rd; adult/child $10/7; 10am-4pm Mon-Thu & school holidays) Hedge your bets at Mintaro Maze as you try to find your way into the middle and back out again. There's a cafe here too.

Sleeping & Eating

Reilly's MODERN AUSTRALIAN $$
(☎08-8843 9013; www.reillyswines.com.au; cnr Hill St & Leasingham Rd; mains $16-28; 10am-4pm) Reilly's started life as a cobbler's shop in 1856. An organic vegie garden out the back supplies the current restaurant, which is decorated with local art and serves creative, seasonal Mod Oz food (antipasto, rabbit terrine, spanikopita). The owners also rent out four gorgeous old stone cottages on Hill St (doubles from $145).

Magpie & Stump Hotel PUB $$
(☎08-8843 9014; www.mintaro.sa.au/eateries; Burra St; mains $12-26; noon-2pm Tue-Sun, 6-8pm Mon-Sat) The old Magpie & Stump was first licensed in 1851, and was a vital rehydration point for the copper carriers travelling between Burra and Port Wakefield. Schnitzels and steaks, log fires, pool table, Mintaro-slate floors and a sunny beer garden out the front – the perfect pub?

DON'T MISS

CLARE VALLEY WINERIES

The Clare Valley's cool micro-climates (around rivers, creeks and gullies) noticeably affect the wines, enabling local whites to be laid down for long periods and still be brilliant. The valley produces some of the world's best riesling, plus grand semillon and shiraz. Our favourite cellar doors:

Skillogalee (☎08-8843 4311; www.skillogalee.com.au; Trevarrick Rd, Sevenhill; 10am-5pm) Skillogalee is a small family outfit known for its spicy shiraz, fabulous food and top-notch riesling. Kick back with a long, lazy lunch on the verandah (mains $20 to $30; book ahead).

Pikes (www.pikeswines.com.au; Polish Hill River Rd, Sevenhill; 10am-4pm) The industrious Pike family set up shop in 1984, and have been producing show-stopping riesling ever since (and shiraz, sangiovese, pinot grigio, viognier...). It also bottles up the zingy 'Oakbank Pilsener' if you're parched.

Knappstein (www.knappstein.com.au; 2 Pioneer Ave, Clare; 9am-5pm Mon-Fri, 11am-5pm Sat, 11am-4pm Sun) Taking a minimal-intervention approach to wine making, Knappstein has built quite a name for itself. Shiraz and riesling steal the show, but it also makes a mighty fine semillon sauvignon blanc blend (and beer!).

Sevenhill Cellars (☎08-8843 4222; www.sevenhill.com.au; College Rd , Sevenhill; 9am-5pm Mon-Fri, 10am-5pm Sat & Sun) Want some religion with your drinking? This place was established by Jesuits in 1851, making it the oldest winery in the Clare Valley (check out the incredible 1866 St Aloysius Church). Oh, and the wine is fine too!

Taylors Wines (www.taylorswines.com.au; Taylors Rd, Auburn; 9am-5pm Mon-Fri, 10am-5pm Sat, 10am-4pm Sun) Sure, it's a massive nationwide operation with a heinous mock-castle cellar door, but the wine here is fit for royalty (love the cab sav).

Clare

POP 5460

Named after County Clare in Ireland, this town was founded in 1842 and is the biggest in the valley, but it's more practical than charming. All the requisite services are here (post, supermarket, fuel, internet etc), but you'll have a more interesting Clare Valley experience sleeping out of town.

Sights & Activities

Riesling Trail Bike Hire BICYCLE HIRE
(☎0418 777 318; www.rieslingtrailbikehire.com.au; 10 Warenda Rd; bike hire per half-/full day $25/40, tandems $40/60) Quality two-wheelers (including two-seaters) right on the Riesling Trail itself.

Clare Valley Cycle Hire BICYCLE HIRE
(☎0418 802 077, 08-8842 2782; www.clarevalleycyclehire.com.au; 32 Victoria Rd; bike hire per half/full day $17/25) Also has baby seats and pull along buggies for the little 'uns.

Spring Gully Conservation Park RESERVE
(www.environment.sa.gov.au; ⊙24hr) About 3km southwest of Sevenhill, the 400-hectare Spring Gully Conservation Park features blue-gum forest, red stringybarks and 18m-high winter waterfalls. There are plenty of bird twitters, critters and trails too.

Old Police Station Museum MUSEUM
(www.nationaltrustsa.org.au; cnr Victoria & Neagles Rock Rd; adult/child $2/0.50; ⊙10am-noon & 2-4pm Sat & Sun) The 1850 cop shop and courthouse is now the Old Police Station Museum, displaying Victorian clothing, old photos, furniture and domestic bits and pieces.

Sleeping

Bungaree Station B&B $
(☎08-8842 2677; www.bungareestation.com.au; Main North Rd; per person $44-99;) About 12km north of Clare, this beautiful 170-year-old homestead is still a working 3000-acre sheep farm. It was once SA's northernmost settlement, with 50 staff, a church and school. Accommodation is in simple, clean, renovated heritage buildings (one to four bedrooms, some with shared bathrooms). You can feed farm animals, take an audio tour (per person from $11) or have a dip in the pool.

Battunga B&B B&B $$
(☎08-8843 0120; www.battunga.com.au; Upper Skilly Rd, Watervale; d/q incl breakfast $195/315;) On an 80-hectare farm over the hills 2km west of Watervale (it's a little hard to find – ask for directions), Battunga has four modern apartments in two stone cottages with Mintaro-slate floors, barbecues, kitchenettes and wood fires. This is beautiful country – undulating farmland studded with huge eucalypts.

Riesling Trail & Clare Valley Cottages B&B $$
(☎0427 842 232; www.rtcvcottages.com.au; 9 Warenda Rd; 1-/2-/3-bed cottage d incl breakfast from $150/230/320;) A newish operation offering seven contemporary cottages, all encircled by country gardens and right on the Riesling Trail. Handily, the owners also run Riesling Trail Bike Hire.

Clare Caravan Park CARAVAN PARK $
(☎08-8842 2724; www.clarecaravanpark.com.au; Main North Rd; unpowered/powered sites from $20/29, cabins from $89;) This huge, efficiently run park 4km south of town towards Auburn has secluded sites, en-suite cabins, a creek and giant gum trees. There's also an inground pool for cooling off post-cycling, and it's a stone's throw from the Clare Valley visitor information centre.

Eating

Taminga Hotel PUB $$
(☎08-8842 2808; www.tamingahotel.com.au; 302 Main North Rd; mains $16-30; ⊙noon-2pm & 6-8pm) The most reliable of Clare's pubs when it comes to food, the tarted-up Taminga looks good. Pub classics are what you're here for: surf 'n' turf, steak-and-kidney pie and schnitzels.

Wild Saffron CAFE $
(☎08-8842 4255; www.wildsaffron.com.au; 288 Main North Rd; mains $7-18; ⊙8.30am-5.30pm Mon-Fri, 8.30am-12.30pm Sat & Sun) We're not sure how much wild saffron grows in the Clare Valley (most of it seems to be 'under vine', as they say), but this new cafe is hugely popular regardless. No surprises on the menu (focaccias, baguettes, BLTs, soup, homemade cakes), but it's simple stuff done well.

Artisans Table MODERN AUSTRALIAN $$
(☎08-8842 1796; www.artisanstable.com.au; Lot 3, Wendouree Rd; mains $28-32; ⊙noon-3pm Sat & Sun, 6-9pm Wed-Sat) This mod, airy, hillside bar-restaurant has a broad, sunny balcony – perfect for a bottle of local riesling and some internationally inspired culinary offerings: a

OFF THE BEATEN TRACK

BURRA

Bursting at the seams with historic sites, Burra (population 1110), 43km northeast of Clare, was a copper-mining boomtown between 1847 and 1877 with a burgeoning Cornish community. Towns like Mintaro and Auburn serviced miners travelling between Burra and Port Wakefield, from where the copper was shipped. The miners had it tough here, excavating dugouts for themselves and their families to live in.

Burra visitor information centre (☎08-8892 2154, 1300 775 540; www.visitburra.com; 2 Market St; ⏲9am-5pm Mon-Fri, 10am-4pm Sat & Sun) sells the self-guided **Burra Heritage Passport** (adult/child $25/free) giving access to eight historic sights and three museums. It also handles bike hire (half-/full day $20/35) and accommodation.

bit of Thai, a bit of Indian, a bit of Brazilian… Lots of seasonal and local produce, and surprisingly good seafood this far inland.

Information

Clare Valley Visitor Information Centre (☎08-8842 2131, 1800 242 131; www.clarevalley.com.au; cnr Spring Gully & Main North Rd; ⏲10am-5pm Mon-Fri, 10am-4pm Sat & Sun) Local info, internet access and valley-wide accommodation bookings.

YORKE PENINSULA

A couple of hours west of Adelaide, boot-shaped Yorke Peninsula (better known as 'Yorkes') bills itself as 'Agriculturally Rich – Naturally Beautiful'. It does have a certain agrarian beauty – deep azure summer skies and yellow wheat fields on hazy, gently rolling hills – but if you're looking for cosmopolitan riches and tourist trappings, you won't find much to engage you.

That said, far-flung Innes National Park on the peninsula's southern tip is well worth visiting. The coastline here is gorgeous, with great surf, roaming emus, kangaroos, ospreys and sea eagles, and southern right whales and dolphins cruising by.

For history buffs, the peninsula's north has a trio of towns called the Copper Triangle: Moonta (the mine), Wallaroo (the smelter) and Kadina (the service town). Settled by Cornish miners, this area drove the regional economy following a copper boom in the early 1860s.

Online, see www.yorkepeninsula.com.au.

Tours

Adjahdura Land INDIGENOUS
(☎0429 367 121; www.adjahdura.com.au; half-/1-/2-day tours $65/130/320) Highly regarded Aboriginal cultural tours of the peninsula, exploring the incredibly long indigenous association with this country. Three- and five-day tours are also available.

Sleeping

There are 15 council-run **camp sites** (☎0408 170 414, 08-8832 0000; www.yorke.sa.gov.au; per night free-$10) around the peninsula. For holiday-house rentals from as little as $90 per night, try **Accommodation on Yorkes** (☎08-8852 2000; www.accommodationonyorkes.com.au) or **Country Getaways** (☎08-8832 2623; www.countrygetaways.info).

Getting There & Around

BUS

Yorke Peninsula Coaches (☎08-8821 2755; www.ypcoaches.com.au) Daily buses run from Adelaide through to Kadina ($32, 2¼ hours), Wallaroo ($32, 2½ hours) and Moonta ($32, three hours), travelling as far south as Yorketown ($48, four hours, daily except Wednesday).

FERRY

SEASA (☎08-8823 0777; www.seasa.com.au; one-way per adult/child/car $35/10/140) Daily vehicle ferry between Wallaroo (Yorke Peninsula) and Lucky Bay (Eyre Peninsula) – a shortcut shaving 350km and several hours off the drive via Port Augusta. The voyage takes around 1¾ hours one way.

West Coast

Fronting Spencer Gulf, the west coast has a string of shallow swimming beaches, plus the Copper Triangle towns, all a short drive from each other. **Kernewek Lowender** (www.kernewek.org), aka the Copper Coast Cornish Festival, happens around here in May in odd-numbered years.

Kadina

POP 4030

Baking-hot, inland Kadina (ka-*dee*-na) has some impressive copper-era civic buildings and a slew of massive old pubs, car yards and petrol stations. The **Copper Coast Visitor Information Centre** (☎08-8821 2333, 1800 654 991; www.yorkepeninsula.com.au; 50 Moonta Rd; ⏰9am-5pm Mon-Fri, 10am-4pm Sat & Sun) is here – the peninsula's main visitor centre. Behind it is an amazing collection of old farming, mining and domestic bits and pieces at the **Farm Shed Museum** (www.nationaltrust.org.au/sa; 50 Moonta Rd; adult/child/family $8/3/20; ⏰9am-5pm Mon-Fri, 10am-3.30pm Sat & Sun), which gives an engaging insight into olden days and ways.

If you're just after a basic, clean place to rest your head, **Kadina Village Motel** (☎08-8821 1920; www.kadinavillagemotel.websyte.com.au; 28 Port Rd; s/d $80/90; ❄📶) is a retro, U-shaped joint on the road to Wallaroo.

Wallaroo

POP 3050

Still a major wheat port, Wallaroo is a town on the up: the Eyre Peninsula ferry is running and the town is full of folks. There's a huge new subdivision north of town, and the shiny new **Copper Cove Marina** (www.coppercove.com.au) is full of expensive boats. The marina also hosts the nautical **Copper Cove Marina Festival** in October.

A stoic 1865 post office houses the **Heritage & Nautical Museum** (www.nationaltrust.org.au/sa; cnr Jetty Rd & Emu St; adult/child $6/3; ⏰10am-4pm Mon-Fri, 2-4pm Sat & Sun), with tales of square-rigged English ships and George the pickled giant squid.

Sleeping & Eating

Sonbern Lodge Motel HOTEL-MOTEL $
(☎08-8823 2291; www.sonbernlodgemotel.com.au; 18 John Tce; s/d/f from $75/90/125; ❄) Once a grand temperance hotel, Sonbern is an old-fashioned charmer, right down to the old wooden balcony and antique wind-up phone. There are basic pub-style rooms upstairs (with bathrooms), and newish motel units out the back.

Wallaroo Marina Apartments HOTEL, APARTMENTS $$
(☎08-8823 4068; www.wallarooapartments.com.au; 11 Heritage Dve; d/apt from $100/174; ❄) The new multistorey Wallaroo Marina Apartments at the marina on the northern edge of town has spiffy suites, plus cold beer, pub meals, marina views and the occasional live band downstairs in the **Coopers Alehouse** (☎08-8823 2488; www.wallaroomarinahotel.com/dining; mains $15-38; ⏰noon-2.30pm & 6-8.30pm).

Moonta

POP 3350

In the late 19th century, the Moonta copper mine was the richest in Australia. These days the town, which calls itself 'Australia's Little Cornwall', maintains a faded glory, with a couple of decent pubs, and shallow Moonta Bay 1km west of the town centre, with good fishing from the jetty and a netted swimming area.

Moonta Visitor Information Centre (☎08-8825 1891; www.moontatourism.org.au; Blanche Tce, Old Railway Station; ⏰9am-5pm) has a smattering of history pamphlets, and details on the Moonta Heritage Site 1.5km east of town. The site includes the excellent **Moonta Mines Museum** (www.nationaltrust.org.au/sa; Verran Tce; adult/child $6/2; ⏰1-4pm Sat-Thu, 10am-4pm Fri), once a grand school with 1100 pupils; the 1946 **Moonta Mines Sweet Shop** (Verran Tce; ⏰10am-4pm) across the road; and a fully restored **Miner's Cottage** (Verco St; adult/child $3/1; ⏰1.30-4pm Wed, Sat & Sun, daily during school holidays).

Sleeping & Eating

Seagate Bistro Motel MOTEL $$
(☎08-8825 3270; www.seagatemoontabay.com.au; 171 Bay Rd; d from $170; ❄📶) The flashy Seagate is an octagonal (or is it a squashed dodecahedron?) motel right by Moonta Bay jetty. The pick of the rooms upstairs have sweeping oceanic views, as does the downstairs bistro (mains $18 to $37, open noon to 2pm and 6pm to 8pm), which serves better-than-average pub grub – perfect for a sunset beer.

Moonta Bay Caravan Park CARAVAN PARK $
(☎08-8825 2406; www.yorkepeninsula.net.au; Foreshore, Moonta Bay; unpowered/powered sites from $30/32, cabins without/with spa from $107/145; ❄📶) This caravan park is handy to the beach and jetty, and has decent luxury cabins with spas. The grassy camping areas are almost on the beach (but wi-fi reception can be a bit patchy down here).

Cornish Kitchen FAST FOOD $
(10-12 Ellen St; items $4-8; ⏲9am-4pm Mon-Fri, 9am-2pm Sat) After a hard day's copper mining, swing your shovel into the Cornish Kitchen for the ultimate Cornish pastie.

Point Turton

For a far-flung Yorkes experience, try Point Turton (population 250) in the southwest. The breezy **Tavern on Turton** (☎08-8854 5063; www.tavernonturton.com; 154 Bayview Rd; mains $18-36; ⏲9am-2pm & 6pm-8pm) is here, and the superfriendly **Point Turton Caravan Park** (☎08-8854 5222; www.pointturtoncp.com.au; Bayview Rd; unpowered/powered sites $22/29, cabins $55-150; ❄📶), with lovely grassy sites and cabins overlooking the sea. You can learn to surf near here with **Neptunes Surf Coaching** (☎0417 839 142; www.neptunes.net.au; 2hr lessons from $45).

East Coast

The east-coast road along Gulf St Vincent traces the coast within 1km or 2km of the water. En route, roads dart east to sandy beaches and holiday towns. Like the suburban Adelaide beaches across the gulf, this is prime crab-fishing territory.

Most of the coastal towns have a pub and a caravan park or camping ground, including unpretentious **Port Vincent** (population 480). The closest thing Yorkes has to a backpackers is the utilitarian **Tuckerway Hostel** (☎08-8853-7285; tuckerway14@bigpond.com; 14 Lime Kiln Rd, Port Vincent; dm from $21; ❄) – a concrete-block bunker uphill from the town containing simple dorms and a large kitchen.

Further south, **Edithburgh** (population 400) is roughly aligned with Adelaide's latitude, and has a **tidal swimming pool** in a small cove. From the cliff-tops, views extend offshore to sandy **Troubridge Island Conservation Park** (www.environment.sa.gov.au). You can stay the night at the **Troubridge Island Lighthouse** (☎08-8852 6290; www.lighthouse.net.au; per adult/child incl transfers $80/30, min charge $320). It sleeps 10; BYO food and linen. Little penguins still live here, but the island is steadily eroding – what the sea wants, the sea will have...

Back on the mainland, the surprisingly hip **Tipper's B&B** (☎08-8852 6181; www.tippersedithburgh.com.au; 35 Blanche St; d from $150; ❄) is on Edithburgh's main street, with two suites occupying an ochre-coloured former blacksmiths (1890s).

South Coast & Innes National Park

The peninsula's south coast is largely sheltered from the Southern Ocean's fury by Kangaroo Island, so there are some great **swimming** beaches along here. The surf finds its way through around Troubridge Point and Cape Spencer, where the **Cutloose Yorkes Classic** surf comp happens every October.

Cape Spencer is part of **Innes National Park** (☎08-8854 3200; www.environment.sa.gov.au; Stenhouse Bay Rd, Stenhouse Bay; per car $10; ⏲visitor centre 10.30am-3pm Wed-Sun), where sheer cliffs plunge into indigo waters and rocky offshore islands hide small coves and sandy beaches. **Marion Bay** (www.marionbay.com.au), just outside the park, and **Stenhouse Bay** and **Pondalowie Bay**, both within the park, are the main local settlements. Pondalowie Bay has a bobbing lobster-fishing fleet and a gnarly surf beach (keep one eye on the swell if you're swimming).

The rusty ribs of the 711-tonne steel barque *Ethel*, which foundered in 1904, arc forlornly from the sands just south of Pondalowie Bay. Follow the sign past the Cape Spencer turn-off to the ghost-town ruins of **Inneston**, a gypsum-mining community abandoned in 1930.

🛏 Sleeping & Eating

★**Marion Bay Motel & Tavern** MOTEL $$
(☎08-8854 4044; www.marionbaymotel.com.au; Jetty Rd, Marion Bay; s/d/tr $120/140/160; ❄📶) This place is the highlight of tiny Marion Bay, with a wing of five spiffy motel rooms out the back (white walls, new TVs, nice linen). The glass-fronted tavern next door (mains $16 to $32, serving noon to 2pm and 6pm to 8pm) looks out over the bay and puts a southeast Asian spin on pub standards (try the Vietnamese chicken salad).

Innes National Park CAMPGROUND, LODGE $
(☎08-8854 3200; www.environment.sa.gov.au; camping per person/car $5/16, lodges $100-170) Innes National Park has seven bushy camp sites. Our favourite spot is Pondalowie, or try Cable Bay for beach access, Surfers for surfing or Browns Beach for fishing. Alternatively, the heritage lodges at Inneston sleep four to 10 people and have showers

and cooking facilities. Book ahead through the park visitor centre; BYO drinking water in summer.

Rhino's Tavern & Innes Park Trading Post PUB $$
(08-8854 4078; www.rhinostavern.com.au; 1 Stenhouse Bay Rd, Stenhouse Bay; mains $18-30; noon-2pm & 6-8pm) This is a one-stop shop for fuel, bait, groceries and takeaway food, or kick back with a beer and a pub meal (laksa and ribs!).

EYRE PENINSULA & THE WEST COAST

The vast, straw-coloured triangle of Eyre Peninsula is Australia's big-sky country, and is considered by galloping gourmands to be the promised land of seafood. Meals out here rarely transpire without the option of trying the local oysters, tuna and whiting. Sublime national parks punctuate the coast, along with world-class surf breaks and lazy holiday towns, thinning out as you head west towards the Great Australian Bight, the Nullarbor Plain and Western Australia.

Eyre Peninsula's photogenic wild-western flank is an important breeding ground for southern right whales, Australian sea lions and great white sharks (the scariest scenes of *Jaws* were shot here). There are some memorable opportunities to encounter these submariners along the way.

Online, visit www.eyrepeninsula.info.

Tours

Wilderness Wanders WILDERNESS
(08-8684 5001; www.wildernesswanders.com.au) One- to eight-day Eyre Peninsula explorations ex-Port Lincoln, with lots of walking, wildlife and wilderness. The epic eight-day 'Walking on Eyre' tour ($2350) includes transport, accommodation, national park entry fees and most meals.

Southern Blue Tours SIGHTSEEING
(08-8683 1330; www.southernblue.travel) Full-day tours to Lincoln National Park ($395), the Coffin Bay region ($245) and half-day Port Lincoln tours ($135).

Getting There & Away

See p783 for info on the car ferry between Yorke Peninsula and Eyre Peninsula.

AIR

Regional Express (Rex; www.regionalexpress.com.au) Daily flights from Adelaide to Whyalla (one way from $140), Port Lincoln (from $99) and Ceduna (from $180).

BUS

Premier Stateliner (www.premierstateliner.com.au) Daily buses from Adelaide to Port Augusta ($54.50, 4¼ hours), Whyalla ($62, 5½ hours), Port Lincoln ($108.50, 9¾ hours), Streaky Bay ($113.50, 10 hours) and Ceduna ($126.50, 11¼ hours).

TRAIN

The famous *Ghan* train connects Adelaide with Darwin via Port Augusta, and the *Indian Pacific* (between Perth and Sydney) connects with the *Ghan* at Port Augusta; see p1091 for details.

Pichi Richi Railway (1800 440 101; www.prr.org.au; one-way adult/child/family $52/19/122) runs between Port Augusta and Quorn (two hours) on Saturdays.

Port Augusta

POP 13,900

At the head of Spencer Gulf, Port Augusta is having an identity crisis: is it the gateway to the outback, or the start of the southern Flinders Ranges? Is it the first town on the Eyre Peninsula, or the last big town until Kalgoorlie? The answer is all of the above. From the 'Crossroads of Australia', highways and railways roll west across the Nullarbor into WA, north to the Flinders Ranges or Darwin, south to Adelaide or Port Lincoln, and east to Sydney. Not a bad position!

The old town centre has considerable appeal, with some elegant old buildings and a revitalised waterfront: locals cast lines into the blue, and indigenous kids back-flip off jetties. The town has had problems with alcoholism (the streets are now a dry zone), but the vibe is rarely menacing.

Sights & Activities

Australian Arid Lands Botanic Garden GARDENS
(www.aalbg.sa.gov.au; Stuart Hwy; tours adult/child $8/5.50; 9am-5pm Mon-Fri, 10am-4pm Sat & Sun, tours 10am Mon-Fri) FREE Just north of town, the excellent (and free!) botanic garden has 250 hectares of sand hills, clay flats and desert flora and fauna. Explore on your own, or take a guided tour. There's a cafe here, too.

Eyre Peninsula & Yorke Peninsula

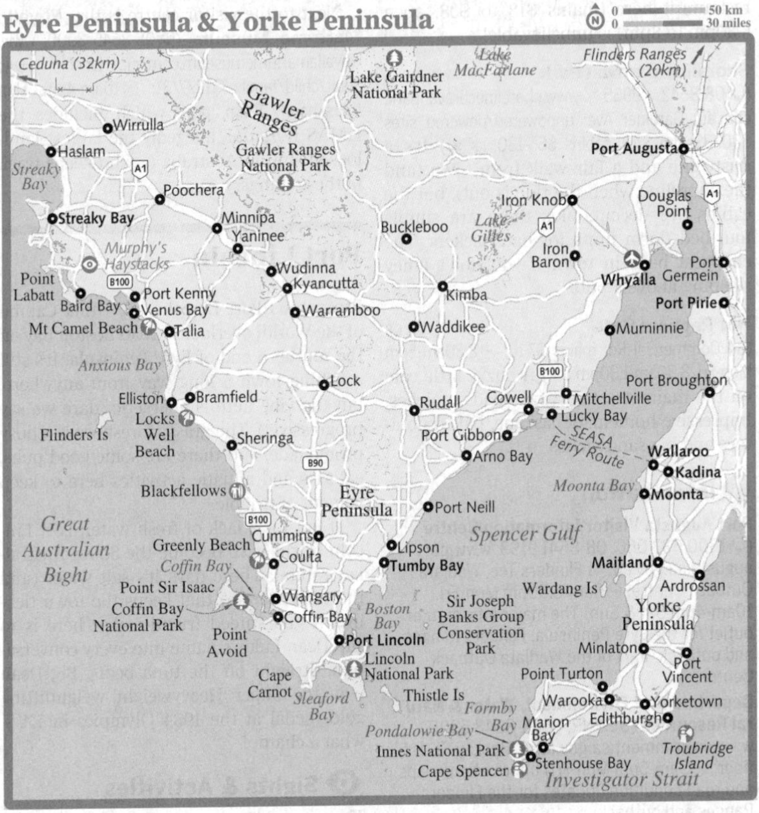

Wadlata Outback Centre MUSEUM
(www.wadlata.sa.gov.au; 41 Flinders Tce; adult/child/family $16.50/10/38.50; ⌚9am-5.30pm Mon-Fri, 10am-4pm Sat & Sun) The highlight at this combined museum/visitor centre is the 'Tunnel of Time', tracing local Aboriginal and European histories using audio-visual displays, interactive exhibits and a distressingly big snake.

Port Augusta Aquatic & Outdoor Adventure Centre OUTDOORS
(☎0427 722 450, 08-8642 2699; www.augustaoutdoors.com.au; 4 El Alamein Rd; ⌚9am-4pm Mon-Fri) Offers lessons and gear rental for kayaking, windsurfing, rock-climbing, abseiling, snorkelling, bushwalking, sailing… Bike hire is $55 per day.

Tours

Flinders & Outback Water Cruises CRUISES
(☎0438 857 001; www.augustawestside.com.au; 3 Loudon Rd; adult/child $50/30) Two-hour morning eco-cruises to the top of the Gulf (any dolphins?).

Sleeping & Eating

Oasis Apartments APARTMENTS $$
(☎08-8648 9000, 1800 008 648; www.majestichotels.com.au; Marryatt St, foreshore; apt $145-215; ❄🛜≋) Catering largely to conventioneers, this group of 75 luxury units (studios to two-bedroom) with jaunty designs is right by the water. All rooms have washing machines, dryers, TVs, fridges, microwaves, fortresslike security and flashy interior design.

Best Western Standpipe MOTEL $$
(☎08-8642 4033; www.standpipe.com.au; cnr Stuart Hwy & Hwy 1; d/2-bedroom apt from $128/233; ❄🛜≋) The sprawling Standpipe attracts government delegates and business types with its 85 reasonably hip units – the best motel in town, hands down. And the Indian

restaurant here (mains $18 to $38, open 5.30pm to 8pm) is unbelievable!

Shoreline Caravan Park   CARAVAN PARK **$**
(☑08-8642 2965; www.shorelinecaravanpark.com.au; Gardiner Ave; unpowered/powered sites $30/33, dm $40, cabins $65-130; ✳✳) It's a dusty site and a fair walk from town (and the shoreline when the tide is out), but the cabins are decent, plus there are simple four-bed dorm units for backpackers. The cheapest beds in town if you don't fancy sleeping above a pub.

Hot Peppers Cafe   CAFE **$**
(34 Commercial Rd; mains $7-16; ☺8.30am-5pm Mon-Fri, 8.30am-1.30pm Sat) A buzzy little cafe on the main street serving salads, quiches, impressive homemade lasagne, baked potatoes and big sandwiches.

ℹ Information

Port Augusta Visitor Information Centre
(☑1800 633 060, 08-8641 9193; www.port augusta.sa.gov.au; 41 Flinders Tce, Wadlata Outback Centre; ☺9am-5.30pm Mon-Fri, 10am-4pm Sat & Sun) The major information outlet for the Eyre Peninsula, Flinders Ranges and outback. Part of the Wadlata Outback Centre.

Department of Environment, Water & Natural Resources (DEWNR; ☑08-8648 5300; www.environment.sa.gov.au; 9 Mackay St, 1st floor; ☺9am-5pm Mon-Fri) Information, maps and road condition updates for the Flinders Ranges and outback.

Whyalla

POP 21,130

An hour's drive south of Port Augusta is Whyalla – the third-biggest city in SA – with a deep-water port sustaining steel mills, oil and gas refineries and a morass of chugging chimneys, portworks and industrial estates. Ugly, yes, but the old town has some good pubs, well-preserved domestic architecture and migrating Giant Australian Cuttlefish in the waters offshore (May to August).

Whyalla Visitor Information Centre (☑08-8645 7900, 1800 088 589; www.whyalla.com; Lincoln Hwy; ☺9am-5pm Mon-Fri, 9.30am-4pm Sat & Sun) can help with cuttlefish info and accommodation listings, or head straight for the utilitarian **Foreshore Motor Inn** (☑08-8645 8877; www.whyallaforeshore.com.au; Watson Tce; d/f from $145/170; ✳🛜✳) down by the wide white sandy expanse of Whyalla's foreshore.

Next to the visitor centre is the **Whyalla Maritime Museum** (☑08-8645 8900; www.whyallamaritimemuseum.com.au; Lincoln Hwy; adult/child/family $12/7/31; ☺10am-4pm, ship tours hourly 10am-2pm), which includes the HMAS *Whyalla*, allegedly the largest land-locked ship in Australia (…who keeps track of these things?).

Port Lincoln

POP 15,000

Prosperous Port Lincoln, the 'Tuna Capital of the World', overlooks broad Boston Bay on the southern end of Eyre Peninsula. It's still a fishing town a long way from anywhere, but the vibe here is energetic (dare we say progressive!). The grassy foreshore is a busy promenade, and there are some good pubs, eateries and aquatic activities here to keep you out of trouble.

If not for a lack of fresh water, Port Lincoln might have become the South Australian capital. These days it's salt water (and the tuna therein) that keeps the town ticking. A guaranteed friend-maker here is to slip Dean Lukin's name into every conversation. Straight off the tuna boats, Big Dean won the Super Heavyweight weightlifting gold medal at the 1984 Olympics in LA – what a champ!

⊙ Sights & Activities

The annual **Tunarama Festival** (www.tunarama.net) on the Australia Day weekend in January celebrates every finny facet of the tuna-fishing industry.

There's good beginner/intermediate **surf**ing at Fisheries Bay, Lone Pine and Wreck Beach. For info visit **Lincoln Surf** (☑08-8682 4428; 1 King St; ☺9am-5.30pm Mon-Fri, 9am-2pm Sat). They're rumoured to be relocating, so phone them if they're not on King St.

If you'd rather be on the water rather than in it, the local **fishing** is outstanding. Ask **Spot On Fishing Tackle** (www.spotonfishing.com.au; 39 Tasman Tce; ☺8.30am-5.30pm Mon-Fri, 8am-4pm Sat & Sun) about what's biting where.

Adventure Bay Charters   ADVENTURE TOUR
(☑08-8682 2979; www.adventurebaycharters.com.au) 🖉 Carbon-neutral Adventure Bay Charters takes you swimming with sea lions (adult/child $195/135) and Port Lincoln's famous tuna ($95/65), which you hand feed in

a fish-farm enclosure. Shark cage dives also available ($295).

Swim With The Tuna ADVENTURE TOUR
(☎1300 788 378; www.swimwiththetuna.com.au; adult/child $80/55) Three-hour boat tours out to a floating tuna enclosure, where you can check out the big fish from an underwater observatory or jump into the brine with them.

Calypso Star Charters ADVENTURE TOUR
(☎08-8682 3939, 1300 788 378; www.sharkcagediving.com.au; 1-day dive $420) Runs cage dives with great white sharks around Neptune Islands. Book in advance.

Kuju Aboriginal Arts GALLERY
(www.visitaboriginalart.com; 30 Ravendale Rd; ⏲10am-5pm Mon-Fri) FREE Stocks exquisite indigenous artworks, and you can meet the artists who work on-site. Aboriginal owned and managed.

Sleeping & Eating

★Tanonga B&B $$$
(☎0427 812 013; www.tanonga.com.au; Charlton Gully; d incl breakfast from $310, minimum 2-night stay; ❄) Two plush, solar-powered, architect-designed ecolodges in the hills behind Port Lincoln. They're both super-private and surrounded by native bush, birdlife and walking trails. Roll in town for dinner, or DIY packs of local produce are available.

Port Lincoln Hotel HOTEL $$
(☎08-8621 2000, 1300 766 100; www.portlincolnhotel.com.au; 1 Lincoln Hwy; d $139-250; ❄☎≋) Bankrolled by a couple of Adelaide Crows AFL footballers, this ritzy seven-storey hotel lifts Port Lincoln above the fray. It's a classy, contemporary affair with switched-on staff. Good on-site bars and eateries too, open all day – play 'Spot Mark Ricciuto' from behind your menu (mains $16 to $37).

Port Lincoln YHA HOSTEL $
(☎08-8682 3605; www.yha.com.au; 24-26 London St; dm/d/f from $36/100/125; ❄@☎) Run by a high-energy couple who have spent a fortune renovating the place, this impressive new 84-bed hostel occupies a 100-year-old house and the former squash courts behind it. Thoughtful bonuses include king-single beds, reading lights, a cafe/bar and power outlets in lockers (for phones!). Can help with booking activities, too.

Pier Hotel PUB $
(☎08-8682 1322; www.portlincolnpier.com.au; 33 Tasman Tce; d/2-bedroom apt from $80/130; ❄) The old Pier has had a facelift, including the dozen en-suite rooms upstairs – bright and clean with polished floorboards and TVs. The bistro downstairs (mains $17 to $33, serving noon to 2pm and 6pm to 8pm) is big on local seafood: oysters, calamari and scallops reign supreme.

Port Lincoln Tourist Park CARAVAN PARK $
(☎08-8621 4444; www.portlincolntouristpark.com.au; 11 Hindmarsh St; unpowered/powered sites $23/35, cabins & units $70-140; ❄@☎) Lincoln's best caravan park is this breezy waterside operation, with some beaut executive cabins by the water and plenty of elbow room. You can fish from the jetty and swim at the beach. BYO linen in the basic cabins.

GLO CAFE $
(☎08-8682 6655; www.goodlivingorganics.net; 23 Liverpool St; items $5-10; ⏲8.30am-5.30pm Mon-Fri, 9am-noon Sat; ✎) A local hang-out a block away from the beach (and thus not on many tourist radars), GLO (Good Living Organics) features cute staff in black T-shirts serving quiches, wraps, salads, falafels, couscous and Port Lincoln's best coffee.

Information

Port Lincoln Visitor Information Centre
(☎08-8683 3544, 1300 788 378; www.visitportlincoln.net; 3 Adelaide Pl; ⏲9am-5pm) Books accommodation and has national parks information and passes, plus the *Port Lincoln & Districts Cycling Guide*. Ask about the local railway, maritime and heritage museums.

Port Lincoln to Streaky Bay

Around Port Lincoln

About 50km north of Port Lincoln, **Tumby Bay** (www.tumbybay.com) is a quiet little town with a beach, jetty, pub, caravan park and motel – serious holiday territory!

About 15km south of Port Lincoln is **Lincoln National Park** (www.environment.sa.gov.au; per car $10), with roaming emus, roos and brush-tailed bettongs, safe swimming coves and pounding surf beaches. Entry is via self-registration on the way in.

If you want to stay the night, the two-bedroom **Donnington Cottage** (per night

$85, 2-night minimum) at Spalding Cove, built in 1899, sleeps six and has photo-worthy views. Book through Port Lincoln visitor information centre; BYO linen and food. The visitor centre can also advise on **bush camping** (per car $17) in the park, including sites at Fisherman's Point, Memory Cove, September Beach and Surfleet Cove.

The Port Lincoln visitor information centre also sells permits to **Mikkira Station & Koala Sanctuary** (www.mikkirakoalas.com; Fishery Bay Rd; day permit/camping $15/25), Eyre Peninsula's first sheep station and home to the endemic Port Lincoln parrot (and some koalas); and **Whalers Way** (24hr pass per car incl 1 night camping $30), a super-scenic 14km coastal drive 32km southwest of Port Lincoln.

Coffin Bay

POP 650

Oyster lovers rejoice! Deathly sounding Coffin Bay (named by Matthew Flinders after his buddy Sir Isaac Coffin) is a snoozy fishing village basking languidly in the warm sun…until a 2500-strong holiday horde arrives every January. Slippery, salty **oysters** from the nearby beds are exported worldwide, but you shouldn't pay more than $1 per oyster around town. Online, see www.coffinbay.net.

Along the ocean side of Coffin Bay there's some wild coastal scenery, most of which is part of **Coffin Bay National Park** (www.environment.sa.gov.au; per car $9), overrun with roos, emus and fat goannas. Access for conventional vehicles is limited: you can get to **Point Avoid** (coastal lookouts, rocky cliffs, good surf and whales passing between May and October) and **Yangie Bay** (arid-looking rocky landscapes and walking trails), but otherwise you'll need a 4WD. There are some isolated **camp sites** (per car $7) within the park, generally with dirt-road access.

Coffin Bay Explorer (☎0428 880 621, 1300 788 378; www.coffinbayexplorer.com; adult/child $85/45) runs half-day wildlife and seafood tours with plenty of oysters and dolphins. See also Earth Adventure (p715).

Sleeping & Eating

To rent out holiday shacks around town from $50 to $300 per night try **Coffin Bay Holiday Rentals** (☎0427 844 568; www.coffinbayholidayrentals.com.au) or **Flinders Keepers** (☎1300 986 849, 08-8685 4063; www.flinderskeepers.com.au).

Coffin Bay Caravan Park CARAVAN PARK $
(☎08-8685 4170; www.coffinbay.net/caravanpark; 91 Esplanade; unpowered/powered sites $24/34, cabins without/with bathroom $75/105, villas $130; ❄) Resident cockatoos, galahs and parrots squawk around the shady she-oak sites here, and the cabins are a reasonable bang for your buck (BYO linen). Lovely two-bedroom family villas, too.

Coffin Bay Hotel MOTEL $
(☎08-8685 4111; www.coffinbay.net/accommodation/hotel.html; cnr Jubilee Dr & Shepperd Ave; s/d $85/95; ❄) The sprawling local pub (built, it seems, to avoid any kind of view) has eight regulation units out the back (all brown brick and teak veneer), and plates up regulation counter meals (mains $16 to $27, serving noon to 2pm and 6pm to 8pm). What will emerge from the building site out the front?

Oysterbeds SEAFOOD $$
(☎08-8685 4000; www.oysterbeds.com.au; 61 Esplanade; mains $18-28; ⏲10.30am-2pm Wed-Sun, 6-8pm Fri & Sat, closed Jun-Aug) A gregarious little food room – all tangerine, sea-blue and shiny liquor bottles – serving the pick of the local seafood. Takeaway oysters shucked/unshucked are $14/10 per dozen.

Coffin Bay to Streaky Bay

There's reliable surf at **Greenly Beach** just south of Coulta, 40km north of Coffin Bay. There's also good salmon fishing along this wild stretch of coast, notably at **Locks Well**, where a long, steep stairway called the **Staircase to Heaven** (283 steps? Count 'em…) leads from the car park down to an awesome surf beach, the deep orange sand strewn with seashells.

About 15km further north, tiny **Elliston** (population 380; www.elliston.com.au) is a small fishing town on soporific Waterloo Bay, with a beautiful swimming beach and a fishing jetty (hope the whiting are biting). Waterside **Waterloo Bay Tourist Park** (☎08-8687 9076; www.visitelliston.net; 10 Beach Tce; unpowered/powered sites $25/29, cabins $60-110; ❄📶) is a smallish operation with decent cabins (aim for one on top of the dunes) and fishing gear for sale.

Just north of Elliston, take the 10km detour to **Anxious Bay** for some anxiety-relieving ocean scenery (billed as Elliston's 'Great Ocean Tourist Drive'). En route you'll pass **Blackfellows**, which boasts some of the west coast's best surf. From here you can eyeball the 36-sq-km **Flinders Island** 35km offshore, where there's a sheep station and a self-contained, nine-bed **holiday house** (☎0428 261 132; www.flindersgetaway.com; per person from $90). To get here you have to charter a plane from Port Lincoln or a boat from Elliston (additional to accommodation costs); ask for details when you book.

At **Venus Bay** there are sheltered beaches (and the not-so-sheltered Mount Camel Beach), a gaggle of pelicans, a small caravan park and the obligatory fishing jetty.

If you feel like taking a plunge and swimming with sea lions and dolphins, stop by Baird Bay and organise a tour with **Baird Bay Ocean Eco Experience** (☎08-8626 5017; www.bairdbay.com; 4hr tours adult/child $140/70; Sep-May). Accommodation is also available.

If you'd rather stay high-and-dry, the road to **Point Labatt**,43km south of Streaky Bay, takes you to one of the few permanent sea-lion colonies on the Australian mainland; ogle them from the cliff-tops (with binoculars).

A few kilometres down the Point Labatt road are the globular **Murphy's Haystacks**, an improbable congregation of 'inselbergs' – colourful, weather-sculpted granite outcrops, which are millions of years old.

Streaky Bay

POP 1150

This endearing little seasider (actually on Blanche Port) takes its name from the streaks of seaweed Matt Flinders spied in the bay as he sailed by. Visible at low tide, the seagrass attracts ocean critters and the bigger critters that eat them – first-class fishing. For tourist info, swing by the **Streaky Bay Visitor Information Centre** (☎08-8626 7033; www.streakybay.com.au; 21 Bay Rd; 9am-12.30pm & 1.30-5pm Mon-Fri).

The **Streaky Bay Museum** (www.nationaltrust.org.au/sa; 42 Montgomery Tce; adult/child $3.50/50c; 2-4pm Tue & Fri, 9am-noon Sat) is inside a 1901 school house, and features a fully furnished pug-and-pine hut, an old iron lung and plenty of pioneering history.

Sleeping & Eating

Streaky Bay Hotel/Motel HOTEL-MOTEL $
(☎08-8626 1008; www.streakybayhotel.com.au; 33 Alfred Tce; hotel s/d $50/65, motel d $110-135, all incl breakfast;) The hotel rooms upstairs at this 1866 brick beauty have rip-snorting water views and a large balcony from which to snort them. The downstairs rooms are sans views but perfectly decent. Motel rooms out the back are unglamorous but have more privacy. Breakfast, lunch and dinner happen in the bistro daily (mains $15 to $30, serving 7am to 9am, noon to 2pm and 6pm to 8.30pm).

Foreshore Tourist Park CARAVAN PARK $
(☎08-8626 1666; www.streakybayftpark.com.au; 82 Wells St; unpowered/powered sites from $23/28, cabins & units $85-110;) Right on Doctors Beach just east of town, this sandy park is overrun with cavorting families in summer. Plenty of space and sea-based things to do.

★**Mocean** CAFE $$
(☎08-8626 1775; www.moceancafe.com.au; 34b Alfred Tce; mains $16-32; 10am-3pm Tue-Sun, 6-8pm Thu-Sat) It looks like a big shipping container from the street, but this jaunty corrugated-iron-clad cafe is the town's social pacemaker, with murals, Moroccan lanterns and water views from the alfresco terrace. Dishes focus on scrumptious local seafood – try the chilli-and-lime squid. There's good coffee, too.

Ceduna

POP 3800

Despite the locals' best intentions, Ceduna remains a raggedy fishing town that just can't shake its tag as a blow-through pit stop en route to WA. But the local oysters love it! **Oysterfest** (www.ceduna.net/site/page.cfm?u=167) in late September is the undisputed king of Australian oyster parties. And if you're heading west in whale season (May to October), Ceduna is the place for updates on sightings at Head of Bight.

For local info, swing by the **Ceduna Visitor Information Centre** (☎08-8625 2780, 1800 639 413; www.cedunatourism.com.au; 58 Poynton St; 9am-5.30pm Mon-Fri, 9.30am-5pm Sat & Sun).

Sights

Ceduna Museum MUSEUM
(www.nationaltrust.org.au/sa; 2 Park Tce; adult/child/family $3.50/2/7; 10am-noon Mon, Tue, Fri & Sat, 2-4pm Wed, 10am-4pm Thu) Little Ceduna Museum has pioneer exhibits, indigenous artefacts and a display on the tragic British nuclear tests at Maralinga.

Ceduna Aboriginal Arts & Culture Centre GALLERY
(www.visitaboriginalart.com; 2 Eyre Hwy; ⊙9am-5pm Mon-Fri) **FREE** The sea-inspired works of local indigenous artists from along the coast steal the show at this casual arts centre.

Sleeping & Eating

Ceduna Foreshore Hotel/Motel MOTEL $$
(☎08-8625 2008; www.cedunahotel.com.au; 32 O'Loughlin Tce; d $150-195, f $220; ❄📶) The renovated 54-room Foreshore is the most luxurious option in town, with water views and a bistro zooming in on west-coast seafood (mains $16 to $32, serving 6.30am to 9am, noon to 2pm and 6pm to 8.30pm). Views from the outdoor terrace look through Norfolk Island pines and out across the bay.

Ceduna Oyster Bar SEAFOOD $
(☎08-8626 9086; www.ceduna.net/site/page.cfm?u=493; Eyre Hwy; 12 oysters $12; ⊙9.30am-5pm Mon-Fri, 10am-4pm Sat) Pick up a box of freshly shucked molluscs and head for the foreshore, or sit by the highway-side here and watch the road trains rumble past. Hours can be sketchy – call in advance.

Ceduna to the Western Australian Border

It's 480km from Ceduna to the WA border. Along the stretch you can get a bed and a beer at Penong (72km from Ceduna), Nundroo (151km), the Nullarbor Roadhouse (295km) near Head of Bight, and at Border Village on the border itself.

Wheat and sheep paddocks line the road to Nundroo, after which you're in mallee scrub for another 100km. Around 20km later, the trees thin to low bluebush as you enter the true Nullarbor (Latin for 'no trees'). Road trains, caravans and cyclists of questionable sanity are your only companions as you put your foot down and careen towards the setting sun.

Turn off the highway at Penong (population 200), and follow the 20km dirt road to Point Sinclair and **Cactus Beach**, which has three of Australia's most famous surf breaks. Caves is a wicked right-hand break for experienced surfers (locals don't take too kindly to tourists dropping in). There's bush camping (per person from $10) on private property close to the breaks; BYO drinking water.

The viewing platforms at **Head of Bight** (☎0407 832 297; www.yalata.org; adult $20, child under/over 15 free/$15; ⊙8am-5pm) overlook a major southern-right-whale breeding ground. Whales migrate here from Antarctica, and you can see them cavorting from May to October. The breeding area is protected by the **Great Australian Bight Commonwealth Marine Reserve** (www.environment.gov.au/coasts/mpa/gab), the world's second-largest marine park after the Great Barrier Reef.

Head of Bight is a part of the Yalata Indigenous Protected Area. Pay your entry fee and get the latest whale information from the White Well Ranger Station on the way in to the viewing area. The signposted turn-off is 14km east of the Nullarbor Roadhouse.

While you're in the Head of Bight area, you can also check out **Murrawijinie Cave**, a large overhang behind the Nullarbor Roadhouse, and have a look at the signposted coastal lookouts along the top of the 80m-high **Bunda Cliffs**.

If you're continuing west into WA, dump all fruit, vegetables, cheese and plants at Border Village (as per quarantine regulations), and watch out for animals if you're driving at night. Note that if you're driving east rather than west, SA's quarantine check point isn't until Ceduna.

Sleeping & Eating

Penong Caravan Park CARAVAN PARK $
(☎08-8625 1111; www.nullarbornet.com.au/towns/penong.html; 5 Stiggants Rd, Penong; unpowered/powered sites $23/27, onsite vans/cabins from $50/78; ❄) A short hop from Ceduna, this well-kept park is rated by some travellers as the best on the Nullarbor. The cabins are in good shape, and the camping area has a laundry and barbecues. Extra charge for linen.

Fowlers Bay Caravan Park CARAVAN PARK $
(☎08-8625 6143; www.nullarbornet.com.au/towns/fowlersBay.html; Fowlers Bay; powered sites $25, units $65-75; ❄) There's basic accommodation, a shop and takeaway food in this almost ghost town, plus heritage buildings, good fishing and rambling dunes. Take the Fowlers Bay turn-off 106km from Ceduna.

Nundroo Hotel/Motel MOTEL $
(☎08-8625 6120; www.nundrooaccommodation.com; Eyre Hwy, Nundroo; unpowered/powered sites $8/20, d $90; ❄📶) If you're heading west, Nundroo has this decent hotel/motel and

the last mechanic until Norseman in WA, 1038km away. There's a very basic dorm, and worn but comfy motel rooms with updated bathrooms. There's a bar/restaurant onsite, open 11am until late (meals $15 to $35).

Nullarbor Roadhouse MOTEL $
(☎08-8625 6271; www.nullarbornet.com.au/towns/nullarbor.html; Eyre Hwy, Nullarbor; unpowered/powered sites $20/25, budget rooms s/d/tr $47/57/67, motel s/d/tr $125/145/165; ❄) Close to the Head of Bight whale-watching area, this roadhouse is a real oasis. The onsite bar/restaurant is open from 7am to 10pm (meals $15 to $30).

Border Village Motel MOTEL $
(☎08-9039 3474; www.nullarbornet.com.au/towns/borderVillage.html; Eyre Hwy, Border Village; unpowered/powered sites $15/20, budget rooms s/d/tr $40/60/70, motel s/d/f from $95/110/120; ❄@🏊) Just 50m from the WA border, this motel has a variety of modern rooms and cabins and a licensed restaurant (meals $13 to $25, serving from noon to 2pm and 6pm to 8pm).

FLINDERS RANGES

Known simply as 'the Flinders', this ancient mountain range is an iconic South Australian environment. Jagged peaks and escarpments rise up north of Port Augusta and track 400km north to Mt Hopeless. The colours here are remarkable: as the day stretches out, the mountains shift from mauve mornings to midday chocolates and ochre-red sunsets.

Before Europeans arrived, the Flinders were prized by the Adnyamathanha peoples for their red ochre deposits, which had medicinal and ritual uses. Sacred caves, rock paintings and carvings exist throughout the region. In the wake of white exploration came villages, farms, country pubs, wheat farms and cattle stations, many of which failed under the unrelenting sun.

The cooler Southern Ranges are studded with stands of river red gums and country hamlets with cherubic appeal. In the arid Northern Ranges, the desert takes a hold: the scenery here is stark, desolate and very beautiful.

Online, see www.flindersoutback.com.

Tours

See Heading Bush (p715).

Bookabee Tours INDIGENOUS
(☎0408 209 593, 08-8235 9954; www.bookabee.com.au; 2-/3-/4-day tours $995/1520/2025) Highly rated indigenous-run tours to the Flinders Ranges and outback, departing Adelaide, including quality accommodation, meals, cultural tours, activities and interpretation.

Swagabout Tours WILDERNESS
(☎0408 845 378; www.swagabouttours.com.au) Dependable Flinders Ranges trips including Quorn and Wilpena (plus Arkaroola on the four-day jaunt), and can be extended to Coober Pedy. Costs per day are around $300/500 with camping/hotel accommodation.

Wallaby Tracks Adventure Tours WILDERNESS
(☎0428 486 655; www.wallabytracks.com; 1-/4-day tours $250/1200) Small-group 4WD tours around the Ranges and Wilpena Pound. One-day tours ex-Quorn or Port Augusta; four-day tours ex-Adelaide.

Adventure Tours Australia WILDERNESS
(☎08-8132 8130, 1300 654 604; www.adventuretours.com.au) Popular small-group tours through the Flinders region and beyond; seven-day Adelaide to Alice Springs tours $1020.

Groovy Grape WILDERNESS
(☎08-8440 1640, 1800 661 177; www.groovygrape.com.au) Adelaide to Coober Pedy and back over four days, via the Flinders Ranges will cost $495.

Getting There & Away

BUS

Premier Stateliner (www.premierstateliner.com.au) Daily buses from Adelaide to Port Pirie ($43, 3¼ hours).

Yorke Peninsula Coaches (☎08-8821 2755; www.ypcoaches.com.au) Runs a Friday bus between Port Augusta and Quorn ($6, 40 minutes), and a Thursday bus between Port Pirie and Melrose ($6, 1¼ hours).

TRAIN

Pichi Richi Railway (p786) has trains between Port Augusta and Quorn (two hours) every Saturday.

Southern Ranges Towns

Port Pirie (population 13,200) is a big lead- and zinc-smelting town on the edge of the Southern Flinders. The Nyrstar smelter dominates the skyline, but the town itself has some pretty old buildings along Ellen St, and is a good spot to stock up on supplies before heading north. The **Port Pirie Regional Tourism & Arts Centre** (☎08-8633 8700, 1800 000 424; www.piriehasitall.com.au; 3 Mary Elie St; ⏰9am-5pm Mon-Fri, 10am-4pm Sat & Sun) has local info.

You enter the Southern Ranges proper near **Laura** (population 550), emerging from the wheat fields like Superman's Smallville (all civic pride and 1950s prosperity). There's not a lot to do here, but the long, geranium-adorned main street has a supermarket, chemist, bakery, bank, post office...even a shoe shop!

The oldest town in the Flinders (1853) is **Melrose** (population 200), snug in the elbow of the 960m Mt Remarkable. It has the perfect mix of well-preserved architecture, a cracking-good pub, quality accommodation and parks with *actual grass*. Don't miss the decaying multistorey ruins of **Jacka's Brewery** (1878) on Mount St, which once employed 40 staff.

Online, see www.southernflindersranges.com.au.

Sleeping & Eating

North Star Hotel PUB $$
(☎08-8666 2110; www.northstarhotel.com.au; 43 Nott St, Melrose; d $110-225, trucks $160; ❄📶) As welcome as summer rain, the North Star Hotel in Melrose is a fabulous 1854 pub renovated in city-meets-woolshed style. Sit under the hessian-sack ceiling and spinning fans for a fresh menu (mains $16 to $30, serving noon to 2pm and 6pm to 8pm), great coffee and cold beer. Accommodation ranges from rooms in Bundaleer Cottage next door (sleeps 16) to plush suites above the pub and surprisingly cool metal-clad cabins built on two old trucks out the back.

Melrose Caravan Park CARAVAN PARK $
(☎08-8666 2060; www.members.westnet.com.au/venhoek/~melrose; Joe's Rd, Melrose; dm $20, unpowered/powered sites $20/25, cabins $60-120; ❄) A small, tidy park with five acres of bush campsites and self-contained cabins salvaged from the 2000 Sydney Olympics (all with TVs and cooking facilities – the cheaper ones are sans bathrooms). The 12km return hike up Mt Remarkable starts on the back doorstep. Next door is a converted agricultural shed with basic dorm facilities.

Old Bakery BAKERY $
(☎08-8663 2165; www.oldbakerystonehut.com.au; 1 Main North Rd, Stone Hut; items $4-10; ⏰7am-6pm) About 10km north of Laura in Stone Hut (population 290) is this amazing bakery, which makes legendary chunky beef pies, slices and quandong tart. There's cabin-style accommodation here too (doubles from $150).

Mt Remarkable National Park

Bush boffins rave about the steep, jaggedy **Mt Remarkable National Park** (www.environment.sa.gov.au; per person/car $4/10) straddling the Southern Flinders. Wildlife and bushwalking are the main lures, with various tracks (including part of the **Heysen Trail**) meandering through isolated gorges.

From the car park at **Alligator Gorge** take the short, steep walk (2km, two hours) down into the craggy gorge (no sign of any 'gators), the ring route (9km, four hours), or walk to **Hidden Gorge** (18km, seven hours) or **Mambray Creek** (13km, seven hours). From Mambray Creek the track to **Davey's Gully** (2.5km, one hour) is (literally and metaphorically) a walk in the park. Peak baggers sweat up the track to the 960m-high summit of **Mt Remarkable** (12km, five hours); the trail starts behind Melrose Caravan Park.

Pay the park entry fee at the **Park Office** (☎08-8634 7068; www.environment.sa.gov.au) at Mambray Creek, off Hwy 1 about 21km north of Port Germein. On the inland route (Main North Rd between Melrose and Wilmington), there's an honesty box at Alligator Gorge. Both stations have park info brochures.

If you want to stay the night there's plenty of **bush camping** (per person/car $6/18), and two lodges: at **Mambray Creek** (sleeps 4, per night from $55) and **Alligator Gorge** (sleeps 10, per night from $150). Both are solar powered; Alligator Gorge has better cooking facilities and showers. Book through the Park Office.

Quorn

POP 1210

Is Quorn a film set after the crew has gone home? With more jeering crows than people, it's a cinematographic little outback town. Wheat farming took off here in 1875, and the town prospered with the arrival of the Great Northern Railway from Port Augusta. Quorn (pronounced 'kworn') remained an

Flinders Ranges

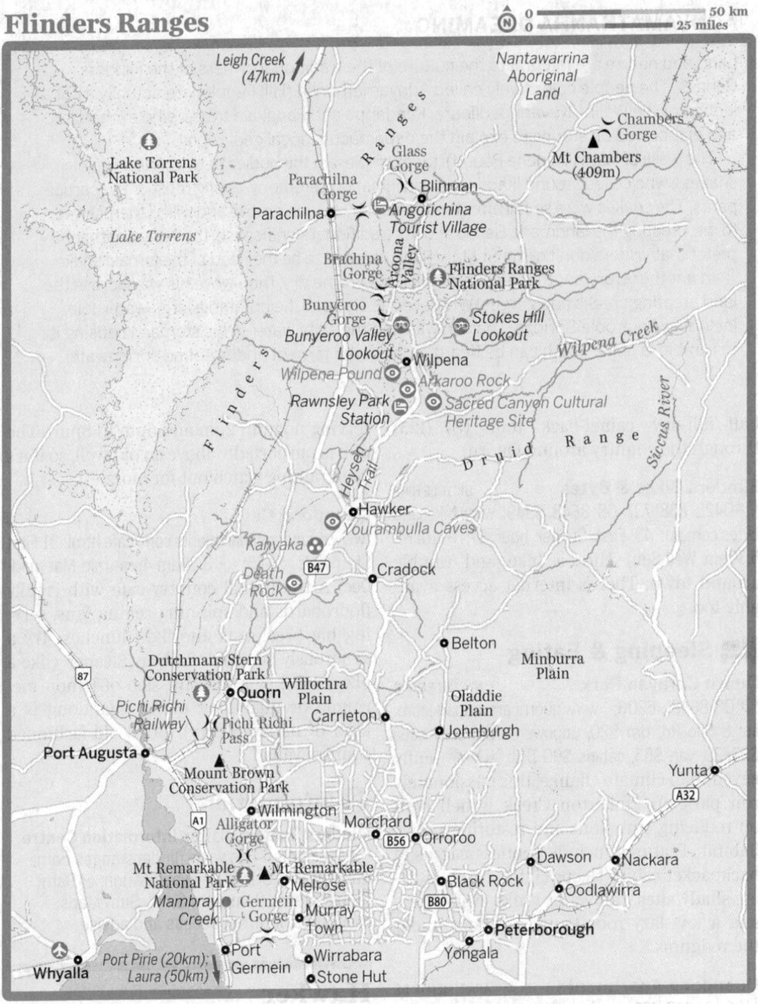

important railroad junction until trains into the Flinders were cut in 1970.

Sights & Activities

Quorn's streetscapes, especially Railway Tce, are a real history lesson, and have featured in iconic Australian films such as *Gallipoli* and *Sunday Too Far Away*. Pick up the *Quorn Historic Buildings Walk* brochure from the visitor centre. A fragment of the long-defunct railway now conveys the Pichi Richi Railway (p786) between Port Augusta and Quorn.

Derelict ruins of early settlements litter the Quorn–Hawker road, the most impressive of which is **Kanyaka**, a once-thriving sheep station founded in 1851. From the homestead ruins (41km from Quorn) it's a 20-minute walk to a waterhole, loomed over by the massive **Death Rock**. The story goes that local Aborigines once placed their dying kinfolk here to see out their last hours.

Pichi Richi Camel Tours CAMEL TOUR
(☎0439 333 257, 08-8648 6640; www.pichirichicameltours.com) Saddle up for two-hour sunset rides ($85), breakfast rides (55), or a longer

ADNYAMATHANHA DREAMING

Land and nature are integral to the culture of the traditional owners of the Flinders Ranges. The people collectively called Adnyamathanha (Hill People) are actually a collection of the Wailpi, Kuyani, Jadliaura, Piladappa and Pangkala tribes, who exchanged and elaborated on stories to explain their spectacular local geography.

The walls of Ikara (Wilpena Pound), for example, are the bodies of two *akurra* (giant snakes), who coiled around Ikara during an initiation ceremony, eating most of the participants. The snakes were so full after their feast they couldn't move and willed themselves to die, creating the landmark. Because of its traditional significance, the Adnyamathanha prefer that visitors don't climb St Mary Peak, reputed to be the head of the female snake.

In another story another *akurra* drank Lake Frome dry, then wove his way across the land creating creeks and gorges. Wherever he stopped, he created a large waterhole, including Arkaroola Springs. The sun warmed the salty water in his stomach causing it to rumble, a noise which can be heard today in the form of underground springwater.

half-/full-day camel-back tour ($75/125) through the country around Quorn.

Flinders Bikes & Bytes BICYCLE HIRE
(☎0428 838 737, 08 8648 6349; www.bikesandbytes.com.au; 43 First St; per hour $7; ⏰10am-5.30pm Wed-Sun) Hire a bike and ramble around town. There's internet access available too.

Sleeping & Eating

Quorn Caravan Park CARAVAN PARK $
(☎08-8648 6206; www.quorncaravanpark.com.au; 8 Silo Rd; dm $20, unpowered/powered sites $23/29, van $65, cabins $90-120; ❄) Fully keyed in to climate change, this passionately run park on Pinkerton Creek is hell bent on reducing emissions and restoring native habitat. Features include spotless cabins, a backpacker cabin (sleeps eight), camp kitchen, shady sites, rainwater tanks everywhere and a few lazy roos lounging about under the redgums.

Quandong Apartments APARTMENTS $$
(☎0432 113 473; www.quandongapartments.com; 31 First St; d $160; ❄) Next door to the Quandong Café (and run by the same folks), these two self-contained apartments have full kitchens, big TVs, quality linen and chintz-meets-Asian touches. Rates come down for stays of two nights or more.

Austral Inn HOTEL-MOTEL $
(☎08-8648 6017; www.australinn.info; 16 Railway Tce; d motel/pub from $90/115; ❄) There's always a few locals here giving the jukebox a workout. The pub rooms are renovated – simple and clean with new linen (nicer than the motel rooms out the back). Try a kangaroo schnitzel in the bistro (mains $15 to $30, serving noon to 2pm and 6pm to 8pm). The pub is purportedly above an old well, so if it's been raining watch out for mozzies.

Quandong Café CAFE $
(www.quandongapartments.com/cafe.html; 31 First St; meals $4-15; ⏰8.30am-4pm mid-Mar–mid-Dec) A traditional country cafe with creaky floorboards and spinning ceiling fans, serving big breakfasts and light lunches. Try a generously adorned 'Railway Sleeper' (like a pizza sub), or a massive slab of lemon meringue or quandong pie (a quandong is a kind of native cherry). Good old-fashioned country value!

Information

Flinders Ranges Visitor Information Centre
(☎08-8648 6419; www.flindersranges.com; Railway Tce, Quorn Railway Station; ⏰9am-5pm Mon-Fri, 9am-4pm Sat & Sun) Maps, brochures, internet access and advice.

Hawker

POP 300

Hawker is the last outpost of civilisation before Wilpena Pound, 55km to the north. Much like Quorn, Hawker has seen better days, most of which were when the old *Ghan* train stopped here. These days Hawker is a pancake-flat, pit-stop town with an ATM and the world's most helpful petrol station.

Sights & Activities

It's not so much what's in Hawker that's interesting – it's more what's around it – but if you like your great outdoors inside (and a little bit eccentric), **Wilpena Panorama** (www.wilpenapanorama.com; cnr Wilpena

& Cradock Rds; adult/child $8/5.50; ⏲9am-5pm Mon-Sat, 9am-4pm Sat, 11am-2pm Sun, closed Jan & Feb) is a large circular room with a painting of Wilpena Pound surrounding you on all sides.

Yourambulla Caves, 12km south of Hawker, have detailed Aboriginal rock paintings (including emu tracks), with three sites open to visitors. **Yourambulla Peak**, a half-hour walk from the car park, is the most accessible spot to check out the paintings.

Around 40km north of Hawker towards Wilpena, **Arkaroo Rock** is a sacred Aboriginal site. The rock art here features reptile and human figures in charcoal, bird-lime and yellow and red ochre. It's a short(ish) return walk from the car park (2km, one hour).

Tours

Derek's 4WD Tours DRIVING TOUR
(☎0417 475 770; www.dereks4wdtours.com; tours half-/full day from $115/170) These are 4WD trips with an environmental bent, including visits to Bunyeroo and Brachina gorges.

Skytrek Willow Springs DRIVING TOUR
(☎08-8648 0016; www.skytrekwillowsprings.com.au) Six-hour self-drive tours on a working sheep station (per vehicle $65), or they can hook you up with a tour operator. Self-contained cabin accommodation is also available (doubles from $100).

Sleeping & Eating

BIG4 Hawker Caravan Park CARAVAN PARK $
(☎08-8648 4006; www.hawkerbig4holidaypark.com.au; cnr Wilpena Rd & Chace View Tce; unpowered/powered sites $26/28, en-suite sites $39-45, cabins $96-162; ❄📶🏊) At the Wilpena end of town, this upbeat, fastidiously maintained acreage has generous gravelly sites and a range of cabins. And there's a pool!

Outback Motel & Chapmanton Holiday Units MOTEL $$
(☎08-8648 4100; www.hawkersa.info/biz/outback.htm; 1 Wilpena Rd; s/d motel $110/125, units $120/150; ❄) Like a transplanted vision from Utah, this orange-brick, drive-up motel offers the best rooms in town. The two-bedroom units are good value for families.

Flinders Ranges Accommodation Booking Service ACCOMMODATION SERVICES $$
(FRABS; ☎08-8648 4022, 1800 777 880; www.frabs.com.au; d $75-225) Bookings for rural cottages and shearers quarters around Hawker.

Old Ghan Restaurant MODERN AUSTRALIAN $$
(☎08-8648 4176; www.hawkersa.info/biz/ghan.htm; Leigh Creek Rd, Old Hawker Railway Station; mains $19-32; ⏲5.30-8pm Wed-Sat, closed Jan) In the *1884 Ghan* railway station on the outskirts of town, this rough-and-ready eatery is about as upmarket as Hawker gets. Expect mains such as kangaroo medallions with wattleseed and mustard, and beer-battered garfish.

Information

Teague's Hawker Motors & Visitor Information Centre (☎1800 777 880, 08-8648 4014; www.hawkervic.info; cnr Wilpena & Cradock Rds; ⏲7.30am-6pm) The town's petrol station (fill up if you're heading north) is also the visitor information centre.

Flinders Ranges National Park

One of SA's most treasured parks, **Flinders Ranges National Park** (www.environment.sa.gov.au; per car $9) is laced with craggy gorges, saw-toothed ranges, abandoned homesteads, Aboriginal sites, native wildlife and, after it rains, carpets of wildflowers. The park's big-ticket drawcard is the 80-sq-km natural basin **Ikara (Wilpena Pound)** – a sunken elliptical valley ringed by gnarled ridges (don't let anyone tell you it's a meteorite crater!).

The Pound is only vehicle accessible on the Wilpena Pound Resort's **shuttle bus** (return adult/child/family $4/2.50/9), which drops you within 1km of the old Hills Homestead, from where you can walk to **Wangarra Lookout**. The shuttle runs at 9am, 11am, 1pm, 3pm and 5pm, dropping people off and coming straight back (so if you take the 5pm shuttle and want more than a cursory look around, you'll miss the return bus). Otherwise it's a three-hour, 8km return walk between the resort and lookout.

The 20km **Brachina Gorge Geological Trail** features an amazing layering of exposed sedimentary rock, covering 120 million years of the Earth's history. Grab a brochure from the visitors centre.

The **Bunyeroo–Brachina–Aroona Scenic Drive** is a 110km round trip, passing by Bunyeroo Valley, Brachina Gorge, Aroona Valley and **Stokes Hill Lookout**. There are plenty of short walks along the way; a stop at **Bunyeroo Valley Lookout** is mandatory. The drive starts north of Wilpena off the road to Blinman.

Just beyond the park's southeast corner, a one-hour, 1km return walk leads to the **Sacred Canyon Cultural Heritage Site**, with Aboriginal rock-art galleries featuring animal tracks and designs.

Sights & Activities

Bushwalking in the Flinders is an unforgettable experience. Before you make happy trails, ensure you've got enough water, sunscreen and a hat, and tell someone where you're going and when you'll be back. Pick up the *Bushwalking in Flinders Ranges National Park* brochure/map from the visitors centre, detailing 19 park walks. Many of the walks kick off at Wilpena Pound Resort.

For a look at Wilpena, the walk up to **Tanderra Saddle** (return 15km, six hours) on the ridge of **St Mary Peak** on the Pound's rim is brilliant, though it's a thigh-pounding scramble at times. The Adnyamathanha people request that you restrict your climbing to the ridge and don't climb St Mary Peak itself, due to its traditional significance to them. If you have time, take the longer outside track for more eye-popping vistas. You can keep going on the round trip (22km, nine hours), camping overnight at Cooinda Camp.

The quick, tough track up to **Mt Ohlssen Bagge** (return 6.5km, four hours) rewards the sweaty hiker with a stunning panorama. Good short walks include the stroll to **Hills Homestead** (return 6.5km, two hours), or the dash up to the **Wilpena Solar Power Station** (return 500m, 30 minutes).

In the park's north (50km north of Wilpena Pound Resort), the **Aroona Ruins** are the launch pad for a few less-trampled walks. The **Yuluna Hike** (return 8km, four hours) weaves through a painterly stretch of the ABC Ranges. The challenging **Aroona–Youngoona Track** (one way 15.5km, seven hours) offers views of the Trezona and Heysen Ranges; cool your boots overnight at Youngoona camp site.

Tours

Wilpena Pound Resort (half-/full day from $180/245) and Rawnsley Park Station (half-/full day from $135/225) both run **4WD tours**. There are also tour companies operating from Hawker.

Air Wilpena Scenic Flights SCENIC FLIGHTS
(☎08-8648 0004; www.wilpenapound.com.au/scenic-flights; flights 20min/30min/1hr $165/190/299) Flights from Wilpena Pound Resort.

Central Air Services SCENIC FLIGHTS
(☎08-8648 0040; www.centralairservices.com.au; flights 20min/30min/1hr $160/180/350) Scenic flights from Rawnsley Park Station.

Sleeping & Eating

Permits for **bush camping** (per person/car $7/13) within the national park (ie outside the resort) are available from either the visitor information centre or self-service booths along the way. Trezona, Aroona and Brachina East have creek-side sites among big gum trees; Youngoona in the park's north is a good base for walks. Remote Wilkawillina is certainly the quietest spot.

★ **Wilpena Pound Resort** RESORT $$$
(☎08-8648 0004, 1800 805 802; www.wilpenapound.com.au; Wilpena Rd via Hawker; unpowered/powered sites $22/32, permanent tent with/without linen $97/75, d $224-288;) Accommodation at this plush resort includes motel-style rooms, upmarket self-contained suites, and a great (although hugely popular) camp site. If you don't have your own camping gear, there are permanent tents sleeping five. Purchase your camping permit at the visitors centre, which also sells petrol and basic (and expensive) groceries. Don't miss a swim in the pool, happy hour at the bar (5pm to 6pm) and dinner at the excellent bistro (mains $19 to $29 – the roo is the best we've ever had!).

Rawnsley Park Station RESORT $$
(☎08-8648 0030, caravan park 08-8648 0008, restaurant 08-8648 0126; www.rawnsleypark.com.au; Wilpena Rd via Hawker; unpowered/powered sites $22/33, hostel s/d/f from $50/75/95, cabins/units/villas from $90/130/370;) This rangy homestead, 35km from Hawker just south of the national park, runs the accommodation gamut from tent sites to luxe eco-villas. There are also some caravan-park cabins set up as dorms, managed by the **YHA** (www.yha.com.au). Also on offer is a range of outback activities including mountain-bike hire (per hour $15), bushwalks (30 minutes to four hours), hot-air ballooning, 4WD tours and scenic flights. The Woolshed Restaurant (mains $10 to $40, open noon to 2pm and 6pm to 8pm) does bang-up bush tucker, plus curries, seafood and pizzas.

Information

Wilpena Pound Visitor Information Centre
(☎08-8648 0048, 1800 805 802; www.wilpenapound.com.au; Wilpena Pound Resort;

⏲8am-5pm) Info on the park and district, internet access and bike hire (per half-/full day $20/40). Also does bookings for scenic flights and 4WD tours, and issues bushwalking advice. You can pay park entry fees here (per car $9).

Blinman & Parachilna

North of Wilpena Pound on a sealed road, ubercute Blinman (population 30) owes its existence to the copper ore discovered here in 1859 and the smelter built in 1903. But the boom went bust and 1500 folks left town. Today Blinman's main claim to fame is as SA's highest town (610m above sea level).

Much of the old **Heritage Blinman Mine** (☎08-8648 4782; www.heritageblinmanmine.com.au; Main St, Blinman; tours adult/child/family $25/10/60; ⏲9.30am-5pm) has been redeveloped with lookouts, audio-visual interpretation and information boards. One-hour tours run at 10am, noon and 2pm (extra tours in winter).

Slate floors, old photos and colonial-style rooms collide at the renovated 1869 **North Blinman Hotel** (☎08-8648 4867; www.blinmanhotel.com.au; Mine Rd, Blinman; unpowered/powered sites $10/20, d motel/hotel $90/155; ❄📶), which has tent sites out the back (...D'oh! They filled in the pool!). The bistro (mains $14 to $30, serving noon to 2pm and 6pm to 8pm) plates up pubby delights.

In an 1883 school building, **Wild Lime Café & Gallery** (☎08-8648 4679; www.wildlimecafe.com; Main St, Old Schoolhouse, Blinman; mains $8-20; ⏲9am-4pm daily Apr-Nov, closed Tue Dec-Mar) serves great coffee, soups, salads, pies, pasties, cakes and bush-inspired dishes such as red roo curry.

The road between Blinman and Parachilna tracks through gorgeous **Parachilna Gorge**, where you'll find free creek-side camping and chill-out spots. The northern end of the **Heysen Trail** starts/finishes here.

'Real people only, no Yuppies' is the slogan at **Angorichina Tourist Village** (☎08-8648 4842; www.angorichinavillage.com.au; Blinman–Parachilna Rd; unpowered/powered sites $22/26, dm $42, cabins from $120; ❄@), 17km west of Blinman in Parachilna Gorge. It's a rambling joint with a mix of accommodation; the store sells fuel. The **Blinman Pools Walk** (12km return, five hours) starts here, following a creek past abandoned dugouts, river red gums and cypress pines.

On the Hawker–Leigh Creek road, Parachilna (population somewhere between four and seven) is an essential Flinders Ranges destination. Aside from a few shacks, a phone booth and some rusty wrecks, the only thing here is the legendary **Prairie Hotel** (☎08-8648 4895, 1800 331 473; www.prairiehotel.com.au; cnr High St & West Tce, Parachilna; powered sites $32, cabins d/f from $80/180, hotel d $195-345; ❄📶). It's a world-class stay with slick suites, plus camping and workers' cabins across the street. Don't miss a meal and a cold beer (or five) in the pub (mains $22 to $35, serving 11.30am to 3pm and 6pm to 8.30pm). Try the feral mixed grill (camel sausage, kangaroo fillet and emu). We arrived at 10.42am: 'Too early for a beer!? Whose rules are those?' said the barman.

Leigh Creek & Copley

In the early 1980s, the previously nonexistent town of Leigh Creek (population 700) was built by the state government: blooming out of the desert, it's an odd, Canberra-like oasis of leafy landscaping and cul-de-sacs. It's a coal-mining town, supplying the Port Augusta power stations. The **Leigh Creek Visitor Information Centre** (☎08-8675 2315; www.loccleighcreek.com.au; Shop 2, Black Oak Dr, Leigh Creek; ⏲8.30am-5.30pm Mon-Fri, 8.30am-2pm Sat) is at Liz's Open Cut Cafe.

The hub of town life, the **Leigh Creek Tavern** (☎08-8675 2025; leighcreektavern@alintaenergy.com.au; Black Oak Dr, Leigh Creek; motel s/d $110/150, cabins s/d/f $90/100/130; ❄) offers jaunty '90s-style motel rooms, basic cabins a few hundred metres from the pub, and miner-sized bistro meals (mains $12 to $24, serving noon to 2pm and 6pm to 8pm).

About 6km north of Leigh Creek is the sweet meaninglessness of little Copley (population 80). **Copley Cabin & Caravan Park** (☎08-8675 2288; www.copleycaravan.com.au; Railway Tce W, Copley; unpowered/powered sites $25/28, cabins d $80-150; ❄) is a going concern: a small, immaculate park. Down the street is **Copley Bush Bakery & Quandong Cafe** (www.copleybushbakery.com.au; Railway Tce, Copley; items $4-6; ⏲8am-4pm), serving decent coffee and delicious quandong pies.

Iga Warta (☎08-8648 3737; www.igawarta.com; Arkaroola Rd; unpowered sites $36, dm & tents per person $36, cabins/safari tents d $104/150), 57km east of Copley on the way into Vulkathunha-Gammon Ranges National Park, is an indigenous-run establishment offering Adnyamathanha cultural experiences ($25 to $75) as well as 4WD and bushwalking tours ($52 to $228). The various onsite accommodation is open to all comers.

Immediately after Iga Warta just before the national park is **Nepabunna**, an Adnyamathanha community that manages the local land.

Vulkathunha-Gammon Ranges National Park

Blanketing 1282 sq km of desert, the remote **Vulkathunha-Gammon Ranges National Park** (www.environment.sa.gov.au) has deep gorges, rugged ranges, yellow-footed rock wallabies and gum-lined creeks. Most of the park is difficult to access (4WDs are near compulsory) and has limited facilities. The rangers hang out at the **Balcanoona Park Office** (☎08-8648 4829, info line 08-8204 1910), 99km from Copley.

The area around Grindells Hut has expansive views and stark ridges all around. You can reach it on a 4WD track off the Arkaroola road, or by walking through **Weetootla Gorge**. It's a 13km return hike – you might want to stay the night at Grindells Hut. Check with the ranger before driving or walking into this area.

The park has six **bush camping** (per person/car $8/5) areas, including Italowie Gorge, Grindells Hut, Weetootla Gorge and Arcoona Bluff. Pick up camping permits at Balcanoona Park HQ. There are two huts that can be booked at the ranger's office: **Grindells Hut** (up to 8 people $145) and **Balcanoona Shearer's Quarters** (d/tr $40/65, exclusive use up to 18 people $265).

Arkaroola

A privately operated wildlife reserve-resort 129km east of Copley on unsealed roads, **Arkaroola Wilderness Sanctuary** (☎08-8648 4848, 1800 676 042; www.arkaroola.com.au) occupies a far-flung and utterly spectacular part of the Flinders Ranges. The **visitor information centre** (9am-5pm) has displays on local natural history, including a scientific explanation of the tremors that often shake things up hereabouts.

The absolute must-do highlight of Arkaroola is the four-hour 4WD **Ridgetop Tour** (adult $120) through wild mountain country, complete with white-knuckle climbs and descents towards the freakish Sillers Lookout. Once you've extracted your fingernails from your seat, look for wedge-tailed eagles and yellow-footed rock wallabies. You can also book guided or tag-along tours (drives and walks) through the area. Most areas are accessible in a regular car, with some hiking to pump up your pulse.

The **resort** (Arkaroola Rd Camp; unpowered/powered sites $18/25, cabins $40, cottages $130-175, motel d $145-175;) includes a motel complex and caravan park. Camp sites range from dusty hilltop spots to creekside corners; the comfortable cabins are a good budget bet. Other facilities include a woody bar-restaurant (mains $15 to $30, serving noon to 2pm and 6pm to 8pm), a supermarket and service station.

OUTBACK

The area north of the Eyre Peninsula and the Flinders Ranges stretches into the vast, empty spaces of SA's outback. If you're prepared, travelling through this sparsely populated and harsh country is utterly rewarding.

Heading into the red heart of Australia on the Stuart Hwy, Woomera is the first pit stop, with its dark legacy of nuclear tests and shiny collection of left-over rockets. Further north, the opal-mining town of Coober Pedy is an absolute one-off: a desolate human aberration amid the blistering, arid plains. If you're feeling gung-ho, tackle a section of the iconic Oodnadatta Track, a rugged outback alternative to the Stuart Hwy tarmac. Along the way are warm desert springs, the gargantuan Lake Eyre (Kati Thanda) and some amazing old outback pubs.

Online, see www.flindersoutback.com.

Tours

For scenic outback flights, see the Coober Pedy, William Creek and Marree listings.

Arabunna Tours INDIGENOUS
(☎08-8675 8351; www.arabunnatours.com.au; 7-day tour ex-Adelaide $1695) Aboriginal-owned company offering cultural tours from Adelaide to the Flinders Ranges, Marree, Oodnadatta Track and Lake Eyre.

Just Cruisin 4WD Tours INDIGENOUS
(☎08-8383 0962; www.justcruisin4wdtours.com.au; 5-day tour ex-Adelaide $3295) Aboriginal cultural tours visiting outback indigenous communities, sites and guides between Adelaide and Coober Pedy.

Getting There & Around

AIR

Regional Express (Rex; www.regionalexpress.com.au) Flies most days between Adelaide and Coober Pedy ($235, two hours).

BUS

Greyhound Australia (www.greyhound.com.au) Daily coaches from Adelaide to Alice Springs ($331, 19½ hours), stopping at Pimba ($122, seven hours), Glendambo ($153, 8¼ hours) and Coober Pedy ($197, 10½ hours). Online fares are cheaper.

CAR

The Stuart Hwy is sealed from Port Augusta to Darwin. In SA, fuel and accommodation are available at Pimba (171km from Port Augusta), Glendambo (285km), Coober Pedy (535km), Cadney Homestead (689km) and Marla (771km). Pimba, Coober Pedy and Marla have 24-hour fuel sales. The Oodnadatta Track, Birdsville Track or Strzelecki Track are subject to closure after heavy rains – check conditions with the Royal Automobile Association in Adelaide, or online at www.dpti.sa.gov.au/OutbackRoads.

TRAIN

The *Ghan* train runs through the SA outback between Adelaide and Alice Springs; see p1091 for details.

Woomera

POP 450

A 6km detour off the Stuart Hwy from Pimba (population 50; 485km from Adelaide), Woomera began in 1947 as HQ for experimental British rocket and nuclear tests at notorious sites like Maralinga. Local indigenous tribes suffered greatly from nuclear fallout. These days Woomera is an eerie, oddly artificial government town that's still an active Department of Defence test site.

Rocket into the **Woomera Heritage & Visitor Information Centre** (☎08-8673 7042; www.woomera.com.au; Dewrang Ave; museum adult/child $6/3; ⊙9am-5pm Mar-Nov, 10am-2pm Dec-Feb), with its displays on Woomera's past and present (plus a bowling alley!). Just across the car park is the **Lions Club Aircraft & Missile Park**, studded with jets and rocket remnants.

Built to house rocket scientists, the **Eldo Hotel** (☎08-8673 7867; www.eldohotel.com.au; Kotara Ave; d from $95; ❄) has comfortable motel-style rooms in a couple of 1960s buildings, and serves à la carte meals in an urbane bistro (mains $16 to $32, serving noon to 2pm and 6pm to 8.30pm). Try the kangaroo bratwurst snags!

Continue north through Woomera for 90km (sealed road) and you'll hit **Roxby Downs** (www.roxbydowns.com), population 4500, a bizarrely affluent desert town built to service the massive Olympic Dam Mine, which digs up untold amounts of copper, silver, gold and uranium.

Woomera to Coober Pedy

Around 115km northwest of Pimba and 245km shy of Coober Pedy, middle-of-nowhere Glendambo (population 30) was established in 1982 as a Stuart Hwy service centre. This is the last fuel stop before Coober Pedy.

You can bunk down at the oasis-like **Glendambo Hotel-Motel** (☎08-8672 1030; Stuart Hwy; unpowered/powered sites $18/22, d $99-120; ❄@≋), which has bars, a restaurant and a bunch of decent motel units. Outside are dusty camp sites; inside are meaty mains at the bistro ($16 to $30, serving noon to 2pm and 6pm to 8pm).

North of Glendambo the Stuart Hwy enters the government-owned Woomera Prohibited Area – the highway itself is unrestricted, but don't go a-wanderin' now, y'hear?

Coober Pedy

POP 3500

Coming into Coober Pedy the dry, barren desert suddenly becomes riddled with holes and adjunct piles of dirt – reputedly more than a million around the township. The reason for all this rabid digging is opals, which have made this small town a mining mecca. This isn't to say it's also a tourist mecca – with swarms of flies, no trees, 50°C summer days, subzero winter nights, cave-dwelling locals and rusty car wrecks in front yards, you might think you've arrived in a wasteland. But it sure is interesting!

> **DESERT PARKS PASS**
>
> To explore the outback environment consider purchasing a **Desert Parks Pass** (☎1800 816 078; http://forms.bizgate.sa.gov.au/deh/parkspasses/desert.htm; per car $150), allowing access to seven outback parks (including camping), with a map and handbook. Pick one up from the DEWNR in Adelaide or Post Augusta, order one online and have it mailed to you (Australia only), or see www.environment.sa.gov.au/parks/park_entry_fees/parks_pass_outlets for regional pass agents in the Flinders Ranges and SA outback.

Coober Pedy

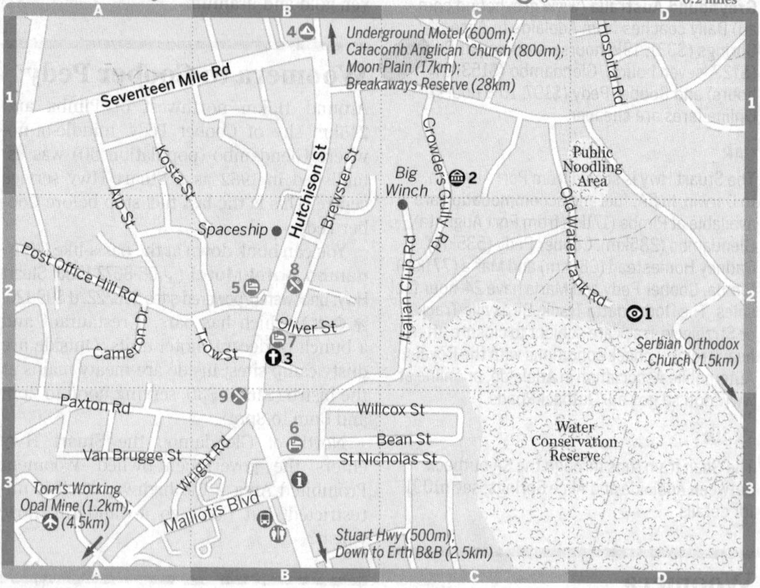

Coober Pedy

Sights

1 Faye's Underground Display Home.....D2
2 Old Timers Mine.....C1
3 St Peter & Paul Catholic Church.....B2

Sleeping

4 BIG4 Oasis Coober Pedy.....B1
5 Desert Cave Hotel.....B2
6 Mud Hut Motel.....B3
7 Radeka Downunder.....B2

Eating

8 John's Pizza Bar.....B2
9 Tom & Mary's Greek Taverna.....B3
Umberto's.....(see 5)

Coober Pedy is actually very cosmopolitan, with 44 nationalities represented. Few locals make their living solely from mining, so there's a lot of 'career diversification' here (...the dude who drives the airport bus also loads the baggage, mans the hotel reception desk and works his opal claim on weekends).

The surrounding desert is jaw-droppingly desolate, a fact not overlooked by international filmmakers who've come here to shoot end-of-the-world epics like *Mad Max III, Red Planet, Ground Zero, Pitch Black* and the slightly more believable *Priscilla, Queen of the Desert.*

Sights & Activities

Opal Mining

There are hundreds of working opal mines around town, the elusive gems at the fore of everyone's consciousness. If you're keen for a fossick, tour operators or locals may invite you out to their claim to 'noodle' through the mullock (waste pile) for stones. Watch out for unmarked shafts, and never wander around the fields at night.

Tom's Working Opal Mine MINE

(www.tomsworkingopalmine.com.au; Lot 1993, Stuart Hwy; tours adult/child/family $25/10/55; ⏲tours 8am, 10am, 2pm & 4pm) The best place to check out a working excavation is Tom's, 3km southwest of town: miners continue their search for the big vein while visitors noodle for small fortunes. Self-guided tours adult/child $10/5.

Old Timers Mine MUSEUM

(www.oldtimersmine.com; 1 Crowders Gully Rd; self-guided tours adult/child $15/1; ⏲9am-5pm) The interesting warren was mined in 1916 but was then hidden by the miners. The mine was rediscovered when a dugout home punched through into the labyrinth of tunnels, which now makes a great tour. There's also a museum, a re-created 1920s underground home, and free mining-equipment demos daily (9.30am, 1.30pm and 3.30pm).

Dugout Homes & Churches

It gets hot here in summer – it makes sense to live underground! Even if it's a stinker outside, subterranean temperatures never rise above 23°C, and air-conditioning isn't necessary. The same goes for churches (miners are big on faith and hope).

Faye's Underground Display Home UNDERGROUND HOME
(Old Water Tank Rd; adult/child $5/2.50; ⌚8am-5pm Mon-Sat Mar-Oct) Faye's was hand dug by three women in the 1960s. It's a little chintzy, but the living-room swimming pool is a winner!

Serbian Orthodox Church CHURCH
(Saint Elijah Dr, off Flinders St; admission $5; ⌚24hr) The largest and most impressive underground church, with rock-wall carvings. It's about 8km south of town.

St Peter & Paul Catholic Church CHURCH
(cnr Halliday Pl & Hutchison St; ⌚10am-4pm) FREE Coober Pedy's first church still has a sweet appeal.

Catacomb Anglican Church CHURCH
(Catacomb Rd; ⌚24hr) FREE Remote sermons beamed onto a big screen.

Other Sights

You can't miss the **Big Winch**, from which there are sweeping views over Coober Pedy and towards the Breakaways. An optimistic 'if' painted on the side of the big bucket sums up the town's spirit.

Leftover sets and props from the movies that have been filmed here are littered around town. Check out the amazing **spaceship** from *Pitch Black*, which has crash landed outside the Opal Cave shop on Hutchison St.

Tours

Arid Areas Tours WILDERNESS
(☎08-8672 3008; www.aridareastours.com; 2/4/6hr tours per 2 people $100/200/420) Offers 4WD tours around town, extending to the Painted Desert and the Breakaways.

Desert Cave Tours SIGHTSEEING
(☎08-8672 5688; www.desertcave.com.au; 4hr tour per person $90) A convenient highlight tour taking in the town, the Dog Fence, Breakaways and Moon Plain. Also on offer are four-hour 'Down 'N' Dirty' opal-digging tours (per person $105).

Mail Run Tour GUIDED TOUR
(☎08-8672 5226, 1800 069 911; www.mailruntour.com) Coober Pedy–based full-day mail-run tours through the desert and along the Oodnadatta Track to Oodnadatta and William Creek return ($195).

Opal Air SCENIC FLIGHTS
(☎08 8670 7997; www.opalair.com.au; flights per person from $470) Half-day scenic flights ex-Coober Pedy winging over Lake Eyre, William Creek and the Painted Desert.

Oasis Tours SIGHTSEEING
(☎08-8672 5169; 3hr tour adult/child $45/22.50) A good budget tour taking in the major town sights plus a little fossicking. Two-hour sunset Breakaways tours ($50/25) also swing by the Dog Fence and the Moon Plain. Run by BIG4 Oasis Coober Pedy caravan park.

Coober Pedy Tours SIGHTSEEING
(☎08-8672 5223; www.cooberpedytours.com; 4hr tour adult/child $70/35) A wandering tour that includes an underground home, fossicking, the Breakaways, an underground church, the Dog Fence and an active opal mine. Stargazing and Breakaways sunset tours also available. Run by Radeka Downunder accommodation.

Sleeping

Down to Erth B&B B&B $$
(☎08-8672 5762; www.downtoerth.com.au; Monument Rd; d incl breakfast $160, extra person $25;) A real dugout gem 4km from town, where you can have your own subterranean two-bedroom bunker. There's a shady plunge pool for cooling off after a day exploring the Earth, and a telescope for exploring the universe.

Underground Motel MOTEL $$
(☎08-8672 5324; www.theundergroundmotel.com.au; Catacomb Rd; s/d/f incl breakfast from $125/135/182;) Choose between standard rooms and suites (with separate lounge and kitchen) at this serviceable spot with a broad Breakaways panorama. It's a fair walk from town, but friendly and affordable.

Desert Cave Hotel HOTEL $$$
(☎08-8672 5688; www.desertcave.com.au; Lot 1 Hutchison St; s & d $250, extra person $35; @) For a much-needed shot of desert

luxury – plus a pool, gym, in-house movies, formidable minibar and the excellent Umberto's restaurant. Staff are supercourteous and there are plenty of tours on offer. Above-ground rooms also available.

Riba's CAMPGROUND $
(☎08-8672 5614; www.camp-underground.com.au; William Creek Rd; underground sites $30, above-ground unpowered/powered sites $20/28, s & d $60; @) Around 5km from town, Riba's offers the unique option of underground camping! Extras include an underground TV lounge, cell-like underground budget rooms and a nightly opal-mine tour (adult $22, free for campers).

Mud Hut Motel MOTEL $$
(☎08-8672 3003; www.mudhutmotel.com.au; St Nicholas St; d/2-bedroom apt $130/220; ❄) The rustic-looking walls here are actually rammed earth, and despite the grubby name this is one of the cleanest places in town. The two-bedroom apartments have cooktops and fridges. Central location.

Radeka Downunder HOSTEL $
(☎08-8672 5223, 1800 633 891; www.radekadownunder.com.au; 1 Oliver St; dm $35, d & tw $85, motel units $130; ❄@) The owners started excavating this place in 1960 – they haven't found much opal, but have ended up with a beaut backpackers! On multiple levels down 6.5m below the surface are Coober Pedy's best budget beds, plus good individual rooms and motel units. The shared kitchen is handy for self-caterers, and there's a bar, barbecue, snooker room and laundry.

BIG4 Oasis Coober Pedy CARAVAN PARK $
(☎08-8672 5169; www.oasiscooberpedy.com.au; Seventeen Mile Rd; unpowered/powered sites $30/33, r/vans from $58/68, cabins $106-126; ❄@) There are a few places to camp in Coober Pedy, but this place is reasonably central (a little way down the main street across from the drive-in cinema) and has the most shade, plus a swimming pool. An affordable tour runs daily.

Eating

John's Pizza Bar ITALIAN $
(☎08-8672 5561; www.johnspizzabarandrestaurant.com.au; Shop 24, 1 Hutchison St; meals $7-31; ⏲9am-10pm) Serving up table-sized pizzas, hearty pastas and heat-beating gelato, you can't go past John's. Grills, salads, burgers, yiros, and fish and chips also available. Sit inside, order some takeaways, or pull up a seat with the bedraggled pot plants by the street.

Tom & Mary's Greek Taverna GREEK $$
(☎08-8672 5622; Shop 4/2 Hutchison St; meals $15-25; ⏲6-9pm) This busy Greek diner does everything from a superb moussaka to yiros, seafood, Greek salads and pastas with Hellenic zing. Sit back with a cold retsina as the red sun sets on another dusty day in Coober Pedy.

Umberto's MEDITERRANEAN $$$
(☎08-8672 5688; www.desertcave.com.au; Lot 1 Hutchison St; mains $28-46; ⏲6-9pm) The Desert Cave Hotel's rooftop restaurant maintains the quality with first-class dishes such as wallaby shanks with vegetables and char-grilled tomato stew, and its 'Essential Tastes of the Outback' platter: char-grilled kangaroo, camel, emu and beef with bush chutney and hand-cut fries.

Information

Coober Pedy Visitor Information Centre (☎08-8672 4617, 1800 637 076; www.opalcapitaloftheworld.com.au; Hutchison St, Council Offices; ⏲8.30am-5pm Mon-Fri, 10am-1pm Sat & Sun) Free 30-minute internet access, history displays and comprehensive tour and accommodation info.

Coober Pedy Hospital (☎08-8672 5009; www.countryhealthsa.sa.gov.au; Lot 89 Hospital Rd; ⏲24hr) Accident and emergency.

24-hour Water Dispenser (Hutchison St; per 30L 20c) Fill your canteens opposite the BIG4 Oasis Coober Pedy caravan park.

Getting There & Around

Budget (☎08-8672 5333; www.budget.com.au; Coober Pedy Airport) Cars, 4WDs and camping vehicles from around $80 per day.

Cedrent (☎08-8672 3003; www.cedrent.com.au; St Nicholas St, Mud Hut Motel) Stationwagons, utes and 4WDs from $125 per day. Based at the Mud Hut Motel.

Coober Pedy to Marla

The **Breakaways Reserve** is a stark but colourful area of arid hills and scarps 33km away on a rough road north of Coober Pedy – turn off the highway 22km west of town. You can drive to a lookout in a conventional vehicle and check out the white-and-yellow mesa called the **Castle**, which featured in *Mad Max III* and *Priscilla, Queen of the Desert*. Entry permits (per person $2.20) are available at the Coober Pedy visitor information centre.

An interesting 70km loop on mainly unsealed road from Coober Pedy takes in the

Breakaways, the **Dog Fence** (built to keep dingos out of southeastern Australia) and the table-like **Moon Plain** on the Coober Pedy–Oodnadatta Rd. If it's been raining, you'll need a 4WD.

If you're heading for Oodnadatta, turning off the Stuart Hwy at Cadney Homestead (151km north of Coober Pedy) gives you a shorter run on dirt roads than the routes via Marla or Coober Pedy. En route you pass through the aptly named **Painted Desert** (bring your camera).

Cadney Homestead (☎08-8670 7994; cadney@bigpond.com; Stuart Hwy; unpowered/powered sites $15/25, d cabin/motel $60/115; ❄@🏊) itself has caravan and tent sites, serviceable motel rooms and basic cabins (no linen, shared facilities), plus petrol, puncture repairs, takeaways, cold beer, ATM, swimming pool...

In mulga scrub about 82km from Cadney Homestead, Marla (population 245) replaced Oodnadatta as the official regional centre when the *Ghan* railway line was rerouted in 1980. **Marla Travellers Rest** (☎08-8670 7001; www.marla.com.au; Stuart Hwy; unpowered/powered sites/cabins $15/25/40, d $100-120; ❄@🏊) has fuel, motel rooms, camp sites, pool, a cafe and a supermarket.

Frontier-style Mintabie (population 250) is an opal field settlement on Aboriginal land 35km west of Marla – there's a general store, restaurant and basic caravan park here.

From Marla the NT border is another 180km, with a fuel stop 20km beyond that in Kulgera.

Oodnadatta Track

The legendary, lonesome Oodnadatta Track is an unsealed, 615km road between Marla on the Stuart Hwy and Marree in the northern Flinders Ranges. The track traces the route of the old Overland Telegraph Line and the defunct Great Northern Railway. **Lake Eyre** (the world's sixth-largest lake and usually dry) is just off the road. The landscape here is amazingly diverse: floodplains south of Marla, saltbush flats around William Creek, dunes and red gibber plains near Coward Springs. Bring a 4WD – the track is often passable in a regular car, but it gets bumpy, muddy, dusty and potholed.

ℹ Information

Before you hit the Oodnadatta – a rough, rocky and sandy track that's subject to closure after rains – check track conditions with the Coober Pedy visitor information centre, the Royal Automobile Association in Adelaide, or online at www.dpti.sa.gov.au/OutbackRoads.

If you're finding the dust and dirt heavy going, there are escape routes to Coober Pedy on the Stuart Hwy from William Creek and Oodnadatta. Fuel, accommodation and meals are available at Marla, Oodnadatta, William Creek and Marree.

See the *Oodnadatta Track – String of Springs* booklet from the South Australian Tourism Commission, and the *Travel the Oodnadatta Track* brochure produced by the Pink Roadhouse for detailed track info.

Oodnadatta to William Creek

Around 209km from Marla, **Oodnadatta** (population 280) is where the main road and the old railway line diverged. Here you'll find the **Pink Roadhouse** (☎08-8670 7822, 1800 802 074; www.pinkroadhouse.com.au; ⏲8am-5.30pm), a good source of track info and meals (try the impressive 'Oodnaburger'). The roadhouse also has an attached **caravan park** (unpowered/powered sites from $22/30, budget cabins d/f from $65/125, self-contained cabins d from $110; ❄@🏊), which has basic camping through to self-contained cabins. Note that one of the roadhouse managers passed away in 2012 – at the time of writing the future of the business was uncertain.

In another 70km you'll hit William Creek (population six), best enjoyed in the weather-beaten **William Creek Hotel** (☎08-8670 7880; www.williamcreekhotel.net.au; William Creek; unpowered/powered sites $25/35, cabins s/d $35/70, hotel $110/140; ❄), an iconic 1887 pub festooned with photos, business cards, old licence plates and money stapled to the walls. There's also a dusty campground and modest cabins and motel rooms. Also on offer are fuel, cold beer, basic provisions, all-day meals (mains $16 to $32) and spare tyres.

William Creek is also a base for **Wrightsair** (☎08-8670 7962; www.wrightsair.com.au; William Creek), which runs scenic flights over Lake Eyre (per adult/child $260/234).

Coward Springs to Marree

Some 130km shy of Marree, **Coward Springs Campground** (☎08-8675 8336; www.cowardsprings.com.au; unpowered sites adult/child $10/5) is the first stop at the old Coward

Springs railway siding. You can soak yourself silly in a **natural hot-spring tub** (per person $2) made from old rail sleepers, or take a six-day **camel trek** (per person $1500) to Lake Eyre from here.

Next stop is the lookout over **Lake Eyre South**, which is 12m below sea level. For a Lake Eyre water-level report, see www.lakeeyreyc.com. About 60km from Marree is the **Mutonia Sculpture Park** (24hr) FREE, featuring a jaunty car-engine hitchhiker and several planes welded together with their tails buried in the ground to form 'Planehenge'.

Marree (population 100) was once a vital hub for Afghan camel teams and the Great Northern Railway, and is the end (or start) of both the Oodnadatta Track and Birdsville Track. The big stone 1883 **Marree Hotel** (08-8675 8344; www.marreehotel.com.au; Railway Tce; unpowered sites free, pub s/d $90/110, cabins $110/130;) has decent pub rooms, brand new en-suite cabins and free camp sites! Marree is also a good place to organise scenic flights (1½ hours around $270): try **GSL Aviation** (1300 475 247; wwwgslaviation.com.au) or **Aus Air Services** (08-8675 8212; www.ausairservices.com.au).

From the air you'll get a good look at **Marree Man**, a 4.2km-long outline of a Pitjantjatjara Aboriginal warrior etched into the desert near Lake Eyre. It was only discovered in 1988, and no-one seems to know who created it. It's eroding rapidly these days.

From Marree it's 80km to Lyndhurst, where the bitumen kicks back in, then 33km down to Copley at the northern end of the Flinders Ranges.

Birdsville Track

This old droving trail runs 517km from Marree in SA to Birdsville, just across the border in Queensland, passing between the Simpson Desert to the east and Sturt Stony Desert to the west. It's one of Australia's classic outback routes. For road conditions see www.dpti.sa.gov.au/OutbackRoads (...a 4WD is the best way to go, regardless).

Strzelecki Track

Meandering through the sand hills of the **Strzelecki Regional Reserve** (www.environment.sa.gov.au), the Strzelecki Track spans 460km from Lyndhurst, 80km south of Marree, to the tiny outpost of Innamincka. Discovery of oil and gas at Moomba (a town closed to travellers) saw the upgrading of the road from a camel track to a decent dirt road, though heavy transport travelling along it has created bone-rattling corrugations. The newer Moomba–Strzelecki Track is better kept, but longer and less interesting than the old track, which follows Strzelecki Creek. Accommodation, provisions and fuel are available at Lyndhurst and Innamincka, but there's nothing in between.

Innamincka

POP 130

On Cooper Creek at the northern end of the Strzelecki Track, Innamincka is near where Burke and Wills' ill-fated 1860 expedition expired. The famous Dig Tree marks the expedition's base camp, and although the word 'dig' is no longer visible you can still see the expedition's camp number. The Dig Tree is over the Queensland border, though memorials and markers – commemorating where Burke and Wills died, and where sole survivor King was found – are downstream in SA. There's also a memorial where AW Howitt's rescue party made its base on the creek.

Cooper Creek only has water in it after heavy rains across central Queensland, but it has deep, permanent waterholes and the semipermanent **Coongie Lakes**, which are part of the **Innamincka Regional Reserve** (www.environment.sa.gov.au). Prior to European settlement the area had a large Aboriginal population, so relics such as middens and grinding stones can be seen around the area.

The **Innamincka Trading Post** (08-8675 9900; www.innamminckatp.com.au; South Tce; 9am-4pm Mar-Nov, 10am-3pm Dec-Feb) sells fuel, Desert Parks passes, camping permits and provisions, including fresh bread and rolls.

The old-fashioned **Innamincka Hotel** (08-8675 9901; www.theoutback.com.au/innaminckahotel; 2 South Tce; s/d $130/155;) has decent motel-style rooms and hefty counter meals (mains $20 to $30, serving noon to 2pm and 6pm to 8pm).

There are plenty of shady **bush camping sites** (per car $25) along Cooper Creek – Innamincka Trading Post sells permits, or you can use a Desert Parks Pass. You can use the hot shower ($2) and toilet outside the Trading Post.

Darwin to Uluru

Includes ➡

Best Places to Eat

- Saffrron (p828)
- Char Restaurant (p827)
- Litchfield Cafe (p839)
- Fernanda's Café & Restaurant (p869)
- Hanuman (p880)

Best Places to Stay

- Kings Creek Station (p888)
- Ormiston Gorge Camping Ground (p887)
- Rum Jungle Bungalows (p838)
- Lakeview Park (p852)
- Mt Bundy Station (p839)

Why Go?

From the tropics to the deserts, the Northern Territory (NT) is a splendid place to be during Australia's winter months. Access is easy, with good roads and air connections; however, the vast distances ensure a good dose of adventure accompanies every visit.

NT's tropical Top End has an undeniable wild side. Crocodiles lurk in the rivers, and the air is alive with birds. Here you will find unparalleled opportunities to experience timeless indigenous culture and behold ethereal rock art. The cosmopolitan capital of Darwin is Australia's doorstep to Asia and celebrates its multicultural mix with delicious fusion cuisine and a relaxed tropical vibe.

The Red Centre is Australia's heartland boasting the iconic attractions of Uluru and Kata Tjuta, plus an enigmatic central desert culture that continues to produce extraordinary abstract art. And delighting travellers with its eccentric offerings, pioneering spirit and weathered mountain setting, is Alice Springs, the city at the centre of a continent.

When to Go

Darwin

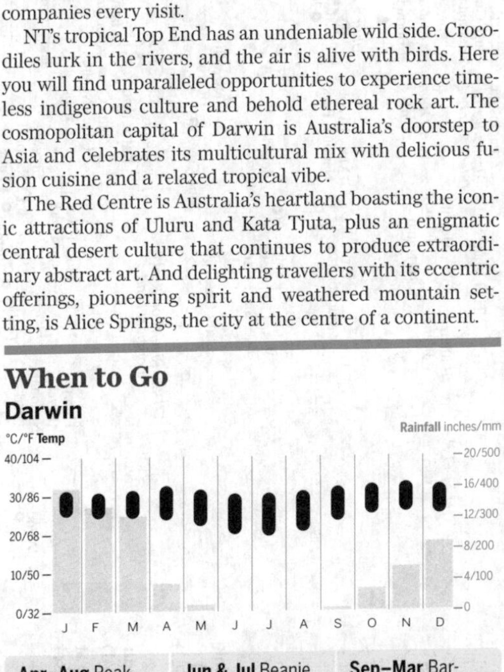

Apr–Aug Peak season with lower humidity up north and cooler temperatures in the Red Centre.

Jun & Jul Beanie Festival and Camel Cup in Alice, Beer Can Regatta and Fringe Festival in Darwin.

Sep–Mar Barramundi fishing heats up as the Wet turns the Top End into a watery wonderland.

Darwin to Uluru Highlights

1. Witness the wonderful **Uluru** (p895) and **Kata Tjuta** (p896) at sunset
2. Paddle a canoe beneath soaring sandstone ramparts in **Nitmiluk (Katherine Gorge) National Park** (p861)
3. Cruise with huge crocodiles at **Kakadu National Park** (p841)
4. Sample a satay at **Mindil Beach Sunset Market** (p830)
5. Hike past prehistoric ferns through bizarre beehive rock formations to **Kings Canyon** (p888)
6. Plunge into a crystal-clear rock pool at **Litchfield National Park** (p838)

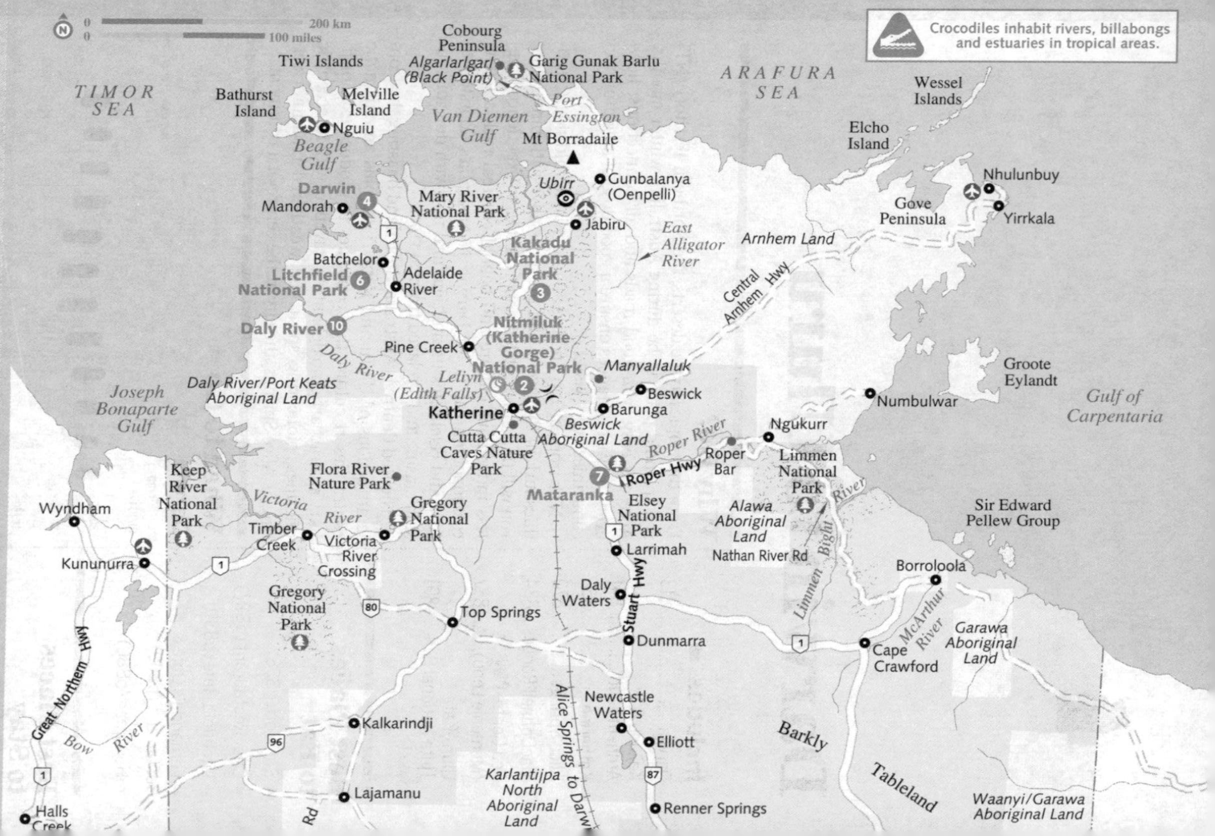

7 Soak in a thermal spring at **Mataranka** (p865)

8 Gaze at ghost gums, budgerigars and wallabies at **West MacDonnell National Park** (p885)

9 Wander among the boulders at **Devil's Marbles Conservation Reserve** (p869)

10 Battle a barra and catch your daily limit at **Daly River** (p839)

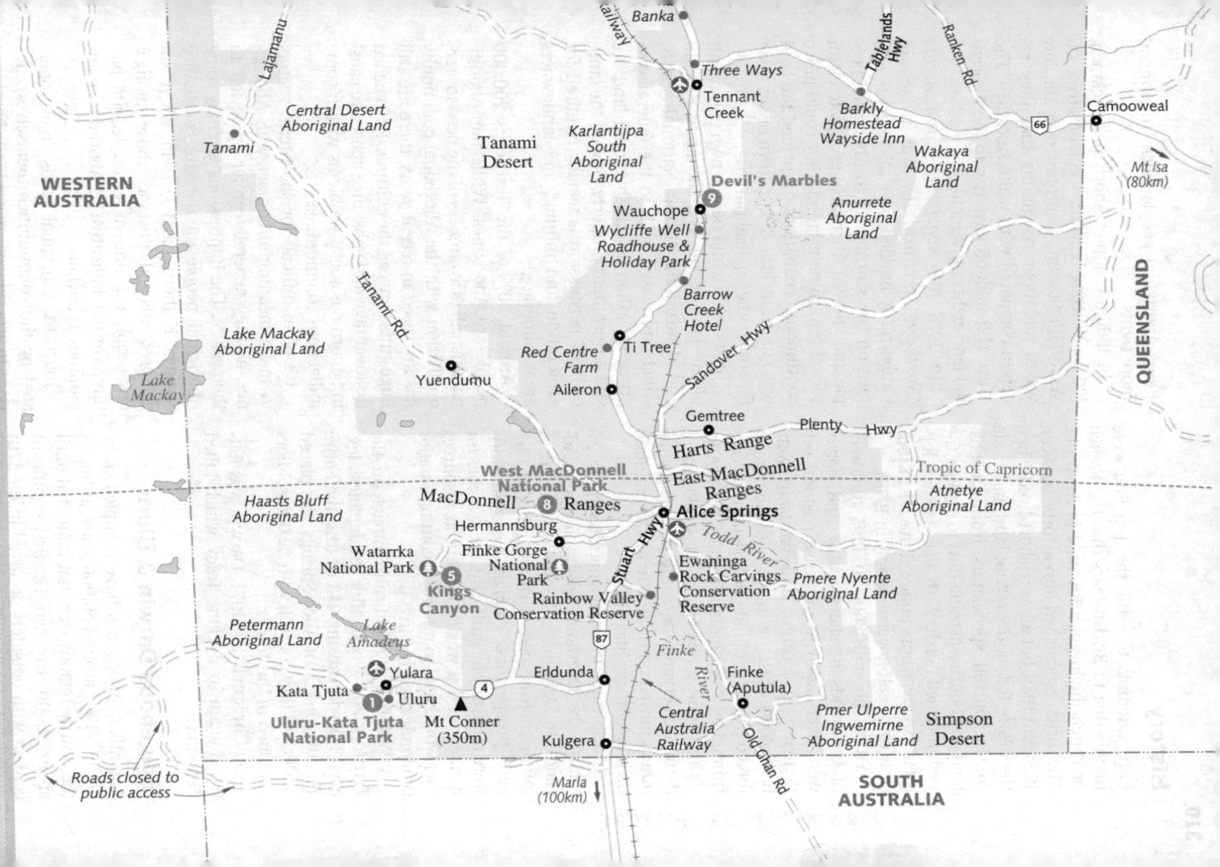

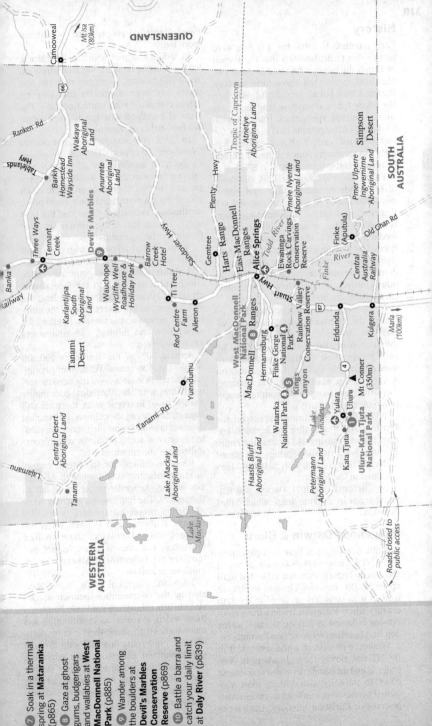

History

Early attempts to settle the Top End were mainly due to British fears that the French or Dutch might get a foothold in Australia. The Brits established three forts between 1824 and 1838, but all were short-lived. Then the desire for more grazing land and trade routes spurred speculators from Queensland and South Australia (SA) to explore the vast untamed north. With an eye to development, SA governors annexed the NT in 1863 (it became self-governing only in 1978).

From the mid-1860s to 1895 hundreds of thousands of sheep, cattle and horses were overlanded to immense pastoral settlements. Dislocation and hardship were bedfellows of the industry, with Aborigines forced from their lands and pastoralists confronted by a swath of difficulties. Some Aborigines took employment as stockmen or domestic servants on cattle stations, while others moved on in an attempt to maintain their customary lifestyle.

In the early 1870s, during digging to establish the Overland Telegraph (from Adelaide to Darwin), gold was discovered. A minor rush ensued, with an influx of Chinese prospectors. Though the gold finds were relatively insignificant, the searches for it unearthed a wealth of natural resources that would lead to mining becoming a major economic presence in SA.

WWII had a significant impact on the Territory. Just weeks after the Japanese levelled Darwin causing 243 deaths, the entire Territory north of Alice Springs was placed under military control, with 32,000 soldiers stationed in the Top End.

On Christmas Eve 1974, Darwin was flattened again by Cyclone Tracy, which killed 71 people.

Indigenous Darwin & Uluru

Australian Aborigines have occupied parts of the NT for around 60,000 years, although the central regions were not inhabited until about 24,000 years ago. The first significant contact with outsiders occurred in the 17th century when Macassan traders from modern-day Sulawesi in Indonesia came to the Top End to collect *trepang* (sea cucumber).

While the process of white settlement in the NT was slower than elsewhere in Australia, it had an equally troubled and violent effect. By the early 20th century, most Aboriginal people were confined to government reserves or Christian missions. During the 1960s Aboriginal people began to demand more rights.

In 1966 a group of Aboriginal stockmen, led by Vincent Lingiari, went on strike on Wave Hill Station, to protest over the low wages and poor conditions that they received compared with white stockmen. The Wave Hill walk-off gave rise to the Aboriginal land-rights movement.

In 1976 the *Aboriginal Land Rights (Northern Territory) Act* was passed in Canberra. It handed over all reserves and mission lands in the NT to Aboriginal people and allowed Aboriginal groups to claim vacant government land if they could prove continuous occupation – provided the land wasn't already leased, in a town or set aside for some other special purpose.

Today, Aboriginal people own about half of the land in the NT, including Kakadu and Uluru-Kata Tjuta National Parks, which are leased back to the federal government. Minerals on Aboriginal land are still government property, though the landowners' permission is usually required for exploration and mining, and landowners are remunerated.

Around 30% of the Territory's 200,000 people are Aborigines. While non-Aboriginal Australia's awareness of the need for reconciliation with the Aboriginal community has increased in recent years, there are still huge gulfs between the cultures. Entrenched disadvantage and substance abuse are causing enormous social problems within some indigenous communities.

It's often difficult for short-term visitors to make meaningful contact with Aborigines, as they generally prefer to be left to themselves. The impressions given by some Aboriginal people on the streets of Alice Springs, Katherine and Darwin, where social problems and substance abuse among a few people can present an unpleasant picture, are not indicative of Aboriginal communities as a whole.

Tours to Aboriginal lands (most operated by the communities themselves) and visits to arts centres are gradually becoming more widely available, as communities feel more inclined to share their culture. Benefits are numerous: financial gain through self-determined endeavour, and educating non-Aboriginal people about their culture and customs, which helps to alleviate the problems caused by the ignorance and misunderstandings of the past.

National Parks

The NT is all about its national parks; it has some of the largest and most famous natural areas in Australia, including Kakadu, Uluru-Kata Tjuta and Nitmiluk. Parks Australia (p48) manages Kakadu and Uluru-Kata Tjuta, while the NT's Department of Natural Resources, Environment, the Arts and Sport (p812) manages the other parks and produces fact sheets, available online or from its various offices.

Activities

Bushwalking

The Territory's national parks offer well-maintained tracks of different lengths and degrees of difficulty that introduce walkers to various environments and wildlife habitats. Carry plenty of water, take rubbish out with you and stick to the tracks.

Top bushwalks include the Barrk Sandstone Bushwalk in Kakadu National Park, the Jatbula Trail in Nitmiluk (Katherine Gorge) National Park, Ormiston Pound in the West MacDonnell Ranges, Trephina Gorge in the East MacDonnell Ranges, and the Valley of the Winds at Kata Tjuta.

Fishing

No permit is required to fish the Territory's waterways, though there are limits on the minimum size and number of fish per person. Travel NT produces the excellent *The EsseNTial Fishing Travel Guide* booklet (free from information centres), and publishes some info online (www.travelnt.com). The **Amateur Fishermen's Association of the Northern Territory** (www.afant.com.au) also has online info.

The feisty barramundi lures most fisherfolk to the Top End, particularly to Borroloola, Daly River and Mary River. Increasingly, the recreational-fishing fraternity encourages catch and release to maintain sustainable fish levels. Loads of tours offer transport and gear and start at $250 per person.

Swimming

The cool waterfalls, waterholes and rejuvenating thermal pools throughout the NT are perfect spots to soak. Litchfield National Park, in the Top End, and the West MacDonnell Ranges, in the Centre, are particularly rewarding.

Saltwater crocodiles inhabit both salt and fresh waters in the Top End, though there are quite a few safe, natural swimming holes. Before taking the plunge, be sure to obey the signs and seek local advice. If in doubt, don't risk it.

Box jellyfish seasonally infest the sea around Darwin; swimming at the city's beaches is safest from May to September.

Wildlife Watching

The best places for guaranteed wildlife sightings, from bilbies to emus, are at the excellent Territory Wildlife Park outside Darwin and the Alice Springs Desert Park.

If you prefer to see wildlife in the wild, there are few guarantees; many of the region's critters are nocturnal. One exception is at Kakadu, where you'll certainly see crocodiles at Cahill's Crossing or Yellow Waters and numerous species of birds at its wealth of wetlands. In the arid Centre you'll see wallabies, reptiles and eagles. Good places to keep an eye out include the West MacDonnell Ranges and Watarrka (Kings Canyon) National Park.

Tours

Even staunch independent travellers entrust some hard-earned time and money to a carefully selected tour. Tours can provide unmatched insights and access to the Territory, and they support local industry. Uluru Aboriginal Tours (p891) offer good tours of the famed rock.

World Expeditions ADVENTURE
(☎1300 720 000; www.worldexpeditions.com) Several Kakadu, Katherine Gorge and Arnhem Land trips ex-Darwin, and various options along the Larapinta Trail ex-Alice Springs.

Kakadu Animal Tracks INDIGENOUS
(www.animaltracks.com.au) Enviro-focused bush-tucker tour in Kakadu; profits support the local Buffalo Farm, which donates food to local communities.

Conservation Volunteers Australia VOLUNTEERING
(CVA; ☎1800 032 501; www.conservationvolunteers.com.au) Nature-based volunteer projects that double as tours: weeding, walking-track maintenance and wildlife surveys. Day trips are free; multiday projects cost from around $50 per night including meals, accommodation and travel.

Magela Cultural & Heritage Tours INDIGENOUS
(www.kakadutours.com.au) Aboriginal owned; runs tours into Arnhem Land and around Kakadu.

Tiwi Tours INDIGENOUS
Trips with local communities to the Tiwi Islands.

Willis's Walkabouts BUSHWALKING
(☎08-8985 2134; www.bushwalkingholidays.com.au) Small-group multiday guided hikes, carrying your own gear, to Kakadu, Litchfield, Watarrka and the West MacDonnells.

Seasonal Work

The majority of working-holiday opportunities in the NT for backpackers are in fruit picking, pastoral station work, labouring and hospitality.

Most work is picking mangoes and melons on plantations between Darwin and Katherine. Mango harvesting employs up to 2000 workers each season (late September to November). Station-work wannabes are generally required to have some skills (ie a trade or some experience), as with labouring and hospitality. Employers usually ask workers to commit for at least a month (sometimes three months).

Information

RESOURCES

Department of Natural Resources, Environment, the Arts and Sport (☎08-8999 5511; www.nretas.nt.gov.au/national-parks-and-reserves/) Details on NT parks and reserves, including fact sheets.

Exploroz (www.exploroz.com) Handy user-generated site for fuel locations and pricing, weather forecasts, road conditions and more.

Road Report (www.ntlis.nt.gov.au/roadreport) Road-conditions report.

Tourism Top End (www.tourismtopend.com.au) Darwin-based tourism body.

Travel NT (www.travelnt.com) Official tourism site.

ABORIGINAL LAND PERMITS

Permits may be required to enter Aboriginal land, unless you are using recognised public roads that cross Aboriginal territory. Permits can take four to six weeks to be processed, although for the Injalak Arts Centre at Gunbalanya (Oenpelli) they are generally issued on the spot in Jabiru.

Central Land Council (www.clc.org.au) Alice Springs (p882); Tennant Creek (☎08-8962 2343; 63 Patterson St, Tennant Creek) Deals with all land south of a line drawn between Kununurra (Western Australia) and Mt Isa (Queensland).

Northern Land Council (www.nlc.org.au) Darwin (☎08-8920 5100; www.nlc.org.au; 45 Mitchell St); Jabiru (☎08-8979 2410; Flinders St, Jabiru; ⏰8am-4.30pm Mon-Fri); Katherine (☎08-8971 9802; 5 Katherine Tce) Responsible for land north of a line drawn between Kununurra (Western Australia) and Mt Isa (Queensland).

Tiwi Land Council (☎08-8919 4305; www.tiwilandcouncil.com) Permits for the Tiwi Islands.

Getting There & Around

AIR

International and domestic flights arrive at and depart from **Darwin International Airport** (www.darwinairport.com.au; Henry Wrigley Dr, Marrara). There are also flights between Darwin, Alice Springs and Uluru. Airlines operating here include:

Airnorth (www.airnorth.com.au) To/from East Timor, and to Arnhem Land, Broome, Perth, Kununurra and the Gold Coast.

Jetstar (www.jetstar.com.au) Services most major Australian cities and several South-East Asian cities.

Qantas (www.qantas.com.au) To/from Asia and Europe, and servicing all major Australian cities.

Virgin Australia (www.virginaustralia.com) Direct flights between Darwin and Brisbane, Melbourne, Perth and Sydney.

BUS

Greyhound Australia (www.greyhound.com.au) regularly services the main road routes throughout the Territory, including side trips to Kakadu and Uluru.

An alternative is tour-bus companies such as AAT Kings, and backpacker buses that cover vast distances while savouring the sights along the way.

CAR

Having your own vehicle in the NT means you can travel at your own pace and branch off the main roads to access less-visited places. To truly explore, you'll need a well-prepared 4WD vehicle and some outback nous. The **Automobile Association of the Northern Territory** (AANT; www.aant.com.au; 79-81 Smith St, Darwin; ⏰9am-5pm Mon-Fri) can advise on preparation and additional resources; members of automobile associations in other states have reciprocal rights.

Many roads are open to conventional cars and campervans, which can be hired in Darwin and Alice Springs and can work out to be quite economical when split by a group.

Some driving conditions are particular to the NT. While traffic may be light and roads dead straight, distances between places are long. Watch out for the four great NT road hazards: speed (maximum speed on the open highway is now 130km/h), driver fatigue, road trains and animals (driving at night is particularly dangerous). Note that some roads are regularly closed during the Wet due to flooding.

Quarantine restrictions require travellers to surrender all fruit, vegetables, nuts and honey at the NT–Western Australia (WA) border.

TRAIN

The famous interstate *Ghan* train is run by **Great Southern Rail** (www.gsr.com.au), grinding between Darwin and Adelaide via Katherine and Alice Springs. The *Ghan* is met in Port Augusta (SA) by the *Indian Pacific*, which travels between Sydney and Perth; and in Adelaide by the *Overland*, which travels to/from Melbourne.

The *Ghan* has three levels of sleeper berths plus a chair class.

DARWIN

POP 127,500

Australia's only tropical capital, Darwin gazes out confidently across the Timor Sea. It's closer to Bali than Bondi, and many from the southern states still see it as some frontier outpost or jumping-off point for Kakadu National Park.

But Darwin is a surprisingly affluent, cosmopolitan, youthful and multicultural city, thanks in part to an economic boom fuelled by the mining industry and tourism. It's a city on the move but there's a small-town feel and a laconic, relaxed vibe that fits easily with the tropical climate. Here non-Aboriginal meets Aboriginal (Larrakia), urban meets remote, and industry meets idleness.

Darwin has plenty to offer the traveller. Boats bob around the harbour, chairs and tables spill out of streetside restaurants and bars, museums celebrate the city's past, and galleries showcase the region's rich indigenous art. Darwin's cosmopolitan mix – more than 50 nationalities are seamlessly represented here – is typified by the wonderful markets held throughout the dry season.

Nature is well and truly part of Darwin's backyard – the famous national parks of Kakadu and Litchfield are only a few hours' drive away and the unique Tiwi Islands are a boat-ride away. For locals the perfect weekend is going fishing for barra in a tinny with an esky full of cold beer.

History

The Larrakia Aboriginal people lived for thousands of years in Darwin, hunting, fishing and foraging. In 1869 a permanent white settlement was established and the grid for a new town was laid out. Originally called Palmerston, and renamed Darwin in 1911, the new town developed rapidly, transforming the physical and social landscape.

The discovery of gold at nearby Pine Creek brought an influx of Chinese, who soon settled into other industries. Asians and Islanders came to work in the pearling industry and on the railway line and wharf. More recently, neighbouring East Timorese and Papuans have sought asylum in Darwin.

During WWII, Darwin was the frontline for the Allied action against the Japanese in the Pacific. It was the only Australian city ever bombed, and official reports of the time downplayed the damage – to buoy Australians' morale. Though the city wasn't destroyed by the 64 attacks, the impact of full-scale military occupation on Darwin was enormous.

More physically damaging was Cyclone Tracy, which hit Darwin at around midnight on Christmas Eve 1974. By Christmas morning, Darwin effectively ceased to exist as a city, with only 400 of its 11,200 homes left standing and 71 people killed. The town was rebuilt to a new, stringent building code and in the past decade has steadily expanded outwards and upwards, with the latest project the multimillion-dollar waterfront development at Darwin Harbour.

Sights

Central Darwin

Crocosaurus Cove ZOO

(Map p818; www.croccove.com.au; 58 Mitchell St; adult/child $30/18; 8am-6pm, last admission 5pm) If the tourists won't go out to see the crocs, then bring the crocs to the tourists. Right in the middle of Mitchell St, Crocosaurus Cove is as close as you'll ever want to get to these amazing creatures. Six of the largest crocs in captivity can be seen in state-of-the-art aquariums and pools. You can be lowered right into a pool with them in the transparent **Cage of Death** (1/2 people $150/220). If that's too scary, there's another pool where you can swim with a clear tank wall separating you from some mildly less menacing baby crocs. Other aquariums feature barramundi, turtles and stingrays, plus there's an enormous reptile house (allegedly

Greater Darwin

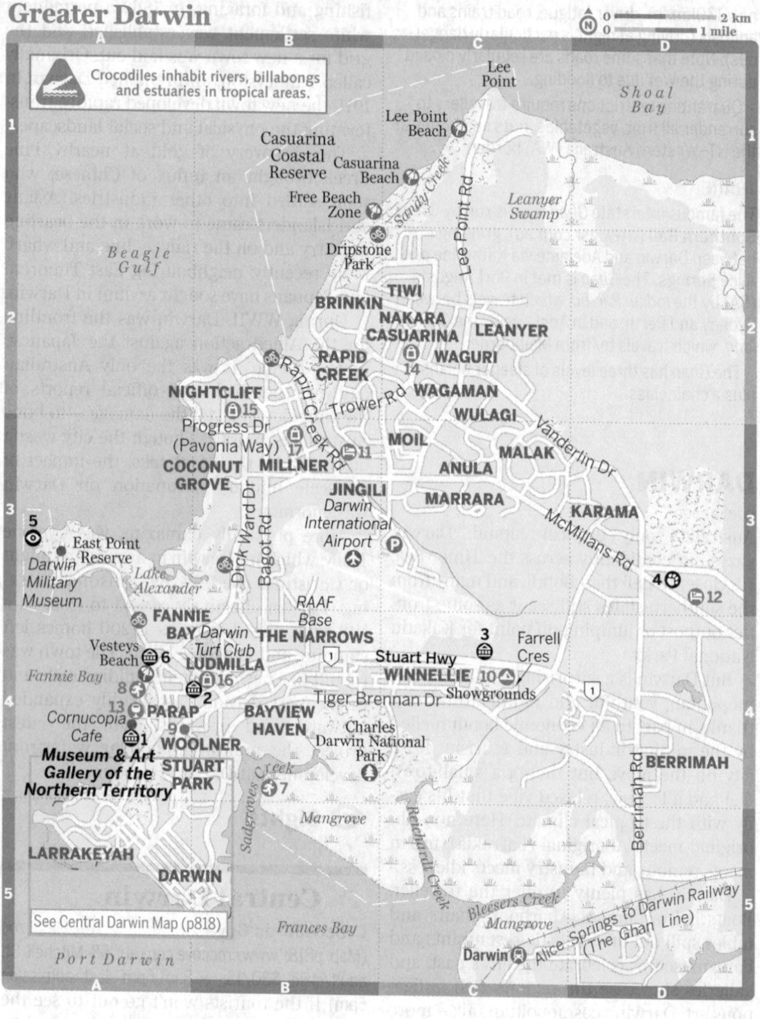

the greatest variety of reptiles on display in the country).

Aquascene AQUARIUM

(Map p818; www.aquascene.com.au; 28 Doctors Gully Rd; adult/child $15/10; ⏲ high tide, check website) At Doctors Gully, an easy walk from the north end of the Esplanade, Aquascene runs a remarkable fish-feeding frenzy at high tide. Visitors, young and old can hand-feed hordes of mullet, catfish, batfish and huge milkfish. Check the website and tourism publications for feeding times.

The Esplanade STREET

Darwin's Esplanade is a long, straight street with flashy hotels on one side and the lush waterside **Bicentennial Park** (Map p818; www.darwin.nt.gov.au; ⏲ 24hr) on the other. The park runs the length of the Esplanade from Doctors Gully to Lameroo Beach, a sheltered cove popular in the '20s when it housed the saltwater baths, and traditionally a Larrakia camp area. Shaded by tropical trees, the park is an excellent place to wander.

At the Herbert St end, there's a **cenotaph** commemorating Australians' service to the country's war efforts. Also honoured

Greater Darwin

Top Sights
1 Museum & Art Gallery of the Northern Territory A4

Sights
2 24HR Art B4
3 Australian Aviation Heritage Centre C4
4 Crocodylus Park D3
5 East Point Reserve A3
6 Fannie Bay Gaol Museum A4

Activities, Courses & Tours
7 Charles Darwin National Park B4
8 Darwin Sailing Club A4
9 Tiwi Land Council A4

Sleeping
10 Aurora Shady Glen Caravan Park C4
11 Feathers Sanctuary B3
12 Grungle Downs B&B D3

Eating
Cyclone Cafe .... (see 16)
Parap Fine Foods .... (see 16)
Saffrron .... (see 2)

Drinking & Nightlife
Darwin Sailing Club .... (see 8)
13 Darwin Ski Club A4

Shopping
14 Casuarina Square C2
15 Nightcliff Market B2
16 Parap Village Market B4
17 Rapid Creek Market B3
Tiwi Art Network .... (see 16)

are **200 Remarkable Territorians**: hand-painted tiles in panels dispersed intermittently along the Esplanade commemorate some of the Territory's 'quiet achievers', including pioneers, publicans and pastoralists.

Lyons Cottage HISTORIC BUILDING
(Map p818; www.aboriginalbushtraders.com; cnr Esplanade & Knuckey St; 9am-3pm) FREE Just across the road from Bicentennial Park, Lyons Cottage was built in 1925. It was Darwin's first stone residence, formerly housing executives from the British Australian Telegraph Company (which laid a submarine cable between Australia and Java). Now it's a museum and retail outlet run by Aboriginal Bush Traders displaying Darwin in photos from the early days.

Parliament House NOTABLE BUILDING
(Map p818; 08-8946 1434; www.nt.gov.au/lant; 8am-6pm) FREE At the southern end of Mitchell St is the elegant, box-like Parliament House, which opened in 1994. Reminiscent of Southeast Asian colonial architecture, it's designed to withstand Darwin's monsoonal climate. Attend a free tour exploring the cavernous interior on Saturday at 9am and 11am. No booking required. The building also houses the **Northern Territory Library**.

George Brown Botanic Gardens GARDEN
(Map p818; www.nretas.nt.gov.au/national-parks-and-reserves/botanic; Geranium St, Stuart Park; 7am-7pm, information centre 8am-4pm Mon-Fri, 8.30am-4pm Sat & Sun) FREE Named after the gardens' curator from 1971 to 1990, these 42-hectare gardens showcase plants from the Top End and around the world – monsoon vine forest, the mangroves and coastal plants habitat, boabs and a magnificent collection of native and exotic palms and cycads.

Many of the plants here were traditionally used by the local Aboriginal people, and self-guiding **Aboriginal plant-use trails** have been set up – pick up a brochure at the gardens' information centre near the Geranium St entry. You'll also find **birdwatching** brochures and garden maps here too.

The gardens are an easy 2km bicycle ride out from the centre of town along Gilruth Ave and Gardens Rd, or there's another entrance off Geranium St, which runs off the Stuart Hwy in Stuart Park. Alternatively, bus 7 from the city stops near the Stuart Hwy/Geranium St corner.

Myilly Point Heritage Precinct HISTORIC SITE
(Map p818) At the far northern end of Smith St is this small but important precinct of four houses built between 1930–39 (which means they survived both the WWII bombings and Cyclone Tracy!). They're now managed by the National Trust. One of them, **Burnett House** (Map p818; www.nationaltrustnt.org.au; admission by donation; 10am-1pm Mon-Sat), operates as a museum. There's a tantalising colonial high tea ($10) in the gardens on Sunday afternoon from 3.30pm to 6pm between April and October.

Chinese Museum & Chung Wah Temple MUSEUM, TEMPLE
(www.chungwahnt.asn.au; 25 Woods St; admission by donation; ⌚museum 10am-2pm, temple 8am-4pm) This excellent little museum explores Chinese settlement in the Top End. The adjacent temple has a hushed interior, punctuated by scarlet lanterns and smouldering incense sticks. The sacred tree in the grounds is rumoured to be a direct descendant from the Bodhi tree under which Buddha sat when he attained enlightenment.

Darwin Waterfront Precinct

The bold redevelopment of the old Darwin Waterfront Precinct (www.waterfront.nt.gov.au) has transformed the city. The multimillion-dollar redevelopment features a cruise-ship terminal, luxury hotels, boutique restaurants and shopping, the Sky Bridge, an elevated walkway and elevator at the south end of Smith St, and a Wave Lagoon.

The old Stokes Hill Wharf (p826) is well worth an afternoon promenade. At the end of the wharf an old warehouse houses a food centre that's ideal for an alfresco lunch, cool afternoon beer or a seafood dinner as the sun sets over the harbour. Several harbour cruises and a jet boat also leave from the wharf.

Wave & Recreation Lagoons WATER PARK
(www.waterfront.nt.gov.au; Wave Lagoon adult/child half-day $5/3.50, full day $8/5; ⌚Wave Lagoon 10am-6pm) The hugely popular Wave Lagoon is a hit with locals and travellers alike. There are 10 different wave patterns produced (20 minutes on with a 10-minute rest in between) and there are lifeguards, a kiosk, and a strip of lawn to bask on. Adjacent is the **Recreation Lagoon** with a sandy beach, lifeguards and stinger-filtered seawater (although the nets and filters are not guaranteed to be 100% effective).

WWII Oil-Storage Tunnels TUNNELS
(Map p818; www.darwintours.com.au/tours/ww2tunnels.html; self-guided tour per person $6; ⌚9am-4pm May-Sep, 9am-1pm Oct-Apr) You can escape from the heat of the day and relive your Hitchcockian fantasies by walking through the **WWII oil-storage tunnels**. They were built in 1942 to store the navy's oil supplies (but never used), and they exhibit wartime photos.

Indo-Pacific Marine Exhibition AQUARIUM
(Map p818; www.indopacificmarine.com.au; 29 Stokes Hill Rd; adult/child $22/10; ⌚10am-4pm) This excellent marine aquarium at the Waterfront Precinct gives you a close encounter with the denizens at the bottom of Darwin Harbour. Each small tank is a complete ecosystem, with only the occasional extra fish introduced as food for some of the predators, such as stonefish or the bizarre angler fish.

Also recommended here is the **Coral Reef by Night** (adult/child $110/55; ⌚7pm Wed, Fri & Sun), which consists of a tour of the aquarium, seafood dinner (on biodegradable plates, no less!) and an impressive show of fluorescing animals.

Fannie Bay

★ **Museum & Art Gallery of the Northern Territory** MUSEUM
(MAGNT; Map p814; www.magnt.nt.gov.au; Conacher St, Fannie Bay; ⌚9am-5pm Mon-Fri, 10am-5pm Sat & Sun) FREE This superb museum and gallery boasts beautifully presented galleries

DARWIN IN...

Two Days

Start with breakfast at **Four Birds** (p826)or **Roma Bar** (p826), while flipping through the *Northern Territory News*. Take a stroll downtown and through **Bicentennial Park** (p814). Don't miss the high-tide action at **Aquascene** (p814) and as the afternoon warms up, head down to the **waterfront precinct** (p816), stopping for a dip in the **Wave Lagoon** (p816). As the sun sets, make your way to **Mindil Beach Sunset Market** (p830), packed with food outlets, buskers and souvenirs.

On day two, hire a bike and head out to the **Museum & Art Gallery of the Northern Territory** (p816). Continue your coastal jaunt to the **East Point Reserve** (p817) and the **Darwin Military Museum** (p817). At night, hit the bars along Mitchell St, or find a quite waterfront restaurant at Cullen Bay and catch a movie under the stars at the **Deckchair Cinema** (p829).

of Top End–centric exhibits. The **Aboriginal art collection** is a highlight, with carvings from the Tiwi Islands, bark paintings from Arnhem Land and dot paintings from the desert.

An entire room is devoted to Cyclone Tracy, in a display that graphically illustrates life before and after the disaster. You can stand in a darkened room and listen to the whirring sound of Tracy at full throttle – a sound you won't forget in a hurry.

The cavernous **Maritime Gallery** houses an assortment of weird and wonderful crafts from the nearby islands and Indonesia, as well as a pearling lugger and a Vietnamese refugee boat.

Pride of place among the stuffed animals undoubtedly goes to **Sweetheart**: a 5m-long, 780kg saltwater crocodile. It became a Top End personality after attacking several fishing dinghies on the Finniss River.

The museum has a good bookshop, and the Cornucopia Cafe is a great lunch spot with views over the sea.

Fannie Bay Gaol Museum MUSEUM

(Map p814; www.ntretas.nt.gov.au/knowledge-and-history/heritage/visit/gaol; cnr East Point Rd & Ross Smith Ave; admission by donation; ⏲10am-3pm) This interesting (if a little grim) museum represents almost 100 years of solitude. Serving as Darwin's main jail from 1883 to 1979, the solid cells contain information panels that provide a window into the region's unique social history. Lepers, refugees and juveniles were among the groups confined here, and you can still see the old cells and the gallows constructed for two hangings in 1952.

East Point Reserve GARDEN

(Map p814; ⏲mangrove boardwalk 8am-6pm) North of Fannie Bay, this spit of land is particularly attractive in the late afternoon when wallabies emerge to feed and you can watch the sun set over the bay.

Lake Alexander, a small, recreational saltwater lake, was created so people could enjoy a swim year-round without having to worry about box jellyfish. There's a good children's playground here and picnic areas with BBQs. A 1.5km **mangrove boardwalk** leads off from the car park.

On the point's northern side is a series of WWII gun emplacements and the fascinating Darwin Military Museum.

Darwin Military Museum MUSEUM

(www.darwinmilitarymuseum.com.au; 5434 Alec Fong Lim Dr; adult/child $14/5.50; ⏲9.30am-5pm)

LOCAL KNOWLEDGE

PARAP VILLAGE MARKET

Parap Village is a foodies heaven with several good restaurants, bars and cafes as well as the highly recommended deli, Parap Fine Foods (p828). However, it's the Saturday morning markets that attract locals like bees to honey. It's got a relaxed vibe as breakfast merges into brunch and then lunch. Between visits to the takeaway food stalls, mostly spicy southeast Asian snacks, shoppers stock up on interesting and amazing tropical fruit and vegetables – all you need to make your own laksa or rendang. The produce is local so you know it'll be fresh.

The **Defence of Darwin Experience** at the Darwin Military Museum is a sobering reminder of Australia's most significant wartime attack. It features personal accounts and an interactive light-and-sound show. Other museum exhibits include an assortment of military hardware. It's on the Tour Tub (p821) route.

24HR Art ART GALLERY

(Map p814; www.24hrart.org.au; Vimy Lane, Parap Shopping Village; ⏲10am-4pm Wed-Fri, 10am-2pm Sat) Changing and challenging exhibitions by the Northern Territory Centre for Contemporary Art.

Outer East

Crocodylus Park ZOO

(Map p814; www.crocodyluspark.com.au; 815 McMillans Rd, Berrimah; adult/child $35/17.50; ⏲9am-5pm, tours 10am, noon, 2pm & 3.30pm) Crocodylus Park showcases hundreds of crocs and a mini-zoo comprising lions, tigers and other big cats, spider monkeys, marmosets, cassowaries and large birds. Allow about two hours to look around the whole park, and you should time your visit with a tour, which includes a feeding demonstration. Croc meat BBQ packs for sale!

The park is about 15km from the city centre. Take bus 5 from Darwin.

Australian Aviation Heritage Centre MUSEUM

(Map p814; www.darwinsairwar.com.au; 557 Stuart Hwy, Winnellie; adult/child $12/7; ⏲9am-5pm) Darwin's aviation museum, about 10km

Central Darwin

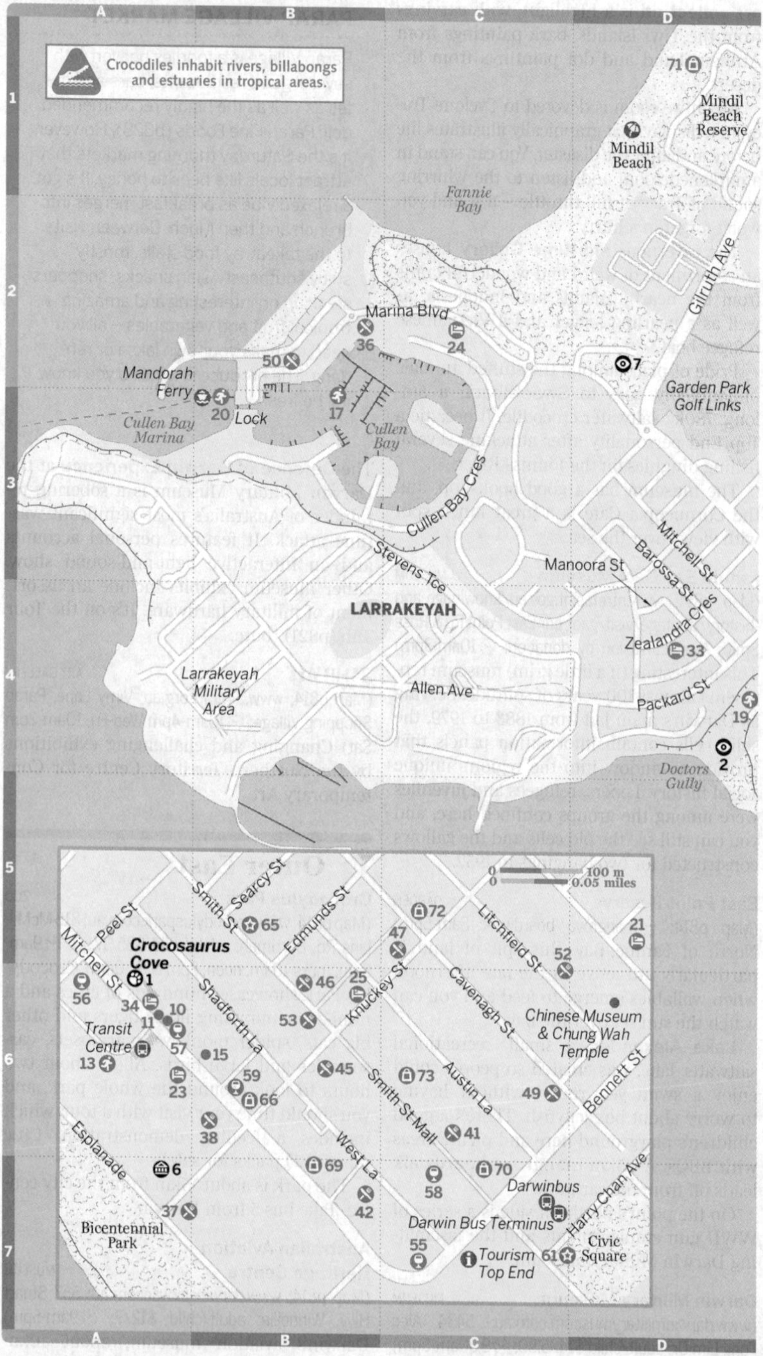

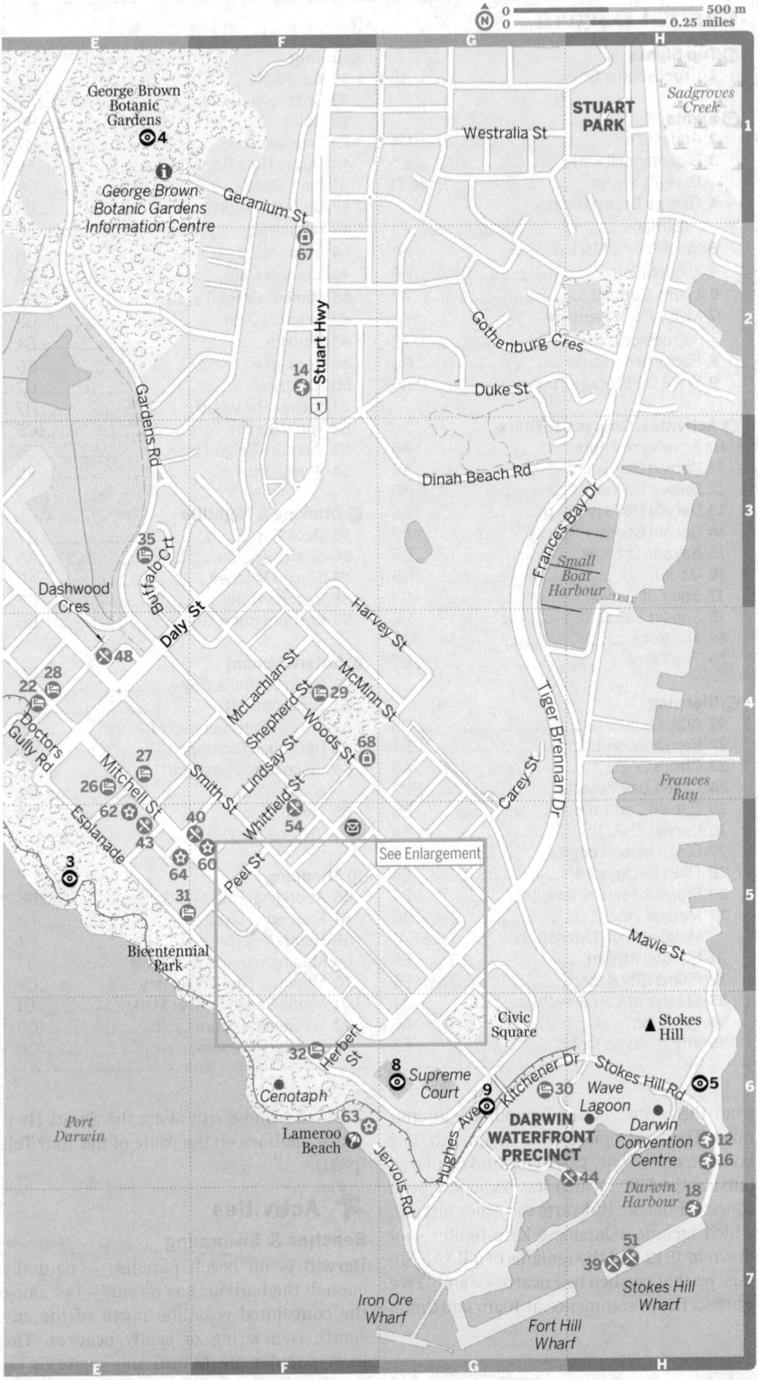
0 500 m
0 0.25 miles
E
F
G
H
1
2
3
4
5
6
7
George Brown Botanic Gardens
4
George Brown Botanic Gardens Information Centre
Geranium St
67
Stuart Hwy
1
14
STUART PARK
Sadgroves Creek
Westralia St
Gothenburg Cres
Duke St
Dinah Beach Rd
Gardens Rd
Frances Bay Dr
Small Boat Harbour
35
Buffalo Crt
Dashwood Cres
Daly St
48
28
22
Doctors Gully Rd
Harvey St
McLachlan St
McMinn St
29
Shepherd St
Woods St
68
Lindsay St
Tiger Brennan Dr
Carey St
Frances Bay
27
26
Mitchell St
62
43
Smith St
Whitfield St
54
40
60
Esplanade
64
3
See Enlargement
Peel St
31
Mavie St
Bicentennial Park
Civic Square
Stokes Hill
32
Herbert St
8
Supreme Court
9
Kitchener Dr
30
Stokes Hill Rd
5
Wave Lagoon
Cenotaph
Port Darwin
63
Lameroo Beach
Hughes Ave
DARWIN WATERFRONT PRECINCT
Darwin Convention Centre
12
16
Jervois Rd
44
Darwin Harbour
18
51
39
Stokes Hill Wharf
Iron Ore Wharf
Fort Hill Wharf

Central Darwin

Top Sights
1 Crocosaurus Cove ... A6

Sights
2 Aquascene ... D4
3 Bicentennial Park ... E5
Burnett House ... (see 7)
4 George Brown Botanic Gardens ... E1
5 Indo-Pacific Marine Exhibition ... H6
6 Lyons Cottage ... A7
7 Myilly Point Heritage Precinct ... D2
8 Parliament House ... G6
9 WWII Oil-Storage Tunnels ... G6

Activities, Courses & Tours
10 Adventure Tours ... A6
11 Darwin Day Tours ... A6
12 Darwin Harbour Cruises ... H6
13 Darwin Holiday Shop ... A6
14 Darwin Scooter Hire ... F2
15 Kakadu Dreams ... B6
16 Oz Jet ... H6
17 Spirit of Darwin ... B3
18 Sunset Sail ... H7
19 The Rock ... D4
20 Tiwi Ferry ... B3

Sleeping
21 Argus ... D5
22 Banyan View Lodge ... E4
23 Chilli's ... A6
24 Cullen Bay Resorts ... C2
25 Darwin Central Hotel ... B6
26 Darwin YHA ... E4
27 Dingo Moon Lodge ... E4
28 Elkes Backpackers ... E4
29 Frogshollow Backpackers ... F4
30 Medina Vibe ... G6
Melaleuca on Mitchell ... (see 34)
31 Novotel Atrium ... E5
32 Palms City Resort ... F6
33 Steeles at Larrakeyah ... D4
34 Value Inn ... A6
35 Vitina Studio Motel ... E3

Eating
36 Buzz Café ... B2
37 Char Restaurant ... A7
38 Coles ... B6
39 Crustaceans ... H7
40 Ducks Nuts Bar & Grill ... F5
41 Four Birds ... C6
42 Go Sushi Train ... B7
43 Hanuman ... E5
44 Il Lido ... H6
45 Istanbul Cafe ... B6
46 Manolis Greek Taverna ... B6
47 Moorish Café ... C5
48 Nirvana ... E4
49 Roma Bar ... C6
50 Seadogs ... B2
51 Stokes Hill Wharf ... H7
52 Tim's Surf 'n' Turf ... C5
53 Vietnam Saigon Star ... B6
54 Woolworths ... F5

Drinking & Nightlife
55 Deck Bar ... C7
56 Shenannigans ... A6
57 Tap on Mitchell ... A6
58 Victoria Hotel ... C7
59 Wisdom Bar & Grill ... B6

Entertainment
60 Birch Carroll & Coyle ... F5
61 Brown's Mart ... C7
62 Darwin Entertainment Centre ... E5
63 Deckchair Cinema ... F6
64 Discovery & Lost Arc ... E5
Nirvana ... (see 48)
65 Throb ... B5
Victoria Hotel ... (see 58)

Shopping
66 Aboriginal Fine Arts Gallery ... B6
67 Framed ... F2
68 Happy Yess Market ... F4
69 Maningrida Arts & Culture ... B7
70 Mbantua Fine Art Gallery ... C7
71 Mindil Beach Sunset Market ... D1
72 NT General Store ... C5
73 Territory Colours ... C6

from the centre, is one for military aircraft nuts. The centrepiece is a mammoth B52 bomber, one of only two of its kind displayed outside the USA, which has somehow been squeezed inside. It dwarfs the other aircraft, which include a Japanese Zero fighter shot down in 1942 and the remains of a RAAF Mirage jet that crashed in a nearby swamp. Free **guided tours** commence at 10am and 2pm.

Buses 5 and 8 run along the Stuart Hwy, and sometimes on the route of the Tour Tub (p821).

Activities

Beaches & Swimming

Darwin is no beach paradise – naturally enough the harbour has no surf – but along the convoluted coastline north of the city centre is a string of sandy beaches. The most popular are **Mindil** and **Vestey's** on

Fannie Bay. Further north, a stretch of the 7km **Casuarina Beach** is an official nude beach. Darwin's swimming beaches tend to be far enough away from mangrove creeks to make the threat of meeting a crocodile very remote. A bigger problem is the deadly box jellyfish, which makes swimming decidedly unhealthy between October and March (and often before October and until May). You can swim year-round without fear of stingers in the western part of **Lake Alexander**, an easy cycle from the centre at East Point (p817), and at the Wave Lagoon (p816), the centre piece of the Darwin Wharf Precinct. Also at the wharf precinct is the Recreation Lagoon (p816), where filtered seawater and nets provides a natural seawater swim.

Sailing

Darwin Sailing Club SAILING
(Map p814; ☎08-8981 1700; www.dwnsail.com.au) A good place to meet local yachties, and to watch the sunset over a beer. Although you can't charter boats here, there is a noticeboard advertising crewing needs and detailing the seasonal race program.

Cycling

Darwin is great for cycling (in winter!). Traffic is light and a series of **bike tracks** covers most of the city, with the main one running from the northern end of Cavenagh St to Fannie Bay, Coconut Grove, Nightcliff and Casuarina. At Fannie Bay, a side track heads out to the East Point Reserve.

Consider heading for **Charles Darwin National Park** (Map p814; www.nt.gov.au/nreta/parks/find/charlesdarwin.html), 5km southeast of the city, with a few kilometres of path around the park's wetlands, woodlands and WWII bunkers.

Some hostels hire out bicycles for $15 to $25 per day for a mountain bike, or try:

Darwin Scooter Hire CYCLING
(Map p818; www.esummer.com.au; 9 Daly St; ⏲8am-5pm Mon-Fri, 9am-3pm Sat) Mountain bikes for $20 a day ($100 deposit required).

Darwin Holiday Shop CYCLING
(Map p818; ☎08-8981 0277; www.darwinholidayshop.com.au; 88 The Esplanade, Shop 2, Mantra on the Esplanade; ⏲9am-5pm Mon-Fri, 9am-1pm Sat) Mountain bikes per half-/full day $20/25.

Rock Climbing

The Rock ROCK CLIMBING
(Map p818; www.rockclimbing.com.au; climbing incl equipment $25; ⏲noon-9pm Tue, Thu & Sat, noon-6pm Wed, Fri & Sun) Inside an old WWII oil-storage tank at Doctors Gully, The Rock is the place to chalk-up your fingers, defy gravity and dangle yourself off a climbing wall.

Jetboating

Oz Jet JETBOATING
(Map p818; ☎1300 135 595; www.ozjetboating.com/darwin; 30min rides adult/child $55/30) If a harbour cruise is too tame, jump on Oz Jet for a white-knuckle ride around the harbour that'll test how long it's been since you had lunch. Departs from Stokes Hill Wharf. Bookings essential; closed during the Wet.

Skydiving

Top End Tandems SKYDIVING
(☎0417 190 140; www.topendtandems.com.au; tandem jumps from $380) Has tandem skydives starting at Darwin Airport and landing at Lee Point Reserve.

Tours

There are dozens of tours in and around Darwin, and lots of combinations covering Kakadu, Arnhem Land, Litchfield and further afield. Tourism Top End (p832) is the best place to start looking and asking questions. Remember that many tours run less frequently (or not at all) in the Wet.

City Tours

Darwin Walking & Bicycle Tours WALKING, CYCLING
(☎08-8981 0227; www.darwinwalkingtours.com.au) Two-hour guided history walks around the city for $25 (children free), plus three-hour bike tours (adult/child $55/40) that take you out to Fannie Bay and East Point.

Tour Tub SIGHTSEEING
(☎08-8985 6322; www.tourtub.com.au; adult/child $45/20; ⏲9am-4pm Apr-Sep) This open-sided hop-on, hop-off minibus tours all around Darwin's big-ticket sights throughout the day. Call for bookings, pick-up times and locations. Pay the driver onboard – cash only.

Sea Darwin ECOTOUR
(☎1300 065 022; www.seadarwin.com; tours adult/child from $35/20) One-, two-, or three-hour eco tours around the city and Darwin Harbour, checking out mangroves, a crocodile trap, a shipwreck and (if you're lucky) dugongs and dolphins.

ABORIGINAL FESTIVALS & EVENTS

Most of the festivals in the Northern Territory's cities and towns have strong Aboriginal components, plus there's a bunch of annual Aboriginal celebrations to attend. Although these festivals are usually held on restricted Aboriginal land, permit requirements are generally waived for them; this applies to most of the festivals listed here. Bear in mind that alcohol is banned in many communities.

Tiwi Grand Final Held at the end of March on Bathurst Island, this sporting spectacular displays the Tiwis' sparkling skills and passion for Aussie Rules football. Thousands come from Darwin for the day, which coincides with the **Tiwi Art Sale** (www.tiwiart.com).

Barunga Festival (www.jawoyn.org/tourism/barunga-festival) For three days over a long weekend in mid-June, Barunga, 80km east of Katherine, displays traditional arts and crafts, dancing, music and sporting competitions. Bring your own camping equipment; alternatively, visit for the day from Katherine.

Merrepen Arts & Sports Festival (www.merrepenfestival.com.au) The Nauiyu community, on the banks of the Daly River, is the venue for this sporty arts festival on the first weekend in June. The Merrepen Arts Centre showcases its string bags, paintings and prints, while locals sweat it out in foot races and basketball and softball matches.

Walking With Spirits (www.djilpinarts.org.au/visit-us/walking-with-spirits) A two-day Indigenous cultural festival in July at Beswick Falls, 130km from Katherine. In a magical setting, traditional dance and music is combined with theatre, films and a light show. Camping is allowed at the site (only during the festival). A 4WD is recommended for the last 20km to the falls, or a shuttle bus runs from Beswick.

Stone Country Festival (www.injalak.com) This open day and cultural festival is held in August in Gunbalanya (Oenpelli) just outside Kakadu National Park. It has traditional music, dancing, and arts and crafts demonstrations, and is the only day you can visit Gunbalanya without a permit. Camping allowed; no alcohol.

Garma Festival (www.yyf.com.au) Also in August, a four-day festival in northeastern Arnhem Land. It's one of the most significant regional festivals, a celebration of Yolngu culture that includes ceremonial performances, bushcraft lessons, a *yidaki* (didgeridoo) master class and an academic forum. Serious planning is required to attend, so start early.

Darwin Day Tours SIGHTSEEING
(Map p818; ☎1300 721 365; www.darwindaytours.com.au; afternoon city tour adult/child $69/55) Runs an afternoon city tour that takes in all the major attractions, including Stokes Hill Wharf, the Museum & Art Gallery and East Point Reserve, and can be linked with a sunset harbour cruise ($144/110).

Harbour Cruises

Between April and October there are plenty of boats based at the Cullen Bay Marina and Stokes Hill Wharf to take you on a cruise of the harbour.

Anniki Pearl Lugger Cruises SAILING
(☎0428 414 000; www.australianharbourcruises.com.au; tours adult/child $70/50) Three-hour sunset cruises on this historical pearling lugger depart at 4.45pm from Cullen Bay Marina and include sparkling wine and nibbles. You might recognise the ship from the film *Australia*.

Sunset Sail SAILING
(Map p818; ☎0408 795 567; www.sailnt.com.au; tours adult/child $70/45) This three-hour afternoon cruise aboard the catamaran *Daymirri 2* departs from Stokes Hill Wharf. Refreshments are included but BYO alcohol.

Darwin Harbour Cruises CRUISES
(Map p818; ☎08-8942 3131; www.darwinharbourcruises.com.au) Variety of cruises from Stokes Hill Wharf. The 20m schooner *Tumlaren* does a 'Tastes of the Territory' sunset cruise (adult/child $70/45), while the 30m schooner *Alfred Noble* has a full-dinner cruise departing at 5.30pm ($110/65).

Spirit of Darwin CRUISES
(Map p818; ☎0417 381 977; www.spiritofdarwin.com.au; tours adult/child $65/20) This fully licensed air-con catamaran runs a two-hour sightseeing cruise at 2pm and a sunset cruise at 5.30pm daily from Stokes Hill Wharf.

Territory Trips

Davidson's Arnhemland Safaris INDIGENOUS
(☎08-8927 5240; www.arnhemland-safaris.com) Experienced operator based at Mt Borradaile, north of Oenpelli. Meals, guided tours including Aboriginal rock art, fishing and accommodation in the comfortable safari camp are included in the daily price of around $750; transfers from Darwin can be arranged.

Tiwi Tours INDIGENOUS
(☎1300 721 365; www.aussieadventures.com.au) Small-group cultural tours out to the nearby Tiwi Islands with indigenous guides (adult/child including flights $498/449). Kakadu and Litchfield tours also available through the company's other brands: Darwin Day Tours (p822) and Aussie Adventure.

Adventure Tours BACKPACKER
(Map p818; ☎08-8132 8230, 1800 068 886; www.adventuretours.com.au) Range of 4WD tours to suit the spirited backpacker crowd. Two-/three-day Kakadu tours $468/663, plus day tours to Litchfield ($119) and Katherine Gorge ($157). Longer tours available.

Northern Territory Indigenous Tours INDIGENOUS
(☎1300 921 188; www.ntitours.com.au) Upmarket indigenous tours to Litchfield National Park stopping off at Territory Wildlife Park (adult/child $249/124).

Sacred Earth Safaris WILDERNESS
(☎08-8981 8420; www.sacredearthsafaris.com.au) Multiday, small-group 4WD camping tours around Kakadu, Katherine and the Kimberley. Two-day Kakadu tour starts at $850; the five-day Top End tour is $2250.

Kakadu Dreams BACKPACKER
(Map p818; ☎1800 813 266; www.kakadudreams.com.au; 50 Mitchell St) Backpacker day tours to Litchfield ($119), and boisterous two-/three-day trips to Kakadu ($387/400).

Wallaroo Tours SIGHTSEEING
(☎08-8983 2699; www.litchfielddaytours.com) Small-group tours to Litchfield National Park ($130).

Festivals & Events

WordStorm LITERARY
(www.wordstorm.org.au) The biannual NT Writers' Festival event, in May (even-numbered years), includes song, storytelling, visual-art collaboration, theatre, performance poetry, history, biography, poetry and fiction.

Arafura Games SPORTS
(www.arafuragames.nt.gov.au) A week-long multisport competition held in May in odd-numbered years, targeting up-and-coming athletes from the Asia-Pacific region. Athletics, basketball, cricket, soccer, swimming, volleyball...

Darwin Blues Festival MUSIC
(www.darwinbluesfestival.com) In late June, venues across Darwin charge up with live blues. Much beer and bending guitar strings.

Beer Can Regatta LOCAL CULTURE
(www.beercanregatta.org.au) An utterly insane and typically Territorian festival that features races for boats made out of beer cans. It takes places at Mindil Beach in July and is a good, fun day.

Royal Darwin Show AGRICULTURAL
(www.darwinshow.com.au) This agricultural show takes place at the showgrounds in Winnellie on the last weekend of July. Plenty of rides, demonstrations, competitions and pampered farm animals.

Darwin Cup Carnival HORSE RACING
(www.darwinturfclub.org.au) The Darwin Cup racing carnival takes place in July and August at the Darwin Turf Club in Fannie Bay. The highlight of the eight-day program is the running of the Darwin Cup, along with the usual fashion and frivolities.

Darwin Aboriginal Art Fair VISUAL ARTS
(www.darwinaboriginalartfair.com.au) Held at the Darwin Convention Centre, this two-day August festival showcases indigenous art from communities throughout the Territory.

Darwin Festival ARTS
(www.darwinfestival.org.au) This mainly outdoor arts and culture festival highlights the cultures of Darwin's large Aboriginal and Asian populations and runs for two weeks in August.

Sleeping

Darwin has a good range of accommodation, most of it handy to the CBD, but finding a bed in the peak May to September period can be difficult at short notice – book ahead, at least for the first night. Accommodation prices vary greatly with the season and demand. Prices given here are for high season, but expect big discounts between November and March, especially for midrange and top-end accommodation.

Backpacker hostels fluctuate the least, and prices differ little between places – concentrated as they are in a small stretch of bar-heavy Mitchell St. If you want a quieter stay, choose somewhere a bit further out – they're still within walking distance of the action. Hostel facilities usually include a communal kitchen, pool and laundry facilities and they all have tour-booking desks. Some offer airport, bus or train station pick-ups with advance bookings, and most give YHA/VIP discounts.

There are a few decent camping/caravan park options within 10km of the city centre. Some campervanners take their chances staying overnight at parking areas along the beach around Fannie Bay and East Point Reserve, but it's officially a no-no and council officers may move you on or dish out fines.

Darwin's larger hotels quote inflated rack rates, but there are all sorts of specials, including stand-by, weekend and internet rates. Most of the big hotels are gathered along the Esplanade.

City Centre

Frogshollow Backpackers HOSTEL $

(Map p818; ☎08-8941 2600, 1800 068 686; www.frogs-hollow.com.au; 27 Lindsay St; dm $24-30, d without/with bathroom $80/100; ❄@🛜🏊) Presiding over a tranquil patch of parkland, Frogshollow is a chilled-out backpackers' choice. A relaxed Euro crew basks by the pool or kicks back in the park across the road. Afternoon balconies drip with pot-plant overflows as dorm-dwellers mooch around the kitchen. Some rooms have air-con; most have fans. Dorms can be a bit cramped.

Dingo Moon Lodge HOSTEL $

(Map p818; ☎08-8941 3444; www.dingomoonlodge.com; 88 Mitchell St; dm $31-36, d & tw $100, all incl breakfast; ❄@🛜🏊) Howl at the moon at the Dingo, a great addition to the Darwin hostel scene. It's a two-building affair with 65 beds – big enough to be sociable but not rowdy. A highlight is the pool, sparkling underneath a massive frangipani tree, and a great outdoor kitchen. No TV room – have a conversation instead.

Melaleuca on Mitchell HOSTEL $

(Map p818; ☎1300 723 437; www.momdarwin.com.au; 52 Mitchell St; dm $31, d without/with bathroom $95/115; ❄@🛜🏊) The highlight at this busy backpackers is the rooftop island bar and pool area overlooking Mitchell St – complete with waterfall spa and big-screen TV. Party heaven! The modern hostel is immaculate but a little sterile, with stark white walls and sparse rooms. Facilities are A1 though and it's very secure. The 3rd floor is female only.

Chilli's HOSTEL $

(Map p818; ☎08-8980 5800, 1800 351 313; www.chillis.com.au; 69a Mitchell St; dm $32, tw & d without bathroom $100; ❄@🛜) Friendly Chilli's is a funky place with a small sundeck and spa (use the pool next door). There's also a pool table and a breezy kitchen/meals terrace overlooking Mitchell St. Rooms are compact but clean.

Darwin YHA HOSTEL $

(Map p818; ☎08-8981 5385; www.yha.com.au; 97 Mitchell St; dm $33, d/f $115/145; ❄@🛜🏊) The Darwin YHA is in a converted motel, so all 34 rooms (including dorms) have en suites, and they're built around a decent pool. The kitchen and TV room are tiny, but next door Globetrotters Bar has cheap meals and entertainment.

Banyan View Lodge HOSTEL $

(Map p818; ☎08-8981 8644; www.banyanviewlodge.org.au; 119 Mitchell St; dm $27-29, s/d without bathroom from $68/78, d with bathroom from $110; ❄@🏊) The Banyan View suits travellers who aren't into the party scene. It's a big, austere, office-block-looking YWCA that welcomes men too. Spacious rooms are clean and well kept – ask for one with a fan rather than air-con if you'd prefer. Bike hire available.

Elkes Backpackers HOSTEL $

(Map p818; ☎1800 808 365; www.elkesbackpackers.com.au; 112 Mitchell St; dm $30, tw & d $85, tr $180; ❄@🛜🏊) Elkes is a friendly, multilingual independent backpackers housed in a shambling cluster of rudimentary timber buildings punctuated by thick copses of vegetation. It's a good place to meet fellow travellers and chill out, but check the room thoroughly before settling in.

Value Inn HOTEL $$
(Map p818; ☎08-8981 4733; www.valueinn.com.au; 50 Mitchell St; d from $140; P❄≋) In the thick of the Mitchell St action but quiet and comfortable, Value Inn lives up to its name, especially out of season. En-suite rooms are small but sleep up to three and have fridge and TV.

Palms City Resort RESORT $$$
(Map p818; ☎08-8982 9200, 1800 829 211; www.citypalms.com; 64 The Esplanade; motel d $195, villas d $285; P❄≋) True to name, this centrally located resort is fringed by palm-filled gardens. If you covet a microwave and have space cravings, the superior motel rooms are worth a bit extra, while the Asian-influenced, hexagonal villas with outdoor spas are utterly indulgent. Butterflies and dragonflies drift between bougainvilleas in the knockout gardens.

Medina Vibe HOTEL $$$
(Map p818; ☎08-8941 0755; www.medina.com.au; 7 Kitchener Dr; d/studio from $215/235, apt from $335; P❄@≋) Two hotels in one building: standard doubles at Vibe, and studios and apartments next door at the Medina. Either way, you're in for an upmarket stay with friendly staff and a great location in the Darwin Waterfront Precinct. The Wave Lagoon is right next door if the shady swimming pool is too placid for you.

★**Darwin Central Hotel** HOTEL $$$
(Map p818; ☎info 1300 364 263, 08-8944 9000; www.darwincentral.com.au; 21 Knuckey St; d from $180; P❄@≋; 🚌4, 5, 8, 10) Right in the centre of town, this plush independent hotel oozes contemporary style and impeccable facilities, including an award-winning restaurant. There are a range of stylish rooms with excellent accessibility for disabled travellers. Rack rates are steep, but internet, weekend, and three-night-stay discounts make it great value.

Argus APARTMENTS $$$
(Map p818; ☎08-8925 5000; www.argusdarwin.com.au; 6 Cardona Ct; 1-/2-/3-bedroom apt from $280/360/590; P❄@≋) In a corner of town awash with apartment towers, the Argus stands out as a quality option. Apartments are *very* spacious, with lovely bathrooms, generous expanses of cool floor tiles, simple balcony living/dining spaces and snazzy kitchens with all the requisite appliances. The pool seems an afterthought, tucked into a corner of the car park, but it's shady and welcoming on a sticky Top End afternoon.

Novotel Atrium HOTEL $$$
(Map p818; ☎08-8941 0755; www.novoteldarwin.com.au; 100 The Esplanade; d from $365, 2-bedroom apt from $485; P❄@≋) OK, OK, we know Novotel is a global chain and we've seen it all before, but what makes this one special are to-die-for ocean views and stylistic standards above the norm: subtle lighting, fresh flowers and interesting indigenous art. Breathe the sea air on your balcony or descend into the kidney-shaped swimming pool, one of the best-looking puddles in Darwin. Off-season rates are a steal.

City Fringe & Suburbs

Aurora Shady Glen Caravan Park CARAVAN PARK $
(Map p814; ☎08-8984 3330, 1800 662 253; www.shadyglen.com.au; cnr Farrell Cres & Stuart Hwy, Winnellie; unpowered/powered sites $34/39, budget r $90, en suite cabins from $110; ❄≋) Well-treed caravan park with immaculate facilities, a camp kitchen, licensed shop and friendly staff. Public bus 8 rolls into downtown Darwin from the corner of the street.

FreeSpirit Resort Darwin CARAVAN PARK $
(☎08-8935 0888; www.darwinfreespiritresort.com.au; 901 Stuart Hwy, Berrimah; unpowered/powered sites $36/42, cabins & units $135-295; ❄@≋) An impressive highway-side park about a 10-minute drive from the city, with loads of facilities (including three pools). During the Dry there are regular nocturnal troubadours and activities including pancake breakfasts and water aerobics.

Vitina Studio Motel MOTEL $$
(Map p818; ☎08-8981 1544; www.vitinastudiomotel.com.au; 38 Gardens Rd; d $149, ste $199; P❄@≋) Vitina is a convenient option providing bright, stylish accommodation in contemporary motel rooms as well as larger studios with kitchenettes. It's right on the city fringe convenient to the Gardens Park golf course, Botanic Gardens and Mindil Beach. Ask about discounts.

Steeles at Larrakeyah B&B $$
(Darwin City B&B; Map p818; ☎08-8941 3636; www.darwinbnb.com.au; 4 Zealandia Cres, Larrakeyah; d from $175, 1-/2-bedroom apt $250/270; ❄≋) Some B&Bs are business and others feel like you're staying with friends; Steeles is one of the latter. With a quiet residential location

midway between the city centre, Cullen Bay and Mindil Beach, the three rooms in this pleasant Spanish Mission–style home are equipped with fridges, flat-screen TVs and private entrances. Breakfast happens in the tropical garden.

Cullen Bay Resorts HOTEL, APARTMENTS **$$**
(Map p818; ☎08-8981 7999, 1800 625 533; www.cullenbayresortsdarwin.com.au; 26-32 Marina Blvd; hotel d $165-190, 1-/2-bed apt from $265/320; P❄🛜🏊) Cullen Bay is (or was, until the Waterfront Precinct came along) Darwin's prime waterfront location, and this pair of twin apartment towers boasts a million-dollar outlook over the marina and harbour. Interiors aren't super-flash, but the views are worth it.

Grungle Downs B&B B&B **$$**
(Map p814; ☎08-8947 4440; www.grungledowns.com.au; 945 McMillans Rd, Knuckey Lagoon; d $140-165, cottage $400; ❄🏊) Set on a two-hectare property, this beautiful rural retreat seems worlds away from the city (but it's only 13km). It's handy to Crocodylus Park and the airport, too. When it's hot outside, hang out in the guest lounge or by the pool. There are four lodge rooms (one with en suite) and a gorgeous two-bedroom cottage (which drops to $200 in the low season).

Feathers Sanctuary BOUTIQUE HOTEL **$$$**
(Map p814; ☎08-8985 2144; www.featherssanctuary.com; 49a Freshwater Rd, Jingili; d incl breakfast $330; ❄🏊) A sublime retreat for twitchers and nature lovers, Feathers has beautifully designed 'Bali-meets-bush' timber-and-iron cottages with semi-open-air bathrooms and luxurious interiors. The lush gardens have a private aviary breeding some rare birds, and a waterhole – more tropical birds than you're ever likely to see in one place again! Gangly free-roaming brolgas and jabirus steal the show.

Eating

Darwin is the glistening pearl in the Territory's dining scene. Eateries make the most of the tropical ambience with alfresco seating, and the quality and diversity of produce tops anywhere else in the Territory.

Darwin has a growing number of cafes serving good coffee and grazing. The city's top restaurants will surprise with exotic and innovative fusion cuisine, while Darwin's famous markets sizzle and smoke with all manner of multicultural delights. Mitchell St pubs also entice backpackers off the pavement with free BBQs and cheap meals to soak up the beer.

On the edge of the CBD, Cullen Bay has a stylish waterfront dining scene with many options, while the food centre at the end of Stokes Hill Wharf provides cheap-and-cheerful fish and chips and Asian stir-fries, and there are also a few gems hidden in the suburbs north of the city.

City Centre

There are two large supermarkets in downtown Darwin: **Coles** (Map p818; 55-59 Mitchell St, Mitchell Centre; ⏰6am-10pm) and **Woolworths** (Map p818; cnr Cavenagh & Whitfield Sts; ⏰6am-10pm)

Four Birds CAFE **$**
(Map p818; 32 Smith St Mall, Shop 2, Star Village; items $4-8; ⏰breakfast & lunch Mon-Fri, plus Sat Jun-Aug) Nooked into the arcade on the site of the old Star Cinema (a '74 cyclone victim), this hole-in-the-wall does simple things very well: bagels, toasted sandwiches, muffins, paninis and coffee (we reckon it's the best in Darwin). Book-reading office types and travellers sit on stools scattered under a burgeoning frangipani tree.

Roma Bar CAFE **$**
(Map p818; www.romabar.com.au; 9-11 Cavenagh St; mains $7-15; ⏰breakfast & lunch; 🛜) Roma is a local institution and meeting place for lefties, literati and travellers. Well away from the craziness of Mitchell St, with free wi-fi, great coffee and juices, and you can get anything from muesli and eggs benedict for breakfast to excellent toasted focaccia and fish curry for lunch.

Stokes Hill Wharf SEAFOOD, FAST FOOD **$**
(Map p818; www.darwinhub.com/stokes-hill-wharf; Stokes Hill Wharf; mains $8-16; ⏰lunch & dinner) Squatting on the end of Stokes Hill Wharf is a hectic food centre with half-a-dozen food counters and outdoor tables lined up along the pier. It's a pumping place for some fish and chips, oysters, a stir-fry, a laksa or just a cold sunset beer.

Vietnam Saigon Star VIETNAMESE **$**
(Map p818; 21 Smith St, Shop 4; mains $12-18; ⏰lunch Mon-Fri, dinner daily; 🖉) Darwin's speediest, shiniest Vietnamese restaurant serves up inexpensive rice-paper rolls, and beef, pork, chicken and seafood dishes with a multitude of sauces. Vegetarians are well

catered for and there are good-value lunch specials.

Istanbul Cafe TURKISH, FAST FOOD **$$**
(Map p818; 12 Knuckey St; mains $11-25; ⏲ breakfast, lunch & dinner) Inside Darwin's old Country Women's Association building (not a scone or pavlova in sight), this Turkish joint serves up quick takeaway kebabs, meaty grills, dip platters, kofte meatballs and kick-arse Turkish coffee.

★**Hanuman** INDIAN, THAI **$$**
(Map p818; ☎08-8941 3500; www.hanuman.com.au; 28 Mitchell St; mains $16-38; ⏲ lunch Mon-Fri, dinner daily; ☑) Ask most locals about fine dining in Darwin and they'll usually mention Hanuman. Sophisticated but not stuffy, enticing aromas of innovative Indian and Thai Nonya dishes waft from the kitchen to the stylish open dining room and deck. The signature dish is oysters bathed in lemon grass, chilli and coriander, but the menu is broad, with exotic vegetarian choices and banquets also available.

Go Sushi Train JAPANESE **$$**
(Map p818; www.darwinhub.com/go-sushi-train; 28 Mitchell St, Shop 5; sushi $4.50-6.50, mains $25-38; ⏲ lunch & dinner Tue-Sat; ☑) Pull up a stool at this hip sushi circuit, hidden down a lane off Mitchell St. Despite the obscure location it's hugely popular, especially on 'Super Sushi Saturday' (all sushi $4 from 10.30am to 3.30pm). Can't get enough of those eel-and-cucumber rolls...

★**Moorish Café** MIDDLE EASTERN **$$**
(Map p818; ☎08-8991 0010; www.moorishcafe.com.au; 37 Knuckey St; tapas $4-12, mains $20-40; ⏲ lunch & dinner Mon-Sat) Seductive aromas emanate from this divine terracotta-tiled cafe fusing North African, Mediterranean and Middle Eastern delights. The lunchtime crowd arrives for tantalising tapas and lunch specials, but it's an atmospheric place for dinner, too – order a tagine of NT prawns, apple cider, local jewfish coconut and lime, or the four-course banquet ($38 per person with a minimum of six diners; booking essential).

Manolis Greek Taverna GREEK **$$**
(Map p818; www.manolisgreektaverna.com.au; Shop 4, 64 Smith St; mains $18-30; ⏲ lunch Tue-Fri, dinner Mon-Sat) Manolis boasts excellent Greek Island inspired dishes in a friendly, family-run restaurant with an unmistakable Greek ambience. There are blue-and-white table cloths and a fresh seafood-dominated menu that features small *mezethes* plates to share. Traditional favourites including fried cheese, lamb yiros, octopus, great salads and amazingly sweet desserts won't disappoint. There's boisterous live bouzouki music on Saturday nights.

Crustaceans SEAFOOD **$$**
(Map p818; ☎08-8981 8658; Stokes Hill Wharf; mains $17-35; ⏲ dinner Mon-Sat) This casual, licensed restaurant features fresh fish, bugs, lobster, oysters, even crocodile, as well as succulent steaks. The nerdy ordering forms detract from the romance, but it's the location, perched right at the end of Stokes Hill Wharf with sunset views over Francis Bay, plus the cold beer and a first-rate wine list that seals the deal.

Tim's Surf 'n' Turf STEAKHOUSE, SEAFOOD **$$**
(Map p818; ☎08-8981 1024; www.timssurfandturf.com.au; 10 Litchfield St; mains $18-40; ⏲ dinner daily) Squirrelled away on a city backstreet, Tim's is a long-standing locals' diner where you can enjoy good-value seafood, steak, schnitzels and pasta on a relaxed, leafy terrace (just ignore the faux waterfall). Mark what you want on the DIY ordering form with a pencil and hand it to the cashier.

Ducks Nuts Bar & Grill MODERN AUSTRALIAN **$$**
(Map p818; ☎08-8942 2122; www.ducksnuts.com.au; 76 Mitchell St; mains $15-25; ⏲ breakfast, lunch & dinner) An effervescent bar/bistro delivering a clever fusion of Top End produce with that Asian/Mediterranean blend we like to claim as Modern Australian. Great lunchtime burgers, light salads such as the warm Thai beef salad, and hearty mains such as lamb shanks. Good brekkies and caffeinated brews, too.

Il Lido ITALIAN **$$$**
(Map p818; ☎08-8941 0900; www.illidodarwin.com.au; Wharf One, f3/19 Kitchener Dr, Waterfront Precinct; tapas $8-18, pizzas $17-27, mains $28-44) Taking pride of place in the Waterfront Precinct is this contemporary Italian restaurant developed by the folks that introduced Hanuman restaurant to Darwin two decades ago. Delightful breakfasts and a simply stunning balcony for sunset drinks and tapas.

Char Restaurant STEAKHOUSE **$$$**
(Map p818; ☎08-8981 4544; www.charrestaurant.com.au; 70 The Esplanade; mains $28-54; ⏲ lunch Wed-Fri, dinner daily) Housed in the grounds of the historic Admiralty House is Char, a

carnivore's paradise. The speciality here is chargrilled steaks – aged, grain-fed and cooked to perfection – but there's also a range of clever seafood creations on the associated 'Jellyfish' menu.

City Fringe & Suburbs

Parap Fine Foods SELF-CATERING $
(Map p814; www.parapfinefoods.com; 40 Parap Rd, Parap; 8am-6.30pm Mon-Fri, 8am-6pm Sat, 9am-1pm Sun) A gourmet food hall in the Parap shopping centre, stocking organic and health foods, deli items and fine wine – perfect for a picnic.

Cyclone Cafe CAFE $
(Map p814; www.parapvillage.com.au; 8 Urquhart St, Parap; meals $7-14; breakfast & lunch Mon-Sat) Some of Darwin's best coffee is brewed at this unassuming Parap haunt. The decor is all rusty corrugated-iron (Cyclone Tracy's favourite projectile), the staff are upbeat, the coffee is strong and aromatic (try the triple-shot 'Hypercino'), and there's some great breakfast and lunch fare: croissants, burritos, cheese melts and bacon-and-egg rolls.

Seadogs ITALIAN $$
(Map p818; 08-8941 2877; Marina Blvd, Cullen Bay; mains $15-27; lunch & dinner Tue-Sun) It may not front the marina, but the meals are cheaper at this popular local restaurant specialising in pizza, pasta, risotto and a few prawn and calamari dishes.

★ **Saffron** INDIAN $$
(Map p814; 08-8981 2383; www.saffrron.com; 34 Parap Rd, Shop 14, Parap; mains $14-26; lunch Tue-Fri, dinner Tue-Sun, brunch Sun;) Saffrron is Darwin's best Indian restaurant, a contemporary but intimate dining experience. The menu spans the subcontinent, from rich butter chicken masala to barramundi *mooli*. Sunday brunch is a South Indian taste adventure. There are plenty of vegetarian choices, traditional Indian sweets, and takeaways available. Rather progressively, it uses biodegradable furniture, cutlery, plates, bowls and takeaway containers.

Nirvana THAI, INDIAN $$
(Map p818; 08-8981 2025; www.nirvanarestaurantdarwin.com; 6 Dashwood Cres; mains $15-30; dinner Mon-Sat;) Excellent Thai, Malaysian and Indian dishes are only part of the story at Nirvana – it's also one of Darwin's best small live-music venues for jazz and blues. It doesn't look much from the outside, but inside is an intimate warren of rooms with booth seating and Oriental decor. Enjoy a Thai green curry or fish masala with your tunes.

Buzz Café MODERN AUSTRALIAN $$
(Map p818; 08-8941 1141; www.darwinhub.com/buzz-cafe; 48 Marina Blv, Cullen Bay; mains $18-40; lunch & dinner daily, breakfast Sun) This chic bar-restaurant furnished in Indonesian teak and Mt Bromo lava has a super multilevel deck overlooking the marina and makes a seductively sunny spot for a lazy lunch and a few drinks. Meals are Mod Oz, with some zingy salads and dishes to share. Aim for a deck table cantilevering out over the water.

Drinking

Drinking is big business in tropical Darwin (cold beer and humidity have a symbiotic relationship), and the city has dozens of pubs and terrace bars that make the most of balmy evenings. Virtually all bars double as restaurants, especially along Mitchell St – a frenzied row of booze rooms full of travellers, all within stumbling distance of one another.

Tap on Mitchell BAR
(Map p818; www.thetap.com.au; 51 Mitchell St) One of the busiest of the Mitchell St terrace bars, the Tap is always buzzing and there are inexpensive meals (nachos, burgers, calamari) to complement a great range of beer and wine.

Darwin Ski Club SPORTS CLUB
(Map p814; www.darwinskiclub.com.au; Conacher St, Fannie Bay) Leave Mitchell St behind and head for a sublime sunset at this laid-back (and refreshingly run-down) water-ski club on Vestey's Beach. The view through the palm trees from the beer garden is a winner, and there are often live bands.

Deck Bar BAR
(Map p818; www.thedeckbar.com.au; 22 Mitchell St) At the nonpartying parliamentary end of Mitchell St, the Deck Bar still manages to get lively with happy hours, pub trivia and regular live music. Blurring the line between indoors and outdoors brilliantly, the namesake deck is perfect for people-watching.

Darwin Sailing Club SPORTS CLUB
(Map p814; www.dwnsail.com.au; Atkins Dr, Fannie Bay) More upmarket than the ski club, the sailing club is always filled with yachties enjoying a sunset beer overlooking the Timor Sea. Tunes on the sound system are surprisingly

un-yacht club (no Christopher Cross or Rod Stewart), and its waterfront bistro is a great place for dinner, too. Sign in as a visitor at the door (bring some ID).

Shenannigans PUB

(Map p818; www.shenannigans.com.au; 69 Mitchell St) It's a long way from Cork, but Darwin has a few Irish-theme pubs. Shenannigans mixes it up with a big Mitchell St terrace, hearty food and big party nights. Guinness aplenty, live music and rugby on the TV.

Wisdom Bar & Grill BAR

(Map p818; www.wisdombar.com.au; 48 Mitchell St) Bright blue walls, velour couches and a streetside terrace with a tree growing out of it add up to a more intimate version of the Tap on Mitchell.

Ducks Nuts Bar & Grill BAR

(www.ducksnuts.com.au; 76 Mitchell St) A big backlit cocktail bar, regular live music and the swanky vodka bar give the Ducks Nuts plenty of cred.

Victoria Hotel PUB

(The Vic; Map p818; www.thevic.com.au; 27 Smith St Mall) The venerable old Vic is a good place for a drink and where locals and travellers can mingle. Seemingly undergoing constant renovations, these days it's more of an all-round backpacker entertainment venue.

☆ Entertainment

Darwin's balmy nights invite a bit of late-night exploration and while there is only a handful of nightclubs, you'll find something on every night of the week. There's also a thriving arts and entertainment scene: theatre, film and concerts.

Off the Leash magazine (www.offtheleash.net.au) lists events happening around town, as does **Darwin Community Arts** (www.darwincommunityarts.org.au). Keep an eye out for bills posted on noticeboards and telegraph poles that advertise dance and full-moon parties.

Live Music

Just about every pub/bar in town puts on some form of live music, mostly on Friday and Saturday nights, and sometimes filling the midweek void with karaoke and DJs.

Victoria Hotel ROCK, DJS

(The Vic; Map p818; www.thevichotel.com; 27 Smith St Mall) The Vic has bags of history – the stone building dates from 1890 – but it's hard to see it these days. This is Darwin's favourite backpacker pub and goes off every night of the week. Dirt-cheap meals draw the travellers to the upstairs bar, and they stay for the pool tables, DJs and dance floor. Downstairs has a pub quiz on Monday, table dancing, live bands and DJs.

Nirvana JAZZ, BLUES

(Map p818; ☎08-8981 2025; www.nirvanarestaurantdarwin.com; 6 Dashwood Cres) Behind an imposing dungeon-like doorway, this cosy restaurant-bar has live jazz/blues every Thursday, Friday and Saturday night and an open-mic jam session every Tuesday. And the Thai/Indian/Malaysian food here is magic.

Clubs

Discovery & Lost Arc NIGHTCLUB

(Map p818; www.discoverydarwin.com.au; 89 Mitchell St; ⏲9pm-4am Fri & Sat) Discovery is Darwin's biggest, tackiest nightclub and dance venue with three levels playing techno, hip hop and R&B. The Lost Arc is the neon-lit chill-out bar (undergoing renovations at the time of writing) opening on to Mitchell St, which starts to thaw after about 10pm.

Throb NIGHTCLUB

(Map p818; www.throbnightclub.com.au; 64 Smith St; ⏲10pm-5am Fri & Sat) Darwin's premier gay- and lesbian-friendly nightclub and cocktail bar, Throb attracts party-goers of all genders and persuasions for its hot DJs and cool atmosphere. Hosts drag shows and touring live acts.

Cinemas

★ **Deckchair Cinema** OUTDOOR CINEMA

(Map p818; ☎08-8981 0700; www.deckchaircinema.com; Jervois Rd, Waterfront Precinct; tickets adult/child $15/7; ⏲box office from 6.30pm Apr-Nov) During the Dry, the Darwin Film Society runs this fabulous outdoor cinema below the southern end of the Esplanade. Watch a movie under the stars while reclining in a deckchair. There's a licensed bar serving food or you can bring a picnic (no BYO alcohol). There are usually double features on Friday and Saturday nights (adult/child $22/10).

Birch Carroll & Coyle CINEMA

(Map p818; www.eventcinemas.com.au; 76 Mitchell St; tickets adult/child $17/13) Darwin's mainstream cinema complex, screening latest-release films across five theatres. Head down on Tropical Tuesday for $12 entry (all day).

DARWIN'S MAGICAL MARKETS

Mindil Beach Sunset Market (Map p818; www.mindil.com.au; off Gilruth Ave; ⌚5-10pm Thu, 4-9pm Sun May-Oct) As the sun heads towards the horizon on Thursday and Sunday, half of Darwin descends on Mindil Beach, with tables, chairs, rugs, grog and kids in tow. Food is the main attraction – Thai, Sri Lankan, Indian, Chinese and Malaysian to Brazilian, Greek, Portuguese and more – all at around $5 to $10 a serve. Don't miss a flaming satay stick from Bobby's brazier. Top it off with fresh fruit salad, decadent cakes or luscious crepes. But that's only half the fun – arts and crafts stalls bulge with handmade jewellery, fabulous rainbow tie-died clothes, Aboriginal artefacts, and wares from Indonesia and Thailand. Peruse and promenade, stop for a pummelling massage or to listen to rhythmic live music. Mindil Beach is about 2km from the city centre; an easy walk or hop on buses 4 or 6 which go past the market area.

Similar stalls (you'll recognise many of the stall holders) can be found at various suburban markets from Friday to Sunday.

Parap Village Market (Map p814; www.parapvillage.com.au; Parap Shopping Village, Parap Rd, Parap; ⌚8am-2pm Sat) This compact, crowded food-focused market is a local favourite with the full gamut of Southeast Asian cuisine, as well as plenty of ingredients to cook up your own tropical storm.

Rapid Creek Market (Map p814; www.rapidcreekshoppingcentre.com.au; 48 Trower Rd, Rapid Creek; ⌚6.30am-1.30pm Sun) Darwin's oldest market is another Asian marketplace, with a tremendous range of tropical fruit and vegetables mingled with a heady mixture of spices and swirling satay smoke.

Nightcliff Market (Map p814; www.nightcliffmarkets.com; Pavonia Way, Nightcliff; ⌚8am-2pm Sun) Another popular community market, north of the city in the Nightcliff Shopping Centre, where you will find lots of secondhand goods and designer clothing.

Happy Yess Market (Map p818; http://happyyess.tumblr.com; 56 Woods St; ⌚2-6pm 1st Sun each month) In association with the Darwin Visual Arts Association, this popular market is a great way to laze away a Sunday afternoon. The stalls are filled with secondhand treasures, tasty treats and whimsical stalls.

Theatre

Darwin Entertainment Centre ARTS CENTRE
(Map p818; ☎08-8980 3333; www.darwinentertainment.com.au; 93 Mitchell St; ⌚box office 10am-5.30pm Mon-Fri & 1hr prior to shows) Darwin's main community arts venue houses the Playhouse and Studio Theatres, and hosts events from fashion-award nights to plays, rock operas, comedies and concerts. Check the website for upcoming shows.

Brown's Mart ARTS CENTRE
(Map p818; ☎08-8981 5522; www.brownsmart.com.au; 12 Smith St) This historic venue (a former mining exchange) features live theatre performances, music and short films.

Shopping

You don't have to walk far along the Smith St Mall to find a souvenir shop selling lousy NT souvenirs: tea towels, T-shirts, stubbie holders and cane-toad coin purses (most of it made in China). Also in oversupply are outlets selling Aboriginal arts and crafts (be informed about reliable operators). However, Darwin's fabulous markets sell unique handcrafted items such as seed-pod hats, shell jewellery, kites, clothing and original photos.

Framed ART, DESIGN
(Map p818; www.framed.com.au; 55 Stuart Hwy, Stuart Park) Surrounded by sex shops, car yards and plumbing supply outlets, Frames presents a surprisingly classy range of NT arts and crafts. The eclectic and always changing range is typically tropical, and includes contemporary Aboriginal art, pottery, jewellery and some exquisitely carved furniture.

Casuarina Square MALL
(Map p814; www.casuarinasquare.com.au; 247 Trower Rd, Casuarina) This massive shopping complex has 170 mainstream retail outlets, plus cinemas and a food court. Good air-con

on sticky afternoons in the Wet. Buses 4 and 5 travel the 20 minutes north of Darwin.

NT General Store OUTDOOR GEAR
(Map p818; 42 Cavenagh St) This casual, corrugated-iron warehouse has shelves piled high with camping and bushwalking gear, as well as a range of maps.

Arts & Crafts

Aboriginal Fine Arts Gallery ART GALLERY
(Map p818; www.aaia.com.au; 1st fl, cnr Mitchell & Knuckey Sts; 9am-5pm) Displays and sells art from Arnhem Land and the Central Desert region.

Maningrida Arts & Culture ART GALLERY
(Map p818; www.maningrida.com; 32 Mitchell St, Shop 1; 9am-5pm Mon-Fri, 11.30am-4.30pm Sat) Features fibre sculptures, weavings and paintings from the Kunibidji community at Maningrida on the banks of the Liverpool River, Arnhem Land. Fully Aboriginal-owned.

Mbantua Fine Art Gallery ART GALLERY
(Map p818; www.mbantua.com.au; 2/30 Smith St Mall; 9am-5pm Mon-Sat) Vivid utopian designs painted on everything from canvasses to ceramics.

Territory Colours ART GALLERY
(Map p818; www.territorycolours.com; 46 Smith St Mall; 10am-5pm Mon-Fri, 10am-3pm Sat & Sun) Contemporary paintings and crafts, including glass, porcelain and wood from local artists; features the work of contemporary indigenous artist Harold Thomas.

Tiwi Art Network ART GALLERY
(Map p814; www.tiwiart.com; 3/3 Vickers St, Parap; 10am-5pm Wed-Fri, 10am-2pm Sat) The office and showroom for three arts communities on the Tiwi Islands.

Information

EMERGENCY

AANT Roadside Assistance (13 11 11; www.aant.com.au)

Ambulance (000; www.stjohnnt.com.au)

Fire (000; www.nt.gov.au/pfes)

Poisons Information Centre (13 11 26; 24hr) Advice on poisons, bites and stings.

Police (000; www.nt.gov.au/pfes)

INTERNET ACCESS

Most accommodation in Darwin provides some form of internet access, and there is free wi-fi available in Smith Street Mall.

Northern Territory Library (1800 019 155; www.ntl.nt.gov.au; Mitchell St, Parliament House; 10am-5pm Mon-Fri, 1-5pm Sat & Sun) Book in advance for free access. Wi-fi also available.

MEDICAL SERVICES

Royal Darwin Hospital (08-8920 6011; www.health.nt.gov.au; Rocklands Dr, Tiwi; 24hr) Accident and emergency services.

Travellers Medical & Vaccination Centre (08-8901 3100; www.traveldoctor.com.au; 43 Cavenagh St, 1st fl; 8.30am-noon & 1.30-5pm Mon-Fri) GPs by appointment.

MONEY

There are 24-hour ATMs dotted around the city centre, and exchange bureaux on Mitchell St.

BUYING ABORIGINAL ART

Taking home a piece of Aboriginal art can create an enduring connection with Australia. For Aboriginal artists, painting is an important cultural and economic enterprise. To ensure you're not perpetuating non-Indigenous cash-in on Aboriginal art's popularity, avoid buying cheap imported fridge magnets, stubbie holders, boomerangs or didgeridoos. Make sure you're buying from an authentic dealer selling original art, and if the gallery doesn't pay their artists upfront, ask exactly how much of your money will make it back to the artist or community.

A good test is to request some biographical info on the artists – if the vendor can't produce it, keep walking. An authentic piece will come with a certificate indicating the artist's name, language group and community, and the work's title, its story and when it was made.

You may also check that the selling gallery is associated with a regulatory body, such as the **Australian Commercial Galleries Association** (www.acga.com.au). Where possible, buy direct from Aboriginal arts centres or their city outlets (see www.ankaaa.org.au or www.aboriginalart.org); this is generally cheaper and ensures authenticity. You also get to view the works in the context in which they were created.

POST

General Post Office (☎13 13 18; www.auspost.com.au; 48 Cavenagh St; ⏰9am-5pm Mon-Fri, 9am-12.30pm Sat) Poste restante.

TOURIST INFORMATION

Tourism Top End (☎08-8980 6000, 1300 138 886; www.tourismtopend.com.au; cnr Smith & Bennett Sts, Darwin, NT; ⏰8.30am-5pm Mon-Fri, 9am-3pm Sat & Sun) Hundreds of brochures; books tours and accommodation.

Getting There & Away

AIR

Apart from the following major carriers arriving at Darwin International Airport (p812), smaller routes are flown by local operators; ask a travel agent.

Airnorth (www.airnorth.com.au) To/from East Timor, and to Broome, Perth, Kununurra and the Gold Coast.

Jetstar (www.jetstar.com) Direct flights to the eastern coast capitals and major hubs, as well as several Southeast Asian cities.

Qantas (www.qantas.com.au) Direct flights to Perth, Adelaide, Canberra, Sydney, Brisbane, Alice Springs and Cairns.

Skywest (www.skywest.com.au) Direct flights to Perth, Kununurra and Broome.

Virgin Australia (www.virginaustralia.com) Direct flights between Darwin and Brisbane, Broome, Melbourne, Sydney and Perth.

BUS

Greyhound Australia (www.greyhound.com.au) operates long-distance bus services from the **Transit Centre** (69 Mitchell St). There's at least one service per day up/down the Stuart Hwy, stopping at Pine Creek ($75, three hours), Katherine ($94, 4½ hours), Mataranka ($132, seven hours), Tennant Creek ($290, 14½ hours) and Alice Springs ($391, 22 hours).

For Kakadu, there's a daily return service from Darwin to Cooinda ($87, 4½ hours) via Jabiru ($62, 3½ hours).

Backpacker buses can also get you to out-of-the-way places:

Adventure Tours (www.adventuretours.com.au)

Oz Experience (www.ozexperience.com)

CAR & CAMPERVAN

For driving around Darwin, conventional vehicles are cheap enough, but most companies offer only 100km free, which won't get you very far. Rates start at around $40 per day for a small car with 100km per day.

There are also plenty of 4WD vehicles available in Darwin, but you usually have to book ahead and fees/deposits are higher than for 2WD vehicles. Larger companies offer one-way rentals plus better mileage deals for more-expensive vehicles. Campervans are a great option for touring around the Territory and you generally get unlimited kilometres even for short rentals. Prices start at around $50 a day for a basic camper or $80 to $100 for a three-berth hi-top camper, to $200-plus for the bigger mobile homes or 4WD bushcampers. Additional insurance cover or excess reduction costs extra.

Most rental companies are open every day and have agencies in the city centre. Avis, Budget, Hertz and Thrifty all have offices at the airport.

Advance Car Rentals (www.advancecar.com.au; 86 Mitchell St) Local operator with some good deals (ask about unlimited kilometres).

Avis (www.avis.com; 89 Smith St)

Mighty Cars & Campervans (www.mightycampers.com.au; 17 Bombing Rd, Winnellie) At the same depot as Britz, this is a budget outfit with small campers and hi-tops at reasonable rates.

Britz Australia (www.britz.com.au; 17 Bombing Rd, Winnellie) Britz is a reliable outfit with a big range of campervans and motorhomes, including 4WD bushcampers.

Budget (www.budget.com.au; cnr Daly St & Doctors Gully Rd)

Europcar (www.europcar.com.au; 77 Cavenagh St)

Hertz (www.hertz.com.au; 55–59 Mitchell St, Shop 41, Mitchell Centre)

Thrifty (www.rentacar.com.au; 50 Mitchell St)

Travellers Autobarn (www.travellers-autobarn.com.au; 13 Daly St) Campervan specialist.

Wicked Campers (www.wickedcampers.com.au; 75 McMinn St) Colourfully painted small campers aimed at backpackers.

TRAIN

The legendary *Ghan* train, operated by **Great Southern Rail** (www.gsr.com.au), runs weekly (twice weekly May to July) between Adelaide and Darwin via Alice Springs. The Darwin terminus is on Berrimah Rd, 15km/20 minutes from the city centre. A taxi fare into the centre is about $35, though there is a shuttle service to/from the Transit Centre for $10.

Getting Around

TO/FROM THE AIRPORT

Darwin International Airport (p812) is 12km north of the city centre, and handles both international and domestic flights. **Darwin Airport Shuttle** (☎08-8981 5066, 1800 358 945; www.darwinairportshuttle.com.au) will pick up or drop off almost anywhere in the centre for $15. When leaving Darwin book a day before departure. A taxi fare into the centre is about $30.

PUBLIC TRANSPORT

Darwinbus (www.nt.gov.au/transport) runs a comprehensive bus network that departs from the **Darwin Bus Terminus** (Harry Chan Ave), opposite Brown's Mart.

A $2 adult ticket gives unlimited travel on the bus network for three hours (validate your ticket when you first get on). Daily ($5) and weekly ($15) travel cards are also available from bus interchanges, newsagencies and the visitor information centre. Bus 4 (to Fannie Bay, Nightcliff, Rapid Creek and Casuarina) and bus 6 (Fannie Bay, Parap and Stuart Park) are useful for getting to Aquascene, the Botanic Gardens, Mindil Beach, the Museum & Art Gallery, Fannie Bay Gaol Museum, East Point Reserve and the markets.

Alternatively, the privately run Tour Tub (p821) is a hop-on, hop-off minibus touring Darwin's sights throughout the day.

SCOOTER

Darwin Scooter Hire (www.esummer.com.au; 9 Daly St) Rents out mountain bikes/50cc scooters/motorbikes for $20/60/180 per day.

TAXI

Taxis wait along Knuckey St, diagonally opposite the north end of Smith St Mall, and are usually easy to flag down. Call **Darwin Radio Taxis** (☎13 10 08; www.131008.com).

AROUND DARWIN

Mandorah

Mandorah is a low-key, relaxed residential beach suburb looking out across the harbour to Darwin. It sits on the tip of Cox Peninsula, 128km by road from Darwin but only 6km across the harbour by regular ferry. The main reason to visit is for the ferry ride across the harbour and a few drinks or dinner at the super-friendly pub. The nearby Wagait Aboriginal community numbers around 400 residents.

The **Mandorah Beach Hotel** (☎08-8978 5044; www.mandorahbeachhotel.bigpondhosting.com; d/f $88/110; ❄@≋) has sublime views over the beach and turquoise water to Darwin. All rooms in the refurbished motel have a fridge, TV and air-con. Even if you don't stay the night, the pub and restaurant (mains $13 to $26, open for lunch to 2pm, and dinner) food is great, and there's live music some weekends in season.

The **Mandorah Ferry** (www.fastferries.com.au; adult/child return $23/12) operates about a dozen daily services (adult/child return $25/12.50), with the first departure from the Cullen Bay Marina in Darwin at 6.30am and the last at 10pm (midnight on Friday and Saturday). The last ferry from Mandorah is at 10.20pm (12.20am Friday and Saturday). Bookings not required.

Tiwi Islands

The Tiwi Islands – **Bathurst Island** and **Melville Island** – lie about 80km north of Darwin, and are home to the Tiwi Aboriginal people. The Tiwis ('We People') have a distinct culture and today are well known for producing vibrant art and the odd champion Aussie Rules football player.

Tourism is restricted on the islands and for most tourists the only way to visit is on one of the daily organised tours from Darwin.

The Tiwis' island homes kept them fairly isolated from mainland developments until the 20th century, and their culture has retained several unique features. Perhaps the best known are the pukumani (burial poles), carved and painted with symbolic and mythological figures, which are erected around graves. More recently the Tiwis have turned their hand to art for sale – carving, painting, textile screen-printing, batik and pottery using traditional designs and motifs. The Bima Wear textile factory was set up in 1969 to employ Tiwi women, and today makes many bright fabrics in distinctive designs.

The main settlement on the islands is **Nguiu** in the southeast of Bathurst Island, which was founded in 1911 as a Catholic mission. On Melville Island the settlements are **Pularumpi** and **Milikapiti**.

Most of the 2700 Tiwi Islanders live on Bathurst Island (there are about 900 people on Melville Island). Most follow a mainly nontraditional lifestyle, but they still hunt dugong and gather turtle eggs, and hunting and gathering usually supplements the mainland diet a couple of times a week. Tiwis also go back to their traditional lands on Melville Island for a few weeks each year to teach and to learn traditional culture. Descendants of the Japanese pearl divers who regularly visited here early this century also live on Melville Island.

Aussie Rules football is a passion among the islanders and one of the biggest events

Around Darwin

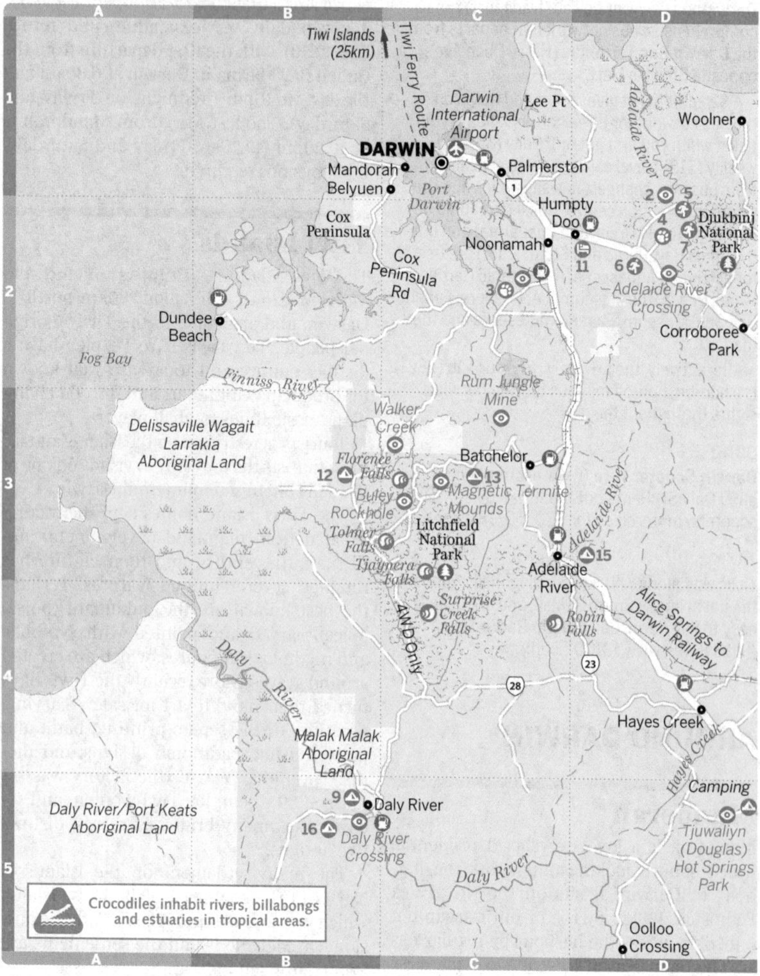

of the year (and the only time it's possible to visit without a permit or on a tour) is the Tiwi football grand-final day in late March. Huge numbers of people come across from the mainland for the event – book your tour/ferry well in advance.

Tours

There's no public transport on the islands, so the best way to see them is on a tour. You can catch the Tiwi Ferry over to Nguiu and have a look around the town without taking a tour or buying a permit, but if you want to explore further you'll need a permit from the Tiwi Land Council (p812).

Tiwi Tours CULTURAL
(☎08-8923 6523, 1300 721 365; www.aussieadventures.com.au; tour adult/child $465/418) Runs fascinating day trips to the Tiwis, although interaction with the local community is limited to your guides and local workshops and showrooms. A one-day tour to Bathurst Island includes a charter flight, permit, lunch, tea and damper with Tiwi women, craft workshops, and visits to the early Catholic-mission buildings, the Patakijiyali Museum

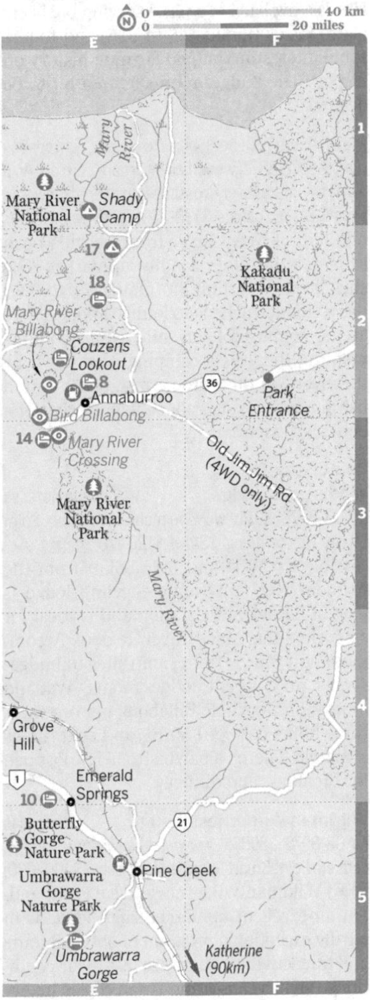

Around Darwin

Sights

1 Berry Springs Nature Park C2
2 Fogg Dam Conservation Reserve D1
3 Territory Wildlife Park C2
4 Window on the Wetlands Visitor Centre D2

Activities, Courses & Tours

5 Adelaide River Cruises D2
6 Adelaide River Queen D2
7 Spectacular Jumping Crocodile Cruise D2

Sleeping

8 Bark Hut Inn E2
9 Daly River Mango Farm B5
10 Emerald Springs Roadhouse E4
11 Humpty Doo Hotel D2
12 Litchfield Safari Camp B3
13 Litchfield Tourist Park C3
14 Mary River Wilderness Retreat E3
15 Mt Bundy Station D3
16 Perry's B5
17 Point Stuart Wilderness Lodge E2
18 Wildman Wilderness Lodge E2

Eating

Litchfield Cafe .... (see 16)

and a pukumani burial site. Tours depart Monday to Friday from March to November.

Tiwi Ferry CULTURAL
(Map p818; ☎0418 675 266; www.tiwiferry.com.au; tour per person $149 plus ferry fare, ferry only return adult/child $180/120) Leaving from Cullen Bay ferry terminal at 7.30am and returning at 5pm, the boat trip takes about two hours, and you spend all of the land time in Nguiu, visiting the church, museum, Tiwi Design and Ngaruwanajirri Art Community. The ferry runs on Mondays, Wednesdays and Fridays.

Arnhem Highway

The Arnhem Hwy (Route 36) branches off towards Kakadu 34km southeast of Darwin. About 10km along the road, in the small agricultural hub of Humpty Doo, the self-proclaimed 'world famous' **Humpty Doo Hotel** (☎08-8988 1372; humptydoohotel@hotmail.com; Arnhem Hwy; d/cabins $120/140; ❄ ☒) is a brawling kinda roadhouse, serving big meals (mains $17 to $30, lunch and dinner). There are unremarkable motel rooms and cabins out the back.

About 15km beyond Humpty Doo is the turn-off to the fecund green carpet of **Fogg Dam Conservation Reserve** (www.foggdamfriends.org). Bring your binoculars – there are ludicrous numbers of waterbirds living here. The dam walls are closed to walkers (due to crocs), but there are a couple of nature walks (2.2km and 3.6km) through the forest and woodlands. Bird numbers are highest between December and July. A further 8km beyond the Window on the Wetlands Visitor Centre is **Adelaide River Crossing**. It's from the murky waters of this river that large crocs are tempted to jump for camera-weilding tourists. See the boxed text (p837).

Window on the Wetlands Visitor Centre WILDLIFE RESERVE
(www.nretas.nt.gov.au/national-parks-andreserves/parks/windowwetlands; Arnhem Hwy; ⏲8am-7pm) FREE Three kilometres past the Fogg Dam turn-off is this dashing-looking structure full of displays (static and interactive) explaining the wetland ecosystem, as well as the history of the local Limilgnan-Wulna Aboriginal people. There are great views over the Adelaide River floodplain from the observation deck, and binoculars for studying the waterbirds on Lake Beatrice.

Mary River Region

Beyond Adelaide River, the Arnhem Hwy passes through the Mary River region with the wetlands and wildlife of the Mary River National Park extending to the north.

Bird Billabong, just off the highway a few kilometres before Mary River Crossing, is a back-flow billabong, filled by creeks flowing off the nearby Mt Bundy Hill during the Wet. It's 4km off the highway and accessible by 2WD year-round. The scenic **loop walk** (4.5km, two hours) passes through **tropical woodlands**, with a backdrop of Mt Bundy granite rocks.

About another 2km along the same road is the emerald-green **Mary River Billabong**, with a BBQ area (no camping). From here the 4WD-only Hardies Track leads deeper into the national park to **Corroboree Billabong** (25km) and **Couzens Lookout** (37km).

Further along and north of the Arnhem Hwy, the partly sealed Point Stuart Rd leads to a number of riverside viewing platforms and to **Shady Camp**. The causeway barrage here, which stops freshwater flowing into saltwater, creates the ideal feeding environment for barramundi, and is the ideal fishing environment.

Sleeping & Eating

There are basic public **camping grounds** (adult/child/family $3.30/1.65/7.70) at Couzens Lookout and Shady Camp, where there are grassy camp sites under banyan trees. Come prepared to ward off armies of mosquitoes.

Bark Hut Inn HOTEL $
(☎08-8978 8988; unpowered/powered site $15/30, budget s/d $65/85, cabins $190) The Bark Hut is a big barn of a place serving big beefy bistro meals (mains $15 to $26) and there's some interesting buffalo farming history on display. The budget rooms leave a bit to be desired.

Mary River Wilderness Retreat RESORT $$
(☎08-8978 8877; www.maryriverpark.com.au; Arnhem Hwy, Mary River Crossing; unpowered/powered sites $22/30, cabins $190-220; ❄📶≋) Boasting 3km of Mary River frontage, this bush retreat is heading steadily upmarket. The slick licensed restaurant (mains $12 to $30) has a wonderful deck to lounge about. There are 26 comfortable en-suite cabins complementing the grassy camping area down by the river. Go on a croc cruise ($45), hire a fishing boat, or ask about fishing charters; bookings essential.

Point Stuart Wilderness Lodge CAMPGROUND, HOTEL $$
(☎08-8978 8914; www.pointstuart.com.au; Point Stuart Rd; camping $34, d $120-170; ❄≋) Accessible by 2WD and only 36km from the Arnhem Hwy, this remote-feeling lodge is part of an old cattle station and is ideal for exploring the Mary River region. Accommodation ranges from camp sites to budget rooms and decent lodge rooms. Wetland cruises on Rockhole Billabong per one/two/three hours cost $40/50/65, and boat hire is available. There's a bar/bistro here too, open for breakfast and dinner.

Wildman Wilderness Lodge RESORT $$$
(☎08-8978 8955; www.wildmanwildernesslodge.com.au; Point Stuart Rd; safari tent/cabin $490/630; ❄≋) Wildman Wilderness Lodge is out-and-out an excellent upmarket safari lodge with a truly exceptional program of optional tours and fun activities. There are just 10 air-conditioned stylish cabins and 15 fan-cooled luxury tents to choose from and the daily tarriff includes breakfast and a three-course dinner.

Stuart Highway to Litchfield National Park

Territory Wildlife Park & Berry Springs Nature Park

The turn-off to the Territory Wildlife Park and Berry Springs is 48km down the Stuart Hwy from Darwin; it's then about 10km to the park.

Sights & Activities

★Territory Wildlife Park WILDLIFE PARK
(www.territorywildlifepark.com.au; 960 Cox Peninsula Rd; adult/child/family $26/13/45.50; ⌚8.30am-6pm, last admission 4pm) This excellent park showcases the best of Aussie wildlife. Highlights include the Flight Deck, where birds of prey display their dexterity (free-flying demonstrations at 11am and 2.30pm daily); the nocturnal house, where you can observe nocturnal fauna such as bilbies and bats; 11 different habitat aviaries; and a huge walk-through aviary, representing a monsoon rainforest. Pride of place must go to the aquarium, where a clear walk-through tunnel puts you among giant barramundi, stingrays, sawfish and saratogas, while a separate tank holds a 3.8m saltwater crocodile. To see everything you can either walk around the 4km perimeter road, or hop on and off the shuttle trains that run every 15 to 30 minutes and stop at all the exhibits.

Berry Springs Nature Park NATURE RESERVE
(www.nretas.nt.gov.au/national-parks-and-reserves/parks/find/berrysprings; ⌚8am-6.30pm) Close by is this beautiful series of spring-fed swimming holes shaded by paperbarks and pandanus palms and serenaded by abundant birds. Facilities include a kiosk, a picnic area with BBQs, toilets, changing sheds and showers.

The turn-off to Berry Springs and Territory Wildlife Park is 48km down the Track from Darwin; it's then 10km to the park.

Batchelor

POP 538

The government once gave Batchelor's blocks of land away to encourage settlement in the little town. That was before uranium was discovered and the nearby **Rum Jungle mine** developed (it closed in 1971 after almost 20 years). These days, Batchelor exists as a gateway and service centre for neighbouring Litchfield National Park, and is home to the **Batchelor Institute for Indigenous Education**.

Opposite the general store, a small, sporadically staffed **visitor information centre** (Tarkarri Rd; ⌚8.30am-5pm) is stocked with fliers, including national-parks info.

Sleeping & Eating

Although most travellers are naturally headed into Litchfield, this gateway town offers

JUMPING CROCS

Few people seem to be able to resist the sight of a 3m-long saltwater crocodile launching itself out of the water towards a hunk of meat. Like a well-trained circus act, these wild crocs know where to get a free feed – and down on the Adelaide River, the croc-jumping show is guaranteed.

Jumping out of the water to grab prey is actually natural behaviour for crocs, usually to take surprised birds or animals from overhanging branches. They use their powerful tails to propel themselves up from a stationary start just below the surface, from where they can see their prey.

There are three operators at different locations along the Adelaide River. The modus operandi is pretty similar – a crew member (or nervous tourist) holds one end of a long stick that has a couple of metres of string attached to the other end. Tied to the end of the string is a very domesticated-looking pork chop – not exactly bush tucker, but the crocs love it. The whole thing is contrived, but it's still an amazing sight. And if you are lucky you will get to see one of the old denizens measuring over 5m. These old fellas aren't as spritely as their children but are a truly awesome sight.

Adelaide River Cruises (☎08-8983 3224; www.adelaiderivercruises.com.au; tours adult/child $35/25; ⌚9am, 11am, 1pm & 3pm May-Oct) On a private stretch of river past the Fogg Dam turn-off. Also runs small-group full-day wildlife cruises.

Adelaide River Queen (☎08-8988 8144; www.jumpingcrocodilecruises.com.au; tours adult/child $40/28; ⌚9am, 11am, 1pm & 3pm, for times Nov-Feb see website) Well-established operator on the highway just before Adelaide River Crossing.

Spectacular Jumping Crocodile Cruise (☎08-8988 9077; www.jumpingcrocodile.com.au; tours adult/child $35/20; ⌚9am, 11am, 1pm & 3pm) Along the Window on the Wetlands access road, this outfit runs one-hour tours. Ask about trips ex-Darwin.

some quality accommodation and a pub. The **Batchelor General Store** (cnr Tarkarri & Nurndina Rds; ⊙6am-6pm) has a well-stocked supermarket, takeaway shop, newsagent and post office.

Rum Jungle Bungalows
B&B $$

(☑08-8976 0555; www.rumjunglebungalows.com.au; 10 Meneling Rd; d $160; ❋▣) Bombarded by fluttering butterflies, these six olive-coloured bungalows are simple, elegant and immaculately clean. Each has a small fridge and en suite, and it's a short walk through tropical gardens (featuring native NT plants and herbs) to the private pool and breezy breakfast room (fresh seasonal fruit, local honey, homemade muesli and hot coffee).

Batchelor Butterfly Farm
RESORT $$

(☑08-8976 0199; www.butterflyfarm.net; 8 Meneling Rd; d $110-160; ❋@⎈▣) This compact retreat divides itself between a low-key tourist attraction and friendly tropical-style resort. The kids will love the butterfly farm (adult/child $10/5) and mini zoo, which is free for staying guests. There are en suite cabins, a large homestay, and a busy all-day cafe/restaurant (mains $12 to $34), featuring Asian-inspired dishes. It's all a bit Zen with Buddha statues, chill music and wicker chairs on the shaded deck.

Historic Retreat B&B
B&B $$

(☑08-8976 0554; www.historicretreat.com.au; 19 Pinaroo Cres; d incl breakfast $120-160; ❋) The beautifully restored former home of Rum Jungle-mine managers is elevated (tropical-style) and has louvred windows, polished floorboards, vintage furniture and plenty of mine memorabilia. The five guest rooms share two bathrooms.

Litchfield Tourist Park
CARAVAN PARK $

(☑08-8976 0070; www.litchfieldtouristpark.com.au; 2916 Litchfield Park Rd; unpowered/powered sites $24/32, bunkhouse $65, en-suite cabins $125-140; ❋@⎈▣) Just 4km from Litchfield, the standout feature of this attractive park is the two-bedroom ranch-style house that you can rent for $30. There's also a breezy, open-sided bar/restaurant here (mains $13 to $22, open breakfast and dinner) where you can get a beer, a burger or a real coffee.

Batchelor Resort
RESORT $$

(☑08-8976 0123; www.batchelor-resort.com; 37-49 Rum Jungle Rd; unpowered/powered sites $30/38, cabins/motel d $130/170; ❋⎈▣) On the edge of town, this sprawling orange-brick complex has a caravan park with en suite sites and cabins, and a separate motel section. It's good for families, with bird feeding, two pools and two restaurants. There's also a bar and a grocery shop.

Litchfield National Park

It may not be as well known as Kakadu, but many Territory locals rate Litchfield even higher. In fact, there's a local saying that goes: 'Litchfield-do, Kaka-don't'. We don't entirely agree – we think Kaka-do-too – but this is certainly one of the best places in the Top End for bushwalking, camping and especially swimming, with waterfalls plunging into gorgeous, safe swimming holes.

The 1500-sq-km national park encloses much of the spectacular Tabletop Range, a wide sandstone plateau mostly surrounded by cliffs. The waterfalls that pour off the edge of this plateau are a highlight of the park, feeding crystal-clear cascades and croc-free plunge pools.

The two routes to Litchfield (115km south of Darwin) from the Stuart Hwy join up and loop through the park. The southern access road via Batchelor is all sealed, while the northern access route, off the Cox Peninsula Rd, is partly unsealed, corrugated and often closed in the Wet.

About 17km after entering the park from Batchelor you come to what looks like tombstones. But only the very tip of these magnetic termite mounds is used to bury the dead; at the bottom are the king and queen, with workers in between. They're perfectly aligned to regulate temperature, catching the morning sun, then allowing the residents to dodge the midday heat. Nearby are some giant mounds made by the aptly named cathedral termites.

Another 6km further along is the turn-off to Buley Rockhole (2km), where water cascades through a series of rock pools big enough to lodge your bod in. This turn-off also takes you to Florence Falls (5km), accessed by a 15-minute, 135-step descent to a deep, beautiful pool surrounded by monsoon forest. Alternatively, you can see the falls from a lookout, 120m from the car park. There's a walking track (1.7km, 45 minutes) between the two places that follows Florence Creek.

About 18km beyond the turn-off to Florence Falls is the turn-off to the spectacular Tolmer Falls, which is for looking only. A

1.6km loop track (45 minutes) offers beautiful views of the valley.

It's a further 7km along the main road to the turn-off for Litchfield's big-ticket attraction, **Wangi Falls** (pronounced *Wong-guy*), 1.6km up a side road. The falls flow year-round, spilling either side of a huge orange-rock outcrop and filling an enormous swimming hole bordered by rainforest. Bring swimming goggles to spot local fish. It's immensely popular during the Dry (when there's a portable refreshment kiosk here), but water levels in the Wet can make it unsafe; look for signposted warnings.

The park offers plenty of bushwalking, including the **Tabletop Track** (39km), a circuit of the park that takes three to five days to complete depending on how many side tracks you follow. You can access the track at Florence Falls, Wangi Falls and Walker Creek. Overnight walkers should register (call ☎1300 650 730); camping fees apply. The track is closed September to March.

Tours

There are numerous Litchfield tours ex-Darwin (p821).

Sleeping & Eating

There is excellent public **camping** (adult/child $6.60/3.30) within the park. Grounds with toilets and fireplaces are located at Florence Falls, Florence Creek, Buley Rockhole, Wangi Falls (better for vans than tents) and Tjaynera Falls (Sandy Creek; 4WD required). A visitor centre and cafe was being built at Wangi Falls at the time of writing. There are more-basic camp sites at Surprise Creek Falls (4WD required) and Walker Creek, with its own swimming hole, where camping involves bushwalking to a series of sublime, isolated riverside sites.

Litchfield Safari Camp CAMPGROUND $
(☎08-8978 2185; www.litchfieldsafaricamp.com.au; Litchfield Park Rd; unpowered/powered sites $30/35, dm $30, d safari tents $130, extra person $10;) Shady grassed sites make this a good alternative to Litchfield's bush camping sites, especially if you want power. The safari tents are great value as they comfortably sleep up to four folks. There's also a ramshackle camp kitchen, a kiosk and a pint-sized pool.

★**Litchfield Cafe** CAFE $$
(www.litchfieldcafe.com.au; Litchfield Park Rd; mains $16-35; ⊙breakfast, lunch & dinner Apr-Sep, lunch only Oct-Mar) Filo parcels (try the chicken, mango and macadamia) make for a super lunch at this superb licensed cafe, or you could go for a meal of grilled local barra or roo fillet, topped-off with a good coffee and some wicked mango cheesecake.

Adelaide River to Katherine

Adelaide River

POP 238

Blink and you'll miss this tiny highway town, 111km south of Darwin, which was once an important point on the Overland Telegraph Line and supply depot during WWII. The **Adelaide River War Cemetery** (Memorial Tce) is an important legacy: a sea of brass plaques commemorating those killed in the 1942–43 air raids on northern Australia.

Sleeping & Eating

Adelaide River Inn PUB $
(☎08-8976 7047; www.adelaideriverinn.com.au; 106 Stuart Hwy; unpowered/powered sites $18/25, budget/motel/cabin d $85/110/140;) An affable little pub (mains $9 to $32, open breakfast, lunch and dinner) hiding behind the BP petrol station. On the corner of the bar stands Charlie the water buffalo, who lived here in relative obscurity until shooting to fame in *Crocodile Dundee*. When he died, the owner had him stuffed for posterity. There is a range of en-suite accommodation including neat cabins across the road.

★**Mt Bundy Station** CAMPGROUND $
(☎08-8976 7009; www.mtbundy.com.au; Haynes Rd; unpowered/powered sites $22/26, s/d $50/85, cottage d $145, safari tent $202;) If you're into horse riding, fishing and country-style hospitality, Mt Bundy Station is the perfect detour, 3km off the highway after Adelaide River. The original station buildings have become spotless guest accommodation, plus there are luxury safari tents. There are 4WD tours and plenty of animals on the property – guided horse rides cost $60 per hour, with overnight treks by arrangement.

Daly River

POP 512

The Daly River is considered some of the best **barramundi fishing** country in the Territory and the hub is this small community

117km southwest of Hayes Creek, reached by a narrow sealed road off the Dorat Rd (Old Stuart Hwy; Rte 23). Most of the population lives in the Nauiyu Nambiyu Aboriginal community, near the Daly River Crossing. A new bridge to replace the old causway was under construction at the time of writing. There's a shop and fuel here and visitors are welcome without a permit, but note that this is a dry community (no alcohol).

Other than fishing, the main attraction here is **Merrepen Arts** (☎08-8978 2533; www.merrepenarts.com.au; ⊙10am-5pm) FREE, a gallery displaying locally made arts and crafts including etchings, screen printing, acrylic paintings, carvings, weaving and textiles. You can usually see artists at work in the mornings. Call in advance to check if they're open.

The **Merrepen Arts & Sports Festival** (www.merrepenfestival.com.au) celebrates arts and music from communities around the district, including Nauiyu, Wadeye and Peppimenarti, with displays, art auctions, workshops and dancing.

Sleeping & Eating

Daly River Mango Farm CAMPGROUND $
(☎08-8978 2464; www.mangofarm.com.au; unpowered/powered sites $30/35, d $100-175, 2-bedroom family cabin $350; ❄≋) The camping ground here, on the Daly River 9km from the crossing, is shaded by a magnificent grove of near-century-old mango trees. Other accommodation includes budget and self-contained cabins. Guided fishing trips and boat hire available.

Daly River Roadside Inn PUB $
(☎08-8978 2418; dalyriverpub@bigpond.com; unpowered/powered sites $15/30, r $100-130; ❄) At Daly River itself is this rowdy pub with basic rooms, a small camping ground and meals (takeaway or pub food from $8 to $20) and fuel available.

Perry's CAMPGROUND $
(☎08-8978 2452; www.dalyriver.com; Mayo Park; unpowered/powered sites $28/24, unit $120; ❄≋) A very peaceful place with 2km of river frontage and gardens where orphaned wallabies bound around. Dick Perry, a well-known fishing expert, operates guided trips, and boat hire is available. The self-contained unit has a deck with a BBQ and if you stay for seven nights you will only pay for six.

Pine Creek

POP 381

A short detour off the Stuart Hwy, Pine Creek was once the scene of a frantic gold rush. The open-cut mine here closed in 1995, but today there's still gold and iron-ore mining and exploration nearby. A few of the 19th-century timber and corrugated-iron buildings still survive. The Kakadu Hwy (Rte 21) branches off the Stuart Hwy here, connecting it to Cooinda and Jabiru, making Pine Creek a useful base for exploring the region.

Sights & Activities

Railway Museum & Stream Train MUSEUM
(Railway Tce; ⊙10am-2pm Mon-Fri May-Sep) FREE Dating from 1889, the Railway Museum has a display on the Darwin-to-Pine Creek railway which ran from 1889 to 1976. The lovingly restored steam engine, built in Manchester in 1877, sits in its own enclosure next to the museum.

Pine Creek Museum MUSEUM
(www.nationaltrustnt.org.au; 11 Railway Tce; adult/child $2.20/free; ⊙11am-5pm Mon-Fri, 11am-1pm Sat) This museum is dedicated to the area's mining history and Chinese population. A one-time hospital, pharmacy and military communications centre, it's the oldest prefab corrugated iron building in Australia, made in England and shipped here in 1889.

Umbrawarra Gorge Nature Park NATURE RESERVE
(www.nretas.nt.gov.au/national-parks-and-reserves/find/umbrawarragorge.html; campground adult/child $3.30/1.65) About 3km south of Pine Creek on the Stuart Hwy is the turn-off to pretty Umbrawarra Gorge, with a safe swimming hole, a little beach and a basic campground. It's 22km southwest on a rugged dirt road (just OK for 2WDs in the Dry; often impassable in the Wet). Bring plenty of water and mozzie repellent.

Lookout LANDMARK
Drive or walk up the short-but-steep hill off Moule St to the lookout over the old open-cut mine, now full of water (135m deep!).

Sleeping & Eating

Lazy Lizard Tourist Park & Tavern CAMPGROUND $
(☎08-8976 1008; www.lazylizardpinecreek.com.au; 299 Millar Tce; unpowered/powered sites $17/25; ≋) The small, well-grassed camping area at the

Lazy Lizard is really only secondary to the pulsing pub next door. The open-sided bar supported by carved ironwood pillars is a busy local watering hole with a pool table and old saddles slung across the rafters. The kitchen serves top-notch pub food (mains $16 to $30, open lunch and dinner), featuring big steaks and barra dishes.

Emerald Springs Roadhouse ROADHOUSE **$**
(☎08-8976 1169; www.emeraldsprings.com.au; Stuart Hwy; unpowered/powered sites $10/20, cabins from $65; ❄☒) About 25km north of Pine Creek, the excellent Emerald Springs Roadhouse (mains $16 to $32) makes an effort to provide more than a regulation roadhouse. You can still get a burger and a beer, but there's also a 'specials' blackboard with many wonderful choices. Out back there's decent accommodation and a great deck on which to sit, sip and savour your steak sanger or wok-tossed vegetables. And the homemade ice cream is awesome!

Pine Creek Railway Resort BOUTIQUE HOTEL **$$**
(☎08-8976 1001; www.pinecreekrailwayresort.com.au; s/d $85/110, cabins $130-150; ❄☒) This charming hotel uses raw iron, steel and wood in its stylish and modern rooms with options for singles, doubles and families. The dining area has been designed with romantic rail journeys of yore in mind and is a scene-stealer with pressed-tin ceilings and elaborate chandeliers. The menu is, however, modern with Asian-inspired dishes, pizzas and more.

KAKADU & ARNHEM LAND

Kakadu and neighbouring Arnhem Land epitomise the remarkable landscape and cultural heritage of the Top End. Each is a treasure house of natural history and Aboriginal art, and both are significant homelands of contemporary indigenous culture.

Kakadu National Park

Kakadu is a whole lot more than a national park. It's also a vibrant, living acknowledgment of the elemental link between the Aboriginal custodians and the country they have nurtured, endured and respected for thousands of generations. Encompassing almost 20,000 sq km (about 200km north–south and 100km east–west), it holds in its boundaries a spectacular ecosystem and a mind-blowing concentration of ancient **rock art**. The landscape is an ever-changing tapestry – periodically scorched and flooded, apparently desolate or obviously abundant depending on the season.

In just a few days you can cruise on billabongs bursting with wildlife, examine 25,000-year-old rock paintings with the help of an indigenous guide, swim in pools at the foot of tumbling waterfalls and hike through ancient sandstone escarpment country.

If Kakadu has a downside – in the Dry at least – it's that it's incredibly popular. Resorts, camping grounds and rock-art sites can be very crowded, but this is a vast park and with a little adventurous spirit you can easily get off the beaten track and be alone with nature.

The Arnhem Hwy and Kakadu Hwy traverse the park; both are sealed and accessible year-round. The 4WD-only Old Jim Jim Rd is an alternative access from the Arnhem Hwy, joining the Kakadu Hwy 7km south of Cooinda.

Note that takeaway alcohol is hideously expensive anywhere in Kakadu – if you want a drink back at the camp site, stock up in Darwin.

Geography

The circuitous Arnhem Land escarpment, a dramatic 30m- to 200m-high sandstone cliff line, forms the natural boundary between Kakadu and Arnhem Land and winds 500km through eastern and southeastern Kakadu.

Creeks cut across the rocky plateau and, in the wet season, tumble off it as thundering waterfalls. They then flow across the lowlands to swamp Kakadu's vast northern flood plains. From west to east, the rivers are the Wildman, West Alligator, South Alligator and East Alligator (the latter forming the eastern boundary of the park). The coastal zone has long stretches of mangrove swamp, important for halting erosion and as a breeding ground for bird and marine life. The southern part of the park is dry lowlands with open grassland and eucalypts. Pockets of monsoon rainforest crop up throughout the park.

More than 80% of Kakadu is savannah woodland. It has more than 1000 plant species, many still used by Aboriginal people for food and medicinal purposes.

Kakadu National Park

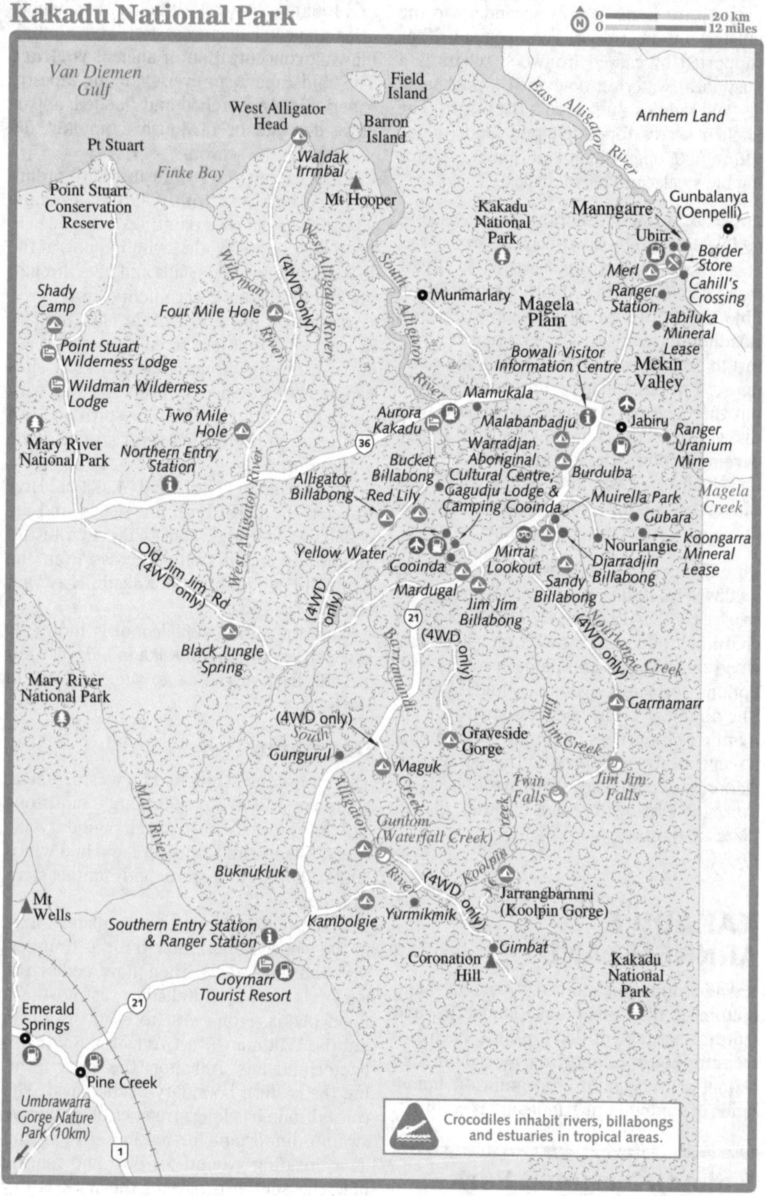

Climate

The average maximum temperature in Kakadu is 34°C, year-round. The Dry is roughly April to September, and the Wet, when most of Kakadu's average rainfall of 1500mm falls, is from October to March. As wetlands and waterfalls swell, unsealed roads become impassable, cutting off some highlights such as Jim Jim Falls.

Local Aboriginal people recognise six seasons in the annual cycle:

Gunumeleng (October to December) is the build-up to the Wet. Humidity increases, the temperature rises to 35°C or more and mosquitoes reach near-plague proportions. By November the thunderstorms have started, billabongs are replenished, and waterbirds and fish disperse.

Gudjewg (January to March) is the Wet proper with violent thunderstorms, and flora and fauna thriving in the hot, moist conditions.

Banggerreng (April) is when storms (known as 'knock 'em down' storms) flatten the spear grass, which during the course of the Wet has shot up to 2m high.

Yegge (May to June) is the season of mists, when the air starts to dry out. The wetlands and waterfalls still have a lot of water and most of the tracks are open. The first firing of the countryside begins.

Wurrgeng (June to mid-August) is the most comfortable time, weather-wise, is the late Dry, beginning in July. This is when animals, especially birds, gather in large numbers around shrinking billabongs, and when most tourists visit.

Gurrung (mid-August to September) is the end of the Dry and the beginning of another cycle.

Wildlife

Kakadu has more than 60 species of mammals, more than 280 bird species, 120 recorded species of reptile, 25 species of frog, 55 freshwater fish species and at least 10,000 different kinds of insect. Most visitors see only a fraction of these creatures (except the insects), since many of them are shy, nocturnal or scarce.

Birds

Abundant waterbirds and their beautiful wetland homes are a highlight of Kakadu. This is one of the chief refuges in Australia for several species, including the magpie goose, green pygmy goose and Burdekin duck. Other fine waterbirds include pelicans, brolgas and the jabiru (or more correctly black-necked stork), Australia's only stork, with distinctive red legs and long beak. Herons, egrets, cormorants, wedge-tailed eagles, whistling kites and black kites are common. The open woodlands harbor rainbow bee-eaters, kingfishers and the endangered bustard. Majestic white-breasted sea eagles are seen near inland waterways. At night, you might hear barking owls calling – they sound just like dogs – or the plaintive wail of the bush stone curlew. The raucous call of the spectacular red-tailed black cockatoo is often considered the signature sound of Kakadu.

At Mamukala, 8km east of the South Alligator River on the Arnhem Hwy, is a wonderful observation building, plus birdwatching hides and a 3km walking track.

Fish

You can't miss the silver barramundi, which creates a distinctive swirl near the water's surface. A renowned sportfish, it can grow to more than 1m in length and changes sex from male to female at the age of five or six years.

Mammals

Several types of kangaroo and wallaby inhabit the park; the shy black wallaroo is unique to Kakadu and Arnhem Land – look for them at Nourlangie Rock, where individuals rest under rocky overhangs. At Ubirr, short-eared rock wallabies can be spotted in the early morning. You may see a sugar glider or a shy dingo in wooded areas in the daytime. Kakadu has 26 bat species, four of them endangered.

Reptiles

Twin Falls and Jim Jim Falls have resident freshwater crocodiles, which have narrow snouts and rarely exceed 3m, while the dangerous saltwater variety is found throughout the park.

Kakadu's other reptiles include the frill-necked lizard, 11 species of goanna, and five freshwater turtle species, of which the most common is the northern snake-necked turtle. Kakadu has many snakes, though most are nocturnal and rarely encountered. The striking Oenpelli python was first recorded by non-Aboriginal people in 1976. The odd-looking file snake lives in billabongs and is much sought after as bush tucker. They have square heads, tiny eyes and saggy skin covered in tiny rough scales (hence 'file'). They move very slowly (and not at all on land), eating only once a month and breeding once every decade.

Rock Art

Kakadu is one of Australia's richest, most accessible repositories of rock art. There are more than 5000 sites, which date from 20,000 years to 10 years ago. The vast majority of these sites are off limits or inaccessible, but two of the finest collections are the easily visited galleries at Ubirr and Nourlangie.

Rock paintings have been classified into three roughly defined periods: Pre-estuarine, which is from the earliest paintings up to around 6000 years ago; Estuarine, which covers the period from 6000 to around 2000 years ago, when rising sea levels brought the coast to its present level; and Freshwater, from 2000 years ago until the present day.

For local Aboriginal people, these rock-art sites are a major source of traditional knowledge and represent their archives. Aboriginal people rarely paint on rocks anymore, as they no longer live in rock shelters and there are fewer people with the requisite knowledge. Some older paintings are believed by many Aboriginal people to have been painted by mimi spirits, connecting people with creation legends and the development of Aboriginal lore.

As the paintings are all rendered with natural, water-soluble ochres, they are very susceptible to water damage. Drip lines of clear silicon rubber have been laid on the rocks above the paintings to divert rain. As the most accessible sites receive up to 4000 visitors a week, boardwalks have been erected to keep the dust down and to keep people at a suitable distance from the paintings.

Tours

There are dozens of Kakadu tours on offer; book at least a day ahead if possible; operators generally collect you from your accommodation. There are plenty of tours departing from Darwin.

Indigenous Tours & Sightseeing

Kakadu Animal Tracks INDIGENOUS
(☎08-8979 0145; www.animaltracks.com.au; tours adult/child $205/135) Based at Cooinda, this outfit runs seven-hour tours with an indigenous guide combining a wildlife safari and Aboriginal cultural tour. You'll see thousands of birds, get to hunt, gather, prepare and consume bush tucker and crunch on some green ants.

Magela Cultural & Heritage Tours INDIGENOUS
(☎08-8979 2548; www.kakadutours.com.au; tours adult/child $245/196) Aboriginal-owned and -operated 4WD day tour into northern Kakadu and Arnhem Land, including Injalak Hill and a cruise on Inkiyu billabong.

Gagudju Adventure Tours SIGHTSEEING
(☎08-8979 0145; www.gagudju-dreaming.com; tours adult/child $195/145) 4WD tours to Jim Jim and Twin Falls from April to October.

Top End Explorer Tours SIGHTSEEING
(☎08-8979 3615, 1300 556 609; www.kakadutours.net.au; tours adult/child $195/150) 4WD tours to Jim Jim Falls and Twin Falls from Jabiru and Cooinda.

Ayal Aboriginal Tours INDIGENOUS
(☎0429 470 384; www.ayalkakadu.com.au; tours adult/child $220/99) Full-day indigenous-run tours around Kakadu, with former ranger and local, Victor Cooper, shining a light on art, culture and wildlife.

Kakadu Air SCENIC FLIGHTS
(☎1800 089 113; www.kakaduair.com.au) Offers 30-minute/one-hour fixed-wing flights for $140/230 per adult. Helicopter tours, though more expensive, give a more dynamic aerial perspective. They cost from $210 (20 minutes) to $460 (45 minutes) per person. Also on offer are one- and two-day tours flying from Darwin that include land and wetland tours in Kakadu.

Wetland & River Trips

Yellow Water Cruises WILDLIFE CRUISES
(☎1800 500 401; www.gagudju-dreaming.com) Cruise the South Alligator River and Yellow Water Billabong spotting wildlife. Purchase tickets from Gagudju Lodge, Cooinda, where a shuttle bus will deliver you to the departure point. Two-hour cruises ($99/70 per adult/child) depart at 6.45am, 9am and 4.30pm; 1½-hour cruises ($68/47) leave at 11.30am, 1.15pm and 2.45pm.

Guluyambi Cultural Cruise INDIGENOUS
(☎1800 895 175; www.kakaduculturaltours.com.au; adult/child $61/40; ⏲9am, 11am, 1pm & 3pm May-Nov) Launch into an Aboriginal-led river cruise from the upstream boat ramp on the East Alligator River near Cahill's Crossing.

Kakadu Culture Camp INDIGENOUS
(☎night cruise 1800 811 633, overnight 0428 792 048; www.kakaduculturecamp.com) Aboriginal-owned and -operated cruises on the Djarradjin Billabong; three-hour night cruise (per adult/child $80/50), and five-hour cruise-plus-dinner tours ($260/180). Tours depart from Muirella Park campground.

(Continued on page 851)

Outback Journeys

You won't find a road sign indicating the start of the legendary Australian outback, nor a map that defines its borders. Nonetheless, the outback of vast distances, lonely roads, red sand, unique wildlife and a mysterious ancient culture is real and recognisable, and it's ready and waiting to be explored.

Contents

Above Kata Tjuta (the Olgas; p896)

1

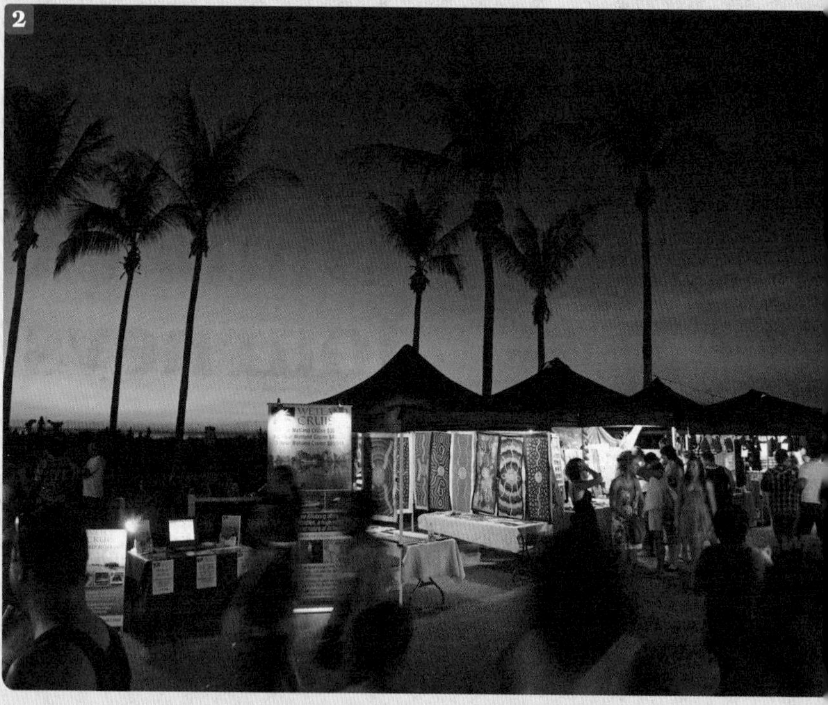
2

LYNN GAIL / GETTY IMAGES ©

1. Wave Lagoon (p816) 2. Mindil Beach Sunset Market (p830) 3. Feeding diamond-scaled mullet, Aquascene (p814)

Darwin

Darwin is a young-at-heart city, vibrant with potential and a can-do attitude as it turns its focus on nearby Asia. Long gone is the frontier outpost of yore. Yet some things never change, and locals are ready to relax with a cool drink at the drop of a hat. Business may be booming but Darwin also takes to R&R with gusto.

Mindil Beach

This palm-lined beach is home to a Darwin institution – sunset markets. As the sausages and satays begin to sizzle, the sultry evening air is spiced with a melting pot of foodie delights and accompanying earthy tunes.

Mitchell Street

This is Darwin's action strip, lined with bars, cafes and restaurants with tables spilling out onto the promenade. The hostels provide a steady stream of backpackers, stopping over on the across-Asia route, that keep the street buzzing. And where else can you swim with a crocodile in the middle of the CBD?

Waterfront Precinct

The perfect place to escape the tropical heat. The Wave Lagoon has a repertoire suitable for boogie boards, body surfing, or just bobbing up and down. Adjacent is the (free) recreation lagoon – a safe place to take a dip in Darwin's harbour waters. There are restaurants on nearby Stokes Wharf and more bordering the lagoon parklands.

Aquascene

There's something decidedly fishy going on down in Doctors Gully. But it only happens at high tide. With the high water comes an army of hungry fish that you can hand feed. Their size, audacity and hunger will amaze.

Indigenous Art & Culture

The intricate and mesmerising art, songs and dances of the various Aboriginal peoples from across the continent resonate with the deep association between Indigenous Australians and the ancient land itself. Through these arts you can immerse yourself in the stories of the Dreaming, be they painted on rocks eons old, or represented in abstract patterns in modern acrylics.

Rock Art

Remarkable evidence of Australia's ancient Indigenous culture can be found at the outdoor rock-art sites scattered across the outback. Highlights include the 5000-plus sites in Kakadu National Park that document a timeline of spirits from the Dreaming, extinct fauna, and remarkable 'contact art', portraying the interaction between Indigenous Australians, Macassan fishermen and early European settlers. Standout Kakadu sites include Ubirr and Nourlangie. More rock art can easily be seen at Nitmiluk and Keep River national parks, the MacDonnell Ranges near Alice, and Uluru.

Contemporary Indigenous Art

Contemporary Australian Indigenous art – the lion's share of which is produced in outback communities – has soared to global heights in recent years. Traditional methods and spiritual significance are fastidiously maintained, but often find a counterpart in Western materials – the results can be wildly original interpretations of traditional stories and ceremonial designs. Dot paintings (acrylic on canvas) are the

1

most recognisable form, but you may also see synthetic polymer paintings, weavings, barks, weapons, boomerangs and sculptures.

You can pay thousands of dollars for pieces in the big cities, but you'll save some money and ensure you're making an ethical purchase if you buy directly from outback Indigenous community centres.

Cultural Tours

The proliferation of Indigenous-owned and -operated cultural tours in places all over Australia is testament to how far Indigenous tourism has come. You can now learn about Country from the people who know it best. Some of the best places to find these truly 'local' guides in the Northern Territory include Darwin, Kakadu National Park and Arnhem Land in the Top End, and Alice Springs and Uluru-Kata Tjuta National Park in the Red Centre.

Indigenous Festivals

For a truly unforgettable experience you should time your outback visit to coincide with a traditional Indigenous festival. These celebrations offer visitors a look at Aboriginal culture in action. Witnessing a timeless dance and feeling the primal beats is a journey beyond time and place. The Northern Territory plays host to several Indigenous festivals and events, including the popular Walking With Spirits in Beswick, Barunga Festival near Katherine, Merrepen Arts & Sports Festival at Daly River, and Arnhem Land's Stone Country Festival.

OLIVER STREWE / GETTY IMAGES ©

2

LEANNE WALKER / GETTY IMAGES ©

1. Dot painting, Northern Territory **2.** Barunga Festival (p822)

Kings Canyon (p888)

Ultimate Outback

'Outback' means different things to different people and in different parts of Australia – deserts, tropical savannah, even wetlands – but what's consistent is the idea that it is far from comforts of the familiar and the crowds of urbanisation. It is 'beyond the black stump' and it holds many surprises.

Uluru (Ayers Rock)

Uluru-Kata Tjuta National Park is the undisputed highlight of Central Australia. There's not much that hasn't been said about Uluru. And not many parts of it that haven't been explored, photographed and documented. Still, nothing can prepare you for its almighty bulk, spiritual stories, remarkable surface and extraordinary colour.

Kata Tjuta (The Olgas)

The tallest dome of Kata Tjuta is taller than Uluru (546m versus 348m), and some say exploring these 36 mounded monoliths is a more intimate, moving experience. Trails weave in among the red rocks, revealing pockets of silent beauty and taking you to a spiritually significant place.

Kings Canyon

In Watarrka National Park, about 300km north of Uluru by road, Kings Canyon is the inverse of Uluru – as if someone had grabbed the big rock, and pushed it into the desert sand. Here, 270m-high cliffs drop away to a palm-lined valley floor, home to 600 plant species and native animals. The 6km canyon rim walk is four hours well spent.

MacDonnell Ranges

The 'Macs' stretch east and west of Alice Springs and in their ancient folds are hidden worlds where rock wallabies and colourful birds can find water even on the hottest days.

(Continued from page 844)

Ubirr & Around

It'll take a lot more than the busloads of visitors here to disturb Ubirr's inherent majesty and grace. Layers of **rock-art paintings**, in various styles and from various centuries, command a mesmerising stillness. Part of the main gallery reads like a menu, with images of kangaroos, tortoises and fish painted in x-ray, which became the dominant style about 8000 years ago. Predating these are the paintings of mimi spirits: cheeky, dynamic figures who, it's believed, were the first of the Creation Ancestors to paint on rock (...given the lack of cherry pickers in 6000 BC, you have to wonder who else but a spirit could have painted at that height and angle). Look out for the yam-head figures, where the head is depicted as a yam on the body of a human or animal; these date back around 15,000 years.

The magnificent **Nardab Lookout** is a 250m scramble from the main gallery. Surveying the billiard-table-green floodplain and watching the sun set and the moon rise, like they're on an invisible set of scales, is glorious, to say the least. **Ubirr** (8.30am-sunset Apr-Nov, from 2pm Dec-Mar) is 39km north of the Arnhem Hwy via a sealed road.

On the way you'll pass the turn-off to Merl Camping Ground (p852), which is only open in the Dry and has an amenities block, and the Border Store (p852), selling groceries and takeaway food (no fuel).

Activities

Bardedjilidji Sandstone Walk WALKING

Starting from the upstream picnic-area car park, this walk (2.5km, 90 minutes, easy) takes in wetland areas of the East Alligator River and some interesting eroded sandstone outliers of the Arnhem Land escarpment. Informative track notes point out features on this walk.

Manngarre Monsoon Forest Walk WALKING

Mainly sticking to a boardwalk, this walk (1.5km return, 30 minutes, easy) starts by the boat ramp near the Border Store and winds through heavily shaded vegetation, palms and vines.

Sandstone & River Rock Holes WALKING

This extension (6.5km, three hours, medium) of the Bardedjilidji Walk features

URANIUM MINING

It's no small irony that some of the world's biggest deposits of uranium lie within one of Australia's most beautiful national parks. In 1953 uranium was discovered in the Kakadu region. Twelve small deposits in the southern reaches of the park were worked in the 1960s, but were abandoned following the declaration of Woolwonga Wildlife Sanctuary.

In 1970 three huge deposits – Ranger, Nabarlek and Koongarra – were found, followed by Jabiluka in 1971. The Nabarlek deposit (in Arnhem Land) was mined in the late 1970s, and the Ranger Uranium Mine started producing ore in 1981.

While all mining in the park has been controversial, it was Jabiluka that brought international attention to Kakadu and pitted conservationists and Indigenous owners against the government and mining companies. After uranium was discovered at Jabiluka, an agreement to mine was negotiated with the local Aboriginal people. The Jabiluka mine became the scene of demonstrations during 1998 that resulted in many arrests. In 2003 stockpiled ore was returned into the mine and the tunnel leading into the deposit was backfilled as the mining company bagan talks with the traditional landowners, the Mirrar people.

In February 2005 the current owners of the Jabiluka mining lease, Energy Resources of Australia (ERA), signed an agreement that gave the Mirrar the deciding vote on any resumption of this controversial mining project. Under the deal, ERA is allowed to continue to explore the lease, subject to Mirrar consent. In 2011 the traditional owners of the Koongarra lease, near Nourlangie, rejected the promise of millions of dollars from French nuclear power conglomerate Areva and requested the land be integrated into the national park. The legal steps necessary for the inclusion of the lease into the park were well underway in 2012. Meanwhile, the Ranger mine – which is officially not part of the national park but is surrounded by it – was transitioning from an open-cut to an underground mine in late 2012. However, expansion of the mine is not guaranteed and under current legislation it is due to close in 2021, with rehabilitation complete by 2026.

sandstone outcrops, paperbark swamps and riverbanks. Closed in the Wet.

🛏 Sleeping & Eating

Merl Camping Ground CAMPGROUND $
(adult/child $10/free) The turn-off to this national parks ground is about 1km before the Border Store. It is divided into a quiet zone and a generator use-zone, each with a block of showers and toilets. It can get mighty busy at peak times and be warned, the mosquitos are diabolical. The site is closed in the Wet.

★ Border Store CAFE $$
(☑ 08-8979 2474; meals $6-26; ⊗ 8am-6pm Mon, 8am-8pm Tue-Sun Apr-Nov) The charming little Border Store is full of surprises, including real coffee, sweet cakes and delicious Thai-cooked Thai food. A real treat if you are camping at nearby Merl. You can book a Guluyambi Cultural Cruise on the East Alligator River or a tour to Arnhem Land, and watch local artists at work outside the cafe. Plans are in place for safari-tent and powered site accommodation.

Jabiru

POP 1129

It may seem surprising to find a town of Jabiru's size and structure in the midst of a wilderness national park, but it exists solely because of the nearby Ranger uranium mine. It's Kakadu's major service centre, with a bank, newsagent, medical centre, supermarket, bakery and service station. You can even play a round of golf here.

🏃 Activities

Ranger Uranium Mine Tour MINE TOUR
(☑ 1800 089 113; adult/child $30/10; ⊗ 9am, 11am & 1pm Mon-Sat) The Ranger Uranium Mine Tour is an opportunity to see one of the park's controversial mining projects up close and learn about some of the issues surrounding uranium mining. Guided tours leave from Jabiru airstrip, 8km east of town.

🛏 Sleeping & Eating

★ Lakeview Park CABINS $$
(☑ 08-8979 3144; www.lakeviewkakadu.com.au; 27 Lakeside Dr; en suite powered sites $35, bungalows/d/cabins $120/130/235; ❄) Although there are no lake views as such, this Aboriginal-owned park is one of Kakadu's best with a range of tropical-design bungalows set in lush gardens. The doubles share

a communal kitchen, bathroom and lounge, and also come equipped with their own TV and fridge, while the 'bush bungalows' are stylish elevated safari designs (no air-con) with private external bathroom that sleep up to four. No pool, but one is planned and Jabiru public pool is only 50m away.

Aurora Kakadu
Lodge & Caravan Park RESORT, CAMPGROUND $$$
(☑ 1800 811 154; www.auroraresorts.com.au; Jabiru Dr; unpowered/powered sites $26/38, cabins from $240; ❄ ❄ ⛱) An impeccable resort/caravan park with shady, grassed sites and a lagoon-style swimming pool (movie nights by the pool on Fridays). Self-contained cabins sleep up to five people but are booked up well in advance. There's also a bar and bistro.

Gagudju Crocodile Holiday Inn HOTEL $$$
(☑ 08-8979 9000; www.gagudju-dreaming.com; 1 Flinders St; d from $285; ❄ ❄ ⛱) Known locally as 'the Croc', this hotel is designed in the shape of a crocodile, which, of course, is only obvious when viewed from the air or Google Earth. The rooms are clean and comfortable if a little pedestrian for the price (which drops considerably during the Wet). Try for one on the ground floor opening out to the central pool. The **Escarpment Restaurant** (mains $24-38; ⊗ breakfast, lunch & dinner) here is the best in Jabiru.

Jabiru Sports & Social Club PUB $$
(☑ 08-8979 2326; Lakeside Dr; mains $16-32; ⊗ lunch & dinner daily) Along with the golf club, this low-slung hangar is the place to meet the locals over a beer. The bistro meals are surprisingly adventurous (try the tempura croc tail with bean salad and chilli ketchup), there's an outdoor deck overlooking the lake and sports on TV.

Kakadu Bakery BAKERY $
(Gregory Pl; meals $5-17; ⊗ breakfast & lunch daily, dinner Mon-Sat) Superb made-to-order sandwiches on home-baked bread walk out the door, plus mean burgers, slices, breakfast fry-ups, pizzas, cakes and basic salads.

Foodland SUPERMARKET $
(Jabiru Plaza; ⊗ 9am-5.30pm Mon-Fri, 9am-3pm Sat, 9am-1pm Sun) The local supermarket.

Nourlangie

The sight of this looming outlier of the Arnhem Land escarpment makes it easy to understand its ancient importance to Aboriginal people. Its long red-sandstone bulk, striped in places with orange, white and black, slopes up from surrounding woodland to fall away at one end in stepped cliffs. Below is Kakadu's best-known collection of Aboriginal **rock art**.

The name Nourlangie is a corruption of *nawulandja,* an Aboriginal word that refers to an area bigger than the rock itself. The 2km looped walking track (open 8am to sunset) takes you first to the **Anbangbang Shelter**, used for 20,000 years as a refuge and canvas. Next is the **Anbangbang Gallery**, featuring Dreaming characters repainted in the 1960s. Look for the virile Nabulwinjbulwinj, a dangerous spirit who likes to eat females after banging them on the head with a yam. From here it's a short walk to **Gunwarddehwarde Lookout**, with views of the Arnhem Land escarpment.

Nourlangie is at the end of a 12km sealed road that turns east off Kakadu Hwy. About 7km south is the turn-off to **Muirella Park** (adult/child $10/free) camping ground at **Djarradjin Billabong**, with BBQs, excellent amenities and the 5km-return **Bubba Wetland Walk**.

Activities

Nawurlandja Lookout WALKING

This is a short walk (600m return, 30 minutes, medium) up a gradual slope, but it gives excellent views of the Nourlangie rock area and is a good place to catch the sunset.

Anbangbang Billabong Walk WALKING

This picturesque, lily-filled billabong lies close to Nourlangie, and the picnic tables dotted around its edge make it a popular lunch spot. The track (2.5km loop, 45 minutes, easy) circles the billabong and passes through paperbark swamp.

Barrk Walk WALKING

This long day walk (12km loop, five to six hours, difficult) will take you away from the crowds on a circuit of the Nourlangie area. Barrk is the male black wallaroo and you might see this elusive marsupial if you set out early. Starting at the Nourlangie car park, this demanding walk passes through the Anbangbang galleries before a steep climb to the top of Nourlangie Rock. Cross the flat top of the rock weaving through sandstone pillars before descending along a wet-season watercourse. The track then follows the rock's base past the Nanguluwur Gallery and western cliffs before re-emerging at the car park. Pick up a brochure from the Bowali Visitor Centre.

Nanguluwur Gallery WALKING

This outstanding rock-art gallery receives far fewer visitors than Nourlangie simply because it's further to walk (3.5km return, 1½ hours, easy) and has a gravel access road. Here the paintings cover most of the styles found in the park, including very early dynamic style work, x-ray work and a good example of 'contact art', a painting of a two-masted sailing ship towing a dinghy.

Jim Jim Falls & Twin Falls

Remote and spectacular, these two falls epitomise the rugged Top End. Jim Jim Falls, a sheer 215m drop, is awesome after rain (when it can only be seen from the air), but its waters shrink to a trickle by about June. Twin Falls flows year-round (no swimming), but half the fun is getting there, involving a little **boat trip** (adult/child $2.50/free, ⏲ running 7.30am to 5pm) and an over-the-water boardwalk.

These two iconic waterfalls are reached along a 4WD track that turns south off the Kakadu Hwy between the Nourlangie and Cooinda turn-offs. Jim Jim Falls is about 56km from the turn-off (the last 1km on foot), and it's a further five corrugated kilometres to Twin Falls. The track is open in the Dry only and can still be closed into late May; it's off limits to most rental vehicles (check the fine print). A couple of tour companies make trips here in the Dry and there's a camping area, **Garrnamarr** (adult/child $5/free) near Jim Jim Falls.

Cooinda & Yellow Water

Cooinda is best known for the cruises (p844) on the wetland area known as Yellow Water, and has developed into a slick resort. About 1km from the resort, the **Warradjan Aboriginal Cultural Centre** (www.kakadu-attractions.com/warradjan; Yellow Water Area; ⏲ 9am-5pm) depicts Creation stories and has a great permanent exhibition that includes clap sticks, sugar-bag holders and rock-art samples. You'll be introduced to the moiety system (law of interpersonal relationships), languages and skin names, and there's a minitheatre with a huge selection of films from which to choose. A mesmeric soundtrack of chants and didgeridoos plays in the background. Warradjan is an easy 2km walk from the Cooinda resort.

Gagudju Lodge & Camping Cooinda (08-8979 0145, 1800 500 401; www.gagudjulodgecooinda.com.au; unpowered/powered sites $36/46, dm $57, budget/lodge r from $155/295;) is the most popular accommodation resort in the park. It's a modern oasis but, even with 380 camp sites, facilities can get very stretched. The budget air-con units share camping ground facilities and are compact and comfy enough (but for this money should be more than glorified sheds). The lodge rooms are spacious and more comfortable, sleeping up to four people. There's also a grocery shop, tour desk, fuel pump and the excellent open-air **Barra Bar & Bistro** (mains $15-36; breakfast, lunch & dinner) here too.

The turn-off to the Cooinda accommodation complex and Yellow Water wetlands is 47km down the Kakadu Hwy from the Arnhem Hwy intersection. Just off the Kakadu Hwy, 2km south of the Cooinda turn-off, is the scrubby **Mardugal camping ground** (adult/child $10/free)– an excellent year-round camping area with shower and toilets.

Cooinda to Pine Creek

This southern section of the park sees far fewer tour buses. Though it's unlikely you'll have dreamy Maguk (Barramundi Gorge; 45km south of Cooinda and 10km along a corrugated 4WD track) to yourself, you might time it right to have the glorious natural pool and falls between just a few of you. Forty-odd kilometres further south is the turn-off to Gunlom (Waterfall Creek), another superb escarpment waterfall, plunge pool and camping area. It's located 37km along an unsealed road, again 4WD recommended. Walk the steep **Waterfall Walk** (1km, one hour) here, which affords incredible views.

Located just outside the park's southern boundary, the **Goymarr Tourist Resort** (08-8975 4564; Kakadu Hwy; unpowered/powered sites $20/30, dm $20, budget/motel d $65/125) has a variety of accommodation options, a bistro and a bar. If you are coming into Kakadu from the south, there's a small information office and art gallery housed in an orange shed where you can buy a park pass.

Activities

Yurmikmik Walks WALKING

On the road to Gunlom is the start of a series of interconnected walks leading first through woodlands and monsoon forest to **Boulder Creek** (2km, 45 minutes), then on to the **Lookout** (5km, 1½ to two hours), with views over rugged ridges, and **Motor Car Falls** (7.5km, four hours).

Information

About 200,000 people visit Kakadu between April and October, so expect some tour-bus action at sites like Ubirr and Yellow Water. Consider spending some time bushwalking and camping in the south of the park – it's less visited but inimitably impressive.

Admission to the park is via a 14-day **Park Pass** (adult/child $25/free): pick one up (along with the excellent *Visitor Guide* booklet) from Bowali visitor information centre, Tourism Top End in Darwin, Gagudju Lodge Cooinda, Goymarr Tourist Resort, or Katherine visitor information centre. Carry it with you at all times, as rangers conduct spot checks (penalties apply for nonpayment). Fuel is available at Kakadu Resort, Cooinda, Goymarr Tourist Resort and Jabiru. Jabiru has a shopping complex with a supermarket, post office, a Westpac bank and newsagency.

Accommodation prices in Kakadu vary tremendously depending on the season – resort rates can drop by as much as 50% during the Wet.

The first-rate **Bowali Visitor Information Centre** (08-8938 1121; www.kakadunationalparkaustralia.com/bowali_visitors_center.htm; Kakadu Hwy, Jabiru; 8am-5pm) has walk-through displays that sweep you across the land, explaining Kakadu's ecology from Aboriginal and non-Aboriginal perspectives. The helpful staffed info booth has details on walks and the plants and animals you might encounter along the way. The 'What's On' flier details where and when to catch a free and informative park ranger talk. The centre is about 2.5km south of the Arnhem Hwy intersection; a 1km walking track connects it with Jabiru.

The Northern Land Council issues permits (adult/child $16.50/free) to visit Gunbalanya (Oenpelli), across the East Alligator River.

Getting There & Around

Many people choose to access Kakadu on a tour, which shuffles them around the major sights with the minimum of hassles. But it's just as easy with your own wheels, if you know what kinds of road conditions your trusty steed can handle (Jim Jim Falls and Twin Falls, for example, are 4WD-access only).

Greyhound Australia (www.greyhound.com.au) runs a daily return coach service from Darwin to Cooinda ($89, 4½ hours) via Jabiru ($65, 3½ hours).

Arnhem Land

Arnhem Land is a vast, overwhelming and mysterious corner of the Northern Territory. About the size of the state of Victoria and with a population of only around 17,000, mostly Yolngu people, this Aboriginal reserve is one of Australia's last great untouched wilderness areas. Most people live on outstations, combining traditional practices with modern Western ones, so they might go out for a hunt and be back in time to watch the 6pm news. Outside commercial interests and visits are highly regulated through a permit system, designed to protect the environment, the rock art and ceremonial grounds. *Balanda* (white people) are unaware of the locations of burial grounds and ceremonial lands. Basically, you need a specific purpose for entering, usually to visit an arts centre, in order to be granted a permit. If you're travelling far enough to warrant an overnight stay, you'll need to organise accommodation (which is in short supply). It's easy to visit Gunbalanya (Oenpelli) and its arts centre, just over the border, either on a tour or independently. Elsewhere, it's best to travel with a tour, which will include the necessary permit(s) to enter Aboriginal lands.

Tours

Arnhemlander Cultural & Heritage Tour SIGHTSEEING
(1800 895 179; www.kakaduculturaltours.com.au; adult/child $229/183) 4WD tours to the Mikinj (Crocodile Nest) Valley and Injalak Art Centre at Gunbalanya (Oenpelli).

Davidson's Arnhemland Safaris SIGHTSEEING
(08-8927 5240; www.arnhemland-safaris.com) Experienced operator taking tours to Mt Borradaile, north of Oenpelli. Meals, guided tours including Aboriginal rock art, fishing and safari camp accommodation are included in the daily price (from $750); transfers from Darwin can be arranged.

Venture North Australia WILDERNESS
(08-8927 5500; www.northernaustralia.com; 4-/5-day tour $2290/2590) 4WD tours to remote areas; features expert guidance on rock art. It also has a safari camp near Smith Point on the Cobourg Peninsula.

Lord's Kakadu & Arnhemland Safaris SIGHTSEEING
(08-8948 2200; www.lords-safaris.com; tours adult/child $215/170) One-day trip into Arnhem Land (Gunbalanya) from Jabiru (or Darwin adult/child $245/195), visiting Oenpelli with an Aboriginal-guided walk around Injalak Hill rock-art site.

Nomad Tours SIGHTSEEING
(08-8987 8085; www.banubanu.com; tours from 3-day $2188) Luxury small-group tours from Nhulunbuy including fishing charters, 4WD and cultural tours.

Gove Diving & Fishing Charters FISHING
(08-8987 3445; www.govefish.com.au) Variety of fishing, diving and snorkelling, and wilderness trips from Nhulunbuy. Half-/full-day fishing trips costs $205/305.

Gunbalanya (Oenpelli)

POP 1121

Gunbalanya is a small Aboriginal community 17km into Arnhem Land across the East Alligator River from the Border Store in Kakadu. The drive in itself is worth it with brilliant green wetlands and spectacular escarpments all around. Road access is only possible between May and October: check the tides at Cahill's Crossing on the East Alligator River before setting out so you don't get stuck on the other side.

A permit is required to visit the town, usually issued for visits to the **Injalak Arts & Crafts Centre** (www.injalak.com; 8am-5pm Mon-Fri, 8.30am-2pm Sat). At this centre, artists and craftspeople produce traditional paintings on bark and paper, plus didgeridoos, pandanus weavings and baskets, and screen-printed fabrics, either at the arts centre or on remote outstations throughout Arnhem Land.

As you walk around the verandah of the arts centre to see the artists at work (morning only), peer out over the wetland at the rear to the escarpment and **Injalak Hill** (Long Tom Dreaming). Knowledgeable local guides lead tours to see the fine rock-art galleries here. The three-hour tours (bookings essential) cost from $150 per group. Although it may be possible to join a tour as a walk-in, it's generally best to book a tour from Jabiru or Darwin.

The **Northern Land Council** (☎08-8938 3000, 1800 645 299; www.nlc.org.au; 3 Government Bldg, Flinders St, Jabiru; ⏲8am-4.30pm Mon-Fri) issues permits (adult/child $16.50/free) to visit Injalak, usually on the spot. It also provides tide times for the East Alligator River, which is impassable at high tide.

Cobourg Peninsula

The wilderness of this peninsula forms the **Garig Gunak Barlu National Park** (www.nretas.nt.gov.au/national-parks-and-reserves/parks/find/gariggunak) which includes the surrounding sea. In the turquoise water you'll likely see dolphins and turtles, and – what most people come for – a threadfin salmon thrashing on the end of your line.

On the shores of Port Essington are the stone ruins and headstones from Victoria settlement – Britain's 1838 attempt to establish a military outpost.

At Algarlarlgarl (Black Point) there's a **ranger station** (☎08-8979 0244) with a visitor information and cultural centre, and the **Garig Store** (☎08-8979 0455; ⏲4-6pm Mon-Sat), which sells basic provisions, ice and camping gas.

Two permits are required to visit the Cobourg Peninsula: for a transit pass ($12.10 per vehicle) to drive through Aboriginal land contact the Northern Land Council (p812); for permission to stay overnight in the national park contact the **Cobourg Peninsula Sanctuary & Marine Park Board** (☎08-8999 4814; www.nretas.nt.gov.au/national-parks-and-reserves/parks/find/gariggunak). The overnight fee is $232.10 per vehicle, which covers up to five people for seven days and includes camping and transit pass.

There are two camping grounds in the park with shower, toilet, BBQs and limited bore water; generators are allowed in one area. Camping fees (per person per day $16.50) are covered by your vehicle permit, but if you fly in you'll have to pay them. Other accommodation is available in pricey fishing resorts.

ℹ Getting There & Away

The quickest route here is by private charter flight, which can be arranged by accommodation providers. The track to Cobourg starts at Gunbalanya (Oenpelli) and is accessible by 4WD vehicles only from May to October. The 270km drive to Black Point from the East Alligator River takes about four hours.

Eastern Arnhem Land

The wildly beautiful coast and country of Eastern Arnhem Land (www.ealta.org) is really off the beaten track. About 4000 people live in the region's main settlement, Nhulunbuy, built to service the bauxite mine here. The 1963 plans to establish a manganese mine were hotly protested by the traditional owners, the Yolngu people; though mining proceeded, the case became an important step in establishing land rights. Some of the country's most respected art comes out of this region too, including bark paintings, carved mimi figures, *yidaki* (didgeridoo), woven baskets and mats, and jewellery.

Nambara Arts & Crafts Aboriginal Gallery (Melville Bay Rd, Nhulunbuy) sells art and crafts from northeast Arnhem Land and often has artists in residence. **Buku Larrnggay Mulka Art Centre & Museum** (www.yirrkala.com; Yirrkala; museum admission $2; ⏲8am-4.30pm Mon-Fri, 9am-noon Sat), 20km southeast of Nhulunbuy in Yirrkala, is one of Arnhem Land's best. No permit is required to visit from Nhulunbuy or Gove Airport.

Overland travel through Arnhem Land from Katherine requires a permit (free) from the Northern Land Council (p812). The **Dhimurru Land Management Aboriginal Corporation** (☎08-8987 3992; www.dhimurru.com.au; Arnhem Rd, Nhulunbuy) issues recreation permits ($35/45 for seven days/two months) for visits to particular recreation areas in Eastern Arnhem Land – check the website for details.

ℹ Getting There & Away

Airnorth (☎1800 627 474; www.airnorth.com.au) and Qantaslink (p832) flies from Darwin to Gove (for Nhulunbuy) daily from $355 one way. Overland, it's a 10-hour 4WD trip and only possible in the Dry. The Central Arnhem Hwy to Gove leaves the Stuart Hwy (Rte 87) 52km south of Katherine.

KATHERINE TO ALICE SPRINGS

The Stuart Hwy from Darwin to Alice Springs is still referred to as 'the Track' – it has been since WWII, when it was a dirt track connecting the Territory's two main towns, roughly following the Overland Telegraph Line. It's dead straight most of the way and gets drier and flatter as you head south, but there are a few notable diversions.

Katherine

POP 9187

Katherine is considered a big town in this part of the world and you'll certainly feel like you've arrived somewhere after the long trip up the highway. Its namesake river is the first permanent running water on the road north from Alice Springs. In the Wet the river swells dramatically and has been responsible for some devastating floods – the worst in memory was Australia Day 1998, when rising waters inundated the surrounding countryside and left a mark up to 2m high on Katherine's buildings.

Katherine is probably best known for the Nitmiluk (Katherine Gorge) National Park to the east, and the town makes an obvious base, with plenty of accommodation and some decent restaurants. It also has quite a few attractions of its own, including a thriving indigenous arts community, thermal springs and a few museums.

The Katherine area is the traditional home of the Jawoyn and Dagoman Aboriginal people. Following land claims they have received the title to large parcels of land, including Nitmiluk National Park. You'll see a lot of Aborigines around town, in from outlying communities for a few days to meet friends and hang out. No one seems too bothered by the disconcerting mix of country and retro pop that pipes into the main street from loudspeakers day and night.

Sights & Activities

Katherine Low Level Nature Park PARK

(www.ourterritory.com/katherine_nt/low_level.htm) The park is a scenic spot on the banks of the babbling Katherine River, just off the Victoria Hwy (Rte 1) 4km from town. It has a popular dry-season swimming hole linked to crystalline **thermal pools** (access via Murray St) and the town by a tree-lined shared cycle way/footpath.

Djilpin Arts ART GALLERY

(www.djilpinarts.org.au; Katherine Tce; 9am-4pm Mon-Fri) This Katherine gallery is Aboriginal owned and represents art from the Ghunmarn Culture Centre, in the remote community of Beswick. Paintings, weavings and termite-bored didjeridoos.

Top Didj Cultural Experience & Art Gallery ART GALLERY

(www.topdidj.com; cnr Gorge Rd & Jaensch Rd; cultural experience adult/child/family $50/28/140; 9am-6pm May-Oct, cultural experience 9.30am & 2.30pm Sun-Fri, 9.30am & 1.30pm Sat) Run by the owners of the Katherine Art Gallery, this is a good place to see Aboriginal artists at work. The cultural experience is hands on with fire sticks, spear throwing, painting and basket weaving.

Katherine Museum MUSEUM

(Gorge Rd; adult/child $7.50/3.50; 9am-4pm) The museum is in the old airport terminal, about 3km from town on the road to the gorge. The original Gypsy Moth biplane flown by Dr Clyde Fenton, the first Flying Doctor, is housed here, along with plenty of interesting old rusty trucks. There's a good selection of historical photos, including a display on the 1998 flood.

School of the Air SCHOOL

(08-8972 1833; www.schools.nt.edu.au/ksa; Giles St; adult/child $5/2; Mar-Nov) At the School of the Air, 1.5km from the town centre, you can listen into a class and see how kids in the remote outback are educated in the virtual world. Guided tours are held at 9am, 10am and 11am Monday to Friday; bookings preferred.

Katherine Public Art & Craft Galley ART GALLERY

(www.ktc.nt.gov.au; Stuart Hwy, Civic Centre; 8am-3pm Mon-Fri) FREE The low-key gallery is home to the Katherine Collection, a community-owned collection of interesting local art. There are a couple of amazing photos from the '98 flood here, too.

Springvale Homestead HOMESTEAD

(www.travelnorth.com.au; Shadforth Rd) Alfred Giles established Springvale Homestead in 1879 after he drove 2000 cattle and horses and 12,000 head of sheep from Adelaide to the site in 19 months. It claims to be the oldest cattle station in the Northern Territory. The stone homestead still stands by the river, about 7km southwest of town, and the surrounding riverside property is now a caravan and camping resort. There's a free homestead tour at 3pm daily (except Saturday) from May to September. Canoe hire per hour/two hours/day costs $20/25/75. There's also accommodation here.

Tours

Gecko Canoeing & Trekking CANOEING, BUSHWALKING

(08-8972 2224, 1800 634 319; www.geckocanoeing.com.au) Offers some exhilarating

Katherine

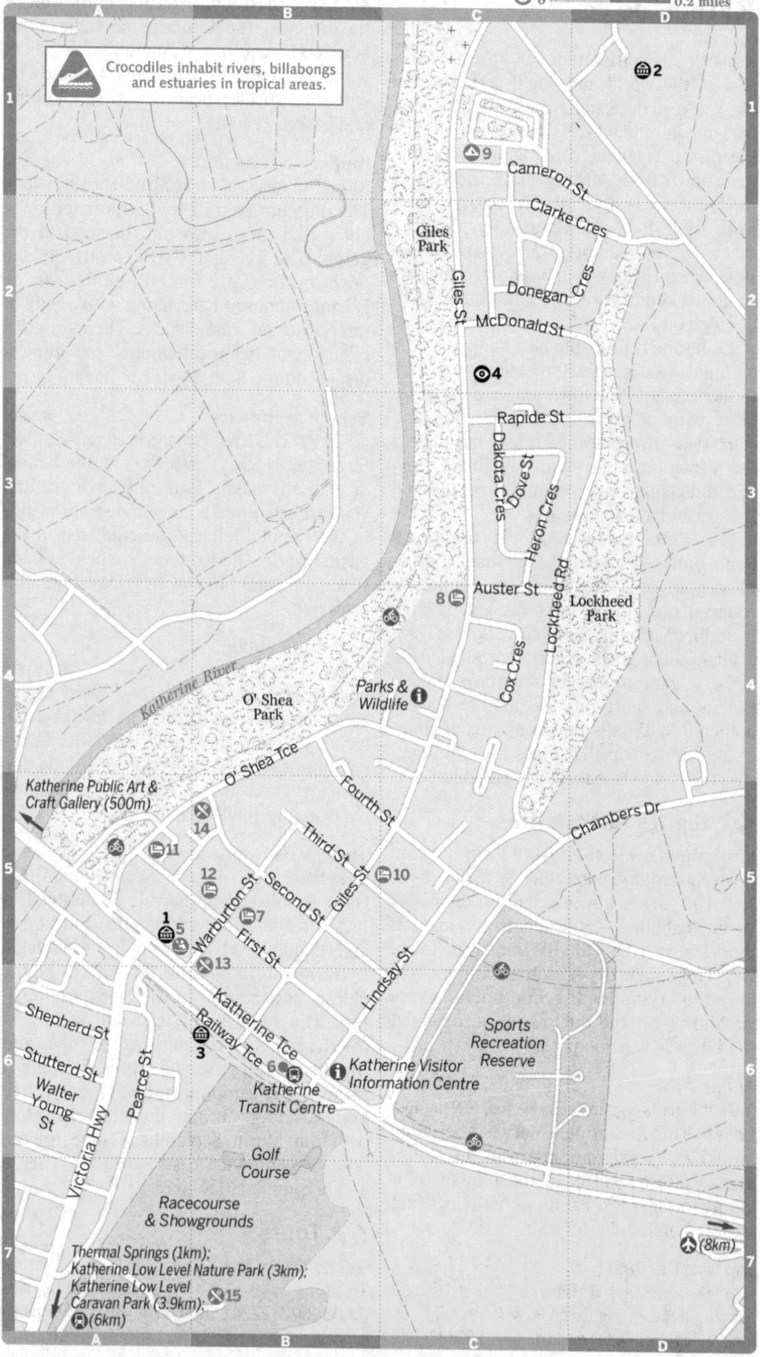
0 400 m
0 0.2 miles
Crocodiles inhabit rivers, billabongs and estuaries in tropical areas.
2
9
Cameron St
Clarke Cres
Giles Park
Giles St
Donegan
Cres
McDonald St
4
Rapide St
Dakota Cres
Dove St
Heron Cres
Lockheed Rd
8
Auster St
Lockheed Park
Katherine River
O' Shea Park
Parks & Wildlife
Cox Cres
O' Shea Tce
Fourth St
Katherine Public Art & Craft Gallery (500m)
14
11
Third St
Chambers Dr
12
Second St
Giles St
10
Warburton St
7
1
5
First St
13
Lindsay St
Katherine Tce
Railway Tce
3
Shepherd St
Stutterd St
Walter Young St
Pearce St
Victoria Hwy
6
Katherine Transit Centre
Katherine Visitor Information Centre
Sports Recreation Reserve
Golf Course
Racecourse & Showgrounds
(8km)
Thermal Springs (1km);
Katherine Low Level Nature Park (3km);
Katherine Low Level Caravan Park (3.9km);
(6km)
15

Katherine

Sights

1	Djilpin Arts	A5
2	Katherine Museum	D1
3	Railway Museum & Stream Train	B6
4	School of the Air	C2

Activities, Courses & Tours

5	Nitmiluk Tours	A5
6	Travel North	B6

Sleeping

7	Coco's International Backpackers	B5
8	Katherine River Lodge Motel	C4
9	Knott's Crossing Resort	C1
10	Palm Court Kookaburra Backpackers	C5
11	Paraway Motel	A5
12	St Andrews Apartments	B5

Eating

13	Coffee Club	B5
14	Katherine Club	B5
15	Katherine Country Club	B7
	Savannah Bar & Restaurant	(see 9)

guided canoe trips on the more remote stretches of the Katherine River. Trips include three days ($810) on the Katherine River and six days ($1390) on the Daly and Flora Rivers. A five-day hike along the Jatbula Trail in Nitmiluk National Park costs $1290. Gecko can also shuttle Jatbula Trail hikers from Edyth Falls back to Katherine ($50) or Nitmiluk National Park HQ ($66). Minimum numbers apply.

Crocodile Night Adventure CRUISE
(☎1800 089 103; www.travelnorth.com.au; cruises adult/child $69/45; ⊙6.30pm May-Oct) At Springvale Homestead, this evening cruise seeks out crocs and other nocturnal wildlife on the Katherine River. Includes BBQ dinner and drinks.

Travel North SIGHTSEEING
(☎08-8971 9999, 1800 089 103; www.travelnorth.com.au; 6 Katherine Tce, Transit Centre) Katherine-based tour operator with a range of tours to Kakadu, Arnhem Land and Litchfield, and full-day Katherine town tours. Also booking agent for the *Ghan* and Greyhound.

Festivals & Events

Katherine Country Music Muster MUSIC
(www.kcmm.com.au) 'We like both kinds of music: country *and* western.' Plenty of live music in the pubs and entertainment at the Tick Market Lindsay St Complex on a weekend in May or June. Check website for actual dates.

Katherine District Show AGRICULTURAL
(www.katherineshow.org.au) Annual agricultural show at the Katherine Showgrounds, with the usual rides, stalls and pungent animals in July.

Sleeping

Coco's International Backpackers HOSTEL $
(☎08-8971 2889; www.21firstst.com; 21 First St; camping per person $18, dm $28) With travellers idly strumming on guitars and swapping outback tales, you'll feel like you've walked into an old Asian overland bolthole here. Coco's is a real backpackers and well-known to those on marathon cycling trips. It's a converted home where the owner chats with the guests and offers sage advice on didgeridoos from his tin shed gallery. Aboriginal artists are often here painting didgeridoos.

Palm Court Kookaburra Backpackers HOSTEL $
(☎08-8972 2722, 1800 626 722; www.palmcourtbackpackers.com; cnr Third & Giles Sts; dm $27, motel d $69, self-contained unit $89; ❄@≋) This well-equipped, welcoming backpackers occupies a retired motel, clad in faux stone in an attempt to resemble some kind of castle. Scruffy international knights and maidens enjoy rooms with bathrooms, fridges and TVs. It's a short walk to town or there's a free shuttle to the Transit Centre.

Katherine Low Level Caravan Park CARAVAN PARK $
(☎08-8972 3962; www.katherinelowlevel.com.au; Shadforth Rd; unpowered/powered sites $37/40, en suite cabin d $175; ❄📶≋) A well-manicured park with plenty of shady sites, a great swimming pool adjoining a bar and an excellent bistro (mains $20 to $25) that is sheltered by a magnificent fig tree. The amenities are first rate, making it the pick of the town's several caravan parks. It's about 5km along the Victoria Hwy from town and across the Low Level bridge.

Springvale Homestead CARAVAN PARK, MOTEL $
(☎1800 089 103, 08-8972 1355; www.travelnorth.com.au; Shadforth Rd; unpowered/powered sites $20/27, d/f $69/79; ❄≋) In a bushland setting by the Katherine River, about 7km west of town, this historic homestead is a lovely place to camp. There's plenty of space, a palm-shaded pool and a bistro open for breakfast

and dinner (mains $19 to $25). Rooms are motel-style (old but clean and good value), and there are free homestead tours at 3pm daily (except Saturday) in the Dry.

Knott's Crossing Resort RESORT **$$**
(08-8972 2511, 1800 222 511; www.knottscrossing.com.au; cnr Cameron & Giles Sts; unpowered/powered sites $27/39, cabin/motel d from $99/149;) Knott's Crossing is more a motel and cabin resort than camping ground, but it's a great spot for caravans and campervans, too. Everything is packed pretty tightly into the tropical gardens here, but it's very professionally run and there's a bar and bistro.

Katherine River Lodge Motel MOTEL **$$**
(08-8971 0266; www.katherineriverlodge.net; 50 Giles St; s/d from $95/105;) One of Katherine's best-value motels (and definitely the friendliest), this large complex (three three-storey blocks) has spotless rooms in a tropical garden. The attached restaurant (mains $18 to $28) plates up filling meals nightly, or you can fire up the BBQ outside. You couldn't say the rooms are contemporary, but they're tidy and clean.

Paraway Motel MOTEL **$$**
(08-8972 2644; www.parawaymotel.com.au; cnr First St & O'Shea Tce; d from $135;) This smart motel is as neat as a pin, and its location is handy to the main street but quiet enough. Standard motel rooms are very clean, with typically tropical tile-and-floral-bedspread decor, plus there are spa rooms and a decent restaurant, too.

St Andrews Apartments APARTMENTS **$$$**
(08-8971 2288, 1800 686 106; www.standrewsapts.com.au; 27 First St; apt $220-260;) In the heart of town, these serviced apartments are great for families or if you're pining for a few home comforts. The two-bedroom apartments sleep four (six if you use the sofa bed), and come with fully equipped kitchen and lounge/dining area. Nifty little BBQ decks are attached to the ground-floor units.

Eating

Coffee Club CAFE **$**
(www.coffeeclub.com.au; cnr Katherine Tce & Warburton St; meals $12-18; 6.30am-5pm Mon-Fri, 7am-4pm Sat & Sun) Albeit a chain, the Coffee Club is the cafe of choice in Katherine, with huge gourmet breakfasts, decent coffee and plenty of options for a light or filling lunch.

Katherine Country Club LICENSED CLUB **$$**
(www.katherinecountryclub.com.au; 3034 Pearce St; mains $15-25; 10am-late) Overlooking Katherine's nine-hole golf course, this boozy bistro is a real locals' haunt. You don't have to be a club member (or even know how to swing a club) – just turn up and enjoy big steaks, burgers and schnitzels, and Aerosmith on the jukebox. 'The burgers are better at the Golfy!'

Savannah Bar & Restaurant MODERN AUSTRALIAN **$$**
(08-8972 2511; www.knottscrossing.com.au/restaurant; Knott's Crossing Resort, cnr Giles & Cameron Sts; mains $24-46; 5.30pm-late) This intimate little bistro at Knott's Crossing Resort is a local fave. Wagyu beef, lobster and prawn pasta, crocodile spring rolls and grilled barramundi grace the menu, and you can eat inside or alfresco by the pool.

Katherine Club LICENSED CLUB **$$**
(www.katherineclubinc.com; cnr Second St & O'Shea Tce; mains $19-32; 11.30am-2pm Mon-Fri, 6.30-8.30pm Mon-Sat) Close to the town centre, the Club ain't fancy, but you can rely on satisfying bistro meals (steak, schnitzel and barra), and the kids are welcome. Tuesday is roast night, Wednesday is pizza and pasta, Thursday it's schnitzels. Sign in as a visitor at the fortress-like front desk, or find a member to tag along with.

Information

Katherine Art Gallery (08-8971 1051; www.katherineartgallery.com.au; 12 Katherine Tce; 9am-6pm daily May-Oct, 10am-5pm Mon-Fri, 10am-2pm Sat Nov-Apr) A commercial indigenous gallery doubling as an internet cafe.

Katherine Hospital (08-8973 9211; www.health.nt.gov.au; Giles St) About 3km north of town, with an emergency department.

Katherine Visitor Information Centre (1800 653 142; www.visitkatherine.com.au; cnr Lindsay St & Stuart Hwy; 8.30am-5pm daily in the Dry, 8.30am-5pm Mon-Fri, 10am-2pm Sat & Sun in the Wet) Modern, air-con information centre stocking information on all areas of the Northern Territory. Pick up the handy *Katherine Region Visitor Guide*.

Parks & Wildlife (08-8973 8888; www.nt.gov.au/nreta/parks; 32 Giles St; 8am-4.20pm) National park information and notes.

Getting There & Around

Katherine is a major road junction: from here the Stuart Hwy tracks north and south, and the Victoria Hwy heads west to Kununurra in WA.

Greyhound Australia (www.greyhound.com.au) has regular services between Darwin and Alice Springs, Queensland or WA. Buses stop at **Katherine Transit Centre** (☎08-8971 9999; 6 Katherine Tce). One-way fares from Katherine include: Darwin ($94, four hours), Alice Springs ($315, 16 hours), Tennant Creek ($207, 8½ hours) and Kununurra ($146, 4½ hours).

The *Ghan* train, operated by **Great Southern Rail** (www.gsr.com.au), travels between Adelaide and Darwin twice a week, stopping at Katherine for four hours – enough for a whistlestop tour to Katherine Gorge! Katherine train station is off the Victoria Hwy, 9km southwest of town. Fares to/from Katherine are the same as per Darwin. **Nitmiluk Tours** (☎1300 146 743; www.nitmiluktours.com.au; Katherine Tce; ⏲9am-5pm Mon-Sat) runs shuttles between the station and town.

Around Katherine

Cutta Cutta Caves Nature Park

About 30km south of Katherine, turn your back on the searing sun and dip down 15m below terra firma into this mazelike limestone cave system. The 1499-hectare **Cutta Cutta Caves Nature Park** (☎08-8972 1940; www.nretas.nt.gov.au/national-parks-and-reserves/parks/find/cuttacuttacaves; tours adult/child $17/8.50; ⏲8.30am-4.30pm, guided tours 9am, 10am, 11am, 1pm, 2pm & 3pm) has a unique ecology and you'll be sharing the space with brown tree snakes and pythons, plus the endangered ghost bats and orange horseshoe bats that they feed on. Cutta Cutta is a Jawoyn name meaning many stars; it was taboo for Aborigines to enter the cave, which they believed was where the stars were kept during the day. Admission by tour only.

Nitmiluk (Katherine Gorge) National Park

Spectacular Katherine Gorge forms the backbone of the 2920-sq-km **Nitmiluk (Katherine Gorge) National Park** (www.nt.gov.au/nreta/parks/find/nitmiluk.html), about 30km from Katherine. A series of 13 deep sandstone gorges have been carved out by the Katherine River on its journey from Arnhem Land to the Timor Sea. It is a hauntingly beautiful place – though it can get crowded in peak season – and a must-do from Katherine. In the Dry the tranquil river is perfect for a paddle, but in the Wet the deep still waters and dividing rapids are engulfed by an awesome torrent that churns through the gorge. Plan to spend at least a full day canoeing or cruising on the river and bushwalking.

The traditional owners are the Jawoyn Aboriginal people who jointly manage Nitmiluk with Parks & Wildlife. Nitmiluk Tours (p862) manages accommodation, cruises and activities within the park.

Sights

Leliyn (Edith Falls) NATURE RESERVE

Reached off the Stuart Hwy 40km north of Katherine and a further 20km along a sealed road, Leliyn is an idyllic, safe haven for swimming and hiking. The moderate **Leliyn Trail** (2.6km loop, 1½ hours) climbs into escarpment country through grevillea and spinifex and past scenic lookouts (Bemang is best in the afternoon) to the Upper Pool, where the moderate **Sweetwater Pool Trail** (8.6km return, three to five hours) branches off. The peaceful Sweetwater Pool has a small **camping ground** (per person $3.30, plus $50 refundable deposit); overnight permits are available at the kiosk.

The main Lower Pool – a gorgeous, mirror-flat swimming lagoon – is a quick 150m dash from the car park. The Parks & Wildlife **camping ground** (☎08-8975 4869; adult/child $12/6) next to the car park has grassy sites, lots of shade, toilets, showers, a laundry and facilities for the disabled. Fees are paid at the **kiosk** (⏲8am-6pm May-Oct, 9.30am-3pm Nov-Apr), which sells snacks and basic supplies. Nearby is a picnic area with BBQs and tables.

Activities

Bushwalking

The park has around 120km of marked walking tracks, ranging from 2km stretches to 66km multinight hikes. Overnight hikers must register at the Nitmiluk Centre. There's a $50 refundable deposit for any overnight walk and a camping fee of $3.30 per person per night. The Nitmiluk Centre has maps and info on the full range of walks.

Barrawei (Lookout) Loop BUSHWALKING

Starting with a short, steep climb this walk (3.7km loop, two hours, moderate difficulty) provides good views over the Katherine River.

Butterfly Gorge BUSHWALKING

A challenging, shady walk (12km return, 4½ hours) through a pocket of monsoon rainforest, often with butterflies, leads to midway along the second gorge and a deep-water swimming spot.

Jawoyn Valley BUSHWALKING

A difficult (40km loop, overnight) wilderness trail leading off the Eighth Gorge walk into a valley with rock outcrops and rock-art galleries.

Jatbula Trail BUSHWALKING

This renowned walk (66km one way, five days, difficult) to Leliyn (Edith Falls) climbs the Arnhem Land escarpment, passing the swamp-fed Biddlecombe Cascades, Crystal Falls, the Amphitheatre and the Sweetwater Pool. This walk can only be done one way (ie you can't walk from Leliyn to Katherine Gorge). It is closed from October to April, and a minimum of two walkers are required. A ferry service ($7) takes you across the gorge to kick things off.

Canoeing

Nothing beats exploring the gorges in your own boat, and lots of travellers canoe at least as far as the first or second gorge. Bear in mind the intensity of the sun and heat, and the fact that you may have to carry your canoe over the rock bars and rapids that separate the gorges. Pick up the *Canoeing Guide* at the Nitmiluk Centre. If you want to use your own canoe you need to pay a registration fee of $5.50 per person, plus a refundable $50 deposit.

Nitmiluk Tours CANOEING

(☎08-8972 1253, 1300 146 743; www.nitmiluktours.com.au) From April to November, Nitmiluk Tours hires out single/double canoes for a half-day ($48/71, departing 8am and 1pm) or full day ($62/90, departing 8am), including the use of a splash-proof drum for cameras and other gear (it's not fully waterproof), a map and a life jacket. The half-day hire only allows you to paddle up the first gorge; with the full day you can get up as far as the third gorge depending on your level of fitness – start early. The canoe shed is at the boat ramp by the main car park, about 500m beyond the Nitmiluk Centre. There's a $50 deposit required for half-day hires.

You also can be a little more adventurous and take the canoes out overnight for $119/133 a single/double, plus $3.30 for a camping permit – there are camp sites at the fifth, sixth, eighth and ninth gorges. Bookings are essential as overnight permits are limited and there is a $60 deposit. Don't take this trip lightly though.

Gorge Cruises

Nitmiluk Tours CRUISES

(☎08-8972 1253, 1300 146 743; www.nitmiluktours.com.au; 2hr cruise adult/child $73/41, 4hr cruise $91/46, breakfast cruise $88/58, sunset cruise $142/126) An easy way to see far into the gorge is on a cruise. Bookings on some cruises can be tight in the peak season; make your reservation a day in advance. The two-hour cruise goes to the second gorge and visits a rock-art gallery (including 800m walk). Departures are at 9am, 11am, 1pm and 3pm daily year-round depending on river level. There's wheelchair access to the top of the first gorge only. The four-hour cruise goes to the third gorge and includes refreshments and a chance to swim. This

GHUNMARN CULTURAL CENTRE

If you're interested in seeing genuine Aboriginal art produced by local communities, it's worth detouring off the Stuart Hwy to this remote cultural centre.

The small community of Beswick is reached via the sealed Central Arnhem Hwy 56km east of the Stuart Hwy on the southern fringes of Arnhem Land. Here you'll find the **Ghunmarn Culture Centre** (☎08-8977 4250; www.djilpinarts.org.au; Beswick; ⌚9.30am-4pm Mon-Fri Apr-Nov), opened in 2007, and displaying local artworks, prints, carvings, weaving and didgeridoos from western Arnhem Land. The centre also features the Blanasi Collection, a permanent exhibition of works by elders from the western Arnhem Land region. Visitors are welcome to visit the centre without a permit – call ahead to check that it's open. If you can't get out here, drop in to Djilpin Arts (p857) in Katherine.

A very special festival at Beswick is Walking With Spirits (p822) – magical performances of traditional corroborees staged in conjunction with the Australian Shakespeare Company. It's held on the first weekend in August. Camping is possible at Beswick Falls over this weekend but advance bookings are essential.

cruise leaves at 9am daily from April to November, plus at 11am and 1pm May to August.

There's also a more leisurely two-hour breakfast cruise, leaving at 7am May to October and a sunset cruise, sailing at 4.30pm on Monday, Wednesday, Friday, Saturday and Sunday from May to December, with a candlelit buffet dinner and champagne.

Scenic Flights

Nitmiluk Tours SCENIC FLIGHTS
(☎1300 146 743; www.nitmiluktours.com.au; flights from $85 per person) Nitmiluk Tours offers a variety of flights ranging from an eight-minute buzz over the first gorge (per person $85) to an 18-minute flight over all 13 gorges ($232). The Adventure Swim Tour ($449) drops you at a secluded swimming hole for an hour or so, and there are broader tours that take in Aboriginal rock-art sites and Kakadu National Park. Book at the Nitmiluk Centre.

Sleeping

There are bush-camping sites for overnight walkers throughout the park, and permanent camping grounds near the Nitmiluk Visitor Centre and at Leliyn (Edith Falls). The exciting new Cicada Lodge is due to open in 2013.

Nitmiluk National Park Campground CAMPGROUND $
(☎08-8972 1253, 1300 146 743; www.nitmiluktours.com.au; unpowered/powered sites $36/40, safari tents $124;) Plenty of grass and shade, hot showers, toilets, BBQs, a laundry and a kiosk by the good-lookin' swimming pool. Wallabies and goannas are frequent visitors. There's a 'tent village' here with permanent safari tents sleeping two people. Book at the Nitmiluk Centre.

Nitmiluk Chalets CABINS $$
(☎08-8972 1253, 1300 146 743; www.nitmiluktours.com.au; 1-/2-bedroom cabins $195/245;) Next door to the caravan park, these cabins are a serviceable choice if you'd rather have a solid roof over your head (and a flat-screen TV). Access to all the caravan park facilities (pool, BBQs, kiosk etc).

Cicada Lodge BOUTIQUE HOTEL $$$
(☎1300 146 743; www.cicadalodge.com.au; Nitmiluk National Park; d inc breakfast $645;) Under construction at the time of research, this luxury lodge, also near the visitor centre, has been architecturally designed to meld modern sophistication and traditional Jawoyn themes. It will have just 18 luxury rooms overlooking the Katherine River. Packages including gorge and dinner cruises will be available.

Information

The **Nitmiluk Centre** (☎08-8972 1253, 1300 146 743; www.nitmiluktours.com.au; ⏲7am-6pm) has excellent displays and information on the park's geology, wildlife, the traditional owners (the Jawoyn) and European history. There's also a restaurant here (snacks and meals $5 to $20), and a desk for **Parks & Wildlife** (☎08-8972 1886), which has information sheets on a wide range of marked walking tracks that start here and traverse the picturesque country south of the gorge. Registration for overnight walks and camping permits ($3.30 per night) is from 8am to 1pm; canoeing permits are also issued. Check at the centre for information on ranger talks.

Getting There & Away

It's 30km by sealed road from Katherine to the Nitmiluk Centre, and a few hundred metres further to the car park, where the gorge begins and the cruises start.

Daily transfers between Katherine and the gorge are run by **Nitmiluk Tours** (☎08-8972 1253, 1300 146 743; www.nitmiluktours.com.au; 27 Katherine Tce, Shop 2, Katherine; adult/child return $27/19), departing from the Nitmiluk Town Booking Office and also picking up at local accommodation places on request. Buses leave Katherine at 7.30am, 12.15pm and 5pm, returning from Nitmiluk at 8am, 1.15pm and 5.30pm.

Katherine to Western Australia

The sealed Victoria Hwy – part of the Savannah Way – stretches 513km from Katherine to Kununurra in WA. It winds through diverse landscapes, with extensive tracts annexed as cattle stations in the 1880s, which became the economy's backbone in the postwar recovery period of the 1950s.

A 4WD will get you into a few out-of-the-way national parks accessed off the Victoria Hwy, or you can meander through semiarid desert and sandstone outcrops until bloated boab trees herald your imminent arrival in WA. All fruits, vegetables, nuts and honey must be left at the quarantine-inspection post on the border. WA time is 1½ hours behind NT time.

Flora River Nature Park

The irradescent bue-green water of the mineral-rich Flora River precipitates calcium carbonate onto roots and fallen branches creating limestone tufa (spongy rock) dams; the effect is a series of pretty cascades. Within **Flora River Nature Park** (www.nretas.nt.gov.au/national-parks-and-reserves/parks/find/florariver) there's a **camping ground** (adult/child $6.60/3.30) at Djarrung with an amenities block. The Flora River has crocs, so there's no swimming. The park will be known as Giwining in the near future.

The park turn-off is 90km southwest of Katherine; the park entrance is a further 32km along a passable dirt road (OK for 2WD cars in the Dry).

Victoria River Crossing

The red sandstone cliffs surrounding this spot where the highway crosses the Victoria River (194km west of Katherine) create a dramatic setting. Much of this area forms the eastern section of Gregory National Park. The **Victoria River Roadhouse Caravan Park** (☎08-8975 0744; fax 08-8975 0819; Victoria Hwy; unpowered/powered sites $15/20, d $125), west of the bridge, has a shop, bar and meals ($12 to $29).

Timber Creek

POP 231

Tiny Timber Creek is the only town between Katherine and Kununurra. It has a pretty big history for such a small place, with an early European exploration aboard the *Tom Tough* requiring repairs to be carried out with local timber (hence the town's name). The expedition's leader, AC Gregory, inscribed his arrival date into a boab; it is still discernable (and is explained in detail through interpretive panels) at **Gregory's Tree**, 15km northwest of town.

The town's **Old Police Station Museum** (www.nationaltrustnt.org.au; adult/child $4/free; ⏲10am-noon Mon-Fri May-Oct), established to smooth relations with pastoralists and indigenous people, is now a museum displaying old police and mining equipment.

A highlight of Timber Creek is the **Victoria River Cruise** (☎08-8975 0850; www.victoriarivercruise.com; adult/child $85/45; ⏲4pm Mon-Sat), which takes you 40km downriver, spotting wildlife and returning in time for a fiery sunset.

The town is dominated by the roadside **Timber Creek Hotel & Circle F Caravan Park** (☎08-8975 0722; www.timbercreekhotel.com.au; Victoria Hwy; unpowered/powered sites $25/27.50, budget r from $66, motel d $95; ❄🏊). Enormous trees shade parts of the camping area, which is next to a small creek where there's croc feeding every evening (5pm). The complex includes the Timber Creek Hotel and Fogarty's Store.

Gregory National Park

The remote and rugged wilderness of the little-visited **Gregory National Park** (www.nretas.nt.gov.au/national-parks-and-reserves/parks/find/gregory) will swallow you up. Covering 12,860 sq km, it sits at the transitional zone between the tropical and semiarid regions. The park, which will eventually be called Judbarra National Park, consists of old cattle country and is made up of two separate sections: the eastern (Victoria River) section and the much larger Bullita section in the west. While some parts of the park are accessible by 2WD, it's the rough-as-guts, dry-season-only 4WD tracks that are the most rewarding; for these you need to be self-sufficient and to register (call ☎1300 650 730).

Parks & Wildlife (☎08-8975 0888; ⏲7am-4.30pm) in Timber Creek can provide park and 4WD notes, and a map to the various walks, camping spots, tracks and the historic homestead and ruggedly romantic original stockyards – a must before heading in. This is crocodile country; swimming isn't safe.

There's 2WD accessible bush camping at **Big Horse Creek** (adult/child $3.30/1.75), 7km west of Timber Creek.

Keep River National Park

The remote **Keep River National Park** (www.nretas.nt.gov.au/national-parks-and-reserves/parks/find/keepriver) is noted for its stunning sandstone formations, beautiful desolation and rock art. Pamphlets detailing walks are available at the start of the excellent trails. Don't miss the **rock-art walk** (5.5km return, two hours) near Jarnem, and the **gorge walk** (3km return, two hours) at Jinumum.

The park entrance is just 3km from the WA border. You can reach the park's main points by conventional vehicle during the Dry. A **rangers station** (☎08-9167 8827) lies 3km into the park from the main road, and there are basic, sandstone-surrounded **camping grounds** (adult/child $3.30/1.65) at Gurrandalng (18km into the park) and Jarnem (32km). Tank water is available at Jarnem.

Mataranka & Elsey National Park

POP 244

With soothing, warm thermal springs set in pockets of palms and tropical vegetation, you'd be mad not to pull into Mataranka for at least a few hours to soak off the road dust. The small settlement regularly swells with towel-toting visitors shuffling to the thermal pool or the spring-fed Elsey National Park. If you see Mataranka referred to as the 'capital of the Never Never', it's a reference to Jeannie Gunn's 1908 autobiographical novel *We of the Never Never,* about life as a pioneering woman on nearby Elsey Station – the deeds of title of which have since been returned to the Mangarayi indigenous owners.

Sights & Activities

Mataranka's crystal-clear **thermal pool**, shrouded in rainforest, is 10km from town beside the Mataranka Homestead Resort. The warm, clear water dappled by filtered light leaking through overhanging palms rejuvenates a lot of bodies on any given day; it's reached via a boardwalk from the resort and can get mighty crowded. About 200m away (keep following the boardwalk) is the Waterhouse River, where you can rent canoes for $10 per hour. **Stevie's Hole**, a natural swimming hole in the cooler Waterhouse River, about 1.5km from the homestead, is rarely crowded.

Elsey Station Homestead HISTORIC BUILDING
(admission by donation; daylight hours) Outside the Mataranka Homestead Resort entrance is a replica of the Elsey Station Homestead, constructed for the filming of *We of the Never Never,* which is screened daily at noon in the resort bar.

Never Never Museum MUSEUM
(120 Roper Tce; adult/child $3.50/1.50; 9am-4.30pm Mon-Fri) Back in town, the Never Never Museum has displays on the northern railway, WWII and local history. Access via the Rural Transaction Centre next door.

Elsey National Park NATURE RESERVE
(www.nretas.nt.gov.au/national-parks-and-reserves/parks/find/elsey) The national park adjoins the thermal-pool reserve and offers peaceful **camping**, **fishing** and **walking** along the Waterhouse and Roper Rivers. Bitter Springs is a serene palm-fringed thermal pool within the national park, 3km from Mataranka along the sealed Martin Rd. The almost unnatural blue-green colour of the 34°C water is due to dissolved limestone particles.

Sleeping & Eating

Jalmurark Camping Area CAMPGROUND $
(John Hauser Dr; adult/child $6.60/3.30) Located at 12 Mile Yards in Elsey National Park, this scrubby camping ground has lots of shade, toilets and showers and access to the Roper River and walking trails. There's a kiosk here in the Dry from which you can hire canoes.

Mataranka Homestead Resort CAMPGROUND $
(08-8975 4544; www.matarankahomestead.com.au; Homestead Rd; unpowered/powered site $24/29, dm/d/cabins $25/89/115;) Only metres from the main thermal pool and with a range of budget accommodation, this is a *very* popular option. The large camping ground is dusty but has a few shady areas and decent amenities. The fan-cooled hostel rooms are very basic (linen provided). The air-con motel rooms (also rudimentary) have fridge, TV and bathroom, while the cabins have a kitchenette and sleep up to six people. Book ahead.

Mataranka Cabins CABINS $$
(08-8975 4838; www.matarankacabins.com.au; 4705 Martin Rd, Bitter Springs; unpowered/powered sites $25/30, cabins $120; @) On the banks of the Little Roper River, only a few hundred metres from Bitter Springs thermal pool, this quiet bush setting has some amazing termite mounds adorning the front paddock. The TV-equipped, open-plan cabins have linen, bathrooms and kitchens, and two can accommodate up to five folks.

Territory Manor Motel & Caravan Park CAMPGROUND, MOTEL $$
(08-89754516; www.matarankamotel.com; Martin Rd; unpowered/powered sites $26/30, s/d $100/115; @) Mataranka's best caravan park with grassy, shaded sites and attractive rammed-earth motel units. Pet barramundi are hand fed in spectacular fashion twice a day. Their

cousins are served up in the licensed bistro (mains $20 to $35) along with steaks, salad etc.

Stockyard Gallery CAFE $
(www.stockyardgallery.com.au; Stuart Hwy; snacks $5-10; ⏲ breakfast & lunch daily May-Oct, lunch only Nov-Apr) This casual cafe is a little gem. There's a delicious range of homemade snacks (focaccia, sandwiches, cakes, muffins) plus fresh espresso coffee and divine mango smoothies. The art gallery here sells Aboriginal art, books and souvenirs.

Barkly Tableland & Gulf Country

East of the Stuart Hwy lies some of the Territory's most remote cattle country, but parts are accessible by sealed road and the rivers and inshore waters of the Gulf coast are regarded as some of the best fishing locales in the country.

Roper Highway

Not far south of Mataranka on the Stuart Hwy, the mostly sealed single-lane Roper Hwy strikes 175km eastwards to Roper Bar, crossing the paperbark- and pandanus-lined Roper River where freshwater meets saltwater. It's passable only in the Dry. Keen fisherfolk stop here, with accommodation, fuel and supplies available at the **Roper Bar Store** (☎ 08-8975 4636; www.roperbar.com.au; unpowered site $20, s/d $95/115; ⏲ 9am-6pm Mon-Sat). Roper Bar is an access point to Borroloola. Head south along the rough-going Nathan River Rd through **Limmen National Park** (www.nt.gov.au/nreta/parks/find/limmen.html) – high-clearance with two spare tyres is required – and into southeastern Arnhem Land.

Continuing east along the highway for 45km leads to the Aboriginal community of Ngukurr, home to about 1000 people from nine different language groups and cultures. This cultural diversity informs the unique works on show and available to buy from the **Ngukurr Arts Centre** (www.ngukurrarts.com.au; ⏲ 9am-2pm Mon-Fri); no permit is required to visit the centre.

Carpentaria & Tablelands Highways

Just south of Daly Waters, the sealed Carpentaria Hwy (Hwy 1) heads 378km east to Borroloola, near the Gulf of Carpentaria, and one of the NT's top barramundi fishing spots. After 267km the Carpentaria Hwy meets the sealed Tablelands Hwy at Cape Crawford. At this intersection is the famous **Heartbreak Hotel** (☎ 08-8975 9928; unpowered/powered sites $16/26, s/d $70/80; ❄). Pitch the tent on the shaded grassy lawn and park yourself on the wide verandah with a cold beer. Breakfast, lunch and dinner (meals $15 to $30) are available.

Cape Crawford Tourism (☎ 0400 156 685; www.capecrawfordtourism.com.au) runs helicopter rides (from $100) to see the otherwise inaccessible Lost City sandstone formations.

From here it's a desolate 374km south across the Barkly Tableland to the Barkly Hwy (Rte 66) and the **Barkly Homestead Roadhouse** (☎ 08-8964 4549; www.barklyhomestead.com.au; unpowered/powered sites $20/28, cabins & motel d $140; ❄ 🏊), a surprisingly upbeat roadhouse. From here it's 210km west to Tennant Creek and 252km east to the Queensland border.

Borroloola

POP 927

On the McArthur River close to the bountiful waters of the Gulf, Borroloola is big news for **fishing** fans, but unless you're keen on baiting a hook (the barramundi season peaks from February to April) or driving the remote (preferably 4WD) Savannah Way to Queensland, it's a long way to go for not much reward.

About three-quarters of the population of Borroloola is indigenous, and the town's colourful history is displayed at the **Borroloola Museum** (www.nationaltrustnt.org.au; Robinson Rd; admission $2; ⏲ 8am-5pm Mon-Fri May-Sep), inside the 1886 police station.

The **Savannah Way Motel** (☎ 08-8975 8883; www.savannahwaymotel.com.au; Robinson Rd; r $80-120, cabins $130; ❄ 🏊), on the main road through town, is clean and comfortable, with cabins, lodge rooms and tropical gardens. If you're with a group you can book the whole lodge for $440. There's a restaurant here, too.

There's also the **McArthur River Caravan Park** (☎ 08-8975 8712; mcarthurcaravanpark.com.au; Robinson Rd; unpowered/powered site $22/28, budget unit s/d $75/85, self-contained unit s/d $98/110), and meals available at the local pub: burgers, chops and mixed grills at the rowdy **Borroloola Hotel** (166 Robinson Rd; meals $10-28; ⏲ lunch & dinner), within a lounge bar reinforced with steel mesh.

Mataranka to Tennant Creek

Larrimah

POP 18

Once upon a time the railway line from Darwin came as far as Birdum, 8km south of tiny Larrimah, which itself is 185km south of Katherine. **Larrimah Museum** (Mahoney St; admission by donation; ⏲7am-9pm), in the former telegraph repeater station opposite the Larrimah Hotel, tells of the town's involvement with the railway, the Overland Telegraph and WWII. The town was built in 1940, essentially as life support for the nearby Gorrie Airfield.

Originally a WWII officers' mess, **Larrimah Hotel** (☎08-8975 9931; unpowered/powered sites $18/22, d $60-75; ❄≋) is a cheerfully rustic and quirky pub offering basic rooms, meals (mains $10 to $29) and a menagerie of animals. **Fran's Devonshire Teahouse** (Stuart Hwy; meals $4-15; ⏲8am-4pm) makes a great lunchtime pit stop. Try a legendary camel or buffalo pie, some roast lamb with damper, or just a Devonshire tea (a long way from Exeter) or fresh coffee.

Daly Waters

POP 25

About 3km off the highway and 160km south of Mataranka is Daly Waters, an important staging post in the early days of aviation – Amy Johnson landed here on her epic flight from England to Australia in 1930. Just about everyone stops at the famous **Daly Waters Pub** (☎08-8975 9927; www.dalywaterspub.com; unpowered/powered sites $14/24, d $60-95, cabins $125-165; ❄≋). Decorated with business cards, bras, banknotes and memorabilia from passing travellers, the pub claims to be the oldest in the Territory (its liquor licence has been valid since 1893) and has become a bit of a legend along the Track, although it may be a bit too popular for its own good. Every evening from April to September there's the popular beef 'n' barra BBQ ($28). Otherwise, hearty meals (mains $10 to $25, open lunch and dinner), including the filling barra burger, are served. Beside the pub is a dustbowl camping ground with a bit of shade – book ahead or arrive early to secure a powered site. Accommodation ranges from basic dongas (small, transportable buildings) to spacious self-contained cabins.

Daly Waters to Three Ways

Heading south, you encounter the fascinating ghost town of Newcastle Waters, 3km west of the highway. Its atmospheric, historic buildings include the Junction Hotel, cobbled together from abandoned windmills in 1932. South of the cattle town of Elliott, the land just gets drier and drier and the vegetation sparser. The mesmerising sameness breaks at Renner Springs, generally accepted as the dividing line between the seasonally wet Top End and the dry Centre, where there is a decent roadhouse.

Banka Banka (☎08-8964 4511; adult/child $10/5) is a historic cattle station 100km north of Tennant Creek, with a grassy camping area (no power), marked walking tracks (one leading to a tranquil waterhole) and a licensed bar and small kiosk selling basic refreshments.

Three Ways, 537km north of Alice Springs, is the junction of the Stuart and Barkly Hwys, from where you can head south to Alice, north to Darwin (988km) or east to Mt Isa in Queensland (643km). **Threeways Roadhouse** (☎08-8962 2744; www.threewaysroadhouse.com.au; Stuart Hwy; unpowered/powered sites $24/32, cabins d $90-113; ❄@≋) is a potential stopover with a bar and restaurant, but Tennant Creek is only 26km further south.

Tennant Creek

POP 3061

Servicing a vast region of cattle stations and remote Aboriginal communities, roughly the size of the UK, Tennant Creek is the only town of any size between Katherine, 680km to the north, and Alice Springs, 511km to the south. It's a good place to break up a long drive and check out the town's few attractions.

Local legend speaks of Tennant Creek being founded on beer: first settled when the drivers of a broken-down beer-laden wagon settled in to consume the freight in the 1930s. The truth is far more prosaic: the town was established as a result of a small gold rush around the same time. While it was short-lived, gold-mining ventures have operated discontinuously depending on metal prices, and exploration continues in the region today.

Tennant Creek is known as Jurnkurakurr to the local Warumungu people and almost half of the population is of Aboriginal descent. When the town is in the news, it's often for the wrong reasons – mainly alcoholism and violence – but there is a lot that is positive happening here and it's worth a stop to experience the wealth of Aboriginal art and culture on offer.

Sights & Activities

Nyinkka Nyunyu   ART GALLERY

(www.nyinkkanyunyu.com.au; Paterson St; tour guide $15; ⊙8am-4pm Mon-Fri, 9am-4pm Sat & Sun) This innovative museum and gallery highlights the dynamic art and culture of the local Warumungu people. The absorbing displays focus on contemporary art, traditional objects (many returned from interstate museums), bush medicine and regional history. The diorama series, or bush TVs as they became known within the community, are particularly special. Nyinkka Nyunyu is located beside a sacred site of the spiky tailed goanna. Learn about bush tucker and Dreaming stories with your personal guide. There's also a gallery store and the lovely Jajjikari Café (⊙8am-3pm), which serves espresso coffee and light meals.

Julalikari Arts Centre   ARTS CENTRE

(North Stuart Hwy; ⊙8am-noon Mon-Thu) It's best to visit the 'Pink Palace', at the entrance to the Ngalpa Ngalpa community (also known as Mulga Camp), mid-morning when the artists are at work painting traditional and contemporary art. You can chat to the artists and purchase directly from them.

Battery Hill Mining Centre   MINE

(Peko Rd; adult/child $25/15; ⊙9am-5pm) Experience life in Tennant Creek's 1930s gold rush at this mining centre, which doubles as the Visitor Information Centre, 2km east of town. There are underground mine tours and audio tours of the 10-head battery. In addition there is a superb Minerals Museum and you can try your hand at gold panning. The admission price gives access to all of the above, or you can choose to visit the Minerals and Social History Museums only (adult/family $7/15), or just go panning (per person $2).

While you're here, ask for the key ($20 refundable deposit) to the old Telegraph Station, which is just off the highway about 12km north of town. This is one of only four of the original 11 stations remaining in the Territory. Just north of the Telegraph Station is the turn-off west to Kundjarra (The Pebbles), a formation of granite boulders like a miniature version of the better-known Devil's Marbles found 100km south. It's a sacred women's Dreaming site of the Warumungu.

Kelly's Ranch   HORSE RIDING

(☑08-8962 2045; www.kellysranch.com.au; 5 Fazaldeen Rd; trail rides per person $150, lesson per person $50) Experience the Barkly from the back of a horse with local Warumungu man Jerry Kelly. His two-hour trail rides start with a lesson and then a ride through some superb outback scenery with bush-tucker stops along the way. Jerry entertains with stories about Aboriginal culture and life on the cattle stations.

Sleeping & Eating

Tourist's Rest Youth Hostel   HOSTEL $

(☑08-8962 2719; www.touristrest.com.au; cnr Leichhardt & Windley Sts; dm/d $26/56; ❄@❄) This small, friendly and slightly ramshackle hostel has bright clean rooms, free breakfast and VIP discounts. The hostel can organise tours of the gold mines and Devil's Marbles and pick-up from the bus stop.

Outback Caravan Park   CAMPGROUND $

(☑08-8962 2459; Peko Rd; unpowered/powered sites $25/33, cabins $60-140; ❄❄) In a town that often feels parched, it's nice to be in the shade of this grassy caravan park about 1km east of the centre. There's a well-stocked kiosk, camp kitchen and fuel. You may even be treated to some bush poetry and bush tucker, courtesy of yarn spinner Jimmy Hooker, at 7.30pm ($5). There are discounts for bookings of more than three nights.

Safari Lodge Motel   MOTEL $

(☑08-8962 2207; safari@switch.com.au; Davidson St; s/d $90/100; ❄@❄) ❂ You should book ahead to stay at this family-run motel where the owners have made steps to gain accreditation as environmentally friendly. Safari Lodge is centrally located next to the best restaurant in town and has clean, fairly standard rooms with phone, fridge and TV.

Desert Sands   MOTEL $$

(☑08-8962 1346; www.desertsands.com.au; 780 Stuart Hwy; s/d from $105/115, extra person $10; ❄@❄) The Desert Sands offers enormous modern units (sleeping three to eight), each with a fully equipped kitchen, TV (with in-house movies) and bathroom with washing machine. The motel is at the southern entrance to Tennant Creek, which makes for a decent walk if you don't have a car (plus it can get a bit rowdy at that end of town at night).

Woks Up CHINESE $$
(☎08-8962 3888; 108 Paterson St; mains $14-24; ⏲5pm-late) An unexpected gem, Woks Up is one of the Territory's best Chinese diners with an immense menu and generous portions in a bright and clean restaurant.

★ **Fernanda's Café & Restaurant** MEDITERRANEAN $$
(☎08-8962 3999; 1 Noble St; mains $18-34; ⏲5.30-9.30pm Mon-Sat; ❄) Tucked inside the Tennant Creek squash courts (yes squash courts) is this surprising Mediterranean-inspired restaurant. A definite Tennant Creek highlight, it is run by the ebullient Fernanda, who serves up tantalising dishes such as Portuguese seafood hotpots.

Tennant Food Barn SUPERMARKET $
(185 Paterson St; ⏲8am-5pm) Opposite the post office, this supermarket has a pretty extensive selection and can supply your self-catering needs.

Information

Leading Edge Computers (☎08-8962 3907; 145 Paterson St; per 20min $2; ⏲9am-5pm Mon-Fri, 9am-noon Sat) Internet access.

Police Station (☎08-8962 4444; Paterson St)

Tennant Creek Hospital (☎08-8962 4399; Schmidt St)

Visitor Information Centre (☎08-8962 3388; www.barklytourism.com.au; Peko Rd; ⏲9am-5.30pm) Located 2km east of town at Battery Hill.

Getting There & Away

All long-distance buses stop at the **Transit Centre** (☎08-8962 2727; 151 Patterson St; 9am-5pm Mon-Fri, 8.30-11.30am Sat), where you can purchase tickets. **Greyhound Australia** (☎1300 473 946; www.greyhound.com.au) has regular buses from Tennant Creek to Alice Springs ($195, six hours), Katherine ($207, 8½ hours), Darwin ($282, 14 hours) and Mount Isa ($165, eight hours).

The weekly *Ghan* rail link between Alice Springs and Darwin can drop off passengers in Tennant Creek, although cars can't be loaded or offloaded. The train station is about 6km south of town so you will need a **taxi** (☎0432 289 369, 08-8962 3626; ⏲6am-5.30pm).

Car hire is available from **Thrifty** (☎08-8962 2207; Davidson St, Safari Lodge Motel), while for tyres and tyre repairs head to **Bridgestone Tyre Centre** (☎08-8962 2361; Paterson St).

Tennant Creek to Alice Springs

The gigantic boulders in precarious piles beside the Stuart Hwy, 105km south of Tennant Creek, are called the **Devil's Marbles**. Karlu Karlu is their Warumungu name, and this registered sacred site has great cultural importance. The rocks are believed to be the eggs of the Rainbow Serpent.

According to scientists, the 'marbles' are the rounded remains of a layer of granite that has eroded over aeons. A 15-minute walk loops around the main site. This geological phenomenon is particularly beautiful at sunrise and sunset, when these oddballs glow warmly. The **camping ground** (adult/child $3.30/1.65) has remarkably hard ground, pit toilets and fireplaces (BYO firewood).

At Wauchope (*war*-kup), 10km south of the Devil's Marbles, you will find Bruce, the gregarious publican of the **Wauchope Hotel** (☎08-8964 1963; www.wauchopehotel.com.au; Stuart Hwy; unpowered/powered sites $14/20, budget s $45, en suite s/d $85/95; ❄☒). His budget rooms are dongas but the costlier rooms are more spacious, with bathrooms. Meals from the **restaurant** (mains $18-33) are more than satisfactory.

At the kooky **Wycliffe Well Roadhouse & Holiday Park** (☎1800 222 195, 08-8964 1966; www.wycliffe.com.au; unpowered/powered sites $34/35, budget s/d from $50/60, s/d cabins with bathroom $110/117; ⏲6.30am-9pm; ❄@☒), 17km south of Wauchope, you can fill up with fuel and food (mains $15 to $20) or stay and spot UFOs that apparently fly over with astonishing regularity. The place is decorated with alien figures and UFO newspaper clippings. The park has a lawn camp site, an indoor pool, kids' playground, a cafe and a range of international beer.

Heading south, you reach the rustic **Barrow Creek Hotel** (☎08-8956 9753; Stuart Hwy; powered camp sites $15, s/d $50/65; ⏲7am-11pm), one of the highway's eccentric outback pubs. In the tradition of shearers who'd write their name on a banknote and pin it to the wall to ensure they could afford a drink when next they passed through, travellers continue to leave notes and photos. Food and fuel are available and next door is one of the original **Telegraph Stations** on the Overland Telegraph Line.

The highway continues through Ti Tree, where you'll find a roadhouse and, off the highway, the Ti Tree Food Store, which has espresso coffee. About 12km south of Ti Tree, the **Red Centre Farm** (Shatto Mango; ☎08-8956 9828; www.redcentrefarm.com; Stuart Hwy; ⏰7am-7pm) sells unique Territory-style wine – made from mangoes. If that sounds a bit hard to swallow, try the other mango products, such as the delicious ice cream.

In the grand Australian tradition of building very big things by the side of the road to pull up drivers, Aileron, 135km north of Alice, has Naked Charlie Quartpot, the 12m Anmatjere (Anmatyerre) man, who cuts a fine figure at the back of the roadhouse along with his larger-than-life family. The **Outback Art Gallery** (☎08-8956 9111; Stuart Hwy; ⏰8am-5pm Mon-Sat, 10am-4pm Sun) sells inexpensive paintings by the local Anmatjere community, as well as works from the Warlpiri community of Yuendumu.

Aileron Hotel Roadhouse (☎08-8956 9703; www.aileronroadhouse.com.au; Stuart Hwy; unpowered/powered sites $10/12, dm $36, s/d $110/120; ⏰5am-9pm; ❄📶) has camp sites (power available until 10pm), a 10-bed dorm and decent motel units. There's an ATM, bar, shop, a licensed restaurant (meals $10 to $25) and not forgetting Bozo the wedge-tail eagle. The owner's large collection of Namatjira watercolours (at least 10 by Albert Namatjira) is displayed around the roadhouse's dining area.

About 70km north of Alice, the Plenty Hwy heads off to the east towards the **Harts Range**. The main reason to detour is to fossick in the gem fields about 78km east of the Stuart Hwy, which are well known for garnets and zircons. You're guaranteed to get lucky at the popular **Gemtree Caravan Park** (☎08-8956 9855; www.gemtree.com.au; Gemtree; unpowered/powered sites $22/30, cabins $85).

For a taste of desert life, time your visit with the annual **Harts Range Races** (last weekend in July), one of the Territory's best outback rodeos.

The Tanami Road

Synonymous with isolated outback driving, the 1000km Tanami Rd connects Alice Springs with Halls Creek in WA and is essentially a short cut between central Australia and the Kimberley. In dry conditions it's possible to make it through the unsealed dust and corrugations in a well-prepared 2WD. Stay alert, as rollovers are common, and stock up with fuel, tyres, food and water.

The NT section is wide and usually well graded, and starts 20km north of Alice Springs. The road is sealed to **Tilmouth Well** (☎08-8956 8777; www.tilmouthwell.com; unpowered/powered sites $25/35, cabins without bathroom $70; ❄@📶) on the edge of Napperby Station which bills itself as an oasis in the desert with a sparkling pool and lush, sprawling lawns.

The next fuel stop is at Yuendumu, the largest remote community in the region and home to the Warlpiri people who were made famous in **Bush Mechanics** (www.bushmechanics.com). It's worth popping in to the **Warlukurlangu Art Centre** (☎08-8956 4133; www.warlu.com; ⏰9am-5pm Mon-Fri), a locally owned venture specialising in acrylic paintings.

From here there is no fuel for another 600km until you cross the WA border and hit **Billiluna** (☎08-9168 8076; www.billiluna.org.au). Note, Rabbit Flat Roadhouse has closed permanently. Another 170km will have you resting your weary bones in Halls Creek.

ALICE SPRINGS

POP 25,186

The Alice, as it's often known, sprang from humble beginnings as a lonely telegraph station on the continent-spanning Overland Telegraph Line (OTL) more than 140 years ago. Although still famous for its far-flung location, Alice Springs is no longer the frontier settlement of legend. Ignited by the boom in adventure tourism, the insatiable interest in contemporary Aboriginal art and improved access, the modernisation of Alice has been abrupt and confronting. Yet the vast surroundings of red desert and burnished ranges still underscore its remoteness.

This ruggedly beautiful town is shaped by its mythical landscapes, vibrant Aboriginal culture (where else can you hear six uniquely Australian languages in the main street?) and tough pioneering past. The town is a natural base for exploring central Australia, with Uluru-Kata Tjuta National Park a relatively close four-hour drive away. The mesmerising MacDonnell Ranges stretch east and west from the town centre, and you don't have to venture far to find yourself among ochre-red gorges, pastel-hued hills and ghostly white gum trees.

To the Arrernte people, the traditional owners of the Alice Springs area, this place is called Mparntwe. The heart of Mparntwe is the junction of the Charles (Anthelke Ulpeye) and Todd (Lhere Mparntwe) Rivers, just north of Anzac Hill (Untyeyetweleye). The topographical features of the town were formed by the creative ancestral beings – known as the Yeperenye, Ntyarlke and Utnerrengatye caterpillars – as they crawled across the landscape from Emily Gap (Anthwerrke), in the MacDonnell Ranges southeast of town. For many travellers, international and Australian, Alice Springs is their first encounter with contemporary indigenous Australia – with its enchanting art, mesmerising culture and present-day challenges.

Sights

Alice Springs Desert Park WILDLIFE PARK
(www.alicespringsdesertpark.com.au; Larapinta Dr; adult/child $25/12.50, nocturnal tour adult/child $25/12.50; ⏲7.30am-6pm, last entry 4.30pm, birds of prey show 10am & 3.30pm, nocturnal tour 7.30pm) If you haven't managed to glimpse a spangled grunter or a marbled velvet gecko on your travels, head to the Desert Park where the creatures of central Australia are all on display in one place. The predominantly open-air exhibits faithfully re-create the animals' natural environment in a series of habitats: inland river, sand country and woodland.

Try to time your visit with the terrific **birds of prey show**, featuring free-flying Australian kestrels, kites and awesome wedge-tailed eagles. To catch some of the park's rare and elusive animals like the bilby, visit the excellent **nocturnal house**. If you like what you see, come back at night and spotlight endangered species on the guided **nocturnal tour** (booking essential).

To get the most out of the park pick up a free audioguide (available in various languages) or join one of the free ranger-led talks held throughout the day.

It's an easy 2.5km cycle out to the park. Alternatively, **Desert Park Transfers** (☎08-8952 1731, 1800 806 641; www.tailormadetours.com.au; adult/child $48/33) operates five times daily during park hours and the cost includes park entry and pick-up and drop-off at your accommodation.

Araluen Cultural Precinct CULTURAL CENTRE
(Map p872; www.araluen.nt.gov.au; cnr Larapinta Dr & Memorial Ave; precinct pass adult/child $15/10) You can wander around freely outside, accessing the cemetery and grounds, but the 'precinct pass' provides entry to the exhibitions and displays for two days (with 14 days to use the pass).

Araluen Arts Centre ART GALLERY
(Map p872) For a small town, Alice Springs has a thriving arts scene and the Araluen Arts Centre is at its heart. There is a 500-seat theatre and four galleries with a focus on art from the central desert region.

The Albert Namatjira Gallery features works by the artist, who began painting watercolours in the 1930s at Hermannsburg. The exhibition draws comparisons between Namatjira and his initial mentor, Rex Battarbee and other Hermannsburg School artists. It also features 14 early acrylic works from the Papunya Community School Collection.

Other galleries showcase local artists, travelling exhibitions and newer works from Indigenous community art centres.

Museum of Central Australia MUSEUM
(Map p872; ⏲10am-5pm, library 10am-4pm Mon-Fri) The natural history collection at this museum recalls the days of megafauna – when hippo-sized wombats and 3m-tall flightless birds roamed the land. Among the displays are meteorite fragments and fossils. There's a free audio tour, narrated by a palaeontologist, which helps bring the exhibition to life.

There's also a display on the work of Professor TGH Strehlow, a linguist and anthropologist born at the Hermannsburg Mission among the Arrernte people. During his lifetime he gathered one of the world's most documented collections of Australian Aboriginal artefacts, songs, genealogies, film and sound recordings. It's upstairs in the **Strehlow Research Centre** which has a library open to the public.

Central Australia Aviation Museum MUSEUM
(Map p872; Memorial Ave; ⏲9am-5pm Mon-Fri, 10am-5pm Sat & Sun) FREE Housed in the Connellan Airways Hangar, Alice's original aerodrome, there are displays on pioneer aviation in the Territory including Royal Flying Doctor (RFDS) planes.

Easily the most interesting exhibit is the wreck of the **Kookaburra**, a tiny plane that crashed in the Tanami Desert in 1929 while searching for Charles Kingsford Smith and his co-pilot Charles Ulm, who had gone down in their plane, the *Southern Cross*. The *Kookaburra* pilots, Keith Anderson

Alice Springs

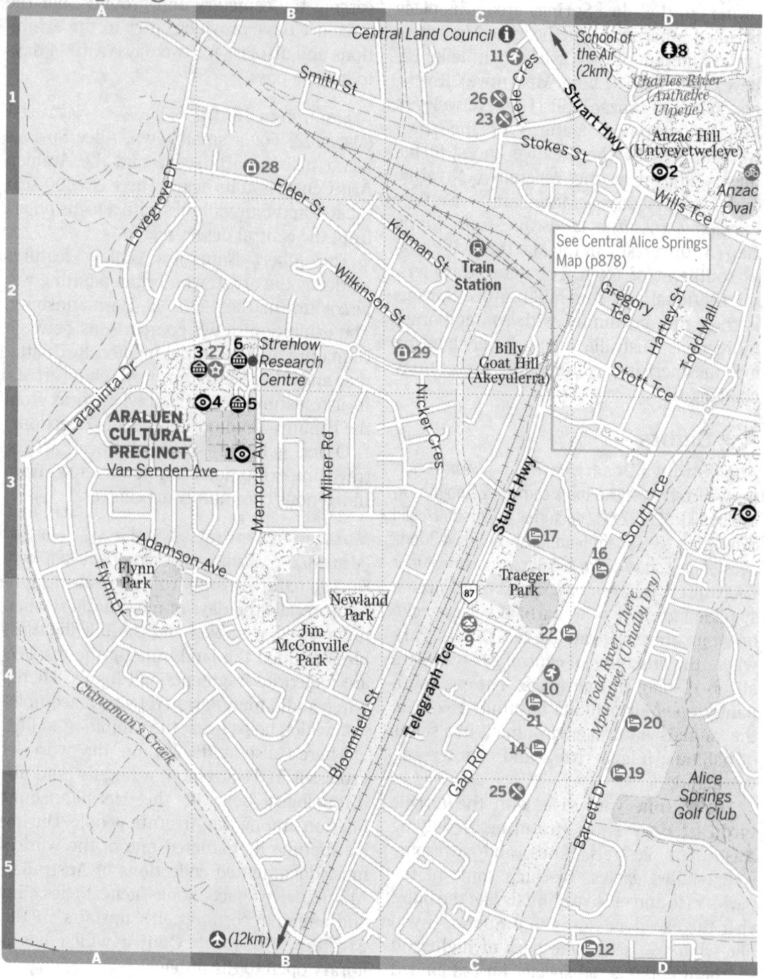

and Bob Hitchcock, perished in the desert, while Kingsford Smith and Ulm were rescued.

Alice Springs Memorial Cemetery CEMETERY

(Map p872) The cemetery is adjacent to the aviation museum and contains the graves of some prominent locals including Albert Namatjira (1902–59) and Harold Lasseter (1880–1931), the eccentric prospector whose fervent search for a folkloric reef of gold (Lasseter's Reef) claimed his life. Anthropologist Olive Pink (1884–1975), who campaigned for Aboriginal rights, is buried facing the opposite direction to the others – a rebel to the end.

Telegraph Station Historical Reserve HISTORIC PARK

(Map p872; adult/child $9/4.50; ⌚8am-9pm, museum 9am-5pm) The old Telegraph Station, which used to relay messages between Darwin and Adelaide, offers a fascinating glimpse of the town's European beginnings. Built along the Overland Telegraph Line in the 1870s, the station continued to operate until 1932. It later served as a welfare home for Aboriginal children of mixed ancestry

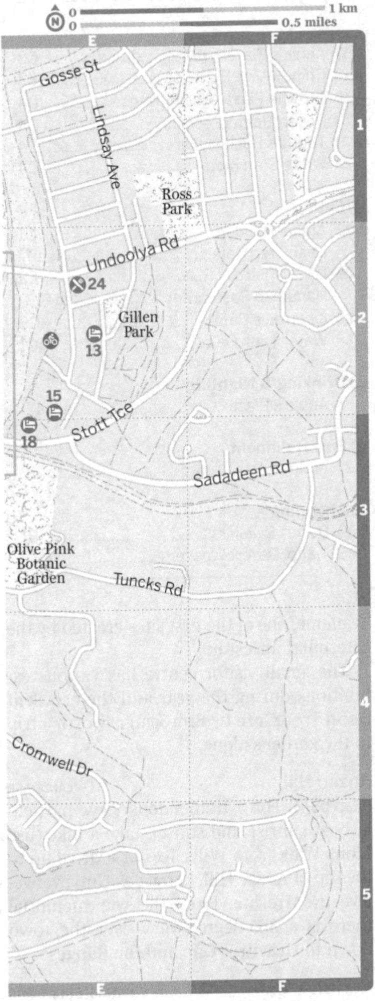

until 1963. The building has been faithfully restored and guided tours operate roughly on the hour between 9am and 4.30pm (April to October). Nearby is the original **'Alice' spring** (Thereyurre to the Arrernte Aboriginal people), a semipermanent waterhole in the Todd River after which the town is named.

It's all set in 450 hectares of shady parkland with free BBQs (alcohol permitted) and walking trails. The best is the 30-minute loop to **Trig Hill**, returning via the original station cemetery.

It's an easy 4km walk or cycle north to the station from Todd Mall; follow the path on the western side of the riverbed.

Royal Flying Doctor Service Base MUSEUM

(RFDS; Map p878; www.flyingdoctor.net; Stuart Tce; adult/child $12/6; ⌚9am-5pm Mon-Sat, 1-5pm Sun, cafe 9am-4.30pm Mon-Sat) This is the home of the Royal Flying Doctor Service, whose dedicated health workers provide 24-hour emergency retrievals across an area of around 1.25 million sq km. Entry to the visitor centre is by a half-hour tour that includes a video presentation, and a look at the operational control room as well as some ancient medical gear and a flight simulator. There's an adjoining giftshop and cafe.

School of the Air SCHOOL

(www.assoa.nt.edu.au; 80 Head St; adult/child $7.50/5; ⌚8.30am-4.30pm Mon-Sat, 1.30-4.30pm Sun) Started in 1951, this was the first school of its type in Australia, broadcasting lessons to children over an area of 1.3 million sq km. While transmissions were originally all done over high-frequency radio, satellite broadband internet and web-cams now mean students can study in a virtual classroom. The guided tour of the centre includes a video. During school term you can view a live broadcast from 8.30am to 2.30pm Monday to Friday. The school is about 3km north of the town centre.

Alice Springs Reptile Centre ZOO

(Map p878; www.reptilecentre.com.au; 9 Stuart Tce; adult/child $14/7; ⌚9.30am-5pm, handling demonstrations 11am, 1pm & 3.30pm) It may be small, but this reptile centre packs a poisonous punch with its impressive collection of venomous snakes, thorny devils and bearded dragons. Inside the cave room are 11 species of NT geckos, and outside there's Terry, a 3.3m saltwater croc plus Bub, a magnificent perentie, Australia's largest lizard. The enthusiastic guides will happily plonk a python around your neck during the handling demonstrations or let you pet a bluetongue lizard.

Alice Springs Transport Heritage Centre MUSEUM

At the MacDonnell siding, about 10km south of Alice and 1km west of the Stuart Hwy, are a couple of museums dedicated to big trucks and old trains. If you want to visit both the museums, consider the **half-day tour** (☎08-8955 5047; tours $55; ⌚10am-2pm), which includes entry, a guide and lunch.

Alice Springs

Sights

1 Alice Springs Memorial Cemetery B3
2 Anzac Hill D1
3 Araluen Arts Centre B2
4 Araluen Cultural Precinct B3
5 Central Australia Aviation Museum B3
6 Museum of Central Australia B2
7 Olive Pink Botanic Garden D3
8 Telegraph Station Historical Reserve D1

Activities, Courses & Tours

9 Alice Aquatic & Leisure Centre C4
10 Dust Bowl C4
11 Ultimate Ride C1

Sleeping

12 Alice in the Territory D5
13 Alice Lodge Backpackers E2
14 Alice on Todd C4
15 Alice's Secret Traveller's Inn E2
16 All Seasons Oasis D3
17 Annie's Place C3
18 Chifley Alice Springs E3
19 Crowne Plaza Alice Springs D4
20 Desert Palms Resort D4
21 Toddy's Backpackers C4
22 White Gum Motel C4

Eating

23 Afghan Traders C1
Bean Tree Cafe .... (see 7)
24 Casa Nostra E2
Hanuman Restaurant .... (see 19)
25 Kwerralye Cafe C5
26 Water Tank Cafe C1

Drinking & Nightlife

Annie's Place .... (see 17)

Entertainment

27 Araluen Arts Centre B2

Shopping

28 Desert Dwellers B1
29 Tjanpi Desert Weavers C2

The **Old Ghan Rail Museum** (1 Norris Bell Ave; adult/child $10/6; ⏲9am-5pm) has a collection of restored *Ghan* locos (originally called the Afghan Express after the cameleers who forged the route). There's also the Old Ghan Tea Rooms and an ad-hoc collection of railway memorabilia in the lovely Stuart railway station.

For a truckin' good time, head to the **National Road Transport Hall of Fame** (www.roadtransporthall.com; 2 Norris Bell Ave; adult/child $15/8; ⏲9am-5pm) which has a fabulous collection of big rigs, including a few ancient road trains. Admission includes entry to the Kenworth Dealer Truck Museum. There are more than 100 restored trucks and vintage cars, including many of the outback's pioneering vehicles.

Olive Pink Botanic Garden — NATURE RESERVE

(Map p872; www.opbg.com.au; Tuncks Rd; admission by donation; ⏲8am-6pm) A network of meandering trails leads through this lovely arid zone botanic garden, which was founded by the prominent anthropologist Olive Pink. The garden has more than 500 central Australian plant species and grows bush foods and medicinal plants like native lemon grass, quandong and bush passionfruit. There's a gentle climb up Meyers Hill with fine views over Alice and Ntyarlkarle Tyaneme, one of the first sites created by the caterpillar ancestors.

The small visitor centre has various exhibitions during the year and the excellent **Bean Tree Cafe** (⏲8am-3pm) is worth a trip to the gardens alone.

Anzac Hill — LANDMARK

(Map p872) For a tremendous view, particularly at sunrise and sunset, take a hike (use Lions Walk from Wills Tce) or a drive up to the top of Anzac Hill, known as Untyeyetweleye in Arrernte. From the war memorial there is a 365-degree view over the town down to Heavitree Gap and the Ranges.

Heritage Walk — NOTABLE BUILDINGS

(admission by donation) To get a feel for early Alice Springs, there are a number of historic-buildings-cum-mini-museums that you can pop into while wandering around town.

On Todd Mall is **Adelaide House** (Map p878; ⏲10am-4pm Mon-Fri, 10am-noon Sat) built in the 1920s by the founding flying doctor Reverend John Flynn as the first hospital in central Australia. Enter a classroom from 1938 at the **Old Hartley Street School** (Map p878; 39 Hartley St; ⏲10.30am-2.30pm Mon-Fri Feb-Nov) or take in the gracious beauty of the **Residency** (Map p878; 12 Parsons St; ⏲10am-2pm Mon-Fri), built in 1927 and a symbol of the town's brief legislative independence from the rest of the NT.

Activities

Ballooning

Outback BALLOONING
(☎1800 809 790; www.outbackballooning.com.au; 30/60min flight $290/385, mandatory insurance $25) Floating above Alice at sunrise is not an experience you will forget in a hurry (though the included picnic champagne breakfast may be). Hotel transfers are included in the price.

Bowling

Dust Bowl BOWLING
(Map p872; ☎08-8952 5051; 29 Gap Rd; per game $11; ⏲10am-late) After the pins are scattered there's a bar serving drinks and a cafe serving burgers. In the same building, the Red Tomato has wood-fired pizzas.

Bushwalking

Experience the bush around Alice with several easy walks radiating from the Olive Pink Botanic Garden and the Telegraph Station, which marks the start of the first stage of the Larapinta Trail.

Alice Springs Bushwalkers Association BUSHWALKING
(http://home.austarnet.com.au/longwalk) A group of local bushwalkers that schedules a wide variety of walks in the area, particularly the West MacDonnell Ranges, from March to November.

Camel Riding

Camels played an integral part in pioneering central Australia before roads and railways, and travellers can relive some of that adventure.

Pyndan Camel Tracks CAMEL RIDING
(☎0416 170 164; www.cameltracks.com; Jane Rd) Local cameleer Marcus Williams offers one-hour rides (adult/child $50/25), as well as half-day jaunts (per person $95).

Cycling & Mountain Bike Riding

Bikes are the perfect way to get around Alice Springs. There are cycle paths along the Todd River to the Telegraph Station, west to the Alice Springs Desert Park and further out to Simpsons Gap. For a map of cycling and walking paths pick up a copy of *Active in Alice* from the visitor information centre.

With its arid rangeland terrain and networks of single tracks, Alice Springs is getting a name for mountain bike riding, with the annual five-day MTB Enduro race a calendar highlight. Trails are easily accessed from town or meet up for a **social sunset ride** (☎08-8952 5800; centralaustralianroughriders.asn.au; Scout Hall, cnr Larapinta & Lovegrove Drs; ride $5; ⏲6pm Wed winter, 5pm summer) with the Central Australian Rough Riders' Club.

Longhorn BIKE HIRE
(☎0439 860 735; half-/full day $20/35) Drop-off/pick-up service with commuter, mountain and tandem bikes available as well as kids' bikes and baby seats.

Ultimate Ride BIKE SHOP
(Map p872; ☎08-8953 7297; 2/30 North Stuart Hwy; ⏲9am-6pm Mon-Fri, 9am-2pm Sat) Home of the Rough Riders, Ultimate Ride sells bicycles, stocks accessories and does repairs. It will also advise on bike tracks.

Swimming

Alice Aquatic & Leisure Centre SWIMMING
(Map p872; ☎08-8953 4633; Speed St; adult/child $5/2.55; ⏲6am-7pm Mon-Fri, 9am-7pm Sat & Sun) With lots of grass for lounging about and views of the Ranges, the Leisure Centre makes a lovely alternative to your hotel pool. The solar-heated indoor pools are open year-round.

Tours

Around Alice & MacDonnell Ranges

Alice Wanderer OUTBACK
(Map p878; ☎1800 722 111; www.alicewanderer.com.au; Gregory Tce) Has the 'hop on, hop off' town tours aboard the Alice Explorer ($44), which continually loops around town stopping at the major sights. Also runs day tours into the West MacDonnell Ranges as far as Glen Helen Gorge, including morning tea and lunch (adult/child $117/72), and a half-day trip to Simpsons Gap and Standley Chasm ($68/42). The office is opposite the visitor information centre.

Dreamtime Tours INDIGENOUS
(☎08-8953 3739; www.rstours.com.au; adult/child $85/42, self-drive $66/33; ⏲8.30-11.30am) Runs the three-hour Dreamtime & Bushtucker Tour, where you meet Warlpiri Aboriginal people and learn a little about their traditions. As it caters for large bus groups it can be impersonal, but you can tag along with your own vehicle.

★ **Foot Falcon** TOWN
(☎0427 569 531; www.footfalcon.com; tours $30; ⏲Mon & Thu 8.30am, Tue, Wed & Fri 4pm, Sun 3pm)

Local historian, author and teacher Linda Wells leads two-hour walks around town with insights into Alice's indigenous and pioneering history.

L'Astragale TOWN
(☎08-8953 6293; eroullet@gmail.com; tours $27) Francophone Evelyne Roullet runs a local walking tour of Alice Springs (or customise tour to your interests) which leaves from the visitor information centre.

Rainbow Valley Cultural Tours INDIGENOUS
(☎1800 011 144; www.rainbowvalleyculturaltours.com; self-drive morning $50/25, afternoon $70/50) Tour beautiful Rainbow Valley with a traditional owner and visit rock-art sites not open to the general public. Sunset self-drive tours can include overnight camping and dinner for an extra $30/20.

RT Tours FOOD
(☎08-8952 0327; www.rttoursaustralia.com; tours $150) Chef and Arrernte guide Bob Taylor runs a popular lunch and dinner tour at Simpsons Gap and the Telegraph Reserve where he whips up a bush-inspired meal. Other tours available.

Trek Larapinta WALKING
(☎1300 133 278; www.treklarapinta.com.au; from 6 days $1895) Guided multiday walks along sections of the Larapinta Trail. Also runs volunteer projects involving trail maintenance and bush regeneration on Aboriginal outstations.

Uluru, Kings Canyon & Palm Valley

Emu Run Tours OUTBACK
(Map p878; ☎1800 687 220, 08-8953 7057; www.emurun.com.au; 72 Todd St) Operates day tours to Uluru ($215) and two-day tours to Uluru and Kings Canyon ($520). Prices include park entry fees, meals and accommodation. There are also recommended small-group day tours through the West MacDonnell Ranges ($110) or Palm Valley ($189), including morning tea, lunch and entrance fees.

The Rock Tour OUTBACK
(☎1800 246 345; www.therocktour.com.au) Backpacker-friendly three-day (two nights) camping safari ($350) which visits Kings Canyon, Curtin Springs, the 'Rock' and Kata Tjuta. Leaves Alice daily at 6am.

Wayoutback Desert Safaris 4WD
(☎08-8952 4324, 1300 551 510; www.wayoutback.com) Small group 4WD safari tours including the excellent two-day Aboriginal-led Culture and Country trip ($670). There are also three-day safaris that traverse 4WD tracks to Uluru and Kings Canyon for $695, and five-day safaris that top it up with the Palm Valley and West MacDonnells for $1125.

Festivals & Events

Alice Springs Cup Carnival HORSE RACING
(www.alicespringsturfclub.org.au) On the first Monday in May, don a hat and gallop down to the Pioneer Park Racecourse for the main event of this five-day carnival.

Finke Desert Race MOTOCROSS
(www.finkedesertrace.com.au) Motorcyclists and buggy drivers vie to take out the title of this crazy June race 240km from Alice along the Old South Rd to Finke; the following day they race back again. Spectators camp along the road to cheer them on.

Alice Springs Beanie Festival ARTS
(www.beaniefest.org) This four-day festival in June/July, held at the Araluen Art Centre, celebrates the humble beanie (knitted woollen hat) – handmade by women throughout the central desert.

Camel Cup CAMEL RACING
(www.camelcup.com.au) A carnival atmosphere prevails during the running of the Camel Cup at Blatherskite Park in mid-July.

Alice Springs Rodeo RODEO
Bareback bull riding, steer wrestling and ladies' barrel races are on the bill at Blatherskite Park in August.

Old Timers Fete FETE
Stock up on doilies and tea towels at this ode to granny arts, held on the second Saturday in August at the Old Timers Village.

Alice Desert Festival ARTS
(www.alicedesertfestival.com.au) A cracker of a festival, including a circus program, music, film, comedy and the highly anticipated Desert Mob art exhibition. It's held every September.

Henley-on-Todd Regatta REGATTA
(www.henleyontodd.com.au) These boat races in September on the dry bed of the Todd River are a typically Australian light-hearted denial of reality. The boats are bottomless; the crews' legs stick through and they run down the course.

🛌 Sleeping

If you are travelling in peak season (June to September) make sure you book ahead, but if you're trying your luck, check the internet for last-minute rates, which often bring top-end places into midrange reach.

Alice Lodge Backpackers HOSTEL $
(Map p872; ☑ 08-8953 1975, 1800 351 925; www. alicelodge.com.au; 4 Mueller St; dm $22-26, d/tr $65/80; ❄ @ 🛜 ⊠) Located in a lovely residential area across the Todd River, an easy 10-minute walk from town, this is a small, highly recommended, low-key hostel. The friendly staff are as accommodating as the variety of room options which include mixed and female, three-, four- and six-bed dorms, as well as comfortable doubles and twins built around a central pool.

Pioneer YHA Hostel HOSTEL $
(Map p878; ☑ 08-8952 8855; www.yha.com.au; cnr Leichhardt Tce & Parsons St; dm $24-31, tw & d $75; ❄ @ ⊠) This YHA is housed in the old Pioneer outdoor cinema and guests can still enjoy nightly screenings of movies under the stars. Location is the biggest bonus here but it's also friendly and well run. The comfortable doubles share bathrooms. There's a good-sized kitchen and a pleasant outdoor area around a small pool. Discounted weekly rates are available.

Alice in the Territory RESORT $
(Map p872; ☑ 08-8952 6100; www.alicent.com. au; 46 Stephens Rd; dm $22.50, s or d $89-99; ❄ @ 🛜 ⊠) This sprawling resort is the best bargain stay in town. The rooms, doubles or four-bed dorms, have tiny bathrooms, but otherwise are bright, spotless and comfortable and offer two free movie channels. The management is enthusiastic and eager to please, there's a great bar and multicuisine restaurant and the big pool sits at the foot of the Ranges.

Alice's Secret Traveller's Inn HOSTEL $
(Map p872; ☑ 08-8952 8686, 1800 783 633; www. asecret.com.au; 6 Khalick St; dm $23-26, s/d/tr $60/65/90; ❄ @ ⊠) Across the Todd River from town, this is a 'non-party' hostel where you can relax around the pool, puff on a didge, or lie in a hammock in the garden. Rooms in the dongas are a bit of a squeeze, and those in the house are simple, comfortable and clean.

Toddy's Backpackers HOSTEL $
(Map p872; ☑ 1800 027 027; www.toddys.com.au; 41 Gap Rd; dm $22-26, d $78; ❄ @ ⊠) Toddy's is a rambling place with a huge variety of rooms from dorms and budget doubles to a motel section. Toddy's is popular with groups and there's a party atmosphere, spurred on by the $8 meals and cheap jugs of beer at the outdoor bar every evening. Although there are plenty of beds, the motel-style rooms can be hard to get, so book ahead. Tariff includes a light breakfast.

Annie's Place HOSTEL $
(Map p872; ☑ 08-8952 1545, 1800 359 089; www. anniesplace.com.au; 4 Traeger Ave; dm $20, d & tw $55-75; ❄ @ ⊠) With its leafy beer garden, popular with travellers and locals, and great poolside area, Annie's is a lively place to hang out any night of the week. This is only a problem if you actually enjoy sleeping. The converted motel rooms (all with bathrooms and some with a fridge) are right on top of the bar and the new management should be on top of the old cleanliness issues.

Heavitree Gap
Outback Lodge CARAVAN PARK $
(☑ 08-8950 4444, 1800 896 119; www.aurorar esorts.com.au; Palm Circuit; unpowered/powered sites $24/30, dm $26, d $130-180; ❄ @ 🛜 ⊠) At the foot of the Ranges and dotted with eucalypts and bounding rock wallabies, Heavitree makes a shady place to pitch or park. Alternatively, there are rooms: four-bed dorms, lodge and very basic kitchenette rooms that sleep six. The lodge offers a free shuttle into the town centre, which is about 4km away. The neighbouring tavern has live country music most nights of the week.

MacDonnell Range
Holiday Park CARAVAN PARK $
(☑ 08-8952 6111, 1800 808 373; www.macrange. com.au; Palm Pl; unpowered/powered sites $39/45, cabins d $84-256; ❄ @ ⊠) Probably Alice's biggest and best kept secret, this park has grassy sites, spotless amenities and a variety of accommodation from simple cabins with shared bathroom to self-contained two-bedroom villas. Not the cheapest option, but you get what you pay for with a roster of daily activities from stargazing to pancake Sundays. Kids can cavort in the adventure playground, BMX track and basketball court, while adults can kick back around the pool.

White Gum Motel MOTEL $$
(Map p872; ☑ 08-8952 5144, 1800 624 110; www.whitegum.com.au; 17 Gap Rd; s/d/tr/q $100/115/130/145; ❄ 🛜 ⊠) This impeccable old-fashioned motel is located about 10 to

Central Alice Springs

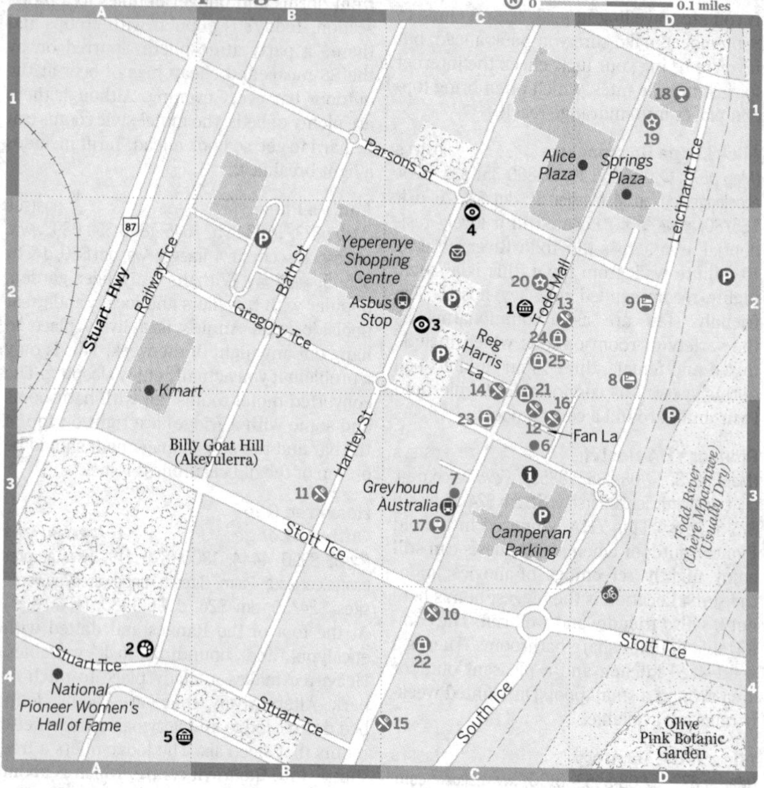

Central Alice Springs

Sights
1 Adelaide House C2
2 Alice Springs Reptile Centre A4
3 Old Hartley Street School C2
4 Residency C2
5 Royal Flying Doctor Service Base A4

Activities, Courses & Tours
6 Alice Wanderer C3
7 Emu Run Tours C3

Sleeping
8 Aurora Alice Springs D2
9 Pioneer YHA Hostel D2

Eating
10 Montes C4
11 Overlanders Steakhouse B3
12 Page 27 Cafe C3
13 Red Ochre Grill C2
14 Soma C2
15 Tea Shrine C4
16 Thai Room C3

Drinking & Nightlife
17 Bojangles C3
18 Todd Tavern D1

Entertainment
19 Alice Springs Cinema D1
20 Sounds of Starlight Theatre C2

Shopping
21 Aboriginal Art World C2
22 Central Australian Aboriginal Media Association C4
23 Mbantua Gallery C3
24 Papunya Tula Artists C2
25 Todd Mall Market C2

15 minutes' walk from the mall, and perfect if you want a reasonably priced room with your own full kitchen. The spacious rooms are self-contained, clean as a whistle, and ideal for families.

Alice on Todd APARTMENTS $$
(Map p872; ☎08-8953 8033; www.aliceontodd.com; cnr Strehlow St & South Tce; studio $128, 1-/2-bedroom apt $156/195, deluxe 1-/2-bedroom apt $170/210;) This attractive and secure apartment complex on the banks of the Todd River offers one- and two- bedroom self-contained units with kitchen and lounge. The balconied units sleep up to six so they're a great option for families. The deluxe apartments are a step up in decor and comfort. The landscaped grounds enclose a BBQ area, playground and a games room.

Chifley Alice Springs HOTEL $$
(Map p872; ☎08-8951 4545; www.chifleyhotels.com.au; 34 Stott Tce; standard/superior/deluxe d $140/190/250;) With a circle of double-storey buildings arranged around a swath of lawns and gum trees, the Chifley has a relaxed country-club vibe. Avoid the standard rooms and go for the recently refurbished superior and deluxe accommodation overlooking the Todd River. There's an attractive pool area with a swim-up bar, plus a seafood restaurant.

All Seasons Oasis HOTEL $$
(Map p872; ☎08-8952 1444; www.allseasons.com.au; 10 Gap Rd; d from $140;) With two swimming pools, the central one shaded by sails and surrounded with palm-shaded lawn, All Seasons convincingly recreates the oasis experience. The rooms are conventional and comfortable enough to keep it busy with tour groups. There's a restaurant, a bar with a couple of pool tables and a happy hour that brings in the locals. The best rates are available from the website.

Desert Palms Resort HOTEL $$
(Map p872; ☎1800 678 037, 08-8952 5977; www.desertpalms.com.au; 74 Barrett Dr; villas $140;) This hotel has a relaxed island vibe with its shady palms, cascading bougainvillea and Indonesian-style villas. The rooms – which have cathedral ceilings, kitchenette, tiny bathroom, TV and private balcony are rather dated, though the island swimming pool is a big hit with kids.

Alice Station Bed & Breakfast B&B $$
(☎08-8953 6600; www.alicestation.com; 25 The Fairway; s/d/ste from $180/195/260;) The host of this lovely B&B, which backs on to the bush, really does have kangaroos in her backyard. Made out of old *Ghan* railway sleepers, the whimsically designed home has a relaxed atmosphere with a communal lounge and stylishly decorated rooms with local Aboriginal art on the walls. Continental breakfasts get the thumbs up, as do the homemade cakes and eight different types of tea.

Crowne Plaza Alice Springs HOTEL $$
(Map p872; ☎08-8950 8000, 1300 666 545; www.crowneplaza.com.au; Barrett Dr; d from $150, ste $188-328;) With its spacious resort-style facilities, this is widely considered Alice's top hotel. Choose from the garden-view rooms or the better mountain range-view rooms – they're decked out with floor-to-ceiling windows, cane furniture and pastel colours. There's a lovely pool and spa, well-equipped gym and sauna, tennis courts and a house peacock. Alice's best restaurant, Hanumans (p880), is in the lobby.

Aurora Alice Springs HOTEL $$$
(Map p878; ☎08-8950 6666, 1800 089 644; www.auroraresorts.com.au; 11 Leichhardt Tce; standard/deluxe/executive d $210/230/299;) Right in the town centre – the 'back' door opens out onto Todd Mall, the front door looks over the Todd River – this modern hotel has a relaxed atmosphere and a great restaurant, Red Ochre Grill (p880). Standard rooms are comfortable and well appointed with fridge, phone and free in-house movies.

Bond Springs Outback Retreat B&B $$$
(☎08-8952 9888; www.outbackretreat.com.au; cottage d $230;) Experience a taste of outback station life at this retreat, about 25km from town. The private self-contained cottage is a refurbished stockman's quarters. A full breakfast is included but the rest is self-catering. Have a game of tennis or mooch around the enormous property including the original station school, which operated through the School of the Air (p873).

Eating

Kwerralye Cafe CAFE $
(Map p872; 6 South Tce; mains $6-12; 7.30am-3pm Mon-Fri) This excellent cafe is part of a program training young indigenous Territorians in all aspects of hospitality. There are

excellent light breakfasts, homemade pies, gourmet salads and daily specials, plus espresso coffee.

Bean Tree Cafe CAFE $
(Map p872; Tuncks Rd, Olive Pink Botanic Garden; mains $9-12; ⏲8am-3pm) Breakfast with the birds at this superb outdoor cafe tucked away in the Olive Pink Botanic Garden. Service can be slow, but it's a relaxing place to sit and the wholesome home-style dishes such as the kangaroo burger and apple crumble are well worth the wait.

Page 27 Cafe CAFE $
(Map p878; Fan Lane; mains $9-16; ⏲7.30am-3pm Tue-Fri, 8am-3pm Sat & Sun; ✎) Alice's locals duck down this arcade for great coffee or fresh juice and wholesome home-style breakfasts (eggs any style, pancakes), pita wraps, pies and salads. Excellent vegetarian menu.

Water Tank Cafe CAFE $
(Map p872; Hele Cres; mains $8-16; ⏲10am-3pm Mon-Fri, 9am-3pm Sat; wi-fi) Tucked away in the Bloomin' Deserts nursery this friendly cafe serves up fresh salads, burgers and homemade cake. Locals sprawl out on the couches and beanbags, sipping potent coffee and making use of the free wi-fi.

Tea Shrine VEGAN $
(Map p878; 113 Todd St; mains $8-15; ⏲9am-4pm Mon-Sat; ✎) Vegetarians may be forgiven for feeling a bit left out in meat-heavy Alice Springs, but not at the Tea Shrine, a vegan Asian restaurant and teahouse. Popular with hippies and health workers, this peaceful cafe has daily specials and a range of yum cha dishes.

★ **Hanuman Restaurant** THAI $$
(Map p872; ☎08-8953 7188; Barrett Dr, Crowne Plaza Alice Springs; mains $18-36; ⏲12.30-2.30pm Mon-Fri, from 6.30pm daily; ✎) You won't believe you're in the outback when you try the incredible Thai- and Indian-influenced cuisine at this stylish restaurant. The delicate Thai entrees are a real triumph as are the seafood dishes, particularly the Hanuman prawns. Although the menu is ostensibly Thai, there are enough Indian dishes to satisfy a curry craving. There are also several vegetarian offerings and a good wine list.

Tinh & Lan Alice Vietnamese Restaurant VIETNAMESE $$
(☎08-8952 8396; 1900 Heffernan Rd; mains $16-30; ⏲11am-2pm & 5-10pm Tue-Sun) This atmospheric Vietnamese restaurant is set in a market garden illuminated with lanterns. All the favourites – rice paper rolls, pho, salt and pepper squid – are deliciously prepared and the ingredients, growing all around you, couldn't be fresher. Follow the signs off Colonel Rose Dr; it's about 14km south of town.

Casa Nostra ITALIAN $$
(Map p872; ☎08-8952 6749; cnr Undoolya Rd & Sturt Tce; mains $14-28; ⏲6-10pm Mon-Sat) Step across the Todd River and into 1970s Italy at this old-school pizza and pasta joint. Madly popular on the weekends (bookings are recommended), it is wonderfully cosy with red and white checked tablecloths and plastic grape vines hanging from the ceiling. Order the famously delectable vanilla slice early as they run out the door. Note that it's BYO wine.

Montes MODERN AUSTRALIAN $$
(Map p878; cnr Stott Tce & Todd St; Mains $12-17; ⏲11am-late) A travelling circus meets outback homestead with a leafy beer garden (and range of beers) or intimate booth seating. Patio heaters keep patrons warm on a cool desert night. It's family friendly with a play area, and the food ranges from gourmet burgers, pizzas and tapas to curries and seafood.

Thai Room THAI $$
(Map p878; Fan Lane; mains $12-20; ⏲11am-2pm Mon-Fri, 6-10pm Mon-Sat) Head to this arcade restaurant for perky Thai dishes and quicker than average service. The modest menu mixes its signature spices with a variety of veggie, meat and seafood dishes. The lunch specials are a bargain and it's BYO.

Soma CAFE $
(Map p878; 64 Todd Mall; mains $12-17; ⏲8am-3pm; ✎) There's excellent people-watching and even better eating to be had at this Todd Mall cafe which offers sophisticated dishes and great coffee. Breakfast is on all day and lunch ranges from a camel panini to a delicious vegan scrambled tofu. There is a focus on organic ingredients and there are a number of gluten-free options.

Red Ochre Grill MODERN AUSTRALIAN $$
(Map p878; Todd Mall; mains $14-32; ⏲6.30am-9.30pm) Offering innovative fusion dishes with a focus on outback cuisine, the menu usually features traditional meats plus locally bred proteins, such as kangaroo and emu, matched with native herbs: lemon myrtle,

pepper berries and bush tomatoes. The all-day brunch in the courtyard turns out more predictable dishes including excellent eggs benedict.

Overlanders Steakhouse STEAKHOUSE $$$
(Map p878; ☎08-8952 2159; 72 Hartley St; mains $21-40; ⏰6pm-late) The place for steaks, big succulent cuts of beef (and crocodile, camel, kangaroo or emu). Amid the cattle station decor (saddles, branding irons and the like) you can take the challenge of the Drover's Blowout, four courses including a platter of the aforementioned Aussie bush meats.

Afghan Traders HEALTH FOOD $
(Map p872; cnr Smith St & Helle Cres; ⏰9am-6pm Mon-Fri, 9am-3pm Sat) Excellent range of organic and wholefoods.

Drinking

Annie's Place BAR
(Map p872; 4 Traeger Ave; ⏰5pm-late) Bustling backpackers bar. Decent music (sometimes live), leafy beer garden, cheap jugs and poolside drinking.

Bojangles BAR
(Map p878; 80 Todd St; ⏰11.30am-late) Behind the swinging saloon doors is a 'Wild West meets Aussie outback' theme complete with cowhide seats, stockman regalia and a live 3m-long carpet python behind the bar. Bo's is beloved of backpacker groups and station ringers and is jumping most nights of the week.

Montes BAR
(cnr Stott Tce & Todd St) Most variety of beers on tap in Alice. Leafy street-front beer garden and plenty of cosy niches. Also good food (p880).

Todd Tavern PUB
(Map p878; www.toddtavern.com.au; 1 Todd Mall; ⏰10am-midnight) This enduring, classically Aussie pub has a lively bar, pokies, decent pub grub and occasional live music on weekends.

Entertainment

The gig guide in the entertainment section of the *Centralian Advocate* (published every Tuesday and Friday) lists what's on in and around town.

Araluen Arts Centre ARTS CENTRE
(Map p872; ☎08-8951 1122; www.araluen.nt.gov.au; Larapinta Dr) The cultural heart of Alice, the 500-seat Araluen Theatre hosts a diverse range of performers, from dance troupes to comedians, while the Art House Cinema screens films every Sunday evening at 7pm (adult/child $15/12). The website has an events calendar.

Sounds of Starlight Theatre LIVE MUSIC
(Map p878; ☎08-8953 0826; www.soundsofstarlight.com; 40 Todd Mall; adult/family $30/90; ⏰8pm Tue, Fri & Sat) This atmospheric 1½-hour musical performance evoking the spirit of the outback with didgeridoo, drums and keyboards, and wonderful photography and lighting is an Alice institution. Musician Andrew Langford also runs free didge lessons (10.30am and 2.30pm Monday to Friday).

Alice Springs Cinema CINEMA
(Map p878; ☎08-8952 4999; Todd Mall; adult/child $17/13, Tue all tickets $12) The place to go for latest-release Hollywood blockbusters.

Shopping

Alice is the centre for Aboriginal arts from all over central Australia. The places owned and run by community art centres ensure that a better slice of the proceeds goes to the artist and artist's community. Look for the black over red Indigenous Art Code (www.indigenousartcode.org) displayed by dealers dedicated to fair and transparent dealings with artists.

Aboriginal Art World INDIGENOUS ART
(Map p878; ☎08-8952 7788; www.aboriginalartworld.com.au; 89 Todd Mall) Specialises in art from about 70 artists living in South Australia and NT central deserts, particularly Pitjantjatjara lands. Most art pieces are sold with a DVD showing the artwork being created.

Central Australian Aboriginal Media Association MUSIC STORE
(CAAMA; Map p878; ☎08-8951 9711; www.caama.com.au; 101 Todd St; ⏰9am-5pm Mon-Fri) Here at the CAAMA studio, which has its own radio network (8KIN FM), you will find most of the CDs recorded by central Australia's Aboriginal musicians.

Desert Dwellers OUTDOOR GEAR
(Map p872; ☎08-8953 2240; www.desertdwellers.com.au; 38 Elder St; ⏰9am-5pm Mon-Fri, 9am-2pm Sat) For camping and hiking gear, head to this shop, which has just about everything you need to equip yourself for an outback jaunt – maps, swags, tents, portable fridges, stoves and more.

Mbantua Gallery INDIGENOUS ART
(Map p878; ☎08-8952 5571; www.mbantua.com.au; 64 Todd Mall; ⏲9am-6pm Mon-Fri, 9.30am-3pm Sat) This privately owned gallery includes a cafe and extensive exhibits of works from the renowned Utopia region, as well as watercolour landscapes from the Namatjira school. The upstairs Educational & Permanent Collection (admission free) is a superb cultural exhibition space with panels explaining Aboriginal mythology and customs.

Papunya Tula Artists INDIGENOUS ART
(Map p878; ☎08-8952 4731; www.papunyatula.com.au; 63 Todd Mall; ⏲9am-5pm Mon-Fri, 10am-2pm Sat) The Western Desert art movement began at Papunya Tula in 1971, and today this Aboriginal-owned gallery displays some of this most sought-after art. Papunya Tula works with around 120 artists, most painting at Kintore in the far west.

Tjanpi Desert Weavers INDIGENOUS ART
(Map p872; ☎08-8958 2377; www.tjanpi.com.au; 3 Wilkinson St; ⏲10am-4pm Mon-Fri) This small enterprise employs and supports Central Desert weavers from 18 remote communities. Their store is well worth a visit to see the magnificent woven baskets and quirky sculptures created from locally collected grasses.

Todd Mall Market MARKET
(Map p878; ⏲9am-1pm 2nd Sun May-Dec) Buskers, craft stalls, sizzling woks, smoky satay stands, Aboriginal art, jewellery and knick-knacks make for a relaxed stroll.

Information

Dangers & Annoyances

Avoid walking alone at night anywhere in town but particularly around Gap Rd. Catch a taxi back to your accommodation if you're out late.

Emergency

Ambulance (☎000)
Police (☎08-8951 8888, 000; Parsons St)

Internet Access

JPG Computers (☎08-8952 2040; Bath St, Coles Complex; per hr $6; ⏲9am-5.30pm Mon-Fri, 10am-2pm Sat)
Water Tank Café (Hele Cres) Free wi-fi at the Bloomin' Deserts nursery.

Medical Services

Alice Springs Hospital (☎08-8951 7777; Gap Rd)
Alice Springs Pharmacy (☎08-8952 1554; 36 Hartley St, shop 19, Yeperenye Shopping Centre; ⏲8.30am-7.30pm)

Money

Major banks with ATMs, such as ANZ, Commonwealth, National Australia and Westpac, are located in and around Todd Mall in the centre.

Post

Main Post Office (☎13 13 18; 31-33 Hartley St; ⏲8.15am-5pm Mon-Fri) All the usual services are available here.

Tourist Information

Central Land Council (☎08-8951 6211; www.clc.org.au; PO Box 3321, 31-33 Stuart Hwy, NT; ⏲8.30am-noon & 2-4pm) For Aboriginal land permits and transit permits.
Tourism Central Australia Visitor Information Centre (☎08-8952 5199, 1800 645 199; www.centralaustraliantourism.com; 60 Gregory Tce; ⏲8.30am-5pm Mon-Fri, 9.30am-4pm Sat & Sun) This helpful centre can load you up with stacks of brochures and the free visitors guide. Weather forecasts and road conditions are posted on the wall, and Mereenie Tour Passes ($3.50) and fossicking permits (free) are issued. National parks information is also available. Tourism Central Australia desks are also found at the airport and train station. Ask about their unlimited kilometre deals if you are thinking of renting a car.

Websites

Alice Online (www.aliceonline.com.au) Wonderful stories, new and old, about central Australia.

Getting There & Away

AIR

Alice Springs is well connected, with **Qantas** (☎08-8950 5211, 13 13 13; www.qantas.com.au) operating daily flights to/from capital cities. Other airlines come and go but were not flying to Alice Springs at the time of research. Airline representatives are based at Alice Springs airport. One-way fares from Alice include Yulara (from $168), Adelaide (from $210), Darwin (from $300), Melbourne (from $280), Sydney (from $280), Brisbane (from $310) and Perth (from $350). Check websites for latest timetables and fare offers.

BUS

Greyhound Australia (☎1300 473 946; www.greyhound.com.au; 113 Todd St, shop 3; ⏲office 8.30-11.30am & 1.30-4pm Mon-Fri) has regular services from Alice Springs (check website for timetables and discounted fares). Buses arrive at, and depart from, the Greyhound office on Todd St.

DESTINATION	ONE-WAY FARE ($)	TIME(HR)
Adelaide	331	20
Coober Pedy	192	8
Darwin	391	22
Katherine	315	16½
Tennant Creek	195	6½

Emu Run (p876) runs the cheapest daily connections between Alice Springs and Yulara (adult/child $215/108) and between Kings Canyon and Alice Springs ($189/95). **Gray Line** (☎1300 858 687; www.grayline.com; Capricornia Centre 9 Gregory Tce) also runs between Alice Springs and Yulara (adult/child $226/113), and offers a one-way option ($156/113).

Backpacker buses roam to and from Alice providing a party atmosphere and a chance to see some of the sights on the way. **Groovy Grape Getaways Australia** (☎1800 661 177; www.groovygrape.com.au) plies the route from Alice to Adelaide on a seven-day, backpacker camping jaunt for $945.

CAR & MOTORCYCLE

Alice Springs is a long way from everywhere. It's 1180km to Mt Isa in Queensland, 1490km to Darwin and 441km (4½ hours) to Yulara (for Uluru). Although the roads to the north and south are sealed and in good condition, these are outback roads, and it's wise to have your vehicle well prepared, particularly as you won't get a mobile phone signal outside Alice or Yulara. Carry plenty of drinking water and emergency food at all times.

All the major companies have offices in Alice Springs, and many have counters at the airport. Prices drop by about 20% between November and April but rentals don't come cheap, as most firms offer only 100km free per day, which won't get you far. Talk to the people at the **visitor centre** (☎08-8952 5199, 1800 645 199) about its unlimited kilometres deal before you book. A conventional (2WD) vehicle will get you to most sights in the MacDonnell Ranges and out to Uluru and Kings Canyon via sealed roads. If you want to go further afield, say to Chambers Pillar, Finke Gorge or even the Mereenie Loop Rd, a 4WD is essential.

Alice Camp 'n' Drive (☎08-8952 0098; www.alicecampndrive.com; 76 Hartley St) Provides vehicles fully equipped for camping with swags (or tents), sleeping bags, cooking gear, chairs etc. Rates include unlimited kilometres and vehicles can be dropped off at your accommodation.

Avis (☎08-8953 5533; www.avis.com.au; Crowne Plaza Hotel) Also has an airport counter.

Britz (☎08-8952 8814; www.britz.com.au; cnr Stuart Hwy & Power St) Campervans and cars; also at the airport. This is also the base for **Maui** (www.maui.com.au) and **Mighty** (www.mightycampers.com.au) campervans.

Budget (☎08-8952 8899, 13 27 27; www.budget.com.au; 79 Todd Mall & airport)

Central Car Rentals (☎08-8952 0098; www.centralcarrentals.com.au; 76 Hartley St) A local operator (associated with Alice Camp 'n' Drive) with 2WD and 4WD vehicles which can be equipped with camping gear. Unlimited kilometre rates are available.

Europcar (☎13 13 90; www.europcar.com.au; airport)

Hertz (☎08-8952 2644; www.hertz.com; 34 Stott Tce & airport)

Territory Thrifty Car Rental (☎08-8952 9999; www.rentacar.com.au; cnr Stott Tce & Hartley St)

TRAIN

A classic way to enter or leave the Territory is by the *Ghan* which can be booked through **Great Southern Rail** (☎13 21 47; www.greatsouthernrail.com.au) or **Travelworld** (☎08-8953 0488; 40 Todd Mall). Discounted fares are sometimes offered, especially in the low season (February to June). Bookings are essential.

The train station is at the end of George Cres off Larapinta Dr.

Getting Around

Alice Springs is compact enough to get to most parts of town on foot, and you can reach quite a few of the closer attractions by bicycle.

TO/FROM THE AIRPORT

Alice Springs airport is 15km south of the town. It's about $40 by taxi. The **airport shuttle** (☎08-8952 2111; Gregory Tce; 1/2 persons one-way $18.50/30 plus $10 each additional person) meets all flights and drops off passengers at city accommodation. Book a day in advance for pick-up from accommodation.

BUS

The public bus service, **Asbus** (☎08-8952 5611), departs from outside the Yeperenye Shopping Centre. Buses run about every 1½ hours from 7am to 6pm Monday to Friday, and from 9am to 12.45pm on Saturday. The adult/child fare for all routes is $2/0.50. There are three routes of interest to travellers: 400/401 has a detour to the cultural precinct, 100/101 passes the School of the Air, and 300/301 passes many southern hotels and caravan parks along Gap Rd and Palm Circuit. The visitor information centre has timetables.

The **Alice Explorer** (☎08-8952 2111, 1800 722 111; www.alicewanderer.com.au; adult/child $44/35; ⏲9am-4pm) is a hop-on, hop-off sightseeing bus that covers 11 major sites, including the Telegraph Station, School of the Air, Old Ghan Rail Museum and Araluen. The ticket is valid for two days and the circuit runs every 70 minutes from opposite the visitor information centre on Gregory Tce. You can arrange to be picked up from your accommodation.

TAXI

Taxis congregate near the visitor information centre. To book one, call 13 10 08 or 08-8952 1877.

MACDONNELL RANGES

The beautiful, weather-beaten MacDonnell Ranges, stretching 400km across the desert, are a hidden world of spectacular gorges, rare wildlife and poignant Aboriginal heritage all within a day's journey from Alice. There's no public transport to either the East or West MacDonnell Ranges; there are plenty of tours from Alice.

East MacDonnell Ranges

Although overshadowed by the more popular West Macs, the East MacDonnell Ranges are no less picturesque and, with fewer visitors, can be a more enjoyable outback experience. The sealed Ross Hwy runs 100km along the Ranges, which are intersected by a series of scenic gaps and gorges. The gold-mining ghost town of Arltunga is 33km off the Ross Hwy along an unsealed road that is usually OK for 2WD vehicles, however access to John Hayes Rockhole (in Trephina Gorge Nature Park), N'Dhala Gorge and Ruby Gap is by 4WD only.

Emily & Jessie Gaps Nature Park

Both of these gaps are associated with the Eastern Arrernte Caterpillar Dreaming trail. **Emily Gap**, 16km out of town, has stylised rock paintings and a fairly deep waterhole in the narrow gorge. Known to the Arrernte as Anthwerrke, this is one of the most important Aboriginal sites in the Alice Springs area; it was from here that the caterpillar ancestral beings of Mparntwe originated before crawling across the landscape to create the topographical features that exist today. The gap is a sacred site with some well-preserved paintings on the eastern wall. **Jessie Gap**, 8km further on, is equally scenic and usually much quieter. Both sites have toilets, but camping is not permitted. And both attract flocks of birds looking for a drink. An 8km unmarked bushwalk leads around the ridge between the two gaps.

Corroboree Rock Conservation Reserve

Past Jessie Gap you drive over eroded flats before entering a valley between red ridges. Corroboree Rock, 51km from Alice Springs, is one of many strangely shaped dolomite outcrops scattered over the valley floor. Despite the name, it's doubtful the rock was ever used as a corroboree area, but it is associated with the Perentie Dreaming trail. The perentie lizard grows in excess of 2.5m, and takes refuge within the area's rock falls. There's a short walking track (15 minutes) around the rock.

Trephina Gorge Nature Park

If you only have time for a couple of stops in the East MacDonnell Ranges, make Trephina Gorge Nature Park (75km from Alice) one of them. The play between the pale sandy river beds, the red and purple gorge walls, the white tree trunks, the eucalyptus-green foliage and the blue sky is spectacular. You'll also find deep swimming holes and abundant wildlife. The **Trephina Gorge Walk** (45 minutes, 2km) loops around the gorge's rim. The **Ridgetop Walk** (five hours, 10km one way) traverses the ridges from the gorge to John Hayes Rockhole; the 8km return along the road takes about two hours.

The delightful **John Hayes Rockhole**, 9km from the Trephina Gorge turn-off (the last 4km is 4WD only) has three basic **camping sites** (adult/child $3.30/1.65). From here, the gorgeous **Chain of Ponds Walk** (1½ hours, 4km loop) leads past rock pools and up to a lookout above the gorge.

There's a **rangers station** (☎08-8956 9765) and **camping grounds** (adult/child $3.30/1.65) with BBQs, water and toilets at Trephina Gorge and the Bluff.

N'Dhala Gorge Nature Park

Shortly before the Ross River Resort, a strictly 4WD-only track leads 11km south to **N'Dhala Gorge**. More than 5900 ancient Aboriginal rock carvings and some rare endemic plants decorate a deep, narrow gorge, although the art isn't easy to spot. There's a small, exposed **camping ground** (adult/child $3.30/1.65) without reliable water.

Ross River

About 9km past the Arltunga turn-off you come to the secluded **Ross River Resort** (☎08-8956 9711; www.rossriverresort.com.au; unpowered & powered sites $36, bunkhouse $25, d/f cabin $120/150; ❄ ≋), built around a historic stone homestead with basic timber cabins encircling a swimming pool. The stunning camp site is grassy and studded with gums. There's a store with fuel, and it's worth grabbing lunch (mains $15 to $20) or a beer in the Stockman's Bar.

Arltunga Historical Reserve

Situated at the eastern end of the MacDonnell Ranges, 110km east of Alice Springs, is the old gold-mining ghost town of Arltunga (40km on unsealed road from the Ross Hwy). Its history, from the discovery of alluvial (surface) gold in 1887 until mining activity petered out in 1912, is fascinating. Old buildings, a couple of cemeteries and the many deserted **mine sites** in this parched landscape give visitors an idea of what life was like for the miners. There are walking tracks and old mines (with bats!) to explore, so bring a torch.

The unstaffed visitor information centre has old photographs of the gold-extracting process, plus a slide show on the area's history, and drinking water and toilets. There's no camping in the reserve itself.

From Arltunga it's possible to loop back to Alice along the Arltunga Tourist Dr, which pops out at the Stuart Hwy about 50km north of town. The road runs past the gracious **Old Ambalindum Homestead** (☎08-8956 9993; www.oldambalindumhomestead.com.au; unpowered/powered sites $25/30, dm $75; ❄ ≋) which offers self-catered accommodation for up to 12 people in the homestead and in the bunkhouse on a working cattle station. Bookings are essential and you need to bring your own food.

Ruby Gap Nature Park

This remote park rewards visitors with wild and beautiful scenery. The sandy bed of the Hale River sparkles with thousands of tiny garnets. The garnets caused a 'ruby rush' here in the 19th century and some miners did well out of it until it was discovered that the 'rubies' were, in fact, virtually worthless. It's an evocative place and is well worth the considerable effort required to reach it – by high-clearance 4WD. The waterholes at **Glen Annie Gorge** are usually deep enough for a cooling dip.

Camping (adult/child $3.30/1.65) is permitted anywhere along the river; make sure to BYO drinking water and a camp cooker. Allow two hours each way for the 44km trip from Arltunga.

West MacDonnell Ranges

With their stunning beauty and rich diversity of plants and animals, the West MacDonnell Ranges are not to be missed. Their easy access by conventional vehicle makes them especially popular with day-trippers. Heading west from Alice, Namatjira Dr turns northwest off Larapinta Dr 6km beyond Standley Chasm and is sealed all the way to Tylers Pass.

Most sites in the West MacDonnell Ranges lie within the West MacDonnell National Park, except for Standley Chasm, which is privately owned. There are ranger stations at Simpsons Gap and Ormiston Gorge.

Larapinta Trail

The 230km Larapinta Trail extends along the backbone of the West MacDonnell Ranges and is one of Australia's great long-distance walks. The track is split into 12 stages of varying difficulty, stretching from the Telegraph Station in Alice Springs to the craggy 1380m summit of Mt Sonder. Each section takes one to two days to navigate and passes many of the attractions in the West MacDonnells:

Section 1 Alice Springs Telegraph Station to Simpsons Gap (23.8km)

Section 2 Simpsons Gap to Jay Creek (24.5km)

Section 3 Jay Creek to Standley Chasm (13.6km)

Section 4 Standley Chasm to Birthday Waterhole (17.7km)

Section 5 Birthday Waterhole to Hugh Gorge (16km)

Section 6 Hugh Gorge to Ellery Creek (31.2km)

Section 7 Ellery Creek to Serpentine Gorge (13.8km)

Section 8 Serpentine Gorge to Serpentine Chalet Dam (13.4km)

Section 9 Serpentine Chalet Dam to Ormiston Gorge (28.6km)

Section 10 Ormiston Gorge to Finke River (9.9km)

Section 11 Finke River to Redbank Gorge (25.2km)

Section 12 Redbank Gorge to Mt Sonder (15.8km return)

Trail notes and maps are available from **Parks & Wildlife** (www.nt.gov.au/nreta/parks/walks/larapinta/index.html). Walkers should register their names and itinerary at ☎1300 650 730. And don't forget to deregister.

There's no public transport out to this area, but transfers can be arranged through the **Alice Wanderer** (☎08-8952 2111, 1800 722 111; www.alicewanderer.com.au); see the website for the various costs. For guided walks, including transport from Alice Springs, go through Trek Larapinta (p876).

Simpsons Gap

Westbound from Alice Springs on Larapinta Dr you come to the **grave of John Flynn**, the founder of the Royal Flying Doctor Service, which is topped by a boulder donated by the Arrernte people (the original was a since-returned Devil's Marble). Opposite the car park is the start of the sealed **cycling track** to Simpsons Gap, a recommended three- to four-hour return ride.

By road, Simpsons Gap is 22km from Alice Springs and 8km off Larapinta Dr. It's a popular picnic spot and has some excellent short walks. Early morning and late afternoon are the best time to glimpse black-footed rock wallabies. The visitor information centre is 1km from the park entrance.

Standley Chasm (Angkerle)

About 50km west of Alice Springs is the spectacular **Standley Chasm** (☎08-8956 7440; adult/concession $10/8, family 2+2 $25, under 12 $5; ⏲8am-5pm, last Chasm entry 4.30pm) which is owned and run by the nearby community of Iwupataka. This narrow corridor slices neatly through the rocky range and in places the smooth walls rise to 80m. The rocky path into the gorge (15 minutes) follows a creek bed lined with ghost gums and cycads. You can continue to a second chasm (one hour return) or head up Larapinta Hill (45 minutes return) for a fine view. There's a cafe, picnic facilities and toilets near the car park.

Namatjira Drive

Not far beyond Standley Chasm you can choose the northwesterly Namatjira Dr (which loops down to connect with Larapinta Dr west of Hermannsburg) or continue along Larapinta Dr. Namatjira Dr takes you to a whole series of gorges and gaps in the range like **Ellery Creek Big Hole**, 91km from Alice Springs, and with a large permanent waterhole – a popular place for a swim on a hot day (the water is usually freezing). About 11km further, a rough gravel track leads to narrow **Serpentine Gorge**, which has a waterhole blocking the entrance and a lookout at the end of a short, steep track, where you can view ancient cycads.

The **Ochre Pits** line a dry creek bed 11km west of Serpentine and were a source of pigment for Aboriginal people. The various coloured ochres – mainly yellow, white and red-brown – are weathered limestone, with iron-oxide creating the colours.

The car park for the majestic **Ormiston Gorge** is 25km beyond the Ochre Pits. It's the most impressive chasm in the West MacDonnells. There's a waterhole shaded with ghost gums, and the gorge curls around to the enclosed **Ormiston Pound**. It is a haven for wildlife and you can expect to see some critters among the spinifex slopes and mulga woodland. There are **walking tracks**, including the **Ghost Gum Lookout** (20 minutes), which affords brilliant views down the gorge, and the excellent, circuitous **Pound Walk** (three hours, 7.5km). There's a **visitor centre** (☎08-8956 7799) and a kiosk which is open 11am to 4pm (closed Wednesday).

About 2km further is the turn-off to **Glen Helen Gorge**, where the Finke River cuts through the MacDonnells. Only 1km past Glen Helen is a good lookout over Mt Sonder; sunrise and sunset here are particularly impressive.

If you continue northwest for 25km you'll reach the turn-off (4WD only) to multi-hued, cathedral-like **Redbank Gorge**. This permanent waterhole runs for kilometres through the labyrinth gorge, and makes for an incredible swimming and scrambling adventure on a hot day. Namatjira Dr then heads south and is sealed as far as **Tylers Pass Lookout**, which provides a dramatic view of **Tnorala** (Grosse Bluff), the legacy of an earth-shattering comet impact.

Sleeping & Eating

There are basic **camping grounds** (adult/child $3.30/1.65) at Ellery Creek Big Hole, Redbank Gorge and 6km west of Serpentine Gorge at Serpentine Chalet (a 4WD or high-clearance 2WD vehicle is recommended to reach the chalet ruins). The ritzy **camping area** (adult/child $6.60/3.30) at Ormiston Gorge has showers, toilets, gas barbecues and picnic tables.

Glen Helen Resort HOTEL $
(08-8956 7489; www.glenhelen.com.au; Namatjira Dr; unpowered/powered sites $24/30, dm/r $30/160;) At the edge of the national park is the popular Glen Helen Resort which has an idyllic back verandah overlooking the spectacular gorge. This comfortable retreat contains a busy restaurant-pub (breakfast and lunch $8 to $20, dinner $30 to $35) that serves hearty meals and showcases live music on the weekend. There are also 4WD tours available and helicopter flights ranging from $55 (five minutes) to $425, with the $145 Ormiston Gorge flight representing the best value for money.

RED CENTRE WAY (MEREENIE LOOP)

The Red Centre Way is the 'back road' from Alice to the Rock. It incorporates an 'inner loop' comprising Namatjira (p886) and Larapinta Drive, plus the rugged Mereenie Loop Rd, the short cut to Kings Canyon. This dusty, heavily corrugated road is not to be taken lightly, and hire car companies won't permit their 2WD to be driven on it.

Larapinta Drive

Continuing south from Standley Chasm, Larapinta Dr crosses the intersection with Namatjira Dr and the Hugh River before reaching the turn-off to the Western Arrernte community of **Wallace Rockhole**, 18km off the main road and 109km from Alice Springs.

You'll be virtually guaranteed seclusion at the **Wallace Rockhole Tourist Park** (08-8956 7993; www.wallacerockholetours.com.au; unpowered/powered sites $20/24, cabins $130;), which has a camping area with good facilities. Tours must be booked in advance and can include a 1½-hour rock-art and bush medicine tour (adult/child $15/13) with billy tea and damper.

About 26km from the Wallace Rockhole turn-off, continuing along Larapinta Dr, you will pass the lonely **Namatjira Monument**, which is about 8km from Hermannsburg.

Hermannsburg

POP 625

The Aboriginal community of Hermannsburg (Ntaria), about 125km from Alice Springs, is famous as the one-time home of artist Albert Namatjira and the site of the Hermannsburg Mission.

The whitewashed walls of the **mission** (08-8956 7402; www.hermannsburg.com; adult/child $10/5; 9am-4pm Mar-Nov, 10am-4pm Dec-Feb) are shaded by majestic river gums and date palms. This fascinating monument to the Territory's early Lutheran missionaries includes a school building, a church and various outbuildings. The 'Manse' houses an art gallery and a history of the life and times of Albert Namatjira as well as work of 39 Hermannsburg artists.

The **Kata-Anga Tea Room** (meals $8-12; 9am-4pm), in the old missionary house, serves yummy apple strudel and Devonshire teas. Distinctive paintings and pottery by the locals is also on display here and is for sale.

West of Hermannsburg is **Namatjira's House**.

Finke Gorge National Park

With its primordial landscape, the Finke Gorge National Park, south of Hermannsburg, is one of central Australia's premier wilderness reserves. The top-billing attraction is **Palm Valley**, famous for its red cabbage palms, which exist nowhere else in the world. These relics from prehistoric times give the valley the feel of a picture-book oasis.

Tracks include the **Arankaia walk** (2km loop, one hour), which traverses the valley, returning via the sandstone plateau; the **Mpulungkinya track** (5km loop, two hours), heading down the gorge before joining the Arankaia walk; and the **Mpaara track** (5km loop, two hours), taking in the Finke River, Palm Bend and a rugged amphitheatre (a semicircle of sandstone formations sculpted by a now-extinct meander of

Palm Creek). There's also a popular **camping ground** (adult/child $6.60/3.30).

Access to the park follows the sandy bed of the Finke River and rocky tracks, so a high-clearance 4WD is essential. If you don't have one, several tour operators go to Palm Valley from Alice Springs. The turn-off to Palm Valley starts about 1km west of the Hermannsburg turn-off on Larapinta Dr.

If you are well-prepared there's a challenging route through the national park along the sandy bed of the Finke River. This is a remote and scenic drive to the Ernest Giles Rd, from where you can continue west to Kings Canyon (and Uluru) or east back to the Stuart Hwy. It pays to travel in a convoy (getting bogged is part of the adventure) and get a copy of the *Finke River 4WD Route* notes (www.nretas.nt.gov.au).

Mereenie Loop Road

From Hermannsburg you can continue west to the turn-off to Areyonga (no visitors) and then take the Mereenie Loop Rd to Kings Canyon. This is an alternative route from Alice to Kings Canyon. The NT Government is planning to seal the road but locals say they'll believe it when they see it. There are deep sandy patches and countless corrugations (call ☎1800 246 199 for latest road conditions) and it's best travelled in a high-clearance 4WD. Be aware that 2WD hire vehicles will not be covered by insurance on this road.

To travel along this route, which passes through Aboriginal land, you need a Mereenie Tour Pass ($3.50), which is valid for one day and includes a booklet with details about the local Aboriginal culture and a route map. The pass is issued on the spot (usually only on the day of travel) at the visitor information centre in Alice Springs, Glen Helen Resort, Kings Canyon Resort and Hermannsburg service station.

Kings Canyon & Watarrka National Park

The main attraction along this route is one of the most spectacular sights in central Australia – the yawning chasm of **Kings Canyon** in Watarrka National Park. The other ways to get here include the unsealed Ernest Giles Rd which heads west off the Stuart Highway 140km south of Alice Springs, and the sealed Luritja Rd which detours off the Lasseter Hwy on the way to Uluru. The latter is the longest route but easily the most popular and comfortable.

Whichever way you get here you will want to spend some time shaking off the road miles and taking in the scenery. Walkers are rewarded with awesome views on the **Kings Canyon Rim Walk** (6km loop, four hours), which many travellers rate as a highlight of their trip to the Centre. After a short but steep climb (the only 'difficult' part of the trail), the walk skirts the canyon's rim before descending down wooden stairs to the **Garden of Eden**: a lush pocket of ferns and prehistoric cycads around a tranquil pool. The next section of the trail winds through a swarm of giant beehive domes: weathered sandstone outcrops, which to the Luritja represent the men of the Kuniya Dreaming.

The **Kings Creek Walk** (2km return) is a short stroll along the rocky creek bed to a raised platform with views of the towering canyon rim.

About 10km east of the car park, the **Kathleen Springs Walk** (one hour, 2.6km return) is a pleasant wheelchair-accessible track leading to a waterhole at the head of a gorge.

The **Giles Track** (22km one way, overnight) is a marked track that meanders along the George Gill Range between Kathleen Springs and the canyon; before starting out register with the **Overnight Walker Registration Scheme** (☎1300 650 730).

Tours

Several tour companies depart from Alice and stop at Kings Canyon on the way to/from Uluru (see p876).

Kings Creek Helicopters HELICOPTER FLIGHT
(☎08-8956 7083; www.kingscreekstation.com.au; flights per person $60-445) Flies from Kings Creek Station, including a breathtaking 30-minute canyon flight for $275.

Professional Helicopter Services HELICOPTER FLIGHT
(PHS; ☎08-8956 7873; www.phs.com.au; flights per person $95-275) Picking up from Kings Canyon Resort, PHS buzzes the canyon for eight/15 minutes ($95/145).

Sleeping & Eating

Kings Creek Station CABINS $$
(☎08-8956 7474; www.kingscreekstation.com.au; Luritja Rd; unpowered/powered sites $17/19, safari

Kings Canyon

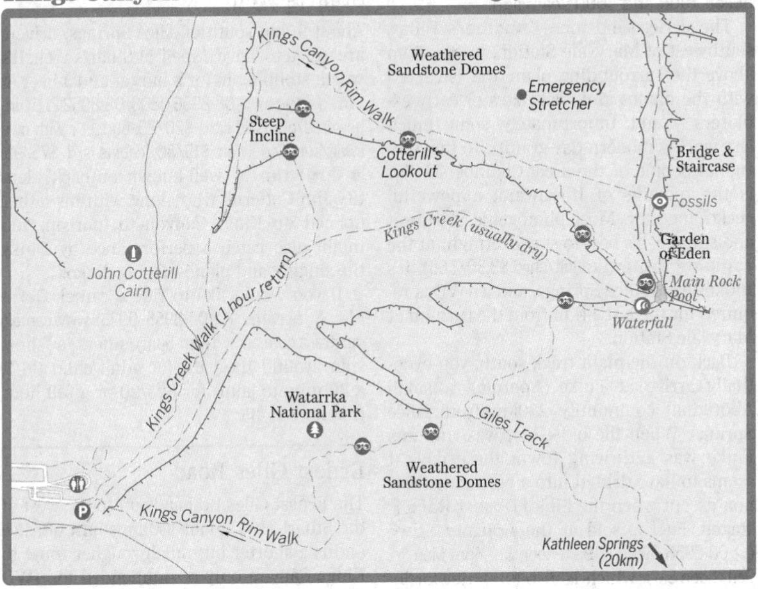

cabins s/d incl breakfast $103/165; @) Located 35km before the canyon, this family-run station offers a bush camping experience among the desert oaks. Cosy safari-style cabins (small canvas tents on solid floors) share amenities and a kitchen-BBQ area. You can tear around the desert on a quad bike (one-hour ride $93) or enjoy the more sedate thrills of a sunset camel ride (one-hour ride $60). Fuel, ice, beer, wine, BBQ packs and meals are available at the shop (open 7am to 7pm). Ask about **Conways' Kids** (www.conwayskids.org.au), a charitable trust set up by the owners to send local indigenous children to school in Adelaide.

Kings Canyon Resort RESORT **$$$**
(1300 863 248; www.kingscanyonresort.com.au; Luritja Rd; unpowered/powered sites $38/42, dm $35, budget d $139, standard/deluxe spa d $279/339; @) Only 10km from the canyon, this well-designed resort boasts a wide range of accommodation from a grassy camp area with its own pool and bar to deluxe rooms with an almost-outdoor spa. Eating and drinking options are as varied, with a cafe, a restaurant for buffet breakfasts and dinner, a bar with pizzas, an outback BBQ for big steaks and live entertainment. **Under the Desert Moon** ($160 per person; Apr-Oct) offers an exclusive six-course candlelit dinner around a campfire. There's a general store with fuel and an ATM at reception.

Kings Canyon Wilderness Lodge RESORT **$$$**
(1800 891 121; www.aptouring.com.au; Luritja Rd; tented cabins s/d $599/740;) In a secret pocket of Kings Creek Station is this luxury retreat with 10 stylish tents offering private en-suite facilities and decks with relaxing bush views. Run by APT, independent travellers may find themselves squeezed in among tour groups. Tariff includes breakfast and dinner.

SOUTH OF ALICE SPRINGS

Old South Road

The Old South Road, which runs close to the old *Ghan* railway line, is pretty rough and really requires a 4WD. It's only 39km from Alice Springs to Ewaninga, where prehistoric Aboriginal petroglyphs are carved into sandstone. The rock carvings found here and at N'Dhala Gorge are thought to have been made by Aboriginal people who lived here before those currently in the region, between 1000 and 5000 years ago.

The eerie, sandstone **Chambers Pillar**, southwest of Maryvale Station, towers 50m above the surrounding plain and is carved with the names and visit dates of early explorers – and, unfortunately, some much less worthy modern-day graffiti. To the Aboriginal people of the area, Chambers Pillar is the remains of Itirkawara, a powerful gecko ancestor. Most photogenic at sunset and sunrise, it's best to stay overnight at the **camping ground** (adult/child $3.30/1.65). It's 160km from Alice Springs, and a 4WD is required for the last 44km from the turn-off at Maryvale Station.

Back on the main track south, you eventually arrive at Finke (Aputula), a small Aboriginal community 230km from Alice Springs. When the old *Ghan* was running, Finke was a thriving town; these days it seems to have drifted into a permanent torpor, except when the **Finke Desert Race** is staged. Fuel is sold at the **Aputula Store** (☑08-8956 0968; ⊙9am-noon & 2-4pm Mon-Fri, 9am-noon Sat), which is also an outlet for local artists' work.

From Finke, you can turn west along the Goyder Stock Rte to join the Stuart Hwy at Kulgera (150km), or east to Old Andado station on the edge of the Simpson Desert (120km). Just 21km west of Finke, and 12km north of the road along a signposted track, is the Lambert Centre. The point marks Australia's geographical centre and features a 5m-high version of the flagpole found on top of Parliament House in Canberra.

Rainbow Valley Conservation Reserve

This series of freestanding sandstone bluffs and cliffs, in shades ranging from cream to red, is one of central Australia's more extraordinary sights. A marked walking trail takes you past claypans and in between the multihued outcrops to the aptly named **Mushroom Rock**. Rainbow Valley is most striking in the early morning or at sunset, but the area's silence will overwhelm you whatever time of day you are here.

The park lies 24km off the Stuart Hwy along a 4WD track that's 77km south of Alice Springs. It has a pretty exposed **camping ground** (adult/child $3.30/1.65) but the setting is perfectly positioned for sunset viewing.

Stuarts Well

About 90km south of Alice Springs, drivers are urged to 'have a spell' at Stuarts Well. It's worth stopping in for a burger and a beer at **Jim's Place** (☑08-8956 0808; 08-8952 2111; unpowered/powered sites $20/25, budget r with own swag/supplied linen $15/30, cabins s/d $75/95; ❄@🏊) run by well-known outback identity Jim Cotterill, who along with his father opened up Kings Canyon to tourism. You might also catch a performance by Dinky the singing and piano-playing dingo.

If you would like to ride a camel, **Camels Australia** (☑08-8956 0925; www.camels-australia.com.au; ⊙7am-5pm) offers a short spin around the yard for adult/child $6/5, a 30-minute jaunt for $25/20 or a full hour ride for $45/35.

Ernest Giles Road

The Ernest Giles Rd heads off to the west of the Stuart Hwy about 140km south of Alice and is a shorter but much rougher route to Kings Canyon only recommended for 4WD vehicles.

HENBURY METEORITE CRATERS

About 11km west of the Stuart Hwy, a corrugated track leads 5km off Ernest Giles Rd to this cluster of 12 small craters, formed after a meteor fell to Earth 4700 years ago. The largest of the craters is 180m wide and 15m deep.

There are no longer any fragments of the meteorites at the site, but the Museum of Central Australia (p871) in Alice Springs has a small chunk that weighs 46.5kg.

There are also some pretty exposed **camp sites** (adult/child $3.30/1.65) available.

Lasseter Highway

The Lasseter Hwy connects the Stuart Hwy with Uluru-Kata Tjuta National Park, 244km to the west from the turn-off at Erldunda. At Erldunda food, fuel and accommodation is available at the **Desert Oaks Resort** (☑08-8956 0984; www.desertoaksresort.com; Stuart Hwy, Erldunda; unpowered/powered sites $22/32, dm $18, motel s/d from $100/118; ❄🏊).

Mt Conner, the large mesa (table-top mountain) that looms 350m out of the desert, is the outback's most photographed red herring – on first sighting many mistake it for Uluru. It has great significance to local Aboriginal people, who know it as Atila.

Curtin Springs Wayside Inn (08-8956 2906; www.curtinsprings.com; Lasseter Hwy; unpowered/powered sites free/$25, s/d $65/95, r with bathroom $150;) is the last stop before Yulara about 80km away, and the closest alternative to staying at Ayers Rock Resort. You can pitch a tent for free (showers $3) or bed down in a well-maintained cabin. There's fuel, a store with limited supplies and takeaway and bistro meals (mains $20 to $32), plus a bar.

ULURU-KATA TJUTA NATIONAL PARK

For many visitors, Australian and international, a visit to Uluru is high on the list of 'must-sees' and the World Heritage–listed icon has attained the status of a pilgrimage. But the park offers much more than just the multidimensional grandeur of Uluru. Along with the equally (some say more) impressive Kata Tjuta (the Olgas) the area is of deep cultural significance to the traditional owners, the Pitjantjatjara and Yankuntjatjara Aboriginal peoples (who refer to themselves as Anangu). The Anangu officially own the national park, which is leased to Parks Australia and jointly administered.

Although many of the 400,000 annual visitors whiz through here in 24 hours, it's recommended to spend at least the three days the entry pass allows. There's plenty to see and do: meandering walks, guided tours, desert culture and contemplating the many changing colours and moods of the great monolith itself.

The only accommodation is Ayers Rock Resort (p896) in the Yulara village, 20km from the Rock, where you can expect premium prices, reflecting the remote locale.

Information

The **park** (www.environment.gov.au/parks/uluru; adult/child $25/free) is open from half an hour before sunrise to sunset daily (varying between 5am to 9pm November to March and 6am to 7.30pm April to October). Entry permits are valid for three days and available at the drive-through entry station on the road from Yulara.

Uluru-Kata Tjuta Cultural Centre (08-8956 1128; 7am-6pm) is 1km before Uluru on the road from Yulara and should be your first stop. Displays and exhibits focus on tjukurpa (Aboriginal law, religion and custom) and the history and management of the national park. The information desk in the Nintiringkupai building is staffed by park rangers who supply the informative *Visitor Guide*, leaflets and walking notes. During the week a local Anangu ranger runs a presentation at 10am each morning on bush foods and Aboriginal history.

The Cultural Centre encompasses the craft outlet **Maruku Arts** (08-8956 2558; www.maruku.com.au; 8.30am-5.30pm), owned by about 20 Anangu communities from across central Australia (including the local Mutitjulu community), selling hand-crafted wooden carvings, bowls and boomerangs. **Walkatjara Art Centre** (08-8956 2537; 9am-5.30pm) is a working art centre owned by the local Mutitjulu community. It focuses on paintings and ceramics created by women from Mutitjulu. **Ininti Cafe & Souvenirs** (08-8956 2214; 7am-5pm) sells souvenirs such as T-shirts, ceramics, hats, CDs and a variety of books on Uluru, Aboriginal culture, bush foods and the flora and fauna of the area. The attached cafe serves ice cream, pies and light meals.

Tours

Bus Tours

Seit Outback Australia BUS TOURS
(08-8956 3156; www.seitoutbackaustralia.com.au) This small group tour operator has numerous options including a sunset tour around Uluru (adult/child $139/110), and a sunrise tour at Kata Tjuta for the same price including breakfast and a walk into Walpa Gorge.

AAT Kings BUS TOURS
(08-8956 2171; www.aatkings.com) Operating the biggest range of coach tours, AAT offers a range of half- and full-day tours from Yulara. Check the website or enquire at the Tour & Information Centre in Yulara.

Camel Tours

Uluru Camel Tours CAMEL TOURS
(08-8956 3333; www.ulurucameltours.com.au; short rides adult/child $15/10; 10.30am-2.30pm) View Uluru and Kata Tjuta from a distance atop a camel ($75, 1½ hours) or take the popular Camel to Sunrise and Sunset tours ($119, 2½ hours).

Cultural Tours

★**Uluru Aboriginal Tours** INDIGENOUS
(0447 878 851; www.uluruaboriginaltours.com.au; guided tours starting from $45 per person) Owned and operated by Anangu from the Mutitjulu community, this company offers a range of trips to give you an insight into the significance of the Rock through the eyes of the traditional owners. Tours operate and

South of Alice Springs

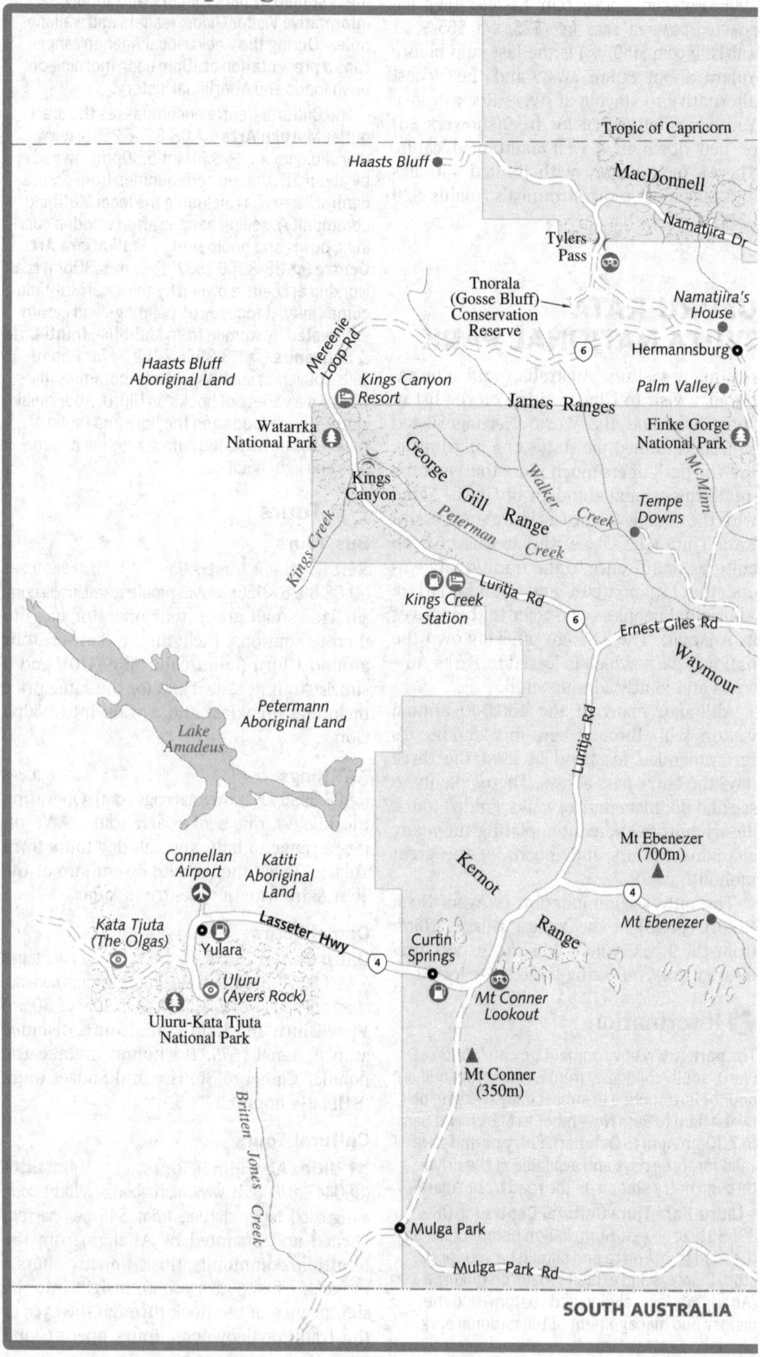

Tropic of Capricorn
Haasts Bluff
MacDonnell
Namatjira Dr
Tylers Pass
Tnorala (Gosse Bluff) Conservation Reserve
Namatjira's House
Hermannsburg
6
Mereenie Loop Rd
Haasts Bluff Aboriginal Land
Kings Canyon Resort
Palm Valley
James Ranges
Watarrka National Park
Finke Gorge National Park
George Gill Range
Walker Creek
McMinn
Kings Canyon
Tempe Downs
Peterman Creek
Kings Creek
Kings Creek Station
Luritja Rd
Ernest Giles Rd
Waymour
Petermann Aboriginal Land
Lake Amadeus
Luritja Rd
Mt Ebenezer (700m)
Kernot Range
Connellan Airport
Katiti Aboriginal Land
4
Mt Ebenezer
Kata Tjuta (The Olgas)
Yulara
Lasseter Hwy
Curtin Springs
Uluru (Ayers Rock)
Mt Conner Lookout
Uluru-Kata Tjuta National Park
Mt Conner (350m)
Britten Jones Creek
Mulga Park
Mulga Park Rd
SOUTH AUSTRALIA

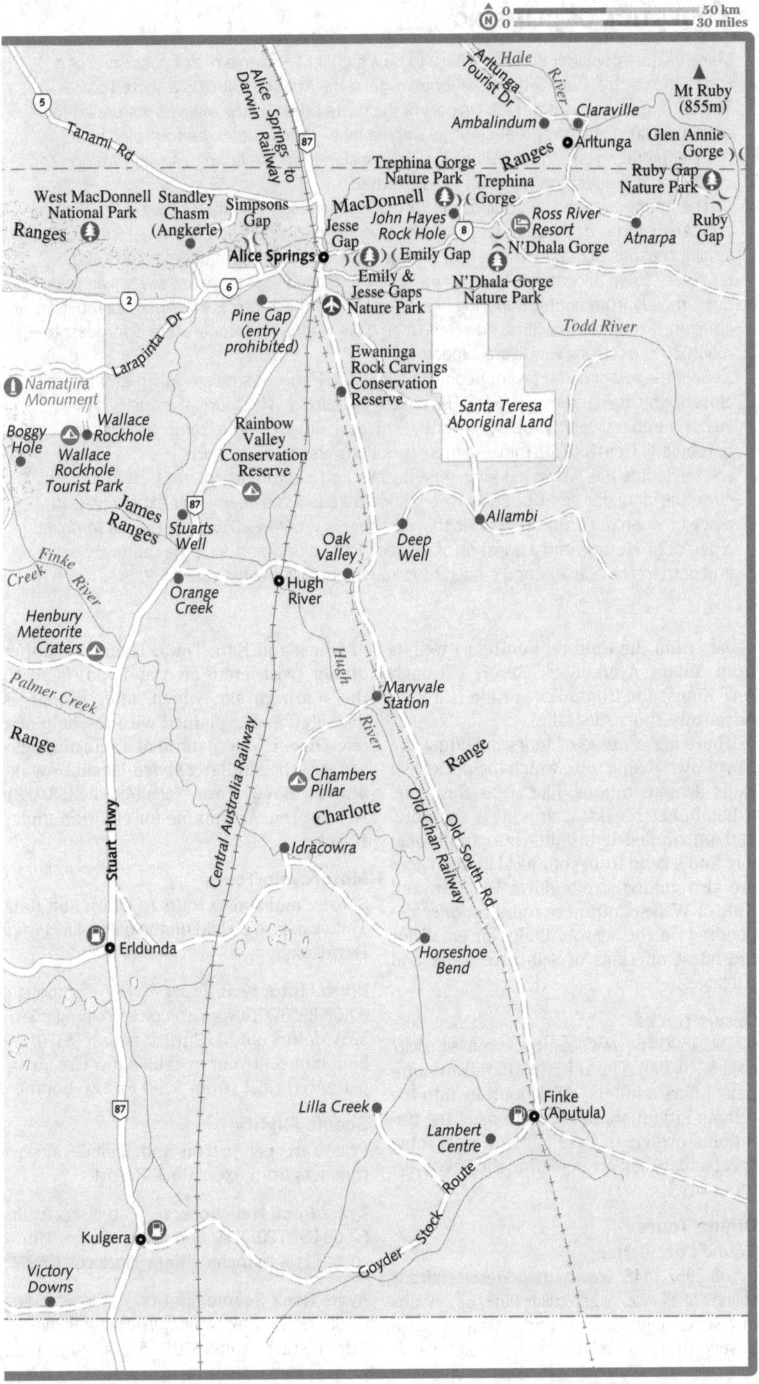

0 50 km
0 30 miles
Arltunga Tourist Dr
Hale River
Mt Ruby (855m)
Claraville
Ambalindum
Arltunga
Glen Annie Gorge
Alice Springs to Darwin Railway
87
5
Tanami Rd
Trephina Gorge Nature Park
Ranges
Ruby Gap Nature Park
Trephina Gorge
West MacDonnell National Park
Standley Chasm (Angkerle)
Simpsons Gap
MacDonnell
John Hayes Rock Hole
Ross River Resort
Ruby Gap
Ranges
Jesse Gap
8
Atnarpa
Alice Springs
Emily Gap
N'Dhala Gorge
Emily & Jesse Gaps Nature Park
N'Dhala Gorge Nature Park
6
2
Pine Gap (entry prohibited)
Todd River
Larapinta Dr
Ewaninga Rock Carvings Conservation Reserve
Namatjira Monument
Santa Teresa Aboriginal Land
Wallace Rockhole
Boggy Hole
Wallace Rockhole Tourist Park
Rainbow Valley Conservation Reserve
87
James Ranges
Stuarts Well
Allambi
Oak Valley
Deep Well
Finke River
Creek
Orange Creek
Hugh River
Henbury Meteorite Craters
Hugh River
Palmer Creek
Maryvale Station
Range
Central Australia Railway
Range
Chambers Pillar
Charlotte
Old Ghan Railway
Old South Rd
Stuart Hwy
Idracowra
Erldunda
Horseshoe Bend
Finke (Aputula)
Lilla Creek
87
Lambert Centre
Route
Stock
Goyder
Kulgera
Victory Downs

A QUESTION OF CLIMBING

Many visitors consider climbing Uluru to be a highlight – even a rite of passage – of a trip to the centre. But for the traditional owners, the Anangu, Uluru is a sacred place. The path up the side of the rock is part of the route taken by the Mala ancestors on their arrival at Uluru and has great spiritual significance – and is not to be trampled by human feet. When you arrive at Uluru you'll see a sign from the Anangu saying 'We don't climb' and a request that you don't climb either.

The Anangu are the custodians of Uluru and take responsibility for the safety of visitors. Any injuries or deaths that occur are a source of distress and sadness to them. For similar reasons of public safety, Parks Australia would prefer that people didn't climb. It's a very steep ascent, not to be taken lightly, and each year there are several air rescues, mostly from people suffering heart attacks. Furthermore, Parks Australia must constantly monitor the climb and close it on days where the temperature is forecast to reach 36°C or strong winds are expected.

So if the Anangu don't want people to climb and Parks Australia would prefer to see it closed, why does it remain open? The answer is tourism. The tourism industry believes visitor numbers would drop significantly – at least initially – if the climb was closed, particularly from visitors thinking there is nothing else to do at Uluru.

The debate has grown louder in recent years and a commitment has been made to close the climb for good, but only when there are adequate new visitor experiences in place or when the proportion of visitors climbing falls below 20%. Until then, it remains a personal decision and a question of respect. Before deciding, visit the Cultural Centre and perhaps take an Anangu guided tour. You might just change your mind.

depart from the Cultural Centre, as well as from Yulara Ayers Rock Resort (through AAT Kings) and from Alice Springs (through Adventure Tours Australia).

There are a range of tours including the New Dawn Rising tour, which includes bush skills demonstrations, like spear throwing, a hot buffet breakfast around a campfire, and unparallelled insights into traditional lore and legend from your local guide. There are also guided strolls down the Liru and Kuniya Walks, and more tours on offer depending on the season. Phone or email for the latest offerings of self-drive tours and packages.

Desert Tracks CULTURAL TOURS
(☎ 0439 500 419; www.deserttracks.com.au; adult/child $249/199) This Pitjantjatjara-run company offers a full-day 4WD journey into the remote Pitjantjatjara Lands to meet the traditional owners of Cave Hill and view some spectacular rock art depicting the Seven Sisters story.

Dining Tours

Sounds of Silence DINING
(☎ 08-8957 7448; www.ayersrockresort.com.au/sounds-of-silence; adult/child $169/87) Waiters serve champagne and canapés on a desert dune with stunning sunset views of Uluru and Kata Tjuta. Then it's a buffet dinner (with emu, croc and roo) beneath the southern sky, which, after dinner, is dissected and explained with the help of a telescope. If you're more of a morning person, try the similarly styled **Desert Awakenings 4WD Tour** (adult/child $158/122). Neither tour is suitable for children under 10 years.

Motorcycle Tours

Sunrise and sunset tours to Uluru and Kata Tjuta can also be had on the back of a Harley Davidson.

Uluru Motorcycle Tours MOTORCYCLE
(☎ 08-8956 2019; www.ulurucycles.com; rides $95-325) Motors out to Uluru at sunset ($170, 1½ hours) or rent your own bike if you're an experienced rider (from $290 for two hours).

Scenic Flights

Prices are per person and include airport transfers from Ayers Rock Resort.

Ayers Rock Helicopters HELICOPTER FLIGHTS
(☎ 08-8956 2077) A 15-minute buzz of Uluru costs $145; to include Kata Tjuta costs $275.

Ayers Rock Scenic Flights SCENIC FLIGHTS
(☎ 08-8956 2345; www.ayersrockflights.com.au) Prices start from $100 for a 20-minute

flight over Uluru. Include Kata Tjuta and it's $200. For $495 you get a two-hour flight that also takes in Lake Amadeus and Kings Canyon.

Uluru (Ayers Rock)

Nothing quite prepares you for the first sight of Uluru on the horizon – it will astound even the most jaded traveller. Uluru is 3.6km long and rises a towering 348m from the surrounding sandy scrubland (867m above sea level). If that's not impressive enough, it's believed that two-thirds of the rock lies beneath the sand. Closer inspection reveals a wondrous contoured surface concealing numerous sacred sites of particular significance to the Anangu. If your first sight of Uluru is during the afternoon, it appears as an ochre-brown colour, scored and pitted by dark shadows. As the sun sets, it illuminates the rock in burnished orange, then a series of deeper reds before it fades into charcoal. A performance in reverse, with marginally fewer spectators, is given at dawn.

Activities

Walking

There are walking tracks around Uluru, and ranger-led walks explain the area's plants, wildlife, geology and cultural significance. All the trails are flat and suitable for wheelchairs. Several areas of spiritual significance are off limits to visitors; these are marked with fences and signs. The Anangu ask you not to photograph these sites.

The excellent *Visitor Guide & Maps* brochure, which can be picked up at the Cultural Centre, gives details on a few self-guided walks.

Base Walk WALKING
This track (10.6km, three to four hours) circumnavigates the rock, passing caves and paintings, sandstone folds and geological abrasions along the way.

Liru Walk WALKING
Links the Cultural Centre with the start of the Mala walk and climb, and winds through strands of mulga before opening up near Uluru (4km return, 1½ hours).

Mala Walk WALKING
From the base of the climbing point (2km return, one hour), interpretive signs explain the tjukurpa of the Mala (hare-wallaby people), which is significant to the Anangu, as well as fine examples of rock art. A ranger-guided walk (free) along this route departs at 10am (8am from October to April) from the car park.

Uluru (Ayers Rock)

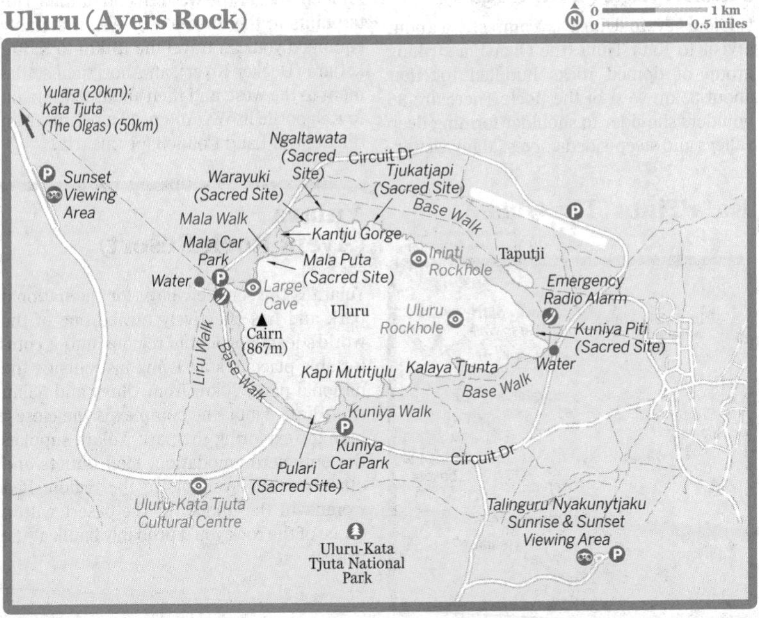

Kuniya Walk WALKING

A short walk (1km return, 45 minutes) from the car park on the southern side leads to the most permanent waterhole, Mutitjulu, home of the ancestral watersnake. Great birdwatching and some excellent rock art are highlights of this walk.

Uluru Climb WALKING

The Anangu ask that visitors respect Aboriginal law by not climbing Uluru. The steep and demanding path (1.6km return, two hours) follows the traditional route taken by ancestral Mala men. The climb is often closed (sometimes at short notice) due to weather and Anangu business. Between January and February the climb is closed at 8am.

Sunset & Sunrise Viewing Areas

About halfway between Yulara and Uluru, the sunset viewing area has plenty of car and coach parking for that familiar postcard view. The Talnguru Nyakunytjaku sunrise viewing area is perched on a sand dune and captures both the Rock and Kata Tjuta in all their glory. It also has two great interpretive walks (1.5km) about women's and men's business. There's a shaded viewing area, toilets and a place to picnic.

Kata Tjuta (The Olgas)

No journey to Uluru is complete without a visit to Kata Tjuta (the Olgas), a striking group of domed rocks huddled together about 35km west of the Rock. There are 36 boulders shoulder to shoulder forming deep valleys and steep-sided gorges. Many visitors find them even more captivating than their prominent neighbour. The tallest rock, **Mt Olga** (546m, 1066m above sea level) is approximately 200m higher than Uluru. Kata Tjuta means 'many heads' and is of great tjukurpa significance, particularly for men, so stick to the tracks.

The 7.4km **Valley of the Winds** loop (two to four hours) is one of the most challenging and rewarding bushwalks in the park. It winds through the gorges giving excellent views of the surreal domes and traversing varied terrain. It's not particularly arduous, but wear sturdy shoes, and take plenty of water. Starting this walk at first light often rewards you with solitude, enabling you to appreciate the sounds of the wind and bird calls carried up the valley.

The short signposted track beneath towering rock walls into pretty **Walpa Gorge** (2.6km return, 45 minutes) is especially beautiful in the afternoon, when sunlight floods the gorge.

There's a picnic and sunset-viewing area with toilet facilities just off the access road a few kilometres west of the base of Kata Tjuta. Like Uluru, Kata Tjuta is at its glorious, blood-red best at sunset.

Kata Tjuta (The Olgas)

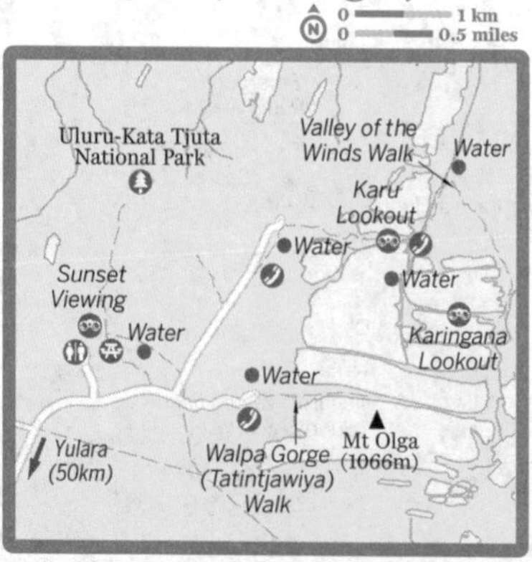

Heading West

A lonely sign at the western end of Kata Tjuta points in the direction of WA. If suitably equipped you can travel the 181km to Kaltukatjara (Docker River), an Aboriginal settlement to the west, and then about 1500km on to Kalgoorlie in WA. You need a permit from the Central Land Council for this trip.

Yulara (Ayers Rock Resort)

POP 887

Yulara is the service village for the national park and has effectively turned one of the world's least hospitable regions into a comfortable place to stay. Lying just outside the national park, 20km from Uluru and 53km from Kata Tjuta, the complex is the closest base for exploring the park. Yulara supplies the only accommodation, food outlets and other services available in the region. If it weren't in the middle of the desert within cooee of the rock you'd probably baulk at the prices.

SUNSET WITH SOLITUDE

Uluru at sunset is a mesmerising experience but it can be hard to escape the crowds and their cameras. Here park rangers share their secrets for a sunset with solitude.

Talinguru Nyakunytjaku Wildly popular at dawn, but at sunset you'll have both Uluru and Kata Tjuta, in silhouette, in the same shot, all to yourself.

Kantju Gorge Head to the end of the Mala Walk in time for a dazzling sunset on the walls of the Rock.

Kata Tjuta Sunset Viewing Take a seat in a private area and watch the colours change to the deepest red.

Mutitjulu Waterhole For profound peace follow the Kuniya Walk to this glorious waterhole.

Sights & Activities

The Ayers Rock Resort conducts numerous free activities throughout the day: from spear, boomerang and didgeridoo classes to dance programs. Pick up a program at your accommodation.

Mulgara Gallery ART GALLERY
(Sails in the Desert Hotel) Quality handmade Australian arts and crafts are displayed here. Each month brings a new artist in residence.

Uluru Outback Sky Journey STARGAZING
(☎08-8956 2563; Tour & Information Centre; adult/child $38/free; ⏲30 min after sunset) Takes an informative one-hour look at the startlingly clear outback night sky with a telescope and an astronomer. Tour starts at the Yulara Town Square.

Sleeping

All of the accommodation in Yulara, including the camping ground and hostel, is owned by the Ayers Rock Resort. And unless the free camping at Curtin Springs station outweighs the risk of driving in the dark for sunrise/sunset at Uluru, there's no other option. Even though there are almost 5000 beds, it's wise to make a reservation, especially during school holidays. Bookings can be made through **central reservations** (☎1300 134 044; www.ayersrockresort.com.au). Substantial discounts are usually offered if you book for two or three nights or more, and you can also save a reasonable amount through internet sites offering discount accommodation.

Ayers Rock Resort Campground CAMPGROUND $
(☎08-8957 7001; camp.ground@ayersrockresort.com.au; unpowered/powered sites $36/41, cabins $150; ❄@≋) A saviour for the budget conscious, this sprawling campground is set among native gardens. There are good facilities, including a kiosk, free BBQs, a camp kitchen and a pool. During the peak season it's very busy and the inevitable pre-dawn convoy heading for Uluru can provide an unwanted wake-up call. The cramped cabins (shared facilities) sleep six people and are only really suitable for a family.

Outback Pioneer Hotel & Lodge HOSTEL $
(☎1300 134 044; dm $38-46, d $220-280; ❄@≋) With a lively bar, BBQ restaurant and musical entertainment, this is the budget choice for noncampers. The cheapest options are the 20-bed YHA unisex dorms and squashy four-bed budget cabins with fridge, TV and shared bathroom. There are also more spacious motel-style rooms that sleep up to four people. Children under 12 stay free, though anyone over 12 is an extra $50 a night.

Emu Walk Apartments APARTMENTS $$$
(☎1300 134 044; 1-/2-bedroom apt from $380/480; ❄) The pick of the bunch for families looking for self-contained accommodation, Emu Walk has comfortable, modern apartments, each with a lounge room (with TV) and a well-equipped kitchen with washer and dryer. The one-bedroom apartment accommodates four people, while the two-bedroom version sleeps six.

Desert Gardens Hotel HOTEL $$$
(☎1300 134 044; r $380-480; ❄@≋) One of Yulara's originals, the standard rooms, particularly the bathrooms, are looking dated but, at the time of research, a major renovation was planned for the near future. Currently the spacious deluxe rooms are the best option, featuring balconies with desert

Yulara (Ayers Rock Resort)

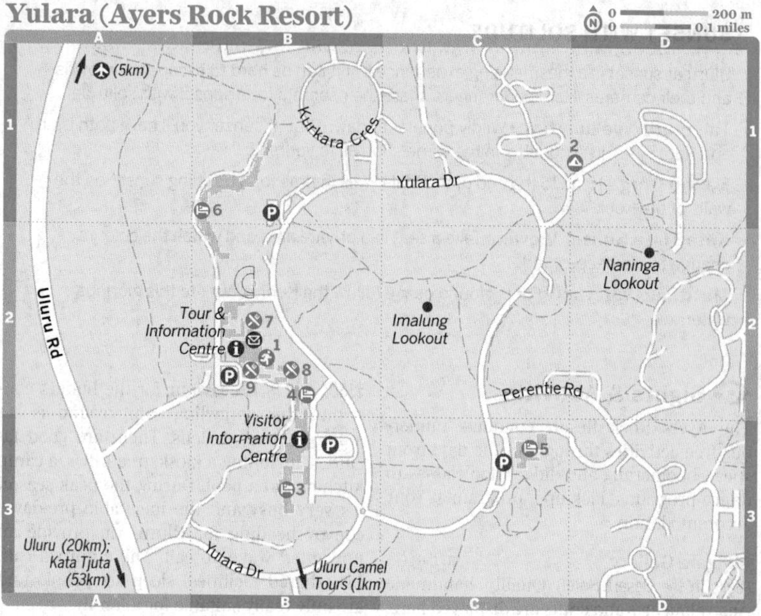

Yulara (Ayers Rock Resort)

Sights

Mulgara Gallery .... (see 6)

Activities, Courses & Tours

1 Uluru Outback Sky Journey B2

Sleeping

2 Ayers Rock Resort Campground D1
3 Desert Gardens Hotel B3
4 Emu Walk Apartments B2
5 Outback Pioneer Hotel & Lodge C3
6 Sails in the Desert B1

Eating

Arngulli Flame Grill .... (see 3)
Bough House .... (see 5)
7 Geckos Cafe B2
Kuniya .... (see 6)
Outback Pioneer Barbecue .... (see 5)
Pioneer Kitchen .... (see 5)
8 Red Rock Deli B2
Rockpool .... (see 6)
White Gums .... (see 3)
Winkiku .... (see 6)
9 Yulara IGA Supermarket B2

Drinking & Nightlife

Bunya Bar .... (see 3)
Pioneer Barbecue Bar .... (see 5)
Tali Bar .... (see 6)

or Uluru views. A big buffet breakfast is served in the restaurant and there's a pleasant pool area shaded with gums.

Sails in the Desert HOTEL $$$

(☎1300 134 044; standard d $400, ste $780; ❄@🛜🏊) Although refurbished in 2011/12, the rooms still seem overpriced and by far the best part of this hotel is the lovely (and exclusive) pool and surrounding lawn shaded by sails and trees. There are also tennis courts, a health spa, several restaurants and a piano bar. The best rooms have balcony views of the rock – request one when you make a booking.

Eating

Red Rock Deli DELI $

(Resort Shopping Centre; snacks $5-10; ⏱8am-4pm) Line up for steaming-hot espresso and croissants in the morning or grab filled paninis and wraps for lunch.

Geckos Cafe MEDITERRANEAN $$

(Resort Shopping Centre; mains $18-28; ⏱11am-9pm; ✍) For great value, warm atmosphere and tasty food head to this buzzing licensed cafe, which, it says, 'cater for everyone'. The wood-fired pizzas, salads and pasta go well with a carafe of sangria, and the courtyard tables are a great place to enjoy the desert night air. There are several veggie and gluten-free options plus meals can be made to takeaway.

Outback Pioneer Barbecue BBQ **$$**
(Outback Pioneer Hotel & Lodge; mains $20-35, salad only $16; ⏲6-9pm) For a fun, casual night out, this lively tavern is the popular choice for everyone from backpackers to grey nomads. Choose between kangaroo skewers, prawns, veggie burgers, steaks and emu sausages and grill them yourself at the communal BBQs. The deal includes a salad bar. In the same complex is the **Pioneer Kitchen** (meals $10-22; ⏲lunch & dinner), doing brisk business in burgers, pizza and kiddie meals.

White Gums BUFFET **$$**
(☎08-8957 7888; Desert Gardens Hotel; buffet $27-33; ⏲6.30-10.30am) Hotel guests enjoy a big hot or cold buffet breakfast here.

Arngulli Flame Grill MODERN AUSTRALIAN **$$**
(Desert Gardens Hotel; 2/3 courses $55/65; ⏲6.30-10.30pm) Featuring fusion cuisine with Asian, Mediterranean and Australian themes, the Arngulli Flame Grill specialises in meat and seafood dinners including Australian native meats such as kangaroo and crocodile.

Rockpool TAPAS **$$$**
(Sails in the Desert; 3 tapas plates $45, plus dessert $50; ⏲11am-10pm) Beside the pool and under the sails, this casual eatery serves Mediterranean and Asian tapas-style dishes and some decadent desserts.

Winkiku BUFFET **$$$**
(Sails in the Desert; breakfast/dinner buffet $38/70; ⏲6.30-10.30am & 6.30-9.30pm) In Yulara's five-star hotel, this casual-yet-stylish restaurant does extravagant seafood buffets with a meat carvery, and all the trimmings and desserts you can imagine. Kids eat free, so it can work out as good value for families. At the time of research a name change was being discussed.

Bough House BUFFET **$$**
(Outback Pioneer Hotel & Lodge; breakfast/dinner buffets $30/52; ⏲6.30-10am & 6.30-9.30pm) This family-friendly, country-style place overlooks the pool at the Outback Pioneer and has buffet spreads for breakfast and dinner. The 'Tastes of Australia' dinner features outback tucker – kangaroo, emu, crocodile and barramundi. Kids under 12 eat free, making this popular with families.

Kuniya MODERN AUSTRALIAN **$$$**
(☎08-8956 2200; Sails in the Desert; mains $45-60; ⏲6.30-9.30pm) Yulara's most sophisticated restaurant, Kuniya is the place for romantic dinners and special occasions. The walls are adorned with contemporary Australian art and the inspired menu features Aussie cuisine infused with native ingredients that complement the extensive Australian wine list. Reservations are essential.

Yulara IGA Supermarket SUPERMARKET **$**
(Resort Shopping Centre; ⏲8am-9pm) This well-stocked supermarket has a delicatessen and sells picnic portions, fresh fruit and vegetables, meat, groceries, ice and camp supplies.

Drinking

Pioneer Barbecue Bar PUB
(Outback Pioneer Hotel & Lodge; ⏲10am-midnight) This rowdy bar is lined with long benches, with plenty of chances to meet other travellers. It has pool tables and live music nightly (usually a touch of twang).

Tali Bar BAR
(Sails in the Desert; ⏲11am-midnight) The cocktails ($18 to $21) at this bar include locally inspired mixes like Desert Oasis. The piano gets a workout most nights during the season from 8pm.

Bunya Bar BAR
(Desert Gardens Hotel; ⏲10.30am-10pm) This is a rather characterless hotel lobby bar, but it knows the importance of well-chilled beer, and the cocktails are several dollars cheaper than at Tali Bar.

Information

The useful *Welcome to Ayers Rock Resort* flier is available at the Visitor Information Centre and at hotel desks. Most of the village's facilities are in the shopping centre, including a post office and a local job vacancies board.

ANZ bank (☎08-8956 2070) Currency exchange and 24-hour ATMs.

Emergency (☎ambulance 0420 101 403, police 08-8956 2166)

Internet Cafe (Outback Pioneer Hotel; per 10min $2; ⏲5am-11pm) In the backpacker common room. Internet access is also available at the Tour & Information Centre and all accommodation.

Post Office (☎08-8956 2288; Resort Shopping Centre; ⏰9am-6pm Mon-Fri, 10am-2pm Sat & Sun) An agent for the Commonwealth and NAB banks. Pay phones are outside.

Royal Flying Doctor Service Medical Centre (☎08-8956 2286; ⏰9am-noon & 2-5pm Mon-Fri, 10-11am Sat & Sun) The resort's medical centre and ambulance service.

Tour & Information Centre (☎08-8957 7324; Resort Shopping Centre; ⏰8am-8pm) Most tour operators and car-hire firms have desks at this centre.

Visitor Information Centre (☎08-8957 7377; ⏰8.30am-4.30pm) Contains displays on the geography, wildlife and history of the region. There's a short audio tour ($2) if you want to learn more. It also sells books and regional maps.

Getting There & Away

AIR

Connellan airport is about 4km north of Yulara. **Qantas** (☎13 13 13; www.qantas.com.au) has direct flights from Alice Springs, Melbourne, Perth, Adelaide and Sydney. **Virgin Australia** (☎13 67 89; www.virginaustralia.com) has daily flights from Sydney.

BUS

Daily shuttle connections (listed as mini tours) between Alice Springs and Yulara are run by **AAT Kings** (☎1300 556 100; www.aatkings.com) and cost adult/child $150/75. Emu Run (p876) runs the cheapest daily connections between Alice Springs and Uluru ($215/108).

CAR & MOTORCYCLE

One route from Alice to Yulara is sealed all the way, with regular food and petrol stops. It's 200km from Alice to Erldunda on the Stuart Hwy, where you turn west for the 245km journey along the Lasseter Hwy. The journey takes four to five hours.

Renting a car in Alice Springs to go to Uluru and back is a reasonably priced option if you make the trip in a group.

Getting Around

A free shuttle bus meets all flights and drops off at all accommodation points around the resort; pick-up is 90 minutes before your flight. Another free shuttle bus loops through the resort – stopping at all accommodation points and the shopping centre – every 15 minutes from 10.30am to 6pm and from 6.30pm to 12.30am daily.

Uluru Express (☎08-8956 2152; www.uluruexpress.com.au) falls somewhere between a shuttle-bus service and an organised tour. It provides return transport from the resort to Uluru (adult/child $50/30, $60/30 for the sunrise and sunset shuttles). Morning shuttles to Kata Tjuta cost $80/45; afternoon shuttles include a stop at Uluru for sunset and cost $90/45. There are also two-day ($170/90) and three-day ($195/90) passes which allow unlimited use of the service. Fares do not include the park entry fee.

Hiring a car will give you the flexibility to visit the Rock and the Olgas whenever you want. **Hertz** (☎08-8956 2244) has a desk at the Tour & Information Centre, which also has direct phones to the **Avis** (☎08-8956 2266) and **Thrifty** (☎08-8956 2030) desks at Connellan Airport.

Bike hire is available at the **Ayers Rock Resort Campground** (☎08-8957 7001; per hr $7, per half-/full day $15/20; ⏰7am-8pm).

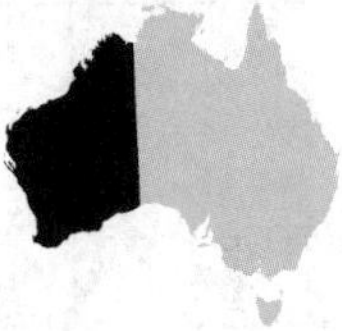

Perth & Western Australia

Includes ➡

Best Places to Eat

- Greenhouse (p918)
- Cantina 663 (p918)
- Pepper & Salt (p955)
- Whalers Restaurant (p996)
- Karijini Eco Retreat (p1003)

Best Places to Stay

- Eight Nicholson (p916)
- Burnside Organic Farm (p945)
- Cape Howe Cottages (p955)
- Gnaraloo Station (p988)
- Mornington Wilderness Camp (p1018)

Why Go?

If you subscribe to the 'life's a beach' school of thought, you'll fall in love with Western Australia (WA) and its 12,500km of spectacular coastline. WA is beyond huge; if it were a separate country, it would be the 10th biggest in the world. You can wander along a beach for hours without seeing a footprint in the sand, be one of a handful of campers stargazing in a national park, or bushwalk for days without seeing a soul.

Up north in the Kimberley, you'll encounter wide open spaces that shrewdly conceal striking gorges, waterfalls and ancient rock formations. At the other end of the state, the south is a playground of white-sand beaches, expanses of springtime wildflowers, lush green forests and world-class wineries. Perth and neighbouring Fremantle are cosmopolitan cities, yet both retain a languorously laid-back feel. Wind down with them and take a walk on the WA side.

When to Go

Perth

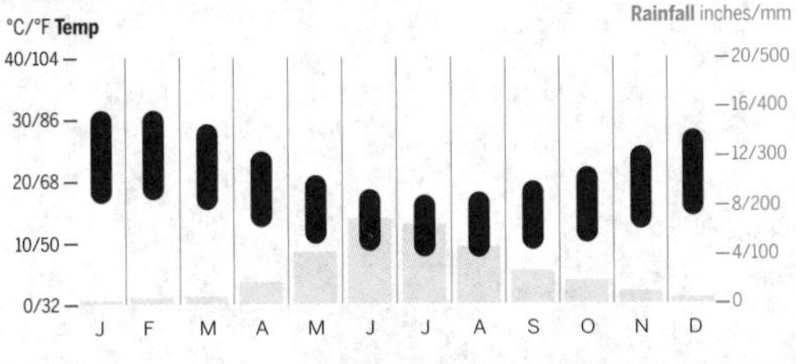

Mar Wet up north but great beach weather elsewhere and not as swelteringly hot in Perth.

Aug Head north for the Dry, south for festivals and flowers, and to Gnaraloo for surf.

Sep The best month statewide: wildflowers, whales and warming weather, and still dry up north.

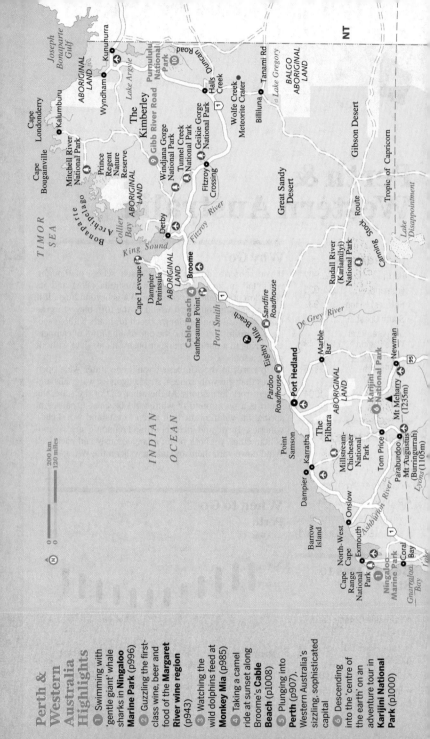

Perth & Western Australia Highlights

1. Swimming with 'gentle giant' whale sharks in **Ningaloo Marine Park** (p996)
2. Guzzling the first-class wine, beer and food of the **Margaret River wine region** (p943)
3. Watching the wild dolphins feed at **Monkey Mia** (p985)
4. Taking a camel ride at sunset along Broome's **Cable Beach** (p1008)
5. Plunging into **Perth** (p907), Western Australia's sizzling, sophisticated capital
6. Descending into the 'centre of the earth' on an adventure tour in **Karijini National Park** (p1000)

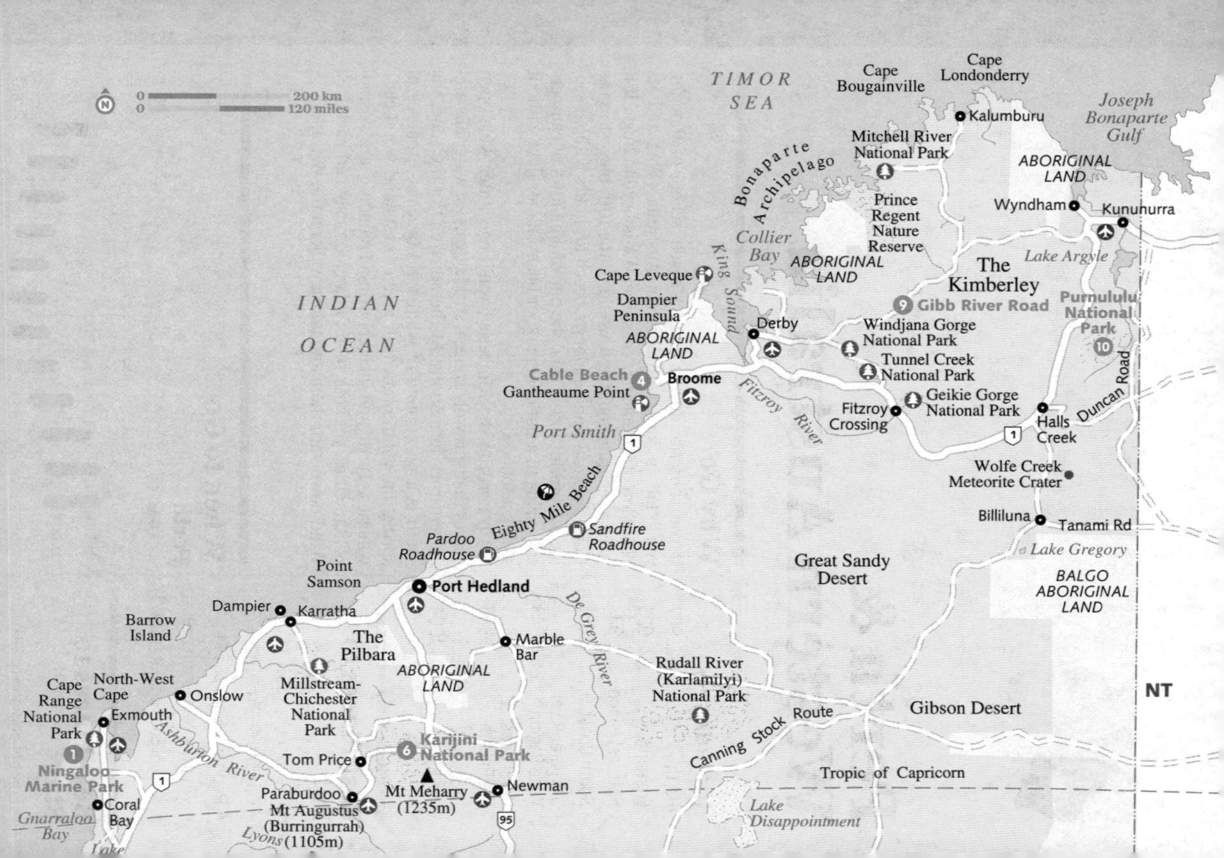

7 Enjoying a sublime sunset over the other-worldly **Pinnacles Desert** (p973)

8 Walking among and above the giant tingle trees on the **Valley of the Giants** (p953) Tree Top Walk

9 Tackling the notorious **Gibb River Road** (p1017) on a 4WD adventure

10 Getting lost among the remarkable orange beehive domes of the Bungle Bungle Range in the **Purnululu National Park** (p1023)

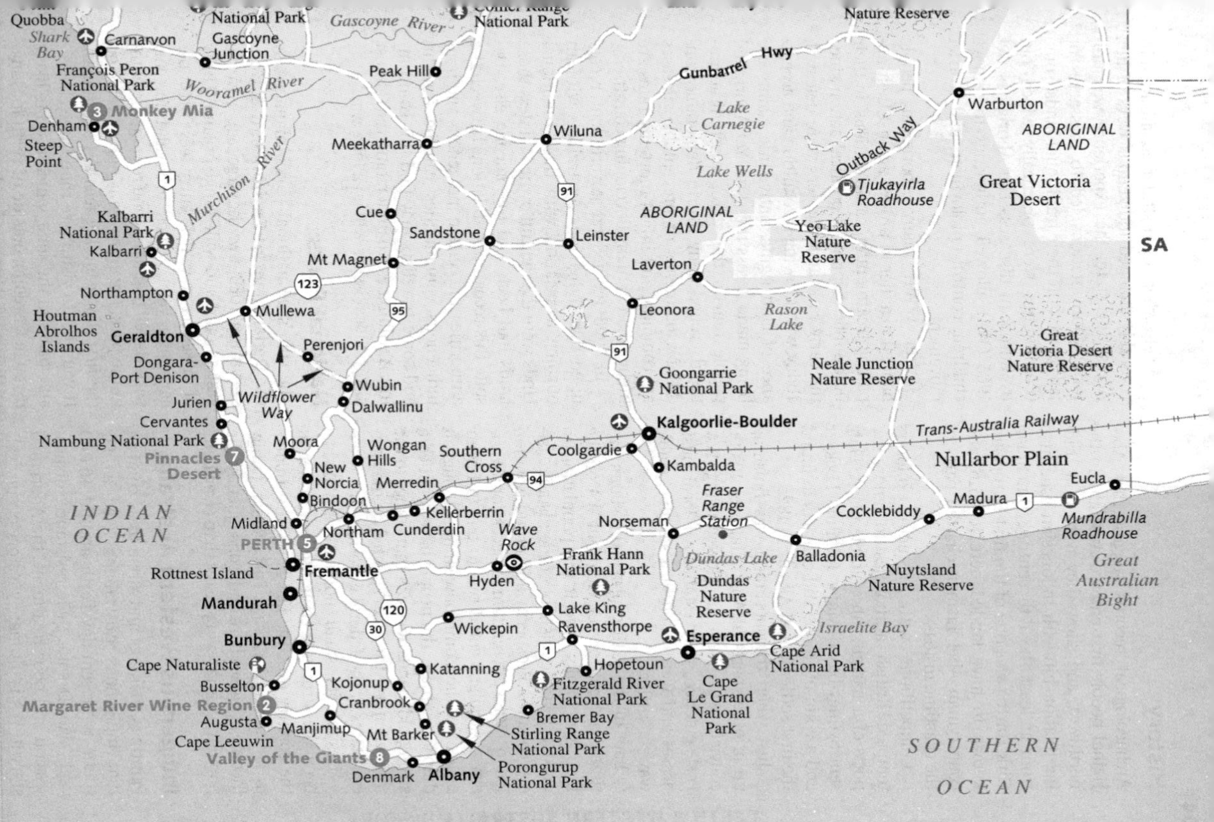

History

Archaeological records suggest that Aboriginal people first entered Australia in the northwest, and show they were in a trading relationship with Indonesian fishermen from at least the 17th century. Dutchman Dirk Hartog was one of the first Europeans known to have landed here in 1616, and countryman Abel Tasman charted parts of the coastline in 1644.

Competition with French explorers tempted British authorities to ignore reports of a barren, inhospitable place. They sent Sydney-based Major Edmund Lockyer and a team of troops and convicts to found the first settlement at Albany in 1826.

Just when transportation was finishing up in other parts of Australia, over 10,000 convicts were sent to slow-growing WA. Post-sentence, they established local businesses and were in effect a sizeable, stable wave of settlers.

Late in the 19th century, the state's fortunes changed forever. Gold put WA on the map and finally gave it the population to make it a viable offshoot of the distant eastern colonies. Prosperity and proud isolation led to a 1933 referendum on secession: Western Australians voted two to one in favour of leaving the Commonwealth. Although it didn't eventuate, the people have retained a strong independent streak that comes to the fore whenever they feel slighted by the eastern states or the federal government.

Despite its small population, WA has been the strongest economic performer in the country over the last few years, thanks to its mining industry. The average family income is higher here and, consequently, the population is growing faster than elsewhere.

Indigenous Western Australia

Paintings, etchings and stone tools confirm that indigenous Australians lived as far south as present-day Perth around 40,000 years ago. Despite their resistance, dispossession and poor treatment, the Aboriginal story in WA is ultimately a story of survival.

With around 72,000 people, WA has one of the largest indigenous communities in Australia today, particularly around the Pilbara and Kimberley regions where in many towns they form the majority. Even in Perth and the southwest, which has the greatest non-indigenous population, the local Noongar people have a more visible presence than, say, Kooris in Sydney.

As elsewhere in Australia, colonisation irrevocably changed indigenous ways of life. Across the state, the experience was uniform: confrontations led to massacres or jail. Forced off their traditional lands, some communities were practically wiped out by European diseases. The Aborigines Act 1905 (WA) allowed authorities to remove children, control employment and restrict movement.

After WWII many Aboriginal people banded together in protest against their appalling treatment on cattle stations, in their first public displays of political action since the early resistance fighters were defeated. Today, with growing recognition and acceptance of land rights, native-title claims are being made across the state. Yet Aboriginal people remain the state's most disadvantaged group. Many live in deplorable conditions, outbreaks of preventable diseases are common, and infant-mortality rates are higher than in many developing countries.

In 1993 the federal government recognised that Indigenous Australians with an ongoing association with their traditional lands were the rightful owners, unless those lands had been sold to someone else. Despite this recognition, relations between the authorities and certain indigenous and non-indigenous communities can be fraught, and some travellers may find this confronting. A willingness to understand the (almost always) local issues will go a long way.

National Parks

The state's 96 national parks, managed by the **Department of Environment & Conservation** (DEC; www.dec.wa.gov.au), cover a vast amount and wide range of land. Thirty of these charge vehicle entry fees ($11/5 per car/motorcycle), which are valid for any park visited that day. If you're camping within the park, the entry fee is only payable on the first day (camping fees are additional). If you plan to visit more than three chargeable parks in the state, which is quite likely if you're travelling outside of Perth for longer than a week, take advantage of the four-week Holiday Pass ($40). All DEC offices sell them and if you've already paid a day-entry fee in the last week (and have the voucher to prove it), you can subtract it from the cost.

Wine Regions

Margaret River is one of Australia's most acclaimed wine regions – and arguably its most beautiful – known for its Bordeaux-style wines. The cool-climate Great Southern wine region covers a vast area, with hubs in Denmark, Mt Barker and Porongurup. Less lauded but more accessible is the Swan Valley, on Perth's eastern fringes.

Activities

Bushwalking

WA is blessed with wonderful bushwalking terrain, from the cool, fertile forests of the southwest, to the rugged, tropical Kimberley in the far north. Get in touch with like-minded souls through **Bushwalking Australia** (www.bushwalkingaustralia.org).

If you've got eight spare weeks up your sleeve, consider trekking the **Bibbulmun Track** (www.bibbulmuntrack.org.au), a long-distance walking trail that winds its way south from Kalamunda, about 20km east of Perth, through virtually unbroken natural environment to Walpole and along the coast to Albany – a total of 963km. Camp sites are spaced at regular intervals, most with a three-sided shelter that sleeps eight to 16 people, plus a water tank and pit toilets. The best time to tackle the track is from late winter to spring (August to October).

Camping

This enormous state provides plenty of opportunity to get back to basics, especially in the national parks, where sleeping in a swag under the stars is almost obligatory.

Cycling

WA has excellent day, weekend and multi-week cycling routes. Perth has an ever-growing network of bike tracks, and you'll find the southwest region good for cycle touring. While there are thousands of kilometres of good, practically traffic-free roads in country areas, the distance between towns makes it difficult to plan – even if the riding is flat.

The most exciting opportunity for mountain bikers is the **Munda Biddi Trail** (www.mundabiddi.org.au), heading 1000km from Mundaring on Perth's outskirts through the southwest forests to Albany.

Diving & Snorkelling

Close to Perth, divers can explore shipwrecks and marine life off the beaches of Rottnest Island, or head south to explore Shoalwater Islands Marine Park or Geographe Bay. A staggering amount of marine life can be found just 100m offshore within the Ningaloo Marine Park, on the Coral Coast, making this pristine area the premier destination for divers and snorkellers.

Surfing & Windsurfing

Beginners, intermediates, wannabe pros and adventure surfers will find excellent conditions to suit their skill levels right along the coast. WA gets huge swells (often over 3m), so it's critical to align where you surf with your ability. Look out for strong currents, huge sharks and territorial local surfers who can be far scarier than a hungry white pointer.

The state's traditional surfing ground is the southwest, particularly the beaches from Yallingup to Margaret River. Heading north, the best-known spots are the left-hand point breaks of Jake's Point near Kalbarri; Gnaraloo Station, 150km north of Carnarvon; and Surfers Beach at Exmouth.

Windsurfers and kitesurfers have plenty of choice spots to try out in WA as well, with excellent flat-water and wave sailing. Kitesurfers in particular will appreciate the long, empty beaches and offshore reefs away from crowds. The premier location is windy Lancelin, north of Perth.

Whale Watching

For most visitors to WA there's no better wildlife watching than seeing the southern right and humpback whales make their way along the coast. There are so many (upwards of 30,000) that it's become known as the Humpback Hwy. From June the gentle giants make their way on their annual pilgrimage from Antarctica to the warm, tropical waters of the northwest coast. They can then be seen again on their slow southern migration down the coast in early summer. Mothers with calves regularly make themselves at home in the bays and coves of King George Sound in Albany from July to October each year.

Wildflowers

When spring has sprung in southern WA, wildflowers abound. From about August to October the bush is ablaze with colour; it's a great time to bushwalk sections of the Bibbulmun Track or to drive through inland national parks such as Stirling Range or Mt Lesueur near Cervantes.

Tours

If you don't feel like travelling solo or you crave a hassle-free holiday where everything is organised for you, dozens of tours cover all tastes and budgets. Some adventure tours include serious 4WD safaris, taking travellers to places they simply couldn't get to on their own without large amounts of expensive equipment. The WA Visitor Centre in Perth has a wide selection of brochures and suggestions for tours all over the state.

AAT Kings Australian Tours BUS, 4WD TOUR
(☎1300 228 546; www.aatkings.com.au) Fully escorted bus trips and 4WD adventures.

Adventure Tours 4WD TOUR
(☎1800 068 886; www.adventuretours.com.au) 4WD bus tours from Perth, Exmouth, Broome and Kununurra.

Outback Spirit LUXURY TOUR
(☎1800 688 222; www.outbackspirittours.com.au) Luxury all-terrain explorations including a Western Wildflowers Discovery tour and exploring the Pilbara, Karijini and Ningaloo Reef regions.

Red Earth Safaris BUS TOUR
(☎1800 501 968; www.redearthsafaris.com.au) Operates a six-day Perth to Exmouth minibus tour.

Seasonal Work

WA is in a labour shortage and a wealth of opportunities exists for travellers for paid work year-round.

INDUSTRY	TIME	REGION
grapes	Feb-Mar	Denmark Margaret River Mt Barker Manjimup
apples/pears	Feb-Apr	Donnybrook Manjimup
prawn trawlers	Mar-Jun	Carnarvon
bananas	Apr-Dec	Kununurra
bananas	year-round	Carnarvon
vegies	May-Nov	Kununurra, Carnarvon
tourism	May-Dec	Kununurra
flowers	Sep-Nov	Midlands
lobsters	Nov-May	Esperance

Information

Tourism Western Australian (www.westernaustralia.com) Comprehensive website for general statewide information.

Getting There & Away

The east coast is the most common gateway for international travellers, although if you're coming from Europe, Asia or Africa it's more convenient and quicker to take any of the 18 airlines flying directly to **Perth Airport** (☎08-9478 8888; www.perthairport.com). Port Hedland has international flights to/from Bali, while Perth, Kalgoorlie, Port Hedland and Broome welcome interstate flights.

The only interstate bus is the daily **Greyhound** (☎1300 473 946; www.greyhound.com.au) service between Darwin and Broome (from $361, 25 hours), via Kununurra, Fitzroy Crossing and Derby.

The only interstate rail link is the famous *Indian Pacific*, run by **Great Southern Railway** (☎13 21 47; www.greatsouthernrail.com.au), which travels to Perth from Kalgoorlie (10 hours), Adelaide (two days), Broken Hill (2¼ days) and Sydney (4352km, three days).

Getting Around

AIR

Airnorth (☎1800 627 474; www.airnorth.com.au) Flies Perth–Kununurra, Karratha–Port Hedland, Karratha–Broome, Port Hedland–Broome and Broome–Kununurra.

Cobham (☎1800 105 503; www.cobham.com.au) Flies between Perth and Kambalda.

Qantas (☎13 13 13; www.qantas.com.au) WA destinations include Perth, Kalgoorlie, Paraburdoo, Newman, Exmouth, Karratha, Port Hedland and Broome.

Skippers Aviation (☎1300 729 924; www.skippers.com.au) Perth–Leonora–Laverton, Perth–Wiluna–Leinster, Perth–Mt Magnet–Meekatharra, Perth–Carnarvon, Perth–Geraldton–Carnarvon and Perth–Kalbarri–Monkey Mia.

Virgin Australia (☎13 67 89; www.virginaustralia.com) Flies to Perth, Busselton, Albany, Esperance, Geraldton, Exmouth (Learmonth), Port Hedland, Kalgoorlie, Karratha, Kununurra, Derby and Broome.

BUS

WA's bus network offers access to substantially more destinations than the railways.

Greyhound (☎1300 473 946; www.greyhound.com.au) Perth–Broome via Geraldton, Carnarvon, Karratha and Port Hedland; Broome–Darwin via the Great Northern Hwy (Rte 1).

Integrity Coach Lines (☎1800 226 339; www.integritycoachlines.com.au) Weekly buses between Perth and Port Hedland via the Great Northern Hwy, and also from Perth to Lancelin, Cervantes, Geraldton and Exmouth.

South West Coach Lines (☎08-9261 7600; www.veoliatransportwa.com.au) From Perth to all the major towns in the southwest – your best choice for Margaret River.

Transwa (☎1300 662 205; www.transwa.wa.gov.au) Perth–Augusta, Perth–Pemberton, Perth–Albany (three routes), Perth–Esperance (two routes), Albany–Esperance, Kalgoorlie–Esperance, Perth–Geraldton (three routes) and Geraldton–Meekathara.

CAR

The best way to really see and explore this enormous state is by car. Bear in mind that WA is not only enormous but also sparsely populated, so make safety preparations if you plan to travel any significant distance. There are many enticing areas of the state that don't have sealed roads, and a 4WD is recommended for many places such as the spectacular Kimberley, even in the Dry.

Department of Aboriginal Affairs (DAA; ☎1300 651 077; www.daa.wa.gov.au; 151 Royal St, East Perth) To travel through Aboriginal land in WA you need a permit. Applications can be lodged on the internet.

Mainroads (☎13 81 38; www.mainroads.wa.gov.au) Provides statewide road-condition reports, updated daily (and more frequently if necessary).

Royal Automobile Club (RAC; ☎13 17 03; www.rac.com.au) Useful advice on statewide motoring, including road safety, local regulations and buying or selling a car.

TRAIN

Transwa (☎1300 662 205; www.transwa.wa.gov.au) services are limited to the *Prospector* (Perth–Kalgoorlie), *AvonLink* (Perth–Northam) and *Australind* (Perth–Bunbury). Transperth's train network reaches as far south as Mandurah.

PERTH

POP 1.8 MILLION

Planted by a river and beneath an almost permanent canopy of blue sky, the city of Perth is a modern-day boom town, stoking Australia's economy from its glitzy central business district. Yet it remains as relaxed as the sleepy Swan River – black swans bobbing atop – which winds past the skyscrapers and out to the Indian Ocean.

About as close to Southeast Asia as to Australia's eastern state capitals, Perth is a combination of big-city attractions and relaxed and informal surrounds, offering an appealing lifestyle for locals and a variety of things to do for visitors. It's a sophisticated, cosmopolitan city with myriad bars, restaurants and cultural activities all vying for attention. And even in its boardrooms, its heart is down at the beach, tossing around in clear ocean surf.

OFF THE BEATEN TRACK

WESTERN AUSTRALIA

It's easy to get off the beaten track pretty well anywhere amid Western Australia's huge expanses, but the following are extra-special destinations definitely worth an intrepid road trip.

- Dryandra Woodland (p971)
- Canning Stock Route (p970)
- Steep Point (p984)
- Marble Bar (p1004)
- Kalumburu (p1020)
- Mt Augustus National Park (p987)
- Duncan Road (p1022)
- Tanami Road (p1025)

History

Modern Perth was founded in 1829 when Captain James Stirling established the Swan River colony on the lands of the Wadjuk, a subgroup of the Noongar people. The discovery of stone implements near the Swan River suggests that the area had already been occupied for around 40,000 years.

Relations were friendly at first, the Noongar believing the British to be the returned spirits of their dead, but competition for resources led to conflict. By 1843 the Wadjuk had been dispossessed of all of their lands around the new city and were forced to camp near the swamps and lakes to the north.

The early settlement grew very slowly until 1850, when convicts alleviated the labour shortage and boosted the population. Convict labour was also responsible for constructing the city's substantial buildings, such as Government House and the town hall. The discovery of gold inland in the 1890s increased Perth's population fourfold in a decade and initiated a building bonanza, mirrored in the current mining and economic boom.

Rumours of a slowdown by the Chinese and Indian economies driving the resources boom continue to bubble away, but obviously no one's told more than a few of the fiscally confident locals.

Perth

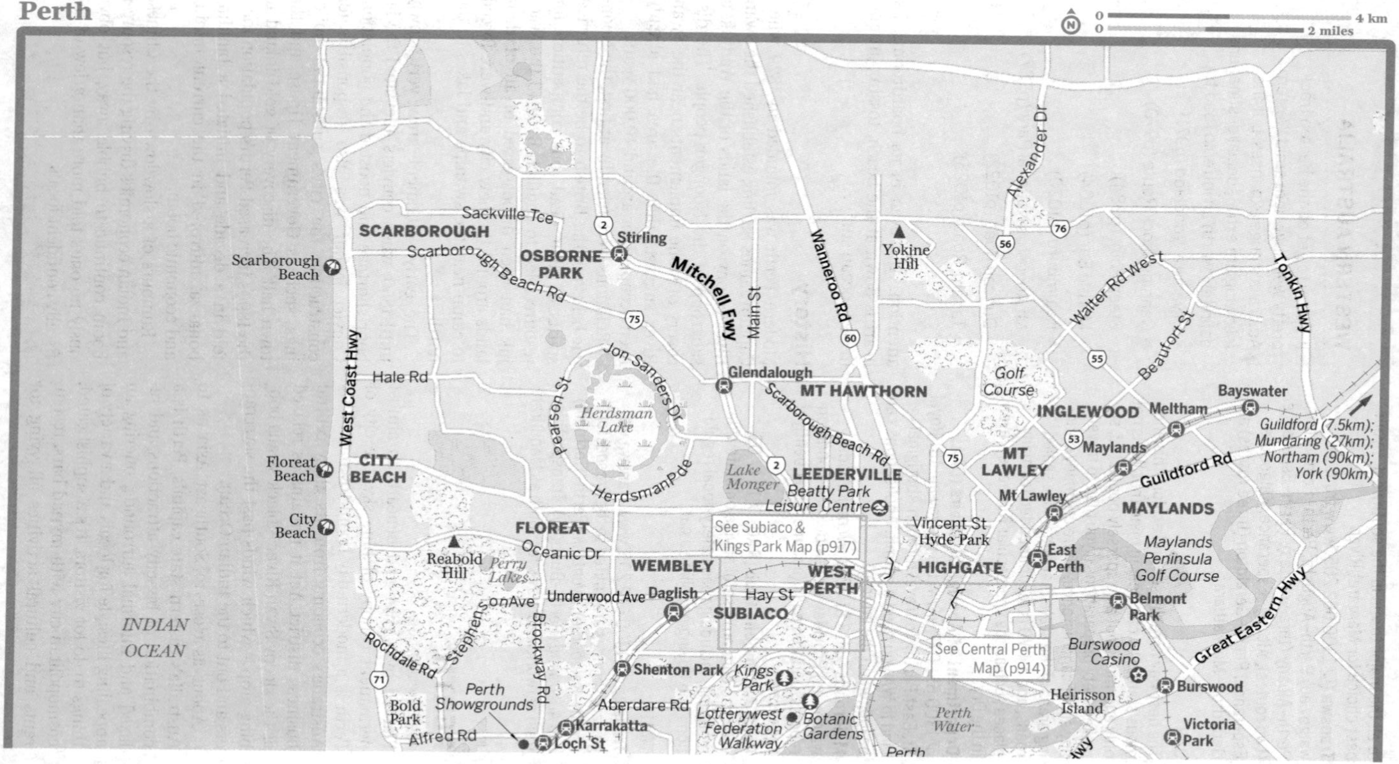
0 4 km
0 2 miles
INDIAN OCEAN
Scarborough Beach
Floreat Beach
City Beach
West Coast Hwy
SCARBOROUGH
Sackville Tce
Scarborough Beach Rd
OSBORNE PARK
Stirling
Mitchell Fwy
Main St
Wanneroo Rd
Yokine Hill
Alexander Dr
Walter Rd West
Beaufort St
Tonkin Hwy
Hale Rd
Jon Sanders Dr
Pearson St
Herdsman Lake
Herdsman Pde
Glendalough
MT HAWTHORN
Scarborough Beach Rd
Golf Course
INGLEWOOD
Meltham
Bayswater
Guildford (7.5km); Mundaring (27km); Northam (90km); York (90km)
Maylands
MT LAWLEY
Guildford Rd
CITY BEACH
Lake Monger
LEEDERVILLE
Beatty Park Leisure Centre
Mt Lawley
MAYLANDS
FLOREAT
Oceanic Dr
See Subiaco & Kings Park Map (p917)
Vincent St
Hyde Park
East Perth
Maylands Peninsula Golf Course
Reabold Hill
Perry Lakes
WEMBLEY
WEST PERTH
HIGHGATE
Underwood Ave
Daglish
Hay St
SUBIACO
Belmont Park
Stephenson Ave
Brockway Rd
Great Eastern Hwy
Rochdale Rd
Shenton Park
Kings Park
See Central Perth Map (p914)
Burswood Casino
Perth Showgrounds
Aberdare Rd
Heirisson Island
Burswood
Bold Park
Lotterywest Federation Walkway
Botanic Gardens
Perth Water
Victoria Park
Alfred Rd
Karrakatta
Loch St
Perth
Hwy

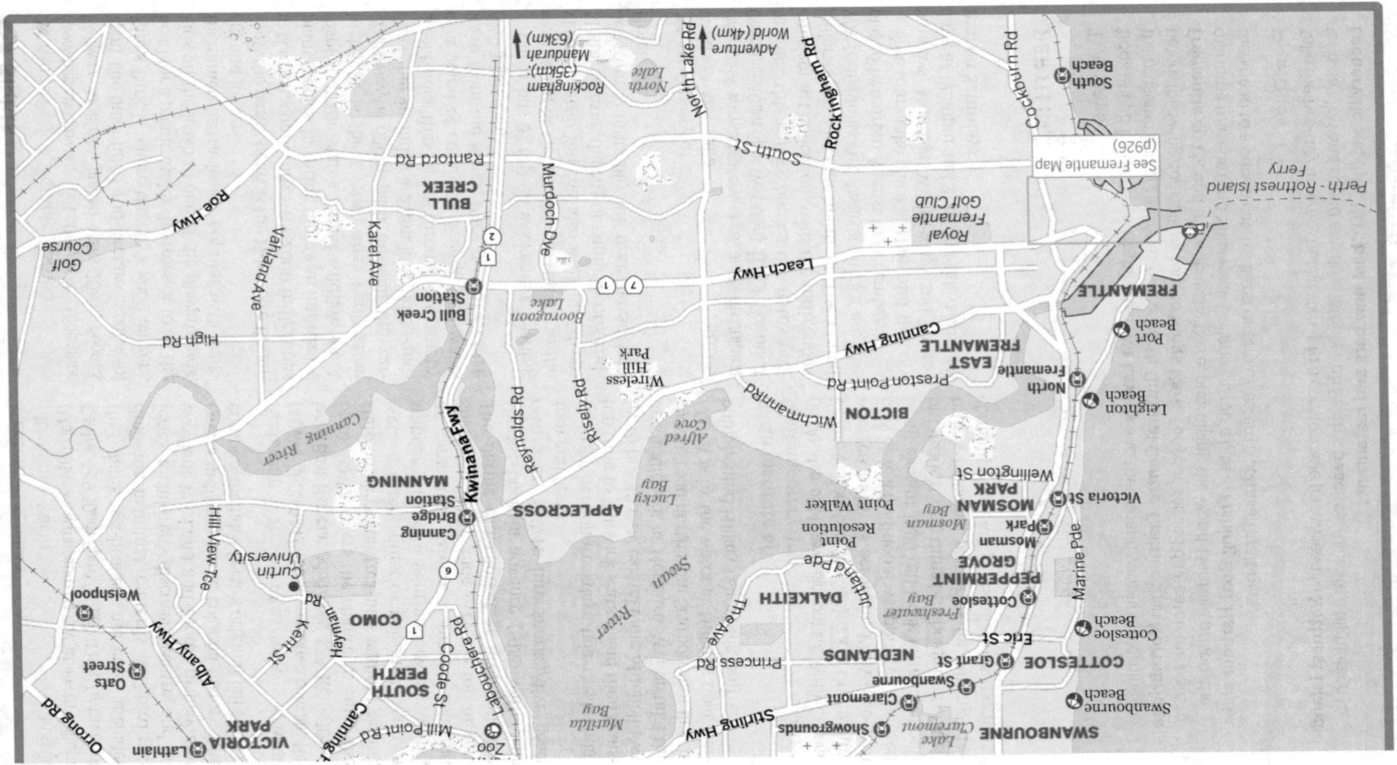
Orrong Rd
Lathlain
VICTORIA PARK
Oats Street
Welshpool
Albany Hwy
Canning Hwy
Mill Point Rd
SOUTH PERTH
Coode St
Labouchere Rd
Zoo
COMO
Hayman Rd
Kent St
Curtin University
Hill View Tce
Canning Bridge Station
MANNING
Canning River
Kwinana Fwy
APPLECROSS
Reynolds Rd
Risely Rd
Matilda Bay
Swan River
Lucky Bay
Alfred Cove
Wireless Hill Park
High Rd
Vahland Ave
Karel Ave
Golf Course
Roe Hwy
Bull Creek Station
BULL CREEK
Ranford Rd
Murdoch Dve
Booragoon Lake
Leach Hwy
Rockingham (35km); Mandurah (63km)
North Lake
North Lake Rd
Adventure World (4km)
Rockingham Rd
South St
Cockburn Rd
South Beach
See Fremantle Map (p926)
Perth - Rottnest Island Ferry
Royal Fremantle Golf Club
FREMANTLE
Port Beach
Canning Hwy
EAST FREMANTLE
North Fremantle
Preston Point Rd
Leighton Beach
Wichmann Rd
BICTON
Wellington St
MOSMAN PARK
Victoria St
Point Walker
Point Resolution
Mosman Bay
Mosman Park
Marine Pde
PEPPERMINT GROVE
Jutland Pde
DALKEITH
Cottesloe
Freshwater Bay
The Ave
Cottesloe Beach
Eric St
NEDLANDS
Princess Rd
Grant St
COTTESLOE
Swanbourne
Swanbourne Beach
Claremont
Stirling Hwy
Showgrounds
Lake Claremont
SWANBOURNE

Sights

★Kings Park & Botanic Garden PARK

(www.bgpa.wa.gov.au; Lotterywest Federation Walkway 9am-5pm, guided walks 10am, noon & 2pm) The bush-filled 400-hectare expanse of Kings Park is where the city's good citizens head for a picnic under the trees or to let the kids off the leash in one of the playgrounds. Its numerous tracks are popular with walkers and joggers.

At the park's heart is the 17-hectare Botanic Garden, containing over 2000 indigenous plant species. In spring there's an impressive display of the state's famed wildflowers. A highlight is the **Lotterywest Federation Walkway**, a 620m path through the gardens that includes a 222m-long, glass-and-steel bridge that passes through the canopy of a stand of eucalypts. Free guided walks leave from the **Kings Park Visitor Centre** (9.30am-4pm).

Catch bus 37 (39 on weekends), heading west along St Georges Tce (S-stand), to the visitor centre. You can also walk up (steep) Mount St from the city or climb Jacob's Ladder from Mounts Bay Rd, near the Adelphi Hotel.

★Art Gallery of Western Australia GALLERY

(Map p914; www.artgallery.wa.gov.au; Perth Cultural Centre; 10am-5pm Wed-Mon) FREE Founded in 1895, this gallery houses the state's pre-eminent art collection, with the indigenous galleries providing the highlight. The annual WA Indigenous Art Awards entries are displayed here from August to December.

Free tours take place at 11am and 1pm on Sundays, Mondays, Wednesdays and Thursdays, at 12.30pm and 2pm on Fridays, and at 1pm on Saturdays.

Western Australian Museum – Perth MUSEUM

(Map p914; www.museum.wa.gov.au; Perth Cultural Centre; 9.30am-5pm) FREE This branch of the state's six-headed museum includes dinosaur, mammal, butterfly and bird galleries, a children's discovery centre, and an excellent WA Land and People display that covers indigenous and colonial history. The complex includes Perth's original jail (1856).

Aquarium of Western Australia AQUARIUM

(AQWA; 08-9447 7500; www.aqwa.com.au; Hillarys Boat Harbour; adult/child $28/16; 10am-5pm) AQWA offers the chance to enjoy the state's underwater treasures without getting wet...or eaten, stung or poisoned. You can wander through a 98m underwater tunnel as gargantuan stingrays, turtles, fish and sharks stealthily glide over the top of you. The daring can snorkel or dive with the sharks; book in advance ($159 with your own gear; $20/40 hire snorkel/dive gear; 1pm and 3pm).

To get here on weekdays, take the Joondalup train to Warwick station and then transfer to bus 423. By car, take the Mitchell Fwy north and exit at Hepburn Ave, or take the coastal road north from Scarborough Beach. AQWA is by the water at Hillarys Boat Harbour, behind Hillarys shopping centre.

Perth Institute of Contemporary Arts GALLERY

(PICA; Map p914; www.pica.org.au; Perth Cultural Centre; 11am-6pm Tue-Sun) FREE Commonly referred to by its acronym, PICA (pee-kah) may have a traditional wrapping (it's housed in an elegant 1896 red-brick former school) but inside it's anything but, being one of Australia's principal platforms for cutting-edge contemporary art – installations, perform-

PERTH IN...

Two Days

Book ahead for dinner in **Highgate** or **Mt Lawley** and then spend your first morning in the museum and art galleries of the **Perth Cultural Centre**. Grab lunch in **Northbridge** before following our walking tour to **Kings Park**. For your second day, catch the train to **Fremantle** and spend the whole day there, prioritising the World-Heritage prison, the maritime museum and Shipwreck Galleries. Grab a bite in **Fishing Boat Harbour** and then head to a pub to catch a band or drink Western Australian craft beer.

Four Days

Take the two-day itinerary but stretch it to a comfortable pace. Head to **Rottnest Island** for a day trip and spend any time left over on Perth's **beaches**. Allocate a night each to **Leederville** and the CBD's **best new bars and restaurants**.

ance, sculpture, video works and the like. It actively promotes new and experimental art, and exhibits graduate works annually.

Bell Tower LANDMARK
(Map p914; www.thebelltower.com.au; adult/child $14/9; ⏲10am-4pm, ringing noon-1pm Sat-Tue & Thu) This pointy glass spire fronted by copper sails contains the royal bells of London's St Martin-in-the-Fields, the oldest of which dates to 1550. They were given to WA by the British government in 1988, and are the only set known to have left England. Clamber to the top for 360-degree views of Perth by the river.

Perth Mint HISTORIC BUILDING
(Map p914; www.perthmint.com.au; 310 Hay St; adult/child $15/5; ⏲9am-5pm) Dating from 1899, the oddly compelling mint displays a collection of coins, nuggets and gold bars. You can fondle a bar worth over $200,000, mint your own coins and watch gold pours (on the hour, starting 10am).

Swan Valley WINERIES, CRAFT BEER
Perthites visit this semirural valley on the city's eastern fringe to partake in booze, nosh and the great outdoors. Perhaps in a tacit acknowledgement that its wines will never compete with the state's more prestigious regions (it doesn't really have the ideal climate), the Swan Valley compensates with galleries, breweries, provedores and restaurants.

The gateway is National Trust–classified **Guildford**, established in 1829. Heritage buildings, one housing the **visitor centre** (☎08-9379 9400; www.swanvalley.com.au; Old Courthouse, cnr Swan & Meadow Sts; ⏲9am-4pm), make it the logical starting place for day trippers. Guildford is 12km from central Perth by suburban trains.

Cottesloe Beach BEACH
The safest swimming, cafes, pubs, pine trees and fantastic sunsets. From Cottesloe station (on the Fremantle line) it's 1km to the beach.

Activities

Kings Park has good bike tracks, and there are cycling routes along the Swan River to Fremantle and along the coast. Bikes can be taken free of charge on ferries any time and on trains outside weekday peak hours (7am to 9am and 4pm to 6.30pm). For route maps, see www.transport.wa.gov.au/cycling. Bike-hire options are listed here.

The whale-watching season runs from mid-September to early December.

Mills Charters WHALE WATCHING
(☎08-9246 5334; www.millscharters.com.au; adult/child $80/65) Informative three- to four-hour trip departing from Hillarys Boat Harbour at 9am on Wednesdays. See Aquarium of Western Australia review for information on getting to Hillarys Boat Harbour.

Surf Sail Australia WINDSURFING, KITESURFING
(Map p917; ☎1800 686 089; www.surfsailaustralia.com.au; 260 Railway Pde; ⏲10am-5pm Mon-Sat) When the afternoon sea breeze blusters in, windsurfers take to the Swan River, Leighton and beaches north of Perth. Hire or buy gear here.

Oceanic Cruises WHALE WATCHING
(Map p914; ☎08-9325 1191; www.whalewatching.com.au; adult/child $77/34) Departs Barrack St Jetty at 8.30am, returning at 5.45pm after spending the afternoon in Fremantle. Daily departures during the school holidays, otherwise Wednesday and Friday to Sunday only.

Cycle Centre BICYCLE RENTAL
(Map p914; ☎08-9325 1176; www.cyclecentre.com.au; 313 Hay St; per day/week $25/65; ⏲9am-5.30pm Mon-Fri, 9am-3pm Sat, 1-4pm Sun) See the website for recommended rides.

About Bike Hire BICYCLE RENTAL
(☎08-9221 2665; www.aboutbikehire.com.au; 1-7 Riverside Dr, Causeway Carpark; per day/week from $36/80; ⏲9am-5pm) Also hires kayaks ($16/65 per hour/day).

Gecko Bike Hire BICYCLE RENTAL
(☎0439 989 610; www.geckobikehire.com.au) Four locations around the city. See the website for route maps.

Australasian Diving Academy DIVING
(☎08-9389 5018; www.ausdiving.com.au; 142 Stirling Hwy) Hires diving gear (full set $75/200 per day/week) and offers diving courses (four-day open-water course $495). Sites in the vicinity include several around Rottnest Island and four wrecks.

Funcats SAILING
(☎0408 926 003; www.funcats.com.au; Coode St Jetty; per hr $40; ⏲Oct-Apr) These easy-to-sail catamarans are for hire on the South Perth foreshore. Each holds up to three people.

Surfschool SURFING
(☎08-9447 5637; www.surfschool.com; Scarborough Beach; adult/child $55/50) Two-hour

lessons at Scarborough Beach, including boards and wetsuits.

WA Skydiving Academy SKYDIVING
(☎1300 137 855; www.waskydiving.com.au; 458 William St; ⊙Mon-Thu) Tandem jumps from 8000/10,000/12,000ft from $300/340/380.

Tours

Indigenous Tours WA INDIGENOUS CULTURE
(www.indigenouswa.com) See Perth through the eyes of the local Wadjuk people. Options include the **Indigenous Heritage Tour** (☎08-9483 1106; adult/child $25/15; ⊙1.30pm) – a 90-minute guided walk around Kings Park – and an indigenous-themed stroll around Fremantle (p929).

Beer Nuts BREWERY TOUR
(☎08-9295 0605; www.beernuts.com.au) Visits five Swan Valley microbreweries and a rum distillery.

City Sightseeing Perth Tour BUS TOUR
(☎08-9203 8882; www.citysightseeingperth.com; adult/child $28/10) Hop-on, hop-off double-decker bus tour, with loop routes taking in the central city, Kings Park and the Burswood Entertainment Complex. Tickets are valid for two days. The Kings Park section can be purchased separately (adult/child $6/3).

Captain Cook Cruises CRUISE
(Map p914; ☎08-9325 3341; www.captaincook-cruises.com.au) Cruises to the Swan Valley or Fremantle.

Golden Sun Cruises CRUISE
(Map p914; ☎08-9325 9916; www.goldensuncruises.com.au) Cheaper and fewer frills than Captain Cook Cruises.

Out & About WINE TASTING
(☎08-9377 3376; www.outandabouttours.com.au) Wine-focused tours of the Swan Valley and historic Guildford.

Swan Valley Tours FOOD, WINE TASTING
(☎03-9274 1199; www.svtours.com.au) Food- and wine-driven tours.

Two Feet & A Heartbeat WALKING TOUR
(☎1800 459 388; www.twofeet.com.au; per person $40-50) Daytime walking tours of Perth, and a popular after-dark 'Small Bar Tour'.

Rottnest Air Taxi SCENIC FLIGHTS
(☎08-9292 5027; www.rottnest.de) Half-hour joy flights over the city, Kings Park and Fremantle ($88 to $115).

Festivals & Events

Perth Cup HORSE RACING
(www.perthracing.org.au) New Year's Day sees Perth's biggest day at the races.

Summadayze MUSIC
(www.summadayze.com) Electronic beeps and beats in early January.

Australia Day Skyworks NATIONAL HOLIDAY
(www.perth.wa.gov.au/skyworks) A day of family entertainment on 26 January, culminating in a 30-minute riverside firework display.

Big Day Out MUSIC
(www.bigdayout.com; Claremont Showgrounds) Australia's biggest music festival, attracts big-name alternative bands and local up-and-comers in early February.

Perth International Arts Festival ARTS
(www.perthfestival.com.au) Artists like Laurie Anderson and Philip Glass perform alongside top local talent. Held over 25 days from mid-February, it spans theatre, classical music, jazz, visual arts, dance, film and literature.

Good Vibrations MUSIC
(www.goodvibrationsfestival.com.au; Claremont Show-ground) One-day festival in late February featuring international acts.

Laneway MUSIC
(http://perth.lanewayfestival.com.au) In early February, Perth's skinny-jean hipsters party to the planet's up-and-coming indie acts.

Kings Park Festival WILDFLOWERS
(www.kingsparkfestival.com.au) Month-long festival including wildflowers, live music every Sunday, guided walks and talks.

Perth Royal Show AGRICULTURE
(www.perthroyalshow.com.au; Claremont Show-ground) A week of fun-fair rides, spun sugar and cute farm animals in late September.

Parklife MUSIC
(www.parklife.com.au; Wellington Sq) Danceable indie bands in late September.

Sleeping

Perth is very spread out, so choose your location carefully. Northbridge is best for those unperturbed by noise. On the other hand, the CBD and Northbridge are close to all forms of public transport, and hopping out to inner-city suburbs such as Leederville and Mt Lawley is simple. If you care most

PERTH FOR CHILDREN

With a usually clement climate and plenty of open spaces and beaches to run around on, Perth is a great place to bring children. Of the beaches, Cottesloe is the safest. If the kids are old enough, take advantage of the bike tracks that stretch along the river and the coast. Kings Park has playgrounds and walking tracks.

The Perth Royal Show (late September) is an ever-popular family outing, all sideshow rides, showbags and proudly displayed poultry. Many of Perth's big attractions cater well for young audiences, especially the Aquarium of Western Australia (AQWA), the WA Museum and the Art Gallery of Western Australia.

Part of the fun of **Perth Zoo** (www.perthzoo.wa.gov.au; 20 Labouchere Rd, South Perth; adult/child $28/14; ⊙9am-5pm) is getting there by ferry. **Scitech** (Map p917; www.scitech.org.au; Sutherland St, City West Centre; adult/child $14/9; ⊙10am-4pm) has over 160 hands-on, large-scale science and technology exhibits.

Adventure World (www.adventureworld.net.au; 179 Progress Dr; adult/child $51/43; ⊙10am-5pm Thu-Mon late Sep-early May, daily in school holidays & Dec) has rides, pools, waterslides and a castle. From Perth, exit the Kwinana Fwy at Farrington Rd, turn right and follow the signs.

At 26 sq km, **Whiteman Park** (www.whitemanpark.com; enter from Lord St or Beechboro Rd, West Swan; ⊙8.30am-6pm) is Perth's biggest, with over 30km of walkways and bike paths, and numerous picnic and barbecue spots. Within its ordered grounds are **Caversham Wildlife Park** (www.cavershamwildlife.com.au; adult/child $23/10; ⊙9am-5.30pm, last entry 4.30pm), **Bennet Brook Railway** (www.whitemanpark.com; adult/child $8/4; ⊙11am-1pm Wed, Thu, Sat & Sun), **tram rides** (www.pets.org.au; adult/child $5/2.50; ⊙noon-2pm Tue & Fri-Sun) and the **Motor Museum of WA** (www.motormuseumofwa.asn.au; adult/child $10/7; ⊙10am-4pm).

Look for the *LetsGoKids* (www.letsgokids.com.au) booklet at the WA Visitor Centre (p924) for loads more kid-friendly information.

for the beach consider staying there, as public transport can be time-consuming.

Fuelled by the ongoing mining boom, Perth is an expensive town for accommodation. Book as early as you can, and note that many hotels are significantly cheaper from Friday to Sunday compared to Monday to Thursday. B&Bs are usually better value than hotels, and another option is to base yourself in better-value Fremantle.

City Centre

Wickham Retreat HOSTEL $
(Map p914; ☎08-9325 6398; www.facebook.com/WickhamRetreatBackpackers; 25-27 Wickham St; dm $35-40, d $70-100; @ 🛜) Located in a residential neighbourhood east of the city centre, Wickham Retreat has a quieter vibe compared to other hostels around town. Most of the guests are international travellers, drawn by the colourful rooms and dorms, and a funky AstroTurf garden.

Perth City YHA HOSTEL $
(Map p914; ☎08-9287 3333; www.yha.com.au; 300 Wellington St; dm $39, r with/without bathroom $120/95; ❄@🛜🏊) Occupying an impressive 1940s art-deco building by the train tracks, the centrally located YHA has a slight boarding-school feel in the corridors, but the rooms are clean and there are good facilities including a gym.

Regal Apartments APARTMENT $$
(Map p914; ☎08-9221 8614; www.regalapartments.com.au; 11 Regal Pl; apt from $230; ❄@) Tucked in behind good-value Asian restaurants east of the city centre, these one- and two-bedroom apartments are spacious and modern. Fully equipped kitchens make them ideal for families watching their dollars.

Medina Executive Barrack Plaza APARTMENT $$
(Map p914; ☎08-9267 0000; www.medina.com.au; 138 Barrack St; apt from $229; ❄🏊) The Medina's meticulously decorated apartment-sized rooms are minimalist yet welcoming. All one-bedrooms have balconies, and rooms on Barrack St have more natural light.

Riverview on Mount Street APARTMENT $$
(Map p914; ☎08-9321 8963; www.riverviewperth.com.au; 42 Mount St; apt from $140; ❄@🛜)

Central Perth

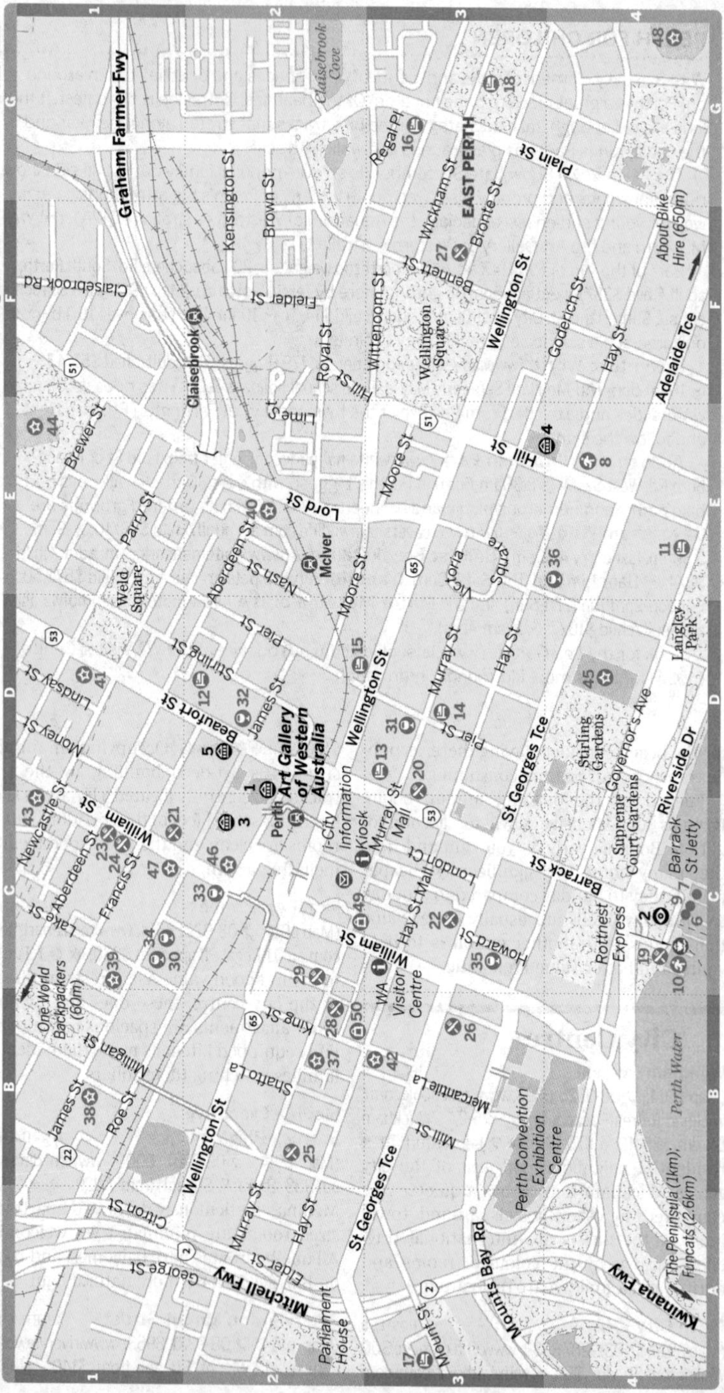

Central Perth

Top Sights
1 Art Gallery of Western Australia D2

Sights
2 Bell Tower C4
3 Perth Institute of Contemporary Arts C2
4 Perth Mint E4
5 Western Australian Museum – Perth D2

Activities, Courses & Tours
6 Captain Cook Cruises C4
7 Captain Cook Cruises C4
8 Cycle Centre E4
9 Golden Sun Cruises C4
10 Oceanic Cruises C4

Sleeping
11 City Waters E4
12 Emperor's Crown D2
13 Medina Executive Barrack Plaza D3
14 Pensione Hotel D3
15 Perth City YHA D2
16 Regal Apartments G3
17 Riverview on Mount Street A3
18 Wickham Retreat G3

Eating
19 Annalakshmi C4
20 Cabin Fever D3
21 Flipside C1
22 Greenhouse C3
23 La Cholita C1
24 Little Willy's C1
25 Mama Tran B2
26 Print Hall B3
27 Restaurant Amusé F3
28 Tiger, Tiger B2
29 Venn Cafe & Bar C2
Viet Hoa .... (see 43)

Drinking & Nightlife
30 Air C1
31 Ambar D3
Bird .... (see 33)
Cheeky Sparrow .... (see 28)
32 Court D2
33 Ezra Pound C2
34 Geisha C1
Greenhouse .... (see 22)
35 Helvetica C3
36 Hula Bula Bar E4
Mechanics Institute .... (see 21)
Wolfe Lane .... (see 28)

Entertainment
37 Amplifier B2
38 Bakery B1
39 Cinema Paradiso C1
40 Devilles Pad E2
41 Ellington Jazz Club D1
42 His Majesty's Theatre B3
43 Moon C1
44 NIB Stadium E1
45 Perth Concert Hall D4
46 State Theatre Centre C2
47 Universal C1
48 WACA G4

Shopping
49 78 Records C2
Perth Map Centre .... (see 49)
Pigeonhole .... (see 20)
50 Wheels & Doll Baby B2

There's a lot of brash new money up here on Mount St, but character-filled Riverview stands out as the best personality on the block. Its refurbished 1960s bachelor pads sit neatly atop a modern foyer and a relaxed cafe.

Pensione Hotel BOUTIQUE HOTEL $$
(Map p914; ☎08-9325 2133; www.pensione.com.au; 70 Pier St; d from $155; ❄ ☜) The Pensione's standard rooms veer to cosy and (very) compact, but classy decor and a good location are two definite pluses in an expensive city.

City Waters MOTEL $$
(Map p914; ☎08-9325 1566; www.citywaters.com.au; 118 Terrace Rd; s/d $130/150; ❄) Rooms are small, simple and face onto the car park, but they're clean, airy and the waterfront location is top-notch. Top-floor rooms are best; river views exist but are difficult to secure.

Northbridge, Highgate & Mt Lawley

Most of Perth's hostels are in Northbridge, and it's possible to walk around and inspect rooms before putting your money down.

Emperor's Crown HOSTEL $
(Map p914; ☎08-9227 1400; www.emperorscrown.com.au; 85 Stirling St; dm $36, r with/without bathroom from $130/110; ❄ @ ☜) One of Perth's best hostels has a great position (close to the Northbridge scene without being in the thick of it), friendly staff and high housekeeping standards.

Witch's Hat HOSTEL $
(☎08-9228 4228; www.witchs-hat.com; 148 Palmerston St; dm/tw/d $34/88/99; ❄@📶) Housed in an interesting 1897 building, Witch's Hat has light and spacious dorms, and there's a red-brick barbecue area out the back.

One World Backpackers HOSTEL $
(☎08-9228 8206; www.oneworldbackpackers.com.au; 162 Aberdeen St; dm $28-30, d $80; @) 🍃 Polished floorboards beam brightly in all the rooms of this nicely restored old house. Dorms are big and sunny, and the kitchen is large and functional.

Durack House B&B $$
(☎08-9370 4305; www.durackhouse.com.au; 7 Almondbury Rd; r inc breakfast $195-215; 📶) Set on a peaceful suburban street, the three rooms here have plenty of old-world charm, paired with modern bathrooms. It's only 250m from Mt Lawley station; turn left onto Railway Pde and then first right.

Pension of Perth B&B $$
(☎08-9228 9049; www.pensionperth.com.au; 3 Throssell St; s/d inc breakfast from $150/165; 🚭❄@📶) Pension of Perth's French belle-époque style lays luxury on thick: *chaise longues*, rich floral rugs, heavy brocade curtains, open fireplaces and gold-framed mirrors. Two doubles with bay windows (and small bathrooms) look out onto the park, and there are two rooms with spa baths. It's adjacent to gorgeous Hyde Park.

Above Bored B&B $$
(☎08-9444 5455; www.abovebored.com.au; 14 Norham St; d inc breakfast $190-200; ❄📶) In a quiet residential neighbourhood, this 1927 Federation house is owned by a friendly TV scriptwriter. Two themed rooms in the main house have eclectic decor, there's also a cosy self-contained cottage with a kitchenette.

Subiaco & Kings Park

★ **Eight Nicholson** BOUTIQUE HOTEL $$$
(☎08-9382 1881; www.8nicholson.com.au; 8 Nicholson Rd; r inc breakfast from $369; ❄📶) This stylish heritage house is one part luxury boutique hotel and one part welcoming B&B. Hip but elegant decor and interesting artworks are evidence of the well-travelled owners' eclectic tastes

Richardson HOTEL $$$
(Map p917; ☎08-9217 8888; www.therichardson.com.au; 32 Richardson St; r from $520; ❄📶🏊) The Richardson offers luxurious rooms, and the whole complex has a breezy, summery feel, with pale marble tiles, creamy walls and interesting art. There's also an in-house spa centre.

Beaches

Ocean Beach Backpackers HOSTEL $
(☎08-9384 5111; www.oceanbeachbackpackers.com; 1 Eric St; dm/s/d $26/70/80; @📶) Offering (some) ocean views, this big, bright hostel in the heart of Cottesloe is just a short skip from the sand. Hire a bike, or use the hostel's free bodyboards and surfboards.

Trigg Retreat B&B $$
(☎08-9447 6726; www.triggretreat.com; 59 Kitchener St; r inc breakfast $190; ❄@📶) Quietly classy, this three-room B&B offers attractive and comfortable queen bedrooms in a modern house a short drive from Trigg Beach.

Other Areas

Discovery Holiday Parks – Perth CAMPGROUND $
(☎08-9453 6877; www.discoveryholidayparks.com.au; 186 Hale Rd; powered sites for 2 people $38-45, units $125-187; ❄@📶🏊) This well-kept holiday park, 15km out of the city, has a wide range of cabins and smart-looking units, many with decks, TVs and DVD players.

Peninsula APARTMENT $$
(☎08-9368 6688; www.thepeninsula.net; 53 South Perth Esplanade; apt from $205; ❄@📶) While only the front few apartments have full-on views, the Peninsula's waterfront location lends itself to lazy ferry rides and sunset riverside strolls. It's a sprawling, older-style complex but kept in good nick.

Eating

While Australia's other state capitals might have few top restaurants charging over $40 a main, in Perth those prices are fast becoming the norm for any establishment that considers itself above average.

Unfortunately, the experience doesn't always match the outlay, and inferior and lax service is more prevalent than it should be. It's still possible to eat cheaply, especially in the Little Asia section of William St, Northbridge. Many restaurants are BYO (bring your own wine; check first). Cafes are good places to go for a midrange meal.

Some establishments listed under Drinking & Nightlife blur the line between bar, cafe and restaurant, and offer good dining as well.

City Centre

Mama Tran VIETNAMESE $

(Map p914; www.mamatran.com.au; 36-40 Milligan St; snacks & mains $8-12; ⏲7am-4pm) The hip Mama Tran does hearty bowls of *pho* (Viet-

Subiaco & Kings Park

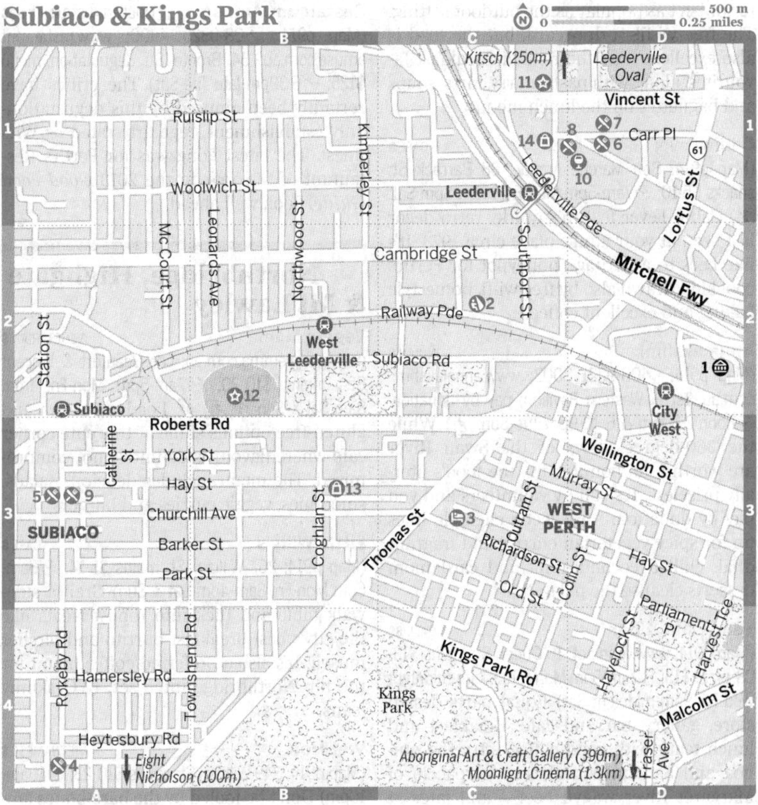

Subiaco & Kings Park

Sights
1 Scitech D2

Activities, Courses & Tours
2 Surf Sail Australia C2

Sleeping
3 Richardson C3

Eating
4 Boucla A4
5 Chutney Mary's A3
6 Duende D1
7 Sayers D1
8 Snags & Sons D1
9 Subiaco Hotel A3

Drinking & Nightlife
10 Honey Lounge D1

Entertainment
11 Luna C1
12 Patersons Stadium B2

Shopping
Atlas Divine .... (see 14)
13 Indigenart B3
14 Oxford St Books C1

namese noodle soup), excellent coffee, fresh rice-paper rolls, and Asian salads.

Tiger, Tiger CAFE $
(Map p914; ☎08-9322 8055; www.tigertigercoffee-bar.com; Murray Mews; mains $8-20; ⊙7am-5pm Mon & Sat, to 8pm Tue-Thu, to midnight Fri; 📶) In a laneway off Murray St, the shabby-chic interior isn't as popular as the outdoor setting. The free wi-fi's a drawcard, but the food is also excellent – all the regular breakfast favourites, along with pasta, curry, tarts, soups and baguettes on the lunch menu.

Cabin Fever CAFE $
(Map p914; Bon Marche Arcade, 88 Barrack St; snacks $5-10; ⊙7am-5pm Mon-Fri, 10am-5pm Sat; 📶) Cabin Fever features quirky retro decor last seen at your aunt's place circa 1973. It's like bees to a heritage honeypot for Perth's cool kids, drawn also by free wi-fi, homestyle baking and excellent coffee.

Annalakshmi INDIAN $
(Map p914; ☎08-9221 3003; www.annalakshmi.com.au; 1st fl, Western Pavilion; pay by donation; ⊙noon-2.30pm & 6.30-9pm Tue-Sun; 🌶) While the 360-degree views of the Swan River are worth a million dollars, the food's literally priceless. It's run by volunteers and you pay by donation. An eclectic clientele lines up for spicy vegetarian curries and fragrant dhal, chilled coconut-milk and cardamom desserts cleanse the palate.

Venn Cafe & Bar CAFE $$
(Map p914; www.venn.net; 16 Queen St; mains $13-28, pizza $15; ⊙7am-5pm Mon & Tue, 7am-midnight Wed-Fri, 9am-midnight Sat) Equal parts design store, gallery, bar and cafe. Breakfast and lunch team with good coffee – try the quinoa and banana pancakes or carpaccio of Margaret River wagyu beef – and later at night pizza and charcuterie combine with wine and craft beers from around Australia.

★**Greenhouse** TAPAS $$
(Map p914; ☎08-9481 8333; www.greenhouseperth.com; 100 St Georges Tce; tapas $10-19; ⊙7am-midnight Mon-Sat) 🍃 Ground-breaking design combines with excellent food at this hip tapas-style eatery. Asian and Middle Eastern influences inform a sustainably sourced menu including spiced lamb with yoghurt and quinoa, or lamb with pistachio and pomegranate.

Print Hall ASIAN, MODERN AUSTRALIAN $$$
(Map p914; www.printhall.com.au; 125 St Georges Tce; snacks $10-18, mains $25-45; ⊙noon-midnight Mon-Fri, 4pm-midnight Sat) This sprawling complex in the Brookfield Pl precinct includes the Apple Daily, featuring Southeast Asian-style street food, and the expansive Print Hall Dining Room, with an oyster bar and grilled WA meat and seafood. Don't miss having a drink in the rooftop Bob's Bar.

Restaurant Amusé MODERN AUSTRALIAN $$$
(Map p914; ☎08-9325 4900; www.restaurantamuse.com.au; 64 Bronte St; degustation menu $125; ⊙6.30pm-late Tue-Sat) The critics have certainly been amused by this degustation-only establishment, regularly rated as WA's finest. The latest gong was for Perth's Restaurant of the Year in the 2013 *Good Food Guide*. Book well ahead.

Northbridge, Highgate & Mt Lawley

Veggie Mama VEGETARIAN $
(www.veggiemma.com.au; cnr Beaufort & Vincent Sts; mains $10-20; ⊙7am-5pm Mon-Fri, from 8am Sat & Sun; 📶🌶) 🍃 Loads of vegan and gluten-free options shine at this cute corner cafe where flavour is definitely not compromised. The menu includes delicious salads, smoothies, veggie curries and burgers.

Little Willy's CAFE $
(Map p914; 267 William St; mains $5-14; ⊙6am-6pm Mon-Fri, 8am-4pm Sat & Sun) Grab a sidewalk table and tuck into robust treats like the city's best breakfast burrito and bircher museli. It's also a preferred coffee haunt for the hip Northbridge indie set. BYO skinny jeans.

Viet Hoa VIETNAMESE $
(Map p914; 349 William St; mains $10-23; ⊙10am-10pm) Don't be fooled by the bare-bones ambience of this corner Vietnamese restaurant – or you'll miss out on the fresh rice-paper rolls and top-notch *pho* (noodle soup).

Flipside BURGERS $
(Map p914; www.flipsideburgerbar.com.au; 222 William St; burgers $10.50-14.50; ⊙11.30am-10pm Tue-Sat, to 9pm Sun) Gourmet burgers with the option of takeout, upstairs to the Mechanics Institute (p920).

★**Cantina 663** MEDITERRANEAN $$
(☎08-9370 4883; www.cantina663.com; 663 Beaufort St; mains lunch $12-28, dinner $26-34; ⊙8am-late Mon-Sat, to 3pm Sun) Spanish, Portuguese and Italian flavours all feature at this chic but casual cantina. Service can be a bit too

cool for school, but it's worth waiting for dishes like Ortiz anchovies with lemon and charred bread.

La Cholita MEXICAN $$
(Map p914; cnr Aberdeen & William Sts; snacks $6-12, mains $26-28; ⏲5pm-late Wed-Sun) La Cholita's energetic combo of Mexican street food, ice-cold *cerveza* (beer) and gutsy tequilas is *muchas* fun. Don't come expecting a quiet romantic evening – you may have to share tables – and there are no reservations, so try and come early in the night.

Beaufort St Merchant CAFE $$
(☎08-9328 6299; www.beaufortmerchant.com; 488 Beaufort St; breakfast $13-22, mains lunch & dinner $24-37; ⏲7am-10pm) Our favourite cafe in Mt Lawley, especially for a leisurely breakfast over the papers and a couple of coffees. Go for the chorizo and manchego-cheese tortilla, and work out what you'd order if you came back for dinner.

★**Namh Thai** THAI $$$
(☎08-9328 7500; 223 Bulwer St; mains $22-40; ⏲6-10pm Mon-Sat) Namh Thai experiments with interesting taste combinations – duck with lychees is the speciality – and serves them in an elegant candlelit dining room. Fridays and Saturdays are given over to banquet-style dining.

Must Winebar FRENCH $$$
(☎08-9328 8255; www.must.com.au; 519 Beaufort St; mains $39-46; ⏲noon-midnight) Not content with being Perth's best wine bar, Must is one of its best restaurants as well. The Gallic vibe is hip, slick and a little bit cheeky, and the menu marries classic French bistro flavours with the best local produce.

Mt Hawthorn & Leederville

Snags & Sons FAST FOOD $
(Map p917; www.snagsandsons.com.au; 749 Newcastle St; sausages $5-10; ⏲11am-10pm Tue-Sat, to 9pm Sun & Mon) It's sausage heaven at Snags & Sons. Tasty spins on the humble snarler – often made from free-range and organic produce – include smoked cheese kransky, Thai red curry or North African lamb. Healthy single-serve salads are also available.

Kitsch ASIAN $$
(www.kitschbar.com.au; 229 Oxford St; small plates $5-19; ⏲5pm-midnight Tue-Sat) Southeast Asian-style street food, Thai beers and an eclectic garden make Kitsch a great spot for a few laid-back hours of tasty grazing. Standout dishes include the son-in-law eggs with tamarind and pork crackling, or the five-spice pork with plums and ginger chilli caramel.

★**Duende** TAPAS $$
(Map p917; ☎08-9228 0123; www.duende.com.au; 662 Newcastle St; tapas & mains $14-29; ⏲7.30am-late) Stellar modern-accented tapas are served, so make a meal of it or call in for a late-night glass of dessert wine and *churros* (Spanish doughnuts). We're also partial to Duende's crab and chorizo omelette for brunch.

Sayers CAFE $$
(Map p917; www.sayersfood.com.au; 224 Carr Pl; mains $10-27; ⏲7am-3pm) This classy cafe has a counter groaning under the weight of an alluring cake selection. The breakfast menu includes eggy treats like a beetroot-cured salmon omelette, and lunch highlights include a zingy calamari, watermelon and fresh mint salad.

Divido ITALIAN $$$
(☎08-9443 7373; www.divido.com.au; 170 Scarborough Beach Rd; mains $33-39, 6-course degustation $95; ⏲6pm-late Mon-Sat) Italian but not rigidly so (the chef's of Croatian extraction), this romantic restaurant serves handmade pasta dishes and delicately flavoured mains. Good-value 'Champagne Mondays' feature three courses and a glass of bubbles for $65.

Subiaco & Kings Park

Boucla CAFE $
(Map p917; www.boucla.com; 349 Rokeby Rd; mains $11-22; ⏲7am-5pm Mon-Fri, to 3.30pm Sat) This Greek- and Levantine-infused haven is pleasingly isolated from the thick of the Rokeby Rd action. Baklava and cakes tempt you from the corner, and huge tarts filled with blue-vein cheese and roast vegetables spill off plates.

Subiaco Hotel GASTROPUB $$
(Map p917; ☎08-9381 3069; www.subiacohotel.com.au; 465 Hay St; mains $19-34; ⏲7am-late) The Subi's buzzy dining room showcases classy fare including Asian-inspired pork belly, perfectly cooked steaks, and excellent fish dishes.

Chutney Mary's INDIAN $$
(Map p917; www.chutneymarys.com.au; 67 Rokeby Rd; mains $15-28; ⊙noon-2.30pm Mon-Sat, 5.30pm-late daily; ✎) The feisty, authentic Indian food here is much loved by locals, and there are loads of vegetarian favourites.

Drinking & Nightlife

Licences to sell alcohol in WA were once tightly restricted and expensive. To recoup the investment, big booze barns became the norm. A recent law change has seen quirky small bars sprouting up all over the place, including in the formerly deserted-after-dark central city. Northbridge also has more idiosyncratic drinking establishments.

One of the by-products of the mining boom has been the rise of the Cashed-Up Bogan (CUB) – young men with plenty of cash to splash on muscle cars, beer and drugs. A spate of fights and glassings in bars has caused many venues, particularly around Northbridge, to step up security. Most pubs now have lockouts, so you'll need to be in before midnight in order to gain entry. You may need to present photo ID to obtain entry, and you should keep your wits about you in pubs and on the streets after dark.

City Centre

Greenhouse COCKTAIL BAR
(Map p914; www.greenhouseperth.com; 100 St Georges Tce; ⊙7am-midnight Mon-Sat) In a city so in love with the great outdoors, it's surprising that nobody's opened a rooftop bar in the central city before now. Hip, eco-conscious Greenhouse is leading the way, mixing up a storm amid the greenery with great cocktails and an interesting beer and wine list.

Helvetica BAR
(Map p914; www.helveticabar.com.au; rear 101 St Georges Tce; ⊙3pm-midnight Tue-Thu, noon-midnight Fri, 6pm-midnight Sat) Clever artsy types tap their toes to alternative pop in this bar named after a typeface and specialising in whisky and cocktails. The concealed entry is off Howard St: look for the chandelier in the lane behind Andaluz tapas bar.

Wolfe Lane COCKTAIL BAR
(Map p914; www.wolfelane.com.au; Wolfe Lane; ⊙4pm-midnight Tue-Sat) Exposed bricks, classic retro furniture and high ceilings create a pretty decent WA approximation of a New York loft. A serious approach to cocktails and wine combines with an eclectic beer selection, and bar snacks include shared plates of cheese and chorizo.

Cheeky Sparrow BAR, CAFE
(Map p914; www.cheekysparrow.com.au; 1/317 Murray St; ⊙11.30am-late Tue-Fri, from 4pm Sat) Cheeky Sparrow's multi-level labyrinth of leather banquettes and bentwood chairs is great for everything from brunch and coffee through to pizza and cheese and charcuterie plates. If you're feeling peckish later at night, pop in for robust bar snacks including chorizo croquettes and chickpea fritters. Access is via Wolfe Lane.

Hula Bula Bar COCKTAIL BAR
(Map p914; www.hulabulabar.com; 12 Victoria Ave; ⊙4pm-midnight Wed-Fri, 6pm-1am Sat; 📶) This tiny Polynesian-themed bar is decked out in bamboo, palm leaves and tikis. A cool but relaxed crowd jams in to sip ostentatious cocktails out of ceramic monkey's heads.

Air CLUB
(Map p914; www.airclub.com.au; 139 James St; ⊙from 9pm Fri & Sat) Nonstop house, techno and trance.

Ambar CLUB
(Map p914; www.boomtick.com.au/ambar; 104 Murray St; ⊙10pm-5am Fri & Sat) Perth's premier club for breakbeat, drum 'n' bass and visiting international DJs.

Geisha CLUB
(Map p914; www.geishabar.com.au; 135a James St; ⊙11pm-6am Fri & Sat) A small-and-pumping DJ-driven, gay-friendly club.

Northbridge, Highgate & Mt Lawley

Northbridge is the rough-edged hub of Perth's nightlife, with dozens of pubs and clubs clustered mainly around William and James Sts. It's so popular, it even has its own website (www.onwilliam.com.au). A few recent openings have lifted the tone of the area.

★**Mechanics Institute** BAR
(Map p914; www.mechanicsinstitutebar.com.au; 222 William St; ⊙noon-midnight Tue-Sun) Negotiate the laneway entrance around the corner on James St to discover one of Perth's most down-to-earth small bars. Share one of the big tables on the deck or nab a stool by the

bar. You can also order in a gourmet burger from Flipside (p918) downstairs.

Five Bar CRAFT BEER, CAFE
(www.fivebar.com.au; 560 Beaufort St; ⊙11am-midnight) More than 50 international and Australian craft beers – and a few interesting ciders – make Mt Lawley's Five Bar worth seeking out by the discerning drinker. Wine lovers are also well catered for, and the menu leans towards classy comfort food.

Ezra Pound BAR
(Map p914; www.epbar.com.au; 189 William St; ⊙1pm-midnight Thu-Tue) Down a much graffitied lane leading off William St, Ezra Pound is favoured by Northbridge's bohemian set. Earnest conversations about Kerouac and Kafka are strictly optional.

Brisbane PUB
(www.thebrisbanehotel.com.au; 292 Beaufort St; ⊙11.30am-late) This classic corner pub (1898) is now a thoroughly modern venue, where each space seamlessly blends into the next. Best of all is the large courtyard where the phoenix palms and ponds provide a balmy holiday feel.

399 BAR
(www.399bar.com; 399 William St; ⊙10am-midnight Mon-Sat, to 10pm Sun; 📶) This friendly neighbourhood bar has artfully crafted cocktails, and there's a serious approach to beer and wine. Good-value tapas are three for $19, and 399 is also a good espresso and wi-fi stop during the day.

Bird BAR
(Map p914; www.williamstreetbird.com; 181 William St; ⊙1pm-midnight) Grungy indie bar that's always worth a look for local bands and DJs. Upstairs there's a brick-lined deck with city views.

Flying Scotsman PUB
(www.theflyingscotsman.com.au; 639 Beaufort St; ⊙11am-midnight) Old-style pub that attracts the Beaufort St indie crowd. A good spot before a gig up the road at the Astor.

Court BAR
(Map p914; www.thecourt.com.au; 50 Beaufort St; ⊙noon-midnight Sun-Thu, to 2am Fri & Sat) A large, rambling complex consisting of an old corner pub and a big, partly covered courtyard with a clubby atmosphere. Wednesday is drag night, with kings and queens holding court in front of a young crowd.

Velvet Lounge BAR
(www.theflyingscotsman.com.au; 639 Beaufort St) Out the back of the Flying Scotsman (p921) is this lounge with ska, punk and indie beats. Upstairs, the Defectors bar channels cocktails and chilled dub and dance beats.

Subiaco & Kings Park

Honey Lounge BAR
(Map p917; 663 Newcastle St; ⊙Tue-Sun) Ladies only on Queen Bee nights the first Thursday of every month.

Beaches

Cottesloe Beach Hotel PUB
(www.cottesloebeachhotel.com.au; 104 Marine Pde; ⊙11am-midnight Mon-Sat, to 10pm Sun) Grab a spot on the lawn in the massive beer garden, or watch the sun set from the balcony. A recent trendy makeover has installed a specialist craft beer bar downstairs.

☆ Entertainment

Live Music

Ellington Jazz Club LIVE MUSIC
(Map p914; www.ellingtonjazz.com.au; 191 Beaufort St; ⊙7pm-1am Mon-Thu, to 3am Fri & Sat, 5pm-midnight Sun) Live jazz nightly in this handsome, intimate venue.

Bakery LIVE MUSIC
(Map p914; www.nowbaking.com.au; 233 James St; ⊙7pm-late) Popular indie gigs are held almost every weekend.

Amplifier LIVE MUSIC
(Map p914; www.amplifiercapitol.com.au; rear 383 Murray St) Live (mainly indie) bands. Adjacent is Capitol, used mainly for DJ gigs.

Moon LIVE MUSIC
(Map p914; www.themoon.com.au; 323 William St; ⊙6pm-late Mon-Tue, 11am-late Wed-Sun) Low-key, late-night cafe with singer-songwriters on Wednesdays, jazz on Thursdays, and poetry on Saturday afternoons.

Universal LIVE MUSIC
(Map p914; www.universalbar.com.au; 221 William St; ⊙7am-late) Much-loved by jazz and blues enthusiasts.

Rosemount Hotel LIVE MUSIC
(www.rosemounthotel.com.au; cnr Angove & Fitzgerald Sts; ⊙noon-late) Local and international bands.

Astor CONCERT VENUE
(www.liveattheastor.com.au; 659 Beaufort St) Local and international bands in glorious art-deco surroundings.

Cabaret & Comedy

Devilles Pad CABARET
(Map p914; www.devillespad.com; 3 Aberdeen St; ⌚6pm-midnight Thu, to 2am Fri & Sat) The devil goes to Vegas disguised as a 1950s lounge lizard in this extremely kooky venue. Punters are encouraged to dress to match the camp interiors (complete with erupting volcano). Burlesque dancers, live bands and assorted sideshow freaks provide the entertainment, and good food is available.

Lazy Susan's Comedy Den COMEDY
(www.lazysusans.com.au; The Brisbane, 292 Beaufort St; ⌚8.30pm Tue, Fri & Sat) Tuesdays offers a mix of first-timers, seasoned amateurs and pros trying out new shtick, Friday is for more established stand-ups, and Saturday is the Big Hoohaa – a team-based comedy wrassle.

Theatre & Classical Music

Check the *West Australian* newspaper for listings. Book through www.ticketek.com.au.

State Theatre Centre THEATRE
(Map p914; www.statetheatrecentrewa.com.au; 174 William St) Includes the Heath Ledger Theatre and the smaller Studio Underground, and home to the Black Swan State Theatre Company and Perth Theatre Company.

His Majesty's Theatre THEATRE
(Map p914; www.hismajestystheatre.com.au; 825 Hay St) Home to the **West Australian Ballet** (www.waballet.com.au) and **West Australian Opera** (www.waopera.asn.au).

Perth Concert Hall CONCERT HALL
(Map p914; www.perthconcerthall.com.au; 5 St Georges Tce) Home to the **Western Australian Symphony Orchestra** (WASO; www.waso.com.au).

Cinema

Somerville Auditorium CINEMA
(www.perthfestival.com.au; 35 Stirling Hwy; ⌚Dec-Mar) The Perth Festival's film program is held on beautiful grounds surrounded by pine trees.

Luna CINEMA
(Map p917; www.lunapalace.com.au; 155 Oxford St) Art-house cinema with Monday double features.

Cinema Paradiso CINEMA
(Map p914; www.lunapalace.com.au; 164 James St) Art-house cinema.

Moonlight Cinema CINEMA
(www.moonlight.com.au; Synergy Parklands, Kings Park) Summer only.

Camelot Outdoor Cinema CINEMA
(www.lunapalace.com.au; 16 Lochee St, Memorial Hall; ⌚Dec-Easter) Seated open-air cinema in Mosman Park.

Sport

In WA 'football' means Aussie Rules and during the AFL (Australian Football League) season it's hard to get locals to talk about anything but the two local teams – the **West Coast Eagles** (www.westcoasteagles.com.au) and the **Fremantle Dockers** (www.fremantlefc.com.au). The *West Australian* has details of all sports games.

Patersons Stadium FOOTBALL
(Subiaco Oval; Map p917; ☎08-9381 2187; www.patersonsstadium.com.au; 250 Roberts Rd) The home of Aussie Rules and huge concerts.

WACA CRICKET
(Western Australian Cricket Association; Map p914; ☎08-9265 7222; www.waca.com.au; Nelson Cres) Test and state cricket.

NIB Stadium SOCCER, RUGBY
(Perth Oval; Map p914; www.nibstadium.com.au; Lord St) Both the **Perth Glory** (www.perthglory.com.au) soccer (football) team and the **Western Force** (www.westernforce.com.au) Super 15 rugby union team play here, and it's the home of WA rugby league.

Challenge Stadium NETBALL
(www.venueswest.wa.gov.au; Stephenson Ave, Mt Claremont) Home to the **West Coast Fever** (www.westcoastfever.com.au) netball team

Shopping

City Centre

Murray St and Hay St Malls are the city's shopping heartland, while King St is the place for swanky boutiques. London Court arcade has opals and souvenirs.

Wheels & Doll Baby CLOTHING
(Map p914; www.wheelsanddollbaby.com; 26 King St; ⌚10am-6pm Mon-Sat, 11am-5pm Sun) Punky rock-chick chic with a bit of baby doll mixed in. Perhaps Perth fashion's coolest export,

and worn by Courtney Love, Katy Perry and Debbie Harry.

78 Records MUSIC
(Map p914; www.78records.com.au; upstairs 255 Murray St Mall; 9am-5pm Mon-Sat, from 11am Sun) Independent record shop with a massive range of CDs and lots of specials. Also good for vinyl and tickets to rock and indie gigs.

Pigeonhole CLOTHING, ACCESSORIES
(Map p914; www.pigeonhole.com.au; Shop 16, Bon Marche Arcade, 80 Barrack St; 10am-5.30pm Mon-Sun) Hip clothing, and stylish retro accessories and gifts. There are five stores around the city – the main store is adjacent to the associated Cabin Fever (p918) cafe in Bon Marche Arcade.

Perth Map Centre BOOKS, MAPS
(Map p914; www.mapworld.com.au; 900 Hay St; 9am-5.30pm Mon-Fri, 10am-3pm Sat) Maps and travel guides.

Northbridge, Highgate & Mt Lawley

William Topp DESIGN
(www.williamtopp.com; 452 William St; 11am-6pm Tue-Fri, to 5pm Sat, to 4pm Sun) Lots of cool knick-knacks.

Future Shelter HOMEWARES
(www.futureshelter.com; 56 Angove St, North Perth; 10am-6pm Mon-Sat) Quirky clothing, gifts and homewares designed and manufactured locally.

Planet BOOKS, MUSIC
(www.planetvideo.com.au; 636-638 Beaufort St; 10am-late) Books, CDs, lots of obscure DVDs and an excellent adjoining cafe.

Leederville

Leederville's Oxford St is the place for groovy boutiques, eclectic music and bookshops.

Atlas Divine CLOTHING
(Map p917; www.atlasdivine.com; 121 Oxford St; 9am-9pm) Hip women's and men's clobber: jeans, quirky tees, dresses etc.

Oxford St Books BOOKSTORE
(Map p917; 119 Oxford St) Knowledgeable staff, great range of fiction and a travel section.

Subiaco & Kings Park

Rokeby Rd and Hay St boast fashion, art and classy gifts.

Indigenart INDIGENOUS ART
(Map p917; www.mossensongalleries.com.au; 115 Hay St; 10am-5pm Mon-Fri, 11am-4pm Sat) Reputable Indigenart carries art from around the country but with a particular focus on WA artists.

Aboriginal Art & Craft Gallery INDIGENOUS ART
(www.aboriginalgallery.com.au; Fraser Ave; 10.30am-4.30pm Mon-Fri, 11am-4pm Sat-Sun) Tends to be more populist than high-end or collectable.

Information

EMERGENCY

Police (13 14 44; www.police.wa.gov.au; 60 Beaufort St)

Sexual Assault Resource Centre (08-9340 1828, freecall 1800 199 888; www.kemh.health.wa.gov.au/services/sarc; 24hr)

INTERNET ACCESS

Plenty of eating and sleeping places offer free wireless internet access. The **State Library of WA** (www.slwa.wa.gov.au; Perth Cultural Centre; 9am-8pm Mon-Thu, 10am-5.30pm Fri-Sun;) offers free wireless and computer terminals.

MEDIA

Free publications include *Your Guide to Perth & Fremantle*.

Drum Media (www.facebook.com/drumperth) Music, film and culture listings.

Go West (www.gowesternaustralia.com.au) Backpacker magazine with WA information and seasonal work opportunities.

Urban Walkabout (www.urbanwalkabout.com) Handy free pocket guides covering hip eating, drinking and shopping spots.

West Australian (www.thewest.com.au) Local newspaper with entertainment and cinema listings.

X-Press Magazine (www.xpressmag.com.au) Live-music information.

MEDICAL SERVICES

Lifecare Dental (08-9221 2777; www.dentistsinperth.com.au; 419 Wellington St; 8am-8pm)

Royal Perth Hospital (08-9224 2244; www.rph.wa.gov.au; Victoria Sq) In the CBD.

Travel Medicine Centre (08-9321 7888; www.travelmed.com.au; 5 Mill St; 8am-5pm Mon-Fri)

POST

Main Post Office (GPO; Map p914; ☎13 13 18; 3 Forrest Pl; ⊙8.30am-5pm Mon-Fri, 9am-12.30pm Sat)

TOURIST INFORMATION

i-City Information Kiosk (Map p914; Murray St Mall; ⊙9.30am-4.30pm Mon-Thu & Sat, to 8pm Fri, 11am-3.30pm Sun) Volunteer-run walking tours.

WA Visitor Centre (Map p914; ☎08-9483 1111, 1800 812 808; www.bestofwa.com.au; 55 William St; ⊙9am-5.30pm Mon-Fri, 9.30am-4.30pm Sat, 11am-4.30pm Sun) Information on all of WA.

USEFUL WEBSITES

www.heatseeker.com.au Gig guide and ticketing.

www.perth.citysearch.com.au Entertainment and restaurants.

www.perthnow.com.au Perth and WA news and restaurant reviews.

www.scoop.com.au Entertainment.

www.whatson.com.au Events and travel information.

Getting There & Away

For details on flights, buses and trains to Perth see p906.

AIR

For details on flights to and from Perth, see the Transport chapter.

TRAIN

Transwa (☎1300 662 205; www.transwa.wa.gov.au) runs the following services:

Australind (twice daily) Perth to Pinjarra ($16, 1¼ hours) and Bunbury ($30, 2½ hours).

AvonLink (thrice weekly) East Perth to Toodyay ($16, 1¼ hours) and Northam ($19, 1½ hours).

Prospector (daily) East Perth to Kalgoorlie-Boulder ($82, seven hours).

Getting Around

TO/FROM THE AIRPORT

The domestic and international terminals of Perth's airport are 10km and 13km east of Perth respectively, near Guildford. Taxi fares to the city are around $40 from the domestic/international terminal, and about $60 to Fremantle.

Connect (☎1300 666 806; www.perthairportconnect.com.au) runs shuttles to and from hotels and hostels in the city centre (one way/return $18/30, every 50 minutes) and Fremantle (one-way/return $33/58, every 2½ hours). Prices are slightly cheaper between Perth and the domestic terminal and are substantially discounted for groups of two to four people (check the website for details). Bookings are essential for all services to the airport and are recommended for services to Fremantle. No bookings are taken for shuttles from the airport to Perth's city centre.

Transperth bus 37 travels to the domestic airport from St Georges Tce, near William St ($4.55, 44 minutes, every 10 to 30 minutes, hourly after 7pm).

CAR & MOTORCYCLE

Driving in the city takes a bit of practice, as some streets are one way and many aren't signed. There are plenty of car-parking buildings in the central city but no free parks. For unmetered street parking you'll need to look well away from the main commercial strips and check the signs carefully.

Some local Perth-based hire companies:

Backpacker Car Rentals (☎08-9430 8869; www.backpackercarrentals.com.au; 235 Hampton Rd, South Fremantle) Good-value local agency.

Bayswater Car Rental (☎08-9325 1000; www.bayswatercarrental.com.au) Local company with four branches in Perth and Fremantle.

Britz Rentals (☎1800 331 454; www.britz.com.au) Hires fully equipped 4WDs fitted out as campervans, popular on the roads of northern WA. Britz has offices in all the state capitals, as well as Perth and Broome, so one-way rentals are possible.

Campabout Oz (☎08-9477 2121; www.campaboutoz.com.au) Campervans, 4WDs and motorbikes with branches in Perth, Broome and Darwin.

Scootamoré (☎08-9380 6580; www.scootamore.com.au; 356a Rokeby Rd, Subiaco; day/3 days/week/month $45/111/200/400) Hires 50cc scooters with helmets (compulsory) and insurance included (for over 21 year olds; $500 excess).

Wicked Campers (☎1800 246 869; www.wickedcampers.com.au) Check the website for good last-minute discounts.

PUBLIC TRANSPORT

Transperth (☎13 62 13; www.transperth.wa.gov.au) operates Perth's public buses, trains and ferries. There are Transperth information offices at Perth Station (Wellington St), Wellington St Bus Station, Perth Underground Station (off Murray St) and the Esplanade Busport (Mounts Bay Rd). There's also a journey planner on the website.

From the central city, the following fares apply for all public transport:

Free Transit Zone (FTZ) Central commercial area, bounded (roughly) by Fraser Ave, Kings Park Rd, Thomas St, Newcastle St, Parry St, Lord St and the river (including City West and

Claisebrook train stations, to the west and east respectively).

Zone 1 City centre and inner suburbs ($2.70).

Zone 2 Fremantle, Guildford and the beaches as far north as Sorrento ($4).

Zone 3 Hillarys Boat Harbour (AQWA), the Swan Valley and Kalamunda ($4.90).

Zone 5 Rockingham ($7.10).

Zone 7 Mandurah ($9.40).

DayRider Unlimited travel after 9am weekdays and all day on the weekend in any zone ($11).

FamilyRider Lets two adults and up to five children travel for a total of $1 on weekends, after 6pm weekdays and after 9am on weekdays during school holidays.

If you're in Perth for a while, it may be worth buying a SmartRider card, which covers you for bus, train and ferry. It's $10 to purchase, then you add value to your card. The technology deducts the fare as you go, as long as you tap in and tap out (touch your card on the electronic reader) every time you travel, including within the FTZ. The SmartRider works out 15% cheaper than buying single tickets and automatically caps itself at the DayRider rate if you're avoiding the morning rush hour.

Bus

As well as regular buses the FTZ is well covered during the day by the three free CAT (Central Area Transit) services. The Yellow and Red CATs operate east–west routes, Yellow sticking mainly to Wellington St and Red looping roughly east on Murray and west on Hay. The Blue Cat does a figure eight through Northbridge and the south end of the city; this is the only one to run late – until 1am on Friday and Saturday nights only. Pick up a copy of the free timetable (widely available on buses and elsewhere) for the exact routes and stops. Best of all, services run every five to eight minutes during weekdays and every 15 minutes on weekends; there are digital displays at the stops telling you when the next bus is due.

The metropolitan area is serviced by a wide network of Transperth buses. Pick up timetables from any of the Transperth information centres or use the 'journey planner' on its website.

Ferry

The only ferry runs every 20 to 30 minutes between Barrack St Jetty and Mends St Jetty in South Perth – use it to get to the zoo or for a bargain from-the-river glimpse of the Perth skyline.

Train

Transperth operates five train lines from around 5.20am to midnight weekdays and until about 2am Saturday and Sunday. Your rail ticket can also be used on Transperth buses and ferries within the ticket's zone. You're free to take your bike on the train in non-peak times. The lines and useful stops:

Armadale Thornlie line Perth, Burswood.

Fremantle line Perth, City West, West Leederville, Subiaco, Shenton Park, Swanbourne, Cottesloe, North Fremantle, Fremantle.

Joondalup line Esplanade, Perth Underground, Leederville.

Mandurah line Perth Underground, Esplanade, Rockingham, Mandurah.

Midland line Perth, East Perth, Mt Lawley, Guildford, Midland.

TAXI

Perth has a decent system of metered taxis, though the distances in the city make frequent use costly and on busy nights you may have trouble flagging a taxi down in the street. There are ranks throughout the city. The two main companies are **Swan Taxis** (☎13 13 30; www.swantaxis.com.au) and **Black & White** (☎13 10 08; www.bwtaxi.com.au), both of which have wheelchair-accessible cabs.

FREMANTLE

POP 28,100

Perth has sprawled to enfold Fremantle within its suburbs, yet the port city maintains its own distinct personality – proud of its nautical ties, working-class roots, bohemian reputation and, especially, its football team. A 20th-century economic slump meant that the city retained an almost complete set of formerly grand Victorian and Edwardian buildings, creating a heritage precinct that's unique among Australia's cities today.

Today's 'Freo' makes a cosy home for performers, professionals, artists and more than a few eccentrics. There's a lot to enjoy here – fantastic museums, edgy galleries, pubs thrumming with live music and a thriving coffee culture.

History

This was an important area for the Wadjuk Noongar people, as it was a hub of trading paths. It was occupied mainly in summer, when the Wadjuk would base themselves here to fish. In winter they would head further inland, avoiding seasonal flooding.

Fremantle's European history began when the HMS *Challenger* landed in 1829. Like Perth, the settlement made little progress until convict labour was used. The port blossomed during the gold rush and many of its

Fremantle

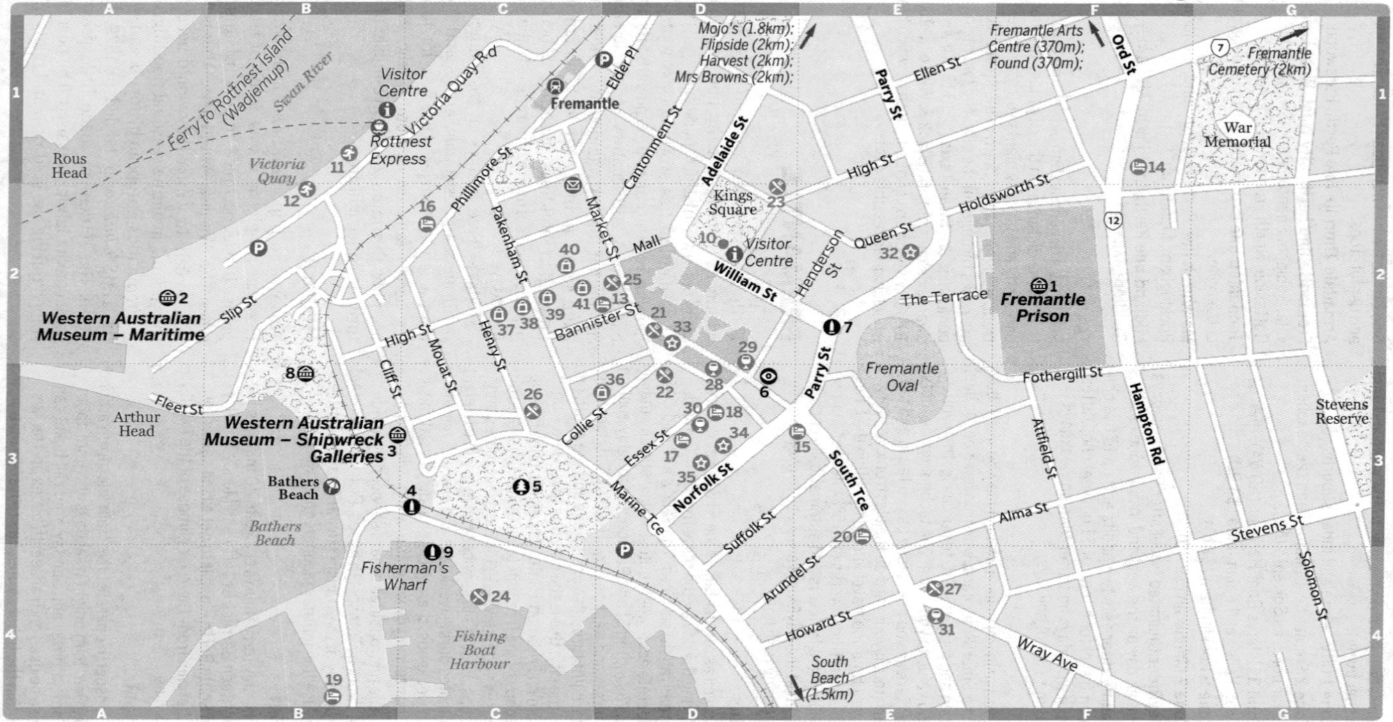
0 200 m
0 0.1 mile
Ferry to Rottnest Island (Wadjemup)
Swan River
Visitor Centre
Victoria Quay Rd
Rottnest Express
Rous Head
Victoria Quay
Fremantle
Elder Pl
Cantonment St
Mojo's (1.8km); Flipside (2km); Harvest (2km); Mrs Browns (2km);
Adelaide St
Parry St
Ellen St
Fremantle Arts Centre (370m); Found (370m);
Ord St
Fremantle Cemetery (2km)
War Memorial
Phillimore St
Pakenham St
Market St
Kings Square
High St
Holdsworth St
Queen St
Mall
Visitor Centre
William St
Henderson St
The Terrace
Fremantle Prison
Western Australian Museum – Maritime
Slip St
Bannister St
Henry St
Mouat St
Cliff St
Fremantle Oval
Fothergill St
Hampton Rd
Stevens Reserve
Fleet St
Arthur Head
Western Australian Museum – Shipwreck Galleries
Collie St
Essex St
Norfolk St
South Tce
Attfield St
Bathers Beach
Marine Tce
Suffolk St
Alma St
Stevens St
Solomon St
Fisherman's Wharf
Arundel St
Howard St
Wray Ave
Fishing Boat Harbour
South Beach (1.5km)

Fremantle

Top Sights
1 Fremantle Prison ... F2
2 Western Australian Museum – Maritime ... A2
3 Western Australian Museum – Shipwreck Galleries ... B3

Sights
4 Bon Scott Statue ... C3
5 Esplanade Reserve ... C3
6 Fremantle Markets ... D3
7 Mark of the Century ... E2
8 Round House ... B3
9 To the Fishermen ... C4

Activities, Courses & Tours
10 Fremantle Tram Tours ... D2
11 Oceanic Cruises ... B1
12 STS Leeuwin II ... B2

Sleeping
13 Bannister Suites Fremantle ... D2
14 Fothergills of Fremantle ... F1
15 Norfolk Hotel ... E3
16 Old Firestation Backpackers ... C2
17 Pirates ... D3
18 Port Mill B&B ... D3
19 Quest Harbour Village ... B4
20 Terrace Central B&B Hotel ... E3

Eating
21 Gino's ... D2
22 iPho ... D3
23 Juicy Beetroot ... D2
24 Little Creatures ... C4
25 Maya ... D2
26 Moore & Moore ... C3
27 Wild Poppy ... E4

Drinking & Nightlife
Little Creatures ... (see 24)
28 Monk ... D3
Norfolk Hotel ... (see 15)
29 Sail & Anchor ... D2
30 Whisper ... D3
31 Who's Your Mumma ... E4

Entertainment
32 Fly by Night Musicians Club ... E2
33 Kulcha ... D2
34 Luna on SX ... D3
35 X-Wray Cafe ... D3

Shopping
36 Chart & Map Shop ... D3
37 Japingka ... C2
38 Jarrahcorp ... C2
39 Love in Tokyo ... C2
40 New Edition ... C2
41 Record Finder ... C2

distinctive buildings date from this period. It wasn't until 1987, when Fremantle hosted the America's Cup, that it transformed itself from a sleepy port town into today's vibrant, artsy city.

Sights

★ Fremantle Prison — HISTORIC BUILDING

(☎08-9336 9200; www.fremantleprison.com.au; 1 The Terrace; Gatehouse free, torchlight tours adult/child $25/15; ⊙9am-5.30pm) With its foreboding 5m-high walls enclosing a nearly 6-hectare site, the old convict-era prison still dominates present-day Fremantle. In 2010 its cultural status was recognised, along with 10 other penal buildings, as part of the Australian Convict Sites entry on the Unesco World Heritage list.

The first convicts were made to build their own prison, constructing it from pale limestone dug out of the hill on which it was built. From 1855 to 1991, 350,000 people were incarcerated here. Of those, 43 men and one woman were executed on site, the last in 1964.

Entry to the gatehouse, including the Prison Gallery, gift shop (where you can purchase fetching arrow-printed prisoner PJs) and Convict Cafe, is free. To enter the prison proper, you'll need to take a tour. During the day there are two fascinating 1¼-hour tours on offer (Doing Time and Great Escapes), timed so you can take one after the other on a combined ticket (single tour adult/child $19/10, combined $26/17).

Bookings are required for the two more intense experiences on offer. Torchlight Tours (1½ hours, adult/child $25/21, Wednesday and Friday evenings) are designed to chill. The 2½-hour Tunnels Tour (adult/child over 12 $60/40) takes you 20m underground to tunnels and includes an underground boat ride.

★ Western Australian Museum – Maritime — MUSEUM

(www.museum.wa.gov.au; Victoria Quay; adult/child museum $10/3, submarine $10/3, museum & submarine $16/5; ⊙9.30am-5pm) Housed in an intriguing sail-shaped building on the harbour, just west of the city centre, this is a fascinating exploration of WA's relationship with the ocean. Various boats are on display and, if you're not claustrophobic, you can take an hour-long tour of the Australian Navy submarine HMAS *Ovens* (departing every half-hour from 10am to 3.30pm).

★ Western Australian Museum – Shipwreck Galleries MUSEUM
(www.museum.wa.gov.au; Cliff St; admission by donation; ⏲9.30am-5pm) Housed in an 1852 commissariat store, the Shipwreck Galleries are considered the finest display of maritime archaeology in the southern hemisphere. The highlight is the Batavia Gallery, where a section of the hull of Dutch merchant ship the *Batavia*, wrecked in 1629, is displayed.

Round House HISTORIC BUILDING
(☎08-9336 6897; www.fremantleroundhouse.com.au; admission by donation; ⏲10.30am-3.30pm) Commenced in 1830, shortly after the founding of the colony, this odd 12-sided stone prison is the oldest surviving building in WA. It was the site of the colony's first hangings and was used for holding Aboriginal people before they were taken to Rottnest Island.

On the hilltop outside is the Signal Station, where at 1pm daily a time ball and cannon blast were used to alert seamen to the correct time. The ceremony is re-enacted daily; book ahead if you want to fire the cannon.

Fremantle Arts Centre GALLERY
(www.fac.org.au; 1 Finnerty St; ⏲10am-5pm) FREE An impressive neo-Gothic building surrounded by lovely elm-shaded gardens, the Fremantle Arts Centre was constructed by convict labourers as a lunatic asylum in the 1860s. Saved from demolition in the 1960s, it houses interesting exhibitions and the excellent Canvas (p930) cafe. During summer, there's concerts, courses and workshops.

Fremantle Markets MARKET
(www.fremantlemarkets.com.au; cnr South Tce & Henderson St; ⏲8am-8pm Fri, to 6pm Sat & Sun) Originally opened in 1897, these colourful markets were reopened in 1975 and today draw slow-moving crowds, combing over souvenirs such as plastic boomerangs and swan-shaped magnets. The fresh produce section is a good place to stock up on snacks.

Gold Rush Buildings HISTORIC BUILDINGS
Fremantle boomed during the WA gold rush in the late 19th century, and many wonderful buildings remain which were constructed during, or shortly before, this period. High St, particularly around the bottom end, has some excellent examples including several old hotels.

Public Sculptures MONUMENTS
Enlivening Fremantle's streets are numerous bronze sculptures, many by local artist Greg James (www.gregjamessculpture.com). Most popular is the statue of **Bon Scott** (1946–80) strutting on a Marshall amplifier in Fishing Boat Harbour. The AC/DC singer moved to Fremantle with his family in 1956 and his ashes are interred in **Fremantle Cemetery** (Carrington St); it's reputedly the most-visited grave in Australia, with many travellers stopping in for 'a beer with Bon'. Enter the cemetery at the entrance near the corner of High St and Carrington St. Bon's plaque is on the left around 15m along the path.

Also in Fishing Boat Harbour is **To The Fishermen** (Fishing Boat Harbour), and another quirky bronze is **Mark of the Century** (Parry St) outside Fremantle Oval.

Esplanade Reserve PARK
(Marine Tce) A large park shaded by Norfolk Island pines between the city and Fishing Boat Harbour.

Bathers Beach BEACH
You could theoretically swim here, but most people save the soaking for beaches further from the port.

South Beach BEACH
Sheltered, swimmable, only 1.5km from the city centre and on the free CAT bus route.

Coogee Beach BEACH
Coogee is 6km further south of South Beach.

Activities

Fremantle Trails WALKING
(www.fremantlewa.com.au) Pick up trailcards from the visitor centre for 11 self-guided themed walking tours.

Oceanic Cruises WHALE WATCHING
(☎08-9325 1191; www.oceaniccruises.com.au; adult/child $67/29; ⏲mid-Sep–early Dec) Departs B Shed, Victoria Quay at 10.15am for a two-hour tour. Days of operation vary by month, so check the website.

STS Leeuwin II SAILING
(☎08-9430 4105; www.sailleeuwin.com; Berth B; adult/child $95/60) Take a trip on a 55m, three-masted tall ship.

Tours

Fremantle Tram Tours CITY
(☎08-9433 6674; www.fremantletrams.com.au; departs Town Hall; adult/child $24/5, Ghostly Tour $70/50, Lunch & Tram $79/42, Triple Tour $85/40, Tram & Prison adult/child $42/13) Looking like a heritage tram, this bus departs from the Town Hall on an all-day hop-on, hop-off circuit around the city. The **Ghostly Tour** runs 6.45pm to 10.30pm Fridays and visits the prison, Round House and Fremantle Arts Centre (former asylum) by torchlight.

Captain Cook Cruises CRUISE
(Map p914; ☎08-9325 3341; www.captaincook-cruises.com.au; C Shed) Cruises between Fremantle and Perth (adult/child $25/15). A three-hour lunch cruise departs at 12.45pm (adult/child $62/41).

Fremantle Indigenous Heritage Tours WALKING TOUR
(☎08-9431 7878; www.indigenouswa.com; adult/child $25/15; ⊙10.30am) Highly regarded tour covering the history of Fremantle and the Nyoongar and Wadjuk people. Book at the Fremantle visitor centre.

Two Feet & A Heartbeat WALKING TOUR
(☎1800 459 388; www.twofeet.com.au; per person $20-40; ⊙10am) Focusing on Fremantle's often rambunctious history. 'Tight Arse Tuesdays' are good value.

Festivals & Events

West Coast Blues 'n' Roots Festival MUSIC
(www.westcoastbluesnroots.com.au) With international acts in late March/early April.

Blessing of the Fleet RELIGIOUS
(Esplanade Reserve, Fishing Boat Harbour) An October tradition since 1948, brought to Fremantle by immigrants from Molfetta, Italy.

Fremantle Festival CULTURE
(www.fremantle.wa.gov.au) Freo's streets and concert venues come alive with parades and performances in November.

Sleeping

Old Firestation Backpackers HOSTEL $
(☎08-9430 5454; www.old-firestation.net; 18 Phillimore St; dm $27-31, d $72; @📶) There's entertainment aplenty in this converted firestation: free internet, foosball, movies and a sunny courtyard. Dorms have natural light and the afternoon sea breeze fluttering in, and there's a female-only section. The hippy vibe culminates in occasional late-night guitar-led singalongs around the campfire.

Pirates HOSTEL $
(☎08-9335 6635; www.piratesbackpackers.com.au; 11 Essex St; dm $29-31, d $65; @📶) Attracting a diverse international crew, this sun- and fun-filled hostel in the thick of the Freo action is a top spot to socialise. Rooms are small and reasonably basic, but the bathrooms are fresh and clean.

Woodman Point Holiday Park CAMPGROUND $
(☎08-9434 1433; www.aspenparks.com.au; 132 Cockburn Rd; sites for 2 people $45, d $135-255; ❄@📶🏊) A particularly pleasant spot, 10km south of Fremantle. It's usually quiet, and its location makes it feel more summer beach holiday than outer-Freo staging post.

Fothergills of Fremantle B&B $$
(☎08-9335 6784; www.fothergills.net.au; 18-22 Ord St; r $175-225; ❄📶) Naked bronze women sprout from the front garden, while a life-size floral cow shelters on the verandah of these neighbouring mansions on the hill. Inside, the decor is in keeping with their venerable age (built 1892), aside from the contemporary art scattered about.

Terrace Central B&B Hotel B&B $$
(☎08-9335 6600; www.terracecentral.com.au; 79-85 South Tce; d $190-215; ❄@📶) Terrace Central may be a character-filled B&B at heart, but its larger size gives it the feel of a boutique hotel. The main section is created from an 1888 bakery and an adjoined row of terrace houses, and there are also modern one- and two-bedroom apartments.

Port Mill B&B B&B $$
(☎08-9433 3832; www.portmillbb.com.au; 3/17 Essex St; r $179-299; ❄📶) One of the most luxurious B&Bs in town, it's clearly the love child of Paris and Freo. Crafted from local limestone (built in 1862 as a mill), inside it's all modern Parisian style, with contemporary French furniture and wrought-iron balconies. French doors open out to the decks.

Norfolk Hotel HOTEL $$
(☎08-9335 5405; www.norfolkhotel.com.au; 47 South Tce; s/d without bathroom $100/140, d with bathroom $180; ❄📶) Far above your standard pub digs; rooms have all been tastefully decorated in muted tones and crisp white linen, and there's a communal sitting room. It can be noisy on weekends, but the bar closes at midnight .

Bannister Suites Fremantle HOTEL $$
(☎08-9435 1288; www.bannistersuitesfremantle.com.au; 22 Bannister St; r from $199; ❄) Modern and fresh, boutiquey Bannisters is a stylish highlight of central Fremantle's accommodation scene. It's worth paying extra for one of the suites with balconies, where you can enjoy views over the rooftops.

Number Six APARTMENT $$
(☎08-9299 7107; www.numbersix.com.au; studios/1-bedroom apt from $105/150; ❄) Self-contained and stylish studios, apartments and houses available for overnight to long-term stays in great locations around Freo.

Quest Harbour Village APARTMENT $$$
(☎08-9430 3888; www.questharbourvillage.com.au; Mews Rd, Challenger Harbour; apt from $292; ❄📶) At the end of a wharf, this attractive, two-storey, sandstone and brick block of one- to three-bedroom apartments makes the most of its nautical setting; one-bedroom units have views over the car park to the Fishing Boat Harbour, while the others directly front the marina.

Eating

City Centre & South Fremantle

★ **Moore & Moore** CAFE $
(www.mooreandmoorecafe.com; 46 Henry St; mains $8-22; ⏲8am-4pm; 📶) An urban-chic cafe that spills into the adjoining art gallery and overflows into a flagstoned courtyard. With great coffee, good cooked breakfasts, pastries, wraps and free wi-fi, it's a great place to linger.

iPho VIETNAMESE $
(1/25 Collie St; mains $12.50-22; ⏲11.30am-9.30pm Tue-Sun) Settle into the mod-Asian decor and multitask your way through the menu including crispy *cha gio* (spring rolls), plump *banh xeo* (crepes), and hearty noodle-filled bowls of *pho*.

Juicy Beetroot VEGETARIAN $
(mains $10-15; ⏲10am-4pm Mon-Fri; ✍) 🍃 This popular meat-free zone serves tasty vego and vegan dishes of the wholefood variety (tofu burgers, curries etc), and zingy fresh juices. It's tucked up an alley off High St with outdoor seating.

Canvas CAFE $$
(www.canvasatfremantleartscentre.com; Fremantle Arts Centre; mains $12-25; ⏲8.30am-4pm) In the Fremantle Arts Centre, Freo's best cafe channels Middle Eastern, Spanish and North African influences. Breakfast highlights are the baked-egg dishes – try the Israeli-style Red Shakshuka or the Spanish eggs Flamenco – and lunch presents everything from citrus-cured salmon to scallops.

Maya INDIAN $$
(☎08-9335 2796; www.mayarestaurant.com.au; 77 Market St; mains $18-29; ⏲6pm-late Tue-Sun, noon-3pm Fri) Maya's white tablecloths and wooden chairs signal classic style without the pomp. Its well-executed meals have made it a popular local spot for years, earning it the reputation of WA's best Indian restaurant.

Wild Poppy CAFE $$
(2 Wray Ave; breakfast $6-16, lunch $16-22; ⏲7am-4pm; 📶) Soup and salad specials team with good coffee, beer and cider, and the chilli eggs are a great way to start the day. For lunch, ask if the Cape Malay fish curry is available.

Gino's CAFE $$
(www.ginoscafe.com.au; 1 South Tce; mains $15-30; ⏲6am-late; 📶) Old-school Gino's is Freo's most famous cafe, and while it's become a tourist attraction in its own right, the locals still treat it as their second living room, only with better coffee.

Fishing Boat Harbour

Little Creatures PUB $$
(www.littlecreatures.com.au; 40 Mews Rd; pizzas $18-34, shared plates $9-24; ⏲10am-midnight) Little Creatures is classic Freo: harbour views, fantastic brews (made on-site) and excellent food. In a cavernous converted boatshed overlooking the harbour, it can get chaotic at times, but a signature Pale Ale with a wood-fired pizza will be worth the wait. More substantial shared plates include chickpea tagine and pork belly with fennel. No bookings.

North Fremantle

Flipside BURGERS $
(www.flipsideburgers.com.au; 239 Queen Victoria St; burgers $10.50-13.50; ⏲5.30-9.30pm Tue-Thu, noon-2.30pm Thu, noon-9pm Fri-Sun) Gourmet

burgers with the option of dining in next door at Mrs Browns.

Harvest MODERN AUSTRALIAN $$$

(☎08-9336 1831; www.harvestrestaurant.net.au; 1 Harvest Rd; mains $38-42; ⏲6pm-late Tue-Thu, noon-late Fri, 8am-late Sat, 8am-3pm Sun) Swing through the heavy, fuchsia-painted metal doors and into the dark-wood dining room lined with artworks and curios. Then settle down to comforting Mod Oz dishes cooked with a dash of panache. Breakfast and lunch are less expensive.

Drinking & Entertainment

Most of Fremantle's big pubs are lined up along South Tce and High St. They've long been incubators for rock kids, turning out WA bands like the John Butler Trio, San Cisco and Tame Impala.

★**Sail & Anchor** PUB

(www.sailandanchor.com.au; 64 South Tce; ⏲11am-midnight Mon-Sat, to 10pm Sun) More than 40 different taps delivering a stunning range of local and international beers. Welcome to the best destination for the travelling beer geek in WA. Occasional live music and decent pub meals complete the picture.

Little Creatures MICROBREWERY

(www.littlecreatures.com.au; 40 Mews Rd, Fishing Boat Harbour; ⏲10am-midnight) Try the Pale Ale and Pilsner, and other beers and ciders under the White Rabbit and Pipsqueak labels. Creatures Loft is an adjacent lounge bar with regular live entertainment and DJs. Live jazz kicks off at 4pm on Sundays.

Who's Your Mumma BAR

(cnr Wray Ave & South Tce; ⏲4pm-late Mon-Thu, 8am-late Fri-Sun) Industrial-chic lightbulbs and polished-concrete floors are softened by recycled timber at the laid-back Who's Your Mumma. An eclectic crew of South Freo locals crowd in for great-value combo specials (around $15) including 'Taco Tuesdays' and 'Schnitzel Mondays'.

Norfolk Hotel PUB

(www.norfolkhotel.com.au; 47 South Tce; ⏲11am-midnight Mon-Sat, to 10pm Sun) Slow down to Freo pace and take your time over one of the many beers on tap at this 1887 pub. Lots of interesting guest brews create havoc for the indecisive drinker, and the pub food and pizzas are very good.

Monk CRAFT BEER

(www.themonk.com.au; 33 South Tce; ⏲11.30am-late) Enjoy occasional guest beers or the the Monk's own brews (kolsch, mild, wheat, porter, rauch, pale ale). The bar snacks and pizzas are also good.

Mrs Browns BAR

(www.mrsbrownbar.com.au; 241 Queen Victoria St, North Fremantle; ⏲4.30pm-late Tue-Thu, 1pm-late Fri-Sun) Exposed bricks and a copper bar combine with retro and antique furniture to create North Fremantle's most atmospheric bar. An eclectic menu of beer, wine and tapas targets the more discerning, slightly older bar hound, and you can order in burgers from Flipside next door.

Whisper WINE BAR

(www.whisperwinebar.com.au; 1/15 Essex St; ⏲noon-late Wed-Sun) In a lovely heritage building, this classy French-themed wine bar also does shared plates of charcuterie and cheese.

Fly by Night Musicians Club LIVE MUSIC

(www.flybynight.org; Parry St) Variety is the key at Fly by Night, a not-for-profit club that's been run by musos, for musos, for years. Many local bands made a start here.

Kulcha LIVE MUSIC, CLUB

(☎08-9336 4544; www.kulcha.com.au; 1st fl, 13 South Tce) World music of all sorts is the focus here. At the time of research the line-up included Gypsy swing, indigenous Australian reggae and rap, and melancholy Portuguese *fado*. Book ahead.

X-Wray Cafe LIVE MUSIC

(www.xwraymusic.tumblr.com; 3-13 Essex St; ⏲10am-11pm Mon-Wed, 9am-midnight Thu-Sat, 8am-9pm Sun) There's something on every night (live jazz, rock, open piano) at this hipster hang-out, comprising a smallish indoor area and a large canvas-covered terrace. Light meals are available.

Mojo's LIVE MUSIC

(www.mojosbar.com.au; 237 Queen Victoria St, North Fremantle; ⏲7pm-late) Mojo's is one of Freo's longstanding live-music venues. Local and national bands and DJs play at this small venue, and there's a sociable beer garden out the back.

Luna on SX CINEMA

(www.lunapalace.com.au; Essex St) Art-house films; set back in a lane between Essex and Norfolk Sts.

Shopping

The bottom end of High St is the place for interesting and quirky shopping. Fashion stores run along Market St, towards the train station. Queen Victoria St in North Fremantle is the place to go for antiques.

Japingka INDIGENOUS ART
(www.japingka.com.au; 47 High St; ⌚10am-5.30pm Mon-Fri, noon-5pm Sat & Sun) Specialising in indigenous fine art, from WA and beyond. Purchases include extensive notes about the the artists that painted them.

Jarrahcorp FURNITURE
(www.jarrahcorp.com.au; cnr High & Pakenham Sts; ⌚11am-4pm Mon-Sat, noon-4pm Sun) Traditional and contemporary furniture and gifts crafted from jarrah and marri timber salvaged from old buildings or ancient logs.

Found ARTS & CRAFTS
(www.fac.org.au; 1 Finnerty St; ⌚10am-5pm) The Fremantle Arts Centre shop stocks an inspiring range of WA art and craft.

Love in Tokyo CLOTHING
(www.loveintokyo.com.au; 61-63 High St; ⌚10am-5pm Mon-Sat, 1-5pm Sun) Local designer turning out gorgeously fashioned fabrics for women.

New Edition BOOKS
(www.newedition.com.au; 82 High St; ⌚7.30am-6pm Mon-Sat, 9am-6pm Sun) A bookworm's dream with comfy armchairs for browsing and a funky cafe attached.

Record Finder MUSIC
(87 High St; ⌚10am-5pm) A treasure trove of old vinyl, including rarities and collectables.

Chart & Map Shop MAPS
(www.chartandmapshop.com.au; 14 Collie St; ⌚10am-5pm) Maps and travel guides.

Information

Fremantle City Library (☎08-9432 9766; www.frelibrary.wordpress.com; Town Hall, Kings Sq; ⌚9.30am-5.30pm Mon, Fri & Sat, to 8pm Tue-Thu; wi-fi) Free wi-fi and internet.

Fremantle Hospital (☎08-9431 3333; www.fhhs.health.wa.gov.au; Alma St)

Post Office (☎13 13 18; 1/13 Market St; ⌚9am-5pm Mon-Fri)

Visitor Centre (☎08-9431 7878; www.fremantlewa.com.au; Town Hall, Kings Sq; ⌚9am-5pm Mon-Fri, 10am-3pm Sat, 11.30am-2.30pm Sun) Free maps and brochures, and bookings for accommodation and tours.

Getting There & Around

Fremantle sits within Zone 2 of the Perth public-transport system, **Transperth** (☎13 62 13; www.transperth.wa.gov.au), and is only 30 minutes away by train. There are numerous buses between Perth's city centre and Fremantle, including routes 103, 106, 107, 111 and 158. There is also a Connect airport shuttle.

Another very pleasant way to get here from Perth is by the 1¼-hour river cruise run by Captain Cook Cruises (p929).

There are numerous one-way streets and parking meters in Freo. It's easy enough to travel by foot or on the free CAT bus service, which takes in all the major sites on a continuous loop every 10 minutes from 7.30am to 6.30pm on weekdays, until 9pm on Fridays, and from 10am to 6.30pm on the weekend.

Bicycles can be rented free from the **Fremantle Visitors Centre** (Kings Sq; ⌚9.30am-4.30pm Mon-Fri, to 3.30pm Sat, 10.30am-3.30pm Sun). It's an ideal way to get around Freo's storied streets. A refundable bond of $200 applies.

AROUND PERTH

Rottnest Island (Wadjemup)

POP 475

'Rotto' has long been the family-holiday playground of choice for Perth locals. Although it's only about 19km offshore from Fremantle, this car-free, off-the-grid slice of paradise, ringed by secluded beaches and bays, feels a million miles from the metropolis.

Cycling round the 11km-long, 4.5km-wide island is a real pleasure; just ride around and pick your own bit of beach to spend the day on. You're bound to spot quokkas on your journey. These are the island's only native land mammals, but you might also spot New Zealand fur seals splashing around off magical **West End**, dolphins; and, in season, whales. King skinks are common, sunning themselves on the roads.

If you fancy further diversions, snorkelling, fishing, surfing and diving are all excellent on the island. In fact, there's not a lot to do here that's not outdoors, so you're better off postponing your day trip if the weather's bad. It can be unpleasant when the wind really kicks up.

Rotto is also the site of annual school leavers' and end-of-uni-exams parties, a time when the island is overrun by kids 'getting blotto on Rotto'. Depending on your age, it's either going to be the best time you've ever had or the worst – check the calendar before proceeding.

History

Wadjuk oral history recalls the island being joined to the mainland before being cut off by rising waters. The fact that modern scientists date that occurrence to before 6500 years ago makes these memories some of the

Around Perth

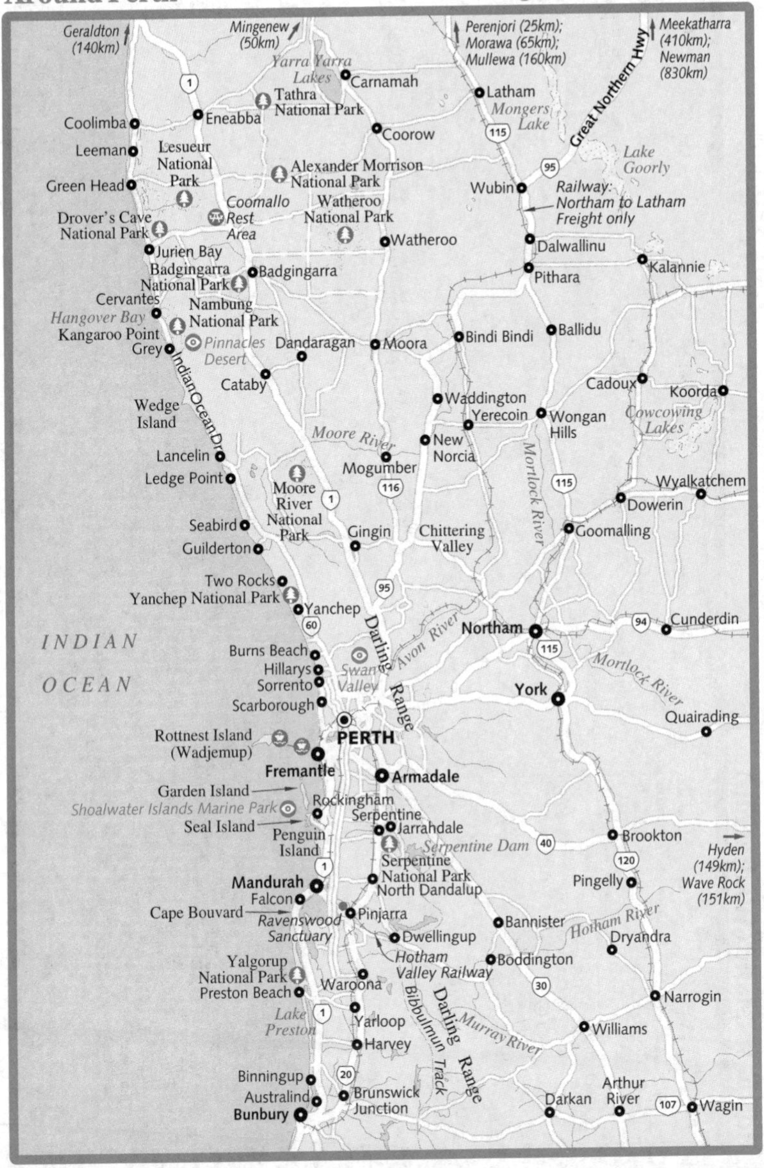

Rottnest Island (Wadjemup)

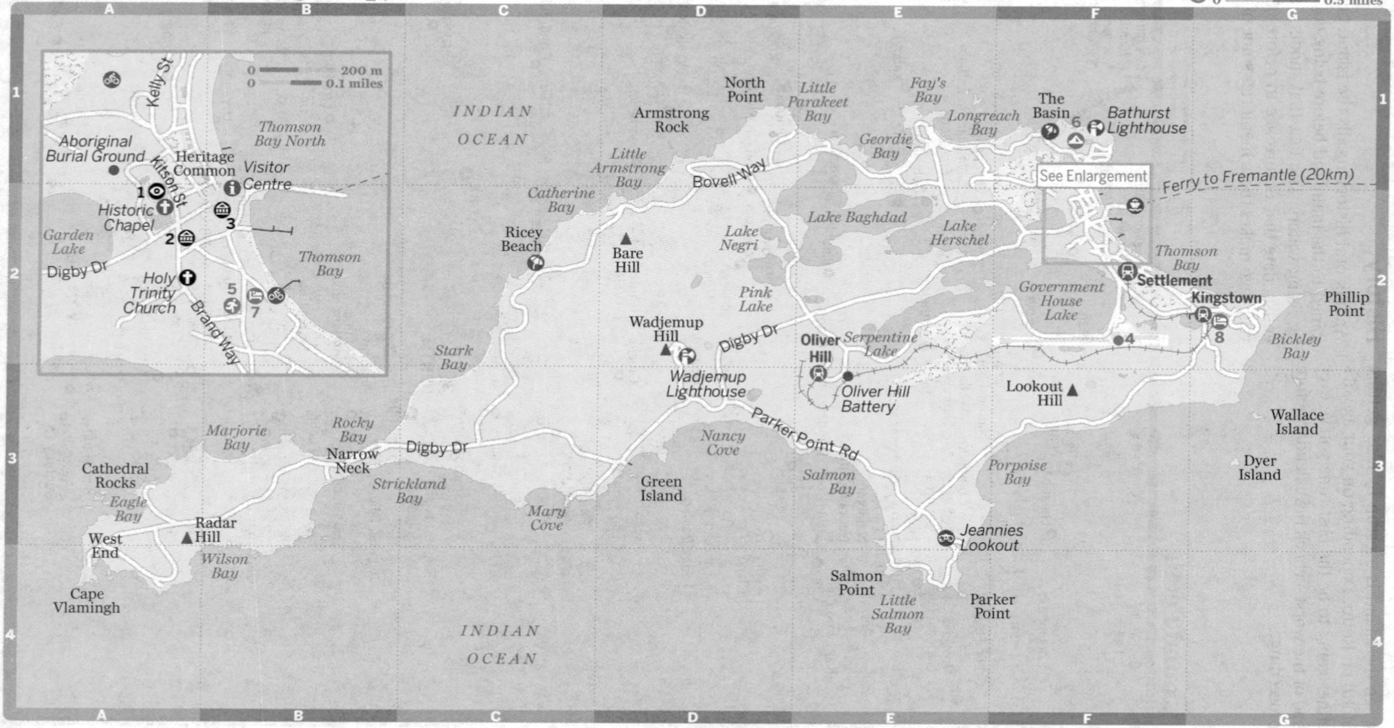

Rottnest Island (Wadjemup)

world's oldest. Archaeological finds suggest that the island was inhabited from 30,000 years ago, but not after it was separated from the mainland.

Dutch explorer Willem de Vlamingh claimed discovery of the island in 1696 and named it Rotte-nest (rat's nest) because of the numerous king-sized 'rats' (which were actually quokkas) he saw there.

From 1838 it was used as a prison for Aboriginal men and boys from all around the state. At least 3670 people were incarcerated here, in harsh conditions, with around 370 dying (at least five hanged). Even before the prison was built, Wadjemup was considered a 'place of the spirits', and it's been rendered even more sacred to indigenous people because of the hundreds of their people who died there. Many avoid it to this day.

Sights

Quod & Aboriginal Burial Ground HISTORIC SITE
(Kitson St) This octagonal 1864 building with a central courtyard was once the Aboriginal prison block but is now part of a hotel. During its time as a prison, several men would sleep in each 3m by 1.7m cell with no sanitation (most of the deaths were due to disease). Immediately adjacent to the Quod is a **wooded area** where hundreds of Aboriginal prisoners were buried in unmarked graves. Plans are underway to convert the area into a memorial, in consultation with Aboriginal elders.

Rottnest Museum MUSEUM
(Kitson St; admission by gold-coin donation; 11am-3.30pm) Housed in the old hay-store building, this little museum tells the island's natural and human history.

Salt Store HISTORIC BUILDING
(Colebatch Ave) FREE A photographic exhibition in this 19th-century building looks at a different chapter of local history: when the island's salt lakes provided all of WA's salt (between 1838 and 1950).

Activities

Excellent visibility in the temperate waters, coral reefs and shipwrecks makes Rottnest a top spot for **scuba diving** and **snorkelling**. There are snorkel trails with underwater plaques at **Little Salmon Bay** and **Parker Point**.

Over a dozen boats have come a cropper on Rottnest's reefs. Marker **plaques** around the island tell the sad tales of how and when the ships sank. The only wreck that is accessible to snorkellers without a boat is at **Thomson Bay**.

The best surfing breaks are at **Strickland**, **Salmon** and **Stark Bays**, at the west end of the island.

Rottnest Island Bike Hire BICYCLE HIRE
(08-9292 5105; www.rottnestisland.com; cnr Bedford Ave & Welch Way; 8.30am-4pm, to 5.30pm summer) Rents masks, snorkels and fins ($20 per day) and surfboards (per day $50).

Tours

Rottnest Voluntary Guides WALKING
(08-9372 9757; www.rvga.asn.au) There are free themed walks leaving from the Salt Store daily. Guides also run tours of Wadjemup Lighthouse (adult/child $7/3) and Oliver Hill Gun & Tunnels (adult/child $8/3.50).

Oliver Hill Train & Tour TRAIN RIDES
(www.rottnestisland.com; adult/child $28/16) This trip takes you by train to Oliver Hill (departing from the train station twice daily) and includes the Gun & Tunnels tour.

Discovery Coach Tour BUS TOUR
(www.rottnestisland.com; adult/child $35/17; departs 11.20am, 1.40pm & 1.50pm) Leaves from

QUOKKAS

Once found throughout the southwest, quokkas are now confined to forest on the mainland and a population of 8000 to 10,000 on Rottnest Island. These little marsupials have suffered a number of indignities over the years. First Dutch explorer Willem de Vlamingh's crew mistook them for rats. Then the British settlers misheard and mangled their name (the Noongar word was probably *quak-a* or *gwaga*). But worst of all, a cruel trend for 'quokka soccer' by sadistic louts in the 1990s saw many kicked to death before a $10,000 fine was imposed.

Thomson Bay three times daily (book at the visitor centre); includes a commentary and a stop at West End.

Rottnest Adventure Tour BOAT TOUR
(www.rottnestexpress.com.au; adult/child $50/25; ⏲late Sep-early Jun) Ninety-minute cruises around the coast with a special emphasis on spotting wildlife, including whales in season from October to November. Packages also available from Perth (adult/child $130/67) and Fremantle ($115/57).

Rottnest Air Taxi SCENIC FLIGHTS
(☎0411 264 547, 1800 500 006; www.rottnest.de) Ten-minute flights over the island ($38).

Sleeping & Eating

Rotto is wildly popular in summer and school holidays, when accommodation is booked out months in advance. Most visitors to Rotto self-cater. The general store is like a small supermarket (and also stocks liquor), but if you're staying a while, you're better to bring supplies with you. You can also pre-order supplies from www.rottnest-generalstore.com.au.

Allison Tentland CAMPGROUND $
(☎08-9432 9111; www.rottnestisland.com; Thomson Bay; sites per person $13) Camping on the island is restricted to this leafy camping ground with barbecues. Be vigilant about your belongings, especially your food – cheeky quokkas have been known to help themselves.

Kingstown Barracks Youth Hostel HOSTEL $
(☎08-9432 9111; www.rottnestisland.com; dm/f $50/106) This hostel is located in an old army barracks has a rather institutional feel, and few facilities. Check in at the visitor centre before you make the 1.8km walk, bike or bus trip to Kingston.

Rottnest Lodge HOTEL $$
(☎08-9292 5161; www.rottnestlodge.com.au; Kitson St; r $190-300; ❄) It's claimed there are ghosts in this comfortable complex, which is based around the former Quod and boys' reformatory school. If that worries you, ask for a room in the new section, looking onto a salt lake.

Rottnest Island Authority Cottages ACCOMMODATION SERVICES $$
(☎08-9432 9111; www.rottnestisland.com; cottages $100-228) There are more than 250 villas and cottages for rent around the island. Some have magnificent beachfront positions and are palatial; others are more like beach shacks. Prices rise by around $60 for Friday and Saturday nights, and they shoot up by up to $120 in peak season (late September to April).

Hotel Rottnest HOTEL $$$
(☎08-9292 5011; www.hotelrottnest.com.au; 1 Bedford Ave; r $270-320; ❄) Based around the former summer holiday pad for the state's governors (built in 1864), the former Quokka Arms has been transformed by a stylish renovation. The whiter-than-white rooms are smart and modern, if a tad pricey. A big glass pavilion creates an open and inviting space, and bistro-style food (mains $19 to $38) is reasonably priced given the location. Bands and DJs regularly boost the laid-back island mood during summer.

Riva SEAFOOD $$
(Rottnest Lodge , Kitson St; mains $27-34; ⏲noon-late) Classy Italian restaurant with a focus on local seafood. Prawns, squid, mussels and oysters all receive an elegant touch of the Med, and there are also wood-fired pizzas and interesting spins on duck, chicken and lamb.

Information

Near the main jetty there's a shopping area with ATMs.

Ranger (☎08-9372 9788)

Visitor Centre (www.rottnestisland.com) Thomson Bay (☎08-9372 9732; ⏲7.30am-5pm Sat-Thu, 7.30am-7pm Fri, extended in summer) Fremantle (☎08-9432 930; E Shed, Victoria Quay) Handles check-ins for all the island authority's accommodation. There's a bookings counter at the Fremantle office, near where the ferry departs.

Getting There & Away

AIR

Rottnest Air-Taxi (☎0411 264 547; www.rottnest.de) Flies from Jandakot airport in four-seater (one way/same-day return/extended return $230/330/430) or six-seater planes (one way/extended return $350/550). Prices include up to three passengers in the four-seater and five passengers in the six-seater.

BOAT

Rottnest Express (☎1300 467 688; www.rottnestexpress.com.au) Fremantle (B Shed, Victoria Quay; adult/child $72.50/40); Northport (1 Emma Pl, Rous Head; adult/child $72.50/40); Perth (Map p914; Pier 2, Barrack St Jetty; adult/child $92.50/50) The prices listed are for return day trips and include the island admission fee; add $10 for an extended return. Ferry schedules are seasonal, though those listed here are roughly the minimum: Perth (1¾ hours, twice daily), Fremantle (30 minutes, five times daily) and North Fremantle (30 minutes, three times daily). Various packages are available, which can add bike hire, snorkelling equipment, meals and tours.

Rottnest Fast Ferries (☎08-9246 1039; www.rottnestfastferries.com.au; adult/child $83/45) Departs from Hillarys Boat Harbour (40 minutes; three times daily). Packages also available. Hillarys Boat Harbour is around 40 minute drive north of Perth. See www.hillarysboatharbour.com.au for public transport details.

Getting Around

Bikes can be booked in advance online or on arrival from **Rottnest Island Bike Hire** (☎08-9292 5105; www.rottnestisland.com; cnr Bedford Ave & Welch Way; per hour/1/2/3/4/5 days $16/28/45/56/67/79; ⏲8.30am-4pm, to 5.30pm in summer). Rottnest Express also hires bikes (per 1/2/3 days $28/41/56).

A free shuttle runs between Thomson Bay and the main accommodation areas. The **Bayseeker** (day pass adult/child $14/6) does an hourly loop around the island.

Rockingham & the Peel District

Taking in swathes of jarrah forest and coastal resorts, this area can easily be tackled as a day trip from Perth or as the first stopping point of a southwest expedition. Entering the Peel District, you're passing out of Wadjuk country and into that of their fellow Noongar neighbours, the Pinjarup.

Rockingham

POP 100,000

This seaside city has some nice beaches and a noticeable British expat community. These characteristics in themselves wouldn't lure travellers 46km south from central Perth if it weren't for the **Shoalwater Islands Marine Park** on the city's doorstep, where you can observe dolphins, sea lions and penguins in the wild.

Just a few minutes' paddle, swim or **ferry ride** (Mersey Point Jetty; per person $12; ⏲hourly 9am-3pm Sep-May) from the mainland is **Penguin Island**, home to about 600 breeding pairs of penguins and several thousand ground-nesting silver gulls. You can also swim and snorkel in the crystal-clear waters. At low tide it's possible to wade the few hundred metres to the island across the sandbar. However, people have drowned after being washed off the bar during strong winds and high tides.

Activities

Rockingham Wild Encounters WILDLIFE TOURS
(☎08-9591 1333; www.rockinghamwildencounters.com.au; cnr Arcadia Dr & Penguin Rd) Runs a variety of low-impact tours; the most popular is the **dolphin swim tour** (departs Val St Jetty; tours $205-225; ⏲8am Sep-May). If you don't fancy getting wet, there are two-hour **dolphin-watch tours** (departs Mersey St Jetty, Shoalwater; adult/child $85/50; ⏲10.45am Sep-May). Pickups can also be arranged from Perth hotels.

There's also a 45-minute **penguin and sea lion cruise** (departs Penguin Island; adult/child $36.50/27.50; ⏲10.15am, 11.15am & 1.15pm Sep-May), which heads around the islands in a glass-bottomed boat.

West Coast Dive Park DIVING
(www.westcoastdivepark.com.au; permits per day/week $25/50) Diving within the marine park became even more interesting after the sinking of the *Saxon Ranger*, a 400-tonne fishing vessel. Contact the Australasian Diving Academy (p911) about expeditions to this and the wrecks of three other boats, two planes and various reefs in the vicinity.

Information

Visitor Centre (☎08-9592 3464; www.rockinghamvisitorcentre.com.au; 19 Kent St; ⏲9am-5pm) Accommodation bookings.

WORTH A TRIP

YALGORUP NATIONAL PARK

Fifty kilometres south of Mandurah is this beautiful 12,000-hectare coastal park, consisting of a succession of 10 tranquil lakes and surrounding woodlands and sand dunes. The park is recognised as a wetland of international significance for seasonally migrating water birds. Amateur scientists can visit the distinctive **thrombolites** of Lake Clifton, descendants of the earliest living organisms on earth. These rock-like structures are most easily seen when the water is low, particularly in March and April. There's a viewing platform on Mt John Rd, off Old Coast Rd.

Getting There & Around

Rockingham sits within Zone 5 of the Perth public-transport system, **Transperth** (13 62 13; www.transperth.wa.gov.au), with regular trains via the Mandurah line to Perth Underground/Esplanade ($7.10, 34 minutes) and Mandurah ($4.90, 18 minutes).

Rockingham station is around 4km southeast of Rockingham Beach and around 6km east of Mersey Point, where the Penguin Island ferries depart; catch bus 551 or 555 to the beach, or stay on the 551 to Mersey Point.

Mandurah

POP 68,300

Shrugging off its fusty retirement-haven image, Mandurah has made concerted efforts to reinvent itself as an upmarket beach resort, taking advantage of its new train link. And while its linked set of redeveloped 'precincts' and 'quarters' may sound a little pretentious, the overall effect is actually pretty cool.

The town spans the Mandurah Estuary, which sits between the ocean and the large body of water known as the Peel Inlet. It's one of the best places in the region for fishing, crabbing, prawning (March to April) and dolphin-spotting.

Sights & Activities

Australian Sailing Museum MUSEUM
(www.australiansailingmuseum.com.au; Ormsby Tce; adult/child $10/5; 9am-5pm) A very cool building housing 200 model yachts and tall ships, as well as a replica of the America's Cup and a cafe.

Hall's Cottage HISTORIC BUILDING
(Leighton Pl, Halls Head; admission by gold-coin donation; 10am-3pm Sun) An 1830s cottage and one of the first dwellings in the state.

Mandurah Ferry Cruises CRUISE
(08-9535 3324; www.mandurahferrycruises.com; Boardwalk) Take a one-hour **Dolphin & Mandurah Waterways Cruise** (adult/child $28/14; on the hour 10am-4pm), or a half-day **Murray River Lunch Cruise** (adult/child $79/49; Sep-May). Other cruise options incorporate catching and cooking Mandurah's famous blue manna crabs.

Mandurah Boat & Bike Hire BOATING, CYCLING
(08-9535 5877; www.mandurahboatandbikehire.com.au; Boardwalk) Hires four-seat dinghy or six-seat pontoons (per hour/day from $50/320), and bikes $10/33.

Eating

Taste & Graze CAFE $$
(www.tasteandgraze.com.au; Shop 3/4, 16 Mandurah Tce; mains $15-30, shared-plate menus per person $45; 9am-4pm Sun-Thu, till late Fri & Sat) In town in 'old' Mandurah, and perfectly located to catch the afternoon sun. Outdoor seating and a versatile modern Australian menu covering breakfast, lunch and shared smaller plates make it a cosmopolitan slice of cafe cool.

Information

Visitor Centre (08-9550 3999; www.visitmandurah.com; 75 Mandurah Tce; 9am-5pm)

Getting There & Away

There are direct trains to Perth Underground/Esplanade ($9.40, 50 minutes) and Rockingham ($7.10, 18 minutes). **Transwa** (1300 662 205; www.transwa.wa.gov.au) and **South West Coach Lines** (08-9261 7600; www.veoliatransportwa.com.au) buses stop here.

Dwellingup

POP 550

Dwellingup is a forest-shrouded township with character, 100km south of Perth. Its reputation as an activity hub has only been enhanced by the hardy long-distance walkers and cyclists passing through on the Bibbulmun Track and the Munda Biddi Trail.

Sights & Activities

Forest Heritage Centre NATURE RESERVE
(www.forestheritagecentre.com.au; 1 Acacia St; adult/child $5.50/2.20; 10am-3pm) Set within

the jarrah forest, this interesting rammed-earth building takes the shape of three interlinked gum leaves. Inside are displays about the forest's flora and fauna, and a shop that sells beautiful pieces crafted by the resident woodwork artists. Short marked trails lead into the forest, including an 11m-high canopy walk.

Hotham Valley Railway HISTORIC TRAIN
(☎08-9221 4444; www.hothamvalleyrailway.com.au; Forest Train adult/child $24/12, Restaurant Train $79, Steam Ranger adult/child $34/17; ⊙Forest Train departs 10.30am & 2pm, Restaurant Train departs 7.45pm, Steam Ranger departs 10.30am) On weekends (and Tuesdays and Thursdays during school holidays), the Dwellingup **Forest Train** chugs along 8km of forest track on a 90-minute return trip. Every Saturday night and some Fridays, the **Restaurant Train** follows the same route, serving up a five-course meal in a 1919 dining car. A third option is the **Steam Ranger**, travelling 14km via Western Australia's steepest rail incline to Isandra Siding. Steam Ranger trains only run on Sundays from May to October.

Dwellingup Adventures KAYAKING, RAFTING
(☎08-9538 1127; www.dwellingupadventures.com.au; 1-person kayaks & 2-person canoes per day $45; ⊙8.30am-5pm) Don't miss the opportunity to get out on the beautiful Murray River. Hire camping gear, bikes, kayaks and canoes, or take an assisted, self-guided paddling (full day, one-person kayak $90) or cycling tour (full day, per one/two/three people $97/124/174). White-water rafting tours are available from June to October (per person $130).

Information

Visitor Centre (☎08-9538 1108; www.murraytourism.com.au; Marrinup St; ⊙9am-3pm) Displays about Dwellingup's 1961 bushfires that destroyed 75 houses but took no lives.

THE SOUTHWEST

The farmland, forests, rivers and coast of the lush southwestern corner of WA contrast vividly with the stark, sunburnt terrain of much of the state. On land, world-class wineries beckon and tall trees provide shade for walking trails and scenic drives, while offshore, bottlenose dolphins and whales frolic, and devoted surfers search for – and often find – their perfect break.

Unusually for WA, distances between the many attractions are short, and driving time is mercifully limited, making it a fantastic area to explore for a few days – you will get much more out of your stay here if you have your own wheels. Summer brings hordes of visitors, but in the wintery months the cosy pot-belly stove rules and visitors are scarce, and while opening hours can be somewhat erratic, prices drop.

History

For 55,000 years this area belonged to the Wardandi, one of the Noongar peoples. They lived a nomadic life linked to the seasons: heading to the coast in summer to fish and journeying inland during the wet winter months.

The French connection to many of the current place names dates from the early 19th-century expedition by the ships *Géographe* and *Naturaliste*, for which the bay and the cape were named. Thomas Vasse, a crewman who was lost at sea, is remembered in several place names. According to local Wardandi, who found and fed him, he made it to shore but later died on the beach waiting for his ship to return.

Getting There & Around

AIR

Virgin Australia (☎136789; www.virginaustralia.com) Flies to Busselton from Perth and Albany.

BUS

Transwa (☎1300 662 205; www.transwa.wa.gov.au) Coach routes include the following:

SW1 East Perth to Bunbury, Busselton, Dunsborough, Margaret River and Augusta. Twelve per week; three per week continue on to Nannup and Pemberton.

SW2 East Perth to Bunbury, Balingup, Bridgetown, Manjimup and Pemberton; thrice weekly.

GS3 Bunbury to Balingup, Bridgetown, Manjimup, Pemberton, Walpole, Denmark and Albany; daily.

South West Coach Lines (☎08-9261 7600; www.veoliatransportwa.com.au) Has the following services:

- Perth (Esplanade Busport) to Bunbury, Busselton, Margaret River and Augusta.
- Perth to Bunbury, Busselton and Dunsborough.
- Bunbury to Balingup, Bridgetown and Manjimup.
- Bunbury to Busselton and Nannup.

The Southwest

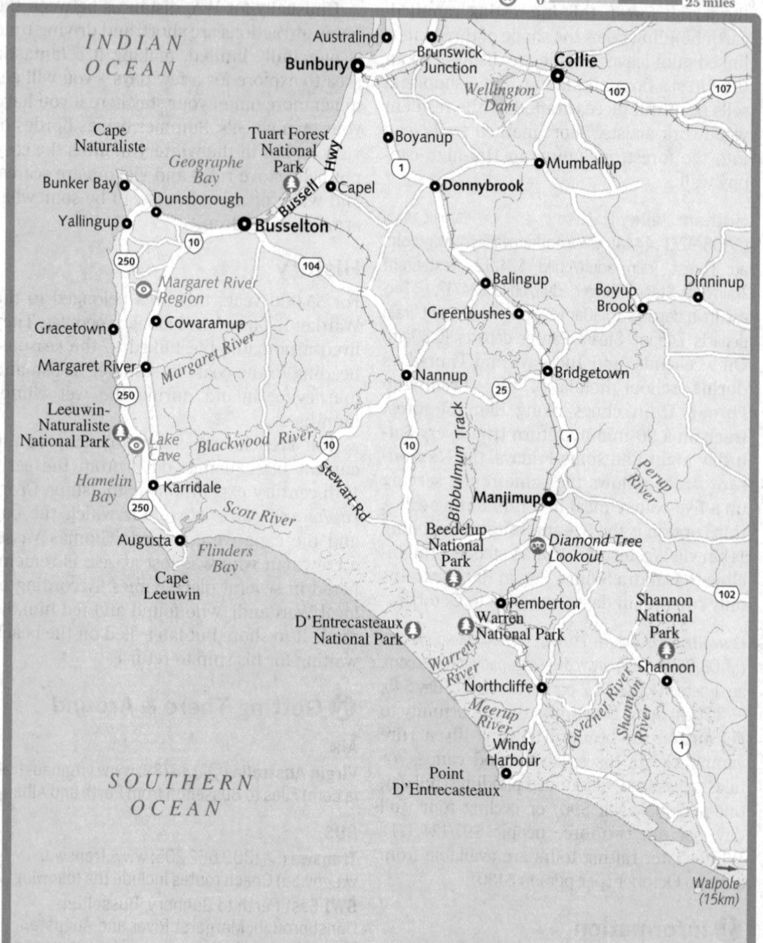

TransBusselton (☎08-9754 1666; 39 Albert St) Bus 903 follows the coast from Busselton to Dunsborough (four daily, Monday to Saturday).

TRAIN

Bunbury is the terminus of the *Australind* train line, with twice-daily services to Perth ($30, 2½ hours).

Geographe Bay

Turquoise waters and white sands are the defining features of this gorgeous bay, lined with 30km of excellent swimming beaches. Positioned between the Indian Ocean and a sea of wine, the beachside towns of Busselton and Dunsborough attract hordes of holidaymakers seeking to spend their vacations with sand between their toes and a glass between their lips.

Bunbury

POP 66,100

The southwest's only city is remaking its image from that of an industrial port into a seaside-holiday destination. Located 170km from Perth, Bunbury has good eateries and a few interesting attractions worthy of a stop.

◉ Sights & Activities

Dolphin Discovery Centre   WILDLIFE RESERVE
(☑08-9791 3088; www.dolphindiscovery.com.au; Koombana Beach; adult/child $10/5; ⊗9am-2pm Jun-Sep, 8am-4pm Oct-May) Around 60 bottle-nose dolphins live in the bay year-round, their numbers increasing to 260 in summer. This centre has a beachside zone where dolphins regularly come to interact with people in the shallows and you can wade in alongside them, under the supervision of trained volunteers.

If you want to up your chances, there are 1½-hour **Eco Cruises** (1½hr cruise adult/child $53/35; ⊗11am Sat & Sun Jun-Sep, 11am & 3pm Oct-May) and three-hour **Swim Encounter Cruises** (3hr cruises $185; ⊗7.30am mid-Oct–Jan, 11.30am mid-Dec–Apr).

Bunbury Wildlife Park   ZOO
(Prince Philip Dr; adult/child $8/5; ⊗10am-5pm) Parrots, kangaroos, wallabies, possums, owls and emus all feature. Across the road, the **Big Swamp** has good wetlands walking tracks and stops for birdwatching.

Bunbury Regional Art Galleries   GALLERY
(www.brag.org.au; 64 Wittenoom St; ⊗10am-4pm) **FREE** Housed in a restored pink-painted convent (1897), this excellent gallery has a collection that includes works by Australian art luminaries Arthur Boyd and Sir Sidney Nolan.

🛏 Sleeping

Dolphin Retreat YHA   HOSTEL $
(☑08-9792 4690; www.dolphinretreatbunbury.com.au; 14 Wellington St; dm/s/d $27/47/68; @ 🛜) Just around the corner from the beach, this small hostel is well located in a rabbit warren of an old house, with hammocks and a barbecue on the back verandah.

Mantra   APARTMENT $$$
(☑08-9721 0100; www.mantra.com.au; 1 Holman St; apt from $209; ❄@🛜🏊) One of the most unusual heritage conversions we've seen, the Mantra has sculpted a set of modern studios and apartments around four grain silos by the harbour. Deluxe rooms have spa baths and full kitchens.

✖ Eating & Drinking

Happy Wife   CAFE $$
(www.thehappywife.com.au; 98 Stirling St; mains $10-20; ⊗6.30am-3.30pm Mon-Fri, 7.30am-2.30pm Sat) Grab a spot in the garden of this Cape Cod–style cottage just a short drive from the centre of town. Excellent home-style baking and regular lunch specials make it worth seeking out.

Café 140   CAFE $$
(140 Victoria St; mains $12-21; ⊗7.30am-4.30pm Mon-Fri, 8am-2pm Sat & Sun) The funky Café 140 is a top spot for good coffee and one of WA's best salmon omelettes. Gourmet burgers and grilled Turkish sandwiches are among the lunchtime stars.

Mash   CRAFT BEER
(www.mashbrewing.com.au; 2/11 Bonnefoi Blvd; ⊗11am-3pm Mon & Tue, to 9pm Wed-Sun) With an absolute waterfront location, this modern microbrewery turns out seven regular beers, plus always interesting seasonal concoctions. Thursday night's 'Pint & Parma' deal ($25) is good value.

ℹ Information

Visitor Centre (☑08-9792 7205; www.visitbunbury.com.au; Carmody Pl; ⊗9am-5pm Mon-Sat, 10am-2pm Sun) Located in the historic train station (1904).

Busselton

POP 15,400

Unpretentious, uncomplicated and with a slightly faded charm, family-friendly Busselton is surrounded by calm waters and white-sand beaches. During school holidays it really bustles – the population increases fourfold and accommodation prices soar.

◉ Sights & Activities

Busselton Jetty   JETTY
(☑08-9754 0900; www.busseltonjetty.com.au; adult/child $2.50/free, return train adult/child $11/6, Interpretive Centre admission free; ⊗Interpretive Centre 9am-5pm) Busselton's 1865 timber-piled jetty is the longest in the southern hemisphere (1841m). A little **train** chugs along to the **Underwater Observatory** (adult/child incl train $29.50/14; ⊗9am-4.25pm), where tours take place approximately 8m below the surface.

Dive Shed   DIVING
(☑08-9754 1615; www.diveshed.com.au; 21 Queen St) Runs regular dive charters along the jetty, to Four Mile Reef (a 40km limestone ledge about 6.5km off the coast) and to the scuttled navy vessel HMAS *Swan* (off Dunsborough).

✤ Festivals & Events

Southbound   MUSIC
(www.southboundfestival.com.au) Start the new
year with three days of alternative music
and camping.

CinéfestOZ   CINEMA
(www.cinefestoz.com.au) Busselton briefly
morphs into St-Tropez in late August with
this oddly glamorous festival of French and
Australian cinema.

🛏 Sleeping

Busselton is packed in the holidays and
pretty much deserted off-season. Accommodation sprawls along the beach for several
kilometres either side of the town, so make
sure you check the location if you don't have
your own wheels.

Beachlands Holiday Park   CARAVAN PARK $
(☑1800 622 107; www.beachlands.net; 10 Earn-
shaw Rd, West Busselton; sites per 2 people $42,
chalets from $132; ❄ 🛜 🌊) This excellent fam-
ily-friendly park offers a wide range of accommodation amid shady trees, palms and
flax bushes.

Blue Bay Apartments   APARTMENT $$
(☑08-9751 1796; www.bluebayapartments.com;
66 Adelaide St; apt from $125; ❄) Close to the
beach, these good-value self-contained
apartments are bright and cheery, each with
private courtyard and barbecue.

🍴 Eating

★Laundry Cafe   CAFE $$
(www.laundrycafe.com.au; 43 Prince St; shared
plates $14-39) Brick walls and a honey-
coloured jarrah bar form the backdrop for
Margaret River beers and wines, great cocktails, and classy shared plates including pan-
ko-crumbed cuttlefish and kangaroo tataki.

Goose   CAFE $$
(www.thegoose.com.au; Geographe Bay Rd; breakfast $11-24, lunch & dinner mains $29-39; ⊙7am-
5pm Mon-Tue, till late Wed-Sun; 🛜) Near the jetty,
this stylish cafe offers an eclectic, interesting
menu and views out to sea. Between meals
it's open for coffee, wine and tapas (from $15
to $20).

ℹ Information

Visitor Centre (☑08-9752 5800; www.geogra-
phebay.com; 38 Peel Tce; ⊙9am-5pm Mon-Fri,
to 4.30pm Sat & Sun)

Dunsborough
POP 3400

Dunsborough is a relaxed, beach-worship-
ping town that goes bonkers towards the
end of November when 7000 'schoolies' descend. When it's not inundated with drunk-
en, squealing teenagers, it's a thoroughly
pleasant place to be. The beaches are better than Busselton's, but accommodation is
more limited.

🏃 Activities

Cape Dive   DIVING
(☑08-9756 8778; www.capedive.com; 222
Naturaliste Tce) There is excellent diving in
Geographe Bay, especially since the decom-
missioned navy destroyer HMAS *Swan* was
purposely scuttled in 1997 for use as a dive
wreck. Marine life has colonised the ship,
which lies at a depth of 30m, 2.5km offshore.

Naturaliste Charters   WHALE WATCHING
(☑0419 186 133; www.whales-australia.com; adult/
child $80/50; ⊙10am & 2pm Sep-Dec) Two-hour
whale-watching cruises from September to
December. From January to March the emphasis switches to an **Eco Wilderness Tour**
showcasing beaches, limestone caves with
indigenous art, and wildlife. Tours also run
from Augusta.

🛏 Sleeping

There are many options for self-contained
rentals in town depending on the season;
the visitor centre has current listings.

Dunsborough Beachouse YHA   HOSTEL $
(☑08-9755 3107; www.dunsboroughbeachouse.
com.au; 205 Geographe Bay Rd; dm $32-34, s/d
$55/80; @ 🛜) On the Quindalup beachfront,
this friendly hostel has lawns stretching languidly to the water's edge; it's an easy 2km
cycle from the town centre.

Dunsborough Central Motel   MOTEL $$
(☑08-9756 7711; www.dunsboroughmotel.com.au;
50 Dunn Bay Rd; r $120-175) Centrally located
in Dunsborough town, this well-run motel
is good value, especially if you can snare an
online midweek discount.

🍴 Eating & Drinking

Samudra   CAFE $$
(www.samudra.com.au; 226 Naturaliste Tce; mains
$14-20; ⊙7.30am-4pm daily, plus 5.30-8pm Fri
& Sat; ☑) 🌱 Mexican, Middle Eastern and
Asian flavours underpin a super-healthy

vegetarian menu of salads, curries, wraps and smoothies, and there are plenty of shady places to sit and read or write. Samudra also offers relaxing and reinvigorating yoga classes and surfing and spa retreats.

Pourhouse BISTRO $$
(www.pourhouse.com.au; 26 Dunn Bay Rd; mains $19-28; 4pm-late) Hip but not pretentious, with comfy couches, regular live bands, and an upstairs terrace for summer. The pizzas are excellent, and top-notch burgers come in a locally baked sourdough bun. A considered approach to beer includes rotating taps from the best of WA's craft breweries.

Information

Visitor Centre (08-9752 5800; www.geographebay.com; Seymour Blvd; 9am-5pm Mon-Fri, 9.30am-4.30pm Sat & Sun) In the same building as the post office.

Cape Naturaliste

Northwest of Dunsborough, Cape Naturaliste Rd leads to the excellent beaches of **Meelup**, **Eagle Bay** and **Bunker Bay**, and on to Cape Naturaliste. Bunker Bay is also home to **Bunkers Beach Cafe** (www.bunkersbeachcafe.com.au; Farm Break Lane; breakfast $14-24, lunch $16-34; 11.30am-4pm), which serves an adventurous menu from a spot only metres from the sand.

The **Cape Naturaliste lighthouse** (adult/child $13/7; tours every 30min 9.30am-4pm), built in 1903, can be visited, and Above and Below packages (adult/child $27/14) incorporate entry to Ngilgi Cave near Yallingup.

Craft beer fans should definitely divert to the **Eagle Bay Brewing Co** (www.eaglebaybrewing.com.au; Eagle Bay Rd, Dunsborough; 11am-5pm) for sublime rural views, great beer and wine, and wood-fired pizzas.

Margaret River Wine Region

With its blissful country roads shaded by mature trees, its crashing surf beaches, and, of course, its excellent chardonnays and Bordeaux-style reds, Margaret River is our favourite Australian wine region and a highlight of any trip to WA. Of course, where there's fine wine, fancy restaurants surely follow – and cheese shops, craft breweries, art galleries and craft stores. Margaret River has all of the predictable trappings of gentrification, yet it still seems to remember that it's in the country, not some swanky corner of Subiaco. The local pub keeps it real and, for the most part, wineries don't charge for tastings.

There are a huge number of tour companies operating in Margaret River; see the visitor centre for all options.

Yallingup & Around

POP 1070

Beachside Yallingup is as much a mecca for surfers as it is for wine aficionados. You're permitted to let a 'wow' escape when the surf-battered coastline first comes into view. Romantics may be encouraged to know that the name Yallingup means 'place of love'.

Sights & Activities

Wardan Aboriginal Centre INDIGENOUS CULTURE
(08-9756 6566; www.wardan.com.au; Injidup Springs Rd, Yallingup; experiences adult/child $20/10; 10am-4pm daily 15 Oct-15 Mar, closed Tue & Sat 15 Mar-15 Oct, experiences Sun, Mon, Wed & Fri) FREE Offers a window into the lives of the local Wardandi people. There's a gallery, an interpretive display on the six seasons which govern the Wardandi calendar (admission $5) and the opportunity to take part in various experiences like stone toolmaking and boomerang and spear throwing. Guided bushwalks explore Wardandi spirituality and the uses of plants for food, medicine and shelter.

Ngilgi Cave CAVING
(08-9755 2152; www.geographebay.com; Yallingup Caves Rd; adult/child $21/11; 9.30am-4.30pm) Between Dunsborough and Yallingup, this 500,000-year-old cave is known for its limestone formations. Entry is by semiguided tours departing depart every half-hour. Check the website for more adventurous caving options. Well-marked bushwalks also start from here.

Sleeping & Eating

Yallingup Beach Holiday Park CARAVAN PARK $
(08-9755 2164; www.yallingupbeach.com.au; Valley Rd; sites per 2 people $32, cabins $100-150;) You'll sleep to the sound of the surf here, with the beach just across the road.

Wildwood Valley Cottages & Cooking School COTTAGE $$
(08-9755 2120; www.wildwoodvalley.com.au; 1481 Wildwood Rd; cottages from $220;) Luxury cottages trimmed by native bush are

arrayed across 120 acres, and the property's main house also hosts the Mad About Food Cooking School with Sioban and Carlo Baldini. The culinary emphasis is Thai or Italian, and classes start at $85 per person.

★**Studio Bistro** MODERN AUSTRALIAN **$$$**
(☎08-9756 6164; www.thestudiobistro.com.au; 7 Marrinup Dr; mains $35, degustation menu with/without wine matches $125/90;) The gallery focuses on Australian artists, while the restaurant showcases subtle dishes like pan-fried fish with cauliflower cream, radicchio, peas and crab meat. Five-course degustation menus are offered on Friday and Saturday nights. Bookings recommended.

Cowaramup & Wilyabrup

POP 990

Cowaramup is little more than a couple of blocks of shops lining Bussell Hwy. That a significant percentage of those are devoted in one way or another to eating or drinking is testament to its position at the heart of the wine region. The rustic area to the northwest known as Wilyabrup is where, in the 1960s, the Margaret River wine industry was born.

Activities

Margaret River Regional Wine Centre WINE SHOP
(www.mrwines.com; 9 Bussell Hwy, Cowaramup; ⏲10am-7pm) A one-stop shop for Margaret River wine, with daily tastings rotating between smaller wineries without cellar doors.

Sleeping

Noble Grape Guesthouse B&B **$$**
(☎08-9755 5538; www.noblegrape.com.au; 29 Bussell Hwy, Cowaramup; s $135-155, d $150-190;) Noble Grape is more like an upmarket motel than a traditional B&B. Rooms offer a sense of privacy and each has a well-tended garden courtyard.

Eating & Drinking

Providore DELI **$**
(www.providore.com.au; 448 Tom Cullity Dr, Wilyabrup; ⏲9am-5pm) Voted one of Australia's Top 100 Gourmet Experiences by *Australian Traveller* magazine – and, given its amazing range of artisan produce including organic olive oil, tapenades and preserved fruits, we can only agree.

Margaret River Chocolate Company CHOCOLATES **$**
(www.chocolatefactory.com.au; Harman's Mill Rd; ⏲9am-5pm) Watch truffles being made, sample chocolate buttons, or grab a coffee.

Vasse Felix WINERY RESTAURANT **$$$**
(☎08-9756 5050; www.vassefelix.com.au; cnr Caves Rd & Harmans Rd S, Cowaramup; mains $29-39; ⏲10am-3pm) Vasse Felix is considered by many to have the finest restaurant in the region. The grounds are peppered with sculptures, while the gallery displaying works from the Holmes à Court collection is worth a trip in itself.

Cullen Wines WINERY RESTAURANT **$$$**
(☎08-9755 5277; www.cullenwines.com.au; 4323 Caves Rd, Cowaramup; mains $33-39; ⏲10am-4pm) Grapes were first planted here in 1966 and Cullen has an ongoing commitment to organic and biodynamic principles in both food and wine. The food is excellent, with many of the fruits and vegetables from Cullen's own gardens.

Cowaramup Brewing Company CRAFT BEER
(www.cowaramupbrewing.com.au; North Treeton Rd, Cowaramup; ⏲11am-5pm) Modern microbrewey with an award-winning Pilsner and a moreish English-style Special Pale Ale. Four other beers and occasional seasonal brews also feature.

Margaret River

POP 4500

Although tourists might outnumber locals much of the time, Margaret River still feels like a country town. The advantage of basing yourself here is that after 5pm, once the surrounding wineries shut up shop, it's one of the few places with any vital signs.

Sleeping

Margaret River Lodge YHA HOSTEL **$**
(☎08-9757 9532; www.mrlodge.com.au; 220 Railway Tce; dm $31-34, r with/without bathroom $74/85;) About 1.5km southwest of the town centre, this clean, well-run hostel has a pool, a volleyball court and a football field. Dorms share a big communal kitchen, and a quieter area with private rooms has its own little kitchen and lounge.

Edge of the Forest MOTEL **$$**
(☎08-9757 2351; www.edgeoftheforest.com.au; 25 Bussell Hwy; r $120-180;) New owners have re-energised this motel a pleasant

stroll from Margaret River township. The six rooms have all been recently renovated, several with a chic Asian theme.

Vintages MOTEL $$
(☎08-9758 8333; www.vintagesmargaretriver.com.au; cnr Willmott Ave & Le Souef St; r $157-220; ❄) Another spotless motel, this one set in tropical gardens.

★**Burnside Organic Farm** BUNGALOWS $$$
(☎08-9757 2139; www.burnsideorganicfarm.com.au; 287 Burnside Rd; d $275; ❄) Rammed-earth and limestone bungalows have spacious decks and designer kitchens, and the surrounding farm hosts a menagerie of animals and organic avocado and macadamia orchards.

Eating & Drinking

Margaret River Farmers Market MARKET $
(www.margaretriverfarmersmarket.com.au; cnr Tunbridge & Farrelly Sts; 8am-noon Sat) The region's organic and sustainable artisan producers come to town. Check the website for your own foodie hit list.

Margaret River Bakery CAFE $
(89 Bussell Hwy; mains $10-18; 7am-4pm Mon-Sat;) Elvis on the stereo, retro furniture, and kitsch needlework 'paintings' – the MRB has a rustic, playful interior. It's the perfect backdrop to the bakery's honest home-style baking, often with a vegie or gluten-free spin.

Settler's Tavern PUB $$
(www.settlerstavern.com; 114 Bussell Hwy; mains $15-29; 11am-midnight Mon-Sat, to 10pm Sun) There's live entertainment Thursday to Sunday at Settler's, so pop in for good pub grub and a beer or wine from the extensive list. Dinner options are limited in Margaret River, and Settler's is often wildly popular with locals and visitors.

Morries Anytime CAFE $$
(www.morries.com.au; 2/149 Bussell Hwy; mains $15-34) Settle into the clubby, cosmopolitan atmosphere of Morrie's, either for breakfast or lunch, or later at night for cocktails and tapas or dinner.

Shopping

Tunbridge Gallery INDIGENOUS ART
(www.tunbridgegallery.com.au; 101 Bussell Hwy; 10am-5pm Mon-Sat, to 3pm Sun) Excellent Aboriginal art gallery featuring mainly WA works.

SURFING THE SOUTHWEST

Known to surfers as 'Yals' (around Yallingup) and 'Margs' (around the mouth of the Margaret River), the beaches between Capes Naturaliste and Leeuwin offer powerful reef breaks, mainly left-handers.

Around Dunsborough, the better locations are between Eagle and Bunker Bays. Near Yallingup there's the Three Bears, Rabbits (a beach break towards the north of Yallingup Beach), Yallingup, Injidup Car Park and Injidup Point. You'll need a 4WD to access Guillotine/Gallows, north of Gracetown. Also around Gracetown are Huzza's, South Point and Lefthanders. The annual surfer pro is held around Margaret River Mouth and Southside ('Suicides').

Information

Visitor centre (☎08-9757 2911; www.margaretriver.com; Bussell Hwy; 9am-5pm) This sleek visitor centre also includes an on-site wine centre.

Getting Around

Margaret River Beach Bus (☎08-9757 9532; www.mrlodge.com.au) Minibus linking the township and the beaches around Prevelly ($10, three daily); summer only, bookings essential.

Around Margaret River

West of the township, the coastline provides spectacular surfing and walks. Prevelly is the main settlement, with a scattering of places to sleep and eat.

Sights & Activities

CaveWorks & Lake Cave CAVE
(www.margaretriver.com; Conto Rd; single cave adult/child $22/10; 9am-5pm, Lake Cave tours hourly 9.30am-3.30pm) Acting as the main ticket office for three of the region's most impressive caves (Lake, Mammoth and Jewel), CaveWorks also has excellent displays about caves, cave conservation and local fossil discoveries.

Behind the centre is Lake Cave, where limestone formations are reflected in an underground stream.

Single cave tickets include entry to CaveWorks. The **Grand Pass** (adult/child $50/22), covering CaveWorks and all three caves, is valid for seven days, while the **Ultimate**

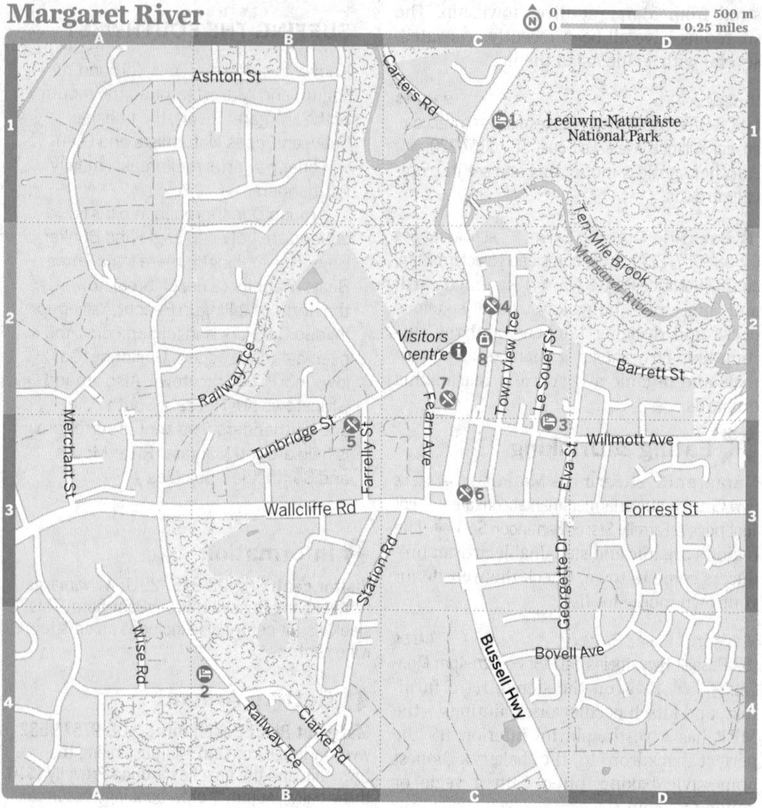

Margaret River

Sleeping

1 Edge of the Forest C1
2 Margaret River Lodge YHA B4
3 Vintages C3

Eating

4 Margaret River Bakery C2
5 Margaret River Farmers Market B3
6 Morries Anytime C3
7 Settler's Tavern C2

Shopping

8 Tunbridge Gallery C2

Pass (adult/child $65/27) also includes Cape Leeuwin lighthouse.

Mammoth Cave CAVE
(www.margaretriver.com; Caves Rd; adult/child $22/10; ⊙9am-4pm) Mammoth Cave boasts fossil remains and the impressive Mammoth Shawl formation. Visits are self-guided, and an MP3 audio player is provided.

Calgardup & Giants Caves CAVES
These two self-guided caves are managed by the Department of Environment and Conservation (DEC), which provides helmets and torches. **Calgardup Cave** (www.dec.wa.gov.au; Caves Rd; adult/child $15/8; ⊙9am-4.15pm) has a seasonal underground lake. **Giants Cave** (www.dec.wa.gov.au; Caves Rd; adult/child $15/8; ⊙9.30am-3.30pm school & public holidays only), further south, is deeper and longer.

Ellensbrook Homestead HISTORIC BUILDING
(www.ntwa.com.au; Ellensbrook Rd; adult/child $4/2; ⊙10am-4pm Sat & Sun) National Trust–

owned Ellensbrook (1857) was the home of pioneer settlers and later served as an Aboriginal mission. The house is more than a little ramshackle, constructed of paperbark, driftwood, timber, lime, dung and hair. A short walk leads to Meekadarribee ('bathing place of the moon'), a grotto set below trickling rapids.

Boranup Drive SCENIC DRIVE
This 14km diversion runs along an unsealed road through Leeuwin-Naturaliste National Park's beautiful karri forest. Near the southern end there's a lookout offering sea views.

Eagles Heritage WILDLIFE
(☎08-9757 2960; www.eaglesheritage.com.au; adult/child $15/7.50; ⊙10am-5pm) Housing Australia's largest collection of raptors, this centre, 5km south of Margaret River, rehabilitates many birds of prey each year. There are free-flight displays at 11am and 1.30pm.

Sleeping

Surfpoint HOSTEL $
(☎08-9757 1777; www.surfpoint.com.au; Reidle Dr, Gnarabup; dm/d $32/105; @🛜🏊) This light and airy place offers the beach on a budget. The rooms are clean and well presented, and there's a very enticing little pool.

National Park Campgrounds CAMPGROUND $
(www.dec.wa.gov.au; sites per adult/child $7/2) DEC has three basic campgrounds within Leeuwin-Naturaliste National Park: **Conto Campground** (Conto Rd), **Boranup Campground** (off Boranup Dr), and **Point Road Campground** (only accessible by foot or 4WD from the northern end of Boranup Dr).

★ **Acacia Chalets** CHALET $$$
(☎08-9757 2718; www.acaciachalets.com.au; 113 Yates Rd; d $250-270; ❄) Private bushland – complete with marsupial locals – conceals three luxury chalets that are well located to explore the region's vineyards, caves and rugged nearby coastline. Limestone walls and honey-coloured jarrah floors feature, and spacious decks are equipped with gas barbecues.

Eating & Drinking

Watershed Premium Wines RESTAURANT $$
(www.watershedwines.com.au; cnr Bussell Hwy & Darch Rd; cafe $17-22, restaurant $38-42; ⊙10am-5pm) Famous for its Awakening cabernet sauvignon, and regularly rated as one of WA's best vineyard restaurants. Dining options include an informal cafe and Watershed's classier restaurant with expansive views of trellised vines.

Voyager Estate WINERY
(☎08-9757 6354; www.voyagerestate.com.au; Stevens Rd; ⊙10am-5pm) There are formal gardens and Cape Dutch–style buildings at Voyager Estate, the grandest of Margaret River's wineries. Tours are available ($25 including tastings).

Leeuwin Estate WINERY
(☎08-9759 0000; www.leeuwinestate.com.au; Stevens Rd; ⊙10am-5pm) Leeuwin's Art Series chardonnay is one of the best in the country. Behind-the-scenes wine tours and tastings take place at 11am, noon and 3pm (adult/child $12.50/4). Big open-air concerts are regularly held here.

Cheeky Monkey Brewery CRAFT BEER
(www.cheekymonkeybrewery.com.au; 4259 Caves Rd; ⊙10am-6pm) Craft beers and ciders stand out at Margaret River's newest microbrewery. Set around a pretty lake, there's also lots of room for the kids to run around.

Augusta & Around

POP 1700

Augusta is positioned at the mouth of the Blackwood River, 5km north of Cape Leeuwin. There are a few vineyards scattered around, but the vibe here is less epicurean, more languid.

Sights & Activities

Cape Leeuwin Lighthouse LIGHTHOUSE
(www.margaretriver.com; adult/child $5/3, tours $17/7; ⊙8.45am-4.45pm) Wild and windy Cape Leeuwin, where the Indian and Southern Oceans meet, is the most southwesterly point in Australia. The lighthouse (1896), WA's tallest, offers magnificent views of the coastline. Tours leave every 40 minutes from 9am to 4.30pm. The **Ultimate Pass** (adult/child $65/27) incorporates admission to the lighthouse with Jewel, Lake and Mammoth Caves.

Jewel Cave CAVE
(www.margaretriver.com; Caves Rd; adult/child $22/10; ⊙tours hourly 9.30am-3.30pm) The most spectacular of the region's caves, Jewel Cave features an impressive 5.9m straw stalactite. It's around 8km north of Augusta.

The nearby **Moondyne Cave** (www.margaretriver.com; Caves Rd; adult/child 12-16yr $150/120; ⏲10am-2pm Tue & Fri Jun-Dec) can be visited on the Moondyne Experience, a subterranean adventure combining overalls, hard hats and torches. Prior booking is essential, and children must be at least 12 years of age.

Naturaliste Charters WHALE WATCHING
(☎0419 186 133; www.whales-australia.com.au; adult/child $80/50; ⏲10am & 2pm Sep-Dec) Two-hour whale-watching cruises from September to December. From January to March the emphasis switches to an Eco Wilderness Tour. Tours also run from Dunsborough.

Absolutely Eco River Cruises CRUISE
(☎08-9758 4003; cdragon@westnet.com.au; adult/child $30/10) Blackwood River; October to May.

Miss Flinders CRUISE
(☎0409 377 809; adult/child $40/15) Blackwood River; October to May.

Sleeping & Eating

Hamelin Bay Holiday Park CARAVAN PARK $
(☎08-9758 5540; www.mronline.com.au/accom/hamelin; Hamelin Bay West Rd; 2-person sites $20-25, cabins $80-180) Absolute beachfront, northwest of Augusta, this secluded place gets very busy during holiday times.

Baywatch Manor YHA HOSTEL $
(☎08-9758 1290; www.baywatchmanor.com.au; 9 Heppingstone View; dm $29, d with/without bathroom $93/73; @ 📶) Clean, modern rooms with creamy brick walls and pieces of antique furniture. There is a bay view from the deck and, in winter, a roaring fire in the communal lounge. Some doubles have compact balconies.

Deckchair Gourmet CAFE, DELI $
(Blackwood Ave; mains $7-16; ⏲8.30am-4pm; 📶) Excellent coffee, delicious food and free wi-fi.

Information

Visitor Centre (☎08-9758 0166; www.margaretriver.com; cnr Blackwood Ave & Ellis St; ⏲9am-5pm)

Southern Forests

The tall forests of WA's southwest are simply magnificent, with towering gums (karri, jarrah, marri) sheltering cool undergrowth. Between the forests, small towns bear witness to the region's history of logging and mining. Many have redefined themselves as small-scale tourist centres where you can take walks, wine tours, canoe trips and trout- and marron-fishing expeditions.

Nannup

POP 500

Nannup's historic weatherboard buildings and cottage gardens have an idyllic bush setting on the Blackwood River. The Noongar-derived name means 'a place to stop and rest', which indeed it still is, although it's also a good base for bushwalkers and canoeists. **Blackwood River Canoeing** (☎08-9756 1209; www.blackwoodrivercanoeing.com; hire per day from $25) provides equipment, basic instruction and transfers for paddle-powered excursions.

Sporadic but persistent stories of sightings of a striped wolflike animal, dubbed the Nannup tiger, have led to hopes that a thylacine (Tasmanian tiger) may have survived in the surrounding bush (the last known one died in Hobart Zoo in 1936). Keep your camera handy and your eyes peeled!

The **Nannup Music Festival** (www.nannupmusicfestival.org) is held in early March, focusing on folk and world music.

Sleeping & Eating

Visitor Centre Caravan Park CARAVAN PARK $
(☎08-9756 1211; www.nannupwa.com; 4 Brockman St; sites s/d from $15/25, cabins $66-77) Contact the visitor centre.

Holberry House B&B $$
(☎08-9756 1276; www.holberryhouse.com; 14 Grange Rd; r incl breakfast $120-190; 📶 🏊) The decor might lean towards granny-chic but this large house on the hill has charming hosts and comfortable rooms. It's surrounded by large gardens dotted with quirky sculptures (open to nonguests for $4).

Nannup Bridge Cafe CAFE $$
(1 Warren Rd; breakfast & lunch $9-18, dinner $16-38; ⏲9am-2pm Tue-Sun, plus 6-8pm Wed-Sat) Right opposite the tourist office, this cool-looking riverfront cafe morphs into a bistro at night. Standout dishes include pork belly and sticky date pudding.

Information

Visitor Centre (☎08-9756 1211; www.nannupwa.com; 4 Brockman St; ⏲10am-4pm) Administers the neighbouring caravan park.

Bridgetown

POP 2400

Spread around the Blackwood River and surrounded by karri forests and farmland, Bridgetown is one of the loveliest little towns in the southwest. Despite being busy most weekends, and overrun with visitors on the second weekend of November during its annual **Blues at Bridgetown Festival** (www.bluesatbridgetown.com), it retains a community feel.

Sleeping & Eating

Bridgetown Hotel HOTEL $$
(☎08-9761 1034; www.bridgetownhotel.com.au; 157 Hampton St; r $165-265, mains $17-29; ❄) You don't expect quirky pizzas (lime and tequila; lamb and tzatziki) or large modern bedrooms with spa baths at an Australian country pub. A recent revamp has left this 1920s gem with both.

Bridgetown Riverside Chalets RENTAL HOUSES $$
(☎08-9761 1040; www.bridgetownchalets.com.au; 1338 Brockman Hwy; chalets from $125) On a rural riverside property, 5km up the road to Nannup, these four stand-alone wooden chalets (complete with pot-bellied stoves and washing machines) sleep up to six in two bedrooms.

Nelsons of Bridgetown MOTEL $$
(☎08-9761 1645; www.nelsonsofbridgetown.com.au; 38 Hampton St; s $95-145, d $130-195; ❄📶🏊) The central location is great, but go for the spacious newer rooms built adjacent to the 1898 Federation-style hotel.

Cidery CAFE $$
(www.thecidery.com.au; 43 Gifford Rd; mains $10-25; ⏰11am-4pm Sat-Thu, to 8pm Fri) Craft beer, cider and light lunches on outdoor tables by the river. On Friday nights from 5.30pm there's live music.

ELVIS SIGHTED IN BOYUP BROOK

The pretty township of Boyup Brook (population 540), 31km northeast of Bridgetown, is the centre of country music in WA. The fantastically over-the-top **Harvey Dickson's Country Music Centre** (www.harveydickson.com.au; adult/child $8/2; ⏰9am-5pm) comes complete with a life-size Elvis and Johnny Cash, an Elvis room and three 13.5m-tall guitar-playing men. It hosts regular rodeos (the big one's in October) and big-name country-music events, as well as the **WA Country Music Festival** (www.countrymusicwa.com.au) in February. Scenic but basic **bush camping** (sites $8) is always available.

Information

Visitor Centre (☎08-9761 1740; www.bridgetown.com.au; 154 Hampton St; ⏰9am-5pm Mon-Fri, 10am-3pm Sat, 10am-1pm Sun)

Pemberton

POP 760

Hidden deep in the karri forests, drowsy Pemberton has taken an epicurean turn, producing excellent wine that rivals Margaret River's for quality if not scale. Wine tourism isn't as developed here, with some of the better names only offering tastings by appointment; grab a free map listing opening hours from the visitor centre.

WORTH A TRIP

D'ENTRECASTEAUX NATIONAL PARK

This quiet gem of a **national park** (entry per car/motorcycle $11/5), named for French Admiral Bruny d'Entrecasteaux, who led an exploratory expedition here in 1792, stretches for 130km along the coast 60km south of Pemberton. It's a complete contrast to the tall forests, with its five rivers and wild stretches of coastal heath, sand dunes, cliffs and beaches.

Sealed roads lead to **Windy Harbour**, a collection of ramshackle holiday shacks with names like 'Wywurk', where you can camp as long as you have all your own provisions. From here, D'Entrecasteaux Dr continues for 6km to Point d'Entrecasteaux, or a 3km wild and windy coastal walk will get you to the same place.

A series of 4WD tracks leads in from the Pemberton–Northcliffe Rd to bush and beach camp sites; check with the DEC in Pemberton (p951) that the roads are open.

The national parks circling Pemberton are impressive. Aim to spend a day or two driving the Karri Forest Explorer, walking the trails and picnicking in the green depths.

◉ Sights & Activities

Salitage Winery
WINERY

(☑08-9776 1195; www.salitage.com.au; Vasse Hwy; ⊙10am-4pm) Salitage's pinot noir has been rated the state's best, while its chardonnay and sauvignon blanc are also very highly regarded. Hour-long vineyard tours leave at 11am; call ahead.

Pemberton Tramway
TRAM RIDES

(☑08-9776 1322; www.pemtram.com.au; adult/child $18/9; ⊙10.45am & 2pm) Built between 1929 and 1933, the route travels through lush karri and marri forests to Warren River. A commentary is provided and it's a fun 1¾-hour return trip, if noisy.

Pemberton Wine Centre
WINE TASTING

(www.marima.com.au; 388 Old Vasse Rd; ⊙noon-4pm Mon-Fri) At the very heart of Warren National Park, this centre offers tastings of local wines and can compile a mixed case of your favourites.

◐ Tours

Pemberton Hiking & Canoeing
HIKING, CANOEING

(☑08-9776 1559; www.hikingandcanoeing.com.au; half-/full day $50/100) Environmentally sound tours in Warren and D'Entrecasteaux National Parks and to the Yeagarup sand dunes. Specialist tours (wildflowers, frogs, rare fauna) are also available, as are night canoeing trips ($75) to spot nocturnal wildlife.

Pemberton Discovery Tours
4WD TOUR

(☑08-9776 0484; www.pembertondiscoverytours.com.au; adult/child $95/50) Half-day 4WD tours to the Yeagarup sand dunes and the Warren River mouth.

Donnelly River Cruises
BOAT TOUR

(☑08-9777 1018; www.donnellyrivercruises.com.au; adult/child $65/35) Cruises through 12km of D'Entrecasteaux National Park to the cliffs of the Southern Ocean.

🛏 Sleeping & Eating

Pemberton has some excellent accommodation choices, and the local culinary specialities are trout and marron, which make their way onto most menus.

Pemberton Backpackers YHA
HOSTEL $

(☑08-9776 1105; www.yha.com.au; 7 Brockman St; dm/s/d $28/62/65; @🖥) The main hostel is given over to seasonal workers, but you'll need to check in here for a room in the separate cottage (8 Dean St) that's set aside for travellers. It's cute and cosy but book ahead as it only has three rooms.

★ Foragers
COTTAGE $$

(☑08-9776 1580; www.foragers.com.au; cnr Roberts & Northcliffe Rds; cottages $160-270; ❋) Choose between very nice, simple karri cottages, or leap to the top of the ladder with the luxury eco-chalets. The latter are light and airy, with elegant, contemporary decor, eco-conscious wastewater systems and

---

WORTH A TRIP

KARRI FOREST EXPLORER

Punctuated by glorious walks, magnificent individual trees, picnic areas and lots of interpretive signage, this tourist drive wends its way along 86km of scenic (partly unsealed) roads through three national parks (vehicle entry $11).

Its popular attractions include the **Gloucester Tree**; if you're feeling fit and fearless, make the 58m climb to the top. The **Dave Evans Bicentennial Tree**, tallest of the 'climbing trees' at 68m, is in Warren National Park, 11km south of Pemberton. The Bicentennial Tree one-way loop leads via **Maiden Bush** to the **Heartbreak Trail**. It passes through 250-year-old karri stands, and nearby Drafty's Camp and Warren Campsite are great for overnighting (sites $7/2 per adult/child).

The enchanting **Beedelup National Park**, 15km west of Pemberton on the Vasse Hwy (Rte 104), shouldn't be missed. There's a short, scenic walk that crosses Beedelup Brook near **Beedelup Falls**. North of town, **Big Brook Arboretum** (admission free) features big trees from all over the world.

The track loops on and off the main roads, so you can drive short sections at a time. Pick up a brochure from Pemberton's visitor centre.

a solar-passive design. You're also right on hand to enjoy culinary treats at the adjacent **Foragers Field Kitchen** (☎08-9776 1503; www.foragers.com.au; cnr Roberts & Northcliffe Rds; dinner $55-75).

Old Picture Theatre Holiday Apartments APARTMENT **$$**
(☎08-9776 1513; www.oldpicturetheatre.com.au; cnr Ellis & Guppy Sts; apt $170-300; ❄ 📶) The town's old cinema has been revamped into well-appointed, self-contained, spacious apartments with lots of jarrah detail and black-and-white movie photos. It offers terrific value for money and the guest laundry and spa are rare treats.

Marima Cottages COTTAGE **$$$**
(☎08-9776 1211; www.marima.com.au; 388 Old Vasse Rd; cottages $225-245) Right in the middle of Warren National Park, these four country-style rammed-earth-and-cedar cottages with pot-bellied stoves and lots of privacy are luxurious getaways.

Forest Fresh Marron SELF-CATERING **$**
(☎0428 887 720; www.forestfreshmarron.com.au; Pump Hill Rd; ⏲10am-5pm Mon-Fri, 4.30-5.30pm Sat & Sun) 🍃 Live sustainably farmed marron for sale. Transport packs – to keep the wee beasties alive for up to 30 hours – and cooking pots are also available. It's 300m left of the caravan park.

Holy Smoke! SELF-CATERING **$**
(www.holysmoke.com.au; 3/19 Brockman St; snacks $5-15; ⏲9am-5pm Mon-Sat) Good coffee, sourdough bread, house-smoked meat, chicken and fish. Pop in for picnic supplies.

Sadie's INTERNATIONAL, INDIAN **$$**
(Ellis St; mains $25-35; ⏲6-9pm) Local trout and marron, and authentically good Indian curries from an authentically good Indian chef. At the Gloucester Motel.

ℹ Information

DEC (☎08-9776 1207; www.dec.wa.gov.au; Kennedy St; ⏲8am-4.30pm) Has detailed information on the local parks and stocks the useful *Pemberton Bushwalks* brochure.

Visitor Centre (☎08-9776 1133; www.pembertonvisitor.com.au; Brockman St; ⏲9am-4pm) Includes a pioneer museum and karri-forest discovery centre.

Shannon National Park

Until 1968, 535-sq-km **Shannon National Park** (entry per car/motorcycle $11/5) was the site of WA's biggest timber mill, and plants including northern hemisphere deciduous trees are reminders of the old settlement.

The 48km **Great Forest Trees Drive** is a one-way loop, split by the highway – tune into 100FM for a commentary. Start at the park day-use area on the north of the highway. From here there's an easy 3.5km walk to Shannon Dam (via a quokka-observation deck) and a steeper 5.5km loop to Mokare's Rock, with a boardwalk and great views. Further along, the 8km-return **Great Forest Trees Walk** crosses the Shannon River. Off the southern part of the drive, boardwalks look over stands of giant karri at **Snake Gully** and **Big Tree Grove**.

There is a sizeable **campground** (sites per adult/child $9/2) with showers in the spot where the original timber-milling town used to be. A self-contained bunkhouse, **Shannon Lodge** (per night $66, bond $150), is available for groups of up to eight people; book through DEC in Pemberton.

> WORTH A TRIP
>
> **MANJIMUP**
>
> To learn more about how the world's most expensive produce is harvested, follow your snout to the **Wine & Truffle Co** (☎08-9777 2474; www.wineandtruffle.com.au; Seven Day Rd; mains $19-35; ⏲10am-4.30pm). On Saturday and Sunday from June to August, you can join a 2½-hour truffle hunt ($95 per person; book ahead), and end with a breakfast of scrambled eggs and truffles. Offerings in the attached restaurant (open year-round) range from a truffle tasting plate to truffle fettuccine. Manjimup is en route from Bridgetown to Pemberton; the turn-off to the Wine & Truffle Co is about 3km south of town.

SOUTH COAST

Standing on the cliffs of the wild south coast as the waves pound below is an elemental experience. And on calm days, when the sea is varied shades of aquamarine and the glorious white-sand beaches lie pristine and welcoming, it's an altogether different type of magnificent. If you're seeking solitude, even busy holiday periods here in the 'Great Southern' are relaxed; it's just that bit too far from Perth for the holiday hordes. Marine

South Coast

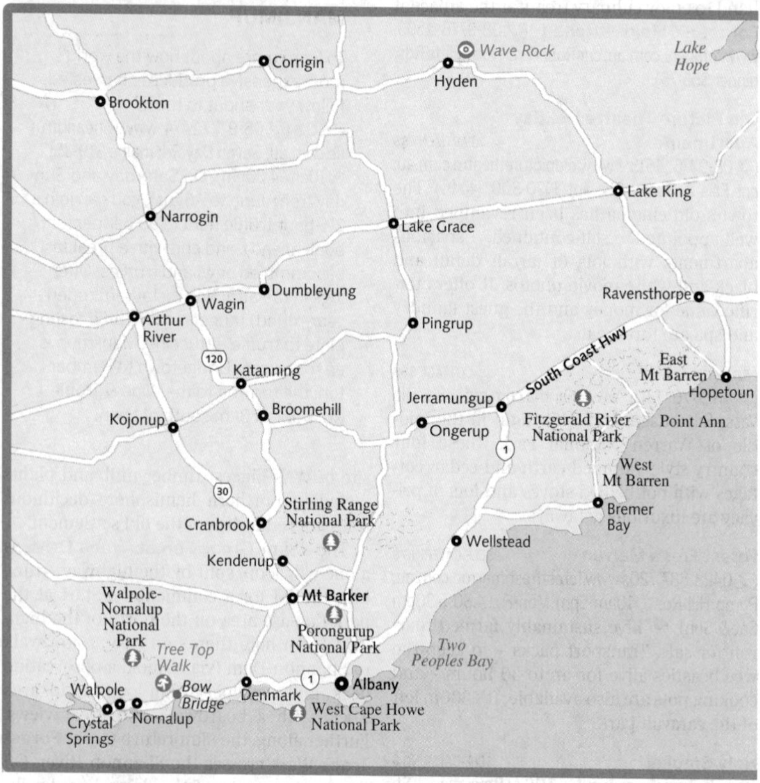

visitors come this way, though: the winter months bring a steady stream of migrating whales.

Getting There & Away

AIR

Virgin Australia (☎ 136789; www.virginaustralia.com) flies daily from Perth to Albany (75 minutes) and Esperance (1¾ hours). It also flies between Albany and Busselton twice a week.

BUS

Transwa (☎ 1300 662 205; www.transwa.wa.gov.au) services include the following:

GS1 & GS2 To/from Perth, Mt Barker and Albany daily.

GS3 To/from Bunbury, Bridgetown, Pemberton, Walpole, Denmark and Albany daily.

GE1 Between Perth and Esperance ($87, 10¼ hours, three times weekly).

GE2 To/from Perth, Hyden and Esperance three times weekly.

GE3 To/from Kalgoorlie, Coolgardie, Norseman and Esperance.

GE4 Between Albany and Esperance ($64, 6½ hours, twice weekly).

Walpole & Nornalup

POP 320 & 50

The peaceful twin inlets of Walpole and Nornalup make good bases from which to explore the heavily forested Walpole Wilderness Area – an immense wilderness incorporating a rugged coastline, several national parks, marine parks, nature reserves and forest-conservation areas – covering a whopping 3630 sq km. Look for DEC's *Exploring the Walpole Wilderness and Surrounding Area* pamphlet.

Walpole is the bigger settlement, and it's here the South Western Hwy (Rte 1) becomes the South Coast Hwy.

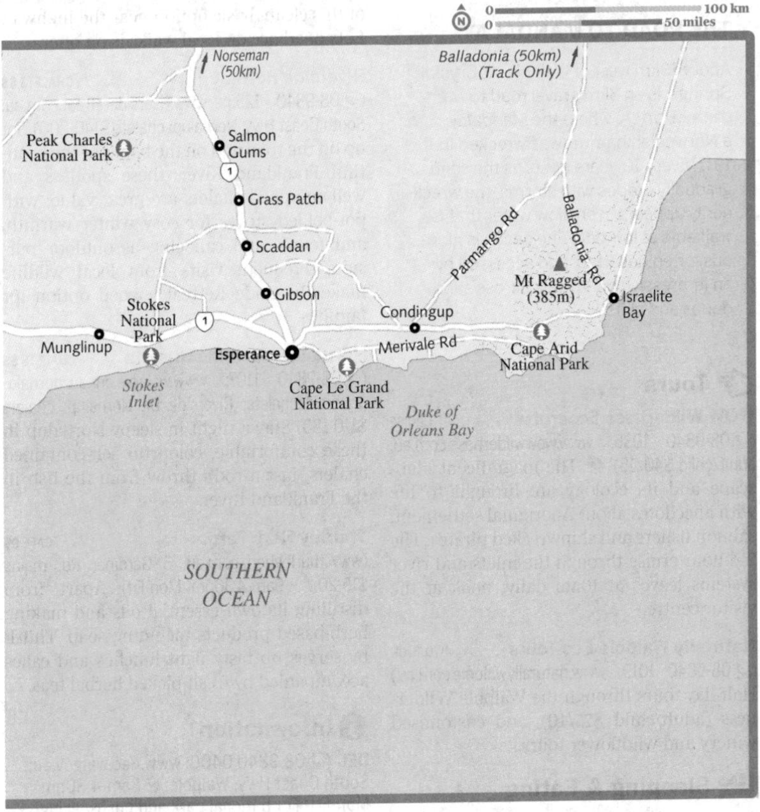

Sights & Activities

Walpole-Nornalup National Park NATURE RESERVE

The giant trees of this park include red, yellow and Rates tingle trees, and, closer to the coast, the red flowering gum.

In the **Valley of the Giants** (www.valleyofthegiants.com.au; Valley of the Giants Tree Top Walk adult/child $12.50/5; Valley of the Giants Tree Top Walk 9am-4.15pm) the **Tree Top Walk** is Walpole's main drawcard. A 600m-long ramp rises from the floor of the valley, allowing visitors access high into the canopy of the giant tingle trees. At its highest point the ramp is 40m above the ground. It's on a gentle incline so it's easy to walk and is even accessible by assisted wheelchair. The ramp is an engineering feat in itself, though vertigo sufferers might have a few problems; it's designed to sway gently in the breeze to mimic life in the treetops. At ground level the **Ancient Empire** boardwalk meanders around and through the base of veteran red tingles, some of which are 16m in circumference.

There are numerous good walking tracks around, including a section of the **Bibbulmun Track**, which passes through Walpole to Coalmine Beach. Scenic drives include the **Knoll Drive**, 3km east of Walpole; the **Valley of the Giants Road**; and through pastoral country to **Mt Frankland**, 29km north of Walpole. Here you can climb to the summit for panoramic views or walk around the trail at its base. Opposite Knoll Dr, Hilltop Rd leads to a **giant tingle tree**; this road continues to the **Circular Pool** on the Frankland River, a popular canoeing spot. You can hire canoes from Nornalup Riverside Chalets (p954).

Midway between Nornalup and Peaceful Bay, check out **Conspicuous Cliffs**. It's a great spot for whale watching from July to November, with a boardwalk, hilltop lookout and steepish 800m walk to the beach.

THE ROAD TO MANDALAY

About 13km west of Walpole, at Crystal Springs, is an 8km gravel road to **Mandalay Beach**, where the *Mandalay*, a Norwegian barque, was wrecked in 1911. Every 10 years or so, as the sand gradually erodes with storms, the wreck eerily appears in shallow water that is walkable at low tide. The beach is glorious, often deserted, and accessed by an impressive boardwalk across sand dunes and cliffs.

Tours

WOW Wilderness Ecocruises CRUISE
(☎08-9840 1036; www.wowwilderness.com.au; adult/child $40/15) The magnificent landscape and its ecology are brought to life with anecdotes about Aboriginal settlement, salmon fishers and shipwrecked pirates. The 2½-hour cruise through the inlets and river systems leaves at 10am daily; book at the visitor centre.

Naturally Walpole Eco Tours 4WD TOUR
(☎08-9840 1019; www.naturallywalpole.com.au) Half-day tours through the Walpole Wilderness (adult/child $75/40), and customised winery and wildflower tours.

Sleeping & Eating

There are bush-camping sites (per adult/child $7/2) in the Walpole Wilderness Area, including at Crystal Springs and Fernhook Falls.

Coalmine Beach CARAVAN PARK $
(☎08-9840 1026; www.coalminebeach.com.au; Coalmine Beach Rd, Walpole; 2-person sites $31-35, cabins $115-180; ❄@📶) You couldn't get a better location than this, under shady trees above the sheltered waters of the inlet.

Walpole Lodge HOSTEL $
(☎08-9840 1244; www.walpolelodge.com.au; Pier St, Walpole; dm/s/d $26/45/65; @📶) This popular place is basic, open-plan and informal, with great info boards around the walls and casual, cheery owners. En suite rooms are excellent value.

Tingle All Over YHA HOSTEL $
(☎08-9840 1041; www.yha.com.au; 60 Nockolds St, Walpole; dm/s/d $31/54/74; @📶) Help yourself to lemons and chillies from the garden of this clean, basic option near the highway. Lots of advice on local walks is on offer.

Riverside Retreat CHALETS $$
(☎08-9840 1255; www.riversideretreat.com.au; South Coast Hwy, Nornalup; chalets $140-200) Set up off the road and on the banks of the beautiful Frankland River, these spotless and well-equipped chalets are great value, with pot-bellied stoves for cosy winter warmth, and tennis and canoeing as outdoor pursuits. Frequent visits from local wildlife make Riverside Retreat a good option for families.

Nornalup Riverside Chalets CHALETS $$
(☎08-9840 1107; www.walpole.org.au/nornaluppriversidechalets; Riverside Dr, Nornalup; chalets $110-180) Stay a night in sleepy Nornalup in these comfortable, colourful self-contained chalets, just a rod's throw from the fish in the Frankland River.

Thurlby Herb Farm CAFE $$
(www.thurlbyherb.com.au; 3 Gardiner Rd; mains $15-20; ⏰9am-4.30pm Mon-Fri) Apart from distilling its own essential oils and making herb-based products including soap, Thurlby serves up tasty light lunches and cakes accompanied by fresh-picked herbal teas.

Information

DEC (☎08-9840 0400; www.dec.wa.gov.au; South Coast Hwy, Walpole; ⏰8am-4.30pm Mon-Fri) For national park and bushwalking information.

Visitor Centre (☎08-9840 1111; www.walpole.com.au; South Coast Hwy, Walpole; ⏰9am-5pm)

Denmark

POP 2800

The first wave of alternative lifestylers landed in idyllic Denmark about 20 years ago, attracted by its beaches, river, sheltered inlet, forested backdrop and rolling hinterland. Farmers, ferals, fisherfolk and families mingle during the town's three market days each year (December, January and Easter), when the population and accommodation prices soar.

The town is located in the cool-climate Great Southern wine region and has some notable wineries, including **Howard Park** (www.howardparkwines.com.au; Scotsdale Rd; ⏰10am-4pm) and **Forest Hill** (www.foresthillwines.com.au; cnr South Coast Hwy & Myers Rd; ⊙10am-5pm).

Denmark was established to supply timber to the early goldfields. Known by the Minang Noongar people as Koorabup ('place of the black swan'), there's evidence of early Aboriginal settlement in the 3000-year-old fish traps found in Wilson Inlet.

Sights & Activities

Surfers and anglers usually waste no time in heading to ruggedly beautiful **Ocean Beach**. If you're keen to try surfing, accredited local instructor Mike Neunuebel gives **surf lessons** (☎0401 349 854; www.southcoastsurfinglessons.com.au; 2hr lessons incl equipment from $50).

To get your bearings, walk the **Mokare Heritage Trail** (3km circuit along the Denmark River) or the **Wilson Inlet Trail** (12km return, starting at the river mouth), which forms part of the longer **Nornalup Trail**. Put everything into perspective at **Mt Shadforth Lookout**, with its view of fine coastal scenery. The lush **Mt Shadforth Road**, running from the centre of town and finishing up on the South Coast Hwy west of town, makes a great scenic drive, as does the longer pastoral loop of **Scotsdale Road**. Potter along these, taking your pick of attractions including alpaca farms, wineries, cheese farms, and art and craft galleries.

William Bay National Park, about 20km west of town, offers sheltered swimming in gorgeous **Greens Pool** and **Elephant Rocks**, and has good walking tracks. Swing by **Bartholomews Meadery** for a post-beach treat of homemade ice cream.

Tours

Out of Sight! 4WD TOUR
(☎08-9848 2814; www.outofsighttours.com) Nature trips into the Walpole Wilderness (three hours, adult/child $90/45), West Cape Howe (six hours, adult/child $150/75) or Stirling Range (eight hours, adult/child $200/100); sightseeing around Denmark (two hours, adult/child $50/25); or sampling tours of the local wineries (full day $100). Visit its Eco-Discovery shop at the Denmark visitor centre to hire canoes and bikes. In 2013 the Munda Biddi Trail was extended to Denmark, completing the trail's total of 1000km.

Denmark Wine Lovers Tour BUS TOUR
(☎0410 423 262; www.denmarkwinelovers.com.au) Full-day tours taking in Denmark wineries ($95), or further afield to Porongurup or Mt Barker (price on application).

Sleeping

Blue Wren Travellers' Rest YHA HOSTEL $
(☎08-9848 3300; www.denmarkbluewren.com.au; 17 Price St; dm/d $27/73) Chooks live under this little timber house and everyone spoils the goofy house dog. Great info panels cover the walls, and it's small enough (just 20 beds) to have a homey feel. Bikes can also be rented – $25 per day or just $15 if you're a guest – and friendly owner Graham is a whiz at bike repairs.

Denmark Rivermouth Caravan Park CARAVAN PARK $
(☎08-9848 1262; www.denmarkrivermouthcaravanpark.com.au; Inlet Dr; 2-person sites $30, cabins & chalets $130-200) Ideally located for nautical pursuits, this caravan park sits along Wilson Inlet beside the boat ramp. Some of the units are properly flash, although they are quite tightly arranged. There's also a kids playground and kayaks for hire.

★**Cape Howe Cottages** COTTAGE $$
(☎08-9845 1295; www.capehowe.com.au; 322 Tennessee Rd S; cottages $170-280; ❄) For a remote getaway, these five cottages in bushland southeast of Denmark really make the grade. They're all different, but the best is only 1.5km from dolphin-favoured Lowlands Beach and is properly plush – with a BBQ on the deck, a dishwasher in the kitchen and laundry facilities.

Eating & Drinking

Mrs Jones CAFE $$
(☎0467 481 878; www.mrsjonescafe.com; 12 Mt Shadforth Rd; breakfast $9-18, lunch $14-21; ⊙7am-4pm) Denmark's best coffee is at this spacious spot with high ceilings and exposed beams. Settle in for interesting cafe fare including Turkish eggs with roasted pumpkin, chorizo and lentils, or Asian-style duck pancakes with a plum sauce.

★**Pepper & Salt** MODERN AUSTRALIAN $$$
(☎08-9848 3053; www.matildasestate.com; 18 Hamilton St, Matilda's Estate; mains $35-40; ⊙noon-10pm) Highlights include chilli-and-coconut prawns, or the great-value tasting platter ($48), which effortlessly detours from Asia to the Middle East. Buy some wine from the adjacent Matilda's Estate before settling in for a foodie's adventure. Bookings recommended.

★Boston Brewery CRAFT BEER
(www.willoughbypark.com.au; Willoughby Park Winery, South Coast Hwy; pizzas $18-23, mains $24-32; ⏲10am-7pm Mon-Thu, to 10pm Fri & Sat, to 9pm Sun) The industrial chic of the brewery gives way to an absolute edge-of-vineyard location, and wood-fired pizzas, meals and bar snacks go well with Boston's four beers. There's also live music from 4pm to 8pm every second Saturday afternoon.

Information

Visitor Centre (☎08-9848 2055; www.denmark.com.au; 73 South Coast Hwy; ⏲9am-5pm) Ask for *The Wine Lovers' Guide to Denmark* brochure and get exploring.

Albany

POP 25,200

Established shortly before Perth in 1826, the oldest European settlement in the state is now the bustling commercial centre of the southern region. Albany is a mixed bag, comprising a stately colonial quarter, a waterfront in the midst of redevelopment and a hectic sprawl of malls and fast-food joints. Less ambivalent is its coastline, which is uniformly spectacular.

The Bibbulmun Track ends (or starts) here, outside the visitor centre.

History

The Minang Noongar people called this place Kinjarling ('place of rain') and believed that fighting Wargals (mystical giant serpents) created the fractured landscape. They set up sophisticated fish traps on Oyster Harbour, the remains of which can still be seen.

Initial contacts with Europeans were friendly, with over 60 ships visiting between 1622 and 1826. The establishment of a British settlement here was welcomed at first as it regulated the behaviour of sealers and whalers, who had been responsible for kidnapping, rape and murder. Yet by the end of that century the Minang were a marginalised group, refused entry into every shop in Albany.

Albany's sheltered harbour made it a thriving whaling port. Later it became a coaling station for British ships and during WWI it was the mustering point for ships heading for Egypt and the Gallipoli campaign.

Sights

★Western Australian Museum – Albany MUSEUM
(www.museum.wa.gov.au; Residency Rd; admission by donation; ⏲10am-4.30pm) This branch of the state museum is split between two neighbouring buildings. The newer Eclipse building has a kids' discovery section, a lighthouse exhibition, a gallery for temporary exhibitions and a gift shop. The restored 1850s home of the resident magistrate illuminates Minang Noongar history, local natural history, and seafaring stories.

Brig Amity SHIP
(www.historicalbany.com.au; adult/child $5/2; ⏲9am-4pm) This full-scale replica of the brig which carried Albany's first British settlers from Sydney in 1826 was completed for the city's 150th anniversary. Self-guided audio tours bring to life the ship's history.

Town Centre HISTORIC BUILDINGS
Take a stroll down historic Stirling Tce – noted for its Victorian shopfronts, **Courthouse** and **Old Post Office** – and up York St to **St John's Anglican Church** and Albany's **Town Hall** (www.albanytownhall.com.au; 217 York St). A guided walking-tour brochure is available from the visitor centre.

Patrick Taylor Cottage MUSEUM
(www.historicalbany.com.au; 39 Duke St; admission $2; ⏲11am-3pm) Believed to be the oldest colonial dwelling in WA, this 1832 wattle-and-daub cottage is packed with antiques, freaky mannequins and displays on its former residents.

Albany Convict Gaol MUSEUM
(www.historicalbany.com.au; Stirling Tce; adult/child $5/2.50; ⏲10am-4pm) The old jail was built in 1851 as a hiring depot for ticket-of-leave convicts but by 1855 most were in private employment. In 1872 the building was extended and reopened as a civil jail, and is now a folk museum.

Princess Royal Fortress HISTORIC SITE
(www.forts.albany.wa.gov.au; Forts Rd; adult/child $12/4.50; ⏲9am-5pm) As a strategic port, Albany was historically regarded as being vulnerable to attack. Built in 1893 on Mt Adelaide, this fort was initially constructed as a defence against potential attacks from the Russians and French. The restored buildings, gun emplacements and views are interesting, and there are also poignant photos of Anzac troops leaving for Gallipoli.

Albany

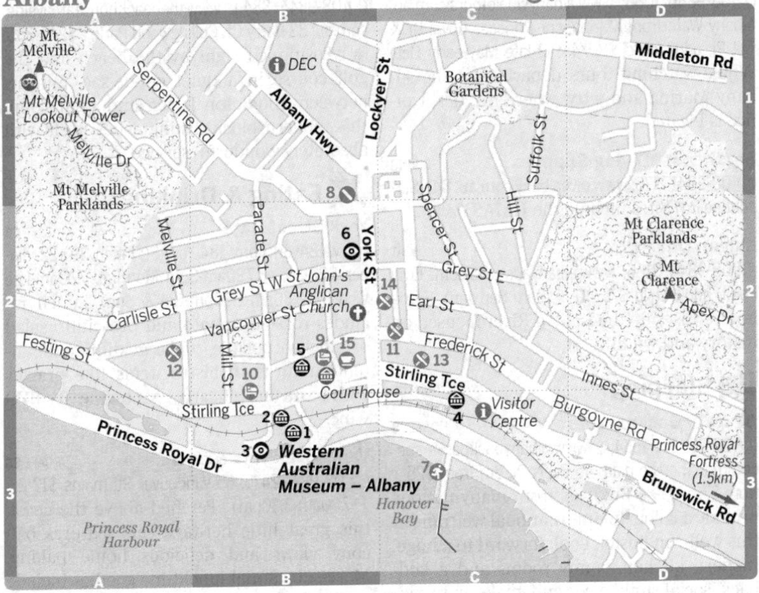

Albany

Top Sights
1 Western Australian Museum – Albany B3

Sights
2 Albany Convict Gaol B3
3 Brig Amity B3
4 Old Post Office C3
5 Patrick Taylor Cottage B2
6 Town Hall B2

Activities, Courses & Tours
7 Albany Whale Tours C3
8 Southcoast Diving Supplies B1

Sleeping
9 1849 Backpackers B2
10 Albany Harbourside B2

Eating
11 14 Peels Place C2
12 Vancouver Cafe & Store A2
13 White Star Hotel C2
14 York Street Cafe C2

Drinking & Nightlife
15 Liberté B2

Middleton & Emu Beaches BEACHES
East of the town centre, these beautiful beaches facing King George Sound share one long stretch of family-friendly sand. In winter you'll often see pods of mother whales and their calves here. Head around Emu Point to Oyster Harbour for swimming pontoons and even calmer waters.

Activities

After whaling ended in 1978, whales slowly began returning to the waters of Albany. You can usually spot them from the beach from July to mid-October, but if you fancy a closer look, contact a recommended operator.

Albany's appeal as a top-class diving destination grew after the 2001 scuttling of the **HMAS Perth** (www.hmasperth.com.au). Natural reefs feature temperate and tropical corals, and are home to the bizarre leafy and weedy sea dragons.

Albany Dolphin & Whale Cruises WHALE WATCHING
(☎0428 429 876; www.whales.com.au; adult/child $80/45; ⊙Jul–mid-Oct) Runs regular whale-watching cruises in season.

Albany Whale Tours
WHALE WATCHING

(☑08-9845 1068; www.albanywhaletours.com.au; Albany Waterfront Marina, cnr Princess Royal Dr & Toll Pl; adult/child $80/45; ⊙late May-early Oct) Whale-watching tours depart from the Albany Marina and jetty, where the ticket office is located.

Southcoast Diving Supplies
DIVING

(☑08-9841 7176; www.divealbany.com.au; 84b Serpentine Rd) Sites include the HMAS *Perth*.

Kalgan Queen
BOAT

(☑08-9844 3166; www.albanyaustralia.com; Emu Point; adult/child $75/40; ⊙9am Sep-Jun) Four-hour cruises up the Kalgan River focused on history and wildlife.

🛏 Sleeping

★1849 Backpackers
HOSTEL $

(☑08-9842 1554; www.albanybackpackersaccommodation.com.au; 45 Peels Pl; dm from $25, r from $70; @ 🛜) Big flags from many nations provide a colourful international welcome at this well-run hostel. Look forward to a huge, modern kitchen, sunny rooms and a laid-back social ambience, and make sure you book in for 1849's free barbecue on Sunday night.

Albany Discovery Inn
GUESTHOUSE $

(☑08-9842 5535; www.discoveryinn.com.au; 9 Middleton Rd, Middleton Beach; s $55, d $80-90; @ 🛜) Guests can mingle in the central conservatory, and the refurbished rooms are colourfully decorated. A recent addition is an on-site cafe offering evening meals for $20. Outside dinner guests are welcome, but book ahead. Rates include a cooked breakfast.

Emu Beach Holiday Park
CARAVAN PARK $

(☑08-9844 1147; www.emubeach.com; 8 Medcalf Pde, Emu Point; 2-person sites from $35, chalets $130-190; ❄) Families love the Emu Beach area and this holiday park, close to the beach, has good facilities, including a BBQ area and a kids' playground. Newly built motel units are spacious and modern.

Albany Harbourside
APARTMENT $$

(☑08-9842 1769; www.albanyharbourside.com.au; 8 Festing St; d $159-219; ❄) Albany Harbourside's portfolio includes spacious and spotless apartments on Festing St, and three other self-contained options arrayed around central Albany. Decor is modern and colourful, and some apartments have ocean views.

Beach House at Bayside
BOUTIQUE HOTEL $$$

(☑08-9844 8844; www.thebeachhouseatbayside.com.au; 33 Barry Ct, Collingwood Park; r $249-335; ❄) Positioned right by the beach and the golf course in a quiet cul-de-sac, midway between Middleton Beach and Emu Point, this modern block distinguishes itself with absolutely wonderful service.

🍴 Eating & Drinking

York Street Cafe
CAFE $$

(www.184york.com; 184 York St; lunch $10-22, dinner $22-36; ⊙7.30am-3pm Mon-Tue, 7.30am-late Wed-Fri, 8.30am-2.30pm Sat & Sun) Lunch includes roasted tomato and prosciutto salad or chicken pot pie, while at dinner the attention turns to bistro items like prawns with pasta and a hearty goat tagine. It's BYO wine.

Vancouver Cafe & Store
CAFE $$

(☑08-9841 2475; 65 Vancouver St; mains $12-25; ⊙7.30am-3.30pm) Perched above the coast, this great little heritage cafe features balcony views and delicious home baking. More substantial lunchtime goodies include garlic-prawn risotto or bangers and mash. Book ahead for its music and pizza events on Thursday nights.

White Star Hotel
PUB $$

(72 Stirling Tce; mains $16-34; ⊙11am-late) With 20 beers on tap (including its own Tanglehead brews) and excellent pub grub, this old pub gets a gold star. Sunday night folk and blues gigs are a good opportunity to share a pint with Albany's laid-back locals.

14 Peels Place
CAFE $$

(14 Peels Pl; breakfast $7-21, lunch $14-22; ⊙8.30am-4pm Mon-Fri, to 1pm Sat & Sun; 🍴) 🌿 A colourful haven for in-the-know local foodies, 14 Peels Place's combo of good coffee and cool jazz is a great way to start the day. Freshly baked cakes include lots of gluten-free options.

Liberté
CAFE, BAR

(London Hotel,162 Stirling Tce; ⊙8.30am-5pm Mon & Tue, till late Wed-Sat) Channelling a louche Parisian cafe and a velvet-trimmed speakeasy, Liberté's Gallic-inspired versatility includes good coffee and cake during the day, and craft beer, potent cocktails and Med-inspired tapas later at night.

ℹ Information

DEC (☑08-9842 4500; 120 Albany Hwy; ⊙8am-4.30pm Mon-Fri) For national park information.

Visitor Centre (☎08-9841 9290; www.amazingalbany.com; Proudlove Pde; ⏰9am-5pm) In the old train station.

Around Albany

Sights

Whale World Museum MUSEUM
(☎08-9844 4019; www.whaleworld.org; Frenchman Bay Rd; adult/child $29/10; ⏰9am-5pm) When the Cheynes Beach Whaling Station ceased operations in November 1978, few could predict its gore-covered decks would eventually be covered in tourists, craning to see passing whales. The museum screens several films about marine life and whaling operations, and displays giant skeletons, harpoons, whaleboat models and scrimshaw (etchings on whalebone). Outside there's the rusting *Cheynes IV* whale chaser and station equipment. Free guided tours depart hourly from 10am to 3pm.

Attached to the complex is the Walk On The Wild Side wildlife park. Entrance is included with admission to Whale World.

Torndirrup National Park NATIONAL PARK
(Frenchman Bay Rd) FREE Covering much of the peninsula enclosing the southern reaches of King George Sound, this national park is known for its windswept, ocean-bashed cliffs. The Gap is a natural cleft in the rock, channelling surf through walls of granite, and close by is the Natural Bridge.

Further east, the spectacular Blowholes are worth the 78 steps down and back up. Steep, rocky, green-water coves like Jimmy Newells Harbour and Salmon Holes are popular with surfers but scary for swimmers. Head instead to Misery Beach or Frenchman Bay on the peninsula's sheltered side.

There's a challenging 10km-return bushwalk (five hours plus) over Isthmus Hill to Bald Head.

Two Peoples Bay NATURE RESERVE
(Two Peoples Bay Rd) Some 20km east of Albany, Two Peoples Bay is a 46-sq-km nature reserve with a good swimming beach and scenic coastline.

Waychinicup National Park NATIONAL PARK
(Cheyne Beach Rd; park admission free, camp sites adult/child $7/3) In a beautiful spot, by the inlet of the Waychinicup River; toilets are provided but there's no fresh water.

Mt Barker

POP 1770

Mt Barker (50km north of Albany) is the gateway town to the Porongurup and Stirling Range National Parks. An increasingly prestigious local wine industry includes **Plantagenet Wines** (www.plantagenetwines.com; Albany Hwy; ⏰10am-4.30pm) in the middle of town.

The town has been settled since the 1830s and the convict-built 1868 police station and jail have been preserved as a **museum** (Albany Hwy; adult/child $5/free; ⏰10am-3pm Sat & Sun).

All 78 types and 24 subtypes of Australia's weird and wonderful banksia plant feature at the **Banksia Farm** (☎08-9851 1770; www.banksiafarm.com.au; Pearce Rd; admission $11; ⏰9.30am-4.30pm Mon-Fri Mar-Jun, daily Aug-Nov). Also on offer are guided tours ($25), morning and afternoon tea, and B&B accommodation (single/double from $95/150).

Head up **Mt Barker**, 5km south of town, for excellent views of the neighbouring ranges. Southwest of Mt Barker on the Egerton-Warburton estate is **St Werburgh's Chapel**, built between 1872 and 1873.

A surprising sight is the authentic Mongolian felt tent – or gert – and gallery of eclectic Mongolian and Chinese art in the grounds of **Nomads Guest House** (☎08-9851 2131; www.nomadsguesthousewa.com.au; 12 Morpeth St; s/d/gers/chalets $70/90/100/110).

Porongurup National Park

The 24-sq-km, 12km-long **Porongurup National Park** (entry per car/motorcycle $11/5) has 1100-million-year-old granite outcrops, panoramic views, beautiful scenery, large karri trees and some excellent bushwalks. The rich forest also supports 65 species of orchid in spring and, in September and October, there are wildflowers among the trees. There are 11 wineries in the immediate vicinity.

Sleeping & Eating

There is no accommodation within the national park, but most places are nearby. Eating options are limited.

Porongurup Village Inn, Shop & Tearooms B&B $
(☎08-9853 1110; www.porongurupinn.com.au; s/d/cottages $30/60/100) This rustic place

also serves home-cooked food (breakfast $5 to $14, lunch $16 to $18) with vegies from the organic garden – try the salmon patties – and there's a trampoline for younger visitors.

Porongurup Range Tourist Park CARAVAN PARK $
(08-9853 1057; www.poronguruprangetouristpark.com.au; 1304 Porongurup Rd; 2-person sites $30, cabins $90-110;) Tidy with good facilities.

Ty-Jarrah CHALET $$
(08-9853 1255; www.tyjarrah.com; 3 Bolganup Rd; 1-/2-bedroom chalets from $125/145) Located in a shady forested setting, these self-contained A-frame chalets are very cosy and comfortable. Twilight visitors include local marsupials.

Maleeya's Thai Cafe THAI $$
(08-9853 1123; www.maleeya.com.au; 1376 Porongurup Rd; mains $25-30; 11.30am-3pm & 6-9pm Fri-Sun;) Curries, soups and stir fries all come studded with fresh herbs straight from Maleeya's garden, and other ingredients are organic and free range. Bookings recommended.

Stirling Range National Park

Rising abruptly from the surrounding plains, this 1156-sq-km national park consists of a single chain of peaks pushed up to form a range 10km wide and 65km long. Bluff Knoll (Bular Mai) is the highest point in the southwest (1095m). Due to the altitude and climate there are many localised plants.

Changing colours of blues, reds and purples captivate photographers during the wildflower season from late August to early December, and it's recognised by the Noongar people as a place of special significance. Every summit has an ancestral being associated with it, so be respectful when visiting.

Park fees are charged at the start of Bluff Knoll Rd (car/motorcycle $11/5). Walkers must be experienced and equipped as the range is subject to sudden drops in temperature, driving rain and sometimes snow; register in and out with the **rangers** (08-9827 9230).

Sleeping & Eating

Options are limited, so stock up on food in Mt Barker.

Stirling Range Retreat CARAVAN PARK $
(08-9827 9229; www.stirlingrange.com.au; 8639 Chester Pass Rd; unpowered/powered 2-person sites $30/32, cabins $55-79, units $145-175;) On the park's northern boundary, this shaded site has accommodation including camp sites, simple cabins and vans, and self-contained rammed-earth units. Wildflower and orchid bus tours and walkabouts (three hours, per person $49) are conducted from mid-August through October.

Mount Trio Bush Camping & Caravan Park CARAVAN PARK $
(08-9827 9270; www.mounttrio.com.au; Salt River Rd; unpowered/powered sites per person $12/14) Rustic bush campground on a farm property close to the walking tracks, north of the centre of the park. Guided walks from two hours to three days are on offer.

Moingup Springs CAMPGROUND $
(Chester Pass Rd; sites per adult/child $7/2) DEC's only campground within the park; no showers or electriity.

Lily COTTAGES $$
(08-9827 9205; www.thelily.com.au; Chester Pass Rd; cottages $139-169) These self-contained cottages 12km north of the park are grouped around a working windmill. Meals ($36) are also available for guests at the neighbouring restaurant. Call to enquire which nights the restaurant is open to the public as hours vary.

Fitzgerald River National Park

Midway between Albany and Esperance, this national park is a Unesco biosphere reserve. Its 3300 sq km contains 22 mammal species, 200 species of bird and 1700 species of plant (20% of WA's described species). Wildflowers are most abundant in spring, but flowers bloom throughout the year.

Walkers will discover beautiful coastline, sand plains, rugged coastal hills and deep river valleys. In season you'll probably see whales and their calves from **Point Ann**, where there's a lookout and a heritage walk following part of the 1164km **No 2 rabbit-proof fence**.

The three main 2WD entry points are from the South Coast Hwy (Quiss Rd and Pabelup Dr), Hopetoun (Hamersley Dr) and Bremer Bay (along Swamp and Murray Rds).

All roads are gravel, and likely to be impassable after rain, so check before you set out.

Bookending the park are **Bremer Bay** (population 250) and **Hopetoun** (population 590), both with white sand and green waters. To the east of Hopetoun is the scenic but in parts extremely rough **Southern Ocean East Drive**, heading to beach camp sites at **Mason Bay** and **Starvation Bay**. If you're in a 2WD, don't head to Esperance this way.

Sleeping

Quaalup Homestead CAMPGROUND $
(08-9837 4124; www.whalesandwildflowers.com.au; Quaalup Rd; sites per person from $12, on-site vans $60, r $90-120) This 1858 homestead is secluded deep within the southern reaches of the park. Electricity is solar, and forget about mobile phone coverage. Sleeping options range from a bush camp site with gas BBQs to cosy units and chalets.

DEC Camp sites CAMPGROUND $
(sites per adult/child $7/2) Of five national-park camp sites only St Mary Inlet (near Point Ann) can be reached by 2WD. The two at Hamersley Inlet and the others at Whale Bone Beach, Quoin Head and Fitzgerald Inlet can only be reached by 4WD or on foot.

Hopetoun Motel & Chalet Village MOTEL $$
(08-9838 3219; www.hopetounmotel.com.au; 458 Veal St; r $140-200;) Rammed-earth complex with comfy beds and quality linen. A larger townhouse ($310) is also available for families.

Esperance

POP 9600

Esperance sits on the Bay of Isles, a seascape of aquamarine waters and squeaky white beaches. Despite its southeastern isolation, Esperance still has devotees who make the intrepid pilgrimage from Perth to melt into the low-key, community-oriented vibe. In Kalgoorlie nobody would question the wisdom of driving 390km to Esperance's beaches, and for travellers taking the coastal route across Australia, it's the last sizeable town before the Nullarbor.

Some of Australia's most picture-perfect beaches are in the more remote national parks to the southeast. Out in the bay, the pristine Recherche Archipelago can be wild and windy, or calm and settled, and its 105 islands are home to fur seals, penguins and sea birds.

History

Esperance's indigenous name, Kepa Kurl ('water boomerang'), refers to the shape of the bay. It received its current name in 1792 when the *Recherche* and *l'Espérance* sailed into the bay to shelter from a storm. In the 1820s and 1830s the Recherche Archipelago was home to Black Jack Anderson – Australia's only pirate. From his base on Middle Island he raided ships and kept a harem of Aboriginal women whose husbands he had killed. He was eventually murdered in his sleep by one of his own men.

The first settlers arrived in 1863, but it wasn't until the 1890s gold rush that Esperance became established as a port. When gold fever subsided, Esperance was quiet until the 1950s when it became an agricultural centre; grain and minerals are still important exports.

Sights & Activities

Esperance Museum MUSEUM
(cnr James & Dempster Sts; adult/child $6/2; 1.30-4.30pm) Glass cabinets are crammed with seashells, frog ornaments, tennis rackets and bed pans. Bigger items include boats, a train carriage and the remains of the USA's spacecraft *Skylab,* which made its fiery re-entry at Balladonia, east of Esperance, in 1979.

Museum Village HISTORIC BUILDINGS
Galleries and cafes occupy restored heritage buildings, and markets are held every second Sunday morning. Aboriginal-run **Kepa Kurl Art Gallery** (www.kepakurl.com.au; cnr Dempster & Kemp Sts; 10am-4pm Mon-Fri & market Sun) has reasonably priced works by local and Central Desert artists.

Lake Warden Wetland System LAKES
Esperance is surrounded by extensive wetlands, which include seven large lakes and over 90 smaller ones. The 7.2km return **Kepwari Wetland Trail** (off Fisheries Rd) takes in **Lake Wheatfield** and **Woody Lake**, with boardwalks, interpretive displays and good birdwatching. **Lake Monjimup**, 14km to the northwest along the South Coast Hwy, is divided by Telegraph Rd into a conservation area and a recreation area. The conservation side has boardwalks over inky black water, while the recreation side has banksia, hakea and grevillea gardens and a hedge maze.

Great Ocean Drive SCENIC DRIVE
Many of Esperance's most dramatic sights can be seen on this well-signposted 40km loop. Starting from the waterfront it heads southwest past breathtaking and popular surfing and swimming spots including **Blue Haven Beach** and **Twilight Cove**. Stop at rugged **Observatory Point** and the lookout on **Wireless Hill**. A turn-off leads to the **wind farm**, supplying 23% of Esperance's electricity. Walking among the turbines is surreal when it's windy.

Tours

Esperance Island Cruises BOAT TOUR
(08-9071 5757; www.woodyisland.com.au; 72 The Esplanade; daily late Sep-May) Tours include Esperance Bay and Woody Island in a power catamaran (half-/full day $95/150), getting close to fur seals, sea lions, Cape Barren geese and (with luck) dolphins. In January there's a ferry to Woody Island (adult/child return $60/30).

Kepa Kurl Eco Cultural Discovery Tours INDIGENOUS CULTURE TOUR
(08-9072 1688; www.kepakurl.com.au; Museum Village) Explore the country from an Aboriginal perspective: visit rock art and waterholes, sample bush food and hear ancient stories (adult/child $105/90; minimum two).

Eco-Discovery Tours 4WD TOUR
(0407 737 261; www.esperancetours.com.au) Runs 4WD tours along the sand to Cape Le Grand National Park (half-/full day $95/165, minimum two/four) and two-hour circuits of the Great Ocean Drive (adult/child $55/40).

Aussie Bight Expeditions 4WD TOUR
(0427 536 674; www.aussiebight.com; half-/full day $90/160; Aug-Apr) 4WD expeditions covering wildflowers and Cape Le Grand National Park. Sandboarding is available from mid-December to April.

Esperance Diving & Fishing DIVING, FISHING
(08-9071 5111; www.esperancedivingandfishing.com.au; 72 The Esplanade) Wreck-diving on the *Sanko Harvest* (two-tank dive including all gear $260) or charter fishing throughout the archipelago.

Sleeping

Woody Island Eco-Stays CAMPGROUND $
(08-9071 5757; www.woodyisland.com.au; sites per person $25, on-site tents $41-61, huts $140-165; late Sep-Apr;) Choose between leafy camp sites or canvas-sided bush huts, a few with a private deck. Power is mostly solar, and rainwater supplies the island. Count on adding on a $60 return ferry transfer as well.

Blue Waters Lodge YHA HOSTEL $
(08-9071 1040; www.yha.com.au; 299 Goldfields Rd; dm/s/d $28/50/70) On the beachfront about 1.5km from the town centre, this rambling place feels a little institutional but it looks out over a tidy lawn to the water. Hire bikes to cycle the waterfront.

Esperance B&B by the Sea B&B $$
(08-9071 5640; www.esperancebb.com; 34 Stewart St; s/d $120/170;) This great-value beach house has a private guest wing and breathtaking views overlooking Blue Haven Beach. It's just a stroll from the ocean and a five-minute drive from Dempster St.

Clearwater Motel Apartments MOTEL $$
(08-9071 3587; www.clearwatermotel.com.au; 1a William St; s $110, d $140-195;) The bright and spacious rooms and apartments here have balconies and are fully self-contained, and there's a well-equipped shared barbecue area. It's just a short walk from both waterfront and town.

Driftwood Apartments APARTMENTS $$
(0428 716 677; www.driftwoodapartments.com.au; 69 The Esplanade; apt $165-220;) Each of these seven smart apartments opposite the waterfront has its own BBQ and outdoor table setting. The two-storey, two-bedroom units have decks and more privacy.

Eating

Taylor's Beach Bar & Cafe CAFE $$
(Taylor St Jetty; lunch $7-24, dinner $24-32; 7am-2pm Wed, to 9pm Thu-Mon;) This attractive, sprawling cafe by the jetty serves cafe fare, tapas, seafood and salads. Locals hang out at the tables or read on the covered terrace. Sandwiches ($6.50 to $9.50) are good value if you're heading for the beach, and it's good for a chilled pint of Little Creatures Pale Ale.

Alimento CAFE $$
(94 Dempster St; mains $13-18; 7am-3pm Mon-Fri, 8am-1pm Sat, 7.30am-11.30am Sun) Excellent coffee and colourful local art feature at this centrally located cafe. Try the tasting platter with homemade hummus and warm Turkish bread, or see what's on for the popular 'Curry of the Day'.

Ocean Blues CAFE $$
(19 The Esplanade; mains $22-34; 9.30am-8.30pm Tue-Sat, 8am-4pm Sun) Wander in sandy-footed

and order burgers, salads and wraps from this unpretentious eatery. Dinners are more adventurous and good value.

Pier Hotel PUB **$$**
(www.pierhotelesperance.net.au; 47 The Esplanade; mains $20-35; ⏲11.30am-late) Lots of beers on tap, wood-fired pizzas and tasty bistro meals conspire to make the local pub a firm favourite.

Information

DEC (☎08-9083 2100; 92 Dempster St) National parks information.

Visitor Centre (☎08-9083 1555; www.visitesperance.com; cnr Kemp & Dempster Sts; ⏲9am-5pm Mon-Fri, to 2pm Sat, to noon Sun)

Around Esperance

Cape Le Grand National Park

An easy day trip from Esperance, this **national park** (entry per car/motorcycle $11/5, camp sites adult/child $9/2) starts 60km to the east and boasts coastal scenery, beautiful beaches and excellent walking tracks. It offers good fishing, swimming and camping at **Lucky Bay** and **Le Grand Beach**, and day-use facilities at gorgeous **Hellfire Bay**. Make the effort to climb **Frenchman Peak** (a steep 3km return, two hours), as the views from the top and through the 'eye', especially late afternoon, are superb.

Rossiter Bay is where the British and Aboriginal duo Edward John Eyre and Wylie fortuitously met the French whaling ship *Mississippi* in the course of their epic 1841 overland crossing and spent two weeks resting onboard. The 15km **Le Grand Coastal Trail** links the bays; you can do shorter stretches between beaches.

Cape Arid National Park

Further east, at the start of the Great Australian Bight and on the fringes of the Nullarbor Plain, **Cape Arid** (entry per car/motorcycle $11/5, camp sites adult/child $7/2) is rugged and isolated, with good bushwalking, camp sites and great beaches.

Whales (in season), seals and Cape Barren geese are seen here. Most of the park is 4WD-accessible only, although the Thomas River Rd, leading to the shire camp site, is accessible to all vehicles. There's a tough walk up **Tower Peak** on Mt Ragged (3km return, three hours), where the planet's most primitive species of ant was found in 1930.

For those heading across the Nullarbor, the extremely rough Balladonia Track and Parmango Rd offer an alternative to the Eyre Hwy but you'll absolutely need a 4WD; check conditions at the Esperance visitor centre before starting out.

Peak Charles National Park

There are no charges to visit or camp at this granite wilderness area, 130km north of Esperance. Only basic facilities are provided (long-drop toilets), and you'll need to be completely self-sufficient.

SOUTHERN OUTBACK

The southern outback is an iconic Australian experience. In summer, heat haze shimmers on the desert, and midyear, a winter chill diffuses the landscape's reds and blues to cool purple and grey. Almost-empty roads run relentlessly towards South Australia (SA) via the Nullarbor Plain, and up to the Northern Territory (NT). This was (and is) goldrush country, with the city of Kalgoorlie-Boulder as its hub, while more-remote and less-sustainable gold towns lie sunstruck and deserted. Aboriginal people have lived for an age in this region, which early colonists found unforgiving until the allure of gold made it worthwhile to stay.

History

Gold was discovered at Southern Cross in 1888, and in one of the world's last great gold rushes, prospectors flocked from other states and nations. Around 50 towns quickly sprouted, but it was a harsh life. Enthusiasm and greed often outweighed common sense, and as typhoid ran through mining camps, inadequate water, housing, food and medical supplies led to many fatalities.

The area's population dwindled along with the gold, and today Kalgoorlie-Boulder is the only real survivor. Explore other diminished towns and prodigious mining structures along the 965km **Golden Quest Discovery Trail** (www.goldenquesttrail.com).

Stretching 560km from the Perth foothills, the 1903 **Golden Pipeline** (www.goldenpipeline.com.au) brought water to the goldfields. It was a lifeline for the towns it passed through and filled Kalgoorlie with the sense of a future, with or without gold. The present-day Great Eastern Hwy follows the pipeline's route, incorporating heritage pumping stations and information signs.

Getting There & Away

AIR

Qantas (13 13 13; www.qantas.com.au) Perth to Kalgoorlie (one hour, two to three daily).

Skippers Aviation (1300 729 924; www.skippers.com.au) Perth–Leonora–Laverton (four weekly) and Perth–Wiluna–Leinster (three weekly).

Virgin Australia (13 67 89; www.virginaustralia.com)

BUS

Transwa (1300 662 205; www.transwa.wa.gov.au) Perth to Kalgoorlie and Esperance three times a week ($56, five hours), via Coolgardie and Norseman.

Goldrush Tours (1800 620 440; www.goldrushtours.com.au) Weekly service from Kalgoorlie to Laverton (via Menzies and Leonora), departing Thursday and returning Friday.

TRAIN

Transwa runs the *Prospector* service from East Perth to Kalgoorlie ($82, seven hours, daily).

Norseman

POP 860

From the crossroads of Norseman go south to Esperance, north to Kalgoorlie, west to Hyden and Wave Rock, or east across the Nullarbor.

THE WORLD'S LONGEST GOLF COURSE

The only water hazard you'll face on this 18-hole, par-72 course is the risk of running out of it. Stretching 1362km from Kalgoorlie south to Norseman and across the desolate Nullarbor Plain to Ceduna, the **Nullarbor Links** (www.nullarborlinks.com; 18 holes $50) is golf, Tiger, but not as we know it.

Purchase your scorecard from the Kalgoorlie, Norseman or Ceduna visitor centres, and follow the directions along the route. Collect stamps along the way to qualify for your completion certificate.

Clubs are available for hire at each hole ($5). If you'd rather use your own, pack your oldest – the parched ground can be as hard as steel.

Stretch your legs at the **Beacon Hill Mararoa Lookout**, where there's a walking trail, and stop at the **Historical Museum** (Battery Rd; adult/child $3/1; 10am-1pm Mon-Sat). Pick up the **Dundas Coach Road Heritage Trail** brochure, for a 50km loop drive with interpretive panels.

Sleeping

Great Western Motel MOTEL $
(08-9039 1633, 1800 755 423; www.goldenchain.com.au; Prinsep St; r $120;) 'Budget' and 'lodge' rooms in an older block are perfectly adequate, but the rammed-earth 'motel' rooms are much nicer. There's a restaurant on-site.

Gateway Caravan Park CARAVAN PARK $
(08-9039 1500; www.acclaimparks.com.au; 23 Prinsep St; sites per 2 people $33-38, cabins $80-131;) Decent cabins and a bushy atmosphere.

Information

Visitor Centre (08-9039 1071; www.norseman.info; 68 Roberts St; 9am-5pm Mon-Fri, 9.30am-4pm Sat & Sun) A great source of information about the Nullarbor.

Eyre Highway (The Nullarbor)

London to Moscow, or Perth to Adelaide? There's not much difference, distance-wise. The 2700km Eyre Hwy crosses the southern edge of the **Nullarbor Plain**, parallel with the **Trans-Australia Railway** to the north.

John Eyre was the first European to cross this unforgiving stretch of country in 1841. After the 1877 telegraph line was laid, miners en route to the goldfields trekked its length under blistering sun and in freezing winter. In 1912 the first car made it across. By 1941 the rough-and-ready road carried a handful of vehicles a day; in 1962 the first cyclist crossed. In 1969 the WA government surfaced the road as far as the SA border. Finally, in 1976, the last stretch was surfaced and runs close to the coast, with the Nullarbor region ending at the cliffs of the Great Australian Bight.

From Norseman it's 725km to the SA border, and a further 480km to Ceduna (meaning 'a place to sit down and rest' in the local Aboriginal language). From Ceduna, it's still another 793km to Adelaide.

NOT NULLAR-BORING AT ALL

'Crossing the Nullarbor' is an iconic Australian trip. It's absolutely about journey as much as destination, so relax and enjoy the big skies and long horizons. Pack plenty of CDs and audiobooks, and stretch out those driving muscles by waving at other drivers, and *(very)* occasional cyclists and walkers. The long-distance Nullarbor Links golf course is also great fun.

All roadhouses sell food and fuel and have accommodation. Room rates given range from budget (often *very* basic) to motel style; camp sites can resemble desolate *Mad Max* landscapes. Free roadside camping – toilets, tables, a bit of shade – is about every 250km. See www.nullarbornet.com.au.

Ensure your vehicle is up to the distance and carry more drinking water than you think you'll need. You may have to sit it out by the roadside for quite a while. This is not the place to run out of fuel: prices are high and there's a distance between fuel stops of about 200km.

Norseman to Eucla

At the 100km mark from Norseman, **Fraser Range Station** (☎08-9039 3210; www.fraserrangestation.com.au; unpowered/powered sites $22/30, budget s/tw/d/f $55/95/95/120, cottage r $155) is the first (or last, depending) and best stop on the Nullarbor. This sheep station's heritage buildings and camping ground are top-notch (though there's no fuel), and you might even score some fresh vegies from the garden. Next is **Balladonia** (193km), where the **Balladonia Hotel Motel** (☎08-9039 3453; www.balladoniahotelmotel.com.au; unpowered/powered sites $19/28, dm $50, r from $130; ❄@≋) has a small museum including debris from Skylab's 1979 nearby return to earth.

Balladonia to Cocklebiddy is some 210km. The first 160km to **Caiguna** includes Australia's longest stretch of straight road – 145km, the so-called Ninety Mile Straight. Caiguna's **John Eyre Motel** (☎08-9039 3459; caigunarh@bigpond.com; unpowered/powered sites $20/25, d $80-115, tr/q $125/135; ❄) is at the end of it. There are shaded picnic tables and a comfortable restaurant at the **Cocklebiddy Wedgetail Inn** (☎08-9039 3462; cocklebiddy@bigpond.com; unpowered/powered sites $15/25, r $70-100; ❄), which runs on Central Western time, 45 minutes ahead of Perth time, and 45 minutes behind Adelaide time.

Birds Australia's **Eyre Bird Observatory** (☎08-9039 3450; www.eyrebirds.org) is in the isolated and lovely 1897 former Eyre Telegraph Station, 50km south of Cocklebiddy. Full board and lodging is good value at $90 per person per night – book ahead. Day visitors are welcome ($10 per vehicle), but the last 10km are soft sand and 4WD accessible only; 2WD travellers who want to stay can arrange pick-up with the wardens. There's no camping.

Tiny **Madura**, 91km east of Cocklebiddy, is close to the Hampton Tablelands (stop for wild wide views at the lookout). The **Madura Pass Oasis Inn** (☎08-9039 3464; maduraoasis@bigpond.com; unpowered/powered sites $15/25, r $105-125; ❄≋) has a green and shady camp site, and a welcome pool.

In **Mundrabilla**, 116km further east, the **Mundrabilla Motel Hotel** (☎08-9039 3465; mundrabilla@bigpond.com.au; unpowered/powered sites $20/25, r $80-110; ❄) has consistently cheaper fuel prices than roadhouses further west.

Just before the SA border is Eucla, surrounded by stunning sand dunes and pristine beaches. Visit the atmospheric ruins of the 1877 **telegraph station**, 5km south of town and gradually being engulfed by the dunes; the remains of the old jetty are a 15-minute walk beyond. Pleasant camp sites and spacious rooms are available at the **Eucla Motor Hotel** (☎08-9039 3468; euclamotel@bigpond.com; unpowered/powered sites $15/20, r $45-110; ❄).

Coolgardie

POP 800

In 1898 sleepy Coolgardie was the third-biggest town in WA, with a population of 15,000, six newspapers, two stock exchanges, more than 20 hotels and three breweries. It all took off just hours after Arthur Bayley rode into Southern Cross in 1892 and dumped 554oz of Coolgardie gold on the mining warden's counter. The only echoes that remain are some historic buildings lining the uncharacteristically wide main road and information panels detailing the glory days.

Sights & Activities

Goldfields Museum & Visitor Centre MUSEUM

(08-9026 6090; www.coolgardie.wa.gov.au; Bayley St, Warden's Court; adult/child $4/2; 8.30am-4.20pm Mon-Fri, 10am-3pm Sat & Sun) Goldfields memorabilia including information about former US president Herbert Hoover's days on the goldfields in Gwalia. Also the fascinating story of Modesto Varischetti, the 'Entombed Miner'.

Warden Finnerty's Residence HISTORIC BUILDING

(2 McKenzie St; adult/child $4/2; 11am-4pm) Built in 1895 for Coolgardie's first mining warden and magistrate, this National Trust house has been beautifully restored.

Sleeping & Eating

Coolgardie Goldrush Motel MOTEL $$

(08-9026 6080; www.coolgardiemotels.com.au; 49-53 Bayley St; r $110-125;) With colourful linen, spotless bathrooms and flat-screen TVs, the Goldrush's small but recently refurbished rooms are very comfortable. The homemade pies and sausage rolls are especially tasty at the attached restaurant, easily the best place in town to eat.

Kalgoorlie-Boulder

POP 28,300

Kalgoorlie-Boulder ('Kal' to the locals), some 600km from Perth, is an outback success story. The town is prosperous, with well-preserved historic buildings and streets wide enough to turn a camel train in – a necessity in turn-of-the-century goldfield towns. The most enduring of WA's gold towns, today it's still the centre for mining in this part of the state.

Historically, mineworkers would come straight to town to spend disposable income at Kalgoorlie's infamous brothels, or at pubs staffed by 'skimpies' (scantily clad female bar staff). Nowadays, the town is definitely more family-friendly – mineworkers must reside in the town and cannot be transient 'fly-in, fly-out' labour – and there are significant New Zealand and Irish populations attracted by the mining industry.

It still feels a bit like the Wild West though – a frontier town where bush meets brash – and the rough and tumble pubs and 'skimpy' bar staff are reminders of a more rambunctious past.

It's undeniably an interesting place, but probably not to everyone's taste. There are plenty of historical and modern mining sites to explore, and it makes a good base for trips out to the ghost towns in the surrounding outback.

History

Long-time prospector Paddy Hannan set out from Coolgardie in search of another gold strike. He stumbled across the surface gold that sparked the 1893 gold rush, and inadvertently chose the site of Kalgoorlie for a township.

When surface sparkles subsided, the miners dug deeper, extracting the precious metal from the rocks by costly and complex processes. Kalgoorlie quickly prospered, and the town's magnificent public buildings, constructed at the end of the 19th century, are evidence of its fabulous wealth.

Despite its slow decline after WWI, Kal is still the largest producer of gold in Australia. What was a Golden Mile of small mining operators' headframes and corrugated-iron shacks is now an overwhelmingly huge Super Pit, which will eventually be 3.8km long, 1.35km wide and 500m deep.

Sights & Activities

Super Pit LOOKOUT

(www.superpit.com.au; Outram St; 7am-7pm) The view is staggering, with building-sized trucks zigzagging up and down the huge hole and looking like kids' toys. It's quite beautiful in its own way, with nature's palette of red, black and grey revealed on the exposed rock faces. Take a tour run by Kalgoorlie Tours & Charters.

Western Australian Museum – Kalgoorlie-Boulder MUSEUM

(www.museum.wa.gov.au; 17 Hannan St; suggested donation $5; 10am-4.30pm) The impressive Ivanhoe-mine headframe marks this excellent museum's entrance; take the lift to look over the city and mines. An underground vault displays giant nuggets and gold bars, and there's also a fantastic collection of trade-union banners. Relocated historic buildings include a miner's cottage and mobile police station (attached to a train). Half-hour guided tours start at 11am.

Hannan St HISTORIC BUILDINGS
The city's main drag, Hannan St has retained many of its original gold-rush-era buildings, including several grand hotels and the imposing **town hall**. Outside is a drinking fountain in the form of a **statue of Paddy Hannan** holding a water bag. Pick up **audiotour** equipment from the visitor centre ($10).

School of Mines Mineral Museum MUSEUM
(cnr Egan & Cassidy Sts; 9am-noon Mon-Fri, closed school holidays) FREE Geology display including replicas of big nuggets discovered locally.

Goldfields Arts Centre GALLERY
(http://gac.curtin.edu.au; Cheetham St; 10am-3pm Mon-Fri, noon-3pm Sun) FREE Interesting exhibitions are held here by local, state and national artists.

Royal Flying Doctor Service VISITOR CENTRE
(RFDS; www.flyingdoctor.org.au; Kalgoorlie-Boulder Airport; admission by donation; 10am-3pm Mon-Fri) See how the flying doctors look after the outback; tours at 10.15am and 2pm.

Hammond Park PARK
(Lyall St; 9am-5pm) A good spot for kids, with playgrounds, aviaries, kangaroos and emus.

Karlkurla Park PARK
This regenerated bushland on the north-western edge of town has 4km of walking trails.

Kalgoorlie Arboretum PARK
(Hawkin St) Twenty-six hectares of parkland managed by DEC with 50 native tree species set around a lake.

Goldfields Oasis Centre AQUATIC CENTRE
(www.goldfieldsoasis.com.au; 99 Johnston Rd; pools adult/child $5.50/3.50; 5.45am-9pm Mon-Fri, 7am-7pm Sat & Sun) When you're baking 390km from the nearest beach, this high-tech aquatic centre may prove irresistible. Hit the **Flowrider** wave pool to surf in the desert; there are also **water slides**.

Tours

Kalgoorlie Tours & Charters BUS TOUR
(08-9021 2211; www.kalgoorlietours.com.au; 250 Hannan St) Here's your chance to explore the Super Pit. Regular 2½-hourtours (adult/child $70/45) leave at 9.30am and 1.30pm Monday to Saturday, and shorter 1½-hour tours ($40/25) run on demand during school holidays. All participants must wear long trousers and enclosed shoes.

Goldrush Tours BUS TOUR
(1800 620 440; www.goldrushtours.com.au) Includes half-day heritage jaunts around Kalgoorlie-Boulder (adult/child $50/25) and day tours to the sculptures on Lake Ballard ($150/75).

Questa Casa HISTORICAL TOUR
(08-9021 4897; www.questacasa.com.au; 133 Hay St; tours $20; tours 3pm) Touring Australia's oldest operating brothel has become de rigueur for many visitors to Kalgoorlie. It's the sole survivor of the many brothels that once lined Hay St. Curious visitors must be 18 years or older.

Festivals & Events

Kalgoorlie Market MARKET
(Hannan St, St Barbara's Sq) First Sunday of the month.

Boulder Market Day MARKET
Third Sunday of the month.

Kalgoorlie-Boulder Racing Round RACING
(www.kbrc.com.au) Locals and a huge influx of visitors dress up to watch horses race in September. Accommodation can be difficult to secure.

Sleeping

Much of the accommodation in Kalgoorlie is targeted towards the mining industry. The smarter places tend to be overpriced for what's offered, while the hostels and pubs are often full of rough-and-tumble long-stayers.

York Hotel PUB $
(08-9021 2337; www.yorkhotel.com.au; 259 Hannan St; s/d/tr $65/89/140) One of Kalgoorlie's most unique heritage buildings, this is a character-filled labyrinth of high-ceilinged rooms, shared bathrooms, wooden staircases and lacework balconies. It's good value, with a light breakfast included.

Kalgoorlie Backpackers HOSTEL $
(08-9091 1482; www.kalgoorliebackpackers.com.au; 166 Hay St; dm/s/d $33/50/75;) Partly located in a former brothel, this hostel is in a central location, and is an excellent place to find out about work opportunities.

Golddust Backpackers YHA
HOSTEL $

(☑08-9091 3737; www.yha.com.au; 192 Hay St; dm/s/d $33/50/70; ✳@☒) A row of boots and hard hats by the front door gives a good indication of the regular clientele. The rooms are clean but basic and communal facilities are good.

Discovery Holiday Parks
CARAVAN PARK $

(www.discoveryholidayparks.com.au; sites $21-41, units $169-199; ✳@☒) Sister complexes with sizeable and well-fitted-out A-frame chalets and cabins, grassy tent sites, and playgrounds and pools. The branch in **Boulder** (☑08-9093 1266; 201 Lane St) is conveniently located at the southern entrance to town; the branch in **Kalgoorlie** (☑08-9039 4800; 286 Burt St) feels slightly less crammed.

Rydges Kalgoorlie
HOTEL $$

(☑08-9080 0800; www.rydges.com; 21 Davidson St; r from $189; ✳@☎☒) Easily the town's best, this resort-style complex is located in a residential area between Kalgoorlie and Boulder. The rooms, set within an oasis of lush native bush, are spacious and very comfortable.

Quest Yelverton Kalgoorlie
APARTMENTS $$

(☑08-9022 8181; www.questkalgoorlie.com.au; 210 Egan St; apt from $195; ✳☎☒) Close to Hannan St but far enough away to get a quiet night's sleep, the Quest offers fully self-contained and serviced apartments.

Railway Motel
MOTEL $$

(☑08-9088 0000; www.railwaymotel.com.au; 51 Forrest St; r/apt $160/250; ✳☒) This complex opposite the train station has bright, spruced-up rooms. Self-contained two-bedroom apartments just up the road are spacious and comfortable.

Langtrees
BOUTIQUE HOTEL $$$

(☑08-9026 2181; www.langtreeshotel.com; 181 Hay St; d $300) Kalgoorlie's newest hotel used to be one of the town's most famous brothels. The slightly eccentric decor is showcased in 10 themed rooms, including an Afghan boudoir or the Holden-On room that's perfect for recovering petrolheads. Less ostentatious rooms are also available.

✖ Eating

Kalgoorlie won't set the gastronomic world alight anytime soon, but if you're a fan of simple, meaty, man-size meals, you won't have any complaints.

★ Relish
CAFE $

(162 Hannan St; breakfast $8-16, lunch $10-14; ⊙6am-3pm Mon-Fri, 7am-2pm Sat & Sun; ☑) ⌀ Seemingly transplanted from cosmopolitan Perth, this excellent cafe has the best coffee in town and interesting lunch snacks like Spanish meatballs, tandoori chicken skewers and vegie frittata. We're big fans of the folded eggs for breakfast. Check out the canvases from local artists lining Relish's whitewashed laneway area.

Hoover's Cafe
PUB $

(www.palacehotel.com.au; 137 Hannan St; mains $10-25; ⊙8am-5pm Mon-Sat; ☎) Attached to the Palace Hotel, this old-fashioned pub dining room serves great-value, tasty food and surprisingly good coffee. Upstairs is the flasher **Balcony Bar & Restaurant** (mains $32-49; ⊙from 6pm Mon-Sat) doing classic spins on steak and seafood.

Hannan Street Gourmet
DELI $

(147 Hannan St; mains around $12; ⊙9.30am-5pm Mon-Fri, 10am-2pm Sat; ☑) Salads, very good sandwiches and daily hot-lunch specials. You can take away, or eat at the tables in the back.

Paddy's Ale House
PUB $$

(Exchange Hotel, 135 Hannan St; mains $17-30; ⊙11am-late) With a wide range of tap beers, Paddy's serves up classic counter meals (such as steaks and bangers-and-mash) to the hordes. It's a good place to catch live TV sport, too.

Lemongrass
ASIAN $$

(5/84-90 Brockman St; mains $19-24; ⊙5.30-10pm) Decent Vietnamese and Thai flavours all delivered with a warm welcome from the friendly family owners; a healthy and lighter option in a town better known for robust pub grub.

☗ Drinking & Entertainment

If you need proof that Kalgoorlie is stuck in a time rift, somewhere between the Wild West and a 1970s mechanic's garage, step into one of the gold-rush-era pubs of Hannan St. Offering an opportunity to quench your anthropological curiosity as much as your thirst, Kal's watering holes are full of hard-drinking blokes and female bar staff clad in underwear, suspenders and high heels. You'll need to pick your pub carefully if you prefer your bar staff fully clothed and not in 'skimpy' attire.

Judd's PUB
(www.kalgoorliehotel.com.au; Kalgoorlie Hotel, 319 Hannan St) With a beer garden and windows that open onto the street, Judd's at the Kalgoorlie Hotel is the place to check out live bands and DJs.

Palace Hotel PUB
(www.palacehotel.com.au; 137 Hannan St) Watch the street life from the relatively demure balcony bar or descend to the depths of the Gold Bar for live bands, DJs and skimpies.

Wild West Saloon PUB
(Exchange Hotel, 135 Hannan St) The front bar at the Exchange Hotel has skimpies (some in cowboy hats), TV sports, live music and mine workers furiously refuelling.

Orana Cinema CINEMA
(☎08-9021 2199; www.oranacinemas.com.au; 26 Oswald St) Movies in air-conditioned comfort.

Goldfields Arts Centre ARTS CENTRE
(☎08-9088 6900; http://gac.curtin.edu.au; Cheetham St) Performing arts with occasional national acts.

Information

DEC (☎08-9080 5555; 32 Brookman St; ⊙8am-5pm Mon-Fri)

Kalgoorlie Regional Hospital (☎08-9080 5888; Piccadilly St)

Visitor Centre (☎08-9021 1966; www.kalgoorlietourism.com; Town Hall, cnr Hannan & Wilson Sts; ⊙8.30am-5pm Mon-Fri, 9am-2pm Sat & Sun)

North of Kalgoorlie-Boulder

Heading north from Kalgoorlie-Boulder, the Goldfields Hwy is surfaced as far as Wiluna (580km north), which is also the starting point for the 4WD Canning Stock Route and Gunbarrel Hwy. Branching east off the highway, the road from Leonora is sealed as far as Laverton (367km northeast), which is the starting point for the unsealed Great Central Rd (Outback Way).

Off the main road you'll see the occasional mining truck, but other traffic is virtually nonexistent – and while many gravel roads are fine for regular cars, rain can quickly close them to all vehicles. All the (non-ghost) towns have pub accommodation, caravan parks (most with on-site cabins), fuel stops and grocery stores.

Kanowna, Broad Arrow & Ora Banda

Easy day trips north from Kalgoorlie include the gold ghost towns of Kanowna (18km northeast), Broad Arrow (38km north) and Ora Banda (65km northwest). Little remains of Kanowna apart from the building foundations of its 16 hotels (!) and other public buildings, but its pioneer cemetery – including a couple of early Japanese graves – is interesting. Broad Arrow was featured in *The Nickel Queen* (1971), the first full-length feature film made in WA. It is a shadow of its former self: at the beginning of the 20th century it had a population of 2400. Now there's just one pub – popular with Kal locals at weekends – and a couple of tumbledown houses. The 1911 **Ora Banda Historical Inn** (☎08-9024 2444; www.orabanda.com.au; sites per 2 people $120-30, r $75-120) has a beer garden, simple accommodation in a donga-style block and a dusty camping area.

Menzies & Lake Ballard

The once thriving but now tiny township of **Menzies**, 132km from Kalgoorlie, is best known as the turn-off for the stunning **Antony Gormley sculptures** on **Lake Ballard**, an eye-dazzling salt lake 51km northwest of town. You can camp here for free; there are toilets and a barbecue area but no showers.

The **Menzies visitor centre** (☎08-9024 2702; www.menzies.wa.gov.au; Shenton St; ⊙9am-4.30pm Mon-Fri, 10am-2pm Sat & Sun) has internet access and information on visiting the sculptures and other local sites, and runs the neighbouring **Caravan Park** (sites per 2 people $20-26). It also houses the **Spinifex Art Gallery**, which exhibits works from the Tjuntjuntjarra community, located deep in the desert 750km to the east.

PERMITS, PLEASE

The Canning Stock Route and Outback Way traverse pockets of Aboriginal land and travellers must obtain a permit from the **Department of Aboriginal Affairs** (DAA; www.daa.wa.gov.au) to cross them. It's usually a quick online process, but if you're planning to stay rather than just pass through, additional approvals are required from the affected community; allow two weeks.

OFF THE BEATEN TRACK

CANNING STOCK ROUTE & GUNBARREL HIGHWAY

Wiluna, 300km north of Leonora, is the start or finish point of two of Australia's most extreme 4WD adventures – the Canning Stock Route and the Gunbarrel Hwy. These rough, remote routes head through unforgiving wilderness for thousands of kilometres. They can only be safely traversed from April to September. Don't attempt them at all without checking with visitor centres and DEC offices first as they're completely weather-dependent. HEMA Maps' detailed *Great Desert Tracks – North West Sheet* is essential.

The **Canning Stock Route** (www.exploroz.com/TrekNotes/WDeserts/Canning_Stock_Route.aspx) runs 2006km northeast to Halls Creek, crossing the Great Sandy and Gibson Deserts, and is a route to be taken very seriously. If you're starting from Wiluna, pick up road and safety information from the **shire office** (☎08-9981 8000; www.wiluna.wa.gov.au; Scotia St). You'll need a permit to cross the Birrilburru native-title area.

Taking the old **Gunbarrel Highway** (www.exploroz.com/TrekNotes/WDeserts/Gunbarrel_Highway.aspx) from Wiluna to Warakurna near the NT border (where it joins the Outback Way) is a long, rough, heavily corrugated trip through lots of sand dunes. Like the Canning, it's suggested that for safety you drive this in convoy with other vehicles, and you need to take all supplies – including fuel and water for the duration – with you. Let the police posts at either end of both tracks know your movements.

Kookynie

Between Menzies and Leonora, a good dirt road leads 25km to Kookynie, another interesting ghost town, where the **Kookynie Grand Hotel** (☎08-9031 3010; s/d $77/93) pulls pints and offers beds. Quiet **Niagara Dam**, 10km from Kookynie, has bush camping.

Leonora

North of Kookynie (237km from Kalgoorlie), this is the area's largest service centre for mining exploration and farming. Check out the old public buildings and pubs on the main street near the **visitor centre** (☎08-9037 7016; Tower St; ⏲9am-4pm Mon-Fri). Just 4km southwest of town, **Gwalia Historic Site** was occupied in 1896 and deserted in 1963, after the pit closed. With houses and household goods disintegrating intact, it's a strangely fascinating ghost town. The **museum** (adult/child $10/5; ⏲9am-4pm) is full of wonderful curios, and there's a good audiotour ($2). **Hoover House** (☎08-9037 7122; www.gwalia.org.au; s $120-140, d $130-150; ❄) – the 1898 mine manager's house, named for Gwalia's first mine manager, Herbert Hoover, who later became the 31st president of the United States – is beautifully restored, and you can B&B in one of its three antique-strewn bedrooms.

Laverton

Laverton crouches on the edge of the Great Victoria Desert. The **visitor centre** (☎08-9031 1361; Augusta St; ⏲9.30am-4.30pm Mon-Fri, 9am-1pm Sat & Sun) is combined with the **Great Beyond – Explorers' Hall of Fame** (adult/child $10/5), which makes use of technology to tell pioneer stories. The not-for-profit **Laverton Outback Gallery** (www.laverton-outback-gallery.com.au; 4 Euro St; ⏲9am-5pm) is a great place to purchase paintings, necklaces, woomeras and boomerangs – 80% of the price goes straight to the Aboriginal artist.

Laverton marks the start of the Outback Way. Expect to overnight and/or stock up on supplies of fuel and water here, and *definitely* check at the visitor centre for current road conditions.

Outback Way (Great Central Road)

The unsealed **Outback Way** (www.outbackway.org.au) – previously known as the Great Central Road – provides rich scenery of red dirt, spinifex, mulga and desert oak. It links Laverton with Winton in central Queensland, via the red centre of the NT. From Laverton it is a mere 1098km to Yulara, 1541km to Alice Springs and 2720km to Winton!

The road can be sandy and corrugated in places, but it's wide and suitable for all vehicles. It can be closed for several days after rain. Diesel is available at roughly 300km intervals on the WA side, and Opal fuel takes the place of unleaded petrol. (Opal is unsniffable, and its provision is one of the measures in place to counteract petrol-sniffing problems in local communities.)

Coming from Laverton, three **WA roadhouses** (www.ngaanyatjarraku.wa.gov.au) all provide food, fuel and limited mechanical services – **Tjukayirla** (☎08-9037 1108; tjukayirlaroadhouse@bigpond.com) at 315km, **Warburton** (☎08-8956 7656) at 567km and **Warakurna** (☎08-8956 7344; warakurnaroadhouse@bigpond.com) at 798km. All have accommodation, from camping (around $15 per person) to budget rooms (around $50) and self-contained units (around $150). Book ahead as rooms are limited. The Tjukayirla roadhouse offers tours to caves with 5000-year-old rock art.

At Warburton visit the **Tjulyuru Cultural & Civic Centre** (☎08-8956 7966; www.tjulyuru.com; ⊙8.30am-4.30pm Mon-Fri), near the roadhouse; the art gallery contains an extensive collection of Ngaanyatjarra Aboriginal paintings. At **Giles**, 231km northeast of Warburton and 105km west of the NT border, there is a meteorological station where weather balloons are released at 9.30am and 2.30pm daily.

Warakurna, Warburton and Giles run on NT time, 1½ hours ahead of WA time.

DRYANDRA TO HYDEN

A beautiful forest, rare marsupials, stunning ancient granite-rock formations, salt lakes, interesting back roads and the unique Wave Rock are the scattered highlights of this widespread farming region.

Getting There & Away

It's much easier with your own vehicle. Wave Rock is a long day trip from Perth.

Transwa (☎1300 662 205; www.transwa.wa.gov.au) Runs sporadic buses between Perth and the south coast.

Western Travel Bug (☎9486 4222; www.travelbug.com.au; tours $175) Offers a one-day tour.

Western Xposure (☎08-9414 8423; www.westernxposure.com.au) Takes in Wave Rock as part of a five-day southwest loop ($750).

Hyden & Wave Rock

Large granite outcrops dot the Central and Southern Wheat Belts, and the most famous is the multicoloured cresting swell of **Wave Rock**, 350km from Perth. Formed some 60 million years ago by weathering and water erosion, Wave Rock is streaked with colours created by run-off from local mineral springs.

To get the most out of Wave Rock, obtain the *Walk Trails at Wave Rock and The Humps* brochure from the **visitor centre** (☎08-9880 5182; www.waverock.com.au; Wave Rock; ⊙9am-5pm). Park at Hippos Yawn (no fee) and follow the shady track back along the rock base to Wave Rock (1km).

Accommodation can fill quickly, so phone ahead for a spot amid the gum trees at **Wave Rock Cabins & Caravan Park** (☎08-9880 5022; www.waverock.com.au; unpowered/powered

OFF THE BEATEN TRACK

DRYANDRA WOODLAND

With small populations of threatened numbats, woylies and tammar wallabies, the Dryandra Woodland, an isolated remnant of eucalypt forest 164km southeast of Perth, hints at what the wheat belt was like before large-scale land clearing and feral predators wreaked havoc on local ecosystems. With numerous walking trails, it makes a great getaway from Perth.

The excellent **Barna Mia Animal Sanctuary**, home to endangered bilbies, boodies, woylies and marla, conducts 90-minute after-dark torchlight tours, providing a rare opportunity to see these creatures up close. Book through the **DEC** (☎weekdays 08-9881 9200, weekends 08-9881 2064; www.dec.wa.gov.au; Hough St, Narrogin; adult/child/family $14/7.50/37.50; ⊙9am-4pm) for post-sunset tours on Monday, Wednesday, Friday and Saturday and book early for peak periods.

While you can hoist your tent at the **Congelin Camp Ground** (☎08-9881 9200; per person $10), Dryandra is one place you should splurge. The **Lions Dryandra Village** (☎08-9884 5231; www.dryandravillage.org.au; adult/child $30/15, 2-/4-/8-12 person cabins $70/90/130) is a 1920s forestry camp offering self-contained, renovated woodcutters' cabins complete with fridge, stove, fireplace, en suite and nearby grazing wallabies. Narrogin, serviced by Transwa buses, is 22km southeast.

DON'T MISS

MULKAS CAVE & THE HUMPS

The superb Mulkas Cave and the Humps are a further 16km from Wave Rock. Mulkas Cave, an easy stroll from the car park, is an important rock-art site with over 450 stencils and hand prints. The more adventurous can choose from two walking tracks. The **Kalari Trail** (1.6km return) climbs up onto a huge granite outcrop (one of the Humps) with excellent views, somehow wilder and more impressive than Wave Rock, while the **Gnamma Trail** (1.2km return) stays low and investigates natural waterholes with panels explaining Noongar culture.

sites from $28/35, cabins from $140, cottages from $160; ❄ ≋).

In **Hyden** (population 190), 4km east of the rock, the '70s brick **Wave Rock Motel** (☎08-9880 5052; www.waverock.com.au; 2 Lynch St; s/d from $105/150; ❄ ≋) has well-equipped rooms, a comfy lounge with fireplace, and an indoor bush bistro.

Transwa runs a bus from Perth to Hyden ($51, five hours) and on to Esperance ($53, five hours) every Tuesday, returning on Thursday.

If heading to/from the Nullarbor, take the unsealed direct **Hyden–Norseman Road**, which will save 100km or so. Look for the brochure *The Granite and Woodlands Discovery Trail* at the Norseman or Wave Rock visitor centres.

SUNSET & TURQUOISE COASTS

The Indian Ocean Drive connects Perth to a succession of beautiful beaches, sleepy fishing villages, extraordinary geological formations, rugged national parks and incredibly diverse flora.

ℹ Getting There & Away

Greyhound (☎1300 473 946; www.greyhound.com.au) Runs to/from Perth stopping at Lancelin, Cervantes, Geraldton and Carnarvon.

Integrity (☎1800 226 339; www.integrity-coachlines.com.au) Buses run from Perth via Lancelin north to Cervantes, Jurien Bay and Geraldton.

Yanchep National Park

The woodlands and wetlands of **Yanchep National Park** (www.dec.wa.gov.au/yanchep; Wanneroo Rd; per car $11; ⏲visitor centre 9.15am-4.30pm) are home to hundreds of species of fauna and flora including koalas, kangaroos, emus and cockatoos. Caves can be viewed on 45-minute tours (adult/child $10/5; five per day). On weekends at 2pm and 3pm, local Noongar guides run excellent **tours** (adult/child $10/5) on indigenous history, lifestyle and culture, and give **didgeridoo and dance performances** (adult/child $10/5).

Guilderton

POP 150

Some 43km north of Yanchep, Guilderton is a popular family-holiday spot. Children paddle safely near the mouth of the Moore River, while adults enjoy the excellent fishing, surfing and sunbathing on the white sands of the ocean beach. The **Guilderton Caravan Park** (☎08-9577 1021; www.guildertoncaravanpark.com.au; 2 Dewar St; 2-person sites $29-40, chalets $165) is the holidaymakers' hub, with self-contained chalets, a cafe and a general store, and there's a volunteer-run **visitor centre** (erratic hours).

Lancelin

POP 670

Afternoon winds and shallows protected by an outlying reef make this sleepy beach perfect for windsurfing and kitesurfing, attracting action seekers from around the world for the **Lancelin Ocean Classic** (www.lancelinoceanclassic.com.au) every January. It's also a great snorkelling spot.

Activities

Surfschool SURFING

(☎1800 198 121, 08-9444 5399; www.surfschool.com.au; 69 Casserley Way; 3/6hr lessons $40/75; ⏲8am) The main beach's gentle waves make it a good place for beginners and there are bigger breaks nearby for more experienced surfers. Three- to six-hour lessons include boards and wetsuits. There are also surf-camp packages, including lessons, transfers from Perth and accommodation.

Makanikai Kiteboarding KITEBOARDING

(☎0406 807 309; www.makanikaikiteboarding.com; lessons/courses from $60/200, rental per hr/

day $20/60) Gear rental and lessons and tuition in kiteboarding. Accommodation packages are also available.

Sleeping & Eating

★Lancelin Lodge YHA HOSTEL $
(08-9655 2020; www.lancelinlodge.com.au; 10 Hopkins St; dm/d/f $30/80/98;) A well-equipped and laid-back hostel, with wide verandahs and lots of relaxed communal spaces. Excellent facilities include a big kitchen, barbecue, wood-fire pizza oven, swimming pool, ping-pong table, volleyball court and free use of bikes and boogie boards.

Endeavour Tavern PUB $$
(58 Gingin Rd; mains $18-34) A classic beachfront Aussie pub with a beer garden overlooking the ocean. The casual eatery serves decent seafood and pub grub classics.

Cervantes & Pinnacles Desert

POP 480

The laid-back crayfishing town of Cervantes makes a pleasant base for exploring the **Pinnacles Desert** and the **Kwongan**, the wildflower-rich inland heathland of **Lesueur** and **Badgingarra National Parks**. There are also some lovely beaches.

Grab a copy of the *Turquoise Coast Self Drive Map* from Cervantes' combined **post office and visitor centre** (08-9652 7700, freecall 1800 610 660; www.visitpinnaclescountry.com.au; Cadiz St; 8am-5pm), which also supplies accommodation and tour information.

Sights & Activities

★Nambung National Park NATURE RESERVE
(per car $11) Situated 19km from Cervantes, Nambung is home to the spectacular

WORTH A TRIP

KWONGAN WILDFLOWERS

Take any road inland from the Turquoise Coast and you'll soon enter the Kwongan heathlands, where, depending on the season, the roadside verges burst with native wildflowers like banksia, grevillea, hakea, calothamnus, kangaroo paw and smokebush. While Lesueur National Park is an obvious choice for all things botanical, consider some of the following options:

Badgingarra National Park Three and a half kilometres of walking trails, kangaroo paws, banksias, grass trees, verticordia and a rare mallee. The back road linking Badgingarra to Lesueur is particularly rich in flora. Obtain details from the Badgingarra Roadhouse. There's also a picnic area on Bibby Rd.

Alexander Morrison National Park Named after Western Australia's first botanist. There are no trails, but you can drive through slowly on the Coorow Green Head Rd, which has loads of flora along its verge all the way from Lesueur. Expect to see dryandra, banksia, grevillea, smokebush, leschenaultia and honey myrtle.

Tathra National Park Tathra has similar flora to Alexander Morrison National Park and the drive between the two is rich with banksia, kangaroo paw and grevillea.

Coomallo Rest Area Orchids, feather flowers, black kangaroo paws, wandoo and river red gums can be found upstream and on the slopes of the small hill.

Brand Highway (Rte 1) The route's not exactly conducive to slow meandering, but the Brand Hwy verges are surprisingly rich in wildflowers, especially either side of Eneabba.

Wildflower Way (Rte 115) From Wongan Hills verticordia to the wreath flower of Mullewa, and the everlastings of Coalseam National Park, the verges and back roads surrounding Rtes 116 and 115 (including Moora and pretty Perenjori) abound with spectacular natives.

If you're overwhelmed and frustrated by not being able to identify all these strange new plants, consider staying at **Western Flora Caravan Park** (08-9955 2030; wfloracp@activ8.net.au; Brand Hwy, North Eneabba; unpowered/powered sites $24/26, d $65, on-site vans $75, chalets $120), where the enthusiastic owners run free two-hour wildflower walks across their 65-hectare property every day at 4.30pm.

Pinnacles Desert, where thousands of limestone pillars rise eerily from the desert floor, their lime-rich sand remnants of compacted seashells that, over millennia, subsequently eroded. A loop-road runs through the formations, but it's more fun to wander on foot, especially at sunset, full moon or dawn when the light is sublime and the crowds evaporate.

Nearby **Kangaroo Point** and **Hangover Bay** make nice picnic spots with BBQs and tables, while stromatolites inhabit the shoreline at **Lake Thetis**, and **Hansen Bay Lookout** has excellent views across the coast. In town, walkways wend along the coastline providing beach access.

Lesueur National Park NATURE RESERVE
(per car $11) This botanical paradise, 50km north of Cervantes, contains a staggering 820 plant species, many of them rare and endemic, such as the pine banksia *(Banksia tricupsis)* and Mt Lesueur grevillea *(Grevillea batrachioides)*. Late winter sees the heath erupt into a mass of colour, and the park is also home to the endangered Carnaby's cockatoo. An 18km circuit drive is dotted with lookouts and picnic areas. Flat-topped **Mt Lesueur** (4km return walk) has panoramic coastal views.

Tours

Many Perth-based companies offer day trips to the Pinnacles.

Turquoise Coast Enviro Tours SIGHTSEEING
(08-9652 7047; www.thepinnacles.com.au; 59 Seville St; 3hr Pinnacles tours $60, full-day Kwongan tours $170) Cervantes local and ex-ranger Mike Newton runs informative morning (8am, three hours) and evening (2½ hours before sunset) Pinnacles trips, as well as a full-day Kwongan tour, including Lesueur National Park and the coast up to Leeman.

Sleeping & Eating

Prices surge during school holidays.

★**Cervantes Lodge & Pinnacles Beach Backpackers** HOSTEL $
(1800 245 232; www.cervanteslodge.com.au; 91 Seville St; dm $30, d with/without bathroom $130/90; @) In a great location behind the dunes, this relaxing hostel has a wide verandah, small and tidy dorms, a nice communal kitchen and cosy lounge area. Bright, spacious en-suite rooms, some with views, are next door in the lodge.

Pinnacles Caravan Park CARAVAN PARK $
(08-9652 7060; www.pinnaclespark.com.au; 35 Aragon St; unpowered/powered sites from $27/32, on-site vans/cabins $50/75;) Fantastic location right behind the beach with plenty of shady, grassy sites and on-site cafe.

★**Amble Inn** B&B $$
(0429 652 401; 2150 Cadda Rd, Hill River; d with/without spa $165/150;) High up on the heathland, about 25km east of Cervantes, this hidden gem as beautiful thick stone walls, cool, wide verandahs and superbly styled rooms. Watch the sun set over the coast from the nearby hill with a glass of your complimentary wine.

Lobster Shack SEAFOOD $$
(08-9652 7010; www.lobstershack.com.au; 11 Madrid St; shop 9am-5pm, lunch 11.30am-2.30pm) Craving for crayfish? They don't come much fresher than at this lobster factory–turned–lunch spot, where a delicious grilled cray, chips and salad will set you back $25. Self-guided tours (adult/child $15/7.50) and takeaway frozen seafood are also available here.

Cervantes Country Club SEAFOOD $$
(08-9652 7123; Aragon St; seafood platters from $55; 6-9pm) The seafood platters at this humble sporting club are legendary, and include prawns, oysters, fish, calamari, crayfish (in season), salad and mountains of chips. Bring a friend.

Getting There & Away

Integrity runs daily to Perth ($26, three hours), Dongara ($28, two hours) and Geraldton ($32, three hours) with a twice-weekly overnight service to Exmouth ($162, 14 hours).

Greyhound runs three times weekly to Perth ($37, three hours) and Dongara ($40, two hours), continuing to Broome ($380, 31 hours). Locally, both buses stop at Jurien Bay (20 minutes), Green Head (40 minutes) and Leeman (55 minutes).

Jurien Bay, Green Head & Leeman

Heading north from Cervantes, sprawling **Jurien Bay** (population 1500) is home to a large fishing fleet and pleasant seaside walks. Holiday houses and apartments can be booked via local **real estate agents** (08-9652 2055; www.jurienbayholidays.com; Shop 1A, 34 Bashford St) while **Jurien Bay**

Tourist Park (☎08-9652 1595; www.jurienbay-touristpark.com.au; Roberts St; unpowered/powered sites $28/33, on-site vans from $90, 1-/2-bedroom chalets $115/145) has comfortable chalets right behind the beach. Next door, the Jetty Cafe (☎08-9652 1999; meals $5-17; ⌚7.30am-5pm) has decent brekkies, burgers and grilled fish.

Tiny Green Head (population 280) has several beautiful bays great for swimming, and nearby Leeman (population 400) is popular with windsurfers.

Green Head has the best sleeping and eating options, including Centrebreak Beach Stay (☎08-9953 1896; www.centrebreak-beachstay.com.au; Lot 402 Ocean View Dr; dm/d/f $35/150/190, meals $14-35;), complete with licensed cafe; the lovely Seaview (☎08-9953 1487; 25 Whiteman St; per person $65) B&B with great views; and the relaxed and shady Green Head Caravan Park (☎08-9953 1131; 9 Green Head Rd; unpowered/powered sites $20/28, on-site vans from $70).

Nearby, leafy Leeman Caravan Park (☎08-9953 1080; 43 Thomas St; unpowered/powered sites $20/25, on-site vans $60, cabins $70-90) has lots of shade, grassy sites and a good camp kitchen all close to the dunes.

If you have a 4WD, Stockyard Gully Caves are 30km away, off the Coorow–Green Head Rd, and you can explore the underground creek and caverns with a torch. Watch out for bees and bats.

★Sea Lion Charters (☎08-9953 1012; http://sealioncharters.biz; 24 Bryant St, Green Head; half-day tours adult/child $120/60) offers a magical experience interacting in shallow water with playful sea lions who mimic your every move. It helps to be a good snorkeller. Wetsuits are $10 extra.

GREAT NORTHERN HIGHWAY

Most travellers avoid the direct route north, preferring the scenic attractions of the coast to the minimalist landscape and mining towns of the interior. Closer to Perth, the peaceful village (and lovely pub) of New Norcia makes for an excellent weekend getaway.

Getting There & Away

AIR

Skippers (☎1300 729 924; www.skippers.com.au) Flies regularly between Perth, Mt Magnet and Meekatharra.

BUS

Integrity (☎1800 226 339; www.integrity-coachlines.com.au) Leaves Perth Wednesday and runs up the Great Northern Hwy (Rte 95) to Mt Magnet ($105, eight hours), Cue ($118, nine hours), Meekatharra ($136, 11 hours) and Newman ($235, 16 hours), before reaching Port Hedland ($255, 22 hours); returns Friday.

Transwa (☎1300 662 205; www.transwa.wa.gov.au) Runs Monday and Thursday from Geraldton to Mt Magnet ($51, four hours), Cue ($61, six hours) and Meekatharra ($73, seven hours) along Rte 123, returning Tuesday and Friday; connections to Perth via Mullewa ($69, seven hours) or Geraldton.

New Norcia

POP 70

The idyllic monastery settlement of New Norcia, 132km from Perth, consists of a cluster of ornate Spanish-style buildings set incongruously in the Australian bush. Founded in 1846 by Spanish Benedictine monks as an Aboriginal mission, today the working monastery holds prayers and retreats, alongside a business producing boutique breads and gourmet goodies.

Guided two-hour town tours (www.newnorcia.wa.edu.au; adult/child $15/10; ⌚11am & 1.30pm) include various chapels and their amazing frescos; purchase tickets from the museum.

At the New Norcia Museum & Art Gallery (☎08-9654 8056; www.newnorcia.wa.edu.au; Great Northern Hwy; combined museum & town tours adult/family $25/60; ⌚10am-4.30pm), you can discover the history of the monastery and marvel at one of the country's largest collections of post-Renaissance religious art. The gift shop sells souvenirs, honey and lovely local bread.

Sleeping

New Norcia Hotel HOTEL $
(☎08-9654 8034; www.newnorcia.wa.edu.au; Great Northern Hwy; s/d $75/95) Sweeping staircases, high ceilings, understated rooms and wide verandahs invoke a more genteel era. An international menu ($15 to $30) is available at the bar or in the elegant dining room (also open for breakfast). Sit outside on the terrace and sample the delicious but deadly New Norcia Abbey Ale.

Monastery Guesthouse GUESTHOUSE $
(☎08-9654 8002; www.newnorcia.wa.edu.au; full board suggested donation $80) The abbey offers

full lodging in the Monastery Guesthouse, within the walls of the southern cloister.

Getting There & Away

Transwa coaches run from Perth ($22, two hours) on Tuesday, Thursday, Saturday and Sunday, returning on Sunday, Tuesday and Thursday. Integrity buses to/from Perth ($26, two hours) stop at ungodly times on Wednesday (northbound) and Saturday (southbound).

New Norcia to Meekatharra

A handful of dusty mining towns lie strung out like nuggets along the thousand parched kilometres between New Norcia and Newman. **Mt Magnet** has a couple of pubs, a supermarket, an airport and a dusty caravan park, as does **Meekatharra**, from where the shortest route to **Mt Augustus** departs.

In between the two is the beautiful goldfields architecture of **Cue**. There's a pub, a B&B – the grand **Queen of the Murchison** (08-9963 1625; www.queenofthemurchisonhotel.com; Austin St; s/d $88/120;) – and a dusty caravan park.

BATAVIA COAST

From tranquil Dongara-Port Denison to the remote, wind-scoured Zuytdorp Cliffs stretches a dramatic coastline steeped in history, littered with shipwrecks and abounding in marine life. While the region proved the undoing of many early European sailors, today modern fleets make the most of a lucrative crayfish industry.

Getting There & Around

AIR

Skippers (1300 729 924; www.skippers.com.au) Services Kalbarri, Geraldton, Shark Bay and Carnarvon.

Qantas (13 13 13; www.qantas.com.au) Perth to Geraldton daily.

Virgin Australia (13 67 89; www.virginaustralia.com) Flies regularly to Geraldton.

BUS

Integrity (1800 226 339; www.integritycoachlines.com.au) Runs a handy daily coastal connection between Perth and Geraldton, and a twice-weekly overnighter to Exmouth.

Greyhound (1300 473 946; www.greyhound.com.au) Runs services three times weekly between Broome and Perth along the coast.

Transwa (1300 662 205; www.transwa.wa.gov.au) Runs regular buses between Perth and Kalbarri, Geraldton and Dongara along the Brand Hwy (Rte 1).

Dongara-Port Denison

POP 3100

Dongara and Port Denison, twin seaside towns 359km from Perth, are known for their beautiful beaches, historic buildings and laid-back atmosphere. Port Denison has most of the beaches and accommodation, while Dongara's main street, shaded by century-old figs, offers banks, internet and food options.

Sights & Activities

Pick up the free *Walk Dongara Denison* brochure from the visitor centre and choose from 12 historic or nature-based rambles, including the scenic **Irwin River Nature Trail** with its resident swans, pelicans and cormorants. The *Heritage Trail* booklet ($2) details a 1.6km route linking buildings such as 1860s **Russ Cottage** (Point Leander Dr) and the **Royal Steam Flour Mill** (Brand Hwy; closed).

Denison Beach Marina brims with boats that haul crayfish, the towns' livelihood, while sunsets are dazzling from nearby **Fishermens Lookout**.

Sleeping & Eating

Public and school holidays attract a surcharge. There is a supermarket, cafes and takeaways on Moreton Tce and a decent bakery on Waldeck St, in Dongara, while the **Port Store** (08-9927 1030; 52 Point Leander Dr; 7.30am-6pm) in Port Denison has most necessities.

Dongara Backpackers HOSTEL $
(Breeze Inn; 08-9927 1332; www.dongarabackpackers.com.au; 32 Waldeck St, Dongara; dm/d/f $30/85/130) The cheapest beds in town look onto a leafy garden at this popular backpackers, which has stylish doubles, rustic dorms (in a vintage railway carriage) and free bike hire for guests.

Dongara Tourist Park CARAVAN PARK $
(08-9927 1210; www.dongaratouristpark.com.au; 8 George St, Port Denison; unpowered/powered sites $25/33, 1-/2-bedroom cabins $105/145;

) The best camping option has shaded, spacious sites behind South Beach. The two-bedroom cabins on the hill have great views, and there's a lush pergola for dining outdoors.

Priory Hotel GUESTHOUSE $
(08-9927 1090; www.prioryhotel.com.au; 11 St Dominics Rd, Dongara; r $70-130, mains $20-32;) There's a touch of *Picnic at Hanging Rock* about this leafy former nunnery and ladies college with its period furniture, polished floorboards, black-and-white photos and wide verandahs.

Port Denison Holiday Units APARTMENTS $$
(08-9927 1104; www.portdenisonholidayunits.com.au; 14 Carnarvon St, Port Denison; d $110-120;) These spotless, spacious, self-catering units, some with views, are just a block from the beach.

Little Starfish CAFE $
(0448 344 215; White Tops Rd, Port Denison; mains $6-18; 8am-4pm Wed-Mon) Hidden away in the South Beach car park, this casual snack shack does coffee, jaffles, winter soups and summer salads.

Dongara Hotel Motel MOTEL $$
(08-9927 1023; www.dongaramotel.com.au; 12 Moreton Tce, Dongara; d $130, mains $20-40; breakfast, lunch & dinner;) Locals love the Dongara's legendary servings of fresh seafood, steaks and 'Asian Corner' curries. The motel rooms, popular with corporates, are adequate if not flash.

Information

Moreton Tce, Dongara, has several banks with ATMs.

Telecentre (Community Resource Centre; 08-9927 2111; 11 Moreton Tce, Dongara; internet per hr $5; 8.30am-4.30pm Mon-Fri)

Visitor Centre (08-9927 1404; www.irwin.wa.gov.au; 9 Waldeck St, Dongara; 9am-5pm Mon-Fri, to noon Sat)

Getting There & Around

Dongara-Port Denison is accessible via the Brand Hwy, Indian Ocean Dr or Midlands Rd (Rte 116).

Greyhound has services to Broome ($356, 29 hours, Monday, Wednesday and Friday) and Perth ($60, five hours, Wednesday, Friday and Sunday). Transwa runs daily to Perth ($53, five hours) and Geraldton ($13, one hour). Integrity runs daily to Perth ($49, five hours) and Geraldton ($16, one hour) and twice weekly overnight to Exmouth ($149, 12 hours). Buses arrive/depart from the visitor centre.

If you need a cab, call **Dongara Taxi** (08-9927 1555).

Geraldton

POP 39,000

Capital of the midwest and surrounded by beaches, sun-drenched 'Gero' offers aquatic opportunities including swimming, surfing, kite-boarding and diving. The largest town between Perth and Darwin has huge wheat-handling and fishing industries, and itinerant workers flood the town during crayfish season. Still a work in progress, Gero blends big-city sophistication with small-town friendliness, offering a strong arts culture, a blossoming foodie scene and some great local music.

Sights

★ **Western Australian Museum – Geraldton** MUSEUM
(08-9921 5080; www.museum.wa.gov.au; 1 Museum Pl; admission by donation; 9.30am-4pm) One of the state's best museums: intelligent multimedia displays relate the area's natural, cultural and indigenous history. The Shipwreck Gallery documents the tragic story of the *Batavia,* while video footage reveals the sunken HMAS *Sydney II.*

Cathedral of St Francis Xavier Church CHURCH
(08-9921 3221; www.geraldtondiocese.org.au; Cathedral Ave; tours 10am Mon & Fri, 4pm Wed) The finest example of the architectural achievements of the Monsignor John Hawes.

Geraldton Regional Art Gallery GALLERY
(08-9964 7170; 24 Chapman Rd; 10am-4pm Tue-Sat, from 1pm Sun) FREE An excellent permanent collection complements provocative contemporary work and touring exhibitions.

HMAS Sydney II Memorial MONUMENT
(Mt Scott; tours free; tours 10am) Commanding the hill overlooking Geraldton, this memorial commemorates the 1941 loss of the *Sydney* and its 645 men after a skirmish with the German raider *Kormoran.*

Activities

While most activities are water-based, Geraldton also has an excellent network of bike paths, including the 10km-long coastal route from **Tarcoola Beach** to **Chapman River**. Grab the *Local Travelsmart Guide* from

Geraldton

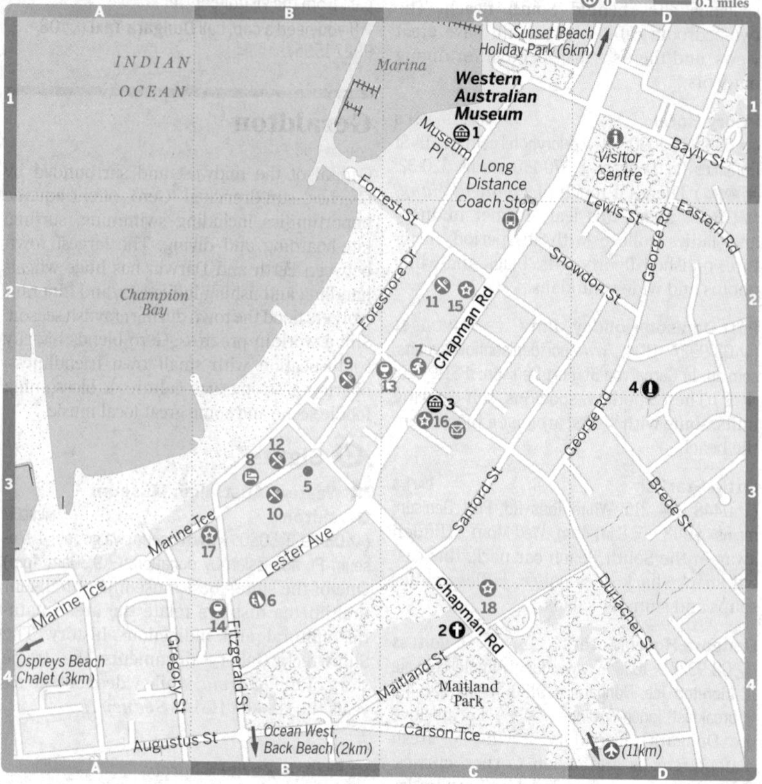

the visitor centre. Bikes can be hired from **Revolutions** (☎08-9964 1399; 1/27 Chapman Rd; bike hire per day $20; ⌚9am-5.30pm Mon-Fri, to noon Sat).

G-Spot Xtreme WINDSURFING
(☎08-9965 5577; www.gspotxtreme.com.au; 241a Lester Ave; hire per day windsurfers $100, paddleboards $100, electric bikes $25) Hire or buy windsurfing equipment here.

Batavia Coast Dive Academy DIVING
(☎08-9921 4229; www.bcda.com.au; 153 Marine Tce; local dives with/without equipment $140/100) Offers open-water courses (full PADI $630) and a range of diving trips, including to the Abrolhos Islands (from $300 per person per day).

KiteWest KITEBOARDING
(☎0449 021 784; www.kitewest.com.au; coaching per hr from $80) Kitesurfing courses and 4WD camping tours.

Sleeping

Expect price hikes for school and public holidays.

Foreshore Backpackers HOSTEL $
(☎08-9921 3275; www.foreshorebackpackers.bigpondhosting.com; 172 Marine Tce; dm/s/d $30/45/65; @) Shambolic, rambling and oozing character, this central hostel is full of hidden nooks, sunny balconies and world-weary travellers. Recently renovated and under new management, it's still the best place to find a job, lift or travel buddy.

Sunset Beach Holiday Park CARAVAN PARK $
(☎1800 353 389; www.sunsetbeachpark.com.au; Bosley St; powered sites $35, cabins $100-152) About 6km north of the CBD, Sunset Beach has roomy, shaded sites just a few steps from a lovely beach, and an ultramodern camp kitchen with the biggest plasma TV on the coast.

Geraldton

Top Sights	
1 Western Australian Museum	C1
Sights	
2 Cathedral of St Francis Xavier Church	C4
3 Geraldton Regional Art Gallery	C3
4 HMAS Sydney II Memorial	D2
Activities, Courses & Tours	
5 Batavia Coast Dive Academy	B3
6 G-Spot Xtreme	B4
7 Revolutions	C2
Sleeping	
8 Foreshore Backpackers	B3
Eating	
9 Go Health Lunch Bar	B2
10 Provincial	B3
11 Saltdish	C2
12 Topolinis Caffe	B3
Drinking & Nightlife	
13 Freemasons Hotel	C2
14 Vibe	B4
Entertainment	
15 Breakers Bar	C2
16 Camel Bar	C3
17 Orana Cinemas	B3
18 Queens Park Theatre	C4

★Ospreys Beach Chalet COTTAGE $$
(0447 647 994; enerhkalm@gmail.com; 40 Bosuns Cr, Point Moore; for 2 persons from $145) Both ospreys and beach are nearby this sustainably restored cottage, which began life as a proof-of-concept. Rainwater tanks and solar panels complement recycled materials in a restoration that doesn't skimp on comfort. There are plenty of outdoor areas and the rear native garden is a gem.

Ocean West APARTMENTS $$
(08-9921 1047; www.oceanwest.com.au; 1 Hadda Way; 1-/3-bedroom apt from $135/215;) Don't let the '60s brick put you off; these fully self-contained units have all been tastefully renovated, making them one of the better deals in town. The wildly beautiful back beach is just across the road.

Eating

Geraldton has great food options including Asian, takeaways, coffee lounges, bakeries and supermarkets. Free BBQs and picnic tables dot the foreshore.

Go Health Lunch Bar CAFE $
(08-9965 5200; 122 Marine Tce; light meals around $10; 8.30am-3pm Mon-Fri, to 1pm Sat;) Vegetarians can rejoice at the choice of fresh juices and smoothies, excellent espresso, healthy burritos, lentil burgers, focaccias and other light meals from this popular lunch bar in the middle of the mall.

★Saltdish CAFE $$
(08-9964 6030; 35 Marine Tce; breakfasts $6-20, lunches $18-30; 7.30am-2.30pm Mon-Sat;) The hippest cafe in town does innovative, contemporary brekkies, light lunches and industrial-strength coffee, and screens films in its courtyard on summer evenings. BYO.

Provincial MODERN AUSTRALIAN $$
(08-9964 1887; www.theprovincial.com.au; 167 Marine Tce; tapas $8-12, pizza $24-30, mains $28-42; 5.30pm-late daily, lunch Fri-Sun, breakfast Sat & Sun) Stencil-art adorns this atmospheric wine bar serving up tapas, wood-fired pizzas and modern Oz/Mediterranean-inspired dishes. Live music Friday nights.

Topolinis Caffe ITALIAN $$
(08-9964 5866; 158 Marine Tce; mains $22-36; 8.30am-late;) This home-style licensed bistro is perfect for an afternoon coffee, cake and wi-fi; a preshow bite; or just a relaxed family feed. The $34 dinner-and-movie deal (Sunday to Thursday) and Monday half-price pasta are popular.

Drinking & Entertainment

Live-music options include **Breakers** (08-9921 8924; 41 Chapman Rd; from 9pm), **Camel Bar** (08-9965 5500; 20 Chapman Rd), **Provincial** and **Freemasons** (08-9964 3457; www.freemasonshotel.com.au; cnr Marine Tce & Durlacher St; 11am-late).There's also a **cinema** (08-9965 0568; www.oranacinemas.com.au; cnr Marine Tce & Fitzgerald St; tickets $16), **theatre** (08-9956 6662; cnr Cathedral Ave & Maitland St) and **nightclub** (08-9921 3700; 38-42 Fitzgerald St; from 11pm Thu-Sun).

Information

The best free wi-fi in town is at the **library** (☎08-9956 6659; library.cgg.wa.gov.au; 37 Marine Tce; wi-fi 1st hr free; ⏰from 9am Tue-Sat, from 1pm Sun & Mon; 📶). There are several banks with ATMs along Marine Tce.

Visitor Centre (☎08-9921 3999; www.geraldtontourist.com.au; Bill Sewell Complex, Chapman Rd; ⏰9am-5pm Mon-Fri, 10am-4pm Sat & Sun) One of the best, with lots of great info sheets and helpful staff who'll book accommodation, tours and transport.

Getting There & Around

AIR

Virgin and Qantas both fly daily to/from Perth. Skippers flies direct to/from Carnarvon several times weekly. The airport is situated 12km from Marine Tce.

BUS

Integrity coaches service Perth ($54, six hours) daily via the coast and run twice weekly to Carnarvon ($99, six hours) and Exmouth ($135, 11 hours). Transwa has daily inland services to Perth ($61, six hours) and thrice-weekly to Kalbarri ($27, two hours). There's also a twice-weekly service to Meekatharra ($73, seven hours). Greyhound runs three times weekly to Perth ($65, six hours) and north to Carnarvon ($105, six hours) and Broome ($350, 27 hours). **Batavia Tickets** (☎08-9964 8881; www.bataviatickets.com.au; ⏰8am-4.30pm Mon-Fri, to 9.30am Sat) sell seats for all long-distance buses from the old railway station; buses leave from outside. **Transgeraldton** (☎08-9923 2225; www.buswest.com.au) operates eight routes to local suburbs.

TAXI

Call **Geraldton Associated Taxis** (☎131 008) for a lift.

Kalbarri

POP 2000

Magnificent red-sandstone cliffs tumble loosely into the Indian Ocean while the beautiful Murchison River snakes through tall, steep gorges, before ending treacherously at Gantheaume Bay. Wildflowers line paths frequented by kangaroos, emus and thorny devils, while whales breach just offshore, and rare orchids struggle in the rocky ground. To the north, the towering line of the limestone Zuytdorp Cliffs remains aloof, pristine and remote.

Kalbarri, in Nhanda country, is surrounded by stunning nature, and there's great surfing, swimming, fishing, bushwalking, horse riding and canoeing both in town and in Kalbarri National Park. While the vibe is mostly low key, school holidays see Kalbarri stretched to the limit.

Sights & Activities

Kalbarri has a network of cycle paths along the foreshore, and you can ride out to **Blue Holes** for snorkelling, **Jakes Point** for its surf and fishing, and **Red Bluff Beach** (5.5km). Any of the lookouts along the coast are perfect for watching the sunset. Look for wildflowers along Siles Rd, River Rd and out near the airport; the visitor centre publishes regular wildflower updates in season.

★**Kalbarri National Park** NATIONAL PARK
(per car $11) With its magnificent river red gums and Tumblagooda sandstone, this rugged park contains almost 2000 sq km of wild bushland, stunning river gorges and savagely eroded coastal cliffs. There's abundant wildlife, including 200 species of birds, and spectacular wildflowers between July and November.

A string of lookouts dot the impressive coast south of town, and the easy **Bigurda Trail** (8km one-way) follows the cliff tops between **Natural Bridge** and **Eagle Gorge**; from July to November you may spot migrating whales. Closer to town are **Pot Alley**, **Rainbow Valley**, **Mushroom Rock** and **Red Bluff**, the last accessible via a walking trail from Kalbarri (5.5km one-way).

The river gorges are east of Kalbarri, off Ajana Kalbarri Rd. Bring lots of water for the unshaded **Loop Trail** (8km return) and don't miss the incredible natural rock arch of **Nature's Window** (1km return). **Z-Bend** has a breathtaking lookout (1.2km return) or you can continue steeply down to the gorge bottom (2.6km return). **Hawk's Head**, back off the main road, has great views and picnic tables, and you can access the river at **Ross Graham**. It's possible to hike 38km from Ross Graham to the Loop in a demanding four-day epic with no marked trails and several river crossings.

Pelican Feeding WILDLIFE WATCHING
(☎08-9937 1104; ⏰8.45am) FREE Kalbarri's most popular attraction.

Kalbarri Boat Hire CANOEING
(☎08-9937 1245; www.kalbarriboathire.com; Grey St; kayak/canoe/surf cat/powerboat per hr $15/15/45/50) If it goes in the water then these guys

Kalbarri

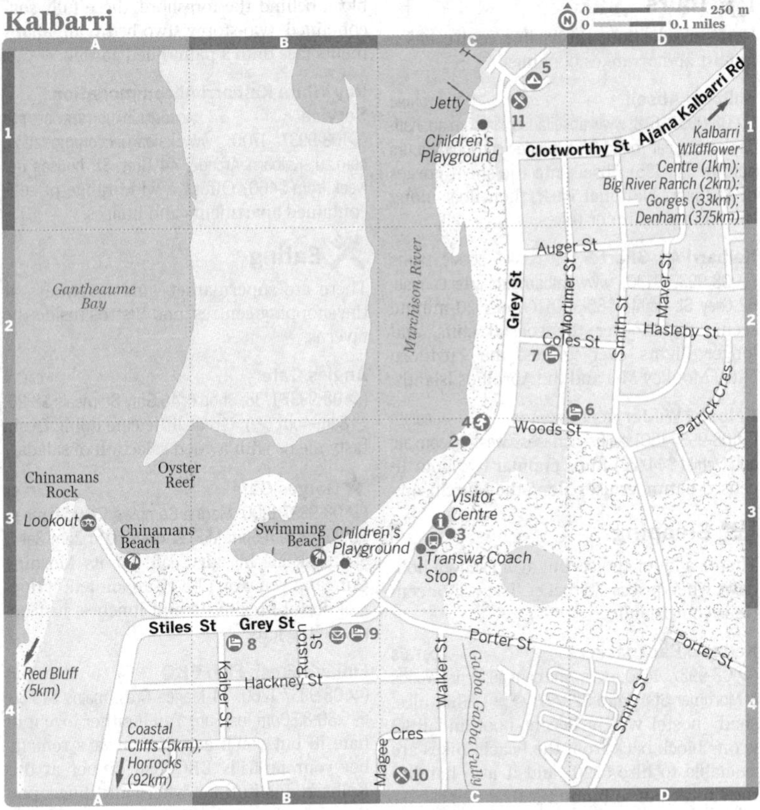

Kalbarri

Activities, Courses & Tours

1 Kalbarri Air Charter C3
2 Kalbarri Boat Hire C3
3 Kalbarri Wilderness Cruises C3
4 Pelican Feeding C3

Sleeping

5 Anchorage Caravan Park C1
6 Kalbarri Backpackers D2
7 Kalbarri Reef Villas C2
8 Pelican Shore Villas B4
Pelican's Nest .... (see 6)
9 Ray White Kalbarri Accommodation Service B4

Eating

Angies Cafe .... (see 9)
10 Finlay's Fresh Fish BBQ C4
11 Gorges Café C1

hire it. They also run four-hour breakfast and lunch canoe trips down the Murchison (adult/child $65/45).

Kalbarri Adventure Tours CANOEING
(☎08-9937 1677; www.kalbarritours.com.au; adult/child $90/70) Combine canoeing, bushwalking and swimming around the park's Z-Bend/Loop area.

Big River Ranch HORSE RIDING
(☎08-9937 1214; www.bigriverranch.net; 90min trail rides $85) Track through the beautiful Murchison River floodplain on horseback. All experience levels catered for, and the overnight rides are the highlight. Camping (camp sites per person $10, powered sites $25) and rustic bunkhouse rooms (per person from $25) available. Off Ajana Kalbarri Rd.

☞ Tours

Here's a selection; the visitor centre has a full list and arranges bookings.

Kalbarri Abseil   CANYONING
(☑08-9937 1618; www.abseilaustralia.com.au; half-day abseil year-round $80, full-day canyoning tours Apr-Nov only 135) Abseil into the sheer gorges of Kalbarri National Park, then float along the bottom on inner tubes.

Kalbarri Air Charter   SCENIC FLIGHTS
(☑08-9937 1130; www.kalbarriaircharter.com.au; 62 Grey St; flights $65-300) Offers 20-minute scenic flights over the coastal cliffs, and longer flights over gorges, the Zuytdorp cliffs, Monkey Mia and the Abrolhos Islands.

Kalbarri Wilderness Cruises   CRUISES
(☑08-9937 1601; kalbarricruises@westnet.com.au; adult/child $44/22) Runs popular two-hour licensed nature cruises along the Murchison.

🛏 Sleeping

There's a lot of choice, but avoid school holidays, when prices skyrocket. The visitor centre is your friend.

Kalbarri Backpackers   HOSTEL $
(☑08-9937 1430; www.yha.com.au; cnr Woods & Mortimer Sts; dm/d $29/77; @☎) This nice, shady hostel with a decent pool and BBQ is one block back from the beach. Bikes are available to hire ($20) and it also handles the shuttle out to Binnu ($41).

Anchorage Caravan Park   CARAVAN PARK $
(☑08-9937 1181; www.kalbarrianchorage.com.au; cnr Anchorage Lane & Grey St; powered sites $34, cabins with/without bathroom $100/70; ☎) The best option for campers, Anchorage has roomy, nicely shaded sites that overlook the river mouth.

★ Pelican's Nest   MOTEL $$
(☑08-9937 1430; www.pelicansnestkalbarri.com.au; 45-47 Mortimer St; d $100-140; ✳@☎) Adjoining Kalbarri Backpackers, the Nest has a selection of neat motel-style rooms (some with kitchenettes), and excellent facilities.

Pelican Shore Villas   APARTMENTS $$
(☑08-9937 1708; www.pelicanshorevillas.com.au; cnr Grey & Kaiber Sts; villas $136-188; ✳☎☎) These beautiful manicured townhouses have all the mod cons, and the best view in town.

Kalbarri Reef Villas   APARTMENTS $$
(☑08-9937 1165; www.reefvillas.com.au; cnr Coles & Mortimer Sts; units $130-180; ✳☎☎) One

block behind the foreshore, these fully self-contained two-storey, two-bedroom apartments face onto a palm-filled garden.

Ray White Kalbarri Accommodation
Service   ACCOMMODATION SERVICES $$$
(☑08-9937 1700; www.kalbarriaccommodation.com.au; Kalbarri Arcade, 44 Grey St; houses per week from $460) Offers a wide range of self-contained apartments and houses.

✗ Eating

There are supermarkets and takeaways at the shopping centres, and bistros inside the taverns.

Angies Cafe   CAFE $
(☑08-9937 1738; Shop 6, 46 Grey St; meals $8-20; ☺8am-4pm; ✎) Great little cafe doing fresh, tasty meals with a good selection of salads.

★ Gorges Café   CAFE $$
(☑08-9937 1200; Marina Complex, Grey St; meals $8-25; ☺7am-5pm Mon & Wed-Fri, to 2pm Sat & Sun) Ask at this airy cafe for its Morning Cure and you won't be disappointed; it does wonderful breakfasts and lunches, just opposite the jetty.

Finlay's Fresh Fish BBQ   SEAFOOD $$
(☑08-9937 1260; 24 Magee Cres; mains $15-30; ☺5.30-8.30pm Tue-Sun) You'll either love it or hate it, but you'll certainly always remember your no-frills BBQ fish dinner at this Kalbarri institution, where the huge portions of fish come with lashings of (usually, but not always) tongue-in-cheek abuse.

ⓘ Information

There are ATMs at the shopping centres on Grey and Porter Sts, while internet can be found at the **CRC** (☑08-9937 1933; Hackney St; internet $5 per hr; ☺9am-3pm Mon-Fri), **Book Nook** (☑08-9937 2676; internet $5 per hr; ☺10am-5pm Mon-Fri, to 4pm Sat & Sun) and the library.

Visitor Centre (☑1800 639 468; www.kalbarri.org.au; Grey St; ☺9am-5pm Mon-Sat) Great wildflower and activities info and can book accommodation and tours. Internet access is available at the library next door.

ⓘ Getting There & Around

Skippers flies to Perth, Shark Bay and Carnarvon several times weekly.

Getting to/from Perth ($76, nine hours) and Geraldton ($27, two hours) by bus is easiest with Transwa at the visitor centre. Heading to/from points further north, Greyhound stops at Binnu on the highway, 77km away – arrange a shuttle from Kalbarri Backpackers. From Binnu you can reach Overlander Roadhouse (for Monkey Mia, $52, two hours), Coral Bay ($106, eight hours) and Broome ($325, 26 hours). Integrity passes through Ajana on the way to Exmouth ($126, 10 hours).

Kalbarri Auto Centre (☎ 08-9937 1290) rents 4WDs and sedans from $60 per day. Both bikes and scooters can be hired from **Kalbarri Air Charter** (☎ 08-9937 1130; 62 Grey St; bikes half-/full day $10/20, scooters half-/full day $45/85), and bikes are also available from the YHA and the **entertainment centre** (☎ 08-9937 1105; 15 Magee Cres). For a taxi call **Kalbarri Taxi Service** (☎ 0419 371 888).

SHARK BAY

World Heritage–listed Shark Bay, with more than 1500km of pristine coastline, barren peninsulas, white-sand beaches and bountiful marine life, draws tourists from around the world. The sheltered turquoise waters and skinny fingers of stunted land at the westernmost edge of the continent are one of WA's most biologically rich habitats.

Lush beds of seagrass and sheltered bays nourish dugongs, sea turtles, humpback whales, rays, sharks and other aquatic life. Ancient stromatolites bask in the salt-rich waters of Hamelin Pool, while endangered marsupials benefit from Project Eden, an ambitious ecosystem-regeneration program that has sought to eradicate feral animals and reintroduce endemic species.

The Malgana, Nhanda and Inggarda peoples originally inhabited the area and visitors can take indigenous cultural tours to learn about the country. Shark Bay played host to early European explorers, and many geographical names show this legacy. In 1616 Dutchman Dirk Hartog famously left a pewter plate at Cape Inscription on the island now bearing his name.

Getting There & Away

Shark Bay airport is located between Denham and Monkey Mia. Skippers flies to Perth six times weekly, with some return flights via Kalbarri.

The closest Greyhound and Integrity approach is the Overlander Roadhouse, 128km away on the North West Coastal Hwy. **Shark Bay Car Hire** (☎ 0427 483 032; www.carhire.net.au; 65 Knight Tce, Denham; shuttle $67, car/4WD hire per day $95/185) runs a connecting shuttle (book ahead!).

Overlander Roadhouse to Denham

Hamelin Pool (the turn-off past Hamelin Station) marine reserve contains the world's best-known colony of **stromatolites**. These squat coral-like formations consist of cyanobacterias, which are almost identical to organisms existing 3.5 billion years ago and considered largely responsible for creating our current atmosphere by using photosynthesis, paving the way for more complex life. There's an excellent boardwalk with information panels, best seen at low tide.

The adjacent 1884 **Telegraph Office** (admission $5.50) houses a fascinating museum containing possibly the only living stromatolites in captivity; check at shop for opening hours. The Postmaster's Residence is also the office for the tiny **Hamelin Pool Caravan Park** (☎ 08-9942 5905; Hamelin Pool; unpowered/powered sites $22/27) and serves Devonshire teas, pies and ice creams.

Nearby **Hamelin Station** (☎ 08-9948 5145; www.hamelinstationstay.com.au; sites per person $12, s/d/f $60/90/120) has lovely rooms in converted shearers quarters, top-class amenities and somewhat arid camp sites. There's great bird life at the nearby waterhole.

As Shark Bay Rd swings north, you'll pass the turn-off for **Useless Loop** (a closed salt-mining town), **Edel Land** and **Steep Point**, the Australian mainland's most westerly tip.

Back on the main road, the compacted cockleshells of **Shell Beach** were once quarried as building material for businesses in Denham.

You'll pass turn-offs to bush camp sites before reaching **Eagle Bluff**, which has spectacular cliff-top views overlooking an azure lagoon. You may spot turtles, sharks or manta rays.

Denham

POP 1500

Beautiful, laid-back Denham, with its aquamarine sea and palm-fringed beachfront, makes a great base for trips to the surrounding Shark Bay Marine Park, nearby François Peron and Dirk Hartog Island National Parks, and Monkey Mia, 26km away.

Australia's westernmost town originated as a pearling base, and the streets were once paved with pearl shell. Knight Tce, the now-tarmac main drag, has everything you need.

Sights & Activities

★ Shark Bay World Heritage Discovery Centre MUSEUM
(☎08-9948 1590; www.sharkbayvisit.com; 53 Knight Tce; adult/child $11/6; ⏰9am-5pm Mon-Fri, 10am-4pm Sat & Sun) Informative and evocative displays of Shark Bay's ecosystems, marine and animal life, indigenous culture, early explorers, settlers and shipwrecks.

Ocean Park AQUARIUM
(☎08-9948 1765; www.oceanpark.com.au; Shark Bay Rd; adult/child $20/12; ⏰9am-5pm) On a headland just before town, this family-run aquaculture farm features an artificial lagoon where a one-hour guided tour observes feeding sharks, turtles, stingrays and fish. The licensed cafe has sensational views.

Tours

Aussie Off Road Tours 4WD
(☎0429 929 175; www.aussieoffroadtours.com.au) Culture, history, wildlife and bush tucker feature in these excellent indigenous-owned and -operated 4WD tours, including twilight wildlife ($90), full day/overnight François Peron National Park ($189/$300) and overnight to Steep Point ($390).

Shark Bay Scenic Flights SCENIC FLIGHTS
(☎0417 919 059; www.sharkbayair.com.au) Offers various scenic flights, including 15-minute Monkey Mia flyovers ($59) and a sensational 40-minute trip over Steep Point and the Zuytdorp Cliffs ($175).

Shark Bay Coaches & Tours SIGHTSEEING
(☎08-9948 1081; www.sbcoaches.com; bus/quad bike $80/$90) Half-day bus tours to all key sights and two-hour quad-bike tours to Little Lagoon.

Sleeping & Eating

Denham has accommodation for all budgets. There's a **pub** (☎08-9948 1203; www.sharkbayhotelwa.com.au; 43 Knight Tce; dinner $22-38; ⏰10am-late), which is Australia's most westerly, a supermarket, bakery, cafes and takeaways on Knight Tce.

★ Bay Lodge HOSTEL $
(☎08-9948 1278; www.baylodge.info; 113 Knight Tce; dm/d from $26/68; ❄@≋) Every room at this YHA hostel has its own en suite, kitchenette and TV/DVD. Ideally located across from the beach, it also has a pool, common kitchen, and a shuttle bus to Monkey Mia.

Denham Seaside Tourist Village CARAVAN PARK $
(☎1300 133 733; www.sharkbayfun.com; Knight Tce; sites unpowered/powered/with bathroom $30/37/45, d cabins $80, 1-/2-bedroom chalets $125/135; ❄) This lovely, shady park on the water's edge is the best in town, though you

OFF THE BEATEN TRACK

WAY OUT WEST IN EDEL LAND

The Australian mainland's westernmost tip is **Steep Point**, just below **Dirk Hartog Island**. It's a wild, wind-scarred, barren cliff top with a beauty born of desolation and remoteness. The **Zuytdorp Cliffs** stretch away to the south, the limestone peppered with blowholes, while leeward, bays with white sandy beaches provide sheltered camp sites. The entire area is known as **Edel Land**, soon to become a national park. Anglers have been coming here for years to game fish off the towering cliffs, but few tourists make the 140km rough drive down a dead-end road.

Access to the area is via Useless Loop Rd, and is controlled by the **Department of Environment and Conservation** (DEC; ☎08-9948 3993; entry permit per vehicle $11, sites per person $7). There is a ranger station at **Shelter Bay**, with camping nearby; at Steep Point (rocky and exposed); and at **False Entrance** to the south. Sites are strictly limited and must be booked in advance. You'll need a high-clearance 4WD as the road deteriorates past the Useless Loop turn-off (approximately 100km from Shark Bay Rd). Tyres should be deflated to 20psi. Ensure you bring ample water and enough fuel to return to the Overlander Roadhouse (185km) or Denham (230km). During winter, a barge runs from Shelter Bay to Dirk Hartog Island (bookings essential). The site www.sharkbay.org.au has all the details and downloadable permits. Hire-car companies will not insure for this road, though (expensive) tours can be arranged from Denham. The drive is pure adventure; Steep Point is probably more easily reached by boat, but then that's not the Point, is it?

will need to borrow its drill for your tent pegs. Cover up at night against the insects and ring first if arriving after 6pm.

Oceanside Village CABINS $$
(☎1800 680 600; www.oceanside.com.au; 117 Knight Tce; cabins $160-200;) These neat self-catering cottages with sunny balconies are perfectly located directly opposite the beach.

★**Old Pearler Restaurant** SEAFOOD $$$
(☎08-9948 1373; 71 Knight Tce; meals $30-49; ⊙dinner Mon-Sat) Built from shell bricks, this atmospheric nautical haven does fantastic seafood. The exceptional platter features local snapper, whiting, cray, oysters, prawns and squid – all grilled, not fried. BYO.

Ocean Restaurant CAFE $$
(www.oceanpark.com.au; Shark Bay Rd; mains $19-32; ⊙9am-5pm;) The most refined lunch in Shark Bay also comes with the best view. Inside Ocean Park, overlooking turquoise waters, choose from mouth-watering tapas, all-day brekkies or tantalising local seafood dishes. Fully licensed.

Information

There are ATMs at Heritage Resort and Shark Bay Hotel, and internet access at the **CRC** (☎08-9948 1787; 67 Knight Tce) and post office.

DEC (☎08-9948 1208; www.dec.gov.au; 89 Knight Tce; ⊙8am-5pm Mon-Fri) Park passes, information and camping permits.

Shark Bay Home Page (www.sharkbay.org.au) Great information, interactive maps and downloadable permits.

Shark Bay Visitor Centre (☎08-9948 1590; www.sharkbayvisit.com; 53 Knight Tce; ⊙9am-5pm Mon-Fri, 10am-4pm Sat & Sun) Located in the Discovery Centre foyer; the very informative staff handle accommodation and tour bookings and issue bush-camping permits for South Peron.

François Peron National Park

Covering the whole peninsula north of Denham is an area of low scrub, salt lakes and red sandy dunes, home to the rare bilby, mallee fowl and woma python. There's a scattering of rough **camp sites** (per person $7) alongside brilliant white beaches, all accessible via 4WD (deflate tyres to 20psi). Don't miss the fantastic **Wanamalu Trail** (3km return), which follows the cliff top between Cape Peron and Skipjack Point, from where you can spot marine life in the crystal waters below. Those with 2WD can enter only as far as the old **Peron Homestead**, where there's a short 'lifestyle' walk around the shearing sheds, and an artesian-bore hot tub to soak in. Park entry is $11 per vehicle. Tours start at around $180 from Denham or Monkey Mia, but if there's a group of you, consider hiring your own 4WD from Denham for the same price.

Monkey Mia

Watching the wild dolphins arrive each morning in the shallow waters of **Monkey Mia** (adult/child/family $8/3/16), 26km north-east of Denham, is a highlight of every traveller's trip. The first feed is around 7.45am, but the dolphins will normally arrive earlier. The pier's a good vantage point. Hang around after the first session, as the dolphins routinely come back a second and sometimes a third time.

You can **volunteer** to work full time with the dolphins for a period of between four and 14 days – it's popular, so apply several months in advance (though sometimes there are last-minute openings). Contact the **volunteer coordinator** (☎08-9948 1366; monkeymiavolunteers@westnet.com.au).

Monkey Mia visitor centre (☎08-9948 1366; ⊙8am-4pm) has a good range of publications and can book tours.

Tours

Wula Guda Nyinda Aboriginal Cultural Tours INDIGENOUS CULTURE
(☎0429 708 847; www.wulaguda.com.au; 90min tours adult/child from $50/25) You'll pick up some local Malgana language and identify bush tucker and indigenous medicine on these amazing bushwalks led by local Aboriginal guide Darren 'Capes' Capewell. The evening 'Didgeridoo Dreaming' tours (adult child $60/30) are magical.

Wildsights ADVENTURE
(☎1800 241 481; www.monkeymiawildsights.com.au) On the small *Shotover* catamaran you're close to the action and wildlife cruises start from $79 (2½ hours).

Aristocat II CRUISES
(☎1800 030 427; www.monkey-mia.net; 1-/2½hr tours $45/80) Cruise in comfort on this large catamaran, and you might see dugongs,

dolphins and loggerhead turtles. You'll also stop off at the **Blue Lagoon Pearl Farm**.

Sleeping & Eating

Monkey Mia is a resort and not a town, so eating and sleeping options are limited to the Monkey Mia Dolphin Resort. Self-catering is a good option.

Monkey Mia Dolphin Resort RESORT **$$$**
(1800 653 611; www.monkeymia.com.au; tent sites per person $15, van sites from $39, dm/d $30/89, garden units $223, beachfront villas $315;) A stunning location, friendly staff and good-value backpacker doubles are the highlights of this resort. Unfortunately it can get seriously crowded and at times sounds like a continuous party. The restaurant has sensational water views but bland, overpriced meals. Don't waste money on the wi-fi.

Getting There & Away

There is no public transport. Denham's Bay Lodge (p984) runs a shuttle for guests on alternate days. Your other options are hiring a car, cycling or hitching.

GASCOYNE COAST

This wild, rugged, largely unpopulated coastline stretches from Shark Bay to Ningaloo, with excellent fishing and waves that bring surfers from around the world. Subtropical Carnarvon, the region's hub, is an important fruit- and vegetable-growing district, and farms are always looking for seasonal workers. The 760km Gascoyne River, WA's longest, is responsible for all that lushness, though it flows underground for most of the year. Inland are huge distances, high temperatures, the ancient eroded rocks of the Kennedy Range, and the massive Mt Augustus.

Carnarvon

POP 9000

On Yinggarda country at the mouth of the Gascoyne River, fertile Carnarvon, with its fruit and vegetable plantations and thriving fishing industry, makes a pleasant stopover between Denham and Exmouth. This friendly, vibrant town has quirky attractions, a range of decent accommodation, well-stocked supermarkets and great local produce. The long picking season from March to January ensures plenty of seasonal work.

Sights & Activities

Established jointly with NASA in 1966, the **OTC Dish** (Mahony Ave) at the edge of town tracked Gemini and Apollo space missions, as well as Halley's Comet, before closing in 1987. Stage One of the small but fascinating **Carnarvon Space and Technology Museum** (Mahony Ave; admission $5; 10am-3pm) is nearby.

Carnarvon's luxuriant plantations along North and South River Rds provide a large proportion of WA's fruit and veg; grab the *Gascoyne Food Trail* brochure (www.gascoynefood.com.au) from the visitor centre. **Bumbak's** (08-9941 8006; 449 North River Rd; 1hr tours $8.80; shop 9am-4pm Mon-Fri, tours 10am Mon, Wed, Fri Apr-Oct) offers tours and sells a variety of fresh and dried fruit, preserves and yummy homemade ice cream. Check out the delicious produce at the **Gascoyne Arts, Crafts & Growers Market** (Civic Centre car park; 8-11.30am Sat May-Oct).

You can walk or ride 2.5km along the old tramway to the **Heritage Precinct** on Babbage Island, once the city's port. **One Mile Jetty** (admission tram/walking $7/4; 9am-4.30pm) provides great fishing and views; walk or take the vintage tram to the end. The nearby **Lighthouse Keepers Cottage** (10am-1pm) has been painstakingly restored; don't miss the view from the top of the creaky water tower in the **Railway Station Museum** (9am-5pm).

Gwoonwardu Mia (08-9941 1989; gahcc@gahcc.com.au; 146 Robinson St; 10am-3pm Mon-Fri), built to depict a cyclone, represents the five local Aboriginal language groups and houses a cultural centre, art gallery, interpretive garden and the hospitality-training Yallibiddi Café.

From September to March windsurfers head to Pelican Point, while novice (or advanced) kiteboarders can learn some new skills from **Kitemix** (0400 648 706; www.kitemix.com; lessons per hr from $80; Sep-Mar).

The palm-lined **walking path** along the side of the Fascine (the body of water at the end of Robinson St) is a pleasant place for a wander, especially at sunset.

Sleeping

Most accommodation, including numerous caravan parks, is spread out along the 5km

OFF THE BEATEN TRACK

MT AUGUSTUS (BURRINGURRAH) NATIONAL PARK

In Wajarri country, the huge monocline of **Mt Augustus** (1105m), twice as large as Uluru (Ayers Rock) and a good deal more remote, rises 717m above the surrounding plains. There are a number of walking trails and Aboriginal rock-art sites to explore, including the superb summit trail (12km return, six hours). In a 2WD it's a rough, unsealed 450km from Carnarvon via **Gascoyne Junction** or 350km from **Meekatharra**. With a 4WD there are at least three other routes including a handy back door to Karijini via **Dooley Downs** and Tom Price. All of these routes see little traffic, so be prepared for the worst. There's no camping in the park, though you can stay at nearby dusty **Mt Augustus Tourist Park** (☎08-9943 0527; www.mtaugustustouristpark.com; unpowered/powered sites $22/33, dongas d $88, units $176; ❄). Worth a look 60km to the west is the historic **Cobra Bangemail Inn** (☎08-9943 9565; sites per person $15, d $160). If you get to Gascoyne Junction and decide to give up, nearby **Bidgemia Station** (☎08-9943 0501; caunt@harboursat.com.au; Gascoyne Junction; sites per person $15, shearers quarters $65) offers shearers quarters and shady camping.

feeder road from the highway. Try to arrive before 6pm.

★Fish & Whistle HOSTEL $
(☎08-9941 1704; 35 Robinson St; dm/s $30/45, motel r $99; ❄@) Travellers love this big, breezy backpackers with its wide verandahs, bunk-free rooms, enormous communal spaces, excellent kitchen and happy vibe. There are air-con motel rooms out back, discounts for longer stays and the revamped **Port Hotel** serving decent beer downstairs.

Capricorn Holiday Park CARAVAN PARK $
(☎08-9941 8153; www.capricornholidaypark.com.au; 1042 North West Coastal Hwy; sites d $36, cabins $120; ❄🛜≋) Out on the highway, this peaceful, friendly park has lots of shade, a covered pool, grassy sites and lovely bougainvillea.

Coral Coast Tourist Park CARAVAN PARK $
(☎08-9941 1438; www.coralcoasttouristpark.com.au; 108 Robinson St; powered sites $35, cabins $75-155; ❄🛜≋) This pleasant, shady park, with tropical pool and grassy sites, is the closest to the town centre. There's a variety of well-appointed cabins, a decent camp kitchen, and bicycles for hire (half-/full day $10/15).

Carnarvon Central Apartments APARTMENTS $$
(☎08-9941 1317; www.carnarvonholidays.com; 120 Robinson St; 2-bedroom apt $140; ❄) Neat, fully self-contained apartments popular with business travellers.

Eating

With all that great produce, self-catering is a good option. There are **free BBQs** along the Fascine and at Baxter Park. Knight Tce has takeaways and some early-opening cafes.

Morel's Orchard MARKET $
(☎08-9941 8368; 486 Robinson St; ⏲8.30am-5.30pm; ✎) A great selection of local fresh fruit and vegetables, as well as natural fruit ice creams.

Yallibiddi Café CAFE $$
(☎08-9941 3127; 146 Robinson St; mains $10-20; ⏲9am-3pm Mon-Fri) Inside Gwoonwardu Mia, this training cafe was previously doing great things with bush tucker, but now seems content to churn out roo burgers and chicken satays.

Waters Edge MODERN AUSTRALIAN $$
(☎08-9941 1181; www.thecarnarvon.com.au; 121 Olivia Tce; mains $25-46; ⏲6-9pm Tue-Sat; ❄) Perfectly situated to capture the sunset over the Fascine, the restaurant out back of the Carnarvon Hotel has a good selection of seafood and steaks. There are also clean, basic rooms.

Hacienda Crab Shack SEAFOOD $$
(☎08-9941 4078; Small Boat Harbour; ⏲9am-4pm, shorter hours Sun) Got an esky? Then fill it full of freshly steamed crabs, prawns, mussels, shucked oysters and fish fillets from this fishmonger.

Information

There's a post office on Camel Lane and ATMs on Robinson St.

Visitor Centre (☎08-9941 1146; www.carnarvon.org.au; Civic Centre, 21 Robinson St; ⏲9am-5pm Mon-Fri, to noon Sat) Very helpful, with information, maps, local books and produce.

Getting There & Around

Skippers flies daily to Perth, and less often to Geraldton, Shark Bay and Kalbarri.

Greyhound buses head to Perth ($175, 13 hours), Broome ($293, 21 hours) and Coral Bay ($37, three hours) three times per week. Integrity runs twice weekly to Exmouth ($79, four hours), Geraldton ($99, six hours) and Perth ($144, 12 hours). All buses depart from the visitor centre.

Bikes can be hired from the Coral Coast Tourist Park (p987).

For a taxi, call **Carnarvon Taxis** (☎131 008).

Point Quobba to Gnarraloo Bay

While the North West Coastal Hwy heads inland, the coast north of Carnarvon is wild, windswept and desolate, a favourite haunt of surfers and fisherfolk.

Blowholes Rd, 12km after the Gascoyne bridge, will get you to the coast (49km). The **blowholes** (waves spraying out of limestone chimneys) are just left of the T-intersection. **Point Quobba**, 1km further south, has beach shacks, excellent fishing, some gritty **camp sites** (sites $5.50), and not much else.

Ten kilometres north of the T-junction (2km past a lonely cairn commemorating HMAS *Sydney II*), on an unsealed road, is **Quobba Station** (☎08-9948 5098; www.quobba.com.au; unpowered/powered sites $11/13.50, cabins per person $25-60), with plenty of rustic accommodation, a small store and legendary fishing.

Still on Quobba, 60km north of the homestead, **Red Bluff** (☎08-9948 5001; www.quobba.com.au; unpowered sites per person $12, shacks per person from $20, bungalows/safari retreats $170/345) is a spectacular headland with a wicked surf break, excellent fishing and the southern boundary of **Ningaloo Marine Park**. Accommodation runs from exposed camp sites and palm shelters to exclusive upmarket tents with balconies and killer views.

The jewel, however, is at the end of the road around 150km from Carnarvon: **Gnaraloo Station** (☎08-9942 5927; www.gnaraloo.com; unpowered sites per person $20, cabins d $130-210; Wi-Fi). Surfers from around the world come every winter to ride the notorious **Tombstones**, while summer brings turtle monitoring and windsurfers trying to catch the strong afternoon sea breeze. There's excellent snorkelling close to shore and the coastline north from **Gnarraloo Bay** is eye-burningly pristine. You can stay in rough camp sites next to the beach at **3-Mile**, or there's a range of options up at the homestead, the nicest being stone cabins with uninterrupted ocean views – great for spotting migrating whales (June to November) and sea eagles. Gnaraloo is dedicated to sustainability and has implemented a number of visionary environmental programs. The station is always looking for willing workers, and there's such a nice vibe happening that many folk come for a night and end up staying months. Who could blame them?

CORAL COAST & THE PILBARA

Lapping on the edge of the Indian Ocean, the shallow, turquoise waters of the Coral Coast nurture a unique marine paradise. World Heritage–listed Ningaloo Reef is one of the very few places you can swim with the world's largest fish, the gentle whale shark. Lonely bays, deserted beaches and crystal-clear lagoons offer superb snorkelling and diving among myriad other sea life including humpback whales, manta rays and loggerhead turtles. Development is low-key, towns few and far between, and seafood and sunsets legendary.

Inland, miners swarm like ants over the high, eroded ranges of the Pilbara, while ore trains snake down to a string of busy ports stretching from Dampier to Port Hedland. But hidden among the hills are two beautiful gems – Karijini and Millstream-Chichester National Parks, home to spectacular gorges, remote peaks, deep, tranquil pools and abundant wildlife.

Getting There & Around

AIR

The following airlines service the Coral Coast and the Pilbara:

Airnorth (☎1800 627 474; www.airnorth.com.au)

Alliance Airlines (☎1300 780 970; www.allianceairlines.com.au) Perth to Karratha.

Qantas (☎13 13 13; www.qantas.com.au)

Virgin Australia (☎13 67 89; www.virginaustralia.com)

BUS

Greyhound (☎1300 473 946; www.greyhound.com.au) Runs three times weekly between Broome and Perth along the coast.

Integrity (☎1800 226 339; www.integrity-coachlines.com.au) Runs weekly between Perth and Port Hedland via Newman on the inland Great Northern Hwy and twice weekly to Exmouth on the coastal route.

Coral Bay

POP 255

Beautifully situated just north of the Tropic of Capricorn, the tiny seaside village of Coral Bay is one of the easiest locations to access the exquisite **Ningaloo Marine Park**. Consisting of only one street and a sweeping white-sand beach, the town is small enough to enjoy on foot, making it popular with families. It's also a great base for outer-reef activities like scuba diving, fishing and whale watching (June to November), and tourists flock here in the winter months to swim with whale sharks (April to July) and manta rays.

As development is strictly limited, expect higher prices for food and accommodation. Exmouth, 118km away, has more options. There are ATMs at the shopping centre and the Peoples Park grocer, and internet access at some of the tour outlets and Fins Cafe. The town is chock-full from April to October.

Sights & Activities

Keep to the southern end of **Bills Bay** when swimming as the northern end (Skeleton Bay) is a breeding ground for reef sharks. There's good snorkelling in the bay, and even better at **Purdy Point**; walk 500m south along the coast until you see the 8km/h marker, then drift with the current back to the bay. You can hire snorkel gear anywhere in town.

Fish feeding occurs on the beach at 3.30pm every day and sunsets are sublime from the lookout above the beach car park.

Ningaloo Kayak Adventures KAYAKING
(☎08-9948 5034; www.ningalookayakadventures.com; 2/3hr tours $50/70) Various length kayak tours with snorkelling are available from the main beach. You can also hire a glass-bottom canoe ($25 per hour), wetsuit and snorkelling gear ($15 per day).

Ningaloo Reef Dive DIVING
(☎08-9942 5824; www.ningalooreefdive.com) This PADI and eco-certified dive crew offers snorkelling with whale sharks ($390, from late March to July) and manta rays ($150, all year), half-day reef dives ($170) and a full range of dive courses (from $380).

Ningaloo Marine Interactions SNORKELLING
(☎08-9948 5190; www.mantaraycoralbay.com.au; 2hr/half-/full day $75/170/210; ⏲Jun-Oct, manta rays all year) Informative and sustainably run tours to the outer reef include two-hour whale watching, half-day manta-ray interaction and full-day wildlife spotting with snorkelling.

Tours

Popular tours from Coral Bay include swimming with whale sharks, spotting marine life (whales, dolphins, dugongs, turtles and manta rays), coral viewing from glass-bottom boats, and quad-bike trips. Tour operators have offices in the shopping centre and caravan parks; this is only a small selection.

Coral Bay Ecotours BOAT
(☎08-9942 5885; www.coralbayecotours.com.au; 1/2/3hr $39/54/75, all day $140) Eco-certified and carbon-neutral tours include glass-bottom boat cruises with snorkelling, and all-day wildlife-spotting trips complete with manta-ray interaction.

Coral Coast Tours 4WD
(☎0427 180 568; www.coralcoasttours.com.au; half-day 4WD adult/child $135/78, snorkelling 2/3hr $55/75) Explore the wildlife along the rugged 4WD coastal tracks of Warroora Station, or try your hand at Blo Karting (sand yachting) on nearby salt lakes ($50 per hour). It also runs reef tours and airport transfers ($80), continuing on to Exmouth ($100).

Sleeping & Eating

Avoid school holidays and book well ahead for peak season (April to October). Holiday houses can be rented online from www.coralbay.org (from $950 per week).

The shopping-centre **bakery** (Robinson St; ⏲6.30am-5.30pm) is the best option for early risers and vegetarians with its muesli and salad rolls. Seriously consider self-catering, as eating out is expensive.

Peoples Park Caravan Village CARAVAN PARK $
(☎08-9942 5933; www.peoplesparkcoralbay.com; sites unpowered $36, powered $42-52, 1-/2-bedroom cabins $240/260, hilltop villas $285; ❄) This excellent park offers grassy, shaded sites and a variety of fully self-contained cabins. The

Coral Coast & the Pilbara

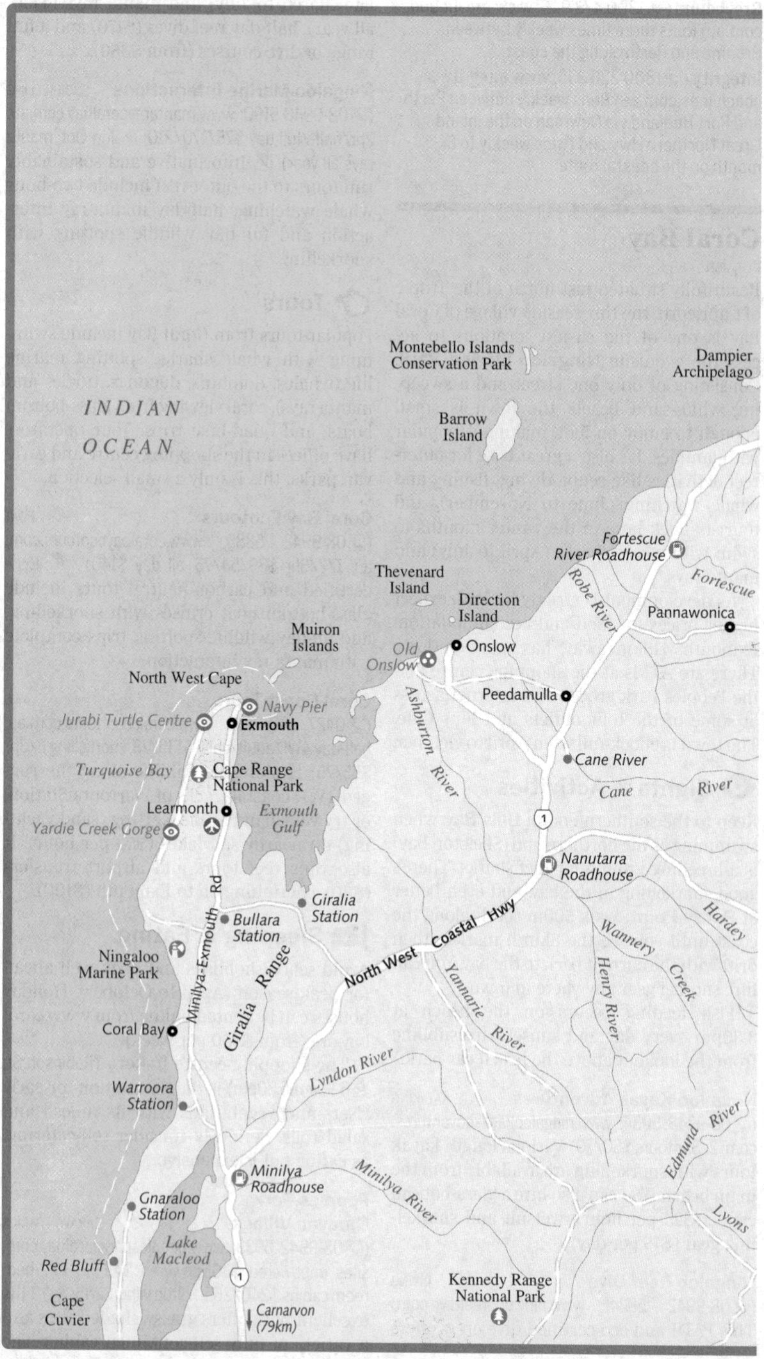
Montebello Islands
Conservation Park
Dampier
Archipelago
INDIAN
OCEAN
Barrow
Island
Fortescue
River Roadhouse
Fortescue
Robe River
Thevenard
Island
Direction
Island
Pannawonica
Muiron
Islands
Old
Onslow
Onslow
North West Cape
Navy Pier
Peedamulla
Jurabi Turtle Centre
Exmouth
Ashburton
River
Turquoise Bay
Cape Range
National Park
Cane River
Cane
River
Learmonth
Exmouth
Gulf
Yardie Creek Gorge
1
Nanutarra
Roadhouse
Rd
Giralia
Station
Bullara
Station
Hardey
Wannery
Creek
Minilya-Exmouth
Range
Ningaloo
Marine Park
North West
Coastal
Hwy
Yannarie
River
Henry River
Giralia
Coral Bay
Lyndon River
Warroora
Station
Edmund
River
Minilya
Roadhouse
Minilya
River
Gnaraloo
Station
Lyons
Lake
Macleod
Red Bluff
1
Kennedy Range
National Park
Cape
Cuvier
Carnarvon
(79km)

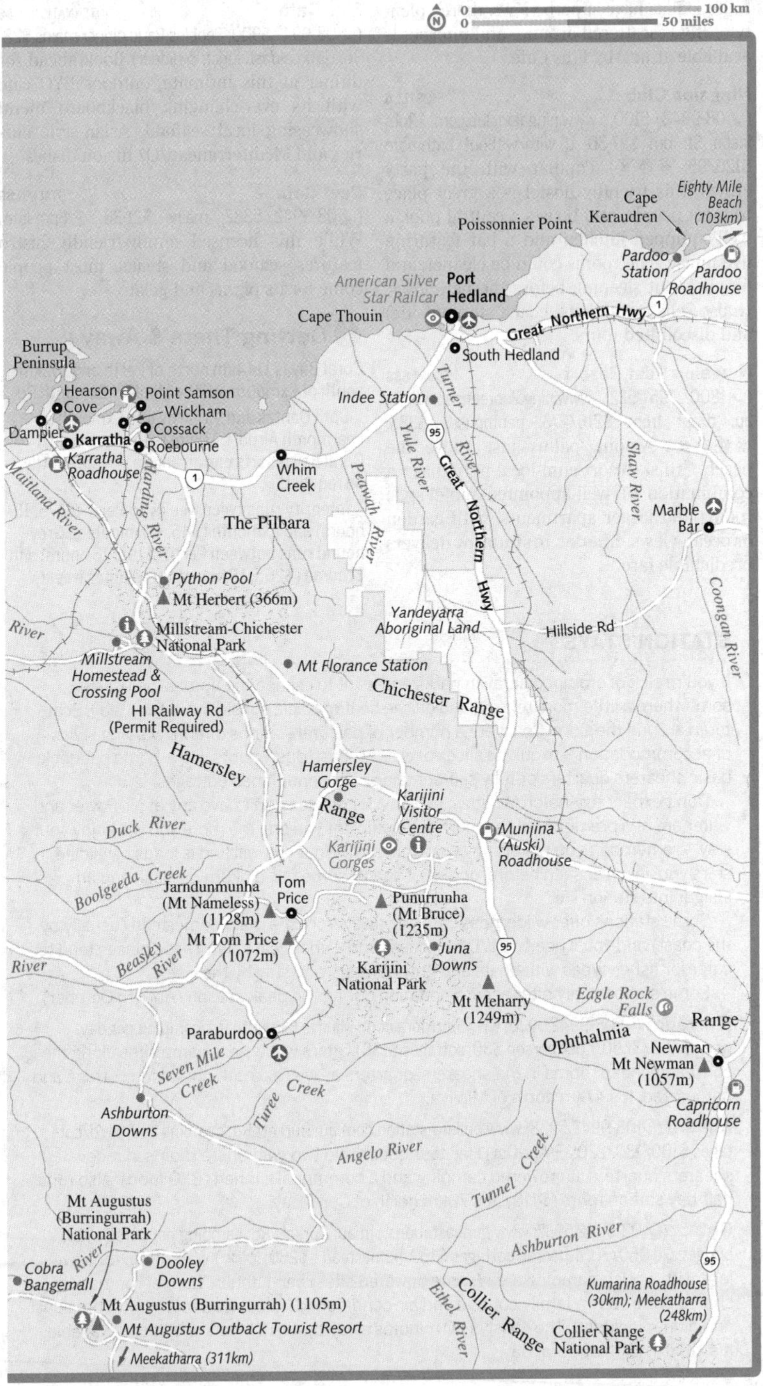
0 100 km
0 50 miles
Eighty Mile Beach (103km)
Cape Keraudren
Poissonnier Point
Pardoo Station
Pardoo Roadhouse
American Silver Star Railcar
Port Hedland
Cape Thouin
Great Northern Hwy
South Hedland
Burrup Peninsula
Hearson Cove
Point Samson
Wickham
Cossack
Dampier
Karratha
Roebourne
Karratha Roadhouse
Indee Station
Turner River
Yule River
Great Northern Hwy
Shaw River
Whim Creek
Peawah River
Maitland River
Harding River
The Pilbara
Marble Bar
Python Pool
Mt Herbert (366m)
Yandeyarra Aboriginal Land
Hillside Rd
Coongan River
River
Millstream-Chichester National Park
Millstream Homestead & Crossing Pool
Mt Florance Station
Chichester Range
HI Railway Rd (Permit Required)
Hamersley
Hamersley Gorge
Range
Karijini Visitor Centre
Munjina (Auski) Roadhouse
Duck River
Karijini Gorges
Boolgeeda Creek
Jarndunmunha (Mt Nameless) (1128m)
Tom Price
Punurrunha (Mt Bruce) (1235m)
Mt Tom Price (1072m)
Juna Downs
River
Beasley River
Karijini National Park
Mt Meharry (1249m)
Eagle Rock Falls
Range
Ophthalmia
Paraburdoo
Newman
Mt Newman (1057m)
Seven Mile Creek
Turee Creek
Ashburton Downs
Capricorn Roadhouse
Angelo River
Tunnel Creek
Mt Augustus (Burringurrah) National Park
Ashburton River
Cobra Bangemall
River
Dooley Downs
Collier Range
Ethel River
Kumarina Roadhouse (30km); Meekatharra (248km)
Mt Augustus (Burringurrah) (1105m)
Mt Augustus Outback Tourist Resort
Collier Range National Park
Meekatharra (311km)

hilltop villas have superb views, there's plenty of BBQs scattered around, and internet is available at nearby Fins Cafe.

Ningaloo Club HOSTEL $
(☎08-9948 5100; www.ningalooclub.com; Robinson St; dm $27-30, d with/without bathroom $120/95; ❄@≋) Popular with the party crowd, this friendly hostel is a great place to meet people, and boasts a central pool, a well-equipped kitchen and a bar featuring live music. The rooms could be cleaner, and forget about sleeping before the bar closes. It also sells bus tickets (coach stop outside) and discounted tours.

Ningaloo Reef Resort RESORT $$$
(☎1800 795 522; www.ningalooreefresort.com.au; d/apt from $216/276, penthouses $385; ❄@☜≋) Among palms just above the beach, this resort-cum-local-pub has a combination of well-appointed motel-style rooms and larger apartments, with garden or ocean views. **Shades restaurant** delivers predictable fare.

Fins Cafe INTERNATIONAL $$
(☎08-9942 5900; Peoples Park; dinner mains $28-36; ⊙breakfast, lunch & dinner) Book ahead for dinner at this intimate, outdoor BYO cafe with its ever-changing blackboard menu showcasing local seafood, Asian-style curries and Mediterranean/Oz fusion dishes.

Reef Cafe ITALIAN $$
(☎08-9942 5882; mains $21-36; ⊙6pm-late) While this licensed family-friendly bistro features seafood and steaks, most people come for its pizzas and gelato.

ℹ Getting There & Away

Coral Bay is 1144km north of Perth and 152km south of Exmouth, off the Minilya–Exmouth Rd.

Both Qantas and Virgin fly into Exmouth's Learmonth Airport, 118km to the north; most Coral Bay resorts can arrange a private shuttle on request.

Integrity runs twice weekly to Perth ($176, 15 hours) and Exmouth ($45, 90 minutes). Greyhound runs between Perth ($198, 16 hours) and Broome ($265, 19 hours) three times weekly.

STATION STAYS

If you're sick of cramped caravan parks and want to escape the hordes, or just stay somewhere a little more relaxed and off the beaten track, consider a station stay. Scattered around the Coral Coast are a number of pastoral stations offering varying styles of accommodation – exquisite slices of empty coast, dusty spots in the home paddock, basic shearers quarters or fully self-contained, air-conditioned cottages.

Don't expect top-notch facilities; in fact, a lot of sites don't have any at all. Power and water are at a premium, so the more self-sufficient you are, the more you will enjoy your stay – remember: you're getting away from it all. What you will find is loads of wildlife, stars you've never seen before, oodles of space, some fair-dinkum outback and an insight into station life.

Some stations offer wilderness camping away from the main homestead (usually by the coast) and you'll need a 4WD for access and a chemical toilet. These places tend to cater for fisher-types with boats and grey nomads who stay by the week.

Some stations only offer accommodation during the peak season (April to October).

Warroora (☎08-9942 5920; www.warroora.com; Minilya Exmouth Rd; camping per day/week $7.50/37.50, r per person $30, cottages $130) Offers wilderness camp sites along the coast and cheap rooms in the shearers' quarters as well as a self-contained cottage and homestead. It's 47km north of Minilya.

Bullara (☎08-9942 5938; www.bullara-station.com.au; Burkett Rd; camping $12, tw/d/cottages $100/130/220; ⊙Apr-Oct) Has four queen and two twin-share rooms in renovated shearers quarters, unpowered camping and a communal kitchen (BYO food). Also runs half-day station tours ($110). It's 70km north of Coral Bay.

Giralia (☎08-9942 5937; www.giraliastation.com.au; Burkett Rd; camping per person $10, budget s/d $60/70, 4-person cottages $160, homestead r $260; ❄≋) Well set up for travellers, with a bush-camping area (some powered sites) and kitchen, budget rooms with shared bathroom, a family cottage and air-conditioned homestead rooms with breakfast and dinner included. The coast is 40 minutes away by 4WD. Meals and liquor available. It's 110km north of Coral Bay.

Exmouth

POP 2500

Exmouth began life during WWII as a US submarine base, though the town didn't flourish until the 1960s with the establishment of the Very Low Frequency (VLF) communications facility at the North West Cape. Fishing (especially prawns) and oil and gas exploration commenced, and both industries are still thriving – the flares of gas platforms are visible from Vlamingh Head at night.

With the protection of pristine Ningaloo Reef, tourism now accounts for the bulk of all visitors, many coming to see the magnificent and enigmatic whale sharks (April to July). Peak season (April to October) sees this laid-back town stretched to epic proportions, but don't be put off, as it's still the best base to explore nearby Ningaloo Marine and Cape Range National Parks. Alternatively, just relax, wash away the dust after a long road trip and enjoy the local wildlife; emus walking down the street, 'roos lounging in the shade, lizards ambling across the highway and corellas, galahs and ringnecks screeching and swooping through the trees.

Sights & Activities

Exmouth is flat, hot and sprawling, with most of the attractions outside town and no public transport. **Town Beach** is an easy 1km walk east, though swimmers and anglers usually head to **Bundegi Beach**, 14km north in the shadow of the VLF antenna array. A set of cycle paths ring the town and continue out to the **Harold E Holt Naval Base** (HEH), where you can follow the road on to Bundegi; watch out for dingos! Bikes can be hired from **Exmouth Minigolf** (08-9949 4644; www.exmouthminigolf.com.au; Murat Rd; bike/kayak/snorkel gear per day $20/50/10; 9am-5pm).

The sewage works and golf course are good places for birdwatching, while turtle volunteering is popular from November to January – check out the excellent **Jurabi Turtle Centre** (JTC; Yardie Creek Rd). Nearby, the hilltop **Vlamingh Head lighthouse** is the spot for whale spotting and sunsets.

Snorkellers and divers head to **Ningaloo Marine Park** or the **Muiron Islands**. You can camp on South Muiron with a permit from Exmouth DEC. Try to find its informative book *Dive and Snorkel Sites in Western Australia*. The **Navy Pier** dive at **Point Murat**, near Bundegi Beach, is world class. Several dive shops in town offer PADI courses.

Surfers flock to **Dunes** on the western cape during winter, while in the summer months windsurfing and kiteboarding are popular.

Ningaloo Kite & Board KITEBOARDING
(08-9949 2770; www.ningalooexcape.com.au; 16 Nimitz St; 2hr lessons $200; 10am-1pm Mon-Sat) Talk to the experts about the best windsurfing and kiteboarding locations, book a lesson or even buy a secondhand kite.

Capricorn Kayak Tours KAYAKING
(0427 485 123; www.capricornseakayaking.com.au; half-/1-/2-/5-day tours $89/169/665/1650) Capricorn offers single- and multi-day kayaking and snorkelling tours along the lagoons of Ningaloo Reef.

Ningaloo Whaleshark-N-Dive DIVING
(1800 224 060; www.ningaloowhalesharkndive.com.au) Offers daily dives to Lighthouse Bay ($165) and the Muiron Islands ($200) as well as longer liveaboard tours. Currently holds the exclusive licence to Navy Pier ($145). Dive courses also available from introductory ($215) to full PADI ($600).

Tours

Adventure tours from Exmouth include swimming with whale sharks, wildlife spotting, diving, sea kayaking, fishing and surf charters, and coral viewing from glass-bottom boats. Some companies only operate during peak season. Check conditions carefully regarding 'no sighting' policies and cancellations.

Outside the whale-shark season, tours focus on manta rays. You need to be a capable snorkeller to get the most out of these experiences. It's normally 30% cheaper if you don't swim. Also be wary of snorkelling on what may essentially be a dive tour – the action may be too deep. Most ocean tours usually depart from Tantabiddi on the western Cape and include free transfers from Exmouth. Here are just a selection of operators – see the visitor centre for a full list.

Kings Ningaloo Reef Tours WILDLIFE
(08-9949 1764; www.kingsningalooreeftours.com.au; snorkeller/observer $385/285) Long-time player Kings still gets rave reviews for its whale-shark tours. It's renowned for staying out longer than everyone else, and has a 'next available tour' no-sighting policy.

Exmouth

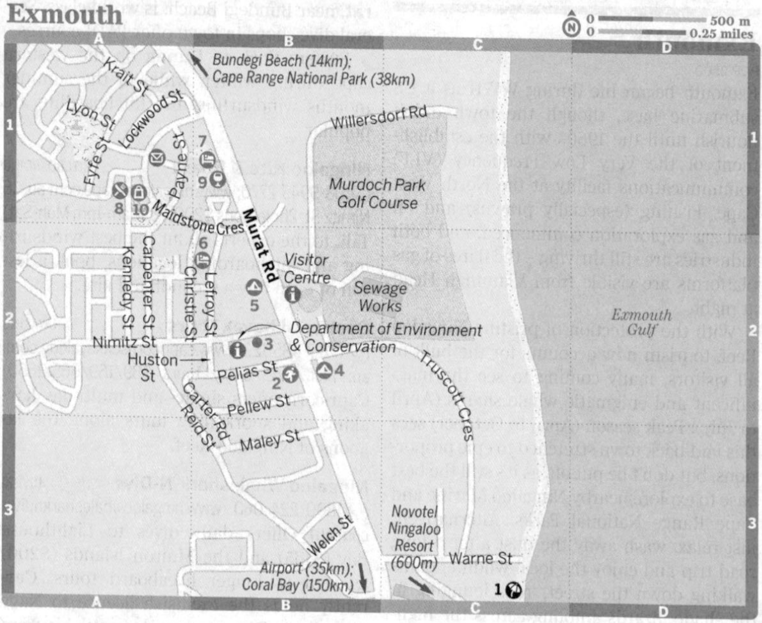

Exmouth

Sights
1 Town Beach C3

Activities, Courses & Tours
2 Exmouth Minigolf B2
3 Ningaloo Kite & Board B2

Sleeping
4 Exmouth Cape Holiday Park B2
Exmouth Holiday Accommodation/Ray White .... (see 10)
5 Exmouth Ningaloo Caravan & Holiday Resort B2
6 Ningaloo Lodge B2
7 Potshot Hotel Resort B1

Eating
8 Ningaloo Health A1
Pinocchio .... (see 5)
Whalers Restaurant .... (see 8)

Drinking & Nightlife
9 Potshot Hotel B1

Shopping
10 Exmouth Shopping Centre A1

Ningaloo Ecology Cruises CRUISE
(☎1800 554 062; www.ningalootreasures.com.au; 1/2½hr $40/60) Has one-hour glass-bottom boat trips (April to October), and longer 2½-hour trips (all year) including snorkelling.

WestTreks 4WD
(☎08-9949 2659; www.westtreksafaritours.com.au; night/half-/full-day 4WD tours $90/$110/$199) Caves, canyons, a boat cruise and snorkelling are only part of these full-day 4WD tours that traverse the Cape Range to the west coast. Perfect for those without their own transport; shorter tours also available.

Sleeping

Accommodation is limited, so it's best to book ahead, especially for the peak season (April to October).

Exmouth Ningaloo Caravan & Holiday Resort CARAVAN PARK $
(☎08-9949 2377; www.exmouthresort.com; Murat Rd; unpowered/powered sites $38/48, dm/d

$39/80, chalets $200; ❄📶🏊) Across from the visitor centre, this friendly, spacious park has grassy sites, self-contained chalets, four-bed dorms, an on-site restaurant and even a pet section. If you're tenting, this is your best bet.

Exmouth Cape Holiday Park CARAVAN PARK $

(Blue Reef Backpackers; ☎1800 621 101; www.aspenparks.com.au; cnr Truscott Cres & Murat Rd; sites unpowered/powered/with bathroom $35/49/76, dm/d $32/100, cabin d $130-297; ❄@🏊) The Cape offers van sites with their own en suites, as well as four-bed dorms, budget twins and a host of different cabin options. There's a good camp kitchen and an excellent pool. The few unpowered tent sites are rather cramped.

Ningaloo Lodge GUESTHOUSE $$

(☎1800 880 949; www.ningaloolodge.com.au; Lefroy St; d $140; ❄📶🏊) These clean, tastefully appointed motel rooms are one of the better deals, with a modern communal kitchen, barbecue, shady pool and free wi-fi all within walking distance of either pub.

Potshot Hotel Resort RESORT $

(☎08-9949 1200; www.potshotresort.com; Murat Rd; dm/d $30/70, motel d $120, studios $225, apt from $245; ❄@📶🏊) A town-within-a-town, this bustling resort has seven-bed dorms, standard motel rooms, luxury Osprey apartments and several bars, catering for all comers. The backpacker rooms can be noisy.

Exmouth Holiday Accommodation/ Ray White RENTAL HOUSES $$

(☎08-9949 1144; www.exmouthholidays.com.au; 3 Kennedy St; per week from $600; ❄) Ray White has a wide range of weekly rentals, from fibro shacks to double-storey mansions.

Novotel Ningaloo Resort RESORT $$$

(☎08-9949 0000; www.novotelningaloo.com.au; Madaffari Dr; d/apt from $275/355; ❄📶🏊) In

NINGA TURTLE GUIDES

Between November and March each year, volunteer turtle-monitoring programs are held along the northwest coast, providing an amazing experience for those with time to spare. You'll be working at strange hours during the hottest season in remote areas with little comfort, but knowing that you're actively taking part in the conservation of these magnificent creatures is incredibly satisfying. Applications usually open around August, but check individual program timelines.

➡ **Exmouth** volunteers need to commit to a five-week period and be prepared to spend most of that time at a remote base. Days start at sunrise with five hours' work collecting data on turtle nesting, habitat and predation, then the rest of the day is free to enjoy the surroundings. Volunteers pay around $1300, which covers all equipment, meals, transport from Exmouth and insurance. Accommodation is usually in tents or swags at a Department of Environment and Conservation (DEC) research station or remote beach. See the website of the **Ningaloo Turtle Program** (NTP; www.ningalooturtles.org.au) for more information.

If you enjoy interaction of the human kind, consider the NTP's Turtle Guide Program. You will need to complete at least the first module of the Exmouth TAFE formal training course, Turtle Tour Guiding, before commencing at the Jurabi Turtle Centre (JTC; p993) and this course gains credits towards a Certificate III in Tourism. The JTC plays an important role in minimising the disturbance to nesting turtles and hatchlings by educating tourists and supervising interaction during the breeding period.

➡ **Port Hedland** volunteers can apply for **Pendoley Environmental's** (www.penv.com.au) tagging program, which works alongside the oil and gas industry at sites like Barrow Island. Typical placements are for 17 days with all expenses covered; there's a strict selection process and you'll be working mostly at night with minimal free time. The environmental group **Care for Hedland** (☎0439 941 431; www.careforhedland.org.au) also runs monitoring programs, and training sessions kick off in November.

➡ Science graduates (any discipline) prepared to commit for six months can apply to Gnaraloo Station's **Turtle Conservation Program** (GTCP; www.facebook.com/pages/Gnaraloo-Turtle-Conservation-Program/108817312525609), where all food, accommodation, transport and training are supplied, and volunteers work at the world's third-largest loggerhead rookery.

the marina, the Novotel Ningaloo is at the pointy end of sophistication (and expense) in Exmouth. The tastefully designed rooms are spacious, well equipped and all include balconies.

Eating & Drinking

There's a supermarket, a bakery and several takeaways at **Exmouth Shopping Centre** (Maidstone Cres).

Graces Tavern and the Potshot Hotel are your drinking options.

Ningaloo Health CAFE $
(☎08-9949 1400; www.ningaloohealth.com.au; 3A Kennedy St; mains $7-19; ⊙7.30am-4pm;) Breakfasts start with a bang at this tiny cafe – try the chilli eggs on blue-vein toast, or a bowl of Vietnamese *pho*. The less brave can dive into a berry pancake stack, bircher muesli or a detox juice. NH also does light lunches, salads, smoothies, takeaway picnic hampers (great for a day trip to Cape Range National Park) and the best coffee around.

★**Whalers Restaurant** SEAFOOD $$
(☎08-9949 2416; www.whalersrestaurant.com.au; 5 Kennedy St; mains lunch $8-24, dinner $29-40; ⊙9am-2pm & 6pm-late) Delicious Creole-influenced seafood is the star attraction at this Exmouth institution. Sit back on the leafy verandah and share a seafood tasting plate with soft-shell crab and local prawns, or try the signature New Orleans gumbo. Non-fishheads can hook into chargrilled kangaroo or Mexican fajitas. The lunch menu is more bistro-like.

Pinocchio ITALIAN $$
(☎08-9949 2577; Murat Rd; mains $16-35; ⊙6-9pm) Located inside the Exmouth Ningaloo Caravan & Holiday Resort, this licensed alfresco *ristorante* is popular with locals and travellers alike. Families are well catered for, there's a pleasant deck by the pool, and the tasty pasta and pizza servings are huge.

Information

Internet access is available at the **library** (☎08-9949 1462; 22 Maidstone Cres; ⊙8.30am-4pm Mon-Thu, to noon Sat), **Exmouth Diner** (Maidstone Cr; internet free with $5 minimum purchase; ⊙4.30-8.30pm;), **Potshot Hotel** (☎08-9949 1200; Murat Rd) and the dive shops.

Cape Conservation Group (www.ccg.org.au) Website listing environmental projects around the cape.

Department of Environment & Conservation (DEC; ☎08-9947 8000; www.dec.wa.gov.au; 20 Nimitz St; ⊙8am-5pm Mon-Fri) Supplies maps, brochures and permits for Ningaloo, Cape Range and Muiron Islands, including excellent wildlife guides. Can advise on turtle volunteering.

Visitor Centre (☎08-9949 1176; www.exmouthwa.com.au; Murat Rd; ⊙9am-5pm Mon-Sat, to 1pm Sun) Tour bookings, bus tickets, accommodation service and parks information.

Getting There & Away

Exmouth's Learmonth Airport is 37km south of town. Both Qantas and Virgin fly to Perth daily. The **airport shuttle** (☎08-9949 4623; $25) meets all flights.

Integrity coaches run to Perth twice weekly ($200, 17 hours) via Coral Bay ($45, 90 minutes). Greyhound no longer visits Exmouth, so if you're heading north it's easiest to depart from Coral Bay via the charter shuttle ($100, two hours). Buses leave from the visitors centre.

Red Earth Safaris (☎1800 501 968; www.redearthsafaris.com.au) offers a weekly Perth express departing Exmouth 7am Sunday (one way $200, 30 hours) with an overnight stop.

Getting Around

Allens (☎08-9949 2403; rear 24 Nimitz St) Cars start from $60 per day with 150 free kilometres; Budget, Avis and Europcar also have agents.

Exmouth Camper Hire (☎08-9949 4050; www.exmouthcamperhire.com.au; 16 Nimitz St; 4 days from $600) Campervans with everything you need to spend time in Cape Range National Park, including solar panels.

Scooters2go (☎08-9949 4488; www.scooters2go.com.au; cnr Murat Rd & Pellew St; per day/week $80/$175) You only need a car licence for these 50cc scooters, which are much cheaper by the week.

Ningaloo Marine Park

Recently extended and World Heritage listed, the Ningaloo Marine Park now protects the full 300km length of the exquisite Ningaloo Reef, from Bundegi Reef on the eastern tip of the peninsula to Red Bluff on Quobba Station far to the south.

Ningaloo is Australia's largest fringing reef, in places only 100m offshore, and it's this accessibility and the fact that it's home to a staggering array of **marine life** that makes it so popular. Sharks, manta rays, humpback whales, turtles, dugongs and dolphins complement more than 500 species of fish.

There's great marine activity year-round:

November to March Turtles – three endangered species nestle and hatch in the dunes.

March Coral spawning – an amazing event seven days after the full moon.

Mid-March to July Whale sharks – the biggest fish on the planet arrive for the coral spawning.

May to November Manta rays – present all year round; their numbers increase dramatically over winter and spring.

June to November Humpback whales – breed in the warm tropics then head back south to feed in the Antarctic.

Over 220 species of hard **coral** have been recorded in Ningaloo, ranging from bulbous brain corals found on bommies to delicate branching staghorns and the slow-growing massive coral. While less colourful than soft corals (which are normally found in deeper water on the outer reef), the hard corals have incredible formations. Spawning, where branches of hermaphroditic coral simultaneously eject eggs and sperm into the water, occurs after full and new moons between February and May, but the peak action is usually six to 10 days after the March full moon.

It's this spawning that attracts the park's biggest drawcard, the solitary speckled **whale shark** *(Rhiniodon typus)*. Ningaloo is one of the few places in the world where these gentle giants arrive like clockwork each year to feed on plankton and small fish, making it a mecca for marine biologists and visitors alike. The largest fish in the world, the whale shark can weigh up to 21 tonnes, although most weigh between 13 and 15 tonnes, and reach up to 18m long. They can live for 70 years.

Upload your amazing whale-shark pics to **Ecocean** (www.whaleshark.org), which will identify and track your whale shark. To learn more about Ningaloo's denizens, grab a copy of DEC's *The Marine Life of Ningaloo Marine Park and Coral Bay.*

Activities

Most travellers visit Ningaloo Marine Park to **snorkel**. Stop at **Milyering visitor centre** (☎08-9949 2808; Yardie Creek Rd; ⌚9am-3.45pm) for maps and information on the best spots and conditions. Check its tide chart and know your limits, as the currents can be dangerous. The shop next to the park office sells and rents snorkelling equipment ($10 per day, $15 overnight).

The most popular snorkel and dive spots:

Lakeside SNORKELLING

Walk 500m south along the beach from the car park then snorkel out with the current before returning close to your original point.

Oyster Stacks SNORKELLING

These spectacular bommies are just metres offshore, but you need a tide of at least 1.2m and sharp rocks make entry/exit difficult. If you tire, don't stand on the bommies; look for some sand.

Turquoise Bay SNORKELLING

The Bay Snorkel Area is suitable for all skill levels and provides myriad fish and corals just off the beach to the right of the Bay car park. Stronger swimmers will want to head to the Drift Snorkel Area: 300m south along the beach from the Drift car park, swim out for about 40m then float face down; the current will carry you over coral bommies and abundant sea life. Get out before the sandy point then run back along the beach and start all over! Beware strong currents and don't miss the exit point or you'll be carried out through the gap in the reef.

Lighthouse Bay SCUBA DIVING

There's great scuba diving at Lighthouse Bay at sites like the Labyrinth, Blizzard Ridge and Mandu Wall. Check out the DEC book *Dive and Snorkel Sites in Western Australia* for other ideas.

Tours

See tours in the Exmouth (p993) and Coral Bay (p989) sections.

Cape Range National Park

The jagged limestone peaks and gorges of rugged 510-sq-km **Cape Range National Park** (per car $11) offer relief from the otherwise flat, arid expanse of the North West Cape, and are rich in wildlife, including the rare black-flanked rock wallaby, five types of bat and over 200 species of bird. Spectacular deep canyons cut dramatically into the range, before emptying out onto the wind-blown coastal dunes and turquoise waters of Ningaloo Reef.

The main park access is via Yardie Creek Rd. Several areas in the east are accessible from unsealed roads off Minilya–Exmouth Rd, south of Exmouth. Milyering visitor centre (p997) has comprehensive natural and cultural displays, maps and publications.

Sights & Activities

On the east coast, 23km south of Exmouth, the scenic and at times incredible **Charles Knife Road** climbs dramatically above the **canyon** of the same name. The road follows the knife-edge ridge up through rickety corners and you'll need frequent stops to take in the breathtaking views.

Don't miss beautiful **Shothole Canyon** (turn-off 16km south of Exmouth), with its colourful walls and pretty picnic area.

On the west coast, spot birds at the **Mangrove Bay Bird Hide**, 8km from the entrance station. **Mandu Mandu Gorge** is a pleasant but dry walk (3km return) from a car park 20km south of the Milyering visitor centre.

Much nicer is the 2km return walk to **Yardie Creek Gorge** with its permanent water, sheer cliffs and excellent views. You can take the relaxing one-hour **Yardie Creek Cruise** (08-9949 2808; adult/child $25/12; 11am daily) up the short, sheer gorge to spot rare black-flanked rock wallabies.

Sleeping

A string of sandy, compact **camp sites** (per person $7) line the coast within the park. Facilities and shade are minimal, though most have toilets. Avoid long peak-season queues (from 7am!) at the park entrance station by pre-booking a site (at least 48 hours ahead) through the **DEC** (www.dec.wa.gov.au/campgrounds). Currently, only certain sites can be booked online, the rest are allocated upon arrival at the entrance station – ask for a generator-free site if you're after quiet.

Ningaloo Lighthouse Caravan Park CARAVAN PARK $$
(08-9949 1478; www.ningaloolighthouse.com; Yardie Creek Rd; unpowered/powered sites $29/35, cabins $95, bungalows $125, lighthouse/lookout chalets $150/245;) Outside the park but superbly located on the western cape under Vlamingh lighthouse near Surfers Beach, the chalets have fantastic views. There are plenty of shady tent sites for lesser mortals.

Sal Salis LUXURY WILDERNESS $$$
(1300 790 561; www.salsalis.com; wilderness tent s/d $1088/1450; Mar-Dec) Want to watch that flaming crimson Indian Ocean sunset from between 500-threadcount pure cotton sheets? Pass the chablis! For those who want their camp without the cramp, there's a minimum two-night stay, three gourmet meals a day, a free bar (!) and the same things to do as the couple over the dune in the pop-up camper.

Dampier to Roebourne

Most travellers skip this mining-services section of the coast as there's not much to see, unless you like huge industrial facilities. Accommodation is ludicrously overpriced and almost impossible to find thanks to the resources boom and the flood of FIFO (fly-in, fly-out) workers. However, the area has good transport, well-stocked supermarkets and booked-out repair shops.

Dampier

POP 1300

Dampier is the region's main port. Spread around King Bay, it overlooks the 42 pristine islands of the **Dampier Archipelago**, and supports a wealth of marine life in its coral waters, but heavy industry has blighted Dampier's shores. The nearby **Burrup Peninsula** contains possibly the greatest number of rock-art petroglyphs on the planet but is under threat from continued industrial expansion (see www.burrup.org.au). The most accessible are at **Deep Gorge** near **Hearson Cove**, where you can also view the Staircase to the Moon; you'll need a 4WD for the rest of the peninsula.

Dampier Transit Caravan Park (08-9183 1109; The Esplanade; unpowered/powered sites $18/22) has a handful of grassy sites overlooking the water.

Karratha

POP 17,000

Most travellers bank, restock, repair stuff and get out of town before their wallet ignites.

From behind the visitor centre, the **Jaburara Heritage Trail** (3.5km one way) takes visitors through significant traditional sites and details the displacement and eventual extinction of the Jaburara people. Bring plenty of water and start early.

The **Karratha visitor centre** (08-9144 4600; www.pilbaracoast.com; Karratha Rd; 9am-5pm Mon-Fri, 10am-1pm Sat & Sun, shorter hours

Nov-Apr) has good local info, supplies Hamersley Iron (HI) road permits, books tours (including mining infrastructure), and may be able to find you a room.

Sleeping & Eating

Accommodation prospects are dire in Karratha; try to stay at beautiful Point Samson instead. Otherwise, search online for last-minute deals or ask at the visitor centre. Due to FIFO, weekends are usually cheaper than midweek.

The shopping centre has most things you'll need, while the **JavaVan** coffee, in the visitor centre car park, is the best in town.

Pilbara Holiday Park CARAVAN PARK $
(08-9185 1855; www.aspenparks.com.au; Rosemary Rd; powered sites $40, motel/studio d $229/220;) Neat, well run with good facilities.

Getting There & Away

Karratha is exceptionally well connected. Virgin, Qantas and Alliance all fly daily to Perth, while Qantas also offers weekly direct flights to most other capitals. Airnorth flies to Broome (with a Darwin connection) and Port Hedland weekly. Greyhound coaches run to Perth ($286, 22 hours), Port Hedland ($61, three hours) and Broome ($168, 11 hours) three times weekly.

Roebourne

POP 850

Roebourne, 40km east of Karratha, is the oldest (1866) Pilbara town still functioning, and sits on Ngaluma country. It's home to a large Aboriginal community; Yindjibarndi is the dominant language group. There are some beautiful old buildings, including the old gaol, which houses the **visitor centre** (Old Gaol; 08-9182 1060; www.pilbaracoast.com/towns/roebourne-visitor-centre; Queen St; 9am-4pm Mon-Fri, to 3pm Sat & Sun, shorter hours Nov-Apr) and museum. Don't miss the mineral display in the courtyard.

Roebourne has a thriving indigenous art scene, and you'll pass the odd gallery on the highway. See www.roebourneart.com.au for more details.

Cossack

The scenic ghost town of Cossack, at the mouth of the Harding River, was previously the district's main port but was usurped by Point Samson and then eventually abandoned. Many of the historic bluestone buildings date from the late 1800s; there's a 6km **Heritage Trail** around the town that links all the major sites (pick up the brochure from Roebourne visitor centre). Attractions include the self-guided **Social History Museum** (adult/child $2/1; 9am-4pm), and the pioneer **cemetery** with a tiny Japanese section dating from Cossack's pearling days. Past the cemetery, **Reader Head Lookout** has great views over the river mouth and of the Staircase to the Moon.

Cossack Budget Accommodation (08-9182 1190; www.roebourne.wa.gov.au/cossack.aspx; d with/without air-con $110/90;) has five basic rooms in the atmospheric old police barracks. BYO food.

Point Samson

POP 300

Point Samson is a small, industrial-free seaside village, home to great seafood and clean beaches, making it the nicest place to stay in the area. There's good **snorkelling** off Point Samson, and the picturesque curved beach of Honeymoon Cove.

Sleeping & Eating

Cove CARAVAN PARK $
(08-9187 0199; www.thecovecaravanpark.com.au; Macleod St; sites $49.50, 1-/2-bedroom units $240/310) It's a bit 'van city', but the modern, clean facilities complement a great location with an easy walk to all attractions.

Samson Beach Chalets COTTAGES $$$
(08-9187 0202; www.samsonbeach.com.au; Samson Rd; chalets $250-600;) Offers beautifully appointed, self-contained chalets (various sizes) just a short walk from the beach. There's a shady pool, free wi-fi and in-house movies.

Samson Beach Bistro SEAFOOD $$
(08-9187 1435; mains $11-44; 11am-8.30pm daily, closed 2-5pm Mon-Fri) Does great seafood on a shady deck overlooking the ocean.

Millstream-Chichester National Park

Among the arid, spinifex-covered plateaus and basalt ranges between Karijini and the coast, the tranquil Millstream waterholes of the Fortescue River form cool, lush oases. Lovely **Crossing Pool** (sites per person $7;), with palms, pelicans and gas barbecues, makes an idyllic camp site, though some may prefer the larger **Milliyanha Campground** (sites per person $7), with its camp kitchen and nearby visitor centre. **Murlamunyjunha Trail** (7km, two hours return) links both areas and features interpretive plaques by the traditional Yindjibarndi owners.

Once the station homestead, the unstaffed **visitor centre** (08-9184 5144; 8am-4pm) houses historical, ecological and cultural displays; as a lifeline for flora and fauna during dry spells, the park is one of the most important indigenous sites in WA. The nearby lily- and palm-fringed **Jirndarwurrunha Pool** is especially significant and swimming is not permitted.

You can swim at **Deep Reach Pool** (Nhangganggunha), believed to be the resting place of the Warlu, the creation serpent; the shady tables and barbecues are perfect for a lazy picnic.

In the park's north are the stunning breakaways and eroded mesas of the **Chichester Range**. Don't miss the amazing panorama from the top of **Mt Herbert** (the viewpoint is a 10-minute walk from the car park) and on the road to Roebourne. You can continue walking to McKenzie Spring (4.5km, one hour return). Lower down the range, **Python Pool** is worth a look, though check for algal bloom before diving in; the pool is linked to Mt Herbert by the Chichester Range Camel Trail (16km, six hours return).

Karijini National Park

Arguably one of WA's most magnificent destinations, **Karijini National Park** (per car $11) reveals itself slowly. Ragged ranges, upthrust and twisted by nature, glow in the setting sun. Wedge-tailed eagles soar above grey-green spinifex and goannas shelter under stunted mulga. Kangaroos and wildflowers dot the plains, criss-crossed by deep, dark chasms emitting the enticing sound of distant water.

While the narrow, breathtaking gorges, with their hidden, sculptured pools, are Karijini's biggest drawcard, the park is also home to a wide variety of fauna and flora, with an estimated 800 plant species, including some 50 varieties of wattle (acacia). Dragon lizards scurry over stones, rock wallabies cling to sheer cliffs and endangered olive pythons lurk on the far side of pools. The park also contains WA's three highest peaks: Mt Meharry, Mt Bruce and Mt Frederick.

Banyjima Dr, the park's main thoroughfare, connects with Karijini Dr at two entrance stations. The eastern access is sealed to the visitor centre and Dales Gorge, while the rest of the park is unsealed. Take extra care driving as tourist rollovers are common. Avoid driving at night.

Choose walks wisely, dress appropriately and never enter a restricted area without a certified guide. Avoid the gorges during and after rain, as flash flooding does occur.

Sights & Activities

Scenic **Dales Gorge** and its campground are 19km from the eastern entrance. A short, sharp descent leads to **Fortescue Falls**, behind which a leafy stroll upstream reveals the beautiful **Fern Pool**; head downstream from Fortescue Falls to picturesque **Circular Pool**; ascend to **Three Ways Lookout** and return along the cliff top.

Wide **Kalamina Gorge**, 24km from the visitor centre, has a small tranquil pool and falls with easy access suitable for families. Joffre Falls Rd leads to stunning **Knox**

TOM PRICE & NEWMAN

Bookending Karijini National Park are the neat, company-built mining towns of Tom Price and Newman. Newman, to the east on the Great Northern Hwy, is the larger of the two, with better transport and accommodation options, although it's a lot further from Karijini. Both have good (ie air-con) supermarkets, fuel and excellent visitor centres which can book you on mine tours if huge holes are your thing. The local libraries have internet access, and Newman's caravan parks are OK to pitch a tent.

Newman Visitor Centre (08-9175 2888; www.newman-wa.org; Fortescue Ave; 8am-5pm, closed Sun Jan) Ask for its mud-map of local sights.

Tom Price Visitor Centre (08-9188 1112; www.tompricewa.com.au; Central Rd; 8.30am-5pm Mon-Fri, to 12.30pm Sat & Sun, shorter hours Nov-Apr) Can supply Hamersley Iron (HI) road permits and book tours.

Karijini National Park

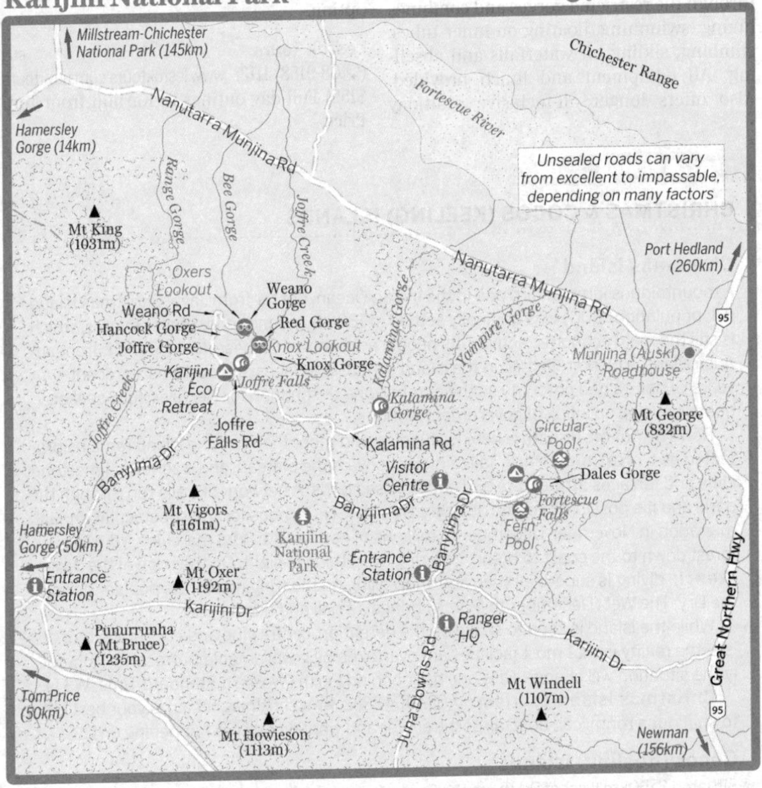

Gorge, passing the lookout over the spectacular **Joffre Falls**. Knox Gorge has several nice swimming holes, fringed by native figs, while in **Joffre Gorge** the frigid pools are perennially shaded.

Weano Rd junction is 32km from the visitor centre, and the **Eco Retreat** is nearby. The final 13km to the breathtaking **Oxers Lookout** can be rough, but it's worth it for the magnificent views of the junction of Red, Weano, Joffre and Hancock Gorges some 130m below.

A steep descent into **Hancock Gorge** (partly on ladders) will bring you first to the sunny **Amphitheatre**, then along the slippery **Spider Walk** to the sublime **Kermits Pool**. On the other side of the car park, a rough track winds down to the surreal **Handrail Pool** in the bowels of **Weano Gorge**. Swimming in these pools is a magical experience, but obey all signs and don't even think about entering a restricted area.

Hamersley Gorge SWIMMING

In Karijini's northwest corner, off Nanutarra-Wittenoom Rd, idyllic swimming holes and a waterfall lie only minutes from the car park.

Punurrunha WALKING

(Mt Bruce) Grab some altitude on WA's second-highest mountain (1235m), a superb ridge walk with fantastic views all the way to the summit. Start early, carry lots of water and allow five hours (9km return). The access road is off Karijini Dr opposite the western end of Banyjima Dr.

Tours

To fully appreciate the magical quality of Karijini's gorges, consider an accredited adventure tour through the restricted areas.

★ **West Oz Active Adventure Tours** ADVENTURE

(☎ 0438 913 713; www.westozactive.com.au; Karijini Eco Retreat; 1-/3-/5-day tours $245/$745/1450;

⌚Apr-Nov) Offers action-packed day trips through the restricted gorges and combines hiking, swimming, floating on inner tubes, climbing, sliding off waterfalls and abseiling. All equipment and lunch provided. Also offers longer all-inclusive multiday tours with airport pickups and a Ningaloo option.

Lestok Tours BUS
(☎08-9188 1112; www.lestoktours.com.au; tours $155) Full-day outings to Karijini from Tom Price.

OFF THE BEATEN TRACK

CHRISTMAS & COCOS (KEELING) ISLANDS

Christmas Island

A mountainous lump of bird poo in the Indian Ocean, not far from Java, Christmas Island (CI; population 1600) was originally settled in 1888 by guano (phosphate) miners, which is still the main economic activity. Its people are a mix of Chinese, Malays and European-Australians, a blend reflected in the island's food, languages and customs. In recent years CI has gained notoriety as the number-one destination for illegal asylum-seeker boats, causing an influx of government workers.

Don't be put off, as nature here is stunning and more than half the island remains protected as **CI National Park**. Tall rainforest covers the plateau, and a series of limestone cliffs and terraces attract rare and endemic sea birds. A network of trails run through the park, and it's possible to camp at **Dolly Beach**. CI is famous for the spectacular annual migration in November-December of millions of **red land crabs** marching from the forest down to the coast to breed, covering everything in sight. On the edge of the **Java Trench**, diving is superb all year, and snorkelling on the fringing reefs is popular during the Dry. The Wet (December to March) brings a swell and decent surf.

While the island is keen to shake off the detention-centre vibe and encourage tourists, the reality is that most facilities are overtaken by government contractors. Hopefully the situation will change. CI is one hour behind Perth (Western Standard Time; WST).

Christmas Island Tourism (☎08-9164 8382; www.christmas.net.au) is your best bet to sniff out a room, car, boat, airport transfer and whatever else is happening on CI.

Cocos (Keeling) Islands

Situated 2750km west of Perth are the Cocos (Keeling) Islands (CKI; population 650), a necklace of 27 idyllic, low-lying islands around a blue lagoon that inspired Charles Darwin's theory of coral-atoll formation. CKI was settled by John Clunies-Ross in 1826 and his family remained in control of the islands and their Malay workers until 1978, when CKI became part of Australia's Indian Ocean territories. Today about 550 Malays and 100 European-Australians live on **Home** and **West Islands**. It's a very low-key place in which to walk, snorkel, dive, fish, windsurf, birdwatch and relax. While most people come on a package, you can visit independently, and camping is allowed at Scout Park on West Island, and on **Direction** and **South Islands**. You will need to bring all your own gear. Bring lots of cash as there are no ATMs, though some places accept credit cards. CKI is 90 minutes behind WST.

Cocos-Keeling Islands (☎08-9162 6790; www.cocos-tourism.cc) Great CKI website includes accommodation, tours and activities.

Cocos Dive (☎08-9162 6515; www.cocosdive.com; per day from $210) Able to arrange single dives, week-long packages or SSI courses.

Getting There & Away

Virgin Australia (☎13 67 89; www.virginaustralia.com.au) flies from Perth to both islands several times weekly. Prices start at around $500 for either island, and at $220 between the two. There's also a return charter flight on Saturday from Kuala Lumpur to CI, bookable through **Island Explorer Holidays** (☎1300 884 855; www.islandexplorer.com.au). Twitchers could consider an all-inclusive tour of both islands from **Birding Tours Australia** (☎02-4927 1808; www.birdingtours.com.au; 14-day tours $3800; ⌚Feb-Mar & Nov-Dec). Australian visa requirements apply, and Australians should bring their passports.

Sleeping & Eating

Dales Gorge CAMPGROUND $
(sites adult/child $7/2) This large DEC campground offers shady, spacious sites with nearby toilets and picnic tables. Forget tent pegs – you'll be using rocks as anchors.

Karijini Eco Retreat RESORT $$$
(☎08-9425 5591; www.karijiniecoretreat.com.au; sites $35, tent d low/high season $177/315) This 100% indigenous-owned retreat is a model for sustainable tourism, and the attached bar and restaurant does fantastic food. Campers get hot showers and the same rocks as the DEC camping ground. Summer is bargain time when the retreat winds down and temperatures soar.

Information

Visitor Centre (☎08-9189 8121; Banyjima Dr; ⏰9am-4pm Apr-Oct, from 10am Nov-Mar) Indigenous-managed with excellent interpretive displays highlighting Banyjima culture and park wildlife, good maps and walks information, a public phone and really great air-con.

Getting There & Away

There's no public transport. The closest airports are at the mining towns of Paraburdoo (101km southwest) and Newman (201km southeast).

Integrity coaches stop at Munjina (Auski) on Thursday (northbound) and Friday (southbound). Munjina is the best place to score a lift.

Port Hedland

POP 16,000

Port Hedland ain't the prettiest place. Confronted by its railway yards, iron-ore stockpiles, salt mountains, furnaces and massive deepwater port, the average tourist might instinctively floor the accelerator. Yet Hedland is not just another bland prefab Pilbara town. With a heritage spanning over 115 years, it's been battered by cyclones, plundered by pearlers and bombed by the Japanese – it's even hosted royalty.

Iron ore plays a huge part in the town's fortunes, and Port Hedland is riding the current resources boom. While this pushes up prices and squeezes accommodation, it's also sparked a renaissance. Old pubs are being renovated, the art and cafe (real coffee!) scenes are expanding, fine dining is flourishing, cocktail and tapas bars are sprouting and cycle paths are spreading along the foreshore. Just don't mind the red dust.

Sights & Activities

Collect the excellent *Port Hedland Cultural & Heritage Sites* brochure from the visitor centre and take a self-guided tour around the CBD, or hire a bicycle and meander along the **Richardson Street Bike Path** to a cold beer at the **Yacht Club** (☎08-9173 1198; Sutherland St; ⏰Thu-Sun).

Between November and February **flatback turtles** nest on nearby beaches. Check at the visitor centre for volunteer options.

Goode St, near Pretty Pool, is handy to observe Port Hedland's **Staircase to the Moon**.

★**Courthouse Gallery** GALLERY
(☎08-9173 1064; www.courthousegallery.com.au; 16 Edgar St; ⏰9am-4pm Mon-Fri, to 2pm Sat & Sun) More than a gallery, this leafy arts HQ is the centre of all goodness in Hedland. Inside are stunning local contemporary and indigenous exhibitions while the shady surrounds host sporadic craft markets. If something is happening, these folks will know about it.

Marapikurrinya Park PARK
The visitor centre publishes shipping times for the ridiculously large tankers passing by. After dark, the park's **Finucane Lookout** provides a view into BHP Billiton's smouldering hot briquetted iron plant on Finucane Island. The park is situated at the end of Wedge St.

Pretty Pool FISHING, PICNIC SPOT
A popular fishing and picnicking spot (beware of venomous stonefish), 7km east of the town centre.

Tours

BHP Billiton IRON-ORE PLANT
(adult/child $26/20; ⏰9.30am Mon, Wed & Fri) This popular iron-ore plant tour departs from the visitor centre.

Sleeping & Eating

Finding a room in Hedland isn't easy or cheap – 80 Mile Beach or Point Samson are better options.

There are supermarkets, cafes and takeaways at both the **Boulevard** (cnr Wilson & McGregor Sts) and **South Hedland** (Throssell Rd) shopping centres or try the all-you-can-eat buffet at the **Esplanade Hotel** (☎08-9173 9700; www.theesplanadeporthedland.com.au; 2-4 Anderson St; d Fri-Sun from $295, Mon-Thu from $495; ⏰dinner from 6pm; ❄@📶).

OFF THE BEATEN TRACK

MARBLE BAR

Marble Bar, population 196 and a long way off everybody's beaten track, has burnt itself into the Australian psyche as the country's hottest town, when back in 1921 the mercury didn't dip below 37.8°C (100°F) for 161 consecutive days. The town is (mistakenly) named after a bar of jasper beside a pool on the Coongan River, 5km southwest.

Most days there's not much to do. You can pore over the minerals at the **Comet Gold Mine** (☎08-9176 1015; Hillside Rd; admission $3; ⏲9am-4pm), 8km out of town, or you can prop at the bar and have a yarn with Foxie at the **Ironclad Hotel** (☎08-9176 1066; 15 Francis St; d $120). This classic outback pub offers comfy motel rooms, decent meals and a welcome to budget travellers.

But come the first weekend in July, the town swells to 10 times its normal size for a weekend of drinking, gambling, fashion crime, country music, nudie runs and horse racing known as the **Marble Bar Cup**. The **caravan park** (☎08-9176 1569; 64 Contest St) overflows and the Ironclad is besieged as punters from far and wide come for a bit of outback knees-up.

The **shire office** (☎08-9176 1008) runs a weekly bus service to Port Hedland and Newman (via Nullagine) and provides tourist information. If you're heading south, the easiest route back to bitumen is the lonely but beautiful Hillside Rd.

Cooke Point Caravan Park CARAVAN PARK $$
(☎08-9173 1271; www.aspenparks.com.au; cnr Athol & Taylor Sts; powered sites $52, d without bathroom $150, unit d from $320; ❄📶🏊) You might be able to snag a dusty van or tent site here, but the other options are usually full. There's a nice view over the mangroves near Pretty Pool and the amenities are well maintained.

★ **Silver Star** CAFE $$
(☎0411 143 663; Edgar St; breakfast $12-18, lunch $18-24; ⏲8am-2pm daily, tapas from 6pm Fri & Sat) Possibly the coolest cafe in the Pilbara, this 1930s American Silver Star railcar sits next to the Courthouse Gallery and serves up decent coffee, brekkies and burgers in the original observation lounge. A tapas selection ($40 per head) is available Friday and Saturday evenings.

ℹ Information

Internet access is available at the visitor centre, the **library** (☎08-9158 9378; Dempster St; ⏲9am-5pm Mon-Fri, 10am-1pm Sat) and the **Seafarers Centre** (☎08-9173 1315; www.phseafarers.org; cnr Wedge & Wilson Sts; ⏲9am-9pm).

Visitor Centre (☎08-9173 1711; www.phvc.com.au; 13 Wedge St; ⏲9am-4pm Mon-Fri, 10am-2pm Sat) Newly refurbished, the centre sells bus tickets, publishes shipping times, arranges iron-ore plant tours, and helps with accommodation and turtle monitoring (November to February). Check here for bicycle hire.

ℹ Getting There & Away

Virgin and Qantas both fly to Perth daily; on Tuesday Qantas also flies direct to Brisbane and Melbourne, and Virgin flies to Broome on Sunday. Airnorth heads to Broome (Tuesday and Friday) with a Darwin connection, and Karratha (Friday).

Greyhound coaches run to Perth ($258, 26 hours) and Broome ($87, eight hours) three times weekly. Integrity departs Perth Wednesday using the quicker ($232, 22 hours) inland route via Newman, returning Friday. Both depart from the visitor centre and South Hedland shopping centre.

ℹ Getting Around

The airport is 13km from town; the **Airport Shuttle Service** (☎08-9173 4554; per person $22) meets every flight, while **Hedland Taxis** (☎08-9172 1010) charge around $35. **Hedland Bus Lines** (☎08-9172 1394) runs limited weekday services between Port Hedland and Cooke Point (via the visitor centre) and on to South Hedland ($3.50). **McLaren Hire** (☎08-9140 2200; www.rawhire.com.au) offers a large range of rental 4WDs. Rent scooters from **Port Hedland Scooter Hire** (☎0450 481 765; www.phsh.com.au; from $45 per day).

BROOME & THE KIMBERLEY

Australia's last frontier is a wild land of remote, spectacular scenery spread over huge distances, with a severe climate, a sparse population and minimal infrastructure. Larger than 75% of the world's countries, the Kimberley is hemmed by impenetrable coastline and unforgiving deserts. In between lie vast boab-studded spinifex plains, palm-fringed gorges, desolate mountains and magnificent waterfalls. Travelling here is a true adventure, and each dry season a steady flow of explorers search for the real outback along the legendary Gibb River Road.

Aboriginal culture runs deep across the region, from the Dampier Peninsula, where neat communities welcome travellers to country, to distant Mitchell Plateau, where ancient Wandjina and Gwion Gwion stand vigil over sacred waterholes.

Swashbuckling Broome, home to iconic Cable Beach, camel-tinged sunsets and amber-hued watering holes, and practical Kununurra, with its irrigation miracle, bookend the region.

Both are great places to unwind, find a job and meet other travellers.

Getting There & Around

AIR

The following airlines service the Kimberley:

Airnorth (☎1800 627 474; www.airnorth.com.au)

Qantas (☎13 13 13; www.qantas.com.au)

Virgin Australia (☎13 67 89; www.virginaustralia.com)

Skippers (☎1300 729 924; www.skippers.com.au) Flies between Broome, Derby, Halls Creek and Fitzroy Crossing.

Slingair (Heliwork; ☎1800 095 500; www.slingair.com.au) Runs helicopters and fixed-wing sightseeing tours across the Kimberley.

KIMBERLEY ART COOPERATIVES

Indigenous art of the Kimberley is unique. Encompassing powerful and strongly guarded Wandjina, prolific and puzzling Gwion Gwion (Bradshaws), bright tropical coastal x-rays, subtle and sombre bush ochres and topographical dots of the western desert, every work sings a story about country.

To experience it firsthand, visit some of these Aboriginal-owned cooperatives; most are accessible by 2WD:

Mowanjum Art & Culture Centre (☎08-9191 1008; www.mowanjumarts.com; Gibb River Rd, Derby; ⏲9am-5pm daily dry season, closed Sat & Sun wet season) Just 4km along the Gibb River Rd, Mowanjum artists recreate Wandjina and Gwion Gwion images in this incredible gallery shaped like their artwork.

Waringarri Aboriginal Arts Centre (p1022) This excellent Kununurra gallery-studio hosts local artists working with ochres in a unique abstract style. It also represents artists from Kalumburu.

Warmun Arts (☎08-9168 7496; www.warmunart.com; Great Northern Hwy, Warmun; ⏲9am-4pm Mon-Fri) Between Kununurra and Halls Creek, Warmun artists create beautiful works, using ochres to explore Gija identity. Phone first from Warmun Roadhouse for a verbal permit.

Laarri Gallery (p1021) This tiny not-for-profit gallery in the back of the community school has interesting contemporary-style art detailing local history. Laarri is 120km west of Halls Creek and 5km from the Great Northern Hwy. Be sure to phone ahead.

Mangkaja Arts (p1020) Fitzroy Crossing gallery where desert and river tribes interact producing unique acrylics, prints and baskets.

Yaruman Artists Centre (☎08-9168 8208; Kundat Djaru) Sitting on the edge of the Tanami, 162km from Halls Creek, Yaruman has acrylic works featuring the many local soaks (waterholes). The weekly mail run from Kununurra stops here (Ringer Soak).

Yarliyil Gallery (p1021) Great new Halls Creek gallery showcasing talented local artists as well as some of the Ringer Soak mob.

Warlayirti Artists Centre (☎08-9168 8960; www.balgoart.org.au; Balgo; ⏲9am-5pm) This centre 255km down the Tanami Track is a conduit for artists around the area and features bright acrylic dot-style as well as lithographs and glass. Phone first to arrange an entry permit.

The Kimberley

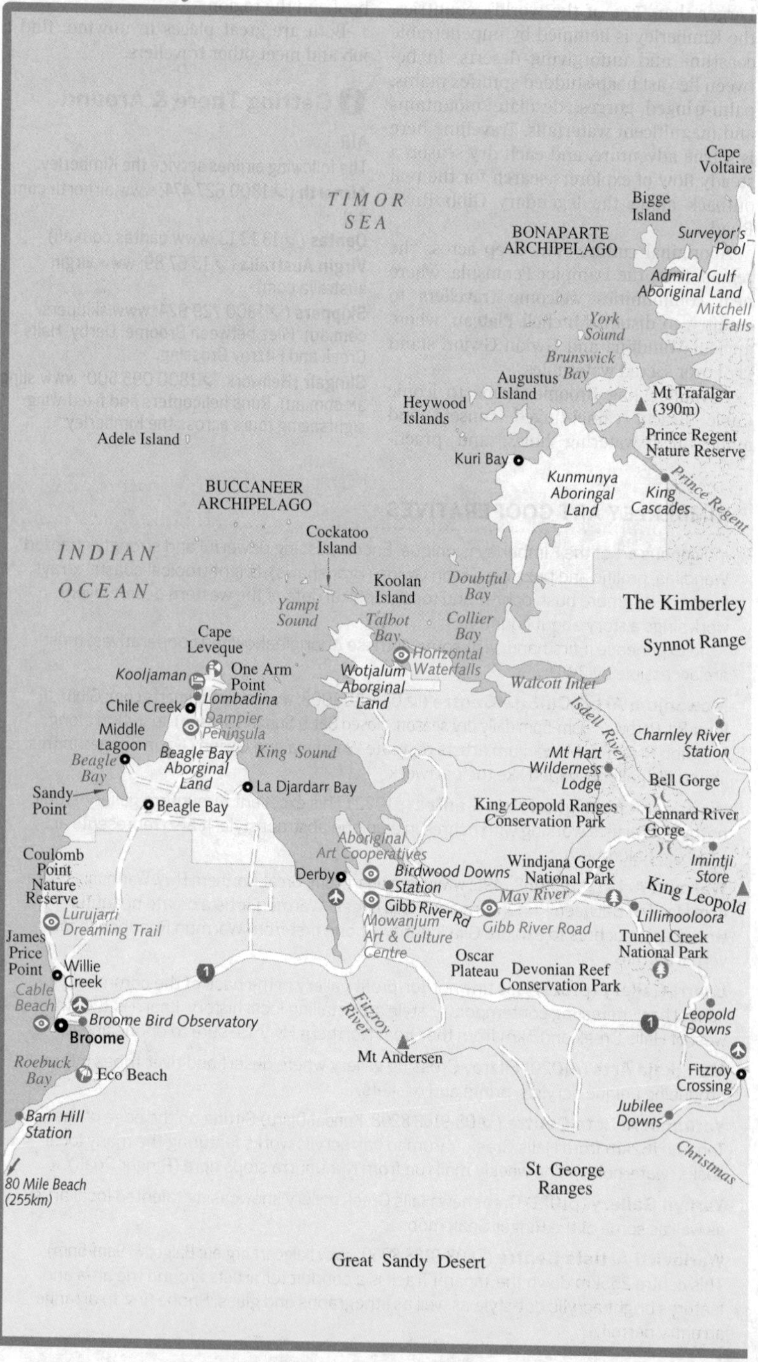
TIMOR SEA
INDIAN OCEAN
Cape Voltaire
Bigge Island
BONAPARTE ARCHIPELAGO
Surveyor's Pool
Admiral Gulf Aboriginal Land
Mitchell Falls
York Sound
Brunswick Bay
Augustus Island
Mt Trafalgar (390m)
Heywood Islands
Prince Regent Nature Reserve
Adele Island
Kuri Bay
Kunmunya Aboringal Land
King Cascades
Prince Regent
BUCCANEER ARCHIPELAGO
Cockatoo Island
Koolan Island
Doubtful Bay
The Kimberley
Yampi Sound
Talbot Bay
Collier Bay
Synnot Range
Cape Leveque
Horizontal Waterfalls
Kooljaman
One Arm Point
Wotjalum Aborginal Land
Walcott Inlet
Lombadina
Chile Creek
Dampier Peninsula
Isdell River
Charnley River Station
Middle Lagoon
Beagle Bay Aborginal Land
King Sound
Mt Hart Wilderness Lodge
Beagle Bay
La Djardarr Bay
Bell Gorge
Sandy Point
Beagle Bay
King Leopold Ranges Conservation Park
Lennard River Gorge
Aboriginal Art Cooperatives
Coulomb Point Nature Reserve
Derby
Birdwood Downs Station
Windjana Gorge National Park
Imintji Store
King Leopold
May River
Gibb River Rd
Lillimooloora
Lurujarri Dreaming Trail
Mowanjum Art & Culture Centre
Gibb River Road
Tunnel Creek National Park
James Price Point
Oscar Plateau
Devonian Reef Conservation Park
Willie Creek
1
Cable Beach
Fitzroy River
Leopold Downs
Broome Bird Observatory
Broome
1
Mt Andersen
Roebuck Bay
Eco Beach
Fitzroy Crossing
Barn Hill Station
Jubilee Downs
Christmas
80 Mile Beach (255km)
St George Ranges
Great Sandy Desert

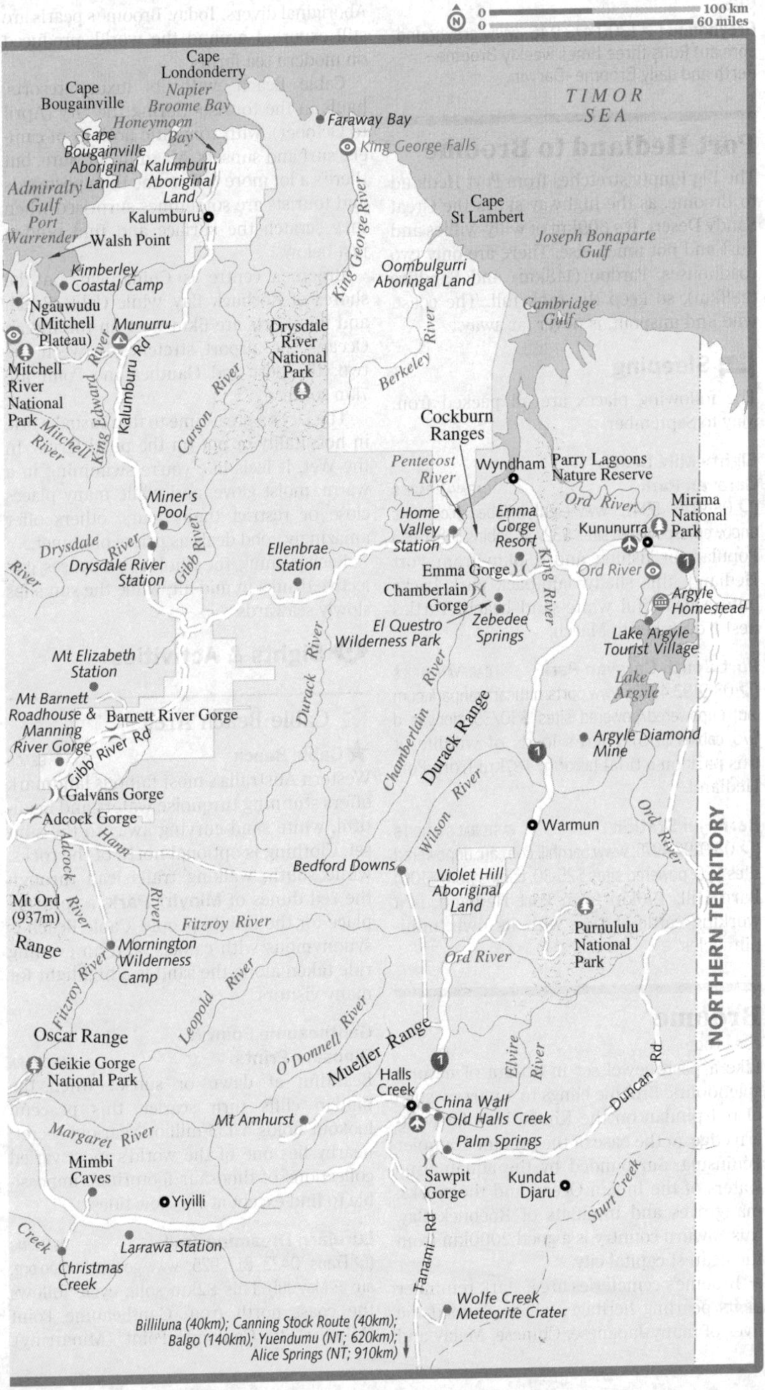

100 km
60 miles
TIMOR SEA
Cape Londonderry
Napier Broome Bay
Cape Bougainville
Honeymoon Bay
Cape Bougainville Aboriginal Land
Kalumburu Aboriginal Land
Admiralty Gulf
Port Warrender
Walsh Point
Kalumburu
Faraway Bay
King George Falls
King George River
Cape St Lambert
Joseph Bonaparte Gulf
Oombulgurri Aboringal Land
Cambridge Gulf
Kimberley Coastal Camp
Ngauwudu (Mitchell Plateau)
Munurru
Mitchell River National Park
Mitchell River
King Edward River
Kalumburu Rd
Carson River
Drysdale River National Park
Berkeley River
Cockburn Ranges
Pentecost River
Wyndham
Parry Lagoons Nature Reserve
Ord River
Mirima National Park
Kununurra
Home Valley Station
Emma Gorge Resort
Emma Gorge
King River
Ord River
Argyle Homestead
Miner's Pool
Gibb River
Drysdale River
Drysdale River Station
Ellenbrae Station
Chamberlain Gorge
El Questro Wilderness Park
Zebedee Springs
Lake Argyle Tourist Village
Lake Argyle
Mt Elizabeth Station
Durack River
Chamberlain River
Durack Range
Mt Barnett Roadhouse & Manning River Gorge
Barnett River Gorge
Gibb River Rd
Argyle Diamond Mine
Galvans Gorge
Adcock Gorge
Wilson River
Warmun
Ord River
Hann River
Adcock River
Bedford Downs
Violet Hill Aboriginal Land
NORTHERN TERRITORY
Mt Ord (937m)
Range
Fitzroy River
Mornington Wilderness Camp
Purnululu National Park
Ord River
Fitzroy River
Leopold River
Oscar Range
O'Donnell River
Mueller Range
Geikie Gorge National Park
Halls Creek
Elvire River
Duncan Rd
China Wall
Old Halls Creek
Mt Amhurst
Margaret River
Palm Springs
Mimbi Caves
Sawpit Gorge
Kundat Djaru
Yiyilli
Sturt Creek
Tanami Rd
Creek
Larrawa Station
Christmas Creek
Wolfe Creek Meteorite Crater
Billiluna (40km); Canning Stock Route (40km); Balgo (140km); Yuendumu (NT; 620km); Alice Springs (NT; 910km)

BUS

Greyhound (☎1300 473 946; www.greyhound.com.au) Runs three times weekly Broome–Perth and daily Broome–Darwin.

Port Hedland to Broome

The Big Empty stretches from Port Hedland to Broome, as the highway skirts the Great Sandy Desert. It's 609km of willy-willies and dust and not much else. There are only two roadhouses, Pardoo (148km) and Sandfire (288km), so keep the tank full. The coast, wild and unspoilt, is never far away.

Sleeping

The following places are all packed from May to September.

Eighty Mile Beach Caravan Park CARAVAN PARK $
(☎08-9176 5941; www.eightymilebeach.com.au; unpowered/powered sites $32/37, cabins $180;) Popular for fishing and 250km from Port Hedland, this shady, laid-back park backs onto a beautiful white-sand beach. Turtles nest November to March.

Port Smith Caravan Park CARAVAN PARK $
(☎08-9192 4983; www.portsmithcaravanpark.com.au; unpowered/powered sites $30/35, dongas d $75, cabins $175) There's loads of wildlife at this park on a tidal lagoon, 487km from Port Hedland.

Barn Hill Station PASTORAL STATION $
(☎08-9192 4975; www.barnhill.com.au; unpowered sites $20, powered sites $25-30, cabins from $100) Barn Hill, 490km from Port Hedland, is a working cattle station with its own 'mini-pinnacles'.

Broome

POP 16,000

Like a paste jewel set in a tiara of natural splendours, Broome clings to a narrow strip of red pindan on the Kimberley's far-western edge, at the base of the pristine Dampier Peninsula. Surrounded by the aquamarine waters of the Indian Ocean and the creeks, mangroves and mudflats of Roebuck Bay, this Yawuru country is a good 2000km from the nearest capital city.

Broome's cemeteries are a stark reminder of its pearling heritage, which claimed the lives of many Japanese, Chinese, Malay and Aboriginal divers. Today, Broome's pearls are still exported around the world, produced on modern sea farms.

Cable Beach, with its luxury resorts, hauls in the tourists during the Dry (April to October), with romantic notions of camels, surf and sunsets. Magnificent, sure, but there's a lot more to Broome than postcards and tourists are sometimes surprised when they scratch the surface and find pindan just below.

Broome's centre is Chinatown, on the shores of Roebuck Bay, while Cable Beach and its resorts are 6km west on the Indian Ocean. The airport stretches between the two; the port and Gantheaume Point are 7km south.

The Dry's a great time to find casual work, in hospitality or out on the pearl farms. In the Wet, it feels like you're swimming in a warm, moist glove, and while many places close or restrict their hours, others offer amazingly good deals as prices plummet.

Each evening, the whole town pauses, collective drinks in mid-air, while the sun slips slowly seawards.

Sights & Activities

Cable Beach Area

★**Cable Beach** BEACH
Western Australia's most famous landmark offers stunning turquoise waters and beautiful, white sand curving away to the sunset. Clothing is optional north of the rocks, while south, walking trails lead through the red dunes of **Minyirr Park**, a spiritual place for the Rubibi people. Cable Beach is synonymous with camels, and an evening ride taken along the sand is a highlight for many visitors.

Gantheaume Point & Dinosaur Prints LANDMARK
Beautiful at dawn or sunset when the pindan cliffs turn scarlet, this peaceful lookout holds a 135-million-year-old secret: nearby lies one of the world's most varied collections of dinosaur footprints, impossible to find except at very low tides.

Lurujarri Dreaming Trail WALKING
(☎Frans 0423 817 925; www.goolarabooloo.org.au; ⊙May-Jul) This 82km song cycle follows the coast north from Gantheaume Point (Minyirr) to Coulomb Point (Minarriny).

The Goolarabooloo organise a yearly guided nine-day trip ($1600), staying at traditional camp sites. Independent walkers should first check with the Goolarabooloo for route conditions as water is scarce.

Chinatown Area

A number of cemeteries testify to Broome's multicultural past; the most striking is the **Japanese Cemetery** (Frederick St), with 919 graves (mostly pearl divers), while **Chinese** (Frederick St) and **Muslim** (Frederick St) cemeteries are nearby. There's a **pioneer cemetery** by Town Beach overlooking the bay.

Town Beach is fine for a dip if it's not stinger season, and the **port** jetty is good for fishing and whale watching.

Sun Pictures HISTORIC BUILDING
(08-9192 1077; www.sunpictures.com.au; 27 Carnarvon St; adult/child $16.50/11.50, History Tours per person $5; History Tours 10.30am & 1pm Mon-Fri) Sink back in a canvas deckchair in the world's oldest operating picture gardens and enjoy the latest movies. The history of the Sun building is the history of Broome itself – don't miss the informative History Tours.

Broome Museum MUSEUM
(08-9192 2075; www.broomemuseum.org.au; 67 Robinson St; adult/child $5/1; 10am-4pm Mon-Fri, to 1pm Sat & Sun Jun-Sep, to 1pm daily Oct-May) Discover Cable Beach and Chinatown's origins as you examine pearling history and WWII bombing in this quirky museum.

★ **Short Street Gallery** GALLERY
(08-9192 2658; www.shortstgallery.com.au; 7 Short St; 10am-5pm Mon-Fri, to 2pm Sat) Broome's oldest gallery is now an art space, though several curated exhibitions still run each year.

Tours

Camels

It's a feisty business, but at last count there were three camel-tour operators running at Cable Beach offering similar trips.

Broome Camel Safaris CAMEL TOUR
(0419 916 101; www.broomecamelsafaris.com.au; 30min afternoon rides $25, 1hr sunset rides adult/child $70/55) Trips offered by Alison, the only female camel-tour operator in Broome.

Red Sun Camels CAMEL TOUR
(1800 184 488; www.redsuncamels.com.au; adult/child 40min morning rides $55/35, 1hr sunset rides $75/55) Red Sun runs both morning and sunset tours, with a shorter trip at 4pm (30 minutes $30).

Ships of the Desert CAMEL TOUR
(08-9192 2958; www.shipsofthedesert.com.au; adult/child 40min morning rides $50/30, 1hr sunset rides $70/50) The original camel tour company offers morning and sunset trips, and a shorter afternoon option (30 minutes $30).

Not Camels

There's a million options; see the visitor centre for the full selection.

Kujurta Buru INDIGENOUS CULTURE
(08-9192 1662; www.kujurtaburu.com.au; adult/child from $77/39; Tue, Thu & Sun) Nagula half-day tours explore Yawuru culture and country, including spear throwing and bush-tucker tasting.

Broome Adventure Company KAYAKING
(1300 665 888; www.broomeadventure.com.au; 3/4hr trips $70/90) Glide past turtles on these eco-certified coastal kayaking trips.

Kimberley Dreamtime Adventure Tours INDIGENOUS CULTURE
(0447 214 681; www.kimberleydreamtimeadventures.com.au; 1-/2-day cultural tours $299/492) Immerse yourself in Nyikina culture and learn bush skills on these amazing tours to Mt Andersen on the Fitzroy River. Longer tours and camel treks also available.

Kimberley Birdwatching BIRDWATCHING
(08-9192 1246; www.kimberleybirdwatching.com.au; 3/5/10hr tours $100/150/290) Join ornithologist George Swann on his Broome nature tours. Overnight trips also available.

Festivals & Events

Dates (and festivals!) vary from year to year. Check with the visitor centre and consult the community website (www.broome.wa.au).

Staircase to the Moon MOON
Three magical nights each month at full moon from March to October.

Gimme Fest MUSIC
(www.goolarri.comy) Showcasing the best of indigenous music in May.

Kullari NAIDOC Week INDIGENOUS CULTURE
(www.goolarri.com) Celebration of Aboriginal and Torres Strait Islander culture usually held late June or July.

Broome

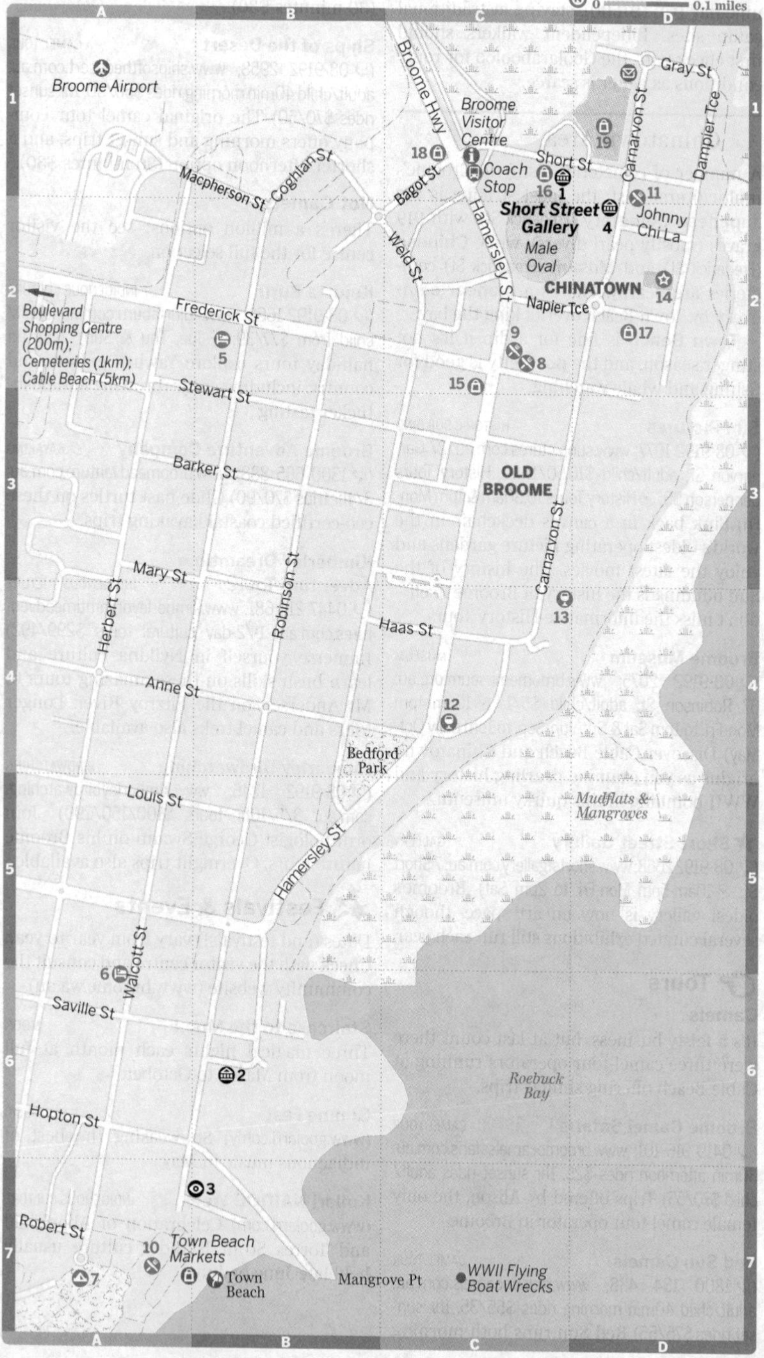
200 m
0.1 miles
Broome Airport
Macpherson St
Coghlan St
Broome Hwy
Bagot St
Weld St
Broome Visitor Centre
Coach Stop
Hamersley St
Short St
Short Street Gallery
Male Oval
Gray St
Carnarvon St
Dampier Tce
Johnny Chi La
CHINATOWN
Napier Tce
Boulevard Shopping Centre (200m); Cemeteries (1km); Cable Beach (5km)
Frederick St
Stewart St
Barker St
OLD BROOME
Mary St
Herbert St
Robinson St
Haas St
Anne St
Bedford Park
Louis St
Mudflats & Mangroves
Hamersley St
Walcott St
Saville St
Roebuck Bay
Hopton St
Robert St
Town Beach Markets
Town Beach
Mangrove Pt
WWII Flying Boat Wrecks

Broome

Top Sights

1 Short Street Gallery C1

Sights

2 Broome Museum B6
3 Pioneer Cemetery B7
4 Sun Pictures D2

Sleeping

5 Kimberley Klub B2
6 Old Broome Guesthouse A6
7 Roebuck Bay Caravan Park A7

Eating

8 Aarli C2
9 Noodlefish C2
10 Town Beach Cafe A7
11 Yuen Wing D1

Drinking & Nightlife

12 Matso's Broome Brewery C4
13 Tides Garden Bar C4

Entertainment

14 Roebuck Bay Hotel D2

Shopping

15 Courthouse Markets C2
16 Gecko Gallery C1
17 Kimberley Bookshop D2
18 Magabala Books C1
19 Paspaley Shopping Centre D1

Environs Annual Art Auction ART
(www.environskimberley.org.au) Environment fundraiser in July auctioning work by Kimberley artists.

Broome Race Round HORSE RACING
(www.broometurfclub.com.au) Kimberley Cup, Ladies Day and Broome Cup are when locals and tourists frock up and party hard. Race season runs over July and August.

Corrugated Lines WRITING
(http://broome.wa.au/events/corrugated-lines) Three-day festival of the written word in August.

Opera Under the Stars OPERA
(www.operaunderthestars.com.au) Opera alfresco, one night only at the Cable Beach Amphitheatre in August.

Shinju Matsuri Festival of the Pearl PEARLS
(www.shinjumatsuri.com.au) Broome's homage to the pearl includes a week of parades, food, art, concerts, fireworks and dragon boat races in late August or September.

Mango Festival MANGOES
A celebration of the fruit in all its forms, held on the last weekend in November.

Sleeping

Accommodation is plentiful, but either book ahead or be flexible. If you're a group, consider an apartment. Prices plummet in the Wet.

Kimberley Klub HOSTEL $
(☎08-9192 3233; www.kimberleyklub.com; 62 Frederick St; dm $26-33, d $95-135; ❄@📶🏊) Handy to the airport, this big, laid-back tropical backpackers is a great place to meet other travellers. Features include poolside bar, games room, massive kitchen, an excellent noticeboard and organised activities most nights.

Tarangau Caravan Park CARAVAN PARK $
(☎08-9193 5084; www.tarangaucaravanpark.com; 16 Millington Rd; unpowered/powered sites $34/42) A quieter alternative to often noisy Cable Beach caravan parks, Tarangau has pleasant grassy sites 1km from the beach, though at times it can be overly officious.

Cable Beach Backpackers HOSTEL $
(☎1800 655 011; www.cablebeachbackpackers.com; 12 Sanctuary Rd; dm $30, d $85; ❄@📶🏊) Within splashing distance of Cable Beach, this relaxed place has a lush tropical courtyard, swimming pool, big communal kitchen and bar.

Roebuck Bay Caravan Park CARAVAN PARK $
(☎08-9192 1366; www.roebuckbaycp.com.au; 91 Walcott St; unpowered sites $28-40, powered sites $37-50, on-site van d $90) Right next to Town Beach, this shady, popular park has several campsite options though sandflies can be menacing.

★ **Beaches of Broome** HOSTEL $$
(☎1300 881 031; www.beachesofbroome.com.au; 4 Sanctuary Rd, Cable Beach; dm $32-45, motel d $140-180; ❄@📶🏊) More resort than hostel; spotless, air-conditioned rooms are complemented by shady common areas, poolside bar and a modern self-catering kitchen. Dorms come in a variety of sizes, and the

motel rooms are beautifully appointed. Scooter hire available.

★ **Old Broome Guesthouse** BOUTIQUE $$$
(08-9192 6106; www.oldbroomeguesthouse.com.au; 64 Walcott St; s/d $265/285;) Exotically appointed rooms with a Southeast Asian aesthetic surround a shady common area and leafy pool. High ceilings, sunken baths, an immaculate common kitchen and drooping palms create a tropical Eden.

Bali Hai Resort & Spa SPA RESORT $$$
(08-9191 3100; www.balihairesort.com; 6 Murray Rd, Cable Beach; d $298-525;) Lush and tranquil, this beautiful small resort has gorgeously decorated studios and villas, each with individual outside dining areas and open-roofed bathrooms. The emphasis is on relaxation, and the on-site spa offers a range of exotic therapies. The off-season prices are a bargain.

Broome Beach Resort APARTMENTS $$$
(08-9158 3300; www.broomebeachresort.com; 4 Murray Rd, Cable Beach; 1-/2-/3-bedroom apt $300/340/375;) Great for families and groups. Large, modest apartments surround a central pool within easy walking distance of Cable Beach.

Eating

Be prepared for 'Broome prices' (exorbitant), 'Broome time' (when it should be open but it's closed) and surcharges: credit cards, public holidays, bad karma. Service can fluctuate wildly, as most staff are just passing through. Most places close in the Wet.

The back lanes of Chinatown, especially around **Johnny Chi Lane**, have cheap weekday lunch options. All pubs and resorts have in-house restaurants; some are good value, at others you're just paying for the view.

Self-caterers can enjoy well-stocked supermarkets and bakeries at Paspaley and Boulevard Shopping Centres and **Yuen Wing** (08-9192 1267; 19 Carnarvon St; 8.30am-5.30pm Mon-Fri, to 2pm Sat & Sun) Asian grocery.

Cable Beach General Store CAFE $
(08-9192 5572; www.cablebeachstore.com.au; cnr Cable Beach & Murray Rds; internet per hr $4; 6am-8.30pm;) Cable Beach unplugged – a typical Aussie corner shop with coffee, pancakes, barra burgers, pies, internet and no hidden charges. You can even play a round of **minigolf** (adult/child/family $7/5/20).

★ **12 Mile Cafe** CAFE $$
(08-9192 8552; 12milecafe@westnet.com.au; 53 Yamashita Rd, 12 Mile; mains $16-30; 8am-4pm Thu-Mon dry season, Sat & Sun wet season;) Out amongst the shady mango plantations of 12 Mile, Asian flavours are fused with local organic produce, sending vegoes to instant heaven, kids to smoothie and pikelet bliss and crusty old hippies to cake nirvana. Reduce, reuse, recycle...

★ **Aarli** TAPAS $$
(08-9192 5529; 2/6 Hamersley St, cnr Frederick St; tapas $13-19, pizzas $20, fish by weight; 8am-late dry season;) Meaning 'fish' in Bardi, the Aarli is cooking up some of the most inventive and tasty titbits in Broome. The Med-Asian fusion tapas are excellent with a cold beer or chilled wine, and the pizzas are simple and scrumptious, but, really, you want to share the signature baked whole fish because it is superb – just check the price first!

Noodlefish ASIAN $$
(08-9192 1697; 6 Hamersley St, cnr Frederick St; mains $21-36; 6-9pm Tue-Sat) This quirky alfresco BYO restaurant is doing fantastic contemporary Asian dishes using classic Kimberley ingredients. Get there early because you can't book; cash only.

Town Beach Cafe CAFE $$
(08-9193 5585; Robinson St; breakfast $11-20, lunch $18-24; 7.30am-2pm Tue-Sun, from 6pm Fri & Sat) With a great view over Roebuck Bay, the alfresco tables of the Town are an ideal spot for an early brekkie.

Wharf Restaurant SEAFOOD $$$
(08-9192 5800; Port of Pearls House, Port Dr; mains $20-42; 11am-11pm) Settle back for a long, lazy seafood lunch with waterside ambience and the chance of a whale sighting. OK, it's pricey but the wine's cold, the sea stunning and the chilli blue swimmer crab is sensational. Just wait until after 2pm before ordering oysters.

Drinking & Entertainment

Check the gig guide on www.broome.wa.au. Avoid wandering around late at night, alone and off your dial; it's not as safe as it may seem.

Tides Garden Bar BAR
(08-9192 1303; www.mangrovehotel.com.au; 47 Carnarvon St) The Mangrove Resort's casual outdoor bar is perfect for a few early bevvies while contemplating Roebuck Bay. Decent

bistro meals, half-price oysters (5.30pm to 6.30pm) and live music (Thursday to Sunday) complement excellent Staircase to the Moon viewing.

Sunset Bar & Grill BAR
(☎ 08-9192 0470; Cable Beach Club Resort, Cable Beach Rd) Arrive around 4.45pm, grab a front-row seat, order a drink and watch the show – backpackers, package tourists, locals, camels and a searing Indian Ocean sunset shaded by imported coconut palms.

Matso's Broome Brewery PUB
(☎ 08-9193 5811; www.matsos.com.au; 60 Hamersley St; ⊙ music 3-6pm Sun) Get a Smokey Bishop into you at this casual backpackers pub and kick back to live music on the verandah. Bring something for the sandflies.

Roebuck Bay Hotel LIVE MUSIC
(☎ 08-9192 1221; www.roebuckbayhotel.com.au; 45 Dampier Tce; ⊙ noon-late) Party central, the Roey's labyrinthine bars offer sports, live music, DJs, cocktails and wet T-shirts until the wee hours.

Diver's Tavern LIVE MUSIC
(☎ 08-9193 6066; www.diverstavern.com.au; Cable Beach Rd; ⊙ noon-midnight) Diver's pumps most nights. Don't miss Wednesday jams and the Sunday Session.

ZeeBar CLUB
(☎ 08-9193 6511; www.zeebar.com.au; 4 Sanctuary Rd; ⊙ 6pm-late) This stylish bar and bistro near Cable Beach mixes up tasty cocktails, great tapas and DJs. Tuesday is trivia night.

Shopping

The old tin shanties of Short St and Dampier Tce are chock-full of extraordinary indigenous art, beautiful, expensive jewellery and cheap, tacky souvenirs.

Gecko Gallery INDIGENOUS ART
(☎ 08-9192 8909; www.geckogallery.com.au; 9 Short St; ⊙ 10am-6pm Mon-Fri, to 2pm Sat & Sun dry season, shorter hours wet season) Gecko specialises in East Kimberley and Western Desert art, including canvases, prints and etchings.

Kimberley Bookshop BOOKS
(☎ 08-9192 1944; www.kimberleybookshop.com.au; 4 Napier Tce; ⊙ 9am-5pm Mon-Fri, 10am-2pm Sat) Extensive range of books on Broome and the Kimberley.

Kimberley Camping & Outback Supplies OUTDOOR EQUIPMENT
(☎ 08-9193 5909; www.kimberleycamping.com.au; cnr Frederick St & Cable Beach Rd) Camp ovens, jaffle irons and everything else you need for a successful expedition.

Magabala Books BOOKS
(☎ 08-9192 1991; www.magabala.com; 1 Bagot St; ⊙ 9am-4.30pm Mon-Fri) Indigenous publishers with selection of novels, social history, biographies and children's literature.

Courthouse Markets MARKET
(Hamersley St; ⊙ mornings Sat, plus Sun Apr-Oct) Local arts, crafts, music and hippy gear.

Information

The hostels, **Fongs** (29 Saville St) and Yuen Wing Asian grocery all have great noticeboards.

INTERNET ACCESS

Broome Community Resource Centre (CRC; ☎ 08-9193 7153; 40 Dampier Tce; per hr $5; ⊙ 9am-5pm Mon-Fri, to noon Sat; wi-fi) Cheap printing and wi-fi.

Galactica DMZ Internet Café (☎ 08-9192 5897; 4/2 Hamersley St; per hr $5; ⊙ 10am-8pm; wi-fi) The usual geek stuff; behind Macca's.

PERMITS

Department of Aboriginal Affairs (DAA; ☎ 1300 651 077; www.daa.wa.gov.au) Apply online for free permits to visit Aboriginal communities. Three-day processing time.

TOURIST INFORMATION

Broome Visitor Centre (☎ 08-9195 2200; www.broomevisitorcentre.com.au; Male Oval, Hamersley St; ⊙ 8.30am-5pm Mon-Fri, to 4.30pm Sat & Sun dry season, shorter hours wet season) On the roundabout entering town. Good info on road conditions, Staircase to the Moon, dinosaur footprints, WWII wrecks and tide times; can book most things.

USEFUL WEBSITES

Broome Community Website (www.broome.wa.au) Gig guide/what's on.

Chunes of Broome (www.chunesofbroome.com.au) Online Kimberley music and DVDs.

Environs Kimberley (www.environskimberley.org.au) Latest environmental issues and projects across the Kimberley.

Getting There & Away

Virgin and Qantas fly daily to Perth, and Qantas also has seasonal direct flights to eastern capitals. Airnorth flies daily to Darwin (except Saturday) and Kununurra, and to Karratha and Port Hedland twice weekly (on Tuesday and Friday). It also has a handy weekly connection to Bali (via Port Hedland). Skippers flies to Fitzroy Crossing, Halls Creek and Port Hedland four times weekly.

Greyhound buses leave the visitor centre daily for Darwin, and Tuesday, Thursday and Saturday for Perth. The local Derby bus (p1017) leaves on Monday, Wednesday and Friday. Broome is a popular destination for car pooling (www.findalift.com.au).

Getting Around

Town Bus Service (☎08-9193 6585; www.broomebus.com.au; adult/child $3.50/1.50, day pass $10) links Chinatown with Cable Beach every hour (7.10am to 6.23pm year-round), plus half-hourly (8.40am to 6.40pm) from May to mid-October. Under 16s ride free with an adult.

No rental-car company offers unlimited kilometres. Local operator **Broome Broome** (☎08-9192 2210; www.broomebroome.com.au; cars/4WDs/scooters from $63/153/40) has cars, 4WDs and scooters. **Britz** (☎08-9192 2647; www.britz.com; 10 Livingston St) hires campervans and 4WD Toyota Land Cruisers (from $176 per day) – essential for the Gibb River Rd.

Broome Cycles (www.broomecycles.com.au) has locations in **Chinatown** (☎08-9192 1871; 2 Hamersley St, Chinatown; per day/week $24/84, deposit $50; ⏲8.30am-5pm Mon-Fri, to 2pm Sat) and **Cable Beach** (☎0409 192 289; Old Crocodile Park car park, Cable Beach; ⏲9am-noon May-Oct).

For a taxi, try **Broome Taxis** (☎131 008) or **Chinatown Taxis** (☎1800 811 772).

Around Broome

Visitors enter through the jaws of a giant crocodile to the 30-hectare **Malcolm Douglas Wilderness Park** (☎08-9193 6580; www.malcolmdouglas.com.au; Broome Hwy; adult/child/family $35/25/95; ⏲2-5pm daily, from 10am dry season), 16km northeast of Broome. The park is home to dozens of crocs (feedings 3pm), as well as kangaroos, cassowaries, emus, dingos, jabirus and numerous birds.

On Roebuck Bay, 25km from Broome, the amazing **Broome Bird Observatory** (☎08-9193 5600; www.broomebirdobservatory.com; Crab Creek Rd; admission by donation, camping per person $15, dongas s/d $50/85, chalets $165; ⏲8am-5pm) is a vital staging post for hundreds of migratory species, some travelling over 12,000km. Tours range from an excellent two-hour walk ($75) to a five-day all-inclusive course ($1090). Self-guided trails, accommodation and binoculars are available. The dirt access road can close during the Wet.

Dampier Peninsula

Stretching north from Broome, the red pindan of the Dampier Peninsula ends abruptly above deserted beaches, secluded mangrove bays and cliffs burnished crimson by the setting sun. This country is home to thriving indigenous settlements of the Ngumbarl, Jabirr Jabirr, Nyul Nyul, Nimanburu, Bardi, Jawi and Goolarabooloo peoples.

Access is by 4WD, along the largely unsealed 215km-long Cape Leveque Rd. Visiting Aboriginal communities requires both a DAA (p1013) permit and one from the community (there are exceptions), payable at the office on arrival. Communities can close suddenly, so always book ahead from the Broome Visitor Centre (p1013; look for the booklet *Ardi – Dampier Peninsula Travellers Guide*). You should be self-sufficient, though limited supplies are available.

On Cape Leveque Rd, turn left after 14km onto Manari Rd, and head north along the spectacular coast. There are **bush camping sites** (no facilities) at Barred Creek, Quandong Point, James Price Point and Coulomb Point, where there is a **nature reserve**. Conventional vehicles should make it to **James Price Point**, the Kimberley's foremost environmental battleground, where there are plans to construct a large LNG facility. See it in its pristine state while you still can.

Back on Cape Leveque Rd, it's 110km to **Beagle Bay** (☎08-9192 4913), notable for the extraordinarily beautiful mother-of-pearl altar at Beagle Bay church, built by Pallottine monks in 1918. There's no accommodation, but fuel is available (weekdays only). Contact the office on arrival.

★**Middle Lagoon** (☎08-9192 4002; www.middlelagoon.com.au; unpowered/powered sites $30/40, beach shelter d $50, cabins d $140-240), 180km from Broome and surrounded by empty beaches, is superb for swimming, snorkelling, fishing and doing nothing. There's plenty of shade and bird life, and the cabins are great value, though the access road is terrible. Other options include quiet **Gnylmarung Retreat** (☎0429 411 241; www.gnylmarung.org.au; sites per person $20, bungalows from $90) and upmarket **Mercedes Cove** (☎08-9192 4687; www.mercedescove.com.au; eco tents/air-con cabins $150/300). Don't miss **Whale Song Cafe** (☎08-9192 4000; Munget; light meals $7-25, campsites per person $20; ⏲9am-3pm Jun-Aug; ☑) at nearby Munget, overlooking exquisite Pender Bay. This eco-cafe serves fabulous mango smoothies, lovingly made pizzas and the best coffee on the peninsula. There's a tiny bush campground with stunning views, a funky outdoor bathroom and not a caravan in sight.

Between Middle Lagoon and Cape Leveque, **Lombadina** (☎08-9192 4936; www.lombadina.com; entry per car $10, s/d $80/150, 4-person cabin $200-260; ⏰office 8am-noon & 1-4pm Mon-Fri), 200km from Broome, is a tree-fringed village offering various tours (requiring a minimum of three people) including fishing, whale watching, 4WD, mudcrabbing, kayaking and walking. Accommodation is in lodge-style rooms and self-contained cabins; there's no camping. Fuel is available weekdays and there are some lovely artefacts for sale at the Arts Centre.

Nearby, tiny **Chile Creek** (☎08-9192 4141; www.chilecreek.com; sites per person $16.50, bush bungalows $100, 4-person safari tents $185), 7km from Lombadina down a disintegrating track, offers basic bush camp sites, and modern en-suite safari tents and renovated bungalows, all just a short stroll to a lovely beach. Ask Roma if she's running her legendary cultural tours.

Cape Leveque is spectacular, with gorgeous white beaches and stunning red cliffs. Eco-tourism award-winner **Kooljaman** (☎08-9192 4970; www.kooljaman.com.au; entry per car $10, unpowered/powered sites d $38/43, dome tents $65, cabins with/without bathroom d $170/145, safari tents d $275; 📶) offers grassy camp sites, driftwood beach shelters, hilltop safari tents with superb views, and stuffy budget tents. There's a minimum two-night stay, and it is packed from June to October. The **restaurant** (☎08-9192 4970; mains $29-38, BBQ packs $22-26; ⏰11.30am-1.30pm & 6pm-late Apr-Oct) opens for lunch and dinner, or grab a takeaway BBQ pack.

If you prefer less bling, there are a couple of outstations offering camp sites between Cape Leveque and Ardiyooloon (One Arm Point). **Goombading** (☎0457 138 027; unpowered/powered sites per person $15/20), with a fantastic water view, is very relaxed, and hosts Unja and Jenny are keen to share Bardi culture, and offer spear-making, fishing and crabbing tours.

You can't camp at **Ardiyooloon** (One Arm Point; per person $10), but you can visit this neat community with a well-stocked store, fuel, a barramundi hatchery and great fishing and swimming with views of the Buccaneer Archipelago.

A handful of other outstations offer camping, fishing and crabbing opportunities.

Chomley's Tours (☎08-9192 6195; www.chomleystours.com.au; 1-/2-day tours $260/490) offers several day and overnight tours (including mudcrabbing) on the peninsula, as well as one-way transfers from Broome (from $110). **Kujurta Buru** (☎08-9192 1662; www.kujurtaburu.com.au) provides transport Sunday, Tuesday and Thursday from Broome to Beagle Bay ($95) and Lombadina, Kooljaman and Ardiyooloon (all $155), returning the same day.

Derby

POP 5000

Late at night while Derby sleeps, the boabs cut loose and wander around town, marauding mobs flailing their many limbs in battle against an army of giant, killer croc-people emerging from the encircling mudflats... If only.

There are crocs hiding in the mangroves, but you're more likely to see birds, over 200 different varieties, while the boabs are firmly rooted along the two main parallel drags, Loch and Clarendon Sts. Derby, sitting on King Sound, is the departure point for tours to the Horizontal Waterfalls and Buccaneer Archipelago, and the western terminus of the Gibb River Rd (GRR). It's also the West Kimberley's administrative centre, and the asylum-seeker detention facility situated at nearby RAAF Curtin brings in hordes of contractors.

Sights & Activities

The visitor centre's excellent town map lists every conceivable attraction.

★Norval Gallery — GALLERY

(Loch St; ⏰hours vary) Kimberley art legends Mark and Mary Norval have set up an exciting gallery-cafe in an old tin shed on the edge of town. Featuring striking artworks, exquisite jewellery, decent coffee and 5000 vinyl records (brought out on themed nights), any visit here is a delight to the senses.

Wharefinger Museum — MUSEUM

(admission by donation) Grab the key from the visitor centre and have a peek inside for atmospheric shipping and aviation displays.

Jetty — LANDMARK

Check out King Sound's colossal 11.5m tides from the circular jetty, 1km north of town, a popular fishing, crabbing, bird-spotting and staring-into-the-distance haunt. Yep, there are crocs in the mangroves.

Kimberley School of the Air SCHOOL
(Marmion St; admission $5) Fascinating look at how school is conducted over the radio for children on remote stations. Times vary, so check with the visitor centre first.

Bird Hide BIRDWATCHING
There's a bird hide in the wetlands (aka sewage ponds) at the end of Conway St.

Old Derby Gaol HISTORICAL BUILDING
(Loch St) Along with the **Boab Prison Tree** (7km south), this old jail is a sad reminder of man's inhumanity to man.

Joonjoo Botanical Trail WALKING
This 2.3km trail, opposite the GRR turn-off, has neat interpretive displays from the local Nyikina people.

Tours

The Horizontal Waterfalls are Derby's top draw and most cruises also include the natural splendours of remote King Sound and the Buccaneer Archipelago. There are many operators to choose from (see the visitor centre for a full list). Most tours only operate during peak season.

Horizontal Falls Seaplane Adventures SCENIC FLIGHT
(☎08-9192 1172; www.horizontalfallsadventures.com.au; 6hr tours from Derby/Broome $695/745) Flights to Horizontal Falls including a speedboat ride through the falls. Also has an overnight stay option (ex-Derby) for $845.

Bush Flight SCENIC FLIGHT
(☎08-9193 2680; www.bushflight.com.au; flights from $352) Horizontal Waterfalls and the Buccaneer Archipelago; you can look but not touch.

Derby Bus Service BUS TOUR, CAMPING
(West Kimberley Tours/Windjana Tours; ☎08-9193 1550; www.derbybus.com.au; day tours $150, camping tours per day from $200) The local bus company runs a full-day tour to Windjana Gorge and Tunnel Creek, and tailored two- to seven-day Kimberley camping trips.

Festivals & Events

Boab Festival MUSIC, CULTURE
(www.derbyboabfestival.org.au) Derby goes off in July with concerts, mud footy, horse and mudcrab races, poetry readings, art exhibitions and street parades. Try to catch the Long Table dinner out on the mudflats.

Sleeping & Eating

Any decent accommodation is normally full of contract workers. Try the visitor centre, but if you're heading to/from the Gibb River Road, consider stopping at Birdwood Downs Station (20km) instead.

There are several takeaways and cafes along Loch and Clarendon Sts.

Kimberley Entrance Caravan Park CARAVAN PARK $
(☎08-9193 1055; www.kimberleyentrancecaravanpark.com; 2 Rowan St; unpowered/powered sites $32/38) You'll always find room here, though not all sites are shaded. There's a nice outdoor area with tables, but expect lots of insects this close to the mudflats.

DON'T MISS

HORIZONTAL WATERFALLS

One of the most intriguing features of the Kimberley coastline is the phenomenon known as 'horizontal waterfalls'. Despite the name, the falls are simply tides gushing through narrow coastal gorges in the Buccaneer Archipelago, north of Derby. What creates such a spectacle are the huge tides, often varying up to 11m. The water flow reaches an astonishing 30 knots as it's forced through two narrow gaps 20m and 10m wide – resulting in a 'waterfall' reaching 4m in height.

Many tours leave Derby (and some from Broome) each Dry, by air, sea or a combination of both. It's become de rigueur to 'ride' the tide change through the gorge on a high-powered speedboat, but this is risky at best, and accidents have occurred. Scenic flights are the quickest and cheapest option, and some seaplanes will land and transfer passengers to a waiting speedboat for the adrenalin hit. If you prefer to be stirred, not shaken, then consider seeing the falls as part of a longer cruise through the archipelago. Book tours at Derby and Broome visitor centres.

Spinifex Hotel RESORT $$
(☎08-9191 1233; www.spinifexhotel.com.au; Clarendon St; dongas/motel r $160/250; ❄@≋) Rising phoenix-like from the ashes of the old Spini, this sleek new resort has corporate-class rooms (some with kitchenettes) and an on-site restaurant.

★**Desert Rose** B&B $$$
(☎08-9193 2813; 4 Marmion St; d $250; ≋) The best sleep in town is worth booking ahead for; spacious, individually styled rooms with a nice shady pool, leadlight windows and a sumptuous breakfast. Host Anne is a font of local information.

Boab Inn PUB $$
(☎08-9191 1044; www.derbyboabinn.com; Loch St; lunches $16-18, dinners $22-39, d $225; ❄📶) Excellent counter meals and free wi-fi make this the lunch stop of choice. The motel-style rooms are clean, comfortable and normally booked out.

Jila Gallery ITALIAN $$
(☎08-9193 2560; 18 Clarendon St; pizzas $19-25, mains $19-35; ⏰10am-2pm & 6pm-late Tue-Fri, 6pm-late Sat) Great wood-fired pizzas, shady alfresco dining and wonderful cakes are the highlights of this friendly trattoria.

Catch SEAFOOD $$
(☎08-9191 2664; meals $18-25; ⏰10am-9pm) Gloriously overlooking the jetty; the (mainly) seafood meals are quite reasonable, though quality can fluctuate. Takeaway also available.

ℹ Information

The supermarket and ATMs are on Loch and Clarendon Sts.

Derby Visitor Centre (☎1800 621 426; www.derbytourism.com.au; 30 Loch St; ⏰8.30am-5pm Mon-Fri, 9am-4pm Sat & Sun) Recently relocated, this super-helpful centre has the low-down on road conditions, accommodation, transport and tour bookings.

ℹ Getting There & Away

Virgin heads to Perth Monday to Friday. Skippers flies to Broome, Fitzroy Crossing and Halls Creek several times weekly. There's an **airport shuttle** (☎08-9193 2568; per person $30) to/from Curtin.

Greyhound buses to Darwin ($350, 25 hours) and Broome ($68, two hours) stop at the visitor centre. **Derby Bus Service** (☎08-9193 1550; www.derbybus.com.au; one way/return $50/80; ⏰Mon, Wed & Fri) runs services to Broome three times weekly, leaving early and returning the same day.

For a taxi, call ☎131 008.

Gibb River Road

Cutting a brown swath through the scorched heart of the Kimberley, the legendary Gibb River Road ('the Gibb' or GRR) provides one of Australia's wildest outback experiences. Stretching some 660km between Derby and Kununurra, the largely unpaved GRR is an endless sea of red dirt, big open skies and dramatic terrain. Rough, sometimes deeply corrugated, side roads lead to remote gorges, shady pools, distant waterfalls and million-acre cattle stations. Rain can close the road any time and permanently during the Wet. This is true wilderness with minimal services, so good planning and self-sufficiency are vital.

Several pastoral stations offer overnight accommodation from mid-April to late October; advance bookings are essential during the peak period of June to August. Hema Maps' *Kimberley Atlas & Guide* provides the best coverage, while visitor centres sell *The Gibb River & Kalumburu Road Guide* ($5).

A high-clearance 4WD (eg Toyota Land Cruiser) is mandatory, with two spare tyres, tools, emergency water (20L minimum) and several days' food in case of breakdown. Britz (p1014) in Broome is a reputable hire outfit. Fuel is limited and expensive, most mobile phones won't work, and temperatures can be life-threatening. Broome and Kununurra are best for supplies.

For just a sniff of outback adventure, try the 'tourist loop' along the GRR from Derby onto Fairfield Leopold Downs Rd to Windjana Gorge and Tunnel Creek National Parks, then exit onto the Great Northern Hwy near Fitzroy Crossing.

☞ Tours

Kimberley Wild Expeditions 4WD
(☎1300 738 870; www.kimberleywild.com.au) Consistent award winner. Tours from Broome range from one- ($250) to nine-day GRR ($2050).

Kimberley Adventure Tours 4WD
(☎1800 083 368; www.kimberleyadventures.com.au) Runs between Broome and Darwin including the GRR and Purnululu National Park ($1825, nine days).

Information

Check out www.gibbriverroad.net and www.kimberleyaustralia.com, and the Derby and Kununurra visitor centre sites.

For maps, take Hema's *Kimberley Atlas & Guide* ($35) or *Regional Map – The Kimberley* ($10).

Department of Environment & Conservation (DEC; www.dec.wa.gov.au) Park permits, camping fees, info. A Holiday Pass ($40) works out cheaper if visiting more than three parks in one month.

Mainroads Western Australia (MRWA; ☎138 138; www.mainroads.wa.gov.au; ⏲24hr) Highway and GRR conditions.

Shire of Derby/West Kimberley (☎08-9191 0999; www.sdwk.wa.gov.au) Information about side road conditions.

Shire of Wyndham/East Kimberley (☎08-9168 4100; www.swek.wa.gov.au) Kalumburu/Mitchell Falls road conditions.

Derby to Wyndham & Kununurra

The first 100km from Derby are sealed.

After only 4km, Mowanjum Art & Culture Centre, with its striking Wandjina and Gwion Gwion images, is well worth a stop. Nine kilometres further, 2000-hectare **Birdwood Downs Station** (☎08-9191 1275; www.birdwooddowns.com; camping $13, savannah huts per person incl breakfast & dinner $135) offers rustic savannah huts and dusty camping. WWOOFers are welcome and it's also the **Kimberley School of Horsemanship**, with lessons, riding camps and trail rides (two-hour sunset rides $99).

At the 40km mark, a rough track heads left 12km to several bush campsites on the **May River**. Windjana Gorge turn-off arrives at the 119km mark – your last chance to head back to the highway. The scenery improves after crossing the Lennard River into Napier Downs Station as the ancient **King Leopold** ranges loom straight ahead. Just after **Inglis Gap** is the turn-off (a rough 50km) to the remote **Mt Hart Wilderness Lodge** (☎08-9191 4645; sites per person $18, r per person incl dinner & breakfast $200; ⏲dry season) with grassy camp sites, pleasant gorges, swimming and fishing holes. Seven kilometres past the Mt Hart turn-off brings the narrow **Lennard River Gorge** (3km return walk).

March Fly Glen, at the 204km mark, despite its name, is a pleasant, shady picnic area ringed by pandanus. Don't miss stunning **Bell Gorge**, 29km down a rough track, with a picturesque waterfall and popular plunge pool; you can camp at **Silent Grove** (adult/child $11/2). Refuel (diesel only) and grab an ice cream at **Imintji Store** (☎08-9191 7471; ⏲7am-4.30pm dry season, shorter hours wet season), your last chance for supplies. Next door is **Over the Range Repairs** (☎08-9191 7887; ⏲8am-5pm dry season), where Neville is your best, if not only, hope of mechanical salvation on the whole Gibb.

Part of the Australian Wildlife Conservancy, the superb **Mornington Wilderness Camp** (☎08-9191 7406; www.awc.org.au; entry fee per vehicle $25, sites adult/child $17.50/8, safari tents incl full board s/d $315/540; ⏲Dry) is as remote as it gets, lying on the Fitzroy River, a very rough, incredibly scenic 95km drive south of the Gibb's 247km mark. Nearly 400,000 hectares are devoted to conserving the Kimberley's endangered fauna and there's excellent canoeing, birdwatching and bushwalking. Choose from shady camp sites or spacious, raised tents with verandahs. The bar and restaurant offers picnic hampers and the best cheese platter this side of Margaret River.

Just 4km past Mornington's turn-off is the entrance to historic **Charnley River Station** (☎08-9191 4646; www.charnleyriverstation.com; camp sites d $35, rondavels & guesthouse incl full board s/d $230/310, day visit $20) and its alluring gorges. Grassy camp sites come with hot showers, or you can opt for full board up at the homestead. Meals and home-grown vegies are available.

Beautiful **Galvans Gorge** with waterfall, swimming hole, rock wallabies and Wandjina art is the most accessible of all gorges, less than 1km from the road. Fuel up at **Mt Barnett Roadhouse** (☎08-9191 7007; ⏲8am-5pm), at the 300km point, and get your camping permit if choosing to stay at **Manning River Gorge** (per person $20), 7km behind the roadhouse. The campground is often full of travellers waiting for fuel but at least there's a good swimming hole and even hot showers. Better still are the free bush camp sites at **Barnett River Gorge**; turn off 29km from the roadhouse – they're several kilometres down a sandy track.

Further up the Gibb (at the 338km mark) is the turn-off to **Mt Elizabeth Station** (☎08-9191 4644; www.mountelizabethstation.com; sites per person $15, s/d incl breakfast & dinner $170/340; ⏲dry season), one of the few remaining private leaseholders in the Kimberley. Peter Lacy's 200,000-hectare property is a good base for exploring the nearby gorges, waterfalls and indigenous rock art – don't

WORTH A TRIP

MITCHELL PLATEAU & DRYSDALE RIVER

In the Dry, Kalumburu Rd is normally navigable as far as **Drysdale River Station** (☎08-9161 4326; www.drysdaleriver.com.au; sites $10-15, d $150; ⏲8am-5pm Apr-Dec), 59km from the Gibb River Road (GRR), where there is fuel, meals and accommodation, and you can check ongoing conditions. Scenic flights to Mitchell Falls operate April to September (from $400 per person).

The **Ngauwudu** (Mitchell Plateau) turn-off is 160km from the GRR, and within 6km a deep, rocky ford crosses the **King Edward River**, formidable early in the season. Another 2km brings pleasant, shady **Munurru Campground** (adult/child $7/2), with excellent nearby rock art. Many people prefer to camp here and visit Mitchell Falls as a day trip. From the Kalumburu Rd it's a rough 87km, past lookouts and forests of *livistona* palms to the dusty camping ground at **Mitchell River National Park** (entry per vehicle $11, camping adult/child $7/2).

Leave early if walking to **Mitchell Falls** (Punamii-unpuu). The easy trail (8.6km return) meanders through spinifex, woodlands and gorge country, dotted with Wandjina and Gwion Gwion rock-art sites, secluded waterholes, lizards, wallabies and brolga. The falls are stunning, whether trickling in the Dry or raging in the Wet (when only visible from the air). You can swim in the long pool above the falls, but swimming in the lower pools is strictly forbidden because of their cultural importance to the Wunambal people. Most people will complete the walk in three hours.

miss the 4WD tag-along tour ($50). Wallabies frequent the camp site, and the home-style three-course dinners ($45) hit the spot.

At 406km you reach the Kalumburu turn-off. Head right on the GRR, and pull into atmospheric **Ellenbrae Station** (☎08-9161 4325; sites per person $15, bungalow d $155) for fresh scones and quirky bungalows. The GRR continues through spectacular country, crossing the mighty Durack River and, at 579km, there are panoramic views of the Cockburn Ranges, Cambridge Gulf and Pentecost River.

The privations of the Gibb are left behind after pulling into amazing **Home Valley Station** (☎08-9161 4322; www.homevalley.com.au; sites adult/child $17/5, 4-person eco tents $190, homestead d from $250; ❄@📶🏊), an indigenous hospitality training resort with a superb range of luxurious accommodation. There are excellent grassy camp sites and motel-style rooms, a fantastic open bistro, tyre repairs and activities including trail rides, fishing and cattle mustering.

At 589km cross the infamous **Pentecost River** – take care as water levels are unpredictable and saltwater crocs lurk nearby. Slightly further is 400,000-hectare **El Questro Wilderness Park** (☎08-9169 1777; www.elquestro.com.au; 7-day park permit $20; ⏲dry season), a vast former cattle station with scenic gorges (Amelia, El Questro) and Zebedee thermal springs (mornings only). Boat tours explore **Chamberlain Gorge** (adult/child $64/34; ⏲3pm) or you can hire your own boat ($70). There are shady camp sites and air-con bungalows at **El Questro Station Township** (sites per person $20-25, bungalows d from $329; ❄) and also an outdoor bar and upmarket **steakhouse** (mains $28-42). There are a million activities to choose from, but you'll pay for most of them.

The rest of the GRR is now sealed. Ten kilometres along is El Questro's **Emma Gorge Resort** (safari cabin d from $289; ⏲dry season; 🏊), where a 40-minute walk reaches a sublime plunge pool and waterfall, one of the prettiest in the whole Kimberley. The resort has an open-air bar and restaurant, though the non-air-con cabins are stuffy and overpriced.

At 630km you cross King River and at 647km you finally hit the highway – turn left for Wyndham (48km) and right to get to Kununurra (53km).

Devonian Reef National Parks

Three national parks with three stunning gorges were once part of a western 'great barrier reef' in the Devonian era, 350 million years ago. Windjana Gorge and Tunnel Creek National Parks are accessed via Fairfield Leopold Downs Rd (linking the Great Northern Hwy with the Gibb River Rd), while Geikie Gorge National Park is just northeast of Fitzroy Crossing.

The walls of beautiful **Windjana Gorge** (per car $11) soar 100m above the Lennard River, which surges in the Wet but is a series of pools in the Dry. Scores of freshwater crocodiles lurk along the banks. Bring plenty of water for the 7km return walk from the **campground** (per person $10).

Sick of the sun? Then cool down underground at **Tunnel Creek** (per car $11, no camping), famous as the hideout of rebel Jandamarra, which cuts through a spur of the Napier Range for almost 1km. In the Dry, the full length is walkable by wading partly through knee-deep water; watch out for bats and take good footwear and a strong torch. Aboriginal paintings exist at both ends and a **tour** (☎08-9191 5355; www.bungoolee.com.au; 2hr adult/child $50/20) is available.

Not-to-be-missed, the magnificent **Geikie Gorge** (⊙Apr-Dec) is 22km north of Fitzroy Crossing. The self-guided trails are sandy and hot, but the **DEC** (☎08-9191 5121; 1hr tour adult/child $30/7.50; ⊙various cruises from 8am May-Oct) runs daily cruises. Local Bunuba guides introduce indigenous culture and bush tucker on the amazingly informative cruises run by **Darngku Heritage Tours** (☎0417 907 609; www.darngku.com.au; adult/child 2hr $65/55, 3hr $80/65, half-day $160/$128; ⊙Apr-Dec). A shorter one-hour cruise (adult/child $30/5) operates during the shoulder season (April and October to December).

Fitzroy Crossing to Halls Creek

Gooniyandi, Bunuba, Walmatjarri and Wangkajungka people populate the small settlement where the Great Northern Hwy crosses the mighty Fitzroy River. There's little reason to stay other than it's a good access point for the Devonian Reef national parks. Check out **Mangkaja Arts** (☎08-9191 5833; www.mangkaja.com; 8 Bell Rd , Fitzroy Crossing; ⊙11am-4pm Mon-Fri) with its unique acrylics, and **Dr Sawfish** (⊙8.30am-4.30pm Mon-Fri, shorter hours Sat & Sun), who makes exquisite glass and ceramics and is located next to the tyre guy. Camping and rooms are available at the atmospheric **Crossing Inn** (☎08-9191 5080; www.crossinginn.com.au; Skuthorpe Rd; unpowered/powered sites $26/30, r from $180; ❄@) and across the river at the upmarket **Fitzroy River Lodge** (☎08-9191 5141; www.fitzroyriverlodge.com.au; Great Northern Hwy; camping per person $15, tent d $155, motel d $199, meals $20-34; ❄@🛜≋), which also does decent counter meals. There's a new supermarket, and the **visitor centre** (☎08-9191 5355; www.sdwk.wa.gov.au; ⊙8.30am-4.30pm Mon-Fri year round, plus 9am-1pm Sat Dry) (and bus stop) is just off the highway.

One of the Kimberley's best-kept secrets is the vast subterranean labyrinth of **Mimbi Caves**, 90km southeast of Fitzroy Crossing. Located within Mt Pierre Station, on Gooniyandi land, the caves house a significant collection of Aboriginal rock art and some of the most impressive fish fossils in the southern hemisphere. Aboriginal-owned **Girloorloo Tours** (adult/child $80/40; ⊙Tue-Sat Apr-Sep) runs trips including an introduction to local Dreaming stories, bush tucker and traditional medicines. Book through Fitzroy Crossing or Halls Creek visitor centres.

Nearby **Larrawa Station** (☎08-9191 7025; Great Northern Hwy; sites $20, s with/without meals $120/70), halfway between Fitzroy Crossing and Halls Creek, makes a pleasant overnight stop, with hot showers, basic camp sites,

OFF THE BEATEN TRACK

KALUMBURU

The road to Kalumburu deteriorates quickly after the Mitchell Plateau turn-off and eventually becomes very rocky. You'll need a permit from the DAA (p1013) to visit Kalumburu and a visitors pass (valid for seven days) on entry from the **Kalumburu Aboriginal Community** (KAC; ☎08-9161 4300; www.kalumburu.org; per car $50). Kalumburu is a picturesque mission nestled beneath giant mango trees and coconut palms with two shops and **fuel** (⊙7.30-11.30am & 1.30-4.30pm Mon-Fri). Ask around if you need any repairs. There's some interesting rock art nearby, and the odd WWII bomber wreck. You can stay at the **Kalumburu Mission** (☎08-9161 4333; kalumburumission@bigpond.com; sites per person $20, dongas s/d $120/175), which has a small **museum** (admission $10; ⊙8.30-10.30am), or obtain a permit from the KAC office to camp at **Honeymoon Bay** (☎08-9161 4378) or **McGowan Island** (☎08-9161 4748; www.mcgowanisland.com.au), 20km further out on the coast – the end of the road. Alcohol is banned at Kalumburu.

WORTH A TRIP

PARRY LAGOONS NATURE RESERVE

This beautiful Ramsar-listed wetland, 15km from Wyndham, teems in the Wet with migratory birds arriving from as far away as Siberia. There's a bird hide and boardwalk at **Marlgu Billabong** (4WD) and an excellent view from **Telegraph Hill**. Back on the highway, steep steps lead down to the **Grotto**, a deep, peaceful pool in a small gorge, perfect for a quiet dip.

Surrounded by nature reserve, tranquil **Parry Creek Farm** (08-9161 1139; www.parrycreekfarm.com.au; unpowered/powered sites $34/37, r $125, cabins $210;), with grassy camp sites, attracts hordes of wildlife. Comfy rooms and air-con cabins are connected by a raised boardwalk above a billabong for easy bird-spotting. The licensed cafe serves excellent baked barramundi, wood-fired pizzas and other gourmet delights.

and shearers rooms. Another 30km towards Halls Creek brings **Yiyilli** with its **Laarri Gallery** (08-9191 7195; yiyilischool@activ8.net.au; 8am-4pm school days).

On the edge of the Great Sandy Desert, **Halls Creek** is a small town with communities of Kija, Jaru and Gooniyandi people. The excellent **visitor centre** (08-9168 6262; www.hallscreektourism.com.au; Great Northern Hwy; 8am-5pm) can book tours to the Bungles and tickets for Mimbi Caves. Check email next door at the **Community Resource Centre** (8.15am-3.45pm Mon-Fri). Across the highway, **Yarliyil Gallery** (08-9168 6723; www.yarliyil.com.au; Great Northern Hwy; 9am-4.30pm Mon-Fri) is definitely worth a look.

Kimberley Hotel (08-9168 6101; www.kimberleyhotel.com.au; Roberta Ave; r from $172, restaurant mains $16-42;) is your best lunch option and you can find a bed there or at **Best Western** (08-9168 9600; www.bestwestern.com.au; d $260;). There's a caravan park, but you're better off heading out of town.

Skippers flies from Fitzroy Crossing and Halls Creek to Broome and Greyhound passes through daily.

Wyndham

POP 900

A gold-rush town fallen on leaner times, Wyndham is scenically nestled between rugged hills and Cambridge Gulf, some 100km northwest of Kununurra. Sunsets are superb from the spectacular **Five Rivers Lookout** on Mt Bastion (325m) overlooking the King, Pentecost, Durack, Forrest and Ord Rivers entering Cambridge Gulf.

A giant 20m croc greets visitors entering town, but you might see the real thing if **Wyndham Crocodile Farm** (08-9161 1124; Barytes Rd; feeding time 11am) is open. The port precinct also contains a small **museum** (08-9161 1857; Old Courthouse; 10am-3pm daily dry season) and the **Wyndham Town Hotel** (08-9161 1202; O'Donnell St; d $143, meals $18-38;) with its legendary meals and overpriced rooms.

In town, **Five Rivers Cafe** (08-9161 2271; 12 Great Northern Hwy; meals $6-16; 6am-3pm Mon-Fri, from 7am Sat & Sun) serves up great coffee, breakfasts and barra burgers, while laid-back **Wyndham Caravan Park** (08-9161 1064; Baker St; unpowered/powered sites $25/30, dongas d $70;) offers grassy, shady camp sites.

Greyhound drops passengers 56km away at the Victoria Hwy junction. Internet is available at the **Telecentre** (CRC; 08-9161 1166; www.wyndham.crc.net.au; 26 Koojarra Rd; 8am-4pm Mon-Fri), and Tuesday/Wednesdays' mail-run flights might get you out to Kununurra. For a taxi, call 0408 898 638.

Kununurra

POP 6000

Kununurra, on Miriwoong country, is a relaxed town set in an oasis of lush farmland and tropical fruit and sandalwood plantations, thanks to the Ord River irrigation scheme. With good transport and communications, excellent services and well-stocked supermarkets, it's every traveller's favourite slice of civilisation between Broome and Darwin.

Kununurra is also the departure point for most of the tours in the East Kimberley, and with all that fruit, there's plenty of seasonal work. Note that there's a 90-minute time difference with the NT.

OFF THE BEATEN TRACK

DUNCAN ROAD

Snaking its way east from Halls Creek before eventually turning north and playing hide and seek with the Northern Territory (NT) border, Duncan Road is the Kimberley's 'other' great outback driving experience. Unsealed for its entire length (445km), it receives only a trickle of travellers compared to the Gibb River Road (GRR), but those who make the effort are rewarded with stunning scenery, beautiful gorges, tranquil billabongs and breathtakingly lonely camp sites.

Technically it's no harder than the Gibb, and while there are several creek and river crossings, the fords are concrete-lined and croc-free. It also makes a nice loop if you've come down the Great Northern Hwy to Purnululu and want to return to Kununurra and/or the NT. There are no services on the entire Duncan, so carry fuel for at least 500km and watch out for road trains. Enquire at Halls Creek or Kununurra visitor centres about road conditions.

Sights & Activities

Across the highway from the township, **Lily Creek Lagoon** is a mini-wetlands with amazing bird life, boating and freshwater crocs. **Lake Kununurra** (Diversion Dam) has pleasant picnic spots and great fishing. Groups could consider hiring their own 'barbie' boat from **Kununurra Self Drive Hire Boats** (☎0409 291 959; Lakeside Resort; per hr from $88).

Self-guided two- or three-day canoe trips run from Lake Argyle along the scenic **Ord River** to Kununurra, overnighting at designated riverside camp sites. Canoes, camping equipment and transport are provided, while you supply your own food and sleeping bag. You can choose to paddle the whole way back, bail out along the way, or take an extra day.

Don't miss the excellent **Waringarri Aboriginal Arts** (☎08-9168 2212; www.waringarri-arts.com.au; 16 Speargrass Rd; ⏰8.30am-4.30pm Mon-Fri, 10am-2pm Sat dry season, weekdays only wet season) centre on Speargrass Rd, opposite the road to **Kelly's Knob**, a popular sunset viewpoint.

Mirima National Park NATIONAL PARK
(per car $11) A stunning area of rugged sedimentary formations like a mini-Bungle Bungles. The eroded gorges of Hidden Valley are home to brittle red peaks, spinifex, boab trees and abundant wildlife. Several walking trails lead to lookouts, and early morning or dusk are the best times for sighting fauna.

Red Rock Art Gallery GALLERY
(☎08-9169 3000; 50 Coolibah Dr; ⏰10am-4pm Mon-Fri) If you're lucky, you might see Indigenous artists in action at this gallery showcasing ochres from the East Kimberley.

Kununurra Historical Society Museum MUSEUM
(Coolibah Dr; admission by gold-coin donation) Old photographs and newspaper articles document Kununurra's history, including the story of a wartime Wirraway aircraft crash and subsequent recovery mission. The museum is opposite the country club exit.

Big Waters CANOEING
(☎1800 650 580; www.bigwaters.com.au; 3 days $185) Self-guided overnight canoe trips on the Ord River.

Go Wild CANOEING, ADVENTURE SPORTS
(☎1300 663 369; www.gowild.com.au; 3-day canoe trips $180) Guide yourself down the Ord by canoe, or join a group caving ($200), abseiling (from $150) or bushwalking (from $40).

Tours

Kununurra Cruises CRUISE
(☎08-9168 1718; www.thebbqboat.com.au; adult/child $95/45) Popular sunset 'BBQ Dinner' cruises on Lily Creek Lagoon and the Ord River. BYO drinks.

Shoal Air SCENIC FLIGHTS
(☎08-9169 3554; www.shoalair.com.au; per person from $295) Various flights around the Bungles, Cambridge Gulf, Kalumburu and majestic Mitchell and King George Falls.

Triple J Tours CRUISE
(☎08-9168 2682; www.triplejtours.net.au; adult/child one-way $165/125, return $150/115) Triple J cruises along the 55km Ord River between Kununurra and Lake Argyle Dam.

Sleeping

There's a great variety of accommodation to choose from, and the more it costs, the more of a discount you'll get in the Wet. Watch out for mozzies if you're camping near the lake.

Hidden Valley Tourist Park   CARAVAN PARK $
(☑ 08-9168 1790; www.hiddenvalleytouristpark. com; 110 Weaber Plains Rd; unpowered/powered sites $24/30, cabin d $125; @ 🛜 🌊) Under the looming crags of Mirima National Park, this excellent little park has nice grassy sites and is popular with seasonal workers. The self-contained cabins are good value.

Kimberley Croc Backpackers   HOSTEL $
(☑ 1300 136 702; www.kimberleycroc.com.au; 120 Konkerberry Dr; dm $27-33, d $89-125; ❄ @ 🛜 🌊) This slick, modern YHA close to the action has a large pool and barbecue area and excellent kitchen facilities. It also runs the nearby **Kimberley Croc Lodge** (dm per week $160) for seasonal workers.

Freshwater   APARTMENTS $$
(☑ 1300 729 267; www.freshwaterapartments.net. au; 19 Victoria Hwy; studio/1-/2-/3-bedroom apts

---

DON'T MISS

PURNULULU NATIONAL PARK & BUNGLE BUNGLE RANGE

Looking like a packet of half-melted Jaffas, the World Heritage **Purnululu National Park** (per car $11; ☺ Apr-Dec) is home to the incredible ochre and black striped 'beehive' domes of the Bungle Bungle Range.

The distinctive rounded rock towers are made of sandstone and conglomerates moulded by rainfall over millions of years. Their stripes are the result of oxidised iron compounds and algae. To the local Kidja people, *purnululu* means sandstone, with Bungle Bungle possibly a corruption of 'bundle bundle', a common grass. Whitefellas only 'discovered' the range during the mid-1980s.

Over 3000 sq km of ancient country contains a wide array of wildlife, including more than 130 bird species. **Kungkalahayi Lookout** has a fine view of the range. Look for tiny bats high on the walls above palm-fringed **Echidna Chasm** (a one-hour return walk) in the north, but it's the southern area comprising aptly named **Cathedral Gorge** (a 45-minute return walk) that's most inspiring. Remote and pristine **Piccaninny Gorge** is best experienced as an overnight round trip (30km return); check with the park's visitor centre for details. The restricted gorges in the northern park can only be seen from the air.

Rangers are based here April to December and the park is closed outside this time. The turn-off is 53km south of Warmun and you'll need a high-clearance 4WD for the 52km twisting, unsealed road to the visitor centre. There are five deep, permanent creek crossings, so allow 2½ hours. **Kurrajong Camp Site** (☺ May-Sep) and **Walardi Camp Site** (☺ Apr-Dec) have fresh water and toilets (sites per person $11). Book campsites online via the **DEC** (www.dec.wa.gov.au/campgrounds), allowing at least 48 hours' notice. Alternatively, **Mabel Downs Station** (Bungle Bungle Caravan Park; ☑ 08-9168 7220; www.bunglebunglecaravanpark.com.au; tent/powered sites $30/45, safari tents with/without bathroom $225/120) offers camping just 1km from the highway (outside the park). Don't expect much privacy: tents are jammed between choppers and ridiculously long trailers.

Tours

Most Kimberley tour operators include Purnululu in multiday tours. You can also pick up tours at Warmun Roadhouse, Halls Creek and Mabel Downs. Helicopters will get you closer than fixed-wing flights.

East Kimberley (☑ 08-9168 2213; www.eastkimberleytours.com.au; tours from $180) Has a wide range of tours from both Kununurra and Warmun.

Sling Air (☑ 1800 095 500; www.slingair.com.au; 18/30/48min flights $225/299/495) Runs helicopter flights from Bellburn airstrip in the park, as well as fixed-wing flights from Warmun and Kununurra.

Bungle Bungle Expeditions (☑ 08-9168 7220; www.bunglebungleexpeditions.com.au; bus day/overnight $250/695, helicopter from $250) Various 4WD bus and helicopter tours run from the caravan park on Mabel Downs, near the highway.

WORTH A TRIP

LAKE ARGYLE

Enormous Lake Argyle, where barren red ridges plunge spectacularly into the deep blue water of the dammed Ord River, is Australia's second-largest reservoir. Holding the equivalent of 18 Sydney Harbours, it provides Kununurra with year-round irrigation, and important wildlife habitats for migratory waterbirds, freshwater crocodiles and isolated marsupial colonies.

You can drive across the dam wall, take a **boat tour** (08-9168 7687; www.lakeargyle-cruises.com; adult/child morning $70/45, afternoon $155/90, sunset $85/50) or just amble nearby. **Lake Argyle Village** (08-9168 7777; www.lakeargyle.com; Lake Argyle Rd; unpowered/powered sites $28/35, cabins $139-199, units from $299;) offers a range of accommodation and incredible views, especially from its **infinity pool**. Nearby, the original **Argyle Homestead** (08-9167 8088; adult/child $4/1; 8am-4pm Apr-Oct) has been turned into a museum.

$218/249/304/399;) Kununurra's newest rooms feature exquisite fully self-contained units with exotic open-roofed showers.

Lakeview Apartments APARTMENTS $$
(08-9168 0000; www.lakeviewapartments.net; 31 Victoria Hwy; 1-/2-/3-bedroom apt $230/280/380;) These spacious, self-contained apartments across from Lily Creek Lagoon have all mod cons, fully equipped kitchens, free wi-fi and cable. There's a weekend minimum two-night stay.

Eating

The big resorts all have restaurants offering similar dining experiences. There are two well-stocked supermarkets and several takeaways. Most places keep shorter hours during the Wet, and you'll struggle finding lunch after 2pm.

★**Wild Mango** CAFE $
(08-9169 2810; 20 Messmate Way; breakfasts $9-23, lunches $6-13; 7.30am-4pm Mon-Fri, 8am-1pm Sat & Sun;) The hippest, healthiest feed in town with curry wraps, mouth-watering pancakes, chai smoothies, real coffee, gelato and free wi-fi. The entrance is in Konkerberry Dr.

Ivanhoe Cafe CAFE $$
(0427 692 775; Ivanhoe Rd; mains $11-20; 8am-4pm Tue-Fri, to 2pm Sat & Sun;) Grab a table under the leafy mango trees and tuck into tasty wraps, salads and burgers, all made from fresh, local produce.

★**PumpHouse** MODERN AUSTRALIAN $$$
(08-9169 3222; www.ordpumphouse.com.au; Lakeview Dr; lunches $18-30, dinners $33-42; 11.45am-1.45pm & 6pm-late Wed-Fri, from 8am Sat & Sun, dinner only Tue;) Idyllically situated on Lake Kununurra, the PumpHouse creates succulent dishes featuring quality local ingredients. Watch the catfish swarm should a morsel slip off the verandah. Or just have a beer and watch the sunset. There's an excellent wine list and free wi-fi.

Shopping

Artlandish INDIGENOUS ART
(08-9168 1881; www.aboriginal-art-australia.com; cnr Papuana St & Konkerberry Dr; 9am-4.30pm Mon-Fri, to 1pm Sat) Stunning collection of Kimberley ochres and Western Desert acrylics to suit all price ranges.

Kununurra Markets MARKET
(Whitegum Park; 8am-noon Sat dry season) In the park opposite the visitor centre; stalls feature local crafts and produce.

Bush Camp Surplus OUTDOOR EQUIPMENT
(08-9168 1476; cnr Papuana St & Konkerberry Dr) The best camping gear between Broome and Darwin.

Information

There are ATMs near the supermarkets and a 24-hour laundromat at the **BP roadhouse.** (Messmate Way). Several cafes have free wi-fi; otherwise try the **library** (08-9169 1227; Mangaloo St; from 8am, Mon-Sat) or **CRC** (08-9169 1868; Coolibah Dr; per hr $6; 8am-5pm Mon-Fri, 9am-1pm Sat;).

DEC (www.dec.wa.gov.au; 08-9168 4200; Lot 248 Ivanhoe Rd; 8am-4.30pm Mon-Fri) Parks information and permits.

Visitor Centre (1800 586 868; www.visitkununurra.com; Coolibah Dr; 8.30am-4.30pm Mon-Fri, 9am-1pm Sat & Sun Apr-Oct, shorter hours Nov-Mar) Check here for accommodation, tours, seasonal work and road conditions.

Getting There & Around

Airnorth flies to Broome and Darwin daily, and to Perth on Saturday. Virgin departs for Perth Sunday through Friday, Broome thrice weekly and Darwin on Monday.

Greyhound has daily buses to Darwin ($191, 13 hours) and Broome ($237, 13 hours) that stop at the BP roadhouse. Destinations include Halls Creek ($86, four hours), Fitzroy Crossing ($181, seven hours), Derby ($212, 10 hours) and Katherine ($129, eight hours).

Avis (08-9168 1999), **Budget** (08-9168 2033) and **Thrifty** (1800 626 515) rental cars are available.

For a taxi, call 13 10 08.

The Tanami Road

With care and extra fuel, 2WD vehicles can normally make the desolate, corrugated 1000km shortcut to Alice Springs, though if you're freaking out by Wolfe Creek, turn around, as it doesn't get any better. See p870 for the full description.

Wolfe Creek Meteorite Crater

According to the local Jaru people, **Kandimalal**, as the crater is traditionally known, marks the spot where a huge rainbow serpent emerged from the ground. The crater (880m across and 60m deep) makes an impressive, if somewhat eerie site, and it's possible to walk down into the centre. **Camp sites** (per person $7) and toilets are provided, but no water, and it's 137km south along the Tanami – the final 23km are quite rough. **Northwest Regional Airlines** (08-9168 5211; www.northwestregional.com.au) offers 70-minute scenic flights from Halls Creek ($270 per person, minimum two people).

Understand Australia

Australia Today

Australia's identity, both geographic and cultural, has been forged by millennia of survival and isolation. Cut from the ancient Gondwanaland continent more than 45 million years ago, this harsh but beautiful landscape continues to survive voracious fires, desperate droughts and unbelievable floods. You'll find resilience too in the Australian people, hiding behind larrikin wit and amicable informality. The Australian economy has also proved robust in recent times, riding out the GFC on the back of a mining boom.

Best on Film

Lantana (director Ray Lawrence; 2001) Mystery for grown-ups: a meditation on love, truth and grief.
Gallipoli (director Peter Weir; 1981) Nationhood in the crucible of WWI.
Mad Max (director George Miller; 1979) Mel Gibson gets angry.
Two Hands (director Gregor Jordan; 1999) Vicious humour in Sydney's criminal underworld.
Ten Canoes (directors Rolf de Heer and Peter Djigirr; 2006) The first Australian film scripted entirely in Aboriginal language.

Best in Print

Dirt Music (Tim Winton; 2002) Guitar-strung Western Australian page-turner.
Oscar & Lucinda (Peter Carey; 1988) Man Booker Prize winner. How to relocate a glass church.
Montebello (Robert Drewe; 2012) Part memoir, part exposé of British nuclear tests in WA.
The Secret River (Kate Grenville; 2005) 19th-century convict life around Sydney.
Death of a River Guide (Richard Flanagan; 1997) The summative thoughts of man drowning in Tasmania.

Talk of the Town

The talk around the country is invariably about the weather, which seems to have gone haywire in recent years. Australia has always been a land of climatic extremes, but a barrage of significant recent events has upped the ante. A decade of drought – the shocking nadir of which were the 2009 'Black Saturday' bushfires in Victoria – came to an end in 2010 with mass flooding across eastern Australia. This continued into 2011 with yet more floods and the sweeping devastation brought by category-five Tropical Cyclone Yasi in Queensland (the same intensity as Hurricane Katrina, which devastated New Orleans in 2005). In 2013 southeast Queensland was again inundated, this time by the tail-end of Tropical Cyclone Oswald, which immersed Bundaberg and parts of Brisbane in river water once again. At the same time Tasmania was being ravaged by bushfires and drought was persisting across parts of Western Australia (WA). It's little wonder people are scratching their heads.

The political landscape is also heating up, with a federal election slated for September 2013. By the time you read this, Australians will have decided on another three years of the left-wing Labor party, or a new start with the right-wing Liberal-National Party Coalition. Internal factional struggles within the governing Labor party saw Julia Gillard lose the prime ministership in June 2013 to Kevin Rudd, whom she herself had ousted in 2010. Will Rudd be able to swing the national political mood back towards Labor and defeat Tony Abbott's conservatives in the election? Time will tell...

States of Mind

Of course, state by state, local issues dominate. In New South Wales (NSW) the limp state of the economy, transport system and general infrastructure is causing ructions. The state Labor government, in power since 1995, was ousted from office in 2011...but has Barry O'Farrell's right-wing Liberal stewardship done any better? Aside from mourning the demise of the kitsch-but-lovable Darling Harbour monorail in 2013, the mood on the street isn't grim. But Sydneysiders are longing for the good ol' days when their No 1 passion – real estate – carried them high on the hog.

Queensland is still wringing itself dry after the 2013 floods closed airports and broke the hearts of many residents who had just rebuilt after the 2011 disaster. His popularity seemingly already on the slide, new conservative premier Campbell Newman has his work cut out for him. His plans to abolish compulsory voting in Queensland and his decision not to introduce daylight savings are raising eyebrows around the country. Meanwhile, Brisbane and the Gold Coast continue to thrive.

In Victoria, conservative premier Ted Ballieu fell on his sword in 2013 after a protracted period of wavering leadership and debate over his bullish communication style. New state premier Denis Napthine has seen it all before – he was conservative leader way back in 2002. Back to the future for Victoria? Meanwhile, the start of the 2013 Australian Football League (AFL) season was marred by allegations of players using performance-enhancing drugs.

In Tasmania, green-minded organisations and government logging and hydro-electric authorities have been at each other's throats for decades. Trees or jobs? Jobs or trees? Can we have both? In 2010 a peace deal was struck between timber company Gunns and forestry conservation groups, resulting in a logging moratorium in Tasmania's native forests. But in 2012 the deal collapsed and Gunns went into voluntary administration. Other than predictably regular bushfires, the future of Tasmania's forests is uncertain, and the state economy continues to falter.

In South Australia (SA) – Australia's driest state – the lower lakes at the mouth of the Murray River have been revived by the effects of the big rains further north. The Murray provides much of Adelaide's drinking water: so confident is the state government of sustained future flows that a $1.8 billion desalination plant built to provide 50% of Adelaide's water has been mothballed. It seems the city's water supply is assured.

In the Northern Territory (NT), the Indigenous population continues its parlous existence. Substance abuse, domestic violence, suicide and infant mortality rates in Indigenous communities remain significantly higher than in the non-Indigenous realm. Here, Indigenous Australians can expect to live for around 10 years less than non-Indigenous Australians. Fuelled by natural-gas export dollars, Darwin is booming, with apartment towers going up apace. Despite a thriving desert arts scene, Alice Springs is feeling a little sad, with quite a few empty shopfronts on Todd St.

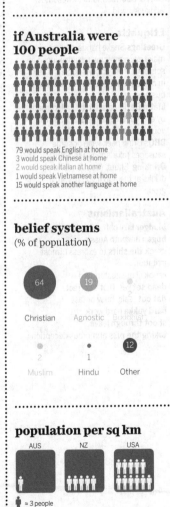

POPULATION: **23 MILLION**

AREA: **7,692,024 SQ KM**

GDP: **US$1.57 TRILLION**

GDP GROWTH: **3.3%**

INFLATION: **2.1%**

UNEMPLOYMENT: **5.2%**

if Australia were 100 people

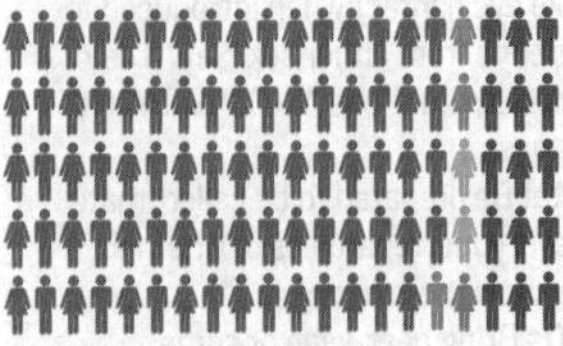

79 would speak English at home
3 would speak Chinese at home
2 would speak Italian at home
1 would speak Vietnamese at home
15 would speak another language at home

belief systems

(% of population)

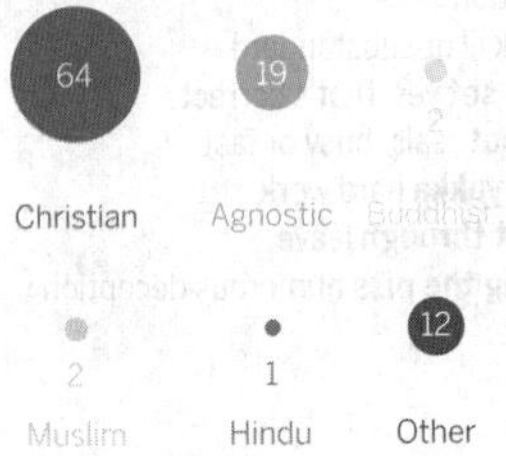

population per sq km

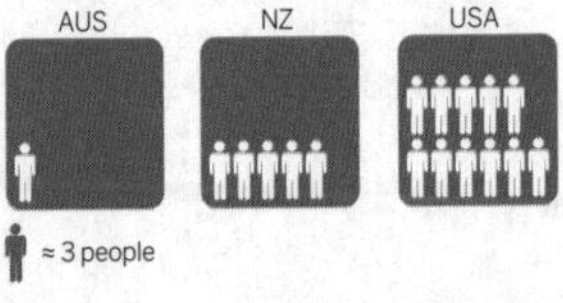

Aussie Bands On the Way Up

The Rubens Bluesy, croony and impossibly catchy: breakthrough track *Lay It Down*.

Boy & Bear Folk-rock Sydney songwriting brilliance.

San Cisco Sunlight-clear indie pop from Fremantle, WA.

Tame Impala Alternately heavy and trippy (both, at their best).

Wolf & Cub Yet another awesome Adelaide band.

Etiquette

Greetings Shake hands, smile and make eye contact when introduced to someone from either sex. Say 'G'day' in casual situations; 'Hello' or 'Hi' if it's business.

Mate! Be prepared to be called 'mate' by everyone, regardless of whether you know them or not.

BBQs Bring beer, wine or some sausages (aka 'snags') to a BBQ.

Drinking 'Shout' (buy) a round of drinks at the pub if you're with a group.

Australianisms

bludger lazy oaf

bogan uncouth Aussie

crack the shits to express utmost irritation

crook ill or substandard

dead set yes, that's correct

flat out really busy or fast

hard yakka hard work

shoot through leave

taking the piss humorous deception

WA is enigmatic: still bound by drought, but blessed with phenomenal mineral wealth that continues to put a rocket under the local (and national) economy. The average family income here is higher than everyone else's over east – to the tune of a carton of beer per week! This translates into oversized homes, shiny boats parked casually on front lawns, and brashly confident locals.

City Life

Australia is an urbanised country: around 90% of Australians live in cities and towns. Cities here are in a constant state of growth, reinvention and flux, absorbing fresh influences from far corners of the globe. The sense that the 'local' is inferior to the foreign – a phenomenon known as 'cultural cringe' – is less prevalent today than it was 30 years ago. Despite a poor Olympic showing in London in 2012, national pride is on the up, manifest in the urban arts and culinary scenes. Multiculturalism prevails and cities here remain distinct: Sydney is a luscious tart, Melbourne an arty glamour puss, Brisbane a blithe playmate, Adelaide a gracious dame and Perth a free spirit. Not to mention bookish Hobart, hedonistic Darwin and museum-fixated Canberra.

History

Michael Cathcart

Australia is an ancient continent – rocks here have been dated back beyond the Archean eon 3.8 billion years ago. Its Indigenous people have been here more than 50,000 years. Given this backdrop, 'history' as we describe it can seem somewhat fleeting...but it sure makes an interesting read!

From the days of struggling convict colonies dotted around the coastline, to inland exploration, gold rushes and independence from Great Britain, the new nation steadily found its feet. Wars in Europe and the Pacific, the Great Depression, and urban, industrial and cultural evolution defined the 20th century. It was during this recent period, more than any other, that the impact of modern Australia on both Australia's ancient landscape and its Indigenous people was thrown into stark relief.

Michael Cathcart teaches history at the Australian Centre, University of Melbourne. He is well known as a broadcaster on ABC Radio National and has presented history programs on ABC TV.

Intruders Arrive

By sunrise the storm had passed. Zachary Hicks was keeping sleepy watch on the British ship *Endeavour* when suddenly he was wide awake. He summoned his commander, James Cook, who climbed into the brisk morning air to a miraculous sight. Ahead of them lay an uncharted country of wooded hills and gentle valleys. It was 19 April 1770. In the coming days Cook began to draw the first European map of Australia's eastern coast. He was mapping the end of Aboriginal supremacy.

Two weeks later Cook led a party of men onto a narrow beach. As they waded ashore, two Aboriginal men stepped onto the sand and challenged the intruders with spears. Cook drove the men off with musket fire. For the rest of that week, the Aboriginal people and the intruders watched each other warily.

Cook's ship *Endeavour* was a floating annexe of London's leading scientific organisation, the Royal Society. The ship's gentlemen passengers included technical artists, scientists, an astronomer and a wealthy botanist named Joseph Banks. As Banks and his colleagues strode about the Indigenous Australians' territory, they were delighted by the mass of new

TIMELINE

80 million years ago

After separating from the prehistoric Gondwana landmass about 120 million years ago, Australia breaks free from Antarctica and heads north.

50,000 years ago

The earliest record of Aboriginal people inhabiting the land. The country is home to giant marsupials including a wombat the size of a rhinoceros, lush forests and teeming lakes.

1616

The Dutch trading route across the Indian Ocean to Indonesia utilises winds called 'the Roaring Forties'. These winds bring Captain Dirk Hartog to the Western Australian coast.

plants they collected. (The showy banksia flowers, which look like red, white or golden bottlebrushes, are named after Banks.)

The local Aboriginal people called the place Kurnell, but Cook gave it a foreign name: he called it 'Botany Bay'. The fertile eastern coastline of Australia is now festooned with Cook's place names – including Point Hicks, Hervey Bay (after an English admiral), Endeavour River and Point Solander (after one of the *Endeavour*'s scientists).

When the *Endeavour* reached the northern tip of Cape York, blue ocean opened up to the west. Cook and his men could smell the sea-route home. And on a small, hilly island ('Possession Island'), Cook raised the Union Jack. Amid volleys of gunfire, he claimed the eastern half of the continent for King George III.

Cook's intention was not to steal land from the Indigenous Australians. In fact he rather idealised them. 'They are far more happier than we Europeans', he wrote. 'They think themselves provided with all the necessaries of Life and that they have no superfluities.' At most, his patriotic ceremony was intended to contain the territorial ambitions of the French, and of the Dutch, who had visited and mapped much of the western and southern coast over the previous two centuries. Indeed, Cook knew the western half of Australia as 'New Holland'.

Members of the Palawa Aboriginal community in Tasmania are attempting to piece together a generic Tasmanian Aboriginal language called 'palawa kani', based on records of Indigenous languages on the island. The last native speaker of original Tasmanian language died in 1905.

Convict Beginnings

Eighteen years after Cook's arrival, in 1788, the English were back to stay. They arrived in a fleet of 11 ships, packed with supplies including weapons, tools, building materials and livestock. The ships also contained 751 convicts and around 250 soldiers, officials and their wives. This motley 'First Fleet' was under the command of a humane and diligent naval captain, Arthur Phillip. As his orders dictated, Phillip dropped anchor at Botany Bay. But the paradise that had so delighted Joseph Banks filled Phillip with dismay. The country was marshy, there was little healthy water, and the anchorage was exposed to wind and storm. So Phillip left his floating prison and embarked in a small boat to search for a better location. Just a short way up the coast his heart leapt as he sailed into the finest harbour in the world. There, in a small cove, in the idyllic lands of the Eora people, he established a British penal settlement. He renamed the place after the British Home Secretary, Lord Sydney.

The intruders set about clearing the trees and building shelters and were soon trying to grow crops. Phillip's official instructions urged him to colonise the land without doing violence to the local inhabitants, but they were shattered by the loss of their lands. Hundreds died of smallpox, and many of the survivors succumbed to alcoholism and despair.

In 1803 English officers established a second convict settlement in Van Diemen's Land (later called Tasmania). Soon, re-offenders filled the grim

David Unaipon (Ngarrindjeri; 1872–1967), the 'Australian Leonardo da Vinci', is remembered as an advocate for Indigenous culture, a writer and an inventor. He took out 19 provisional patents, including drawings for a pre-WWI, boomerang-inspired helicopter. His portrait is on the Australian $50 note.

1770

Captain James Cook is the first European to map the eastern coast, which he names 'New South Wales'. He returns to England having found an ideal place for settlement at 'Botany Bay'.

ANDREW HOLT / GETTY IMAGES ©

➡ Captain Cook statue, Sydney

1788

The First Fleet brings British convicts and officials to the lands of the Eora people, where Governor Arthur Phillip establishes a penal settlement. He calls it 'Sydney'.

1789

An epidemic of smallpox devastates the Aboriginal groups around Sydney. British officers report that Indigenous Australians' bodies are rotting in every bay of the harbour.

prison at Port Arthur on the beautiful and wild coast near Hobart. In time, others would endure the senseless agonies of Norfolk Island prison in the remote Pacific.

So miserable were these convict beginnings, that Australians long regarded them as a period of shame. But things have changed: today most white Australians are inclined to brag a little if they find a convict in their family tree. Indeed, Australians annually celebrate the arrival of the First Fleet at Sydney Cove on 26 January 1788 as 'Australia Day'. It's no surprise that Indigienous Australians refer to the day as 'Invasion Day'.

From Shackles to Freedom

At first, Sydney and the smaller colonies depended on supplies brought in by ship. Anxious to develop productive farms, the government granted land to soldiers, officers and settlers. After 30 years of trial and error, the farms began to flourish. The most irascible and ruthless of these new landholders was John Macarthur. Along with his spirited wife Elizabeth, Macarthur pioneered the breeding of merino sheep on his verdant property near Sydney.

Macarthur was also a leading member of the 'Rum Corps', a clique of powerful officers who bullied successive governors (including William Bligh of *Bounty* fame) and grew rich by controlling much of Sydney's trade, notably rum. But the Corps' racketeering was ended in 1810 by a tough new governor named Lachlan Macquarie. Macquarie laid out the major roads of modern-day Sydney, built some fine public buildings (many of which were designed by talented convict-architect Francis Greenway) and helped to lay the foundations for a more civil society.

Convict History Hot-Spots

- Port Arthur, Tasmania
- Parramatta, Sydney
- Rottnest Island, Western Australia
- Hyde Park Barracks, Sydney

BENNELONG

Among the Indigenous Australians Governor Philip used as intermediaries was an influential Eora man named Bennelong, who adopted many white customs and manners. After his initial capture, Bennelong learnt to speak and write English and became an interlocutor between his people and the British, both in Australia and on a trip to the United Kingdom in 1792; his 1796 letter to Mr and Mrs Philips is the first known text in English by an Indigenous Australian.

For many years after his return to Sydney, Bennelong lived in a hut built for him on the finger of land now known as Bennelong Point, the site of the Sydney Opera House. He led a clan of 100 people and advised then Governor Hunter. Although accounts suggest he was courageous, intelligent, feisty, funny and 'tender with children', in his later years Bennelong's health and temper were affected by alcohol. He was buried in the orchard of his friend, brewer James Squire, in 1813.

1804
In Van Diemen's Land (now called Tasmania), David Collins moves the fledgling convict colony from Risdon Cove to the site of modern Hobart.

1820s
In Van Diemen's Land, Aboriginal people and settlers clash in the Black Wars. The bloody conflict devastates the Aboriginal population. Only a few survive.

1829
Captain James Stirling heads a private company that founds the settlement of Perth on Australia's west coast. The surrounding land is arid, retarding development of the colony.

1835
John Batman sails from Van Diemen's Land to Port Phillip and negotiates a land deal with elders of the Kulin Nation. The settlement of Melbourne follows that same year.

By now, word was reaching England that Australia offered cheap land and plenty of work, and adventurous migrants took to the oceans in search of their fortunes. At the same time the British government continued to transport prisoners.

In 1825 a party of soldiers and convicts established a penal settlement in the territory of the Yuggera people, close to modern-day Brisbane. Before long this warm, fertile region was attracting free settlers, who were soon busy farming, grazing, logging and mining.

The website www.portarthur.org.au is a vital guide for visitors to this powerful historical site, with a tragic history spanning from the 1830s to the infamous 1996 massacre.

Two New Settlements: Melbourne & Adelaide

In the cooler grasslands of Tasmania, the sheep farmers were also thriving. In the 1820s they waged a bloody war against the island's Aboriginal people, driving them to the brink of extinction. Now these settlers were hungry for more land. In 1835 an ambitious young man named John Batman sailed to Port Phillip Bay on the mainland. On the banks of the Yarra River, he chose the location for Melbourne, famously announcing 'This is the place for a village'. Batman persuaded local Indigenous Australians to 'sell' him their traditional lands (a whopping 250,000 hectares) for a crate of blankets, knives and knick-knacks.

At the same time, a private British company settled Adelaide in South Australia (SA). Proud to have no links with convicts, these folks instituted a scheme under which their company sold land to settlers, and used the revenue to assist poor British labourers to emigrate. When these worthies earned enough to buy land from the company, that revenue would in turn pay the fare of another shipload of labourers. This theory collapsed in a welter of land speculation and bankruptcy, and in 1842 the South Australian Company yielded to government administration. By then miners had found deposits of silver, lead and copper at Burra, Kapunda and the Mt Lofty Ranges, and the settlement began to pay its way.

A brilliant biography of Cook is JC Beaglehole's *The Life of Captain James Cook* (1974). Beaglehole also edited Cook's journals. There are several biographies online, including the excellent www.en.wikipedia.org/wiki/james_cook.

The Search for Land Continues

Each year, settlers pushed deeper into Aboriginal territories in search of pasture and water for their stock. These men became known as squatters (because they 'squatted' on Aboriginal lands) and many held this territory with a gun. To bring order and regulation to the frontier, from the 1830s the governments permitted the squatters to stay on these 'Crown lands' for payment of a nominal rent. Aboriginal stories tell of white men slaughtering groups of Aboriginal people in reprisal for the killing of sheep or settlers. Later, across the country, people would also tell stories of black resistance leaders, including Yagan of Swan River, Pemulwuy of Sydney, and Jandamarra, the outlaw-hero of the Kimberley.

1836

Colonel William Light chooses the site for Adelaide on the banks of the River Torrens in the lands of the Kaurna people. Unlike Sydney, settlers here are free, willing immigrants.

1851

Prospectors find gold in central Victoria, triggering a great rush of youthful settlers from across the world. At the same time, the eastern colonies exchange the governor's rule for democracy.

1854

Angered by the hefty cost of licences, gold miners stage a protest at the Eureka Stockade near Ballarat. Several rebels are killed; others are charged with treason. Public opinion supports the rebels.

1861

The explorers Burke and Wills become the first Europeans to cross the continent from south to north. Their expedition is an expensive debacle that costs several lives, including their own.

In time, many of the squatters reached a compromise with local tribes. Indigenous Australians took low-paid jobs on sheep and cattle stations as drovers and domestics. In return they remained on their traditional lands, adapting their cultures to their changing circumstances. This arrangement continued in outback pastoral regions until after WWII.

The newcomers had fantasised about the wonders waiting to be discovered from the moment they arrived. Before explorers crossed the Blue Mountains west of Sydney in 1813, some credulous souls imagined that China lay on the other side. Then explorers, surveyors and scientists began trading theories about inland Australia. Most spoke of an Australian Mississippi. Others predicted desert. An obsessive explorer named Charles Sturt (there's a fine statue of him looking lost in Adelaide's Victoria Sq) believed in an almost mystical inland sea.

The explorers' expeditions inland were mostly journeys into disappointment. But Australians made heroes of explorers who died in the wilderness (Ludwig Leichhardt, and the duo of Burke and Wills, are the most striking examples). It was as though the Victorian era believed that a nation could not be born until its men had shed their blood in battle – even if that battle was with the land itself.

Best History Museums

Rocks Discovery Museum, Sydney

Western Australian Museum, Perth

Museum of Sydney

Commissariat Store, Brisbane

Gold & Rebellion

Transportation of convicts to eastern Australia ceased in the 1840s. This was just as well: in 1851 prospectors discovered gold in New South Wales (NSW) and central Victoria. The news hit the colonies with the force of a cyclone. Young men and some adventurous women from every social class headed for the diggings. Soon they were caught up in a great rush of prospectors, entertainers, publicans, sly-groggers (illicit liquor-sellers), prostitutes and quacks from overseas. In Victoria, the British governor was alarmed – both by the way the Victorian class system had been thrown into disarray, and by the need to finance law and order on the goldfields. His solution was to compel all miners to buy an expensive monthly licence, partly in the hope that the lower orders would return to their duties in town.

But the lure of gold was too great. In the reckless excitement of the goldfields, the miners initially endured the thuggish troopers who enforced the government licence. After three years, however, the easy gold at Ballarat was gone, and miners were toiling in deep, water-sodden shafts. They were now infuriated by a corrupt and brutal system of law which held them in contempt. Under the leadership of a charismatic Irishman named Peter Lalor, they raised their own flag, the Southern Cross, and swore to defend their rights and liberties. They armed themselves and gathered inside a rough stockade at Eureka, where they waited for the government to make its move.

Tasmania's Aboriginal people were separated from the mainland when sea levels rose after the last Ice Age. They subsequently developed their own utterly distinct languages and cultures.

1872

Engineer Charles Todd builds a telegraph line from Adelaide to Darwin. It joins an undersea cable to Java, linking Australia to Europe. The age of electronic information is born.

1880

Police capture the notorious bushranger Ned Kelly at the Victorian town of Glenrowan. Kelly is hanged as a criminal – and remembered by the people as a folk hero.

1895

Publication of AB 'Banjo' Paterson's ballad *The Man from Snowy River*. Paterson and his rival Henry Lawson lead the literary movement that creates the legend of the Australian bush.

1901

The Australian colonies form a federation of states. The federal parliament sits in Melbourne, where it passes the Immigration Restriction Act – the 'White Australia policy'.

In the predawn of Sunday, 3 December 1854, a force of troopers attacked the stockade. It was all over in 15 terrifying minutes. The brutal and one-sided battle claimed the lives of 30 miners and five soldiers. But democracy was in the air and public opinion sided with the miners. When 13 of the rebels were tried for their lives, Melbourne juries set them free. Many Australians have found a kind of splendour in these events: the story of the Eureka Stockade is often told as a battle for nationhood and democracy – again illustrating the notion that any 'true' nation must be born out of blood. But these killings were tragically unnecessary. The eastern colonies were already in the process of establishing democratic parliaments, with the full support of the British authorities. In the 1880s Peter Lalor himself became speaker of the Victorian parliament.

In remote parts of Australia, and in centres like Alice Springs and Darwin, many Aboriginal people still speak their traditional languages rather than English. Many people are multilingual – there were once over 300 Aboriginal language groups on mainland Australia.

The gold rush had also attracted boatloads of prospectors from China. These Asians sometimes endured serious hostility from whites, and were the victims of ugly race riots on the goldfields at Lambing Flat (now called Young) in NSW in 1860–61. Chinese precincts soon developed in the backstreets of Sydney and Melbourne, and popular literature indulged in tales of Chinese opium dens, dingy gambling parlours and brothels. But many Chinese went on to establish themselves in business and, particularly, in market gardening. Today the busy Chinatowns of the capital cities and the presence of Chinese restaurants in towns across the country are reminders of the vigorous role of the Chinese in Australia since the 1850s.

Gold and wool brought immense investment and gusto to Melbourne and Sydney. By the 1880s they were stylish modern cities, with gaslights in the streets, railways, electricity and that great new invention, the telegraph. In fact, the southern capital became known as 'Marvellous Melbourne', so opulent were its theatres, hotels, galleries and fashions. But the economy was overheating. Many politicians and speculators were engaged in corrupt land deals, while investors poured money into wild and fanciful ventures. It could not last.

The hard-fought biennial 'Ashes' Test cricket series between Australia and England has been played since 1882. Despite long periods of dominance by both sides, the ledger stands at 31 series wins to Australia, 30 to England. Tell us what happens in 2013.

Meanwhile, in the West...

Western Australia (WA) lagged behind the eastern colonies by about 50 years. Though Perth was settled by genteel colonists back in 1829, their material progress was handicapped by isolation, Aboriginal resistance and the arid climate. It was not until the 1880s that the discovery of remote goldfields promised to gild the fortunes of the isolated colony. At the time, the west was just entering its own period of self-government, and its first premier was a forceful, weather-beaten explorer named John Forrest. He saw that the mining industry would fail if the government did not provide a first-class harbour, efficient railways and reliable water supplies. Ignoring the threats of private contractors, he appointed

1915

On 25 April the Australian and New Zealand Army Corps (the Anzacs) joins an ambitious British attempt to invade Turkey. The ensuing military disaster at Gallipoli spawns a nationalist legend.

PHILLIP HAYSON / GETTY IMAGES ©

➡ Anzac Bridge, Sydney

1919

Australian aviators Ross and Keith Smith become national heroes after they fly their Vickers Vimy biplane from England to Australia. Both receive knighthoods for their efforts.

1932

NSW firebrand premier Jack Lang is upstaged when a right-wing activist named Francis de Groot, wearing military uniform and riding a horse, cuts the ribbon to open the Sydney Harbour Bridge.

the brilliant engineer CY O'Connor to design and build each of these as government projects.

Growing Nationalism

By the end of the 19th century, Australian nationalists tended to idealise 'the bush' and its people. The great forum for this 'bush nationalism' was the massively popular *Bulletin* magazine. Its politics were egalitarian, democratic and republican, and its pages were filled with humour and sentiment about daily life, written by a swag of writers, most notably Henry Lawson and AB 'Banjo' Paterson.

The 1890s were also a time of great trauma. As the speculative boom came crashing down, unemployment and hunger dealt cruelly with working-class families in the eastern states. However, Australian workers had developed a fierce sense that they were entitled to share in the country's prosperity. As the depression deepened, trade unions became more militant in their defence of workers' rights. At the same time, activists intent on winning legal reform established the Australian Labor Party (ALP).

Nationhood

On 1 January 1901 Australia became a federation. When the bewhiskered members of the new national parliament met in Melbourne, their first aim was to protect the identity and values of a European Australia from an influx of Asians and Pacific Islanders. Their solution was a law which became known as the White Australia policy. It became a racial tenet of faith in Australia for the next 70 years.

For whites who lived inside the charmed circle of citizenship, this was to be a model society, nestled in the skirts of the British Empire. Just one year later, white women won the right to vote in federal elections. In a series of radical innovations, the government introduced a broad social welfare scheme and it protected Australian wage levels with import tariffs. Its radical mixture of capitalist dynamism and socialist compassion became known as the 'Australian settlement'.

Meanwhile, most Australians lived on the coastal 'edge' of the continent. So forbidding was the arid, desolate inland that they called the great dry Lake Eyre 'the Dead Heart' of the country. It was a grim image – as if the heart muscle, which should pump the water of life through inland Australia, was dead. But one prime minister in particular, the dapper Alfred Deakin, dismissed such talk. He led the 'boosters' who were determined to triumph over this tyranny of the climate. Even before Federation, in the 1880s, Deakin championed irrigated farming on the Murray River at Mildura. Soon the district was green with grapevines and orchards.

Two very different, intelligent introductions to Australian history are Stuart Macintyre's *A Concise History of Australia* and Geoffrey Blainey's *A Shorter History of Australia*.

1936

The last captive Thylacine (aka Tasmanian Tiger) dies in a Hobart zoo. It's possible thylacines survived in the wild until the 1960s, but extensive searches have failed to deliver credible evidence.

1939

Prime Minister Robert Menzies announces that Britain has gone to war with Hitler's Germany and that 'as a result, Australia is also at war'.

1941

The Japanese attack Pearl Harbor and sweep through Southeast Asia. Australia discovers that it has been abandoned by traditional ally Britain. Instead, it welcomes US forces, based in Australia.

1945

The war ends. Australia adopts a new slogan, 'Populate or Perish'. Over the next 30 years more than two million immigrants arrive. One-third are British.

Entering the World Stage

Living on the edge of a dry and forbidding land, and isolated from the rest of the world, most Australians took comfort in the knowledge that they were a dominion of the British Empire. When war broke out in Europe in 1914, thousands of Australian men rallied to the Empire's call. They had their first taste of death on 25 April 1915, when the Australian and New Zealand Army Corps (the Anzacs) joined thousands of British and French troops in an assault on the Gallipoli Peninsula in Turkey. It was eight months before the British commanders acknowledged that the tactic had failed. By then 8141 young Australians were dead. Before long the Australian Imperial Force was fighting in the killing fields of Europe. By the time the war ended, 60,000 Australian men had died. Ever since, on 25 April, Australians have gathered at war memorials around the country for the sad and solemn services of Anzac Day.

The most accessible version of the Anzac legend is Peter Weir's Australian epic film *Gallipoli* (1981), with a cast that includes a fresh-faced Mel Gibson.

In the 1920s Australia embarked on a decade of chaotic change. Cars began to rival horses on the highway. In the new cinemas, young Australians enjoyed American movies. In an atmosphere of sexual freedom not equalled until the 1960s, young people partied and danced to American jazz. At the same time, popular enthusiasm for the British Empire grew more intense – as if imperial fervour were an antidote to grief. As radicals and reactionaries clashed, Australia careered wildly through the 1920s until it collapsed into the abyss of the Great Depression in 1929. World prices for wheat and wool plunged. Unemployment brought its shame and misery to one in three households. Once again working people experienced the cruelty of a system which treated them as expendable. For those who were wealthy – or who had jobs – the Depression was hardly noticed. In fact, the extreme deflation of the economy actually meant that the purchasing power of their wages was enhanced.

The year 1932 saw accusations of treachery on the cricket field. The English team, under their captain Douglas Jardine, employed a violent

PHAR LAP'S LAST LAP

In the midst of the Depression-era hardship, sport brought escape to Australians in love with games and gambling. A powerful chestnut horse called Phar Lap won race after race, culminating in an effortless and graceful victory in the 1930 Melbourne Cup (this annual event is still known as 'the race that stops a nation'). In 1932 the great horse travelled to the racetracks of America, where he mysteriously died. In Australia, the gossips insisted that the horse had been poisoned by envious Americans. And the legend grew of a sporting hero cut down in his prime. Phar Lap was stuffed and is a revered exhibit at the Melbourne Museum; his skeleton has been returned to his birthplace, New Zealand.

1948

Cricketer Don Bradman retires with an unsurpassed test average of 99.94 runs. South African batsman Graeme Pollock is next in line, having retired in 1970 with a relatively paltry average of 60.97.

1956

The Olympic Games are held in Melbourne. The Olympic flame is lit by running champion Ron Clarke, and Australia finishes third on the medal tally with an impressive 13 golds.

1965

Prime Minister Menzies commits Australian troops to the American war in Vietnam, and divides the nation. A total of 426 Australians were killed in action, with a further 2940 wounded.

1967

White Australians vote to grant citizenship to Indigenous Australians. The words 'other than the aboriginal race in any State' are removed from citizenship qualifications in the Australian Constitution.

new bowling tactic known as 'bodyline'. The aim was to unnerve Australia's star batsman, the devastatingly efficient Donald Bradman. The bitterness of the tour provoked a diplomatic crisis with Britain, and became part of Australian legend. And Bradman batted on. When he retired in 1948 he had an unsurpassed career average of 99.94 runs.

During WWII, Darwin in the Northern Territory was comprehensively bombed in 64 Japanese air raids (1942–43). Contrary to reports of 17 deaths, 243 people were killed, hundreds were injured and half the population fled to Adelaide River. Darwin was also flattened by Cyclone Tracy on Christmas morning, 1974.

War with Japan

After 1933, the economy began to recover. The whirl of daily life was hardly dampened when Hitler hurled Europe into a new war in 1939. Though Australians had long feared Japan, they took it for granted that the British navy would keep them safe. In December 1941 Japan bombed the US Fleet at Pearl Harbor. Weeks later, the 'impregnable' British naval base in Singapore crumbled, and before long thousands of Australians and other Allied troops were enduring the savagery of Japanese prisoner-of-war camps.

As the Japanese swept through Southeast Asia and into Papua New Guinea, the British announced that they could not spare any resources to defend Australia. But the legendary US commander General Douglas MacArthur saw that Australia was the perfect base for American operations in the Pacific. In a series of fierce battles on sea and land, Allied forces gradually turned back the Japanese advance. Importantly, it was the USA, not the British Empire, that saved Australia. The days of the alliance with Britain alone were numbered.

Visionary Peace

When WWII ended, a new slogan rang through the land: 'Populate or Perish!' The Australian government embarked on an ambitious scheme to attract thousands of immigrants. With government assistance, people flocked from Britain and from non-English-speaking countries. They included Greeks, Italians, Slavs, Serbs, Croatians, Dutch and Poles, followed by Turks, Lebanese and many others. These 'new Australians' were expected to assimilate into a suburban stereotype known as the 'Australian way of life'.

Many migrants found jobs in the growing manufacturing sector, in which companies such as General Motors and Ford operated with generous tariff support. In addition, the government embarked on audacious public works schemes, notably the mighty Snowy Mountains Hydro-Electric Scheme in the mountains near Canberra. Today, environmentalists point out the devastation caused by this huge network of tunnels, dams and power stations. But the Snowy scheme was an expression of a new-found optimism and testifies to the cooperation among the men of many nations who laboured on the project.

The massive Murray River spans three states (New South Wales, Victoria and South Australia) and is navigable for 1986 of its 2756km: for half a century from 1853 it acted as a watery highway into inland Australia.

1973

After a conflict-ridden construction which included the sacking of Danish architect Jørn Utzon, the Sydney Opera House opens for business. This iconic building was granted World Heritage status in 2007.

1975

Against a background of radical reform and uncontrolled inflation, Governor-General Sir John Kerr sacks Labor's Whitlam government and orders a federal election, which the conservatives win.

1983

Tasmanian government plans for a hydroelectric dam on the wild Franklin River dominate a federal election campaign. Supporting a 'No Dams' policy, Labor's Bob Hawke becomes prime minister.

1992

Directly overturning the established principal of 'terra nullius', the High Court of Australia recognises the principle of native title in the Mabo decision.

British scientists detonated seven nuclear bombs at Maralinga in remote South Australia in the 1950s and early 1960s, with devastating effects on the local Maralinga Tjarutja people. Lesser-known are the three nuclear tests carried out in the Montebello Islands in Western Australia in the '50s: a good read on the subject is Robert Drewe's *Montebello* (2012).

This era of growth and prosperity was dominated by Robert Menzies, the founder of the modern Liberal Party and Australia's longest-serving prime minister. Menzies was steeped in British history and tradition, and liked to play the part of a sentimental monarchist. He was also a vigilant opponent of communism. As Asia succumbed to the chill of the Cold War, Australia and New Zealand entered a formal military alliance with the USA – the 1951 Anzus security pact. When the USA hurled its righteous fury into a civil war in Vietnam, Menzies committed Australian forces to the battle, introducing conscription for military service overseas. The following year Menzies retired, leaving his successors a bitter legacy. The antiwar movement split Australia.

There was a feeling among many artists, intellectuals and the young that Menzies' Australia had become a rather dull, complacent country, more in love with American and British culture than with its own talents and stories. In an atmosphere of youthful rebellion and new-found nationalism, the Labor Party was elected to power in 1972 under the leadership of a brilliant, idealistic lawyer named Gough Whitlam. In just four short years his government transformed the country. He ended conscription and abolished all university fees. He introduced a free universal health scheme, no-fault divorce, the principle of Aboriginal land rights and equal pay for women. The White Australia policy had been gradually falling into disuse; under Whitlam it was finally abandoned altogether. By now, around one million migrants had arrived from non-English-speaking countries, and they had filled Australia with new languages, cultures, foods and ideas. Under Whitlam this achievement was embraced as 'multiculturalism'.

By 1975 the Whitlam government was rocked by a tempest of inflation and scandal. At the end of 1975 his government was controversially dismissed from office by the governor-general. But the general thrust of Whitlam's social reforms was continued by his successors. The principle of Aboriginal land rights was expanded. From the 1970s Asian immigration increased, and multiculturalism became a new Australian orthodoxy. China and Japan far outstripped Europe as major trading partners – Australia's economic future lay in Asia.

In Melbourne you can find out about others who have come to Australia at the excellent Chinese museum (www.chinesemuseum.com.au) and Immigration museum (www.museumvictoria.com.au/immigrationmuseum).

Challenges

Today Australia faces new challenges. In the 1970s the country began dismantling its protectionist scaffolding. New efficiency brought new prosperity. At the same time, wages and working conditions, which were once protected by an independent tribunal, became more vulnerable as egalitarianism gave way to competition. And after two centuries of development, the strains on the environment were starting to show – on water supplies, forests, soils, air quality and the oceans.

2000

The Sydney Olympic Games are a triumph of spectacle and good will. Aboriginal running champ Cathy Freeman lights the flame at the opening ceremony and wins gold in the 400m event.

2007

Kevin Rudd is elected Australian prime minister. Marking a change of direction from his conservative predecessor, Rudd says 'sorry' to Indigenous Australians and ratifies the Kyoto Protocol on climate change.

OLIVER STREWE / GETTY IMAGES ©

➡ Sorry Day

2009

On 7 February Australia experiences its worst loss of life in a natural disaster when 400 bushfires kill 173 people in country Victoria. The day is known thereafter as 'Black Saturday'.

Under the conservative John Howard, Australia's second-longest-serving prime minister (1996–2007), the country grew closer than ever to the USA, joining the Americans in the war in Iraq. The government's treatment of asylum seekers, its refusal to acknowledge the reality of climate change, its anti-union reforms and the prime minister's lack of empathy with Indigenous Australians dismayed left-leaning Australians. But Howard presided over a period of economic growth that emphasised the values of self-reliance and won him continuing support in middle Australia.

In 2007 Howard was defeated by the Labor Party's Kevin Rudd, an ex-diplomat who immediately issued a formal apology to Indigenous Australians for the injustices they had suffered over the past two centuries. Though it promised sweeping reforms in environment and education, the Rudd government found itself faced with a crisis when the world economy crashed in 2008; by June 2010 it had cost Rudd his position. Incoming Prime Minister Julia Gillard, along with other world leaders, now faced three related challenges – climate change, a diminishing oil supply and a shrinking economy. This difficult landscape, shrinking popularity and ongoing agitations to return Rudd to the top job saw Gillard toppled and Rudd reinstated in June 2013.

Australia's first female prime minister – Labor's Julia Gillard – held the position from 2010 to 2013. In 1895, her home state of South Australia was the first colony to give women the right to run for parliament.

2010

Australia's first female prime minister, Julia Gillard, is sworn in. Born in Wales, Gillard and her family emigrated to Australia's warmer climate due to her poor health as a child.

2011

Category 5 Tropical Cyclone Yasi makes landfall at Mission Beach on the north Queensland coast, causing mass devastation to property, infrastructure and crops.

2012

Despite lofty expectations, Australia's gold medal tally at the London Olympics is a meager seven, following on from 14 in Beijing 2008, 17 in Athens 2004, and 16 in Sydney 2000. National pride is significantly dented.

2013

Prime Minister Julia Gillard announces a federal election eight months in advance – but is replaced by Kevin Rudd as prime minister before she can contest the election.

Aboriginal Australia

Cathy Craigie

A visit to Australia would not be complete without experiencing the rich cultures of Aboriginal and Torres Strait Islander people. Visitors have an opportunity to learn from the oldest continuous cultures in the world and share a way of life that has existed for over 50,000 years. From the cities to the bush, there are opportunities to get up close with Australia's Indigenous people. Visit an art gallery, a museum or book a tour of Aboriginal lands. There is so much on offer for a truly unique Australian experience.

Cathy Craigie is a Gamilaroi/ Anaiwon woman from northern New South Wales. She is a freelance writer and cultural consultant and has extensive experience in Aboriginal Affairs.

Aboriginal Culture

Aboriginal cultures have evolved over thousands of years with strong links between the spiritual, economic and social lives of the people. This heritage has been kept alive from one generation to the next by the passing of knowledge and skills through rituals, art, cultural material and language. Aboriginal people originally had an oral tradition and so language played an important part in preserving Aboriginal cultures.

Today there is a national movement to revive Aboriginal languages and a strong Aboriginal art sector. Traditional knowledge is being used in science, natural resource management and government programs. Aboriginal culture has never been static, and continues to evolve with the changing times and environment. New technologies and mediums are now used to tell Aboriginal stories and there are cultural tourism and hospitality ventures where visitors can experience an Aboriginal perspective. You can learn about ancestral beings at natural landmarks, look at rock art that is thousands of years old, taste traditional foods or attend an Aboriginal festival or performance. There are many opportunities open to the public, advertised in Aboriginal and mainstream media.

Government support for cultural programs is sporadic and depends on the political climate at the time. However, Aboriginal people are determined to maintain their links with the past and to also use their cultural knowledge to shape a better future.

Land

Aboriginal land ethic is based on humans fitting into the ecology and not living outside of it. Everything is connected and not viewed as just soil and rocks but as a whole environment that sustains the spiritual,

TORRES STRAIT ISLANDERS

Aboriginal societies are diverse, not one homogenous group but several hundred different sovereign nations. Torres Strait Islanders are a Melanesian people with a separate culture from that of Aboriginal Australians but have a shared history with Aboriginal people, and together these two groups form Australia's Indigenous peoples. While this chapter touches on broader Indigenous issues relating to both peoples, it focuses primarily on mainland Australia, which is Aboriginal land.

economic and cultural lives of the people. In turn, Aboriginal people have sustained the land by conducting ceremonies, rituals, songs and stories. This interrelation was developed and practised over thousands of years. For Aboriginal people land is intrinsically connected to identity and spirituality. All land in Australia is reflected in Aboriginal lore but particular places may be significant for religious and cultural beliefs. Some well-known sites are the Three Sisters in the Blue Mountains, and Warreen Cave in Tasmania with artefacts dated from around 40,000 years old.

Sacred sites can be parts of rocks, hills, trees or water and are associated with an ancestral being or an event that occurred. Often these sites are part of a Dreaming story and link people across areas. The ranges around Alice Springs are part of the caterpillar Dreaming with many sites including Akeyulerre (Billy Goat Hill), Atnelkentyarliweke (Anzac Hill) and rock paintings at Emily Gap. The most well known are Uluru and Kata Tjuta, which is the home of the snake Wanambi. His breath is the wind that blows through the gorge. Pirla Warna Warna, a significant site in the Tanami Desert for Warlpiri people, is 270 miles northwest of Alice and is where several Walpiri Dreaming stories meet.

Cultural tours offer visits to Aboriginal sites, learning about plants and animals, hunting and fishing trips and even workshops on bushfood or dance.

Please note that many Aboriginal sites are protected by law and are not to be disturbed in any way.

The Arts

Aboriginal art has impacted the Australian landscape and is now showcased at national and international events and is celebrated as a significant part of Australian culture. Exhibited in state institutions, independent theatres and galleries, Aboriginal art has slowly grown in its visibility. It still retains the role of passing on knowledge but today it is also important for economic, educational and political reasons. Art has been used to raise awareness of issues such as health and has been a primary tool for the reconciliation process in Australia. In many communities art has become a major source of employment and income.

Visual Arts

It is difficult to define Aboriginal art as one style because form and practice vary from one area to another. From the original art forms of rock art, carving and body decoration, a dynamic contemporary art industry has grown into one of the success stories of Aboriginal Australia.

Rock Art

Rock art is the oldest form of human art and Aboriginal rock art stretches back thousands of years. Rock art is found in every state of Australia and many sites are thousands of years old. For Aboriginal people, rock art is a direct link with life before Europeans. The art and

KEY EVENTS

1928

Anthony Martin Fernando, the first Aboriginal activist to campaign internationally against racial discrimination in Australia, is arrested for protesting outside Australia House in London in 1928.

26 January 1938

To mark the 150th anniversary of the arrival of the British, the Aborigines Progressive Association holds a meeting in Australia Hall in Sydney, called 'A Day of Mourning and Protest'.

15 August 1963

A bark petition is presented to the House of Representatives from the people of Yirrikala in the Northern Territory, objecting to mining on their land, which the federal government had approved without consultation.

27 May 1967

A federal referendum allows the Commonwealth to make laws on Aboriginal issues and include them in the national census. They will now have the same citizen rights as other Australians.

12 July 1971

The Aboriginal flag first flies on National Aborigines Day in Adelaide. Designed by Central Australian Harold Thomas, the flag is a unifying symbol of identity for Aboriginal people.

26 January 1972

The Aboriginal Tent Embassy is set up on the lawns of Parliament House in Canberra to oppose the treatment of Aboriginal people and the Government's recent rejection of a proposal for Aboriginal Land Rights.

THE IMPORTANCE OF STORYTELLING

Aboriginal people had an oral culture so storytelling was an important way to learn. Stories gave meaning to life and were used to teach the messages of the spirit ancestors. Although beliefs and cultural practices vary according to region and language groups, there is a common world-view that these ancestors created the land, the sea and all living things. This is often referred to as the Dreaming and Aboriginal people attribute their origins and existence to these ancestors. Through stories, the knowledge and beliefs are passed on from one generation to another and set out morals to live by. They also recall events from the past. Today artists have continued this tradition but are using new mediums such as film and writing. The first Aboriginal writer to be published was David Unaipon, a Ngarrindjeri man from South Australia (SA) who was a writer, scientist and advocate for his people. Born in 1872, he published *Aboriginal Legends* in 1927 and *Native Legends* in 1929.

Other early published writers were Oodgeroo Noonuccal, Kevin Gilbert and Jack Davis. Contemporary writers of note are Alexis Wright, Kim Scott, Anita Heiss and Ali Cobby Eckerman. Award-winning novels to read are Kim Scott's *Deadman Dancing* (Picador Australia) and *Benang* (Fremantle Press), Alexis Wright's *Carpentaria* (Giramando) and Ali Cobby Eckerman's *Little Bit Long Time* (Picaro Press) and *Ruby Moonlight* (Magabala Books).

the process of making it are part of songs, stories and customs that connect the people to the land. There are a number of different styles of rock art across Australia. These include engravings in sandstone and stencils, prints and drawings in rock shelters. Aboriginal people carried out rock art for several reasons including as part of a ritual or ceremony and to record events.

In the 1980s acclaimed Papunya Tula artists were invited to submit work for the new Parliament House in Canberra. Michael Nelson Jagamarra's 'Possum and Wallaby Dreaming' is embedded in the mosaic forecourt.

Some of the oldest examples of engravings can be found in the Pilbara in Western Australia (WA) and in Olary in South Australia (SA) where there is an engraving of a crocodile. This is quite amazing as crocodiles are not found in this part of Australia. The Kimberley rock art centres on the Wandjina, the ancestral creation spirits. All national parks surrounding Sydney have rock engravings and can be easily accessed and viewed. At Gariwerd (the Grampians) in Victoria there are handprints and hand stencils. Aboriginal-owned tour company Guurrbi Tours (p459) guides visitors to the Wangaar-Wuri painted rock-art sites near Cooktown in Queensland.

In the Northern Territory (NT) many of the rock-art sites have patterns and symbols that appear in paintings, carvings and other cultural material. Kakadu National Park has over 5000 recorded sites but many more are thought to exist. Some of these sites are 20,000 years old. Kakadu is World Heritage listed and is internationally recognised for its cultural significance.

When Europeans first saw a corroboree they described it as a 'bush opera'. These festive social events combined music, dance and drama with body art. One of the first recorded corroborees was in 1791 at Bennelong Point, now the site of the Sydney Opera House.

In central Australia rock paintings still have religious significance. Here, people still retouch the art as part of ritual and to connect them to the stories. In most other areas people no longer paint rock images but instead work on bark, paper and canvas.

If you visit rock-art sites, please do not touch or damage the art, and respect the sites and the surrounding areas.

Contemporary Art

The contemporary art industry started in a tiny community called Papunya in central Australia. It was occupied by residents from several language groups who had been displaced from their traditional lands. In 1971 an art teacher at Papunya school encouraged painting and some senior men took interest. This started the process of transferring sand and body drawings onto modern mediums and the 'dot and circle' style of contemporary painting began. The emergence of 'dot' paintings has been described as the greatest art movement of the 20th century and Papunya Tula artists became a model for other Aboriginal communities.

The National Gallery of Australia in Canberra has a fantastic collection, but contemporary Aboriginal art can also be viewed at any public art gallery or in one of the many independent galleries dealing in Aboriginal work. Contemporary artists work in all mediums and Aboriginal art has appeared on unconventional surfaces such as a BMW car and a Qantas plane. The central desert area is still a hub for Aboriginal art and Alice Springs is one of the best places to see and buy art. Cairns is another hot spot for innovative Aboriginal art.

If you are buying art make sure that provenance of the work is included. This tells the artist's name, community/language group they come from and the story of the work. If it is an authentic work, all proceeds go back to the artist. Australia has a resale royalty scheme.

Music

Music has always been a vital part of Aboriginal culture. Songs were important for teaching and passing on knowledge and musical instruments were often used in healing, ceremonies and rituals. The most well-known instrument is the Yidaki or didgeridoo, which was traditionally only played by men in northern Australia. Other instruments included clapsticks, rattles and boomerangs; in southern Australia animal skins were stretched across the lap to make a drumming sound.

This rich musical heritage continues today with a strong contemporary music industry. Like other art forms, Aboriginal music has developed into a fusion of new ideas and styles mixed with strong cultural identity. Contemporary artists such as Dan Sultan and Jessica Mauboy have crossed over successfully into the mainstream – they have won major music awards and can be seen regularly on popular programs and at major music festivals. Aboriginal radio is the best and most accessible way to hear Aboriginal music.

Performing Arts

Dance and theatre are a vital part of social and ceremonial life and are important elements in Aboriginal culture. Historically, dances often told stories to pass on knowledge. Styles varied from one nation to the next and depended on whether the dance was for social or ritual reasons. Imitation of animals, birds and the elements was common across Australia but dance movements such as set arm, leg and body movements differed greatly. Ceremonial or ritual dances were highly structured and were distinct from the dancing that people did socially at corroborees. Like other artforms, dance has adapted to the modern world and contemporary dance companies and groups have merged traditional forms into a modern interpretation. The most well-known dance company is the internationally acclaimed Bangarra Dance Theatre.

10 August 1987
A Royal Commission into Aboriginal deaths in custody investigates the high number of Aboriginal deaths in jails. Aboriginal people are still over-represented in the criminal system today.

3 June 1992
The previous legal concept of terra nullius is overturned by the Australian High Court in its landmark decision in the Mabo case, declaring Australia was occupied before the British settlement.

26 January 1988
As Australia celebrates its bicentenary, 40,000 Aboriginal people and supporters march in Sydney to mark the 200-year anniversary of invasion.

28 May 2000
Over 300,000 people walk together across Sydney Harbour Bridge to highlight the need for reconciliation between Aboriginal people and other Australians.

21 June 2007
The federal government suspends the Racial Discrimination Act to implement a large-scale intervention, the Northern Territory Emergency Response, to address child abuse in NT Aboriginal communities.

13 February 2008
The Prime Minister of Australia makes a national apology to Aboriginal people for the forced removal of their children and the injustices that occurred.

10 July 2010
Aboriginal leader Yagan is put to rest in a Perth park bearing his name. He was murdered in 1833 and his head sent to England. Aboriginal people have campaigned for decades to repatriate their people's remains.

Theatre also draws on the storytelling tradition. Currently there are two major Aboriginal theatre companies: Ilbijerri in Melbourne and Yirra Yakin in Perth. In addition there are several mainstream companies that specialise in Aboriginal stories. These companies have had several successes with productions here and overseas. Australia has a thriving Aboriginal theatre industry and many Aboriginal actors and writers work in or collaborate with mainstream productions. Traditionally drama and dance came together in ceremonies or corroborees and this still occurs in many contemporary productions.

TV, Radio & Film

Aboriginal people have quickly adapted to electronic broadcasting and have developed an extensive media network of radio, print and television services. There are over 120 Aboriginal radio stations and programs operating across Australia in cities, rural areas and remote communities. Program formats differ from location to location. Some broadcast only in Aboriginal languages or cater to a specific music taste.

There is a thriving Aboriginal film industry and in recent years feature films including *The Sapphires*, *Bran Nue Day* and *Samson and Delilah* have had mainstream success. Since the first Aboriginal television channel, NITV, was launched in 2007, there has been a growth in the number of filmmakers wanting to tell their stories.

Most Australians celebrate 26 January as Australia Day in recognition of British settlement, but for Aboriginal people it is known as 'Invasion Day', 'Survival Day' or 'Day of Mourning'.

History of Aboriginal Australia

Before the coming of Europeans to Australia, culture was the common link for Aboriginal people across Australia. There were many aspects that were common to all groups in Australia and it was through these commonalities that Aboriginal people were able to interact with each other. In post-colonial Australia it is also the shared history that binds Aboriginal people.

THE STOLEN GENERATIONS

When Australia became a Federation in 1901, a government policy known as the 'White Australia policy' was put in place. It was implemented to restrict non-white immigration to Australia but the policy also impacted Aboriginal Australians. Assimilation into the broader society was 'encouraged' by all sectors of government with the intent to eventually fade out the Aboriginal race. A policy of forcibly removing Aboriginal and Torres Strait Islander children from their families was official from 1909 to 1969, although the practice was happening before and after those years. Although accurate numbers will never be known, it is estimated that around 100,000 Aboriginal children were taken from their families.

A government agency, the Aborigines Protection Board, was set up to manage the policy and had the power to remove children without consent from families or without a court order. Many children never saw their families again and those that did manage to find their way home often found it difficult to maintain relationships. The generations of children who were taken from their families became known as the stolen generations.

In the 1990s the Australian Human Rights Commission held an inquiry into the practice of removing Aboriginal children. The 'Bring Them Home' report was tabled in parliament in May 1997 and told of the devastating impact that these polices had on the children and their families. Governments, churches and welfare bodies all took part in the forced removal. Sexual and physical abuse and cruelty was common in many of the institutions where children were placed. Today many of the stolen generations still suffer trauma associated with their early lives.

On 13 February 2008 the then prime minister of Australia offered a national apology to the stolen generations. For many Aboriginal people it was the start of a national healing process and today there are many organisations working with the stolen generations.

First Australians

Many academics believe Aboriginal people came from somewhere else, and scientific evidence places Aboriginal people on the continent at least 40,000 to 50,000 years ago. However, Aboriginal people believe they have always inhabited the land.

At the time of European contact the Aboriginal population was grouped into 300 or more different nations with distinct languages and land boundaries. Most Aboriginal people did not have permanent shelters but moved within their territory and followed seasonal patterns of animal migration and plant availability. The diversity of landscapes in Australia meant that each nation varied in their lifestyles and cultures. Although these nations were distinct cultural groups, there were also many common elements. Each nation had several clans or family groups who were responsible for looking after specific areas. For thousands of years Aboriginal people lived within a complex kinship system that tied them to the natural environment. From the desert to the sea Aboriginal people shaped their lives according to their environments and developed different skills and a wide body of knowledge on their territory.

The *Macquarie PEN Anthology of Aboriginal Literature* (www.macquariepen-anthology.com.au) offers over 200 years of Aboriginal culture, history and life. It starts with Bennelong's letter in 1796 and includes works from some of Aboriginal Australia's best writers.

Colonised

The effects of colonisation started immediately after the Europeans arrived. It started with the appropriation of land and water resources and an epidemic of diseases. Smallpox killed around 50% of the Sydney Harbour natives. A period of resistance occurred as Aboriginal people fought back to retain their land and way of life. As violence and massacres swept the country, many Aboriginal people were pushed away from their traditional lands. Over a century, the Aboriginal population was decimated by 90%.

By the late 1800s most of the fertile land had been taken and most Aboriginal people were living in poverty on the fringes of settlements or on land unsuitable for settlement. Aboriginal people had to adapt to the new culture but were treated like second-class citizens. Employment opportunities were scarce and most worked as labourers or domestic staff. This disadvantage has continued and even though successive government policies and programs have been implemented to assist Aboriginal people, most have had little effect on improving lives.

YABUN

Yabun is held every year on Australia Day (26 January) at Victoria Park in Sydney and is a free festival celebrating the survival of Aboriginal cultures. The cultural program includes music, dance, visual arts and crafts, storytelling, politics and games.

Rights & Reconciliation

The relationship between Aboriginal people and other Australians hasn't always been an easy one. Over the years several systematic policies have been put in place, but these have often had an underlying purpose including control over the land, decimating the population, protection, assimilation, self-determination and self-management.

The history of forced resettlement, removal of children and the loss of land and culture can't be erased, even with governments addressing some of the issues. Current policies focus on 'closing the gap' and centre on better delivery of essential services to improve lives, but there is still great disparity between Aboriginal people and other Australians, including lower standards of education, employment, health and living conditions high incarceration and suicide rates and a lower life expectancy.

Throughout all of this, Aboriginal people have managed to maintain their identity and link to country and culture. Although there is a growing recognition and acceptance of Aboriginal people's place in this country, there is still a long way to go. Aboriginal people have no real political or economic wealth, but their struggles for legal and cultural rights continue today and are always at the forefront of politics. Any gains for Aboriginal people have been hard won and initiated by Aboriginal people themselves in bringing the issues to public notice.

Environment
Tim Flannery

Australia's plants and animals are just about the closest things to alien life you are likely to encounter on earth. That's because Australia has been isolated from the other continents for a very long time – around 80 million years. Unlike those on other habitable continents that have been linked by land bridges, Australia's birds, mammals, reptiles and plants have taken their own separate and very different evolutionary journey and the result today is the world's most distinct – and one of the most diverse – natural realms.

Tim Flannery is a scientist, explorer and writer. He has written several award-winning books including *The Future Eaters*, *Throwim Way Leg* (an account of his work as a biologist in New Guinea) and *The Weather Makers*. He lives in Sydney where he is a professor in the faculty of science at Macquarie University.

The first naturalists to investigate Australia were astonished by what they found. Here the swans were black – to Europeans this was a metaphor for the impossible – and mammals such as the platypus and echidna were discovered to lay eggs. It really was an upside-down world, where many of the larger animals hopped and where each year the trees shed their bark rather than their leaves.

If you are visiting Australia for a short time, you might need to go out of your way to experience some of the richness of the environment. That's because Australia is a subtle place, and some of the natural environment – especially around the cities – has been damaged or replaced by trees and creatures from Europe. Places like Sydney, however, have preserved extraordinary fragments of their original environment that are relatively easy to access. Before you enjoy them though, it's worthwhile understanding the basics about how nature operates in Australia. This is important because there's nowhere like Australia, and once you have an insight into its origins and natural rhythms, you will appreciate the place so much more.

A Unique Environment

There are two important factors that go a long way towards explaining nature in Australia: its soils and its climate. Both are unique.

Soils

In recent geological times, on other continents, processes such as volcanism, mountain building and glacial activity have been busy creating new soil. Just think of the glacier-derived soils of North America, north Asia and Europe. The rich soils of India and parts of South America were made by rivers eroding mountains, while Java in Indonesia owes its extraordinary richness to volcanoes.

All of these soil-forming processes have been almost absent from Australia in more recent times. Only volcanoes have made a contribution, and they cover less than 2% of the continent's land area. In fact, for the last 90 million years, beginning deep in the age of dinosaurs, Australia has been geologically comatose. It was too flat, warm and dry to attract glaciers, its crust too ancient and thick to be punctured by volcanoes or folded into mountains. Look at Uluru and Kata Tjuta. They are the stumps of mountains that 350 million years ago were the height of the Andes. Yet for hundreds of millions of years they've been nothing but nubs.

Under such conditions no new soil is created and the old soil is leached of all its goodness by the rain, and is blown and washed away. Even if just 30cm of rain falls each year, that adds up to a column of water 30 million kilometres high passing through the soil over 100 million years, and that can do a great deal of leaching! Almost all of Australia's mountain ranges are more than 90 million years old, so you will see a lot of sand here, and a lot of country where the rocky 'bones' of the land are sticking up through the soil. It is an old, infertile landscape and life in Australia has been adapting to these conditions for aeons.

Climate

Australia's misfortune in respect to soils is echoed in its climate. In most parts of the world outside the wet tropics, life responds to the rhythm of the seasons – summer to winter, or wet to dry. Most of Australia experiences seasons – sometimes severe ones – yet life does not respond solely to them. This can clearly be seen by the fact that although there's plenty of snow and cold country in Australia, there are almost no trees that shed their leaves in winter, nor do any Australian animals hibernate. Instead there is a far more potent climatic force that Australian life must obey: El Niño.

El Niño is a complex climatic pattern that can cause major weather shifts around the South Pacific. The cycle of flood and drought that El Niño brings to Australia is profound. Our rivers – even the mighty Murray River, the nation's largest river, which runs through the southeast – can be miles wide one year, yet you can literally step over its flow the next. This is the power of El Niño, and its effect, when combined with Australia's poor soils, manifests itself compellingly.

Uluru (Ayers Rock) is often thought to be the world's largest monolith. In fact, it only takes second prize. The biggest is Burringurrah (Mt Augustus) in Western Australia, which is 2½ times the size of Uluru.

Fauna & Flora

Australia's wildlife and plant species are as diverse as they are perfectly adapted to the country's soils and climate.

Mammals

Kangaroos

Australia is, of course, famous as the home of the kangaroo (roo) and other marsupials. Unless you visit a wildlife park, such creatures are not easy to see as most are nocturnal. Their lifestyles, however, are exquisitely attuned to Australia's harsh conditions. Have you ever wondered

ENVIRONMENT & CONSERVATION GROUPS

- The **Australian Conservation Foundation** (ACF; www.acfonline.org.au) is Australia's largest nongovernment organisation involved in protecting the environment.
- **Bush Heritage Australia** (www.bushheritage.org.au) and **Australian Wildlife Conservancy** (AWC; www.australianwildlife.org) allow people to donate funds and time to conserving native species.
- Want to get your hands dirty? **Conservation Voluntweers Australia** (www.conservationvolunteers.com.au) is a nonprofit organisation focusing on practical conservation projects such as tree planting, walking-track construction, and flora and fauna surveys.
- **Ecotourism Australia** (www.ecotourism.org.au) has an accreditation system for environmentally friendly and sustainable tourism in Australia, and lists ecofriendly tours, accommodation and attractions by state.
- The **Wilderness Society** (www.wilderness.org.au) focuses on the protection of wilderness and forests.

why kangaroos, alone among the world's larger mammals, hop? It turns out that hopping is the most efficient way of getting about at medium speeds. This is because the energy of the bounce is stored in the tendons of the legs – much like in a pogo stick – while the intestines bounce up and down like a piston, emptying and filling the lungs without needing to activate the chest muscles. When you travel long distances to find meagre feed, such efficiency is a must.

Koalas

Marsupials are so energy-efficient that they need to eat one-fifth less food than equivalent-sized placental mammals (everything from bats to rats, whales and ourselves). But some marsupials have taken energy efficiency much further. If you visit a wildlife park or zoo you might notice that faraway look in a koala's eyes. It seems as if nobody is home – and this in fact is near the truth. Several years ago biologists announced that koalas are the only living creatures that have brains that don't fit their skulls. Instead they have a shrivelled walnut of a brain that rattles around in a fluid-filled cranium. Other researchers have contested this finding, however, pointing out that the brains of the koalas examined for the study may have shrunk because these organs are so soft. Whether soft-brained or empty-headed, there is no doubt that the koala is not the Einstein of the animal world, and we now believe that it has sacrificed its brain to energy efficiency. Brains cost a lot to run. Koalas eat gum leaves, which are so toxic that they use 20% of their energy just detoxifying this food. This leaves little energy for the brain, fortunately living in the treetops where there are so few predators means that they can get by with few wits at all.

AUSTRALIAN MUSEUM

The website of the Australian Museum (www.australianmuseum.net.au) holds a wealth of info on Australia's animal life from the Cretaceous period till now. Kids can get stuck into online games, fact files and movies.

Wombats

The peculiar constraints of the Australian environment have not made everything dumb. The koala's nearest relative, the wombat (of which there are three species), has a large brain for a marsupial. These creatures live in complex burrows and can weigh up to 35kg, making them the largest herbivorous burrowers on earth. Because their burrows are effectively air-conditioned, they have the neat trick of turning down their metabolic activity when they are in residence. One physiologist, who studied their thyroid hormones, found that biological activity ceased to such an extent in sleeping wombats that, from a hormonal point of view, they appeared to be dead! Wombats can remain underground for a week at a time, and can get by on just one-third of the food needed by a sheep of equivalent size. One day, perhaps, efficiency-minded farmers will keep wombats instead of sheep. At the moment, however, that isn't possible;

BIRDS IN BED

Relatively few of Australia's birds are seasonal breeders, and few migrate. Instead, they breed when the rain comes and a large percentage are nomads, following the rain across the breadth of the continent.

So challenging are environmental conditions in Australia that its birds have developed some extraordinary habits. Kookaburras, magpies and blue wrens – to name just a few – have developed a breeding system called 'helpers at the nest'. The helpers are the young adult birds of previous breedings, which stay with their parents to help bring up the new chicks. Just why they should do this was a mystery, until it was realised that conditions in Australia can be so harsh that more than two adult birds are needed to feed the nestlings. This pattern of breeding is very rare in places like Asia, Europe and North America, but it is common in many Australian birds.

A WHALE OF A TIME

A driving economic force across much of southern Australia from the time of colonisation, whaling was finally banned in Australia in 1979. The main species on the end of the harpoon were humpback, blue, southern right and sperm whales, which were culled in huge numbers in traditional breeding grounds such as Sydney Harbour, the Western Australia coast around Albany, and Hobart's Derwent River estuary. The industry remained profitable until the mid-1800s, before drastically depleted whale numbers, the lure of inland gold rushes and the emergence of petrol as an alternative fuel started to have an impact.

Over recent years (and much to locals' delight), whales have made cautious returns to both Sydney Harbour and the Derwent River. Ironically, whale watching has emerged as a lucrative tourist activity in migratory hot spots such as Head of Bight in South Australia, Warrnambool in Victoria, Hervey Bay in Queensland and out on the ocean beyond Sydney Harbour.

the largest of the wombat species, the northern hairy-nose, is one of the world's rarest creatures, with only about 150 surviving in a remote nature reserve in central Queensland.

Other Mammals

Among the more common marsupials you might catch a glimpse of in the national parks that are situated around Australia's major cities are the species of antechinus. These nocturnal, rat-sized creatures lead an extraordinary life. The males live for just 11 months, the first 10 of which consist of a concentrated burst of eating and growing. The day comes when their minds turn to sex, and in the antechinus this becomes an obsession. As they embark on their quest for females they forget to eat and sleep. By the end of August – just two weeks after they reach 'puberty' – every male is dead, exhausted by sex and by carrying around swollen testes.

R Strahan's *The Mammals of Australia* is a comprehensive survey of Australia's somewhat cryptic mammals. Every species is illustrated, with individual species descriptions penned by the nation's experts.

Two unique monotremes (egg-laying mammals) live in Australia: the bumbling echidna, something akin to a hedgehog; and the platypus, a bit like an otter, with webbed feet and a ducklike bill. Echidnas are common along bushland trails, but platypuses are elusive, seen at dawn and dusk in quiet rivers and streams.

Reptiles

One thing you will see lots of in Australia are reptiles. Snakes are abundant, and they include some of the most venomous species known in the world. Where the opportunities to feed are few and far between, it is best not to give your prey a second chance, hence their potent venom. Snakes will usually leave you alone if you do not fool with them. Observe, back quietly away and try not to panic, and most of the time you will be fine.

Some visitors mistake lizards for snakes, and indeed some Australian lizards look bizarre. One of the more abundant is the sleepy lizard. These creatures, which are found in the southern arid region, look like animated pine cones. They are the Australian equivalent of tortoises, and are harmless. Other lizards are much larger. Unless you visit the Indonesian island of Komodo you will not see a larger lizard than the desert-dwelling perentie. These creatures, with their leopardlike blotches, can grow to more than 2m long, and are efficient predators of introduced rabbits, feral cats and the like.

Feeling right at home in Kakadu National Park, the saltwater crocodile is the world's largest living reptile – old males can reach an intimidating 6m long.

If you're interested in Australian reptiles (or exist in a state of mortal fear), H Cogger's *Reptiles and Amphibians of Australia* is a cold-blooded bible. This hefty volume will allow you to identify sundry species (or you can wield it as a defensive weapon if necessary!).

Flora

Australia's plants can be irresistibly fascinating. If you happen to be in the Perth area in spring it's well worth taking a wildflower tour. The best flowers grow on the arid and monotonous sand plains, and the blaze of colour produced by the kangaroo paws, banksias and similar native plants can be dizzying. The sheer variety of flowers is amazing, with 4000 species crowded into the southwestern corner of the continent. This diversity of prolific flowering plants has long puzzled botanists. Again, Australia's poor soils seem to be the cause. The sand plain is about the poorest soil in Australia – it's almost pure quartz. This prevents any single fast-growing species from dominating. Instead, thousands of specialist plant species have learned to find a narrow niche and so coexist. Some live at the foot of the metre-high sand dunes, some on top, some on an east-facing slope, some on the west and so on. Their flowers need to be striking in order to attract pollinators, for nutrients are so lacking in this sandy world that even insects such as bees are rare.

If you do get to walk the wildflower regions of the southwest, keep your eyes open for the sundews. Australia is the centre of diversity for these beautiful, carnivorous plants. They've given up on the soil supplying their nutritional needs and have turned instead to trapping insects with the sweet globs of moisture on their leaves, and digesting them to obtain nitrogen and phosphorus.

If you are very lucky, you might see a honey possum. This tiny marsupial is an enigma. Somehow it gets all of its dietary requirements from nectar and pollen, and in the southwest there are always enough flowers around for it to survive. But no one knows why the males need sperm larger even than those of the blue whale, or why their testes are so massive. Were humans as well endowed, men would be walking around with the equivalent of a 4kg bag of potatoes between their legs!

Offical Floral Emblems

- Common Heath (Victoria)
- Cooktown Orchid (Queensland)
- Red and Green Kangaroo Paw (WA)
- Royal Bluebell (ACT)
- Tasmanian Blue Gum (Tasmania)
- Sturt's Desert Pea (SA)
- Sturt's Desert Rose (NT)
- Waratah (NSW)

Environmental Challenges

The European colonisation of Australia, commencing in 1788, heralded a period of catastrophic environmental upheaval. The result today is that Australians are struggling with some of the most severe environmental problems to be found anywhere in the world. It may seem strange that a population of just 23 million, living in a continent the size of the USA minus Alaska, could inflict such damage on its environment, but Australia's long isolation, its fragile soils and difficult climate have made it particularly vulnerable to human-induced change.

Environmental damage has been inflicted in several ways, the most important include the introduction of pest species, the destruction of forests, overstocking range lands and interference with water flows.

SHARKY

Shark-o-phobia ruining your trip to the beach? Despite media hype, Australia has averaged just one shark-attack fatality per year since 1791. There are about 370 shark species in the world's oceans – around 160 of these swim through Australian waters. Of these, only a few pose any threat to humans: the usual suspects are oceanic white tip, great white, tiger and bull sharks.

It follows that where there are more people, there are more shark attacks. NSW, and Sydney in particular, have a bad rep. Attacks here peaked between 1920 and 1940, but since shark-net installation began in 1937 there's only been one fatality (1963), and dorsal-fin sightings are rare enough to make the nightly news. Realistically, you're more likely to get hit by a bus – so get wet and enjoy yourself!

Beginning with the escape of domestic cats into the Australian bush shortly after 1788, a plethora of vermin – from foxes to wild camels and cane toads – have run wild in Australia, causing extinctions in the native fauna. One out of every 10 native mammals living in Australia prior to European colonisation is now extinct, and many more are highly endangered. Extinctions have also affected native plants, birds and amphibians.

The destruction of forests has also had an effect on the environment. Most of Australia's rainforests have suffered clearing, while conservationists fight with loggers over the fate of the last unprotected stands of 'old growth'.

Many Australian range lands have been chronically overstocked for more than a century, the result being the extreme vulnerability of both soils and rural economies to Australia's drought and flood cycle, as well as the extinction of many native species. The development of agriculture has involved land clearance and the provision of irrigation; again the effect has been profound. Clearing of the diverse and spectacular plant communities of the Western Australia wheat belt began just a century ago, yet today up to one-third of that country is degraded by salination of the soils.

Just 1.5% of Australia's land surface provides over 95% of its agricultural yield, and much of this land lies in the irrigated regions of the Murray-Darling Basin. This is Australia's agricultural heartland, yet it too is under severe threat from salting of soils and rivers. Irrigation water penetrates into the sediments laid down in an ancient sea, carrying salt into the catchments and fields. The Snowy River in New South Wales and Victoria also faces a battle for survival.

Despite the enormity of the biological crisis engulfing Australia, governments and the community have been slow to respond. It was in the 1980s that coordinated action began to take place, but not until the '90s that major steps were taken. The establishment of **Landcare** (www.landcareaustralia.com.au), an organisation enabling people to effectively address local environmental issues, and the expenditure of over $2 billion through the federal government initiative **Caring for our Country** (www.nrm.gov.au) have been important national initiatives. Yet so difficult are some of the issues the nation faces that, as yet, little has been achieved in terms of halting the destructive processes.

So severe are Australia's environmental problems that it will take a revolution before they can be overcome, for sustainable practices need to be implemented in every arena of life – from farms to suburbs and city centres. Renewable energy, sustainable agriculture and water use lie at the heart of these changes, and Australians are only now developing the road map to sustainability that they so desperately need if they are to have a long-term future on the continent.

Current Environmental Issues

Headlining the environmental issues facing Australia's fragile landscape at present are climate change, water scarcity, nuclear energy and uranium mining. All are interconnected. For Australia, the warmer temperatures resulting from climate change spell disaster to an already fragile landscape. A 2°C climb in average temperatures on the globe's driest continent will result in an even drier southern half of the country and greater water scarcity. Scientists also agree that hotter and drier conditions will exacerbate bushfire conditions and increase cyclone intensity.

Australia is a heavy greenhouse-gas emitter because it relies on coal and other fossil fuels for its energy supplies. The most prominent and also contentious alternative energy source is nuclear power, which creates less greenhouse gases and relies on uranium, in which Australia is

BUSHFIRES

Australia has seen some devastating bushfires in recent times: the 'Black Saturday' fires in Victoria in 2009 claimed 173 lives, while in 2013 fires in Tasmania killed a firefighter and destroyed hundreds of buildings.

World Heritage Wonders

- *Great Barrier Reef, Queensland*
- *Southwest Wilderness, Tasmania*
- *Uluru-Kata Tjuta National Park, NT*
- *Kakadu National Park, NT*

MALAISE OF THE MURRAY-DARLING

The Murray-Darling Basin is Australia's largest river system, flowing through Queensland, NSW, the ACT, Victoria then SA, covering an area of 1.05 million sq km – roughly 14% of Australia. Aside from quenching around a third of the country's agricultural and urban thirsts, it also irrigates precious rainforests, wetlands, subtropical areas and scorched arid lands.

But drought, irrigation and climate change have depleted Murray-Darling flows. Wetland areas around the Darling River that used to flood every five years are now likely to do so every 25 years, and prolific species are threatened with extinction. That the entire system will become too salty and unusable is a very real danger.

Rains and widespread flooding across eastern Australia since 2010 (especially in 2011) have increased flows, but finding the delicate balance between agricultural and environmental water allocations continues to cause political and social turmoil across five states and territories.

rich. But the radioactive waste created by nuclear power stations can take thousands of years to become harmless. Moreover, uranium is a finite energy source (as opposed to yet-cleaner and renewable energy sources such as solar and wind power), and even if Australia were to establish sufficient nuclear power stations now to make a real reduction in coal-dependency, it would be years before the environmental and economic benefits were realised.

Uranium mining also produces polarised opinions. Because countries around the world are also looking to nuclear energy, Australia finds itself in a position to increase exports of one of its top-dollar resources. But uranium mining in Australia has been met with fierce opposition, not only because the product is a core ingredient of nuclear weapons, but also because much of Australia's uranium supplies sit beneath sacred Indigenous land. Supporters of increased uranium mining and export suggest that the best way to police the use of uranium is to manage its entire life cycle; that is to sell the raw product to international buyers, and then charge a fee to accept the waste and dispose of it. Both major political parties consider an expansion of Australia's uranium export industry to be inevitable for economic reasons.

The Coastal Studies Unit at the University of Sydney has deemed there to be an astonishing 10,685 beaches in Australia (their definition of a beach being a stretch of sand more than 20m long which remains dry at high tide).

National & State Parks

Australia has more than 500 national parks – nonurban protected wilderness areas of environmental or natural importance. Each state defines and runs its own national parks, but the principle is the same throughout Australia. National parks include rainforests, vast tracts of empty outback, strips of coastal dune land and rugged mountain ranges.

Public access is encouraged as long as safety and conservation regulations are observed. In all parks you're asked to do nothing to damage or alter the natural environment. Camping grounds (often with toilets and showers), walking tracks and information centres are often provided for visitors. In most national parks there are restrictions on bringing in pets.

State parks and state forests are owned by state governments and have fewer regulations. Although state forests can be logged, they are often recreational areas with camping grounds, walking trails and signposted forest drives. Some permit horses and dogs.

Watching Wildlife

Some regions of Australia offer unique opportunities to see wildlife, and one of the most fruitful is Tasmania. The island is jam-packed with wallabies, wombats and possums, principally because foxes, which have decimated marsupial populations on the mainland, were slow to reach the island state (the first fox was found in Tasmania only as recently as 2001!). It is also home to the Tasmanian devil. They're common on the island, and in some national parks you can watch them tear apart road-killed wombats. Their squabbling is fearsome, their shrieks ear-splitting. It's the nearest thing Australia can offer to experiencing a lion kill on the Masai Mara. Unfortunately, Tassie devil populations are being decimated by the devil facial tumour disease.

For those intrigued by the diversity of tropical rainforests, Queensland's World Heritage Sites are well worth visiting. Birds of paradise, cassowaries and a variety of other birds can be seen by day, while at night you can search for tree-kangaroos (yes, some kinds of kangaroo do live in the treetops). In your nocturnal wanderings you are highly likely to see curious possums, some of which look like skunks, and other marsupials that are restricted to a small area of northeast Queensland.

Australia's deserts are a real hit-and-miss affair as far as wildlife is concerned. If you're visiting in a drought year, all you might see are dusty plains, the odd mob of kangaroos and emus, and a few struggling trees. Return after big rains, however, and you'll encounter something close to a Garden of Eden. Fields of white and gold daisies stretch endlessly into the distance. The salt lakes fill with fresh water, and millions of water birds – pelicans, stilts, shags and gulls – can be seen feeding on the superabundant fish and insect life of the waters. It all seems like a mirage, and like a mirage it will vanish as the land dries out, only to spring to life again in a few years or a decade's time. For a more reliable birdwatching spectacular, Kakadu is worth a look, especially towards the end of the dry season around November.

The largest creatures found in the Australian region are marine mammals such as whales and seals, and there is no better place to see them than South Australia. During springtime southern right whales crowd into the head of the Great Australian Bight. You can readily observe them near the remote Aboriginal community of Yalata as they mate, frolic and suckle their young. Kangaroo Island, south of Adelaide, is a fantastic place to see seals and sea lions. There are well-developed visitor centres to facilitate the viewing of wildlife, and nightly penguin parades occur at some places where the adult blue penguins make their nest burrows. Kangaroo Island's beaches are magical places, where you're able to stroll among fabulous shells, whale bones and even jewel-like leafy sea dragons amid the sea wrack.

The fantastic diversity of Queensland's Great Barrier Reef is legendary, and a boat trip out to the reef from Cairns or Port Douglas is unforgettable. Just as extraordinary but less well known is the diversity of Australia's southern waters; the Great Australian Bight is home to more kinds of marine creatures than anywhere else on earth.

Some of Australia's most beautiful national parks and important sites are included on the World Heritage Register, a UN register of natural and cultural places deemed to be universally significant: see http://whc.unesco.org for listings.

Walk Amongst the Tall Timber

- *Valley of the Giants Tree Top Walk, WA*
- *Tahune Airwalk, Tasmania*
- *Otway Fly, Victoria*
- *Illawarra Fly Tree Top Walk, NSW*

Food & Wine

In a decade not long ago, Australians proudly survived on a diet of 'meat and three veg'. Fine fare was a Sunday roast, and lasagne was considered exotic. Fortunately the country's cuisine has evolved, and these days Australian gastronomy is keen to break rules, backed up by world-renowned wines, excellent coffee and a growing craft beer scene.

Top Food Festivals

The Taste (p634), Hobart, Tasmania

Melbourne Food & Wine Festival (p500), Melbourne, Victoria

Clare Valley Gourmet Weekend (p779), Clare Valley, South Australia

Mod Oz (Modern Australian)

The phrase Modern Australian (Mod Oz) has been coined to classify contemporary Australian cuisine: a melange of East and West; a swirl of Atlantic and Pacific Rim; a flourish of authentic French and Italian.

Immigration has been the key to this culinary concoction. An influx of immigrants since WWII, from Europe, Asia, the Middle East and Africa, introduced new ingredients and new ways to use staples. Vietnamese, Japanese, Fijian – no matter where it's from, there are expat communities and interested locals keen to cook and eat it. You'll find Jamaicans using Scotch bonnet peppers and Tunisians making tajine.

As the Australian appetite for diversity and invention grows, so does the food culture surrounding it. Cookbooks and foodie magazines are bestsellers and Australian celebrity chefs – highly sought overseas – reflect Australia's multiculturalism in their backgrounds and dishes.

If all this sounds overwhelming, never fear. The range of food in Australia is a true asset. You'll find that dishes are characterised by bold and interesting flavours and fresh ingredients. All palates are catered for: the chilli-metre spans gentle to extreme, seafood is plentiful, meats are full-flavoured, and vegetarian needs are considered (especially in the cities).

Fresh Local Food

Australia is huge (similar in size to continental USA), and it varies so much in climate, from the tropical north to the temperate south, that at any time of the year there's an enormous array of produce on offer. Fruit is a fine example. In summer, kitchen bowls overflow with nectarines, peaches and cherries, and mangoes are so plentiful that Queenslanders get sick of them. The Murray River gives rise to orchards of citrus fruits, grapes and melons. Tasmania's cold climate means its strawberries and stone fruits are sublime. The tomatoes of South Australia (SA) are the nation's best. Local supermarkets stock the pick of the bunch.

Seafood is always freshest close to the source; on this big island it's plentiful. Oysters are popular: connoisseurs prize Sydney rock oysters, a species that actually lives right along the New South Wales (NSW) coast. Excellent oysters are grown in seven different regions in SA, and Tasmania is known for its Pacific oysters. Australia's southernmost state is also celebrated for its trout, salmon and abalone.

An odd-sounding delicacy from these waters is bugs – shovel-nosed lobsters without a lobster's price tag (try the Balmain and Moreton Bay varieties). Marron are prehistoric-looking freshwater crayfish from Western Australia (WA), with a subtle taste that's not always enhanced by the heavy dressings that seem popular. Prawns in Australia are incredible, particularly sweet school prawns or the eastern king (Yamba) prawns found along the northern New South Wales coast. You can sample countless wild fish species, including prized barramundi from the Northern Territory (NT), but even fish that are considered run-of-the-mill (such as snapper, trevally and whiting) taste fabulous simply barbecued.

There's a growing boutique cheese movement across the country's dairy regions; Tasmania alone now produces 50 cheese varieties.

Restaurant Dining

A restaurant meal in Australia is a relaxed affair. You'll probably order within 15 minutes and see the first course (entrée) 20 minutes later. The main course will arrive about half an hour after that. Even at the finest restaurants a jacket is not required (but certainly isn't frowned upon).

If a restaurant is BYO, you can bring your own alcohol. If it also sells alcohol, you can usually only bring your own bottled wine (no beer, no cask wine) and a corkage charge is added to your bill. The cost is either per person or per bottle, and can be up to $20 per bottle in fine-dining places.

Tipping is not mandatory in Australia, but is appreciated when service comes with a smile. Around 5% to 10% is the norm (perhaps more if your kids have gone crazy and trashed the dining room).

Quick Eats

In the big cities, street vending is on the rise – coffee carts have been joined by vans selling tacos, burritos, baked potatoes, burgers... Elsewhere around the cities you'll find fast-food chains, gourmet sandwich bars, food courts in shopping centres and market halls, bakeries, and sushi, noodle and salad bars. Beyond the big smoke the options are more limited and traditional, such as milk bars (known as delis in SA and WA). These corner stores often serve old-fashioned hamburgers (with bacon, egg, pineapple and beetroot!) and other takeaway foods.

There are almost a million Aussies with Italian heritage: it follows that pizza is (arguably) the most popular Australian fast food. Most home-delivered pizzas are of the American style (thick crusts and with lots of toppings) rather than the Italian style. However, wood-fired, thin, Neapolitan-style pizza can still be found, even in country towns.

Fish and chips are still hugely popular, the fish most often a form of shark (often called flake; don't worry, it's delicious), either grilled or dipped in batter and fried.

If you're at a rugby league or Aussie rules football match, a beer and a meat pie are as compulsory as wearing your team's colours.

BUSH TUCKER: AUSTRALIAN NATIVE FOODS *JANELLE WHITE*

There are around 350 food plants that are native to the Australian bush. Bush foods provide a real taste of the Australian landscape. There are the dried fruits and lean meats of the desert; shellfish and fish of the coast; alpine berries and mountain peppers of the high country; and citrus flavours, fruits and herbs of the rainforests.

This cuisine is based on Indigenous Australians' expert understanding of the environment, based on cultural knowledge handed down over generations. Years of trial and error have ensured a rich appreciation of these foods and mastery of their preparation.

The harvesting of bush foods for commercial return has been occurring for about 30 years. In central Australia it is mainly carried out by middle-aged and senior Aboriginal women. Here and in other regions, bush meats such as kangaroo, emu and crocodile; fish such as barramundi; and bush fruits including desert raisins, quandongs, riberries, and Kakadu plums are seasonally hunted and gathered for personal enjoyment, as well as to supply local, national and international markets.

Janelle White is an applied anthropologist currently completing a PhD on Aboriginal people's involvement in a variety of desert-based bush produce industries – including bush foods, bush medicines and bush jewellery. She splits her time between Adelaide and the land 200km northwest of Alice Springs.

Eating with the Locals

Most Aussies eat cereal, toast and/or fruit for breakfast, often extending to bacon and eggs on weekends, washed down with tea and coffee. They devour sandwiches, salads and sushi for lunch, and then eat anything and everything in the evening.

The iconic Australian barbecue (BBQ or barbie) is a near-mandatory cultural experience. In summer locals invite their mates around at dinnertime and fire-up the barbie, grilling burgers, sausages (snags), steaks, seafood, and veggie, meat or seafood skewers (if you're invited to a BBQ, bring some meat and cold beer). Year-round the BBQ is wheeled out at weekends for quick-fire lunches. There are coin-operated and free BBQs in parks around the country – a terrific traveller-friendly option.

Cafes & Coffee

Cafes in Australia generally serve good-value food: you can get a decent meal for around $15. Kids are usually more than welcome.

If you're invited to someone's house for dinner, always take a gift (even if the host dissuades you): a bottle of wine, a six-pack of beer, some flowers or a box of chocolates.

Coffee has become an Australian addiction. There are Italian-style espresso machines in virtually every cafe, boutique roasters are all the rage and, in urban areas, the qualified barista is ever-present (there are even barista-manned cafes attached to petrol stations). Sydney and Melbourne have given rise to a whole generation of coffee snobs, the two cities battling for bragging rights as Australia's coffee capital. The cafe scene in Melbourne is particularly artsy; the best way to immerse yourself in it is by wandering the city centre's cafe-lined laneways. You'll also find decent places in the other big cities and towns, and there's now a sporting chance of good coffee in many rural areas.

Pubs & Drinking

No matter what your poison, you're in the right country if you're after a drink. Long recognised as some of the finest in the world, Australian wines are one of the nation's top exports. As the public develops a more sophisticated palate, local beers are rising to the occasion, with a growing wealth of microbrewed flavours and varieties.

Beers have an alcohol content between 3.5% and 5.5%, less than European beers but more than most in North America. Light beers contain under 3% alcohol and are favoured by people observing Australia's stringent drink-driving laws.

FOOD: WHEN, WHERE & HOW

- Budget eating venues usually offer main courses for under $15, midrange places are generally between $15 and $32, with top-end venues charging over $32.
- Cafes serve breakfasts from around 8am on weekends – a bit earlier on weekdays – and close around 5pm.
- Pubs and bars usually open around lunchtime and continue til at least 10pm – later from Thursday to Saturday. Pubs usually serve food from noon to 2pm and 6pm to 8pm.
- Restaurants generally open around noon for lunch, 6pm for dinner. Australians usually eat lunch shortly after noon; dinner bookings are usually made between 7pm and 8pm, though in big cities some restaurants stay open past 10pm.
- Vegetarian eateries and vegetarian selections in non-veg places (including menu choices for vegans and for coeliac sufferers) are common in large cities. Rural Australia continues its dedication to meat.
- Smoking is banned in cafes, restaurants, clubs, pubs and an increasing number of ity malls.

WINE REGIONS

Most Australian states now nurture wine industries, some almost 200 years old. Many wineries have tastings for free or a small fee. Although plenty of good wine comes from big wineries with economies of scale on their side, the most interesting wines are often made by small producers. The following rundown should give you a head start.

South Australia

South Australia's wine industry is a global giant, as a visit to the National Wine Centre in Adelaide will attest. Cabernet sauvignon from Coonawarra, riesling from the Clare Valley, sauvignon blanc from the Adelaide Hills, and shiraz from the Barossa Valley and McLaren Vale are world-renowned.

New South Wales & the Australian Capital Territory

Dating from the 1820s, the Hunter Valley is Australia's oldest wine region. The Lower Hunter is known for shiraz and unwooded semillon. Upper Hunter wineries specialise in cabernet sauvignon and shiraz, with forays into verdelho and chardonnay. Further inland are award-winning wineries at Griffith, Mudgee and Orange. Canberra's surrounds have a growing number of excellent wineries.

Western Australia

Margaret River is synonymous with superb cabernets and chardonnays. Among old-growth forest, Pemberton wineries produce cabernet sauvignon, merlot, pinot noir, sauvignon blanc and shiraz. The south coast's Mt Barker is another budding wine region.

Victoria

Victoria has more than 500 wineries. Just out of Melbourne, the Yarra Valley produces excellent chardonnay and pinot noir, as does the Mornington Peninsula. Wineries in Rutherglen produce superb fortified wines as well as shiraz and durif.

Tasmania

Try the Pipers River Region and the Tamar Valley in the north, and explore the burgeoning wine industry in the Coal River Valley around Richmond near Hobart. Cool-climate drops are the name of the game here: especially pinot noir and sauvignon blanc.

Queensland

The Darling Downs is the heartland of Queensland's boutique wine industry. Stanthorpe is its centre, though you'll find a few cellar doors at Tamborine Mountain near Brisbane.

The terminology used to order beer varies from state to state. In NSW you ask for a schooner (425mL) if you're thirsty and a middy (285mL) if you're not quite so dry. In Victoria the 285mL measure is called a pot; in Tasmania it's called a 10-ounce. Pints can either be 425mL or 568mL, depending on where you are. Mostly you can just ask for a beer and see what turns up.

Shouting is a revered custom where people take turns to pay for a round of drinks. At a toast, everyone should touch glasses and look each other in the eye as they clink – failure to do so is purported to result in seven years' bad sex.

Pub meals (often referred to as counter meals) are usually hefty and good value; standards such as sausages and mash or schnitzel and salad go for $15 to $25.

A competitively priced place to eat is at a club – Returned and Services League (RSL) or Surf Life Saving clubs are solid bets. You order at the kitchen, take a number and wait until it's called out over the counter or intercom. You pick up the meal yourself, saving the restaurant on staffing costs and you on your total bill.

Delicious (www.taste.com.au/delicious) is a monthly magazine published by the Australian Broadcasting Corporation (ABC) listing recipes, restaurant reviews, food and wine trends, and foodie-related travel articles.

Sport

Whether they're filling stadiums, glued to the big screen at the pub or on the couch in front of the TV, Australians invest heavily in sport – both fiscally and emotionally. The federal government kicks in more than $300 million every year – enough cash for the nation to hold its own against formidable international sporting opponents. Despite slipping to 10th spot on the 2012 London Olympics medal tally, Australia is looking forward to redemption at the 2016 Rio Olympics.

'Footy' in Australia can mean a number of things: in NSW and Queensland it's usually rugby league, but the term is also used for Aussie rules, rugby union and soccer.

Australian Rules Football

Australia's most attended sport, and one of the two most watched, is Australian Rules football (Aussie rules). While traditionally embedded in the Victorian culture and identity, the Australian Football League (AFL) has gradually expanded its popularity into all states, including rugby-dominated New South Wales (NSW) and Queensland. Long kicks, high marks and brutal collisions whip crowds into frenzies and the roar of 50,000-plus fans yelling 'Baaall!!!' upsets dogs in suburban backyards for miles around.

Rugby

The **National Rugby League** (www.nrl.com.au) is the most popular football code north of the Murray River, the season highlight being the annual State of Origin series between NSW and Queensland. To witness an NRL game is to appreciate all of Newton's laws of motion, in bone-crunching style!

The national rugby union team, the Wallabies, won the Rugby World Cup in 1991 and 1999 and was runner-up in 2003, but hasn't made the final since. Australia, New Zealand and South Africa compete in the super-popular **Super 15s** (www.superxv.com) competition, which includes five Australian teams: the Waratahs (Sydney), the Reds (Brisbane), the Brumbies (Australian Capital Territory, or ACT), the Force (Perth) and the Rebels (Melbourne).

Soccer

Australia's national soccer team, the Socceroos, qualified for the 2006 and 2010 World Cups after a long history of almost-but-not-quite getting there. Regardless, national pride in the team remains undiminished. The national **A-League** (www.a-league.com.au) has enjoyed increased popularity in recent years, successfully luring a few big-name international players to bolster the home-grown talent pool.

Cricket

The Aussies dominated both test and one-day cricket for much of the noughties, holding the No 1 world ranking for most of the decade. But the subsequent retirement of once-in-a-lifetime players like Shane Warne and Ricky Ponting sent the team into an extended rebuilding mode. Series losses in 2009 and 2011 to arch-enemies England have caused nationwide misery. This biennial series is known as 'The Ashes' and the

SURF'S UP!

Australia has been synonymous with surfing ever since the Beach Boys effused about 'Australia's Narrabeen', one of Sydney's northern beaches, in *Surfin' USA*. Other surfing hot spots such as Bells Beach, Margaret River, the Pass at Byron Bay, and Burleigh Heads on the Gold Coast also resonate with international wave addicts. Iron Man and Surf Life Saving competitions are also held on beaches around the country, attracting dedicated fans to the sand.

Few Australian surfers have attained 'World Champion' status. Legendary surfers include Mark Richards, Tom Carroll, 2012 champ Joel Parkinson, Wendy Botha, seven-time champion Layne Beachley and 2012 champ (and five-time winner) Stephanie Gilmore.

unofficial trophy is a tiny terracotta urn containing the ashen remnants of an 1882 cricket bail (the perfect Australian BBQ conversation opener: ask a local what a 'bail' is).

Despite the Australian cricket team's bad rep for sledging (verbally dressing down one's opponent on the field), cricket is still a gentleman's game. Take the time to watch a match if you never have – such tactical cut-and-thrust, such nuance, such grace.

Tennis

Every January in Melbourne, the **Australian Open** (www.australianopen.com) attracts more people to Australia than any other sporting event. The men's competition was last won by an Australian, Mark Edmondson, back in 1976 – and while Lleyton Hewitt has been Australia's great hope for the last decade, the former world No 1's best playing days are behind him (but he looks set for a career as a commentator). In the women's game, Australian Sam Stosur won the US Open in 2011 and has been hovering around the top-10 player rankings ever since.

Swimming

Girt by sea and pock-marked with pools, Australia's population can swim. Australia's greatest female swimmer, Dawn Fraser, known simply as 'our Dawn', won the 100m freestyle gold at three successive Olympics (1956–64), plus the 4 x 100m freestyle relay in 1956. Australia's greatest male swimmer, Ian Thorpe (known as Thorpie or the Thorpedo), retired in 2006 aged 24 with five Olympic golds swinging from his neck. In early 2011, Thorpe announced his comeback, his eye fixed on the 2012 London Olympics – but he failed to make the team in the selection trials, and left the pool again to finish his autobiography.

Australia's Big Bash League (www.bigbash.com.au), the Twenty20 form of cricket, is gaining ground on the traditional five-day and one-day forms of the game. Fast, flashy and laced with pyrotechnics, it makes for a fun night out.

Horse Racing

Australians love to bet on the 'nags' – in fact, betting on horse racing is so mainstream and accessible that it's almost a national hobby! There are racecourses all around the country and local holidays for racing carnivals in Victoria, Tasmania and South Australia.

Australia's biggest race – the 'race that stops a nation' – is the **Melbourne Cup** (www.racingvictoria.net.au), which occurs on the first Tuesday in November. The most famous Melbourne Cup winner was the New Zealand-born Phar Lap, who won in 1930 before dying of a mystery illness (suspected arsenic poisoning) in America. Phar Lap is now a prize exhibit in the Melbourne Museum. The British-bred (but Australian-trained) Makybe Diva is a more recent star, winning three cups in a row before retiring in 2005.

Tennis

Swimming

Horse Racing

Survival Guide

Deadly & Dangerous

If you're the pessimistic type, you might choose to focus on the things that can bite, sting, burn, freeze, drown or rob you in Australia. But chances are the worst you'll encounter are a few pesky flies and mosquitoes. Splash on some insect repellent and boldly venture forth!

Where the Wild Things Are

Australia's profusion of dangerous creatures is legendary: snakes, spiders, sharks, crocodiles, jellyfish... Travellers needn't be alarmed, though – you're unlikely to see many of these creatures in the wild, much less be attacked by one.

Crocodiles

Around the northern Australian coastline, saltwater crocodiles (salties) are a real danger. They also inhabit estuaries, creeks and rivers, sometimes a long way inland. Observe safety signs or ask locals whether that inviting-looking waterhole or river is croc-free before plunging in.

Jellyfish

With venomous tentacles up to 3m long, box jellyfish (aka sea wasps or stingers) inhabit Australia's tropical waters. You can be stung during any month, but they're most common during the wet season (October to March) when you should stay out of the sea in many places. Stinger nets are in place at some beaches, but never swim unless you've checked. 'Stinger suits' (full-body Lycra swimsuits) prevent stinging, as do wetsuits. If you are stung, wash the skin with vinegar then get to a hospital.

The box jellyfish also has a tiny, lethal relative called an irukandji though, to date, only two north-coast deaths have been directly attributed to it.

MAINTAINING PERSPECTIVE

There's approximately one shark-attack and one croc-attack fatality per year in Australia. Blue-ringed-octopus deaths are rarer – only two in the last century. Jellyfish do better – about two deaths annually – but you're still more than 100 times more likely to drown. Spiders haven't killed anyone in the last 20 years. Snake bites kill one or two people per year, as do bee stings, but you're about a thousand times more likely to perish on the nation's roads.

Sharks

Despite extensive media coverage, the risk of shark attack in Australia is no greater than in other countries with extensive coastlines. Check with surf life-saving groups about local risks.

Snakes

There's no denying it: Australia has plenty of venomous snakes. Most common are brown and tiger snakes, but few species are aggressive. Unless you're messing around with or accidentally standing on one, it's extremely unlikely that you'll get bitten. The golden rule: if you see a snake, do a Beatles and *let it be*. If you are bitten, prevent the spread of venom by applying pressure to the wound and immobilising the area with a splint or sling before seeking medical attention.

Spiders

Australia has several poisonous spiders, bites from which are usually treatable with antivenins. The deadly funnel-web spider lives in New South Wales (including Sydney) – bites are treated as per snake bites (pressure and immobilisation before transferring to a hospital). Redback spiders live throughout Australia; bites cause pain, sweating and nausea. Apply ice or cold packs, then transfer to hospital. White-tailed spider bites may cause an ulcer that's slow and difficult to heal. Clean the wound and seek medical assistance. The disturbingly large huntsman spider is harmless, though seeing one can affect your blood pressure and/or underpants.

Out & About

At the Beach

Undertows (or rips) are a problem in the surf, but popular beaches are patrolled by surf life-savers. Patrolled areas are indicated by red-and-yellow flags. If you find yourself being carried out by a rip, swim parallel to the shore until you're out of the rip, then head for the beach.

Several people are paralysed every year by diving into shallow waves and hitting sand bars: look before you leap.

Bushfires

Bushfires happen regularly across Australia. In hot, dry and windy weather and on total-fire-ban days, you should be extremely careful with naked flames (including cigarette butts) and don't use camping stoves, campfires or BBQs. Bushwalkers should delay trips until things cool down. If you are out in the bush and you see smoke, take it seriously: find the nearest open space (downhill if possible). Forested ridges are dangerous places to be.

Cold Weather

More bushwalkers in Australia die of cold than in bushfires. Even in summer, particularly in highland Tasmania, Victoria and NSW, conditions can change quickly, with temperatures dropping below freezing and blizzards blowing in. Hypothermia is a real risk. Early signs include the inability to perform fine movements (eg doing up buttons), shivering and a bad case of the 'umbles' (fumbles, mumbles, grumbles, stumbles). Get out of the cold, change out of wet clothing and into dry stuff, and eat and drink to warm up.

Crime

Australia is a relatively safe place to visit, but you should still take reasonable precautions. Avoid walking around alone at night, don't leave hotel rooms or cars unlocked, and don't leave valuables visible through car windows.

Some pubs in Sydney and other big cities post warnings about drugged or 'spiked' drinks: play it safe if someone offers you a drink in a bar.

Infectious Diseases

You'll be unlucky to pick any of these up in your travels, but the following are a few diseases that do crop up around Australia.

Dengue Fever

Dengue fever occurs in northern Queensland, particularly during the wet season. Causing severe muscular aches, it's a viral disease spread by a day-feeding species of mosquito. Most people recover in a few days, but more severe forms of the disease can occur.

Giardiasis

Giardia is widespread in Australian waterways. Drinking untreated water from streams and lakes is not recommended. Use water filters, and boil or treat this water with iodine to help prevent giardiasis. Symptoms consist of intermittent bad-smelling diarrhoea, abdominal bloating and wind. Effective treatment is available (tinidazole or metronidazole).

Hepatitis C

This is still a growing problem among intravenous-drug users. Blood-transfusion services fully screen all blood before use.

Human Immunodeficiency Virus (HIV)

In Australia HIV rates have stabilised and levels are similar to other Western countries. Clean needles and syringes are widely available at all chemists.

Meningococcal Disease

A minor risk if you have prolonged stays in dormitory-style accommodation. A vaccine exists for some types of this disease (meningococcal A, C, Y and W), but there's no vaccine available for viral meningitis.

Ross River Fever

The Ross River virus is widespread in Australia, transmitted by marsh-dwelling mosquitoes. In addition to fever, it causes headache, joint and muscular pain, and a rash that resolves after five to seven days.

Tick Typhus

Predominantly occurring in Queensland and NSW, tick typhus involves a dark area forming around a tick bite, followed by a rash, fever, headache and lymph-node inflammation. The disease is treatable with antibiotics (doxycycline).

Viral Encephalitis

This mosquito-borne disease is most common in northern Australia (especially during the wet season), but poses minimal risk to travellers. Symptoms include headache, muscle pain and sensitivity to light. Residual neurological damage can occur and no specific treatment is available.

Directory A–Z

Accommodation

Australia offers everything from the tent-pegged confines of camping grounds and the communal space of hostels, to gourmet breakfasts in guesthouses, chaperoned farmstays and everything-at-your-fingertips resorts, plus the full gamut of hotel and motel lodgings.

During the high season over summer (December to February) and at other peak times, particularly school holidays and Easter, prices are usually at their highest. Outside these times you'll find useful discounts and lower walk-in rates. Notable exceptions include central Australia, the Top End and Australia's ski resorts, where summer is the low season and prices drop substantially.

B&Bs

Local bed-and-breakfast options include everything from restored miners' cottages, converted barns, rambling old houses, upmarket country manors and beachside bungalows to a simple bedroom in a family home. In areas that attract weekenders – historic towns, wine regions, accessible forest regions such as the Blue Mountains in New South Wales and the Dandenongs in Victoria – B&Bs are often upmarket, charging small fortunes for weekend stays in high season. Tariffs are typically in the midrange bracket, but can be higher. Local tourist offices can usually provide a list of places. Online resources for accommodation include:

Bed & Breakfast Accommodation in Australia (BABS; www.babs.com.au)

Hosted Accommodation Australia (www.australianbedandbreakfast.com.au)

OZ Bed & Breakfast (www.ozbedandbreakfast.com)

SLEEPING PRICE RANGES

The following price ranges refer to a double room with bathroom in high season (summer):

- **$** less than $100
- **$$** $100 to $200
- **$$$** more than $200

Expect to pay $20 to $50 more in expensive areas – notably Sydney, Perth and parts of northern Western Australia.

Camping & Caravanning

The cheapest accommodation lies outdoors, where the nightly cost of camping for two people is usually between $15 and $30, slightly more for a powered site. Camping in the bush is a highlight of travelling in Australia: in the outback and northern Australia you often won't even need a tent, and nights spent around a campfire under the stars are unforgettable.

Seasons Bear in mind that camping is best done during winter (the dry season) across the north of Australia, and during summer in the south of the country.

Costs Unless otherwise stated, prices for camp sites are usually for two people. Staying at designated sites in national parks normally costs between $7 and $15 per person.

Facilities Almost all caravan or holiday parks are equipped with hot showers, flushing toilets and laundry facilities, and frequently a pool. Most have cabins, powered caravan sites and tent sites. Cabin sizes and facilities vary, but expect to pay $70 to $80 for a small cabin with a kitchenette and up to $170 for a two- or three-bedroom cabin with a fully equipped kitchen, lounge room, TV and beds for up to six people.

Locations Note that most city camping grounds usually lie several kilometres from the town centre – only convenient if you have wheels. Caravan parks are popular along coastal areas: book well in advance for travel during summer and Easter. If you're doing a lot of caravanning/camping, consider joining one of the major chains, which offer member discounts.

Resources Get your hands on **Camps Australia Wide** (www.campsaustraliawide.com), a handy publication containing maps and information about camp sites across Australia.

Permits These days, applications for national park camping permits are often handled online by state departments (eg in Queensland it's via the Department of National Parks, Recreation, Sport & Racing website – www.nprsr.qld.gov.au; in WA it's via the Department of Environment & Conservation website – www.dec.wa.gov.au/campgrounds). Regional sleeping listings in this book contain this booking info.

Major chains

Big 4 (www.big4.com.au)

Discovery Holiday Parks (www.discoveryholidayparks.com.au)

Top Tourist Parks (www.toptouristparks.com.au)

Holiday Apartments

Costs For a two-bedroom flat, you're looking at anywhere from $140 to $200 per night, but you will pay much more in high season and for serviced apartments in major cities.

Facilities Self-contained holiday apartments range from simple, studio-like rooms with small kitchenettes, to two-bedroom apartments with full laundries and state-of-the-art entertainment systems: great value for multinight stays. Sometimes they come in small, single-storey blocks, but in tourist hot spots such as the Gold Coast expect a sea of high-rises.

PRACTICALITIES

- **Currency** The Australian dollar comprises 100 cents. There are 5c, 10c, 20c, 50c, $1 and $2 coins, and $5, $10, $20, $50 and $100 notes.
- **DVDs** Australian DVDs are encoded for Region 4, which includes Mexico, South America, Central America, New Zealand, the Pacific and the Caribbean.
- **Newspapers** Leaf through the daily *Sydney Morning Herald*, Melbourne's *Age* or the national *Australian* broadsheet newspapers.
- **Radio** Tune in to ABC radio; check out www.abc.net.au/radio.
- **Smoking** Banned on public transport, in pubs, bars and eateries, and in some public outdoor spaces.
- **TV** The main free-to-air TV channels are the government-sponsored ABC, multicultural SBS and the three commercial networks – Seven, Nine and Ten – plus numerous additional channels from these main players.
- **Weights and measures** Australia uses the metric system.

Hostels

Backpacker hostels are exceedingly popular in Australian cities and along the coast, but in the outback and rural areas you'll be hard pressed to find one. Highly social affairs, they're generally overflowing with 18- to 30-year-olds, but some have reinvented themselves to attract other travellers who simply want to sleep for cheap.

Costs Typically a dorm bed costs $25 to $35 per night, and a double (usually without bathroom) $70 to $90.

Facilities Hostels provide varying levels of accommodation, from the austere simplicity of wilderness hostels to city-centre buildings with a cafe-bar and en-suite rooms. Most of the accommodation is in dormitories (bunk rooms), usually ranging in size from four to 12 beds. Many hostels also provide twin rooms and doubles. Hostels generally have cooking facilities, a communal area with a TV, laundry facilities and sometimes travel offices and job centres.

Bed linen Often provided; sleeping bags are not welcome due to hygiene concerns.

HOSTEL ORGANISATIONS & CHAINS

The **Youth Hostels Association** (YHA; ☎02-9261 1111; www.yha.com.au) is part of **Hostelling International** (HI; www.hihostels.com), and has around 60 Australian hostels. If you're already a member in your own country, you're entitled to member rates at YHA Australia hostels (10% to 15% discount). Preferably, visitors to Australia should purchase an HI card in their country of residence, but once you're in Australia you can also buy memberships online, at state offices or major YHA hostels. A 12-month membership costs $42/32 if you're over/under 26; see the HI or YHA websites for details.

BOOK YOUR STAY ONLINE

For more accommodation reviews by Lonely Planet authors, check out http://hotels.lonelyplanet.com. You'll find independent reviews, as well as recommendations on the best places to stay. Best of all, you can book online.

Other international organisations with Australian hostels:

Base Backpackers (www.stayatbase.com)

Nomads Backpackers (www.nomadsworld.com)

VIP Backpacker (www.vipbackpackers.com)

Hotels

Hotels in Australian cities or well-touristed places are generally of the business or luxury-chain variety (midrange to top end), with comfortable, anonymous, mod-con-filled rooms in multistorey blocks. For these hotels we quote 'rack rates' (official advertised rates – usually more than $150 a night), though significant discounts can be offered when business is quiet.

Motels

Drive-up motels offer comfortable midrange accommodation and are found all over Australia. They rarely offer a cheaper rate for singles, so are better value for couples or groups of three. You'll mostly pay between $100 and $150 for a simple room with a kettle, fridge, TV, air-con and bathroom.

Pubs

Hotels in Australia – the ones that serve beer – are commonly known as pubs (from the term 'public house'). Many were built during boom times, so they're often among the largest, most extravagant buildings in town. Some have been restored but, generally, rooms remain small and weathered, with a long amble down the hall to the bathroom. They're usually central and cheap – singles/doubles with shared facilities from $50/80, more if you want a private bathroom – but if you're a light sleeper, avoid booking a room above the bar and check whether a band is playing downstairs that night.

Rental & Long-Term Accommodation

If you're in Australia for a while (visas permitting), then a rental property or room in a shared flat or house will be an economical option. Delve into the classified advertisement sections of the daily newspapers; Wednesday and Saturday are usually the best days. Noticeboards in universities, hostels, bookshops and cafes are also useful. Properties listed through a real-estate agent necessitate at least a six-month lease, plus a bond and first month's rent up front.

CityHobo (www.cityhobo.com) Matches your personality with your ideal suburb in Melbourne, Adelaide, Brisbane, Perth or Sydney.

Couch Surfing (www.couchsurfing.com) Connects spare couches with new friends around the world.

Flatmate Finders (www.flatmatefinders.com.au) Long-term share accommodation listings.

Gumtree (www.gumtree.com.au) Flat shares, jobs and other classifieds in capital cities.

Stayz (www.stayz.com.au) Holiday rentals.

Other Accommodation

There are lots of less-conventional and, in some cases, uniquely Australian accommodation possibilities scattered across the country.

Country farms sometimes offer a bed for a night, while some remote outback stations allow you to stay in homestead rooms or shearers' quarters and try activities such as horse riding. Check out **Hosted Accommodation Australia** (www.australianbedandbreakfast.com.au) and **Farmstay Camping Australia** (www.farmstaycampingaustralia.com.au) for options. State tourist offices can also help.

Back within city limits, it's sometimes possible to stay in the hostels and halls of residence normally occupied by university students, though you'll need to time your stay to coincide with the longer university holiday periods.

Children

If you can survive the long-haul distances between cities, travelling around Australia with the kids can be a real delight. There's oodles of interesting stuff to see and do, both indoors and outdoors.

Lonely Planet's *Travel with Children* contains plenty of useful information.

Practicalities

Accommodation Many motels and the better-equipped caravan parks have playgrounds and swimming pools, and can supply cots and baby baths – motels may also have in-house children's videos and child-minding services. Top-end hotels and many (but not all) midrange hotels are well versed in the needs of guests with children. B&Bs, on the other hand, often market themselves as kid-free.

Change rooms and breastfeeding All cities and most major towns have centrally located public rooms where parents can go to nurse their baby or change a nappy;

check with the local tourist office or city council for details. Most Australians have a relaxed attitude about breastfeeding and nappy changing in public.

Child care Australia's numerous licensed child-care agencies offer babysitting services. Check under 'Baby Sitters' and 'Child Care Centres' in the Yellow Pages telephone directory, or phone the local council for a list. Licensed centres are subject to government regulations and usually adhere to high standards; avoid unlicensed operators.

Child safety seats Major hire-car companies will supply and fit child safety seats, charging a one-off fee of around $25. Call taxi companies in advance to organise child safety seats. The rules for travelling in taxis with kids vary from state to state: in most places safety seats aren't legally required but must be used if available.

Concessions Child concessions (and family rates) often apply to accommodation, tours, admission fees and transport, with some discounts as high as 50% of the adult rate. However, the definition of 'child' varies from under 12 to under 18 years. Accommodation concessions generally apply to children under 12 years sharing the same room as adults.

Eating out Many cafes and restaurants offer kids' meals, or will provide small serves from the main menu. Some also supply high chairs.

Health care Australia has high-standard medical services and facilities, and items such as baby formula and disposable nappies are widely available.

Customs Regulations

For detailed information on customs and quarantine regulations, contact the **Australian Customs & Border Protection Service** (☎1300 363 263, 02-6275 6666; www.customs.gov.au) and the **Department of Agriculture, Fisheries & Forestry** (www.daff.gov.au).

When entering Australia you can bring most articles in free of duty provided that customs is satisfied they are for personal use and that you'll be taking them with you when you leave. Duty-free quotas per person:

Alcohol 2.25L (over the age of 18)

Cigarettes 50 cigarettes (over the age of 18)

Dutiable goods Up to the value of $900 ($450 for people under 18)

Narcotics, of course, are illegal, and customs inspectors and their highly trained hounds are diligent in sniffing them out. Quarantine regulations are strict, so you must declare all goods of animal or vegetable origin – wooden spoons, straw hats, the lot. Fresh food (meat, cheese, fruit, vegetables etc) and flowers are prohibited. There are disposal bins located in airports where you can dump any questionable items if you don't want to bother with an inspection. You need to declare currency in excess of $10,000 (including foreign currency).

Discount Cards

Travellers over 60 with some form of identification (eg a Seniors Card – www.seniorscard.com.au) are often eligible for concession prices. Overseas pensioners are entitled to discounts of at least 10% on most express-bus fares with Greyhound.

The internationally recognised **International Student Identity Card** (ISIC; www.isic.org) is available to full-time students aged 12 and over. The card gives the bearer discounts on accommodation, transport and admission to various attractions. The same organisation also produces the International Youth Travel Card (IYTC), issued to people under 26 years of age who are not full-time students, and has benefits equivalent to the ISIC. Also similar is the International Teacher Identity Card (ITIC), available to teaching professionals. All three cards are chiefly available from student travel companies.

Electricity

Embassies & Consulates

The main diplomatic representations are in Canberra. There are also consulates in other major cities, particularly for countries with a strong link to Australia, such as the USA, the UK and New Zealand, or in cities with important connections, such as Darwin, which has an Indonesian consulate.

Yellow Pages phone directories offer more complete listings of offices.

Canadian Embassy Canberra (☎02-6270 4000; www.australia.gc.ca; Commonwealth Ave, Yarralumla, ACT); Sydney

(☎02-9364 3000; L5, 111 Harrington St, Sydney, NSW)

Chinese Embassy (☎02-6273 4780; http://au.china-embassy.org; 15 Coronation Dr, Yarralumla, Canberra, ACT)

Dutch Embassy Canberra (☎02-6220 9400; www.netherlands.org.au; 120 Empire Circuit, Yarralumla, ACT); Sydney (☎02-9387 6644; L23, Westfield Tower 2, 101 Grafton St, Bondi Junction, NSW)

French Embassy Canberra (☎02-6216 0100; www.ambafrance-au.org; 6 Perth Ave, Yarralumla, ACT); Sydney (☎02-9268 2400; L26, 31 Market St, Sydney, NSW)

German Embassy Canberra (☎02-6270 1911; www.canberra.diplo.de; 119 Empire Circuit, Yarralumla, ACT); Sydney (☎02-9328 7733; 13 Trelawney St, Woollahra, NSW); Melbourne (☎9864 6888; www.melbourne.diplo.de; 480 Punt Rd, South Yarra)

Irish Embassy (☎02-6214 0000; www.embassyofireland.au.com; 20 Arkana St, Yarralumla, Canberra, ACT)

Japanese Embassy Canberra (☎02-6273 3244; www.au.emb-japan.go.jp; 112 Empire Circuit, Yarralumla, ACT); Sydney (☎02-9250 1000; L12, 1 O'Connell St, Sydney, NSW)

Malaysian Embassy (☎02-6120 0300; www.malaysia.org.au; 7 Perth Ave, Yarralumla, Canberra, ACT 2600)

New Zealand Embassy Canberra (☎02-6270 4211; www.nzembassy.com; Commonwealth Ave, Yarralumla, ACT); Sydney (☎1300 559 535; L10, 55 Hunter St, Sydney, NSW)

Singaporean Embassy (☎02-6271 2000; www.mfa.gov.sg/canberra; 17 Forster Cres, Yarralumla, ACT)

South African Embassy (☎02-6272 7300; www.sahc.org.au; cnr Rhodes Pl & State Circle, Yarralumla, ACT)

Thai Embassy Canberra (☎02-6206 0100; http://canberra.thaiembassy.org; 111 Empire Circuit, Yarralumla, ACT); Sydney (☎02-9241 2542; www.thaiconsulatesydney.org; L8, 131 Macquarie St, Sydney NSW)

UK Embassy Canberra (☎02-6270 6666; www.ukinaustralia.fco.gov.uk; Commonwealth Ave, Yarralumla, ACT); Sydney (☎02-9247 7521; L16, Gateway Bldg,1 Macquarie Pl, Sydney, NSW); Melbourne (☎03-9652 1600; L17, 90 Collins St, Melbourne, VIC)

US Embassy Canberra (☎02-6214 5600; http://canberra.usembassy.gov; 1 Moonah Pl, Yarralumla, ACT); Sydney (☎02-8278 1420; L10, MLC Centre, 19-29 Martin Pl, Sydney, NSW); Melbourne (☎03-9526 5900; L6, 553 St Kilda Rd, Melbourne, VIC)

Food

Eating reviews in this guide use the following price ranges to refer to a standard main course:

- **$** less than $15
- **$$** $15 to $32
- **$$$** more than $32

Gay & Lesbian Travellers

Australia is a popular destination for gay and lesbian travellers, with the so-called 'pink tourism' appeal of Sydney especially big, thanks largely to the city's annual, high-profile and spectacular Sydney Gay & Lesbian Mardi Gras. In general, Australians are open-minded about homosexuality, but the further into the country you get, the more likely you are to run into overt homophobia.

Throughout the country, but particularly on the east coast, there are tour operators, travel agents and accommodation places that make a point of welcoming gay men and lesbians.

Same-sex acts are legal in all states but the age of consent varies.

Major Gay & Lesbian Events

Midsumma Festival (www.midsumma.org.au; ⏲Jan-Feb) Melbourne's annual gay-and-lesbian arts festival features more than 100 events from mid-January to mid-February, with a Pride March finale.

Sydney Gay & Lesbian Mardi Gras (www.mardigras.org.au) The highlight of this world-famous, month-long festival is the over-the-top, sequined Oxford St parade. February to March.

Pridefest (www.pridewa.asn.au) In October in Perth.

Feast Festival (www.feast.org.au) Three weeks in November in Adelaide, with a carnival, theatre, dialogue and dance.

Publications & Contacts

Major cities have gay newspapers, available from clubs, cafes, venues and newsagents. Gay and lesbian lifestyle magazines include *DNA*, *Lesbians on the Loose (LOTL)* and the Sydney-based *SX*. In Melbourne look for *MCV*; in Queensland look for *Queensland Pride*. Perth has the free *OutinPerth* and Adelaide has *Blaze*.

Gay and Lesbian Counselling & Community Services of Australia (GLCCS; www.glccs.org.au) Telephone counselling.

Gay & Lesbian Tourism Australia (GALTA; www.galta.com.au) A wealth of information about gay and lesbian travel in Australia.

Same Same (www.samesame.com.au) News, events and lifestyle features.

Health

Healthwise, Australia is a remarkably safe country in which to travel, considering that such a large portion of it lies in the tropics. Few travellers to Australia will experience anything worse than an upset stomach or a bad hangover and, if you do fall ill, the standard of hospitals and health care is high.

Vaccinations

Visit a physician four to eight weeks before departure. Ask your doctor for an International Certificate of Vaccination (aka the 'yellow booklet'), which will list the vaccinations you've received.

If you're entering Australia within six days of having stayed overnight or longer in a yellow-fever-infected country, you'll need proof of yellow-fever vaccination. For a full list of these countries visit **Centers for Disease Control & Prevention** (www.cdc.gov/travel).

The **World Health Organization** (WHO; www.who.int/wer) recommends that all travellers should be covered for diphtheria, tetanus, measles, mumps, rubella, chicken pox and polio, as well as hepatitis B, regardless of their destination. While Australia has high levels of childhood vaccination coverage, outbreaks of these diseases do occur.

Insurance

Health insurance is essential for all travellers, see p1072.

Internet Resources

There's a wealth of travel health advice on the internet: **Lonely Planet** (www.lonelyplanet.com) is a good place to start. The **World Health Organization** (WHO; www.who.int/ith) publishes *International Travel and Health*, revised annually and available free online. **MD Travel Health** (www.mdtravelhealth.com) provides complete travel health recommendations for every country, updated daily. A selection of government travel health websites:

- **Australia** (www.smartraveller.gov.au)
- **Canada** (www.hc-sc.gc.ca)
- **UK** (www.nhs.uk/livewell/travelhealth)
- **USA** (www.cdc.gov/travel)

Availability & Cost of Health Care

Facilities Australia has an excellent health-care system. It's a mixture of privately run medical clinics and hospitals alongside a system of public hospitals funded by the Australian government. There are also excellent specialised public-health facilities for women and children in major centres.

Medicare This system covers Australian residents for some health-care costs. Visitors from countries with which Australia has a reciprocal health-care agreement are eligible for benefits specified under the Medicare program. Agreements are currently in place with Finland, Italy, Malta, the Netherlands, Norway, Sweden and the UK – check the details before departing these countries. For further details, visit www.humanservices.gov.au/customer/enablers/medicare/medicare-card/new-arrivals-and-visitors-to-australia.

Medications Painkillers, antihistamines for allergies, and skincare products are widely available at chemists throughout Australia. You may find that medications readily available over the counter in some countries are only available in Australia by prescription. These include the oral contraceptive pill, some medications for asthma and all antibiotics.

Health Care in Remote Areas

In Australia's remote locations, it is possible there'll be a significant delay in emergency services reaching you in the event of serious accident or illness. Do not underestimate the vast distances between most major outback towns; an increased level of self-reliance and preparation is essential. The **Royal Flying Doctor Service** (www.flyingdoctor.net) provides an important back-up for remote communities.

Consider taking a wilderness first-aid course, such as those offered by **Wilderness First Aid Consultants** (www.equip.com.au). Take a comprehensive first-aid kit that is appropriate for the activities planned.

Ensure that you have adequate means of communication. Australia has extensive mobile-phone coverage, but additional radio communication is important for remote areas.

At the Beach

Check with local surf lifesaving organisations and be aware of your own expertise and limitations before entering the surf. Always use SPF30+ sunscreen (or higher); apply it 30 minutes before going into the sun and repeat applications regularly.

Heat Exhaustion & Heatstroke

Symptoms of heat exhaustion include dizziness, fainting, fatigue, nausea or vomiting. The skin is usually pale, cool and clammy. Treatment consists of rest in a cool, shady place and fluid replacement with water or diluted sports drinks.

Heatstroke is a severe form of heat illness and is a true medical emergency, with heating of the brain leading to disorientation, hallucinations and seizures. Prevent heatstroke by maintaining an adequate fluid intake to ensure the continued passage of clear and copious urine, especially during physical exertion.

Insect-Borne Illnesses

Various insects in Australia may be the source of specific diseases (dengue fever, Ross River fever, viral encephalitis). For protection wear loose-fitting, long-sleeved clothing, and apply 30% DEET to all exposed skin.

Travellers' Diarrhoea

Tap water is universally safe in Australia. All other water should be boiled, filtered or chemically disinfected (with iodine tablets) to prevent travellers' diarrhoea and giardiasis.

If you develop diarrhoea (more than four or five stools a day), drink plenty of fluids – preferably an oral rehydration solution containing lots of salt and sugar. You should also begin taking an antibiotic (usually a quinolone drug) and an antidiarrhoeal agent (such as loperamide). If diarrhoea is bloody, persists for more than 72 hours or is accompanied by fever, shaking, chills or severe abdominal pain, seek medical attention.

Medical Checklist

- acetaminophen (paracetamol) or aspirin
- antibiotics
- antidiarrhoeal drugs (eg loperamide)
- antihistamines (for hayfever and allergic reactions)
- anti-inflammatory drugs (eg ibuprofen)
- antibacterial ointment in case of cuts or abrasions
- steroid cream or cortisone (for allergic rashes)
- bandages, gauze, gauze rolls
- adhesive or paper tape
- scissors, safety pins, tweezers
- thermometer
- pocket knife
- DEET-containing insect repellent for the skin
- permethrin-containing insect spray for clothing, tents and bed nets
- sunscreen
- oral rehydration salts
- iodine tablets or water filter (for water purification)

Insurance

Worldwide travel insurance is available at www.lonelyplanet.com/travel_services. You can buy, extend and claim online anytime – even if you're already on the road.

Level of cover A good travel insurance policy covering theft, loss and medical problems is essential. Some policies specifically exclude designated 'dangerous activities' such as scuba diving, skiing and even bushwalking. Make sure the policy you choose fully covers you for your activity of choice.

Health You may prefer a policy that pays doctors or hospitals directly rather than requiring you to pay on the spot and claim later. If you have to claim later make sure you keep all documentation. Check that the policy covers ambulances and emergency medical evacuations by air.

Internet Access

Accessing Terminals

There are fewer internet cafes around these days than there were five years ago (thanks to the advent of iPhones/iPads and wi-fi) but you'll still find them in most sizable towns. Hourly costs range from $6 to $10. Most youth hostels have both internet kiosks and wi-fi, as do many hotels and caravan parks.

Most public libraries have internet access, but generally it's provided for research needs, not for travellers to check Facebook – so book ahead or tackle an internet cafe.

BYO

ISPs If you're bringing your palmtop or laptop, check with your Internet Service Provider (ISP) for access numbers you can dial into in Australia. Some major Australian ISPs:

- **Australia On Line** (☎1300 650 661; www.ozonline.com.au)
- **Dodo** (☎13 36 36; www.dodo.com)
- **iinet** (☎13 19 17; www.iinet.net.au)
- **iPrimus** (☎13 17 89; www.iprimus.com.au)
- **Optus** (www.optus.com.au)
- **Telstra BigPond** (☎13 76 63; www.bigpond.com)

Plugs Australia primarily uses the RJ-45 telephone plugs although you may see Telstra EXI-160 four-pin plugs – electronics shops such as Tandy and Dick Smith can help.

Modem Keep in mind that your PC-card modem may not work in Australia. The safest option is to buy a reputable 'global' modem before you leave home or buy a local PC-card modem once you get to Australia.

Wi-fi

It's still rare in remote Australia, but wireless internet access is increasingly the norm in Australia's big-city accommodation, with cafes, bars and even some public gardens also providing wi-fi access (often free for customers/guests). For locations, visit www.freewifi.com.au.

Legal Matters

Most travellers will have no contact with Australia's police or legal system; if they do, it's most likely to be while driving.

Driving There's a significant police presence on central Australian roads, and police have the power to stop your car, see your licence (you're required to carry it), check your vehicle for roadworthiness, and insist that you take a breath test for alcohol (and sometimes illicit drugs).

Drugs First-time offenders caught with small amounts of illegal drugs are likely to receive a fine rather than go to jail, but the recording of a conviction against you may affect your visa status.

Visas If you remain in Australia beyond the life of your visa, you'll officially be an 'overstayer' and could face detention and then be prevented from returning to Australia for up to three years.

Arrested? It's your right to telephone a friend, lawyer or relative before questioning begins. Legal aid is available only in serious cases; for Legal Aid office info see www.nla.aust.net.au. However, many solicitors do not charge for an initial consultation.

INTERSTATE QUARANTINE

When travelling within Australia, whether by land or air, you'll come across signs (mainly in airports and interstate train stations and at state borders) warning of the possible dangers of carrying fruit, vegetables and plants from one area to another. Certain pests and diseases (fruit fly, cucurbit thrips, grape phylloxera...) are prevalent in some areas but not in others: authorities would like to limit them spreading.

There are quarantine inspection posts on some state borders and occasionally elsewhere. While quarantine control often relies on honesty, many posts are staffed and officers are entitled to search your car for undeclared items. Generally they will confiscate all fresh fruit and vegetables, so it's best to leave shopping for these items until the first town past the inspection point.

Money

In this book, prices refer to the (very stable) Australian dollar.

ATMs & Eftpos

ATMs Australia's 'big four' banks – ANZ, Commonwealth, National Australia Bank and Westpac – and affiliated banks have branches all over Australia, and many provide 24-hour automated teller machines (ATMs). But don't expect to find ATMs *everywhere*, certainly not off the beaten track or in small towns. Most ATMs accept cards issued by other banks (for a fee) and are linked to international networks.

Eftpos Most service stations, supermarkets, restaurants, cafes and shops have Electronic Funds Transfer at Point of Sale (Eftpos) facilities these days, allowing you to make purchases and even draw out cash with your credit or debit card. Just don't forget your PIN (Personal Identification Number)!

Fees Bear in mind that withdrawing cash via ATMs or Eftpos may attract significant fees – check the associated costs with your bank first.

Opening a Bank Account

Within six weeks If you're planning on staying in Australia a while (on a Working Holiday visa for instance) it makes sense to open a local bank account. This is easy enough for overseas visitors provided it's done within six weeks of arrival. Simply present your passport and provide the bank with a postal address and they'll open the account and send you an ATM card.

After six weeks ...it becomes much more complicated. A points system operates and you need to score a minimum of 100 points before you can have the privilege of letting the bank take your money. Passports or birth certificates are worth 70 points; an international driving licence with photo earns you 40 points; and minor IDs, such as credit cards, get you 25 points. You must have at least one ID with a photograph. Once the account is open, you should be able to have money transferred from your home account (for a fee, of course).

Before you arrive It's possible to set up an Australian bank account before you embark on your international trip and applications can be made online; check bank websites for details:

ANZ (www.anz.com.au)

Commonwealth Bank (www.commbank.com.au)

National Australia Bank (NAB; www.nab.com.au)

Westpac (www.westpac.com.au)

Credit Cards

Credit cards such as Visa and MasterCard are widely accepted for everything from a hostel bed or a restaurant meal to an adventure tour, and are pretty much essential (in lieu of a large deposit) for hiring a car. They can also be used to get cash advances over the counter at banks and from many ATMs, depending on the card, though these transactions incur immediate interest. Diners Club and American Express (Amex) are not as widely accepted.

Lost credit-card contact numbers:

American Express (☎1300 132 639; www.americanexpress.com.au)

Diners Club (☎1300 360 060; www.dinersclub.com.au)

MasterCard (☎1800 120 113; www.mastercard.com.au)

Visa (☎1800 450 346; www.visa.com.au)

Debit Cards

A debit card allows you to draw money directly from your home bank account using ATMs, banks or Eftpos machines. Any card connected to the international banking network – Cirrus, Maestro, Plus and Eurocard – should work with your PIN. Expect substantial fees.

Companies such as Travelex offer debit cards (Travelex calls them 'Cash Passport' cards) with set withdrawal fees and a balance you can top up from your personal bank account while on the road.

Exchanging Money

Changing foreign currency or travellers cheques is usually no problem at banks throughout Australia, or at licensed moneychangers such as Travelex or AmEx in cities and major towns.

Taxes & Refunds

The goods and services tax (GST) is a flat 10% tax on all goods and services – accommodation, eating out, transport, electrical and other goods, books, furniture, clothing etc. There are exceptions, such as basic foods (milk, bread, fruit and vegetables etc). By law the tax is included in the quoted or shelf price, so all prices are GST-inclusive.

International air and sea travel to and from Australia is GST-free, as is domestic air travel when purchased outside Australia by nonresidents.

If you purchase new or secondhand goods with a total minimum value of $300 from any one supplier no more than 30 days before you leave Australia, you are entitled under the Tourist Refund Scheme (TRS) to a refund of any GST or WET (wine equalisation tax) that you paid. The scheme doesn't apply to all goods, and those that do qualify must be worn or taken as hand luggage onto the plane or ship. Also note that the refund is valid for goods bought from more than one supplier, but only if at least $300 is spent in each. For more details of the refund, see the website of the **Australian Customs & Border Protection Service** (☎1300 363 263, 02-6275 6666; www.customs.gov.au).

Visitors pay tax on earnings made within Australia, and must lodge a tax return with the Australian Taxation Office (ATO). If too much tax was withheld from your pay, you will receive a refund. See the **Australian Taxation Office** (ATO; www.ato.gov.au) website for details.

Travellers Cheques

➡ The ubiquity and convenience of internationally linked credit and debit card facilities in Australia means that travellers cheques are virtually redundant.

➡ AmEx and Travelex will exchange their associated travellers cheques, and major banks will change travellers cheques also.

➡ In all instances you'll need to present your passport for identification when cashing them.

Opening Hours

Business hours do vary from state to state, but use the following as a guide. Note that nearly all attractions across Australia are closed on Christmas Day; many also close on New Years Day and Good Friday.

Banks 9.30am to 4pm Monday to Thursday; until 5pm on Friday. Some large city branches open 8am to 6pm weekdays; a few also till 9pm Friday.

Cafes Usually open from around 7am until around 5pm, or continuing their business into the night.

Petrol stations and roadhouses Usually open 8am to 10pm. Some urban service stations open 24 hours.

Post offices 9am to 5pm Monday to Friday; some from 9am to noon on Saturday. You can also buy stamps from newsagents and some delis.

Pubs Usually serve food from noon to 2pm and from 6pm to 8pm. Pubs and bars often open for drinking at lunchtime and continue well into the evening, particularly from Thursday to Saturday.

Restaurants Open around noon for lunch and from 6pm for dinner, typically serving until at least 2pm and 8pm respectively, often later. Big-city eateries keep longer hours.

Shops and businesses 9am to 5pm or 6pm Monday to Friday, until either noon or 5pm on Saturday. Sunday trading operates in major cities, urban areas and tourist towns. There is late-night shopping till 9pm in major towns (usually Thursday or Friday night).

Supermarkets Generally open from 7am until at least 8pm; some open 24 hours. Delis (general stores) also open late.

Photography

Availability and printing Digital cameras, memory sticks and batteries are sold prolifically in cities and urban centres. Try electronics stores (Dick Smith, Tandy) or the larger department stores. Many internet cafes, camera stores and large stationers (Officeworks, Harvey Norman) have printing and CD-burning facilities.

Books Check out Lonely Planet's *Travel Photography* guide.

Etiquette As in any country, politeness goes a long way when taking photographs; ask before taking pictures of people. Particularly bear in mind that for indigenous Australians, photography can be highly intrusive: photographing cultural places, practices and images, sites of significance and ceremonies may also be a sensitive matter. Always ask first.

Post

Australia Post (www.auspost.com.au) runs national and world-wide services; the website has info on international letter and parcel delivery zones and rates. Post offices will hold mail for visitors: you must provide identification (such as a passport or driver's licence) to collect mail.

Public Holidays

Timing of public holidays can vary from state to state: check locally for precise dates (* indicates holidays that are only observed locally within each state).

National

New Year's Day 1 January

Australia Day 26 January

Easter (Good Friday to Easter Monday inclusive) late March/early April

Anzac Day 25 April

Queen's Birthday (except WA) Second Monday in June

Queen's Birthday (WA) Last Monday in September

Christmas Day 25 December

Boxing Day 26 December

Australian Capital Territory

Canberra Day Second Monday in March

Bank Holiday First Monday in August

Labour Day First Monday in October

New South Wales

Bank Holiday First Monday in August

Labour Day First Monday in October

Northern Territory

May Day First Monday in May

Show Day* (Alice Springs) First Friday in July; (Tennant Creek) second Friday in July; (Katherine) third Friday in July; (Darwin) fourth Friday in July

Picnic Day First Monday in August

Queensland

Labour Day First Monday in May

Royal Queensland Show Day* (Brisbane) Second or third Wednesday in August

South Australia

Adelaide Cup Day Third Monday in May

Labour Day First Monday in October

Proclamation Day Last Monday or Tuesday in December

Tasmania

Regatta Day* (Hobart) 14 February

Launceston Cup Day* Last Wednesday in February

Eight Hours Day First Monday in March

Bank Holiday Tuesday following Easter Monday

King Island Show* First Tuesday in March

Launceston Show Day* Thursday preceding second Saturday in October

Hobart Show Day* Thursday preceding fourth Saturday in October

Recreation Day* (Northern Tasmania) First Monday in November

Victoria

Labour Day Second Monday in March

Melbourne Cup Day First Tuesday in November

Western Australia

Labour Day First Monday in March

Foundation Day First Monday in June

School Holidays

- The Christmas/summer school holiday season runs from mid-December to late January.
- Three shorter school holiday periods occur during the year, varying by a week or two from state to state. They fall roughly from early to mid-April, late June to mid-July, and late September to early October.

Safe Travel

Australia is a relatively safe place to travel by world standards – crime- and war-wise at any rate – but natural disasters have been wreaking havoc of late. Bushfires, floods and cyclones regularly decimate parts of most states and territories, but if you pay attention to warnings from local authorities and don't venture into affected areas, you should be fine.

Telephone

Australia's main telecommunication companies:

Telstra (www.telstra.com.au) The main player – landline and mobile phone services.

GOVERNMENT TRAVEL ADVICE

The following government websites offer travel advisories and information about current hot spots around the world.

- **Australian Department of Foreign Affairs & Trade** (www.smarttraveller.gov.au)
- **British Foreign & Commonwealth Office** (www.gov.uk/fco)
- **Government of Canada** (www.travel.gc.ca)
- **US State Department** (www.travel.state.gov)

Optus (www.optus.com.au) Telstra's main rival – landline and mobile phone services.

Vodafone (www.vodafone.com.au) Mobile phone services.

Virgin (www.virginmobile.com.au) Mobile phone services.

Toll-Free & Information Calls

➡ Many businesses have either a toll-free 1800 number, dialled from anywhere within Australia for free, or a 13 or 1300 number, charged at a local call rate. None of these numbers can be dialled from outside Australia.

➡ To make a reverse-charge (collect) call from any public or private phone, dial 1800 738 3773 or 12 550.

➡ Numbers starting with 190 are usually recorded information services, charged at anything from 35c to $5 or more per minute (more from mobiles and payphones).

International Calls

From payphones Most payphones allow International Subscriber Dialling (ISD) calls, the cost and international dialling code of which will vary depending on which international phonecard provider you are using. International phone cards are readily available from internet cafes and convenience stores.

From landlines International calls from landlines in Australia are also relatively cheap and often subject to special deals; rates vary with providers.

Codes When calling overseas you will need to dial the international access code from Australia (0011 or 0018), the country code and then the area code (without the initial 0). So for a London telephone number you'll need to dial 0011-44-20, then the number. In addition, certain operators will have you dial a special code to access their service. If dialling Australia from overseas, the country code is 61 and you need to drop the 0 in state/territory area codes. Other country codes:

COUNTRY	CODE
France	33
Germany	49
Ireland	353
Japan	81
Netherlands	31
New Zealand	64
UK	44
USA & Canada	1

Local Calls

Calls from private phones cost 15c to 30c, while local calls from public phones cost 50c; both involve unlimited talk time. Calls to mobile phones attract higher rates and are timed.

Long-Distance Calls & Area Codes

Long-distance calls (over around 50km) are timed. Australia uses four Subscriber Trunk Dialling (STD) area codes. These STD calls can be made from any public phone and are cheaper during off-peak hours (generally between 7pm and 7am, and on the weekends). Broadly, the main area codes are as follows.

STATE/ TERRITORY	AREA CODE
ACT	02
NSW	02
NT	08
QLD	07
SA	08
TAS	03
VIC	03
WA	08

Area code boundaries don't necessarily coincide with state borders; for example some parts of NSW use the neighbouring states' codes.

Mobile (Cell) Phones

Numbers Numbers with the prefix 04xx belong to mobile phones.

Networks Australia's GSM and 3G mobile networks service more than 90% of the population but leave vast tracts of the country uncovered. Australia's digital network is compatible with GSM 900 and 1800 (used in Europe), but generally not with the systems used in the USA or Japan.

Reception The east coast, southeast and southwest get good reception, but elsewhere (apart from major towns) it can be haphazard or nonexistent. Things are improving, however.

New accounts It's easy and cheap enough to get connected short-term, with prepaid mobile systems offered by the main providers.

Phonecards & Public Phones

A variety of phonecards can be bought at newsagents, hostels and post offices for a fixed dollar value (usually $10, $20 etc) and can be used with any public or private phone by dialling a toll-free access number and then the PIN number on the card.

Most public phones use phonecards; some of them also accept credit cards. Old-fashioned coin-operated public phones are becoming increasingly rare (and if you do find one, chances are the coin slot will be gummed up or vandalised beyond function).

Time

Zones Australia is divided into three time zones: Western Standard Time (GMT/UTC plus eight hours), covering WA; Central Standard Time (plus 9½ hours), covering NT and SA; and Eastern Standard Time (plus 10 hours), covering Tasmania, Victoria, NSW, the ACT and Queensland. There are minor exceptions – Broken

Hill (NSW), for instance, is on Central Standard Time. For international times, see www.timeanddate.com/worldclock.

Daylight saving Clocks are put forward an hour. This system operates in some states during the warmer months (October to early April), but things can get pretty confusing, with WA, NT and Queensland staying on standard time, while in Tasmania daylight saving starts a month earlier than in SA, Victoria, ACT and NSW.

Toilets

- Toilets in Australia are sit-down Western style (… though you mightn't find this prospect too appealing in some remote outback pit-stops).
- See www.toiletmap.gov.au for public toilet locations.

Tourist Information

The **Australian Tourist Commission** (ATC; www.australia.com) is the national government tourist body, and has a good website for pre-trip research. The website also lists reliable travel agents in countries around the world to help you plan your trip, plus visa, work and customs information.

Within Australia, tourist information is disseminated by various regional and local offices. Almost every major town in Australia seems to maintain a tourist office of some type and in many cases they are very good, with chatty staff (often retiree volunteers) providing local info not readily available from the state offices. If booking accommodation or tours from local offices, bear in mind that they often only promote businesses that are paying members of the local tourist association.

Travellers with Disabilities

- Disability awareness in Australia is high and getting higher.
- Legislation requires that new accommodation meets accessibility standards for mobility-impaired travellers, and discrimination by tourism operators is illegal.
- Many of Australia's key attractions, including many national parks, provide access for those with limited mobility and a number of sites also address the needs of visitors with visual or aural impairments. Contact attractions in advance to confirm the facilities.
- Tour operators with vehicles catering to mobility-impaired travellers operate from most capital cities.
- Facilities for wheelchairs are improving in accommodation, but there are still many older establishments where the necessary upgrades haven't been done.

Resources

Deaf Australia (www.deafau.org.au)

Easy Access Australia (www.easyaccessaustralia.com.au) A publication by Bruce Cameron available from various bookshops. Details accessible transport, accommodation and attraction options.

e-Bility (www.ebility.com) Classifieds, links and resources for travellers with disabilities.

National Information Communication & Awareness Network (NICAN; www.nican.com.au) Australia-wide directory providing information on access issues, accessible accommodation, sporting and recreational activities, transport and specialist tour operators.

National Public Toilet Map (www.toiletmap.gov.au) Lists more than 14,000 public toilets around Australia, including those with wheelchair access.

Spinal Cord Injuries Australia (SCIA; www.spinalcordinjuries.com.au)

Vision Australia (www.visionaustralia.org.au)

Air Travel

Qantas (www.qantas.com.au) entitles a disabled person and the carer travelling with them to a discount on full economy fares; contact NICAN for eligibility and an application form. Guide dogs travel for free on **Qantas**, **Jetstar** (www.jetstar.com.au) and **Virgin Australia** (www.virginaustralia.com), and their affiliated carriers. All of Australia's major airports have dedicated parking spaces, wheelchair access to terminals, accessible toilets, and skychairs to convey passengers onto planes via airbridges.

Train Travel

In NSW, CountryLink's XPT trains have at least one carriage (usually the buffet car) with a seat removed for a wheelchair, and an accessible toilet. Queensland Rail's *Tilt Train* from Brisbane to Cairns has a wheelchair-accessible carriage.

Melbourne's suburban rail network is accessible and guide dogs and hearing dogs are permitted on all public transport in Victoria. **Metlink** (PTV; ☎1800 800 007; http://ptv.vic.gov.au; Southern Cross Station; 🚉Southern Cross) offers a free travel pass to visually impaired people for transport in Melbourne.

Visas

All visitors to Australia need a visa – only New Zealand nationals are exempt, and even they sheepishly receive a 'special category' visa on arrival. Application forms for the several types of visa are available from Australian diplomatic missions overseas, travel agents or the website of the **Department of Immigration & Citizenship** (www.immi.gov.au).

eVisitor (651)

Many European passport holders are eligible for a free eVisitor visa, allowing stays in Australia for up to three months within a 12-month period. eVisitor visas must be applied for online (www.immi.gov.au/e_visa/evisitor.htm). They are electronically stored and linked to individual passport numbers, so no stamp in your passport is required. It's advisable to apply at least 14 days prior to your proposed date of travel to Australia.

Electronic Travel Authority (ETA; 976)

Passport holders from eight countries which aren't part of the eVisitor scheme – Brunei, Canada, Hong Kong, Japan, Malaysia, Singapore, South Korea and the USA – can apply for either a visitor or business ETA. ETAs are valid for 12 months, with stays of up to three months on each visit. You can apply for the ETA online (www.eta.immi.gov.au), which attracts a nonrefundable service charge of $20.

Tourist Visas (676)

Short-term tourist visas have largely been replaced by the eVisitor and ETA. However, if you are from a country not covered by either, or you want to stay longer than three months, you'll need to apply for a tourist visa. Standard tourist visas (which cost $115) allow one (in some cases multiple) entry, for a stay of up to 12 months, and are valid for use within 12 months of issue. For online applications see www.immi.gov.au/e_visa/e676.htm.

Visa Extensions

If you want to stay in Australia for longer than your visa allows, you'll need to apply for a new visa (usually a tourist visa 676) through the Department of Immigration & Citizenship at www.immi.gov.au/visitors/tourist. It's best to apply at least two or three weeks before your visa expires. Application fee $290.

Working Holiday Visas (417)

Young (aged 18 to 30) visitors from Belgium, Canada, Cyprus, Denmark, Estonia, Finland, France, Germany, Hong Kong, Ireland, Italy, Japan, South Korea, Malta, Netherlands, Norway, Sweden, Taiwan and the UK are eligible for a working holiday visa, which allows you to visit for up to one year and gain casual employment.

The emphasis of this visa is on casual and not full-time employment, so you're only supposed to work for any one employer for a maximum of six months. A first working holiday visa must be obtained prior to entry to Australia: see www.immi.gov.au/visitors/working-holiday. You can't change from a tourist visa to a working holiday visa once you're in Australia.

You can apply for this visa up to a year in advance. Conditions include having a return air ticket or sufficient funds for a return or onward fare. Application fee $365.

Second Working Holiday Visa

Visitors who have worked as a seasonal worker in regional Australia for a minimum of three months while on their first working holiday visa are eligible to apply for a second working holiday visa while still in Australia. 'Regional Australia' encompasses the vast majority of the country, excepting major cities; the definition of 'seasonal work' is a little more specific. For information see www.immi.gov.au/visitors/working-holiday/417/eligibility-second.htm. Application fee $365.

Work & Holiday Visas (462)

Nationals from Argentina, Bangladesh, Chile, Indonesia, Malaysia, Thailand, Turkey and the USA aged between the ages of 18 and 30 can apply for a work and holiday visa prior to entry to Australia. Once granted, this visa allows the holder to enter Australia within three months of issue, stay for up to 12 months, leave and re-enter Australia any number of times within that 12 months, undertake temporary employment to supplement a trip, and study for up to four months. For details see www.immi.gov.au/visitors/working-holiday/462. Application fee $365.

Volunteering

Lonely Planet's *Volunteer: A Traveller's Guide to Making a Difference Around the World* provides useful information about volunteering.

Australian Volunteers International (www.australianvolunteers.com) Places skilled volunteers into indigenous communities in northern and central Australia (mostly long-term placements). Occasional short-term unskilled opportunities too, helping out at community-run roadhouses.

Conservation Volunteers Australia (CVA; www.conservationvolunteers.com.au) Nonprofit organisation involved in tree planting, walking-track construction, and flora and fauna surveys.

Earthwatch Institute Australia (www.earthwatch.org) Volunteer expeditions that focus on conservation and wildlife.

Go Volunteer (www.govolunteer.com.au) National website listing a variety of volunteer opportunities.

i to i Volunteering (www.i-to-i.com) Conservation-based volunteer holidays in Australia.

Responsible Travel (www.responsibletravel.com) Volunteer travel opportunities.

STA (www.statravel.com.au) Volunteer holiday opportunities in Australia – click on 'Planning' on their website then the volunteer link.

Volunteering Australia (www.volunteeringaustralia.org) Support, advice and volunteer training.

Willing Workers on Organic Farms (WWOOF; www.wwoof.com.au) 'WWOOFing' is where you do a few hours' work each day on a farm in return for bed and board, often in a family home. As the name states, the farms are supposed to be organic (including permaculture and biodynamic growing), but that isn't always so. Some places aren't even farms – you might help out at a pottery or do the books at a seed wholesaler. Whether participants in the scheme have a farm or just a vegie patch, most are concerned to some extent with alternative lifestyles. Most places have a minimum stay of two nights. You can join online or through various WWOOF agents (see the website for details) for a fee of $65. You'll get a membership number and a booklet that lists participating enterprises. If you need these posted overseas, add another $5.

Women Travellers

Australia is generally a safe place for women travellers, although the usual sensible precautions apply.

Night-time Avoid walking alone late at night in any of the major cities and towns – keep enough money aside for a taxi back to your accommodation.

Pubs Be wary of staying in basic pub accommodation unless it looks safe and well managed.

Sexual harassment Rare, though some macho Aussie males still slip – particularly when they've been drinking.

Rural areas Stereotypically, the further you get from the big cities, the less enlightened your average Aussie male is probably going to be about women's issues. Having said that, many women travellers say that they have met the friendliest, most down-to-earth blokes in outback pubs and remote roadhouse stops.

Hitchhiking Hitching is not recommended for anyone. Even when travelling in pairs, exercise caution at all times.

Drugged drinks Some pubs in Sydney and other big cities post warnings about drugged or 'spiked' drinks: probably not cause for paranoia, but play it safe if someone offers you a drink in a bar.

Work

Work visas If you come to Australia on a tourist visa then you're not allowed to work for pay: you'll need a working holiday visa (417) or work and holiday visa (462) – visit www.immi.gov.au for more details.

Finding work Backpacker magazines, newspapers and hostel noticeboards are good places to source local work opportunities. Casual work can often be found during peak season at the major tourist centres: places such as Alice Springs, Cairns and resort towns along the Queensland coast, and the ski fields of Victoria and NSW are all good prospects during holiday season. Other possibilities for casual employment include factory work, labouring, bar work, waiting tables, domestic chores at outback roadhouses, nanny work, working as a station hand and collecting for charities. People with computer, secretarial, nursing and teaching skills can find work temping in the major cities by registering with a relevant agency.

Employment Websites

Career One (www.careerone.com.au) General employment site; good for metropolitan areas.

Gumtree (www.gumtree.com.au) Great classified site with jobs, accommodation and items for sale.

MyCareer (www.mycareer.com.au) Website for general employment; good for metropolitan areas.

Seek (www.seek.com.au) General employment site; good for metropolitan areas.

Travellers at Work (www.taw.com.au) Excellent site for working travellers in Australia.

Seasonal Work Resources

Seasonal fruit-picking (harvesting) relies on casual labour – there's always something that needs to be picked, pruned or farmed somewhere in Australia all year round. It's definitely hard work, involving early morning starts, and you're usually paid by how much you pick (per bin, bucket, kilo etc). Expect to earn about $50 to $60 a day to start with; more when your skills and speed improve. Some work, such as pruning or sorting, is paid at around $15 per hour.

Call the **National Harvest Telephone Information Service** (☎1800 062 332) for more information about when and where you're likely to pick up this sort of work.

Grunt Labour (www.gruntlabour.com) Specialises in mining, manufacturing and agricultural-based recruitment, plus seasonal fruit picking.

Harvest Trail (www.jobsearch.gov.au/harvesttrail) Harvest jobs around Australia.

QITE (www.qite.com.au) Nonprofit Queensland employment agency operating around Cairns, Innisfail and the Atherton Tablelands.

Viterra (www.viterra.com.au) Seasonal grain harvest jobs in Victoria and South Australia (October to January).

Workabout Australia (www.workaboutaustralia.com.au) Gives a state-by-state breakdown of seasonal work opportunities.

Seasonal Work Hot Spots

NSW The NSW ski fields have seasonal work during the ski season, particularly around Thredbo. There's also harvest work around Narrabri and Moree, and grape picking in the Hunter Valley. Fruit picking happens near Tenterfield, Orange and Young.

NT The majority of working-holiday opportunities in the Northern Territory for backpackers are in fruit picking, station handing, labouring and hospitality.

Queensland Queensland has vast tracts of farmland and orchards: there's fruit picking work to be found around Stanthorpe, Childers, Bundaberg and Cairns. Those looking for sturdier (and much better-paying) work should keep an eye on mining opportunities in growth mining towns such as Weipa and Cloncurry.

SA Good seasonal-work opportunities can be found on the Fleurieu Peninsula, Coonawarra region and Barossa Valley (wineries), and along the Murray River around Berri (fruit picking).

Tasmania The apple orchards in the south, especially around Cygnet and Huonville, are your best bet for work in Tassie.

Victoria Harvest work in Mildura and Shepparton.

WA In Perth, plenty of temporary work is available in tourism and hospitality, administration, IT, nursing, child care, factories and labouring. Outside of Perth, travellers can easily get jobs in tourism and hospitality, plus a variety of seasonal work. For grape-picking work, head for the vineyards around Margaret River.

Tax

TAX FILE NUMBER

If you have a working holiday visa, you should apply for a Tax File Number (TFN). Without it, tax will be deducted at the maximum rate from any wages you receive. Apply for a TFN online via the **Australian Taxation Office** (ATO; www.ato.gov.au); it takes up to four weeks to be issued.

PAYING TAX & TAX REFUNDS

Even with a Tax File Number, nonresidents (including working holiday visa holders) pay a considerably higher rate of tax than most Australian residents. For a start, there's no tax-free threshold – you pay tax on every dollar you earn.

Because you have been paid wages in Australia, you must lodge a tax return with the ATO: see the website for info on how to do this, including getting a Payment Summary (an official summary of your earnings and tax payments) from your employer, timing/dates for lodging your tax return, and how to receive your Notice of Assessment.

Bear in mind that you're not entitled to a refund for the tax you paid – you will only receive a refund if too much tax was withheld from your pay. If you didn't pay enough while you were working then you will have to pay more. You are, however, entitled to any superannuation that you have accumulated.

Transport

GETTING THERE & AWAY

Australia is a long way from just about everywhere – getting there usually means a long-haul flight. If you're short on time on the ground, consider internal flights – they're affordable (compared with petrol and car-hire costs), can usually be carbon offset, and will save you some *looong* days in the saddle. Flights, tours and rail tickets can be booked online at www.lonelyplanet.com/bookings.

Entering the Country

Arrival in Australia is usually straightforward and efficient, with the usual customs declarations. There are no restrictions for citizens of any particular foreign countries entering Australia – if you have a current passport and visa, you should be fine.

Air

High season (with the highest prices) for flights into Australia is roughly over the country's summer (December to February); low season generally tallies with the winter months (June to August), though this is actually peak season in central Australia and the Top End. Australia's international carrier is **Qantas** (www.qantas.com.au), which has an outstanding safety record (...as Dustin Hoffman said in Rainman, 'Qantas never crashed').

International Airports

Australia has numerous international gateways, with Sydney and Melbourne being the busiest. Other than the big-city airports listed here, some smaller cities (notably the Gold Coast) also offer international flights.

Adelaide Airport (www.aal.com.au)

Brisbane Airport (www.bne.com.au)

Cairns Airport (www.cairnsairport.com)

Darwin Airport (www.darwinairport.com.au)

Melbourne Airport (Tullamarine; www.melbourneairport.com.au)

Perth Airport (www.perthairport.net.au)

Sydney Airport (Kingsford Smith; www.sydneyairport.com.au)

Sea

It's possible (though by no means easy or safe) to make your way between Australia and countries such as Papua New Guinea, Indonesia, New Zealand and the Pacific islands by hitching rides or crewing on yachts – usually you have to at least contribute towards food. Ask around at marinas and sailing clubs in places like Coffs Harbour, Great Keppel Island, Airlie

CLIMATE CHANGE & TRAVEL

Every form of transport that relies on carbon-based fuel generates CO_2, the main cause of human-induced climate change. Modern travel is dependent on aeroplanes, which might use less fuel per kilometre per person than most cars but travel much greater distances. The altitude at which aircraft emit gases (including CO_2) and particles also contributes to their climate change impact. Many websites offer 'carbon calculators' that allow people to estimate the carbon emissions generated by their journey and, for those who wish to do so, to offset the impact of the greenhouse gases emitted with contributions to portfolios of climate-friendly initiatives throughout the world. Lonely Planet offsets the carbon footprint of all staff and author travel.

Beach, the Whitsundays, Darwin and Cairns. April is a good time to look for a berth in the Sydney area.

Alternatively, **P&O Cruises** (www.pocruises.com.au) operates holiday cruises between Brisbane, Melbourne or Sydney and destinations in New Zealand and the Pacific. Even more alternatively, some freighter ships allow passengers to travel on-board as they ship cargo to/from Australia: check out websites such as www.freighterexpeditions.com.au and www.freighter-cruises.com for options.

GETTING AROUND

Air

Airlines in Australia

Australia's main (and highly safe and professional) domestic airlines are **Qantas** (www.qantas.com.au) and **Virgin Australia** (www.virginaustralia.com), servicing all the main centres with regular flights. **Jetstar** (www.jetstar.com.au; a subsidiary of Qantas) and **Tiger Airways** (www.tigerairways.com) (partially owned by Singapore Airlines) are generally a bit cheaper and fly between most Australian capital cities. See regional chapters for info on airlines operating locally within Australia's states and territories.

Air Passes

Qantas offers a discount-fare **Walkabout Air Pass** for passengers flying into Australia from overseas with Qantas or American Airlines. The pass allows you to link up around 80 domestic Australian destinations for less than you'd pay booking flights individually.

Bicycle

Australia has much to offer cyclists, from bike paths winding through most major cities, to thousands of kilometres of good country roads where you can wear out your sprockets. There's lots of flat countryside and gently rolling hills to explore and, although Australia is not as mountainous as, say, Switzerland or France, mountain bikers can find plenty of forest trails and high country. If you're really keen, outback cycling might also be an option.

Hire Bike hire in cities is easy, but if you're riding for more than a few hours or even a day, it's more economical to invest in your own wheels.

Legalities Bike helmets are compulsory in all states and territories, as are white front-lights and red rear-lights for riding at night.

Maps You can get by with standard road maps, but to avoid low-grade unsealed roads, the government series is best. The 1:250,000 scale is suitable, though you'll need lots of maps if you're going far. The next scale up is 1:1,000,000 – widely available in map shops.

Weather In summer carry plenty of water. Wear a helmet with a peak (or a cap under your helmet), use sunscreen and avoid cycling in the middle of the day. Beware summer northerlies that can make a north-bound cyclist's life hell. South-easterly trade winds blow in April, when you can have (theoretically) tail winds all the way to Darwin. It can get very cold in Victoria, Tasmania, southern South Australia and the New South Wales mountains, so pack appropriate clothing.

Transport If you're bringing in your own bike, check with your airline for costs and the degree of dismantling or packing required. Within Australia, bus companies require you to dismantle your bike and some don't guarantee that it will travel on the same bus as you.

Information

The national cycling body is the **Bicycle Federation of Australia** (www.bicycles.net.au). Each state and territory has a touring organisation that can also help with cycling information and put you in touch with touring clubs.

Bicycle Network Victoria (www.bicyclenetwork.com.au)

Bicycle NSW (www.bicyclensw.org.au)

Bicycle Queensland (www.bq.org.au)

Bicycle SA (www.bikesa.asn.au)

Bicycle Tasmania (www.biketas.org.au)

Bicycle Transportation Alliance (www.btawa.org.au) In WA.

Cycling Northern Territory (www.nt.cycling.org.au)

Pedal Power ACT (www.pedalpower.org.au)

Buying a Bike

If you want to buy a reliable, new road or mountain bike, your bottom-level starting price will be around $600. Throw in all the requisite on-the-road equipment (panniers, helmet etc), and your starting point becomes around $1600. Secondhand bikes are worth checking out in the cities, as are the post-Christmas sales and mid-year stocktakes, when newish cycles can be heavily discounted.

To sell your bike (or buy a secondhand one), try hostel noticeboards or online at **Trading Post** (www.tradingpost.com.au) or **Gumtree** (www.gumtree.com.au).

Boat

There's a hell of a lot of water around Australia, but unless you're fortunate enough to hook up with a yacht, it's not a feasible way of getting around. Other than short-hop regional ferries (eg to Kangaroo Island in SA, Rottnest

Island in WA, Bruny Island in Tasmania, North Stradbroke Island in Queensland), the only long-range passenger services are the two high-speed, vehicle-carrying **Spirit of Tasmania** (www.spiritoftasmania.com.au) boats between Melbourne and Devonport on Tasmania's northwest coast.

Bus

Australia's extensive bus network is a reliable way to get around, though bus travel isn't always cheaper than flying and it can be tedious over huge distances. Most buses are equipped with air-con, toilets and videos; all are smoke-free. There are no class divisions on Australian buses (very democratic), and the vehicles of the different companies all look pretty similar.

Small towns eschew formal bus terminals for a single drop-off/pick-up point (post office, newsagent, corner shop etc).

Greyhound Australia (www.greyhound.com.au) runs a national network (notably not across the Nullarbor Plain, between Adelaide and Perth). Book online for the cheapest fares. Other operators:

Firefly Express (www.fireflyexpress.com.au) Runs between Sydney, Canberra, Melbourne and Adelaide.

Premier Motor Service (www.premierms.com.au) Runs along the east coast between Cairns and Melbourne.

V/Line (www.vline.com.au) Connects Victoria with NSW, SA and the ACT.

Bus Passes

Greyhound offers a slew of passes geared towards various types and routes of travel: see www.greyhound.com.au/australia-bus-pass for details. Many proffer a 10% discount for members of YHA, VIP, Nomads and other approved organisations.

KILOMETRE PASS

Under the banner of 'Oz-Flexi Travel', these are the simplest passes, giving you specified amounts of travel starting at 500km ($108), going up in increments of 1000km to a maximum of 25,000km ($2600). A 5000km pass costs $814; 10,000km is

Principal Bus Routes & Railways

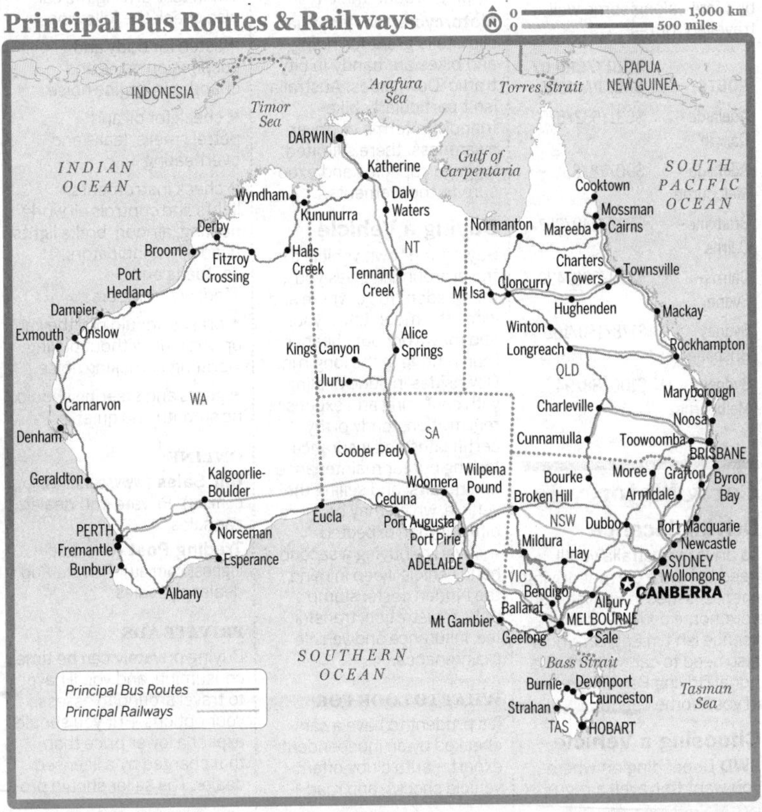

$1397. Passes are valid for 12 months (90 days for 500km and 1000km passes), and you can travel where and in what direction you please, stopping as many times as you like. Use the online kilometre chart to figure out which pass suits you. Phone at least a day ahead to reserve your seat.

MINI TRAVELLER PASSES

In the 'Oz-Choice Travel' pass category, these 90-day, hop-on, hop-off passes allow you to traverse a couple of dozen popular routes, mostly along the east coast. Travel is in one direction. Melbourne to Cairns costs $450; Perth to Broome is $405; Sydney to Brisbane is $147.

Costs

Following are the average, non-discounted, one-way bus fares along some well-travelled routes:

ROUTE	ADULT/CHILD/ BACKPACKER
Adelaide–Darwin	$631/532/575
Adelaide–Melbourne	$90/78/83
Brisbane–Cairns	$292/249/267
Cairns–Sydney	$470/398/430
Sydney–Brisbane	$178/150/162
Sydney–Melbourne	$100/88/94

Car & Motorcycle

Driving Licence

To drive in Australia you'll need to hold a current driving licence issued in English from your home country. If the licence isn't in English, you'll also need to carry an International Driving Permit, issued in your home country.

Choosing a Vehicle

2WD Depending on where you want to travel, a regulation 2WD vehicle might suffice. They're cheaper to hire, buy and run than 4WDs and are more readily available. Most are fuel efficient, and easy to repair and sell. Downsides: no off-road capability and no room to sleep!

4WD Four-wheel drives are good for outback travel as they can access almost any track you get a hankering for. And there might even be space to sleep in the back. Downsides: poor fuel economy, awkward to park and more expensive to hire/buy.

Campervan Creature comforts at your fingertips: sink, fridge, cupboards, beds, kitchen and space to relax. Downsides: slow and often not fuel-efficient, not great on dirt roads and too big for nipping around the city.

Motorcycle The Australian climate is great for riding, and bikes are handy in city traffic. Downsides: Australia isn't particularly bike-friendly in terms of driver awareness, there's limited luggage capacity, and exposure to the elements.

Buying a Vehicle

Buying your own vehicle to travel around in gives you the freedom to go where and when the mood takes you, and may work out cheaper than renting in the long run. Downsides include dealing with confusing and expensive registration, roadworthy certificates and insurance; forking out for maintenance and repairs; and selling the vehicle, which may be more difficult than expected.

If you're buying a second-hand vehicle, keep in mind the hidden costs: stamp duty, registration, transfer fee, insurance and vehicle maintenance.

WHAT TO LOOK FOR

It's prudent to have a car checked by an independent expert – auto clubs offer vehicle checks, and road transport authorities have lists of licensed garages – but if you're flying solo, here are some things to check:

- tyre tread
- number of kilometres
- rust damage
- accident damage
- oil should be translucent and honey-coloured
- coolant should be clean and not rusty in colour
- engine condition: check for fumes from engine, smoke from exhaust while engine is running, and engines that rattle or cough
- exhaust system should not be excessively noisy or rattly when engine is running
- windscreen should be clear with no cracks or chip marks

When test-driving the car, also check the following:

- listen for body and suspension noise and changes in engine noise
- check for oil and petrol smells, leaks and overheating
- check instruments, lights and controls all work: heating, air-con, brake lights, headlights, indicators, seatbelts and windscreen wipers
- brakes should pull the car up straight, without pulling, vibrating or making noise
- gears and steering should be smooth and quiet

ONLINE

Car Sales (www.carsales.com.au) Private and dealer car sales.

Trading Post (www.tradingpost.com.au) Private and dealer car sales.

PRIVATE ADS

Buying privately can be time consuming, and you'll have to travel around to assess your options. But you should expect a lower price than that charged by a licensed dealer. The seller should provide you with a roadworthy certificate (if required in the state you're in), but you won't get a cooling-off period or a statutory warranty.

It's your responsibility to ensure the car isn't stolen and that there's no money owing on it: check the car's details with the **Personal Property Securities Register** (☎1300 007 777; www.ppsr.gov.au).

BACKPACKERS & RIDE-SHARING

Hostel noticeboards and the Thorn Tree travel forum at lonelyplanet.com are good places to find vehicles for sale. Tour desks also often have noticeboards.

Ride-sharing is also a good way to split costs and environmental impact with other travellers. Noticeboards are good places to find ads; also check online classifieds:

Catch A Lift (www.catchalift.com)

Coseats (www.coseats.com)

Need A Ride (www.needaride.com.au)

DEALERS

Licenced car dealers are obliged to guarantee that no money is owing on the car and you're often allowed a cooling-off period (usually three days). Depending on the age of the car and the kilometres travelled, you may also receive a statutory warranty. You will need to sign an agreement for sale; make sure you understand what it says before you sign. Some dealers will sell you a car with an undertaking to buy it back at an agreed price, but don't accept verbal guarantees – get it in writing.

TRAVELLERS' MARKETS

Cairns, Sydney, Darwin and Perth (cities where travellers commonly begin or finish their travels) are the best places to buy or sell a vehicle, especially Cairns.

There are a couple of big backpacker car markets in Sydney. It's possible these

Sydney to Melbourne via the Princes Hwy

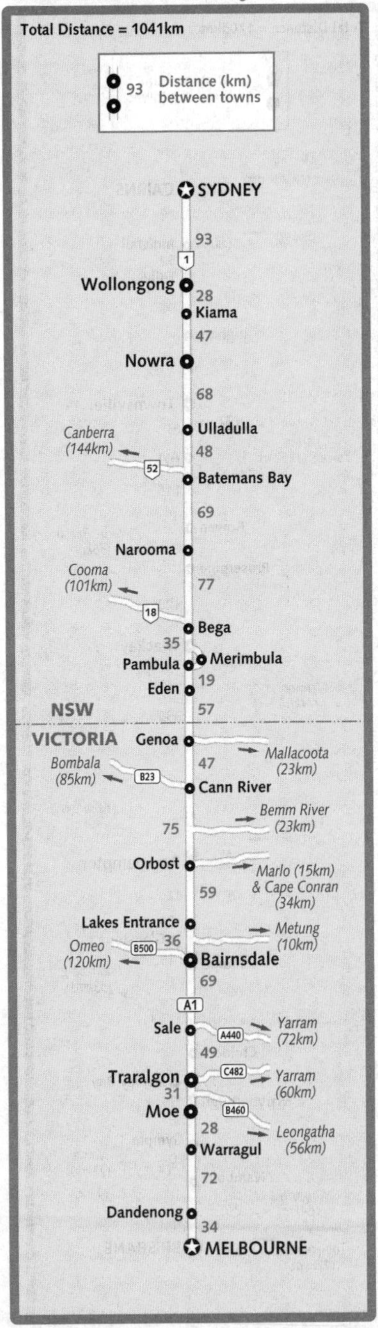

Brisbane to Cairns via the Bruce Hwy

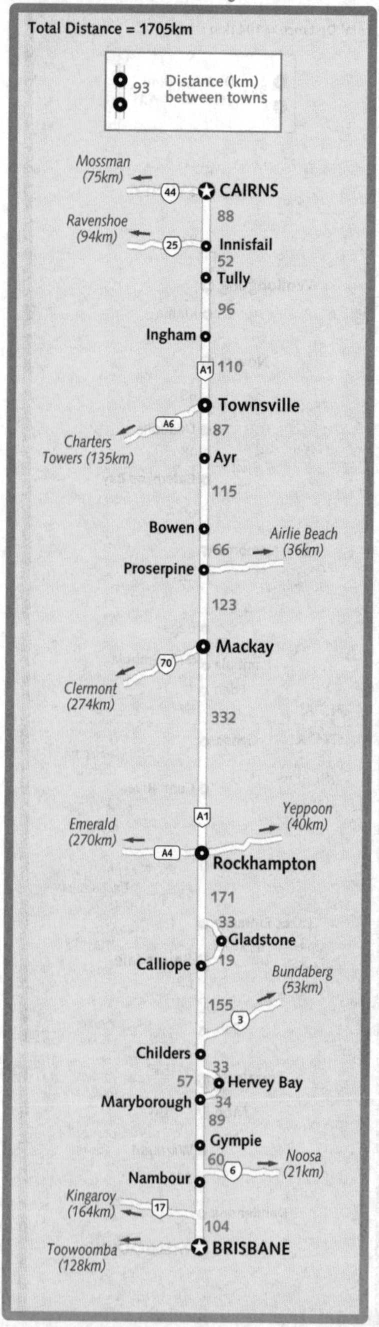

cars have been around Australia several times, so it can be a risky option.

Kings Cross Car Market (☎1800 808 188; www.carmarket.com.au; 110 Bourke St, Woolloomooloo; ⏰9am-5pm)

Sydney Travellers Car Market (☎02-9331 4361; www.sydneytravellerscarmarket.com.au; L2, Ward Ave Car Park, Kings Cross; ⏰9am-5pm Mon-Sat)

PAPERWORK

Registration When you buy a vehicle in Australia, you need to transfer the registration into your own name within 14 days. Each state has slightly different requirements and different organisations that do this. Similarly, when selling a vehicle you need to advise the state or territory road-transport authority of the sale and change of name.

In NSW, NT, Queensland, Tasmania, Victoria and WA, the buyer and seller need to complete and sign a Transfer of Registration form. In the ACT and SA there is no form, but the buyer and seller need to complete and sign the reverse of the registration certificate.

Roadworthy certificate Sellers are required to provide a roadworthy certificate when transferring registration in the following situations:

- ACT – once the vehicle is six years old
- NSW – once the vehicle is five years old
- NT – once the vehicle is three years old
- Queensland – Safety Certificate required for all vehicles
- Victoria – Certificate of Roadworthiness required for all vehicles
- WA, SA and Tasmania – no inspections/certificates required in most circumstances

If the vehicle you're considering doesn't have a

roadworthy certificate, it's worth having a roadworthiness check done before you buy it. This can cost upwards of $100 but can save you money on hidden costs. Road-transport authorities have lists of licensed vehicle testers.

Gas certificate In Queensland, if a vehicle runs on gas, a gas certificate must be provided by the seller in order to transfer the registration. In the ACT, vehicles running on gas require an annual inspection.

Immobiliser fitting In WA it's compulsory to have an approved immobiliser fitted to most vehicles (not motorcycles) before transfer of registration; this is the buyer's responsibility.

Changing state of registration Note that registering a vehicle in a different state to the one it was previously registered in can be difficult, time-consuming and expensive.

Renewing registration Registration is paid annually Australia-wide, but most states/territories also give you the option of renewing it for six and sometimes three months.

ROAD TRANSPORT AUTHORITIES

For more information about processes and costs:

Rego ACT (☎13 22 81; www.rego.act.gov.au) ACT

Transport, Roads & Maritime Services (☎13 27 01; www.rta.nsw.gov.au) NSW

Department of Transport (☎1300 654 628; www.transport.nt.gov.au; 🐾) NT

Department of Transport & Main Roads (☎13 23 80; www.tmr.qld.gov.au) Queensland

Department of Transport, Planning & Infrastructure (☎13 10 84; www.dpti.sa.gov.au) SA

Department of Infrastructure, Energy & Resources (☎1300 135 513; www.transport.tas.gov.au) Tasmania

VicRoads (☎13 11 71; www.vicroads.vic.gov.au) Victoria

Department of Transport (☎13 11 56; www.transport.wa.gov.au) WA

Renting a Vehicle

Larger car-rental companies have drop-offs in major towns and cities. Most companies require drivers to be over the age of 21, though in some cases it's 18 and in others 25.

Suggestions to assist in the process:

➡ Read the contract cover to cover.

➡ Bond: some companies may require a signed credit-card slip, others may actually charge your credit card; if this is the case, find out when you'll get a refund.

➡ Ask if unlimited kilometres are included and, if not, what the extra charge per kilometre is.

➡ Find out what excess you'll have to pay if you have a prang, and if it can be lowered by an extra charge per day (this option will usually be offered to you whether you ask or not). Check if your personal travel insurance covers you for vehicle accidents and excess.

➡ Check for exclusions (hitting a kangaroo, damage on unsealed roads etc) and whether you're covered on unavoidable unsealed roads (eg accessing campgrounds). Some companies also exclude parts of the car from cover, such as the underbelly, tyres and windscreen.

➡ At pick-up inspect the vehicle for any damage. Make a note of anything on the contract before you sign.

➡ Ask about breakdown and accident procedures.

➡ If you can, return the vehicle during business hours and insist on an inspection in your presence.

The usual big international companies all operate in Australia (Avis, Budget, Europcar, Hertz, Thrifty). The following websites offer last-minute discounts:

Carhire.com (www.carhire.com.au)

Drive Now (☎1300 547 214; www.drivenow.com.au)

Webjet (www.webjet.com.au)

4WDS

Having a 4WD is essential for off-the-beaten-track driving into the outback. The major car-hire companies have 4WDs.

Renting a 4WD is affordable if a few people get together: something like a Nissan X-Trail (which can get you through most tracks) costs around $100 to $150 per day; for a Toyota Landcruiser you're looking at around $150 up to $200, which should include unlimited kilometres.

Check the insurance conditions, especially the excess (which can be up to $5000), as they can be onerous and policies might not cover damage caused when travelling off-road. A refundable bond is also often required – this can be as much as $7500.

CAMPERVANS

Companies for campervan hire – with rates from around $90 (two-berth) or $150 (four-berth) per day, usually with minimum five-day hire and unlimited kilometres – include the following:

Apollo (☎1800 777 779; www.apollocamper.com)

Britz (☎1800 331 454; www.britz.com.au)

Jucy Rentals (☎1800 150 850; www.jucy.com.au)

Maui (☎1300 363 800; www.maui.com.au)

Mighty Cars & Campers (☎1800 670 232; www.mightycampers.com)

Spaceships (☎1300 132 469; www.spaceshipsrentals.com.au)

Travel Wheels (☎1800 289 222; www.travelwheels.com.au)

Sydney to Brisbane via the Pacific Hwy

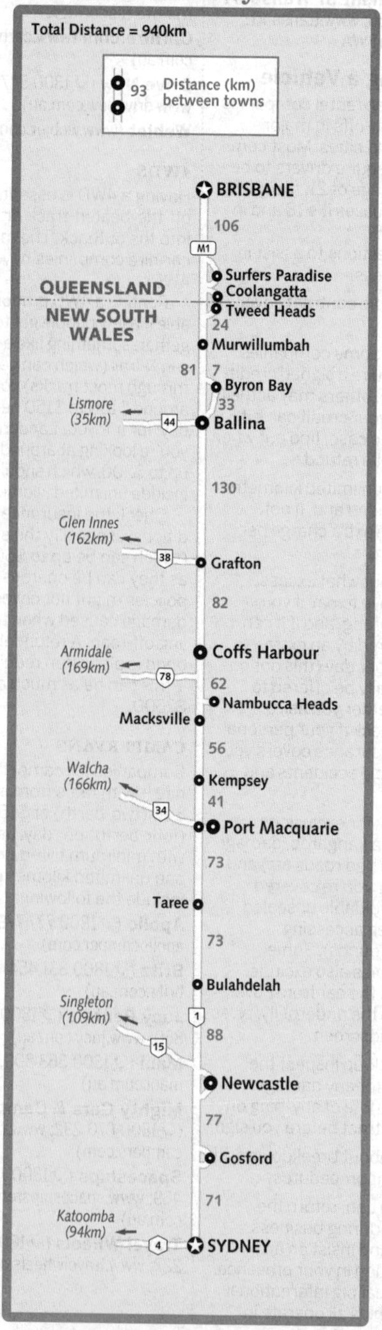

Wicked Campers (☎1800 246 869; www.wickedcampers.com.au)

ONE-WAY RELOCATIONS

Relocations are usually cheap deals, although they don't allow much time flexibility. Most of the large hire companies offer deals, or try the following operators. See also:

Drive Now. (☎1300 547 214; www.drivenow.com.au)

Relocations2Go (☎1800 735 627; www.relocations2go.com)

Standbycars (☎1300 789 059; www.standbycars.com.au)

Transfercar (☎02-8011 1870; www.transfercar.com.au)

Insurance

Third-party insurance With the exception of NSW, third-party personal-injury insurance is included in the vehicle registration cost, ensuring that every registered vehicle carries at least minimum insurance (if registering in NSW you'll need to arrange this privately). We recommend extending that minimum to at least third-party property insurance – minor collisions can be amazingly expensive.

Rental vehicles When it comes to hire cars, understand your liability in the event of an accident. Rather than risk paying out thousands of dollars, consider taking out comprehensive car insurance or paying an additional daily amount to the rental company for excess reduction (this reduces the excess payable in the event of an accident from between $2000 and $5000 to a few hundred dollars).

Exclusions Be aware that if travelling on dirt roads you usually will not be covered by insurance unless you have a 4WD (read the fine print). Also, many companies' insurance won't cover the cost of damage to glass (including the windscreen) or tyres.

Auto Clubs

Under the auspices of the **Australian Automobile Association** (AAA; ☎02-6247 7311; www.aaa.asn.au) are automobile clubs in each state, handy when it comes to insurance, regulations, maps and roadside assistance. Club membership (around $100 to $150) can save you a lot of trouble if things go wrong mechanically. If you're a member of an auto club in your home country, check if reciprocal rights are offered in Australia. The major Australian auto clubs generally offer reciprocal rights in other states and territories.

AANT (Automobile Association of the Northern Territory; ☎08-8925 5901; www.aant.com.au)

NRMA (☎13 11 22; www.mynrma.com.au) NSW and the ACT.

RAC (Royal Automobile Club of WA; ☎13 17 03; www.rac.com.au)

RACQ (Royal Automobile Club of Queensland; ☎13 19 05; www.racq.com.au)

RACT (Royal Automobile Club of Tasmania; ☎13 27 22; www.ract.com.au)

RACV (Royal Automobile Club of Victoria; ☎13 72 28; www.racv.com.au)

Road Rules

Australians drive on the left-hand side of the road and all cars are right-hand drive.

Give way An important road rule is 'give way to the right' – if an intersection is unmarked (unusual) and at roundabouts, you must give way to vehicles entering the intersection from your right.

Speed limits The general speed limit in built-up and residential areas is 50km/h (or sometimes 40km/h). Near schools, the limit is usually 25km/h in the morning and afternoon. On the highway it's usually 100km/h or 110km/h; in the NT it's either 110km/h or 130km/h. Police have speed radar guns and cameras and are fond of using them in strategic locations.

Seatbelts and car seats It's the law to wear seatbelts in the front and back seats; you're likely to get a fine if you don't. Small children must be belted into an approved safety seat.

Drink-driving Random breath-tests are common. If you're caught with a blood-alcohol level of more than 0.05% expect a fine and the loss of your licence. Police can randomly pull any driver over for a breathalyser or drug test.

Mobile phones Using a mobile phone while driving is illegal in Australia (excluding hands-free technology).

Hazards & Precautions

Fatigue Be wary of driver fatigue; driving long distances (eg in hot weather) can be exhausting. Falling asleep at the wheel is not uncommon. On a long haul, stop and rest every two hours – do some exercise, change drivers or have a coffee.

Road trains Be careful overtaking road trains (trucks with two or three trailers stretching for as long as 50m); you'll need distance and plenty of speed. On single-lane roads get as far off the road as possible when one approaches.

Unsealed roads Unsealed road conditions vary wildly and cars perform differently when braking and turning on dirt. Don't exceed 80km/h on dirt roads; if you go faster you won't have time to respond to a sharp turn, stock on the road or an unmarked gate or cattle grid.

ANIMAL HAZARDS

➡ Roadkill is a huge problem in Australia, particularly in the NT, Queensland, NSW, SA and Tasmania. Many Australians avoid travelling once the sun drops because of the risks posed by nocturnal animals on the roads.

➡ Kangaroos are common on country roads, as are cows and sheep in the unfenced outback. Kangaroos are most active around dawn and dusk and often travel in groups: if you see one hopping across the road, slow right down, as its friends may be just behind it.

➡ If you hit and kill an animal while driving, pull it off the road, preventing the next car from having a potential accident. If the animal is only injured and is small, perhaps an orphaned joey (baby kangaroo), wrap it in a towel or blanket and call the relevant wildlife rescue line.

Department of Environment & Conservation (☎08-9474 9055; www.dec.wa.gov.au) WA

Department of Environment & Heritage Protection (☎1300 130 372; www.ehp.qld.gov.au) Queensland

Fauna Rescue of South Australia (☎08-8289 0896; www.faunarescue.org.au)

NSW Wildlife Information, Rescue & Education Service (WIRES; ☎1300 094 737; www.wires.org.au)

CARBON OFFSETTING

Various organisations use 'carbon calculators' that allow travellers to offset the greenhouse gases they are responsible for with financial contributions.

Carbon Neutral (www.carbonneutral.com.au)

Carbon Planet (www.carbonplanet.com)

Elementree (www.elementree.com.au)

Greenfleet (www.greenfleet.com.au)

ROAD DISTANCES (KM)

	Adelaide	Albany	Alice Springs	Birdsville	Brisbane	Broome	Cairns	Canberra	Cape York	Darwin	Kalgoorlie	Melbourne	Perth	Sydney	Townsville
Albany	2649														
Alice Springs	1512	3573													
Birdsville	1183	3244	1176												
Brisbane	1942	4178	1849	1573											
Broome	4043	2865	2571	3564	5065										
Cairns	3079	5601	2396	1919	1705	4111									
Canberra	1372	4021	2725	2038	1287	5296	2923								
Cape York	4444	6566	3361	2884	2601	5076	965	3888							
Darwin	3006	5067	1494	2273	3774	1844	2820	3948	3785						
Kalgoorlie	2168	885	3092	2763	3697	3052	5234	3540	6199	4896					
Melbourne	728	3377	2240	1911	1860	4811	3496	637	4461	3734	2896				
Perth	2624	411	3548	3219	4153	2454	6565	3996	7530	4298	598	3352			
Sydney	1597	4246	3109	2007	940	5208	2634	289	3599	3917	3765	862	3869		
Townsville	3237	5374	2055	1578	1295	3770	341	2582	1306	2479	4893	3155	5349	2293	
Uluru	1559	3620	441	1617	2290	3012	2837	2931	3802	1935	3139	2287	3595	2804	2496

	Bicheno	Cradle Mountain	Devonport	Hobart	Launceston
Cradle Mountain	383				
Devonport	283	100			
Hobart	186	296	334		
Launceston	178	205	105	209	
Queenstown	443	69	168	257	273

These are the shortest distances by road; other routes may be considerably longer. For distances by coach, check the companies' leaflets.

NT Wildlife Rescue Wildlife Rescue Darwin (☎0409 090 840; www.wildlifedarwin.com.au); Katherine Wildlife Rescue Service (☎0407 934 252; www.fauna.org.a); Wildcare Inc Alice Springs (☎0419 221 128; www.fauna.org.au)

Wildlife Care (☎03-6233 6556; www.fnpw.org.au) Tasmania

Wildlife Victoria (☎1300 094 535; www.wildlifevictoria.org.au)

Fuel

Fuel types Unleaded and diesel fuel is available from service stations sporting well-known international brand names. LPG (liquefied petroleum gas) is not always stocked at more remote roadhouses; if you're on gas it's safer to have dual-fuel.

Costs Prices vary from place to place, but at the time of writing unleaded was hovering between $1.30 and $1.50. Out in the country, prices soar – in outback NT, WA and Queensland you can pay as much as $2.20.

Availability In cities and towns petrol stations proliferate, but distances between fill-ups can be long in the outback. On main roads there'll be a small town or roadhouse roughly every 150km to 200km. Many petrol stations, but not all, are open 24 hours.

Resources

Australian Bureau of Meteorology (www.bom.gov.au) Weather information.

Green Vehicle Guide (www.greenvehicleguide.gov.au) Rates Australian vehicles based on greenhouse and air-pollution emissions.

Live Traffic NSW (☎13 27 01; http://livetraffic.rta.nsw.gov.au) NSW road conditions.

Main Roads Western Australia (☎13 81 38; www.mainroads.wa.gov.au) WA road conditions.

Motorcycle Riders Association of Australia (MRAA; www.mraa.org.au)

Road Report (☎1800 246 199; www.roadreport.nt.gov.au) NT road conditions.

Traffic & Travel Information (☎13 19 40; http://highload.131940.qld.gov.au) Queensland road conditions.

Department of Planning, Transport & Infrastructure (☎1300 361 033; www.transport.sa.gov.au) SA road conditions.

Hitching

Hitching is never entirely safe in any country in the world, and we don't recommend it. Travellers who decide to hitch should understand that they are taking a small but potentially serious risk. People who choose to hitch will be safer if they travel in pairs and let someone know where they are planning to go.

Local Transport

All of Australia's major towns have reliable, affordable public bus networks, and there are suburban train lines in Sydney, Melbourne, Brisbane, Adelaide and Perth. Melbourne also has trams, and Sydney has harbour ferries and a light rail line. Taxis operate Australia-wide.

Tours

Backpacker-style and more formal bus tours offer a convenient way to get from A to B and see the sights on the way. The following listings are multi-state operators; see regional chapters for smaller companies operating within individual states.

AAT Kings (☎1300 556 100; www.aatkings.com) Big coach company (popular with the older set) with myriad tours all around Australia.

Adventure Tours Australia (☎1800 068 886; www.adventuretours.com.au) Affordable tours in all states. A two-day Red Centre tour starting/finishing in Alice Springs via Uluru, Kata Tjuta and Kings Canyon costs $490. Ten days from Perth to Broome costs $1645.

Autopia Tours (☎03-9391 0261; www.autopiatours.com.au) Three-day trips along the Great Ocean Road from Melbourne to Adelaide, or Melbourne to Sydney for $425.

Groovy Grape Getaways Australia (☎1800 661 177; www.groovygrape.com.au) Small-group, SA-based operator. Tours include three days Melbourne to Adelaide via the Great Ocean Road ($425), and Adelaide to Alice Springs via Uluru ($975).

Nullarbor Traveller (☎1800 816 858; www.the-traveller.com.au) Small, eco-certified company running relaxed minibus trips across the Nullarbor. Ten days Adelaide to Perth costs $1495, including bushwalking, surfing, whale watching, meals and national-park entry fees.

Oz Experience (☎1300 300 028; www.ozexperience.com) Sociable hop-on, hop-off services covering eastern Australia. Travel is one-directional and passes are valid for up to 12 months with unlimited stops. A Sydney–Cairns pass is $669; the 'Fish Hook' pass from Sydney to Darwin via Melbourne, Adelaide and Uluru is $2465.

Train

Long-distance rail travel in Australia is something you do because you really want to – not because it's cheap, convenient or fast. That said, trains are more comfortable than buses, and there's a certain long-distance 'romance of the rails' that's alive and kicking. Shorter-distance rail services within most states are run by state rail bodies, either government or private.

The three major interstate services in Australia are operated by **Great Southern Rail** (☎13 21 47; www.gsr.com.au), namely the *Indian Pacific* between Sydney and Perth, the *Overland* between Melbourne and Adelaide, and the *Ghan* between Adelaide and Darwin via Alice Springs. There's also the *Sunlander* service between Brisbane and Cairns, operated by **Queensland Rail** (☎1800 872 467; www.queenslandrail.com.au). Trains from Sydney to Brisbane, Melbourne and Canberra are operated by **CountryLink** (www.countrylink.info).

Costs

Following are standard internet-booked one-way train fares. Note that cheaper seat fares are readily available but are generally nonrefundable with no changes permitted. Backpacker discounts are also available.

Adelaide–Darwin Adult/child seated $862/403; from $2290/1582 in a cabin

Adelaide–Melbourne Adult/child seated $116/60

Adelaide–Perth Adult/child seated $553/310; from $1750/1202 in a cabin

Brisbane–Cairns Adult/child seated from $269/135; from $349/215 in a cabin

Sydney–Brisbane Adult/child seated $130/65; cabin $271/180**Sydney–Canberra** Adult/child seated $57/28

Sydney–Melbourne Adult/child seated $130/65; cabin $271/180

Sydney–Perth Adult/child seated $783/575, from $2178/1936 in a cabin.

Train Passes

For international visitors only, the **Ausrail Pass** offered by Great Southern Rail permits unlimited travel on the interstate rail network (including CountryLink and *Sunlander* services) over a three- or six-month period (seated, not in cabins). The three-/six-month pass costs $795/1045 per adult – inexpensive considering the amount of ground you could cover. Present your passport to qualify.

Great Southern Rail offers international visitors a couple of other passes, the pick of which is probably the **Rail Explorer Pass**, costing $495/649 per adult for three/six months. Travel is on the *Ghan*, the *Overland* and the *Indian Pacific* (again, seated, not in cabins).

CountryLink offers several passes covering various regions, some utilising Great Southern Rail services. The **East Coast Discovery Pass** allows one-way economy travel between Melbourne and Cairns (in either direction) with unlimited stopovers, and is valid for six months – the full trip costs $450, while Sydney to Cairns is $370 and Brisbane to Cairns is $280. The **Backtracker Pass**, available only to international visitors, permits travel on the entire CountryLink network and has four versions: a 14-day/one-/three-/six-month pass costing $232/275/298/420.

Behind the Scenes

SEND US YOUR FEEDBACK

We love to hear from travellers – your comments keep us on our toes and help make our books better. Our well-travelled team reads every word on what you loved or loathed about this book. Although we cannot reply individually to postal submissions, we always guarantee that your feedback goes straight to the appropriate authors, in time for the next edition. Each person who sends us information is thanked in the next edition – the most useful submissions are rewarded with a selection of digital PDF chapters.

Visit **lonelyplanet.com/contact** to submit your updates and suggestions or to ask for help. Our award-winning website also features inspirational travel stories, news and discussions.

Note: We may edit, reproduce and incorporate your comments in Lonely Planet products such as guidebooks, websites and digital products, so let us know if you don't want your comments reproduced or your name acknowledged. For a copy of our privacy policy visit lonelyplanet.com/privacy.

OUR READERS

Many thanks to the travellers who used the last edition and wrote to us with helpful hints, useful advice and interesting anecdotes:

Sylvie Addor, Melissa-Kate Ashwell-Meijer, Dennis Balemans, Bettina Bergmann-Remy, Aida Bour, Nicola Broderick, Nico Bryant-Stevens, Raymond Chan, Jane Coffey, Patricia Collé, Nicolas Combremont, Florian Cottez, Colin Davies, Richard Devlin, Anke Dijkstra, Silvia Disch, Missy Dugan, Lacroix Elodie, Maurici Espinar, Robert Eustace, Orly Flax, Stephen Gates, Sarah Hatherell, Len Kirby, Yero Kuethe, Irina Kulina, Ellen Lemson, Jane Luckraft, Megan Mann, Jeroen Martens, Molly Massingham, Bruce McKay, Javier Mendez, Charlotte Middleton, Erica Minarik, Dagmar Moehring, Domitille Motte, Konrad Nerger, Kim Niggemeyer, Kim Price, Christian Proulx, Summer Read, Michael Reeves, Ilona Renwick, Bo Rud Nielsen, Elisabeth Schiske, Marianne Schmid, Trevor Scott, Rob Seabourne, Justyn Shaw, Stine Skovgaard, Kevin Smythe, Heather Stafford, Johanna Teichmann, Steve Tervet, Marie Umbricht, Corrine Van Vliet, Jeroen van Heeren, Melissa Verrier Daunais, Timothy Wei, Alastair Weston, Jay Wiener, Malcolm Wilcock, Pennie Williams, Hansie Wong

AUTHOR THANKS

Charles-Rawlings Way

Huge thanks to Maryanne for the gig, and to our highway-addled coauthors, who covered a helluva lot of kilometres in search of the perfect review. Thanks also to the all-star inhouse LP production staff, and in Brisbane thanks to Christian, Lauren, Rachel, Brett and all the kids. Special thanks as always to Meg, my road-trippin' sweetheart, and our daughters Ione and Remy who provided countless laughs, unscheduled pitstops and ground-level perspectives along the way.

Meg Worby

Thank you Maryanne, for the gig! Big ups to the in-house team at LP for turning our many weeks of exploration into a useful thing you can hold in your hand. In Brisbane: huge thanks to Lauren, Christian, Orlando, Ilaria and friends for great company and insider tips. To our little daughters, Ione and Remy, it was the smoothest trip yet – nice work pulling your own suitcases! Love, as ever, to Charles – away and at home, you make hard work seem easy.

Brett Atkinson

Thanks to the keen and professional staff at WA's visitor centres who smoothed the way for information gathering, allowing me to focus on the vital task of taste testing the craft breweries of Margaret River. In Perth, thanks to Amanda Keenan for the pre-trip hit list. Special thanks to my fellow scribe Steve Waters, and also to the Lonely Planet inhouse team, especially Maryanne Netto for her support. Final thanks to Carol for holding the fort back home in Auckland.

Lindsay Brown

Thanks to Lizzie and Phoebe in Alice, and Jenny, Sinead and Pat at home. Cheers to all the national parks rangers that put up with my questions and the great staff at all the Northern Territory visitor centres. Finally, thanks to Meg, Charles and Maryanne for getting this whole show on the road.

Jayne D'Arcy

Sharik D'Arcy – you've done it again. Thanks for making all this possible and for letting me take little Ruby and big Miles on the adventure. Thanks for coming along, too. Thanks Miles for reminding me how cool koalas and penguins are! Dave Carswell, James Smith and Matt Holden, kudos for sharing your Melbourne with me, and all the wonderful folk who made travelling a joy. Thanks to my coauthor Paul, and Maryanne for commissioning me.

Anthony Ham

Thanks to Maryanne Netto for sending me to such wonderful places, to David Andrew for so many wise wildlife tips and to every person I met along the road – from knowledgeable and patient tourist office staff to other travellers. Thanks to Ron and Jan for their infinite hospitality and patience. And to Marina, Carlota and Valentina – home is wherever you are.

Paul Harding

Thanks to those who put me up or helped with tips and advice. Brian, Kerry, Martyn and Braidyn in Swan Hill; Matt, Simone, Xavier and Remy in Yack; Chad, Kylie, Amy, Parker Will; Phil, Ashleigh and Dan in central Vic; mum and dad in Castlemaine. Thanks to coauthor Jayne. But mostly to my occasional travel partners, Hannah and Layla.

Shawn Low

Thanks always to the crew at LP. Maryanne for opening the door and Charles and Meg for illuminating the path through it. Of course, thanks to the production staff, the heart of everything LP! Cheers to innumerable travellers I met on the road: your tips, company and advice were much appreciated. Of course, thanks to Wyn for being so amazing.

Virginia Maxwell

Many thanks to Maryanne Netto, Diana von Holdt, Charles Rawlings-Way, Meg Worby, Elizabeth Maxwell, Matthew Clarke, Bridget Smyth, Christopher Procter, Peter Handsaker and Max Handsaker.

Tom Spurling

Thanks to Maryanne Netto for getting me to go around again. High fives to Bob and Bulldog for their political wisdom and for reminding me of my roots. To Adam D and

THIS BOOK

Lonely Planet's guide to Australia was first published in 1977, when the company's cofounder Tony Wheeler covered the entire country on his own. In the 36 years since then we've sent literally hundreds of authors around Australia to check every dusty nook and cranny of the world's largest island for Lonely Planet guidebooks. This 17th edition of the Australia guide combined the efforts of 11 fabulous Lonely Planet writers. To see who did what, see Our Writers (p1112). We'd also like to thank the following people for their contributions to this guide: Dr Michael Cathcart, Dr Tim Flannery and Cathy Craigie. Andrew Tudor wrote the Where to Surf section in the Australia Outdoors chapter. This guidebook was commissioned in Lonely Planet's Melbourne office, and produced by the following:

Commissioning Editor Maryanne Netto
Coordinating Editor Alison Ridgway
Senior Cartographers Julie Sheridan, Diana Von Holdt
Coordinating Layout Designer Carlos Solarte
Managing Editors Barbara Delissen, Martine Power
Managing Layout Designer Chris Girdler
Assisting Editors Susie Ashworth, Penny Cordner, Andrea Dobbin, Lauren Hunt, Anne Mason, Alan Murphy, Jenna Myers, Kirsten Rawlings, Gabbi Stefanos
Assisting Cartographers Enes Bašić, Fatima Bašić, Jeff Cameron, Mick Garrett, Corey Hutchison
Internal Image Research Kylie McLaughlin
Thanks to Sasha Baskett, Nicholas Colicchia, Brigitte Ellemor, Ryan Evans, Larissa Frost, Jane Hart, Martin Heng, Trent Holden, Errol Hunt, Genesys India, Jouve India, Ali Lemer, James Maffesconi, Katherine Marsh, Virginia Moreno, Catherine Naghten, Karyn Noble, Darren O'Connell, Trent Paton, Suzannah Shwer, Rebecca Skinner, Kerrianne Southway, Marg Toohey, Sam Trafford, Tasmin Waby, Gerard Walker, Jeanette Wall

family for the mad pancakes. To Goose and Pop for hanging out Noosa-style. To all the Queenslanders who helped us along without any fuss. And to Lucy, Oliver and Poppy, who needs a holiday? Just keep on movin'. xo

Steve Waters

Thanks to Karen from RACWA for not hanging up, Mick for the tow, Leonie and Nev for beer and watermelons, Dave and Thuman of Djarindjin for the sand rescue, Travis for the drive shaft, John in the Subie for the WD40, Colleen and Karen for dinner and great conversation, Trace and Heath, Brodie, Abbidene, Meika and Kaeghan for EVERYTHING, Roz, Megan and Batty for caretaking, Friz and Ian for putting up with me, and the Bung-Bung crew for, well, Bung-Bung.

ACKNOWLEDGMENTS

Illustration p118-19 by Javier Zarracina.
Cover photograph: Surfer, Tamarama Beach, New South Wales, Kokkai Ng, Getty Images ©.

Index

Map Pages **000**
Photo Pages **000**

C

Map Pages **000**
Photo Pages **000**

D

E

Map Pages **000**
Photo Pages **000**

N

Map Pages **000**
Photo Pages **000**

Q

R

S

Map Pages **000**
Photo Pages **000**

Map Pages **000**
Photo Pages **000**

Map Legend

Sights
- Beach
- Buddhist
- Castle
- Christian
- Hindu
- Islamic
- Jewish
- Monument
- Museum/Gallery
- Ruin
- Winery/Vineyard
- Zoo
- Other Sight

Activities, Courses & Tours
- Diving/Snorkelling
- Canoeing/Kayaking
- Skiing
- Surfing
- Swimming/Pool
- Walking
- Windsurfing
- Other Activity/ Course/Tour

Sleeping
- Sleeping
- Camping

Eating
- Eating

Drinking
- Drinking
- Cafe

Entertainment
- Entertainment

Shopping
- Shopping

Information
- Post Office
- Tourist Information

Transport
- Airport
- Border Crossing
- Bus
- Cable Car/ Funicular
- Cycling
- Ferry
- Metro
- Monorail
- Parking
- S-Bahn
- Taxi
- Train/Railway
- Tram
- Tube Station
- U-Bahn
- Other Transport

Routes
- Tollway
- Freeway
- Primary
- Secondary
- Tertiary
- Lane
- Unsealed Road
- Plaza/Mall
- Steps
- Tunnel
- Pedestrian Overpass
- Walking Tour
- Walking Tour Detour
- Path

Boundaries
- International
- State/Province
- Disputed
- Regional/Suburb
- Marine Park
- Cliff
- Wall

Population
- Capital (National)
- Capital (State/Province)
- City/Large Town
- Town/Village

Geographic
- Hut/Shelter
- Lighthouse
- Lookout
- Mountain/Volcano
- Oasis
- Park
- Pass
- Picnic Area
- Waterfall

Hydrography
- River/Creek
- Intermittent River
- Swamp/Mangrove
- Reef
- Canal
- Water
- Dry/Salt/ Intermittent Lake
- Glacier

Areas
- Beach/Desert
- Cemetery (Christian)
- Cemetery (Other)
- Park/Forest
- Sportsground
- Sight (Building)
- Top Sight (Building)

Contributing Authors

Michael Cathcart Michael teaches history at the Australian Centre, University of Melbourne. He is well known as a broadcaster on ABC Radio National and has presented history programs on ABC TV. Michael wrote the History chapter.

Cathy Craigie Cathy is a Gamilaroi/Anaiwon woman from northern New South Wales. She is a freelance writer and cultural consultant and has extensive experience in Aboriginal Affairs. Cathy wrote the Aboriginal Australia chapter.

Tim Flannery Tim is a scientist, explorer and writer. He has written several award-winning books including *The Future Eaters*, *Throwim Way Leg* (an account of his work as a biologist in New Guinea) and *The Weather Makers*. He lives in Sydney where he is a professor in the faculty of science at Macquarie University. Tim wrote the Environment chapter.

Jayne D'Arcy
Melbourne & Victoria Melbourne strikes a new pose every day and Jayne does her best to snap it in words and photos. A fan of cycling around the city, she's learnt that you can't look at anything in Melbourne at face value, you've got to look up (for the rooftop bars) down (for the graffiti) and along that grimy laneway (for the glitzy restaurant). Jayne's lived on the Mornington Peninsula and Great Ocean Road but is now happier than ever in Melbourne.

Anthony Ham
Sydney & New South Wales Anthony was born in Melbourne, grew up in Sydney and spent much of his adult life travelling the world. He recently returned to Australia after 10 years living in Madrid. In NSW he found a perfect fit for his passion for wild landscapes – coastal rainforests, vast sweeps of sand and the endless outback horizon reminded him just how much he missed the land of his birth. He brings to the book the unique perspective of knowing the land intimately and yet seeing it anew as if through the eyes of an outsider.

Paul Harding
Melbourne & Victoria Growing up in Victorian goldrush town, Castlemaine, Paul was nicely placed to explore his home state, spending childhood summer holidays in the Gippsland Lakes, and later camping trips to the Murray River and winter skiing in the High Country. As a freelance travel writer he has since seen a good part of the world but now lives in Melbourne, where he's again well placed to explore Victoria. Paul has contributed to more than 40 Lonely Planet guidebooks, including many Australian titles.

Shawn Low
Queensland & the Great Barrier Reef, Your Reef Trip Good things come to those who wait. So the cliché goes. After missing out on a chance to work on the previous edition of the Australia guide, Shawn filled in his time with research trips to Singapore, Korea and China instead. His patience was rewarded and aside from a wicked tan, Shawn's now got a new bag load of travel stories to enthral (or bore) his mates with at the next pub session. Find out where he's currently travelling viaTwitter @shawnlow.

Virginia Maxwell
Sydney & New South Wales, Canberra & Around Despite being born, bred and based in Melbourne, Virginia knows Sydney well and loves it to bits. Having lived there in the past and visited frequently ever since, she has a good grasp of where to swim, sightsee, sleep and party. She resolutely refuses to engage in the age-old Sydney vs Melbourne rivalry – both are wonderful cities, especially now that Sydney has finally added a vibrant coffee culture to its many charms.

Tom Spurling
Queensland & the Great Barrier Reef Tom Spurling has written 10 guidebooks for Lonely Planet on five continents. He lives dangerously close to a trotting track in Perth, Western Australia. For this book he returned to Queensland with his wife and two children, driving 3000km of near-coastal highway and nonstop nursery rhymes. He escaped just days before mass floods. Tom also drove through the Outback with his dad who snored a lot but bought most of the beer.

Steve Waters
Perth & Western Australia From the corrugations of the Tanami to Nambung's ghostly Pinnacles, Steve covered 15,000km in Ezy, his Subaru L-series. Driving-lights dropped off, shockers, tyres, drive-shafts all shattered and they both almost drowned entering Purnululu. It only caught fire once. Slept in, eaten on, buried in Dampier Peninsula pindan, covered in Pilbara dust, pulled over by Cervantes cops, Ezy kept going. Steve's also co-authored previous editions of *Australia*, *Indonesia* and *Great Adventures*, and while not on the road, frequents LP's Melbourne office.

OUR STORY

A beat-up old car, a few dollars in the pocket and a sense of adventure. In 1972 that's all Tony and Maureen Wheeler needed for the trip of a lifetime – across Europe and Asia overland to Australia. It took several months, and at the end – broke but inspired – they sat at their kitchen table writing and stapling together their first travel guide, *Across Asia on the Cheap*. Within a week they'd sold 1500 copies. Lonely Planet was born.

Today, Lonely Planet has offices in Melbourne, London and Oakland, with more than 600 staff and writers. We share Tony's belief that 'a great guidebook should do three things: inform, educate and amuse'.

OUR WRITERS

Charles Rawlings-Way

Coordinating Author, Queensland & the Great Barrier Reef, Adelaide & South Australia As a likely lad, Charles suffered in shorts through Tasmanian winters, and in summer counted the days til he visited his grandparents in Adelaide. With desert-hot days, cool swimming pools, pasties with tomato sauce squirted into the middle and four TV stations, this flat South Australian city held paradisiacal status. Little did he know that southeast Queensland was just as alluring – a fact confirmed by more recent encounters with Brisbane's bookshops, bars and band rooms. An underrated rock guitarist and proud father of daughters, Charles has penned 20-something guidebooks for Lonely Planet.

Meg Worby

Coordinating Author, Queensland & the Great Barrier Reef, Adelaide & South Australia Meg's first foray into Queensland introduced her to a green turtle, face-to-face underwater. Twenty-eight years and six trips later, Queensland's inhabitants are still as naturally charming and a shell-load more cosmopolitan. Meanwhile, writing about South Australia was an honour as always. A former member of Lonely Planet's languages, editorial and publishing teams, this is Meg's seventh Australian guidebook for Lonely Planet.

Brett Atkinson

Tasmania, Perth & Western Australia Brett's previous visits to Western Australia involved museum- and bar-hopping in Fremantle, and taking on the mighty Nullarbor Plain. This time he expanded his WA horizons by immersing himself in Perth's restaurants and cafes, 'researching' craft breweries in the Swan Valley, and jumping from beach to forest and back to beach throughout Margaret River and the southwest. Brett's covered more than 45 countries as a guidebook author and travel and food writer. See www.brett-atkinson.net for where he's travelling to next.

Lindsay Brown

Darwin to Uluru, Your Outback Trip A former conservation biologist and publishing manager of outdoor activity guides at Lonely Planet, Lindsay enjoys nothing more than heading into the outback in his trusty old 4WD to explore and photograph Australia's heartland. As a Lonely Planet author, Lindsay has contributed to several titles including *Australia, Central Australia, Northern Territory, Queensland & the Great Barrier Reef, East Coast Australia, Sydney & New South Wales* and *Walking in Australia*.

OVER PAGE MORE WRITERS

Published by Lonely Planet Publications Pty Ltd
ABN 36 005 607 983
17th edition – Nov 2013
ISBN 978 1 74220 423 9

10 9 8 7 6 5 4 3 2 1
Printed in Singapore